Cases and Materials on Torts

Cases and Materials on Torts

Geoffrey Samuel

LawMatters
PUBLISHING

Cover Plate
A Child Bomb-Victim Receiving Penicillin Treatment
by Ethel Leontine Gabain, 1944
Reproduced with permission of The Imperial War Museum, London

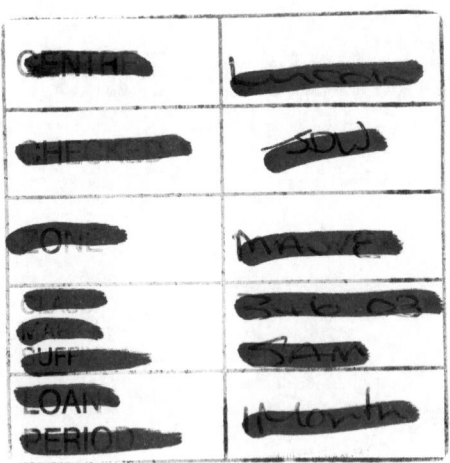

Published by Law Matters Publishing
Law Matters Limited
33 Southernay East
Exeter EX1 1NX
Tel: 01392 215577
www.lawmatterspublishing.co.uk

© 2006 Geoffrey Samuel

British Cataloguing-in-Publication Data

A catalogue record for this book is available from the British Library.

ISBN   10: 1 84641 016 9
ISBN   13: 978 1 84641 016 1

Typeset by Pantek Arts Ltd, Maidstone, Kent

Printed by Ashford Colour Press Ltd, Gosport, Hampshire

Contents

Abbreviations   ix
Dedication   xi
Preface   xiii
Acknowledgments   xv
Table of cases   xvii
Table of statutes   xxvii

1   Definition and Scope of the Law of Tort   1
    1.1   Historical considerations   1
    1.2   Definitional approaches   9
    1.3   Liability and remedies   14
    1.4   Province and scope of tort   16
    1.5   Tort and methodology   30
    1.6   European considerations   40

2   Purpose and Policy of Tort   44
    2.1   Aims and philosophy of the law of tort   44
    2.2   Compensation and loss-spreading   49
    2.3   Deterrence   55
    2.4   Protecting rights   59
    2.5   Protecting interests   70
    2.6   Tort and insurance   71

3   Liability for Individual Acts (1): Harm Intentionally Caused   76
    3.1   Intention and interests   76
    3.2   Assault and battery   91
    3.3   False imprisonment   95
    3.4   Harassment   99
    3.5   Fraud and lies   101
    3.6   Abuse of public power   102
    3.7   Abuse of the judical process   110

4   Liability for Individual Acts (2): Harm Negligently Caused   112
    4.1   Negligence as a cause of action   112
    4.2   Breach of duty   118

4.3	Duty of care	134
4.4	Causation and remoteness	155
4.5	Negligence and unlawfulness	155

5   Liability for Things (1): Moveable Things   **157**

5.1	Historical and conceptual considerations	157
5.2	Dangerous products	158
5.3	Dangerous industrial equipment	163
5.4	Motor vehicles	169
5.5	Animals	174
5.6	Aircraft	179
5.7	Liability for dangerous things in general	184

6   Liability for Things (2): Immovable Things   **187**

6.1	Liability for land and structures (1): on the land	188
6.2	Liability for land and structures (2): off the land	200
6.3	Public and private interests	211
6.4	Liability for dangerous things brought onto land	216

7   Liability for People   **225**

7.1	Three-party situations: general considerations	225
7.2	Liability for employees	230
7.3	Liability for non-employees	246
7.4	Liability for children	252

8   Liability for Words   **255**

8.1	General considerations: words and interests	255
8.2	Defamation (1): general liability	264
8.3	Defamation (2): defences	275
8.4	Misrepresentation and misstatement	286
8.5	Professional liability	290
8.6	Threats	293

9   Liability of Public Bodies   **294**

9.1	Public and private law	294
9.2	Central government	302
9.3	Local authorities	304
9.4	Police and prosecution service	315
9.5	Emergency services	319
9.6	National Health Service	320
9.7	Financial institutions	323

10 Causation and General Defences   324

    10.1   Approaches and theories   324
    10.2   Actionability   327
    10.3   Factual causation   335
    10.4   Remoteness of damage   358
    10.5   Damages   364

11 Remedies   369

    11.1   Actions and remedies   369
    11.2   Damages (1): general considerations   379
    11.3   Damages (2): personal injury   386
    11.4   Damages (3): non-personal injury damage   401
    11.5   Debt and similar claims   411
    11.6   Injunction   415
    11.7   Self-help   415
    11.8   Final word   418

Index   421

Abbreviations

AC	Appeal Cases (Third Series)
AJCL	American Journal of Comparative Law
All ER	All England Law Reports (Butterworths & Co)
App Cas	Appeal Cases (Second Series)
BGB	Bürgerliches Gesetzbuch (German Civil Code)
C	Code of Justinian
CA	Court of Appeal
CC	Code civil (French Civil Code)
Ch	Chancery Division (Third Series)
Ch D	Chancery Division (Second Series)
CLJ	Cambridge Law Journal
CLP	Current Legal problems
CLR	Commonwealth Law Reports
CUP	Cambridge University Press
D	Dalloz (also Digest of Justinian)
ECHR	European Court of Human Rights
ECJ	European Court of Justice
EHRR	European Human Rights Reports
ER	English Reports
FLR	Family Law Reports
G	Institutes of Gaius
HL	House of Lords
ICLQ	International and Comparative Law Quarterly
IECL	International Encyclopedia of Comparative Law
J	Institutes of Justinian/Justice (High Court)
JCP	Jurisclasseur périodique (La Semaine Juridique)
KB	King's Bench (Third Series)
LC	Lord Chancellor
LJ	Lord Justice (Court of Appeal)
LJCP	Law Journal Common Pleas
LJ Ex	Law Journal Exchequer
LJQB	Law Journal Queen's Bench
Ll Rep	Lloyd's List Law Reports
LQR	Law Quarterly Review
LR...CP	Common Pleas Cases (First Series)
LR...Eq	Equity Cases (First Series)
LR...Ex	Exchequer Cases (First Series)
LR...HL	English and Irish Appeals (First Series)
LR...QB	Queen's Bench Cases (First Series)
LS	Legal Studies
LT	Law Times Reports

MLR	Modern Law Review
NILQ	Northern Ireland Legal Quarterly
OJLS	Oxford Journal of Legal Studies
OUP	Oxford University Press
P	Probate Division (Third Series)
PC	Privy Council
PECL	Principles of European Contract Law
PETL	Principles of European Tort Law
PL	Public Law
QB	Queen's Bench (Third Series)
QBD	Queen's Bench (Second Series)
WLR	Weekly Law Reports

This book is dedicated to my sister, and to her courage and humour, whose life would have been devastated had it not been for the devotion of our parents and the great skill of Sir Alexander Fleming

Preface

A colleague and I once stated in the preface to a small tort casebook that we compiled many years ago that modest-sized casebooks tend to be judged by what they omit. The same remark can be made in respect of this sourcebook. Much has had to be omitted in order to meet a strict word limit. In addition one can legitimately ask whether such sourcebooks should be compiled at all, given that short extracts might be seen as encouraging laziness amongst its users. My response to this point is to argue that, if short textbooks (that is to say introductory books) are acceptable, then modest sourcebooks should be equally valid.

At all events, the purpose of this book is to provide a relatively solid introduction to the main areas of undergraduate tort law through the words of a range of those who are responsible for the modern development of the subject. Such an introductory sourcebook should be valuable when used alongside tort lectures. It ought not to replace library (or Internet) research which, of course, remains the essential foundation for success in the subject. But it will hopefully act as a stimulating bridge between classroom and library source material. If any specific characteristics are to be associated with this new sourcebook, perhaps the European orientation and the emphasis on method in tort might be the ones to gain attention. They have been my guide. I have chosen what I think is a modest selection of extracts from the law reports, statute book and academic publications available to me up to the end of 2004. But I have without doubt overlooked some important source material for which I apologise in advance. In terms of my own method, it might be useful for me to point out that I have been motivated more by the spirit of enquiry rather than of authority.

I would like to thank some of my colleagues here at Kent for spending time commenting on chapters. Their observations have been invaluable. Many thanks also to my family for their patience. I should very much like to thank my sister and the Imperial War Museum for allowing me to use the painting by Ethel Gabain of Gillian on the front cover of this book. The painting was rediscovered by us only recently and of course is of itself a tribute both to Sir Alexander Fleming and to Gillian who had to remain on the ward during V-1 attacks. What makes the painting pertinent for this book is that she was, in truth, a victim of a road accident and not bomb damage. Sir Alexander took my sister as a test patient and penicillin saved her leg.

Geoffrey Samuel
Kent Law School
January 2006

Acknowledgments

The publisher and author would like to thank the following for permission to reproduce extracts:

Brill NV – Extracts from F Stone, International Encyclopedia of Comparative Law, Vol XI, Ch 5; A Honoré, International Encyclopedia of Comparative Law, Vol XI, Ch 7; A Tunc, International Encyclopedia of Compartive Law, Vol XI, Ch 1.

Cambridge University Press – Extracts from P Winfield, *The Province of the Law of Tort* (1930); S Waddams, *Dimensions of Private Law* (2003).

Hart Publishing Ltd – Extract from P Cane, *The Anatomy of Tort Law*, reproduced with kind permission of the author and Hart Publishing Ltd.

The Incorporated Council of Law Reporting for England and Wales – Extracts from The Law Reports, The Weekly Law Reports and The Industrial Cases Reports reproduced by permission of The Incorporated Council of Law Reporting for England and Wales, Megarry House, 119 Chancery Lane, London WC2A 1PP.

Jordan Publishing – The kind permission of Jordan Publishing to reproduce the extract from *Z v United Kingdom* [2001] 2 FLR 612 in Family Law Reports is gratefully acknowledged.

LexisNexis Butterworths – Extracts from *Bamford v Turnley* (1862) 122 ER 27 Ex Ch; *Berkoff v Burchill* [1996] 4 All ER 1008, CA; *Bird v Jones* (1845) 115 ER 668, QB; *Bradford Building Society v Borders* [1941] 2 All ER 205, HL; *McKew v Holland & Hannen & Cubitts Ltd* [1969] 3 All ER 1621, HL (Scotland); *Thomas v Countryside Council for Wales* [1994] 4 All ER 853, QBD.

London Review of Books and Bernard Rudden – Extract from B Rudden, 'The Battle of Manywells Spring', 19 June 2003.

NI Syndication – Extract from *Hatton and Others v United Kingdom* (2003) *The Times*, 10 July.

Oxford University Press – Extracts from C von Bar, *The Common European Law of Torts*, Vol 2 (2000); D Ibbetson, *A Historical Introduction to the Law of Obligations* (1999); M Jones, *Textbook on Torts* (8th edn, 2002); P Cane, *Tort Law and Economic Interests* (2nd edn, 1996).

Pluto Press – Extract from J Conaghan and W Mansell, *The Wrongs of Tort* (1999).

PUF – Extracts from A Demichel and P Lalumière, *Le Droit Public* (1996); J Moreau, *La responsabilité administrative* (1986).

Société de legislation comparée – Extract from Tony Weir, 'Recent developments in causation in English tort law' in *De tous horizons, Mélanges Xavier Blanc-Jouvan*, Paris (2005).

Sweet and Maxwell – Extracts from Tony Weir, 'Government Liability' [1989] Public Law 40; S Waddams, 'Johanna Wagner and the Rival Opera Houses' (2001) 117 Law Quarterly Review 431.

Every effort has been made to contact individual copyright holders for their permission to reproduce extracts contained in this book. Apologies are offered for any errors or omissions, which will be rectified in future editions.

Table of Cases

A v National Blood Authority [2001] 3 All ER 289 163

Adams v Bracknell Forest BC [2005] 1 AC 76 54, 77

Akenzua v Home Secretary [2003] 1 WLR 741 303–4

Alcock v Chief Constable of South Yorkshire Police [1992] 1 AC 310 143–4, 146, 150

Allan v Liverpool Overseers (1874) LR 9 QB 180 370

Allen v Flood [1898] AC 1 79, 86–7, 106

Allen v Gulf Oil Refining Ltd [1981] AC 1001 296

Alton v Midland Railway (1865) 19 C B (N S) 213; 34 LJCP 292 18

Anderton v Clwyd County Council (see *Phelps v Hillingdon London Borough Council*)

Anns v Merton London Borough Council [1978] AC 728 33, 135, 136, 153, 305

Anufrijeva v Southwark LBC [2004] QB 1124 410–11

Appah v Parncliffe Investments Ltd [1964] 1 WLR 1064 370

Arthur J.S Hall and Co. v Simons [2002] 1 AC 615 19–21, 117

Ashby v White (1703) 92 ER 126 105

Attorney-General v Bastow [1957] 1 QB 514 69

Attorney-General v Blake [2001] 1 AC 268 26, 30, 47, 52, 385

Attorney-General v PYA Quarries Ltd [1957] 2 QB 169 68–9, 172, 201

Attorney General v Tod Heatley [1897] 1 Ch 560 201

Baker v Market Harborough Industrial Cooperative Society [1953] 1 WLR 1472 321

Baker v Willoughby [1970] AC 467 346, 347–8

Bamford v Turnley (1862) 3 B & S 62, 122 ER 27 210, 211–212, 220

Banque Bruxelles Lambert SA v Eagle Star Insurance Co Ltd [1997] AC 191 335–6

Barber v Somerset CC [2004] 1 WLR 1089 128

Barclays Bank plc v Fairclough Building Ltd [1995] QB 214 365

Barker v Herbert [1911] 2 KB 633 202

Barrett v Enfield London Borough Council [2001] 2 AC 550 305–6, 311

Barrett v Ministry of Defence [1995] 1 WLR 1217 154

Beaudesert Shire Council v Smith (1966) 120 CLR 145 106

Behrens v Bertram Mills Circus Ltd [1957] 2 QB 1 174, 179

Benjamin v Storr (1874) LR 9 CP 400 2, 19, 7, 34

Berkoff v Burchill [1996] 4 All ER 1008 266–8

Best v Samuel Fox & Co Ltd [1952] AC 716 137, 141–2, 393

Beswick v Beswick [1968] AC 58 263

Bird v Jones (1845) 115 ER 668 95–6

Birmingham CC v Oakley [2001] 1 AC 617 36

Birse Construction Ltd v Haiste Ltd [1996] 1 WLR 675 114, 414

Black v Yates [1992] QB 526 21

Blackpool & Fylde Aero Club Ltd v Blackpool BC [1990] 1 WLR 1195 30

Blake v Galloway [2004] 1 WLR 2844 95

Blue Circle Industries v Ministry of Defence [1999] Ch 298 224

Blyth v Proprietors of the Birmingham Waterworks (1856) 11 Exch 781, 156 ER 1047 118–19

Boddington v British Transport Police [1999] 2 AC 143 28

Bolam v Friern Hospital Management
    Committee [1957] 1 WLR 582
    130–1
Bolitho v City and Hackney Health
    Authority [1998] AC 232 131–2
Bolton v Stone [1951] AC 850 119–21,
    198–9
Bone v Seale [1975] 1 WLR 797
    803–804, 407
Bourgoin SA v Ministry of Agriculture,
    Fisheries and Food [1986] QB 716
    105
Bourhill v Young [1943] AC 92 143, 150
Bradford Building Society v Borders
    [1941] 2 All ER 205 101, 287
Bradford Corporation v Pickles [1895] AC
    587 9, 11, 24, 60–1, 77, 79–80, 87,
    106, 298
Bridlington Relay Ltd v Yorkshire
    Electricity Board [1965] Ch 436 206
British Celanese v AH Hunt Ltd [1969] 2
    All ER 1253 216
Brooks v Commissioner of Police for the
    Metropolis [2005] 1 WLR 1495 37,
    316
Broome v Cassell Co Ltd [1972] AC 1027
    49, 56–7, 409
Brunswick (Duke of) v Harmer (1830) 14
    QB 185 273
Bryanston Finance v de Vries [1975] QB
    703 272
Bryant v Herbert (1877) 3 CPD 389 2,
    13, 16
Buchanan v Motor Insurers' Bureau
    [1955] 1 WLR 488 50
Burnie Port Authority v General Jones Pty
    Ltd (1994) 179 CLR 520 221
Burris v Azadani [1995] 1 WLR 1372
    22, 23, 30, 375–6, 415
Burton v Winters [1993] 1 WLR
    1077 415

Calveley v Chief Constable of the
    Merseyside Police [1989] AC 1228
    106, 313
Cambridge Water Co v Eastern Counties
    Leather plc [1994] 2 AC 264 69,
    209–10, 218–19, 221
Camelot Group v Centaur
    Communications [1999] QB 124
    285
Campbell v MGN Ltd [2003] QB 633 64

Campbell v Paddington Corporation
    [1911] 1 KB 869 21
Campbell v Spottiswoode (1863) 3 B & S
    769, 122 ER 288 276–7
Caparo Industries plc v Dickman [1990]
    2 AC 605 135–6, 140–1, 146,
    149, 306
Capital & Counties plc v Hampshire CC
    [1997] QB 1004 154
Carmarthenshire CC v Lewis [1955] AC
    549 253
Carslogie SS Co v Royal Norwegian
    Government [1952] AC 292 342–3,
    346
Cartledge v E Jopling & Sons Ltd [1963]
    AC 758 402–3
Cassidy v Ministry of Health [1951] 2 KB
    343 234–5, 321
Cattle v Stockton Waterworks Co (1875)
    LR 10 QB 453 138
Caxton Publishing Co Ltd v Sutherland
    Publishing Co [1939] AC 178 23
Chadwick v British Railways Board
    [1967] 1 WLR 912 146, 148
Chaplin v Hicks [1911] 2 KB 786 77,
    352, 356
Chester v Afshar [2005] 1 AC 134
    352–4
Christie v Davey [1893] 1 Ch D 316 79
Christie v Leachinsky [1947] AC 573 98
Clarke v Dickson (1858) 120 ER 463
    287
Clay v AJ Crump & Sons Ltd [1964] 1 QB
    533 293
Close v Steel Co of Wales [1962] AC 367
    165
Coggs v Bernard (1703) 92 ER 107 24
Cole v Turner (1704) 6 Mod Rep 149, 90
    ER 958 3
Colwell v Corrective Services Commission
    of New South Wales (1988) 13
    NSWLR 714 82
Cooper v Wandsworth Board of Works
    (1863) 14 CBNS 180; 143 ER 414
    27, 301
Copeland v Smith [2000] 1 WLR 1371
    39
Coxall v Goodyear Great Britain Ltd
    [2003] 1 WLR 536 126–8
Cutler v Wandsworth Stadium Ltd [1949]
    AC 398 155

D v East Berkshire NHS Trust [2005] 2
    AC 373 149–51, 259, 263, 310–14

Danby v Lamb (1861) 31 LJCP 19 18
Dann v Hamilton [1939] 1 KB 509 128
Darbishire v Warran [1963] 1 WLR 1067
 367–8
Davey v Spelthorne Borough Council
 [1984] AC 262 297, 299
Davidson v Chief Constable of North
 Wales [1994] 2 All ER 597 99
Davie v New Merton Board Mills Ltd
 [1959] AC 604 163, 167
Davies v Snead (1870) LR 5 QB 608 278
Davis v Bromley Corporation [1908] 1 KB
 170 105
Davis v Radcliffe [1990] 1 WLR 821
 106
Delaware Mansions Ltd v Westminster
 CC [2002] 1 AC 321 209, 211
Dennis v Ministry of Defence [2003]
 EWHC 793 180–2, 211
Denton v United Counties Omnibus Co
 (1986) The Times 6 May 247
Derbyshire County Council v Times
 Newspapers Ltd [1993] AC 534 30,
 64, 270
Derry v Peek (1887) 37 Ch D 541 (CA);
 (1889) 14 App Cas 337 (HL) 115,
 287
Donoghue v Folkestone Properties Ltd
 [2003] QB 1008 197, 198
Donoghue v Stevenson [1932] AC 562
 112–13, 115, 134, 135, 136, 140,
 152, 157, 159, 210, 222, 293
Dooley v Cammell Laird [1951] 1
 Lloyd's Rep 271 145
Dorset Yacht Co Ltd v Home Office
 [1970] AC 1004 135, 152, 296,
 305
Douglas v Hello! [2001] QB 967 76
Dubai Aluminium Co Ltd v Salaam
 [2003] 2 AC 366 413
Dulieu v White & Sons [1901] 2 KB 669
 143
Dunlop v Woollahra Municipal Council
 [1982] AC 158 84, 105
Dunne v North Western Gas Board
 [1964] 2 QB 806 302
Dymond v Pearce and Others [1972] 1
 QB 496 172–4

E v United Kingdom (2002) 36 EHRR
 519 311
Electrochrome Ltd v Welsh Plastics Ltd
 [1968] 2 All ER 205 138

Elguzouli-Daf v Commissioner of Police
 of the Metropolis [1995] QB 335
 315–16
Elliott Steam Tug Co Ltd v Shipping
 Controller [1922] 1 KB 137
Elsee v Smith (1822) 2 Chit 304 110
Emerald Construction Co v Lowthian
 1966] 1 WLR 691 89
English v Dedham Vale Properties [1978]
 1 WLR 93 30
Eshugbayi Eleko v Officer Administering
 the Government of Nigeria [1931]
 AC 662 27
Esso Petroleum Co Ltd v Southport
 Corporation [1953] 3 WLR 773
 (QBD), [1954] 2 QB 182 (CA),
 [1956] AC 218 (HL) 4–5, 34, 68,
 69, 76, 172, 233
European Commission v UK [1997] All
 ER (EC) 481; [1997] 3 CMLR 923
 163
Everett v Ribbands [1952] 2 QB 198
 110

F (In re) (Mental Patient: Sterilisation)
 [1990] 2 AC 1 67, 68
Fagan v Metropolitan Police
 Commissioner [1969] 1 QB 439
 92–3
Fairchild v Glenhaven Funeral Services
 Ltd [2003] 1 AC 32 40, 42–3,
 348–51, 353–4
Fayed v United Kingdom (1994) 18
 EHRR 393 271
Femis-Bank Ltd v Lazar [1991] Ch 391
 111
Fitzgerald v ED and AD Cooke Bourne
 (Farms) Ltd [1964] 1 QB 249 174
Fowler v Lanning [1959] 1 QB 426 3
Francovich v Italy (Case C–6/90) [1991]
 ECR I–5357 36
Freeman v Home Office (No 2) [1984] QB
 524 114
Frost v Aylesbury Dairy Co Ltd [1905] 1
 KB 608 114

Galoo Ltd v Bright Grahame Murray
 [1994] 1 WLR 1360 141
Gaunt v Fynney (1873) LR 8 Ch App 8
 79
Gautret v Egerton (1867) LR 2 CP 371
 134

Geddis v Proprietors of Bann Reservoir
(1878) 3 App Cas 430 300
Ghaidan v Godin-Mendoza [2004] 2 AC
557 36
Gibbs v Rea [1998] AC 786 110, 317
Godfrey v Demon Internet Ltd [2001]
QB 201 273
Goldman v Hargrave [1967] AC 645
214, 224, 299
*Goodwill v British Pregnancy Advisory
Service* [1996] 1 WLR 1397 33, 136
Gorringe v Calderdale MBC [2004] 1
WLR 1057 170, 263, 299–300,
304, 315
Gorris v Scott (1874) LR 9 Ex 125 155
*Governors of Peabody Donation Fund v
Sir Lindsay Parkinson & Co Ltd*
[1985] AC 210 135
Grainger v Hill (1838) 132 ER 769 111
Grant v Australian Knitting Mills Ltd
[1936] AC 85 104, 114, 140,
159–60
Gregg v Scott [2005] 2 AC 176 355–7
Groves v Lord Wimborne [1898] 2 QB
402 155, 164–5
Gulf Oil (GB) Ltd v Page [1987] Ch 327
91, 111
*Gwilliam v West Hertfordshire Hospital
NHS Trust* [2003] 3 QB 443 123–4,
157, 194

H West & Son Ltd v Shepard [1964] AC
326 397–8
Haigh v Charles W Ireland [1973] 3 All
ER 1137 36
Hall (Inspector of Taxes) v Lorimer [1992]
1 WLR 939 (QBD); [1994] 1 All ER
250 (CA) 236
Hall (Arthur JS) and Co. v Simons (see
Arthur J.S Hall and Co. v Simons)
Halsey v Esso Petroleum Co Ltd [1961] 1
WLR 683 205
*Halsey v Milton Keynes General NHS
Trust* [2004] 1 WLR 3002 348
*Hammersmith and City Railway Co v
Brand* (1867) LR 2 QB 223 220
*Harbutt's 'Plasticine' Ltd v Wayne Tank
and Pump Co Ltd* [1970] 1 QB 447
403
Hargrave v Goldman (1963) 110 CLR 40
152
Haseldine v CA Daw & Son Ltd [1941] 2
KB 343 293

Hatton v UK (2003) 37 EHRR 611
183–4, 216
Hayley v London Electricity Board [1965]
AC 778 124–5
Haynes v Harwood [1935] 1 KB 146 345
Heap v Ind Coope and Allsopp Ltd [1940]
K B 476 203
*Hedley Byrne & Co v Heller & Partners
Ltd* [1964] AC 465 19, 30, 115,
118, 135, 138, 139, 140, 255–6,
263
Heil v Rankin [2001] QB 272 399–400
Henderson (ex p) [1997] PIQR 413 128
Henderson v HE Jenkins & Sons Ltd
[1970] AC 282 170, 223
Henderson v Merrett Syndicates Ltd
[1995] 2 AC 145 2, 10, 17, 18
Herring v Boyle (1834) 1 CM & R 377,
149 ER 1126 98
Herrington v British Railways Board
[1972] AC 877 195, 199
Hertel v Switzerland (1999) 28 EHRR
534 271
*Hill v Chief Constable of West York*shire
[1989] AC 53 36–7, 40, 68, 135,
296, 311, 316
Hodgson v Trapp [1989] 1 AC 807 389,
395
*Holbeck Hall Hotel Ltd v Scarborough BC
(No 2)* [2000] QB 836 209
Holgate-Mohammed v Duke (see
Mohammed-Holgate v Duke)
Holliday v National Telephone Co [1899]
2 QB 392 249
Hollins v Fowler (1875) LR 7 HL 757 62
Hollywood Silver Fox Farm Ltd v Emmett
[1936] 2 KB 468 24, 79, 208
Home Office v Dorset Yacht Co Ltd
[1970] AC 1004 23, 31, 134,
226–7, 303
Honeywill & Stein Ltd v Larkin Bros
[1934] 1 KB 191 249
Hope v Evered (1886) 17 QBD 338 110
Horrocks v Lowe [1975] AC 135 264,
280, 282
Hughes v Lord Advocate [1963] AC 837
362, 363
Hunt v Severs [1994] 2 AC 350 391,
393
Hunter v Canary Wharf Ltd [1997] AC
655 64, 80–1, 206–8, 211, 407–8

Hussain v Lancaster CC [2000] 1 QB 1 315

Hussain v New Taplow Paper Mills Ltd [1988] AC 514 528, 393

Huth v Huth [1915] 3 KB 32 272

Inland Revenue Commissioners v Hambrook [1956] QB 641 137

Inverugie Investments Ltd v Hackett [1995] 1 WLR 713 25–6

Island Records (ex p) [1978] Ch 122 84, 91

Jackson v Horizon Holidays [1975] 1 WLR 1468 263

Jaggard v Sawyer [1995] 1 WLR 269 30, 66

Janvier v Sweeney [1919] 2 KB 316 65

Jefford v Gee [1970] 2 QB 130 395

Jobling v Associated Dairies Ltd [1982] AC 794 347–8

John Summers v Frost [1955] AC 740 165

John v MGN Ltd [1997] QB 586 404, 408–9

Jolley v London Borough of Sutton [2000] 1 WLR 1082 362, 362–3

Jones v Berkshire Area Health Authority (1986) (unreported) 2 July 46

Jones v Swansea City Council [1990] 1 WLR 54 106

Joyce v Sengupta [1993] 1 WLR 337 101–2

Junior Books Ltd v Veitchi Co Ltd [1983] 1 AC 520 140

Keeble v Hickeringill (1809) 11 East 574, 103 ER 1127, 90 ER 906 79

Keegan v Chief Constable of Merseyside [2003] 1 WLR 2187 110, 317–18

Kennaway v Thompson [1981] QB 88 16, 181

Kent v Griffiths [2001] QB 36 311, 319

Keppel Bus Co Ltd v Sa'ad bin Ahmad [1974] 1 WLR 1082 242

Khorasandjian v Bush [1993] QB 727 64

King (ex parte) [1984] 3 All ER 897 36

King v Phillips [1953] 1 QB 429 138

Kirkham v Boughey [1958] 2 QB 338 137

Kitchen v Royal Air Force Association [1958] 1 WLR 563 356

Kleinwort Benson Ltd v Glasgow CC [1999] 1 AC 153 24, 25

Knightley v Johns [1982] 1 WLR 349 296

Kuddus v Chief Constable of Leicestershire [2002] 2 AC 122 384–6

L (A Child) v Reading Borough Council [2001] 1 WLR 1575 311

Lagden v O'Connor [2003] 3 WLR 1571 402–3

Lamb v Camden LBC [1981] QB 625 74

Latimer v AEC Ltd [1953] AC 643 121

Law Society v KPMG [2000] 1 WLR 1921 141

Leakey v National Trust [1980] QB 485 214

Lennon v Commissioner of Police for the Metropolis [2004] 1 WLR 2594 19

Letang v Cooper [1965] 1 QB 232 3, 76

Lewis v Daily Telegraph [1964] AC 234 268–70

Liesbosch (the) [1933] AC 449 402–403

Lim Poh Choo v Camden and Islington Area Health Authority [1980] AC 174 379, 389

Linden Gardens Trust Ltd v Lenesta Sludge Disposals Ltd [1994] 1 AC 85 262

Lingens v Austria (1986) 8 EHRR 407 271

Lippiatt v South Gloucestershire Council [2000] 1 QB 51 314

Lister v Hesley Hall Ltd [2002] 1 AC 215 231–2, 242–4

Lister v Romford Ice & Cold Storage Co Ltd [1957] AC 555 19, 52–3, 56, 232, 415

Livingstone v Rawyards Coal Co (1880) 5 App Cas 25 380, 389

London Artists Ltd v Littler [1969] 2 QB 375 277

London Passenger Transport Board v Upson [1949] AC 155 156

Lonrho Ltd v Shell Petroleum Co Ltd (No 2) [1982] AC 173 83, 91, 106, 155

Loutchansky v Times Newspapers Ltd (Nos 2–5) [2002] QB 783 273–4, 284–5

Lumley v Gye (1853) 2 E & B 216; 118 ER 749 89

Lumley v Wagner (1852) 1 De GM & G
  604; 42 ER 687 89
Lupton v FA & AB Ltd [1972] AC 634
  32

M v Newham London Borough Council
  [1995] 2 AC 633 310–11, 312
*McDermid v Nash Dredging and
  Reclamation Co* [1987] AC 906
  250–1
McFarlane v Tayside Health Board [2000]
  2 AC 59 45–6, 377–8
McIlgrew v Devon County Council [1995]
  PIQR 66 389
*McKew v Holland & Hannen & Cubitts
  Ltd* [1969] 3 All ER 1621 339
McLoughlin v O'Brian [1983] 1 AC 410
  143–4
McPherson v Daniels (1829) 10 B & C
  263, 109 ER 448 275
McWilliams v Sir William Arrol & Co
  [1962] 1 WLR 295 342
*Majrowski v Guy's and St Thomas's NHS
  Trust* [2005] 2 WLR 1503 245
*Malone v Metropolitan Police
  Commissioner* [1979] Ch 344 64
Manchester Airport plc v Dutton [2000] 1
  QB 133 370, 415
Mansfield v Weetabix Ltd [1998] 1 WLR
  1263 169
Marc Rich & Co v Bishop Rock Ltd [1996]
  1 AC 211 18, 136–7, 149, 154,
  291–3
Marcic v Thames Water Utilities Ltd
  [2004] 2 AC 42 69, 213–14,
  215–16
*Margarine Union GmbH v Cambay Prince
  SteamshipCo Ltd* [1969] 1 QB 220
  137
*Market Investigations Ltd v Ministry of
  Social Security* [1969] 2 QB 173
  236–7
*Markt Intern Verlag GmbH and Beerman
  v Germany* (1989) (1989) 12 EHRR
  161 271
Martin v Watson [1996] AC 74 102–4
Mattis v Pollock [2003] 1 WLR 2158
  227, 245–6
Maynard v West Midlands Regional HA
  [1984] 1 WLR 634 131–2
*Mediana (Owners of Steamship) v Comet
  (Owners of Lightship)* [1900] AC 113
  25, 404

*Meering v Grahame-White Aviation Co
  Ltd* (1920) 122 LT 44 98
*Meridian Global Funds Management v
  Securities Commission* [1995] 2 AC
  500 232
Merkur Island Shipping Corpn v Laughton
  [1983] 2 AC 570 90
Merlin v British Nuclear Fuels plc [1990]
  2 QB 557 36
*Mersey Docks and Harbour Board
  Trustees v Gibbs* (1866) LR 1 HL 93
  296
*Mersey Docks and Harbour Board v
  Coggins and Griffith (Liverpool) Ltd*
  [1947] AC 1 238–9
Millard v Serck Tubes Ltd [1969] 1 WLR
  211 165
Miller v Jackson [1977] QB 966 14–15,
  30, 49, 66, 181, 211, 415
Mint v Good [1951] 1 KB 517 202–3
Mirvahedy v Henley [2003] 2 AC 491
  34–5, 174–7, 178
Mitchell v Ealing LBC [1979] QB 1 23
*Mogul Steamship Co v McGregor, Gow &
  Co* (1889) 23 QBD 598 (CA),
  [1892] AC 25 (HL) 84–5, 87
Mohammed Holgate v Duke [1984] AC
  437 323
Moorgate Mercantile Co Ltd v Twitchings
  [1977] AC 890 23, 62, 248
Morgan Crucible v Hill Samuel [1991]
  Ch 295 141
Morgans v Launchbury [1973] AC 127
  72, 169, 170, 248
Morris v CW Martin & Sons Ltd [1966] 1
  QB 716 23–4, 229, 230, 241, 243,
  244
Morris v Ford Motor Co Ltd [1973] 1 QB
  792 63
Morris v KLM Royal Dutch Airlines
  [2002] QB 100 36
Morris v Network Rail [2004] All ER (D)
  342 210, 211
*Morrison Steamship Co Ltd v Greystoke
  Castle (Cargo Owners)* [1947] AC
  265 138
Morton v Wheeler (1956) January 31,
  1956, CA; Bar Library Transcript
  No 33 173
Mullin v Richards [1998] 1 WLR 1304
  129–30
Murphy v Brentwood DC [1991] 1 AC
  398 304

Murray v Ministry of Defence [1988] 1
WLR 692 98–9

National Telephone Co v Baker [1893] 2
Ch 186 32
Nettleship v Weston [1971] 2 QB 691
128–9, 170
New York Times Co. v Sullivan (1964)
376 US 254 281
Nichols v Marsland (1876) 2 Ex D 1 344
Nor-Video Services Ltd v Ontario Hydro
(1978) 84 DLR (3d) 221 206
Northern Territory v Mengel (1995) 69
AJLR 527 83–4, 106

OBG Ltd v Allan [2005] QB 762 91
O'Reilly v Mackman [1983] 2 AC 237
30, 297
The Oropesa [1943] P 32 338
Osman v United Kingdom (1998) 29
EHRR 245 308, 311
*Overseas Tankship (UK) Ltd v Miller
Steamship Co Pty Ltd (The Wagon
Mound No 2)* [1967] 1 AC 617 121
*Overseas Tankship (UK) Ltd v Morts Dock
& Engineering Co (The Wagon
Mound No 1)* [1961] AC 388
359–60, 361, 363

Page v Smith [1996] 1 AC 155 143, 148
Paris v Stepney BC [1951] AC 367 126
*Parkinson v St James and Seacroft
University Hospital NHS Trust* [2002]
QB 266 377
Parry v Cleaver [1970] AC 1 393
Peek v Derry (see *Derry v Peek*)
Peek v Gurney (1873) LR 2 QB 580 287
Performance Cars Ltd v Abraham [1962]
1 QB 33 343, 346, 348
Perry v Kendricks Transport [1956] 1
WLR 85 223–4
*Phelps v Hillingdon London Borough
Council* [2001] 2 AC 619 77, 228,
229, 306, 308–9, 311
*Phillips v Britannia Hygienic Laundry Co
Ltd* [1923] 2 KB 832 155, 156,
171–2
Phipps v Rochester Corporation [1955] 1
QB 450 192
*Photo Production Ltd v Securicor
Transport Ltd* [1980] AC 827
229–30, 232, 243, 244

Pitts v Hunt [1991] 1 QB 24 23
Polemis (In re) [1921] 3 KB 560 358–9,
360
*Post Office v Norwich Union Fire
Insurance Society Ltd* [1967] 2 QB
363 63
Poussard v Spiers & Pond (1876) 1 QBD
410 89

Qualcast (Wolverhampton) Ltd v Haynes
[1959] AC 743 132
Quinn v Leathem [1901] AC 495 87

*R (Beer) v Hampshire Farmers' Markets
Ltd* [2004] 1 WLR 233 301
*R (McCann) v Crown Court at
Manchester* [2001] 1 WLR 1084 22,
23
R (Munjaz) v Mersey Care NHS Trust
[2004] QB 395 322–3
R v Bowden [1996] 1 WLR 98 106
*R v Chief Constable of Sussex, ex p
International Trader's Ferry Ltd*
[1999] 2 AC 418 305
*R v Deputy Governor of Parkhurst Prison,
ex p Hague* [1992] 1 AC 58 322
R v Dytham [1979] QB 722 296
*R v Governor of Blundeston Prison, ex p
Gaffney* [1982] 1 WLR 696 27
*R v Governor of Brockhill Prison, ex p
Evans (No 2)* [2001] 2 AC 19 27–8,
67, 82–3, 99
R v Lloyd (1800) 170 ER 691 69
R v Rimmington [2005] 3 WLR 982 21,
201
*R v Secretary of State for the Environment,
Transport and the Regions, ex p
Spath Holme Ltd* [2001]
2 AC 349 36
R v Self [1992] 1 WLR 657 99, 416
R v Somerset CC, ex p Fewings [1995] 1
WLR 1037 298
*R v Transport Sec, ex p Factortame Ltd
(No 7)* [2001] 1 WLR 942 40–1,
155
Racz v Home Office [1994] 2 AC 45 106
Rahman v Arearose [2001] QB 351
412–13
Ratcliff v McConnell [1999] 1 WLR 670
197
Ratcliffe v Evans [1892] 2 QB 524 81
Rawlinson v Rice [1997] 2 NZLR 651
107

Read v J Lyons & Co [1947] AC 156 14, 48, 184–6, 217, 218, 219, 223

Rees v Darlington Memorial Hospital NHS Trust [2004] 1 AC 309 47, 377–9, 380

Reeves v Commissioner of Police for the Metropolis [2000] 1 AC 360 154, 199, 317, 336–7, 340–1, 365–6

Reid v Rush & Tompkins plc [1990] 1 WLR 212 50–1, 170

Revill v Newbery [1996] QB 567 416–17

Reynolds v Commissioner of Police of the Metropolis [1985] QB 881 110

Reynolds v Times Newspapers Limited [2001] 2 AC 127 265, 275–6, 276–7, 278, 280–4

RH Willis & Son v British Car Auctions Ltd [1978] 1 WLR 438 62–3

Ricket v Metropolitan Railway Co (1865) 5 B & S 149, (1867) LR 2 HL 175 (HL) 58

Rigby v Chief Constable of Northamptonshire [1985] 1 WLR 1242 30, 296

Riverstone Meat Co Pty Ltd v Lancashire Shipping Co Ltd [1961] AC 807 251–2

Robinson v Balmain New Ferry Co Ltd [1910] AC 295 96–7

Robinson v Kilvert (1889) 41 Ch D 88 210, 211

Robinson v Post Office [1974] 1 WLR 1176 361

Roe v Minister of Health [1954] 2 QB 66 132, 235, 320–1

Roles v Nathan [1963] 1 WLR 1117 193–4

Rondel v Worsley [1969] 1 AC 191 37

Rookes v Barnard [1964] AC 1129 88, 293, 384, 385

Ross v Caunters [1980] Ch 297 260–1, 262

Rowe v Herman [1997] 1WLR 1390 252

Rowling v Takaro Properties Ltd [1988] AC 473 135

Roy v Prior [1971] A.C. 470 110

Rutter v Palmer [1922] 2 KB 87 116

Ruxley Electronics and Construction Ltd v Forsyth [1996] AC 344 407

Rylands v Fletcher (1866) LR 1 Exch 265 (1868) LR 3 HL 330 32, 74, 157, 185, 187–8, 217, 221–2, 302

S v Gloucestershire County Council [2001] Fam 313 311

St. Helen's Smelting Co v Tipping (1865) 11 HL Cas 642, 11 ER 1483 208, 408

Salsbury v Woodland [1970] 1 QB 324 248–9

Sandhar v Department of Transport [2005] 1 WLR 1632 304

Searle v Wallbank [1947] AC 341 175

Sedleigh-Denfield v O'Callaghan [1940] AC 880 5, 6, 214

Shelfer v City of London Electric Lighting Company [1894] 1 Ch 287 181

Sidaway v Bethlem Royal Hospital [1985] 1 AC 871 131

Silkin v Beaverbrook Newspapers Ltd [1958] 1 WLR 743 277

Simpson & Co v Thomson (1877) 5R (HL) 40 137

Slater v Clay Cross Co Ltd [1956] 2 QB 264 128

Slim v Daily Telegraph Ltd [1968] 2 QB 157 265

Smedleys Ltd v Breed [1974] AC 839 163

Smith and Grady v United Kingdom [1999] 29 EHRR 493 184

Smith New Court Securities Ltd v Scrimgeour Vickers Ltd [1997] AC 254 288–9

Smith v Leech Brain & Co Ltd [1962] 2 QB 405 361

Smith v Littlewoods Organisation Ltd [1987] AC 241 223–4, 229

Smith v Stages [1989] AC 928 240

Snelling v Whitehead (1975) *The Times*, 31 July 169

Société Anonyme de Remorquage à Hélice v Bennetts [1911] 1 KB 243 138

Spartan Steel & Alloys Ltd v Martin & Co (Contractors) Ltd [1973] 1 QB 27 11, 37, 40, 54–5, 137–9, 404

Spath Holme Ltd (ex p) (see R v. Secretary of State for the Environment, Transport and the Regions, ex p Spath Holme Ltd)

Speed Seal Products v Paddington [1985] 1 WLR 1327 111

Spring v Guardian Assurance plc [1995] 2 AC 296 101, 102, 117, 255, 257–9, 352

St Aubyn v Att-Gen [1952] AC 15 36
Stapley v Gypsum Mines Ltd [1953] AC
 663 129
Staveley Iron & Chemical Co v Jones
 [1956] AC 627 232–3
Steel and Morris v United Kingdom
 (2005) (Application no 68416/01),
 ECtHR 42, 270–2
Stoke-on-Trent City Council v WJ Wass
 Ltd [1988] 1 WLR 1406 25
Stonedale (No 1) (the) [1956] AC 1 52
Stovin v Wise [1996] AC 923 58, 59,
 136, 152–4, 170, 296
Strand Electric & Engineering Ltd v
 Brisford Entertainments Ltd [1952] 2
 QB 246 27
Street v Mountford [1985] AC 809 370
Stubbings v Webb [1993] AC 498 10
Sturges v Bridgman (1879) 11 Ch D 852
 211
Swinney v Chief Constable of
 Northumbria [1997] QB 464
 316–17

Tai Hing Cotton Mill Ltd v Liu Chong
 Hing Bank Ltd [1986] AC 80 18
Tarry v Ashton (1876) 1 QBD 314 202
Taylor v Caldwell (1863) 3 B & S 826,
 122 ER 309 43
Taylor v Manchester, Sheffield &
 Lincolnshire Railway Co [1895] 1
 QB 134 18
Tesco Supermarkets Ltd v Nattrass [1972]
 AC 153 232
Thackwell v Barclays Bank plc [1986] 1
 All ER 676 38
Thomas v Countryside Council for Wales
 [1994] 4 All ER 853 367
Thompson-Schwab v Costaki [1956] 1
 WLR 335 69, 206–7
Thompson v Commissioner of Police of
 the Metropolis [1998] QB 498
 405–6
Thorne v Motor Trade Association [1937]
 AC 797 91
Three Rivers District Council v Governor
 and Company of The Bank of
 England (No 3) [2003] 2 AC 1
 83–4, 105–7, 299, 303–4
Tinsley v Milligan [1994] 1 AC 340 38
Tolstoy Miloslavsky v United Kingdom
 (1995) 20 EHRR 442 271

Tomlinson v Congleton BC [2004] 1 AC
 46 195, 197–9, 314
Toogood v Spyring (1834) 1 CM & R
 181, 149 ER 1044 278
Topp v London Country Bus (South West)
 Ltd [1993] 1 WLR 976 246–8
Torquay Hotel Co v Cousins [1969] 2 Ch
 106 86, 89–90
TP and KM v United Kingdom (2001) 34
 EHRR 42 310, 312
Transco plc v Stockport Metropolitan
 Borough Council [2004] 2 AC 1 58,
 74, 188, 220–2
Trotman v North Yorkshire County
 Council [1999] LGR 584 243
Turner v Sterling (1671) 2 Vent 24, 86
 ER 287 105

Vellino v Chief Constable of Greater
 Manchester Police [2002] 1 WLR
 218 22, 23, 38, 317
Voli v Inglewood Shire Council (1963)
 110 CLR 74 293

W v Essex County Council [2001] 2 AC
 592 311
Wadey v Surrey CC [2000] 1 WLR 820
 52, 394–6
The Wagon Mound (No 1) (see *Overseas*
 Tankship (UK) Ltd v Morts Dock &
 Engineering Co)
The Wagon Mound (No 2) (see *Overseas*
 Tankship (UK) Ltd v Miller
 Steamship Co Pty Ltd)
Wainwright v Home Office [2004] 2 AC
 406 8, 28, 64–5, 77, 81, 109, 317
Wandsworth LBC v Railtrack plc [2002]
 QB 756 200–1, 204
Ward v James [1966] 1 QB 273 118,
 379
Waters v Commissioner of Police of the
 Metropolis [2000] 1 WLR 1607 311
Watt v Longsdon [1930] 1 KB 130 279
Weller & Co v Foot and Mouth Disease
 Research Institute [1966] 1 QB 569
 138
Wells v Cooper [1958] 2 QB 265 122
Wells v Wells [1999] 1 AC 345 389
Wheat v E Lacon & Co Ltd [1966] AC
 552 190–1
Wheeler v JJ Saunders Ltd [1996] Ch 19
 69, 212–13

White (Frost) v Chief Constable of South Yorkshire [1999] 2 AC 455 146–8

White v Jones [1995] 2 AC 207 11, 19, 33, 40, 47, 118, 136, 257, 260–3, 292

Wilchick v Marks and Silverstone [1934] 2 KB 56 203

Wildtree Hotels Ltd v Harrow LBC [2001] 2 AC 1 58, 212, 220

Wilkinson v Downton [1897] 2 QB 57 7–8, 28, 65, 77, 289

Williams v Humphrey (1975) (unreported) February 1975 94 [Wilson v Pringle]

Wilson v National Coal Board 1981 SC (HL) 9 395

Wilson v Pringle [1987] QB 237 94

Wilsons and Clyde Coal Co Ltd v English [1938] AC 57 166–7

Withers v Perry Chain Co [1961] 1 WLR 1314 127–8

Wong Mee Wan v Kwan Kin Travel Services [1996] 1 WLR 38 229

Wong v Parkside Health NHS Trust [2003] 3 All ER 932 65

Wright v British Railways Board [1983] 2 AC 773 379, 387–8

Wringe v Cohen [1940] 1 KB 229 6, 201–2, 203, 252

X (Minors) v Bedfordshire County Council [1995] 2 AC 633 21, 29, 106, 155, 296, 299, 304, 306–7, 309, 310, 311–12

Yorkshire Electricity Board v British Telecom [1986] 1 WLR 1029 52

Youssoupoff v MGM Pictures (1934) 50 TLR 581 264

Yuen Kun-Yeu v Attorney-General of Hong Kong [1988] AC 175 106, 135

Z v United Kingdom (2001) 34 EHRR 97, [2001] 2 FLR 612 42, 68, 306–7, 310, 312

Table of Statutes

Animals Act 1971 174–8
  ss 1–6 178
  s 2 178
  s 2(1) 157, 174–5, 179
  s 2(2) 31, 34–5, 175, 179
  s 4 175
  s 5 176
  s 5(3) 175
  s 6(2)b 179
  s 8 177
  s 8(2) 175

Children Act 1989 306
Civil Aviation Act 1982
  s 76 180, 184
  s 76(2) 157
  s 77 180
Civil Evidence Act 1968
  s 11 22
Civil Liability (Contribution) Act 1978
  412, 414, 415
Coal Mines Act 1911 166
Code Civil 60, 63
  art 31 375
  art 1382 76, 134
  art 1383 76
  art 1384 157, 230–1, 252
Common Law Procedure Act 1852 2
Commons Registration Act 1965 177
Competition Act 1998 86
  s 57 278
Congenital Disabilities (Civil Liability)
  Act 1976 374–5
Consumer Protection Act 1987 40,
  114, 157, 160–2, 168
  s 1(1) 163
  s 4(1)(e) 163, 219
Contract (Rights of Third Parties) Act
  1999 160
Countryside and Rights of Way Act
  2000 189, 196
Courts and Legal Services Act 1990
  409

Crime and Disorder Act 1998
  s 1 22
Criminal Injuries Compensation Act
  1995 22, 411
Criminal Justice Act 2003 417

Damages Act 1996 34
  s 1 390
  s 2 388
Damages (Scotland) Act 1976 160
Data Protection Act 1998 64
Defamation Act 1952 81, 102, 276
  s 7 281
  s 16 264
Defamation Act 1996 278
  s 1 273, 274
  s 2 285, 285–6
  s 3 286
  s 4 286
  s 14(1) 278
  s 15 281
Defective Premises Act 1972 188,
  203–4

Employers' Liability (Compulsory
  Insurance) Act 1969 51
Employers' Liability (Defective
  Equipment) Act 1969 157, 168
Environmental Protection Act 1990
  s 79 70
European Communities Act 1972 40
  s 2(1) 41
European Convention for the
  Protection of Human Rights
  42, 216
  art 3 307
  art 5 83
  art 5(4) 411
  art 6 307
  art 8 28, 29, 66, 183–4, 314, 410
  art 10 282
  art 13 183–4, 307

European Group on Tort Law
  art 1:101 8
  art 2:102 70
  art 3:101 325
  art 3:102 325
  art 3:103 326
  art 3:104 326, 346
  art 3:105 326
  art 3:106 326
  art 3:201 326
  art 4:102 119, 226
  art 4:103 225, 227
  art 5:101 222
  art 6:102 226
  art 8:107 229
  art 10:101 379, 380
  art 10:102 379
  art 10:201 389
  art 10:202 387
  art 10:301 387

Factories Act 1961 165
Factory and Workshop Act 1878 164
Fatal Accidents Act 1846 142
Fatal Accidents Act 1976 34, 160, 340
  s 1(1) 150, 372
  s 1(2) 372
  s 1(3) 372
  s 1(4) 372
  s 1(6) 372
  s 1A 150, 371, 373, 388
  s 3 400–1
  s 4 401
Financial Services and Markets Act
    2000 323
Fires Prevention (Metropolis) Act 1774
  s 86 223

Health and Safety at Work Act 1974
  s 47(2) 165
Human Rights Act 1998 28, 29, 44,
    60, 68, 108–9, 182
  s 2(1) 40
  s 3 36
  s 6 215
  s 6(1) 42, 108
  ss 6–8 301
  s 7 109
  s 8 410
  s 8(1) 42
  s 12 282

Inquiries Act 2005
  s 37 278

Judicature Act 1873 4

Latent Damage Act 1986 17
Law Reform (Contributory Negligence)
    Act 1945 364–5
Law Reform (Married Women and
    Tortfeasors) Act 1935 413
Law Reform (Miscellaneous Provisions)
    Act 1934 340, 371
Law Reform (Personal Injuries) Act
    1948
  s 2(1) 394–5
Libel Amendment Act 1888 281
Limitation Act 1980 40
  s 2 41
  s 11 77
Local Government Act 2000
  s 74 278

Mental Health Act 1983 323
Mineral Workings (Off-Shore
    Installations) Act 1971 51
Mines and Quarries Act 1954 165
Misrepresentation Act 1967
  s 2 290
Motor Cars (Use and Construction)
    Order 1904 171
Motor Insurer's Bureau agreement
    1946 50

National Parks and Access to the
    Countryside Act 1949 189
Negligence (Psychiatric Illness) Bill
    (Law Com No 249), cl l(3)(b) 145
Noise Act 1996
  s 10(2) 22
Nuclear Installations Act 1965 224

Occupiers' Liability Act 1957 188–9,
    190, 314
  s 1(2) 195, 197
  s 2(3)b 192–3
Occupiers' Liability Act 1984 195–6,
    197
  s 1(3) 198
Offences against the Person Act 1861
    416
Offices, Shops and Railway Premises
    Act 1963 165

Police Act 1996 231
Police and Criminal Evidence Act 1984
    67, 99, 416

Proceeds of Crime Act 2002 21, 52
Protection from Harassment Act 1997
    22, 64, 65, 255
    c. 40 100
    s 7 293

Rehabilitation of Offenders Act 1974
    276
Road Traffic Act 1988 299, 300

Sale of Goods Act 1979
    s 14 19, 159
    s 16 60
Social Security Act 1975 395
Social Security Act 1989 395
Social Security (Recovery of Benefits)
    Act 1997 34, 395–6

Supply of Goods and Services Act 1982
    s 13 19, 115
Supreme Court Act 1981 375

Terrorism Act 2000 99
Theatres Act 1968
    s 4 264
Torts (Interference with Goods) Act
    1977 63
Trade Union and Labour Relations
    (Consolidation) Act 1992 91

Unfair Contract Terms Act 1977 188
UNIDROIT
    art 5.4 19

Chapter 1

Definition and Scope
of the Law of Tort

The purpose of this first chapter is to look at attempts to define the law of tort (or torts) in the common law world. This is an exercise that does not prove easy, partly because it can be approached from a variety of perspectives each of which tends to result in a rather different definition. There is also a danger here for those keen to draw comparisons with the legal systems of the UK's continental EU partners. Although the law of torts can be seen as roughly equivalent to delictual or civil liability, such comparison can mask as much as it can reveal since differences of structure, mentality and methodology profoundly affect the perception, role and context of tort *vis-à-vis* non-contractual liability in the European codes.

1.1 Historical considerations

The first perspective from which tort can be approached and defined is that of history. In the civil law world the history of the fundamental legal categories is tied up with the history of Roman law; the forms of legal thinking had been determined and defined by the great classical jurists and these categories were transported to the modern world in Justinian's *Institutes*. Liability was *ex contractu, quasi ex contractu, ex delicto* or *quasi ex delicto*. In the common law there was no such blueprint. Both the system of courts and the system of liability developed in a haphazard fashion according to the empirical needs of the time. The result was a structural foundation – in effect a list or personal actions – very different from that of Roman law.

1.1.1 Forms of action

The historical basis of liability in the common law is to be found in a series of writs which were in effect a list of categories of personal action into which one had to fit one's claim. These writs were not 'based on substantive legal categories or any legal plan'; and if 'there was a plan behind it all, it was merely to create an adequate royal remedy for a number of very common wrongs, which upset society and with which the existing courts dealt in too slow, cumbersome and incalculable a way' (RC van Caenegem, History of European Civil Procedure, IECL, vol XVI, Ch 2, n° 22). Very simply, the English 'law of obligations' (a Roman category now in vogue in English law) was not divided up into contract and tort, but into trespass, debt, detinue, trover, nuisance and so on. A useful overview is to be found in the extract from one of Lord Goff's judgments.

Henderson v Merrett Syndicates Ltd [1995] 2 AC 145, HL

(For facts see p 17)

Lord Goff: ... The situation in common law countries, including of course England, is exceptional, in that the common law grew up within a procedural framework uninfluenced by Roman law. The law was categorised by reference to the forms of action, and it was not until the abolition of the forms of action by the Common Law Procedure Act 1852 (15 & 16 Vict c 76) that it became necessary to reclassify the law in substantive terms. The result was that common lawyers did at last separate our law of obligations into contract and tort, though in so doing they relegated quasi-contractual claims to the status of an appendix to the law of contract, thereby postponing by a century or so the development of a law of restitution. Even then, there was no systematic reconsideration of the problem of concurrent claims in contract and tort. We can see the courts rather grappling with unpromising material drawn from the old cases in which liability in negligence derived largely from categories based upon the status of the defendant. In a sense, we must not be surprised; for no significant law faculties were established at our universities until the late 19th century, and so until then there was no academic opinion available to guide or stimulate the judges...

NOTE

Another reason why the idea of a law of obligations is misleading is that English law does not rigidly distinguish between real rights (in rem) and personal rights (in personam), the former being the objects of the law of property and the latter objects of the law of obligations. The action of debt, for example, was as much a proprietary claim as 'contractual' (D Ibbetson, *A Historical Introduction to the Law of Obligations* (OUP, 1999), 18). Equally many 'torts' like trover or detinue (although detinue even in the nineteenth century was being seen as more 'contractual' in nature) were not really, from a Romanist viewpoint, dealing with relations between persons. They were part of the law of property. The forms of action were abolished in 1852 (as Bramwell LJ indicates in the next extract) and this had the effect of opening up the system in as much as it became much easier for a substantive law to free itself from the procedural forms which had dominated legal thinking in the common law.

Bryant v Herbert (1877) 3 CPD 389, CA

Bramwell LJ: ... [The Common Law Procedure Acts 1852-1860] did not abolish forms of action in words. The Common Law Commissioners recommended that: but it was supposed that, if adopted, the law would be shaken to its foundations; so that all that could be done was to provide as far as possible that, though forms of actions remained, there never should be a question what was the form. This was accomplished save as to this very question of costs in actions within the county court jurisdiction. Until the passing of the statute [County Courts Act] we are discussing, it was necessary to see if an action was *assumpsit*, case &c. But the Common Law Procedure Act having passed, and the forms of actions being practically abolished, the legislature pass this Act dropping the words '*assumpsit*, case', &c., and using the words 'founded on contract', 'founded on tort'. This shows to me that the substance of the matter was to be looked at. One may observe there is no middle term; the statute supposes all actions are founded either on contract or on tort. So that it is tort, if not contract, contract if not tort...

NOTE

Lawyers throughout Europe distinguish today between jurisdiction, procedure and substantive rights. What one has to remember with regard to the forms of action is that they did not make these distinctions; each form defined whether or not a common law court had jurisdiction, the procedure that attached to a claim and the 'right' in issue.

1.1.2 Causes of action

The effect of the abolition of the forms of action was not to dispense with centuries of legal thinking overnight. The old forms of personal action at common law became causes of action; that is to say they moved from being procedural structures that obliquely defined substantive ideas to become a list of substantive ideas underpinning liability. Thus, while debt and *assumpsit* got swallowed up by a general theory of contract (although not completely), trespass, nuisance, trover (conversion), detinue and the like became 'torts'. They became little more than 'wrongs' that could not be accommodated by the category of contract. Tort, in other words, is not in its origin some rationally conceived category of liability; it is, or was, simply a category into which claims which could not be classified elsewhere were housed (or dumped). As the next case indicates, history is still in the making.

Letang v Cooper [1965] 1 QB 232, CA

Mrs Letang brought an action for damages against Mr Cooper after she had been run over by the latter while sunbathing in a hotel car park. However, as the action was brought more than three years after the accident, there was a problem with respect to the limitation period. Statute states that 'in the case of actions for damages for negligence, nuisance or breach of duty', where the damage consists of 'personal injuries', the limitation period is three years (instead of six with respect to other kinds of damage). Mrs Letang tried to get around this limitation bar by pleading the case in trespass to the person, claiming that the statute did not apply to trespass. This argument was rejected by the Court of Appeal (Lord Denning MR, Danckwerts LJ and Diplock LJ).

Lord Denning MR: ... The truth is that the distinction between trespass and case is obsolete. We have a different sub-division altogether. Instead of dividing actions for personal injuries into trespass (direct damage) or case (consequential damage), we divide the causes of action now according as the defendant did the injury intentionally or unintentionally. If one man intentionally applies force directly to another, the plaintiff has a cause of action in assault and battery, or, if you so please to describe it, in trespass to the person. 'The least touching of another in anger is a battery,' per Holt CJ in *Cole v Turner*. If he does not inflict injury intentionally, but only unintentionally, the plaintiff has no cause of action today in trespass. His only cause of action is in negligence, and then only on proof of want of reasonable care. If the plaintiff cannot prove want of reasonable care, he may have no cause of action at all. Thus, it is not enough nowadays for the plaintiff to plead that 'the defendant shot the plaintiff.' He must also allege that he did it intentionally or negligently. If intentional, it is the tort of assault and battery. If negligent and causing damage, it is the tort of negligence.

The modern law on this subject was well expounded by Diplock LJ in *Fowler v Lanning* with which I fully agree. But I would go this one step further: when the injury is not

▶

inflicted intentionally, but negligently, I would say that the only cause of action is negligence and not trespass. If it were trespass, it would be actionable without proof of damage; and that is not the law today.

In my judgment, therefore, the only cause of action in the present case, where the injury was unintentional, is negligence and is barred by reason of the express provision of the statute...

Diplock LJ: ... A cause of action is simply a factual situation the existence of which entitles one person to obtain from the court a remedy against another person. Historically, the means by which the remedy was obtained varied with the nature of the factual situation and causes of action were divided into categories according to the 'form of action' by which the remedy was obtained in the particular kind of factual situation which constituted the cause of action. But that is legal history, not current law ... The Judicature Act, 1873 abolished forms of action. It did not affect causes of action; so it was convenient for lawyers and legislators to continue to use, to describe the various categories of factual situations which entitle one person to obtain from the court a remedy against another, the names of the various 'forms of action' by which formerly the remedy appropriate to the particular category of factual situation was obtained. But it is essential to realise that when, since 1873, the name of a form of action is used to identify a cause of action, it is used as a convenient and succinct description of a particular category of factual situation which entitles one person to obtain from the court a remedy against another person. To forget this will indeed encourage the old forms of action to rule us from their graves...

NOTE

As a category tort 'provided few answers to the substantive questions that might have been asked' (Ibbetson, above, at 57) and this is still true today. 'Tort' (unlike contract) is not itself the basis of a cause of action; it is only a generic category containing a list of specified causes of action and before liability in tort can be established a plaintiff must base his claim on one of these causes, as the next case illustrates.

Esso Petroleum Co Ltd v Southport Corporation [1953] 3 WLR 773, QBD, [1954] 2 QB 182, CA, [1956] AC 218, HL

Southport Corporation brought an action for damages against an oil company in respect of a tanker that had run aground and whose cargo of oil, when deliberately released from the stricken ship by the captain in order to avoid endangering his crew, had polluted the Corporation's beaches. The Corporation pleaded the following causes of action: (i) trespass; (ii) private nuisance; (iii) public nuisance; and (iv) negligence of the captain (for which the employer would be vicariously liable). Devlin J at first instance held that the oil company was not liable since the captain had not acted negligently. This decision was reversed in the Court of Appeal. The oil company then appealed to the House of Lords (Earl Jowitt, Lords Normand, Morton, Radcliffe and Tucker), but in turn the Corporation tried to add a further cause of action to the list, namely that the oil company were in breach of a direct duty to the plaintiff in putting to sea an unseaworthy ship. The Corporation were not allowed to add this new cause of action and the oil company was held not to be liable.

Denning LJ (Court of Appeal): This is one of those cases, rare nowadays, where much depends on ascertaining the proper cause of action, particularly with regard to the burden of proof... The judge seems to have thought that it did not matter much what was the proper cause of action; it all came back in the end to the universal tort of negligence... I do not share this view,...

(1) *Trespass to land* ... I am clearly of opinion that the Southport Corporation cannot here sue in trespass. This discharge of oil was not done directly on to their foreshore, but outside in the estuary. It was carried by the tide on to their land, but that was only consequential, not direct. Trespass, therefore, does not lie.

(2) *Private nuisance*. In order to support an action on the case for a private nuisance the defendant must have used his own land or some other land in such a way as injuriously to affect the enjoyment of the plaintiffs' land. 'The ground of responsibility', said Lord Wright in *Sedleigh-Denfield v O'Callaghan*, 'is the possession and control of the land from which the nuisance proceeds'. Applying this principle, it is clear that the discharge of oil was not a private nuisance, because it did not involve the use by the defendants of any land, but only of a ship at sea.

(3) *Public nuisance*. The term 'public nuisance' covers a multitude of sins, great and small ... Suffice it to say that the discharge of a noxious substance in such a way as to be likely to affect the comfort and safety of Her Majesty's subjects generally is a public nuisance...

Applying the old cases to modern instances, it is, in my opinion, a public nuisance to discharge oil into the sea in such circumstances that it is likely to be carried on to the shores and beaches of our land to the prejudice and discomfort of Her Majesty's subjects. It is an offence punishable by the common law. Furthermore, if any person should suffer greater damage or inconvenience from the oil than the generality of the public, he can have an action to recover damages on that account, provided, of course, that he can discover the offender who discharged the oil. This action would have been described in the old days as an action on the case, but it is now simply an action for a nuisance...

(4) *Burden of proof*. One of the principal differences between an action for a public nuisance and an action for negligence is the burden of proof. In an action for a public nuisance, once the nuisance is proved and the defendant is shown to have caused it, then the legal burden is shifted on to the defendant to justify or excuse himself. If he fails to do so, he is held liable, whereas in an action for negligence the legal burden in most cases remains throughout on the plaintiff. In negligence, the plaintiff may gain much help from provisional presumptions like the doctrine of *res ipsa loquitur*, but, nevertheless, at the end of the case the judge must ask himself whether the legal burden is discharged. If the matter is left evenly in the balance, the plaintiff fails. But in public nuisance, as in trespass, the legal burden shifts to the defendant, and it is not sufficient for him to leave the matter in doubt. He must plead and prove a sufficient justification or excuse.

(5) *Justification or excuse*. The defendants seek to justify themselves by saying that it was necessary for them to discharge the oil because their ship was in danger. She had been driven by rough seas on to the revetment wall, and it was necessary to discharge the oil in order to get her off. If she had not done so, lives might have been lost. This is, no doubt, true at that stage in the story, but the question is, how came she to get upon

▶

the wall? If it was her own fault, then her justification fails, because no one can avail himself of a necessity produced by his own default. Where does the legal burden rest in this respect? Must the Southport Corporation prove that the ship was at fault in getting on to the wall, or must the ship prove that she herself was not at fault? In my opinion the burden is on the ship. She does not justify herself in law by necessity alone, but only by unavoidable necessity, and the burden is on her to show it was unavoidable.

Public nuisance is, in this respect, like unto a trespass, as to which it was said by the Court of King's Bench as long ago as 1616 in *Weaver v Ward*, that no man shall be excused 'except it may be judged utterly without his fault' ...

Those were, it is true, cases in trespass; but the same principle applies to cases of public nuisance. That is shown by *Tarry v Ashton*, where a lamp which projected over the Strand fell on to a passer-by. This was described by Lord Wright as private action for a public nuisance: see *Sedleigh-Denfield v O'Callaghan*. Another example is *Wringe v Cohen*, where the gable of a house next the highway was blown down in a storm (which was treated by this court as a public nuisance). In both cases the defendant was held liable because his premises were in a defective state. He did not know of the defect, and he was not negligent in not knowing, but, nevertheless, he was liable because he did not prove any sufficient justification or excuse. He did not prove inevitable accident...

Earl Jowitt (House of Lords): ... In the present case every allegation of negligence has been answered by the finding of the judge, and there was no allegation of unseaworthiness. That being so, I do not think that the present appellants, the owners of the *Inverpool*, can be held responsible because they did not negative some possible case which had never been alleged against them in the pleadings or made against them in the course of the trial...

Lord Radcliffe (House of Lords): My Lords, I think that this case ought to be decided in accordance with the pleadings. If it is, I am of opinion, as was the trial judge, that the respondents failed to establish any claim to relief that was valid in law. If it is not, we might do better justice to the respondents – I cannot tell, since the evidence is incomplete – but I am certain that we should do worse justice to the appellants, since in my view they were entitled to conduct the case and confine their evidence in reliance upon the further and better particulars of the statement of claim which had been delivered by the respondents. It seems to me that it is the purpose of such particulars that they should help to define the issues and to indicate to the party who asks for them how much of the range of his possible evidence will be relevant and how much irrelevant to those issues. Proper use of them shortens the hearing and reduces costs. But if an appellate court is to treat reliance upon them as pedantry or mere formalism, I do not see what part they have to play in our trial system...

NOTES

1. Although Denning LJ's judgment was overturned in the House of Lords it remains very valuable from a methodological point of view. Liability in tort is a matter of going through the various heads of liability and applying each one to the facts in order to see if there is a 'fit'. If one does fit the facts, the defendant is liable; if not, then there is no liability in tort. According to this approach, tort consists of distinct causes of action with the result that one takes an alphabetical approach to liability (B Rudden, 'Torticles' (1991-92) 6/7 Tulane Civil Law Forum 105).

2. Note also how the law of procedure was instrumental in preventing the Corporation from succeeding in its tort claim. Had it been allowed to add the fifth cause of action, the oil company might well have been liable on the basis that they were in breach of a direct duty owed to the claimant not to put to sea an unseaworthy ship. This is where Denning LJ's approach was most perceptive: he effectively achieved the same result through his interpretation of the tort of public nuisance.

3. Damage arising from oil contamination at sea is now covered by statute and, to an extent, by a voluntary scheme: see Cane, *Tort Law and Economic Interests* (2nd edn, OUP, 1996), 433–5.

QUESTIONS

1. Read the case of *Benjamin v Storr* (1874). Could this case have been of help to the Corporation? Should the Corporation's lawyers have impressed it on the House of Lords in their arguments? Can you draft such an argument using the case?

2. Procedure was reformed in 1998 (see Civil Procedure Rules 1998). Would these new rules now allow a new cause of action to be added at an appeal stage?

1.1.3 General principles of liability

The abolition of the forms of action opened up the common law to the development of forms of liability based upon general principles and this is a process that is still continuing. At the end of the nineteenth century a general principle of liability was established in respect of physical harm intentionally caused (*Wilkinson*) and this was extended to negligently caused physical harm during the early part of the twentieth century (*Donoghue*). One can, now, more or less say that any *physical* damage (personal injury and actual damage to property) intentionally or negligently caused will give rise to tortious liability (*Letang*).

Wilkinson v Downton [1897] 2 QB 57, QBD

Wright J: In this case the defendant, in the execution of what he seems to have regarded as a practical joke, represented to the plaintiff that he was charged by her husband with a message to her to the effect that her husband was smashed up in an accident, and was lying at The Elms at Leytonstone with both legs broken, and that she was to go at once in a cab with two pillows to fetch him home. All this was false. The effect of the statement on the plaintiff was a violent shock to her nervous system, producing vomiting and other more serious and permanent physical consequences at one time threatening her reason, and entailing weeks of suffering and incapacity to her as well as expense to her husband for medical attendance. These consequences were not in any way the result of previous illhealth or weakness of constitution; nor was there any evidence of predisposition to nervous shock or any other idiosyncrasy...

...The defendant has, as I assume for the moment, wilfully done an act calculated to cause physical harm to the plaintiff – that is to say, to infringe her legal right to personal safety, and has in fact thereby caused physical harm to her. That proposition without more appears to me to state a good cause of action, there being no justification alleged for the act. This wilful injuria is in law malicious, although no malicious purpose to cause the harm which was caused nor any motive of spite is imputed to the defendant...

QUESTION

Is this a trespass or a negligence case? (Cf *Wainwright v Home Office* (2004) at § 47.)

NOTE

The development of general principles continued during the twentieth century as the next extracts indicate.

Donoghue v Stevenson [1932] AC 562, HL (Scotland)

(See p 112)

Lord Goff, 'The Search for Principle'
Maccabaean Lecture in Jurisprudence, 1983

...[P]erhaps ... one of Lord Denning's principal contributions will be perceived to have been his loosening of the reins of a doctrine of precedent which had become too strict. When I was a student, there appeared to exist some judges who saw the law almost as a deductive science, a matter of finding the relevant authorities and applying them to the facts of the particular case. This is no longer so; and there is now a readiness among judges, not of course to disregard or ignore precedents by which they are bound, but, where they are at liberty to do so, to adopt or qualify them – not simply to achieve a personally desired result, but to ensure that principles are so stated as to embrace the legally just result on facts possibly not foreseen by those who had previously formulated them...

NOTE

It would be a mistake to think that the old categories of liability have disappeared, even if the onward march of negligence, with its empirical notion of reasonable behaviour, is infecting the law of tort as a whole (T Weir, 'The Staggering March of Negligence', in P Cane and J Stapleton (eds), *The Law of Obligations: Essays in Celebration of John Fleming* (OUP, 1998), 97–138). Trespass, nuisance, defamation, conversion, the rule in *Rylands v Fletcher* and so on remain distinct causes of action with the result that one can still take an alphabetical approach to the law of torts (see Rudden, above). What is important, however, about this movement towards general principle is that it poses a question about whether common lawyers should be talking about a law of 'torts' or a law of 'tort'.

European Group on Tort Law *Principles of European Tort Law* (2003)

Article 1:101. Basic norm

(1) A person to whom damage to another is legally attributable is liable to compensate that damage.

(2) Damage may be attributed in particular to the person
    (a) whose behaviour constituting fault has caused it; or
    (b) whose abnormally dangerous activity has caused it; or
    (c) whose auxiliary has caused it within the scope of his functions.

QUESTION

Read the case of *Bradford Corporation v Pickles* (p 60). If art 1:101 became part of English tort law would *Bradford*, if it arose again, have to be decided differently?

1.2 Definitional approaches

There are, very broadly, two main approaches to defining tort and these can be expressed in two questions. What *is* the law of tort? And what does the law of tort *do*? The first question approaches the subject from what might be called a formalist viewpoint and thus invites a formalist definition (for example: 'the law of tort arises from a breach of duty...'). The second question is one that goes to the *function* of the law of tort and, accordingly, attracts functional definitions (for example: 'the law of tort is about obtaining a remedy for harm caused...'). Formalism and functionalism are not, however, absolute or alternative categories; they are schemes of approach or understanding. They are broad templates for viewing an object called 'tort'. Not only may some definitions display both formalist and functionalist tendencies, but formalism and functionalism hide a range of other analytical templates of analysis.

1.2.1 Formalist definitions

Perhaps the leading formalist definition is the one fashioned by Winfield.

Percy Winfield, *The Province of the Law of Tort* (CUP, 1932), 32, 229, 231

Tortious liability arises from the breach of a duty primarily fixed by the law: such duty is towards persons generally and its breach is redressible by an action for unliquidated damages...

The words 'primarily fixed by the law' serve to distinguish liability in tort from that arising on breach of contract, and from breach of bailment.

The statement that the duty is 'towards persons generally' marks off tort from contract, bailment, and quasi-contract...

The last requisite in the definition is that tort is remediable by 'an action for unliquidated damages'. This distinguishes it from crime and from breach of trust, though... trusts are more conveniently separated from the law of tort by the historical gulf which lies between them and the Common Law rather than by the narrow line of a particular legal remedy...

Of course, an action for damages is not the only remedy for tort. Other remedies are self help, injunctions, and actions for the specific restitution of property...

NOTE

1. Winfield's definition of tort is now seen by many as either obsolete or circular, yet it remains valuable as an example of a definition based on a structural or

systems approach. The category of 'tort' is identified in terms of its relations with other categories of law such as 'contract', 'bailment' and 'crime'. It is part of a 'system' of law. This view of law is in many ways more than just a view; a systems approach is an essential part of legal knowledge itself and has roots going back to Roman law (thus see D.44.7.4 for a Roman definition of liability for wrongs). The Romans structured their law around the three focal points of 'persons', 'things' and 'actions' and each of these three generic categories was in turn divided into sub-categories. Areas of law became part of a grand system – subsequently given expression in continental Europe by civil codes – and this system provided one means of definition.

2. Winfield's definition is also valuable because it emphasises two other important aspects of legal knowledge, namely 'duty' and 'remedy'. In fact it now seems that he was being over-optimistic in trying to reduce all of tort law to a matter of duty (*Stubbings v Webb* (1993), at 508). Yet as we have seen (*Merrett Syndicates*, below, p 17) if one replaces 'duty' by 'obligation' one captures the general normative (what one *ought* to do) dimension to civil liability. Tort law is part of the 'law of obligations'.

Peter Cane, *The Anatomy of Tort Law*
(Hart Publishing, 1997), 1

As its name implies, this book is about the structure of tort law. Its starting point is the proposition that the law of tort can be viewed as a system of ethical rules and principles of personal responsibility for conduct. This approach is in contrast to the traditional one of seeing tort law as made up of a number of discrete 'torts', that is, legal formulae which can be used to obtain remedies from courts or as bargaining counters in out-of-court negotiations. I see tort law as a collection of causes of action (or 'heads of liability') each made up of three main components: an interest protected by the law, some conduct which the law sanctions, and a remedy or sanction by which the interest is protected and the conduct is sanctioned. The structure of causes of action in tort is 'correlative'; that is, every cause of action in tort is a two-sided affair made up of elements relating to the plaintiff and elements relating to the defendant...

NOTES

1. Cane is a leading and respected contemporary commentator on tort law and although he is not attempting a formal definition as such, his 'starting point' is valuable in that it emphasises what one might call an 'actionist' and 'causal' approach to tort. It focuses on the individual in society (actor) and analyses damage in terms of a relationship between an individual who suffers damage and an actor who causes it. Of course this causal relation is often not enough in itself to establish liability and thus the harmed individual may well have to establish some ethical reason as to why the actor should be liable. From Roman law times, one central ethical reason is *fault*; an actor is liable if his culpable behaviour causes damage.

2. In fact, in English (and for example German) law, damage, fault and cause are not enough to establish liability in tort (but cf French law: CC art 1382). Something more is required as Cane indicates. The damage must also amount to the invasion of a legally protected 'interest'. Accordingly certain types of damage

such as pure economic loss or psychological harm, if caused negligently, may not give rise to liability (see eg *Spartan Steel*, below, p 137). This notion of an 'interest' is particularly useful as an analytical tool in tort law, but it is equally a very subversive word in that it appears to be purely *descriptive* (factual). That is to say, unlike 'duty' or 'right', it seemingly carries no *normative* (ought) implication. In practice it often proves to be a more subtle analytical and reasoning tool (see Chapter 11).

3. Cane also makes use of a 'structural' scheme of analysis when he relates 'heads of liability' to the claimant and to the defendant. He is attempting to define tort by its internal structure. As one will see, this proves necessary in that there are occasions when even damage, fault, cause and interest prove inadequate to explain certain cases. A further concept, either a 'right' or a 'duty', will need to be brought into the structural scheme of tort elements to explain cases like *Bradford v Pickles* (p 60) (*damnum sine injuria*: damage without any legal wrong) or those cases where proof of damage is unnecessary (eg defamation) (*injuria sine damno*: legal wrong without damage). Thus the great value of the Winfield and the Cane view is that the former provides an *external* structural definition while the latter provides an *internal* structural view. Cane sees tort liability as involving the interplay of a number of elements, notions and concepts. Persons, ethical principles, interests, rights, duties, causes of action and remedies are key elements when it comes to analysing factual problems and the student should try to identify them in every tort case (note for example the interplay of ethics or 'practical justice', interest, damage, duty and remedy in *White v Jones*, below, p 260).

1.2.2 Functional definitions

A functional approach defines a system or category of knowledge, not so much in terms of the internal structure of the system or category, but in respect of its *purpose*. Perhaps it is misleading to describe the extracts that follow below as definitional, but they do indicate how tort can be approached and understood as a category of legal knowledge through reference to its purpose. These aims and objectives are probably more important than pure formal definitions, although if one sees tort law in terms of the pursuit of 'justice', the position becomes more complex since justice can attach to the internal and (or) external mechanisms of a category of law.

**John G Fleming, *An Introduction to the Law of Torts*
(2nd ed, OUP, 1985,) 1 (footnotes omitted)**

The toll on life, limb, and property exacted by today's industrial operations, methods of transport, and many another activity benignly associated with the 'modern way of life' has reached proportions so staggering that the economic cost of accidents represents a constant and mounting drain on the community's human and material resources. The task of the law of torts is to play an important regulatory role in the adjustment of these losses and the eventual allocation of their cost...

Michael A Jones, *Textbook on Torts*
(8th edn, OUP, 2002), 1

The law of tort is primarily concerned with providing a remedy to persons who have been harmed by the conduct of others. In any society conflicts of interest are bound to lead to the infliction of losses, a process that, not surprisingly, tends to increase with the level of social interaction. The allocation, and in some instances the prevention, of these losses is the principal function of tort law...

Tony Weir, *Governmental Liability*
[1989] Public Law 40, pp 62–3

We have had several compendious theories as to the law of tort. Lynx-eyed predecessors who noticed that a tort suit often resulted in a transfer of funds from the defendant to the plaintiff inferred that it was the purpose of tort law to effect such transfers: the more transfers the better, or tort was being false to its purpose. This was especially true if the defendant could spread the loss, very thinly like jam so that no one could taste it...

An appropriate basis for discriminating between plaintiffs would be according to whether they were the victims of misfortune or of mismanagement, of bad luck or of bad behaviour, that is, whether they have just a pain or a grievance as well, whether we can say of them that, the world being what it is, they should not have been hurt... The purpose of fault would be to determine not who must pay but who may claim, to distinguish between plaintiffs rather than between defendants. And we would also distinguish according to the nature of the harm in issue, and make the law reflect society's proper value-judgments by letting people recover more easily in respect of personal injury than financial harm, and for property damage only if it also represented financial loss to them

NOTE

The purpose and policy of the law of torts will be pursued in a separate chapter (**Chapter 2**). Suffice it to stress here, once again, that a too rigid separation between definition and function can be both helpful and misleading. Schemes of analysis can focus on individual things (eg acts of individuals) or on holistic elements (activities like driving or manufacturing). If one says that the law of tort is concerned only with acts, it is likely that key elements of liability will be behaviour, duty, right, responsibility and the like. But if tort were to focus on activities – for example driving and industry (see Fleming, above) – it could well be that a rather different set of liability elements will come into play such as risk, costs and loss-spreading. Justice, as we shall see, can attach to act or activity and that is why there can be definitional and functional tension even at the moral level. There is no right answer, just different schemes of analysis and different types of justice.

1.2.3 Definitional scepticism

The sceptical approach to defining tort has one great strength: it reflects the historical construction of the subject that, as we have seen, is a matter of different forms of action. These forms of action, before the nineteenth century, were not categorised under the labels of 'contract' and 'tort'. This classification did not happen until the abolition of the forms of action in 1852 (see *Bryant v Herbert*, above, p 2). Perhaps the dialectical scheme is the appropriate one here in as much as tort is the result of the development of a general theory of 'contract'; any 'form' (later 'cause') of action that could not be categorised under 'contract' usually had to be put into the open-ended category of 'tort'. If it is not contract it must be tort. And this is why the next writer is able to describe tort as a 'ragbag'.

Tony Weir, *Tort Law*
(OUP, 2002), ix (Preface)

... The Dean of an American Law School once asked me over lunch 'And what is your normative theory of tort?' It was rather a poor lunch and, as I thought, a very stupid question. Tort is what is in the tort books, and the only thing holding it together is the binding. In contract matters the courts may be predominantly a debt-collecting agency (it can now be done on the Internet), but, in tort they function as a complaints department – though the claimant, unlike the customer, is not always right. The complaints are of such different kinds that very different reactions may be appropriate, and though there are horses for courses, the tort course sports quite a lot of horses, and they are of very different breeds and speeds. In any case before producing a 'normative theory' or even discussing the purpose of 'tort', it is surely desirable to become familiar with what that ragbag actually contains: otherwise we shall be like adolescents spending all night discussing the meaning of life before, perhaps instead of, experiencing it...

NOTE

Some writers adopt a more political orientation.

Joanne Conaghan and Wade Mansell, *The Wrongs of Tort*
(2nd edn, Pluto Press,1999), 3

Conventional texts such as *Winfield & Jolowicz on Tort* proceed on the basis that tort law consists of a basically uncontentious and apolitical body of principles. This encourages a view of tort law as 'largely common sense' and often corresponds closely with many students' perception of what is just and fair. This tendency to take the common sense of tort for granted impedes the development of a reflective and critical approach to the subject. Tort law appears apolitical because it is experienced as largely uncontentious and because it is uncontentious we do not tend to question its politics. But the politics are there. It is vital to understand that tort, its texts and its syllabuses, are inherently political and this is no less true because the politics are hidden. The foundation of tort law reflects a particular ideological and philosophical perspective (essentially captured by the principle of individual rather than societal responsibility for the misfortune of others) which is, in our view, highly contentious...

NOTE

Perhaps an example of this kind of 'apolitical' thinking is to be found in the next extract.

Read v J Lyons & Co [1947] AC 156, HL

(For facts see p 185)

Lord Simonds: ... Here is an age-long conflict of theories which is to be found in every system of law. 'A man acts at his peril', says one theory. 'A man is not liable unless he is to blame', answers the other. It will not surprise the students of English law or of anything English to find that between these theories a middle way, a compromise, has been found... There is not one principle only which is to be applied with rigid logic to all cases. To this result both the infinite complexity of human affairs and the historical development of the forms of action contribute... Yet I would venture to say that the law is that, subject to certain specific exceptions which I will indicate, a man is not in the absence of negligence liable in respect of things, whether they are called dangerous or not, which he has brought or collected or manufactured upon his premises, unless such things escape from his premises...

QUESTION

In the Court of Appeal Scott LJ stated that 'our law of torts is concerned not with activities but with acts' ((1945) at p 228). Is this an ideological statement? Having digested the cases in this and the following chapters, consider how our law of tort might be different if its concern had been with activities rather than acts.

1.3 Liability and remedies

It is easy to think that in any one situation there is just one rule (or set of rules) that will apply to the facts. But legal knowledge is more complex because rules attach to particular institutions which, as the Roman lawyers observed, were threefold. Rules could attach to *persons*, to *things* or to *actions* (remedies) and it is this plurality of possibilities that Lord Denning exploits in the next case.

Miller v Jackson [1977] QB 966, CA

This was an appeal by a cricket club against the granting of an injunction by a High Court judge ordering the club not to play cricket on a piece of land adjacent to the claimants' house. The claimants had sought the injunction because at weekends, when cricket was played, cricket balls sometimes landed in their garden; the fear of injury from the balls resulted in the claimants being unable to use their garden on days when there were matches. A majority of the Court of Appeal (Lord Denning MR and Cumming-Bruce LJ; Geoffrey Lane LJ dissenting) allowed the appeal.

Lord Denning MR: ... The case here was not pleaded by either side in the formulae of the 19th century. The plaintiffs did not allege trespass... The case was pleaded in negligence or alternatively nuisance...

The tort of nuisance in many cases overlaps the tort of negligence... But there is at any rate one important distinction between them. It lies in the nature of the remedy sought. Is it damages? Or an injunction? If the plaintiff seeks a remedy in damages for injury done to him or his property, he can lay his claim either in *negligence* or in *nuisance*. But, if he seeks an injunction to stop the playing of cricket altogether, I think he must make his claim in nuisance. The books are full of cases where an injunction has been granted to restrain the continuance of a nuisance. But there is no case, so far as I know, where it has been granted so as to stop a man being negligent. At any rate in a case of this kind, where an occupier of a house or land seeks to restrain his neighbour from doing something on his own land, the only appropriate cause of action, on which to base the remedy of an injunction, is nuisance... He must have been guilty of the fault, not necessarily of negligence, but of the unreasonable use of land...

I would, therefore, adopt this test: is the use by the cricket club of this ground for playing cricket a reasonable use of it? To my mind it is a most reasonable use...

On taking the balance, I would give priority to the right of the cricket club to continue playing cricket on the ground, as they have done for the last 70 years. It takes precedence over the right of the newcomer to sit in his garden undisturbed. After all he bought the house four years ago in mid-summer when the cricket season was at its height. He might have guessed that there was a risk that a hit for six might possibly land on his property. If he finds that he does not like it, he ought, when cricket is played, to sit in the other side of the house or in the front garden, or go out; or take advantage of the offers the club have made to him of fitting unbreakable glass, and so forth. Or, if he does not like that, he ought to sell his house and move elsewhere. I expect there are many who would gladly buy it in order to be near the cricket field and open space. At any rate he ought not to be allowed to stop cricket being played on this ground.

This case is new. It should be approached on principles applicable to modern conditions. There is a contest here between the interest of the public at large and the interest of a private individual. The *public* interest lies in protecting the environment by preserving our playing fields in the face of mounting development, and by enabling our youth to enjoy all the benefits of outdoor games, such as cricket and football. The *private* interest lies in securing the privacy of his home and garden without intrusion or interference by anyone. In deciding between these two conflicting interests, it must be remembered that it is not a question of damages. If by a million-to-one chance a cricket ball does go out of the ground and cause damage, the cricket club will pay. There is no difficulty on that score. No, it is a question of an injunction. And in our law you will find it repeatedly affirmed that an injunction is a discretionary remedy. In a new situation like this, we have to think afresh as to how discretion should be exercised... As between their conflicting interests, I am of opinion that the public interest should prevail over the private interest ... In my opinion the right exercise of discretion is to refuse an injunction; and, of course, to refuse damages in lieu of an injunction. Likewise as to the claim for past damages. The club were entitled to use this ground for cricket in the accustomed way. It was not a nuisance, nor was it negligence... So if the club had put it to the test, I would have dismissed the claim for damages also. But as the club very fairly say that they are willing to pay for any damage, I am content that there should be an award of £400 to cover any past or future damage...

NOTE

The tort of nuisance, as we shall see (**Chapter 6**), attaches to a thing (land) and this land rule favoured the claimants (although Lord Denning, unlike the other two judges, thought that it did not). However the two majority judges out-flanked this rule by putting the accent on the rule that attached to the *remedy*, namely the injunction (cf **Chapter 11**). This discretion rule allowed Lord Denning to bring into the analysis the notion of a 'public interest' which he can play off against the 'private interest'. This is a classic piece of legal reasoning, even if, in the end, it is wrong (since the tort of private nuisance by definition tends to put the private interest before the public: *Kennaway v Thompson* (1981)). In addition it shows how important the remedy can be in the establishment of liability (cf **Chapter 11**). In any contract and tort case the reader should always ask: what remedy is the claimant seeking?

QUESTION

If one of the claimants had been hit on the head by a cricket ball could he or she have sued the club for damages? (Read Lord Denning's judgment in full in the law reports.)

1.4 Province and scope of tort

A structural or systems approach to tort sees this category as being defined by its relationship with other legal categories. Winfield talked in terms of the province of the law of tort: 'no clear-cut exclusive definition of tort is possible until the complementary task of settling the limits of other fields of the law has been accomplished' (*The Province of the Law of Tort* (CUP, 1931), 6). These relations are particularly difficult in the common law tradition because no category of law is either clearly defined as a matter of internal theory or properly systematised one with another as a matter of legal (that is say Romanist) legal science. In fact, in no European legal system, can tort or its equivalent be considered these days in isolation of contract, crime, property and public law. There is another reason for examining tort in relation to contract, crime, property and public law. These areas now impact on the law of tort – or one should say impact upon sets of facts categorised as primarily falling within tort – in such a way that they cannot be ignored as a matter of tort law itself.

1.4.1 Tort and contract

Given the central role of the remedy of damages in tort law, one ought perhaps to start with the subject's relationship with the other great area where damages are important, the law of contract (although perhaps one should bear in mind that statistically most actions in contract are in debt). Indeed tort liability was once defined in terms of its not being contractual (*Bryant v Herbert*, p 2).

Henderson v Merrett Syndicates Ltd [1995] 2 AC 145, HL

This was an action for damages brought by underwriting members at Lloyds' (known as 'names') against underwriting agents. The former claimed that the latter had been negligent in the handling of their affairs. Some of the names had specific contractual relationships with the defendants while others did not; and the question arose, on a preliminary issue, as to whether a duty of care was owed in tort by all the defendants, even where there was a specific contractual regime in place. The question was important because of the more liberal limitation period in tort. The lower courts held that concurrent contract and tort duties were owed and an appeal to the House of Lords (Lords Keith, Goff, Browne-Wilkinson, Mustill and Nolan) was dismissed.

Lord Goff: ... All systems of law which recognise a law of contract and a law of tort (or delict) have to solve the problem of the possibility of concurrent claims arising from breach of duty under the two rubrics of the law. Although there are variants, broadly speaking two possible solutions present themselves: either to insist that the claimant should pursue his remedy in contract alone, or to allow him to choose which remedy he prefers... France has adopted the former solution in its doctrine of non cumul, under which the concurrence of claims in contract and tort is outlawed (see Tony Weir in XI Int.Encycl.Comp.L., ch. 12, paras. 47-72, at paragraph 52). The reasons given for this conclusion are (1) respect for the will of the legislator, and (2) respect for the will of the parties to the contract (see paragraph 53). The former does not concern us; but the latter is of vital importance. It is however open to various interpretations. For such a policy does not necessarily require the total rejection of concurrence, but only so far as a concurrent remedy in tort is inconsistent with the terms of the contract. It comes therefore as no surprise to learn that the French doctrine is not followed in all civil law jurisdictions, and that concurrent remedies in tort and contract are permitted in other civil law countries, notably Germany (see paragraph 58). I only pause to observe that it appears to be accepted that no perceptible harm has come to the German system from admitting concurrent claims...

I think it is desirable to stress at this stage that the question of concurrent liability is by no means only of academic significance. Practical issues, which can be of great importance to the parties, are at stake. Foremost among these is perhaps the question of limitation of actions. If concurrent liability in tort is not recognised, a claimant may find his claim barred at a time when he is unaware of its existence. This must moreover be a real possibility in the case of claims against professional men, such as solicitors or architects, since the consequences of their negligence may well not come to light until long after the lapse of six years from the date when the relevant breach of contract occurred. Moreover the benefits of the Latent Damage Act 1986, under which the time of the accrual of the cause of action may be postponed until after the plaintiff has the relevant knowledge, are limited to actions in tortious negligence. This leads to the startling possibility that a client who has had the benefit of gratuitous advice from his solicitor may in this respect be better off than a client who has paid a fee. Other practical problems arise, for example, from the absence of a right to contribution between negligent contract-breakers; from the rules as to remoteness of damage, which are less restricted in tort than they are in contract; and from the availability of the opportunity to obtain leave to serve proceedings out of the jurisdiction. It can of course be argued that the principle established in respect of concurrent liability in contract and tort should not be tailored to

▶

mitigate the adventitious effects of rules of law such as these, and that one way of solving such problems would no doubt be to rephrase such incidental rules as have to remain in terms of the nature of the harm suffered rather than the nature of the liability asserted (see Tony Weir, XI Int Encycl Comp L ch.12, para 72). But this is perhaps crying for the moon; and with the law in its present form, practical considerations of this kind cannot sensibly be ignored.

Moreover I myself perceive at work in these decisions not only the influence of the dead hand of history, but also what I have elsewhere called the temptation of elegance. Mr Tony Weir (XI Int Encycl Comp L ch.12, para 55) has extolled the French solution for its elegance; and we can discern the same impulse behind the much-quoted observation of Lord Scarman when delivering the judgment of the Judicial Committee of the Privy Council in *Tai Hing Cotton Mill Ltd v Liu Chong Hing Bank Ltd* [1986] AC 80, 107...

It is however my understanding that by the law in this country contracts for services do contain an implied promise to exercise reasonable care (and skill) in the performance of the relevant services; indeed, as Mr Tony Weir has pointed out (XI Int Encycl Comp L. ch. 12, para 67), in the 19th century the field of concurrent liabilities was expanded 'since it was impossible for the judges to deny that contracts contained an implied promise to take reasonable care, at the least, not to injure the other party.' My own belief is that, in the present context, the common law is not antipathetic to concurrent liability, and that there is no sound basis for a rule which automatically restricts the claimant to either a tortious or a contractual remedy. The result may be untidy; but, given that the tortious duty is imposed by the general law, and the contractual duty is attributable to the will of the parties, I do not find it objectionable that the claimant may be entitled to take advantage of the remedy which is most advantageous to him, subject only to ascertaining whether the tortious duty is so inconsistent with the applicable contract that, in accordance with ordinary principle, the parties must be taken to have agreed that the tortious remedy is to be limited or excluded. ...

NOTES

1. *Definition*. Several points emerge from the relationship. Tort and contract have been distinguished not only in the common law but equally by statute, in particular the old County Court Acts; this legislation forced the courts to state whether an action was 'founded on contract' or 'founded upon tort' (*Taylor v MS & LR Co* (1895), 138). When forced to choose between the two, contract was said to be based on a breach of promise (*assumpsit*) whereas tort became based on a 'wrong' (see eg *Danby v Lamb* (1861)).

2. *Absence of a rule of non-cumul*. The frontier between the two never became rigid. In the nineteenth century the courts and Bar accepted that parties could often choose between the two forms of liability on many sets of facts (see *Alton v Midland Ry* (1865)). And today an action for damages arising out of a single set of facts can still be based either on a breach of contract or on say the tort of negligence (*Henderson v Merrett*). It may well be however that the courts will not allow tort to be used to undermine well-established contractual structures in certain types of commercial situations (*Marc Rich & Co v Bishop Rock Marine Co Ltd*, below, p 291).

3. *Adjunct to contract.* In other situations the courts may use tort to fill certain gaps in the law of contract. Thus the absence of consideration in support of a statement that causes damage will not necessarily mean that an action for damages will fail; if the relationship between the parties is close, then the statement might give rise to tortious liability (*Hedley Byrne v Heller*, below, p 115; and see eg *Lennon v Comr of Police for the Metropolis* (2004)). Another area where tort has aided contract was (statute has now intervened) where the rule of privity of contract prevented a third party from suing (*White v Jones*, below, p 260).

4. *Strict liability and negligence.* One area where the frontier between contract and tort can be important is where a single set of facts discloses both a liability based on negligence and a stricter liability based on breach of an implied term to warrant a result (similar to the *obligation de moyens* and *obligation de résultat* dichotomy in French law; and see UNIDROIT art 5.4). In the case of a contract for services, negligence can indifferently give rise to liability in contract (Supply of Goods and Services Act 1982, s 13) and in the tort of negligence; but in contracts to supply goods there may be a stricter form of liability (eg under Sale of Goods Act 1979, s 14) and this will bring into play different rules as to remoteness of damage and contributory negligence (see **Chapter 10**).

5. *Complex liabilities.* Contract and tort can intertwine in situations where there are multiple grounds of claim, not just in respect of one party (concurrence), but where two or more parties may have claims against a single other party or vice versa (see **11.5**). This produces inherent complexity (Weir, *Complex Liabilities*, IECL, vol XI, Ch 12, § 73). The growth of liability insurance (contract) and subrogation (restitution) have been a major factor in this development of complex liabilities since it is usually insurance companies, subrogated to the rights of parties, that are behind the recourse actions; these (contractual) actions in turn can on occasions undermine the loss-spreading aim of the law of tort (see eg *Lister v Romford Ice & Cold Storage Co*, below, p 52).

1.4.2 Tort and crime

The relationship between tort and crime is also difficult because the two were not easily distinguished in early Roman and common law. The distinction today is, from a practical point of view, based on entirely separate procedures: the criminal process involves one set of courts, the civil process another. However there are various points at which the two areas meet and interrelate.

Arthur J.S Hall and Co. v. Simons [2002] 1 AC 615, HL

A series of claims (and counter-claims) for damages were brought by clients against firms of solicitors for negligence. The judge at first instance decided that in all of the actions the solicitors enjoyed advocate's immunity and struck out the claims. The Court of Appeal restored the claims and an appeal to the House of Lords (Lords Steyn, Browne-Wilkinson, Hoffmann, Hope, Hutton, Hobhouse and Millett) was dismissed. All of the Law Lords agreed that the public interest no longer required that advocates should have immunity from negligence claims and a majority (Lords Hope and Hobhouse dissenting) concluded that immunity was not required where the disputed proceeding were criminal.

▶

Lord Hobhouse (dissenting in part): ... All of your Lordships are in favour of dismissing the appeals; the solicitors are not entitled to the immunity which they claim in the present cases. Your Lordships agree that on any view the immunity claimed in these cases falls outside the recognised immunity afforded to advocates. The Court of Appeal arrived at the right conclusion. Further, all your Lordships would be prepared to arrive at the same conclusion on the basis that there is no longer an adequate justification for continuing to recognise a general immunity for advocates engaged in civil litigation.

But that is the limit of the unanimity. Some of your Lordships would be prepared to declare that the immunity should also no longer be recognised for advocates engaged in criminal litigation. Other of your Lordships, among whom I number myself, would not be prepared to take that step on the present appeals...

The civil process

...The character of civil litigation is that it involves the assertion by one party that the other has infringed his rights; he seeks a remedy, normally a monetary remedy but sometimes a remedy of declaration of right or specific implement. The court, therefore, has essentially to make a decision between two conflicting parties and determining their respective rights inter se. It is primarily the provision by the state of a service similar to the provision of arbitration services. The public interest does not normally come into it save in so far as the provision of a system of civil dispute resolution and the enforcement of civil rights is a necessary part of a society governed by the rule of law not by superior force.

It is a system of relative justice. It exists in economic terms. The plaintiff complains that he has suffered loss and damage; he claims that the defendant should be required to pay monetary damages to compensate him; the remedy is a redistribution of wealth between the parties. Or he may assert a property right and ask that the court should assist him enforce it against the defendant...

The criminal process

Even though the criminal process is formally adversarial, it is of a fundamentally different character to the civil process. Its purpose and function are different. It is to enforce the criminal law. The criminal law and the criminal justice system exists in the interests of society as a whole. It has a directly social function. It is concerned to see that the guilty are convicted and punished and those not proved to be guilty are acquitted. Anyone not proved to be guilty is to be presumed to be not guilty. It is of fundamental importance that the process by which the defendant is proved guilty shall have been fair and it is the public duty of all those concerned in the criminal justice system to see that this is the case. This is the public interest in the system.

The criminal trial does not exist to protect private interests. It exists as part of the enforcement of the criminal law in the public interest. Those who take part in the trial do so as a public duty whether in exchange for remuneration or the payment of expenses. The purpose of all is, or should be, to see justice done and to play their appropriate part in achieving that end...

It follows from these fundamentals that the salient features of this procedure exist to serve the public interest, not to serve any private interest...

The legitimate interest of the citizen charged with a criminal offence is that he should have a fair trial and only be convicted if his guilt has been proved. It is not an economic interest. His interest like his potential liability under the criminal law stems from his membership of the society to which he belongs – his citizenship. If the charge against him has not been proved, he should be acquitted. If he has been wrongly convicted, his appeal against conviction should be allowed. If he has been wrongly or excessively sentenced, his punishment should be remitted or reduced. His only remedy lies within the criminal justice system. This is appropriate. The civil courts do not have any part to play in such matters. The relevance of what the advocate does during the criminal trial is to the issues at that trial, not the remoter economic consequences of the outcome of that trial...

NOTES

1. *Introduction.* Although Lord Hobhouse's judgment is a dissenting one (at least on the criminal proceedings point), it is extracted here because it is instructive in the way it exhaustively distinguishes between civil and criminal proceedings.

2. *Action civile.* There is no equivalent to the French *action civile* in English law whereby a victim can use the criminal proceedings to pursue a civil remedy (see *Black v Yates* (1992)). The victim of, say, a theft can sue in conversion and/or trespass to goods while the victim of an attack will sue in trespass to the person (assault); the victim of fraud can sue in deceit. But this civil process has to be pursued quite separately from the criminal proceedings (although there is statutory power to make compensation orders in criminal proceedings; and see Proceeds of Crime Act 2002).

3. *Public nuisance.* At the level of substance the relationship between tort and crime can be more complex because certain crimes can also be torts if they cause damage to an individual. One important tort here is public nuisance which is not just a crime but also a tort if any individual suffers special damage (*Campbell v Paddington Corporation* (1911)). (See also *R v Rimmington* (2005)).

4. *Breach of statutory duty.* Another crime which can, in certain circumstances, amount to a tort is where a person causes damage in breach of a statutory provision. Not all breaches will give rise to torts and this is why this area is complex; but the general principles have been set out by Lord Browne-Wilkinson in the *X (Minors)* case (see below pp 29, 155)

5. *Trespass.* Facts which give rise to the tort of trespass to the person will often equally give rise to the crime of assault (or causing bodily harm). However, unlike public nuisance and breach of statutory duty, it is not the crime itself which gives rise to the tort; the facts which constitute the crime also constitute the tort and thus may be the subject of two quite different processes. One might note that the standard of proof is not so high in the civil courts and thus failure to establish the crime of assault in the criminal court will not necessarily mean that a claim in the civil court for damages for trespass will fail. (Authoritarian Home Secretaries dream of introducing the civil standard of proof into the criminal process, which, were it ever to be successful, would no doubt fill the prisons with ever more, possibly innocent, people.)

6. *Evidence.* However if a defendant is successfully convicted of a crime whose facts also constitute a tort (for example driving without due care and attention,

assault, theft), the conviction can be used as evidence in the civil proceedings (Civil Evidence Act 1968, s 11).

7. *Defence of illegality*. The criminal law can also be of importance when it comes to defences in tort: if the claimant was involved in a criminal act when he suffered tortious damage he may be prevented from suing by the defence of illegality (see eg *Pitts v Hunt*, p 333). This rule, namely *ex turpi causa non oritur actio*, was originally a rule that applied only to contractual liability, but it has been adopted in more recent years by the law of tort. See also *Vellino v Chief Constable of Greater Manchester* (2002)

8. *Injunctions*. One might note that the remedy of an injunction can play a role in respect of certain kinds of behaviour that are not in themselves tortious but which may be unlawful according to the criminal law. Even if the unlawful behaviour does not give rise to the tort of breach of statutory duty, the court may nevertheless issue an injunction (*Burris v Azadani*, p 375); once issued the case could become a precedent establishing a new tort. Sometimes statute might intervene to confirm both the crime and the tort (see Protection from Harassment Act 1997) (see p 100).

9. *Anti-social behaviour*. These injunctions for anti-social behaviour are now supplemented by public law remedies which are quasi-criminal in nature. That is to say they are remedies that are civil in form but essentially criminal in substance (*R (McCann) v Crown Court at Manchester* (2001)). Thus the victim of a nuisance can ask a local authority to act against either the things (Noise Act 1996, s 10(2)) or the persons causing the nuisance (Crime and Disorder Act 1998, s 1).

10. *Criminal injuries compensation*. A person who suffers personal injury as a result of a crime can of course sue the criminal in tort for damages. But the victim can also claim compensation from the State under a government scheme (Criminal Injuries Compensation Act 1995 and regulations made under it). Such a scheme was once as generous as damages in tort, but this is no longer true. The scheme does not cover property damage and thus if a victim (or his insurance company) want compensation they will have to use the law of tort (see eg *Home Office v Dorset Yacht Co*, below, pp 31, 29, 226).

EXERCISE

Compare and contrast in *Arthur Hall* the different types of interest employed in the analysis:
(a) public interest;
(b) private interest;
(c) legitimate interest;
(d) interests of society;
(e) economic interests.

1.4.3 Tort and property

Tort also provides causes of action and remedies for the protection of property and thus the borderline between tort and property is another area of difficulty. These difficulties, it must be stressed again, are not just academic; they can create structural problems which then emerge in the reasoning of judges and in questions of the existence, the non-existence and (or) the level of any duty. The problem is often one between 'owning' and 'owing' or between obligation and right: does an owner of an expensive car, who carelessly leaves his keys in the vehicle while purchasing some fresh pasta, owe a duty of care to any subsequent good faith acquirer who might obtain it after it has been stolen by an opportunist thief? Here the tort of negligence finds itself confronting the rights of ownership (*Moorgate Mercantile Ltd v Twitchings* (1977)). Or take the local authority that gratuitously agrees to look after the claimant's property which is subsequently stolen by an employee of the authority. If one applies rules of tort, it might well be arguable that an employer should not be liable for an act which does not form part of the employee's duties; the law of property might take a different view (*Mitchell v Ealing LBC* (1979)). As Diplock LJ explains in the next case, bailment creates its own duties that are independent of the law of tort. Where tort is relevant is in respect of the remedies used by a bailor against a bailee (the tort of detinue up until 1977 and now the tort of conversion).

Morris v CW Martin & Sons Ltd [1966] 1 QB 716, CA

The owner of a mink stole brought an action against a firm of cleaners for its value. She had sent it to Beder, a furrier, for cleaning and Beder, with the owner's consent, sent it to the defendants for the actual cleaning. The defendants' employee who was supposed to clean it stole it instead. The trial judge held the defendants not liable, but an appeal to the Court of Appeal (Lord Denning MR, Diplock LJ and Salmon LJ) was allowed.

Diplock LJ: ... Duties at common law are owed by one person to another only if there exists a relationship between them which the common law recognises as giving rise to such duty. One of such recognised relationships is created by the voluntary taking into custody of goods which are the property of another. By voluntarily accepting from Beder the custody of a fur which they knew to be the property of a customer of his, they brought into existence between the plaintiff and themselves the relationship of bailor and bailee by sub-bailment. The legal relationship of bailor and bailee of a chattel can exist independently of any contract, for the legal concept of bailment as creating a relationship which gives rise to duties owed by a bailee to a bailor is derived from Roman law and is older in our common law than the legal concept of parol contract as giving rise to legal duties owed by one party to the other party thereto. The nature of those legal duties, in particular as to the degree of care which the bailee is bound to exercise in the custody of the goods and as to his duty to redeliver them, varies according to the circumstances in which and purposes for which the goods are delivered to the bailee. But we are concerned here with conversion. This is a breach of a particular duty common to all classes of bailment. While most cases of bailment today are accompanied by a contractual relationship between bailee and bailor which may modify or extend the common law duties of the parties that would otherwise arise from the mere fact of bailment, this is not necessarily so – as witness gratuitous bailment or bailment by finding ...

One of the common law duties owed by a bailee of goods to his bailor is not to convert them, ie not to do intentionally in relation to the goods an act inconsistent with the bailor's right of property therein. (See *Caxton Publishing Co Ltd v Sutherland Publishing Co*, per Lord Porter.) This duty, which is common to all bailments as well as to other relationships which do not amount to bailment, is independent of and additional to the other common law duty of a bailee for reward to take reasonable care of his bailor's

▶

goods. Stealing goods is the simplest example of conversion; but, perhaps because in his classic judgment in *Coggs v Bernard* Sir John Holt CJ discusses the circumstances in which bailees are liable to their bailors for the loss of goods stolen not by the servant of the bailee but by a stranger, some confusion has, I think, arisen in later cases through failure to recognise the co-existence of the two duties of a bailee for reward; to take reasonable care of his bailor's goods and not to convert them – even by stealing.

If the bailee in the present case had been a natural person and had converted the plaintiff's fur by stealing it himself, no one would have argued that he was not liable to her for its loss. But the defendant bailees are a corporate person. They could not perform their duties to the plaintiffs to take reasonable care of the fur and not to convert it otherwise than vicariously by natural persons acting as their servants or agents. It was one of their servants to whom they had entrusted the care and custody of the fur for the purpose of doing work upon it who converted it by stealing it. Why should they not be vicariously liable for this breach of their duty by the vicar whom they had chosen to perform it? Sir John Holt, I think, would have answered that they were liable 'for seeing that someone must be the loser by this deceit it is more reason that he who employs and puts a trust and confidence in the deceiver should be the loser than a stranger': *Hern v Nichols...*

NOTE

The use and enjoyment of land equally raises questions about the relationship between the exercise of property rights and any damage this exercise might cause to others. A person who *unreasonably* uses his land will normally be liable for any harm that this unreasonable use causes to his neighbour's use and enjoyment of property (*Hollywood Silver Fox Farm v Emmett*, below, p 79); but the *unreasonable* exercise of an actual property *right* could well result in no liability, English law having no general principle of an abuse of a right (*Bradford Corporation v Pickles*, below, p 60).

1.4.4 Tort and restitution

Another frontier that can cause problems, again because of the traditional law of remedies approach, is the one between tort and unjust enrichment. Until relatively recently the only two categories of liability were contract and tort, but the House of Lords has now recognised the law of restitution as a separate category (*Kleinwort Benson Ltd v Glasgow CC* (1999)). Restitution differs from tort in that its focal point is the defendant's *enrichment* rather than the claimant's *harm* and consequently liability in restitution is not measured by the claimant's loss. Where there is overlap between tort and restitution is in the area of profits arising out of wrongs and this can give rise to a conflict of purpose. Should the court be focusing on the claimant's loss or the defendant's profit? Sometimes this can have very real practical effects, as the next case illustrates.

Inverugie Investments Ltd v Hackett [1995] 1 WLR 713, PC

Lord Lloyd: This is in form an ordinary claim for mesne profits, that is to say a claim for damages for trespass to land. But the facts are unusual, since the land consists of 30 specified apartments in a much larger hotel. The hotel is owned by the defendants, Inverugie Investments Ltd. The plaintiff, the late Mr Richard Hackett, was the lessee of the apartments under a lease dated 5 June 1970 for a term of 99 years. On 25 November 1974 the plaintiff was ejected by the defendants. On 6 March 1975 he brought proceedings for possession. Those proceedings culminated on 19 December 1984 when the Board dismissed the defendants' appeal against a decision of the Court of Appeal of the Commonwealth of the Bahamas in favour of the plaintiff. Despite a further order granted by Malone J on 23 June 1986 requiring the defendants to give up possession forthwith, they did not do so until 12 April 1990. The trespass thus lasted for a continuous period of 15 years. The question for decision is the appropriate measure of damages...

Before stating their own conclusions on the facts, their Lordships should say a brief word on the law. The cases to which they have already referred establish, beyond any doubt, that a person who lets out goods on hire, or the landlord of residential property, can recover damages from a trespasser who has wrongfully used his property whether or not he can show that he would have let the property to anybody else, and whether or not he would have used the property himself...

It is sometimes said that these cases are an exception to the rule that damages in tort are compensatory. But this is not necessarily so. It depends how widely one defines the 'loss' which the plaintiff has suffered. As the Earl of Halsbury LC pointed out in *Mediana (Owners of Steamship) v Comet (Owners of Lightship)* [1900] AC 113, 117, it is no answer for a wrongdoer who has deprived the plaintiff of his chair to point out that he does not usually sit in it or that he has plenty of other chairs in the room.

In *Stoke-on-Trent City Council v WJ Wass Ltd* [1988] 1 WLR 1406 Nicholls LJ called the underlying principle in these cases the 'user principle.' The plaintiff may not have suffered any actual loss by being deprived of the use of his property. But under the user principle he is entitled to recover a reasonable rent for the wrongful use of his property by the trespasser. Similarly, the trespasser may not have derived any actual benefit from the use of the property. But under the user principle he is obliged to pay a reasonable rent for the use which he has enjoyed. The principle need not be characterised as exclusively compensatory, or exclusively restitutionary; it combines elements of both.

If this is the correct principle, how does it apply to the facts of the present case?...

The point is not altogether easy. But their Lordships have concluded that Mr Mowbray's argument is to be preferred. If a man hires a concrete mixer, he must pay the daily hire, even though he may not in the event have been able to use the mixer because of rain. So also must a trespasser who takes the mixer without the owner's consent. He must pay the going rate, even though in the event he has derived no benefit from the use of the mixer. It makes no difference whether the trespasser is a professional builder or a do-it-yourself enthusiast.

▶

The same applies to residential property. In the present case the defendants have had the use of all 30 apartments for 15 years. Applying the user principle, they must pay the going rate, even though they have been unable to derive actual benefit from all the apartments for all the time. The fact that the defendants are hotel operators does not take the case out of the ordinary rule. The plaintiff is not asking for an account of profits. The chance of making a profit from the use of the apartments is not the correct test for arriving at a reasonable rent.

It follows that their Lordships cannot agree with the judgment of the majority in the court below...

NOTE

Perhaps one difference between tort and restitution is to be found in the distinction between obligations and property as the next extract suggests. However the nature of the remedy is another focal point of distinction.

Attorney-General v Blake [2001] 1 AC 268, HL

Lord Hobhouse (dissenting): ... The concepts of restitution and compensation are not the same though they will on occasions fulfil the same need. Restitution is analogous to property: it concerns wealth or advantage which ought to be returned or transferred by the defendant to the plaintiff. It is a form of specific implement. Its clearest form is an order for the return or transfer of property which belongs in law or in equity to the plaintiff. Property includes an interest in property. Then there are rights recognised in equity such as those which arise from a fiduciary relationship. These rights give rise to restitutionary remedies including the remedy of account which, depending on the circumstances, could also derive from a common law relationship such as agency. Then, again, there are the rights now grouped under the heading of the law of restitution or unjust enrichment. These are still truly restitutionary concepts leading to restitutionary remedies. Typically they require the payment of money by the person unjustly enriched to the person at whose expense that enrichment has taken place. In so far as the appropriate remedy is the payment of money or the delivery up of a chattel or goods is concerned the common law could provide it; insofar as it required some other remedy or the recognition of an equitable right, the chancery jurisdiction had to be invoked.

The essential of such rights and their enforcement was the procuring by the courts of the *performance* by the defendant of his obligations. The plaintiff recovers what he is actually entitled to not some monetary substitute for it. If what the plaintiff is entitled to is wealth expressed in monetary terms, the order will be for the payment of money but this does not alter the character of the remedy or of the right being recognised. He gets the money because it was his property or he was in some other way entitled to it. It is still the enforced performance of an obligation. The same is the case where an injunction is granted or a decree of specific performance or the ordering of an account.

QUESTION

'If a wrongdoer has made use of goods for his own purpose, then he must pay a reasonable hire for them, even though the owner has in fact suffered no loss ...

The claim for a hiring charge is ... not based on the loss to the plaintiff, but on the fact that the defendant has used the goods for his own purposes. It is an action against him because he has had the benefit of the goods. It resembles, therefore, an action for restitution, rather than an action of tort' (Denning LJ in *Strand Electric & Engineering Ltd v Brisford Entertainments Ltd* (1952), at pp 254–5). Given that damages are designed to compensate for loss, would it not be better to see an action for a hiring charge, or sometimes an action for damages in trespass, as a claim in debt? Would the equitable remedy of account of profits (mentioned by Lord Lloyd in *Inverugie*) be a more suitable remedy? (Cf *Att-Gen v Blake* (2001).)

1.4.5 Tort and constitutional law

We have already seen that tort (especially trespass and conversion) plays an important role in protecting property rights and as a result tort and property law overlap. The same is true for constitutional law since trespass (and other torts) can be used against the police or any other local or central government agency that assaults or imprisons a person, or deliberately damages property, without legal justification (see **Chapter 9**). Thus where a house owner saw his home, built without planning permission, knocked down without notice by the local Board of Works, the owner succeeded in trespass against the Board (*Cooper v Wandsworth Board of Works* (1863)).

R v Governor of Brockhill Prison, ex p Evans (No 2) [2001] 2 AC 19, HL

(See also p 82)

Lord Steyn: My Lords, the applicant was kept in prison for 59 days longer than she should have been. The Governor was blameless. He relied on a Home Office explanation of the legal position of prisoners in the position of the applicant. The Home Office was also blameless. The Home Office view of the position was founded on a clear line of Divisional court decisions, starting with *Reg v Governor of Blundeston Prison, Ex parte Gaffney* [1982] WLR 696. But the courts had erred. On the applicant's application for judicial review the Divisional court overruled the earlier decisions: *Reg v Brockhill Prison, Ex parte Evans* [1997] QB 443. It was held that the applicant was unlawfully detained. The governor immediately released the applicant. The applicant pursued claim for false imprisonment against the Governor. Collins J dismissed the claim but in the event that he was wrong, assessed damages at £2,000. By a majority the Court of Appeal allowed the appeal of the applicant, and increased the assessment to £5,000: [1999] QB 1043. The majority (Lord Woolf, MR and Judge LJ) took the view that a defendant may be liable for false imprisonment of a plaintiff in circumstances where the defendant acts in good faith on a view of the law which appears to be settled by precedent but which subsequently turns out to have been wrong...

On balance I think the arguments of the applicant outweigh those of the Solicitor-General. In *Eshugbayi Eleko v Officer Administering the Government of Nigeria* [1931] AC 662, a habeas corpus case, Lord Atkin observed, at p. 670, that 'no member of the executive can interfere with the liberty or property of a British subject except on the condition that he can support the legality of his action before a court of justice.' Recently, with the approval of other members of the House, I cited Lord Atkin's observation in the

▶

Eleko case: *Boddington v British Transport Police* [1999] 2 AC 143, 173F. It represents the traditional common law view. It points to a decision in the present case that the respondent is entitled to recover compensation on the ground of false imprisonment where the executive can no longer support the lawfulness of the detention...

[Lords Slynn, Browne-Wilkinson, Hope and Hobhouse agreed that the defendant was liable for false imprisonment.]

NOTE

The Human Rights Act 1998, which incorporated the European Convention for the Protection of Human Rights and Fundamental Freedoms, creates a direct legislative connection between tort and constitutional law. However the Act does not necessarily import Convention rights directly into English law.

Wainwright v Home Office [2004] 2 AC 406, HL

This was an action for damages by a mother and her son against the Home Office in respect of a prison visit during which they were both strip-searched. The searches were not conducted according to prison rules, and were thus not covered by statutory authority, and both claimants alleged that they had been humiliated and stressed. In addition the son, who had physical and learning difficulties, claimed damages for post-traumatic stress disorder. The damages claims were based upon trespass to the person and upon infringement of the right of privacy (subsequently protected by article 8 of the European Convention for the Protection of Human Rights and Fundamental Freedoms). The trial judge found that the touching of the son's penis during the search amounted to a battery and awarded the son damages. The judge also found that the authorities were liable under a form of trespass extended by the principle of *Wilkinson v Downton* (1897) and accordingly awarded damages to the mother as well. The Court of Appeal considered that the prison authorities had not committed any trespass save the battery to the son and thus reduced the damages to the son and quashed those awarded to the mother. The House of Lords (Lords Bingham, Hoffmann, Hope, Hutton and Scott) dismissed an appeal and asserted that there was no tort of an invasion of privacy.

Lord Hoffmann: ... **7** The conclusion of both the judge and the Court of Appeal was... that the searches were not protected by statutory authority. But that is not enough to give the Wainwrights a claim to compensation. The acts of the prison officers needed statutory authority only if they would otherwise have been wrongful, that is to say, tortious or in breach of a statutory duty. People do all kinds of things without statutory authority. So the question is whether the searches themselves or the manner in which they were conducted gave the Wainwrights a cause of action...

Lord Scott: ... **62** The important issue of principle is not, in my opinion, whether English common law recognises a tort of invasion of privacy. As Lord Hoffmann has demonstrated, whatever remedies may have been developed for misuse of confidential information, for certain types of trespass, for certain types of nuisance and for various other situations in which claimants may find themselves aggrieved by an invasion of what they conceive to be their privacy, the common law has not developed an overall remedy for the invasion of privacy. The issue of importance in the present case is whether the infliction of humiliation and distress by conduct calculated to humiliate and cause distress, is without more, tortious at common law. I am in full agreement with the reasons that have been given by Lord Hoffmann for concluding that it is not. Nor, in my opinion, should it be. Some institutions, schools, university colleges, regiments and the like (often bad ones) have initiation ceremonies and rites which newcomers are expected to undergo. Ritual humiliation is often a part of this. The authorities in charge of these institutions usually object to these practices and seek to put an end to any excesses. But why, absent any of the traditional nominate torts such as assault, battery, negligent causing of harm etc, should the law of tort intrude? If a shop assistant or a bouncer or barman at a club is publicly offensive to a customer, the customer may well be humiliated and distressed. But that is no sufficient reason why the law of tort should be fashioned and developed with a view to providing compensation in money to the victim.

63 Whether today, the Human Rights Act 1998 having come into effect, conduct similar to that inflicted on Mrs Wainwright and Alan Wainwright, but without any element of battery and without crossing the line into the territory of misfeasance in public office, should be categorised as tortious must be left to be decided when such a case arises. It is not necessary to decide now whether such conduct would constitute a breach of article 8 or of article 3 of the Convention...

(For further extracts see pp 64, 81, 109)

1.4.6 Tort and administrative law

In tort itself there is no formal distinction between public and private bodies (cf **Chapter 9**). A local authority can be just as liable as the manufacturer of ginger beer in the tort of negligence, nuisance, trespass or whatever. Equally the local authority can sue the private person or commercial corporation for damages under one of these heads (*Esso v Southport*, above pp 4, 34). Nevertheless at the level of remedies tort claims must be distinguished from actions for judicial review.

X (Minors) v Bedfordshire County Council [1995] 2 AC 633, HL

Lord Browne-Wilkinson: ... The question is whether, if Parliament has imposed a statutory duty on an authority to carry out a particular function, a plaintiff who has suffered damage in consequence of the authority's performance or non-performance of that function has a right of action in damages against the authority. It is important to distinguish such actions to recover damages, based on a private law cause of action, from actions in public law to enforce the due performance of statutory duties, now brought by way of judicial review. The breach of a public law right by itself gives rise to no claim for damages. A claim for damages must be based on a private law cause of action. The distinction is important because a number of earlier cases (particularly in the field of education) were concerned with the enforcement by declaration and injunction of what would now be called public law duties...

NOTE

Probably only when it comes to defamation will there be a restriction on a government body's right to sue (*Derbyshire CC v Times Newspapers* (1993)). Sometimes an aggrieved citizen might well decide to sue in private law for damages rather than to seek the quashing of a decision in administrative law; and unless this procedure amounts to an abuse of process (*O'Reilly v Mackman* (1983)) it will be perfectly valid (see eg *Blackpool & Fylde Aero Club Ltd v Blackpool BC* (1990)). There is, however, one very important qualification to this right to sue. Although in form a public body like a local authority or the police can be sued for negligence (see *Rigby v Chief Constable of Northamptonshire*, p 334), in substance the judges have a number of weapons that they can use to protect a public authority. To succeed in negligence the claimant must establish a duty of care and so a court can simply declare that no such duty exists, say on the ground that the claimant or the damage is unforeseeable or that there are policy reasons against the existence of a duty (see **Chapter 9**).

1.4.7 Tort and equity

The frontier between tort and equity is to be found mainly (but not exclusively) at the level of remedies. The common law remedy of damages needs to be distinguished not just from the equitable remedy of injunction (see *Miller v Jackson*, p 14 and *Burris v Azadani*, p 375 but also from the equitable remedy of account of profits (*English v Dedham Vale Properties* (1978); *Att-Gen v Blake* (2001)). However just to complicate things further there is also an equitable form of damages which, thanks to statute, can be awarded in lieu of an injunction (see generally *Jaggard v Sawyer* (1995)). Equitable ideas can also influence tort thinking: see eg *Hedley Byrne v Heller*, p 115.

1. 5 Tort and methodology

It was once believed, at least on the continent, that application of a rule was merely a matter of syllogistic logic: the judge was little more than a computer mechanically applying legal rules (major premise) to sets of facts (minor premise), the solution flowing deductively from the juxtaposition of the two premises. This methodology was shown to be a myth even before it was discovered that one cannot produce a computer programme that thinks like a judge. All the same, if we assume (in fact a dangerous assumption) that having knowledge of a particular area of law is knowing the rules said to fall within that area, then tort rules come in two sorts. There are those arising out of legal precedents and those set out in statutes.

1.5.1 Tort and precedent

Knowing the rules is not, however, enough. The tort lawyer must know how to discover their scope and extent and how to apply them to particular factual situations. When the rule has its source in case law, what counts is the ratio decidendi. But what exactly is the ratio of a case in which there are several judgments each one saying something slightly different? And what role do the facts of a precedent play when applying such a precedent to a new situation? Statute might appear more straightforward in that the rule is clearly stated in writing;

however it may not be clearly expressed (see eg Animals Act 1971, s 2(2), pp 34, 175) with the result that applying it to certain sets of facts can be extremely problematic. In fact, knowing tort law is knowing how to reason like a tort lawyer and in this sense the whole subject could be said to be one of method rather than rules. Nevertheless there are a number of methodological points that can be usefully absorbed at this introductory and definitional stage. These are set out in the following extracts.

Home Office v Dorset Yacht Co Ltd [1970] AC 1004, HL

(For facts and further extracts see p 226

Lord Diplock: ... The method adopted at this stage of the process is analytical and inductive. It starts with an analysis of the characteristics of the conduct and relationship involved in each of the decided cases. But the analyst must know what he is looking for; and this involves his approaching his analysis with some general conception of conduct and relationships which ought to give rise to a duty of care. This analysis leads to a proposition which can be stated in the form: 'In all the decisions that have been analysed a duty of care has been held to exist wherever the conduct and the relationship possessed each of the characteristics A, B, C, D etc, and has not so far been found to exist when any of these characteristics were absent.'

For the second stage, which is deductive and analytical, that proposition is converted to: 'In all cases where the conduct and relationship possess each of the characteristics A, B, C, D etc, a duty of care arises.' The conduct and relationship involved in the case for decision is then analysed to ascertain whether they possess each of these characteristics. If they do the conclusion follows that a duty of care does arise in the case for decision.

But since *ex hypothesi* the kind of case which we are now considering offers a choice whether or not to extend the kinds of conduct or relationships which give rise to a duty of care, the conduct or relationship which is involved in it will lack at least one of the characteristics A, B, C, or D etc. And the choice is exercised by making a policy decision ... which ... will be influenced by the same general conception of what ought to give rise to a duty of care as was used in approaching the analysis. The choice to extend is given effect to by redefining the characteristics in more general terms so as to exclude the necessity to conform to limitations imposed by the former definition which are considered to be inessential...

Inherent in this methodology, however, is a practical limitation which is imposed by the sheer volume of reported cases. The initial selection of previous cases to be analysed will itself eliminate from the analysis those in which the conduct or relationship involved possessed characteristics which are obviously absent in the case for decision. The proposition used in the deductive stage is not a true universal. It needs to be qualified so as to read: 'In all cases where the conduct and relationship possess each of the characteristics A, B, C and D etc, but do not possess any of the characteristics Z, Y or X etc, which were present in the cases eliminated from the analysis, a duty of care arises.' But this qualification, being irrelevant to the decision of the particular case, is generally left unexpressed...

QUESTION

What do you think is the most important focal point in Lord Diplock's analysis of legal reasoning:

(a) induction;
(b) deduction; or
(c) policy?

NOTE

It is very tempting to think that legal method is a question of inducing a rule or principle out of a set of previous cases and then applying this rule in a deductive manner whereby the rule acts as the major premise, the facts of the case to be decided as the minor premise, the solution seemingly following as a matter of syllogistic logic. However legal method is not so simple, as indeed Lord Diplock indicated with his reference to policy. The next extract shows how even the formal reasoning method is more complex than just induction and deduction.

Lupton v FA & AB Ltd [1972] AC 634, HL

Lord Simon: ... A judicial decision will often be reached by a process of reasoning which can be reduced into a sort of complex syllogism, with the major premise consisting of a pre-existing rule of law (either statutory or judge-made) and with the minor premise consisting of the material facts of the case under immediate consideration. The conclusion is the decision of the case, which may or may not establish new law – in the vast majority of cases it will be merely the application of existing law to the facts judicially ascertained. Where the decision does constitute new law, this may or may not be expressly stated as a proposition of law: frequently the new law will appear only from subsequent comparison of, on the one hand, the material facts inherent in the major premise with, on the other, the material facts which constitute the minor premise. As a result of this comparison it will often be apparent that a rule has been extended by an analogy expressed or implied. I take as an example ... *National Telephone Co v Baker* [1893] 2 Ch 186. Major premise: the rule in *Rylands v Fletcher* (1866) LR 1 Exch 265, (1868) LR 3 HL 330. Minor premise: the defendant brought and stored electricity on his land for his own purpose; it escaped from the land; in so doing it injured the plaintiff's property. Conclusion: the defendant is liable in damages to the plaintiff (or would have been but for statutory protection). Analysis shows that the conclusion establishes a rule of law, which may be stated as 'for the purpose of the rule in *Rylands v Fletcher* electricity is analogous to water' or 'electricity is within the rule in *Rylands v Fletcher*'. That conclusion is now available as the major premise in the next case, in which some substance may be in question which in this context is not perhaps clearly analogous to water but is clearly analogous to electricity. In this way, legal luminaries are constituted which guide the wayfarer across uncharted ways.

NOTE

Although Lord Simon puts the emphasis on the syllogism, the real key to the solution in *National Telephone* is reasoning by analogy: electricity is analogous to water. This technique of analogy is fundamental to tort law as the next cases show.

Goodwill v British Pregnancy Advisory Service [1996] 1 WLR 1397, CA

The claimant brought an action for damages, in respect of her unwanted pregnancy, against an organisation which had arranged a vasectomy for a man with whom the claimant subsequently had sexual relations which resulted in the pregnancy. The Court of Appeal (Peter Gibson LJ and Thorpe LJ) held that the action should be struck out.

Peter Gibson LJ: The law of negligence, and in particular that part relating to the recovery of damages for economic loss caused by negligent statements or advice, has undergone a number of shifts in direction. The attempt in *Anns v. Merton London Borough Council* [1978] AC 728 to lay down a principle of general applicability did not find favour for long. Instead, whilst certain key ingredients of the tort, such as foreseeability, proximity, assumption of responsibility and reliance have been identified, it has been held that the law should develop incrementally by reference to or analogy with established categories of situations where the law has recognised that a duty of care arises and a plaintiff may recover for his loss. The situation in the present case, it is accepted on behalf of the plaintiff, does not fall within an established category, but, it is suggested, it requires only a modest step from an established category and one which should on the favoured incremental approach now be taken to afford the plaintiff a remedy in tort. That is challenged by the defendants who say that it requires a giant and impermissible leap from an established category and that not even arguably was any duty of care owed by these defendants to this plaintiff in the circumstances of this case...

Miss Booth also relied on *White v Jones* [1995] 2 AC 207 as providing an example of an analogous situation in which a duty of care has been recognised. In that case a solicitor who was instructed to prepare a will but delayed in carrying out his instructions was held to owe a duty of care to the intended beneficiaries. She submitted that a woman who had a sexual relationship with Mr MacKinlay is in an analogous position to the intended beneficiaries under the will, because just as the solicitor was employed to confer a benefit (in the form of bequests) on a particular class of people (the beneficiaries), so the doctor is employed to confer a benefit (not getting pregnant) on a particular class of people (women who have sexual relationships with Mr MacKinlay). I admire the ingenuity of the suggested analogy, but I have to say that I am wholly unpersuaded that the analogy is real...

NOTES

1. Principles are never to be abstracted from the particular factual situations of the precedents in which they are latent. For 'what constitutes binding precedent is the ratio decidendi of a case and this is almost always to be ascertained by an analysis of the material facts of the case – that is, generally, those facts which the tribunal whose decision is in question itself holds, expressly or implicitly, to be material' (Lord Simon in *Lupton*). Precedent, therefore, is as much a question of analogy between factual situations as induction and deduction from some pre-existing proposition of law. Previous cases can always be 'distinguished' (avoided) on their facts. As Lobban has observed of the early nineteenth century, 'precedents were not absolute, nor did they create precise rules. Rather, they acted as a source of legal analogy... Since precedent was unclear, and worked only by rough analogies from decided cases, the law could be favourable to flexibility and certainty at the same time' (Lobban, *The Common Law and English Jurisprudence 1760-1850* (OUP, 1991), 83, 86).

2. Lord Hoffmann has observed that the 'common law develops from case to case in harmony with statute' and its 'principles are generalisations from detailed rules, not abstract propositions from which those rules are deduced' (*In re McKerr* (2004), § 71).

Esso Petroleum Co Ltd v Southport Corporation, [1953] 3 WLR 773, QBD, [1954] 2 QB 182, CA, [1956] AC 218, HL

(See p 4)

Devlin J (Queen's Bench Division): ... [I]f one seeks an analogy from traffic on land, it is well established that persons whose property adjoins the highway cannot complain of damage done by persons using the highway unless it is done negligently: ... These cases amplify the principle in *Holmes v Mather* which dealt with collisions on the highway itself and which is the foundation of the modern practice whereby a plaintiff in a running-down action sues for negligence and not for trespass ...

NOTE

Denning LJ in the Court of Appeal (see above p 5) drew quite a different analogy. The discharge of oil into the sea was analogous to an adjoining neighbour's horses polluting the street and harming the claimant's café business (*Benjamin v Storr* (1874)). A difference of analogy led to a difference of result (although not for long since the House of Lords reinstated Devlin J's decision).

1.5.2 Tort and statute

The foundational source of the law of torts is the common law (precedent). However legislative intervention and the methods that attach to the interpretation of statutes cannot now be ignored in tort even if the intervention is relatively modest. In the remedial field of damages the intervention is such that the texts have become one starting point in personal injury claims (see Fatal Accidents Act 1976, Damages Act 1996, Social Security (Recovery of Benefits) Act 1997 etc). And in the area of liability for defective premises (occupiers' liability) the foundation is almost entirely statutory as will be seen in a later chapter. Animals in tort are now governed by a statutory regime as the next case illustrates.

Animals Act 1971 (c 22)

(For extract see p 75)

Mirvahedy v Henley [2003] 2 AC 491, HL

This was an action for damages brought by a car driver against the owner of a horse that had escaped from a field in a panic and collided with the claimant's car causing him severe personal injury. The trial judge found that the escape had not been due to any negligence on the part of the defendant and the sole question, therefore, was whether liability could be established under the Animals Act 1971, s 2(2). A majority of the House of Lords (Lords Nicholls, Hobhouse and Walker; Lords Slynn and Scott dissenting) held that there was liability.

Lord Hobhouse: ... Horses are not normally in a mindless state of panic nor do they normally ignore obstacles in their path. These characteristics are normally only found in horses in circumstances where they have been very seriously frightened. It is only in such circumstances that it becomes likely that, due to these characteristics, the horse will cause severe damage. This case clearly comes within the words of s 2(2)(b). There is no ambiguity either about the facts of this case or about the meaning of paragraph (b)...

The statute, in this respect following the recommendation of the Law Commission, had to reflect a choice as to the division of risk between the keeper of an animal and members of the general public. Neither is blameworthy but it is the member of the public who suffers the injury or damage and it is the keeper who knows of the characteristics of the animal which make it dangerous and liable to cause such injury or damage. The element of knowledge makes the choice a coherent one but it, in any event, was a choice which it was for the Legislature to make...

Lord Scott (dissenting): ... A clear answer to the question as to the proper construction of paragraph (b) cannot, in my opinion, be obtained from the actual language of the provision, nor from a perusal of Hansard, nor from examining the contents of the Law Commission Report of 1967 on which the 1971 Act was in part based. The answer depends upon identifying what Parliament appears to have been trying to achieve. It seems to me that Parliament was trying to draw a distinction between animals that in normal circumstances behaving normally are dangerous and those that in normal circumstances behaving normally are not. As to the former, they belong to a dangerous species and there was to be strict liability for damage; as to the latter they do not belong to a dangerous species and strict liability was to be limited to damage caused by the animal displaying abnormal characteristics that it was known by its keeper to possess. This seems to me to be a coherent policy. In respect of damage for which no strict liability was imposed, a remedy in negligence would always be available if the keeper of the animal had failed to exercise reasonable care to see that the animal did not cause damage. The keeper's knowledge of the circumstances in which and times at which the animal might be likely to become dangerous and cause damage would, of course, be highly relevant in determining the standard of care required to be observed by the keeper. A standard of care can, in appropriate circumstances, be placed so high as to require the person subject to it to become virtually an insurer against damage...

(See also extracts on pp 174, 178)

NOTES

1. The methods applied to the interpretation and application of statutory texts are traditionally seen as being rather different from the application of precedents since the starting point is not analogy with pre-existing factual situations. The method is 'hermeneutical' in the more traditional sense of working directly on a text (signifier) to discover what Parliament 'intended' (signified). But this 'intention' is normally to be gauged only from the words of the text and reasoning by analogy is excluded (see Weir, *Tort Law* (OUP, 2002), 10). Thus the s 2(1) strict

liability under the Animals Act 1971 cannot be extended by analogy from a dangerous animal to a dangerous non-living thing.

2. In the past the approach towards statutes was often quite literal, the judges stopping at the text itself and not considering the contextual situation (see eg *Haigh v Charles W Ireland* (1973)). It is not what the legislature aims at but what it hits that counts (*St Aubyn v Att-Gen* [1952] AC at 32; Weir, above, at 8). But among some judges (although not all) the approach has become more flexible in recent years (see Lord Nicholls in *ex p Spath Holme Ltd* (2001)). Thus where the statute is ambiguous the judges have abandoned their rule that they could never look at the *travaux préparatoires* (see the Court of Appeal judgment in *Mirvahedy v Henley* at § 24).

3. In addition, where human rights are involved, the judges are now under a statutory duty to interpret in such a way that, if at all possible, the Act in question is compatible with European Convention rights (Human Rights Act 1998, s 3; cf *Ghaidan v Godin-Mendoza* (2004)). However, artificial distinctions are still to be found especially in cases where for example the judges feel they are being forced to make policy decisions which would be better made by Parliament, especially if there are huge financial implications (*Birmingham CC v Oakley* (2001)). Moreover traditional distinctions such as those between physical and mental injury (cf *Morris v KLM Royal Dutch Airlines* (2002)) and physical and pure economic damage (*Merlin v British Nuclear Fuels plc* (1990)) can, sometimes at least, still influence the way texts are interpreted.

1.5.3 Tort and policy

Legal theorists in the UK tend to present law as a body of rules. Yet the actual case law perhaps tells a rather different story from those presented by rule-theorists. Thus one finds in the judgments comments such as the common law often prefers pragmatism to logic (see eg *ex p King* (1984), at p 903). Direct appeals to policy are now particularly prevalent in the law of tort.

Hill v Chief Constable of West Yorkshire [1989] AC 53, HL

This was an action for damages brought against the police by the estate of the last victim of the notorious 'Yorkshire Ripper' (Peter Sutcliffe). The claimant alleged in the writ that the police had been negligent in failing to apprehend the murderer thus leaving him free to murder the claimant. The judge ordered that the claim should be struck out and a final appeal to the House of Lords (Lords Keith, Brandon, Templeman, Oliver and Goff) was dismissed.

Lord Keith: ... [I]n my opinion there is another reason why an action for damages in negligence should not lie against the police in circumstances such as those of the present case, and that is public policy.... Potential existence of such liability may in many instances be in the general public interest, as tending towards the observance of a higher standard of care in the carrying on of various different types of activity. I do not, however, consider that this can be said of police activities. The general sense of public duty which motivates police forces is unlikely to be appreciably reinforced by the imposition of such liability so far as concerns their function in the investigation and suppression of crime. From time to time they make mistakes in the exercise of that function, but it is not to be doubted that they apply their best endeavours to the performance of it. In some instances the imposition of liability may lead to the exercise of a function being carried on in a detrimentally defensive frame of mind. The possibility of this happening in relation to the investigative operations of the police cannot be excluded. Further it would be reasonable to expect that if potential liability were to be imposed it would be not uncommon for actions to be raised against police forces on the ground that they had failed to catch some criminal as soon as they might have done, with the result that he went on to commit further crimes. While some such actions might involve allegations of a simple and straightforward type of failure – for example that a police officer negligently tripped and fell while pursuing a burglar – others would be likely to enter deeply into the general nature of a police investigation, as indeed the present action would seek to do. The manner of conduct of such an investigation must necessarily involve a variety of decisions to be made on matters of policy and discretion, for example as to which par-ticular line of inquiry is most advantageously to be pursued and what is the most advantageous way to deploy the available resources. Many such decisions would not be regarded by the courts as appropriate to be called in question, yet elaborate investi-gation of the facts might be necessary to ascertain whether or not this was so. A great deal of police time, trouble and expense might be expected to have to be put into the preparation of the defence to the action and the attendance of witnesses at the trial. The result would be a significant diversion of police manpower and attention from their most important function, that of the suppression of crime. Closed investigations would require to be reopened and retraversed, not with the object of bringing any criminal to justice but to ascertain whether or not they had been competently conducted. I there-fore consider that Glidewell LJ, in his judgment in the Court of Appeal [1988] QB 60, 76 in the present case, was right to take the view that the police were immune from an action of this kind on grounds similar to those which in *Rondel v Worsley* [1969] 1 AC 191 were held to render a barrister immune from actions for negligence in his conduct of proceedings in court.

QUESTIONS

1. Ought judges to be concerned with policy reasons or should they confine themselves only to legal rights and duties?

2. The judges have now recognised that the blanket immunity given to advo-cates by *Rondel v Worsley* is no longer acceptable (see *Arthur Hall*, above, p 19). Do you think that one day the same will be said of the immunity given to the police? Is there any actual empirical evidence to support Lord Keith's opinions or is much of what he says simply his own intuitive feelings? (Cf *Brooks v Comr of Police for the Metropolis* (2005).)

NOTE

Policy was used as one of the main reasons behind the economic loss rule in the tort of negligence (see *Spartan Steel*, p 54, 137). It would appear, however, that there are limits to policy reasoning as the next extract powerfully shows.

Vellino v Chief Constable of Greater Manchester Police [2002] 1 WLR 218, CA

Sedley LJ (dissenting): ... The House of Lords in *Tinsley v Milligan* [1994] 1 AC 340 rejected the 'public conscience' test articulated by Hutchison J in *Thackwell v Barclays Bank plc* [1986] 1 All ER 676 as a filter on claims with a criminal dimension. We are not now required, in other words, to look over our shoulders at what we fear the press will make of our decisions in this already difficult field. The public conscience, an elusive thing, as often as not turns out to be an echo-chamber inhabited by journalists and public moralists. To allow judicial policy to be dictated by it would be as inappropriate as to let judges dictate editorial policy. It is not difficult, for example, to visualise how some sections of the media would choose to report a decision along the lines which I have proposed. The Law Commission's scholarly and constructive working paper has so far been reported under the headline 'Law paves way for thugs to sue victims' ('Daily Express', 30 June 2001) and has earned the Law Commission the soubriquet 'Enemy of the people' ('Sunday Times', 1 July 2001). In a free society such comment is perfectly permissible and its influence on public opinion no doubt considerably greater than that of a judgment or a Law Commission paper. The public may one day have to decide through the democratic process whether it wants the law to legitimise the use of firearms against intruders in a society which at present has a gun homicide rate 150 times lower than the United States. But to expect a judiciary to modify its decisions as to what the law and justice require because of what it fears the media would make of them is to ask for the surrender of judicial independence. The 'fair, just and reasonable' test is now the established judicial control on ground-breaking in tort. If the law were ever to revert to an exogenous test, it should be one which gauges the response of people who actually know what the court's reasoning is; and no court which has confidence in its own reasoning should be worried about that...

QUESTION

Read this case in the law reports. What do you think is the difference between the 'public conscience' test and the 'fair, just and reasonable' test? Are they both not tests rooted in what the public are imagined to perceive as what is 'just'?

1.5.4 Tort and argumentation

Several other methodological points need to be stressed. One important point is that it is not just the judges who are the sources of law; they make their decisions on the basis of arguments presented to them by the parties' barristers. Indeed, the judges rely on the barristers to research the law. The presentation of these arguments is itself dialectical because of the nature of the legal process; thus nearly all English judgments consider in turn the arguments presented first by the claimant's counsel and then by the defendant's. The judge then decides between them, sometimes after a lengthy analysis of the precedents (and/or the statutory provisions) and (or) sometimes after a detailed consideration of the factual context.

Tony Weir, 'Recent Developments in Causation in English Tort Law', in B Fauvarque-Cosson, E Picard and A Voinnesson (eds), *De tous horizons: Mélanges Xavier Blanc Jouvan* (Société de Législation Comparée, 2005), 883, 890

The importance in the common law of the arguments of counsel is frequently over-looked by comparative lawyers. They are important because of the way our judges are selected. Until very recently all our senior judges had spent most of their lives as barristers. Now whereas barristers are successful enough to be appointed judges only if they specialise in a particular area of law, once they are raised to the bench they instantly become generalists having to deal with cases of all kinds... Consequently the judges are often not at all familiar with the area of law being discussed before them by the barristers: in England the maxim *curia novit jura* is more a joke than a principle... It may perhaps be added that in difficult cases counsel are tempted to try every argument at all plausible, and that the judges who have to respond to them are sometimes less dismissive of feeble arguments than they might be, perhaps out of deference to their future colleagues. Again it may happen that the spokesman for the party that ought to win on the merits may not adduce the best arguments in their client's favour, with the effect that the judges, who usually reach the correct result, may not be able to give the best reasons for it.

QUESTION

What if a barrister fails to present to the court an accurate account of the law?

Copeland v Smith [2000] 1 WLR 1371, CA

Buxton LJ: ... Although the matter does not arise for decision because it is now conceded, I cannot draw back from expressing my very great concern that the judge was permitted by those professional advocates to approach the matter as if it were free from authority when there was a recently reported case in this court directly on the point, which was reported not in some obscure quarter but in the official law reports. It is, of course, not only extremely discourteous to the judge not to inform him properly about the law, but it has also been extremely wasteful of time and money in this case, because not only did the judge have to deal with the matter, but it has also formed an issue in the appeal to this court. I have, I fear, to say that the advocates who appeared below did not discharge their duty properly to the court in that they apparently failed to be aware of the existence of that authority...

Brooke LJ: ... The English system of justice has always been dependent on the quality of the assistance that advocates give to the bench. This is one of the reasons why, in contrast to systems of justice in other countries, English judges are almost invariably in a position to give judgment at the end of a straightforward hearing without having to do their own research and without the state having to incur the cost of legal assistance for judges because they cannot rely on the advocates to show them the law they need to apply....

NOTE

Decisions are often supported by a series of justifications (arguments) that may use reasoning internal to the law (eg the interpretation and application of a precedent or text) or external to strict positive law (eg arguments of policy or morality: see *Hill v Chief Constable*, above). Recourse to metaphor is not unusual (see eg *Spartan Steel*, below, p 404); and in one tort case the majority based its decision on the notion of 'practical justice' (*White v Jones* (1995), below, p 260).

1.6 European considerations

European law, in the sense of law having its direct or indirect source in continental Europe, impacts on tort law in three main ways. First, there is EU law which finds expression in regulatory texts, European Directives and in European Court of Justice decisions. UK courts must have regard to this law (European Communities Act 1972); and failure to implement a Directive may give an individual the right to sue in tort. Secondly, there is human rights law where the UK courts are under a statutory duty to 'take into account' any decisions of the European Court of Human Rights or opinion or decision of the Commission (Human Rights Act 1998, s 2(1)). Thirdly there are the continental legal systems themselves which produce not just their own legal decisions on 'tort' problems but much academic writing on the law of obligations within the member states of the EU. These court decisions are in no way binding on UK courts, but judges sometimes take note of developments in the civil law systems (see eg *Fairchild v Glenhaven Funeral Services Ltd*, extracted later in this chapter). In addition, several unofficial groups of (mainly) continental jurists are working on the codification of tort law (see, eg, *Principles of European Tort Law*) and, while these codes are unlikely to replace English law in the foreseeable future, they ought not to be ignored by today's UK law student.

1.6.1 European union

One important European source is the Directive. These are texts that are not as such directly enforceable as a statute and thus they need to be implemented. One such implementation that is of importance to tort lawyers is the Consumer Protection Act 1987 (see p 160) which implements the Council Directive of 25 July 1985 on liability for defective products. However failure to implement a Directive can give rise to a tort on behalf of individuals.

R v Transport Sec, Ex p Factortame Ltd (No 7) [2001] 1 WLR 942, QBD

This was an action for damages brought by Spanish fishermen against the United Kingdom for breach of European Community law. On a preliminary issue a question arose as to whether certain new parties and new claims could be added to the proceedings or whether they were statute-barred under the Limitation Act 1980. A further question arose as to whether the claimants were entitled to damages for injury to feelings and distress. The judge held that the new parties and claims were statute-barred and that damages were limited strictly to economic losses.

Judge John Toulmin QC: ... **56**. It was not until the *Francovich* case [1995] ICR 722 that the European Court of Justice gave a right to individuals to recover damages against the state for the state's failure to implement a directive, provided the appropriate conditions were fulfilled.

57. The court said, at p 772, para 41: 'Those conditions are sufficient to give rise to a right on the part of individuals to obtain reparation, a right founded directly on Community law.'

58. This finding must be read in the light of the explanation given in *Factortame 4* [1996] QB 404, 455, at para 42, that individuals derive their rights from Community law, but the means of enforcing those rights are derived from the principle that an unlawful act or omission of the member states gives rise to an obligation to make good the damage caused...

145. An action for breach of English statutory duty is properly classified as an action founded on tort. It is argued that this can be properly extended to breaches of Community law by the government in these circumstances. The breach relied on in relation to breaches of the Treaty is the government's breach of its obligations under section 2(1) of the European Communities Act 1972, which requires domestic law to give effect to all rights, powers, liabilities, obligations and restrictions arising out of the Treaties and provides that where there is an enforceable Community right it should be enforceable as a matter of domestic law...

148. [The authorities do] not address the fundamental problem of whether or not an action by an individual against a government for breach of Community law can properly be described as an action founded on tort. Nevertheless, giving the statute the widest construction in accordance with its purpose, a combination of a breach of article 52 of the Treaty (now article 43 EC) and section 2(1) of the European Communities Act 1972 does amount to a breach of statutory duty which is within section 2 of the Limitation Act 1980.

149. This does not absolve me from answering the fundamental question. I start from the fact that the term 'action founded on tort' is not defined in section 2 of the 1980 Act and that it is within the purpose of the Act that the words should be given a wide construction.

150. Following the approach suggested by Lord Hoffmann in the *Banque Bruxelles Lambert* case [1997] AC 191, 211, I define a tort as a breach of non-contractual duty which gives a private law right to the party injured to recover compensatory damages at common law from the party causing the injury.

151. This covers not only the present case but those few torts in English law where violation of a plaintiff's interest without proof of actual damage is sufficient to found a claim in tort...

NOTE

Note the formalist definition of tort based on duty, right and remedy.

1.6.2 Human rights

The incorporation of the European Convention of Human Rights and Fundamental Freedoms into English law by the Human Rights Act 1998 (see p 108) is a constitutional event of immense importance to the law of tort. The Convention and Act impact on English law in a direct (vertical) way in as much as the Act creates a new form of liability (Human Rights Act 1998, s 6(1)) which will give rise to 'such relief or remedy... as [a court] considers just and appropriate' (s 8(1)). They also impact in an indirect (horizontal) way in as much as the Convention rights – together with decisions of the European Court of Human Rights – are modifying existing areas of tort law such as negligence, nuisance and defamation. *Z v United Kingdom* (see pp 306, 310) is a good example of the importance of the European Court jurisprudence on the English tort of negligence (see *Barrett v Enfield LBC*, p 305). Another decision that ought in principle to be of importance both to tort and to constitutional law is *Steel & Morris v UK* (see p 270).

1.6.3 Influence of civil law

Finally mention must be made of the indirect influence of European law on English tort. In this context 'European law' refers not just to the case law (jurisprudence) of France, Germany and other continental systems but also Roman law (read Lord Rodger in the law report).

Fairchild v Glenhaven Funeral Services Ltd [2002] 3 WLR 89, HL

(For facts see p 348)

Lord Bingham: ... **32.** ... Development of the law in this country cannot of course depend on a head-count of decisions and codes adopted in other countries around the world, often against a background of different rules and traditions. The law must be developed coherently, in accordance with principle, so as to serve, even-handedly, the ends of justice. If, however, a decision is given in this country which offends one's basic sense of justice, and if consideration of international sources suggests that a different and more acceptable decision would be given in most other jurisdictions, whatever their legal tradition, this must prompt anxious review of the decision in question. In a shrinking world (in which the employees of asbestos companies may work for those companies in any one or more of several countries) there must be some virtue in uniformity of outcome whatever the diversity of approach in reaching that outcome...

Lord Rodger: ... **156.** I derive support for that conclusion from what has been done in other legal systems. In the course of the hearing counsel for both sides referred to authorities from a number of different jurisdictions. It would be impossible to do justice to all of them in this opinion. Broadly speaking, they appear to me to demonstrate two things: first, that other systems have identified the need to adopt special rules or principles to cope with situations where the claimant cannot establish which of a number of wrongdoers actually caused his injury; secondly, that there are considerable divergences of view and indeed uncertainty as to the proper area within which any such special rules or principles should apply. I have simply selected a few among the many authorities cited by counsel...

NOTE

It might be tempting to think that this judicial interest in Europe is a recent phenomenon. It is not. Over a century ago, particularly after the abolition of the forms action in 1852, the English judges seriously started to look over the Channel for guidance in particular areas of private law (see eg *Taylor v Caldwell* (1863); and see generally G Samuel, *Law of Obligations and Legal Remedies* (2nd edn, Cavendish,2001), 99–111). The two World Wars discouraged this process, but the impact of these events is receding, at least in the minds of some, with the result that a number of common lawyers are interesting themselves once again with Europe and with comparative law.

Chapter 2

Purpose and Policy
of Tort

A major definitional perspective of the law of tort is, as we have seen, from the position of its function. The category having been established as an historical fact, one can ask what are its aims or what is its purpose? In truth this may involve a number of different viewpoints within functionalism depending upon differences of method, philosophy and (or) policy.

2.1 Aims and philosophy of the Law of Tort

Yet defining tort from the position of its purpose and function is by no means easy. The subject's fragmentary basis in a wide range of old forms (now causes) of action is at the heart of the problem since this fragmentation is equally reflected in its functions. Moreover the lack of any formal distinction between public and private law – between administrative and civil liability – means that tort ends up playing an important administrative and constitutional law role (cf **Chapter 9**). This constitutional role has become increasingly acute, and in some ways more complex, with the incorporation of the European Convention for the Protection of Human Rights and Fundamental Freedoms into English Law (Human Rights Act 1998). The absence of any strict divisions, at the level of remedies at any rate, between property and obligations, and between personal and patrimonial rights, results in yet further roles for tort. It ends up as the category providing remedies for the 'vindication' of property rights and of personal rights such as privacy (to the extent that it actually protects this interest). This said, it must be remembered that statistically the great majority of tort claims are for personal injury arising out of accidents on the road or in the factory. Personal injury thus dominates the purpose and policy dimension. All these differing aims and functions have created, as the next extract suggests, an atmosphere of 'crisis'.

André Tunc, *Introduction*, Torts, *International Encyclopedia of Comparative Law* vol XI, Ch 1 (footnotes omitted)

1. ... The law of tort ... is in a state of crisis. It may have reached its zenith; at the very moment where it occupies a position without precedent, it is impregnated and surrounded by institutions which deeply modify its traditional working and put into question its functions and its domain. Inherited from a time when there was neither social security nor insurance, it is now threatened by the rise of these institutions of loss distribution. Furthermore, it has been designed to govern individuals and it now

mainly applies to private and public enterprises. The notions according to which western societies have lived for centuries are no longer true: it is no longer true that we are liable for the harm we have done by a tort, since it is likely that we will be either employed or insured; by reason of social security it is no longer true that no-one can recover for the damage he suffers as a consequence of his own fault. In certain respects man is more responsible than ever; his power to cause harm (as is his power to help his fellow men) is multiplied by increased industrialization and by the general development of technology. In other respects, as a result of the emergence of social security and insurance, his responsibility disappears.

Clearly, the law of tort needs a deep reconsideration...

QUESTION

These words were written over thirty years ago. Why is it that the law of tort seems, to date, not to have been subject to any serious reconsideration?

NOTE

In a famous article published half a century ago Professor Glanville Williams identified a number of differing aims of the law of tort ((1951) 4 CLP 137; and see also Glanville Williams and BA Hepple, *Foundations of the Law of Tort* (2nd edn, Butterworths, 1984), 27–30). The most important of these aims are:

(a) compensation;
(b) deterrence; and
(c) protecting constitutional rights.

Other aims include:

(d) protecting expectation interests;
(e) preventing unjust enrichment and;
(f) determining status. Behind these aims is, as the next extract suggests, the philosophy of justice, the major dichotomy being that between distributive and corrective justice.

McFarlane v Tayside Health Board [2000] 2 AC 59, HL

This was an action for damages by a husband and wife to recover the cost of bringing up a healthy and normal child born to the wife. The couple alleged they followed negligent advice on the effect of a vasectomy performed on the husband. The House of Lords (Lords Slynn, Steyn and Hope; Lords Millett and Clyde dissenting in part) rejected the claim.

Lord Steyn: My Lords, A surgeon wrongly and negligently advised a husband and wife that a vasectomy had rendered the husband infertile. Acting on his advice they ceased to take contraceptive precautions. The wife became pregnant and gave birth to a healthy child. The question is what damages, if any, the parents are in principle entitled to recover...

▶

It is possible to view the case simply from the perspective of corrective justice. It requires somebody who has harmed another without justification to indemnify the other. On this approach the parents' claim for the cost of bringing up Catherine must succeed. But one may also approach the case from the vantage point of distributive justice. It requires a focus on the just distribution of burdens and losses among members of a society. If the matter is approached in this way, it may become relevant to ask commuters on the Underground the following question: Should the parents of an unwanted but healthy child be able to sue the doctor or hospital for compensation equivalent to the cost of bringing up the child for the years of his or her minority, i.e. until about 18 years? My Lords, I am firmly of the view that an overwhelming number of ordinary men and women would answer the question with an emphatic 'No.' And the reason for such a response would be an inarticulate premise as to what is morally acceptable and what is not. Like Ognall J in *Jones v Berkshire Area Health Authority* (unreported) 2 July 1986 they will have in mind that many couples cannot have children and others have the sorrow and burden of looking after a disabled child. The realisation that compensation for financial loss in respect of the upbringing of a child would necessarily have to discriminate between rich and poor would surely appear unseemly to them. It would also worry them that parents may be put in a position of arguing in court that the unwanted child, which they accepted and care for, is more trouble than it is worth. Instinctively, the traveller on the Underground would consider that the law of tort has no business to provide legal remedies consequent up upon the birth of a healthy child, which all of us regard as a valuable and good thing.

My Lords, to explain decisions denying a remedy for the cost of bringing up an unwanted child by saying that there is no loss, no foreseeable loss, no causative link or no ground reasonable restitution is to resort to unrealistic and formalistic propositions which mask the real reasons for the decisions. And judges ought to strive to give the real reasons for their decision. It is my firm conviction that where courts of law have denied a remedy for the cost of bringing up an unwanted child the real reasons have been grounds of distributive justice. That is, of course, a moral theory. It may be objected that the House must act like a court of law and not like a court of morals. That would only be partly right. The court must apply positive law. But judges' sense of the moral answer to a question, or the justice of the case, has been one of the great shaping forces of the common law. What may count in a situation of difficulty and uncertainty is not the subjective view of the judge but what he reasonably believes that the ordinary citizen would regard as right...

In my view it is legitimate in the present case to take into account considerations of distributive justice. That does not mean that I would decide the case on grounds of public policy. On the contrary, I would avoid those quick sands. Relying on principles of distributive justice I am persuaded that our tort law does not permit parents of a healthy unwanted child to claim the costs of bringing up the child from a health authority or a doctor. If it were necessary to do so, I would say that the claim does not satisfy the requirement of being fair, just and reasonable.

This conclusion is reinforced by an argument of coherence...

QUESTIONS

1. How does Lord Steyn in *McFarlane* know what people on the underground might think? Is this a helpful or useful way of deciding cases?

2. Lord Steyn in *McFarlane* denies that he is deciding the case on grounds of public policy. Do you agree? (Cf MA Jones, *Textbook on Torts* (8th edn, OUP, 2002) 15–18.)

3. What do you consider to be the most powerful motivating reason behind the decision in *McFarlane*: (a) the 'no business' thesis of the traveller on the underground; (b) distributive justice theory; (c) the discomfort felt by the judges that the NHS should be paying out to families with healthy children; (d) practical justice? Would you classify (c) as a policy argument?

4. The judgment of Lord Steyn in *McFarlane* has been deliberately cut off after his opening paragraph statement about coherence. What do you imagine this coherence argument to be about?

NOTES

1. See now *Rees v Darlington Memorial Hospital NHS Trust* (pp 329, 377, 380).

2. Another form of justice, namely 'practical justice', has also been identified by the English judiciary.

Attorney-General v Blake [2001] 1 AC 268, HL

Lord Steyn: ... I bear in mind that the enduring strength of the common law is that it has been developed on a case-by-case basis by judges for whom the attainment of practical justice was a major objective of their work. It is still one of the major moulding forces of judicial decision-making. These observations are almost banal: the public would be astonished if it was thought that judges did not conceive it as their prime duty to do practical justice whenever possible. A recent example of this process at work is *White v Jones* [1995] 2 AC 207 where by a majority the House of Lords held that a solicitor who caused loss to a third party by negligence in the preparation of a will is liable in damages. Subordinating conceptual difficulties to the needs of practical justice a majority, and notably Lord Goff of Chieveley, at pp. 259G-260H, upheld the claim...

QUESTION

How does 'practical justice' differ from other forms of justice? Do the public have a well-developed notion of practical justice? If they do, do you think this accords with the judicial view of practical justice?

NOTE

In addition to the doctrinal work on the purpose, policy and aims of the law of tort, there is a huge body of literature, especially American, devoted to the theory and philosophy behind tort liability (see eg Owen, *Philosophical Foundations of Tort Law* (OUP, 1995)). Indeed, there is enough to fill a whole course on the subject. Some theories are based directly on particular notions of justice; thus an emphasis on individual *corrective justice* usually focuses on the balance between individuals in society and the moral imperative behind the obligation to pay damages. Theories of *distributive justice* often emphasise the statistical cost (human and economic) of certain activities and the unrealistic nature of moral imperatives in a legal structure where most defendants are insured and accidents statistics are predictable. These theories motivate the debate between fault and no-fault liability. In the USA the law and economics school has been particularly active in the area of tort law (see **2.3**), but old ideas about individual responsibility and freedom to act are by no means dead as the next extracts indicate.

Read v J Lyons & Co Ltd [1947] AC 156, HL

(For facts see p 185)

Lord Macmillan: ...In my opinion the appellant's statement of claim discloses no ground of action against the respondents. The action is one of damages for personal injuries. Whatever may have been the law of England in early times I am of opinion that as the law now stands an allegation of negligence is in general essential to the relevancy of an action of reparation for personal injuries. The gradual development of the law in the matter of civil liability is discussed and traced by the late Sir William Holdsworth with ample learning and lucidity in his *History of English Law*, vol 8, pp. 446 et seq, and need not here be rehearsed. Suffice it to say that the process of evolution has been from the principle that every man acts at his peril and is liable for all the consequences of his acts to the principle that a man's freedom of action is subject only to the obligation not to infringe any duty of care which he owes to others. The emphasis formerly was on the injury sustained and the question was whether the case fell within one of the accepted classes of common law actions; the emphasis now is on the conduct of the person whose act has occasioned the injury and the question is whether it can be characterized as negligent. I do not overlook the fact that there is at least one instance in the present law in which the primitive rule survives, namely, in the case of animals ferae naturae or animals mansuetae naturae which have shown dangerous proclivities. The owner or keeper of such an animal has an absolute duty to confine or control it so that it shall not do injury to others and no proof of care on his part will absolve him from responsibility. But this is probably not so much a vestigial relic of otherwise discarded doctrine as a special rule of practical good sense. At any rate, it is too well established to be challenged. But such an exceptional case as this affords no justification for its extension by analogy...

Lord Simonds: ... Here is an age-long conflict of theories which is to be found in every system of law. 'A man acts at his peril,' says one theory. 'A man is not liable unless he is to blame,' answers the other. It will not surprise the students of English law or of anything English to find that between these theories a middle way, a compromise, has been found...

NOTE

Given the discursive nature of common law judgments, the policy, aims and philosophy questions remain important in the understanding of the case law itself. Different judgments can reveal differing theoretical perspectives. However the judges themselves do tend to agree on one thing; that English tort law has committed itself to no single theory.

Broome v Cassell & Co Ltd [1972] AC 1027, HL

Lord Wilberforce (dissenting): ... English law does not work in an analytical fashion;... That is why the terminology used is empirical and not scientific. And there is more than merely practical justification for this attitude. For particularly over the range of torts for which punitive damages may be given (trespass to person or property, false imprisonment and defamation being the commonest) there is much to be said before one can safely assert that the true or basic principle of the law of damages in tort is compensation, or, if it is, what the compensation is for (if one says that a plaintiff is given compensation because he has been injured, one is really denying the word its true meaning) or, if there is compensation, whether there is not in all cases, or at least in some, of which defamation may be an example, also a delictual element which contemplates some penalty for the defendant. It cannot lightly be taken for granted, even as a matter of theory, that the purpose of the law of tort is compensation, still less that it ought to be, an issue of large social import, or that there is something inappropriate or illogical or anomalous (a question-begging word) in including a punitive element in civil damages, or, conversely, that the criminal law, rather than the civil law, is in these cases the better instrument for conveying social disapproval, or for redressing a wrong to the social fabric, or that damages in any case can be broken down into the two separate elements. As a matter of practice English law has not committed itself to any of these theories: it may have been wiser than it knew...

...Take a common case: a man is assaulted, or his land is trespassed upon, with accompanying circumstances of insolence or contumely. He decides to bring an action for damages, he need not further specify the claim. Is he suing for compensation, for injury to his feelings, to teach his opponent a lesson, to vindicate his rights, or 'the strength of the law,' or for a mixture of these things? Most men would not ask themselves such questions, many men could not answer them. If they could answer them, they might give different answers. The reaction to a libel may be anything from 'how outrageous' to 'he has delivered himself into my hands.' The fact is that the plaintiff sues for damages, inviting the court to take all the facts into consideration, and, if he wins, he may ascribe his victory to all or any of the ingredients...

QUESTION

Is Lord Wilberforce in truth committing himself to a theory?

2.2 Compensation and loss spreading

One broad way of defining tort in terms of its purpose and policies is through the remedies associated with this category (cf **Chapter 11**). By far the most important of these is damages; only the equitable remedy of injunction has any other real claim and this remedy is more or less limited to certain specific torts (*Miller v Jackson* (1977), p 14). However the deterrence effect of forcing a defendant to pay damages is now in question.

Reid v Rush & Tompkins plc [1990] 1 WLR 212, CA

This was an action for damages by an employee against his employer. The facts are well-summarised by Ralph Gibson LJ: 'The plaintiff on 26 January 1984 suffered severe injuries while driving the defendant's Landrover vehicle on a road in Ethiopia in the course of his employment by the defendant as a quarry foreman on the Armati Diversion Project. His injuries were caused by a collision between the Landrover and a lorry which was being driven along the road in the opposite direction by some person whose identity is not known. The defendant was in no way responsible for the happening of the accident of which the sole cause was the negligence of the lorry driver. The plaintiff has alleged that the defendant was in breach of its duty of care as employer in failing either to insure the plaintiff so as to provide suitable benefits to him in the event of his being injured, as a result of the negligence of a third party, in such a traffic accident or to advise the plaintiff to obtain such insurance cover for himself. His case is that if he had been so advised he would have obtained personal accident cover'. The Court of Appeal (Ralph Gibson LJ, May LJ and Neill LJ) held the employer not liable.

Ralph Gibson LJ: ... The defendant, apart from submitting that the law leaves to employees the responsibility for deciding whether they need personal accident insurance, has not contended that the special risk is not sufficiently special or unusual to provide an arguable case for the plaintiff if he can surmount the legal barriers which, on the defendant's submissions, justify striking out his claim. The defendant recognises, rightly in my view, that assessment of the nature and extent of the risk, for the purposes of the plaintiff's case, must be made, if the case is to proceed, when the evidence is before the court. It was for that reason that detailed submissions were not made by either side as to the extent of the risk in this country of suffering injury which may go uncompensated. Nevertheless, before considering the points of law raised in the submissions before the court, it is useful to describe, and to put into context, the special risk upon which the plaintiff's case depends.

It is, of course, not the case under the law of this country that in respect of all injuries, caused by the fault of another, a claimant will be able actually to recover the compensation which the law would award in respect of his injuries. The person responsible may have no money. For some 50 years the law has dealt with one of the most common causes of serious injury by the requirement of compulsory third party insurance in respect of the use on the public roads of a motor vehicle. Effective cover, in the event of the driver in breach of the law having no insurance cover, was provided by means of the Motor Insurers' Bureau agreement in 1946, and was extended to the case of the untraced driver in 1969. A description of the terms and of the wording of the MIB agreements can be found in *Charlesworth & Percy on Negligence*, 7th ed (1983), c 17, pp. 1036–1042. Effective cover, however, is by no means complete even for traffic accidents: a pedestrian or a cyclist may be solely to blame for an accident in which a driver or other persons are seriously hurt and there is no compulsory insurance or scheme like that of the MIB to cover such accidents. Further the MIB is not liable where the accident occurred in some place which was not a public road: see *Buchanan v Motor Insurers' Bureau* [1955] 1 WLR 488.

As to accidents which a servant may suffer in the course of his employment as a result of the fault of the master, or of a fellow servant, actual recovery of the compensation to which the servant was in law entitled was for many years not certain because the master might have no money and no insurance to cover his liability. Compulsory insurance against liability to employees was required by the Employers' Liability (Compulsory Insurance) Act 1969 – which came into force on 1 January 1972 – but the requirement applies only to 'liability for bodily injury or disease sustained by his employees, and arising out of and in the course of their employment in Great Britain': see section 1(1). Insurance for liability for 'injury or disease suffered or contracted outside Great Britain' is only compulsory when required by regulations. According to the note to the Act of 1969 in *Halsbury's Statutes of England and Wales*, 4th ed., vol 16 (1986), p 181, the Act of 1969 has been applied to employers of persons working on or from off-shore installations in designated areas of the continental shelf and territorial waters by the Offshore Installation (Application of the Employers' Liability (Compulsory Insurance) Act 1969) Regulations 1975 (S.I. 1975 No. 1289) made under the Mineral Workings (Off-Shore Installations) Act 1971. Failure to insure as required by the Act of 1969 is a criminal offence: see section 5. There is, however, no scheme equivalent to that of the MIB to ensure recovery of compensation by a servant in respect of injury suffered in this country if, in breach of law, the employer has failed to take out insurance cover.

Next, it is to be noted that the insurance required by the Act of 1969 applies only to liability to employees. Liability to members of the public is, I think, usually covered by a public liability policy in the case of responsible employers whose activities expose members of the public to risk of injury but the law imposes no statutory duty to have such insurance cover and serious injury might be suffered without compensation by a servant in the course of his employment as a result of the wrongdoing of a third party not concerned with the use of a motor vehicle on a public road.

Another common form of injury for which the victim cannot normally recover substantial compensation from the wrongdoer is criminal injury. The Criminal Injuries Compensation Scheme, which came into operation in 1964, enabled the Criminal Injuries Compensation Board to make ex gratia payments in respect of personal injury directly attributable to a crime of violence, to an arrest of an offender, to the prevention of an offence, or to the giving of help to a constable engaged on making an arrest or preventing an offence. Details of the current scheme as revised in 1979 are now contained in the 21st Report of the Board (Cmnd. 9684). Two matters must be noted: first, the scheme applies only to injuries suffered in this country or upon a British ship or aircraft and not to criminal injuries suffered abroad, and, secondly, the scheme provides no compensation for property or economic loss caused by crime save for such loss resulting from a criminal injury within the scheme.

From this limited survey it can be seen that in a number of cases it is possible for someone to suffer personal injury in this country, caused by the wrongdoing of another, for which the victim may well not recover the compensation which the law would award. Further, in respect of injury suffered or disease contracted outside this country by a person normally resident here, or employed abroad by an employer based in this country, there is in general no protection of compulsory employers' insurance and, in respect of the special claims of injury arising from road accidents or criminal activity, there is no protection from any body such as the MIB or the Criminal Injuries Compensation Board...

NOTES

1. Viewed from the position of damages one can talk of the law of tort as being concerned with compensation, but several qualifications must be made here. First, to talk in terms of compensation is to view tort from the position of the claimant; tort can, and must, equally be viewed from the position of the defendant. From this position tort can be seen in terms of freedom of action; or, put another way, tort equally aims to promote initiative and risk-taking, important to the economic welfare of society. Thus one might add that tort can equally be viewed from the perspective of society and from this perspective a number of conflicting aims come into play.

2. Secondly, the rise of insurance has impacted on tort (and contract) in a number of ways. It goes far in undermining the deterrence aim in as much as the wrongdoer is not the one who must shoulder the burden of the damages. Yet it also provides a means of loss-spreading.

3. Thirdly, an award of damages in tort is not the only means of securing help and compensation for harm. Private insurance, social security, criminal injuries compensation, family support, charity and of course the National Health Service (NHS) are other support systems. Tort needs to be considered in relation to these other systems and not just because this contextual perspective is an accepted part of any tort course. These other systems are also of importance because they can directly influence the actual reasoning and decisions of the judges (see eg *Wadey v Surrey CC*, p 394).

4. Fourthly, damages as a remedy has a variety of aims and functions not all of which are compensatory (see **Chapter 11**). These differing functions are directly reflected back into the causes of action that give rise to the remedy and thus compensation has to be distinguished, for example, from restitution and from deterrence (cf Proceeds of Crime Act 2002). In other words damages as a common law monetary remedy needs to be distinguished from other monetary claims such as an action for debt, an action for account or a claim for damages in equity. Indeed, some claims for 'damages' are in substance really 'debt' (see eg *The Stonedale (No 1)* (1956); *Yorkshire Electricity Board v British Telecom* (1986)) or account actions (see eg *Att-Gen v Blake* (2001)) and as a result they belong in substantive categories different from tort.

QUESTION

Do the courts always fully appreciate these differing aims and functions of the law of tort?

Lister v Romford Ice & Cold Storage Co Ltd [1957] AC 555, HL

This was an action in damages and (or) debt by an insurance company, subrogated to the rights of an assured employer, against an employee who had, while driving a lorry, negligently injured a fellow-employee. The fellow-employee had obtained damages, paid by the insurance company, on the basis that the employer was vicariously liable for the fault of its lorry driving employee. The insurance company based their claims on breach of an implied term of the employee's contract of employment (damages) and (or) on statutory rights of contribution and indemnity (debt). A majority of the House of Lords (Viscount

Simonds, Lord Morton and Lord Tucker; Lords Radcliffe and Somerville dissenting) gave judgment for the insurance company.

Viscount Simonds: ... [referring to Denning LJ's dissenting judgment in the Court of Appeal] ... [H]e says: 'This shows that there is an implied term in these cases whereby, if the employer is insured, he will not seek to recover contribution or indemnity from the servant.'

It will be observed that the implied term which thus commended itself to the learned Lord Justice is limited in its scope. The driver is to be relieved from liability if his master is covered by insurance against the claim. If he is not covered, for instance, because the accident takes place not on a road but on private premises and the law does not require him to insure against such a risk, and he has not done so, then under this plea the driver must bear the consequences of his negligence if he is himself sued. This consideration led counsel to yet another variation of the plea. This was that the driver was entitled to be indemnified not only if the employer was in fact insured or was required by law to be insured, but also if he ought, as a reasonable and prudent man, to have been insured against the risk in question...

My Lords, undoubtedly there are formidable obstacles in the path of the appellant ... First, it is urged that it must be irrelevant to the right of the master to sue his servant for breach of duty that the master is insured against its consequences. As a general proposition it has not, I think, been questioned for nearly 200 years that in determining the rights *inter se* of A and B the fact that one or other of them is insured is to be disregarded ... And this general proposition no doubt, applies if A is a master and B his man. But its application to a case or class of case must yield to an express or implied term to the contrary, and, as the question is whether that term should be implied, I am not constrained by an assertion of the general proposition to deny the possible exception. Yet I cannot wholly ignore a principle so widely applicable as that a man insures at his own expense for his own benefit and does not thereby suffer any derogation of his rights against another man...

Here, it was said, was a duty alleged to arise out of the relation of master and servant in this special sphere of employment which was imposed by the common law. When, then, did it first arise? Not, surely, when the first country squire exchanged his carriage and horses for a motor car or the first haulage contractor bought a motor lorry. Was it when the practice of insurers against third-party risk became so common that it was to be expected of the reasonable man or was it only when the Act of 1930 made compulsory and therefore universal what had previously been reasonable and usual?...

Lord Radcliffe (dissenting): ... Now, the insurance policy required [by the Road Traffic Act 1930] could not come into existence of its own motion. One of the two parties, employer and employed, had to assume responsibility for taking it out or keeping it running and for paying up the necessary premiums to buy the cover. To which of them ought we to attribute that responsibility, having regard to the relationship of the parties? In my view, to the employer. I cannot suppose that, short of special stipulation, any other answer would be given in such a case...

Then it is sought to show that the term in question cannot exist in law because it has never been heard of before this case. When did it first enter into the relations of employer and employed? Could it really have existed since the Road Traffic Act, 1930, if it did not exist before it? My Lords, I do not know because I do not think that I need to know. After all we need not speak of the master's action against his servant for negligence as if it had been common fare at the law for centuries. Economic reasons alone would have made the action a rarity. If such actions are now to be the usual practice I think it neither too soon nor too late to examine afresh some of their implications in a society which has been almost revolutionised by the growth of all forms of insurance...

Lord Somerville (dissenting): ... Romer LJ [in the Court of Appeal], at the end of his judgment said that it was not in the public interest that drivers should be immune from the financial consequences of their negligence. The public interest has for long tolerated owners being so immune, and it would, I think, be unreasonable if it was to discriminate against those who earned their living by driving. Both are subject to the sanction of the criminal law as to careless or dangerous driving. The driver has a further sanction in that accidents causing damage are likely to hinder his advancement...

QUESTIONS

1. The real claimant in this case was the insurance company. Do you think it right that they should be able to escape from a risk that they had been paid to take?

2. Is the remedy of subrogation based on principles of tort, contract, equity or restitution (unjust enrichment)? Do you think adequate consideration was given to this question in *Lister*? (Cf *Morris v Ford Motor Co* (1973).)

3. 'Commentators and judges should think twice before making off-hand comments that insurance should be relevant to the scope of tort liability, that judges should take into account 'the realities of insurance' or that they should address the comparative insurability of parties' (Stapleton (1995) 58 MLR 820, 843). Why should they think twice?

4. 'There is no doubt that insurance profoundly influences the practical operation of the law of tort' (Lewis (2005) 25 LS 85, 86). How? (Cf **2.6**.)

NOTE

Another point that must be stressed is that *damages* and *damage* are not the same (see eg *Adams v Bracknell Forest BC*, p 77). Not all damage will attract compensation (damages) and thus a second descriptive concept, that of an *interest*, needs to be brought into the model. As the next case illustrates, tort can be seen as a matter of protected and unprotected interests.

Spartan Steel & Alloys Ltd v Martin & Co (Contractors) Ltd [1973] 1 QB 27, CA

(For facts and further extract see p 137)

Lord Denning MR: ... The second consideration is the nature of the hazard, namely, the cutting of the supply of electricity. This is a hazard which we all run. It may be due to a short circuit, to a flash of lightning, to a tree falling on the wires, to an accidental cutting of the cable, or even to the negligence of someone or other. And when it does happen, it affects a multitude of persons; not as a rule by way of physical damage to them or their property, but by putting them to inconvenience, and sometimes to economic loss. The supply is usually restored in a few hours, so the economic loss is not very large. Such a hazard is regarded by most people as a thing they must put up with – without seeking compensation from anyone. Some there are who install a stand-by system. Others seek refuge by taking out an insurance policy against breakdown in the supply. But most people are content to take the risk on themselves. When the supply is cut off, they do not go running round to their solicitor. They do not try to find out whether it was anyone's fault. They just put up with it. They try to make up the economic loss by doing more work next day. This is a healthy attitude which the law should encourage...

2.3 Deterence

The deterrence aspect of the law of tort manifests it two main ways. First, there is the direct deterrence effect of imposing damages as a sanction; paying for the harm one causes through bad behaviour is supposed to deter such behaviour. The problem here is that most tort claims arise out of accidents on the road or in the workplace and both these sources attract compulsory insurance. There is, however, a second and more subtle manifestation of the deterrence theory. The law and economics school uses the notion of economic efficiency both as a criterion for analysing case law decisions and as a normative principle for determining the outcome of tort litigation.

2.3.1 Damages as deterrence

Fault, damages and deterrence come together in the following extract.

Lister v Romford Ice & Cold Storage Co Ltd [1957] AC 555, HL

(See p 52)

Viscount Simonds: ... It was contended, too, that a term should not be implied by law of which the social consequences would be harmful. The common law demands that the servant should exercise his proper skill and care in the performance of his duty: the graver the consequences of any dereliction, the more important it is that the sanction which the law imposes should be maintained. That sanction is that he should be liable in damages to his master: Other sanctions there may be, dismissal perhaps and loss of character and difficulty of getting fresh employment, but an action for damages, whether for tort or for breach of contract, has, even if rarely used, for centuries been available to the master, and now to grant the servant immunity from such an action would tend to create a feeling of irresponsibility in a class of persons from whom, perhaps more than any other, constant vigilance is owed to the community...

QUESTIONS

1. Does an employee undertake never to make a mistake in the performance of his duties? Ought employees to take out insurance against injuring either their employer or their employer's insurance company?

2. Should car drivers be made personally liable for any tort damages they have to pay to victims of their bad driving? What would be the disadvantages, from an aims of the law of tort perspective, of such a rule?

3. A company deliberately commits a tort hoping that the profit it will make from the tortious act will be much greater than any damages it will have to pay to the tort victim. Should the victim be able to sue the tortfeasor in damages only for the amount of his loss?

Broome v Cassell & Co [1972] AC 1027, HL

This was an appeal by publishers of a book (written by David Irving), known by them to be libellous before publication, against an award of punitive (exemplary) damages made by the jury. A majority of the House of Lords (Lords Hailsham LC, Reid, Morris and Kilbrandon; Viscount Dilhorne and Lords Wilberforce and Diplock dissenting) upheld the award.

Lord Reid: ... It was argued that to allow punitive damages in this case would hamper other publishers or limit their freedom to conduct their business because it can always be inferred that publishers publish any book because they expect to profit from it. But punitive damages could not be given unless it was proved that they knew that passages in the book were libellous and could not be justified or at least deliberately shut their eyes to the truth. I would hope that no publisher would publish in such circumstances. There is no question of curtailing the freedom of a reputable publisher.

Lord Kilbrandon: ... If a publisher knows, or has reason to believe, that the act of publication will subject him to compensatory damages, it must be that, since he is actuated by the profit-motive, he is confident that by that publication he will not be the loser. Some deterrent, over and above compensatory damages, may in these circumstances be called for.

Lord Diplock (dissenting): ... The award of damages as the remedy for all civil wrongs was in England the creature of the common law. It is a field of law in which there has been but little intervention by Parliament. It is judge-made law par excellence. Its original purpose in cases of trespass was to discourage private revenge in a primitive society inadequately policed, at least as much as it was to compensate the victim for the material harm occasioned to him...

No one would today suggest this as a justification for rewarding the victim of a tort for refraining from unlawful vengeance on the wrong-doer. Conversely, the punishment of wrong-doers today is regarded as the function of the state to be exercised subject to safeguards for the accused assured to him by the procedure of the criminal law and with the appropriate punishment assessed by a dispassionate judge and not by a jury roused to indignation by partisan advocacy. One of the most significant and humane developments in English law over the past century and a half has been the increasing protection accorded to the accused under our system of criminal justice. As my noble and learned friend, Lord Reid has pointed out no similar protection is available to a defendant as a party to a civil action.

So the survival into the latter half of the twentieth century of the power of a jury in a civil trial to impose a penalty on a defendant simply to punish him had become an anomaly which it lay within the power of this House in its judicial capacity to restrict or to remove; though it would have been anticipating by two years the recent change in the practice of this House if to have done so would have involved overruling one of its own previous decisions.

NOTE

See **Chapter 11**.

QUESTIONS

1. Should the victim have any remedy additional to, or in the place of, a remedy in damages? (Cf *Att-Gen v Blake* (2001).)

2. Does the fear of having to pay high damages deter publication of certain newspaper stories? If so, is this deterrence a legitimate function of tort?

2.3.2 Economic efficiency and deterrence

A more subtle version of the deterrence theory is to be found in the work of the law and economics school.

Michael A Jones, *Textbook on Torts* (8th edn, OUP, 2002), 20–1

Economic efficiency as an objective of tort is a variant of deterrence. It has been argued, for example, that to the extent that an activity imposes costs on others for which it does not have to pay, the activity is being subsidised and its price does not reflect its true cost. This distorts the market mechanism, because the activity is underpriced, and this leads to inefficiency. The solution is to require activities to 'internalise' these external costs by imposing strict liability for the damage caused by the specific risks created by a particular activity. This increases the price, thereby reducing the level of the activity and hence the amount of damage associated with it. The object is not to eliminate all damage but to achieve an efficient amount, taking into account the costs of prevention. In other words, tort should aim to minimise the sum of accident costs and the costs of preventing accidents...

This theory is known as general deterrence because it seeks to influence behaviour through the pricing of activities, rather than deterring individuals from specific acts. Other theories rely on the deterrent effect of liability rules on individuals. For example, it has been suggested that the tort of negligence leads to efficient results because the standard of reasonable care encourages people to take only those precautions that are justified on the ground of cost, whereas strict liability might lead people to devote more resources to damage prevention than is warranted by the risk...

Ultimately, all economic theorising about tort rests on assumptions about the deterrent effect of liability rules, which have not been empirically tested...

NOTE

The influence of the economics can now be detected in the reasoning of some judges.

Wildtree Hotels Ltd v Harrow LBC [2001] 2 AC 1, HL

Lord Hoffmann: ... The construction of the railways, which gave rise to most of the 19th century cases on injurious affection, involved massive changes in the urban and rural landscape of the United Kingdom and the disruption of the lives and businesses of very large numbers of people. It is not surprising that strong views were held about the respective claims of the winners and losers in this revolution and the judicial decisions often reveal the opinions of individual judges on questions of economic and social policy. Some were in favour of full compensation for all whose property had been adversely affected by the railway and others thought that the public interest required that liability should be kept within narrow bounds...

In modern economic terms, Bramwell B thought that the railways should not create externalities; that is, costs involuntarily borne by other people which were not taken into account in assessing the profitability of the enterprise. The contrary view is exemplified by Erle CJ in *Ricket v Metropolitan Railway Co* (1865) 5 B & S 149, 163, 169... Judges who took this view tended to rely upon a floodgates argument: unless the right to compensation was rigidly confined, everyone whose economic interests had been damaged by the construction of the railways would be entitled to compensation. Post houses and coaching inns were favourite examples.

My Lords, I mention these ancient controversies not only because they still have some resonance today but also because they are an aid to the understanding of the old cases to which your Lordships were referred in the course of the argument. The 19th century authorities on this subject do not display a steady development of the law but the shifting ascendancies of one view or the other...

NOTES

1. See also Lord Hoffmann's judgments in *Stovin v Wise* (pp 136, 152, 296) and *Transco plc v Stockport MBC* (pp 74, 220).

2. One conceptual focal point between economics and law is the notion of an 'interest'. It is the key concept in economic science because it allows everything, even morality, to become a matter of economic calculation. Only the behaviour of individuals and not their intentions is of importance. Everything becomes a matter of loss and gain. One can understand the attraction of this key concept for the law of damages since interest can act – and indeed has acted since Roman times (see D.9.2.23.4) – as the bridge between damage and damages. Damages are awarded only to compensate for invasions of recognised interests. If there is no legal interest there is no damage(s) (for a Roman example of an interest that was too speculative see D.9.2.29.3). Equally if one can turn an economic interest into a legal interest, the easier it becomes to demand compensation for its invasion. This interest aspect of tort law will be investigated further in various parts of this book.

3. An economic analysis is valuable, also, because it seemingly provides an empirical justification for an existing legal rule and (or) solution to a case. This is particularly evident in *Stovin* where Lord Hoffmann uses the 'externalities' argument to justify the non-liability for a mere omission in the tort of negligence. What must not be forgotten, however, is that economic science is not like physics or zoology. It is not a knowledge discipline capable of validation, in part at least, by reference to external realities. There is a large ideological dimension to economic science. For example, is society to be viewed as a mass of interests attaching to individuals or should one be thinking more in terms of group interests? The point to be made, therefore, is that economic science is similar to law in as much as it is in many ways a normative discipline: it is less about providing a theory that explains and predicts and more about what those in positions of political and commercial power *ought* to do. Viewed in this light, justifying one normative rule (mere omissions as in *Stovin*) with another normative rule (externalities) begins to look like a boot-strap argument.

QUESTIONS

1. The basic methodological paradigm underpinning law is authority. One arrives at decisions based on the authority of a statute or a precedent. Is an appeal to economics simply an attempt to provide lawyers with an alternative authority? Why should economists be more authoritative than philosophers or bishops or, indeed, jurists?

2. Should privacy be protected by the law of tort only if it can be shown that privacy is an interest capable of having an economic value? If it can be shown to have such a value, would it then become a property interest to be protected like any other item of value? Or is privacy some kind of special interest?

3. Imagine that the case of *Miller v Jackson* (see p 14) had come before a Court of Appeal consisting entirely of judges devoted to the law and economics school of legal analysis. Do you think the reasoning and the result would be very different from the actual reasoning and result in the case?

2.4 Protecting rights

The concept of a 'right' fulfils several functions. First and foremost it is a way of viewing law from the position of the individual subject rather than from an objective system of rules. Often a 'right' is seen as the correlative of 'duty' and when the two are put together each individual is said to have both rights (claims to things or on other people) and duties (obligations to others). Secondly, the word 'right' is used as a means of expressing a strict form of liability; here the term is closely associated with the idea of ownership and so when a claimant asserts that he has a right he is asserting a claim against a thing. 'That is mine, please return it'. It should be noted here that behaviour is irrelevant to ownership: a claimant in a proprietary action need assert, in principle, only that the defendant has interfered with his title. In the law of tort there are several causes of action which have this proprietary flavour – trespass, conversion and defamation being good examples – and this is the reason why these torts can be seen as protecting rights. Thirdly, the term right has acquired a constitutional flavour. In many ways this public law aspect is simply the appropriation of the property relationship between person and thing (ownership) by constitutional lawyers to give expression to the relationship between the individual and the state. Yet it is an effective appropriation in as much as the Latin for ownership is *dominium* and this reflects the political and social power inherent in the term. To say that citizens have rights against the State is a way of counterbalancing the idea that all law (and thus all rights) flow from the State. The Human Rights Act 1998 goes some way, therefore, in recognising the individual as a source of law, as a source of rights.

2.4.1 Property rights

In French law ownership is famously defined in the *Code civil* as 'the right to enjoy and to dispose of things in the most absolute manner, provided that one does not use them in a way prohibited by statute or regulations' (art 544). In English law (and Roman law) it is nowhere defined; and, indeed, it is arguable that English law needs neither a definition nor ownership itself since what is protected is the best right to *possession*. Thus tort and contract (see Sale of Goods Act 1979, s 16) may talk about interference with ownership (or 'property') but in terms of remedies tort looks to the immediate right to possess. Nevertheless, as the next extracts indicate, tort remedies do seem to give indirect expression to ownership.

Bradford Corporation v Pickles [1895] AC 587, HL

This was an action for an injunction brought by a local authority against a landowner who, so it was alleged, was deliberately interfering with the natural supply of water to the corporation's waterworks by digging holes on his land. The landowner, it seemed, was trying to bring pressure on the corporation to purchase his land. The House of Lords (Lords Halsbury LC, Ashbourne, Macnaghten and Watson) gave judgment for the landowner.

Lord Halsbury LC: ... The acts done, or sought to be done, by the defendant were all done upon his own land, and the interference whatever it is, with the flow of water is an interference with water, which is underground and not shown to be water flowing in any defined stream, but is percolating water, which, but for such interference, would undoubtedly reach the plaintiff's works, and in that sense does deprive them of the water which they would otherwise get. But although it does deprive them of water which they would otherwise get, it is necessary for the plaintiffs to establish that they have a right to the flow of water, and that the defendant has no right to do what he is doing...

The very question was ... determined by this House, [in *Chasemore v Richards*], and it was held that the landowner had a right to do what he had done whatever his object or purpose might be, and although the purpose might be wholly unconnected with the enjoyment of his own estate...

The only remaining point is the question of fact alleged by the plaintiffs, that the acts done by the defendant are done, not with any view which deals with the use of his own land or the percolating water through it, but is done, in the language of the pleader, 'maliciously'...

This is not a case in which the state of mind of the person doing the act can affect the right to do it. If it was a lawful act, however ill the motive might be, he had a right to do it. If it was an unlawful act, however good his motive might be, he would have no right to do it...

Lord Macnaghten: ... But the real answer to the claim of the corporation is that in such a case motives are immaterial. It is the act, not the motive for the act, that must be regarded. If the act, apart from motive, gives rise merely to damage without legal injury, the motive, however reprehensible it may be, will not supply that element...

NOTE

This great case is the subject of a whole book: M Taggart, *Private Property and Abuse of Rights in Victorian England* (OUP, 2002). The case is important from a rights point of view for several reasons. First, because it indicates how rights can trump 'obligations' or 'wrongful' (in the social sense) behaviour. The House of Lords was not applauding the behaviour of the defendant; it is just that his behaviour did not amount to a legal wrong (*injuria*) and it did not amount to such a wrong because he had the 'right' to do it. Secondly, the case is interesting from a comparative law viewpoint. Had these facts arisen in France the landowner would probably have been held legally liable for his behaviour; this liability would result, not from a failure by the law to recognise that a landowner had rights, but because the land owner was abusing his rights. Abuse of rights is, in other words, a tort in civil law thinking (see Taggart, pp 145–66). Thirdly, the case is important because it establishes that merely to intend certain types of damage is not enough to give rise to liability. This of course can be described as a refusal to recognise a doctrine of abuse of rights, but it is in some ways more subtle as the next extracts indicate.

Bernard Rudden, 'The Battle of Manywells Spring'
London Review of Books, 19 June 2003, 24

In a perfect world of rational economic actors a problem of [the *Bradford v Pickles*] kind would be solved by agreement. Transaction costs are low, since there are only two players and they are neighbours. If the water rights are valued more by Bradford than they are by Pickles, the town will buy him out. If less, it will not. But in either case the normal process of bargaining should ensure that the resource ends up with one who values it most. In this way litigation is avoided, but even if it takes place, the end of a lawsuit can restart negotiation. If the court forbids Pickles to cut off the water, he can still buy the right to do so if he values it at more than the town does. If, on the other hand, the town loses the lawsuit, it can always offer more money. And even if this fails, the town can apply for an Act authorising compulsory purchase at a price fixed, if necessary, by a jury. Thus the overall system provides for three possible stages of decentralised dispute settlement, all of which require the public utility to pay monetary compensation for its intrusion into others' private property rights. Unless, of course, the others are so saintly as to cede them for nothing.

In all-too-human West Yorkshire nothing like this happened...

QUESTIONS

1. Do you think that *Bradford* is a much cited case?

2. Do you think that *Bradford* is a much criticised case?

3. How would an adherent to the law and economics school have decided *Bradford*?

PROBLEM

D deliberately lets his garden get overgrown to annoy his neighbour C and to block out some of the light to C's kitchen. Can C sue D for damages? What if D deliberately played loud music to annoy C? (Cf *Hollywood Silver Fox Farm v Emmett*, below, p 79.)

NOTE

Bradford involved land. The next case concerns moveable property.

RH Willis & Son v British Car Auctions Ltd [1978] 1 WLR 438, CA

This was an action for damages in the tort of conversion by a finance company against a firm of car auctioneers. The auctioneers had sold a car for a client not knowing that the client had no right to sell the vehicle because the car was on hire purchase from the claimant finance company. The auctioneers had taken reasonable steps to check the client's statement that he was owner of the car, but the Court of Appeal (Lord Denning MR, Roskill LJ and Brown LJ) nevertheless held the auctioneers liable.

Lord Denning MR: ... The question that arises is the usual one: which of the two innocent persons is to suffer? Is the loss to fall on the owners? They have been deprived of the £275 due to them on the car. Or on the auctioneers? They sold it believing that Mr. Croucher was the true owner. In answering that question in cases such as this, the common law has always acted on the maxim nemo dat quod non habet. It has protected the property rights of the true owner. It has enforced them strictly as against anyone who deals with the goods inconsistently with the dominion of the true owner. Even though the true owner may have been very negligent and the defendant may have acted in complete innocence, nevertheless the common law held him liable in conversion. Both the 'innocent acquirer' and the 'innocent handler' have been hit hard. That state of the law has often been criticised. It has been proposed that the law should protect a person who buys goods or handles them in good faith without notice of any adverse title, at any rate where the claimant by his own negligence or otherwise has largely contributed to the outcome. Such proposals have however been effectively blocked by the decisions of the House of Lords in the last century of *Hollins v Fowler* (1875) LR 7 HL 757, and in this century of *Moorgate Mercantile Co Ltd v Twitchings* [1977] AC 890, to which I may add the decision of this court in *Central Newbury Car Auctions Ltd v Unity Finance Ltd* [1957] 1 QB 371.

In some instances the strictness of the law has been mitigated by statute, as for instance, by the protection given to private purchasers by the Hire-Purchase Acts. But in other cases the only way in which the innocent acquirers or handlers have been able to protect themselves is by insurance. They insure themselves against their potential liability. This is the usual method nowadays. When men of business or professional men find themselves hit by the law with new and increasing liabilities, they take steps to insure themselves, so that the loss may not fall on one alone, but be spread among many. It is a factor of which we must take account: see *Post Office v Norwich Union Fire Insurance Society Ltd* [1967] 2 QB 363, 375 and *Morris v Ford Motor Co Ltd* [1973] 1 QB 792, 801.

Sales under the hammer

The position of auctioneers is typical. It is now, I think, well established that if an auctioneer sells goods by knocking down with his hammer at an auction and thereafter delivers them to the purchaser – then although he is only an agent – then if the vendor has no title to the goods, both the auctioneer and the purchaser are liable in conversion to the true owner, no matter how innocent the auctioneer may have been in handling the goods or the purchaser in acquiring... This state of the law has been considered by the Law Reform Committee in its 12th Report, Transfer of Title to Chattels (1966), Cmnd. 2958, as to innocent acquirers (see paragraph 39 as to 'Liability of Auctioneers'); and in its 18th Report (Conversion and Detinue) (1971), Cmnd. 4774 as to innocent handlers: paragraphs 46-50. But Parliament has made no change in it: no doubt it would have done so in the Torts (Interference with Goods) Act 1977 if it had thought fit to do so...

QUESTIONS

1. Why should it be the auctioneers and not the owner of the car (particularly a finance company) who are charged with the burden of insuring against fraud? (Cf *Shogun Finance v Hudson* (2003).)

2. Who profits from hire-purchase? Who is in the best position to guard against fraud? Are these points taken account of in *Willis*?

3. What if the owner had carelessly failed to register with an information service (Hire Purchase Information) that this particular car was on hire-purchase and that the claimant was the owner? (Cf *Moorgate Mercantile v Twitchings* (1977).)

4. The torts of trespass to goods and conversion protect moveable property rights. What amounts to 'property' for this purpose? Does conversion apply only to tangible property or can it be used to claim damages for the interference with an intangible property right? Can one, for example, convert a contractual right? (Cf *OBG Ltd v Allan* (2005).)

2.4.2 Personality rights

Personality rights in civil law thinking are different from patrimonial (property and obligation) rights in that the former belong to the law of persons and the latter to the law of things. This distinction, which goes back to Roman legal classification, is to be found in the modern codes. Thus for example invasions of privacy and dignity are rights located not in the 'tort' section of the *Code civil* (Book 3 Title IV) but in the section on Persons (Book I). Personality rights are, accordingly, distinguished from obligation rights simply by their location in the institutional system. English law has no imposed structure and thus has no easy means of distinguishing between different kinds of right; all claims for invasion of non-contractual rights tend to end up as 'tort' or property problems as the next case indicates.

Wainwright v Home Office [2004] 2 AC 406, HL

(For facts see p 28)

Lord Hoffmann: ... **18** The need in the United States to break down the concept of 'invasion of privacy' into a number of loosely-linked torts must cast doubt upon the value of any high-level generalisation which can perform a useful function in enabling one to deduce the rule to be applied in a concrete case. English law has so far been unwilling, perhaps unable, to formulate any such high-level principle. There are a number of common law and statutory remedies of which it may be said that one at least of the underlying values they protect is a right of privacy. Sir Brian Neill's well known article 'Privacy: a challenge for the next century' in *Protecting Privacy* (ed B Markesinis, 1999) contains a survey. Common law torts include trespass, nuisance, defamation and malicious falsehood; there is the equitable action for breach of confidence and statutory remedies under the Protection from Harassment Act 1997 and the Data Protection Act 1998. There are also extra-legal remedies under Codes of Practice applicable to broadcasters and newspapers. But there are gaps; cases in which the courts have considered that an invasion of privacy deserves a remedy which the existing law does not offer. Sometimes the perceived gap can be filled by judicious development of an existing principle. The law of breach of confidence has in recent years undergone such a process: see in particular the judgment of Lord Phillips of Worth Matravers MR in *Campbell v MGN Ltd* [2003] QB 633. On the other hand, an attempt to create a tort of telephone harassment by a radical change in the basis of the action for private nuisance in *Khorasandjian v Bush* [1993] QB 727 was held by the House of Lords in *Hunter v Canary Wharf Ltd* [1997] AC 655 to be a step too far. The gap was filled by the 1997 Act.

19 What the courts have so far refused to do is to formulate a general principle of 'invasion of privacy' (I use the quotation marks to signify doubt about what in such a context the expression would mean) from which the conditions of liability in the particular case can be deduced. The reasons were discussed by Sir Robert Megarry V-C in *Malone v Metropolitan Police Comr* [1979] Ch 344, 372–381...

31 There seems to me a great difference between identifying privacy as a value which underlies the existence of a rule of law (and may point the direction in which the law should develop) and privacy as a principle of law in itself. The English common law is familiar with the notion of underlying values – principles only in the broadest sense – which direct its development. A famous example is *Derbyshire County Council v Times Newspapers Ltd* [1993] AC 534, in which freedom of speech was the underlying value which supported the decision to lay down the specific rule that a local authority could not sue for libel. But no one has suggested that freedom of speech is in itself a legal principle which is capable of sufficient definition to enable one to deduce specific rules to be applied in concrete cases. That is not the way the common law works.

32 Nor is there anything in the jurisprudence of the European Court of Human Rights which suggests that the adoption of some high level principle of privacy is necessary to comply with article 8 of the Convention. The European Court is concerned only with whether English law provides an adequate remedy in a specific case in which it considers that there has been an invasion of privacy contrary to article 8(1) and not justifiable under article 8(2)...

41 Commentators and counsel have nevertheless been unwilling to allow *Wilkinson v Downton* to disappear beneath the surface of the law of negligence. Although, in cases of actual psychiatric injury, there is no point in arguing about whether the injury was in some sense intentional if negligence will do just as well, it has been suggested (as the claimants submit in this case) that damages for distress falling short of psychiatric injury can be recovered if there was an intention to cause it. This submission was squarely put to the Court of Appeal in *Wong v Parkside Health NHS Trust* [2003] 3 All ER 932 and rejected. Hale LJ said that before the passing of the Protection from Harassment Act 1997 there was no tort of intentional harassment which gave a remedy for anything less than physical or psychiatric injury. That leaves *Wilkinson v Downton* with no leading role in the modern law...

44 I do not resile from the proposition that the policy considerations which limit the heads of recoverable damage in negligence do not apply equally to torts of intention. If someone actually intends to cause harm by a wrongful act and does so, there is ordinarily no reason why he should not have to pay compensation. But I think that if you adopt such a principle, you have to be very careful about what you mean by intend. In *Wilkinson v Downton* Wright J wanted to water down the concept of intention as much as possible. He clearly thought, as the Court of Appeal did afterwards in *Janvier v Sweeney* [1919] 2 KB 316, that the plaintiff should succeed whether the conduct of the defendant was intentional or negligent. But the *Victorian Railway Comrs* case 13 App Cas 222 prevented him from saying so. So he devised a concept of imputed intention which sailed as close to negligence as he felt he could go.

46 Even on the basis of a genuine intention to cause distress, I would wish, as in *Hunter's* case [1997] AC 655, to reserve my opinion on whether compensation should be recoverable. In institutions and workplaces all over the country, people constantly do and say things with the intention of causing distress and humiliation to others. This shows lack of consideration and appalling manners but I am not sure that the right way to deal with it is always by litigation. The Protection from Harassment Act 1997 defines harassment in section 1(1) as a 'course of conduct' amounting to harassment and provides by section 7(3) that a course of conduct must involve conduct on at least two occasions. If these requirements are satisfied, the claimant may pursue a civil remedy for damages for anxiety: section 3(2). The requirement of a course of conduct shows that Parliament was conscious that it might not be in the public interest to allow the law to be set in motion for one boorish incident. It may be that any development of the common law should show similar caution.

47 In my opinion, therefore, the claimants can build nothing on *Wilkinson v Downton* [1897] 2 QB 57. It does not provide a remedy for distress which does not amount to recognised psychiatric injury and so far as there may a tort of intention under which such damage is recoverable, the necessary intention was not established. I am also in complete agreement with Buxton LJ [2002] QB 1334, 1355-1356, paras 67–72, that *Wilkinson v Downton* has nothing to do with trespass to the person...

NOTES

1. Privacy and harassment caused difficulties for several reasons. First, because there existed no specific cause of action for either; facts involving one or the other had to be squeezed into one of the existing torts and if this proved impossible

there was obviously a presumption of no liability. Statute has now intervened to modify the law. In the case of privacy, the statute in question is the Human Rights Act 1998 which has incorporated art 8 of the European Convention into UK law. One should note, however, that it is by no means evident that art 8(2) covers invasion by a non-public authority. So this gives rise to a problem about the so-called 'horizontal effect' of the Convention. Is privacy a right to be protected from any invasion or only from an invasion by 'a public authority'? One way around this problem is to use the remedy of an injunction to develop the law. Equity would always grant an injunction to protect an existing right and so a claimant could now go to court and, instead of trying to fit the complaint into an existing cause of action, simply point to art 8. The right exists as part of English law and equity should protect it. The next step is to award equitable damages in lieu of an injunction (see *Jaggard v Sawyer* (1995)). Finally equitable and common law thinking could be merged into a new tort of privacy. As for harassment, this now has its own specific legislation which is no doubt one reason why the judges felt able to resist developing the case law in this area.

2. A second reason why harassment and privacy caused difficulties is to be found in the nature of the damage. Mental distress is less well protected in English tort law than more obvious forms of personal injury. Thus the woman harassed by cricket balls in *Miller v Jackson* (see p 14) attracted no sympathy from judges whereas had she suffered the same fate as Miss Stone (see p 119) she would probably have recovered damages (although Miss Stone did not). A third reason for the difficulties arising from harassment and privacy is reflected in the questions posed below.

QUESTIONS

1. Ought English law to develop a law of persons as a separate category from the law of things? Or, if not separate categories, should English law recognise that personality rights are very different from patrimonial rights?

2. If English law were to develop privacy as a tort would this have serious constitutional implications for a free press? Would it lead to a restriction of the constitutional right of free speech? Why is it that in France few newspapers could, and still cannot, expose the full political and moral corruption of one of its former presidents? Would a privacy law provide a useful source of revenue for politicians who like to cheat on their partners?

3. Do you think that the tort of defamation (see **Chapter 8**) should be seen as protecting personality rights or patrimonial rights?

4. Are personality 'rights' in reality only 'values' in the eyes of the common law?

5. Does *Wainwright* in effect mean that public officials have the right to humiliate members of the public provided they commit no actual trespass?

6. Where is the line to be drawn between behaviour designed to humiliate and harassment?

2.4.3 Constitutional rights

Distinguishing personality and constitutional rights is not always easy since there is a considerable overlap. Indeed human rights are as much a constitutional as a personality question. Some torts such as trespass have, as we saw in

R v Governor of Brockhill Prison, ex p Evans (No 2) (pp 27, 82), an old and important constitutional role in as much as they act as a restraint on governmental power. In the area of medical law personality and constitutional rights continue to overlap as the next case illustrates.

In re F (Mental Patient: Sterilisation) [1990] 2 AC 1, HL

This was an action for a declaration by the mother of a 36-year-old mentally incapable woman that it would be lawful for doctors to sterilise the mentally retarded woman. Evidence was submitted that the woman would be unable to cope with pregnancy and that any other form of contraception would be ineffective or dangerous. The House of Lords (Lords Bridge, Brandon, Griffiths, Goff and Jauncey) upheld the decisions of the lower courts granting the declaration.

Lord Brandon: ... At common law a doctor cannot lawfully operate on adult patients of sound mind, or give them any other treatment involving the application of physical force however small ('other treatment'), without their consent. If a doctor were to operate on such patients, or give them other treatment, without their consent, he would commit the actionable tort of trespass to the person. There are, however, cases where adult patients cannot give or refuse their consent to an operation or other treatment. One case is where, as a result of an accident or otherwise, an adult patient is unconscious and an operation or other treatment cannot be safely delayed until he or she recovers consciousness. Another case is where a patient, though adult, cannot by reason of mental disability understand the nature or purpose of an operation or other treatment. The common law would be seriously defective if it failed to provide a solution to the problem created by such inability to consent. In my opinion, however, the common law does not so fail. In my opinion, the solution to the problem which the common law provides is that a doctor can lawfully operate on, or give other treatment to, adult patients who are incapable, for one reason or another, of consenting to his doing so, provided that the operation or other treatment concerned is in the best interests of such patients. The operation or other treatment will be in their best interests if, but only if, it is carried out in order either to save their lives, or to ensure improvement or prevent deterioration in their physical or mental health...

NOTES

1. Although English law thinks more in terms of liberties rather than rights, the starting point for the tort of trespass to the person (and often trespass to land and to goods) is simple enough. The body is inviolable and thus any *intentional* interference with the person (or his or her things) is prima facie a trespass (see **Chapter 3**). This is an important constitutional principle because it means that no person can be arrested, imprisoned or otherwise molested without legal justification (although they can be humiliated). If jailers or policemen cannot show justification they can be sued for damages in trespass by their victims (but cf *Wainwright*, pp 28, 64, 81, 109). In the field of public law most of the justifications used by agents of the State are granted by legislation and this means that many trespass actions end up as statutory interpretation cases (see in particular the Police and Criminal Evidence Act 1984). Strict liability has a vital function here; and thus the importance of *Brockhill* (see pp 27, 82) is that it indicates clearly that justification and reasonableness are quite different notions.

2. Reasonableness suggests the tort of negligence. What, then, if a person's body (goods) are negligently invaded by a public authority? In this situation a quite different tort comes into play and it may be that the function of protecting constitutional rights gives way to policy considerations that favour the State over the individual (see eg *Hill v Chief Constable of West Yorks*, above, pp 36, 296 and **Chapter 9**). However it was this very conflict between rights and reasonableness that once made the boundary between trespass and negligence a difficult one (see eg *Esso v Southport*, above, pp 4, 34). And this conflict between rights on the one hand and policy and reasonableness on the other has been brought back into play by the Human Rights Act 1998 (see eg *Z v UK*, below, pp 306, 310).

3. In the case of medical treatment, consent is what usually negates any liability in trespass, but Lord Goff in *Re F* indicated how necessity is another important defence (see pp 67, 335). Note also the important role in *Re F* of the concept of an 'interest'.

QUESTIONS

1. What or whose interests is sterilisation really protecting?

2. Is it ever in a patient's best interest that they be allowed to die? (Cf *Airedale NHS Trust v Bland* (1993).)

2.4.4 Environmental rights

Environmental rights present particular conceptual difficulties for many European legal systems both because they concern 'right holders' who may not yet exist (future generation) and because they do not attach to the individual. The rights attach to humans as a class whereas tort law thinking tends to start out from the individual with a particular interest to protect. Nevertheless the law of tort is not completely impotent as the next case indicates.

Attorney-General v PYA Quarries Ltd [1957] 2 QB 169, CA

This was a relator action brought by a local authority in the name of the Attorney-General for an injunction to stop a quarry owner from causing a nuisance through its activities. Local residents complained of flying stones, dust and vibration. The owner claimed that its activities did not affect a sufficient number of people to amount to a public nuisance, but the Court of Appeal (Denning LJ, Romer LJ and Parker LJ) upheld the injunctions.

Romer LJ: ... I do not propose to attempt a more precise definition of a public nuisance than those which emerge from the textbooks and authorities to which I have referred. It is, however, clear, in my opinion, that any nuisance is 'public' which materially affects the reasonable comfort and convenience of life of a class of Her Majesty's subjects. The sphere of the nuisance may be described generally as 'the neighbourhood'; but the question whether the local community within that sphere comprises a sufficient number of persons to constitute a class of the public is a question of fact in every case. It is not necessary, in my judgment, to prove that every member of the class has been injuriously affected; it is sufficient to show that a representative cross-section of the class has been so affected for an injunction to issue.

Denning LJ: ... I decline to answer the question how many people are necessary to make up Her Majesty's subjects generally. I prefer to look to the reason of the thing and to say that a public nuisance is a nuisance which is so widespread in its range or so indiscriminate in its effect that it would not be reasonable to expect one person to take proceedings on his own responsibility to put a stop to it, but that it should be taken on the responsibility of the community at large.

Take the blocking up of a public highway or the non-repair of it. It may be a footpath very little used except by one or two householders. Nevertheless, the obstruction affects everyone indiscriminately who may wish to walk along it. Take next a landowner who collects pestilential rubbish near a village or permits gypsies with filthy habits to encamp on the edge of a residential neighbourhood. The householders nearest to it suffer the most, but everyone in the neighbourhood suffers too. In such cases the Attorney-General can take proceedings from injunction to restrain the nuisance: and when he does so he acts in defence of the public right, not for any sectional interest: see *Attorney-General v Bastow*. But when the nuisance is so concentrated that only two or three property owners are affected by it, such as the three attornies in Clifford's Inn, then they ought to take proceedings on their own account to stop it and not expect the community to do it for them: see *Rex v Lloyd*, and the precedent in Chitty's *Criminal Law* (1826), vol III, pp 664-665.

Applying this test, I am clearly of opinion that the nuisance by stones, vibration and dust in this case was at the date of the writ so widespread in its range and so indiscriminate in its effect that it was a public nuisance...

NOTES

1. A local authority can now bring such a claim in its own name: Local Government Act 1972, s 222.

2. See also *Esso Petroleum v Southport Corporation* (pp 4, 34); *Wheeler v Saunders* (p 212); *Marcic v Thames Water* (p 213); *Cambridge Water v Eastern Counties Leather* (p 218).

3. There is no doubt that one function of tort is to protect property not just from direct interference (trespass) but also from indirect ones. Where such an interference is indirect and it affects a neighbouring landowner or occupier, the tort of private nuisance is the main cause of action (see **Chapters 5 and 6**). If the interference is more widespread, then, as Denning LJ suggested, the tort of public nuisance might be relevant (see **6.2.1**). Difficulties arise when the environmental interest of a group of individuals comes into conflict with the economic interests of commerce. The question then becomes one of where the public interest is said to lie. Here damage is important: if the interference causes physical damage to person or property it may be easier to sue in tort than when the damage is noise or smell pollution. All the same, offensive sights might amount to 'pollution' (see *Thompson-Schwab v Costaki* (1956)).

QUESTIONS

1. To what extent ought English law to give expression to the principle that it is the polluter who should pay for environmental damage? (Cf *Cambridge Water*, p 218.)

2. Does the law of tort go far enough in providing remedies in respect of mental distress caused by noise pollution? Do individuals have a human right not to suffer such distress? (Cf *Hatton v UK*, p 183.)

3. If the community benefits as a whole from an economic activity (public interest), why should the community not pay for the burden this activity may cause to individuals who suffer from the activity? (Cf *Dennis v MOD*, p 181.)

PROBLEM

One northern city in the UK is often plagued by a ghastly smell emanating from an industrial bone-boiling farm on its perimeter. This undoubtedly amounts to a prima facie 'statutory nuisance' under s 79 of the Environmental Protection Act 1990. Read s 80 of this Act and explain why you think it is that the local authority has not been able to use this statute to eliminate the smell. Advise local residents if they could use the torts of public or private nuisance to obtain an injunction (see generally **6.2**).

2.5 Protecting interests

We have already mentioned in passing that tort can be analysed in terms of interests. These have been helpfully set out by the European Group on Tort Law in its draft code.

European Group on Tort Law, *Principles of European Tort Law* (2003)

Art. 2:102. Protected interests

(1) The scope of protection of an interest depends on its nature; the higher its value, the precision of its definition and its obviousness, the more extensive is its protection.

(2) Life, bodily or mental integrity and liberty enjoy the most extensive protection.

(3) Extensive protection is granted to property rights, including those in intangible property.

(4) Protection of pure economic interests or contractual relationships may be more limited in scope. In such cases, due regard must be had especially to the proximity between the actor and the endangered interest, or to the fact that the actor is aware of the fact that he will cause damage even though his interests are necessarily valued lower than those of the victim.

(5) The scope of protection may also be affected by the nature of liability, so that an interest may receive more extensive protection against intentional harm than in other cases.

(6) In determining the scope of protection, the interests of the actor, especially in liberty of action and in exercising his rights, as well as public interests also have to be taken into consideration.

NOTE

These principles are offered as a guide to the cases in this book. They should be continually referred to and readers should reflect upon whether they accurately reflect English tort law.

2.6 Tort and insurance

The existence of insurance impacts upon the law of tort in a number of ways, some of which have already been discussed. However, one important question is the extent to which insurance should affect the function of the law of tort.

Richard Lewis, 'Insurance and the Tort System' 2005, *Legal Studies,* vol 25, 85, 86, 89, 116 (footnotes omitted)

There is no doubt that insurance profoundly influences the practical operation of the law of tort. Liability insurance is not merely an ancillary device to protect the insured, but is the 'primary medium for the payment of compensation, and tort law [is] a subsidiary part of the process'. Although the majority of defendants in tort are individual people, they are almost all insured... Insurers determine how the defence is to be conducted and, for example, commonly make admissions without the consent of the insured, and settle cases in spite of the policyholder's objection...

Insurers' influence upon settlements is even more pronounced than it is upon decided cases. For the lawyer asked by his client to advise on the merits of a case it is the realities of the litigation system that are of concern rather than the formal rules of law. Practitioners would agree... that the textbook rules of tort are often transformed when they come to be used in the system in three ways: first, they are simplified; secondly, they are made more liberal; and thirdly, they are made more inequitable...

... Much more difficult to assess is the potential for insurance to affect the outcome of individual claims. Proving that the facts of cases have been moulded to fit the deeper pocket of insurers cannot be done by resort to the law reports alone, but it remains the suspicion of many a practitioner. Although it is easier to assess the influence of insurance upon the rules of tort, rather than the facts found in individual cases, the picture is by no means clear...

QUESTIONS

1. Why and how is insurance capable of transforming the textbook rules of tort law?

2. As the above extracted article makes clear (this useful article should be read in full in the journal), the insurance question is given added importance once one remembers that public law requires that both the main factual sources of personal injury litigation, the road and the workplace, be covered by liability insurance. Should insurance now replace fault as the main criterion of liability?

JA Jolowicz, 'Liability for Accidents' [1968] *Cambridge Law Journal 50*

It is submitted that a suitable criterion is to be found in the concept of risk and that a satisfactory body of legal rules could quite rapidly be developed by the courts if in every case they were to pose the question, 'Whose risk was it that this damage might occur?' in place of the present 'Whose fault was it that this damage did occur?' It is essential, however, that the traditional refusal of the courts to consider the factor of insurance be reversed. It is perhaps this refusal of the courts to face up to the facts of contemporary life which has led them to overlook loss distribution as it already exists and to insist on fault as the criterion of liability as if every defendant had to find the damages from his own pocket....

NOTE

The judges remain to be convinced.

Morgans v Launchbury [1973] AC 127, HL

This was an action for damages by passengers injured in a car accident against the owner of the car they were using for their pub-crawl. The owner had lent the car to her husband on condition that he got a friend to drive if he got too drunk. The husband did get too drunk, but the friend he got to drive drove carelessly causing a collision. If the friend was acting as an 'agent' of the owner when the collision occurred the owner's insurance would be liable to the injured passengers for the careless driving. In the Court of Appeal, Lord Denning MR had 'sought to extend the liability of a car owner for negligent driving of his car by other persons, because the car owner is the person who has or ought to have a motor insurance policy' (Lord Pearson). However, the House of Lords (Lords Wilberforce, Pearson, Cross and Salmon and Viscount Dilhorne), reversing a majority decision of the Court of Appeal, held the owner not liable on this 'agency' ground.

Lord Pearson: ... It seems to me that these innovations [of Lord Denning MR], whether or not they may be desirable, are not suitable to be introduced by judicial decision. They raise difficult questions of policy, as well as involving the introduction of new legal principles rather than extension of some principle already recognised and operating. The questions of policy need consideration by the government and Parliament, using the resources at their command for making wide inquiries and gathering evidence and opinions as to the practical effects of the proposed innovations. Apart from the transitional difficulty of current policies of insurance being rendered insufficient by judicial changes in the law, there is the danger of injustice to owners who for one reason or another are not adequately covered by insurance or perhaps not effectively insured at all (for example, if they have forgotten to renew their policies or have taken out policies which are believed by them to be valid but are in fact invalid, or have taken their policies from an insolvent insurance company). Moreover, lack of insurance cover would in some cases defeat the object of the proposed innovation, because uninsured or insufficiently insured owners would often be unable to pay damages awarded against them in favour of injured plaintiffs. Any extension of car owners' liability ought to be accompanied by an extension of effective insurance cover. How would that be brought about? And how would it be paid for? Would the owner of the car be required to take out a policy for the benefit of any person who may drive the car? Would there be an exception for some kinds of unlawful driving? A substantial increase in premiums for motor insurance would be likely to result and to have an inflationary effect on costs and prices. It seems to me that, if the proposed innovations are desirable, they should be introduced not by judicial decision but by legislation after suitable investigation and full consideration of the questions of policy involved...

NOTE

Some academics are equally sceptical about insurance as a criterion of liability.

Peter Cane, *Tort Law and Economic Interests* (2nd edn, OUP, 1996), 427–9 (foot-notes omitted)

The insurability argument purports to be an argument about where the law ought to place the loss; but it is quite inconsistent with notions of personal responsibility and corrective justice which underlie the common law of obligations. To take an extreme case, it is not possible to insure against liability for intentional wrongdoing, but this fact provides no good argument for not imposing liability for such wrongdoing; nor, conversely, does the fact that property can easily be protected from theft by loss insurance provide a good reason for not imposing tort liability on thieves. The real weakness of the insurance argument is that insurance is essentially a group or social phenomenon, whereas the common law of obligations is concerned with individuals. Disputes between individuals do not provide a good medium through which to decide what is the best pattern of insurance in a particular area ... As Weinrib says, the invocation of insurance in tort disputes undermines the conception of tort law as concerned with the immediate personal interaction of the doer and the sufferer of harm...

QUESTIONS

1. Are Cane's two extreme cases really relevant in any argument attacking Jolowicz's risk and insurability thesis (see above p 71)?

2. Would it be that difficult to discover the insurability position in the following cases: *Read v J Lyons* (pp 14, 185); *Jolley v Sutton LBC* (p 362); *The Wagon Mound* (No 1) (pp 359, 363)? What about the following contract (but with a tort aspect) cases: *The Moorcock* (1889); *Shogun Finance v Hudson* (2003)?

NOTES

1. This comment by Cane is valuable in the way that it highlights the structural, more than the functional, difficulty of attempting to marry tort and insurance. The model of private law from Roman to modern times is strictly individualist in its design; it is based on relations between individual persons with individual things (property) and between one individual and another individual (obligations). In short, it sees society as consisting strictly of individuals and society itself is little more than the sum of these parts (cf environmental rights). Of course this model has been distorted by the recognition that certain groups of individuals, if the group has legal personality, are treated as if it (they) were an individual; a large multinational corporation is just an ordinary person according to the legal institutional model. Thus insurance can impact on this model only in terms of adding a new relational dimension: the defendant, if held liable, can deflect the burden towards a third party. However this third party can in turn demand to 'stand in the shoes' of the assured and take over any legal rights he may have against others (subrogation) and this may have an unfortunate distorting effect on loss-spreading (*Lister v Romford Ice* (1957), p 52).

2. Insurance can be important, according to Jolowicz, for potential claimants as well. If the party suffering damage were the one in the better position to shoulder the risk of this damage, then he, she or it would not be able to demand compensation from the party that caused the harm, even if this latter party had been negligent. One example to be found in the law reports of this kind of

approach is *Lamb v Camden LBC* (1981). Jolowicz's approach is not above criticism as Cane indicates. Nevertheless, whatever the weakness of Jolowicz's thesis, it does have one very positive feature: it provides an alternative viewpoint for analysing cases.

3. Recently the role of insurance has been raised by the judiciary in a case involving property damage and the strict liability rule in *Rylands v Fletcher* (p 217). The difference between the two Law Lords indicates that the debate is by no means settled.

Transco plc v Stockport Metropolitan Borough Council [2004] 2 AC 1, HL

(For facts see p 220)

Lord Hoffmann: ... **46** Secondly, so far as the rule [in *Rylands v Fletcher*] does have a residuary role to play, it must be borne in mind that it is concerned only with damage to property and that insurance against various forms of damage to property is extremely common. A useful guide in deciding whether the risk has been created by a 'non-natural' user of land is therefore to ask whether the damage which eventuated was something against which the occupier could reasonably be expected to have insured himself. Property insurance is relatively cheap and accessible; in my opinion people should be encouraged to insure their own property rather than seek to transfer the risk to others by means of litigation, with the heavy transactional costs which that involves. The present substantial litigation over £100,000 should be a warning to anyone seeking to rely on an esoteric cause of action to shift a commonplace insured risk...

Lord Hobhouse: ... **60** Thirdly, it is argued that the risk of property damage is 'insurable', just as is public liability. It is then said that, since insurers are likely to be the real parties behind any litigation, the rule has become unnecessary. This is an unsound argument for a number of reasons. It is historically unsound: in the second half of the 19th century there already existed in England, as the common law judges were well aware, a developed insurance market. The existence of an insurance market does not mean that such insurance is available free of charge: premiums have to be paid. Some risks may only be insurable at prohibitive rates or at rates which for the proposer are not commercially viable and so make the risk, for him, commercially uninsurable. (Indeed, in recent times it has been the experience that some insurers will not cover certain risks at all, *eg* loss or damage caused by flooding.) The rationale, he who creates the risk must bear the risk, is not altered at all by the existence of an insurance market. It is an application of the same concept, an acknowledgement of risk. The economic burden of insuring against the risk must be borne by he who creates it and has the control of it. Further, the magnitude of the burden will depend upon who ultimately has to bear the loss: the rule provides the answer to this. The argument that insurance makes the rule unnecessary is no more valid than saying that, because some people can afford to and sensibly do take out comprehensive car insurance, no driver should be civilly liable for his negligent driving. It is unprincipled to abrogate for all citizens a legal rule merely because it may be unnecessary as between major corporations...

QUESTIONS

1. Should tort textbooks now have a chapter entitled 'Esoteric Torts'? What would be the criteria for inclusion in this chapter?

2. 'Without insurance, it is probable that tort liability itself could not survive' (Richard Lewis). Discuss.

Chapter 3

Liability for Individual Acts (1): Harm Intentionally Caused

Continental civil lawyers tend to divide delictual (tort) liability into two categories: damage arising from fault (*culpa*) and damage arising from risk. All blameworthy acts – whether they arise from intention, recklessness, gross fault or mere carelessness – amount to fault for this purpose. For example, if D deliberately pushes C into a ditch causing him serious personal injury, C will be able to sue D in France for damages on the basis of art 1382 of the *Code civil* which states that any 'human act whatever which causes damage to another obliges him by whose fault it occurred to make reparation'. However even if D only carelessly knocked C into the ditch, C would still be able to use art 1382 to claim damages for his injuries. As art 1383 makes clear, fault for this purpose includes negligence and imprudence. The same was true of Roman law: the identical form of action for wrongful damage was available whether the defendant wilfully caused the damage or whether he was guilty of the slightest *culpa* (*culpa levissima*) (D.9.2.44pr).

English law, in contrast, tends to divide tortious liability into three behavioural categories. It has a broad category of strict liability where fault is not normally an essential element; and, with respect to fault liability, it distinguishes between damage arising out of intentional acts and damage arising out of negligent behaviour. Thus, in the ditch example, if D deliberately pushed C, the cause of action would lie in trespass; but if he only carelessly knocked C, the cause of action would be in negligence (see *Letang v Cooper*, above, p 3). This chapter and the next reflect this distinction between intentionally and negligently caused damage. However it has to be said at the outset that English law does not in fact frame liability specifically around the idea of intention to damage; liability depends upon the existence of a cause of action (see eg *Esso v Southport*, pp 4, 34 and *Douglas v Hello!* (2001)). And so if a claimant, despite being wilfully harmed, cannot establish such a cause of action he cannot in theory succeed. This said, wilful and abusive behaviour can be a powerful ingredient.

3.1 Intention and interests

It would be tempting to think that any wilfully caused damage ought to be actionable. Indeed, such behaviour, if it caused harm, would prima facie appear to fall within art 1382 of the CC. Yet a moment's reflection should soon convince one that matters are not quite so simple. Deliberately causing physical harm is one thing, but intentionally inflicting other kinds of damage can be more problematic. For example, if D wishes to prevent C winning a bicycle race and places a log in the road in order to cause him to crash, there is little problem not just about liability for any physical injury but also about liability for the loss of a chance of winning (*Chaplin v Hicks* (1911)). But it would be quite different if D decided, being an excellent cyclist himself, to enter the race with the sole motive of depriving C of the chance of winning. Lawyers tend to analyse this latter situation by saying that there is no *injuria*; that is to say there is no legal wrong despite the existence of intention and of damage (*Bradford Corp v Pickles*, above, p 60). Yet part of the problem is also the nature of the harm itself. And so it is not possible simply to focus upon behaviour: it is necessary to link it to the interest invaded.

3.1.1 Health interest

Where a person deliberately causes physical (as opposed to mental) personal injury this will normally amount to a trespass unless of course the act is covered by consent (eg operating surgeon). One traditional source for this trespass liability is *Wilkinson v Downton* (p 7); but the authority of this precedent as a trespass (as opposed to negligence) case has now been put into question by *Wainright v Home Office* (pp 28, 64, 109). Another difficulty, on occasions, is actually defining the health interest, as the next extract shows.

Adams v Bracknell Forest BC [2005] 1 AC 76, HL

This was an action for damages brought by a 30-year-old dyslexic against an education authority for its failure to detect, and ameliorate, his condition when he was at school. The claimant had always experienced difficulties in reading and writing and found that these difficulties were causing him severe problems in his employment. However, although he had consulted doctors about his depression and lack of self-esteem, he had always been too embarrassed to disclose his literary problems during consultancies. The defendant pleaded that the action was statute-barred under s 11 of the Limitation Act 1980 in that it was a claim for personal injuries and was suffered more than three years prior to the issuing of proceedings. The question arose as to whether dyslexia was a form of personal injury damage. The House of Lords (Lords Hoffmann, Phillips, Scott and Walker and Baroness Hale) held that it was and that the claim was therefore barred. The House also decided that the claimant had constructive knowledge of his condition before the three-year limitation period (per s 14(3) of the 1980 Act).

Lord Scott: ... **67** It is important when considering the first issue to keep in mind that the alleged negligence of the educational authorities did not cause the respondent's dyslexia. His complaint is that they failed to take steps to counteract its effect, to 'ameliorate' his difficulties (see para 7 of the particulars of claim). He seeks damages for the consequences of that failure. Subject to the Limitation Act point I would be in no doubt but that if the respondent can establish that in failing to teach him to read the schools were in breach of the duty they owed him he would be entitled at least to general damages. The ability to read is a benefit that nobody who is able to read would dream of undervaluing. It is not simply a benefit of economic value leading to enhanced employment prospects, although it certainly is that. It is a benefit that transforms the whole quality of life of the person who acquires it.

68 But although the deprivation of the benefit of literacy may, if brought about by a breach of duty, entitle the victim to general damages it does not, to my mind, fit com-

▶

fortably within the concept of a 'personal injury'. It is not, in my view, in itself an impairment of a physical or mental state. The alleged consequences of the deprivation, however, ie 'panic attacks', 'social phobia' and 'depression', might well be regarded as impairments of the mental state of the sufferer.

69 There is some authority on this point. In *Anderton v Clwyd County Council* (reported as *Phelps v Hillingdon London Borough Council* [2001] 2 AC 619) this House had to consider whether pre-action discovery could be claimed pursuant to section 33(2) of the Supreme Court Act 1981. The section has since been amended but at that time pre-action discovery could only be sought by a person likely to be a party to proceedings in which 'a claim in respect of personal injuries to a person ... is likely to be made' (section 33(2)). Section 35(5) of the Act said that 'personal injuries' included 'any impairment of a person's physical or mental condition', a definition identical to that in section 38(1) of the Limitation Act 1980. The potential claimant in *Anderton* was dyslexic. Her problem had not been diagnosed while she was at school and consequently no remedial teaching had been provided. She said that this had led to psychological problems. This House, disagreeing with the Court of Appeal, took the view that her proposed claim was a claim for 'personal injuries'. Lord Slynn of Hadley [2001] 2 AC 619, 664 said that it would be wrong to adopt an over-legalistic view of what were 'personal injuries' and 'a failure to mitigate the adverse consequences of a congenital defect is capable of being "personal injuries to a person" within the meaning of the rules'.

70 If the proposed claim in *Anderton* was a 'personal injuries' claim then so too must the respondent's claim in the present case be, or at least include, a 'personal injuries' claim. The first issue must be decided in favour of the respondent.

The second issue

71 As to the second issue ... The reference in section 14(3) to 'knowledge which he might reasonably have been expected to acquire' should, in my opinion, be taken to be a reference to knowledge which a person in the situation of the claimant, ie an adult who knows he is illiterate, could reasonably be expected to acquire. Personal characteristics such as shyness and embarrassment, which may have inhibited the claimant from seeking advice about his illiteracy problems but which would not be expected to have inhibited others with a like disability, should be left out of the equation. It is the norms of behaviour of persons in the situation of the claimant that should be the test.

72 One of the problems in the present case is that, for entirely understandable reasons, the Limitation Act issue was directed to be dealt with as a preliminary point. As Lord Hoffmann has noted, at para 50 of his opinion, there was no evidence before the court justifying the conclusion that Mr Adams' inhibitions, to which his failure to disclose to his medical adviser his illiteracy problem was attributed, were inhibitions which other people with that problem would be expected to share. My own, non-expert, inclination would be to think that a person of average intelligence (Mr Adams was rated as above average intelligence) who knew himself to be illiterate, knew that his illiteracy was at the back of problems such as stress, depression etc and who consulted a doctor about those problems, could reasonably be expected to inform the doctor about the illiteracy. Expert evidence to the contrary could lead to a different conclusion but in the present case there has been no evidence to the contrary...

QUESTIONS

1. Does this decision mean that every person afflicted with dyslexia has a health problem?

2. Is Lord Scott saying that the issue of the reasonableness of a person's inhibitions is related to the level of his intelligence? Is such a connection reasonable?

3.1.2 Property interest

Deliberate physical damage inflicted *directly* on the property of another will prima facie be a trespass. However, deliberate damage inflicted *indirectly* is more problematic as *Bradford Corporation v Pickles* (p 60) shows. Nevertheless the law of tort is not always impotent.

Hollywood Silver Fox Farm Ltd v Emmett [1936] 2 KB 468, KBD

This was an action for an injunction and for damages brought by the breeder of silver foxes against his neighbour who had carried out a threat to fire a shotgun, on his own land, but close to where the foxes were kept. Vixens are extremely nervous during the breeding season and a loud noise will deter them from breeding and possibly make them kill their young. The defendant claimed he was shooting rabbits on his own land, but Macnaghten J granted the remedies.

Macnaghten J: ... In *Christie v Davey* the plaintiffs, Mr and Mrs Christie, and the defendant lived side by side in semi-detached houses in Brixton. Mrs Christie was a teacher of music, and her family were also musical, and throughout the day sounds of music pervaded their house and were heard in the house of their neighbour. The defendant did not like the music that he heard, and by way of retaliation he took to making noises himself, beating trays and rapping on the wall. The action came on for trial before North J, who delivered judgment in favour of the plaintiffs and granted an injunction restraining the defendant from causing or permitting any sounds or noises in his house so as to vex or annoy the plaintiffs or the occupiers of their house. In the course of his judgment, he said at page 326, after dealing with the facts as he found them, 'The result is that I think I am bound to interfere for the protection of the plaintiffs. In my opinion the noises which were made in the defendant's house were not of a legitimate kind. They were what, to use the language of Lord Selborne in *Gaunt v Fynney*, "ought to be regarded as excessive and unreasonable." I am satisfied that they were made deliberately and maliciously for the purpose of annoying the plaintiffs.' Then come the significant words: 'If what has taken place had occurred between two sets of persons both perfectly innocent, I should have taken an entirely different view of the case. But I am persuaded that what was done by the defendant was done only for the purpose of annoyance, and in my opinion it was not a legitimate use of the defendant's house to use it for the purpose of vexing and annoying his neighbours.'...

The cases to which I have referred were decided before the decision of the House of Lords in *Bradford Corporation v Pickles*; and the question therefore arises whether those cases must now be considered as overruled. It is to be observed that in *Allen v Flood* Lord Watson discussed fully the case of *Keeble v Hickeringill* and said with reference to that case: 'No proprietor has an absolute right to create noises upon his own land,

▶

because any right which the law gives him is qualified by the condition that it must not be exercised to the nuisance of his neighbours or of the public. If he violates that condition he commits a legal wrong, and if he does so intentionally he is guilty of a malicious wrong, in its strict legal sense.'

In my opinion the decision of the House of Lords in *Bradford Corporation v Pickles* has no bearing on such cases as this. I therefore think that the plaintiff is entitled to maintain this action. I think also that in the circumstances an injunction should be granted restraining the defendant from committing a nuisance by the discharge of firearms or the making of other loud noises in the vicinity of the Hollywood Silver Fox Farm during the breeding season – namely, between January 1 and June 15 – so as to alarm or disturb the foxes kept by the plaintiffs at the said farm, or otherwise to injure the plaintiff company.

NOTE

One important aspect of this case is that the harm to the claimant's foxes was caused indirectly and that was why the claim was framed in nuisance. Had the defendant directly shot the foxes he would have been liable in trespass and had he negligently caused their damage he might have had to pay damages through liability in the tort of negligence (see **Chapter 4**).

QUESTIONS

1. What if the defendant had no desire to cause damage to his neighbour's silver foxes; he just felt that he had to shoot rabbits on his land to protect his own crops?

2. What if the defendant had held a firework party to mark his wedding anniversary?

3.1.3 Mental health interest

The deliberate infliction of mental distress (rather than severe psychological damage) is not of itself actionable. The claimant has to fit such a claim into an existing cause of action, although statute has provided some help here.

Hunter v Canary Wharf Ltd [1997] AC 655, HL

Lord Hoffmann:... The perceived gap in *Khorasandjian v Bush* was the absence of a tort of intentional harassment causing distress without actual bodily or psychiatric illness. This limitation is thought to arise out of cases like *Wilkinson v Downton* [1897] 2 QB 57 and *Janvier v Sweeney* [1919] 2 KB 316. The law of harassment has now been put on a statutory basis (see the Protection from Harassment Act 1997) and it is unnecessary to consider how the common law might have developed. But as at present advised, I see no reason why a tort of intention should be subject to the rule which excludes compensation for mere distress, inconvenience or discomfort in actions based on negligence: see *Hicks v Chief Constable of the South Yorkshire Police* [1992] 2 All ER 65. The policy considerations are quite different. I do not therefore say that *Khorasandjian v Bush* was wrongly decided. But it must be seen as a case on intentional harassment, not nuisance...

NOTE

Lord Hoffmann has now added the following qualification.

Wainwright v Home Office [2004] 2 AC 406, HL

(For facts see p 28)

Lord Hoffmann: ... **45** If... one is going to draw a principled distinction which justifies abandoning the rule that damages for mere distress are not recoverable, imputed intention will not do. The defendant must actually have acted in a way which he knew to be unjustifiable and intended to cause harm or at least acted without caring whether he caused harm or not...

NOTE

While it remains true that any deliberate infliction of personal injury will be a trespass, *Wilkinson* has now been re-interpreted as a negligence case: see Lord Hoffmann in *Wainwright* at § 44 (above pp 64, 65).

3.1.4 Reputation interest

Where the mental distress is caused by an untrue statement which in turn can be seen as invading a person's reputation, then the tort of defamation may be relevant (see **Chapter 8**). A deliberate lie that invades a person's business reputation may also be actionable according to the following precedent.

Ratcliffe v Evans [1892] 2 QB 524, CA

This was an action for damages brought by the owner of a business against a person who had published in a local weekly newspaper that the claimant's firm had gone out of business. The plaintiff claimed that his business had suffered general loss as a result of the publication. The jury found that although the words were not defamatory they were not published in good faith and awarded £120 in damages. The Court of Appeal (Lord Esher MR, Fry LJ and Bowen LJ) dismissed an appeal.

Bowen LJ: ... That an action will lie for written or oral falsehoods, not actionable per se nor even defamatory, where they are maliciously published, where they are calculated in the ordinary course of things to produce, and where they do produce, actual damage, is established law. Such an action is not one of libel or of slander, but an action on the case for damage wilfully and intentionally done without just occasion or excuse, analogous to an action for slander of title. To support it, actual damage must be shewn, for it is an action which only lies in respect of such damage as has actually occurred...

NOTE

See now s 3 of the Defamation Act 1952.

3.1.5 Constitutional interest

The deliberate imprisonment of a person without lawful justification will amount to the tort of false imprisonment, a species of trespass.

R v Governor of Brockhill Prison, ex p Evans (No 2) [2001] 2 AC 19, HL

(See also p 27)

Lord Steyn: ... It is common ground that the tort of false imprisonment involves the infliction of bodily restraint which is not expressly or impliedly authorised by the law. The plaintiff does not have to prove fault on the part of the defendant. It is a tort of strict liability. These propositions are also common ground. There the agreement ends. The parties invoke competing principles of law. The Solicitor-General argued that the question whether the governor had authority to detain the respondent for an extra 59 days must be determined on the basis of the law as it then stood. He said that the governor was obliged to obey the law. Consequently, he submitted, that his conduct was authorised by law and he did not commit the tort of false imprisonment. And he said that the principled arguments underpinning his case are reinforced by the injustice of holding the governor liable in tort.

Counsel for the applicant took as his starting point that the tort of false imprisonment is one of strict liability. He submitted that once the applicant's imprisonment for the 59 days was held to be unlawful that is determinative of the issue. Relying on the declaratory theory of judicial decisions – that the law has always been as it is now expounded – he said that legal principle ruled out any defence by the Governor of having relied on the earlier and incorrect view of the law. He said these principles are reinforced by the injustice of leaving the victim of a substantial period of unlawful imprisonment without a remedy.

My Lords, the principles of law invoked by the two sides pull in opposite directions. I am advisedly speaking of principles as opposed to rules. As *Dworkin, Taking Rights Seriously: with a reply to critics* (1977), pp 24-26 observed, rules have an 'all or nothing' quality: they are either determinative or irrelevant. On the other hand, principles are general norms which may be in competition: the dimension and weight of principles need to be considered. In a sense therefore principles have a function not widely different from the role of analogies in the law: *MacCormick, Legal Reasoning and Legal Theory* (1994), pp. 231–232. It is a matter of judgment how the weight of the competing principles in the present case should be assessed. Similarly, both sides assert that the justice of the case – to the wrongly detained woman and to the governor doing his job in accordance with law – favour their particular interpretation. Again, one must consider the comparative potency of these claims to the just solution of the case...

It is also instructive that on remarkably similar facts the New South Wales Court of Appeal in *Colwell v Corrective Services Commission of New South Wales* (1988) 13 NSWLR 714 came to the same conclusion ... that the Commission could be liable for unlawful imprisonment in spite of the fact that those responsible for the detention acted in good faith in accordance with the law as they understood it: see also Fordham, 'False Imprisonment in Good Faith' (2000) Tort L Rev 53. This decision provides support for the view of the majority in the present case from an important common law jurisdiction.

Finally, article 5 of the European Convention for the Protection of Human Rights and Fundamental Freedoms (1953) (Cmd. 8969) provides as follows:

'1. Everyone has the right to liberty and security of person. No one shall be deprived of his liberty save in the following cases and in accordance with a procedure pre-scribed by law: (a) the lawful detention of a person after conviction by a competent court;... 5. Everyone who has been the victim of arrest or detention in contravention of the provisions of this article shall have an enforceable right to compensation.'

In my view these provisions rule out the defence that the Governor acted in accor-dance with the law as it was understood at the time. Article 5 reinforces the view which I have accepted...

Finally, the appellant challenged the Court of Appeal's decision to increase the dam-ages to £5,000. The period of unlawful detention was substantial. This decision was well within the power of the Court of Appeal and I have no reason to doubt the appropriateness of the substituted award.

My Lords, I would uphold the decision and reasoning of the majority in the Court of Appeal. I would dismiss the appeal.

[The appeal was dismissed.]

NOTE

The defendant in the above case did not act in bad faith. What if a public official deliberately, and in bad faith, injures a citizen?

Three Rivers District Council v Governor and Company of The Bank of England (No 3) [2003] 2 AC 1, HL

(For facts see p 105)

Lord Hobhouse: ... I will start by putting the tort in its legal context. Typically, a tort involves the invasion by the defendant of some legally protected right of the plaintiff, for example, trespass to property or trespass to the person. Conversion is another exam-ple. Such conduct on the part of the defendant is actionable as such and the belief of the defendant as to the legality of what he did is irrelevant. It is no defence for the defendant to say that he believed that he had statutory or other legal authority if he did not. The legal justification must actually exist otherwise he is liable in tort. (*Northern Territory v Mengel* 69 AJLR 527, 547)

On the other hand, where the plaintiff is not entitled to complain of the invasion of such a right but bases his claim on some loss which he has suffered consequentially upon some act of the defendant which the defendant mistakenly believed was authorised by the law, the defendant's honest belief provides him with an answer to the plaintiff's claim notwithstanding any actual illegality. Thus the holder of a public office who acts honestly will not be liable to a third party indirectly affected by something which the official has done even if it turns out to have been unlawful. Illegality without more does not give a cause of action. (*Lonrho Ltd v Shell Petroleum Co Ltd* (No 2) [1982] AC 173, 189;

Dunlop v Woollahra Municipal Council [1982] AC 158, 172; *Mengel* at p 546) There is no principle in English law that an official is the guarantor of the legality of everything he does; but he is liable if he injures another by an act which is itself tortious if not justified and he is unable to justify it, however honestly he may have acted.

The subject matter of the tort of misfeasance in public office operates in the area left unoccupied by these limits...

NOTE

The importance of this extract from Lord Hobhouse is that it distinguishes between torts protecting rights and torts arising from wrongs. From the claimant's viewpoint, the latter are more concerned with protected interests.

3.1.6 Trade and business interest

The distinction made by Lord Hobhouse is valuable for understanding legal reasoning. If one wants to grant a legal remedy for the invasion of a particular interest, it can be a useful ploy to turn the 'interest' into a 'right'. Lord Denning does just this in the next extract.

Ex p Island Records [1978] Ch 122, CA

Lord Denning MR: ... The question ... becomes this: has the plaintiff a particular right which he is entitled to have protected? To this the answer which runs through all the cases is: a man who is carrying on a lawful trade or calling has a right to be protected from any unlawful interference with it ... It is a right which is in the nature of a right of property ... [The Attorney-General] has, we are told, refused his consent to a relator action – presumably because no public rights are involved. So perforce if the law is to be obeyed – and justice to be done – the courts must allow a private individual himself to bring an action against the offender – in those cases where his private rights and interests are specially affected by the breach [of the criminal law]. This principle is capable of extension so as to apply not only to rights of property or rights in the nature of it, but to other rights or interests...

NOTE

Lord Denning's analysis is perhaps over-optimistic. Not all deliberate invasions of another's lawful trade are actionable.

Mogul Steamship Co v McGregor, Gow & Co (1889) 23 QBD 598, CA, [1892] AC 25, HL

This was an action for damages brought by one shipping firm against an association of other shipping firms which it was alleged had conspired to keep the claimant out of the tea trade. The association had lowered their own freight rates to below an economic figure; they refused contracts to anyone who booked space on non-combination ships; they gave rebates to those who used only combination vessels; and they shadowed any non-combination ship with the object of 'stealing' its trade. The claimant was soon ruined. The claimant's action was dismissed and appeals to the Court of Appeal and House of Lords (Lords Halsbury LC, Watson, Bramwell, Macnaghten, Morris, Hannen and Field) were also dismissed.

Bowen LJ (Court of Appeal): We are presented in this case with an apparent conflict or antinomy between two rights that are equally regarded by the law – the right of the plaintiffs to be protected in the legitimate exercise of their trade, and the right of the defendants to carry on their business as seems best to them, provided they commit no wrong to others. The plaintiffs complain that the defendants have crossed the line which the common law permits; and inasmuch as, for the purposes of the present case, we are to assume some possible damage to the plaintiffs, the real question to be decided is whether, on such an assumption, the defendants in the conduct of their commercial affairs have done anything that is unjustifiable in law...

What, then, are the limitations which the law imposes on a trader in the conduct of his business as between himself and other traders? There seem to be no burdens or restrictions in law upon a trader which arise merely from the fact that he is a trader, and which are not equally laid on all other subjects of the Crown. His right to trade freely is a right which the law recognises and encourages, but it is one which places him at no special disadvantage as compared with others. No man, whether trader or not, can, however, justify damaging another in his commercial business by fraud or misrepresentation. Intimidation, obstruction, and molestation are forbidden; so is the intentional procurement of a violation of individual rights, contractual or other, assuming always that there is no just cause for it... [The defendants] have done nothing more against the plaintiffs than pursue to the bitter end a war of competition waged in the interest of their own trade. To the argument that a competition so pursued ceases to have a just cause or excuse when there is ill-will or a personal intention to harm, it is sufficient to reply (...) that there was here no personal intention to do any other or greater harm to the plaintiffs than such as was necessarily involved in the desire to attract to the defendants' ships the entire tea freights of the ports, a portion of which would otherwise have fallen to the plaintiffs' share. I can find no authority for the doctrine that such a commercial motive deprives of 'just cause or excuse' acts done in the course of trade which would but for such a motive be justifiable. So to hold would be to convert into an illegal motive the instinct of self-advancement and self-protection, which is the very incentive to all trade. To say that a man is to trade freely, but that he is to stop short at any act which is calculated to harm other tradesmen, and which is designed to attract business to his own shop, would be a strange and impossible counsel of perfection... To attempt to limit English competition in this way would probably be as hopeless an endeavour as the experiment of King Canute. But on ordinary principles of law no such fetter on freedom of trade can in my opinion be warranted...

Lord Bramwell: My Lords, the plaintiffs in this case do not complain of any trespass, violence, force, fraud, or breach of contract, nor of any direct tort or violation of any right of the plaintiffs, like the case of firing to frighten birds from a decoy; nor of any act, the ultimate object of which was to injure the plaintiffs, having its origin in malice or ill-will to them...

The Master of the Rolls says the lowering of the freight far beyond a lowering for any purpose of trade was not an act done in the exercise of their own free right of trade, but for the purpose of interfering with the plaintiffs' right to a free course of trade; therefore a wrongful act as against the plaintiffs' right; and as injury to the plaintiffs followed, they had a right of action. I cannot agree. If there were two shopkeepers in a village and one sold an article at cost price, not for profit therefore, but to attract customers or cause his rival to leave off selling the article only, it could not be said he was liable to an action. I cannot think that the defendants did more than they had a legal right to do...

NOTE

This tea-clipper case must be treated with caution since the commercial liberty protected by the House of Lords has long since gone thanks to European competition law and the Competition Act 1998. Yet it still has an important conceptual relevance in as much as it confirms the principle that the infliction of deliberate economic damage is not in itself actionable. Something more must be shown. If the defendants had been guilty of trespass, nuisance, direct intimidation or some other established wrong (see eg *Torquay Hotel* (1969), below), then the invasion of the claimant's economic interest would have been actionable. The point to be stressed of course is that Lord Denning's assertion in *Island Records* (1978) is too wide: he was trying to turn a commercial interest into a property interest.

QUESTION

Tea clippers often raced and one of the great races, China to London, took place in 1866 between *Taeping* and *Ariel*. The winner would get 10 shillings a ton bonus. The two ships arrived in London docks within 10 minutes of each other: what happened with the prize bonus? What if (which was not the case) one of the ships had taken an illegal short cut and as a result had secured the prize money: could the owner of the ship which came in second sue the winner and, if so, for how much?

3.1.7 Employment interest

A person who loses a job is of course losing his or her means of income (if only temporarily). What is the position if one person deliberately engineers the dismissal of another person?

Allen v Flood [1898] AC 1, HL

This was an action for damages by two woodworkers, who had once done ironwork, against the representative of the ironworkers union. The representative, reflecting the discontent of ironworkers working in a dockyard with the two woodworkers who had once done ironwork, had gone to the employers and informed them that the ironworkers would not turn up for work the next day and thereafter until the two woodworkers were dismissed. The employees were on day-to-day contracts and thus refusing to turn up for work would not have amounted to a breach of any of the employment contracts. The employers dismissed the woodworkers who succeeded in their action against the representative at first instance and in the Court of Appeal. The case was reargued before seven Law Lords and opinions were taken from judges summoned to attend (a procedure no longer current). A majority of the House of Lords (Lords Watson, Herschell, Macnaghten, Shand, Davey and James; Lords Halsbury LC, Ashbourne and Morris dissenting) allowed an appeal. (A majority of the judges who had delivered opinions to the Law Lords were in favour of the claimants.)

Lord Halsbury LC (dissenting): ... I see it is suggested by one of your Lordships that the action for malicious prosecution is supposed to be an exception. I am not quite certain that I understand what is the proposition to which it is an exception. If it means that there is no other form of procedure known to the law wherein malice may make the distinction between a lawful and an unlawful act, I am unable to agree. Maliciously procuring a person to be made a bankrupt, maliciously and without reasonable or probable cause presenting a petition to wind up a company, or maliciously procuring an arrest, are equally cases wherein the state of mind of the person procuring the arrest may affect the question of the lawfulness or unlawfulness of the act done....

Lord Watson: ... Although the rule may be otherwise with regard to crimes, the law of England does not, according to my apprehension, take into account motive as constituting an element of civil wrong. Any invasion of the civil rights of another person is in itself a legal wrong, carrying with it liability to repair its necessary or natural consequences, in so far as these are injurious to the person whose right is infringed, whether the motive which prompted it be good, bad, or indifferent. But the existence of a bad motive, in the case of an act which is not in itself illegal, will not convert that act into a civil wrong for which reparation is due. A wrongful act, done knowingly and with a view to its injurious consequences, may, in the sense of law, be malicious; but such malice derives its essential character from the circumstance that the act done constitutes a violation of the law. There is a class of cases which have sometimes been referred to as evidencing that a bad motive may be an element in the composition of civil wrong; but in these cases the wrong must have its root in an act which the law generally regards as illegal, but excuses its perpetration in certain exceptional circumstances from considerations of public policy. These are well known as cases of privilege, in which the protection which the law gives to an individual who is within the scope of these considerations consists in this – that he may with immunity commit an act which is a legal wrong and but for his privilege would afford a good cause of action against him, all that is required in order to raise the privilege and entitle him to protection being that he shall act honestly in the discharge of some duty which the law recognises, and shall not be prompted by a desire to injure the person who is affected by his act. Accordingly, in a suit brought by that person, it is usual for him to allege and necessary for him to prove an intent to injure in order to destroy the privilege of the defendant. But none of these cases tend to establish that an act which does not amount to a legal wrong, and therefore needs no protection, can have privilege attached to it; and still less that an act in itself lawful is converted into a legal wrong if it was done from a bad motive...

Lord Herschell: ... I can imagine no greater danger to the community than that a jury should be at liberty to impose the penalty of paying damages for acts which are otherwise lawful, because they choose, without any legal definition of the term, to say that they are malicious. No one would know what his rights were. The result would be to put all our actions at the mercy of a particular tribunal whose view of their propriety might differ from our own...

NOTES

1. The holding in this case did not survive for very long, for the judges a few years later developed the tort of conspiracy: *Quinn v Leathem* (1901). Nevertheless it should be seen as one of a trilogy of cases, all decided at the end of the nineteenth century, marking the limits of liability for damage intentionally caused. The other two cases are, of course, *Mogul SS* (p 84) and *Bradford Corporation v Pickles* (p 60).

2. If the deliberate act which results in another's loss of a job is of itself a wrong, then the actor may be liable to a claim in damages.

Rookes v Barnard [1964] AC 1129, HL

This was an action for damages brought by a draughtsman, who had been dismissed from his job at BOAC, against the union officials who had told BOAC that unless the claimant was sacked there would be a strike. If there had been a strike by BOAC skilled draughtsman this would have amounted to a breach of their contracts of employment which incorporated a no-strike clause. Thus the plaintiff claimed that that the strike warning amounted to a threat to do a wrongful act. The trial judge instructed the jury to award exemplary damages, which they did, but his decision was reversed by the Court of Appeal. An appeal to the House of Lords (Lords Reid, Evershed, Hodson, Devlin and Pearce) was allowed.

Lord Reid: ... This case... raises the question whether it is a tort to conspire to threaten an employer that his men will break their contracts with him unless he dismisses the plaintiff, with the result that he is thereby induced to dismiss the plaintiff and cause him loss...

...A person is no more entitled to sue in respect of loss which he suffers by reason of a tort committed against someone else than he is entitled to sue in respect of loss which he suffers by reason of breach of a contract to which he is not a party. What he sues for in each case is loss caused to him by the use of an unlawful weapon against him – intimidation of another person by unlawful means. So long as the defendant only threatens to do what he has a legal right to do he is on safe ground. At least if there is no conspiracy he would not be liable to anyone for doing the act, whatever his motive might be, and it would be absurd to make him liable for threatening to do it but not for doing it. But I agree with Lord Herschell (*Allen v Flood*) that there is a chasm between doing what you have a legal right to do and doing what you have no legal right to do, and there seems to me to be the same chasm between threatening to do what you have a legal right to do and threatening to do what you have no legal right to do. It must follow from *Allen v Flood* that to intimidate by threatening to do what you have a legal right to do is to intimidate by lawful means. But I see no good reason for extending that doctrine. Threatening a breach of contract may be a much more coercive weapon than threatening a tort, particularly when the threat is directed against a company or corporation, and, if there is no technical reason requiring a distinction between different kinds of threats, I can see no other ground for making any such distinction...

Lord Devlin: ... I find... nothing to differentiate a threat of a breach of contract from a threat of physical violence or any other illegal threat. The nature of the threat is immaterial, because, as Professor Hamson points out, its nature is irrelevant to the plaintiff's cause of action. All that matters to the plaintiff is that, metaphorically speaking, a club has been used. It does not matter to the plaintiff what the club is made of – whether it is a physical club or an economic club, a tortious club or an otherwise illegal club. If an intermediate party is improperly coerced, it does not matter to the plaintiff how he is coerced.

I think, therefore, that at common law there is a tort of intimidation and that on the facts of this case each of the respondents has committed it, both individually (since the jury has found that each took an overt and active part) and in combination with others...

QUESTION

Is there really no difference between a threat to commit violence and a threat to break a contract?

3.1.8 Contract interest

A person's employment is of course a contractual right. Yet it is also a kind of 'property' in that it is an identifiable asset, if only an abstract one. Is the same true of contracts in general?

Torquay Hotel Co v Cousins [1969] 2 Ch 106, CA

This was an action for an interlocutory injunction brought by a hotel against a trade union that had issued threats to the hotel's oil suppliers warning them not to supply oil to the hotel. The hotel alleged that the union's threats amounted to an attempt to induce a breach of contract between the hotel and the oil suppliers even though this contract contained an exception clause covering labour disputes. The Court of Appeal (Lord Denning MR, Russell LJ and Winn LJ) upheld the grant of the injunction.

Lord Denning MR: ... It is plain that, if delivery was hindered or prevented by labour disputes, as, for instance, because their drivers would not cross the picket line, Esso could rely on that exception clause as a defence to any claim by Imperial. They would not be liable in damages. And I am prepared to assume that Esso would not be guilty of a breach of contract. But I do not think that would exempt the trade union officials from liability if they unlawfully hindered or prevented Esso from making deliveries. The principle of *Lumley v Gye* extends not only to inducing breach of contract, but also to preventing the performance of it. That can be shown by a simple illustration taken from the books. In *Lumley v Gye*, Miss Wagner, an actress, was engaged by Mr Lumley to sing at Her Majesty's Theatre. Mr Gye, who ran Covent Garden, procured her to break her contract with Mr Lumley by promising to pay her more: see *Lumley v Wagner*. He was held liable to Mr Lumley for inducing a breach of contract. In *Poussard v Spiers & Pond* Madam Poussard was under contract with Spiers to sing in an opera at the Criterion Theatre. She fell sick and was unable to attend rehearsals. Her non-performance, being occasioned by sickness, was not a breach of contract on her part: but it was held to excuse the theatre company from continuing to employ her. Suppose now that an ill-disposed person, knowing of her contract, had given her a potion to make her sick. She would not be guilty of a breach herself. But undoubtedly the person who administered the potion would have done wrong and be liable for the damage suffered by them. So here I think the trade union officials cannot take advantage of the *force majeure* or exception clause in the Esso contract. If they unlawfully prevented or hindered Esso from making deliveries, as ordered by Imperial, they would be liable in damage to Imperial, notwithstanding the exception clause...

... [T]he common law would be seriously deficient if it did not condemn such interference. It is this very case. The principle can be subdivided into three elements:

First, there must be interference in the execution of a contract. The interference is not confined to the procurement of a breach of contract. It extends to a case where a third person prevents or hinders one party from performing his contract, even though it be not a breach.

Second, the interference must be deliberate. The person must know of the contract or, at any rate, turn a blind eye to it and intend to interfere with it: see *Emerald Construction Co v Lowthian*.

▶

Third, the interference must be direct. Indirect interference will not do. Thus, a man who 'corners the market' in a commodity may well know that it may prevent others from performing their contracts, but he is not liable to an action for so doing...

Conclusion

Other wrongs were canvassed, such as conspiracy and intimidation, but I do not think it necessary to go into these. I put my decision on the simple ground that there is evidence that the defendants intended to interfere directly and deliberately with the execution of the existing contracts by Esso and future contracts by Alternative Fuels so as to prevent those companies supplying oil to the Imperial Hotel. This intention was sufficiently manifest to warrant the granting of an injunction...

Winn LJ: ... For my part I think that it can at least be said, with confidence, that where a contract between two persons exists which gives one of them an optional extension of time or an optional mode for his performance of it, or of part of it, but, from the normal course of dealing between them, the other person does not anticipate such postponement, or has come to expect a particular mode of performance, a procuring of the exercise of such an option should, in principle, be held actionable if it produces material damage to the other contacting party ...

NOTE

This case is regarded as a sound precedent (see *Merkur Island Shipping Corpn v Laughton* (1983); *OGB Ltd v Allan* (2005) at § 45), yet it has attracted criticism on the ground that it extends the tort of inducing breach of contract too far.

SM Waddams, 'Johanna Wagner and the Rival Opera Houses' (2001) 117 Law Quarterly Review 431, 454 (footnotes omitted)

I would suggest... that it is not desirable to treat inducement of every breach of contract as a wrong. It is not possible to specify precisely the kinds of contract in respect of which inducement of breach should be tortious, because attention must be given to several concepts simultaneously. In general terms it may be suggested that inducing breach of contract should be wrongful when, but only when, it enables the defendant to take something that belongs to the plaintiff. This concept cannot be precise, but it is likely to include those classes of case where the plaintiff has a special interest in performance such as would not be adequately protected by an award of compensatory damages, that is, as the *Lumley* cases themselves demonstrate, the very kind of case in which the court is likely to favour specific relief, where also the court is likely to categorise the plaintiff's interest as proprietary, and to order profits derived from the breach to be restored to the plaintiff (either by the contract-breaker or by the third party, or both). The concepts tend to support each other in a way that is circular, but not empty of content, nor lacking in persuasive power. Of course, this conclusion is untidy, but it may be said in response that interdependent legal arguments of this kind are very frequent, and that conceptual tidiness is not the highest object of the law.

NOTES

1. Much of the area of trade union liability and industrial disputes is governed by statute and falls outside most foundational tort courses: see now Trade Union and Labour Relations (Consolidation) Act 1992.

2. The main difficulty with these economic torts (see **3.1.6** to **3.1.8**) is to define their limits (see now *OBG v Allan* (2005)). As far as the common law of tort is concerned, not every intentional injury causing economic loss will be actionable otherwise all industrial action by ill-treated workers would be tortious (although much of it can be, thanks now to complex legislation) and all calls to boycott certain products would equally be actionable (although anyone calling for such a boycott now runs the risk of being subject to an Anti-Social Behaviour Order). One notion developed by the courts is that of 'legitimate interest' as related to the behaviour of the defendant. Thus if the defendant is acting to protect a well-established interest, this may give rise either to the non-existence of any economic tort or to a defence based on justification. For example, a trade association can impose fines on its members and any threat of expulsion for non-payment will not amount to blackmail or an economic tort (*Thorne v Motor Trade Association* (1937)). Even behaviour that is illegal might not be actionable at common law if it was not aimed at the claimant (*Lonrho v Shell Petroleum Co Ltd (No 2)* (1982)). However if a defendant intentionally damages a claimant in circumstances where he has no interest of his own to protect, it may be that the damage will be actionable even if the behaviour itself does not actually fit into any civil or criminal wrong category (*Gulf Oil (GB) Ltd v Page* (1987)). It is of course these latter cases that make this area so complex, particularly where the remedy sought is an interlocutory (emergency) injunction rather than damages. Probably no principle is foolproof (and industrial action is governed by statute) but if one is able to add a proprietary dimension – the defendant is interfering with the claimant's 'property right' – it sometimes gives further conceptual strength to the granting of a remedy (see *Ex p Island Records* (1978); and Waddams, above).

3. In *OGB Ltd v Allan* (2005) Peter Gibson LJ stated that 'an interference with contractual performance that causes no breach of contractual obligation on principle cannot be tortious... but cases such as *Torquay Hotel* and *Merkur Island* breach that purist principle'. He was, accordingly, reluctant to extend the tort any further especially where 'intention is lacking' and 'where the interference is not directed at preventing or hindering the performance of any obligation imposed by a contract' (§ 47).

3.2 Assault and battery

An intentional attack on another amounts to an assault which is both a crime and a tort (trespass). The intentional touching of another without justification amounts in theory to a battery (trespass); in practice of course the law has to tolerate some intentional touching. Trespass normally requires a direct invasion. Just what amounts to 'direct' can sometimes give rise to problems as the next case illustrates.

Fagan v Metropolitan Police Commissioner [1969] 1 QB 439, QBD

This was an appeal by way of case stated against a conviction for assaulting a police officer in the execution of his duty. The defendant was directed by a policeman to park his car in a particular spot, but the car, seemingly accidentally, came to rest on the policeman's foot. When the latter asked the defendant to remove the car he received an abusive reply. However, after several more requests, the defendant reluctantly reversed the vehicle off the policeman's foot. The appeal was dismissed by the Divisional Court (Lord Parker CJ and James J; Bridge J dissenting).

James J: ... In our judgment the question arising, which has been argued on general principles, falls to be decided on the facts of the particular case. An assault is any act which intentionally – or possibly recklessly – causes another person to apprehend immediate and unlawful personal violence. Although 'assault' is an independent crime and is to be treated as such, for practical purposes today 'assault' is generally synonymous with the term 'battery' and is a term used to mean the actual intended use of unlawful force to another person without his consent. On the facts of the present case the 'assault' alleged involved a 'battery.' Where an assault involves a battery, it matters not, in our judgment, whether the battery is inflicted directly by the body of the offender or through the medium of some weapon or instrument controlled by the action of the offender. An assault may be committed by the laying of a hand upon another, and the action does not cease to be an assault if it is a stick held in the hand and not the hand itself which is laid on the person of the victim. So for our part we see no difference in principle between the action of stepping on to a person's toe and maintaining that position and the action of driving a car on to a person's foot and sitting in the car whilst its position on the foot is maintained.

To constitute the offence of assault some intentional act must have been performed: a mere omission to act cannot amount to an assault. Without going into the question whether words alone can constitute an assault, it is clear that the words spoken by the appellant could not alone amount to an assault: they can only shed a light on the appellant's action. For our part we think the crucial question is whether in this case the act of the appellant can be said to be complete and spent at the moment of time when the car wheel came to rest on the foot or whether his act is to be regarded as a continuing act operating until the wheel was removed. In our judgment a distinction is to be drawn between acts which are complete – though results may continue to flow – and those acts which are continuing. Once the act is complete it cannot thereafter be said to be a threat to inflict unlawful force upon the victim. If the act, as distinct from the results thereof, is a continuing act there is a continuing threat to inflict unlawful force. If the assault involves a battery and that battery continues there is a continuing act of assault.

For an assault to be committed both the elements of actus reus and mens rea must be present at the same time. The 'actus reus' is the action causing the effect on the victim's mind (see the observations of Park B in *Regina v St George*). The 'mens rea' is the intention to cause that effect. It is not necessary that mens rea should be present at the inception of the actus reus; it can be superimposed upon an existing act. On the other hand the subsequent inception of mens rea cannot convert an act which has been completed without mens rea into an assault.

In our judgment the Willesden magistrates and quarter sessions were right in law. On the facts found the action of the appellant may have been initially unintentional, but the time came when knowing that the wheel was on the officer's foot the appellant (1) remained seated in the car so that his body through the medium of the car was in contact with the officer, (2) switched off the ignition of the car, (3) maintained the wheel of the car on the foot and (4) used words indicating the intention of keeping the wheel in that position. For our part we cannot regard such conduct as mere omission or inactivity.

There was an act constituting a battery which at its inception was not criminal because there was no element of intention but which became criminal from the moment the intention was formed to produce the apprehension which was flowing from the continuing act. The fallacy of the appellant's argument is that it seeks to equate the facts of this case with such a case as where a motorist has accidentally run over a person and, that action having been completed, fails to assist the victim with the intent that the victim should suffer.

We would dismiss this appeal

Bridge J (dissenting): I fully agree with my Lords as to the relevant principles to be applied. No mere omission to act can amount to an assault. Both the elements of actus reus and mens rea must be present at the same time, but the one may be superimposed on the other. It is in the application of these principles to the highly unusual facts of this case that I have, with regret, reached a different conclusion from the majority of the court. I have no sympathy at all for the appellant, who behaved disgracefully. But I have been unable to find any way of regarding the facts which satisfies me that they amounted to the crime of assault. This has not been for want of trying. But at every attempt I have encountered the inescapable question: after the wheel of the appellant's car had accidentally come to rest on the constable's foot, what was it that the appellant did which constituted the act of assault? However the question is approached, the answer I feel obliged to give is: precisely nothing. The car rested on the foot by its own weight and, remained stationary by its own inertia. The appellant's fault was that he omitted to manipulate the controls to set it in motion again.

Neither the fact that the appellant remained in the driver's seat nor that he switched off the ignition seem to me to be of any relevance. The constable's plight would have been no better, but might well have been worse, if the appellant had alighted from the car leaving the ignition switched on. Similarly I can get no help from the suggested analogies. If one man accidentally treads on another's toe or touches him with a stick, but deliberately maintains pressure with foot or stick after the victim protests, there is clearly an assault. But there is no true parallel between such cases and the present case. It is not, to my mind, a legitimate use of language to speak of the appellant 'holding' or 'maintaining' the car wheel on the constable's foot. The expression which corresponds to the reality is that used by the justices in the case stated. They say, quite rightly, that he 'allowed' the wheel to remain.

With a reluctantly dissenting voice I would allow this appeal and quash the appellant's conviction.

NOTES

1. Although a criminal case, the judgments are equally relevant for tort since an assault and a battery are both forms of trespass to the person. One might note how the old adage that 'not doing is no trespass' still has a resonance in the modern law. However, the line between act and omission can be difficult to draw on occasions and depends on how one sees the world. Was the act of coming to rest on the constable's foot and the subsequent reluctance to reverse off it a single act? Or was it two distinct acts? It matters in cases where intention is a constituent of liability since the guilty mind (mens rea) and criminal act (actus reus) must coincide. Thus if D sets out to kill V in stormy weather, but on arriving at V's house finds him trapped under a fallen tree and returns home without aiding him or calling the emergency services, D will probably not at common law be guilty of unlawful killing.

2. One of the difficulties in saying that any unlawful touching of another amounts to a trespass is that ordinary horseplay which results in unintentional injury appears actionable without proof of fault. Would it not be better if this kind of case was dealt with as a negligence problem?

Wilson v Pringle [1987] QB 237, CA

This was an action for damages by one schoolboy against another in respect of an injury arising out of horseplay in a school corridor. The defendant pulled at a bag being carried by the claimant causing the latter to fall and sustain a serious injury. The claimant sought summary judgment on the ground that the defendant's admission that he pulled at the bag amounted in itself to the tort of trespass (battery) and the trial judge agreed. However the Court of Appeal (O'Connor LJ, Croom-Johnson LJ and Balcombe LJ) allowed an appeal on this point and gave leave for the defendant to defend the action.

Croom-Johnson LJ: ... The defendant in the present case has sought to add to the list of necessary ingredients. He has submitted that before trespass to the person will lie it is not only the touching that must be deliberate but the infliction of injury. The plaintiff's counsel, on the other hand, contends that it is not the injury to the person which must be intentional, but the act of touching or battery which precedes it: as he put it, what must be intentional is the application of force and not the injury...

...[W]hat does entitle an injured plaintiff to sue for the tort of trespass to the person? Reference must be made to one further case: *Williams v Humphrey* (unreported), 12 February 1975, a decision of Talbot J. There the defendant, a boy just under 16, pushed the plaintiff into a swimming pool and caused him physical injury. The judge found the defendant acted negligently and awarded damages. But there was another claim in trespass. Talbot J rejected the submission that the action would not lie unless there was an intent to injure. He held that it was sufficient, if the act was intentional, that there was no justification for it. In the present Order 14 [summary judgment] proceedings the judge relied upon that decision. The reasoning in *Williams v Humphrey* is all right as far as it goes, but it does not go far enough. It did not give effect to the reasoning of the older authorities, such as *Tuberville v Savage*... that for there to be either an assault or a battery there must be something in the nature of hostility. It may be evinced by anger, by words or gesture. Sometimes the very act of battery will speak for itself, as where somebody uses a weapon on another...

QUESTIONS

1. When people push others into swimming pools do they not intend some harm? Is such behaviour not a practical joke? Are not practical jokes that end in serious injury a matter of trespass rather than negligence? (Cf *Wainwright v Home Office*, pp 28, 64, 81, 109)

2. D deliberately travels on the underground in London during the rush hour because he likes to find himself in physical contact with others. Is he continually committing a trespass while travelling?

3. A surgeon operates upon a patient without the latter's consent: can the patient sue in trespass or only in negligence? (Cf *Sidaway v Bethlem Royal Hospital* (1985).)

NOTE

In *Blake v Galloway* (2004) a group of teenagers were involved in good-natured and high-spirited horseplay that involved the throwing of twigs and pieces of wood at each other. The claimant was hit, and seriously injured, in the eye by a piece of bark thrown by the defendant. The claim for damages in negligence and trespass was rejected by the Court of Appeal. Dyson LJ stated: 'By participating in this game, the claimant must be taken to have impliedly consented to the risk of a blow on any part of his body, provided that the offending missile was thrown more or less in accordance with the tacit understandings or conventions of the game' (§ 24). Indeed, he added that the victims of horseplay 'will usually not be able to recover damages unless they can show that the injury has been caused by a failure to take care which amounts to recklessness or a very high degree of carelessness, or that it was caused deliberately (ie with intent to cause harm)' (§ 25). See also *Mullin v Richards* (p 129)

3.3 False imprisonment

False imprisonment also amounts to the tort of trespass and thus is an action of considerable importance in constitutional law since it is often the police that imprison. Nevertheless the tort has a role in private law.

Bird v Jones (1845) 115 ER 668, QB

Patteson J:. ... Now the facts of this case appear to be as follows. A part of Hammersmith Bridge which is ordinarily used as a public footway was appropriated for seats to view a regatta on the river, and separated for that purpose from the carriage way by a temporary fence. The plaintiff insisted on passing along the part so appropriated, and attempted to climb over the fence. The defendant, being clerk of the Bridge Company, seized his coat, and tried to pull him back: the plaintiff, however, succeeded in climbing over the fence. The defendant then stationed two policemen to prevent and, they did prevent, the plaintiff from proceeding forwards along the footway; but he was told that he might go back into the carriage way, and proceed to the other side of the bridge, if he pleased. The plaintiff would not do so, but remained where he was above half an hour: and then, on the defendant still refusing to suffer him to go forwards along the footway, he endeavoured to force his way, and, in so doing, assaulted the defendant: whereupon he was taken into custody...

▶

I have no doubt that, in general, if one man compels another to stay in any given place against his will, he imprisons that other just as much as if he locked him up in a room: and I agree that it is not necessary, in order to constitute an imprisonment, that a man's person should be touched. I agree, also, that the compelling a man to go in a given direction against his will may amount to imprisonment. But I cannot bring my mind to the conclusion that, if one man merely obstructs the passage of another in a particular direction, whether by threat of personal violence or otherwise, leaving him at liberty to stay where he is or to go in any other direction if he pleases, he can be said thereby to imprison him. He does him wrong, undoubtedly if there was a right to pass in that direction, and would be liable to an action on the case for obstructing the passage, or of assault, if, on the party persisting in going in that direction, he touched his person, or so threatened him as to amount to an assault. But imprisonment is, as I apprehend, a total restraint of the liberty of the person, for however short a time, and not a partial obstruction of his will, whatever inconvenience it may bring on him. The quality of the act cannot, however, depend on the right of the opposite party. If it be an imprisonment to prevent a man passing along the public highway, it must be equally so to prevent him passing further along a field into which he has broken by a clear act of trespass...

Coleridge J:. ... I am of opinion that there was no imprisonment. To call it so appears to me to confound partial obstruction and disturbance with total obstruction and detention. A prison may have its boundary large or narrow, visible and tangible, or, though real, still in the conception only; it may itself be moveable or fixed: but a boundary it must have; and that boundary the party imprisoned must be prevented from passing; he must be prevented from leaving that place, within the ambit of which the party imprisoning would confine him, except by prison-breach. Some confusion seems to me to arise from confounding imprisonment of the body with mere loss of freedom: it is one part of the definition of freedom to be able to go whithersoever one pleases; but imprisonment is something more than the mere loss of this power; it includes the notion of restraint within some limits defined by a will or power exterior to our own.

[Willimas J was of the opinion that there was no imprisonment; Lord Denman CJ dissented.]

QUESTION

The imprisonment must be total. But what if the defendant demands money before allowing the claimant to leave an enclosure?

Robinson v Balmain New Ferry Co Ltd [1910] AC 295, PC

This was an action for damages for false imprisonment against a ferry company. The Privy Council (Lords Loreburn LC, Macnaghten, Collins and Sir Arthur Wilson) held the company not liable.

Lord Loreburn LC: ... The plaintiff paid a penny on entering the wharf to stay there till the boat should start and then be taken by the boat to the other side. The defendants were admittedly always ready and willing to carry out their part of this contract. Then the plaintiff changed his mind and wished to go back. The rules as to the exit from the wharf by the turnstile required a penny for any person who went through. This the plaintiff refused to pay, and he was by force prevented from going through the turnstile. He then claimed damages for assault and false imprisonment.

There was no complaint, at all events there was no question left to the jury by the plaintiff's request, of any excessive violence, and in the circumstances admitted it is clear to their Lordships that there was no false imprisonment at all. The plaintiff was merely called upon to leave the wharf in the way in which he contracted to leave it. There is no law requiring the defendants to make the exit from their premises gratuitous to people who come there upon a definite contract which involves their leaving the wharf by another way; and the defendants were entitled to resist a forcible passage through their turnstile.

The question whether the notice which was affixed to these premises was brought home to the knowledge of the plaintiff is immaterial, because the notice itself is immaterial.

When the plaintiff entered the defendants' premises there was nothing agreed as to the terms on which he might go back, because neither party contemplated his going back. When he desired to do so the defendants were entitled to impose a reasonable condition before allowing him to pass through their turnstile from a place to which he had gone of his own free will. The payment of a penny was a quite fair condition, and if he did not choose to comply with it the defendants were not bound to let him through. He could proceed on the journey he had contracted for...

QUESTIONS

1. The notice mentioned by Lord Loreburn stated: 'Notice. A Fare of One Penny Must Be Paid on Entering or Leaving the Wharf. No Exception Will Be Made to This Rule Whether the Passenger has Travelled by the Ferry or Not'. Do you really think the notice was immaterial? What if there had been evidence that the company did on occasions refund money to those who did not use the ferry?

2. Why were the defendants entitled to impose a reasonable condition before allowing a person to pass through their turnstile?

3. What if the plaintiff, having entered the wharf, suddenly got a severe attack of sickness and could not face the crossing?

4. What if a child, without money, had entered and had then been refused exit until he paid? What if the inability of the child to return home for twelve hours had caused his parents to suffer severe psychological damage?

5. A group of miners refuse to continue working underground because they consider conditions to be unsafe. The manager of the mine refuses to take them to the surface until the time stipulated in their contracts of employment which in effect means that they have to remain underground for over two hours. Is this false imprisonment? (Cf. *Herd v Weardale Colliery* (1915).)

6. Must the imprisoned person have been aware of his or her imprisonment? And if imprisoned by the authorities, must the imprisoned person be informed of the reasons for the imprisonment?

Murray v Ministry of Defence [1988] 1 WLR 692, HL

This was an action for damages for false imprisonment brought against the MOD by a woman whose house was searched by soldiers in Northern Ireland. The soldiers arrived at 7am and a corporal accompanied the claimant upstairs so that she could get dressed. When they returned downstairs about half an hour later the corporal formerly arrested the claimant. The woman argued that she was falsely imprisoned between 7am and the time she was formerly arrested and one of the legal issues that arose was whether it would still be false imprisonment even if she had been unaware that she was being restrained while getting dressed. The House of Lords (Lords Keith, Templeman, Oliver, Jauncey and Griffiths) held that the arrest was not unlawful as it had been reasonable under the emergency legislation to delay formal arrest until the premises had been searched.

Lord Griffiths: ... The question remains, however, whether the failure to tell the plaintiff that she was being arrested until the soldiers were about to leave the house renders the arrest unlawful. It has been well-settled law, at least since *Christie v Leachinsky*, that a person must be informed of the reason for his arrest at or within a reasonable time of the arrest. There can be no doubt that in ordinary circumstances, the police should tell a person the reason for his arrest at the time they make the arrest. If a person's liberty is being restrained, he is entitled to know the reason. If the police fail to inform him, the arrest will be held to be unlawful, with the consequence that if the police are assaulted as the suspect resists arrest, he commits no offence, and if he is taken into custody, he will have an action for wrongful imprisonment. However, it is made plain in the speeches in *Christie v Leachinsky* that there are exceptions to this general rule...

Although on the facts of this case I am sure that the plaintiff was aware of the restraint on her liberty from 7.00 a.m., I cannot agree with the Court of Appeal that it is an essential element of the tort of false imprisonment that the victim should be aware of the fact of denial of liberty. The Court of Appeal relied upon *Herring v Boyle*, for this proposition which they preferred to the view of Atkin LJ to the opposite effect in *Meering v Grahame-White Aviation Co Ltd*,...

In the first place it is not difficult to envisage cases in which harm may result from unlawful imprisonment even though the victim is unaware of it. Dean William L Prosser gave two examples in his article in the Columbia Law Review, vol. 55 (June 1955), p 847 ('False Imprisonment: Consciousness of Confinement'), in which he attacked section 42 of the *Restatement of Torts* which at that time stated the rule that 'there is no liability for intentionally confining another unless the person physically restrained knows of the confinement.' Dean Prosser wrote, at p 849:

'Let us consider several illustrations. A locks B, a child two days old, in the vault of a bank. B is, of course, unconscious of the confinement, but the bank vault cannot be opened for two days. In the meantime, B suffers from hunger and thirst, and his health is seriously impaired; or it may be that he even dies. Is this no tort? Or suppose that A abducts B, a wealthy lunatic, and holds him for ransom for a week. B is unaware of his confinement, but vaguely understands that he is in unfamiliar surroundings, and that something is wrong. He undergoes mental suffering affecting his health. At the end of the week, he is discovered by the police and released without ever having known that he has been imprisoned. Has he no action against B? ... If a child of two is kidnapped, confined, and deprived of the care of its mother for a month, is the kidnapping and the confinement in itself so minor a matter as to call for no redress in tort at all?'

The Restatement of Torts has now been changed and requires that the person confined 'is conscious of the confinement or is harmed by it' (*Restatement of the Law, Second, Torts 2d* (1965), section 35, p 52).

If a person is unaware that he has been falsely imprisoned and has suffered no harm, he can normally expect to recover no more than nominal damages, and it is tempting to redefine the tort in the terms of the present rule in the American Restatement of Torts. On reflection, however, I would not do so. The law attaches supreme importance to the liberty of the individual and if he suffers a wrongful interference with that liberty it should remain actionable even without proof of special damage...

NOTES

1. See also *R v Governor of Brockhill Prison, ex p Evans* (No 2) (2001) (pp 27, 82).
2. Police, security guards, store detectives and the like are only liable if they detain someone whom they suspect of a crime if they have detained unlawfully. Powers to stop and search and to arrest are to be found principally in the Police and Criminal Evidence Act 1984 (PACE) but the new legislation is giving the police ever more powers. See also ss 40 and 43 of the Terrorism Act 2000. Some of the technicalities of arrest under PACE can be found in *Davidson v Chief Constable of North Wales* (1994). Note also the remedy of self-help: *R v Self* (see p 416).

QUESTION

What if a person finds himself lawfully imprisoned but the lawful imprisonment is the result of police and Crown Prosecution Service carelessness with respect to the evidence? If both had done their jobs properly both would have realised that the person imprisoned had nothing to do with the crime for which he was being held. Should the person imprisoned be able to sue for damages? If so, in what tort? (Cf *Elguzouli-Daf v Commissioner of Police for the Metropolis*, p 315; *Brooks v Comr of Police for the Metropolis* (2005).)

3.4 Harassment

We have already seen that there is no tort of harassment at common law: *Wainwright v Home Office* (pp 28, 64, 81, 109). However under statute harassment can give rise to a civil remedy.

Protection from Harassment Act 1997 (c. 40)

1 Prohibition of harassment

(1)   A person must not pursue a course of conduct—
     (a) which amounts to harassment of another, and
     (b) which he knows or ought to know amounts to harassment of the other.

(2)   For the purposes of this section, the person whose course of conduct is in ques-
     tion ought to know that it amounts to or involves harassment of another if a
     reasonable person in possession of the same information would think the course
     of conduct amounted to or involves harassment of the other.

(3)   Subsection (1) or (1A) does not apply to a course of conduct if the person who
     pursued it shows—
     (a) that it was pursued for the purpose of preventing or detecting crime,
     (b) that it was pursued under any enactment or rule of law or to comply with any
          condition or requirement imposed by any person under any enactment, or
     (c) that in the particular circumstances the pursuit of the course of conduct was
          reasonable.

(1A) A person must not pursue a course of conduct—
     (a) which involves harassment of two or more persons, and
     (b) which he knows or ought to know involves harassment of these persons, and
     (c) by which he intends to persuade any person (whether or not one of those
          mentioned above)—
          (i) not to do something that he is entitled or required to do, or
          (ii) to do something that he is not under any obligation to do.

3 Civil remedy

(1) An actual or apprehended breach of section 1(1) may be the subject of a claim in
    civil proceedings by the person who is or may be the victim of the course of con-
    duct in question.

(2) On such a claim, damages may be awarded for (among other things) any anxiety
    caused by the harassment and any financial loss resulting from the harassment...

3A Injunctions to protect persons from harassment within section 1(1A)

...

(2) In such a case—
(a) any person who is or may be a victim of the course of conduct in question, or
(b) any person who is or may be a person falling within section 1(1A)(c), may apply to
    the High Court or a county court for an injunction...

QUESTIONS

1. Will an employer be liable for harassment of one of his employees by another
employee? (See Chapter 7 and *Majrowski v Guy's & St Thomas's NHS Trust* (2005).)

2. Does section 1A destroy any right to picket or even to demonstrate? (Cf p 293)

3.5 Fraud and lies

Several torts can be relevant where one causes deliberate damage through false statements. Much depends upon the nature of the statement, the intention of the author, whether it was published, and the interest invaded.

3.5.1 Deceit

The elements of the tort of deceit are set out in *Bradford Building Society v Borders* (p 287). The main obstacle facing a claimant wishing to use the tort of deceit is that fraud must be proved. This is often not easy, but it may be possible for a victim to use the tort of negligence instead: see eg *Spring v Guardian Insurance* (pp 257, 352).

3.5.2 Defamation and malicious falsehood

If there is no fraud as such but still a deliberate lie that harms another, the torts of defamation and malicious prosecution may be available.

Joyce v Sengupta [1993] 1 WLR 337, CA

This was an action for damages, brought by a woman who had worked as a maid in the royal household, against a newspaper and journalist, in respect of an article published in the paper which made very serious allegations about the claimant. Legal aid was not available for defamation and so the claimant based her action on the tort of malicious falsehood. The trial judge struck out the claim as an abuse of process, but an appeal against this decision was allowed by the Court of Appeal (Sir Donald Nicholls V-C, Butler-Sloss LJ and Sir Michael Kerr).

Sir Donald Nicholls V-C: ... Before turning to the issues raised by the appeal I should comment briefly on the difference between defamation and malicious falsehood. The remedy provided by the law for words which injure a person's reputation is defamation. Words may also injure a person without damaging his reputation. An example would be a claim that the seller of goods or land is not the true owner. Another example would be a false assertion that a person has closed down his business. Such claims would not necessarily damage the reputation of those concerned. The remedy provided for this is malicious falsehood, sometimes called injurious falsehood or trade libel. This cause of action embraces particular types of malicious falsehood such as slander of title and slander of goods, but it is not confined to those headings.

Falsity is an essential ingredient of this tort. The plaintiff must establish the untruth of the statement of which he complains. Malice is another essential ingredient. A genuine dispute about the ownership of goods or land should not of itself be actionable. So a person who acted in good faith is not liable. Further, since the object of this cause of action is to provide a person with a remedy for a false statement made maliciously which has caused him damage, at common law proof of financial loss was another essential ingredient. The rigour of this requirement was relaxed by statute. I shall have to return to the question of damages at a later stage. For present purposes it is sufficient to note that if a plaintiff establishes that the defendant maliciously made a false statement which has caused him financial damage, or in respect of which he is relieved from

▶

proving damage by the Defamation Act 1952, the law gives him a remedy. The false statement may also be defamatory, or it may not. As already mentioned, it need not be defamatory. Conversely, the fact that the statement is defamatory does not exclude a cause of action for malicious falsehood, although the law will ensure that a plaintiff does not recover damages twice over for the same loss...

So far as the statement of claim is concerned I am satisfied that, although open to criticism here and there, it does disclose the essentials of a cause of action for malicious falsehood...

NOTE

This case is not as such an action for fraud since the motive of the defendants was not criminal profiteering (just unpleasant profiteering). The relevant tort for fraud is deceit. Nevertheless the tort of malicious falsehood might be a valuable alternative on occasions where fraud itself cannot easily be proved but malice and recklessness can. *Joyce* reaffirms the point that the existence of one cause of action within a set of facts will not exclude others. For another case where a claimant uses a tort other than defamation to obtain damages for false statements see *Spring v Guardian Assurance* (pp 257, 352). These cases of deliberate wrongdoing often raise questions of exemplary damages (see **11.2.3**).

QUESTIONS

1. What was the main interest being protected in *Joyce* (1993)?

2. Is it true to say that maliciously causing mental distress is actionable in tort? (Cf *Wainwright v Home Office*, pp 28, 64, 81, 109.)

3.6 Abuse of public power

We have already seen that the tort of trespass is of central importance to victims of abusive behaviour by public officials that directly interferes with the physical and constitutional well-being of the victim. But where the interference and damage from abusive behaviour is more indirect, or where the interference itself might be lawful but the motive malicious, other torts become relevant. Two common law torts in particular apply to public authorities: malicious prosecution and misfeasance in public office. Added to these two there is now a statutory action created by the Human Rights Act 1998. Other torts, such as malicious falsehood and defamation, might equally be available on occasions depending on the facts.

3.6.1 Malicious prosecution

The main elements of the tort of malicious prosecution are set out in the next case.

Martin v Watson [1996] AC 74, HL

Lord Keith of Kinkel: My Lords, the background to the proceedings which give rise to this appeal is a long history of mutual antagonism between neighbours. The appellant plaintiff, Mr Martin, and the respondent defendant, Mrs Watson, lived next door to each other in Orpington. The garden of each dwelling abutted on that of the other. Relations between the parties and their respective spouses were acrimonious for many years, for reasons which need not be gone into. Eventually the defendant began to make accusations that the plaintiff had indecently exposed himself to her... [T]he plaintiff was arrested and taken to the police station, where he was interviewed and bailed to attend court the next day upon a charge related to the events of 20 July 1989. He duly did so but the Crown Prosecution Service offered no evidence and he was discharged.

In the circumstances the plaintiff brought this action for malicious prosecution against the defendant in Bromley County Court. On 13 July 1992 Judge Goodman, after trial, gave judgment in favour of the plaintiff and awarded him damages of £3,500. The defendant was granted leave to appeal to the Court of Appeal, which on 21 January 1994 by a majority (Ralph Gibson and Hobhouse LJJ, McCowan LJ dissenting) [1994] QB 425 allowed the appeal and set aside the judgment of Judge Goodman. The plaintiff now appeals, with leave given by the Court of Appeal, to your Lordships' House.

It is common ground that the ingredients of the tort of malicious prosecution are correctly stated in *Clerk & Lindsell on Torts*, 16th ed. (1989), p. 1042, para. 19-05:

'In action of malicious prosecution the plaintiff must show first that he was prosecuted by the defendant, that is to say, that the law was set in motion against him on a criminal charge; secondly, that the prosecution was determined in his favour; thirdly, that it was without reasonable and probable cause; fourthly, that it was malicious. The onus of proving every one of these is on the plaintiff.'

Judge Goodman found that all four of these ingredients had been proved...

The question at issue is whether or not the defendant is properly to be regarded, in all the circumstances, as having set the law in motion against the plaintiff. Curiously enough, there appears to be no reported English decision dealing with the situation where the defendant in a malicious prosecution action has falsely and maliciously accused the plaintiff to a police officer of having committed an offence, with the result that a prosecution has been initiated by the police officer. A number of decisions in other Commonwealth countries have, however, considered such a state of affairs...

...Where an individual falsely and maliciously gives a police officer information indicating that some person is guilty of a criminal offence and states that he is willing to give evidence in court of the matters in question, it is properly to be inferred that he desires and intends that the person he names should be prosecuted. Where the circumstances are such that the facts relating to the alleged offence can be within the knowledge only of the complainant, as was the position here, then it becomes virtually impossible for the police officer to exercise any independent discretion or judgment, and if a prosecution is instituted by the police officer the proper view of the matter is that the prosecution has been procured by the complainant...

▶

Mr Munby, for the defendant, mounted a powerful argument to the effect that considerations of policy pointed against a decision in favour of the plaintiff in the present case. Such a decision, so it was maintained, would tend to discourage members of the public from bringing criminal activities to the notice of the police, lest they should find themselves harassed by actions of malicious prosecution in the event that the alleged perpetrator of the offence were acquitted. The logical result, if this argument were accepted, would be to stultify completely the tort of malicious prosecution since the rationale would apply not only to those giving information which resulted in a police prosecution but also to those who themselves signed the charge sheet or laid the information. There is no good ground here for making a distinction between persons who procure a police prosecution and those who are technically prosecutors. It is said that victims of sexual assaults would be particularly discouraged from complaining. This, however, could not be so where the alleged perpetrator was a stranger to the complainant, and where the parties are known to each other a prosecution is unlikely to follow unless there is some evidence other than that of the complainant herself. Further, false accusations of sexual offences are by no means unknown, and there are many other types of offences of which a person may be falsely accused. It is to be kept in mind also that in actions for malicious prosecution the onus lies on the plaintiff to prove malice and want of reasonable cause. This would not be possible in the case of genuine complaints. It is suggested that adequate remedies for false accusations are available by way of prosecution for attempting to pervert the course of justice or wasting the time of the police, and also by way of prosecution for perjury if the complainant has actually given false evidence. But none of these remedies affords any compensation to a person who may have been arrested and imprisoned and perhaps subjected to the ordeal of a trial...

...To deny any remedy to a person whose liberty has been interfered with as a result of unfounded and malicious accusations in such circumstances would constitute a serious denial of justice.

My Lords, for these reasons I would set aside the order of the Court of Appeal [1994] QB 425 and restore the judgment of Judge Goodman. The defendant must pay the plaintiff's costs in the Court of Appeal. The defendant was legally aided before your Lordships' House but the plaintiff was not. The plaintiff will be entitled to his costs here against the legal aid fund, subject to the usual opportunity for objection.

[Lords Slynn, Lloyd, Nicholls and Steyn agreed with Lord Keith.]

NOTE

The actual person guilty of abusing public power was, in this case, not a public official. Normally in malicious prosecution cases it is a police officer that is the defendant, but, as this case shows, the tort is not confined to public officials. Perhaps the defendant in this case should be seen as a kind of temporary public official the moment she brought the public prosecution machinery into play in her dealings with her next-door neighbour.

3.6.2 Misfeasance in public office

The tort of misfeasance in public office has been reviewed and restated recently in a major House of Lords decision.

Three Rivers District Council v Governor and Company of The Bank of England (No 3) [2003] 2 AC 1, HL

This was an action for damages brought against the Bank of England by a large group of depositors who had lost money when the Bank of Credit and Commerce International (BCCI) collapsed. The cause of action was the tort of misfeasance in public office. The 'plaintiffs allege that named senior officials of the Banking Supervision Department of the Bank, but not two successive Governors of the Bank, acted in bad faith (a) in licensing BCCI in 1979, when they knew that it was unlawful to do so; (b) in shutting their eyes to what was happening at BCCI after the licence was granted; and (c) in failing to take steps to close BCCI when the known facts cried out for action at least by the mid 80s' (Lord Steyn). The defendants successfully argued before the trial judge and a majority of the Court of Appeal that the action should be struck out. The House of Lords, having restated the tort of misfeasance in public office, sent the case back to the trial judge for a further hearing.

Lord Steyn: ... The present appeal to the House, described as the plaintiffs' legal appeal, is brought by the plaintiffs with the leave of the Court of Appeal given on 21 January 1999. The order of the Court of Appeal contemplated that the House would determine 'the legal issues as to the correct test for misfeasance in public office... before any consideration of whether the facts alleged or capable of being alleged are capable of meeting that test'...

Misfeasance in public office

The early history

The history of the development of the tort has been described by Clarke J and in the judgments in the Court of Appeal: see also *Arrowsmith, Civil Liability and Public Authorities*, (1992), pp. 226–234. It is traceable to the 17th century: *Turner v Sterling* (1671) 2 Vent 24. But the first solid basis for this new head of tort liability, based on an action on the case, is to be found in *Ashby v White* (1703), best reported in 1 *Smith's Leading Cases* (13th ed) 253. The view ultimately prevailed that an action would lie by an elector who was wilfully denied a right to vote by a returning officer. Despite the recognition of the tort in a number of cases in the 18th and 19th centuries, the Court of Appeal in 1907 denied the existence of the tort in *Davis v Bromley Corporation* [1908] 1 KB 170. But by 1981 the Privy Council described the tort as 'well established:' *Dunlop v Woollahra Municipal Council* [1982] AC 158, at 172F. An examination of the ingredients of the tort was still required. The first step towards that goal was the judgments in the Court of Appeal in *Bourgoin SA v Ministry of Agriculture, Fisheries and Food* [1986] QB 716. The present case is the first occasion on which the House has been called on to review the requirements of the tort in a comprehensive manner. Your Lordships are however not asked to prepare an essay on the tort of misfeasance in public office but to state the ingredients of the tort so far as it may be material to the concrete disposal of the issues arising on the pleadings in this case.

The matrix of the tort

The coherent development of the law requires the House to consider the place of the tort of misfeasance in public office against the general scheme of the law of tort. It is well established that individuals in the position of the depositors cannot maintain an action for compensation for losses they suffered as a result of the Bank's breach of statutory

▶

duties: *Yuen Kun-Yeu v Attorney-General of Hong Kong* [1988] AC 175 (PC); *Davis v Radcliffe* [1990] 1 WLR 821 (PC). Judicial review is regarded as an adequate remedy. Similarly, persons in the position of the depositors cannot sue the Bank for losses resulting from the negligent licensing, supervision or failure to withdraw a licence: *Yuen Kun-Yeu v Attorney-General of Hong Kong; Davis v Radcliffe*. The availability of the tort of misfeasance in public office has been said to be one of the reasons justifying the non-actionability of a claim in negligence where there is an act of maladministration: *Calveley v Chief Constable of the Merseyside Police* [1989] AC 1228, at 1238F. It is also established that an ultra vires act will not per se give rise to liability in tort: *X (Minors) v Bedfordshire County Council* [1995] 2 AC 633. And there is no overarching principle in English law of liability in tort for 'unlawful, intentional and positive acts': see *Lonrho Ltd v Shell Petroleum Co Ltd (No 2)* [1982] AC 173, 187G in which the House refused to follow *Beaudesert Shire Council v Smith* (1966) 120 CLR 145, which was subsequently overruled by the Australian High Court in *Northern Territory v Mengel* (1995) 69 AJLR 527. The tort of misfeasance in public office is an exception to 'the general rule that, if conduct is presumptively unlawful, a good motive will not exonerate the defendant, and that, if conduct is lawful apart from motive, a bad motive will not make him liable': *Winfield and Jolowicz on Tort*, 15th ed, (1998), p. 55; *Bradford Corporation v Pickles* [1895] AC 587; *Allen v Flood* [1898] AC 1. The rationale of the tort is that in a legal system based on the rule of law executive or administrative power 'may be exercised only for the public good' and not for ulterior and improper purposes: *Jones v Swansea City Council* [1990] 1 WLR 54, 85F, per Nourse LJ; a decision reversed on the facts but not on the law by the House of Lords: [1990] 1 WLR 1453, at 1458. The tort bears some resemblance to the crime of misconduct in public office: *Reg v Bowden* [1996] 1 WLR 98.

The ingredients of the tort

It is now possible to consider the ingredients of the tort. That can conveniently be done by stating the requirements of the tort in a logical sequence of numbered paragraphs.

(1) The defendant must be a public officer

It is the office in a relatively wide sense on which everything depends. Thus a local authority exercising private-law functions as a landlord is potentially capable of being sued: *Jones v Swansea City Council*. In the present case it is common ground that the Bank satisfies this requirement.

(2) The second requirement is the exercise of power as a public officer

This ingredient is also not in issue. The conduct of the named senior officials of the Banking Supervision Department of the Bank was in the exercise of public functions. Moreover, it is not disputed that the principles of vicarious liability apply as much to misfeasance in public office as to other torts involving malice, knowledge or intention: *Racz v Home Office* [1994] 2 AC 45.

(3) The third requirement concerns the state of mind of the defendant

The case law reveals two different forms of liability for misfeasance in public office. First there is the case of targeted malice by a public officer ie conduct specifically intended to injure a person or persons. This type of case involves bad faith in the sense of the exercise of public power for an improper or ulterior motive. The second form is where a public officer acts knowing that he has no power to do the act complained of and that the act will probably injure the plaintiff. It involves bad faith inasmuch as the public officer does not have an honest belief that his act is lawful...

The basis for the action lies in the defendant taking a decision in the knowledge that it is an excess of the powers granted to him and that it is likely to cause damage to an individual or individuals. It is not every act beyond the powers vesting in a public officer which will ground the tort...

...This is an organic development, which fits into the structure of our law governing intentional torts. The policy underlying it is sound: reckless indifference to consequences is as blameworthy as deliberately seeking such consequences. It can therefore now be regarded as settled law that an act performed in reckless indifference as to the outcome is sufficient to ground the tort in its second form...

Initially, counsel for the plaintiffs argued that in this context recklessness is used in an objective sense... The difficulty with this argument was that it could not be squared with a meaningful requirement of bad faith in the exercise of public powers which is the raison d'être of the tort. But, understandably, the argument became more refined during the oral hearing and counsel for the plaintiffs accepted that only reckless indifference in a subjective sense will be sufficient. This concession was rightly made. The plaintiff must prove that the public officer acted with a state of mind of reckless indifference to the illegality of his act: *Rawlinson v Rice* [1997] 2 NZLR 651. Later in this judgment I will discuss the requirement of reckless indifference in relation to the consequences of the act.

(4) Duty to the plaintiff

The question is who can sue in respect of an abuse of power by a public officer... It would be unwise to make general statements on a subject which may involve many diverse situations. What can be said is that, of course, any plaintiff must have a sufficient interest to found a legal standing to sue. Subject to this qualification, principle does not require the introduction of proximity as a controlling mechanism in this corner of the law. The state of mind required to establish the tort, as already explained, as well as the special rule of remoteness hereafter discussed, keeps the tort within reasonable bounds. There is no reason why such an action cannot be brought by a particular class of persons, such as depositors at a bank, even if their precise identities were not known to the bank...

(5) Causation

Causation is an essential element of the plaintiffs' cause of action. It is a question of fact. The majority in the Court of Appeal and Auld LJ held that it is unsuitable for summary determination. That is plainly correct. This conclusion disposes of agreed issue 3 so far as it relates to the tort of misfeasance.

(6) Damage and Remoteness

The claims by the plaintiffs are in respect of financial losses they suffered. These are, of course, claims for recovery of consequential economic losses. The question is when such losses are recoverable. It would have been possible, as a matter of classification, to discuss this question under paragraph 3 in which the required state of mind for this tort was examined. It is, however, convenient to consider it under the traditional heading of remoteness...

(See p 83 for further extract.)

QUESTIONS

1. Prison officials release a highly dangerous criminal from prison knowing that they have no lawful power to do so. The prisoner, while free, kills a member of the public. Can the victim (or more precisely his estate) sue the Home Office in damages for misfeasance in public office? (Cf *Akenzua v Home Secretary*, p 303.)

2. Must physical or economic damage be proved before a claimant can succeed in the tort of misfeasance in public office? Or, put another way, what interests are protected by this tort? (Cf *Watkins v Home Secretary* (2005).)

3.6.3 Abuse of a human right

There is no tort at common law of invading or abusing a human right. However statute has established the possibility of an action against a 'public authority'.

Human Rights Act 1998 (c 42)

6.   Acts of public authorities

(1) It is unlawful for a public authority to act in a way which is incompatible with a Convention right.

(2) Subsection (1) does not apply to an act if—
  (a) as the result of one or more provisions of primary legislation, the authority could not have acted differently; or
  (b) in the case of one or more provisions of, or made under, primary legislation which cannot be read or given effect in a way which is compatible with the Convention rights, the authority was acting so as to give effect to or enforce those provisions.

(3) In this section 'public authority' includes—
  (a) a court or tribunal,...

7.   Proceedings

(1) A person who claims that a public authority has acted (or proposes to act) in a way which is made unlawful by section 6(1) may—
  (a) bring proceedings against the authority under this Act in the appropriate court or tribunal,

or

  (b) rely on the Convention right or rights concerned in any legal proceedings,

but only if he is (or would be) a victim of the unlawful act...

(8) Nothing in this Act creates a criminal offence.

8.   Judicial remedies

(1) In relation to any act (or proposed act) of a public authority which the court finds is (or would be) unlawful, it may grant such relief or remedy, or make such order, within its powers as it considers just and appropriate.

(2) But damages may be awarded only by a court which has power to award damages, or to order the payment of compensation, in civil proceedings.

(3) No award of damages is to be made unless, taking account of all the circumstances of the case, including—
 (a) any other relief or remedy granted, or order made, in relation to the act in question (by that or any other court), and
 (b) the consequences of any decision (of that or any other court) in respect of that act,

the court is satisfied that the award is necessary to afford just satisfaction to the person in whose favour it is made.

(4) In determining—
 (a) whether to award damages, or
 (b) the amount of an award,

the court must take into account the principles applied by the European Court of Human Rights in relation to the award of compensation under Article 41 of the Convention.

NOTE

The scope of s 7 may be more limited than it might first appear.

Wainwright v Home Office [2004] 2 AC 406, HL

(For facts see p 28)

Lord Hoffmann: ... **51** Article 8 is more difficult. Buxton LJ thought [2002] QB 1334, 1352, para 62, that the Wainwrights would have had a strong case for relief under section 7 if the 1998 Act had been in force. Speaking for myself, I am not so sure. Although article 8 guarantees a right of privacy, I do not think that it treats that right as having been invaded and requiring a remedy in damages, irrespective of whether the defendant acted intentionally, negligently or accidentally. It is one thing to wander carelessly into the wrong hotel bedroom and another to hide in the wardrobe to take photographs. Article 8 may justify a monetary remedy for an intentional invasion of privacy by a public authority, even if no damage is suffered other than distress for which damages are not ordinarily recoverable. It does not follow that a merely negligent act should, contrary to general principle, give rise to a claim for damages for distress because it affects privacy rather than some other interest like bodily safety: compare *Hicks v Chief Constable of South Yorkshire Police* [1992] 2 All ER 65.

NOTE

This extract illustrates once again how (a) the difference between intention and unintentional behaviour and (b) the nature of the interest invaded are vital components in assessing liability. A deliberate invasion of privacy is one thing while a negligent invasion is another.

3.7 Abuse of the judical process

The tort of malicious prosecution indicates that the common law has long regarded the deliberate misuse of the judicial process as capable of giving rise to an action for damages. To what extent is the common law prepared to extend the law beyond malicious prosecution? The next case indicates that there may be a more general tort.

Gibbs v Rea [1998] AC 786, PC

This was an action for damages brought against a drugs squad police officer for the malicious procurement of a search warrant. The defendant had obtained the warrant to search the claimant's home and workplace, but there was no documented evidence indicating grounds for suspicion. Indeed the claimant was able to show that there was no reasonable grounds for suspecting him of drug-trafficking and the defendant was unable to rebut this evidence. The trial judge dismissed the claim but the Court of Appeal of the Cayman Islands allowed an appeal and awarded the claimant damages. The Privy Council (Lords Steyn and Hutton and Gault J; Lords Goff and Hope dissenting) dismissed an appeal.

Gault J (delivering the judgment of the Privy Council): ... On the first issue their Lordships agree with the conclusions reached by the courts below and accepted by counsel. That it is an actionable wrong to procure the issue of a search warrant without reasonable cause and with malice has long been recognised though seldom successfully prosecuted: *Elsee v Smith* (1822) 2 Chit. 304, *Hope v Evered* (1886) 17 Q.B.D. 338, 340, *Everett v Ribbands* [1952] 2 Q.B. 198, 205, *Reynolds v Commissioner of Police of the Metropolis* [1985] Q.B. 881, 886. Generally any damage will arise from execution rather than issue of a warrant but there may be special circumstances in which it can be shown that the issue of the warrant will itself cause harm. It is the essential element of malice that distinguishes the cause of action from that of trespass where entry is made without authority or on the authority of a warrant invalid on its face. It is akin to malicious prosecution which is a well established tort and to the less common tort of maliciously procuring an arrest: *Roy v Prior* [1971] A.C. 470. The true foundation of each is intentional abuse of the processes of the court. Malice in this context has the special meaning common to other torts and covers not only spite and ill-will but also improper motive. In the present context the requirement of improper motive would be satisfied by proof of intent to use the process of the court for granting a warrant for a purpose other than to search in the permitted circumstances...

NOTES

1. In *Keegan v Chief Constable of Merseyside* (2003) Ward LJ noted that there are four ingredients of the tort. These are '(1) that there was a successful application for the search warrant; (2) that the defendant did not have reasonable and probable cause to make the application; (3) that the defendant acted with malice; and (4) that the damage resulted from the issue or execution of the warrant' (§ 26).

2. It may be that there is a more general tort of abuse of the court process.

Speed Seal Products v Paddington [1985] 1 WLR 1327, CA

This was a counterclaim for damages brought by a defendant against a plaintiff who sought an injunction for breach of confidence. The defendant had worked for the plaintiff on the design of oil-pipe couplings but had left to set up his own business. The defendant alleged that the injunction action was not brought in good faith and thus amounted to the tort of abuse of court process. The Court of Appeal (Fox LJ and Lloyd LJ and Sir George Waller) agreed with the trial judge that the defendant's counterclaim should not be struck out as he had an arguable case.

Fox LJ: ... But quite apart from these contentions, the defendants advance a further argument. They say that there is a tort of abuse of process of the court established by *Grainger v Hill*...

It is clear that the court distinguished the case from one of malicious prosecution, and accordingly rejected the arguments based upon non-determination of the original proceedings. They regarded the wrong as abuse of the process. And the abuse, as I understand it, was that the purpose of the original proceeding was not the recovery of the debt (which was not due) but the extortion of the register...

It seems to me that if the allegations of fact pleaded in the draft countercliam are established at the trial, the decision in *Grainger v Hill* provides a basis for an arguable case that there has been an actionable abuse of the process of the court. I express no view as to the strength of the defendant's case. It is enough to say that I think that a sufficiently argualbe case has been demonstrated to justify giving leave to amend the defence by adding a counterclaim as asked. It will be open to the defendants to support it by such arguments as may be available, whether based on *Grainger v Hill* or not...

NOTE

This case is probably as close as English law will get to a general doctrine of abuse of rights since it goes some way in saying that intentionally causing economic loss to another might be actionable where the actor is pursuing no legitimate interest (and see *Gulf Oil Ltd v Page* (1987); cf *Femis-Bank Ltd v Lazar* (1991)). Thus the case needs to be read alongside the economic torts cases extracted earlier in the chapter (and see Taggart, *Private Property and Abuse of Rights in Victorian England* (OUP), 145–66) and cases like *White & Carter (Councils) v McGregor* (1962) where Lord Reid hints at an abuse of process where a person sues in debt with no legitimate interest in play). But *Speed Seal* is not laying down any normative principle in the abstract, for the absence of a legitimate interest is not enough. The abuse still needs to be inserted into an existing specific category: abuse of legal process, nuisance, economic tort, malicious prosecution and so on. There is, in other words, no general duty not intentionally to cause loss (and how could there be?).

Chapter 4

Liability for Individual Acts (2): Harm Negligently Caused

In the last chapter, which attempted to bring together all the torts based upon harm intentionally caused, the fragmented nature of that area of law was evident from the outset. It is a matter of bringing together a range of diverse torts (causes of action). The main reason for this fragmentation is that behaviour is not enough; the nature of the harm – or the interest invaded – is a fundamental constituent of liability because intentionally causing physical loss is not the same as intentionally causing economic harm. Moreover the notion of 'intention' is itself difficult. With respect to damage negligently caused, the position at first sight looks very different. The area seems dominated by a single tort, itself, perhaps, governed by a single principle (the 'neighbour principle'). This is the tort of negligence with its principle of liability based upon a common duty of care. In truth the position turns out to be more complex since the nature of the harm (interest) does prove important even if this has to be concealed within the tort of negligence itself (rather than expressed via separate causes of action). This said, harm caused by careless behaviour is not completely confined to the single tort of negligence since unreasonable behaviour can be an ingredient of other torts such as nuisance. In addition, some take the view that the tort of breach of statutory duty is a form of statutory negligence, although it is probably more helpful to say that it is based on *unlawful* behaviour.

4.1 Negligence as a cause of action

Negligence as an independent tort was established by the following decision.

Donoghue v Stevenson [1932] AC 562, HL

This was an action for damages brought by the consumer of a bottle of ginger beer against the manufacturer of the drink. The consumer, Mrs Donoghue, alleged that she had gone to a café with a friend who had bought her a bottle of ginger beer, some of which she poured over an ice-cream and then consumed. When Mrs Donoghue poured some more of the beer out of the opaque bottle, she claimed that a decomposed snail emerged with the liquid and that she suffered physical and psychological damage as a result. Mrs Donoghue asserted that the manufacturer owed her a legal duty to keep such foreign bodies out of his products, but the latter agued in return that, even if he had been careless, he owed her no legal duty of care. A preliminary question of law was thus raised as to whether, as a matter of law, a legal duty was owed by the manufacturer to Mrs Donoghue.

A bare majority of the House of Lords (Lords Atkin, Macmillan and Thankerton; Lords Buckmaster and Tomlin dissenting) held that such a duty did exist.

Lord Atkin: ... At present I content myself with pointing out that in English law there must be, and is, some general conception of relations giving rise to a duty of care, of which the particular cases found in the books are but instances. The liability for negligence, whether you style it such or treat it as in other systems as a species of 'culpa', is no doubt based upon a general public sentiment of moral wrongdoing for which the offender must pay. But acts or omissions which any moral code would censure cannot in a practical world be treated so as to give a right to every person injured by them to demand relief. In this way rules of law arise which limit the range of complainants and the extent of their remedy. The rule that you are to love your neighbour becomes in law, you must not injure your neighbour; and the lawyer's question, who is my neighbour? receives a restricted reply. You must take reasonable care to avoid acts or omissions which you can reasonably foresee would be likely to injure your neighbour. Who, then, in law is my neighbour? The answer seems to be – persons who are so closely and directly affected by my act that I ought reasonably to have them in contemplation as being so affected when I am directing my mind to the acts or omissions which are called in question. This appears to me to be the doctrine of *Heaven v Pender* ... There will no doubt arise cases where it will be difficult to determine whether the contemplated relationship is so close that the duty arises. But in the class of case now before the court I cannot conceive any difficulty to arise. A manufacturer puts up an article of food in a container which he knows will be opened by the actual consumer. There can be no inspection by any purchaser and no reasonable preliminary inspection by the consumer. Negligently, in the course of preparation, he allows the contents to be mixed with poison. It is said that the law of England and Scotland is that the poisoned consumer has no remedy against negligent manufacturer. If this were the result of the authorities, I should consider the result a grave defect in the law, and so contrary to principle that I should hesitate long before following any decision to that effect which had not the authority of this House. I would point out that, in the assumed state of the authorities, not only would the consumer have no remedy against manufacturer, he would have none against any one else, for in the circumstances alleged there would be no evidence of negligence against any one other than the manufacturer; and, except the case of a consumer who was also a purchaser, no contract and no warranty of fitness, and in the case of the purchase of a specific article under its patent or trade name, which might well be the case in the purchase of some articles of food or drink, no warranty protecting even the purchaser-consumer ... I do not think so ill of our jurisprudence as to suppose that its principles are so remote from the ordinary needs of civilised society and the ordinary claims it makes upon its members as to deny a legal remedy where there is so obviously a social wrong...

In my opinion several decided cases support the view that in such a case as the present the manufacturer owes a duty to the consumer to be careful...

NOTES

1. This case is the starting point for the modern UK tort of negligence. Despite being a Scottish case, it is equally an English precedent because the House of Lords stated that they were declaring the law of England as well. Just why the case

is so important is to be found in a number of factors. First it extended 'contract' in that the original seller, if also the manufacturer, could be liable to an ultimate consumer of the product despite the absence of any direct contractual relationship between the two. If Mrs Donoghue had bought the beer herself she could have sued the café owner in contract without having to prove fault (*Frost v Aylesbury Dairy Co Ltd*, p 159). In allowing her to sue the manufacturer she has to prove fault, but this is less of a burden than it might seem thanks to a later case establishing that the defect itself is prima facie evidence of negligence (*Grant v Australian Knitting Mills Ltd*, p 159). Legislation has further improved the position of the third-party consumer (Consumer Protection Act 1987, below p 160).

2. Secondly it established a general principle of liability. Normally a case is rarely much of an authority beyond its own material facts, but Lord Atkin famously stated his neighbour principle. This is what lifts negligence liability out of its imprisonment within specific factual categories and establishes the tort as a general cause of action prima facie applicable, seemingly, to any set of facts where damage is caused, by a careless act, to anyone within the 'neighbour' range of 'proximity'. However the neighbour principle was not to be as abstract as it might first have appeared. One material fact was the damage suffered by Mrs Donoghue which was physical illness. Later cases, citing earlier ones, identified the 'interest' forming the object of manufacturer's duty as the threat to health, not the threat to the pocket (see Consumer Protection Act 1987, s 5(2)). Put another way, the physical injury suffered by Mrs Donoghue and her economic loss (loss of a bottle of drinkable beer) are two quite different types of 'damage' (*Birse Construction Ltd v Haiste Ltd* (1996), p 414).

3. Thirdly, it was never proved whether or not there was a snail in the ginger beer bottle (*Freeman v Home Office (No 2)* (1984), at pp 555–6). This is because the case never went to trial. The appeal that reached the House of Lords was a 'striking out' action; that is to say the defendant asked the court on a preliminary question of law to strike out the case as disclosing no cause of action. Even if, argued the defendant, all the facts, including negligence, were proved by the claimant, these facts would still not make him liable since they disclosed no duty of care. What the House of Lords had to decide, then, was whether they did disclose a duty of care and, in order to decide this question, it was assumed that there was a snail in the bottle. Having lost the preliminary question of law action, Stevenson settled the case (see Rodger (1988) 41 CLP 1). Many subsequent duty of care cases are striking out claims and some have proved problematic from a human rights position (see *Barrett v Enfield LBC*, below, p 305, and *Z v UK*, below, pp 306, 310).

QUESTIONS

1. Imagine that the friend who purchased the ginger beer in the café for Mrs Donoghue had run out of the premises before paying for the drink but after Mrs Donoghue had drunk some of the contents. Could the café owner demand that Mrs Donoghue pay for the beer? If your answer to this question is 'yes', does this mean that *Donoghue v Stevenson* went to the House of Lords on a false premise?

2. Is every decision in the tort of negligence since 1932 based on the premise that the thing that does the damage to the claimant is analogous (or not) to a bottle of ginger beer?

FURTHER NOTE

The next major development in the tort of negligence was the decision in *Hedley Byrne*. This decision extended liability to damage done by careless words (misrepresentation) and although it looks at first sight a major extension of *Donoghue v Stevenson* it is probably more accurate to see the case as a development in the area of the tort of deceit (see *Peek v Derry* (1887) CA; cf (1889) HL), perhaps with the idea of filling gaps in the law of contract rather than in extending *Donoghue* as such (cf Supply of Goods and Services Act 1982, s 13).

Hedley Byrne & Co v Heller & Partners Ltd [1964] AC 465, HL

This was an action for damages brought by a firm of advertising agents against a bank in respect of financial loss incurred by the agents when one of their clients, to whom they had extended credit, went into liquidation. The advertising agents had extended the credit on the basis of a credit reference supplied by the defendant bank. The bank denied liability on the ground that they owed no duty of care to the agency and that they were protected by an exclusion clause. The House of Lords (Lords Reid, Morris, Hodson, Devlin and Pearce), while giving judgment for the bank on the basis of the clause, nevertheless decided that such facts could give rise to a duty of care.

Lord Reid: ... The appellants' first argument was based on *Donoghue v Stevenson*. That is a very important decision, but I do not think that it has any direct bearing on this case. That decision may encourage us to develop existing lines of authority, but it cannot entitle us to disregard them. Apart altogether from authority, I would think that the law must treat negligent words differently from negligent acts. The law ought so far as possible to reflect the standards of the reasonable man, and that is what *Donoghue v Stevenson* sets out to do. The most obvious difference between negligent words and negligent acts is this. Quite careful people often express definite opinions on social or informal occasions even when they see that others are likely to be influenced by them; and they often do that without taking that care which they would take if asked for their opinion professionally or in a business connection. The appellant agrees that there can be no duty of care on such occasions, and we were referred to American and South African authorities where that is recognised, although their law appears to have gone much further than ours has yet done. But it is at least unusual casually to put into circulation negligently made articles which are dangerous. A man might give a friend a negligently-prepared bottle of home-made wine and his friend's guests might drink it with dire results. But it is by no means clear that those guests would have no action against the negligent manufacturer.

Another obvious difference is that a negligently made article will only cause one accident, and so it is not very difficult to find the necessary degree of proximity or neighbourhood between the negligent manufacturer and the person injured. But words can be broadcast with or without the consent or the foresight of the speaker or writer. It would be one thing to say that the speaker owes a duty to a limited class, but it would be going very far to say that he owes a duty to every ultimate 'consumer' who acts on those words to his detriment. It would be no use to say that a speaker or writer owes a duty but can disclaim responsibility if he wants to. He, like the manufacturer, could make it part of a contract that he is not to be liable for his negligence: but that contract would not protect him in a question with a third party, at least if the third party was unaware of it.

▶

So it seems to me that there is good sense behind our present law that in general an innocent but negligent misrepresentation gives no cause of action. There must be something more than the mere misstatement. I therefore turn to the authorities to see what more is required. The most natural requirement would be that expressly or by implication from the circumstances the speaker or writer has undertaken some responsibility, and that appears to me not to conflict with any authority which is binding on this House...

A reasonable man, knowing that he was being trusted or that his skill and judgment were being relied on, would, I think have three courses open to him. He could keep silent or decline to give the information or advice sought: or he could give an answer with a clear qualification that he accepted no responsibility for it or that it was given without that reflection or inquiry which a careful answer would require: or he could simply answer without any such qualification. If he chooses to adopt the last course he must, I think, be held to have accepted some responsibility for his answer being given carefully, or to have accepted a relationship with the inquirer which requires him to exercise such care as the circumstances require...

The appellants founded on a number of cases in contract where very clear words were required to exclude the duty of care which would otherwise have flowed from the contract. To that argument there are, I think, two answers. In the case of a contract it is necessary to exclude liability for negligence, but in this case the question is whether an undertaking to assume duty to take care can be inferred: and that is a very different matter. And, secondly, even in cases of contract general words may be sufficient if there was no other kind of liability to be excluded except liability for negligence: the general rule is that a party is not exempted from liability for negligence 'unless adequate words are used' – per Scrutton LJ in *Rutter v Palmer*. It being admitted that there was here a duty to give an honest reply, I do not see what further liability there could be to exclude except liability for negligence: there being no contract there was no question of warranty.

I am therefore of opinion that it is clear that the respondents never undertook any duty to exercise care in giving their replies. The appellants cannot succeed unless there was such a duty and therefore in my judgment this appeal must be dismissed.

Lord Morris: ... My Lords, I consider that it follows and that it should now be regarded as settled that if someone possessed of a special skill undertakes, quite irrespective of contract, to apply that skill for the assistance of another person who relies upon such skill, a duty of care will arise. The fact that the service is to be given by means of or by the instrumentality of words can make no difference. Furthermore, if in a sphere in which a person is so placed that others could reasonably rely upon his judgment or his skill or upon his ability to make careful inquiry, a person takes it upon himself to give information or advice to, or allows his information or advice to be passed on to, another person who, as he knows or should know, will place reliance upon it, then a duty of care will arise...

Lord Devlin: ... [T]he distinction is now said to depend on whether financial loss is caused through physical injury or whether it is caused directly. The interposition of the physical injury is said to make a difference of principle. I can find neither logic nor common sense in this. If irrespective of contract, a doctor negligently advises a patient that he can safely pursue his occupation and he cannot and the patient's health suffers and he loses his livelihood, the patient has a remedy. But if the doctor negligently advises him that he cannot safely pursue his occupation when in fact he can and he loses his livelihood, there is said to be no remedy. Unless, of course, the patient was a private patient and the doctor accepted half a guinea for his trouble: then the patient can recover all. I am bound to say my Lords, that I think this to be nonsense. It is not the sort of nonsense that can arise even in the best system of law out of the need to draw nice distinctions between borderline cases. It arises, if it is the law, simply out of a refusal to make sense. The line is not drawn on any intelligible principle. It just happens to be the line which those who have been driven from the extreme assertion that negligent statements in the absence of contractual or fiduciary duty give no cause of action have in the course of their retreat so far reached...

I think ... that there is ample authority to justify your Lordships in saying now that the categories of special relationships which may give rise to a duty to take care in word as well as in deed are not limited to contractual relationships or to relationships of fiduciary duty, but include also relationships which in the words of Lord Shaw in *Nocton v Lord Ashburton* are 'equivalent to contract', that is, where there is an assumption of responsibility in circumstances in which, but for the absence of consideration, there would be a contract. Where there is an express undertaking, an express warranty as distinct from mere representation, there can be little difficulty. The difficulty arises in discerning those cases in which the undertaking is to be implied. In this respect the absence of consideration is not irrelevant. Payment for information or advice is very good evidence that it is being relied upon and that the informer or adviser knows that it is. Where there is no consideration, it will be necessary to exercise greater care in distinguishing between social and professional relationships and between those which are of a contractual character and those which are not. It may often be material to consider whether the adviser is acting purely out of good nature or whether he is getting his reward in some indirect form. The service that a bank performs in giving a reference is not done simply out of a desire to assist commerce. It would discourage the customers of the bank if their deals fell through because the bank had refused to testify to their credit when it was good...

Lord Pearce: ... To import such a duty the representation must normally, I think, concern a business or professional transaction whose nature makes clear the gravity of the inquiry and the importance and influence attached to the answer...

NOTE

Those suffering loss as a result of a misstatement need no longer prove fraud provided they can establish a *special relationship*. Thus, in the words of Lord Steyn, 'the rule was established that irrespective of contract, if someone possessed of a special skill undertakes to apply that skill for the assistance of another person who relies upon such skill, a duty of care will arise' (*Arthur JS Hall & Co v Simons* (2002) at p 676). The case extends the tort of negligence into the realm of protecting a pure economic interest. However there must normally be (a) a misstatement and (b) a *voluntary assumption* of responsibility by the defendant together with (c) *reliance* by the claimant. Yet it may be that 'reliance' will be interpreted quite generously when the duty problem is closely associated, directly or indirectly, with a contractual relationship. Thus liability can attach to a reference from an ex-employer (*Spring v Guardian Assurance* (1995), below, pp 257, 352) and to a breach of contract by a solicitor where only a third party (and not the contracting party) suffers loss as a result of the breach (*White v Jones*, below, p 260). What is particularly important about *Hedley Byrne* is its central place in the law of obligations in as much as it straddles the divide between contract and tort.

QUESTIONS

1. Could a person who negligently withdraws a contractual offer before it has been accepted by the offeree ever be liable for any financial loss caused to the offeree by the withdrawal?

2. C asks D, a solicitor, at a cocktail party if it is OK for him, C, to be a witness to his friend's will under which the friend has bequeathed to him his house. D, who has had a few drinks, replies that it 'is perfectly legal'. After the friend's death C learns that he cannot inherit because he is a witness to the will. Can C sue D for damages for a lost house?

3. Can the principle of *Hedley Byrne* cover a failure to take action? (Cf *Customs & Excise Commissioners v Barclays Bank* (2005).)

4.2 Breach of duty

The tort of negligence traditionally requires three questions to be answered in the positive. Did the defendant owe the claimant a duty of care? Was the defendant in breach of this duty? Did the breach cause the claimant's damage? It may seem odd to put the breach of duty question before the question about the actual existence of a duty. However there is good reason for doing this in as much as the breach of duty question is the major question of fact. Was the defendant on the facts of the case as presented to the court actually careless? If there was no negligence then there cannot even be the beginnings of any liability under the neighbour principle.

   The reason why the breach and the duty questions are separate is to be found in the history of the common law. All questions of fact in the courts of common law were, until the end of the nineteenth century, decided by a jury. Questions of law were decided by the judge. The breach question, being a question of fact, was for the jury. Whether or not a duty existed was for the judge. The result was that if a jury found for the plaintiff on the negligence question, the judge could still deny liability on the basis of no duty. In other words, the existence or non-existence of a duty of care is in reality a 'control device'. Juries have disappeared from negligence cases thanks to statute and an important case (*Ward v James* (1966)) and so it is the trial judge who now renders a verdict on the facts. Yet this change has had an important consequence. Juries did not give reasons for their verdicts and thus their decisions could never form part of the precedent system. Judges, in contrast, have to give reasons; and even if answers to questions of fact do not in theory form precedents, in practice breach of duty cases easily appear as authoritative. Great care must be taken not to intermix breach, duty and causal questions, although judges often do allow concepts from one question to carry over into the other questions.

4.2.1 Defining negligence

The classic definition of negligence was given by Alderson B in *Blyth v Proprietors of the Birmingham Waterworks* (1856). 'Negligence', he said, 'is the omission to do something which a reasonable man, guided upon those considerations which ordinarily regulate the conduct of human affairs, would do, or doing something which a prudent and reasonable man would not do'. The point must be made again that this is a definition of negligence and not the tort of negligence. The distinction is crucial because the mere causing of harm by a negligent act was, and is, never capable of giving rise to liability in itself; there has to be a pre-existing duty to take care and it is the breach of this duty – the negligent act or omission – which legally creates the liability. The European Group on Tort Law has also proposed a definition.

European Group on Tort Law
Principles of European Tort Law **(2003)**

Art. 4:102. Required standard of conduct

(1) The required standard of conduct is that of the reasonable person in the circumstances, and depends, in particular, on the nature and value of the protected interest involved, the dangerousness of the activity, the expertise to be expected of a person carrying it on, the foreseeability of the damage, the relationship of proximity or special reliance between those involved, as well as the availability and the costs of precautionary or alternative methods.

(2) The above standard may be adjusted when due to age, mental or physical disability or due to extraordinary circumstances the person cannot be expected to conform to it.

(3) Rules which prescribe or forbid certain conduct have to be considered when establishing the required standard of conduct.

4.2.2 Ordinary standard of care

The general test of negligence is founded on a single expression, that of 'reasonableness'.

Bolton v Stone [1951] AC 850, HL

This was an action for damages by a person who had been standing on a public highway against a cricket club for an injury sustained after being struck by a cricket ball. The ball had been hit out of the cricket ground by a visiting batsman and the claimant argued that the club had been negligent in failing to build a fence that was sufficiently high so as to prevent such escapes. An appeal by the cricket club was allowed by the House of Lords (Lords Reid, Radcliffe, Porter, Normand and Oaksey).

Lord Oaksey: ... Cricket has been played for about ninety years on the ground in question and no ball has been proved to have struck anyone on the highways near the ground until the respondent was struck, nor has there been any complaint to the appellants. In such circumstances was it the duty of the appellants, who are the committee of the club, to take some special precautions other than those they did take to prevent such an accident as happened? The standard of care in the law of negligence is the standard of an ordinarily careful man, but in my opinion an ordinarily careful man does not take precautions against every foreseeable risk. He can, of course, foresee the possibility of many risks, but life would be almost impossible if he were to attempt to take precautions against every risk which he can foresee. He takes precautions against risks which are reasonably likely to happen. Many foreseeable risks are extremely unlikely to happen and cannot be guarded against except by almost complete isolation. The ordinarily prudent owner of a dog does not keep his dog always on a lead on a country highway for fear it may cause injury to a passing motor cyclist, nor does the ordinarily prudent pedestrian avoid the use of the highway for fear of skidding motor cars. It may very well be that after this accident the ordinarily prudent committee man of a similar cricket ground would take some further precaution, but that is not to say that he would have taken a similar precaution before the accident...

Lord Reid: My Lords, it was readily foreseeable that an accident such as befell the respondent might possibly occur during one of the appellants' cricket matches. Balls had been driven into the public road from time to time and it was obvious that, if a person happened to be where a ball fell, that person would receive injuries which might or might not be serious. On the other hand it was plain that the chance of that happening was small...

This... raises sharply the question what is the nature and extent of the duty of a person who promotes on his land operations which may cause damage to persons on an adjoining highway. Is it that he must not carry out or permit an operation which he knows or ought to know clearly can cause such damage, however improbable that result may be, or is it that he is only bound to take into account the possibility of such damage if such damage is a likely or probable consequence of what he does or permits, or if the risk of damage is such that a reasonable man, careful of the safety of his neighbour, would regard that risk as material?

I do not know of any case where this question has had to be decided or even where it has been fully discussed. Of course there are many cases in which somewhat similar questions have arisen, but generally speaking if injury to another person from the defendants' acts is reasonably foreseeable the chance that injury will result is substantial and it does not matter in which way the duty is stated. In such cases I do not think that much assistance is to be got from analysing the language which a judge has used. More assistance is to be got from cases where judges have clearly chosen their language with care in setting out a principle, but even so, statements of the law must be read in light of the facts of the particular case. Nevertheless, making all allowances for this, I do find at least a tendency to base duty rather on the likelihood of damage to others than on its foreseeability alone...

It would take a good deal to make me believe that the law has departed so far from the standards which guide ordinary careful people in ordinary life. In the crowded conditions of modern life even the most careful person cannot avoid creating some risks and accepting others. What a man must not do, and what I think a careful man tries not to do, is to create a risk which is substantial. Of course there are numerous cases where special circumstances require that a higher standard shall be observed and where that is recognized by the law. But I do not think that this case comes within any such special category. It was argued that this case comes within the principle in *Rylands v Fletcher*, but I agree with your Lordships that there is no substance in this argument. In my judgment the test to be applied here is whether the risk of damage to a person on the road was so small that a reasonable man in the position of the appellants, considering the matter from the point of view of safety, would have thought it right to refrain from taking steps to prevent the danger...

...But I think that this case is not far from the borderline. If this appeal is allowed, that does not in my judgment mean that in every case where cricket has been played on a ground for a number of years without accident or complaint those who organize matches there are safe to go on in reliance on past immunity. I would have reached a different conclusion if I had thought that the risk here had been other than extremely small, because I do not think that a reasonable man considering the matter from the point of view of safety would or should disregard any risk unless it is extremely small...

Lord Radcliffe: My Lords, I agree that this appeal must be allowed. I agree with regret, because I have much sympathy with the decision that commended itself to the majority of the members of the Court of Appeal. I can see nothing unfair in the appellants being required to compensate the respondent for the serious injury that she has received as a result of the sport that they have organized on their cricket ground at Cheetham Hill. But the law of negligence is concerned less with what is fair than with what is culpable, and I cannot persuade myself that the appellants have been guilty of any culpable act or omission in this case...

NOTE

This case is foundational for several reasons. First, it keeps separate the two concepts of reasonable (question of fact) and foreseeable (often a question of law, or at least one for the judge). Thus just because an accident is foreseeable this does not necessarily make failing to guard against it unreasonable (note the opening words in the extract from Lord Reid's judgment). The breach of duty question is, therefore, always this: did the defendant behave *unreasonably*? In answering this question the court will of course look at the likelihood of a particular accident occurring, but it is utterly wrong to say that Miss Stone failed in her claim because her injury was *unforeseeable*. Secondly, as a result of this emphasis on reasonableness, economic considerations can come into play. The risk of injury can be measured against the costs of guarding against it: see eg *Latimer v AEC Ltd* (1952). See also Lord Reid's judgment in *The Wagon Mound (No 2)* (1967).

QUESTIONS

1. Does *Bolton v Stone* effectively mean that it is the victims of risky activities who must bear the burden of the risk rather than those undertaking the activity? Can employers base safety considerations simply on the equation between cost and risk or could profitability of the firm's activity be a consideration? (Cf *Latimer v AEC* (1952).)

2. Imagine that a local authority was the owner of the cricket ground at Cheetham Hill and the authority was worried about the safety of the road users. Could the local authority have ordered the club to vacate the premises? (Cf *Wheeler v Leicester CC* (1985).) If the local authority was not the owner of the

ground, could it have nevertheless sought an injunction to prevent the playing of cricket? (Cf *Miller v Jackson*, above p 14.)

3. Would it not have been reasonable for the cricket club to insure against injury to any person outside the ground and the law to reflect this fact by making the club strictly liable for any such injury?

FURTHER NOTE

The reasonable man text is one that applies to the population in general. Given that many people undertake weekend DIY jobs, what standard is expected of their work?

Wells v Cooper [1958] 2 QB 265, CA

This was an action for damages by a visitor to the defendant's house injured when a door handle came away from the back door. The defendant had fixed the handle to the door himself, but the trial judge held he had not been negligent in his work. The claimant's appeal to the Court of Appeal (Jenkins LJ, Parker LJ and Pearce LJ) failed.

Jenkins LJ: ... [W]e think the standard of care and skill to be demanded of the defendant in order to discharge his duty of care to the plaintiff in the fixing of the new handle in the present case must be the degree of care and skill to be expected of a reasonably competent carpenter doing the work in question. This does not mean that the degree of care and skill required is to be measured by reference to the contractual obligations as to the quality of his work assumed by a professional carpenter working for reward, which would, in our view, set the standard too high. The question is simply what steps would a reasonably competent carpenter wishing to fix a handle such as this securely to a door such as this have taken with a view to achieving that object...

...There is no doubt that he was doing his best to make the handle secure and believed that he had done so. Accordingly, he must be taken to have discharged his duty of reasonable care, unless the belief that three-quarter inch screws would be adequate was one which no reasonably competent carpenter could reasonably entertain, or, in other words, an obvious blunder which should at once have been apparent to him as a reasonably competent carpenter. The evidence adduced on the plaintiff's side failed, in the judge's view, to make that out...

QUESTIONS

1. Was such an accident foreseeable? Does it matter if it was?

2. If the handle had been fixed by a professional carpenter employed by the defendant could the claimant have successfully sued the carpenter?

3. Can you think of any reason why a court *might* today hold such a householder liable (although this is not to suggest that it actually would)?

NOTE

In *Wells* the occupier was an ordinary human householder undertaking the activity (DIY job) himself. What if an occupier invites another person to carry out an activity or a job on the occupier's land?

Gwilliam v West Hertfordshire Hospital NHS Trust [2003] 3 QB 443, CA

This was an action for damages by a visitor to a hospital injured on a fund-raising day as a result of the negligence of an independent contractor hired by the hospital to run a 'splat-wall'. The claimant had been injured while using this entertainment described by Waller LJ as an 'inherently risky' activity (para 42). The claimant sought to recover damages from the independent contractor but it transpired that his insurance had lapsed and so she settled for a low figure fearing that he would not be able to meet any higher award. The claimant then sued the hospital for the outstanding amount of damages. The Court of Appeal (Lord Woolf CJ and Waller LJ; Sedley LJ dissenting) held by majority that although the hospital owed her a duty to check that the contractor had insurance, it had done enough to discharge this duty and so was not in breach.

Lord Woolf CJ: ... **15** ... In these circumstances, on the facts of this case (and these issues are fact specific), in the absence of any other credentials, it seems to me that, in order to discharge the common duty of care, Mr Wynne was under an obligation to enquire into the insurance position of Club Entertainments so as to confirm the firm's suitability to be entrusted with the supply and operation of the 'splat-wall'....

16 Mr Wynne did enquire as to the insurance position although it is true that he did not ask to see the policy. However, as the judge found, 'Mr Wynne had no reason to believe that insurance was not in force'. This last conclusion is one which I am prepared to accept on the limited evidence called. If the position was to be otherwise, it would involve finding that the hospital would not only be required to inquire into the insurance position, they would be required to check the terms of the insurance policy. This I would regard as being an unreasonable requirement...

17 In the result, therefore, I consider that the judge came to the right decision, not because there was no duty but because the duty had been fulfilled.

Waller LJ: ... **45** This is an aspect which the judge did not consider. However, it is at this stage where it seems to me that the claimant has serious difficulties. If there was a duty to inspect the insurance certificate of Club Entertainments then the hospital would obviously be in breach of it. But as it seems to me the only duty is to act reasonably. In the context of this case Mr Wynne checked whether there was insurance and indeed made a contract for that insurance to be in place. To impose a duty that goes further than that would, as it seems to me, be unreasonable. Thus it is that, in my view, the appeal of the appellant must fail.

Sedley LJ (dissenting) ... **58** Even accepting that this case affects only the liability of an occupier, occupiers are a large and heterogeneous class, and the duty owed by them to their visitors is not a special duty but the common duty of care. What is there, in a legal system which offers equality before the law by seeking to treat like cases alike, to contain this case in a category peculiar to its own facts? If the ambit of a public institution's duty to its visitors embraces an obligation to check on contractors' insurance, why will a private person whose garden is used for a local fete not equally be liable to pay a sum representing full personal injury damages to a visitor injured, perhaps badly, by the negligent supervision of a coconut shy or a greasy pole by an uninsured stallholder? Or why will a householder who fails to check that his or her builder is insured not have to pay heavy damages to a neighbour who has been unable to make a worthwhile claim against

▶

the builder when a nail through a water pipe brings the neighbour's ceiling down or a carelessly handled blowtorch bums their house down. None of these scenarios, as the courts well know, is in the least fanciful; and we cannot say in advance whether – and if so, why – it will be a differentiating factor that the host of local fete is not raising money for herself, or that the stallholder is a volunteer rather than a contractor, or that the victim of fire or flood is a neighbour rather than a visitor. The scenarios are made worse, not better, if the difference between a potentially ruinous tort liability and no liability at all can lie in a perfunctory enquiry met by a casual and verifiably negligent answer...

QUESTIONS

1. What if the defendant had not been a hospital but a commercial enterprise holding an open day for local families to promote the benefits of genetically modified crops? Would the court have found the enterprise liable?

2. If the defendant in *Wells v Cooper* (1958) (above) had decided to have all his door handles renewed by a professional carpenter, would he have been under a duty to check that the carpenter had liability insurance? What if it was a hospital which decided to employ a professional to renew its door handles?

3. Is it right that an occupier might be able to disclaim responsibility for some dangerous activity on his land, and from which he profits, simply by saying that the activity is being carried out by an independent contractor?

4.2.3 Vulnerable victims

One term that recurs in this breach of duty question is that of guarding against a 'risk'. Is this to be measured simply in terms of the activity in question or must one take into account the needs of specific individuals, or classes of individuals, likely to affected by the activity?

Hayley v London Electricity Board [1965] AC 778, HL

This was an action for damages by a blind pedestrian against the LEB which had excavated a trench in the street and erected a two-foot high barrier consisting of a long-handled hammer to protect the public. The claimant, being blind, had not seen the barrier, had tripped over it, and had fallen into the hole sustaining injury. The trial judge and the Court of Appeal held that the defendants had not been negligent, but an appeal to the House of Lords (Lords Reid, Morton, Evershed, Hodson and Guest) was allowed.

Lord Reid: ... In deciding what is reasonably foreseeable one must have regard to common knowledge. We are all accustomed to meeting blind people walking alone with their white sticks on city pavements. No doubt there are many places open to the public where for one reason or another one would be surprised to see a blind person walking alone, but a city pavement is not one of them. And a residential street cannot be different from any other. The blind people we meet must live somewhere and most of them probably left their homes unaccompanied. It may seem surprising that blind people can avoid ordinary obstacles so well as they do, but we must take account of the facts. There is evidence in this case about the number of blind people in London and it appears from Government publications that the proportion in the whole country is near one in 500. By no means all are sufficiently skilled or confident to venture out alone but the number who habitually do so must be very large. I find it quite impossible to say that it is not reasonably foreseeable that a blind person may pass along a particular pavement on a particular day.

No question can arise in this case of any great difficulty in affording adequate protection for the blind. In considering what is adequate protection again one must have regard to common knowledge. One is entitled to expect of a blind person a high degree of skill and care because none but the most foolhardy would venture to go out alone without having that skill and exercising that care. We know that in fact blind people do safely avoid all ordinary obstacles on pavements; there can be no question of padding lamp posts as was suggested in one case. But a moment's reflection shows that a low obstacle in an unusual place is a grave danger: on the other hand, it is clear from the evidence in this case and also, I think, from common knowledge that quite a light fence some two feet high is an adequate warning. There would have been no difficulty in providing such a fence here. The evidence is that the Post Office always provide one, and that the respondents have similar fences which are often used. Indeed the evidence suggests that the only reason there was no fence here was that the accident occurred before the necessary fences had arrived...

I can see no justification for laying down any hard-and-fast rule limiting the classes of persons for whom those interfering with a pavement must make provision. It is said that it is impossible to tell what precautions will be adequate to protect all kinds of infirm pedestrians or that taking such precautions would be unreasonably difficult or expensive. I think that such fears are exaggerated, and it is worth recollecting that when the courts sought to lay down specific rules as to the duties of occupiers the law became so unsatisfactory that Parliament had to step in and pass the Occupiers' Liability Act, 1957. It appears to me that the ordinary principles of the common law must apply in streets as well as elsewhere, and that fundamentally they depend on what a reasonable man, careful of his neighbour's safety, would do having the knowledge which a reasonable man in the position of the defendant must be deemed to have...

QUESTIONS

1. Were the defendants in effect arguing that from an economic perspective the risk of injury to blind people, with respect to street works, should be borne by the blind people themselves?

2. Those carrying out work on the public highways are expected to be aware of disabled members of the public, especially if precautions are inexpensive when measured against the risk. Does an employer have to be similarly aware of employees with special disabilities?

Paris v Stepney BC [1951] AC 367, HL

This was an action for damages by an employee against his employer. The employee, who had been blind in one eye, worked as a fitter in the defendant's garage; while using a hammer to remove a bolt on a vehicle a chip of metal flew into the employee's one good eye and he was rendered totally blind. The employer had not supplied goggles to employees and there was evidence to the effect that it was not usual to supply them in trades of this nature. The employee claimed that the defendant had been negligent in not supplying goggles and a majority of the House of Lords (Lords Normand, Oaksey and MacDermott; Lords Simonds and Morton dissenting), reversing the Court of Appeal, accepted his argument.

Lord Normand: ... It may be said that, if it is obvious that goggles should have been supplied to a one-eyed workman, it is scarcely less obvious that they should have been supplied to all the workmen, and therefore that the judgment rests on an unreal or insufficient distinction between the gravity of the risk run by a one-eyed man and the gravity of the risk run by a two-eyed man. I recognize that the argument has some force but I do not assent to it. Blindness is so great a calamity that even the loss of one of two good eyes is not comparable; and the risk of blindness from sparks of metal is greater for a one-eyed man than for a two-eyed man, for it is less likely that both eyes should be damaged than that one eye should, and the loss of one eye is not necessarily or even usually followed by blindness in the other...

Lord Oaksey: ... The duty of an employer towards his servant is to take reasonable care for the servant's safety in all the circumstances of the case. The fact that the servant has only one eye if that fact is known to the employer, and that if he loses it he will be blind, is one of the circumstances which must be considered by the employer in determining what precautions if any shall be taken for the servant's safety. The standard of care which the law demands is the care which an ordinarily prudent employer would take in all the circumstances. As the circumstances may vary infinitely it is often impossible to adduce evidence of what care an ordinarily prudent employer would take. In some cases, of course, it is possible to prove that it is the ordinary practice for employers to take or not to take a certain precaution, but in such a case as the present, where a one-eyed man has been injured, it is unlikely that such evidence can be adduced. The court has, therefore, to form its own opinion of what precautions the notional ordinarily prudent employer would take...

QUESTION

Assuming that an employer must act reasonably towards a vulnerable employee, are there limits as to what the employer is expected to do?

Coxall v Goodyear Great Britain Ltd [2003] 1 WLR 536, CA

This was an action for damages by an employee against his employer in respect of asthma contracted while he was working as a paint operator in the defendants' factory. Although the system of work was reasonable, it was discovered that the claimant had a mild predisposition to contracting asthma and the works doctor wrote a memo to the employer saying that the claimant should not continue as a paint operator. The memo did not reach the relevant team manager and the claimant, although he knew of the memo and its content, continued as a paint operator only subsequently to be taken seriously ill. The trial judge held that the defendants were in breach of their duty of care and this decision was upheld by the Court of Appeal (Simon Brown LJ and Brooke LJ).

Simon Brown LJ: ... **25** For my part, I readily acknowledge that conflicting principles, perhaps even philosophies, are here in play. On the one hand is the principle expressed by Sellers LJ in *Withers* [1961] 1 WLR 1314, 1317 that 'imposing a restriction on the freedom of the individual ... is foreign to the whole spirit of the common law of our country' (or, as Devlin LJ put it, at p 1320, 'The relationship between employer and employee is not that of a schoolmaster and pupil'). On the other hand employers clearly must bear some overall responsibility for the health and safety of their workforce.

26 How, then, is the undoubted tension between these principles to be resolved? To my mind this can only be achieved by reference to the individual facts of each case. Powerfully though Mr Beard's [counsel for the defendants] arguments were advanced, I think in the end they go too far and prove too much. I simply cannot accept the *Withers* principle in quite the absolute terms he suggests, namely as a principle in no way dependent upon the magnitude of the risk in question. If the defendants' argument here were sound, it would follow that employers would be immune from liability even, say, if they retained as spidermen employees whom they knew to suffer intermittently from vertigo or epileptic fits. That cannot, I think, be right.

27 Rather it seems to me that the principal consideration in determining whether or not any particular case falls within the *Withers* principle must be the actual nature and extent of the known risk. The risk in *Withers* itself, be it noted, was variously described in the judgments as 'some risk' (Sellers LJ: 'there may be some risk'), 'a slight risk' and 'a small risk'. *Kossinski* 15 KIR 225 concerned only a tennis elbow. The plaintiff in *Henderson* [1997] PIQR P413 had not even been advised by her own doctor to stop work.

28 How then do matters stand in the present case? I confess I have not found it an altogether easy one. For my part I regard the *Withers* principle as no less effective today than when it was first adumbrated. True it is that employers' responsibilities towards their workforce have grown down the years. But society's increasing respect for an employee's autonomy to my mind represents a countervailing consideration. And the risk of precipitating claims for unfair dismissal is by no means to be discounted.

29 All that said, however, cases will undoubtedly arise when, despite the employee's desire to remain at work notwithstanding his recognition of the risk he runs, the employer will nevertheless be under a duty in law to dismiss him for his own good so as to protect him against physical danger. The spiderman example I have given above is an obvious one. The present case, of course, is very much less obvious. I conclude, however, that in this instance too the duty arose. It is a striking feature of this case that all three of the defendants' staff most directly concerned with the claimant's welfare (the works doctor, the line manager and the health and safety manager) all thought that he should cease work...

30 It follows that, in my judgment, whilst the judge was wrong to decide (if, indeed, he did) that the *Withers* principle was not binding upon him, he was nevertheless correct in concluding that the defendants were negligent in having failed to follow their own doctor's advice (because, of course, they had not received it) and failed 'either to move or in the final analysis to dismiss' the claimant...

NOTE AND QUESTIONS

1. Compare this decision with *Withers v Perry Chain Co* (1961) (read it in the law report). In *Barber v Somerset CC* (2004) Lord Rodger, on the basis of *Withers*, said: 'where the risk is small, the common law has taken the view that the employee can decide whether to run it ... I draw particular attention to Devlin LJ's view that the employer is under no common law obligation to offer alternative safe employment' (§ 30). *Barber's* case involved an action for damages by a school-teacher against his local authority employer for stress caused by overwork: do you think the claim was successful?

2. What if the employer had sound evidence to believe that dismissing the employee would cause him greater physical harm than continuing to employ him in the paint plant?

3. To what extent has the *Withers'* principle been modified by *Coxall*? Is it really helpful to talk here of a 'principle' if the facts of each case are crucial?

4. Does *Coxall* indicate a changing philosophy with respect to the duties of employers towards their workforce?

4.2.4 Inexperienced defendants

Where an inexperienced person undertakes an activity such as learning to drive, what standard is expected: that of a reasonably experienced person (ie normal driver) or that of the reasonably inexperienced driver (reasonable learner driver)?

Nettleship v Weston [1971] 2 QB 691, CA

This was an action for damages for personal injury by a (non-professional) driving instructor against an inexperienced learner driver. The trial judge dismissed the claim, but an appeal to the Court of Appeal (Lord Denning MR, Megaw LJ and Salmon LJ) was allowed, although damages were reduced by 50% for contributory negligence.

Lord Denning MR: ... The driver owes a duty of care to every passenger in the car, just as he does to every pedestrian on the road: and he must attain the same standard of care in respect of each. If the driver were to be excused according to the knowledge of the passenger, it would result in endless confusion and injustice... The knowledge of the passenger may go to show that he was guilty of contributory negligence in ever accepting the lift – and thus reduce his damages – but it does not take away the duty of care, nor does it diminish the standard of care which the law requires of the driver: see *Dann v Hamilton* [1939] 1 KB 509 and *Slater v Clay Cross Co Ltd* [1956] 2 QB 264, 270...

The special factor in this case is that Mr. Nettleship was not a mere passenger in the car. He was an instructor teaching Mrs. Weston to drive. Seeing that the law lays down, for all drivers of motor cars, a standard of care to which all must conform, I think that even a learner driver, so long as he is the sole driver, must attain the same standard towards all passengers in the car, including an instructor... He may, of course, be guilty of contributory negligence and have his damages reduced on that account. He may, for instance, have let the learner take control too soon, he may not have been quick enough to correct his errors, or he may have participated in the negligent act himself:

see *Stapley v Gypsum Mines Ltd* [1953] AC 663. But, apart from contributory negligence, he is not excluded unless it be that he has voluntarily agreed to incur the risk...

Megaw LJ: ... In my judgment, in cases such as the present it is preferable that there should be a reasonably certain and reasonably ascertainable standard of care, even if on occasion that may appear to work hardly against an inexperienced driver, or his insurers. The standard of care required by the law is the standard of the competent and experienced driver: and this is so, as defining the driver's duty towards a passenger who knows of his inexperience, as much as towards a member of the public outside the car; and as much in civil as in criminal proceedings...

NOTES

1. The idea that an inexperienced road user should be liable for negligence even if he was doing his best is not new. A Roman law text states that people have no business undertaking tasks in which they know or ought to know that their inexperience will be a danger to others (D.9.2.8.1).

2. Children are almost by definition inexperienced. Moreover they tend to indulge in child-like activities such as horse-play (see eg *Wilson v Pringle*, p 94). What if it goes wrong? What standard is expected of (a) the children involved and/or (b) any adult supervisor?

Mullin v Richards [1998] 1 WLR 1304, CA

This was an action for damages for personal injuries brought by one 15-year-old schoolgirl against another and against the local education authority. Both had been having a mock sword fight with plastic rulers in the classroom when one of the rulers broke and a piece went into the claimant's eye. The trial judge dismissed the claim against the education authority but awarded damages against the schoolgirl subject to a reduction for contributory negligence. The Court of Appeal (Hutchison LJ, Sir John Vinelott and Butler-Sloss LJ) held the schoolgirl not liable.

Hutchison LJ: ... The argument centres on foreseeability. The test of foreseeability is an objective one; but the fact that the first defendant was at the time a 15-year-old schoolgirl is not irrelevant. The question for the judge is not whether the actions of the defendant were such as an ordinarily prudent and reasonable adult in the defendant's situation would have realised gave rise to a risk of injury, it is whether an ordinarily prudent and reasonable 15-year-old schoolgirl in the defendant's situation would have realised as much...

...This was in truth nothing more than a schoolgirls' game such as on the evidence was commonplace in this school and there was, I would hold, no justification for attributing to the participants the foresight of any significant risk of the likelihood of injury. They had seen it done elsewhere with some frequency. They had not heard it prohibited or received any warning about it. They had not been told of any injuries occasioned by it. They were not in any sense behaving culpably. So far as foresight goes, had they paused to think they might, I suppose, have said: 'It is conceivable that some unlucky injury might happen,' but if asked if there was any likelihood of it or any real possibility of it, they would, I am sure, have said that they did not foresee any such possibility...

▶

... I have to say that I appreciate that this result will be disappointing to the plaintiff for whom one can have nothing but sympathy, because she has suffered a grave injury through no fault of her own. But unfortunately she has failed to establish in my view that anyone was legally responsible for that injury and, accordingly, her claim should have failed.

QUESTIONS

1. Does the argument centre on foreseeability in breach of duty questions? Did Hutchison LJ actually base his decision on foreseeability?

2. Are there special standards for different age groups?

3. What if the 15-year-old had been learning to drive a sit-on lawnmower and had run over the gardener?

4. If the claimant had been poked in the eye during the swordfight by the other girl could she have sued in trespass?

5. Did the schoolgirl not consent to the injury? (Cf *Blake v Galloway* (2004), noted above, p 95.)

4.2.5 Professional skills

Where the defendant is a professional person alleged to have been negligent in the exercise of his or her professional skill the reasonable man test is inappropriate. The test for professional negligence is set out in the next case which, although a first instance decision (and note the jury), is nevertheless regarded as the *locus classicus* (see eg *A v Essex CC* (2004) at § 57).

Bolam v Friern Hospital Management Committee [1957] 1 WLR 582, QBD

This was an action for damages by a patient against a hospital in respect of injuries received while undergoing electro-convulsive therapy. The claimant alleged that the doctor had been negligent in the way he carried out the treatment. The trial took place before McNair J and a jury; a verdict was given for the defendant.

McNair J: Members of the jury, it is now my task to try to help you to reach a true verdict, bearing in mind that you take the law from me and that the facts are entirely a matter for your consideration. You will only give damages if you are satisfied that the defendants have been proved to be guilty of negligence...

... I must tell you what in law we mean by 'negligence.' In the ordinary case which does not involve any special skill, negligence in law means a failure to do some act which a reasonable man in the circumstances would do, or the doing of some act which a reasonable man in the circumstances would not do; and if that failure or the doing of that act results in injury, then there is a cause of action. How do you test whether this act or failure is negligent? In an ordinary case it is generally said you judge it by the action of the man in the street. He is the ordinary man. In one case it has been said you judge it by the conduct of the man on the top of a Clapham omnibus. He is the ordinary man. But where you get a situation which involves the use of some special skill or competence, then the test as to whether there has been negligence or not is not the test of the man on the top of a Clapham omnibus, because he has not got this special skill. The test is the standard of the ordinary skilled man exercising and professing to have that special skill. A man need not possess the highest expert skill; it is well established law that it is sufficient if he exercises the ordinary skill of an ordinary competent man exercising that particular art...

NOTE

McNair J also said that a doctor would not be guilty of negligence 'if he had acted in accordance with a practice accepted as proper by a responsible body of medical men skilled in that particular art'. Thus if a defendant could show that there was a section of medical opinion that would have done or omitted to do what the doctor had done, he would seemingly not have been negligent. Although the *Bolam* test was approved by the House of Lords in *Sidaway v Bethlem Royal Hospital* (1985), the 'responsible body of medical men' aspect arose for consideration in the next case.

Bolitho v City and Hackney Health Authority [1998] AC 232, HL

This was an action for damages by a parent, suing in her own right and as administratrix of her dead child's estate, against a health authority. The claimant alleged that her child's death was the result of the negligence of a doctor who had failed to attend the child when he had a breathing crisis while in hospital. A competent doctor, it was argued, would have arranged for an intubation. The judge held that the doctor had been negligent in failing to attend but that even if she had attended she would not have organised an intubation. Thus the mere failure to attend was not necessarily the cause of the child's death. The question then became one of whether it would have been negligent for the doctor not to have arranged for an intubation. On this question the judge, having heard from an expert witness that intubation would have been inappropriate, decided that any decision not to have organised an intubation would not have been negligent. The hospital was thus held not liable. This decision was upheld by the House of Lords (Lords Browne-Wilkinson, Slynn, Nolan, Hoffmann and Clyde).

Lord Browne-Wilkinson: ... The locus classicus of the test for the standard of care required of a doctor or any other person professing some skill or competence is the direction to the jury given by McNair J in *Bolam v Friern Hospital Management Committee*...

My Lords, I agree... the court is not bound to hold that a defendant doctor escapes liability for negligent treatment or diagnosis just because he leads evidence from a number of medical experts who are genuinely of opinion that the defendant's treatment or diagnosis accorded with sound medical practice. In the *Bolam* case itself, McNair J [1957] 1 WLR 583, 587 stated that the defendant had to have acted in accordance with the practice accepted as proper by a 'responsible body of medical men.' Later, at p 588, he referred to 'a standard of practice recognised as proper by a competent reasonable body of opinion.' Again, in the passage which I have cited from *Maynard's* case [1984] 1 WLR 634, 639, Lord Scarman refers to a 'respectable' body of profes-

▶

sional opinion. The use of these adjectives – responsible, reasonable and respectable – all show that the court has to be satisfied that the exponents of the body of opinion relied upon can demonstrate that such opinion has a logical basis. In particular in cases involving, as they so often do, the weighing of risks against benefits, the judge before accepting a body of opinion as being responsible, reasonable or respectable, will need to be satisfied that, in forming their views, the experts have directed their minds to the question of comparative risks and benefits and have reached a defensible conclusion on the matter...

... In my judgment that is because, in some cases, it cannot be demonstrated to the judge's satisfaction that the body of opinion relied upon is reasonable or responsible. In the vast majority of cases the fact that distinguished experts in the field are of a particular opinion will demonstrate the reasonableness of that opinion. In particular, where there are questions of assessment of the relative risks and benefits of adopting a particular medical practice, a reasonable view necessarily presupposes that the relative risks and benefits have been weighed by the experts in forming their opinions. But if, in a rare case, it can be demonstrated that the professional opinion is not capable of withstanding logical analysis, the judge is entitled to hold that the body of opinion is not reasonable or responsible...

Even if this is to put too favourable a meaning on the judge's judgment, when the evidence is looked at it is plainly not a case in which Dr Dinwiddie's views can be dismissed as illogical. According to the accounts of Sister Sallabank and Nurse Newbold, although Patrick had had two severe respiratory crises, he had recovered quickly from both and for the rest presented as a child who was active and running about. Dr Dinwiddie's view was that these symptoms did not show a progressive respiratory collapse and that there was only a small risk of total respiratory failure. Intubation is not a routine, risk-free process. Dr Roberton, a consultant paediatrician at Addenbrooke's Hospital, Cambridge, described it as 'a major undertaking – an invasive procedure with mortality and morbidity attached – it was an assault.' It involves anaesthetising and ventilating the child. A young child does not tolerate a tube easily 'at any rate for a day or two' and the child unless sedated tends to remove it. In those circumstances it cannot be suggested that it was illogical for Dr Dinwiddie, a most distinguished expert, to favour running what, in his view, was a small risk of total respiratory collapse rather than to submit Patrick to the invasive procedure of intubation...

NOTES

1. This case is seen as important in as much as Lord Browne-Wilkinson seems to be qualifying the *Bolam* test. Not only must there be a respectable body of opinion supporting a particular medical practice in order to escape an accusation of negligence but this opinion must have a 'logical basis'. In other words the mere existence of the body of medical opinion is no longer enough.

2. See also *Roe v MOH* (p 320) for another classic medical case on breach of duty.

QUESTIONS

1. How can judges know if a body of medical opinion has a logical basis? If the opinion is held by a respectable number of medical experts, does this not in itself suggest that there is a basis in logic? And, anyway, what is actually meant

by 'logic' in this situation? Is there a difference in this context between 'logical basis' and 'reasonable'?

2. Is it 'logical' to believe (a) in witchcraft, (b) in God, and/or (c) in aliens from outer space?

3. Is it negligent for a doctor to make an error of judgment? (Cf *Whitehouse v Jordan* (1981).)

4. Is it negligent for a driver to make an error of judgment?

5. C enters hospital for an operation but the surgeon, acting in what he believed C's best interests, decides not to inform C that there is a 1% risk of a serious spinal injury associated with the operation. The risk materialises. Can C sue the hospital for (a) trespass, or (b) negligence? (Cf *Sidaway v Bethlem Royal Hospital* (1985).)

4.2.6 Breach of duty and precedent

It is tempting to treat the cases extracted under this breach of duty question as binding precedents. They are not and nor can they be, as the Law Lord in the next case explains.

Qualcast (Wolverhampton) Ltd v Haynes [1959] AC 743, HL

This was an action for damages by an employee against an employer for an injury suffered in the latter's iron foundry when molten metal spilt onto his boots. The employee was not wearing protective spats or boots, although they were available from the employer. The trial judge thought that he was bound as a question of law to hold the defendants liable since precedent appeared to indicate that an employer is under a duty to urge its employees to wear safety equipment. However the House of Lords (Lords Radcliffe, Keith, Somerville and Denning; Lord Cohen dissenting in part) held the employers not liable.

Lord Somervell: ... I hope it may be worth while to make one or two general observations on the effect on the precedent system of the virtual abolition of juries in negligence actions. Whether a duty of reasonable care is owed by A to B is a question of law... When negligence cases were tried with juries the judge would direct them as to the law ... The question whether on the facts in that particular case there was or was not a failure to take reasonable care was a question for the jury. There was not, and could not be, complete uniformity of standard. One jury would attribute to the reasonable man a greater degree of prescience than would another. The jury's decision did not become part of our law citable as a precedent. In those days it would only be in very exceptional circumstances that a judge's direction would be reported or be citable. So far as the law is concerned they would all be the same. Now that negligence cases are mostly tried without juries, the distinction between the functions of judge and jury is blurred. A judge naturally gives reasons for the conclusion formerly arrived at by a jury without reasons. It may sometimes be difficult to draw the line, but if the reasons given by a judge for arriving at the conclusion previously reached by a jury are to be treated as 'law' and citable, the precedent system will die from a surfeit of authorities ...

NOTE

Lord Denning's judgment is also worth reading (in the law report).

QUESTION

If these facts arose again today and came before the two judges in *Coxall v Goodyear* (2003) (above), do you think that they would have found the employer negligent?

4.2.7 Proof of breach

The doctrine of res ipsa loquitur (the thing speaks for itself) may give rise to a situation where the defendant will need to provide an explanation as to how the accident happened: see *Cassidy v MOH* (p 234); *Roe v MOH* (p 320). If no such explanation is forthcoming the court may presume negligence: *Ward v Tesco* (1976); *Henderson v HE Jenkins* (p 170).

4.3 Duty of care

In French law culpable behaviour, provided it causes damage, is of itself enough to generate liability (CC art 1382). In English law, in contrast, it is not a negligent act that generates a liability to pay damages in tort; it is a breach of a duty of care and so if there was no duty there can be no damages action (*Gautret v Egerton* (1867)). The importance of this duty requirement is that it was a question of law to be decided by judges and not juries. Until 1932 the main duty underpinning damages claims was either contractual or one arising out of some particular set of circumstances where the law imposed an obligation. The importance of the great case of *Donoghue v Stevenson* (1932) (p 112) was that it elevated the non-contractual 'duty of care' to a new level of abstraction; duty was no longer confined to specific categories of fact. However, this can mask as much as it can reveal since the old specific liabilities approach has not been completely abandoned; it has, to an extent, been incorporated into the tort of negligence under the heading of 'duty of care'. Thus duty can be broken down into a number of categories: economic loss; psychological harm; pure omissions; and public bodies. This last category is not equivalent to the other three since it cuts across them in as much as many of the public body duty cases can equally be categorised as pure economic loss, psychological harm or omission problems. Yet public bodies do raise special policy problems as we have seen (*Hill*, above, p 36, 296); and they will be considered in a separate chapter (**Chapter 9**). Equally, negligent words as opposed to acts can be problematic (see **Chapter 8**). Accordingly, duty of care will be considered in this chapter only in its basic outline; other duty cases will appear in other chapters.

4.3.1 Methodological approach

Duty of care is not just a matter of applying a rule; it is as much a question of method and approach. This has been described by Lord Diplock in *Home Office v Dorset Yacht Co* (see p 31; for facts see p 226) as an 'analytical and inductive process' recalling the methodology set out by Lord Simon (see above p 32). But care must be taken here as the next case indicates.

Caparo plc v Dickman [1990] 2 AC 605, HL

(For facts see below p 140)

Lord Bridge: ... The most comprehensive attempt to articulate a single general principle is reached in the well known passage from the speech of Lord Wilberforce in *Anns v Merton London Borough Council* [1978] AC 728, 751-752:

> 'Through the trilogy of cases in this House – *Donoghue v Stevenson* [1932] AC 562, *Hedley Byrne & Co Ltd v Heller & Partners Ltd* [1964] AC 465, and *Dorset Yacht Co Ltd v Home Office* [1970] AC 1004, the position has now been reached that in order to establish that a duty of care arises in a particular situation, it is not necessary to bring the facts of that situation within those of previous situations in which a duty of care has been held to exist. Rather the question has to be approached in two stages. First one has to ask whether, as between the alleged wrongdoer and the person who has suffered damage there is a sufficient relationship of proximity or neighbourhood such that, in the reasonable contemplation of the former, careless-ness on his part may be likely to cause damage to the latter – in which case a prima facie duty of care arises. Secondly, if the first question is answered affirmatively, it is necessary to consider whether there are any considerations which ought to negative, or to reduce or limit the scope of the duty or the class of person to whom it is owed or the damages to which a breach of it may give rise: see *Dorset Yacht case* [1970] AC 1004 per Lord Reid at p 1027.'

But since the *Anns* case a series of decisions of the Privy Council and of your Lordships' House, notably in judgments and speeches delivered by Lord Keith of Kinkel, have emphasised the inability of any single general principle to provide a practical test which can be applied to every situation to determine whether a duty of care is owed and, if so, what is its scope: see *Governors of Peabody Donation Fund v Sir Lindsay Parkinson & Co Ltd* [1985] AC 210, 239f-241c; *Yuen Kun Yeu v Attorney-General of Hong Kong* [1988] AC 175, 190e-194f; *Rowling v Takaro Properties Ltd* [1988] AC 473, 501d-g; *Hill v Chief Constable of West Yorkshire* [1989] AC 53, 60b-d. What emerges is that, in addition to the foreseeability of damage, necessary ingredients in any situation giving rise to a duty of care are that there should exist between the party owing the duty and the party to whom it is owed a relationship characterised by the law as one of 'proximity' or 'neighbourhood' and that the situation should be one in which the court considers it fair, just and reason-able that the law should impose a duty of a given scope upon the one party for the benefit of the other. But it is implicit in the passages referred to that the concepts of proximity and fairness embodied in these additional ingredients are not susceptible of any such precise definition as would be necessary to give them utility as practical tests, but amount in effect to little more than convenient labels to attach to the features of different specific situations which, on a detailed examination of all the circumstances, the law recognises pragmati-cally as giving rise to a duty of care of a given scope. Whilst recognising, of course, the importance of the underlying general principles common to the whole field of negligence, I think the law has now moved in the direction of attaching greater significance to the more traditional categorisation of distinct and recognisable situations as guides to the existence, the scope and the limits of the varied duties of care which the law imposes...

Lord Oliver: ... Perhaps, therefore, the most that can be attempted is a broad categori-sation of the decided cases according to the type of situation in which liability has been established in the past in order to found an argument by analogy...

NOTE

The difference of approach between Lord Wilberforce in *Anns* and the judges in *Caparo* is of historical and conceptual importance. Lord Wilberforce (who knew something of French law) was trying to steer English law towards a more civilian approach to liability. That is to say, he was trying to see the ratio decidendi of *Donoghue*, as (re)interpreted by *Hedley Byrne* and *Dorset Yacht*, as a general principle of liability abstracted from any particular factual situation. *Caparo* has put a stop to this and returned to the categories of liability approach. Of course these categories are not as rigid as those of the old forms of action; but the material facts of negligence cases retain their precedent force and thus reasoning is by analogy rather than deduction. See also *Goodwill v British Pregnancy Advisory Service* (p 33).

QUESTIONS

1. Compare and contrast the method of Lord Diplock in *Home Office v Dorset Yacht* (1970) (pp 31, 226) with the method advocated in *Caparo*. Are they very different? Will each method lead to a different result?

2. What is the difference between 'proximity', 'foreseeability' and 'duty'?

3. Does it all come down, in the end, to policy (cf Lord Denning in *Spartan Steel* (1973), pp 54, 137) or to 'fairness' and 'reasonableness'? Or do the terms 'proximity' and 'relationship' still have a certain normative force?

Stovin v Wise [1996] AC 923, HL

(For facts see p 152)

Lord Nicholls (dissenting): ... The *Caparo* tripartite test elevates proximity to the dignity of a separate heading. This formulation tends to suggest that proximity is a separate ingredient, distinct from fairness and reasonableness, and capable of being identified by some other criteria. This is not so. Proximity is a slippery word. Proximity is not legal shorthand for a concept with its own, objectively identifiable characteristics. Proximity is convenient shorthand for a relationship between two parties which makes it fair and reasonable one should owe the other a duty of care. This is only another way of saying that when assessing the requirements of fairness and reasonableness regard must be had to the relationship of the parties....

NOTE

One must not forget reasoning by analogy (see also above p 33).

Marc Rich & Co v Bishop Rock Marine Co Ltd [1996] 1 AC 211, HL

(For facts see p 291)

Lord Steyn: ... In the course of their submissions counsel took your Lordships on a tour of many of the landmark cases on negligence from *Donoghue v Stevenson* [1932] AC 562 to *White v Jones* [1995] 2 WLR 187. In this area the common law develops incrementally on the basis of a consideration of analogous cases where a duty has been recognised or desired. But none of the cases cited provided any realistic analogy to be used as a springboard for a decision one way or the other in this case. The present case can only be decided on the basis of an intense and particular focus on all its distinctive features, and then applying established legal principles to it. No doubt those principles are capable of further development but, for present purposes, the applicable principles can readily be identified and require no re-examination.

QUESTION

What do you think these 'distinctive features' might be?

4.3.2 Pure economic loss

Establishing new duty situations may be a matter of method, but there are some types of damage which themselves have defined the limits of duty. Pure economic loss is one such form of damage.

Spartan Steel & Alloys Ltd v Martin & Co (Contractors) Ltd [1973] 1 QB 27, CA

This was an action for damages by the owners of a factory against a firm of contractors for damage and loss suffered when the supply of electricity was cut off as a result of the contractors, while excavating with a mechanical shovel on the highway, carelessly cutting through an electric cable. The factory owners claimed damages under three heads: (i) damage to metal in a furnace when the power failed; (ii) loss of profit on the ruined metal in the furnace; and (iii) loss of profit on four other metal melting operations that could have been carried out if the electricity had not been off. A majority of the Court of Appeal (Lord Denning MR and Lawton LJ; Edmund Davies LJ dissenting) held that the plaintiffs could recover under heads (i) and (ii), but not under head (iii).

Lord Denning MR: ... At bottom I think the question of recovering economic loss is one of policy. Whenever the courts draw a line to mark out the bounds of duty, they do it as matter of policy so as to limit the responsibility of the defendant. Whenever the courts set bounds to the damages recoverable – saying that they are, or are not, too remote – they do it as matter of policy so as to limit the liability of the defendant.

In many of the cases where economic loss has been held not to be recoverable, it has been put on the ground that the defendant was under no duty to the plaintiff. Thus where a person is injured in a road accident by the negligence of another, the negligent driver owes a duty to the injured man himself, but he owes no duty to the servant of the injured man – see *Best v Samuel Fox & Co Ltd*: nor to the master of the injured man – *Inland Revenue Commissioners v Hambrook*: nor to anyone else who suffers loss because he had a contract with the injured man – see *Simpson & Co v Thomson*: nor indeed to anyone who only suffers economic loss on account of the accident: see *Kirkham v Boughey*. Likewise, when property is damaged by the negligence of another, the negligent tortfeasor owes a duty to the owner or possessor of the chattel, but not to one who suffers loss only because he had a contract entitling him to use the chattel or giving him a right to receive it at some later date: see *Elliott Steam Tug Co Ltd v Shipping Controller* and *Margarine Union GmbH v Cambay Prince Steamship*.

▶

In other cases, however, the defendant seems clearly to have been under a duty to the plaintiff, but the economic loss has not been recovered because it is too remote. Take the illustration given by Blackburn J in *Cattle v Stockton Waterworks Co*, when water escapes from a reservoir and floods a coal mine where many men are working. Those who had their tools or clothes destroyed could recover: but those who only lost their wages could not. Similarly, when the defendants' ship negligently sank a ship which was being towed by a tug, the owner of the tug lost his remuneration, but he could not recover it from the negligent ship: though the same duty (of navigation with reasonable care) was owed to both tug and tow: see *Société Anonyme de Remorquage à Hélice v Bennetts*. In such cases if the plaintiff or his property had been physically injured, he would have recovered: but, as he only suffered economic loss, he is held not entitled to recover. This is, I should think, because the loss is regarded by the law as too remote: see *King v Phillips*.

On the other hand, in the cases where economic loss by itself has been held to be recoverable, it is plain that there was a duty to the plaintiff and the loss was not too remote. Such as when one ship negligently runs down another ship, and damages it, with the result that the cargo has to be discharged and reloaded. The negligent ship was already under a duty to the cargo owners: and they can recover the cost of discharging and reloading it, as it is not too remote: see *Morrison Steamship Co Ltd v Greystoke Castle (Cargo Owners)*. Likewise, when a banker negligently gives a reference to one who acts on it, the duty is plain and the damage is not too remote: see *Hedley Byrne & Co Ltd v Heller & Partners Ltd*.

The more I think about these cases, the more difficult I find it to put each into its proper pigeon-hole. Sometimes I say: 'There was no duty'. In others I say: 'The damage was too remote'. So much so that I think the time has come to discard those tests which have proved so elusive. It seems to me better to consider the particular relationship in hand, and see whether or not, as a matter of policy, economic loss should be recoverable, or not. Thus in *Weller & Co v Foot and Mouth Disease Research Institute* it was plain that the loss suffered by the auctioneers was not recoverable, no matter whether it is put on the ground that there was no duty or that the damage was too remote. Again in *Electrochrome Ltd v Welsh Plastics Ltd*, it is plain that the economic loss suffered by the plaintiffs' factory (due to the damage to the fire hydrant) was not recoverable, whether because there was no duty or that it was too remote...

Edmund Davies LJ (dissenting): ... For my part, I cannot see why the £400 loss of profit here sustained should be recoverable and not the £1,767. It is common ground that both types of loss were equally foreseeable and equally direct consequences of the defendants' admitted negligence, and the only distinction drawn is that the former figure represents the profit lost as a result of the physical damage done to the material in the furnace at the time when power was cut off. But what has that purely fortuitous fact to do with legal principle? In my judgment, nothing...

(For a further extract see p 54.)

NOTES

1. This rather dated decision from the Court of Appeal is hardly the latest word on duty of care and economic loss. Nevertheless it retains a certain vitality for

several reasons. First, because Lord Denning's judgment gives a flavour of the historical background to what might be described as the economic loss rule. His judgment refers to several of the main authorities. Secondly, because his judgment also is frank – perhaps too frank – about the policy aspect to the rule (see above p 54). One cannot imagine a House of Lords judge (although Lord Denning was once there) talking about running around to one's solicitor but one knows what he meant. Thirdly, because the case neatly emphasises the boundary between physical damage and pure economic loss and to this extent it remains an important authority. Many of the later economic loss cases fall more (although not always completely) within the sphere of *Hedley Byrne* whose facts were rather different since there was no physical damage whatsoever (save perhaps some sleepless nights for some sensitive media types).

2. *Spartan* also indicates that the economic loss rule in negligence can be applied even to claimants who had suffered physical injury; if the court could make a clear distinction between *damnum emergens* (consequential loss) and *lucrum cessans* (failure to make a gain) the latter could be excluded as a head of damages. However care must be taken here. Economic loss could and can always be recovered in the tort of negligence as part of the loss consequential to the physical harm; thus in *Spartan* damages were recoverable in respect of the loss of profits on the ruined 'melt' because this was an economic 'interest' that attached to damaged tangible property. It was only the 'pure' economic loss that attached to no item of damaged property that could not be recovered (loss of a 'pure' economic expectation). Equally economic interests attaching to the claimant as a person can be recovered if the claimant has suffered personal injuries and this economic loss will include loss of earnings past, present and future; indeed damages are sub-divided into non-pecuniary and pecuniary (see **11.3**).

3. The so-called economic loss rule – which it must be noted applies for the main part only to the tort of negligence plus, on occasions, to breach of statutory duty (see eg *Merlin v British Nuclear Fuels plc* (1990)) – has been justified in a number of ways. Lord Denning has said it is a matter of policy (*Spartan Steel*) while Weir argues that people and tangible things are more important interests than money (*A Casebook on Tort* (10th edn, Sweet & Maxwell, 2004), 6). Whatever the justification the rule is breaking down, and at one point nearly disappeared (*Junior Books Ltd v Veitchi Co Ltd* (1983)). The approach is now this. The causing of physical damage has universally to be justified whereas the infliction of pure economic loss does not (*Murphy v Brentwood DC* (1991)). Yet even although the logic of the rule suggests that where a defendant does carelessly cause physical damage to property there must, almost by definition, be a duty of care, it may be that a duty will be denied if policy and (or) fairness demand such a denial, say because of the insurance position *(Marc Rich & Co v Bishop Rock Marine Co Ltd* (1996), below, p 291). One can still talk of an economic loss rule in negligence, but one is forced back, these days, to the circumstances of each case. The rule is subject to exceptions, if only, sometimes, because the distinction between the physical and economic is not always an easy one (*Murphy*; and see *McFarlane v Tayside HB*, above, p 45).

4. The first important major exception to the economic loss rule was the decision in *Hedley Byrne* (above, p 115). Yet, as the next case shows, it is not always easy for a claimant to recover (and see also *Mutual Life Citizens Assurance Co v Evatt* (1971)).

Caparo plc v Dickman [1990] 2 AC 605, HL

The claimant company brought an action for damages against a firm of account-ants which had audited the accounts of another company which the claimant had taken over. The successful take-over bid was based upon published accounts that showed a healthy profit when, according to the claimants, it should have showed a loss. The claimants thus argued that they suffered financial loss in paying much more for the shares than they would have had to pay if the accounts had been accurate. The House of Lords (Lords Bridge, Roskill, Ackner, Oliver and Jauncey) dismissed the claim: the accountants owed no duty of care to the claimant company either as a potential investor or as a shareholder.

Lord Oliver: ... For my part, however, I can see nothing in the statutory duties of a com-pany's auditor to suggest that they were intended by Parliament to protect the interests of investors in the market and I see no reason in policy or in principle why it should be either desirable or appropriate that the ambit of the special relationship required to give rise to liability in cases such as the present should be extended beyond those limits which are deducible from the cases of *Hedley Byrne* and *Smith v Eric S Bush*. Those limits appear to me to be correctly and admirably stated in the passages from the judg-ment of Richmond P in the *Scott Group* case to which I have already referred. In particular, I see no reason why any special relationship should be held to arise simply from the circumstance that the affairs of the company are such as to render it suscepti-ble to the attention of predators in the market who may be interested in acquiring all or the majority of the shares rather than merely a parcel of shares by way of addition to portfolio. It follows that I would dismiss the respondents' cross-appeal...

In seeking to ascertain whether there should be imposed on the adviser a duty to avoid the occurrence of the kind of damage which the advisee claims to have suffered it is not, I think, sufficient to ask simply whether there existed a 'closeness' between them in the sense that the advisee had a legal entitlement to receive the information upon the basis of which he has acted or in the sense that the information was intended to serve his interest or to protect him. One must, I think, go further and ask, in what capacity was his interest to be served and from what was he intended to be protected? A com-pany's annual accounts are capable of being utilised for a number of purposes and if one thinks about it it is entirely foreseeable that they may be so employed. But many of such purposes have absolutely no connection with the recipient's status or capacity, whether as a shareholder, voting or non-voting, or as a debenture-holder. Before it can be concluded that the duty is imposed to protect the recipient against harm which he suffers by reason of the particular use that he chooses to make of the information which he receives, one must, I think, first ascertain the purpose for which the information is required to be given. Indeed the paradigmatic *Donoghue v Stevenson* case of a manu-factured article requires, as an essential ingredient of liability, that the article has been used by the consumer in the manner in which it was intended to be used: see *Grant v Australian Knitting Mills Ltd* [1936] AC 85, 104 and *Junior Books Ltd v Veitchi Co Ltd* [1983] 1 AC 520, 549, 552...

In my judgment, accordingly, the purpose for which the auditors' certificate is made and published is that of providing those entitled to receive the report with information to enable them to exercise in conjunction those powers which their respective proprietary interests confer upon them and not for the purposes of individual speculation with a view to profit. The same considerations as limit the existence of a duty of care also, in my judgment, limit the scope of the duty and I agree... that the duty of care is one owed to the shareholders as a body and not to individual shareholders.

To widen the scope of the duty to include loss caused to an individual by reliance upon the accounts for a purpose for which they were not supplied and were not intended would be to extend it beyond the limits which are so far deducible from the decisions of this House. It is not, as I think, an extension which either logic requires or policy dictates and I, for my part, am not prepared to follow the majority of the Court of Appeal in making it. In relation to the purchase of shares of other shareholders in a company, whether in the open market or as a result of an offer made to all or a majority of the existing shareholders, I can see no sensible distinction, so far as a duty of care is concerned, between a potential purchaser who is, vis-à-vis the company, a total outsider and one who is already the holder of one or more shares....

NOTE

This case is *not* authority for the proposition that accountants can never be liable to those who rely upon their accounts: see *Morgan Crucible v Hill Samuel* (1991); *Galoo Ltd v Bright Grahame Murray* (1995); *Law Society v KPMG* (2000). The key concept is 'interest': ought the accountants to have had the claimant's particular interest in mind when the accounts (or whatever) were published? 'Interest' here does not of course stand alone; it attaches to the status and capacity of the claimant and so at a descriptive level 'proximity' will depend upon all three notions. In addition, in order to be able to jump from 'proximity' (descriptive) to 'duty' (normative), it must be 'fair, just and reasonable that the law should impose a duty' (Lord Bridge). When analysing a set of facts these descriptive tools are vital.

QUESTION

Traditionally there were three requirements before liability could be established in the tort of negligence: duty, breach and causation. Is there now a fourth requirement of fair and reasonable? Or is this fourth requirement only applicable in certain types of duty cases? Could it ever be applicable in cases of physical damage?

PROBLEM

A claimant seeking a large sum of money from the defendant successfully applies for a freezing injunction to freeze the bank account of the defendant. However the bank, which had been notified of the injunction, carelessly fails to take action and the defendant is able to move all his money in the account out of the UK jurisdiction. Can the claimant sue the bank for an amount equivalent to the sum he hoped to get from the defendant? (Cf *Customs & Excise Commissioners v Barclays Bank* (2005).)

4.3.3 Psychological harm

In addition to pure economic loss, psychological harm is another type of damage that gives rise to duty problems.

Best v Samuel Fox & Co Ltd [1952] AC 716, HL

This was an action for damages by the wife of an employee against her husband's employer. The husband had been injured as a result of the negligence of his employers and he had recovered damages from his employers; his injuries, however, rendered him incapable of sexual intercourse and so his wife sued on her own behalf for her mental distress at the loss of both sexual relations and the chance of having children. The House of Lords (Lords Porter, Goddard, Oaksey, Morton and Reid) rejected her claim.

Lord Porter: ... The salient fact, as I see it, is that the wife had herself suffered no physical injury and could only base her claim on the circumstance that she had lost the consortium of her husband by reason of the injury to him. Such a claim was put forward on the analogy of the enticement cases ... In that class of case, however, the wrong is a deliberate action taken with the object of inducing the wife to leave her husband or the husband to leave his wife – malicious because it is their mutual duty to give consortium to one another, and the defendant has persuaded the errant spouse not to fulfil that duty...

On behalf of the appellant it is urged that a husband can bring an action for the loss of the consortium of his wife by reason of any tort which deprives him of that consortium and that in the circumstances prevailing today a wife must have a similar right. Even, however, if it be assumed that in enticement cases the husband and wife have equal rights it does not follow that today they have equal rights and liabilities one towards the other in all respects. I do not think it possible to say that a change in the outlook of the public, however great, must inevitably be followed by a change in the law of this country. The common law is a historical development rather than a logical whole, and the fact that a particular doctrine does not logically accord with another or others is no ground for its rejection...

Lord Goddard: ... Negligence, if it is to give rise to legal liability must result from a breach of duty owed to a person who thereby suffers damage. But what duty was owed here by the employers of the husband to the wife? If she has an action in this case so must the wife of any man run over in the street by a careless driver. The duty there which gives rise to the husband's cause of action arises out of what may for convenience be called proximity; the driver owes a duty not to injure other persons who are using the road on which he is driving. He owes no duty to persons not present except to those whose property may be on or adjoining the road which it is his duty to avoid injuring. It may often happen that an injury to one person may affect another; a servant whose master is killed or permanently injured may lose his employment, it may be of long standing, and the misfortune may come when he is of an age when it would be very difficult for him to obtain other work, but no one would suggest that he thereby acquires a right of action against the wrongdoer. Damages for personal injury can seldom be a perfect compensation, but where injury has been caused to a husband or father it has never been the case that his wife or children whose style of living or education may have radically to be curtailed have on that account a right of action other than that which, in the case of death, the Fatal Accidents Act, 1846, has given...

QUESTIONS

1. Why did Mrs Best's claim fail? Was it because of the type of damage she suffered or was it because her damage was not foreseeable? What if the injury to her husband had been the result of a deliberate assault by (a) a policeman attempting to arrest the husband, or (b) a car driver motivated by road-rage?

2. What if Mrs Best had suffered a similar level of mental agony on seeing the family home go up in flames as a result of the negligence of heating engineers working in the house under a contract made with her husband? (Cf *Attia v British Gas* (1988).)

NOTES

1. *Best* is not authority for the proposition that mental distress is an unprotected interest in the law of obligations (see eg *Farely v Skinner* (2001)). Nor does it mean that members of a victim's family can never sue in their own right (as Lord Goddard indicates at the end of the extract). As Lord Porter observes, the common law is not a logical whole.

2. It is not just the nature of the damage that is the cause of the duty problem. It is the structure of the various relationships, for psychological damage usually arises in three-party situations (tortfeasor, victim and third party claimant suffering shock). In standard two-party situations psychological damage, seemingly, gives rise to no conceptual difficulty.

Page v Smith [1996] 1 AC 155, HL

This was an action for damages by a car driver in respect of chronic fatigue syndrome (or ME) triggered by an accident in which the claimant suffered no other personal injury. His claim was allowed by a majority of the House of Lords (Lords Ackner, Browne-Wilkinson and Lloyd; Lords Keith and Jauncey dissenting).

Lord Keith: (dissenting) ...The defendant can be liable only if the hypothetical reasonable man in his position should have foreseen that the plaintiff, regarded as a person of normal fortitude, might suffer nervous shock leading to an identifiable illness. For this purpose the nature of the accident is to be taken into account. The collision which occurred between the two cars is described by the trial judge as one of 'moderate severity.' No one involved sustained any bodily injury whatever. The plaintiff was able to drive his car home after the accident, though the damage to the car was such that owing to its age it was not economic to repair it, so that it was written off... Whether this recrudescence was attributable to the accident is debatable... In my opinion a reasonable man in the position of the defendant would not have foreseen that an accident of the nature that he actually brought about might inflict on a person of normal susceptibility such mental trauma as to result in illness. There is no question of the plaintiff having been terrified by his experience, as the plaintiff foreseeably was in *Dulieu v White & Sons* [1901] 2 KB 669, or having suffered an 'acute emotional trauma,' to use the expression of Lord Bridge of Harwich in *McLoughlin v O'Brian* [1983] 1 AC 410, 433...

Lord Lloyd: This is the fourth occasion on which the House has been called on to consider 'nervous shock.' On the three previous occasions, *Bourhill v Young* [1943] AC 92, *McLoughlin v O'Brian* [1983] 1 AC 410 and *Alcock v Chief Constable of South Yorkshire*

▶

Police [1992] 1 AC 310, the plaintiffs were, in each case, outside the range of foreseeable physical injury. Thus, in *Bourhill v Young* [1943] AC 92 the plaintiff was 'not in any way physically involved in the collision:' see per Lord Russell of Killowen, at p 101. The defendant's motor cycle was already some 45 feet past the plaintiff when he collided with a motor car, and was killed. The plaintiff was on the far side of a tramcar, and so shielded from the physical consequences of the accident. If, therefore, liability was to be established, it could only be on the basis that the defendant should have foreseen injury by nervous shock. The plaintiff did, in fact, suffer injury to her health as a result of the shock which she sustained. But as the defendant could not reasonably foresee that she would suffer injury by shock, it was held that she could not recover.

Likewise, in *McLoughlin v O'Brian* [1983] 1 AC 410, the plaintiff was at home two miles away when her husband and three children were involved in a road accident. When she reached the hospital about two hours later, she heard that her daughter had been killed and saw the extent of her son's injuries. The shock which she suffered resulted in psychiatric illness. It was held by this House, reversing the Court of Appeal and the trial judge, that the plaintiff could recover damages, since it was reasonably foreseeable that, unlike Mrs. Bourhill, she would suffer nervous shock as a result of injuries to her family.

Alcock v Chief Constable of South Yorkshire Police [1992] 1 AC 310 was the case arising out of the disaster at the Hillsborough football stadium. A number of plaintiffs brought actions for damages for nervous shock. Two of the plaintiffs were present at the stadium. Others saw the disaster on television. They all failed either because the relationship between the plaintiffs and the victims was not sufficiently close, or because watching the scene on television did not create the necessary degree of proximity.

In all these cases the plaintiff was the secondary victim of the defendant's negligence. He or she was in the position of a spectator or bystander. In the present case, by contrast, the plaintiff was a participant. He was himself directly involved in the accident, and well within the range of foreseeable physical injury. He was the primary victim. This is thus the first occasion on which your Lordships have had to decide whether, in such a case, the foreseeability of physical injury is enough to enable the plaintiff to recover damages for nervous shock.

The factual distinction between primary and secondary victims of an accident is obvious and of long-standing...

Suppose, in the present case, the plaintiff had been accompanied by his wife, just recovering from a depressive illness, and that she had suffered a cracked rib, followed by an onset of psychiatric illness. Clearly, she would have recovered damages, including damages for her illness, since it is conceded that the defendant owed the occupants of the car a duty not to cause physical harm. Why should it be necessary to ask a different question, or apply a different test, in the case of the plaintiff? Why should it make any difference that the physical illness that the plaintiff undoubtedly suffered as a result of the accident operated through the medium of the mind, or of the nervous system, without physical injury? If he had suffered a heart attack, it cannot be doubted that he would have recovered damages for pain and suffering, even though he suffered no broken bones. It would have been no answer that he had a weak heart...

Nor in the case of a primary victim is it appropriate to ask whether he is a person of 'ordinary phlegm.' In the case of physical injury there is no such requirement. The negligent defendant, or more usually his insurer, takes his victim as he finds him. The same should apply in the case of psychiatric injury. There is no difference in principle ... Since the number of potential claimants is limited by the nature of the case, there is no need to impose any further limit by reference to a person of ordinary phlegm. Nor can I see any justification for doing so...

In conclusion, the following propositions can be supported. 1. In cases involving nervous shock, it is essential to distinguish between the primary victim and secondary victims. 2. In claims by secondary victims the law insists on certain control mechanisms, in order as a matter of policy to limit the number of potential claimants. Thus, the defendant will not be liable unless psychiatric injury is foreseeable in a person of normal fortitude. These control mechanisms have no place where the plaintiff is the primary victim. 3. In claims by secondary victims, it may be legitimate to use hindsight in order to be able to apply the test of reasonable foreseeability at all. Hindsight, however, has no part to play where the plaintiff is the primary victim. 4. Subject to the above qualifications, the approach in all cases should be the same, namely, whether the defendant can reasonably foresee that his conduct will expose the plaintiff to the risk of personal injury, whether physical or psychiatric. If the answer is yes, then the duty of care is established, even though physical injury does not, in fact, occur. There is no justification for regarding physical and psychiatric injury as different 'kinds of damage.' 5. A defendant who is under a duty of care to the plaintiff, whether as primary or secondary victim, is not liable for damages for nervous shock unless the shock results in some recognised psychiatric illness. It is no answer that the plaintiff was predisposed to psychiatric illness. Nor is it relevant that the illness takes a rare form or is of unusual severity. The defendant must take his victim as he finds him....

NOTES

1. It is in three-party situations that duty problems are encountered. The starting point is that a third party (C) who witnesses an accident in which a victim (V) is injured or killed by the careless act of the defendant (D) will not have an action in negligence for nervous shock (*Bourhill v Young* (1943)). C is said to be too remote and owed no duty of care (the unforeseeable claimant). There were, however, exceptions to this rule based upon a relationship between V and C. The most important of these relationships was, and remains, a family one, now described as 'a close tie of love and affection' (Law Commission, Draft Negligence (Psychiatric Illness) Bill (Law Com No 249), cl l(3)(b)). Thus if V is injured or killed by D's negligent act and the accident is witnessed by C, his mother (or probably any family member in the draft Negligence (Psychiatric Illness) Bill, cl 3(4)), then D will be liable to C for C's nervous shock. And this will be true even if C does not witness the actual accident but sees the victim in a bad state in the hospital shortly (but how long?) after the accident (*McLoughlin v O'Brien* (1983)). Two other relationships were once of importance. If V and C were co-employees and C witnessed an accident at the workplace attributable to the employer's negligence, there was some authority that this might allow C to sue for nervous shock (*Dooley v Cammell Laird* (1951); cf *Hunter v British Coal* (1998)). Equally, if C was a rescuer who intervened to help after an accident

caused by D's negligence, it seemed that C would have an action against D for nervous shock (*Chadwick v British Railways Board* (1967)). The symmetry once seemed fairly clear: a nervous shock claimant would no longer be 'unforeseeable' if there existed some relationship between the victim and claimant that brought him or her into the range of proximity and thus duty. However this is no longer the legal position.

2. The symmetry was fundamentally modified in two important cases arising out of the dreadful Hillsborough stadium tragedy in which the police were negligent. In the first case relatives or friends of those killed who witnessed, either directly or indirectly on television or radio, the events claimed damages for nervous shock; their claims were dismissed on the ground that they were outside the scope of proximity (*Alcock* (1992)). Either there was not a sufficient close tie of love and affection or, if there was, the claimants were too far removed from the accident. Basically secondary claimants (three-party situations) must (a) have a close tie of love and affection with victims; (b) be close to the incident; and (c) witness the accident *directly* (sight and sound), although there might be some *very limited* exceptions. In the second case police officers who had been present at the stadium brought claims for psychiatric injury on the basis that they were both rescuers and employees of the police force; the Court of Appeal allowed their claims. The case then went to the House of Lords.

White (Frost) v Chief Constable of South Yorkshire [1999] 2 AC 455, HL

This was an action for damages by a group of police officers against their employer for psychiatric damage suffered while tending the victims of the Hillsborough tragedy. The police authority admitted negligence but contested liability in respect of the psychiatric harm suffered by these particular employees. The House of Lords held that liability in respect of this psychiatric damage on the basis either of an employer's duty of care relationship (Lords Browne-Wilkinson, Griffiths, Steyn and Hoffmann; Lord Goff dissenting) or a rescuer relationship (Lord Griffiths dissenting) could not be established.

Lord Steyn: ... The contours of tort law are profoundly affected by distinctions between different kinds of damage or harm: see *Caparo Industries plc v Dickman* [1990] 2 AC 605 at 618E per Lord Bridge of Harwich....

Policy considerations and psychiatric harm

Policy considerations have undoubtedly played a role in shaping the law governing recovery for pure psychiatric harm. The common law imposes different rules for the recovery of compensation for physical injury and psychiatric harm. Thus it is settled law that bystanders at tragic events, even if they suffer foreseeable psychiatric harm, are not entitled to recover damages: *Alcock v Chief Constable of South Yorkshire Police* [1992] 1 AC 310. The courts have regarded the policy reasons against admitting such claims as compelling...

I do not doubt that public perception has played a substantial role in the development of this branch of the law. But nowadays we must accept the medical reality that psychiatric harm may be more serious than physical harm. It is therefore necessary to consider whether there are other objective policy considerations which may justify differ-ent rules for the recovery of compensation for physical injury and psychiatric harm. And in my view it would be insufficient to proceed on the basis that there are unspecified policy considerations at stake. If, as I believe, there are such policy considerations it is necessary to explain what the policy considerations are so that the validity of my assumptions can be critically examined by others.

My impression is that there are at least four distinctive features of claims for psychiatric harm which in combination may account for the differential treatment. Firstly, there is the complexity of drawing the line between acute grief and psychiatric harm: see Hedley, Nervous Shock: Wider Still and Wider, 1997 CLJ 254... Secondly, there is the effect of the expansion of the availability of compensation on potential claimants who have wit-nessed gruesome events. I do not have in mind fraudulent or bogus claims. In general it ought to be possible for the administration of justice to expose such claims. But I do have in mind the unconscious effect of the prospect of compensation on potential claimants. Where there is generally no prospect of recovery, such as in the case of injuries sustained in sport, psychiatric harm appears not to obtrude often... The litigation is sometimes an unconscious disincentive to rehabilitation...

The third factor is important. The abolition or a relaxation of the special rules governing the recovery of damages for psychiatric harm would greatly increase the class of per-sons who can recover damages in tort... Fourthly, the imposition of liability for pure psychiatric harm in a wide range of situations may result in a burden of liability on defen-dants which may be disproportionate to tortious conduct involving perhaps momentary lapses of concentration, e.g. in a motor car accident...

The police officers' claims

In the present case, the police officers were more than mere bystanders. They were all on duty at the stadium. They were all involved in assisting in the course of their duties in the aftermath of the terrible events. And they have suffered debilitating psychiatric harm. The police officers therefore argue, and are entitled to argue, that the law ought to pro-vide compensation for the wrong which caused them harm. This argument cannot be lightly dismissed. But I am persuaded that a recognition of their claims would substan-tially expand the existing categories in which compensation can be recovered for pure psychiatric harm. Moreover, as the majority in the Court of Appeal was uncomfortably aware, the awarding of damages to these police officers sits uneasily with the denial of the claims of bereaved relatives by the decision of the House of Lords in *Alcock*. The decision of the Court of Appeal has introduced an imbalance in the law of tort which might perplex the man on the Underground...

Thus far and no further

My Lords, the law on the recovery of compensation for pure psychiatric harm is a patchwork quilt of distinctions which are difficult to justify. There are two theoretical solu-tions. The first is to wipe out recovery in tort for pure psychiatric injury. The case for such a course has been argued by Professor Stapleton. But that would be contrary to precedent and, in any event, highly controversial. Only Parliament could take such a step. The second solution is to abolish all the special limiting rules applicable to psychi-

▶

atric harm. That appears to be the course advocated by *Mullany and Handford*, *Tort Liability for Psychiatric Damage*. They would allow claims for pure psychiatric damage by mere bystanders: see (1997) 113 LQR 410, at 415. Precedent rules out this course and, in any event, there are cogent policy considerations against such a bold innovation. In my view the only sensible general strategy for the courts is to say thus far and no further. The only prudent course is to treat the pragmatic categories as reflected in authoritative decisions such as the *Alcock* case [1992] 1 AC 310 and *Page v Smith* [1996] AC 155 as settled for the time being but by and large to leave any expansion or development in this corner of the law to Parliament. In reality there are no refined analytical tools which will enable the courts to draw lines by way of compromise solution in a way which is coherent and morally defensible. It must be left to Parliament to undertake the task of radical law reform...

Lord Griffiths (dissenting on the rescuer point) ... If the rescuer is in no physical danger it will only be in exceptional cases that personal injury in the form of psychiatric injury will be foreseeable for the law must take us to be sufficiently robust to give help at accidents that are a daily occurrence without suffering a psychiatric breakdown. But where the accident is of a particularly horrifying kind and the rescuer is involved with the victims in the immediate aftermath it may be reasonably foreseeable that the rescuer will suffer psychiatric injury as Mr Chadwick did when trying to bring relief and comfort to the victims of the Lewisham train disaster. Mr Chadwick suffered his injury because of the terrible impact on his mind of the suffering he witnessed in his rescue attempt, and not because of any fear for his own safety: see *Chadwick v British Railways Board* [1967] 1 WLR 912. What rescuer ever thinks of his own safety? It seems to me that it would be a very artificial and unnecessary control, to say a rescuer can only recover if he was in fact in physical danger. A danger to which he probably never gave thought, and which in the event might not cause physical injury...

NOTE

If psychiatric injury were to be treated as physical injury, all claimants would be primary victims and all could bring actions for their damage in the normal way against the tortfeasor. The law does not do this except (a) when the shock claimant was present at the scene of the accident and (b) either suffered some physical injury or was immediately threatened with such injury (see *Page v Smith* p 143). Rescuers are on the whole secondary victims and thus must prove the three *Alcock* conditions before they can recover; however, if their lives were immediately threatened by say falling masonry or whatever, they will be treated as primary victims (*Chadwick* (1967)). In *Frost* the police were not so threatened and thus had to prove the *Alcock* conditions, which they could not. Note, with regard to this complexity, that bereavement has its own rule (Fatal Accidents Act 1976, s 1A).

QUESTION

Can 'lesser' forms of psychological damage ever be recovered in the tort of negligence?

D v East Berkshire NHS Trust [2005] 2 AC 373

This was an action for damages in negligence by parents against a local authority. The House of Lords (Lords Nicholls, Steyn, Rodger and Brown; Lord Bingham dissenting) held, on a preliminary question of law, that the parents were owed no duty of care. The general question for consideration in the House of Lords is set out by Lord Bingham.

Lord Bingham (dissenting): **1** My Lords, the question in this appeal is whether the parent of a minor child falsely and negligently said to have abused or harmed the child may recover common law damages for negligence against a doctor or social worker who, discharging professional functions, has made the false and negligent statement, if the suffering of psychiatric injury by the parent was a foreseeable result of making it and such injury has in fact been suffered by the parent...

Lord Rodger: ... **100** In the field of negligence the common law 'develops incrementally on the basis of a consideration of analogous cases where a duty has been recognised or desired': *Marc Rich & Co AG v Bishop Rock Marine Co Ltd* [1996] AC 211, 236B–C, per Lord Steyn. The test to be applied is whether the situation is one 'in which the court considers it fair, just and reasonable that the law should impose a duty of a given scope upon the one party for the benefit of the other': *Caparo Industries plc v Dickman* [1990] 2 AC 605, 618A, per Lord Bridge of Harwich. In applying that test, the court has regard to analogous cases where a duty of care has, or has not, been held to exist. On the other hand, when applying the test, I do not actually find it helpful to bear in mind – what is in any event obvious – that the public policy consideration which has first claim on the loyalty of the law is that wrongs should be remedied. Harm which constitutes a 'wrong' in the contemplation of the law must, of course, be remedied. But the world is full of harm for which the law furnishes no remedy. For instance, a trader owes no duty of care to avoid injuring his rivals by destroying their long-established businesses. If he does so and, as a result, one of his competitors descends into a clinical depression and his family are reduced to penury, in the eyes of the law they suffer no wrong and the law will provide no redress – because competition is regarded as operating to the overall good of the economy and society. A young man whose fiancée deserts him for his best friend may become clinically depressed as a result, but in the circumstances the fiancée owes him no duty of care to avoid causing this suffering. So he too will have no right to damages for his illness. The same goes for a middle-aged woman whose husband runs off with a younger woman. Experience suggests that such intimate matters are best left to the individuals themselves. However badly one of them may have treated the other, the law does not get involved in awarding damages.

101 Other relationships are also important. We may have children, parents, grandparents, brothers, sisters, uncles and aunts – not to mention friends, colleagues, employees and employers – who play an essential part in our lives and contribute to our happiness and prosperity. We share in their successes, but are also affected by anything bad which happens to them. So it is – and always has been – readily foreseeable that if a defendant injures or kills someone, his act is likely to affect not only the victim but many others besides. To varying degrees, these others can plausibly claim to have suffered real harm as a result of the defendant's act. For the most part, however, the policy of the law is to concentrate on compensating the victim for the effects of his injuries while doing little or nothing for the others. In technical language, the defendants owe a duty of care to the victim but not to the third parties, who therefore suffer no legal wrong.

▶

102 So, when someone negligently kills another, at common law his relatives have no right to recover damages for the distress and loss which this causes them. Of course, sections 1(1) and 1A of the Fatal Accidents Act 1976 modify the common law by providing that the wrongdoer is liable to certain dependants for the loss they suffer due to the death of the victim, and to certain relatives for their bereavement. But the defendant is liable only if he would have been liable to the victim if he had lived. The statute thus remains true to the common law position that the tortfeasor owed a duty of care to the victim but not to the dependants. So, for instance, a surgeon operating on a child will readily foresee that, if he is careless and the child dies, her parents will suffer extreme distress which may well make them ill. Nevertheless, her parents will have no common law right to damages for that distress or illness. They may have a claim for bereavement damages under section 1A of the 1976 Act – but only because the surgeon owed a duty of care to their daughter, as his patient.

104 ... In the present case it is apposite to recall that, a fortiori, the common law does not give damages 'for the mental anguish and even illness which may flow from having lost a wife, parent or child or from being compelled to look after an invalid': [1992] 1 AC 310, 409G-H, per Lord Oliver. So, for instance, if a doctor carelessly fails to diagnose a child's illness and, as a result, her distraught parents, who have to nurse her over many months, suffer psychiatric harm, they recover nothing by way of damages – because, in the contemplation of the law of tort, the doctor and the patient's parents are not in a relationship of sufficient proximity or directness as to give rise to a duty of care to them on the part of the doctor.

105 For the most part, then, the settled policy of the law is opposed to granting remedies to third parties for the effects of injuries to other people. The appellants are seeking to introduce an exception to that approach.

106 The defendants now accept that the doctors owed a duty of care to the children whom they examined and assessed. As the precedents show, it by no means follows that they owed any similar duty of care to the parents. Here the appellants formulate the alleged duty in this way: the doctors were under a duty not to cause harm to a parent foreseeably at risk of suffering harm by failing to exercise reasonable and proper care in making a diagnosis of child abuse. Despite the terms of the alleged duty, counsel for the appellants was at pains to argue that in substance it was the same as the duty which the doctors already owed to the child: if they performed their duty to the child, they would ipso facto perform their duty to the parents. As I shall suggest in a moment, assimilating the two duties in this way tends to conceal the real nature of the appellants' complaint. But, even on counsel's formulation, the similarity in the content of the two duties is no reason for holding that the supposed duty was owed to the parents. The content of a duty of care and the range of persons to whom it is owed are quite separate matters, the latter raising issues of proximity. For instance, when riding his motorbike, John Young owed certain other road users a duty of care to avoid injuring them, but he did not owe that duty to Mrs Bourhill alighting on the other side of the tram – even though, in substance, any duty of care to her in the way he drove his motorbike would have been the same as the one he already owed to the other road users: *Bourhill v Young* [1943] AC 92. In *Alcock v Chief Constable of South Yorkshire Police* the House dismissed the plaintiffs' claims, even although, again, as a practical matter the content of the duty which they said was owed to them was no different from the content of the duty which the chief constable admittedly owed to the people killed or injured in the crush. The plaintiffs were simply not persons to whom he owed that duty...

108 That being so, on the assumption that the appellants are claiming the same duty of care as was owed to their children, it seems to me that there would have to be some factor, over and above the foreseeable harm which the parents suffered, before the law would hold that the doctors and parents were in sufficient proximity to give rise to a duty of care. Mr Langstaff suggested that the necessary degree of proximity could be found in the fact that the parents themselves had taken the children to see the doctor. That is indeed what happened in these cases. But in itself this can hardly be a criterion for attaching liability to the defendants. For example, there is nothing in the nervous shock cases to suggest that taking the child to the hospital would, in itself, create the necessary proximity for a successful claim by her parents. Something more, by way of actually experiencing the critical event, is required. More generally, it would in my view be unacceptable for a doctor to be liable in damages to a father who took his daughter to the surgery, but not to a father whose daughter happened to be taken by someone else who was looking after her for the day when her symptoms developed. If that supposed distinction is rejected, I am unable to see why it would be fair, just and reasonable for the doctors to owe the parents a duty of care of this kind when, for instance, a defendant who negligently injures a child travelling in his car owes no duty of care to the parents who may foreseeably develop a psychiatric illness as a result of the strain of caring for her. I would therefore reject the appellants' submission that the defendants owed substantially the same duty of care to the parents as to the children…

Lord Nicholls: … **85** In my view the Court of Appeal reached the right conclusion on the issue arising in the present cases. Ultimately the factor which persuades me that, at common law, interference with family life does not justify according a suspected parent a higher level of protection than other suspected perpetrators is the factor conveniently labelled 'conflict of interest'. A doctor is obliged to act in the best interests of his patient. In these cases the child is his patient. The doctor is charged with the protection of the child, not with the protection of the parent. The best interests of a child and his parent normally march hand-in-hand. But when considering whether something does not feel 'quite right', a doctor must be able to act single-mindedly in the interests of the child. He ought not to have at the back of his mind an awareness that if his doubts about intentional injury or sexual abuse prove unfounded he may be exposed to claims by a distressed parent…

Lord Brown: … **136** … The point to be made … is that the public interest in law enforcement and the administration of justice does sometimes require potential liabilities to be excluded notwithstanding that those 'wronged' are left uncompensated…

138 I … readily [acknowledge] the legitimate grievances of these particular appellants, against whom no suspicions whatever remain, sufferers from a presumed want of professional skill and care on the part of the doctors treating their children. It is they, I acknowledge, who are paying the price of the law's denial of a duty of care. But it is a price they pay in the interests of children generally. The well-being of innumerable children up and down the land depends crucially upon doctors and social workers concerned with their safety being subjected by the law to but a single duty: that of safeguarding the child's own welfare. It is that imperative which in my judgment must determine the outcome of these appeals. For these reasons, together with those given by my noble and learned friends, Lord Nicholls of Birkenhead and Lord Rodger of Earlsferry, I would dismiss them.

(For further extract see p 310)

QUESTIONS

1. Did the parents fail because of the type of damage they suffered?

2. Is it in the best interests of the child to have clinically depressed parents?

3. Why should it be the non-professional individual and not the professionals who have to bear the price of professional failure?

4.3.4 Omissions

Another complex area of duty of care is where a defendant's negligence consists, not in a positive act which causes damage, but in a failure to act. Here the direct cause is either an event of nature (eg flood or landslide) or the act of a person other than the defendant (eg thief or a builder whose incompetence is not noticed by local authority inspector). In principle there is no liability for such a mere omission on the basis of an absence of duty.

Stovin v Wise [1996] AC 923, HL

This was an action for damages for personal injury brought by a motorist against another driver and a local authority. It was alleged that the local authority had been in breach of statutory duty and negligent in failing to take steps to make a particular road junction, known to be dangerous, safe. The judge held both the defendant driver and the local authority liable, but on appeal to the House of Lords (Lords Goff, Jauncey and Hoffmann; Lords Nicholls and Slynn dissenting) a majority held that the local authority was not liable.

Lord Hoffmann: ... The judge made no express mention of the fact that the complaint against the council was not about anything which it had done to make the highway dangerous but about its omission to make it safer. Omissions, like economic loss, are notoriously a category of conduct in which Lord Atkin's generalisation in *Donoghue v Stevenson* [1932] AC 562 offers limited help. In the High Court of Australia in *Hargrave v Goldman* (1963) 110 CLR 40, 66, Windeyer J drew attention to the irony in Lord Atkin's allusion, in formulating his 'neighbour' test, to the parable of the Good Samaritan [1932] AC 562, 580:

> 'The priest and the Levite, when they saw the wounded man by the road, passed by on the other side. He obviously was a person whom they had in contemplation and who was closely and directly affected by their action. Yet the common law does not require a man to act as the Samaritan did.'

A similar point was made by Lord Diplock in *Dorset Yacht Co Ltd v Home Office* [1970] AC 1004, 1060. There are sound reasons why omissions require different treatment from positive conduct. It is one thing for the law to say that a person who undertakes some activity shall take reasonable care not to cause damage to others. It is another thing for the law to require that a person who is doing nothing in particular shall take steps to prevent another from suffering harm from the acts of third parties (like Mrs Wise) or natural causes. One can put the matter in political, moral or economic terms. In political terms it is less of an invasion of an individual's freedom for the law to require him to consider the safety of others in his actions than to impose upon him a duty to rescue or protect. A moral version of this point may be called the 'why pick on me?' argument. A duty to prevent harm to others or to render assistance to a person in danger or distress may apply to a large and indeterminate class of people who happen to be able to do something. Why should one be held liable rather than another? In economic terms, the efficient allocation of resources usually requires an activity should bear its own costs. If it benefits from being able to impose some of its costs on other people (what economists call 'externalities,') the market is distorted because the activity appears cheaper than it really is. So liability to pay compensation for loss caused by negligent conduct acts as a deterrent against increasing the cost of the activity to the community and reduces externalities. But there is no similar justification for requiring a person who is not doing anything to spend money on behalf of someone else. Except in special cases (such as marine salvage) English law does not reward someone who voluntarily confers a benefit on another. So there must be some special reason why he should have to put his hand in his pocket...

In terms of public finance... [i]t is one thing to provide a service at the public expense. It is another to require the public to pay compensation when a failure to provide the service has resulted in loss. Apart from cases of reliance, which I shall consider later, the same loss would have been suffered if the service had not been provided in the first place. To require payment of compensation increases the burden on public funds. Before imposing such an additional burden, the courts should be satisfied that this is what Parliament intended...

In my view the creation of a duty of care upon a highway authority, even on grounds of irrationality in failing to exercise a power, would inevitably expose the authority's budgetary decisions to judicial inquiry. This would distort the priorities of local authorities, which would be bound to try to play safe by increasing their spending on road improvements rather than risk enormous liabilities for personal injury accidents. They will spend less on education or social services. I think that it is important, before extending the duty of care owed by public authorities, to consider the cost to the community of the defensive measures which they are likely to take in order to avoid liability. It would not be surprising if one of the consequences of the *Anns* case and the spate of cases which followed was that local council inspectors tended to insist upon stronger foundations than were necessary. In a case like this, I do not think that the duty of care can be used as a deterrent against low standards in improving the road layout. Given the fact that the British road network largely antedates the highway authorities themselves, the court is not in a position to say what an appropriate standard of improvement would be. This must be a matter for the discretion of the authority. On the other hand, denial of liability does not leave the road user unprotected. Drivers of vehicles must take the highway network as they find it. Everyone knows that there are hazardous bends, intersections and junctions. It is primarily the duty of drivers of vehicles to take due care. And if, as in the case of Mrs Wise, they do not, there is compulsory insurance to provide compensation to the victims. There is no reason of policy or justice which requires the highway authority to be an additional defendant. I would therefore allow the appeal.

(For further extract see p 136.)

Lord Nicholls (dissenting): ... [T]he recognised legal position is that the bystander does not owe the drowning child or the heedless pedestrian a duty to take steps to save him. Something more is required than being a bystander. There must be some additional reason why it is fair and reasonable that one person should be regarded as his brother's keeper and have legal obligations in that regard. When this additional reason exists, there is said to be sufficient proximity. That is the customary label. In cases involving the use of land, proximity is found in the fact of occupation. The right to occupy can reasonably be regarded as carrying obligations as well as rights.

The council was more than a bystander. The council had a statutory power to remove this source of danger, although it was not under a statutory duty to do so...

...[I]t may be debatable whether there is anything to be gained, any social utility, in shifting the financial loss from road users to a highway authority. But there can be no room for doubt when the injured road user has no such claim. This may well happen. Then it does seem eminently fair and reasonable that the loss should fall on the highway authority and not the hapless road user. And if the existence of a duty of care in all cases, in the shape of a duty to act as a reasonable authority, has a salutary effect on tightening administrative procedures and avoiding another needless road tragedy, this must be in the public interest...

(For a further extract see p 136)

QUESTIONS

1. What if economists were to declare that Lord Hoffmann had completely misunderstood economic theory: would this undermine his analysis and his conclusion?

2. Read *East Suffolk Rivers Catchment Board v Kent* (1941) in the law report. If the facts of the case arose again today would it be decided in the same way?

3. Ought a person to be under a duty to save a drowning child in situations presenting no danger to a rescuer? If a child trespasser falls into your garden pond, and is in danger of drowning, are you under a duty to try to rescue him? If so, why?

4. What if it could be shown that positive action by local authorities to make their roads safer has a measurable effect on the accidents statistics. Would this be an argument in favour of imposing a duty of care in *Stovin*-type cases?

5. If the real claimant in *Stovin* was an insurance company taking over the rights of the accident victim by subrogation, would (or should) this be a reason in itself for denying a duty of care?

NOTE

As with shock, there are exceptions to the no duty principle for mere omissions, usually based upon some pre-existing relationship between claimant (C) and the person failing to act (D). Thus if D owed a pre-existing duty to C, then there might be liability (*Reeves v Commissioner of Police for the Metropolis*, pp 336, 340); equally once D has intervened he may be liable if he makes matters worse (*Barrett v Ministry of Defence* (1995)). On the whole such defendants are usually public bodies and much may depend upon the nature of the statutory duty that D has failed to perform (see **Chapter 9**). Sometimes a range of factors may point one way or the other: nature of the damage, status of the defendant, insurance position, contractual relations and so on (see *Marc Rich* (1996), below, p 291; but cf *Capital & Counties plc v Hampshire CC* (1997)).

4.4 Causation and remoteness

The third fundamental requirement of the tort of negligence is that there is suffi-cient causal connection between the defendant's careless act and the claimant's damage. If there is an insufficient causal link the claim will fail. This causal aspect will be dealt with in a separate chapter (**Chapter 10**), but it might be helpful to note here that this causal requirement broadly divides into three cate-gories: (a) cause in fact (which used to be a question for the jury); (b) cause in law or remoteness of damage (a question of law for the judge); and (c) defences based on causation such as contributory negligence and mitigation. The causal issue can attach to the damage as a whole or it can on occasions attach to just certain categories of damage (see eg *Spartan Steel*, above, pp 54, 137).

4.5 Negligence and unlawfulness

English tort law distinguishes between careless and unlawful acts which cause damage. The first falls within the realm of the tort of negligence and the second within the tort of breach of statutory duty (and also public nuisance).

X (Minors) v Bedfordshire County Council [1995] 2 AC 633, HL

Lord Browne-Wilkinson: ... The principles applicable in determining whether such statu-tory cause of action exists are now well established, although the application of those principles in any particular case remains difficult. The basic proposition is that in the ordi-nary case a breach of statutory duty does not, by itself, give rise to any private law cause of action. However a private law cause of action will arise if it can be shown, as a matter of construction of the statute, that the statutory duty was imposed for the protection of a limited class of the public and that Parliament intended to confer on members of that class a private right of action for breach of the duty. There is no general rule by reference to which it can be decided whether a statute does create such a right of action but there are a number of indicators. If the statute provides no other remedy for its breach and the Parliamentary intention to protect a limited class is shown, that indicates that there may be a private right of action since otherwise there is no method of securing the protection the statute was intended to confer. If the statute does provide some other means of enforcing the duty that will normally indicate that the statutory right was intended to be enforceable by those means and not by private right of action: *Cutler v Wandsworth Stadium Ltd* [1949] AC 398; *Lonrho Ltd v Shell Petroleum Co Ltd (No 2)* [1982] AC 173. However, the mere existence of some other statutory remedy is not necessarily decisive. It is still possible to show that on the true construction of the statute the protected class was intended by Parliament to have a private remedy. Thus the specific duties imposed on employers in relation to factory premises are enforceable by an action for damages, notwithstanding the imposition by the statutes of criminal penalties for any breach: see *Groves v Wimborne (Lord)* [1898] 2 QB 402...

NOTES

1. See also *Groves v Wimborne* (p 164); *Phillips v Britannia Hygienic Laundry* (p 171); *R v Transport Secretary, ex p Factortame Ltd* (No 7) (p 40). *Gorris v Scott* (p 329)

2. At one time negligence and breach of statutory duty were seen as quite separate causes of action (*London Passenger Transport Board v Upson* (1949)) and this is probably still true today at the formal level. In substance, however, breach of statutory duty has become more closely associated with negligence in a number of ways. It is seen by some as a form of statutory negligence; it is often a concurrent claim in employment liability cases (but not of course in the other great source of tort claims, car accidents: *Phillips*, p 171); and in actions against public bodies the two torts can become intertwined in as much as a body such as a local authority can act only pursuant to statutory authority (see X (*Minors*)). Breach of statutory duty is important when it comes to an employer's liability for dangerous plant and equipment (see **5.3**).

Chapter 5

Liability for Things (1): Moveable Things

The idea of a liability for things, where liability attaches more to a physical object than to a person, finds its fullest expression in art 1384 of the French Civil Code. A person is liable for damage done by things under his control. This is, it must be said, quite a unique provision in civil law systems since strict liability – that is to say liability without fault – is normally based upon risk arising from dangerous activities rather than upon a general liability attaching to a thing, although the two ideas tend to overlap (for example with respect to dangerous animals, buildings and products).

English law recognises such a strict (no fault) liability attaching to things only in a few specific instances such as dangerous products (Consumer Protection Act 1987), dangerous animals (Animals Act 1971, s 2(1)) and things falling off aeroplanes (Civil Aviation Act 1982, s 76(2)). In certain circumstances the owner and (or) the occupier of land might also be strictly liable for damage caused by things on or attaching to the land. However, it is also possible to talk about a liability for things where the duty is at the same level as that of the ordinary tort of negligence or, in certain circumstances, actually lower. It is still a liability for a thing since this is what actually causes the damage. Thus an employer is now deemed liable for the fault of the manufacturer where injury is caused by a defective tool supplied by the employer (Employers' Liability (Defective Equipment) Act 1969); and of course *Donoghue v Stevenson* (1932) (p 112) itself was a liability attaching to a defective product. Where damage has been caused by things on land the position becomes complex because the sources of such liability are complex. Statute plays a fundamental role; however not only are several different statutes to be considered, but the common law continues to have a background role as well (*Gwilliam v West Herts NHS Trust* (2002), §§ 35–44).

5.1 Historical and conceptual considerations

The idea of a law of things, although not a formal category of liability in common law thinking, is nevertheless a useful analytical framework for problem solving. It directs analysis towards 'active' (in the causal sense) things that cause damage and sometimes these active things in themselves bring into play specific statutory rules or common law causes of action. For example, as we have indicated, damage caused by a product, animal or workplace tool will be governed (although not necessarily exclusively) by a specific statutory regime. More generally, damage arising from the unreasonable use of land ought to direct thinking towards private nuisance and where a dangerous thing escapes from land this will bring into play a particular rule arising from *Rylands v Fletcher* (1868) (p 217). In fact the notion of a liability for things bring into play a whole spectrum of ideas as the following extract indicates.

Ferdinand Stone, *Liability For Damage Caused By Things*, Torts, *International Encyclopedia of Comparative Law* vol XI, Ch 5 (footnotes omitted)

1. In tracing the history of liability for damage caused by things, one sees the whole spectrum of ideas concerning legal responsibility. One begins with primitive law's concept of thing responsibility, whereby vengeance was wrought upon the thing itself which caused the damage, as if it were possessed of demons. Later, we find the shift to personal responsibility for the damage, based either on the notion of personal fault or negligence with regard to the thing, eg in controlling or guarding it, or on the notion of vicarious liability for the thing's 'fault'. Later still, there emerged the modern doctrine which imposes strict liability on persons and enterprises for such damage, either as a 'price' for carrying on the activity or possessing the thing, or on the theory that the activity, being ultra-hazardous, is carried on at one's peril, or on the ground that public policy favours the imposition of strict liability upon the one conducting the activity or having the thing, in view of the general availability of insurance against such risk of damage. This modern doctrine goes by various names: 'liability without fault', 'negligence without fault', 'presumed responsibility', 'fault *per se*', 'objective liability' or 'risk liability'...

NOTE

Of course, as this extract implies, this idea of a liability for things should not be the only regime that comes into play since tort liability is based upon specific causes of action and these tend to be arranged as a list (breach of statutory duty, negligence, nuisance, trespass and so on). The nature of the interest invaded (personal injury, physical damage to property and pure economic loss) can be equally important. But a liability for things does help focus the mind on risk as well as fault and thus is a most useful template. Indeed, land (including buildings and structures) is an important formal 'thing' in English tort law in that nearly all textbooks have a chapter on occupiers' liability and so it is certainly not unreasonable to talk in terms of a law of things when it comes to persons suffering damage on property under the occupation of another. When occupiers' liability (see **Chapter 6**) is combined with the specific regimes dealing with moveable property, the French idea of a liability based upon the relationship between person and thing is perhaps not so alien after all.

5.2 Dangerous products

Dangerous products that cause personal injury are now the subject of a specific statutory regime, itself the result of a European Directive (Council Directive 85/374/EEC). One might recall, also, that the whole of the tort of negligence is based on a case about a dangerous product (*Donoghue v Stevenson* (1932), p 112) and this decision remains important in that it indicates that where a defective product does cause damage there is a presumption that the defect is the result of carelessness in its manufacture.

Grant v Australian Knitting Mills Ltd [1936] AC 85, PC

This was an action for damages brought by a consumer against both the retailer and the manufacturer of underpants for injury caused to a purchaser by underpants which had not been properly decontaminated of chemicals before leaving the factory. The Privy Council (Viscount Hailsham, Sir Lancelot Sanderson and Lords Wright, Macmillan and Blanesburgh) upheld the claims against both defendants.

Lord Wright: ... The principle of *Donoghue's* case can only be applied where the defect is hidden and unknown to the consumer, otherwise the directness of cause and effect is absent: the man who consumes or uses a thing which he knows to be noxious cannot complain in respect of whatever mischief follows, because it follows from his own conscious volition in choosing to incur the risk or certainty of mischance.

If the foregoing are the essential features of *Donoghue's* case they are also to be found, in their Lordships' judgment, in the present case. The presence of the deleterious chemical in the pants, due to negligence in manufacture, was a hidden and latent defect, just as much as were the remains of the snail in the opaque bottle: it could not be detected by any examination that could reasonably be made. Nothing happened between the making of the garments and their being worn to change their condition. The garments were made by the manufacturers for the purpose of being worn exactly as they were worn in fact by the appellant: it was not contemplated that they should be first washed. It is immaterial that the appellant has a claim in contract against the retailers, because that it a quite independent cause of action, based on different considerations, even though the damage may be the same. Equally irrelevant is any question of liability between the retailers and the manufacturers on the contract of sale between them. The tort liability is independent of any question of contract.

It was argued, but not perhaps very strongly, that *Donoghue's* case was a case of food or drink to be consumed internally, whereas the pants here were to be worn externally. No distinction, however, can be logically drawn for this purpose between a noxious thing taken internally and a noxious thing applied externally: the garments were made to be worn next to the skin: indeed Lord Atkin specifically puts as examples of what is covered by the principle he is enunciating things operating externally, such as 'an ointment, a soap, a cleaning fluid or cleaning powder' ...

The decision in *Donoghue's* case did not depend on the bottle being stoppered and sealed: the essential point in this regard was that the article should reach the consumer or user subject to the same defect as it had when it left the manufacturer. That this was true of the garment is in their Lordships' opinion beyond question. At most there might in other cases be a greater difficulty of proof of the fact ...

NOTES

1. Liability for defective products is an area where contract and tort meet and overlap. In *Grant* the claimant not only succeeded against the manufacturer but also against the seller of the product. This latter liability was not, however, in negligence but in contract where a term as to quality is implied by statute (Sale of Goods Act 1979, s 14). The tort and contract duties differ in as much as the former is dependent upon the existence of negligence while the latter is strict; if

the goods, objectively, are not reasonably fit for their purpose and (or) of satis-factory (formerly merchantable) quality, the seller will be strictly liable. If a consumer wishes, then, to sue the manufacturer carelessness must be proved. However dangerous goods 'speak for themselves' (*res ipsa loquitur*) and thus the chemically infected underpants were in themselves evidence of negligence and the manufacturers' evidence that only one pair in a million was contaminated did not save them from liability.

2. Another distinction between tortious and contractual liability is that the former is limited to physical damage. A product that turns out to be defective, but which does no physical damage to anything other than to itself, will not result in liability in the tort of negligence. Poor quality goods, in other words, are regarded as a bad bargain resulting in pure economic loss (cf **4.3.2**). The purchaser of such a poor product can of course sue the seller in contract for his pure economic loss, but a third party in receipt of the goods (eg as a birthday present) will have no direct contractual action, unless the sale contract specifically confers a right to enforce the implied term (Contract (Rights of Third Parties) Act 1999).

3. The contract (strict liability) and tort (negligence) dichotomy has now been eclipsed, where goods cause physical injury, by statute.

Consumer Protection Act 1987 (c 43)

1.   Purpose and construction of Part I

(1) This Part shall have effect for the purpose of making such provision as is necessary in order to comply with the product liability Directive and shall be construed accordingly.

(2) In this Part, except in so far as the context otherwise requires—

[...]

'dependant' and 'relative' have the same meanings as they have in, respectively, the Fatal Accidents Act 1976 and the Damages (Scotland) Act 1976;

'producer', in relation to a product, means—

(a) the person who manufactured it;
(b) in the case of a substance which has not been manufactured but has been won or abstracted, the person who won or abstracted it;
(c) in the case of a product which has not been manufactured, won or abstracted but essential characteristics of which are attributable to an industrial or other process having been carried out (for example, in relation to agricultural produce), the person who carried out that process;

'product' means any goods or electricity and (subject to subsection (3) below) includes a product which is comprised in another product, whether by virtue of being a component part or raw material or otherwise...

2.   Liability for defective products

(1) Subject to the following provisions of this Part, where any damage is caused wholly or partly by a defect in a product, every person to whom subsection (2) below applies shall be liable for the damage.

(2) This subsection applies to—
   (a) the producer of the product;
   (b) any person who, by putting his name on the product or using a trade mark or other distinguishing mark in relation to the product, has held himself out to be the producer of the product;
   (c) any person who has imported the product into a member State from a place outside the member States in order, in the course of any business of his, to supply it to another...

3. Meaning of 'defect'

(1) Subject to the following provisions of this section, there is a defect in a product for the purposes of this Part if the safety of the product is not such as persons generally are entitled to expect; and for those purposes 'safety', in relation to a product, shall include safety with respect to products comprised in that product and safety in the context of risks of damage to property, as well as in the context of risks of death or personal injury.

(2) In determining for the purposes of subsection (1) above what persons generally are entitled to expect in relation to a product all the circumstances shall be taken into account, including—
   (a) the manner in which, and purposes for which, the product has been marketed, its get-up, the use of any mark in relation to the product and any instructions for, or warnings with respect to, doing or refraining from doing anything with or in relation to the product;
   (b) what might reasonably be expected to be done with or in relation to the product; and
   (c) the time when the product was supplied by its producer to another;

and nothing in this section shall require a defect to be inferred from the fact alone that the safety of a product which is supplied after that time is greater than the safety of the product in question.

4. Defences

(1) In any civil proceedings by virtue of this Part against any person ('the person proceeded against') in respect of a defect in a product it shall be a defence for him to show—
   (a) that the defect is attributable to compliance with any requirement imposed by or under any enactment or with any Community obligation; or
   (b) that the person proceeded against did not at any time supply the product to another; or
   (c) that the following conditions are satisfied, that is to say—
      (i) that the only supply of the product to another by the person proceeded against was otherwise than in the course of a business of that person's; and
      (ii) that section 2(2) above does not apply to that person or applies to him by virtue only of things done otherwise than with a view to profit; or
   (d) that the defect did not exist in the product at the relevant time; or
   (e) that the state of scientific and technical knowledge at the relevant time was not such that a producer of products of the same description as the product in question might be expected to have discovered the defect if it had existed in his products while they were under his control; or

(f) that the defect—
    (i) constituted a defect in a product ('the subsequent product') in which the product in question had been comprised; and
    (ii) was wholly attributable to the design of the subsequent product or to compliance by the producer of the product in question with instructions given by the producer of the subsequent product.

5. Damage giving rise to liability

(1) Subject to the following provisions of this section, in this Part 'damage' means death or personal injury or any loss of or damage to any property (including land).

(2) A person shall not be liable under section 2 above in respect of any defect in a product for the loss of or any damage to the product itself or for the loss of or any damage to the whole or any part of any product which has been supplied with the product in question comprised in it.

(3) A person shall not be liable under section 2 above for any loss of or damage to any property which, at the time it is lost or damaged, is not—

(a) of a description of property ordinarily intended for private use, occupation or consumption; and

(b) intended by the person suffering the loss or damage mainly for his own private use, occupation or consumption.

(4) No damages shall be awarded to any person by virtue of this Part in respect of any loss of or damage to any property if the amount which would fall to be so awarded to that person, apart from this subsection and any liability for interest, does not exceed £275.

(5) In determining for the purposes of this Part who has suffered any loss of or damage to property and when any such loss or damage occurred, the loss or damage shall be regarded as having occurred at the earliest time at which a person with an interest in the property had knowledge of the material facts about the loss or damage...

6. Application of certain enactments

(7) It is hereby declared that liability by virtue of this Part is to be treated as liability in tort for the purposes of any enactment conferring jurisdiction on any court with respect to any matter...

7. Prohibition on exclusions from liability

The liability of a person by virtue of this Part to a person who has suffered damage caused wholly or partly by a defect in a product, or to a dependant or relative of such a person, shall not be limited or excluded by any contract term, by any notice or by any other provision.

NOTES AND QUESTIONS

1. The key words in this legislation are: 'where any damage is caused wholly or partly by a defect in a product' the producer 'shall be liable for the damage' (s 2).

And: 'there is a defect in a product... if the safety of the product is not such as persons generally are entitled to expect' (s 3). The central question is thus likely to focus upon what consumers are 'entitled to expect'. What are consumers entitled to expect with regard to products such as medicines, tobacco, alcohol, microwave ovens, tins of peas containing a caterpillar (cf *Smedleys Ltd v Breed* (1974)) and the like? What will be the basis of 'entitled'? Will it reflect the economic interest of the consumer or of the producer?

2. Another ambiguous point that arises from this legislation is the extent to which it takes consumer protection beyond the position at common law (negligence and contract). One point of contention is s 4(1)(e) whose words can be compared with those in the Directive which states that the 'producer shall not be liable... if he proves:... that the state of scientific and technical knowledge at the time when he put the product into circulation was not such as to enable the existence of the defect to be discovered' (art 7(e)). The European Commission took the view that s 4(1)(e) was not compatible with art 7(e), but the European Court of Justice held that the two were not necessarily incompatible (*European Commission v UK*, Case C-300/95). The European Court of Justice stated that it is not just a matter of the wording in the text but how national courts actually interpret the legislation and on this point the court noted s 1(1) of the 1987 Act.

3. What is the position if someone receives infected blood in a transfusion? Is blood a 'product'? What if there was no medical test in existence capable of detecting the infection in the blood? (Cf *A v National Blood Authority* (2001).)

LIBRARY RESEARCH PROBLEM

Research the following cases in the law reports: (a) *Wyngrove's Curator Bonis v Scottish Omnibuses Ltd* (1966); (b) *Ingham v Emes* (1955); (c) *Reed v Dean* (1949); (d) *Square v Model Farm Dairies* (1939); (e) *Read v Croydon Corporation* (1938). If the facts of these cases occurred again today could each of the claimants succeed against the producer under the 1987 Act?

5.3 Dangerous industrial equipment

Injury caused to an employee by a dangerous product supplied by an employer might well give rise to a liability on the part of the manufacturer of the defective item of equipment. But it was held at common law that there is no liability of the employer unless the employer himself was negligent or in breach of a statute with respect to the dangerous tool or equipment (*Davie v New Merton Board Mills* (1959)). This non-liability was criticised (see eg Hamson [1959] CLJ 157) and statute stepped in to remedy the situation. Before looking at this specific statutory extension of liability, it is necessary first to consider the position at common law.

5.3.1 General considerations

The industrial revolution created a new social problem that was to impact upon the law of tort throughout Europe. Accidents in the workplace became increasingly frequent with devastating results not just for the victim but often for his family (cf Fatal Accidents Act 1976, p 372). Many of these accidents resulted from dangerous things such as unfenced factory machinery and gradually

Parliament intervened with factory legislation. Equally (and interestingly) the courts responded by creating a strict liability action in tort where such safety legislation was breached by an employer. The 'liability for things' perspective is well expressed in the extract below.

Ferdinand Stone, *Liability For Damage Caused By Things*, Torts, *International Encyclopedia of Comparative Law* vol XI, Ch 5 (footnotes omitted)

17. Professor *Lawson* has pointed out that in the pre-Industrial Revolution society the dominant precept was that people should not act dangerously and if they did and damage resulted therefrom compensation or restitution should be made. But the Industrial Revolution illustrated dramatically that using dangerous things such as machinery might be meritorious even though some damage resulted. Thus in this period jurists sought ways by which the meritorious use of dangerous things might be encouraged at the same time that deleterious effects might in proper cases be avoided or repaired...

18. In response to the needs of this changed society, jurists turned to and developed the concept of negligence ... However, as the risk-producing capacity of an industrialized society increased and as it became more and more difficult for either party to an accident to prove specific facts indicating negligence, machines and factory processes having become exceedingly complex, courts and jurists began to search for a theory or theories of liability which would on the one hand permit the compensation of worthy claims without on the other hand opening the floodgates of liability and litigation to fictitious and fraudulent demands. Out of this search was developed the concept of strict liability...

5.3.2 Tort of breach of statutory duty

These observations by Stone ought to be borne in mind when reading the next case. This is one of the key cases of strict liability in English law and is the foundational precedent for the tort of breach of statutory duty in the context of employer's liability.

Groves v Lord Wimborne [1898] 2 QB 402, CA

AL Smith LJ: In this case the plaintiff sues the defendant, who is the occupier of the Dowlais Iron Works, for breach of a duty to fence certain machinery imposed upon him as such occupier by the Factory and Workshop Act, 1878, by reason of which breach of duty the plaintiff sustained personal injuries. The learned judge at the trial gave judgment for the defendant, being of opinion that no action lay for the breach of duty alleged by the plaintiff. The Act in question, which followed numerous other Acts in pari material, is not in the nature of a private legislative bargain between employers and workmen, as the learned judge seemed to think, but is a public Act passed in favour of the workers in factories and workshops to compel their employers to do certain things for their protection and benefit ... In the present case it is admitted that machinery on the defendant's premises which came within these provisions was not fenced as required by the Act, and that injury was thereby occasioned to the plaintiff, a boy employed on the works.

On proof of a breach of this statutory duty imposed on the defendant, and injury resulting to the plaintiff therefrom, prima facie the plaintiff has a good cause of action ...
[U]nless it appears from the whole 'purview' of the Act, to use the language of Lord
Cairns in the case of *Atkinson v Newcastle Waterworks Co*, that it was the intention of
the Legislature that the only remedy for breach of the statutory duty should be by proceeding for the fine imposed by s 82, it follows that, upon proof of a breach of that duty
by the employer and injury thereby occasioned to the workman, a cause of action is
established. The question therefore is whether the cause of action which prima facie is
given by s 5 is taken away by any provisions to be found in the remainder of the Act...
In dealing with the question whether this was the intention of the Legislature, it is material, as Kelly CB pointed out in giving judgment in the case of *Gorris v Scott*, to consider
for whose benefit the Act was passed, whether it was passed in the interests of the
public at large or in those of a particular class of persons. The Act now in question, as I
have said, was clearly passed in favour of workers employed in factories and workshops, and to compel their employers to perform certain statutory duties for their
protection and benefit. It is to be observed in the first place that under the provisions of
s 82 not a penny of the fine necessarily goes to the person injured or his family. The provision is only that the whole or any part of it may be applied for the benefit of the injured
person or his family, or otherwise, as a secretary of state determines ... [I]t cannot have
been the intention of the Legislature that the provision which imposes upon the
employer a fine as a punishment for neglect of his statutory duty should take away the
prima facie right of the workman to be fully compensated for injury occasioned to him
by that neglect ... I cannot read this statute in the manner in which it is sought to be
read by the defendant. I think that s 5 does give to the workman a right of action upon
the statute for injury caused by a breach of the statutory duty thereby imposed, and that
he is not relegated to the provisions for the imposition of a fine on the employer, or it
may be a workman, as his sole remedy...

[Rigby LJ and Vaughan Williams LJ delivered judgments agreeing with AL Smith LJ.]

NOTE

The Factories Act 1961, which provided that dangerous machinery had to be
fenced, gave rise to a considerable body of case law. Once it had been determined that a machine was 'dangerous' within the meaning of the Act, it was no
defence that fencing would render the machine unusable (*John Summers v Frost*
(1955)). The fact that the accident happened in an unforeseeable way was,
equally, no defence (*Millard v Serck Tubes* (1969)). However the courts would look
at the purpose of the legislation and so, for example, the object of the fencing
provision was to keep the worker out and not bits of the machine in (*Close v
Steel Co of Wales* (1962)). Other workplace statutes such as the Mines and
Quarries Act 1954 and the Offices, Shops and Railway Premises Act 1963 were
also important sources of litigation. All of these Acts have now been replaced by
Regulations made under the Health and Safety at Work Act 1974. This piece of
primary legislation specifically states that breach 'of a duty imposed by health
and safety regulations [...] shall, so far as it causes damage, be actionable except
in so far as the regulations provide otherwise' (s 47(2)).

5.3.3 Negligence liability

An employee injured in the workplace is not restricted to suing in the tort of breach of statutory duty. He or she can equally claim that the employer was in breach of his common law duty to take care.

Wilsons and Clyde Coal Co Ltd v English [1938] AC 57, HL

This was an action for damages by an employee at a coalmine, against his employer, for injury suffered when some haulage plant was put into motion while he was making his way along one of the underground roads. The claimant argued that the employers had been negligent in allowing the haulage plant to be in motion at a time when the day shift men were being raised to the surface. The defendants responded in saying that they had delegated their duty to maintain a safe system of work by appointing a qualified manager to deal with the technical management of the mine in accordance with the Coal Mines Act 1911. The House of Lords (Lords Atkin, Thankerton, Macmillan, Wright and Maugham) rejected this defence.

Lord Macmillan: ... Now I take it to be settled law that the provision of a safe system of working in a colliery is an obligation of the owner of the colliery. He cannot divest himself of this duty, though he may – and, if it involves technical management and he is not himself technically qualified, must – perform it through the agency of an employee. It remains the owner's obligation, and the agent whom the owner appoints to perform it performs it on the owner's behalf. The owner remains vicariously responsible for the negligence of the person whom he has appointed to perform his obligation for him, and cannot escape liability by merely proving that he has appointed a competent agent. If the owner's duty has not been performed, no matter how competent the agent selected by the owner to perform it for him, the owner is responsible...

Lord Wright: ... This House held that... the statutory duty was personal to the employer, in this sense that he was bound to perform it by himself or by his servants. The same principle, in my opinion, applies to those fundamental obligations of a contract of employment... and for the performance of which employers are absolutely responsible. When I use the word absolutely, I do not mean that employers warrant the adequacy of plant, or the competence of fellow-employees, or the propriety of the system of work. The obligation is fulfilled by the exercise of due care and skill. But it is not fulfilled by entrusting its fulfilment to employees, even though selected with due care and skill. The obligation is threefold – 'the provision of a competent staff of men, adequate material, and a proper system and effective supervision';...

There is perhaps a risk of confusion if we speak of the duty as one which can, or cannot, be delegated. The true question is, What is the extent of the duty attaching to the employer? Such a duty is the employer's personal duty, whether he performs or can perform it himself, or whether he does not perform it or cannot perform it save by servants or agents. A failure to perform such a duty is the employer's personal negligence. This was held to be the case where the duty was statutory, and it is equally so when the duty is one attaching at common law. A statutory duty differs from a common law duty in certain respects, but in this respect it stands on the same footing...

NOTE

This case is important in that it translates Lord Atkin's neighbour principle (see **4.1**) into an employer's duty towards its employees. The duty is usually regarded as tortious, but in theory it can equally be seen as an implied term of the contract of employment. The case is important, also, because it shows that this duty is a direct and non-delegable duty. An employer cannot escape liability by saying that it had fulfilled its duty of care in appointing, say, a safety officer.

5.3.4 Liability for defective equipment

However the position is not quite the same when it comes to supplying a tool. At common law the duty is summed up in the short extract below.

Davie v New Merton Board Mills Ltd [1959] AC 604, HL

Lord Reid: My Lords, the facts of this case are very simple. The appellant was a maintenance fitter employed by the respondents. In the course of his work he was using in a proper manner a wedged-shaped tool called a drift which was supplied to him by the respondents: he was hammering it for the purpose of separating two pieces of metal. A chip flew off it and struck his eye so that he lost the sight of that eye. The drift was not safe for use because it was much too hard and brittle, and the cause of this was negligence of the manufacturers of the drift, or their servants. The respondents had bought the tool from a reputable merchant, who had in turn bought it from the manufacturers...

... The appellant's contention is that the respondents are liable to him in damages because of the negligence of the manufacturers or their servants...

The conclusion to which I have come is that an employer, besides being liable to his servant for injury caused by the negligence of his own servants, is in some cases liable in respect of the negligence of others. Where, then, is the line to be drawn? On the one hand it appears that an employer is liable for the negligence of an independent contractor whom he has engaged to carry out one of what have been described as his personal duties on his own premises and whose work might normally be done by the employer's own servant – at least if the negligent workmanship is discoverable by reasonable inspection. On the other hand for the reasons which I have given, I am of opinion that he is not liable for the negligence of the manufacturer of an article which he has bought, provided that he has been careful to deal with a seller of repute and has made any inspection which a reasonable employer would make...

[Viscount Simonds and Lords Morton, Tucker and Keith delivered judgment in favour of the defendants.]

QUESTION

Should the employer have supplied goggles?

NOTE

The House of Lords could have held that an employer contractually warrants via an implied term that the equipment supplied would not be defective. It failed to do this and so Parliament stepped in.

Employer's Liability (Defective Equipment) Act 1969 (c 37)

1. Extension of employer's liability for defective equipment.

(1) Where after the commencement of this Act—
  (a) an employee suffers personal injury in the course of his employment in consequence of a defect in equipment provided by his employer for the purposes of
  the employer's business; and
  (b) the defect is attributable wholly or partly to the fault of a third party (whether
  identified or not),

  the injury shall be deemed to be also attributable to negligence on the part of the
  employer (whether or not he is liable in respect of the injury apart from this subsection), but without prejudice to the law relating to contributory negligence and
  to any remedy by way of contribution or in contract or otherwise which is available to the employer in respect of the injury.

(2) In so far as any agreement purports to exclude or limit any liability of an employer
  arising under subsection (1) of this section, the agreement shall be void.

(3) In this section—

  'business' includes the activities carried on by any public body;

  'employee' means a person who is employed by another person under a contract of
  service or apprenticeship and is so employed for the purposes of a business carried
  on by that other person, and 'employer' shall be construed accordingly;

  'equipment' includes any plant and machinery, vehicle, aircraft and clothing;

  'fault' means negligence, breach of statutory duty or other act or omission which
  gives rise to liability in tort in England and Wales or which is wrongful and gives rise
  to liability in damages in Scotland; and

  'personal injury' includes loss of life, any impairment of a person's physical or mental
  condition and any disease...

NOTE

This statute is very much a liability attaching to a 'thing' (equipment) since the
thing itself acts as the means of extending liability from the manufacturer to the
employer. The key words in this statute are 'fault' (s 1(1)(b)) and its definition (s
1(3)). This definition is wider than carelessness and includes 'or other act or
omission which gives rise to liability in tort'. Thus an employer will presumably
be deemed liable if the producer of a defective product is liable under the
Consumer Protection Act 1987.

QUESTIONS

1. Is a ship 'equipment' within the meaning of the 1969 Act? (Cf *Coltman v
Bibby Tankers* (1988).)

2. Is a flagstone 'equipment'? What about a brick? (Cf *Knowles v Liverpool CC*
(1993).)

5.4 Motor vehicles

One social reason for imposing liability on employers for defective equipment is, as we have seen, that the workplace is one of two major factual sources of tort claims. The other major source is road accidents. Damage caused by motor vehicles has, however, not given rise to any special liabilities, except in one rather limited way where an owner lends his or her car to another (see *Morgans v Launchbury*, p 72). The position can be contrasted with France which, since 1985, has had a special statutory regime covering road accidents; and even before 1985, cars fell within the strict liability provision of art 1384 of the CC thanks to a famous decision in 1930.

5.4.1 Tort of negligence

In England, as the case below reaffirms, a road accident victim must normally prove fault in order to recover damages.

Mansfield v Weetabix Ltd [1998] 1 WLR 1263, CA

This was an action for damages by the owners of a shop against the employer and personal representative of a lorry driver whose lorry crashed into their shop. The trial judge held the defendants liable on the ground that the lorry driver had been negligent, but an appeal against this judgment was allowed by the Court of Appeal (Leggatt, Aldous and Sir Patrick Russell LJJ).

Leggatt LJ: ... In my judgment, the standard of care that Mr Tarleton was obliged to show in these circumstances was that which is to be expected of a reasonably competent driver unaware that he is or may be suffering from a condition that impairs his ability to drive. To apply an objective standard in a way that did not take account of Mr Tarleton's condition would be to impose strict liability. But that is not the law. As Lord Wilberforce said in *Snelling v Whitehead*, The Times, 31 July 1975, a transcript of the speeches in which is before the court:

'The case is one which is severely distressing to all who have been concerned with it and one which should attract automatic compensation regardless of any question of fault. But no such system has yet been introduced in this country and the courts, including this House, have no power to depart from the law as it stands. This requires that compensation may only be obtained in an action for damages and further requires, as a condition of the award of damages against the [driver], a finding of fault, or negligence, on his part... it is... not disputed that any degree of fault on the part of the [driver], if established, is sufficient for the [plaintiff] to recover. On the other hand, if no blame can be imputed to the [driver], the action, based on negligence, must inevitably fail.'

In the present case the plaintiffs may well have been insured. Others in their position may be less fortunate. A change in the law is, however, a matter for Parliament. Meanwhile, since in my judgment Mr Tarleton was in no way to blame, he was not negligent. I would therefore allow the appeal.

QUESTION

Leggatt LJ observes that the claimant in this case may well have been insured. Is this the reason why he was prepared to give judgment for the defendants? Which insurance policy should carry the risk of accidental damage to a building: the one attaching to a car or the one attaching to the building?

NOTE

Insurance has proved to be a factor in a number of cases involving damage done by motor vehicles. Note how it is also a factor in the road accident cases extracted elsewhere in the book: *Reid v Rush & Tompkins* (p 50); *Stovin v Wise* (pp 136, 152, 296); *Morgans v Launchbury* (p 72); and *Nettleship v Weston* (p 128). See also *Gorringe v Calderdale MBC* (p 299) and Lewis (2005) 25 LS 85. In the next case insurance may also have been a factor: those who put lorries on the road for profit ought to take the risk of damage they cause even in respect of virtually latent defects. The case remains a negligence case, but it shows how by manipulating the burden (or at least standard) of proof (cf **4.2.7**) the courts can sometimes get close to a strict liability for things (motor vehicles).

Henderson v HE Jenkins & Sons Ltd [1970] AC 282, HL

This was an action in damages under the Fatal Accidents Act by a widow against the owners of a runaway lorry that had killed her husband. The owners claimed that the lorry's brakes had failed because of a latent defect undiscoverable by the use of reasonable care and this defence was upheld by the trial judge and Court of Appeal. However a bare majority of the House of Lords (Lords Reid, Donovan and Pearson; Lord Guest and Viscount Dilhorne dissenting) allowed an appeal.

Lord Donovan: ... [The defendants] proved that the pipe in question was visually inspected *in situ* once a week; that the brake pedal was on these occasions depressed to check for leaks from the pipe and none seen; that nothing more than such visual inspection of the pipe was required by Ministry of Transport rules or the maker's advice...

Yet the kind of load this lorry had been carrying in the past was something which had to be known in order to assess the measure of the duty of reasonable care resting on the [defendants]. For the corrosion of the pipe was caused by some chemical agent. Had the lorry, therefore, been carrying chemicals of any kind? Or had it operated under conditions where salt (also a corrosive agent) might come in contact with the pipe? Or had it at some time been adapted for carrying cattle and done so? If any of these things were the case then clearly visual inspection of the pipe *in situ* would not have been enough. It should have been removed at intervals so that the whole of it, and not merely part of it, could be examined...

It was, therefore, incumbent on the [defendants], if they were to sustain their plea of latent defect undiscoverable by the exercise of ordinary care, to prove where the vehicle had been and what it had been carrying whilst in their service and in what conditions it had operated. Only then could the standard of reasonable care be ascertained, and their conduct measured against it...

QUESTION

Is this case an example of what Stone (see p 158) has called 'negligence without fault'?

5.4.2 Tort of breach of statutory duty

One reason why the courts have had to manipulate the rules of evidence within the tort of negligence to achieve a stricter liability is because the judges failed to develop the tort of breach of statutory duty beyond industrial accidents. They had their opportunity as the next case shows.

Phillips v Britannia Hygienic Laundry Co Ltd [1923] 2 KB 832, CA

Bankes LJ: This is an appeal from the Divisional Court reversing the county court judge in an action brought by the plaintiff for damage done to his motor van. The axle of the defendants' motor lorry broke and caused the damage. The action in the county court was founded on an alleged breach of a statutory provision contained in the Motor Cars (Use and Construction) Order 1904 and alternatively on the alleged negligence of the defendant. The county court judge absolved the defendant from negligence in relation either to the management of the motor lorry or to the state of its axle, but he found negligence on the part of the repairers to whom the motor lorry had been sent, in not having executed the repairs efficiently, and gave judgment for the plaintiff on the ground that the lorry was not in the condition required by cl 6 of art II of the Order. On an appeal by the defendants the Divisional Court reversed this judgment. The plaintiff appeals to this court.

I agree with the conclusion of the Divisional Court. If the judgment of the county court judge were to stand it would have very far-reaching consequences...

We have not to consider the case of a person injured on the highway. The injury here was done to the appellant's van; and the appellant, a member of the public, claims a right of action as one of a class for whose benefit cl 6 was introduced. He contends that the public using the highway is the class so favoured. I do not agree. In my view the public using the highway is not a class; it is itself the public and not a class of the public. The clause therefore was not passed for the benefit of a class or section of the public. It applies to the public generally, and it is one among many regulations for breach of which it cannot have been intended that a person aggrieved should have a civil remedy...

Atkin LJ: ... This is an important question, and I have felt some doubt upon it, because it is clear that these regulations are in part designed to promote the safety of the public using highways. The question is whether they were intended to be enforced only by the special penalty attached to them in the Act. In my opinion, when an Act imposes a duty of commission or omission, the question whether a person aggrieved by a breach of the duty has a right of action depends on the intention of the Act. Was it intended to make the duty one which was owed to the party aggrieved as well as to the State, or was it a public duty only ?... I have come to the conclusion that the duty they were intended to impose was not a duty enforceable by individuals injured, but a public duty only, the sole remedy for which is the remedy provided by way of a fine... In particular it is not likely that the legislature intended by these means to impose on the owners of vehicles an absolute obligation to have them roadworthy in all events even in the absence of negligence...

[Younger LJ agreed]

NOTE

The principles of the tort of breach of statutory duty have been set out in the extract of the judgment of Lord Browne-Wilkinson in *X (Minors) v Bedfordshire CC* (1995) at the end of Chapter 4 (p 155). Suffice it to say here that *Phillips* is very much a missed opportunity to introduce a form of strict liability into the second main source of personal injury claims, namely road accidents. Had the result of *Phillips* been different, there would have been a symmetry between industrial and road accidents.

QUESTION

Phillips was not of course a personal injury claim, a point made by Bankes LJ. If it had been, do you think Bankes LJ would have given judgment for the claimant?

5.4.3 Tort of public nuisance

Another attempt to introduce strict liability into highway accidents was made through the tort of public nuisance whose principles are set out in *Esso* (pp 4, 34) and *Att-Gen v PYA Quarries* (p 68).

Dymond v Pearce and Others [1972] 1 QB 496, CA

This was an action for damages by a motor cycle passenger against the employers of a lorry driver (second defendant) in respect of personal injuries suffered by the passenger when the motor cycle ran into the back of the parked lorry. The lorry driver had parked his vehicle with the tail lights on, beneath a street lamp on a dual carriageway, and there was a clear view of the lorry for at least 200 yards. The crash occurred when the driver of the motor cycle (first defendant) was looking behind him at girls on the pavement. The Court of Appeal (Sachs, Edmund Davies and Stephenson LJJ) upheld a judgment that the accident was wholly the fault of the motor cyclist.

Sachs LJ: ... The leaving of a large vehicle on a highway for any other purpose for a considerable period (it is always a matter of degree) otherwise than in a lay-by *prima facie* results in a nuisance being created, for it narrows the highway. With all respect to the views expressed by the learned trial judge as to the ways of life today, I am unable to accept his conclusion that the parking for many hours for the driver's own convenience of a large lorry on a highway of sufficient importance to have a dual carriageway did not result in the creation of a nuisance...

But the mere fact that a lorry was a nuisance does not render its driver or owner liable to the plaintiff in damages unless its being in that position was a cause of the accident...

[The trial judge found] that the sole cause of the accident was the first defendant's negligence ... It entails a parallel conclusion that the nuisance was not a cause of the plaintiff's injuries; that, indeed, in the vast majority of cases is an inevitable conclusion once negligence on the part of a driver of a stationary vehicle is negatived, for only rarely will that which was found not to be a foreseeable cause of an accident also be found to have been in law the actual cause of it...

It is thus not necessary to decide a further point inherent in much that was canvassed before us as to the ingredients of nuisance of the category under consideration. What would be the position if, even though the third defendant had not been negligent in leaving the lorry as it was in fact left, yet there had occurred some unexpected supervening happening – such as an onset of heavy weather, sea mist or fog, or, for instance, a sudden rear light failure (potent cause of fatalities) – which had so affected the situation that the lorry became the cause of an accident? Should the risk fall entirely on those using the highway properly? Or should some liability attach to the person at fault in creating a nuisance? It may well be that, as I am inclined to think, he who created the nuisance would be under a liability ... If he was thus liable this might be the only class of case in which an action in nuisance by obstruction of the highway could succeed where one in negligence would fail...

Edmund Davies LJ: ... Where a vehicle has been left parked on the highway for such a length of time or in such other circumstances as constitute it an obstruction amounting to a public nuisance, I remain of the view I expressed in *Parish v Judd* that, in order that a plaintiff who in such proceedings as the present may recover compensation for personal injuries caused by a collision with that obstruction, he must establish that the obstruction constituted a danger...

[He then cited Denning LJ in *Morton v Wheeler*, as to what constitutes a danger – 'whether injury may reasonably be anticipated'.] It goes without saying, however, that the person creating a highway obstruction must be alert to such sudden and unpredicted weather changes as those to which we are subject in this country at most seasons, to the possibility that the vehicular or highway lighting may fail or be interfered with in these days of rampant vandalism, and to other circumstances which may convert what was originally a danger-free obstruction into a grave traffic hazard. If he fails to exercise ordinary intelligence in those and similar respects, he can make no proper claim reasonably to have anticipated the probable shape of things to come, and he must expect his conduct to be subjected to the most critical scrutiny in the event of an accident occurring...

It is true that in the result, as Denning LJ said in *Morton v Wheeler*, 'Inasmuch as the test of danger is what may reasonably be foreseen, it is apparent that cases of public nuisance ... have an affinity with negligence.' Nevertheless, as he went on to point out: 'There is a real distinction between negligence and nuisance. In an action for private damage arising out of a public nuisance, the court does not look at the conduct of the defendant and ask whether he was negligent. It looks at the actual state of affairs as it exists in or adjoining the highway without regard to the merits or demerits of the defendant. If the state of affairs is such as to be a danger ... the person who created it is liable unless he can show sufficient justification or excuse.'

NOTES AND QUESTIONS

1. Compare Denning LJ's observation (in Edmund Davies LJ's judgment) with his analysis of public nuisance and negligence in *Esso v Southport* (pp 4, 34). From a factual position, it would seem that public nuisance will be relevant mainly (only?) in situations where motor vehicles obstruct the highway. Could a moving vehicle ever constitute a nuisance? Could *Henderson v Jenkins* (above, p 170) be reanalysed as a public nuisance case?

2. What public nuisance shares with breach of statutory duty is that they are both torts arising out of unlawful (criminal) behaviour.

3. Is 'public nuisance' being used in the same way as res ipsa loquitur (cf **4.2.7**)?

5.5 Animals

With regard to motor vehicles, it is in some ways difficult to talk about a specific liability for things since claims are in theory founded upon the careless behaviour of the road user. It is a personal liability of the individual based upon his or her individual act. With respect to animals, however, one can certainly talk in terms of a liability for things since the statutory regime that now governs liability is founded on the relationship between defendant (keeper) and animal (thing). Of course liability is still personal to the defendant; the keeper cannot escape liability (as one could in Roman law) by handing over the offending animal to the victim. The relevant statutory scheme is set out in this section, but sandwiched between extracts of speeches from a recent House of Lords decision. These extracts provide a useful introduction to, and commentary on, the Act.

Mirvahedy v Henley [2003] 2 AC 491, HL

(For facts and main extracts see pp 34, 178)

Lord Walker: ... **134** It is not necessary to go far into the old common law rules which imposed strict liability for wild animals (animals ferae naturae) or for tame or domesticated animals with a known vicious propensity (the scienter basis of liability). The old rules were both questionable in their foundations and uncertain in their limits. That appears from two cases decided not very long before the Act, *Behrens v Bertram Mills Circus Ltd* [1957] 2 QB 1 (the case of the trained Burmese elephant which was more docile than many horses until harassed by a small dog) and *Fitzgerald v ED and AD Cooke Bourne (Farms) Ltd* [1964] 1 QB 249 (the case of an unbroken filly in a field crossed by a public footpath). The Goddard Committee (which reported in 1953) (Report of the Committee on the Law of Civil Liability for Damage done by Animals (Cmd 8746)) proposed to abolish strict liability for damage caused by animals, but the Law Commission in its Report on Civil Liability for Animals (published in 1967 (Law Com No 13) as one of the Law Commission's earliest reports) took a different view. The Law Commission recommended that the principle of strict liability should not be abolished, but should be modified and simplified. It is clear that in enacting the Act, Parliament was (in the most general terms) following the Law Commission's recommendations to retain the principle in a modified form. It is unfortunately far from clear that Parliament achieved the objective of simplification...

135 Part of the problem is that section 2 of the Act is expressed in very general terms. It is notable that the Law Commission inquired into the prevalence of particular types of damage caused by animals. Its report contains some detailed statistics about road accidents in which animals were involved. But in section 2 Parliament has not chosen to identify or make specific provision for the varying circumstances in which animals do most commonly cause damage. In practice section 2(1) has a very narrow scope, being almost entirely limited to incidents in (or following escapes from) zoos or circuses.

Section 2(2) has to cover the whole range of incidents involving animals of species classified as non-dangerous (which I will call domesticated animals, although that is not an entirely accurate term). That range includes (i) physical injury to humans by biting (especially by dogs) or kicking or knocking down (especially by horses); (ii) injuries caused to livestock (such as a dog worrying a neighbour's sheep, or a cat killing a neighbour's chickens); (iii) road traffic accidents, especially those caused by animals straying on the highway; (iv) damage caused by livestock getting out on to neighbouring land and destroying crops or gardens; and (v) injury or damage caused by the spread of animal infection or by the smell or noise of animals (a class which shades off into cases normally classified as nuisance). So section 2(2) has a lot of work to do. It is expressed in general, abstract terms and it has to be applied to a wide range of disparate incidents.

136 Other sections of the Act do contain more specific provisions. The case of livestock trespassing on private land is covered by section 4, and there is a special provision as to guard dogs injuring trespassers (section 5(3)). But the only special provision made for animals straying on the highway is the abolition by section 8 (subject to qualifications in section 8(2)) of the old common law rule which gave immunity: see *Searle v Wallbank* [1947] AC 341...

Animals Act 1971 (c 22)

2. Liability for damage done by dangerous animals.

(1) Where any damage is caused by an animal which belongs to a dangerous species, any person who is a keeper of the animal is liable for the damage, except as otherwise provided by this Act.

(2) Where damage is caused by an animal which does not belong to a dangerous species, a keeper of the animal is liable for the damage, except as otherwise provided by this Act, if—
   (a) the damage is of a kind which the animal, unless restrained, was likely to cause or which, if caused by the animal, was likely to be severe; and
   (b) the likelihood of the damage or of its being severe was due to characteristics of the animal which are not normally found in animals of the same species or are not normally so found except at particular times or in particular circumstances; and
   (c) those characteristics were known to that keeper or were at any time known to a person who at that time had charge of the animal as that keeper's servant or, where that keeper is the head of a household, were known to another keeper of the animal who is a member of that household and under the age of sixteen.

3. Liability for injury done by dogs to livestock.

Where a dog causes damage by killing or injuring livestock, any person who is a keeper of the dog is liable for the damage, except as otherwise provided by this Act.

4. Liability for damage and expenses due to trespassing livestock

(1) Where livestock belonging to any person strays on to land in the ownership or occupation of another and—
   (a) damage is done by the livestock to the land or to any property on it which is in the ownership or possession of the other person; or

(b) any expenses are reasonably incurred by that other person in keeping the livestock while it cannot be restored to the person to whom it belongs or while it is detained in pursuance of section 7 of this Act, or in ascertaining to whom it belongs;

the person to whom the livestock belongs is liable for the damage or expenses, except as otherwise provided by this Act.

(2) For the purposes of this section any livestock belongs to the person in whose possession it is.

5. Exceptions from liability under sections 2 to 4.

(1) A person is not liable under sections 2 to 4 of this Act for any damage which is due wholly to the fault of the person suffering it.

(2) A person is not liable under section 2 of this Act for any damage suffered by a person who has voluntarily accepted the risk thereof.

(3) A person is not liable under section 2 of this Act for any damage caused by an animal kept on any premises or structure to a person trespassing there, if it is proved either—
(a) that the animal was not kept there for the protection of persons or property; or
(b) (if the animal was kept there for the protection of persons or property) that keeping it there for that purpose was not unreasonable.

(4) A person is not liable under section 3 of this Act if the livestock was killed or injured on land on to which it had strayed and either the dog belonged to the occupier or its presence on the land was authorised by the occupier.

(5) A person is not liable under section 4 of this Act where the livestock strayed from a highway and its presence there was a lawful use of the highway.

(6) In determining whether any liability for damage under section 4 of this Act is excluded by subsection (1) of this section the damage shall not be treated as due to the fault of the person suffering it by reason only that he could have prevented it by fencing; but a person is not liable under that section where it is proved that the straying of the livestock on to the land would not have occurred but for a breach by any other person, being a person having an interest in the land, of a duty to fence.

6. Interpretation of certain expressions used in sections 2 to 5.

(1) The following provisions apply to the interpretation of sections 2 to 5 of this Act.

(2) A dangerous species is a species—
(a) which is not commonly domesticated in the British Islands; and
(b) whose fully grown animals normally have such characteristics that they are likely, unless restrained, to cause severe damage or that any damage they may cause is likely to be severe.

(3) Subject to subsection (4) of this section, a person is a keeper of an animal if—
(a) he owns the animal or has it in his possession; or
(b) he is the head of a household of which a member under the age of sixteen owns the animal or has it in his possession;

and if at any time an animal ceases to be owned by or to be in the possession of a person, any person who immediately before that time was a keeper thereof by virtue of the preceding provisions of this subsection continues to be a keeper of the animal until another person becomes a keeper thereof by virtue of those provisions.

(4) Where an animal is taken into and kept in possession for the purpose of preventing it from causing damage or of restoring it to its owner, a person is not a keeper of it by virtue only of that possession.

(5) Where a person employed as a servant by a keeper of an animal incurs a risk incidental to his employment he shall not be treated as accepting it voluntarily...

8. Duty to take care to prevent damage from animals straying on to the highway.

(1) So much of the rules of the common law relating to liability for negligence as excludes or restricts the duty which a person might owe to others to take such care as is reasonable to see that damage is not caused by animals straying on to a highway is hereby abolished.

(2) Where damage is caused by animals straying from unfenced land to a highway a person who placed them on the land shall not be regarded as having committed a breach of the duty to take care by reason only of placing them there if—
   (a) the land is common land, or is land situated in an area where fencing is not customary, or is a town or village green; and
   (b) he had a right to place the animals on that land...

11. General interpretation.

In this Act—

'common land', and 'town or village green' have the same meanings as in the Commons Registration Act 1965;

'damage' includes the death of, or injury to, any person (including any disease and any impairment of physical or mental condition);

'fault' has the same meaning as in the Law Reform (Contributory Negligence) Act 1945;

'fencing' includes the construction of any obstacle designed to prevent animals from straying;

'livestock' means cattle, horses, asses, mules, hinnies, sheep, pigs, goats and poultry, and also deer not in the wild state and, in sections 3 and 9, also, while in captivity, pheasants, partridges and grouse;

'poultry' means the domestic varieties of the following, that is to say, fowls, turkeys, geese, ducks, guinea-fowls, pigeons, peacocks and quails; and

'species' includes sub-species and variety.

QUESTION

What if the courts decided to interpret the word 'animal' very widely? Can you think of a range of scenarios to which the Act might apply that were not perhaps foreseen by Parliament?

NOTE

Extracts below provide some useful judicial commentary on the Act.

Mirvahedy v Henley [2003] 2 AC 491, HL

(For facts and main extracts see pp 34, 174)

Lord Nicholls: ... **9** The purpose of the 1971 Act was to simplify the law. Sections 1 to 6 of the Act made new provision regarding strict liability for damage done by animals. They replace the old rules of the common law. Section 2 contains provisions relating to liability for damage done by dangerous animals. Unfortunately the language of section 2(2) is itself opaque. In this instance the parliamentary draftsman's zeal for brevity has led to obscurity. Over the years section 2(2) has attracted much judicial obloquy.

10 Section 2 places all animals into one or other of two categories, according to their species. Animals either belong to a dangerous species, or they do not. The circumstances in which the keeper of an animal is liable for damage caused by his animal depend upon the category to which the animal belongs.

11 A dangerous species of animal is a species which meets two requirements, set out in section 6(2). A species can include a sub-species or a variety: see section 11. The first requirement (a) is that the species is not commonly domesticated in the British Islands. The second requirement (b) is that fully grown animals of the species 'normally have such characteristics that they are likely, unless restrained, to cause severe damage or that any damage they may cause is likely to be severe'. In short, they are dangerous animals.

12 A tiger satisfies both requirements. It is not commonly domesticated in this country, and it is dangerous. A horse does not satisfy the first requirement. Unlike tigers, horses are commonly domesticated here. So tigers, satisfying both requirements, are a dangerous species of animals. Horses, which do not satisfy the two requirements, are not...

Lord Hobhouse: ... **66** The Act was a reforming act and followed from Report No 13 of the Law Commission on Civil Liability for Animals. Without adopting all the recommendations of the Law Commission, the Act completely recasts the previous law but has retained a recognisable structure derived from the previous law. Thus it retains a distinct category for wild animals 'not commonly domesticated in the British Islands', sections 6(2)(a) and 2(1); and has a residual category which makes use of the former scienter rule based on the keeper's knowledge of the particular animal's actual characteristics: section 2(2)(c).

67 Another feature of the Act is that it uses a double-barrelled concept of dangerousness with alternative criteria either of which suffices. The first is the familiar characteristic that the animal or its species is, unless restrained, likely to cause severe damage; this corresponds to what has sometimes been called a vicious propensity. The second is directed not to the animal's propensities, be they vicious or benign, but to the consequences of anything it may do. Thus the alternative criterion is that it is an animal of which it can be said that 'any damage [it] may cause is likely to be severe': section 6(2)(b). These two alternative criteria are used in conjunction with the criterion of non-domestication to define what is a dangerous species of animal in section 6(2). Using the first alternative, a tiger is a dangerous animal. It is likely, unless restrained, to cause severe injuries to humans: that is its nature. Using the second alternative, an Indian elephant is a dangerous animal, not because it is likely to injure any one, but because, if it does, the injury is likely, as a result of its weight and bulk, to be severe: cf *Behrens v Bertram Mills Circus Ltd* [1957] 2 QB 1. This is a statement about its physical capacity to injure and its inability to limit the consequences of that capacity not about its inclination to injure. In section 2(1) there is a strict liability for damage caused by dangerous animals as defined in section 6(2). In section 2(2) there is a scienter liability for any damage caused by any other animal which is, inter alia, damage of a kind which the animal in question was, unless restrained, likely to cause or which, if caused by that animal, was likely to be severe: section 2(2)(a)...

Lord Walker: ... **136** ... It has not been contended in your Lordships' House (although it was contended at first instance) that section 8 has the effect of excluding possible liability under section 2(2)...

QUESTIONS

1. If D's cat eats his neighbour's pet canary will D be liable under the 1971 Act?

2. Do the facts of *Mirvahedy* fall under s 8 rather than s 2? Or do they fall under s 8 in addition to s 2? Does it matter?

5.6 Aircraft

Aircraft attract their own regime for several reasons. First, legislation excludes any right of action in trespass in respect of aircraft over-flying private property. Secondly, material loss or damage caused by aircraft to person or property is governed by a statutory strict liability provision. And thirdly, aircraft can give rise to a specific conflict of interest: the mental distress to individuals resulting from aircraft noise conflicts with the general public benefit arising from air transport and air defence.

5.6.1 Statute

The starting point of liability for damage caused by aircraft is statute. The 1982 Act, set out below, suppresses certain actions at common law, but establishes a kind of statutory trespass claim.

Civil Aviation Act 1982 (c 16)

76. Liability of aircraft in respect of trespass, nuisance and surface damage.

(1) No action shall lie in respect of trespass or in respect of nuisance, by reason only of the flight of an aircraft over any property at a height above the ground which, having regard to wind, weather and all the circumstances of the case is reasonable, or the ordinary incidents of such flight, so long as the provisions of any Air Navigation Order and of any orders under section 62 above have been duly complied with and there has been no breach of section 81 below.

(2) Subject to subsection (3) below, where material loss or damage is caused to any person or property on land or water by, or by a person in, or an article, animal or person falling from, an aircraft while in flight, taking off or landing, then unless the loss or damage was caused or contributed to by the negligence of the person by whom it was suffered, damages in respect of the loss or damage shall be recoverable without proof of negligence or intention or other cause of action, as if the loss or damage had been caused by the wilful act, neglect, or default of the owner of the aircraft.

(3) Where material loss or damage is caused as aforesaid in circumstances in which—
   (a) damages are recoverable in respect of the said loss or damage by virtue only of subsection (2) above, and
   (b) a legal liability is created in some person other than the owner to pay damages in respect of the said loss or damage,

   the owner shall be entitled to be indemnified by that other person against any claim in respect of the said loss or damage.

77. Nuisance caused by aircraft on aerodromes.

(1) An Air Navigation Order may provide for regulating the conditions under which noise and vibration may be caused by aircraft on aerodromes and may provide that subsection (2) below shall apply to any aerodrome as respects which provision as to noise and vibration caused by aircraft is so made.

(2) No action shall lie in respect of nuisance by reason only of the noise and vibration caused by aircraft on an aerodrome to which this subsection applies by virtue of an Air Navigation Order, as long as the provisions of any such Order are duly complied with.

PROBLEM

A number of inhabitants of a village suffer severe psychiatric injury when they witness a plane crashing nearby. Are they entitled to damages under s 76(2) of the 1982 Act? And, if so, ought an analogy to be made with *Wilkinson v Downton* (p 7) or with *Frost v Chief Constable of S Yorks* (p 146)? (Cf *Glen v Korean Airlines* (2003).)

5.6.2 Common law (tort of private nuisance)

Despite the statutory defence in ss 76 and 77 of the 1982 Act, the tort of private nuisance still has an important role to play in respect of mental distress damage caused by aircraft.

Dennis v Ministry of Defence [2003] EWHC 793, QBD

Buckley J: 1 This case concerns the effect of noise from Harrier jet fighters on the 1st Claimant's neighbouring estate. It is alleged to constitute a nuisance at common law and/or to infringe his human rights, and also to infringe the human rights of his wife, the 2nd Claimant. A declaration and damages are sought, alternatively damages of some £10,000, 000...

Nuisance at Common Law

30 This case raises an important and problematic point of principle in the law of nuisance. Namely, whether and in what circumstances a sufficient public interest can amount to a defence to a claim in nuisance. In several cases the point has arisen in a less dramatic form than here. For example, the local cricket club case: *Miller v Jackson* [1977] QB 966 and *Kennaway v Thompson* [1981] QB 88 in which the Court of Appeal affirmed the principle in *Shelfer v City of London Electric Lighting Company* [1894] 1 Ch 287, namely, the fact that the wrong doer is in some sense a public benefactor has never been considered a sufficient reason to refuse an injunction. (See Lindley LJ. At 315/6). *Clerk and Lindsell* concludes that public interest is 'not in itself a defence, but a factor in assessing reasonableness of user'. 18th Edition paragraph 19.72. *Fleming The Law of Torts* 9th Edition at 471 points out that some weight is accorded to the utility of the defendant's conduct, but suggests that the argument 'must not be pushed too far.' He cites Bohlen Studies 429:

'If the public be interested let the public as such bear the costs.'

He points out this can be achieved by holding the defendant liable and leaving him to include the cost in charges to the public, or by statutory authority with provision for compensation. The former suggestion, of course, would only apply to a service provider capable of raising charges...

45 Where there is a real public interest in a particular use of land, I can see no objection in principle to taking that public interest into account, in one way or another, in deciding what is best to be done...

46 The problem with putting the public interest into the scales when deciding whether a nuisance exists, is simply that if the answer is no, not because the claimant is being over sensitive, but because his private rights must be subjugated to the public interest, it might well be unjust that he should suffer the damage for the benefit of all. If it is to be held that there is no nuisance, there can be no remedy at common law. As this case illustrates, the greater the public interest, the greater may be the interference. If public interest is considered at the remedy stage and since the court has a discretion, the nuisance may continue but the public, in one way or another, pays for its own benefit... Allowing a human rights claim but denying a remedy in nuisance would, of course, be another solution, but it would be one that reflected adversely on the flexibility of the common law...

47 The principles or policy underlying these considerations are that public interest should be considered and that selected individuals should not bear the cost of the public benefit. I am in favour of giving effect to those principles. I believe it is necessary

▶

to do so if the common law in this area is to be consistent with the developing jurisprudence on human rights.

48 I therefore hold that a nuisance is established but that the public interest clearly demands that RAF Wittering should continue to train pilots...

49 I do not believe that the conclusion at which I have arrived is prohibited by authority. The facts of this case are extreme and not analogous to others to which I was referred. I am conscious that there is no authority directly in point which supports my solution. However, save where it may be considered more appropriate to leave the matter to legislation, the common law should develop in line with European decisions on human rights, which I consider later...

QUESTIONS

1. Is the nuisance liability for the aircraft noise attaching to the use of aircraft or to the use of the land?

2. Has *Dennis* been put into question by the House of Lords' decision in *Marcic v Thames Water* (p 213)?

5.6.3 Human rights

As Buckley J suggests, an alternative head of claim by the victims of aircraft noise might now be available thanks to Human Rights Act 1998.

Dennis v Ministry of Defence [2003] EWHC 793, QBD

(See above p 181)

Buckley J: ... **55**. The claims here are on behalf of both Claimants (Mr and Mrs Dennis). It is alleged that the aircraft noise constitutes an interference with their human rights under the Human Rights Act 1998....

61 In view of my findings on the extent of noise interference and the agreed fact that it significantly reduces the market value of the Estate, I am satisfied there is an interference both with Article 1 and Article 8 rights....

63 ... In my view, common fairness demands that where the interests of a minority, let alone an individual, are seriously interfered with because of an overriding public interest, the minority should be compensated. To its credit the MOD appears to accept that principle since it operates the voluntary schemes to which I have referred...

QUESTION

What are the rights and remedies of those living near a commercial airport?

Hatton v UK (2003) *The Times*, 10 July, ECHR (Grand Chamber)

THE COURT: ... **3** The applicants alleged that Government policy on night flights at Heathrow airport gave rise to a violation of their rights under Article 8 of the Convention and that they were denied an effective domestic remedy for this complaint, contrary to Article 13 of the Convention...

6 On 7 November 2000 the Chamber delivered its judgment in which it held, by five votes to two, that there had been a violation of Article 8 of the Convention and by, six votes to one, that there had been a violation of Article 13. The Chamber also decided, by six votes to one, to award compensation for non-pecuniary damage of 4,000 pounds sterling ('GBP') to each applicant, and a global sum of GBP 70,000 in respect of legal costs and expenses...

7 On 19 December 2001 the Government requested, pursuant to Article 43 of the Convention and Rule 73, that the case be referred to the Grand Chamber. The Panel of the Grand Chamber accepted this request on 27 March 2002...

84 The applicants complained that the Government policy on night flights at Heathrow introduced in 1993 violated their rights under Article 8 of the Convention...

96 Article 8 protects the individual's right to respect for his or her private and family life, home and correspondence. There is no explicit right in the Convention to a clean and quiet environment, but where an individual is directly and seriously affected by noise or other pollution, an issue may arise under Article 8...

98 Article 8 may apply in environmental cases whether the pollution is directly caused by the State or whether State responsibility arises from the failure properly to regulate private industry. Whether the case is analysed in terms of a positive duty on the State to take reasonable and appropriate measures to secure the applicants' rights under paragraph 1 of Article 8 or in terms of an interference by a public authority to be justified in accordance with paragraph 2, the applicable principles are broadly similar. In both contexts regard must be had to the fair balance that has to be struck between the competing interests of the individual and of the community as a whole; and in both contexts the State enjoys a certain margin of appreciation in determining the steps to be taken to ensure compliance with the Convention. Furthermore, even in relation to the positive obligations flowing from the first paragraph of Article 8, in striking the required balance the aims mentioned in the second paragraph may be of a certain relevance...

125 Whether in the implementation of that regime the right balance has been struck in substance between the Article 8 rights affected by the regime and other conflicting community interests depends on the relative weight given to each of them. The Court accepts that in this context the authorities were entitled, having regard to the general nature of the measures taken, to rely on statistical data based on average perception of noise disturbance...

126 As to the economic interests which conflict with the desirability of limiting or halting night flights in pursuance of the above aims, the Court considers it reasonable to assume that those flights contribute at least to a certain extent to the general economy...

▶

130 There has accordingly been no violation of Article 8 of the Convention...

139 As the Chamber found, Section 76 of the [Civil Aviation] 1982 Act prevents actions in nuisance in respect of excessive noise caused by aircraft at night. The applicants complain about the flights which were permitted by the 1993 Scheme, and which were in accordance with the relevant regulations. No action therefore lay in trespass or nuisance in respect of lawful night flights...

140 The question which the Court must address is whether the applicants had a remedy at national level to 'enforce the substance of the Convention rights ... in whatever form they may happen to be secured in the domestic legal order' (*Vilvarajah and Others v United Kingdom*) ... In... its judgment in the case of *Smith and Grady v United Kingdom*, the Court concluded that judicial review was not an effective remedy on the grounds that the domestic courts defined policy issues so broadly that it was not possible for the applicants to make their Convention points regarding their rights under Article 8 of the Convention in the domestic courts.

141 The Court recalls that judicial review proceedings were capable of establishing that the 1993 Scheme was unlawful because the gap between Government policy and practice was too wide (see *R v Secretary of State for Transport, ex parte Richmond LBC (No. 2)* [1995] Environmental Law Reports p. 390). However, it is clear, as noted by the Chamber, that the scope of review by the domestic courts was limited to the classic English public law concepts, such as irrationality, unlawfulness and patent unreasonableness, and did not at the time (that is, prior to the entry into force of the Human Rights Act 1998) allow consideration of whether the claimed increase in night flights under the 1993 Scheme represented a justifiable limitation on the right to respect for the private and family lives or the homes of those who live in the vicinity of Heathrow airport.

142 In these circumstances, the Court considers that the scope of review by the domestic courts in the present case was not sufficient to comply with Article 13. There has therefore been a violation of Article 13 of the Convention...

QUESTIONS

1. If s 76 of the Civil Aviation Act 1982 prevents actions in nuisance (see para 139 in *Hatton*), why were the claimants in *Dennis* able to succeed in nuisance?

2. Is it fair and just that a burden (or price) associated with a public good that benefits everyone in a particular society should fall on the shoulders of just a few individuals in that society?

5.7 Liability for dangerous things in general

In this final section on damage caused by moveable things a general question can be posed. Does English law recognise a strict form of liability, perhaps based on risk (and perhaps analogous to dangerous animals), for damage done by a dangerous thing under the control of another? A definitive answer to this question has been given by the House of Lords.

Read v J Lyons & Co [1947] AC 156, HL

This was an action for damages for personal injury brought by a Ministry of Supply factory inspector (the appellant) against the operators of a munitions factory (the respondents) where she had been directed to work. The appellant was injured by an unexplained explosion in the shell shop and in her action she did not plead or prove negligence; the trial judge accordingly treated her action as based on the rule in *Rylands v Fletcher* (on which see p 217 below). He held the respondents liable. However his decision was overturned by the Court of Appeal whose judgment was upheld by the House of Lords (Viscount Simon and Lords Macmillan, Porter, Simonds and Uthwatt).

Viscount Simon: ... Now, the strict liability recognised by this House to exist in *Rylands v Fletcher* is conditioned by two elements which I may call the condition of 'escape' from the land of something likely to do mischief if it escapes, and the condition of 'non-natural use' of the land... It is not necessary to analyse this second condition on the present occasion, for in the case now before us the first essential condition of 'escape' does not seem to me to be present at all...

Lord Macmillan: ... In my opinion the appellant's statement of claim discloses no ground of action against the respondents. The action is one of damages for personal injuries. Whatever may have been the law of England in early times I am of opinion that as the law now stands an allegation of negligence is in general essential to the relevancy of an action of reparation for personal injuries... The emphasis formerly was on the injury sustained and the question was whether the case fell within one of the accepted classes of common law actions; the emphasis now is on the conduct of the person whose act has occasioned the injury and the question is whether it can be characterised as negligent. I do not overlook the fact that there is at least one instance in the present law in which the primitive rule survives, namely, in the case of animals *ferae naturae* or animals *mensuetae naturae* which have shown dangerous proclivities. The owner or keeper of such an animal has an absolute duty to confine or control it so that it shall not do injury to others and no proof of care on his part will absolve him from responsibility. But this is probably not so much a vestigial relic of otherwise discarded doctrine as a special rule of practical good sense. At any rate, it is too well established to be challenged. But such an exceptional case as this affords no justification for its extension by analogy...

In an address characterised by much painstaking research Mr Paull for the appellant sought to convince your Lordships that there is a category of things and operations dangerous in themselves and that those who harbour such things or carry on such operations in their premises are liable apart from negligence for any personal injuries occasioned by these dangerous things or operations. I think that he succeeded in showing that in the case of dangerous things and operations the law has recognised that a special responsibility exists to take care. But I do not think that it has ever been laid down that there is absolute liability apart from negligence where persons are injured in consequence of the use of such things or the conduct of such operations... Should it be thought that this is a reasonable liability to impose in the public interest it is for Parliament so to enact...

▶

Your Lordships' task in this House is to decide particular cases between litigants and your Lordships are not called upon to rationalise the law of England. That attractive if perilous field may well be left to other hands to cultivate. It has been necessary in the present instance to examine certain general principles advanced on behalf of the appellant because it was said that consistency required that these principles should be applied to the case in hand. Arguments based on legal consistency are apt to mislead for the common law is a practical code adapted to deal with the manifold diversities of human life, and as a great American judge has reminded us, 'the life of the law has not been logic; it has been experience.' For myself, I am content to say that in my opinion no authority has been quoted from case or textbook which would justify your Lordships, logically or otherwise, in giving effect to the appellant's plea. I would accordingly dismiss the appeal.

Lord Porter: ... Normally at the present time in an action of tort for personal injuries if there is no negligence there is no liability...

It was urged upon your Lordships that it would be a strange result to hold the respondents liable if the injured person was just outside their premises but not liable if she was just within them. There is force in the objection, but the liability is itself an extension of the general rule and, in my view, it is undesirable to extend it further...

Lord Uthwatt: ... In substance the appellant was on the respondents' premises in performance of a statutory duty incumbent on her as a citizen, but it is, I think, obvious that this circumstance did not alter the nature of the duty which the respondents owed to her as a person who with their consent was present on their premises on business bent...

Is there any good reason consistent with respect for the rights of dominion and user incident to the occupation of land, and with an appreciation of the position of an invitee, for subjecting the occupier carrying on a dangerous but lawful business to an absolute duty to safeguard the invitee from harm?...

QUESTIONS

1. How would you answer Lord Uthwatt's question?

2. How would a case such as this have been decided in France? (Cf p 301.)

3. Is the whole result of this case premised on the categorisation of the appellant as a 'visitor' or 'invitee' and the respondents as an 'occupier'? Are such status categories realistic given the actual occupations of each party?

Chapter 6

Liability for Things (2):
Immovable Things

In this second chapter on liability for things the emphasis will be on land. This emphasis will embrace not just damage caused by the land itself (landslips, lakes and the like) together with buildings and other structures that give rise to liability, but harm resulting from activities on the land to people on and off the premises. Again it must be stressed that English law does not really start off from the idea of a liability for things; liability depends upon establishing particular causes of action such as public nuisance, private nuisance, trespass and (or) negligence. However a number of dichotomies can be mentioned at the outset. As we shall see, English law distinguishes between damage to persons on the premises and damage to persons off the premises. It also distinguishes between harm directly caused by the occupier of land (for example knocking down a neighbour's fence or cutting down his trees) (see **Chapter 3**) and harm indirectly caused (for example smoke or fumes resulting from activities on the land). In addition the dichotomy between fault and strict liability is ever present in problems arising out of acts and omissions on land and it tends to express itself in conceptual arguments about the distinction between negligence and nuisance. Yet another dichotomy is the one between statutory and common law liability. The duty of care owed by an occupier of land to persons on his premises may seem to have its roots in Lord Atkin's neighbour principle (above p 113), but the duty is statute based. This is why occupiers' liability attracts its own chapters in many tort textbooks.

Emphasising land as the foundation of liability means that the various actors involved can get lost behind the props so to speak. This must be rectified in that the problem-solver must move from the land to the various persons who are associated with the property. In terms of potential defendants one tends to think of the owners, yet absentee landlords will indicate immediately that the possessor or occupier of the land or building might be just as relevant. As for potential claimants, these can embrace people lawfully on the property of another (visitors) or indeed people unlawfully on the land (trespassers). Passers-by and neighbours are other groups of potential claimants. In short the class, or 'status', of the various persons associated with land are important focal points when it comes to analysing factual situations.

Finally, one should note by way of introduction that one particular cause of action, liability for the escape of a dangerous thing brought onto land, is based upon a single nineteenth-century precedent. Yet the case of *Rylands v Fletcher* (1868) can be seen as something more than a mere extension of the tort of nuisance. Like art 1384 of the CC it had the potential for a wide-ranging liability for dangerous things based upon the notion of risk or hazardous activity. The case, therefore, could have been one that transcended this chapter on immovable property to act as a rallying point for a liability for things in general. It is now clear, however, that it has lost this potential (*Transco plc v Stockport MBC*, p 220).

6.1 Liability for land and structures (1): on the land

Liability for damage caused by land and things on or attached to land is complex for a variety of reasons. First, it is governed primarily by four statutes: the Occupiers' Liability Act 1957; the Occupiers' Liability Act 1984; the Defective Premises Act 1972; and the Unfair Contract Terms Act 1977. The first two statutes apply only in relation to damage to victims incurred on the premises and this is the justification for distinguishing between 'on the land' and 'off the land' (see **6.2**). Secondly, the statutes differentiate between various classes of persons and so for example 'occupiers' must be distinguished from non-occupiers and perhaps from 'landlords'. Equally 'visitors' must be differentiated from 'trespassers'. Thirdly, as in other areas of tort law, the nature of the damage can be vital; the distinction between personal injury, physical damage to property and pure economic loss must be kept in mind when analysing problems. Finally, it may be important on occasions to distinguish between damage occurring as a result of the state of the land, buildings or other natural and man-made structures and damage resulting from activities on the land.

6.1.1 Occupier's duty to visitors

The duty of an occupier of land to persons on the premises was once very complex because the occupier owed differing duties depending upon the status of the person entering the property. All this changed in 1957.

Occupiers' Liability Act 1957 (5 & 6 Eliz. II, c 31)

1. Preliminary.

(1) The rules enacted by the two next following sections shall have effect, in place of the rules of the common law, to regulate the duty which an occupier of premises owes to his visitors in respect of dangers due to the state of the premises or to things done or omitted to be done on them.

(2) The rules so enacted shall regulate the nature of the duty imposed by law in consequence of a person's occupation or control of premises and of any invitation or permission he gives (or is to be treated as giving) to another to enter or use the premises, but they shall not alter the rules of the common law as to the persons on whom a duty is so imposed or to whom it is owed; and accordingly for the purpose of the rules so enacted the persons who are to be treated as an occupier and as his visitors are the same (subject to subsection (4) of this section) as the persons who would at common law be treated as an occupier and as his invitees or licensees.

(3) The rules so enacted in relation to an occupier of premises and his visitors shall also apply, in like manner and to the like extent as the principles applicable at common law to an occupier of premises and his invitees or licensees would apply, to regulate—

(a) the obligations of a person occupying or having control over any fixed or move-able structure, including any vessel, vehicle or aircraft; and

(b) the obligations of a person occupying or having control over any premises or structure in respect of damage to property, including the property of persons who are not themselves his visitors.

(4) A person entering any premises in exercise of rights conferred by virtue of:—

(a) section 2(1) of the Countryside and Rights of Way Act 2000, or

(b) an access agreement or order under the National Parks and Access to the Countryside Act, 1949,

is not, for the purposes of this Act, a visitor of the occupier of those premises.

2. Extent of occupier's ordinary duty.

(1) An occupier of premises owes the same duty, the 'common duty of care', to all his visitors, except in so far as he is free to and does extend, restrict, modify or exclude his duty to any visitor or visitors by agreement or otherwise.

(2) The common duty of care is a duty to take such care as in all the circumstances of the case is reasonable to see that the visitor will be reasonably safe in using the premises for the purposes for which he is invited or permitted by the occupier to be there.

(3) The circumstances relevant for the present purpose include the degree of care, and of want of care, which would ordinarily be looked for in such a visitor, so that (for example) in proper cases—

(a) an occupier must be prepared for children to be less careful than adults; and

(b) an occupier may expect that a person, in the exercise of his calling, will appreci-ate and guard against any special risks ordinarily incident to it, so far as the occupier leaves him free to do so.

(4) In determining whether the occupier of premises has discharged the common duty of care to a visitor, regard is to be had to all the circumstances, so that (for example)—

(a) where damage is caused to a visitor by a danger of which he had been warned by the occupier, the warning is not to be treated without more as absolving the occupier from liability, unless in all the circumstances it was enough to enable the visitor to be reasonably safe; and

(b) where damage is caused to a visitor by a danger due to the faulty execution of any work of construction, maintenance or repair by an independent contractor employed by the occupier, the occupier is not to be treated without more as answerable for the danger if in all the circumstances he had acted reasonably in entrusting the work to an independent contractor and had taken such steps (if any) as he reasonably ought in order to satisfy himself that the contractor was competent and that the work had been properly done.

(5) The common duty of care does not impose on an occupier any obligation to a visitor in respect of risks willingly accepted as his by the visitor (the question whether a risk was so accepted to be decided on the same principles as in other cases in which one person owes a duty of care to another).

(6) For the purposes of this section, persons who enter premises for any purpose in the exercise of a right conferred by law are to be treated as permitted by the occupier to be there for that purpose, whether they in fact have his permission or not.

6.1.2 Occupier

One of the first questions to arise out of this statute is this. Who is an 'occupier'?

Wheat v E Lacon & Co Ltd [1966] AC 552, HL

This was an action for damages by a paying guest against an owner of a public house. The House of Lords (Viscount Dilhorne and Lords Denning, Morris, Pearce and Pearson) dismissed the claim but held that the owners were an occupier of the premises.

Lord Denning: My Lords, The 'Golfers' Arms' at Great Yarmouth is owned by the brewery company, E Lacon & Co Ltd. The ground floor was run as a public-house by Mr Richardson as manager for the brewery company. The first floor was used by Mr and Mrs Richardson as their private dwelling. In the summer Mrs Richardson took in guests for her private profit. Mr and Mrs Wheat and their family were summer guests of Mrs Richardson. About 9 pm one evening, when it was getting dark, Mr Wheat fell down the back staircase in the private portion and was killed. Winn J held that there were two causes: (i) the handrail was too short because it did not stretch to the foot of the stairs; (ii) someone had taken the bulb out of the light at the top of the stairs.

The case raises this point of law: did the brewery company owe any duty to Mr Wheat to see that the handrail was safe to use or to see that the stairs were properly lighted? That depends on whether the brewery company was 'an occupier' of the private portion of the 'Golfers' Arms,' and Mr Wheat its 'visitor' within the Occupiers' Liability Act, 1957: for, if so, the brewery company owed him the 'common duty of care.'...

In the Occupiers' Liability Act, 1957, the word 'occupier' is used in the same sense as it was used in the common law cases on occupiers' liability for dangerous premises. It was simply a convenient word to denote a person who had a sufficient degree of control over premises to put him under a duty of care towards those who came lawfully on to the premises. Those persons were divided into two categories, invitees and licensees: and a higher duty was owed to invitees than to licensees. But by the year 1956 the distinction between invitees and licensees had been reduced to vanishing point. The duty of the occupier had become simply a duty to take reasonable care to see that the premises were reasonably safe for people coming lawfully on to them: and it made no difference whether they were invitees or licensees: see *Slater v Clay Cross Co Ltd*. The Act of 1957 confirmed the process. It did away, once and for all, with invitees and licensees and classed them all as 'visitors'; and it put upon the occupier the same duty to all of them, namely, the common duty of care. This duty is simply a particular instance of the general duty of care which each man owes to his 'neighbour.'... Translating this general principle into its particular application to dangerous premises, it becomes simply this: wherever a person has a sufficient degree of control over premises that he ought to realise that any failure on his part to use care may result in injury to a person coming lawfully there, then he is an 'occupier' and the person coming lawfully there is his 'visitor': and the 'occupier' is under a duty to his 'visitor' to use reasonable care. In order to be an 'occupier' it is not necessary for a person to have entire control over the premises. He need not have exclusive occupation. Suffice it that he has some degree of control. He may share the control with others. Two or more may be 'occupiers.' And whenever this happens, each is under a duty to use care towards persons coming lawfully on to the premises, dependent on his degree of control. If each fails in his duty, each is liable to a visitor who is injured in consequence of his failure, but each may have a claim to contribution from the other.

In *Salmond on Torts*, 14th ed (1965), p. 372, it is said that an 'occupier' is 'he who has the immediate supervision and control and the power of permitting or prohibiting the entry of other persons.' This definition was adopted by Roxburgh J in *Hartwell v Grayson, Rollo and Clover Docks Ltd* and by Diplock LJ in the present case. There is no doubt that a person who fulfils that test is an 'occupier.' He is the person who says 'come in.' But I think that test is too narrow by far. There are other people who are 'occupiers,' even though they do not say 'come in.' If a person has any degree of control over the state of the premises it is enough...

What did the common duty of care demand of each of these occupiers towards their visitors? Each was under a duty to take such care as 'in all the circumstances of the case' is reasonable to see that the visitor will be reasonably safe. So far as the brewery company are concerned, the circumstances demanded that on the ground floor they should, by their servants, take care not only of the structure of the building, but also the furniture, the state of the floors and lighting, and so forth, at all hours of day or night when the premises were open. But in regard to the private portion, the circumstances did not demand so much of the brewery company. They ought to see that the structure was reasonably safe, including the handrail, and that the system of lighting was efficient. But I doubt whether they were bound to see that the lights were properly switched on or the rugs laid safely on the floor. The brewery company were entitled to leave those day-to-day matters to Mr and Mrs Richardson. They, too, were occupiers. The circumstances of the case demanded that Mr and Mrs Richardson should take care of those matters in the private portion of the house. And of other matters, too. If they had realised the handrail was dangerous, they should have reported it to the brewery company.

We are not concerned here with Mr and Mrs Richardson. The judge has absolved them from any negligence and there is no appeal. We are only concerned with the brewery company. They were, in my opinion, occupiers and under a duty of care. In this respect I agree with Sellers LJ and Winn J, but I come to a different conclusion on the facts. I can see no evidence of any breach of duty by the brewery company...

NOTE

The occupiers were held not liable because there was no breach of the s 2 common duty of care. In other words, they had on the facts not been careless.

6.1.3 Visitor

Having defined an occupier, the next question is to determine who is a 'visitor'.

Phipps v Rochester Corporation [1955] 1 QB 450, QBD

This was an action for damages by a young boy, five years old at the time of the accident, who was injured on the defendants' land when he fell into a trench dug on the land to lay a pipe. The defendants knew that people crossed the land and seemingly did not object; the child was accordingly an invitee (visitor) and not a trespasser. However the judge held the corporation not liable.

Devlin J: ... A licensor who tacitly permits the public to use his land without discriminating between its members must assume that the public may include little children. But as a general rule he will have discharged his duty towards them if the dangers which they may encounter are only those which are obvious to a guardian or of which he has given a warning comprehensible by a guardian. To every general rule there are, of course, exceptions. A licensor cannot divest himself of the obligation of finding out something about the sort of people who are availing themselves of his permission and the sort of use they are making, of it. He may have to take into account the social habits of the neighbourhood. No doubt there are places where little children go to play unaccompanied. If the licensor knows or ought to anticipate that, he may have to take steps accordingly. But the responsibility for the safety of little children must rest primarily upon the parents; it is their duty to see that such children are not allowed to wander about by themselves, or at the least to satisfy themselves that the places to which they do allow their children to go unaccompanied are safe for them to go to. It would not be socially desirable if parents were, as a matter of course, able to shift the burden of looking after their children from their own shoulders to those of persons who happen to have accessible bits of land. Different considerations may well apply to public parks or to recognized playing grounds where parents allow their children to go unaccompanied in the reasonable belief that they are safe...

NOTE

This case was decided before the 1957 Act and thus the issue to be determined was whether the child was a 'licensee'. However it remains relevant because a 'licensee' is a 'visitor' and thus the occupier of the land, had this case occurred after 1957, would owe a s 2 common duty of care to the child. The occupier was not liable because he had 'discharged his duty', that is to say he had not been negligent. Where Devlin J is confusing is that he justifies this discharge on the basis of a parental 'duty'. This is fair enough in one sense, but care must be taken to keep the existence of a duty and its breach quite separate.

QUESTION

Given that Devlin J's decision remains of relevance in relation to the 1957 Act, are different types of duty being reintroduced under the guise of breach?

6.1.4 Independent contractor

The 1957 Act specifically states in s 2(3)(b) that an occupier is entitled to expect that a person who enters in the exercise of a calling will appreciate any risks with respect to this calling. This section was considered in the next case.

Roles v Nathan [1963] 1 WLR 1117, CA

Lord Denning MR: This case arises out of a tragic accident which took place on Friday, December 12, 1958, when two chimney sweeps were overcome by fumes, and died in the basement of the Manchester Assembly Rooms. Their widows bring the action against the occupier, Mr Nathan, claiming that he was at fault and in breach of the duty of care which is now laid down by the Occupiers' Liability Act, 1957...

The occupier now appeals and says that it is not a case of negligence and contributory negligence, but that, on the true application of the Occupiers' Liability Act, 1957, the occupier was not liable at all...

...[T]he Act goes on to give examples of the circumstances that are relevant. The particular one in question here is in subsection (3) of section 2...

...The risk of a defective window is a special risk, but it is ordinarily incident to the calling of a window cleaner, and so he must take care for himself, and not expect the householder to do so. Likewise in the case of a chimney sweep who comes to sweep the chimneys or to seal up a sweep-hole. The householder can reasonably expect the sweep to take care of himself so far as any dangers from the flues are concerned. These chimney sweeps ought to have known that there might be dangerous fumes about and ought to have taken steps to guard against them. They ought to have known that they should not attempt to seal up a sweep-hole whilst the fire was still alight. They ought to have had the fire withdrawn before they attempted to seal it up, or at any rate they ought not to have stayed in the alcove too long when there might be dangerous fumes about. All this was known to these two sweeps; they were repeatedly warned about it, and it was for them to guard against the danger. It was not for the occupier to do it, even though he was present and heard the warnings. When a householder calls in a specialist to deal with a defective installation on his premises, he can reasonably expect the specialist to appreciate and guard against the dangers arising from the defect. The householder is not bound to watch over him to see that he comes to no harm. I would hold, therefore, that the occupier here was under no duty of care to these sweeps, at any rate in regard to the dangers which caused their deaths. If it had been a different danger, as for instance if the stairs leading to the cellar gave way, the occupier might no doubt be responsible, but not for these dangers which were special risks ordinarily incidental to their calling.

Even if I am wrong about this point, and the occupier was under a duty of care to these chimney sweeps, the question arises whether the duty was discharged by the warning that was given to them...

...I am quite clear that the warnings which were given to the sweeps were enough to enable them to be reasonably safe. The sweeps would have been quite safe if they had heeded these warnings. They should not have come back that evening and attempted to seal up the sweep-hole while the fire was still alight. They ought to have waited till next morning, and then they should have seen that the fire was out before they attempted to seal up the sweep-hole. In any case they should not have stayed too long in the sweep-hole. In short, it was entirely their own fault. The judge held that it was

▶

contributory negligence. I would go further and say that under the Act the occupier has, by the warnings, discharged his duty.

I would therefore be in favour of allowing this appeal and entering judgment for the defendants.

[Harman LJ agreed that the appeal should be allowed; Pearson LJ dissented.]

QUESTIONS

1. Could this case be explained in terms of causation? (Cf **Chapter 10.**)

2. What if an independent contractor, while working on the occupier's land, injures another visitor on the same property? If the independent contractor turns out to have no insurance, might the occupier be liable under the 1957 Act?

Gwilliam v West Hertfordshire Hospital NHS Trust [2002] 3 WLR 1425, CA

(For facts and other extracts see p 123)

Waller LJ: ... **40** If one goes back to the wording of section 2(4)(b) of the 1957 Act it will be seen that there are two obligations on the employer of an independent contractor, one is 'to act reasonably in entrusting the work to an independent contractor' and the other is to take steps to satisfy himself about the competence etc. If a hospital reasonably wishes to have a somewhat hazardous activity on its land in order to raise money, but wishes to entrust the operation of that activity to an independent contractor, has the hospital acted 'reasonably' in the selection of that independent contractor if it has not checked the viability and/or insurance position so far as that independent contractor is concerned? In my view, the language of that section of the 1957 Act allows for consideration of the viability of the independent contractor. It might be said that the section only related to work of 'construction, maintenance or repair' but I would suggest that the concepts identified by the section also reflect the position at common law and that, thus, if someone like the hospital seeks to use an independent contractor for carrying out the sort of activities that are the subject of this case, it may be held not to act reasonably if it does not check the viability of that independent contractor...

43 I would emphasise that I am not saying that, in relation to every independent contractor employed, there is a duty to check the insurance or viability. It is the nature of the activities which, if not extra-hazardous, were hazardous, in which people were being invited by the hospital to take part, which to my mind distinguishes this case from other cases involving independent contractors...

6.1.5 Occupier's duty to trespassers

The 1957 Act established a common duty of care between occupier and visitor; it said nothing about the person who entered land as a trespasser. Logically, therefore, one could conclude that, up until 1984, no duty was owed to the trespasser. But, as the extract below indicates, the legal situation was not quite so simple. In 1984 the position was amended by statute and this Act immediately follows the judicial extract below.

Tomlinson v Congleton BC [2004] 1 AC 46, HL

(For facts see below p 197)

Lord Hoffmann: ... **6** The 1957 Act was passed to amend and codify the common law duties of occupiers to certain persons who came upon their land. The common law had distinguished between invitees, in whose visit the occupier had some material interest, and licensees, who came simply by express or implied permission. Different duties were owed to each class. The Act, on the recommendation of the Law Reform Committee (Third Report: Occupiers' Liability to Invitees, Licensees and Trespassers (1954) (Cmd 9305)), amalgamated (without redefining) the two common law categories, designated the combined class 'visitors' (section 1(2)) and provided that (subject to contrary agreement) all visitors should be owed a 'common duty of care'...

8 ... At common law the only duty to trespassers was not to cause them deliberate or reckless injury, but after an inconclusive attempt by the House of Lords to modify this rule in *Herrington v British Railways Board* [1972] AC 877, the Law Commission recommended the creation of a statutory duty to trespassers: see its Report on Liability for Damage or Injury to Trespassers and Related Questions of Occupiers' Liability (1976) (Law Com No 75) (Cmnd 6428). The recommendation was given effect by the 1984 Act...

Occupiers' Liability Act 1984 (c 3)

1. Duty of occupier to persons other than his visitors.

(1) The rules enacted by this section shall have effect, in place of the rules of the common law, to determine—
    (a) whether any duty is owed by a person as occupier of premises to persons other than his visitors in respect of any risk of their suffering injury on the premises by reason of any danger due to the state of the premises or to things done or omitted to be done on them; and
    (b) if so, what that duty is.

(2) For the purposes of this section, the persons who are to be treated respectively as an occupier of any premises (which, for those purposes, include any fixed or movable structure) and as his visitors are—
    (a) any person who owes in relation to the premises the duty referred to in section 2 of the Occupiers' Liability Act 1957 (the common duty of care), and
    (b) those who are his visitors for the purposes of that duty.

(3) An occupier of premises owes a duty to another (not being his visitor) in respect of any such risk as is referred to in subsection (1) above if—
    (a) he is aware of the danger or has reasonable grounds to believe that it exists;
    (b) he knows or has reasonable grounds to believe that the other is in the vicinity of the danger concerned or that he may come into the vicinity of the danger (in either case, whether the other has lawful authority for being in that vicinity or not); and

▶

(c)   the risk is one against which, in all the circumstances of the case, he may reasonably be expected to offer the other some protection.

(4)   Where, by virtue of this section, an occupier of premises owes a duty to another in respect of such a risk, the duty is to take such care as is reasonable in all the circumstances of the case to see that he does not suffer injury on the premises by reason of the danger concerned.

(5)   Any duty owed by virtue of this section in respect of a risk may, in an appropriate case, be discharged by taking such steps as are reasonable in all the circumstances of the case to give warning of the danger concerned or to discourage persons from incurring the risk.

(6)   No duty is owed by virtue of this section to any person in respect of risks willingly accepted as his by that person (the question whether a risk was so accepted to be decided on the same principles as in other cases in which one person owes a duty of care to another).

(6A) At any time when the right conferred by section 2(1) of the Countryside and Rights of Way Act 2000 is exercisable in relation to land which is access land for the purposes of Part I of that Act, an occupier of the land owes (...) no duty by virtue of this section to any person in respect of—
       (a)   a risk resulting from the existence of any natural feature of the landscape, or any river, stream, ditch or pond whether or not a natural feature, or
       (b)   a risk of that person suffering injury when passing over, under or through any wall, fence or gate, except by proper use of the gate or of a stile...

(7)   No duty is owed by virtue of this section to persons using the highway, and this section does not affect any duty owed to such persons.

(8)   Where a person owes a duty by virtue of this section, he does not, by reason of any breach of the duty, incur any liability in respect of any loss of or damage to property.

(9)   In this section—

       'highway' means any part of a highway other than a ferry or waterway;

       'injury' means anything resulting in death or personal injury, including any disease and any impairment of physical or mental condition; and

       'movable structure' includes any vessel, vehicle or aircraft.

NOTE

The relationship between the Act of 1957 and that of 1984 is dealt with in the following extracts.

Tomlinson v Congleton BC [2004] 1 AC 46, HL

(For facts see below)

Lord Hoffmann: ... **38** ... Parliament has made it clear that in the case of a lawful visitor, one starts from the assumption that there is a duty whereas in the case of a trespasser one starts from the assumption that there is none.

Lord Hobhouse: ... **68** The two Acts apply the same general policy and the 1984 Act is a supplement to the 1957 Act... The 1984 Act made provision for when a duty of care should be owed to persons who were not visitors (I will for the sake of convenience call such persons 'trespassers') and what the duty should then be, that is, a duty of care in the terms of section 1(3), more narrow than that imposed by the 1957 Act. Thus the duty owed to visitors and the lesser duty which may be owed to trespassers was defined in appropriate terms. But, in each Act, there are further provisions which define the content of the duty and, depending upon the particular circumstances, its scope and extent...

NOTE

Many of the cases that have arisen since 1984 have involved trespassers entering property and diving into pools, lakes or sea with tragic results. Two cases that came before the Court of Appeal seemed to go in different directions, but the matter now appears to have been settled on appeal from one of these cases to the House of Lords.

Tomlinson v Congleton BC [2004] 1 AC 46, HL

This was an action for damages by a teenager who had entered land owned by the local authority and dived into a lake on the property suffering severe injury when his head struck the bottom. The defendant local authority was aware that people were attracted by the lake and prominent notices declared that swimming was prohibited. The defendants were equally aware that these notices were often ignored and they intended, when finances permitted, to plant vegetation around the lake that would physically prevent people from entering the water. However at the time of the accident the vegetation plan had not been executed. A majority of the Court of Appeal gave judgment for the teenager, but this was reversed by the House of Lords (Lords Nicholls, Hoffmann, Hobhouse and Scott; Lord Hutton dubitante).

Lord Hoffmann: ... **4** It is a terrible tragedy to suffer such dreadful injury in consequence of a relatively minor act of carelessness. It came nowhere near the stupidity of Luke Ratcliff, a student who climbed a fence at 2.30 a m on a December morning to take a running dive into the shallow end of a swimming pool (see *Ratcliff v McConnell* [1999] 1 WLR 670) or John Donoghue, who dived into Folkestone Harbour from a slipway at midnight on 27 December after an evening in the pub: *Donoghue v Folkestone Properties Ltd* [2003] QB 1008. John Tomlinson's mind must often recur to that hot day which irretrievably changed his life. He may feel, not unreasonably, that fate has dealt with him unfairly. And so in these proceedings he seeks financial compensation: for the

▶

loss of his earning capacity, for the expense of the care he will need, for the loss of the ability to lead an ordinary life. But the law does not provide such compensation simply on the basis that the injury was disproportionately severe in relation to one's own fault or even not one's own fault at all. Perhaps it should, but society might not be able to afford to compensate everyone on that principle, certainly at the level at which such compensation is now paid. The law provides compensation only when the injury was someone else's fault. In order to succeed in his claim, that is what Mr Tomlinson has to prove...

The scope of the duty under the 1984 Act

25 The conditions in section 1(3) of the 1984 Act determine whether or not a duty is owed to 'another' in respect of 'any such risk as is referred to in subsection (1)'. Two conclusions follow from this language. First, the risks in respect of which the Act imposes a duty are limited to those mentioned in subsection (1)(a) – risks of injury 'by reason of any danger due to the state of the premises or to things done or omitted to be done on them'. The Act is not concerned with risks due to anything else. Secondly, the conditions have to be satisfied in respect of the claimant as 'another'; that is to say, in respect of a class of persons which includes him and a description of risk which includes that which caused his injury...

28 Mr Braithwaite was inclined to accept the difficulty of establishing that the risk was due to the state of the premises... Ward LJ said that the water was 'a siren call strong enough to turn stout men's minds'. In my opinion this is gross hyperbole. The trouble with the island of the Sirens was not the state of the premises. It was that the Sirens held mariners spellbound until they died of hunger. The beach, give or take a fringe of human bones, was an ordinary Mediterranean beach. If Odysseus had gone ashore and accidentally drowned himself having a swim, Penelope would have had no action against the Sirens for luring him there with their songs. Likewise in this case, the water was perfectly safe for all normal activities. In my opinion 'things done or omitted to be done' means activities or the lack of precautions which cause risk, like allowing speedboats among the swimmers. It is a mere circularity to say that a failure to stop people getting into the water was an omission which gave rise to a duty to take steps to stop people from getting into the water.

29 It follows that in my opinion, there was no risk to Mr Tomlinson due to the state of the premises or anything done or omitted upon the premises. That means that there was no risk of a kind which gave rise to a duty under the 1957 or 1984 Acts. I shall nevertheless go on to consider the matter on the assumption that there was...

Free will

44 The second consideration, namely the question of whether people should accept responsibility for the risks they choose to run, is the point made by Lord Phillips of Worth Matravers MR in *Donoghue v Folkestone Properties Ltd* [2003] QB 1008, 1024, para 53 and which I said was central to this appeal. Mr Tomlinson was freely and voluntarily undertaking an activity which inherently involved some risk. By contrast, Miss Bessie Stone (*Bolton v Stone* [1951] AC 850), to whom the House of Lords held that no duty was owed, was innocently standing on the pavement outside her garden gate at 10 Beckenham Road, Cheetham when she was struck by a ball hit for six out of the Cheetham Cricket Club ground. She was certainly not engaging in any activity which involved an inherent risk of such injury. So compared with *Bolton v Stone*, this is an a fortiori case.

45 I think it will be extremely rare for an occupier of land to be under a duty to prevent people from taking risks which are inherent in the activities they freely choose to undertake upon the land. If people want to climb mountains, go hang-gliding or swim or dive in ponds or lakes, that is their affair. Of course the landowner may for his own reasons wish to prohibit such activities. He may think that they are a danger or inconvenience to himself or others. Or he may take a paternalist view and prefer people not to undertake risky activities on his land. He is entitled to impose such conditions, as the Council did by prohibiting swimming. But the law does not require him to do so.

46 My Lords, as will be clear from what I have just said, I think that there is an important question of freedom at stake. It is unjust that the harmless recreation of responsible parents and children with buckets and spades on the beaches should be prohibited in order to comply with what is thought to be a legal duty to safeguard irresponsible visitors against dangers which are perfectly obvious. The fact that such people take no notice of warnings cannot create a duty to take other steps to protect them. I find it difficult to express with appropriate moderation my disagreement with the proposition of Sedley LJ [2003] 2 WLR 1120, 1135, para 45, that it is 'only where the risk is so obvious that the occupier can safely assume that nobody will take it that there will be no liability'. A duty to protect against obvious risks or self-inflicted harm exists only in cases in which there is no genuine and informed choice, as in the case of employees, or some lack of capacity, such as the inability of children to recognise danger (*Herrington v British Railways Board* [1972] AC 877) or the despair of prisoners which may lead them to inflict injury on themselves: *Reeves v Comr of Police of the Metropolis* [2000] 1 AC 360...

Lord Scott: ... **91** In the present case it seems to me unreal to regard Mr Tomlinson's injury as having been caused while he was a trespasser. His complaint, rejected by the trial judge but accepted by the majority in the Court of Appeal, was that the council ought to have taken effective steps to discourage entry by visitors into the waters of the lake. The notices were held to be inadequate discouragement. But, if there was this duty, it was a duty owed to visitors. The people who read the notices, or who could have read them but failed to do so, would have been visitors. These were the people to be discouraged. The alleged duty was a 1957 Act duty...

94 ... [The claimant] was a high-spirited young man enjoying himself with his friends in a pleasant park with a pleasant water facility. If he had set out to swim across the lake, it might have been relevant to speak of his taking an obvious risk. If he had climbed a tree with branches overhanging the lake and had dived from a branch into the water he would have been courting an obvious danger. But he was not doing any such thing. He was simply sporting about in the water with his friends, giving free rein to his exuberance. And why not? And why should the council be discouraged by the law of tort from providing facilities for young men and young women to enjoy themselves in this way? Of course there is some risk of accidents arising out of the joie-de-vivre of the young. But that is no reason for imposing a grey and dull safety regime on everyone. This appeal must be allowed.

QUESTIONS

1. Did the House of Lords hold in *Bolton v Stone* (1951 (p 119)) that the cricket club owed no duty of care to Miss Stone?

2. Which of the following reasons best explains the decision in *Congleton*: (a) the claimant was the cause of his own misfortune; (b) the local authority was not in breach of its duty; (c) a holding for the claimant would result, ultimately, in fewer recreational facilities for the rest of the population; (d) the local authority owed no duty to the claimant in respect of the damage that actually occurred? What if the claimant had been a boy of 10 years of age?

3. Can Congleton BC now abandon its plan to plant vegetation around the lake?

6.2 Liability for land and structures (2): off the land

The distinction between duties owed by an occupier and (or) owner to persons on the land and off the land is alluded to in s 1(7) of the Occupiers' Liability Act 1984. As one might expect, the main reason for such a difference of duty is to be found in different causes of action. The duty owed by an occupier to his visitor is, of course, one that arises out of the tort of negligence ('common duty of care'). However, liability for the state of the premises to persons on the highway predates the establishment of a general tort of negligence and sounded in the tort of public nuisance. This tort is often regarded as one of strict liability. Where the victim is on neighbouring private land, rather than the highway, the tort of private nuisance is relevant provided that there is some degree of continuity with respect to the nuisance. A single escape from land of a dangerous thing could give rise to a claim under the rule in *Rylands v Fletcher* (1868) (p 217). Again these last two torts are often regarded as strict liability, although negligence is gradually invading their territory. Statute has also created some extra duties.

6.2.1 Liability to persons on the highway (public nuisance)

Liability in public nuisance to persons off the premises can arise, as the next three extracts show, either from activities being carried out on the land or from the state of the premises or other man-made (?) structures on the land.

Wandsworth LBC v Railtrack plc [2002] QB 756, CA

Chadwick LJ: 29 I agree that this appeal should be dismissed.

30 Wandsworth London Borough Council is the highway authority in respect of that part of Balham High Road which adjoins Balham station. The street is crossed by a railway bridge which is now vested in Railtrack plc as part of its undertaking. The construction of the railway bridge is such that it provides a convenient roost to the numerous feral pigeons attracted to the area by the ready availability of food in the vicinity. The obvious consequences of pigeon infestation ensue, to the annoyance and inconvenience of pedestrians using the highway beneath the bridge. The judge found, 'as a matter of fact and degree' that the pigeon infestation and the fouling caused by it amounted to a nuisance; that is to say that there was a substantial interference with the comfort and convenience of the public or a significant class of the public who use the footpaths or pavements. There is no challenge to that finding. Nor could there be; the evidence was overwhelming.

31 It is the duty of the council, as local highway authority, to assert and protect the rights of the public to the use and enjoyment of Balham High Road, including the pavements provided for pedestrian use: see section 130(1) of the Highways Act 1980. In furtherance of that duty the council has brought these proceedings against Railtrack plc as the owners of the bridge. The issue on this appeal is whether the judge was right to find, as he did, that Railtrack were liable for the public nuisance arising from the pigeon infestation.

32 The liability of a landowner for a public nuisance on or emanating from his land was recognised by this court over one hundred years ago in *Attorney General v Tod Heatley* [1897] 1 Ch 560.... Liability in public nuisance arises where the landowner has knowledge of the existence of a nuisance on or emanating from his land, where there are means reasonably open to him for preventing or abating it, and where he fails to take those means within a reasonable time...

33 The three elements of knowledge, means to abate and failure to take those means are all present in the present case. In my view, the judge was plainly correct to find that liability in public nuisance had been established. I agree, also, that he was entitled to make an order for the payment of damages in addition to the declaration which he granted.

[Kennedy LJ delivered a judgment dismissing the appeal and Rougier LJ agreed with the judgments.]

QUESTION

An old tree on D's land collapses onto the highway and destroys C's parked car. Assuming the collapse was caused by a latent disease in the roots, will D be liable to C? (Cf *Caminer v Northern and London Investment Trust* (1951).)

NOTES

1. See also *Att-Gen v PYA Quarries* (p 68) and *R v Rimmington* (2005) (especially paras 5–7).

2. *Wandsworth* dealt with a nuisance to those on the highway. The next case concerns a dangerous state of affairs that injures a neighbouring property.

Wringe v Cohen [1940] 1 KB 229, CA

This was an action for damages by the owner of a shop against the landlord of a neighbouring property for damage caused to the shop when the gable end of the defendant's house collapsed during a storm. The Court of Appeal (Slesser and Luxmoore LJJ and Atkinson J) dismissed an appeal from a county court judgment holding the defendant liable.

Atkinson J: ... In our judgment if, owing to want of repair, premises on a highway become dangerous and, therefore, a nuisance, and a passer-by or an adjoining owner suffers damage by their collapse, the occupier, or the owner if he has undertaken the

▶

duty of repair, is answerable whether he knew or ought to have known of the danger or not. The undertaking to repair gives the owner control of the premises, and a right of access thereto for the purpose of maintaining them in a safe condition. On the other hand, if the nuisance is created, not by want of repair, but, for example, by the act of a trespasser, or by a secret and unobservable operation of nature, such as a subsidence under or near the foundations of the premises, neither an occupier nor an owner responsible for repair is answerable, unless with knowledge or means of knowledge he allows the danger to continue. In such a case he has in no sense caused the nuisance by any act or breach of duty. I think that every case decided in the English Courts is consistent with this view.

By common law it is an indictable offence for an occupier of premises on a highway to permit them to get into a dangerous condition owing to non-repair. It was not and is not necessary in an indictment to aver knowledge or means of knowledge ...

QUESTIONS

1. Was the defendant held liable in public or private nuisance?

2. What is the level of duty owed by an occupier to a passer-by? Does the next case give a clear answer?

Mint v Good [1951] 1 KB 517, CA

This was an action for damages by a boy against the owner of premises for injury sustained by the boy on a public highway when a wall on the premises collapsed onto him. The trial judge dismissed the action against the owner on the ground that the owner, who had let the premises to tenants, had not reserved the right of entry to make repairs. An appeal to the Court of Appeal (Somervell, Denning and Birkett LJJ) was allowed.

Denning LJ: ... The law of England has always taken particular care to protect those who use a highway. It puts on the occupier of adjoining premises a special responsibility for the structures which he keeps beside the highway. So long as those structures are safe, all well and good; but if they fall into disrepair, so as to be a potential danger to passers-by, then they are a nuisance, and, what is more, a public nuisance; and the occupier is liable to anyone using the highway who is injured by reason of the disrepair. It is no answer for him to say that he and his servants took reasonable care; for, even if he has employed a competent independent contractor to repair the structure, and has every reason for supposing it to be safe, the occupier is still liable if the independent contractor did the work badly: see *Tarry v Ashton*.

The occupier's duty to passers-by is to see that the structure is as safe as reasonable care can make it; a duty which is as high as the duty which an occupier owes to people who pay to come on to his premises. He is not liable for latent defects, which could not be discovered by reasonable care on the part of anyone, nor for acts of trespassers of which he neither knew, nor ought to have known: see *Barker v Herbert*; but he is liable when structures fall into dangerous disrepair, because there must be some fault on the part of someone or other for that to happen; and he is responsible for it to persons using the highway, even though he was not actually at fault himself. That principle was laid down in this court in *Wringe v Cohen*, where it is to be noted that the principle is confined to 'premises on a highway' ...

The question in this case is whether the owner, as well as the occupier, is under a like duty to passers-by. I think he is. The law has shown a remarkable development on this point during the last sixteen years. The three cases of *Wilchick v Marks and Silverstone*, *Wringe v Cohen* and *Heap v Ind Coope and Allsopp Ltd* show that the courts are now taking a realistic view of these matters. They recognise that the occupying tenant of a small dwelling-house does not in practice do the structural repairs, but the owner does; and that if a passer-by is injured by the structure being in dangerous disrepair, the occupier has not the means to pay damages, but the owner has, or, at any rate, he can insure against it. If a passer-by is injured by the structure falling on him, he should be entitled to damages from someone, and the person who ought to pay is the owner, because he is in practice responsible for the repairs...

That is sufficient for the decision of this case, but I venture to doubt in these days whether a landlord can exempt himself from liability to passers-by by taking a covenant from a tenant to repair the structure adjoining the highway ... The liability of the owner is a liability in tort and cannot be affected by the terms of the agreement between himself and his tenant. Just as a manufacturer who is liable under the principle in *Donoghue v Stevenson* cannot exempt himself from liability to the public by the terms of his contract with the wholesaler, so also I should doubt whether a property owner could exempt himself by the terms of his contract with the tenant...

QUESTION

Is Denning LJ holding the landlord liable in negligence or public nuisance? Does it matter? (Cf Denning LJ's judgment in *Esso v Southport Corpn*, pp 4, 34.)

NOTE

A landlord's duty in respect of demised premises is now subject to a statutory duty.

Defective Premises Act 1972 (c 35)

3. Duty of care with respect to work done on premises not abated by disposal of premises.

(1) Where work of construction, repair, maintenance or demolition or any other work is done on or in relation to premises, any duty of care owed, because of the doing of the work, to persons who might reasonably be expected to be affected by defects in the state of the premises created by the doing of the work shall not be abated by the subsequent disposal of the premises by the person who owed the duty...

▶

4. Landlord's duty of care in virtue of obligation or right to repair premises demised.

(1) Where premises are let under a tenancy which puts on the landlord an obligation to the tenant for the maintenance or repair of the premises the landlord owes to all persons who might reasonably be expected to be affected by defects in the state of the premises a duty to take such care as is reasonable in all the circumstances to see that they are reasonably safe from personal injury or from damage to their property caused by a relevant defect.

(2) The said duty is owed if the landlord knows (whether as the result of being notified by the tenant or otherwise) or if he ought in all the circumstances to have known of the relevant defect...

QUESTION

Is this statutory duty of care in s 4 a lower duty than the one in (a) *Wringe v Cohen* and (b) *Mint v Good*?

6.2.2 Liability to neighbours (private nuisance)

Where an activity on land, or the state of the property, causes injury to a neighbouring occupier or landowner, a different cause of action comes into play. It is a matter of private rather than public nuisance. The distinction between public nuisance, private nuisance and negligence is explained in the first short extract. And this is followed by decisions setting out the main elements of private nuisance.

Wandsworth LBC v Railtrack plc [2002] QB 756, CA

(For facts and decision see p 200)

Kennedy LJ: ... **6** Public nuisance is also a crime, and a person is said to be guilty if he does an act not warranted by law or omits to discharge a legal duty if the effect of the act is to endanger the life, health, property, morals or comfort of the public, or to obstruct the public in the exercise or enjoyment of rights common to all: see *Archbold, Criminal Pleading, Evidence and Practice*, 2001 ed, para 31–40. Private nuisance is different. It is the wrongful interference with another's use or enjoyment of land, or of some right over or in connection therewith, and negligence arises where the relationship between the parties is such as to give rise to a duty of care...

NOTE

The overlap of public and private nuisance is to be found in the next case as well. However, before turning to this case, it may be useful to examine, once again, the basic elements of public and private nuisance in Denning LJ's judgment in *Esso v Southport* (p 4). More detailed principles with respect to private nuisance are contained in the case extracted below.

Halsey v Esso Petroleum Co Ltd [1961] 1 WLR 683, QBD

This was an action for damages and an injunction against an oil company in respect of a nuisance associated with one of the company's oil distribution depots in London. The claimant complained of acid smuts from the depot's chimneys which caused damage to his washing in his garden and car parked on the highway; of a pungent and nauseating smell; of noise from the boilers; and of noise at night from road tankers coming and going from the depot. The judge held there was a public nuisance in respect of the damage to the car and of the noise at night; and a private nuisance with regard to the washing and the boiler noise. The acid smuts also gave rise to a liability under *Rylands v Fletcher* (see p 217).

Veale J: ... So far as the present case is concerned, liability for nuisance by harmful deposits could be established by proving damage by the deposits to the property in question, provided of course that the injury was not merely trivial. Negligence is not an ingredient of the cause of action, and the character of the neighbourhood is not a matter to be taken into consideration. On the other hand, nuisance by smell or noise is something to which no absolute standard can be applied. It is always a question of degree whether the interference with comfort or convenience is sufficiently serious to constitute a nuisance. The character of the neighbourhood is very relevant and all the relevant circumstances have to be taken into account. What might be a nuisance in one area is by no means necessarily so in another. In an urban area, everyone must put up with a certain amount of discomfort and annoyance from the activities of neighbours, and the law must strike a fair and reasonable balance between the right of the plaintiff on the one hand to the undisturbed enjoyment of his property, and the right of the defendant on the other hand to use his property for his own lawful enjoyment. That is how I approach this case...

It is said by the defendants that since the public highway is for the use of everyone, the plaintiff cannot complain if all the defendants do is to make use of their right to use the public highway. I agree, if that is all that the defendants have done. If a person makes an unreasonable use of the public highway, for instance, by parking stationary vehicles on it, a member of the public who suffers special damage has a cause of action against him for public nuisance. Similarly, in my view, if a person makes an unreasonable use of the public highway by concentrating in one small area of the highway vehicles in motion and a member of the public suffers special damage, he is equally entitled to complain, although in most cases concentration of moving as opposed to stationary vehicles will be more likely to be reasonable. This is a question of reasonable user...

NOTES

1. This case brings out two important points. First, the difference between public (damage to car on the highway) and private (damage to washing) nuisance, but there may be an overlap where the nuisance can be associated with both private land (depot) and public highway (road tankers). Secondly, the role of the character of the locality: this is only relevant in respect of intangible damage (noise and smell).

2. Private nuisance is a tort arising out of the use of land. It is, in other words, a liability that attaches to real property. This real property dimension affects claimants as well, as the next case confirms.

Hunter v Canary Wharf Ltd [1997] AC 655, HL

This case concerned two damages actions for nuisance, brought by two groups of claimants, in respect of a large building known as Canary Wharf. The first group complained of interference with their television reception caused by the building, while the second group complained of excessive amounts of dust caused by construction work associated with the building. The House of Lords (Lords Goff, Hoffmann, Lloyd and Hope; Lord Cooke dissented in part) dismissed the actions.

Lord Goff: ... In both actions, Judge Fox-Andrews QC made orders for the trial of a number of preliminary issues of law. Of the issues of law in the first action, two have survived to reach your Lordships' House, viz. (1) whether interference with television reception is capable of constituting an actionable nuisance, and (2) whether it is necessary to have an interest in property to claim in private nuisance and, if so, what interest in property will satisfy this requirement. In the second action, the only issue to reach your Lordships' House is the latter of these two issues...

Interference with television signals

I turn first to consider the question whether interference with television signals may give rise to an action in private nuisance. This question was first considered over 30 years ago by Buckley J in *Bridlington Relay Ltd v Yorkshire Electricity Board* [1965] Ch 436... Certainly it can be asserted with force that for many people television transcends the function of mere entertainment, and in particular that for the aged, the lonely and the bedridden it must provide a great distraction and relief from the circumscribed nature of their lives. That interference with such an amenity might in appropriate circumstances be protected by the law of nuisance has been recognised in Canada, in *Nor-Video Services Ltd v Ontario Hydro* (1978) 84 DLR (3d) 221, 231.

However, as I see the present case, there is a more formidable obstacle to this claim. This is that the complaint rests simply upon the presence of the defendants' building on land in the neighbourhood as causing the relevant interference...

As a general rule, a man is entitled to build on his own land, though nowadays this right is inevitably subject to our system of planning controls. Moreover, as a general rule, a man's right to build on his land is not restricted by the fact that the presence of the building may of itself interfere with his neighbour's enjoyment of his land. The building may spoil his neighbour's view (...); in the absence of an easement, it may restrict the flow of air on to his neighbour's land (...); and, again in the absence of an easement, it may take away light from his neighbour's windows (...): nevertheless his neighbour generally cannot complain of the presence of the building, though this may seriously detract from the enjoyment of his land... From this it follows that, in the absence of an easement, more is required than the mere presence of a neighbouring building to give rise to an actionable private nuisance. Indeed, for an action in private nuisance to lie in respect of interference with the plaintiff's enjoyment of his land, it will generally arise from something emanating from the defendant's land. Such an emanation may take many forms – noise, dirt, fumes, a noxious smell, vibrations, and suchlike. Occasionally activities on the defendant's land are in themselves so offensive to neighbours as to constitute an actionable nuisance, as in *Thompson-Schwab v Costaki* [1956] 1 WLR 335, where the sight of prostitutes and their clients entering and leaving neighbouring premises were held to fall into that category. Such cases must however be relatively rare…

For these reasons I would dismiss the appeal of the plaintiffs in the first action on this issue.

Right to sue in private nuisance

I turn next to the question of the right to sue in private nuisance. In the two cases now under appeal before your Lordships' House, one of which relates to interference with television signals and the other to the generation of dust from the construction of a road, the plaintiffs consist in each case of a substantial group of local people. Moreover they are not restricted to householders who have the exclusive right to possess the places where they live, whether as freeholders or tenants, or even as licensees. They include people with whom householders share their homes, for example as wives or husbands or partners, or as children or other relatives. All of these people are claiming damages in private nuisance, by reason of interference with their television viewing or by reason of excessive dust…

It follows that, on the authorities as they stand, an action in private nuisance will only lie at the suit of a person who has a right to the land affected. Ordinarily, such a person can only sue if he has the right to exclusive possession of the land, such as a freeholder or tenant in possession, or even a licensee with exclusive possession… But a mere licensee on the land has no right to sue.

The question therefore arises whether your Lordships should be persuaded to depart from established principle, and recognise such a right in others who are no more than mere licensees on the land. At the heart of this question lies a more fundamental question, which relates to the scope of the law of private nuisance. Here I wish to draw attention to the fact that although, in the past, damages for personal injury have been recovered at least in actions of public nuisance, there is now developing a school of thought that the appropriate remedy for such claims as these should lie in our now fully developed law of negligence, and that personal injury claims should be altogether excluded from the domain of nuisance. The most forthright proponent of this approach has been Professor Newark, in his article 'The Boundaries of Nuisance' 65 LQR 480 from which I have already quoted. Furthermore, it is now being suggested that claims in respect of physical damage to the land should also be excluded from private nuisance: see, eg, the article by Mr Conor Gearty on 'The Place of Private Nuisance in a Modern Law of Torts' [1989] CLJ 214. In any event, it is right for present purposes to regard the typical cases of private nuisance as being those concerned with interference with the enjoyment of land and, as such, generally actionable only by a person with a right in the land. Characteristic examples of cases of this kind are those concerned with noise, vibrations, noxious smells and the like. The two appeals with which your Lordships are here concerned arise from actions of this character.

For private nuisances of this kind, the primary remedy is in most cases an injunction, which is sought to bring the nuisance to an end, and in most cases should swiftly achieve that objective. The right to bring such proceedings is, as the law stands, ordinarily vested in the person who has exclusive possession of the land. He or she is the person who will

▶

sue, if it is necessary to do so. Moreover he or she can, if thought appropriate, reach an agreement with the person creating the nuisance, either that it may continue for a certain period of time, possibly on the payment of a sum of money, or that it shall cease, again perhaps on certain terms including the time within which the cessation will take place. The... efficacy of arrangements such as these depends upon the existence of an identifiable person with whom the creator of the nuisance can deal for this purpose. If anybody who lived in the relevant property as a home had the right to sue, sensible arrangements such as these might in some cases no longer be practicable...

Lord Hoffmann: ... Nuisance is a tort against land, including interests in land such as easements and profits. A plaintiff must therefore have an interest in the land affected by the nuisance...

Once it is understood that nuisances 'productive of sensible personal discomfort' (*St Helen's Smelting Co v Tipping*, 11 HL Cas 642, 650) do not constitute a separate tort of causing discomfort to people but are merely part of a single tort of causing injury to land, the rule that the plaintiff must have an interest in the land falls into place as logical and, indeed, inevitable...

Lord Cooke (dissenting in part): ... Inhabitants of the Isle of Dogs and many another concentrated urban area might react with incredulity, and justifiably so, to the suggestion that the amenity of television and radio reception is fairly comparable to a view of the surroundings of their homes. Neither in nature nor in value is that so. It may be suspected that only a lawyer would think of such a suggestion....

NOTE

The television aspect of this case is obviously an important point. But *Hunter* is a key case because it re-emphasises the difference between the torts of negligence and private nuisance. The latter attaches to land and both the claimant and the defendant must have legal connections (interest) in real property; nuisance is, in this respect, a true liability for things (land), although it extends to activities (unreasonable) on such property. Negligence in contrast attaches to a careless act of an individual. Fault, of course, may be relevant in assessing whether an activity on land amounts to an unreasonable use. Thus deliberately to annoy a neighbour will give rise to liability in private nuisance: *Hollywood Silver Fox Farm v Emmett* (see p 79).

6.2.3 Nuisance by omission (nuisance and negligence)

Liability in nuisance is not restricted to unreasonable activities on land. It can arise out of the state of the land itself or something on it. Even if the defendant did not cause the nuisance, he may become liable if he adopts it or fails to remedy a continuing nuisance.

Delaware Mansions Ltd v Westminster CC [2002] 1 AC 321, HL

This was an action for damages by the owner of a building adjoining the highway against a highway authority for the latter's failure to remove a tree whose roots were causing damage to the claimants' land and buildings. The House of Lords (Lords Steyn, Browne-Wilkinson, Cooke, Clyde and Hutton) held the authority liable for continuing a nuisance.

Lord Cooke: 3 My Lords, this case raises an issue, on which there is surprisingly little authority in English law, about the recoverability of remedial expenditure incurred after encroachment by tree roots...

29 ... I think that the answer to the issue falls to be found by applying the concepts of reasonableness between neighbours (real or figurative) and reasonable foreseeability which underlie much modern tort law and, more particularly, the law of nuisance...

31 In both the second *Wagon Mound* case and *Goldman v Hargrave* the judgments, which repay full rereading, are directed to what a reasonable person in the shoes of the defendant would have done. The label nuisance or negligence is treated as of no real significance. In this field, I think, the concern of the common law lies in working out the fair and just content and incidents of a neighbour's duty rather than affixing a label and inferring the extent of the duty from it.

33 Approaching the present case in the light of those governing concepts and the judge's findings, I think that there was a continuing nuisance... Having regard to the proximity of the plane tree to Delaware Mansions, a real risk of damage...

NOTE AND QUESTIONS

In *Holbeck Hall Hotel Ltd v Scarborough BC* (2000) Stuart-Smith LJ said the 'duty arises when the defect is known and the hazard or danger to the claimants' land is reasonably foreseeable, that is to say it is a danger which a reasonable man with knowledge of the defect should have foreseen as likely to eventuate in the reasonably near future. It is the existence of the defect coupled with the danger that constitutes the nuisance; it is knowledge or presumed knowledge of the nuisance that involves liability for continuing it when it could reasonably be abated' (§ 42). Does this test suggest that the key to liability for nuisance by omission (unreasonable use of land) is actually similar to the test for liability in negligence (unreasonable behaviour)? Perhaps the key is in the nature of the damage as the next extract suggests.

Cambridge Water Co v Eastern Counties Leather plc [1994] 2 AC 264, HL

(For facts see p 218)

Lord Goff: ... Of course, although liability for nuisance has generally been regarded as strict, at least in the case of a defendant who has been responsible for the creation of a nuisance, even so that liability has been kept under control by the principle of reasonable user – the principle of give and take as between neighbouring occupiers of land, under which 'those acts necessary for the common and ordinary use and occupation of land and houses may be done, if conveniently done, without subjecting those who do

▶

them to an action': see *Bamford v Turnley* (1862) 3 B & S 62, 83, per Bramwell B. The effect is that, if the user is reasonable, the defendant will not be liable for consequent harm to his neighbour's enjoyment of his land; but if the user is not reasonable, the defendant will be liable, even though he may have exercised reasonable care and skill to avoid it. Strikingly, a comparable principle has developed which limits liability under the rule in *Rylands v Fletcher*. This is the principle of natural use of the land...

It is, of course, axiomatic that in this field we must be on our guard, when considering liability for damages in nuisance, not to draw inapposite conclusions from cases concerned only with a claim for an injunction. This is because, where an injunction is claimed, its purpose is to restrain further action by the defendant which may interfere with the plaintiff's enjoyment of his land, and *ex hypothesi* the defendant must be aware, if and when an injunction is granted, that such interference may be caused by the act which he is restrained from committing. It follows that these cases provide no guidance on the question whether foreseeability of harm of the relevant type is a prerequisite of the recovery of damages for causing such harm to the plaintiff... Here, as I have said, it is still the law that the fact that the defendant has taken all reasonable care will not of itself exonerate him from liability, the relevant control mechanism being found within the principle of reasonable user. But it by no means follows that the defendant should be held liable for damage of a type which he could not reasonably foresee; and the development of the law of negligence in the past 60 years points strongly towards a requirement that such foreseeability should be a prerequisite of liability in damages for nuisance, as it is of liability in negligence. For if a plaintiff is in ordinary circumstances only able to claim damages in respect of personal injuries where he can prove such foreseeability on the part of the defendant, it is difficult to see why, in common justice, he should be in a stronger position to claim damages for interference with the enjoyment of his land where the defendant was unable to foresee such damage...

NOTE

In *Morris v Network Rail* (2004) Buxton LJ said that 'it is difficult to see any further life in some particular rules of the law of nuisance, such as for instance the concept of 'abnormal sensitiveness' drawn from *Robinson v Kilvert* (1889)... It is very difficult not to think that such particular rules are now subsumed under the general view of the law of nuisance expressed in *Delaware Mansions*: not dissimilarly to the way in which the generalisation of the law of negligence initiated by *Donoghue v Stevenson* has rendered obsolete the previous categories of dangerous chattels; duties of occupiers of land; duties attaching to specific trades; and the like' (§ 35).

PROBLEM

The owner of a sound studio suffers severe financial harm resulting from loss of trade caused by electronic interference, emanating from the signalling system used by the nearby railway, with the sound recording process. When the signalling system was introduced the railway company was unaware that it would cause such problems. Can the owner of the sound studio sue the railway company in nuisance for (a) damages for the financial loss and/or (b) an injunction to stop the interference? (Cf *Morris v Network Rail* (2004).)

6.3 Public and private interests

One particular problem associated with nuisance, hinted at by Lord Hoffmann in *Hunter v Canary Wharf* (1997), is the clash of interests that can arise when it comes to socially useful activities that nevertheless cause harm or annoyance to neighbours. Should the public interest be allowed to override the private interest? This problem was at the heart of *Miller v Jackson* (see p 14) and *Dennis v MOD* (p 181) and it also brings into play an economic analysis of tort (see **2.3.2**).

6.3.1 Private nuisance and public benefit

Two nuisance points should be noted with respect to *Miller v Jackson*. The first is that undue sensitivity used to be a defence to a nuisance claim and thus if a defendant's activity caused damage to the claimant's stock of paper only because the claimant had particularly sensitive paper on his land there was no liability (*Robinson v Kilvert* (1889)). One can understand why the cricket-loving judges ('manly sport') were keen to brand the wife as ultra-sensitive. However, as we have seen above, it has recently been asserted that this sensitivity defence is no longer relevant now that foreseeability has become a central test in nuisance (*Delaware* (2002), p 209). An unduly sensitive activity interfered with by the defendant land user will probably be 'unforeseeable' (see Buxton LJ in *Morris v Network Rail* (2004), above, p 210).

Secondly, coming to the nuisance is no defence (*Sturges v Bridgman* (1879)). This precedent seems to have been treated in rather a cavalier way by Lord Denning MR, although the dissenting judge thought he was bound by it. In *Dennis* the principle that the judge applied is more profound than it might first seem. The costs of a public benefit should not be allowed to fall on a few individual shoulders but should be borne by the community as a whole (through the payment of damages by the State). What if such a principle were to be applied more widely? (Cf *Dunne v NW Gas Board*, p 302.)

6.3.2 Cost of activities

The idea that a defendant should pay for his activity is not new as the next extract indicates.

Bamford v Turnley (1862) 122 ER 27 Ex Ch

This was an action for damages by a householder against a neighbour whose brickworks caused unpleasant smoke and smells. The jury gave a verdict for the defendant and this was upheld by the Court of Queen's Bench. A further appeal by the claimant to Exchequer Chamber was allowed (Pollock CB dissenting).

Bramwell B: ... I am of opinion that this judgment should be reversed. The defendant has done that which, if done wantonly or maliciously, would be actionable as being a nuisance to the plaintiff's habitation by causing a sensible diminution of the comfortable enjoyment of it. This, therefore, calls on the defendant to justify or excuse what he has done. And his justification is this: He says that the nuisance is not to the health of the inhabitants of the plaintiff's house, that it is of a temporary character, and is necessary for the beneficial use of his, the defendant's land, and that the public good requires he should be entitled to do what he claims to do...

▶

But it is said that, temporary or permanent, it is lawful because it is for the public benefit. Now, in the first place, that law to my mind is a bad one which, for the public benefit,
inflicts loss on an individual without compensation...It is for the public benefit there
should be railways, but it would not be unless the gain of having the railway was sufficient to compensate the loss occasioned by the use of the land required for its site; and
accordingly no one thinks it would be right to take an individual's land without compensation to make a railway. It is for the public benefit that trains should run, but not unless
they pay their expenses...

NOTE

See also Lord Hoffmann in *Wildtree Hotels v Harrow LBC* (2001) (p 58).

6.3.3 Statutory authority

One way of allowing the public interest to override the private interest is for
Parliament to provide a statutory defence to any claims in trespass and (or) nuisance (see eg Civil Aviation Act 1982 (p 180)). But what if Parliament provides a
statutory planning regime: will the grant of planning permission act in itself as a
defence to a nuisance claim?

Wheeler v JJ Saunders Ltd [1996] Ch 19, CA

This was an action for an injunction and for damages by a veterinary surgeon
and his wife against a farm in respect of a number of acts and activities including the smell from pigs said to constitute a nuisance. The judge having awarded
damages and an injunction, the defendants appealed arguing that since they
had obtained planning permission for the pig farm they should not have been
held liable in nuisance. The Court of Appeal (Staughton LJ, Peter Gibson LJ and
Sir John May LJ) upheld the judge's decision on the nuisance aspect of the case.

Staughton LJ: ... I do not consider that planning permission necessarily has the same
effect as statutory authority. Parliament is sovereign and can abolish or limit the civil
rights of individuals... The planning authority... has only the powers delegated to it by
Parliament. It is not in my view self-evident that they include the power to abolish or limit
civil rights in any or all circumstances. The process by which planning permission is
obtained allows for objections by those who might be adversely affected, but they have
no right of appeal if their objections are overruled. It is not for us to say whether the private bill procedure in Parliament is better or worse. It is enough that it is different...

It would in my opinion be a misuse of language to describe what has happened in the
present case as a change in the character of a neighbourhood. It is a change and
abuse of a very small piece of land, a little over 350 square metres according to the
dimensions on the plan, for the benefit of the applicant and to the detriment of the
objectors in the quiet enjoyment of their house. It is not a strategic planning decision
affected by considerations of public interest. Unless one is prepared to accept that any
planning decision authorises any nuisance which must inevitably come from it, the argument that the nuisance was authorised by planning permission in this case must fail. I

am not prepared to accept that premise. It may be – I express no concluded opinion – that some planning decisions will authorise some nuisances. But that is as far as I am prepared to go. There is no immunity from liability for nuisance in the present case. I would dismiss the second part of this appeal.

Peter Gibson LJ: ... I am not prepared to accept that the principle applied in the *Gillingham* case must be taken to apply to every planning decision. The court should be slow to acquiesce in the extinction of private rights without compensation as a result of administrative decisions which cannot be appealed and are difficult to challenge...

Sir John May: ... Further, if a planning permission could authorise a nuisance, then so also could it in an appropriate case license a trespass. But in planning cases where, in addition to permission, a way-leave is for instance required for electric cables, or a highway has to be stopped up or opened, then the permission alone is never enough and the procedures to obtain a way-leave or to interfere with the highway have to be followed...

QUESTION

What if, in *Halsey v Esso* (1961) (above p 205), the oil company's depot had been specifically authorised by the grant of local authority planning permission: would the claimant have been debarred from suing for all his various heads of damage?

NOTE

Planning regimes are not the only form of possible statutory authority as the next case indicates.

Marcic v Thames Water Utilities Ltd [2004] 2 AC 42, HL

This was an action for damages by a householder against a water company in respect of damage caused to the claimant's premises by flooding. This flooding resulted from inadequate sewers. The Court of Appeal held that the householder had a claim in private nuisance and under the Human Rights Act 1998. However an appeal to the House of Lords (Lords Nicholls, Steyn, Hoffmann, Hope and Scott) was allowed.

Lord Nicholls: 1 My Lords, this appeal concerns flooding of a particularly unpleasant kind: from foul water sewers as well as surface water sewers. Sewer flooding is a nationwide environmental problem, arising largely from the building of ever more houses to meet the housing demand. Sewers and drains, sufficient when laid in the 19th century or later, are no longer adequate to cope with the volume of surface water entering the public drainage system in times of heavy rainfall. Overloaded surface water sewers spill into the foul water sewers. As a result, all too often water and untreated sewage overflow at the lower levels of the drainage system, causing misery for the people living there...

34 In my view the cause of action in nuisance asserted by Mr Marcic is inconsistent with the statutory scheme. Mr Marcic's claim is expressed in various ways but in practical terms it always comes down to this: Thames Water ought to build more sewers. This is the only way Thames Water can prevent sewer flooding of Mr Marcic's property...

▶

35 The difficulty I have with this line of argument is that it ignores the statutory limitations on the enforcement of sewerage undertakers' drainage obligations...

42 In the present case the interests Parliament had to balance included, on the one hand, the interests of customers of a company whose properties are prone to sewer flooding and, on the other hand, all the other customers of the company whose properties are drained through the company's sewers. The interests of the first group conflict with the interests of the company's customers as a whole in that only a minority of customers suffer sewer flooding but the company's customers as a whole meet the cost of building more sewers. As already noted, the balance struck by the statutory scheme is to impose a general drainage obligation on a sewerage undertaker but to entrust enforcement of this obligation to an independent regulator who has regard to all the different interests involved. Decisions of the director are of course subject to an appropriately penetrating degree of judicial review by the courts...

Lord Hoffmann: ... **61** Why should sewers be different? If the *Sedleigh-Denfield* case [1940] AC 880 lays down a general principle that an owner of land has a duty to take reasonable steps to prevent a nuisance arising from a known source of hazard, even though he did not himself create it, why should that not require him to construct new sewers if the court thinks it would have been reasonable to do so?

62 The difference in my opinion is that the *Sedleigh-Denfield*, *Goldman* and *Leakey* cases were dealing with disputes between neighbouring land owners simply in their capacity as individual land owners. In such cases it is fair and efficient to impose reciprocal duties upon each landowner to take whatever steps are reasonable to prevent his land becoming a source of injury to his neighbour. Even then, the question of what measures should reasonably have been taken may not be uncomplicated. As Lord Wilberforce said in *Goldman's* case [1967] 1 AC 645, 663, the court must (unusually) have regard to the individual circumstances of the defendant. In *Leakey's* case [1980] QB 485, 526 Megaw LJ recoiled from the prospect of a detailed examination of the defendant's financial resources and said it should be done on a broad basis.

63 Nevertheless, whatever the difficulties, the court in such cases is performing its usual function of deciding what is reasonable as between the two parties to the action. But the exercise becomes very different when one is dealing with the capital expenditure of a statutory undertaking providing public utilities on a large scale. The matter is no longer confined to the parties to the action. If one customer is given a certain level of services, everyone in the same circumstances should receive the same level of services. So the effect of a decision about what it would be reasonable to expect a sewerage undertaker to do for the plaintiff is extrapolated across the country. This in turn raises questions of public interest. Capital expenditure on new sewers has to be financed; interest must be paid on borrowings and privatised undertakers must earn a reasonable return. This expenditure can be met only by charges paid by consumers. Is it in the public interest that they should have to pay more? And does expenditure on the particular improvements with which the plaintiff is concerned represent the best order of priorities?

64 These are decisions which courts are not equipped to make in ordinary litigation. It is therefore not surprising that for more than a century the question of whether more or better sewers should be constructed has been entrusted by Parliament to administrators rather than judges...

QUESTION

The Law Lords seem to be treating the water company as a public utility balancing the public interest against the private. But, being a private company, would not their profit interest be a major consideration? What if they thought that the building of extra sewers would not go down well with the shareholders?

6.3.4 Nuisance and human rights

The Human Rights Act 1998 has introduced a whole new dimension into nuisance cases, that is to say into cases where home life is invaded by an activity of a neighbour. For the European Convention of Human Rights and Fundamental Freedoms guarantees in art 8 'the right to respect for his private and family life, his home and his correspondence'. This article is considered in the following nuisance case.

Marcic v Thames Water Utilities Ltd [2004] 2 AC 42, HL

(For facts see p 213)

Lord Nicholls: ... **37** I turn to Mr Marcic's claim under the Human Rights Act 1998. His claim is that as a public authority within the meaning of section 6 of the Human Rights Act 1998 Thames Water has acted unlawfully. Thames Water has conducted itself in a way which is incompatible with Mr Marcic's Convention rights under article 8 of the Convention and article 1 of the First Protocol to the Convention. His submission was to the following effect. The flooding of Mr Marcic's property falls within the first paragraph of article 8 and also within article 1 of the First Protocol. That was common ground between the parties. Direct and serious interference of this nature with a person's home is prima facie a violation of a person's right to respect for his private and family life (article 8) and of his entitlement to the peaceful enjoyment of his possessions (article 1 of the First Protocol). The burden of justifying this interference rests on Thames Water. At the trial of the preliminary issues Thames Water failed to discharge this burden. The trial judge found that the system of priorities used by Thames Water in deciding whether to carry out flood alleviation works might be entirely fair. The judge also said that on the limited evidence before him it was not possible to decide this issue, or to decide whether for all its apparent faults the system fell within the wide margin of discretion open to Thames Water and the director: [2002] QB 929, 964, para 102.

38 To my mind the fatal weakness in this submission is the same as that afflicting Mr Marcic's claim in nuisance: it does not take sufficient account of the statutory scheme under which Thames Water is operating the offending sewers. The need to adopt some system of priorities for building more sewers is self-evident. So is the need for the system to be fair. A fair system of priorities necessarily involves balancing many intangible factors. Whether the system adopted by a sewerage undertaker is fair is a matter inherently more suited for decision by the industry regulator than by a court. And the statutory scheme so provides. Moreover, the statutory scheme provides a remedy where a system of priorities is not fair. An unfair system of priorities means that a sewerage undertaker is not properly discharging its statutory drainage obligation so far as

▶

those who are being treated unfairly are concerned. The statute provides what should happen in these circumstances. The director is charged with deciding whether to make an enforcement order in respect of a sewerage undertaker's failure to drain property properly. Parliament entrusted this decision to the director, not the courts.

Lord Hoffmann: ... **71** That leaves only the question of whether the remedies provided under the 1991 Act do not adequately safeguard Mr Marcic's Convention rights to the privacy of his home and the protection of his property. The judge, who found for Mr Marcic on this ground, did not have the benefit of the decision of the Grand Chamber of the European Court of Human Rights in *Hatton v United Kingdom* (Application No 36022/97) The Times, 10 July 2003. That decision makes it clear that the Convention does not accord absolute protection to property or even to residential premises. It requires a fair balance to be struck between the interests of persons whose homes and property are affected and the interests of other people, such as customers and the general public. National institutions, and particularly the national legislature, are accorded a broad discretion in choosing the solution appropriate to their own society or creating the machinery for doing so. There is no reason why Parliament should not entrust such decisions to an independent regulator such as the director. He is a public authority within the meaning of the 1998 Act and has a duty to act in accordance with Convention rights. If (which there is no reason to suppose) he has exceeded the broad margin of discretion allowed by the Convention, Mr Marcic will have a remedy under section 6 of the 1998 Act. But that question is not before your Lordships. His case is that he has a Convention right to have the decision as to whether new sewers should be constructed made by a court in a private action for nuisance rather than by the director in the exercise of his powers under the 1991 Act. In my opinion there is no such right...

NOTE AND QUESTION

Two other important cases, already extracted, are *Dennis v MOD* (p 181) and *Hatton v UK* (p 83). What will be the effect, if any, of *Hatton* and (or) *Marcic* or *Dennis*?

6.4 Liability for dangerous things brought onto land

Nuisance normally involves some kind of continuing state of affairs arising out of an activity or the state of the property. A single isolated noise or smell will not ground liability in nuisance however annoying. Sometimes, however, a single escape of a thing can cause serious damage to a neighbour and while there is some authority that such an incident might amount to a nuisance (see eg *British Celanese v AH Hunt Ltd* (1969)), the escape can give rise to an independent cause of action in tort.

6.4.1 Dangerous things

The precedent for this independent cause of action is set out next.

Rylands v Fletcher (1866) LR 1 Ex 265, Ex Ch, (1868) LR 3 HL 330, HL

This was an action for damages by a landowner against his neighbour in respect of damage done by water escaping from a reservoir on the defendant's land. The escape occurred as a result of negligent work carried out by the contractors who constructed the reservoir. The Court of Exchequer Chamber gave judgment for the claimant and an appeal to the House of Lords (Lords Cairns and Cranworth) was dismissed.

Blackburn J (Court of Exchequer Chamber): ... We think that the true rule of law is, that the person who for his own purposes brings on his lands and collects and keeps there anything likely to do mischief if it escapes, must keep it in at his peril, and, if he does not do so, is *prima facie* answerable for all the damage which is the natural consequence of its escape. He can excuse himself by showing that the escape was owing to the plaintiff's default; or perhaps that the escape was the consequences of *vis major*, or the act of God; but as nothing of this sort exists here, it is unnecessary to inquire what excuse would be sufficient...

Lord Cairns LC (House of Lords): ... [I]f, in what I may term the natural user of that land, there had been any accumulation of water, either on the surface or underground, and if, by the operation of the laws of nature, that accumulation of water had passed off into the close occupied by the plaintiff, the plaintiff could not have complained that the result had taken place...

On the other hand if the defendants, not stopping at the natural use of their close, had desired to use it for any purpose which I may term a non-natural use ... then it appears to me that that which the defendants were doing they were doing at their own peril; and, if in the course of their doing it, the evil arose to which I have referred, the evil, namely, of the escape of the water and its passing away to the close of the plaintiff and injuring the plaintiff, then for the consequence of that, in my opinion, the defendants would be liable...

QUESTION

Why were there seemingly only two Law Lords in this House of Lords decision? (Cf Heuston (1970) 86 LQR 160.)

NOTE

This great case has become less important than it deserves thanks to the failure of English judges to develop its potential. Just as *Donoghue v Stevenson* (1932) (p 112) became the basis for negligence liability, so *Rylands* could have become the fundamental starting point for a strict liability for things. Blackburn J's rule was, admittedly, not as abstract as art 1384 of the CC, yet it could have acted as the foundation for a liability for dangerous things analogous to the strict liability for dangerous animals. This opportunity was lost when the House of Lords rendered its judgments in *Read v Lyons* (1947) (p 185). Matters were not helped by Lord Cairns, whose rewording of Blackburn J's 'not naturally there' with 'non-natural use' meant that later judges could restrict the precedent within narrow limits. Another opportunity was lost more recently, as the next case indicates.

Cambridge Water Co v Eastern Counties Leather plc [1994] 2 AC 264, HL

This was an action for damages by a water utilities company against a tanning factory in respect of contamination caused by a solvent known as per-chloroethene (PCE) used by the defendants in the process of degreasing pelts at its tanning works. The PCE had seeped into the ground beneath the defendants' works and was conveyed in percolating water in the direction of the claimant's borehole. The damages action was based on three causes of action: negligence, nuisance and the rule in *Rylands v Fletcher* (1868). The judge dismissed the claims but the Court of Appeal allowed an appeal. An appeal to the House of Lords (Lords Templeman, Goff, Jauncey, Lowry and Woolf) was allowed.

Lord Goff: ... It can be argued that the rule in *Rylands v Fletcher* should not be regarded simply as an extension of the law of nuisance, but should rather be treated as a developing principle of strict liability from which can be derived a general rule of strict liability for damage caused by ultra-hazardous operations on the basis of which persons conducting such operations may properly be held strictly liable for the extraordinary risk to others involved in such operations. As is pointed out in Fleming on *The Law of Torts*, pp 327–328, this would lead to the practical result that the cost of damage resulting from such operations would have to be absorbed as part of the overheads of the relevant business rather than be borne (where there is no negligence) by the injured person or his insurers, or even by the community at large. Such a development appears to have been taking place in the United States, as can be seen from paragraph 519 of the *Restatement of Torts* (2d) vol 3 (1977). The extent to which it has done so is not altogether clear; and I infer from paragraph 519, and the Comment on that paragraph, that the abnormally dangerous activities there referred to are such that their ability to cause harm would be obvious to any reasonable person who carried them on.

I have to say, however, that there are serious obstacles in the way of the development of the rule in *Rylands v Fletcher* in this way. First of all, if it was so to develop, it should logically apply to liability to all persons suffering injury by reason of the ultra-hazardous operations; but the decision of this House in *Read v J Lyons & Co Ltd* [1947] AC 156, which establishes that there can be no liability under the rule except in circumstances where the injury has been caused by an escape from land under the control of the defendant, has effectively precluded any such development. Professor Fleming has observed that 'the most damaging effect of the decision in *Read v J Lyons & Co Ltd* is that it prematurely stunted the development of a general theory of strict liability for ultra-hazardous activities' (see Fleming on *Torts*, p 341). Even so, there is much to be said for the view that the courts should not be proceeding down the path of developing such a general theory. In this connection, I refer in particular to the *Report of the Law Commission on Civil Liability for Dangerous Things and Activities* (1970) (Law Com No 32). In paragraphs 14–16 of the Report, the Law Commission expressed serious misgivings about the adoption of any test for the application of strict liability involving a general concept of 'especially dangerous' or 'ultra-hazardous' activity, having regard to the uncertainties and practical difficulties of its application. If the Law Commission is unwilling to consider statutory reform on this basis, it must follow that judges should if anything be even more reluctant to proceed down that path.

Like the judge in the present case, I incline to the opinion that, as a general rule, it is more appropriate for strict liability in respect of operations of high risk to be imposed by

Parliament, than by the courts. If such liability is imposed by statute, the relevant activities can be identified, and those concerned can know where they stand. Furthermore, statute can where appropriate lay down precise criteria establishing the incidence and scope of such liability.

It is of particular relevance that the present case is concerned with environmental pollution. The protection and preservation of the environment is now perceived as being of crucial importance to the future of mankind; and public bodies, both national and international, are taking significant steps towards the establishment of legislation which will promote the protection of the environment, and make the polluter pay for damage to the environment for which he is responsible – as can be seen from the WHO, EEC and national regulations to which I have previously referred. But it does not follow from these developments that a common law principle, such as the rule in *Rylands v Fletcher*, should be developed or rendered more strict to provide for liability in respect of such pollution. On the contrary, given that so much well-informed and carefully structured legislation is now being put in place for this purpose, there is less need for the courts to develop a common law principle to achieve the same end, and indeed it may well be undesirable that they should do so.

Having regard to these considerations, and in particular to the step which this House has already taken in *Read v J Lyons & Co Ltd* [1947] AC 156 to contain the scope of liability under the rule in *Rylands v Fletcher*, it appears to me to be appropriate now to take the view that foreseeability of damage of the relevant type should be regarded as a prerequisite of liability in damages under the rule...

The facts of the present case

Turning to the facts of the present case, it is plain that, at the time when the PCE was brought onto [the defendants'] land, and indeed when it was used in the tanning process there, nobody at [the defendants' works] could reasonably have foreseen the resultant damage which occurred at CWC's borehole at Sawston ...

In the result, since those responsible at [the defendant company] could not at the relevant time reasonably have foreseen that the damage in question might occur, the claim of [the claimant] for damages under the rule in *Rylands v Fletcher* must fail...

NOTE

The introduction of foreseeability does not, of course, mean that the rule in *Rylands v Fletcher* is no longer in the category of a liability for things since the foresight attaches as much to the thing as to the act of bringing it onto land. There must be an awareness of the risk and it is possible that foreseeability in this context is analogous to the state of scientific knowledge in s 4(1)(e) of the Consumer Protection Act 1987 (p 160). However, as *Cambridge* itself indicates, the requirement weakens the idea both that it is the polluter who should pay and that liability for a dangerous thing should be fully strict. The latest decision on *Rylands* has possibly weakened the cause of action even further. However this latest decision subjects the cause of action to a wide-ranging review.

Transco plc v Stockport Metropolitan Borough Council [2004] 2 AC 1, HL

This was an action for damages by a gas-pipe owner against a local authority in respect of damage done to a gas pipe by the escape of water from premises owned by the local authority. The escape of water was caused by the failure of a water supply pipe on the local authority's land, but both the failure and the escape were not due to any negligence on the part of the defendants. The claimant based his action on the rule in *Rylands v Fletcher*, but the House of Lords (Lords Bingham, Hoffmann, Hobhouse, Scott and Walker) held that the local authority was not liable.

Lord Hoffmann: ... **29** It is tempting to see, beneath the surface of the rule [in *Rylands v Fletcher*], a policy of requiring the costs of a commercial enterprise to be internalised; to require the entrepreneur to provide, by insurance or otherwise, for the risks to others which his enterprise creates. That was certainly the opinion of Bramwell B, who was in favour of liability when the case was before the Court of Exchequer: (1865) 3 H & C 774. He had a clear and consistent view on the matter: see *Bamford v Turnley* (1862) 3 B & S 62, 84–85 and *Hammersmith and City Railway Co v Brand* (1867) LR 2 QB 223, 230–231. But others thought differently. They considered that the public interest in pro-moting economic development made it unreasonable to hold an entrepreneur liable when he had not been negligent: see *Wildtree Hotels Ltd v Harrow London Borough Council* [2001] 2 AC 1, 8–9 for a discussion of this debate in the context of compensa-tion for disturbance caused by the construction and operation of works authorised by statutory powers. On the whole, it was the latter view – no liability without fault – which gained the ascendancy. With hindsight, *Rylands v Fletcher* can be seen as an isolated victory for the internalisers. The following century saw a steady refusal to treat it as laying down any broad principle of liability...

Where stands the rule today?

39 I pause at this point to summarise the very limited circumstances to which the rule has been confined. First, it is a remedy for damage to land or interests in land. As there can be few properties in the country, commercial or domestic, which are not insured against damage by flood and the like, this means that disputes over the application of the rule will tend to be between property insurers and liability insurers. Secondly, it does not apply to works or enterprises authorised by statute. That means that it will usually have no application to really high risk activities. As Professor Simpson points out ([1984] 13 J Leg Stud 225) the Bradfield Reservoir was built under statutory powers. In the absence of negligence, the occupiers whose lands had been inundated would have had no remedy. Thirdly, it is not particularly strict because it excludes liability when the escape is for the most common reasons, namely vandalism or unusual natural events. Fourthly, the cases in which there is an escape which is not attributable to an unusual natural event or the act of a third party will, by the same token, usually give rise to an inference of negligence. Fifthly, there is a broad and ill-defined exception for 'natural' uses of land. It is perhaps not surprising that counsel could not find a reported case since the second world war in which anyone had succeeded in a claim under the rule. It is hard to escape the conclusion that the intellectual effort devoted to the rule by judges and writers over many years has brought forth a mouse.

Is it worth keeping?

40 In *Burnie Port Authority v General Jones Pty Ltd* (1994) 179 CLR 520 a majority of the High Court of Australia lost patience with the pretensions and uncertainties of the rule and decided that it had been 'absorbed' into the law of negligence. Your Lordships have been invited by the respondents to kill off the rule in England in similar fashion. It is said, first, that in its present attenuated form it serves little practical purpose; secondly, that its application is unacceptably vague ('an essentially unprincipled and ad hoc subjective determination' said the High Court (at p 540) in the *Burnie* case) and thirdly, that strict liability on social grounds is better left to statutory intervention.

41 There is considerable force in each of these points.

43 But despite the strength of these arguments, I do not think it would be consistent with the judicial function of your Lordships' House to abolish the rule. It has been part of English law for nearly 150 years and despite a searching examination by Lord Goff of Chieveley in the *Cambridge Water* case [1994] 2 AC 264, 308, there was no suggestion in his speech that it could or should be abolished. I think that would be too radical a step to take...

49 In my opinion the Court of Appeal was right to say that it was not a 'non-natural' user of land. I am influenced by two matters. First, there is no evidence that it created a greater risk than is normally associated with domestic or commercial plumbing. True, the pipe was larger. But whether that involved greater risk depends upon its specification. One cannot simply assume that the larger the pipe, the greater the risk of fracture or the greater the quantity of water likely to be discharged. I agree with my noble and learned friend Lord Bingham of Cornhill that the criterion of exceptional risk must be taken seriously and creates a high threshold for a claimant to surmount. Secondly, I think that the risk of damage to property caused by leaking water is one against which most people can and do commonly insure. This is, as I have said, particularly true of Transco, which can be expected to have insured against any form of damage to its pipe. It would be a very strange result if Transco were entitled to recover against the council when it would not have been entitled to recover against the Water Authority for similar damage emanating from its high pressure main.

50 I would therefore dismiss the appeal.

Lord Hobhouse: ... **56** This approach was entirely in keeping with the economic and political culture of the 19th Century, *laissez faire* and an understanding of the concept of risk. During the 20th Century and particularly during the second half, the culture has changed. Government has increasingly intervened to limit the freedom of a landowner to use his land as he chooses, *eg* through the planning laws, and has regulated or forbidden certain dangerous or antisocial uses of land such as the manufacture or storage of explosives or the emission of noxious effluents. Thus the present state of the law is that some of the situations where the rule in *Rylands v Fletcher* applies are now also addressed by the first type of solution. But this does not deprive the rule of its utility. The area of regulation is not exhaustive; it does not necessarily give the third party affected an adequate or, even, any say; the Government decision may give priority to some national or military need which it considers must over-ride legitimate individual interests; it will not normally deal with civil liability for damage to property; it does not provide the third party with adequate knowledge and control to evaluate and protect himself from the consequent risk and insurance cost. As Lord Goff pointed out in *Cambridge Water*

▶

(...), the occasions where *Rylands v Fletcher* may have to be invoked by a claimant may be reducing but that is not to say that it has ceased to be a valid part of English law. The only way it could be rendered obsolete is by a compulsory strict public liability insurance scheme for all persons using their land for dangerous purposes. However this would simply be to re-enact *Rylands v Fletcher* in another guise.

57 *Rylands v Fletcher* was unremarkable in the mid 19th century since there was then nothing peculiar about strict liability. There were many other fields in which strict liability existed, for example conversion. For those following a 'common' calling, such as common carriers or common inn-keepers, liability was also strict. Although the origins were already present in the 19th century in the defence of 'inevitable accident' in trespass cases, it was only later that the generalised criterion of negligence was developed, culminating in *Donoghue v Stevenson* [1932] AC 562. That is a fault – *ie*, breach of a duty of care – not a risk concept. But, where the situation arises as between landowners and arises from the dangerous use of his land by one of them, the risk concept remains relevant. He who creates the relevant risk and has, to the exclusion of the other, the control of how he uses his land, should bear the risk. It would be unjust to deny the other a risk based remedy and introduce a requirement of proving fault...

(For further extracts see p 74.)

QUESTION

Do you think that Blackburn J thought that he was conceiving a mouse?

6.4.2 Dangerous activities

Rylands v Fletcher was a genuine liability for things in that liability attached to the escape of a thing rather than from a dangerous activity. However some US jurisdictions have used this English precedent to develop a rule of strict liability arising from ultra-hazardous activities. One might note European tort thinking as well.

European Group on Tort Law, *Principles of European Tort Law* (2003)

Article 5:101. Abnormally dangerous activities

(1) A person who carries on an abnormally dangerous activity is strictly liable for damage characteristic to the risk presented by the activity and resulting from it.

(2) An activity is abnormally dangerous if
   (a) it creates a foreseeable and highly significant risk of damage even when all due care is exercised in its management and
   (b) it is not a matter of common usage.

(3) A risk of damage may be significant having regard to the seriousness or the likelihood of the damage.

(4) This Article does not apply to an activity which is specifically subjected to strict liability by any other provision of these Principles or any other national law or international convention.

NOTE

The decision in *Read v Lyons* (1947) (p 185) would suggest that this European code principle does not represent English law. Nevertheless a reversal of the burden of proof within negligence (*res ipsa loquitur*: see **4.2.7**) might go far in achieving a measure of strict liability in practice (and see *Henderson v Jenkins*, p 170).

6.4.3 Liability for the escape of fire

One 'thing' around which a liability for things and a liability for dangerous activities can coalesce is fire. Liability for the spread of fire is complex first because it can bring into play a range of heads of liability such as *Rylands v Fletcher*, negligence and nuisance. And, secondly, because there is a statutory defence 'against any person in whose house, chamber, stable, barn or other building, or in whose estate any fire shall *accidentally* begin' (Fires Prevention (Metropolis) Act 1774, s 86 (emphasis added)). The word 'accidentally' has been construed narrowly with the result that defendants have been held liable in the heads mentioned above. Moreover risk can also have its role as the next judicial extract indicates.

Smith v Littlewoods Organisation Ltd [1987] AC 241, HL (Scotland)

This was an action for damages by the owner of a café against a neighbouring owner of a derelict cinema in respect of damage done by a fire deliberately started in the empty cinema by vandals who had broken into the premises. The action failed in the House of Lords (Lords Keith, Brandon, Griffiths, Mackay and Goff).

Lord Goff: ... It is, in my opinion, consistent with the existence of such liability that an occupier who negligently causes or permits a source of danger to be created on his land, and can reasonably foresee that third parties may trespass on his land and, interfering with the source of danger, may spark it off, thereby causing damage to the person or property of those in the vicinity, should be held liable to such a person for damage so caused to him. It is useful to take the example of a fire hazard, not only because that is the relevant hazard which is alleged to have existed in the present case, but also because of the intrinsically dangerous nature of fire hazards as regards neighbouring property. Let me give an example of circumstances in which an occupier of land might be held liable for damage so caused. Suppose that a person is deputed to buy a substantial quantity of fireworks for a village fireworks display on Guy Fawkes night. He stores them, as usual, in an unlocked garden shed abutting onto a neighbouring house. It is well known that he does this. Mischievous boys from the village enter as trespassers and, playing with the fireworks, cause a serious fire which spreads to and burns down the neighbouring house. Liability might well be imposed in such a case; for, having regard to the dangerous and tempting nature of fireworks, interference by naughty children was the very thing which, in the circumstances, the purchaser of the fireworks ought to have guarded against.

But liability should only be imposed under this principle in cases where the defender has negligently caused or permitted the creation of a source of danger on his land, and where it is foreseeable that third parties may trespass on his land and spark it off, thereby damaging the pursuer or his property. Moreover, it is not to be forgotten that, in ordinary households in this country, there are nowadays many things which might be

▶

described as possible sources of fire if interfered with by third parties, ranging from matches and firelighters to electric irons and gas cookers and even oil-fired central heating systems. These are commonplaces of modern life; and it would be quite wrong if householders were to be held liable in negligence for acting in a socially acceptable manner. No doubt the question whether liability should be imposed on defenders in a case where a source of danger on his land has been sparked off by the deliberate wrongdoing of a third party is a question to be decided on the facts of each case, and it would, I think, be wrong for your Lordships' House to anticipate the manner in which the law may develop: but I cannot help thinking that cases where liability will be so imposed are likely to be very rare.

There is another basis upon which a defender may be held liable for damage to neighbouring property caused by a fire started on his (the defender's) property by the deliberate wrongdoing of a third party. This arises where he has knowledge or means of knowledge that a third party has created or is creating a risk of fire, or indeed has started a fire, on his premises, and then fails to take such steps as are reasonably open to him (in the limited sense explained by Lord Wilberforce in *Goldman v Hargrave* [1967] 1 AC 645, 663–664) to prevent any such fire from damaging neighbouring property. If, for example, an occupier of property has knowledge, or means of knowledge, that intruders are in the habit of trespassing upon his property and starting fires there, thereby creating a risk that fire may spread to and damage neighbouring property, a duty to take reasonable steps to prevent such damage may be held to fall upon him. He could, for example, take reasonable steps to keep the intruders out. He could also inform the police; or he could warn his neighbours and invite their assistance. If the defender is a person of substantial means, for example, a large public company, he might even be expected to employ some agency to keep a watch on the premises. What is reasonably required would, of course, depend on the particular facts of the case. I observe that, in *Goldman v Hargrave*, such liability was held to sound in nuisance; but it is difficult to believe that, in this respect, there can be any material distinction between liability in nuisance and liability in negligence ...

NOTE

In the firework example given by Lord Goff liability under the rule in *Rylands v Fletcher* might be avoided thanks to the decision in *Perry v Kendricks Transport* (1956) which laid down that an act of a third party facilitating the escape is a defence for the occupier of the land.

6.4.4 Liability for the escape of nuclear radiation

A range of pollution situations arising from the escape of noxious material is now governed by statute. With respect to nuclear radiation the relevant legislation is the Nuclear Installations Act 1965 whose provision about causing 'injury to any person or damage to any property' (s 7(1)(a)) has given rise to difficulty. Where is the line to be drawn between damage (to property) and pure financial loss? See now *Blue Circle Industries v Ministry of Defence* (1999).

Chapter 7

Liability for People

We have already seen how, in addition to fault liability given expression in art 1382 of the CC, French law also has a field of strict liability based on the relationship between persons and things. Yet art 1384 of the CC is even wider: it states that one 'is liable not only for the damage that one causes by one's own act, but also for that which is caused by the act of persons for whom one is responsible'. In other words, there is, besides the liability for things, also a liability for persons. More generally in European law – and indeed in English law – the idea of a liability for people is based upon two separate ideas. These are given expression in the articles from the *Principles of European Tort Law* extracted in **7.1.1**. In terms of structure, whereas a liability for things is based on a person-thing-person pattern, liability for persons is founded on three-party situations. These are claimant-actor-defendant, and one obvious focal point is the relationship between actor (the person who actually causes the damage to the claimant) and the defendant. Yet again, however, this structure can become hidden in English law behind the forms of liability (nuisance, negligence, vicarious liability etc) and other conceptual focal points such as 'duty' and 'causation'.

7.1 Three-party situations: general considerations

The starting point for understanding liability for people is to look at the various principles upon which such liability is based. These are, evidently, principles of liability; yet one needs to go beyond these principles because institutional structures such as the legal person (corporation) and contract have an important role to play in understanding why liability is imposed in certain situations.

7.1.1 Foundational tort principles

The foundational principles set out below do not necessarily fully represent English law but they certainly come quite close to capturing its structure.

European Group on Tort Law, *Principles of European Tort Law* (2003)

Article 4:103. Duty to protect others from damage

A duty to act positively to protect others from damage may exist if law so provides, or if the actor creates or controls a dangerous situation, or when there is a special relationship between parties or when the seriousness of the harm on the one side and the ease of avoiding the damage on the other side point towards such a duty.

▶

Article 6:102. Liability for auxiliaries

(1) A person is liable for damage caused by his auxiliaries acting within the scope of their functions provided that they violated the required standard of conduct (Art. 4:102).

(2) An independent contractor is not regarded as an auxiliary for the purposes of this Article.

NOTE

Two quite different principles can give rise to a liability for a tortious act committed by another. The first is based on a direct duty of care and is illustrated by the next extract.

Home Office v Dorset Yacht Co Ltd [1970] AC 1004, HL

This was an action for damages by the owners of a yacht (in truth their insurance company subrogated to their rights) against the Home Office in respect of damage done to the yacht by escaping borstal boys. It was claimed that the three officers supervising the boys had been negligent and that the Home Office was to be vicariously liable for the officers' behaviour. The Home Office, on a preliminary question of law, claimed that the facts disclosed no duty of care. A majority of the House of Lords (Lords Reid, Morris, Pearson and Diplock; Viscount Dilhorne dissenting) disagreed with the Home Office.

Lord Reid: ... *Donoghue v Stevenson* may be regarded as a milestone, and the well-known passage in Lord Atkin's speech should I think be regarded as a statement of principle. It is not to be treated as if it were a statutory definition. It will require qualification in new circumstances. But I think that the time has come when we can and should say that it ought to apply unless there is some justification or valid explanation for its exclusion...

It is argued that it would be contrary to public policy to hold the Home Office or its officers liable to a member of the public for this carelessness – or, indeed, any failure of duty on their part. The basic question is: who shall bear the loss caused by that carelessness – the innocent [plaintiff] or the Home Office, who are vicariously liable for the conduct of their careless officers? ... [His Lordship then discussed the American case of *Williams v State of New York* where the State was held not liable for the negligence of prison warders on the ground of public policy.] ... It may be that public servants of the State of New York are so apprehensive, easily dissuaded from doing their duty and intent on preserving public funds from costly claims that they could be influenced in this way. But my experience leads me to believe that Her Majesty's servants are made of sterner stuff. So I have no hesitation in rejecting this argument. I can see no good ground in public policy for giving this immunity to a government department...

Lord Pearson: ... The borstal boys were under the control of the Home Office's officers, and control imports responsibility ...

Lord Diplock: My Lords, this appeal is about the law of negligence. Regrettably, as I think, it comes before your Lordships' House upon a preliminary question of law which is said to arise upon the facts pleaded in the statement of claim. This makes it necessary to identify the precise question of law raised by those facts which are very summarily pleaded. Some of them relate to the acts of seven youths undergoing sentences of Borstal training; others relate to the acts and omissions of persons concerned in the management of Borstals and, in particular, to the acts and omissions of three officers of the Portland Borstal.

It is alleged and conceded that the defendant, the Home Office, is vicariously responsible for the tortious acts of the three Borstal officers and any other persons concerned in the management of Borstals. It is not contended that the Home Office is vicariously liable for any tortious acts of the youths undergoing sentences of Borstal training...

Viscount Dilhorne (dissenting): ... I think that it is clear that the *Donoghue v Stevenson* principle cannot be regarded as an infallible test of the existence of a duty of care, nor do I think that, if that test is satisfied, there arises any presumption of the existence of such a duty...

I, of course, recognise that the common law develops by the application of well established principles to new circumstances but I cannot accept that the application of Lord Atkin's words, which, though they applied in *Deyong v Shenburn*, and might have applied in *Commissioner for Railways v Quinlan*, were not held to impose a new duty on a master to his servant or on an occupier to a trespasser, suffices to impose a new duty on the Home Office and on others in charge of persons in lawful custody of the kind suggested...

The absence of authority shows that no such duty now exists. If there should be one, that is, in my view, a matter for the legislature and not for the courts...

QUESTION

Ought an insurance company (the real claimant in *Dorset*) to be able to recoup its money from the public purse? Who was paid to take the risk of damage to, or theft of, property?

NOTES

1. The two ideas set out in the extract from the *Principles of European Tort Law* (PETL) can both be found in the facts of this case. The first idea, given expression in art 6.102 of the PETL, is called vicarious liability in English law. An employer will be automatically liable for a tort committed by its employee acting in the course of his employment (see **7.2**). Thus if one of the prison officers was in breach of a duty of care towards the claimant, then the Home Office would be liable under the principle of vicarious liability (see Lord Diplock).

2. There is, however, a second idea that could arise out of these facts. That is whether the Home Office, as a legal person, owed a direct duty of care to the claimant. If so, and the Home Office itself was in breach of this duty, then the Home Office would be directly liable to the claimant under the *Donoghue v Stevenson* neighbour principle (see **4.1**). This idea is given expression in art 4.103 of the PETL and see *Mattis v Pollock* (p 245).

3. Note also a third idea mentioned by Lord Diplock. Could one argue that the Home Office is vicariously liable for the acts of the borstal boys? This is unlikely because the boys were not employees (see§ 7.2.3). But it is an interesting question all the same and probably one that would be dealt with as part of the second idea mentioned above.

4. This idea of two duties of care (one owed by the employee and the other owed by the employer) towards the claimant is specifically discussed in the next extract.

Phelps v Hillingdon LBC [2001] 2 AC 619, HL

This was a claim by a local authority to strike out various actions for damages brought against it. The House of Lords (Lords Slynn, Jauncey, Lloyd, Nicholls, Clyde, Hutton and Millett) refused to allow the striking out of the claims.

Lord Slynn: My Lords, the appeals in these four cases were heard together. They all raise questions as to the liability of a local education authority for what is said to have been a failure, either by the local authority or by employees for whom the local authority was vicariously liable, in the provision of appropriate educational services for children at school...

I do not, rule out the possibility of a direct claim in all situations where the local authority is exercising its powers...

Since the authority can only act through its employees or agents, and if they are negligent vicarious liability will arise, it may rarely be necessary to invoke a claim for direct liability. After the argument in these cases, I do not, however, accept the absolute statement that an education authority 'owes no common law duty of care ... in the exercise of the powers ... relating to children with special educational needs' under the Act of 1981...

Lord Nicholls: ... So far I have been considering the duties owed to a child by individual educational psychologists and teachers, and the resultant vicarious liability of local education authorities. This leaves unresolved the question whether the education authority itself owes a duty of care to the children in its schools. It was common ground, and rightly so, that the educational obligations imposed on local education authorities by statute cannot give rise to a (private law) action for damages for breach of statutory duty at the suit of pupils in their schools. But does an education authority owe to school pupils a duty at common law to take reasonable care in discharging its educational functions, either as regards children with special educational needs or generally?

This is an exceedingly difficult question. One of the difficulties lies in identifying satisfactorily what are the types of case which would be left without remedy if direct liability, as distinct from vicarious liability, were excluded. This, in turn, makes it difficult to evaluate the validity of drawing a distinction between direct liability and vicarious liability of local education authorities in this context...

(For further extracts see p 308.)

7.1.2 Liability based on property interests

Liability for the acts of others – or apparent acts of others – can arise from legal ideas other than those outlined above. One fundamental idea is the property relationship. This can manifest itself in a number of ways, but a relationship of bailment is of particular importance. In *Morris v Martin* (p 23) the defendant was liable, at least according to Diplock LJ, because it was a bailee and this relationship in itself can give rise to liability. Although enforced through a tort remedy (once detinue but now conversion), bailment is a proprietary rather than a personal relationship; and so the claimant in *Morris* was in essence demanding the return of her property and it was no answer for the defendant to say that it was not he who stole the stole. But, this said, the case is also seen as a vicarious liability precedent, the court deciding that the employee who stole the stole was not acting outside the course of his employment (or the scope of his function to use the PETL expression). Bailment involves only moveable property, yet real property can also create liabilities on the part of occupiers and (or) landlords for acts done by third parties: see *Smith v Littlewoods* (p 223).

7.1.3 Local authorities

Nuisance and negligence are two torts that can arise in three-party situations and, as the previous extracts indicate, local authorities are particularly vulnerable to such actions (see eg *Phelps v Hillingdon* (2001), above, p 228). The position of such public bodies will be examined in detail in Chapter 9. Suffice it to note for the present that the three-party negligence cases involving local authorities or other governmental agencies often raise the duty questions of a mere omission (see eg *Stovin v Wise* (1996), pp 136, 152, 296) and (or) pure economic loss (*Murphy v Brentwood DC* (1991)).

7.1.4 Contract

Liability of one person for the acts of another can also arise in situations where there is a contractual relationship between the claimant and the defendant. Here the relevant principle is summed up in art 8.107 of the *Principles of European Contract Law*: 'A party who entrusts performance of the contract to another person remains responsible for performance'. One Privy Council decision giving expression to this principle is *Wong Mee Wan v Kwan Kin Travel Services* (1996). Another case forms the next extract.

Photo Production Ltd v Securicor Transport Ltd [1980] AC 827, HL

This was an action for damages brought by the owners of a factory (or more precisely their insurance company) against a security company in respect of a fire deliberately started by one of the security company's patrolmen. The fire completely destroyed the claimants' factory, but the security company resisted liability on the basis of a clause in the contract which stipulated that 'under no circumstances' were the defendants to be 'responsible for any injurious act or default by any employee unless such act or default could have been foreseen and avoided by the exercise of due diligence on the part of the [defendants] as his employer; nor, in any event, [were the defendants to] be held responsible for any loss suffered by the [claimants] through fire or any other cause, except in so far as such loss [was]

▶

solely attributable to the negligence of the [defendants'] employees acting within the course of their employment.' The trial judge gave judgment for the security company; the Court of Appeal reversed this decision. Although an appeal to the House of Lords (Lords Wilberforce, Diplock, Salmon, Keith and Scarman) was allowed, the Law Lords made it clear that, but for the exclusion clause, the security company would be liable for the deliberate act of their patrolman.

Lord Diplock: ... My Lords, it is characteristic of commercial contracts, nearly all of which today are entered into not by natural legal persons, but by fictitious ones, ie companies, that the parties promise to one another that some thing will be done; for instance, that property and possession of goods will be transferred, that goods will be carried by ship from one port to another, that a building will be constructed in accordance with agreed plans, that services of a particular kind will be provided. Such a contract is the source of primary legal obligations upon each party to it to procure that whatever he has promised will be done is done. (I leave aside arbitration clauses which do not come into operation until a party to the contract claims that a primary obligation has not been observed.)

Where what is promised will be done involves the doing of a physical act, performance of the promise necessitates procuring a natural person to do it; but the legal relationship between the promisor and the natural person by whom the act is done, whether it is that of master and servant, or principal and agent, or of parties to an independent sub-contract, is generally irrelevant. If that person fails to do it in the manner in which the promisor has promised to procure it to be done, as, for instance, with reasonable skill and care, the promisor has failed to fulfil his own primary obligation. This is to be distinguished from 'vicarious liability' – a legal concept which does depend upon the existence of a particular legal relationship between the natural person by whom a tortious act was done and the person sought to be made vicariously liable for it. In the interests of clarity the expression should, in my view, be confined to liability for tort...

QUESTION

Could the security company have been held liable to the factory owner in trespass?

NOTE

The reference to *Morris v Martin* was probably unnecessary since there was a contractual relationship between the factory owner and the security company (cf **7.3.1**). The security company, which could only act through its employees, failed to perform this contract and thus (but for the exclusion clause) would be liable for breach of contract. However only Lord Diplock seemed fully to discuss this point.

7.2 Liability for employees

English law, like French law (see art 1384 of the CC), has a very clear rule with regard to damage caused by employees. An employer (master) will be vicariously liable for torts committed by an employee (servant) acting in the course of his employment. Such liability is strict in the sense that once the employee would be personally liable to the claimant the employer will be automatically liable as well. The claimant, when suing the employer, has in other words to prove only (a) that there was a tort (b) committed by an employee (c) acting in the course of his employment. Each of these requirements will be examined below after an introductory section looking at the background and theory basis to vicarious liability.

7.2.1 Vicarious liability: general considerations

The rule, as we have seen, is easily stated as the following statutory extract indicates.

Police Act 1996 (c 16)

88. Liability for wrongful acts of constables.

(1) The chief officer of police for a police area shall be liable in respect of any unlawful conduct of constables under his direction and control in the performance or purported performance of their functions in like manner as a master is liable in respect of any unlawful conduct of his servants in the course of their employment ...

QUESTION

What if a police officer maliciously abuses his power: can the victim of such an abuse of power sue under s 88? (Cf *Racz v Home Office* (1994).)

NOTE

Although the rule of vicarious liability, set out above, is well established and uncontroversial as a principle of liability, its theoretical basis is by no means clear. Various explanations have been proposed, but none completely explains all the cases. The following extract examines this basis.

Lister v Hesley Hall Ltd [2002] 1 AC 215, HL

(For facts and further extracts see p 242)

Lord Millett: ... **65** Vicarious liability is a species of strict liability. It is not premised on any culpable act or omission on the part of the employer; an employer who is not personally at fault is made legally answerable for the fault of his employee. It is best understood as a loss-distribution device: see Cane's edition of *Atiyah's Accidents, Compensation and the Law* 6th ed (1999), p 85 and the articles cited by Atiyah in his monograph on *Vicarious Liability in the Law of Torts*, at p 24. The theoretical underpinning of the doctrine is unclear. Glanville Williams wrote ('Vicarious Liability and the Master's Indemnity' (1957) 20 MLR 220, 231):

'Vicarious liability is the creation of many judges who have had different ideas of its justification or social policy, or no idea at all. Some judges may have extended the rule more widely or confined it more narrowly than its true rationale would allow; yet the rationale, if we can discover it, will remain valid so far as it extends'.

▶

Fleming observed (*The Law of Torts*, 9th ed (1998), p 410) that the doctrine cannot parade as a deduction from legalistic premises. He indicated that it should be frankly recognised as having its basis in a combination of policy considerations, and continued: 'Most important of these is the belief that a person who employs others to advance his own economic interest should in fairness be placed under a corresponding liability for losses incurred in the course of the enterprise...' Atiyah, *Vicarious Liability in the Law of Torts* wrote to the same effect. He suggested, at p 171: 'The master ought to be liable for all those torts which can fairly be regarded as reasonably incidental risks to the type of business he carries on'. These passages are not to be read as confining the doctrine to cases where the employer is carrying on business for profit. They are based on the more general idea that a person who employs another for his own ends inevitably creates a risk that the employee will commit a legal wrong. If the employer's objectives cannot be achieved without a serious risk of the employee committing the kind of wrong which he has in fact committed, the employer ought to be liable. The fact that his employment gave the employee the opportunity to commit the wrong is not enough to make the employer liable. He is liable only if the risk is one which experience shows is inherent in the nature of the business...

NOTE

As we saw in the *Photo Production* (1980) case (above, p 229), a company can only act through its human 'agents' and rules of vicarious liability should be viewed within this context. The principle of vicarious liability is not just a tort rule; it is equally part of company law in that it deems some acts as company acts (see further Lord Hoffmann in *Meridian Global Funds Management v Securities Commission* (1995)). Nevertheless the whole notion of a company as a fictional person (*persona ficta*) gives rise to structural oddities. In one sense company employees remain 'persons' separate from the 'person' of the company and thus a company may have a defence in criminal law when one of its employees, in carrying out his employment duties, commits a crime: see *Tesco v Nattrass* (1972). Equally the company, held liable under the vicarious liability rule, can sue the employee who actually committed the tort either in debt for contribution (see **11.6**) or in damages for breach of his contract of employment: *Lister v Romford Ice & Cold Storage Co* (1957) (pp 52, 55).

7.2.2 Tort

Three requirements have to be fulfilled before an employer can be held vicariously responsible for the act of another. The first requirement is that there was an actual tort.

Staveley Iron & Chemical Co v Jones [1956] AC 627, HL

This was an action for damages by an employee against his employer for an injury sustained due, so it was alleged, to the negligence of a fellow employee crane driver. Denning LJ in the Court of Appeal appeared to have suggested that the employer would be vicariously liable to the employee even if the latter could not actually prove negligence on the part of the crane driver. The House of Lords (Lords Morton, Porter, Reid, Tucker and Cohen) disagreed with Denning LJ on this point but held that the crane driver had been negligent.

Lord Morton: ... My Lords, what the court has to decide in the present case is: Was the crane driver negligent? If the answer is 'Yes,' the employer is liable vicariously for the negligence of his servant. If the answer is 'No,' the employer is surely under no liability at all. Cases such as this, where an employer's liability is vicarious, are wholly distinct from cases where an employer is under a personal liability to carry out a duty imposed upon him as an employer by common law or statute. In the latter type of case the employer cannot discharge himself by saying: 'I delegated the carrying out of this duty to a servant, and he failed to carry it out by a mistake or error of judgment not amounting to negligence.' To such a case one may well apply the words of Denning LJ: '[The employer] remains responsible even though the servant may, for some reason, be immune.' These words, however, are, in my view, incorrect as applied to a case where the liability of the employer is not personal but vicarious. In such a case if the servant is 'immune,' so is the employer. See, for instance, *Esso Petroleum Co Ltd v Southport Corporation*...

Although I have felt bound to express my dissent from this passage in the judgment of Denning LJ I am glad to find myself in agreement with the views expressed by him and by his colleagues that the crane driver was negligent...

Lord Reid: ... The Court of Appeal reversed the decision of Sellers J, but different views were expressed on the law. Denning LJ, as I read his judgment, did not find it necessary to hold that the crane driver was herself negligent. He said: 'The employer is made liable, not so much for the crane driver's fault, but rather for his own fault committed through her ... He acts by his servant; and his servant's acts are, for this purpose, to be considered as his acts. Qui facit per alium facit per se. He cannot escape by the plea that his servant was thoughtless or inadvertent or made an error of judgment. If he takes the benefit of a machine like this, he must accept the burden of seeing that it is properly handled. It is for this reason that the employer's responsibility for injury may be ranked greater than that of the servant who actually made the mistake.'

My Lords, if this means that the appellants could be held liable even if it were held that the crane driver was not herself guilty of negligence, then I cannot accept that view. Of course, an employer may be himself in fault by engaging an incompetent servant or not having a proper system of work or in some other way. But there is nothing of that kind in this case. Denning LJ appears to base his reasoning on a literal application of the maxim qui facit per alium facit per se, but, in my view, it is rarely profitable and often misleading to use Latin maxims in that way. It is a rule of law that an employer, though guilty of no fault himself, is liable for damage done by the fault or negligence of his servant acting in the course of his employment. The maxims respondeat superior and qui facit per alium facit per se are often used, but I do not think that they add anything or that they lead to any different results. The former merely states the rule baldly in two words, and the latter merely gives a fictional explanation of it...

...Hodson and Romer LJJ do not follow Denning LJ on this point and they appear to me to base their judgments on the crane driver having been negligent. I think she was negligent. The system was that there were two safety checks. Jones was supposed to see to the first, centring, and the crane driver was responsible for the second, pausing after taking the weight of the load. The first was not done but, as I have said, there is insufficient evidence to find that Jones was guilty of contributory negligence. But the fact that the first check was omitted is no excuse for failure to carry out the second, and the crane driver gave no reason to explain her failure. I am therefore of opinion that this appeal should be dismissed.

QUESTIONS

1. Is this case an example of the House of Lords deciding a question of pure fact?

2. Is the use of Latin phrases useful? (Cf Kidner (1995) 15 LS 47, 56ff.)

3. Could not negligence have been presumed, the employer only escaping liability if it could prove an absence of fault?

4. Can an employer be liable for a breach of duty which is of a type that is imposed on the employee rather than upon the employer? (Cf *Majrowski v Guy's and St Thomas's NHS Trust* (2005).)

7.2.3 Employee

The second requirement is that the tort must have been committed by an employee. However distinguishing an employee from an independent contractor is by no means easy.

Cassidy v Ministry of Health [1951] 2 KB 343, CA

This was an action for damages in respect of the negligent performance of an operation in one of the defendant's NHS hospitals. The claimant had entered the hospital for an operation on his left hand because he could not use it very well; however when he left he could not use it at all. The claimant alleged that someone must have been careless – the doctor, surgeon or a nurse – but he could not point to whom it was. The trial judge dismissed the action because the claimant had failed to prove that anyone had been negligent, but an appeal to the Court of Appeal (Somervell, Singleton and Denning LJJ) was allowed.

Denning LJ: ... The truth is that, in cases of negligence, the distinction between a contract of service and a contract for services only becomes of importance when it is sought to make the employer liable, not for a breach of his own duty of care, but for some collateral act of negligence of those whom he employs. He cannot escape the consequences of a breach of his own duty, but he can escape responsibility for collateral or casual acts of negligence if he can show that the negligent person was employed, not under a contract of service but only under a contract for services. Take first an instance when an employer is under no duty himself: he is riding passively in a car along a road; he is not under any duty of care himself to road-users, but the driver is. If the driver is a chauffeur employed under a contract of service, the employer is liable for his negligence: but if the driver is a taximan employed under a contract for services, the employer is not liable.

Take now an instance where an employer is under a duty himself:- Suppose an employer has a lamp which overhangs his shop door; he is himself under a duty to his customers to use reasonable care to see that it is safe, and he cannot escape that duty by employing an independent contractor to do it. He is liable, therefore, if the independent contractor fails to discover a patent defect which any careful man should have discovered, and in consequence the lamp falls on a customer; but he is not liable if the independent contractor drops a hammer on the head of the customer, because that is not negligence in the employer's department of duty. It is collateral or casual negligence by one employed under a contract for services. The employer would, however, have been liable if he had got his servant to mend the lamp and his servant dropped the hammer; because that would be negligence by one employed under a contract of service...

Turning now to the facts in this case, this is the position: the hospital authorities accepted the plaintiff as a patient for treatment, and it was their duty to treat him with reasonable care. They selected, employed, and paid all the surgeons and nurses who looked after him. He had no say in their selection at all. If those surgeons and nurses did not treat him with proper care and skill, then the hospital authorities must answer for it, for it means that they themselves did not perform their duty to him. I decline to enter into the question whether any of the surgeons were employed only under a contract for services, as distinct from a contract of service. The evidence is meagre enough in all conscience on that point. But the liability of the hospital authorities should not, and does not, depend on nice considerations of that sort. The plaintiff knew nothing of the terms on which they employed their staff: all he knew was that he was treated in the hospital by people whom the hospital authorities appointed; and the hospital authorities must be answerable for the way in which he was treated.

This conclusion has an important bearing on the question of evidence. If the plaintiff had to prove that some particular doctor or nurse was negligent, he would not be able to do it. But he was not put to that impossible task: he says, 'I went into the hospital to be cured of two stiff fingers. I have come out with four stiff fingers, and my hand is useless. That should not have happened if due care had been used. Explain it, if you can'. I am quite clearly of opinion that that raises a prima facie case against the hospital authorities: see per Goddard, LJ, in *Mahon v Osborne*. They have nowhere explained how it could happen without negligence. They have busied themselves in saying that this or that member of their staff was not negligent. But they have called not a single person to say that the injuries were consistent with due care on the part of all the members of their staff. They called some of the people who actually treated the man, namely Dr Fahrni, Dr Ronaldson, and Sister Hall, each of whom protested that he was careful in his part; but they did not call any expert at all, to say that this might happen despite all care. They have not therefore displaced the prima facie case against them and are liable to damages to the plaintiff...

NOTE

See also *Roe v Minister of Health* (1954) (p 320).

QUESTION

How should one approach this employee issue in terms of method?

Hall v Lorimer [1992] 1 WLR 939, QBD

Mummery J: ... In order to decide whether a person carries on business on his own account it is necessary to consider many different aspects of that person's work activity. This is not a mechanical exercise of running through items on a check list to see whether they are present in, or absent from, a given situation. The object of the exercise is to paint a picture from the accumulation of detail. The overall effect can only be appreciated by standing back from the detailed picture which has been painted, by viewing it from a distance and by making an informed, considered, qualitative appreciation of the whole. It is a matter of evaluation of the overall effect of the detail, which is not necessarily the same as the sum total of the individual details. Not all details are of equal weight or importance in any given situation. The details may also vary in importance from one situation to another.

[Mummery J's decision was upheld by the Court of Appeal.]

NOTE

The question of who is an employee has arisen in cases that are not actually vicarious liability problems, for the term is used in national insurance and tax legislation. These cases have, however, a precedent value for tort (but cf Kidner (1995) 15 LS 47).

Market Investigations Ltd v Ministry of Social Security [1969] 2 QB 173, QBD

Cooke J: The appellant company in this case, Market Investigations Ltd, are engaged in the field of market research. In addition to their permanent staff at the headquarters office, they employ interviewers for about eight to ten thousand interviews annually to provide information for the company's customers about the habits and opinions of members of the general public, retailers or other people in commerce, industry and the professions...

... The sole issue for determination in the appeal is whether, as the company say, Mrs Irving was employed during the relevant period under a series of contracts for services or, as the Minister says, she was employed during that period under a series of contracts of service...

I think it is fair to say that there was at one time a school of thought according to which the extent and degree of the control which B was entitled to exercise over A in the performance of the work would be a decisive factor. However, it has for long been apparent that an analysis of the extent and degree of such control is not in itself decisive...

The observations of Lord Wright, of Denning LJ and of the judges of the Supreme Court suggest that the fundamental test to be applied is this: 'Is the person who has engaged himself to perform these services performing them as a person in business on his own account?' If the answer to that question is 'yes,' then the contract is a contract for services. If the answer is 'no,' then the contract is a contract of service. No exhaustive list has been compiled and perhaps no exhaustive list can be compiled of the considerations which are relevant in determining that question, nor can strict rules be laid down as to the relative weight which the various considerations should carry in particular cases. The most that can be said is that control will no doubt always have to be considered, although it can no longer be regarded as the sole determining factor; and that factors which may be of importance are such matters as whether the man performing the services provides his own equipment, whether he hires his own helpers, what degree of financial risk he takes, what degree of responsibility for investment and management he has, and whether and how far he has an opportunity of profiting from sound management in the performance of his task...

In the present case it is clear that on each occasion on which Mrs Irving engaged herself to act as an interviewer for a particular survey she agreed with the company, in consideration of a fixed remuneration, to provide her own work and skill in the performance of a service for the company. I therefore proceed to ask myself two questions: First, whether the extent and degree of the control exercised by the company, if no other factors were taken into account, be consistent with her being employed under a contract of service. Second, whether when the contract is looked at as a whole, its nature and provisions are consistent or inconsistent with its being a contract of service, bearing in mind the general test I have adumbrated...

It is apparent that the control which the company had the right to exercise in this case was very extensive indeed. It was in my view so extensive as to be entirely consistent with Mrs Irving's being employed under a contract of service. The fact that Mrs Irving had a limited discretion as to when she should do the work was not in my view inconsistent with the existence of a contract of service... Nor is there anything inconsistent with the existence of a contract of service in the fact that Mrs Irving was free to work for others during the relevant period. It is by no means a necessary incident of a contract of service that the servant is prohibited from serving any other employer. Again, there is nothing inconsistent with the existence of a contract of service in the master having no right to alter the place or area within which the servant has agreed to work. So far as concerns practical limitations on a master's power to give instructions to his servant, there must be many cases when such practical limitations exist. For example, a chauffeur in the service of a car hire company may, in the absence of radio communication, be out of reach of instructions for long periods...

...The opportunity to deploy individual skill and personality is frequently present in what is undoubtedly a contract of service. I have already said that the right to work for others is not inconsistent with the existence of a contract of service. Mrs Irving did not provide her own tools or risk her own capital, nor did her opportunity of profit depend in any significant degree on the way she managed her work.

Taking all the factors into account... I am clearly of opinion that on the facts of this case the Minister was right in concluding that Mrs Irving was employed by the company under a series of contracts of service, and the appeal accordingly must fail.

QUESTION

Are the following 'employees' for the purposes of vicarious liability: (a) casual workers fruit picking on a farm; (b) taxi drivers who own their own cars and who work when they want directed to clients by a radio call centre; (c) borstal boys doing prison work; (d) a young person helping his local milkman do the milk rounds; (e) a young person doing a paper round every morning; (f) a lorry driver working in company uniform but whose contract with the company specifically states that he is an independent contractor who must purchase his own uniform and lorry (out of an interest free loan provided by the company)? (Cf Kidner (1995) 15 LS 47.)

7.2.4 Transferred employee

One particular problem that can arise in vicarious liability is that of the transferred employee. For example, a crane-hire firm hires out one of its cranes, together with a driver, to a construction company for a longish period during which the crane driver carelessly injures someone on the site. The issue here is not one of whether or not the driver is an employee; it is a matter of which 'employer' – the crane-hire firm or the construction company – is to be liable to the victim.

Mersey Docks and Harbour Board v Coggins and Griffith (Liverpool) Ltd [1947] AC 1, HL

This was an action for damages by a dockyard employee against a harbour authority in respect of personal injuries suffered when he was run over by a crane carelessly driven by a man called Newall. The harbour authority had hired out the crane and its driver, Newall, to a firm of stevedores and it was stipulated that drivers would be employees of anyone hiring such a crane. Newall himself, when asked in court from whom he took his orders, replied 'I take no orders from anybody'. The trial judge held that the crane driver was the employee of the harbour board when the accident occurred and appeals to the Court of Appeal and House of Lords (Lords Porter, Uthwatt, Simon, Macmillan and Simonds) were dismissed.

Lord Macmillan: ... [I]t is always open to an employer to show, if he can, that he has for a particular purpose or on a particular occasion temporarily transferred the services of one of his general servants to another party so as to constitute him pro hac vice the servant of that other party with consequent liability for his negligent acts. The burden is on the general employer to establish that such a transference has been effected. Agreeing as I do with the trial judge and the Court of Appeal, I am of opinion that, on the facts of the present case, Newall was never so transferred from the service and control of the appellant board to the service and control of the stevedores as to render the stevedores answerable for the manner in which he carried on his work of driving the crane. The stevedores were entitled to tell him where to go, what parcels to lift and where to take them, that is to say, they could direct him as to what they wanted him to do; but they had no authority to tell him how he was to handle the crane in doing his work. In driving the crane, which was the appellant board's property confided to his charge, he was acting as the servant of the appellant board, not as the servant of the stevedores. It was not in consequence of any order of the stevedores that he negligently ran down the plaintiff; it was in consequence of his negligence in driving the crane, that is to say, in performing the work which he was employed by the appellant board to do...

... Reference was also made to art 6 of the appellant board's regulations which states that drivers provided by the appellant board 'shall be the servants of the applicants,' that is, of the parties to whom they are hired. But this does not mean that the appellant board's drivers cease to be the servants of the appellant board when they accompany cranes, which the appellant board lets out on hire. Servants cannot be transferred from one service to another without their consent and even where consent may be implied there will always remain a question as to the extent and effect of the transfer. Here the driver became the servant of the stevedores only to the extent and effect of his taking directions from them as to the utilization of the crane in assisting their work, not as to how he should drive it. Many reported cases were cited to your Lordships but where, as all agree, the question in each case turns on its own circumstances, decisions in other cases are rather illustrative than determinative. So far as attempts have been made to formulate a criterion of general application it cannot be said that these attempts have been very successful...

Lord Porter: ... Many factors have a bearing on the result. Who is paymaster, who can dismiss, how long the alternative service lasts, what machinery is employed, have all to be kept in mind. The expressions used in any individual case must always be considered in regard to the subject matter under discussion but amongst the many tests suggested I think that the most satisfactory, by which to ascertain who is the employer at any particular time, is to ask who is entitled to tell the employee the way in which he is to do the work upon which he is engaged. If someone other than his general employer is authorized to do this he will, as a rule, be the person liable for the employee's negligence. But it is not enough that the task to be performed should be under his control, he must also control the method of performing it. It is true that in most cases no orders as to how a job should be done are given or required: the man is left to do his own work in his own way. But the ultimate question is not what specific orders, or whether any specific orders, were given but who is entitled to give the orders as to how the work should be done. Where a man driving a mechanical device, such as a crane, is sent to perform a task, it is easier to infer that the general employer continues to control the method of performance since it is his crane and the driver remains responsible to him for its safe keeping. In the present case if the appellants' contention were to prevail, the crane driver would change his employer each time he embarked on the discharge of a fresh ship. Indeed, he might change it from day to day, without any say as to who his master should be and with all the concomitant disadvantages of uncertainty as to who should be responsible for his insurance in respect of health, unemployment and accident. I cannot think that such a conclusion is to be drawn from the facts established. I would dismiss the appeal.

7.2.5 Course of employment

The third requirement of vicarious liability is that the employee must have been acting in the course of his employment when the tort was committed. Thus a van driver supplied with a company van might well be acting on 'a frolic of his own' if he carelessly injures another road user while using the van one Sunday for a family picnic.

Smith v Stages [1989] AC 928, HL

This was an action for damages for personal injuries by a car passenger named Machin against a co-employee, who was driving the car, called Stages. The employer of the two men was joined as second defendant. The personal injuries resulted from a car accident which occurred when the men were returning from a job to which they had been sent by their employer. The car accident had been caused by Stages' negligence, but it turned out that he was uninsured and thus Machin argued that the employer was vicariously liable for Stages' negligence. The employer claimed that Stages was not acting in the course of his employment when the accident occurred. The House of Lords (Lords Goff, Lowry, Keith, Brandon and Griffiths) held the employer liable.

Lord Goff: ... We can begin with the simple proposition that, in ordinary circumstances, when a man is travelling to or from his place of work, he is not acting in the course of his employment. So a bank clerk who commutes to the City of London every day from Sevenoaks, is not acting in the course of his employment when he walks across London Bridge from the station to his bank in the City. This is because he is not employed to travel from his home to the bank; he is employed to work at the bank, his place of work, and so his duty is to arrive there in time for his working day. Nice points can arise about the precise time, or place, at which he may be held to have arrived at work; but these do not trouble us in the present case. Likewise, of course, he is not acting in the course of his employment when he is travelling home after his day's work is over. If however a man is obliged by his employer to travel to work by means of transport provided by his employer, he may be held to be acting in the course of his employment when so doing...

I approach the matter as follows. I do not regard this case as an ordinary case of travelling to work. It would be more accurate to describe it as a case where an employee, who has for a short time to work for his employers at a different place of work some distance away from his usual place of work, has to move from his ordinary base to a temporary base (here lodgings in Pembroke) from which he will travel to work at the temporary place of work each day. For the purpose of moving base, a normal working day was set aside for Stages' journey, for which he was paid as for an eight hour day. In addition to his day's pay he was given a travel allowance for his journey, and an allowance for his lodgings at his temporary base in Pembroke. In my opinion, in all the circumstances of the case, Stages was required by the employers to make this journey, so as to make himself available to do his work at the Pembroke Power Station, and it would be proper to describe him as having been employed to do so...

I turn to Stages' journey back. Another ordinary working day, Tuesday, 30 August, was made available for the journey, with the same pay, to enable him to return to his base in the Midlands to be ready to travel to work on the Wednesday morning. In my opinion, he was employed to make the journey back, just as he was employed to make the journey out to Pembroke. If he had chosen to go to sleep on the Monday morning and afternoon for eight hours or so, and then to drive home on the Monday evening so that he could have Tuesday free (as indeed Mr Pye expected him to do), that would not have detracted from the proposition that his journey was in the course of his employment. For this purpose, it was irrelevant that Monday was a bank holiday. Of course, it was wrong for him to succumb to the temptation of driving home on the Monday morning, just after he had completed so long a spell of work; but once again that cannot alter the fact that his journey was made in the course of his employment...

QUESTIONS

1. Did Stages' lack of insurance put him in breach of his contract of employment? Did it put him in breach of any duty towards Machin?

2. What if the employers had specifically instructed both men not to travel by car: if they had disobeyed this instruction would this mean that, while in the car, they were automatically outside the course of their employment?

3. What if they had given a lift to a hitch-hiker: if he had been injured in the accident would he have been able to sue the employer?

4. What if Stages and Machin carelessly left the car with the keys in the ignition while they went for a cup of tea and a thief knocked down and injured a passer-by while driving off in the car: could the passer-by sue the employer?

NOTE

In considering the above questions, read *Rose v Plenty* (1976) in the law report.

7.2.6 Criminal act

One of the most difficult problems in the course of employment requirement is where the employee's tortious act is also a criminal act. Does this automatically take the act outside the course of employment?

Morris v CW Martin & Sons Ltd [1966] 1 QB 716, CA

(For facts and further extract see p 23)

Salmon LJ: ... A bailee for reward is not answerable for a theft by any of his servants but only for a theft by such of them as are deputed by him to discharge some part of his duty of taking reasonable care. A theft by any servant who is not employed to do anything in relation to the goods bailed is entirely outside the scope of his employment and cannot make the master liable. So in this case, if someone employed by the defendants in another depot had broken in and stolen the fur, the defendants would not have been liable. Similarly in my view if a clerk employed in the same depot had seized the opportunity of entering the room where the fur was kept and had stolen it, the defendants would not have been liable. The mere fact that the master, by employing a rogue, gives him the opportunity to steal or defraud does not make the master liable for his depredations: *Ruben v Great Fingall Consolidated*. It might be otherwise if the master knew or ought to have known that his servant was dishonest, because then the master could be liable in negligence for employing him...

NOTE

This case is important for vicarious liability because it established that a criminal act of an employee would not necessarily take him outside the course of his employment (and see *Photo Production* (1980), p 229). The test was whether the employee was doing what he was employed to do (a test that has now been modified as will be seen). In *Morris* he was employed to handle the stole, which no doubt he did rather too well, and this *authorised contact* with the thing in issue was enough to keep his criminal act within the scope of his employment. Nevertheless this test had its limits: see eg *Keppel Bus Co Ltd v Sa'ad bin Ahmad* (1974) (read it in the law report). In *Keppel* the Privy Council held that the employer of a bus conductor who deliberately injured a passenger was not liable for this damage. But the problem with cases like *Keppel* was that it seemed an affront to common sense that because the conductor's behaviour was worse than careless, the company could escape liability (for if the conductor had negligently injured the passenger with his ticket machine the bus company would of course have been liable). The next case, perhaps now the major leading precedent on course of employment, has gone some way in recognising this latter criticism.

Lister v Hesley Hall Ltd [2002] 1 AC 215, HL

This was an action for damages against the employer of a warden of a boarding house in which the claimants had been resident when young teenagers. The claimants had been sexually abused by the warden while in residence and they claimed damages from the employer on the basis both of a breach of a direct duty of care and of vicarious liability. The judge dismissed the direct claims against the employer and held that the employer could not be vicariously liable for the warden's torts against the boys. However, he held that the employers were vicariously liable for the warden's failure to report the abuses. An appeal by the employers was allowed by the Court of Appeal, but this was overturned on further appeal to the House of Lords (Lords Steyn, Clyde, Hutton, Hobhouse and Millett).

Lord Steyn: My Lords, ... **1** The central question before the House is whether as a matter of legal principle the employers of the warden of a school boarding house, who sexually abused boys in his care, may depending on the particular circumstances be vicariously liable for the torts of their employee...

14 Vicarious liability is legal responsibility imposed on an employer, although he is himself free from blame, for a tort committed by his employee in the course of his employment. Fleming observed that this formula represented 'a compromise between two conflicting policies: on the one end, the social interest in furnishing an innocent tort victim with recourse against a financially responsible defendant; on the other, a hesitation to foist any undue burden on business enterprise': *The Law of Torts*, 9th ed (1998), pp 409–410.

15 For nearly a century English judges have adopted Salmond's statement of the applicable test as correct. Salmond said that a wrongful act is deemed to be done by a 'servant' in the course of his employment if 'it is either (a) a wrongful act authorised by the master, or (b) a wrongful and unauthorised mode of doing some act authorised by the master': *Salmond on Torts*, 1st ed (1907), p 83; and *Salmond and Heuston on Torts*, 21st ed (1996), p 443...

16 It is not necessary to embark on a detailed examination of the development of the modern principle of vicarious liability. But it is necessary to face up to the way in which the law of vicarious liability sometimes may embrace intentional wrongdoing by an employee. If one mechanically applies *Salmond's* test, the result might at first glance be thought to be that a bank is not liable to a customer where a bank employee defrauds a customer by giving him only half the foreign exchange which he paid for, the employee pocketing the difference. A preoccupation with conceptualistic reasoning may lead to the absurd conclusion that there can only be vicarious liability if the bank carries on business in defrauding its customers. Ideas divorced from reality have never held much attraction for judges steeped in the tradition that their task is to deliver principled but practical justice. How the courts set the law on a sensible course is a matter to which I now turn...

19 The classic example of vicarious liability for intentional wrong doing is *Morris v C W Martin & Sons Ltd* [1966] 1 QB 716...

22 The Court of Appeal treated the *Morris v CW Martin & Sons Ltd* [1966] 1 QB 716 line of authority as applicable only in bailment cases. That was the Court of Appeal's answer to the argument that, in the context of vicarious liability, the law ought not to incur the reproach of showing greater zeal in protecting jewellery than in protecting children. My Lords, I trust that I have already shown that Morris's case cannot be so easily dismissed. It is only necessary to add that in *Photo Production Ltd v Securicor Transport Ltd* [1980] AC 827 the House of Lords took the view that the principles enunciated in *Morris's* case by Diplock and Salmon LJ are of general application...

24 It is useful to consider an employer's potential liability for non-sexual assaults. If such assaults arise directly out of circumstances connected with the employment, vicarious liability may arise: see Rose, 'Liability for an employee's assaults' (1977), 40 MLR 420, 432–433. Butler-Sloss LJ considered this analogy... If I correctly understand [her] passage, it appears to be indicating that there could not be vicarious liability by an employer for a brutal assault, or serious sexual misconduct, whatever the circumstances. That appears to be a case of saying 'The greater the fault of the servant, the less the liability of the master': *Morris v CW Martin & Sons Ltd* [1966] 1 QB 716, 733, per Diplock LJ. A better approach is to concentrate on the relative closeness of the connection between the nature of the employment and the particular tort.

25 In my view the approach of the Court of Appeal in *Trotman v North Yorkshire County Council* [1999] LGR 584 was wrong. It resulted in the case being treated as one of the employment furnishing a mere opportunity to commit the sexual abuse. The reality was that the county council were responsible for the care of the vulnerable children and employed the deputy headmaster to carry out that duty on its behalf. And the sexual abuse took place while the employee was engaged in duties at the very time and place demanded by his employment. The connection between the employment and the torts was very close. I would overrule *Trotman v North Yorkshire County Council*...

Lord Millett: ... **79** ... [I]t is no answer to say that the employee was guilty of intentional wrongdoing, or that his act was not merely tortious but criminal, or that he was acting exclusively for his own benefit, or that he was acting contrary to express instructions, or that his conduct was the very negation of his employer's duty. The cases show that where an employer undertakes the care of a client's property and entrusts the task to an employee who steals the property, the employer is vicariously liable. This is not only in accordance with principle but with the underlying rationale if Atiyah has correctly identified it. Experience shows that the risk of theft by an employee is inherent in a business

▶

which involves entrusting the custody of a customer's property to employees. But the theft must be committed by the very employee to whom the custody of the property is entrusted. He does more than make the most of an opportunity presented by the fact of his employment. He takes advantage of the position in which the employer has placed him to enable the purposes of the employer's business to be achieved. If the boys in the present case had been sacks of potatoes and the defendant, having been engaged to take care of them, had entrusted their care to one of its employees, it would have been vicariously liable for any criminal damage done to them by the employee in question, though not by any other employee. Given that the employer's liability does not arise from the law of bailment, it is not immediately apparent that it should make any difference that the victims were boys, that the wrongdoing took the form of sexual abuse, and that it was committed for the personal gratification of the employee...

82 In the present case the warden's duties provided him with the opportunity to commit indecent assaults on the boys for his own sexual gratification, but that in itself is not enough to make the school liable. The same would be true of the groundsman or the school porter. But there was far more to it than that. The school was responsible for the care and welfare of the boys. It entrusted that responsibility to the warden. He was employed to discharge the school's responsibility to the boys. For this purpose the school entrusted them to his care. He did not merely take advantage of the opportunity which employment at a residential school gave him. He abused the special position in which the school had placed him to enable it to discharge its own responsibilities, with the result that the assaults were committed by the very employee to whom the school had entrusted the care of the boys... I would hold the school liable...

84 I would hold the school vicariously liable for the warden's intentional assaults, not (as was suggested in argument) for his failure to perform his duty to take care of the boys. That is an artificial approach based on a misreading of *Morris v Martin*. The cleaners were vicariously liable for their employee's conversion of the fur, not for his negligence in failing to look after it. Similarly in *Photo Production v Securicor Transport Ltd* the security firm was vicariously liable for the patrolman's arson, not for his negligence. The law is mature enough to hold an employer vicariously liable for deliberate, criminal wrongdoing on the part of an employee without indulging in sophistry of this kind. I would also not base liability on the warden's failure to report his own wrongdoing to his employer, an approach which I regard as both artificial and unrealistic. Even if such a duty did exist, on which I prefer to express no opinion, I am inclined to think that it would be a duty owed exclusively to the employer and not a duty for breach of which the employer could be vicariously liable. The same reasoning would not, of course, necessarily apply to the duty to report the wrongdoing of fellow employees, but it is not necessary to decide this...

NOTE

This case is an important precedent because it has gone some way in developing, if not expanding, the course of employment test in situations where the employee's wrongful act was criminal. The test is now this: there will be liability 'where the unauthorised acts of the employee are so *connected with* acts which the employer has authorised that they may properly be regarded as being within the scope of his employment'. Or, to quote a more recent observation: 'What matters is the closeness of the connection between the offending conduct of the employee with the nature and circumstances of that employment... It is the breach of the duty, as much as the duty itself, which is caught by the new test' (Auld LJ in *Majrowski v Guy's and St Thomas's NHS Trust* (2005) § 38). In short, the key word is 'connection'. The effect of *Lister* can be felt in the next case.

Mattis v Pollock [2003] 1 WLR 2158, CA

This was an action for damages, by the victim of a serious assault, against the owner of a nightclub which had employed the doorman who had carried out the attack. The doorman, while on duty, had become involved in a dispute in which he instigated a violent confrontation with a group wishing to enter the club. The group fought back and the doorman escaped to his flat. Later the doorman reappeared with a knife and attacked the claimant, for which he was later convicted and imprisoned. The claimant based his action on the breach of a direct duty of care with respect to the hiring of the doorman and on the vicarious liability of the owner for the tort of the doorman. The trial judge dismissed the claim but the Court of Appeal (Judge and Dyson LJJ and Pumfrey J) allowed an appeal.

Judge LJ (delivering judgment of the court): ... **19** The essential principle we derive from the reasoning in the *Lister* and *Dubai Aluminium* cases is that Mr Pollock's vicarious liability to Mr Mattis for Cranston's attack requires a deceptively simple question to be answered. Approaching the matter broadly, was the assault 'so closely connected' with what Mr Pollock authorised or expected of Cranston in the performance of his employment as doorman at his nightclub, that it would be fair and just to conclude that Mr Pollock is vicariously liable for the damage Mr Mattis sustained when Crantson stabbed him...

30 Cranston was indeed employed by Mr Pollock to keep order and discipline at the nightclub. That is what bouncers are employed to do. Moreover, however, he was encouraged and expected to perform his duties in an aggressive and intimidatory manner, which included physical man-handling of customers. In our judgment, this aspect of the evidence was not sufficiently addressed by Judge Seymour QC. He suggested that the evidence went no further than a single incident of inappropriate violence (on 18 July) which would not have justified immediate dismissal. Whether, taking Cranston's behaviour as a whole, it would have been appropriate to dismiss him, is a moot point. The reality was that Mr Pollock should not have been employing Cranston at all, and certainly should not have been encouraging him to perform his duties as he did. It was not perhaps anticipated that Cranston's behaviour would be counter-productive, and that by way of self-defence, and indeed revenge, his behaviour would provoke a violent response. That is because the customers with whom he tangled were supposed to be intimidated, and to go quietly. The whole point of any physical confrontation with Mr Pollock's customers in the nightclub, whether engineered by Cranston or not, was that he should win it.

31 Judge Seymour QC accurately noted that the incident might have ended at a number of different stages before Mr Mattis was stabbed. Nevertheless, that did not of itself provide the definitive answer to the question whether Mr Pollock should be held vicariously liable for the stabbing... Cranston was still in his working hours, and if he had

▶

not found an immediate target on whom to vent his anger outside the club, it seems probable that he would have returned inside the club to ascertain whether any of his attackers were still there. If so, on the facts found here, we have little doubt that he would have been violent within the premises, as he was outside them. In any event his return to the immediate vicinity was motivated by a need to revenge the physical injuries and public humiliation he had sustained inside the club. The incident had wholly undermined his reputation and status as the doorman Mr Pollock expected him to be. And the words he used as he stabbed Mr Mattis demonstrated that he had Mr Mattis's intervention in defence of Mr Cook in the forefront of his mind, and that his actions were directly linked to the incident which had taken place earlier in the club.

33 The issue of Mr Pollock's personal, as opposed to vicarious liability, was not closely canvassed in argument. Judge Seymour QC's robust approach to this aspect of his decision derived from his conclusion that personal liability would not survive the reasoning which had led him to conclude that the claim based on vicarious liability must fail. In the circumstances of this case we accept the validity of this approach adding, however, that personal liability would not necessarily and always follow the establishment of vicarious liability. In the present case, however, it does. Mr Pollock chose to employ Cranston, knowing and approving of his aggressive tendencies, which he encouraged rather than curbed, and the assault on Mr Mattis represented the culmination of an incident which began in Mr Pollock's premises and involved his customers, in which his employee behaved in the violent and aggressive manner which Mr Pollock expected of him.

34 Given the particular circumstances in which we have found that vicarious liability is established, if we had to decide the point, Mr Pollock's personal liability would also follow.

QUESTION

Can you modify these facts as to time and place so as to produce a factual situation in which the nightclub owner would not be liable for the revenge attack by the doorman?

7.3 Liability for non-employees

Vicarious liability comes into play only when the actor who commits the tort is an employee of the defendant. What is the position if the actor is not actually an employee?

7.3.1 Unauthorised user

For example, what is the position if a stranger (or other unauthorised user) injures someone while using the defendant's property?

Topp v London Country Bus (South West) Ltd [1993] 1 WLR 976, CA

Dillon LJ: ... The claim is a claim for damages arising out of the death of the plaintiff's wife, Mrs Jacqueline Topp, on 25 April 1988... The defendants run a bus service in the region of Epsom, and one of their buses was hijacked by a third party, who has never been identified, at about 11 pm on 25 April. Very shortly afterwards the bus, driven by the hijacker, knocked down and killed Mrs Topp as she was cycling home from work in Dorking Road, Epsom...

In accordance with usual practice, the driver, Mr Green, left the bus in that lay-by at the bus stop at about 2.35 p.m. on 24 April 1988. He left it unlocked, with the ignition key in it. He had then a 40-minute rest period before resuming his duties driving a different bus... It was taken by somebody who has never been traced just before 11.15 at night, driven for a relatively short distance until the point where Mrs Topp was knocked down and killed, and it was abandoned round the corner from there.

In these circumstances, the plaintiff's claim is founded in negligence on the basis that the bus company, knowing that there must be a threat that a bus left ready to be driven away might be stolen and that whoever stole it, a joyrider, might drive dangerously and kill or injure someone else or damage property, was in breach of duty in failing to collect the bus or see that it was locked, without an ignition key and not capable of being driven away.

...[I]t seems to me, as it did to May J, that there is no valid distinction between the present case and a decision of another division of this court (Stephen Brown, Nourse and Balcombe LJJ) in *Denton v United Counties Omnibus Co*. In that case, an omnibus owned by the defendants was unlawfully taken, by some person whose identity was never discovered, in the early hours of the morning from the defendants' bus station in the centre of Northampton. It was driven about a mile from the bus station and it collided with the plaintiff's motor car, which he had parked in a road near to his dwelling house, causing substantial damage to the car. Fortunately for the plaintiff in that case, the consequences of the unlawful taking of the bus were not so grave as in the present case.

...It was held by this court that the bus company owed no duty of care to the plaintiff and that the plaintiff's claim for damages must therefore be dismissed. All these cases in a certain sense depend on their own facts, but it is inevitable that there should be careful consideration of what, if any, valid distinctions there may be between cases which it is said should be decided differently.

I cannot see any valid distinction between the present case and *Denton's* case...

Rose LJ: I agree. I doubt whether, for my part, I would have found, as the judge did, that there was in the circumstances of this case a relationship of proximity between the defendants and Mrs Topp. But I entirely agree with the judge that no duty of care is shown either in principle or having regard to the authority of this court in *Denton v United Counties Omnibus Co*, which seems to me, for the reasons given by Dillon LJ, to be indistinguishable from the present case.

Peter Gibson J: I also agree and I share with Rose LJ the doubt as to whether the judge was right in finding that the label of proximity could be attached to the relationship between Mrs Topp and the defendants.

NOTE AND QUESTION

This is a typical example of the reluctance of English law to hold one person liable for torts committed by another person (a point often made by Tony Weir). Moreover, English law takes the view that owners of vehicles are entitled to be careless with their property if they wish (*Moorgate Mercantile v Twitchings* (1977)). Yet such a rule is probably fine where the damage is financial or at least of a type amenable to insurance protection. But is it right that the Topp family should have to bear the burden of a devastating accident arising from a train of events that is perfectly foreseeable? Do sensible vehicle owners leave their vehicles on a public highway unlocked and with the keys in the ignition? One might argue that the driver left the keys in the ignition so that a relief driver could use the bus without having to search out the first driver. Yet is this a safe system of operation? The decision in *Topp* is, with respect, a scandal (see **7.3.4** below).

7.3.2 Authorised car driver

However, where a car owner lends his or her car to another, the common law will hold the car owner liable provided that he or she has an interest in the journey: see *Morgans v Launchbury* (1973) (p 72). Normally, of course, many insurance policies cover drivers named by the owner.

7.3.3 Independent contractors

The logic of vicarious liability is inescapable. If the doctrine applies only in cases where the tortious act is committed by an employee, then a tort committed by an independent contractor (by definition not an employee) cannot implicate the employer in liability. This logic was reconfirmed in the next extracted case.

Salsbury v Woodland [1970] 1 QB 324, CA

This was an action for damages by a bystander in the street who had been watching a tree-felling operation on the defendant's land. The defendant occupier had employed an independent contractor to cut down the tree, but owing to a 'near miracle of incompetence' (Sachs LJ) the contractor allowed the tree to fall into the road taking with it some telephone wires. A car approached this scene too fast and the claimant, sensing the inevitable collision, dived out of the way and, in doing so, injured himself. The Court of Appeal (Widgery, Harman and Sachs LJJ) held that the occupier was not liable.

Widgery LJ: ... It is trite law that an employer who employs an independent contractor is not vicariously responsible for the negligence of that contractor. He is not able to control the way in which the independent contractor does the work, and the vicarious obligation of a master for the negligence of his servant does not arise under the relationship of employer and independent contractor. I think that it is entirely accepted that those cases – and there are some – in which an employer has been held liable for injury done by the negligence of an independent contractor are in truth cases where the employer owes a direct duty to the person injured, a duty which he cannot delegate to the contractor on his behalf. The whole question here is whether the occupier is to be judged by the general rule, which would result in no liability, or whether he comes within one of the somewhat special exceptions – cases in which a direct duty to see that care is taken rests upon the employer throughout the operation...

In truth, according to the authorities there are a number of well-determined classes of case in which this direct and primary duty upon an employer to see that care is taken exists. Two such classes are directly relevant for consideration in the present case. The first class concerns what have sometimes been described as 'extra-hazardous acts' – acts commissioned by an employer which are so hazardous in their character that the law has thought it proper to impose this direct obligation on the employer to see that care is taken. An example of such a case is *Honeywill & Stein Ltd v Larkin Bros (London's Commercial Photographers) Ltd* [1934] 1 KB 191. Other cases which one finds in the books are cases where the activity commissioned by the employer is the keeping of dangerous things within the rule in *Rylands v Fletcher* (1868) LR 3 HL 330 and where liability is not dependent on negligence at all.

I do not propose to add to the wealth of authority on this topic by attempting further to define the meaning of 'extra-hazardous acts'; but I am confident that the act commissioned in the present case cannot come within that category. The act commissioned in the present case, if done with ordinary elementary caution by skilled men, presented no hazard to anyone at all.

The second class of case, which is relevant for consideration, concerns dangers created in a highway. There are a number of cases on this branch of the law, a good example of which is *Holliday v National Telephone Co* [1899] 2 QB 392. These, on analysis, will all be found to be cases where work was being done in a highway and was work of a character which would have been a nuisance unless authorised by statute. It will be found in all these cases that the statutory powers under which the employer commissioned the work were statutory powers which left upon the employer a duty to see that due care was taken in the carrying out of the work, for the protection of those who passed on the highway. In accordance with principle, an employer subject to such a direct and personal duty cannot excuse himself, if things go wrong, merely because the direct cause of the injury was the act of the independent contractor.

This again is not a case in that class. It is not a case in that class because in the instant case no question of doing work in the highway, which might amount to a nuisance if due care was not taken, arises. In my judgment, the present case is clearly outside the well defined limit of the second class to which I have referred...

QUESTIONS

1. What if the tree-felling independent contractor did not have liability insurance? Could the bystander sue the employer of the contractor?

2. A militrary hospital is closed down in order to save the army money and its activities are handed over to the private sector. A soldier injured on active service is negligently treated in the private hospital and suffers further harm. Can he sue the MOD for damages for this further harm? (Cf *A (A Child) v Minister of Defence* (2004).)

7.3.4 Non-delegable duty

There do appear to be some cases where an employer is held liable for torts committed by an independent contractor. However, as the next extracts will indicate, a close examination of these cases will reveal that they are not actually vicarious liability decisions. The defendant is in breach of a direct duty to the claimant and such a duty cannot be delegated to an independent contractor.

McDermid v Nash Dredging and Reclamation Co [1987] AC 906, HL

This was an action for damages by a deckhand on a tug against his employer for an injury received from mooring ropes which entrapped him when the tug moved off without warning. The accident was caused by the negligence of the captain of the tug, but as the captain was not actually employed by the defendants it was argued that he was not an employee and thus could not involve the defendants in liability. The House of Lords (Lords Bridge, Hailsham, Brandon, Mackay and Ackner) dismissed an appeal against a decision holding the defendants liable.

Lord Brandon: ... My Lords, the Court of Appeal regarded the case as raising difficult questions of law on which clear authority was not easy to find. With great respect to the elaborate judgment of that court, I think that they have treated the case as more difficult than it really is. A statement of the relevant principle of law can be divided into three parts. First, an employer owes to his employee a duty to exercise reasonable care to ensure that the system of work provided for him is a safe one. Secondly, the provision of a safe system of work has two aspects: (a) the devising of such a system and (b) the operation of it. Thirdly, the duty concerned has been described alternatively as either personal or non-delegable. The meaning of these expressions is not self-evident and needs explaining. The essential characteristic of the duty is that, if it is not performed, it is no defence for the employer to show that he delegated its performance to a person, whether his servant or not his servant, whom he reasonably believed to be competent to perform it. Despite such delegation the employer is liable for the non-performance of the duty.

In the present case the relevant system of work in relation to the plaintiff was the system for unmooring the tug *Ina*. In the events which occurred the defendants delegated both the devising and the operating of such system to Captain Sas, who was not their servant. An essential feature of such system, if it was to be a safe one, was that Captain Sas would not work the tug's engines ahead or astern until he knew that the plaintiff had completed his work of unmooring the tug. The system which Captain Sas devised was one under which the plaintiff would let him know that he had completed that work by giving two knocks on the outside of the wheelhouse. I have already said that I agree with the Court of Appeal that there was scope, on the evidence, for a finding that that system was not a safe one. I shall assume, however, in the absence of any contrary finding by Staughton J, that that system, as devised by Captain Sas, was safe. The crucial point, however, is that, on the occasion of the plaintiff's accident, Captain Sas did not operate that system. He negligently failed to operate it in that he put the tug's engines astern at a time when the plaintiff had not given, and he, Captain Sas, could not therefore have heard, the prescribed signal of two knocks by the plaintiff on the outside of the wheelhouse. For this failure by Captain Sas to operate the system which he had devised, the defendants, as the plaintiff's employers, are personally, not vicariously, liable to him.

It was contended for the defendants that the negligence of Captain Sas was not negligence in failing to operate the safe system which he had devised. It was rather casual negligence in the course of operating such system, for which the defendants, since Captain Sas was not their servant, were not liable. I cannot accept that contention. The negligence of Captain Sas was not casual but central. It involved abandoning the safe system of work which he had devised and operating in its place a manifestly unsafe system. In the result there was a failure by the defendants, not in devising a safe system of work for the plaintiff, but in operating one.

On these grounds, which while not differing in substance from those relied on by the Court of Appeal are perhaps more simply and directly expressed, I agree with that court that the defendants are liable to the plaintiff...

NOTE

The defendant employer was held liable because he was in breach of a direct duty to the employee to provide a safe system of work. This duty is non-delegable. Equally a carrier of goods by sea is under a direct, non-delegable duty to the owner of the goods to provide a seaworthy ship.

Riverstone Meat Co Pty Ltd v Lancashire Shipping Co Ltd [1961] AC 807, HL

This was an action for damages by the owner of a cargo in respect of its damage while being transported in the defendants' unseaworthy ship. The ship was unseaworthy because it had been negligently repaired by a firm of independent contractors employed by the defendant. The defendants argued that they were not to be liable for the cargo damage because they had fulfilled their obligations towards the owner by hiring a firm of competent contractors. The trial judge and Court of Appeal dismissed the owner's action, but an appeal to the House of Lords (Lords Radcliffe, Merriman, Hodson and Keith and Viscount Simonds) was allowed.

Lord Radcliffe: ... I see no ground ... for saying that the carriers themselves were negligent in anything that they did...

But there is, on the other hand, a way of looking at the intrinsic nature of the obligation that is materially different from this. It is to ask the question, when there has been damage to cargo and that damage is traceable to unseaworthiness of the vessel, whether that unseaworthiness is due to any lack of diligence in those who have been implicated by the carriers in the work of keeping or making the vessel seaworthy...

Such general considerations as occur to me appear to favour the cargo owner's claim. He is not in any sense behind the scenes with regard to what is done to the vessel or how or when it is done. His concern with it begins and ends with the loading and discharge of his goods. The carrier, on the other hand, must have some form of ownership of the vessel and some measure of responsibility for seeing that it is fit and in proper condition for the carriage undertaken. He may qualify that responsibility by stipulation, if the law allows him to; or the law may write out the terms of his responsibility for him; but within those limits the responsibility is there. I should regard it as unsatisfactory, where a

▶

cargo owner has found his goods damaged through a defect in the seaworthiness of the vessel, that his rights of recovering from the carrier should depend on particular circumstances in the carrier's situation and arrangements with which the cargo owner has nothing to do; as, for instance, that liability should depend upon the measure of control that the carrier had exercised over persons engaged on surveying or repairing the ship or upon such questions as whether the carrier had, or could have done, whatever was needed by the hands of his own servants or had been sensible or prudent in getting it done by other hands. Carriers would find themselves liable or not liable, according to circumstances quite extraneous to the sea carriage itself...

Lord Keith: ... We are not faced with a question in the realm of tort, or negligence. The obligation is a statutory contractual obligation. The novelty, if there is one, is that the statutory obligation is expressed in terms of an obligation to exercise due diligence, etc. There is nothing, in my opinion, extravagant in saying that this is an inescapable personal obligation. The carrier cannot claim to have shed his obligation to exercise due diligence to make his ship seaworthy by selecting a firm of competent ship repairers to make his ship seaworthy. Their failure to use due diligence to do so is his failure. The question, as I see it, is not one of vicarious responsibility at all...

QUESTION

If a carrier has to warrant the seaworthiness of his ship, why did the House of Lords decide in *Davie v New Merton Board Mills* (1959) (p 167) that an employer does not warrant the safety of equipment supplied to an employee? Are things more important than people in the eyes of the law?

NOTES

1. The carrier was of course a bailee of the cargo and thus the case could well be seen as falling, today, within Diplock LJ's analysis in *Morris v Martin* (pp 23, 241).

2. By way of analogy to the carrier, an occupier and a landlord can be under a non-delegable duty to users of the highway in respect to the state of the property: see eg *Wringe v Cohen* (1940) (p 201). This duty is given expression through the tort of public nuisance. Nevertheless there are occasions when the owner or occupier can escape liability under the independent contractor principle: see eg *Rowe v Herman* (1997).

7.4 Liability for children

Vicarious liability in French law extends beyond employees and includes children (CC, art 1384). Parents have, accordingly, been held strictly liable for a traffic accident caused by their teenage son riding his moped. In English law there is no such vicarious liability; victims injured by the act of a child will prima facie have to sue the child, who will probably have neither assets nor insurance. However, the victim may be able to sue the parents or guardian if they owed him or her a direct duty of care in respect of the child.

Carmarthenshire CC v Lewis [1955] AC 549, HL

This was an action for damages by the widow of a lorry driver against a local authority in respect of an accident caused by the escape of a child from a nursery school. A majority of the House of Lords (Lords Goddard, Reid, Tucker and Keith; Lord Oaksey dissenting) held the authority liable.

Lord Reid: ... In these circumstances, two questions arise for decision. In the first place, was the escape of the child David into the street attributable to negligence of the appellants or of those for whom they are responsible? If it was, then it appears to me to be obvious that his being there alone might easily lead to an accident, and if the child had been killed or injured the appellants would have been liable in damages, for they certainly owed a duty to the child to protect him from injury. But then a second question is raised by the appellants. They say that, although they owed a duty to the child, they owed no duty to other users of the highway, and that even if they were negligent in letting the child escape onto the street they cannot be held responsible for damage to others caused by the action of the child when there.

On the first question I am of opinion that the appellants were negligent... The actions of a child of this age are unpredictable, and I think that it ought to have been anticipated by the appellants or their responsible officers that in such a case a child might well try to get out onto the street and that if it did a traffic accident was far from improbable...

I turn now to the second question, which is one of novelty and general importance. If the appellants are right it means that no matter how careless the person in charge of a young child may be, and no matter how obvious it may be that the child may stray into a busy street and cause an accident, yet that person is under no liability for damage to others caused solely by the action of the child because his only duty is towards the child under his care...

...There is no absolute duty; there is only a duty not to be negligent, and a mother is not negligent unless she fails to do something which a prudent or reasonable mother in her position would have been able to do and would have done. Even a housewife who has young children cannot be in two places at once and no one would suggest that she must neglect her other duties, or that a young child must always be kept cooped up. But I think that all but the most careless mothers do take many precautions for their children's safety and the same precautions serve to protect others. I cannot see how any person in charge of a child could be held to have been negligent in a question with a third party injured in a road accident unless he or she had failed to take reasonable and practicable precaution for the safety of the child...

...Moreover, a person who brings his animal onto a road or street and then negligently fails to look after it there is not free from liability. Counsel for the appellants did not argue that this rather illogical distinction should be applied to children, and it would be strange if a person in charge of a child were under a different duty according to whether he let the child stray from his house or garden or took the child onto the road and then let it stray there. Counsel took the only logical course and argued that even if a person takes a child into the street and then takes no care of it he cannot be held liable for damage suffered by a third party as a result of its actions, and that argument gains no support from the rules which apply to animals...

QUESTIONS

If a master is to be liable for torts committed by his servant, why should a parent not be strictly liable for torts committed by their child? Would such a liability materially increase household insurance premiums? Should car accidents be excluded (or at least subject to a separate insurance regime)?

Chapter 8

Liability for Words

The idea of a liability for persons and for things is well established in civilian thinking if not in the common law mind. The category of a liability for words is rather different since this is something that probably does make more sense in English law than it does in continental thinking. Harm arising from words not only has attracted its own tort, that of defamation, but has also given rise to its own sub-category within the law of negligence. Negligent misrepresentation is both an offshoot from the neighbour principle and something of an independent area within tort thanks to the requirement of a particular type of duty of care based upon a special relationship (*Hedley Byrne v Heller* (1964), p 115). Defamation and negligence are not the only torts of relevance in this area. The tort of deceit (fraudulent misrepresentation) is of course important and so are some of the economic torts since they can often involve verbal threats. Even trespass can be relevant (see eg *Wilkinson v Downton*, p 7; but cf *Wainwright*, pp 28, 64, 81, 109) and this tort is now supplemented by a statutory tort of harassment (see Protection from Harassment Act 1997, p 100). In short, words are an important vehicle for causing damage and in English law they can act as a focal point for a number of torts.

8.1 General considerations: words and interests

To talk in terms of a coherent law of liability arising from words is impossible, just as it is to talk of a fully comprehensive liability for things or liability for persons. These broad terms are, in English law at least, organising ideas and no more (although useful ones). Other categories and concepts need to be brought into play. This is true even for a well-defined category like the tort of negligence; notions such as duty and interest (personal injury, economic etc) are equally important when it comes to analysing a litigation problem arising out of carelessly caused harm. The first extract in this chapter will thus raise the issue of the relationship between words and protected interests as well as introducing the two main torts associated with harm arising from words.

Peter Birks, 'Equity in the Modern Law: An Exercise in Taxonomy' (1996) 26 The University of Western Australia Law Review 1, 5–6 (footnotes omitted)

The House of Lords recently decided *Spring v Guardian Assurance* [see below pp 251, 352]. An employer wrote a reference which made incorrect assertions of fact about a former employee and thus caused that employee pure economic loss. Was the employer liable in negligence? The answer was yes. This is somewhat surprising. The reference was a communication which was subject to qualified privilege having been written as a matter of duty to a person with an interest to receive it. In defamation the

▶

employer could not therefore have been liable without proof of malice. One commentator asks whether, if the case had been argued in defamation, the House of Lords would have changed the law applicable to that tort. Since the law seemingly was that such a defendant could not be liable except for malice, and since the law is that he can be liable for negligence, one might equally put the question differently. Has not the decision in negligence changed the law of defamation?

This is a conundrum of disorderly categories. It is a species of problem which disfigures the law. It is discreditably elementary. Two categories intersect. Defamation is a wrong, like inducing breach of contract or interference with chattels, which is manifestly named by reference to the interest infringed. Defamation is an infringement of the interest in reputation. Negligence is a wrong named by reference to a kind of fault. It follows that the two categories must intersect. In other words infringement of the interest in reputation will often be negligent. Is there then one wrong or two? My canary is yellow and eats seeds. If all birds are seed-eaters, yellow, or others, my canary counts twice. Are there two birds or one? If there come to be two birds, the double-vision is due to bent classification. There is only one bird.

... The whole law of tort is bedevilled by the same essentially trivial problem. The law cannot tolerate, or should not be able to tolerate, torts named so as to intersect...

NOTES

1. Sadly, Professor Birks died recently. An obituary recording his enormous contribution to academic law can be found in *The Guardian*, 16 July 2004, 31.

2. This extract from Birks is important in a number of ways. First, it shows how particular torts can be linked to particular interests: defamation is a tort protecting the reputation interest. Secondly it emphasises in outline the difference, in the area of liability for words, between the torts of defamation and negligence. Thirdly, it suggests that law and legal method should be one of deduction; solutions to legal problems are not to be found by searching amongst the facts to see if they can be fitted within some tort or other (cf eg *Esso v Southport* (1956) per Denning LJ, p 4). It is a matter of logical inference from a carefully constructed reasoning model of non-intersecting categories. Nevertheless the assumptions that Professor Birks makes are open to challenge. One might start by asking what interests negligence protects. If one reasonable response is to say that, where there has been a misrepresentation, it will protect economic interests, one could argue that the House of Lords was thus justified in applying *Hedley Byrne v Heller* (1964) (p 115) to the facts of *Spring v Guardian Assurance* (1995) (see below p 257). After all Mr Spring suffered severe economic loss as a result of the incorrect reference letter (as various newspapers reported at the time). But a further challenge can also be mounted, as the next extract will indicate.

Stephen Waddams, *Dimensions of Private Law*
CUP, 2003), 12–14 (footnotes omitted)

A related problem is the absence of uniformity in the reasoning and conclusions of judges, both within particular jurisdictions and from one jurisdiction to another. Thus in *White v Jones* [see below p 260] ... where loss was caused to an intended beneficiary by a lawyer's failure to prepare a will in due time, the three majority judges and the two dissenting judges all took different approaches. A differently constituted panel of English judges could very well have reached the opposite conclusion, as has indeed occurred on this question in other common law jurisdictions. This diversity also tends to impede a close analogy between judicial reasoning and the mapping of geographical territory...

Another obstacle to conceptual organization has been the complexity of the relation between facts and law. The facts of a case are defined in relation to legal principles, but the principles themselves are formulated in relation to facts, real or hypothetical. Facts may be stated at countless levels of particularity, and legal issues and legal rules may be formulated at countless levels of generality. No map or scheme could possibly classify all imaginable facts, for there is no limit whatever to the number of facts that may be postulated of a sequence of human events. The selection of legally relevant facts is a matter not of empirical investigation but of judgment, and not wholly separable from the formulation of the applicable legal rule. Facts are selected and marshalled to fit perceived rules of law, but the rules themselves change in response to facts, often by deploying concepts and categories that had not formerly been supposed to be applicable...

NOTES

1. These important and insightful paragraphs from Professor Waddams could well have been located at the very beginning of this book. But they are particularly apt here because, as we have seen from the Professor Birks' extract, the law has been developing quite rapidly for half a century. Moreover, situations where harm is said to arise from words are particularly complex not just because the meaning of language is complex but equally because of 'the cumulative weight of a number of legal concepts operating concurrently' (Waddams, above). Duty, right, interest, fault, damage and so on are often competing within the judgments in complex misrepresentation and defamation cases.

2. It might be useful to turn by way of introduction to the law itself to short extracts from the two cases that have stimulated the above debate between academic writers.

Spring v Guardian Assurance plc [1995] 2 AC 296, HL

In this action for damages by an employee against an ex-employer, in respect of economic loss arising out of an inaccurate reference, a majority of the House of Lords (Lords Goff, Lowry, Slynn and Woolf; Lord Keith dissenting) gave judgment for the employee.

Lord Goff: ... The central issue in this appeal is whether a person who provides a reference in respect of another who was formerly engaged by him as a member of his staff (at this point I use a deliberately neutral term) may be liable in damages to that other in

▶

respect of economic loss suffered by him by reason of negligence in the preparation of the reference...

Prima facie (ie, subject to the point on defamation, which I will have to consider later), it is my opinion that an employer who provides a reference in respect of one of his employees to a prospective future employer will ordinarily owe a duty of care to his employee in respect of the preparation of the reference. The employer is possessed of special knowledge, derived from his experience of the employee's character, skill and diligence in the performance of his duties while working for the employer... The provision of such references is a service regularly provided by employers to their employees; indeed, references are part of the currency of the modern employment market. Furthermore, when such a reference is provided by an employer, it is plain that the employee relies upon him to exercise due skill and care in the preparation of the reference before making it available to the third party. In these circumstances, it seems to me that all the elements requisite for the application of the *Hedley Byrne* principle are present. I need only add that, in the context under consideration, there is no question of the circumstances in which the reference is provided being, for example, so informal as to negative an assumption of responsibility by the employer...

... Since, for the reasons I have given, it is my opinion that in cases such as the present the duty of care arises by reason of an assumption of responsibility by the employer to the employee in respect of the relevant reference, I can see no good reason why the duty to exercise due skill and care which rests upon the employer should be negatived because, if the plaintiff were instead to bring an action for damage to his reputation, he would be met by the defence of qualified privilege which could only be defeated by proof of malice. It is not to be forgotten that the Hedley Byrne duty arises where there is a relationship which is, broadly speaking, either contractual or equivalent to contract. In these circumstances, I cannot see that principles of the law of defamation are of any relevance...

Lord Keith (dissenting): ... In my opinion the same grounds of public policy are applicable where the claim is based not on defamation as such but on negligence associated with the making or publication of an untrue statement, where the occasion on which that was done was a privileged one in the sense in which that expression is used in the context of defamation law. If liability in negligence were to follow from a reference prepared without reasonable care, the same adverse consequences would flow as those sought to be guarded against by the defence of qualified privilege. Those asked to give a reference would be inhibited from speaking frankly lest it should be found that they were liable in damages through not taking sufficient care in its preparation. They might well prefer, if under no legal duty to give a reference, to refrain from doing so at all. Any reference given might be bland and unhelpful and information which it would be in the interest of those seeking the reference to receive might be withheld....

Lord Slynn: ... [T]he starting-point in my view is that the suggested claim in negligence and the torts of defamation and injurious and malicious falsehood do not cover the same ground, as Mr Tony Weir shows in his note in [1993] CLJ 376. They are separate torts, defamation not requiring a proof by the plaintiff that the statement was untrue (though justification may be a defence) or that he suffered economic damage, but being subject to defences quite different from those in negligence, such as the defence of qualified privilege which makes it necessary to prove malice. Malicious falsehood requires proof that the statement is false, that harm has resulted and that there was express malice. Neither of these involves the concept of a duty of care. The essence of a claim in defamation is that a person's reputation has been damaged; it may or not involve the loss of a job or economic loss. A claim that a reference has been given negligently is essentially based on the fact, not so much that reputation has been damaged, as that a job, or an opportunity, has been lost. A statement carelessly made may not be defamatory – a statement that a labourer is 'lame,' a secretary 'very arthritic,' when neither statement is true, though they were true of some other employee mistakenly confused with the person named.

I do not for my part consider that to recognise the existence of a duty of care in some situations when a reference is given necessarily means that the law of defamation has to be changed or that a substantial section of the law relating to defamation and malicious falsehood is 'emasculated' (Court of Appeal, at p. 437). They remain distinct torts. It may be that there will be less resort to these torts because a more realistic approach on the basis of a duty of care is adopted. If to recognise that such a duty of care exists means that there have to be such changes – either by excluding the defence of qualified privilege from the master-servant situation or by withdrawing the privilege where negligence as opposed to express malice is shown – then I would in the interests of recognising a fair, just and reasonable result in the master–servant situation accept such change...

NOTES

1. This case is ideal for anyone who wishes to approach liability from the position of damage done by words. First, Lord Goff sets out the requirements of liability under the *Hedley Byrne* principle (cf p 115). These are special relationship, reliance and professional (rather than informal) context. Secondly, the majority take a step towards a more general idea of a liability for words in refusing to erect liability barriers between those various independent torts – defamation, malicious falsehood and negligence – which can apply in factual situations involving reference letters (see **3.5.2** for the tort of malicious falsehood).

2. The case is also important for some points made in observations that have not been extracted above (for want of space). For example, Lord Woolf specifically said the case was about the balancing of *interests* between employers and employees (for an analogous type of interest analysis see *D v East Berks NHS Trust*, p 149). In other words, the nature and severity of the damage vis-à-vis the behaviour of the writer of the reference are vital focal points. Furthermore, Lord Woolf also made the point that the claim was for pure economic loss; this is the typical damage that arises from misstatements. In addition, two judges stressed the importance and role of the particular facts in arriving at the decision as to whether principle (*Hedley Byrne*) and policy dictate liability. In short, the decision confirms Professor Waddams' analysis of the common law mentality.

3. But Professor Waddams specifically mentions another case. This decision, set out below, can be seen as extending the *Hedley Byrne* principle (either directly or by way of analogy) and thus it could be relevant in establishing the idea of a 'misstatement' by silence or inaction.

White v Jones [1995] 2 AC 207, HL

This was an action for damages in negligence brought against a firm of solicitors by two disappointed daughters who expected to benefit under their late father's will. They did not benefit as a result of the solicitors' negligence. The House of Lords (Lords Goff, Browne-Wilkinson and Nolan; Lords Keith and Mustill dissenting) allowed their claim.

Lord Goff: My Lords, in this appeal, your Lordships' House has to consider for the first time the much discussed question whether an intended beneficiary under a will is entitled to recover damages from the testator's solicitors by reason of whose negligence the testator's intention to benefit him under the will has failed to be carried into effect… In the present case, the testator's solicitors negligently delayed the preparation of a fresh will in place of a previous will which the testator had decided to revoke, and the testator died before the new will was prepared. The plaintiffs were the two daughters of the testator who would have benefited under the fresh will but received nothing under the previous will which, by reason of the solicitors' delay, remained unrevoked…

… [T]he question is one which has been much discussed, not only in this country and other common law countries, but also in some civil law countries, notably Germany… In Germany a disappointed beneficiary may be entitled to claim damages from the testator's negligent solicitor under the principle known as contract with protective effect for third parties (*Vertrag mit Schutzwirkung für Dritte*)… It also appears that a similar conclusion would be reached in France…, which appears to be based on the broad principle that a notary is responsible, even as against third parties, for all fault causing damage committed by him in the exercise of his functions. On facts very similar to those of the present case, the Court of Appeal of Amsterdam has held a notary liable in negligence to the intended beneficiary…

The conceptual difficulties

Even so, it has been recognised on all hands that *Ross v Caunters* raises difficulties of a conceptual nature, and that as a result it is not altogether easy to accommodate the decision within the ordinary principles of our law of obligations…

It is right however that I should immediately summarise these conceptual difficulties. They are as follows.

(1) First, the general rule is well established that a solicitor acting on behalf of a client owes a duty of care only to his client…

(2) A further reason is given which is said to reinforce the conclusion that no duty of care is owed by the solicitor to the beneficiary in tort. Here, it is suggested, is one of those situations in which a plaintiff is entitled to damages if, and only if, he can establish a breach of contract by the defendant… Such a claim falls within the exclusive zone of contractual liability; and it is contrary to principle that the law of tort should be allowed to invade that zone…

(3) A third, and distinct, objection is that, if liability in tort was recognised in cases such as *Ross v Caunters*, it would be impossible to place any sensible bounds to cases in which such recovery was allowed…

(4) Other miscellaneous objections were taken, though in my opinion they were without substance...

(5) There is however another objection of a conceptual nature, which was not adumbrated in argument before the Appellate Committee. In the present case, unlike *Ross v Caunters* itself, there was no act of the defendant solicitor which could be characterised as negligent. All that happened was that the solicitor did nothing at all for a period of time ... As a general rule, however, there is no liability in tortious negligence for an omission, unless the defendant is under some pre-existing duty. Once again, therefore, the question arises how liability can arise in the present case in the absence of a contract...

The impulse to do practical justice

Before addressing the legal questions which lie at the heart of the present case, it is, I consider, desirable to identify the reasons of justice which prompt judges and academic writers to conclude ... that a duty should be owed ... to a disappointed beneficiary. The principal reasons are, I believe, as follows.

(1) In the forefront stands the extraordinary fact that, if such a duty is not recognised, the only persons who might have a valid claim (ie the testator and his estate) have suffered no loss, and the only person who has suffered a loss (ie the disappointed beneficiary) has no claim ... It can therefore be said that, if the solicitor owes no duty to the intended beneficiaries, there is a lacuna in the law which needs to be filled. This I regard as being a point of cardinal importance in the present case.

(2) The injustice of denying such a remedy is reinforced if one considers the importance of legacies in a society which recognises (...) the right of citizens to leave their assets to whom they please, and in which, as a result, legacies can be of great importance to individual citizens, providing very often the only opportunity for a citizen to acquire a significant capital sum; or to inherit a house, so providing a secure roof over the heads of himself and his family; or to make special provision for his or her old age...

(3) There is a sense in which the solicitors' profession cannot complain if such a liability may be imposed upon their members. If one of them has been negligent in such a way as to defeat his client's testamentary intentions, he must regard himself as very lucky indeed if the effect of the law is that he is not liable to pay damages in the ordinary way...

(4) That such a conclusion is required as a matter of justice is reinforced by consideration of the role played by solicitors in society...

A contractual approach

It may be suggested that, in cases such as the present, the simplest course would be to solve the problem by making available to the disappointed beneficiary, by some means or another, the benefit of the contractual rights (such as they are) of the testator or his estate against the negligent solicitor, as is for example done under the German principle of *Vertrag mit Schutzwirkung für Dritte*. Indeed that course has been urged upon us by Professor Markesinis in 'An Expanding Tort Law' (1987) 103 LQR 354 at

396-397, echoing a view expressed by Professor Fleming in 'Comparative Law of Torts' (1986) 4 OJLS 235 at 241. Attractive though this solution is, there is unfortunately a serious difficulty in its way. The doctrine of consideration still forms part of our law of contract, as does the doctrine of privity of contract which is considered to exclude the recognition of a *jus quaesitum tertio*. To proceed as Professor Markesinis has suggested may be acceptable in German law, but in this country could be open to criticism as an illegitimate circumvention of these long-established doctrines; and this criticism could be reinforced by reference to the fact that, in the case of carriage of goods by sea, a contractual solution to a particular of transferred loss, and to other cognate problems, was provided only by recourse to Parliament. Furthermore, I myself do not consider that the present case provides a suitable occasion for reconsideration of doctrines so fundamental as these...

The tortious solution

I therefore return to the law of tort for a solution to the problem. For the reasons I have already given, an ordinary action in tortious negligence on the lines proposed by Megarry V-C in *Ross v Caunters* [1980] Ch 297 must, with the greatest respect, be regarded as inappropriate, because it does not meet any of the conceptual problems which have been raised. Furthermore, for the reasons I have previously given, the *Hedley Byrne* principle cannot, in the absence of special circumstances, give rise on ordinary principles to an assumption of responsibility by the testator's solicitor towards an intended beneficiary. Even so, it seems to me that it is open to your Lordships' House, as in *Linden Gardens Trust Ltd v Lenesta Sludge Disposals Ltd* [1994] 1 AC 85, to fashion a remedy to fill a lacuna in the law and so prevent the injustice which would otherwise occur on the facts of cases such as the present. In the *Lenesta Sludge* case, as I have said, the House made available a remedy as a matter of law to solve the problem of transferred loss in the case before them. The present case is, if anything, *a fortiori*, since the nature of the transaction was such that, if the solicitors were negligent and their negligence did not come to light until after the death of the testator, there would be no remedy for the ensuing loss unless the intended beneficiary could claim. In my opinion, therefore, your Lordships' House should in cases such as these extend to the intended beneficiary a remedy under the *Hedley Byrne* principle by holding that the assumption of responsibility by the solicitors towards his client should be held in law to extend to the intended beneficiary who (as the solicitor can reasonably foresee) may, as a result of the solicitor's negligence, be deprived of his intended legacy in circumstances in which neither the testator nor his estate will have a remedy against the solicitor ... I only wish to add that, with the benefit of experience during the 15 years in which *Ross v Caunters* has been regularly applied, we can say with some confidence that a direct remedy by the intended beneficiary against the solicitor appears to create no problems in practice. That is therefore the solution which I would recommend to your Lordships...

Lord Keith of Kinkel (dissenting): ... To admit the plaintiffs' claim in the present case would in substance, in my opinion, be to give them the benefit of a contract to which they were not parties.

Further, there is, in my opinion, no decided case the grounds of decision in which are capable of being extended incrementally and by way of analogy so as to admit of a remedy in tort being made available to the plaintiffs...

Upon the whole matter I have found the conceptual difficulties involved in the plaintiffs' claim, which are fully recognised by all your Lordships, to be too formidable to be resolved by any process of reasoning compatible with existing principles of law...

I would therefore allow the appeal.

Lord Mustill (dissenting): ... Here ... to enable the estate, in title of the deceased testator, to recover a sum equivalent to the disappointed expectations of the beneficiaries would be to compensate it for a loss which it not only had not, but could not have, suffered. The plaintiffs' complaint and the consequent damage are quite different from the complaint and the damage to which the estate succeeded on the death of the testator. To allow them to be treated as if they were the same would extend the boundaries of a contractual obligation far further than has ever been previously contemplated; and, I suspect further than has been contemplated even in the majority of those jurisdictions where concepts of privity are less rigorous than in our own.

Furthermore, even if the doctrine [of transferred loss] were to be fully received into English law I am unable to visualise how it could help the plaintiffs here. As its name denotes it is concerned with the transfer of loss to the claimant from someone else. In the present case the intended beneficiaries do not need such a transfer, for they already have a loss. Their problem is to find a cause of action, and to achieve this a quite different kind of transfer would be required...

NOTES

1. This case is obviously an important precedent, but it is not that easy to decide exactly what the precedent is. The view seems to be that the courts fashioned a remedy for a particular set of circumstances on the ground of practical justice (see eg Lord Steyn in *Att-Gen v Blake* (2001), above, pp 26, 47). And so one can seemingly predict that the case is an important professional liability authority (see **8.5**), at least where the professional defendant is a solicitor. But what are the wider implications? It may be that the principle of liability for negligent misstatement as established by *Hedley Byrne v Heller* (1964) (p 115) is capable of extension not just directly but also by analogy. However, in *White v Jones* all the ingredients of *Hedley Byrne* seemed to be weak or missing: there was, it seems, no misstatement as such, no reliance, and no special relationship. Yet, as Professor Waddams indicates (see above, p 257), much depends on how one views the facts. If one talks of a 'family' solicitor it becomes possible to argue that such a solicitor owes a duty not just to individuals but to the family as a whole. One relies upon the family solicitor and it is a professional relationship that could be said to be special vis-à-vis each of the testator's immediate family. Perhaps, then, the facts do have something compelling in them, just as in the family case of *Jackson v Horizon Holidays* (1975) where the Court of Appeal also achieved a kind of 'practical justice'. One might note, equally, how the House of Lords 'fashioned' a remedy to aid a family member in *Beswick v Beswick* (1968). But cf *D v East Berks NHS Trust* (pp 149, 310).

2. For a case where the claimant argued that a local authority was negligent in failing to put up warning words, see *Gorringe v Calderdale MBC* (2002) (p 299).

3. Can a person be liable for economic loss for a failure to issue instructions? (Cf *Customs & Excise Commissioners v Barclays Bank* (2005).)

8.2 Defamation (1): general liability

One of the key torts giving rise to a liability for words is the tort of defamation. This, at a very abstract level, is an easy tort to comprehend once one appreciates how it neatly falls into two parts, namely elements of liability (this section) and defences (see **8.3**). Perhaps one should add a third part, that of damages, since they have given rise to their own rules and legislative intervention (see **11.4.5**). At a more detailed level it is exceptionally complex. This complexity results from a number of factors: the meaning of language, the ever-more detailed procedural refinements (including jury trial), the plethora of case law and, now, the human rights dimension. This latter point helps emphasise that defamation extends beyond the category of tort and into the realm of constitutional law. It is a central topic in freedom of expression.

8.2.1 Introduction to defamation

The following extracts are intended to provide a number of general observations on the tort of defamation.

Horrocks v Lowe [1975] AC 135, HL

Lord Diplock: ... My Lords, as a general rule English law gives effect to the ninth commandment that a man shall not speak evil falsely of his neighbour. It supplies a temporal sanction: if he cannot prove that defamatory matter which he published was true, he is liable in damages to whomever he has defamed, except where the publication is oral only, causes no damage and falls outside the categories of slander actionable per se. The public interest that the law should provide an effective means whereby a man can vindicate his reputation against calumny has nevertheless to be accommodated to the competing public interest in permitting men to communicate frankly and freely with one another about matters in respect of which the law recognises that they have a duty to perform or an interest to protect in doing so. What is published in good faith on matters of these kinds is published on a privileged occasion. It is not actionable even though it be defamatory and turns out to be untrue. With some exceptions... the privilege is not absolute but qualified. It is lost if the occasion which gives rise to it is misused. For in all cases of qualified privilege there is some special reason of public policy why the law accords immunity from suit – the existence of some public or private duty, whether legal or moral, on the part of the maker of the defamatory statement which justifies his communicating it or of some interest of his own which he is entitled to protect by doing so. If he uses the occasion for some other reason he loses the protection of the privilege...

NOTES

1. Defamation divides into two sub-torts, slander and libel. The distinction was once easier enough to comprehend: slander was concerned with verbal defamation while libel dealt with written defamation. However, newer forms of communication have created ambiguous areas: see eg *Youssoupoff v MGM Pictures* (1934); Defamation Act 1952, s 16; Theatres Act 1968, s 4.

2. Defamation is not only a tort of strict liability – reputation being treated as equivalent to a property right (D Ibbetson, *A Historical Introduction to the Law of Obligations*, OUP, 1999, 186) – but libel (words in permanent form) does not require proof of any actual damage. It is actionable per se. This latter point is not true of slander (spoken words) save in certain situations.

3. The strict nature of defamation has given rise to much criticism, some of which is reflected in Lord Steyn's observation in the next extract. However Lord Nicholls defends the need to protect the reputation interest.

Reynolds v Times Newspapers Limited [2001] 2 AC 127, HL

(For facts and further extracts see pp 275, 276, 278, 280)

Lord Steyn (dissenting): ... *Weir, A Casebook on Tort*, 8th ed., (1996) describes defamation as 'the oddest' of the torts. He explains (at p. 525):

'he (the plaintiff) can get damages (swingeing damages!) for a statement made to others without showing that the statement was untrue, without showing that the statement did him the slightest harm, and without showing that the defendant was in any way wrong to make it (much less that the defendant owed him any duty of any kind)'

Weir, at p. 530, observes that 'the courts could arguably have done more to prevent the law becoming as absurd, complex and unfair as it is, without resigning themselves to saying, as Diplock LJ did, that the law of defamation "has passed beyond redemption by the courts" ' (*Slim v. Daily Telegraph Ltd.* [1968] 2 QB 157, 179). Weir states that 'the law of England is certainly stricter than that of any free country...' at p. 528. The argument for addressing the chilling effect of our defamation law on political speech and for striking a better balance between freedom of speech and defamation is strong: see Eric Barendt and others, *Libel and the Media: The Chilling Effect*, (1997), Clarendon Press, Oxford, pp. 191–192...

Lord Nicholls: ... Reputation is an integral and important part of the dignity of the individual. It also forms the basis of many decisions in a democratic society which are fundamental to its well-being: whom to employ or work for, whom to promote, whom to do business with or to vote for. Once besmirched by an unfounded allegation in a national newspaper, a reputation can be damaged for ever, especially if there is no opportunity to vindicate one's reputation. When this happens, society as well as the individual is the loser. For it should not be supposed that protection of reputation is a matter of importance only to the affected individual and his family. Protection of reputation is conducive to the public good. It is in the public interest that the reputation of public figures should not be debased falsely. In the political field, in order to make an informed choice, the electorate needs to be able to identify the good as well as the bad. Consistently with these considerations, human rights conventions recognise that freedom of expression is not an absolute right. Its exercise may be subject to such restrictions as are prescribed by law and are necessary in a democratic society for the protection of the reputations of others...

8.2.2 Defamatory statements

The first substantive question in defamation concerns its definition. As we shall see, the standard definition – the publication of a statement which tends to lower a person in the estimation of right-thinking members of society – turns out to be meaningless and thus a more practical question is this: what amounts to a defamatory statement?

Berkoff v Burchill [1996] 4 All ER 1008, CA

Neill LJ: This appeal raises questions as to the meaning of the word 'defamatory' and as to the nature of an action for defamation. The facts can be stated quite shortly. The plaintiff, Mr Steven Berkoff is an actor, director and writer who is well known for his work on stage, screen and television. The first defendant, Miss Julie Burchill, is a journalist and writer who at the material times was retained to write articles about the cinema for the Sunday Times. The second defendants, Times Newspapers Limited, are the publishers of the Sunday Times.

In the issue of the Sunday Times dated 30 January 1994 Miss Burchill wrote a review of the film 'The Age of Innocence'. In the course of the review, in a general reference to film directors, Miss Burchill wrote:

'... film directors, from Hitchcock to Berkoff are notoriously hideous-looking people.'

Nine months later Miss Burchill returned to the same theme in a review of the film 'Frankenstein'. In this review, which was published in the issue of the Sunday Times dated 6 November 1994, Miss Burchill described a character in the film called 'the Creature'. She wrote:

'The Creature is made as a vessel for Waldman's brain, and rejected in disgust when it comes out scarred and primeval. It's a very new look for the Creature – no bolts in the neck or flat-top hairdo – and I think it works; its a lot like Stephen Berkoff, only marginally better-looking.'...

It will be seen from this collection of definitions that words may be defamatory, even though they neither impute disgraceful conduct to the plaintiff nor any lack of skill or efficiency in the conduct of his trade or business or professional activity, if they hold him up to contempt scorn or ridicule or tend to exclude him from society. On the other hand insults which do not diminish a man's standing among other people do not found an action for libel or slander. The exact borderline may often be difficult to define....

It is trite law that the meaning of words in a libel action is determined by the reaction of the ordinary reader and not by the intention of the publisher, but the perceived intention of the publisher may colour the meaning. In the present case it would in my view be open to a jury to conclude that in the context the remarks about Mr Berkoff gave the impression that he was not merely physically unattractive in appearance but actually repulsive. It seems to me that to say this of someone in the public eye who makes his living, in part at least, as an actor, is capable of lowering his standing in the estimation of the public and of making him an object of ridicule.

I confess that I have found this to be a far from easy case, but in the end I am satisfied that it would be wrong to decide this preliminary issue in a way which would withdraw the matter completely from the consideration of a jury.

Millett LJ (dissenting): Many a true word is spoken in jest. Many a false one too. But chaff and banter are not defamatory, and even serious imputations are not actionable if no one would take them to be meant seriously. The question, however, is how the words would be understood, not how they were meant, and that issue is pre-eminently one for the jury. So, however difficult it may be, we must assume that Miss Julie Burchill might be taken seriously. The question then is: is it defamatory to say of a man that he is 'hideously ugly'?...

The submission illustrates the danger of trusting to verbal formulae. Defamation has never been satisfactorily defined. All attempted definitions are illustrative. None of them is exhaustive. All can be misleading if they cause one to forget that defamation is an attack on reputation, that is on a man's standing in the world...

The line between mockery and defamation may sometimes be difficult to draw. When it is it should be left to the jury to draw it. Despite the respect which is due to the opinion of Neill LJ, whose experience in this field is unrivalled, I am not persuaded that the present case could properly be put on the wrong side of the line. A decision that it is an actionable wrong to describe a man as 'hideously ugly' would be an unwarranted restriction on free speech. And if a bald statement to this effect would not be capable of being defamatory, I do not see how a humorously exaggerated observation to the like effect could be. People must be allowed to poke fun at one another without fear of litigation. It is one thing to ridicule a man; it is another to expose him to ridicule. Miss Burchill made a cheap joke at Mr Berkoff's expense; she may thereby have demeaned herself, but I do not believe that she defamed Mr Berkoff.

If I have appeared to treat Mr Berkoff's claim with unjudicial levity it is because I find it impossible to take it seriously. Despite the views of my brethren, who are both far more experienced than I am, I remain of the opinion that the proceedings are as frivolous as Miss Burchill's article. The time of the Court ought not to be taken up with either of them. I would allow the appeal and dismiss the Action.

Phillips LJ: ... Where the issue is whether words have damaged a Plaintiff's reputation by exposing him to ridicule, that question cannot be answered simply by considering whether the natural and ordinary meaning of the words used is defamatory per se. The question has to be considered in the light of the actual words used and the circumstance in which they are used. There are many ways of indicating that a person is hideously ugly, ranging from a simple statement of opinion to that effect, which I feel could never be defamatory, to words plainly intended to convey that message by way of ridicule.

The words used in this case fall into the latter category. Whether they have exposed the Plaintiff to ridicule to the extent that his reputation has been damaged must be answered by the Jury. The preliminary point raised by the Defendant cannot be answered in the affirmative and this appeal should be dismissed.

NOTE

This case is 'important' in that it indicates that almost any statement critical of another, however frivolous, can be defamatory. Furthermore it perhaps gives some support to the following editorial comment: 'Libel is often played as farce. Vain pop stars, self-important actresses and – yes – even editors can cut comic figures as they seek to protect their precious reputations in the mock Gothic majesty of the High Court. But the dishonest use of libel laws to suppress legitimate reporting activities of people in public life is no joke' (Editorial, *Guardian*, 9 June 1999, 21). This editorial was written after yet another politician had been exposed as a liar, cheat and perjurer in defamation proceedings initiated by the politician (hoping to get a tax-free windfall).

QUESTIONS

1. It so happened that in 1994 there were two academics at Lancaster University with the name 'Geoffrey Samuel'. What would have been the position if a newspaper had printed a defamatory article about Geoffrey Samuel of Lancaster University believing, wrongly, that the defamatory allegation was true of one of the academics (and not knowing of the existence of the second academic)? Could both academics sue? (Cf *Newstead v London Express Newspapers* (1940).)

2. What is the position if a magazine prints a serious story about a named woman raped by a named man. The story is based on a true experience but the names of the woman and the man are changed to fictional names. However, it so happens that there are real people with these names. Can they both sue the magazine for defamation? (Cf *Hulton & Co v Jones* (1910).)

3. An Internet pornography site advertises itself using the photograph of a model. However, the model has a very similar face to a respectable vicar and there is some gossip among the parishioners. Can the vicar sue the Internet site publisher for defamation? (Cf *O'Shea v MGN* (2001).)

4. Millett LJ talks of a 'man's standing in the world'. What about a woman's?

8.2.3 Innuendo

What if a journalist had written of an actor that he made the Frankenstein Creature look handsome? In other words, what if the journalist had made disparaging marks by innuendo? As the next case shows, innuendo can amount to defamation but there are some limits.

Lewis v Daily Telegraph [1964] AC 234, CA

This was an action for damages in defamation brought by a company and its chairman against two newspapers. The newspapers had published columns headed 'Fraud Squad Probe Firm' and 'Inquiry on Firm by City Police' and went on to state that the police were inquiring into the affairs of the claimant company. The claimants alleged that the words were defamatory in that they suggested that the two claimants were guilty of fraud. The trial judge directed the jury that the words were capable of bearing the alleged defamatory innuendo and the jury returned verdicts in favour of the claimants. They awarded damages of £25,000 to the chairman and £75,000 to the company against one newspaper and £17,000 and £100,000 against the other newspaper (very large sums indeed in 1964). On appeal the House of Lords (Lords Reid, Jenkins, Hodson and Devlin; Lord Morris dissenting) held that the words were not capable of bearing the alleged defamatory meaning and ordered new trials. The majority also indicated that they would have ordered a new trial on the ground that the damages awarded were excessive.

Lord Reid: ... The gist of the two paragraphs is that the police, the City Fraud Squad, were inquiring into the appellants' affairs. There is no doubt that in actions for libel the question is what the words would convey to the ordinary man: it is not one of construction in the legal sense. The ordinary man does not live in an ivory tower and he is not inhibited by a knowledge of the rules of construction. So he can and does read between the lines in the light of his general knowledge and experience of worldly affairs. I leave aside questions of innuendo where the reader has some special knowledge which might lead him to attribute a meaning to the words not apparent to those who do not have that knowledge. That only arises indirectly in this case...

What the ordinary man would infer without special knowledge has generally been called the natural and ordinary meaning of the words. But that expression is rather misleading in that it conceals the fact that there are two elements in it. Sometimes it is not necessary to go beyond the words themselves, as where the plaintiff has been called a thief or a murderer. But more often the sting is not so much in the words themselves as in what the ordinary man will infer from them, and that is also regarded as part of their natural and ordinary meaning. Here there would be nothing libellous in saying that an inquiry into the appellants' affairs was proceeding: the inquiry might be by a statistician or other expert. The sting is in inferences drawn from the fact that it is the fraud squad which is making the inquiry. What those inferences should be is ultimately a question for the jury, but the trial judge has an important duty to perform.

Generally the controversy is whether the words are capable of having a libellous meaning at all, and undoubtedly it is the judge's duty to rule on that...

What the ordinary man, not avid for scandal, would read into the words complained of must be a matter of impression. I can only say that I do not think that he would infer guilt of fraud merely because an inquiry is on foot. And, if that is so, then it is the duty of the trial judge to direct the jury that it is for them to determine the meaning of the paragraph but that they must not hold it to impute guilt of fraud because as a matter of law the paragraph is not capable of having that meaning. So there was here, in my opinion, misdirection of the two juries sufficiently serious to require that there must be new trials.

... Then it is said that if that is so there can be no difference between an allegation of suspicious conduct and an allegation of guilt. To my mind, there is a great difference between saying that a man has behaved in a suspicious manner and saying that he is guilty of an offence, and I am not convinced that you can only justify the former statement by proving guilt. I can well understand that if you say there is a rumour that X is guilty you can only justify it by proving that he is guilty, because repeating someone else's libellous statement is just as bad as making the statement directly...

Lord Devlin: ... Just as a bare statement of suspicion may convey the impression that there are grounds for belief in guilt, so a bare statement of the fact of an inquiry may

▶

convey the impression that there are grounds for suspicion. I do not say that in this case it does; but I think that the words in their context and in the circumstances of publication are capable of conveying that impression. But can they convey an impression of guilt? Let it be supposed, first, that a statement that there is an inquiry conveys an impression of suspicion; and, secondly, that a statement of suspicion conveys an impression of guilt. It does not follow from these two suppositions that a statement that there is an inquiry conveys an impression of guilt. For that, two fences have to be taken instead of one. While, as I have said, I am prepared to accept that the jury could take the first, I do not think that in a case like the present, where there is only the bare statement that a police inquiry is being made, it could take the second in the same stride. If the ordinary sensible man was capable of thinking that where ever there was a police inquiry there was guilt, it would be almost impossible to give accurate information about anything: but in my opinion he is not. I agree with the view of the Court of Appeal...

NOTES

1. This leading case is important not just for the innuendo point. It indicates that companies, as well as humans, have reputations that the tort will protect. (Do companies also have human rights?) It was once held that even local authorities could sue in defamation but this has been overruled by the House of Lords in *Derbyshire CC v Times Newspapers* (1993) and this decision probably extends to all government institutions (see eg *Goldsmith v Bhoyrul* (1998)). Furthermore the case is important in helping one to understand why defamation is a complex tort: procedural niceties are vital not just because of juries but equally because of the various preliminary, striking out defences that are often raised. In addition the *Lewis* case is important in as much as it illustrates the daft level of damages that juries can award (cf **Chapter 11**).

2. Although a company can, it seems, sue for defamation (being a legal person) a loose group of persons cannot if the group is defamed. Thus to say that 'all lawyers are thieves' is not defamatory of every lawyer who is not.

QUESTION

Should large corporations have the legal right to pursue those who criticise their products, even if the factual basis of the criticisms turns out to be inaccurate?

Steel and Morris v United Kingdom (2005) (Application no 68416/01), ECtHR

This case arose out of a successful claim for damages in defamation by a large multi-national corporation (McDonalds) against two individual environmental campaigners who had distributed leaflets containing many allegations about the corporation's products, some of which were found by the English courts to be defamatory. The two campaigners were ordered by the English court to pay large damages to the corporation, but they successfully argued that there had been an infringement of their human rights.

88 The Court must weigh a number of factors in the balance when reviewing the proportionality of the measure complained of. First, it notes that the leaflet in question

contained very serious allegations on topics of general concern, such as abusive and immoral farming and employment practices, deforestation, the exploitation of children and their parents through aggressive advertising and the sale of unhealthy food. The Court has long held that 'political expression', including expression on matters of public interest and concern, requires a high level of protection under Article 10 (see, for example, *Thorgeir Thorgeirson v Iceland*, judgment of 25 June 1992, Series A no. 239, and also *Hertel v Switzerland*, judgment of 25 August 1998, *Reports* 1998-VI, § 47)...

94 The Court... does not consider that the fact that the plaintiff in the present case was a large multinational company should in principle deprive it of a right to defend itself against defamatory allegations or entail that the applicants should not have been required to prove the truth of the statements made. It is true that large public companies inevitably and knowingly lay themselves open to close scrutiny of their acts and, as in the case of the businessmen and women who manage them, the limits of acceptable criticism are wider in the case of such companies (see *Fayed v the United Kingdom*, judgment of 21 September 1994, Series A no. 294-B, § 75). However, in addition to the public interest in open debate about business practices, there is a competing interest in protecting the commercial success and viability of companies, for the benefit of shareholders and employees, but also for the wider economic good. The State therefore enjoys a margin of appreciation as to the means it provides under domestic law to enable a company to challenge the truth, and limit the damage, of allegations which risk harming its reputation (see *Markt Intern Verlag GmbH and Beerman v Germany*, judgment of 20 November 1989, Series A no. 165, §§ 33–38).

95 If, however, a State decides to provide such a remedy to a corporate body, it is essential, in order to safeguard the countervailing interests in free expression and open debate, that a measure of procedural fairness and equality of arms is provided for. The Court has already found that the lack of legal aid rendered the defamation proceedings unfair, in breach of Article 6 § 1. The inequality of arms and the difficulties under which the applicants laboured are also significant in assessing the proportionality of the interference under Article 10. As a result of the law as it stood in England and Wales, the applicants had the choice either to withdraw the leaflet and apologise to McDonalds, or bear the burden of proving, without legal aid, the truth of the allegations contained in it. Given the enormity and complexity of that undertaking, the Court does not consider that the correct balance was struck between the need to protect the applicants' rights to freedom of expression and the need to protect McDonalds' rights and reputation. The more general interest in promoting the free circulation of information and ideas about the activities of powerful commercial entities, and the possible 'chilling' effect on others are also important factors to be considered in this context, bearing in mind the legitimate and important role that campaign groups can play in stimulating public discussion (see, for example, *Lingens v Austria*, judgment of 8 July 1986, Series A no. 103, § 44, *Bladet Tromsø* § 64, *Thorgeir Thorgeirson* § 68). The lack of procedural fairness and equality therefore gave rise to a breach of Article 10 in the present case.

96 Moreover, the Court considers that the size of the award of damages made against the two applicants may also have failed to strike the right balance. Under the Convention, an award of damages for defamation must bear a reasonable relationship of proportionality to the injury to reputation suffered (see *Tolstoy Miloslavsky v. the United Kingdom*, judgment of 13 July 1995, Series A, No. 316-B, § 49). The Court notes on the one hand that the sums eventually awarded in the present case (GBP 36,000 in the case of the first applicant and GBP 40,000 in the case of the second applicant) although relatively moderate by contemporary standards in defamation cases in England and Wales, were very substantial when compared to the modest incomes and resources of the two applicants. While accepting, on the other hand, that the statements in the leaflet which were found to be untrue contained serious allegations, the Court observes that not only were the plaintiffs large and powerful corporate entities but that, in accordance with the principles of English law, they were not required to, and did not, establish that they had in fact suffered any financial loss as a result of the publication of the 'several thousand' copies of the leaflets found to have been distributed, by the trial judge (see paragraph 45 above and compare, for example, *Hertel v Switzerland*, cited above, § 49).

97 While it is true that no steps have to date been taken to enforce the damages award against either applicant, the fact remains that the substantial sums awarded against them have remained enforceable since the decision of the Court of Appeal. In these circumstances, the Court finds that the award of damages in the present case was disproportionate to the legitimate aim served.

98 In conclusion, given the lack of procedural fairness and the disproportionate award of damages, the Court finds that there has been a violation of Article 10...

109 The Court has found violations of Articles 6 § 1 and 10 based, principally, on the fact that the applicants had themselves to carry out the bulk of the legal work in these exceptionally long and difficult proceedings to defend their rights to freedom of expression. In these circumstances the applicants must have suffered anxiety and disruption to their lives far in excess of that experienced by a represented litigant, and the Court also notes in this connection the medical evidence submitted by Ms Steel. It awards compensation for non-pecuniary damage of EUR 20,000 to the first applicant and EUR 15,000 to the second applicant.

NOTE

Should a corporate person be able to obtain substantial damages in defamation without having to prove damage? (Cf *Jameel (Yousef) v Dow Jones & Co* (2005); *Jameel (Mohammed) v Wall Street Journal Europe* (2005).)

8.2.4 Publication

Defamation is strictly a three-party tort: there has to be publication of the statement defamatory of the claimant to a third party. If there is no publication there can be no action. In other words, defamation is not a tort of insult (unlike the Roman law *injuria*); and so if Miss Burchill (above, p 266) had simply sent her comments to Mr Berkoff in a private letter, or had insulted him out of the hearing of anyone else, the latter would have no claim (but cf *Bryanston Finance v de Vries* (1975)). Indeed, even if the letter had been opened by one of Mr Berkoff's employees there would probably be no publication, unless perhaps Miss Burchill should have known that a secretary or the like would open the letter (see *Huth v Huth* (1915)). No doubt if Miss Burchill had written her comments on a postcard things would not be so simple. New forms of communication are, however, creating challenges for the law of defamation as the next extract indicates.

Loutchansky v Times Newspapers Ltd (Nos 2-5) [2002] 2 QB 783, CA

This was an action in damages by a claimant whom a newspaper had alleged to be a member of the Russian mafia. Various issues arose, one of which was limitation in relation to publication of the article as archive material on the Internet. The Court of Appeal's view (Lord Phillips MR, Simon Brown and Tuckey LJJ) is set out in Lord Phillips' judgment of the court.

Lord Phillips MR: ... **57** It is a well established principle of the English law of defamation that each individual publication of a libel gives rise to a separate cause of action, subject to its own limitation period. *Duke of Brunswick v Harmer* 14 QB 185 provides a striking illustration of this principle. On 19 September 1830 an article was published in the 'Weekly Dispatch'. The limitation period for libel was then six years. The article defamed the Duke of Brunswick. Seventeen years after its publication an agent of the Duke purchased a back number containing the article from the 'Weekly Dispatch' office. Another copy was obtained from the British Museum. The Duke sued on those two publications. The defendant contended that the cause of action was time-barred, relying on the original publication date. The Court of Queen's Bench held that the delivery of a copy of the newspaper to the plaintiff's agent constituted a separate publication in respect of which suit could be brought.

58 In *Godfrey v Demon Internet Ltd* [2001] QB 201 the plaintiff brought an action in defamation against the defendants, who were Internet service providers. They had received and stored on their news server an article, defamatory of the plaintiff, which had been posted by an unknown person using another service provider. The issue was whether the defendants had a defence under section 1(1) of the Defamation Act 1996. The judge held that they did not. He observed, at pp 208-209:

'In my judgment the defendants, whenever they transmit and whenever there is transmitted from the storage of their news server a defamatory posting, publish that posting to any subscriber to their ISP who accesses the newsgroup containing that posting. Thus every time one of the defendants' customers accesses soc.culture.thai and sees that posting defamatory of the plaintiff there is a publication to that customer.'

59 This decision was consistent with the *Duke of Brunswick* case 14 QB 185 and Lord Lester did not suggest to the contrary...

74 We do not accept that the rule in the *Duke of Brunswick* case imposes a restriction on the readiness to maintain and provide access to archives that amounts to a disproportionate restriction on freedom of expression. We accept that the maintenance of archives, whether in hard copy or on the Internet, has a social utility, but consider that the maintenance of archives is a comparatively insignificant aspect of freedom of expression. Archive material is stale news and its publication cannot rank in importance with the dissemination of contemporary material. Nor do we believe that the law of defamation need inhibit the responsible maintenance of archives. Where it is known that archive material is or may be defamatory, the attachment of an appropriate notice warning against treating it as the truth will normally remove any sting from the material.

75 Turning to the defendants' wider argument, it is true that to permit an action to be based on a fresh dissemination of an article published long ago is at odds with some of the reasons for the introduction of a 12-month limitation period for defamation. But the scale of such publication and any resulting damage is likely to be modest compared with that of the original publication. In the present case, as the judge observed, the action based on the Internet publication is subsidiary to the main action.

76 The change in the law of defamation for which the defendants contend is a radical one. In our judgment they have failed to make out their case that such a change is required. The Internet single publication appeal is therefore dismissed.

QUESTIONS

1. Is Lord Phillips' proposition in para 74 really practical or does it show a lack of understanding both of the workings of the Internet and of the role of archives? (cf. *Guardian* 27 December 2005, 15.)

2. A celebrity slanders the claimant's business in the hearing of several other people and these people report the slander to the press. The press widely publishes the slander and the claimant's business suffers as a result. Can the claimant claim damages for this business loss from (a) the celebrity and (b) the press?

8.2.5 Liability for publication

The position at common law is that it is not only the author of the defamatory material who can be held liable in defamation. Printers, publishers and distributors can also be sued. The position has now been modified by statute.

Defamation Act 1996 (c 31)

1 Responsibility for publication.

(1) In defamation proceedings a person has a defence if he shows that—
  (a) he was not the author, editor or publisher of the statement complained of,
  (b) he took reasonable care in relation to its publication, and
  (c) he did not know, and had no reason to believe, that what he did caused or contributed to the publication of a defamatory statement…

(3) A person shall not be considered the author, editor or publisher of a statement if he is only involved—
  (a) in printing, producing, distributing or selling printed material containing the statement
  (b) in processing, making copies of, distributing, exhibiting or selling a film or sound recording (as defined in Part I of the Copyright, Designs and Patents Act 1988) containing the statement
  (c) in processing, making copies of, distributing or selling any electronic medium in or on which the statement is recorded, or in operating or providing any equipment, system or service by means of which the statement is retrieved, copied, distributed or made available in electronic form
  (d) as the broadcaster of a live programme containing the statement in circumstances in which he has no effective control over the maker of the statement

(e) as the operator of or provider of access to a communications system by means of which the statement is transmitted, or made available, by a person over whom he has no effective control.

In a case not within paragraphs (a) to (e) the court may have regard to those provisions by way of analogy in deciding whether a person is to be considered the author, editor or publisher of a statement…

(5) In determining for the purposes of this section whether a person took reasonable care, or had reason to believe that what he did caused or contributed to the publication of a defamatory statement, regard shall be had to—
(a) the extent of his responsibility for the content of the statement or the decision to publish it,
(b) the nature or circumstances of the publication, and
(c) the previous conduct or character of the author, editor or publisher…

QUESTION

Why did the law not extend this reasonable care defence to the author, editor and publisher? Might it be because the law treats reputation as akin to a property right? Ought reputation to be part of the law of property?

8.3 Defamation (2): defences

Given that almost any critical statement made of another can be defamatory, the defences are of major constitutional importance since they are the only effective means of protecting freedom of speech. There are three traditional defences (if one excludes death as a 'defence', for a defamation claim dies with the defamed person). These three defences are justification or truth, fair comment and privilege. In addition to these three defences there is now a statutory offer of amends defence.

8.3.1 Justification

Truth is a complete defence to an action in defamation, as the next extracts indicate.

Reynolds v Times Newspapers Limited [2001] 2 AC 127, HL

(For facts and further extracts see pp 265, 276, 278, 280)

Lord Nicholls: … Historically the common law has set much store by protection of reputation. Publication of a statement adversely affecting a person's reputation is actionable. The plaintiff is not required to prove that the words are false. Nor, in the case of publication in a written or permanent form, is he required to prove he has been damaged. But, as Littledale J said in *McPherson v Daniels* (1829) 10 B & C 263, 272, 'the law will not permit a man to recover damages in respect of an injury to a character which he does not or ought not to possess'. Truth is a complete defence. If the defendant proves the substantial truth of the words complained of, he thereby establishes the

▶

defence of justification. With the minor exception of proceedings to which the Rehabilitation of Offenders Act 1974 applies, this defence is of universal application in civil proceedings. It avails a defendant even if he was acting spitefully...

Defamation Act 1952 (15 & 16 Geo. VI & 1 Eliz. III, c 66)

5   Justification.

In an action for libel or slander in respect of words containing two or more distinct charges against the plaintiff, a defence of justification shall not fail by reason only that the truth of every charge is not proved if the words not proved to be true do not materially injure the plaintiff's reputation having regard to the truth of the remaining charges.

NOTE

The onus is on the defendant to prove truth and thus a reasonable belief that the allegation is true is not enough. However proof of conviction of a crime is enough to establish justification even if the defamed convicted person believes that the conviction was a miscarriage of justice (Civil Evidence Act 1968, s 13).

8.3.2 Fair (honest) comment

Fair comment honestly held on a matter of fact is also a defence.

Defamation Act 1952 (15 & 16 Geo. VI & 1 Eliz. III, c 66)

6   Fair comment.

In an action for libel or slander in respect of words consisting partly of allegations of fact and partly of expression of opinion, a defence of fair comment shall not fail by reason only that the truth of every allegation of fact is not proved if the expression of opinion is fair comment having regard to such of the facts alleged or referred to in the words complained of as are proved.

NOTE

The Act uses the expression 'fair'. However, as the next extract shows, this term is no longer accurate.

Reynolds v Times Newspapers Limited [2001] 2 AC 127, HL

(For facts and further extracts see pp 265, 275, 278, 280)

Lord Nicholls: ... One established exception is the defence of comment on a matter of public interest. This defence is available to everyone, and is of particular importance to the media. The freedom of expression protected by this defence has long been regarded by the common law as a basic right, long before the emergence of human rights conventions. In 1863 Crompton J observed in *Campbell v. Spottiswoode* (1863) 3

B & S 769, 779, that 'it is the right of all the Queen's subjects to discuss public matters'. The defence is wide in its scope. Public interest has never been defined, but in *London Artists Ltd. v. Littler* [1969] 2 QB 375, 391, Lord Denning MR rightly said that it is not to be confined within narrow limits. He continued:

> 'Whenever a matter is such as to affect people at large, so that they may be legiti-mately interested in, or concerned at, what is going on; or what may happen to them or others; then it is a matter of public interest on which everyone is entitled to make fair comment.'

Traditionally one of the ingredients of this defence is that the comment must be fair, fair-ness being judged by the objective standard of whether any fair-minded person could honestly express the opinion in question. Judges have emphasised the latitude to be applied in interpreting this standard. So much so, that the time has come to recognise that in this context the epithet 'fair' is now meaningless and misleading. Comment must be relevant to the facts to which it is addressed. It cannot be used as a cloak for mere invective. But the basis of our public life is that the crank, the enthusiast, may say what he honestly thinks as much as the reasonable person who sits on a jury. The true test is whether the opinion, however exaggerated, obstinate or prejudiced, was honestly held by the person expressing it: see Diplock J in *Silkin v. Beaverbrook Newspapers Ltd.* [1958] 1 WLR 743, 747.

It is important to keep in mind that this defence is concerned with the protection of comment, not imputations of fact. If the imputation is one of fact, a ground of defence must be sought elsewhere. Further, to be within this defence the comment must be recognisable as comment, as distinct from an imputation of fact. The comment must explicitly or implicitly indicate, at least in general terms, what are the facts on which the comment is being made: see the discussion in *Duncan and Neill on Defamation*, 2nd ed. (1983), pp. 58–62.

One constraint does exist upon this defence. The comment must represent the honest belief of its author. If the plaintiff proves he was actuated by malice, this ground of defence will fail...

NOTES

1. The comment must be 'fair' and the facts upon which it is based must be accurate. Thus if Miss Burchill (above, p 266) had described a character in a film or play acted by Mr Berkoff as being hideously ugly or less good looking than the Frankenstein Creature, it may be that Miss Burchill would have had the defence of fair comment. She is entitled to comment on a public fact such as a film or public performance. She equally could have described his acting in derogatory terms, just as he would be entitled to criticise, say, the literary quality of her newspaper columns. However, the defence of fair comment will fail if actuated by malice, proof of which rests on the claimant.

2. The distinction between fact and comment is, of course, more complex than Lord Nicholls would seem to admit and this is yet another reason why defama-tion as a tort is so complex. Could Miss Burchill (p 266) have claimed that she was simply stating a fact when she described Mr Berkoff in the way she did? If

ugliness is a question of opinion, what if a weather forecaster describes a day as 'dull'? Or what if she talks of an 'ugly storm'? A doctor states that a patient is displaying the symptoms of a particular disease: is this a statement of fact or opinion? What if the patient demands a 'second opinion'?

8.3.3 Privilege (1): absolute privilege

The law recognises, as the next extract indicates, that there are some situations where the public interest and (or) the interests of justice require that statements, even if defamatory, should be published to persons having an interest in receiving the statement. There are two forms of privilege, absolute and qualified.

Reynolds v Times Newspapers Limited [2001] 2 AC 127, HL

(For facts and further extracts see pp 265, 275, 280)

Lord Nicholls: ... The defence of honest comment on a matter of public interest, then, does not cover defamatory statements of fact. But there are circumstances, in the famous words of Parke B. in *Toogood v. Spyring* (1834) 1 CM & R 181, 193, when the 'common convenience and welfare of society' call for frank communication on questions of fact. In *Davies v. Snead* (1870) LR 5 QB 608, 611, Blackburn J spoke of circumstances where a person is so situated that it 'becomes right in the interests of society' that he should tell certain facts to another. There are occasions when the person to whom a statement is made has a special interest in learning the honestly held views of another person, even if those views are defamatory of someone else and cannot be proved to be true. When the interest is of sufficient importance to outweigh the need to protect reputation, the occasion is regarded as privileged.

Sometimes the need for uninhibited expression is of such a high order that the occasion attracts absolute privilege, as with statements made by judges or advocates or witnesses in the course of judicial proceedings...

NOTE

Some forms of absolute privilege are based in statute.

Defamation Act 1996 (c 31)

14   Reports of court proceedings absolutely privileged.

(1) A fair and accurate report of proceedings in public before a court to which this section applies, if published contemporaneously with the proceedings, is absolutely privileged...

NOTE

See also the Competition Act 1998, s 57; Local Government Act 2000, s 74; Inquiries Act 2005, s 37.

8.3.4 Privilege (2): qualified privilege

One of the classic statements of privilege is to be found in the next case.

Watt v Longsdon [1930] 1 KB 130, CA

This was an action for damages in defamation brought by a director of a company against another director of the same company in respect of a letter written by a foreign manager of the company. The letter accused the claimant of gross immorality. The defendant director, before obtaining further evidence against the claimant, showed the letter to the chairman and to the claimant's wife, the latter commencing divorce proceedings as a result. The allegations in the letter were unfounded but the defendant believed them to be true. The Court of Appeal (Scrutton Greer and Russelll LJJ) held that the publication of the letter to the chairman of the board was privileged but the publication to the wife was not. The court also held that in the publication to the wife there was evidence of malice which ought to be left to the jury.

Scrutton LJ: ... By the law of England there are occasions on which a person may make defamatory statements about another which are untrue without incurring any legal liability for his statements. These occasions are called privileged occasions. A reason frequently given for this privilege is that the allegation that the speaker has 'unlawfully and maliciously published,' is displaced by proof that the speaker had either a duty or an interest to publish, and that this duty or interest confers the privilege. But communications made on these occasions may lose their privilege: (1) they may exceed the privilege of the occasion by going beyond the limits of the duty or interest, or (2) they may be published with express malice, so that the occasion is not being legitimately used, but abused... The question whether the occasion was privileged is for the judge, and so far as 'duty' is concerned, the question is: Was there a duty, legal, moral, or social, to communicate? As to legal duty, the judge should have no difficulty; the judge should know the law; but as to moral or social duties of imperfect obligation, the task is far more troublesome. The judge has no evidence as to the view the community takes of moral or social duties. All the help the Court of Appeal can give him is contained in the judgment of Lindley LJ in *Stuart v Bell*: 'The question of moral or social duty being for the judge, each judge must decide it as best he can for himself ...' ... It is not surprising that with such a standard both judges and text-writers treat the matter as one of great difficulty in which no definite line can be drawn...

NOTE

Qualified privilege differs from absolute privilege in that it can be rebutted by proof of malice as Lord Nicholls goes on to explain in the next extract.

Reynolds v Times Newspapers Limited [2001] 2 AC 127, HL

This was an action for damages for defamation by a former Irish Prime Minster against a newspaper which had implied that he had lied to the Irish Parliament. At the trial the jury ruled that the words were not true, but the newspaper also argued that the article should be covered by qualified privilege. This latter argument was rejected by the trial judge. On appeal the Court of Appeal set aside the jury verdict and the judgment and ordered a new trial; it also decided that the defendant could not rely upon qualified privilege. The House of Lords (Lords Nicholls, Cooke and Hobhouse; Lords Steyn and Hope dissenting), by a majority, dismissed an appeal, although they reassessed the scope of qualified privilege in the light of the coming into force of the Human Rights Act 1998.

Lord Nicholls: ... Sometimes the need for uninhibited expression is of such a high order that the occasion attracts absolute privilege, as with statements made by judges or advocates or witnesses in the course of judicial proceedings. More usually, the privilege is qualified in that it can be defeated if the plaintiff proves the defendant was actuated by malice.

The classic exposition of malice in this context is that of Lord Diplock in *Horrocks v Lowe* [1975] AC 135, 149. If the defendant used the occasion for some reason other than the reason for which the occasion was privileged he loses the privilege. Thus, the motive with which the statement was made is crucial. If desire to injure was the dominant motive the privilege is lost. Similarly, if the maker of the statement did not believe the statement to be true, or if he made the statement recklessly, without considering or caring whether it was true or not...

Over the years the courts have held that many common form situations are privileged. Classic instances are employment references, and complaints made or information given to the police or appropriate authorities regarding suspected crimes. The courts have always emphasised that the categories established by the authorities are not exhaustive. The list is not closed. The established categories are no more than applications, in particular circumstances, of the underlying principle of public policy...

The requirement that both the maker of the statement and the recipient must have an interest or duty draws attention to the need to have regard to the position of both parties when deciding whether an occasion is privileged. But this should not be allowed to obscure the rationale of the underlying public interest on which privilege is founded. The essence of this defence lies in the law's recognition of the need, in the public interest, for a particular recipient to receive frank and uninhibited communication of particular information from a particular source. That is the end the law is concerned to attain. The protection afforded to the maker of the statement is the means by which the law seeks to achieve that end. Thus the court has to assess whether, in the public interest, the publication should be protected in the absence of malice.

In determining whether an occasion is regarded as privileged the court has regard to all the circumstances...

Statutory privilege

Many, if not all, of the common law categories of case where reports of proceedings attract privilege are now the subject of statutory privilege. Successive statutes have extended the categories. The Law of Libel Amendment Act 1888 granted qualified privilege to fair and accurate reports published in newspapers of a limited range of public meetings. In 1948 the Report of the Committee on the Law of Defamation (Cmd 7536), chaired by Lord Porter, recommended that the classes of reports subject to qualified privilege should be extended, and that they should be re-classified into two categories: those where statements were privileged without explanation or contradiction, and those where privilege was conditional on publication on request of a letter or statement by way of explanation or contradiction. The Defamation Act 1952 gave effect to these recommendations. Among the publications having qualified privilege without explanation or contradiction was a fair and accurate report of proceedings in public of the Irish legislature. Until abandoned, this was one of the defendants' pleaded defences in the present proceedings.

In 1975 the committee on defamation chaired by Faulks J considered a proposal that a statutory qualified privilege should be created to protect statements made, whether in a newspaper or elsewhere, if the matter was of public interest and the publisher believed the statement of facts was true and he had taken reasonable care in relation to such facts. In its report (Cmnd. 5909) the committee did not accept this proposal. The committee considered this would seriously alter the balance of the law of defamation against a defamed plaintiff. The committee noted that the common law defence of qualified privilege was available to the media as much as anyone else, and referred to the *Cox v Feeney* line of cases.

In 1991 the Supreme Court Procedure Committee, chaired by Neill LJ, in its Report on Practice and Procedure in Defamation considered that fair and accurate coverage by the British media of statements and proceedings abroad ought to be protected by qualified privilege in circumstances which would attract privilege if comparable statements or proceedings occurred in this country. The committee recommended this result should be achieved by statute. The committee regarded the 'duty' test as too stringent in modern conditions and productive of too much uncertainty. The committee was opposed to the introduction of a defence similar to the 'public figure' defence enunciated by the United States Supreme Court in *New York Times Co. v Sullivan* (1964) 376 US 254.

The Defamation Act 1996 broadly gave effect to the Neill committee recommendations. The Act contained an extended list of categories of statutory qualified privilege. In the Act of 1996 and the Act of 1952 statutory privilege was additional to any common law privilege, but did not protect publication of any matter which was not of public concern and the publication of which was not for the public benefit: see section 15 of the Act of 1996 and section 7 of the Act of 1952...

A new category of privileged subject-matter?

I turn to the appellants' submissions. The newspaper seeks the incremental development of the common law by the creation of a new category of occasion when privilege derives from the subject-matter alone: political information...

These are powerful arguments, but I do not accept the conclusion for which the newspaper contended. My reasons appear from what is set out below.

▶

My starting point is freedom of expression. The high importance of freedom to impart and receive information and ideas has been stated so often and so eloquently that this point calls for no elaboration in this case. At a pragmatic level, freedom to disseminate and receive information on political matters is essential to the proper functioning of the system of parliamentary democracy cherished in this country. This freedom enables those who elect representatives to Parliament to make an informed choice, regarding individuals as well as policies, and those elected to make informed decisions. Freedom of expression will shortly be buttressed by statutory requirements. Under section 12 of the Human Rights Act 1998, expected to come into force in October 2000, the court is required, in relevant cases, to have particular regard to the importance of the right to freedom of expression. The common law is to be developed and applied in a manner consistent with article 10 of the European Convention for the Protection of Human Rights and Fundamental Freedoms (Cmd. 8969), and the court must take into account relevant decisions of the European Court of Human Rights (sections 6 and 2). To be justified, any curtailment of freedom of expression must be convincingly established by a compelling countervailing consideration, and the means employed must be proportionate to the end sought to be achieved.

Likewise, there is no need to elaborate on the importance of the role discharged by the media in the expression and communication of information and comment on political matters. It is through the mass media that most people today obtain their information on political matters. Without freedom of expression by the media, freedom of expression would be a hollow concept. The interest of a democratic society in ensuring a free press weighs heavily in the balance in deciding whether any curtailment of this freedom bears a reasonable relationship to the purpose of the curtailment. In this regard it should be kept in mind that one of the contemporary functions of the media is investigative journalism. This activity, as much as the traditional activities of reporting and commenting, is part of the vital role of the press and the media generally...

The crux of this appeal ... lies in identifying the restrictions which are fairly and reasonably necessary for the protection of reputation. Leaving aside the exceptional cases which attract absolute privilege, the common law denies protection to defamatory statements, whether of comment or fact, proved to be actuated by malice, in the *Horrocks v Lowe* [1975] AC 135 sense. This common law limitation on freedom of speech passes the 'necessary' test with flying colours. This is an acceptable limitation. Freedom of speech does not embrace freedom to make defamatory statements out of personal spite or without having a positive belief in their truth...

Conclusion

My conclusion is that the established common law approach to misstatements of fact remains essentially sound. The common law should not develop 'political information' as a new 'subject-matter' category of qualified privilege, whereby the publication of all such information would attract qualified privilege, whatever the circumstances. That would not provide adequate protection for reputation. Moreover, it would be unsound in principle to distinguish political discussion from discussion of other matters of serious public concern. The elasticity of the common law principle enables interference with freedom of speech to be confined to what is necessary in the circumstances of the case. This elasticity enables the court to give appropriate weight, in today's conditions, to the importance of freedom of expression by the media on all matters of public concern.

Depending on the circumstances, the matters to be taken into account include the following. The comments are illustrative only.

1. The seriousness of the allegation. The more serious the charge, the more the public is misinformed and the individual harmed, if the allegation is not true.

2. The nature of the information, and the extent to which the subject-matter is a matter of public concern.

3. The source of the information. Some informants have no direct knowledge of the events. Some have their own axes to grind, or are being paid for their stories.

4. The steps taken to verify the information.

5. The status of the information. The allegation may have already been the subject of an investigation which commands respect.

6. The urgency of the matter. News is often a perishable commodity.

7. Whether comment was sought from the defendant. He may have information others do not possess or have not disclosed. An approach to the defendant will not always be necessary.

8. Whether the article contained the gist of the plaintiff's side of the story.

9. The tone of the article. A newspaper can raise queries or call for an investigation. It need not adopt allegations as statements of fact.

10. The circumstances of the publication, including the timing.

This list is not exhaustive. The weight to be given to these and any other relevant factors will vary from case to case. Any disputes of primary fact will be a matter for the jury, if there is one. The decision on whether, having regard to the admitted or proved facts, the publication was subject to qualified privilege is a matter for the judge. This is the established practice and seems sound. A balancing operation is better carried out by a judge in a reasoned judgment than by a jury. Over time, a valuable corpus of case law will be built up.

In general, a newspaper's unwillingness to disclose the identity of its sources should not weigh against it. Further, it should always be remembered that journalists act without the benefit of the clear light of hindsight. Matters which are obvious in retrospect may have been far from clear in the heat of the moment. Above all, the court should have particular regard to the importance of freedom of expression. The press discharges vital functions as a bloodhound as well as a watchdog. The court should be slow to conclude that a publication was not in the public interest and, therefore, the public had no right to know, especially when the information is in the field of political discussion. Any lingering doubts should be resolved in favour of publication.

Privilege and the facts of this case

The appellant newspaper's primary submission was that they never had the opportunity of pleading and proving a case that the 'circumstantial test' was satisfied, because this

▶

test had not been formulated until the Court of Appeal gave judgment. I am not persuaded by this line of argument...

Was the information in the 'Sunday Times' article information the public was entitled to know? The subject matter was undoubtedly of public concern in this country. However, these serious allegations by the newspaper, presented as statements of fact but shorn of all mention of Mr Reynolds' considered explanation, were not information the public had a right to know. I agree with the Court of Appeal this was not a publication which should in the public interest be protected by privilege in the absence of proof of malice. The further facts the defendants wish to assert and prove at the retrial would make no difference, either on this point or overall. I would dismiss this appeal.

NOTE

There is no doubt that this case is one of the most important decisions on defamation in recent years. It has clearly expanded the defence of qualified privilege in the light of the Human Rights Act 1998. It is not, however, a radical decision. It offers some protection to the press, but, as the next extracts show, not too much.

Loutchansky v Times Newspapers Ltd (Nos 2–5) [2002] QB 783, CA

This was an action in damages by a claimant whom a newspaper had alleged to be a member of the Russian mafia. Various issues arose, one of which was limitation (see above p 273) and another was the defence of qualified privilege. The Court of Appeal's view on qualified privilege is set out in Lord Phillips' judgment of the court.

Lord Phillips MR: ... **41** In deciding in any given case whether the standard of responsible journalism has been satisfied, the following considerations are likely to feature prominently in the court's thinking.

(i)   If the publication is held privileged, that, to all intents and purposes, will provide the publishers with a complete defence. In this class of case, as already observed, a finding of privilege will effectively pre-empt a finding of malice...

(ii)   Setting the standard of journalistic responsibility too low would inevitably encourage too great a readiness to publish defamatory matter. Journalists should be rigorous, not lax, in their approach. It is in the interests of the public as well as the defamed individual that, wherever possible, truths and not untruths should be told. This is in the interests of the media too: once untruths can be published with impunity, the public will cease to believe any communications, true or false.

(iii)   Setting the standard too high, however, would be no less damaging to society. This would deter newspapers from discharging their proper function of keeping the public informed. When determining in respect of any given article whether or not it should attract qualified privilege, the court must bear in mind the likely impact of its ruling not only upon the case in hand but also upon the media's practices generally. Qualified privilege ordinarily falls to be judged as a preliminary issue and before, therefore, the truth or falsity of the communication is established. The question to be posed is accordingly whether it was in the public interest to publish the article, true or false, rather than whether it was in the public interest to publish an untruth. Even, moreover, when the untruth of the article is established (or when, as here, it is not formally disputed), it is important to remember that the defence of qualified privilege tolerates factual inaccuracy for two purposes: first so as not to deter the publication sued upon (which might have been true); and secondly so as not to deter future publications of truthful information...

NOTE

The effect of *Reynolds* is to introduce into defamation via the defence of qualified privilege an element of fault focused on the 'reasonable journalist' (Lord Phillips). This has been necessary because, as Lord Nicholls indicated, the European Convention of Human Rights and Fundamental Freedoms guarantees freedom of expression in art 10. The problem is that the judges have allocated to themselves the job of reviewing editorial decisions founded on criteria (Lord Nicholls' ten points) that are possibly more intrusive than the criteria they apply when it comes to judicial review of administrative decisions. The effect of the *Reynolds* decision is to introduce into English law a power to review media decisions. This may be no bad thing, of course; but the judicial track record to date, when it comes to the press, is somewhat depressing (see eg *Camelot Group v Centaur Communications* (1999)).

QUESTION

Sedley LJ has stated that it is not for judges to determine the editorial policy of the press (see above p 38). Does not the notion of the reasonable journalist in fact allow the judges to do just this?

8.3.5 Offer of amends

Legislation now offers a new, if somewhat limited, defence.

Defamation Act 1996 (c 31)

2   Offer to make amends.

(1) A person who has published a statement alleged to be defamatory of another may offer to make amends under this section.

(2) The offer may be in relation to the statement generally or in relation to a specific defamatory meaning which the person making the offer accepts that the statement conveys ('a qualified offer')...

(4) An offer to make amends under this section is an offer—
  (a) to make a suitable correction of the statement complained of and a sufficient apology to the aggrieved party,
  (b) to publish the correction and apology in a manner that is reasonable and practicable in the circumstances, and

▶

(c) to pay to the aggrieved party such compensation (if any), and such costs, as may be agreed or determined to be payable...

3 Accepting an offer to make amends.

(1) If an offer to make amends under section 2 is accepted by the aggrieved party, the following provisions apply.

(2) The party accepting the offer may not bring or continue defamation proceedings in respect of the publication concerned against the person making the offer, but he is entitled to enforce the offer to make amends...

4 Failure to accept offer to make amends.

(1) If an offer to make amends under section 2, duly made and not withdrawn, is not accepted by the aggrieved party, the following provisions apply.

(2) The fact that the offer was made is a defence (subject to subsection (3)) to defamation proceedings in respect of the publication in question by that party against the person making the offer.

A qualified offer is only a defence in respect of the meaning to which the offer related.

(3) There is no such defence if the person by whom the offer was made knew or had reason to believe that the statement complained of—
   (a) referred to the aggrieved party or was likely to be understood as referring to him, and
   (b) was both false and defamatory of that party

but it shall be presumed until the contrary is shown that he did not know and had no reason to believe that was the case.

(4) The person who made the offer need not rely on it by way of defence, but if he does he may not rely on any other defence.

If the offer was a qualified offer, this applies only in respect of the meaning to which the offer related.

(5) The offer may be relied on in mitigation of damages whether or not it was relied on as a defence.

NOTE

Careful reading of these provisions will soon indicate they do not offer much protection for the press.

8.4 Misrepresentation and misstatement

The case of *Spring v Guardian Assurance* (1995) (above p 257) has already indicated how defamation and the tort of negligent misstatement (*Hedley Byrne v Heller* (1964), p 115) can overlap. Yet misstatement and misrepresentation are governed by rules that are very different from defamation: the basis of liability is the defendant's fault and even proof of carelessness will not be enough in itself to establish liability. The claimant must also prove a special relationship. Defamation, in contrast, arises simply out of the invasion of the claimant's reputation interest and fault, if it has any role at all, is restricted to certain defences; liability, in other words, is strict. Negligence and defamation are not, however, the only torts relevant to damage done by words. Where there has been an intentional misrepresentation – a deliberate lie – the tort of deceit will come into play and even a completely innocent misrepresentation, where it has led to a contract, may attract the equitable remedy of rescission (*Redgrave v Hurd* (1881)). This latter remedy takes one outside tort and into contract, but misrepresentation in general is a field of liability that often operates at the frontier between tort and contract.

8.4.1 Deceit

The first distinction that needs to be made is between fraudulent and negligent misstatement. Where the defendant has told a deliberate lie and this results in loss to another the tort of deceit may be available. Its elements of liability are neatly summarised in the next extract.

Bradford Building Society v Borders [1941] 2 All ER 205, HL

Viscount Maugham: ... My Lords, we are dealing here with a common law action of deceit, which requires four things to be established. First, there must be a representation of fact made by words, or, it may be, by conduct. The phrase will include a case where the defendant has manifestly approved and adopted a representation made by some third person. On the other hand, mere silence, however morally wrong, will not support an action of deceit: *Peek v Gurney* per Lord Chelmsford, and per Lord Cairns, and *Arkwright v Newbold*. Secondly, the representation must be made with a knowledge that it is false. It must be wilfully false, or at least made in the absence of any genuine belief that it is true: *Derry v Peek* and *Nocton v Ashburton (Lord)*. Thirdly, it must be made with the intention that it should be acted upon by the plaintiff, or by a class of persons which will include the plaintiff, in the manner which resulted in damage to him: *Peek v Gurney* and *Smith v Chadwick*. If, however, fraud be established, it is immaterial that there was no intention to cheat or injure the person to whom the false statement was made: *Derry v Peek*, and *Peek v Gurney*. Fourthly, it must be proved that the plaintiff has acted upon the false statement and has sustained damage by so doing: *Clarke v Dickson*. I am not, of course, attempting to make a complete statement of the law of deceit, but only to state the main facts which a plaintiff must establish ...

NOTE

The main difficulty facing any claimant wishing to sue in deceit is that fraud must be proved. And this is by no means easy. Nevertheless, if the claimant succeeds he can expect the courts to be more generous when it comes to assessing compensation.

Smith New Court Securities Ltd v Scrimgeour Vickers Ltd [1997] AC 254, HL

This was an action for damages in the tort of deceit against a defendant who had induced, by fraudulent misrepresentation, the claimants to buy shares at a price which, soon after the purchase, dropped considerably. The trial judge awarded damages of over £10 million, but this was reduced to just over £1 million by the Court of Appeal. The House of Lords (Lords Browne-Wilkinson, Keith, Mustill, Slynn and Steyn) reinstated the trial judge's award.

Lord Browne-Wilkinson: ... In sum, in my judgment the following principles apply in assessing the damages payable where the plaintiff has been induced by a fraudulent misrepresentation to buy property: (1) the defendant is bound to make reparation for all the damage directly flowing from the transaction; (2) although such damage need not have been foreseeable, it must have been directly caused by the transaction; (3) in assessing such damage, the plaintiff is entitled to recover by way of damages the full price paid by him, but he must give credit for any benefits which he has received as a result of the transaction; (4) as a general rule, the benefits received by him include the market value of the property acquired as at the date of acquisition; but such general rule is not to be inflexibly applied where to do so would prevent him obtaining full compensation for the wrong suffered; (5) although the circumstances in which the general rule should not apply cannot be comprehensively stated, it will normally not apply where either (a) the misrepresentation has continued to operate after the date of the acquisition of the asset so as to induce the plaintiff to retain the asset or (b) the circumstances of the case are such that the plaintiff is, by reason of the fraud, locked into the property. (6) In addition, the plaintiff is entitled to recover consequential losses caused by the transaction; (7) the plaintiff must take all reasonable steps to mitigate his loss once he has discovered the fraud.

In the circumstances, it would not in my judgment compensate Smith for the actual loss they have suffered (ie the difference between the contract price and the resale price eventually realised) if Smith were required to give credit for the shares having a value of 78p on 21 July 1989. Having acquired the shares at 82p for stock Smith could not commercially have sold on that date at 78p. It is not realistic to treat Smith as having received shares worth 78p each when in fact, in real life, they could not commercially have sold or realised the shares at that price on that date. In my judgment, this is one of those cases where to give full reparation to Smith, the benefit which Smith ought to bring into account to be set against its loss for the total purchase price paid should be the actual resale price achieved by Smith when eventually the shares were sold...

Lord Steyn: ... That brings me to the question of policy whether there is a justification for differentiating between the extent of liability for civil wrongs depending on where in the sliding scale from strict liability to intentional wrongdoing the particular civil wrong fits in. It may be said that logical symmetry and a policy of not punishing intentional wrongdoers by civil remedies favour a uniform rule. On the other hand, it is a rational and defensible strategy to impose wider liability on an intentional wrongdoer. As *Hart and Honoré, Causation in the Law*, 2nd ed. (1985), p 304 observed, an innocent plaintiff may, not without reason, call on a morally reprehensible defendant to pay the whole of the loss he caused. The exclusion of heads of loss in the law of negligence, which reflects considerations of legal policy, does not necessarily avail the intentional wrong-doer. Such a policy of imposing more stringent remedies on an intentional wrongdoer serves two purposes. First it serves a deterrent purpose in discouraging fraud. Counsel for Citibank argued that the sole purpose of the law of tort generally, and the tort of deceit in particular, should be to compensate the victims of civil wrongs. That is far too narrow a view. Professor Glanville Williams identified four possible purposes of an action for damages in tort: appeasement, justice, deterrence and compensation: see 'The Aims of the Law of Tort' (1951) 4 CLP 137. He concluded, at p 172:

> 'Where possible the law seems to like to ride two or three horses at once; but occa-sionally a situation occurs where one must be selected. The tendency is then to choose the deterrent purpose for tort of intention, the compensatory purpose for other torts.'

And in the battle against fraud civil remedies can play a useful and beneficial role. Secondly, as between the fraudster and the innocent party, moral considerations militate in favour of requiring the fraudster to bear the risk of misfortunes directly caused by his fraud. I make no apology for referring to moral considerations. The law and morality are inextricably interwoven. To a large extent the law is simply formulated and declared morality. And, as *Oliver Wendell Holmes*, *The Common Law* (ed. M De W Howe), p 106, observed, the very notion of deceit with its overtones of wickedness is drawn from the moral world...

QUESTIONS

1. Is this case authority for the proposition that 'bad people pay more' (Weir)?

2. Is this case authority for the proposition that morality is formally part of the law of tort?

8.4.2 Negligence

Before 1964 damages actions at common law for damage done by words had to be based either on a breach of contract or on the torts of defamation, deceit or one of the economic torts. The position was changed by the *Hedley Byrne* case (1964) (see p 115). Other cases of importance are: *Caparo Industries v Dickman* (1990) (p 140); *Spring v Guardian Assurance* (1995) (p 257); *White v Jones* (1995) (p 260). For a case of misstatement causing personal injury see *Wilkinson v Downton* (1897) (p 7).

8.4.3 Statute

Where a person suffers loss as a result of entering a contract induced by a mis-representation, damages used to be recoverable only if the claimant could prove, before 1964, fraud and, after 1964, negligence. This position has now been amended by statute.

Misrepresentation Act 1967 (c 7)

2   Damages for misrepresentation

(1) Where a person has entered into a contract after a misrepresentation has been made to him by another party thereto and as a result thereof he has suffered loss, then, if the person making the misrepresentation would be liable to damages in respect thereof had the misrepresentation been made fraudulently, that person shall be so liable notwithstanding that the misrepresentation was not made fraudulently, unless he proves that he had reasonable ground to believe and did believe up to the time the contract was made that the facts represented were true.

(2) Where a person has entered into a contract after a misrepresentation has been made to him otherwise than fraudulently and he would be entitled, by reason of the misrepresentation, to rescind the contract, then, if it is claimed, in any proceedings arising out of the contract, that the contract ought to be or has been rescinded, the court or arbitrator may declare the contract subsisting and award damages in lieu of rescission, if of opinion that it would be equitable to do so, having regard to the nature of the misrepresentation and the loss that would be caused by it if the contract were upheld, as well as to the loss that rescission would cause to the other party.

(3) Damages may be awarded against a person under subsection (2) of this section whether or not he is liable to damages under subsection (1) thereof, but where he is so liable any award under the said subsection (2) shall be taken into account in assessing his liability under the said subsection (1).

QUESTION

Are damages under s 2(1) to be awarded according to the principles of the tort of negligence or the tort of deceit?

NOTE

For a judicial analysis of s 2 see *Witter Ltd v TBP Industries* (1996)

8.5 Professional liability

Many of the negligent misstatement cases can be classified not only under the tort of negligence or under liability for words. They can equally be seen as professional liability cases since a great many of them involve professional defendants such as bankers, solicitors, surveyors and the like. A category of 'professional liability' is valuable because the breach of duty test is not one dependent upon the reasonable man test (see **4.2.4**). It is dependent upon the reasonable man exercising the particular professional skill in question. Another reason why professional liability is a useful category is because it acts as a meeting point for contractual and non-contractual obligations which, as the next case shows, can directly influence the outcome of a litigation problem. Often the damage in these professional liability questions (except of course in the case of medical negligence) is pure economic loss and this is another factor that makes them problematic (**4.3.2**). However, another interesting aspect of the next extracted case is that the damage was physical.

Marc Rich & Co v Bishop Rock Ltd [1996] 1 AC 211, HL

This was an action for damages by owners of a cargo lost at sea against a firm of ship surveyors. The action was dismissed by the House of Lords (Lords Steyn, Keith, Jauncey and Browne-Wilkinson; Lord Lloyd dissenting).

Lord Steyn: ... In this case the question is whether a classification society owed a duty of care to a third party, the owners of cargo laden on a vessel, arising from the careless performance of a survey of a damaged vessel by the surveyor of the classification society which resulted in the vessel being allowed to sail and subsequently sinking. It is a novel question. In England no classification society, engaged by owners to perform a survey, has ever been held liable to cargo owners on the ground of a careless conduct of any survey. Your Lordships have also been informed that there is apparently no reported case in which such a duty has been recognised in any foreign court. Given the fact that surveyors of classification societies have regularly performed occasional surveys of laden vessels for over a century and a half the novel nature of the problem may not be entirely without significance. Ultimately, however, the problem must be considered in accordance with our tort law as it now stands without any a priori disposition for or against the legal sustainability of such a claim...

(a) Direct physical loss?

Counsel for the cargo owners argued that the present case involved the infliction of *direct* physical loss. At first glance the issue of directness may seem a matter of terminology rather than substance. In truth it is a material factor. The law more readily attaches the consequences of actionable negligence to directly inflicted physical loss than to indirectly inflicted physical loss. For example, if the NKK surveyor had carelessly dropped a lighted cigarette into a cargo hold known to contain a combustible cargo, thereby causing an explosion and the loss of the vessel and cargo, the assertion that the classification society was in breach of a duty of care might have been a strong one. That would be a paradigm case of directly inflicted physical loss... In the present case the shipowner was primarily responsible for the vessel sailing in a seaworthy condition. The role of the NKK was a subsidiary one. In my view the carelessness of the NKK surveyor did not involve the direct infliction of physical damage in the relevant sense. That by no means concludes the answer to the general question. But it does introduce the right perspective on one aspect of this case...

(f) Policy factors

Counsel for the cargo owners argued that a decision that a duty of care existed in this case would not involve wide ranging exposure for NKK and other classification societies to claims in tort. That is an unrealistic position...

At present the system of settling cargo claims against shipowners is a relatively simple one. The claims are settled between the two sets of insurers. If the claims are not settled, they are resolved in arbitration or court proceedings. If a duty is held to exist in this case as between the classification society and cargo owners, classification societies would become potential defendants in many cases. An extra layer of insurance would become involved. The settlement process would inevitably become more complicated and expensive. Arbitration proceedings and court proceedings would often involve an

▶

additional party. And often similar issues would have to be canvassed in separate pro-ceedings since the classification societies would not be bound by arbitration clauses in the contracts of carriage. If such a duty is recognised, there is a risk that classification societies might be unwilling from time to time to survey the very vessels which most urgently require independent examination. It will also divert men and resources from the prime function of classification societies, namely to save life and ships at sea. These factors are, by themselves, far from decisive. But in an overall assessment of the case they merit consideration.

Is the imposition of a duty of care fair, just and reasonable?

Like Mann LJ in the Court of Appeal [1994] 1 WLR 1071, 1085H, I am willing to assume (without deciding) that there was a sufficient degree of proximity in this case to fulfil that requirement for the existence of a duty of care. The critical question is therefore whether it would be fair, just and reasonable to impose such a duty. For my part I am satisfied that the factors and arguments advanced on behalf of cargo owners are decisively out-weighed by the cumulative effect, if a duty is recognised, of the matters discussed [earlier]... and the other considerations of policy. By way of summary, I look at the matter from the point of view of the three parties concerned. I conclude that the recognition of a duty would be unfair, unjust and unreasonable as against the shipowners who would ultimately have to bear the cost of holding classification societies liable, such conse-quence being at variance with the bargain between shipowners and cargo owners based on an internationally agreed contractual structure. It would also be unfair, unjust and unreasonable towards classification societies, notably because they act for the col-lective welfare and unlike shipowners they would not have the benefit of any limitation provisions. Looking at the matter from the point of view of cargo owners, the existing system provides them with the protection of the Hague Rules or Hague-Visby Rules. But that protection is limited under such Rules and by tonnage limitation provisions. Under the existing system any shortfall is readily insurable. In my judgment the lesser injustice is done by not recognising a duty of care. It follows that I would reject the pri-mary way in which counsel for the cargo owners put his case...

Lord Lloyd (dissenting): ... How... does the position of a surveyor, called in by shipown-ers because the vessel is leaking, differ from that of the shiprepairer? The answer is that it differs not at all. If it is fair, just and reasonable to hold a shiprepairer liable to an unlim-ited extent for damage to cargo on board caused by his negligence, even though the damage does not occur until after the vessel has sailed, why should it not be fair, just and reasonable in the case of a surveyor? Suppose in the case of the inspection cover, the surveyor negligently tells the fitter that four bolts are sufficient to secure the cover, instead of the usual six, how could it be fair, just and reasonable that the surveyor should not be liable? On what principle would the fitter be liable in such circumstances, when he acts unadvised, but not the surveyor who advises him? No 'coherent system of law' to use the language of Sir Donald Nicholls V-C in *White v Jones* [1993] 3 WLR 730, 740, should permit such a result...

Conclusion

The overriding consideration in the present case is that the cargo owners, as we are asked to assume, have suffered physical damage to their cargo, and such damage was caused by Mr Ducat's negligence, for which NKK are responsible on ordinary principles of respondeat superior... We are not here asked to extend the law of negligence into a new field. We are not even asked to make an incremental advance. All that is required is a straightforward application of *Donoghue v Stevenson*. The ground is already marked out by cases such as *Haseldine v CA Daw & Son Ltd* [1941] 2 KB 343, *Clay v AJ Crump & Sons Ltd* [1964] 1 QB 533, *Voli v Inglewood Shire Council* (1963) 110 CLR 74 and *Muirhead v Industrial Tank Specialities Ltd* [1986] QB 507, 532. In physical damage cases proximity very often goes without saying. Where the facts cry out for the imposition of a duty of care between the parties, as they do here, it would require an exceptional case to refuse to impose a duty on the ground that it would not be fair, just and reasonable. Otherwise there is a risk that the law of negligence will disintegrate into a series of isolated decisions without any coherent principles at all, and the retreat from *Anns* will turn into a rout...

QUESTION

Is this a case where policy defeated the logical application of a rule? Do you think that the claimants regarded the cargo as anything more than an economic asset?

8.6 Threats

Threats are a means of causing damage by words and threats of violence aimed directly at a victim can amount in themselves to trespass (*Read v Cocker* (1853); and see Protection from Harassment Act 1997 s 4). But many threats are of an economic kind and this takes one into the realm of the economic torts (or trade, business and labour relations torts). This is a complex area often outside many foundational tort courses, but some of the basic cases are to be found in Chapter 3. One leading economic tort case involving damage arising out of a threatening statement is *Rookes v Barnard* (p 88). Note also that harassment is now actionable (see p 100)

Protection from Harassment Act 1997 (c. 40)

7   Interpretation of this group of sections

...

(2) References to harassing a person include alarming the person or causing the person distress.

(3) A 'course of conduct' must involve—
   (a) in the case of conduct in relation to a single person (see section 1(1)), conduct on at least two occasions in relation to that person, or
   (b) in the case of conduct in relation to two or more persons (see section 1(1A)), conduct on at least one occasion in relation to each of those persons...

(4) 'Conduct' includes speech.

Chapter 9

Liability of Public Bodies

In continental European systems the distinction between public and private law is fundamental and this reflects itself in tort law in the difference between civil and administrative liability. In other words the tortious liability of State bodies or officials is part of administrative rather than private law. Now, according to traditional English constitutional theory, a separate chapter on the liability of public bodies in tort ought to be superfluous since the common law recognises no formal distinction between public and private law. Everybody, public or private, is subject to the same rules. The position, however, proves in substance to be a little more complex.

9.1 Public and private law

The distinction between public and private law has generated much literature both in continental Europe (as one might expect given that it is a division that goes back to Roman law) and in the United Kingdom. Something thus needs to be said about the nature of the distinction and its relevance to the common law.

9.1.1 Nature of the distinction

The first, and still the most influential, definition was given by the Roman jurist Ulpian who was assassinated in 223 (or 228) AD.

Justinian, *Digest*, Book 1 Title 1

1: ULPIAN ... 2. There are two branches of this subject: public law and private law. Public law is that which pertains to the position of the Roman state (*status rei Romanae*), private that which pertains to individual interests (*utilitates*): for certain matters are of public interest others of private. Public law consists of religious rites, the priesthood and public offices. Private law is tripartite, for it derived from the rules of natural law, the *ius gentium* and civil law.

NOTE

Public law is concerned with the interests of the State – with the public interest – private law with the interests of individuals. However, this does not give the whole picture even with respect to Roman law itself. Another basis for the distinction is to be found in the difference between two types of power relations upon which much of Roman law might be said to be based. This is the difference between *dominium* (ownership) and *imperium* (sovereignty). Private law might be said to be about ownership (and its satellite institutions) while public law is about sovereignty (and associated concepts). However in medieval feudal Europe the distinction had little meaning since political power (*imperium*) was based upon the grant of land (*dominium*). With the decline of feudalism and the rise of the Nation State the Roman model once again became the basis of legal and political thinking.

9.1.2 Theoretical and practical considerations

One recurring problem with the public/private distinction is the isolation of a definitional and practical theory upon which the distinction can be based.

André Demichel & Pierre Lalumière, *Le droit public*
(7th edn, Presses Universitaires de France, 1996), 6–11
(translation Geoffrey Samuel)

The distinction [between public and private law] is made up of several elements which are superimposed on each other without always overlapping.

1. The factual distinction. – The factual distinction between public and private law rests on a simple idea: public law being the law applicable to the state and to administrative officials, the distinction criterion between public and private law will be the intervention of the state in legal relations. As soon as this intervention takes place, the law applicable will have the character of public law. Thus public law will be the law dealing with the organisation of the state and its relation with individuals; private law will be just the law dealing with relations between private individuals.

2. The formal distinction. – Public and private law can be distinguished from a formal viewpoint, through technique. In this sense, as soon as concepts and legal techniques foreign to the ordinary law of private relationships are used, there is public law...

3. The functional distinction. – The functional distinction refers to the respective objectives of public and private law rules. The latter would protect only private interests while public law rules would be destined to safeguarding the public interest (*l'intérêt général*)...

At the end of the day, none of the possible criteria of distinction has in itself an absolute value. Can then the three criteria taken together permit the putting of a given fact into public or private law? In fact, even this cumulative use cannot give a definitive character to a distinction which has, in essence, a relative character...

QUESTIONS

1. How might privatisation of public utilities fit within the above schemes?

2. Is human rights law part of public or private law?

3. Should a private corporate body ever be treated as a 'public authority'? If so, upon what test? (Cf *R (Beer) v Hampshire Farmers' Markets Ltd* (2004).)

9.1.3 Traditional common law position

The common law, perhaps because of its feudal past, does not in form distinguish between civil and administrative liability as the following extracts clearly indicate.

Hill v Chief Constable of West Yorkshire [1989] AC 53, HL

(For facts and other extract see p 36)

Lord Keith: ... There is no question that a police officer, like anyone else, may be liable in tort to a person who is injured as a direct result of his acts or omissions. So he may be liable in damages for assault, unlawful arrest, wrongful imprisonment and malicious prosecution, and also for negligence. Instances where liability for negligence has been established are *Knightley v Johns* [1982] 1 WLR 349 and *Rigby v Chief Constable of Northamptonshire* [1985] 1 WLR 1242. Further, a police officer may be guilty of a criminal offence if he wilfully fails to perform a duty which he is bound to perform by common law or by statute: see *Reg v Dytham* [1979] QB 722, where a constable was convicted of wilful neglect of duty because, being present at the scene of a violent assault resulting in the death of the victim, he had taken no steps to intervene...

Stovin v Wise [1996] AC 923, HL

(For facts and other extract see p 152)

Lord Hoffmann: ... Since *Mersey Docks and Harbour Board Trustees v Gibbs* (1866) LR 1 HL 93 it has been clear law that in the absence of express statutory authority, a public body is in principle liable for torts in the same way as a private person. But its statutory powers or duties may restrict its liability. For example, it may be authorised to do something which necessarily involves committing what would otherwise be a tort. In such a case it will not be liable: *Allen v Gulf Oil Refining Ltd* [1981] AC 1001. Or it may have discretionary powers which enable it to do things to achieve a statutory purpose notwithstanding that they involve a foreseeable risk of damage to others. In such a case, a bona fide exercise of the discretion will not attract liability: *X (Minors) v Bedfordshire County Council* [1995] 2 AC 633 and *Dorset Yacht Co Ltd v Home Office* [1970] AC 1004...

Tony Weir, Governmental Liability
[1989] PL 40, 47–8

From the point of view of the tort lawyer, local government is much more important than central government. Local government may decide less, but it does more, and tort liability attaches to people who do rather than to people who decide ... The liability of central government may admittedly be impressive in amount ... But generally, apart from the prisons and to a smaller extent the military, central government does not seem to be very vulnerable to tort suits. They do not occupy schools, though they seek increasingly to control them; and they do not mend the sidewalks, they only deny the ha'porth of tar required to mend them. Quite different is local government. Everyone sues them, even the Minister for Local Government himself...

NOTE

Another reason why English law does not easily distinguish between public and private law is to be found in the next extract.

Davey v Spelthorne Borough Council [1984] AC 262, HL

Lord Wilberforce: ... The expressions 'private law' and 'public law' have recently been imported into the law of England from countries which, unlike our own, have separate systems concerning public law and private law. No doubt they are convenient expressions for descriptive purposes. In this country they must be used with caution, for, typically, English law fastens not on principles but on remedies. The principle remains intact that public authorities and public servants are, unless clearly exempted, answerable in the ordinary courts for wrongs done to individuals...

9.1.4 Changing attitudes

As Lord Wilberforce hinted, the public/private division was beginning to find its way into common law thinking in the 1980s. Indeed in *O'Reilly v Mackman* (1983) Lord Diplock appeared formally to accept the distinction. The use of 'private' law remedies to enforce 'public' law rights could, said Lord Diplock, amount to an abuse of process. However, as the next extract shows, the importation was to cause as many problems as it solved.

Mercury Communications Ltd v Director General of Telecommunications
[1996] 1 WLR 48, HL

Lord Slynn:... The recognition by Lord Diplock [in *O'Reilly v Mackman* [1983] 2 AC 237] that exceptions exist to the general rule may introduce some uncertainty but it is a small price to pay to avoid the over-rigid demarcation between procedures reminiscent of earlier disputes as to the forms of action and of disputes as to the competence of jurisdictions apparently encountered in civil law countries where a distinction between public and private law has been recognised. It is of particular importance, as I see it, to retain some flexibility as the precise limits of what is called 'public law' and what is called 'private law' are by no means worked out. The experience of other countries seems to show that the working out of this distinction is not always an easy matter. In the absence of a single procedure allowing all remedies – quashing, injunctive and declaratory relief, damages – some flexibility as to the use of different procedures is necessary. It has to be borne in mind that the overriding question is whether the proceedings constitute an abuse of the process of the court...

NOTE

Despite these reservations, the distinction can prove useful when it comes to constitutionally sensitive matters.

R v Somerset CC, ex p Fewings [1995] 1 WLR 1037, CA

This was an action for judicial review to quash a local authority decision to ban hunting on land owned by the authority. A majority of the Court of Appeal (Sir Thomas Bingham MR and Swinton Thomas LJ; Simon Brown LJ dissenting) upheld the judge's decision to quash the decision.

Sir Thomas Bingham MR: ... The point is often made that unelected unrepresentative judges have no business to be deciding questions of potentially far-reaching social concern which are more properly the preserve of elected representatives at national or local level. In some cases the making of such decisions may be inescapable, but in general the point is well made. In the present case it certainly is. The court has no role whatever as an arbiter between those who condemn hunting as barbaric and cruel and those who support it as a traditional country sport more humane in its treatment of deer or foxes (as the case may be) than other methods of destruction such as shooting, snaring, poisoning or trapping. This is of course a question on which most people hold views one way or the other. But our personal views are wholly irrelevant to the drier and more technical question which the court is obliged to answer. That is whether the county council acted lawfully in making the decision it did on the grounds it did. In other words, were members entitled in reaching their decision to give effect to their acceptance of the cruelty argument?

In seeking to answer that question it is, as the judge very clearly explained, at pp 523-525, critical to distinguish between the legal position of the private landowner and that of a land-owning local authority. To the famous question asked by the owner of the vineyard ('Is it not lawful for me to do what I will with mine own?' St. Matthew, chapter 20, verse 15) the modern answer would be clear: 'Yes, subject to such regulatory and other constraints as the law imposes.' But if the same question were posed by a local authority the answer would be different. It would be: 'No, it is not lawful for you to do anything save what the law expressly or impliedly authorises. You enjoy no unfettered discretions. There are legal limits to every power you have.' As Laws J put it, at p 524, the rule for local authorities is that any action to be taken must be justified by positive law...

NOTE

This case emphasises the distinction between *dominium* and *imperium*. The local authority was indeed the owner of the land and an ordinary private owner has the right do as he wishes with or on his own property (see *Bradford Corporation v Pickles* (1895), p 60). However a local authority is not an ordinary owner since it must exercise the rights of ownership, not in its own 'private' interests, but in the 'public' interests of the community. What the public/private distinction is doing here is to subject the power of *dominium* to principles that apply to *imperium*, for the authority was in substance exercising public rather than private power. *Fewings* indicates why the result of *Bradford Corporation* would have been different if the parties had been reversed; if the corporation had been digging holes on its land deliberately to harm a private citizen the latter could probably have had the decision to dig holes quashed through a judicial review action in administrative law.

9.1.5 Public and private remedies

Lord Wilberforce indicated in *Davey v Spelthorne* (1984) (see **9.1.3**) that English law tends to fasten onto remedies rather than rights. In actions against public bodies the form of the remedy is of particular importance: if the claimant wants damages a cause of action in tort must be established: see *X (Minors) v Bedfordshire County Council* (1995) (pp 29, 155); *Three Rivers District Council v Governor and Company of The Bank of England (No 3)* (1996) (p 105); and the next case.

Gorringe v Calderdale MBC [2004] 1 WLR 1057, HL

This was an action for damages by a car driver against a local authority in respect of personal injuries suffered in a serious car accident. The claimant's 'case is, first, that the absence of suitable road signage constituted a failure "to maintain" the road in such a condition as to be safe for use; and, secondly, that the council's common law duty of care required it to put into effect safety measures that included the positioning of the road signs in order to discharge its section 39 [of the Road Traffic Act 1988] duty' (Lord Scott). The House of Lords (Lords Steyn, Hoffmann, Scott, Rodger and Brown) dismissed the claim.

Lord Steyn: ... **2** There are ... a few remarks that I would wish to make about negligence and statutory duties and powers. This is a subject of great complexity and very much an evolving area of the law. No single decision is capable of providing a comprehensive analysis. It is a subject on which an intense focus on the particular facts and on the particular statutory background, seen in the context of the contours of our social welfare state, is necessary. On the one hand the courts must not contribute to the creation of a society bent on litigation, which is premised on the illusion that for every misfortune there is a remedy. On the other hand, there are cases where the courts must recognise on principled grounds the compelling demands of corrective justice or what has been called 'the rule of public policy which has first claim on the loyalty of the law: that wrongs should be remedied': *M (A Minor) v Newham London Borough Council* and *X (Minors) v Bedfordshire County Council* [1995] 2 AC 633, 663, per Sir Thomas Bingham MR. Sometimes cases may not obviously fall in one category or the other. Truly difficult cases arise...

Lord Hoffmann: ... **17** The alternative claim is for common law negligence... If the highway authority at common law owed no duty other than to keep the road in repair and even that duty was not actionable in private law, it is impossible to contend that it owes a common law duty to erect warning signs on the road. It is not sufficient that it might reasonably have foreseen that in the absence of such warnings, some road users might injure themselves or others. Reasonable foreseeability of physical injury is the standard criterion for determining the duty of care owed by people who undertake an activity which carries a risk of injury to others. But it is insufficient to justify the imposition of liability upon someone who simply does nothing: who neither creates the risk nor undertakes to do anything to avert it. The law does recognise such duties in special circumstances: see, for example, *Goldman v Hargrave* [1967] 1 AC 645 on the positive duties of adjoining landowners to prevent fire or harmful matter from crossing the boundary. But the imposition of such a liability upon a highway authority through the law of negligence would be inconsistent with the well established rules which have always limited its liability at common law...

38 My Lords, I must make it clear that this appeal is concerned only with an attempt to impose upon a local authority a common law duty to act based solely on the existence of a broad public law duty. We are not concerned with cases in which public authorities

▶

have actually done acts or entered into relationships or undertaken responsibilities which give rise to a common law duty of care. In such cases the fact that the public authority acted pursuant to a statutory power or public duty does not necessarily negative the existence of a duty. A hospital trust provides medical treatment pursuant to the public law duty in the 1977 Act, but the existence of its common law duty is based simply upon its acceptance of a professional relationship with the patient no different from that which would be accepted by a doctor in private practice. The duty rests upon a solid, orthodox common law foundation and the question is not whether it is created by the statute but whether the terms of the statute (for example, in requiring a particular thing to be done or conferring a discretion) are sufficient to exclude it. The law in this respect has been well established since *Geddis v Proprietors of Bann Reservoir* (1878) 3 App Cas 430...

Lord Scott: ... **70** ... The reason why damages in a private action for breach of the statutory duty imposed by section 39 [of the Road Traffic Act 1988] cannot be recovered is because section 39, correctly construed, does not impose a duty owed to any individual. It imposes a duty owed to the public as a whole. It forms part of the corpus of public law, not private law, and can only be enforced by the procedures and remedies available for enforcing public law duties...

Lord Rodger: ... **93** If traffic authorities carry out their duties under section 39, this should help to make the roads safer by informing their decisions as to the repairs and modifications, including the placing of warning signs, that should be carried out. In the exercise of their public law powers and duties, highway authorities do often, or even usually, warn of prospective dangers at junctions or crests in the road, but drivers cannot rely on them always having done so. Drivers must take care for themselves and drive at an appropriate speed, irrespective of whether or not there is a warning sign. By insisting that drivers always look out for dangers themselves and not rely on others, the common law supports the overall policy of promoting road safety. If drivers fail to drive carefully and others are injured, the others can recover compensation from the drivers' insurers or from the Motor Insurers' Bureau. Neither the drivers nor their passengers, nor indeed their insurers, can recover damages from the highway authorities for not having placed a warning sign. If that settled pattern is to be changed, it is for Parliament to make the change and to approve the additional funding needed by the authorities to handle and meet the claims...

Lord Brown: ... **100** I agree with the reasons given in the speech of my noble and learned friend, Lord Hoffmann, for distinguishing that line of authority – essentially because the common law duty of care in those cases was found or suggested to have arisen not by reference to the existence of the respective authorities' statutory powers and duties but rather from the relationships in fact created between those authorities and the children for whom in differing ways they had assumed responsibility. I would add, moreover, this further distinction. Unless in those cases the court were to find the authority's various responsibilities capable of giving rise to a common law duty of care, those wronged children, themselves wholly blameless, would go uncompensated, however inadequately their interests had been safeguarded. In the highway context, by contrast, the claimant (or some other road user involved in the accident) will almost inevitably himself have been at fault. In these circumstances it seems to me entirely reasonable that the policy of the law should be to leave the liability for the accident on the road user who negligently caused it rather than look to the highway authority to protect him against his own wrong...

NOTE

A sort of distinction between public and private law has always existed in common law at the level of remedies (cf Lord Scott above). The old prerogative writs, now amalgamated into the action for judicial review, were for the most part available only against public bodies (although habeas corpus was an exception and was used in family law). Today judicial review lies only against public and quasi-public bodies. Of course the distinction was not watertight because the 'private' law forms of action such as trespass were available against public bodies (see eg *Cooper v Wandsworth Board of Works* (1863)). Today this remains true of the causes of action in tort. However, some of these causes of action, like abuse of public office, are available only against public officials. Note also that liabilty under the Human Rights Act 1998, ss 6–8 applies only to a 'public authority' (see *R (Beer) v Hampshire Farmers' Markets Ltd (2004)*).

9.1.6 Individual and the community

One theme to be found at the heart of French public law is the dichotomy between the individual and the community.

Jacques Moreau, *La responsabilité administrative*
(Presses Universitaires de France, 1986), 108–10
(Translation Geoffrey Samuel)

Indeed, at first sight the choice made by the Conseil d'État to apply the system of liability without fault seems to be explicable by the idea of risk. It is because the administration has created certain exceptional risks, in exposing its officials for service reasons, that in the case of accident the latter are compensated without having to prove fault by the service; it is because of the special risks for third parties caused by 'dangerous things' or 'dangerous methods' that the victims can obtain compensation as soon as they show abnormal and special damage together with a causal link. Interpreting this case law certain writers… have seen in it the ratification of what they call the 'socialisation of risk'.

This idea is not wrong, but it has only a limited explanatory value. For a start, many public works (roads, bridges, canals, walls…) do not in themselves harbour particular dangers, and the basis of liability which might be valuable for a hydro-electric or nuclear power station loses all *raison d'être* in the majority of public works damages cases. Furthermore, the application of strict liability to those who voluntarily or occasionally assist in public service tallies only imperfectly with the idea of danger… Finally, except by distorting the sense of language, the caselaw of *Couitéas*, on the refusal of intervention of the police force and *Sté La Fleurette*, with its recent developments concerning the application of administrative regulations, are difficult to reconcile with any notion of 'social risk' or 'legislative risk', even if certain specialists have constructed elaborate structures here!

In the… cases just cited, the justification of liability without fault is rather that a certain equilibrium has been broken – and must be re-established by the award of damages – between, on the one hand, a behaviour of the administration that is taken to be inspired

▶

by the general interest aim (it is, among other things a part of the definition of the notion of public works) and which 'benefits everyone' and, on the other hand, a 'burden', a relatively serious injury which falls only upon certain persons (adjoining owners, those who assist the administration, public officials exposed to risk, those destined to be affected by certain administrative regulations). The sought-after basis of liability is, then, *the equality of citizens before public burdens*, as the frequent conclusions of the *commissaires de gouvernement* and the judgments of certain cases indicate more and more clearly…

QUESTION

How would the *Conseil d'État* have decided *Read v Lyons* (1947) (pp 14, 48, 185)?

NOTE

In English law this community (equality) principle mentioned by Professor Moreau seems to have been used to arrive at exactly the opposite result.

Dunne v North Western Gas Board [1964] 2 QB 806, CA

This was an action for damages in respect of personal injuries suffered by the claimant as a result of a gas explosion in the street. The claimant based his claim in nuisance and on the strict liability rule in *Rylands v Fletcher* (see p 217). The Court of Appeal (Sellers, Danckwerts and Davies LJJ) dismissed the claim.

Sellers LJ: … Gas, water and also electricity services are well-nigh a necessity of modern life, or at least are generally demanded as a requirement for the common good, and one or more are being taken with considerable despatch to every village and hamlet in the country with either statutory compulsion or sanction. It would seem odd that facilities so much sought after by the community and approved by their legislators should be actionable at common law because they have been brought to places where they are required and have escaped without negligence by an unforeseen sequence of mishaps. A sequence of events may be just as unforeseeable and unavoidable and as extraneous to an individual or a supplier of services as an act of God is recognised to be…

QUESTIONS

1. How might this case have been decided under French law?

2. Does the judge in *Dennis v MOD* (p 181) start out from a different premise or does he simply draw a different conclusion?

9.2 Central government

Continental European systems often view the state as a corporate legal person but this is not the case in English common law. There is no developed legal notion of the State as a juridical entity capable of suing and being sued. Central government consists, instead, of various government departments and agencies and when things go wrong, resulting in injury, damage or loss to another, the department may well have to answer either for the act of its employee (vicarious liability) or breach of a non-delegable duty: see *Home Office v Dorset Yacht Co* (1970) (p 226). However, negligence is not, of course, the only tort of relevance to central government liability.

Akenzua v Home Secretary [2003] 1 WLR 741, CA

The estate of a victim of a murder brought an action for damages for abuse of public office against the Home Department and the Commissioner of Police in respect of the act of one of their officials who had deliberately set free from custody a man known to be a murderer. While free the man murdered the victim. The defendants sought to have the action struck out and were successful at first instance; but an appeal against the striking out by the claimant was allowed by the Court of Appeal (Simon Brown, Sedley and Scott Baker LJJ).

Sedley LJ: ... **9** The tort of misfeasance in public office originates, at least so far as the law reports take us, in electoral corruption cases beginning in the late 17th century. The right to vote was then a property right, and subsequent cases have likewise typically concerned deprivation of property. There is no reported case where the consequence of the misfeasance has been personal injury or death. But while this may, as Mr Freeland for the Commissioner suggests, be indicative of the historical nature of the tort it cannot be definitive of it. Moreover, no reported decision deals frontally with the question of law which we have to decide. The nature of the tort, however, is now authoritatively described in the decision of the House of Lords in the *Three Rivers* case and it is from this source that the answer to the present appeal has to be derived...

16 Before turning to the arguments, let me put two paradigm cases which were put by the court in argument in varying forms to counsel.

(A) A public official corruptly arranges the liberation of a man serving a sentence for attempting to murder his wife, knowing that he will make a further attempt to kill her if allowed to do so. On his release the man finds his wife and kills her.

(B) A public official corruptly arranges the liberation of a man serving a sentence of imprisonment for terrorist bombings, knowing that he will resume his activities if allowed to do so. On his release the man places a bomb in a public place and kills several people.

17 All parties accept that no principle of law excludes the action for misfeasance in public office purely because the consequence is personal injury or death rather than loss of or damage to property. Any other doctrine would give life to the old reproach that the law of England and Wales was more concerned with property than with people. The question is then whether the decision of their Lordships' House in the *Three Rivers* case excludes the action where the predictable victim is neither an identifiable individual nor an identifiable group of individuals.

18 Neither defendant's counsel has been able to explain either the logic or justice of making case A actionable and case B not; yet both counsel submit, in the light of the *Three Rivers* decision, that it is so. Mr Blake, for the claimants, submits that if, as is conceded, case A is actionable as misfeasance in public office at the suit of the victim, so must case B be; and in my judgment he is right. The purpose of the 'class' category of liability is to enlarge case A, not to exclude case B...

21 It follows that the averment that the deceased was a member of a class – any class – is an immaterial averment. Denton killed a single person in the period of his arranged liberty. If he had predictably murdered or maimed more than one person they would form a class for present purposes. What matters is not the predictability of his killing the deceased but the predictability of his killing someone. That is my understanding of the effect of the reasoning in the *Three Rivers* case. It is also case B of my examples. Put another way, but again using the *Three Rivers* taxonomy, Denton's single known victim stands in the same situation as each of those claimants who at the time of the alleged misfeasance in the *Three Rivers* case were only potential depositors; that is to say, she too was a potential victim. The alternative analysis, that the material class was all Denton's potential victims, among whom it is sufficient to be able now to identify the deceased, is feasible but seems to me artificial to the point of torture. On none of these views is the claimants' pleading demurrable...

QUESTION

Could the Home Department also be liable in the tort of negligence?

NOTES

1. The *Three Rivers* case (1996) can be found on pp 83, 105.

2. The highway authorities have attracted litigation in respect of the mainte-nance of public roads: see *Sandhar v Department of Transport* (2005) and *Gorringe v Calderdale* (2004) (p 299).

9.3 Local authorities

As Tony Weir points out in an extract at **9.1.3**, local authorities find themselves as regular targets of tort claims (see eg *Gorringe v Calderdale* (2004), above p 299). The most important of these claims may appear to be those founded on the tort of negligence, but local authorities can equally find themselves facing actions in nuisance and even trespass.

9.3.1 Negligence

Leaving aside the ordinary type of accident claim (where for example a local authority employee drops a hammer on the head of a passer-by), the difficult negligence cases often give rise to two broad types of duty problems. The first is technical; many of the factual situations can display problems of pure economic loss (*Murphy v Brentwood DC* (1991)) and/or mere omissions (*Stovin v Wise* (1996), pp 136, 152, 296). The second type of duty problem is perhaps rooted in the public/private division: the courts have held that there are policy reasons for refusing to hold that the authority owes a duty of care (*X (Minors) v Bedfordshire CC* (1995)). Of course, in the majority of the cases the technical and the policy become intermixed. The duty of care aspect tends to endow these local authority cases with another characteristic: many are striking out claims in which the authority seeks to put an end to the legal claim at a preliminary stage. This procedure has of itself created problems and as a result the House of Lords seems to have changed direction, as the next case illustrates.

Barrett v Enfield LBC [2001] 2 AC 550, HL

This was an action for damages in negligence against a local authority brought by a person who had been in the local authority's care for most of his pre-adult life. He claimed that the local authority had been in breach of its duty to exercise the standard of care of a reasonable parent; and as a result of this breach of duty he suffered physical and psychological injury. The local authority sought to have the action struck out for disclosing no reasonable cause of action. The House of Lords (Lords Browne-Wilkinson, Slynn, Nolan, Steyn and Hutton), reversing the Court of Appeal, refused to strike out the claim.

Lord Slynn: ... It is obvious from previous cases and indeed is self-evident that there is a real conflict between on the one hand the need to allow social welfare services exercising statutory powers to do their work in what they as experts consider is the best way in the interests first of the child, but also of the parents and of society, without an unduly inhibiting fear of litigation if something goes wrong, and on the other hand the desirability of providing a remedy in appropriate cases for harm done to a child through the acts or failure to act of such services.

[The] distinction which is sometimes drawn between decisions as to 'policy' and as to 'operational acts' sounds more promising. A pure policy decision where Parliament has entrusted the decision to a public authority is not something which a court would normally be expected to review in a claim in negligence. But again this is not an absolute test. Policy and operational acts are closely linked and the decision to do an operational act may easily involve and flow from a policy decision. Conversely, the policy is affected by the result of the operational act: see *Reg v Chief Constable of Sussex, Ex parte International Traders' Ferry Ltd* [1998] 3 WLR 1260).

Where a statutory power is given to a local authority and damage is caused by what it does pursuant to that power, the ultimate question is whether the particular issue is justiciable or whether the court should accept that it has no role to play. The two tests (discretion and policy/operational) to which I have referred are guides in deciding that question. The greater the element of policy involved, the wider the area of discretion accorded, the more likely it is that the matter is not justiciable so that no action in negligence can be brought... Moreover, I share Lord Browne-Wilkinson's reluctance to introduce the concepts of administrative law into the law of negligence, as Lord Diplock appears to have done [in *Dorset Yacht*]. But in any case I do not read what either Lord Reid or Lord Wilberforce in the *Anns* case (and in particular Lord Reid) said as to the need to show that there has been an abuse of power before a claim can be brought in negligence in the exercise of a statutory discretion as meaning that an action can never be brought in negligence where an act has been done pursuant to the exercise of the discretion. A claim of negligence in the taking of a decision to exercise a statutory discretion is likely to be barred, unless it is wholly unreasonable so as not to be a real exercise of the discretion, or if it involves the making of a policy decision involving the balancing of different public interests; acts done pursuant to the lawful exercise of the

▶

discretion can, however, in my view be subject to a duty of care, even if some element of discretion is involved. Thus accepting that a decision to take a child into care pursuant to a statutory power is not justiciable, it does not in my view follow that, having taken a child into care, an authority cannot be liable for what it or its employees do in relation to the child without it being shown that they have acted in excess of power. It may amount to an excess of power, but that is not in my opinion the test to be adopted: the test is whether the conditions in the *Caparo* case have been satisfied...

...I consider also that the question whether it is just and reasonable to impose a liability of negligence is not to be decided in the abstract for all acts or omissions of a statutory authority, but is to be decided on the basis of what is proved. The comment of Andenas and Fairgrieve that one of the problems about the uncertainty of the law in this area is that many cases are decided on an application to strike out or on a preliminary issue on assumed facts as stated in the Statement of Claim – 'Dealing with such hypothetical facts deprives the courts of the opportunity to apply the operational-policy distinction to concrete facts. It is likely to exacerbate the formulation of clear statements of principle.' – is to be borne in mind. See, also the discussion of the facts in *Phelps v Hillingdon London Borough Council* [1997] 1 WLR 500 where the importance of investigating the precise nature of the service provided was made clear...

Accordingly, I consider that this claim should not be struck out. This does not mean that I think that the appellant must or will win. He faces considerable difficulties, but with great respect to the experience and judgment of the members of the Court of Appeal, I consider that he is entitled to have these matters investigated and not to have them summarily dismissed. I would accordingly allow the appeal.

NOTE

Subsequent to this decision the European Court of Human Rights delivered its judgment on the *X (Minors)* case.

Z v United Kingdom [2001] 2 FLR 612, ECtHR

THE COURT: ... **44** The applicants appealed to the House of Lords. On 29 June 1995, the House of Lords rejected their appeal, finding that no action lay against the local authority in negligence or breach of statutory duty concerning the discharge of their duties relating to the welfare of children under the Children Act 1989 in respect of child care. The case is reported as *X and Others v. Bedfordshire County Council* [1995] 3 AER 353....

60 The decision in *X and Others v. Bedfordshire County Council* ([1995] 3 AER 353) is the leading authority in the United Kingdom in this area. It held that local authorities could not be sued for negligence or for breach of statutory duty in respect of the discharge of their functions concerning the welfare of children...

61 Since the *X and Others* case, there have been two further significant judgments regarding the extent of liability of local authorities in child care matters...

95 The Court observes, firstly, that the applicants were not prevented in any practical manner from bringing their claims before the domestic courts. Indeed, the case was litigated with vigour up to the House of Lords...

96 Moreover, the Court is not persuaded that the House of Lords' decision that as a matter of law there was no duty of care in the applicants' case may be characterised as either an exclusionary rule or an immunity which deprived them of access to court...

99 Furthermore, it cannot be said that the House of Lords came to its conclusion without a careful balancing of the policy reasons for and against the imposition of liability on the local authority in the circumstances of the applicants' case...

101 The applicants may not therefore claim that they were deprived of any right to a determination on the merits of their negligence claims. Their claims were properly and fairly examined in light of the applicable domestic legal principles concerning the tort of negligence. Once the House of Lords had ruled on the arguable legal issues that brought into play the applicability of Article 6 § 1 of the Convention (...), the applicants could no longer claim any entitlement under Article 6 § 1 to obtain any hearing concerning the facts. As pointed out above, such a hearing would have served no purpose, unless a duty of care in negligence had been held to exist in their case. It is not for this Court to find that this should have been the outcome of the striking out proceedings since this would effectively involve substituting its own views as to the proper interpretation and content of domestic law.

102 It is nonetheless the case that the interpretation of domestic law by the House of Lords resulted in the applicants' case being struck out. The tort of negligence was held not to impose a duty of care on the local authority in the exercise of its statutory powers. Their experiences were described as 'horrific' by a psychiatrist (...) and the Court has found that they were victims of a violation of Article 3 (...). Yet the outcome of the domestic proceedings they brought is that they, and any children with complaints such as theirs, cannot sue the local authority in negligence for compensation, however foreseeable – and severe – the harm suffered and however unreasonable the conduct of the local authority in failing to take steps to prevent that harm. The applicants are correct in their assertions that the gap they have identified in domestic law is one that gives rise to an issue under the Convention, but in the Court's view it is an issue under Article 13, not Article 6 § 1...

111 The Court finds that in this case the applicants did not have available to them an appropriate means of obtaining a determination of their allegations that the local authority failed to protect them from inhuman and degrading treatment and the possibility of obtaining an enforceable award of compensation for the damage suffered thereby. Consequently, they were not afforded an effective remedy in respect of the breach of Article 3 and there has, accordingly, been a violation of Article 13 of the Convention.

For these reasons, The Court

1. *Holds* unanimously that there has been a violation of Article 3 of the Convention.

2. *Holds* unanimously that no separate issue arises under Article 8 of the Convention.

3. *Holds* by twelve votes to five that there has been no violation of Article 6 of the Convention.

4. *Holds* by fifteen votes to two that there has been a violation of Article 13 of the Convention...

QUESTION

The court held that there had been no violation of art 6 but there was a violation of art 13 (as well as art 3). The difference of article is crucial as far as English law is concerned. Why? (Cf Human Rights Act 1998, s 1.)

NOTE

The question of striking out actions of negligence against local authorities has again come before the House of Lords.

Phelps v Hillingdon LBC [2001] 2 AC 619, HL

(See also p 228)

Lord Clyde: ... The present group of four appeals raises questions as to the liability of those engaged in the education of young persons for negligent acts and omissions which have caused loss, injury or damage to their students. In only one of them has the matter been taken to trial. That is the case of *Phelps*. There the claimant sought damages for the negligence of an educational psychologist who had examined her and had failed to diagnose her dyslexia... The basic point of principle which is common to all these cases is whether there is a duty of care owed by the employees of a local education authority to the students of whatever age they may be in the meeting of their educational needs...

There is no question that a teacher owes a duty of care for the physical safety of a child attending school under the charge of that teacher. The teacher has a duty to take reasonable care that the child does not come to harm through any danger which may arise during the course of the child's attendance at the school. But the present case is different in certain respects from that situation... The loss claimed may be purely of an economic character. But the mental or psychological effects of negligent advice may in themselves be able to constitute a proper head of damages, such as a post-traumatic stress disorder or a psychological illness. Dyslexia is a condition which may in itself become worse through the absence of an appropriate educational regime, and the frustration of an inappropriate regime may cause psychological stress and injury. The consequences of negligent advice regarding the future treatment of a child with some special educational need may take a variety of forms and may be extensive...

The test for the existence of a duty of care which looks to what the court considers is fair, just and reasonable is of a different order from the test of proximity or neighbourhood with its further ingredient of foreseeability. The test of fairness is a test which may principally involve considerations of policy... Thus in *Osman v UK* [1999] 1 FLR 193, (para. 151) the European Court of Human Rights required account to be taken of such matters as the gravity of the negligence in question, the assumption of responsibility by the police for the safety of the eventual victim, and the seriousness of the harm sustained. Even where sound policy reasons can be put forward for excluding a claim it is not thereby necessarily to be excluded.

In the present case I am not persuaded that there are sufficient grounds to exclude these claims even on grounds of public policy alone. It does not seem to me that there is any wider interest of the law which would require that no remedy in damages be available. I am not persuaded that the recognition of a liability upon employees of the education authority for damages for negligence in education would lead to a flood of claims, or even vexatious claims, which would overwhelm the school authorities, nor that it would add burdens and distractions to the already intensive life of teachers. Nor should it inspire some peculiarly defensive attitude in the performance of their professional responsibilities. On the contrary it may have the healthy effect of securing that high standards are sought and secured. If it is thought that there would only be a few claims and for that reason the duty should not be recognised, the answer must be that if there are only a few claims there is the less reason to refuse to allow them to be entertained. As regards the need for this remedy, even if there are alternative procedures by which some form of redress might be obtained, such as resort to judicial review, or to an ombudsman, or the adoption of such statutory procedures as are open to parents, which might achieve some correction of the situation for the future, it may only be through a claim for damages at common law that compensation for the damage done to the child may be secured for the past as well as the future...

The present claims all arise in the public sector where there is a very obvious statutory context. The education authorities are creatures of statute and operate to a considerable extent under the provisions of the Education Acts. The question arises whether the common law duty can or cannot stand in the face of the statutory context. But while no common law can stand in contradiction of some statutory provision, and it may be hard to impose a duty of care in the exercise of a statutory power (*Stovin v Wise* [1996] AC 923, 954) the existence of a statutory background against which the professionals are exercising their particular skills should not inhibit the existence of a common law duty of care...

A distinction may be suggested between on the one hand matters of policy or discretion and on the other hand matters of an operational or administrative character. But this kind of classification does not appear to provide any absolute test for determining whether the case is one which allows or excludes a duty of care. The classification may provide some guide towards identifying some kinds of case where a duty of care may be thought to be inappropriate... But it was recognised by Lord Browne-Wilkinson in *X (Minors) v Bedfordshire County Council* [1995] 2 AC 633, 738 that even in matters of a discretionary character the authority may be liable in damages if its decision falls without the ambit of the discretion, as where the action taken is so totally unreasonable as to amount to an abuse of the discretion...

[Lords Steyn, Jauncey, Lloyd, Nicholls, Hutton and Millett were also of the view that a duty of care might be owed.]

QUESTION

Could any of the reasons used by Lord Clyde for imposing a duty be used, equally, for not imposing a duty?

NOTE

1. See also *Stovin v Wise* (1996) (pp 136, 152, 296).

2. The position of local authorities in these child abuse cases has now been summed up by the House of Lords.

D v East Berkshire NHS Trust [2005] 2 AC 373

(For facts and other extracts see p 149)

Lord Bingham (dissenting): ... **3** The courts below have concluded that in such a situation no duty of care can be owed by the doctor or the social worker to the parent, that accordingly no claim may lie and that these claims brought by the parents must be dismissed with no evidence called and no detailed examination of the facts. In the second appeal there is also a claim by the child, but that has been treated differently. I understand that a majority of my noble and learned friends agree with this conclusion, for which there is considerable authority in the United Kingdom and abroad. But the law in this area has evolved very markedly over the last decade. What appeared to be hard-edged rules precluding the possibility of any claim by parent or child have been eroded or restricted. And a series of decisions of the European Court of Human Rights has shown that application of an exclusionary rule in this sensitive area may lead to serious breaches of Convention rights for which domestic law affords no remedy and for which, at any rate arguably, the law of tort should afford a remedy if facts of sufficient gravity are shown.

4 I would not, for my part, strike out these claims but would allow them to go to trial. A judgment can then be made on the liability of the respective defendants on facts which have been fully explored. At present, we have only an agreed statement of what is, at this stage and for the purpose of legal argument, to be assumed. I take no account of additional factual allegations made by the appellants in their written case which, if true, may well be significant, but which have not been agreed. The facts which have been agreed are important and must be summarised...

22 In *X v Bedfordshire County Council* itself, five child plaintiffs complained that they had been the victims of maltreatment and neglect which had been brought to the notice of the defendant council but on which, for a long time, the council had failed to act. The facts, only assumed when the strike-out application was heard in this country but established or accepted when the claimants took their complaint to Strasbourg, were very strong. An experienced and highly respected child psychiatrist described the children's experiences as 'to put it bluntly, "horrific" ' and added that it was the worst case of neglect and emotional abuse that she had seen in her professional career: *Z v United Kingdom* (2001) 34 EHRR 97, para 40. It was accepted in Strasbourg that the neglect and abuse suffered by the four child applicants reached the threshold of inhuman and degrading treatment (para 74) and a violation of article 3 of the European Convention was found, arising from the failure of the system to protect the child applicants from serious, long-term neglect and abuse (paras 74-75). The court awarded compensation amounting to £320,000, a substantial figure by Strasbourg standards. Yet the local authority's failure to intervene, which had permitted the abuse and neglect to continue, was held by the Court of Appeal and the House of Lords to afford the children no tortious remedy in negligence against the local authority in English law.

23 The facts of *M v Newham London Borough Council* [1995] 2 AC 633 were less stark than in *X v Bedfordshire County Council*, but they were disturbing enough. There was reason to believe that M, aged about four, had been sexually abused. In the course of interview by healthcare professionals the child was thought to identify her mother's current partner as the abuser. In fact, it seems, the child identified a cousin who had earlier lived in the house and who had the same first name. The child was removed from the mother's care for a period of almost a year, during which time the mother was refused sight of the video and transcript made of the child's earlier interview. It was only when the video and transcript were seen by the mother's solicitors that it became clear that the healthcare professional had mistaken the identity of the alleged abuser. Both the mother and the child claimed damages for negligence against the employers of the healthcare professionals involved, but in the domestic proceedings the mother's claim was unanimously dismissed by the Court of Appeal and the House of Lords and the child's claim by a majority of the Court of Appeal and a unanimous House. At Strasbourg, both succeeded in establishing a violation of article 8, a finding based not on the decision to remove the child from the mother's care but on a failure to disclose to the mother immediately thereafter the matters relied on as showing that the child could not be returned safely to her care: if this had been done, it would have avoided the period of separation which followed and was said to have caused psychiatric disorder to both mother and child: *TP and KM v United Kingdom* (2001) 34 EHRR 42, paras 30, 80–83, 115–117. This was, again, a violation for which the English law of tort afforded no remedy…

25 But mention should first be made of the European court decision in *Osman v United Kingdom* (1998) 29 EHRR 245. That case concerned the liability in negligence of the police towards a person claiming to have suffered as the result of a failure to apprehend a suspected criminal. To that extent its factual subject matter resembled that of *Hill v Chief Constable of West Yorkshire* [1989] AC 53, a decision which the domestic court had applied. The court found a violation of article 6 of the Convention because, as it held in para 151 of its judgment, the domestic court's application of the law had served to confer a blanket immunity on the police for their acts and omissions during the investigation and suppression of crime and therefore unjustifiably restricted a claimant's right to have his claim determined on the merits. See also the concurring judgment of Sir John Freeland, at pp 321–322. This decision was the subject of compelling criticism by Lord Browne-Wilkinson in *Barrett v Enfield London Borough Council* [2001] 2 AC 550, 558–560. In that case, the claimant, who had spent his childhood in foster care, claimed damages against a local authority for decisions made and not made during that period. The judge's decision to strike out the claim had been upheld by the Court of Appeal but was unanimously reversed by the House. There are four points worthy of note for present purposes. First, it was accepted that a claim may lie against a local authority arising from childcare decisions in certain circumstances: see pp 557, 573, 575, 587–590. Secondly, the general undesirability of striking out claims arising in uncertain and developing areas of the law without full exploration of the facts was emphasised: pp 557–558, 575. This was a point made in the *Bedfordshire* case, at pp 740–741, and is a point strongly echoed in later cases such as *Waters v Comr of Police of the Metropolis* [2000] 1 WLR 1607, 1613; *W v Essex County Council* [2001] 2 AC 592, 598; *Phelps v Hillingdon London Borough Council* [2001] 2 AC 619, 659–660; and *L (A Child) v Reading Borough Council* [2001] 1 WLR 1575, 1587. Thirdly, the notion of an exclusionary rule conferring immunity on particular classes of defendant was rejected: pp 559, 570, 575. This rejection has been echoed with approval in later cases such as *Kent v Griffiths* [2001] 1 QB 36, para 38; *S v Gloucestershire County Council* [2001] Fam 313, 338; and *E v United Kingdom* (2002) 36 EHRR 519. Fourthly, it was

▶

not considered that the policy factors which had weighed with the House in *X v Bedfordshire County Council* and *M v Newham London Borough Council* had the same weight where complaints related to acts and omissions after a child had been taken into care: [2001] 2 AC 550, 568, 575. The argument that imposition of a duty might lead to defensiveness and excessive caution was discounted, the remedies available to the claimant were not thought to be as efficacious as recognition of a common law duty of care and it was not accepted that imposition of a duty made no contribution to the maintenance of high standards: pp 568, 575. There was nothing to displace the general rule, recognised in the *Bedfordshire* and *Newham* case, at pp 663 and 749, that the public policy consideration which had first claim on the loyalty of the law was that wrongs should be remedied: p 588...

30 In the light of all this authority, coupled with *Z v United Kingdom* 34 EHRR 97 and *TP and KM v United Kingdom* 34 EHRR 42 it could not now be plausibly argued that a common law duty of care may not be owed by a publicly-employed healthcare professional to a child with whom the professional is dealing...

Lord Nicholls: ...**70** There are two cardinal features in these cases. One feature is that a parent was suspected of having deliberately harmed his or her own child or having fabricated the child's medical condition. The other feature, which is to be assumed, is that the ensuing investigation by the doctors was conducted negligently. In consequence, the suspected parent's family life was disrupted, to greater or lesser extent, and the suspected parent suffered psychiatric injury.

71 It is the combination of these features which creates the difficult problem now before the House. In the ordinary course the interests of parent and child are congruent. This is not so where a parent wilfully harms his child. Then the parent is knowingly acting directly contrary to his parental responsibilities and to the best interests of his child. So the liability of doctors and social workers in these cases calls into consideration two countervailing interests, each of high social importance: the need to safeguard children from abuse by their own parents, and the need to protect parents from unnecessary interference with their family life.

72 The first of these interests involves protection of children as the victims of crime. Child abuse is criminal conduct of a particularly reprehensible character: children are highly vulnerable members of society. Child abuse is also a form of criminal conduct peculiarly hard to combat, because its existence is difficult to discover. Babies and young children are unable to complain, older children too frightened. If the source of the abuse is a parent, the child is at risk from his primary and natural protector within the privacy of his home. This both increases the risk of abuse and means that investigation necessitates intrusion into highly sensitive areas of family life, with the added complication that the parent who is responsible for the abuse will give a false account of the child's history.

73 The other, countervailing interest is the deep interest of the parent in his or her family life. Society sets much store by family life. Family life is to be guarded jealously. This is reflected in article 8 of the European Convention on Human Rights. Interference with family life requires cogent justification, for the sake of children and parents alike. So public authorities should, so far as possible, cooperate with the parents when making decisions about their children. Public authorities should disclose matters relied upon by them as justifying interference with family life. Parents should be involved in the decision-making process to whatever extent is appropriate to protect their interests adequately.

74 The question raised by these appeals is how these countervailing interests are best balanced when a parent is wrongly suspected of having abused his child. Public confidence in the child protection system can only be maintained if a proper balance is struck, avoiding unnecessary intrusion in families while protecting children at risk of significant harm: see the Preface to 'Working Together' (1991). Clearly, health professionals must act in good faith. They must not act recklessly, that is, without caring whether an allegation of abuse is well founded or not. Acting recklessly is not acting in good faith. But are health professionals liable to the suspected parents if they fall short of the standards of skill and care expected of any reasonable professional in the circumstances? Are they exposed to claims by the parents for professional negligence? Put differently and more widely, what is the appropriate level of protection for a person erroneously suspected of child abuse? Should he be protected against professional negligence by those charged with protecting the child? Or only against lack of good faith?...

77 Stated in this broad form, this is a surprising proposition. In this area of the law, concerned with the reporting and investigation of suspected crime, the balancing point between the public interest and the interest of a suspected individual has long been the presence or absence of good faith. Good faith is required but not more. A report, made to the appropriate authorities, that a person has or may have committed a crime attracts qualified privilege. A false statement ('malicious falsehood') attracts a remedy if made maliciously. Misfeasance in public office calls for an element of bad faith or recklessness. Malice is an essential ingredient of causes of action for the misuse of criminal or civil proceedings. In *Calveley v Chief Constable of the Merseyside Police* [1989] AC 1228, 1238, Lord Bridge of Harwich observed that 'where no action for malicious prosecution would lie, it would be strange indeed if an acquitted defendant could recover damages for negligent investigation'. This must be equally true of a person who has been suspected but not prosecuted.

78 This background accords ill with the submission that those responsible for the protection of a child against criminal conduct owe suspected perpetrators the duty suggested. The existence of such a duty would fundamentally alter the balance in this area of the law. It would mean that if a parent suspected that a babysitter or a teacher at a nursery or school might have been responsible for abusing her child, and the parent took the child to a general practitioner or consultant, the doctor would owe a duty of care to the suspect. The law of negligence has of course developed much in recent years, reflecting the higher standards increasingly expected in many areas of life. But there seems no warrant for such a fundamental shift in the long established balance in this area of the law...

NOTES AND QUESTIONS

1. Lord Bingham's dissenting speech is extracted here because he gives a concise history of the duty of care litigation, in the domestic courts and in the human rights court, involving public bodies.

2. Lord Nicholl's speech is extracted at some length because of its conceptual importance. He bases his reasoning on the conflict of two interests, those of the children with those of the parents. But are these the only interests to be considered? Is there not a separate family interest which has been invaded by the state? In § 78 Lord Nicholls clearly thinks that no duty should be owed by the doctor to the suspect; but why should such a duty not be owed given the devastating effect that a child-abuse allegation can have on such a person? Why should there not be some regime of administrative responsibility? Why must it always be the individual that has to pay the cost of administrative incompetence? Is this really in the 'public interest'?

3. Lord Nicholls distinguishes between negligence and good faith. Are the two notions always so different? Could it not be said that the negligence of the officials in *Elguzouli-Daf v Commissioner of Police* (1995) (see p 315) amounted to bad faith given that they should have known that any carelessness on their part would result in imprisonment? Do you think that *Elguzouli-Daf* is still good law? (Cf *Brooks v Comr of Police for the Metropolis* (2005).)

9.3.2 Nuisance

Local authorities are important landowners and thus they can find themselves facing claims arising out of the use and occupation of land. These claims can of course be in common law negligence or founded upon the Occupiers' Liability Act 1957 or 1984 (see in particular *Tomlinson v Congleton BC*, p 197). But nuisance (public and private) can be an important cause of action.

Lippiatt v South Gloucestershire Council [2000] 1 QB 51, CA

This was an action for an injunction and damages brought by farmers against a local authority for damage done by travellers who had occupied land belonging to the council. The judge struck out the claim, but an appeal was allowed by the Court of Appeal (Evans and Mummery LJJ and Sir Christopher Staughton).

Mummery LJ: ... It is reasonably arguable that the continuing presence of the travellers on the council's land constituted a nuisance to the plaintiffs' use and enjoyment of their rights in their land, even though the travellers' activities involved using the council's land as a launching pad for repeated acts of trespass on the plaintiffs' land.

It is not, contrary to the submission of Mr Spens for the council, a case of the plaintiffs seeking to make the council vicariously liable for individual acts of trespass committed by uncontrolled third parties (ie the travellers) on the plaintiffs' land. It is rather a complaint of a continuing and potentially injurious state of affairs on the council's land, ie the presence of the travellers who, as the council were made aware, repeatedly behaved in the way complained of by the plaintiffs. The council let that state of affairs continue to exist on its land notwithstanding the complaints of the plaintiffs; and that state of affairs was capable of constituting a nuisance for which the council was liable, even if individual acts of the travellers of which the plaintiffs complained occurred on the plaintiffs' land...

NOTES

1. In *Hussain v Lancaster CC* (1999) the resident owner of a shop on a housing estate brought an action for damages in negligence and nuisance against a local authority. The owner claimed that the authority had failed to prevent him from being seriously harassed by other tenants on the estate. The Court of Appeal held that the master was right to strike out the action and a petition to appeal to the House of Lords was subsequently refused. Might Mr Hussain be more successful today given the coming into force of the Human Rights Act 1998?

2. In *Gorringe v Calderdale MBC* (p 299) Lord Scott said: 'a highway authority may be liable at common law for damage attributable to dangers that it has introduced, or, in the case of dangers introduced by some third party, that it has unreasonably failed to abate. Members of the public who drive cars on the highways of this country are entitled to expect that the highways will be kept properly in repair. They are entitled to complain if damage is caused by some obstruction or condition of the road or its surroundings that constitutes a public nuisance. And they are, of course, entitled to complain if they suffer damage by the negligence of some other user of the highway. But an overriding imperative is that those who drive on public highways do so in a manner and at a speed that is safe having regard to such matters as the nature of the road, the weather conditions and the traffic conditions. Drivers are first and foremost themselves responsible for their own safety' (§ 76).

9.4 Police and prosecution service

Like local authorities, the police find themselves in a position where they can attract claims in tort. Here the torts tend to fall into two distinct categories. There is what might be called the constitutional torts, that is to say claims arising out of the invasion of constitutional rights (see **2.4.1** and **3.6.1**). And there are those arising out of negligence. However, the two cases extracted below might be said to fall within both categories.

Elguzouli-Daf v Commissioner of Police of the Metropolis [1995] QB 335, CA

This was a claim for damages brought against the Crown Prosecution Service (CPS) by two men who had been arrested for two quite different serious crimes. The CPS discontinued proceedings against them, but not before the two men had been held in prison for 22 and 85 days respectively. The men claimed that had the CPS not been negligent in respect of investigating the evidence against them, they would not have been detained for such long periods. The Court of Appeal (Steyn, Rose and Morritt LJJ) confirmed the trial judge's decision to strike out the claims.

Steyn LJ: ... That brings me to the policy factors which, in my view, argue against the recognition of a duty of care owed by the CPS to those it prosecutes. While it is always tempting to yield to an argument based on the protection of civil liberties, I have come to the conclusion that the interests of the whole community are better served by not imposing a duty of care on the CPS. In my view, such a duty of care would tend to have an inhibiting effect on the discharge by the CPS of its central function of prosecuting crime. It would in some cases lead to a defensive approach by prosecutors to their mul-

▶

tifarious duties. It would introduce a risk that prosecutors would act so as to protect themselves from claims of negligence. The CPS would have to spend valuable time and use scarce resources in order to prevent law suits in negligence against the CPS. It would generate a great deal of paper to guard against the risks of law suits. The time and energy of CPS lawyers would be diverted from concentrating on their prime function of prosecuting offenders. That would be likely to happen not only during the prosecution process but also when the CPS is sued in negligence by aggrieved defendants. The CPS would be constantly enmeshed in an avalanche of interlocutory civil proceedings and civil trials. That is a spectre that would bode ill for the efficiency of the CPS and the quality of our criminal justice system…

NOTE

This kind of reasoning has been applied to the police as well as to the CPS (see *Hill v Chief Constable of West Yorkshire* (1988), p 36; *Brooks v Comr of Police of the Metropolis* (2005)). But there may be occasions where the proximity is close enough to give rise to a duty.

Swinney v Chief Constable of Northumbria [1997] QB 464, CA

This was an action for damages for personal injury and loss brought against the police by two claimants who had been severely threatened and intimidated by an alleged criminal. The claimants had given confidential information about the alleged criminal to the police, but their names and address had, so they alleged, been carelessly left in a police car which had then been broken into, allowing their names and address to end up in the hands of the alleged criminal. The police applied to have the action struck out but were unsuccessful in the Court of Appeal (Hirst, Peter Gibson and Ward LJJ).

Ward LJ: … The greater public good rightly outweighs any individual hardship. On the other hand, it is incontrovertible that the fight against crime is daily dependent upon information fed to the police by members of the public, often at real risk of villainous retribution from the criminals and their associates. The public interest will not accept that good citizens should be expected to entrust information to the police, without also expecting that they are entrusting their safety to the police. The public interest would be affronted were it to be the law that members of the public should be expected, in the execution of public service, to undertake the risk of harm to themselves without the police, in return, being expected to take no more than reasonable care to ensure that the confidential information imparted to them is protected. The welfare of the community at large demands the encouragement of the free flow of information without inhibition. Accordingly, it is arguable that there is a duty of care, and that no consideration of public policy precludes the prosecution of the plaintiffs' claim, which will be judged on its merits later…

Hirst LJ: … I wish to end this judgment by stressing a point with which I began, namely that I am upholding no more than the arguability of the plaintiffs' case on these two grounds. It by no means follows that they will succeed on either of them at the trial. Nor, for that matter, does it follow that the plaintiffs will establish, when all the evidence is considered, the necessary substratum of fact as pleaded in the statement of claim on which their whole case depends…

NOTES

1. Hirst LJ's reservation proved a valuable warning: the claimants ultimately lost their case at the trial. For another case where the police were held liable for the breach of a specific duty of care see *Reeves v Commissioner of Police for the Metropolis* (p 340).

2. See also *Vellino v Chief Constable of Greater Manchester Police* (2002).

3. When the police or prison authorities act maliciously they may find themselves having to answer a claim in trespass, malicious prosecution, abuse of the legal process or abuse of public office. Nevertheless it would appear that merely being offensive is not necessarily enough to give rise to a tort: *Wainwright v Home Office* (pp 28, 64, 81, 109). Also the private interest needs to be weighed against the public interest as the next extract clearly suggests.

Gibbs v Rea [1998] AC 786, PC

(For facts and further extracts see p 110)

Lord Goff and Lord Hope (dissenting): ... In our opinion the greatest care must always be taken to strike the right balance between the public interest in the investigation of crime and the rights of the individual who is seeking to pursue a private law remedy. On the one hand there are the evils of drug trafficking. The offences which lie within this field vary greatly in their character and gravity throughout the complex and clandestine network which links the consumer to the source of the supply. The gathering of evidence against those who are involved in it is often difficult, and it may also be dangerous both for the informant and for the investigator. The court has a responsibility to ensure that the rights of the individual are respected at all times, but it must be careful also not to hamper the police in their legitimate endeavours to seek out and to identify the criminal. The risk that if things go wrong the police will be exposed to a claim of damages for having acted maliciously is just one of the many hazards which they must face. But we should not like to see too easy a resort to this remedy...

NOTE

These comments come from a dissenting opinion, but they still represent a policy view that underpins the law of tort when it is dealing with constitutional interests as the next case implicitly indicates.

Keegan v Chief Constable of Merseyside [2003] 1 WLR 2187, CA

This was an action for damages by the occupants of a house against the police in respect of a search of the house carried out by the police in the early hours of the morning. The police had obtained a search warrant to search this particular council house on the basis of information given by a suspect who had once lived there. The police did not check with the utility companies or with the local authority as to whether the house was still occupied by the suspect or members of his family. The damages claim was based upon (i) malicious procurement of a search warrant and (ii) trespass; but the trial judge rejected the first claim on the

▶

ground that the police did have reasonable cause to obtain a search warrant and did not act with targeted malice or in bad faith. The trespass claim was also dismissed because the entry was lawful. An appeal to the Court of Appeal (Lord Phillips MR, Kennedy and Ward LJJ) was dismissed.

Ward LJ: ... **33** That causes me concern. Here a law-abiding family have had their front door smashed by battering ram in the early hours of the morning whilst they were still asleep. It seems to have caused terror and some distress and perhaps even the psychiatric harm upon which a substantial part of the claim is based. Given the inefficiency of the police investigation, the family gain my sympathy. If malice can be inferred from the lack of reasonable and probable cause to believe that stolen cash was on the premises, why should the case not be remitted to the county court to determine whether or not malice can be established in the light of the finding in the claimant's favour on ingredient number 2? I have given that question anxious consideration.

34 Not without a measure of reluctance, I conclude that the prospects of eventual success are so slender that it is better that this case ends here. The police may have been negligent but it is practically impossible to say that any officer acted without a bona fide belief that he was placing, or allowing another officer of the squad to place before the justices material sufficient to meet the conditions for the issue of the search warrant. It is difficult to see any improper motive for the police action.

35 That an Englishman's home is said to be his castle reveals an important public interest, but there is another important public interest in the detection of crime and the bringing to justice of those who commit it. These interests are in conflict in a case like this and on the law as it stood when these events occurred, which is before the coming into force of the Human Rights Act 1998, which may be said to have elevated the right to respect for one's home, a finding of malice on the part of police is the proper balancing safeguard.

36 Upon careful reflection, I agree with Lord Phillips of Worth Matravers MR and Kennedy LJ that it is inevitable that malice will not be proved in this case.

Trespass

37 I agree that as the warrant on the face of it was lawful, entry pursuant to it was lawful and thus not a trespass upon the property.

Conclusion

38 Sympathy for the claimants is not enough. I agree that the appeal must be dismissed.

QUESTION

Could the occupiers have sued the police in negligence? If not, why not?

9.5 Emergency services

A number of cases have arisen involving allegations of damage caused by carelessness on the part of an emergency service. In some of the cases the courts have refused to impose liability, but in others the public service (police, fire or ambulance) have been held liable in tort.

Kent v Griffiths [2001] QB 36, CA

This was an action for damages for negligence by a patient against an ambulance service in respect of the late arrival of an ambulance. The patient had suffered an asthma attack and her doctor called an ambulance at 4.25pm; however the ambulance did not arrive until 5.05pm. Before arrival at the hospital the claimant suffered a respiratory arrest which caused brain damage. The judge found that had the ambulance arrived on time there was a high probability that the arrest would have been averted. He also found that there was no satisfactory explanation for the late arrival of the ambulance and that the crew had falsified the record with respect to the time of arrival. The judge held the ambulance service liable and an appeal to the Court of Appeal (Lord Woolf MR, Aldous and Laws LJJ) was dismissed.

Lord Woolf MR: 1 The issue on this appeal is whether an ambulance service can owe any duty of care to a member of the public on whose behalf a 999 telephone call is made if, due to carelessness, it fails to arrive within a reasonable time...

45 Here what was being provided was a health service. In the case of health services under the 1977 Act the conventional situation is that there is a duty of care. Why should the position of the ambulance staff be different from that of doctors or nurses? In addition the arguments based on public policy are much weaker in the case of the ambulance service than they are in the case of the police or the fire service. The police and fire services' primary obligation is to the public at large. In protecting a particular victim of crime, the police are performing their more general role of maintaining public order and reducing crime. In the case of fire the fire service will normally be concerned not only to protect a particular property where a fire breaks out but also to prevent fire spreading. In the case of both services, there is therefore a concern to protect the public generally. The emergency services that can be summoned by a 999 call do, in the majority of situations, broadly carry out a similar function. But in reality they can be very different. The ambulance service is part of the health service. Its care function includes transporting patients to and from hospital when the use of an ambulance for this purpose is desirable. It is therefore appropriate to regard the LAS as providing services of the category provided by hospitals and not as providing services equivalent to those rendered by the police or the fire service. Situations could arise where there is a conflict between the interests of a particular individual and the public at large. But, in the case of the ambulance service in this particular case, the only member of the public who could be adversely affected was the claimant. It was the claimant alone for whom the ambulance had been called.

47 An important feature of this case is that there is no question of an ambulance not being available or of a conflict in priorities. Again I recognise that where what is being attacked is the allocation of resources, whether in the provision of sufficient ambulances

▶

or sufficient drivers or attendants, different considerations could apply. There then could be issues which are not suited for resolution by the courts. However, once there are available, both in the form of an ambulance and in the form of manpower, the resources to provide an ambulance on which there are no alternative demands, the ambulance service would be acting perversely 'in circumstances such as the present', if it did not make those resources available. Having decided to provide an ambulance an explanation is required to justify a failure to attend within reasonable time...

49 ... On the findings of the judge it was delay which caused the further injuries. If wrong information had not been given about the arrival of the ambulance, other means of transport could have been used...

NOTE AND QUESTION

The importance of this case is that it illustrates that the question of liability in negligence will depend upon the circumstances of each case. Why exactly was Lord Woolf prepared to impose liability on the facts of this case? Is there one single fact that is important or are there several?

9.6 National Health Service

Actions for damages in negligence against the NHS are now a specialist area of tort liability. Such claims have an important public interest dimension since money paid out in damages cannot be used to provide or improve medical services.

Roe v Minister of Health [1954] 2 QB 66, CA

Denning LJ: No one can be unmoved by the disaster which has befallen these two unfortunate men. They were both working men before they went into the Chesterfield Hospital in October 1947. Both were insured contributors to the hospital, paying a small sum each week, in return for which they were entitled to be admitted for treatment when they were ill. Each of them was operated on in the hospital for a minor trouble, one for something wrong with a cartilage in his knee, the other for a hydrocele. The operations were both on the same day, 13th October 1947. Each of them was given a spinal anaesthetic by a visiting anaesthetist, Dr Graham. Each of them has in consequence been paralysed from the waist down.

The judge has said that those facts do not speak for themselves, but I think that they do. They certainly call for an explanation. Each of these men is entitled to say to the hospital: 'While I was in your hands something has been done to me which has wrecked my life. Please explain how it has come to pass'. The reason why the judge took a different view was because he thought that the hospital authorities could disclaim responsibility for the anaesthetist, Dr Graham: and, as it might be his fault and not theirs, the hospital authorities were not called upon to give an explanation. I think that that reasoning is wrong. In the first place, I think that the hospital authorities are responsible for the whole of their staff, not only for the nurses and doctors, but also for the anaesthetists and the surgeons. It does not matter whether they are permanent or tem-

porary, resident or visiting, whole-time or part-time. The hospital authorities are responsible for all of them. The reason is because, even if they are not servants, they are the
agents of the hospital to give the treatment. The only exception is the case of consult-
ants or anaesthetists selected and employed by the patient himself. I went into the
matter with some care in *Cassidy v Ministry of Health* and I adhere to all I there said. In
the second place, I do not think that the hospital authorities and Dr Graham can both
avoid giving an explanation by the simple expedient of each throwing responsibility on to
the other. If an injured person shows that one or other or both of two persons injured
him, but cannot say which of them it was, then he is not defeated altogether. He can
call on each of them for an explanation: see *Baker v Market Harborough Industrial Cooperative Society*.

I approach this case, therefore, on the footing that the hospital authorities and Dr
Graham were called on to give an explanation of what has happened. But I think that
they have done so. They have spared no trouble or expense to seek out the cause of the
disaster. The greatest specialists in the land were called to give evidence. In the result,
the judge has found that what happened was this. [His lordship discussed how the accident had occurred: disinfectant had seeped into the anaesthetic by means of invisible
cracks in the ampoules; the anaesthetic was thus contaminated when used.] ... That is
the explanation of the disaster, and the question is: were any of the staff negligent? I
pause to say that once the accident is explained, no question of *res ipsa loquitur* arises.
The only question is whether on the facts as now ascertained anyone was negligent ... If
the anaesthetists had foreseen that the ampoules might get cracked with cracks that
could not be detected on inspection they would no doubt have dyed the phenol a deep
blue; and this would have exposed the contamination. But I do not think that their failure
to foresee this was negligence. It is so easy to be wise after the event and to condemn
as negligence that which was only a misadventure. We ought always to be on our guard
against it, especially in cases against hospitals and doctors. Medical science has conferred great benefits on mankind, but these benefits are attended by considerable risks.
Every surgical operation is attended by risks. We cannot take the benefits without taking
the risks. Every advance in technique is also attended by risks. Doctors, like the rest of
us, have to learn by experience; and experience often teaches in a hard way. Something
goes wrong and shows up a weakness, and then it is put right. That is just what happened here. Dr Graham sought to escape the danger of infection by disinfecting the
ampoule. In escaping that known danger he unfortunately ran into another danger. He
did not know that there could be undetectable cracks, but it was not negligent for him
not to know it at that time. We must not look at the 1947 accident with 1954 spectacles.
The judge acquitted Dr Graham of negligence and we should uphold his decision...

One final word. These two men have suffered such terrible consequences that there is a
natural feeling that they should be compensated. But we should be doing a disservice
to the community at large if we were to impose liability on hospitals and doctors for
everything that happens to go wrong. Doctors would be led to think more of their own
safety than of the good of their patients. Initiative would be stifled and confidence
shaken. A proper sense of proportion requires us to have regard to the conditions in
which hospitals and doctors have to work. We must insist on due care for the patient at
every point, but we must not condemn as negligence that which is only a misadventure.
I agree with my Lord that these appeals should be dismissed.

[Somervell and Morris LJJ also delivered judgments dismissing the appeal.]

QUESTIONS

1. 'We cannot take the benefits without taking the risks. Every advance in technique is also attended by risks. Doctors, like the rest of us, have to learn by experience; and experience often teaches in a hard way'. Was it actually the doctors that had to learn the hard way? Why should it be the two individuals who are left to carry the risks?

2. 'Forget the stiff upper lip, this groundswell of litigation is turning us into grasping whingers and self-pitying milksops... Citizens should be discouraged from exploiting public services: suing should become shameful' (Polly Toynbee, *Guardian*, 21 April 1999, 18). Were the plaintiffs in *Roe* whingers and self-pitying milksops who ought to be ashamed of themselves?

NOTES

1. See also *Goodwill v British Pregnancy Advisory Service* (p 33); *McFarlane v Tayside HA* (p 45); *Gwilliam v West Herts Hospital NHS Trust* (p 123); *Bolam v Friern Hospital Management Committee* (p 130); *Bolitho v City and Hackney HA* (p 131); *Cassidy v MOH* (p 234); *Rees v Darlington Memorial Hospital NHS Trust* (pp 329, 377, 386).

2. Where a victim suffers personal injury as a result of a medical mishap negligence is now virtually the exclusive tort (*Sidaway v Bethlem Royal Hospital* (1985)). However in mental care cases other torts may be relevant as the next extract indicates.

R (Munjaz) v Mersey Care NHS Trust [2003] 3 WLR 1505, CA

This was an action for judicial review brought by two detained psychiatric patients who claimed that they had been unlawfully placed in secluded confinement. The Court of Appeal (Lord Phillips MR, Hale and Latham LJJ) in its judgment discussed what private law remedies might be available to patients in such a situation and the manner in which these remedies might be restricted by legislation.

Hale LJ: ... **49** As the authorities currently stand, merely confining a detained patient to a particular room or part of the hospital will not amount to the tort of false imprisonment. False imprisonment is the deprivation of liberty without lawful justification. A person who has been deprived of his liberty in pursuance of a lawful power to detain cannot through the medium of the tort of false imprisonment complain about the conditions in which he is detained, at least by those who are lawfully detaining him. This was decided by the House of Lords in *R v Deputy Governor of Parkhurst Prison, Ex p Hague* [1992] 1 AC 58, although their Lordships accepted that unauthorised persons, such as other prisoners, might indeed be guilty of false imprisonment if they confined another prisoner within the prison. We shall return to whether this decision requires to be revisited in the light of the Convention.

50 However, that does not mean that the patient is without a remedy if other torts have been committed against him. If the breach of a duty of care towards the patient causes him physical or psychiatric harm, he has a remedy in the tort of negligence. The use of physical restraint upon a patient, or the administration of physical treatment, without lawful justification will amount to the tort of assault and/or battery which is actionable without proof of harm. This will include the use of excessive force or the use of force to enforce a decision which was unlawful in public law terms: see *Mohammed Holgate v Duke* [1984] AC 437. Evidentially, however, neither will be easy to prove. Where physical restraint is employed in an emergency to prevent an escape or to protect others from harm, the court will not find it easy to criticise the decisions made by those who were there at the time. It was acknowledged by the experts in S's case that they were not as well placed as the doctors and nurses on the ward at the time to judge the degree of danger which S presented to staff and patients and those outside the hospital.

51 A further qualification is that individuals acting in pursuance of the 1983 Act cannot be sued, even in respect of acts without lawful justification, unless they are shown to have acted in bad faith or without reasonable care: section 139(1) of the 1983 Act. The leave of a High Court judge must first be obtained: section 139(2). This section does not apply to actions against health authorities and NHS trusts: section 139(4). Nor does it apply to judicial review, which in any event requires the permission of a High Court judge: see *Ex p Waldron* [1986] QB 824.

52 It follows that there are circumstances in which the use of seclusion will involve the commission of a tort against the patient for which the ordinary tortious remedies will be available. But these will not cover the use of seclusion in itself, or even every use of seclusion of which legitimate complaint might be made, and certainly not every use of seclusion which does not comply with the Code of Practice...

9.7 Financial institutions

See Financial Services and Markets Act 2000, s 102 and *Three Rivers District Council v Governor and Company of The Bank of England* (No 3) (2000) (pp 88, 105). Note also *Yuen Kun Yeu v Att-Gen of Hong Kong* (1988)

Chapter 10

Causation and General Defences

It would perhaps be cynical to describe this chapter as dealing with the question of how to escape from liability. Yet there is a certain truth in such an assertion. Even when carelessness and duty can be shown, it is still possible to avoid liability on the basis that it 'is axiomatic that the law will not impose liability to pay compensation for damage unless there is a relevant causal connection between the damage and the defendant's tort, breach of contract or statutory duty' (Lord Hoffmann in *Fairchild v Glenhaven Funeral Services* (2002), § 48). The problem, however, is 'what amounts to a relevant causal connection'? As Lord Hoffmann has observed, everyone 'agrees that there is no scientific or philosophical touchstone for determining the relevant causal connection in any particular case' and so the 'relevance of a causal connection depends upon the purpose of the inquiry' (*ibid.*, § 49).

10.1 Approaches and theories

Causation is intrinsically a complex subject and as a result has attracted the attention of theorists both from within and from without the law and, as the extract from Professor Honoré will suggest, no single theory is satisfactory.

10.1.1 Theories of causation

Causation is a means of analysing physical and social facts and is based on the idea that any event or phenomenon is caused by an earlier event or phenomenon. The regression is of course endless and science fiction writers have long developed themes about time travel and the problems that might be created for the contemporary world if a time-traveller, while venturing into the past, kills a life form. When applied to legal events causation is about linking the phenomenon of harm with anterior events and theory is important in two main ways. First, theory is required to distinguish between what one might call potent and non-potent causal events; in other words a theoretical model is needed to distinguish those events that will be regarded as a cause and those that will not. However, given that many judges (at least in England) faced with difficult causation cases will tend to rely upon 'common sense', a second role for theory is to explain the precedents. In short, theory is necessary to explain the past cases and to predict how future cases will be decided. However, the next extract suggests that the isolation of a single theory is elusive.

AM Honoré, *Causation and Remoteness of Damage, Torts, International Encyclopedia of Comparative Law* **vol XI, Ch 7**

1. ... [I]t is very difficult to construct a theory of causation and remoteness of damage which will at the same time explain the meaning of the terms involved and constitute a useful guide to decision. The theories tend to induce a feeling of frustration, because they either have little empirical content and so fail to point the way, or are clear-cut but apply to only a segment of the circle of problems which present themselves.

It is not surprising, then, that in many legal systems there are competing theories, that often a theory is officially adopted but not consistently applied, and that in one and the same system different theories are applied to different types of case. This is a wholesome phenomenon, but it makes the standard method of comparison, in which each solution is represented by a single system, unworkable...

105 ... But in any case the problems to be answered are so various that they cannot be solved by a single formula which remains at all meaningful... It would be unsound to adopt any theory of causation if by it a court was committed to the view that there is only one ground on which the tortfeasor's responsibility can properly be limited. The real function of the theories is rather to emphasize a particular technique of limitation while not rigidly excluding the use of others... But though forensically the vaguest formula may often be the best, from the standpoint of legal science it is important to recognize that just as there are several different grounds for imposing a duty to compensate, so there are several different grounds for limiting compensation...

10.1.2 European approaches

The idea that there are various competing theories of causation is specifically confirmed in the next text which, although not having the force of positive law, at least reflects the main models employed in European legal systems. It thus provides an excellent reference point for tort lawyers.

Principles of European Tort Law (2003)
European Group on Tort Law

Chapter 3. Causation

Section 1. Conditio sine qua non and qualifications

Article 3:101. Conditio sine qua non

An act or omission (hereafter: activity) is a cause of the victim's damage if, in the absence of the activity, the damage would not have occurred.

Article 3:102. Concurrent causes

In case of multiple activities, where each of them alone would have caused the damage at the same time, each activity is regarded as a cause of the victim's damage.

▶

Article 3:103. Alternative causes

(1) In case of multiple activities, where each of them alone would have been sufficient to cause the damage, but it remains uncertain which one in fact caused it, each activity is regarded as a cause to the extent corresponding to the likelihood that it may have caused the victim's damage.

(2) If, in case of multiple victims, it remains uncertain whether a particular victim's damage has been caused by an activity, while it is likely that it did not cause the damage of all victims, the activity is regarded as a cause of the damage suffered by all victims in proportion to the likelihood that it may have caused the damage of a particular victim. Regard is to be had to the background risk and the specific circumstances of each victim.

Article 3:104. Potential causes

(1) If an activity has definitely and irreversibly led the victim to suffer damage, a subsequent activity which alone would have caused the same damage is to be disregarded.

(2) A subsequent activity is nevertheless taken into consideration
   a) if it has led to additional or aggravated damage, or
   b) if it has led to continuous damage, but only starting from the time that it also would have caused it.

Article 3:105. Minimal causation

In the case of multiple activities, when it is certain that none of them has caused the entire damage or any determinable part thereof, those that are likely to have minimally contributed to the damage are presumed to have caused equal shares thereof.

Article 3:106. Alternative and potential causes within the victim's sphere

If an activity, occurrence or other circumstance, including natural events, within the sphere of the victim may have caused the damage, the victim has to bear his loss to the extent that the cause may lie within his own sphere.

Section 2. Scope of Liability

Article 3:201. Scope of liability

Where causation has been established under Section 1 of this Chapter, whether and to what extent damage may be attributed to a person depends on factors such as

(a) the foreseeability of the damage to a reasonable person at the time of its occurrence, taking into account in particular the closeness in time or space between the damaging activity and its consequence, or the magnitude of the damage in relation to the normal consequences of such an activity;

(b) the nature and the value of the protected interest (Art. 2:102);

(c) the basis of liability (Art. 1:101);

(d) the extent of the ordinary risks of life; and

(e) the protective purpose of the rule that has been violated.

10.1.3 Common law approaches to causation

Perhaps because of the complexity the common law has tended to diffuse the topic of causation behind a range of different concepts and levels of approach. For example, in addition to the requirement of cause and connection between tortious behaviour and damage, causation is to be found behind concepts as wide-ranging as duty of care, contributory negligence, remoteness of damage, mitigation and so on. The approach that will therefore be adopted in this chapter is to distribute the problem of causation between various levels of operation; these are actionability (where causation forms part of the definition of the cause of action), factual causation (where the jury once decided if cause and connection existed in fact), legal causation (alternatively known as remoteness of damage and is a question of law for the judge) and finally damages (which includes the defences of contributory negligence and mitigation).

10.2 Actionability

The first level at which causation operates is actionability. This is to say there are some causes of action specifically requiring a particular type of cause and connection before an action can get off the ground so to speak.

10.2.1 Trespass

Perhaps the leading tort here is trespass. The reason why a causal requirement came to determine actionability is explained in the extract below.

David Ibbetson, *A Historical Introduction to the Law of Obligations*
(OUP, 1999), p (footnotes omitted)

The upshot of this was that by 1700 it was established as a rule, almost certainly introduced by analogy with Roman law, that where the plaintiff had been directly injured by the defendant's act the correct action was trespass, and where the injury was merely consequential case was appropriate... An alternative way of putting the same point was that, if the defendant's act was an invasive interference – a trespass, a wrong – the plaintiff should bring trespass, any consequential loss being recovered in damages; if the act was not in itself a trespass, then the correct form was case...

NOTE

The directness rule still has a role in the modern tort of trespass.

Harnett v Bond [1925] AC 669, HL

This was an action for damages in trespass brought against one of the Commissioners at the offices of the Commissioner of Lunacy. The claimant had been confined in a mental asylum but when granted leave went to the offices of the Commissioner to try to prove his sanity. The defendant (Dr Bond), however, came to the conclusion that the claimant was not sane and locked him in a room until the doctor in charge of the asylum (Dr Adam) could come to take him back into custody. The claimant was detained for another nine years before escaping and being found to be perfectly sane. The question arose as to whether the defendant (Dr Bond) should be liable in trespass for the nine years' detention which followed the imprisonment in the locked room. The House of Lords (Viscount Cave LC and Lords Dunedin, Atkinson, Sumner and Buckmaster) held that the defendant was not to be so liable.

Viscount Cave LC: ... The defendants having applied to the Court of Appeal for a new trial or judgment, that Court (...) unanimously set aside the judgment of Lush J and ordered a new trial as against Dr Bond and that judgment should be entered for Dr Adam. As to Dr Bond, the learned Lords Justices held that the chain of causation had been broken, not only when Dr Adam decided to retain the appellant after his return to Malling Place, but at 'innumerable points' after that date, and that it was plainly not permissible for the jury in assessing damages to treat the whole period of the appellant's captivity as directly caused by the events of December 14, 1912...

My Lords, as regards Dr Bond, I feel no doubt whatever that the Court of Appeal was right in ordering a new trial...

NOTE

Before an action in trespass will be available the damage must have been directly caused. Indirect damage might give rise to another tort such as nuisance or negligence, but it cannot give rise to trespass: see *Esso v Southport* (1956) (pp 4, 34). The case of *Wilkinson v Downton* (1897) (p 7) might appear to be an exception; however this decision has recently been held not to be a trespass case (*Wainwright*, pp 28, 64, 81, 109). Some duty of care cases can be seen in terms of actionability; thus a mere omission could be said to give rise to no duty of care because there is not a sufficient cause and connection: see *Stovin v Wise* (1996) (pp 136, 152, 296). Duty of care is a question of actionability.

QUESTION

What if the defendant in *Harnett* had locked the claimant in the room knowing that he was perfectly sane?

10.2.2 Breach of statutory duty

In another strict liability tort, breach of statutory duty, there is also an important causal requirement which must be fulfilled before there can be an action for damages. Cause and connection between the actual damage suffered and the breach of the statute has to be shown and thus if the damage is independent of the breach there can be no claim.

Gorris v Scott (1874) 9 LR Exch 125, Court of Exchequer

Kelly CB: This is an action to recover damages for the loss of a number of sheep which the defendant, a shipowner, had contracted to carry, and which were washed overboard and lost by reason (as we must take it to be truly alleged) of the neglect to comply with a certain order made by the Privy Council, in pursuance of the Contagious Diseases (Animals) Act, 1869. The Act was passed merely for sanitary purposes, in order to prevent animals in a state of infectious disease from communicating it to other animals with which they might come in contact. Under the authority of that Act, certain orders were made; amongst others, an order by which any ship bringing sheep or cattle from any foreign port to ports in Great Britain is to have the place occupied by such animals divided into pens of certain dimensions, and the floor of such pens furnished with battens or foot holds. The object of this order is to prevent animals from being overcrowded, and so brought into a condition in which the disease guarded against would be likely to be developed. This regulation has been neglected, and the question is, whether the loss, which we must assume to have been caused by that neglect, entitles the plaintiffs to maintain an action...

But, looking at the Act, it is perfectly clear that its provisions were all enacted with a totally different view; there was no purpose, direct or indirect, to protect against such damage; but, as is recited in the preamble, the Act is directed against the possibility of sheep or cattle being exposed to disease on their way to this country... That being so, if by reason of the default in question the plaintiffs' sheep had been overcrowded, or had been caused unnecessary suffering, and so had arrived in this country in a state of disease, I do not say that they might not have maintained this action. But the damage complained of here is something totally apart from the object of the Act of Parliament, and it is in accordance with all the authorities to say that the action is not maintainable...

[Barons Pigott, Pollock and Amphlett were of the same opinion.]

NOTE

This is a causation case in that the breach of duty could be said not to have caused the loss of the sheep. See also *Bailey v Ayr Engineering Co Ltd* (1958).

10.2.3 Negligence

Causation and actionability can often be found in the duty of care question as the next extract indicates.

Rees v Darlington Memorial Hospital NHS Trust [2003] 3 WLR 1091, HL

(For facts see p 377)

Lord Millett ... 107 Each of those cases raised an issue of causation. In neither case was it a factual issue, for there was no doubt that the loss was sustained as a direct result of the negligent information which the defendant had supplied. But the law does not hold a person liable for all the foreseeable consequences of his actions. So the question in each case was one of responsibility: was the defendant legally responsible for the loss which his negligence had caused? There was nothing unusual, however, in the nature of the loss; indeed it was commonplace-financial loss arising from a bad investment. The difficulty arose from the causal relationship between the defendant's negligence and the loss sustained by the plaintiff. The solution lay in recognising that a person is only liable for loss which falls within the scope of his duty of care.

108 The problem in a case of wrongful pregnancy is not the same. There is no difficulty about causation, whether as a matter of fact or of legal responsibility. The pregnancy and birth of a child are the very things which the defendants are employed to prevent. It is impossible to say that consequential loss falls outside the scope of their duty of care. They are accordingly liable for the normal and foreseeable heads of loss, such as the mother's pain and suffering (and where appropriate loss of earnings) due to the confinement and delivery. The novelty of the claim in *McFarlane* lay in one particular head of damage – the cost of bringing up a healthy child. The House considered it to be morally repugnant to award damages for the birth of a healthy child. It makes for easier exposition to identify the issue by reference to the head of damage rather than the duty of care. It also has the added advantage that identifying the ratio of *McFarlane* in this way may make it simpler to find the answer to the question raised by the present case...

NOTE AND QUESTION

In the end, then, the Law Lord thought that this was not a causal problem that functioned at the level of actionability. It was a matter of damages. But what if a child had been born severely disabled and the hospital had carelessly failed to inform the mother of this possibility soon after conception: could the child sue for damages claiming that it would have been better to have been aborted? Would this be a causal problem?

10.2.4 Consent to injury

A person may be prevented from bringing an action for damages on the basis that he consented to the risk of incurring damage. Or, put another way, his injury is not caused by the defendant but by his own willingness to accept the risk of incurring the damage: *volenti non fit injuria*. However, the defence is rarely successful since the courts have long made a distinction between mere knowledge of a risk and actual consent to the injury. Moreover, being a complete defence to an action, the courts have often preferred to apply the damages defence of contributory negligence (see **10.5.1**).

Morris v Murray [1991] 2 QB 6, CA

This was an action for damages brought by a passenger in a light aeroplane against the estate of the pilot of the aircraft. The pilot and the passenger had spent the afternoon drinking alcohol after which the pilot suggested that they go for a flight. The aircraft crashed owing to the negligence of the pilot and as a result the pilot was killed and the passenger injured. The Court of Appeal (Fox and Stocker LJJ and Sir George Waller) held that the passenger had consented to the risk of injury and thus that he had no action.

Fox LJ: ... I think that in embarking upon the flight the plaintiff had implicitly waived his rights in the event of injury consequent on Mr. Murray's failure to fly with reasonable care. The facts go far beyond *Dann v Hamilton* [1939] 1 K.B. 509; *Nettleship v Weston* [1971] 2 Q.B. 691 and *Slater v Clay Cross Co Ltd* [1956] 2 Q.B. 264. It is much nearer to the dangerous experimenting with the detonators in *Imperial Chemical Industries Ltd v Shatwell* [1965] A.C. 656. I would conclude, therefore, that the plaintiff accepted the risks and implicitly discharged Mr. Murray from liability for injury in relation to the flying of the plane. The result, in my view, is that the maxim volenti non fit injuria does apply in this case. The judge appears to have been influenced by the fact that Mr. Murray managed to get the plane airborne. He did, but the take off downwind was irregular and the bizarre movements of the plane in flight must raise the greatest doubts whether he was in proper control of it. The judge thought that the case was analogous to *Owens v Brimmell* [1977] Q.B. 859. But the volenti defence was not in issue in that case.

Considerations of policy do not lead me to any different conclusion. Volenti as a defence has, perhaps, been in retreat during this century – certainly in relation to master and servant cases. It might be said that the merits could be adequately dealt with by the application of the contributory negligence rules. The judge held that the plaintiff was only 20 per cent. to blame (which seems to me to be too low) but if that were increased to 50 per cent. so that the plaintiff's damages were reduced by half, both sides would be substantially penalised for their conduct. It seems to me, however, that the wild irresponsibility of the venture is such that the law should not intervene to award damages and should leave the loss where it falls. Flying is intrinsically dangerous and flying with a drunken pilot is great folly. The situation is very different from what has arisen in motoring cases.

I should mention that the defence of volenti has been abrogated in relation to passengers in motor vehicles covered by comprehensive insurance: section [149(3) the Road Traffic Act 1988]. It is not suggested, however, that there is any similar enactment relating to aircraft and applicable to this case...

QUESTION

Might this decision be based upon a concern about who should end up the defendant's assets?

NOTES

1. *ICI v Shatwell* (1965) should be read in the law reports.

2. The defence of *volenti* is to be found in a range of statutes: see eg Occupier's Liability Act 1957, s 2(5); Animals Act 1971, s 5(2); Occupiers' Liability Act 1984, s 1(6).

3. A person can also be deemed to consent to damage via a contractual exclusion clause or a notice. However, statute lays down certain restrictions.

Unfair Contract Terms Act 1977 (c 50)

1 Scope of Part I

(1) For the purposes of this Part of this Act, 'negligence' means the breach—
   (a) of any obligation, arising from the express or implied terms of a contract, to take reasonable care to exercise reasonable skill in the performance of the contract;
   (b) of any common law duty to take reasonable care or exercise reasonable skill (but not any stricter duty);
   (c) of the common duty of care imposed by the Occupiers' Liability Act 1957 or the Occupiers' Liability Act (Northern Ireland) 1957.

(2) This Part of this Act is subject to Part III; and in relation to contracts, the operation of sections 2 to 4 and 7 is subject to the exceptions made by Schedule 1.

(3) In the case of both contract and tort, sections 2 to 7 apply (except where the contrary is stated in section 6(4)) only to business liability, that is liability for breach of obligations or duties arising—
   (a) from things done or to be done by a person in the course of a business (whether his own business or another's); or
   (b) from the occupation of premises used for business purposes of the occupier;

and references to liability are to be read accordingly [but liability of an occupier of premises for breach of an obligation or duty towards a person obtaining access to the premises for recreational or educational purposes, being liability for loss or damage suffered by reason of the dangerous state of the premises, is not a business liability of the occupier unless granting that person such access for the purposes concerned falls within the business purposes of the occupier].

(4) In relation to any breach of duty or obligation, it is immaterial for any purpose of this Part of this Act whether the breach was inadvertent or intentional, or whether liability for it arises directly or vicariously.

2 Negligence liability

(1) A person cannot by reference to any contract term or to a notice given to persons generally or to particular persons exclude or restrict his liability for death or personal injury resulting from negligence.

(2) In the case of other loss or damage, a person cannot so exclude or restrict his liability for negligence except in so far as the term or notice satisfies the requirement of reasonableness.

(3) Where a contract term or notice purports to exclude or restrict liability for negligence a person's agreement to or awareness of it is not of itself to be taken as indicating his voluntary acceptance of any risk.

QUESTIONS

1. What would be the effect of this statute on *Ashdown v Samuel Williams* (1957) and *White v Blackmore* (1972)?

2. How does this 1977 Act relate to the Occupiers' Liability Act 1984, s 1(5)?

PROBLEM

A commercial company owns and occupies a piece of land on which is a dilapidated building that sometimes attracts trespassers. The company erects notices stating: 'Danger: Do Not Enter. Dilapidated and Dangerous Building. Trespassers enter entirely at their own risk and are deemed to have consented to, and to be the cause of, any injury'. A homeless teenager enters the land and is injured while sleeping in the building when part of the roof collapses. Can the teenager sue the commercial company for damages?

10.2.5 Ex turpi causa non oritur actio

This maxim states that no action can arise out of an illegal cause. Accordingly if the claimant is injured while participating in a criminal activity he may be denied a claim for damages.

Pitts v Hunt [1991] 1 QB 24, CA

This was an action for damages by a pillion passenger on a motor-cycle driven by the defendant in respect of personal injuries suffered when the motor-cycle was involved in a collision with another vehicle. The claimant and the defendant had been drinking before the journey and the former knew that the latter had no licence or insurance. In addition the claimant had encouraged the defendant to drive in a reckless and dangerous manner. The Court of Appeal (Dillon, Balcombe and Beldam LJJ) held that the claimant was precluded from bringing an action on the ground of illegality.

Beldam LJ: ... On the facts found by the judge in this case the plaintiff was playing a full and active part in encouraging the young rider to commit offences which, if a death other than that of the young rider himself had occurred, would have amounted to manslaughter. And not just manslaughter by gross negligence, on the judge's findings. It would have been manslaughter by the commission of a dangerous act either done with the intention of frightening other road users or when both the plaintiff and the young rider were aware, or but for self-induced intoxication would have been aware, that it was likely to do so, and nevertheless they went on and did the act regardless of the consequences. Thus on the findings made by the judge in this case I would hold that the plaintiff is precluded on grounds of public policy from recovering compensation for the injuries which he sustained in the course of the very serious offences in which he was participating. On a question on which, as Bingham LJ said in *Saunders v Edwards* [1987] 1 WLR 1116, 1134, the courts have tended to adopt a pragmatic approach, I do not believe that it is desirable to go further in an attempt to categorise the degree of seriousness involved in offences which will preclude recovery of compensation. I would, however, add that the public attitude to driving a motor vehicle on a road when under the influence of drink has, I believe, changed markedly with the increasing number of serious accidents and the dreadful injuries which are the consequence of such driving. The public conscience is ever increasingly being focused not only on those who commit the offence but, in the words of recent publicity, those who ask the driver to drink and drive...

NOTE

See also *Vellino v Chief Constable of Greater Manchester Police* (2002).

QUESTION

Is there really a need for a separate doctrine of illegality? Could not the cases be solved using the notions of factual causation, *volenti* and/or contributory negligence?

10.2.6 Necessity

A legal action may prove impossible in situations where the defendant's act was prompted by necessity. In medical liability problems the value of necessity is apparent given that the medical profession is under a duty to save lives (cf *Re F*, p 67). But what if the police have to destroy a private person's house or shop in order to subdue a dangerous criminal?

Rigby v Chief Constable of Northamptonshire [1985] 1 WLR 1242, QBD

Taylor J: On 17 December 1977, the Sportsman's Lodge, a gunsmiths shop in Northampton owned by the first plaintiff, Michael Rigby, was burned out. The cause of the fire was most unusual. A young psychopath had broken into the premises and armed himself. The police laid siege to the shop. Eventually they fired in a canister of CS gas to smoke out the intruder. The canister set the shop ablaze. The first plaintiff now sues the Chief Constable of Northamptonshire for damages for loss and damage to the premises and contents. The second plaintiff makes a small claim for damage to his guns which were in the first plaintiff's custody in the shop...

There is a surprising dearth of authority as to the nature and limits of necessity as a defence in tort. Mr Machin referred me to three cases. *Cope v Sharpe (No 2)* [1912] 1 KB 496 was a case of alleged trespass where the defendant had sought to prevent a heather fire from spreading. *Creswell v Sirl* [1948] 1 KB 241 was a case of alleged trespass to a dog which the defendant had shot to prevent it worrying sheep. In each case the defence prevailed...

I therefore hold that a defence of necessity is available in the absence of negligence on the part of the defendant creating or contributing to the necessity. In this case there was a dangerous armed psychopath whom it was urgently necessary to arrest. I have already found that it was not negligent of the defendant to be without Ferret. It is conceded that the only alternative was to fire in a CS gas canister, which was done. I therefore find that the defence of necessity prevails and that the cause of action in trespass fails...

Mr O'Brien, whilst accepting that necessity can apply to *Rylands v Fletcher* liability, sought to argue that it has a more limited scope there than in answer to alleged trespass. He based this on the decision in *West v Bristol Tramways Co* [1908] 2 KB 14, the creosote case. However, there the defence was statutory authority and I do not think Mr O'Brien made his submission good. In the result, I conclude that if, which I doubt, this case falls to be considered at all under *Rylands v Fletcher*, necessity would provide a good defence as it does in trespass...

This leads me to consider the remaining allegation of negligence....

... Mr O'Brien argues the probability that a fire appliance (for example the Wellingborough Green Goddess which in fact came later) could have been brought to

the scene and would have arrived before 9.20. Bearing all these matters in mind, I conclude that the defendant by his officers was negligent in failing to react to the departure
of the Green Goddess by seeking other help, and in using the canister without any fire-
fighting equipment...

I am not asked to consider the issue of damages. Suffice it to say, therefore, that in the
upshot I find the defendant liable in negligence to both plaintiffs. The damages issue
must be tried by another tribunal unless agreed.

QUESTIONS

1. How might these facts have been decided in France? (See Moreau, p 301.)

2. If the real plaintiff in *Rigby* was the shop owner's building insurance company, would you still consider it right that the police should have to pay the
company damages?

NOTE

In the case of *In re F* (above p 67) Lord Goff said (at 74) 'That there exists in the
common law a principle of necessity which may justify action which would otherwise be unlawful is not in doubt'.

10.3 Factual causation

Factual causation is perhaps the most complex level. In the past this question
would have been decided by a jury who would not have given reasons. These days
it is a matter for the judge who is expected to motivate his or her conclusions.

10.3.1 Introductory

Such motivations can take one away from strict questions of fact as the extract
from Lord Hoffmann illustrates.

Banque Bruxelles Lambert SA v Eagle Star Insurance Co Ltd [1997] AC 191, HL

Lord Hoffmann: ... There is no reason in principle why the law should not penalise
wrongful conduct by shifting on to the wrongdoer the whole risk of consequences
which would not have happened but for the wrongful act. Hart and Honoré, in
Causation in the Law, 2nd ed (1985), p 120, say that it would, for example, be perfectly
intelligible to have a rule by which an unlicensed driver was responsible for all the consequences of his having driven, even if they were unconnected with his not having a
licence. One might adopt such a rule in the interests of deterring unlicensed driving. But
that is not the normal rule...

Rules which make the wrongdoer liable for all the consequences of his wrongful conduct are exceptional and need to be justified by some special policy. Normally the law
limits liability to those consequences which are attributable to that which made the act
wrongful. In the case of liability in negligence for providing inaccurate information, this
would mean liability for the consequences of the information being inaccurate.

▶

I can illustrate the difference between the ordinary principle and that adopted by the Court of Appeal by an example. A mountaineer about to undertake a difficult climb is concerned about the fitness of his knee. He goes to a doctor who negligently makes a superficial examination and pronounces the knee fit. The climber goes on the expedition, which he would not have undertaken if the doctor had told him the true state of his knee. He suffers an injury which is an entirely foreseeable consequence of mountaineering but has nothing to do with his knee...

Your Lordships might, I would suggest, think that there was something wrong with a principle which, in the example which I have given, produced the result that the doctor was liable. What is the reason for this feeling? I think that the Court of Appeal's principle offends common sense because it makes the doctor responsible for consequences which, though in general terms foreseeable, do not appear to have a sufficient causal connection with the subject matter of the duty. The doctor was asked for information on only one of the considerations which might affect the safety of the mountaineer on the expedition. There seems no reason of policy which requires that the negligence of the doctor should require the transfer to him of all the foreseeable risks of the expedition.

NOTE

Lord Hoffmann may well be talking about liability and factual causation but two non-factual notions emerge from his discussion: they are the notions of deterrence and policy. These aims and policy aspects, when combined with various technical causal terms, only increase the complication, as the next extract illustrates.

Reeves v Commissioner of Police for the Metropolis [2000] 1 AC 360, HL

(For facts and further extracts see pp 340, 365)

Lord Hobhouse (dissenting): ... My Lords, causation as discussed in the authorities has been complicated both by conflicting statements about whether causation is a question of fact or of law or, even, 'common sense' and by the use of metaphor and Latin terminology, eg, *causa sine qua non*, *causa causans*, *novus actus* and *volenti*, which in themselves provide little enlightenment and are not consistently used.

At one level causation is purely a question of fact. It is a question of fact whether event 'a' was a cause of event 'x'. To simplify, it is a factual question whether event 'x' would still have occurred if event 'a' had not. However facts are not that simple. Virtually every event will have a number of antecedent facts which satisfy such a factual test. The ordinary use of language then distinguishes between them, choosing some and discarding others. The presence of oxygen is a necessary cause of combustion yet it is not normally treated as being a cause. This is because it is part of the normal environment and therefore is disregarded when identifying the cause of some abnormal event. (In certain circumstances, oxygen is not or should not be part of the normal environment, eg in tanks used for the sea carriage of petroleum, in which case its presence would be identified as a cause.) The ordinary use of language makes a distinction, independent of any legal concept, between the normal and the abnormal in describing something as a cause.

This use of language is most easily observed in relation to physical events but is also applied to human conduct. Reasonable human responses to situations are not treated as causative; they are a normal consequence of the antecedent event and it is that event which is described as the cause. Thus the reasonable response of a rescuer to an accident caused by the negligence of another would not without more be described as a cause of an injury suffered by the rescuer. Similarly, to act reasonably on the faith of some misinformation is normally described as a consequence not as a cause. Human conduct, which is not entirely reasonable, for example, where it is itself careless, but is within the range of human conduct that is foreseeable and normally contemplated as not unlikely, may add a further cause of the relevant subsequent event but would not normally mean that an earlier relevant event ceased also to be a cause of that later event. Careless conduct may ordinarily be regarded as being within the range of normal human conduct when reckless conduct ordinarily would not.

Any disputed question of causation (factual or legal) will involve a number of factual events or conditions which satisfy the 'but for' test. A process of evaluation and selection has then to take place. It may, for example, be necessary to distinguish between what factually are necessary and sufficient causes. It may be necessary to distinguish between those conditions or events which merely provide the occasion or opportunity for a given consequence and those which in the ordinary use of language would (independently of any imposed legal criterion) be said to have caused the relevant consequence. Thus certain causes will be discarded as insignificant and one cause may be selected as the cause. It is at this stage that legal concepts may enter in, either in a way that is analogous to the factual assessment – as for 'proximate' cause in insurance law – or, in a more specifically legal manner, in the attribution of responsibility (bearing in mind that responsibility may not be exclusive). In the law of tort it is the attribution of responsibility to humans that is the relevant legal consideration…

NOTE

A number of points emerge from this extract. Yet perhaps the most important at a technical level is that factual causation can be classified into various sub-categories depending upon the actual causal agency or event. Thus one important Latin tag is *novus actus interveniens* which gives expression to the idea of a new intervening cause. For example D negligently injures C but, while C is being taken to hospital in an ambulance, the ambulance driver carelessly crashes the vehicle causing further injury to C. Is D to be liable for this further injury?

10.3.2 Intervention by a third party

One might start therefore with the causal situation where the new intervening event (*novus actus interveniens*) is by a third party.

The Oropesa [1943] P 32, CA

This was an action for damages by the parent of one of the crew members of the *Manchester Regiment* who died when a lifeboat capsized. The *Manchester Regiment* had been involved in a collision with the *Oropesa* caused partly through the negligence of the *Oropesa*. The captain of the *Manchester Regiment* decided to confer with the captain of the *Oropesa* and set out, with various crew members including the claimant's son, in the fatal lifeboat. The owners of the *Oropesa* claimed they were not liable for the death because the act of the captain in setting out in the lifeboat had broken the chain of causation. This defence was rejected by the trial judge and an appeal to the Court of Appeal (Lord Wright, Scott and MacKinnon LJJ) was dismissed.

Lord Wright: ... If... the test is whether what was done was reasonable, there can be no question that the actions of both the master and the deceased were reasonable. Whether the master took exactly the right course is another matter. He may have been guilty of an error of judgment, but, as I read the authorities, that would not affect the question whether the action he took and its consequences flowed directly from the negligence of the *Oropesa*... Having regard to the situation of the *Manchester Regiment* and those on board her, I think that the hand of the casualty lay heavily on her and that the conduct both of the master and of the deceased was directly caused by and flowed from it. There was an unbroken sequence of cause and effect between the negligence which caused the *Oropesa* to collide with the *Manchester Regiment*, and their action, which was dictated by the exigencies of the position. It cannot be severed from the circumstances affecting both ships. To that must be joined the duty which they were under in their positions as captain and sixth engineer.

There are some propositions which are beyond question in connection with this class of case. One is that human action does not per se sever the connected sequence of acts. The mere fact that human action intervenes does not prevent the sufferer from saying that injury which is due to that human action as one of the elements in the sequence is recoverable from the original wrongdoer... The question is not whether there was new negligence, but whether there was a new cause... To break the chain of causation it must be shown that there is something which I will call ultroneous, something unwarrantable, a new cause which disturbs the sequence of events, something which can be described as either unreasonable or extraneous or extrinsic... Here it may be said that, even if the master of the *Manchester Regiment* was not doing quite the right thing, his mistake might be regarded as the natural consequence of the emergency in which he was placed by the negligence of the *Oropesa*...

The real difficulty in the present case is the application of the principle, which is a question of fact. I agree entirely with Langton J in the way in which he has dealt with the question. I am not prepared to say in all the circumstances that the fact that the deceased's death was due to his leaving the ship in the lifeboat and to the unexpected capsizing of that boat prevented his death being a direct consequence of the casualty. It was a risk, no doubt, but a boat would not generally capsize in those circumstances. In my opinion, the appeal should be dismissed.

NOTE

The test applied was one of reasonableness. Such a test is not surprising given that factual causation was once a question for the jury. However 'reasonableness' in this context is not the same as in the duty of care question (cf *Bolton v Stone* (1951), p 119). The captain, in setting off in the small boat, may have been unreasonable in the sense that it could have been a careless thing to do (the present author's late father-in-law, a highly experienced merchant navy captain, decorated for bravery, who was a passenger on the *Oropesa* at the time of this accident, certainly thought it was pretty daft). But it does not follow that such duty of care unreasonableness is equivalent to causal unreasonableness. The tests are quite different.

10.3.3 Intervention by the claimant

The *novus actus interveniens* can result from the claimant's own act.

McKew v Holland & Hannen & Cubitts Ltd [1969] 3 All ER 1621, HL (Scotland)

This was an action for damages by an employee against his employer in respect of two injuries, one sustained at work and one sustained while visiting a block of flats. In the second accident the plaintiff was descending some steep stairs when his leg gave way (a result of the first accident) and he tried to jump the rest of the way in order to land in an upright position. However he succeeded only in severely fracturing his ankle. The House of Lords (Lords Reid, Hodson, Guest, Upjohn and Viscount Dilhorne) held that the employer was not liable for this second injury.

Lord Reid: … In my view the law is clear. If a man is injured in such a way that his leg may give way at any moment he must act reasonably and carefully. It is quite possible that in spite of all reasonable care his leg may give way in circumstances such that as a result he sustains further injury. Then that second injury was caused by his disability which in turn was caused by the defender's fault. But if the injured man acts unreasonably he cannot hold the defender liable for injury caused by his own unreasonable conduct. His unreasonable conduct is novus actus interveniens. The chain of causation has been broken and what follows must be regarded as caused by his own conduct and not by the defender's fault or the disability caused by it. Or one may say that unreasonable conduct of the pursuer and what follows from it is not the natural and probable result of the original fault of the defender or of the ensuing disability. I do not think that foreseeability comes into this. A defender is not liable for a consequence of a kind which is not foreseeable. But it does not follow that he is liable for every consequence which a reasonable man could foresee. What can be foreseen depends almost entirely on the facts of the case, and it is often easy to foresee unreasonable conduct or some other novus actus interveniens as being quite likely. But that does not mean that the defender must pay for damage caused by the novus actus. It only leads to trouble if one tries to graft on to the concept of foreseeability some rule of law to the effect that a wrongdoer is not bound to foresee something which in fact he could readily foresee as quite likely to happen. For it is not at all unlikely or unforeseeable that an active man who has suffered such a disability will take some quite unreasonable risk. But if he does he cannot hold the defender liable for the consequences.

NOTES AND QUESTION

1. Compare the above decision with *Sayers v Harlow UDC* (1958) and *Wieland v Cyril Lord Carpets Ltd* (1969). Why was *Wieland* decided differently from *McKew*?

2. What is particularly important about Lord Reid's judgment in this case is that he clearly restates (a) the test as one of 'reasonableness' and (b) that this test is quite different from 'foreseeability'. This latter test, as we shall see, is relevant only to remoteness of damage and not factual causation. The flexibility of the reasonableness test in factual causation is tested to the limit by the next case.

Reeves v Commissioner of Police for the Metropolis [2000] 1 AC 360, HL

This was an action for damages brought under the Fatal Accidents Act 1976 and Law Reform (Miscellaneous Provisions) Act 1934 against the police by a dependant of a man who had committed suicide while in police custody. The police were adjudged negligent but the judge held that the man, in taking his own life, was the sole cause of his damage. An appeal to the Court of Appeal was allowed, a majority holding that the claimant was entitled to full damages. A further appeal to the House of Lords (Lords Hoffmann, Mackay, Jauncey and Hope; Lord Hobhouse dissenting) was allowed: a majority held that the claimant was entitled to damages reduced by 50% on the basis of contributory negligence.

Lord Jauncey: ... Mr Pannick submitted that the deceased's death was caused not by the negligence of the police officers but by the voluntary act of the deceased while of sound mind. This act broke the chain of causation between the Commissioner's breach of duty and the death...

> My Lords, I consider that this argument is flawed. Professor Glanville Williams in his *Joint Torts and Contributory Negligence* (1951) stated at para. 2–24 that:

> 'If a particular consequence of the defendant's wrongdoing is attributable to some independent act or event which supersedes the effect of the tortious conduct, the defendant's responsibilities may not extend to the consequences of the supervening act or event.'

He went on to state that the *novus actus interveniens* 'must constitute an event of such impact that it rightly obliterates the wrongdoing of the defendant.' The reference to an independent act superseding the effect of the tortious conduct must, in my view, relate to an act which was outwith the contemplated scope of events to which the duty of care was directed. Where such a duty is specifically directed at the prevention of the occurrence of a certain event I cannot see how it can be said that the occurrence of that event amounts to an independent act breaking the chain of causation from the breach of duty, even although it may be unusual for one person to come under a duty to prevent another person deliberately inflicting harm on himself. It is the very thing at which the duty was directed...

The individual's right of self determination is irrelevant here for two reasons. In the first place it is not a defence to a breach of duty but rather an argument against the existence of a duty at all. If an individual can do to his own body what he wills, whether by positive act or neglect then there can be no duty on anyone else to prevent his so doing. In this case, however, it is accepted that the commissioner owed a duty of care to the deceased. In the second place the cases in which the principle has been recognised and to which your Lordships have been referred were cases in which prevention of injury to health or death would have involved an unlawful physical invasion of the individual's rights. In this case performance of the duty of care by closing the flap would have involved no invasion of any rights of the deceased...

Lord Hobhouse (dissenting): ... The attribution of human responsibility is often a complex exercise since it involves an examination of the legally relevant features of the consequence in question and the legally relevant features of the conduct complained of (eg *The Empire Jamaica* [1957] AC 386) in conjunction with or in contrast to other human conduct which may also be factually relevant. Legal criteria (maybe fact sensitive) have to be applied. At this level causation is a question of law. Now is not the time to enter upon an exhaustive examination of the legal criteria. For present purposes two categories are directly relevant.

Before examining these two categories, however, I would stress three points. First, a distinction is drawn between natural and human phenomena. Save in theologically inspired language now long discarded, responsibility is not attached to natural events. The only consideration to which they give rise is remoteness. Secondly, human conduct in contrast can have a double relevance, both to remoteness and to attracting legal and moral responsibility. But, for most purposes in the law, and in particular in the law of tort, all a plaintiff need prove is that the defendant's tort was a cause of the loss in respect of which the plaintiff claims. If two or more tortfeasors have each contributed to causing the plaintiff's loss, each of them is severally liable for that loss. Remoteness is, again, the only relevant consideration. Unless the conduct of one tortfeasor has been such as to take the consequence out of the scope of another's tortious duty and render it too remote, the liability of one does not preclude the claim of the plaintiff against each.

Thirdly and most importantly in the present context, there is a radical distinction between the conduct of the plaintiff and the conduct of third parties. To overlook this distinction will inevitably lead to error. At one level where it merely involves some lack of care or breach of duty it reduces but does not negative the plaintiff's right of recovery; this is the position (now) where there is contributory negligence. Failure to mitigate can be similarly analysed (though it can also be analysed pro tanto in terms of remoteness or causation). Where deliberate voluntary conduct of the plaintiff is involved in the knowledge of what the defendant has done, the plaintiff cannot disclaim responsibility for the consequence: he has caused his own loss. His conduct has a different impact to that of a third party...

QUESTION

If the majority had followed the dissenting opinion of Lord Hobhouse, would the police's duty of care towards the prisoner have been empty of content?

NOTE

Reeves can be compared with the next case. And see also pp 336, 365

McWilliams v Sir William Arrol & Co [1962] 1 WLR 295, HL (Scotland)

This was an action for damages by a widow against the employer of her late husband. The House of Lords (Viscount Kilmuir LC, Viscount Simonds and Lords Reid, Morris and Devlin) dismissed the claim.

Lord Devlin: My Lords, the appellant is the widow of a steel erector who was killed by a fall in the course of his employment by the first respondents. She alleges that the employers were in breach of their duty at common law to the deceased in that they failed to provide him with a safety belt, and failed to instruct him to wear it. The courts below have held that the employers were in breach of their duty in failing to provide a safety belt, but that that was not the cause of the deceased's death since he would not have worn it if it had been provided. They have held also that there was no duty on the employers to instruct the deceased to wear it... [Lord Devlin went on to dismiss the appeal.]

Lord Reid: ... If I prove that my breach of duty in no way caused or contributed to the accident I cannot be liable in damages. And if the accident would have happened in just the same way whether or not I fulfilled my duty, it is obvious that my failure to fulfil my duty cannot have caused or contributed to it. No reason has ever been suggested why a defender should be barred from proving that his fault, whether common law negligence or breach of statutory duty, had nothing to do with the accident.

QUESTIONS

1. Did the deceased suffer the loss of a chance not to be killed? If so, what was the cause of the loss of this chance not to be killed? Could one raise a similar question in respect of *Barnett v Chelsea and Kensington Hospital Management Committee* (1969) (read in law report)?

2. Ought the employer to have been under a duty not only to supply safety belts but to ensure they were used? Would *McWilliams* be decided the same way today?

10.3.4 Intervention by nature

Sometimes the intervention is not by human hand but by an 'Act of God' or an 'Act of Nature'.

Carslogie SS Co v Royal Norwegian Government [1952] AC 292, HL

This was an action for damages by one ship owner against another in respect of damage to a ship arising out of a collision caused by the defendants' negligence. After the collision the claimant's ship was temporarily rendered seaworthy in England but she needed longer term repairs in the USA. While crossing the Atlantic for these repairs she encountered heavy weather which rendered her once again unseaworthy. The claim for damages for the loss of use of the ship was unsuccessful in the House of Lords (Viscount Jowitt and Lords Normand, Morton, Tucker and Asquith).

Lord Morton: My Lords, the *Heimgar* was detained in New York for nearly 50 days. At an early stage in the speech of counsel for the appellants, I asked whether it was common ground between the parties that, if the collision between the *Heimgar* and the *Carslogie* had never happened, the *Heimgar* would have been detained in New York for the same period of 50 days. The answer was in the affirmative...

My Lords, I agree with this answer, and if it is the correct answer I can see no ground upon which the respondents can recover the damages which they claim for the detention of their ship. If the *Heimgar* had not encountered heavy weather on her voyage across the Atlantic, I entertain no doubt that the respondents could have recovered damages for her detention in New York for the period of 10 days which would have been required to repair the collision damage. In that event they would have lost the use of their profit-earning chattel for a period of 10 days and the negligence of the appellants would have been the cause of that loss; but in the events which happened the respondents have failed to prove that any loss of the use of their profit-earning chattel resulted from the negligence of the appellants...

NOTES

1. See also *Perfomance Cars v Abrahams* (1961) (read in the law report).

2. These property cases (*Carslogie* and *Performance Cars*) can perhaps be seen as examples of the rule that a defendant must take his victim as he finds him. Normally this rule operates in favour of the claimant and so for example it is no defence that a victim has a particular susceptibility to injury ('egg-shell skull' principle) (see eg *Smith v Leech Brain & Co Ltd* (1962)). Equally an impecunious claimant might be able to claim special damages caused as a result of this impecuniousness (*Lagden v O'Connor*, p 402)). In *Performance Cars* the rule operated in favour of the defendant in the second action: he had damaged an already damaged car and so the first damage absorbed the second so to speak. Yet much depends upon how the issue is framed. By focusing on the respray it is possible to say that this head of damage did not 'exist' when the second accident occurred. But, as we shall see later, if one attempts to extend this principle by analogy to personal injury damage, the courts may not be so generous to defendants because it is not so easy to isolate personal injury damage into discrete heads.

QUESTIONS

1. In *Carslogie*, did the second (weather) damage obliterate the first?

2. What was the nature of the damage in issue in this case: was it physical damage to the ship or economic loss arising out of the loss of use of a profit-earning thing?

3. What if the cause of action is not negligence but a strict liability tort?

Nichols v Marsland (1876) 2 Ex D 1, CA

This was an action for damages, based on Rylands v Fletcher (see p 217), brought by a county surveyor against a landowner in respect of damage to bridges caused by flooding. The defendant kept on her land ornamental pools containing large quantities of water and these pools burst their banks during a period of exceptionally heavy rainfall. The Court of Exchequer gave judgment for the defendant and this decision was confirmed by the Court of Appeal (Mellish and James LJJ, Cockburn CJ and Baggallay JA).

Mellish LJ (delivering judgment of the court): ... Now, with respect to the first question, the ordinary rule of law is that when the law creates a duty and the party is disabled from performing it without any default of his own, by the act of God, or the King's enemies, the law will excuse him; but when a party by his own contract creates a duty, he is bound to make it good notwithstanding any accident by inevitable necessity. We can see no good reason why that rule should not be applied to the case before us. The duty of keeping the water in and preventing its escape is a duty imposed by the law, and not one created by contract. If, indeed, the making a reservoir was a wrongful act in itself, it might be right to hold that a person could not escape from the consequences of his own wrongful act. But it seems to us absurd to hold that the making or the keeping a reservoir is a wrongful act in itself...

It was indeed ingeniously argued for the appellant that at any rate the escape of the water was not owing solely to the act of God, because the weight of the water originally in the reservoirs must have contributed to break down the dams, as well as the extraordinary water brought in by the flood. We think, however, that the extraordinary quantity of water brought in by the flood is in point of law the sole proximate cause of the escape of the water. It is the last drop which makes the cup overflow.

QUESTIONS

1. Why should the public have to shoulder the risk of flooding caused by another landowner's acts of self-indulgence?

2. What does *Nichols* have in common with *Bradford Corp v Pickles* (1895) (p 60)?

10.3.5 Intervention by a rescuer

One particular form of causal intervention that raises a special policy question is where an intervener performs an act of rescue. For example, a passer-by dives into a river in an attempt to rescue the defendant who, through his (or a third party's) negligence, has got himself into difficulties. If the rescuer is injured as a result of the rescue attempt, will the defendant, or his estate, be liable to the claimant or the claimant's dependants? Two possible arguments could be raised to deny liability. It could be argued that the claimant was the cause of his own injury or it could be said that he consented to the risk of injury. Not surprisingly the courts are slow to accept such arguments as the next case indicates.

Haynes v Harwood [1935] 1 KB 146, CA

This was an action for damages by a policeman against the owner of a van and horses whose employee had carelessly left the van unattended in the street. A passing boy threw a stone at the horses and they bolted. The policeman, realising that a woman and some children were in danger, managed to halt the horses but at the cost of personal injury to himself. The trial judge held in favour of the claimant and this decision was upheld by the Court of Appeal (Greer, Maugham and Roche LJJ).

Greer LJ: ... If what is relied upon as novus actus interveniens is the very kind of thing which is likely to happen if the want of care which is alleged takes place, the principle embodied in the maxim is no defence. The whole question is whether or not, to use the words of the leading case, *Hadley v Baxendale*, the accident can be said to be 'the natural and probable result' of the breach of duty. If it is the very thing which ought to be anticipated by a man leaving his horses, or one of the things likely to arise as a consequence of his wrongful act, it is no defence; it is only a step in the way of proving that the damage is the result of the wrongful act.

There can be no doubt in this case that the damage was the result of the wrongful act in the sense of being one of the natural and probable consequences of the wrongful act. It is not necessary to show that this particular accident and this particular damage were probable; it is sufficient if the accident is of a class that might well be anticipated as one of the reasonable and probable results of the wrongful act....

Maugham LJ: ... In deciding whether such a rescuer is justified in putting himself into a position of such great peril, the law has to measure the interests which he sought to protect and the other interests involved. We have all heard of the reasonable man whom the law postulates in certain circumstances; the reasonable man here must be endowed with qualities of energy and courage, and he is not to be deprived of a remedy because he has in a marked degree a desire to save human life when in peril. So regarded, the present plaintiff was not acting unreasonably in the risks he took...

NOTE

Maugham LJ said that one has to balance the various interests in play. This is important in understanding the decision, for the horses were threatening members of the public; thus the *novus actus interveniens* was not just reasonable but admirable. If the horses had bolted into a field and were threatening no one the result might have been different: see *Cutler v United Dairies* (1933).

QUESTION

What if a member of the public, on seeing the horses running amok, had suffered severe psychological damage: could he or she have recovered damages from the defendant? Could he or she recover if the facts occurred today?

10.3.6 Overlapping damage

One of the more general problems that can emerge out of these *novus actus interveniens* cases is that of overlapping damage. D tortiously causes damage to C, but before judgment C suffers further damage which either aggravates the first damage or obliterates it completely. To what extent is D liable for this second damage? Where the damage is property damage two cases are important: *Carslogie SS Co v Royal Norwegian Government* (1952) (p 342) and *Performance Cars v Abrahams* (1961). And these decisions can be compared with art 3:104 of the *Principles of European Tort Law*. But what if the damage is personal injury?

Baker v Willoughby [1970] AC 467, HL

The claimant brought an action for damages against a car driver in respect of a leg injury. After the accident but before the trial the claimant was shot in the injured leg by robbers and as a result the leg had to be amputated. The car driver argued 'that the second injury removed the very limb from which the earlier disability had stemmed, and that therefore no loss suffered thereafter [could] be attributed to the [car driver's] negligence'. In other words 'the second injury submerged or obliterated the effect of the first and that all loss thereafter must be attributed to the second injury' (Lord Reid). The trial judge rejected this argument, but it was accepted by the Court of Appeal. A further appeal to the House of Lords (Lords Reid, Guest, Donovan, Pearson and Viscount Dilhorne) was allowed.

Lord Reid: ... If it were the case that in the eye of the law an effect could only have one cause then the respondent might be right. It is always necessary to prove that any loss for which damages can be given was caused by the defendant's negligent act. But it is a commonplace that the law regards many events as having two causes: that happens whenever there is contributory negligence for then the law says that the injury was caused both by the negligence of the defendant and by the negligence of the plaintiff. And generally it does not matter which negligence occurred first in point of time.

I see no reason why the appellant's present disability cannot be regarded as having two causes ...

We were referred to a number of shipping cases where the question was who must pay for demurrage or loss of profit when a vessel damaged by two mishaps was in dock to have both sets of damage repaired at the same time. It would seem that much depends on which mishap rendered the vessel unseaworthy or no longer a profit-earning machine. I get no help from these cases because liability for personal injury cannot depend on which mishap renders the man 'unseaworthy' or 'not a profit-earning machine.' ...

These cases [including *Performance Cars*] exemplify the general rule that a wrongdoer must take the plaintiff (or his property) as he finds him: that may be to his advantage or disadvantage. In the present case the robber is not responsible or liable for the damage caused by the respondent: he would only have to pay for additional loss to the appellant by reason of his now having an artificial limb instead of a stiff leg...

Lord Pearson: ... I think a solution of the theoretical problem can be found in cases such as this by taking a comprehensive and unitary view of the damage caused by the original accident. Itemisation of the damages by dividing them into heads and sub-heads is often convenient, but is not essential...

QUESTIONS

1. Was it right in *Baker* to make the defendant pay for the lost leg when there exists a state scheme to compensate victims of violent crime (Criminal Injuries Compensation Scheme)?

2. Is *Baker* an example of the application of the theory of concurrent causes as defined in art 3:102 of the *Principles of European Tort Law*? If so, is the next case correct in saying that such a theory is often 'unsatisfactory' (Lord Wilberforce)?

Jobling v Associated Dairies Ltd [1982] AC 794, HL

An employee brought an action for damages against his employer in respect of a back injury suffered at work in 1973 which reduced his earning capacity by 50%. Before the trial, in 1976, the employee contracted a serious disease, quite unconnected with his work accident, which left him totally unfit to work. The House of Lords (Lords Wilberforce, Keith, Bridge, Edmund-Davies and Russell) held that the employer was liable to compensate the employee for reduced earning capacity only for the years between 1973 and 1976.

Lord Wilberforce: ... **1.** Causation arguments. The unsatisfactory character of these is demonstrated by *Baker v Willoughby* [1970] A.C. 467. I think that it can now be seen that Lord Reid's theory of concurrent causes even if workable on the particular facts of *Baker v Willoughby* (where successive injuries were sustained by the same limb) is as a general solution not supported by the authority he invokes (*Harwood v Wyken Colliery Co* [1913] 2 K.B. 158) nor workable in other cases...

In the present, and in other industrial injury cases, there seems to me no justification for disregarding the fact that the injured man's employer is insured – indeed since 1972 compulsorily insured – against liability to his employees. The state has decided, in other words, on a spreading of risk. There seems to me no more justification for disregarding the fact that the plaintiff – presumably, we have not been told otherwise – is entitled to sickness and invalidity benefit in respect of his myelopathy the amount of which may depend on his contribution record, which in turn may have been affected by his accident. So we have no means of knowing whether the plaintiff would be over-compensated if he were, in addition, to receive the assessed damages from his employer, or whether he would be under-compensated if left to his benefit. It is not easy to accept a solution by which a partially incapacitated man becomes worse off in terms of damages and benefit through a greater degree of incapacity. Many other ingredients, of weight in either direction, may enter into individual cases. Without any satisfaction I draw from this the conclusion that no general, logical, or universally fair rules can be stated which will cover, in a manner consistent with justice, cases of supervening events whether due to tortious, partially tortious, non-culpable or wholly accidental events. The courts can only deal with each case as best they can in a manner so as to provide just and sufficient but not excessive compensation, taking all factors into account. I think that this is what *Baker v Willoughby* did – and indeed that Lord Pearson reached his decision in this way: the rationalisation of the decision as to which I at least have doubts, need and should not be applied to other cases. In the present case the Court of Appeal reached the unanswerable conclusion that to apply *Baker v*

▶

Willoughby to the facts of the present case would produce an unjust result, and I am willing to accept the corollary that justice, so far as it can be perceived, lies the other way and that the supervening myelopathy should not be disregarded. If rationalisation is needed, I am willing to accept the 'vicissitudes' argument as the best available. I should be more firmly convinced of the merits of the conclusion if the whole pattern of benefits had been considered, in however general a way. The result of the present case may be lacking in precision and rational justification, but so long as we are content to live in a mansion of so many different architectures, this is inevitable...

QUESTIONS

1. Is this case an example of the application of the causal theory expressed in art 3:106 of the *Principles of European Tort Law*?

2. If the employee had been left totally unfit for work in 1976 as a result of being shot by robbers, would the House of Lords have arrived at the same decision?

NOTE

Performance Cars v Abrahams (1961) has recently not only been confirmed as good authority but also applicable to personal injury cases: *Halsey v Milton Keynes General NHS Trust* (2004). In *Halsey* the Court of Appeal said: 'In the present case, the question is whether the second tortfeasor is responsible for the consequences of the first injury. To that question, the answer can only be: no. It is true that, but for the first accident, the second accident would have caused the same damage as the first accident. But that is irrelevant. Since the claimant had already suffered that damage, the second defendant did not cause it. This is not a case of concurrent torfeasors' (§ 70)

10.3.7 Proof of causation

In order for a tortfeasor to be held liable for a particular type of damage the victim has to prove that the defendant is the actual cause of the actual harm in issue. Sometimes such proof can be difficult either because no definitive causal link can be established as a matter of say medical science or because there may be several possible defendants who might be the cause. For example, just because there is a statistically higher rate of cancer among those living near electric pylons this does not *prove* an actual causal connection between pylons and cancer (see *Guardian*, 3 June 2005, 10). The problem of multiple defendants is illustrated by the next case.

Fairchild v Glenhaven Funeral Services Ltd [2002] 3 WLR 89, HL

This was an action for damages by three appellants suffering from cancer (mesothelioma) as a result of being exposed to asbestos. The appellants had worked for more than one employer each of whom, in breach of a duty of care, had exposed the employees to asbestos; however the appellants could not prove which exposure had actually triggered the cancer and so the Court of Appeal dismissed their claims against all the tortfeasors on the ground of a lack of proof of causation. The House of Lords (Lords Bingham, Nicholls, Hoffmann, Hutton and Rodger) allowed the three appeals.

Lord Bingham: ...9 The issue in these appeals does not concern the general validity and applicability of that requirement, which is not in question, but is whether in special circumstances such as those in these cases there should be any variation or relaxation of it. The overall object of tort law is to define cases in which the law may justly hold one party liable to compensate another. Are these such cases? A and B owed C a duty to protect C against a risk of a particular and very serious kind. They failed to perform that duty. As a result the risk eventuated and C suffered the very harm against which it was the duty of A and B to protect him. Had there been only one tortfeasor, C would have been entitled to recover, but because the duty owed to him was broken by two tortfeasors and not only one, he is held to be entitled to recover against neither, because of his inability to prove what is scientifically unprovable. If the mechanical application of generally accepted rules leads to such a result, there must be room to question the appropriateness of such an approach in such a case...

Policy

33 The present appeals raise an obvious and inescapable clash of policy considerations. On the one hand are the considerations powerfully put by the Court of Appeal ([2002] 1 WLR 1052 at 1080, para 103)... The Court of Appeal had in mind that in each of the cases discussed in paras 14–21 above (*Wardlaw, Nicholson, Gardiner, McGhee*) there was only one employer involved. Thus there was a risk that the defendant might be held liable for acts for which he should not be held legally liable but no risk that he would be held liable for damage which (whether legally liable or not) he had not caused. The crux of cases such as the present, if the appellants' argument is upheld, is that an employer may be held liable for damage he has not caused. The risk is the greater where all the employers potentially liable are not before the court. This is so on the facts of each of the three appeals before the House, and is always likely to be so given the long latency of this condition and the likelihood that some employers potentially liable will have gone out of business or disappeared during that period. It can properly be said to be unjust to impose liability on a party who has not been shown, even on a balance of probabilities, to have caused the damage complained of. On the other hand, there is a strong policy argument in favour of compensating those who have suffered grave harm, at the expense of their employers who owed them a duty to protect them against that very harm and failed to do so, when the harm can only have been caused by breach of that duty and when science does not permit the victim accurately to attribute, as between several employers, the precise responsibility for the harm he has suffered. I am of opinion that such injustice as may be involved in imposing liability on a duty-breaking employer in these circumstances is heavily outweighed by the injustice of denying redress to a victim. Were the law otherwise, an employer exposing his employee to asbestos dust could obtain complete immunity against mesothelioma (but not asbestosis) claims by employing only those who had previously been exposed to excessive quantities of asbestos dust. Such a result would reflect no credit on the law. It seems to me, as it did to Lord Wilberforce in *McGhee* [1973] 1 WLR 1 at 7, that

> 'the employers should be liable for an injury, squarely within the risk which they created and that they, not the pursuer, should suffer the consequence of the

▶

impossibility, foreseeably inherent in the nature of his injury, of segregating the precise consequence of their default.'

Conclusion

34 ... [I]t seems to me just and in accordance with common sense to treat the conduct of A and B in exposing C to a risk to which he should not have been exposed as making a material contribution to the contracting by C of a condition against which it was the duty of A and B to protect him. I consider that this conclusion is fortified by the wider jurisprudence reviewed above. Policy considerations weigh in favour of such a conclusion. It is a conclusion which follows even if either A or B is not before the court. It was not suggested in argument that C's entitlement against either A or B should be for any sum less than the full compensation to which C is entitled, although A and B could of course seek contribution against each other or any other employer liable in respect of the same damage in the ordinary way. No argument on apportionment was addressed to the House... It would be unrealistic to suppose that the principle here affirmed will not over time be the subject of incremental and analogical development. Cases seeking to develop the principle must be decided when and as they arise. For the present, I think it unwise to decide more than is necessary to resolve these three appeals which, for all the foregoing reasons, I concluded should be allowed...

Lord Nicholls: 36 My Lords, I have no hesitation in agreeing with all your Lordships that these appeals should be allowed. Any other outcome would be deeply offensive to instinctive notions of what justice requires and fairness demands. The real difficulty lies in elucidating in sufficiently specific terms the principle being applied in reaching this conclusion. To be acceptable the law must be coherent. It must be principled. The basis on which one case, or one type of case, is distinguished from another should be transparent and capable of identification. When a decision departs from principles normally applied, the basis for doing so must be rational and justifiable if the decision is to avoid the reproach that hard cases make bad law. I turn therefore to consider the departure from the normal, and the basis of that departure, in the present appeals...

Lord Hoffmann: ... **60** The problem in this appeal is to formulate a just and fair rule. Clearly the rule must be based upon principle. However deserving the claimants may be, your Lordships are not exercising a discretion to adapt causal requirements to the individual case. That does not mean, however, that it must be a principle so broad that it takes no account of significant differences which affect whether it is fair and just to impose liability.

61 What are the significant features of the present case? First, we are dealing with a duty specifically intended to protect employees against being unnecessarily exposed to the risk of (among other things) a particular disease. Secondly, the duty is one intended to create a civil right to compensation for injury relevantly connected with its breach. Thirdly, it is established that the greater the exposure to asbestos, the greater the risk of contracting that disease. Fourthly, except in the case in which there has been only one significant exposure to asbestos, medical science cannot prove whose asbestos is more likely than not to have produced the cell mutation which caused the disease. Fifthly, the employee has contracted the disease against which he should have been protected.

62 In these circumstances, a rule requiring proof of a link between the defendant's asbestos and the claimant's disease would, with the arbitrary exception of single-employer cases, empty the duty of content. If liability depends upon proof that the conduct of the defendant was a necessary condition of the injury, it cannot effectively exist. It is however open to your Lordships to formulate a different causal requirement in this class of case. The Court of Appeal was in my opinion wrong to say that in the absence of a proven link between the defendant's asbestos and the disease, there was no 'causative relationship' whatever between the defendant's conduct and the disease. It depends entirely upon the level at which the causal relationship is described. To say, for example, that the cause of Mr Matthews' cancer was his significant exposure to asbestos during two employments over a period of eight years, without being able to identify the day upon which he inhaled the fatal fibre, is a meaningful causal statement. The medical evidence shows that it is the only kind of causal statement about the disease which, in the present state of knowledge, a scientist would regard as possible. There is no a priori reason, no rule of logic, which prevents the law from treating it as sufficient to satisfy the causal requirements of the law of negligence. The question is whether your Lordships think such a rule would be just and reasonable and whether the class of cases to which it applies can be sufficiently clearly defined.

63 So the question of principle is this: in cases which exhibit the five features I have mentioned, which rule would be more in accordance with justice and the policy of common law and statute to protect employees against the risk of contracting asbestos-related diseases? One which makes an employer in breach of his duty liable for the claimant's injury because he created a significant risk to his health, despite the fact that the physical cause of the injury may have been created by someone else? Or a rule which means that unless he was subjected to risk by the breach of duty of a single employer, the employee can never have a remedy? My Lords, as between the employer in breach of duty and the employee who has lost his life in consequence of a period of exposure to risk to which that employer has contributed, I think it would be both inconsistent with the policy of the law imposing the duty and morally wrong for your Lordships to impose causal requirements which exclude liability...

(For further extracts see p 42)

NOTE

This major decision of the House of Lords represents a triumph of justice over cynicism. The decision of the Court of Appeal whereby neither wrongdoer was to be liable because it could not be established which of the two actually caused the fatal illness raised a serious question about the quality of common law decision-making. One might note that in their search for justice the members of the House of Lords did not confine themselves to the common law; the Law Lords asked counsel to look at the civil law systems as well (see above p 42). Most textbooks in England on the law of tort rigidly confine themselves to common law precedents (although there are one or two exceptions); *Fairchild* ought to act as a wake-up call. Knowledge of tort law is no longer confined by European frontiers; indeed, it would seem from Lord Rodger's judgment, that this knowledge is not confined by time-barriers either since he quotes extensively from Roman law. *Fairchild* is truly a leading case and one that will be celebrated by common lawyers and by civilians.

10.3.8 Loss of a chance

Another way of circumventing the difficulty raised in *Fairchild* is to rethink the nature of the damage. Instead of focusing on the physical harm itself one can ask if the tortious behaviour of the defendant deprived the claimant of a chance of not contracting the damage in question. The starting point in English law of a loss of a chance damage is to be found in the contract case of *Chaplin v Hicks* (1911) where the defendant's breach of contract deprived the claimant of a chance of winning a competition. The Court of Appeal confirmed that the loss of a chance to win the beauty contest was a form of damage for which damages could be claimed. One can equally recall the *Spring* case.

Spring v Guardian Assurance plc [1995] 2 AC 296, HL

(See p 257)

Lord Lowry: ... Once the duty of care is held to exist and the defendants' negligence is proved, the plaintiff only has to show that by reason of that negligence he has lost a reasonable chance of employment (which would have to be evaluated) and has thereby sustained loss: *McGregor on Damages*, 14th ed (1980), pp 198–202, paras. 276–278 and *Chaplin v Hicks* [1911] 2 KB 786. He does not have to prove that, but for the negligent reference, Scottish Amicable would have employed him...

QUESTIONS

1. C contracted dermatitis which he believed was caused by the hot and dusty conditions of his workplace. C sues D, his employer, for damages but cannot prove conclusively that his dermatitis was caused by D's workplace conditions. Can C claim, instead, that D's behaviour has deprived C of a chance of being free of dermatitis? (Cf *McGhee v NCB* (1973).)

2. C fell out of a tree and the resulting injury had, at the time of the actual accident, a 75% chance of developing into a permanent disability. The hospital, however, carelessly failed to diagnose the correct problem and proper treatment was delayed increasing the chance of permanent disability to 100%. Can C claim that the negligence of the hospital has deprived him of a 25% chance of recovery from permanent disability? (Cf *Hotson v East Berkshire HA* (1987).)

3. Would your answer to questions 1 and/or 2 immediately above be different after the *Fairchild* case?

Chester v Afshar [2005] 1 AC 134

This was an action for damages by a claimant, who had reluctantly undergone a surgical operation to cure a back pain, against the surgeon in respect of serious neurological damage arising as a result of the operation. The claimant asserted that the surgeon had been negligent in not warning her of the small risk of neurological damage that accompanied such operations. The judge found as a fact that had the claimant been warned of the risk she would not have undergone the operation at the time she did; however he made no finding that she would never have had the operation. A majority of the House of Lords (Lords Steyn, Hope and Walker; Lords Bingham and Hoffmann dissenting) held that the claimant was entitled to damages.

Lord Steyn: ... **16** A surgeon owes a legal duty to a patient to warn him or her in general terms of possible serious risks involved in the procedure. The only qualification is that there may be wholly exceptional cases where objectively in the best interests of the patient the surgeon may be excused from giving a warning. This is, however, irrelevant in the present case. In modern law medical paternalism no longer rules and a patient has a prima facie right to be informed by a surgeon of a small, but well established, risk of serious injury as a result of surgery.

17 Secondly, not all rights are equally important. But a patient's right to an appropriate warning from a surgeon when faced with surgery ought normatively to be regarded as an important right which must be given effective protection whenever possible.

18 Thirdly, in the context of attributing legal responsibility, it is necessary to identify precisely the protected legal interests at stake. A rule requiring a doctor to abstain from performing an operation without the informed consent of a patient serves two purposes. It tends to avoid the occurrence of the particular physical injury the risk of which a patient is not prepared to accept. It also ensures that due respect is given to the autonomy and dignity of each patient. Professor Ronald Dworkin (*Life's Dominion: An Argument about Abortion and Euthanasia*, 1993) explained these concepts at p 224:

> 'The most plausible [account] emphasizes the integrity rather than the welfare of the choosing agent; the value of autonomy, on this view, derives from the capacity it protects: the capacity to express one's own character – values, commitments, convictions, and critical as well as experiential interests – in the life one leads. Recognizing an individual right of autonomy makes self-creation possible. It allows each of us to be responsible for shaping our lives according to our own coherent or incoherent – but, in any case, distinctive – personality. It allows us to lead our lives rather than be led along them, so that each of us can be, to the extent a scheme of rights can make this possible, what we have made of ourselves. We allow someone to choose death over radical amputation or a blood transfusion, if that is his informed wish, because we acknowledge his right to a life structured by his own values.'

19 Fourthly, it is a distinctive feature of the present case that but for the surgeon's negligent failure to warn the claimant of the small risk of serious injury the actual injury would not have occurred when it did and the chance of it occurring on a subsequent occasion was very small. It could therefore be said that the breach of the surgeon resulted in the very injury about which the claimant was entitled to be warned.

20 These factors must be considered in combination. But they must also be weighed against the undesirability of departing from established principles of causation, except for good reasons. The collision of competing ideas poses a difficult question of law...

23 It is true that there is no direct English authority permitting a modification of the approach to the proof of causation in a case such as the present. On the other hand, there is the analogy of *Fairchild v Glenhaven Funeral Services Ltd* [2003] 1 AC 32 which reveals a principled approach to such a problem.... The *Fairchild* case is, of course, very different from the facts of the present case. A modification of causation principles as

▶

was made in *Fairchild* will always be exceptional. But it cannot be restricted to the particular facts of *Fairchild*...

24 Standing back from the detailed arguments, I have come to the conclusion that, as a result of the surgeon's failure to warn the patient, she cannot be said to have given informed consent to the surgery in the full legal sense. Her right of autonomy and dignity can and ought to be vindicated by a narrow and modest departure from traditional causation principles.

25 On a broader basis I am glad to have arrived at the conclusion that the claimant is entitled in law to succeed. This result is in accord with one of the most basic aspirations of the law, namely to right wrongs. Moreover, the decision announced by the House today reflects the reasonable expectations of the public in contemporary society...

Lord Hoffmann (dissenting): ... **31** In my opinion this argument is about as logical as saying that if one had been told, on entering a casino, that the odds on No 7 coming up at roulette were only 1 in 37, one would have gone away and come back next week or gone to a different casino. The question is whether one would have taken the opportunity to avoid or reduce the risk, not whether one would have changed the scenario in some irrelevant detail. The judge found as a fact that the risk would have been precisely the same whether it was done then or later or by that competent surgeon or by another.

32 It follows that the claimant failed to prove that the defendant's breach of duty caused her loss. On ordinary principles of tort law, the defendant is not liable. The remaining question is whether a special rule should be created by which doctors who fail to warn patients of risks should be made insurers against those risks.

33 The argument for such a rule is that it vindicates the patient's right to choose for herself. Even though the failure to warn did not cause the patient any damage, it was an affront to her personality and leaves her feeling aggrieved.

34 I can see that there might be a case for a modest solatium in such cases. But the risks which may eventuate will vary greatly in severity and I think there would be great difficulty in fixing a suitable figure. In any case, the cost of litigation over such cases would make the law of torts an unsuitable vehicle for distributing the modest compensation which might be payable.

35 Nor do I agree with Professor Honoré's moral argument for making the doctor an insurer, namely that his act caused the damage. That argument seems to me to prove both too much and too little. Too much, because it is an argument for making a doctor the insurer of any damage which he causes, whether the patient knew of the risk or not. Too little, because it would excuse the doctor in a case in which he had a duty to warn but the actual operation was perfectly properly performed by someone else, for example, by his registrar...

QUESTION

Is Lord Steyn locating his decision within the law of persons (personality rights) rather than within the law of things (personal injury damage)? Does Lord Hoffmann appear to think this is the case?

NOTE

As Professor Waddams has observed (see above p 257), a differently constituted court may well have reached the opposite decision. This point is well illustrated by the next case.

Gregg v Scott [2005] 2 AC 176

This was an action for damages for negligence brought by a patient against a doctor in respect of the latter's failure to diagnose an under arm lump as cancerous. By the time the patient had received a correct diagnosis, the cancer had spread into his chest leaving him with a poor chance of survival. The patient claimed that had he received the correct diagnosis from the defendant doctor his chance of survival would have been high, whereas it was now below 50%. However, statistical evidence, accepted by the trial judge as fact, indicated that even if he had received the correct diagnosis from the defendant his chance of survival would have been only 42% and, given the relapses he had suffered, his actual chance was only 25%. The trial judge held that although there had been a breach of duty by the defendant doctor, there could be no liability because on the balance of probabilities the claimant would not have survived even if treated promptly. The patient had, in other words, failed to show that he would have been, percentage-wise, in a materially different position from the position he would have been in had the defendant correctly diagnosed the lump. The House of Lords (Lord Hoffmann, Lord Phillips and Baroness Hale; Lords Nicholls and Hope dissenting) upheld this decision.

Lord Nicholls (dissenting): ... **24** Given this uncertainty of outcome, the appropriate characterisation of a patient's loss in this type of case must surely be that it comprises the loss of the chance of a favourable outcome, rather than the loss of the outcome itself. Justice so requires, because this matches medical reality. This recognises what in practice a patient had before the doctor's negligence occurred. It recognises what in practice the patient lost by reason of that negligence. The doctor's negligence diminished the patient's prospects of recovery. And this analysis of a patient's loss accords with the purpose of the legal duty of which the doctor was in breach. In short, the purpose of the duty is to promote the patient's *prospects* of recovery by exercising due skill and care in diagnosing and treating the patient's condition.

25 This approach also achieves a basic objective of the law of tort. The common law imposes duties and seeks to provide appropriate remedies in the event of a breach of duty. If negligent diagnosis or treatment diminishes a patient's prospects of recovery, a law which does not recognise this as a wrong calling for redress would be seriously deficient today. In respect of the doctors' breach of duty the law would not have provided an appropriate remedy. Of course, losing a chance of saving a leg is not the same as losing a leg: see Tony Weir, *Tort Law* (2002), p 76. But that is not a reason for declining to value the chance for whose loss the doctor was directly responsible. The law would rightly be open to reproach were it to provide a remedy if what is lost by a professional adviser's negligence is a financial opportunity or chance but refuse a remedy where what is lost by a doctor's negligence is the chance of health or even life itself. Justice requires that in the latter case as much as the former the loss of a chance should constitute actionable damage...

Lord Hoffmann: ... **90** ... [A] wholesale adoption of possible rather than probable causation as the criterion of liability would be so radical a change in our law as to amount to a legislative act. It would have enormous consequences for insurance companies and the National Health Service. In company with my noble and learned friends Lord Phillips of Worth Matravers and Baroness Hale of Richmond, I think that any such change should be left to Parliament...

Lord Hope (dissenting): ... **117** The key to the decision in this case lies, I think, in the way in which the appellant's cause of action is identified. The description of it as a claim for the loss of a chance is invited by the approach which the pleader has taken to the issue of damages. The description is apt in cases where the claim is for an economic loss or the loss of something to which the claimant has a right, such as in *Chaplin v Hicks* [1911] 2 KB 786 and *Kitchen v Royal Air Force Association* [1958] 1 WLR 563. But that is not what this claim is about. It is, in essence, a claim for the loss and damage caused by the enlargement of the tumour due to the delay in diagnosis. It is for the loss and damage caused, in other words, by a physical injury which the appellant would not have suffered but for the doctor's negligence. The fact that there was a physical injury has been proved on a balance of probabilities. So too has the fact that, in addition to pain and suffering, it caused a reduction in the prospects of a successful outcome. I would hold that, where these factors are present, the way is open for losses which are consequential on the physical injury to be claimed too. I do not think that those consequences of the physical injury should be treated as if they were the product of a separate cause of action from the pain and suffering. I see the reduction in the prospects of a successful outcome as one element among several in the claim for which there is a single cause – the enlargement of the tumour. This was a physical injury, the avoidance or minimisation of which was within the scope of the doctor's duty of care when the appellant consulted him...

Baroness Hale: ... **195** If it is more likely than not that the defendant's carelessness caused me to lose a leg. I do not want my damages reduced to the extent that it is less than 100% certain that it did so. On the other hand, if it is more likely than not that the defendant's carelessness did *not* cause me to lose the leg, then the defendant does not want to have to pay damages for the 20% or 30% chance that it did. A 'more likely than not' approach to causation suits both sides

223 Until now, the gist of the action for personal injuries has been damage to the person. My negligence probably caused the loss of your leg: I pay you the full value of the loss of the leg (say £100,000). My negligence probably did not cause the loss of your leg. I do not pay you anything. Compare the loss of a chance approach: my negligence probably caused a reduction in the chance of your keeping that leg: I pay you the value of the loss of your leg, discounted by the chance that it would have happened anyway. If the chance of saving the leg was very good, say 90%, the claimant still gets only 90% of his damages, say £90,000. But if the chance of saving the leg was comparatively poor, say 20%, the claimant still gets £20,000. So the claimant ends up with less than full compensation even though his chances of a more favourable outcome were good. And the defendant ends up paying substantial sums even though the *outcome* is one for which by definition he cannot be shown to be responsible.

224 Almost any claim for loss of an outcome could be reformulated as a claim for loss of a chance of that outcome. The implications of retaining them both as alternatives would be substantial. That is, the claimant still has the prospect of 100% recovery if he can show that it is more likely than not that the doctor's negligence caused the adverse outcome. But if he cannot show that, he also has the prospect of lesser recovery for loss of a chance. If (for the reasons given earlier) it would in practice always be tempting to conclude that the doctor's negligence had affected his chances to some extent, the claimant would almost always get something. It would be a 'heads you lose everything, tails I win something' situation. But why should the defendant not also be able to redefine the gist of the action if it suits him better?

225 The [claimant] in this case accepts that the proportionate recovery effect must cut both ways. If the claim is characterised as loss of a chance, those with a better than evens chance would still only get a proportion of the full value of their claim. But I do not think that he accepts that the same would apply in cases where the claim is characterised as loss of an outcome. In that case there is no basis for calculating the odds. If the two are alternatives available in every case, the defendant will almost always be liable for something. He will have lost the benefit of the 50% chance that causation cannot be proved. But if the two approaches cannot sensibly live together, the claimants who currently obtain full recovery on an adverse outcome basis might in future only achieve a proportionate recovery. This would surely be a case of two steps forward, three steps back for the great majority of straightforward personal injury cases. In either event, the expert evidence would have to be far more complex than it is at present. Negotiations and trials would be a great deal more difficult. Recovery would be much less predictable both for claimants and for defendants' liability insurers. There is no reason in principle why the change in approach should be limited to medical negligence. Whether or not the policy choice is between retaining the present definition of personal injury in outcome terms and redefining it in loss of opportunity terms, introducing the latter would cause far more problems in the general run of personal injury claims than the policy benefits are worth...

226 Much of the discussion in the cases and literature has centred round cases where the adverse outcome has already happened. The patient has lost his leg. Did the doctor's negligence cause him to lose the leg? If not, did it reduce the chances of saving the leg? But in this case the most serious of the adverse outcomes has not yet happened, and (it is to be hoped) may never happen. The approach to causation should be the same for both past and future events. What, if anything, has the doctor's negligence caused in this case? We certainly do not know whether it has caused this outcome, because happily Mr Gregg has survived each of the significant milestones along the way. Can we even say that it reduced the chances of a successful outcome, given that Mr Gregg has turned out to be one of the successful minority at each milestone? This is quite different from the situation in *Hotson*, where the avascular necrosis had already happened, or in *Rufo v Hosking*, where the fractures had already happened. Mr Gregg faced a risk of an adverse outcome which happily has not so far materialised, serious though the effects of his illness, treatment and prognosis have been. The complexities of attempting to introduce liability for the loss of a chance of a more favourable outcome in personal injury claims have driven me, not without regret, to conclude that it should not be done...

QUESTIONS

1. A claimant must prove his case on a balance of probabilities. Can this balance truly be reduced to a mathematical model or is this recourse to percentage numbers just a form of rhetoric?

2. What is the present status of loss of a chance in personal injury cases in general? Is the 'principle' in *Gregg v Scott* to be limited to medical negligence cases?

3. How would you characterise the reasoning in *Gregg*: (a) causal (mathematical); (b) functional (policy); (c) interpretative (meaning of 'loss'); or (d) bits of all three?

10.4 Remoteness of damage

Even if cause and connection can be established, as a question of fact, between tortious act and damage a claimant can still fail if the court decides, as a question of law, that the damage is too remote. One of the main questions that have preoccupied the courts is the appropriate rule or test to be applied.

10.4.1 Directness test

The test established in the nineteenth century was one of directness. Once the defendant had been found to have committed a tort he was to be liable for all the damage directly flowing from the wrong. This test was confirmed in the case set out below.

In re Polemis and Furness, Withy & Co [1921] 3 KB 560, CA

Bankes LJ: By a time charterparty dated February 21, 1917, the respondents chartered their vessel to the appellants. Clause 21 of the charterparty was in these terms. [The Lord Justice read it.] The vessel was employed by the charterers to carry a cargo to Casablanca in Morocco. The cargo included a quantity of benzine or petrol in cases. While discharging at Casablanca a heavy plank fell into the hold in which the petrol was stowed, and caused an explosion, which set fire to the vessel and completely destroyed her. The owners claimed the value of the vessel from the charterers, alleging that the loss of the vessel was due to the negligence of the charterers' servants. The charterers contended that they were protected by the exception of fire contained in clause 21 of the charterparty, and they also contended that the damages claimed were too remote... To speak of 'probable' consequence is to throw everything upon the jury. It is tautologous to speak of 'effective' cause or to say that damages too remote from the cause are irrecoverable, for an effective cause is simply that which causes, and in law what is ineffective or too remote is not a cause at all. I still venture to think that direct cause is the best expression. Proximate cause has acquired a special connotation through its use in reference to contracts of insurance. Direct cause excludes what is indirect, conveys the essential distinction, which causa causans and causa sine qua non rather cumbrously indicate, and is consistent with the possibility of the concurrence of more direct causes than one, operating at the same time and leading to a common result...

In the present case the arbitrators have found as a fact that the falling of the plank was due to the negligence of the defendants' servants. The fire appears to me to have been directly caused by the falling of the plank. Under these circumstances I consider that it is immaterial that the causing of the spark by the falling of the plank could not have been reasonably anticipated... Given the breach of duty which constitutes the negligence, and given the damage as a direct result of that negligence, the anticipations of the person whose negligent act has produced the damage appear to me to be irrelevant. I consider that the damages claimed are not too remote...

Warrington LJ: ... The result may be summarised as follows: The presence or absence of reasonable anticipation of damage determines the legal quality of the act as negligent or innocent. If it be thus determined to be negligent, then the question whether particular damages are recoverable depends only on the answer to the question whether they are the direct consequence of the act. Sufficient authority for the proposition is afforded by *Smith v London and South Western Ry Co*...

Scrutton LJ: ... To determine whether an act is negligent, it is relevant to determine whether any reasonable person would foresee that the act would cause damage; if he would not, the act is not negligent. But if the act would or might probably cause damage, the fact that the damage it in fact causes is not the exact kind of damage one would expect is immaterial, so long as the damage is in fact directly traceable to the negligent act, and not due to the operation of independent causes having no connection with the negligent act, except that they could not avoid its results. Once the act is negligent, the fact that its exact operation was not foreseen is immaterial...

NOTE

The method adopted by the judges in this case was to focus exclusively on the connection between act and damage. Once it was judged that the act (letting fall the plank) was careless, foresight was no longer relevant. Legal causation was closely intertwined with factual causation.

QUESTION

D moves C's bicycle without C's permission so that D can park his own bike in the space where C's bike was parked. In its new position, under a large tree, C's bike is destroyed when the tree is struck by lightning. Is D liable to C for the full value of the bicycle?

10.4.2 Foreseeability text

The directness test came in for criticism and in 1961 it was rejected by the Privy Council.

Overseas Tankship (UK) Ltd v Morts Dock & Engineering Co (The Wagon Mound No 1) [1961] AC 388, PC

This was an action for damages by the owners of a wharf against the charterers of a ship from which oil had carelessly been discharged while the ship was in Sydney harbour. The oil had spread to the claimants' wharf and they halted their welding operations until assured by expert scientific opinion that oil on water would not ignite. Subsequently, when a spark from the claimants' welding fell on to a piece of floating rag, the oil did ignite and their wharf was destroyed in the ensuing fire. The Australian courts held that the destruction of the wharf was the direct but unforeseeable consequence of the spilling of the oil; they held the charterers were liable. The charterers' appeal to the Privy Council (Lords Reid, Radcliffe, Tucker, Morris and Viscount Simonds) was allowed.

▶

Viscount Simonds: ... Enough has been said to show that the authority of *Polemis* has been severely shaken though lip-service has from time to time been paid to it. In their Lordships' opinion it should no longer be regarded as good law. It is not probable that many cases will for that reason have a different result, though it is hoped that the law will be thereby simplified, and that in some cases, at least, palpable injustice will be avoided. For it does not seem consonant with current ideas of justice or morality that for an act of negligence, however slight or venial, which results in some trivial foreseeable damage the actor should be liable for all consequences however unforeseeable and however grave, so long as they can be said to be 'direct.' It is a principle of civil liability, subject only to qualifications which have no present relevance, that a man must be considered to be responsible for the probable consequences of his act. To demand more of him is too harsh a rule, to demand less is to ignore that civilised order requires the observance of a minimum standard of behaviour...

Their Lordships conclude this part of the case with some general observations. They have been concerned primarily to displace the proposition that unforeseeability is irrelevant if damage is 'direct.' In doing so they have inevitably insisted that the essential factor in determining liability is whether the damage is of such a kind as the reasonable man should have foreseen. This accords with the general view thus stated by Lord Atkin in *Donoghue v Stevenson*: 'The liability for negligence, whether you style it such or treat it as in other systems as a species of "culpa," is no doubt based upon a general public sentiment of moral wrongdoing for which the offender must pay.' It is a departure from this sovereign principle if liability is made to depend solely on the damage being the 'direct' or 'natural' consequence of the precedent act. Who knows or can be assumed to know all the processes of nature? But if it would be wrong that a man should be held liable for damage unpredictable by a reasonable man because it was 'direct' or 'natural,' equally it would be wrong that he should escape liability, however 'indirect' the damage, if he foresaw or could reasonably foresee the intervening events which led to its being done: cf *Woods v Duncan*. Thus foreseeability becomes the effective test. In reasserting this principle their Lordships conceive that they do not depart from, but follow and develop, the law of negligence as laid down by Baron Alderson in *Blyth v Birmingham Waterworks Co*...

NOTE

It has been said that the change of test from directness to foreseeability was more a change of name than a change of substance. But this is not strictly accurate. The change is one of method in that the focus is no longer on the *connection* between act and damage but on the *actor* as a 'reasonable man'. This is quite a different focal point giving rise to quite a different way of envisaging a factual situation (actional rather than causal). A 'reasonable man' is in effect now allowed to behave carelessly provided that his wrongful act does not give rise to any damage that a reasonable man might foresee. The problem of course is that the reasonable man ought not to indulge in careless behaviour in the first place (a point that seemed rather obvious to the judges in *Re Polemis* (1921)).

QUESTIONS

1. Does the foreseeability test apply only to the tort of negligence?

2. In a subsequent claim arising out of the same fire which destroyed the wharf in *The Wagon Mound* (No 1), owners of ships moored alongside the wharf also sought damages from the same defendants. Do you think this claim equally failed? If not, why not? (Cf *The Wagon Mound* (No 2).)

10.4.3 Personal injury and foreseeability

The test of foreseeability was, almost immediately, to give rise to new arguments for escaping from liability. Sometimes these worked, but sometimes they were unsuccessful as the next case indicates. The rule that a tortfeasor must 'take his victim as he finds him' appeared not to have been suppressed by the foreseeability test.

Robinson v Post Office [1974] 1 WLR 1176, CA

This was an action for damages by an employee, who cut his knee when he slipped off an oily ladder, against his employer. The employee went to the doctor who administered an anti-tetanus injection but who carelessly failed to give a test dose; the employee was allergic to the serum and contracted encephalitis which left him partially handicapped. The employer admitted negligence but claimed they were not liable for the encephalitis. The Court of Appeal (Davies, Buckley and Orr LJJ) held that they were liable for the full damage.

Orr LJ: ... Mr Newey's main argument, however, was that the onset of encephalitis was not reasonably foreseeable and that on the basis of the decision of the Privy Council in *Overseas Tankship (UK) Ltd v Morts Dock and Engineering Co Ltd (The Wagon Mound)* [1961] AC 388, the Post Office should not be held liable for that consequence of the injury. In answer to this argument the plaintiff relied on the judgment of Lord Parker CJ in *Smith v Leech Brain & Co Ltd* [1962] 2 QB 405. In that case an employee already suffering from premalignant changes had, as a result of his employers' negligence, sustained a burn which the judge found to have been the promoting agent in the development of cancer from which the employee died, and in a fatal accident claim by his widow it was argued for the defendant employers that the development of cancer was unforeseeable and that on the basis of *The Wagon Mound* decision the claim should be dismissed. Lord Parker CJ, however, rejected this argument [on the basis that it 'has always been the law of this country that a tortfeasor takes his victim as he finds him']...

In the present case the judge held that it was plainly foreseeable (1) that if oil was negligently allowed to escape on to a ladder a workman was likely to slip and sustain the type of wound in question; and (2) that such injury might well require medical treatment; and on this basis alone he was prepared to hold the defendants liable for the encephalitis; but he held in addition that, having regard to the nature of the plaintiff's work and the area in which he was working, it was also foreseeable that some form of anti-tetanus prophylactic would be deemed necessary. In the result he concluded that every relevant matter was foreseeable except the terrible extent of the injury which was due to the plaintiff's allergy to a second dose of ATS, in which respect the Post Office must take their victim as they found him...

... In our judgment, however, there was no missing link and the case is governed by the principle that the Post Office had to take their victim as they found him, in this case with an allergy to a second dose of ATS...

▶

10.4.4 Typical damage

Nevertheless the foreseeability rule was at first to prove effective when it came to the type of damage suffered. Thus in one case the defendant negligently allowed his farm to become infested with rats with the result that an employee suffered what was then a very rare illness, namely Weil's disease contracted from rats' urine. Had the employee suffered illness from a rat's bite there would have been no problem with respect to liability, but the trial judge held the farmer not liable since Weil's disease was unforeseeable (*Tremain v Pike* (1969)). In other words 'untypical damage' (Weir) may be unforeseeable. Much of course depends upon the question posed. Does one have to foresee the actual species of damage which occurs or is foreseeability of the genus of damage enough? This question may now have been settled by the next case.

Jolley v Sutton London Borough Council [2000] 1 WLR 1082, HL

This was an action for damages for personal injury against a local authority for negligence and for breach of the Occupiers' Liability Act 1957. The Court of Appeal held that the authority was not liable, but this decision was overturned by the House of Lords (Lords Browne-Wilkinson, Mackay, Steyn, Hoffmann and Hobhouse).

Lord Steyn: My Lords, on 8 April 1990, in the grounds of a block of council flats owned and occupied by the London Borough of Sutton, Justin Jolley, then a schoolboy aged 14, sustained serious spinal injuries in an accident. It arose when a small abandoned cabin cruiser, which had been left lying in the grounds of the block of flats, fell on Justin as he lay underneath it while attempting to repair and paint it. As a result he is now a paraplegic. He claimed damages in tort from the council. At trial the claim was primarily based on a breach of the Occupiers' Liability Acts 1957 and 1984. After a seven day trial in 1998 Mr Geoffrey Brice QC, a Deputy High Court Judge, gave judgment for Justin but reduced the damages by 25 per cent by virtue of a finding of contributory negligence. The judge awarded damages in the sum of £621,710, together with interest: *Jolley v London Borough of Sutton* [1998] 1 Lloyds' Rep. 433. The council appealed. The Court of Appeal unanimously reversed the judge's conclusions on the merits and entered judgment for the council: *Jolley v Sutton LBC* [1998] 1 WLR 1546...

The law

Very little needs to be said about the law. The decision in this case has turned on the detailed findings of fact at first instance on the particular circumstances of this case. Two general observations are, however, appropriate. First, in this corner of the law the results of decided cases are inevitably very fact-sensitive. Both counsel nevertheless at times invited your Lordships to compare the facts of the present case with the facts of other decided cases. That is a sterile exercise. Precedent is a valuable stabilising influence in our legal system. But, comparing the facts of and outcomes of cases in this branch of the law is a misuse of the only proper use of precedent, viz to identify the relevant rule to apply to the facts as found.

Secondly, Lord Woolf MR made an observation casting doubt on part of Lord Reid's speech in *Hughes v Lord Advocate* [1963] AC 837. The defendants left a manhole uncovered and protected only by a tent and paraffin lamp. A child climbed down the hole. When he came out he kicked over one of the lamps. It fell into the hole and caused an explosion. The child was burned. The Court of Session held that there was no liability. The House of Lords reversed the decision of the Court of Session...

Lord Woolf MR observed that he had difficulty in reconciling... remarks [made by Lord Reid in Hughes] with the approach in *The Wagon Mound (No 1)* [1961] AC 388. It is true that in *The Wagon Mound (No 1)* Viscount Simonds at one stage observed, at p. 425E:

> 'If, as admittedly it is, B's liability (culpability) depends on the reasonable foreseeability of the consequent damage, how is that to be determined except by the foreseeability of the damage which in fact happened – the damage in suit?'

But this is to take one sentence in the judgment in *The Wagon Mound (No 1)* out of context. Viscount Simonds was in no way suggesting that the precise manner of which the injury occurred nor its extent had to be foreseeable. And Lord Reid was saying no more. The speech of Lord Reid in *Hughes v Lord Advocate* [1963] AC 837 is in harmony with the other judgments. It is not in conflict with *The Wagon Mound (No 1)*. The scope of the two modifiers – the precise manner in which the injury came about and its extent – is not definitively answered by either *The Wagon Mound (No 1)* or *Hughes v Lord Advocate*. It requires determination in the context of an intense focus on the circumstances of each case: see John Fleming, *The Law of Torts*, 9th ed, (1998), pp. 240–243.

Conclusion

My Lords, I would restore the wise decision of Mr Geoffrey Brice QC, the Deputy High Court judge. I would allow the appeal. I would further remit the case to the Court of Appeal to enable it to consider what course it should adopt on any application in regard to the determination of any issue relating to quantum of damages.

Lord Hoffmann: ... It is... agreed that what must have been foreseen is not the precise injury which occurred but injury of a given description. The foreseeability is not as to the particulars but the genus. And the description is formulated by reference to the nature of the risk which ought to have been foreseen. So, in *Hughes v Lord Advocate* [1963] AC 837 the foreseeable risk was that a child would be injured by falling in the hole or being burned by a lamp or by a combination of both. The House of Lords decided that the injury which actually materialised fell within this description, notwithstanding that it involved an unanticipated explosion of the lamp and consequent injuries of unexpected severity...

I think that in a case like this, analogies from other imaginary facts are seldom helpful. Likewise analogies from real facts in other cases: I entirely agree with my noble and learned friend Lord Steyn in deploring the citation of cases which do nothing to illuminate any principle but are said to constitute analogous facts. In the present case, the rotten condition of the boat had a significance beyond the particular danger it created. It proclaimed the boat and its trailer as abandoned, res nullius, there for the taking, to make of them whatever use the rich fantasy life of children might suggest...

QUESTIONS

1. If Lord Hoffmann is right (genus and not species), does this mean that the decision in the Weil's disease case (*Tremain v Pike* (1969)) must now be in question?

2. Does *Jolley* go some way in resurrecting the directness test?

3. Is it really possible, in a case like *Jolley*, for counsel not to draw analogies with the facts of previous cases? How else do you argue the case in a precedent-based system given that the ratio decidendi always includes the material facts of the precedent?

4. In *Morris v Network Rail* (2004) Buxton LJ asserted 'no more in nuisance than in negligence is it possible to base a claim on liability in the air, in the sense that the defendant is liable for conduct, or for a state of affairs, just because it will foreseeably cause some harm to some person. What must be foreseen is relevant damage to this plaintiff or to a category of persons into which he falls, a requirement that subsumes the tests both of duty in fact and of remoteness of damage' (§ 34). Does this statement actually accord with Lord Hoffmann's view in *Jolley*? What does Buxton LJ mean when he says that foreseeability subsumes the tests of duty in fact and of remoteness?

10.5 Damages

The final level at which causation can operate is the level of the remedy of damages. The details of this remedy will be pursued in the next chapter, but there are several rules which might usefully be discussed under the general heading of causation. These rules are contributory negligence, mitigation and remoteness of a particular head of damage.

10.5.1 Contributory negligence

Contributory negligence was once a question of factual causation: if the claimant was guilty of contributing by his own negligence to his damage this would amount to a complete *novus actus interveniens* isolating the defendant from liability (cf *McWilliams v Sir William Arrol & Co* (1962), p 342). This position was considered unjust and was alleviated by statutory intervention. The effect of this statute was to move contributory negligence from the level of factual causation to the level of damages. Contributory negligence is, on the whole, no longer a matter of liability but an issue of the amount of damages payable.

Law Reform (Contributory Negligence) Act 1945 (8 & 9 Geo VI, c 28)

1   Apportionment of liability in case of contributory negligence.

(1) Where any person suffers damage as the result partly of his own fault and partly of the fault of any other person or persons, a claim in respect of that damage shall not be defeated by reason of the fault of the person suffering the damage, but the damages recoverable in respect thereof shall be reduced to such extent as the court thinks just and equitable having regard to the claimant's share in the responsibility of the damage...

4   Interpretation.

...

'damage' includes loss of life and personal injury ...

'fault' means negligence, breach of statutory duty or other act or omission which gives rise to liability in tort or would, apart from this Act, give rise to the defence of contributory negligence.

NOTE

One of the questions that plagued the courts is whether the Act applies to breaches of contract. The next extract, in addition to giving a brief background to the 1945 Act, concludes that it does not, unless the facts also disclose a tort.

Barclays Bank plc v Fairclough Building Ltd [1995] QB 214, CA

Beldam LJ: ... The common law rule that in an action in tort a plaintiff whose own fault contributed with the defendant's to cause his damage could recover nothing was perceived to be unfair and, as a result of the Law Revision Committee's Eighth Report (Contributory Negligence) (1939) (Cmnd 6032), the Law Reform (Contributory Negligence) Act 1945 was passed. Its purpose was to enable a court in actions of tort to apportion responsibility for the damage suffered by the plaintiff where there had been fault by both parties...

In my judgment... in the present state of the law contributory negligence is not a defence to a claim for damages founded on breach of a strict contractual obligation. I do not believe the wording of the Law Reform (Contributory Negligence) Act 1945 can reasonably sustain an argument to the contrary. Even if it did, in the present case the nature of the contract and the obligation undertaken by the skilled contractor did not impose on the plaintiff any duty in its own interest to prevent the defendant from committing the breaches of contract. To hold otherwise would, I consider, be equivalent to implying into the contract an obligation on the part of the plaintiff inconsistent with the express terms agreed by the parties. The contract clearly laid down the extent of the obligations of the plaintiff as architect and of the defendant. It was the defendant who was to provide appropriate supervision on site, not the architect...

NOTE

The word 'fault' has also given rise to difficulties where the act of the claimant was intentional rather than careless.

Reeves v Commissioner of Police for the Metropolis [2000] 1 AC 360, HL

(For facts see p 340)

Lord Jauncey: ... Mr Blake QC for the plaintiff submitted that the act of suicide could not amount to contributory negligence on the part of the deceased inasmuch as it did not amount to fault by him within the meaning of section 4 of the Law Reform (Contributory Negligence) Act 1945. Section 1(1) of that Act provides that where A suffers damage 'as the result partly of his own fault and partly of the fault' of B, the damages recoverable may be reduced 'having regard to the claimant's share in the responsibility for the damage.' Fault is defined in section 4 as meaning 'negligence, breach of statutory duty or other act or omission which gives rise to a liability in tort or would, apart from this Act, give rise to the defence of contributory negligence.' Mr Blake contended that since an act which was intentional not only as to its performance but also as to its consequences would not have amounted to contributory negligence at

▶

common law it followed that the deceased's act of suicide was not 'fault' within the meaning of section 4...

My Lords, no United Kingdom authority has been cited in support of Mr Blake's contention so far as the period before 1945 is concerned. This is perhaps not altogether surprising in view of the fact that the effect of contributory negligence at that time was identical to that of the defence of *volenti non fit injuria*. The authorities from New Zealand and the United States do not suggest that an act intentional both as to performance and consequences can never amount to contributory negligence. If the law is to retain the respect of the public it should where possible walk hand in hand with common sense. There are, of course, occasions where legislation both domestic and European appear to make this impossible but where there is no such legislative inhibition the law should be interpreted and applied so far as possible to produce a result which accords with common sense. To take an example A working beside a tank of boiling liquid which is inadequately guarded negligently allows his hand to come in contact with the liquid and suffers damage; B for a dare plunges his hand into the same liquid to see how long he can stand the heat. It would be bordering on the absurd if A's entitlement to damages were reduced but B could recover in full for his own folly. B's responsibility for the damage which he suffered is undeniable. I see no reason to construe section 4 of the Act of 1945 to produce such a result and I agree with the Lord Chief Justice that the word 'fault' in that section is wide enough to cover acts deliberate as to both performance and consequences. An individual of sound mind is no less responsible for such acts than he is for negligent acts and it is his share of responsibility for the damage which reduces the damages recoverable.

In this case the open flap was not a danger to an occupant of the cell acting normally with reasonable regard for his own safety. It only became a danger when it was deliberately used by the deceased as part of the mechanism whereby he strangled himself. The act of the deceased was accordingly a substantial cause of his own demise and any damages recoverable by the plaintiff should be reduced to reflect this.

Were I sitting alone I would have apportioned the blame as to one third to the commissioner and as to two thirds to the deceased. However, I understand that the majority of your Lordships favour a 50/50 division of responsibility and I do not feel inclined to dissent from that view.

In all the circumstances I would allow the appeal and make the same order as that proposed by my noble and learned friend Lord Hoffmann.

QUESTION

Does contributory negligence mean that a person owes a duty of care to him or herself? Or is it a duty owed to others? (Cf *Froom v Butcher* (1976).)

10.5.2 Mitigation of damage

The principle of mitigation of damage is explained in the next short extract.

Thomas v Countryside Council for Wales [1994] 4 All ER 853, QBD

Rougier J: ... Under the normal law of contract and tort the fundamental basis for the measure of damages is compensation for pecuniary loss which directly and naturally flows from the breach ... There is, however, a qualification that a plaintiff suing for breach of contract or, for that matter, for tort cannot call upon a defendant to pay the full direct consequences unless he himself has acted reasonably to mitigate the loss. It is sometimes loosely described as a plaintiff's duty to mitigate...

If he wishes to claim the full measure of his loss, a plaintiff must act reasonably, but, as was recently pointed out in ... *The Solholt* ... a plaintiff is under no duty to mitigate his loss. He is completely free to act as he judges to be in his best interests. The significance of his failure to act in a reasonable manner is merely that he cannot then call upon the defendant to pay for losses which he might have avoided had he taken reasonable steps to do so...

NOTE

The idea that mitigation is no longer a question of 'duty' is valuable to the extent that it re-emphasises the causation aspect. Nevertheless to redefine it terms of an interest does nothing to change the normative aspect of the mitigation rule. A claimant who wishes to be compensated for losses 'has to' behave not just reasonably but, according to the next case, as the 'reasonable businessman'.

Darbishire v Warran [1963] 1 WLR 1067, CA

The claimant brought an action for damages against another driver who had negligently caused serious damage to his Lea Francis shooting brake. The county court judge had assessed the value of the shooting brake at £80, but had allowed the claimant to recover damages of £180 because the claimant had had the shooting brake repaired at this cost. The defendant did not contest liability but argued that the claimant should be allowed to recover only the £80 (adjusted to £85) and not the £180. The Court of Appeal (Harman and Pearson LJJ and Pennycuick J) held that the claimant was not entitled to the cost of repairing the shooting brake.

Pearson LJ: ... For the purposes of the present case it is important to appreciate the true nature of the so-called 'duty to mitigate the loss' or 'duty to minimise the damage.' The plaintiff is not under any actual obligation to adopt the cheaper method: if he wishes to adopt the more expensive method, he is at liberty to do so and by doing so he commits no wrong against the defendant or anyone else. The true meaning is that the plaintiff is not entitled to charge the defendant by way of damages with any greater sum than that which he reasonably needs to expend for the purpose of making good the loss. In short, he is fully entitled to be as extravagant as he pleases but not at the expense of the defendant...

In my view it is impossible to find from the evidence that the plaintiff took all reasonable steps to mitigate the loss, or did all that he reasonably could do to keep down the cost. He was fully entitled to have his damaged vehicle repaired at whatever cost because he

▶

preferred it. But he was not justified in charging against the defendant the cost of repairing the damaged vehicle when that cost was more than twice the replacement market value and he had made no attempt to find a replacement vehicle...

...It is vital, for the purpose of assessing damages fairly between the plaintiff and the defendant, to consider whether the plaintiff's course of action was economic or uneconomic, and if it was uneconomic it cannot (at any rate in the absence of special circumstances, of which there is no evidence in this case) form a proper basis for assessment of damages. The question has to be considered from the point of view of a business man. It seems to me the practical business view is that if the cost of repairing your damaged vehicle is greatly in excess of the market price, you must look around for a replacement and you would expect to find one at a cost not far removed from the market price, although unless you were lucky you might have to pay something more than the standard market price to obtain a true equivalent of a well-maintained and reliable vehicle.

QUESTION

Will the reasonable business man test apply to all types of property damage?

Chapter 11

Remedies

The Roman jurist Gaius, writing in the second century AD, stated that all law is about persons (*persona*), things (*res*) and actions (*actiones*). The last category got lost from civilian private law in the sixteenth century thanks to the French humanist jurists who replaced 'actions' with 'obligations'. The modern structure of civilian private law thus consists of the law of persons, the law of property and the law of obligations. However 'actions', or remedies, has not completely disappeared from English liability law. Of course the English forms of actions – trespass, debt, case etc – were a very different set of remedies from the Roman *actiones*, just as Chancery's remedies of injunction, specific performance, rescission etc, were only partly shaped by Roman thinking.

Remedies thinking remains vibrant, and useful, in the common law for several reasons. First, because the forms of action approach – that is to say thinking in terms of lists of categories of liability – never completely disappeared from the law of torts even after the abolition of the forms of action (see eg *Esso v Southport* (1956), p 4). Secondly, because both common law remedies (debt and damages) and equitable remedies (injunction etc) still act as institutional focal points for their own specific rules. There are thus textbooks devoted to damages, injunctions and specific performance.

A third reason why the remedy or *actio* remains active is that it is still a most useful perspective from which to view liability. This is particularly true when third parties are affected by a tortfeasor's infliction of damage on a victim. When a negligent car driver or employer carelessly kills or injures the father of a family, do the other family members have an action against the tortfeasor? Does a child in the womb have an action against a tortfeasor who injures the mother? These questions can, of course, be seen in terms of substantive liability; yet starting out from the availability of an action is often most helpful in terms of a structural analysis.

11.1 Actions and remedies

Remedies are thus important in that they act as a focal point for some fundamental practical questions. Who can bring an action and for what?

11.1.1 Types of remedies

As far as the tort lawyer is concerned, remedies can usefully be classified into three main groups: there are (a) monetary remedies; (b) non-monetary remedies; and (c) self-help remedies. Very broadly the monetary and non-monetary remedies reflect the difference between common law and equity; however the symmetry is not perfect. There are some equitable monetary remedies and the common law has long been prepared to order repossession of land.

Manchester Airport plc v Dutton [2000] 1 QB 133, CA

Laws LJ: I gratefully adopt the account of the facts set out in the judgment of Chadwick LJ. As there appears, the defendants or others (to whom I will compendiously refer as 'the trespassers') entered Arthur's Wood and set up their encampments before the grant of the licence by the National Trust to the airport company. Moreover it appears (and I will assume it for the purpose of the appeal) that the airport company has not to date gone into occupation of the land under the licence.

In those circumstances, the question which falls for determination is whether the airport company, being a licensee which is not de facto in occupation or possession of the land, may maintain proceedings to evict the trespassers by way of an order for possession...

In my judgment the true principle is that a licensee not in occupation may claim possession against a trespasser if that is a necessary remedy to vindicate and give effect to such rights of occupation as by contract with his licensor he enjoys. This is the same principle as allows a licensee who is in de facto possession to evict a trespasser. There is no respectable distinction, in law or logic, between the two situations. An estate owner may seek an order whether he is in possession or not. So, in my judgment, may a licensee, if other things are equal. In both cases, the plaintiff's remedy is strictly limited to what is required to make good his legal right. The principle applies although the licensee has no right to exclude the licensor himself. Elementarily he cannot exclude any occupier who, by contract or estate, has a claim to possession equal or superior to his own. Obviously, however, that will not avail a bare trespasser.

In this whole debate, as regards the law of remedies in the end I see no significance as a matter of principle in any distinction drawn between a plaintiff whose right to occupy the land in question arises from title and one whose right arises only from contract. In every case the question must be, what is the reach of the right, and whether it is shown that the defendant's acts violate its enjoyment. If they do, and (as here) an order for possession is the only practical remedy, the remedy should be granted. Otherwise the law is powerless to correct a proved or admitted wrongdoing; and that would be unjust and disreputable. The underlying principle is in the Latin maxim (for which I make no apology), 'ubi jus, ibi sit remedium.'...

For all the reasons I have given, I would dismiss this appeal.

Kennedy LJ: delivered a judgment dismissing the appeal.

Chadwick LJ (dissenting): ... It has long been understood that a licensee who is not in exclusive occupation does not have title to bring an action for ejectment. The position of a non-exclusive occupier was explained by Blackburn J. in *Allan v Liverpool Overseers* (1874) LR 9 QB 180, 191-192, in a passage cited by Davies LJ in this court in *Appah v Parncliffe Investments Ltd* [1964] 1 WLR 1064, 1069–1070 and by Lord Templeman in the House of Lords in *Street v Mountford* [1985] AC 809, 818...

That passage, as it seems to me, provides clear authority for the proposition that an action for ejectment – the forerunner of the present action for recovery of land – as well as an action for trespass can only be brought by a person who is in possession or who has a right to be in possession. Further, that possession is synonymous, in this context, with exclusive occupation – that is to say occupation (or a right to occupy) to the exclusion of all others, including the owner or other person with superior title (save in so far as he has reserved a right to enter)...

I would have allowed this appeal.

NOTE

This case is of interest because it raises a distinction that was fundamental to Roman law, namely the distinction between an *actio in rem* and an *actio in personam*. The former was a claim against a thing and was brought to enforce a property right while the latter was against another person and gave expression to liability in the law of obligations. The Romans, and indeed modern civil lawyers, kept the two types of claim strictly separate; English law, in contrast, seems to allow the two to become intermixed which in turn causes conceptual difficulties when it comes to trying to isolate an English 'law of obligations' (dealing strictly with personal rights). The claimant was asserting a contractual right (*ius in personam*), yet he was effectively allowed to succeed in an *actio in rem*. In order to be able to assert a *ius in rem*, he would, as Chadwick LJ pointed out, have to show that he was in possession (ie he had a real right or interest in the land) (see also P Cane, *The Anatomy of Tort Law* (Hart, 1997), 75).

QUESTION

Could the claimant in *Manchester* have sued for damages? If so, what would be the basis of his claim?

11.1.2 Legal subject (*persona*) and remedy (*actio*)

When one focuses on the remedy (*actio*) it leads one to think about which persons (*personae*) are entitled to sue. Normally it is people who sue, but what if such people are either dead or unborn?

Law Reform (Miscellaneous Provisions) Act 1934 (24 & 25 Geo V c 41)

1 Effect of death on certain causes of action

(1) Subject to the provisions of this section, on the death of any person after the commencement of this Act all causes of action subsisting against or vested in him shall survive against, or, as the case may be, for the benefit of, his estate. Provided that this subsection shall not apply to causes of action for defamation...

(1A) The right of a person to claim under section 1A of the Fatal Accidents Act 1976 (bereavement) shall not survive for the benefit of his estate on his death.

(2) Where a cause of action survives as aforesaid for the benefit of the estate of a deceased person, the damages recoverable for the benefit of the estate of that person:—
(a) shall not include—
 (i) any exemplary damages;
 (ii) any damages for loss of income in respect of any period after that person's death;...

QUESTION

Does this Act create an artificial person (or ghost?) called an 'estate'?

NOTE

The 1934 Act keeps the *actio* alive in respect of the dead victim (for many claims), yet the victim's immediate family can also incur loss if the victim was the bread-winner. At common law they had no claim, but this was altered by statute.

Fatal Accidents Act 1976 (c 30)

1 Right of action for wrongful act causing death

(1) If death is caused by any wrongful act, neglect or default which is such as would (if death had not ensued) have entitled the person injured to maintain an action and recover damages in respect thereof, the person who would have been liable if death had not ensued shall be liable to an action for damages, notwithstanding the death of the person injured.

(2) Subject to section 1A(2) below, every such action shall be for the benefit of the dependants of the person ('the deceased') whose death has been so caused.

(3) In this Act 'dependant' means—
(a) the wife or husband or former wife or husband of the deceased;
(aa) the civil partner or former partner of the deceased
(b) any person who—
    (i) was living with the deceased in the same household immediately before the date of the death; and
    (ii) had been living with the deceased in the same household for at least two years before that date; and
    (iii) was living during the whole of that period as the husband or wife or civil partner of the deceased;
(c) any parent or other ascendant of the deceased;
(d) any person who was treated by the deceased as his parent;
(e) any child or other descendant of the deceased;
(f) any person (not being a child of the deceased) who, in the case of any marriage to which the deceased was at any time a party, was treated by the deceased as a child of the family in relation to that marriage;
(fa) any person (not being a child of the deceased) who, in the case of any civil partnership in which the deceased was at any time a civil partner, was treated by the deceased as a child of the family in relation to that civil partnership;
(g) any person who is, or is the issue of, a brother, sister, uncle or aunt of the deceased...

(4) In deducing any relationship for the purposes of subsection (3) above—
(a) any relationship by marriage or civil partnership shall be treated as a relationship by consanguinity, any relationship of the half blood as a relationship of the whole blood, and the stepchild of any person as his child, and
(b) an illegitimate person shall be treated as the legitimate child of his mother and reputed father.

(6) Any reference in this Act to injury includes any disease and any impairment of a person's physical or mental condition.

1A   Bereavement

(1) An action under this Act may consist of or include a claim for damages for bereavement.

(2) A claim for damages for bereavement shall only be for the benefit—
(a) of the wife or husband or civil partner of the deceased; and
(b) where the deceased was a minor who was never married or a civil partner—
    (i) of his parents, if he was legitimate; and
    (ii) of his mother, if he was illegitimate.

(3) Subject to subsection (5) below, the sum to be awarded as damages under this section shall be [£10,000].

(4) Where there is a claim for damages under this section for the benefit of both the parents of the deceased, the sum awarded shall be divided equally between them (subject to any deduction falling to be made in respect of costs not recovered from the defendant).

(5) The Lord Chancellor may by order made by statutory instrument, subject to annulment in pursuance of a resolution of either House of Parliament, amend this section by varying the sum for the time being specified in subsection (3) above.

QUESTIONS

1. Is s 1A really a compensatory damages provision or is it more like a statutory debt? What is the policy behind the section?

2. Does s 1A mean that bereavement is a very different head of damage from either severe psychological damage (nervous shock) or mental distress?

NOTE

The 1934 and the 1976 Acts deal with the physical disappearance of the human person and the effect that this disappearance has in the legal plan. A symmetrical problem arises with respect to 'persons' who have not yet come into existence, the most important of which is the conceived but unborn child. It has been a general rule in all Western legal systems that legal personality attaches to the human person only when they are born, although the law will strive to protect the interests of the unborn child. The complexity is reflected in the next extract.

Congenital Disabilities (Civil Liability) Act 1976 (c 28)

1 Civil liability to child born disabled

(1) If a child is born disabled as the result of such an occurrence before its birth as is mentioned in subsection (2) below, and a person (other than the child's own mother) is under this section answerable to the child in respect of the occurrence, the child's disabilities are to be regarded as damage resulting from the wrongful act of that person and actionable accordingly at the suit of the child.

(2) An occurrence to which this section applies is one which—
   (a) affected either parent of the child in his or her ability to have a normal, healthy child; or
   (b) affected the mother during her pregnancy, or affected her or the child in the course of its birth, so that the child is born with disabilities which would not otherwise have been present.

(3) Subject to the following subsections, a person (here referred to as 'the defendant') is answerable to the child if he was liable in tort to the parent or would, if sued in due time, have been so; and it is no answer that there could not have been such liability because the parent suffered no actionable injury, if there was a breach of legal duty which, accompanied by injury, would have given rise to the liability.

(4) In the case of an occurrence preceding the time of conception, the defendant is not answerable to the child if at that time either or both of the parents knew the risk of their child being born disabled (that is to say, the particular risk created by the occurrence); but should it be the child's father who is the defendant, this subsection does not apply if he knew of the risk and the mother did not.

(5) The defendant is not answerable to the child, for anything he did or omitted to do when responsible in a professional capacity for treating or advising the parent, if he took reasonable care having due regard to then received professional opinion applicable to the particular class of case; but this does not mean that he is answerable only because he departed from received opinion.

(6) Liability to the child under this section may be treated as having been excluded or limited by contract made with the parent affected, to the same extent and subject to the same restrictions as liability in the parent's own case; and a contract term which could have been set up by the defendant in an action by the parent, so as to exclude or limit his liability to him or her, operates in the defendant's favour to the same, but no greater, extent in an action under this section by the child.

(7) If in the child's action under this section it is shown that the parent affected shared the responsibility for the child being born disabled, the damages are to be reduced to such extent as the court thinks just and equitable having regard to the extent of the parent's responsibility.

[...]

2   Liability of woman driving while pregnant

A woman driving a motor vehicle when she knows (or ought reasonably to know) herself to be pregnant is to be regarded as being under the same duty to take care for the safety of her unborn child as the law imposes on her with respect to the safety of other people; and if in consequence of her breach of that duty her child is born with disabilities which would not otherwise have been present, those disabilities are to be regarded as damage resulting from her wrongful act and actionable accordingly at the suit of the child.

QUESTIONS

1. Why did the Act simply not declare that a duty of care is owed to the unborn child? Are such unborn children owed such a duty at common law?

2. Can a child born terribly handicapped argue that it would have been better not to have been born at all? In other words, can he claim that his or her very birth is a form of damage in itself?

11.1.3 Remedy (*actio*), right and interest

The French Code of Civil Procedure states that the *actio* is available 'to all those who have a legitimate interest to the success or rejection of a claim' (art 31). English law does not seem to have quite such a clear rule, but the notion of an interest is still of considerable importance in the law of actions. Normally the 'interest' dimension of a remedy is combined with the question whether or not the claimant has suffered damage.

Burris v Azadani [1995] 1 WLR 1372, CA

This was an appeal by a man who had been imprisoned for failing to respect an injunction issued against him for his 'intolerable history of harassment and molestation'. The injunction had been obtained by the woman who had been the victim of this harassment. The Court of Appeal (Sir Thomas Bingham MR, Millett and Schiemann LJJ) upheld the injunction.

Sir Thomas Bingham MR: ... The power of the High Court is found in section 37(1) of the Supreme Court Act 1981, which provides:

'(1) The High Court may by order (whether interlocutory or final) grant an injunction... in all cases in which it appears to the court to be just and convenient to do so.'

It is of course quite clear that the court cannot properly grant an injunction unless the plaintiff can show at least an arguable cause of action to support the grant, but subject to this overriding requirement section 37, as has often been observed, is cast in the widest terms.

If an injunction may only properly be granted to restrain conduct which is in itself tortious or otherwise unlawful, that would be a conclusive objection to term (c) of the 28

▶

January 1994 injunction, since it is plain that Mr Azadani would commit no tort nor otherwise act unlawfully if, without more, he were to traverse Mandrake Road without any contact or communication with Miss Burris, exercising his right to use the public highway peacefully in the same way as any other member of the public. I do not, however, think that the court's power is so limited...

Neither statute nor authority in my view precludes the making of an 'exclusion zone' order. But that does not mean that such orders should be made at all readily, or without very good reason. There are two interests to be reconciled. One is that of the defendant. His liberty must be respected up to the point at which his conduct infringes, or threatens to infringe, the rights of the plaintiff. No restraint should be placed on him which is not judged to be necessary to protect the rights of the plaintiff. But the plaintiff has an interest which the court must be astute to protect. The rule of law requires that those whose rights are infringed should seek the aid of the court, and respect for the legal process can only suffer if those who need protection fail to get it. That, in part at least, is why disobedience to orders of the court has always earned severe punishment. Respect for the freedom of the aggressor should never lead the court to deny necessary protection to the victim.

Ordinarily, the victim will be adequately protected by an injunction which restrains the tort which has been or is likely to be committed, whether trespass to the person or to land, interference with goods, harassment, intimidation or as the case may be. But it may be clear on the facts that if the defendant approaches the vicinity of the plaintiff's home he will succumb to the temptation to enter it, or to abuse or harass the plaintiff; or that he may loiter outside the house, watching and besetting it, in a manner which might be highly stressful and disturbing to a plaintiff. In such a situation the court may properly judge that in the plaintiff's interest – and also, but indirectly, the defendant's – a wider measure of restraint is called for...

QUESTIONS

1. Could the woman have sued the harasser for damages? (Cf above p 100)

2. Can a court issue an injunction whenever it thinks it 'just and convenient' to do so? If so, given that there is statutory power for a court to award damages in lieu of such an injunction (see *Jaggard v Sawyer* (1995)), can a court award damages whenever it thinks it just and convenient to do so?

11.1.4 Remedies and damage

As we have already suggested, interest can merge with damage. This merging is illustrated by the next case.

Rees v Darlington Memorial Hospital NHS Trust [2003] 3 WLR 1091, HL

This was an action for damages by a blind woman in respect of the birth of a healthy child born after she had undergone a sterilisation operation. She had undergone sterilisation because she felt that her disability would make the bringing up of a child particularly onerous. The operation had been negligently performed and the claimant sought damages for the costs of providing for the child. The judge held that the mother was not entitled to damages under this head, but the Court of Appeal allowed her appeal in part. On a further appeal, the House of Lords (Lords Bingham, Nicholls, Millett and Scott; Lords Steyn, Hope and Hutton dissenting) held that the claimant was not entitled to damages for the costs of bringing up a normal healthy child. However she was entitled to a conventional award of £15,000.

Lord Bingham: 1 My Lords, in *McFarlane v Tayside Health Board* [2000] 2 AC 59 a husband and wife, themselves healthy and normal, sought to recover as damages the cost of bringing up a healthy and normal child born to the wife, following allegedly negligent advice on the effect of a vasectomy performed on the husband. Differing from the Inner House of the Court of Session 1998 SLT 307, the House unanimously rejected this claim. A factual variant of that case reached the Court of Appeal in *Parkinson v St James and Seacroft University Hospital NHS Trust* [2002] QB 266: the mother, who had undergone a negligently performed sterilisation operation, conceived and bore a child who was born with severe disabilities. Following *McFarlane* the Court of Appeal held that the mother could not recover the whole cost of bringing up the child; but it held that she could recover the additional costs she would incur so far as they would be attributable to the child's disabilities. There was no appeal from that decision. The present case raises a further factual variant of *McFarlane*. The claimant in these proceedings (Ms Rees) suffers a severe and progressive visual disability, such that she felt unable to discharge the ordinary duties of a mother, and for that reason wished to be sterilised. She made her wishes known to a consultant employed by the appellant NHS Trust, who carried out a sterilisation operation but did so negligently, and the claimant conceived and bore a son. The child is normal and healthy but the claimant's disability remains. She claimed as damages the cost of rearing the child. The Court of Appeal (Robert Walker and Hale LJJ, Waller LJ dissenting) held that she was entitled to recover the additional costs she would incur so far as they would be attributable to her disability: [2003] QB 20. The appellant NHS Trust now challenges that decision as inconsistent with *McFarlane*. The claimant seeks to uphold the decision, but also claims the whole cost of bringing up the child, inviting the House to reconsider its decision in *McFarlane*...

7 I am of the clear opinion, for reasons more fully given by my noble and learned friends, that it would be wholly contrary to the practice of the House to disturb its unanimous decision in *McFarlane* given as recently as four years ago, even if a differently constituted committee were to conclude that a different solution should have been adopted. It would reflect no credit on the administration of the law if a line of English authority were to be disapproved in 1999 and reinstated in 2003 with no reason for the change beyond a change in the balance of judicial opinion. I am not in any event persuaded that the arguments which the House rejected in 1999 should now be accepted, or that the policy considerations which (as I think) drove the decision have lost their potency. Subject to one gloss, therefore, which I regard as important, I would affirm and adhere to the decision in *McFarlane*.

▶

8 My concern is this. Even accepting that an unwanted child cannot be regarded as a financial liability and nothing else and that any attempt to weigh the costs of bringing up a child against the intangible rewards of parenthood is unacceptably speculative, the fact remains that the parent of a child born following a negligently performed vasectomy or sterilisation, or negligent advice on the effect of such a procedure, is the victim of a legal wrong. The members of the House who gave judgment in *McFarlane* recognised this by holding, in each case, that some award should be made to Mrs McFarlane (although Lord Millett based this on a ground which differed from that of the other members and he would have made a joint award to Mr and Mrs McFarlane). I can accept and support a rule of legal policy which precludes recovery of the full cost of bringing up a child in the situation postulated, but I question the fairness of a rule which denies the victim of a legal wrong any recompense at all beyond an award immediately related to the unwanted pregnancy and birth. The spectre of well-to-do parents plundering the National Health Service should not blind one to other realities: that of the single mother with young children, struggling to make ends meet and counting the days until her children are of an age to enable her to work more hours and so enable the family to live a less straitened existence; the mother whose burning ambition is to put domestic chores so far as possible behind her and embark on a new career or resume an old one. Examples can be multiplied. To speak of losing the freedom to limit the size of one's family is to mask the real loss suffered in a situation of this kind. This is that a parent, particularly (even today) the mother, has been denied, through the negligence of another, the opportunity to live her life in the way that she wished and planned. I do not think that an award immediately relating to the unwanted pregnancy and birth gives adequate recognition of or does justice to that loss. I would accordingly support the suggestion favoured by Lord Millett in *McFarlane*, at p 114, that in all cases such as these there be a conventional award to mark the injury and loss, although I would favour a greater figure than the £5,000 he suggested (I have in mind a conventional figure of £15,000) and I would add this to the award for the pregnancy and birth. This solution is in my opinion consistent with the ruling and rationale of *McFarlane*. The conventional award would not be, and would not be intended to be, compensatory. It would not be the product of calculation. But it would not be a nominal, let alone a derisory, award. It would afford some measure of recognition of the wrong done. And it would afford a more ample measure of justice than the pure *McFarlane* rule...

Lord Steyn (dissenting): ... **46** Like Lord Hope I regard the idea of a conventional award in the present case as contrary to principle. It is a novel procedure for judges to create such a remedy. There are limits to permissible creativity for judges. In my view the majority have strayed into forbidden territory. It is also a backdoor evasion of the legal policy enunciated in *McFarlane*. If such a rule is to be created it must be done by Parliament. The fact is, however, that it would be a hugely controversial legislative measure. It may well be that the Law Commissions and Parliament ought in any event, to consider the impact of the creation of a power to make a conventional award in the cases under consideration for the coherence of the tort system...

Lord Hope (dissenting): ... The award of a conventional sum is familiar in the field of damages for personal injury. Conventional sums are awarded as general damages for typical injuries such as the loss of a limb or an eye or for the bereavement that results from the loss of a child or parent in the case of a fatal accident. This is the means by which the court arrives, as best it can, at a figure for the damage suffered which is incapable of being calculated arithmetically: *Kemp & Kemp, The Quantum of Damages*, vol 1, para 1-003. The sum which it awards has been described by Lord Denning MR in *Ward v James* [1966] 1 QB 273, 303 as 'basically a conventional figure derived from experience and from awards in comparable cases': see also *Wright v British Railways Board* [1983] 2 AC 773, 777D, per Lord Diplock. The award is conventional in the sense that there is no pecuniary guideline which can point the way to a correct assessment: *Lim Poh Choo v Camden and Islington Area Health Authority* [1980] AC 174, 189G-H per Lord Scarman. But financial loss does not present the same problem. It is capable of assessment in money. So it has never been the practice to resort to a conventional sum as a means of compensating the claimant for that part of the loss that falls under the head of special damages...

QUESTIONS

1. Are the £15,000 damages awarded in this case compensatory? If so, what is the principle of compensation that underpins the award?

2. Is this a policy decision? If so, what is the policy? (Reading in full the judgments of Lord Bingham and Lord Steyn, in the law report, will be valuable.)

11.2 Damages (1): general considerations

Statistically speaking, by far the greatest number of tort actions consist of personal injury claims. The remedy here is damages. This is a remedy that has attracted its own rules and principles and to explain the law in detail requires a large textbook in itself. Monographs could be written on personal injury damages and on property damage claims. Thus damages actions can be classified into various different categories.

11.2.1 Compensatory damages

The basic principle of damages is to be found in the following extracts.

European Group on Tort Law, *Principles of European Tort Law* (2003)

Article 10:101. Nature and purpose of damages

Damages are a money payment to compensate the victim, that is to say, to restore him, so far as money can, to the position he would have been in if the wrong complained of had not been committed. Damages also serve the aim of preventing harm.

Article 10:102. Lump sum or periodical payments

Damages are awarded in a lump sum or as periodical payments as appropriate with particular regard to the interests of the victim.

Article 10:103. Benefits gained through the damaging event

When determining the amount of damages benefits which the injured party gains through the damaging event are to be taken into account unless this cannot be reconciled with the purpose of the benefit.

NOTE

These three principles more or less represent English law, as we shall see. The principle in art 10:101 is to be found in the next extract.

Livingstone v Rawyards Coal Co (1880) 5 App Cas 25, HL

Lord Blackburn: ... [W]here any injury is to be compensated by damages, in settling the sum of money to be given for reparation of damages you should as nearly as possible get at that sum of money which will put the party who has been injured, or who has suffered, in the same position as he would have been in if he had not sustained the wrong for which he is now getting his compensation or reparation.

NOTE

This principle was reformulated a century later by Lord Diplock who said 'The general rule in English law today as to the measure of damages recoverable for the invasion of a legal right, whether by breach of a contract or by commission of a tort, is that damages are compensatory. Their function is to put the person whose right has been invaded in the same position as if it had been respected so far as the award of a sum of money can do so ...' (Lord Diplock in *The Albazero* (1977), 841). However, much depends on the nature of the damage suffered.

QUESTION

Is there a difference between an award of damages for breach of contract and for tort?

Rees v Darlington Memorial Hospital NHS Trust [2003] 3 WLR 1091, HL

(For facts see above p 377)

Lord Scott: ... **130** In applying this [*Livingstone*] principle there is often, however, a difference depending on whether the claim is a contractual one or a claim in tort. In general, where a claim is based on a breach of contract, the claimant is entitled to the benefit of the contract and entitled, therefore, to be placed in the position, so far as money can do so, in which he would have been if the contractual obligation had been properly performed. But where the claim is in tort, there being no contract to the benefit of which the claimant is entitled, the claimant is entitled to be placed in the position in which he would have been if the tortious act, the wrong, had not been committed. The difference in approach is often important in cases where the claim is based on negligent advice or negligent misrepresentation. If the defendant was under a contractual obligation to give competent advice, the claimant is entitled to be put in the position he would have been in if competent advice had been given. But if the defendant owes no contractual obligation to the claimant and the case is brought in tort, the claimant must be put in the position he would have been in if no advice had been given at all...

QUESTION

What if the misrepresentation is fraudulent: is the victim better off suing in contract or in tort?

11.2.2 Damage, damages and interests

The basic principle is thus to translate 'damage' into 'damages'. However, it has to be appreciated that the two are not synonymous; there are certain types of damage which the law will not compensate (see eg *Best v Samuel Fox*, p 142). One key concept for translating damage into damages is that of an 'interest'. The harm suffered by a claimant is split into various heads of damage or particular interests; some of these interests – for example pure financial loss in some negligence cases – might be disregarded and this is why damage and damages are not the symmetrical.

Christian von Bar, *The Common European Law of Torts*, vol 2, (OUP, 2000), 4, 6–7 (footnotes omitted)

1 The law of delict [tort] can only operate as an effective, sensible and fair system of compensation if excessive liability is avoided. It is important to prevent it from becoming a disruptive factor in an economic sense. No law based on rational principles can impose damages on each and every act of carelessness...

3 We must therefore start by looking carefully at the term 'damage', the centrepiece of all delict law. European codifications have rarely attempted a detailed legal definition, whether general or particular, ie from a delict point of view. In English law damage is even defined separately for each tort. Here, damage as a general term represents the detriment the duty of care was intended to avoid. Damages, on the other hand, are the sum which the tortfeasor must pay to the injured party. Special damages (ie expenses incurred which can be, and therefore have to be, proven) and general damages (the amount of which is determined by the judge) are distinguished.... Not everything considered as harm or loss by the individual, not even everything an impartial by-stander would qualify as harm or loss, merits compensation, even if negligently inflicted on another.... Therefore, someone who used to enjoy watching a specific type of bird which has stopped coming to the area due to environmental changes undeniably suffers considerable detriment. That this loss does not qualify as damage is undisputed in all European legal systems....

QUESTION

Is a system of law which gives much higher damages for the invasion of reputation than for serious personal injury one based on rational principles? (Cf *John v MGN Ltd*, below p 408.)

NOTE

The idea that damage is defined separately for each tort indicates, from a remedies position, how English tort law is concerned with protecting particular interests. This is why the notion of an 'interest' is so central to tort law. As the next extract shows, it brings together the various aspects of law, that is to say persons (legal subjects), things (assets) and actions (causes of action and remedies). One might note that French lawyers do not talk of *les dommages* (damages) but *les dommages-intérêts*.

Peter Cane, *Tort Law and Economic Interests* (2nd edn, OUP,, 1996), 3–5 (footnotes omitted)

...[I]t is worth noting some nuances in the use of the word 'interest'. When we speak of someone having, for instance, a 'property interest', we mean that the person has some sort of claim over or right in some tangible or intangible thing; and when we speak of someone having a 'contractual interest' we mean that the person has some claim or right by reason of a contract. In such instances the word 'interest' is more or less synonymous with the word 'right' or 'claim'... On the other hand, we often speak of a person's interests or of the public interest in a broader sense to mean simply objectives or states of affairs which are, or would be, to the person's or the public's advantage: for example, the public interest in the due administration of justice ... While it is clear that both types of interest may be 'legal' in the sense of 'recognized and protected by law', interests of the former type are, on the whole, better protected than those of the latter type, at least in the sense that interests of the former type often constitute legal 'swords', whereas those of the latter type are often only effective as 'shields'...

NOTE

One should note Cane's distinction between the different meanings of 'interest'. Sometimes it is a *normative* (an 'ought') term almost interchangeable with the word 'right'; sometimes it is descriptive. In the law of damages it is descriptive in as much as it is used to divide up factual damage into different types (physical injury, mental injury, economic loss); yet it can be manipulated in the hands of some judges to have something of an 'ought' (normative) flavour ('the claimant has an interest that ought to be protected...').

Tony Weir, *A Casebook on Tort* (10th edn, Sweet & Maxwell, 2004), 6

There are several good things in life, such as liberty, bodily integrity, land, possessions, reputation, wealth, privacy, dignity, perhaps even life itself. Lawyers call these goods 'interests'. These interests are all good, but they are not all *equally* good. This is evident when they come into conflict (one may jettison cargo to save passengers, but not vice versa, and one may detain a thing, but not a person, as security for a debt). Because these interests are not equally good, the protection afforded to them by the law is not equal: the law protects the better interests better: murder and rape are, after all, more serious crimes than theft. Accordingly, the better the interest invaded, the more readily does the law give compensation for the ensuing harm. In other words, whether you get the money you claim depends on what you are claiming it for. It would be surprising if it were otherwise.

NOTE

The law can give expression to the existence or non-existence of an interest in two ways. First, it can grant a cause of action directly to protect the interest in question; equally the absence of a cause of action suggests that the interest is not one that is to be fully protected. Secondly, it can give expression through the law of remedies. Certain types of mental distress may not give rise to a direct cause of action, but the distress may attract damages if the victim is able to establish liability through say negligence or breach of contract (see *Jackson v Horizon Holidays* (1975) for an interesting case where a third party's interest was protected via the law of damages).

Geoffrey Samuel, The Notion of an Interest as a Formal Concept in English and in Comparative Law, in Guy Canivet, Mads Andenas & Duncan Fairgrieve (eds), *Comparative Law Before the Courts*, British Institute of International & Comparative Law, 2004, 263, 289 (footnotes omitted)

[The] Roman contribution to the law of damages was of immense importance for two reasons. First, it provided a 'scientific' means of assessing compensation: damages would be payable only if an interest could be indentified and valued. 'Interest', on other words, was the means by which one could link descriptive categories of harm to normative principles of what a defendant ought to pay. Secondly, it provided a means of giving concrete expression to intangible 'goods', such as loss of an expected profit, or intangible 'harms', such as depreciation of a collective group of objects through the destruction of a single item. 'Interest' in this sense became a form of property, an intangible thing (*res incorporalis*) that in turn endowed the whole idea of an obligation with its proprietary character. These ideas in turn helped transform the law of delict (tort) from a quasi-criminal law of actions, where a person who had caused harm paid a fine or penalty, to a law of actions founded on a relationship between two individuals where the idea was to re-establish harmony between two patrimonies. The development of the notion of an 'interest', in short, was virtually synonymous with the development of a sophisticated private law…

QUESTION

Does not the reduction of 'harms' and 'invasions' to 'interests' suggest that everything in the end has an economic value? Can interests such as liberty or privacy be traded?

11.2.3 Non-compensatory damages

Damages can also be non-compensatory. There are three categories: (a) exemplary damages which are awarded to punish a defendant; (b) restitutionary damages which are awarded, not to compensate the claimant, but to deprive a defendant of an unjust profit (although exemplary damages may also be used to deprive a defendant of a profit as the next extract indicates); and (c) nominal damages which are awarded in situations where either the claimant has suffered no recognisable damage or the court is of the view that the claimant merits such an award.

Rookes v Barnard [1964] AC 1129, HL

(For facts see p 88)

Lord Devlin: ... The first category [for an award of exemplary damages] is oppressive, arbitrary or unconstitutional action by servants of the government. I should not extend this category ... Where one man is more powerful than another ... he is not to be punished simply because he is the more powerful. In the case of the government it is different, for the servants of the government are also servants of the people and the use of their power must always be subordinate to their duty of service ... Cases in the second category are those in which the defendant's conduct has been calculated by him to make a profit for himself which may well exceed the compensation payable to the plaintiff ... Exemplary damages can properly be awarded whenever it is necessary to teach a wrongdoer that tort does not pay.

NOTE

The role of exemplary damages has been given further consideration by the House of Lords in a more recent case.

Kuddus v Chief Constable of Leicestershire [2002] 2 AC 122, HL

Lord Slynn: ... 2 The relevant pleaded facts are short. The appellant plaintiff told a police constable that he had come back to his flat where a friend had been staying to find that a lot of property was missing. The officer said that the matter would be investigated but some two months later he forged the plaintiff's signature on a written statement withdrawing the complaint of theft. Accordingly the police investigation ceased.

3 The defendant Chief Constable admits the forgery and that the officer's conduct amounts to misfeasance in a public office. He successfully contended, however, that exemplary damages are not recoverable for the tort of misfeasance by a public officer so that that part of the claim should be struck out. He accepts that there is a viable claim for aggravated damages for such misfeasance...

27 So on the present appeal the question is whether the exemplary damages claimed are on the basis of facts which if established fall within the first category. For the purpose of the strike-out application, it is accepted that they do so fall. The claim is not excluded because it is not shown that a case on the basis of misfeasance in a public office had been decided before 1964. I would therefore allow the appeal. The claim for exemplary damages should not have been struck out on the basis argued before the House. The question whether in principle the Chief Constable can be vicariously liable has not been argued and I do not think it right to discuss or to rule on it in this case.

Lord Nicholls: ... **50** Exemplary damages are a controversial topic, and have been so for many years. Over-simplified, the matter may be summarised thus. Awards of damages are primarily intended to compensate for loss, whether pecuniary or non-pecuniary. Non-pecuniary loss includes mental distress arising from the circumstances in which the tort was committed, such as justified feelings of outrage at the defendant's conduct. Damages awarded for this type of loss are sometimes called aggravated damages, as the defendant's conduct aggravates the injury done. Sometimes damages may also be measured by reference, not to the plaintiff's loss, but to the profit obtained by the defendant from his wrongdoing: see the discussion in *Attorney General v Blake* [2001] 1 AC 268, 278–280.

51 Exemplary damages or punitive damages, the terms are synonymous, stand apart from awards of compensatory damages. They are additional to an award which is intended to compensate a plaintiff fully for the loss he has suffered, both pecuniary and non-pecuniary. They are intended to punish and deter...

66 In *Rookes v Barnard* [1964] AC 1129, 1226 , Lord Devlin drew a distinction between oppressive acts by government officials and similar acts by companies or individuals. He considered that exemplary damages should not be available in the case of non-governmental oppression or bullying. Whatever may have been the position 40 years ago, I am respectfully inclined to doubt the soundness of this distinction today. National and international companies can exercise enormous power. So do some individuals. I am not sure it would be right to draw a hard-and-fast line which would always exclude such companies and persons from the reach of exemplary damages. Indeed, the validity of the dividing line drawn by Lord Devlin when formulating his first category is somewhat undermined by his second category, where the defendants are not confined to, and normally would not be, government officials or the like.

67 Nor, I may add, am I wholly persuaded by Lord Devlin's formulation of his second category (wrongful conduct expected to yield a benefit in excess of any compensatory award likely to be made). The law of unjust enrichment has developed apace in recent years. In so far as there may be a need to go further, the key here would seem to be the same as that already discussed: outrageous conduct on the part of the defendant. There is no obvious reason why, if exemplary damages are to be available, the profit motive should suffice but a malicious motive should not...

Lord Hutton: ... **79** In my opinion the power to award exemplary damages in such cases serves to uphold and vindicate the rule of law because it makes clear that the courts will not tolerate such conduct. It serves to deter such actions in future as such awards will bring home to officers in command of individual units that discipline must be maintained at all times. In my respectful opinion the view is not fanciful, as my noble and learned friend Lord Scott of Foscote suggests, that such awards have a deterrent effect and such an effect is recognised by Professor Atiyah in the passage from his work on *Vicarious Liability* cited by Lord Scott of Foscote in his speech. Moreover in some circumstances where one of a group of soldiers or police officers commits some outrageous act in the course of a confused and violent confrontation it may be very difficult to identify the individual wrongdoer so that criminal proceedings may be brought against him to punish and deter such conduct, whereas an award of exemplary damages to mark the court's condemnation of the conduct can be made against the

▶

Minister of Defence or the Chief Constable under the principle of vicarious liability even if the individual at fault cannot be identified...

Lord Scott: ... **110** Whatever may have been the position in 1964, when *Rookes v Barnard* [1964] AC 1129 was decided, or in 1972, when *Broome v Cassell & Co Ltd* [1972] AC 1027 was decided, there is, in my opinion, no longer any need for punitive damages in the civil law...

122 Faced with the unattractive alternatives of leaving the cause of action test in place or removing it, I would, for my part, favour a pragmatic solution under which, on the one hand, the cause of action test were removed but, on the other, exemplary damages were declared to be unavailable in cases of negligence, nuisance and strict liability, and also liability for breach of statutory duty except where the statute in question had expressly authorised the remedy. In this way the main objections to the cause of action test would be met and tedious research into pre-1964 case law would be avoided but existing authority as to cases where exemplary damages cannot be claimed would be left broadly unaltered. It will be noticed that I have not included deceit among the nominate torts where, on authority, exemplary damages cannot be claimed. This is because if, which I regret, exemplary damages are to be retained and reformed, rather than abolished, deceit practised by a government or local authority official, or by a police officer, on a citizen ought, it seems to me, to be allowed in a suitable case to attract them...

[Appeal allowed.]

NOTE

Exemplary damages must be distinguished from aggravated damages: the latter are compensatory while the former are not.

QUESTION

Does the existence of exemplary damages mean that the separation between tort and criminal law is not yet complete?

11.3 Damages (2): personal injury

Physical health and bodily wholeness is an interest protected by the law of tort. Indeed, statistically, it is the most important interest since the great majority of tort claims are for personal injuries. The *summa divisio* within this broad interest is between the non-economic and economic (sub) interests associated with personal injury. (Note that in a number of the case extracts that follow in this section the facts are not given since they are not considered relevant to the subject matter of the judicial observation extracted.)

11.3.1 General introduction to personal injury damages

The general principle with respect to personal injury damages is given expression in the following code extract.

European Group on Tort Law, Principles of European Tort Law (2003)

Article 10:202. Personal injury and death

(1) In the case of personal injury, which includes injury to bodily health and to mental health amounting to a recognized illness, pecuniary damage includes loss of income, impairment of earning capacity (even if unaccompanied by any loss of income) and reasonable expenses, including the cost of medical care.

(2) In the case of death, persons such as family members whom the deceased maintained or would have maintained if death had not occurred are treated as having suffered recoverable damage to the extent of loss of that support.

Article 10:301. Non-pecuniary damage

(1) Considering the scope of its protection (Art 2:102), the violation of an interest may justify compensation of non-pecuniary damage. This is the case in particular where the victim has suffered personal injury; or injury to his liberty, or other personality rights. Non-pecuniary damage can also be recovered by persons having a close relationship with a victim suffering a fatal or very serious non-fatal injury.

(2) In general, in the assessment of such damages, all circumstances of the case, including the gravity, duration and consequences of the grievance, have to be taken into account. The degree of the tortfeasor's fault is to be taken into account only where it significantly contributes to the grievance of the victim.

(3) In cases of personal injury, non-pecuniary damage corresponds to the suffering of the victim and the impairment of his bodily or mental health. In assessing damages (including damages for persons having a close relationship to deceased or seriously injured victims) similar sums should be awarded for objectively similar losses.

NOTE

The above European code provisions do not necessarily reflect with complete accuracy the present state of English law since damages for personal injury is a technical and complex topic. Yet this complexity makes it important to try to keep in mind the general principles that operate in this area together with an overview of the main interests protected. The next extract thus considers the broad approach to be adopted by the English courts.

Wright v British Railways Board [1983] 2 AC 773, HL

Lord Diplock: ... My Lords, claims for damages in respect of personal injuries constitute a high proportion of civil actions that are started in the courts in this country. If all of them proceeded to trial the administration of civil justice would break down; what prevents this is that a high proportion of them are settled before they reach the expensive and time-consuming stage of trial, and an even higher proportion of claims, particularly the less serious ones, are settled before the stage is reached of issuing and serving a writ. This is only possible if there is some reasonable degree of predictability about the sum of money that would be likely to be recovered if the action proceeded to trial.

▶

The principal characteristics of actions for personal injuries that militate against pre-dictability as to the sum recoverable are, first, that the English legal system requires that any judgment for tort damages, not being a continuing tort, shall be for one lump sum to compensate for all loss sustained by the plaintiff in consequence of the defendant's tortious act whether such loss be economic or non-economic, and whether it has been sustained during the period prior to the judgment or is expected to be sustained there-after. The second characteristic is that non-economic loss constitutes a major item in the damages. Such loss is not susceptible of measurement in money. Any figure at which the assessor of damages arrives cannot be other than artificial and, if the aim is that justice meted out to all litigants should be even-handed instead of depending on idiosyncrasies of the assessor, whether jury or judge, the figure must be 'basically a conventional figure derived from experience and from awards in comparable cases'...

As regards assessment of damages for non-economic loss in personal injury cases, the Court of Appeal creates the guidelines as to the appropriate conventional figure by increasing or reducing awards of damages made by judges in individual cases for vari-ous common kinds of injuries. Thus so-called 'brackets' are established broad enough to make allowance for circumstances which make the deprivation suffered by an individ-ual plaintiff in consequence of the particular kind of injury greater or less than in the general run of cases, yet clear enough to reduce the unpredictability of what is likely to be the most important factor in arriving at settlement of claims ...

NOTES

1. The principle of a lump-sum award is now being increasingly modified by statute: see s 2 of the Damages Act 1996. This section allows a court in a personal injury action to award damages in the form of periodical payments, but the con-sent of the parties is required. It is likely that future legislation will remove this consent requirement.

2. English law approaches personal injury damages by reducing the damage to a number of categories. The *summa divisio* is between (a) pecuniary and (b) non-pecuniary loss. Pecuniary loss is sub-divided into (a) expenses incurred in restoring the plaintiff back to a normal life or at least as normal as possible; (b) actual loss of earnings; and (c) loss of future earnings or earning capacity. Non-pecuniary loss is sub-divided into (a) pain and suffering and (b) loss of amenities. The pain and suffering (mental distress) applies to the victim and not the dependants, but one exception is to be found in the Fatal Accidents Act 1976 s 1A. There are some other categories that are of importance: in particular the problems caused by (a) collateral benefits and (b) death of the victim.

11.3.2 Pecuniary loss

Pecuniary damage can be defined as follows.

European Group on Tort Law, *Principles of European Tort Law* (2003)

Article 10:201. Nature and determination of pecuniary damage

Recoverable pecuniary damage is a diminution of the victim's patrimony caused by the damaging event. Such damage is generally determined as concretely as possible but it may be determined abstractly when appropriate, for example by reference to a market value.

NOTE

The principle may seem clear enough, but translating it into practice is another matter, as Lord Steyn has indicated.

Wells v Wells [1999] 1 AC 345, HL

This case involved several actions for damages for severe personal injuries where liability was admitted. The question to be decided was the rate of return on investment of damages. The House of Lords (Lords Lloyd, Steyn, Hope, Clyde and Hutton) held that an injured claimant was not in the same position as an ordinary prudent investor and was entitled to a greater security in respect of the damages sum to be invested. This security could be achieved through investment in index-linked government securities for which the then current discount rate was 3%.

Lord Steyn: ... The premise of the debate was that as a matter of law a victim of a tort is entitled to be compensated as nearly as possible in full for all pecuniary losses. For present purposes this mainly means compensation for loss of earnings and medical care, both past and future. Subject to the obvious qualification that perfection in the assessment of future compensation is unattainable, the 100 per cent. principle is well established and based on high authority: *Livingstone v. Rawyards Coal Co.* (1880) 5 App.Cas. 25, 39; *Lim Poh Choo v. Camden and Islington Area Health Authority* [1980] AC 175, at 187E, *per* Lord Scarman. The technique employed to achieve this result is to provide an annuity of an annual amount equivalent to the streams of future losses of earnings and cost of future expenses: *Hodgson v. Trapp* [1989] AC 807, *per* Lord Oliver of Aylmerton, at 826D-E.

It must not be assumed that the 100 per cent. principle is self evidently the only sensible compensation system. Judges have to a limited extent tried to control the size of awards for pecuniary losses in personal injury cases. Thus judges have in practice imposed a limit of 18 years in fixing a multiplier and, having done their sums in the context of the facts of a case, they have resorted to the so-called judicial discount for uncertainties. The first tendency is illustrated by *McIlgrew v. Devon County Council* [1995] PIQR 66, at 74, *per* Sir John May, and the second by the judicial discount applied in the case of *Thomas*. Moreover, the 100 per cent. principle has been criticised by commentators, notably in *Atiyah's Accidents, Compensation and the Law*, 5th ed. (1993) edited by Peter Cane, 1993. About the hundred per cent. principle Professor Atiyah states (at 131):

▶

'...most other compensation systems, especially social security systems (and in other countries, worker's compensation laws) generally reject the 100 per cent. principle. Our own social security system generally pays benefits well below the full amount of lost earnings. Similarly, the New Zealand Accident Compensation Act provides for benefits of 80 per cent. of lost earnings; and the Australian Committee of Inquiry recommended benefits equal to 85 per cent. of lost earnings. Moreover, in most compensation systems there are minimum loss qualifications. Thus, no social security benefits are payable in this country for the first three days' loss of earnings; no criminal injuries compensation benefits are payable if the compensation would amount to less than £1,000, and so on.

Clearly, such arguments are stronger in the case of loss of future earnings than in respect of the cost of future medical care. Rhetorically, Professor Atiyah asks 'why should different accident victims be compensated for the same injury on a scale which varies according to their previous level of earnings?' and 'if . . . two people are killed in similar accidents, what justification is there for compensating their dependants at different rates?': at pp. 127–129. The author gives two main reasons for rejecting the 100 per cent. principle. The first is the cost involved. The second is that it reduces the victim's incentive to return to work. The second consideration is not relevant to the appellants in the present appeals but may arguably be relevant in other personal injury cases. Not only do these arguments contemplate a radical departure from established principle, but controversial issues regarding resources and social policy would be at stake. Such policy arguments are a matter for Parliament and not the judiciary...

Lord Clyde: ... In order to calculate the appropriate capital sum which will secure such an annuity one has to ascertain the appropriate rate of return which is appropriate for such a notional annuity. That depends upon the choice of investment to be adopted. Here one can only look to the markets for a solution. Between the rival suggestions put forward in the present appeals, namely investment in equities or investment in index-linked government stocks, it seems to me plain that the latter are the preferred choice. The problem which has been of concern in past years of meeting the risk of inflation, a problem which cannot reasonably be wholly disregarded for the future, is substantially met by the nature of an index-linked investment... It was suggested that the present issues of index-linked government stock could not cover all the various periods which might be required in different cases. But the shortfall on an early maturity could reasonably be supposed to be covered by a cash investment from the remaining proceeds of the notional investment and in any event it may well be that future issues of index-linked stock will be made so that a greater variety of periods can be covered more precisely...

NOTES

1. The discount rate is now set by statutory instrument: see s 1 of the Damages Act 1996. The lower the discount rate, the higher the damages: See Tony Weir, *Tort Law* (OUP, 2002), 193.

2. Calculating the future loss of earnings is not the only difficulty facing the courts. A severely injured claimant may well have to rely upon family members or friends.

Hunt v Severs [1994] 2 AC 350, HL

This was an action for damages by the pillion passenger against the driver of a motor-cycle for severe personal injury arising out of the driver's negligence. The passenger claimed damages for the caring services rendered to her by the defendant driver who, after the accident, married the claimant. The House of Lords (Lords Keith, Bridge, Jauncey, Browne-Wilkinson and Nolan) held that, although damages could in principle be claimed by a victim for the cost of services rendered by a family member (the money to be held on trust by the victim for the carer), damages could not be claimed for a carer who was also the defendant.

Lord Bridge: My Lords, a plaintiff who establishes a claim for damages for personal injury is entitled in English law to recover as part of those damages the reasonable value of services rendered to him gratuitously by a relative or friend in the provision of nursing care or domestic assistance of the kind rendered necessary by the injuries the plaintiff has suffered. The major issue which arises for determination in this appeal is whether the law will sustain such a claim in respect of gratuitous services in the case where the voluntary carer is the tortfeasor himself...

The action was tried in April 1992 by Mr. David Latham Q.C., sitting as a deputy judge of the Queen's Bench Division [1993] PIQR Q43. He delivered judgment on 15 April 1992 awarding the plaintiff a total sum of £617,004 made up as follows:

	£
General damages for pain and suffering and loss of amenity	90,000
Special damages	90,094
Future loss	412,104
Interest on general damages	6,588
Interest on special damages	18,218
	£617,004

Included in the award of special damages was a sum of £4,429 representing the defendant's travelling expenses incurred in visiting the plaintiff while she was in hospital and a sum of £17,000 representing the value of the past services rendered by the defendant in caring for the plaintiff when she was at home. Included in the award for future loss was a sum of £60,000 representing the estimated value of the services which would be rendered by the defendant in caring for the plaintiff in future. The basis on which the judge approached the assessment of the several elements which went to make up the plaintiff's estimated future loss, subject to a number of detailed adjustments which it is unnecessary for present purposes to examine, was to apply a multiplier of 14 to the estimated future annual losses...

The law with respect to the services of a third party who provides voluntary care for a tortiously injured plaintiff has developed somewhat erratically in England. The voluntary carer has no cause of action of his own against the tortfeasor. The justice of allowing the injured plaintiff to recover the value of the services so that he may recompense the voluntary carer has been generally recognised, but there has been difficulty in articulating a consistent juridical principle to justify this result.

... I accept that the basis of a plaintiff's claim for damages may consist in his need for services but I cannot accept that the question from what source that need has been

▶

met is irrelevant. If an injured plaintiff is treated in hospital as a private patient he is entitled to recover the cost of that treatment. But if he receives free treatment under the National Health Service, his need has been met without cost to him and he cannot claim the cost of the treatment from the tortfeasor. So it cannot, I think, be right to say that in all cases the plaintiff's loss is 'for the purpose of damages ... the proper and reasonable cost of supplying [his] needs.'...

Thus, in both England and Scotland the law now ensures that an injured plaintiff may recover the reasonable value of gratuitous services rendered to him by way of voluntary care by a member of his family... I would think it appropriate for the House to take the opportunity... [of] adopting the view of Lord Denning M.R. in *Cunningham v Harrison* [1973] Q.B. 942 that in England the injured plaintiff who recovers damages under this head should hold them on trust for the voluntary carer.

By concentrating on the plaintiff's need and the plaintiff's loss as the basis of an award in respect of voluntary care received by the plaintiff, the reasoning in *Donnelly v Joyce* diverts attention from the award's central objective of compensating the voluntary carer. Once this is recognised it becomes evident that there can be no ground in public policy or otherwise for requiring the tortfeasor to pay to the plaintiff, in respect of the services which he himself has rendered, a sum of money which the plaintiff must then repay to him...

The case for the plaintiff was argued in the Court of Appeal without reference to the circumstance that the defendant's liability was covered by insurance. But before your Lordships Mr McGregor, recognising the difficulty of formulating any principle of public policy which could justify recovery against the tortfeasor who has to pay out of his own pocket, advanced the bold proposition that such a policy could be founded on the liability of insurers to meet the claim. Exploration of the implications of this proposition in argument revealed the many difficulties which it encounters. But I do not think it necessary to examine these in detail. The short answer, in my judgment, to Mr McGregor's contention is that its acceptance would represent a novel and radical departure in the law of a kind which only the legislature may properly effect. At common law the circumstance that a defendant is contractually indemnified by a third party against a particular legal liability can have no relevance whatever to the measure of that liability...

QUESTIONS

1. It might seem perfectly logical within the two-party structure (claimant-defendant) for the carer head of damages to be refused since, within this structure, the claimant would be obtaining money from the defendant which she would then have to pay back to the defendant. But the reality is that road accident claims involve three parties, the third party being the defendant's insurance company. Ought the House of Lords to have recognised this reality?

2. A claimant is injured by the defendant's negligence and can no longer spend 77 hours a week looking after his disabled brother. He can only devote 35 hours of care, the rest being provided by his mother. Can the claimant sue for this loss? Can he also sue for loss of employment capacity given that he was unemployed before the accident only because he cared for his brother? (See *Lowe v Guise* (2002).)

NOTE

Hunt v Severs illustrates once again how the paradigm idea of one individual suing another (corrective justice) is an inadequate model, for it is not just the claimant victim who incurs damage; members of his or her family also suffer harm (cf *Best v Samuel Fox* (1952), p 142). Where the victim is killed outright as a result of a tort the family members who were dependent upon the victim have, thanks to statute, their own damages claims (Fatal Accidents Act 1976, pp 372, 400). But if the victim is not killed the family members will not have a claim, even if the victim's life is shortened. The objectives of a damages claim, where the victim is suing, thus can turn out to be wider than compensating the victim's own interests. A lump sum damages award must often reflect the interests of others. Where the victim's life is shortened as a result of the tort, the interests of the family are now given some expression in the law of damages (*Pickett v British Rail Engineering* (1980)).

11.3.3 Collateral benefits

A victim of an accident may receive money from a number of sources. He or she may have taken out private insurance or may benefit from money donated by the public or by friends or by a charity. If the victim sues a tortfeasor for compensation the question arises as to whether or not collateral benefits should be deducted from any damages awarded.

Hunt v Severs [1994] 2 AC 350, HL

(For facts see above p 391)

Lord Bridge: ... The starting point for any inquiry into the measure of damages which an injured plaintiff is entitled to recover is the recognition that damages in the tort of negligence are purely compensatory. He should recover from the tortfeasor no more and no less than he has lost. Difficult questions may arise when the plaintiff's injuries attract benefits from third parties. According to their nature these may or may not be taken into account as reducing the tortfeasor's liability. The two well established categories of receipt which are to be ignored in assessing damages are the fruits of insurance which the plaintiff himself has provided against the contingency causing his injuries (which may or may not lead to a claim by the insurer as subrogated to the rights of the plaintiff) and the fruits of the benevolence of third parties motivated by sympathy for the plaintiff's misfortune. The policy considerations which underlie these two apparent exceptions to the rule against double recovery are, I think, well understood: see, for example, *Parry v Cleaver* [1970] AC 1, 14, and *Hussain v New Taplow Paper Mills Ltd* [1988] AC 514, 528. But I find it difficult to see what considerations of public policy can justify a requirement that the tortfeasor himself should compensate the plaintiff twice over for the self-same loss. If the loss in question is a direct pecuniary loss (eg loss of wages), *Hussain's* case is clear authority that the defendant employer, as the tortfeasor who makes good the loss either voluntarily or contractually, thereby mitigates his liability in damages pro tanto...

QUESTIONS

1. What do you think are the public policy considerations which led to the 'two well established categories' being ignored in assessing damages? (See *Parry v Cleaver* (1970).)

2. Does a victim of a tort, for measure of damages purposes, have to use the National Health Service or can the victim use private medical care? If the victim does use the NHS, can he or she nevertheless claim private medical expenses? (See Law Reform (Personal Injuries) Act 1948, s 2; Administration of Justice Act 1982, s 5.)

NOTE

A victim may be entitled to social security benefits simply as a result of his or her disability. The sums received are no longer deducted from damages but are recouped by the Secretary of State. The history of the various schemes is set out in the judgments below.

Wadey v Surrey CC [2000] 1 WLR 820, HL

Lord Hope: My Lords, these appeals, one from the Inner House of the Court of Session in Scotland and the other from the Court of Appeal, Civil Division, in England, both raise the same question. It is whether, in an action for damages for personal injuries, social security benefits received by the injured person that are disregarded in the assessment of special damages must be disregarded when interest is being calculated on those damages. All parties are agreed that this question should receive the same answer in Scotland and in England...

The recovery of benefits – history

The original scheme for the recovery of social security benefits was set out in section 2(1) of the Law Reform (Personal Injuries) Act 1948. It had been recognised as a general principle by Beveridge that an injured person should not be compensated twice over for the same loss: *Social Insurance and Allied Services*, Cmnd. 6404 (1942), p. 101, para. 260. He suggested that this principle could be preserved if the claimant repaid the benefits to the Ministry when he was awarded damages or the benefits which he received were taken into account in the assessment of damages. When the Monkton Committee came to examine this issue the general principle was recognised, but there was disagreement as to how it was to be applied under the new scheme: *Departmental Committee on Alternative Remedies*, Cmnd. 6860 (1946), para. 38. The majority recommended that the general principle on which legislation should be framed was that the claimant should not recover more by way of damages and benefits than he could have recovered from either source alone: p. 18, para. 38. Two members dissented, on the view that the scheme for national insurance was very little different from private insurance so the claimant's benefits should be left out of account altogether in the assessment of damages.

Section 2(1) of the Act of 1948 appears to have been arrived at as a compromise between these two views. It provided that there was to be taken into account in the assessment of damages for any loss of earnings or profits accruing to the injured person from his injuries one half of the benefits which he had received during the period of five years beginning with the time when the cause of action accrued. But this system did not extend to the full range of welfare benefits. Only those specified in section 2(1) of the Act as amended from time to time were subject to the statutory rule that one half of the benefits received was to be offset in the calculation of damages. These were sickness benefit, invalidity benefit, non-contributory invalidity pension, severe disablement allowance, sickness benefit (formerly injury benefit) and disablement benefit. Attendance allowance and mobility allowance, family credit (formerly family income supplement), income supplement (formerly supplementary benefit), redundancy payments, reduced earnings allowance, statutory sick pay, and unemployment benefit were not subject to the statutory rule. In a series of decisions in both England and Scotland it was held that the whole of sums received in respect of benefits which were not subject to the rule must be deducted. This is in accordance with the general principle that damages are intended to be purely compensatory, and that what the court must measure is the net consequential loss and expense which has been incurred in arriving at the measure of the claimant's damages: see *Wilson v. National Coal Board*, 1981 SC (HL) 9; *Hodgson v. Trapp* [1989] 1 AC 807, 822A-823D *per* Lord Bridge of Harwich.

In the application of this scheme in assessing damages only one half of the listed benefits was regarded as compensation for the loss of income or loss of profits due to the accident. That half was taken into account in the calculation by deducting it from the loss of income or profits to arrive at the net loss. The other half was disregarded in the same way as if it had been received from charity or under a private insurance policy. Awards of interest followed the same pattern. The one half of the benefits which was taken into account in the calculation did not bear interest. As it had been deducted from the principal sum awarded as damages, it reduced by the same amount the net loss on which interest was to be payable. But the disregarded half bore interest along with the rest of the award. As Lord Sutherland said in *Wisely's* case at p. 918G, it was never suggested in Scotland that interest should not be payable on the whole of the loss of earnings so calculated even though the pursuer had received, during the relevant period, half of the benefits. In *Wadey's* case Simon Brown L.J. said at p. 1620H that *Jefford v. Gee* [1970] 2 Q.B. 130 made it plain that the plaintiff (whilst, of course, he received no interest on the moiety for which he gave credit against damages) did not have to give credit in the interest calculation in respect of his windfall receipt of the other moiety of the benefits paid.

The recommendation by Beveridge that the full amount of the benefits received by the injured person or his dependants as the result of an injury should be deducted in the assessment of damages was adopted when the whole subject of compensation for personal injury was considered by the Pearson Commission: *Royal Commission on Civil Liability and Compensation for Personal Injury*, Cmnd. 7054-1 (1978), ch. 13. It recommended that the full amount should be deducted, and this view was accepted in principle by the government: *Social Security Act 1975: Reform of the Industrial Injuries Scheme* Cmnd. 8402 (1981), ch. 8. But it was concluded that a workable scheme for the direct recovery of this amount from the injured person or his dependants would not be practicable in view of its cost and the large number of cases which were settled extrajudicially. It was not until 1989, when the Social Security Act 1989 was enacted, that a system was introduced for the recovery in full of the benefits received from the compensation paid to the injured person under a court order or an agreed settlement...

The Scheme of the Act of 1997

The principal features of the scheme introduced by the Act of 1989 are reproduced in the Act of 1997. It enables the Secretary of State to recover the whole amount of any listed benefits paid to a person in consequence of any accident, injury or disease during the relevant period where that person also receives a compensation payment for that

▶

accident, injury or disease from a third party. The compensator is liable to pay to the Secretary of State the whole amount of the listed benefits received by the claimant for the relevant period. He is then entitled to deduct that amount from the compensation which he is to make to the injured party. But there are some important differences. Under the new scheme the reduction in respect of recoverable benefits is restricted to particular heads of the compensation payment, with the result that other heads – in particular damages for pain and suffering – are insulated from, or ring-fenced against, the deduction. According to a system of calculation which is set out in section 8 and Schedule 2, the only heads of compensation which are affected by it are those for loss of earnings, cost of care and loss of mobility during the relevant period against which are to be set the amount of any recoverable benefit which is attributed to those heads. There is no small payments limit under the new scheme, and a new procedure for appeals against certificates of recoverable benefit has been introduced...

Lord Clyde: ... The new regime was significantly different from the former scheme. Essentially while under the former scheme the wrongdoer or tortfeasor was relieved from paying the whole of the patrimonial loss, since one half of the benefits was to be set against the sum in the award, under the new scheme the Secretary of State is able to recover from the person paying the damages, referred to as the 'compensator,' a sum representing the benefits paid to the injured person and the compensator is then entitled to offset that sum against the amount which he is bound to pay to the injured person under the court's order and is to that extent discharged from satisfying the order. Under the language of the Act a payment made to a person in consequence of an accident, injury or disease is a 'compensation payment.' By virtue of section 1(3) of the Act of 1997 voluntary payments as well as payments under a court order are included. For this purpose of the scheme the Act sets out in Schedule 2 various heads of loss which may be found within a compensation payment and a list of the particular benefits to which each head is to relate. Any of the benefits in the list which have been or are likely to be paid in respect of the accident, injury or disease, during a period defined in detail in section 3 and referred to as the 'relevant period,' constitutes a 'recoverable benefit.' In paying the person entitled to a compensation payment the compensator is entitled to offset against the heads of loss specified in Schedule 2 the recoverable benefits relative to each of those respective heads...

What seems to me very evident from the new scheme is that a separation is being made between the court's function in the assessing and awarding of damages and the quite distinct mechanism for the recovery of the recoverable benefits from the wrongdoer. The latter process is managed independently of the court. It operates after the court has made its order. It concerns particularly the time of payment to the pursuer, not the time of the making of any order or decree by the court. It affects not the terms of the order but the satisfaction of the order by the compensator. It has its own procedures for the resolution of disputes, which may involve reference to a medical appeal tribunal. Under section 14 of the Act and regulation 11 of the Social Security (Recovery of Benefits) Regulations 1997 (SI 1997 No. 2205) if it is found that the amount of the recoverable benefit has been over calculated and too much has been paid to the Secretary of State, then the balance is to be repaid by the Secretary of State to the compensator, the compensation payment is recalculated and the increase if any is paid to the person to whom the compensation payment was made. Nothing in that process touches upon the award made by the court. It is managed outwith the court processes...

QUESTION

1. If the State is entitled to recoup money paid to an injured person, why should a private insurance company not be able to do the same?

2. Is the Secretary of State's right to recover benefits a public or a private law right? Upon what principle do you think the right is based?

11.3.4 Non-pecuniary loss

General damages for pain and suffering and loss of amenity are, as we have seen, awarded to a victim suffering personal injury. This interest can be seen as a species of mental distress, but what if the victim is permanently unconscious?

H West & Son Ltd v Shepard [1964] AC 326, HL

The question that arose in this case was whether a person who had been reduced to permanent unconsciousness by the tortious act, or was otherwise unaware of his or her condition, could recover damages for loss of amenity. A majority of the House of Lords (Lords Tucker, Morris and Pearce; Lords Reid and Devlin dissenting) held that awareness of the loss was not a factor to be taken into account in awarding personal injury damages for non-pecuniary loss.

Lord Pearce: ... The loss of happiness of the individual plaintiffs is not, in my opinion, a practicable or correct guide to reasonable compensation in cases of personal injury to a living plaintiff. A man of fortitude is not made less happy because he loses a limb. It may alter the scope of his activities and force him to seek his happiness in other directions. The cripple by the fireside reading or talking with friends may achieve happiness as great as that which, but for the accident, he would have achieved playing golf in the fresh air of the links. To some ancient philosophers the former kind of happiness might even have seemed of a higher nature than the latter, provided that the book or the talk were such as they would approve. Some less robust persons, on the other hand, are prepared to attribute a great loss of happiness to a quite trivial event. It would be lamentable if the trial of a personal injury claim put a premium on protestations of misery and if a long face was the only safe passport to a large award. Under the present practice there is no call for a parade of personal unhappiness. A plaintiff who cheerfully admits that he is happy as ever he was, may yet receive a large award as reasonable compensation for the grave injury and loss of amenity over which he has managed to triumph. I venture to think that an alteration of the current principles of assessing damages for personal injury would be an embarrassment to a practice which in spite of its difficulties does in the main produce a just result. Common law courts should not lightly abandon a method of estimation that works reasonably well and achieves a certain amount of precision, for a method that is nebulous, variable and subjective...

Lord Morris: ... My Lords, leaving aside for the moment the question as to whether the amount is, as an amount, excessive I can see no fault in the approach of the learned judge. It is necessary to have in mind the matters for which he was awarding these general damages. Accepting the estimate as to the plaintiff's expectation of life, damages were to be given to cover a period of over seven years. At the age of 41 everything that life held for her was taken away from her. For a period of about seven years instead of

▶

having life's activities and amenities she will have mere existence but little else, save that, to the extent that I have described, she may have the torment of a realisation of her helplessness. If in some degree she has processes of thought she has the agony and frustration of being unable to convey her thoughts or to give them expression. All these matters constitute grave and sombre deprivations for which in my view she is entitled to receive substantial compensation.

Lord Reid (dissenting): ... To my mind there is something unreal in saying that a man who knows and feels nothing should get the same as a man who has to live with and put up with his disabilities, merely because they have sustained comparable physical injuries. It is no more possible to compensate an unconscious man than it is to compensate a dead man. The fact that the damages can give no benefit or satisfaction to the injured man and can only go to those who inherit the dead man's estate would not be a good reason for withholding damages which are legally due. But it is, in my view, a powerful argument against the view that there is no analogy between a dead man and a man who is unconscious and that a man who is unconscious ought to be treated as if he were fully conscious.

It is often said that it is scandalous that it should be cheaper to kill a man than to maim him, and that it would be monstrous if the defendant had to pay less because in addition to inflicting physical injuries he had made the plaintiff unconscious. I think that such criticism is misconceived. Damages are awarded not to punish the wrongdoer but to compensate the person injured, and a dead man cannot be compensated. Loss to his estate can be made good, and we can give some compensation to those whom he leaves behind. Perhaps we should do more for them – but not by inflating the claim of the dead man's executor, for then the money may go to undeserving distant relatives or residuary legatees or even to the Treasury if he dies intestate and without heirs. And it is already the case that it may benefit the defendant to injure the plaintiff more severely. If he is injured so severely that he can only live a year or two at most the damages will be much less than if he is less severely injured so that he may survive for many years. And that brings me to the other matter of loss of expectation of life...

Lord Devlin (dissenting): ... I can see no distinction, logical or otherwise, between sudden death and death preceded by a period of unconsciousness, long or short. The injury that mortifies the limbs and cuts off the faculties has in both cases the same effect on the power of enjoyment; in each case the deprivation is absolute. Death is often preceded by some period of unconsciousness. For how long must the period last in order that the victim's estate may benefit by the higher measure? For days, for weeks or for months? I find it, with respect, repugnant to common sense and to justice that if the victim dies at once the estate benefits only by a few hundreds but if the body is kept alive and inert when the mind is dead, the amount should grow and grow until it reaches a sum such as £15,000...

QUESTIONS

1. What if a victim of a tort knows that he is going to die within a year or so because of the accident for which the tortfeasor is responsible: should the victim be awarded damages for this knowledge? If so, should he be awarded damages for the foreshortening of his life even if he does not know it has been foreshortened?

2. A victim is reduced to a living vegetable as a result of the defendant's negligence and a judge in the family division decides that it is in the victim's 'best interests' that the hospital no longer artificially keep the victim alive (*Airedale NHS Trust v Bland* (1993)). What are the implications for the law of damages?

3. The Law Commission has recommended that the amount awarded for pain and suffering should be increased. Can Parliament only implement this recommendation or can the judges do it? (Cf next case.)

Heil v Rankin [2001] QB 272, CA

These were actions for damages in which the claimants disputed the awards made for pain and suffering and loss of amenity. The Law Commission in its Report on Damages for Personal Injury: Non-Pecuniary Loss (Law Com No 257, 1999) had recommended substantial increases in the damages to be awarded under these non-pecuniary heads. The Court of Appeal (Lord Woolf MR, Beldam, Otton and May LJJ and Nelson J) held that the awards should be increased in the case of awards currently above £10,000 but not to the levels recommended by the Law Commission.

Lord Woolf MR (delivering judgment of the Court): ... **1** In June 1995 the then Lord Chancellor announced the Law Commission's ('Commission') sixth programme of law reform. The programme included an examination of: 'the principles governing and the effectiveness of the present remedy for damages for monetary and non-monetary loss, with particular regard to personal injury litigation'. A matter for specific consideration was 'the award of damages for pain and suffering and other forms of non-pecuniary loss'.

2 In January 1996 the Commission published a Consultation Paper (No. 140) Damages for Personal Injury: Non-Pecuniary Loss. This was followed by the publication of the Commission Report (No. 257) which was ordered by the House of Commons to be printed on 19 April 1999. Included among the recommendations was a recommendation that the level of damages for non-pecuniary loss for personal injuries should be increased. The recommendation was set out in the Summary of Recommendations contained in the report in the following terms :

'(1) Damages for non-pecuniary loss for serious personal injury should be increased. We recommend that :

(1) in respect of injuries for which the current award for non-pecuniary loss for the injury alone would be more than £3,000, damages for non-pecuniary loss (that is for pain and suffering and loss of amenity) should be increased by a factor of at least 1.5, but by not more than a factor of 2;

(2) in respect of injuries for which the current award for non-pecuniary loss for the injury alone would be in the range £2,001 to £3,000, damages for non-pecuniary loss (that is for pain and suffering and loss of amenity) should be increased by a series of tapered increases of less than a factor of 1.5 (so that, for example, an award now of £2,500 should be uplifted by around 25 per cent);

(3) Finally, if the increases recommended by us are not implemented until over a year after publication of this report, the recommended increases should be adjusted to take into account any change in the value of money since the publication of this report. (paragraphs 3.40 and 3.110)'.

▶

...

48 In summary, our conclusion is... that it is appropriate for the Court to consider the Commission's recommendation. What is involved is part of the traditional role of the courts. It is a role in which juries previously were involved. Now it is the established role of the judiciary. It is a role which, as a result of their accumulated experience, the judiciary is well qualified to perform. Parliament can still intervene. It has, however, shown no inclination that it intends to do so. If it should decide to do so then the fact that the courts have already considered the question will be of assistance to Parliament. Until Parliament does so, the courts cannot avoid their responsibility. While a public debate on this subject would no doubt be salutary, the contribution which it could make to the actual decision of the Court is limited. The Court has the report of the Commission. It also has the other material which the parties have placed before it. It is in as good a position as it is likely to be to make a decision in the context of the present appeals. We see no reason to accede to Mr Havers' submission that we should postpone doing so. To postpone would be to neglect our responsibility to provide certainty in this area as soon as it is practical to do so...

QUESTION

1. Is this case an example of judicial activism?

2. Is the Law Commission now a source of English law?

11.3.5 Damages arising out of death

Where the victim is killed as a result of the tort, two potential claimants can sue. There is the estate of the victim which survives as a legal subject thanks to legislation (see above p 371) and there are the dependants.

Fatal Accidents Act 1976 (c 30)

3   Assessment of damages

(1) In the action such damages, other than damages for bereavement, may be awarded as are proportioned to the injury resulting from the death to the dependants respectively.

(2) After deducting the costs not recovered from the defendant any amount recovered otherwise than as damages for bereavement shall be divided among the dependants in such shares as may be directed.

(3) In an action under this Act where there fall to be assessed damages payable to a widow in respect of the death of her husband there shall not be taken account the re-marriage of the widow or her prospects of re-marriage.

(4) In an action under this Act where there fall to be assessed damages payable to a person who is a dependant by virtue of section 1(3)(b) above in respect of the death

of the person with whom the dependant was living as husband or wife or civil partner there shall be taken into account (together with any other matter that appears to
the court to be relevant to the action) the fact that the dependant had no enforceable right to financial support by the deceased as a result of their living together.

(5) If the dependants have incurred funeral expenses in respect of the deceased, damages may be awarded in respect of those expenses...

4 Assessment of damages: disregarded benefits

In assessing damages in respect of a person's death in an action under this Act, benefits which have accrued or will or may accrue to any person from his estate or otherwise
as a result of his death shall be disregarded.

QUESTION

What is the policy consideration behind s 3(3)?

NOTE

In *H v S* (2003) Kennedy LJ said 'In my judgment, in the light of the authorities,
the position is reasonably clear. Where, as here, infant children are living with
and are dependent on one parent, with no support being provided by the other
parent, in circumstances where the provision of such support in the future seems
unlikely, and the parent with whom they are living is killed, in circumstances
giving rise to liability under the Fatal Accidents Act 1976, after which the other
parent (who is not the tortfeasor) houses and takes responsibility for the children, the support which they enjoy after the accident is a benefit which has
accrued as a result of the death and, pursuant to section 4 of the 1976 Act, it
must be disregarded, both in the assessment of loss and in the calculation of
damages' (§ 29).

11.4 Damages (3): non-personal injury damage

It might be thought that calculating damages for damage other than personal
injury harm would be relatively straightforward. Sometimes it can be, but there
are many situations where the calculation can prove extremely difficult and
sometimes controversial. Damages for intangible harm to reputation is one obvious example. Yet even physical damage to property can prove difficult when the
thing damaged is for instance a profit-earning chattel. Physical damage is not
the only type of interference with another person's thing; wrongful use or complete deprivation are other forms of harm.

11.4.1 Property damage

The economic consequences of damage to property can prove difficult in a range
of situations.

Lagden v O'Connor [2003] 3 WLR 1571, HL

This was an action for damages by the owner of a car damaged by the negligence of the defendant. The unemployed claimant was unable to afford to hire a replacement car while his was off the road and so he signed an agreement with a credit company whereby it provided the claimant with a car, at no cost to him personally, recouping the money from the defendant's insurance company. Such a car hire arrangement was more expensive than if the claimant had been able to hire a car himself from a hire company. The defendant admitted liability but disputed the cost of the credit company charges. The trial judge and the Court of Appeal held that the impecunious claimant was entitled to damages for the credit hire package since he had no other option; an appeal to the House of Lords (Lords Nicholls, Slynn and Hope; Lords Scott and Walker dissenting) was dismissed.

Lord Nicholls: ... **6** My Lords, the law would be seriously defective if in this type of case the innocent motorist were, in practice, unable to obtain the use of a replacement car. The law does not assess damages payable to an innocent plaintiff on the basis that he is expected to perform the impossible. The common law prides itself on being sensible and reasonable. It has regard to practical realities. As Lord Reid said in *Cartledge v E Jopling & Sons Ltd* [1963] AC 758, 772, the common law ought never to produce a wholly unreasonable result. Here, as elsewhere, a negligent driver must take his victim as he finds him. Common fairness requires that if an innocent plaintiff cannot afford to pay car hire charges, so that left to himself he would be unable to obtain a replacement car to meet the need created by the negligent driver, then the damages payable under this head of loss should include the reasonable costs of a credit hire company. Credit hire companies provide a reasonable means whereby innocent motorists may obtain use of a replacement vehicle when otherwise they would be unable to do so. Unless the recoverable damages in such a case include the reasonable costs of a credit hire company the negligent driver's insurers will be able to shuffle away from their insured's responsibility to pay the cost of providing a replacement car. A financially well placed plaintiff will be able to hire a replacement car, and in the fullness of time obtain reimbursement from the negligent driver's insurers, but an impecunious plaintiff will not. This cannot be an acceptable result.

7 The conclusion I have stated does not mean that, if impecunious, an innocent motorist can recover damages beyond losses for which he is properly compensatable. What it means is that in measuring the loss suffered by an impecunious plaintiff by loss of use of his own car the law will recognise that, because of his lack of financial means, the timely provision of a replacement vehicle for him costs more than it does in the case of his more affluent neighbour. In the case of the impecunious plaintiff someone has to provide him with credit, by incurring the expense of providing a car without receiving immediate payment, and then incur the administrative expense involved in pursuing the defendant's insurers for payment.

8 In your Lordships' House the appellant sought to derive assistance from *Owners of Liesbosch Dredger v Owners of SS Edison (The Liesbosch)* [1933] AC 449 and Lord Wright's much discussed observations, at pp 460-461, regarding not taking into account a claimant's want of means when assessing the amount of his loss. For the reasons given by my noble and learned friends, Lord Hope of Craighead and Lord

Walker of Gestingthorpe, these observations, despite the eminence of their source, can no longer be regarded as authoritative. They must now be regarded as overtaken by subsequent developments in the law.

9 There remains the difficult point of what is meant by 'impecunious' in the context of the present type of case. Lack of financial means is, almost always, a question of priorities. In the present context what it signifies is inability to pay car hire charges without making sacrifices the plaintiff could not reasonably be expected to make. I am fully conscious of the open-ended nature of this test. But fears that this will lead to increased litigation in small claims courts seem to me exaggerated. It is in the interests of all concerned to avoid litigation with its attendant costs and delay. Motor insurers and credit hire companies should be able to agree on standard enquiries, or some other means, which in practice can most readily give effect to this test of impecuniosity. I would dismiss this appeal.

Lord Hope: ... **32** In *Harbutt's 'Plasticine' Ltd v Wayne Tank and Pump Co Ltd* [1970] 1 QB 447 the plaintiffs' factory, which was in an old mill, was destroyed by fire as a result of defects in the design of equipment supplied by the defendants and its having been switched on and the plant left unattended. A new factory had to be built. The plaintiffs had no other option if they were to continue their business of making plasticine. They were not allowed to rebuild the old mill, so they had to put up a new factory. A question was raised as to the measure of damages. The defendants said that it should be limited to the difference in the value of the old mill before and after the fire and that the plaintiffs should not be allowed the cost of replacing it with a new building. This argument was rejected...

34 Of course, the facts in these two cases were quite different from those in this case. But I think that the principles on which they were decided are of general application, and it is possible to extract this guidance from them. It is for the defendant who seeks a deduction from expenditure in mitigation on the ground of betterment to make out his case for doing so. It is not enough that an element of betterment can be identified. It has to be shown that the claimant had a choice, and that he would have been able to mitigate his loss at less cost. The wrongdoer is not entitled to demand of the injured party that he incur a loss, bear a burden or make unreasonable sacrifices in the mitigation of his damages. He is entitled to demand that, where there are choices to be made, the least expensive route which will achieve mitigation must be selected. So if the evidence shows that the claimant had a choice, and that the route to mitigation which he chose was more costly than an alternative that was open to him, then a case will have been made out for a deduction. But if it shows that the claimant had no other choice available to him, the betterment must be seen as incidental to the step which he was entitled to take in the mitigation of his loss and there will be no ground for it to be deducted...

QUESTIONS

1. Is this a causation case?

2. Is the *Liesbosch Dredger* case (1933) still of any relevance to the law of damages?

3. Has precedent now lost its force (cf para 8 above)?

NOTES

1. Certain heads of damage (eg loss of profit) can sometimes be refused on the ground of remoteness (see eg *Spartan Steel* (1973), pp 54, 137) or mitigation (see *Darbishire v Warran* (1963), p 367) or indeed causation (*The Liesbosch* (1933)).

2. In *Spartan Steel* (1973) (see pp 54, 137) Lord Denning MR said: 'I do not like this doctrine of 'parasitic damages'. I do not like the very word 'parasite'. A 'parasite' is one who is a useless hanger-on sucking the substance out of others. 'Parasitic' is the adjective derived from it. It is a term of abuse. It is an opprobrious epithet. The phrase "parasitic damages" conveys to my mind the idea of damages which ought not in justice to be awarded, but which somehow or other have been allowed to get through by hanging on to others. If such be the concept underlying the doctrine, then the sooner it is got rid of the better.' Lord Denning was commenting upon counsel's attempt to attach, in the negligence action, the claim for the loss of profits to the claim for the physical damage to the metal.

3. In *The Mediana* (1900) the Earl of Halsbury LC said this: 'Now, in the particular case before us ... the broad proposition seems to me to be that by a wrongful act of the defendants the plaintiffs were deprived of their vessel. When I say deprived of their vessel, I will not use the phrase "the use of the vessel". What right has a wrongdoer to consider what use you are going to make of your vessel? More than one case has been put to illustrate this: for example, the owner of a horse, or of a chair. Supposing a person took away a chair out of my room and kept it for 12 months, could anybody say you had a right to diminish the damages by showing that I did not usually sit in that chair, or that there were plenty of other chairs in the room? The proposition so nakedly stated appears to me to be absurd.'

11.4.2 Damages for trespass to property

See *Inverugie Investments v Hackett* (1995) (p 25).

QUESTION

With respect to the Earl of Halsbury's comment in 11.4.1 (in *The Mediana* (1900)), would it be absurd to award full loss of use damages (as if it were midsummer) to a deck-chair hiring company at a seaside resort deprived of the use of a few of its deckchairs during the winter season?

11.4.3 Damages for trespass to the person

Where a defendant causes deliberate personal injury the normal rules applicable to personal injury damages will obviously apply. However, many trespass claims are brought against the police and thus involve, also, an invasion of the claimant's constitutional rights. Awards are often made by juries, but judges have been given statutory power to modify any awards (see *John v MGN Ltd* (1997), p 408)

Thompson v Commissioner of Police of the Metropolis [1998] QB 498, CA

This case involved two actions for damages against the police. In the first case the claimant had been awarded by the jury £1,500 compensatory and £50,000 exemplary damages for false imprisonment and malicious prosecution. In the second case the claimant had been awarded £20,000 compensatory (including aggravated) and £200,000 exemplary damages for trespass. The Court of Appeal (Lord Woolf MR, Auld LJ and Sir Brian Neill) substituted an award of £10,000 compensatory and £25,000 exemplary damages in the first case and reduced the award of exemplary damages, in the second case, to £15,000.

Lord Woolf MR: This is the judgment of the court. In a number of recent cases members of the public have been awarded very large sums of exemplary damages by juries against the Commissioner of Police of the Metropolis for unlawful conduct towards them by the police. As a result these two appeals have been brought by the commissioner. The intention is to clarify the directions which a judge should include in a summing up to assist the jury as to the amount of damages, particularly exemplary damages, which it is appropriate for them to award a plaintiff who is successful in this type of action. As similar appeals are pending any guidance given by us on this subject should influence the out-come of those appeals in addition to providing guidance for the future...

... Part of the claim can have, as in both of these appeals, a personal injury element which makes the experience in ordinary personal injury cases directly relevant. A differ-ence in the awards for compensation for the same injury, ignoring any question of aggravation, cannot be justified because the award is by a jury in a small minority of cases (the false imprisonment cases) while in the majority of cases (the other personal injury cases) the award is by a judge. If this court would intervene in one situation it should do so in the other. There is no justification for two tariffs. Furthermore even where what is being calculated is the proper compensation for loss of liberty or the damaging effect of a malicious prosecution the analogy with personal injuries is closer than it is in the case of defamation. The compensation is for something which is akin to pain and suffering. There is also recognition today that the uncertainty produced by the lack of consistency as to the damages which will be awarded in cases of this sort results in increased costs.

We have already referred to what was said in his judgment in *John v MGN Ltd* [1997] QB 586 by Sir Thomas Bingham MR as to the effect of excessive awards of damages in defamation cases on the public perception of civil justice. In this category of case the reaction could understandably be stronger since the excessive awards are being paid out of public money (though police forces other than the Metropolitan do take out insur-ance) and could well result in a reduction in the resources of the police available to be used for activities which would benefit the public. The Law Commission's Consultation Paper to which we have already made reference considers whether the power to award aggravated and exemplary damages should be abolished. The Law Commission's pro-visional views expressed in their consultation paper is that the power should be retained. However it is counterproductive to give juries an impossible task. It must at present be very difficult for a jury to understand the distinction between aggravated and exemplary damages when there is such a substantial overlap between the factors which provide the sole justification for both awards. The extent to which juries fluctuate in the

▶

awards which they make (which the present appeals demonstrate) indicates the difficulties which they have. On the other hand there are arguments which can be advanced to justify the retention of the use of juries in this area of litigation. Very difficult issues of credibility will often have to be resolved. It is desirable for these to be determined by the plaintiff's fellow citizens rather than judges, who like the police are concerned in maintaining law and order. Similarly the jury because of their composition, are a body which is peculiarly suited to make the final assessment of damages, including deciding whether aggravated or exemplary damages are called for in this area of litigation and for the jury to have these important tasks is an important safeguard of the liberty of the individual citizen.

As the Court of Appeal has usually the responsibility for determining the level of damages when it allows an appeal its decisions should indicate what is the appropriate level for damages in these actions. A standard will be established with which jury awards can be compared. This will make it easier to determine whether or not the sum which the jury has awarded is excessive. To not provide juries with sufficient guidance to enable them to approach damages on similar lines to those which this court will adopt will mean the number of occasions this court will be called on to intervene will be undesirably frequent. This will be disadvantageous to the parties because it will result in increased costs and uncertainty. It will also have adverse consequences for the reputation of the jury system. It could be instrumental in bringing about its demise...

(5) In a straightforward case of wrongful arrest and imprisonment the starting point is likely to be about £500 for the first hour during which the plaintiff has been deprived of his or her liberty. After the first hour an additional sum is to be awarded, but that sum should be on a reducing scale so as to keep the damages proportionate with those payable in personal injury cases and because the plaintiff is entitled to have a higher rate of compensation for the initial shock of being arrested...

(6) In the case of malicious prosecution the figure should start at about £2,000 and for prosecution continuing for as long as two years, the case being taken to the Crown Court, an award of about £10,000 could be appropriate. If a malicious prosecution results in a conviction which is only set aside on an appeal this will justify a larger award to reflect the longer period during which the plaintiff has been in peril and has been caused distress...

(10) We consider that where it is appropriate to award aggravated damages the figure is unlikely to be less than a £1,000. We do not think it is possible to indicate a precise arithmetical relationship between basic damages and aggravated damages because the circumstances will vary from case to case. In the ordinary way, however, we would not expect the aggravated damages to be as much as twice the basic damages except perhaps where, on the particular facts, the basic damages are modest...

(13) Where exemplary damages are appropriate they are unlikely to be less than £5,000. Otherwise the case is probably not one which justifies an award of exemplary damages at all. In this class of action the conduct must be particularly deserving of condemnation for an award of as much as £25,000 to be justified and the figure of £50,000 should be regarded as the absolute maximum, involving directly officers of at least the rank of superintendent...

QUESTIONS

1. From the citizen's point of view, does it matter whether his or her constitutional rights are invaded by a constable or a by superintendent?

2. What is the object of the award of damages in false imprisonment and malicious prosecution cases: is it the invasion of the constitutional right or the mental distress of the victim? Have constitutional rights been 'devalued' by *Thompson*?

11.4.4 Damages for nuisance

Private nuisance is a tort that attaches to land and thus damages are measured prima facie with reference to the *res* (thing) rather than to the persons (*personae*) who occupy the property.

Hunter v Canary Wharf Ltd [1997] AC 655, HL

(See pp 80, 206)

Lord Hoffmann:... I cannot... agree with Stephenson LJ in *Bone v Seale* [1975] 1 WLR 797, 803-804 when he said that damages in an action for nuisance caused by smells from a pig farm should be fixed by analogy with damages for loss of amenity in an action for personal injury. In that case it was said that 'efforts to prove diminution in the value of the property as a result of this persistent smell over the years failed.' I take this to mean that it had not been shown that the property would sell for less. But diminution in capital value is not the only measure of loss. It seems to me that the value of the right to occupy a house which smells of pigs must be less than the value of the occupation of an equivalent house which does not. In the case of a transitory nuisance, the capital value of the property will seldom be reduced. But the owner or occupier is entitled to compensation for the diminution in the amenity value of the property during the period for which the nuisance persisted. To some extent this involves placing a value upon intangibles. But estates agents do this all the time. The law of damages is sufficiently flexible to be able to do justice in such a case: compare *Ruxley Electronics and Construction Ltd v Forsyth* [1996] AC 344.

There may of course be cases in which, in addition to damages for injury to his land, the owner or occupier is able to recover damages for consequential loss. He will, for example, be entitled to loss of profits which are the result of inability to use the land for the purposes of his business. Or if the land is flooded, he may also be able to recover damages for chattels or livestock lost as a result. But inconvenience, annoyance or even illness suffered by persons on land as a result of smells or dust are not damage consequential upon the injury to the land. It is rather the other way about: the injury to the amenity of the land consists in the fact that the persons upon it are liable to suffer inconvenience, annoyance or illness.

It follows that damages for nuisance recoverable by the possessor or occupier may be affected by the size, commodiousness and value of his property but cannot be increased merely because more people are in occupation and therefore suffer greater collective discomfort. If more than one person has an interest in the property, the damages will have to be divided among them. If there are joint owners, they will be jointly

▶

entitled to the damages. If there is a reversioner and the nuisance has caused damage of a permanent character which affects the reversion, he will be entitled to damages according to his interest. But the damages cannot be increased by the fact that the interests in the land are divided; still less according to the number of persons residing on the premises.... Once it is understood that nuisances 'productive of sensible personal discomfort' (*St. Helen's Smelting Co. v Tipping*, 11 HL Cas 642, 650) do not constitute a separate tort of causing discomfort to people but are merely part of a single tort of causing injury to land, the rule that the plaintiff must have an interest in the land falls into place as logical and, indeed, inevitable...

QUESTIONS

1. Does it really make sense to say that the victim of a nuisance is the land rather than the people on it?

2. An occupier of a terraced house deliberately plays loud music at 3 am in order to annoy the families on each side of him. In one family several children do badly in their GCSE exams probably as a result of the noise; in the other family only one child does badly in the exams probably as a result of the noise. If you were the solicitor acting for both the victim families would you advise them that each family could only be awarded more or less the same amount of damages?

11.4.5 Damages for defamation

Invasion of a person's reputation interest has given rise to particular difficulties in the law of damages as the next extract indicates.

John v MGN Ltd [1997] QB 586, CA

In an action for damages for defamation against *The Sun* newspaper, the entertainer Elton John was awarded £75,000 compensatory and £275,000 exemplary damages by a jury. The Court of Appeal (Sir Thomas Bingham MR, Neill and Hirst LJJ) reduced the figure to £25,000 compensatory and £50,000 exemplary damages.

Sir Thomas Bingham MR: ... The successful plaintiff in a defamation action is entitled to recover, as general compensatory damages, such sum as will compensate him for the wrong he has suffered. That sum must compensate him for the damage to his reputation; vindicate his good name; and take account of the distress, hurt and humiliation which the defamatory publication has caused. In assessing the appropriate damages for injury to reputation the most important factor is the gravity of the libel; the more closely it touches the plaintiff's personal integrity, professional reputation, honour, courage, loyalty and the core attributes of his personality, the more serious it is likely to be. The extent of publication is also very relevant: a libel published to millions has a greater potential to cause damage than a libel published to a handful of people. A successful plaintiff may properly look to an award of damages to vindicate his reputation: but the significance of this is much greater in a case where the defendant asserts the truth of the libel and refuses any retraction or apology than in a case where the defendant acknowledges the falsity of what was published and publicly expresses regret that the libellous publication took place. It is well established that compensatory damages may and should compensate for additional injury caused to the plaintiff's feelings by the defendant's conduct of the action, as when he persists in an unfounded assertion that the publication was true, or refuses to apologise, or cross-examines the plaintiff in a wounding or insulting way. Although the plaintiff has been referred to as 'he' all this of course applies to women just as much as men.

There could never be any precise, arithmetical formula to govern the assessment of general damages in defamation, but if such cases were routinely tried by judges sitting alone there would no doubt emerge a more or less coherent framework of awards which would, while recognising the particular features of particular cases, ensure that broadly comparable cases led to broadly comparable awards. This is what has happened in the field of personal injuries since these ceased to be the subject of trial by jury and became in practice the exclusive preserve of judges. There may be even greater factual diversity in defamation than in personal injury cases, but this is something of which the framework would take account...

...A series of jury awards in sums wildly disproportionate to any damage conceivably suffered by the plaintiff has given rise to serious and justified criticism of the procedures leading to such awards. This has not been the fault of the juries. Judges, as they were bound to do, confined themselves to broad directions of general principle, coupled with injunctions to the jury to be reasonable. But they gave no guidance on what might be thought reasonable or unreasonable, and it is not altogether surprising that juries lacked an instinctive sense of where to pitch their awards. They were in the position of sheep loosed on an unfenced common, with no shepherd...

Following enactment of section 8(2) of the Courts and Legal Services Act 1990 and the introduction of RSC, Ord 59, r 11(4) in its present form the Court of Appeal was for the first time empowered, on allowing an appeal against a jury's award of damages, to substitute for the sum awarded by the jury such sum as might appear to the court to be proper....

...[T]here is continuing evidence of libel awards in sums which appear so large as to bear no relation to the ordinary values of life. This is most obviously unjust to defendants. But it serves no public purpose to encourage plaintiffs to regard a successful libel action, risky though the process undoubtedly is, as a road to untaxed riches. Nor is it healthy if any legal process fails to command the respect of lawyer and layman alike, as is regrettably true of the assessment of damages by libel juries. We are persuaded by the arguments we have heard that the subject should be reconsidered....

In the passage from the judgment of the court in the *Rantzen* case [1994] QB 670... the Court of Appeal essentially adopted the approach of Lord Hailsham LC in *Broome v Cassell Co Ltd* [1972] AC 1027 in concluding that there was no satisfactory way in which conventional awards in actions for damages for personal injuries could be used to provide guidance for an award in an action for defamation. Much depends, as we now think, on what is meant by guidance: it is one thing to say (and we agree) that there can be no precise equiparation between a serious libel and (say) serious brain damage; but it is another to point out to a jury considering the award of damages for a serious libel that the maximum conventional award for pain and suffering and loss of amenity to a plaintiff suffering from very severe brain damage is about £125,000 and that this is something of which the jury may take account...

QUESTIONS

1. Have the awards of damages in defamation cases been brought under control?

2. Could the amounts awarded in defamation cases ever give rise to human rights issues?

11.4.6 Damages for deceit

Damages awarded in the tort of deceit for fradulent misrepresentation may be more generous than would be the case if the misrepresentation had been negligent. See *Smith New Court Securities Ltd v Scrimgeour Vickers Ltd* (1997) (p 288).

11.4.7 Damages for breach of a human right

Under the Human Rights Act 1998 damages may be awarded (s 8) for an unlawful act which breaches a Convention right (s 6(1)).

Anufrijeva v Southwark LBC [2004] 2 WLR 603, CA

This case concerned a number of actions for damages against public authorities under s 8 of the Human Rights Act 1998 by persons seeking asylum in the UK. The claimants argued that the authorities had breached their rights, under art 8 of the Convention for the Protection of Human Rights and Fundamental Freedoms, to respect for their private and family life. The Court of Appeal (Lord Woolf CJ, Lord Phillips MR and Auld LJ) held that on the facts of each claim there had been no breach of art 8 but that, had there been such a breach, modest damages could have been awarded.

Lord Woolf (delivering judgment of the court): ... **50** As we shall see, whereas damages are recoverable as of right in the case of damage caused by a tort, the same is not true in the case of a claim brought under the HRA for breach of the Convention. The language of the HRA and the jurisprudence of the Court of Human Rights make this clear...

57 Section 8(4) of the HRA requires the court to take into account the principles applied by the Court of Human Rights when deciding whether to award damages and the amount of an award. Both the decisions of that court and the HRA make it plain that when damages are required to vindicate human rights and to achieve just satisfaction, damages should be awarded. Our approach to awarding damages in this jurisdiction should be no less liberal than those applied at Strasbourg or one of the purposes of the HRA will be defeated and claimants will still be put to the expense of having to go to Strasbourg to obtain just satisfaction. The difficulty lies in identifying from the Strasbourg jurisprudence clear and coherent principles governing the award of damages...

59 Despite these warnings it is possible to identify some basic principles the Court of Human Rights applies. The fundamental principle underlying the award of compensation is that the court should achieve what it describes as restitutio in integrum. The applicant should, in so far as this is possible, be placed in the same position as if his Convention rights had not been infringed. Where the breach of a Convention right has clearly caused significant pecuniary loss, this will usually be assessed and awarded... The problem arises in relation to the consequences of the breach of a Convention right which are not capable of being computed in terms of financial loss...

72 An infringement of a Convention right may have similar consequences to a tort giving rise to a claim under our domestic law – indeed the same act may constitute both a tort and a breach of a Convention right... Where a breach of article 5(4) results in a patient continuing to be detained in a hospital where he would otherwise have been released, the consequence of the breach bears close comparison with the consequences of the tort of false imprisonment. Should the English court, when awarding damages under the HRA, use the damages awarded for the tort of false imprisonment as a model?...

74 We have made plain that the discretionary exercise of deciding whether to award compensation under the HRA is not to be compared to the approach adopted where damages are claimed for breach of an obligation under civil law. Where, however, in a claim under the HRA, the court decides that it is appropriate to award damages, the levels of damages awarded in respect of torts as reflected in the guidelines issued by the Judicial Studies Board, the levels of awards made by the Criminal Injuries Compensation Board and by the Parliamentary Ombudsman and the Local Government Ombudsman may all provide some rough guidance where the consequences of the infringement of human rights are similar to that being considered in the comparator selected. In cases of maladministration where the consequences are not of a type which gives rise to any right to compensation under our civil law, the awards of the ombudsman may be the only comparator.

75 We have indicated that a finding of a breach of a positive obligation under article 8 to provide support will be rare, and will be likely to occur only where this impacts severely on family life. Where such a breach does occur, it is unlikely that there will be any ready comparator to assist in the assessment of damages. There are good reasons why, where the breach arises from maladministration, in those cases where an award of damages is appropriate, the scale of such damages should be modest. The cost of supporting those in need falls on society as a whole. Resources are limited and payments of substantial damages will deplete the resources available for other needs of the public including primary care. If the impression is created that asylum seekers whether genuine or not are profiting from their status, this could bring the HRA into disrepute...

QUESTIONS

1. Is an action for damages under s 8 of the HRA 1998 a true claim in tort or is it a rather different type of substantive claim? (See *R(Greenfield) v Home Secretary* (2005), § 19.)

2. Is this case authority for the proposition that the measure of damages in the law of obligations should take account not only of the claimant's interests but also those of the defendant?

11.5 Debt and similar claims

The great majority of claims in tort are damages actions by a victim against a single tortfeasor. Yet on occasions damage can be attributable to more than one wrongdoer and when this is the case the victim is entitled to claim the whole of his damages from any single defendant (unless the 'damage' is split up and apportioned causally to different actors: *Rahman v Arearose* (2001)). However, the defendant who pays is entitled under statute to reclaim, provided certain conditions are fulfilled, contribution, if not a complete indemnity, from other tortfeasors. These claims are not really damages actions since they are based more on the principle of unjust enrichment. Conceptually therefore it might be better to see such claims for specific amounts as recourse 'debt' actions (although whether they are technically debt claims is open to discussion).

Civil Liability (Contribution) Act 1978 (c 47)

1 Entitlement to contribution

(1) Subject to the following provisions of this section, any person liable in respect of any damage suffered by another person may recover contribution from any other person liable in respect of the same damage (whether jointly with him or otherwise)...

(3) A person shall be liable to make contribution by virtue of subsection (1) above notwithstanding that he has ceased to be liable in respect of the damage in question since the time when the damage occurred, unless he ceased to be liable by virtue of the expiry of a period of limitation or prescription which extinguished the right on which the claim against him in respect of the damage was based...

2 Assessment of contribution

(1) Subject to subsection (3) below, in any proceedings for contribution under section 1 above the amount of the contribution recoverable from any person shall be such as may be found by the court to be just and equitable having regard to the extent of that person's responsibility for the damage in question.

(2) Subject to subsection (3) below, the court shall have power in any such proceedings to exempt any person from liability to make contribution, or to direct that the contribution to be recovered from any person shall amount to a complete indemnity...

6 Interpretation

(1) A person is liable in respect of any damage for the purposes of this Act if the person who suffered it (or anyone representing his estate or dependants) is entitled to recover compensation from him in respect of that damage (whatever the legal basis of his liability, whether tort, breach of contract, breach of trust or otherwise)...

NOTE

The background to this statute is explained in the next two extracts.

Rahman v Arearose [2001] QB 351, CA

Law LJ: ... **18** The reason for the rule that each concurrent tortfeasor is liable to compensate for the whole of the damage is not hard to find. In any such case, the claimant cannot prove that either tortfeasor singly caused the damage, or caused any particular part or portion of the damage. Accordingly his claim would fall to be dismissed, for want of proof of causation. But that would be the plainest injustice; hence the rule. However, the rule was a potential source of another injustice. A defendant against whom judgment had been given, under the rule, for the whole of the claimant's damages had at common law no cause of action against his fellow concurrent tortfeasor to recover any part of what he had to pay under the judgment; so that the second tortfeasor, if for whatever reason he was not sued by the claimant, might escape scot free. Hence the 1978 Act and its predecessor the Law Reform (Married Women and Tortfeasors) Act 1935. It provides a right of contribution between concurrent tortfeasors. The expression 'same damage' in section 1(1) therefore means (and means only) the kind of single indivisible injury as arises at common law in a case of concurrent torts...

QUESTION

The facts of the above case are interesting both from a contribution and a causation point of view. The claimant had been attacked by two youths while working in the King's Cross branch of Burger King and subsequently had to undergo an eye operation as a result. However, the operation was negligently performed and the claimant lost the sight in that eye. In addition to the hospital's negligence, the employer had also been at fault in not providing the employee with sufficient security at his workplace. This loss of an eye was not the only damage suffered; there was also pain and suffering, loss of future earnings and severe psychological harm. Should each defendant (employer and hospital) be separately liable for the whole of the claimant's damage or should each defendant be liable only for parts of the overall damage? (Cf Weir (2004) 78 *Tulane L R* 511.)

Dubai Aluminium Co Ltd v Salaam [2003] 2 AC 366, HL

Lord Hobhouse: ... **71** In a simple case, say, injury to a passenger arising from a collision between two cars, both to blame, no problem arises. The court apportions the liability between the two drivers. But where, as in the present case, there has been a conspiracy to defraud involving a number of individuals, complications can arise. Only some of them may be before the court; some may be beyond the practical reach of the law; some may be insolvent; the routes by which liability has arisen may differ.

72 Section 2 of the statute requires the court to order contribution in an amount which is 'just and equitable having regard to the extent of that person's responsibility for the damage in question', the 'person' being the person being ordered to contribute and the 'damage in question' being the damage suffered by the victim for which the persons claiming and paying contribution were both liable. The concept of what is just and equitable corresponds to the restitutionary principles applied elsewhere in the law, for example, contributions between sureties or between insurers. The right to a contribution arises from the fact that one person has borne a disproportionate burden which it is just that another should share (or even bear in full, section 2(3)). Likewise responsibility includes both the degree of fault and the causative relevance of that fault. The power given to the court is principled but not otherwise restricted. It is this power which the court must use to solve any problems and arrive at a just and equitable outcome...

QUESTION

What is meant by 'the same damage' in s 1(1) of the 1978 Act?

Birse Construction Ltd v Haiste Ltd [1996] 1 WLR 675, CA

This was an action for damages by a reservoir construction company (Birse) against consulting engineers (Haiste) in respect of the building of a defective reservoir for a water company (Anglian). Birse assumed responsibility for the defective reservoir and agreed to build a new reservoir at its own expense for Anglian. Haiste in turn brought a statutory contribution claim against a third party (Newton), an employee of the water company who was advising on the reservoir project, on the basis that the third party had been negligent and in breach of contract. The question arose as to whether the damage suffered by Anglian in having a defective reservoir was the 'same damage' as the damage suffered by Birse in having to build, at its own expense, a new reservoir. The Court of Appeal (Sir John May, Roch and Nourse LJJ) held that they were not the same since one was physical damage while the other was economic loss.

Roch LJ: I agree. A person liable for damage suffered by another may recover contribution from any other person liable in respect of the same damage under section 1(1) of the Civil Liability (Contribution) Act 1978, subject to the following provisions of the section. The liability of the person claiming contribution, Haiste, and the liability of the person from whom contribution is claimed, Mr Newton, does not have to be joint (section 1(1)), nor does the legal basis of the liability of Haiste have to be the same as the basis of the liability of Mr Newton: see section 6(1) of the Act.

The word 'damage' in the phrase 'the same damage' in section 1(1) does not mean 'damages.' This is demonstrated by other sections of the Act, for example section 2(3). By section 6(1) 'damage' is the harm suffered by the 'another person,' to use the phrase in section 1(1), for which that person is entitled to recover compensation; it is not the compensation which is recoverable although in cases of purely financial loss it may be commensurate with it.

For there to be an entitlement to claim contribution the damage for which the person who claims contribution and the person from whom contribution is claimed has to be the same damage, that is to say the sufferer must be the same person or some person representing his estate or dependants. This is because the person who is entitled to recover compensation for the damage has to be the person who suffered the damage. I disagree with Judge Cyril Newman QC that this interpretation of the Act requires the addition of section 1(1) of the Act of words that are not there. In my view, this is the correct construction to be placed on section (1) when the Act is construed as a whole.

The damage suffered by Anglian in this case was the physical defects in the reservoir. The damage suffered by Birse was the financial loss of having to construct a second reservoir for Anglian. Anglian and Birse did not suffer the same damage. Consequently, I, too, would answer the question raised in the summons in the negative.

QUESTION

Did Anglian suffer physical damage or did it suffer only financial loss in not getting as good a 'product' as it expected under the construction contract? If Anglian's damage was only financial would this mean that it was the same damage as that suffered by Birse?

NOTE

This right to contribution is not unproblematic and can on occasions give rise to unfortunate results in terms of loss-spreading, one reason being that the central concept is fault. When fault (tort) finds itself in the same arena, so to speak, as unjust enrichment (restitution), one concept tends to lose out: see eg *Lister v Romford Ice Co* (1957) (pp 52, 55); and for a brief but perceptive discussion see Tony Weir, *Tort Law* (OUP, 2002), 107–13. As Weir observes (at 112), the 1978 Act 'permits a party who should bear the loss through his liability insurance to throw this loss or part of it onto a person, public or private, who would never have been sued by the primary victim'.

11.6 Injunction

Although the normal claim in a tort action is for damages, there are occasions – for example where the cause of action is harassment or nuisance – when the remedy of damages is insufficient. What is required is a court order to prohibit the defendant from continuing his activity. Such a remedy is the injunction, but being equitable it brings into play its own particular principles that attach to the *actio* itself. See in particular *Miller v Jackson* (1977) (p 14) and *Burris v Azadani* (1995) (p 375). Note that interlocutory (emergency) injunctions are subject to special principles that can make them particularly valuable as a means of developing existing, or even new, causes of action. But note also that *Manchester Airport plc v Dutton* (p 370) is not an injunction case; it was an order for repossession. Could the claimant in the case have sought repossession by injunction?

11.7 Self-help

There are occasions when a victim of a tort can 'take the law into his own hands' and use self-redress. However this 'is a summary remedy, which is justified only in clear and simple cases, or in an emergency' (Lloyd LJ in *Burton v Winters* (1993) at 1082). Perhaps the most famous example of self-help is self-defence, which of course is a self-redress remedy used to resist a trespass. And this self-help resistance often arises in constitutional 'rights' cases: can a person unlawfully arrested escape conviction for assaulting a police officer on the basis that the assault was justified as self-defence?

R v Self [1992] 1 WLR 657, CA

Garland J: ... This matter comes before the court by leave of the single judge on a point of law. There is one point central to the appeal. It is this. Since the appellant was acquitted of theft neither Mr Frost nor Mr Mole were entitled by virtue of section 24 of the Police and Criminal Evidence Act 1984 to effect a citizen's arrest. If they were not entitled to do that then this appellant could not be convicted of an assault with intent to resist or prevent the lawful apprehension or detainer of himself, that is to say his arrest...

The view of this court is that little profit can be had from taking examples and trying to reduce them to absurdity. The words of the statute are clear and applying those words to this case there was no arrestable offence committed. It necessarily follows that the two offences under section 38 of the Offences against the Person Act 1861 could not be committed because there was no power to apprehend or detain the appellant.

It follows also, that that being the law, as this court sees it, the convictions on counts 2 and 3 must be quashed and this appeal allowed.

QUESTIONS

1. Could the defendant now sue Mr Frost and Mr Mole for damages in tort?

2. What if the defendant had been arrested by a policeman? (Cf Police and Criminal Evidence Act 1984, s 25.)

3. Under what circumstances could Mr Frost and Mr Mole have lawfully arrested the defendant? (Cf Police and Criminal Evidence Act 1984, s 24.)

NOTE

Any force used however must not be excessive.

Revill v Newbery [1996] QB 567, CA

This was an action for damages by a burglar injured when shot by the owner of a shed into which he was trying illegally to enter. The Court of Appeal (Neill, Evans and Millett LJJ) upheld an award of damages suitably reduced for contributory negligence.

Neill LJ: ... Each case must depend on its own facts. There may well be cases where in order to frighten a burglar away a gun is discharged in the air and the burglar is injured because unexpectedly he is on the roof. That, however, is not this case. I have carefully considered what weight should be given to the fact that the defendant thought that the intruder was at the window rather than at the door. I have come to the conclusion, however, that the judge was entitled to treat the discharge of the gun not merely as a warning shot but as a shot which was likely to strike anyone who was in the vicinity of the door. Although the intruder may have been at the window a person in the defendant's position could reasonably have anticipated that if the window were shuttered, as it was, the intruder might move to the door. The hole through which the gun was discharged was at body height and, as I understand it, the gun was fired more or less horizontally.

It is right to emphasise, as did the judge, that the defendant certainly did not intend to hit the plaintiff. Nevertheless I am satisfied that on the facts of this case the judge was entitled to find that the plaintiff was a person to whom the defendant owed some duty and that the defendant was in breach of that duty. The finding of a substantial proportion of contributory negligence was more than justified.

I would dismiss the appeal.

Millett LJ: For centuries the common law has permitted reasonable force to be used in defence of the person or property. Violence may be returned with necessary violence. But the force used must not exceed the limits of what is reasonable in the circumstances. Changes in society and in social perceptions have meant that what might have been considered reasonable at one time would no longer be so regarded; but the principle remains the same. The assailant or intruder may be met with reasonable force but no more; the use of excessive violence against him is an actionable wrong.

It follows, in my opinion, that there is no place for the doctrine ex turpi causa non oritur actio in this context. If the doctrine applied, any claim by the assailant or trespasser would be barred no matter how excessive or unreasonable the force used against him.

I agree that, for the reasons given by Neill LJ, the judge was entitled to find that the defendant's conduct was not reasonable. It was clearly dangerous and bordered on reckless. I would dismiss the appeal.

QUESTIONS

1. Is the defendant liable to the claimant in the tort of trespass or negligence?

2. Is this case authority for the proposition that one should never try to defend oneself, one's family or one's property against a burglar, for there is always a risk that one will have to pay him or her damages?

3. Why is it not possible to say that a burglar who enters another's property takes the risk of the householder behaving, perhaps out of fear, irrationally?

4. A householder shoots and kills a professional burglar. The wife of the burglar sues the householder for damages under the Fatal Accidents Act 1976. Can she claim compensation for the 'earnings' that her late husband would have made from his 'professional' activity had he not been wrongfully killed?

NOTES

1. See now *Criminal Justice Act 2003* S 329

2. Abatement is a self-help remedy against a nuisance, see: M Jones, *Textbook on Torts* (8th edn, OUP, 2002), 376–7.

11.8 Final word

Stephen Waddams, 'Classification of Private Law in Relation to Historical Evidence: Description, Prescription, and Conceptual Analysis' in A Lewis and M Lobban (eds), *Law and History: Current Legal Issues 2003* vol 6 (OUP, 2004), 265, 284

Conceptual analysis, description of the past, and prescription for the future have been closely interrelated in legal analysis. One reason for the association is that an assessment of what the law is at the time of assessment, or of what it has been at any past time (not entirely distinguishable, because Anglo-Amercian law has always been conscious of its own past), is itself a complex enterprise, involving elements of historical enquiry, prediction, judgment, synthesis, and argument. So, when a writer assesses what the current law is on any question, she includes elements not only of a historical account of the past, but also of judgment, supported by argument of what is desirable, together with a prediction of what the courts will do in the future. It is practically inevitable for these considerations to merge, because eventual acceptance by the courts is naturally predicted of arguments found persuasive by writer and reader...

The same can be said of many other accounts at many different levels of theory: an account may be correct from its own particular conceptual perspective despite, or rather just because of, its not undertaking to describe the past. But then it should not be mistaken for a historical account. Historical enquiry, conceptual analysis, and prescriptions or aspiration for the future are interrelated, and each has had an important place in legal analysis, but there is good reason for distinguishing among them, for each has limitations: historical enquiry alone cannot tell us what kinds of legal rules might be logical, elegant, or otherwise desirable, and neither conceptual analysis nor aspirations for the future can supply an account of the past.

QUESTION

Does 'tort' gain its normative force from: (a) legal history; (b) black-letter positive rules; (c) moral philosophy; (d) social policy; (e) economic policy; (f) tort's own internal symmetry; (g) a mixture of philosophical, social, political and economic arguments brought to bear on particular factual situations; (h) analogies with the facts of previous cases; (i) or some other source?

NOTE

The great temptation is to conclude a book on tort by referring, favourably or critically, to its function or its internal structure. Does tort achieve what it is supposed to achieve? Is it a philosophically coherent subject or an incoherent mess? (And so on.) This temptation has been resisted in this present student book, not, it must be said at once, because these functional or structural questions are irrelevant (they are not). The temptation has been resisted because one of the most difficult aspects of tort is arguably its reasoning methodology; there are seemingly very few rules as such (compare with contract) and considerable argumentation, much of it based on 'policy'. Theory, in its turn, meanders between extreme individualism and communitarian holism, punctuated by attempts to base tort on some moral or economic perspective. Professor Waddams offers an insight into legal method and his comments are offered here, as a final note, as a prism in which the materials in this casebook can be reviewed. His comments are worth reflecting upon since they offer a real insight into English legal reasoning (judical and academic); and tort is a subject very dependent upon the reasoning to be found in the judgments.

Index

abatement 417
'abnormal sensitiveness' 210
absolute privilege 278
Accidents, Compensation and the Law
    (Atiyah) 389–90
accidents, liability for 71–2
actio 375
actio in personam 371
actio in rem 371
action civile 21
actionability 327–35
actiones 369
actionist approach 10
acts of God/acts of Nature 342–4
acts/omissions 94
administrative law 29–30
aggravated damages 386, 406
aims and philosophy of tort 44–9
'The Aims of Tort Law' (Williams) 289
Air Navigation Orders 180
aircraft 157, 179–84
Alderson, B 118–19
alternative causes 326
alternative remedies 394
ambulance service 319–20
amends, offer of 285–6
analogy *32–4, 135, 136–7*
The Anatomy of Tort Law (Cane) 10–11
animals 157, 174–9, 185
annuities 390
anti-social behaviour 22
argumentation and tort 38–40
assault and battery 91–5
assaults by employees 242–6
assumpsit 2, 3
Atiyah, Professor 231–2, 385, 389–90
*Atiyah's Accidents, Compensation and
    the Law* 231
Atkin, Lord
    constitutional law 27–8
    motor vehicles 171
    negligence 113
    neighbour principle 152

Atkinson, J 201–2
auctioneers 63
authorised users 248
auxiliaries, liability for 226

bailment 9, 23, 229, 252
balance of probabilities 355, 357
Bank of Credit and Commerce
    International 105–7
Bankes, LJ 171, 358
Banque Bruxelles Lambert case [1997]
    AC 191, 211 41
Barendt, Eric 265
'The Battle of Manywells Spring'
    (Rudden) 61
behavioural categories 76
Beldam, LJ 365
benevolence 393
bereavement 148, 150, 371, 373, 378,
    400
Bingham, Lord
    child abuse 310–12
    damages for defamation 408–9
    European law 42
    injunctions 375–6
    proof of causation 349–50
    psychological harm 149
    public/private law 298
    remedies and damage 377–8
Birks, Peter 255–6
Blackburn, J 217, 380
blameworthy acts 76
Bowen, LJ 81, 85
Bramwell, LJ 2, 85, 211–12
Brandon, Lord 67, 250–1
breach of bailment 9
breach of confidence 64
breach of contract 9, 365, 380
breach of duty
    inexperienced defendants 126–30
    negligence defined 118–19
    and precedent 133–4
    professional skills 130–3

proof of breach 134
standard of care 119–24
test 290
vulnerable victims 124–6
breach of statutory duty
causation 328–9
crime and tort 21
dangerous equipment 164–5
motor vehicles 171–2
negligence and 156
Bridge, J 93
Bridge, Lord
collateral benefits 393
duty of care 135
pecuniary loss 391–2
broadcasters' Code of Practice 64
Brooke, LJ 39
Brown, Lord 151, 300
Brown, Simon, LJ 127
Browne-Wilkinson, Lord 21, 29,
    131–2, 155, 288
Buckley, J 180–2
burden of proof 5
business interest 84–6
Buxton, LJ 39

Cairns, Lord, LC 217
Cambridge Law Journal 71
Cane, Peter 10–11, 73, 382
care, ordinary standard of 119–24
careless words
    see misrepresentation
A Casebook on Tort (Weir) 265, 382
causal approach 10
causation
    actionability 327–35
    causes of action 1–3
    damages 364–8
    factual causation 335–58
    negligence 155
    remoteness of damage 358–64
    theories 324–7
Causation and Remoteness (Honoré)
    325
Causation in the Law (Hart and
    Honoré) 288–9, 335
central government liability 302–4
*Central Newbury Car Auctions Ltd v
    Unity Finance Ltd* [1957] 1 QB 371
    62
Chadwick, LJ 200–1, 370
chance, loss of 352–8

Charlesworth & Percy on Negligence 50
children
    born disabled 374–5
    in care 306
    child abuse 310–14
    inexperienced defendants 129–30
    liability for 252–3
    local authorities' liability 306–14
civil law, influence of 42–3, 351
Civil Liability for Animals 174, 178
claimant intervention 339–42
Clark & Lindsell on Torts 103
Classification of Private Law (Waddams)
    418, 419
Clyde, Lord 308–9, 390, 396
coal mines 166
Code Civil
    actio 375
    action civile 21
    blameworthy acts 76
    children 252
    damage 76, 134
    damages 157, 382
    duty of care 134
    employees 230–1
    individual/community 301–2
    obligations 19
    ownership 60
    privacy 63
    road accidents 169
    things 157
    words and interests 260
Coleridge, J 96
collateral benefits 393–7
Columbia Law Review 98
The Common European Law of Torts
    (von Bar) 381
common law
    aircraft 180–2
    causation 327
    dangerous equipment 163
    facts 118
    premises on a highway 202
    public/private law 296–7, 299–300
    remedies 369
The Common Law (Holmes) 289
community principle 301–2
companies, defamation and 270
'Comparative Law of Torts' (Fleming)
    262
compensation and loss spreading
    49–55

compensatory damages 379–81
competition 86, 278
complex liabilities 19
Conaghan, Joanne 13
conditio sine qua non 325–6
congenital disabilities 374
consent to injury 330–3
consequential loss/failure to make a
    gain 139
consideration, doctrine of 262
constitutional interest 82–4
constitutional law 27–9, 44
constitutional rights 66–8, 315–17
contracts
    breach of contract 9, 365, 380
    contract interest 89–91
    privity of contract 262
    three-party situations 160, 229–30,
        261–2
    and tort 16–19, 159–60
    unfair 188
contributory negligence 364–6
'Conversion and Detinue' 63
Cooke, Lord 208, 209, 236–7
corrective justice 47
cost of activities 211–12
crime and tort 19–22, 241–6
criminal injuries compensation 22
Criminal Injuries Compensation Board
    51
Criminal Injuries Compensation
    Scheme 51
Criminal Law (Chitty) 69
crisis of tort 44–5
Croom-Johnson, LJ 94
curia novit jura 39

damages
    causation 364–8
    contributory negligence 364–6
    'damage' 364, 381–3
    as deterrence 55–7
    discount rates 390
    general considerations 379–86
    interests and 381–3
    level of 406, 409, 411, 413
    mitigation of damage 366–8
    non-compensatory 383–6
    non-personal injuries 401–11
    personal injuries 34, 386–401
    remedies and 376–9
damnum emergens/lucrum cessans 139

damnum sine injuria 11
dangerous activities 218, 222–3
dangerous animals 178–9
dangerous equipment 163–8
dangerous products 157, 158–63
dangerous things
    brought onto land 216–24
    in general 184–6
data protection 64
Davies, Edmund, LJ 138, 173
death
    on cause of action 371–3
    damages 393, 400–1
debt 3, 411–15
deceit 101, 255, 287–9, 410
defamation
    damages 408–9
    defamatory statements 266–8
    defences 275–86
    general liability 264–75
    innuendo 268–72
    justification 275–6
    malicious falsehood 101–2
    negligence and 255–6
    proof of malice 255
    publication 272–5
    reputation interest 81
defective equipment 157, 167–8
defective premises 188, 203–4
defective products 40, 161
definition and scope of tort
    definitional approaches 9–14
    European considerations 40–3
    historical considerations 1–9
    liability and remedies 14–16
    methodology 30–40
    province and scope 16–30
definitional approaches 9–14
delictual liability 76
Demichel, André 295
Denning, Lord
    analogy 34
    causes of action 3, 5–6
    compensation 54–5
    contract interest 89
    economic loss 137, 139
    employee/independent contractor
        234–5
    fair comment 277
    independent contractors 193–4
    inexperienced defendants 128–9
    interest/right 84

motor vehicles 173
NHS 320–1
occupiers 190–1
persons on the highway 202–3
precedent 8
property rights 62–3
public nuisance 69
remedies 14–15
vicarious liability 232–3
Departmental Committee on Alternative Remedies 394
deterrence 49, 52, 55–9, 336–7
detinue 2, 3
Devlin, Lord
  analogy 34
    causes of action 4
  employment interest 88
  exemplary damages 384
  innuendo 269–70
  intervention by the claimant 342
  negligence 116–17
  visitors 192
Dilhorne, Viscount 227
Dillon, LJ 247
Dimensions of Private Law (Waddams) 257
Diplock, Lord
  causes of action 3–4
  damages 380
  defamation 264
  deterrence 56
  duty of care 134
  omissions 152
  precedent 31
  property 23–4
  public/private law 297
  three-party situations 226–7, 230
'direct' invasion 91
directness test 358–9
discount rates 390
distress 65, 66
distributive justice 47–8
dogs 175
dominium 295, 298
dommages-intérêts 382
Donovan, Lord 170
Le Droit Public (Demichel & Lalumière) 295
Duncan and Neil on Defamation 277
duty of care
  dangerous equipment 166–7
  history 310–12

methodological approach 134–7
obligations and 10
omissions 152–5
psychological harm 141–52
public/private law 304–5
pure economic loss 137–41
two duties of care 228
visitors 188–9, 195
Dworkin, Ronald 82, 353
Dyson, LJ 95

economic efficiency 55, 57–9
economic loss 137–41, 160, 255–6
emergency services liability 319–20
employees, liability for 230–46
  compulsory insurance 51
  course of employment 239–41
  criminal acts 241–6
  dangerous equipment 163–8
  defective equipment 157, 167–8
  defective premises 188, 203–4
  employee/independent contractor 234–8
  general considerations 231–2
  tort 232–4
  transferred employees 238–9
employment, acting in the course of 239–46
employment interest 86–7
environmental rights 68–70
equity 30, 66, 369
'Equity in the Modern Law' (Birks) 255–6
Erle, CJ 58
'estates' 371
ethics 11
European approaches to causation 325–6
European considerations 40–3
European Convention for the Protection of Human Rights
  commercial airports 183–4
  damages 410, 411
  false imprisonment 83
  family life 314
  freedom of expression 282
  'horizontal effect' 66
  incorporation 28, 42
  negligence 307
  privacy 216
European Court of Human Rights 183–4, 216, 306–7, 308

European Court of Justice 163
European Directives 158, 163
European Group on Tort Law
  auxiliaries 226
  causation 325–6, 346
  damages 379, 380, 389
  dangerous activities 222
  liability 8
  non-pecuniary damage 387
  personal injuries 387
  protected interests 70
  standard of conduct 119
  vicarious liability 225, 227
'European law', influence of 42–3
evidence 21–2
ex turpi causa non oritur actio 333–4
exemplary damages 102, 383–6, 406
'An Expanding Tort Law' (Markesinis)
  261–2
'externalities' 59

facts 118, 257, 277–8
factual causation 335–58
  claimant intervention 339–42
  introductory 335–7
  loss of a chance 352–8
  nature intervention 342–4
  overlapping damage 345–8
  proof of causation 348–51
  rescuer intervention 344–5
  third party intervention 337–9
fair comment 276–8
false imprisonment 82–3, 95–100,
  322, 406
'False Imprisonment in Good Faith'
  (Fordham) 82
'False Imprisonment' (Prosser) 98–9
family life 314–15, 410
Faulks Committee 1975 281
'fault' 168, 364, 365
'fault *per se*' 158
ferae naturae 185
feudalism 295
fictional persons 232
financial institutions liability 323
fire, escape of 223–4
Fleming, John G. 11, 262
Fleming on Torts 218, 242
foreseeability
  children 129
  'foreseeable' 121
  personal injury 361

pollution 219
proximity 135, 340
  reasonableness and 119, 120–1
  test 359–61
  typical damage 362–4
  vulnerable victims 124
formalist definitions 9–11, 41
forms of action 1–3, 13, 43, 369
Foundations of the Law of Tort (Williams
  and Hepple) 45
Fox, LJ 111
France
  see Code Civil
fraud 101–2
fraudulent misrepresentation 255
free will 198–9
freedom of expression 282–5
freedom of speech 64
functional definitions 11–13, 44–9

gain, failure to make 139
Gaius 369
Garland, LJ 416
Gault, J 110
Germany 260, 261–2
Gibson, Peter, LJ 33, 213, 247
Gibson, Ralph, LJ 50
Goddard, Lord 142
Goddard Report 1953 174
Goff, Lord
  common law 2
  contract and tort 17
  course of employment 240
  dangerous things 218
  defamation 257–8
  fire, escape of 223–4
  police liability 317
  precedent 8
  private nuisance 206–8
  reasonableness 209–10
  words and interests 260–2
good faith/negligence 313, 314
Good Samaritan 152
Governmental Liability (Weir) 12, 296
Greer, LJ 345
Griffiths, Lord 148
guard dogs 175
Guardian 268

Hague-Visby Rules 292
Hale, LJ 322–3, 356–7
Halsbury, LC 25, 60, 86–7, 404

happiness 397
harassment 22, 65–6, 99–100, 255,
  375–6
Hart 335
health and safety 165
health interest 77–8
Hepple, BA 45
Herschell, Lord 87
highway, liability to persons on
  200–4, 249
hiring charges 27
Hirst, LJ 316–17
historical considerations 1–9
A Historical Introduction to the Law of
  Obligations (Ibbetson) 265
History of English Law (Holdsworth) 48
Hobhouse, Lord
  animals 35, 178–9
  causation 336–7
  constitutional interest 83–4
  crime and tort 20
  damages 413
  dangerous things 221–2
  insurance 74
  intervention by the claimant 341
  restitution 26
  visitors 197
Hoffman, Lord
  causation 324, 350–1, 352–8
  common law 34
  dangerous things 220
  economic efficiency 58
  'externalities' 59
  human rights 28, 109, 216
  insurance 74
  loss of a chance 354, 355–6
  mental health interest 80–1
  nuisance 208, 214, 407–8
  occupiers' duties 195
  omissions 152
  personality rights 64–5
  proof of causation 350–1
  public/private law 296
  remedies 299
  tort definition 41
  trespassers 197–8
  typical damage 363
  visitors 197
Holdsworth, Sir William 48
Holmes, Oliver Wendell 289
Holt, CJ 24
honest comment 276–8

Honoré, AM 325, 335
Hope, Lord 317, 356, 378–9, 394–6
horseplay 94
human rights
  abuse by public authority 301
  aircraft 182–4
  commercial airports 183–4
  damages 410, 411
  damages for breach 410–11
  false imprisonment 83
  family life 314
  freedom of expression 282
  'horizontal effect' 66
  incorporation 28, 42, 44
  negligence 307
  nuisance 215–16
  policy and 36
  privacy 216
  public authorities and 108–9
humiliation 67
hundred per cent principle 389–90
Hutchison, J 38, 129–30
Hutton, Lord 385–6

Ibbetson, D 265
illegality defence 22
immunity from negligence 19–21
imperium 295, 298
independent contractors
  auxiliaries and 226
  employee/independent contractor
    234–8
  liability for 248–9
  non-delegable duty 249–52
  risks 192–4
indirect interference 69, 79
individual/community 301–2
Industrial Revolution 163–4
inexperienced defendants 128–30
injunctions 15, 22, 375–6, 415
injuria 272
injuria sine damno 11
innuendo 268–72
Institutes (Justinian) 1
insult 272
insurance
  collateral benefits 393
  compulsory insurance 50–1
  loss spreading 52
  road accidents 170
  tort and 71–4
'Insurance and the Tort System'
  (Lewis) 71

intangible goods 383
intentionally caused harm
   abuse of judicial process 110–11
   abuse of public power 102–9
   assault and battery 91–5
   constitutional interest 82–4
   contract interest 89–91
   employment interest 86–7
   false imprisonment 95–9
   fraud and lies 101–2
   harassment 99–100
   health interest 77–8
   and interests 76–91
   mental health interest 80–1
   property interest 79–80
   reputation interest 81
   trade and business interest 84–6
interests
   damages and 381–3
   economics 58
   and intention 76–91
   'interest' 68, 382
   invasion of 10–11
   protection of 70
   public and private 211–16
   remedies and 375–9
   rights and 84
   and words 255–63
International Encyclopedia of
   Comparative Law 44–5, 158, 164,
   325
intervention by a rescuer 344–5
intervention by a third party 337–9
intervention by nature 342–4
intervention by the claimant 339–42
An Introduction to the Law of Torts
   (Fleming) 11
invasion of dignity 63
invasion of privacy 28–9, 63, 64

jailers 67
James, J 92
Jauncey, Lord 340–1, 365–6
Jenkins, LJ 122
'Johanna Wagner and the Rival Opera
   House' (Waddams) 90
Joint Torts and Contributory Negligence
   (Williams) 340
Jolowicz, JA 71, 73, 74
Jones, Michael A. 12, 57, 417
Jowitt, Earl 6
Judge, LJ 245–6

judges 39
judicial process, abuse of 110–11
Judicial Studies Board 411
juries 118, 409
justification or excuse 5–6, 67
Justinian 1, 294

Keith, Lord
   defamation 258
   malicious prosecution 103
   non-delegable duty 252
   policy 36–7
   psychological harm 143
   public/private law 296
   three-party situations 262–3
Kennedy, LJ 204
Kilbrandon, Lord 56

Lalumière, Pierre 295
land and structures
   duty to visitors 188–9
   on the land 188–99
    land as 'thing' 158
   off the land 200–10
   use 24
Law Commission 145, 174, 218, 399
Law, LJ 412–13
Law of Obligations and Legal Remedies
   (Samuel) 43
The Law of Torts (Fleming) 181, 232
Law Quarterly Review 90
Law Reform Committee 63
Laws, LJ 370
legal person 225, 227, 371–5
Leggatt, LJ 169
Lewis, Richard 71
liability 6, 7–9, 14–16
'Liability for Accidents' (Jolowicz) 71
'Liability for an Employee's Assaults'
   (Rose) 243
Liability for Damage Caused by Things
   (Stone) 158, 164
'Liability of Auctioneers' 63
'liability without fault' 158
libel 264–5
Libel and the Media (Barendt) 265
licensees 192, 195
lies 101–2
Life's Dominion (Dworkin) 353
limitation 3, 40, 41, 77
livestock 175–6
Lloyd, Lord 143, 292

local authorities
  defamation 270
  environmental rights 69
  negligence 304–14
  nuisance 314–15
  three-party situations 229
local education authorities 228
Local Government Ombudsman 411
London Review of Books 61
Loreburn, Lord 96–7
loss of a chance 352–8
loss-spreading 49–55, 415
Lowry, Lord 352
Loyd, Lord 25

Maccabaean Lecture in Jurisprudence,
  1983 8
*MacCormick, Legal Reasoning and Legal
  Theory* 82
McGregor on Damages 352
Macmillan, Lord 48, 166, 185–6,
  238–9
Macnaghten, Lord 61, 79
McNair, J 130–1
malicious falsehood 101–2, 259, 313
malicious prosecution 102–4, 406
Mansell, Wade 13
Markesinis, Professor 262
master/servant compensation 50
Maugham, LJ 287, 345
May, Sir John 213
media, Codes of Practice 64
medical treatment, consent to 68
Megaw, LJ 129
Mellish, LJ 344
mensuetae naturae 185
mental health interest 80–1, 322–3
methodology 30–40
Millett, Lord 231–2, 243–4, 267, 417
minimal causation 326
misfeasance 84, 104–7, 303
misrepresentation 255, 286–90
misstatement 286–90
mitigation of damage 366–8
monetary remedies 369
Monkton Committee 394
Moreau, Jacques 301–2
Morris, Lord 116, 397–8
Morton, Lord 233, 343
Motor Cars (Use and Construction)
  Order 1904 171
Motor Insurer' Bureau agreement 1946
  50

motor vehicles 169–74
  authorised users 248
  local authorities 315
  pregnancy, driving during 375
  public/private law 299–300
  unauthorised users 246–8
Mummery, LJ 236, 314
Mustill, Lord 263

nature, intervention by 342–4
necessity 68, 334–5
negligence
  to beneficiaries 260–3
  burden of proof 5
  as a cause of action 112–18
  contributory negligence 364–6
  dangerous equipment 166–7
  defined 118–19
  good faith and 313, 314
  liability for words 289
  local authorities 304–14
  misrepresentation 255
  motor vehicles 169
  nuisance and 14–15, 208–11
  rights of ownership and 23
  trespass and 68
  unlawfulness 155
  'without fault' 158
negligently caused harm
  breach of duty 118–34
  causation and remoteness 155
  duty of care 134–55
  negligence as a cause of action
    112–18
  unlawfulness 155–6
neighbour principle 113, 114, 152,
  167, 259
neighbours, liability to 204–8
Neil Committee 1991 281
Neil, LJ 64, 266–7, 416–17
newspapers, Code of Practice 64
NHS 320–3
Nicholls, LJ
  absolute privilege 278
  child abuse 312–13, 314
  defamation 101–2, 265, 275
  duty of care 136
  exemplary damages 385
  fair comment 276–7
  human rights 215–16
  loss of a chance 355
  omissions 153–4

private nuisance 213–14
privilege 280–4
proof of causation 350
property damage 402–3
psychological harm 151
user principle 25
vicarious liability 228
noise 22
nominal damages 383
non-compensatory damages 383–6
non-cumul, absence of 18
non-delegable duty 249–52
non-employees, liability for 246–52
non-monetary remedies 369
non-pecuniary loss 387, 397–400
Normand, Lord 126
The Notion of an Interest (Samuel) 383
novus actus interveniens 336, 337–9,
    340, 345
nuclear radiation, escape of 224
nuisance
    abatement 417
    aircraft 180–2
    damages 407–8
    human rights 215–16
    land rule 16
    local authorities 314–15
    negligence and 14–15
    by omission 208–11
    reasonableness 214

Oaksey, Lord 119–20, 126
'objective liability' 158
obligations
    duty and 10
    in France 19, 43
    law of obligations 1–2
    property and 26
occupiers
    defined 190–1
    duty to others 195–6
    duty to tresspassers 194–9
    duty to visitors 188–9
off-shore installations 51
offer of amends 285–6
Ognall, J 46
Oliver, Lord 135, 140
omissions 152–4, 229, 261
ordinary standard of care 119–24
Orr, LJ 361
overlapping damage 345–8

Parliamentary Ombudsman 411

patrimonial rights 63
Patterson, J 95–6
Pearce, Lord 117, 397
Pearson Commission 395
Pearson, Lord 72, 226, 346, 367–8
pecuniary loss, personal injuries
    388–93
permanent vegetative state 397–8
persona 369
persona ficta 232
personae 371–5
personal injuries
    collateral benefits 393–7
    death 400–1
    dominance of 44
    foreseeability 361–4
    general considerations 386–8
    non-pecuniary loss 397–400
    pecuniary loss 388–93
personality rights 63–6
Phillips, LJ 267
Phillips, Lord, MR 273, 284–5
philosophy of tort 44–9
physical damage 7–8
planning permission 212–13
police
    abuse of judicial process 110–11
    liability 315–19
    public/private law 296
    trespass to the person 67, 404–7
    vicarious liability 231
policy
    factual causation 336–7
    operational acts 305, 309
    proof of causation 349–50
    and tort 36–8, 68
political comment 281–2
pollution 218–19, 224
Porter Committee 1948 281
Porter, Lord 23, 142, 186, 239
potential causes 326
practical justice 47, 261, 263
precedent 8, 30–4, 133–4
pregnancy, driving during 375
prerogative writs 301
'presumed responsibility' 158
primary/secondary victims 144
Principles of European Tort Law
    see European Group on Tort Law
privacy 28–9, 63, 64–6
Privacy (Neil) 64
private interest 15–16, 211–16

private law 294–302
private life 410
private nuisance
    aircraft 180–2
    liability to neighbours 204–8
    public benefit and 211–12
    right to sue 207–8
    ship at sea 4–5
    statutory authority 212–15
Private Property and Abuse of Rights
    (Taggart) 61
privilege 278–85
privity of contract, doctrine of 262
professional liability 261–3, 290–3
professional skills 130–3
proof of breach 134
proof of causation 348–51
property
    damage 401–11
    interests 79–80, 229
    rights 2, 60–3
    tort and 22–4
prosecution service liability 315–19
Prosser, DWL 98–9
protected interests 70
The Province of the Law of Tort
    (Winfield) 9
proximity 119, 135
psychological harm 141–2
public body liability
    central government 302–4
    emergency services 319–20
    financial institutions 323
    local authorities 304–15
    NHS 320–3
    police and prosecution service
        315–19
    public liability policies 51
    public office 84, 102–9
    public/private law 294–302
    see also local authorities
public interest
    fair comment 276–7
    nuisance 181–2
    private interest and 15–16
    private interests and 211–16
public nuisance
    crime and tort 21
    motor vehicles 172–4
    numbers of people 68–9
    persons on the highway 200–4
    pollution 4, 5, 6

private nuisance and 204–5
public/private law 294–302
publication 272–5
pure economic loss 137–41, 160,
    255–6
pursuit of justice 11

qualified privilege 259, 279–85
The Quantum of Damages (Kemp)
    378–9
quarrying 68–9

Radcliffe, Lord 6, 53–4, 121, 251–2
real rights/personal rights 2
'reasonable journalist' 285
reasonableness
    factual causation 338–9
    intervention by the claimant 340
    justification and 67
    negligence 210
    ordinary standard of care 119–24
    public bodies and 68
references 255–9
Reid, Lord
    children 253
    damages as deterrence 56
    employment interest 88
    innuendo 269
    intervention by the claimant 339,
        342
    negligence 115
    non-pecuniary loss 398
    overlapping damage 346
    standard of care 120–1, 124–5
    three-party situations 226
    vicarious liability 233
remedies
    actions and 369–79
    formalist definitions 9
    liability and 14–16
    public and private 299–301
    types of 369–71
remoteness 155, 358–64, 404
repossession of land 370
reputation interest 81, 255–6, 265,
    270
res 369
res incorporalis 383
res ipsa loquitur 160, 223
rescuers, intervention by 344–5
La Responsabilité Administrative
    (Moreau) 301–2

Restatement of the Law 98–9
Restatement of Torts 98–9
restitution 2, 24–7, 52, 383
rights
    concepts of 59–60
    protecting 59–70
    'right holders' 68
rights of way 189, 196
'risk liability' 158
risks, responsibility for 198–9
road accidents
    see motor vehicles
Roch, LJ 414
Rodger, Lord 42, 149, 300
Roman law
    actiones 369, 371
    basis of 294–5
    blameworthy acts 76
    damages 383
    focal points 10
    history of 1–2
    injuria 272
Romer, LJ 68
Rose, LJ 247
Rougier, J 367
Rudden, Bernard 61

Sachs, LJ 172–3
safety 163–8, 251
Salmon, LJ 241
Salmond on Torts 191, 242–3
Samuel, G 43, 383
Scarman, Lord 18, 131–2
scepticism 13–14
school children 228
scope of liability 326
Scotland 160
Scott, Lord
    animals 35
    damages 380
    exemplary damages 386
    health interest 77
    privacy 28–9
    public/private law 300
    trespassers 199
Scrutton, LJ 279, 359
seaworthiness 251–2
Sedley, LJ 38, 123–4, 303–4
self-help remedies 369, 415–17
sexual abuse 242–4
Simon, Lord 32, 185
Simonds, Lord 14, 48, 53, 55, 360

slander 264–5
Slynn, Lord 228, 258–9, 305, 384
Smith, AL, LJ 164–5
Social Insurance and Allied Services 394
social security benefits 394–6
Somerville, Lord 54, 133
'speak for themselves' 160
special relationships 117
speech, threats by 293
standard of care 119–24
standard of conduct 119
statute, tort and 34–6
statutory nuisance 70
statutory privilege 280–1
Staughton, LJ 212–13
sterilisation 67
Steyn, Lord
    analogy 136–7
    constitutional interest 82–3
    constitutional law 27–8
    deceit 288–9
    defamation 265
    distributive justice 45–6
    loss of a chance 353
    misfeasance in public office 105–7
    pecuniary loss 389–90
    practical justice 47
    professional liability 291–2
    prosecution service liability 315–16
    psychological harm 146
    remedies 299, 378
    typical damage 362
    vicarious liability 242
Stone, Ferdinand 158, 164
strangers 246–8
strict liability 19, 67, 157, 158, 163–5,
    172, 174
structural approach 11, 73
Supreme Court Procedure Committee
    281
Sutcliffe, Peter 36–7
systems approach to law 10, 12

Taggart, M. 61
Taking Rights Seriously (Dworkin) 82
television signals, interference with
    206–8
Textbook on Torts (Jones) 12, 57, 417
things, immovable 188–99
things, moveable
    aircraft 179–84
    animals 174–9

dangerous equipment 163–8
dangerous products 158–63
dangerous things in general 184–6
historical considerations 157–8
motor vehicles 169–74
third parties
  benevolence 393
  contract 160
  defamation 272
  factual causation 337–9
  foundational principles 225–8
  interests 383
  motor vehicles 392
  negligence 115, 118
  omissions 152
  psychological harm 143, 145, 149
threats 293
Tort Law and Economic Interests (Cane)
    73, 382
Tort Law (Weir) 13, 415
Tort Liability for Psychiatric Damage
    (Mullany and Handford) 148
'tort'/'torts' 8
Toulmin, Judge John, QC 41
trade and business interest 84–6
'Transfer of Title to Chattels' 63
transferred employees 238–9
transferred loss 263
trespass
  actionability 327–8
  aircraft 180
  animals 175
  crime and tort 21
  occupiers' duties 194–9
  to the person 3, 67, 404–7
  to property 404
trover 2, 3
truth as defence 275–6
Tunc, André 44–5
typical damage 362–4

Ulpian 294
unauthorised users 246–8
unborn children 374–5
UNIDROIT 19
*The University of Western Australia Law
    Review* 255–6
unlawfulness 155
USA 48
user principle 25
Uthwatt, Lord 186

Veale, J 205

Vertrag mit Schutzwirkung für Dritte
    260, 261–2
vicarious liability 227, 228
  see also employees, liability for
'Vicarious Liability and the Master's
    Indemnity' (Williams) 231–2
Vicarious Liability in the Law of Torts
    (Atiyah) 231–2, 385
victims, primary and secondary 144
visitors 188–9, 191–2, 195
von Bar, Christian 381
vulnerable victims 124–8

Waddams, Stephen 90, 257, 259, 355,
    418, 419
Walker, Lord 174–5, 179
Waller, LJ 123, 194
Ward, LJ 110, 316, 318
Warrington, LJ 359
Watson, Lord 87
Weir, Tony
  defamation 265
  economic loss 139
  France 18
  'interests' 382
  judges 39
  local authorities 296, 304
  loss-spreading 415
  tort 12, 13
Widgery, LJ 248–9
Wilberforce, Lord 49, 135, 297, 299,
    347–8
Williams, Glanville 45, 231–2, 289,
    340
wills 260–3
Winfield & Jolowicz on Tort 13, 106
Winfield, Percy 9
Winn, LJ 90
Woolf, Lord
  damages for breach of human rights
      410–11
  emergency services liability 319–20
  non-pecuniary loss 399
  standard of care 123
  trespass to the person 405–6
  typical damage 363
words and interests 255–63
Wright, Lord 7, 159, 166, 338
wrongful arrest 406
The Wrongs of Tort (Conaghan and
    Mansell) 13

'Yorkshire Ripper' 36–7

PSYCHOLOGY

for **A2 Level**

Mike Cardwell

Liz Clark

Claire Meldrum

Published by HarperCollins *Publishers* Limited
77–85 Fulham Palace Road
Hammersmith
London W6 8JB

www.**Collins**Education.com
On-line Support for Schools and Colleges

British Library Cataloguing in Publication Data
A catalogue record for this publication
is available from the British Library.

ISBN 0 00 711512 1

Commissioned by Emma Dunlop and Peter Langley
Project managed by Hugh Hillyard-Parker
Edited by Rosamund Connelly, Carol Schaessens
Picture research and permissions by Rebecca Green
Illustrations by Vicky Squires, Squires Graphics, Cambridge
Typesetting by Hugh Hillyard-Parker
Text and cover design by Patricia Briggs
Cover artwork by Terry Bambrook
Printed and bound by Scotprint

You might also like to visit:

www.**fire**and**water**.com
The book lover's website

Contents

Note: numbers in green italics are the equivalent page numbers of the chapters in the complete Collins *Psychology for A Level.*

Acknowledgements		v
Editor and author biographies		vii
Introduction		ix

SOCIAL PSYCHOLOGY

1 Social cognition 1 *201*

Mike Cardwell

Attribution of causality	1	*201*
Social perception	10	*210*
Prejudice and discrimination	18	*218*

2 Relationships 29 *229*

Paul Humphreys

Attraction and the formation of relationships	30	*230*
Maintenance and dissolution of relationships	36	*236*
Cultural and subcultural differences in relationships	45	*245*

3 Pro- and antisocial behaviour 55 *255*

Mike Cardwell

Nature and causes of aggression	55	*255*
Altruism and bystander behaviour	64	*264*
Media influences on pro- and antisocial behaviour	78	*278*

PHYSIOLOGICAL PSYCHOLOGY

4 Brain and behaviour 91 *291*

Simon Green

Methods used to investigate brain function	91	*291*
Localization of function in the human brain	99	*299*
Lateralization of function in the cerebral cortex	105	*305*

5 Biological rhythms, sleep and dreaming 113 *313*

Simon Green

Biological rhythms	113	*313*
Sleep	118	*318*
Dreaming	124	*324*

6 Motivation and emotion 133 *333*

Simon Green

Brain mechanisms of motivation	133	*333*
Theories of motivation	138	*338*
Emotion	144	*344*

COGNITIVE PSYCHOLOGY

7 Attention and pattern recognition 155 *355*

Jane Willson

Focused attention	156	*356*
Divided attention	164	*364*
Pattern recognition	174	*374*

8 Perceptual processes and development 185 *385*

Jane Willson

The visual system	185	*385*
Perceptual organization	193	*393*
Perceptual development	206	*406*

9 Language and thought 219 *419*

Jane Willson

Language and culture	219	*419*
Language acquisition	228	*428*
Problem-solving and decision-making	234	*434*

DEVELOPMENTAL PSYCHOLOGY

10 Cognitive development 247 *447*

Cara Flanagan

The development of thinking: three theories of cognitive development	247	*447*
The development of measured intelligence	260	*460*
The development of moral understanding	267	*467*

11 Social and personality development 279 *479*

Cara Flanagan

What is personality?	279	*479*
Gender development	288	*488*
Adolescence	295	*495*

12 Adulthood   303   *503*

Alison Wadeley

Early and middle adulthood   305   *505*
Family and relationships in adulthood   312   *512*
Cognitive changes in late adulthood   318   *518*

COMPARATIVE PSYCHOLOGY

13 Determinants of animal behaviour   329   *529*

Mike Cardwell

Evolutionary explanations of animal behaviour   329   *529*
Classical and operant conditioning   339   *539*
Social learning in nonhuman animals   348   *548*

14 Animal cognition   357   *557*

Mike Cardwell

Animal navigation   357   *557*
Animal communication and language   365   *565*
Memory in nonhuman animals   375   *575*

15 Evolutionary explanations of human behaviour   381   *581*

John Cartwright

Human reproductive behaviour   381   *581*
Evolutionary explanations of mental disorders   392   *592*
The evolution of intelligence   397   *597*

INDIVIDUAL DIFFERENCES

16 Issues in the classification and diagnosis of psychological abnormality   405   *605*

Paul Humphreys, Roger Cocks, Pamela Prentice

Classificatory systems   405   *605*
Multiple-personality disorder (dissociative identity disorder)   413   *613*
Culture-bound syndromes   419   *619*

17 Psychopathology   429   *629*

Pamela Prentice

Anxiety disorders   429   *629*
Depression (unipolar disorder)   440   *640*
Schizophrenia   447   *647*

18 Treating mental disorders   459   *659*

Pamela Prentice

Biological (somatic) therapies   459   *659*
Behavioural therapies   466   *666*
Alternatives to biological and behavioural therapies   469   *669*

PERSPECTIVES

19 Issues and debates in psychology   485   *685*

Mike Cardwell

Gender bias in psychological theory and research   485   *685*
Cultural bias in psychological theory and research   490   *690*
Ethical issues in research with human participants   492   *692*
The use of nonhuman animals in research   499   *699*
Free will versus determinism   510   *710*
Reductionism   513   *713*
Psychology as a science   516   *716*
Nature and nurture   520   *720*

20 Approaches in psychology   527   *727*

Phil Banyard

The biological approach   528   *728*
The evolutionary approach   531   *731*
The psychodynamic approach   535   *735*
The behavioural approach   539   *739*
The cognitive approach   543   *743*
Other approaches in psychology   545   *745*

EXAM PREPARATION AND COURSEWORK

21 Preparing for the A2 examination   549   *749*

Mike Cardwell

Examination preparation   549   *749*
Examination performance   556   *756*
Examination marking   557   *757*

22 Coursework   561   *761*

Graham Davies

Exam board documents   561   *761*
The project brief   562   *762*
Organizing and presenting your coursework report   562   *762*
Ethical considerations   563   *763*
Writing up a coursework report   564   *764*

23 Statistical analysis for coursework   573   *773*

Graham Davies

Calculating the standard deviation   573   *773*
Inferential statistics   576   *776*

Glossary   599

References   611

Checklist of synoptic issues   645

Index   651

Acknowledgements

Mike Cardwell would like to thank the three people who really matter – his wife, Denise, who makes him happy, and his children Chris and Alex, who continue to make him proud. Liz Clark would like to thank Charley for infinite support and patience that never cease to calm and restore balance when seemingly impossible deadlines loom. Also for the inspiration of a niece and nephew who are both considering psychology for their AS/A-level studies. Claire Meldrum would like to thank Stuart who, as always, showed tolerance and understanding of the obsessive preoccupation which seems to be the inevitable result of working on such a project. Thanks also go to colleagues and friends for their support and cheerful encouragement.

Our thanks also to the Collins staff, and particularly to Patricia Briggs for her helpful prompts and invaluable contributions, and to Pete Langley, who took over partway through the project. As cheerful but highly focused ringmaster, he has played a key role in bringing this book to completion and on schedule.

Last, but by no means least, we are, as ever, deeply indebted to Hugh Hillyard-Parker, who, along with Patricia, is responsible for the design of the book. He has remained serenely unflappable throughout, always offering constructive comments and soothing words whenever required.

Mike Cardwell, Liz Clark, Claire Meldrum
March 2000

Editor and author biographies

Mike Cardwell BSc, PGCE, MEd, is Senior Lecturer in Psychology at Bath Spa University College, where he teaches courses in social psychology, and Chief Examiner for the AQA (Specification A) AS- and A2-level psychology. Mike's other publications include *The Complete A–Z Psychology Handbook* (Hodder & Stoughton) and the *A-Level Revision Guide* (Longman). Mike is also an Editor of the journal *Psychology Review* and a regular contributor to student conferences. Although psychology takes up most of his time, he still avidly follows the fortunes of his home town football teams, Premier League Liverpool and Marine of the Unibond League.

Although a psychologist at heart and also by training, and someone who is passionate about education and good teaching, **Liz Clark** has worked in nurse education for the past 15 years. She is currently Head of Distance Learning at the Royal College of Nursing, where she is involved in developing and running a range of flexible-learning programmes. The experience of creating effective and highly accessible learning resources, that can be studied by distance-learning students with the minimum of teacher support, contributed to the original ideas and vision behind the first edition of this book. The publisher and editors believe that A-Level students deserve texts that intrigue, challenge and support, and above all that kindle their curiosity to find out more.

Claire Meldrum MA, MSc, PGCE, is a part-time Lecturer at City College, Norwich. She has nearly 20 years of psychology teaching experience on A-level, degree and 'Access to Higher Education' courses. She has also been an A level examiner for psychology, and is a member of the British Psychological Society, with particular interests in social and health psychology. Claire has published in the field of education, as well as having co-edited *Psychology for Nurses and Health Care Professionals* (1996). She has also contributed more recently to *Psychology and Social Care* (Messer & Jones 1999) and acts as consultant for the National Extension College. When time and weather allow, Claire enjoys gardening, the theatre and cinema.

Phil Banyard is Associate Senior Lecturer at The Nottingham Trent University where he teaches on introductory psychology and health psychology courses. He is Chair of Examiners for GCSE Psychology (with OCR) and Chief Examiner for A-level Psychology (also with OCR). He has written books and articles on psychology, most recently *Controversies in Psychology* (1999), *Introducing Psychological Research: Seventy studies that shape psychology* (2000) and *Applying Psychology to Health* (1996). When he is not writing, he can usually be found watching Nottingham Forest or catching up on the adventures of Xena Warrior Princess. Many think he should get out more.

John Cartwright, BSc, MSc, is a Principal Lecturer at Chester College of Higher Education, where he teaches courses on Darwinian psychology, environmental science and the history of science. He has worked as an examiner for the NEAB and is the author of *Evolution and Human Behaviour* (Macmillan 2000) as well as various journal articles on the history of science and psychology.

Roger Cocks is a Senior Lecturer in Psychology at University College Worcester. He is a chartered Educational Psychologist and his specialist teaching areas are abnormal psychology, learning theory and perception. He has an interest in teaching using new technology and has contributed to the development of supplementary CD-ROM resources for well-known psychology textbooks. His interests include squash, swimming, tennis and golf with a little gardening on the side.

Graham Davies, BA, MSc, PGCE, is a Lecturer at Eastbourne College of Arts and Technology and from 1997–2000 was Principal Examiner for the AQA AS/A-level psychology module on Perspectives and Research Methods. He was previously the Principal Moderator for A-level psychology coursework and remains one of the team of Regional Coursework Advisers. He has written various journal articles and has been a speaker and workshop leader at a number of psychology conferences. He is an Honorary Life Member and former Chair of the Association for the Teaching of Psychology, for whom he edited the journal *Teaching Psychology* for some years. A keen mountain climber, he also thoroughly enjoys watching Wimbledon football club beat more fashionable opposition!

Cara Flanagan has published an array of A-level psychology books, such as the Letts *A-level Revision Guides*, as well as various teacher and student work packs, and articles for *Psychology Review*. Her most recent publications include *Early Socialisation* (1999), a book in the Routledge Modular Series of which she is an editor, and *Practicals for Psychology* (1998). Cara has recently been appointed Reviser for the new AS/A-level examinations, and is closely involved with the examining process. She also lectures part-time at Inverness College, living as she does in a remote part of the British Isles where she can see snow-covered mountains.

Simon Green, BSc, PhD, is Head of the School of Psychology at Birkbeck College, University of London. He was the Chief Examiner for AEB psychology between 1983 and 1986 and remains a Senior Examiner today. He is the author of *Principles of Biopsychology* and a contributor to several other psychology books. Simon has also written articles for a number of journals, including the *Psychology Review*. His main interest is finding better ways of managing stress.

Paul Humphreys is Senior Lecturer in Psychology at University College Worcester. His teaching and research interests include social relationships, sexualities, psychology and the media, and (ab)normality. He has been Chief Examiner for psychology at every pre-undergraduate level (O level 1983–88; AS level 1989–91; A level 1992–7) and is now Principal Examiner for the new A2 examination. Paul is the author of several books and in 1997 was conferred Honorary Life Membership of the Association for the Teaching of Psychology for his services to psychology.

Pamela Prentice, BA, MEd, C.Psychol, AFBPsS, is Programme Manager for Humanities, including psychology, at Filton College, Bristol. She teaches A-level psychology and counselling up to HND level, and is an experienced AEB A-level examiner and OCN Moderator. She served five years on the committee for the ATP and two years on the BPS committee for the Division for Teachers and Researchers in Psychology. Her background, prior to teaching, was as a Counselling Psychologist with the NHS. She has written a number of articles for *Psychology Review*. Pam's interests include Le Roc Jive dancing, bridge and general partying.

Alison Wadeley, BSc, PGCE, MPhil, is Senior Lecturer in Psychology at Bath Spa University College. She taught GCSE, AS- and A-level psychology for 20 years and has had long experience as an Examiner, Principal Coursework Moderator, Reviser and adviser for the AEB. She continues to work as a Regional Coursework adviser for AS- and A-level Psychology. Alison has published a number of textbooks and revision guides for GCSE, AS-, A- and undergraduate level psychology. She is also a commissioning co-editor for *Psychology Review* for which she also regularly contributes articles.

Jane Willson is Director of Studies for the A-level programme at City College, Norwich. She has many years' teaching experience in schools and FE and currently teaches psychology at A level and at degree level. She is a team leader for the AEB psychology A level and is a member of the ATP. She has written several other publications for A-level students and has also co-authored a book based on a research project about children's interaction with screen-based technology.

Introduction

'Studies serve for delight, for ornament, and for ability.'

Francis Bacon (1625) *Of Studies*

'... that is what learning is. You suddenly understand
something you've understood all your life,
but in a new way.'

Doris Lessing (1969) *The Four-Gated City*

Since *Psychology for A Level* was first published in 1996, some major changes have occurred concerning the education of students over the age of 16 years. Among these are changes related to the study of psychology beyond GCSE level. In September 2000, a new Advanced Subsidiary (AS level) Psychology course was introduced with qualifications first awarded in August 2001. Students taking this course may use it as a final qualification or as 50 per cent of an Advanced Level qualification, which must be finished before an Advanced Level award can be made. The second part of the new Advanced Level award involves an A2 course of study. The first Advanced Level awards are to be made in August 2002.

Owing to these changes, and with the continuing developments in psychology, we knew the time was right for a new, thoroughly revised second edition of *Psychology for A Level*. This new book, published in Spring 2000, provides a detailed coverage of all aspects of the new **AS and A Level Psychology** courses offered by the **Assessment and Qualifications Alliance (AQA)**, **Specification A**. Some students, of course, will study psychology only to AS level and in this case *Psychology for AS Level*, also published in Spring 2000, will cover all their requirements. For those who decide to continue on to A level, but who have already purchased an AS textbook, this *Psychology for A2 Level* text will provide all that is needed to complete the A2 course.

The material covered in *Psychology for A2 Level* exactly matches the A2 chapters in *Psychology for A Level*, with the addition of **an important new feature**, namely a **checklist of synoptic issues** (pp. 645–50), which gives suggestions as to how issues in the relevant chapters can be used for synoptic assessment.

In *Psychology for A2 Level*, we have maintained our reader-friendly approach but also managed to provide the greater detail required for A2 study. The contributing authors are all teachers and/or examiners of psychology and, consequently, have a clear understanding of the needs of students. We have responded positively to the constructive suggestions made by readers of the first edition of *Psychology for A Level* as to how to improve the book. The first thing you will notice is the increased coverage given to topics. The book provides plentiful descriptive and evaluative detail to help you cope with the requirements of the new examinations. The chapter summaries have also been extended and additional advice is given on how to tackle exam-type questions. Many features of the first edition have been retained as we have been told they are useful to both students and teachers.

Using the book

The book provides the usual features you would expect to find in any textbook. There is an **Index**, a comprehensive list of **References** and a **Glossary** of specification and examination terms. The additional features within each chapter that facilitate the use of the book and make it easier to relate to the requirements of the AQA specifications include the following:

◆ A **Preview** at the start of each chapter, and a **Chapter summary** at the end, will enable you to get a quick idea of the topics covered.

◆ **Activities**, within each chapter, are designed to help you test your knowledge, apply psychological findings, carry out practical exercises and discuss ethical implications.

◆ **In Focus** boxes are used to highlight particularly important research studies or areas of special interest.

◆ **Diagrams**, **tables** and **pictures** help make the psychological material even more accessible.

◆ A new and invaluable feature in this edition is the **Exam summaries** written by the Chief Examiner. These will be a real boon to students. Each major topic area is summarized by taking you through how to answer a carefully constructed exam-type question in this area.

◆ At the end of each chapter, there are recommended **Further resources**, which include books, research articles and, where appropriate, website addresses.

Because this book is designed specifically to meet the requirements of the A2 part of the psychology course offered by AQA (specification A), its contents correspond very closely to those parts of the specification. Nevertheless, because the specifications cover such a wide range of psychological topics and issues, the book deals with many areas of psychology that will interest students studying other courses involving psychology. For those of you studying the AQA courses and using this book as part of your study programme, it is worth spending some time carefully assessing what is required of you. Detailed accounts of the specifications and information about the examinations and coursework assessments are available from AQA (address given at end of this introduction). We shall provide only a brief outline here.

The specifications and the examinations

The AQA (A) A-level course is organised into six *modules,* which mysteriously change their name to *units* when we deal with their assessment. Thus, you will be *taught* a module on Cognitive and Developmental psychology, but *examined* on a unit of the same topics – simple really! The AS-level course consists of three modules and a further three A2 modules make up the full A-level course.

The specification entries are very carefully worded and questions will reflect that wording. We have endeavoured to use the same wording as the specification wherever possible to make it easier for you to track your route through each topic. It is worth remembering that when questions are set, the question-setter will attempt to sample (eventually) all areas of the specification. It is, therefore, unwise to leave out any areas – even small ones – simply because they do not appeal to you.

The examinations will test your *knowledge and understanding* (known as 'Assessment Objective 1' or simply AO1), and your *analysis and evaluation* (known as AO2) skills, together with your ability to *design, conduct and report* (in the Research methods and coursework section, and known as AO3). As we stress in the exam guidance chapter (21), AO2 questions are

really quite different to AO1 questions and require you to *engage* with the subject material in the topic areas. We have attempted to show you how you might address each of these skills in the Exam summaries at the end of each chapter. Although these exam summaries are comprehensive accounts of what is required in each area, they should not take the place of the subject specification that is published by AQA.

Several entries on the AQA specification are preceded by the words 'including' or 'e.g.'. Although the word 'including' indicates prescribed material on which questions may be asked, the use of e.g. is merely illustrative of appropriate subject material. We have covered all *prescribed* material in this book, and have endeavoured, wherever appropriate, to cover all the examples mentioned in the specification as well.

The AQA (A) AS specification

Details of this part of the specification can be obtained from AQA (address given at end of Introduction). Outlines are also given in *Psychology for AS Level* and in *Psychology for A Level*. Those of you using this book, however, will have completed the AS course, and so we move on to outlining the requirements of the A2 specification.

The AQA (A) A2 specification

The A2 part of the specification (Units 4 to 6) allows you to focus on certain topics in more depth, to make links between different perspectives, approaches and methodologies, and to put your study of the subject into practice by completing your own psychological investigation. The A2 units are summarized below, but you need to read Chapter 21 to find detailed guidance on the Assessment of Units 4 and 5, and Chapter 22 for coursework.

Unit 4 allows you to specialize in some of the areas of psychology you sampled in the AS part of the course. Assessment takes the form of three essays from at least two different sections. This means you will need to study a minimum of two of the following:

◆ Social Psychology

◆ Physiological Psychology

◆ Cognitive Psychology

◆ Developmental Psychology

◆ Comparative Psychology.

Every A level must contain what is known as a *synoptic element.* This is the module where students are asked to pull together the different parts of the course to show their grasp of the subject as a whole. This is covered in Unit 5 of the AQA (A) specification, which is worth slightly more as a proportion of your total A level than the other units. Here, in addition to studying *Individual differences* in more depth than was possible in the AS part of the course, you will look at important *Issues and debates* in psychology and be asked to apply different theoretical and/or methodological approaches to a situation or case study provided in the exam.

Unit 6 is a coursework module that gives you the chance to conduct your own psychological study. The investigation needs to be carefully planned using a Project brief, then carried out and reported on in a maximum of 2,000 words. Chapter 22 contains advice and guidelines to help you make the most of this part of the course.

By examining theories, concepts and research studies, those who read this book should acquire an understanding of the different perspectives and methods used by psychologists and gain some insight into the ethical and cultural issues that concern those working in psychology today. While we hope that this book will provide all that is needed for you to complete the A2 part of your psychology course, we have provided a list of *Further resources* at the end of each chapter for those who wish to supplement the information given here.

It is very helpful for us to have feedback from readers, and some teachers have already indicated that they would like supplementary material to accompany the book; this will be available from Spring 2001. Once again we invite you to write to us, care of the Publisher, to let us know how well *Psychology for A2 Level* meets your requirements.

Mike Cardwell, Liz Clark, Claire Meldrum

For details about specifications or any other documents concerning AS- or A-level psychology, contact: AQA Publications Department, Stag Hill House, Guildford, Surrey GU2 5XJ

Permissions

The Publisher and editors would like to acknowledge the contribution made to this book by the following authors of the first edition: David Clarke, David Messer, Lesley Messer, Peter Hayes, George Balfour, Pat Hasan and Roger Davies.

The Publisher, authors and editors would also like to thank the organizations listed below for permission to reproduce material from their publications.

Full bibliographic information for all sources is given in the 'References' section at the end of the book.

30	Table 2.1	Cambridge University Press
35	Table 2.2	Penguin Books Ltd
38	Table 2.4	John Wiley; extract from *Close Relationships* by Kelley *et al.* (c) 1983 by W.H. Freeman & Company. Used with permission
70	Table 3.2	© 1968 by the American Psychological Association. Adapted with permission
71	Table 3.3	Blackwell Publishers
73	Fig. 3.6	Simon and Schuster
76	In Focus	Reproduced with permission from the *British Journal of Psychology* © The British Psychological Society
123	Fig. 5.3	Allyn & Bacon
129	In Focus	The Times
186	In Focus	Fourth Estate Ltd
188	Fig. 8.3	Scientific American Inc.
192	Fig. 8.6	Scientific American Inc.
203	In Focus	Harcourt Brace & Co Ltd
208	Fig. 8.22	Scientific American Inc.
222	Fig. 9.1	The Americal Psychological Association
262	Table 10.8	*Science*
264	Table 10.9	*Child Development*
271	Table 10.11	Holt, Rinehart & Winston
274	Table 10.12	© 1983 by the American Psychological Association. Adapted with permission
307	Fig. 12.1	Sterling Lord
309	Table 12.4	Simon & Schuster
315	Table 12.7	Holt, Rinehart & Winston
316	Table 12.8	Doubleday Transworld Publishers Ltd
319	Table 12.9	With permission, from the *Annual Review of Sociology*, Vol. 8 © 1982 by Annual Reviews
322	Table 12.10	Macmillan (Kübler-Ross); With permission from *OMEGA – Journal of Death and Dying*, 1(1), pp. 23–8, © 1970 Baywood Publishing Co. Inc. (Fulton); Tavistock Publications Ltd (Murray-Parkes)
408	In Focus	*Science*
409	Table 16.3	© 1988 Routledge
412	In Focus	John Wiley & Sons Limited. Reproduced with permission
425	Table 16.12	© 1985 Kluwer Academic Publishers. With kind permission of Kluwer Academic Publishers
430	Table 17.1	Penguin Books Ltd
438	Fig. 17.3	© 1985 by the American Psychological Association. Adapted with permission
444	Table 17.3	The Royal Society of Medicine Press Limited
449	In Focus	*Abnormal Psychology*
455	Table 17.5	Chapman & Hall Ltd
460	Table 18.1	© 1992 The Association for the Teaching of Psychology. The ATP exists to support the teaching of pre-degree psychology in schools and colleges, and can be contacted via the British Psychological Society, St Andrews House, 48 Princess Road East, Leicester LE1 7DR
470	Fig. 18.1	Phillip Allan Publisher Ltd; *Journal of Rational-Emotive and Cognitive-Behaviour Therapy*
486	Activity 1	*Personality and Social Psychology Bulletin*
490	Table 19.1	Sage
491	In Focus	© 1993 Pearson Education Limited
497	Table 19.2	© 1988 by the American Psychological Association. Adapted with permission
501	Table 19.3	*The Psychologist*
503	Fig. 19.1	*Animal Behaviour*
507	Fig. 19.2	*New Scientist*
511	In Focus	© Toby Andrew, *The Independent*
589	Appendix 3	With permission of the McGraw-Hill Companies
592	Appendix 4	© 1963 R.A. Fisher and F. Yates. Reprinted by permission of Pearson Education Limited
593	Appendix 5	Reprinted with permission from the *Journal of the American Statistical Association* © 1965 by the American Statistical Association. All rights reserved
595	Appendix 7	Reprinted with permission from the *Journal of the American Statistical Association*. ©1972 by the American Statistical Association. All rights reserved.

PHOTOGRAPHS

2	Michael Stephens/PA Photos
16	Larry Bray/Telegraph Colour Library
59	Massimo Sambucetti/Associated Press
66	Risto Bozovic/Associated Press
331	Max Gibbs/Oxford Scientific Films/www.osf.uk.com
332	David Parker/Science Photo Library
337	Rudie Kuiter/Oxford Scientific Films/www.osf.uk.com
338	Michael Leach/Oxford Scientific Films/www.osf.uk.com
349	John Paling/Oxford Scientific Films/www.osf.uk.com
351	Flip Schulke/Telegraph Colour Library
352	Telegraph Colour Library
355	E.R. Degginger/Oxford Scientific Films/www.osf.uk.com
359	Siegfried Rath/Oxford Scientific Films/www.osf.uk.com
361	Lon E. Lauber/Oxford Scientific Films/www.osf.uk.com
362	John Downer/Oxford Scientific Films/www.osf.uk.com
366	Daniel J. Cox/Oxford Scientific Films/www.osf.uk.com
369	Rafi Ben-Shahar/Oxford Scientific Films/www.osf.uk.com
392	Bridgeman Art Library

Part 1: Social Psychology

A2

SOCIAL COGNITION

Mike Cardwell

RELATIONSHIPS

Paul Humphreys

PRO- AND ANTISOCIAL BEHAVIOUR

Mike Cardwell

Chapter 1

Social cognition

Mike Cardwell

Preview

In this chapter we shall be looking at:

◆ explanations of the attribution of causality, including errors and biases in the attribution process

◆ social and cultural influences on our perception of the social world, including social representations and stereotyping

◆ the origins and maintenance of prejudice and discrimination, and explanations and research relating to the reduction of prejudice and discrimination.

Introduction

Social cognition refers to the area of social psychology that is concerned with how people think about other people or groups of people. Although this field shares many similarities with the field of cognitive psychology, there is an assumption that the way in which we think about other people (i.e. our *social* world) differs in important ways to the way in which we think about the physical world.

In this chapter we will be examining some of the important issues that have interested psychologists working in this field.

The attribution of causality – seeking explanations for our own behaviour and the behaviour of others – is probably the area closest to a popular understanding of psychology. Through painstaking research, different theorists have attempted to unravel the rules that we use

to make causal attributions about each other's behaviour. This is not as clear cut as it might appear when we read the literature, as much of our attributional thinking is biased in ways that both reflect a particular perspective and also serve our own best interests.

The tendency to take mental short cuts in processing information from our social world is illustrated by the process of stereotyping – mentally placing people into pre-existing categories – which enables us to apply general evaluations based on our existing 'knowledge' about that category and its members. In recent years, social psychology has moved increasingly away from the laboratory to an exploration of the truly *social* aspects of human behaviour. Social representations theory represents our attempt to discover how common-sense representations of the world become so widely spread and shared by most members of a culture. Rooted in a tradition of European social psychology, this theory is characteristic of attempts to develop a *sociological* (rather than *psychological*) social psychology.

One of the inevitable consequences of the process of categorization is the fact that we will judge some people more negatively than others. Theorists have puzzled over the problems of prejudice and discrimination for many years and, at various times, have explained this tendency in terms of personality differences, the pressures of intergroup competition and the need to preserve a positive social identity. Attempts to reduce prejudice have not always met with success, but this does not stop us looking for solutions to this most insidious aspect of social cognition.

Attribution of causality

People have an overwhelming desire to form a coherent understanding of their world and to control their social environment. One aspect which is fundamental to this is that of *causality* – that is, what causes particular events or behaviours to occur. An *attribution* is the end result of a process in which people use available information to make inferences about the causes of a particular behaviour. Attribution theory is concerned

with explanations of how each of us attributes causes for our own and others' behaviour. In this section we will look at what research tells us about the attributions we make about our own behaviour and that of other people. When we process social information, we are apt to take short cuts and consequently, we do not process information as accurately or completely as we could. In other words we might be seen as *cognitive misers*.

As a result of this tendency, *biases* may occur in the attribution process.

According to attribution theorists, our explanations for a person's behaviour will generally refer either to factors stemming from within that person or to factors that are external to that person, such as their environment.

◆ When we explain people's behaviour in terms of it being a result of 'something about them' (such as their 'nature' or mood), we are making a *dispositional attribution*.

◆ When behaviour is explained in terms of something about the environment or social world (such as the weather or the influence of a third person), we are making a *situational attribution*.

Quiz shows – easy questions or bright contestants? Who wants to be a millionaire? host, Chris Tarrant, and successful contestant, Jonathan Green.

Activity 1: Explaining behaviours

Imagine two members of your class. One of them is habitually late (although, you note, she is never late for sociology). Everyone else makes the class on time. The second student grumbles constantly about the poor standard of the teaching. Mind you, so does everybody else in the class, and yet everybody seems to love sociology.

How would you explain these two behaviours? What do you think has caused each of them?

Attribution theories

A number of attribution theories have been developed. These include the *correspondent inference theory* (Jones and Davies 1965), Kelley's (1967) *co-variation model*, and his subsequent (1972) refinement to it, the *causal schemata model*, and Weiner's *model of achievement attribution* (1979). Rather than being seen as competitors, each seeking to explain the same thing in the best way, it is more fruitful to see attribution theories as being complementary. They differ according to the kind of explanation that is required and the information that is available to the person doing the explaining. In this chapter the models of Kelley (1967 and 1972) and Weiner (1979) will be discussed.

The co-variation model

Kelley's co-variation model applies to the explanations we give for the behaviour of people we know. Kelley argues that when we make such attributions we take our information from two sources. The first of these is what we know about the person and their previous behaviour. The second is the way in which the person's behaviour compares with that of other people. According to the principle of co-variation, we take three types of causal information into account when arriving at an explanation, the first two derived from the previous behaviour of the person, and the third from the behaviour of other people. The extent to which these three types of information co-vary results in us making a dispositional (or internal) attribution, a situational (or external) attribution, or a combination of the two. The three types of information are about:

◆ *Consensus* – This refers to the extent to which other people behave in the same way towards the same stimulus as the person whose behaviour we are trying to explain. For example, suppose that we are asked to explain why a person is afraid of a dog. If most people are afraid of this particular dog, then consensus is high. However, if few people are afraid of the dog, consensus is low.

◆ *Consistency* – This refers to the extent to which the person in question has behaved in the same way in the past towards the stimulus in question. If the person has been afraid of the dog on other occasions, consistency is high. However, if the person has not shown fear before, then consistency is low.

◆ *Distinctiveness* – This refers to the extent to which the person behaves in the same or a similar way to other stimuli. If, for example, the person is not afraid of other dogs, then the behaviour of being afraid of this dog is a highly distinctive one. Thus, distinctiveness is high. If the person is afraid of all other dogs and, perhaps, all other animals, then the behaviour of being afraid of this dog is not particularly distinctive. Hence we can say that distinctiveness is low.

Kelley argued that if consensus was low, consistency was high, and distinctiveness was low, then we would tend to make a dispositional (or internal) attribution for behaviour. So, if Rob was afraid of the dog and we knew that very few other people were afraid of the dog (low consensus), that Rob had been afraid of the dog before (high consistency), and that Rob was afraid of other dogs as well as this one (low distinctiveness), we would tend to explain his behaviour in terms of 'something about him'. Perhaps, for example, we might describe him as being 'timid'.

If consensus, consistency and distinctiveness were all high, Kelley argued that an attribution to the 'entity' would be made. For example, suppose that Chris had failed to win a prize on a particular radio quiz show; everyone else he knew had failed to win a prize on the same quiz; he had also failed to win a prize on the quiz when he had taken part in it before and he had won prizes on other quiz shows. We would explain his behaviour in terms of the quiz show. Perhaps, for example, his failure could be explained in terms of the quiz being very difficult.

In circumstances, however, when consensus is low, consistency is low, but distinctiveness is high, Kelley argued that the cause of behaviour would be most likely to be attributed to a particular set of special circumstances. For example, suppose that Alex makes a donation to a particular charity. No one else makes a donation, Alex has not donated to this charity before, and she does not usually give her money away. In this case, Alex might be making her contribution because of some special circumstances. Perhaps she has seen a TV programme describing the plight of the people being helped by this particular charity. See Table 1.1 for a summary of the co-variation model.

Evaluation of the co-variation model

Kelley's theory has been tested in a number of experiments in which people are given a behaviour to explain (such as 'David laughed at the comedian')

along with information about consensus, consistency and distinctiveness. Generally, the results of such experiments have supported Kelley's proposals and shown that when the three types of information are manipulated, people tend to make the attributions predicted by Kelley.

There are, however, several problems with this model. For example, Garland *et al.* (1975) have shown that when given a choice about the information necessary to arrive at an attribution, some people choose information about things like 'personality' and/or the context in which the behaviour is occurring rather than consensus, consistency or distinctiveness information. Indeed, in one study, it was discovered that people only use information about distinctiveness and consistency when no information about context or situation is available. Other research (e.g. Alloy and Tabachnik 1984) has shown that even when information about consensus, consistency and distinctiveness is available, people are not particularly adept at using it in a systematic way, and therefore its usefulness in making accurate attributions is diminished.

We should also note that Kelley's theory is *cognitively expensive*, as it takes a great deal of mental effort to assess information on consensus, consistency, and distinctiveness (even when these sources of information are readily available). Just because people's attributions seem to fit the predictions made by the co-variation model, does not mean that people are actually calculating the co-variation between consensus, consistency, and distinctiveness in their heads. As noted before in this chapter, we tend to act as 'cognitive misers' and rather than spend time searching for information, we often jump to 'quick and easy' conclusions regarding the causes of behaviour.

Hilton and Slugoski (1986) offer a simpler interpretation of the way in which people might use information about consensus, consistency and distinctiveness. In their *abnormal conditions focus model*, they suggest that each type of information 'goes with' a particular type of attribution. Consensus information affects primarily internal attributions, distinctiveness has an important role in situational

Table 1.1	Summary of the co-variation model		
	Attribution to the person (internal)	*Attribution to the 'entity' (external)*	*Attribution to special circumstances (external)*
Consensus	Low	High	Low
Consistency	High	High	Low
Distinctiveness	Low	High	High

Source: Kelley (1967)

(external) attributions, and consistency affects attributions according to circumstance. Hilton and Slugoski describe how people would make attributions according to information that 'stands out' (i.e. is 'abnormal'). For example, if Mark is the only person to order fish (i.e. low consensus), this stands out and we are likely to make an internal attribution (he likes fish). If he only eats fish at this particular restaurant and never orders it elsewhere (i.e. high distinctiveness), then this too stands out and we are more likely to make an external attribution (the fish must be particularly good in this restaurant).

Causal schemata

Largely because of the criticisms that were made of the co-variation model, Kelley advanced a second attribution theory. The *causal schemata model* applies to behaviour observed on a single occasion and about which there is no consensus, consistency or distinctiveness information. Kelley argued that if we do not know a person and have no information about their previous behaviour, then we can only rely on our causal schemata. Causal schemata are, according to Kelley (1972), 'general conceptions a person has about how certain kinds of causes interact to produce a specific kind of effect'. He proposed that causal schemata, along with the processes of *discounting* and *augmenting* are used as follows:

◆ One type of causal schema is that of *multiple sufficient causes*. This applies when a behaviour may have a number of causes for it and when we are satisfied that any one of them is a sufficient explanation of it. For example, suppose that your neighbours have just moved house. They might have moved because they want to live in a larger or smaller house, because they want a bigger garden, because the house is about to be repossessed or because they do not like you playing music loudly and having rowdy parties. Each cause is sufficient in itself to explain the behaviour of moving house.

◆ On some occasions, however, we may have reason to favour one in particular of these sufficient explanations, which leads us to add weight to it and dismiss or discount the others. Kelley calls this the *discounting principle*. For example, suppose that a well-known celebrity appears on television advertising a particular brand of crisps. The celebrity may really like the crisps and be advertising them for that reason. He may, however, be doing the manufacturer a favour because of a personal friendship with the head of the company. It might even be the case that the celebrity had been paid £100,000 to endorse the crisps. It is likely that most of us would discount two of the three sufficient

causes presented above, and opt for the last one. The discounting principle demonstrates that people tend towards simplicity in their social perceptions.

◆ A second type of causal schemata is that of *multiple necessary causes*. These apply when two or more factors are necessary for an attribution to be made to explain a particular behaviour. For example, in order to be successful in the London Marathon, it is not sufficient to wear running shoes; the runner must also be fit. Both of these conditions are necessary for successful performance, and if the marathon was completed, we would conclude that the runner not only wore running shoes, but was also a physically fit athlete.

◆ The *augmentation principle* applies to both multiple sufficient and multiple necessary causal schemata. It proposes that the role of a given cause is *augmented* (increased) if the effect occurs in the presence of an inhibitory cause. For example, someone who does well in an examination despite poor teaching and prolonged illness is more likely to have their success confidently attributed to their ability and hard work (i.e. dispositional factors). The strength of this conviction will be increased by the fact that such difficult circumstances must be overcome in order to succeed.

Evaluation of the causal schemata model

Causal schemata are important for three main reasons (Manstead *et al.* 1995):

1 They help the perceiver to make attributions even when information is incomplete.

2 They are general ideas of causes and effects that may apply across different content areas.

3 They provide the perceiver with a form of 'causal shorthand' so they can carry out complex attribution inferences quickly and easily.

According to Fiedler (1982) however, the research in support of causal schemata is highly artificial and although the theory is plausible, it lacks much empirical support.

Weiner's model of achievement attribution

Weiner (1979) was interested in the sorts of attribution that people make when determining the reasons for success and failure on a task (such as in a driving test or psychology examination). Weiner believed that when explaining success or failure, we attribute it to one or more of four basic causes – ability, effort, task difficulty and luck. We arrive at a causal attribution for success or failure by considering where a particular event lies along three different dimensions:

◆ *Internal/external* – the locus of the cause may be something about the person (i.e. internal) or about the situation (external). For example, ability and effort are internal causes of an event, but help from friends or bad luck are external causes.

◆ *Stable/unstable* – the degree to which the cause is likely to change or stay as an enduring feature. For example, intelligence may be seen as an enduring and therefore stable feature, whereas mood is more changeable and therefore unstable.

◆ *Controllable/uncontrollable* – the extent to which a person has control over the cause. For example, students have a good deal of control over the amount of effort they put into their revision, but very little over how difficult the exam is going to be.

These three dimensions then produce eight different types of explanation for the event being explained (see Table 1.2). For example, failure to pass a driving test might be attributed to the weather (bottom right in Table 1.2), if a person considered themselves a good driver and the weather conditions were unusually bad. In this example, failure is *external* (because it is not about their driving ability and weather conditions were bad, i.e. unstable and uncontrollable).

According to this theory, people first assess whether someone – or they themselves – have succeeded or failed at some task. This leads to either a positive or negative emotion (if we succeed at something we generally feel pleased, if we fail we are disappointed or upset). Following our causal attribution, we then experience more specific emotions. For example, we may feel pity for a person's homelessness if we feel that their plight was beyond their control.

Each of the three dimensions has different consequences for future behaviour:

◆ The stability dimension is important in shaping our expectancies of how well someone might perform in the future. If we believe that someone's poor performance in a sports event is due to their lack of ability, we would expect them to continue to perform poorly in similar events in the future. We may consequently wonder why a football manager continues to select a player whom we have branded as 'useless'.

◆ The internal/external dimension determines the rewards or punishments that might follow an event. If we believe that someone's success has been a product of their hard work, we might reward them for their efforts. If they failed through lack of effort, we might exercise our right to punish for the same reasons. However, if success or failure was perceived to be the product of external forces, then we are more likely to withhold any rewards and restrain from punishing the person who has failed.

◆ The controllability dimension concerns the potential for change in the future. If a person's failure is perceived to have been caused by something uncontrollable (e.g. their lack of ability), then we will be more sceptical about their chances of succeeding in the future, no matter how hard they try. Similarly, if we believe our success to be a matter of good fortune (i.e. uncontrollable), we may not feel confident about predicting similar success in the future.

Evaluation of Weiner's model

Weiner's model has received considerable empirical support. Research has shown that category-based expectancies (e.g. male/female, Black/White) may affect the attributions that are made. For example, members of both sexes are more likely to attribute a woman's success to temporary factors but to attribute a man's success to his ability (Deaux 1976). Similarly, White Americans were more likely to see ability as responsible for success in a White than in a Black person (Yarkin *et al.* 1982).

The model can also be applied to our behaviour when working at a task. Adults and children who attribute their failure in a task to an internal, stable cause (such as a lack of ability or a character defect) are less likely to persist with it. For example, if we can

Table 1.2	Weiner's achievement model of attribution (Weiner 1979)			
	Internal		*External*	
	Stable	*Unstable*	*Stable*	*Unstable*
Controllable	Typical effort	Unusual effort	Consistent help or hindrance from others (e.g. friends)	Unusual help or hindrance from others (e.g. strangers)
Uncontrollable	Ability	Mood	Task difficulty	Luck

attribute our failure to land a favoured job to unfair selection practices or the ignorance of the interviewer (i.e. uncontrollable external causes), we are likely to continue to apply for similar jobs in the future (Crocker and Major 1989).

Weiner's model recognized the importance of dimensions, beyond the simple internal/external dimension, that are significant in the process of attribution. For example, a person's failure in an examination or in a sporting event may be attributed to lack of ability or lack of effort, both internal attributions. The consequences, however, that follow these attributions may be very different, since lack of ability is a stable characteristic whereas lack of effort may be unstable (and therefore changeable).

Of all the attribution theories, Weiner's is the one that has been most extensively studied in different cultural settings. Several studies have shown that at least some aspects of Weiner's model apply to non-Western as well as Western cultures. In one study (Schuster et al. 1989), participants in Belgium, Germany, India, South Korea and England were given details of a person who had failed to get a particular job. Participants rated each of 22 causes for the person's failure to get the job (i.e. their ability, effort, interest, luck and so on) on the dimensions of control (to what extent was it controllable by the person?), stability (to what extent was it changeable?) and locus (did it exist internally or externally to the person?). Schuster and colleagues found considerable consistency across the different cultures in how controllable, stable and internal/external each of these 22 causes was perceived to be. The one exception to this was the Indian sample who consistently rated all causes as being more uncontrollable, unstable and external than samples from the other four cultures. Moghaddam (1998) suggests that this finding (which is also evident in studies by other researchers) might be explained by the fact that Indians are more 'fatalistic'.

Although there is a great deal of empirical support for Weiner's views on attribution, there is some doubt over whether everybody uses his three dimensions in quite the same way. For example, Krantz and Rude (1984) found considerable variation in the ways in which participants classified a particular cause along these dimensions. Intelligence, for example, may be seen as a stable characteristic by some people but a highly changeable characteristic by others. What this research suggests, then, is that we all perceive human attributes in very different ways and this in turn affects the attributions that we make.

Kelley's and Weiner's theories, along with others we have not discussed, assume that we are motivated to explain the behaviour of others in a logical and rational manner. Because these theories describe the ways in which we should normally make attributions, they are referred to as *normative* models of the attribution process. However, as we have stressed on a number of occasions, people do not process every piece of social information in a logical and rational manner. The short cuts we take when arriving at explanations for behaviour lead to biases in our processing of information. It is to biases in the attribution process that we turn next.

Biases in the attribution process

Psychologists have discovered that people can be biased in a number of ways when they make attributions. An attributional bias can be defined as a distortion in perception or judgement about the causes of our own or other people's behaviour. This section looks at several of these biases.

The fundamental attribution error

Ross (1977) defines the *fundamental attribution error* (FAE) as 'the tendency to underestimate the importance of situational determinants and overestimate the degree to which actions and outcomes reflect the actor's dispositions'. What this means is that we have a tendency to make internal (or dispositional) attributions for people's behaviour even when external (or situational) attributions are equally likely to explain the behaviour. For example, if someone was to spill coffee over us, our explanation of their behaviour would probably be in terms of 'being clumsy', even when a situational explanation (the person had been pushed by somebody else) was equally likely. It has been suggested that our 'miserly' approach to cognitive processing leads us to ignore situational influences unless we are directly alerted to them. This results in our emphasizing factors concerned with the person. If we are satisfied that our dispositional attribution is adequate, then we feel we have no need to make matters more complex by considering additional information.

Support for this view was obtained by Ross et al. (1977). In their experiment, participants were randomly assigned to be either questioners or contestants in a general knowledge quiz. The questioners were allowed to make up questions based on their own specialized knowledge which, of course, would mean that contestants would often struggle to provide correct answers. The 'quiz' was observed by other participants and at the end of it the observers, questioners, and contestants were asked to rate the general knowledge of the questioners and contestants.

Both the observers and contestants considered the questioners to have superior knowledge. The questioners, however, did not consider themselves to have superior knowledge. Ross and his colleagues argued that the observers and contestants had ignored the fact that the questioners had an unfair situational advantage (they had compiled the questions) and had overestimated dispositional factors in making their judgements. In another experiment, Bierbrauer (1979) had participants watch a film of Milgram's obedience experiments in which one participant (the 'teacher') apparently gives a series of increasingly severe electric shocks to another (the 'learner'). When asked to explain the behaviour of the teacher, participants underestimated situational factors (such as the presence of the experimenter) in favour of dispositional ones (such as 'the teacher was cruel') in their explanations.

Two explanations of the fundamental attribution error are outlined below:

◆ An interesting explanation of the FAE concerns the role of linguistic factors. Nisbett and Ross (1980) suggest that the English language is constructed in such a way that it is relatively easy to describe an action and the actor in the same way. For example, we may speak of someone as being kind or honest, but it is more difficult to describe a situation in those terms.

◆ When we perceive a particular behaviour, we focus on the person who is behaving, not the situation. It is not surprising, therefore, that the actor is overrated as causally important. When people are primed, however, to pay attention to situational factors, the FAE is less likely (Rholes and Pryor 1982).

Although the FAE has been demonstrated in a number of studies, it has been argued that it is neither fundamental nor an error. According to Fiske and Taylor (1992), there are circumstances in which the FAE does not occur. One of these is when the discounting principle (see p. 4) is used. Rather than use the term 'error', Fiske and Taylor have argued that the word 'bias' is more appropriate since the FAE refers to a systematic distortion of our cognitions rather than to something that is actually wrong.

From a cultural perspective, the fundamental attribution error might be seen as an indication of the pervasive individualism of modern Western societies (Moghaddam 1998). Moghaddam also believes that rather than the FAE being an 'error', it is in fact a cultural 'bias' to perceive causes as internal rather than external to individuals. Support for this assertion comes from Miller (1984) who found that whereas children growing up in Western cultures tend to attribute causes of others' behaviour to dispositional factors, children growing up in India show the opposite trend, attributing them more to situational factors, i.e. things that were outside their control. This was particularly evident when children were asked to explain the actions of someone who had done something wrong.

The FAE may arise in a slightly different form when we are making causal attributions about in-group and out-group behaviours. When it operates at the group level, this form of attributional bias is known as the *ultimate attribution error* (Pettigrew 1979). It involves perceiving desirable actions by one's own group arising as a result of group (internal) characteristics, and undesirable actions being a product of external forces. Conversely, desirable actions performed by other groups are 'explained away' in terms of situational factors (e.g. 'they were lucky') rather than being seen as a product of dispositional characteristics of the group. Undesirable actions, however, are seen as reinforcing our stereotype of the out-group and are therefore attributed to the inherent group characteristics. As a lifelong supporter of Liverpool Football Club, I tend to explain any unruly behaviour among Liverpool fans as being the result of provocation or media hysteria, but am equally quick to condemn the disgraceful behaviour of the hooligans who support other teams!

Actor/observer biases

Before we look at the actor/observer bias, try Activity 2.

---

in focus

The fundamental attribution error

The FAE has a number of implications. One of these is that once a dispositional attribution has been made, it is difficult to reverse. For example, Ross *et al.* (1974) led female students to believe that they had done either quite well or quite poorly on a novel problem-solving task. The students were then debriefed and were told that their scores had been falsified and that what they had been told previously was not necessarily correct. Later, the students were asked to rate their ability at the task, estimate how many correct responses they had made, and predict how well they thought they would do on the task in the future. The results showed that those initially told they had done quite well gave themselves higher ratings and estimates than those initially told they had done poorly. This occurred even though all participants had been told that the initial information they had been given was not necessarily correct.

The FAE occurs when we are explaining the behaviour of other people. Thus, when we are observers of behaviour, we tend to make dispositional attributions about causes rather than situational ones. For example, when we see someone trip up whilst walking down the street, we tend to explain that behaviour in dispositional terms ('what a clumsy person!'). Suppose, however, that we were to trip up whilst walking down a street. Would we explain our own behaviour in dispositional terms? According to the evidence, the answer is 'no'; when we are the actors, we tend to explain our behaviour in situational terms. In the case of tripping up whilst walking down the street, we might explain our behaviour in terms of 'uneven paving stones'.

Some explanations of actor/observer differences are outlined below:

◆ Jones and Nisbett (1971) have argued that one reason for the differences between actors' and observers' attributions is that different aspects of information are available to those concerned. The actor, who has performed the behaviour, has more direct information available about the event than does the observer. The observer may be at some distance from the actor and may not be able to see the actual situational cause (in the example we used above, the uneven paving stone). The actor also knows more about their own previous behaviour than does the observer (i.e. we have more *privileged* information about ourselves than does an observer). We may know, for example, that we have very rarely tripped up while walking down the street. The observer, by contrast, does not have this knowledge and may assume that the behaviour is typical of the person observed.

◆ The *focus of attention* is different for the actor and observer. Actors focus outwards away from themselves towards the situation (and therefore cannot 'see' themselves behaving) and so are likely to locate the cause of their behaviour there (actor bias). Observers, on the other hand, focus their attention on the actor, bypassing situational factors, and are, therefore, more likely to attribute the cause of behaviour to the actor (observer bias).

◆ Research has highlighted the importance of *prominence* in causal attributions. McArthur and Post (1977) found that observers tended to make more dispositional attributions when the actor was strongly illuminated than when they were dimly illuminated.

Although there is a great deal of support for the actor/observer effect, the effect is not always consistent and can be reversed. An analysis of such cases where this is found suggests that the effect is actually influenced by the cultural norms of presenting oneself as 'positive' and 'autonomous' (Moghaddam 1998). For example, actors have been found to attribute their own positive behaviours to dispositional factors and their negative behaviours more to situational factors (Chen *et al.* 1988).

It appears that evidence cannot support a 'strong' view of either the fundamental attribution error or the actor/observer effect. However, a 'weak' form of both is consistent with the research findings. In this, observers do not make either a dispositional or a situational attribution, but use both dispositional and situational factors when determining the cause of events around them. They may rely on one relatively more than the other, depending on their particular perspective of events. Cross-cultural evidence suggests that people must learn the attributional accounts that are favoured by that particular culture. This learning then becomes so efficient that particular attributional accounts become automatic and unthinking (Augoustinos and Walker 1995).

Attributions of success and failure: self-serving biases

Although the actor/observer bias suggests that we emphasize situational factors in explaining our own behaviour, there are occasions on which this bias can be overturned. One of these is when we are asked to explain why we were successful at something, such as passing an examination. The actor/observer bias suggests that such behaviour would be explained in situational terms, such as 'an easy examination paper'. As we know, though, most people do not explain their successes in this way. People who pass exams usually explain their success by reference to all the hard work they did, how intelligent they are, and so on. These, of course, are dispositional attributions.

It seems, then, that we are quite happy to make dispositional attributions for behaviour when we are successful, and this has been termed the *self-enhancing bias*. However, we tend to avoid taking responsibility when we are unsuccessful (the *self-protecting bias*). Miller and Ross (1975) use the general term *self-serving bias* to describe both these biases, which have been demonstrated in a number of experiments. For example, Johnson *et al.* (1964) asked teachers to attribute responsibility for the performance of their pupils. The researchers found that teachers saw poor performance by their pupils as the responsibility of the pupils. However, this view changed when the children improved over time, such that the teachers saw themselves as being responsible for their pupils' improved performance!

Reasons why the self-enhancing and self-protecting biases should operate include the following:

◆ Taking responsibility for success allows us to present ourselves in the best possible light to others (the *impression management* explanation). Denying responsibility for unsuccessful outcomes allows us to protect our self-esteem, whereas taking responsibility for success enhances it.

◆ An implicit assumption of the self-enhancement explanation is that it is normal and biologically adaptive to maintain a positive self-esteem (Augoustinos and Walker 1995). One of the adverse consequences of a chronically low self-esteem is depression, which may be marked by feelings of helplessness and hopelessness. A large number of research studies have now firmly established a link between attributional style and depression. It is argued that depressives possess a particular attribution style in which failures and other negative events are attributed to internal, stable and global (i.e. all-embracing) causes (Augoustinos and Walker 1995). This finding has led to the development of attributional retraining programmes in which depressives are taught how to make more self-serving attributions for their own behaviour. Interestingly enough, some evidence (e.g. Lewinsohn *et al.* 1980) suggests that relative to non-depressed people, depressives tend to make more realistic attributions about their own performances. As a result of attributional retraining, the realism of this self-view tends to diminish, to be replaced by the 'illusory warm glow in which one sees oneself more positively than others see one' (Lewinsohn *et al.* 1980). Perhaps this is a small price to pay for a positive sense of self-worth!

Evidence suggests that the pattern of self-serving biases found in individualist societies such as the United States and Great Britain is not always found in other societies (such as Japan and China) where interdependence is more highly valued than independence. In such societies, individuals learn that they are more likely to be positively evaluated by others if they present themselves in ways that are more self-effacing than self-enhancing. For example, a study of Japanese and American students found that Japanese students estimated that 50 per cent of their peers were intellectually more capable than themselves, but American students estimated that only 30 per cent of their peers were superior to them (Markus and Kitayama 1991).

Self-handicapping

One extension of the self-serving bias is what is called *self-handicapping* (Berglas and Jones 1978). Before we look at this, answer the questions in Activity 3.

Activity 3: Self-handicapping

Think about the time immediately before an examination when you are waiting to go into the examination room. Your fellow students are all there and you begin talking about your prospects in the exam. What sorts of things do you and your fellow students talk about? Do you talk about how little revision you've done and how, as a result of this, your chances in the exam are very slim? Are there any other reasons people come up with for possible failure in the exam?

In some cases we might accept responsibility for failure if it can be attributed to a factor that is evident to others, and we know that we can control that factor and thus improve our performance at a later date. However, when this is not possible, we may invent reasons for the failure before the event has taken place. This is called self-handicapping. Self-handicapping is a strategy we use to maintain an image of competence when things go wrong. In exams, for example, we may know that we don't have the ability to pass. By self-handicapping, we are able to provide a creditable explanation for likely failure in situational rather than dispositional terms.

Exam summary: Attribution of causality

The AQA examination will test your understanding of the following areas:

◆ theories and research studies of attribution (pp. 2–6)

◆ errors and biases in attribution (pp. 6–9).

Example question

The question below is typical of one drawn from the material above, and should take you 30 minutes to answer:

(a) Outline two errors or biases in the attribution process. *(12 marks)*

(b) Assess the extent to which these errors/biases have been supported by research studies. *(12 marks)*

Suggested answer structure

The AO1 requirement for this question is all in part (a) and the AO2 requirement is all in part (b). As questions such as this are 30 minutes in total, the response time for this question should be split into two 15-minute parts (for the two parts of the question). Each part can then be further split as *two* errors (or biases) are required. We have looked at three types of attributional bias (the terms 'error' and 'bias' are used synonymously here) in this chapter – the fundamental attribution error (pp. 6–7), actor/observer biases (pp. 7–8) and self-serving biases (pp. 8–9). Only two of these are required in the first part of this question, and it is important to remember that only an *outline* (or précis) is required here. It is wise, when describing an attributional bias, not to be seduced by the many examples that are available in the text. You should be able to describe what is involved in a particular error: 'when we are observers of behaviour we tend to make dispositional attributions about causes rather than situational ones; when we are the actors, we tend to explain our behaviour in situational terms' (actor/ observer bias –

p. 8). You might then illustrate this bias by offering some of the major explanations (e.g. the different focus of attention for actor and observer).

The second part of this question is the AO2 component, and so it is important that research studies are used in an evaluative way. It is insufficient merely to catalogue research studies in this area (i.e. simply *describe* them), but these should be used in a more active and engaging way. For example, you might point out, when assessing the research support for actor/ observer differences, that evidence cannot support a 'strong' version of this bias, but a 'weak' form of the bias is consistent with the research findings (p. 8). Likewise, research studies of the self-serving bias have not always found evidence of this type of bias in collectivist societies (such as China and Japan), where interdependence is more highly valued than independence (p. 9).

Social perception

To understand social perception, we need to look first at the structure and mechanisms we use to perceive our social world. We also need to look at the processes by which we acquire information about other people and the ways in which we apply this information. *Schema theory* will help us achieve the first objective, and the use of *heuristics* and *social categorization* the second.

Schema theory

Fiske and Taylor (1992) have defined a *schema* as a cognitive structure that represents a person's general knowledge about a given concept or *stimulus domain*. A schema can be seen as a prior expectation about an event which determines what aspects of that event we attend to, what we categorize for further use, and what we discard as unimportant. *Schemata* (the plural of schema) serve a number of useful functions. For example, they simplify detail, speed up processing, help us to interpret and remember, and allow us to evaluate new information. Many social schemata exist. These include *self schemata, role schemata, person schemata* and *script schemata*. (Try Activity 4 now.)

Script schemata, for example, are schemata about events. According to Schank and Abelson (1977), they are a sort of 'mental program' of how we ourselves and others are likely to behave in a particular situation. For example, there is a likely sequence of events that occurs when we go to a restaurant for a meal. First, we are seated by a waiter who then brings us a menu. After looking at the menu, we order some food from it and, possibly, a drink. When the food has been cooked and served, we eat it. Finally, we pay for what we have eaten and drunk. We know how we are likely to behave in

Activity 4: Social schemata

This activity involves making a number of lists:

1 First, list ten characteristics that summarize you as a person. What do you think is individual and special about you? In order to do this, you will need to consult your *self schemata*.

2 List five characteristics which you feel are characteristic of (a) your mother or father and (b) your best friend. How are they similar and how are they different? To construct these lists, you will need to consult your *person schemata*.

3 List five characteristics which you feel are typical of (a) a teacher and (b) a policeman. How are they similar and how are they different? These lists require you to access your *role schemata*.

this situation and we know how those who are with us and those who are serving us are likely to behave. The 'going to the restaurant' script schema thus provides us with the means for successfully interacting with others in society because we understand what they are likely to do – and this understanding allows us to predict their likely behaviour.

As Hamilton (1981) has observed, we also have schemata for members of an identifiable group, and we call these *stereotypes*. According to Aronson (1988), to stereotype someone is 'to assign identical characteristics to any person in a group, regardless of the actual variation among members of that group'. As we will see when we look at prejudice and discrimination, stereotypes are often negative. However, we should also remember that they can be positive or, indeed, neutral.

We mentioned earlier that schemata are concerned with how knowledge is represented in memory. Unfortunately, the information that is stored in memory is so vast and complex that it is impossible for us to have all of it available and ready for use all of the time. According to Fiske and Taylor (1992), when we apply the knowledge in our memory to the perception of our social world, we act as *cognitive misers* – that is, we take short cuts in order to process social information more efficiently. The two main types of short cut are called *heuristics* and *categorization*.

Heuristics

According to Stratton and Hayes (1993), heuristics are 'problem-solving strategies which involve taking the most probable or likely option ... [heuristics] provide a way of reducing a complex task to a manageable set of tasks'. For Tversky and Kahneman (1974), heuristics are short cuts and strategies that we use to modify and reduce complex information about the social world. Whereas schemata contain our knowledge, heuristics help us to *apply* that knowledge.

One type of heuristic is that of *representativeness*. This is what we use to compare whether or not a new *stimulus* matches an existing schema. Representativeness helps us to decide quickly whether a person is a member of a particular group because they match a typical example (or *prototype*) of that group. If an individual possesses one or more matching features, then we conclude that they belong to that group. Suppose, for example, that we hold a particular stereotype about nurses, and we are told that a given individual is a female who is caring. If we were asked to guess that person's occupation, we might be inclined to select nursing because of the two important elements in our stereotype of nurses which that person possesses. Using such short cuts often results in accurate conclusions about people. However, in some cases such short cuts lead to inaccurate conclusions.

A second heuristic is *availability* which is the characteristic that comes to mind first from all other possibilities. If, for example, you were asked to describe a politician, one of the features that might be most readily available (at least to some of us) is an inability to be truthful!

Both representativeness and availability serve a useful function in that they enable us to rate the likelihood or frequency of something being the case in a shorthand way. A more detailed discussion of heuristics can be found in Fiedler (1996).

Categorization

Another way in which we take short cuts in processing social information is by categorizing incoming information into meaningful units that can be stored for future use. A *category* is a set of objects that (are perceived to) have in common one or more characteristics (Hewstone *et al.* 1996). In interpersonal perception, we use categories such as male/female, young/old, and Black/White. No matter how little information we have or how contradictory it may be, and no matter how many times our initial impressions have been wrong, we still categorize.

Such categories include prototypes, which, as we noted above, are typical examples of what we expect someone in a category to be like. For example, if you are asked to imagine a librarian, rugby player, or grandmother, you could probably conjure up prototypical images of these people – that is, images that best represent the category in question. Although categorization into meaningful units is efficient in that it allows us to process a great deal of information in a relatively short period of time and with a minimum amount of effort, the generalizations involved inevitably contain an element of distortion. This is because it is not possible to process *every* item of social data. This distortion manifests itself in the form of biases and errors in judgement.

Two of these errors are the *confirmatory bias* and the *false consensus bias*. The former is the tendency to seek information that is consistent with existing categories. For example, if we are told that a nurse is female and this matches our stereotype for nurses, we may seek other information that confirms our stereotyped notions about nurses, perhaps ignoring other non-confirming information. The false consensus bias is where we assume that if we know something about our own attitudes and behaviours, then we also know about the attitudes and behaviour of others. Thus, we tend to assume that other people behave and think as we do. Both of these biases are evident in many cognitive processes.

Social and cultural stereotyping

Start your work on this section by trying Activity 5 on p. 12.

The notion of *stereotypes* can be traced back to Lippmann (1922), who believed that these 'pictures in the head' represented an '...ordered, more or less consistent picture of the world, to which our habits, our tastes, our capacities, our comforts, and our hopes have adjusted themselves'.

A stereotype is a mental representation of a social group and its members (Hamilton and Sherman 1994). Research on stereotypes has helped us to understand

Activity 5: Stereotypes

In an early study, Katz and Braly (1933) demonstrated the existence of stereotypes about members of different ethnic groups. Subsequent research showed that whilst certain stereotypes had changed over time, they were still prevalent (Karlins *et al.* 1969).

From the list of words below, select five that you think are typical of:

(a) Americans (b) Germans (c) West Indians (d) Chinese.

Place them in order, putting the word you think is most typical first. You may use the same words to describe the members of different nationalities.

Superstitious	Industrious	Sly
Intelligent	Musical	Scientifically minded
Materialistic	Ignorant	Stolid
Methodical	Ambitious	Loyal to family
Impulsive	Passionate	Lazy
Religious	Sportsmanlike	Sensual
Happy-go-lucky	Tradition-loving	

Now compare your responses with those of other people. Do you see any similarities? Karlins and colleagues found that in 1969, Americans were mostly seen as 'materialistic', whereas 'industrious' was the stereotype most typical of Germans. West Indians were seen as 'musical' and the Chinese as 'loyal to family'.

how different groups see each other, e.g. the 'humourless German' or the 'careful Scot'. Stereotypes and stereotyping is of interest to social psychologists because stereotypes are frequently and easily activated, and this activation influences how we react to group members – in particular members of disliked groups.

Stereotyping and prejudice

Stereotypes have received much attention from social psychologists because of their social consequences, which are often negative, and which may lead to prejudice and discrimination. We noted earlier that, because it is impossible to process every aspect of incoming information individually, we take short cuts and categorize information. When asked to recall a person's characteristics, we may do so according to the general category in which we placed them, that is, we tend to recall through stereotypes. We also tend to accept information which confirms the stereotype and refute information which challenges it. For example, when a prejudiced person meets a pleasant or likeable member of a rejected group, that member is perceived

to be 'an exception to the rule' rather than as evidence of a misconception. As a result, our stereotypes remain unchanged, the bias in our processing becomes self-confirming, and prejudice is maintained.

According to Billig (1985), social cognition theories see stereotyping as an almost inevitable consequence of social information processing. Although Billig accepts that it is functional for us to categorize, he points out that we have the ability to particularize. In Billig's view, the focus of research attention should be 'category selection', that is, identifying the categories used by prejudiced and non-prejudiced thinkers.

The functions of stereotypes

Stereotypes also serve the important cognitive function of organizing incoming information, directing our attention towards some events and away from others, and, in so doing, they colour the retrieval of that information.

Augoustinos and Walker (1995) argue that stereotypes are a form of *schema*, that is they direct our mental resources, guide the encoding and retrieval of information, and save cognitive energy. We will now consider each of these in turn.

◆ *Stereotypes direct attention* – We are unable, or unwilling to attend to more than a small proportion of the vast amount of information that we receive from our social environment. We do not even deal with those stimuli we do attend to as if they were unique, but rather we categorize them and process them accordingly. For example, in a study carried out by Taylor *et al.* (1978), participants who were asked to identify which member of a mixed group made a particular comment tended to recall the *category* they were from (e.g. it was a *woman* or a *Black* person) rather than which individual had made the comment. This supports the idea that our attention is directed at category-based stereotypes rather than individuals within those categories.

◆ *Stereotypes guide the encoding of information* – Stereotypes and stereotyping are by their very nature social, since they are about a social category (such as women, students, Australians), and are shared by a large proportion of our own culture. In this sense, they might be considered to be a *social representation* – but more about that later.

◆ *Stereotypes guide the retrieval of information* – A number of studies have reported that participants tend to recall more information about target groups when that information is congruent with their prior impressions of the group. Although many of these studies have used artificial (i.e. fictitious) groups, some using real groups (such as football fans or salesmen) have also confirmed this. The degree to which information about a target group fits with a previously held stereotype will influence the likelihood of that information being remembered (Cano *et al.* 1991).

◆ *Stereotypes save cognitive energy* – We saw earlier that schemas 'simplify detail and speed up processing', or put another way, they conserve mental energy. By using stereotypes, we effectively free up cognitive resources that would otherwise have to be spent processing information about the object of the stereotype (Augoustinos and Walker 1995).

Explaining stereotyping

We may ask where a stereotype originated from in the first place. One explanation is t*he 'grain of truth' hypothesis* – that for at least some members of the target group, the stereotypes are actually true. Social psychologists have not always been keen to tackle this idea, partly because of the fact that many of the negative stereotypes are associated with groups who are already victimized within society. To carry out such research, argue Sieber and Stanley (1988), would be to 'lend scientific integrity to the prevailing prejudice'. The fact that stereotypes might indeed contain a grain of truth is explained by Augoustinos and Walker (1995). They suggest that instead of stereotypes being seen as an intrinsic part of the group themselves, they reflect the social and economic position of the group at the time the stereotype was formed. They give an example purportedly written by Cicero to Atticus during the time of the Roman invasion of Britain:

> 'Do not obtain your slaves from Britain, because they are so stupid and so utterly incapable of being taught that they are not fit to form part of a civilized household.'

Another explanation of stereotypes relates to *illusory correlations* – i.e. perceiving relationships between two events when, in fact, none exists. For example, people may perceive a relationship between a particular ethnic group and violent crime or between travellers and petty crime even though none exists. Hamilton and Gifford (1976) have argued that we perceive a correlation between two such events because they are both unusual and therefore distinctive. When both events occur together, we tend to assume that they are linked (see Fig. 1.1). In their research they presented participants with scenarios depicting desirable and undesirable actions of hypothetical groups. They found that participants typically overestimated the number of undesirable actions from members of the smaller (minority) group.

Illusory correlations may play a key part in the development of prejudice because they lead people to assume that the relationship between two events (particularly if one is negative) is higher than it actually is. They may also lead people to ignore the many other factors that may be responsible for the relationship that have nothing to do with any inherent qualities of the target group. For example, it may well be true that members of a particular minority group commit a disproportionate percentage of violent crimes, but this may be due more to other social factors such as unemployment or antagonism by majority group members, rather than the inherent qualities of the group.

Stereotypes are not always used as a basis for social judgement. Manstead *et al.* (1995) argue that in their role as 'cognitive energy conserving' devices, they are more likely to be employed in situations that are cognitively demanding. Likewise, when perceivers are in extreme emotional states, their information processing capacity is reduced and they are more likely to rely on stereotypes. However, when perceivers are motivated to make individual judgements about others or are held accountable for their perceptions, stereotypes are less likely to be used.

Despite the widespread persistence of illusory correlations, they are not inevitable. If perceivers are able to direct careful attention to information about two events, or if they are distracted from giving it much attention, then the likelihood of illusory correlations is reduced. They are most likely to occur when perceivers have a moderate amount of cognitive resources for

Figure 1.1 Illusory correlations

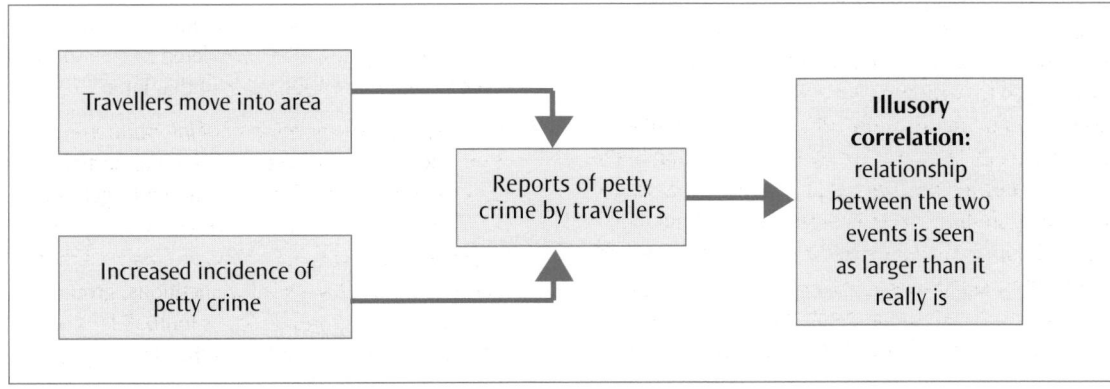

in focus

Stereotype threat

Scottish actor Robbie Coltrane once described the experience of entering a London pub with a Glasgow accent as like 'walking in with a loaded shotgun', such was the effect it had on people. An overstatement perhaps, but you may have experienced something similar walking behind someone late at night, or simply when 'lurking' in a shop doorway. If you have ever felt uncomfortable about doing something simply because you may be eliciting a stereotype in someone who witnesses your behaviour, then you may have experienced 'stereotype threat'. A stereotype threat is 'the event of a negative stereotype about a group to which one belongs becoming self-relevant, usually as a plausible interpretation for something one is doing ... or for a situation one is in, that has relevance to one's self-definition' (Steele 1997). Although for most of us the experience of a stereotype threat is usually short-lived, Steele suggests that for many members of ethnic minorities the threat is ever present. He argues that a stereotype threat is a 'threat in the air' – something 'out there' that is a feature of the culture, and as such it is extremely difficult to change at the individual level. Only cultural reform, argues Steele, can change the pervasive effects of such negative stereotypes.

processing information about the two events. Unfortunately, argue Baron and Byrne (1994), individuals appear to operate at exactly that critical level. They pay just enough attention to information they receive to form erroneous perceptions of the social world. For example, an employer who believes that 'being blonde' and 'having fun' are related, may believe also that blondes are poor employment prospects for responsible jobs because they are too busy having fun (Baron and Byrne 1994).

The traditional view of stereotypes sees them as generally incorrect. This view has been strengthened by research evidence which has exposed significant biases in the way we see and make judgements about our social world. Moghaddam (1998) suggests that a suitable way of summing up our current view of the accuracy of stereotypes is to see them as '... generally inaccurate and systematically biased'.

A more social view of stereotypes sees them from a different perspective. A social perspective acknowledges that stereotypes serve important functions for society as well as for cognitively slothful individuals. Jost and Banaji (1994) suggest at least three important functions for stereotypes:

◆ *ego justification*, i.e. protecting our own status

◆ *group justification*, i.e. protecting the status of our own group

◆ *system justification*, i.e. legitimizing existing status hierarchies so that those with high status are seen as superior to those with low status, who are seen in a more negative light.

Social representations

The nature of social representations

One of the consequences of taking a truly *social* view of human behaviour is to discover that whole cultures often share the same view of the world around them. These shared or *social representations*, passed from person to person in everyday language and embellished by the popular media, allow ordinary people to turn the unfamiliar into the familiar and the complex into the more easily understood. They rapidly become established as unquestioned, common-sense explanations which are shared by, and shape the understanding of, members of a particular group or culture. Social representations therefore have two main functions – to enable us to make sense of our world, and to aid communication within it.

The theory of social representations (Moscovici 1981) emerged out of the need to reintroduce a *social* focus to social psychology, and in particular to understand an individual's psychological functioning by placing them in their social and cultural context. Moscovici's theory was largely based on Durkheim's (1898) idea of 'collective representations'. Collective representations were seen as those views and beliefs that were widely shared by members of a society, that were social in origin and were generally about society. These representations, such as myths, legends and traditions, were phenomena with their own distinctive characteristics, independent from the individuals who expounded them, and which required explanation at the sociological, or societal, level (Lukes 1975).

Moscovici's ideas about social representation, whilst sharing many of the features of Durkheim's collective representations, differ in two important ways. First, social representations are seen as dynamic and constantly changing, and second, many different types of representation exist within the subgroups and other collectives that make up Western society. The role of these representations is to 'conventionalize' objects, persons and events by locating them within a familiar categorical context. Once formed, these representations become prescriptive in nature, determined by tradition and convention and imposing themselves on the way we think about the world around us. Because we are often unaware of the shared prejudices and social determination of our thought, we may choose instead to explain our way of perceiving the world as 'common sense'. Indeed, Moscovici suggested that social representations may be the contemporary equivalent of common sense (Moscovici 1981). What makes social representations truly *social* is their creation and generation through the continued social interaction and communication by individuals and groups. Social representations, therefore, are the ...

'... ideas, thoughts, images and knowledge which members of a collectivity share: consensual universes of thought which are socially created and socially communicated to form part of a "common consciousness". Social representations refer to the stock of common-sense theories about the social world. They are comprised of both conceptual and pictorial elements. Through these, members of a society are able to construct social reality.'
(Augoustinos and Walker 1995, p. 135)

Anchoring and objectification

Two central ideas in Moscovici's view of social representations are *anchoring* and *objectification*. These two processes help us to transform unfamiliar objects or events into something more familiar. Moscovici believed we are motivated to perform this transformation because, if we can make sense of and understand an unfamiliar object, then it becomes less threatening and frightening.

Anchoring refers to the tendency to classify and name unfamiliar objects and events by comparing them with our existing stock of familiar categories. To accomplish this, we compare an unfamiliar object with a prototype (i.e. something that typifies a more familiar object or event). If it fits, or can be adjusted to fit this prototype, then its similarity to it renders us able to predict other characteristics based on our knowledge of the prototype. For example, faced with somebody behaving in a bizarre manner in a public place, we may be relieved when someone explains that they are 'mentally ill'. By classifying and naming this event, we are then able to recognize and understand it within our own representation of the term 'mental illness'.

Objectification is the process by which unfamiliar and abstract notions, ideas and images are transformed into more concrete and objective common-sense realities (Augoustinos and Walker 1995). Moscovici's (1961) own research looked at the way in which psychoanalytic concepts such as 'neurosis' and 'complex' were represented throughout French society. He showed how lay people adopted these terms and used them to explain their own behaviour and the

behaviour of others. In the course of establishing these social representations of Freudian psychology, abstract constructs such as 'unconscious' and 'ego' were perceived as physical entities, and 'complexes' and 'neuroses' as objective conditions that afflict people.

According to social representations theory, as humans, we have the tendency to simplify complex information into a core of pictorial and cognitive elements that are stored in memory and accessed when required (Augoustinos and Walker 1995). This popularization of scientific concepts has been accelerated through the mass media. Media representations enable people with little scientific training to discuss issues such as the greenhouse effect, schizophrenia or the ozone layer.

Knowledge may be 'objectified' into a social representation through three different processes:

◆ *Personification* of knowledge links an idea or concept to a particular person. For example, describing someone as a 'Blairite', or linking together a theory (e.g. psychoanalysis) to one person (e.g. Freud) gives the concept a concrete existence.

◆ *Figuration* is the process by which we use a metaphorical image to help us understand an abstract notion. For example, during the 1980s, food surpluses within the European Community were described as 'milk lakes' or 'butter mountains', and during the Gulf War in the early 1990s, Saddam Hussein's hostages were described as 'human shields' (Augoustinos and Walker 1995).

◆ *Ontologizing* is the process by which an abstract notion is interpreted as a material phenomenon. For example, the abstract notions of a 'mind' or a 'neurosis' may be better understood if they are interpreted in some concrete and physically meaningful way (such as describing someone as 'mechanically minded' or having a 'nervous breakdown').

Social representations research

Critics of social representations have argued that the concept of social representations is too vague and loosely defined, and therefore difficult to translate into scientific research. Moscovici himself (1985) suggests that he has somehow violated a taboo of scientific psychology by not attempting to imitate the rigour of standard scientific theories, and by instead presenting his ideas as a series of essays and speculations.

However, there are a number of important studies that have been carried out within the social representations tradition. One of the most widely cited is Herzlich's (1973) study of the representations of health and illness in France in the 1960s. She interviewed 80 people, half of whom were described as professional

in
focus

'It isn't big and it isn't clever' – social representations of smoking in adolescent girls

Relatively few studies have attempted to describe adolescents' social representations of young cigarette smokers and non-smokers. Kevin Lucas and Barbara Lloyd studied a large group of 11- to 14-year-old adolescents from secondary schools in East Sussex to find out whether the social representations of smoking were different for smokers and non-smokers, and whether this might explain why they identified with one group rather than another. Qualitative data was gathered from girls recruited from friendship groups in years 7 and 9, and their perceptions of smokers and non-smokers noted. Each group was homogeneous in their smoking behaviour: either all members of the group smoked or all members did not smoke.

Among groups of non-smokers, girls who belonged to smoking groups were consistently described as being more active (e.g. smoking was seen as a way of attracting boys), predatory (they are seen as applying pressure to make others smoke) and demanding conformity in their smoking behaviour (non-smoking members were not tolerated). Smoking itself was represented by non-smokers as being analogous to a highly contagious disease. A smoking 'outbreak' is described thus:

> 'It was then they started, in year 8, I think, that they started going to clubs and then more girls started. Just recently, more girls started smoking 'cos a big group of them go down to the leisure centre, and then one started smoking who came to this school just recently, and then they all started smoking.'

Non-smoking groups identified two ways in which this 'infection' was transmitted to others. The first involved an experimental episode, resulting largely from curiosity, the second, and more likely, was predation by a smoking group. Many reasons were given for avoiding smokers, but all represented smokers as having 'gone bad' in some way.

In contrast, smokers noted the desire to be active and out in the world with their friends rather than being bored. Smoking gave them the opportunity to 'go off to the woods and have a laugh'. Despite the fact that

adolescents are often told that smoking for the first time is unpleasant, girls in groups of regular smokers did not always describe the experience as such. Smokers tend to be seen by their peers as fun-loving and non-conformist, and cigarettes are seen as a passport to an exciting and popular lifestyle.

Although it is evident that adolescent girls who never smoke have incorporated and accepted the representations of smoking and non-smoking by the age of 17, there are still substantial numbers who share quite different representations which resist conventional attempts to change their behaviour.

Source: Lucas and Lloyd (1999)

Smoking – a passport to an exciting lifestyle or a contagious disease?

people, and the other half as middle class. Most of the respondents lived in Paris, although 12 lived in a small village in Normandy. Using an interview method structured around themes identified in an earlier pilot study, Herzlich discovered the dominant view that the urban way of life was a primary cause of illness. Living in a city was seen as resulting in fatigue and nervous tension, and as a direct cause of mental disorders, heart disease and cancer. Respondents made frequent references to the 'constraining' noise and rhythm of urban life which were forced upon the individual who was powerless to change them. In contrast, life in the country was seen as healthier, with water and air being cleaner, and the pace of life slower and calmer. Whether or not an individual could resist the onset of illness and remain healthy was, by contrast, seen as a product of internal factors such as the individual's predisposition to illness or their temperament. Illness was, therefore, seen as generated by an external environment, with the individual being the source of health. However, in a cautious postscript to this study, Farr (1977) warns against reading too much into its findings. He claimed that the finding that illness is associated with society and health with the individual is an artefact of the self-serving bias discussed earlier in this chapter. Farr suggests that whenever respondents are asked to explain favourable (i.e. health) as opposed to unfavourable (i.e. illness) accounts, there is a strong tendency to adopt such an attributional bias.

Evaluation of social representations theory

Social representations theory provides a plausible explanation for many of the attributional biases discussed earlier in this chapter. We noted that there are clear cultural differences in the way in which people from different cultures explain their own behaviour and the behaviour of others. In Western cultures, we show a preference for dispositional over situational causes, whereas the reverse is true for many other societies (Slugoski 1998). Slugoski argues that this might be explained in terms of the shared social representations of persons within these different societies. In the West, we tend to see the individual as the primary causative agent in behaviour, whereas in non-Western cultures, shared representations tend to emphasize the social and contextual embeddedness of all human activity. Indeed, as we have seen, the 'fundamental attribution error' appears to be primarily a Western phenomenon, shared, we are led to believe, by all members of Western cultures.

Parker (1987) criticizes Moscovici's concept of social representations because, unlike Durkheim's notion of collective representations, social representations are cognitive structures that reside in the mind of each individual, making subjective meaning more important than the socially shared nature of the content. Parker is also critical of the tendency for social psychologists to use sociological theory to override the problems that have traditionally plagued social psychology since its days as an experimental science. He argues that the theory of social representations can easily be absorbed by mainstream psychology rather than being seen as more 'social' and therefore distinct from it. To critics such as Parker, the cognitive focus of social representations strips them of any true social or collective character.

A final problem with social representations theory is in determining the degree to which social representations are truly *consensual* (i.e. shared by all members of a group). The consensual nature of social representations is at the very heart of social representations theory, because of its importance in establishing a group identity. Critics such as Potter and Litton (1985) argue that empirical studies (such as the Herzlich study discussed earlier) assume consensus and ignore diversity. They argue that it is essential to differentiate between different levels of consensus.

In their analysis of social representations that emerged during the St Paul's riots in Bristol in 1980, they found considerable consensus regarding the range of explanations that could account for the riots (Litton and Potter 1985). However, there also appeared to be considerable variation as to whether people fully accepted, partially accepted or rejected these accounts as having any legitimate explanatory power. Litton and Potter draw an important distinction between the 'use' of an explanation and the 'mention' of an explanation. The former is used to make sense of an event, and implies acceptance by the person using it. The latter refers to an explanation that is not actually used, but is referred to as an available explanation. Many of the people interviewed following the St Paul's riots revealed their preferred explanations whilst also mentioning other explanations that they might have rejected. Litton and Potter suggest that rather than demonstrating consensus, studies such as this actually demonstrate both conflicting and contradictory social representations.

Exam summary: Social perception

The AQA examination will test your understanding of the following areas:

◆ social and cultural influences on social perception (pp. 10–17)

◆ social and cultural stereotyping (pp. 11–14)

◆ social representations (pp. 14–17).

Example question

The question below is typical of one drawn from the material above, and should take you 30 minutes to answer:

◆ Discuss social and/or cultural influences on social perception.   *(24 marks)*

Suggested answer structure

This 'general' question gives you considerable freedom over what you might include in an answer. You might choose to answer questions set to this theme in terms of either of the topics that follow it (i.e. stereotyping or social representations), or in some other way that illustrates how social and/or cultural factors influence the way in which we perceive our social world. In the AQA specification, the latter two topics are preceded by the word 'including', which specifies that they may be prescribed in an examination question, but this question offers the opportunity to use them in a rather different way. It is important, however, given the fact that you only have 30 minutes to answer this question, that you are not too adventurous with your content. The appropriate content for this question spans eight pages of text in this chapter, so it is unlikely that you would be able to reproduce more than a small percentage of that here; any attempt to do that would result in an essay that was ridiculously superficial.

It would be inappropriate to suggest the 'correct' response to this question, but one possibility would be to answer solely in terms of social representations (pp. 14–17). If you think of your social representations answer as having four distinct parts, each being about 150 words in length, it gives you an opportunity to plan your answer strategically.

You may, therefore, describe the nature of social representations (p. 14) and the underlying processes of anchoring and objectification (p. 15), review research evidence that supports or challenges social representations theory (p. 16), and offer an evaluation of the central ideas (p. 17).

This is only one way to address this question. Whatever approach you take, be prepared to support your answer with research evidence, and remember that half your marks are awarded for critical commentary.

Prejudice and discrimination

Zimbardo et al. (1995) have defined prejudice as 'a learned attitude toward a target object, involving negative affect (dislike or fear) and negative beliefs (stereotypes) that justify the attitude'. They define discrimination as 'the behavioural intention to avoid, control, dominate or eliminate those in the target group'.

There is no doubting the existence of prejudice in modern society, and many people have been victims of prejudiced attitudes because of their sex, age, disability, physical appearance and/or membership of an ethnic group. Some people have also been victims of discrimination. Much of the early research in this area of social psychology was conducted by Allport (1954), who outlined five behavioural stages of ethnic prejudice. These are:

◆ antilocution or verbal denigration such as the telling of racist jokes

◆ avoidance of the ethnic group by, for example, segregation

◆ discrimination, or the inequitable treatment or exclusion of those belonging to an ethnic group

◆ physical attack, that is, actual violence against people and their property

◆ extermination of the ethnic group, as, for example, in the case of the attempts by Nazis to exterminate the Jewish race.

Prejudice is an example of an attitude and, as such, has three components:

◆ The affective component refers to our feelings or emotions towards the target group.

◆ The cognitive component refers to the beliefs, thoughts and ideas we have about the members of the target group.

◆ The behavioural component is our predisposition to behave in certain ways towards the target group.

Usually, these three components are in balance: for example, if our beliefs about the target group are negative, our feelings and behaviours are also negative. This is because we prefer consistency in our social world and this allows us to interact successfully in it.

In some cases, however, the components may not be in balance. In their theory of 'reasoned action', Fishbein and Ajzen (1975) argued that although attitudes are frequently correlated with both behavioural intentions and actual behaviour, this is not always the case. Thus, a person may hold prejudiced beliefs but may not necessarily apply those beliefs by engaging in discrimination. Equally, discrimination may occur without this reflecting prejudice. In many schools, for example, physical education is taught separately to boys and girls, an example of discrimination without prejudice.

In this section we will focus on racism, which is one of the most pervasive forms of prejudice and discrimination. Racism can be defined as any attitude, action or institutional structure that exerts power unjustly over others because of their race. It is important to note that our definition includes reference to both individual and institutional racism, where, as Cray (1995) has observed, the political and economic structure of an organization is such that it discriminates. Jobanputra (1995) has argued that psychology itself has always been affected by the racism of society in general. For Bhavnani and Phoenix (1994) three forms of racism in psychology are most evident:

◆ Biological racism – This assumes that some groups are naturally inferior to others, and has been most clearly demonstrated through the use of IQ testing in which attempts have been made to demonstrate White superiority.

◆ Common-sense racism – This refers to work on social identity theory in which it is often assumed that members of the in-group will automatically discriminate against the out-group (a point we will return to later on in this chapter).

◆ *New or modern racism* – This does not view other groups as being explicitly deficient in physical or intellectual terms (as is the case in biological racism), but attempts to justify inequalities in more subtle ways, such as viewing people as being 'different' in terms of their culture and in espousing non-traditional values. For Jobanputra (1995), this type of racism is the most harmful because it can be cleverly disguised and therefore be more difficult to detect and 'prove'.

Origins and maintenance of prejudice and discrimination

Personality theories of prejudice

A popular explanation of prejudice is to attribute it to a particular type of personality. The best-known attempt to link prejudice with personality was Adorno et al.'s (1950) *authoritarian personality theory*. This theory explained why some people were more receptive than others to racist or fascist ideas that may be common in society at that time.

Adorno and colleagues believed that these personality differences could be traced back to the family in which the child was socialized. Parents who imposed a strict regime and were overly concerned with 'good behaviour', and who used harsh disciplinary measures to punish transgressions, produced children who harboured retaliatory urges towards them. As the child's aggression could not be directed towards the parents (because of the obvious consequences), it had to be displaced onto substitute targets. These 'scapegoats' were inevitably those who were seen as weaker than the individual themselves, and were thought to include members of minority ethnic groups or any other socially devalued group.

Adorno and colleagues also believed that this personality syndrome shaped the way in which prejudiced attitudes were constructed and expressed. As a direct result of the parents' strict conventional morality, the child developed a simplistic way of thinking about the world. People and their actions were rigidly categorized into 'right or wrong'. This tendency was thought to develop into a cognitive style where there was little 'fuzziness' between categories (such as social groups), and where the development of distinctive and immutable stereotypes about them was almost inevitable. As a result, the authoritarian personality, overly deferential towards authority figures (who symbolically represented the parents), at the same time saw the rest of the world in black and white, and was overtly hostile to anyone who was not an in-group member.

The development of a personality inventory (the F scale) subsequently established reliable correlations between authoritarianism (as measured by the F scale) and anti-Black prejudice (Pettigrew 1959), ethnocentrism – considering one's group to be at the centre of everything (Meloen *et al.* 1988) – and sexual aggression towards women (Walker *et al.* 1993). Some of the items appearing on the questionnaire are shown below. Respondents are asked to indicate if they agree or disagree with them:

◆ 'Most of our social problems would be solved if we could somehow get rid of the immoral, crooked and feeble-minded people.'

◆ 'Obedience and respect for authority are the most important virtues a child should learn.'

◆ 'An insult to our honour should always be punished.'

◆ 'It is only natural and right that women be restricted in ways in which men have more freedom.'

Problems with authoritarian personality theory

Some of the fundamental problems associated with the notion of an authoritarian personality approach arise from the instruments used to measure the degree of authoritarianism in the first place. Adorno and colleagues' F scale contained 30 items, all worded in such a way that agreement with them indicated an authoritarian response. Brown (1965) suggested that any authoritarianism so measured by the F scale could not be distinguished from the more general tendency to agree with authoritative-sounding statements.

Adorno and colleagues' concept of the authoritarian personality is also criticized because it only deals with right-wing authoritarianism. The theory (and the F Scale) dealt only with prejudice towards 'conventional' targets such as Communists, Jews and other 'deviant' or minority groups (Brown 1995). Rokeach (1956) developed the alternative hypothesis that some people were more *dogmatic* or close-minded and were therefore more predisposed toward prejudice than more open-minded people. Dogmatic individuals are those who have a highly organized set of attitudes which are resistant to change in the light of new information. They are, therefore, rigid and intolerant thinkers. The rejection of Trotskyites by supporters of Stalin in the 1930s is a prime example of how intolerance and mental rigidity can also be observed in extreme left-wing political groups.

Locating prejudice within the individual means that it is seen as a 'personal pathology... rather than a social pathology' (Wetherell and Potter 1992). Prejudiced individuals are seen as irrational and illogical, and requiring 'rehabilitation'. Wetherell and Potter argue that this has the effect of 'deflecting attention from the political necessity of societal and structural change'.

Realistic conflict theory

It has long been recognized that, as well as the needs and personalities of individual group members, the common goals and interests of the group as a whole are potent influences on behaviour (Vivian and Brown 1995). If members of one group believe that their interests can only be satisfied at the expense of some other group, then hostility develops between the groups concerned. When groups are engaged in reciprocally competitive and frustrating activities, each group will develop negative stereotypes about and enmity towards the other group (the out-group). The theory was first formulated by Muzafer Sherif (1966) and colleagues who carried out some of the earliest studies in this area. The initial hypotheses of the theory were validated by the first stage of the Robbers' Cave experiment (Sherif and Sherif 1953) involving 11- to 12-year-old boys at a summer camp (see *In Focus*). As a result of this experiment, Sherif concluded that intergroup bias and hostility develops through competition and can be reduced through cooperation in pursuit of superordinate goals. Although Sherif and Sherif's study has been replicated in a number of different cultural settings, a study by Tyerman and Spencer (1983) failed to produce the same degree of intergroup conflict in a scout group in the UK. They also found that it was relatively easy to increase cooperation between different scout patrols, even in the absence of a superordinate goal. Tyerman and Spencer suggest that this may be due to the fact that, unlike the groups in Sherif and Sherif's experiment, the scout group already possessed an existing superordinate goal (i.e. being members of the larger scout movement and subscribing to its values and goals).

The power of conflict in shaping and developing prejudicial attitudes can be demonstrated in many different studies. For example, Brewer and Campbell (1976) carried out a study of 30 tribal groups in East Africa. Of these, the vast majority rated their own group more favourably than other groups. The degree of bias and hostility towards other groups was determined by the proximity of the groups being rated. Groups that were geographically closer were rated less favourably than those further away. This finding is consistent with realistic conflict theory, as groups in close proximity with each other would be more likely to be involved in disputes over territory and access to scarce resources such as water and grazing rights.

Evaluation of realistic conflict theory

Realistic conflict theory has a number of advantages over other explanations of prejudice. Particularly important in this respect is its ability to explain the 'ebb and flow' of prejudice over time or different social contexts – these can be attributed to changes in the political or economic relations between the groups concerned (Brown 1995). One could usefully apply realistic conflict theory to the conflict between Serbs and Croats or, more recently, between Russia and Chechnya. There are, however, a number of problems with the theory which, Brown suggests, means it is unlikely by itself to provide a complete explanation for all forms of prejudice (Brown 1995):

◆ A number of experiments have demonstrated that in-group bias is extremely difficult to eradicate even when both groups have a vested interest in its elimination. Whilst it is not difficult to understand

Intergroup conflict (Sherif *et al.* 1961)

In a classic study, Sherif *et al.* (1961) demonstrated just how easy it is for intergroup conflict to develop. In the first stage of their study, boys who had arrived at a summer camp were randomly divided into two groups. For the first week, each group worked separately and on their own. One of the groups called themselves 'the Rattlers' and the other called themselves 'the Eagles'. In the second stage of the study, the groups were set against each other. Although the researchers had planned to introduce intergroup rivalry through various tasks, the tasks were not needed. For example, when the Rattlers won a tug of war competition, the Eagles responded by burning the Rattlers' flag! The Rattlers retaliated by raiding the Eagles' camp, damaging their property.

By the end of the second week, the two teams were arch enemies. Support for their own group (the in-group) was high. In written tests, those in the in-group were considered to be 'friendly', 'tough' and 'brave'. Those in the out-group, however, were perceived in strongly negative ways and were described as 'sneaky', 'bums' and 'cowards' (strong terms for the 1950s). In a very short time, then, the competitive structure created by the Sherifs had led to hostility between the groups. In a subsequent condition of the experiment, researchers were able to reduce the hostility between the groups by replacing the competitive goals with goals that could only be achieved by members of the two groups *cooperating* together.

the resilience of such favouritism when groups are engaged in competition for some scarce resource, it is harder to explain when no such competition exists.

◆ A second problem concerns the fact that competition does not even appear to be necessary for in-group favouritism to develop. In Sherif and Sherif's studies, the different groups were already trying to assert their dominance long before the competitive activities were introduced. It appears that people will favour their group over another merely as a result of being categorized in that group rather than another (Tajfel *et al.* 1971). This finding gave rise to a number of experiments which demonstrated that simply belonging to a group was sufficient to produce strong and resilient prejudices for one's own group and against members of other groups (see next section and Fig. 1.2).

◆ A final problem concerns whether conflict between groups must, by necessity, be concrete and real, or whether it can be more abstract or imagined. Brown (1995) points out that racial prejudice often takes the form of 'they (immigrants) are taking all our jobs/houses, etc.', even though rates of unemployment and homelessness might be considerably higher among immigrant groups than among the host community.

Social identity theory and prejudice

Tajfel (1982) believes there are three aspects to prejudice:

◆ *Assimilation* – This is when children learn about and absorb the attitudes and values of the society in which they live.

◆ *Search for coherence* – This involves a need to understand and make sense of our social world. One way of achieving this is through social representations discussed earlier in the chapter.

◆ *Categorization* – According to Tajfel, the mere categorization of people into groups is sufficient for

Figure 1.2 A social identity theory explanation of prejudice and discrimination

discrimination to occur, irrespective of any individual differences within the group.

The theory of social representations suggests that prejudiced explanations derive from the norms of the community or other social institutions of which a person is a part. People are inclined to modify their attitudes so that they come into line with those held by the people with whom they identify (e.g. peer and reference groups). If our reference groups hold prejudiced attitudes, we may adopt these in order to be accepted. This is the process of *assimilation*.

If people conform to the norms of the society they are in, prejudice may maintain itself by becoming part of a cultural ideology. As well as varying from country to country, such ideologies also vary within regions of the same country. For example, Middleton (1976) has shown that there is a difference between the northern and southern states of America; those from the latter show more extreme prejudice against Black people than those from the former.

Social identity theory suggests that we use *categorization* in order to enhance our self-esteem. Within this system of social categorization, people locate themselves and others. The sum total of where they are located with respect to each category constitutes their social identity. Our social identity, therefore, consists of how we define ourselves in each social category (e.g. gender, class, profession, ethnic group, geographical location). The basis of this theory is that people strive for a *positive* social identity. As this is derived from our group membership, a positive social identity is the outcome of favourable social comparisons made between the in-group and other social groups. When we compare ourselves with others, we highlight any qualities which support our own in-group values (termed 'in-group favouritism') and we point out any weaknesses that may appear to exist in the out-group (termed 'negative out-group bias'). *Ethnocentrism* occurs when the in-group considers itself to be at the centre of everything, and any out-group is judged according to the in-group's standards. In relation to mental illness, for example, the White in-

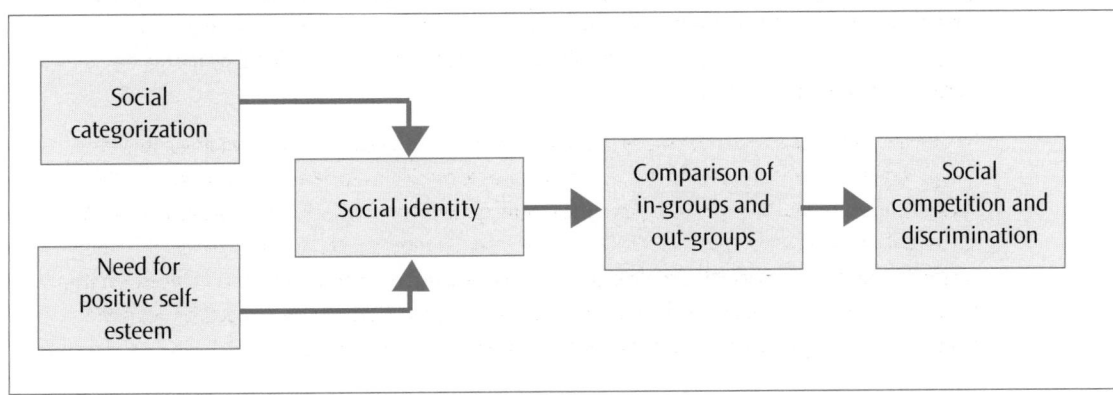

group has adopted a Eurocentric approach in defining mental illness in terms of the norms of White European cultures. For Pettigrew (1979), ethnocentrism is the ultimate attributional bias because group members see their own desirable behaviour as being dispositional and stable, whilst for any out-group, desirable behaviour is attributed to situational factors. The reverse of this is true in the case of undesirable behaviour.

Contrary to the claims of realistic conflict theory, the mere fact that two distinct groups exist seems sufficient for the creation of group identities which take precedence over group members' individual identities. Social identity theory assumes that we are motivated to understand and evaluate ourselves and to enhance our self-esteem. As long as membership in a particular group enables us to do this, we will remain a member of that group. But, Tajfel (1978) argues, if the group fails to satisfy this requirement, the individual may:

◆ try to change the structure of the group (*social change*)

◆ seek a new way of comparison which would favour their group, and thus reinforce their own social identity – an example of this *social creativity* would be the 'Black is beautiful' movement in the USA in the late 1960s

◆ leave the group with the desire to join the 'better' one.

Tajfel also suggests that it is difficult for a member of a minority group to achieve a positive social identity, given that minority groups always have an inferior status compared to the majority. Minority groups do not, therefore, tend to contribute to their members' self-esteem (Turner 1982). Tajfel has even observed that a significant proportion of minority group members may exhibit high levels of self-hatred (Tajfel 1981).

Support for social identity theory

◆ Does group membership have implications for one's social identity?

This assumption has been demonstrated in a number of studies, both in the laboratory and in more natural settings. An example of the latter type of study comes from Cialdini *et al.* (1976). He observed supporters of an American college football team on the days immediately following intercollegiate games. If their team had won, college scarves and insignia were much more in evidence than if they had lost. This suggests that one's willingness to be associated with a group is associated with the group's fortunes in intergroup encounters (Brown 1995).

◆ Do people evaluate their group in terms of intergroup comparison?

There is a great deal of evidence that people will engage in comparisons of this sort when asked to do so, but little evidence of spontaneous comparisons as predicted by the theory. An exception to this is the study carried out by Haeger (1993) who asked participants (as part of a survey) from six European countries to write whatever came into their mind when they thought of their own country. Analysis of their responses showed that 20 per cent had spontaneously included references to other

---

The minimal group paradigm

Tajfel (1970) has demonstrated how easily people will discriminate against others whom they perceive to be in a different group. Some schoolboys from Bristol were placed into groups in a purely random fashion. There was no face-to-face contact between any of the boys. Under the pretext that they were participating in an experiment on decision-making, the boys were required to allocate points, which could later be converted to money, to both their own group (the in-group) and another group (the out-group). In-group favouritism was shown with the boys allocating more points to their own group. Most interestingly, the boys maximized the *differentials* between the groups, even when this meant disadvantaging their own group in terms of the absolute number of points allocated.

Although it is tempting to conclude that the very act of categorizing people as members of even the most nominal (minimal) group is sufficient to cause in-group favouritism and out-group discrimination, the minimal group paradigm has been criticized. For example, the members of the groups in Tajfel's studies may have been subjected to 'demand characteristics' and felt that they had little choice but to discriminate against the out-group members. Nevertheless, the findings from minimal group studies are remarkably robust, having been replicated many times in several countries and using adult as well as child participants.

countries when judging their own: for example, 'people are free and have a comfortable standard of living compared to other countries'.

Social identity theory and the minimal group paradigm

We saw in the previous section how simply *being* in a group is sufficient to develop bias towards one's own group (the in-group) and against other groups (the out-groups). In the absence of anything but a category label (hence the expression 'minimal groups'), one would imagine that these conditions would be insufficient to contribute towards the social identity of their members, so would the identity, comparison and evaluation process take place? Tajfel's research on minimal groups (see *In Focus*, 'The minimal groups paradigm') clearly shows that they do. Mere categorization was sufficient to elicit intergroup discrimination.

Reducing prejudice

The reduction of prejudice is clearly an important goal for society. Traditionally, the way to reduce prejudice was to take one of two approaches:

◆ social education (or socialization)

◆ intergroup contact.

Reducing prejudice through social education

Changing attitudes through targeting children at home has, unfortunately, not met with much success.

Targeting the home can only work when parents realize that their views are prejudiced – and often they think such views are justified. So what can be done? One possibility is to enrich the school curriculum to enable children to be exposed to other viewpoints (see *In Focus* below for an account of one study using experiential learning).

Another classroom-based study was carried out by Aronson *et al.* (1978). These researchers believed that the competitive nature of school ensures children will not learn to like and understand each other. Aronson and colleagues argued that rather than compete, children must cooperate in the pursuit of common goals. In the *jigsaw technique*, each member of a group is given a different section of material to learn. Group members have to interact with each other, learning their part and communicating it to the others. The parts then combine to produce a whole.

In a study by Harris *et al.* (1992), 7- to 10-year-old children were required to complete a variety of tasks (such as building a Lego tower and colouring pictures). Half of the boys had been diagnosed as hyperactive, and were paired with non-hyperactive children with whom they were previously unacquainted. Of the non-hyperactive children, half were told of their partner's 'condition' (that he disrupted the class, talked a lot and got into trouble) and half were not. Results were as expected. Boys who had been told of their partner's hyperactivity were less friendly towards them. As a result, their partners enjoyed the task less, and took

in focus

Verona High School, New Jersey, USA

Over the past few years, Verona High School has achieved national, state and local recognition as a leader in the fields of prejudice reduction. The objectives of the programme are:

◆ to provide students, teachers and staff with sufficient opportunity to discuss equity issues

◆ to understand that equity and diversity represent challenges and opportunities for individuals and society as a whole

◆ to align the specific content area of instruction with equity issues: disability, race, gender, religion, ethnicity or age.

The programme helps prepare students to live effectively in a society that is culturally and ethnically diverse.

Martin Luther King Jr day is set aside for the purpose of this programme. Called Diversity day, classes are dedicated to the programme. Challenging questions are asked of the students concerning how they would react to specific situations involving bias and other ethical issues involving diversity. Each year places a different theme on the day to focus the studies.

The entire high school staff has been trained by the Anti-Defamation League's 'World of Difference' Programme to become aware of stereotyping and biases, and to enhance their ability to work with students cross-culturally.

Source: http://www.veronaschools.org/vhs/activities/prej_red/prej_red.html

less credit for any task success. Harris and colleagues also found that being with a known hyperactive partner also meant that the non-hyperactive children also enjoyed the task less than the children who had not been told of their partner's hyperactivity. Prejudice, it seems, is a two-edged sword, with not only the victims being harmed but also those who are the instigators of prejudice. Baron and Byrne (1997) suggest that educating parents about these harmful effects may well make them think twice before exposing their children to their own prejudiced views. Parents might also encourage self-examination in their children, and stress the importance of seeing people as *individuals* rather than *group representatives* (Hogg and Vaughan 1998).

Evaluation of reduction of prejudice through education

◆ Aronson and his colleagues found that whilst it took some children longer than others to realize the value of cooperation, children from different ethnic groups cooperated and learned from each other when exposed to the jigsaw technique. The strategy appeared to be effective because it made the children mutually interdependent as well as teaching them about cooperation.

◆ The jigsaw method also ensures that children from different ethnic groups are of equal status during the task (see next section on the contact hypothesis). Without this equality of status, the jigsaw method would not be as effective.

◆ The Harris *et al.* study confirmed that negative and stereotypical reactions to prejudiced individuals may be part of a mental 'knee-jerk'. If children could be taught to see others as complex individuals rather than as stereotypes, then these stereotypical reactions might be reduced. Langer *et al.* (1985) supported this idea in the context of young children's attitudes towards disabled people. Children who had been specially trained to be more aware of others as *people* were more positive about disabled people as a result.

The contact hypothesis: reducing prejudice through intergroup contact

The second major approach to the reduction of prejudice is that of enhancing intergroup contact. The aim of this approach is to increase contact between different groups. As in the case with the jigsaw approach (which also involves contact), research indicates that mere contact between groups is not sufficient, and that it must be interdependent and cooperative rather than competitive.

Early studies showed that when contact is increased, prejudice is reduced. For example, Stouffer *et al.* (1949) showed that mixed race units in the American army produced less prejudice than segregated race units. This occurred because actual contact allowed negative stereotypes to be removed, increased cooperation rather than competition, and led to the formation of a single in-group fighting a common enemy. Effects were not generalized, however, to situations beyond the army. In another study, Deutsch and Collins (1951) showed that a group of White residents, moved to an integrated housing programme, showed less prejudice towards Blacks than White residents who moved to a segregated housing programme. Note that the residents in the integrated housing were of equal status and no conflicts existed between them prior to the start of the programme.

---

in focus

Brown eyes, blue eyes

A classroom-based study conducted by Elliott (1977) attempted to show children what it was like to be discriminated against. One day Elliott, a school teacher, told her pupils that blue-eyed children were 'inferior'. Within a day, the blue-eyed children in the class were doing poorly at their work and described themselves as 'sad', 'bad', 'stupid' and 'mean'. In the meantime, the brown-eyed pupils in the class had become what Elliott described as 'nasty, vicious, discriminating little third graders'. Fights broke out because one child called another 'blue eyes'. The following day, Elliott told the children that she had made a mistake and it was actually brown-eyed children who were inferior and not those with blue eyes. Within a very short time, attitudes and behaviours reversed completely! On the third day, the children were told the truth of the matter.

Studies such as Elliott's give children direct experience of what it is like to be discriminated against. It was believed that the effects of the experience would be temporary because school-based studies are done in isolation from the home environment. However, in a ten-year follow-up of the original pupils in her class, Elliott (1990) found that they were more tolerant of group differences and were actively opposed to prejudice.

The results of studies such as these led other researchers to set up situations in which people could be manipulated into being prejudiced and were then exposed to strategies designed to reduce prejudice. Consider, for example, the study conducted by Sherif *et al.* (see p. 20). The researchers found that bringing the leaders of the two groups of boys together did not produce any effect, nor did bringing the groups together. For example, when the groups were invited to eat together they simply threw food at one another. Mere contact, then, was not enough to reduce prejudice.

What did seem to be effective was the creation of superordinate goals, i.e. goals which can only be achieved through cooperation. Thus, when the water supply was damaged and the two groups had to work together to repair it, and when a truck 'broke down' and both groups had to pull it with ropes to get it restarted, the prejudiced feelings that had developed were significantly reduced. Indeed, at the end of the summer camp a party took place which was enjoyed by both groups together.

So how do these approaches relate to social cognition and categorization? We have already pointed out that through equal-status contact, people have the opportunity to gain direct experience of other groups. However, unless this is prolonged (as in the case of an integrated housing project), it has been found that negative stereotypes will actually be reinforced rather than reduced.

Increased contact can help to reduce prejudice, however, in three ways:

♦ It can lead to the recognition of similarities between groups.

♦ Negative stereotypes can be changed if sufficient information about a group is provided.

♦ The out-group homogeneity effect may be challenged (i.e. all out-group members are *not* the same).

According to Fiske (1989), when people are instructed to pay close attention to others, they do perceive those others in terms of personal rather than stereotypical attributes. In fact, Fiske and Neuberg (1990) suggest that we can engage in a number of strategies, ranging from total dependence on stereotypes (least cognitive effort involved) to dependence on the unique features of a person (most cognitive effort involved). Dependence on the unique features of a person matches Billig's idea of particularization (see p. 12). What is important is to address how we prevent people from taking short cuts in their cognitions and focus instead on individual differences.

If intergroup contact is possible, then new in-groups may form, but contact alone is not enough. According to Cook (1978), five factors are necessary for prejudice reduction:

♦ *Equal-status participants* – Prejudice will continue if one group regards itself as being superior. If members of different groups can be brought together on equal terms, a basis for cooperative action is provided and prejudiced attitudes may be revised.

♦ *Exposure to non-stereotypical individuals* – The more people we meet who do not fit into our stereotypes about their group, the more likely that our prejudices about the group will change, provided that we perceive the individuals as *typical* of the group, and not just *exceptions* to it.

♦ *Personal acquaintance* – Getting to know someone on a personal basis may reduce the out-group homogeneity effect; this, in turn, may help us to appreciate members of the so-called out-group as individuals.

♦ *Environmental support for intergroup contact* – Contact can only be effective if there is support from the authorities and the community. For example, racial prejudice is less likely to find expression in a workforce where a company has a well-publicized policy of equal opportunities and antiracism which is implemented openly from the top down.

♦ *Cooperation between groups* – If the groups are placed in a position where there is a common (or superordinate) goal and the group members are mutually interdependent (see Sherif study), then prejudice will be reduced.

Studies that have developed from these five principles have also shown support for the effectiveness of increased contact in reducing prejudice. For example, a study of the attitudes of Hindu and Muslim students towards each other was carried out in Bangladesh (Islam and Hewstone 1993). Included in the questionnaire were questions about the frequency of contact with members of the other group and the quality of this contact (e.g. equal status or not, cooperative or competitive). Islam and Hewstone found that both the quantity and quality of interaction were directly related to a more positive attitude toward the out-group.

A major problem in this area of research is that reducing intergroup conflict can only be achieved if it is possible for both groups to have their needs satisfied. According to Deaux *et al.* (1993), it is necessary to look at the reward structure when considering the interaction between two individuals or two groups. A competitive reward structure, for example, is totally inappropriate for prejudice reduction since success for one person must therefore mean failure for the other. Much more appropriate for the reduction of prejudice is a cooperative reward structure. In this, an individual or a group can only achieve success if the other individual or group also achieves success. A cooperative reward structure was employed by Aronson and his colleagues in their jigsaw technique study, and by Sherif *et al.* when they devised superordinate goals for their groups.

Social identity theory and the reduction of prejudice

New variations of the contact hypothesis have been developed, which have their origins in social identity theory. These new models recognize that group memberships become incorporated into a person's self-concept, and this has important consequences for the person's behaviour towards members of other groups. For example, Brewer and Miller (1984) suggest that, as intergroup discrimination and stereotyping are frequently dependent on social categories becoming psychologically prominent, if boundaries between groups can be made less rigid, then all contact would be at an interpersonal rather than an intergroup level. In this 'personalized' form of contact, they argue, people would be more likely to attend to information about the individual rather than group-based (i.e. stereotypical) information. With repeated contacts of this kind, the usefulness of category identity as a basis for future interactions is undermined, and permanent changes would occur in both the cognitive and motivational aspects of their social interaction with out-group members (Brewer and Miller 1984).

Research support for this model has been encouraging. In one study (Bettencourt *et al.* 1992), two artificial participant categories were created and then members of the two categories were brought together into cooperative work groups so that both categories were represented in each group. Groups were given different instructions, with one group being encouraged to focus on each other 'to find out what other team members really are like' and the other being told to concentrate solely on the task in hand. The dependent measure in this study was the degree to which participants would, once the task was completed, assign rewards to other members of their group and also to members of another group, unknown to them and shown only on a short video clip. In line with the predictions of the model, participants who had been encouraged to 'focus on each other' were far more likely to share the rewards fairly within their own group and also between the two groups. Conversely, participants who had simply been told to 'concentrate on the task' showed a significant bias towards their own category and their own group.

Whereas Brewer and Miller see *decategorization* as the best way of reducing intergroup prejudice, Gaertner *et al.* (1993) suggest that drawing the in-group and out-group together into a new superordinate category (i.e. a process of *recategorization*) would be more effective.

To test this assumption Gaertner and colleagues have carried out a number of experiments which have created artificial categories, then varied the amount of interdependence between the groups. Typically, they have found that where the participants perceive the situation as one in which there was one superordinate group (such as 'students'), they show far less intercategory bias than when they judged the situation as one in which there were two groups (such as 'arts and engineering' students) (Gaertner *et al.* 1990). After the terrible earthquake in India in 1993, both Hindus and Muslims helped each other. A typical response, from a Hindu helping dig out a Muslim family from beneath their collapsed house was: 'That is not a Hindu or a Muslim down there; it is a human being.'

Exam summary: Prejudice and discrimination

The AQA examination will test your understanding of the following areas:

◆ theories of the origins and maintenance of prejudice and discrimination (pp. 18–23)

◆ explanations and research studies relating to their reduction (pp. 23–6).

Example question

The question below is typical of one drawn from the material above, and should take you 30 minutes to answer:

◆ 'A substantial body of research has now shown that the reduction of prejudice is possible.'

Discuss two explanations for the reduction of prejudice. *(24 marks)*

Suggested answer structure

The quotation is included in this question merely to guide you towards the possibility of including research evidence in your answer. This might serve an important evaluative role in this answer. This is not required as such, and as there is no explicit instruction to do so, you need not refer to the quotation in your answer. The question asks for two explanations, and so, as we frequently remind you, your time should be apportioned accordingly.

This chapter has dealt with a number of explanations of how we might reduce prejudice. These include education (such as the jigsaw technique, pp. 23–4), increased intergroup contact (pp. 24–6), and explanations derived from social identity theory (p. 26). When selecting your two explanations, it is appropriate to select two 'macro' level explanations (such as 'education' and 'social identity theory'), or explanations which are more specific within those. For example, you may choose two explanations that are both derived from social identity theory.

It is important when answering a question such as this, not to be seduced into providing long, drawn-out explanations that have more to do with the origins of prejudice than its reduction. There is some relevance to material about origins of prejudice, as many of the problems faced when trying to reduce prejudice are a consequence of the reasons why people are prejudiced

in the first place. However, this material should be used carefully, and is more helpful as a point of critical commentary on the effectiveness of a particular strategy.

It is always a good idea in questions like this, to be strategic about the use of your time. You should be able to describe your first explanation in about 150 words, evaluate it in about the same, and then repeat this pattern for the second explanation. This ensures that each explanation is given the same priority, and that both skills (AO1 and AO2) are addressed with equal importance.

Chapter summary

- Attributions **of causality** of our own behaviour and the behaviour of others may be dispositional (something about the person) or situational (something about the environment).

- **Kelley's co-variation theory** stresses the way that we reach causal decisions when we have information about the person and their previous behaviour, and about the behaviour of others in the same situation. For instance, when someone acts consistently across time and across similar situations, and when others do not respond in the same way, a dispositional attribution is made. When someone acts differently in one situation compared to how they act in other similar situations, and when everybody else acts in the same way, a situational attribution is made.

- **Kelley's causal schemata model** explains how people reach causal attributions based on more limited information. When there are a number of possible causes and one is present, other possible causes may be discounted. If more than one cause is necessary to complete a task, the presence of one is taken to indicate the concurrent action of the other.

- **Weiner's model of achievement attribution** sees causal attributions for success or failure being a product of where an event lies along the dimensions of internal/external, stable/unstable and controllable/uncontrollable. These three dimensions produce different types of explanation for the event being explained.

- **Attributional biases** are distortions in perception or judgement concerning the causes of our own or other people's behaviour. These include the **fundamental attribution error** (FAE) (over-estimating the importance of dispositional factors), actor/observer differences (seeing the causes of others' behaviour in dispositional terms, but our own in situational terms) and **self-serving biases**

which internalize the causes of success but externalize the causes of failure.

- **Social perception** involves the use of social schemata such as heuristics (problem-solving strategies which involve taking the most likely option) and categorization (categorizing incoming information into meaningful units).

- Stereotypes are mental representations of a group and its members. Because they are often negative, **social and cultural stereotyping** may lead to prejudice and discrimination. Stereotypes may also serve an important cognitive function, in that by directing and guiding the encoding and retrieval of information, they save considerable cognitive effort.

- **Social representations** allow us to make sense of our social world and to communicate with others about social issues. They make up a 'common-sense' view of the world that is shared by most members of a group.

- Personality explanations of **prejudice** have explained prejudice as rooted in the individual. Adorno's 'authoritarian personality' model sees prejudice as one possible consequence of a particular type of socialization experience and the individual's subsequent reaction to it.

- **Realistic conflict theory** explains prejudice in terms of competition between groups, usually over some scarce resource. When groups are engaged in competitive and frustrating activities, each group develops negative stereotypes about the other group.

- **Social identity theory** explains prejudice as being a consequence of our search for positive self-esteem. This may be achieved by comparing our own group (the in-group) with other groups and their members (the out-group). In order to achieve a positive self-esteem, these comparisons tend to see the in-group as superior and the out-group as inferior, which can lead to **discriminatory** consequences for the out-group.

◆ Attempts to **reduce prejudice** have met with mixed success. Educational interventions have stressed the importance of cooperation (the jigsaw method) in pursuit of **common goals** and direct experience of prejudice.

◆ Increased intergroup contact (**contact hypothesis**) may be successful if the contact is interdependent

and cooperative, rather than competitive. Increased contact can help to reduce prejudice if it leads to the recognition of similarities between groups, and if sufficient positive information is provided about the target group.

◆ Social identity theory suggests prejudice can be reduced by 'decategorizing' (concentrating on the individual rather than the category) and drawing the in-group and out-group together into a new superordinate category.

Further resources

Hogg, M.A. and Vaughan, G.M. (1998) *Social Psychology*, London: Prentice Hall.

> *A comprehensive and readable text that covers all the issues in this chapter in detail.*

Moghaddam, F.M. (1998) *Social Psychology: Exploring Universals across Cultures*, New York: W.H. Freeman.

> *This text integrates a comprehensive coverage with fascinating insights about cultural diversity in social behaviour*

Pennington, D.C., Gillen, K. and Hill, P. (1999) *Social Psychology*, London: Arnold.

> *An ideal extension text for the material in this chapter.*

Websites

http://www.socialpsychology.org

> *Social psychology network – a searchable database with links to lots of other social psychology sites on the web.*

http://mentalhelp.net/psyhelp/

> *An interesting self-help guide, with Chapter 7 having a good section on explaining and reducing prejudice.*

Chapter 2

Relationships

Paul Humphreys

Preview

In this chapter we shall be looking at:

◆ interpersonal attraction and the formation of relationships, including sociobiological and reward/need satisfaction theories

◆ maintenance and dissolution of relationships, including exchange and equity theories, and psychological explanations of love

◆ cultural and subcultural differences in relationships, including 'understudied' relationships with a focus upon gay/lesbian relationships and CMC (computer mediated communication).

Introduction

If we think about the times in our lives which we associate with great happiness and great sadness, it is highly likely that the majority of them have involved other people. They might include falling in love, a moment of support or help from a close friend when we most needed it, the loss of a loved one, the birth of our children, the pain of a divorce or being told that our parents were splitting up. Even the significant moments in our personal histories which we might think of as personal triumphs or disasters (e.g. getting good A-level results, missing a critical volley in the final of a tennis competition) involve at least some social dimension (e.g. the class you studied with or your opponent in the tennis final). It follows from this that one of the most important aspects of psychology – and social psychology, in particular – is the study of the relationships we have with others.

Much research into relationships in the past has focused on what we might call their 'bright' side – what Duck (1999a) disparagingly calls 'the deliriously cheerful emphasis on the delights of relationships'. He continues, however, to point out:

> 'Research of recent years has discovered the dark side of life generally and of relationships in particular, including consideration of ... relational anger and shame and the management of the daily routine relational hassles that we all experience or the drag of long-term relational obligations.' (Duck 1999a, p. 4)

in focus

The study of social relationships within psychology

It is only relatively recently in the history of psychology that this topic has been regarded as worthy of study. Relationships were once regarded as being too much 'of the real world' or too 'populist' (just as media analysts for many years regarded soap operas as unworthy of study). But times have changed. The area of social relationships now has its own journals, conferences and handbooks. Styles of research have also changed greatly since the early days of research into attraction in the 1960s. Social psychologists today are much more interested in studying relationships as something people 'do' in their everyday lives, rather than as contrived abstractions studied in the psychology laboratory.

> 'Nowadays scholars are more inclined to look at real people doing real things in real life, instead of controlled studies of special people doing special things, though to our discredit we still do plenty of that also.' (Duck 1999a, p. 6)

Finally, let us not lose sight of individual differences. As Bradshaw (1998) points out, the delights of interpersonal relationships are not delights for everyone. In fact, for some, the prospect of meeting and interacting with new people is something they dread rather than desire.

We should note that relationships that are working perfectly well may also have their 'dark' moments too.

We may define a *social relationship* as an 'encounter with another person or with other people which endures through time'. It is likely to be characterized by many features, such as expectations, responsibilities, rules, roles, and giving and taking. It may be institutionalized (as in the case of marriage). It may be permanent or impermanent, formal or informal. One thing we can say with confidence is that at least some of our relationships with others will constitute the most important aspects of our social lives.

So why do we engage in relationships? What do we get out of it for ourselves and what do we give to others? Why do we seek to begin some relationships and end others? What determines which are the relationships from which we derive the most, or least, satisfaction?

These are just some of the questions which psychologists have considered in their attempts to build general explanatory models of relationships. Some writers (e.g. Moghaddam *et al.* 1993, Smith and Bond 1998) have argued that the questions which have most typically been asked, may themselves reflect cultural and gender biases. This point of view will be revisited in the section on cultural and subcultural differences in relationships later in the chapter.

As a starting point we may consider the different theories in terms of their level of analysis. Doise (1986) has argued that psychological analysis may be carried out on four levels (see Table 2.1).

There is an interesting cross-cultural difference worth noting here. According to Smith and Bond (1998), social psychological research in the USA has tended to move towards the 'lower', intrapersonal level in recent years, whereas European research, including that carried out in Eastern Europe, focuses on the 'higher' levels. This reflects the highly individualistic nature of North American society. We will return to the distinction between individualistic and collectivist cultures later.

In 'real-world' relationships, it may well be that relationships are located at several levels (even at the same time). For example, I may have a loving relationship with someone who satisfies my sexual needs (1), with whom I share mutual pleasures of domestic companionship (2), who provides me with the support of a new family (3) and to whom I am married (4). Therefore, to understand or explain this relationship, one needs to analyse its function at each level.

Table 2.1	Levels of psychological analysis
1 *Intrapersonal* (i.e. within a person)	e.g. personality factors, cognitive styles
2 *Interpersonal* (i.e. between people)	e.g. helping others such as family and loved ones
3 *Positional* (i.e. between groups)	e.g. displaying hostility towards an out-group
4 *Ideological* (i.e. at a societal or cultural level)	e.g. belief in a dominant cultural value, such as romantic love

Source: adapted from Doise (1986)

Attraction and the formation of relationships

Explanations and research studies relating to interpersonal attraction

Much of the psychological research into social and interpersonal relationships has focused on romantic relationships. This is not surprising, given that much of the research has been carried out in North America, where a high value is placed on romantic attachment as a basis for marriage and cohabitation. A number of specific factors have been investigated by researchers as possibly important in the formation of relationships.

Activity 1: Your experience of attraction

In your life you will have felt attracted to many people; some may have returned your feelings, others will not have. Think of three people whom you have felt particularly attracted to. What, if anything, did they have in common? When you reach the end of this section on attraction, ask yourself how well you feel the psychological explanations and research described match your subjective experience of being attracted to other people.

Physical attractiveness

Few readers will need to be told that in Western culture, at least, physical attractiveness is very highly valued. A vast array of American studies has shown that it is one of the major determinants of whether we express a wish to develop a relationship (romantic or platonic) with another person. However, there have been criticisms of many of these studies as they tend to concentrate exclusively upon *dyadic* (two-person) and very short-term (e.g. one meeting or 'date') relationships. In the latter, it could be argued that the partners have very little else to go on, other than what they can see.

Two groups of studies in particular illustrate the *zeitgeist* (spirit of the times) of social psychological research into attraction in the mid/late 1960s and the early 1970s:

◆ Walster *et al.* (1966) and Walster and Walster (1969) on dating preferences of North American college students

◆ Murstein (1972) on the perceived attractiveness of 'engaged or steady' couples.

The first of these studies suggested that we try to find the most attractive partner (or date, to be strictly accurate), whereas the second and third supported the so-called *matching hypothesis* (Huston 1973).

The studies have become classics in the field of attraction, not only for what they did but also for the criticisms they attract from many psychologists working in the field of social relationships today.

In the Walster *et al.* study (1966), known as the computer dance study, 752 'fresher' students at the University of Minnesota took part. They initially had to fill out a questionnaire. They were then told that on the basis of the data gathered from these, each student had been allocated an ideal partner for the evening of the dance. In fact, the pairings had been made at random.

Unbeknown to the students, they were all rated for their physical attractiveness. Most contemporary researchers would quake at the prospect of doing this – whose ideal of beauty should one use to make such judgements? What about ethical considerations (would you like to be judged in this manner?). Students were asked how much they had liked their 'date' and how much they wanted to go out with them again. Physical attractiveness was the single biggest predictor of how much each date had been liked (by both males and females), and the desire for another date was determined by the attractiveness of the woman, irrespective of the attractiveness of the male. Clearly the males wanted the best lookers, whatever their own rating in the beauty stakes!

The original 'computer dance' study was criticized for its lack of relevance for real-life relationships because people in North America are rarely ascribed dating partners (unlike arranged marriages in some Asian cultures, as we shall see later). Consequently, in 1969 Walster and Walster carried out another 'computer dance' study, but this time the students were able to meet each other first and state what kind of dating partner they wanted (in terms of physical attractiveness). This made a critical difference. This time the students chose someone of comparable physical attractiveness to themselves, supporting the matching hypothesis, which Cardwell (1996) defines as the tendency for people to select partners who are alike in physical attractiveness, background or education, for example.

A study carried out by Murstein (1972) also supports the matching hypothesis. In this study, photographs of the faces of 'steady or engaged' couples were compared with random couples (i.e. pairs of individuals who were only together for the purpose of the photograph). The real couples were consistently judged to be more similar to each other in physical attractiveness than the random pairs. Murstein summarized the findings of the study thus:

> 'Individuals with equal market value for physical attractiveness are more likely to associate in an intimate relationship such as engagement than individuals with disparate values.'

So much for faces, what about the rest of us? Franzoi and Herzog (1987) asked American college students about body shapes and found that the most attractive quality in men was the upper body (whereas Beck *et al.* (1976) had found that firm buttocks and large chests were the most attractive feature in a man), while overall weight was most important in judgements about women. One should note, of course, that there is likely to be considerable cross-cultural variation in what is deemed to be physically attractive. The thinness currently so fashionable in the West is not considered attractive at all in many Islamic cultures, for example.

One criticism that is frequently made about the research carried out into physical attractiveness until the mid-1980s was its artificiality. Steve Duck has frequently made a plea for research to be relocated into the everyday world of people living their everyday lives. The following is a good illustration of such research.

How do people placing advertisements in the personal columns try to sell themselves and what do they look for in the responses they receive? Cameron *et al.* (1977) found that men tended to sell themselves on characteristics relating to status (e.g. income, job), whereas women mentioned appearance more often. Harrison and Saeed (1977) found that women stressed the need for sincerity and genuineness in replies and tended to seek dates with men older than themselves, whereas men sought attractive women who were younger than themselves. Much of this fits neatly with predictions from sociobiological theory (see p. 33).

However, Koestner and Wheeler (1988) suggest that, at least in personal ads, people tend to offer the attributes that their culture suggests will be attractive to the opposite sex. Duck (1999a) put it thus:

'Advertisers have to present their positive side in a way that is easy to assimilate and economical in terms of space. What is actually going on is that such needs encourage people to play concisely towards cultural norms and stereotypes. On the whole people get plenty of messages from their culture about things that matter in relating to others, and so they develop reasonably clear ideas about the sorts of cues that should be mentioned in ads.' (p. 32)

Frequency of interaction

Much of the early work into friendship and attraction (e.g. Festinger *et al.* 1950) emphasized the importance of proximity (physical/geographical closeness) and the frequency of interaction, which is very often associated with this. A later study illustrated the power of familiarity which arises out of continued contact: Saegert *et al.* (1973) found that women who were simply in the company of certain other women as part of a series of drink-tasting studies, came to prefer them to those whom they met only once.

Despite the wealth of supportive evidence showing the importance of this factor, which Zajonc (1968) calls 'exposure', there does appear to be ambivalence about the direction of the effect. Do we like people more because we spend time with them, or do we spend more time with them because we like them?

Furthermore, frequency of interaction does not always lead to greater liking. Warr (1965) demonstrated that it can also produce more disliking. Thus it may be that frequency of interaction results in greater intensity of feelings between people, but that these feelings may be either positive or negative.

Similarity

There is considerable evidence to support the view that 'alikes' rather than 'opposites' attract. It would appear that similarity of values, attitudes, beliefs and ways of thinking are common indicators of strong friendships and attraction (e.g. Lea and Duck 1982).

In one survey study, it was found that the more similar a husband and wife, the more satisfied they tended to be with their marriage (Caspi and Herbener 1990). See *In Focus* for the results from two other studies looking at the importance of similarity.

Rubin (1973) gives the following reasons why we are attracted to those who are similar to us:

◆ We are 'drawn' to the possibility of engaging in the same activities.

◆ We seek social validation of our beliefs.

◆ If we like ourselves, it should logically follow that we will like others who are similar to us.

◆ It may facilitate communication if certain fundamentals are shared.

◆ We may presume that people who are similar to us will like us.

In arguing for the view that opposites attract, Kerckhoff and Davis's *filter theory of mate selection* (1962) takes a longitudinal view of relationships and contends that in the early stages of a relationship, similarity in values may be important, but in the later stages of an established relationship, complementarity of needs is more important.

Evaluation of attraction and relationship formation research

The following evaluation is based on Duck (1999a), Duck (1999b), Goodwin (1999) and Moghaddam *et al.* (1993):

◆ Much of the research is highly artificial and 'leaves out most of the ... things people do in everyday life' (Duck 1999a). Furthermore, in the case of some studies, the artificiality of the situation is so 'rigged' that physical attraction is all the participants had to go on.

◆ A lot of the research has also focused on 'things in people's heads' (such as attitudes and dispositions) rather than factors that emerge between people.

Similarity in friendship and attraction

Researchers offered free accommodation to male students, who were strangers to each other and who volunteered to let the researchers allocate them to their living quarters for the year. Students were randomly allocated a room mate. The most stable friendships developed between room mates who came from similar backgrounds and who shared similar attitudes (Newcomb 1961).

Boyden *et al.* (1984) found that gay men who scored highly on stereotypical male traits desired a partner who was most of all logical (a stereotypical masculine trait). On the other hand, gay men who scored highly on stereotypical female traits desired a partner who was expressive (a stereotypical feminine trait).

In other words, the approaches were insufficiently social.

♦ Much of the research, especially that carried out in the 1960s and 1970s, focused too heavily on snapshots of relationships (as if frozen at a moment in time) and this takes insufficient account of change and variability. We all have bad days, even in good relationships.

♦ No characteristics or attributes are absolute; all are relative. For example, a characteristic we find attractive in someone at one point in a relationship may be viewed negatively at another time. We may adore someone's unpredictability when we fall in love with them, but see it as irresponsibility when we are falling out of love with them.

♦ By focusing upon the individual or the couple, a lot of the earlier research failed to take account of third parties, such as parents or friends who may have enormous influence upon whom we form relationships with. Furthermore, there needs to be clearer recognition of the fact that relationships do not 'stand alone'. In the real world, as opposed to the psychology laboratory, all of us engage in several relationships simultaneously. In polygynous cultures, for example, a man will have sexual relationships with several wives concurrently. Even in monogamous Western cultures, this occurs when people have extramarital affairs.

♦ There has been too much emphasis upon romantic relationships at the expense of cross-sex and same-sex platonic friendships, for example, which figure largely in the lives of most people.

♦ Attraction may be to a *role*, not a particular person. For example, in the film *Muriel's Wedding*, Muriel just wanted to be married – to whom was a wholly secondary consideration!

♦ Few of us would deny the importance of physical attractiveness but, equally likely, most of us will have encountered physically attractive people who repel rather than attract because of their vanity and self-obsession.

Theories of attraction and relationship formation

Two general theories are particularly applicable to the area of attraction and relationship formation:

♦ sociobiological theory
♦ reward/need satisfaction.

Sociobiological theory

Sociobiology refers to the use of evolutionary ideas to explain the social behaviour of animals (Cardwell 1996). In nonhuman relationships, such as those found among insects or birds, much is genetically programmed. However, the further we move up the phylogenetic (evolutionary) scale, the less this appears to be the case. Some efforts have been made to explain in purely genetic terms aspects of relationships between people, such as lovemaking – usually called mating in this context! – and dominance. Wilson (1975) argues that human sexual attraction and behaviour may be explained through an understanding of 'survival efficiency'. He argues that there is a 'bargaining' between men and women which characterizes and defines their sexual relationships (see *In Focus*). It is, he says, in the 'interests' of the male to impregnate as many women as possible, as this increases the chances of his genes being handed down as copiously as possible into the next generation. The reasons for this lie in the vast number of sperm that a man is capable of producing in his lifetime. Conversely, a woman may produce only one egg per month.

in focus

Personal ads: what men and women say

Dunbar and Waynforth (cited in Dunbar 1995) analysed nearly 900 ads in four USA newspapers. Forty-two per cent of male advertisers sought a youthful mate, as opposed to only 25 per cent of female advertisers. Forty-four per cent of males sought a physically attractive partner, whereas only 22 per cent of women stated this. There were also consistent differences, again consistent with sociobiological explanations, in how men and women tried to 'sell' themselves. In the wording of their ads, 50 per cent of women used terms such as 'pretty', 'curvaceous' and 'gorgeous', but only 34 per cent of males used comparable terms (such as 'handsome'). Men were more likely to advertise their economic status and earning power.

Dunbar and McGuiness (cited in Dunbar 1995) found similar outcomes when they analysed 600 ads in two London magazines. For example, 68 per cent of women advertisers described their physical attractiveness compared to 51 per cent of the men. These results support those found by Cameron *et al.* (1977) and Harrison and Saeed (1977) described earlier.

Whereas the male is capable of fathering an almost infinite number of children in a relatively short period of time, the woman usually carries just one pregnancy at a time. The best chance of her genes surviving into the next generation is for her to ensure the healthy survival of the (relatively) few offspring that she is capable of producing during her reproductive lifetime. This, it is claimed, explains why men are what Woody Allen called 'ever-ready cocksmen', whereas women focus their energies on 'getting a good man and tying him down'!

Evaluation of the sociobiological theory

There are several key points to make about sociobiological theory:

◆ There is always a danger in generalizing from nonhumans to humans.

◆ The above theory presumes that sexual attraction and behaviour is about reproduction. For many people most sexual unions are not directed towards bearing children. Many people now elect to be childless.

◆ The theory presumes heterosexuality.

◆ The theory is both deterministic and reductionist. (Free-will/determinism and reductionism are two key debates in psychology and are discussed at length in Chapter 19. If you are unfamiliar with the terms, read the definitions given there.) The theory accords little importance to our self-awareness, free will and the way in which we regulate most of our behaviours.

◆ There is an ethical concern that the sociobiological theory may be seen to support gender stereotypes which are divisive and to endorse behaviours which perpetuate the so-called 'double standard', allowing men sexual 'privileges' and freedoms which women are denied.

Some psychologists take the view that the old sociobiological explanation may once have suited male/female relationships, but that it would not necessarily suit those of today, or even that sociobiological needs have changed. For example, Lord (1997, p. 347) says:

> 'The world today ... is a far different environment than existed millions of years ago. In the past, it might have been adaptive for men to mate with every attractive woman and for women to prefer dominant men who controlled resources. It may not be as adaptive to do so today (Ickes 1993). In today's world, sex-typed men [i.e. men whose behaviour matches the sex-role expectations for their own gender] often have unsatisfactory personal relationships (Antill 1983) ... It might have been effective in the past for men to acquire resources and women to stay home and feed babies. This division of labor may not be the most effective today (Eagly 1987). Both men and women in technologically advanced cultures can learn how to do both – amass resources and feed babies. If human beings understand the evolutionary and cultural influences that led to the world we live in, they can change modern culture by socializing women to be acquisitive, competitive, and power-hungry as men have traditionally been. Alternatively, they can socialize men to be as nurturing, caring, and closeness-oriented as women have traditionally been (Gilligan 1982, Hatfield and Rapson 1996).'

Reward and need satisfaction

It is possible that the reason why we spend so much of our time in social relationships is that we find them rewarding (i.e. positively reinforcing) or that we find life alone unpleasant and unrewarding. This explanation is based on the idea of conditioning (see Chapter 13).

In a classic study carried out in 1950, Jennings studied 400 girls in a reformatory and found that the most popular girls were those who helped, protected, cheered and encouraged others. Argyle (1992) points out that individuals who are rewarding are liked most, i.e. those who are friendly, helpful and cheerful. Positive nonverbal signals, such as smiling, are signs of liking and are particularly important.

The affect-centred model of attraction

Some research has suggested that people may be liked (found rewarding) because they happen to be associated with something pleasant. For example, May and Hamilton (1980) asked female students to say how much they liked the look of male strangers whose photographs they had. While some students looked at the photographs, pleasant music was played. Others looked at the same photographs while unpleasant music was played. A comparison (control) group viewed the same pictures but no music was played. As predicted, the students who had heard the pleasant music while looking at the photographs liked the men best and rated them as better looking. This and many other experiments (e.g. Cunningham 1988) have shown that positive affect (feeling) can lead to attraction. This is known as the *affect-centred model of attraction* (outlined in Baron and Byrne 1997).

Table 2.2	Human needs affecting social behaviour
Needs/motives	*How relationships help meet needs*
Biological needs	e.g. collective eating and drinking behaviours
Dependency	e.g. being comforted or nurtured
Affiliation	e.g. seeking the company and approval of others
Dominance	e.g. making decisions for other people, being 'bossy'
Sex	e.g. flirting, making love
Aggression	e.g. engaging in football violence
Self-esteem and ego identity	e.g. being valued by others

Source: adapted from Argyle (1994)

Of course, the reinforcements that a person can employ in social relationships may be more than affirmation and approval. People can distribute many other 'rewards' including love, sex, respect, status, information, help, money or goods (Foa and Foa 1975).

A different way of looking at how relationships may be reinforcing is to consider how they may satisfy our social needs. Argyle (1994) has identified motivational systems which he claims are at the roots of social behaviour (see Table 2.2). Read through the table and think about how far you agree with Argyle.

Evaluation of reward and social needs explanations

◆ Most of the general criticisms which can be levelled against behaviourist models (e.g. environmental determinism and failure to credit consciousness and free will) apply here.

◆ Hays (1985) found that in examining student friendships, as much value was given to rewarding the other person as being rewarded oneself. The key factor was the totality of both giving and receiving, not merely the latter in isolation.

◆ Participants in relationships are often more concerned with equity and fairness in rewards and demands than with the desire to maximize their own benefits (see later section on equity theory).

◆ Many social relationships which are more commonly found in non-Western, collectivist cultures show little concern for the receipt of reinforcements. For example, Hill (1970) showed that kinship bonds are very influential, resilient and are not dependent upon reinforcement. (See p. 45 for more on individualist and collectivist cultures.)

◆ There is evidence of gender as well as cultural differences. It has been shown that in many cultures women are socialized into being more attentive to the needs of others (such as husbands and children), rather than being oriented towards the gratification of their own needs (Lott 1994). It could be argued, of course, that this 'meeting the needs of others' might in itself be reinforcing. Many feminist scholars, however, would take issue with this on many levels including a moral/ethical one.

Activity 2: Your social relationships

Note down three important social relationships in which you are involved. Under each of the three, list the social needs you feel are met by these different relationships. In being explicit in this way and producing lists, you may be surprised at the similarities and differences in these relationships.

Exam summary: Attraction and the formation of relationships

The AQA examination will test your understanding of the following areas:

◆ explanations and research studies of interpersonal attraction (pp. 30–3)

◆ theories and research studies of the formation of relationships (pp. 33–5).

Example question

The question below is typical of one drawn from the material above, and should take you 30 minutes to answer:

◆ Discuss psychological research which has been carried out into interpersonal attraction.

(24 marks)

Suggested answer structure

This question asks for a discussion of psychological *research*, which allows you to write about either theoretical (i.e. explanations of attraction) or *empirical* (i.e. research studies) insights into interpersonal attraction. There is no specified number of explanations and/or research studies, and so you are free to structure your response in whatever way you find most effective. You should resist the temptation to include too much (this is only a 30-minute question) – aim instead for a compromise between *depth* and *breadth* in your answer.

We have covered explanations based on *physical attractiveness* (pp. 31–2), *frequency of interaction* (p. 32) and *similarity* (p. 32). If you were to include all three of these in your answer, you would need to choose only representative studies that illustrated the main assumptions of a particular explanation. For example, we are told that in Western cultures, physical attractiveness is very highly valued (p. 31), and this point is amply illustrated in the Walster *et al.* study. The fact that people tend to choose partners who are of comparable physical attractiveness (the matching hypothesis) is illustrated by the Murstein (1972) study. The same process of careful selection (my selections are fairly arbitrary, yours may be different) may then be applied to the other two areas.

Remember that half your marks are available for *evaluation* (the AO2 component of the question), so this should also guide your choice of material. For example, Walster's study was criticized because it bore little relationship to the more voluntary process of dating experienced in the West, and research into interpersonal attraction is criticized because of its concentration on romantic relationships, rather than cross-sex and same-sex platonic relationships (p. 33). Research *studies* may play a useful role in demonstrating the degree to which a particular explanation is *supported* or *challenged* by its related research. For example, research by Cameron *et al.* (1977), and Harrison and Saeed (1977) on p. 31 *supports* the claims made by sociobiological theorists about the evolutionary basis of male and female mate choice.

Maintenance and dissolution of relationships

Activity 3: How you maintain relationships

As we noted at the beginning of the chapter, even the best relationships have their 'dark' moments. Think of the ways in which you have worked on these relationships to ensure that they are maintained and survive. What strategies did you use? Which ones have been the most successful? Did you find that you had to use different strategies for different people/relationships?

Maintaining relationships

Many studies of relationship maintenance assume that the people involved are committed to the survival of the relationship. The problem of this assumption is highlighted by a study carried out by Ayres (1983), who was also concerned with the strategies people use to maintain their relationships. The study showed that the strategies vary according to the direction the people want the relationship to move in: escalation, reduction or no change.

in focus

Maintenance strategies

Dindia and Baxter (1987) interviewed 50 married couples and asked about their maintenance strategies. Partly because of the nature of the questions asked and partly because of the behaviours of the couples, two types of strategies emerged: *maintenance* and *repair*. Repair strategies are those used to make good damage, as discussed in Activity 3. Maintenance strategies may be likened to preventive medicine.

Dindia and Baxter identified a total of 49 different strategies. The maintenance ones – e.g. 'spending time together in the evenings', 'talking about the day', 'telephoning when I'm away' – tended to focus on doing things together, whereas the repair strategies – e.g. 'talking over the problem' or 'issuing an ultimatum' – tended to focus on the nature or mechanics of the relationships itself, and thus were more inward-looking and analytical.

There were interesting differences in the responses given by the couples that had been married for long periods compared to those who had only recently married. The former reported using fewer maintenance strategies than the relatively newly-wed couples. There are a number of possible explanations for this:

◆ It may be related to the beneficial effects of familiarity (knowing the other so well) – a lot of the groundwork will already have been done and the relationship will 'run itself'.

◆ There may be a negative 'taking-for-grantedness' in the relationship.

◆ It may be an issue of awareness: perhaps the long-term partners are so used to the relationship and the things that they do within it, that maintenance becomes 'second nature' and somewhat invisible to them, and, therefore, it was not reported to the researchers.

- *Avoidance strategies* tended to be used by those people resisting an attempt by the other to change the relationship, so they might pretend that the other person's concerns are mistaken or trivial, or they might just refuse to talk about them at all (e.g. 'It's just all in your imagination, there's nothing wrong').

- *Balance strategies*, such as putting in more or less effort, were used by those who wanted a relationship to change. The level of effort depended on the desired direction of change.

- *Directness* usually involved talking about issues and was generally associated with a desire for the status quo.

The ending (dissolution) of a relationship

The ending of a relationship can be one of the most emotionally demanding times of our lives. We must, however, be mindful of the different needs of the people in the relationship. While for some, the end of a relationship may be a catastrophe, for others it can be a liberating restart. It can also be the case, of course, that a relationship ends even though both partners wish it to continue or even develop (e.g. lovers thwarted by parental prohibition, geographical separation or the death of one of the partners).

There are many reasons for relationships ending. Some of those studied by psychologists are listed in Table 2.3.

Table 2.3   Reasons for relationships ending

- conflict (overt disagreement or dispute over an issue such as financial priorities)
- breaking agreed rules (e.g. about confidentiality, support, fidelity)
- dissatisfaction or boredom with the relationship
- lack of stimulation or novelty
- an attractive alternative relationship (see exchange models)
- costs outweighing rewards (see exchange models)
- perceived changes in the relationship (for example, one partner believing that they no longer share key common interests)
- interference from other relationships
- problems of abuse (e.g. alcohol, sexual, monetary)
- changes in self or other person
- falling out of love
- saving face (e.g. finishing a relationship before the other person does).

Duck (1981) offered two categories of causes for relationships breaking down:

- *predisposing personal factors,* such as distasteful personal habits or emotional instability
- *precipitating factors*, such as:
  - exterior influences on breakdown (e.g. a rival)
  - process/behavioural/management features (e.g. incompatible working hours)
  - emergent properties of relationships that cause decline (e.g. 'the relationship was going nowhere' or 'it just got too intense')
  - attributions of blame (e.g. 'what went wrong?', 'who was to blame'?).

Activity 4: Your experience of relationship endings

Think of the relationships in which you have been involved and which you ended. Were there common reasons or was each one different?

Now think of relationships which the other person ended. Were there common reasons or was each one different? If there was a common reason, what does this tell you about yourself?

Duck (1988) has developed a four-phase model of the termination of close or intimate relationships:

1 The *intra-psychic* phase – This is where one of the partners or friends becomes increasingly dissatisfied with the relationship. If the dissatisfaction is sufficiently great there is 'progression' to the next phase.

2 The *dyadic* phase – Here the other person becomes involved. If the dissatisfaction is not acceptably resolved, there is progression to the next phase.

3 The *social* phase – This is where the break-up is 'aired' and made public, for example to friends and family. It is also where the social implications (such as care of children) are negotiated. If the relationship is not saved here (perhaps by the intervention of family), it goes to the final stage.

4 The *grave-dressing* phase – Here the ex-partners begin the organization of their post-relationship lives and begin publicizing their own accounts of the breakdown and what (if any) is the nature of the new relationship with the ex-partner. Partners who develop their own versions of where the blame for breakdown actually lies, frequently employ the self-serving attributional bias (see Chapter 1, p. 8).

Theories of relationship maintenance and breakdown

Two of the most influential theories which have been used to help us understand why we maintain certain relationships and close others down are *social exchange theory* and *equity theory*. They are known as *economic* theories of social relationships.

Since their introduction in the late 1950s, economic theories have been highly influential and have generated a great deal of empirical research. They are so called because they assume a view of social relationships analogous to economic activity, such as cost/benefit analysis: What do I gain? What do I lose? What do I give? What do I receive?

Economic theorists argue that we run our relationships according to a balance sheet principle – we aim to maximize our gains or profits and minimize our losses. The majority of these theories are exchange theories because they employ a metaphor of typical marketplace activity where we haggle/negotiate and try to drive the best bargain we can. We exchange the rewards we give to others for the ones that we wish them to give to us, whilst at the same time trying to 'stay ahead' (receiving more than we give). Blau (1964) argued that our social interactions are 'expensive' (they take energy, time, commitment and other 'valuable', finite personal resources) and so what we get out of the relationships must at least pay us back in equal amount (but preferably give us a profit).

Social exchange theory

This was the first of the economic theories and was developed by Thibaut and Kelley (1959). The theory was concerned with the construction of so-called *payoff matrices*. These are the calculations of the possible activities a couple could engage in and the profits and losses for each person for all the possible permutations of activities.

On the basis of this, Thibaut and Kelley proposed a four-stage model of long-term relationships (see Table 2.4). Thibaut and Kelley also saw the importance of influences beyond an analysis of the relationship itself (called the *reference relationship*). They introduced two 'reference' levels: comparison level (CL) and comparison level for alternatives (CL alt.). CL is concerned with the past and the present; that is, the comparison made is between the rewards and costs of the reference (current) relationship and what we have been used to. If the reference relationship compares favourably, we are motivated to stay in the relationship. CL alt., on the other hand, is concerned with possible alternative relationships. Here we compare the reference relationship with others which we could be in. If we feel that we could do better in another relationship, we may be motivated to finish the current one (see *In Focus*, 'The investment model of relationships').

The social exchange model was modified in several respects by Homans (e.g. 1974) and a major redrawing of social exchange theory began to take shape, which eventually resulted in equity theory.

Equity theory

Equity does not necessarily mean equality; rather it refers to balance and stability. Furthermore, equity may be defined by each member of the social relationship or by outsiders, and these definitions may, of course, differ. Walster *et al.* (1978) offered four principles of equity theory:

◆ People try to maximize their rewards and minimize negative experiences within any relationship.

◆ The distribution of rewards is negotiated to ensure fairness. This may be achieved through trade-offs or compensations (i.e. a 'favour' or 'privilege' for one person is paid back by an equivalent favour or privilege).

◆ Unfair (or inequitable) relationships produce dissatisfaction. Not surprisingly, the dissatisfaction is felt most acutely by the 'loser' and the greater the degree of perceived unfairness, the greater is the sense of dissatisfaction.

◆ As long as the 'loser' feels there is a chance of restoring equity and is motivated to save the relationship, he or she will endeavour to re-establish the equity. Furthermore, the greater the degree of inequity the loser perceives, the greater will be the effort at realignment.

Table 2.4	Thibaut and Kelley's four-stage model of long-term relationship
1 *Sampling*	The couple explore the rewards and costs in a variety of relationships.
2 *Bargaining*	The couple 'cost out' the relationship and identify sources of profit and loss.
3 *Commitment*	The couple settle into a relationship. The exchange of rewards becomes relatively predictable.
4 *Institutionalization*	The interactions are established. The couple have 'settled down'.

Source: adapted from Thibaut and Kelley (1959), Kelley *et al.* (1983)

The investment model of relationships

Caryl Rusbult (1983) found that when people were deciding whether to end a relationship, not only did they weigh up the rewards and costs of the relationship and the possible alternative relationships available to them, but they also considered how much they had invested in the relationship. She defines *investment* as 'anything a person puts into a relationship that will be lost if they leave it'. This may include such things as possessions, children's welfare and emotional energy. To test this hypothesis, Rusbult asked college students in heterosexual relationships to complete questionnaires over a 7-month period. They kept notes about how satisfactory their relationship was, how it compared with possible alternatives and how much they had invested in it. Students also noted how committed they felt to the relationship and whether it had ended. The graph shows the results:

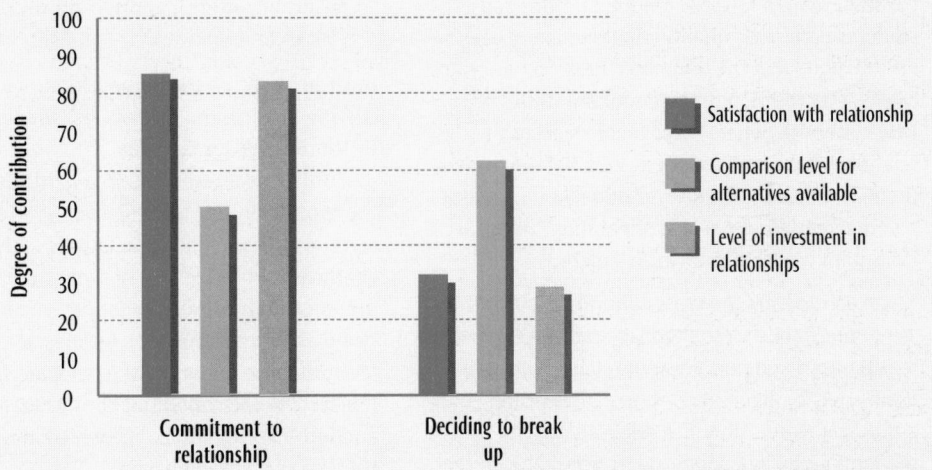

We can see, therefore, that satisfaction, comparison and investment all contributed to commitment and to break-up. High satisfaction and investment are important in committed relationships. The existence of an attractive alternative features large in deciding to end a relationship.

More recently, Rusbult and Martz (1995) applied this model to abusive relationships. They asked women who were living in refuges why they had stayed with abusive partners instead of leaving as soon as the abuse began. As predicted by the model, women had felt the greatest commitment to their relationship when their economic alternatives were poor and when their investment was great.

Evaluation of economic exchange theories

◆ Many of the studies associated with exchange theories have been characterized by rather contrived methodologies, which have little ecological (real-world) validity. Argyle (1988) points out that social exchange theory 'has led mainly to very artificial experiments ... Research on real-life relationships has been hampered by the difficulty of scaling rewards' (p. 224).

◆ The majority of methods and techniques used to test exchange theories were short-term and did not examine the dynamics of relationships through time (i.e. only fairly immediate effects and consequences were identified). See, however, the relatively longitudinal study of Rusbult (*In Focus*).

◆ There is a lack of consistent empirical support. For example, Clark and Mills (1979) have identified two different styles of couples: the *communal couple* and the *exchange couple*. In the former, giving is motivated by concern and positive regard for the other; only in the latter is there the kind of 'score-keeping' predicted by exchange theory. People in communal relationships do have some concerns over equity, but they are more relaxed over what it comprises. They tend to think that eventually in a relationship, rewards and costs balance out and equity is achieved.

◆ There is no clear agreement amongst the research studies on equity theory. For example, Hatfield *et al.* (1979) showed that equity might be more important for females than for males, and Murstein *et al.* (1977) (quoted in Gross 1992) also showed that equity is an issue of concern only in 'problematic' marriages. Both of these factors (i.e. gender and 'health' of relationship) were confirmed as important more recently in a longitudinal study of 736 married couples, carried out by Van Yperen and Buunck (1990).

◆ Work carried out in societies other than North America tends to give little support for equity theory. For example, Lujansky and Mikula (1983) found no equity effects upon romantic relationships in Austria, while Gergen *et al.* (1980) found that whereas American students preferred equity (a constant ratio of rewards to inputs), European students preferred equality. Moghaddam *et al.* (1993) argue that the emphasis upon exchange and equity is a reflection of the dominant values of North America, where these theories of social relationships were developed. They claim that these theories reflect the highly individualistic, capitalist and marketplace economic orientation, and Protestant work ethic of North America.

◆ Again considering the cross-cultural validity of the 'economic' models, Moghaddam *et al.* (1993) believe that Western and non-Western relationships are dominated by different concerns and features. They argue that North American relationships are predominantly individualistic (concerned with the needs of the self rather than those of a broad group of people), voluntary (rather than determined by kin or family) and temporary (with the majority of relationships able to be terminated). Conversely, most non-Western relationships are collective, obligatory and permanent. They argue that the economic/exchange theories are only relevant in Western cultures.

Psychological explanations of love

Romeo and Juliet, Antony and Cleopatra, David Beckham and Posh Spice – all legends of love. But what, exactly, do we mean by the term 'love'?

Beall and Sternberg (1995) say: 'It is difficult, if not impossible, to answer the question "What is love?" because any answer must reflect its time, period and place.' Lord (1997) traces the history of love, in its

Activity 5: These you have loved

Think of three people you have loved. Think of them for a moment as Persons A, B and C. How would you explain your feelings for them? Are the feelings the same or different for A and B? A and C? B and C?

various and changing socially acceptable forms all the way back to Athenian Greece and Ancient Rome, but we can be fairly confident that it will have been a characteristic of human life since the dawn of our species' existence. And yet, as we shall see, even at the dawn of the twenty-first century, what people understand by the term 'love' and how they interpret its experience vary considerably.

> 'Most North Americans believe that romantic love is natural, desirable and necessary for marriage. However, most Chinese words for love have negative connotations: infatuation, unrequited love, sorrow. In China ... romantic love is viewed with some suspicion, as illicit and socially disruptive.' (Smith and Mackie 2000, p. 447)

In Urdu literature the highest form of loving is a striving towards the love of God through human relationships (Gupta 1976).

Furthermore, even within a particular relationship, the expression and form of love may – and almost certainly does – change. Relatively early stages may be characterized by feelings of sheer exhilaration in the presence of the other, perhaps even panic at barely being able to control one's feelings and perspiration levels! But the fireworks of passionate sex may be replaced by the contentment of lifelong partnerships, and intimacy and exchange which may be more psychological than physical.

Romantic and companionate love

Hatfield and Walster (1981) differentiate, as many other psychologists have done since then, between *passionate* (or *romantic*) love and *companionate* love. Hatfield (1987, p. 676) puts it thus:

> 'Passionate love is an intensely emotional state and confusion of feelings: tenderness, sexuality, elation and pain, anxiety and relief, altruism and jealousy. Companionate love, on the other hand, is a less intense emotion, combining feelings of friendly affection and deep attachment. It is characterized by friendship, understanding, and a concern for the welfare of the other.'

Hogg and Vaughan (1995, p. 425) give the following account of romantic love which really seems to capture its essence:

> '... thinking of the lover constantly, wanting to spend as much time as possible with him or her and often being unrealistic in judgements about the lover. This usually results in the lover becoming the focus of the person's life, to the exclusion of other friends. It is perceived as a very intense emotion, and, moreover, one over which the individual has very little control. We speak of "falling" in love as though

Study of romantic love among girls (Simon *et al.* 1992)

Simon *et al.*'s study was concerned with the ways in which girls talked about the centrality of romantic love in their lives, how these norms were communicated and negotiated between the girls, and how they were 'policed'.

The study is a particularly intriguing one as it shows the process of 'enculturation', or 'how the work of culture is done'. Critics of macro-social psychology often argue that culture and ideology should be studied by sociologists rather than psychologists, but this study demonstrates clearly how culture is enacted and negotiated at Doise's personal and interpersonal levels (see Table 2.1).

The study was carried out in a school in mid-western USA. Data were collected over a period of three years by a variety of methods, including participant observation, audio- and video-recording, and in-depth group interviews. Most of the time, the focus of the study was upon the naturally occurring conversations of the girls.

On analysing their huge amount of data, the researchers identified five norms:

◆ Romantic relationships should be important, but not everything, in life.

◆ One should have romantic feelings only for someone of the opposite sex.

◆ One should not have romantic feelings for a boy who is already attached.

◆ One should have romantic feelings for only one boy at a time.

◆ One should always be in love.

The 'assimilation' of culture is not automatic and may be resisted. Whereas some of the norms were highly developed and generally accepted (e.g. the norms of heterosexuality and monogamy), others were not held by all group members and were still being negotiated.

Finally, the study shows the 'techniques' used for norm-establishment and dealing with nonbelievers:

◆ Humour was frequently used to introduce and 'test out' new ideas – through joking and teasing the girls pointed out their friends' norm violations in an indirect, nonthreatening manner.

◆ The norms were always 'on the agenda' because of their inclusion in day-to-day conversation.

◆ Confrontation (with consequential tension and conflict) was used if the other strategies did not work.

None the less, there were girls who did not wholly 'buy into the package'. Thus we see the negotiation of ideology through human activity in social relationships.

it is some sort of accident, something that happens to us rather than some process in which we actively participate.'

Liebowitz (1983) showed that the physiological arousal associated with passionate love is comparable to the 'rush' of excitement produced by such drugs as amphetamine and cocaine. Furthermore, 'withdrawal' symptoms may also be comparable. Perhaps it is possible to understand Romeo and Juliet at a physiological level too!

Contrast all of this with what Lord (1997 p. 354) says about companionate love:

'[It] is fueled by rewards and positive associations. People who are in companionate love enjoy intimacy and care about each other's wellbeing. They want to get close to each other, to explore

similarities and differences in their personal histories, values, hopes and fears. They reveal themselves to one another, feel responsible for each other, and quietly display their gentle, tender feelings for each other.'

Hatfield and Walster's (1981) Three-factor theory of love

According to Hatfield and Walster (1981), three factors need to be present in order for us to 'fall' in (romantic) love:

◆ *Physiological arousal* – Schachter and Singer's (1962) classic studies have shown that, in certain circumstances at least, emotions are determined by a general arousal state which the individual then interprets in a certain way by 'referring' the source of the arousal to external factors or cues. We may feel angry or sexually aroused, according to this explanation, according to whether we are in the presence of an enemy or a desired lover, even though the physiological arousal itself may be very similar in both situations. The term 'being turned on' seems to fit this component very nicely!

◆ *Appropriate love object* – Feeling aroused is all very well, but in order to fall in love (as opposed to being merely 'turned on'), we need a recipient for our desires. Feelings of passion and arousal may disappear quite rapidly unless we have someone appropriate to direct them towards. The key term here is 'appropriate'. As we shall see later in this chapter, people in Western, individualistic cultures tend to believe in a 'Cupid's arrow' scenario of love, whereas in many other cultures, partners are chosen by others. People may be inappropriate for many reasons: we may find them insufficiently attractive (or too attractive! – refer back to the matching hypothesis); they may already be committed to someone else; they may be of an inappropriate class or caste.

◆ *Cultural exposure* – Our culture needs to have a model of love for us to use in order to make sense of our experience (many non-Western ones do not). These cultural beliefs point our attention and perceptions in certain directions. One only tends to see what one is looking for. Research has shown that the more you think about love, the more likely you are to fall in love (Tesser and Paulhus 1976), and the more you believe in there being such a thing as 'love at first sight', the more likely it is that it will happen to you (Averill and Boothroyd 1977).

Is the theory a good one? Hogg and Vaughan (1995, pp. 427–8) appraise its worth wittily when they say:

'It would be difficult to dispute the involvement of these factors in love. However, though they may be necessary for the state of love to occur, they do not seem to be sufficient. If they were, love could easily be taken into the laboratory. The ingredients required would be that Peter's culture includes a concept of love, and Olivia provides arousal by being attractive, or by chasing Peter around the room, or by paying him a compliment – and hey presto, "love".'

The model also focuses largely upon one form of love. Let us now turn our attention to two other models.

Sternberg's 'Triangular theory of love'

According to Sternberg (1986, 1988), types of love are determined by three points of a triangle (see Fig. 2.1) with the points being:

◆ *Passion* – the hot point of love, e.g. arousal, intense feelings, physical attraction, sexual consummation

◆ *Intimacy* – the warm point of love, e.g. close and bonded feelings, helping, depending on, supporting, caring and sharing

◆ *Decision/commitment* – the cool point of love. A deliberate choice about loving, and staying with, someone.

When love has only passion, we often refer to it as infatuation; when it has only intimacy, we may think of it as liking; and when it has only commitment, it may be seen as contractual or economic/market love.

Sternberg identifies another kind of love, consummate love, which occurs when all three of the above operate. Hogg and Vaughan (1995) show how, by combining the points of the triangle in different ways, different types of love can be identified (see Table 2.5).

Problems clearly will arise when, for example, one person has romantic love for another who has companionate love for them.

Hendrick and Hendrick's Six styles of love

Hendrick and Hendrick's (1986) model focuses on the types of love styles that people enter relationships with:

◆ *Game-playing* – treating love like a game, a sport or a competition

◆ *Possessive* – trying to tie the partner into a long-term relationship

◆ *Logical* – treating love as a practical, logical decision-making process

◆ *Altruistic* – making sacrifices; putting the other person's happiness above everything your own

◆ *Companionate* – loving affection and friendship which develops over time

◆ *Erotic* – hedonism and sexual pleasure.

Research has shown that real-life couples show much similarity in their love styles and that lasting romantic relationships scored high on erotic love, but low on game-playing (Hendrick and Hendrick 1992).

Figure 2.1 Sternberg's triangle of love

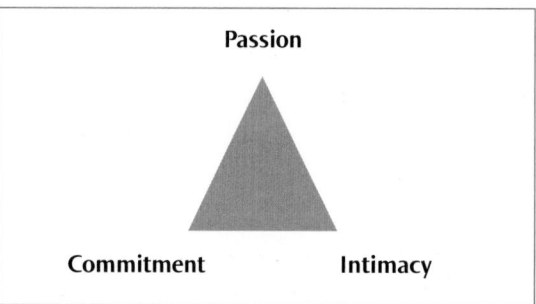

Table 2.5   Hogg and Vaughan's variations of love

	Passion	Commitment	Intimacy
Infatuation	Present	Absent	Absent
Empty love	Absent	Present	Absent
Liking	Absent	Absent	Present
Fatuous love	Present	Present	Absent
Romantic love	Present	Absent	Present
Companionate love	Absent	Present	Present
Consummate love	Present	Present	Present
No love	Absent	Absent	Absent

Activity 6: Your experience of attraction

Hendrick and Hendrick (1986) studied differences in the frequency with which men and women were positively disposed to, and displayed such love 'styles' in the USA in the mid-1980s. Have a go at predicting the sex biases they found. We can think of gender differences as an example of subcultural differences (i.e. differences *within* a culture, such as the USA, as opposed to differences *between* two or more cultures). Other examples of subculture differences include class and ethnicity.

Answers to Activity 6 are given at the end of the chapter.

All three of the theories discussed above were developed in North America. How well would they stand up under a cross-cultural scrutiny? Let us now turn our attention to differences between cultures on the nature of love.

Differences in love between cultures

Lee (1973) developed six love styles which map on with little effort to the Hendrick and Hendrick typology above:

◆ Game-playing love is called *Ludus*.

◆ Possessive love is called *Mania*.

◆ Logical love is called *Pragma*.

◆ Altruistic love is called *Agape*.

◆ Companionate or friendship love is called *Storge*.

◆ Erotic/romantic love is called *Eros*.

A number of studies have been carried out to examine whether there are differences between culture groups and the different love styles. An important point to note

is that most of the research in cultural variation has taken place with different ethnic groups within North America. Here is a summary of the key findings (adapted from Goodwin 1999):

◆ Asian (oriental) students were found to be more storgic (companionate) and pragmatic (logical), and less erotic (romantic) than Black or White US students (Hendrick and Hendrick 1986 – replicated by Dion and Dion 1993 in Canada).

◆ Hispanics were more likely to support emotional types of love (e.g. Eros) than were Caucasians (Rechtien and Fiedler 1988).

◆ Hong Kong Chinese students were found to be more pragmatic (logical) and agapic (altruistic) and less erotic (romantic) than British students (Goodwin and Findlay 1997).

◆ When comparing North American, Japanese and Russian students (Sprecher *et al.* 1994), Americans were higher on erotic (romantic) and storgic (companionate) love. There was also an interesting gender effect here: in the American sample men were more ludic (game-playing) and manic (possessive) but this subcultural difference was not found in the Russian and Japanese samples.

Fiske (1991) developed a cross-cultural model of interpersonal relationships, which identifies four styles (examined in more detail later in the chapter):

◆ *Communal sharing* – People share without expecting specific 'repayment'.

◆ *Equality matching* – People take turns, making equal contributions.

◆ *Authority ranking* – People of lower status are deferential to those of higher status so that the higher status people will look after and protect them.

◆ *Market pricing* – People exchange 'commodities' on an economic or trading basis.

Haslam (1994) has shown that when asked to characterize their two-person (or dyadic) relationships, many people use criteria very similar to these and notable cross-cultural differences have been found. Cultures/countries in Western Europe, North America, Australia and New Zealand emphasize market pricing views of relationships, whereas Asian and Pacific nations emphasize authority-ranking. These have much to do with the distinction between individualist and collectivist cultures, as we shall shortly see.

Cultures have been shown to vary enormously in their accepted love and sexual practices. Consider the following contrasts:

- The Marquesans of Polynesia encourage children to be sexually experienced by the age of 10 (Suggs 1966), whereas Silwa Egyptians discourage sexual activity severely by surgically mutilating young girls' genitals so that they may never enjoy sexual pleasure (Ammar 1954).

- Some cultures encourage child marriages, but men in the Tiwi tribe of Northern Australia are discouraged from marrying before the age of 40 (Hart and Pillig 1960).

- Many cultures have arranged marriages in which partners are given little, if any, choice. By contrast, men and women of the Fon of Dahomey (West Africa) not only choose their partner but which of 13 types of marriage they want (differences relate to control over property, who can initiate a divorce and sexual arrangements).

- In most of North America and Western Europe, it is believed that women have the same 'right' to derive pleasure from sexual activities as men, but the Chiricahua Apache Indians believe that it is wrong for women to show any emotion before or during sexual intercourse (Ford and Beach 1951). Men in the Tepoztlan village of Mexico try to avoid sexually arousing their wives as they believe that a sexually passive wife is more likely to be faithful (Lewis 1960).

- In many countries, homosexuality is still illegal. In East Bay, Melanesia, it is positively encouraged during adolescence when fathers choose an older male partner for their sons, to educate them in sexual techniques (Davenport 1965).

- Psychological writings abound with the notion that sexual motivation is a key human drive that influences much of our thinking and behaviour (think of the Eros instinct in Freudian psychology, for example). In the Dani society of western New Guinea, however, there is indifference to sexual activity (Heider 1976). Premarital and extramarital affairs are rare, and married couples usually wait about two years after marriage before having intercourse.

In contrast, however, consistent cross-cultural similarities have also been found. David Buss (1994), for example, has frequently found that in partner choice, men tend to value physical attractiveness and prefer younger partners, whereas women value status (e.g. economic status) and prefer older partners. This finding is wholly consistent with the sociobiological and evolutionary explanations of attraction.

Exam summary: Maintenance and dissolution of relationships

The AQA examination will test your understanding of the following areas:

- theories and research studies of the maintenance and dissolution of relationships (pp. 36–40)

- psychological explanations of love (pp. 40–4).

Example question

The question below is typical of one drawn from the material above, and should take you 30 minutes to answer:

(a) Outline **two** theories which relate to the maintenance and/or breakdown of relationships.
(24 marks)

(b) Evaluate these two theories of maintenance and/or breakdown of relationships. *(24 marks)*

Suggested answer structure

The AQA specification entry clearly discriminates between theories and research relating to the *formation* of relationships, and theories and research which are more relevant to their *maintenance* and *dissolution* (breakdown). You should draw upon the latter in your answer to this question. Drawing a distinction between explanations of *maintenance* and *dissolution* is less clear cut, and so the question is allowing either or both. The question asks for a *description* of theories in part (a) and an *evaluation* of the same theories in part (b). This makes your choice of theory very important. You should try to select two theories that you also feel confident about evaluating. In other words, when answering part (a) of this question, think ahead to what you might also be able to write in part (b).

This section has dealt with a number of theories that explain the maintenance and dissolution of relationships. These include *social exchange theory* (p. 38), in which people calculate the 'profits and losses' of their relationships, and *equity theory* (p. 38), where relationships are evaluated by each partner in terms of 'fairness'. It is also possible to include Duck's four-phase model of the termination of relationships (p. 37), although this may prove harder to evaluate. Duck's model is a *descriptive* account of the dissolution of relationships which, although potentially relevant here, would be less relevant if the question asked for theories that *explained* the maintenance and/or dissolution of relationships.

Evaluation of social exchange theory and equity theory explanations of relationship maintenance and breakdown (i.e. the economic exchange theories) can be found on pp. 39–40. There are a number of factors that limit the credibility of these theories. For example, they tend to focus more on the short-term effects of relationships rather than studying the long-term dynamics of stable relationships; 'score-keeping' (a key aspect of both theories) may be evident in only certain types of couples (i.e. 'exchange' couples), and the emphasis on exchange and equity may be a characteristic of Western cultures more than it is a characteristic of relationships in non-Western cultures. It is important to remember that the theories that you choose to evaluate in this second part of the question must be the same as the ones that you described in the first.

Cultural and subcultural differences in relationships

Subcultural differences are those which are found within a particular culture, society or country. In contemporary Britain they include, for example, differences between: men and women; gays and straights; Asians, African-Caribbeans and Whites; old and young. Culture has been defined by Hofstede (1994) by way of a computing analogy when he says it is 'the collective programming of the mind which distinguishes one group or category of people from another'. It also 'travels' through time and physical distance (although cultural values do, of course, change too) to provide relatively stable sets of values and rules by which people live their lives. Culture may be largely 'land-locked' within a particular country, especially before the advent of modern travel and communication, or it may not be (such as with Jewish culture).

Differences in relationships: explanations and research

Moghaddam *et al.* (1993) contend that whereas social relationships in Western cultures tend to be individualistic, voluntary and temporary, those in non-Western cultures tend to be collective, obligatory and permanent. It follows from this distinction that a great deal of what we have just been considering is simply not applicable or relevant to non-Western cultures. Moghaddam and colleagues go on to say:

> 'The cultural differences in interpersonal relationships remind us that scientists, like everyone else, are socialized within a given culture. As a result, their theories and research are inevitably affected by this cultural experience. The cultural values and environmental conditions in North America have led North American social psychologists to be primarily concerned with first-time acquaintances, friendships, and intimate relationships, primarily because these appear to be the relationships most relevant to the North American urban cultural experience.' (p. 103).

They suggest that in non-Western cultures where people cannot enter and leave relationships at will, key questions might be very different indeed.

Categorizing cultures

Let us begin our journey into cultural and subcultural differences in relationships by examining how different cultures may be classified.

In some of the largest studies ever carried out in the social sciences, Hofstede (between 1980 and 1994) analysed data on work experience from over 100,000 employees, working in 50 different countries. On the basis of the analysis, he contended that over half of the variance between countries was accounted for by four dimensions:

1 *Individualism/collectivism*

In individualistic cultures, the emphasis is upon the individual person and his or her rights, goals, behaviours, etc. Individual performance and achievement are praised and dependence on others is not seen as particularly desirable. People in individualist cultures strive for autonomy and there is emphasis on the 'I' rather than the 'we'. When there is conflict between the individual and the collective (for example, the group or the family), individual desires are deemed more important by the individual. In contrast, collectivist cultures value the 'we' over the 'I'. Ties between, and responsibilities to collective units (for example, the family or the community) are seen as more important than the desires of particular individuals. Thus, for example, a marriage is seen as a union between families as much – if not more – than between individuals.

What is it that makes some cultures individualistic and others collectivist? Goodwin (1999) offers the following possibilities:

◆ *Economic wealth* – In affluent countries there are likely to be many avenues for individuals to pursue personal economic security and autonomy, whereas in poorer countries people may have to pool resources far more and be more dependent upon others. More developed (and probably richer) countries may have broader social networks and geographical freedom to roam; this may lead to individuals moving away from pre-existing community groups.

◆ *Religion* – The ancient Eastern philosophy of Confucianism puts a very high value upon collective harmony and wellbeing, whereas Christian churches may put more emphasis on individuals making their own unique relationship with God.

◆ *Geographical proximity* – Individualism and collectivism tend to cluster globally. Amongst other factors this may be related to climate. For example, Hofstede (1994) argues that in colder climates, survival may be largely down to individual initiative.

2 *Power-distance*

This concerns the extent to which members of a culture accept that power in an organization or institution should be distributed unequally between its members. High power-distance cultures are characterized by a belief that power is properly vested in formal positions which reflect status differentials. People in low power-distance cultures believe that power should only be deployed when it is necessary and can be justified. Individualistic cultures tend to be low on power-distance, and collectivist cultures high.

3 *Masculinity and femininity*

Even cultures can be sexed/gendered. Hofstede (1983) describes masculine cultures as reflecting 'a preference for achievement, heroism, assertiveness, and material success', as opposed to feminine cultures which show 'a preference for relationships, modesty, caring for the weak and the quality of life'.

4 *Uncertainty avoidance*

This reflects 'the extent to which members of a culture feel threatened by uncertain or unknown situations' (Hofstede 1994). In high uncertainty-avoidance cultures, there is emphasis on consensus, predictability and planning. There tend to be clear and explicit rules for dealing with deviance from acceptable behaviour. In low uncertainty-avoidance cultures, unpredictability and 'voyages into the unknown' are viewed with curiosity and interest, rather than with fear and apprehension.

Bond (1988), working with Chinese social scientists, found a fifth dimension that emerged from his analysis: *Confucian dynamism*. This tends to be characteristic of collectivist cultures and concerns long-term perspectives, perseverance, strict social ordering, thrift and a sense of shame in the context of social responsibility to one's self and others.

Based on Hofstede (1994), Goodwin (1999) gives us the following table on the highest- and lowest-scoring countries on the five cultural categories (see Table 2.6).

Evaluation of the culture classification model

◆ Apart from Confucian dynamism, the categories have been based on concepts which have emerged largely from Western research.

◆ Schwartz (1997) has been critical about the 'purity' of the categories. He argued that there are many variations within, as well as between, cultures.

◆ The model can be said to fail to account sufficiently for situational or contextual variables. We can be

Table 2.6 Highest- and lowest-scoring countries according to five cultural categories					
	*Individualism/ collectivism**	*Power-distance*	*Masculinity/ femininity***	*Uncertainty avoidance*	*Confucian dynamism*
Highest three countries (in order)	USA Australia Britain	Malaysia Guatemala Panama	Japan Austria Venezuela	Greece Portugal Guatemala	China Hong Kong Taiwan
Lowest three countries (in order)	Guatemala Ecuador Panama	Austria Israel Denmark	Sweden Norway Holland	Singapore Jamaica Denmark	Pakistan Nigeria Philippines

* Individualism scores high; collectivism scores low. Therefore, USA was most individualistic; Guatemala was most collectivist.

** Masculinity scores high; femininity scores low. Therefore, Japan was most masculine; Sweden was most feminine.

individualistic in certain situations and collectivist in others (Schneider *et al.* 1997).

◆ Tables such as Table 2.6 focus on the statistical average of people's responses within a particular culture, but there is considerable room for individual variation and diversity (Cha 1994).

Voluntary and involuntary relationships

Marriage 'arrangements' around the globe range from those where partners have no choice whatsoever in whom they marry, to those where the choice is totally determined by the partners themselves. Rosenblatt and Anderson (1981) contend there are few societies characterized by such extremes; the majority have variable characteristics of both. While many Western countries subscribe to the Cupid's Arrow model of love (we 'fall' in love; it is something that 'happens' to us), in many non-Western, collectivist cultures the marriage is seen as a match between families.

It is worth noting, however, that in Western cultures people increasingly say that it is important to love someone before marrying them. Simpson *et al.* (1986) compared responses to the question: 'If a man (woman) had all the qualities you desired, would you marry this person if you were not in love with him (her)?' The biggest changes were between the first two samples for both men and women. In 1967, just over 60 per cent of men responded 'no'; the figure rose to over 80 per cent in 1976 and then fell back slightly in 1984. Slightly over 20 per cent of women responded 'no' to the question in 1967. By 1976, this figure had approximately quadrupled, and further increased (slightly) in 1984 by which time men and women responded almost identically (Hogg and Vaughan 1998).

The most common form of marriage partner selection worldwide is by arrangement, with parents having the most significant say, although family and friends are also often influential (Ingoldsby 1995). There is considerable variation in how much weight is given to the views of the potential partners themselves.

Marital choice among British Asians

How, if at all, do British immigrant families adapt their cultural values and lifestyles to those of their new society? The results of some interesting recent research are summarized below:

◆ In a study looking at Sikhs, Hindus and Muslims living in Britain and Canada, it was found that the practice of arranged marriages was common. Marriages were determined by families and intermediaries with the chief criteria being caste, social class and religion. Asian parents were particularly protective of daughters and this was leading to cross-generational conflict as the young people in the Westernized cultures valued individual partner choice far higher than their family (Ghuman 1994).

◆ Hindus and Sikhs were more likely to accept arranged marriages than Muslims.

◆ In a study of 70 Hindu Gujarati couples living in Leicester, it was found that only 8 per cent had completely 'arranged' marriages. Three-quarters had been introduced by a third-party and had been given the option of refusing their partner. Often they had met each other at large social events (although they had been given little opportunity for close interaction). Hindu Gujaratis had a considerable choice about the timing of their marriage (Goodwin *et al.* 1997).

Permanent or impermanent? The issue of divorce

Almost all cultures have provision for divorce, although there is greater taboo and stigma attached to divorce in cultures with traditional arranged marriages. Betzig (1996) studied divorce in 160 countries and found that the most common ground for divorce was infidelity,

The bride-price and dowry systems

In two-thirds of the world's societies, a man (or his family) must pay (*a bride-price*) to marry a woman (Stephens 1963). It is particularly common in Africa where the bride's family are paid by the groom's family 'in return for her labour and reproductive powers' (Goodwin 1999). Mwamwenda and Monyooe (1997) found considerable support (88 per cent) for the bride-price system amongst Xhosa-speaking graduate students in South African universities. It was seen as a statement of appreciation by the groom about the value of the bride and her dignity.

The *dowry* has been a feature of arranged marriages in Europe and some Asian cultures. Here the bride brings gifts with her from her family, often to help 'set up' the new home. This is seen as an exchange for the groom's earning power. Dowries often operate in societies which have traditionally accorded relatively low status to women.

particularly women's infidelity rather men's. The second most common ground was sterility and the third was cruelty and/or maltreatment (usually of the husband towards the wife).

Other writers have argued that economic and social developments are the factors which put most strain on marriages. Changes in the roles of women have led to increases in divorce rates in many cultures (McKenry and Price 1995).

There is considerable cross-cultural variation in reasons for marital breakdown and divorce. The following are some of those discussed by Goodwin (1999):

◆ In Poland, where divorce rates are low compared to most of Europe, it is usually women who file for divorce, mainly due to maltreatment caused by husbands' alcohol abuse.

◆ In China, the divorce rate is very low (less than 4 per cent) and carries shame for both parties and the family. This is a clear example of collectivist cultural values in operation. In a historical analysis, Simmel (1971) argues that individualism is associated with higher divorce levels as it encourages the individual constantly to seek their ideal partner.

◆ Political unrest has been cited as a major cause of the rising divorce rate in Iran (McKenry and Price 1995). Couples rushed into marriage during the Islamic revolution but many found it difficult to live within the strict Islamic value system.

◆ In African societies such Ghana and Nigeria, social and economic changes such as industrialization, increased urbanization and greater education for women have led to increases in divorce rates (McKenry and Price 1995).

◆ In Saudi Arabia, a man does not have to give a reason for divorcing his wife, but the wife can only initiate a divorce if this is specifically stated in their marriage contract as being allowed. After divorce, the children remain with the father who stays in the family house. The wife returns to her parents' house (Minai 1981).

The collectivist/individualist dimension is well illustrated in a study by Brodbar-Nemzer (1986) of more than 4,000 Jewish households in New York. He asked participants about their denomination (orthodox or liberal); their behaviour (e.g. attending synagogue) and their friendship networks (the proportion of their closest friends who were Jewish). He found a strong link between Jewish commitment and disinclination to divorce, attributing this to a stronger sense of social integration and more favourable attitudes towards the family found in the more 'committed' members of the Jewish community.

Evaluation of cross-cultural research

◆ There can be communication difficulties. For example, literal translations of studies may fail to take into account differences in emphasis or nuance, which can often be important.

◆ There is a danger of making cross-cultural psychology just 'doing psychology in exotic places', i.e. taking issues and phenomena which are of interest to (dominant) Western Psychology and seeing if they replicate in other cultures. Clearly this agenda-setting takes no account of what is important in that 'other' culture. Kim and Berry (1993) address this problem with a call for indigenous psychologies

---

Social class differences in relationships

Work by many psychologists has demonstrated clear and consistent class differences in relationships in Britain. Argyle (1994) includes the following:

◆ Friendship is more important to the middle classes than the working classes, for whom there is more emphasis on kin.

◆ Differences in the nature of friendship: 'Middle-class friends have similar interests and attitudes, and come from work, leisure groups, voluntary work or other activities. Working-class friends are chosen more because they live nearby and can provide help when needed, they form tight-knit groups with neighbours, and see each other in social clubs and pubs.' (p. 157)

◆ Middle-class marriages are more symmetrical with more shared friends and leisure and decision-sharing.

◆ Middle-class families are more child-centred, with the father playing a more significant part than in working-class families.

◆ Working-class families are more authoritarian in child-rearing practices, whereas middle-class families are more egalitarian.

which study factors which have developed/emerged *within* particular cultures and are seen as important and functional to those cultures (rather than risking a psychology of North American self-interest).

Understudied relationships

Gay and lesbian relationships

This section does not aim to address the question: what makes a person homosexual? This is because no one really knows – it is highly likely that there are multiple determinants (Garnets and Kimmel 1991) – but most significantly because of the need to avoid anything that encourages pathologization of any kind of sexuality other than heterosexuality. How many people who are straight have been asked what makes them heterosexual or why they are not homosexual? The converse, however, is a common and recurrent event for many gays and lesbians. Furthermore, unlike most ethnic minority groups, gays and lesbians often grow up surrounded by negative stereotypes held about them by their own families and friends.

Homosexuality is still illegal in many countries in the world today and only as recently as 1973 was it removed from the DSM. It is still a part of the ICD (see Chapter 16). However, there are certain cultures where homosexual practice is positively encouraged (although often only in certain, prescribed situations – see p. 44), and there have been historical periods, such as that of the classic Greco-Roman civilization, where homosexuality was considered quite normal practice. Things are not that easy for gay men and lesbians, even in the liberal West at the turn of a new century. Many politicians and people in the public eye (such as entertainers) have had their careers effectively ruined on being 'outed' (Humphreys 1997).

Among the pressures experienced by gay people that may affect their relationships are:

◆ the psychological effects of growing up in a (heterosexual) society that characterizes homosexuality and lesbianism as unacceptable

◆ the unequal age of consent for gay men (in the process of being changed as this book goes to press)

◆ the way few happy and successful gay relationships are presented by the media; gay characters tend to be secondary to the plot (unless it is a 'gay drama') and gay relationships are often presented as superficial, unstable or problematic.

Greene (1994, p. 10) sums up the position:

'Many [gays and lesbians] endure painful isolation from their families of origin who do not accept their identity, as well as the painful process of rejection that often precedes it. They face internalized

homophobia in themselves, which can negatively affect their psychological adjustment ... 92 per cent of lesbians and gay men report being targets of antigay verbal abuse or threats, and ... 24 per cent report physical attacks, of which some result in death (Herek 1989). Both lesbians and gay men face the realistic potential for physical abuse and violent attack (gay bashing) that can be life threatening.'

It is almost impossible to establish a reliable figure of the number of people who are gay or lesbian – estimates for North America range from 4 per cent to 17 per cent. But estimations are made almost hopelessly tenuous because identification depends wholly upon self-ascription. There is evidence to suggest that for many people sexuality categorization is shifting and impermanent, where one orientation may be adopted after a lengthy adult experience of another. Money (1988) called this sequential bisexuality.

We should note that there is often an (erroneous) presumption of a unitary homosexual culture. This is not the case; homosexuality cuts across all human divides: class, culture, racial, age and so on.

Homosexual people are said to 'pass' when they do not 'correct' people's assumptions about their heterosexuality or when they otherwise conceal their sexuality. Concealing a homosexual identity is also known as being *closeted*. As gay men and lesbians do not differ in appearance from straight people, they are usually presumed to be heterosexual and are treated as such. Their invisibility allows them to 'pass' as heterosexuals – an invaluable survival strategy at times and sites of political intolerance (such as Hitler's Nazi Germany). However, passing may come at a great cost. Gay men and lesbians who do this have to 'seal off' and hide away whole sections of their lives and, if partnered, live in constant dread of being discovered.

One great difficulty for gay men and lesbians, then, is recognizing each other. One practical solution is the gay bar:

'... inside it's a cavernous room filled to the rim with other gay men. Some are there to meet with friends. Some are there to drink, make new friends and conversation. Others are there for sex. Some passively observe the environment while others actively participate in it. Whatever the reason one goes to a gay bar, there is common solace and excitement in the fact that it is one of the few places in society where by their mere presence all patrons can be assumed gay.' (Shaw 1997, pp. 136–7)

For many gay men and lesbians, it is a lose/lose situation. If they are 'out', they may be marginalized and rejected. If they are not, their invisibility will also be problematic. They will not be able to share the joys of openly loving and being companionate, which heterosexuals can enjoy. This will carry many additional burdens such as:

◆ being thrown back on the constant support and sympathy of the (hidden) partner

◆ the fear of being 'outed' – whether deliberately or by accident (e.g. a confidant lets something slip)

◆ family members and friends' unrealistic expectations about the possibility of their developing heterosexual relationships

◆ difficulties in personal counselling if one turns to a professional for help – Markowitz (1991) says that many therapists will impose female/male models on gay/lesbians as there are no equivalents for same-sex pairs. Peplau (1991) lists a number of commonly heard stereotypes about gay/lesbian couples, e.g. that they are incapable of sustaining a long-term relationship and experience inferior versions of heterosexual relationships. Greene (1994) says 'such stereotypes are tenaciously held by many therapists despite the absence of any credible evidence to support them'.

For obvious reasons many gay men and lesbians choose to spend most of their social lives in the company of other gay people, but for those who have children, this option in not so easily available. They have to negotiate a world of schools and child-orientated networks. In all of this they are faced with the task of safeguarding the integrity of their living arrangements, protecting their privacy and also being supportive to the needs of their child(ren).

> 'Those who are involved in shared custody arrangements with a former heterosexual spouse often face the realistic danger of having the courts remove their children from their custody if the true nature of their relationship is exposed. The problem of maintaining secrecy in families in which a gay or lesbian parent is not out is complex.' (Greene 1994, p. 15)

Electronic friendships and computer-mediated communication (CMC)

To start this section, read the *In Focus* about 'Joan'.

Computer-mediated communication (CMC) can take many forms, such as e-mail, virtual notice boards, chat rooms, e.g. IRC (Internet Relay Chat), and the relatively sophisticated MUDs, MOOs and MUSHs (computer programs where users assign themselves a character and then are able to navigate around a metaphorical building or neighbourhood, instigating conversations and joining in – or just listening to – on-going discussions in the 'rooms').

CMC relationships can be contrasted with *corporeal* or face-to-face relationships ('corporeal' means 'bodily, physical, material'). The term corporeal emphasizes physicality, one of the things which CMC most clearly does not have, as the case study of Joan illustrates so dramatically (see *In Focus*).

---

in focus **'Joan'**

'Joan ... was a New York neuropsychologist in her late twenties, who had been severely disfigured in a car accident that was the fault of a drunken driver. The accident had killed her boyfriend. Joan herself spent a year in the hospital being treated for brain damage which affected both her speech and her ability to walk. Mute, confined to a wheelchair, and frequently suffering intense back and leg pain, [she] had at first been so embittered about her disabilities that she didn't want to live. [Then she was given] a computer ... to be used specifically to make friends on-line.

'... Joan could type ... and she had a sassy, bright, generous personality that blossomed in a medium where physicality doesn't count. Joan became enormously popular ... Over the next two years, she became a monumental on-line presence who served both as a support for other disabled women and as an inspiring stereotype-smasher to the able-bodied. Through her many intense friendships and (in some cases) her on-line romances, she changed the lives of dozens of women.

'Thus it was a huge shock when, through a complicated series of events, Joan was revealed as being not disabled at all. More to the point, Joan, in fact, was not a woman. She was really a man ... a prominent New York psychiatrist in his early fifties engaged in a bizarre, all-consuming experiment to see what it felt like to be female, and to experience the intimacy of female friendship.' (Van Gelder 1985, cited in Lea and Spears 1995, pp. 197–8)

Shocked? Most people are. Leaving aside the appalling ethics of what the American psychiatrist did, this case study tells us a good deal about CMCs. Perhaps Cherny (1998) put it best when she said 'what you see is what I say'.

There have been many kinds of noncorporeal interaction before the advent of CMC (e.g. letters and pen-pals, telegrams, faxes and, of course, the telephone). But what has become clear (e.g. Shaw 1997, Reid 1998) is that CMC is often chosen as a preference over corporeality, even when the latter is available. That is to say, many people have been found to initiate, maintain and develop relationships via CMC even when there is an easy opportunity to meet face to face. On the other hand, some people do chose to 'meet the person' with results ranging from the wonderful to the truly woeful.

Activity 7: Your experience of CMC relationships

Are you a regular computer-user and e-mailer? Think of someone you have both a face-to-face and CMC relationship with:

◆ How differently do you interact with the person in these two modes?
◆ Are there things you say in e-mail but would not say face-to-face (or vice versa)?
◆ Is e-mail easier or harder than face-to-face talk?

CMC can provide opportunities for *friendship and support*. Simply because people have not met face to face does not make CMC relationships any less 'real' or significant. Two people who met on Presbynet (a conferencing resource provided by the Presbyterian church) said that after two months on-line 'I know some of these people better than some of my oldest and best friends' and 'I'm constantly amazed at the companionship and warmth one can find at the

computer terminal' (Wilkins 1991). A person on another service said 'I have talked to some people for years without knowing where they live or their real names. Yet they are as much a presence in my life as if they were right in the room' (Kerr 1982).

Context is also important in CMC as the following example given by Reid (1998) clearly illustrates. JennyMUSH was a virtual help centre for people who had been sexually assaulted or abused. Users developed a strong common bond. However, one person was able to destroy all the trust which had been built up and inflict further trauma on the members of the community. After only being in the system for two weeks, this user was able to transform himself into a virtual manifestation of every other user's fears. He changed his initial virtual gender to male (he had joined as a woman) and his name to 'Daddy' and then by using the 'Shout' command, was able to send obscene messages to all other users, describing assaults in graphic and violent terms. Many took the most direct form of defence and logged off the system, but others stayed and tried to stop the attacks. Many pleaded, others used threats, but all of them were powerless.

The administrators of JennyMUSH eventually took charge of the system once they saw what was happening. Daddy was isolated but where there had previously been trust and privacy, there was suspicion, distrust and wariness. JennyMUSH did not survive and was closed down in 1995.

CMC also provides a context for *sexual relationships*. A Wired Top 10 survey carried out in 1994 of the ten most populated chatrooms created by America On-Line (the biggest provider in the USA) showed that three were gay, one was lesbian, one was 'swingers or groups'

---

in focus · Gay men and CMC

Shaw (1997) interviewed twelve gay men about their CMC. Some were interviewed by Internet Relay Chat, others by e-mail, others by telephone. He says: 'While my sample does not purport to be statistically significant, my research role ... afforded me the opportunity to establish a bond of trust with the users (and produced) some keen insights.' Most of the men said they averaged 10 to 15 hours per week on IRC.

He draws the following intriguing parallels between CMC and the (corporeal) gay bar (see p. 49).

> 'Entering the (on-line) community via the gaysex channel, users find themselves in a large "room" with as many as seventy other gay men. Not all of the men ... are contributing to the dialogue: some "lurk" (observing and waiting for the right moment to join it), and some "whisper" (sending private messages to one another). For those participating in the dialogue there is political talk, ... GIFs (electronically scanned photographs sent over the Internet) being exchanged, advice seeking, and just about everything else imaginable. As texts scroll up their screens, users can eavesdrop on many conversations at once. While heterosexuals wander into the channel from time to time, ... there is comfort in the fact that the regulars are gay men ... The results are a mixed bag of excitement and disgust, promise and letdown, nonchalance and embarrassment.' (pp. 136 and 140)

and the remaining five were heterosexual. CMCers also have one-to-one sexual relationships on-line, exchanging sexual banter and simulating sex. 'Julie' (*Marie-Claire* 1993, p. 26) said:

> 'Typing back and forth is as far as I want to go for now. I'm a lot bolder than I would be in person; I'd never do that kind of taking face-to-face, or get into any of my fantasy roles. What I enjoy is that they'll never know who I am, yet we can talk about the most personal and specific things'.

CMC has only really developed over the last decade but it is here to stay. One of the intriguing tasks for social psychologists is to see just how different the experiences, rules and rewards of CMC and face-to-face relationships turn out to be.

Exam summary: Cultural and subcultural differences in relationships

The AQA examination will test your understanding of the following areas:

◆ explanations and research studies of the differences in relationships between Western and non-Western cultures (pp. 45–9)

◆ understudied relationships (pp. 49–52).

Example question

The question below is typical of one drawn from the material above, and should take you 30 minutes to answer:

◆ Discuss the insights which cross-cultural psychological research has given us into the diversity of human relationships. *(24 marks)*

Suggested answer structure

At first glance, this seems like an open invitation simply to list all the different ways that cultures differ in their attitudes to interpersonal relationships. You should resist this temptation and look instead at how research into the diversity of relationships has informed psychologists about the processes that underlie the formation, maintenance and breakdown of relationships in different cultures. A convenient way of classifying cultures is on the dimension of individualism/ collectivism (pp. 45–7). This provides a framework for your essay, and gives you a base from which to explore the various claims concerning the *voluntary/involuntary* (p. 47) and *permanent/impermanent* (p. 48) aspects of relationships in different cultures or cultural groups. For example, in the West the belief that people marry for love has been supported by research which shows that an increasing number of both men and women were unwilling to marry without love even if their prospective partner had all the other qualities desired (p. 47).

It is important to remember that the question asks for insights from *cross-cultural* research, and so material on understudied relationships would not be relevant unless it in some way reflected cross-cultural differences in these practices.

It is always better to integrate your material within some underlying theme. The individualism/collectivism theme is ideal for this. On p. 48, the point is made that individualism may be associated with higher divorce levels because people are encouraged constantly to seek their ideal partner.

As the question also requires you to *evaluate* these insights, you should allow half of your time for critical commentary. This may be achieved by an evaluation of the underlying classification of individualism/ collectivism – for example, the point that this division fails to account for the many variations that exist *within* cultures as well as between cultures (pp. 46–7), or perhaps through evaluation of the research itself. For example, research in other cultures may be limited by communication and translation difficulties (p. 48) or might be criticized as simply studying aspects of experience that are important in Western cultures, but may be less important in the culture being studied (p. 49). An example of this might be the failure of studies outside of North America and Europe to give support to the equity model of human relationships (p. 40).

Chapter summary

◆ Psychological research into **interpersonal attraction** in the US in the 1960s and 70s concentrated on **physical attraction** and resulted in the **matching hypothesis**. However, much research was seen as unlike real life. Research using dating advertisements found culture-specific ideas of attractiveness in use. Frequency of interaction and similarity of values were also found to be important, at least in short-term relationships. Variety between and within relationships is often not taken into enough consideration.

◆ **Sociobiological theory** uses evolutionary ideas to explain human behaviour, favouring stereotypical gender roles and determinism. **Reward and need satisfaction** gives a conditioning explanation for attraction and **formation of relationships**, but fails to take into account cultural, gender and individual differences.

♦ People use different strategies within relationships to **maintain them**. These vary according to whether the participants want the relationship to strengthen, weaken or stay unchanged.

♦ We looked at some of the reasons why relationships are **ended** and considered **a stage model of breakdown**. Two theories of relationship maintenance/breakdown – **social exchange** and **equity** – were described and appraised.

♦ Psychologists have studied many reasons for the **dissolution of relationships**; Duck has developed a four-phase model of these terminations. The **maintenance** and breakdown of relationships have been described by **social exchange** and **equity theories** as analogous to economic cost/benefit situations, with investment, satisfaction, comparisons with others and principles of equity as important factors. However, these theories are difficult to test in real-life and long-term situations. They also appear to reflect predominantly North American values.

♦ Hatfield and Walster's **psychological explanations** divide love into passionate (**romantic**) and **companionate**, with various factors needed for love to occur. Sternberg also includes consummate love and sees love as determined by the various combinations of passion, intimacy and commitment. Hendrick and Hendrick's model focused on the love styles that people enter relationships with.

♦ Comparisons of cultural groups and love styles show support for Lee's six basic love styles, though with variations within and between **cultures** and **subcultures**. While there are some cross-cultural,

similarities, cultures have also been shown to vary enormously in their accepted love and sexual practices.

♦ Hofstede categorized countries along four dimensions, with a fifth added later; the most important being **individualistic/collectivist**. Research has shown a vast array of marriage arrangements in **Western** and **non-Western cultures** from extremes of partners having no choice to partners having total choice of whom they marry. Even in the most common form of marriage, parental arrangement, there is a considerable range from **voluntary** to **involuntary**, as research among British Asians has shown. The issue of **permanence/impermanence** in relationships has been studied through the cross-cultural variations in reasons for, and prevalence of, divorce.

♦ We must remember that much of the research into relationships has itself been conducted from a Western cultural standpoint, and it has often not taken into consideration internal, individual and cultural variation and diversity, nor necessarily understood the nuances of the other cultures and subcultures it has investigated.

♦ It is difficult to make comparisons in '**understudied' relationships** such as **gay and lesbian relationships**, which are by the nature of many societies' laws and prejudices, relatively hidden. However, misconceptions about stereotypes and a unitary culture have been investigated by, for example, Markowitz, Money and Greene. **Electronic friendships** are a newer area of study, with interesting comparisons to be made with face-to-face relationships, especially in the areas of support, potential for harm, disguise and freedom of expression.

Further resources

Duck, S. (1999) *Relating to Others* (2nd edn), Buckingham, Open University Press.

A highly readable yet scholarly account of recent research by the professor who has done most to establish the credentials of relationships as a topic for serious psychological study.

Goodwin, R. (1999) *Personal Relationships Across Cultures,* London: Routledge.

An up-to-date and through account of cultural and subcultural differences (and similarities!) in this complex field of human relationships. An excellent eye-opener.

Greene, B. and Herek, G.M. (1994) *Lesbian and Gay Psychology: Theory, Research and Clinical Applications.,* Thousand Oaks, CA: Sage.

A book which offers a multi-faceted approach to the psychological study of people who are nonheterosexual. Long overdue.

Gackenbach, J. (ed.) (1998) *Psychology and the Internet,* San Diego, CA: Academic Press.

A fascinating set of articles on the new area of psychology which is currently sparsely resourced.

Websites

www.ascusc.org/jcmc/

The Web site of the Journal of Computer Mediated Communication, *and* On-theWeb Quarterly. *Edited*

by McLaughlin and Rafaeli out of Annenberg, School for Communication, University of Southern California. Topics covered since it began in June 1995 include play and performance in CMC, virtual environments and persistent conversation.

Answers to activities

Answer to Activity 6

◆ Game-playing – Men used this type more often than women.

◆ Possessive – Women's lives were more characterized by this type of love than were men's.

◆ Logical – More characteristic of women than men.

◆ Altruistic – No difference found between men and women.

◆ Companionate – Valued slightly higher by women than men.

◆ Erotic – No difference found between men and women.

Chapter 3

Pro- and antisocial behaviour

Mike Cardwell

Preview

In this chapter we shall be looking at:

◆ social psychological theories of aggression (including social learning theory, deindividuation and relative deprivation) and the effects of environmental stressors on aggressive behaviour

◆ explanations of human altruism, including explanations of bystander behaviour and cultural differences in helping behaviour

◆ media influences on pro- and antisocial behaviour.

Introduction

People often do favours for one another: they help, sacrifice, share and even save other people's lives. Such help may involve great risk, with little or no gain to the helper. Sometimes, on the other hand, people behave in distinctly unpleasant ways: they injure, rob, rape and even murder other people. Why do people behave in either prosocial or antisocial ways? Some social psychologists propose that the society in which we live and features of modern life determine our behaviours. Another explanation is that behaviour results from an interaction of physiological arousal (e.g. how alert/emotional we are) and cognitive processing (e.g. how we assess a situation). Some psychologists think that our propensity to behave in a pro- or antisocial way is inherited (part of our genetic make-up), while others believe we learn all our behaviour (whether pro- or antisocial) from parents and significant others. An important consideration in this area of study is the extent to which the media influence our behaviour. A number of studies have shown that exposure to television violence is positively correlated with violent behaviour. Other studies suggest that any relationship is weak and that viewers can discriminate between real-life and fictional violence. It is also argued by some that television can be used to reduce aggression and encourage prosocial behaviour.

Nature and causes of aggression

Antisocial behaviour

'Antisocial acts are those that show a lack of feeling and concern for the welfare of others' (Baron and Richardson 1994). Successful social interaction and the smooth running of society can only exist if most people do not behave antisocially. Most societies, therefore, have laws, enforced via a police force and a legal system, to discourage, condemn and punish antisocial acts. Aggressive acts are usually viewed as one of the most disturbing types of antisocial behaviour.

Defining aggression

Different types of aggressive behaviour have been identified:

◆ *antisocial aggression* – defined by Penrod (1983) as 'all behaviour that is intended to inflict physical or psychological harm on another individual who does not want to be so treated'

◆ *prosocial aggression* – e.g. when the police shoot a terrorist who has murdered hostages and is threatening others

◆ *sanctioned aggression* – such as self-defence, e.g. when a woman injures a rapist while defending herself.

A further distinction is made between aggressive *behaviours* which are overt, and aggressive *feelings*, such as anger, which are covert. Frustration frequently makes people angry, but angry people do not always behave aggressively.

Social psychological theories of aggression

There are many ways of explaining aggressive behaviour in humans. Some theories view aggression as an important part of our evolutionary heritage, others as an imbalance in hormones or neurotransmitters in the brain. Early psychological theories of aggression explained aggressive behaviour as an automatic consequence of personal frustration. Social psychological theories see the cause of our aggressive behaviour as arising out of our interactions with others in our social world. We will now look at three very different ways in which social psychologists explain aggressive behaviour.

Social learning theory

According to Berkowitz (1989) and Bandura (1965), although the aggressive behaviour of nonhuman animals can be explained in terms of instinctual drives, aggression in humans is the product of learning. They claim that aggressive behaviour is learned either through direct experience or by observing others.

◆ *Learning by direct experience* is derived from Skinner's principles of operant reinforcement (see Chapter 13). In other words, if a child pushes another child and as a result gets something they want, the action is *reinforced* and is more likely to occur in similar situations in the future.

◆ Learning by vicarious experience is a contribution made specifically by social learning theorists. This form of *observational learning* occurs when a child sees a role model behaving in a particular way and reproduces that behaviour. The child is then said to be *imitating* the behaviour of the model.

Social learning theorists emphasize that for behaviour to be imitated, it must be seen to be rewarding in some way. The likelihood of a person behaving aggressively in a particular situation is determined by:

◆ their previous experiences of aggressive behaviour – both their own and that of others

◆ the degree to which their aggressive behaviour was successful in the past

◆ the current likelihood of their aggressive behaviour being rewarded or punished

◆ other cognitive, social and environmental factors that are operating at the same time – aggressive behaviour may increase under hostile environmental conditions (e.g. very noisy situations), but fear of retaliation from the 'victim' may inhibit the expression of aggression.

Bandura and his colleagues carried out a series of experiments involving children exposed to the aggressive behaviour of an adult model (see *In Focus*). By varying the conditions under which the model was viewed, as well as the consequences for the model's

 in focus

Do children learn aggression?

Bandura *et al.* (1963) divided 66 nursery school children into three groups. All three groups watched a film where an adult model kicked and punched a Bobo doll (see illustration).

◆ Condition 1: Children saw the adult model being rewarded by a second adult.

◆ Condition 2: Children saw a second adult telling off the adult model for the aggressive behaviour.

◆ Condition 3: The adult model was neither rewarded nor punished.

The children were then allowed to play in the room with the Bobo doll whilst experimenters watched through a one-way mirror.

Results showed that children in Condition 1 behaved most aggressively, and those in Condition 2 behaved least aggressively. However, an important distinction must be made between learning and performance. All the children *learnt* how to behave aggressively, but those in Condition 2 did not *perform* as many aggressive acts until later, when they were offered rewards to do so. When this happened, they quickly showed that they had learned (acquired) as many aggressive techniques as the children in Condition 1.

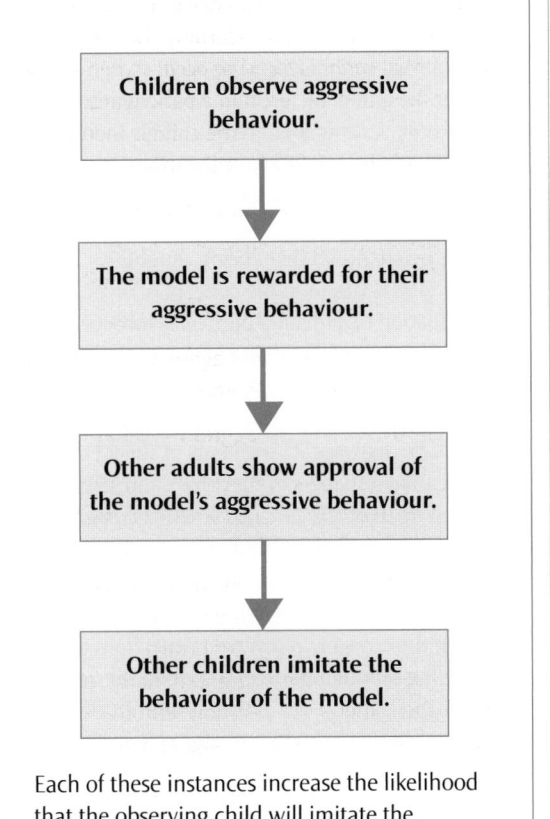

Figure 3.1 The social learning view of aggression
Source: Bandura (1965)

aggressive behaviour, Bandura was able to develop a social learning model of aggression. He found that children were more likely to imitate the aggressive behaviour of a model if:

◆ the model was seen to be rewarded after behaving aggressively

◆ other adults showed approval for the aggressive behaviour of the model

◆ other children were seen to imitate the behaviour of the model (see Fig. 3.1).

Social learning theory leads us to consider the various ways in which children might be exposed to aggressive models. In particular, this has meant a consideration of television as a powerful source of imitative learning. Huesmann (1988) suggests that children may use television models as a source of *scripts* that act as a guide for their own behaviour. For example, if they see a movie hero (e.g. Schwarzenegger) beat up the bad guys that get in his way, this may become a script for any situation in which it might be deemed appropriate. These scripts are stored in memory, and strengthened and elaborated through repetition and rehearsal.

The relationship between observation of aggression in the media and subsequent aggressive behaviour is a complex one (see later in this chapter for a discussion of this). It appears to be influenced by several variables (Manstead *et al.* 1995):

◆ If the observed violence is thought to be real behaviour (e.g. in more 'believable' story lines and 'domestic' drama), it is more likely to elicit aggression than if it is considered to be fictional or fantasy violence.

◆ If viewers identify with the aggressor in some way, they are subsequently more aggressive than if they do not identify with the aggressive model. Heroes are therefore more powerful models than are villains.

◆ Aggression that is identified as being motivated by a desire for revenge is more likely to elicit aggression than aggressive behaviour that is instrumental in the attainment of other goals.

◆ Aggression that is seen as being justified in the context in which it occurs elicits more aggression than aggressive behaviour that is seen as unjustified in that situation.

◆ The observation of unsuccessful aggression, in which the aggressor is punished, does not elicit aggressive behaviour in the observer, but tends to inhibit it.

Evaluation of social learning theory

Social learning theories of aggression rely heavily on experimental evidence and field studies of observational learning. There are, however, some methodological problems in the experiments described by Bandura *et al.* A Bobo doll is not, after all, a living person. Other investigators have also cast doubt on the conclusion that Bandura's child subjects had learned their aggressive behaviour from watching an aggressive model on film. In one study, nursery school children who behaved most violently towards the doll were also rated by their teachers and peers as being more violent generally (Johnston *et al.* 1977).

Social learning explanations can also account for the lack of consistency in people's aggressive behaviour. If someone is assertive and domineering at home but meek and submissive at work, it means they are *reinforced* differently in the two situations. They have *learned* to behave differently in the two situations because assertiveness brings rewards in one context but not in the other.

Social learning theory explanations have also led to an increased focus on the effects of the visual media on both children and adults. If violence is learned, as claimed by supporters of this position, then exposure to successfully aggressive models may lead people to imitate them (Hogg and Vaughan 1998). Aggression can, therefore, be passed across generations, as each new generation observes and imitates what it perceives to be appropriate and successful behaviours of the preceding generation.

Biological explanations of aggression, on the other hand, have stressed factors quite unrelated to social learning. Higher levels of the male hormone testosterone, has been cited as a primary causal agent in aggressive behaviour. Premenstrual syndrome has even been cited in criminal trials as a reason for aggressive behaviour (Flanagan 2000). These, together with other biological explanations, cast doubt on aggression being purely a *learned* behaviour. In defence of this position, however, social learning theorists point to societies that have no aggressive behaviour (such as the Amish in the USA) as powerful evidence of the dominant role played by learning over biology. Interestingly, in most societies where nonaggressive behaviour is more prevalent than aggressive behaviour (such as the Arapesh of New Guinea and the Pygmies of central Africa), there are few distinctions made between males and females. Although differences between the roles of males and females do exist in these societies, no attempt is made to project an image of brave, aggressive masculinity (Deaux *et al.* 1993).

Deindividuation

'When darkness fell excitement kissed the crowd
   and made them wild
In the atmosphere of freaky holiday.
When the spotlight hit the boy the crowd began
   to cheer
He flew away ... '

Paul Simon (1968)

Hogg and Vaughan (1998) define deindividuation as: 'a process whereby people lose their sense of socialized individual identity and engage in unsocialized, often antisocial behaviours'.

People normally refrain from acting in an aggressive and selfish manner in part because they are easily identifiable in societies that have strong norms against such 'uncivilized' behaviour. In certain situations such as in crowds, these restraints may become relaxed and we may engage in 'an orgy of aggressive, selfish and antisocial behaviour' (Hogg and Vaughan 1998).

Zimbardo (1969) distinguished between *individual* behaviour which is rational and conforms to acceptable social standards, and *deindividuated* behaviour, which is based on primitive urges and does not conform to society's norms. According to Zimbardo, being part of a crowd can diminish awareness of individuality. In a large crowd, each person is faceless and anonymous. There is diminished fear of retribution and a diluted sense of

guilt. Conditions that increase anonymity serve to minimize concerns about evaluation by others and thus weaken normal controls based on guilt, shame or fear. The larger the group, the greater the anonymity and the greater the difficulty in identifying a single individual. Malamuthand Check (1981) questioned male students at an American university and found that almost one-third admitted that there was a chance they would rape if there was no chance of them being caught.

Mann (1981) has used the concept of deindividuation to explain a particular form of collective behaviour, the 'baiting crowd'. The 'baiting' or taunting crowd has been reported in some American studies and lends support to the notion of the crowd as a mob. Mann analysed 21 incidents of suicides reported in American newspapers in the 1960s and 1970s. He found that in 10 of the 21 cases where a crowd had gathered to watch, baiting had occurred (i.e. the crowd urged the potential suicide to jump). These incidents tended to occur at night, when the crowd was large and when the crowd was some distance from the person being taunted (particularly when the 'jumper' was high above them). All of these features, claimed Mann, were likely to produce a state of deindividuation in the individual member of the crowd.

The concept of deindividuation can also be applied to the victim of aggression. Milgram (1965) found that participants were more likely to give higher levels of shock when they could not see their victim. When the 'victim' was in the same room, the participants were more reluctant to deliver high levels of shock to someone they could see (and who could see them).

More recent developments of the concept of deindividuation have distinguished between the effects of reduced public self-awareness (being anonymous to others) and reduced private self-awareness. A person who is self-focused tends to act according to internalized attitudes and moral standards. If the person submerges themselves within a group, they may lose this focus and become less privately self-aware. It is this reduction in private self-awareness that is associated with increased antisocial behaviour rather than the anonymity of public self-awareness (Prentice-Dunn and Rogers 1989).

Evaluation of deindividuation

Although much of the early evidence for deindividuation was supportive, the concept is not without its problems, not least of which is the finding in some studies that deindividuation may produce increases in *prosocial* behaviour (e.g. expressions of collective good will at religious rallies) rather than antisocial behaviour (Diener 1980).

Researchers have often failed to distinguish between the effects of anonymity of those being aggressed

in focus

Deindividuation in an aggressor

A variation of deindividuation in the aggressor can occur when the victim, rather than the aggressor, is anonymous or dehumanized in some way, so that the aggressor cannot so easily see the personal pain and injury suffered by the victim. This can weaken any control extended by feelings of shame and guilt.

Many examples of this phenomenon have been documented, such as the violent treatment of psychiatric patients, and prisoners either kept naked or dressed identically so that they are indistinguishable as individuals. Having faceless and deindividuated victims in violent films has been shown to have a disinhibiting effect on some people, encouraging them to imitate the violent acts (Bandura 1986).

Cohen (1987) has presented a revealing analysis of the ways in which military personnel 'sanitize' and thereby justify the use of nuclear weapons by semantics which dehumanize the likely or actual victims, referring to them as 'targets', 'the aggressed' or even 'collateral damage'.

In 1993, Bosnian Serbs, in what was once part of Yugoslavia, referred to acts of genocide against the Muslim population as 'ethnic cleansing'. The media, also, can unwittingly lessen the impact of the horror of large-scale killing. A phrase used often on television during the Allied bombing campaigns in Iraq in 1991 was the 'theatre of war', inviting the audience to sit back and be entertained.

Source: Hogg and Vaughan (1998)

against, e.g. when we aggress against a 'faceless' enemy or victim, as opposed to those doing the aggressing, e.g. hooded terrorists who cannot be identified by their victims. This also raises the question of whether 'identifiability' is in respect of the in-group or out-group. In other words, does the likelihood of aggression increase if our *in-group* cannot recognize us, or if the *out-group* cannot. Manstead *et al.* argue that anonymity among the in-group does not really reflect the reality of most crowd situations (Manstead *et al.* 1995).

The deindividuation perspective argues that our submergence in a group undermines the influence of social norms. This is in sharp contrast to social psychological research that has demonstrated the strong normative hold that groups have on individual members. Rather than individuals pursuing behaviour 'based on primitive urges and not conforming to

society's norms', they might be seen as conforming to a 'local' group norm (Manstead *et al.* 1995). This norm need not necessarily be antisocial, and could thus account for some apparently contradictory findings (e.g. Diener 1980)

It is tempting to apply the concept of deindividuation to crowd violence in British football. Stereotypical images of football fans on the rampage make all too familiar reading in the press and do suggest a faceless crowd engaged in an 'orgy of aggressive, selfish and antisocial behaviour'. A study of football hooliganism by Marsh *et al.* (1978) tells quite a different story. Marsh and colleagues found that what might appear to be an undisciplined mob on match days can actually consist of several different groups, each with their status. By serving an apprenticeship of ritualized aggression over a period of time, young supporters can be 'promoted' into a higher group and can thus continue a 'career' of football violence. Marsh discovered that in most cases this behaviour is highly ritualized, rather than physically violent. For example, it is common after a match to chase rival supporters, who are threatened with shouts of what aggressive actions will take place when they are caught, but on most occasions the aggression remains verbal.

In most cases, crowd behaviour is highly ritualized rather than physically violent

Relative deprivation theory

The root cause of conflict, according to relative deprivation theory (Stouffer *et al.* 1949), is the unacceptable discrepancy between what people think they have a right to expect (e.g. a good education and comfortable standard of living) and what, given current social conditions, they estimate they are realistically capable of attaining. This is accentuated by comparing our own position to that of others whom we feel are not so deprived. The gap between what we feel we have a right to and what we actually get is frequently described as *perceived* relative deprivation, because what a person believes subjectively may be more important than measurable objective criteria.

If people feel deprived of something to which they feel entitled, they feel frustration. Berkowitz (1972) claimed that subjective frustration due to perceived relative deprivation can incite aggression. This relative deprivation will be felt most keenly in modern industrialized societies where the life opportunities and comparative wealth of one sector of society may be markedly and visibly different to the conditions enjoyed by less privileged groups within these societies. The 1992 riots in Los Angeles, which resulted in more than 50 deaths, was an example of this scenario. The spark for these riots was the acquittal by an all-White jury of four Los Angeles police officers who had been accused of beating a Black motorist. With a background of rising unemployment and increasing disadvantage, this was seen as an expression of the low value placed by White America on American Blacks. In one chilling incident at the height of the riots, millions watched on live TV as a White trucker was dragged from his cab and brutally beaten (Hogg and Vaughan 1998).

The discrepancy between what people feel they deserve and will realistically achieve tends not to be as great in traditionally agricultural societies. For most people in these societies, expectations tend not to exceed achievements and so do not result in feelings of relative deprivation. As a result, they are adjusted to their life and do not suffer from an unacceptable amount of relative deprivation. Indeed, many anthropologists have reported a relative lack of violence in such societies compared to modern complex societies.

A sense of perceived relative deprivation can also come about as a *result* of improvement in the resources and opportunities made available to a group. One aspect of human nature seems to be that when things do get better, we expect even greater improvements. Although conditions might be improving, expectations increase even faster. Consider what happened at the end of the Cold War, when countries, once Soviet-controlled, became independent. Expectations rose faster than improvements and in many cases violence and crime have been widespread.

Runciman (1966) has drawn a distinction between two different types of relative deprivation:

◆ *Egoistic relative deprivation* – experienced if an individual feels deprived relative to other similar individuals. If our colleagues all seem to be better off than we are, we may well feel deprived in comparison to them. An important part of this process is that comparisons are realistic. Comparing our standard of living with the rich and famous is a pretty futile exercise, and these unrealistic exercises do not leave us with enduring feelings of relative deprivation.

◆ *Fraternalistic relative deprivation* – experienced when members of one group compare themselves to members of another group. If the general conditions in the two groups are such that one group feels that they are worse off than the other, feelings of relative deprivation may arise.

Evaluation of relative deprivation theory

Runciman's distinction between egoistic and fraternalistic relative deprivation is an important one. Many studies have supported the belief that social unrest and aggression are more a product of the latter rather than the former. For example, Abèles (1976) found that Black militancy in the USA was closely associated with intergroup comparisons between Blacks and Whites. Abèles also found that levels of militancy tend to be greatest in Blacks with the highest socioeconomic and educational status. Remember that relative deprivation is a *subjective* rather than an *objective* experience. These individuals were more acutely aware of the discrepancies between the group (i.e. Blacks) as a whole and the dominant White group with whom they compare (i.e. fraternalistic relative deprivation). Walker and Mann (1987) in a study of unemployed workers in Australia, found that they were more likely to engage in militant protest (such as destruction of private property) when they felt that their group had not attained what they deserved relative to other groups. Those workers who felt more egoistically deprived reported symptoms of stress (headaches, sleeplessness) rather than militancy and aggression.

These studies are useful for showing how egoistic and fraternalistic relative deprivation have quite different outcomes. Relative deprivation theory is also useful in explaining when hostility will emerge between groups (Vivian and Brown 1995). Members of groups tend to share the same notions of justice, as these reflect the norms and values of the group or culture. The shared sense of injustice that follows perceptions of relative deprivation would then explain the uniformity of behaviour that we observe in mass action.

The effects of environmental stressors on aggressive behaviour

The idea that aggression may be a product of aspects of the physical environment is not a new one. Seeing aggression as a response to environmental stressors such as heat, noise and crowding is part of the scientific psychologist's search for causal influences on our behaviour. Environmental stressors (also known as *ambient* stressors) may causes an increase in arousal (a generalized state of physiological and psychological excitation) which may in turn evoke negative emotions and thus hostile thoughts and even aggressive behaviour. These environmental stressors may cause stimulus overload, interfering with whatever a person is trying to accomplish, and therefore leading to frustration. Several stressors in the environment have been shown to relate to aggressive behaviour. We will now examine three of these: temperature, noise and crowding.

Temperature

> *'I pray thee, good Mercutio, let's retire;*
> *The day is hot, the Capulets abroad,*
> *And, if we meet, we shall not 'scape a brawl;*
> *For now, these hot days, is the mad blood stirring.'*

Romeo and Juliet, Act III, scene 1 (cited in Moghaddam 1998)

The effects of high temperatures on aggression have been demonstrated in a number of studies, both in the laboratory and also in the natural environment. Hotter regions of the world tend to have more aggression than cooler regions, and hotter years, seasons and days tend to have more incidents of violent crimes than cooler ones (Anderson 1989). Other studies have demonstrated the effects of high temperatures on drivers' aggression. In one (Kenrick and MacFarlane 1986) drivers honked their horns more in response to a car blocking the road at a traffic light as the temperatures rose.

Laboratory studies of the relationship between heat and aggression have tended to yield a slightly different finding. Halpern (1995) in a review of studies of this area, found evidence for an 'inverted-U' relationship between heat and aggression. In other words, maximum aggression is elicited by moderate temperatures (see Fig. 3.2). As temperature rises, so does aggression, but only to a certain level, after which it begins to decline. It is possible to explain this in terms of the action of two different motives, each linked to changes in temperature. Over the low to moderate temperature range, the motivation to engage in aggressive behaviour (even if this is only thinking hostile thoughts) increases as we experience an increase in our negative emotions. At higher

temperatures, however, the motivation to escape replaces the motivation to aggress.

Comments on the temperature–aggression relationship

◆ Field research has established a relationship between hotter regions and aggression. Moghaddam (1998) warns against taking these results too literally. He quotes studies by Lombroso (1911) who found higher murder rates in southern Italy, and Brearley (1932) who found similar trends in the southern United States, each compared to the northern areas of these countries. Moghaddam argues that the northern and southern regions of Italy and the USA differ in many other ways, each of which might feasibly explain the different rates in murder and other violent crimes.

◆ Other field studies have suggested that seasonal temperature variations appear to be related to increases in violent crime. One possible alternative explanation for this relationship is that during the hot summer months, people tend to be out of doors more, and therefore are more likely to come into contact with each other. This 'social contact' explanation might be challenged by the fact that domestic violence is also at its peak during the summer months, despite the fact that families tend to be indoors together more in the colder winter months. However, given that for most of us, indoor temperatures tend not to vary significantly over the year, it suggests that increases in temperature are unlikely to be responsible for the concurrent rise in aggressive behaviour. This conclusion is also supported by the American homicide statistics, which show that there are two peak periods in homicide rates – late summer, and December, (around Christmas time, when people are more likely to be socially active) (Moghaddam 1998).

◆ Laboratory studies have failed to establish a clear-cut relationship between temperature and aggression. Some studies have found an increase in aggression

Figure 3.2 The relationship between heat and aggression

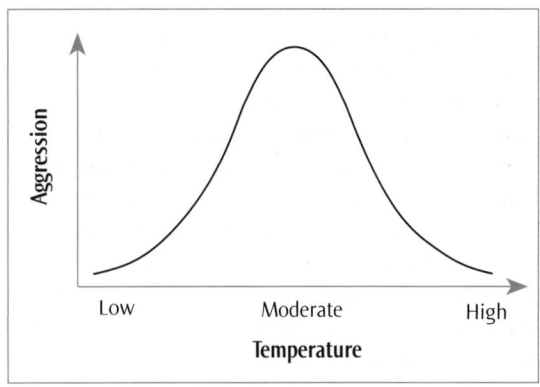

with increasing temperatures, and others have found a decrease in aggressive behaviour. Some studies that have attempted to incorporate anger as a variable into this relationship have found that participants who are cold and angry display more aggressive behaviour than those who are hot and angry (Baron and Bell 1976).

◆ In an analysis of research findings in this area, Moghaddam (1998) suggests that the most important general conclusion that can be drawn is that high temperatures can change the way in which people interpret ambiguous situations, and may, therefore, predispose a person towards an aggressive response.

Noise

Intense levels of noise may also act as an antecedent of aggression. Noise may adversely affect a person's ability to deal with frustration, especially if they must invest considerable effort (e.g. having to speak louder or straining to hear others) trying to adjust to the noise (Manstead et al. 1995). Noise may also increase aggression simply because it raises a person's level of arousal. This is particularly evident if the noise is experienced after the person has become ready to aggress because of some prior provocation.

In a study of this relationship, participants were initially angered by a confederate of the experimenter and then given the opportunity to give electric shocks to them. In one condition they gave the shocks whilst in a quiet room, in a second condition they were in a noisy room, and in the third they were in a noisy room, but were able to stop the noise by pressing a button. Results showed that these participants gave much higher levels of shock when they had no control over the noise levels (Donnerstein and Wilson 1976). This is consistent with the general finding that stress levels are increased when we have no control over the stressor.

Following the finding that controllable noise is less aversive (unpleasant) and arousing than uncontrollable noise, then if participants believed they had control over noise levels, would the noise be less aversive and therefore less likely to produce an aggressive response? Donnerstein and Wilson carried out a second experiment to test this. As participants worked on maths problems, they were exposed either to no artificial noise, to 95db of unpredictable and uncontrollable noise, or to 95db of unpredictable noise that they believed they could terminate at any time. All noise was stopped when the participants moved on to the shock phase of the experiment, so that only the after-effects of the noise could influence aggression. As in the previous experiment, participants were given the chance to give shocks to someone who had angered

them. Results showed that the unpredictable and uncontrollable noise increased aggression (the intensity of the shocks given), whereas the same noise did not increase aggression if participants believed they had control over it.

Comments on the noise–aggression relationship

◆ These experiments suggest that under circumstances in which noise might be expected to increase arousal, aggression is increased. However, when the noise does not appreciably increase arousal (as when the individual has control over it), or when the individual is not already predisposed to aggress, noise appears to have little or no effect on aggression.

◆ Evans et al. (1998) have provided compelling evidence for the stressful effects of long-term exposure to uncontrolled noise. They looked at 7- to 8-year-old children in rural areas 22 miles from Munich, Germany, before and after the opening of a new airport. About half the children lived in an area under the flight path of the new international airport; the others lived in quiet areas. The children were tested for blood pressure, stress hormone levels and quality of life six months before the airport was completed as well as six and 18 months after it opened. The children in the chronic noise group experienced significant increases in blood pressure and significant increases in stress hormones, while the children in the quiet areas experienced no significant changes. Eighteen months after the airport opened, the children exposed to the chronic aircraft noise also reported a significant decline in their quality of life.

Crowding

Crowding refers to the psychological state of discomfort and stress associated with the spatial aspects of the environment (Sears et al. 1988). If our expectations on the use of space are violated by the presence of others, the feeling of crowding is induced. As a result of this, emotional distress may arise and a number of behavioural adjustments aimed at preserving one's personal space may occur (Kaya and Erkíp 1999). High density usually affects social interaction between individuals. When an increase in social density is seen as undesirable, social outcomes are generally negative and more aggression and less cooperation occurs (Horn 1994). Individuals subjected to high density often respond by withdrawing from social interaction and avoiding social contact (you may see this taking place next time you travel in a crowded lift).

Although the role of crowding or population density has also been proposed as an environmental stressor, the evidence is not particularly strong. There is some evidence that increased density of people (e.g. in heavily congested traffic routes) and violations of personal space may produce an aggressive response (Geen 1990).

One research approach which has examined the relationship between crowding and aggression has been to explore the effects of density on children's play. The results have been inconclusive. Some studies have found that increased density leads to more aggression, others have found the reverse, while yet others have found no effect at all. Loo (1978) has suggested that density affects children in a curvilinear fashion, with moderately high density leading to increased aggression in males while very high density led to decreased aggressiveness.

A second line of research has shown more consistent results. Research into the relationship between increased density and adult aggression has shown that increased density is related to increased aggression in males but not in females. For example, Stokols *et al.* (1973) studied same-sex groups of eight in either a small room or a large room, and found that males rated themselves as more aggressive in the small room whereas the opposite was true for females. In another study by Schettino and Borden (1975), using a ratio of people in a classroom to total number of seats as a measure of density, males reported an increase in feelings of aggression as density increased. Again the opposite was true for females.

Stokols (1976) identified three conceptual perspectives that might explain why crowding might lead to increased levels of aggression. These are as follows:

◆ *Stimulus overload* – high density can be aversive because it may cause us to be overwhelmed by sensory inputs. When the amount of stimulation produced by high density exceeds our ability to deal with it, negative consequences occur.

◆ *Behavioural constraint* – high density is aversive because it may lead to reduced behavioural freedom (e.g. waiting in a queue for the ladies, or being stuck in a traffic jam). Whether or not we experience negative effects depends on what we want to do and whether high density constrains us from doing it.

◆ *Ecological model* – this assumes that high density will produce negative consequences since it may result in insufficient resources for people in that setting (e.g. fighting for food at a famine relief centre). Resources are broadly defined and may include both materials (such as food) and privacy.

One element that is common to all three of these perspectives is that conditions that produce a loss of control are more likely to produce negative consequences.

Comments on the crowding–aggression relationship

◆ Research into the effects of crowding on aggression allow us to draw several tentative conclusions. First,

higher densities of people may lead to less liking for both people and places, and greater withdrawal. This effect appears to be stronger for males than for females.

◆ Research into this area has produced inconsistent results suggesting only a weak relationship between high densities and aggressive behaviour. Researchers have also found that the effects of changes in social density (number of people in a space) are more aversive than changes in spatial density (amount of space available) (Paulus 1977). Specifically, high social density will produce negative effects more consistently than high spatial density and while social density manipulations are generally aversive, spatial density manipulations are only problematic among males in same-sex groups (Paulus 1977).

◆ Some studies have shown that cities contain more stressful environmental features. A number of potential stressors that might be more prevalent in cities have already been identified (e.g. increased temperature, noise, crowding and inconvenience). Urban dwellers typically report being affected far more adversely by these physical stressors than do rural dwellers. Although studies have frequently noted the stressful nature of urban life, few have demonstrated the more relaxing nature of the rural environment (see *In Focus*, 'The view from the road', for a description of one study that does).

Activity 1: Your experience of noise and crowding

1 Write down some recent occasions when you have been exposed to prolonged and intense levels of noise. How did it make you feel? Did it make you feel any different if you had some degree of control over the noise?

2 Write down some recent occasions where you have experienced the feeling of 'crowding'. How did it make you feel? Was it desirable (e.g. at a party) or undesirable (e.g. in a shop)? Did that make a difference to the way you felt?

Exam summary: Nature and causes of aggression

The AQA examination will test your understanding of the following areas:

◆ social psychological theories and research studies of aggression (pp. 56–60)

◆ research into the effects of environmental stressors and behaviour (pp. 61–3).

The view from the road – the calming effects of the roadside environment

The value of a 'drive in the country' has, according to popular folklore, always been a good way of winding down from the pressures of urban life. Apart from the pressures of getting stuck behind a slow-moving caravan on narrow country roads, research has finally shown that this really is the case. A team of researchers based in Texas showed participants one of four simulated drives through different outdoor environments immediately before and immediately after a mildly stressful event (a gory film about workplace accidents). Those participants who viewed 'nature-dominated' drives (such as forests and golf courses) recovered more quickly from the stressful event than those who viewed a drive through more urban landscapes. Participants who viewed the nature drives before the stressful event were less affected by it than those who had viewed the urban drives. In other words, they appeared to be 'immunized' against its adverse effects. These findings suggest that roadside scenery and man-made artefacts may well influence the psychological and physiological wellbeing of drivers and their passengers, irrespective of any other characteristics of commuter routes.

Source: Parsons et al. (1998)

Example question

The question below is typical of one drawn from the material above, and should take you 30 minutes to answer:

◆ Outline and evaluate research relating to the effects of **two** environmental stressors on aggressive behaviour. *(24 marks)*

Suggested answer structure

This chapter has covered three types of environmental stressor – temperature, noise and crowding. The AQA specification does not specify any particular environmental stressors, and so you are free to choose any combination of these three. The question instructs you to outline and evaluate *research* relating to their effects, so your response to the question should be guided by the research that does just that. There is no optimum number of research studies that should be included in a question of this type, but you should aim for a balance of depth and breadth of coverage in your answer.

Studies of the effects of temperature (pp. 61–2) have tended to show that high temperatures are more associated with increasing levels of aggression,

although laboratory studies have shown that at very high temperatures, the motivation to aggress is replaced by the motivation to escape from the heat. Likewise, research into the effects of noise has shown that intense levels of noise may act as an antecedent of aggressive behaviour, although this is moderated by an individual's degree of perceived control over the source of the noise. Research on crowding has suggested that increases in aggression as a result of crowding are more likely if the increased social density is seen as undesirable rather than desirable.

The AO2 component of each of these areas is covered under the heading 'Comments on ...'. Remember that half of the marks for this question are available for your ability to *evaluate* the research you have chosen to illustrate the effects of each of these environmental stressors. This is another question where you need to pay very careful attention to the requirements and the time available. The term 'outline' (the AO1 requirement) means you are being asked to describe research in précis form, and the amount of detail you give should reflect this. Likewise, you will need to divide your time more or less equally between the four different components (two types of stressor, outlined *and* evaluated).

Altruism and bystander behaviour

A man approached the gates of Heaven and asked to be admitted. 'Tell me one good thing you have ever done in your life,' said St Peter.

'Well,' said the man. 'I saw a group of skinheads harassing an elderly lady and so I went over and kicked the leader in the shin.'

Impressed, St Peter asked when this act of bravery had occurred.

'About 40 seconds ago,' came the response.

Now consider the following real-life examples of behaviour.

◆ Shortly after Christmas in 1981, while postwoman Karen Green was at work she was assaulted by three men and two women, all of whom were drunk. While she spent 15 minutes struggling, people telephoned the police several times but no one directly intervened. Finally, she was forced into a car and driven away. Her body was found two days later. Why did no one help directly?

◆ In the case above, people at least telephoned for help. In 1964, New Yorker Kitty Genovese was returning home from work. As she neared home, a man jumped out of the shadows, attacked and killed her. She screamed and tried to defend herself. Although 38 people heard her screams and many looked out of their windows and saw the attack, which lasted for over 40 minutes, no one went to her rescue and no one called the police. Why not?

◆ On 13 January 1982, moments after take-off in Washington DC, a commercial jet hit a crowded bridge and plunged into the icy waters of the Potomac river. A 28-year-old man named Lenny Skutnik stopped and watched from the shore as rescuers tried to pull survivors out of the river. When Priscilla Tirado lost her grip on a helicopter lifeline and started to sink, Skutnik risked his own life by jumping into the water and pulling her to safety. Why did he behave in this prosocial way?

Activity 2: Your response to distressing situations

1   Imagine you are sitting watching your 5-year-old son playing the part of a shepherd in the school nativity play. He has just one line to say, but when his time comes, he freezes. Everybody waits, but nothing comes out. And then, imperceptibly to everybody but you, he begins to cry.

    What do you feel like doing?

2   You are flicking through a magazine when you come across a story about a terrible famine in East Africa. The article is accompanied by disturbing photographs of emaciated children and adults.

    Are you haunted by those images for the rest of the day, or do you quickly turn the page to escape the distressing situation?

What is prosocial behaviour? A definition of terms is important:

◆ *Helping* is a general term, which describes giving assistance to another person.

◆ *Altruism* is more specific and considers the motives for helping. Walster and Piliavin (1972) define altruism as 'helping behaviour that is voluntary, costly to the altruist and motivated by something other than the expectation of material or social reward'. Altruism is therefore different from helping,

in that there is a regard for the interest of others, without apparent concern for one's self-interest.

◆ Both altruism and helping are forms of *prosocial behaviour* which can be defined as 'any actions that benefit another regardless of the benefits or self-sacrifices of the actor' (Wispe 1972).

Altruism

Altruism is a form of prosocial behaviour in which a person will voluntarily help another at some cost to themselves. The primary motivation for altruistic behaviour is seen as a desire to improve the welfare of another person rather than the anticipation of some reward or for any other reason that might indicate self-interest (Cardwell 1996). One of the major problems for psychologists has been determining what is truly *altruistic* and what might better be explained in terms of *egoism* (i.e. self-interest). Consider a child who helps to clear snow off an elderly neighbour's drive, and is then given money as a reward. How can an observer know if the child's helpful behaviour was altruistic or egoistic? *Social learning* explanations of altruistic behaviour suggest that young children tend to be motivated by material rewards and punishments (*extrinsic motivation*), older children by social approval (also extrinsic) and adolescents by *intrinsic motivation* (e.g. it makes them feel good about themselves) for helping. From this perspective, people who are motivated by the desire for extrinsic rewards are less likely to help others (such as strangers) when these rewards are less likely (Grusec 1991).

Weiner (1986) proposed an attributional framework where the perceived causes of why someone needs help are analysed in terms of attribution of responsibility (see Chapter 1). These attributions then create an emotional experience, which motivates action or inaction. Attribution to uncontrollable causes (e.g. illness or disability) produces *sympathy*, which in turn produces *helping*. Attribution to controllable causes (e.g. lack of effort, drunkenness) produces *anger*, which in turn inhibits helping. From this perspective, helping an elderly neighbour would be more likely if we consider them unable to clear their own driveway rather than if we feel they are too lazy (or drunk!) to do so. Weiner's theory is only one of many that have tried to explain the basis of altruistic behaviour in human beings. The two models that follow are among the ones that seem best able to do just that.

Batson's empathy-altruism hypothesis

Batson's empathy-altruism hypothesis (Batson 1991) explains altruistic behaviour as a consequence of *empathy*. Empathy involves feeling an emotional response that is consistent with another's emotional state or condition (i.e. feeling sad when we meet someone who is sad). For the purposes of this model, Batson added that this empathy will also result in feelings of sorrow, concern or compassion *for the other person*. Witnessing another person in distress, therefore, will create empathic concern (e.g. sympathy) and helpers would then be motivated to help alleviate the other person's distress. Empathy consists of a number of different components, including *perspective taking* (the ability to take another person's point of view), *personal distress* (experiencing emotions such as alarm or sadness) and *empathic concern*. It is perspective taking, that leads to empathic concern. If the perspective of the other person is not taken, this does not happen, and we experience only personal distress, rather than empathic concern. Any actions we take to reduce this will be based on egoistic motives (i.e. to reduce our own personal distress). It is important to distinguish between empathic concern and personal distress. Personal distress is an aversive emotional reaction commonly experienced when we see someone else suffering and is coupled with self-oriented concerns to diminish it rather than altruistic concerns for the other person (see Fig. 3.3).

Research in this area has found that people high in empathic concern are more likely to help another person even when they are in a position to escape from this responsibility (see *In Focus*).

Evaluation of empathy-altruism explanation

This view of altruistic behaviour is particularly important because:

'Not only does it contradict the common assumption in psychology that all motivation is ultimately directed toward the egoistic goal of increasing our own welfare, but it also contradicts the underlying assumption that

Why do we help – out of compassion or self-interest?

human nature is fundamentally self-serving.' (Batson and Oleson 1991)

In these initial studies, Batson and his colleagues showed that people help for reasons other than the reduction of their own personal distress. Indeed, recent research (Roker *et al.* 1998, cited in Pennington *et al.* 1999) on adolescent altruism has found that British adolescents show a high level of altruistic and helping behaviour, often unbeknown to their parents.

It is possible that people who help in such situations do so to avoid punishment, such as social disapproval, that might arise as a result of not helping. However, in further research where the potential for negative social evaluation was manipulated, concern for the disapproval of others

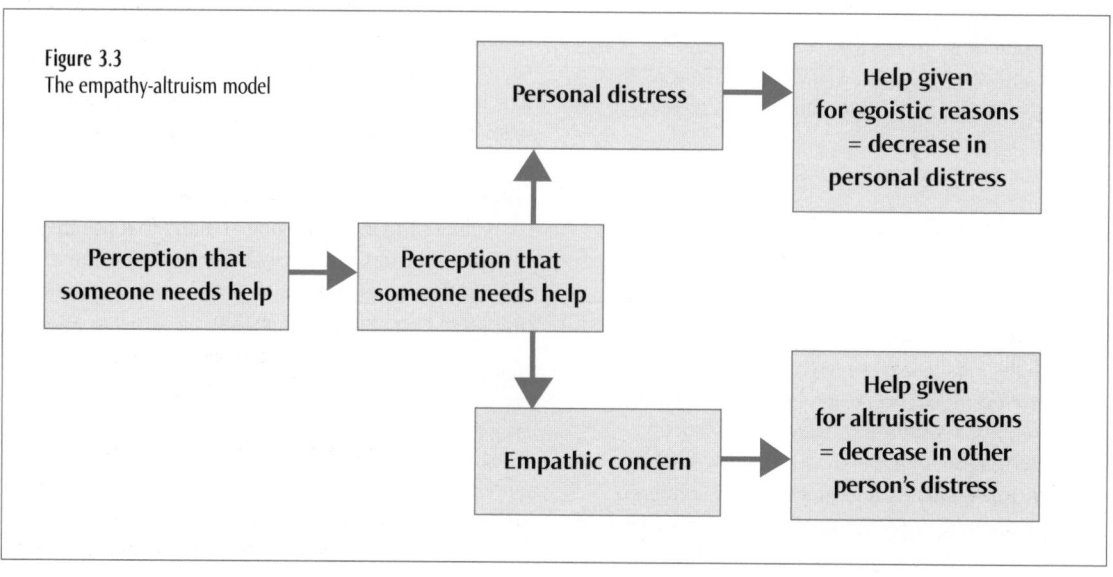

Figure 3.3
The empathy-altruism model

in
focus
Batson *et al.'s* study of the 'empathy condition'

In one intriguing study, Batson *et al.* (1981) had female college students watch up to ten trials while another student (actually a confederate of the experimenter) received random electric shocks. To manipulate emotional reactions, participants were told either that they were very similar to the student receiving the shocks (high-empathy condition) or that they were very dissimilar to the student receiving the shocks (low-empathy/personal distress condition).

In addition, half of the participants from each condition were told they would be free to go after watching two trials. The other half were told they could go only after watching all ten trials. After two trials, the confederate appeared to become distressed and revealed a childhood fear of electric shocks. Participants were then faced with a difficult decision – take her place (showing empathic concern) or leave (showing desire to alleviate personal distress). Batson and colleagues found that those in the high-empathy condition were more likely to take her place. Additionally, those in this condition who were free to leave after the second trial were more likely to stay and take the confederate's place. Among the 'personal distress' participants, only those who had been told they had to watch all ten trials tended to offer to replace the confederate. Those in this condition who were free to leave after two trials tended to take the easy way out, and left. (See Fig. 3.4 for a summary of the results.)

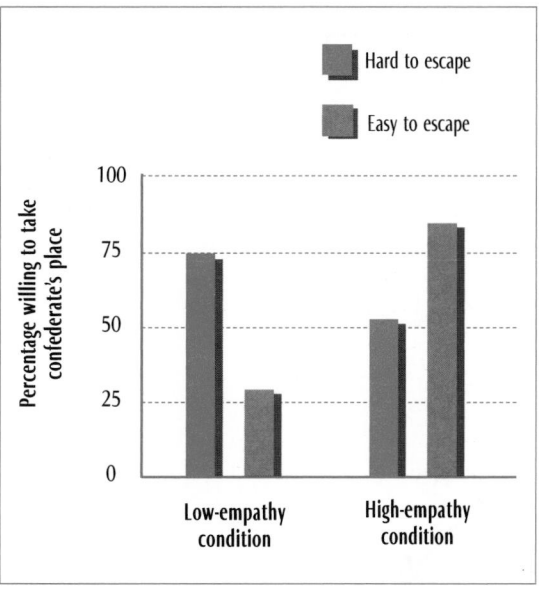

Figure 3.4
Results of Batson *et al.'s* 1981 study

did not appear to explain why empathic concern motivated helping (Fultz *et al.* 1986).

It is also possible that people help simply to avoid feeling bad about themselves. In a study to test for this possibility, Batson *et al.* (1988) contrived another situation where a participant (again a confederate of the experimenter) appeared unable to continue taking electric shocks as part of the study. This time the observers were told they could help the confederate by taking the remainder of the shocks only if they performed well on a numerical test. Half of the observers were told that the test was easy and most people passed it whereas the other half were told the test was difficult and few people passed it. The researchers reasoned that those participants who were high in empathy (achieved by stressing their similarity with the confederate) would take the test and try as hard as they could to do well in order to help the suffering confederate. Those who were high in personal distress might use the alleged difficulty of the test as a reason to decline even attempting it, or even to take it and not try their best. The results of this study are shown in Table 3.1.

What Batson and colleagues discovered was that there was little difference in the percentage of participants who subsequently offered to help the confederate between the two conditions when the test had been introduced as 'easy'. However, when the test was introduced as 'difficult', there was a significant difference between the percentage of high-empathy and high-personal-distress participants who offered to help. What is particularly interesting is

Table 3.1	Results of Batson *et al.'s* 1988 study	
	Percentage offering to help	*Score on test*
'Easy test'		
High-empathy participants	86	9.90
High-personal-distress participants	73	11.30
'Difficult test'		
High-empathy participants	65	13.00
High-personal-distress participants	28	8.25

that the scores on the test showed that under the 'difficult' test condition, high-empathy participants tried much harder to win the right to take the victim's electric shocks for them! It is also revealing that, consistent with the predictions of the researchers, participants in the high-personal-distress condition performed less well when the test was 'difficult' than when it was 'easy' (there was, of course, no difference in the test taken by the different participants).

Studies such as this cast doubt on the claim that people who show empathic concern help others in order to escape social or self-disapproval, and, as claimed earlier, it 'also contradicts the underlying assumption that human nature is fundamentally self-serving' (Batson 1991).

The negative-state relief model (Cialdini et al. 1987)

The negative-state relief model suggests that when we are experiencing negative states (such as sadness or guilt), we are motivated to alleviate this condition by helping others (which is personally rewarding and thus eliminates the negative state). People learn during childhood that helping others in need is a positive behaviour that will make them feel good about themselves. According to this view, therefore, the motivation for helping is egoistic, depending on the anticipated emotional consequences. For example, we may see someone begging for money while we are out Christmas shopping. This might make us feel guilty, so we hand over a pound and feel better.

According to the negative-state relief hypothesis, the primary objective in any behaviour that appears altruistic is actually the enhancement of our own mood. If we are experiencing negative emotions, we may be motivated to help someone else as a way of relieving these emotions. It doesn't really matter whether the emotions are already present *before* the opportunity to help arises, or are aroused by the situation itself. Either way, helping someone in need offers a powerful antidote to whatever negative feelings we may be experiencing. If we are offered a less costly route to the same end result however, we should, according to this hypothesis, take it (see Fig. 3.5).

Cialdini *et al.* (1987) carried out a study in much the same way as Batson had done to test his empathy-altruism hypothesis. Participants were again given instructions designed to create high- or low-empathy conditions and then put into a situation where they might help another person who was receiving electric shocks. This time, however, just before the request for

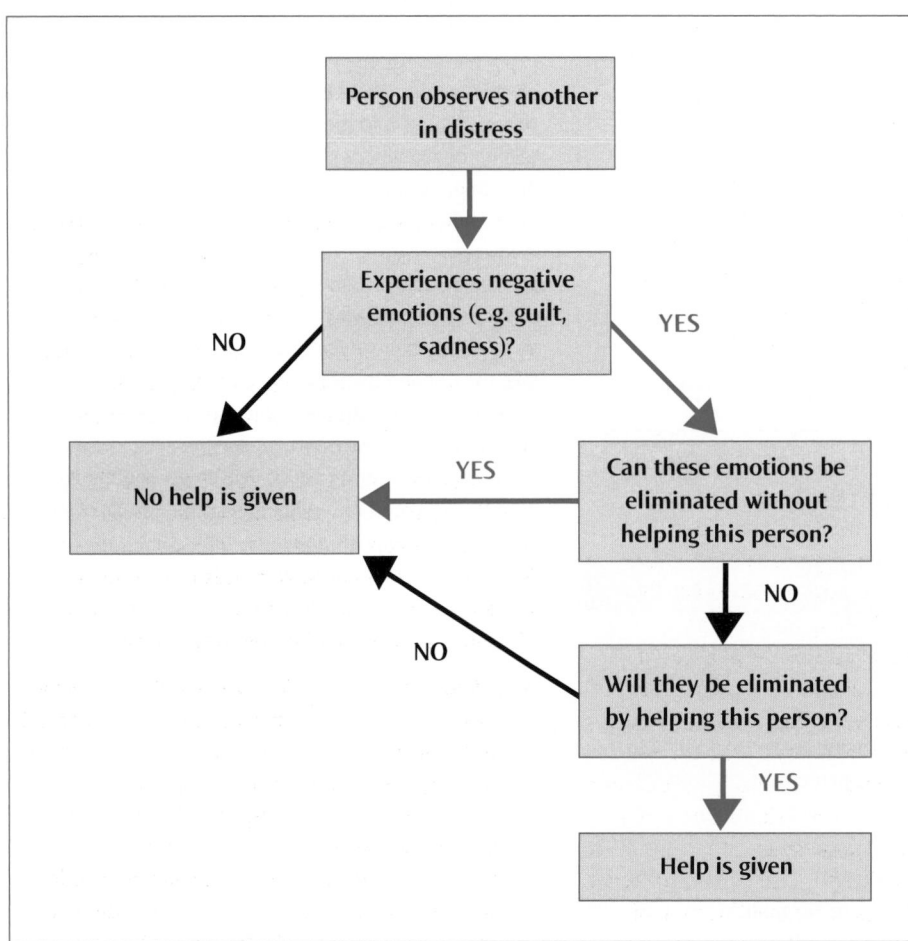

Figure 3.5
The negative-state relief model

help was made, the researchers either offered a surprise monetary 'bonus' or heaped lavish praise on the participants. According to the empathy-altruism hypothesis, highly empathic participants should help regardless of any attempts to elevate their mood by other means. Cialdini and colleagues found that when participants were given the surprise 'bonus', there was no difference between the likelihood of high-empathy and low-empathy participants helping when the request for help was made. Those participants who received unexpected lavish praise, however, were still motivated to help when later requested to do so. This study demonstrates that under some conditions, experiencing a mood-lifting event (in this case receiving money) may lessen our motivation to relieve our negative state by helping others. However, it also demonstrates that sometimes people experiencing empathy help primarily to relieve another person's suffering. In another study by the same researchers (Cialdini *et al.* 1987), participants who were led to believe that they had been given a 'mood fixing' drug (they hadn't of course) were less motivated to help another participant, presumably because they believed that helping would not improve their current mood state.

Evaluation of the negative-state relief model

Both Batson and Cialdini agree that when we come across someone in need we are likely to feel sad, and after helping them we are likely to feel happier. The subtle difference between the two hypotheses lies in *why* we help. Cialdini's view is that we help people in need primarily in order to feel better about ourselves, whereas Batson's view is that we help others because the victim needs help and, by helping, we then feel better about ourselves. Cialdini's research, although showing some evidence of helping for egoistic reasons, does also seem to lend support for Batson's more optimistic view of human altruism.

In support of the negative-state relief model, Cialdini *et al.* (1987) found that when a person feels empathy for another person in need, they also feel sadness. When these researchers manipulated these two emotions independently, they found that higher levels of sadness produced more helping, whereas increasing the amount of empathy was not accompanied by increasing likelihood of helping the other person.

The problem of whether people help others in distress for altruistic or egoistic reasons is not yet resolved. Batson (1991) does suggest one way in which these conflicting findings might be explained. He argues that we are more likely to feel empathic concern when we feel a close attachment with the person in need (as any parent who has witnessed their loved one desperately trying to remember their lines in the school nativity will testify!). It is possible that this form of altruism has developed as a result of kin selection, the

tendency to help members of one's own kin because they carry many of the same genes as you. Research by Batson *et al.* (1983) has established that people are more likely to help others when their similarity to the observer is stressed. On the other hand, we may feel only distress when we have no particular attachment or relationship with the person in need. In these conditions we may reduce our distress either by helping, or simply leaving the scene of the distress. You might like to try Activity 3 in order to examine your reasons for helping – or not helping – on different occasions.

Activity 3: Your reasons for helping/not helping

1 Think of a situation where you gave help. What were your feelings at the time? Why did you help? How did you feel afterwards.

2 Think of a situation where you did not give help. What were your feelings that time? Why did you not help and how did you feel afterwards?

3 Which of the two models you have just read about best describes your feelings on each of these occasions?

Bystander behaviour

The influence of others (bystander effects)

In the Kitty Genovese incident described on p. 65, there were 38 witnesses to her murder, yet no one helped or called the police. Some residents did turn on their lights, and it is possible that one shouted from a window. This did not deter the attacker, who, despite the cries for help from his victim, continued his attack and killed her. Why had nobody helped in this situation? A large number of people witnessed the attack, which lasted over 40 minutes.

Darley and Latané (1968) suspected that the fact that the number of possible helpers was so large might actually have contributed to their lack of intervention. They proposed two possible processes that might explain the reluctance of others to 'get involved' in situations such as the Kitty Genovese incident:

◆ *Diffusion of responsibility* – When only one person is present then that person is 100 per cent responsible for giving help. When there are two people present then responsibility is divided. If there are ten bystanders, the onus of responsibility is diffused amongst all ten. In the Kitty Genovese case, witnesses assumed someone else had phoned for the police. Support for the notion of diffusion of responsibility comes not only from Latané and

Darley's own research, but also from 'social loafing' research (Latané *et al.* 1979) where it has been demonstrated that the more people who are present, the less effort each individual makes.

◆ *Pluralistic ignorance* – When making a decision whether or not to help, we look to see what other bystanders are doing. If one person defines the situation as an emergency and helps, we are likely to follow and give assistance. If no one offers to give help, then we may conclude that the situation is not an emergency and do nothing. In effect, each bystander looks to the behaviour of others as a guide to his or her own behaviour. In the Kitty Genovese case, since no one was seen to be intervening, this tended to define the situation as one not requiring intervention from anyone (see also *In Focus*).

Bystander effects in the laboratory

In their 'epileptic seizure' study, Darley and Latané (1968) used male students seated in cubicles connected by an intercom system. They had volunteered to take part in a discussion on college life. The students were led to believe that they were either alone with one other participant, who later would be heard to have an epileptic seizure, or that they were joined by either one *or* four other participants besides the apparent seizure victim. Therefore, there were three conditions in the experiment. Once the discussion was underway, the victim clearly announced that he was experiencing a seizure. Help was less likely and slower to happen when participants believed that other potential helpers were present (see Table 3.2 for results).

Bystander effects in the natural environment

Latané and Darley (1970) found that when a person dropped some books in a lift, the probability of receiving help decreased with the number of people present: 40 per cent were offered help when there was one other passenger, but only 15 per cent when there were six others. Not all studies carried out in a natural environment, however, have found that large numbers mean little helping.

Piliavin *et al.* (1969) conducted a study to investigate the effects on helping of the type of person who is in need. They looked at the effect on help offered of (a) the victim appearing ill or drunk, and (b) the race of the victim (Black or White). During a seven-and-a-half minute journey on a busy New York subway train, the 'victim' accomplice collapsed on the floor of the train and remained there until someone helped. The major findings of the study are as follows:

◆ Those appearing to be ill were more likely to be helped than those appearing to be drunk.

◆ The race of the 'victim' had little effect on the helping.

◆ The expected diffusion of responsibility effect (mentioned earlier) did not occur.

Table 3.2 Bystander effects			
Group size (no. of people)	% responding during fit	% responding at any point	Average response time (in seconds)
1	85	100	52
2	62	85	93
5	31	62	166

Source: Darley and Latané (1968)

Why was this? It is suggested by Piliavin and colleagues that in the laboratory studies, participants could *hear* but not *see* the 'victim', whereas in this study, participants could both see and hear the 'victim'. Participants could also see what bystanders were *actually* doing.

One of the intriguing questions that came out of these research

---

in focus

If people won't help others in emergencies, will they help themselves?

Latané and Darley (1970) performed another study, the 'smoke-filled room experiment', which demonstrates the power of the bystander effect. In this study, whilst participants are in the waiting room completing questionnaires, smoke begins to fill the room. This continues until the room is full of thick, white smoke. In the condition where experimental accomplices are present with the participants, of all those tested, only one took any action! One possible explanation is that this result is a product of the experimental situation – some participants reported that they thought the smoke was introduced to see how it affected their ability to fill in the questionnaires! Most, however, looked to the others present in the room for some guidance as to how to act. Since the accomplices did nothing, the participants did nothing – a powerful demonstration of the bystander effect.

studies was whether we decide to give help to someone in distress because of the type of person we are or because of the type of person the victim appears to be?

Characteristics of the person in need

Undoubtedly we perceive certain types of people to be more deserving of help than others. We help those to whom we are related and those for whom we feel responsible. For example, you may recall that in 1995 Philip Lawrence went to the aid of one of his pupils who was being bullied by youths from another school. One attacker stabbed Philip Lawrence who died from the wounds inflicted. More generally, research (e.g. Piliavin *et al.* 1981) has shown that:

◆ We are more likely to help those who are perceived to be similar to ourselves.

◆ We are more likely to help those we perceive as less able to help themselves, e.g. children and elderly people.

◆ We are more likely to help those to whom we are physically attracted.

◆ We are less likely to help those who are not attractive, particularly those who are disfigured (unless we are also disfigured).

◆ We are less likely to help those whom we perceive as responsible for their own plight.

A number of research studies have found that men are more likely than women to help a member of the opposite sex, despite consistent findings that women generally show more empathy than men (Eagly and Crowley 1986). A study by Przybyla (1985) provided one explanation for this discovery. Male and female student participants were shown an erotic (sexually explicit) videotape, a nonerotic videotape, or none at all. When leaving the laboratory, the participants passed either a male or female student who had accidentally knocked over a pile of papers. Results showed that the men who had seen the erotic videotape were much more likely to stop and help the female student than those in the other two conditions,

and spent an average of 5 minutes doing so, compared to an average of 30 seconds when helping a male student. In contrast, the female participants who had seen the erotic videotape did not show higher levels of helping behaviour. Przybyla suggested that male helping behaviour is confounded with a desire to 'be romantic', whereas women are less likely to initiate such interactions with opposite-sex strangers.

Characteristics of the potential helper

Is there a helping personality? In an attempt to answer this question, Bierhoff *et al.* (1991) compared the personal characteristics of those who witnessed a road traffic accident and provided first aid with those who witnessed such an accident and did not provide help. The results of this study are shown in Table 3.3.

Other research has concentrated on more transitory psychological states, such as the *mood* someone is in when they encounter another person in need. Being in a good mood may lead to helping if the consequences of helping are likely to be pleasant and where there is little ambiguity about help being needed. If, however, the need is ambiguous and the consequences of helping are likely to be unpleasant, then people in a good mood tend not to help. According to Isen (1984), this is because they do not want to spoil the good mood they are currently enjoying. Likewise, being in a bad mood may help or hinder prosocial behaviour. There is the possibility that the bad mood, if it is due to guilt, might be alleviated by helping someone (the negative-state relief hypothesis). However, if people are focused on their own worries, they may be less responsive to the needs of others (e.g. Cialdini *et al.* 1982).

Steele and Southwick (1985) have shown that the consumption of *alcohol* leads to helping behaviour, because the alcohol reduces inhibitions and awareness of potential dangers. McGovern (1976) suggested that people who fear *embarrassment* are less likely to help, while Satow (1975) found that when others are watching, people who scored high on '*need for approval*' were more likely to help than those with low scores. The relationship between helper characteristics and the

Table 3.3 Components of the helping personality	
Characteristics of those who help	*Characteristics of those who do not help*
◆ had high internal locus of control (see p. 76)	◆ had low internal locus of control
◆ held belief in a 'just world'	◆ held less belief in a 'just world'
◆ felt socially responsible	◆ felt less socially responsible
◆ possessed ability to empathize	◆ possessed less ability to empathize
◆ were less egocentric	◆ were more egocentric

Source: adapted from Bierhoff *et al.* (1991)

likelihood of helping is a complex one. The characteristics of the situation, the request for help and the personal characteristics of the helper interact in complex ways that determine whether or not help will be given.

Characteristics of the situation

Milgram (1970) proposed a *stimulus overload* theory, suggesting that people from cities are so familiar with emergency situations that they treat them as everyday occurrences – these situations are less likely to attract interest and so people do not help. According to this view, urban residents restrict their attention to personally relevant events – the needs of strangers may therefore go unnoticed. People from small towns, however, do not witness emergencies very often, so that when these situations occur, their novelty is more likely to attract attention and help. This claim is supported in numerous studies (e.g. Gelfand *et al.* 1973) which show that people with small town backgrounds are more likely to help in an emergency than those from larger cities. Urban dwellers may also decline from offering help because of respect for the emotional and social privacy of others, as physical privacy is so hard to achieve (Milgram 1977).

Explaining bystander effects

Latané and Darley's cognitive model

Latané and Darley (1970) formulated a five-stage model to explain why bystanders at emergencies sometimes do and sometimes do not offer help. At each stage in the model the answer 'No' results in no help being given, while the answer 'Yes' leads the individual closer to offering help (see Fig. 3.6). Latané and Darley argued that helping responses may be inhibited at any stage of the process. These *inhibitions* and the stages they affect are:

◆ The bystander may not notice the situation (Stage 1).

◆ The situation may be ambiguous and not readily interpretable as an emergency (Stage 2). In this case the bystander may try to interpret the situation by observing the behaviour of other bystanders (*informational influence*).

◆ The person may avoid taking responsibility by assuming that someone else will (Stage 3). This process is known as *diffusion* and is likely to happen if the bystander sees danger in helping or if others are perceived as better able to offer help.

◆ Should the person wish to take responsibility for helping (Stage 4), they may not do so because they are neither trained nor competent to do so.

◆ Competent people may not help in an emergency (Stage 5) because they perceive that it is against

their interests to do so. For example, the recipient of help may be hostile (such as in domestic violence situations), or the situation itself may be dangerous (such as assault cases).

Evaluation of the Latané and Darley model

Several studies support the existence of these decision-making stages. Shotland and Huston (1979) have identified five characteristics which lead us to perceive that an event is an emergency requiring our assistance:

◆ Something happens which is sudden and unexpected.

◆ There is clear threat of harm to the victim.

◆ The harm will persist or worsen if no one intervenes.

◆ The victim is helpless and needs outside assistance.

◆ Some form of effective assistance is possible.

Bickman (1972) has shown that the more ambiguous the situation, the less likely it is that help will be offered. For example, Latané and Nida (1981) found that the helping response is inhibited when situations are manipulated to increase their ambiguity.

As would be expected, people who have the responsibility of group leadership, or are trained and competent to deal with emergency situations, are more likely to help. Maruyama *et al.* (1982) found that increasing personal responsibility leads to an increase in helping, whereas when people are in a group with a leader, group members tend to believe that the leader should be the one to act.

Clark and Word (1974) have demonstrated the importance of necessary skills, and found that those with 'electrical' experience helped those who had apparently suffered an electric shock. Likewise, participants who were told that they were good at handling rats were more likely to help recapture a possibly dangerous laboratory rat (Shwartz and David 1976).

It has been shown, however, that where there are no other people present, individuals will still help despite their lack of competence. Where other people are present, a new set of factors apply in determining whether or not help will be given, (the 'bystander effects' discussed earlier).

One well-established finding is that the presence of other observers reduces the likelihood that any one person will proffer a helping response (Latané and Nida 1981). This is consistent with the diffusion concept, suggested by Latané and Darley (1970). However, this effect does not appear to hold if a helping response is first modelled by an observer. Bryan and Test (1967) showed that people were more likely to help a person in distress if the specific behaviour has previously been modelled to them. This finding is interesting because it seems to be inconsistent with the notion that the presence of

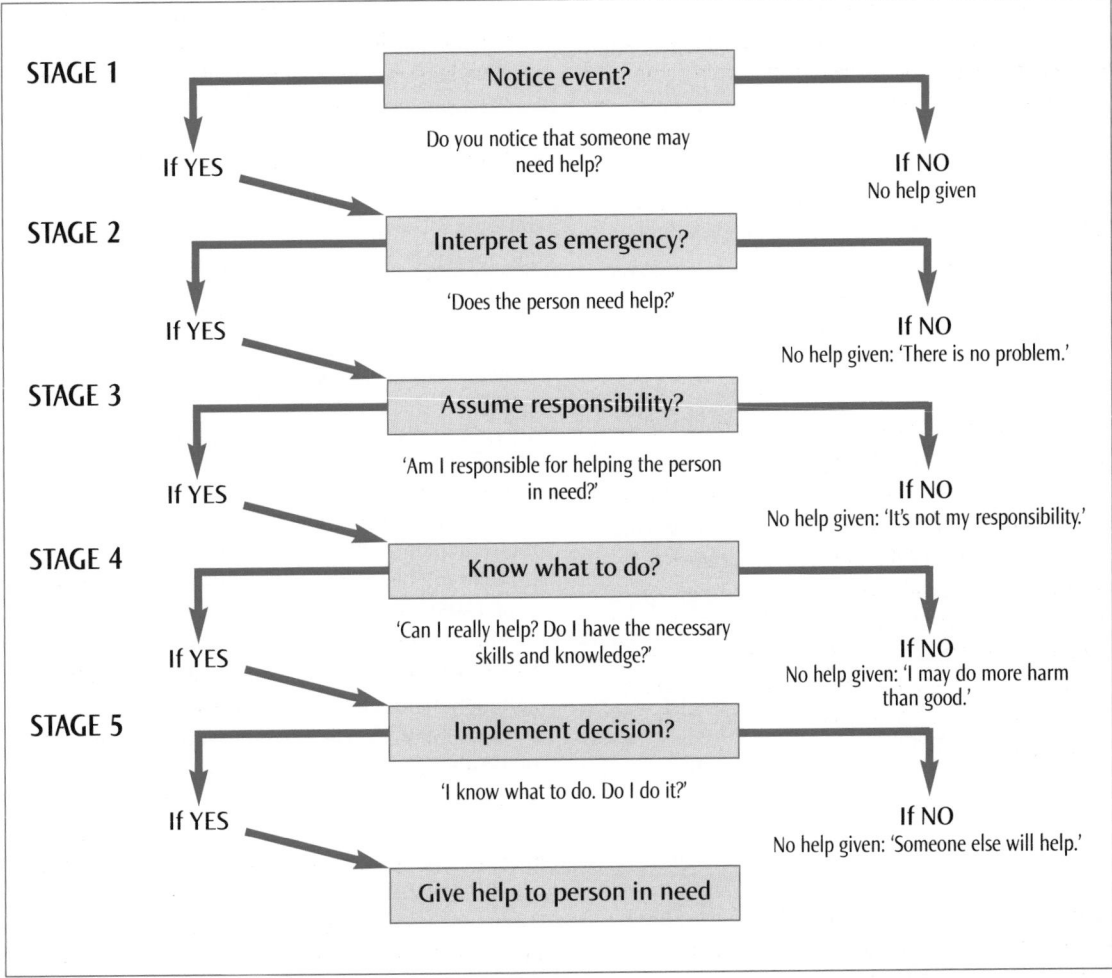

STAGE 1

Notice event?

Do you notice that someone may need help?

If YES

If NO
No help given

STAGE 2

Interpret as emergency?

'Does the person need help?'

If YES

If NO
No help given: 'There is no problem.'

STAGE 3

Assume responsibility?

'Am I responsible for helping the person in need?'

If YES

If NO
No help given: 'It's not my responsibility.'

STAGE 4

Know what to do?

'Can I really help? Do I have the necessary skills and knowledge?'

If YES

If NO
No help given: 'I may do more harm than good.'

STAGE 5

Implement decision?

'I know what to do. Do I do it?'

If YES

If NO
No help given: 'Someone else will help.'

Give help to person in need

Figure 3.6 Latané and Darley (1970) The cognitive model of bystander intervention

others inhibits helping. This may be explained by a process of conformity to social norms. According to this explanation, people use the actions of other people as cues to decide what an appropriate response to specific situations should be. When others help, this should stimulate helping behaviour, but when they do not help, this should inhibit helping behaviour.

The arousal:cost-reward model

Latané and Darley's model was an example of a *cognitive* approach to explaining bystander behaviour. An alternative theory is the arousal:cost-reward model, developed by Piliavin *et al.* (1981) to explain the results of their 'subway Samaritan study' (discussed on p. 70). This theory suggests that when people come across someone in need, they work their way through three stages before they respond or walk away:

◆ *Physiological arousal* – When we see someone in distress, we become physiologically aroused. The greater the arousal in emergencies, the more likely it

is that a bystander will help. Gaertner and Dovidio (1977) found a strong correlation between the speed at which participants responded to an 'emergency' in a laboratory, and their heart rate. Physiological arousal has also been shown to increase with the perceived severity and clarity of a victim's plight (Geer and Jarmecky 1973).

◆ *Labelling the arousal* – Physiological arousal does not automatically produce specific emotions. Our cognitions about that arousal play a critical role in determining the actual emotion that we feel. As we saw in the previous section on altruism, seeing someone else in distress elicits two kinds of responses, *personal distress* and *empathic concern*. Piliavin believed that physiological arousal was more likely to be labelled by bystanders as personally distressing, especially if they did not have a close personal relationship with the person in need of help.

◆ *Evaluating the consequences of helping* – Whether one helps or not depends on the outcome of weighing up both the costs and benefits of helping.

The *costs of helping* may include:

- effort: e.g. helping may be physically demanding
- time: e.g. one may be late for work or an appointment
- loss of resources: e.g. one may damage clothes or lose earnings
- risk of harm: e.g. one may risk life and limb
- negative emotional response: e.g. one may feel physically sick.

All these factors are weighed against the *benefits of helping* such as:

- social approval: e.g. thanks from victim (and crowd, if there is one)
- self-esteem: e.g. feeling that one is a kind person
- positive emotional response: e.g. feelings (such as elation) elicited by successful rescue.

It is argued by Piliavin and colleagues that such a cost/benefit analysis is performed to reduce negative emotional arousal, and in addition to the above factors, the *costs of not helping* must also be assessed. These may include:

- disapproval: e.g. no rewards from victim or crowd

- damaged self-esteem: e.g. feelings that one is not a kind person
- negative emotional response: e.g. not helping may cause feelings of guilt.

The Piliavin *et al.* model has been supported by a number of studies which demonstrated that increasing various costs will lead to a decrease in helping, whilst increasing the benefits will lead to an increase in helping. Some examples of situations that might be explained by this model are described in Fig. 3.7.

Evaluation of the arousal:cost-reward model

There is considerable support for the claim that people are both subjectively and physiologically aroused by the distress of others. These reactions appear quite early developmentally and appear across many different cultures leading to the suggestion that this is a biologically inherited capacity (Manstead *et al.* 1995).

There is also support for the claim that arousal increases the likelihood of helping in an emergency although there is less agreement about the nature of the emotion that arises from this arousal and its specific motivating properties. Piliavin and colleagues believed

Figure 3.7 How Piliavin *et al.*'s model might explain some real-life situations

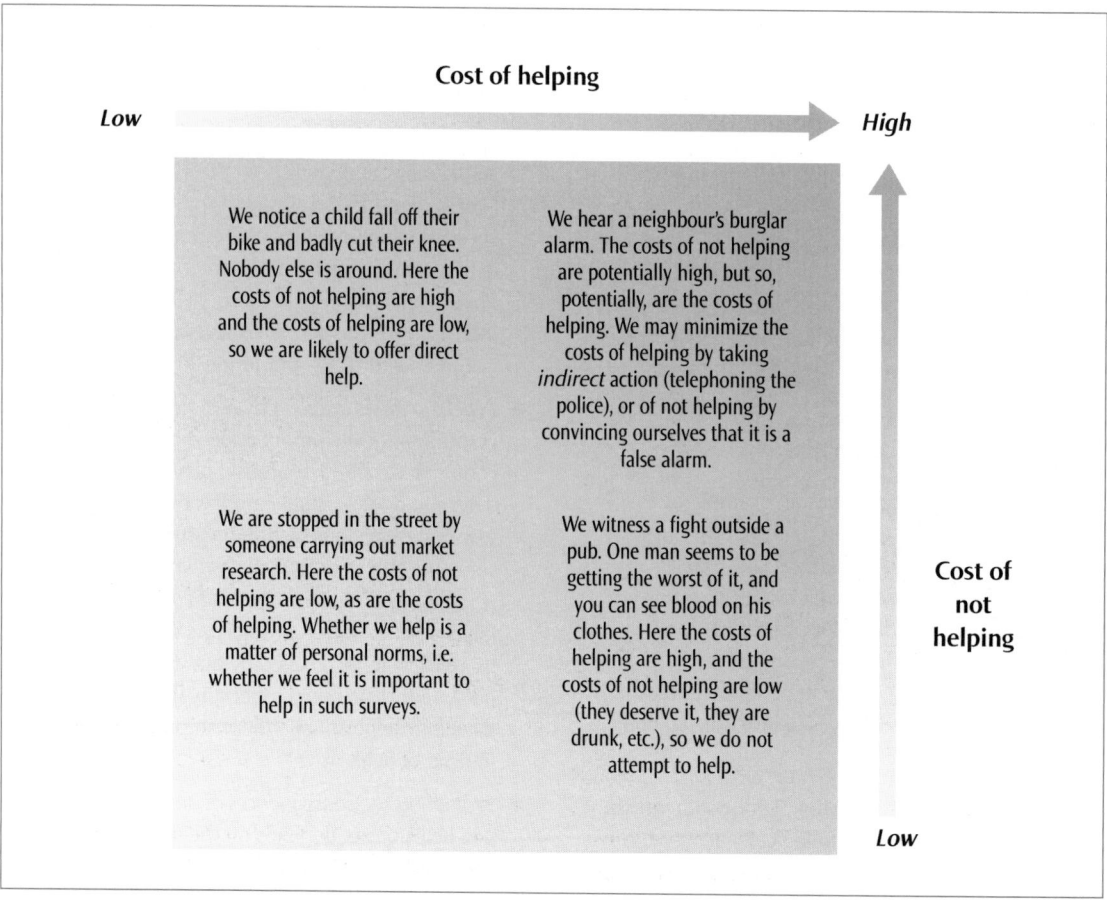

that bystanders help because of their personal distress. Batson *et al.* (1981), however, have argued that when bystanders believe they are similar to the victim, and identify with them, they are more likely to help out of empathic concern rather than out of the egoistic need to reduce their own distress.

Weiner (1986) has proposed an attributional explanation of when we are likely to help another person in distress (see p. 65). When we come across someone in distress, we search for possible causes of their plight. If we decide their plight is a product of uncontrollable causes (e.g. an accident), we feel sympathy and are more likely to help. On the other hand, if we feel their plight is more a product of controllable causes (e.g. their drunkenness), we feel anger or irritation, and are less likely to help.

More recent developments of this model have acknowledged the unnecessarily mechanistic nature of the earlier model, and have suggested that, contrary to the belief that helping must be due to purely egoistic reasons, 'true altruism – acting with the goal of benefiting another – does exist and is part of human nature' (Piliavin and Chang 1990).

Cultural differences in prosocial behaviour

Comparisons of different cultures concerning their prosocial behaviour typically focus on the individual versus the communal. Individualist societies tend to stress the need for individual achievement and recognition, whilst collectivist (communal) societies stress interlocking family-like connections in which individuals depend on each other. Thus, some behavioural differences of individuals may be interpreted in terms of the dominant cultural characteristics of a given society (see Chapter 2, *Relationships*, for more information on individualist and collectivist (communal) cultures).

Cultural perspectives on prosocial behaviour place it within a much larger moral system that binds people together in social relationships (Miller and Bersoff 1994). An example of the role that prosocial behaviour, or specifically helping behaviour, plays in the establishment of social relationships can be found in the Chinese custom of *guanxixue* (guan-shee-shwe), meaning 'doing favours for people' (Moghaddam 1998). This involves 'the exchange of gifts, favours, and banquets; the cultivation of personal relationships and networks of mutual dependence; and the manu-facturing of obligations and indebtedness' (Yang 1994).

Through *guanxixue*, individuals can create extensive social networks involving many others who are morally obligated to them. A cultural perspective of prosocial behaviour, therefore, allows us to see that helping and

being helped involves much more than just instrumental benefits. Culture also provides the rules and norms concerning when it is appropriate to seek and to offer help. If the objective of prosocial behaviour was simply to maximize benefits, then we would expect people to seek help and take it whenever it is offered. We can now turn to the factors that might determine when people seek and give help.

Seeking and giving help

◆ *Liking* – Miller and Bersoff (1998) investigated the importance of liking on perceived responsibilities to help someone in need. The study varied the type of relationship involved (e.g. helping a child, sibling or colleague), and compared the reactions of Indian and American adults to helping within these relationships. American participants were less likely to take responsibility for helping someone they did not like, compared to someone they did like. Liking had no impact on Indian participants' perceptions of their moral responsibility to help in any of the relationships under consideration. They were as likely to help those they did not like as those they did.

◆ *Gender* – Cultural rules governing gender relations may also determine how likely it is that individuals seek help. These may account for the fact that, in most cultures, women seek help more than do men (Moghaddam 1998). Cultural rules allow women to present themselves as 'in need' whereas male concerns for 'toughness' and 'independence' may prevent them from seeking the help of others. In Britain and the US, for example, twice the number of women than men seek help for their depression (Weissman *et al.* 1991), whereas male alcoholics (perhaps a male response to depression) outnumber female alcoholics by the same proportion (Nolen-Hoeksema 1990).

◆ *Communal versus individualistic* – Nadler (1986) compared Israeli urban dwellers with those living on a kibbutz, in terms of whether they would be willing to seek (and whether they would receive)

Activity 4: Individualism, collectivism and rewards

Read through the *In Focus* on p. 76.

◆ What are the main conclusions of this study?

◆ Do these results show evidence of an equity rule, an equality rule or both in operation in these two cultures?

◆ How would you respond if you were the person responsible for the reward allocation?

Individualism, collectivism and reward allocation: a cross-cultural study

Underlying much of the theorizing about individualism and collectivism is the idea that collectivism involves the equal sharing of rewards from collaborative efforts, whilst individualism entails the maximization of personal gain.

Recent studies carried out in Hong Kong and other collectivist Asian cultures have found evidence for a distribution of rewards based on *equality* (i.e. rewards are shared equally regardless of the amount of any one individual's contribution), whereas for members of individualist cultures, the *equity* rule is favoured (those who contribute the most deserve the most rewards).

Members of collectivist cultures do not, however, appear to apply the equality rule beyond the confines of their own group but, on the contrary, make greater use of an equity rule. Members of individualist cultures tend to apply the equity rule both to in-group members *and* out-group members, demonstrating the priority of personal goals over in-group goals. Russia is a country which historically has embodied the values of collectivism, therefore it might be hypothesized that Russians would behave in similar ways to members of other collectivist cultures in their preferred patterns of reward allocation.

This study compared British and Russian participants with respect to their use of equity and equality rules when sharing rewards after a hypothetical collaborative task. The researchers predicted that the British participants would be influenced only by the levels of task performance, allocating more rewards for more work (the equity rule). In contrast, they expected the Russian participants to be influenced by the levels of task performance (i.e. an *equity* rule) only when the co-worker was a stranger. When the hypothetical co-worker was a friend, they would be more likely to share any rewards equally with them *regardless of the amount they had contributed to the task* (the *equality* rule). The main results are described in the table below: Note that each of these percentages refers to the allocation that the participants allocated to themselves. The levels of task performance were always manipulated so that the person doing the allocating either contributed 80 per cent of the task involvement (high performance) or 20 per cent (low performance). Therefore, if participants made equitable distributions they would allocate 80 per cent of the reward to themselves under the high performance condition, and 20 per cent under the low performance condition.

	Britain	Russia
	% given to self	% given to self
High performance		
Friend as co-worker	68.25	58.00
Stranger as co-worker	64.00	73.00
Low performance		
Friend as co-worker	33.15	20.10
Stranger as co-worker	33.30	19.60

As a conclusion to this study, Tower and colleagues gathered qualitative data from focus group discussions with the two sets of participants. The following explanations were typical of responses from the two groups.

'She is my very close friend. Situations and circumstances might differ. One day I might need some help and understanding too. I trust my close friends.' (Russian participant)

'What you put in is what you get out – this is fair. If the mate was a close friend, I'm sure that he/she would understand.' (British participant)

Source: Tower *et al.* (1997)

help. Nadler found that those who had been raised communally were more likely to help than those raised individualistically in a city, especially when the help was seen to benefit the group rather than just the individual. In order to test whether these results really were the product of individualist or collectivist experiences, Nadler (1993) compared these two groups with recent immigrants to Israel, one group from the US (an individualist culture and one from the Soviet Union (generally considered a collectivist culture). As before, the kibbutz dwellers were most likely to seek help, and the US immigrants and Israeli city dwellers less likely to do so. The Soviet immigrants were least likely to seek help – within the former Soviet Union, people tended only to seek help from those to whom they felt close and intimate, avoiding interactions outside this small circle of family and friends.

The meaning of helping behaviour in different cultures

Fiske (1991) suggests that the meaning of 'helping' behaviour may vary between cultures. Feldman (1968) found that foreigners who asked a favour in Greece were more likely to receive help than if they were locals. The reverse was true in Paris and Boston. Collett and O'Shea (1976) had foreigners ask directions to nonexistent sites and two that did exist. In Tehran (Iran) they were frequently given directions to the nonexistent sites, but this did not happen in London. Thus, in Iran, the *format* of helpfulness was preserved, even though the directions were not particularly helpful. Collett and O'Shea conclude that in some collectivist cultures, foreigners may be treated differently to locals because they are seen as in some way more important and worthy of help.

In conclusion, it is worth noting the conflicting results from laboratory and field studies of helping behaviour. Laboratory studies (particularly those involving American participants) tend to emphasize that people will go out of their way to avoid seeking help from others, yet field studies (particularly those involving participants from Asian cultures) emphasize that people go out of their way to seek help (Wills 1992). This contrast in results may not simply be the product of cultural differences alone. American participants (typically undergraduates) may interpret the testing situation very differently from participants in more natural settings. They may well try to prove that they *can* accomplish a task without the help of others. Also, laboratory-based studies tend to lack the *social* context of help seeking. Faced with a limited time period with anonymous fellow participants, there would seem little point in trying to develop a social relationship in such a context. In the real world, however, people actively seek out the help of others to *extend* their social relationships (Moghaddam 1998).

Exam summary: Prosocial behaviour

The AQA examination will test your understanding of the following areas:

◆ explanations and research studies of altruism (pp. 65–9)

◆ explanations and research studies of bystander behaviour (pp. 69–75)

◆ cultural differences in bystander behaviour (pp. 75–7).

Example question

The question below is typical of one drawn from the material above, and should take you 30 minutes to answer:

◆ Discuss research relating to bystander behaviour.
(24 marks)

Suggested answer structure:

When we look at 'bystander behaviour', we are considering a special case of helping behaviour: helping someone in an emergency. We have looked at two different models that explain this process: Latané and Darley's *cognitive model* (pp. 72–3) and Piliavin *et al.*'s *arousal:cost-reward model* (pp. 73–5), as well as the more general points about diffusion of responsibility and pluralistic ignorance (p. 72). Latané and Darley's model focuses on our cognitive interpretation of an incident and our possible role in helping, whereas Piliavin's *et al.*'s model emphasizes a more egoistic concern with the costs and benefits of helping. Each of these explanations may be evaluated in terms of the research studies that support or challenge it.

We have also examined a number of research studies that have explored specific aspects of bystander behaviour, such as the characteristics of the person in need (p. 71), the characteristics of the potential helper (pp. 71–2) and the characteristics of the situation (p. 72). As the question asks for 'research' relating to bystander behaviour, it would be appropriate to answer in terms of theoretical (i.e. the explanations) or empirical (i.e. the research studies) insights, as these are both part of the scientific cycle of research (see Chapter 19).

Although the examples given at the start of this section (such as the case of New Yorker Kitty Genovese) are undoubtedly examples of bystander behaviour (referred to as bystander *apathy* when bystanders do not choose to help), they do not really have a place in an essay of this kind. With just 30 minutes to write your response to this question, you should be careful about what finds itself into your essay. Examples of real-life emergencies such as those involving Kitty Genovese, Karen Green and Lenny Skutnik are fascinating insights into the very different ways in which people respond to emergencies, but they are not *research*. Social psychologists have certainly been influenced by events such as these, and it possible to explain each instance by using the research that follows, but this should be done extremely carefully, if at all.

Media influences on pro- and antisocial behaviour

Media influences on prosocial behaviour

The late 1950s and early 1960s produced a growing concern over the portrayals of violence on television, and its potential effects, particularly on the behaviour of children. While the majority of the literature has focused on the effects of viewing violent behaviour, there has been a substantial number of studies that have provided evidence for the potential value of the media for the development and expression of prosocial behaviour. These studies have demonstrated that children imitate forms of prosocial behaviour such as altruism, helping, delay of gratification and positive interaction with others when exposed to models who display such behaviours. Hearold (1986), carried out a meta-analysis (a statistical review) of over 100 studies of the prosocial effects of television and found that:

> 'Although fewer studies exist on prosocial effects, the effect size is so much larger, holds up better under more stringent experimental conditions and is consistently higher for both boys and girls, that the potential for prosocial overrides the small but persistent effects of antisocial programmes.'
> (Hearold 1986, p135)

Comstock (1989) has explained Hearold's findings thus: prosocial messages are generally designed to have an influence on viewers, whereas antisocial messages are not specifically designed for that purpose. One of the problems faced by researchers is that if television is to teach socially acceptable attitudes and behaviours, these messages must be conveyed effectively or prosocial programmes will fail to achieve their goals (Yates 1999). If a message is not understood, then any effort to teach prosocial behaviour in this way is futile.

Lovelace and Huston (1983) have identified three modelling strategies used by researchers for the transmission of prosocial messages:

◆ *prosocial only* – only prosocial behaviours are modelled

◆ *prosocial conflict resolution* – prosocial behaviours are presented alongside antisocial behaviours

◆ *conflict without resolution* – problems are presented that *suggest* prosocial solutions.

Although these strategies have the potential to have a prosocial effect on adults, most of the attention has been directed towards their effect on children. Each of these strategies is based on *social learning theory*, which holds that viewing modelled behaviours, particularly if the consequences of such behaviours are personally desirable, results in an imitation of those behaviours. We will turn to these different strategies.

Prosocial behaviour only

Research using this strategy has focused on media models who show prosocial or courageous behaviour.

In one such study (Bryan and Bryan 1970), 6- to 9-year-old children were shown a specially recorded film of a character bowling and winning gift certificates. In one version of the film the character gave some of his gift certificates to charity, in the other he kept them for himself. In some conditions of the study he also preached the merits of giving to charity. After watching the film, children were placed in a similar situation, and observed to see if they too would give to charity. Results showed that those children who had seen the character being generous were also likely to display generosity, whilst those who saw him behave selfishly were less generous in their own donations. Interestingly, it was the *actions* of the character that were most influential, as his words made little difference to how the children behaved. However, later research by Rushton and Owen (1975) suggested that the effects of such prosocial manipulations of children's generosity tend to wear off in a week or two.

Several other studies (e.g. Sprafkin *et al.* 1975) have also demonstrated the positive effects of prosocial models on television on children's helping behaviour. In particular, these studies have found that children's willingness to help can be increased through viewing a televised example of a *specific* prosocial behaviour. This supports the predictions of social learning theory, that the effects of a televised example will be mediated by specific modelling cues rather than the general prosocial format of the show.

Comments on the 'prosocial only' model

◆ From their review of studies that had used this approach, Lovelace and Huston (1983) concluded that television extracts that contained *only* a prosocial message were effective in producing prosocial behaviour in viewers.

◆ Programmes made in this way have the advantage of presenting prosocial messages clearly and unambiguously. However, disadvantages include the reliance on brief segments that are often produced specially for use in a laboratory setting.

◆ The measures of prosociality are likewise taken in an artificial and contrived environment, limiting their application to children's behaviour in real-life settings. Thus, generalizations to other situations may be limited.

◆ It is also evident that many of the effects that have been produced by these interventions have been very short-lived (Rushton and Owen 1975).

◆ The value of prosocial programmes can, however, be demonstrated clinically. Specially prepared television material can help lonely, self-conscious children to make friends more readily. Children who have difficulty getting on with their peers can watch fictional scenarios in which they see how to mix with others in various social situations (O'Connor 1969, cited in Gunter and McAleer 1997).

Prosocial conflict resolution

Television programmes that present only prosocial behaviour are rare. Typically, prosocial behaviour is presented alongside or in contrast to antisocial behaviour. Several studies have investigated the effectiveness of prosocial messages when they are presented in this context.

Paulson (1974) investigated the effects of modelling prosocial alongside antisocial behaviour. This was part of a *Sesame Street* programme designed to teach cooperation (a prosocial behaviour). Findings of this study, which took place over a six-month period, indicated that children who saw the programmes recognized cooperation when they saw it, and subsequently scored higher on measures of cooperation compared to children who had not seen the programmes. Unfortunately, the researchers found no evidence of an increase in the general level of these children's prosocial behaviour during free play. Experiments involving *Mr Rogers' Neighbourhood* have demonstrated that preschool children do show significant increases in prosocial behaviours such as nurturance and cooperation when the show is used as part of an intervention programme for children from low socioeconomic backgrounds (Friedrich and Stein 1973).

A US television series designed to reduce sex-role stereotypes among children has been shown to be particularly effective in changing children's stereotypical beliefs about males and females. In *Freestyle*, characters initially choose to perform a nonstereotypic sex-role behaviour, but are faced with difficulties as a result. In the end, the character manages to master the nonstereotypic behaviour, overcomes the difficulties and is rewarded for so doing (Johnston and Ettema 1986).

Comments on the prosocial conflict resolution model

◆ Lovelace and Huston (1983) conclude from the research literature for studies using this strategy that prosocial behaviour may be learned in this way, but these behaviours tend not to be generalized to children's everyday behaviour. Short segments of instruction, such as those portrayed in *Sesame Street* have been shown to be useful for cognitive learning, but dramatic story lines, such as those in *Mr Rogers' Neighbourhood* and *Freestyle* are more effective in helping children generalize the prosocial behaviours they model to their own life.

◆ It is also possible that children might adopt the antisocial behaviours that are modelled alongside the prosocial behaviours in such programmes. In fact, some research studies have found increases in assertiveness and aggression when children have been exposed to *Mr Rogers' Neighbourhood* as part of a 'Headstart' intervention programme (Friedrich-Cofer *et al.* 1979). It appears that the conflict resolution strategy is more effective when the greater proportion of a programme is devoted to prosocial behaviour and when discussion and postviewing rehearsal of the behaviours is possible (Yates 1999).

◆ Lovelace and Huston (1983) also observed that negative effects might occur if the prosocial behaviours were not shown in clear contrast to the antisocial behaviours. A study by Liss and Reinhardt (1979) supported this conclusion. They found an increase in aggressive behaviour in children who had watched a cartoon series *Superfriends*. Although both prosocial and antisocial behaviours were modelled in this series, characters usually demonstrated some justification for their aggressive behaviour, and so legitimized it for those watching.

Conflict without resolution

In the third type of modelling strategy, unresolved conflicts are presented to children via the media. Programme content frequently deals with problems that are likely to be encountered when growing up, such as parental pressure, male/female relationships, privacy and friendship. A character is seen as struggling with a particular problem (for example, should she continue seeing someone of whom her parents clearly disapprove), but no decision is made. Children are encouraged to discuss how they would resolve the problem faced by the central character. Conflicts such as these, as well as many of the less pleasant aspects of growing up (bullying, divorce, death of a loved one), are frequently presented to young viewers through the medium of the soaps. Messenger-Davies (1989) describes how her own daughter (then aged 8) came to terms with the violent death of Damon Grant, the young son of one of the central families in *Brookside*.

'We all agreed (older siblings too) that Elinor should be allowed to continue to watch *Brookside*, with its harrowing, and brilliantly acted, scenes of family mourning and recrimination – and that we

would support her through them. She found her own ways of dealing with her emotion.'
(Messenger-Davies 1989)

Because of her familiarity with the soap opera genre, Elinor was able to put the death of one of her favourite characters in perspective, suggesting alternative ways that the character might have been 'written out' of the series.

Comments on conflict without resolution

◆ Some research has indicated that children do understand and learn the programme content and are able to generate prosocial rather than antisocial solutions to the problems faced in the plot (Rockman 1980).

◆ Other studies have indicated limited potential for prosocial change with this kind of programme, and that children younger than 8 might not benefit from this type of modelling as effectively as older children (Lovelace and Huston 1983).

Activity 5: Prosocial television programmes

Either individually or in a small group, make a list of television programmes that you feel have a significant 'prosocial' content.

◆ Which of the categories just described best fits each of these programmes?

◆ What are the prosocial messages being portrayed in each of these programmes?

◆ Are some types of character in these programmes typically portrayed as more prosocial than others (e.g. women rather than men)?

Media influences on antisocial behaviour

'There can be no longer any doubt that heavy television violence is one of the causes of aggressive behaviour, crime and violence ... Television violence affects youngsters of all ages, of both genders, at all socio-economic levels and all levels of intelligence ... The causal effect of television violence on aggression, even though it is not large, exists.' (Eron 1992)

'What, then, can be seen as the "different" factor that has entered the lives of countless children and adolescents in recent years? This has to be recognized as the easy availability to children of gross images of violence on video.' (Newson 1994)

These statements, from influential psychologists either side of the Atlantic give you an idea of the way in which many people, psychologists included, view the media/violence debate. For many, there is simply no question about television and other forms of media being responsible for the violent behaviour in society today, particularly in children. For others, the debate is far from clear. In this next section we will look at the evidence and examine critically the claims of such a 'media effects' model.

Studies into the effects of exposure to television violence

Correlational studies

The weight of evidence from correlational studies is fairly consistent: viewing and/or preference for violent television is *related* to aggressive attitudes, values and behaviours.

◆ Robinson and Bachman (1972) found a relationship between the number of hours of television viewed

---

in focus

Moral panics

As Pearson (1984) points out, there has been a long history of moral panics about the harmful effects of popular culture such as comics and popular theatre in the nineteenth century, followed by the cinema, television, video and computer games. These panics are largely fuelled by the popular press and their claim that things are getting worse. The last major moral panic about video nasties was in 1983 when a report was produced claiming that half of junior school children had seen banned videos (Barlow and Hill 1985). This produced banner headlines: 'the rape of children's minds' and so on. When we obtained the questionnaire, it became obvious how such an inflated figure could have arisen. The key questions about film titles covered the last five pages of a lengthy questionnaire and listed 113 titles which children had to rate if they had seen them on video. We suspected children would forget the instructions and to test this, faithfully reproduced the questionnaire but substituted nonexistent film titles instead of the video nasties. The results from five classes of 11 year olds indicated that 68 per cent of children claimed to have seen films which do not exist (Cumberbatch 1994)!

Source: Cumberbatch (1997)

National Television Violence Study (MediaScope Inc: February 1996)

This is the largest study of media content ever undertaken. It is the first of three reports to assess violence on cable television in the USA. Rather than narrowing the focus to specific acts of violence, this study broadens the research to cover three areas:

◆ the amount and context of violence on cable

◆ the effectiveness of ratings systems for films (e.g. '18' and 'PG')

◆ the success of antiviolent messages.

Key findings:

◆ The context in which most violence is presented on television poses risks for viewers.

◆ Perpetrators go unpunished in 73 per cent of all violent scenes.

◆ The negative consequences of violence are not often portrayed in violent programming.

◆ One out of four violent interactions involves the use of handguns.

◆ Only 4 per cent of violent programmes emphasize an antiviolent theme.

◆ Children's programmes are the least likely of all genres to show the long-term negative consequences of violence (only 5 per cent were found to do this).

and adolescent self-reports of involvement in aggressive or antisocial behaviour.

◆ Atkin *et al.* (1979) used a different measure of aggressive behaviour. They gave 9- to 13-year-old boys and girls situations such as the following: 'Suppose that you are riding your bicycle down the street and some other child comes up and pushes you off your bicycle. What would you do?' The response options included physical or verbal aggression along with options to reduce or avoid conflict. These investigators found that physical or verbally aggressive responses were selected by 45 per cent of heavy television violence viewers compared to only 21 per cent of those who watched little television violence.

◆ Phillips (1983) investigated the effects of the portrayal of suicides in television soap operas on the suicide rate in the United States using death records compiled by the National Center for Health Statistics. He found, over a six-year period, that whenever a major soap opera character committed suicide on TV, within three days there was a significant increase in the number of female suicides across the USA.

Although these studies suggest a link between watching television violence and engaging in violent behaviour, they do not demonstrate a *causal* relationship between the two. To investigate this, psychologists must choose methods which give them more control over the conditions in which violence is viewed and the behavioural measurement of violence.

Experimental studies

◆ Bandura *et al.* (1963) (see *In Focus*, p. 56) showed that children who had viewed an aggressive model on film were more aggressive in their play than those who had not observed the aggressive model. Early studies such as this were criticized on the grounds that the aggressive behaviour was not meaningful within the social context and that the stimulus materials were not representative of available television programming.

◆ Liebert and Baron (1972) investigated young children's willingness to hurt another child after viewing videotaped sections of aggressive or neutral television programmes. The boys and girls were in two age groups: 5 to 6, and 8 to 9. The aggressive programme consisted of segments of *The Untouchables*, while the neutral programme featured an athletics race. The main findings were that the children who viewed the aggressive programme demonstrated a greater willingness to hurt another child.

It is clear from experimental studies such as these that we can produce an increase in aggressive behaviour following a fairly brief exposure to televised violence, but the question remains over whether the heightened aggression observed in the laboratory would spill over into everyday life. To investigate this it is necessary to study the impact of violence in the media in more natural settings.

Field experiments

Concerns about external (ecological) validity have stimulated researchers to employ field experiments. Field experiments retain the advantages of experimental design, but avoid the problem of demand cues since subjects do not usually know they are being studied. In the typical field experiment, the investigator presents television programmes in the normal viewing setting and observes behaviour where it naturally occurs. The investigator typically controls the television diet of the participants by arranging a special series of programmes.

Stein and Friedrich (1972) presented 97 preschool children with a diet of either 'antisocial', 'prosocial' or 'neutral' television programmes during a four-week viewing period. The antisocial diet consisted of 12 half-hour episodes of *Batman* and *Superman* cartoons. The prosocial diet was composed of 12 episodes of *Mr Rogers' Neighbourhood* (a programme that stresses such themes as sharing possessions and cooperative play). The neutral diet consisted of children's programming which was neither violent nor prosocial. The children were observed through a nine-week period, which consisted of three weeks of pre-viewing baseline, four weeks of television exposure and two weeks of postviewing follow-up. All observations were conducted in a naturalistic setting while the children engaged in daily school activities. The observers recorded various forms of behaviour that could be regarded as prosocial (helping, sharing, cooperative play) or antisocial (i.e. pushing, arguing and breaking toys). The overall results indicated that children who were judged to be initially somewhat aggressive became significantly more so as a result of viewing the *Batman* and *Superman* cartoons. Moreover, the children who had viewed the prosocial diet of *Mr Rogers' Neighbourhood* were less aggressive, more cooperative and more willing to share with other children.

Parke *et al.* (1977) found similar heightened aggression among both American and Belgian teenage boys following exposure to aggressive films. In the Belgian study, teenage boys living in a minimum-security institution were presented with a diet of either aggressive or neutral films. This study included a one-week baseline observation period, followed by one week of film viewing, and a one-week postviewing observation period. There were four cottages involved. Two cottages contained boys with high levels of aggressive behaviour; two contained boys with low levels of aggression. One of each pair of cottages was assigned to the aggressive film condition, while the other two viewed the neutral films. Only the boys in the initially high-aggressive cottage who saw the aggressive movies increased their level of aggression. Those who were exposed to the neutral films reduced their level of aggression.

The results of field experiments have been examined in at least three meta-analyses. Hearold's (1986) revealed an effect for laboratory experiments but no effect for field experiments. Wood *et al.*'s meta-analysis (1991) found that adolescents and child participants engaged in more aggression following exposure to violent films, while in seven studies participants in the control group engaged in more aggression. In five of the studies there was no difference between control and experimental groups.

Natural experiments

These studies take advantage of the fact that television was introduced at different times in different locations. They assume that people who are exposed to television will also be exposed to a high dose of television violence. This is probably a reasonable assumption given the extremely high correlation between television viewing and exposure to television violence (Milavsky *et al.* 1982).

◆ Hennigan *et al.* (1982) compared crime rates in American cities that already had television with those that did not. No effect of the presence or absence of television was found on violent crime rates in a comparison of the two kinds of cities. Furthermore, when cities without television obtained it, there was no increase in violent crime. There *was* an increase in the incidence of robberies, which the authors attributed to the relative deprivation suffered by viewers observing affluent people on television.

◆ Williams (1986) had the opportunity to evaluate the impact of televised violence on the behaviour of children before and after the introduction of television in a Canadian community. They compared children living in the before/after television town with their peers in two other towns where television was well established. The three towns were called Notel (no television reception), Unitel (receiving only the government-owned commercial channel, CBC) and Multitel (receiving the CBC and three American commercial networks). Children in all three towns were evaluated at Time 1 when Notel did not receive a television signal and again at Time 2 when Notel had had television for two years (it had received CBC). Results indicated that there were no differences across the three towns at Time 1, but at Time 2 the children from the former Notel town were significantly more aggressive, both physically and verbally, than the children in the Unitel or Multitel towns. Moreover, only children in the Notel town manifested any significant increase in physical and verbal aggression from Time 1 to Time 2.

◆ Centerwall (1989) examined the relationship between murder rates and the introduction of television in three countries: South Africa, Canada and the United States. Television was introduced in South Africa in 1975, about 25 years after Canada and the United States. The murder rate among Whites increased dramatically in the United States and Canada about 15 years after the introduction of television, when the first generation of children who had access to television were entering adulthood. The murder rate among Whites declined slightly in South Africa in the 15 years after the introduction of television. While Centerwall ruled out some confounding factors (e.g. differences in economic development), it is difficult to explain these findings, given the many differences between the countries involved. In addition, Centerwall could not determine at the time he wrote whether the level of violence had increased 15 years after the introduction of television in South Africa; thus an important piece of evidence was missing (Felson 1996).

The methodological limitations of these studies make it difficult to have confidence in a causal inference about media effects. The substantial differences between the comparison groups increase the risk that the relationship between the introduction of television and increases in aggression is spurious.

Longitudinal studies

We get a clearer picture about the extent of television violence effects when we examine exposure over a much longer period. The long-term influence of television has not been extensively investigated but there is evidence from several major studies.

◆ Lefkowitz et al. (1972) were able to demonstrate long-term effects in a group of children followed up over a ten-year period. In an initial study, Researchers had previously demonstrated a relationship between preference for violent media

and the aggressive behaviour of these children at the age of 8. The investigators obtained peer-rated measures of aggressive behaviour and preferences for various kinds of television, radio and comic books when the children were 8 years old. Ten years later, when the members of the group were 18 years old, the investigators again obtained measures of aggressive behaviour and television programme preferences. The results for boys indicated that preference for television violence at age 8 was significantly related to aggression at age 8, but that preference for television violence at age 18 was not related to aggression at age 18. A second important finding was the significant relationship, for boys, between preference for violent media at age 8 and aggressive behaviour at age 18. Preference for violent television programmes at 18, however, was not related to aggressive behaviour in early childhood.

◆ A study by Belson (1978) helped to pin down which types of programme would have the most influence. Belson interviewed 1,565 youths who were a representative sample of 13- to 17-year-old boys living in London. These boys were interviewed on several occasions concerning the extent of their exposure to a selection of violent television programmes broadcast during the period 1959 to 1971. The level and type of violence in these programmes were rated by members of the BBC viewing panel. It was thus possible to obtain, for each boy, a measure of both the magnitude and type of exposure to televised violence (realistic, fictional, etc.). When Belson compared the behaviour of boys who had higher exposure to televised violence to those who had a lower exposure, he found that the high-violence viewers were more involved in serious violent behaviour. Moreover, he found that serious interpersonal violence is increased by the long-term exposure to (in descending order of importance):

MTV's Video Violence

Of over 500 music videos sampled in a US study, a significantly high percentage contained one or more episodes of overt violence or weapon-carrying. In fact, over one quarter of MTV music videos contained images of 'overt violence'. Rock and rap videos were most likely to contain violent imagery, with young Black men 'over-represented [and] engaging in these violent behaviours'. Although African Americans make up just 15 per cent of the US population, the study found Black characters depicted in over half of the videos that were classified as violent or weapons oriented. The authors believe that although teenagers crave 'anti-establishment' messages from their music idols, 'these videos reinforce negative stereotypes about violence and weapon carrying among adolescent and young adult African-American males'.

Source: *Archives of Pediatric and Adolescent Medicine* (1997, 151, pp. 441–2)

1 plays or films in which personal relationships are a major theme and which feature verbal or physical violence

2 programmes in which violence seems to be thrown in for its own sake or is not necessary to the plot

3 programmes featuring fictional violence of a realistic nature

4 programmes in which the violence is presented as being in a good cause

5 violent westerns.

It is notable that no significant relationships between early viewing exposure and later aggression were obtained for girls.

The mediating effects on TV violence

While the effects of television violence are not simple and straightforward, meta-analyses and reviews of a large body of research suggest that there are clear reasons for concern and caution about the impact of televised violence. There are many factors that moderate the relationship between viewing violence and aggressive behaviour.

A study by Brown and Pennell (1998) discovered some of these important moderating variables. This study was interested not in the simple question of whether television influenced violent behaviour, but in the *reasons* why sometimes it did and sometimes it did not. Groups of offenders and nonoffenders were shown a violent film and then monitored over a ten-month period after the film. The main results were as follows:

◆ More differences were found between offenders and nonoffenders than between violent offenders and nonviolent offenders in terms of film viewing preferences and reactions to violent films.

◆ Offenders spent longer watching video films than nonoffenders. Violent offenders were more likely than nonviolent offenders to prefer violent films.

◆ Ten months after viewing a violent video, twice as many offenders as nonoffenders recalled and identified with vindictively violent characters.

◆ Offenders had a lower level of moral development than nonoffenders, were less able to empathize with others, and were more likely to have aggressive temperaments and distorted perceptions about violence.

◆ The findings suggest that individuals from violent families are more prone to offending behaviour and having a preference for violent films.

Studies such as this suggest that although media violence may be demonstrated to have an effect in

some people, this is more a result of other factors related to the viewers themselves. These include an individual's perception of and preference for violence; level of the viewer's moral development and their family background.

Some possible explanations of media effects

Cognitive priming

Aggressive ideas in violent films can activate other aggressive thoughts in viewers through their association in memory pathways (Berkowitz 1984). Immediately after a violent film, the viewer is primed to respond aggressively because a network of memories involving aggression is retrieved. Huesmann (1982) suggests that children learn problem-solving scripts in part from their observations of others' behaviour. These scripts are cognitive expectations about a sequence of behaviours that may be performed in particular situations. Frequent exposure to scenes of violence may lead children to store scripts for aggressive behaviour in their memories, and these may be recalled in a later situation if any aspect of the original situation – even a superficial one – is present.

Television viewing as a routine activity

Crime should be less frequent when the routine activities of potential offenders and victims reduce their opportunities for contact. Since people watch television at home, the opportunities for violence, at least with people outside the family, are probably reduced. Messner (1986) found that cities with high levels of television viewing have lower rates of both violent and nonviolent crime.

Theoretical explanations involving socialization

It is widely believed that people are more violent because they learn to be violent from their parents, their peers and the mass media. There are a variety of reasons why one might expect viewers to learn aggressive behaviour from the media (Bandura 1986). These are expanded below.

◆ *Learning novel forms of behaviour* – Bandura has argued that television can shape the forms that aggressive behaviour takes. Television can teach skills that may be useful for committing acts of violence, and it can direct the viewer's attention to behaviours that they may not have considered. For example, young people may mimic martial arts moves, or they may learn effective tactics for committing violent crime. There is frequent anecdotal evidence that bizarre violent events have followed soon after their depiction on television, suggesting a form of copycat behaviour (see *In Focus*).

◆ *Vicarious reinforcement and legitimations* – Bandura also suggested that television might inform viewers of the positive and negative consequences of violent behaviour. Audiences can be expected to imitate violent behaviour that is successful in gaining the model's objectives in fictional or nonfictional programmes. When violence is justified or left unpunished on television, the viewer's guilt or concern about consequences is reduced. It is not at all clear, however, what message is learned from viewing violence on television. In most plots, the hero uses violence for legitimate ends while the villain engages in illegitimate violence. The consequences of the illegitimate violence portrayed in fictional television and film are more negative than the consequences of illegitimate violence in real life. In real life, violent people often evade punishment, while in television, the villain is almost always punished. Thus, one could argue that television violence might reduce the incidence of criminal violence, since crime doesn't pay for TV criminals.

◆ *Creating unrealistic fear* – Bandura (1986) claims that television distorts knowledge about the dangers and threats present in the real world. Research shows that heavy television viewers are more distrustful of others and overestimate their chances of being criminally victimized (Gunter 1994). The assumption is that these fears will lead viewers to perceive threats that do not exist and to respond aggressively. It is just as plausible, however, that such fears would lead viewers to avoid aggressive behaviour against others, if they feel it is dangerous. If viewing television violence increases fear, it might decrease the level of violence.

◆ *Desensitization* – This argument assumes that anxiety about violence inhibits its use. Frequent viewing of television violence may cause viewers to be less anxious and sensitive about violence. Therefore, someone who becomes desensitized to violence may perceive it as more 'normal' and be more likely to engage in violence themselves. However, if viewers are exposed to a heavy diet of television violence, one might also argue that they will be less aroused by violence and therefore less likely to engage in violent behaviour themselves. If viewers become desensitized to violent behaviour on television, they may become indifferent to its message. Desensitization could therefore *weaken* the effect of a heavy diet of television violence.

Problems with the effects model of media violence

The media effects model tackles the problem of explaining violent behaviour 'backwards', beginning with the media content and using that to explain the behaviour of offenders. To explain violence in society, researchers should, perhaps, begin with those who perpetrate it.

Hagell and Newburn (1994) found that young offenders watched *less* television and video than their nonoffending counterparts, had less access to the

---

in focus

Violent video games

There has been a great deal of debate about the violent content of many video games and their potential to influence children's aggressive behaviour. From a theoretical point of view, violent video games might promote aggressive tendencies (a prediction of social learning theory) because they offer children the opportunity to imitate what they have seen on screen. An alternative perspective (known as catharsis theory) would suggest that violent video games offer a channel to express aggressive tendencies through game play, and therefore would lower levels of aggressive behaviour in real life. Griffiths (1998) suggests that the actual evidence offers a less than clear-cut confirmation of either perspective. Experimental studies (e.g. Lynch 1994) have tended to focus on fantasy aggression (i.e. involving aggression against fantasy characters) rather than real aggression. The increased levels of fantasy aggression found in these studies is consistent with the catharsis explanation, but the fact that laboratory studies cannot study *real* aggressive behaviour (for obvious ethical reasons) limits their usefulness in this debate.

Observational studies (e.g. Irwin and Gross 1995) do seem to suggest that playing violent video games increases a child's aggressive behaviour, at least in the short term, a finding that lends more support to social learning theory. Griffiths argues that violent video games have a more pronounced effect on young children, but far less an effect on teenagers and no apparent effect on adults. The fact that most studies have discovered only short-term effects has also limited the clarity of the debate. Research on the long-term effects of exposure to violent video games is noticeably lacking and at present, argues Griffiths, entirely speculative.

technology in the first place and had no particular interest in specifically violent programmes.

Psychological research into media effects has tended to represent young media users as 'the inept victims of products, which ... can trick children into all kinds of ill-advised behaviour' (Gauntlett 1998). Research which seeks to establish exactly what children can and do understand about the media has shown that children are able to talk intelligently (and cynically) about the media (Buckingham 1996) and that children as young as 7 are able to make thoughtful, critical and 'media literate' productions themselves.

Whilst it is undoubtedly true that gratuitous depictions of violence could be seen as unpleasant and unnecessary, it cannot be assumed that violence is always shown for 'bad reasons' or in an uncritical light. Even the most obviously gratuitous acts of violence (such as those committed by Beavis and Butthead) can be interpreted as 'rationally resistant reactions to an oppressive world which has little to offer them' (Gauntlett 1997).

Because effective studies of media effects require significant amounts of time and money, many studies are limited to much simpler investigations which are usually characterized by elements of artificiality. Some of these studies take place in a laboratory setting or in a 'natural' setting where the researcher has conspicuously manipulated some aspect of the viewing environment. Research participants are then shown specially selected or recorded clips, which lack the narrative meaning present in everyday TV productions.

Many other studies that do not rely on experimental manipulations show inconsistencies and contradictions in their interpretation of the data they have achieved. For example, Eron *et al.* (1972) found that the media had a marginal effect for boys but no effect for girls, yet a study by the same researchers (Huesmann *et al.* 1984) found the exact opposite (no effect on boys, but a small effect on girls). Another misuse of methodology comes about when studies which merely show a correlation between two factors are treated as if one has caused the other.

The kinds of media violence which are typically condemned by the effects model are limited to fictional programmes. The acts of violence that appear daily on our television screens on news programmes are somehow exempt from this condemnation. There is an inconsistency to this argument. If the antisocial acts that are shown in television drama have such a profound effect on viewers, it is puzzling that the antisocial activities that are so frequently in the news and other documentaries do not have similar effects. This is even more puzzling when we consider the fact that in fictional drama, the majority of antisocial acts have negative consequences for the perpetrator, but in documentary

depictions of violent acts there are few apparent negative consequences for those who perform them.

The basic question of why the media should induce people to imitate its content has never been answered. Likewise, the question of how merely seeing a violent act in the media would prompt an individual to behave in a similar way is just as unresolved, particularly as violent acts in the media more often than not produce negative consequences for the perpetrator.

The lack of a firm theory that might explain *why* the media would have such effects has led to the effects model being based on the variety of assumptions detailed above – that the media (not violent people) should be the starting point for research; that children will be unable to 'cope' with violent media; that the model's predictions are verifiable by scientific research; that screen fiction is of concern whilst news pictures are not. Each of these assumptions has been shown to be problematic and has exposed the failure of media effects commentators to embed their model in any coherent theory (Gauntlett 1998).

Activity 6: **Researching media violence**

Use the Center for Media Literacy's website given at the end of this chapter. Visit a number of sites concerned with media violence. Gather together some arguments for and against the view that the media influences aggressive behaviour in children.

Exam summary: Media influences on pro- and antisocial behaviour

The AQA examination will test your understanding of the following areas:

◆ explanations and research studies of media influences on prosocial behaviour (pp. 78–80)

◆ explanations and research studies of media influences on antisocial behaviour (pp. 80–6).

Example question

The question below is typical of one drawn from the material above, and should take you 30 minutes to answer:

◆ Discuss the view that the media might influence antisocial behaviour. *(24 marks)*

Suggested answer structure:

This question invites you to consider carefully the proposition that the media somehow influences the antisocial behaviour of those who are exposed to it. Although we have concentrated mostly on television and video, the definition of media is much wider than that and would include computer games, pornography and even cartoons. We have also defined antisocial behaviour in terms of aggression, although there are many other forms of antisocial behaviour (such as discrimination or selfishness) that may also be influenced by exposure to the media. There is such a lot to write about that careful planning is essential if you are not to become embroiled in the wide choice of literature available. You cannot include everything, and so you must be *selective*, remembering that the highest marks are given for answers that show a balance between depth and breadth of coverage.

We have examined a number of different research 'types', such as *correlational studies* (p. 80–1), *experimental studies in the laboratory* (p. 81), *field experiments* (p. 82), *natural experiments* (pp. 82–3) and *longitudinal studies* (pp. 83–4). We have also looked at more recent studies that have investigated the mediating effects on TV violence.

As well as examining research studies of the media/antisocial behaviour, we have also covered some possible explanations of media effects. These include the notion of *cognitive priming* (p. 84), *television viewing as routine activity* (p. 84), and a range of theoretical explanations involving various aspects of *socialization* (pp. 84–5).

As the term 'discuss' also requires you to offer some *evaluation* of the explanations and research studies offered, you should allow half of your writing time for just that. Evaluation of the media effects model (i.e. the view that the media directly *affects* the behaviour of those who watch it) can be found on pp. 85–6, although evaluation of media research can also be found in the various *In Focus* boxes in this section. In 'Moral panics' (p. 80), Guy Cumberbatch takes issue with some of the research studies that have claimed a link between media violence and violent behaviour in children. In 'Violent video games' (p. 85), Mark Griffiths suggests that research evidence relating to the effects of playing violent video games has failed to confirm that this has noticeable harmful *or* beneficial effects, and concludes that research on the long-term effects of exposure to this medium is entirely speculative.

Chapter summary

◆ **Social psychological theories of aggression** stress the role of factors outside the organism in determining aggressive behaviour.

◆ The **social learning theory** of aggression sees aggressive behaviour as being learned either through direct experience or by observing others who model it.

◆ **Deindividuation theory** explains aggression as a result of a temporary loss of personal identifiability which may result in an increased tendency to act in antisocial ways.

◆ **Relative deprivation theory** explains aggression as being the result of an unacceptable discrepancy between what people think they have the right to expect and what they realistically are likely to achieve.

◆ Aggression may be a response to **stressors in the environment**. These include temperature, noise and crowding. Although research is inconclusive concerning the negative effects of these stressors, it does suggest that they are more likely if people feel they do not have control over the source of the stress.

◆ Explanations of **human altruism** differ according to whether prosocial behaviour is seen as a product of personal distress (egoistic behaviour) or empathic concern (altruistic behaviour). Cialdini *et al.*'s

negative-state relief model is an example of the former, and Batson's **empathy-altruism** model an example of the latter.

◆ The tendency to help in an emergency may be lessened by the presence of others if diffusion of responsibility occurs.

◆ Theoretical explanations of **bystander behaviour** focus on the decision-making stages that bystanders must go through before deciding whether to help. Latané and Darley's model focuses on the cognitive interpretation of the incident and our possible role in helping, whereas Piliavin *et al.*'s arousal:cost-reward model emphasizes a more egoistic concern with the costs and benefits of helping.

◆ Comparisons of **different cultures** concerning their **prosocial behaviours** have typically focused on the differences between individualist and collectivist cultures. The behavioural differences of individuals may be interpreted in terms of the dominant cultural characteristics of their society.

◆ Although the vast majority of research studies have focused on the **antisocial influences of the media**, a number of studies have suggested the **media's potential as a source of prosocial socialization**. The effectiveness of the media in this role is determined by the way in which prosocial behaviours are modelled.

◆ Research into the potential antisocial effects of the media has not always produced consistent results, although many do suggest a relationship between exposure to media violence and violent behaviour.

◆ Possible explanations of the media–violence relationship include the idea that children learn aggressive scripts from television or they become desensitized as a result of their exposure to violence in the media.

◆ The media effects model is criticized for being based on problematic assumptions about the media and its viewers.

Further resources

Hogg, M.A. and Vaughan, G.M. (1998) *Social Psychology* (2nd edn) London: Prentice Hall.

Although this is an undergraduate text on social psychology, it is very readable and provides a lot of extra detail on the topics in this chapter.

Moghaddam, F.M. (1998) *Social Psychology: Exploring Universals across Cultures*, New York: W.H. Freeman.

A good source of information on aggression and prosocial behaviour, particularly on cultural differences in prosocial behaviour.

Gunter, B. and McAleer, J. (1997) *Children and Television* (2nd edn), London: Routledge.

A comprehensive text dealing with both the antisocial and prosocial effects of television.

Websites

http://search.britannica.com

A searchable site that will take you to lots of fascinating information, definitions and news articles relating to aggressive and altruistic behaviour.

http://www.medialit.org/Violence/indexviol.htm

This is part of the Center for Media Literacy's website, and has numerous links to other sites that are relevant to the media violence debate.

Part 2: Physiological Psychology

A2

BRAIN AND BEHAVIOUR

Simon Green

BIOLOGICAL RHYTHMS, SLEEP AND DREAMING

Simon Green

MOTIVATION AND EMOTION

Simon Green

Chapter 4

Brain and behaviour

Simon Green

Preview

In this chapter we shall be looking at:

◆ various methods used to investigate how the brain works, including invasive and noninvasive methods

◆ the localization of function in the cerebral cortex, including the primary motor, sensory and association areas, and alternative approaches, including distribution functions

◆ the lateralization of functions, such as language, in the cerebral cortex.

Introduction

The functions of the cortex represent the final frontier for neuroscientists. It is the most complex of brain structures, containing over 90 per cent of all the neurons of the forebrain, and is involved in all our higher cognitive abilities, as well as attributes such as consciousness and personality. Although we know a reasonable amount about some functions, such as sensation, perception and language, others remain mysterious. It is also unusual in that some aspects of cortical organization are specifically human, related to the evolution of language, while others, such as sensation and perception, can be modelled using findings from work with animals.

In this chapter we cover some of the methods used to investigate the brain and then review the distribution of functions across the cortex. This is followed by a detailed description of the lateralization of some brain functions, including the pioneering work of Sperry on the split-brain.

Methods used to investigate brain function

How do you know where you are?

Many of the procedures used today by brain researchers involve implanting electrodes (usually made of very thin wire) accurately into the brain. In other areas, too, such as neurosurgery (performing operations on the brain), there is a need to know exactly where structures are located within the brain. For humans and all experimental animals, we now have stereotaxic atlases; when the skull is fixed (painlessly) in a rigid steel frame, or *stereotax,* the atlas can be used to provide three-dimensional coordinates for any brain structure. The surgeon or researcher can then carry out their procedure confident that they are in the correct area.

The two basic processes underlying information transmission in the nervous system are electrical conduction along the neuron, and chemical transmission across the synapse. In order to better understand methods used to investigate the brain, we will briefly review these processes.

Neurons and electrical transmission

Neurons are usually elongated (see Fig. 4.1), with a set of short processes on one side of the cell body (the *dendrites*) and a single longer branching process on the other (the *axon*). The cell body contains the *nucleus,* in which we find the *chromosomes,* the genetic material. Every cell in the body contains an identical set of chromosomes, and, besides allowing us to pass characteristics on to our offspring, the genetic material controls the activity of the cell containing it.

The outer covering of the neuron is the cell membrane. This is a complicated layered structure made up of protein and fat molecules, and is crucial to information transmission. The fluid inside the neuron (*cytoplasm*) and the fluid surrounding it (*extra-cellular fluid*) contain concentrations of electrically charged particles known as ions, and which include positively charged ions such as potassium and sodium, and negatively charged ions such as chloride. When the membrane is in its resting state, the high concentration of potassium ions inside, and the high concentration of

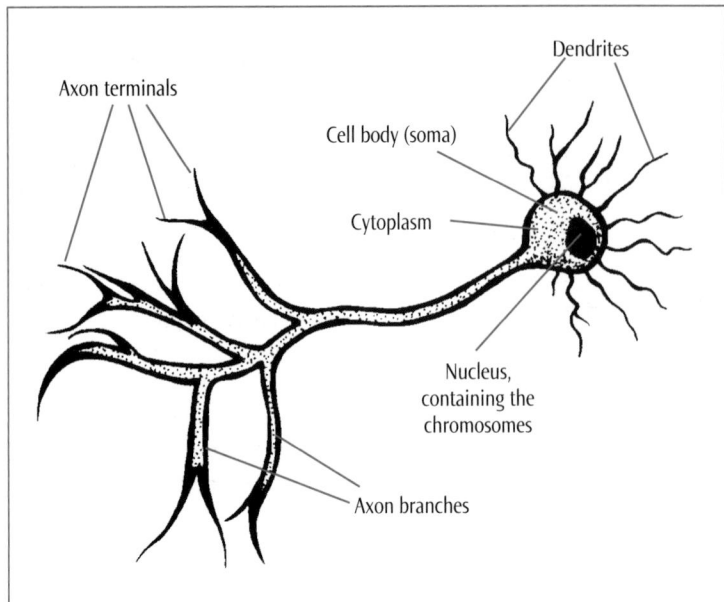

Figure 4.1 Standard neuron

sodium and chloride ions outside, produce an imbalance in the electrical charge across the membrane. This is called the *resting electrical potential*, and is measured at −70 millivolts (a millivolt is a thousandth of a volt).

When the membrane is disturbed, channels within it open and sodium ions rush into the neuron from outside to in. This causes a sudden and radical shift in the resting potential from −70 to +40 millivolts (see Fig. 4.2); after peaking at +40 mv, the membrane returns to its resting state, the whole process taking about 4 milliseconds. This rapid and violent swing in the membrane potential is called the *action potential* or *nerve impulse*. It is another feature of the structure of the cell membrane that when an action potential is produced by some sort of stimulation at one point on the membrane, it automatically travels along the membrane, a process called *propagation*. A thin wire or glass electrode can be used to record the action potential at one point on the cell membrane as a momentary blip of electrical potential. Before and after the action potential or nerve impulse, that point on the membrane is at its resting potential. If nerve impulses are repeatedly stimulated, they travel in sequence along the membrane, and will be recorded by our electrode as a

sequence of blips. As each nerve impulse disturbs the membrane for about 4 msecs, then the maximum rate of impulse transmission is about 250 per second.

Many neurons in the nervous system operate in this way. However, others have become modified to allow even higher rates of transmission. These neurons, including most of those in the brain, have axons covered in a fatty layer called a *myelin sheath* (see Fig. 4.3). At intervals in the sheath the axon membrane is exposed: these points are called *Nodes of Ranvier*, and by complicated electrical processes the nerve impulse can 'jump' from node to node. This is known as *saltatory conduction*, and is much faster than conventional propagation of impulses along the neuronal membrane. Faster transmission clearly increases the rate of information processing, and myelination was an important step in the evolution of advanced brains.

Each impulse, wherever recorded, has exactly the same electrical properties as any other. This is important as we know that information handled by the nervous system, which is in effect everything it does, including sensation and perception, memory, language, thought, emotion, personality, movement, and control of the body's physiological systems, is coded by these

Figure 4.2 Action potential

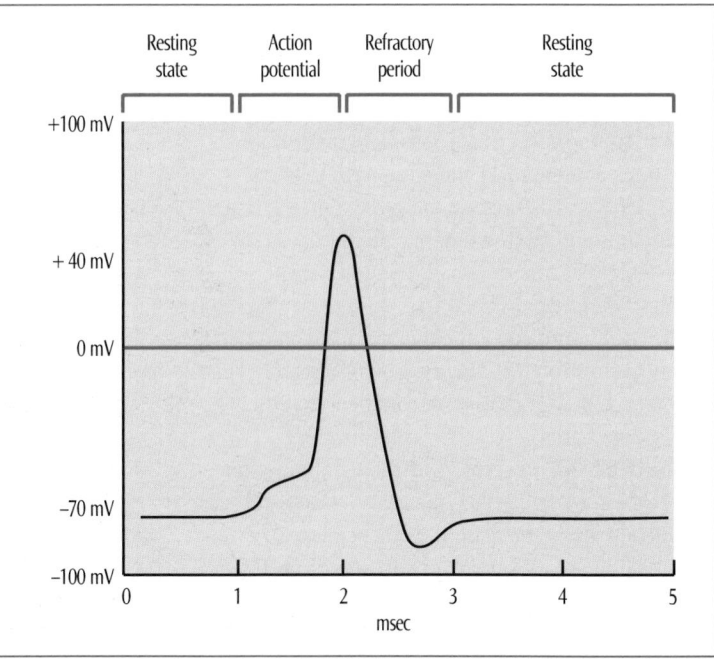

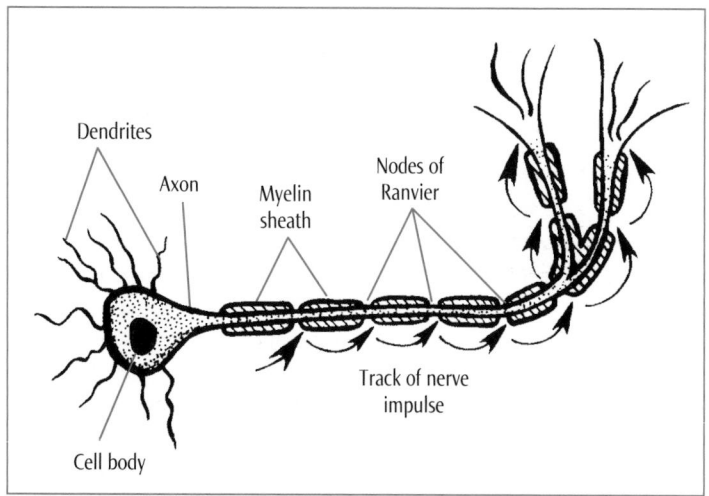

Figure 4.3 Myelinated neuron (saltatory conduction)

The synapse

These gaps between neurons, usually separating the end of an axonal branch from a dendritic surface, are minute. Only visible under the electron microscope, they are measured in microns (billionths of a metre), but even so they represent a physical gap which the electrical nerve impulse cannot cross. Conduction or transmission across the synapse has to involve other processes, and these are chemical in nature.

Within the end of each axon branch (the presynaptic terminal) are sets of *vesicles*, spherical structures containing molecules of chemicals called neurotransmitters (see Fig. 4.4). When nerve impulses travelling along the axon reach the presynaptic terminal, vesicles are stimulated to move to the end membrane of the terminal. Their chemical structure allows them to merge with the membrane, and as they do so their contents, the neurotransmitters, are released into the synaptic gap. Because the gap is so small, the molecules of neurotransmitter can drift or diffuse over to the membrane of the dendrite. On this postsynaptic membrane we find *receptors*. These are molecules attached to the membrane, with a structure that matches that of the neurotransmitter molecule in the same way that the shape of keys fits the appropriate lock. Neurotransmitter molecules attach themselves to receptors and, although the combination is very brief, this is sufficient to disturb the postsynaptic membrane,

signals. As they are electrically identical, then different types of information must be coded by the frequency and patterning of impulses (i.e. whether they come in steady streams or in bursts of activity), and where in the nervous system they occur.

Information in the nervous system is carried along neurons in the form of trains or sequences of nerve impulses. In the nervous system there are something of the order of a hundred billion neurons, most of them in the brain. If these neurons were physically connected, nerve impulses would automatically travel to all parts of the system, as neurons are specialized to transmit impulses and the whole system would be one enormous electrical circuit. This would not allow specialized processing in different parts of the brain, for instance, and it doesn't happen because in between neurons there is a tiny gap, called the *synapse*.

Figure 4.4 Synapse

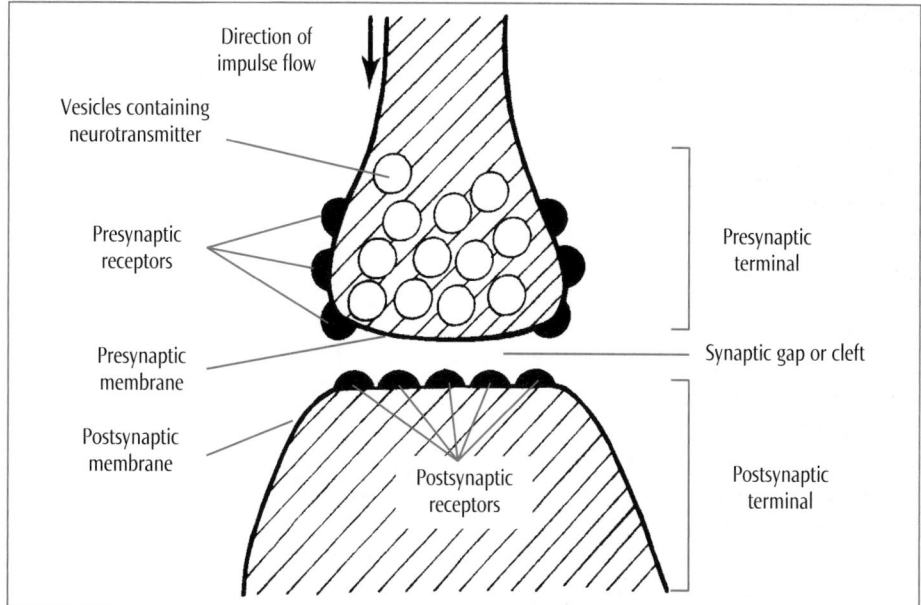

allowing ions to pass through it. This passage of ions is the basis of the nerve impulse, as described earlier, but the combination of a single molecule with a single receptor is not enough to shift the membrane potential very far from its resting state, and a nerve impulse is not stimulated.

For this to happen, a minimum number of combinations must take place in the same region of the postsynaptic membrane, which then disturbs the resting potential sufficiently for an action potential to be triggered. Action potentials, or nerve impulses, are all-or-none events in the sense that they either happen or do not happen. For the minimum number of combinations to occur, there must be an adequate frequency of nerve impulses arriving at the presynaptic terminal in a short space of time, so releasing the necessary amount of neurotransmitter. If a nerve impulse is not triggered in the postsynaptic neuron, then the information coded by activity in the presynaptic neuron is lost.

Activity in the postsynaptic neuron cannot easily be predicted by activity in the presynaptic neuron, and we can see that this change in the frequency and patterning of impulses as they cross (or do not cross) the synapse is a vital aspect of information processing in the brain. It is an opportunity for information, in the form of nerve impulses, to be integrated with other pathways, lost (when they do not cross the synapse), or processed in other complex ways. It is also important to remember that although a single synapse can seem fairly straightforward in operation, their overall organization is not. The 100 billion or so neurons in the nervous system make on average about a thousand synaptic connections each, so the complications of the neuronal network are almost unimaginable.

A final important aspect of chemical conduction across the synapse is the nature of the neurotransmitters. As a general rule, each neuron contains only one of these chemicals, and across all the neurons and synapses in the nervous system there are only about 20 to 30 of them. The ones of most interest to psychologists are those linked to particular aspects of behaviour, and there are about ten of these. You will meet some of them in other parts of the course, for instance, the relationship between schizophrenia and the neurotransmitter dopamine (see Chapter 17).

This outline of electrical and chemical neurotransmission in the nervous system serves as a background to the types of methods used in investigating brain function. We begin with those techniques directly linked to electrical activity.

Electrical stimulation and recording

There are by now many examples of how thin wire electrodes can be used to stimulate brain neurons artificially in order to produce effects on behaviour. The currents used have to be in the range found in the brain (thousandths of an amp), but as the brain does not possess pain receptors, this technique can be used in conscious human patients as well as in nonhuman animals. For instance, Penfield (1958) stimulated the temporal lobe in humans and some patients reported experiencing very vivid memories from their childhood. Stimulation in the visual cortex can produce a sensation of flashes of light; similarly, auditory cortex stimulation may lead to a 'buzzing' sound sensation. Movement of skeletal muscles can be produced by electrical stimulation of the motor cortex.

Besides trying to mimic the brain's natural electrical activity, we can also record it. Thin electrodes can record the activity of single neurons (single unit recording), a procedure which has proved invaluable in the study of, for instance, the visual cortex. Larger electrodes record from clusters of thousands or millions of neurons and often involve measuring evoked potentials (nowadays referred to as *event-related potentials* or ERPs). These are neuronal responses correlated with the regular presentation of stimuli such as light flashes or auditory tones. As there is so much background electrical 'noise' in the brain, the response to a single stimulus does not stand out, so a computer is used to analyse the responses evoked by a series of stimuli and the characteristic evoked potential emerges from this analysis. This can be used to identify areas of the brain involved in sensory processes and selective attention.

The *electroencephalograph* (EEG), introduced by Berger in 1929, records the electrical activity of billions of cortical neurons using a number of small metal electrodes on the surface of the skull. This has the advantage of being a *noninvasive* procedure, with no need to penetrate brain tissue itself. The disadvantage is that we are still not sure how the activity of all those neurons combines to produce the final EEG pattern. In addition, the electrical signals from neurons are distorted as they pass through the skull to be recorded by the electrodes, making interpretation more difficult.

We do know that an EEG can be *synchronized*, with a recognizable and repeated wave form, or *desynchronized* with an apparently random pattern of waves and spikes. It also has a frequency, or number of waves or spikes per second (measured as hertz). Certain patterns correlate highly with behavioural states; alertness and activity produce a fast desynchronized EEG, while drowsiness leads to a synchronized pattern called the *alpha rhythm*, with a frequency of 8 to 12 hertz. Wave frequency gradually slows as you fall asleep, but is then interrupted by the faster desynchronized EEG of REM sleep (see Chapter 5 for more detail).

Strengths and limitations of electrical stimulation and recording

Since the early 1900s, electrical stimulation and recording have provided a huge amount of information on brain function. The invasive procedures of single unit recording and stimulating have mainly involved nonhuman animals, and there is always the problem of extrapolating to the human brain. Where the visual system, for instance, is concerned, work on nonhuman primates has been largely confirmed by studies of humans with visual defects, and much of our knowledge of our sensory and motor systems has come from animal work. However, in the area of cognitive functions, such as memory, planning and problem-solving, our capabilities are so different from other animals that extrapolating is far less justified.

As procedures in humans have, for ethical reasons, to be noninvasive, only the event-related potential and the EEG are regularly recorded in human participants. These have provided insights into such areas as sleep and attentional processes. Electrical recording has the advantage that it is in 'real time'; as neurons produce electrical impulses, so they are directly recorded and we have a moment-by-moment picture of brain activity. This is why ERPs can be used to investigate the rapid processing underlying selective attention. However, a problem with interpretation is that in the case of the EEG, we do not know how the electrical activity of populations of neurons combines to form the overall EEG recording. So localizing observed EEG phenomena to particular regions of the brain is virtually impossible.

Event-related potentials are more specific, and in fact by presenting trains of stimuli and recording the responses in different areas of the brain, we can generate models of where in the brain different aspects of attention and perception occur. Precise localization is still difficult, and the need to present stimuli repeatedly in order to identify ERPs means that this technique is only suitable for certain types of study: for instance, investigating sensory processes.

Chemical stimulation and recording

Earlier, we briefly reviewed chemical conduction across the synapse. Many of the most dramatic effects of drugs on behaviour can be explained by our knowledge of how they act at the synapse. As a given synapse will involve a specific neurotransmitter and its specialized postsynaptic receptors, we can design drugs which are highly specific for particular categories of these synaptic receptors; either they can stimulate the receptor (*stimulants* or *agonists* – these drugs usually have a structure very similar to the natural neurotransmitter), or, by combining with the receptor, they inactivate it (*blockers* or *antagonists*). So if we wish to investigate the

role of dopamine synapses in behaviour, we can give animals drugs which specifically stimulate or block dopamine receptors. By observing the behavioural effects, we can then draw some conclusions on what the dopamine system may be doing. Similarly, if we suspect that the acetylcholine system is involved in memory, drugs which stimulate cholinergic receptors should improve memory and learning in animals, while cholinergic antagonists, which block the receptors, should impair memory and learning. In Alzheimer's disease, known technically as *senile dementia, Alzheimer-type* (SDAT), a fairly common dementia (general breakdown in cognitive and emotional functioning) in old people, amnesia (memory failure) is a key symptom. Autopsy studies of brains of patients with SDAT show a dramatic loss of the neurotransmitter acetylcholine. It was also known from laboratory studies that acetylcholine antagonists could produce amnesia in animals such as rats and monkeys. It was then predicted that giving acetylcholine stimulant drugs to patients with SDAT might improve their memories, and this type of drug (examples include Tacrine and Aricept) is now a regular treatment for SDAT. Unfortunately, these drugs are not consistently effective, possibly because the acetylcholine neurons in the SDAT brain have degenerated too much, and the drugs do not have enough acetylcholine synapses and receptors to work on.

Another chemically-based technique is to measure levels of neurotransmitters in the brain. This is technically very difficult to do and the procedure is not common. One example in relation to Alzheimer's disease was given above and another would be the attempt to measure levels of dopamine in the brains of schizophrenics. The brain is removed at autopsy and the dopamine extracted and measured, to test the theory that schizophrenia is associated with high levels of dopamine. Few positive results have been reported, partly because most of the patients have been on drug therapy for years, which could itself upset dopamine activity. More recently, attempts have been made to use computer-based techniques such as PET scans (see later) to measure, for instance, numbers of dopamine receptors in the living brain. This would seem a more promising approach, as schizophrenic patients can be studied before they are put on drug therapy.

Strengths and limitations of chemical stimulation and recording

As discussed earlier, chemical conduction across the synapse is the second major principle of neuronal transmission of information. So you could argue that to gain a complete picture of brain function, we need to investigate the chemistry of neurotransmitters. Although the majority of the work is again on nonhuman animals, advances in our knowledge over the last 30 years have been dramatic. The recently-introduced antidepressant drugs such as Prozac (from the drug group known as selective serotonin reuptake inhibitors, or SSRIs) were developed on the basis of our increased understanding of the involvement of serotonin synapses in depression, based on the methods outlined above.

We can try to confirm our ideas on neurotrans-mitters and behaviour by observing the effects of drugs in humans; for example, observing the effectiveness of antipsychotic drugs (all of which are dopamine antagonists) in schizophrenia can help to confirm or contradict the dopamine model of schizophrenia. However, direct studies of neurotransmitters in humans are rare. Apart from the PET scanners mentioned above, studies would have to be invasive and there is no technique for doing this in living people. Thus, direct investigations of links between behaviour and neurotransmitters in humans have been scarce. Extrapolating results from nonhuman animals is one of the underpinning problems in this area.

More positively, we now have a greater understanding of how drugs work in the brain, including drugs of abuse such as alcohol, heroin, and ecstasy. This may allow us to understand their appeal, and also the problems of dependence and its treatment.

Physical destruction of brain tissue

This was the original approach to the experimental study of brain function in nonhuman animals and is still popular. At first, techniques were primitive, using needle points or knife cuts. Nowadays, localized areas of damage, or *lesions*, are usually performed using thin wire electrodes. A current is passed through which heats the tip of the electrode and the heat creates a small sphere of destruction around the tip.

Several decades ago large lesions, or *ablations*, were popular and the frontal *lobotomy* (destruction of the frontal lobe) was even used in humans as a 'treatment' for schizophrenia. As more was discovered about the links between brain structure and behaviour, interest shifted to smaller units of the brain. Whereas in the past we might have ablated the whole amygdala, now we

---

Activity 1: Lesion experiments

Lesions to the hippocampus in rats can prevent maze learning. List some of the psychological processes involved in memory and learning, such as perception, short-term and long-term memory, and retrieval. Do you think it is justified to conclude from lesion experiments that the hippocampus is the site of memory in rats?

---

would confine damage to small areas within the amygdala such as the central nucleus. One of the latest lesion techniques used in research with nonhuman animals involves chemicals called *neurotoxins*. These are specific to particular neurotransmitters, so, when injected into a part of the brain, they destroy only those neurons releasing that neurotransmitter at their synapses.

Strengths and limitations of lesion studies

The main criticism of lesion studies is that the simple notion that the effects of brain damage can be identified with the area of brain damaged is unjustified. One analogy is that of sticking a potato up a car exhaust. This stops the engine, but to conclude that the exhaust makes the engine go is obviously incorrect. However, if you perform lots of studies on car engines – remove the distributor, carburettor, pistons, etc. – and see what happens, you might eventually produce a model of how all the components interact. This is the justification for lesion studies.

The brain is infinitely more complicated that a car engine. Even a small lesion destroys not just neurons at that site, but perhaps axonal pathways travelling through. Even the destroyed neurons have connections to many other neurons, and these in turn will be affected by the damage. All neurons are part of intricate circuits, and so lesion effects are never restricted to the site of damage. Interpreting findings has to take this complexity into account.

On the other hand, lesion studies in nonhuman animals and the study of the brain-damaged human have contributed massively to our models of brain function. Broca's work on aphasia (see later), locating a speech planning area to the frontal lobe, served as a basic model of language. Building on that, we now know that other areas may be involved, partly because we now have a much better idea of the intricate nature of the interconnections of Broca's area. We pick this problem up later when we look at localization of function in the brain.

Modern noninvasive procedures

Like the EEG, these are procedures which do not require direct interference with brain tissue. The era began with computed axial tomography, or the CAT scanner, in the early 1970s. This procedure uses multiple X-rays and a computer to produce pictures of horizontal sections through the brain. A later technique was magnetic resonance imaging or MRI scanning (see Fig. 4.5). The procedure involves placing the head in a powerful magnetic field and bombarding the brain with radio waves.

Molecules in the brain vibrate in response to the radio waves and emit radio waves of their own. These are recorded, computerized and assembled into a three-

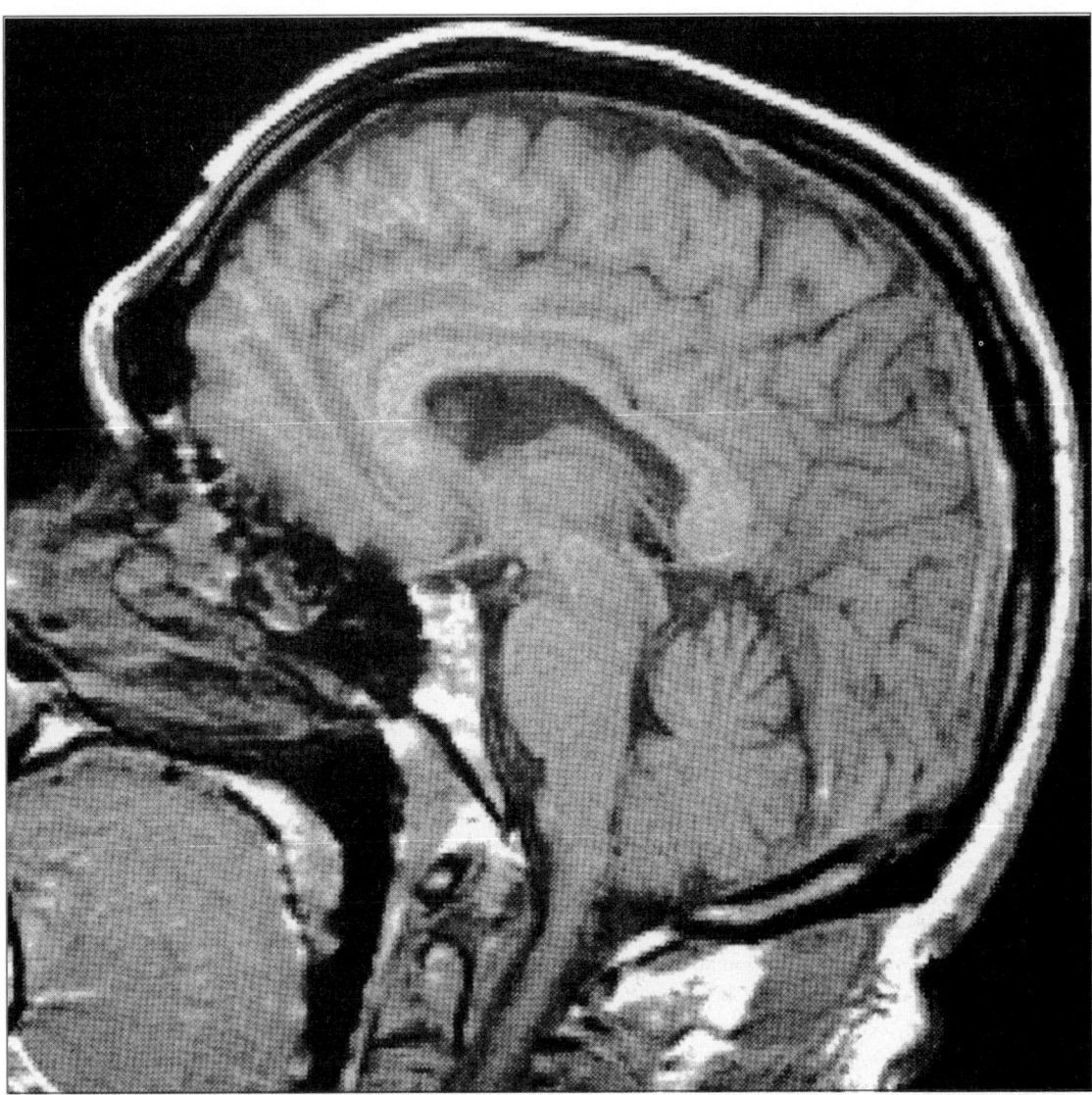

Figure 4.5 A sagittal section of a human brain using MRI scanning

dimensional picture of brain structures. The level of detail is on the whole better than with the CAT scanner and it also avoids subjecting the patient to X-rays. A more complicated but more valuable procedure is *positron emission tomography* (PET scanning). The usual procedure involves injecting radio-active glucose into the bloodstream. This reaches the brain and, as glucose is used as an energy source by cells, it is taken up by neurons. The brain is then scanned by a battery of detectors which pick up the radioactivity emitted by the glucose (doses of radioactivity are tiny and harmless); parts of the brain which are more active take up more glucose and emit more radioactivity and a computer can then draw up an activity map of the brain. The procedure can be used to identify, for instance, those parts of the brain which are most active during speech, or problem solving, or recognizing faces, etc. This ability to correlate activity in different brain areas with psychological functions makes PET scanning

the most useful of current computer-based techniques. It can also be used with radioactive chemicals which combine with synaptic receptors; measuring receptor activity can tell something about neurotransmitter function in the brain. An example would be studies of changes in dopamine and serotonin receptor numbers in schizophrenia.

One of the early problems with scanning techniques was that they took so long (up to half an hour) to produce a picture of the brain that fast psychological processes, such as those involved in selective attention or emotional reactions, could not be studied. Technical advances mean that changes in the brain correlated with psychological reactions of a few seconds can now be studied, using modern PET scanners or *functional MRI* (fMRI). A very recent addition to the battery of scanning techniques is MEG. This stands for *magnetoenecephalography*, and involves recording the tiny magnetic fields produced by active neurons. One clear advantage MEG has over other scanning techniques is that the magnetic fields are produced by nerve impulse activity so that the MEG scan reflects moment by moment neural activity in the brain, down to thousandths of a second.

Strengths and limitations of scanning techniques

It is almost impossible to overestimate the significance of scanning. Up to the early 1970s, neuropsychology and psychobiology were dominated by work with nonhuman animals. The introduction of the first scanners meant that it became possible to investigate the human brain in living participants. Initially, studies were limited to structural pictures, such as X-rays, which could show up tumours, areas of large damage after cerebral haemorrhage, or the degeneration seen in Alzheimer patients. Now we can look at function as well as structure, using PET, fMRI and MEG, and our knowledge of human brain function has increased dramatically in parallel with these technical developments. This eliminates the ethical problems of using nonhuman animals, and practical issues such as extrapolation.

The spatial resolution (i.e. how small an area of brain tissue can be identified) of scanning techniques is still not ideal, with localization only possible to the level of relatively large areas of cortical or subcortical tissue. However, this is improving significantly every year. Temporal resolution (what frequency of brain activity can be identified) has been a problem when studying the brain, which operates in milliseconds. As discussed above, the introduction of fMRI and MEG means that we can now study brain events taking place over milliseconds rather than minutes, which radically increases the range of psychological processes which we can investigate.

Other problems of scanners are more practical. PET, MRI and fMRI scanners involve recording over long periods (usually hours) with the participant's head enclosed in the tube-like scanning machine. Procedures are highly technical, expensive and time-consuming, involving as many as 30 people in a given study. MEG recording uses a net of recording electrodes over the skull, and so does away with the scanning tube. However, it is exquisitely sensitive to environmental magnetic fields and recording has to take place in magnetically-shielded laboratories, preferably at night.

Exam summary: Methods used to investigate brain function

The AQA examination will test your understanding of the following areas:

- methods used to investigate the brain, including invasive (pp. 94–6) and noninvasive methods (pp. 96–8)
- strengths and limitations of these methods.

Example question

The question below is typical of one drawn from the material above, and should take you 30 minutes to answer.

- Critically consider one invasive and one noninvasive method used to investigate the brain.   *(24 marks)*

Suggested answer structure

This section has covered three *invasive* methods of studying the brain. These are:

- *electrical stimulation and recording* (pp. 94–5)
- *chemical stimulation and recording* (pp. 95–6)
- *physical destruction of brain tissue* (p. 96).

Electrical stimulation has been used to mimic brain function, while recordings can be made from single neurons or from clusters of thousands of neurons. The electroencephalograph (EEG) records activity from the cortex. Chemical stimulation uses drugs or specially designed chemicals, while recording concentrates on measuring levels of neurotransmitters. Physical destruction of brain tissue using electrical lesions is less common now and involves only small areas.

Coverage of noninvasive techniques (pp. 96–8) has concentrated on *computed axial tomography* (CAT scanning), *magnetic resonance imaging* (MRI) and *positron emission tomography* (PET scanning). These recently developed, noninvasive procedures produce pictures of the living brain and reduce our reliance on animal-based research.

As this question has a *plurality* requirement (i.e. it requires more than one method), you need to be very careful in your use of time. You only have 30 minutes to answer this question, and that is divided between the two methods in equal measures. For each method, you are required to consider the *strengths and limitations* of the method in question. The injunction *critically consider* has a very specific AO2 requirement, and you would lose marks if you failed to address both aspects. If you are not sure about the specific requirements of each injunction, check Table 21.1 on p. 551.

The strengths and limitations of each method are covered under the content area for that method. However, you might like to try the websites at the end of this chapter to show just how useful noninvasive procedures can be (remember that you must offer a balanced evaluation of each of your two methods).

Localization of function in the human brain

Although it may seem obvious that behavioural functions should be localized to particular structures and regions of the brain, there is, in fact, no particular reason why they should be. If we approached the brain knowing only the arrangement of neurons and how they worked, we would have no immediate way of knowing, for instance, how language might be organized. Would it be spread over large regions of cortex, or would it be restricted to small, highly specialized areas?

The principle of *localization of function* states that psychological functions are located in specialized areas, so that damage to the relevant area causes a drastic loss of that function. It can be contrasted with the view that functions are widespread, or distributed across large regions of the brain, so that damage to any one small area causes only minimal loss of function.

Of course, we have by now collected a huge amount of experimental data which goes a long way towards answering this question. The organization of the hypothalamus suggests a structure which has important specialized functions localized within it, and there is no suggestion that temperature control, for instance, is distributed across large amounts of brain. In fact, many of the more physiological functions of the brain are strictly localized and it is only when we consider the higher cognitive functions of the cerebral cortex that the picture becomes more confused.

Karl Lashley (see *In Focus*) demonstrated that there was a vague localization of maze memory to the visual cortex, although he was working only with memory and other cognitive functions may be organized differently. He did show that the extreme localization found, for instance, in the hypothalamus did not necessarily hold for functional localization in association cortex.

Functional organization of the cortex

The cortex contains most of the neurons in the forebrain and controls many complex functions. The simplest way to approach the organization of these functions is to divide them into different categories:

◆ *Sensory functions*, such as vision and hearing, are related to the processing of sensory input.

◆ *Motor functions* are concerned with the planning and execution of movement.

◆ There is a large category of *cognitive functions*, such as language, thought, planning and problem-solving, personality, and so on, which together make up our higher cognitive abilities.

A practical reason for dividing functions into these categories is that we have known for many years that sensory and motor functions are localized in specialized areas of the cortex, so much so that we can categorize these areas as sensory and motor cortex respectively. As we shall see, labelling areas of cortex as sensory or motor leaves a lot of cortex to be described. These areas of cortex are called *association cortex*, an old-fashioned term based on the idea that the functions of these areas in some way 'associate' sensory input with motor output.

in focus

Lashley's laws of cortical organization

In the 1920s and 30s, Karl Lashley was investigating the brain mechanisms of memory in the rat. He called the physical basis of memory the *engram* and spent many years searching for the site within the brain where the engram was located. For instance, he would train rats to learn a complicated maze and then show that a lesion taking out most of the visual cortex would remove the memory, or engram, so that the rat would no longer remember the maze. So the engram was presumably somewhere in the visual cortex. He then repeated the study several times, each time removing only a small part of the visual cortex, reasoning that the engram must be in one of these smaller zones. In fact, none of these smaller lesions affected memory for the maze and Lashley had to conclude that the engram does not exist in a highly localized form but is spread across cortical regions. He summarized his findings in two laws of cortical organization (Lashley 1929):

◆ The *Law of Mass Action* states that lesions affect memory in proportion to their size, as the cortex works together as a whole.

◆ The *Law of Equipotentiality* states that all areas of the cortex have equal roles in memory storage, so that damage to different areas has similar effects.

Sensory and motor functions

It has been known since the early years of the century that electrical stimulation or lesions of various parts of the cortex in animals can affect sensory and motor abilities. This has been confirmed by the effects of accidental damage to the cortex in humans, or by some rare cases where electrical stimulation has been carried out on human patients (this is usually to check that a subsequent surgical procedure will not damage, or impair, important functions).

The result of all this work is that we can map these sensory and motor functions on to the cortical surface of the hemispheres. Figure 4.6 shows such a map. In each of the areas, electrical stimulation will mimic the function to a greater or lesser extent, while damage will impair the function. You will immediately notice that our most complex and important sensory abilities, vision and hearing, have specialized cortical areas dedicated to them; this is because visual and auditory (hearing) processing is far more sophisticated than, say, the perception of touch or taste and requires more neuronal material. Stimulation in these areas produces either visual sensation (e.g. a flash of brightness) or auditory sensation (e.g. a buzzing noise), while damage may impair vision or hearing.

The *somatosensory* cortex in the *postcentral gyrus* (so-called because it lies behind the central fissure, one of the brain's main anatomical landmarks) contains our general body senses, mainly dealing with stimuli on the skin such as touch, pressure, heat, cold and some aspects of pain. Stimulation here gives rise to the experience of touch or pressure on part of the skin. It seems that there is a point-for-point representation of the body surface on the cortical surface, an arrangement called a topographical map; as you stimulate parts of the somatosensory cortex, so the reported sensation of touch moves up and down the body. The map is upside down, with the skin of feet and legs dealt with by the cortex at the top of the brain. Damage to somatosensory cortex leads to a loss of sensation (anaesthesia) from the body.

Visual, auditory and somatosensory cortex represent the target zones for neuronal pathways carrying sensory information from receptors into the central nervous system. As the receiving areas for these pathways they are called primary sensory cortex. Of course there are a number of stages between basic sensation and complex perception. After arrival at primary cortex, sensory information is passed on to secondary and even tertiary cortical areas where increasingly complex processing occurs. Auditory, visual and somatosensory cortex are surrounded by these secondary and tertiary areas, where sensation becomes perception. You can see this transition in the effects of brain damage. If the primary visual cortex is involved, loss can be profound, as without primary areas the visual input cannot be transmitted on for further processing. If secondary or tertiary areas are involved, basic visual abilities may be intact, but some high level ability, such as face recognition, may be lost.

The study of such syndromes (patterns of symptoms) seen after damage to cortical areas outside primary cortex is called *cognitive neuropsychology*. It aims to use the pattern of cognitive loss after brain damage to build models of how normal cognitive functions are organized.

The *precentral gyrus* in the frontal lobe (Fig. 4.6) contains motor cortex. This is the origin of pathways running eventually to the muscles of the skeleton to produce movement. Damage here can lead to paralysis, while stimulation can produce movement of individual muscle fibres. As with somatosensory cortex, motor cortex contains a topographical map of the body, also upside-down, with muscles of the feet and legs controlled from areas at the top of motor cortex. As our most complex muscular control involves

Figure 4.6
Side view of left hemisphere showing sensory and motor areas

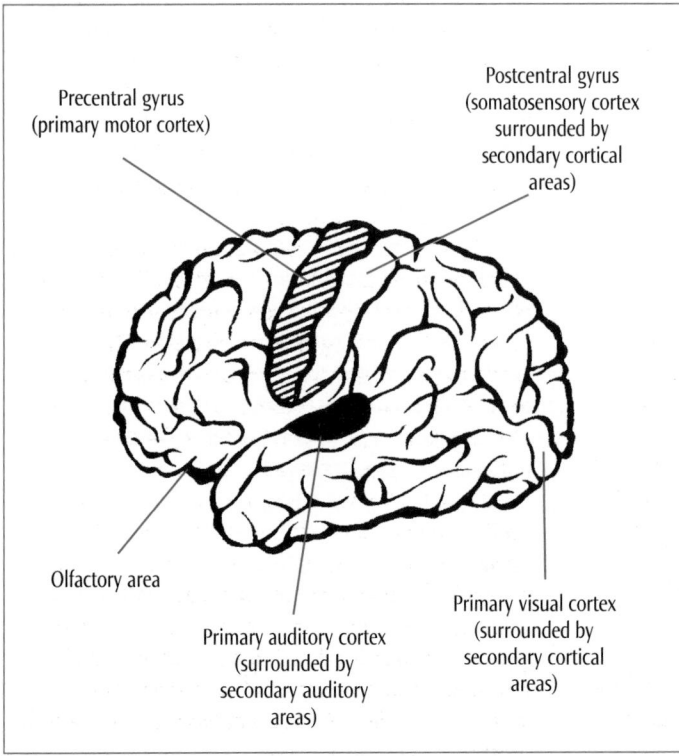

Precentral gyrus (primary motor cortex)

Postcentral gyrus (somatosensory cortex surrounded by secondary cortical areas)

Olfactory area

Primary auditory cortex (surrounded by secondary auditory areas)

Primary visual cortex (surrounded by secondary cortical areas)

the muscles of the throat, larynx, pharynx and tongue used in speech, this area takes up proportionately more cortical surface. It is also important to remember that there are other parts of the motor system. The cerebellum and the basal ganglia have important roles in integrating and fine-tuning movement; damage to those areas impairs smooth control but does not eliminate movement completely.

A note on pathways

Figure 4.6 shows only the left hemisphere. However, a map of the sensory and motor functions of the right hemisphere would look exactly the same, only the other way round. Humans, like all mammals, are what is called bilaterally (bilateral means two-sided) symmetrical; if divided vertically, you end up with two mirror-image halves. The presence of two legs, two arms and two cerebral hemispheres reflects this bilateral symmetry, which also explains why we usually find brain structures in pairs, one on each side.

The arrangement of sensory and motor pathways connecting the hemispheres with the body is determined by this fundamental organizational principle. Motor and somatosensory pathways connect each hemisphere with only one side of the body. For reasons which are unknown, these pathways are crossed, with the left hemisphere connecting to the right side of the body and the right hemisphere to the left. Cortical damage to the left hemisphere therefore produces a right-sided paralysis and loss of sensation. This arrangement is called a crossed or contralateral pathway.

The visual and auditory systems have a more complicated arrangement. Each eye and ear has pathways connecting it with both hemispheres, i.e. a combination of crossed (*contralateral*) and uncrossed (*ipsilateral* – meaning 'same side') pathways. This means that damage to only one hemisphere will not destroy vision or hearing completely, as the other hemisphere is still functionally connected to both eyes or ears. We discuss the visual pathways in more detail later.

Despite vision and hearing having crossed and uncrossed pathways, in relation to the hemispheres themselves the arrangements are perfectly symmetrical. For sensory and motor functions the two hemispheres have similar organizations, i.e. they show functional symmetry and describing one effectively describes the other.

The two hemispheres also show significant localization of function, with small areas of cortex carrying out specialized and specific functions. However, the problems of localization met by Lashley were in the area of memory, so it is to such higher cognitive functions we now turn.

Activity 2: Muscle controls

Lift your left arm. Which hemisphere is controlling the movement? Now raise your right leg and answer the same question. Now read the last sentence. Is it easy to work out which hemisphere is controlling your lips, tongue, larynx and pharynx when you talk? Probably not. These are muscles controlled from the motor cortex, but their role in speech means that control must be highly detailed and fine-tuned. Because of this, they are the only examples where control of muscles on both sides of the body is located in one hemisphere. Can you guess which? Because of the left-hemisphere role in language, the left-hemisphere motor cortex has taken over control of our speech musculature on both sides of the body.

Cortical organization of cognitive functions

Taking out the sensory and motor cortical areas leaves large parts of the cortex unaccounted for (see Fig. 4.6). As mentioned above, these are referred to as association cortex and it is here that we assume that higher cognitive functions will be located.

Broca, Wernicke and language

The search for these began in the earliest days of brain research in the nineteenth century, when the systematic study of brain-damaged patients started. Two of the most remarkable observations were made by Paul Broca and by Karl Wernicke, who were interested in how language was organized in the brain. In 1861, Broca reported on a patient admitted to hospital after suffering a stroke. Tests showed that although he could understand speech, following instructions and answering simple questions with head movements, the only recognizable word he could actually say was 'tan'. There was no fluent speech at all. Broca found eight similar cases with similar symptoms of a lack of speech production coupled with normal speech understanding or comprehension. This syndrome is called *Broca's aphasia*; aphasia is the technical term for any speech problem encountered after brain damage. Alternative terms for Broca's aphasia are *expressive* or *motor aphasia*.

At roughly the same time Wernicke (1874), using similar methods, identified a syndrome with the opposite pattern of symptoms: patients did not seem to comprehend speech, but could produce reasonably well-organized sequences of speech. As they could not understand speech, what they said was unrelated to any question or comment spoken to them. This syndrome is called *Wernicke's aphasia*, or alternatively *sensory* or *receptive aphasia*.

Broca and Wernicke were interested in the brain mechanisms of language and so the brains of the patients were examined after they had died. Broca consistently found that his patients had suffered damage to an area low down in the cortex of the frontal lobe, now known as *Broca's area* (see Fig. 4.7).

Wernicke's patients had damage to an area in the temporal lobe close to the primary auditory cortex (Fig. 4.7), now called *Wernicke's area*. Work since then, right up to recent studies using PET scans, generally confirms the original findings of Broca and Wernicke: damage to Broca's area severely impairs speech but leaves the comprehension of speech intact, while damage to Wernicke's area affects comprehension but leaves speech production quite fluent.

It seems that Wernicke's area in the temporal lobe contains a store of the sound representations of words which we use to recognize incoming speech. Broca's area is thought to contain the motor plans for words, i.e. the pattern of muscle movements of the throat and tongue, etc., which are specific to each word. When we wish to speak, instructions are passed from Wernicke's area to Broca's area to activate the relevant motor plans, which are then transmitted the short distance to the motor cortex in the prefrontal cortex, which sends instructions down the motor pathways to the muscles themselves. When Wernicke's area is damaged we lose

the store of word representations and so cannot recognize incoming speech, but as Broca's area is intact motor plans can still be activated and speech produced. I am sure you can work the opposite pattern out for yourselves.

Besides the significant finding that speech production and comprehension seemed to be localized to particular areas of the cortex, Broca and Wernicke also confirmed a suggestion that had been made earlier in the century, that brain damage affecting language usually involved the left hemisphere. Damage to the right hemisphere rarely had any effect on language. The conclusion was that our language mechanisms are found only in the left hemisphere.

Thousands of research studies since those pioneering observations have confirmed this general pattern, with some exceptions which we meet later in the chapter. The significance of the finding was that, in contrast to sensory and motor functions, language was not organized symmetrically across the two hemispheres of the brain, but represented a hemisphere asymmetry of function. From these beginnings, the study of hemisphere asymmetries of function has become one of the main research themes in psychology. Before looking at some of the findings, however, we should have a more general look at other functions of association cortex.

Figure 4.7 Language mechanisms in the left hemisphere

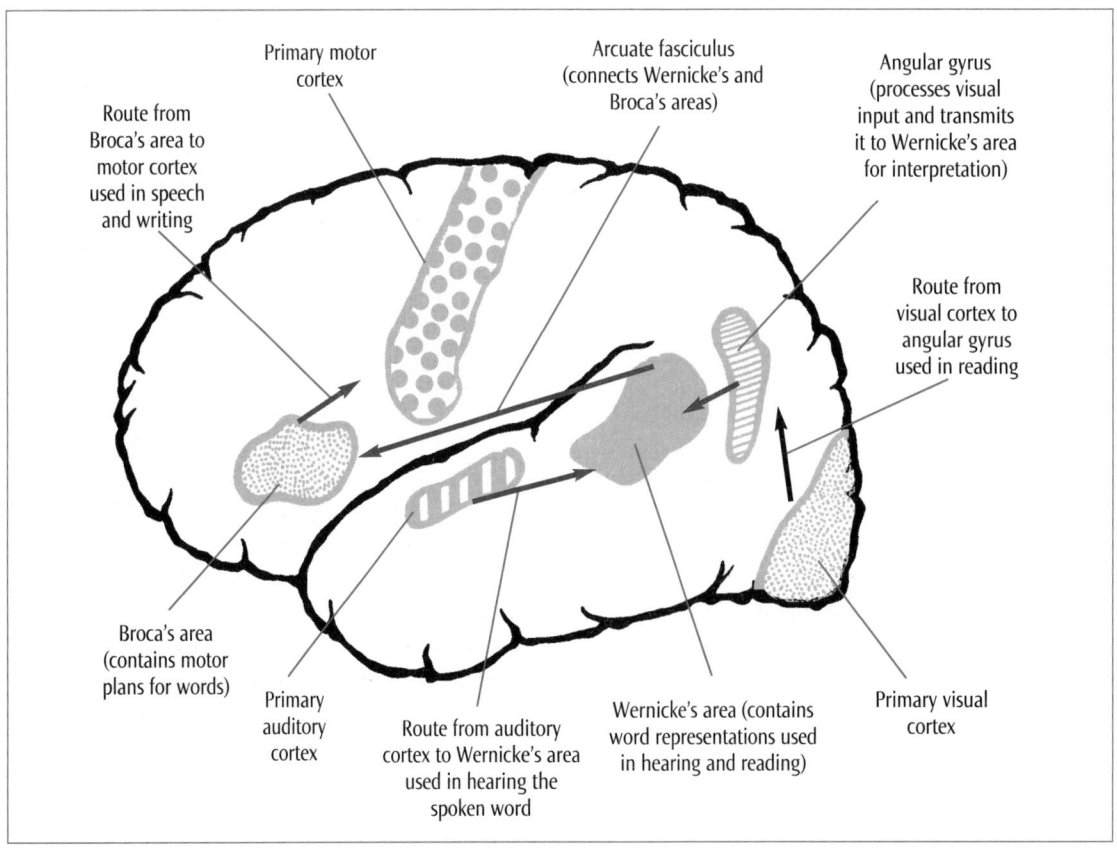

Other studies of association cortex

Studies of damage to the frontal lobes (see *In Focus*) has led to the idea of a frontal lobe syndrome, with symptoms of impulsivity, a failure to plan ahead or to follow plans through to a conclusion, perseveration (repeating the same actions) and sometimes apathy and indecision. There can be a loss of creative or abstract thought. However, the frontal cortex is such a large area that it may well contain a wide range of complex functions and it might be better to map the whole area in detail rather than to study the effects of major damage. Generally, it seems to control our capacity for forward planning and goal-directed behaviour. In relation to hemisphere asymmetries, apart from Broca's area, usually found only in the left frontal cortex, there is little evidence for asymmetries of other frontal functions.

The association cortex of the parietal lobe contains many functions related to perception. Damage can lead to problems with object recognition and *apraxias*, which are particular problems with skilled sequences of actions, for instance in assembling a set of parts into a complete object.

In the right-hemisphere parietal lobe, there appears to be an area specialized for face recognition, while damage to other areas in the right parietal cortex can lead to unilateral neglect. This is a bizarre syndrome in which patients ignore the space on their left, i.e. on the opposite side to the lesion. They will draw only one half of a clock, with all the numbers crowded together, or only dress one side of their body. It seems that the parietal lobe is concerned with our perception of and orientation within the surrounding space.

Another important language structure found in the parietal lobe is the *angular gyrus* (Fig. 4.7). This area of cortex is vital to the visual aspects of language involved in reading and writing, as it works with Wernicke's area to convert the visual input into the brain's language code.

Damage can lead to a loss of both reading and writing, while damage which disconnects the angular gyrus from the visual cortex (which, of course, is where visual input, including the words you are reading, first reaches the cortex) produces a strange syndrome known as *alexia* (absence of reading) without *agraphia* (absence of writing), or pure word blindness. Because the written word cannot reach the angular gyrus, it cannot be read. However, as the gyrus itself is intact, together with the pathways running to Wernicke's area and on to Broca's area, the planning and production of writing can still happen. So patients can write, but not read back what they have written! Although the angular gyrus can be identified in the right hemisphere, the loss of language function occurs only after damage to the left hemisphere.

It is important to remember that these syndromes observed after brain damage happen even though basic sensory and motor pathways are working properly. For instance, testing shows that patients with aphasia or dyslexia have normal vision and motor control, so the symptoms must be due to difficulties with higher level cognitive processes. It is these that the psychologist is interested in.

The temporal lobe association cortex contains the secondary and tertiary auditory cortex and Wernicke's area, described earlier. It also contains regions of secondary and tertiary visual cortex, radiating out from the visual cortex of the occipital lobe. Damage to the temporal lobe can therefore affect auditory perception (e.g. identifying sounds or voices), language, referred to previously, and high level visual perception such as identifying and categorizing stimuli, e.g. being able to recognize that the object seen is an apple and that an apple is a fruit.

These are functions of the cortical surface of the temporal lobe. Under the surface are subcortical structures, while buried within the temporal lobe are parts of the limbic system such as the hippocampus

in focus

The case of Phineas Gage

The frontal lobes contain the largest proportion of association cortex of any of the lobes making up the hemispheres. One of the earliest and most dramatic cases of frontal lobe damage studied was that of Phineas Gage. In 1848, he was working on the construction of the American railroad, where his job was to tamp down the explosive charges used to blow rocks out of the way. One of the charges exploded prematurely and blew the tamping iron (a metal rod, several feet long) through his cheekbone and out through the top of the skull. Gage suffered severe injuries, losing much of his frontal association cortex. Amazingly Gage not only survived (he only lost consciousness for a few minutes and actually signed off from work before going to the doctor), but lived for 13 years afterwards. Even the behavioural effects were less than you might expect after losing so much brain tissue. His general cognitive functions such as memory, attention and perception, were intact. He was, however, more impulsive, less conscientious and had fewer social inhibitions than before. Planning ahead was impossible and he found it difficult to hold down a job, even for a time becoming an exhibit in a circus.

and the amygdala. Besides other functions, the limbic system plays an important role in relation to emotion. Because of the links between the limbic system and temporal lobe cortex, damage to the cortex alone can affect not just how we identify stimuli but also weaken our emotional response to it. Responses become distant and strictly neutral. The association cortex of the occipital lobe is almost completely dedicated to visual processing, so much so that occipital cortex is often simply referred to as visual cortex. Organization of the visual system does lead us to a reconsideration of localization of function in the brain.

Localization versus distributed functions

Even when neuropsychologists discuss higher cognitive functions, they still speak in terms of localization. The frontal lobe syndrome occurs after damage to the frontal lobe, not to the parietal lobe, and vice versa for problems with face recognition. However, two developments mean that these descriptions can be seen as acceptable simplifications. One is the increased awareness of the complexity of psychological functions.

Lashley studied the localization of 'memory'. What do we now mean by 'memory'? Even a simple analysis reveals processes such as short-term memory, transfer to long-term memory, and retrieval from short-term and long-term stores. Add in different types of memory, such as episodic, semantic and procedural, and perhaps memory for different types of material, such as visual and auditory, and you can quickly see that to talk of one 'memory' location in the brain is just plain silly. Each of these aspects may be handled in different ways in different parts or circuits within the brain, so while each may be 'localized', overall the brain must handle memory in a 'distributed' fashion. The efficient functioning of our memory system must involve the integration of neural activity across many distinct areas, regions, or pathways.

Language is an equally sophisticated cognitive process, with many subprocesses going to make up the skills of reading, writing, hearing and speaking. Broca's and Wernicke's areas are still incorporated into models of language, but even with these there is evidence that Broca's aphasia, for instance, is only produced if there is damage to cortical and subcortical areas extending beyond Broca's classical region in the frontal lobe. Ojemann (1983) has shown that electrical stimulation of brain cortex in areas dispersed well outside the classical language centres can interfere with speech production and comprehension. As with memory, the conclusion would be that while small subroutines may be localized, high level cognitive functions are distributed across large areas of cortex.

The best evidence for this comes from the visual system (covered in detail in Chapter 8, see p. 185). It turns out that our visual system processes different characteristics of the visual stimulus independently. Starting with the reception of stimuli on the retina of the eye, shape, colour, and movement follow parallel but independent pathways through visual processing. Damage to separate cortical areas can affect colour vision (the person sees the world only in black and white), or movement (in this strange situation the person can see objects only when they are still; they disappear when they move). Our experience is of seeing whole objects with shape, colour, and movement integrated. But to achieve this the brain has to combine the results of this 'parallel distributed processing' of the separate characteristics. How it does this is one of the many great mysteries of brain function

Exam summary: Localization of function in the human brain

The AQA examination will test your understanding of the following areas:

◆ the functional organization of the cerebral cortex – the primary motor, sensory (pp. 99–101) and association areas (pp. 101–4).

◆ distributed functions in the cerebral cortex (p. 104).

Example question

The question below is typical of one drawn from the material above, and should take you 30 minutes to answer.

(a) Outline some of the ways in which the human cerebral cortex is organized according to function.
(12 marks)

(b) Assess the extent to which research supports the idea of localized rather than distributed functions in the cerebral cortex. *(12 marks)*

Suggested answer structure

Although this question effectively covers all of the content of this section, this does not necessarily make it any easier. The first part of the question constitutes the AO1 component of the question, but has a potentially massive amount of information that could be included. This includes information about the sensory and motor functions of the cerebral cortex (pp. 100–1) and the association areas (pp. 101–4). Each hemisphere has areas dedicated to the motor control and general body senses of the opposite side of the body. Studies of association cortex began with Broca and Wernicke's work on language, which they located to the left hemisphere in the first demonstration of an asymmetry of hemisphere function. Damage to association cortex produces high-level loss of cognitive abilities, such as aphasias, apraxias, the frontal lobe syndrome and perceptual problems.

The problem with all this information is that you only have a meagre 15 minutes (abut 300 words) to represent all these insights into localization of cortical functioning. The question appears to be sympathetic to this and gives hints that you only need to offer a representative sample of the topic area. The injunction *outline* is used to tell you that you need only present a summary description (i.e. a précis) of your chosen material.

As a second generous gesture, the question asks for an outline of *some* of the ways that the cerebral cortex is organized according to function. Perhaps this doesn't help, as you still have to decide what to put in and what to leave out. Well, the final consideration should be the marking criteria for a question of this type (see Table 21.4 on p. 558). You will see that the high marks are given for answers that are well detailed and offer both breadth *and* depth of material. This means that you should choose material that you feel offers a representative view of cerebral organization, and that you feel you can 'do justice to' given the time constraints of the question.

The second part of the question does not present the same problem. Coverage of this topic (localized versus distributed functions) is covered more concisely (p. 104) and so is easier to précis down to just 300 words. The gist of this section is that although small subroutines of cortical processing may be localized, high-level cognitive functions are distributed across large areas of the cortex.

Lateralization of function in the cerebral cortex

Split-brain studies

The historical work of Wernicke, Broca and others demonstrated that some of the functions of association cortex, such as language, seemed to be located in only one hemisphere; this is called an *asymmetry of function*, in comparison to sensory and motor functions which are organized symmetrically across the hemispheres. Since then, a vast number of experimental studies on normal and brain-damaged patients has reinforced and extended these original findings. One of the most dramatic series of studies was that of Roger Sperry (1982), which began in the 1950s and continued until his death in 1980.

Sperry's subjects were patients suffering from epilepsy. Epilepsy comes in many forms, but always involves an uncontrolled discharge of electrical activity in the brain. The discharge may originate in an area of scar tissue following accidental brain damage, often at birth, or during brain surgery, or perhaps from a developing cyst or tumour; when such a point of origin can be identified, it is called a focus and sometimes it can be removed surgically. In other cases of epilepsy there is no clear focus, but probably some imbalance in excitatory and inhibitory influences in the brain.

Whatever the cause, once the discharge begins it is automatically transmitted along neuronal pathways, as this is what they are specialized to do. Severe epilepsy can involve many brain circuits and lead to convulsions and loss of consciousness and a patient may have several attacks a week or even a day. It is therefore a disabling condition. Nowadays we have many drugs for the control of epilepsy, although there are still patients who do not respond and are very handicapped. In the 1940s there were far fewer drugs and many more patients suffering severely from the effects of epilepsy.

It is a feature of most types of epilepsy that the attack usually begins in one hemisphere or the other. Connecting the hemispheres is the largest pathway in the brain, the corpus callosum, consisting of some 300 million neuronal fibres. This pathway interconnects areas of the cortex in each hemisphere, ensuring that the hemispheres communicate with each other and synchronize their activities. The corpus callosum also allows epileptic discharges to spread to the other hemisphere and in the 1940s an operation was devised to prevent this spread; the corpus callosum was cut. In this way the epilepsy was confined to only one hemisphere and its effects reduced.

Strangely, the operation (technically called a *commissurotomy* as the corpus callosum is the largest of the commissures, those pathways travelling between the hemispheres rather than contained within one of them) seemed to have little effect on the patient. Sensory, motor and cognitive functions continued as before, but there was an improvement in their epilepsy.

Sperry was intrigued by this; surely the largest pathway in the brain must have important functions and its removal should affect behaviour. He decided to study these patients using careful experimental procedures based on the anatomy of the visual pathways. These are outlined in Fig. 4.8. Light strikes the retina at the back of the eye, which contains millions of visual receptor cells (these processes are dealt with in detail later in this chapter). The receptors trigger activity in axons making up the optic nerve (see Fig. 4.8), which runs via the thalamus on to primary visual cortex in the occipital lobe.

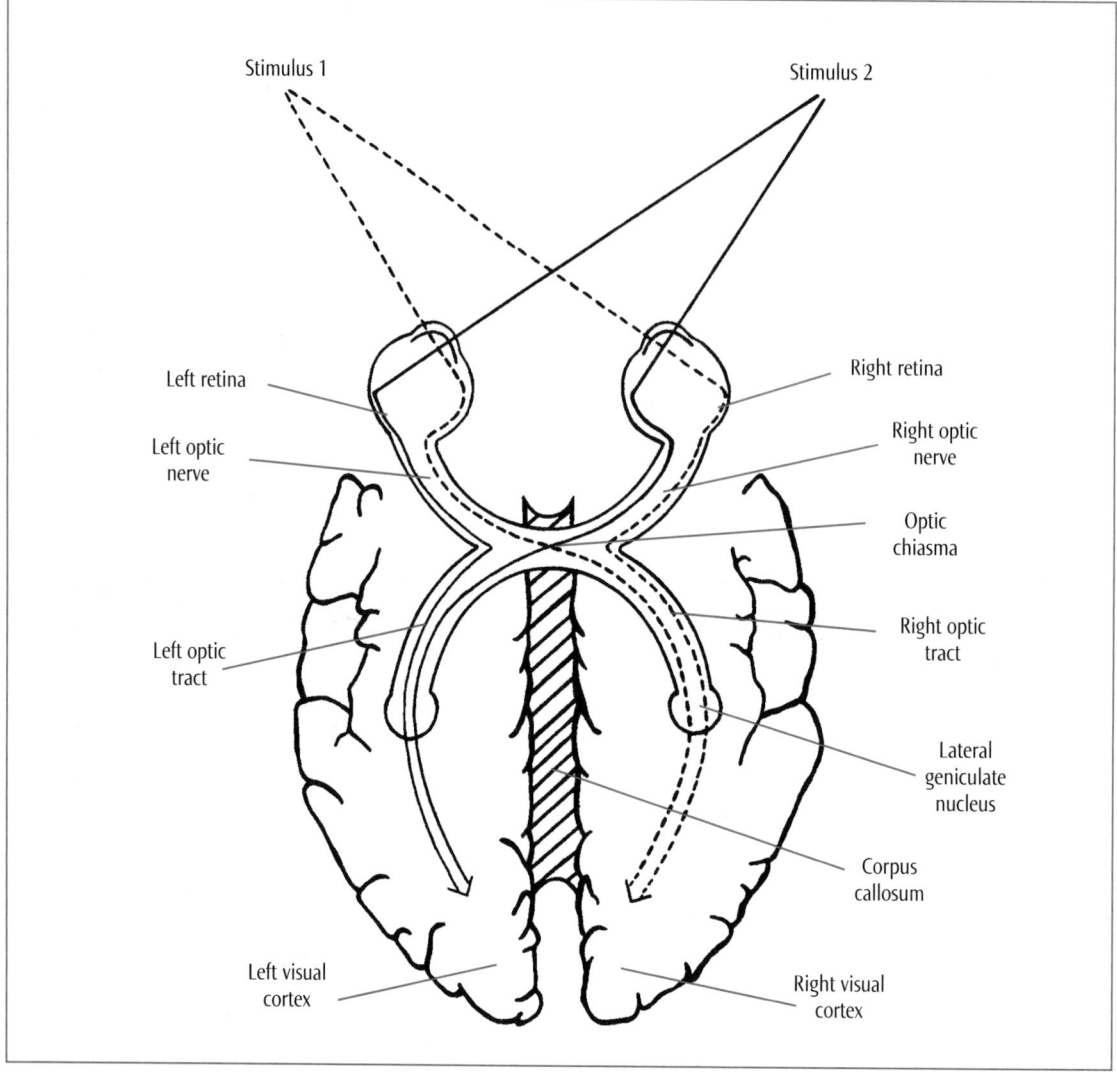

Figure 4.8 Visual pathways in relation to split brain

As Fig. 4.8 shows, it is a feature of the retina of each eye that the receptors in the outer half connect with fibres running to the visual cortex in the hemisphere on the same side of the brain – an ipsilateral (same-side) pathway. Receptors contained within the inner half of each retina project to the visual cortex in the opposite hemisphere – a contralateral (crossed) pathway. So each retina projects in a systematic way to both hemispheres, with the crossed pathways passing from one side to the other at the optic chiasma. Figure 4.8 also shows how a stimulus presented out to the right of the patient (known as the right visual field, or RVF) is picked up. With the eyes pointing (or fixated) straight ahead, it hits the left side of the left eye and the left side of the right eye; look carefully and you will see that these parts of each retina both project to the visual cortex of the left hemisphere. So a stimulus in the RVF, with both eyes fixated straight ahead, is seen first by the left hemisphere and by the same geometrical argument a stimulus out to the left of the subject (in the left visual field, LVF) is seen first by the right hemisphere.

In normal participants, any information reaching one hemisphere first is rapidly and automatically transferred to the other hemisphere via the corpus callosum. In patients who have had a commissurotomy, known informally as split-brain patients, the information cannot pass to the other hemisphere as the corpus callosum has been cut. So this experimental procedure, referred to as the divided field, enabled Sperry to present visual stimuli and know that they would be confined to the hemisphere to which they were transmitted. What sort of things could he demonstrate?

The split-brain patient sits in front of a screen. A word is flashed up briefly in the subject's RVF (if the exposure of the stimulus is too long, the eyes automatically move towards the stimulus, which may then be seen by both hemispheres). The word is transmitted to the left hemisphere and if you ask the patient to report what they saw, they will say the word. Repeat the study with the LVF. The word travels to the right hemisphere. When asked to report what they have seen, the patient denies having seen anything. Can you work out the explanation?

The left hemisphere in most people contains the language system, i.e. it can read words and speak. The word presented in the RVF goes to the left hemisphere, is read and reported by the patient. The word presented in the LVF goes to the right hemisphere, which does not have a highly developed language system and certainly cannot speak. Therefore the subject has nothing to report. In fact the experiment involves a spoken response which itself has to emerge from the left hemisphere; with the corpus callosum cut, the left hemisphere does not know what is going on in the right hemisphere, so the patient's left-hemisphere language system cannot comment on stimuli presented to the right hemisphere.

This type of early study allowed Sperry to confirm that the left hemisphere controls reading and speech and that the right hemisphere apparently could not process verbal stimuli at all. But he was worried that as long as he used verbal questions and responses – 'What was the stimulus you saw?' – he was not giving the right hemisphere a fair chance; if it could not talk, it could not respond at all, so in fact he had no idea what was going on in it. So he introduced a variation.

You may remember that the motor pathways are completely crossed, with each hemisphere controlling the muscles of the opposite side of the body. The right hemisphere controls the left arm and hand, and so it was this system that Sperry used to test the right hemisphere. The experiment described above is repeated, except that in this case the left hand is placed behind a screen (so the subject cannot see what it is doing) among a collection of different objects. A word such as 'orange' is presented in the RVF. It goes to the left hemisphere and when the patient is asked whether they saw anything, they say 'orange'. Then 'banana' is presented in the LVF. This goes to the right hemisphere and when asked for a spoken response the patient denies seeing anything. However, the left hand behind the screen emerges triumphantly holding a banana it has selected from the range of objects!

It appears that the right hemisphere can understand simple concrete nouns and understand their meaning. This has activated the left hand, controlled by the right hemisphere, to select out the appropriate object. Meanwhile the left hemisphere, which can talk but has no access to the right hemisphere, has not seen the word and does not know why the left hand is holding a banana. When asked what is going on, the patient, using their left hemisphere to produce a spoken reply, will seem confused, or sometimes even deny that the

left hand is theirs! The split brain represents a disconnection syndrome, in which brain damage disconnects normally integrated functions. Ask a normal participant, with their eyes shut, to say whether two objects, one in each hand, are the same and they can do it easily. Ask a split-brain patient and they cannot even say whether they have an object in the left hand.

Using the left-hand response system meant that Sperry and other researchers could test the right hemisphere with various types of stimulus, while the left hemisphere could continue using its language mechanisms. Sperry concluded that the right hemisphere had some simple reading ability, in that it could read concrete nouns (i.e. object names) but not abstract words and could not produce language (writing or speaking). However, it was better at recognizing pictures and shapes, especially faces.

Work on the split brain demonstrated that although the right hemisphere may not be very linguistic, it had important functions related to processing pictures and shapes, or visuo-spatial stimuli. This division of the hemispheres into a verbal and linguistic left and a visuo-spatial right has become a basic model of brain function, supported in general by many thousands of subsequent studies with normal participants. Before looking at some of this later work, there are some problems with the split brain that should be mentioned.

Evaluation of split-brain studies

◆ Because it is such a drastic treatment, very few commissurotomies have ever been done – only about 80 overall – and they are extremely rare nowadays. Only about 20 have been given much psychological testing and most of the data has come from fewer than ten of them. Can we base models of brain function on such a small sample?

◆ Epilepsy is caused by some sort of brain abnormality and patients have to live with it for many years before surgery takes place. They are also likely to be on drug therapy and it is hard to argue that these were 'normal' participants before surgery. In fact, some of the later patients showed good evidence of right-hemisphere expressive language, by writing with the left hand. So do we conclude that bilateral (two-sided) language organization is the norm, or that these particular brains have been reorganized because of the presence of some sort of abnormality and should not be used to model the normal brain?

◆ There are too many uncontrolled variables for the split-brain patients to be considered a uniform group. Patients vary in sex, age of onset of epilepsy, cause of the epilepsy, age at which surgery was performed and age at testing.

For the reasons listed above, it is unjustified to use experimental findings only from split-brain patients to build models of normal brain function. However, they have been very important, for various reasons:

◆ From Sperry's earliest work it seemed probable that the right hemisphere, previously thought to be unimportant compared to the verbal left hemisphere, did contain important cognitive functions related to visuo-spatial stimuli.

◆ The split-brain patient shows the central role of language in our conscious self-awareness. When asked to comment on their situation, the patient always refers to the experiences of the left hemisphere. Only under special experimental conditions can the right hemisphere clearly express itself.

◆ Sperry was intrigued by the role of the corpus callosum in brain function. The disconnection syndromes seen in the split-brain patient suggest that the role of this major pathway is to enable each hemisphere to be aware of activities in the other. Each hemisphere seems to have its own specialized functions and, in the intact brain, the corpus callosum allows these to be coordinated and integrated, producing an integrated personality. Thus we can reflect (using left-hemisphere language) on our visuo-spatial abilities (in the right hemisphere).

◆ One underestimated contribution of Sperry's was his development of the divided visual field technique to test the hemispheres separately. As we shall see, this has become one of the most used procedures.

How split-brain people manage

Before discussing work with non-split-brain people, you may wonder how the split-brain patient manages in everyday life and the answer is, much better than you might imagine. The key is the organization of the visual system. Each eye projects to both hemispheres and if the eyes are moved to scan the whole visual field, all the stimuli will be transmitted to both hemispheres. When reading, for instance, head movements are exaggerated as all the text must be seen by the left side of each retina (Fig. 4.8) so it goes to the left-hemisphere language mechanisms. A problem can arise with coordinating the hands, for instance in striking a match. With eyes shut, the person would not know that the left hand held the matchbox, as explained above, so coordination is dependent on the eyes. The most bizarre problem reported is a tendency for the right-hemisphere/left-hand system to have its own views; one patient selected some trousers to wear and then found her left hand independently choosing a second pair!

Hemisphere asymmetries: studies with normal participants

In parallel with the split-brain work, thousands of studies were carried out on normal participants. Many of these relied on two basic techniques: Sperry's divided field and dichotic listening. As normal participants have an intact corpus callosum, the divided field cannot be used unmodified, as a single stimulus presented to one hemisphere is rapidly communicated to the other. The simple modification is to present two stimuli at once, one in each visual field. With brief exposure (less than 100 milliseconds), usually only one is reported by the participant. If words are used, the word presented in the RVF and going directly to the left hemisphere and its language mechanisms would be the one registered by the subject; this is called an RVF superiority. If pictures or faces are used, then the one in the LVF going first to the right hemisphere is reported. This hemisphere is better at analysing such stimuli and although the results have to be passed to the left hemisphere to be verbally reported, this is faster than the processing of the stimulus in the RVF going to the left hemisphere, which cannot deal with it and has to pass it across to the right hemisphere to be analysed. Visuo-spatial stimuli therefore give an LVF advantage.

The results of the many studies done with the divided visual field are reasonably consistent:

◆ Words, letters and digits give an RVF advantage, indicating superior processing by the left hemisphere.

◆ Recognizing faces and patterns, discriminating brightness and colours and depth perception, all give an LVF advantage, indicating right-hemisphere processing.

Dichotic listening is a similar procedure for the auditory system. A pair of sounds is presented simultaneously through headphones. Although each ear projects to both hemispheres, the crossed, contralateral, pathway is dominant, so stimuli in the left ear are processed by the right hemisphere and vice-versa. If words are used, the one in the right ear going to the left hemisphere is usually reported, giving a right-ear advantage (REA). If nonverbal sounds, such as animal noises, are used (a sort of auditory equivalent of visuo-spatial stimuli), then the one in the left ear tends to be the one identified and reported; this is a left-ear advantage, or LEA.

To summarize findings from dichotic listening studies:

◆ Spoken words, digits, normal and backwards speech and nonsense syllables all give an REA (left-hemisphere advantage).

Table 4.1 Suggested characteristics of the two hemispheres	
Left hemisphere	**Right hemisphere**
Verbal	Visuo-spatial
Sequential processing	Simultaneous, parallel positioning
Analytic	Gestalt, holistic
Rational	Emotional
Deductive	Intuitive, creative
Convergent thought	Divergent thought
Scientific	Artistic

◆ Recognizing environmental sounds and most aspects of music perception give an LEA (right-hemisphere advantage).

So the pattern of visual field superiorities and ear advantages can give us a picture of how the hemispheres process a range of stimuli. Table 4.1 summarizes some of the findings.

Attempts have been made to characterize the hemispheres on the basis of such findings. As words and digits come in as a sequence of stimuli spread over time, the left hemisphere is seen as better at sequential or time-based processing and at segmenting and analysing input into its component parts (think of understanding speech, where we take in the sequence of sounds, but to understand them we need to identify each unit, be it phoneme or whole word, and then put the sentence together after analysing the parts). Pictures and faces are usually identified as one whole stimulus with all the features processed immediately in parallel; so the right hemisphere is seen as better at *Gestalt* or *parallel processing*. 'Gestalt' means an integrated whole stimulus, not just a collection of parts.

Some theorists have gone further, seeing the left hemisphere as analytic, scientific and rational and the right hemisphere as creative, artistic and emotional. There is little solid experimental evidence for these speculations. As the role of the corpus callosum is to coordinate the activities of the two hemispheres, it is unlikely that any complicated human activity involves only one of them independently. Science, for instance, involves producing hypotheses and theories, which is clearly a creative enterprise.

Although the original work of Wernicke and Broca, and Sperry's experiments on the split brain, can be criticized for studying too few participants and involving uncontrolled variables, the basic picture of hemisphere specialization that emerged has been confirmed by later, better controlled studies. Language is localized to the left hemisphere, while the right hemisphere is specialized for the processing of visuo-spatial stimuli, of which the best example is faces.

Other approaches, such as assessing the effects of *lateralized* (one-sided) brain damage, give further support. Left-hemisphere damage through a stroke or accidental brain injury can affect language, leaving face recognition intact, while right-hemisphere damage can produce the opposite pattern. What emerges is the picture of a 'standard' brain, with left-hemisphere language and right-hemisphere visuo-spatial ability. But how standard is this brain? The left hemisphere controls language and the right hand, the dominant hand in most people; do left-handers show the same pattern of asymmetries? Does gender make any difference?

Activity 3: How balanced are you?

If you are right-handed, close your eyes and stand on your right leg. Now repeat the exercise while talking (recite a poem, or describe the functions of the cerebral hemispheres!).

Some people find standing on the right leg more difficult if they are simultaneously talking; in theory, both right-leg balancing and talking are left-hemisphere functions and interfere with each other.

What type of task might interfere with left-leg balancing? If you are left-handed, what result would you predict?

Handedness, gender and hemisphere asymmetries

Depending on precisely how it is assessed, around 10 to 15 per cent of the population are left-handed. As right-handers seem to have a left hemisphere which controls language and the right hand, it would seem logical that left-handers should have right-hemisphere language, i.e. the reverse pattern. In fact the picture is more complicated. Around 70 per cent of left-handers have left-hemisphere language, around 15 per cent have language in the right hemisphere and in 15 per cent language seems to involve both hemispheres, i.e. bilateral representation. In general, left-handers are less lateralized in regard to language than right-handers.

Does this have any implications for cognitive abilities? There were early suggestions that left-handers might be worse at visuo-spatial tasks than right-handers, because the spread of language into the right hemisphere somehow interferes with visuo-spatial abilities. However, there is no convincing evidence for overall differences in cognitive abilities between left- and right-handers. Interestingly, left-handers are over represented amongst mathematicians and architects, but also amongst people with dyslexia and those suffering from mental retardation. There are speculations that these observations are related to the unusual pattern of hemisphere development in left-handers.

There is some evidence that females show a different pattern of hemisphere asymmetries to males, specifically a higher frequency of bilateral representation. This has been used to explain the superiority of females in language-based intelligence tests and their poorer performance on visuo-spatial tasks. The increased development of verbal skills, involving both hemispheres, it is argued, interferes with the development of visuo-spatial skills in the right hemisphere. Although this biological argument has become popular, there is little experimental evidence for it and it ignores the wide range of social and cultural pressures during development which can influence cognitive abilities. For instance, there is a powerful correlation, regardless of sex, between academic performance in a particular subject and previous experience of that subject. This does not seem surprising, but learning experience is often ignored by biological theorists.

As left-handers and females can show patterns of reduced asymmetry for language, you might argue that female left-handers should be the least asymmetrical of all. This is not consistently the case. Performance on tests of hemisphere asymmetries, such as the divided field and dichotic listening, seems to involve a complicated interaction between gender and handedness. It also reflects the fact that differences in hemisphere organization between any two individuals, regardless of handedness or gender, are probably greater than any systematic differences between groups of left- and right-handers, or between males and females.

Exam summary: Lateralization of function in the cerebral cortex

The AQA examination will test your understanding of the following areas:

- ◆ lateralization of function in the cerebral cortex (pp. 105–10)

- ◆ the organization of language in the brain (pp. 101–2 and 108–10)

- ◆ other hemispheric asymmetries of function (pp. 108–10).

Example question

The question below is typical of one drawn from the material above, and should take you 30 minutes to answer.

- ◆ Discuss research relating to the organization of language in the brain. *(24 marks)*

Suggested answer structure:

Although this question has a specific requirement to discuss research relating to the organization of *language* in the brain, it taps into much of the most significant research carried out in the area of hemisphere asymmetries. The relevant material for this question is spread over this section (pp. 108–10) and the previous section (pp. 101–2). Broca and Wernicke discovered that brain damage affecting language usually affected the left hemisphere. Damage to the right hemisphere rarely had any effect on language. The significance of this finding was that language was not organized symmetrically across the brain, but represented a hemisphere asymmetry of function (p. 102). More recently, however, research has suggested that Broca's aphasia is only produced if there is damage to cortical and subcortical areas extending beyond Broca's area in the frontal lobe (p. 104).

Sperry's split brain studies (pp. 105–8) also provide valuable insights into the organization of language in the brain. Sperry was able to confirm the earlier finding that language was lateralized to the left hemisphere, but also discovered that the right hemisphere had some rudimentary language skills as well (p. 107) although it was more important in the processing of visuo-spatial information.

Research on handedness (pp. 109–10) has also given us insights into the cerebral organization of language. Although right-handers have their language skills centred in the left hemisphere, a proportion of left-handers have theirs in the right hemisphere, and others have language in both hemispheres (bilateral representation). There is a higher frequency of bilateral representation among females than among males, leading to the suggestion that this might account for the superiority of females on language-based intelligence tests and their relatively poorer performance on visuo-spatial tests (p. 110).

Chapter summary

◆ There are **many methods used to investigate the brain**. **Invasive** techniques include **electrical stimulation** (implanting electrodes into the brain to record nerve impulses and to stimulate brain neurons artificially); **chemical stimulation** (using drugs which mimic the activity of neurotransmitters, or which stimulate or block synaptic receptors); and physical destruction of brain tissue (**lesions** affect localized regions, **ablations** remove larger areas of the brain). The results of these interventions are interpreted by studying their effects on behaviour.

◆ The **main limitation of** invasive experimental methods is that for ethical reasons most of the work has been done on non-human animals, leading to the problem of extrapolating results to the human brain. In addition, specifically human functions such as language cannot be studied with these methods.

◆ **Noninvasive** techniques for studying the brain include **the EEG** (recording the electrical activity of billions of cortical neurons using electrodes on the skull surface; these recordings can be related to the general arousal state of the brain). **CAT scans** use multiple X-rays and computerised analysis to produce pictures of sections through the brain. **MRI and fMRI scans** involve bombarding the brain with radio waves, eventually producing high-definition pictures of brain structures. **PET scans** record the radioactivity emitted by labelled glucose injected into the bloodstream and taken up by brain structures, creating an activity map of the brain. Finally, **MEG scans** reflect moment-by-moment neural activity by recording the tiny magnetic fields produced by neuronal activity.

◆ **Sensory** and **motor functions** are localized to particular areas of the cortex. Each hemisphere is associated with the opposite side of the body, and the arrangement of sensory and motor functions within and across the hemispheres is identical and symmetrical. Motor and sensory pathways are therefore crossed (contralateral). Visual and auditory systems have pathways connecting to both hemispheres (a combination of contralateral and uncrossed or ipsilateral pathways), although the arrangement is perfectly symmetrical.

◆ Higher cognitive functions such as language are located in **association** cortex and can be **asymmetrically** organized across the hemispheres. **Broca's studies** of stroke patients who had little speech but could understand words spoken to them (Broca's, expressive, or motor aphasia), and **Wernicke's** studies of patients apparently without comprehension but able to produce speech (Wernicke's, sensory, or receptive aphasia), both helped to map the localized areas and routes underlying speech production and comprehension. Modern scanning techniques have generally confirmed their findings, locating language mechanisms in the left hemisphere of the brain.

◆ Association cortex also controls other cognitive abilities such as the capacity for forward planning, goal-directed behaviour, perception (such as object recognition), sequences of action, face recognition, visual aspects of language, and auditory perception. Damage to association cortex can produce aphasias, apraxias and problems with perception even though basic sensory and motor processes are intact. The study of these syndromes is known as cognitive neuropsychology.

◆ Lashley's work on memory showed that the cortex could work as a whole (Law of Mass Action), with all areas having equal roles in memory storage (Law of Equipotentiality). This, together with the sophisticated cognitive processes involved in language and the complex processing of visual stimuli, suggests that while individual subroutines may be localized, high-level cognitive functions are **distributed** across large areas of the cortex.

◆ **Sperry** studied epileptic patients who had undergone a commissurotomy, effectively disconnecting the two hemispheres of the brain. He devised experimental techniques such as the divided field to show that in these **split-brain** patients, the right hemisphere had superior visuo-spatial abilities, while the left hemisphere contained **language** mechanisms. In normal intact people the corpus callosum allows the two hemispheres to coordinate and integrate their functions.

◆ Subsequent studies using divided field and dichotic listening experiments in intact people have confirmed the **lateralization of functions**: the left hemisphere being an analytical sequential processor, while the right hemisphere processes whole stimuli such as pictures and faces in parallel. However, studies of left-handedness and gender differences show some variation in patterns of hemisphere asymmetries, although the practical significance of this is unclear.

Further resources

Green, S. (1994) *Principles of Biopsychology*, Hove: Erlbaum.

Gives clear and comprehensive coverage of all the areas covered in this chapter.

Springer, S.P. and Deutsch, G. (1997) *Left Brain, Right Brain* (5th edn), New York: Freeman.

Besides covering hemisphere functional asymmetries in great detail, this text also contains topics such as methodology in brain research, language disorders and some speculations on the nature of consciousness.

Websites

http://www.brain.com/

A major searchable site for all aspects of brain and behaviour.

http://www.nimh.nih.gov/hotsci/mri.htm

A chance to see what an MRI scan looks like in a comparison of the brain of a schizophrenic and a non-schizophrenic individual. Also some useful information about the usefulness of MRI scans.

http://www.nimh.nih.gov/events/petscan.htm

PET scans of schizophrenics versus controls on a memory task.

Chapter 5

Biological rhythms, sleep and dreaming

Simon Green

Preview

In this chapter we shall be looking at:

◆ types of bodily rhythms and internal body clocks, and the consequences of disrupting bodily rhythms

◆ the evolution and functions of sleep, including ecological and restoration accounts, and the implications from the findings of total and partial sleep deprivation studies

◆ the nature of dreaming and theories of the functions of dreaming, including neurobiological and psychological theories.

Introduction

About one third of our lives is spent in the state of sleep, which represents one of our basic biological rhythms. The first part of the chapter introduces bodily rhythms and the interaction between endogenous (internal) pacemakers and *exogenous* (external or environmental) *zeitgebers*, and considers some effects of disrupting these rhythms. The second part describes the phenomena, evolution, and possible functions of sleep. In the final part, various approaches to the study of dreaming are discussed, including the relationship between dreaming and the stages of sleep, and physiological and psychological theories of the functions of dreaming.

Biological rhythms

The natural world is full of rhythms, such as the regular cycle of the seasons, the rise and fall of the tides, and the rising and the setting of the sun. The body also has its rhythms – some obvious, such as the menstrual cycle and the alternation of sleeping and waking, others less obvious, such as the regular variations in body temperature over a single day.

Many of these rhythms are clearly related to the physical properties of the world we live in. The cycle of the seasons depends on the earth's orbit around the sun. The alternation of day and night is due to the earth's rotation about its axis, and tidal flow reflects the gravitational influence of the moon on the earth. It would therefore be logical to assume that the rhythms we observe in living organisms are directly controlled by these external stimuli. In fact, the situation is more complicated than that. For instance, beach-living algae (single-celled plants) stay under the sand at high tide, burrow to the surface as the water recedes to allow for photosynthesis in the sunshine, and then tunnel back under just before the tide returns. Is this regular rhythm controlled by tidal flows? A simple way to test this is to keep the algae in a laboratory with constant light and no tides. Despite the absence of environmental stimuli,

they still burrow to the surface just after the time of high tide at their home beach and tunnel back under just before the tide returns.

The heliotrope (literally, 'sunseeking') plant opens its leaves during the day and closes them at night. It shows this pattern even if kept indoors in the dark, in time with the actual day/night cycle outside. In countries with fierce winters, the squirrel population hibernates. If these squirrels are kept in a laboratory in a constant warm environment, with alternating 12-hour periods of light and dark, they go through the hibernation routine at the appropriate time of year, increasing food intake and body weight and decreasing body temperature. In addition, they awake as spring approaches in the world outside.

These examples suggest that rhythmic activities can be inbuilt, or endogenous, so that they persist even when the environmental stimuli are absent. Algae are single cells and the controlling pacemaker is probably in the genetic material of the cell nucleus. Squirrels are mammals with complex brains, and hibernation is a complex activity probably controlled from pacemakers in the brain. However, even with these endogenous pacemakers, behaviour in the real world has to be adapted to external events such as winter or night-time, so that leaf opening or hibernation occurs at exactly the right time. Where external events have a role in rhythmic activities, they are called *zeitgebers* (literally, 'time-givers') and much of the research into biological rhythms has been aimed at unravelling the relationship between endogenous pacemakers and these exogenous *zeitgebers*.

Types of rhythm

As already mentioned, there are many biological rhythms in the natural world. A general classification divides them into four groups:

◆ *ultradian* rhythms

◆ *circadian* rhythms

◆ *infradian* rhythms

◆ *circannual* rhythms.

Ultradian rhythms

Ultradian rhythms have a frequency of more than one complete cycle every 24 hours. An example we meet later is the oscillation between sleep stages during a single night's sleep. Ultradian rhythms are also seen in other behaviours, such as foraging and hormone release.

They are also found in many complex human behaviours. For example, when human participants perform tasks that require alertness, EEG measures of alertness appear to vary with an ultradian rhythm. Destruction of the brain mechanisms that control circadian rhythms in animals does not appear to affect behaviours that have an ultradian rhythm. However, they are affected by lesions to specific areas of the hypothalamus (Rosenzweig *et al.* 1999). The periods of ultradian rhythms appear to be correlated with brain and body size: smaller animals tend to have more rapid cycles (Gerkema and Dann 1985).

Circadian rhythms

Circadian rhythms occur once every 24 hours. The human sleep/waking cycle is a good example and many other physiological systems, such as body temperature, operate to the same rhythm. The opening and closing of the heliotrope's leaves is also a circadian rhythm. These rhythms are particularly important to animals because they synchronize behaviour and body states to changes in the environment. The cycle of light and dark, for example, has great significance for survival. Nocturnal animals can avoid predators during the day by remaining hidden. Diurnal animals, on the other hand, are adapted to forage during the day. An endogenous pacemaker (or biological clock) enables these animals to anticipate periodic events, such as the coming of darkness or of sunrise, and engage in appropriate behaviour that adapts them to these environmental changes.

Infradian rhythms

Infradian rhythms occur less than once every 24 hours, for instance hibernation in squirrels and the human menstrual cycle. Some infradian rhythms occur on a seasonal basis and are therefore also known as circannual rhythms.

Circannual rhythms

Circannual rhythms occur on a yearly basis. Examples include migration in birds and hibernation in squirrels and bears. Some of these changes in behaviour are driven by *exogenous* factors, such as temperature or food availability. Many of these rhythms (such as seasonal fluctuations in body weight) will, however, still be maintained in the constant conditions of the laboratory. As with circadian rhythms, animals show a free-running annual rhythm of approximately 365 days, suggesting the existence of an endogenous, circannual oscillator or clock.

Research by Zucker *et al.* (1983) explored the operation of both circadian and circannual rhythms in ground squirrels. These researchers measured activity levels, reproductive cycles and body weight in animals who had free-running circadian and circannual rhythms. Lesions in the SCN (we will explore the role of this later) disrupted circadian activity cycles, but tended not to have any effect on changes that operated on a circannual rhythm, such as body weight and reproductive status. This finding suggests that circannual rhythms are more than a transformation of circadian rhythms (i.e. they do not simply arise by counting 365 circadian cycles) and must, therefore, involve a different underlying mechanism.

Seasonal changes in behaviour are also evident in human beings. For some people, winter brings a particularly low period which may become a profound depression. This winter depression may alternate with a summer mania (Blehar and Rosenthal 1989). In winter, people affected by this fluctuation in mood become depressed, slow down, sleep a lot and overeat. When summer comes, they become elated, energetic and thinner (Rosenzweig *et al.* 1999). This syndrome has become known as seasonal affective disorder (SAD). Some studies have suggested a correlation between latitude (northern latitudes have more prolonged periods of winter darkness) and frequency of SAD, although a recent study in Iceland, a country with a far northern latitude, did not confirm this suggestion (Magnusson and Stefansson 1993). One important function of light is that it suppresses melatonin, a hormone that may have an important role in the regulation of sleep. Exposure to darkness stimulates the synthesis of melatonin whereas light suppresses it. People with SAD are thought to have a high threshold for melatonin suppression, and, although oral administration of melatonin does not appear to affect this disorder, one therapy that is effective in a proportion of SAD cases is light treatment. This involves exposure to bright white light for at least an hour or so every morning. This must be influencing the activity of the suprachiasmatic nucleus, the pineal and the release of melatonin, but the precise mechanisms of this antidepressant action are not understood. Serotonin may also have an important role in SAD as a seasonal rhythm has been demonstrated for this neurotransmitter. We have lower levels of serotonin in the winter and spring than in summer and autumn (Egrise *et al.* 1986).

Activity 1: Your own sleep patterns

Think about your own sleep patterns.

◆ Do you sleep early and rise early, sleep late and rise late, or some combination?

◆ Do you need 6, 8 or 10 hours' rest at night? Or more, or fewer?

◆ Are you a 'morning' person, functioning more effectively soon after waking, or an 'evening' person, ready for action when twilight comes?

◆ Do you sometimes nap during the day?

Compare your pattern with someone else you know and you will find differences. Although inbuilt and generally similar across people, biological rhythms show individual differences in their precise patterning.

Pacemakers

Endogenous pacemakers, sometimes referred to as biological clocks, probably represent an inherited genetic mechanism. For example, regular rhythms of activity and rest can be measured in the unborn human embryo which has never been exposed to the outside world. But, as pointed out earlier, these rhythms have to respond to *zeitgebers* if the behaviour they control is to be fully coordinated with the external world. One of the most influential *zeitgebers* is light, and its role in fine-tuning bodily rhythms has been reasonably well mapped out.

Probably the most important pacemaker in the brain of birds and reptiles is the *pineal gland*. This structure contains light receptors which respond to external light, penetrating the thin layer of skull that lies above the pineal. In turn, these light receptors

influence the activity of neurons in the pineal. These neurons have a natural rhythmic activity and also convert the neurotransmitter serotonin into the hormone melatonin. Melatonin is then released into the general circulation, acts on many of the body's organs and glands, and seems to be responsible for the rhythmic nature of many activities. For instance, it acts on brainstem sleep mechanisms to help synchronize the phases of sleep and waking, and it has been shown that injections of melatonin can produce sleep in sparrows. The manufacture and release of melatonin is regulated by the amount of light falling on the pineal, decreasing as light increases. Research has shown, for instance, that chickens wake and become active as dawn breaks and melatonin secretion falls (Binkley 1979). This also means that their waking, although controlled by the biological clock in the pineal, is adjusted to the actual time that morning begins, which of course varies throughout the year.

In mammals, including humans, the pathways are more complicated. The main biological clock seems to be a small area in the hypothalamus, the suprachiasmatic nucleus (SCN), whose neurons have an inbuilt circadian rhythmic firing pattern. This nucleus regulates the manufacture and secretion of melatonin in the pineal gland via an interconnecting pathway. Another pathway connects the retina of the eye to the SCN. This allows the amount of light falling on the retina to influence the activity of SCN neurons and, indirectly, the release of melatonin from the pineal. So the link between light and melatonin production is maintained. One recent discovery is that light can reach the brain without passing through the eyes. Campbell and Murphy (1998) applied light to the back of the knees in human subjects and were able to shift the circadian rhythm in body temperature and melatonin secretion.

The pineal and the SCN function jointly as endogenous pacemakers or biological clocks in the brain. There are many bodily rhythms, and it is likely that there are other structures involved in maintaining their regularity, as we shall see later in relation to sleep. Research has shown, for example, that animals fed on a regular basis soon become active just before their feeding time. This happens even in the absence of environmental cues, and therefore must rely on some sort of internal clock. Rosenwasser *et al.* (1981) found that rats still showed this anticipation after their SCN was destroyed, so another internal clock must be able to perform this function.

Although the SCN has a vital role in 24-hour rhythms, it has also been found to have important functions in rhythms much longer than 24 hours. Male hamsters show annual rhythms of testosterone secretion, and these appear to be based on the amount of light that occurs each day. The hamsters' breeding season begins as the days lengthen and ends when the days get shorter again. Lesions of the SCN destroy these annual breeding cycles, and male hamsters secrete testosterone all year (Rusak and Zucker 1975). Presumably, these lesions disrupt these annual cycles because they destroy the 24-hour clock against which daily light levels are measured to determine the season. If the period of light is less than 12 hours, it must be winter; if more than 12 hours, it must be summer (Carlson 1994).

The sensitivity of the pineal and SCN to light, and the role of melatonin in controlling sleep and activity amongst other things, mean that despite the endogenous nature of the clocks, their activity is synchronized with the light/dark rhythm of the world outside. Occasionally, slightly bizarre studies have allowed us to look at the effects of removing light as a *zeitgeber* and allowing these biological clocks to run free (see *In Focus*).

Such studies show that subjects with free-running biological clocks settle to a rhythmic sleeping/waking pattern of about 25 hours, i.e. slightly longer than under normal conditions. So we can draw two conclusions:

◆ Our endogenous mechanisms can control sleep/waking cycles in the absence of light.

◆ The presence of light as a *zeitgeber* is necessary to reset the clock every day so that the biological rhythm is perfectly coordinated with the external world.

As mentioned earlier, light affects melatonin secretion in chickens, triggering the chicken's waking routine. Something similar may well be happening in humans.

Such studies indicate how we use stimuli around us to coordinate our biological clocks. The gradual lengthening and shortening of the days is reflected in gradual shifts in rhythms of activity and sleep/waking cycles. These biological processes are also influenced by other stimuli, such as outside temperature and social patterns. Eskimos have regular sleep/waking cycles, even though they have continuous daylight in summer and continuous darkness in winter, showing

that for them the social rhythms of life are the dominant *zeitgebers*.

Usually *zeitgebers*, such as light or social behaviour patterns, change only slowly, if at all. However, there are times when they change radically and quickly, and the usual coordination between our biological rhythms and the outside world breaks down. Modern civilization has led to two common examples: jet travel and shift work.

Jet lag

If you travel by plane from England to the East coast of the USA, leaving at noon, you arrive at about 7 p.m. UK-time, but it would be 2 p.m. USA-time. All your physiological rhythms are working to UK-time, so that at 6 p.m. USA-time, you are ready to sleep, with a falling body temperature and decreasing bodily arousal. This dislocation of our physiological rhythms from the outside world produces the sensation of jet lag that many people experience and which lasts as long as it takes for them to resynchronize. Studies have shown that the quickest way to achieve this is to follow the local *zeitgebers* rather than your body, i.e. in the example above you should force yourself to stay awake until 11 p.m. USA-time and also adjust your meal times and socializing patterns. If you follow your biological clocks, adjustment takes much longer.

Strangely, jet lag is more severe travelling West to East (USA to the UK), than from East to West. This may be because it is easier to adjust the body clocks when they are ahead of local time (called 'phase delay') than when they are behind (a situation when they have to 'phase advance'). Because of its role in controlling body rhythms, melatonin has been studied as a possible treatment for jet lag and other desynchronization problems and although nothing very systematic has yet emerged, it may eventually lead to an effective therapy.

Shift work

Organizations and industries that work around the clock require their employees to do shift work. A classic pattern is to divide the day into three eight-hour shifts: midnight to 8 a.m., 8 a.m. to 4 p.m., 4 p.m. to midnight. Switching shifts obviously disrupts links between

Michel Siffre's free-running biological clock

The most famous study of free-running biological clocks involved a French cave explorer, Michel Siffre, who in 1972 spent six months in an underground cave in Texas separated from natural light/dark cycles. He was wired up so that various body functions could be recorded. When he was awake, the experimenters put his lights on; when he went to bed, they turned the lights off. He ate and slept whenever he wanted. At first his sleep-waking cycle was very erratic, but it settled down to a fairly regular pattern with a periodicity of between 25 and 30 hours. When he emerged, it was the 179th day, but by his 'days', it was only the 151st.

zeitgebers (light/dark, meals, social life, etc.) and biological rhythms and, as with jet lag, some time is necessary for readjustment. Many shift patterns require a turn around every week, with workers moving back one shift every time. The work with jet lag suggests that a week is barely enough time to allow for such a major resynchronization, so that workers are in a permanent state of 'jet lag', impairing performance and increasing stress. The backwards movement is the same as West to East jet travel, leading to the more difficult phase-advance situation. There is suggestive anecdotal evidence that performance, especially vigilance, is lowered at times when biological rhythms are pushing for sleep – both the near nuclear accident at Three Mile Island and the actual accident at Chernobyl occurred because of decision failures made in the early hours of the morning.

Experimental support comes from Czeisler *et al.* (1982), studying a Utah Chemical plant. There was a high rate of health problems, sleep difficulties and work-related stress in staff employed on short rotation shifts. Czeisler persuaded them to change to a phase-delay system (moving a shift forwards every time) and to increase the shift rotation from seven days to 21 days, allowing more time for adjustment. After nine months of the new system, worker satisfaction was significantly increased and factory output was higher.

The problems of jet lag and shift work are due to the way we have artificially dislocated the normal coordination between our biological clocks and the external world. We are the results of a long evolutionary history, in which the alternation of day and night has shaped the lives of all organisms. It is, therefore, no surprise that we should still be under the same influence, and suffer consequences when we interfere with things. Coren (1996) has pointed out that a culture shift occurred at the beginning of the last century when electric lighting became widely available. Now factories and offices could operate around the clock, introducing widespread shift work and longer working hours. Social life also could extend late into the night, if you were lucky. Coren estimates that on average we sleep for around one and a half hours less than we did a century ago, so that many of us are in a constant state of mild sleep deprivation.

Exam summary: Biological rhythms

The AQA examination will test your understanding of the following areas:

◆ research studies of circadian, infradian, and ultradian rhythms (pp. 114–15)

◆ the role of endogenous pacemakers and exogenous *zeitgebers* (pp. 115–16)

◆ the consequences of disrupting biological rhythms (pp. 116–17).

Example question

The question below is typical of one drawn from the material above, and should take you 30 minutes to answer:

(a) Outline research studies into two types of biological rhythm. *(12 marks)*

(b) Assess the impact of disrupting biological rhythms in humans. *(12 marks)*

Suggested answer structure

(a) The first thing to remember is that parted questions require very careful time management. You would have 30 minutes to answer this question, and so 15 minutes to answer this part. There are three very important instructions in the question. First, you are asked to write about research studies of biological rhythms, rather than just describing what these rhythms are. Second, you are only required to outline these studies, so a long drawn-out description would not be appropriate. Third, you are asked to write about *two* types of rhythm, so resist the temptation to write about more than two.

The previous section introduced you to four types of rhythm: ultradian, infradian, circadian and circannual rhythms. In the next part of this chapter you will learn that the alternation between different sleep stages (see pp. 118–19) is an example of an ultradian rhythm, so research related to this area would be relevant to this part of the question. Remember also that circannual rhythms, although not mentioned specifically in the specification requirements, are examples of infradian rhythms. Research studies of endogenous pacemakers (such as the SCN) and exogenous *zeitgebers* (pp. 115–16) are examples of how psychologists have investigated circadian rhythms.

(b) This part of the question (which should also take you 15 minutes to answer) asks you to assess the impact of disrupting biological rhythms. There are two especially important points to remember here. First, this part of the question is the AO2 component of the question (see Chapter 21 for an explanation of this), so requires something more than simply a description of the different ways in which behaviour might be affected by disrupting biological rhythms. This is an important point – don't waste time detailing lots of examples of disruption, but spend your time in a more considered (and therefore more effective) way. You should aim for a 'considered appraisal' of evidence that disruption has detrimental effects. This might include explaining why disruption of rhythms has such a detrimental effect (pp. 116–17), looking at the research evidence for such claims (p. 117) or perhaps assessing the consequences of disruption over the longer term (e.g. Coren's claim that we are permanently in a state of mild sleep deprivation).

The second important point about this question is that it does not tie you to the same two biological rhythms that you outlined in the first part of the question. Your response might be specific to one particular type of rhythm (the use of the plural 'rhythms' here does not require more than this) or more general, taking in more than one type of rhythm.

Sleep

The 24-hour cycle of sleeping and waking is our most obvious biological rhythm. We spend around 30 per cent of our lives sleeping, and for centuries have wondered about its function. Other bodily processes, such as body temperature, urine flow and release of hormones from the pituitary and adrenal glands, also show a circadian rhythm, with one peak and one trough every 24 hours. However, it is the sleep/waking cycle that has been most studied. One of the features of sleep is that there are several different identifiable types of sleep which we move between throughout the night in a regular pattern (see Fig. 5.1). This is an example of an ultradian rhythm.

One of the earliest debates in this area was whether sleep was simply the state the body fell into when it was not active, i.e. sleep as a passive process. You have probably read enough now to see that this is unlikely. The brain contains biological clocks which actively regulate physiological and behavioural processes. In the cave studies, sleep/waking patterns settled down to a consistent pattern despite the absence of *zeitgebers*, while states such as hibernation are induced by the brain at the appropriate time of year. Biological rhythms in general reflect active control by brain mechanisms and sleep is unlikely to be different. The problem is to identify the specific brain mechanisms involved in sleep and to explain how they interact with the world outside. This may give us some idea of the functions of sleep.

Sleep – stages and types

The introduction of the electroencephalograph (EEG) in the 1930s was a crucial step in the investigation of sleep. Using it, Dement and Kleitman in the 1950s were able to demonstrate that sleep, far from being a quiet and peaceful phenomenon, consisted of clearly differentiated stages of brain activity (Dement and Kleitman 1957). There are various approaches to defining the stages, but whichever is used, the EEG observations themselves are similar.

Figure 5.1 Pattern of sleep over one night

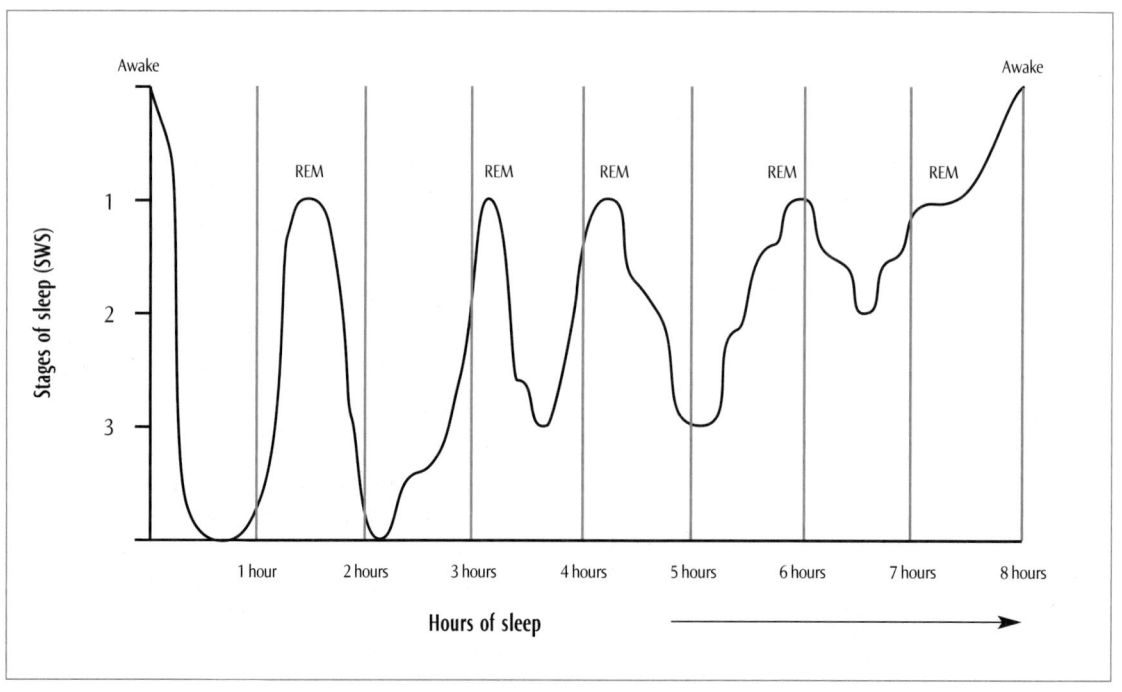

◆ Chapter 4 describes how the EEG pattern can be either synchronized or desynchronized. When it is synchronized, there is a repeated wave form with a particular frequency (measured as cycles per second, or Herz, Hz); when desynchronized, there is no consistent wave form.

◆ The waking, alert EEG consists of fast desynchronized activity.

◆ As we relax prior to sleep, the EEG becomes synchronized and alpha waves appear with a characteristic frequency of 8 to 12 Hz. Heart rate slows, muscle tension reduces and body temperature begins to fall.

◆ In stage 1 of sleep proper, the alpha waves disappear to be replaced by slower and smaller desynchronized activity.

◆ In stage 2, the EEG becomes synchronized with larger and slower waves interrupted by bursts of fast spiking activity, the sleep spindles. These last for a second or two and consist of high frequency (12 to 16 Hz) waves.

◆ Stage 3 is dominated by large slow delta waves (1 to 3 Hz), with spindles becoming less common. Heart rate, respiration and metabolic rate continue to fall.

◆ Finally, in stage 4 the EEG consists only of delta waves, metabolic rate is at its lowest and the arousal threshold (how difficult it is to wake the subject up) is very high.

These are known as the stages of slow-wave sleep or SWS, as the EEG is characterized by synchronized slow-wave activity.

REM sleep

However, sleep is a dynamic process and, after 30 minutes or so in stage 4 SWS, we ascend through the sleep stages to the light SWS of stage 2. At this point, about an hour and a half after sleep onset, the EEG suddenly shifts into the fast, desynchronized pattern of the aroused subject. Here, arousal thresholds are also very high (the participant is hard to awaken) and the skeletal muscles completely relax leaving the person effectively paralysed. Heart rate and respiration increase and rapid movements of the eyes occur. For this reason, this stage of sleep is called rapid eye movement sleep, or REM. It is sometimes also referred to as paradoxical sleep, as it combines features of bodily relaxation with an aroused EEG and the rapid eye movements.

After 15 minutes or so in REM, we move back into light SWS and then descend into the deeper stages 3 and 4. This cyclical pattern (Fig. 5.1) repeats itself every ninety minutes or so (the ultradian rhythm mentioned earlier), giving five or six cycles per night. Towards morning, we spend more time in light SWS, which seems to trigger more phases of REM. As we shall see, REM is associated with dreams and so we tend to dream more as morning approaches.

As mentioned earlier in the chapter, cycles of rest and activity can be recorded in the developing embryo and it has been shown that the sleep cycle of the newborn baby does not vary much over the first year. The rhythms of sleep are controlled by our endogenous biological clocks, although, as the baby grows, the activity of the clocks will become synchronized with the outside world, especially the light–dark cycle. The sleep/waking cycle and the patterning of the stages of sleep are fundamental biological rhythms. So, what are their functions?

Functions of sleep

There is no simple explanation for the functions of sleep and there are many hypotheses based on a wide range of observations and experiments. Sleep is found throughout the animal kingdom, although it can be hard to recognize in reptiles and other cold-blooded animals, since arousal states in these groups depend so much on external temperature that it can be difficult to distinguish sleep from inactivity brought on by the cold. In addition, the EEG recordings used to identify sleep stages in mammals come from the cerebral cortex, which is poorly developed in reptiles, so we are not even sure what reptilian sleep would look like in EEG terms. Sleep is clearly identifiable in birds and mammals and this alone suggests that it must have some function. There are humans who can get by on very little sleep – in rare cases less than an hour – but,

---

Activity 2: How loss of sleep affects you

Think back to a time when you experienced significant sleep deprivation – perhaps at an all-night party or foolishly revising during the night before an examination.

◆ Did you notice any effects the following day? These could have been feelings of tiredness, problems with concentration and perhaps difficulties with memory.

◆ The following night, did you sleep for much longer than usual, or only a little?

Excitement and stress can override our biological pacemakers and keep us awake when the body wants to sleep, and arousal can minimize the psychological effects of sleep deprivation. Eventually, we do have to recover some of the lost sleep, but usually only a fraction of what was lost.

in general, we all need between 6 and 8 hours. If it is universal, what happens if animals are deprived of it?

Rats deprived of sleep for around 21 days die, but this is complicated by the very stressful procedures they are put through in order to keep them awake. There have been many studies of voluntary sleep deprivation in humans and these provide more reliable data.

Sleep deprivation and restoration explanations

Most people, if asked why they sleep, would answer that they sleep because they are tired. This simple explanation of the functions of sleep suggests that the purpose of sleep is somehow to restore the body to its full 'waking' capacity, and make up for all the wear and tear of the day's activities. A specific way in which the body 'restores' the materials of the day comes from the finding that growth hormone is released through SWS. As well as being involved in growth processes, growth hormone has an important role in the metabolism of proteins. Protein synthesis is an important aspect of the restoration of body tissue, and as these are relatively fragile, they must be constantly renewed and replaced during sleep. The highest concentrations of growth hormone in the blood are found in SWS, particularly in stages 3 and 4.

In a thorough review of the area, Horne (1988) concludes that studies of sleep deprivation in normal subjects show only the range of effects seen in the schoolboy, Randy Gardner (see *In Focus*), together with some sleep recovery concentrated in stage 4 SWS and REM. Although the effects of sleep deprivation are not dramatic, they do involve cognitive abilities such as perception, attention and memory, while the recovery of stage 4 SWS and REM suggests that these are the critical phases. Horne therefore proposes that, in humans, core sleep, consisting of stage 4 SWS and REM, is essential for normal brain functioning, while the lighter stages of SWS are not essential and he refers to them as optional sleep. During core sleep the brain recovers and restores itself after the activities of the day (some details of what is being restored are covered later).

This hypothesis is similar to the restoration model put forward by Oswald (1980). He suggests that the high level of brain activity seen in REM reflects brain recovery, while an increase in the body's hormone activities during SWS reflects restoration and recovery in the body. They both agree that REM is essential for brain repair and this is supported by the high proportion of REM seen in the newborn baby, where it makes up 50 to 60 per cent of sleep time, gradually falling to the normal proportion of about 25 per cent as the child grows. The months before and after birth are a time of rapid brain growth and development so that, if REM is a time when such processes occur, it is logical that the baby should show increased REM sleep (see Fig. 5.2).

The difference between the two approaches lies in the proposed functions of slow-wave sleep. As total sleep deprivation produces few obvious effects on the body, Horne (1988) thinks that body restoration is not the purpose of sleep. He suggests that this occurs during periods of relaxed wakefulness, leaving core sleep to provide for the brain. However, Horne is specifically discussing human studies and it is quite possible that the sort of division put forward by Oswald could apply to non-human animals. As there are significant differences between species in the precise details of the sleep/waking cycle, it is possible that no single hypothesis could cover them all.

Evaluation of restoration theories

Somewhat surprisingly, the view that sleep has a vital restorative function is only weakly supported by research. One way of testing this hypothesis is by looking at the effects of presleep activities on the duration of sleep. According to the restorative perspective, intense metabolic expenditure during the day should increase the duration of sleep in order to restore the materials used. For most people, intense exercise may cause them to fall asleep more quickly, but it does not cause them to sleep for longer (Rosenzweig *et al.* 1999).

Sleep deprivation record

The record for total sleep deprivation is held by a 17-year-old schoolboy, Randy Gardner, who in 1964 stayed awake for 264 hours (11 days). If sleep is a critical function, you might expect such deprivation to have severe effects. In fact Gardner did have blurred vision and incoherent speech, some perceptual disturbances such as imagining objects were people and a mild degree of paranoia, imagining that others thought him stupid because of his cognitive problems. He did not suffer from psychosis (a complete breakdown of mental functioning) and recovered quickly when he eventually slept. The first night he slept for 15 hours and, in fact, over that and the following nights he recovered only about a quarter of his lost sleeping time. Recovery was specific to particular stages, as two-thirds of stage 4 SWS and a half of REM sleep were recovered, but little of the other SWS stages.

Figure 5.2
Changes in proportions of SWS and REM sleep with age

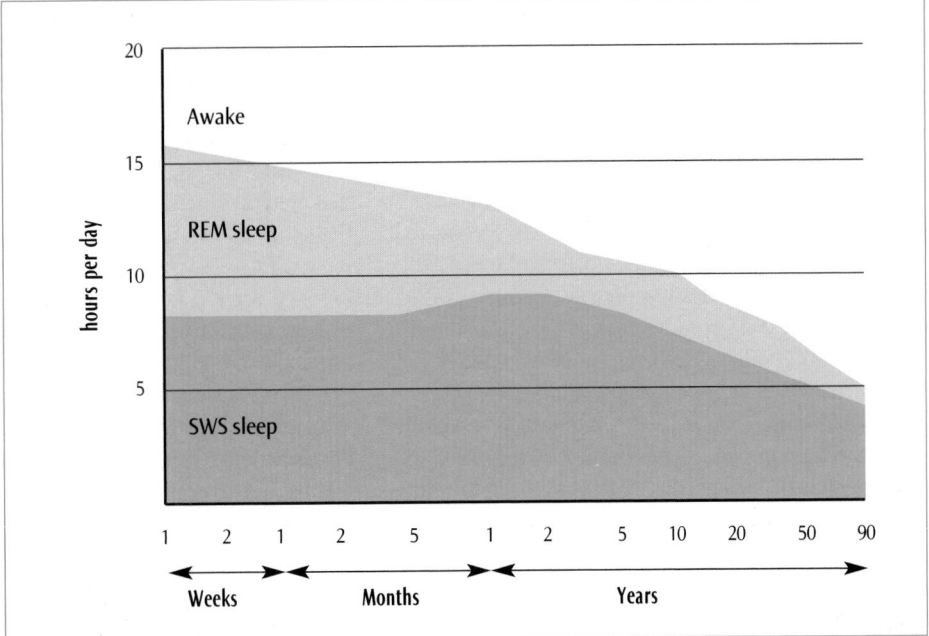

Sleep deprivation studies have failed to provide conclusive evidence that sleep is necessary to keep the body functioning normally. Horne (1978) reviewed 50 studies in which humans had been deprived of sleep. He found that very few of them reported that sleep deprivation had interfered with the participants' ability to perform physical exercise. Neither was there any evidence of a physiological stress response to the sleep deprivation. However, prolonged sleep deprivation in rats appears to cause them to increase their metabolic rate, lose weight and, within an average of 19 days, die (Everson *et al.* 1989). Allowing these animals to sleep within that time prevents their death. Animal studies such as this suffer the problem that it is difficult to separate the effects of sleep deprivation from the methods used to keep the animals awake. In order to keep animals awake they must be constantly stimulated, and hence stressed.

Studies to isolate which organs are most affected by chronic sleep deprivation have failed to isolate one specific system that is affected to the exclusion of others. It is most likely that sleep deprivation in animal studies interferes with the immune system which then leads to death. It is possible that sleep provides the only opportunity for tissue restoration in some species. For example, when rats are awake, they generally spend all their time foraging, seeking mates or avoiding predators. Humans, on the other hand, are capable of resting during the day. In fact, our metabolic activity when we are in a state of quiet restfulness is only 9 per cent higher than it is when we are asleep. Some humans have a rare inherited defect that prevents them sleeping normally. People with this disorder, called *fatal familial insomnia*, sleep normally until middle age

when they simply stop sleeping, leading to death within two years. Autopsies have revealed a degeneration of the thalamus, which may well be responsible for the onset of the insomnia.

One of the most important claims for the restorative function of sleep was that growth hormone is released during SWS and that this has an important role in protein synthesis. Horne (1988) points out, however, that as amino acids (the constituents of proteins) are only freely available for five hours after a meal, and most people eat several hours before going to bed, then for most of the night, the supply of available amino acids is low, which implies that not much protein synthesis would go on during sleep.

REM sleep deprivation and neurochemical explanations

Besides total sleep deprivation, many studies have investigated specific (or partial) deprivation of REM sleep. In rats and cats, this involved the now discredited 'flowerpot technique'. The animal was placed on an upturned flowerpot surrounded by water, with no possibility of escape. It would fall asleep and then pass into a phase of REM. You will recall that in REM the skeletal muscles relax. In the flowerpot animal, as the neck muscles relax, the head falls into the water and the animal wakes up. Over a long period, the animal becomes deprived of sleep in general and REM in particular. It is also permanently wet and highly stressed, which is why any results were very unreliable (and why the procedure is no longer used).

In humans, REM deprivation is achieved by monitoring the EEG recordings and waking the participants up when they enter a phase of REM. One of the earliest observations was that, after some nights of REM deprivation, there would be some REM rebound, i.e. an increase in REM sleep which partially compensated for the lost REM. This is entirely consistent with the findings from Randy Gardner and other studies of total sleep deprivation.

This observation can be combined with those concerning the effects of drugs in the treatment of depression. Drugs (described in Chapter 18) such as the monoamine oxidase inhibitors (MAOIs) and tricyclics, besides their antidepressant action, also cause a drastic reduction in REM sleep. More interestingly, when drug treatment is discontinued, there is no REM rebound as you normally find after REM deprivation.

A possible explanation for this is that REM rebound occurs because the subject has been deprived of whatever it is that occurs during REM sleep and needs to make up the loss. If there is no rebound, perhaps it is because the treatment causing the loss of REM is itself providing whatever is necessary. What do the drugs do in the brain? Although they may have different mechanisms of action, antidepressants always increase levels of the neurotransmitters noradrenaline and serotonin. Therefore, it has been proposed by Stern and Morgane (1974) that the normal function of REM sleep is to enable levels of neurotransmitters to be restored after the day's exertions. An ordinary person deprived of REM suffers a loss of neurotransmitters that they make up when allowed to sleep normally by increasing the amount of REM sleep – REM rebound. A depressed person given antidepressants shows a decrease in REM because the drugs are themselves increasing neurotransmitter levels, removing the need for REM sleep and for any REM rebound when drug treatment stops.

This account is closely related to the restoration hypotheses of Oswald and Horne. REM sleep restores neurotransmitter levels, while REM deprivation causes a loss of noradrenaline and serotonin, and this also causes problems with any behavioural functions in which they are involved, such as perception, memory and attention. Total sleep deprivation would have similar effects, because REM is also lost under these conditions. We return to neurotransmitters and sleep later, but for now we need to look at a very different approach.

Evolutionary and ecological approaches

Although sleep can be identified, with difficulty, in reptiles, it is found in its characteristic complexity only in birds and mammals. Even in mammals, there are profound differences in total sleep time, amounts of SWS and REM, and cyclical organization. Many variables contribute to these differences, such as primitiveness (assessed in terms of brain development), body size and ecological niche (i.e. lifestyle). This variety has led to a number of hypotheses on the general functions of sleep across the animal kingdom.

Meddis (1979) proposes that sleep evolved to keep animals inconspicuous and safe from predators when normal activities were impossible. The importance of the predator or prey status is emphasized by the observation that predators (lions, tigers, etc.) sleep for much longer than prey animals (cattle, gazelle, etc.). It is as though the more dangerous your world, the less time you can afford to spend sleeping and vulnerable. One slight complication is that prey animals tend to be herbivores, needing to spend huge amounts of time grazing in order to take in sufficient food and simply have less time to sleep, although, of course, it still makes sense to be as inconspicuous as possible when not feeding.

The precise ecological niche an animal occupies can also affect the organization of sleep. Aquatic mammals such as dolphins and porpoises have particular problems, because prolonged sleep under water is dangerous, given that they are air breathers. The Indus dolphin gets around this by apparently sleeping for seconds at a time repeatedly throughout the 24-hour day (Pilleri 1979). Other marine mammals have adapted to the need for sleep in different ways. The bottlenose dolphin and the porpoise both display an ability to 'switch off' one of their cerebral hemispheres at a time (Mukhametov 1984). This strategy allows one hemisphere to be alert at all times while the other catches up on its sleep. During these periods of 'unilateral sleep', the animals continue to come up to the surface to breathe, so their sleep is not characterized by complete motor paralysis. Fig. 5.3 shows the EEG records from the two hemispheres, and clearly demonstrates that slow-wave sleep occurs independently in the two hemispheres. The lengths animals go to in order to sleep is a powerful argument in favour of sleep being an essential function.

In land mammals, total sleep time is also related to body weight. Squirrels and shrews, for instance, sleep for about 14 hours a day, cows and sheep for about four. The smaller an animal is, the greater its metabolic rate. Metabolic rate is an index of the activity in the body's physiological systems and the higher it is, the faster the body uses up energy resources. So, sleep in smaller mammals may be important for conserving these resources as well as keeping them safe from predators.

Because of the way sleep duration and patterning seems to depend on brain development, body size, life style, etc., it is unlikely that any single explanation could account for the function of sleep in all animals. The giant sloth is relatively large and not the most active of animals, and should not 'need' much sleep, yet it sleeps for around 20 hours a day; this goes against the body size correlation and restoration ideas. As sleep

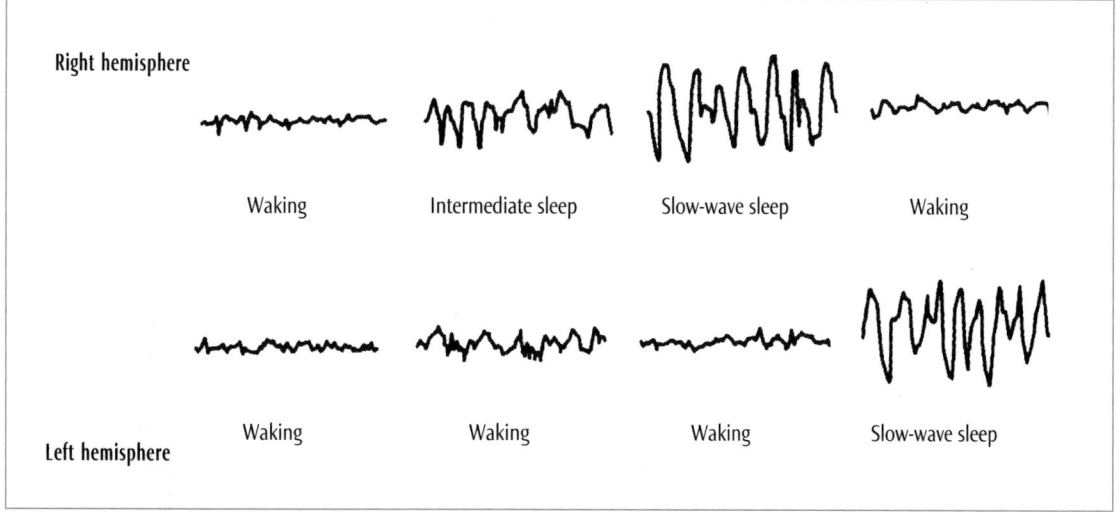

Figure 5.3 Sleep in a dolphin. The two hemispheres sleep independently, presumably so that the animal remains alert
Source: Carlson (1994, p. 261)

itself has many stages, it is even likely that different stages have different functions. For instance, REM sleep is most clearly identifiable in birds and mammals, which are warm-blooded (homiotherms), and not in reptiles, which are cold-blooded (poikilotherms). It has therefore been suggested that REM, during which brain metabolism is increased, evolved as a means of maintaining the brain's temperature during a period when it might otherwise fall to dangerous levels. The peculiar characteristics of REM sleep have generated much interest and a number of detailed hypotheses.

Like all biological and behavioural phenomena, sleep is subject to evolutionary pressures, especially perhaps the ecological niche the animal occupies. Although there seems to be a fundamental drive to sleep, the precise patterning and organization of sleep may then become tailored to the particular lifestyle of the species.

Evaluation of evolutionary and ecological explanations

The basis of these explanations is that sleep serves an important adaptive function, particularly because sleep prevents animals from attracting the attention of predators. Although this seems a very plausible explanation, it is difficult to evaluate what kinds of evidence would support this proposition. It is also not clear why such a complex physiological mechanism as sleep would evolve simply to keep vulnerable animals out of harm's way, when a state of behavioural activity would serve much the same purpose. Many animals do, of course, 'play possum' by freezing when threatened by predators. An opposite view is that more vulnerable animals sleep less, because of their decreased sensitivity to external stimuli (e.g. predators) during sleep. As we have seen, prey animals seen to sleep less than

predators. This is not really a theory of the functions of sleep, but rather an explanation of the factors that limit sleep. This hypothesis is supported by the negative correlation between the amounts of both slow-wave and REM sleep, and predatory danger.

A persuasive argument against the view that sleep serves an important adaptive function is the fact that sleep is found in species who would seem to be better off without it (Carlson 1994). For example, the Indus dolphin lives in the muddy waters of the Indus River in Pakistan. This animal has, over the years, become blind, as given the extremely poor visibility of its environment, good eyesight is somewhat unnecessary. It does, however, have an excellent sonar system, which it uses to navigate and find prey. Despite the dangers of falling asleep (i.e. potential injury from floating debris and passing river traffic), sleep has not disappeared. Although the Indus dolphin never stops swimming, it does sleep for about 7 hours each day, in short naps of 4 to 60 seconds each. If sleep served merely an adaptive function, then surely it would have been eliminated (as was vision) through the process of natural selection (Carlson 1994).

Exam summary: Sleep

The AQA examination will test your understanding of the following areas:

◆ ecological theories of the function of sleep and research studies relating to these explanations (pp. 122–3)

◆ restoration theories of the function of sleep and research studies relating to these explanations (pp. 120–1)

◆ the implications of total and partial sleep deprivation studies for explanations of sleep (pp. 121–2).

Example question

The question below is typical of one drawn from the material above, and should take you 30 minutes to answer:

◆ Describe and evaluate one theory of the functions of sleep.   *(24 marks)*

Suggested answer structure

This section you have just read covers a number of different theories about the functions of sleep. These include restoration theories (pp. 120–1) and ecological theories (pp. 122). Note that it would be perfectly acceptable to cover either a particular perspective (such as restoration) or a particular theory (such as Oswald or Horne) in response to this question.

It is important to remember that there are two components to this question. The term 'describe' invites you to demonstrate your knowledge and understanding of your chosen theory, and the term 'evaluate' invites you to make a judgement about the 'value' of that particular theory. For example, if you chose to write about the evolutionary theory of sleep, you might include the central proposals of this theory (e.g. that sleep evolved to keep animals inconspicuous and safe from predators when normal activities were impossible; and that sleep is subject to evolutionary pressures, especially the ecological niche the animal occupies). These central ideas should then be elaborated, perhaps by the use of appropriate examples to illustrate their importance. For example, how do aquatic air-breathing mammals get over the problem of both sleeping and breathing when asleep?

There are a number of ways in which you can evaluate the evolutionary perspective on sleep. Evolutionary explanations propose that sleep serves an important adaptive function, but is there evidence for this? Sleep is seen as a way of keeping vulnerable animals from the attention of predators, but as we have seen, it seems unlikely that such a complex mechanism would evolve when waking inactivity would do the same job. As evolutionary explanations stress adaptation through natural selection, you might mention the case of the Indus dolphin which sleeps despite the dangers of sleeping in its specific ecological niche. Remember that evaluation involves you actively engaging with your written material – constantly challenging assumptions, critically examining evidence (does it support or challenge a particular point of view?) and suggesting alternative interpretations.

Dreaming

Dreaming and REM

The most distinctive feature of REM sleep is dreaming. Although people woken up during non-REM sleep may report dreaming, they are much more likely to do so if they are woken during a phase of REM. Dreams can be bizarre and dramatic phenomena, and it is easy to assume that they must have some deep meaning. Before looking at some of the possibilities, we must first draw a distinction between REM sleep and dreaming. REM sleep is a physiological state of the brain and body, defined using measures of the EEG, eye movements, muscle tone, etc. The pioneering work of Aserinsky and Kleitman (1953) supported a close association between REM and dreaming, so much so that for years afterwards it was perfectly acceptable to refer to REM as 'dreaming sleep'. If REM and dreaming were the same thing, we could call them *isomorphic*, and talking about one would be the same as talking about the other. However, we now know that they are not isomorphic. Although REM is a physiological state defined by EEG recordings, eye movements, and changes in muscle tone, it could still be isomorphic if dreams occurred whenever we went into REM and only if we went into REM sleep.

However, dreaming also occurs in non-REM sleep (NREM), and although on the whole NREM dreams are less intense, less emotional, and less vivid than REM dreams, sometimes they are indistinguishable (Moffitt *et al.* 1993). So REM and dreaming are not identical. In fact, some of the ideas discussed earlier on restoration of neurotransmitter levels during REM are purely physiological with no role for dreams at all. But, as a generalization, most researchers agree that there is a special relationship between REM and dreaming, and increasingly theories of the function of REM sleep include a role or at least an explanation for the dream imagery that accompanies it.

Dreams are often thought of as a series of visual images, although these are merely one part of the dream experience. We may also experience actions and emotions in our dreams. Congenitally blind people also have dreams that are no less vivid even though they see nothing (Oswald 1980). The term 'nightmare' tends to be used for those dreams that occur during REM sleep in which a series of events are associated with anxiety. When a person awakes from a nightmare, they are frequently aware of the muscle paralysis that accompanies REM sleep. Nightmares occur unpredictably during sleep but become more frequent when the person has experienced considerable anxiety during their waking hours. Likewise, people who are depressed by day tend to have dreams that contain themes of failure and loss (Oswald 1980).

Theories of the functions of dreaming

Early work on the significance and functions of dreaming was dominated by the ideas of psychoanalysts such as Freud and Jung. This was mainly because the highly subjective nature of dream content meant that it was impossible to use objective scientific methods. Psychology sees itself as a science, and therefore had no way of investigating dreams. The discovery of the relationship between REM and dreaming in the 1950s introduced the possibility of linking the scientific study of REM (using the EEG) to hypotheses on the nature of dream content. Gradually, theories of the function of REM began to include speculations on the role of dream imagery. This process was galvanized by rapid developments in computer science, which led to an increasing use of computer analogies to explain psychological phenomena, including REM and dreams.

We therefore have a wide range of hypotheses, ideas, and speculations on the nature and functions of dreaming. After reviewing some of these, we will return to the methodological problems involved in dream research.

There is no particularly neat division of theories of dreaming into categories. Even the earliest ideas from Aristotle in 350 BC and Artemidorus in 200 AD are echoed in contemporary approaches, such as the dependence of dream imagery on the day's experiences. Freud and Jung concentrated on the use of dreams to analyse relationships between our conscious and unconscious minds, but again the idea of dream imagery as reflecting the interface between our daily experiences and our stored memories is also found in theories from modern experimental psychology. We will review some of these approaches, and then summarize some general conclusions on the nature and functions of dreams.

First we will look at some models based on the brain's activity during REM, in which interpreting dream imagery is secondary to explaining the underlying cognitive function of REM. Then we will consider psychological approaches which take the dream itself as subject matter.

Neurobiological theories

Crick and Mitchison

Computer metaphors, popular for describing the brain, have also been applied to dreams. Crick and Mitchison

(1983) propose that during dreaming, the brain is 'off line'; during this phase it sifts through the information gathered during the day's waking activities and throws out unwanted material. According to this model, we dream to forget by a process of 'reverse learning'. The cortex cannot cope with the amount of information received during the day without developing 'parasitic' thoughts, which would disrupt the efficient organization of memory. During REM, these unwanted connections in cortical networks are erased by impulses bombarding the cortex from subcortical areas. The actual content of dreams represents these parasitic thoughts as they are wiped out from memory.

One piece of indirect evidence used for this is from studies of the spiny anteater, echidna. This primitive egg-laying mammal, from a group known as the monotremes, has no REM sleep (incidentally indicating that REM evolved at a point when placental mammals such as humans diverged from the monotremes), but does have a hugely enlarged frontal cortex. Crick and Mitchison argue that it needed this excessive cortical development to store both adaptive memories and parasitic memories, which in more highly evolved animals are disposed of in REM sleep.

One problem for the model is that dreams are often organized into clear narratives (stories). If they consisted only of disposable, parasitic thoughts, why should they be so organized? Later, they in fact restricted their model to apply only to dreams with bizarre imagery.

Hobson and McCarley

Dreaming is associated mostly with REM sleep and it is one of the striking characteristics of REM that during this phase, the brain is as physiologically active as when we are awake. This activity has stimulated the idea that during REM and dreaming something important must be happening, as in the model of Crick and Mitchison outlined above. A similar approach is taken by Hobson and McCarley, whose activation-synthesis hypothesis of dreaming, in contrast to some other researchers, is based on many years of intricate electrophysiological research into the brain mechanisms of REM (Hobson 1988).

The activation component of the hypothesis concerns the regular switching on of REM sleep as part of the endogenous cycle of sleep stages. The REM mechanism is based in the brainstem and when activated, it inhibits skeletal muscles (producing the characteristic 'paralysis' of REM) and excites activity in the forebrain via pathways ascending from the brainstem. As part of this forebrain activation, sensory and motor information is internally and automatically aroused and forms the bases for our dream experience. The dream itself represents a synthesis, or organization into a coherent structure, of this sensory and motor information, with a considerable input from the individual's past experiences and expectations.

The activation-synthesis hypothesis states that dreaming is an automatic part of the brain's sleep mechanisms and can be seen as an endogenous, or inbuilt, process with a large genetic component. It may have no significance beyond the brain's natural drive to organize material into coherent streams. However, activation-synthesis also allows for the brain to integrate sensory and motor information with individual memories and expectations, and this can happen in novel and creative ways. For example, when neurons fire in the part of the brain that handles balance, the cortex may generate a dream about falling. Likewise, when signals occur that would ordinarily produce running, the cortex may create a dream about being chased (Tavris and Wade 1995). In this way, the model can also account for any narrative aspect of dreams.

As stated previously, REM sleep is initiated by cells in the brainstem, and these appear to be sensitive to the neurotransmitter acetylcholine. In support of this idea, Hobson points out that when sleeping volunteers are injected with drugs that increase the action of acetylcholine, both REM and dreaming increase. When volunteers are injected with a drug that blocks the action of acetylcholine, on the other hand, REM sleep and dreaming decrease (Gillin *et al.* 1985).

The model proposed by Hobson is similar in some ways to the approaches mentioned earlier, but differs in its breadth and in the way it is based on extensive experimental work. In fact, its breadth is a major problem in trying to validate it. Since dreams can be either meaningless or creative, it faces the difficulty of being able to explain any type of dream experience, i.e. it has little predictive power. This is not a problem confined to this model; dream research always runs up against the need for subjective interpretation of dream

symbolism and it is virtually impossible to do this in a scientifically rigorous way. However, Hobson does provide a convincing account of the brain mechanisms underlying REM and dreaming and by basing psychological interpretation on the physiology of REM and dream states, makes it that much more convincing.

Psychological theories

Dreaming, REM and learning

Ever since anecdotal stories of problem-solving during dreaming sleep emerged, an association between this phase of sleep and learning and/or memory has been a popular suggestion. The chemist Kekule apparently confirmed the structure of the benzene molecule (a ring) by dreaming of a snake biting its own tail; during REM sleep, his daytime attempts at solving the problem were carried to completion. Such stories are endearing, but hopeless as reliable evidence.

In 1994, Karni trained participants on a perceptual speed task (Karni *et al.* 1994). They had to report whether the pattern serving as background to a letter in the centre of a computer screen was made up of vertical or horizontal lines; response times were around 100 milliseconds, and did not improve with practice. However, after a night's sleep, performance had improved by about 15 milliseconds, an improvement that was sustained over months. However, if participants were woken each time they entered REM sleep, so that they were effectively REM-deprived, no improvement occurred. This would suggest that REM sleep is essential for the improvement in performance, and responsible for the delayed learning. Stickgold (1998) was interested in whether other stages of sleep were important in this task, but his technique was to allow participants to sleep normally and simply to measure the amount of time they spent in each stage. It turned out that those who improved most had the greatest amount of REM in the last two hours of sleep, but also the most slow-wave sleep in the first two hours. He suggests that this sort of learning is a two-stage process involving both slow-wave sleep and REM. He also demonstrated that participants have to sleep within 24 hours of training for this delayed learning to occur.

In similar studies, Smith (1999) used two tasks. In one, participants had to trace between the double outline of a triangle, and in the other they had to do the task while looking in a mirror ('reversed mirror-image drawing'). They were deprived either of slow-wave sleep or REM on the night following training. Smith found that stage 2 SWS deprivation affected only the simple version, while REM deprivation affected the more complex task. He concludes that simple learning, involving only slight modifications of previously

---

Activity 3: Assessing your own dreams

Think back to dreams you have had. Are they usually coherent and understandable, or are they bizarre and intriguing or even frightening? Do you assume they are significant in some way, perhaps dealing with current anxieties or telling you the winner of the 3.30 at Kempton Park?

Compare them with a friend's; do you share similar imagery and do you have the same attitude towards them? Try to slot your experiences into one of the theories discussed above. Which offers the most convincing explanation?

acquired skills, involves stage 2 SWS, but that learning new tasks requires REM sleep.

These studies provide direct evidence that some forms of admittedly very simple learning involve phases of sleep, especially REM. Stickgold points out that participants often report dream imagery that includes elements of the task being learnt, and so both dreams and the brain's electrical activity during REM reflect the learning process.

Many investigators have noticed that during the phases of sleep, there is a huge amount of two-way communication (exchange of nerve impulses) between the cortex and the hippocampus. During SWS it runs from the hippocampus to the cortex, and during REM from cortex to hippocampus. An emerging view is that memories of the day's events are stored initially in the hippocampus, and then during sleep they are integrated with experiences permanently stored in the cortex. The, sometimes bizarre, imagery of dreams reflects these attempts to link recent memories with past ones. One result of this may be improved learning of simple tasks, but the outcome could be more complicated.

Winson

The work of Winson (1997) points to a more complicated picture. He works with non-human animals such as rabbits, cats, and rats, which show a characteristic theta rhythm of six cycles per second in EEG recordings from the hippocampus during REM sleep. This rhythm is also recorded when the animal is awake and engaging in what Winson calls species-specific survival behaviour, such as exploring new territory in rats, predating in cats, or when alert and apprehensive in rabbits. Winson's proposal is that theta rhythm during REM is the reactivation of these memories, stored in the hippocampus, so that they can be integrated with previous experiences stored in the cortex and new survival strategies developed. He speculates that humans have moved beyond behaviours such as simple exploration as a vital survival function, to a world where threats and anxieties are more complex – relationships, examinations, careers, etc. But the role of REM has remained the same, as a time when the day's experiences are reactivated and incorporated with earlier memories, and new coping strategies are evolved. Dream imagery would then depend on the nature of the problems, individual coping strategies, and previous experiences, but would often clearly reflect the day's experiences.

Winson also addresses the problems of the spiny anteater's forebrain and the proportionately large amount of REM found in a new-born child. The spiny anteater does not have REM, and so needs to integrate new information with stored memories while it is awake. To develop more effective survival strategies by processing more information, the frontal cortex would have to increase in size; the evolution of REM meant that this function could be performed 'off line' and so reduce demands on the cortex.

The infant is bombarded with information which is processed into basic memory structures which form the cognitive framework with which later experiences have to be integrated. Forming this bedrock of memories requires large amounts of REM sleep, which then declines as our basic cognitive structures emerge. From then, REM takes on its lifelong function of integrating the day's experiences with this basic structure.

Dreams and problem-solving

Winson's model suggests a major role for REM in developing new coping strategies. The research is based on non-human animals, and so there is no defined role for dream imagery (the rabbit cannot report on its dreams). However, similar ideas have been proposed by other researchers working with humans, looking not so much at learning as problem-solving, and with more of an emphasis on dream imagery. Cartwright believes that dreams help in the adjustment to major life changes, threats, and problems. In one study with divorced women (Cartwright 1984), she found that in the group not depressed by the divorce, dreams were longer, reflected the negative emotions aroused by the situation, and story-lines often involved the dreamer in marital roles. In the depressed group, dreams were shorter, usually with no reference to the divorce, and with less emphasis on marriage as such. As their mood improved, their dreams also began to resemble those of the non-depressed group. Cartwright makes the point that moderate emotional reactions to life changes lead to more adaptive dreams, while strong emotional reactions seem to inhibit the adaptive role of dreaming.

As we move further away from the electrophysiology of REM, through psychological approaches such as Cartwright's, we end up with the psychodynamic approaches of Freud and Jung. These may appear rather unusual participants in a chapter on aspects of biopsychology. However, the recent emphasis in experimental psychology on the interplay between REM and dream imagery, and especially how dream imagery may reflect the possible role of REM in integrating the day's experiences with previous memories, make for a logical link between the two traditions.

Freud and dreams

Freud always felt that his work on the interpretation of dreams was fundamental to his whole psychodynamic approach: 'the interpretation of dreams is the royal road to a knowledge of the unconscious activities of the mind' (Freud 1955). More specifically, a dream was the disguised fulfilment of a repressed desire. It had to be disguised because the repressed desires could be sexual or aggressive urges unacceptable to the dreamer when awake. In that sense, the two functions of dreams are to protect the sleeper, but simultaneously to allow some expression of these latent urges.

Because of this, the dream has a manifest content, which the dreamer reports and which the analyst has to interpret in order to reveal the latent content which directly reflects the repressed urges. The transformation of deep-seated desires and anxieties into the manifest symbolism of the dream is called the 'dream work'. Several mechanisms can be involved, such as condensation, displacement, and considerations of representability:

◆ *Condensation* refers to the way a particular dream symbol acts as a focus for several different latent thoughts or anxieties. A particular character from the past may have several different meanings – your relationship with your father, problems at primary school, perhaps a recent dispute at work or college.

◆ *Displacement* occurs particularly with emotions. Sometimes in a dream the emotional reaction to a particular event is out of all proportion to the event itself. Freud would say that the emotion in fact is attached to some latent wish or thought, and has been displaced onto the dream image.

◆ Considerations of *representability* involve the visual nature of dreams. Latent thoughts have to be translated into a visual code, so that a sense of panic, running from an unknown terror, may represent the latent fear of instinctual sexual urges.

As Freud points out, the whole point of the dream work is to prevent the dreamer becoming aware of the latent thoughts and anxieties, and the role of the analyst is to interpret the imagery and reverse the condensation, displacement, etc., and to reveal the latent meaning of the dream. To help interpretation, Freud had a vocabulary of dream symbols. Drawing on cultural symbols found in stories, mythology, jokes, etc., he proposed that, for instance, dreams of flying represented sexual intercourse. He also emphasized that dream imagery usually contained representations of the previous day's events, which, although in themselves neutral, could be used to disguise the latent content. And, of course, he was happy to accept that sometimes dream imagery could be accepted at face value – sometimes a cigar is just a cigar!

Although Freud's theory of the nature and function of dreams has become more a part of popular culture than serious psychology, recent research with patients with brain damage in the cortical-limbic circuit in the forebrain has shown that dream content may indeed reflect our unconscious wishes and desires as predicted by Freud (see *In Focus*).

Jung and dreams

In the early days of psychoanalysis, Freud and Jung were close collaborators (on one trip across the Atlantic, they spent the time interpreting each other's dreams!), but had a major falling out over future directions for the new field, in part because of their different ideas on dreaming.

Jung did not agree with the distinction between manifest and latent content. To him, dreams had no deliberately disguised meaning, but directly reflected the mind's current state. Their content included thoughts, memories, and emotions from the day's conscious events, and images reflecting our unconscious world. They could seem bizarre, because the waking conscious mind cannot interpret the symbolic language used by the unconscious. The job of the therapist is to work with the client to interpret this language in the light of the basic functions of dreams. To Jung these were twofold:

◆ *Compensation* – In Jung's view of the mind, psychological health requires a balance between the conscious and the unconscious. In dreams, imagery may reflect repressed material that needs to be identified and resolved before this balance can be achieved. This is the function of compensation.

◆ *Prospective vision* – Although dreams could not predict the future, Jung felt that they could suggest possible future directions and developments.

A major difference between Jung and Freud, therefore, was that whereas Freud emphasized the dark and destructive nature of unconscious influences on dream imagery, Jung emphasized the positive and constructive nature of these influences.

Like Freud, though, Jung's approach to interpretation was through the analysis of dream imagery and symbolism. However, he worked within a very different framework. Although each dreamer and dream was unique, within dreams you could regularly identify certain archetypal symbols. These are universal images found across all cultures and developed during the course of human evolution. Jung claimed to have identified archetypes through an analysis of the mythology, folk stories and religious symbolism from prehistory onwards. Archetypes are part of our *collective unconscious*, a dimension of the mind that exists below personal consciousness and unconsciousness, and is common to all people. It represents patterns of universal wisdom created over the course of evolution, and which influences and structures our thoughts and behaviour in the present.

in focus

Dream on, Freud

Sigmund Freud's idea that in our dreams we see our true desires, stripped of the polite concealments that social life imposes, has had a fairly rough ride from scientists. For all his influence in everyday life, the founder of psychoanalysis has not been take seriously by neurologists for a generation or more. But results reported at the American Association for the Advancement of Science (AAAS) in Anaheim, California suggest that Freud may not have been so wide of the mark after all.

Until now, scientists have seen dreams as the manifestation of a period of paradoxical sleep in which the sleeper's brain is aroused even though he or she is sound asleep. Because the eyes are moving, this type of sleep is known as REM, or rapid-eye movement sleep. On an average night we spend about a quarter of our sleeping hours in this condition. When woken from REM sleep, 70 to 95 per cent of people report dreams, whereas only 5 to 10 per cent do so when woken from non-REM sleep.

Dr Mark Solms, of St Bartholomew's and Royal London Hospital School of Medicine, told the conference that this is why REM sleep is seen as the physiological concomitant of dreaming. If so, then dreaming is merely an accidental by-product of REM sleep with no greater significance.

His own work with nine patients suffering a particular type of brain damage led him to doubt this. Seven had suffered cancers, one had an abscess, and the other a stab wound. In each case a circuit in the forebrain called the cortical-limbic circuit had been damaged or destroyed. The patients reported to him that the result of the brain damage was to deprive them of dreams, but sleep studies showed that they still had normal REM sleep.

This sent Dr Solms back to the huge literature on the effect of prefrontal lobotomies, a once fashionable operation in which this very circuit was deliberately severed in order to treat mental disorders. He found what everybody else had forgotten, which was that 70 to 90 per cent of lobotomy patients reported loss of dreams. Since it is known that REM sleep is controlled from an entirely different part of the brain, in the brainstem rather than the forebrain, it became clear to him that REM sleep and dreams, though they may often coincide, are not one and the same.

The effect of a lobotomy was to make the patients listless and apathetic, because the circuit that was cut is connected with motivation and goal-seeking behaviour. It is particularly active in people with addictions to drugs, alcohol or even tobacco. This implies that dreaming is linked to the circuits in the brain which control our wishes and desires, strikingly close to what Freud himself claimed. Not surprisingly, Dr Solms's results have made him popular with Freudians.

At the conference, he also found support from brain-imaging studies by Dr Allen Braun, of the US National Institute on Deafness and Other Communication Disorders, who concluded: 'Rather than implying that dream content is random, meaningless, this pattern suggests that it may constitute direct, albeit distorted, access to unconscious processes.'

Freud lives!

Source: Nigel Hawkes, *The Times*, 27 January 1999

Examples of Jungian archetypes are:

◆ *Persona* – the drive to present yourself in the best possible light. Dreams of anxiety and panic in social situations might represent a weak persona.

◆ *Anima/Animus* – the female aspect of the male and the male aspect of the female. Jung anticipated much contemporary work on androgyny by proposing that we carry within us aspects of the opposite gender, and that their appearance in

dreams helps to balance our masculine and feminine sides.

◆ *Self* – the drive towards wholeness, similar to Maslow's self-realization (see Chapter 6). This is the ultimate expression of the perfect balance between unconscious and conscious worlds, and is rarely achieved. This drive is often represented by the appearance in dreams of Mandala symbols: complex symmetrical patterns in the shape of circles or crosses.

Working on an equal footing with the client, Jung would analyse dream symbolism and help the client understand imbalances between conscious and unconscious levels of the mind. To him, dreams were only obscure because we do not understand the symbolic language they use. Once this is understood, dreams can be seen as direct reflections of the current balance within that individual between unconscious and conscious worlds.

Although Freud and Jung differ in their ideas on the nature and meaning of dream symbolism, they both see dreams as significant in their own right. Dreams are an amalgam of current events and emotions carried over from the day's experiences, mixed in with material from the unconscious. In a way, this is not so far from some contemporary models of REM from experimental psychology, which emphasize the integration of current experiences with earlier memories. Of course, the psychodynamic framework is very different, but the problem of deciding which interpretation of dream imagery is correct is virtually impossible whichever theory you follow. When dealing with dreams, methodology has hardly varied – you have to rely on the subjective report of the dreamer – and those modern psychologists more interested in dream content than in REM as such are using the same methods pioneered by Freud and Jung.

Evaluation of dream research

Much of the research on REM and dreaming takes place in a sleep laboratory. The participant comes into the laboratory, is wired up with recording EEG electrodes, and then allowed to sleep. Not surprisingly, the dreams reported under such conditions can differ significantly from those reported under normal conditions. They tend to be shorter, less dramatic, and with less emotional intensity; nightmares are virtually never experienced. They often incorporate elements of the laboratory setting, such as wires, people in white coats and large complex machines (Van de Castle 1994). This 'laboratory effect' makes it impossible to argue that dreaming under these conditions represents dreams in the real world, although the effect can be lessened by allowing the participants to sleep through one night in the laboratory before recording takes place.

To interpret dream imagery, whether you are a cognitive psychologist or a Jungian analyst, means that you have to rely on the subjective report of the dreamer. This goes against the 'scientific method' adopted by modern day psychology, which normally requires that behaviour should be observable and objective. But since dreams are personal and inaccessible to others, dream researchers simply have to trust their participants.

Many studies on dreaming are done in which humans and other animals are deprived of stages of sleep, usually REM. Work on human problem-solving during REM discussed earlier uses exactly this approach. But we have to accept that waking animals up at intervals during sleep may well have other effects, causing, for instance, nonspecific stress and anxiety, and disrupting other biological rhythms, e.g. secretion of hormones and brain neurotransmitters. Results may therefore be due to these nonspecific effects, rather than to selective REM deprivation.

Exam summary: Dreaming

The AQA examination will test your understanding of the following areas:

◆ research into the nature of dreams (pp. 124–5)
◆ theories of the functions of dreaming – neurobiological (pp. 125–6) and psychological accounts (pp. 126–30).

Example question

The question below is typical of one drawn from the material above, and should take you 30 minutes to answer:

◆ Outline and evaluate one neurobiological theory and one psychological theory of the functions of dreaming. *(24 marks)*

Suggested answer structure

The first thing to remember is that a question such as this needs very careful time management, as you only have 30 minutes writing time. If you divide up that time proportionately, you would have 15 minutes to write about your neurobiological theory, and 15 minutes to write about your psychological theory. As you are also obliged both to 'outline' and to 'evaluate' these theories, you would divide your time again, giving you 7.5 minutes outlining the neurological theory, 7.5 minutes evaluating it, and so on. That translates to approximately 150 words for each 'component' of the essay, and about 600 words in total.

Two neurobiological theories are included in the chapter: Crick and Mitchison's theory (pp. 125) and Hobson's theory (pp. 125–6). Psychological theories include Cartwright's views on dreams and problem-solving (pp. 127), as well as Freud (pp. 127–9) and Jung's (pp. 128–9) psychodynamic theories of the nature and function of dreams. With these latter two theories, the amount of detail that could be included is potentially enormous, so it is worth remembering that the question only requires a summary description (or précis) of these theories. You should not fill your answer with descriptive detail when the question requires an equal amount of evaluative commentary. The 'evaluation of dream research' on p. 130 can be used as generic evaluation of all dream research, although because of the highly theoretical nature of Freudian and Jungian explanations of dreams, it would be less directly relevant there. A critical point that is relevant to all theories of dreams is that as dreams are not observable, researchers must rely on the subjective reports of the dreamer.

Chapter summary

◆ **Biological** rhythms are found throughout the natural world, in both plants and animals, and may be classified into **ultradian**, **infradian** and **circadian biological rhythms**. (Circannual rhythms are examples of infradian rhythms.) Evidence suggests that these rhythms are natural, controlled by **endogenous pacemakers** or biological clocks.

◆ These clocks can be set by external stimuli, referred to as **exogenous *zeitgebers***, such as light and dark. In mammals, the main biological clock is the suprachiasmatic nucleus, which responds to light falling on the eye by altering the release of melatonin from the pineal gland.

◆ Bodily rhythms can be disrupted by jet travel and **shift work**, leading to behavioural disorganization and stress. Day-length changes are involved in seasonal affective disorder, which can be treated by exposure to bright artificial light during the day.

◆ Using the EEG, we can identify four stages of slow-wave sleep (SWS) and a stage of REM or paradoxical sleep. **Restoration accounts** of the function of sleep concentrate on body, brain and hormonal recovery. Sleep deprivation studies show that stage 4 of SWS and REM sleep are important for normal growth and function of the brain. Neurochemical approaches show that REM sleep is important for the functioning of brain neurotransmitter pathways.

◆ Sleep patterns also depend on lifestyle and ecological niche, and **evolutionary** approaches concentrate on the variations between different species. Overall, there is unlikely to be a single explanation for the functions of sleep.

◆ Dreams occur mainly in REM sleep but are not the same thing as REM sleep which is defined physiologically. Research into the **nature of dreams** has looked at their **relationship with stages of sleep**, **duration** and **content**.

◆ Theories of **the functions of** dreaming range from those that see them as meaningless, to those that associate them with learning, problem-solving, and integrating the day's experiences with stored memories.

◆ **Neurobiological approaches** often use computer metaphors to describe the brain's activity during dreaming, e.g. for 'reverse learning': wiping out unwanted information (**Crick and Mitchison**). **Hobson and McCarley** used electrophysiological research into brain mechanisms to forumlate his activation-synthesis hypothesis. Modern **psychological accounts** include studies of dreams in relation to improvements in learning, survival strategies and emotional reactions to life changes.

◆ In all theories of dreams, researchers have to rely on the subjective reports of dreamers. Despite their emphasis on the unconscious, the approach of Freud and Jung has similarities with modern ideas from cognitive psychology.

Further resources

Horne, J. (1988) *Why We Sleep*, Oxford: Oxford University Press.

Excellent review of restoration hypotheses and deprivation studies of sleep in humans.

Coren, S. (1996) *Sleep Thieves*, New York: The Free Press.

Very readable account of the mechanisms of sleep and how biological rhythms can conflict with modern life.

Winson, J. (1997) 'The meaning of dreams', *Scientific American*, Special Issue: *Mysteries of the Mind*, 7 (1), pp. 58–67.

Reviews some modern information-processing theories of dreams.

continued on p. 132

Websites

http://www.sleepnet.com/

A very comprehensive guide to sleep and sleep disorders, including links to the latest research on sleep.

http://www.asdreams.org

The home page for the Association for the Study of Dreams, giving links to lots of other dream-related sites on the web.

http://www.dreamgate.com

A searchable site which includes a full text online version of Freud's classic *Interpretation of Dreams*.

http://www.circadian.com/

A very useful site devoted to circadian rhythms. Includes useful material about the effects of shiftwork, and a comprehensive glossary of terms.

Chapter 6

Motivation and emotion

Simon Green

Preview

In this chapter we shall be looking at:

◆ brain mechanisms involved in motivation, and theories and research relating to the role of brain structures

◆ physiological, psychological, and combined approaches to explaining motivation

◆ emotion, including:

– the role of brain structures in emotional behaviour and experience

– physiological approaches to emotion

– combined models of emotional behaviour and experience.

Introduction

Motivation and emotion are often discussed together in psychology textbooks. They are both terms which are used to explain large areas of human experience, particularly the arousing and directing of behaviour. Everybody has a general idea what the terms mean. Unfortunately, psychology has to define terms in ways that are clear and unambiguous, and this sometimes produces research and theories which can seem a long way from everyday life. Much of the work on the physiology of motivation and emotion has been done with nonhuman animals, and so we also have to consider whether applying the results to humans is justified.

The first part of the chapter looks at brain structures and mechanisms involved in some motivational states, and the second part considers some of the theories of motivation used in psychology. In the third part, emotion is discussed from the perspective of brain structures, and then theoretical approaches to emotion using physiological, psychological and combined models are described.

Brain mechanisms of motivation

Motivation is that area of psychology concerned with the arousing and directing of behaviour. An extreme view would be that all behaviour has some purpose, i.e. it is directed towards some particular goal. Sometimes the purpose seems obvious, such as making and eating a meal when hungry, or revising hard to prepare for an exam. Sometimes the motivation for a particular behaviour is less clear; walking the Derbyshire dales or listening to old Beatles records would be examples of simple behaviours with no easily defined motivation (such as hunger or academic success). The clearest examples of motivated behaviour come from the study of primary or physiological drives, and are associated with the concept of *homeostasis*, a term introduced by Cannon (1932) to describe the stable equilibrium of body systems. As we shall see, homeostasis involves both general physiological systems and their interaction with brain structures.

Claude Bernard (1856) in the nineteenth century was the first to emphasize the importance to survival of the maintenance of a constant internal environment. The internal environment of the body consists of such systems as the oxygen content of the blood, the concentration of various nutrients such as glucose, the water balance of the body, and body temperature. All of these systems can only fluctuate within narrow limits if health and survival are to be maintained.

As a system departs from the stable state – for instance, as we expend energy or go out into the cold – the body tries to restore homeostatic equilibrium through physiological and behavioural mechanisms. For instance, if we have not eaten for some time, we develop a bodily or tissue need for food. This need leads to a drive to eat, and eating reduces the drive and restores homeostasis. This sequence is a simple example of behaviour motivated by a primary physiological drive

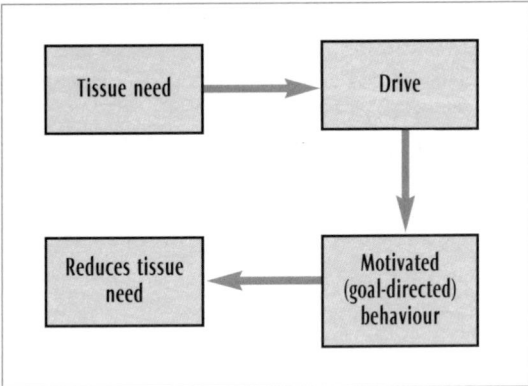

Figure 6.1
A simple model of motivation: homeostatic drive-reduction

aroused by a tissue need, and a whole class of motivated behaviours is represented by these homeostatic primary drives (see Fig. 6.1). In fact, many approaches to motivation try to explain more complicated behaviours using similar models, in which the behaviour is driven by an internal state of 'need'. More recent approaches place emphasis on the *environment* we live in, and the role it plays in arousing and guiding our behaviour. It has even been shown that the behaviour associated with basic homeostatic drives, such as food-seeking, can be influenced by the environment, and that they are not always entirely biological. Homeostatic drives represent the *physiological* approach to the study of motivation. The simple picture of a tissue deficiency leading to a specific need, which in turn arouses the appropriate behaviour, is very appealing, and many thousands of experiments have been done to see if this is indeed the case. Most of these have been done on nonhuman animals, especially rats, and hunger has been the drive most studied.

Hunger

We go without food for some hours, we feel hungry, we eat, the hunger drive disappears. The overall picture looks simple, but even at this level there are complications. Our diet is made up of carbohydrates such as sugar, proteins, fats and small amounts of trace elements and amino acids vital to cellular function throughout the body. So, when we feel hungry, what do we feel hungry for? The most important need is for the foods we use for energy, in particular carbohydrates and fats. The energy content of these foods is measured in calories, and the best index of caloric intake is body weight, as calories taken in but not immediately used in cellular and muscular activity are stored as fat.

One of the most impressive aspects of food intake regulation is that body weight is usually maintained within fairly narrow limits, apart from the dynamic phases of growth and during pregnancy (although it is fair to say that, at least in the West, obesity is now

becoming a widespread problem). So, although we need a balanced diet, research has focused on the regulation of caloric intake and body weight.

This regulation seems to anticipate needs, as we take meals according to routines set by social and cultural patterns (breakfast, lunch, dinner). Again talking about relatively prosperous societies, we do not wait until we feel desperately hungry before eating. This anticipatory function is a departure from the simple homeostatic model. Meals themselves are usually short-lasting, and certainly end before the food can have been fully absorbed with an effect on body weight. This last observation means that although body weight may be important in the long-term regulation of food intake, it does not decide the size of individual meals. There must be other factors which determine food intake in the short-term, and these include the presence of food in the mouth, stomach, and small intestine. They are jointly referred to as peripheral factors.

Short-term regulation of food intake

♦ *Presence of food in the mouth* – In one study, participants swallowed a rubber tube and could then press a button to inject a liquid diet directly into the stomach. After a few days, they established a regular intake which maintained body weight, but they found the meals unsatisfying and wanted to taste and chew the food (Spiegel 1973), implying that taste is an important feature but not strictly necessary for regulation of meal size. This is supported by a study of sham-feeding using rats. Everything the rats swallowed passed out of the oesophagus (via a tube) before it could reach the stomach. In these circumstances, rats ate far more than they normally would, showing that the presence of food in the mouth is not itself sufficient to regulate intake.

♦ *Presence of food in the stomach* – The Spiegel study shows efficient regulation of food injected directly into the stomach. The earliest suggestion that the stomach is central to food intake regulation was by Cannon (Cannon and Washburn 1912). Stomach contractions were recorded in humans using a balloon swallowed by participants and then inflated so that contractions altered the air pressure of the balloon. The hunger pangs reported by the participants correlated with stomach contractions. A more direct study by Deutsch *et al.* (1978) in rats used a reversible block of the passage between the stomach and the small intestine. Rats with the block in place, nevertheless, ate a normal sized meal, even though food did not pass beyond the stomach. This demonstrates that signals of fullness (or satiety as it is technically known) travel from the stomach to the brain, probably via the vagus nerve. The system is sensitive to the quality of food as well as quantity, as the rats would eat less bulk of a high calory food but more of a low calory food. Although the presence of food in the stomach is an important part of our regulatory apparatus, there is no evidence that patients with substantial parts of the stomach removed, because of ulceration or cancer, suffer problems with food intake. There must be alternative regulatory mechanisms.

◆ *Cholecystokinin (CCK)* – CCK is a hormone released into the bloodstream from the duodenum (that part of the small intestine immediately following the stomach) in response to the presence of food in the duodenum. Injections of CCK shorten meal size in rats and humans (Antin *et al.* 1978, Pi-Sunyer *et al.* 1982), and it has been put forward as a satiety hormone. Intriguingly, CCK also functions as a synaptic neurotransmitter in the brain, and it is tempting to see its effect on satiety and meal size as involving brain pathways. However, there is no direct evidence for this and it is more likely that CCK operates in combination with other factors such as the presence of food in the stomach (McHugh and Moran 1985).

The taste of food in the mouth and the presence of food in the stomach and small intestine all contribute in varying degrees to the regulation of food intake. After passing through the gastro-intestinal system, the products of digestion diffuse into the blood supply.

Blood glucose and hunger

One of the main products of carbohydrate digestion is the sugar glucose, and blood glucose levels have been a popular choice for the regulation of food intake. It is unlikely that changes in blood glucose occur fast enough to affect the size of a single meal, but they may certainly affect the feelings of hunger that develop between meals.

Levels of glucose in the blood are controlled by food intake and by the hormone insulin, released from the pancreas gland. Insulin promotes the conversion of glucose to fats and the storage of fats in fat storage cells called *adipocytes*. Therefore, the levels of blood glucose are closely related to levels of insulin; if insulin levels are low, as in diabetes, less glucose is stored in cells and blood levels are high (very high levels lead to hyperglycaemic coma, one of the dangers of diabetes). However, when blood insulin rises, more glucose is stored and less circulates in the bloodstream. Artificial increases in blood glucose via injections decrease food intake (Tordoff *et al.* 1982). Insulin levels are lowest at night, when appetite decreases, and higher during the day, causing lower blood glucose levels and increasing appetite (LeMagnen 1981).

Effects of glucose on appetite depend upon specialized receptors called glucoreceptors, found in the lining of blood vessels, in the liver and in the brain, especially the hypothalamus. In this way, the brain is constantly aware of blood glucose levels. However, this neat relationship between appetite and glucose is probably not the whole answer. In normal people, levels of glucose in the blood do not vary dramatically even after long periods without food. Part of homeostasis involves maintaining steady levels, so that if less is eaten, stored fats are converted to glucose in the bloodstream; if more sugar is taken in the diet, insulin activity increases to convert blood glucose into stored fats in cells. It is unlikely that glucose levels change often enough and regularly enough to explain our eating patterns. Probably of more importance are the central mechanisms of hunger and feeding.

Brain structures: the hypothalamus and feeding centres

In 1942, Hetherington and Ranson demonstrated that lesions of part of the hypothalamus called the ventro-medial (VMH) nucleus caused dramatic overeating in rats, so that they became massively obese. A few years later Anand and Brobeck (1951) showed that lesions of the lateral nucleus of the hypothalamus (LH) inhibited eating so that rats lost weight. These two studies and many others since suggest that the hypothalamus contains two centres, one in the ventromedial nucleus which normally stops feeding at the appropriate time – a satiety centre – and one in the lateral hypothalamus which normally stimulates feeding – a feeding centre.

Although these centres are obviously critical in the control of feeding, they can only act if they know the state of the body's energy reserves, so that feeding is related to need. Glucoreceptors alert them to levels of blood glucose, and this probably plays a part. More popular in recent years has been the concept of body weight set-point. This is the idea that our feeding systems try to maintain our body weight around a set-point or target weight. The best index of body weight is the amount of fat stored in the adipocytes (fatty tissue), and Nisbett (1972) suggested that the hypothalamus monitors (through sensory nerves) fat levels and maintains them around a set level. Lesions to the hypothalamus shift this body weight set-point: VMH lesions raise the level, so that rats overeat and become obese, while LH lesions lower it, so that rats stop eating to reduce their body weight.

The body weight set-point seems to be determined by inherited factors and early nutritional experience. Nisbett's model therefore implies that the obese human is not showing weakness of will or self-indulgence, but simply working to maintain a high target weight. While this is undoubtedly true of some, there are many other factors involved (see *In Focus*), and even in animals

in focus
Obesity and anorexia

A peculiarity of the VMH obese rat is that it is not more motivated to eat, and in fact will eat less of a peculiar-tasting food than hungry controls. Schachter (1971) performed an experiment with obese humans to see how motivated they were. Normal-weight and obese participants were allowed equal access to shelled and unshelled almond nuts. The controls ate roughly similar amounts of both types, but obese participants ignored the unshelled nuts and ate only the shelled. Schachter concluded that when food is accessible, the obese rat or human eats more than normal, but when it is hard to get at, they eat less.

Although human obesity may reflect specific brain mechanisms, it is much more likely to represent general physiological variables, as discussed earlier in the chapter, or psychological variables. The opposite syndrome, anorexia nervosa, is found most commonly in females between 12 and 18. It appears to be a pathological desire to be thin and has no simple explanation. The most convincing explanations are psychological, involving self-concept and family dynamics, plus the influence of idealized female forms seen in the media. The most effective treatments are behavioural or psychodynamic therapies, but they have to overcome the problem that many anorexics refuse to see themselves as being abnormally thin.

there is little direct experimental evidence for the model. However, the impressive regulation of body weight in most people and animals does point to some kind of set-point, and Nisbett's ideas are the most convincing in this area (see Fig. 6.2 on p. 139). More recently, the discovery of leptin has helped to clarify the body's system for signalling body weight to the brain.

The role of leptin

Since the 1950s, a genetic mutation in mice has been known to lead to extreme obesity, with mice overeating and having high levels of insulin. In 1994, Zhang et al. finally identified the cause. Mice with the mutation were not producing a protein called leptin. This is normally produced by the fat storage cells, the adipocytes, in proportion to the amount of fat they contain. It acts as a hormone, travelling via the bloodstream to the hypothalamus where it acts to decrease food intake. This was confirmed by studies where leptin was injected into the obese mice lacking the leptin gene; food intake and body weight fell dramatically over a few weeks (Halaas et al. 1995). It seems likely that leptin may be the key chemical signal, telling the hypothalamus and its feeding regulation centres about the state of fat storage in the body.

We have dealt with hunger in some detail. It is a classic homeostatic drive, but there is no simple relationship between need and intake. Diet depends on inherited factors, habit, taste, gastro-intestinal factors, brain structures and mechanisms, and energy expenditure. Although basically physiological, psychological variables influence food selection in normal individuals and may be heavily involved in abnormal states such as obesity and anorexia. Control is centered in brain structures, especially the

hypothalamus, but regulation of feeding depends on a complicated interaction between physiological and psychological factors.

Brain structures and thirst

Like hunger, thirst represents a complicated interaction between the body's physiological systems and central control by brain structures. Regulation of the body's water content is absolutely basic to survival, and involves several neural and hormonal systems.

Water is found both within cells (intracellular) and outside cells (extracellular). The extracellular component, making up about 33% of our water content, is divided into interstitial fluid, which surrounds and bathes all of the body's cells, and the blood plasma, which is that part of the blood which is not red or white blood cells.

Water contains dissolved substances, many of which are salts, including sodium chloride. The concentration of dissolved salts gives the solution an osmotic pressure, with pressure proportional to the concentration of salts. When two solutions are separated by a semipermeable membrane, that is, a barrier which allows water through but not the dissolved salts, water passes from the solution with the lower osmotic pressure to the one with the higher pressure, until the pressures are equal. This is the position with regard to intracellular and extracellular water, as the cell membrane functions as a semipermeable membrane. Drinking is aimed at maintaining the appropriate dynamic balance between the two water compartments.

Osmotic thirst

We usually lose water regularly, through sweating, urination, breathing and evaporation through the mouth, and defaecation. We replace it through drinking, while our diet may also contain foods high in salts. If, through a combination of these effects, the osmotic pressure of the extracellular water compartment increases (through water loss and intake of salts), water will pass from the intracellular compartment through the semipermeable cell membrane to try and equalize the pressures of intracellular and extracellular components. This also means that intracellular pressure will rise (less water, but the same salt content).

The brain's neurons, although highly specialized, are still cells of the body, and they react in the same way to water loss. In the preoptic area of the hypothalamus, a group of neurons function as *osmoreceptors*. When their osmotic pressure rises through water loss, they react by directly stimulating drinking, and by connections from the hypothalamus to the pituitary gland they stimulate the release of the hormone ADH (antidiuretic hormone) into the bloodstream. ADH travels to the kidneys, where it acts on the kidney tubules to promote water recovery from the urine. So by these two effects – direct stimulation of drinking and water intake, and decreased water loss in the urine – the balance between intracellular and extracellular water compartments is restored.

Experimental studies have shown that injecting concentrated salt solutions into the preoptic area of the hypothalamus stimulates drinking and the release of ADH from the pituitary. Injections of pure water decrease drinking and ADH production. This demonstrates that the preoptic osmoreceptors have a central role in controlling the body's water balance. Compared with hunger and feeding, where the brain needs a signal such as leptin reflecting the body's energy reserves, we do not have to search for an indicator of water balance that signals the brain when to start drinking; the preoptic neurons of the hypothalamus react to water loss in the same way as all the other cells of the body.

Hypovolemic thirst

Thirst can also be produced by sudden and dramatic loss of water from the extracellular compartment. This can be caused by haemorrhage (bleeding) through cuts or internal damage, or perhaps heavy menstrual flow. Besides water, dissolved salts are also lost. This is known as *hypovolemic* (low volume) thirst, and involves additional regulatory systems to those described above.

Low blood volume stimulates specialized pressure receptors known as baroreceptors in the walls of blood vessels. These send messages to the hypothalamus to stimulate drinking behaviour and to increase the release of ADH. Reductions in blood volume also stimulate the kidneys directly to stimulate the release of

the hormone renin which is the starting point for a cascade of chemical events. Renin converts a large protein found in the blood, angiotensinogen, into angiotensin I. This is rapidly converted in turn to angiotensin II, which acts to constrict (narrow) blood vessels and so increase blood pressure. Angiotensin II also sustains the release of ADH, possibly by a direct action on the preoptic area of the hypothalamus. Injection of angiotensin II into the preoptic area also stimulates drinking behaviour even in rats who are not water deprived (Epstein *et al.* 1970).

Another control system also comes into play to cope with hypovolemic thirst. When salt levels fall, the cortex of the adrenal gland, just above the kidneys, releases yet another hormone, aldosterone. This stimulates the kidneys to re-absorb salt from the urine, so together ADH and aldosterone reduce water and salt loss from the kidneys and help restore the extracellular water compartment to balance. It has been noted that a correlate of hypovolemic thirst is an increased appetite for salty foods, and this may be stimulated through the effects of aldosterone.

Brain structures involved in thirst and regulation of drinking focus on the preoptic area of the hypothalamus. However, we also know that other areas and circuits may be involved. As long ago as 1962, Fisher and Coury showed that injecting drugs which increased the activity of the neurotransmitter acetylcholine could produce drinking in nondeprived rats. The effective sites included the preoptic area, but also covered areas in the limbic system (see p. 145). They concluded that drinking was controlled by a limbic circuit of pathways which used acetylcholine as a neurotransmitter, and it has become referred to as the *cholinergic theory of drinking*.

Like eating, drinking usually anticipates states of thirst, and in fact drinking is highly correlated with

Activity 1: Your own eating and drinking habits

Think about your own eating and drinking habits.

◆ When were you last very hungry or thirsty?
◆ Have you eaten anything in the last few hours that you didn't really need?
◆ What was the attraction of it?
◆ If you eat chocolate, do you eat it for dietary reasons or because of the sweet taste?
◆ Why do you think that people sometimes drink when they are not thirsty?

Clearly, our diet is not only determined by basic homeostatic drives.

meals; taking in water with food prevents sudden changes in osmotic pressure in the body, as the salts in the food are diluted by the water. We also take in more of favourite drinks, and an evening in the pub is not a reaction to osmotic or hypovolemic thirst. So drinking, like eating, has psychological as well as physiological aspects to it, and drinking circuits outside the hypothalamus may be more involved in these psychological aspects.

Exam summary: Brain mechanisms of motivation

The AQA examination will test your understanding of the following areas:

◆ theories and research studies of the role of brain structures in motivational states (pp. 133–8).

Example question

The question below is typical of one drawn from the material above, and should take you 30 minutes to answer.

◆ Discuss research relating to the role of brain structures in motivational states. *(24 marks)*

Suggested answer structure

Although the words structure and mechanisms appear independently, it is perfectly acceptable to include information pertaining to the latter in questions about the former (i.e. a brain structure works through brain mechanisms). This section has examined the role of brain structures in hunger (pp. 134–6) and thirst (pp. 136–8).

Meal size, or short-term regulation of food intake, is controlled by the presence of food in the mouth and stomach, the release of CCK from the small intestine, and possibly changes in blood glucose levels (pp. 134–5). Long-term regulation of body weight involves feeding and satiety centres in the hypothalamus. Feeding behaviour is designed to maintain a fairly constant body set-point. The hypothalamus responds to signals of current body weight. These may include blood glucose levels, although recent evidence points to the hormone leptin, released by the fat storage cells (pp. 135–6).

Drinking aims to maintain a balance between intracellular and extracellular water components. In response to osmotic thirst, osmoreceptors in the preoptic area of the hypothalamus stimulate drinking behaviour and water recovery from the kidney through the release of the hormone ADH from the pituitary gland (pp. 136–7). Hypovolemic thirst stimulates the release of renin from the kidneys, which in turn leads to a rise in blood levels of angiotensin II. This hormone raises blood pressure by constricting blood vessels, stimulates drinking, and increases release of ADH. Aldosterone is released by the adrenal gland and promotes the reabsorbtion of salt by the kidneys (pp. 137–8).

Finding AO2 in physiological psychology questions can be quite tricky, but there are many ways that you can satisfy this component of the question. For example, you might appraise a particular explanation – 'It is unlikely that changes in blood glucose occur fast enough to affect the size of a single meal' (p. 135). On the other hand, you can look at alternative explanations, such as 'We take in more of our favourite drinks, and an evening in the pub is not a reaction to osmotic or hypovolemic thirst' (p. 138). The use of empirical evidence to support a particular explanation can also serve a valuable evaluative function, e.g. 'This was confirmed by studies where leptin was injected into the obese mice ...' (p. 136).

Theories of motivation

Physiological approaches: homeostatic drives

The previous section detailed the relationship between goal-seeking behaviour and tissue needs, such as hunger and thirst (Fig. 6.2). The satisfaction of these primary physiological drives is probably the best known and simplest example of motivated behaviour that we know; the animal has to maintain homeostasis to survive, and the primary motivation has to be to satisfy needs related to homeostasis. As we shall see later in relation to Hull's drive-reduction approach to motivation, homeostatic drive-reduction can also be used as a building block for more ambitious theories. However, in its basic form it applies to the satisfaction of physiological needs only, and as was pointed out at the start of the chapter, humans in particular lead complex lives full of complex psychological motivations. To account for these, a number of psychological theories have been developed.

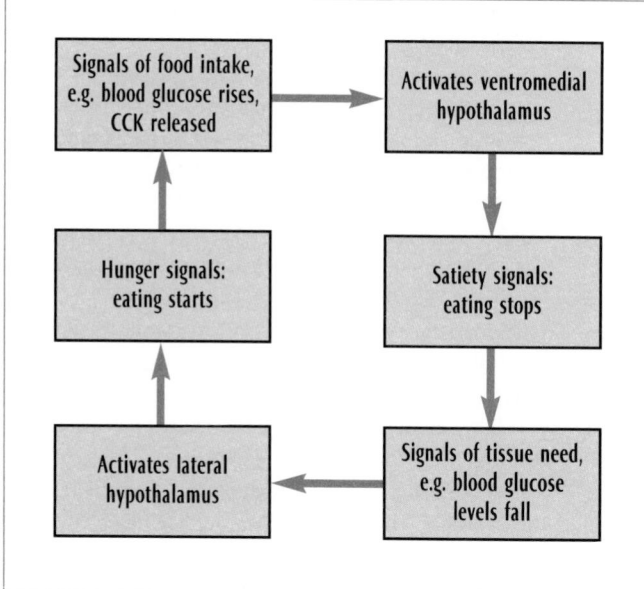

Figure 6.2 Dual centre control of feeding: ventromedial hypothalamus (VMH) and lateral hypothalamus function as satiety and feeding centres

Nonhomeostatic drives and optimal arousal theory

Even in nonhuman animals, behaviour is not always obviously related to homeostasis. Monkeys prefer to watch a roomful of other monkeys rather than an empty room, and will do manipulative puzzles endlessly with no obvious external reward (Hebb 1958). Rats will learn to press the bar in a Skinner box (see p. 344) just to switch on a light (Tapp 1969). If we call each of these behaviours a drive, we end up with long lists – curiosity, manipulative, exploratory drives, etc. – which do not really explain the behaviour; rats run around a maze because they have an exploratory drive. How do we know? Because they run around mazes ... the argument is totally circular.

To break out of this circularity, the concept of *optimal arousal level* was introduced. This states that a major motivation for animals is to maintain an optimal level of arousal, neither too high nor too low. If they are underaroused, they will seek stimulation to increase levels, for instance by doing puzzles, exploring, or playing. If they are overaroused, they will avoid stimulation (Fowler 1965).

This approach is parallel to homeostatic drive theory, with animals seeking to maintain a constant level of arousal, and it copes very well with, for example, the bored monkey doing puzzles. However, it is very general and even in nonhuman animals clearly ignores the particular demands of each situation. For instance, rats do not explore only out of curiosity. Tolman (1948) was the first to suggest that rats build up a 'cognitive map' while they explore a maze. We now know that this 'spatial map' of the world is located

in the hippocampus of the limbic system (O'Keefe and Nadel 1978). It seems clear that animals explore in order to find out about their environment, i.e. exploration has a cognitive function related to survival, and simply to account for it in terms of optimal arousal level misses its main purpose.

Children play with toys. This too seems to fit optimal arousal theory, as it apparently has no obvious purpose. But again it can be fitted into a picture of motor and cognitive development; the child is practising and learning skills which it will need later in life (see, for instance, Piaget's stages of play and its role in cognitive development, in Chapter 10). Simply to see play in general terms of arousal level ignores its most important aspects.

Expectancy or incentive approaches

In the earlier section on hunger and feeding, it was pointed out that the sight, smell, and taste of food are important in deciding what we eat. On the whole, children and rats prefer chocolate biscuits to muesli, and rats will press bars for hours to obtain a nonnutritious but sweet-tasting saccharine solution (Valenstein 1967). These food-related stimuli are capable of producing goal-directed behaviour even though they may not represent a balanced diet or even satisfy the primary drive of hunger.

Stimuli that can produce, or 'elicit', goal-directed behaviour without requiring an internal physiological need for them are called *incentives*, and play the central role in expectancy models of motivation.

Incentives

These are important in that they emphasize the ability of stimuli to 'pull' or elicit behaviour, rather than seeing behaviour as 'pushed' or driven by internal bodily states. Unfortunately, they can be hard to disentangle from conventional drive-reduction approaches. Going to work is often quoted as an example of an expectancy approach; we go because work is there, and we 'expect' certain rewards which then reinforce going to work. But some classic incentive studies, such as monkeys doing puzzles or rats pressing bars to turn lights on, do not involve clear-cut rewards. It is, in any case, difficult to associate the 'reward' of a light coming on with a pay packet at the end of the week or rapid career progress. Complex human behaviours would seem to require equally complicated models, such as Maslow's hierarchy (see later).

The most convincing models of the incentive or expectancy approach to motivation are based in nonhuman animals (Bolles 1967). The fundamental idea is that neutral stimuli acquire arousing and rewarding properties by association with primary rewards such as food. So the sight, taste, and smell of food become 'incentives' through their association with food itself. Rats press a bar for hours for saccharine even though saccharine does not reduce hunger; however, the taste has been linked to nutritive foods, so saccharine becomes an incentive stimulus, capable of arousing and rewarding behaviour.

One feature of some incentive stimuli is that the behaviour does not extinguish easily. If a rat is pressing a bar for nutritious food, responding fades as the hunger drive is satisfied. If pressing is not rewarded with food, it extinguishes. Responding for saccharine does not reduce hunger, yet it can be very persistent (Valenstein 1967). One possible explanation for this involves one of the strangest phenomena in the area of motivation; electrical self-stimulation of the brain.

Electrical self-stimulation of the brain (ESB)

In 1954, James Olds and Peter Milner were doing some brain stimulation studies in rats. They noticed that with one particular brain site, the rat would always move to the area of the cage where it was stimulated, as though the stimulation was reinforcing. The stimulating electrode turned out to be in the septal area, part of the limbic system (see p. 145), and in fact, ironically, it wasn't even the spot they had been aiming for! They then rigged up a Skinner box so that a rat could press the bar to deliver electric stimulation to the same area, and found that the animal would press the bar rapidly (up to 500 presses per minute) for hours on end. They called the phenomenon *rewarding electrical self-stimulation of the brain* (ESB).

It turned out that many areas of the brain, including the septal area, amygdala and hypothalamus, would support high rates of ESB. It was powerfully rewarding, as hungry rats would prefer it to feeding, and thirsty rats would press for ESB rather than drinking. Another peculiarity was that ESB did not extinguish; even though there was no obvious external reward, animals would press the bar, sometimes only stopping when exhausted. This suggested that ESB was very different to natural rewards such as food and water; these can produce powerful behaviour, but the behaviour stops when the animal is full or satiated.

Following up on the work of Olds and Milner, it turned out that one particular pathway in the brain contained most of the effective ESB sites. This was the median forebrain bundle (MFB), a network of fibres in the brain running through structures such as the septal area and hypothalamus. The MFB has become known as the brain's reward pathway.

It therefore seems that the brain has a reward system, which when stimulated gives rise to feelings of pleasure and satisfaction. What may be happening is that whenever animals, including humans, experience pleasure then the MFB is activated. The particular source of pleasure – eating when hungry, drinking, sex, alcohol, etc. – arouses its own control systems in the brain (such as the ventromedial and lateral hypothalamus for hunger), but also arouses the reward pathways of the MFB. The feelings of pleasure ensure that the behaviour is learnt and repeated.

But what would happen if the reward pathways were activated independently of primary drives and reinforcers such as food and drink? As the activation is pleasurable, whatever led to it would be repeated, and as it was not linked to a primary drive such as hunger, it would not satiate as usually happens when we eat. This could be what is happening with ESB. The stimulating electrode is plugged directly into the reward pathways, producing activity which is usually associated with feeding or drinking but which in this case is independent of any other behaviour. As there is nothing to satiate, the behaviour is purely pleasurable and continues as long as the animal has the strength to press the bar.

This also has relevance to theories of expectancy and incentive. Neutral signals associated with rewards (such as the sight, taste, and smell of food) become signals that reward is coming, and eventually can independently arouse reward pathways. So saccharine, whose sweet taste comes to mean 'food', arouses the reward pathways of the brain and so becomes a powerful reward in its own right without being a nutritious food and satisfying a primary drive. Perhaps, for humans, the expectation of a reward for, for instance, going to work, comes to arouse reward pathways and ensures that the behaviour is learnt and sustained.

Reward pathways in the brain may also be involved in some of the most persistent human motivations, those involved in addictive behaviours. The neurons that make up the MFB use noradrenaline and, especially, dopamine as neurotransmitters, and some of the most potent drugs of abuse, such as ecstasy and cocaine, increase the activity of these neurotransmitters. If these drugs activate the brain's reward systems directly, it would explain their pleasurable effects and the difficulty of breaking the habit. It also seems that other addictive drugs, such as heroin, indirectly increase dopamine activity in the brain's reward systems.

ESB is a bizarre phenomenom but it did lead to the discovery of reward pathways in the brain. Although they are independent of psychological models, reward pathways can provide a physiological explanation for the effects of expectation and incentive. Other models of motivation have deliberately linked physiological and psychological approaches.

A combined approach: Hull and drive-reduction

Hull (1943) produced one of the grandest theories in the whole of psychology. It represents a combination of physiological homeostatic drives as described and discussed above, and psychological principles of learning based on drive-reduction. It could thus be classified as a half-way house between purely physiological and purely psychological approaches to motivation. His central thesis is that all behaviour is motivated, and that all motivation originates in the satisfaction of homeostatic drives such as hunger, thirst and temperature control. Homeostatic drives are reduced by the appropriate stimulus, e.g. food, water, warmth. These stimuli serve to reinforce the behaviour that led to them, and the animal learns the behaviour because it is reinforced. Thus Hull's is a theory of motivation and learning through drive-reduction.

An obvious question is how such a theory could cope with complex human behaviour. This requires the introduction of secondary reinforcers. Imagine a baby being fed by its mother. The food she provides satisfies the homeostatic drive of hunger and is called a primary reinforcer. However, because of her constant association with food, the mother acquires reinforcing properties of her own, and becomes a secondary reinforcer to the baby. The child then learns to behave in ways which bring contact with the secondary reinforcer, i.e. mum. It is then a short step to seeing the mother's approval as an important reinforcer for behaviour, and, although it may seem silly now, to see Alexander the Great's motivation for conquering the known world as a way of seeking his mother's approval. This view of motivation was taken seriously by psychologists for many years (in fact, in this respect Hull has a lot in common with Freud!).

Actually Hull's theory failed through more basic weaknesses. His fundamental prediction was that animals do not learn unless there are drives which are reduced through reinforcement. Rats will not learn their way through a maze unless they are, for instance, hungry and find food at the end. As early as 1932, Tolman had shown that rats learn mazes by developing cognitive maps without drive-reduction or reinforcement (Tolman 1948). We also now know that spatial learning is a highly developed cognitive ability in most animals and does not depend on drives and reinforcements (Olton 1976). The work outlined above

on expectation and incentive also falls outside Hull's theory.

Hull failed to address the complexity of human motivations (virtually all his work was on rats) and placed too much emphasis on homeostatic drives and too little on higher cognitive processes. This was not entirely his fault. At the time he was working, psychology was dominated by Skinner's behaviourism, and cognitive psychology did not exist as a discipline. To deal with motivation properly, we have to look at psychological approaches.

Psychological approaches to motivation

An old-fashioned view of motivation divided it into extrinsic and intrinsic motives. With extrinsic motives, you could identify a clear reward or reinforcement for the behaviour. Behaviourists have shown, especially in rats, that almost any behaviour can be learnt on the basis of reward. Other behaviours, even in rats, seem to have no obvious external reward and these are referred to as intrinsically motivated. Monkeys will learn to open a closed window simply to see out for 30 seconds (Butler 1953), or will do wire puzzles for hours on end with no extrinsic reward (Harlow 1950). As discussed earlier, these behaviours are clearly distinct from homeostatic drives. There is no tissue deficiency leading to a drive state, and no obvious physiological explanation.

Similarly, in humans there are many behaviours without a close link to physiology, and various psychological theories have been put forward to explain them.

Murray's needs

One major problem with drives such as curiosity and manipulation is that they are simply descriptions of the behaviour, and in theory anyone could make up their own list of drives or motives. Murray (1938) used his Thematic Apperception Test (TAT) to provide a more reliable set of human social motives. The TAT, still used in personality testing today, consists of twenty pictures of people in various situations. The participant is asked to use his or her imagination to write a story about each picture, and then the stories are analysed in terms of the types of motivation represented. From these analyses, Murray produced a list of twenty social motives, or psychogenic needs, as he called them. These include:

◆ *achievement* – to accomplish difficult tasks, to overcome obstacles, to rival and overcome others

◆ *affiliation* – to cooperate and win affection from others

◆ *aggression* – to overcome others forcefully, by attacking, injuring or killing

◆ *deference* – to admire and support a superior

- *nurturance* – to protect, console, comfort and nurse the weak, ill or disabled
- *play* – to behave for fun, with no other purpose, especially in games and sports
- *understanding* – to seek or give answers to problems, and to analyse and theorize.

Murray's list sounds convincing and it is based on the TAT. But this itself is a projective test and relies on Murray's own analysis. No one would question that these motives are ones which humans would recognize as important, but it would be more convincing if other evidence was available to give them objective validity. In fact, Achievement motivation has been extensively studied by McClelland (1961), who developed original ways of assessing levels of Need for Achievement (nAch) in the stories children write. Using a rating scale, he measured achievement imagery in these stories (e.g. references to ambition, successful careers at school, college and in work), and related levels to, for instance, child-rearing practices, showing that mothers of high nAch boys placed earlier demands on the boy's self-reliance and independence.

On a grander scale, McClelland measured levels of nAch in children's reading books from 1925 across forty countries and found a significant correlation with economic growth between 1929 and 1950. He proposed that a society's future economic progress could be predicted by the achievement imagery used in its children's literature; adult levels of nAch are decided partly by the achievement imagery they are exposed to as a child.

McClelland's work has given nAch more validity as one of the central human motives. Others in Murray's list have not been studied so intensively and so lack a degree of validity. This lack of experimental verification is a consistent feature of models of human motivation. However, Maslow has at least tried to describe the relationships between different types of motive or need.

Maslow's hierarchy of needs

Maslow (1954) proposed that there are two sets of human needs. One set concerns basic survival needs, such as those related to homeostasis, physiological needs and physical safety. The second set concerns self-actualization, the realization of an individual's full potential, especially as shown in creativity and use of the intellect.

Maslow arranged the various needs in a hierarchy (Fig. 6.3), as he stated that the basic survival needs had to be satisfied before you could ascend the hierarchy and begin to satisfy creative and intellectual drives. Also, the higher up the hierarchy you go, the more difficult it is to satisfy the needs, as they become psychological rather than physiological, and long-term rather than short-term. In fact, Maslow would argue

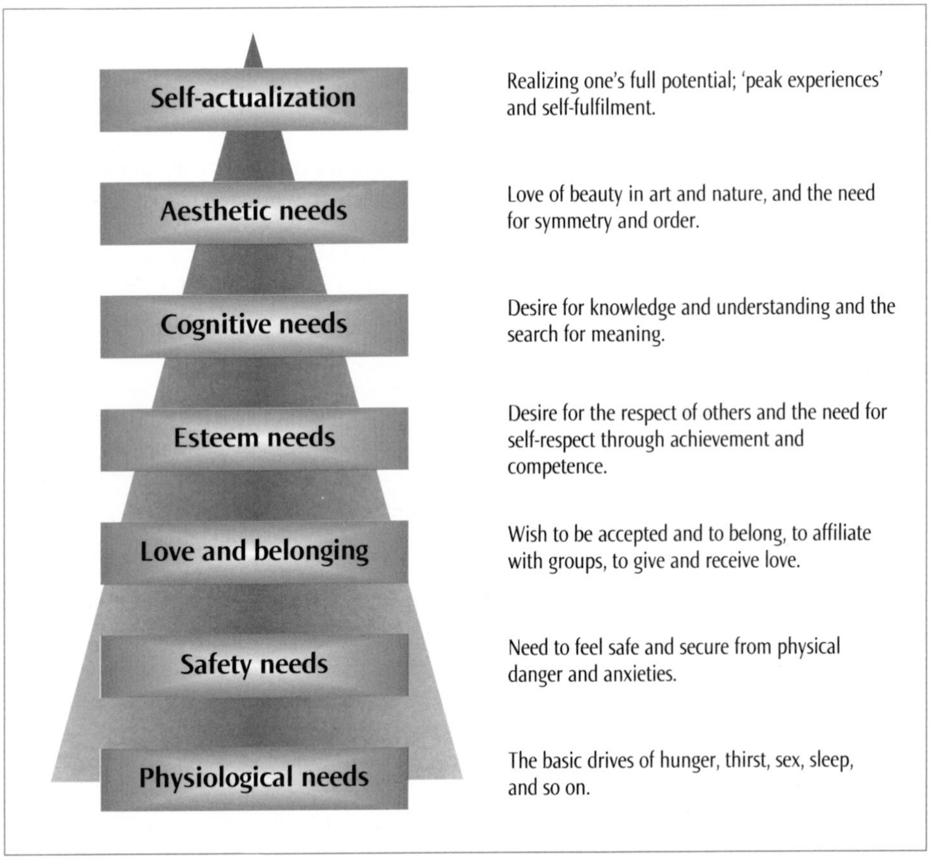

Figure 6.3 Maslow's hierarchy of needs

- **Self-actualization** — Realizing one's full potential; 'peak experiences' and self-fulfilment.
- **Aesthetic needs** — Love of beauty in art and nature, and the need for symmetry and order.
- **Cognitive needs** — Desire for knowledge and understanding and the search for meaning.
- **Esteem needs** — Desire for the respect of others and the need for self-respect through achievement and competence.
- **Love and belonging** — Wish to be accepted and to belong, to affiliate with groups, to give and receive love.
- **Safety needs** — Need to feel safe and secure from physical danger and anxieties.
- **Physiological needs** — The basic drives of hunger, thirst, sex, sleep, and so on.

that many of us do not reach our full human potential, or self-actualize, and as his examples of successful self-actualizers include Einstein and Abraham Lincoln, it is not too surprising!

He does associate 'peak experiences' with self-actualization. These are the moments when individuals are totally lost in themselves and are oblivious to other needs or to other people. Such moments are usually confined to the activity of the moment (work, sport, childbirth, etc.) and are difficult to reach consistently.

Maslow's approach has positive and negative features:

◆ It has a uniquely human emphasis; only humans can self-actualize or engage in high-level cognitive and aesthetic activities. In this way, it is an advance on the largely animal-based physiological and reward-based models of motivation.

◆ There is no evidence that the needs operate as a strict hierarchy. In fact, it is a cliché that great artists like Van Gogh would paint rather than eat or earn the money to eat, and some activities such as pot-holing or mountain climbing deliberately flirt with risk and danger.

◆ There is little direct empirical evidence for the model, and indeed it is hard to imagine how one would collect such evidence.

◆ It provides a framework for discussing the richness and complexity of human motivation that goes beyond homeostatic models and the simple lists of Murray.

Motivation: physiological and psychological approaches

We have discussed various approaches to the study of motivation and now we can draw some general conclusions:

◆ Much behaviour is aimed at satisfying primary physiological drives such as hunger and thirst. However, the link between the drive and behaviour is not always direct. Eating, for instance, is influenced by psychological factors and by the sight, taste and smell of food, as well as by tissue need. We also eat according to habit and custom, and usually anticipate need rather than respond to it.

◆ Physiological theories are limited to behaviours related to survival and have great problems with even simple nonphysiological behaviours such as curiosity and manipulation. Explanations involving secondary reinforcers are clumsy and unconvincing.

◆ Psychological approaches, such as Murray's and Maslow's, try to understand complex human

motivations in a realistic way. Their major weakness is the lack of objective experimental data, but they provide more convincing descriptions of human motivation than does the biological approach.

Activity 2: Your own motivation

Think about your own life.

◆ Why are you studying at college?

◆ Do you have a long-term plan that motivates you?

Look at Maslow's hierarchy.

◆ Can you identify with the types of drives he describes, and can you imagine or have you experienced self-actualizing?

◆ Do you believe the hierarchy is a realistic model of your own motivational structure?

Exam summary: Theories of motivation

The AQA examination will test your understanding of the following areas:

◆ physiological approaches to motivation (pp. 138–41)

◆ psychological approaches to motivation (pp. 141–3)

◆ combined approaches to motivation (e.g. drive-reduction theory) (p. 141).

Example question

The question below is typical of one drawn from the material above, and should take you 30 minutes to answer.

◆ Outline and evaluate one physiological and one psychological approach to motivation.   *(24 marks)*

Suggested answer structure

As frequently mentioned in other chapters, questions such as this require very careful reading and even more careful planning. Reading this question tells you that you are required to write about two approaches, but one of these must be a physiological approach, and the other a psychological approach of motivation. Note that the question does not ask for theories but merely approaches. Second, you are asked to outline these two approaches. This involves a summary description rather than the more detailed description with other AO1 injunctions such as 'describe' or 'consider'. Finally, you are also asked to evaluate your chosen approaches, the AO2 component of this question. This effectively gives us four 'chunks' of answer, each one taking up

7.5 minutes of writing time, approximately equivalent to 150 words for each chunk.

Homeostatic drive reduction (pp. 133–9) is the simplest example of motivated behaviour, but applies only to straightforward physiological drives. It is also based on experiments with nonhuman animals, but this research has provided clear evidence on the role of brain mechanisms in motivation. Optimal arousal theory (p. 139) has been used to account for nonphysiological drives such as curiosity and exploration. Although useful as a general description, it ignores the cognitive aspects and specific aims of these behaviours. Incentive or expectancy approaches to motivation (pp. 139–40) emphasize the ability of environmental stimuli to elicit goal-directed behaviour. Anticipated reward outcomes help establish the behaviour. In other situations the association of neutral stimuli with primary rewards may lead to them becoming incentives.

Electrical self-stimulation of the brain (ESB) (p. 140) led to the discovery of the brain's reward pathways.

Activation of these pathways may account also for the effects of incentive stimuli and for the rewarding effects of drugs of abuse. Hull's drive-reduction model combined physiological and psychological approaches. However, he failed to account for complex human motivations, and his essentially behaviouristic approach ignores cognitive aspects of animal behaviour.

Psychological approaches, such as Murray's and Maslow's try to understand complex human motivations in a realistic way. Murray (pp. 141–2) produced a list of twenty social motives, or psychogenic needs based on his Thematic Apperception Test (TAT), itself a projective test that also relied on Murray's own analysis. Maslow (pp. 142–3) proposed two sets of human needs, one set concerned with basic survival needs and the other concerned with self-actualization: the realization of an individual's full potential. The major weakness of these psychological approaches is the lack of valid experimental data, but they provide more convincing descriptions of human motivation than does the physiological approach.

Emotion

We all experience emotions, and we all know what they are – fear, anger, love, sorrow, etc. We can work out that they have different aspects. We feel angry, we act angrily, and our arousal level goes up; emotions involve subjective experience (the 'feeling'), behaviour and physiological changes. But can you define 'emotion'? Kleinginna and Kleinginna (1981) reviewed a variety of definitions and came up with a synthesis:

> 'Emotion is a complex set of interactions among subjective and objective factors, mediated by neural (nervous) and hormonal systems which can (a) give rise to feelings of arousal, pleasure/displeasure; (b) generate cognitive processes; (c) activate widespread physiological adjustments to the arousal conditions; and (d) lead to behaviour that is often, but not always, expressive, goal-directed, and adaptive.'

Besides being so general as to be not of much practical use, there are problems in using this definition to compare, for example, anger and sorrow. Anger fits the definition quite well, but does sorrow involve 'widespread physiological adjustments', and does it lead to behaviour that may be goal-directed and adaptive? Arnold (1960) suggested a sequence of events in emotional situations:

◆ *perception* of the situation

◆ *appraisal* – an assessment of the situation as beneficial or potentially harmful

◆ *emotion* – a 'felt' tendency towards a beneficial stimulus or away from a harmful stimulus

◆ *expression* – physiological changes in the body associated with the emotion

◆ *action* – behavioural approach or withdrawal.

To make sense of research into emotion, psychologists have sensibly left the problem of a concise definition on the sidelines, and concentrated on other, clearer questions. These involve the relationships between the subjective experience or feeling, the behaviour associated with the emotion along with physiological changes in the body, cognitive processes such as perception and appraisal, and brain structures associated with emotion. We will start by looking at the long tradition of research investigating the role of brain structures.

Brain structures and emotion

As long ago as the 1920s and 1930s lesion and stimulation studies in nonhuman animals had shown that extreme emotions, such as rage and aggression, were controlled from brain structures. Stimulation in sites such as the midbrain, hypothalamus, and thalamus could produce threat and attack behaviour in cats (reviewed in Flynn 1976). Removal of the cerebral cortex led to 'decorticate rage', where aggressive behaviour was easily triggered by the mildest stimulus, showing that the behaviour was organized by systems

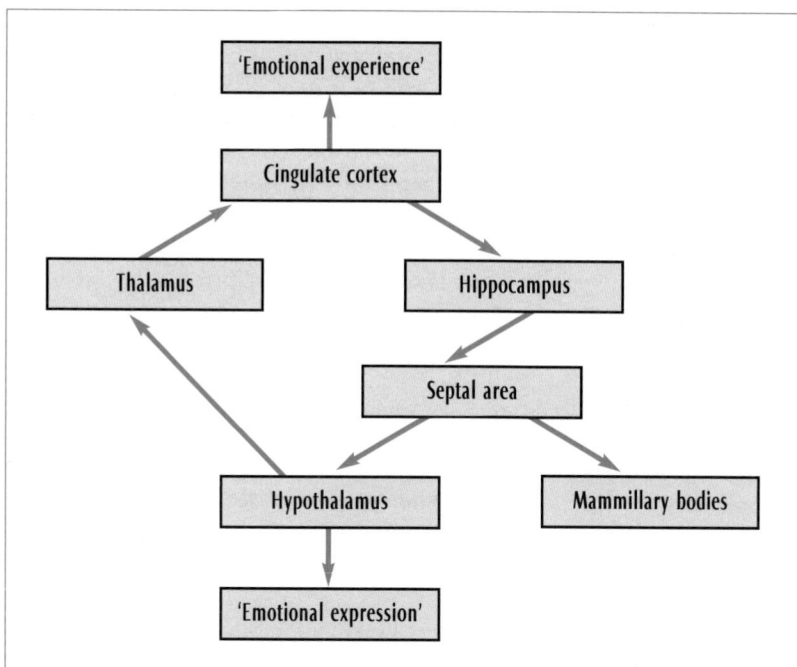

Figure 6.4
The limbic system
(formely the Papez circuit)

outside the cortex but that cortical structures controlled whether it was exhibited or not.

One of the most dramatic syndromes was demonstrated by Kluver and Bucy in 1939. They removed the temporal lobes in Rhesus monkeys and produced a pattern of behaviour that included extreme placidity (reduced fear and aggression), over-sexuality, and 'orality' a tendency to place everything they picked up in their mouths. The temporal lobes contain various structures, but follow-up work showed conclusively that the critical one for the Kluver-Bucy syndrome was the amygdala.

Eventually Papez (1937) proposed a systematic model of brain structures and emotion. Papez was influenced by the ideas of Cannon and Bard (see later) on the role of the hypothalamus in emotional expression (the observed behavioural and physiological signs of emotion) and their finding that the cortex was responsible for the subjective experience (emotional 'feeling'). Papez was also impressed by the heightened emotional behaviour of people with rabies (typically increased anger and rage), an infection which in particular damages the hippocampus.

Papez proposed that, while the hypothalamus was responsible for emotional expression, emotional feeling involved the limbic system. This is a network of structures in the forebrain linked by neural pathways. It includes the hypothalamus, thalamus, hippocampus, septum, and cingulate cortex (see Fig. 6.4). The amygdala has extensive connections with the limbic system and is often included with it.

MacLean (1949) developed Papez's model, using the limbic system as one of three major divisions of the brain. The brainstem (the 'reptilian' brain according to

MacLean) was responsible for essential physiological functions; the limbic brain ('old mammalian') was involved in emotional feeling and behaviour; while the 'new mammalian' cortex looked after higher cognition functions. The Papez-MacLean model of emotion has been very influential, with the limbic system still referred to as our emotional or 'feeling' system. However, while many studies have confirmed that damage or stimulation of limbic system structures affects emotions, there are many problems:

◆ Most of the experimental work has been done on nonhuman animals, and therefore can only study emotional expression, the outward signs of emotion. They cannot be used to investigate emotional feeling, a vital part of the human experience of emotion.

◆ As animals are used, the range of emotions studied is severely limited, usually to the most dramatic ones such as rage, fear, and aggression.

◆ The human brain is more highly evolved and complex than the brains of rats, cats, and even monkeys. While our limbic system is certainly involved in emotion, it is unjustified to extrapolate directly from studies with nonhuman animals.

Psychosurgery

Despite the problems of extrapolating to humans, the work of Papez, MacLean and others has been used to justify the use of brain surgery to treat so-called emotional disorders in humans. Up until the 1970s, lesions to the amygdala were used to try and reduce aggressive behaviour in adults and even children (Kiloh *et al.* 1974). Even more popular in the 1940s was the frontal lobotomy used to treat schizophrenia. Frontal lobe lesions had been shown to 'calm' chimpanzees, and so the frontal lobotomy was introduced as a method of tranquillizing schizophrenic patients, i.e. making them more manageable. There is no evidence that the operation improved the specific symptoms of schizophrenia, and it largely disappeared once the antipsychotic drugs came into use in the 1950s.

As the ethical climate surrounding psychology and psychiatry changed during the 1960s and 70s, so it became clear that performing psychosurgery on patients (adults and children) who were often unable to give informed consent was completely unethical, and often unjustified in terms of its effects, i.e. while it might calm patients, there could be side effects such as dramatic changes in personality. Although largely discredited, psychosurgery hasn't completely disappeared. It is sometimes a treatment of very last resort (after psychological therapies, drugs and electroconvulsive therapy) for disabling psychiatric conditions, such as severe depression or obsessive-compulsive disorder. In 1999, the former child singing star Lena Zavaroni died from complications following psychosurgery. She had suffered for years from anorexia and depression.

Brain structures clearly play a vital role in emotional expression and behaviour. There are, however, other research traditions which have emphasized the body's physiological and arousal systems, and have the advantage of studying emotions in humans. We now turn to these physiological theories.

Physiological and cognitive theories

James-Lange theory of emotion

Working independently, William James (1884) and a Danish psychologist named Lange (1885) put forward similar models of emotion, now known jointly as the James-Lange theory. The theory is counter-intuitive. Their idea was that the perception of an emotion-arousing stimulus (for instance, a hungry bear) leads to a behavioural response, probably running away. This response involves changes in the body's physiological systems (increased arousal in the autonomic nervous system and in skeletal muscles). The brain detects these physiological changes and interprets them as the emotion of fear. In the classic phrase, we do not run because we are scared; we are scared because we run (see Fig. 6.5).

This sequence of events goes against commonsense, which would say that the perception and appraisal of the bear leads *simultaneously* to the feeling of fear and the response of running away. What the James-Lange theory is emphasizing is the central role of feedback to the brain of peripheral physiological arousal in generating emotional states, and it is on this particular aspect that it has been most heavily criticized.

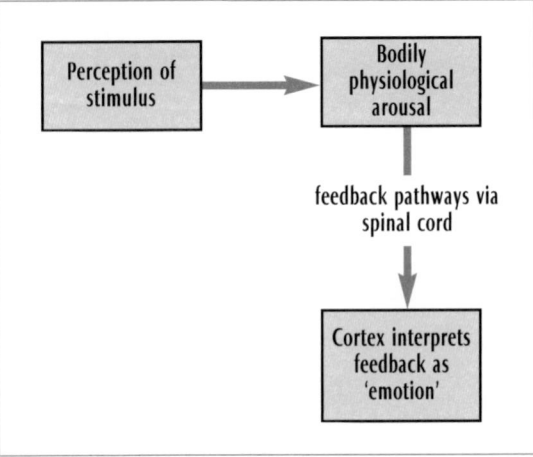

Figure 6.5 James-Lange's model of emotion

Cannon (1929) presented several major criticisms:

◆ If the emotion felt depends upon bodily arousal, then each separate emotion would have to be associated with a different pattern of arousal. Although extreme emotions such as anger and fear can be distinguished on the basis of physiological changes, usually such differences between emotions are subtle, if they exist at all.

◆ Physiological changes occur too slowly following perception of the stimulus to account for the emotional feeling, which occurs almost instantaneously.

◆ Feedback from the body passes to the brain through the spinal cord. If the spinal cord is damaged, bodily changes and feedback are prevented, so there should be no emotional experience. Cannon quotes a study (Dana 1921) of a patient with spinal damage who reported a normal range of emotions. However, Hohmann (1966) reported on 25 such patients who did experience reductions in feelings of anger and fear, in line with predictions from the James-Lange theory.

◆ If bodily arousal was necessary and sufficient to produce emotion, then physical exercise or taking stimulant drugs should produce emotional feelings. Running up the stairs is not usually an emotional experience, but work on drugs is less clear cut. Cannon quotes a study by Maranon (1924), who injected participants with the drug adrenaline (known as epinephrine in the USA) which produces bodily physiological arousal. None of the 210 participants felt real emotions, although 29 per cent reported that they felt 'as if' they were afraid or angry. Cannon concluded that the James-Lange theory was contradicted, as the induced arousal did not produce real emotions as the theory predicted.

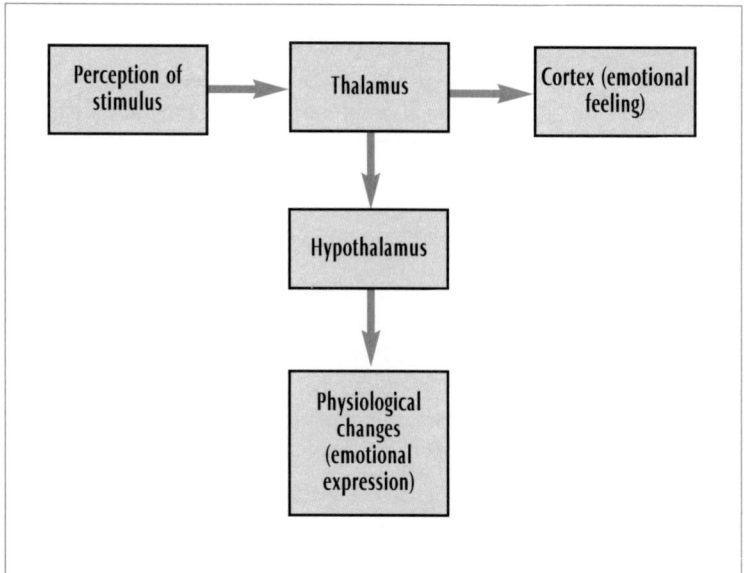

Figure 6.6 Cannon-Bard's model of emotion

Cannon-Bard theory

As an alternative to the James-Lange model, Cannon proposed a central theory of emotions (see Fig. 6.6).

This theory proposes that peripheral arousal is unnecessary for emotional feelings. Incoming stimuli are processed through the thalamus in the brain. Messages then pass from the thalamus upwards to the cortex, which is where conscious emotional experience occurs, and messages are also sent downwards to the hypothalamus and then on to the body, producing physiological arousal and muscular activity. If the spinal cord is damaged, messages cannot reach the body from the brain and arousal does not occur, but messages still ascend from the thalamus to the cortex and so emotional feelings are preserved.

Although not taken seriously today, the Cannon-Bard theory did anticipate limbic models of emotion (see p. 145). It also left unresolved the problem of whether bodily arousal played a role in emotional states. Remember that Maranon's participants experienced 'as if' emotional states, so the arousal induced by the injection of adrenaline did not just produce a pattern of generalized arousal, but led to specific reactions, even if they were not 'real' emotions. To try and clarify the situation Schachter and Singer (1962) performed one of the most famous studies in psychology.

A combined approach: cognitive labelling theory

Schachter and Singer proposed that the debate about the role of arousal in emotional states had largely ignored the important role of cognitive factors. When we feel emotional, it is always about something,

whether it is an external stimulus or internal thoughts and memories. A crucial stage in any emotional experience is therefore *cognitive appraisal*, when a stimulus is perceived and evaluated.

Perception of the stimulus may also lead to bodily physiological arousal and, according to Schachter and Singer, it is the *combination* of arousal and cognitive appraisal that leads to the experience of emotion. For instance, if the arousal is produced by the sight of a grizzly bear, the cognitive appraisal of the situation leads us to interpret the arousal as the emotion of fear. If the arousal is produced by your brother dyeing your favourite T-shirt brown, cognitive appraisal leads to the interpretation of the arousal as the emotion of anger.

In Schachter and Singer's view, physiological arousal is *necessary* for emotional experience, but needs to be *labelled* or interpreted by cognitive appraisal of the situation. So they follow James-Lange in emphasizing the role of arousal, although they do not propose that patterns of arousal vary between emotions. We feel different emotions because of cognitive labelling, and the same pattern of arousal can occur in different emotional states. If we see cognitive appraisal as based in the brain, Schachter and Singer are also emphasizing central mechanisms in emotion, so their position is a combination of the James-Lange bodily arousal theory and the Cannon-Bard central theory.

One clear prediction from the cognitive labelling theory is that if a state of unexplained bodily arousal is induced in participants, they will look around and try to explain it in terms of their environment. If this cognitive appraisal involves an emotional element, then they will label their state of arousal as an emotional experience. This may sound similar to Maranon's experiment mentioned earlier, but don't forget that those people knew they had been injected with adrenaline, and so had a cognitive interpretation for their arousal state that did not involve emotions. Schachter and Singer intended to induce a completely unexpected and unexplained state of arousal, and then manipulate the environment to try and produce different emotional states.

As in Maranon's study, adrenaline was used to produce a physiological arousal state, but Schachter and Singer deceived their male participants by telling them they were receiving a vitamin supplement called 'suproxin' as part of an experiment on vision. There was also a control group receiving a nonactive placebo, but which was otherwise treated in the same way as the experimental groups. Participants given injections of adrenaline were either told to expect the real physiological consequences, such as increased heart-rate, dry mouth and palpitations, were misinformed as to the physical effects of the injection, or were left ignorant. The experimental situation was manipulated in two ways. In the euphoria condition, accomplices of the experimenters acted in a manically happy way, flying paper aeroplanes and playing with balls of paper. In the anger condition, an accomplice of the experimenter became progressively more angry as he and the participant filled in a highly personal questionnaire ('Do members of your family require psychiatric care?').

The emotional state of the participants was assessed using observers watching through one-way mirrors and by self-reports after the episodes with the accomplices, i.e. measures of emotional behaviour and emotional experience. The main predictions were:

◆ The group told to expect physiological arousal after the injection would have a cognitive explanation of their state, and would not need to explain it using the behaviour of the accomplices. This is similar to Maranon's study, and changes in emotion would not be predicted.

◆ The group given the inactive placebo would not experience bodily arousal and therefore would have no arousal state to explain or label. They should not report changes in emotion.

◆ The group given adrenaline but left ignorant as to the effects *would* experience an unexplained state of bodily arousal. To interpret it they would use cognitive appraisal of the environment; if they were with an accomplice behaving euphorically, they should label their state as euphoria, and if they were with an angry accomplice, they should label the state as anger.

The critical predictions Schachter and Singer make are that more emotional change should be seen in the adrenaline-ignorant group than in the placebo group, and that the emotion experienced would depend on which accomplice the participant was with. (The misinformed group were included for complex control reasons and will not be considered further here.)

Schachter and Singer reported results in line with their predictions. Participants given no explanation for the arousing effects of the injection showed more emotional change than the placebo group, reacting more euphorically or angrily in line with their accomplice's behaviour.

This seems a neat combination of the James-Lange and Cannon-Bard positions. Bodily arousal is necessary but not sufficient for emotion, which depends upon an interaction between bodily arousal and the central processes of cognitive appraisal. Therefore, emotion is produced by a combination of peripheral and central factors.

There are, however, problems with this classic study:

◆ The first statistical analyses produced significant differences between adrenaline-ignorant and placebo groups only for the observer ratings in the Anger condition. (Remember that there are four predicted differences, for observer ratings and self-reports in the two conditions of anger and euphoria.)

◆ When Schachter and Singer eliminated participants in the adrenaline-ignorant group who they thought had worked out that the injection was responsible for their state of arousal, they found just one more significant difference, for observer ratings for the euphoria condition.

◆ No significant differences were found for the self-report data on participants' emotional feelings (observer ratings are of emotional behaviour).

◆ Therefore, adrenaline may simply make participants more likely to imitate an accomplice's behaviour, without changing the actual emotional state.

◆ There was no assessment of participants' emotional state before the study, which may have interacted with the experimental manipulations.

◆ Unexplained bodily arousal is an unusual state in real life, and so is drug-induced arousal. The study is far removed from natural emotions, and this reduces its validity.

◆ Attempts to replicate the experiment (which for largely ethical reasons have been rare) have been unsuccessful (Marshall and Zimbardo 1979, Maslach 1979).

Schachter and Singer's study therefore does not settle the dispute on the role of arousal and cognition in emotion. On the positive side, it did emphasize the major role of cognitive processes such as perception and appraisal.

Activity 3: Your emotions and arousal

Consider some of your own emotions. Try to rank them in order of the bodily arousal associated with them. Are there any independent of arousal? Think of a clear emotional experience; do you think it is possible for the bodily reaction to occur before you feel the emotion?

Ekman and the facial feedback model

Paul Ekman (1992) has for many years studied the evolution of emotional behaviour and its role in social interaction. He believes that the facial expressions associated with different emotions do not merely communicate the way you are feeling to others, but directly influence your emotional state. This idea is based on several linked observations:

◆ Emotional expressions are universally recognized.

◆ Emotions are innately programmed.

◆ Emotions involve cognition, facial expression, and bodily arousal.

◆ Each emotion involves a specific pattern of changes in the brain, in facial expression, and in bodily arousal.

◆ Feedback from the pattern of muscle activity and facial blood flow associated with a particular facial expression directly influences the emotion you experience.

Experimental support comes from studies where participants mimic facial expressions and then report on their emotional state. Participants clenching a pencil between their teeth (i.e. 'smiling') rated cartoons as funnier than participants holding a pencil between their lips ('frowning') (Strack *et al.* 1988). As you will see from Fig 6.7, participants adopting happy or angry faces when watching emotional slides reported feeling happier when making a happy face and angrier when making an angry face (Rutlidge and Hupka 1985). One interesting prediction from these results is that you

Activity 4: Putting on a happy face

Get together a few friends or classmates and try out Rutlidge and Hupka's procedure. Be careful about the kind of material you ask people to look at. You could choose pictures carefully from national newspapers. Find out if your results differ when participants know the purpose of the investigation. Don't forget to try this yourself first. Did you succeed in modifying your emotional state?

should be able to modify your own emotional state by adopting a particular emotional expression!

Exactly what sort of feedback from facial expression is critical in these effects is unclear. Possibilities include changes in muscle patterns and in blood flow. Either way, this model has similarities with the James-Lange approach, in that peripheral feedback is vital in emotional experience. But Ekman also emphasizes cognitive appraisal as the basis for facial expression, and so has some slight connection with the cognitive labelling hypothesis.

The debate on the role of arousal and cognition in emotion continues (see *In Focus* on p. 150), with some researchers taking extreme positions. Lazarus (1984), for instance, defines emotions as depending upon cognitive appraisal of the environment, while Zajonc (1984) proposes that cognitive processes and emotions can be independent. He gives the example of babies who can show emotions such as fear and disgust in the

Figure 6.7
The effect of facial expression on the experience of emotion

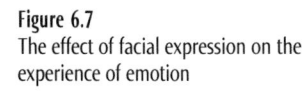
Put on a happy face?

Participants reported feeling more happy and less angry when they viewed slides while making a happy face, and less happy and more angry when they viewed slides while making an angry face.

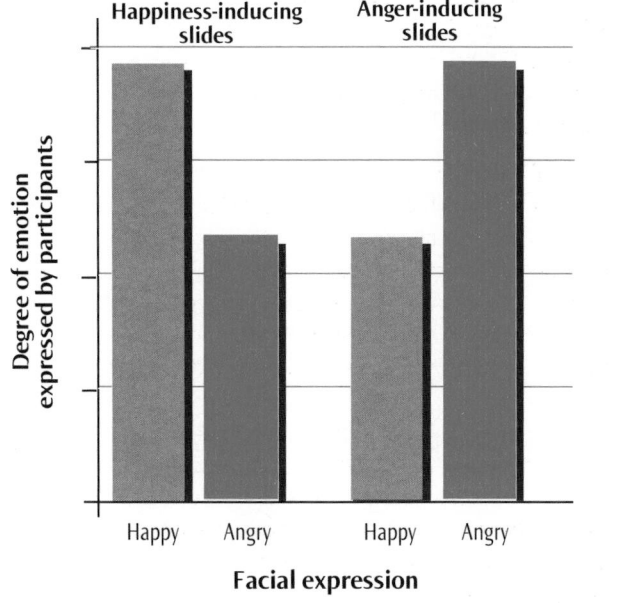

in focus

Bodily arousal and attraction

In 1974 Dutton and Aron reported their suspension bridge study. Male participants visiting a Canadian canyon were questioned by an attractive female on their reactions to the scenery. As part of the interview, they were asked to make up a story about an ambiguous picture of a woman. The level of sexual imagery in the story was scored, and it was found that participants interviewed on a high suspension bridge included more sexual imagery in their stories than those interviewed on a stable wooden bridge. The interpretation was that the bodily arousal produced by the fear and anxiety of the high suspension bridge had intensified the sexual attractiveness of the interviewer, and this was reflected in the stories. Accepting that the sexual imagery of the story is an indirect way of measuring sexual attraction, the study does suggest that arousal can intensify emotions.

absence of high-level cognitive abilities. However, babies are scared or disgusted by something which they have sensed or perceived, and it seems to be splitting hairs to say that their emotions do not depend on some cognitive assessment of their environment. Strongman (1987) gives some general conclusions:

◆ Bodily physiological arousal can be important, intensifying emotional experience in states such as fear and anger, but it is not necessary for all emotional experience. Emotions such as sadness occur in the absence of arousal.

◆ Cognitive processes such as perception and appraisal are basic and necessary for emotion.

◆ The huge range of human emotions means that simple models of the links between emotion, arousal and cognition are unrealistic.

Exam summary: Emotion

The AQA examination will test your understanding of the following areas:

◆ the role of brain structures in emotion (pp. 144–6)

◆ physiological approaches to the explanation of emotion (pp. 146–7)

◆ combined approaches to the explanation of emotion (e.g. Shachter's cognitive labelling theory) (pp. 147–8).

Example question

The question below is typical of one drawn from the material above, and should take you 30 minutes to answer.

◆ Discuss the role of brain structures in emotion.

(24 marks)

Suggested answer structure

This question is effectively the 'mirror' of the question on motivation that we discussed in an earlier section,

therefore the same comments about mechanisms and structures apply here.

There are many components to emotion, including appraisal, feeling, physiological changes, and behaviour. Work mainly with nonhuman animals has identified brain structures of the limbic system as important in emotional behaviours such as rage, fear, and aggression. Extrapolation to the complex human brain can only be done cautiously (pp. 144–5). Despite this, psychosurgery for human psychological disorders was based on the animal work. It has now largely died out, because of the severe ethical issues involved and its general lack of effectiveness (pp. 145–6). The James-Lange theory of emotion (p. 146) proposed that emotions depend on bodily physiological arousal. Cannon (pp. 146–7) criticised their ideas and instead developed a central model which located emotions in brain structures such as the thalamus and hypothalamus.

As this question asks for brain structures in the plural, you should try to include reference to more than one structure in your answer. The limbic system does not count as one structure, but many, as it includes the thalamus and hypothalamus, and has extensive connections to the amygdala. All of these structures have been implicated in the explanation of human emotions.

For the AO2 component of this question, as well as the techniques outlined in the first exam summary of this chapter, you might offer judgement of these explanations, e.g. 'While our limbic system is certainly involved in emotion, it is unjustified to extrapolate directly from studies with nonhuman animals' (p. 145). Alternatively, you might examine the applications of an explanation, e.g. 'Papez was also impressed by the heightened emotional behaviour of people with rabies, an infection which in particular damages the hippocampus' (p. 145). Finally, you might consider the consequences of a particular explanation or action, e.g. '... while it might calm patients, there could be side effects such as dramatic changes in personality' (p. 146).

Chapter summary

◆ Behaviour linked to **homeostatic drives** such as **hunger and thirst** provide the simplest models of **motivation**. Research in these areas has identified **brain structures of motivation** which centre on the **hypothalamus**.

◆ Approaches such as optimal arousal theory have tried to account for nonhomeostatic motivation, but ignore the cognitive aspects of these behaviours.

◆ **Expectancy** and incentive models emphasize the role of environmental stimuli in arousing and directing behaviour.

◆ Activation of reward pathways in the brain can explain incentive effects, and also addiction to drugs of abuse.

◆ Hull's **drive-reduction theory combined physiological** and **psychological** approaches, but over-emphasized homeostatic drives and largely ignored cognitive aspects of motivation.

◆ Murray and Maslow tried to explain complex human motivations, but their theories lack convincing experimental support, although they provide better descriptions of human behaviour than the physiological approach.

◆ **Emotion** involves physiological changes, feelings, and cognitive appraisals. Work with animals has identified the structures of the **limbic system** as central to basic emotional states.

◆ The **James-Lange theory** of emotions emphasized the role of bodily **physiological** changes. This was powerfully criticized by Cannon, who instead proposed that emotion depended upon brain structures such as the **thalamus** and **hypothalamus**.

◆ **Schachter and Singer** combined bodily arousal and central cognitive appraisal in their **cognitive labelling theory**. Although their main study is flawed, they correctly emphasized the importance of cognitive processes in emotional states.

◆ Human emotions are many and varied, and no single model is likely to explain all of them. Cognitive appraisal is central to emotional states, but the significance of physiological arousal varies from emotion to emotion. Ekman's approach emphasizes specific feedback from facial expressions in producing emotional feelings, and has some experimental support.

Further resources

Rosenzweig, M.R., Leiman, A.L. and Breedlove, S.M. (1996) *Biological Psychology*, Sunderland, MA, Sinauer Associates.

Excellent coverage of homeostatic drives and models of emotion.

Strongman, K.T. (1996) *The Psychology of Emotion* (4th edn), Chichester: Wiley.

Definitive coverage of theories of emotion.

Part 3: Cognitive Psychology

A2

ATTENTION AND PATTERN
RECOGNITION

Jane Willson

PERCEPTUAL PROCESSES AND
DEVELOPMENT

Jane Willson

LANGUAGE AND THOUGHT

Jane Willson

Chapter 7

Attention and pattern recognition

Jane Willson

Preview

In this chapter we will be looking at:

◆ research into focused attention, including early-selection and late-selection models

◆ research into divided attention, including controlled and automatic processing

◆ research into pattern recognition, including the role of biological mechanisms and of context, and theories of face recognition.

Introduction

In everyday speech, we use the word attention to refer to several different kinds of mental activity. If you give your whole attention to something, for example taking an exam, you block out everything else that is going on around you. If you are waiting for an important telephone call, you will listen out attentively for the sound of the phone ringing. If you are speaking on the phone while standing in a noisy room, you will focus on the voice at the end of the line and ignore all the competing voices and sounds around you. There are certain familiar things in our environment to which we pay so little attention that we are scarcely aware of them, such as the weight of this book in your hands or the feel of clothes on your body. However, you can turn your attention to them if you choose to. Attention is clearly not a unitary concept and psychologists do not agree on a definition. An all-purpose definition of attention is that it is a focused concentration of mental activity.

In this chapter, we will be looking at two particular types of attention:

1 *focused* or *selective attention* in which we manage to focus on one thing at a time to the exclusion of other competing stimuli

2 *divided attention* whereby we manage to do more than one attentional task at once.

These two types of attention are obviously related and the means of investigating them have been similar, i.e. giving people two tasks to do and seeing how successful they are. However, psychologists have traditionally studied them separately, so we will consider them in separate sections of the chapter.

In the final section of the chapter, we will look at the topic of pattern recognition: the process whereby we transform the raw and unprocessed information arriving from the senses into a recognizable form. This involves comparing the sensory input with information already stored in our long-term memories. Auditory pattern recognition occurs when, for example, we recognize a set of musical notes as a distinct melody, such as the opening bars of the National Anthem. However, in this chapter, the discussion will be limited to visual pattern recognition. We are usually quite competent at distinguishing between various visual stimuli, but psychologists have not been able to explain this ability fully. Various theories have been proposed and we shall look at two of these – template theory and feature detection theory. We shall then consider the role of the biological mechanisms that underpin pattern recognition, and also look at the effects of context on our interpretation of visual stimuli.

One particular type of pattern recognition that has interested psychologists is face recognition; the chapter ends with a look at research in this area.

Focused attention

Modern research on focused attention began in the 1950s and developed from a question raised by Colin Cherry (1953). He was interested in the answer to what he called '*the cocktail party problem*', i.e. the ability to follow just one conversation when others are going on all around. Cherry devised an ingenious experimental technique called the dichotic listening task, in which two simultaneous messages are played to the two ears via headphones. In an artificial replication of the cocktail party situation, participants are asked to pay attention to one of the inputs and ignore the other. This technique made use of the new multi-channel tape recorders that were becoming available at that time and accounts for the fact that much of the early research into selective attention concentrated on auditory stimuli. Typically, the participant is asked to repeat back (shadow) the message heard in one ear.

Activity 1: A 'cocktail party' experiment

You probably do not have access to the kind of sophisticated auditory equipment which would be needed to replicate laboratory studies, but you can investigate the shadowing technique in a cruder fashion by recording two different messages on two separate tape recorders. Play these simultaneously to a willing participant and ask them to repeat out loud one of the messages.

You will find that the dichotic listening task is extremely demanding and requires enormous concentration. You will probably find that your participant repeats the shadowed message in a monotone without the usual rise and fall of normal speech because they are concentrating so hard on simply keeping up. Afterwards, ask what, if anything, they can recall from this message. You will almost certainly find that recall is limited for the shadowed message and non-existent for the other message.

Cherry (1953) carried out several studies in which he investigated the so-called cocktail party effect and reported some interesting findings:

◆ Participants seemed to recall very little about the message played to the unattended ear.

◆ They could recall no words from it.

◆ They did not know whether the message consisted of isolated words or continuous prose.

◆ They were not even aware that the language had switched from English to German.

◆ They did not usually notice if the message was played backwards.

Moray (1959) conducted another study in which the content of the unattended channel was a list of seven words repeated many times. After the shadowing task, participants were given a list of words on a printed sheet and asked to tick those that had been presented on the unattended ear. In spite of the fact that each of the seven words had been repeated 35 times, participant performance on this word recognition task was no better than would have been expected by chance.

However, participants clearly do not block the unattended ear completely. In Cherry's studies, they were able to notice if the voice on the unattended ear changed from male to female, from loud to soft, from high- to low-pitched, or if a pure musical tone replaced a human voice. In other words, they were able to recognize certain physical characteristics of the unattended message, but were oblivious to semantic aspects, i.e. the meaning of the words. However, not all experimental data confirmed this conclusion. Moray (1959) and later Wood and Cowan (1995), using more controlled conditions, found that 35 per cent of participants would hear their own name if it were played on the unattended channel. This is another aspect of the cocktail party phenomenon – even if you are engaged in one conversation at a party, you are likely to hear your own name if it is mentioned in a nearby conversation. This seems to make sense intuitively – in evolutionary terms, it would make sense for us to be equipped with a mechanism which would allow us to switch our attention to something of greater importance, e.g. the sound of a predator approaching. Any adequate theory of attention must be able to account for both these aspects of the cocktail party situation, that is:

◆ the ability to focus on one stimulus input and block out most of the information from others

◆ the ability to switch attention to other messages if necessary.

Early-selection theories

An essential feature of theories of selective attention is that the human brain is unable to analyse all the information that impinges on our senses, so all theories include some mechanism/filter that selects certain inputs and rejects others. The filter is often seen as a

in focus

Broadbent's (1954) split-span procedure

Broadbent's split-span procedure involved participants recalling digits presented simultaneously in pairs, with one digit going to one ear and the other digit going to the other ear. Between the presentation of each pair of digits there was an interval of half a second. Following the presentation, participants were asked to recall the digits in one of two ways:

◆ 'pair by pair' – reporting the first pair of digits presented, then the second and finally the third

◆ 'ear by ear' – reporting the three digits heard by one ear followed by the three digits heard by the other ear.

Broadbent found that 'ear-by-ear' reports were easier for participants, and produced more accurate responses, than 'pair-by-pair' reports. This procedure is illustrated in Fig. 7.1.

On the basis of these findings, Broadbent argued that the ears act as separate channels which can only be attended to one at a time. He suggested that in the pair-by-pair condition the participants had to switch between channels more often than in the ear-by-ear condition. Subsequently, Broadbent presented the first filter model of selective attention (see Fig. 7.2).

Figure 7.1
Broadbent's (1954) split-span procedure

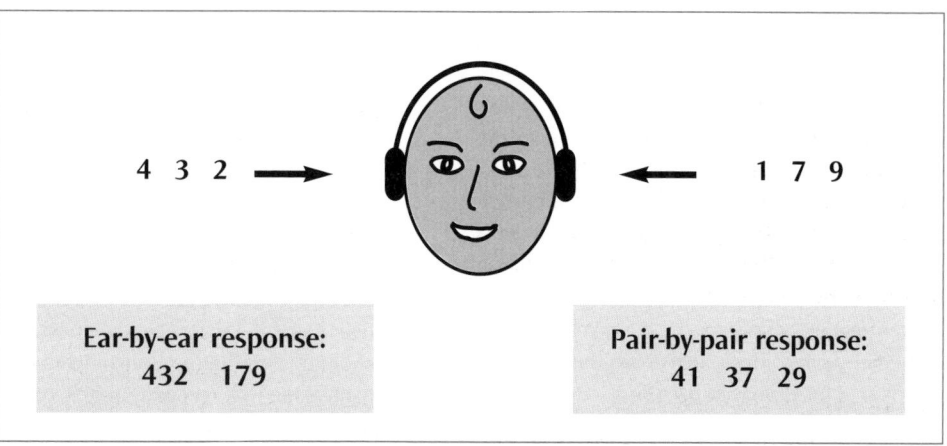

bottleneck where parallel processing stops and serial processing begins. Attention theorists differ in their ideas about the precise location of the bottleneck. Some, like Broadbent and Treisman, place it fairly early in the attentional process, whereas others, such as Deutsch and Deutsch, place it later. We will look first at early-selection theories.

Broadbent's Filter Model of Selective Attention

Broadbent (1958) proposed the first major theory of selective attention. He carried out his own investigations using a particular type of dichotic listening task called the split-span procedure (see *In Focus*).

On the basis of such findings, Broadbent reached the following conclusions:

◆ Two messages presented simultaneously to the two ears can be processed in parallel and gain access to a temporary staging post which he called the sensory buffer store (parallel processing).

◆ One of these messages is then selected on the basis of its physical properties and enters a filter mechanism while the other message waits its turn in the buffer. The buffer has a limited duration and material left there will be lost if it is not passed on quickly.

◆ The filter acts as a 'bottleneck' to prevent too much information flooding the attentional system. Beyond the filter is a limited capacity processor that can only operate on inputs one at a time (serial processing). It is only at this stage that the input can be analysed for meaning.

These conclusions led Broadbent to produce the first comprehensive model of selective attention, in which he represented a sequence of processing stages in the form of a computer flow diagram shown in Fig. 7.2. This use of the computer as an analogy for human thinking processes is called the information-processing approach. Cognitive psychologists working within this framework see the human brain, just like a computer,

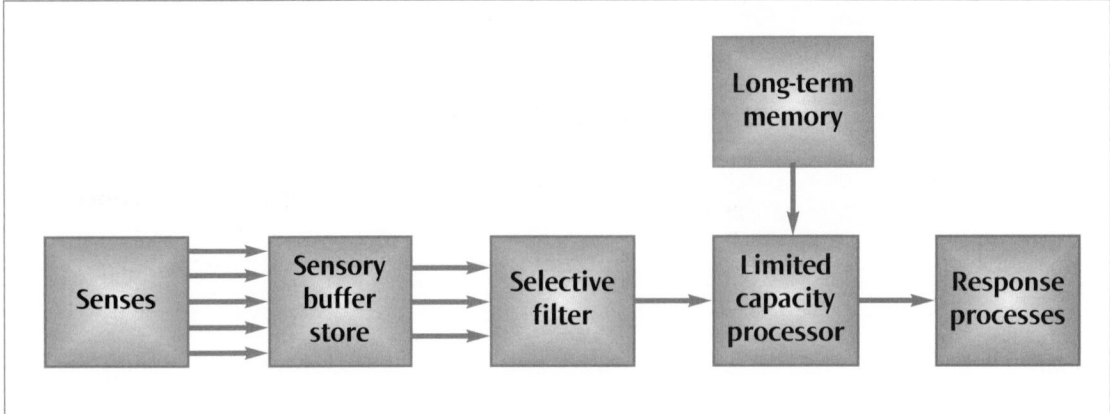

Figure 7.2
Broadbent's (1958) filter model of selective attention

as being required to handle large amounts of incoming information. These inputs frequently exceed the capacity of the brain (or computer) to process them effectively and so inputs have to be prioritized and processed selectively in order to avoid overload.

In Broadbent's model each ear represents a separate channel and the brain can only fully process one channel at a time. This means that one of the two channels has to be selected for further processing. A key aspect of this model is that inputs are selected at the filter stage on the basis of physical properties. This idea will be easier to understand if you think of what happens in a noisy room full of people having separate conversations. Imagine that you are trying to concentrate on what someone is saying in your immediate group. There are certain things that will help you to focus on that person:

◆ the distinctive sound of their voice (i.e. its pitch, rhythm and tone)

◆ the sound intensity (i.e. how loud or soft)

◆ the location of the sound (i.e. where the voice is coming from – you often tend to turn one ear towards the person who is speaking).

By attending to these physical properties of the person's speech, you can identify the conversation which you want to follow (i.e. process for meaning) and avoid being distracted by the semantic content of other conversations going on around you.

Evaluation of Broadbent's model

One of Broadbent's main contributions was that he was the first to make use of the information-processing framework and to present human mental processes in the form of a computer flow diagram. One advantage of this approach is that it suggests suitable tests of its accuracy and the model did, indeed, stimulate considerable research interest in this topic area.

Broadbent's model can account for Cherry's basic findings that unattended messages receive minimal processing. It can also account for Broadbent's own findings from his split-span procedure. If attention needs to be divided between the two ears in order to be able to monitor both messages at once, the filter can switch rapidly between channels on the basis of physical characteristics (in this case, the spatial location). The three items from one ear are reported back, while the items from the second ear are held in the buffer. These latter items can only be reported when the filter switches to the other channel.

However, the model cannot account so easily for other findings. One immediate challenge to the theory came from the study by Moray (1959) mentioned above. He found that listeners often recognized their own name if it was repeated on the unshadowed channel. This finding is incompatible with Broadbent's contention that recognition only occurs after selection on the basis of physical characteristics. Moray's results suggest that there is more analysis of the unattended channel than Broadbent proposed.

Gray and Wedderburn (1960) used a variation of the split-span procedure in which they simultaneously presented material from two categories – digits and words (see Fig. 7.3). Participants had to report either 'ear by ear' or 'category by category'. Gray and Wedderburn found that if the material in either ear was semantically related, as in 'Dear cousin Albert', participants reported this relationship as easily as they reported the ear-by-ear presentation.

This finding created serious problems for Broadbent's model because it suggests that selection can occur on the basis of meaning.

Another problem for the model includes the finding that practice improves the rate of target detection on a non-shadowed message. Underwood (1974) asked participants to shadow one message while an unrelated message was played to the non-shadowed ear. In addition, they were asked to detect particular digits that could be played to either ear. Novices at the task

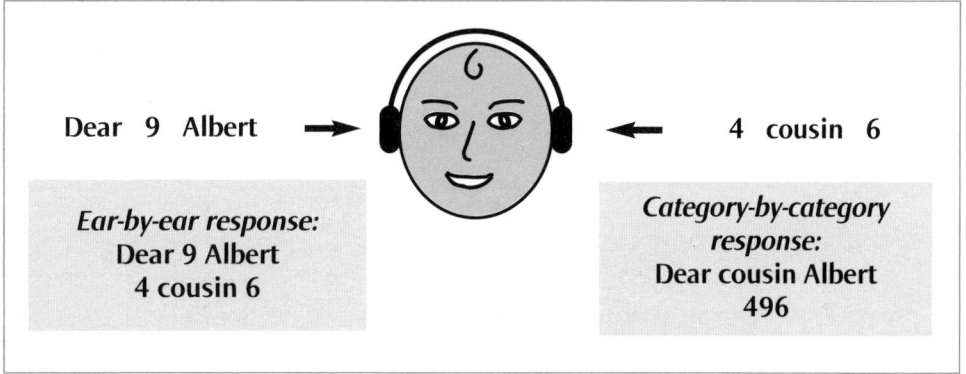

Figure 7.3
Gray and Wedderburn's (1960) version of the split-span procedure

detected on average 8 per cent of the targets, but a highly practised participant was able to detect 67 per cent. This practice effect is difficult to accommodate within Broadbent's model.

It seems, then, that Broadbent's simple model of selective attention is unable to accommodate all the available experimental data. The model has also been criticized because there is no precise definition of the concept of a channel. The notion of separate channels is easy to understand in the context of a dichotic listening task – each ear acts as a separate channel. However, it is not so clear what constitutes a channel in less artificial settings such as listening to some singing on the radio and being able to pick out the words of the singer or the different instruments in the backing music.

Treisman's Attenuator Theory

Anne Treisman (1960) was interested in the findings from studies such as Moray's which suggested that there could be some breakthrough of content from the unattended channel. She set out to investigate how the meaning of auditory input might affect the selection mechanism. In one of her experiments, she used bilingual participants. These participants had to shadow a message in one ear, which was presented in English, while ignoring a message in the other ear, which was presented in the participant's second language, French. In fact, both messages had the same meaning, even though, of course, they sounded completely different. About 50 per cent of participants noticed that both messages were semantically identical, which suggests that the meaning of a message can be recognized prior to any focusing of attention.

In another study, Treisman (1960) asked participants to shadow a story (story 1) in one ear and to ignore another story (story 2) which was being played into the other ear. During the shadowing task, story 1 was switched, without warning, to the other ear and story 2 ceased. A completely new story (story 3) replaced story 1 on the attended ear. Broadbent's model would predict that participants would have their filter tuned to the attended ear and would, therefore, have no awareness

of the semantic content of the unattended channel. Accordingly, they would be expected to begin shadowing story 3 as soon as the switch was made. What participants actually did was to 'follow' story 1 by switching suddenly to shadowing the other ear. Treisman concluded that it is difficult to ignore the non-shadowed channel if it continues the meaningful content of the attended message.

In a further series of studies, Treisman (1964) investigated factors affecting the ability to select one message on the basis of its content. She asked her participants to shadow one message and ignore the other. The shadowed message was always a passage read from a novel by a female voice. However, she varied the content of the unattended message, which was sometimes presented in the same female voice and sometimes not. The unattended message consisted variously of:

◆ a passage from the same novel

◆ a passage from a biochemical text

◆ a passage in a foreign language

◆ a set of nonsense syllables.

The ability of the participants to shadow the attended message was significantly affected by the content of the non-shadowed channel. The most difficult condition for the participants was when both messages were passages from the same novel and read in the same female voice. The more the non-shadowed message differed from the shadowed, both in semantic and physical terms, the easier the task became for the participants. These findings are inconsistent with a filter that operates solely on the physical aspects of the input.

As a result of these and similar findings, Treisman proposed an alternative model of attention. This revised model is shown in Fig. 7.4.

Treisman had shown in her studies that breakthroughs from the unattended channel did sometimes occur during dichotic listening tasks. However, she also noted that such breakthroughs

Figure 7.4
Treisman's (1964) attenuator model of selective attention

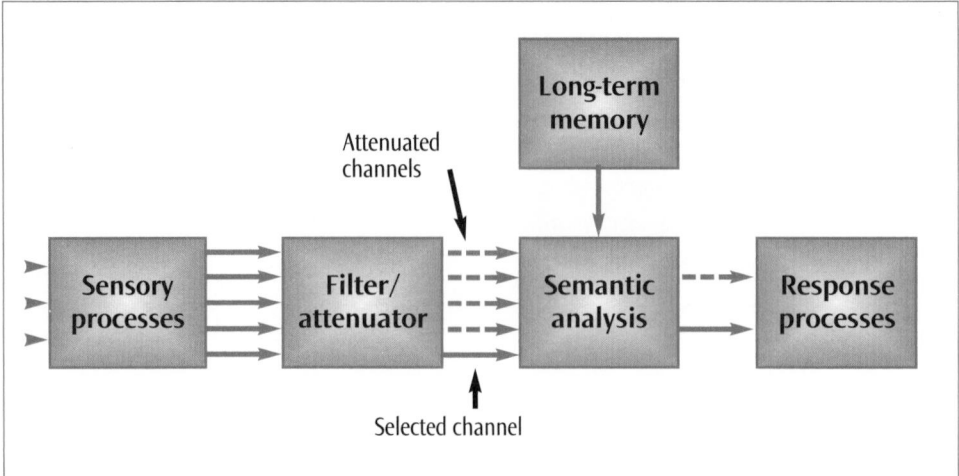

happen only occasionally and only under certain circumstances. She, therefore, suggested that the filter mechanism must operate rather differently from the one in Broadbent's model. She believed that the filter selects one channel on the basis of physical properties and passes it on for semantic analysis. However, instead of blocking unattended channels completely, the filter allows them through in weakened (attenuated) form. For this reason, Treisman's theory is known as an attenuator model. So, Broadbent's all-or-nothing filter, which selects one input and blocks all others, is replaced in Treisman's model with a more flexible filter, which selects one input strongly, but lets others through in attenuated form. This means that all inputs gain access to the limited capacity processor where semantic analysis takes place. At this stage, another selection process takes place – this time, on the basis of meaning. The way in which selection occurs at this stage is shown in Fig. 7.5, which is an enlarged detail of the limited capacity processor (where semantic analysis takes place) shown in Fig. 7.4.

Treisman proposed that the nervous system contains a collection of dictionary units which come into operation at the semantic analysis stage.

Each dictionary unit corresponds to a single word and has a different recognition threshold depending on its salience to the individual. The threshold of a dictionary unit is the minimum intensity a word needs in order for its corresponding dictionary unit to be triggered. Particularly salient words such as your own name, or words with potential survival value such as 'danger' probably have permanently low firing thresholds. However, many dictionary units will have fluctuating thresholds depending on their immediate relevance. For example, think of what happens when you listen to someone talking to you. The first words they speak in a sentence will set up an expectation of what is to follow. If the sentence begins 'I heard an owl...', you will expect the next word to be something like 'screeching' or 'hooting'. This expectation, based on your semantic knowledge, will prime the dictionary units for the expected words and so temporarily lower their firing threshold.

In a shadowing task, where participants are required to follow a message in the attended ear, breakthrough from the unattended channel is only likely to occur if that message contains words whose dictionary units have particularly low firing thresholds. In this case, even

Figure 7.5
Enlarged detail of the limited capacity processor, where semantic analysis takes place (shown in Fig. 7.4)

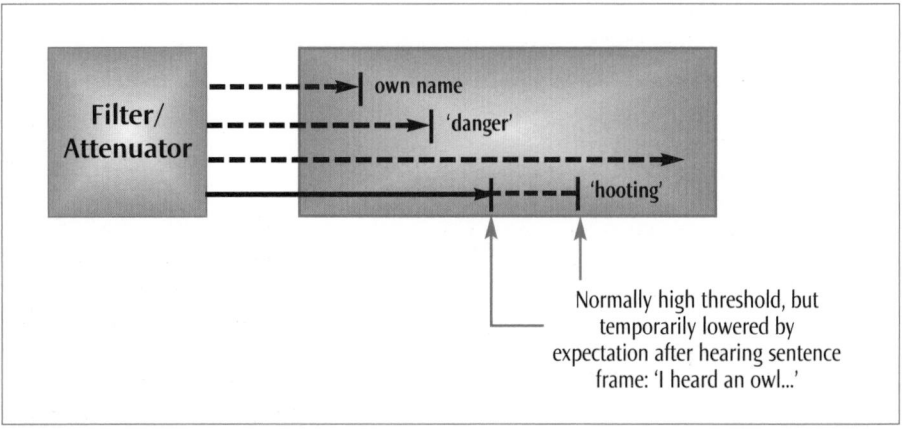

Figure 7.6
The Deutsch–Norman late selection model of selective attention

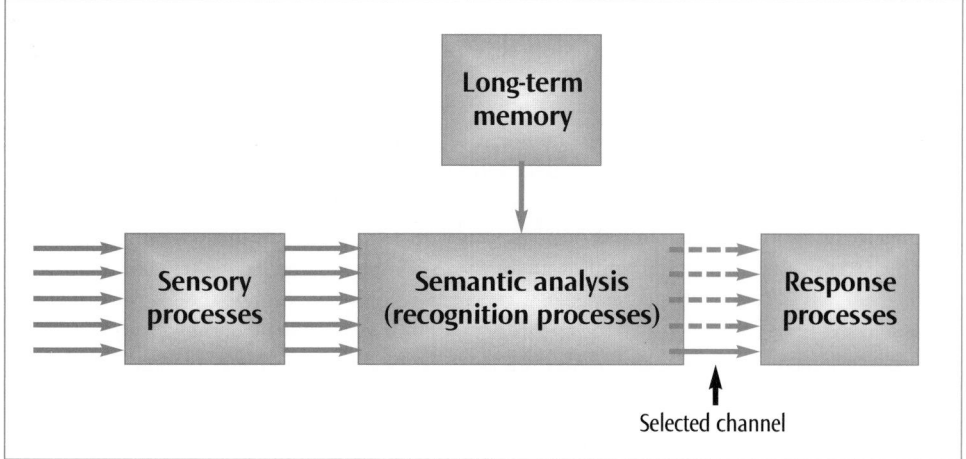

though the message is coming through in attenuated form, its dictionary unit will be triggered before that of the attended message and so will take precedence.

Evaluation of Treisman's model

Treisman's model, although similar to Broadbent's, differs in the flexibility of the selection mechanism. Treisman's notion that selection takes place effectively in two stages accounts for much of the data that Broadbent could not explain. If unattended channels are not totally blocked, then attenuated information which is consistent with expectation (e.g. the continuation of the stories in Treisman's shadowing studies), or which is personally salient (e.g. the participant's name in Moray's 1959 study) will be recognized at the semantic analysis stage. The attenuator theory can successfully account for the breakthrough of certain unattended inputs, but it also accounts for the fact that, most of the time, unattended inputs will not be recognized because they do not come through at sufficient intensity to trigger their dictionary units.

In spite of the fact that Treisman's model is able to provide a neat account of the available experimental data, it has not escaped criticism. One problem concerns the precise meaning of the term attenuation. It is erroneous to think of attenuation as being a process akin to turning down the volume on a radio. Attenuation seems rather to involve a reduction in the amount of information that is passed on from the filter stage. Treisman has not specified exactly how this process works and, since attenuation is the key concept in her model, this lack of explanation is a major weakness. It has also been suggested that her explanation of dictionary units is too vague and that it cannot account for the extensive semantic processing which would be needed, for example, to recognize that a French message on the unattended channel was a direct translation of the attended English message.

Late-selection theories

Deutsch and Deutsch's theory of selective attention

Deutsch and Deutsch (1963) were also interested in studies that demonstrated the breakthrough of information from the unattended channel, but they accounted for the semantic effects of the unattended message in a rather different way from Treisman.

They argued that both attended and unattended inputs are fully analysed for meaning, and that it is only at this late stage that one input is selected and reaches conscious awareness. This means that the bottleneck occurs much later in the system than suggested by Broadbent. Selection at this point is said to depend on the salience or pertinence of the input. Norman (1968) later refined these views and so this late selection theory is often referred to as the Deutsch–Norman model (see Fig. 7.6).

Evaluation of Deutsch and Deutsch's theory

It has proved quite difficult to evaluate this theory because of the problem of demonstrating unconscious processing, but some studies have been reported which appear to offer support. Lewis (1970) presented single words to participants in a shadowing task. Some words on the unattended channel were semantically related to those being shadowed while others were completely unrelated. After the experiment, participants were unable to recall anything from the unattended ear just as would be predicted by early selection models. However, participants took longer to start shadowing a word on the attended channel if a semantically related word was presented simultaneously in the other ear. This suggests, as the Deutsch–Norman model would predict, that unconscious semantic processing of the non-shadowed input slowed down the processing of the shadowed words.

Corteen and Wood (1972) and Corteen and Dunn (1973) conducted a series of studies making use of the galvanic skin response (GSR). GSR measures changes in skin resistance, which occur in response to heightened arousal or anxiety. Corteen and colleagues conditioned participants to expect an electric shock every time they heard an example from a list of words pertaining to cities. The participants were then given a shadowing task to complete while measuring equipment was attached to the palms of their hands in order to record any GSR. Occasionally, one of the words from the list that had been associated with electric shock was played to the non-shadowed ear. In spite of the fact that participants denied recognizing any words from the non-shadowed ear, shock-associated words produced a GSR. In a variation of the study, participants were played some words into the non-shadowed ear, which had not appeared on the original list, but pertained to cities. These, too, provoked a GSR, suggesting that the unconscious processing of the non-shadowed channel could also involve semantic generalization.

In another example of a shadowing task, MacKay (1973) presented participants with ambiguous sentences such as 'They threw stones at the bank yesterday'. At the same time, either the word 'money' or 'river' was presented to the non-shadowed ear. Each of these words suggests a rather different interpretation of the word 'bank' in the shadowed message. After the shadowing task, MacKay gave participants a recognition test in which they had to identify the sentence that most closely resembled the one they had previously shadowed. They were given a choice between:

(a) They threw stones towards the side of the river yesterday.

and:

(b) They threw stones towards the savings and loan association yesterday.

As would be predicted by the Deutsch–Norman model, participants were more likely to pick the sentence that fitted the disambiguating word they had received on the unattended channel even though they denied hearing it. Again, this suggests that unconscious processing of all inputs is occurring. However, later studies (e.g. Dawson and Schell 1983) have reported a momentary stumbling or error in the shadowing when such processing appears to be going on. This would suggest that the semantic processing of the two inputs is not occurring in parallel, but arises as a result of a momentary shift in attention.

All the studies outlined above all seem to provide evidence that selective processing in attention can occur after the meaning of words has been accessed. However, it is difficult to assess whether all inputs are routinely fully processed as the Deutsch–Norman model suggests, or whether there is attenuation of the

unattended channels, which might or might not lead to semantic recognition, as Treisman suggests. Treisman and Geffen (1967) challenged the late selection theory with a study in which participants were required not only to shadow a message played to one ear, but also to tap their hand on the table when they heard particular target words on either channel. Treisman's own theory would predict much lower target recognition rates on the unattended ear because this input would only progress through the filter in attenuated form. The Deutsch–Norman model, on the other hand, would predict equal rates of target recognition for the two inputs, because there is supposed to be full semantic analysis of all incoming stimuli. Findings supported the Treisman model in that detection rates on the attended channel were 87 per cent compared to 8 per cent on the unattended channel.

Johnston and Heinz's theory

It soon became obvious that both early and late selection processes may be involved in selective attention. Johnston and Heinz (1978) put forward evidence suggesting that selective attention is more flexible than either the Treisman or the Deutsch–Norman model allows. They proposed that attention may be focused at various stages of processing and that selection will occur as early as possible depending on the task demands. They tested this idea in a study (1979) where two words were presented simultaneously to participants over headphones. The task was to shadow certain target words, i.e. to repeat the target word every time it was heard on whichever channel. In one condition (high sensory discriminability), the target words were always spoken in the same male voice while the non-target words were always spoken in a distinctive female voice. Thus, target and non-target items were always quite distinctive in physical terms even though participants did not know on which ear to expect them. In the second condition (low sensory discriminability), both target and non-target words were spoken in the same male voice. Thus, the items could not be distinguished in physical terms. Participants were more successful at shadowing in the high-discriminability condition, presumably because they were simply listening out for the male voice (i.e. selecting on the basis of physical properties), and so were easily able to pick out the target items. However, in a subsequent unexpected recall task, participants in the low-discriminability condition were able to recall considerably more non-target items than participants in the high-discriminability condition. This suggests that non-target words needed to be more thoroughly processed in the low-discriminability condition. In the high-discriminability condition, non-target words could be selected out at an early stage of processing on the basis of physical properties. In the low-discriminability condition, target and non-target words were indistinguishable at the early stage, so non-target words could only be selected out once they had been recognized at a later stage of processing. These findings support the view that the nature of the task determines the extent of processing and the point at which selection takes place.

Evaluation of Johnston and Heinz's theory

This theory is certainly the most flexible model described so far and it does seem to account for much of the available data. However, as Styles (1997) has written:

> 'It began to seem as if the bottleneck metaphor was wearing thin. As soon as the bottleneck can be moved around, or can be hypothesized to be located at either end or almost anywhere in the processing continuum, perhaps it ceases to be a bottleneck after all.'

Researchers began to see that the concept of a single channel processor was insufficient to explain attentional processes. Interest shifted to the idea of an attentional system limited not by structural constraints, but by the amount of processing resources available at any one time. We will look at such capacity-based models in the next section.

Exam summary: Focused attention

The AQA examination will test your understanding of the following areas:

◆ explanations and studies of early-selection models of focused attention (pp. 156–61)

◆ explanations and studies of late-selection models of focused attention (pp. 161–3).

Example question

The question below is typical of one drawn from the material above, and should take you 30 minutes to answer.

◆ Outline and evaluate one early-selection model of focused attention (e.g. Broadbent), and one late-selection model (e.g. Deutsch and Deutsch).

(24 marks)

Suggested answer structure

This question makes a quite specific request. You are required to write about two models of focused attention. However, the question requires that these should be one *early-selection* model and one *late-*

selection model. The question gives examples of appropriate models, but these are not prescriptive. Early-selection models, such as Broadbent's Filter model and Treisman's Attenuation theory, are covered on the pp. 157–61. Likewise, the late-selection models, such as those by Deutsch and Deutsch, and Johnston and Heinz's theory, are covered on pp. 161–3.

As you only have 30 minutes to answer this question, this would mean only 15 minutes per theory. As well as this division of time, you have a further division to consider, that of the AO1 and AO2 components of the question. Notice that this question uses the injunction *outline* (see Chapter 21). The AO1 and AO2 components of this question need to be addressed in equal measures.

Your essay plan might look something like this:

◆ outline description of Broadbent's model (7.5 minutes and about 150 words)

◆ evaluation of Broadbent's model (7.5 minutes and 150 words)

◆ outline description of Deutsch and Deutsch's model (7.5 minutes and 150 words)

◆ evaluation of Deutsch and Deutsch's model (7.5 minutes and 150 words)

Remember, it is very easy to start off with the best will in the world, only to find that you are still *describing* the first theory (or model) 20 minutes into your answer!

Early research into attention suggested that our processing system was limited in its ability to deal with parallel tasks. Broadbent (1958) proposed the first information-processing model of selective attention, in which he suggested that incoming stimuli were processed in parallel in terms of their physical properties. A filter mechanism then selected a single channel to be passed onto a limited capacity processor which was only capable of handling inputs one at a time.

Broadbent's model was immediately challenged by findings that suggested that there is much more analysis of unattended inputs than he envisaged. Such studies were interpreted in a rather different way by Treisman (1964), and Deutsch and Deutsch (1963). Treisman (pp. 159–61) believed that the data could be explained by replacing Broadbent's all-or-nothing filter with a more flexible attenuator. Deutsch and Deutsch (pp. 161–2) believed, rather more radically, that all inputs are fully analysed for meaning. Treisman's theory, on balance, appears to be able to account more economically for the available experimental data. It also seems, as Johnston and Heinz (pp. 162–3) suggest, that the precise nature of the attentional task might be a factor in determining when selection takes place.

Divided attention

The bottleneck models we considered in the first section all rest on the assumption that full attention can only be paid to one input channel at a time. However, in our everyday life, we know that we can often successfully divide our attention between two or more tasks. Try Activity 2 before you read on.

Activity 2: Doing several things at the same time

Think of some of the things you find easy to do at the same time. Now think of some of the things you find difficult to do at the same time. Are there any patterns of similarities and differences in the tasks you have identified? Is this pattern consistent or does it change as a result of other factors, such as how you are feeling at any particular time?

Examples might include driving and having a conversation, washing up and listening to the radio, listening to music and reading the newspaper, etc. However, there are some circumstances that prevent us from carrying out these activities simultaneously. For example, a driver will stop contributing to the conversation if something unexpected occurs, such as a flashing blue light appearing in the rear view mirror, and learner drivers find it almost impossible to do anything other than concentrate on the driving task. There are also some activities which we seem never able to combine successfully – for example, reading a novel and simultaneously following a news broadcast on television. Such common-sense findings have led psychologists to suggest that there are various factors that can influence our ability to do more than one thing at a time. In order to investigate these factors, researchers have made use of an experimental technique called the dual-task method. Participants are given concurrent tasks and their performance is monitored. If performance on both tasks is as good as when each is performed singly, it suggests that the two tasks do not interfere with one another and that they are probably making use of distinct processing mechanisms. If performance on one or other of the two tasks is impaired, the inference is that the tasks do interfere with one another and are, therefore, competing for the same processing mechanisms.

Research into dual-task performance

Allport et al. (1972) asked participants to shadow a continuous prose message played over headphones to both ears and, at the same time, to study a set of pictures depicting complex visual scenes, which were entirely unrelated to the content of the auditory message. In a later recognition task, participants were asked to identify these pictures from a larger set. There was no difference in the level of performance on the shadowing and the recognition task than when each of the tasks was performed singly. Allport and colleagues concluded that visual processing calls upon different processing mechanisms from those involved in monitoring auditory speech inputs.

In a second study, Allport et al. (1972) used participants who were all skilled piano players. They were asked to sight-read examination pieces for the piano at the same time as shadowing prose delivered at the rate of 150 words per minute. With very little practice, these participants were able to complete both tasks as competently and accurately as they could when asked to perform either of them separately. Again, the implication of these results is that the two tasks – in this study, speech processing and reading music – make use of different processing mechanisms. Allport and colleagues used the findings from such studies as evidence against a single channel for attentional processing.

Evaluation of dual-task performance studies

Such studies seem to suggest that simultaneous, dual-task processing is possible if the tasks make use of distinct processing mechanisms. Broadbent (1982) has criticized this interpretation and believes that there is evidence for decrements in performance on the concurrent tasks when the data are inspected more closely. He also believes that the findings can be explained in terms of task sharing, rather than simultaneous processing. He suggests that tasks such as shadowing prose and sight-reading music involve a degree of redundancy. Redundancy is a concept borrowed from information theory, which refers to the amount of predictability in communication systems such as language. If you are trying to read a scribbled piece of handwriting, you will make use of your knowledge about English words to help you make sense of it. For example, 'q' is always followed by 'u'. In other words the 'u' is redundant because it is predicted by the 'q'. Broadbent says that, both prose and music contain information which allows the speaker/player to guess what is coming next. This means that, at moments of high predictability in either of the tasks, the participant can switch attention momentarily to the other task. According to this explanation then, dual-task performance is accomplished by rapid switching between attentional channels rather than by parallel processing. It is difficult to demonstrate unequivocally which explanation is correct. Shaffer (1975) reported a study in which he asked a skilled typist to copy type a piece of German prose presented visually whilst simultaneously shadowing an auditorily presented English prose passage. The typist was able to do the two tasks concurrently quite accurately, although there was a slight decrement in performance compared to her accuracy on the tasks when done separately. In this case, it is unlikely that redundancy could have helped her on the copy-typing task because she had no knowledge of the German language, and so could have no expectations about predictable sequences of letters and words.

In another study, Shaffer (1975) demonstrated that tasks which call on the same types of processing, cannot be performed concurrently. A skilled typist was require to shadow an English prose message played over headphones to one ear while simultaneously typing a different English prose message played to the other ear. Her inability to carry out the two tasks simultaneously can be explained in terms of interference – both tasks make use of the auditory modality and so cannot be done in parallel. In a variation on this study, Shaffer asked the same typist to type a message presented auditorily, whilst simultaneously reading aloud from a visually presented text. This, too, proved almost impossible, but the findings cannot be explained simply in terms of competition for the same modality. Audio typing depends on auditory input and motor output whereas reading aloud from written text requires visual input and articulatory output. On the face of it, then, it does not seem as if the same processing mechanisms are being used. The explanation for the interference between these two tasks seems to lie in the similarity of the tasks because they both require a response to the same kind of material, i.e. meaningful language.

Practice in dual-task performance

It seems clear from the research discussed above, that factors such as task similarity and competition for the same processing mechanisms affect the ability to divide attention. It also seems likely that practice may be a contributory factor. Remember that Allport *et al.* (1972) and Shaffer (1975) used only highly skilled practitioners – pianists and typists respectively – in their studies. Spelke *et al.* (1976) conducted a study specifically to investigate this factor. They persuaded two college students to spend five hours per week practising doing two tasks at once. They were required to read short stories whilst simultaneously writing down unrelated words which were dictated to them. The students found this very difficult at first and both tasks were performed

poorly. However, after six weeks regular practice, they were both able to read as quickly, and with the same level of comprehension, as when reading without dictation. However, although they could accurately write down the dictated words, their subsequent recall was minimal. Spelke and colleagues then changed the dictation task, so that the students now had to write down the category to which the word belonged, instead of writing the dictated word. This was obviously a much more demanding task and the students' reading and writing performance suffered. Again, however, after several weeks training, the students were able to carry out the more difficult dictation task without any impairment in their reading comprehension. These findings suggest that learning and practice can affect the ability to divide attention. The results of such a study should, however, be treated with some caution. The fact that only two participants took part makes any definitive interpretation difficult. It could be argued that students willing to give up approximately 12 weeks to such a project are likely to be fairly untypical in a number of ways. It is also unclear from this study what precise strategies were being learned to accomplish the tasks simultaneously. The findings can be explained either by the possibility that the participants had learned to switch rapidly between writing and listening, or by the possibility that the writing task had become so automatic, through practice, that it no longer required any attentional capacity.

It seems, then, that practice facilitates dual-task performance although it is not entirely clear how. Eysenck and Keane (1995) suggest three reasons why practice might have an effect:

◆ Participants may develop new strategies for performing each of the tasks, and so minimize task interference.

◆ The demands that a task makes on attentional or other central resources may be reduced as a function of practice.

◆ A task may initially require the use of several specific processing resources, but, with practice, may become more economical and rely on fewer resources.

Capacity models of divided attention

It seems clear from research into divided attention that the human information processing system is limited in the number and complexity of tasks that can be effectively carried out at any one time. It also seems likely that various external variables can influence our ability to divide our attention. Revelle (1993) has reported on a number of factors, such as heat, noise, anxiety, motivation, lack of sleep, and personality, that affect performance on attentional tasks. Such findings are compatible with capacity or resource allocation models of attention. Instead of the structural bottleneck in information processing suggested by Broadbent, capacity theorists have proposed that we possess a pool of processing resources that we can allocate according to task demands and environmental factors. According to this approach, interference in the tasks will happen only if the demands of one, or both, of the tasks exceed the attentional capacity. This could occur at any stage in the processing and not at a fixed point (bottleneck) in the sequence.

Kahneman's capacity/resource allocation model

One of the best-known capacity models of attention was put forward by Kahneman (1973). This model is shown in Fig. 7.7.

Kahneman believes that attention is controlled by a central processor which coordinates and allocates a limited pool of resources. Although there is an overall limit on the total amount of attention available, the precise amount of attentional capacity can vary

according to factors such as arousal. Kahneman's model also includes the concept of mental effort, which refers to the level of attentional processing required by a particular task.

The key characteristics of the model are as follows:

◆ The total amount of attention available is limited.

◆ Arousal levels can affect the total capacity – capacity increases with moderately high levels of arousal.

◆ More than one task can be performed at one time, provided that the combined mental effort required does not outweigh capacity.

◆ Some tasks require more mental effort than others. More difficult tasks require more mental effort.

◆ Practice can render some tasks automatic (e.g. driving) so that they require less mental effort.

◆ If the amount of mental effort required starts to exceed demand, the central processor, which carries out constant monitoring, must determine which task takes precedence.

◆ In deciding between tasks, the central processor is affected by momentary intentions and enduring dispositions.

Figure 7.7
Kahneman's capacity model of attention
Source: Kahneman (1973)

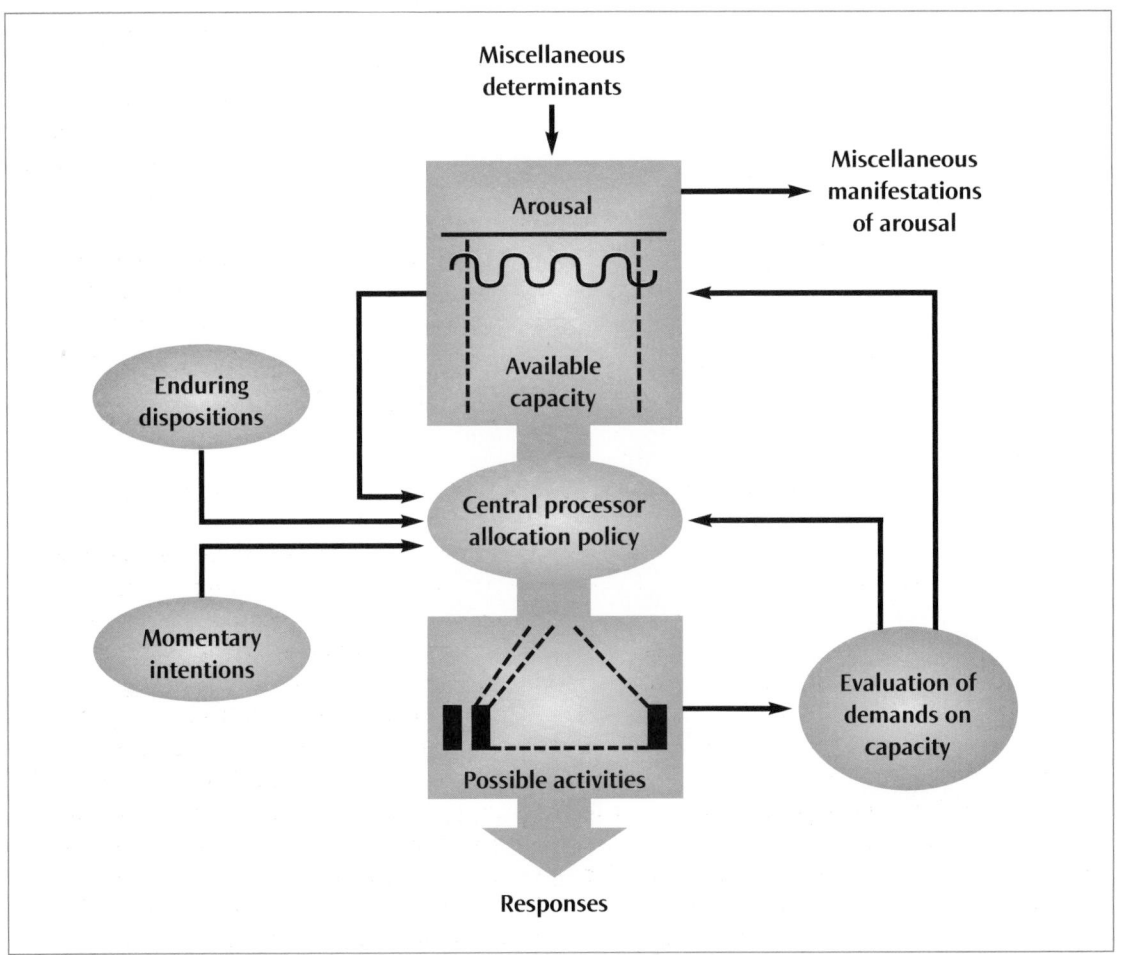

Momentary intentions are voluntary shifts in attention such as deliberately paying attention to the right rather than the left ear in a dichotic listening task.

Enduring dispositions are responses to external stimuli, which are outside voluntary control, such as shifting your attention to a nearby conversation when your name is unexpectedly mentioned.

Evaluation of Kahneman's model

Kahneman's (1973) model moved away from the structural limitations of the single channel models of attention and offered a more flexible account. For example, Kahneman could explain findings from dichotic listening tasks. He assumed that shadowing one of two inputs is a task that demands almost all of the available resources. There is very little attentional capacity left over to process the other channel in anything more than a superficial way. However, because of the effect of enduring dispositions, there is sometimes breakthrough from the non-shadowed message. The capacity model also accounts satisfactorily for many of the dual-task studies.

There are, however, some serious problems with the theory and it has been criticized for vagueness, notably by Allport (1980, 1989). Allport believes that it is too easy to explain dual-task performance in terms of central capacity. In other words, if two tasks can be performed concurrently, it is because the tasks do not exceed the central capacity; if the tasks cannot be performed concurrently, it is because the combined effort required to accomplish them exceeds capacity. The problem here is that there is no independent definition of central processing capacity. There is also a problem with the role of arousal in Kahneman's model. As Revelle (1993) has pointed out, it is difficult to define arousal precisely. It is also a well-established finding that performance increases along with arousal up to an optimum point, after which, further increases in arousal are associated with decrements in performance. This is known as the Yerkes–Dodson law (Yerkes and Dodson 1908). The Kahneman model, on the other hand, would predict a continued increase of performance with increased arousal. Another prediction from the model is that the capacity required by a task will depend on the nature of that particular task, i.e. difficult tasks use up more capacity than simple tasks. Segal and Fusella (1970) gave participants the task of detecting a faint visual or auditory stimulus while simultaneously forming either a visual or auditory mental image. They found that the auditory imaging task impaired performance on the auditory signal detection task more than the visual imaging task. Capacity theorists would explain this finding by saying that the auditory imaging task must, therefore, be more difficult than the visual imaging task. However, Segal and Fusella found that

the auditory imaging task was less disruptive than the visual imaging task on a visual detection task. The inference seems to be that there is no difference in the inherent difficulty of the auditory or visual imaging tasks. The problems of concurrent performance seem to lie in the fact that similar tasks (i.e. tasks depending on the same modality) are competing for the same cognitive processors. This finding cannot be explained by Kahneman's capacity model.

Norman and Bobrow (1975) refined Kahneman's idea of capacity limitation by introducing the concept of resource-limited, and data-limited, processes. A task such as processing the non-shadowed message in dichotic listening is thought to be difficult because the shadowing task is already taking up most of the available capacity. If more resources were available, the non-shadowed message could be processed. This is said to be a resource-limited process. However, if you are asked to listen to a message against a background of loud noise, it would not matter how many resources were at your disposal – the externally imposed limitation of loud noise prevents successful processing of the target message. In this kind of example, performance is said to be data-limited. This distinction between two types of processing can explain some experimental data. For example, you will remember from studies on focused attention that pure tones can be detected on the unattended channel, whereas words usually are not recognized. If we assume that the detection of a tone requires less processing than the recognition of a word, it could be argued that we have sufficient surplus capacity in a dichotic task to pick up a tone, but not a word. Norman and Bobrow would claim that the word identification is resource-limited, while the tone recognition task is only data-limited and will be detected unless the background noise is too strong. However, this theory is as circular in its definitions as Kahneman's theory. There is no independent way of measuring whether a task is resource- or data-limited.

Modular theories of divided attention

Allport (1980) has criticized the capacity models for their lack of explanatory power. Experimental data, such as that provided by Segal and Fusella above, led Allport to believe that the limitation on dual-task performance arose because the tasks were competing for the same processing mechanisms. He suggested that humans possess several different processing mechanisms or modules. Each of these is specialized for handling particular tasks and, although each module has limited capacity, there is no overriding, central processor. When tasks are similar (e.g. they both involve the auditory modality), they are assumed to be competing for the same module and so concurrent performance becomes difficult or even impossible. However, dissimilar tasks (e.g. shadowing speech involving auditory and articulatory modalities) and memorizing pictures (visual modality) can be combined with no decrement in performance because they use different modules and so are not in competition with one another for the same resource.

Evaluation of modular theories

There is support for the modular theory from various experiments that have looked at performance on concurrent tasks in the same and different modalities. However, there are problems with this theoretical approach. Allport has not specified the precise number of these modules, nor has he described their precise mode of functioning. The model can explain virtually any findings from divided attention research simply by postulating the addition of a further processing module. This kind of post hoc explanation is unsatisfactory. It is also unclear how such a large number of independent modules could be coordinated to work effectively and efficiently in parallel.

Research into controlled and automatic processing

The idea of automatic processing is crucial to the notion of divided attention. Posner and Snyder (1975) suggest that performance on a task is automatic if it can occur without the intention or awareness of the performer and does not interfere with other mental activities.

Some activities, such as driving or riding a bike, although difficult to master in the first instance, become automatic with practice. Automacity is clearly helpful in carrying out everyday skills, but it is sometimes difficult to undo once learned. Try Activity 3 before you read any further.

Activity 3: Counting Fs

Read the following sentence and count the number of 'F's.

FISH FINGERS ARE THE PRODUCT
OF MANY YEARS OF DEVELOPMENT
IN THE AREA OF FOOD PROCESSING.

You should have counted six 'F's in the sentence. However, do not worry if you missed some because people often find tasks such as this quite difficult. People often miss the 'F's in the word 'of', which occurs three times in the sentence. Try this out with friends and family.

There are a number of reasons why this task might create problems for readers. People could be automatically converting the visual representation of letters into phonological representations. Therefore, the 'ofs' sound like 'ovs' and people fail to detect the 'f's. Another explanation could be that, in reading, we automatically process frequently occurring words such as 'of' as whole units and find it difficult to focus on component letters. Healy (1976) found support for this latter explanation when she asked participants to read a piece of English prose at normal reading speed while circling the letter 't' whenever it appeared in the passage. Participants were far more likely to detect the letter 't' in uncommon than common words. They were particularly likely to miss the 't' in 'the' which is the most common word in the English language. This suggests that our reading of high frequency words becomes automatic and that we recognize them as whole units rather than by their constituent letters.

The *Stroop Effect* (Stroop 1935) is another example of the powerfully automatic nature of reading words and how this can interfere with other tasks. Stroop found that people have difficulty screening out meaningful information even when it is irrelevant to the task. He asked participants to read out a list of colour words (e.g. green, blue, red, yellow) printed in black ink. This is obviously a very simple task for skilled readers and presented no difficulties. He then presented a list of colour words printed in conflicting coloured inks (e.g. the word 'blue' printed in red) and asked participants to name the colour of the ink. This should also have been a simple colour-recognition task. However, participants took considerably longer to complete this second task than the straightforward reading task. It seems that words provoke an automatic reading response and, although conscious control can prevent this response being articulated aloud, there is a time delay while the correct response, i.e. ink naming, is activated.

Shiffrin and Schneider (1977), in their two-process theory, differentiated between controlled and automatic processes (see *In Focus*). Most of their studies were based on visual rather than auditory attention tasks. In a typical study, participants would be required to search for a fixed set of target items (e.g. the letters N, T and K) amongst a set of distractor items (e.g. the digits 1 to 9). On the first trials, target detection times depended on the number of distractors – the more distractors, the longer it took to find the targets. However, after considerable practice, search times became faster and appeared to become relatively independent of the number of distractors. Shiffrin and Schneider concluded that searching for targets begins as a serial search under conscious control, but that, after much practice, it becomes automatic.

Shiffrin and Schneider's (1977) distinction between controlled and automatic processing

Shiffrin and Schneider (1977) reported a series of studies which explored the nature of automatic, or non-conscious, information processing. Their investigations led them to differentiate between two general modes of human information processing: controlled and automatic. They suggested that the two modes of processing have the following general features.

Controlled processing	*Automatic processing*
These processes are of limited capacity and require focused attention.	These processes are not hindered by capacity limitations.
These processes are serial in nature and, in line with single channel theories, each has to be dealt with singly.	These processes are fast, can operate in parallel and many processes can be active at any one time.
Tasks which are tackled using controlled processing can be learnt quickly and can be modified relatively easily.	Tasks only reach automatic status through considerable practice and are difficult to modify once learnt.
Controlled processes are usually consciously directed to a task.	Automatic processing usually takes place at a non-conscious level.
	Automatic processing is unavoidable; it always occurs when an appropriate stimulus is present.

Poltrock *et al.* (1982) have found similar effects in an auditory detection task, suggesting that automatic and controlled processing may occur in modalities other than vision.

Evaluation of research into controlled and automatic processing

The theoretical distinction between controlled and automatic processing has been useful, but the two-process theory has been criticized for its lack of explanatory power. Shiffrin and Schneider claim that practice leads to automaticity, but they do not explain exactly how this is achieved. It could, for example, be that practice simply speeds up the processes needed to accomplish the task. Neisser (1976) believes that practice does not simply lead to a switch from controlled to automatic processing, but involves the development of skill. This is similar to the idea of 'restructuring' proposed by Cheng (1985). She believes that practice allows the development of new and more efficient strategies for completing tasks.

Another problem for the theory is that there seems to be no clear-cut distinction between automatic and controlled processes. Certain aspects of a task may be automatic whilst others may require attention. Making a cup of instant coffee, for example, involves mainly automatic processing, whereas preparing a three-course meal involves constant checking and monitoring even though some of the subprocesses, such as peeling

the vegetables, may be automatic. This suggests that controlled and automatic processing operate on a continuum rather than as distinct, discrete entities. This idea was incorporated into a theory proposed by Norman and Shallice (1986), as discussed below.

Slips associated with automatic processing

Norman and Shallice (1986) were interested in how attentional activities are controlled and why this control occasionally breaks down, leading to errors. They distinguished between three different types of processing:

◆ fully automatic processing

◆ partially automatic processing

◆ controlled processing.

They believe that certain habitual tasks can be carried out without any need for deliberate attentional processing because they automatically activate a schema (a model of the external world stored in memory) which triggers the appropriate response. Novel tasks, where there is no existing schema, or tasks which involve some degree of calculation, require controlled processing which is facilitated by a mechanism called the supervisory attentional system (SAS). Such tasks would:

- require planning or judgement
- involve elements of problem-solving
- be poorly learned or contain novel factors
- be judged to be risky or technically difficult
- require the suppression of a strong learned response.

Imagine that you are an experienced driver going home along a familiar route. Driving has become an automated skill and is occurring without much conscious thought. It is possible to drive competently while talking to a passenger, listening to the radio, or planning what you are going to do later that evening. However, if something unexpected or potentially dangerous occurs, such as a child running into the road or sudden envelopment in fog, you will turn your full attention to the driving and stop talking, etc. Norman and Shallice believe that this switch from fully automatic processing is brought about by a mechanism known as contention scheduling. This involves invoking some simple rules about the relative importance of events and it can be operated automatically. However, they believe that there are instances where we need to act according to will, i.e. we need to be in control of our attentional processes. Imagine that on your route home there is a junction where you always turn left. Today, you can see roadworks along this road and note that they are causing tailbacks. You have to decide whether to make your habitual response of turning left and risk waiting in a long queue, or to turn right and take a longer, but possibly quicker route home. According to Norman and Shallice, the SAS can interrupt and modify your habitual behaviour in such circumstances and allow you to alter your normal habitual response. However, in some instances, an automatic response is allowed to run on, even where it is inappropriate and errors can then occur.

Evaluation of Norman and Shallice's theory

Norman and Shallice's (1986) theory seems to account for experimental data more successfully than the two-process model of Shiffrin and Schneider (1977). There is also some support for the notion of the SAS from neurological studies. Norman and Shallice believe that the SAS mechanism is located in the frontal lobes of the brain and that patients with damage to this area, experience difficulties which could reflect malfunctioning of the SAS. Baddeley (1986) reports on R.J. (a patient with frontal lobe damage) who seems unable to use appropriate controlled responses. He was asked to measure out a length of string so that it could be cut later. He immediately picked up a pair of scissors and cut the string even though he was simultaneously saying 'Yes, I know I'm not to cut it'. It seems that he was operating according to the schema that had most

strongly been activated by environmental cues, i.e. the instructions, coupled with the presence of the scissors. It is not entirely clear exactly how the SAS operates but, according to Styles (1997), 'Certainly, there is good evidence that people act as if they have an SAS and can behave in goal-directed ways, initiating and changing behaviours, apparently at will'.

Reason's research into action slips

It seems likely from our understanding of theories of attention, that action slips arise from a failure to pay attention appropriately. Cognitive psychologists have used a number of techniques in their study of action slips. For example, questionnaires can be used to assess the frequency with which certain things are forgotten. Another method, which also relies on self-assessment, is the diary study technique. In diary studies, participants are asked to keep daily records of the memory errors they make. One important diary study in this area was carried out by Reason (1979) (see *In Focus*).

Activity 4: Errors and slips you make

Over a two-week period, try to keep a written record of all the slips of action you make. If possible you could also try to get one or two members of your family and/or one or two friends to keep a record of their attentional errors. At the end of the period, try to categorize the errors in the same way as Reason, and consider whether your errors fit into his classification system.

If you have carried out Activity 4, you will realize that there are several difficulties associated with diary studies. There is always the problem of accuracy. We cannot know how many slips have gone unreported – either because they were simply undetected, or because diarists were too embarrassed to record them. It is also possible that certain types of slip are more noticeable than others and are, therefore, more likely to be recorded. The distinctions between some of the categories are unclear, and so some of the slips may be wrongly classified. On the other hand, some slips, which have been classified together because of a superficial similarity, may reflect quite different underlying mechanisms. Grudin (1983) looked at videotapes of typists' fingers on keypads and noted any errors. The typists sometimes struck the wrong key which, on the face of it, would appear to be a single class of error. However, Grudin noted that, in some cases, the correct finger slipped on to an adjacent key whereas, in other cases, the appropriate finger for that key struck the incorrect key. He concluded that the first

> **in focus**
>
> ## Reason's (1979) diary study of slips of action
>
> Reason (1979) conducted a diary study in which 35 participants kept a diary record of their slips of action over a two-week period. The study revealed 400 errors and Reason divided them into five categories:
>
> ◆ Storage failures (40 per cent of total errors): forgetting that an action had already been performed and doing it again (e.g. putting the sugar in a cup of tea twice).
>
> ◆ Test failures (20 per cent of total errors): forgetting the goal of a sequence of actions and switching to a different goal (e.g. starting off making a cup of tea and ending up making a cup of coffee).
>
> ◆ Subroutine failures (18 per cent of total errors): component actions of a sequence being omitted, or wrongly ordered (e.g. putting the boiling water in the tea pot without having put in the tea).
>
> ◆ Discrimination failures (11 per cent of the errors): confusing the objects involved in different actions (e.g. taking a fork instead of a spoon to stir your tea).
>
> ◆ Programme assembly failures (5 per cent of total errors): wrongly combining actions from different sequences (e.g. opening a new packet of tea and placing the wrapping in the teapot and tea in the waste bin).
>
> The remaining 6 per cent of errors were unclassifiable.

error was due to faulty execution of the action, whereas the second error was due to faulty assignment of the finger. As Eysenck and Keane (1995) point out, we need rather more information than is available from diary studies to pick up such subtle differences in underlying mechanisms.

Reason (1992) attempted to respond to some of the criticisms of diary studies by devising an experimental technique to provoke action slips in the laboratory. He asked participants to respond as quickly as possible to a series of questions requiring a one-word answer. In all cases, the most likely answer rhymed with 'oak'. (For example: 'What do we call a funny story?' = 'joke'; 'What is another word for cape?' = 'cloak'.) The last question of the series was 'What do you call the white of an egg?' to which 85 per cent of the participants wrongly replied 'yolk' (the correct answer is albumen). Only 5 per cent of a control group, who were only given the last question, replied 'yolk'. Although this is quite an ingenious technique, it does not seem to produce the kind of slips that are typical of those that occur in everyday situations.

Theories of action slips

Reason explained the error patterns by arguing that attentional processing works at three levels:

◆ a superficial level concerned with routine automatic tasks which require little conscious thought (the majority of errors seem to occur at this level)

◆ a deeper level of processing involving a realization that a routine is incorrect and that more attention and knowledge is required to correct the situation (errors can occur at this level if you misread a

situation and then realize that your actions do not fit the current context)

◆ an even deeper level of processing in which you have to bring all your knowledge to bear and use all your conscious control to solve a problem (a further problem at this level is that by now you might have reached a critical point and fear or panic may not allow clear thinking).

Reason has used these ideas to look at disasters such as Chernobyl, and has concluded that, unless an understanding of the nature of human errors is allowed for in the design of new technology, these accidents are not only possible, but inevitable.

Dual-task limitations

A key finding from the Reason study is that the majority of errors seem to occur in highly practised, over-learned, routines. These action sequences often involve automatic processing and are carried out with little conscious monitoring. Therefore, they are less prone to dual-task limitations (see p. 164 on dual-task monitoring). Automatic actions have the advantage of releasing attentional resources to be used in the performance of parallel activities. However, they can also lead to errors. There is a tendency for a more commonly performed task to take over from one performed less often, particularly if both tasks share a component stage. Slips of action often occur at junctions between stages when there can be a switch over to an incorrect procedure, e.g. walking or driving in the wrong direction because that is the way most often taken. In addition to these 'habit intrusions', people can also lose track of a sequence of actions resulting in actions being repeated or omitted. Some people are more prone to these kinds of errors than others, and everyone finds that slips and lapses can increase with tiredness and stress. Norman (1981) has proposed an explanation of attentional slips and lapses based directly on one of the most important theoretical ideas in cognitive psychology, known as schema theory.

Schema theory

The notion of schemas was first put forward by Bartlett (1932). They can be thought of as organized sets of mental representations which incorporate all our knowledge of particular objects, concepts or events. According to schema theory, if the same incoming information is experienced repeatedly, it eventually becomes incorporated into a generalized schematic representation. Schema theory attempts to explain how we organize knowledge from past experience to help us interpret, or guide, new information coming in from the senses. Rumelhart and Norman (1983) list five main characteristics of schemas:

◆ Schemas incorporate all the knowledge we have acquired through past experiences, including generalizations and learnt facts (e.g. our knowledge of what to do in exams).

◆ Schemas represent knowledge of all kinds ranging from simple feature knowledge (e.g. the features of a triangle) to more complex abstract knowledge (e.g. the meaning of justice).

◆ Schemas can be linked together into related systems containing other schemas and subschemas (e.g. a schema for chairs can be a subschema of a schema for 'items used for sitting on', which in turn can be part of a general schema for furniture).

◆ Schemas have slots which can be filled with fixed or variable values (e.g. a fixed value for a car could be that it has an engine and a variable value could be the size of the engine). Furthermore, variable values can be filled by the most probable value (default value) if any information is not given or is missing (e.g. you might assume a car has four wheels if you do not know it is a Reliant Robin).

◆ Various schemas at different levels may be engaged in recognizing new inputs (e.g. in your first week at university you might incorporate various schemas of educational and social experience to help you with new found independence and the transition into higher education). A good example of the influence of schemas in human information processing can be seen in a study carried out by French and Richards (see *In Focus*).

Norman's model of attentional slips and lapses

According to Norman's (1981) model of attentional slips and lapses, action sequences are controlled by schemas. He suggests that several schemas can be activated simultaneously and linked into related sets. The highest level, or parent schema, corresponds to the overall intention, or goal (e.g. going to school). Subordinate, or child, subschemas correspond to the

French and Richards' (1993) study of schema-driven attentional errors

In this experiment, French and Richards had three conditions.

◆ Condition 1: participants were shown a clock with roman numerals and asked to study the clock for one minute. After the time had elapsed, the clock was taken away and participants were then asked to draw the clock from memory.

◆ Condition 2: the same procedure was followed with the exception that participants were told they would be required to draw the clock from memory.

◆ Condition 3: the clock was left in full view of the participants and they were instructed merely to produce a drawn copy of the clock.

In the standard form of roman numerals the number four is represented as IV, but on clocks with roman numerals the four is almost invariably represented as IIII. French and Richards found that in both the conditions in which participants had to draw the clock from memory, a significant majority reverted to the conventional IV notation. In Condition 3, however, all the participants used the correct IIII notation. French and Richards explained these results in terms of schema theory and the strong influence of schematic knowledge on the way people process information. In Conditions 1 and 2, the strong influence of schematic knowledge of roman numerals appeared to have affected participants' memory retrieval.

component actions in the sequence (e.g. going to the bus stop, catching the bus, getting off the bus and walking to school). Each schema, or subschema, has its own activation level which is determined by both external (the current situation) and internal events (plans and intentions). Each schema also has a set of triggering conditions, and a given schema is activated if the activation level is sufficiently high and the current situation matches the triggering conditions. According to Norman, slips can occur as a result of faulty specification of the overall intention (another schema has a higher level of activation than the one associated with the original intention) or faulty triggering (the current situation, or context, triggers an alternative schema). An example of faulty specification might be starting off going to visit an aunt you have not seen for some time and ending up around the corner at a friend's house which you visit more frequently. An example of faulty triggering could be deciding to walk to school instead of catching the bus, but, as you are passing the bus stop, the bus arrives and before you have realized what you are doing, you are on the bus.

Evaluation of Norman's model

Norman's model provides a useful explanation of attentional slips and errors, but it is not without problems. As with Reason's classifications, some errors do not fall neatly into either category and may result from a combination of factors (e.g. a combination of both faulty specification and faulty triggering). There is also the problem that schema theory relies heavily on the distinction between controlled and automatic processing and, as we have seen above, this is not yet fully understood. In particular, the factors that determine the mode of control in a given situation have not been clearly specified. Action slips usually occur in everyday, highly practised activities and this is entirely compatible with schema theory. However, as Eysenck and Keane (1995) point out, the incidence of action slips is greater in relatively trivial activities than in activities that could have more serious consequences. They give circus performers as an example, whose routines are highly practised, but, because of their dangerous nature, these routines are rarely subject to attentional error. Current theories cannot provide an adequate explanation of such observations.

Exam summary: Divided attention

The AQA examination will test your understanding of the following areas:

◆ explanations of divided attention (pp. 164–8)

◆ research into controlled and automatic processing, including slips associated with automatic processing (pp. 168–73).

Example question

The question below is typical of one drawn from the material above, and should take you 30 minutes to answer.

◆ Discuss one or more explanations of divided attention. *(24 marks)*

Suggested answer structure

This question covers the specification entry for explanations of divided attention (pp. 164–8). The question explicitly asks for one or more *explanations* of divided attention. Much of the material on pp. 164–5 is focused on research studies rather than explanations. This section has covered two main types of explanation for divided attention. Kahneman (1973) believes that attention is controlled by a central processor which coordinates a limited pool of resources. The overall capacity of the pool is limited but can vary according to factors such as arousal. His theory is more flexible than the earlier single-channel models, but it is unable to account for all the data. In particular, it is unable to explain the fact that tasks which use the same modality cannot usually be combined, even if both tasks are simple. Modular theories, such as that proposed by Allport (1980), can explain such findings, but are criticized, in their turn, for being too vague. It is unclear, for example, how a large number of independent modules could be coordinated to work effectively and efficiently in parallel (Kahneman's theory is discussed on pp. 166–7, and modular theories are discussed on pp. 167–8).

This question gives you the option of either writing about one theory in detail (this would probably be Kahneman's theory) or more than one in less detail. It is worth remembering that marks in essays such as this are awarded for both breadth and depth of material. Therefore, when deciding which route to take, you should consider whether you could do each of your chosen theories full justice. The terms *theory* and *model* are often used interchangeably within psychology. For example, Kahneman's theory is sometimes referred to as a *theory*, and sometimes as a *model*. When answering this question, you are not required to make a distinction between the two. Remember, when *assessing*, to cover research that *supports* localization and research that *challenges* it.

Pattern recognition

In the previous sections, we have seen how humans seek to cope with a bombardment of sensory stimuli. They sometimes focus selectively on particular inputs while ignoring others, but, in certain circumstances, they are able to share their attentional resources between tasks. Once our attention has been engaged by a stimulus, we need to be able to identify and make sense of it. So, in the case of auditory speech input, we have to match incoming sounds to vocabulary items stored in our long-term memories so that we can understand the semantic content of the message.

In this section, we are concerned with making sense of visual information. Look around you now. Whether you are in a classroom or at home, you are almost certainly surrounded by visual objects such as tables, chairs, books, pens, windows, doors, etc. Equally likely, you will have no difficulty in naming these objects and understanding their uses. Object recognition seems such an effortless task that you may be wondering why it is a subject of interest for psychologists. In fact, object recognition is a rather more complex activity than it may at first seem. For example, you are able to identify a chair, even if it is partially obscured behind a table, is some distance from you, or is in shadow. Our ability to make sense of our visual environment regardless of such situational factors as lighting, angle and viewing distance, will be explored in more detail in the section on perceptual organization in Chapter 8. For the moment, we will restrict discussion to the topic of pattern recognition, which is the process by which we transform and organize the raw information provided by our sensory receptors into a meaningful whole. Identifying a particular combination of musical notes as, for example, the National Anthem, is a form of pattern recognition, but, in this chapter, we will concentrate on visual patterns. Much of the research into pattern recognition has focused on how we identify two-dimensional patterns such as letters of the alphabet and digits. Consider the examples in Fig. 7.8.

You will have no difficulty in recognizing all the shapes in Fig. 7.8 as the letter 'b', even though they are quite different in size, typeface and orientation. Any adequate theory of pattern recognition will need to be able to account for this ability to recognize the same overall pattern in spite of it being represented quite differently.

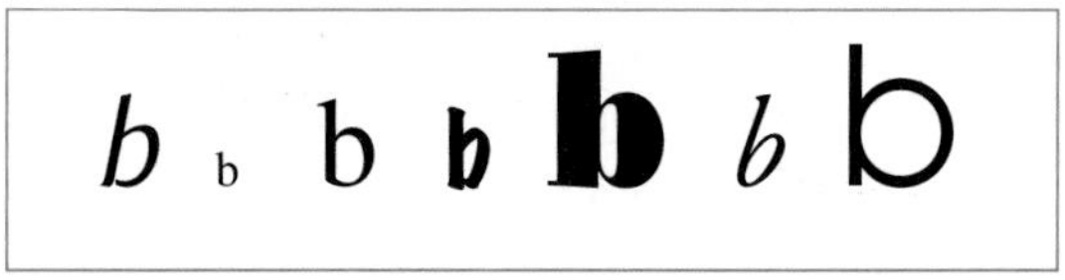

Template theory

The simplest kind of theory is to propose the existence of a set of miniature templates (or copies) of patterns which are stored in long-term memory. When you see the letter 'b', for example, you compare it to your set of stored templates until you find the correct fit. Just as you have to find a piece of exactly the right shape to fit the available space in a jigsaw, so you have to find the correct match amongst your templates. So, the letter 'E' will not fit the template for 'F' because of the extra horizontal bar at the bottom. This template matching works extremely well for computerized recognition systems, which depend on unambiguous identification of digits or symbols. It is the basis for barcode scanning in supermarkets and it is the way bank sorting systems recognize the distinctively shaped digits on the bottom of cheques. Forensic scientists also use it as a method of matching fingerprints.

Evaluation of template theory

As an explanation for human pattern recognition, template theory has several drawbacks. The letters in Fig. 7.8 are all recognizable as the letter 'b', but they are certainly not identical in form. So, given the requirement for an exact match, we would have to assume that there is a separate template stored for every possible presentation of the letter 'b'. This would be very inefficient in storage terms and, even if such a huge set of templates were feasible, it does not explain how we are able to recognize a letter 'b' for the first time in a typeface we have never actually seen before. Another problem for the theory is its inability to account for the recognition of patterns viewed from non-standard angles. If you turn your textbook upside down and look at Fig. 7.8 again, you will still find it easy to recognize the letter 'b'. Jolicoeur and Landau (1984) found that humans require only 15 milliseconds of extra processing time to recognize rotated letters. It seems highly unlikely that we should have stored templates of rotated letters, so it is unclear from template theory how we are able to accomplish this task so quickly. It is clear, then, that there are problems for the theory even in accounting for the relatively simple task of letter and digit recognition. It is even more difficult for template-matching theory to account for our ability to make sense of the complex visual scenes that we encounter in everyday life.

Figure 7.8 Variations on the letter 'b'

Prototype theories

These theories are rather more flexible versions of the template-matching approach. A prototype is an abstract model stored in long-term memory, which embodies the most typical features of an object or pattern. When we see an object, we compare it to our set of prototypes and identify the stimulus as soon as we have a reasonably close match. Unlike original template-matching theory, the match does not have to be exact for recognition to occur. You may have a stored prototype for each of your teachers which includes details such as height, build, facial features, etc. However, if a teacher suddenly came into class wearing glasses for the first time, you would still be able to recognize them because the match would be close enough to your stored prototype for that person.

Evaluation of prototype theories

Prototype-matching theory is more flexible and economical than the original template-matching theory and it can account for the ability to recognize different pictorial representations of the same basic shape. Several studies have shown that prototypes can be helpful in recognizing patterns such as geometric shapes (Posner and Keele 1968) and simple line drawings of faces (Reed 1972). Solso and McCarthy (1981) also demonstrated their importance in the recognition of police identikit pictures used for witness identification. However, the theory does not adequately explain how the prototypes are stored in memory. Nor does it explain how we are able to recognize objects that are partially obscured.

Feature detection theories

An alternative explanation of pattern recognition can be found in feature detection theories. According to these theories, we process images in terms of their basic constituent parts. In other words, we match features of a pattern to features stored in memory, rather than attempt to match a whole pattern to a template or prototype. One of the first feature models was devised as a computer program by Selfridge (1959). It was called the Pandemonium Model because it was based on the metaphor of a hierarchy of demons, each with their own specific contributions to the pattern recognition task.

Imagine being presented with the written letter 'E'. The image of this symbol will fall as a pattern of light on the retina where it will be passed on by an image or data demon to a set of feature or computational demons. Each feature demon has the task of looking out for a specific feature such as a straight vertical line, oblique line, continuous curve, acute angle, etc. If its particular feature is present in the visual image, the demon will 'shout'. The volume of the shouting is determined by the prominence of the feature. So, for example, the letter 'E' will provoke the demons responsible for horizontal lines and for right angles, which will shout more loudly than the vertical line demon because their features are more numerous. The shouting is relayed to the next layer of the hierarchy, where cognitive demons shout out possible matches for the combination of features that have been recognized by the feature demons. It is possible, at this stage, for cognitive demons to be shouting 'F', or even 'L', as well as 'E'. At the top of the hierarchy is the decision demon, which has the task of deciding, on the basis of the accumulated information and the volume of the shouting, which letter has the most matching features – in this case 'E'. The notion of a crowd of demons shouting away inside our heads may seem bizarre, but Selfridge intended it only as a metaphor to represent some of the uncertainty contained in feature processing. Other formulations of feature theory do not make use of demons, but they all rest on the assumption that we recognize patterns by matching them against a set of distinctive features that we have stored in memory.

Evaluation of feature detection theories

There is support for the feature detection approach from both psychological and physiological evidence. Try Activity 5 before you read any further.

Activity 5: Feature detection

Scan through Lists 1 and then 2 until you find the letter Z

LIST 1	LIST 2
GCDROQ	IVEFXW
OQURCG	FWVYMN
QDOPUC	IWXNEV
COPQUG	MNWXIE
GCOUQP	VWXYMF
QOCUGD	FXWYIM
UGCOZQ	IVXNZM
QGUOPC	VWXMNI
CUODQG	WIYXMVF
CGQOODU	IEVYWX
DUQOGC	VYWMNX
CQUGOD	MNWEFI
OCQPUR	XVYWMI
RPQOUC	WXNMIY
GUOCQP	YFEIVM

You probably found the letter 'Z' in list 1 more quickly than the one in list 2. See the text below for an explanation.

Neisser (1964) used arrays of letters similar to those in Activity 5 and asked participants to find certain target letters. He compared the time taken to detect the letter 'Z' when the surrounding letters consisted of straight lines and when the surrounding letters consisted of curved features. Target detection was faster in the second condition because the letter 'Z' has few features in common with the curved letters and so stands out more readily. Similar findings were presented by Gibson (1969) who found that participants take longer to decide whether letters such as 'P' and 'R' are different from one another than letters such as 'G' and 'M'. Garner (1979) found that decision speed increases as a consequence of the number of shared features of the letters. This lends support to the idea that some kind of stage-by-stage feature analysis process is taking place.

There is also some support for the feature models from biological studies carried out by Hubel and Wiesel (1959) (see *In Focus*).

It seems reasonable to accept that feature detection plays some part in the process of pattern recognition,

Figure 7.9 Feature criteria of the capital letter 'T'

but there are some problems. One difficulty is that the theories simply list a set of features, but make no attempt to describe the relationship between features. For example, look at Fig.7.9.

All of the figures illustrated above meet the feature criteria for the capital letter 'T' – i.e. one vertical line, one horizontal line and two right angles – but none of them represent a real 'T'. We also need a structural description that gives information about the relationship between the features. Feature theory also fails to take into account that some features of a visual stimulus are more important than others.

An assumption of the feature model is that recognition of a pattern depends on analysis and synthesis. In other words, the visual system first identifies individual features of a stimulus and then combines these features to decide what the whole

---

◆ **in focus**

Biological mechanisms in pattern recognition

There are over 100 million neurons in the visual cortex – the area of the brain primarily responsible for the processing of visual information – and only the tiniest fraction of these have been systematically studied. Hubel and Wiesel undertook much of the pioneering work in this field in the late 1950s and they were awarded the Nobel Prize in 1981 for their research. Biological aspects of perception will be covered more thoroughly in Chapter 8. We will focus here on biological research specifically relevant to pattern recognition.

Hubel and Wiesel (1962, 1979) inserted microelectrodes into various regions of the visual system in anaesthetized cats and monkeys. They then presented a variety of visual stimuli on a large screen in front of the animals and recorded signals detected by the microelectrodes. They found that the cortical neurons made no response to spots of light, but that they were most responsive to bar-like stimuli with specific orientations. They found three main types of cortical cells, each tuned to detecting the presence of particular features such as edges, light and dark areas, slits of light, orientation and direction of motion. These three types of cell were named simple, complex and hypercomplex cells.

◆ Simple cells respond selectively to lines, edges, bars and slits in specific retinal areas and at a particular orientation. Some simple cells respond best to a vertical stimulus, while others respond best to bars with horizontal or vertical orientations.

◆ Complex cells respond to similar stimuli, but respond best to moving lines in a particular direction of movement.

◆ Hypercomplex or end-stopped cells fire to bars of specific length or to moving corners and angles.

Since these cells identified by Hubel and Wiesel appear to respond differentially to specific features of the stimulus such as orientation, direction and movement, they are sometimes called feature detectors.

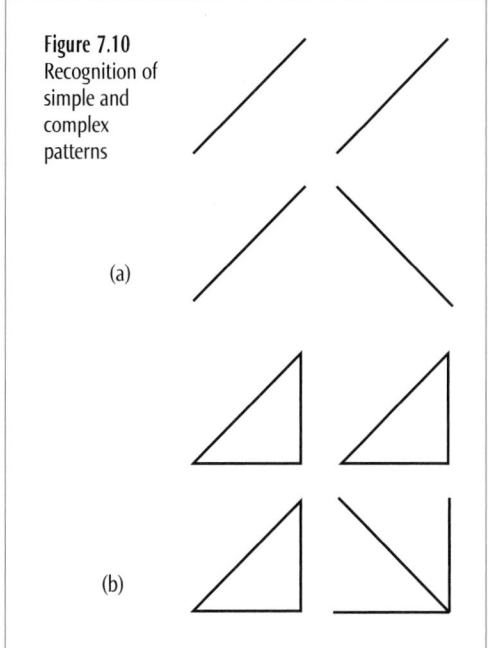

Figure 7.10
Recognition of simple and complex patterns

(a)

(b)

Recognition-by-components theory

The problem of how we recognize objects that are more complex than digits or letters has been addressed by a more recent theoretical approach called the recognition-by-components theory (RBC). It is based on the notion that objects can be represented by a non-arbitrary set of parts or modules and it combines some aspects of prototypes and distinctive features. Biederman (1987, 1990) has suggested that visual objects can be represented as a configuration of simple shapes called geons. These geons (geometric ions) are three-dimensional shapes including cylinders, rectangular solids, arcs, etc. Biederman believed that we are able to construct an infinite number of different objects from just 36 basic geons. Each of these geons is quite distinct from any other and is distinguishable from any viewing angle. Three geons can usually provide enough information for accurate object recognition although sometimes only two are needed (see Fig. 7.11).

Biederman's own research (1987) suggests that RBC can offer an adequate explanation for human shape recognition even when the object is complex, degraded or presented without much detail. He suggests that we find it difficult to identify an object viewed from an unusual angle because we are unable to see its basic geons. However, provided that we have sufficient visual information to identify the basic geons, we will also be able to identify the object. Biederman (1987) flashed line drawings of objects constructed from geons onto a screen and asked participants to identify them as quickly as possible. He found that most people were able to identify objects in less than one second even if the objects were incomplete (see Fig. 7.12).

Evaluation of Biederman's RBC theory

One of the main strengths of Biederman's approach is that he can explain how it is possible to recognize a wide range of objects on the basis of a relatively small number of stored shapes. It is, therefore, much more

pattern represents. The model would, therefore, predict that complex patterns should take longer to identify than simple ones. Pomerantz (1981) showed that this is not always the case. He showed participants stimulus figures similar to those shown in Figs 7.10 (a) and 7.10 (b) and asked them, in each case, to pick the stimulus that was different from the others.

Participants were faster to identify the odd one out in 7.10 (b), even though these stimuli are more complex variations of the stimuli in 7.10 (a). It seems that the provision of additional features in 7.10 (b) – i.e. making the stimuli into familiar triangle figures – provided contextual cues that speeded up identification. We will explore the effects of context later in this section.

Feature theory seems to provide a reasonable, if not complete, explanation of how we recognize simple patterns such as letters and digits. As with template and prototype theories, however, it is too simplistic to explain how we recognize more complex objects.

Figure 7.11
Some examples of geons
Source: Goldstein (1999), based on Biederman (1987)

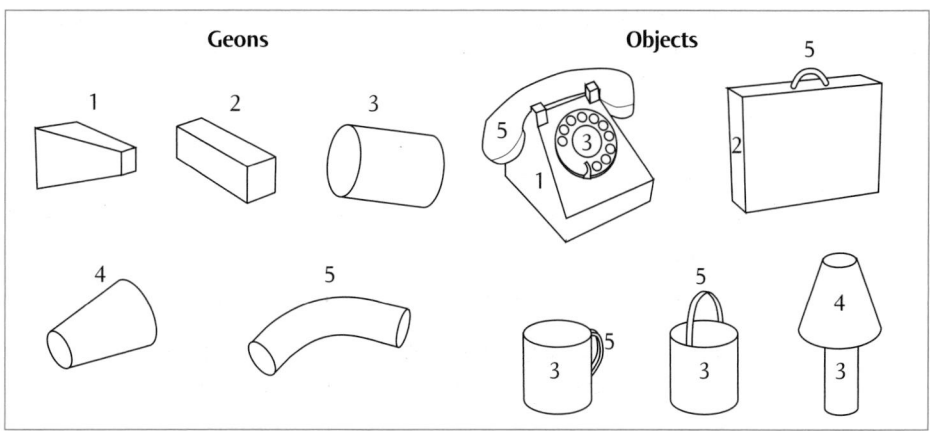

Geons

Objects

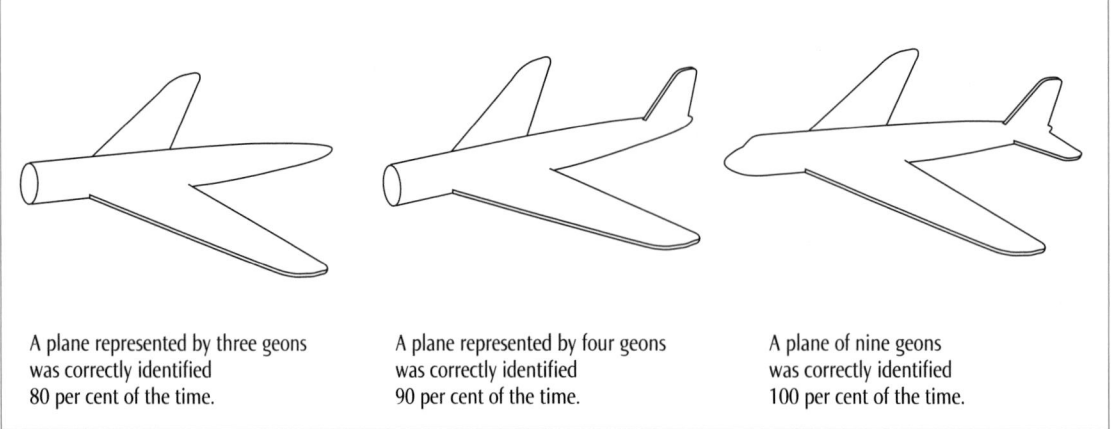

A plane represented by three geons was correctly identified 80 per cent of the time.

A plane represented by four geons was correctly identified 90 per cent of the time.

A plane of nine geons was correctly identified 100 per cent of the time.

Figure 7.12 Partial and complete versions of a nine-component object (airplane) *Source:* Biederman (1987)

economical in storage terms than earlier theories. The theory also seems to be compatible with evidence from people who have specific visual deficits (Banks and Krajicek 1991). However, it is not without flaws. It accounts well for our ability to identify general instances of objects, e.g. chairs, telephones, cups. It is less able to explain how we recognize our favourite chair or how we distinguish between two makes of car, even though the basic geon construction is the same for both of them. Similarly, it cannot adequately explain our recognition of objects with more amorphous shapes, such as clouds.

Another problem for the theory is that it predicts that objects will be recognized purely on the basis of constituent geons. This prediction has been questioned by Cave and Kosslyn (1993) who gave participants pictures similar to those in Fig. 7.13. Line drawings of everyday objects were broken into either geon-consistent parts or more arbitrary parts. Participants identified both types of drawing equally quickly, suggesting that they were recognizing the overall shape, rather than analysing the drawings in their constituent parts. This finding is not compatible with RBC.

RBC is a promising model, but it cannot explain all aspects of pattern recognition, and Biederman himself

Figure 7.13 A pair of scissors broken down into (a) geon-consistent parts and (b) random parts
Source: Cave and Kosslyn (1993)

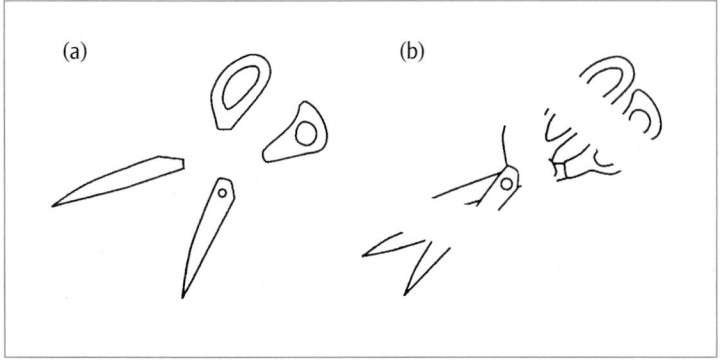

(a)   (b)

admits that more work is necessary to refine the theory. It cannot account for the fact that human perceivers, in their everyday activities, are constantly bombarded with complex visual scenes made up of dozens of objects, and yet are easily able to distinguish those objects and understand the relationships between them. In particular, the theory cannot account for the effects of context and prior expectation.

The role of context

Most of the theories we have looked at so far are based on the assumption that object recognition begins with the analysis of component parts. This kind of analysis of sensory inputs is known as bottom-up processing, a term which comes from the information-processing approach. This is based on the analogy of the human mind as a machine which manipulates information through a series of processing stages. Bottom-up processing, or data-driven processing, stresses the importance of the stimulus in pattern recognition. An example comes from the early work of Hubel and Wiesel (1962) (see *In Focus*). This research indicated that the retinal image is analysed through layers of the cortex in increasingly complex ways until the output of the hypercomplex cells is integrated to form a whole perceptual representation of the visual stimulus. The idea, then, is that visual information is transmitted from the bottom level (i.e. initial sensory input) through a series of stages to the higher levels of analysis where information is synthesized.

It is clear that physical properties, such as areas of light and shade, changes in direction and orientation, size, structural relationships, etc., are important factors in the object-recognition process. However, there is another important contribution to object recognition that is called top-down or conceptually driven processing. According to this approach, the process of object recognition is guided primarily by expectations that are based on the context in which the stimulus is embedded, and on our knowledge about the world. In other words, we expect certain objects to be in certain locations and these expectations aid rapid object recognition. Look at Activity 6 before you read any further.

Activity 6: Reading recognition

Try reading the following fragmented sentence:

Sk-lled re-d-rs f-nd it e-sy to r-ad se-t-nc-s ev-n if t-ey a-e inco-pl-te.

You probably found it relatively easy to read the sentence above, even if it took slightly longer than reading a complete sentence. The fact that we can make sense of fragmented script suggests that reading cannot simply be a bottom-up processing task relying on stimulus information alone. According to Matlin (1998), the typical reader would need to make about 5,000 feature detections a minute if reading involved identification of each component letter in terms of its distinctive features. This is obviously highly unlikely.

The idea that past experience and knowledge can influence perception was first put forward by Helmholtz in the nineteenth century, in the form of his likelihood principle, i.e. we will perceive the object which is most likely to occur in that particular situation. Palmer (1975) illustrated this principle by presenting participants with a picture of a familiar scene, such as a kitchen. He then very briefly flashed a drawing of an individual item onto the screen and asked participants to identify it. The rate of correct identification was 84 per cent for objects that might be expected from the context (e.g. a loaf of bread). However, performance fell to below 50 per cent for unexpected objects such as a letterbox. It seems that prior exposure to a kitchen scene primes recognition of associated objects.

Palmer (1975) provided another illustration of the effect of context on pattern recognition. He used drawings similar to those in Figs 7.14 (a) and 7.14 (b).

The shapes in Fig.7.14 (a) are not recognizable out of context, but become instantly identifiable if they are embedded in the context of a face.

A more recent formulation of the likelihood principle is to be found in Gregory's (1973) idea that perception is governed by hypothesis testing. Gregory believes that human perceivers act like intuitive

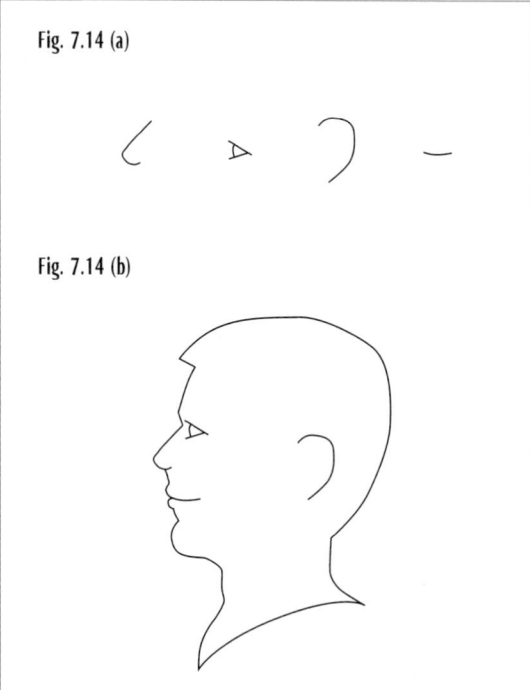

Fig. 7.14 (a)

Fig. 7.14 (b)

Figure 7.14 Recognizing shapes in context
Source: Palmer (1975)

scientists, i.e. they formulate and test hypotheses about the world. Sometimes these hypotheses are wrong and this can lead us to experience visual illusions (see Chapter 8), but they can often help us to identify stimuli that are ambiguous or degraded. A good example is when we are able to decipher poor handwriting. Expectations arise from the context and allow hypotheses to be generated so that we can read quite degraded script provided it makes sense.

Try reading the sentence in Fig. 7.15. You should have no difficulty in deciphering that it says: 'Unfortunately the 5.00pm class is cancelled today'. However, if you now look closely, you will see that the '5' and the 's' at the end of 'class' are written in exactly the same way, the 'U' of 'Unfortunately' is the same as the 'll' of 'cancelled' and the 'cl' of 'class' is the same as the 'd' at the end of 'cancelled' – it is only the context that allows us to differentiate between them.

In practice, perception involves a combination of top-down and bottom-up processing.

Figure 7.15

Unfortunately the 5.00pm class is cancelled today.

Research studies and theories of face recognition

One of the most active, current research areas in pattern recognition concerns the perception of faces. Recognizing faces is very important for human social functioning. It can help us to form relationships, recognize a friend in a crowd and give us non-verbal cues about what a person is thinking and feeling.

All faces have eyes, nose and mouth placed in the same relative locations and yet we are able to identify thousands of different faces that we come across in everyday life. Furthermore, we are able to recognize a particular face, e.g. the face of a best friend, regardless of the expression – angry, sad, amused, etc.

One of the most obvious ways of discriminating between faces seems to be on the basis of gender. Bruce et al. (1993) took photos of large numbers of men and women who were wearing swimming hats to conceal their hairstyles. The women wore no make-up and the men were closely shaven. In spite of the lack of obvious gender cues, observers were 96 per cent

Figure 7.16 Examples of faces similar to those used by Bradshaw and Wallace (1971). Face pairs were constructed showing differences in two, four or seven facial features
Source: Roth and Bruce (1995, p. 144)

accurate in sorting the photos into appropriate gender piles.

According to many of the pattern recognition theories discussed earlier, analysis occurs in a bottom-up fashion. Psychologists have suggested that we might also recognize faces using a feature detection approach, i.e. we might use information about individual features such as eye colour or mouth shape to build up a representation of the face. This approach is the basis of Identikit – a system used by some police forces to build up the face of a criminal on a feature-by-feature basis. Bradshaw and Wallace (1971) used Identikit to construct pairs of faces that shared a number of features, but differed in others (see Fig. 7.16). Participants were asked to decide as quickly as possible whether pairs of faces were the same or different. The more differences there were between the two faces, the faster the judgements.

Bradshaw and Wallace (1971) concluded that participants were processing facial features independently and in serial fashion. Using sequential comparison of features, participants would encounter differences between the two faces sooner if there were several features that differed. However, these data can be interpreted differently. Sergent (1984) pointed out that the faces that differed in several features were also very different in terms of their overall configuration and that it may have been this factor which allowed participants to make speedy judgements. Sergent (1984) conducted her own study based on Identikit pictures and found that the faces were being processed in a holistic form, rather than as a set of independent features. In another study, Young et al. (1987) supported the idea that we recognize faces by processing information about the overall configuration of the face, rather than by analysing individual features. They combined photos of the top half of one celebrity face with the bottom half of another. When the two halves were closely aligned to create a single face, participants experienced great difficulty in identifying the top half. This task became much easier when the two halves were misaligned or when the top half was presented

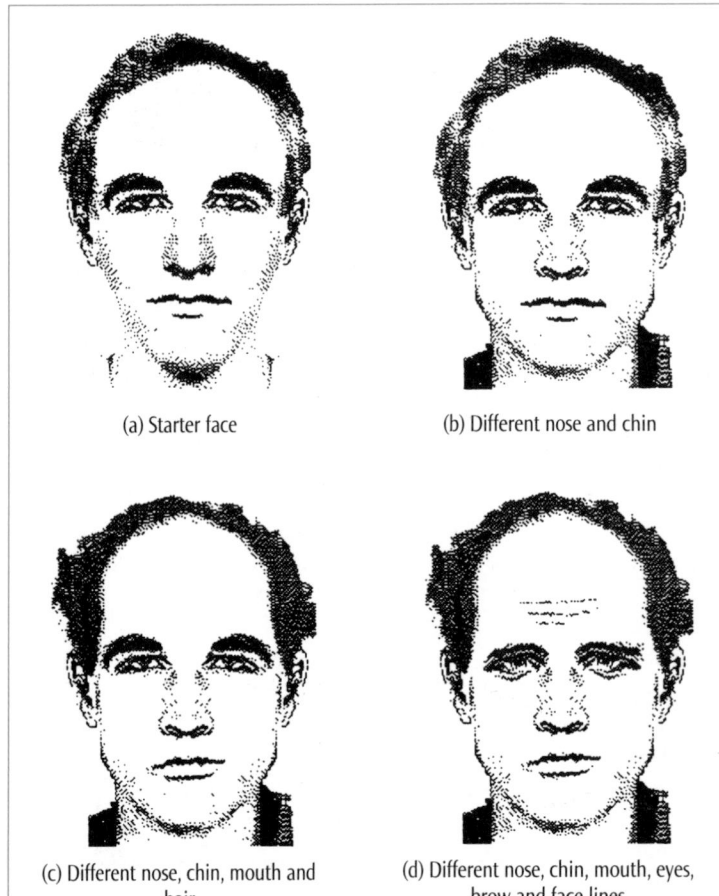

(a) Starter face

(b) Different nose and chin

(c) Different nose, chin, mouth and hair

(d) Different nose, chin, mouth, eyes, brow and face lines

in isolation. This seems to suggest that the close alignment in the first condition produced a novel configuration that interfered with recognition.

It seems likely that we process faces rather differently from other visual stimuli. Tanaka and Farah (1993) showed participants a set of six visual stimuli that included pictures of houses and pictures of faces. Once participants had become familiar with the items, they were given various recognition tests. For example, on some trials, they were asked to choose which of two face parts they had seen before, e.g. two noses. On other trials, they were asked to select which of two whole faces they had seen before. On these trials, the faces usually differed only by one feature, e.g. they had a different nose. There were similar trials showing pictures of whole houses or individual features, e.g. windows. Tanaka and Farah found that participants were far more accurate at recognizing facial features when they appeared in the context of a whole face, rather than in isolation. However, in the house trials, they were just as accurate for the house features presented in isolation, as for the house features appearing in the context of the whole house.

One well-established finding is that faces are more difficult to recognize if viewed upside down. Try Activity 7 to demonstrate this yourself.

Activity 7: Upside-down facial recognition

Find a magazine, e.g. a TV guide, that contains lots of photos of famous people. Turn the magazine upside down and leaf through. How many celebrities are you able to identify? People who would be instantly recognizable in the upright position become much harder to identify.

Yin (1969) found that recognition for faces is far superior to recognition for buildings, but that this superiority is reversed when the pictures are turned upside down. The explanation for such findings seems to be that normal recognition of upright faces depends on holistic processing, but that this configuration of facial features is lost when the face is turned upside down.

Theories of face recognition

Bruce and Young (1986) have put forward an influential model of face recognition. Their model incorporated aspects of earlier formulations by Hay and Young (1982) and Ellis (1986) (see Fig. 7.17).

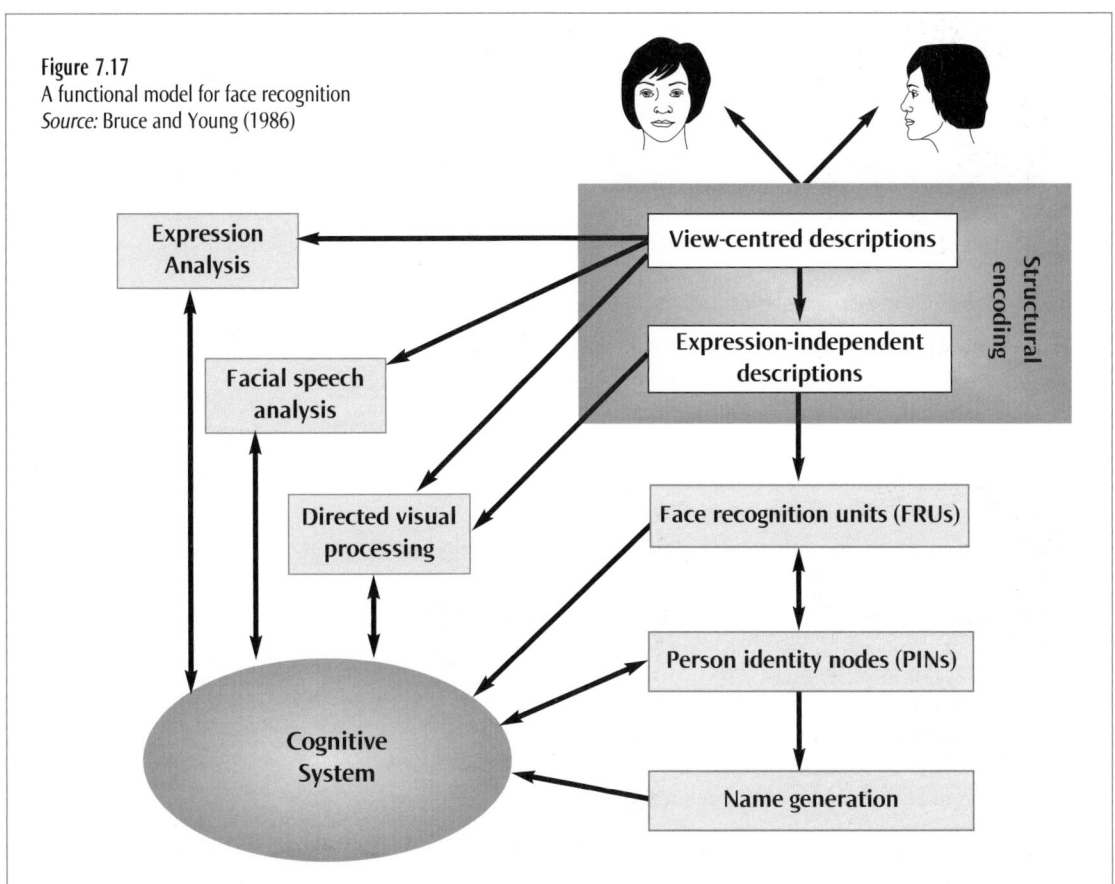

Figure 7.17
A functional model for face recognition
Source: Bruce and Young (1986)

The model includes a number of different processing modules that are linked in sequence and in parallel.

◆ Structural encoding – separate stages of representation of the facial image.

◆ Expression analysis – drawing inferences about a person's emotional state from an analysis of their facial features.

◆ Facial speech analysis – making use of visual information from the face when deciphering speech. Bruce and Young sometimes refer to this as lip-reading.

◆ Directed visual processing – allows for certain kinds of face processing to occur without the necessity for recognizing the identity of the person, e.g. seeing whether or not the individual has a moustache.

◆ Face recognition units – stored structural descriptions of familiar faces.

◆ Person identity nodes (PINs) – provide personal details about an individual who is already known to the observer, e.g. their occupation or interests.

◆ Name generation – the name of the individual is stored separately from their other details.

◆ Cognitive system – this seems to hold additional information that might be of use in face recognition. For example, imagine you see someone in a local shop who looks like the Queen. The cognitive system would evaluate the likelihood of seeing her in such a context and save you from the potential embarrassment of misidentification. It also seems to play a part in determining which components of the system need to be activated.

Evaluation of theories of face recognition

The Bruce and Young model assumes that there are independent routes involved in processing facial expressions, facial speech and the identification of specific individuals, and there is considerable empirical evidence to support this view. Much of the evidence comes from clinical studies, i.e. studies of people with neurological defects that disrupt normal perception. Young et al. (1993) investigated face perception in 34 ex-service men who had received missile wounds to the posterior regions of the brain. Some were selectively poor at familiar face recognition, whereas others only experienced difficulties in matching unfamiliar faces. Others found it difficult to decipher facial expressions accurately. Sergent and Signoret (1992) conducted a study in which healthy individuals were given similar tasks to do while undergoing a PET scan. The three different activities were found to activate

slightly different locations in the brain. These findings provide compelling evidence for the independence of these three functions.

The model has been influential and seems to account successfully for certain aspects of face recognition. However, some of the components in the model have been less well explained than others. In particular, the role of the cognitive system is not clearly specified. Bruce and Young (1986) have recognized this weakness and admitted that the cognitive system 'serves to catch all those aspects of processing not reflected in other components of our model'.

Burton et al. (1990) and Burton and Bruce (1993) have revised the original model and implemented aspects of it using an artificial intelligence model. The major differences in the new formulation are as follows:

◆ There is no separate store for names.

◆ Decisions about the familiarity of a particular face are made at the person-identity nodes, instead of at the face recognition units.

◆ The model has been made more precise and has been demonstrated in a computer simulation.

This model is being extended and updated and seems to provide plausible accounts of many aspects of face recognition. It cannot, however, account for the processes that allow new faces to be learned and for new identities to be stored in memory.

Progress in the field of face recognition research has been rapid over the past 10 years and it is likely that Bruce (1995) is correct when she predicts '...in only a few years time we should have several further pieces of the puzzle in place'.

Exam summary: Pattern recognition

The AQA examination will test your understanding of the following areas:

◆ explanations of pattern recognition (pp. 174–8)

◆ biological mechanisms in pattern recognition (p. 176)

◆ role of context in pattern recognition (pp. 178–9)

◆ research studies and theories of face recognition (pp. 180–2).

Example question

The question below is typical of one drawn from the material above, and should take you 30 minutes to answer.

◆ Outline and evaluate two theories of pattern recognition.
(24 marks)

Suggested answer structure

As this whole section has been concerned with pattern recognition, there is no shortage of material for you to choose from. *Template theory* (p. 174) provided an early explanation for pattern recognition, but was soon found to be inadequate. *Prototype theory* (p. 175) proved more flexible and economical, but was still unable to account for the complexity of human pattern recognition. There is some evidence that pattern recognition occurs as a result of feature analysis, whereby we match the component features of a visual stimulus to features stored in memory. This idea is supported by biological research (e.g. Hubel and Weisel 1962) which has identified feature-detector cells in the visual cortex of the brain. *Feature-detection theory* (pp. 175–7) offers a reasonable explanation of how we recognize fairly simple patterns, but is too simplistic to account for the recognition of more complex objects. Biederman (1987) has proposed a more recent theoretical approach. His *recognition-by-components* model (pp. 177–8) combines aspects of prototype and feature-detection theories. He believes that objects can be represented as combinations of a limited set of simple shapes called geons. This is an

economical and flexible approach that can explain how we recognize a wide range of objects. Although this is a promising approach, in its current form it is unable to account for the full complexity of human pattern recognition.

Theoretical explanations of face recognition (pp. 180–2) are also relevant for this question, as these are *specialized* theories that explain one particular aspect of pattern recognition. Bruce and Young (1986) have produced an influential model of face recognition based on three independent processes: facial expression, facial speech and identity (pp. 181–2). There has been some support for their theory, but some of the components of the model have not yet been fully explained.

When dealing with the AO2 components of this question, you might evaluate in terms of the weaknesses of a particular theory (e.g. the claim that Bruce and Young's model does not fully specify the role of the cognitive system) or the degree of research support for any chosen theory. So, when evaluating a particular theory, research studies can be used as evidence for *support* or as a *challenge* to the main theoretical assumptions.

Chapter summary

- In this chapter, we have considered various aspects of attention. Early research in this field, iniated by **Cherry** (1953), concentrated particularly on **focused** or **selective attention**, whereby we focus on one input to the exclusion of all other competing inputs.

- **Broadbent** (1958) proposed an influential model of focused attention. This was a single channel, **early-selection** model in which one input was selected at a very early stage in the processing on the basis of physical properties and then passed on in serial fashion for semantic analysis. There were immediate challenges to the theory and **Treisman** (1964) put forward a more flexible model that was able to account for new experimental data.

- **Deutsch and Deutsch** (1963), in their so-called **late-selection model**, proposed that all inputs are fully analysed for meaning and, that only then is a single input selected for conscious awareness.

- On balance, Treisman's early-selection theory seems better able to account for all the experimental data. During the 1970s, researchers began to see the limitations of the single channel models and started investigating the idea that attention is limited by capacity.

- It is clear that we are often able to divide our attention between tasks. Psychologists have investigated the circumstances under which this is possible, looking at factors such as task difficulty, task similarity and practice

- One of the first theories put forward to explain **divided attention** was proposed by **Kahneman**. His **capacity resource allocation model** of attention rested on the assumption that the overall amount of attentional **resource** is limited. However, factors such as arousal and mental effort can affect available capacity. Capacity theories are reasonably flexible, but they cannot satisfactorily account for all experimental findings.

- Modular theories, such as that proposed by Allport, can account for some of the findings that have proved incompatible with capacity theories. However, they are also criticized for being vague and descriptive rather than explanatory.

- Tasks seem to be easier to combine if one of them has become automatic. Shiffrin and Schneider (1977) have distinguished between **automatic** and **controlled processing** although the distinction is not always entirely clear-cut.

◆ **Action slips**, which can sometimes occur during the course of carrying out a well-learned or **automatic** activity, have been investigated by a number of psychologists including **Reason** (1979). There is currently no complete theoretical explanation of such errors, although Norman (1981) has proposed an explanation based on schema theory.

◆ In the last section of the chapter, we looked at a rather different kind of processing involving the recognition of visually presented stimuli. There have been various theories of **pattern recognition** ranging from simple **template** matching to the more complex recognition-by-components theory. **Feature detection theories** have received some support from **biological** research such as that carried out by **Hubel and Wiesel**. However, none of these theories provides a comprehensive account of human pattern recognition. They are based on **bottom-up processing** and do not account for the important effects of **context** and past experience (**top-down processing**).

◆ Face perception is a special kind of pattern recognition that has attracted considerable research interest over the last few years. **Bruce and Young** have put forward an influential theory of **face recognition** that has been supported by a number of studies. However, it has not proved adequate and Burton and Bruce have made modifications. This formulation looks promising and has been shown to operate effectively in computer models. This is a rapidly developing field and new theories are likely to emerge in the near future.

Further resources

Eysenck, M.W. and Keane, M.T. (1995) *Cognitive Psychology: A Student's Handbook* (3rd edn), Hove: Lawrence Erlbaum Associates.

This is a good, all-round textbook on cognitive psychology. It has excellent sections on all the topics covered in this chapter and, although aimed at undergraduates, the style is reasonably accessible and straightforward for A-level students.

Styles, E.A. (1997) *The Psychology of Attention*, Hove: Psychology Press.

This is an excellent and comprehensive text on the field of attention. It is intended for undergraduates and contains some material that is beyond the scope of the A-level syllabus. However, it is clearly written and the appropriate sections are quite accessible for students wishing to research the area in more detail.

Chapter 8

Perceptual processes and development

Jane Willson

Preview

In this chapter we shall be looking at:

◆ the structure and function of the visual system and research into the nature of visual processing

◆ theories of perceptual organization, including constructivist and direct theories, and their explanations of perceptual organization

◆ explanations of perceptual development and studies of the development of perceptual abilities.

Introduction

Perception is an important area of study for psychologists because everything we know about the external world must first come in through our senses. The world around us is filled with people and objects which we can see, hear, touch, smell or taste. We receive this information as sensations arriving at sense organs in the body, such as the eyes, ears and nose. These sense organs contain sensory receptors which detect the physical properties of the world around us, such as light and sound, and pass this information to the brain and the central nervous system (CNS). This information is then converted through a number of processes into our perceptual experience of the world. Cognitive psychologists are interested in explaining the mental activity required to convert physical information from the environment into the psychological experience of perception. There has been a huge amount of research into perceptual processing, but most of it has concentrated on visual perception and that will be the focus of this chapter.

Although perception occurs within the brain, our first contact with the external visual world is through our sense organs. It is, therefore, important to understand the physical make-up of the eye and visual pathways in the brain. We will look at the structure and function of the visual system and consider some of the research into the nature of visual information processing. We will then consider two rather different theories of perception. Gibson (e.g. 1979) first coined the term *direct perception* to convey the idea that we pick up sufficient information from the visual environment to be able to form a conscious percept and that we do not need to make use of higher level cognitive processing in order to make sense of the visual world. An alternative view, which originated with Helmholtz in the nineteenth century, but which survives today in the work of researchers such as Gregory and Rock, is called the constructivist approach (or *intelligent perception*). According to this view, we often need to go beyond the information contained in the visual stimulus and use stored memories based on our previous experience to help us build or construct our conscious experience of the world. In particular, we will consider how these two approaches have helped us to understand the ways in which perception is organized.

The last section in this chapter will focus on perceptual development and, in particular, on the nature–nurture debate, i.e. the question of whether adult perceptual skills are innate or develop as a result of learning through experience.

The visual system

The starting point for visual perception is light. Light is a narrow band of the electromagnetic spectrum with a wavelength of between 380 and 760 nanometers (1 nm is a billionth of a metre) which is visible to humans. Other types of electromagnetic energy such as ultraviolet radiation, gamma rays and x-rays are not visible to the human eye.

The reason that we are able to see various objects and people around us is that light is reflected from these things into our eyes. This reflected light is focused to create an image in the eye, which, in turn, causes electrical signals to trigger a chain of events in the brain which lead to conscious perception. Light falls on the back of the eyes as two small, upside-down, two-dimensional images, but what we actually 'see' is a coherent, colourful, three-dimensional world that is the right way up. We need to consider how this transformation occurs (see *In Focus*).

Structure and functions of the visual system

The eye

Look at the cross-section of the eye in Fig. 8.1 before reading any further.

The eye is an extremely delicate organ and, for protection, lies within a bony socket in the skull. It is protected externally by the eyelid which keeps out dust and dirt from the atmosphere and which closes in an automatic reflex action at the sudden approach of an object or movement towards the eye. The outer covering or 'white' of the eye is a strong elastic membrane called the *sclera* which is opaque and cannot admit light. The sclera bulges forward at the front of the eye to form a clear, domed window called

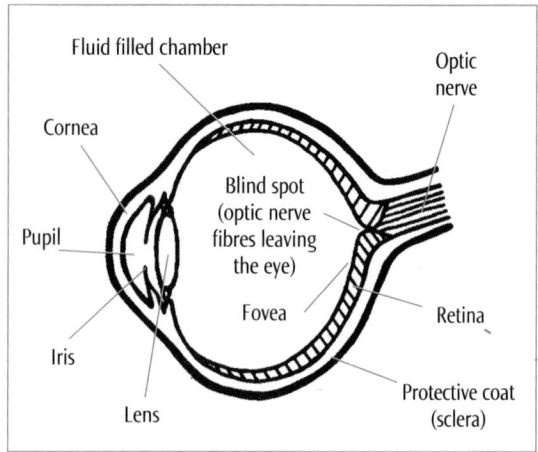

Figure 8.1 Cross-section through the eye

the *cornea*. It is the first optically active element in the eye and its function is to gather and concentrate light reflected from objects in the environment. Because it has to remain completely transparent, the cornea cannot be nourished by blood vessels and so oxygen

---

The fallacy of the internal mental picture

Many people make the assumption that seeing simply involves scanning an internal mental picture. V.S. Ramachandran, an internationally renowned neuroscientist, provides a simple explanation of why this idea is a misconception. He uses the example of looking at a champagne glass.

'The idea that there's a screen somewhere inside the brain where images are displayed embodies a serious fallacy. For, if you were to display an image of a champagne glass on an internal neural screen, you'd need another little person inside the brain to see that image. And that won't solve the problem either because you'd then need yet another, even tinier person inside his head to view that image, and so on and so forth, ad infinitum. You'd end up with an endless regress of eyes, images and little people without really solving the problem of perception.

'So the first step in understanding perception is to get rid of the idea of images in the brain and to begin thinking about symbolic descriptions of objects and events in the external world. A good example of a symbolic description is a written paragraph like the ones on this page. If you had to convey to a friend in China what your apartment looks like, you wouldn't have to teletransport it to China. All you'd have to do would be to write a letter describing your apartment. Yet the actual squiggles of ink – the words and paragraphs in the letter – bear no physical resemblance to your bedroom. The letter is a symbolic description of your bedroom.

'What is meant by a symbolic description in the brain? Not squiggles of ink, of course, but the language of nerve impulses. The human brain contains multiple areas for processing images, each of which is composed of an intricate network of neurons that is specialized for extracting certain types of information from the image. Any object evokes a pattern of activity – unique for each object – among a subset of these areas. For example, when you look at a pencil, a book or a face, a different pattern of nerve activity is elicited in each case, 'informing' higher brain centres about what you are looking at. The patterns of activity symbolize or represent visual objects in much the same way as squiggles of ink on the paper symbolize or represent your bedroom. As scientists trying to understand visual processes, our goal is to decipher the code used by the brain to create these symbolic descriptions, much as a cryptographer tries to crack an alien script.'

Source: Ramachandran and Blakeslee (1999, p. 66)

and nutrients are provided by a watery substance called the *aqueous humour* which fills the small chamber behind the cornea. Behind the chamber is a variable aperture – the *pupil* – which is controlled by a ring of coloured muscles called the *iris*. The colour of the iris seems to be determined genetically and can vary from blue, green, violet, brown to almost black. The function of the iris is to regulate the size of the pupil in response to external stimuli. Bright light will cause the pupil to constrict to as little as 2 mm in diameter, but, under dim light conditions, the pupil can dilate to up to 8 mm. This process of contraction and dilation occurs automatically and is not under conscious control.

The lens is situated directly behind the pupil and its function is to complete the process begun in the cornea of bringing light into focus on the *retina* at the back of the eye. The natural shape of the lens is spheroid, but, through a process called *accommodation*, it can change its shape to bring objects at various distances into focus. To focus on nearby objects, the lens becomes fatter and, to focus on more distant objects, the lens becomes thinner. Accommodation occurs automatically in adults, but does not seem possible for newborn infants whose focus appears fixed at about 19 cm (i.e. the approximate distance of the mother's face from the baby's during feeding). Babies usually develop the ability to accommodate by about 8 weeks, but this ability declines with age. The lens loses elasticity as people grow older and they often become long-sighted (i.e. they have to hold a book at arm's length in order to be able to focus on the print) and they may need to wear corrective glasses. The lens has a slight yellow pigment which acts to screen out some of the ultraviolet light coming into the eye. This yellow tint becomes more pronounced with age and can affect experience of colour, particularly the distinction between blues and greens. To demonstrate accommodation, try Activity 1.

The retina

Light then passes through a large chamber filled with a jelly-like substance called *vitreous humour*, which helps to maintain the spherical shape of the eye, and falls on the retina. The retina effectively works as a screen that covers most of the interior of the eye and it is here that light is changed or transduced into a neural response. It consists of three main layers of neural tissue:

◆ the outermost layers contain *photoreceptors*

◆ the middle layer consists of three types of cell: *amacrine*, *horizontal* and *bipolar cells*

◆ the third layer contains *ganglion cells*.

Activity 1: The process of accommodation

Close one of your eyes and focus on an object, for example, a picture on the wall, about 6 or 7 metres away. Continue to focus on that object and, at the same time, pick up a pen and bring it slowly towards your face. If you maintain focus on the distant object, you will find that the tip of the pen becomes blurred and you will start to see double. Now, keeping one eye closed, hold the pen at a distance of about one foot from you and focus on it. You should find that the distant object has become blurred although the pen is now clearly in focus. Now bring the pen closer to your face and notice how difficult it is to maintain it in focus. The point at which you can no longer bring it into focus no matter how hard you try, is called the near point.

You can see from this activity that it is possible to focus on objects that are distant and close, but that you cannot do both at the same time. In your normal everyday activities, the lens is constantly changing shape to focus on objects at different distances, and the process of accommodation works so quickly and efficiently that you probably feel that everything in the visual scene is in focus simultaneously. You have also demonstrated that accommodation ceases to work when an object is too close to your face.

See Fig. 8.2 for a schematic diagram of the retina.

The photoreceptors consist of two different types of cell – *rods* and *cones* – and these appear to differ in both function and distribution. There are about 5 million cones in each retina and about 50,000 (i.e. about 1 per cent of the total number) are packed into the small central area called the *fovea* (Tyler 1997) (see

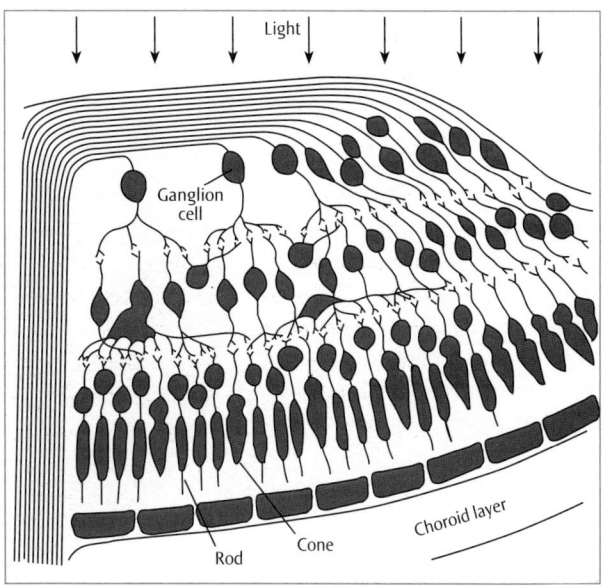

Figure 8.2 Schematic diagram of the retina
Source: Atkinson *et al.* (1983)

Fig. 8.1). The fovea is a small depression at the centre of the retina no bigger than the size of this 'o' which is responsible for our most detailed and accurate vision. The other cones are in the peripheral retina where they are outnumbered by rods by a ratio of about 20 to 1. All 120 million rods are in the peripheral retina. Rods are believed to be responsible for vision under dim light conditions (*scotopic system*) and cones are responsible for vision under bright conditions (*photopic system*) and also for the experience of colour vision. Having these two different functional systems allows human observers to see over a wide range of light intensities.

The photoreceptor cells release neurotransmitter molecules to the bipolar cells which, in turn, connect to the ganglion cells. Axons from the ganglion cells then pass from the eye into the brain. The back-to-front arrangement of the three cell layers in the retina (i.e. with the photoreceptors at the back facing away from the light) means that light has to pass through the other two layers first. This poses no problem because the bipolar and ganglion cells are transparent. The arrangement could, however, present a difficulty for the ganglion cell axons leaving the retina because the photoreceptors would block their exit. This problem is overcome by having a small area at the back of the retina which is completely free of photoreceptors, thus leaving a gap where one million ganglion cell fibres can leave the eye to form the optic nerve. However, the absence of photoreceptors at this point means that a blind spot is created. Try Activity 2 now.

Ramachandran (1999) reports that King Charles II used to amuse himself by 'decapitating' courtiers and ladies in waiting using his blind spot. You can try this rather more gruesome demonstration with one of your friends. Stand about 10 feet away from your chosen victim and, closing your right eye, look at his/her head with your left eye. Slowly move your left eye horizontally towards the right away from the person's head and you will find that your blind spot becomes directly in line with his/her head and, at this point, his head should disappear!

We are not usually aware of the blind spot. This is partly because we have two eyes and so, if the image falls on the blind spot of one eye, it will be picked up by receptors in the other eye. It also seems to be the case that, via some mechanism which is not yet fully understood, we compensate for the blind spot by 'filling in' the place from which the information has disappeared (Churchland and Ramachandran 1996).

Activity 2: Demonstration of the blind spot

Hold the book out at arm's length in front of you. Close your right eye and focus with your left eye on the cross in Fig. 8.3. Gradually move the page towards you. At some point, the centre of the wheel will fall on your blind spot. You may need to do this several times before the centre disappears. However, once you locate your blind spot, you do not experience a void. The brain seems to 'fill in' the missing information and, according to Ramachandran (1992), you are likely to see the spokes of the wheel fill in the hole.

The visual pathways

The nerve impulses that travel along the optic nerve are no longer in the form of raw sense data because a great deal of neural processing has already taken place in the retina. The optic nerves from each eye come together at the base of the brain to form the optic chiasm (see Fig. 4.8 on p. 106).

The optic nerve fibres from the nasal retinas (the parts of the retina closest to the nose) cross to the opposite side of the brain at this point, while the fibres from the temporal retinas (the parts of the retina closest to the temples) continue on the same side of the brain. After they pass through the optic chiasm, the axons of the ganglion cells are called the *optic tract*. Most of the optic tract axons lead to the *lateral geniculate nucleus* (LGN) which is part of the thalamus. Here they form optic radiations which lead to the primary visual cortex (or striate cortex) where additional processing is carried out. However, each module of the primary visual cortex only sees what is happening in one tiny section of the visual field. Information from these modules is

Figure 8.3 Wheel used to demonstrate the blind spot
Source: Ramachandran (1992)

combined in the visual association cortex so that we can experience whole objects and complete visual scenes. Once it arrives in the visual association cortex, the pathway diverges into two streams which seem to have different functions:

◆ One terminates in the *parietal lobe* (the part of the brain just above the ears) and seems to provide information about visually guided movements. It probably allows people to detect the direction of moving targets, to judge the distance of approaching and retreating objects and to reach out and grab objects.

◆ The other one terminates in the *temporal lobe* (the part of the brain beneath the temples) and seems to provide information about the nature of the thing that is being observed, i.e. whether it is a dog, a chair, or a carrot; if it is something to be welcomed or feared, etc.

If either of these pathways is damaged, it causes severe problems for perception. Ramachandran and Blakeslee (1999) report on a recent study carried out by Kluver and Bucy. They removed the pathway in the temporal lobe from monkeys who were then able to walk around without bumping into one another or the walls of their cage (i.e. they still had spatial awareness), but who had real difficulties in recognizing objects and understanding their function. In the intact brain, these two pathways work in tandem and it is hard to separate out their contributions to the perceptual experience. It is possible, however, to devise experimental techniques to show that, even in neurologically normal individuals, the two systems sometimes work independently. Aglioti *et al.* (1994) made use of the size-contrast illusion to demonstrate this. Look at Fig. 8.4.

Although the central circles in Fig. 8.4 are identical in size, there is a powerful illusion that the one on the left is considerably larger. This illusion persists, even

when the observer is told that the two circles are the same. Instead of two-dimensional drawings, Aglioti and colleagues used physical objects (dominoes) to replicate this effect. They placed two equal-sized dominoes on a table and surrounded one of them with larger dominoes and the other one with smaller dominoes. In other words, they replicated the circles illusion with three-dimensional objects. An observer 'saw' the domino surrounded by smaller ones as significantly larger than the domino surrounded by larger ones, just as would be predicted. The observer was then asked to reach out and pick up first one central domino and then the other and he was filmed while doing so. If you reach out to pick up a small object, you will find that your thumb and forefinger are spaced in order to match the approximate size of the object. If the object is small like a grape, your finger and thumb will be close together, but if the object is larger like, for example, a slice of cake, your finger and thumb will be more widely spaced as they move towards it. Since the observer in this study clearly perceived one central domino to be larger than the other, it would be expected that his finger and thumb would be more widely spaced as he approached the 'larger' domino. Frame-by-frame analysis of the videotape, however, showed that the finger and thumb of the reaching hand moved apart exactly the same for each central domino, even though one had been 'seen' as larger. This suggests that the illusion is only experienced in the temporal pathway, but that it does not fool the parietal pathway.

Research into the nature of visual information processing

It is clear from the previous section that the visual system is not a passive recipient of visual input, but that it actively transforms the original stimulus input into a meaningful perceptual experience. One characteristic of all the sensory systems is the ability to adapt to a change in the environment. Sensory adaptation refers to a temporary decrease in sensitivity that occurs when a sensory system is exposed to a particular stimulus for a period of time and the temporary increase in sensitivity that occurs when a sensory system is not stimulated for a time. For example, if you dive into an unheated swimming pool, the water is likely to strike you as very cold at first, but after a while, your body adapts and you are said to have shifted to a new *adaptation level*. This means that you now have a new point of reference for cold/hot judgements. At this new adaptation level, an ice cube would now feel less cold on your skin than under normal conditions. Conversely, a cup with a hot drink would feel

Figure 8.4 Size-contrast illusion using circles

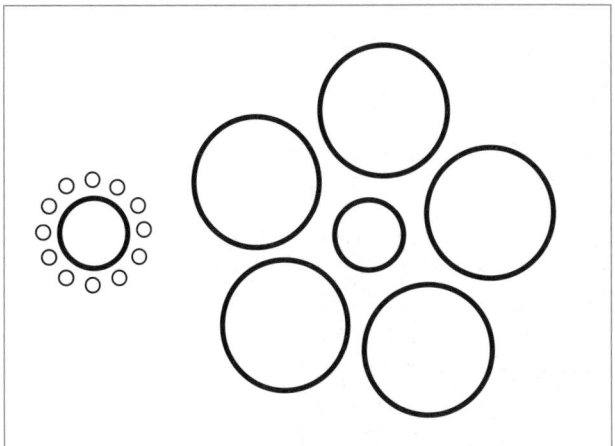

hotter in your hand than usual. However, once you get out of the pool and dry yourself off in the sun, your body will adapt to this warmer environment and so, you will reach a different adaptation level. Sensory adaptation appears to occur without conscious control and does not seem to depend on learning or experience. If you go back into the water after an hour of sunbathing, your body will go through the same process of adaptation and will take about the same length of time. Sensory adaptation probably has evolutionary significance – once stimuli have been observed and recognized as posing no threat, they are of less significance for survival and need less attention. This means that sensory systems can be alert to changes in the environment.

One example of sensory adaptation in vision occurs when the visual system has to adjust to a sudden change in conditions from light to dark. Many motorists find driving in twilight conditions quite difficult because, although both rods and cones are operating, neither is operating at full effectiveness. It is even more difficult to cope if the change from light to darkness occurs more suddenly as, for example, when you go into a dark cinema from the brightly lit foyer. In these circumstances, you feel that you are groping for a seat without really being able to see where you are going. After a few minutes, your eyes become accustomed to the dark conditions (dark adaptation) and you are able to see other people in the cinema even though the lighting conditions have not changed. Similarly, if you come in from the dark into a bright room, you often squint or even shut your eyes briefly while they adjust to the change in light intensity. This is called *light adaptation* and usually occurs more quickly than *dark adaptation*.

Both kinds of photoreceptors contain *photopigments*, which each consist of a molecule derived from vitamin A and a protein molecule. When struck by a particle of light (a photon), photopigments split into their two constituent molecules. This splitting marks the beginning of the process of transduction whereby light is changed into a neural response. Intact photopigments have a characteristic colour – for example, the photopigment rhodopsin is a pinkish-red. Once the action of light causes the photopigment to split, the colour breaks down and becomes bleached. The molecules rapidly recombine so that the photopigment is ready to be bleached again. Each photoreceptor cell contains thousands of molecules of photopigment, but the number of unbleached molecules present at any one moment depends on the relative rate at which they are being split by incoming photons and then re-combined. The number of bleached molecules increases the brighter the light because there are so many photons striking the

photopigments. In very bright conditions, the rate of recombination of the molecules lags behind the rate of the bleaching process so that very few intact photopigment molecules remain. If you then go into a room with very dim levels of light, the likelihood of a photon striking an intact photopigment is very low. However, after a while, the regeneration of the photopigment overcomes the effects of the bleaching and the rods become full of unbleached rhodopsin so that incoming photons are much more likely to find an intact target. This is the process of dark adaptation.

Activity 3: Demonstration of dark adaptation

To demonstrate dark adaptation, carefully blindfold one eye by taping a pad of soft cloth over it. Wait for about 30 minutes and then go into a darkened room. Take the blindfold off and compare the performance of your two eyes by alternately shutting one eye at time. You will find that the dark-adapted eye can see quite well in the gloomy conditions, but that the other eye will be almost blind at first.

Contrast processing

In order to be able to see clearly, it is important to have visual acuity, i.e. the ability to discern fine detail. However, visual acuity is not enough for excellent vision. It is also important to be able to detect brightness differences as well. Visual contrast refers to the difference in brightness levels between adjoining areas. Brightness is not an actual quantity of light intensity, but rather, our impression of light intensity. You can see this by looking at Fig. 8.5.

You probably experience the central grey square in (a) to be the brightest although all four central squares are actually exactly the same. The brightness of the grey patch seems to depend on the difference between the contrasting regions so that it seems brighter the darker the background. This is known as the *simultaneous lightness contrast*. The physiological mechanism underlying simultaneous lightness contrast was first investigated by Hartline and colleagues (1956). They used the limulus or horseshoe crab because the make-up of its eye renders investigation easier than in the human eye. They monitored responses from a cell that is functionally similar to a human ganglion cell. Stimulation of the receptor attached to this cell caused increased activity in the cell, but this activity decreased if the researchers then illuminated another receptor located a short distance away. This suggested that illumination of neighbouring receptors inhibits the firing of the original receptor. They called this *lateral*

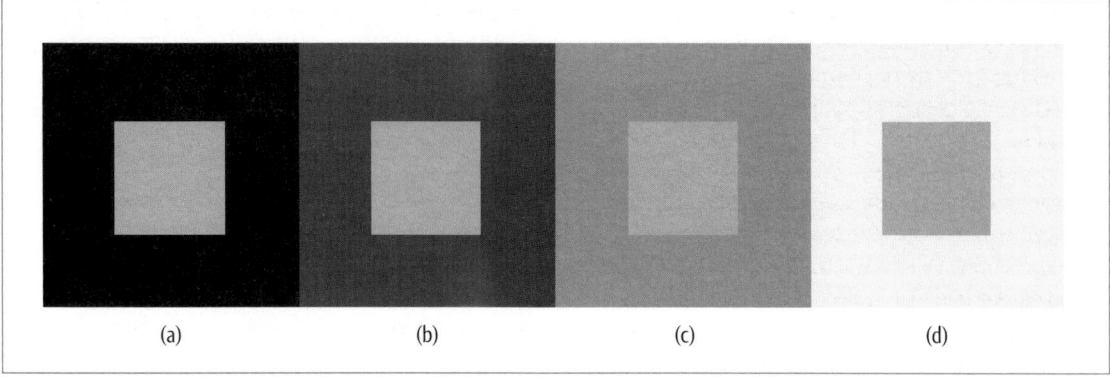

(a)   (b)   (c)   (d)

Figure 8.5 Demonstration of the simultaneous lightness contrast

inhibition because its effects seem to be transmitted laterally, or sideways, across the retina. The amount of inhibition depends on the strength of stimulation any one receptor is receiving. The more a cell is stimulated and the closer it is to an adjacent cell, the more it will inhibit the activity of the other. This explains the simultaneous contrast effect experienced when looking at Fig. 8.5. The receptors exposed to the central square in (d) are illuminated by a light of moderate intensity while the receptors exposed to the surround in (d) are stimulated by light of high intensity. Since the receptors exposed to the surround are more intensely stimulated, they exert strong inhibition on the receptors exposed to the central square. This reduces their neural response rate and causes the central square to appear dimmer. The receptors exposed to the dark surround in (a) are not exposed to light of high intensity and so their inhibitory effect on their neighbouring cells is not strong. Since there is only minimal inhibition, the receptors exposed to the central square are not turned down so fiercely as for the square in (d) and so it is perceived to be brighter. So, even though the two central squares in (a) and (d) reflect exactly the same amount of light into our eyes, the differences in the amount of inhibition they receive from their surrounds make them seem to differ in terms of brightness.

Colour processing

In physical terms, what we refer to as colour should strictly speaking be termed *hue*, i.e. the wavelength of light reflected from an object. People with normal colour vision are able to see light waves of various hues within the visible electromagnetic spectrum. The shortest wavelengths we can see are violet (400 nm) and the longest are red (700 nm). Hue alone cannot explain all our experience of colour because saturation is also a factor. Saturation refers to the purity or richness of a colour so that saturated hues seem to be vivid while desaturated hues look pastel or washed out. The average human observer can reliably discriminate among at least 200 different hues. We need to look at how this remarkable level of achievement comes about.

An early theory of colour processing was proposed by Thomas Young in 1802 and then modified by the German physiologist von Helmholtz (1896). They believed that the human eye contains three kinds of colour receptor, each sensitive to a different hue (red, green and blue) and that the brain combines information from all three receptors and is thus able to synthesize any colour. Yellow, for example is produced when red and green receptors are stimulated simultaneously and white is produced when all three receptor types are stimulated simultaneously. This is known as the *trichromatic theory*. There is some support for this theory and more recent studies have confirmed that there are three kinds of light-sensitive pigments in the cones. These do not correspond exactly to the Young–Helmholtz distinctions – one is primarily sensitive to wavelengths in the blue band, one is sensitive to green and the third is sensitive to the yellowish-red part of the spectrum – but they do confirm the existence of three types of cone. However, the Young–Helmholtz theory has not been able to account for some of the data from studies of colour-blindness. People with red/green colour-blindness have no difficulty in recognizing yellow, and yet trichromatic theory suggests that yellow perception is dependent on stimulation of red and green receptors. Hering in 1870 tried to address this problem. He believed that people tend to behave as if there are four and not three, primary colours and that yellow is seen alongside red, green and blue as a pure colour. This has been confirmed in later studies, e.g. Fuld *et al.* (1981). Hering noted that certain colour combinations, such as yellowish blue or greenish red are never reported and this led him to speculate that the four primary colours are arranged in opposing pairs. One opponent process would operate for red and green, while a separate opponent process would operate for yellow and blue. In other words, the activity of a single neuron would be increased by the presence of the colour red but decreased by green. Since it is impossible for a cell's activity to increase and decrease simultaneously, it would be impossible to experience reddish green. This so-called *opponent process theory* of colour vision was later formalized by Hurvich and Jameson (1957) who also postulated a black–white opponent process to account for brightness perception. When Hering first proposed the opponent process theory, there was no neurological support for his hypothesis. It is now known that cells with this pattern of activity occur in the retinal ganglion cells and in cells within the lateral geniculate. Opponent process theory also accounts for the afterimage effect you experience if you stare at a coloured patch for a period of time and then look at a blank sheet of white paper. You will tend to see an afterimage of the same patch, but in its opponent colour.

It seems that colour vision is at least a two-stage process incorporating elements of both these early theories. The retina contains three types of cones which respond differentially to lights of different wavelengths. Certain cells further along the visual system respond with a burst of impulses when stimulated by short wavelengths, but are inhibited when stimulated by long wavelengths, while, for other cells, it is the other way round. This suggests an opponent process operating at this level. It seems likely, in the future, that elements of the trichromatic and the opponent-process theories will be synthesized to form a new, comprehensive theory of colour vision, but, as yet, there is no satisfactory complete explanation

Feature processing

Brightness and colour are obviously important characteristics of human vision, but we also need to be able to detect contours in order to be able to recognize objects in our perceptual world. Contours can be curved or straight and can be oriented in various directions, e.g. vertical, horizontal, angled upwards, etc. Hubel and Wiesel (1959), who were pioneers in the field of single-cell recording studies in the brain, traced the path of neurons from the receptors in the retina through the ganglion cells and into the visual cortex. They identified several types of cell in the visual cortex which appear to respond to lines and edges of particular orientations. They called these *simple cells, complex cells* and *hypercomplex cells*. A simple cell responds to a line or straight edge in a particular orientation and which falls on a specific part of the retina. This cell will cease to fire if the line is tilted out of its orientation or is moved so that its image falls on a different part of the retina (see Fig. 8.6).

Complex cells also respond to a line in a particular orientation, but will continue to fire if the line moves (provided it maintains its orientation). Hypercomplex cells respond to lines in a particular orientation and of a particular length. Because these cells respond to particular lines and edges, they are called *feature detectors*. More recent research (e.g. DeValois and

DeValois 1980, Shapley and Lennie 1985 has found feature detectors that respond to corners and angles.

Exam summary: The visual system

The AQA examination will test your understanding of the following areas:

◆ the structure of the visual system (pp. 186–9)

◆ the functions of the visual system (pp. 186–9)

◆ research into the nature of visual information processing (pp. 189–92).

Example question

The question below is typical of one drawn from the material above, and should take you 30 minutes to answer.

◆ Describe and evaluate research into visual information processing.   *(24 marks)*

Suggested answer structure

It is one of the comforting aspects of this specification that questions frequently make use of the same phrases and terms as the specification entry. This is a case in

Figure 8.6 Feature detectors
This shows the response of a single cell in the visual cortex to a bar of light. There is no response to a horizontal bar, a slight response to a bar tilted at 45°, but a very strong response to the vertical bar, to which this cell is maximally responsive. *Source:* Hubel (1963)

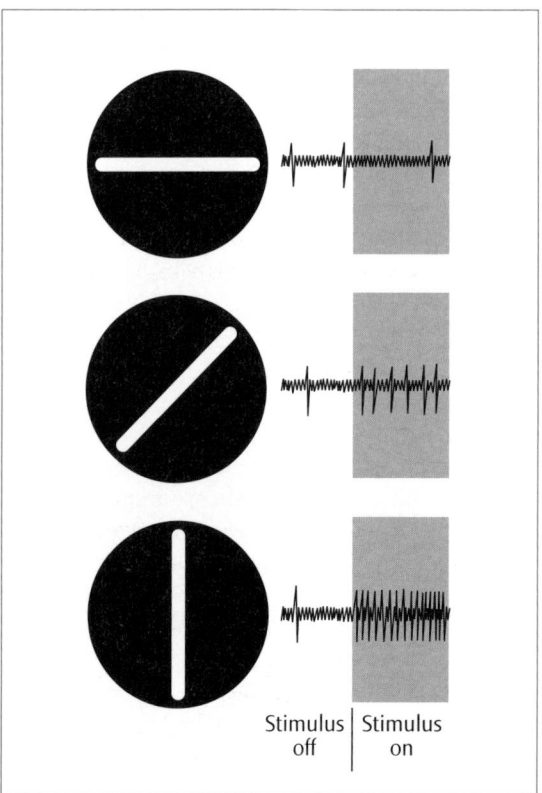

Stimulus off	Stimulus on

point, as the specification uses the same words as the question given here. The specification also gives *examples* of appropriate areas of visual information processing research. This includes research into sensory adaptation (covered on pp. 189–90), contrast processing (covered on pp. 190–1), colour processing (covered on pp. 191–2) and feature processing (covered on p. 192).

The question does not specify how many of these areas you should cover, nor which ones. This latter point is an important one. Specification entries that are preceded by the words *for example* (or e.g.) are merely illustrative, and give you some idea of the *type* of research that would be suitable for this question. As for how many of these areas you would cover, that is very much up to you. Look again at the marking criteria in Table 21.4 on p. 558. You will see there that for the higher mark bands, answers must be *well detailed*, with evidence of breadth *and* depth (for AO1) and with *informed and effective* commentary (for AO2). Given the constraints of a 30-minute question, it is doubtful that

you could manage this degree of detail and effective commentary if you included all four research areas. By the same token, your answer may lack a certain degree of breadth if you stick to just one area (such as colour processing). The question can be answered perfectly well by including just two of these research areas. This would be a suitable compromise between the depth and breadth required by the question.

There is one more helpful gesture from AQA with regard to questions of this type. Note that the question makes reference to *research* rather than research *studies*. This is an important distinction. The AQA *Glossary of Terms* (see Table 21.2 on p. 552) defines *research* as follows:

'The process of gaining knowledge and understanding either through theory construction and examination, or through empirical data collection.'

This allows you to discuss insights from *theories* (or other explanations) of visual information processing as well as the empirical research studies. *Research*, when used in this context, is a very friendly term!

Perceptual organization

So far in this chapter, we have been looking at the physiological mechanisms underlying perception and these are clearly very important. Damage or disease at any point in the visual system can cause severe problems for perception. A clouded lens (*cataract*), for example, can cause blindness while damage to other parts of the brain can result in visual *agnosias* in which individuals have difficulty in recognizing objects. While appreciating the crucial contribution of physiological research, cognitive psychologists have been more interested in investigating the psychological processes involved in perception. In other words, how do we make sense of the myriad of visual stimuli that bombard the sensory system? How do we recognize objects and how do we understand the spatial relationships between them?

Theories of perception tend to fall into two categories:

◆ bottom-up theories

◆ top-down theories.

These terms derive from the information processing approach – a theoretical perspective within cognitive psychology in which the human mind is compared to a computer. According to this view, the human mind manipulates and transforms information through a series of processing stages and these can be represented schematically in flow diagrams which show the direction of the flow of information through the system (see Fig. 8.7).

Bottom-up theories are based on the assumption that the process of perception begins with the physical properties of visual stimuli, e.g. patterns of light reflected from objects in the environment. It is thought that there is sufficient information in the sensory stimulus to allow the individual to make sense of his or her environment without the involvement of stored knowledge or problem-solving skills. The incoming information triggers a response in the retina, which in turn triggers a response higher up in the visual pathways and so on. Bottom-up processing, then, is concerned with physiological processing from the

Figure 8.7 A simple flow diagram to represent processing stages

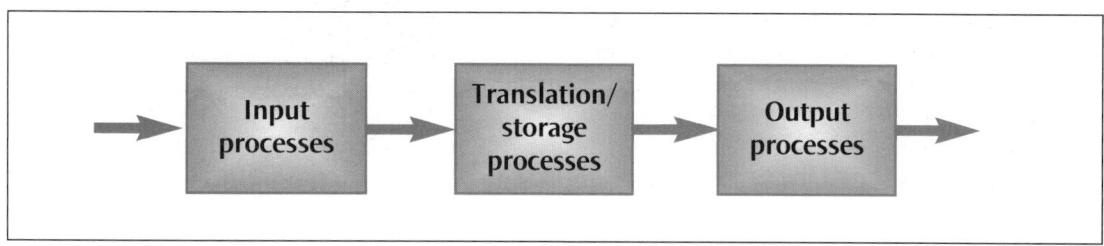

senses, processed upwards in the direction of the cognitive system. Theories based on this are sometimes also known as *data-driven* because the data (sensory input) received by the sensory receptors determines or 'drives' perception. Direct theories of perception are based on bottom-up processing.

Top-down theories, on the other hand, emphasize the involvement of context and prior knowledge in interpreting information derived from the sensory system. This approach stresses the importance of higher cognitive processing right from the beginning of the perceptual process. This kind of processing is also called *concept-driven processing* because prior knowledge (stored mental concepts) determines (drives) the interpretation of the sensory data. Constructivist theories of perception are based on top-down processing.

These two types of processing are not mutually exclusive and it seems likely that we use both in our everyday life. The particular kind of processing used will probably depend on the nature of the visual stimulus. Palmer (1975) carried out a study which demonstrates the way in which bottom-up and top-down processes interact. Look at Fig. 7.14 (a) on p. 179. In themselves the drawings consist of little more than lines on the page. Palmer found that participants in his study were usually unable to recognize the objects depicted in them.

However, when he showed the participants the drawing shown in Fig. 7.14 (b) , they were easily able to identify the same 'squiggles' as facial features because they were embedded in a face. In Fig. 7.14 (a), there is very little information available to us in the actual stimulus and there is no context to help us – we have to rely completely on bottom-up processing. In Fig. 7.14 (b), however, we can use both bottom-up and top-down processing – the facial features remain exactly the same (bottom-up), but now we have the context of a surrounding face (top-down) and so we have no difficulty in identifying the whole face and its constituent parts.

Direct theories of perception

According to these theories, the array of information in our sensory receptors is all that we need in order to perceive and there is no necessity to call upon stored knowledge or past experience to mediate between sensory experience and perception.

Gibson's theory of direct perception

J.J. Gibson (1950, 1966, 1979) is the best known champion of direct perception. He defined direct perception as follows:

'Saying perception of the environment is direct means it is not mediated by retinal pictures, neural pictures, or mental pictures. Direct perception is the activity of getting information from the ambient array of light.' (Gibson 1979, p.147)

Gibson felt strongly that it was important to study perception in real-world environments instead of in the artificial surroundings of a laboratory and, for this reason, he sometimes referred to his theory as an 'ecological approach'. For example, during World War II, he was concerned with developing training programmes for pilots. One of the most difficult tasks for a pilot is to land the plane and, to accomplish this successfully, he or she requires good depth perception. However, Gibson found that traditional training measures designed to help pilots make use of depth information were of little use. This finding led him to review contemporary ideas of perception and to formulate his own theory. Gibson's theory is complex and was developed over a period of more than 30 years so we can only offer a simplified version here. According to Goldstein (1999), the theory is based on four major assumptions:

- the pattern of light reaching the eye can be thought of as an *optic array* and contains all the information necessary for perception

- important information is provided by the *movement* of the observer

- the optic array contains *invariant information*, i.e. information that remains constant as the observer moves

- this invariant information leads directly to *perception*.

The optic array

Gibson believed that the starting point for perception is the structure of the light that reaches the observer. Light alone is insufficient for perception to occur – as you will see if you try Activity 4.

To perceive objects, then, rather than blank nothingness, the light has to be structured by the presence of objects, surfaces and textures (the optic array). The structure is immensely complex because there are rays of light converging on the observer from every part of the surrounding environment and, furthermore, this structure will change every time the observer moves. Look at the person shown in Fig. 8.8.

The person sitting at the desk can perceive the objects, surfaces and textures in the scene because of the way the light rays (solid lines) reaching him are structured by those objects, surfaces and textures. If the observer stands up, the structure of the light rays changes (dotted lines), so that the whole optic array is transformed, thus providing new information for the observer about the environment.

Activity 4: Create your own Ganzfeld

A Ganzfeld is a visual field that consists of diffuse, unstructured light, i.e. there are no luminance changes and so no contours. You can create your own Ganzfeld quite simply. First, look towards a light source (e.g. a table lamp), then take two white plastic spoons and, holding the handles out to the side, place the bowl of a spoon over each eye. Stay like this for a couple of minutes and register any changes in your conscious perceptual experience. Your field of view will initially be flooded with unstructured light, but, if the light originally had a tint, you will probably find that the colour fades and takes on a greyish look. After a while, you will feel that you cannot see at all. This is similar to the experience of snow blindness, which can afflict people in polar regions where the environment contains nothing but snow and ice. If you ask a friend to move something in front of your eyes, however, you will find that vision will recur, because structure has been introduced.

The importance of movement

As the example in Fig. 8.8 shows, the optic array changes as we move around. If you think about it, most of our perception occurs as we move relative to our environment. Even if we are not actually walking, running, driving, etc., we move our eyes and heads in order to observe things going on around us. Gibson was particularly interested in describing elements in the optic array that convey information to the moving observer. According to Gibson, this information remains invariant regardless of the movements of the observer.

Figure 8.8 The optic array and how it is transformed by movement
Source: Gibson (1966)

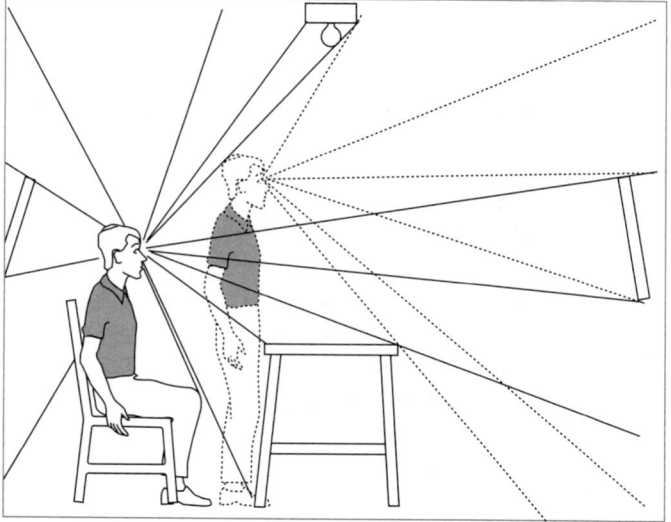

Invariant information

There are various sources of invariant information available to the observer. We will look at three of these sources:

1 *Texture gradient* is of fundamental importance in Gibson's theory. According to Gibson, our perceptual world is made up of surfaces of different textures, and these textures can be used to aid the perception of depth and orientation. A visual texture can be broadly defined as a collection of objects in the visual field, and the gradient refers to the change in the relative size and compactness of these object elements. Look at Fig. 8.9 on p. 196.

Figure 8.9 (a) has a uniform texture and so appears like a representation of something flat like, for example, an upright garage door. In Fig. 8.9 (b), however, the compacted lines at the top of the picture give the impression of depth, perhaps of some decking stretching out in front of us. There is an even stronger impression of depth when the gradient appears in both the horizontal and vertical placing of the object elements as in Fig. 8.9 (c). To understand why Gibson describes texture gradient as an invariant, try to imagine walking along a wide expanse of deserted beach. As you set out on your walk, there may be several depth cues available to you. For example, there may be two breakwaters up ahead and the image of one cuts off part of the other (the cue of overlap – see p. 200). This provides depth and distance information in that you will realize that the 'whole' breakwater is nearer to you than the partially obscured one. You will also have the cue of texture gradient, in that pebbles in the distance will look smaller and more densely packed than pebbles at your feet. As you walk closer to the first breakwater, however, the cue of overlap will disappear and, you will be left just with the cue of texture gradient provided by the pebbles on the beach, which will remain for as long as you are on the beach. So, while some depth cues, such as overlap, cease to provide information if the observer changes his or her position, the information from texture gradient remains invariant.

In addition to providing information about depth and distance, texture gradient also indicates the orientations of surfaces. Sudden changes in the texture often signal a change in the direction of a surface. Figure 8.10, for example, shows how the gradient change indicates a shift from floor to upright wall.

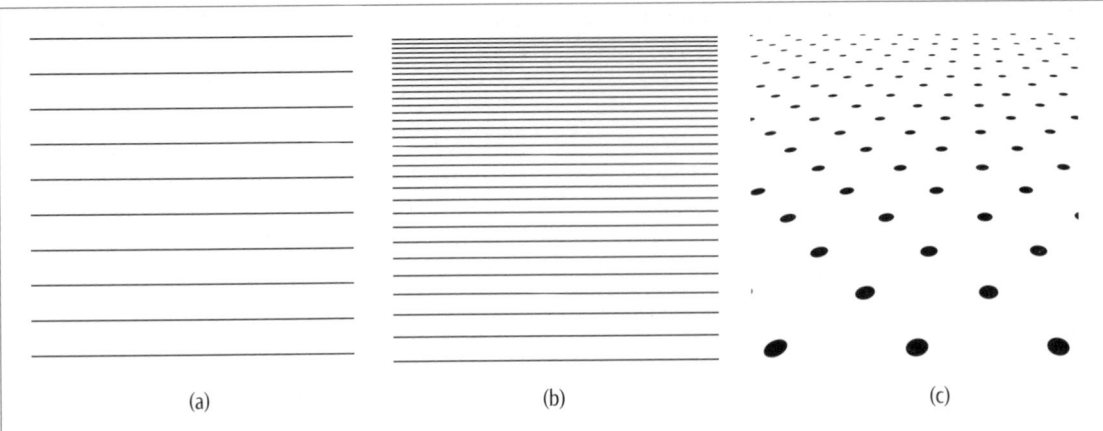

(a)   (b)   (c)

Figure 8.9 Texture gradient

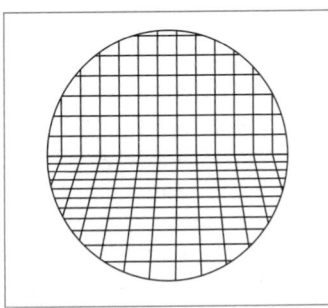

Figure 8.10
Change in texture gradient, showing, for example, a change from floor to wall

2   *Horizon ratio* is another perceptual invariant and refers to the fact that all objects of the same height, whatever their distance from the observer, are cut by the horizon in the same ratio. Objects of different sizes, but at the same distance from the observer, however, have different horizon ratios – see Fig. 8.11. Although the size of the tree may become larger as an observer approaches it, the proportion of the tree that is above or below the horizon will remain the same.

3   *Flow patterns* are created as objects in the visual environment flow past a moving observer. The nature of the flow provides information to the observer about position and depth. Consider how it feels to be the driver or front passenger in a car going along a straight road like a motorway. You are faced with an expanding visual field in which elements that begin in the middle of the visual field pass around you as you move forward. For example, a motorway sign, first seen as a distant spot on the horizon, eventually passes to the left of you as you drive forward; a petrol station seen up ahead actually turns out to be on the other carriageway and will pass you on the right hand side as you advance; a flyover will pass right over your head. If you sit in the back seat of the car and look out of the rear window, the situation will be reversed and you will be faced with a contracting flow field. The sign you have just passed on the right will shift towards the centre of the field as it fades into the distance. So, the nature of the flow field – i.e. expanding or contracting – will provide information to the observer about whether

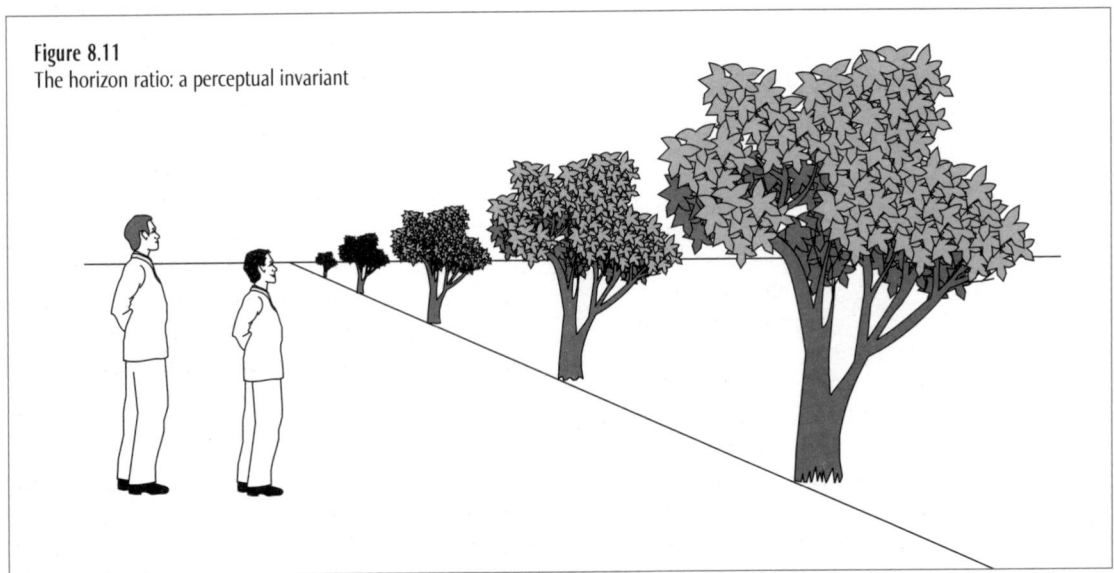

Figure 8.11
The horizon ratio: a perceptual invariant

they are moving forward or backwards. Looking out of the side window of a car will produce yet another type of optic flow pattern. Objects close to the observer, such as fence posts, appear to be moving very fast in a backwards direction, while objects further away (e.g. trees on the horizon) appear to be moving much more slowly and in a forwards direction (motion parallax).

Gibson was particularly interested in the role of optic flow patterns (OFPs) for pilots when landing aircraft. He believed that they provided unambiguous information about the direction, speed and altitude of the plane.

Direct perception

We have looked at the way in which Gibson has sought to explain our ability to understand depth and spatial relationships between objects in the environment, but have not yet explored his ideas about how we attach meaning to what we see. How is it, for example, that we know that the object we are looking at is something to eat, sit on, grasp, etc.? Gibson rejected the notion of top-down processing and suggested, instead, that the uses of objects are perceived directly. All objects in the world have behavioural significance for animals and humans. They offer (afford) certain responses to be made so a door handle affords turning, a chair affords sitting, a bed affords lying down. The *affordance* of an object depends on the particular circumstances in which it is encountered. For example, a chair affords 'sitting down' if you are tired, but 'stepping on' if you want to reach a book on the top shelf. The same object can offer different affordances for different species. For example, a washing line affords hanging out clothes for a human, but perching for a bird.

Evaluation of Gibson's theory

Gibson's theory has attracted considerable criticism, but it has stimulated useful debate in the field of visual perception. His insistence on studying perception in the real environment has shown that traditional laboratory methods have underestimated the richness of information available in the stimulus input. In particular, he has shown how important it is to take into account the movement of the observer. Gibsonian principles have been successfully applied to real-life situations. His work with training programmes for pilots has already been mentioned and airports are now constructed with the best possible lighting and markings to enhance optical flow patterns for incoming pilots. Another practical application can be seen on approach roads to busy roundabouts where a set of parallel lines is painted on the road surface. The lines are painted closer and closer together as the road

approaches the roundabout so that the driver gets the erroneous impression that they are accelerating. Without being given explicit instructions to do so, drivers tend to slow down automatically. As Hampson and Morris (1996) have pointed out, this traffic control technique changes perception by changing the structure of the perceived world, not by appealing to internal perceptual or cognitive mechanisms with a 'Reduce Speed' sign.

However, there are problems with the theory. Gibson emphasized the importance of interaction with the environment and this is undoubtedly a crucial aspect of perception, but his notion of affordance is seen as a weakness in his theory. Bruce and Green (1990) have suggested that the concept of affordance may be able to account for the visually guided behaviour of insects which have no need for a conceptual representation of the environment, but that this an inadequate explanation for human perception. Humans function in an environment where knowledge about objects and their uses are influenced by cultural expectation and values.

Another difficulty for the theory concerns visual illusions (see p. 203). These are situations where an observer's perception of a stimulus does not correspond to the physical properties of the stimulus and so demonstrate that perception can sometimes be inaccurate. Gibson believed that studies based on the perception of illusions are carried out in highly artificial laboratory conditions and so have little relevance to real-life situations. However, in spite of the artificiality of some of the studies, visual illusions remain a phenomenon of perception which need to be explained and Gibson has been unable to provide an adequate account.

In spite of the criticisms, there has been a recent revival of interest in his theory from cognitive psychologists. Greeno (1994), for example, has been developing an approach called *situation theory* which makes use of some of Gibson's ideas. There has also been some support from studies which suggest that there may be some underlying physiological mechanisms which could account for certain aspects of direct perception. For example, neurons have been identified which learn from visual experience to perceive specific forms (Logothetis and Pauls 1995) and others have been identified which might account for our ability to perceive constancies (Tovee *et al.* 1994) (see pp. 202–3 for psychological explanations of constancies).

Constructivist theories

A much older, but still current, approach to perception is found in the *constructivist* theories. The theories are so called because of their emphasis on the combination of several sources of information required to build or construct our conscious perception of the visual world. They originated with the German psychologist, Helmholtz (1821–94) and survive in the work of researchers such as Rock (1983) and Gregory (1980). This approach equates perception with a logical process like reasoning. In addition to the information available in the sensory stimulus, we need to use higher cognitive processes to interpret it appropriately. Look at Fig. 7.15 on p. 179) and read the message. Then read the paragraphs above it, starting at 'Try reading the sentence in Fig. 7.15'.

You were not conscious of having to solve a problem when you read this sentence, but at some level, you were applying problem-solving strategies to this ambiguous piece of handwriting. So, you know that 'class' is an English word and, moreover, that it fits appropriately into this sentence frame. You also know that there is no such word as 'dass', so you automatically read the word correctly. Although it is recognized by constructivists that much of the top-down processing that occurs in perception is unconscious, it is still considered an indirect process because information cannot be picked up directly from the stimulus input, as Gibson suggested. It is a central tenet of constructivist theories that successful perception requires intelligence and reasoning in combining sensory information with knowledge based on previous experience. For this reason, it is sometimes referred to as *intelligent perception*.

Allport (1955) introduced the concept of perceptual set, which is also influenced by top-down processes and refers to the expectancies or predispositions that an observer brings to a perceptual situation. Carry out Activity 5 now.

An experimental study which examined the effects of perceptual set was carried out by Palmer (1975). He presented a picture of a familiar scene like the one in Fig. 8.12. He then briefly flashed a picture of one of the

Activity 5: Seeing what we expect to see

Look at the extract of an article below and read aloud the emboldened words in the centre.

counters, CDC tabulates a prevalence rate of 5% giving a total of between 125,000 and 375,000 additional men positive for HIV.

The AIDS epidemic continues to focus on the the established risk groups.

Users of intravenous drugs are the second largest group of HIV-infected individuals, and the one that gives public health workers

Did you miss the fact that the word 'the' appeared twice before 'established'? This is an easy mistake to make – even the proof-reader for the highly respected journal in which this mistake appeared missed it. We tend to read what we expect to be there and often pay little attention to words like 'the'.

objects – A, B or C – and asked participants to identify it. Participants were much more successful at identifying the picture that fitted the context, i.e. picture A, than either of the other two. Exposure to the first picture seemed to prime them to expect an object compatible with a kitchen scene.

Gregory's theory of perception

Although a constructivist, Gregory acknowledges the contribution made by Gibson to our understanding of perception. In particular, he appreciated the importance of cues such as texture gradient and motion parallax. However, he is not able to accept Gibson's key assertion that perception occurs directly without any intervention from higher cognitive processes. Gregory maintains that our perceptual representation of the world around us is much richer and

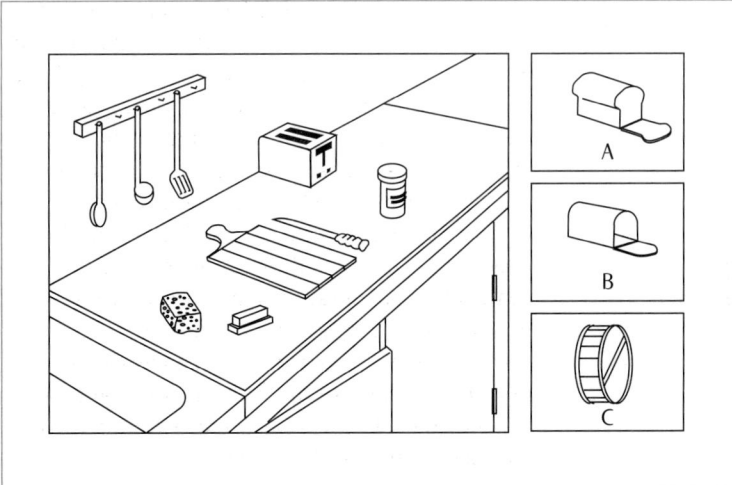

Figure 8.12
The effects of contextual scene on the identification of objects
Source: Palmer (1975)

more detailed than might be expected if we were simply relying on the information contained in the visual stimulus. We are often presented with degraded and ambiguous stimuli which lack detailed information and yet we usually manage to make sense of them. Gregory suggests that we use visual stimuli as a starting point for making informed guesses about their meaning. He explains this idea as follows:

> 'Perception is not determined simply by the stimulus patterns; rather it is a dynamic searching for the best interpretation of the available data. The data are sensory signals, and also knowledge of the many characteristics of objects ... It seems clear that perception involves going beyond the immediately given evidence of the senses: the evidence is assessed on many grounds and generally we make the best bet, and see things more or less correctly. But the senses do not give us a picture of the world directly; rather they provide evidence for the checking of hypotheses about what lies before us. Indeed, we may say that the perception of an object is an hypothesis, suggested and tested by the sensory data.' (Gregory 1990, p.13)

To illustrate this approach, look at the figure called the Necker cube in Fig. 8.13.

You will have no difficulty in identifying a cube, but, if you stare at it for long enough, you will find that the cube seems to pop in and out and you cannot stop it happening. Gregory explains this in terms of hypothesis testing. The figure is ambiguous, i.e. the small circle could be on the inside back wall of the cube or the bottom left-hand corner of the front face of the cube. In other words, the picture could depict a cube resting on a flat surface or a cube mounted against a wall. Gregory believes that we test first one hypothesis and then the other and, because there is no surrounding context to tell us which interpretation is correct, we switch between the two. In the real visual world, Gregory believes that there are usually enough contextual clues

Figure 8.13 The Necker Cube

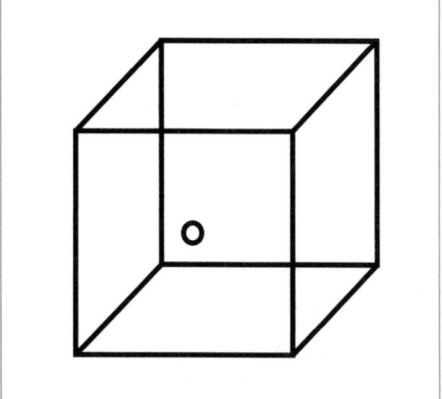

to remove ambiguity and to allow us to confirm a single hypothesis.

One of the consequences of the assumption that perception involves hypothesis testing is that we will sometimes make errors. Gregory has been particularly interested in perceptual errors and we will return to his views when we consider visual illusions on p. 203.

Evaluation of constructivist theories

It seems clear that we often use top-down processes to help us make perceptual sense of our visual environment. However, there are some problems with a strong constructivist position. For example, there is an emphasis in constructivist theories on perceptual errors whereas, in fact, most people see the world accurately most of the time.

Gibson criticized the constructivist view because he felt that laboratory studies were highly artificial and did not reflect real-world perception. It is true that many of the studies that appear to support the constructivist position involve the presentation of ambiguous and fragmented information and, typically, as in Palmer's (1975) experiment, presentations are extremely brief. Under these circumstances, it would be very difficult to rely on bottom-up processing. It could be, then, that the effects of context and experience are magnified in constructivist studies because of the nature of the stimulus material and that they may not be so important in our normal rich visual environment.

It seems likely that we use a combination of information from the sensory input and from our past experience and knowledge.

Depth perception

Imagine that you are looking out of the window at a busy road. You will have no difficulty in seeing one lamp-post as nearby and one on the other side of the road as being further away, nor of understanding that the space between the two has depth. How do we achieve this three-dimensional experience when the image falling on our retina is flat and two-dimensional? We have already seen how Gibson explained depth perception in terms of cues, such as texture gradient and motion parallax, picked up from the optic flow. Other psychologists have also seen the importance of cues and have identified a number of different types. Whereas direct perception theorists believe that these cues are picked up directly from the visual array, constructivists would suggest that they are learned through past experience with objects around us. It is likely that both views are tenable. It is possible, for example, that we have an innate ability to make use of depth cues, but that we learn through experience to use them more rapidly and efficiently.

Some depth cues are based on the fact that each eye receives a slightly different view of the scene in front of us. These are called *binocular depth cues*. Other cues seem to be effective even when one eye is closed and these are called *monocular cues*.

Binocular depth cues

Binocular depth cues include:

♦ *Convergence* – When you rotate your eyes so that the image of an object straight in front of you falls directly on the fovea, each eye has to turn inwards slightly. The closer the object, the more the eyes have to turn. Feedback from the eye muscles helps us to determine the distance of objects.

♦ *Binocular disparity* – This refers to the slight discrepancy in the viewpoint of each eye. You can demonstrate this by doing Activity 6. The process by which these disparate views is merged into a single percept is called *fusion*. The closer the object is to the viewer, the greater the disparity between the two images presented to each eye.

Activity 6: The process of fusion

Hold a pen or pencil with the tip pointing towards you and angled slightly downwards towards your nose. Now close each eye in turn and you will find that the pen seems to jump. With both eyes open, the image is fused and you see a pen straight ahead of you.

Monocular cues

There are several monocular cues and, because they are frequently used by artists to imply depth in paintings, they are also called *pictorial cues*. They are listed below:

♦ Overlap – When one object partially blocks the view of another, the blocked object is perceived to be further away.

♦ Linear perspective – Parallel lines, such as those at the side of a road or a railway appear to converge in the distance.

♦ Relative height – Objects with their bases below the horizon are seen as more distant if they are higher in the visual plane (see, for example, the trees in Fig. 8.11); objects above the horizon are seen as more distant if they are lower in the visual field.

♦ Relative size – As an object moves further away, its retinal image diminishes in size. Smaller objects, therefore, are perceived to be further away.

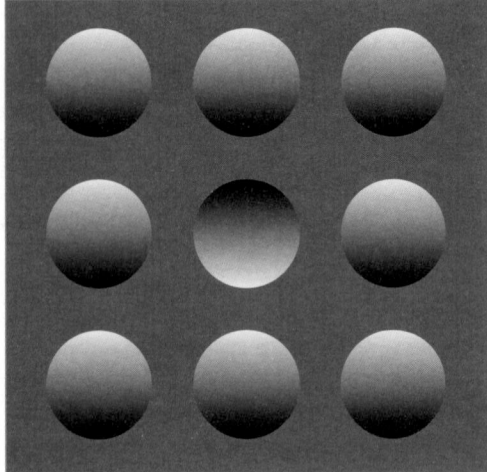

Figure 8.14
Shading gives the impression of dents or bumps. The circle in the middle appears to be a dent, while the other eight circles all appear to be bumps. If you turn this page upside down, you will find the shadow pattern is reversed.

♦ Aerial perspective – The image of a very distant object, e.g. a mountain in the distance, will appear slightly bluer in hue and less distinct than closer objects.

♦ Shadowing – Light usually travels in straight lines. This means that surfaces facing a light source will be relatively bright and surfaces away from the light source will be in shadow (see Fig. 8.14).

♦ Texture gradient – A change in the relative size and density of objects when viewed from different distances, e.g. pebbles on the beach look smaller and more closely packed the further away they are.

There is one further monocular depth cue, but this cannot be conveyed in pictures and so is not called a pictorial cue. Motion parallax is a cue that depends on movement. If you are sitting on a train looking out of the window, you will have the feeling that objects close to the track are moving very swiftly in the opposite direction, and that objects in the distance are moving much more slowly and in the same direction as you.

None of these cues are particularly strong on their own, but, in combination, they can provide powerful cues to depth and distance.

Perceiving movement

We take it for granted that we can perceive movement, so you probably cannot imagine what it would be like not to be able to do so. See *In Focus* for an account of a patient who suffers from *motion agnosia* (i.e. an inability to perceive motion).

Motion agnosia

This is an account of a female patient who was admitted to hospital with damage to part of her cerebral cortex that is known to be associated with the perception of movement.

'She had difficulty, for example, in pouring tea or coffee into a cup because the fluid appeared to be frozen, like a glacier. In addition, she could not stop pouring at the right time since she was unable to perceive the movement in the cup when the fluid rose. Furthermore, the patient complained of difficulties in following a dialogue because she could not see the movements of the face, and, especially, the mouth of the speaker. In a room where more than two people were walking she felt very insecure and unwell, and usually left the room immediately, because "people were suddenly here or there but I have not seen them moving." The patient ... could not cross the street because of her inability to judge the speed of a car, but she could identify the car itself without difficulty. "When I'm looking at the car at first, it seems far away. But then, when I want to cross the road, suddenly the car is very near."'
(Zihl *et al.* 1983, p. 315)

You can see from the *In Focus* just how important the perception of movement is for our everyday functioning, even though we take it for granted. Motion perception can also help us to draw inferences about form and pattern that cannot be picked up from static objects. Johannson (1975), for example, used actors dressed completely in black clothes and attached about ten small lights to key points on their bodies, e.g. wrists, ankles, elbows, hips. (He called them *point light walkers*.) He then filmed them in a darkened room so that only the lights were visible. When the actors remained stationary, observers reported seeing only a meaningless, two-dimensional pattern of lights. However, as soon as the actors began to walk or run, observers instantly recognized the movement as being produced by a moving person. Recent research using positron emission tomography (PET) has shown that there is an increase in activity in the human superior temporal sulcus when observers are presented with point light walkers (Bonda *et al.* 1996).

There is now a considerable body of research that has investigated the neural mechanisms underlying motion perception, but in this section, we are concentrating on psychological explanations. We will look at two factors that affect movement perception:

◆ environmental information

◆ the effect of context.

Environmental information

Gibson, as we have already seen, believed that environmental information provides the basis for perception. He identified two factors which are important in recognizing movement:

◆ *Local movement signal* – This occurs when a certain object moves in the environment while other objects remain stationary. Imagine that you are sitting on a quiet river-bank looking straight ahead at a house on the other side. A boat comes into view and sails past you, from left to right, providing a local movement signal by temporarily covering and uncovering parts of the distant (stationary) house. If you avert your attention from the house and start to follow the boat with your eyes, you will continue to receive a local movement signal. In this case, the crucial information for movement perception is still the local motion of the boat relative to its background. Although the boat will now remain as a stationary image on your retina, you will experience the background as moving from right to left. This means that the boat will continue to cover and uncover different parts of the background.

◆ *Global optic flow* – This occurs when the observer him or herself is moving – under these conditions, everything in the visual environment moves as well. Imagine that you get up from your seat by the river and start to walk along the towpath. The images of all the visual stimuli around you (e.g. trees, boats, houses, etc.) will slide across your retina. According to Gibson, this information tells you that it is you who are moving and not the stationary objects in the background.

Gibson's explanation of movement perception seems quite plausible in situations where the environmental background is clearly visible. However, he could not account for the fact that, under certain circumstances, human observers perceive movement when there is no physical motion of the target and no background information (apparent motion). The autokinetic effect is a powerful illusion in which observers, viewing a stationary point of light in a darkened room, erroneously believe that the light is moving. Another illusion of movement is the *phi phenomenon*, which

A constructivist explanation of the phi phenomenon

According to the constructivist position or inference approach, the brain seems to be unwilling to accept that the disappearance of one stimulus should be followed so swiftly by the sudden and, apparently unconnected, appearance of an identical stimulus in a nearby location. The most logical 'best guess', therefore, is that the first stimulus has moved to new location. In order to experience the phi phenomenon, it is important for the two stimuli to be at the appropriate critical distance from one another and for the timing to be at the critical interval. Rock (1995, p.196) explains this as follows:

'For apparent movement to be seen, the temporal interval between A and B must be neither too short nor too long. Although this fact has been known since apparent motion was first discovered, the reasons behind it have never been clear. The inference approach, however, may help to explain it. If the temporal interval is too brief, we tend to perceive both A and B simultaneously. This fact is based on the persistence of vision. If A is still visible when B appears, the perceptual system can hardly infer that A has moved to B! If the interval is too long, A must be inferred to be moving rather slowly across the intervening space. After all, the object must be assumed to be moving at a speed such that it reaches B just as B appears. If an object were to be moving slowly, it ought to be visible between A and B. Only at fast speeds does the perceptual system 'expect' the object to be little more than a blur between A and B. Therefore, if the speed is inferred to be slow and the object is invisible, the inference that the object is really moving is rejected.'

occurs when two small, adjacent lights are alternately turned on and off in a darkened room. An observer will not be aware that one light is turned off and another is turned on. Instead, there will be strong impression that a single light is on all the time and moving backwards and forward between the two positions. This effect is often used in neon sign displays to convey the impression of movement. The existence of such illusions shows that the perception of movement cannot always occur as Gibson suggested. See *In Focus* for a constructivist explanation of the phi phenomenon.

There are several studies which seem to support the idea of high-level cognitive processes being involved in the perception of apparent movement. For example, Berbaum and Lenel (1983) showed that, if they placed an object in the path of the apparent movement, observers would perceive the movement as being deflected around the barrier. Shepard and Zare (1983) found that they could induce the perceived motion of a curved pathway, if they first briefly flashed a curved path between two alternating stimuli, thereby setting up this expectation in observers.

Visual constancies

One remarkable aspect of perception is that our world remains stable in spite of the constantly changing image on our retinas as we move around, or dart our eyes about. If we took our retinal image at face value, objects and people would appear to shrink and grow as they moved towards or away from us; objects would change shape if we viewed them from different angles; and

colours would alter in response to different levels of illumination. The fact that we do not experience such wild fluctuations depends on the perceptual constancies.

Size constancy

Size constancy is the perception that an object stays the same size regardless of the size of the image on the retina. The same object will provide differently sized retinal images depending on the distance of that object from the observer. If you are talking to a friend, for example, and she then walks away from you down the road, her image will become smaller and smaller on your retina as she moves further away. You do not, however, believe that she is shrinking. According to constructivists, size constancy depends on past experience and stored knowledge. We know from experience that people do not grow and shrink rapidly in the real world so, when our retinal image of a familiar person is very small, we infer that she is standing at a distance from us. If the image starts to grow, we infer that she must be walking towards us. The cue of familiarity is obviously important, but it cannot be the only explanation because size constancy also seems to operate with unfamiliar objects.

Another suggestion is that we also make use of the cue of relative size. In other words, we always judge the size of one object in the context of its surroundings. If you look at the phone as you go to answer it, you will find its retinal image gets larger as you walk towards it. However, the table on which it stands will also get larger as will the phone book lying next to it, so the ratio of the various objects remains constant. Thus, objects appear to stay the same as we walk around because they maintain the same size relative to other objects around them.

This fits in with Gibson's view that all the information necessary for size constancy was located within the stimulus. In other words, he believed that we make use of invariants such as texture gradient to judge the size of objects. You can demonstrate his ideas for yourself if you can find a large paved or tiled area where the tiles are of equal size. Find two equally sized books or magazines and place them in a line at 1 m and at 5 m from your starting point. Return to your starting point and look ahead of you at the two books. The further one will form a smaller image on your retina, but it will cover exactly the same proportion of tile (i.e. the same number of texture units) as the nearer one. According to Gibson, this simple stimulus information will tell you that the two books are the same size without you needing to have recourse to higher level cognitive processes. It seems likely that size constancy depends on a mixture of these factors.

Shape constancy

Shape constancy is the ability to perceive objects as having a stable shape in spite of changes in orientation. Imagine looking at a door as someone opens it and comes into the room. The retinal image of the door will change from being a rectangle to a trapezoid as it swings open, and yet you will not think that the door is changing shape. Constructivists say that we depend on our past experience of doors opening and infer that it remains the same shape. According to direct theory, there is sufficient information in the background and in the unchanging texture elements on the door (wood-grain, panels, etc.), to recognize directly that we are looking at the same door. As usual, the direct theory

has difficulty in accounting for perceptual errors (see *In Focus*).

Lightness constancy

Lightness constancy means that we perceive an object as being evenly illuminated despite differences in the amount of light reaching our eyes. If you are reading from a book with black print on a white page, you do not experience the page turning from white to grey and yet there will probably be shading across various parts of the page because of the angle of lighting. Again, constructivists explain this in terms of our past experience with books whereas direct theorists explain it in terms of the relative illuminance of one object to another.

Colour constancy

Colour constancy refers to our ability to perceive an object as maintaining the same colour despite variations in the wavelength of the light falling on it. Constructivist theorists say that we use cues about the nature of the light falling on an object to allow us to make corrections for colour shifts. They also stress the importance of our stored knowledge about the objects in our environment – for example, we know that cherries are red and they will continue to appear red whatever the illumination. Direct perception explanations are quite complex, but are based largely on the ratio principle.

Visual illusions

We have seen in previous sections what complex mechanisms are involved in perception and yet, for most of the time, we maintain a remarkably stable view of the world and make very few perceptual errors.

---

in focus

Size constancy and shape constancy

Coren *et al.* (1999) give the following example of the close relationship between size and shape constancy, which is hard to explain in terms of direct perception. Look at the two shapes in Fig. 8.15 and consider the two box tops. Do you think they are the same shape? Now look at the two sides labelled (a) and (b). Which side is longer?

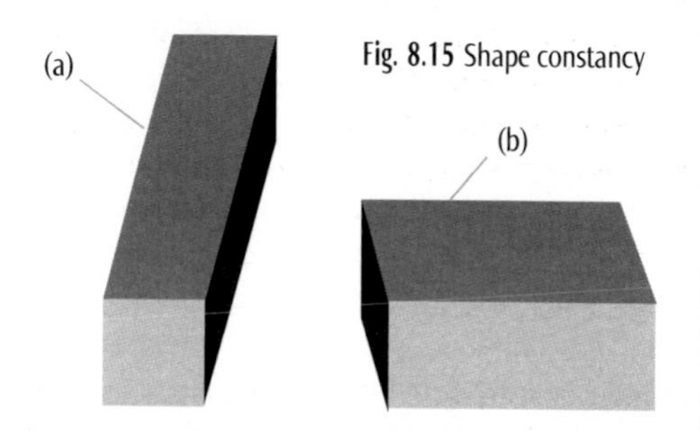

Fig. 8.15 Shape constancy

Now take a ruler and measure the two sides. You will probably be surprised to find that they are exactly the same length. If you were to trace the top of the box on the left and, after rotating it, place it on the top of the other box, you would also find that the shapes of the two tops were exactly the same.

Source: adapted from Coren *et al.* (1999, p. 338)

Veridical perception is the term for perception which matches the physical situation. It occurs when viewing conditions are good and there is rich and detailed information available in the environment. However, under poor viewing conditions, e.g. bad lighting or adverse weather conditions, we can make mistakes. Most of the illusions that have been studied by psychologists are artificial ones that have been devised specifically for experimental purposes so that investigators can uncover some of the reasons why we might misperceive in real-life situations. Gregory (1978) has taken a particular interest in perceptual illusions and has identified four major categories:

◆ *Ambiguous figures* – These are figures like the Necker cube (see p. 199) which can be interpreted in two equally plausible ways. In the absence of any contextual information to reduce the ambiguity, the brain switches backwards and forwards between the two. In other words, the same input results in two different perceptions.

◆ *Paradoxical figures* – these are figures which look perfectly normal at first glance, but which would be impossible to reproduce as a three-dimensional object, e.g. the Penrose triangle in Fig. 8.16.

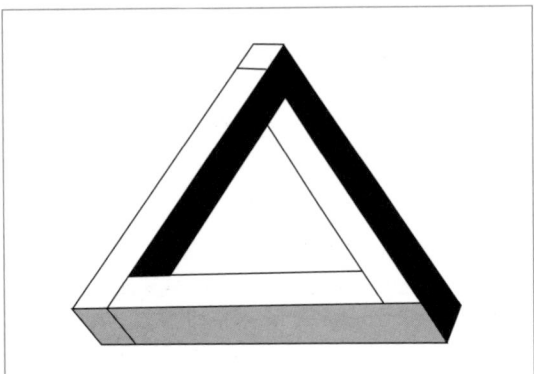

Figure 8.16 The Penrose triangle

◆ *Fictitious figures* – These are illusory figures which do not actually exist. In other words, we perceive a shape in the absence of appropriate sensory data. An example is the Kanizsa triangle in Fig. 8.17, where we 'see' a white triangle with its apex pointing upwards superimposed on another triangle with its apex pointing downwards. Each point of this illusory triangle appears to be obscuring a segment from each of three black 'circles'.

◆ *Distortions* – These are figures which appear to elicit a genuine misperception, e.g. the Müller-Lyer illusion where the two identical vertical lines appear to differ in length, or the Ponzo illusion where the upper horizontal line seems to be longer than the lower horizontal line (see Fig. 8.18).

Figure 8.17 The Kanizsa triangle

The perceptual illusion which has probably attracted the most attention from researchers is the Müller-Lyer illusion, so we will focus on the various explanations which have been proposed to account for this. Gregory has explained this in terms of misapplied size constancy. In other words, we try to apply constancy mechanisms, which usually serve us well, in circumstances where it is not appropriate. Gregory has suggested that, at least in Western cultures, we are used to interpreting two-dimensional drawings as three-dimensional objects and that we attempt to do this when presented with the Müller-Lyer lines. He thinks that we 'see' the left-hand drawing as the inside corner of a room and the right-hand drawing as the outside corner of a building (see Fig. 8.19). Our retinal image of the two vertical lines is identical, but, because the

Figure 8.18 Examples of line illusions

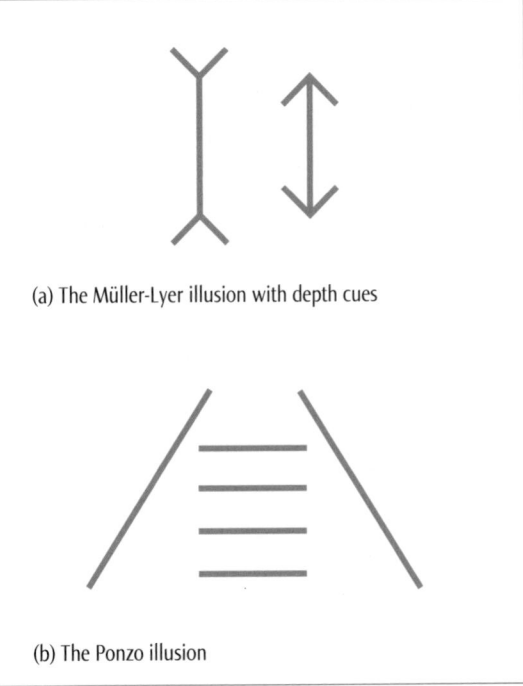

(a) The Müller-Lyer illusion with depth cues

(b) The Ponzo illusion

Figure 8.19 The Müller-Lyer illusion

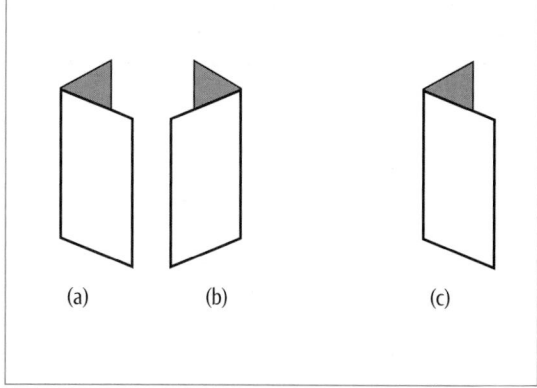

Figure 8.21
Illustration of a three-dimensional Müller-Lyer illusion

inside corner appears to be more distant than the outside corner, we assume that the left-hand line is longer.

It may seem unlikely to you that you should make this assumption about three-dimensional structures when you look at the Müller-Lyer illusion. Gregory, however, believes that this constancy scaling occurs unconsciously because of our ingrained past experience in interpreting drawings. There is some evidence to support his view from cross-cultural studies (see p. 213), but not all psychologists have agreed with him.

One challenge to his theory is that the illusion persists, even when the depth cues provided by the fins are lost as, for example, in Fig. 8.20.

DeLucia and Hochberg (1991) demonstrated that the illusion persists even in a three-dimensional situation. They placed three two-foot high wooden 'fins' on the floor as in Fig. 8.21, so that the distance between the upright edges was the same.

Figure 8.20
The Müller-Lyer illusion without depth cues

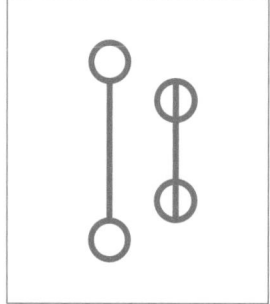

Observers erroneously reported that the distance between fins (b) and (c) was greater than that between (a) and (b). In this three-dimensional model, unlike the conventional two-dimensional drawing, it is clear that the spaces between the two sets of fins are not at different depths and yet the illusion of different lengths is powerful. It is difficult for Gregory to account for this finding.

Day (1990) has rejected the idea that we use depth information and has proposed an alternative explanation, which he has called *conflicting cues theory*. He suggests that we use two separate cues when judging the length of lines like those in the Müller-Lyer illusion:

◆ the actual length of the line

◆ the overall length of the figure.

In the Müller-Lyer illusion, the actual length of both the lines is the same, but the left-hand one is part of a considerably longer figure (i.e. the outward pointing fins make the overall length greater). Day believes that we try to integrate these two pieces of conflicting information by forming a compromise perception of length and deciding that the left-hand line is longer than the right-hand.

Gibson was unable to provide a satisfactory explanation for the experience of perceptual illusions. He dismissed laboratory studies of illusions as highly artificial and believed that they had little relevance in everyday viewing conditions.

There is, as yet, no satisfactory, single explanation for the experience of perceptual illusion and it seems likely that they occur as a result of a combination of factors. However, any comprehensive theory of perception needs to be able to offer some account for these intriguing phenomena.

Exam summary: Perceptual organization

The AQA examination will test your understanding of the following areas:

◆ constructivist theories of visual perception (p. 194 and pp. 197–9)

◆ direct theories of visual perception (pp. 194–7)

◆ perceptual organization (pp. 199–205).

Example question

The question below is typical of one drawn from the material above, and should take you 30 minutes.

(a) Outline one theory of visual perception. *(6 marks)*

(b) Outline and evaluate how this theory might explain two areas of perceptual organization (e.g. depth and movement). *(18 marks)*

Suggested answer structure

Questions that are parted in this way require very careful reading, particularly when there is an uneven mark distribution as here. First of all, we know that the AO1 component is worth 12 marks, as is the AO2 component (see Chapter 21 for an explanation of this). Part (a) is only worth 6 marks, and is all AO1 (*Outline* is an AO1 injunction), therefore that leaves 6 marks which would be accounted for in the AO1 component of part (b). If you were to write around 600 words as a total response to this question, AO1 would require around 300 words, as would AO2. If half of the AO1 content is

in part (a) and half in part (b), that means 150 words of AO1 in part (a) and the remaining 150 in part (b). That leaves 300 words (AO2) that must all appear in part (b), as *evaluate* is an AO2 injunction (see Chapter 21). This may seem obvious, but it does help you to plan your response to the question in the most effective and productive way in order to maximize your marks.

The first of the two main theories we considered is Gibson's direct theory (pp. 194–7), which is based on the assumption that perception is a bottom-up process. He believed that there is sufficiently rich and detailed information in the visual environment for us to perceive directly. An alternative approach is found in Gregory's constructivist theory (pp. 198–9), which emphasizes the importance of top-down processing. Gregory believed that perception involves the use of past experience and stored knowledge. This theory can explain how we maintain reasonably accurate perceptions under poor or ambiguous viewing conditions.

The second part of the question asks you to apply your chosen theory to *two* different aspects of perceptual organization. These include depth perception (pp. 199–200), movement perception (pp. 200–2), visual constancies (pp. 202–3) and visual illusions (pp. 203–5). You should remember that the only AO2 content required in this question is in this second part. However, as you are *using* your chosen theory to explain perceptual organization (i.e. you are *applying* it), it would be appropriate to offer evaluation of the *theory* as an important aspect of the evaluation of its *application*.

Perceptual development

So far in this chapter, we have looked at the normal perceptual abilities of the average human adult. Psychologists have also been interested in finding out about the ways in which our perceptual skills develop. The nature–nurture question reflects a longstanding debate about the relative importance of innate and environmental factors in the acquisition of psychological abilities. As far as perception is concerned, the extreme nativist view holds that we are born with certain perceptual abilities which develop through a genetically programmed process of maturation and which owe nothing to learning. Empiricists, on the other hand, believe that we are born with only the most basic sensory capacity and that our perceptual abilities develop through experience and interaction with our environment. It is unlikely that our acquisition of perceptual skills can be fully explained by either one of these extreme views. It seems much more likely that perceptual skills develop as a result of an interaction between innate and environmental factors.

Neonate research

The most direct method of investigating the nature–nurture debate is to observe human neonates (newborn infants). If perceptual abilities are inborn, they should be apparent in neonates. If perceptual skills are developed through learning and experience with the environment, they would be absent in young babies. However, this is not as easy to establish as it might at first seem. Some of the difficulties of neonate research are given below:

◆ There are ethical and practical difficulties in obtaining permission from parents to run experiments with human neonates.

◆ Young babies tend to spend much of their time sleeping and crying. It is difficult to attract their attention and even more difficult to hold it.

◆ Some abilities (see below) are not present at birth but emerge during the first few weeks of life. It can be difficult to disentangle the effects of maturation of the visual system from the effects of experience with the visual environment.

◆ Because of physical and cognitive constraints, babies produce only a limited range of observable behaviours. It seems relatively easy to show that a baby cannot do something, but it may simply be that babies do not have the behavioural repertoire to demonstrate all their abilities.

◆ Babies cannot understand instructions from the experimenter and cannot answer verbal questions.

◆ Psychologists have devised a number of experimental techniques to overcome some of these difficulties and these are outlined in Table 8.1 below.

As a result of using some of these techniques, psychologists now know that babies have considerably more sophisticated perceptual skills than was previously thought. We will look at some of these abilities.

Table 8.1   Table of techniques used in neonate research

Technique	Description	Explanation
Preferential looking (PL)	The experimenter presents two distinctive visual stimuli together on a screen and monitors how long the baby looks at each of them.	If the baby looks at one for longer than at the other, the experimenter assumes that the baby can distinguish between them and has a preference for one over the other.
Eye-movement monitoring	The experimenter photographs babies' eye movements while they are viewing patterns on a screen.	If the infant appears only to focus on certain features of the stimulus (e.g. areas of light–shade contrast), it suggests that the whole stimulus cannot be perceived.
Habituation	A single stimulus is presented to the infant, who will normally spend time looking at it. As time passes, the infant becomes so familiar with it (habituates to it) that she loses interest and looks away. At this point, a new stimulus is presented.	If there is renewed interest in this novel stimulus, the experimenter infers that the infant has recognized that something has changed. This renewed interest is called dishabituation.
Sucking rate	The infant is given a dummy to suck and the intensity of sucking is measured. Infants tend to suck at a faster rate if they are interested in something. Once the infant habituates to a stimulus, sucking rate declines.	If the sucking rate increases again when a novel stimulus is presented, it can be assumed that the infant is able to distinguish between the old and the new stimulus.
Conditioning	The baby is rewarded (e.g. by the experimenter playing peek-a-boo) every time she turns her head towards a specific visual stimulus. The infant usually learns rapidly to respond to the visual stimulus.	If the baby continues to show a preference for this particular stimulus, even when it is embedded in an array of other visual stimuli, it is assumed that the baby can distinguish it.
Heart and breathing rate	Heart and/or breathing rate is/are measured for changes when various visual stimuli are presented.	If there are changes in rate when novel stimuli are presented, it is assumed that the baby can distinguish between them.
Positron-emission tomography (PET)	Electrodes are attached to the baby's scalp which detect electrical activity in the brain. Certain patterns known as VEPs occur in response to visual stimuli.	The experimenter can assume that the baby differentiates between two stimuli if each stimulus provokes a different pattern of VEPs.
Visually evoked potentials (VEPs) and functional magnetic resonance imaging (fMRI)	These are advanced techniques which allow mapping of brain function.	If different patterns of infant brain activity are recorded in response to different visual stimuli, it is assumed that the infant can distinguish between them.

Acuity and contrast

Visual acuity refers to the ability to perceive visual details and it is poorly developed at birth (Courage and Adams 1996). The level of acuity found in new-borns seems to vary slightly with the technique used to measure it, but it is generally considered to be about 20/800. This means that the infant must view a stimulus from 20 feet in order to perceive it in the same detail as a normally sighted adult at 800 feet. However, it seems to develop rapidly over the first few months and reaches the adult level of 20/20 shortly after the age of 12 months (Haith 1990). Low acuity in infancy seems to be accounted for by physiological factors. Conel (1951), for example, has demonstrated that the rapid development of neurons in the visual cortex, which occurs at the ages of 3 and 6 months coincides with the parallel rapid development of visual acuity. Abramov et al. (1982) have also shown that the fovea (see p. 188) contains widely spaced and poorly developed cone-receptors in the new-born and this could also be an important factor in constraining visual acuity in the early weeks of life.

Infants are unable to perceive contrast in the same way that adults do and it has been estimated that the vision of 1-month-old infants is slightly worse than adult night vision (Pirchio et al. 1978). This can be explained in terms of the undeveloped fovea, which forces the infant to rely mainly on her rod-dominant peripheral retina. However, in spite of the low acuity and poor contrast sensitivity, a 2-day-old infant can recognize her mother's face at close range (see In Focus).

Tracking

Tracking is the ability to follow a moving object with the eyes and it is fairly inefficient in new-born babies. Aslin (1987) has demonstrated that infants can track objects for brief periods of time provided that the objects are moving slowly, but that this ability improves rapidly from the age of approximately 2 to 3 months.

Colour vision

Colour vision is determined by the action of cone receptors in the retina and we have seen already that these are poorly developed in the new-born infant. However, colour vision seems to develop rapidly and infants appear to be able to distinguish between the long and middle wavelengths of light (red and green) as early as the first week of life (Adams 1995). The ability to perceive short-wavelength (blue) appears to develop a bit later although Varner and colleagues (1985) demonstrated that infants have functioning short-wavelength cones by the age of 2 to 3 months.

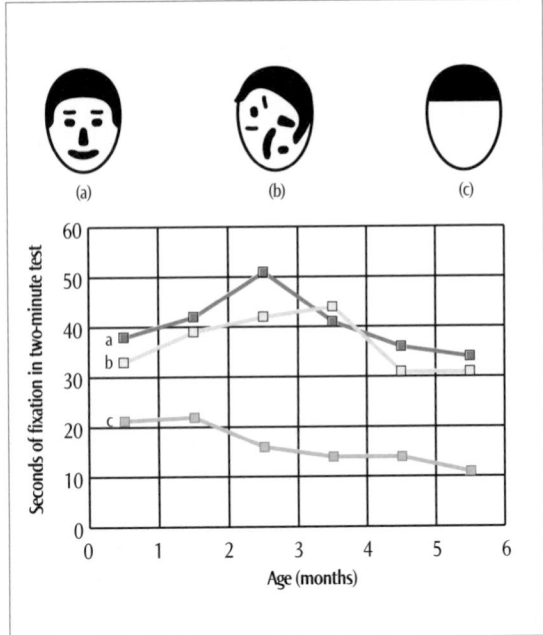

Figure 8.22 Looking time for Fantz's (1961) face stimuli

So, basic visual skills seem to be quite well developed at an early stage and there appears to be a particularly rapid development from about the age of 2 to 3 months. This seems to coincide with physiological changes, e.g. the rapid proliferation of synapses and the growth of dendrites in the cortex (Nowakowski 1987) and with changes in the structure of the eye itself (Abramov et al. 1982). It seems likely, then, that such developments occur as a result of maturational processes.

One area of particular interest in the nature–nurture debate has been the emergence of the ability of babies to recognize faces (see In Focus opposite for a discussion of this research).

Depth and distance perception

Depth perception, as we saw in the previous section, is a complex skill. Babies need it from an early age in order to carry out what appear, on the surface, to be quite simple tasks, e.g. to reach out for a toy, to aim a spoon accurately at a bowl of food or to decide whether it is safe to roll onto the floor from the sofa. Babies seem to be able to start making these kinds of judgement from the age of about 3 months and are often quite skilled by the age of about 6 to 7 months. This coincides with the time that many babies learn to crawl (Bornstein et al. 1992). The interesting question for psychologists is whether depth perception is innate or learned.

A classic experiment investigating this question was carried out by Gibson and Walk in 1960 (see In Focus, p. 210).

Face recognition

Fantz (1961) conducted studies which seemed to demonstrate that face recognition was an innate ability. He presented 4-day to 6-month-old infants with stimuli similar to those in Fig 8.22.

◆ Stimulus (a) is a representation of a human face

◆ Stimulus (b) depicts exactly the same black features, but not configured to look like a face.

◆ Stimulus (c) has the same amount of black shading, but presented as one solid block of colour.

Babies of all ages showed a slight, but distinctive preference for (a) over (b) and most of them paid little attention to stimulus (c). This suggested to Fantz that human babies possess an innate preference for human faces over other visual objects. Other researchers have criticized Fantz' conclusions saying that the stimuli were artificial and bore little resemblance to the real, animated and mobile faces that infants would encounter in the real world. Haith (1980) has suggested that infants in Fantz' study preferred stimulus (a) because it contained more contour than the other stimuli. This interpretation is reinforced by a study conducted by Flavell (1985) who found that babies, presented with faces and other stimuli with similar amounts of movement and contour, show no preference for faces. So, he concluded that, although infants clearly like looking at faces, this may be explained by their interest in contour and movement rather than by an innate preference for faces.

A more recent suggestion (Johnson and Morton 1991) is that babies possess a specific device that contains information about the structural features of human faces. Johnson and Morton referred to this device as 'conspec' and located it in the superior colliculus, a structure in the subcortex. Support for this hypothesis was provided by Umilta and colleagues (1996) who presented new-borns with a variety of face-like stimuli and found a distinct preference for those stimuli which most resembled a correctly structured face.

Whether or not babies have an innate preference for faces, it now seems that they are able to distinguish their mother's face at a very early stage. Walton and her colleagues (1992) videoed 12 faces of new mothers and then videoed 12 other women's faces which were matched in terms of hair and eye colour, complexion and hair-style. Neonates were then showed pairs of videos – one of their mother and one of the matched individual. By sucking on a dummy, the neonates were able to maintain the preferred video on the screen. Babies as young as one day old clearly sucked longer to keep their own mother's picture in view. This study has demonstrated not only that very young babies can discriminate between different faces, but that they also show a preference for their own mother. In order to recognize faces, babies seem to depend on the contrast information provided by the border between the hairline and the skin tone of the forehead. When Pascalis and colleagues (1995) showed babies pictures of their mothers and of strangers but covered the hairline with flesh-coloured hair scarves, the preference for the mother disappeared.

In another intriguing study, Langlois *et al.* (1991), used a variety of life-sized photos of the faces of babies, men and women from both Caucasian and African-American backgrounds, which had previously been rated as either attractive or unattractive by a group of independent judges. Young infants of about 2 months consistently preferred the more attractive pictures. As Bee (1999) has pointed out: 'It is hard to imagine what sort of learning experiences could account for such a preference in a 2-month old. Instead, these findings raise the possibility that there is some inborn template for the 'correct' or most 'desired' shape and configuration for members of our species and that we simply prefer those who match this template better.'

It seems, then, that many perceptual abilities are present in the new-born baby or appear in the first weeks of life. It is highly likely that most of the abilities discussed above arise from maturational changes in the visual system and owe little to experience and learning. The distinction between innate and environmental factors is rather less clear-cut in the area of depth perception and the acquisition of the visual constancies.

The visual cliff experiment (Gibson and Walk 1960)

Gibson and Walk constructed a glass-topped table with two halves. One half of the table had glass covering a checkerboard design immediately below the glass, and the other half had the same design four feet below the glass. The depth cues from the apparatus gave the impression of a deep 'drop' (visual cliff) on one side of the table, even though the glass top continued, in reality, to provide a solid continuous surface. Gibson and Walk were unable to use infants under the age of 6 months because they needed to have babies who were independently mobile. They tested 36 babies by placing them individually on the 'shallow' side of the apparatus and encouraged them to crawl over the 'cliff' to the 'deep' side by having their mothers to call to them. In spite of this encouragement from their mothers, most of the babies would not crawl over the perceived drop (see Fig. 8.23).

Figure 8.23
Gibson and Walk's (1960) 'visual cliff' study

Gibson and Walk concluded that depth perception is an innate ability, but critics argued that babies of 6 months could have learned this ability through experience. Gibson and Walk responded to these criticisms by repeating the experiment using new-born animals such as lambs, kittens and chicks which are independently mobile from birth. These animals refused to cross over the cliff and, if placed on the 'deep' side, showed signs of distress. This suggests that depth perception in such animal species is innate, but there are too many differences between humans and animals for us to be able to generalize this finding. More convincing evidence came from a study by Campos and co-workers (1970). They compared the heart rates of 2-month-old babies when placed on the 'shallow' and the 'deep' side of the apparatus. Heart rates decreased slightly on the deep side suggesting that babies were able to make a distinction between the two sides. However, older babies (approx. 9 months) showed an increased heart rate when placed on the deep side, which is an indicator of anxiety. It may be that depth perception is innate since it can be demonstrated in such young babies, but that avoidance behaviour (i.e. recognizing the danger associated with certain situations) can only be learned through experience. However, babies as young as 2 months have shown avoidance behaviour when a rather different technique is used to test depth perception.

This technique involves showing babies a video of an object which appears to be moving towards them on a direct collision course. If depth perception is present, the baby should flinch, blink or move her head to one side. Such avoidance behaviour has been demonstrated in babies between 2 and 3 months (Yonas and Owsley 1987) suggesting that some awareness of depth perception is present in these very young babies. An earlier study by Yonas (1981) lends weight to the nativist argument. He compared two groups of 6-week-old infants – one group of infants had been born on time, but the other group had been born four weeks late. The post-term babies were significantly more likely to respond to looming objects with an avoidance reaction than the normal term babies, even though both groups had been exposed to environmental influences for the same time (i.e. six weeks).

The use of pictorial cues discussed on p. 200 appears to emerge rather later and probably means that they depend on experience with the environment rather than on the maturation of physiological maturation. Granrud and Yonas (1985), for example, investigated infants' ability to perceive depth from the cue of overlap. They showed babies two-dimensional cardboard cut-outs like the ones in Fig. 8.24.

Infants have a tendency to reach out for objects which seem nearer to them and so, Granrud and Yonas reasoned that they were more likely to reach out for picture (a) (which has the impression of depth provided by overlap cues) than for either (b) or (c). This proved to be the case for 7-month-old babies, but not for 5-month-old babies, which suggests that the ability to use the pictorial cue of overlap emerges around the seventh month.

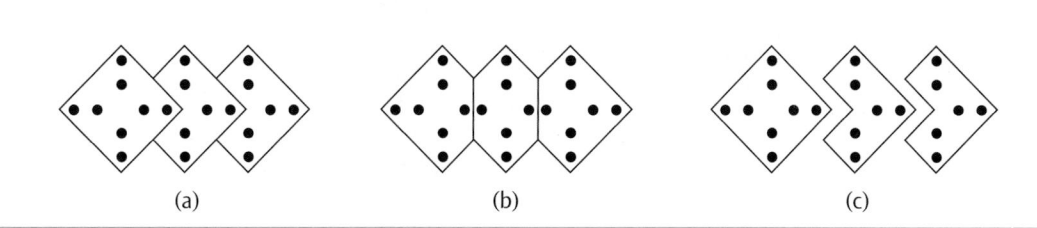

Figure 8.24 Stimuli used in Granrud and Yonas' (1985) experiment

Visual constancies

You will recall from the previous section that constancies are an important means of maintaining a stable visual environment. The central question for developmental psychologists again concerns the nature–nurture debate. We will look at size and shape constancy since these are the ones which have attracted the most research interest.

Size and shape constancy

Bower (1965) conducted the classic study into size constancy in infants (see *In Focus*, p. 212).

Bower (1966) also investigated shape constancy and found that 2- month-old infants responded to a tilted rectangle as if it were the same as the original rectangle, even though a rectangle viewed from such an angle projects a trapezoid on to the retina. More recently, Slater and Morrison (1985) demonstrated shape constancy in new-born infants using the habituation method.

Babies seem to be able to match visual shapes to a shape that they have experienced through touch or feel. Kaye and Bower (1994) put one of two different types of dummy in the mouths of day-old infants. Once the baby started sucking, an image of the dummy would appear on a computer screen in front of the baby. If the baby paused in sucking, the dummy would disappear from the screen and be replaced by an image of the other dummy (which the baby had not experienced sucking). Once the baby started to suck again, the first dummy would reappear on the screen. In this way, the baby was able to control which image appeared on the screen. Babies consistently controlled their sucking to keep the image on the screen of the dummy in their mouth. This suggests that new-born infants are capable of sensing the shape of a dummy in their mouth and then generalizing this perception from the tactile to the visual modality. It is not clear what mechanism underlies this ability, but it seems clear that it is innate rather than learned.

Explanations of perceptual development

We began this section by introducing the nature–nurture debate, and it seems that both innate and learned factors have a role to play in the development of perceptual skills. With the development of ingenious experimental techniques, psychologists have been able to show that human infants possess remarkable perceptual abilities. Many of these are present at birth or appear in the first few weeks of life as the nervous system matures. However, there is also evidence that we need at least some minimal level of experience with the environment to develop our perceptual abilities to their full potential. Much of this evidence comes from studies carried out on non-human animals where animals are deprived of certain environmental stimuli. For example, Riesen (1965) reared chimpanzees in the dark and found that nerve cells in the retina and visual cortex began to atrophy without any light stimulation. In order to avoid this destruction of nerve cells, Riesen conducted further studies in which he allowed chimpanzees and monkeys to experience some light stimulation by wearing translucent goggles from birth. At about 3 months, the animals were able to distinguish brightness and size like normal members of their species, but were unable to follow a moving object with their eyes or discriminate shapes. It is difficult to generalize these findings to humans and it would clearly be unethical to carry out such studies on human neonates, but it does suggest that perceptual abilities depend, to an extent, on interacting with the environment. This conclusion is supported by studies of children who have suffered deprivation for some reason or another. Dennis (1960) studied babies in Iranian orphanages who had been kept in highly impoverished environments with no stimulation or opportunity to move around. He found that these children showed major deficits in perceptual and motor skills.

It seems, then, that both innate and learned factors are involved in perceptual development and psychologists have started to look beyond the nature–nurture debate. They are now beginning to ask how such factors are combined to produce a whole perceptual experience and what patterns of systematic change occur over time in the development of perceptual skills. One prominent researcher who has adopted this approach and has looked for patterns of change in children's development of perceptual strategies is Eleanor Gibson (Gibson 1969, Gibson and Spelke 1983)

Bower's size constancy study (1965)

Bower conditioned nine infants between the ages of 40 and 60 days by rewarding them every time they turned their head in response to the presentation of a 30 cm cube. The reward was a peek-a-boo response by an adult who popped up in front of the baby, smiled and tickled her and then disappeared from view again (see Fig. 8.25). Once the baby had clearly learnt to respond to this particular cube, Bower introduced new stimuli:

◆ the original 30 cm cube placed 3 m away from the infant (i.e. smaller retinal image than the original).

◆ a 90 cm cube placed 1 m away from the infant (i.e. larger retinal image as the original)

◆ a 90 cm cube placed 3 m away (i.e. same retinal image as the original)

Bower recorded the number of times the babies reacted with a conditioned response to the stimuli. The results are shown in the table below.

	Original stimulus	Test stimulus 1	Test stimulus 2	Test stimulus 3
Size	30 cm	Same – 30 cm	Different – 90 cm	Different – 90 cm
Distance	1 m	Different – 3 m	Same – 1 m	Different – 3 m
Retinal image		Different	Different	Same

Bower found, as he had predicted, that retinal size was not the crucial factor and that babies looked least at the stimulus which had the same retinal image, but which differed from the original both in terms of size and distance. He concluded that babies have innate size constancy.

Bower was interested in finding out what cues the babies were using in order to gauge the distance of the cubes. Several types of cue are known to assist in depth perception and these include texture gradient, motion parallax and retinal disparity (see pp. 199–200). Using three ingenious variations on his original experimental technique, Bower (1965) again tested nine infants for size constancy.

◆ condition 1: cues available = texture gradient and motion parallax

◆ condition 2: cues available = texture gradient

◆ condition 3: cues available = retinal disparity and texture gradient.

In condition 2, infants no longer seemed able to judge distance or the real size of the cubes, suggesting that texture gradient was not being used as a guide to distance. Performance in condition 1, however, was at the same level as in the original experiment where babies seemed to understand distance and size constancy. Since texture gradient did not seem to be an important cue, Bower concluded that they were relying on motion parallax. Performance in condition 3 was intermediate between the two other conditions, suggesting that retinal disparity was being used to a limited extent to judge distance.

On the basis of this series of experiments, Bower suggested that infants between the ages of 6 to 8 weeks have some degree of depth perception and size constancy and that this ability depends mainly on the cue of motion parallax. Retinal disparity provides an additional but weaker cue and texture gradient is not yet being used. However, the results have proved difficult to replicate and his conclusions have not been universally accepted by other psychologists. It is not easy to obtain a conditioned response in babies as young as this and their behaviour and body movements can often be misinterpreted.

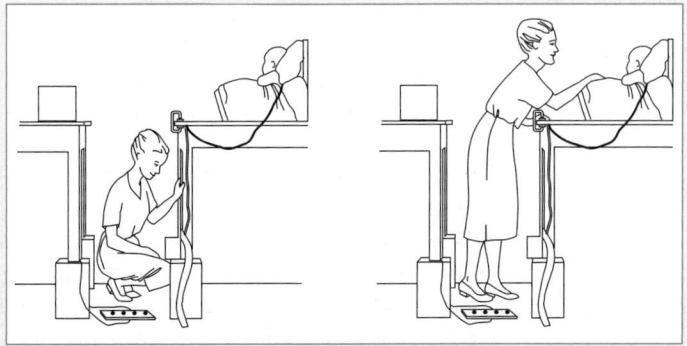

Figure 8.25 The set-up in Bower's (1965) study

Cross-cultural studies

We have seen how perception is shaped by an interaction of biological and environmental factors. Given that there appears to be at least some requirement for experience with the visual environment in order for the visual system to develop normally, psychologists and anthropologists have been interested in finding out the role of cultural background in the development of perceptual skills. People from different cultures may differ from one another in two important ways:

◆ biological

◆ ecological.

Biological differences depend on factors such as genetic inheritance, diet, disease patterns within the culture, etc. While such factors could influence perceptual abilities, there has been little research interest in these areas. Researchers have been far more interested in *ecological* factors such as local environment, cultural history and education. Do people who live in dense forest for example, develop different perceptual skills from people who live in open plains? Do people from cultural backgrounds with no tradition of drawing find it difficult to understand the pictorial cues found in paintings and drawings from other cultures?

Much of the research in this area has centred on the experience of visual illusions (see p. 203). In a classic study, Segall *et al.* (1963, 1966) showed various straight-line illusions including the Müller-Lyer illusion (see p. 204) to nearly 2,000 adult and child participants. There were 14 non-European groups, mostly from Africa, but also from the Philippines and three so-called European groups (actually from South Africa and North America). The researchers found clear cultural differences: the European groups were considerably more susceptible to the Müller-Lyer illusion than the non-European groups. Segall and colleagues explain their findings in terms of the *carpentered world hypothesis*. According to the carpentered world hypothesis, many people live in an environment which is full of lines and angles and rectangular objects. Unless these objects are viewed from exactly the right angle, they will project a non-rectangular image on to the retina and yet we continue to perceive them as rectangular. Segall and colleagues believe that this tendency to interpret trapezoid shapes on the retina is so pervasively reinforced in people who live in carpentered environments that it becomes automatic and unconscious from a very early age. People who live in environments with few straight lines and angles are less used to interpreting acute and obtuse angles on the retina as representations of right angles in the real world. When presented with a drawing of the Müller-Lyer illusion, the Europeans were likely to try to perceive it as a two-dimensional representation of a three-dimensional object. In other words they would interpret the drawings as, for example, the outside corner of a building and the inside corner of a room. Using misapplied size constancy, they would then perceive the apparently closer line to be shorter than the line that was apparently further away. The non-Europeans from non-carpentered environments were much more likely to take the drawing at face value.

Pollack (1963), however, suggested that there might be a biological rather than environmental explanation for these findings. He had noted findings from several studies that susceptibility to the Müller-Lyer illusion declines with age. Since older people also experience increasing difficulty in detecting contours, Pollack hypothesized that there might be a functional relationship between these two abilities. Pollack and Silvar (1967) demonstrated that there was such a relationship – the harder people found it to detect contour, the less susceptible they were to the Müller-Lyer illusion. Silvar and Pollack (1967) then took this idea a stage further and demonstrated in a second study that there is a relationship between contour detection and retinal pigmentation – the denser the pigmentation, the poorer the contour detection. Pollack suggested that retinal pigmentation, which may be denser in dark-skinned people, might have been responsible for the reduced susceptibility to the Müller-Lyer illusion found among the non-European samples in the study by Segall and colleagues. In other words, biological rather than cultural differences might be responsible for the different responses to visual illusions. There was some support for the Pollack hypothesis from Berry (1971) and Jahoda (1971), but both studies have been criticized on methodological grounds. However, Stewart (1973), conducted a well-controlled study which strongly challenged Pollack's hypothesis and, instead, provided support for the environmental view (see *In Focus* on p. 214).

There is other evidence that lack of experience with certain environmental depth cues can impair perceptual abilities such as size constancy. A well-known study by Turnbull (1961) illustrates this. He observed the behaviour of a group of Bambuti Pygmies who lived in dense forest. They have little opportunity to look far into the distance because their environment is enclosed by trees and vegetation. Turnbull reported on a particular occasion when he accompanied his guide, Kenge, out of the forest for the first time in his life. On their journey, they crossed a broad, open plain and could see a herd of grazing buffalo a few miles way in the distance. The guide was puzzled and asked what kind of insects they were and laughed when he was

Susceptibilty to illusions

Stewart (1973) used two illusions: the Müller-Lyer and the Sander illusion (an illusion in which one diagonal line within a parallelogram appears longer than another – see Fig. 8.26).

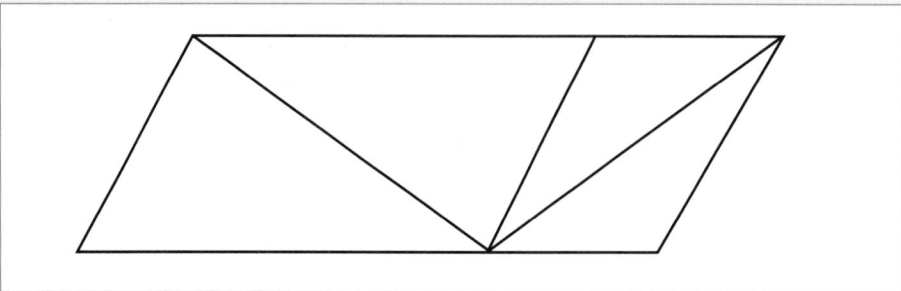

Fig. 8.26 The Sander illusion

She administered them to two completely different groups:

◆ Group 1 – 60 black and 60 white children selected randomly from three schools in a town in Illinois (i.e. children from different ethnic backgrounds, but all living in a carpentered environment)

◆ Group 2 – 432 black children from two regions in Zambia – one group came from the uncarpentered environment of the Zambezi Valley and the other came from the carpentered environment of the capital city, Lusaka (i.e. children from the same ethnic background, but living in different environments).

Stewart found that susceptibility to the two illusions rose as a function of environment rather than ethnic type (see the following table).

Mean number of responses showing susceptibility to the illusions

	Zambezi Valley	Lusaka	Illinois (black)	Illinois (white)
Müller-Lyer	4.63	5.81	6.10	6.10
Sander	4.24	5.33	5.59	5.40

This study seems to undermine Pollack's biological hypothesis and lend support to the ecological hypothesis.

told that they were buffalo. As they drove towards the herd in the car, Kenge seemed alarmed, although his anxiety disappeared once they had got very close and he could verify that they were indeed buffalo. However, he continued to be confused about what had happened and wondered how the buffalo had grown larger as they approached and whether some kind of witchcraft or trickery were involved. This kind of report suggests that the environment we grow up in can influence the way in which we perceive new stimuli. A forest dweller who has only experienced very limited vistas, for example, will find it difficult to understand certain aspects of depth perception and size constancy.

Another area of cross-cultural research into perception has centred on the interpretation of two-dimensional drawings, pictures and photographs. In Western cultures, we are inundated with pictorial images in books, newspapers, television, advertising hoardings, posters, etc. from a very early age. We usually have no difficulty in recognizing objects and in understanding the spatial relations between objects depicted in pictures and yet, pictures rarely reflect an accurate representation of the real-world scene – for example, they are flat, whereas the real world is three-dimensional and they are often in black and white. Some people (e.g. Gombrich 1972) have suggested that we can only understand and interpret pictures drawn according to Western artistic tradition because we are aware of a set of conventions agreed within that culture. If this were true, it would follow that people from other cultures would not readily be able to understand Western pictorial convention.

Hochberg and Brooks (1962) carried out a rather bold experiment on one of their own children. They shielded their son from any sort of pictures for the first 19 months of his life. They made sure that there were no pictures, magazines, newspapers or television in the child's vicinity. They even removed all the labels from tins and packages of food. At the end of this period, they showed him simple line drawings of everyday objects such as shoes. In spite of his restricted upbringing, the child had no difficulty in identifying all these objects. If we can generalize this finding, we can assume that the recognition of objects in pictures is not a learned convention. There is evidence from cross-cultural studies that individuals are able to recognize objects in pictures even if they have never seen examples of Western pictures before. Hagen and Jones (1978) found that coloured photographs were readily understood by people who had never experienced pictures. It seems, however, that less realistic pictures, e.g. black and white photographs or line drawings present more problems. Deregowski (1980) has collected a number of reports from anthropologists and missionaries which suggest that spontaneous object identification can be difficult under these circumstances. It should be noted that these findings derive from anecdotal evidence rather than from rigorously conducted scientific study. One report from a missionary working in Malawi tells of the initial puzzlement of local people when shown a line drawing of an ox and a dog. However, after carefully pointing out individual features such as the nose and ear of the dog and the horns and tail of the ox, recognition dawned. This suggests that object recognition can occur very quickly if attention is directed appropriately and so supports the idea that learning via prolonged exposure is unnecessary.

It seems, then, that the ability to identify objects does not depend on learning or cultural background. There may be more of a problem, however, in interpreting spatial relationships within two-dimensional pictures and this ability may well reflect different cultural conventions. Western artists have long made use of monocular pictorial cues (see p. 200) to imply three dimensions in their paintings. However, there is no binocular disparity between elements in the picture, and all objects require the same degree of accommodation and convergence. This means, as Pick (1987) points out, that, in order to perceive a flat, two-dimensional picture as a scene in three dimensions, we need to pay attention to some depth cues and ignore the absence of others. Perhaps people who have no experience of Western art will find it difficult to use pictorial cues in this way.

Hudson (1960, 1962) showed pictures containing various pictorial depth cues to groups of people in South Africa. Figure 8.27 shows an example of the type of picture he used.

In this picture, the cue of overlap tells us that the hunter and the antelope are standing in front of the rocks and are, therefore, closer to us. The cue of familiar size tells us that the elephant must be furthest away from us because, although it is casting a smaller image on our retina, we know that it is actually larger than either a man or an antelope. Hudson's technique was to ask observers first of all to name all the objects in the picture. Observers were then asked questions such as 'What is the man doing?' and 'What is closer to the man?' Results from Hudson's own study and from subsequent studies conducted in various parts of Africa reported by Deregowski (1980), indicated that non-Western observers had difficulty seeing pictorial depth. However, as Rock (1995) has commented, the cues are quite weak in this picture and, even for Westerners, there is likely to be some ambiguity.

There is some evidence that formal education using picture books and drawings can increase the ability to perceive depth in two-dimensional pictures (Pick 1987). Hagen and Jones (1978) have also demonstrated that certain cues, such as aerial perspective and texture gradient seem to enhance the ability to perceive depth in pictures. It may be the case that some pictorial cues are more helpful and familiar to non-Westerners than others.

Non-Western cultures with no experience of pictures seem to find particular difficulty in perceiving implied movement in drawings. Look at the pictures in Fig. 8.28.

Figure 8.27
Picture used in Hudson's studies
Source: Deregowski (1972)

Figure 8.28 Illustrations implying movement

The artist in these pictures has used a technique to imply movement that is familiar to Western observers from as young as 4 years of age (Friedman and Stevenson 1975). Duncan *et al.* (1973) showed a cartoon picture to a group of rural African children in which a boy's head was shown in three different positions to imply rapid movement of the head. The children did not understand the implied motion and, several of them reported that the boy must be deformed. However, the ability to understand implied motion in line drawings is another skill that can be obtained through education, urbanization and exposure to pictures (Friedman and Stevenson 1980).

Evaluation of cross-cultural studies

Cross-cultural studies have been important in trying to investigate the effects of physical environment and cultural background on perceptual abilities, but findings are often ambiguous and difficult to interpret. Some conclusions have been based on early observations by missionaries and anthropologists which were not conducted under controlled conditions.

Figure 8.29 Drawings of elephants used in Hudson's studies

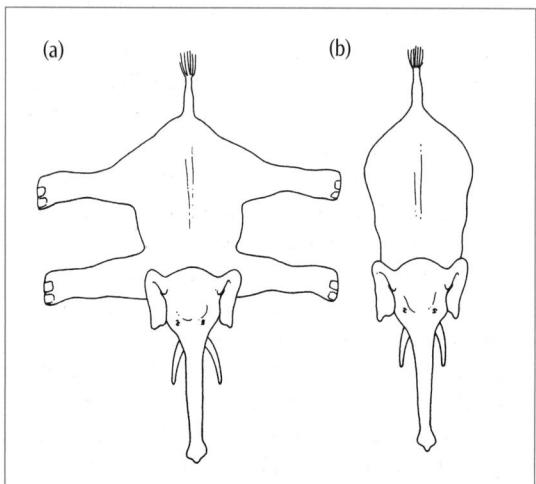

Later, more rigorous studies can still often be criticized for experimenter bias and for underestimating perceptual abilities. There has been very little empirical research in this area in recent years, but, as Segall *et al.* (1990) comment in a review of cross-cultural susceptibility to illusions:

> 'After a quarter century of cross-cultural research on visual perception, it may be stated with confidence that people perceive in ways that are shaped by the inferences they have learned to make in order to function most effectively in the particular ecological settings where they live ... we learn to perceive in the ways we need to perceive.' (p. 88)

The issue of pictorial art is rather more complex. It is possible that the difficulties people from other cultures experience with Western art reflect aesthetic rather than perceptual factors. Hudson (reported in Deregowski 1972) asked groups of African adults and children who had not been exposed to Western culture to choose their preferred picture of an elephant from the two shown in Fig. 8.29.

As you can see, (b) shows a realistic, aerial view of an elephant as it would appear in a photograph taken from above. However, the split-elephant drawing in (a) was overwhelmingly the preferred choice in spite of its unnatural pose. Deregowski maintains that split drawings are preferred by children from all cultures, but that in Western societies, such preferences are suppressed. This is because drawings using perspective cues convey more information than split drawings and so are thought to have more practical use. However, certain societies, where this preference has not been suppressed, have developed the split drawing technique to a high artistic level. It is possible, then, that initial puzzlement with Western-style drawings reflects unfamiliarity with the artistic convention rather than lack of perceptual ability.

Exam summary: Perceptual development

The AQA examination will test your understanding of the following areas:

◆ explanations of perceptual development including nature versus nurture (pp. 206–12)

◆ neonate studies of perceptual development (pp. 206–11)

◆ cross-cultural studies of perceptual development (pp. 213–6).

Example question

The question below is typical of one drawn from the material above, and should take you 30 minutes to answer.

◆ Describe and evaluate research findings from neonate *and* cross-cultural studies of perceptual development. *(24 marks)*

Suggested answer structure

This is another one of those questions where the distribution of marks should determine how much time you spend on each component of the question. If we 'deconstruct' this question, we can see it actually has four distinct parts, each effectively worth 7.5 minutes of writing time:

◆ description of research findings from neonate studies

◆ evaluation of research findings from neonate studies

◆ description of research findings from cross-cultural studies

◆ evaluation of research findings from cross-cultural studies.

When we take a question apart like this, it becomes far more obvious how tight your time is, and how you need to be very strict about apportioning time for each part of the answer. As the average essay length for a 30-minute answer is around 600 words, that means that each one of these parts above would be answered in around 150 words. This calls for the skill of précis, because there is a great deal more than 150 words to choose from in each of these areas.

Neonate research is covered on pp. 206–12, although the *findings* from such research are restricted to pp. 208–12. Cross-cultural research is covered on pp. 213–16. It should be obvious from the previous paragraph that you would have to be selective in your choice of material. Remember that to get high marks you need detail, breadth *and* depth (AO1), and elaboration and *effective* commentary (AO2). Many students worry that they cannot include everything they read in a textbook. This is obviously impossible in 30 minutes, and this question is clearly asking for a *sample* of material that illustrates the insights available from these different research approaches. You might, therefore, include research on depth perception (pp. 208 and 210) and size constancy (pp. 211–12) to illustrate neonate studies, and research on illusions (pp. 213–14) and constancies (pp. 213–14) to illustrate cross-cultural research.

The methodological difficulties involved in testing human neonates makes it difficult to draw firm conclusions about the precise interaction of innate/environmental factors. What does seem very clear from the evidence is that human infants need to engage actively with their visual environment if they are to develop mature perceptual abilities. There are also methodological difficulties and problems of interpretation in cross-cultural studies, but it does seem that our geographical environment and cultural background may have some effect on the ways in which we view the world.

Chapter summary

◆ In this chapter, we have looked at various aspects of perception, starting with the **structure** and **functions** of the **visual system**.

◆ The **eye** is the sense organ for vision and it is here that the process of visual perception begins. Light enters the cornea from the environment and is brought into focus via the lens onto the screen at the back of the eye called the **retina**. This consists of a dense network of nerve cells which are responsible for transforming the incoming light energy into neural impulses. These impulses are then carried along the **visual pathways** to particular areas of the cortex for further processing and integration.

◆ We considered some of the important processes that occur during perception, such as **sensory adaptation**. This is the process whereby we adapt to changes in the environment (e.g. light to dark conditions) and it has probably evolved for survival reasons.

◆ We also looked at the process of **contrast processing** – our ability to differentiate between the brightness levels of adjoining areas. Two further perceptual abilities – **colour** and **feature processing** – both involve highly complex mechanisms, which are not yet fully understood.

◆ In the next section, we considered two main types of theory of **perceptual organization**. **Gibson** proposed the **direct theory** of perception, which is based on the assumption that we 'pick up' information directly from the rich, detailed visual array that surrounds us. In other words, he saw perception as a bottom-up process. **Constructivist** theories, on the other hand, are based on top-down processing. Theorists adopting this approach, e.g. **Gregory**, believe that our perceptual representation of the world is generally much richer and more detailed than could be expected if we were simply relying on information contained in the visual stimulus. They believe, instead, that information from the visual stimulus is combined, often unconsciously, with stored knowledge in a problem-solving approach to perception.

◆ Both theories have been influential, but both have been criticized in various ways. It seems likely that perception is a combination of top-down and bottom-up processing.

◆ We also considered some important aspects of **perceptual organization** which have been explained with varying degrees of success by both types of theory. **Depth perception** is an important way in which we transform the two-dimensional image on our retina into our three-dimensional perceptual world. It is also vital for normal perception that we are able to detect and interpret **movement** in the environment around us. **Perceptual constancies** are a means of maintaining a stable perception, even though the images of objects and people are constantly sliding across our retina as we move around. Finally, we considered some of the **visual illusions** which have been investigated by psychologists as a means of understanding normal perceptual processes.

◆ In the final section of this chapter, we looked at **perceptual development**. One of the central issues in this area is the relative importance of innate and learned factors in the development of perceptual abilities. This is known as the **nature–nurture** debate.

◆ It seems that many perceptual abilities are present in human **neonates** from birth or emerge very shortly afterwards. This suggests that many aspects of perception depend on innate, maturational factors rather than on learning from the environment. The infant ability to perceive **depth and distance** and to apply **visual constancies** has also been investigated. It is less clear, in these areas, whether the skills are inborn or depend on experience. The methodological difficulties of studying human neonates make it difficult to draw firm conclusions. However, it seems likely that babies need to interact with the environment in order for their perceptual abilities to develop normally.

◆ Another way of investigating the relative importance of innate and environmental factors is to conduct **cross-cultural** studies. As with neonate research, there are certain methodological difficulties and it is not always easy to draw clear inferences. On the whole, evidence from cross-cultural research does seem to suggest that our geographical environment and cultural history may well affect our perception to some degree. However, it seems that, in certain circumstances, any such perceptual bias can be changed by exposure to a new environment or cultural setting. These findings suggest quite an important role for learning in the development of mature perceptual abilities.

Further resources

Carlson, N.R. (1998) *Physiology of Behaviour* (6th edn), Boston: Allyn & Bacon.

An up-to-date text on physiological psychology aimed at undergraduates, but the sections on vision are fairly easy to understand and will provide much more detailed coverage of the visual system than is possible in this chapter.

Eysenck, M. and Keane, M. (1995) *Cognitive Psychology: A Student's Handbook* (3rd edn), Hove: Psychology Press.

A comprehensive text aimed mainly at undergraduates, but accessible for A-level students. It contains readable and clear information on most of the topics covered in the last two sections of this chapter.

Rookes, P. and Willson, J. (2000) *Perception: Theory, Development and Organization*, London & New York: Routledge.

This text is aimed at A-level students and is written in a readable, accessible style. It contains more detail on many of the aspects covered in this chapter.

Chapter 9

Language and thought

Jane Willson

Preview

In this chapter we shall be looking at:

◆ research into the relationship between language and thought

◆ research relating to language acquisition

◆ research into problem-solving and errors in reasoning.

Introduction

In this chapter we will consider the nature of human language and thought and look at some of the ways in which psychologists have sought to investigate these topics. Language is a highly complex system of communication based on words that have meaning. These words can be strung together according to a set of grammatical rules and used to create an infinite number of sentences. The flexibility, richness and complexity of human language sets it apart from other animal communication systems, but that very complexity poses an enormous challenge to psychologists attempting to explain the underlying processes of acquisition and everyday use.

Just as humans have developed a highly sophisticated system of languages, they have also outstripped other species in their ability to think and reason. All the processes involved in memory, attention and perception could be legitimately regarded as thought processes. However, when cognitive psychologists refer to thought, they usually mean particular types of goal-directed thinking, such as problem-solving, reasoning and decision-making, and so discussion will be limited to those areas in this chapter.

Language and culture

We will begin the first section by looking at theoretical attempts to establish the links between language and thought, and will then consider some of the social and cultural aspects of language use.

Research into the relationship between language and thought

There has been considerable interest in the question of the relationship between thought and language and the similarities and differences that exist in thinking between members of different language communities. Behaviourists in the early part of this century believed that thought was nothing more than internalized language. Watson (1913), the founder of behaviourism, wrote that 'thought processes are really motor habits in the larynx'. It is certainly true that we often subvocalize when we are engaged in working out a problem – you are probably aware of this yourself when you are planning an essay, for example, or thinking of the best way to get to a friend's house. Early studies (e.g. Jacobsen 1932) appeared to confirm Watson's belief by detecting small movements in the throat muscles when participants were instructed to think. However, a later study (Smith *et al.* 1947) demonstrated in a rather dramatic way that thought *can* occur in the absence of subvocalization. Smith allowed himself to be injected with curare, a highly dangerous drug, which paralyses all the voluntary muscles in the body. After the effects of the drug had worn off, he reported that he had been able to think and to solve problems even though he had been completely incapable of moving any of the muscles in his speech apparatus.

It is clear, then, that there is more to thought than simply moving our vocal muscles and that language may not be essential for thought and problem-solving. Non-human animals can certainly undertake basic problem-solving activities without language and, in spite of considerable recent advances in teaching gorillas and chimpanzees human language (e.g. Savage-Rumbaugh and Lewin 1994), there is no convincing evidence that this language competence improves their performance on other cognitive tasks. However, it is wrong to conclude from animal studies that *all* thinking takes place independently of language. Animals can certainly solve problems without language, but their cognitive abilities are severely limited. Perhaps, as Harley (1995) suggests, language is a tool that sets us further apart from animals because it allows novel and more advanced types of thinking.

As you can see, the relationship between language and thought is not straightforward and psychologists are divided in their explanations of that relationship. There are three main views, which we will consider in the following section:

◆ Language determines thought (the linguistic relativity hypothesis or *Sapir–Whorf hypothesis*).

◆ Cognitive development determines language development (*Piaget's viewpoint*).

◆ Language and thought begin independently, but become interdependent processes (*Vygotsky's viewpoint*).

There is a fourth position taken by Chomsky (1968), and latterly by Pinker (1994), that language and thought are independent processes. We shall consider Chomsky's views in the section on language acquisition.

The linguistic relativity hypothesis

The linguistic relativity hypothesis focuses on the differences between languages and on the influence that languages have on the way native speakers think and perceive the world. This idea was first investigated by Edward Sapir (1921), a respected linguist, who studied various North American languages and noted their different constructions, both from one another and from English. He reported, for example, how English speakers need to consider aspects of time when they make the decision as to whether to add the suffix 'ed' ending to a verb (e.g. 'they walked to the river' instead of 'they walk to the river'). Wintu Indians, on the other hand, do not change verb endings to indicate tense, but, instead, use suffixes to indicate whether the knowledge they are imparting has been gained first-hand or by hearsay. Such differences in grammatical structures led Sapir to suggest that speakers of different languages need to pay attention to different aspects of reality in order to put together meaningful sentence structures. Benjamin Whorf (1956) later conducted his own analysis of North American languages and drew a more radical conclusion than Sapir. He believed that the language we use is directly responsible for shaping our thoughts about the world.

The contention that language and thought are causally related (the *linguistic relativity hypothesis*) came to be known as the Sapir–Whorf hypothesis, even though the two men worked independently and had rather different views. Sapir suggested that language might *influence* thinking, whereas Whorf took the more extreme view that the language people speak *determines* the way they think about the world. These two variants of the hypothesis are known respectively as the weak and the strong version.

Both forms of the hypothesis are difficult to test, not least because the terms 'language' and 'thought' are not precisely defined. It has proved difficult to find unequivocal support for either the strong or weak form of this hypothesis because, even where cognitive differences are found in different language communities, it is impossible to isolate language as the only influence. Education, intelligence, age, experience and environment may all be contributory factors. Much of the evidence cited in support of the theory comes from observations that certain words and grammatical forms exist in some languages, but not in others.

Whorf studied the languages of the North American Indians and argued that each language imposes a particular worldview on its native speakers. He noted that the Hopi have a single term to denote a flying object, whereas English distinguishes between birds, insects, planes, helicopters, etc. Similarly, he wrote that Eskimos have several words for snow, whereas English has only one. The implicit assumption of Whorf's observations is that a huge choice of words allows native speakers to perceive and remember specialized categories of objects in a way that is impossible for native speakers of other languages which lack the appropriate vocabulary. However, the basis on which some of these claims are made is dubious. Pinker (1994) debunks what he calls 'the Great Eskimo Vocabulary Hoax' as follows:

'Contrary to popular belief, the Eskimos do not have more words for snow than do speakers of English. ... One dictionary puts the figure at two. Counting generously, experts can come up with about a dozen, but by such standards English would not be far behind, with snow, sleet, slush, blizzard, avalanche, hail, hardpack, powder, flurry, dusting ...'.

It is, in any case, an enormous inferential leap to assume that people are unable to conceptualize something in the absence of an appropriate linguistic label. A gardening expert, for example, has labels for subspecies of plants that most other people in the same language community do not need to know. These latter individuals, however, are just as capable of perceiving differences between the plants and could learn the labels if they chose to do so. Nor can we assume that the existence of a verbal label ensures complete understanding of a particular concept. Try Activity 1 now to illustrate this point.

It was not only individual words that differentiated
languages according to Whorf, but also their grammars.
He translated passages of Apache language (for
example, he stated that the sentence 'the boat is
grounded on the beach' must be expressed in Apache
as 'it is on the beach pointwise as an event of canoe
motion') and concluded 'How utterly unlike our way of
thinking!' (Whorf 1956). However, there are real flaws
with Whorf's analysis. Lenneberg and Roberts (1956)
responded immediately to Whorf's paper with two
major criticisms:

1 Whorf did not interview any Apaches in the course
   of his study and based all his assumptions about
   their worldview on an analysis of their grammar. He
   believed that Apaches think differently because they
   speak differently, but he had no independent
   evidence of this. Whorf's argument is circular, i.e. he
   notes that a language is different from our own and,
   therefore, infers that speakers of that language think
   differently. He then concludes that the differences in
   thinking stem from differences in the language. In
   fact, differences between languages prove *only* that
   languages differ. Without an independent measure
   of the thought patterns themselves, there is no
   evidence for a causal relationship between language
   and thought.

2 Whorf translated Apache phrases literally into
   English, which inevitably sounds stilted. Mark Twain,
   an excellent German speaker, illustrated this by
   writing a literal English translation of a speech he
   gave in German. A small extract from the translation
   will demonstrate the point: 'I would only the
   language method – the luxurious, elaborate
   construction compress, the eternal parenthesis
   suppress, do away with, annihilate; the introduction
   of more than thirteen subjects in one sentence forbid;
   the verb so far to the front pull that one it without a
   telescope discover can' (from Brown 1958).

The language in this passage is obviously constructed
differently from English and a direct translation sounds
ridiculous and alien. However, if the passage had been
translated sensitively into syntactically correct English,
the ideas would have been perfectly comprehensible.

Germans construct their sentences differently from
native English speakers, but this does not mean that
they think in an essentially different way.

Similarly, Whorf stated that the Hopi Indians had no
words or grammatical forms to convey the idea of time
or to express the concept of past and future. Whorf
believed that this meant that the Hopi had no
conception of time. However, the anthropologist
Malotki (1983), in an extensive study of the Hopi, found
that they kept quite sophisticated records including
various methods of dating events and that they
estimated time using the principle of the sundial.
Moreover, Malotki demonstrated that the Hopi
language contained vocabulary for units of time (e.g.
days, weeks, months) and also that the verbs could be
changed to indicate past and future tenses.

*Other research supporting the linguistic relativity
hypothesis*

Whorf's data are clearly rather unreliable and not based
on rigorous research, so we need to consider if there is
any support for his theory from more controlled
studies. While there is little evidence for Whorf's
extreme version of the linguistic relativity hypothesis,
there is some modest support for the weaker form.
Research has been conducted in several areas:

◆ how verbal labels affect recall

◆ whether colour coding words affect colour
   discrimination

◆ bilingual participants and national stereotypes

◆ the cognitive effects of grammatical differences
   between languages.

In a classic experiment, Carmichael *et al.* (1932) looked
at the effects of learning *verbal labels* on the recall of
ambiguous line drawings (see Figure 9.1). Results
showed that the label that had been attached at the
first presentation affected recall.

There has also been some support from studies on
colour coding. Brown and Lenneberg (1954) and Lantz
and Stefflre (1964) found that people are better able to
remember colour chips if they have a simple colour
name (e.g. red, blue) rather than a composite name like
'bled'. Berlin and Kay (1969) found that languages
differ in the number of terms they have for colours.
Some languages only have two basic colour words but,
where this is the case, the two terms always correspond
to black and white. If there are three colour words, the
third will be red and so on. In other words, Berlin and
Kay found that colour terms occur in different
languages in a hierarchical form – it is only as the
number of colour words increases, that less basic
colours such as pink and grey are represented in the
vocabulary. They found that English, for example, has

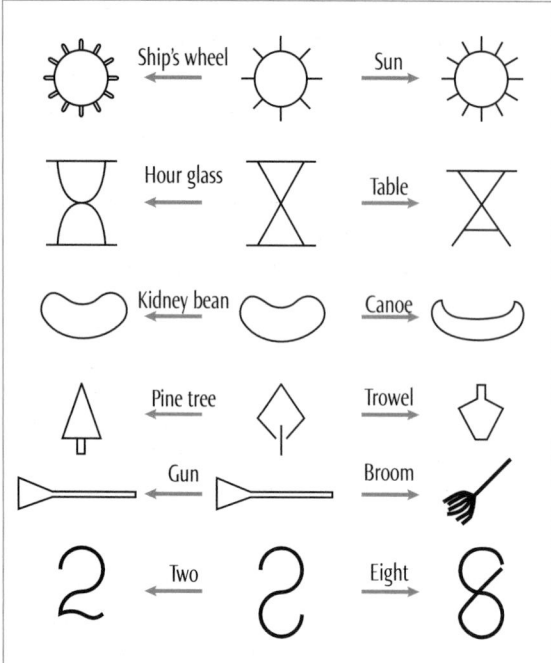

Figure 9.1 Some examples of stimuli and responses showing the effect of verbal labels
Source: adapted from Carmichael *et al.* (1932)

11 basic colour words and that each of these has one generally agreed 'best' colour. This is known as the *focal colour* and English speakers find it easier to remember focal rather than non-focal colours. However, this does not mean that people without appropriate colour labels are unable to distinguish between colours. Laws, Davies and Andrews (1995) showed that English speakers discriminate between shades of light and dark blue just as Russian speakers do, even though Russian, unlike English, has specific verbal labels for these shade variations. Heider (1972) taught the Dani people of New Guinea, who have just two colour words (black and white), some new words for other colours. She found that the Dani learned names more easily for focal colours than for non-focal colours even though they had no native words for any of the colours. Bornstein (1985) found that babies as young as 4 months, who have no language, respond more to the focal colours of red and blue than to non-focal colours. It seems likely, then, that our ability to discriminate between colours depends on innate, biological factors rather than the language that we speak.

There has been some research using *bilingual participants* to see whether the particular language they speak at any one time affects their thought patterns. Ervin-Tripp (1964) found that Japanese–American bilinguals given word association tests in Japanese produced responses that were typical of Japanese monolinguals. The same individuals, however, responded like American monolinguals when

the test was in English. Although this appears to lend support for the Whorfian hypothesis, factors such as the nationality of the listener and the nature of the topics were also found to be influential, so language cannot be isolated as the causal factor. A similar type of study was conducted by Hoffman *et al.* (1986), who gave English–Chinese bilingual participants descriptions of fictional individuals which were written in Chinese and English versions. These descriptions included characters that fitted with particular national stereotypes. For example, they included one type called in Chinese 'sh i gu'. This single word, for which there is no English equivalent, specifically describes a person who is, according to the researchers, 'worldly, experienced, socially skilful, devoted to his/her family and somewhat reserved'. Participants were then asked to write down their own interpretation of the passages they had just read. Findings showed that bilinguals using Chinese were more likely to recall Chinese stereotypes such as the 'sh i gu' character, and bilinguals using English were more likely to emphasize English stereotypes in their descriptions. This study suggests that language exerts some influence on the way people think about issues.

Attempts to investigate the possible effects of *grammatical differences* between languages have produced inconclusive evidence. Carroll and Casagrande (1958) investigated the effect of a particular class of verbs in the Navaho language on the performance of cognitive tasks. In Navaho there are certain verbs that refer to handling (e.g. to carry) and the endings for these verbs must be changed depending on the form of the object being handled. (For example: 'hand over a piece of rope' (a long, thin, flexible object) = san*leh*; 'hand over a stick' (a long, rigid object) = san*tiih*; 'hand over a piece of paper' (a flat, flexible object) = san*ilcoos* and so on). Navaho children have usually learned to use these forms appropriately by the age of 3 or 4 years. Since Navaho speakers have to pay attention to shape in this way, Carroll and Casagrande expected them to group objects according to form rather than to, say, colour. Their participants were Navaho children between the ages of 3 and 10 years, who were presented with two objects (e.g. a blue stick and a yellow piece of rope). They were then offered a third object (e.g. a blue rope) and asked to say which of the two original objects went best with the third one. All the children were at least partially bilingual so they were divided into Navaho-dominant and English-dominant groups. In line with the researchers' expectations, the Navaho-dominant children did, indeed, show a greater tendency to group according to form rather than colour. This would appear to support the weak Whorfian hypothesis, except that the results were confounded by some unexpected additional data from a control group of white American children who showed an even greater tendency to group by form than the Navaho-dominant children. This finding ran totally counter to experimental expectations. One possible explanation arises from what we know about Western children's normal cognitive development. Young children (3–6 years) tend to group objects more on the basis of colour rather than form, but, with increasing age, move towards form rather than colour. When the results of this experiment are analysed in terms of age, it can be seen that there is a greater tendency to group according to form as the age of the child increases, but that this increase begins earlier in the Navaho-dominant group. This suggests that the Navaho linguistic requirement to pay attention to form may facilitate the emergence of the ability to group by form, but does not actually cause it to happen. If this interpretation of the data is correct, it still only provides weak support for the linguistic relativity hypothesis.

Another example of research into the cognitive effects of different grammatical forms has been provided by Bloom (1981). He argued that because English speakers have a subjunctive mood, they find it easy to reason counter-factually (e.g. '*If* she had taken the bus, she *would have* arrived on time'). There is no subjunctive mood in Chinese and so Chinese speakers should find counter-factual reasoning more difficult. Bloom wrote some stories containing a series of events that would have happened if an original event had taken place: for example, 'Bier could not read Chinese, but if he had been able to do so, he would have discovered A; what would most have influenced him would have been B', and so on. He gave these stories to both Chinese and American students and asked them whether A, B, etc. had actually occurred. Bloom found that American students gave the correct answer 98 per cent of the time, but Chinese students got them right only 7 per cent of the time. He concluded that Chinese speakers find it difficult to understand counter-factual reasoning because of the constraints of their language. However, Au (1983) argued that Bloom's findings resulted from the unidiomatic nature of the Chinese versions of the stories. When Au repeated the experiment using more idiomatic Chinese, the Chinese students had no problems in answering the questions correctly. Liu (1985) also refuted Bloom's findings, arguing that such reasoning is possible in Chinese, but might take longer to formulate. While this casts doubt on the strong version of the linguistic relativity hypothesis, it does suggest that the facility within a language to express a concept in simple terms reduces processing time.

Evaluation of the linguistic relativity hypothesis

The evidence from studies investigating the linguistic relativity hypothesis has sometimes been difficult to interpret because of the problem of disentangling the language component from other possible influences. Whorf's own research has largely been discredited because of its subjective quality and there appears to be no support for the strong version of the hypothesis. There is some evidence for the weak version since language does seem to influence some habits of thought and also the facility and efficiency with which certain thoughts can be expressed, although research findings have not always been clear-cut. You may have noticed that much of the research cited in this section is quite old and this reflects the fact that psychologists began to view the weak version of the hypothesis as too vague to be useful. There has, however, been some renewed interest in the idea of linguistic relativity. For example, Hunt and Agnoli (1991) have tried to explain the hypothesis in cognitive terms. They believe that there are bound to be significant, if slight, differences in the performance and acquisition of cognitive tasks between speakers of languages if an idea, which is readily expressible in one language cannot be so easily expressed in the other. In their review of the Whorfian hypothesis, they cite examples that seem to support the idea of different cognitive styles arising from different language bases. Chinese, for example, has only 14 basic number terms (0–10, 100, 1000, and 10,000). All intervening numbers are expressed using combinations of those terms e.g. 12 = 10 and 2. However, English-speaking children have to learn special words for the numbers between 10 and 20 and Hunt and Agnoli contend that they take longer to learn to count in this 10–20 range than Chinese children.

If causal links do exist between thought and language, they are likely to be bi-directional. We sometimes invent new words to meet a need and these new words, in turn, might come to affect the way we think. So, for example, 'chairperson' has been coined in order to provide a less gender-specific term than 'chairman', and those who introduced it hoped that its regular use would change views about gender roles. It seems that there is a constant interaction between thought and language within a cultural context. English, for example, is a dynamic language with new words and expressions being added all the time and it is also used extensively by people for whom it is not the native language. It has been estimated that English has a vocabulary that is three times greater than any other language and this gives rise to the scope for a greater range of expression. While this does not, of itself, guarantee more sophisticated levels of thought than are possible for speakers of more impoverished languages, it may perhaps provide a more flexible tool for thinking.

It seems likely, then, that the properties of certain languages can have consequences for cognitive performance. Harley (1995) suggests, for example, that the lack of irregular words in languages such as

Italian and Serbo-Croat have consequences for children learning to read, compared to children learning to read a language such as English, which has many irregular spellings. He also points out that differences in languages can lead to differences in the effects of brain damage. For example, Japanese has two kinds of written script – Kana which is phonetic and Kanji which is picture-based. Kana gives the reader information about how the word should be pronounced whereas Kanji gives no such information. Damage to the left hemisphere of the brain disrupts the reading of Kana, but recognition of Kanji remains intact because the right hemisphere handles this. The study of dyslexia in other languages is still at quite an early stage, but it is likely to provide some important insights.

In summary, although there is no evidence for the strong version of the linguistic relativity hypothesis that language controls or determines thought, the weaker version of the hypothesis remains a useful concept.

Piaget and the cognition hypothesis

Unlike Whorf, who was concerned with differences between cultures, Piaget was interested in universal patterns that occur in all children's thought regardless of their native language. He saw language as just one type of symbolic function much like symbolic play and symbolic imagery. He believed that early language is egocentric and characterized by three distinct types of speech:

◆ *echolalia* – where children simply repeat utterances

◆ *monologues* – where children appear to be thinking out loud

◆ *collective monologues* – where two or more children give the appearance of engaging in dialogue, but are, in fact, simply producing monologues.

He recognized that language could have a facilitating effect on thinking, but that an understanding of underlying concepts was required *before* the appropriate verbal tag could be applied. Piaget's theory of cognitive development is explained in Chapter 10. Here we will look briefly at research concerned with his *cognition hypothesis*, i.e. that language requires some cognitive competence before it can develop.

For example, Piaget believed that children need to acquire object permanence (i.e. the ability to understand that objects and people continue to exist even if they are not currently visible – see Chapter 10 for a detailed explanation) before they can acquire language concepts such as nouns. He felt that this explained the fact that the vocabulary of children dramatically increases around the age of 18 months (i.e. when object permanence develops). There is some research (e.g.

McCune-Nicolich 1981) which suggests that the child's use of relational words (e.g. 'no', 'down', 'gone') is related to the concept of object permanence. Tomasello and Farrar (1986) found that relational words such as 'up' and 'move' (relating to objects still present) are used before words such as 'all gone' (relating to objects which are absent from the visual field).

One way of testing the cognition hypothesis is to look at the development of children with learning difficulties. If Piaget is correct in assuming that language is dependent on cognitive competence, it would follow that children with learning difficulties should also show delayed or impaired language development. There is certainly evidence that spoken language is often delayed and limited in such children (Johnson and Ramsted 1983). However, this does not always have to be the case. Yamada (1990) has reported a case study of an individual known as 'Laura'. In spite of severe cognitive impairment and restricted short-term memory capacity, she is able to construct complex, grammatically correct sentences and complete other linguistic tasks, even though her overall language competence is not completely normal. Yamada suggests that such cases refute the idea that it is necessary to acquire certain cognitive concepts before language can develop. The study of a rare genetic disorder called Williams syndrome also provides a counter-argument to Piaget. Bellugi *et al.* (1991) have reported that affected individuals, who have very low IQs, show completely normal language competence and seem to take a particular interest in unusual vocabulary.

Evaluation of Piaget and the cognition hypothesis

There seems to be little, unequivocal evidence to support the cognition hypothesis. Children develop some limited language before they develop object permanence and the rapid expansion of vocabulary that takes place around the age of 18 months seems to have little direct relationship with the development of the object concept. However, Bates *et al.* (1987) have suggested that language is delayed in children whose symbolic play and imitation are normally also delayed. They have also shown that children who are early to develop particular kinds of sequence-gesturing in their play (e.g. pouring pretend milk into a cup, drinking from it and then wiping their mouth) are also the first to start using two- and three-word sentences. Such findings have led Bloom (1993) to suggest, much as Piaget had many years before, that 'words a child hears from others will be learned if they connect with what the child is thinking and feeling'.

Evidence from research on children with learning difficulties is mixed but, in general, lends support to the idea that language and thinking are separate, independent processes, rather than that cognition precedes language. Some psychologists believe that language training can actually improve performance on cognitive tasks, although Sinclair-de-Zwart (1969) showed that such training has only an indirect and temporary effect. Best (1973), however, found that deaf children were more likely to do well at cognitive tasks if they had a high level of competence in sign language. This suggests that their language ability facilitated their thinking.

There is not much recent research on the cognition hypothesis and psychologists have tended to become more interested in looking at the social rather than cognitive factors that seem to affect language development (these are discussed in the next section).

Vygotsky and the interdependence of language and thought

A rather different view has been put forward by Vygotsky (1934). He believed that language and thinking have different roots and develop independently in infancy. At first, any attempts by an infant to use language are for social purposes and not linked to inner thoughts. Language at this stage is fairly basic and consists of vocalizations designed to attract attention. Thinking, which starts to develop during this same period, is also at a fairly basic level and occurs in the absence of language, i.e. it depends on images. Vygotsky suggested that, around the age of 2 years, social speech and thought without language begin to merge and language starts to play a major role in the child's intellectual and social development. He believed that egocentric speech becomes internalized as inner speech and continues to play an important role in regulating and planning cognitive operations. In other words, unlike Piaget, he believed that cognitive development from this age is partly controlled by language. From the age of about 2 years, language has two functions:

◆ monitoring and directing thought

◆ communicating with other people.

At first, children find it difficult to disentangle these two functions and often engage in egocentric speech, i.e. they speak their thoughts aloud and do not always communicate effectively. By the age of approximately 7 years, the child has learned the distinction.

Evaluation of Vygotsky's views

Vygotsky conducted his own research to support his ideas, but his work is problematic to evaluate because he reported it in such a way that makes it difficult to replicate. His theory has yet to be elaborated or tested rigorously.

Social and cultural aspects of language use

Language is a tool for social communication but, even within the same language-speaking community, individuals do not all speak in the same way. These differences within a particular language are called *dialects* and are often seen as indicators of real or imagined differences in class, ethnic origin, religion or other aspects of life. Dialects usually arise when a particular group of individuals converse more amongst themselves than with people from the larger community outside the group. Profession, age, geography, social class and ethnic origin are all factors that can contribute to the use of dialect. Sometimes a single speaker will use a different dialect depending on the context. In Greece, for example, there are two forms of the Greek language – High Greek is used in formal settings (e.g. in courts of law, educational institutions, government offices) and Low Greek is used between friends and families. There is no such clear-cut division in English, but people writing an official letter or delivering a public speech will use a more formal style of expression than people chatting to friends.

Social aspects of language use

Basil Bernstein, a British sociologist, studied the differences between the language use of different social classes and concluded that these differences had 'cognitive consequences' (Bernstein 1971). In other words, he subscribed to the weak form of the linguistic relativity hypothesis. He made a distinction between 'restricted code' and 'elaborated code':

◆ Restricted code is a pattern of speech that uses fairly basic vocabulary and contains mainly concrete description. It can usually only be understood when set in context.

◆ Elaborated code is not context-bound and uses more complex grammatical structures and more abstract vocabulary.

Bernstein believed that working-class children use only restricted code whereas most middle-class children can use both, even though they have a greater tendency to adopt the elaborated. Hawkins (1973) asked 5-year-old children to tell a story depicted in a set of pictures. Middle-class children used elaborated code to link the events and people in the pictures and so were able to build up a coherent story that could be understood by listeners without reference to the pictures. Working-class children, on the other hand, were limited by restricted code and only listeners who had access to the pictures could understand their stories.

Bernstein believed that restricted code arises as a function of socialization within working-class family life. Status is unequivocally defined in terms of age, gender and family relationship and so there needs to be no discussion or verbal elaboration to clarify roles. Because the father is in an unambiguous position of authority, he can give an order, e.g. 'Stop it' and will simply expect to be obeyed. In middle-class families, however, members tend to relate to one another more as individuals and the status of individuals within the family is much less clear-cut. As a result, the meaning of communications has to be made much more explicit and there is often discussion and negotiation about decisions and rules. This mode of communication requires a more elaborate form of language. According to Bernstein, the class system restricts access to the elaborated code and, since most teachers are middle class, working-class children cannot understand or be understood by them properly, which exacerbates their problems at school. Bernstein believed that the use of a restricted code in working-class children was related to their low academic attainment compared to middle-class children.

Evaluation of Bernstein's work

Bernstein's conclusions have been the subject of considerable criticism, in particular by the American sociolinguist, William Labov (1970). Labov identified three major criticisms:

◆ Bernstein contended that the verbal IQ of working-class children was lower than their visuospatial IQ. However, verbal IQ is measured by tests of verbal analogy (e.g. toe is to foot as finger is to —) and verbal IQ, by this definition, seems to bear no relation to the linguistic abilities which vary between elaborated and restricted code.

◆ Bernstein produced no evidence of a causal relationship between low academic achievement and the use of a restricted language code.

◆ Bernstein's methods for collecting data may have influenced the samples of language. He used middle-class researchers to collect samples from both working- and middle-class children. The differences in the language samples collected may have reflected the working-class children's difficulty in relating to the interviewers.

Cultural aspects of language use

These criticisms are similar to those levelled at Whorf – namely that the differences he attributed to language might actually have arisen from differences in culture.

There is little evidence that elaborated and restricted codes actually exist as separate entities. Bernstein did not record detailed transcripts to illustrate the two types of speech, and linguists such as Gordon (1981) regard his defining criteria for the two codes as unsatisfactory. There is also little evidence that different family types talk in distinctly different codes. Wells (1985), in a review of relevant research, found that most children of school age have been exposed to a similar range of syntax and language use. Tizard and Hughes (1984) found class differences in amounts of questioning, vocabulary, use of books and imaginative play in pre-school children, but the differences were not large and there were wider variations within classes than between them.

One of the most widespread non-standard dialects is that spoken by black people, both in America and the UK and this has been another area of interest for sociolinguists. This dialect is commonly referred to as 'Black English', although researchers such as Labov (1972) prefer the term Black English Vernacular (BEV). From a linguistic point of view, BEV does not vary significantly from Standard English. However, Labov (1970) has made an extensive study of the dialect and outlined some of the differences. Some of the grammatical rules are different so, for example, agreement between a subject and a verb is not always obligatory in BEV, e.g. 'She have a daughter' or 'They was going'. Similarly, BEV does not appear to have a past tense form for some strong verbs, e.g. 'come', 'see'. This is the kind of finding which might have led Whorf to conclude that speakers of BEV have no concept of the past. This would be a totally erroneous conclusion, however, because the tenses are negated differently: 'I don't see it' is the present tense while 'I ain't see it' is the past. In addition to certain syntactic differences, there are distinct vocabularies. Some BEV words such as 'rap' and 'right-on' have been appropriated by speakers of Standard English, but certain other terms remain distinctively BEV e.g. 'crib' for house (Burling 1973).

Evaluation of cultural aspects of language use

There has been a tendency to see ethnic dialects as somehow inferior and as evidence of a failure on the part of speakers to master the standard dialect. It is sometimes suggested that low academic achievement in black children is directly attributable to impoverished language skills. It is, of course, possible that some black children experience problems in language development just as some white children do. It seems likely that poverty or other social factors retard many aspects of cognitive development. However, it is important not to confuse racial differences with social class differences. Labov (1970) produced a critical analysis of some of the so-called deficits in children speaking BEV, and found that many instances of reported impoverished speech were artefacts of the method of collecting data. It is also important to note that many examples of illogical speech from black children are simply misunderstood dialect differences. For example, the use of the double negative e.g. 'He don't know nothing' is often cited as an example of poor logic in black children. In fact, the double negative is found in other standard languages such as Russian and Old English. Modern English is simply one of those languages that uses a single negative form. Neither form is correct – both forms convey a precise meaning as long as the listener knows the underlying rules. It is simply wrong to assume that non-standard dialects are deficient grammatically.

Gender differences in language use

There has also been some interest in the question of gender differences in language use. For example, in a study of Edinburgh schoolchildren, Romaine (1984) found that most children could differentiate between what he called 'polite' and 'rough' forms of speech, but that girls began to alter their speech patterns as they grew older. The girls used fewer non-standard forms than the boys did and their pronunciation and syntax were closer to 'polite' speech.

Gender differences have also been found in the content of speech. Young adult males have been shown to talk more about their opinions, preferences and sources of personal pride whereas young women preferred to talk about their feelings and their fears (Rubin *et al.* 1980). Tannen (1990, 1993) has conducted research into the different conversational style of men and women. She believes that males and females have different goals for conversation – males prefer to inform whereas females prefer to consult – and that this can lead to serious misunderstandings between them, both in personal relationships and in the workplace.

There have been a number of studies that have shown differences in the way that males and females use language, but it is clearly not the case that all men and women differ in their speech patterns. Nor is it likely that males and females are incapable of changing the way that they speak if they choose to. As Tannen (1995) herself says:

'If women and men talk differently, it is not because they can't talk any other way but because they don't want to. Our ways of talking reflect the way we assume a good person talks – and we get our sense of how we should be a good person by observing the others we talk to *with whom we identify*.'

She illustrates this point with an anecdote from the anthropologist, Keith Basso (1979), who spent most of his career working with the Western Apache. He recalls an occasion when he heard what sounded to him like a group of 'typical white men' conversing behind him. He turned to find that it was a group of young Apache men who told him that they were imitating 'white speech'. They were perfectly capable of doing this convincingly although they usually chose not to because they believed it was a shallow, insincere way to talk, and not their way.

Exam summary: Language and culture

The AQA examination will test your understanding of the following areas:

◆ research into relationship between language and thought (pp. 219–25)
◆ linguistic relativity hypothesis (pp. 220–4)
◆ investigations into the social and cultural aspects of language (pp. 225–7).

Example question

The question below should take you 30 minutes.

◆ 'We see and hear and otherwise experience very largely as we do because the language habits of our community predispose certain choices of interpretation.' (Sapir 1921)

Describe the linguistic relativity hypothesis and assess the extent to which this statement about it is supported by research evidence. *(24 marks)*

Suggested answer structure

This question, unlike most other questions you will have met so far, contains a quotation. It is worth stressing how to go about dealing with them. First, some quotations are there simply as devices to direct you towards the right topic area. This quotation certainly does that: it offers a helpful 'aide memoire' about the main assumptions of the linguistic relativity hypothesis. However, this one requires you to engage with it in your response. You are asked to what extent this statement is supported by research evidence. This should help you to structure your answer so that you are doing exactly that. It also helps to refer to the quotation from time to time, e.g. 'Whorf (1956) later conducted his own analysis of North American languages and drew a more radical conclusion than Sapir ...' (p. 220).

This question is specifically related to the linguistic relativity hypothesis, covered on pp. 220–4. There is a great deal here, and you only have 30 minutes to answer all the question's requirements, so make every sentence count. The AO1 component requires you to describe the linguistic relativity hypothesis, and the AO2 component then requires an assessment of the extent to which the theory is supported by research evidence. This involves more than simply describing research studies in this area. You should attempt to weigh up the evidence from studies that challenge its assumptions as well as those which support it (the assess injunction requires this – see Chapter 21). You should then round up this assessment by reaching conclusions based on the weight of empirically informed argument you have presented (pp. 223–4).

Language acquisition

Language acquisition is one of the most remarkable of human achievements. Clark (1991) has estimated that an average child has acquired a vocabulary of 14,000–15,000 words by the age of 6. In this section we will look at the process of language acquisition and then consider various explanations of how language develops in children.

Research into the process of language acquisition

Before a child can use language, the child needs to be able to discriminate between speech sounds. This is a more complex ability than you might at first imagine. The child has to distinguish, for example, not only the difference between the sounds of 'd' and 't', but also to recognize that a 't' spoken by a deep male voice is the same sound as a 't' spoken by a much higher-pitched voice. It has been demonstrated that this remarkable ability is present either right from birth or very soon afterwards (Bates *et al.* 1992). At first, babies seem able to distinguish a whole range of speech sounds but, as they get older, they seem to 'tune in' more to the speech sounds of the native language to which they are continually exposed. Werker and Tees (1984) found that babies raised in English-speaking homes were able to distinguish between two forms of 't' found in Hindi, but not in English. By the age of 10–12 months, however, this ability had almost disappeared.

Speech perception appears to be quite well developed in young infants, but in order to use language, babies need to be able to *produce* speech sounds. There are clear stages in language production, which seem to be universal. At around the age of 2 months, babies begin to coo, i.e. they utter vowel sounds like 'uuu' and 'aaa'. These sounds show considerable variation in tone, volume and pitch. Consonant sounds do not tend to appear until the age of 6 to 8 months, when babies combine them with vowels to form sound patterns like 'dadadada', 'babababa', etc. This babbling accounts for about half of a baby's non-crying sounds between the ages of 6 and 12 months (Mitchell and Kent 1990). At first, babbling includes sounds that are not heard in the baby's native language but, at around 9 to 10 months, as with speech perception, the range seems to become restricted to the repertoire of surrounding speakers (Oller 1981). At this so-called *pre-linguistic phase*, babies appear to understand the meaning of words even though they cannot yet produce them. In other words, their receptive language outstrips their expressive language. Fenson *et al.* (1994) conducted a large-scale survey of

mothers to find out about their babies' language comprehension. They found that 10-month-old babies could understand about 30 words while 13-month-olds recognized as many as 100 words.

The first real words are usually uttered around the child's first birthday and tend to refer to people and objects (Clark 1993). Although children can vary tremendously in the rate at which they learn new words, Fenson *et al.* (1991) found, in a large-scale study, that the average rate was 12 words at 12 months, 179 words at 20 months and 380 words at 28 months. This explosion from about the age of 16 months may be due to several factors. Bates *et al.* (1992) have suggested that it is linked to rapid increases in synaptic connections in the brain. Another factor that facilitates vocabulary acquisition is what de Villiers and de Villiers (1992) have called 'fast mapping'. This is the ability to use context to make a reasonable guess about a word's meaning after just one or two exposures. This contrasts with the early period of acquisition (around 12 to 16 months) when a child typically learns words slowly and after many repetitions.

At the one-word stage, children typically overgeneralize so that they use 'dog', for example, to refer to various types of four-legged animals or 'daddy' for all men including the postman. One spoken word, often combined with physical gestures, is used to convey a sentence-like meaning. For example, 'ball' accompanied by outstretched arms and cupped fingers may mean 'throw me the ball'. This is called a *holophrase* and occurs commonly in the speech of 12- to 18-month-olds. The first sentences are usually produced around the age of 18 months. These usually consist of only two or three words and are very simple. Brown (1973) has described this as *telegraphic speech* because it resembles the kind of abbreviated sentences used by adults when writing telegrams or short advertisements in the newspaper.

Children at this stage do not use inflections (i.e. grammatical markers such as the plural 's', the verb endings 'ing' and 'ed', or auxiliary verbs such as 'be' and 'do'). So, young children are likely to say 'dog run' rather than 'the dog runs' or 'Mummy sing' rather than 'Mummy is singing'. However, children seem to master how to use such grammatical markers fairly quickly and, by the age of approximately 3-and-a-half years, can use endings such as 's', 'ing' and 'ed' appropriately (Kuczaj 1977). Once children are able to use the regular forms of the plural and past tense, they tend to apply these regular forms inappropriately, e.g. 'goed' and 'sheeps'. This tendency is called *overregularization* although Pinker (1990) has found that children who have learned the 'ed' rule make errors on fewer than 5 per cent of irregular verbs. His data show that children often produce a correct and an incorrect irregular verb in the same sentence, e.g. 'They *went* and *singed* in church.' This suggests that the common irregular verbs are mastered before ones that are heard more rarely.

Children also have to come to grips with syntax – the rules that govern word order, sentence structure and the relationship between words – when they start combining words. As with the acquisition of vocabulary, there seems to be a sudden and rapid expansion after a slow start. Fenson *et al.* (1994) have shown that there is a very high correlation between the size of a child's vocabulary and the complexity of its sentence structures. It is not yet clear whether a large vocabulary encourages syntactic competence or whether increased understanding of the rules of sentence construction allows for easier learning of new words. It could be that both increases are due to the growing capacity of the child's working memory.

Another important aspect of language learning is *pragmatics*. This refers to the social, rather than the grammatical, rules of language. For example, children have to learn quite early how to make requests in a socially acceptable way, e.g. 'can I?' and 'may I?'. Ervin-Tripp *et al.* (1990) have shown that children learn to phrase a question in a different way if the first attempt provokes no response. They also need to learn the conventions of turn-taking in a conversation that involves quite complex language understanding. Children have to anticipate when their conversational partner is about to finish speaking and this seems to be a skill that develops with experience. McTear (1985) showed that 2-year-olds take on average 1.5 seconds to respond to a conversational partner whereas adults take only about 0.8 seconds. Children also seem to learn from an early age that they have to adapt their language to suit the listener. Four-year-olds use simpler language when they are talking to 2-year-olds than when they are chatting to an adult (Tomasello and Mannle 1985). An important aspect of adult conversation involves non-verbal communication such as smiling, head nodding, eye contact, etc. Miller *et al.* (1985) recorded children talking to adults on various topics and noted the degree of non-verbal communication in the children. They found that the number of such gestures increased with the child's age, suggesting that children learn this aspect of conversation through experience.

Research has provided us with a reasonable if not complete picture of the way language develops in young children. A much greater challenge for psychologists has been to explain *how* language develops. We will now look at some of the theories that have attempted to explain language acquisition.

Explanations of language development

We will consider three rather different types of explanation provided by:

◆ environmental theories

◆ nativist theories

◆ interactionist theories.

Environmental theories

The earliest attempts to explain language acquisition were largely founded on the common-sense notion that it was a relatively uncomplicated process dependent on imitation and reinforcement. A formal, learning theory of language acquisition based on this idea was put forward by Skinner (1957). He referred to language acquisition as 'verbal behaviour' because he believed that it was acquired by exactly the same mechanisms of conditioning and reinforcement that governed all other aspects of human behaviour. According to this theory, infants, motivated by a survival need to communicate, begin by emitting random verbal sounds. If adults reinforced these (e.g. by smiling or nodding approval), the sounds will be repeated, but if they are not reinforced, they will extinguish. In addition, children sometimes use echoic responses, i.e. they simply try to imitate what they have heard and these imitations are also reinforced. Through a process of selective reinforcement, adults gradually shape children's language into correct usage. This extreme form of learning theory has a number of serious flaws:

◆ Most children achieve language competence even though their environments are very different.

◆ Language seems to be learnt at roughly the same rate and in the same sequence, regardless of environment.

◆ Adults generally correct only truth and meaning in children's utterances, not syntax and, on the occasions when they do attempt to correct grammar, it usually has little effect (see *In Focus*).

◆ Certain words (e.g. 'no!') are clearly understood by children well before they try to produce the words themselves.

◆ The pattern of acquisition of irregular verb and noun forms does not occur as learning theory would predict. There is often a U-shaped development where performance begins well, becomes temporarily worse, and then improves again. It is as though the child has to learn the general rules and then learn exceptions to those rules (Kolota 1987).

◆ Children often produce new utterances that they have never heard before and Skinner's theory cannot account for this creativity.

in focus

Transcripts of child language

Much of the research into child language has been based on tapes and transcripts of children talking. This has produced a rich source of material and provided many insights into the pattern of language development although there are difficulties with this approach. It is important, for example, to note the context as well as just the words. When a child says, 'Mummy coat' it could mean 'That's mummy's coat', 'Mummy has put her coat on', 'Put your coat on, mummy', etc. An adequate description of the child's language would have to include the range of relationships that are being expressed. It is also important to obtain a large sample of speech in order to avoid hasty conclusions about a child's competence. Adam, a child studied extensively by Roger Brown (1973), often used the expression 'just checking'. It would be tempting to conclude that he had acquired an understanding of how to use the morpheme 'ing'. However, it was clear from analysing many of his utterances that he never used 'ing' except in this phrase, so the likely explanation was that he had simply picked up the whole phrase through imitation. Similarly, it is too simplistic to assume that a child who regularly uses a particular word or construction is actually using it in the way an adult would. Young children, for example, frequently use the conjunction 'because', but mean 'and then' rather than 'as a result of', e.g. 'I fell off the swing because I hurt my leg'.

In spite of some of the difficulties of interpretation, child language transcripts have provided some useful insights. Some extracts are reproduced below which illustrate what happens when adults attempt to correct grammar.

Interviewer: Adam, which is right, 'two shoes' or 'two shoe'?

Adam: Pop goes the weasel.
(Brown and Bellugi 1964)

. . . . .

Child: Want other one spoon, daddy.

Daddy: You mean you want the other spoon.

Child: Want other one spoon, please, daddy.

Daddy: Can you say 'the other spoon'?

Child: Other one spoon.

Daddy: Say 'other'.

Child: Other.

Daddy: 'Spoon'.

Child: Spoon.

Daddy: 'Other spoon'.

Child: Other spoon. Now give me other one spoon.
(Braine 1971)

. . . . .

Child: Nobody don't like me.

Mother: No, say 'Nobody likes me'.

Child: Nobody don't like me.

*(This sequence is repeated **8** times.)*

Mother: Now listen carefully, say 'NOBODY LIKES ME.'

Child: Oh! Nobody don't likes me.
(McNeil 1966)

. . . . .

Child: My teacher holded the rabbits and we patted them.

Adult: Did you say teacher held the baby rabbits?

Child: Yes

Adult: What did you say she did?

Child: She holded the baby rabbits and we patted them.

Adult: Did you say she held them tightly?

Child: No, she holded them loosely.
(Bellugi 1970)

. . . . .

More usually, adults correct meaning rather than syntax:

Child: Doggie (pointing at a horse)

Adult: No, that's a horsie.
(Brown and Hanlon 1970)

While Skinner's extreme view of language acquisition receives little support, there is some evidence that the type of language the child hears spoken does have an effect on development. Children who listen to more spoken language are known to develop vocabulary faster than those who hear less (Engel *et al.* 1975). It also seems that children whose carers use language responsively show more rapid language development (Olsen *et al.* 1986). One particular type of parental language that has attracted interest is the use of *motherese* (Snow 1994). This is a simplified way of talking to children using shorter, slower, clearly segmented speech which includes more repetition and redundancy than is usual in adult speech and is delivered in a higher pitch than normal adult language. The term is something of a misnomer since fathers and other adults use it too (Hladik and Edwards 1984) and even children themselves use it when talking to younger children (Shatz and Gelman 1973), so it is sometimes called *child directed speech* (CDS) instead.

Activity 2: Talking to children

Try to 'listen in' to a carer (usually, but not always, a mother) talking to a young child. A queue at a supermarket checkout is often a good location to do this if you have no other access to a young family. See if you notice anything about the tone, pitch, choice of words, sentence structure, and so on, that is different from language used between adults.

CDS gradually fades as the child gets older and levels of comprehension improve. The evidence concerning the role of CDS in language development is not entirely clear, but it seems likely that it is helpful, at least in the early stages. Certainly babies seem to like to listen to motherese and, from only a few days old, show a preference for it over normal adult speech (Cooper and Aslin 1994). Indeed, Werker and her colleagues (1994) have demonstrated that English and Chinese babies show a preference for CDS regardless of whether it is spoken in English or Chinese. CDS is found in most cultures even though Lieven (1994) has suggested that the style of the speech differs quite widely between language communities. The fact that some form of CDS is almost universal and that babies show a very early preference for it suggests that it has an important developmental function. Gleason and Ratner (1993) believe that the rhythm and simplicity of CDS serves to break speech down into major syntactic constituents so that it is more comprehensible to infants.

Evaluation of environmental theories

While learning theory undoubtedly offers an explanation for certain aspects of language acquisition, such as pronunciation and understanding of word meanings, it is too simplistic to account for the complexity and rapidity of the achievement. As far as CDS is concerned, it does not, on its own, explain the process of language acquisition since children who are not exposed to it still manage to learn a complex grammar, even if they do so at a slower rate. It seems reasonable to conclude that CDS is not necessary for language development, but that it might facilitate the process.

Nativist theories

Given that language development appears to follow a very similar pattern across cultures, it would seem likely that the ability is somehow 'wired in'. The best-known theorist to adopt this position is Chomsky (1957) although, more recently, the cognitive psychologist, Steven Pinker (1989, 1994) has also written in support of this view. Chomsky argued that children learn language by acquiring a set of rules or grammar. He maintained that this could not occur as a result of environmental exposure alone because much of what they hear spoken is 'degenerate output'. In other words, the adults surrounding them produce language which consists of false starts, hesitations, slips of the tongue and blurred word boundaries (i.e. it is not clear where one word ends and the other begins). He also believed that language acquisition could not be dependent on intelligence or experience because it occurs at a time when the child is incapable of complex cognitions. Chomsky thought that children acquire language readily because they are biologically equipped to do so and possess an innate mechanism that is programmed to recognize grammatical structure. This *language acquisition device* (LAD) is not specific to a particular language, such as English or Arabic, but rather it sets limits on what is permissible in any language. Chomsky believes that there are linguistic universals that are features common to all languages, for example, phonological elements such as vowels and syllables and syntactic structures such as nouns, verbs, plurals and tenses. These similarities between languages exist at what Chomsky calls 'the deep structure' level, whereas differences between languages exist at 'surface structure' level (see *In Focus*).

Children have an innate ability to use transformational rules that allow them to transform deep structure into surface structure and vice versa. In Chomsky's early writings in the fifties, the LAD was not described in any great detail and he replaced it later with the idea of 'a universal grammar'. This

Deep and surface structures

Chomsky believed that we possess an innate understanding of grammar that allows us to distinguish between acceptable sentence structure and meaningless strings of words. One aspect of our grammar is a set of rewrite rules which enables us to analyse sentences into their lowest level constituents (e.g. noun phrases, verb phrases, nouns, verbs). A constituent is a unit of language that can be replaced with a single word without altering the basic grammatical structure of the sentence although it might alter the meaning. For example, in the sentence 'The friendly, little girl spoke to the grumpy, old woman', 'the friendly, little girl' is a constituent because it could be replaced with 'Emma' while 'the friendly, little' is not a constituent because it cannot be replaced by one word; 'spoke to the grumpy, old woman' can be replaced simply by 'spoke' so this, too, is a constituent, whereas 'to the' is not. We can use these constituents to generate novel sentences and to avoid producing non-sentences. However, this phrase-structure grammar alone cannot account for all our linguistic competence and in 1965 Chomsky revised his theory to include the concept of *transformational grammar*, which converts *deep structure* (the underlying meaning of a sentence) into *surface structure* (the actual words that are written or spoken). Chomsky recognized that sentences could have different surface structures but similar deep structures. For example:

> The boy ate the apple.

> The apple was eaten by the boy.

On the other hand, sentences can have similar surface structures but quite different deep structures. For example:

> He is easy to please.

> He is eager to please.

Occasionally, a sentence can have one surface structure but two underlying deep structures (as in the case of an ambiguous sentence). For example:

> Teachers should stop drinking in classrooms.

> Visiting relatives can be a nuisance.

Chomsky proposed that people use transformational rules to convert surface structure to deep structure when trying to understand language, and to convert deep structure into surface structure when producing language.

slightly revised formulation of Chomsky's original ideas has been termed *principles and parameters theory* (PPT). Although all languages share many common features (*linguistic principles*), they can differ greatly in superficial ways (*parametric variation*). Children have to learn the particular details of their own native language; Chomsky (1981) calls this *parameter setting*. In order to acquire language, children have to identify the correct parameter from a range of possibilities. There is, for example, only a limited range of ways in which languages allow questions to be formed. In other words, the universal grammar sets constraints on question formation and the child must pick the correct parameter within that innately specified range. This process has been likened to a set of switches that constrain the grammatical possibilities

of language; exposure to a particular language will set the switches to a particular position.

Some researchers believe that all the principles and parameters are available from birth, but factors such as limited memory capacity prevent infants from using them straightaway. According to this *continuity hypothesis*, language develops as such factors are overcome (Clahsen 1992). The alternative *maturation hypothesis* (Felix 1992) suggests that children cannot access their inherited linguistic ability in the early months of life and can only do so as they grow older.

There is other evidence, too, which favours an innate basis for language. Bickerton (1984), for example, has reported on pidgin and creole languages. Pidgin is a highly simplified form of English, which was originally developed in order to communicate with black slaves in areas such as the Caribbean. Creole, on the other hand, is a language that has become the native tongue of children of pidgin speakers. Creole languages are much richer semantically and syntactically than the original pidgin and seem to demonstrate that there is an innate drive to develop syntax even if it is not present in the language of one's parents. Pinker (1994) has shown that even hearing-impaired children develop a creole sign language if they are exposed to signing pidgin.

Some support is also emerging from the relatively new research field of genetic linguistics. Gopnik and Crago (1991) have found that specific language impairment (SLI) runs in families and their study of a particular British family has led geneticists working with them to suggest that a single dominant gene is involved. As Pinker (1994) points out, 'This single gene is not, repeat not, responsible for all the circuitry underlying grammar ... Remember that a single defective component can bring a complex machine to a halt even when the machine needs many properly functioning parts to work.' However, this evidence does suggest that there is some pattern of genetically programmed events in the development of the brain that is specialized for the 'wiring in' of language competence.

Evaluation of nativist theories

Most of the arguments cited earlier against learning theory can be used in support of Chomsky's theory:

◆ Most children achieve language competence and progress through the same developmental stages of language regardless of their environment and culture.

◆ Adults rarely correct grammar and yet children rapidly develop accurate syntax.

◆ Children produce novel utterances that they have never heard before. Sometimes they are incorrect (e.g. he goed), but they demonstrate an awareness of underlying grammatical rules.

The nativist view of language acquisition seems able to explain more aspects of the process than the learning theory account, but there are still a number of criticisms:

◆ Learning must play some part; otherwise, for example, children would not progress from saying 'gived' to 'gave'.

◆ Exposure to spoken language would seem a necessary prerequisite.

◆ It largely ignores social and cognitive factors.

◆ There is some evidence (e.g. Akiyama 1984) that world languages are not as similar as Chomsky supposed.

The slightly revised version of Chomsky's view – PPT – has been quite influential in providing a framework for the acquisition of language and an impetus for research, but it is subject to many of the same criticisms. In particular, it raises questions about how bilingual children are able to acquire two different languages to the same level of competence. As Messer (1999) has pointed out, it seems unlikely that the same parameter can be set in different positions for two different languages.

Interactionist theories

Most contemporary researchers have rejected the extreme forms of both the learning and the environmental approaches and have opted instead for an integrative view that stresses the role of innate factors *and* experience.

Cognitive theory

According to theorists such as Piaget, language is dependent on other cognitive and perceptual processes and follows the stages of cognitive development. His views are relevant to the issue of linguistic relativity and were covered earlier in the chapter. We will just emphasize here that a feature of the cognitive approach is its emphasis on the child as an active learner. Flavell (1985) has suggested that children seem to be constantly formulating and testing hypotheses about the rules and properties of language. Such rule-searching behaviour is apparent in other areas of development and this lends weight to the argument that language learning is simply part of a wider cognitive process. The cognitive theory is not too far removed from the ideas of the nativist theorist, Slobin (1985). The difference centres mainly on whether the rules are innate or whether they arise from the child's active analysis and exploration of the environment. There is little current research in this area and interest has focused more on the social interactionist approach.

Social interactionist theory

While accepting that certain biological and cognitive processes may be necessary for language development, social interactionists believe that these processes alone are not sufficient. They feel that the linguists' preoccupation with grammar obscures the main function of language, which is interpersonal communication. Bruner (1983) contrasted the idea of the LAD with that of the LASS (*language acquisition socialization system*). He believed that the mother–child relationship serves to develop important social skills, such as turn-taking and mutual gaze, which then play a part in conversational language. Support for the necessity of exposure to language in a social context comes from studies of deprived children. Sachs *et al.*

(1981) reported the case of 'Jim' whose parents were both deaf and unable to speak. Television provided his only exposure to spoken language up to the age of 3. Although he produced speech, it was grammatically idiosyncratic and poorly articulated, which suggests that exposure alone is insufficient – there must be some social interaction as well.

It seems irrefutable that language development needs to occur in a social context to be completely effective. The social interactionist theory cannot, however, explain all the features of language acquisition.

Exam summary: Language acquisition

The AQA examination will test your understanding of the following areas:

◆ research into language acquisition (pp. 228–9)

◆ explanations of language development (pp. 229–34)

◆ environmental explanations of language development (pp. 229–31 and pp. 233–4)

◆ nativist theories of language acquisition (pp. 231–4).

Example question

The question below is typical of one drawn from the material above, and should take you 30 minutes to answer.

◆ Discuss how psychological research has helped us to understand the process of language acquisition.

(24 marks)

Suggested answer structure

We have looked at research into the process of language acquisition on pp. 228–9. This is a nice, friendly question that asks you to describe and evaluate research in this area. It pays to reflect upon this for a moment. First of all, the term research allows us to take a fairly liberal interpretation of what is required. The AQA Glossary of Terms (see Table 21.2 on p. 552) defines 'research' as:

> 'The process of gaining knowledge and understanding either through theory construction and examination, or through empirical data collection'.

This is a very helpful definition, as it tells us that writing about theoretical insights is every bit as relevant as are actual research studies (i.e. empirical data collection). This opens up all sorts of possibilities for this question. You could, for example, describe and evaluate specific research studies that have focused on language acquisition (pp. 228–9), or you could examine the various theories and associated research studies that have been proposed to explain this same process. A number of theories have been proposed to account for the acquisition of language, including environmental (pp. 229–31), nativist (pp. 231–3) and interactionist approaches (pp. 233–4), although none has yet been offered that provides a satisfactory explanation for all the features of this complex process.

Note that the question does not say 'describe research that has helped us to understand...', but 'describe *how* research has helped us to understand'. This is an important point: examiners will be more impressed if, in your evaluation, you draw out the degree to which a particular explanation or a particular research study has contributed to this understanding, and exactly how this has been achieved.

Problem-solving and decision-making

Research into problem-solving, including theories of problem-solving

Problem-solving is an everyday activity which is often taken for granted and yet it is a highly complex skill. It is used whenever we need to reach a goal that is not readily available. There is, for example, no problem to be solved in the equation $x = 5 + 2$, because this can be found in a single step (i.e. the goal is readily available). Real problem-solving involves greater complexity. Given the wide diversity of tasks that come under the heading of problem-solving – anything from solving the Northern Ireland situation to working out the best route to an unfamiliar destination – it is not surprising that there is no single adequate theory to explain how we solve all our problems. One early theoretical account of problem-solving was offered by a group of German psychologists collectively known as the *Gestalt School*.

The Gestalt approach to problem-solving

According to Gestalt psychologists, problem-solving requires *structural understanding*, which is the ability to understand how all the parts of the problem fit together to meet the goal. A key requirement is the *reorganization* of the different elements of the problem in such a way that the problem can be solved. Gestaltists believed that people often get stuck when they try to solve problems because they cannot change their *problem-solving set*, i.e. they cannot immediately see how to reorganize the elements in a novel way. Try Activity 3 before you read on.

Activity 3: The matchstick problem

Take six small sticks of equal length (match sticks or toothpicks are suitable for this).

Arrange them in such a way that they form four equilateral triangles (an equilateral triangle has sides of equal length) with each side only one stick long.

Don't worry if you cannot do this – most people find it very difficult. Look to the end of the chapter for the solution.

Once given the clue provided in the answer, most people solve the problem quite quickly because they break free of their usual way of thinking about it. This new way of thinking is called *insight* by the Gestaltists and is sometimes referred to as the 'aha! phenomenon' because the pieces of the problem suddenly fall into place after a period of intense thinking. Wolfgang Kohler (one of the founders of the Gestalt school of psychology) investigated this type of problem-solving in apes. He spent some time during the First World War in Tenerife at an animal research station and published his findings in 1925. A typical problem was to provide a caged chimpanzee with a stick, a number of crates and a banana hanging well out of reach from the ceiling. Typically, Kohler reported that the apes spent a long period of time in intense thinking, followed by a flash of insight that led them to pile the crates on top of one another in a series of steps and then climb up and hook down the banana with the stick.

The Gestaltists called this kind of thinking, which depends on creating a novel solution, *productive thinking*. They contrasted this with *reproductive* or *trial and error thinking* in which people simply reproduce old habits or behaviours. Wertheimer (1945) reported on a study in which students were taught to solve a problem (finding the area of a parallelogram) using one or other of two teaching methods. One teaching method required the students to understand the structural relations in the figure, i.e. that the parallelogram could be rearranged as a rectangle by moving the triangular shape from one end of the figure to the other (see Fig. 9.2 (a)). The students already knew how to find the area of a rectangle so they could easily find the area of the parallelogram once they had re-organized it. A second group of students were simply taught the formula required to solve the problem (see

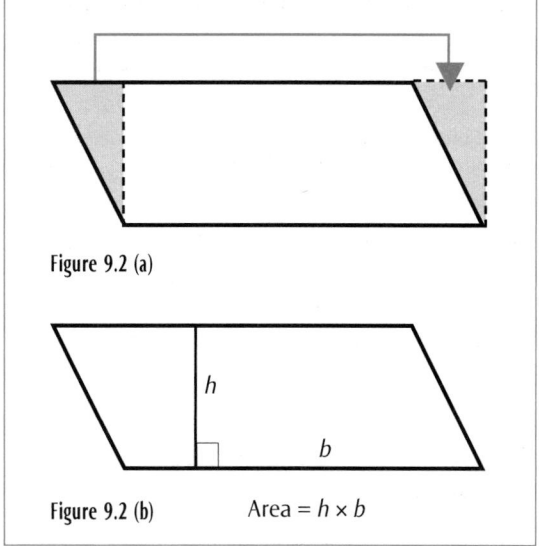

Figure 9.2 (a)

Figure 9.2 (b)   Area = $h \times b$

Fig. 9.2 (b)). They, too, were able to apply this new knowledge and could calculate the area by using the formula. There was no difference in performance between the groups when given a series of similar problems. However, when asked to calculate the areas of unusual parallelograms or novel shapes (*transfer tasks*), the first group was successful, whereas the second group typically said things like, 'We haven't covered that yet'.

This kind of finding suggests that people are more likely to be able to solve novel problems if they are able to reorganize them according to Gestalt principles. Gestalt studies are often criticized because of their lack of clear definitions and absence of statistical analysis. However, some support for Wertheimer's findings was provided by Hilgard and colleagues (1953) who undertook a more controlled study and found that the '*understanding*' group performed significantly better on a series of transfer tasks than the '*rote-learning*' group.

The Gestalt psychologists believed that people often fail to think productively because they are locked into reproductive thinking habits. Duncker (1935) referred to this inhibition as *functional fixedness*. In a well-known study, he asked people to fix a candle to a wall so that it would not drip when lit. Each participant was given various objects including a candle and a box of drawing pins. The only successful solution was to empty the box, fix it to the wall with drawing pins, and stand the candle in it. However, Duncker found that few participants hit on this solution because they were 'fixated' on the usual function of the box (i.e. to hold pins) and, therefore, were unable to see it as a potential holder for the candle. In a variation of the study, Duncker found that participants were more likely to solve the problem when the box was presented separately and *not* as a container for pins.

Maier (1931) conducted a similar kind of study. He took individual participants into a room where two ropes were hanging down from the ceiling. A variety of other objects were lying in the room including a large pair of pliers. The task for participants was to tie the two ropes together. This is not as straightforward as it sounds because it was not possible to reach one rope while holding the other one. The intended solution was to attach the heavy pliers to the bottom of one rope and set it swinging, i.e. to use the pliers as a pendulum. Participants, according to the Gestalt explanation, were 'fixated' on the normal function of pliers and could not see how they could be used to solve the problem of the ropes. After a few minutes, when participants seemed completely at a loss, Maier 'accidentally' brushed past one of the ropes and set it swinging. Although they later claimed not to have noticed Maier's action, many of the participants then went on to use the pendulum solution. Maier believed that his clue had allowed the participants to restructure the problem and think about it in a novel (productive) way.

More recently, researchers have cast doubt on the effectiveness of such hints. Weisberg *et al.* (1978) repeated Duncker's candle experiment, but preceded it with a word-pair memory test that included the pair *candle – box*. Participants presented with the candle task were no more likely to solve it than people who had not previously undertaken the memory test, *unless* they were explicitly told beforehand that one of the word-pairs was relevant to the problem.

A related idea to functional fixedness is that of *set*, in which people get locked into a specific way of tackling problems that has been useful in the past, even when a solution could be reached in a simpler way. The *In Focus* outlines a well-known experiment on mental set conducted by Luchins (1942).

Evaluation of the Gestalt approach

Gestalt ideas have been influential in the field of thinking and reasoning. They demonstrated that reproductive thinking is not sufficient for certain kinds of problem-solving and that past experiences can be detrimental when searching for novel solutions. Their ideas also stimulated research into ways of improving problem-solving skills. However, the theory has been criticized because some of the concepts, such as insight, are too vague to be testable. Early research was often poorly controlled and did not provide a precise explanation of the processes that underlie productive thinking.

Attempts to provide such explanations arose from research conducted within the information-processing framework and this is what we shall look at next.

The information-processing approach to problem-solving

The information-processing approach provides a common framework within which to study problem-solving. This approach arises from the work of Newell *et al.* (1958) which divides problems into a set of stages progressing from the original to the goal state. The stages involve:

◆ representing the problem

◆ selecting and implementing operators to tackle the problem

◆ evaluating progress to assess whether or not the goal state has been achieved.

Luchins' Water Jar Problem

Participants were asked to imagine that they had three jars A, B and C and an unlimited supply of water. For each problem, Luchins supplied a list of the capacities of all three jars and also specified a particular amount of water to be measured out. The task for the subjects was to use all or some of the jars to measure out the required (goal) amount of water. Try this exercise yourself before you read any further.

Problem	A	B	C	Goal
1	22	150	4	120
2	18	125	16	75
3	17	97	9	62
4	39	129	22	46
5	15	66	11	29
6	41	89	7	34

The best way to solve Problem 1 is to fill Jar B and then remove from it one jarful using jar A and then two jarfuls using jar C. The first five problems are all solved best in this way and most people continue to apply this method for the whole exercise. However, in this instance past experience works to the solver's disadvantage because, for Problem 6, there is a more direct method. It is easily solved by subtracting one jarful of C from A. Did you recognize this easier solution?

These stages are flexible and allow the solver to go back to previous states or to set a series of subgoals by which the final goal can be achieved. This approach has the advantage that it provides a broad framework that can then be elaborated to provide more detailed analysis of the specific processes involved in solving particular problems.

Computer modelling of problem-solving has developed from the information-processing approach and this has proved useful in several ways – for example, by providing information about the nature of strategies, the importance of a knowledge base and the crucial nature of the representation stage in problem-solving. In 1972, Newell and Simon developed a computer program called the General Problem Solver (or GPS), in which they attempted to mimic the processes used by humans in tackling problems, including the means-ends analysis approach. The GPS was used extensively to study a number of different problems, but it was eventually discarded by Newell and Simon because it was not as applicable to human problem-solving as they had first assumed, particularly as far as tackling ill-defined problems was concerned.

Problem-solving strategies

Newell and Simon (1972) suggested that problem-solving consisted of searching through the *problem space* which is made up of a number of linked *states* leading to the *goal state*. The solver crosses the problem space by using a range of *permissible operators* that transform one state to another. One way of searching through the problem space which guarantees a solution is to use the *algorithmic method*. This involves a systematic random search in which all possible solutions are tried until the correct one is found. However, this approach can be time-consuming and inefficient, and it is more usual for human problem-solvers to adopt a *heuristic* approach. This is a rule of thumb involving a selective search that looks only at those parts of the problem space that are most likely to produce a solution (see Activity 4).

Psychological research has focused more on heuristics than on algorithms, largely because we use heuristics far more frequently. There are several different kinds of heuristic strategies available to us. We will consider two: means-ends analysis and analogy strategy.

Means-ends analysis

This heuristic is the main problem-solving strategy used in computer simulations of human thinking. It involves breaking a problem into a number of subproblems which are solved in turn and which greatly reduce the difference between the original state and the goal state.

In means-ends analysis, the solver always works on one goal at a time. If that goal is not directly achievable

Activity 4: Solving anagarams heuristically

Try solving the following anagram and think about the way you tackled it:

g w n i l k a

An algorithmic method would guarantee a solution but it is highly unlikely that you applied that method. The anagram has seven letters which means that there are $7 \times 6 \times 5 \times 4 \times 3 \times 2 \times 1$ (= 5040) possible permutations. It is more likely that you used a heuristic method. For example, you might have picked out 'ing' because you recognized this as a familiar combination found at the end of English words. You are then left with a much smaller problem space 'w l k a' and the solution 'walking' now becomes quite easy to find.

in one move, the solver must set a subgoal that will remove the obstacles. At each stage the solver needs to ask the following questions:

◆ What is my goal?

◆ What obstacles are in my way?

◆ What operators are available to me for overcoming these obstacles?

Newell and Simon (1972) gave the following example of using means-ends analysis in everyday life.

'I want to take my son to nursery school. What's the difference between what I have and what I want? One of distance. What changes distance? An automobile. My automobile won't work. What is needed to make it work? A new battery. What has new batteries? An auto repair shop. I want the repair shop to put in a new battery: but the shop doesn't know I need one. What is the difficulty? One of communication. What allows communication? A telephone.... And so on.'

Although this heuristic technique is widely used in computer simulations, the question arises whether humans establish such subgoals in their problem-solving. There is certainly evidence that people pause at intervals during the problem and work out their strategy for the next few moves. Greeno (1974) gave subjects the Hobbits-and-Orcs problem (illustrated in Activity 5) and found that they did not proceed at a steady pace but, instead, took a long time at the beginning and then, again, before two other critical moves. It seems that they were tackling a subproblem at these stages and needed to organize a group of moves. Try to solve the problem in Activity 5 before you read any further.

Activity 5: The Hobbits-and-Orcs Problem

Three Hobbits and three Orcs are standing at the side of a river bank. They all want to cross the river but there is just one small boat available which can only carry up to two creatures at a time. The boat cannot be pushed back empty to the other side and always requires one creature to steer it. If Orcs are ever allowed to outnumber the Hobbits, they will attack them and gobble them up. Your task is to find a way of transporting all the creatures across the river while never leaving more Orcs than Hobbits on any river bank.

The solution can be found at the end of the chapter.

Source: adapted from Thomas (1974)

In dealing with certain problems it is sometimes appropriate actually to increase the difference between the original state and the goal state by temporarily moving backwards. For example, in the Hobbits-and-Orcs problem, solvers tend to concentrate on reducing the difference between the original state (all creatures on the left side) and the goal state (all creatures on the right side) and so think only of moving them from left to right. This means that they ignore the crucial step that they need to solve the problem, i.e. of moving creatures backward across the river. So, it is sometimes necessary temporarily to violate the difference-reduction strategy of the means-ends approach in order to reach a solution. Thomas (1974) found that solvers were often able to make a rapid jump to the goal state once they had realized this, which suggests that human problem-solvers do not always set as many subgoals as a strict application of means-ends analysis would require.

The means-ends analysis approach may well be a useful problem-solving strategy, particularly given the constraints of our working memory capacity. It certainly enables humans to solve puzzles such as the Hobbits-and-Orcs problem. However, in real life, factors such as knowledge and experience affect both the way we represent problems and the way in which we solve them. These factors are considered as part of the *analogy heuristic strategy.*

Analogy strategy

In everyday life, problems are often poorly defined and novel and we need to rely on existing knowledge and experience to find a solution. One heuristic that can be used in these circumstances is analogy. In other words, we use a solution to an earlier problem to help us solve

a new one. This would seem to be a useful approach, but research shows that problem-solvers frequently fail to notice a potential analogy and that, even when they do, they often make errors in their interpretation.

Novick and Holyoak (1991) have suggested four processes that are required for successful problem-solving using analogies:

◆ Locating the appropriate analogical problem (source problem).

◆ Making the appropriate correspondence between parts of the source problem and parts of the target problem.

◆ Adapting the procedures that were helpful in the source problem.

◆ Developing an abstract schema for the whole class of problems that the source and target problems represent.

If these processes are prerequisites for the successful use of the analogy technique, it is, perhaps, not surprising that Novick (1988) found experts using analogies more frequently than novices. The superiority that Novick found for experts over novices has been demonstrated in several studies. Experts differ from novices in many ways – for example, their memory for task-related information, their knowledge base, their method of problem representation, their self-monitoring abilities and their speed and efficiency.

Computer simulations used in the means-ends approach to problem-solving have provided precise theories which can be scientifically tested. However, although computer programs may effectively simulate human thinking, it does not mean that they accurately reflect the underlying human cognitive processes.

Practical issues relating to research in decision-making

There are other types of thinking such as judgement, reasoning and decision-making that have interested psychologists. Decision-making is a particular kind of reasoning that involves making choices and sometimes taking risks. Decision-making can be relatively simple, such as deciding whether to walk or catch the bus to school, or highly complex as when a government has to decide between intervening in a foreign war or remaining neutral.

Risk-taking behaviour in decision-making

Making any kind of decision usually involves weighing up the costs against the benefits. Walking to school has the advantage of saving on the bus fare, but the disadvantages that you have to get up earlier and you will get wet if it rains. More serious decisions can obviously have much more serious and far-reaching consequences. In most decisions, there is a degree of uncertainty or risk and the decision-maker has to decide whether it is a risk worth taking.

Neumann and Morgenstern (1947) suggested that we work out the expected utility of each option using a simple equation:

Expected utility = (probability of a particular outcome) x (utility of the outcome)

Imagine that you are trying to decide whether to buy a £5 lottery ticket which offers you a 1 in 100 chance of winning £250. The equation would work like this:

0.01 (probability) x £250 (utility of the outcome) = £2.50 (the expected utility)

In this case, you probably would not take the risk because the ticket is being sold for double its worth.

However, this so-called *utility theory* in which we seek to gain as much as we can of those things we value (i.e. to maximize utility), does not adequately explain how we make more complex decisions where multiple factors have to be taken into consideration. In any case, research has shown that we do not always operate on the principle of maximizing utility when making decisions. Consider the following example used by Tversky and Kahneman (1987). For each of the two choices below, select the option you prefer.

◆ *CHOICE 1*

Assume that you are richer by $300 than you are today. You now have to choose between:

– a sure gain of $100

– 50 per cent chance to gain $200 and 50 per cent chance to gain nothing.

◆ *CHOICE 2*

Assume that you are richer by $500 than you are today. You have to choose between:

– a sure loss of $100

– 50 per cent chance to lose nothing and 50 per cent chance to lose $200

If you think about this logically, both Choice 1 and Choice 2 are identical (i.e. the utilities are the same in both). In both cases, the first option leaves you with $400 and the second option gives you an even chance of either $300 or $500. There is no right or wrong answer – the option chosen by participants simply reflects their willingness to take a risk. You would expect, then, that people opting for the first option in Choice 1 would also opt for the first one in Choice 2. However, Tversky and Kahneman found that most participants went for the first option in Choice 1, but the second option in Choice 2. In other words, they

contradicted themselves by preferring the sure thing in Choice 1 and the risk in Choice 2. Tversky and Kahneman explain this in terms of the *framing* of the question. In this case, people are influenced by the use of the negative word *loss* in Choice 2 against the positive word *gain* in Choice 1. When offered a sure gain, they seem to be averse to taking risks and prefer to hold on to what they have. When faced with a loss, they seem more ready to take a risk, presumably with the intention of trying to avoid or at least reduce the loss. The interesting point about these findings is not that people differ in their willingness to take risks – this is only to be expected given differing temperaments and circumstances – but that the *same* people differ in their risk-taking strategy depending on the language in which the risk is expressed.

You may think that the study described above is artificial and so cannot be a reliable indicator of how people make decisions in real life. However, the framing effect has been demonstrated in more realistic settings. For example, Johnson (1987) found that people are more likely to choose minced beef that is labelled 80 per cent lean rather than 20 per cent fat and several studies (e.g. McNeil *et al.* 1982 and McNeil *et al.* 1988) have shown that the framing effect can also affect choice of medical treatment. Another study also highlights the importance of framing. Huber *et al.* (1987) asked students on an organizational behaviour course to look at 20 job applications for the post of a computer technician's assistant. The students were asked to draw up a suitable shortlist and were told that the cost of interviewing each candidate would be $300. Some of the students were told to accept applicants who were high on the selection criteria, and other students were instructed to reject applicants who were low on the selection criteria. The first group selected on average six applicants whereas the other group chose to call an average of 10 applicants to interview. The students who were asked to *accept* applicants (i.e. an implication of gain) showed risk aversion and preferred not to interview any risky candidates. Those who were told to *reject* unsuitable candidates (i.e. an implication of loss) were more likely to be risk-seeking and to interview some of the more borderline candidates.

Errors in thinking about probability

It is wrong to assume that people are incapable of making reasoned decisions. Generally speaking, the decision-making strategies available to us are perfectly adequate for handling a wide range of choices. However, people clearly do make errors of judgement and these tend to occur when they use a normally useful strategy in an inappropriate situation. (Note the parallels here with mental set and functional fixedness in problem-solving.) One type of strategy open to us is to use decision-making heuristics. When we make inappropriate decisions, it may be that we have tried to use these heuristics in situations that are beyond their range. We will look at three types of heuristic:

◆ the representativeness heuristic (similarity)
◆ the availability heuristic
◆ the anchoring and adjustment heuristic.

The representativeness heuristic (similarity)

This heuristic is based on the assumption that every instance of a particular category will resemble the prototype for that category (Pitz and Sachs 1984), i.e. it is based on *similarity*. So, for example, if people are given a description of someone and asked to decide whether that person is a librarian or an astronaut, they will base their decision on whether the description is typical of what they think librarians and astronauts are like. While this reliance on similarity and assumption of homogeneous categories can be helpful, it can also lead to error if the decision-maker ignores other factors such as sample size. One well-known error of this type is known as the gambler's fallacy (i.e. that a run of losses *must* be followed by a run of wins). Consider the following example. When a coin is tossed six times, which is the most likely sequence?:

◆ H T H T T H
◆ H H H H H H

Most people pick the first because they know that coin tossing usually produces heads and tails in random order and they think that the first sequence looks more random than the second. In fact, this is a fallacy and both sequences are equally probable. The coin itself has no memory and has no way of knowing that it is time for tails to come up. The likelihood of a tail on the next toss is 50:50, just as it was on the first, second and every toss. So, why do most people choose the first sequence as being most likely? The explanation is based on inappropriate use of the representativeness heuristic. We know that, over a long series of coin tosses, a coin will produce equal numbers of heads and tails. We, therefore, assume that even a small number of tosses will show the same characteristics (i.e. a small sample will be representative of the whole category of 'coin tossing'). In the example above, we believe that the first sequence is a more prototypical example of coin tosses than the second. Hill and Williamson (1998) have found that such biases are evident in the way people choose numbers for the National Lottery. The tendency to choose numbers that have rarely come up before is an example of the gambler's fallacy. Similarly, Hill and Williamson found that people erroneously believed scattered numbers to be more random than adjacent numbers.

Kahneman and Tversky (1972) have carried out a number of experimental studies to demonstrate the inappropriate use of the representativeness heuristic.

They asked people to make probability judgements about birth sequences in large families. Their participants judged the sequence (G = girl and B = boy) G B B G B G more likely than B B B G G G although, in reality, both sequences are equally likely. Another study by Kahneman and Tversky is outlined in Activity 6. Try it yourself before you read any further.

Activity 6: Assessing probability

A local town is served by two hospitals. About 45 babies are born every day in the larger hospital whereas about 15 babies are born each day in the smaller hospital. Approximately 50 per cent of all babies born are boys. However, the exact percentage of babies who are boys will vary from day to day. Some days it will be higher than 50 per cent and other days it might be lower. For a period of one year both hospitals recorded the number of days on which more than 60 per cent of the babies born were boys. Which hospital do you think recorded more such days?

(a) the larger hospital
(b) the smaller hospital
(c) about the same.

Most people respond 'about the same', but this answer is statistically incorrect. We are given the information that 50 per cent of babies in the total population are boys. The larger the sample we have available, the more likely it is to be similar to the total population. On the other hand, a small sample is much less likely to be representative of the total population so the answer to this question should be (b). In this problem, as in the gambler's fallacy, people do not seem to take sample size into account. Most people do not intuitively understand this fundamental statistical concept, so misconceptions are not limited to naive participants. Tversky and Kahneman (1971) found that a group of experienced research psychologists could also be fooled by what the researchers called 'the law of small numbers'. This small-sample fallacy can have important consequences. For example, it can lead to the selection of samples of inadequate size in research studies and thus lead to unwarranted, generalized conclusions. Hamilton and Sherman (1994) have shown that it can also lead to stereotyping where individuals form a detrimental view of a whole group of people, based on their impressions of just a small number of group members. However, it has been shown that people with experience of working out probabilities in particular areas (Kunda and Nisbett 1986) and people who have received training in small-sample theory (Fong *et al.* 1986) do not succumb to the small-number fallacy.

There are other factors that lead to errors in thinking about probability such as the *base-rate fallacy* in which people ignore information about the prior odds of a situation occurring. Kahneman and Tversky (1973) provided participants with brief descriptions of five people and told them that the descriptions had been drawn randomly from a batch of 100. They gave half the participants the base rate information that the total group consisted of 70 lawyers and 30 engineers. The other half were told that the proportions were the other way round, i.e. 70 engineers and 30 lawyers. Participants had to decide on the probability that the particular description they had been given was of a lawyer or an engineer. Some of the descriptions tallied with a picture of an individual which was similar to a general stereotype of an engineer, but quite dissimilar from a stereotype of a lawyer, for example:

> 'Jack is a 45-year-old man. He is married and has four children. He is generally conservative, careful and ambitious. He shows no interest in political and social issues and spends most of his free time on his many hobbies, which include home carpentry, sailing and mathematical puzzles.'

Participants from both base-rate groups responded to this description by suggesting that there was an approximately 90 per cent probability that this description was of an engineer. In other words, they ignored the base-rate information (70:30 or vice versa) and made their decision purely on the basis of representativeness. When they were presented with a completely neutral description, they estimated the probability of the person being an engineer to be 50 per cent whereas they should have estimated it in line with their given base-rates, i.e. either 70 or 30 per cent.

In a later study, Tversky and Kahneman (1982) demonstrated probability errors caused by the *conjunction fallacy*. Participants were asked to rate the likelihood of certain events happening in a particular year. In one example, they were asked the following:

> Suppose Björn Borg reaches the Wimbledon finals in 1981. Please rank in order the following outcomes, from most likely to least likely.
>
> (a) Borg will win the match.
> (b) Borg will lose the first set.
> (c) Borg will win the first set but lose the match.
> (d) Borg will lose the first set but win the match.

Many people rated statement (d) as more probable than statement (a). They failed to realize that the combined probability of Borg losing the first set and winning the match is less likely than the probability of just one of those events being true.

The availability heuristic

It is not surprising that people make mistakes when estimating probability, because it is quite a difficult task. Sometimes people rely on the *availability heuristic* to help them make decisions about probability. This means that they judge the frequency of an event by thinking of readily available examples of that event. If examples spring easily to mind, it is assumed that the event is more frequent than if examples are hard to recall from memory. So, the availability of items determines our judgement of probability. The availability heuristic is often quite accurate, but it can lead to errors when subjective availability does not match true, objective frequency.

Tversky and Kahneman (1973) asked people to assess whether there were more English words beginning with the letter k than having k as their third letter. Using the availability heuristic, most people say that words with an initial k are more common. It is much easier to think of words beginning with k (e.g. king, kettle, etc.) than words like rake where k is the third letter. In fact, there are three times as many English words with k as the third letter than as the initial letter.

Studies like this can be criticized for artificiality. However, there are a number of other studies that suggest that people make errors based on the availability heuristic in real-life decisions. Weber *et al.* (1993), for example, have found that doctors are more likely to make a particular diagnosis if they have recently diagnosed a similar case. MacLeod and Campbell (1992) found that people who were encouraged to think about pleasant events from their past were more likely to expect good things to happen in the future than people who had been encouraged to recall unpleasant events. This could have implications for psychotherapy. There are also instances where people's judgements about the likelihood of events are influenced by the pattern of coverage in the media. Deaths arising from murder or accident are much more frequently reported than deaths from disorders such as asthma or diabetes and so people tend to overestimate their occurrence. Slovic *et al.* (1982) demonstrated that people significantly overestimated the frequency of death caused by such things as murder, road traffic accidents and fire, and significantly underestimated the number of deaths caused by stroke, asthma, tuberculosis and smallpox vaccination. These are all examples of availability bias and it seems that people rarely compensate for this even though they realize that there is a degree of media bias in reporting.

The anchoring and adjusting heuristic

The difficulty in setting aside faulty reasoning is evident in another kind of heuristic identified by Tversky and Kahneman (1973). The so-called *anchoring and adjustment heuristic* refers to the tendency to make judgements by taking an initial value (anchor) and adjusting it. For example, they asked people to estimate the percentage of African nations in the United Nations (UN). Different groups were given arbitrary numbers such as 10 per cent or 65 per cent as a starting point and asked to say whether these figures were under- or overestimates. The mean estimates for groups given the above figures were 25 per cent and 45 per cent respectively. So, a number, which had no meaningful relationship to the original question, was used by participants as an anchor from which they then adjusted on the basis of their knowledge of information about UN nations. However, in almost all cases, participants were too conservative in their adjustments.

There are potentially serious consequences of relying too heavily on the anchoring and adjustment heuristic in real life. Holtgrave *et al.* (1994), for example, have considered the task of risk assessors calculating the possibility of a disaster on a North Sea oil rig. Their risk estimate would be very skewed if they based their calculation on data from the Gulf of Mexico without adjusting accurately for the very different climatic and construction differences. Fortunately, it seems that experienced professionals are not usually influenced by the anchoring and adjustment heuristic when making judgements in their own sphere of expertise. For example, Smith and Kida (1991) have shown that experts in their own field (in this particular case, accountants) are not significantly influenced by the anchoring and adjustment heuristic, and seem to be able to adjust their original estimates to accommodate new information. However, Northcraft and Neale (1987) asked estate agents to value a property based on a 10-page document giving details and pictures of the house, and also based on a tour. Some were given a guide price of approximately $66,000 and others were given a price of about $84,000. Those given the lower anchor set their minimum acceptable price at $65,000, while those given the higher anchor set their minimum at $73,000. In this case, then, professional people were being influenced by the anchoring heuristic. Perhaps this reflects the fact that the housing market is rather volatile and that there are few objective criteria for pricing. However, even when there is uncertainty, there appear to be limits on the influence of the anchoring heuristic. Chapman and Johnson (1994) have demonstrated that people are not influenced if the anchor is wildly implausible.

Although experts tend to be able to make appropriate adjustments in the light of new information, lay people are more likely to ignore new information. Shiloh (1994) has investigated the area of genetic counselling. People who seek advice about the risks of passing on familial disorders are more likely to base their final risk assessment on their own original estimates, without taking into account the information from the genetic counsellor.

Exam summary: Problem-solving and decision-making

The AQA examination will test your understanding of the following areas:

◆ research into problem-solving, including problem-solving strategies and means of representation (pp. 234–8)

◆ practical issues in research in decision-making, including risk taking (pp. 238–9) and errors in thinking about probability (pp. 239–42).

Example question

The question below is typical of one drawn from the material above, and should take you 30 minutes to answer.

(a) Outline two studies of problem-solving. *(12 marks)*

(b) Evaluate how such studies have helped us to understand how humans solve problems.
(12 marks)

Suggested answer structure

Research into problem-solving is covered on pp. 234–8. We have covered two major approaches in this section. One of the earliest theoretical accounts of problem-solving was provided by the Gestalt school (pp. 234–6), and their ideas have been influential. They described some of the ways in which problem-solving can be hampered (e.g. through functional fixedness) and this has stimulated interest in investigating methods for improving problem-solving skills. However, they have been criticized for lack of rigour in experimental studies and also because some of their key concepts are poorly defined.

A more testable approach to problem-solving has been provided by the information-processing approach (pp. 236–8) which compares human mental processing to that of a computer. According to this model, people break problems down into constituent parts (means-ends analysis) and make use of strategies such as analogies and heuristics. While such strategies can be helpful and provide short cuts to problem solution, they are not always successful.

When answering this question, you should remember that you are not being asked to describe these approaches, but rather the research studies that are associated with them. This is in contrast to the question at the end of the previous section, where the use of the term *research* allowed for a more liberal interpretation. The use of the term *studies* is more restricting (see Table 21.2 on p. 552). There are a number of research studies associated with the two approaches summarized above. These include Dunckner's research investigation of functional

fixedness (p. 235) and Novick's research on the use of analogies in problem-solving (p. 238). The second part of this question asks for a more general evaluation of how studies such as these contribute to our understanding of how humans solve problems. Note that this is not an instruction to evaluate only the two studies outlined in the first part of the question. This gives you the opportunity to cover far more ground, and look at how studies from these two approaches (i.e. Gestalt and the information-processing approach) have contributed to this understanding.

Chapter summary

◆ Interest in the relationship between language and culture stimulated research into the notion that language determines thought: the **linguistic relativity hypothesis** or the Sapir–Whorf hypothesis. There has been some support for the weak version of this, but even where differences in thinking can be demonstrated in different language communities, it is impossible to infer that language is the sole factor that distinguishes one group from another.

◆ Researchers such as Bernstein and Labov have been interested in the **social and cultural aspects** of language use. **Bernstein** investigated social class differences and described two distinct speech codes – restricted and elaborated. However, there is little evidence to support this distinction and more recent research suggests that all children of school age have been exposed to a similar range of language. **Labov** investigated Black English and found that, far from being an impoverished dialect, it has its own distinctive grammar and is capable of conveying a rich variety of meaning.

◆ **Language acquisition** is one of the most remarkable of human achievements. Children appear to progress rapidly and in similar ways through a series of distinct stages in their acquisition of language: discriminating speech sounds, producing speech-like sounds, developing a vocabulary and acquiring syntactical competence.

◆ Psychologists have developed a good understanding of the way in which humans acquire language. There is less agreement about the precise mechanism whereby **language develops**. **Environmental theories** suggest that language is learned through the joint processes of reinforcement and imitation. **Nativist theories** appear to account for data which are inconsistent with the learning approach. Given that language development

appears to follow a very similar pattern across cultures, **Chomsky** believed that language ability is somehow 'wired in', i.e. depends on innate mechanisms. The evidence for this approach is fairly strong but it fails to take into account various social and cognitive factors that probably affect language development. There is not yet a complete theory of language acquisition which adequately accounts for all the data. It seems likely that learning, innate mechanisms, cognitive and social factors all contribute, but the precise ways in which these various elements combine and interact is not yet fully understood.

◆ **Problem-solving** is an everyday activity which seems deceptively simple, but which actually involves quite complex skills. **Gestalt psychologists** believed that the various elements of a problem needed to be reorganized so that a solution would become clear. Their ideas have stimulated interest in research which considers ways of improving problem-solving skills. However, concepts such as 'insight' have been seen as too vague and the lack of empirical support has also been seen as a weakness. The information-processing approach, a more testable account of problem-solving, argues that we adopt various heuristics, including **means-ends analysis**, to break problems down into stages which we solve systematically. Computer programs have been designed which effectively solve problems using these strategies. This does not mean, however, that they accurately reflect the strategies used by humans.

◆ In **decision-making**, as with problem-solving, it seems likely that we make use of heuristics. While such strategies usually help us to make decisions and judgements in our everyday life, they can let us down, especially when combined with a lack of understanding or faulty understanding of probability.

Further resources

Garnham, A. and Oakhill, J. (1994) *Thinking and Reasoning*, Oxford UK and Cambridge USA: Blackwell.

This book includes a wide range of research into all aspects of thinking and reasoning. It is aimed primarily at undergraduates, but the clear, lucid style will make it accessible to A-level students who would like to cover the topic in greater depth.

Harley, T.A. (1995) *The Psychology of Language: From Data to Theory*, Hove: Erlbaum (UK), Taylor & Francis.

This is a comprehensive and up-to-date account of the psychology of language. It is an undergraduate text, but it is accessible for A-level students who would like more detailed coverage.

Mayer, R.E. (1992) *Thinking, Problem-solving, Cognition* (2nd edn), New York: W.H. Freeman & Co.

This clearly written text covers many aspects of thinking and reasoning. It goes well beyond the A-level syllabus but has good, relevant chapters which include some clear examples and illustrations.

Answers to activities

Activity 3

Most people take four sticks and form a square from them. They then make an X from the remaining two sticks and try to place them inside the square (see Fig. 9.3 (a). However, this is not an acceptable solution because the diagonal sticks are not long enough to complete the triangles, which would in any case not be equilateral. It is necessary to reorganize the elements of the problem and think in three dimensions (see Fig. 9.3 (b).

Figure 9.3 (a)

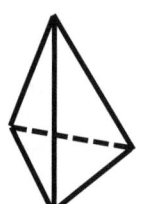

Figure 9.3 (b)

Activity 5

There are several steps involved in the Hobbits and Orcs problem. L represents the left bank and R represents the right bank:

1   Move 2 Orcs, L to R.

2   Move 1 Orc, R to L.

3   Move 2 Orcs, L to R.

4   Move 1 Orc, R to L.

5   Move 2 Hobbits, L to R.

6   Move 1 Orc, 1 Hobbit, R to L.

7   Move 2 Hobbits, L to R.

8   Move 1 Orc, R to L.

9   Move 2 Orcs, L to R.

10   Move 1 Orc, R to L.

11   Move 2 Orcs, L to R.

Part 4: Developmental Psychology

A2

COGNITIVE DEVELOPMENT

Cara Flanagan

SOCIAL AND PERSONALITY DEVELOPMENT

Cara Flanagan

ADULTHOOD

Alison Wadeley

Chapter 10

Cognitive development

Cara Flanagan

Preview

In this chapter we shall be looking at:

◆ the development of thinking: theories of cognitive development (Piaget, Vygotsky and information-processing approaches) and the practical application of these theories to education

◆ the development of measured intelligence: research into the factors that affect the development of intelligence test performance, including a consideration of genetic, environmental and cultural influences

◆ the development of moral understanding: theories of moral understanding (Piaget and Kohlberg) and prosocial reasoning (Eisenberg), and individual (gender) and cultural variations.

Introduction

'Cognitive' is the word psychologists use to refer to mental activities. So 'cognitive development' is the study of how our mental activities develop. The way that children think is different from the way that adults think, and the way younger children think is different from the way that older children think. But in what way is it different? Consider some examples:

◆ 'A sentence is a big word with holes in it.'

◆ 'A is greater than B, B is greater than C; therefore A is greater than C.'

◆ 'Mary didn't mean to hurt Anne; therefore she shouldn't be punished.'

People of different ages express themselves differently and this probably reflects that they *think* differently. How does child-like thought develop into more adult-like thought? Do adults just know more things and think faster? Or is the way they think qualitatively different?

Some psychologists believe that thought changes as children get older – that young children use quite a different sort of logic than adults and are less capable of abstract thought. Other psychologists believe that cognitive development occurs through building up more complex mental routines that become more efficient the more you use them.

A further question is whether these changes are the result of experience or whether they are inborn. Psychologists call this the nature/nurture debate – 'nurture' refers to experience and 'nature' is the outcome of a person's biological or genetic make-up. It is what you are born with or what develops due to maturation during your lifetime? In the seventeenth century, the English philosopher John Locke suggested that a child was born '*tabula rasa*', i.e. with a mind like a blank writing slate. It was assumed that the child's environment determined what was written on the slate. The opposite view taken by, for example, hereditarians is that we inherit our abilities from our parents. In terms of intelligence, the nature/nurture debate asks to what extent your intelligence is innate and unchangeable, or is due to experience so that it is your teachers and friends who might influence the outcome.

Cognitive activity involves more than just problem-solving and reasoning. It includes perception, memory, language, attitudes and so on. In this chapter we will also consider the development of a particular kind of thinking – moral understanding.

The development of thinking: three theories of cognitive development

Piaget's theory

Jean Piaget (1896–1980) is probably the best-known psychologist, after Sigmund Freud. He was born in Switzerland and initially trained as a zoologist – the first

thing he published (at the age of 10) was on molluscs. His interest in cognitive development started when, in the early 1920s, he worked on some of the first intelligence tests. Piaget became intrigued by the replies he got from children when he asked them questions. Piaget noticed that children of the same age tended to make similar kinds of errors. He thought that younger children might be following rather different logical rules from older children. Their errors were quite predictable and could, therefore, be described in terms of a stage theory. In other words, the errors made at certain ages formed a kind of stage of development, and these stages formed a sequence. Piaget suggested that children's thought changes *qualitatively* as they pass through the stages.

The structure of the intellect

Before we look in detail at the stages in cognitive development, we should first consider the central principles of Piaget's theory. Piaget (1926, 1954, 1960) noted that all babies are born with similar biological 'equipment' (Piaget used the term 'structures'). These biological structures were the senses, the brain and reflexes (such as sucking and grasping). At the start of life, an infant has a set of basic reflexes and also a set of innate schema. Piaget introduced the term 'schema' to mean a psychological structure that represented everything that the infant or child knew about an object or an action built up from basic reflexes. An example of an innate schema would be a mental representation of a human face – there is evidence that infants are born with an innate ability to recognize faces (Flanagan 1999; Fantz 1961). From birth onwards, the infant's schemas develop as a result of interactions with the environment. New experiences lead to new schemas being developed. For example, infants learn separate schemas for the faces of people they know.

What is the exact process by which schemas become more complex? Piaget proposed two ways in which this might happen:

◆ *assimilation* – the process of fitting new information and experiences into existing schemas

◆ *accommodation* – the process of changing the existing schemas when new information cannot be assimilated.

For example, a child may have the schema 'four legs, fur and wet nose (dog)'. Every new instance of a creature with the same characteristics is assimilated into this schema. However, one day someone uses the word 'cat' and this challenges the current schema. This new information cannot be assimilated into the existing schema, instead the child's schemas must alter to accommodate the new information and a new schema is formed.

The driving force behind these changes or 'adaptation' is the principle of equilibrium. The intellect strives to maintain equilibrium or a sense of balance. If an experience cannot be assimilated into existing schemas then there is a state of imbalance. Cognitive development is the result of adaptation between the individual's existing schema and environmental 'demands' for change, such as new experiences which don't fit existing schema.

Stages in development

A new stage in development is reached when two things happen:

1 The child's brain must have matured to a point of 'readiness'.

2 Some new information or experiences that cannot be assimilated challenge the child's thinking.

Table 10.1 Piaget's stages of cognitive development

1 *The sensorimotor stage* (0 to 2 years):	The infant's knowledge is limited to what they can experience through their senses (sensory) and their attempts to coordinate this new knowledge with what they can do (motor).
2 *The pre-operational stage* (2 to 7 years):	The child can now use symbols (as in language), but their concepts are general (preconceptual), for example 'Daddy owns a blue car – therefore all blue cars are called "Daddy's car" '. The child's reasoning is pre-operational (it lacks adult logic).
3 *The concrete operational stage* (7 to 11 years):	Children now use logical mental rules, but only in the context of concrete rather than abstract information. For example, they cannot cope with the problem 'Mary is taller than Susan, Susan is taller than Anne. Who is tallest'?' unless the problem is presented using dolls (i.e. in concrete form).
4 *The formal operational stage* (11+ years):	Abstract and systematic thought becomes possible, as distinct from more random problem-solving methods.

Note that even though age ranges are given, these are not fixed – they are only guides. It is the sequence that is important. Children pass through all stages, though there is some debate as to whether everyone reaches the final stage of formal operations.

When the child is 'ready', new experiences will lead to a major reorganization of schemas, so that a new and qualitatively different stage of cognitive development is reached. Each stage is characterized by a coherent structure of principles that operate during that time. These stages are outlined in Table 10.1.

We will now look briefly at the empirical evidence related to each stage.

The sensorimotor stage

Piaget's descriptive account of the sensorimotor stage is based on his detailed observation of young infants, mainly his own three children. He suggested that early movements are uncoordinated. The infant in the cot comes to realize that the object waving back and forth in front of their eyes is in fact their own hand. They coordinate sensory information with motor information and construct new schemas. In total there are six substages within the sensorimotor stage (reflexes, primary circular reactions, secondary circular reactions, coordination of schema, tertiary circular reactions and mental combinations). The concept of 'circular reactions' describes the infant's repetition of actions in order to learn new schema.

One crucial development during the sensorimotor stage is that of 'object permanence' – the realization that objects continue to exist even when they cannot be seen. Up to about eight months, 'out of sight' seems to be 'out of mind', as babies do not search for objects that are hidden from view as they watch. By the age of one, object permanence is quite securely developed and infants will search for an object where it was last seen, expressing surprise if it is not there.

Not everyone, however, has accepted Piaget's claims about object permanence. For example, Bower (1981) showed that if an object disappeared behind a screen and then the screen was lifted, babies as young as five months would show surprise if the object was not there. This suggests that they did expect the object to be there. However, the issue is not so much at what age these changes occur, but that they occur and Bower's evidence merely suggests that Piaget may have underestimated what infants could do.

The pre-operational stage

Piaget named this stage pre-operational because the child is still unable to use 'operations'. Operations are logical mental rules, such as rules of arithmetic. Pre-operational thought is guided more by external appearances than internal consistency or logic. This is not to say that children of this age are not using rules, but that their reasoning lacks logic.

Piaget divided the pre-operational stage into two substages. The preconceptual stage from 2 to 4 years and the intuitive stage from 4 to 7 years. The term 'preconceptual' was used to describe the fact that the child does not yet have fully formed concepts – for example, a young child might call all men 'Daddy'. Another characteristic of children at this stage is 'animism' – a willingness to give lifelike qualities to inanimate things (e.g. 'The moon wants to hide behind the clouds').

The intuitive substage describes the fact that children of this age base their knowledge on what they feel or sense is true, but they cannot explain the underlying principles. Piaget has highlighted some fundamental weaknesses in pre-operational children's thought (see Table 10.2).

Egocentrism is perhaps the most serious limitation in pre-operational children's thinking. The pre-operational child finds it hard to take on the perspective of another. Piaget's classic 'three mountains task' (see Fig. 10.1) demonstrated such egocentrism. Pre-operational children were asked to describe the view seen by a doll. Typically, pre-operational children confidently said that the scene would look just the same as from their own viewpoint. This was the case wherever the doll was positioned.

Figure 10.1
The three mountains were differently coloured and could also be distinguished because there was snow on the top of one, a cross on the top of another, and a house on the top of the third. The child was asked to say what the doll could see.
Source: Davenport (1994)

Table 10.2	Some limitations in pre-operational thought	
1	Egocentrism:	This means viewing the world and thinking about it from one's own point of view and being unaware that others may have different points of view or thoughts.
2	Irreversibility:	Reversible means 'can be returned to the original state'. For example, pouring liquid from one glass beaker to another can be reversed by simply pouring it back again. Pre-operational children lack this flexible reversibility of thought.
3	Centration:	This refers to the pre-operational child's tendency to focus or centre attention on only one aspect of a task, and ignore other relevant aspects.

Concrete operational stage

At the concrete operational stage intuition is replaced by a confident use of logical rules. Yet children's understanding is still limited because it only deals with the actual 'concrete' world. Piaget thought concrete operational children had difficulty in considering ideas that were hypothetical or abstract. Table 10.3 shows two such important abilities associated with this stage.

One of Piaget's most famous ways of assessing children's thinking was to present them with conservation tasks. 'Conservation' refers to the logical rule that quantity does not change even when a display is transformed. Figure 10.2 gives examples of the different types of conservation tasks that Piaget used. To succeed at a task, a child must realize, for example, that the number of counters in a row does not change even when the row is more spaced out. Pre-operational children fail at this task because they cannot conserve quantity, whereas the concrete operational child comprehends the rule and applies it to this concrete situation.

Piaget's conservation experiments have been criticized in terms of the methodology he used. For instance, Rose and Blank (1974) suggested that Piaget's use of *two* questions might have confused younger children. In the original experiment the children were shown the first display and asked 'Are the two displays the same?', and then asked the same question after the transformation. A pre-operational child might think 'if the question is being asked again, even though nothing has changed, perhaps there is a different answer'. This is called a 'demand characteristic' because it leads the child to behave in a particular way. Rose and Blank tried asking just one question, after the transformation, and found that pre-operational children could cope better. However, there were still age differences.

Donaldson and colleagues raised a second criticism of the conservation tasks (Donaldson 1978). They suggested that another demand characteristic of Piaget's experiments was that the deliberate change of the display suggested to the child that the experimenter was looking for a different response. If the change was accidental, the children should focus more on the actual transformation. McGarrigle and Donaldson (1974) tested this by using a 'naughty teddy' glove puppet that 'accidentally' spread out one row of beads in the standard Piagetian conservation task. The children's ability to conserve was much improved compared to performance on Piaget's original version of the task.

However, more recent research suggests that Donaldson may also have been mistaken. It is possible that the children were so absorbed in the 'naughty teddy' routine that they didn't actually notice the transformation. Moore and Frye (1986) tested this possibility by seeing how children would respond if the 'naughty teddy' made an actual change (a counter is added or taken away for the second display). This time children answered that no change had taken place, suggesting that 'naughty teddy' was indeed a distraction.

Table 10.3	Some concrete operational abilities	
Seriation:		This cognitive operation allows the child to order a set of items in terms of dimensions like height, or width or both together. For example, when given a set of dolls of different heights, the child can arrange the dolls in order so that the tallest doll is at one end, followed by the second tallest doll and so on, down to the shortest doll at the other end of the row.
Transitivity:		This is the ability to recognize logical relationships within a series. For example, if David is taller than John, and John is taller than Mike, then it follows logically that David is taller than Mike.

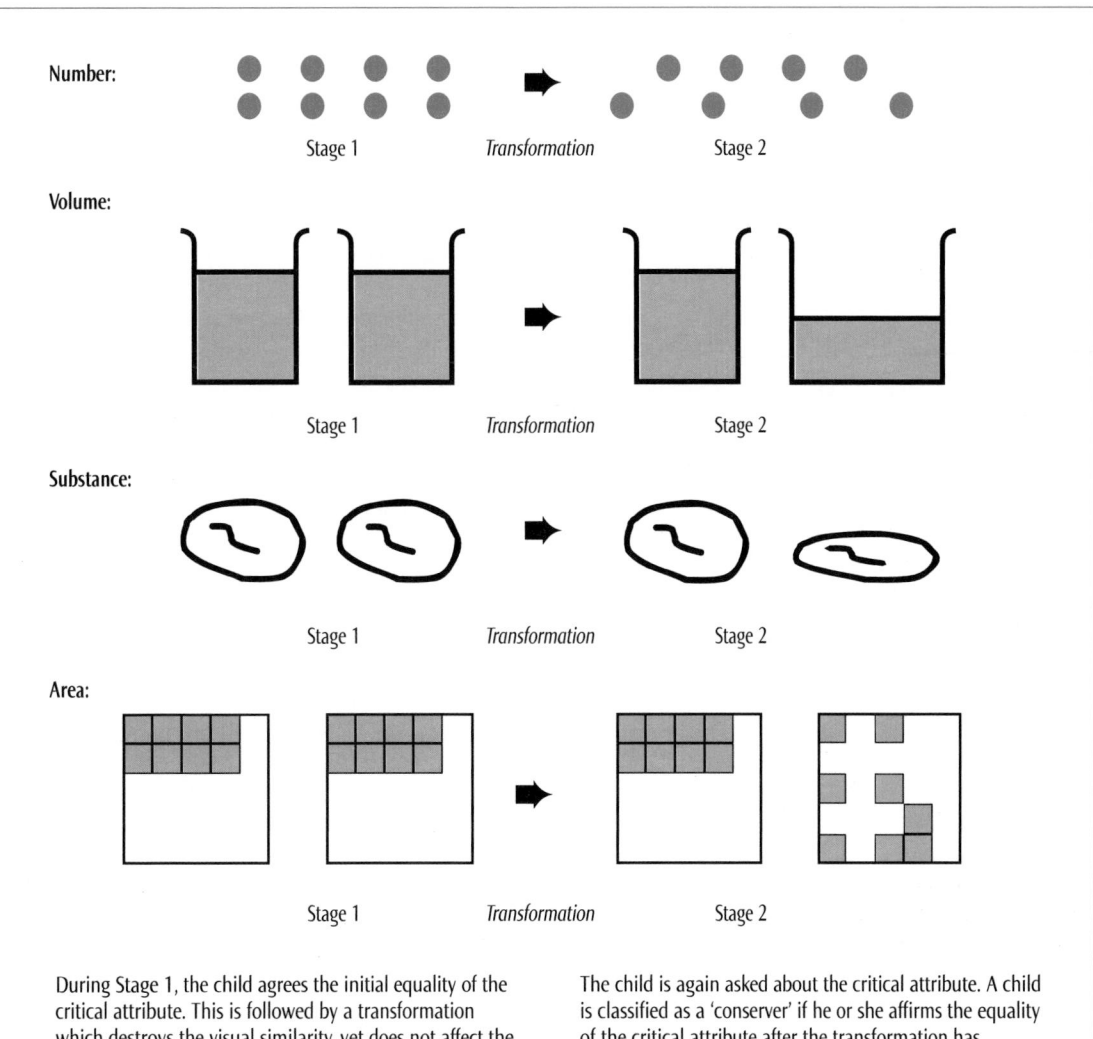

Figure 10.2
Examples of different types of conservation involving
number, volume, substance and area

During Stage 1, the child agrees the initial equality of the critical attribute. This is followed by a transformation which destroys the visual similarity, yet does not affect the critical attribute (number, volume, etc.).

The child is again asked about the critical attribute. A child is classified as a 'conserver' if he or she affirms the equality of the critical attribute after the transformation has occurred.

Activity 1: Trying out Piaget's tasks

Carry out Piaget's conservation of volume task with a child aged between 5 and 8 years.

Present two identical glasses with equal amounts of water in them and get the child's agreement that they contain the same amount of water. Then pour the water from one glass into another differently shaped glass. Ask the child 'Does the glass have more water or is there the same amount in each glass?'

Ask the child to explain their response and try to explore the child's reasoning with follow-up questions. If you can, repeat the task again with a child at a different age. Afterwards, consider whether using different words might have affected the child's replies, and how you might change the task to see if the child's responses change. If you tested two children, how did their responses differ, if at all?

Formal operational stage

Formal operational thinkers are capable of abstract and systematic thought. If children are asked to conduct an investigation, the concrete operational child will not usually have a systematic plan. In contrast, formal operational thinkers typically develop an overall plan. For example, when solving a problem they keep all the variables constant except one in order to determine its effect, and in this way systematically explore all the possibilities.

Piaget and Inhelder (1956) demonstrated this with the 'beaker problem'. Participants were given four beakers of colourless liquids and asked to find out which combination will produce a yellow liquid. The younger children tried all sorts of random combinations and may or may not have found the answer. The older children took a more systematic approach and systematically excluded possibilities until they found the correct solution. They used abstract deductive reasoning: forming a principle, deriving a hypothesis and testing this to confirm the hypothesis.

The main criticism of this stage is that it may not be universal. Piaget assumed that everyone reaches this level, which may be a reflection of his own experience of working with highly intelligent individuals and not universally true.

In summary, there are two strands to Piaget's theory:

◆ an account of *what changes* during development: concrete to abstract thinking, pre-operational to operational thought (i.e. the cognitive activities at each stage)

◆ an account of the *causes* of developmental changes (adaptation).

It is a mistake to become too focused on 'ages and stages' and overlook the part of Piaget's theory that is concerned with a child's innate drive for coherence and equilibrium. Piaget's theory emphasized the role of experience in cognitive development, but at heart it is a biological theory because it is based on the idea of the maturation of innate forces and structures.

Criticisms of Piaget's theory

A key criticism made of Piaget's theory is that he underestimated the age at which children could do things. This may be because he failed to distinguish between *competence* (what a child is capable of doing) and *performance* (how a child performs on a particular task). Piaget's studies tested performance and then he assumed that a child who failed simply lacked the underlying cognitive structures that he believed were needed to succeed on that task. Subsequent research suggests that a child may have these competencies earlier than Piaget suggested. A study by Borke (1975) (see *In Focus*) shows that several factors are important in assessing the competence of young children.

However, simply to focus on age limits is to miss the central point of Piaget's theory that universal, qualitative, biologically regulated cognitive changes occur during development. This is supported by cross-cultural research that has replicated Piaget's findings (Smith *et al.* 1998).

A second criticism relates to the concept of biological maturation or 'readiness'. If the development of cognitive structures is related to maturity, then practice should not improve performance. In other words, if a person is not biologically ready to move on

Borke (1975)

A study by Borke (1975) incorporated many factors that are related to young children's ability to succeed in tests of egocentrism. Children aged 3 and 4 were shown three-dimensional displays after a practice session where they became familiar with turning a red fire engine on a turntable so that it fitted the view of Grover, a popular character from *Sesame Street* (an educational TV programme). The three experimental displays were:

1 Piaget's three mountains scene

2 a scene with a lake, boat, horse, cow and house

3 a visually more complex scene involving people and animals in natural settings.

As Grover drove along and stopped to look, the children had to turn their copy of the display on their turntable, so that it matched Grover's view.

Results

Display	Per cent correct responses	
	3 year olds	4 year olds
1	42	67
2	80	80
3	79	95

Only 31 per cent of errors were *egocentric* errors.

It seems that the children's performance, even in the difficult version of the tasks, was improved by several factors including:

◆ practice, familiarity and interest in the task

◆ how the child's choice is shown (by turning the display rather than by choosing a picture)

◆ by the visual discriminability of the scenes – lots of easy-to-recognize, familiar objects provided good cues.

Given these helpful conditions, 3- and 4-year-old children can overcome egocentrism.

to the next stage then no amount of practice should get them there. However, there is evidence to suggest that practice can make a difference. For example, Bryant and Trabasso (1971) trained children under the age of 7 so that they could cope with using logical mental rules, such as those in the example for transitivity given in Table 10.3. The children practised simple comparisons, using five coloured rods of different lengths, and eventually the children were able to cope with abstract tasks. Danner and Day (1977) coached students aged 10, 13 and 17 in three formal operational tasks. The effects were limited with the younger participants, but very marked at 17 years, showing that training can make a difference, but is still related to cognitive maturation.

Piaget did not deny the role of experience. He used the concept of 'horizontal décalage' to explain why it is that not all aspects of the same stage appear at the same time; for example, the ability to conserve number and volume may not appear at the same time, but one after the other. He suggested that uneven cognitive performance is probably due to different learning experiences.

A third criticism of Piaget's theory relates to the role of language and social factors. Piaget did not feel that language influenced cognitive development. This was supported by an experiment by one of his co-workers, Sinclair-de-Zwart (1969). In an earlier experiment she found that children who were non-conservers differed in terms of the language they used from children classed as conservers. Non-conservers mainly used absolute rather than comparative terms such as 'big' rather than 'larger'. They also used a single term for different dimensions such as 'small' to mean 'short', 'thin', or 'few'. These findings suggest that cognitive and linguistic development is tied together, but which comes first? In a further experiment, Sinclair-de-Zwart tried to teach appropriate verbal skills to the non-conservers. However, 90 per cent of these children were still unable to conserve. This supports Piaget's view that cognitive maturity is a prerequisite for linguistic development (see also Chapter 9).

Evaluation of Piaget's theory

◆ Piaget produced the first comprehensive theory of children's cognitive development. The theory has been more extensively developed than any other. It has changed our ideas about children and has had a general influence on educational practice.

◆ All good theories should generate research and Piaget's theory has certainly done so.

◆ Piaget may have underestimated children's abilities and overestimated adult capacity for formal operational thought.

◆ The theory underemphasizes the role of language and social interaction in cognitive development.

◆ Critics tend to take the model too rigidly, and supporters suggest it should be viewed as a metaphor. The stages are not fact, but a useful model for understanding behaviour and generating research.

Vygotsky's theory

Vygotsky believed that cultural input was fundamental to development. Lev Semenovich Vygotsky (1896–1934) was born in pre-Revolutionary Russia and, like Piaget, had a chequered early career. He took a law degree, wrote about literature, and eventually became interested in the psychology of human development. He contracted tuberculosis at the age of 24 and was sickly throughout the rest of his short life. Notice that Piaget and Vygotsky were contemporaries, though they never met.

The influence of culture

Vygotsky suggested that the intellect consisted of 'elementary' and 'higher' mental functions. Elementary functions are innate capacities such as attention and sensation. These will develop to a limited extent through experience, but cultural influences are required to transform them into higher mental functions, such as problem-solving and thinking. Without culture, an individual would not progress further than the elementary functions. When Vygotsky used the concept of 'culture', he was referring to the body of knowledge which is held by, for example, books and 'experts' (persons with greater knowledge), and which is largely transmitted through language. Therefore cultural knowledge is the means by which cognitive development takes place.

If higher mental functions depend on cultural influences, then we would expect to find different higher mental functions in different cultures. Gredler (1992) recorded an example of this. Children in Papua, New Guinea are taught a counting system which begins on the thumb of one hand and proceeds up the arm and down to the other fingers, ending at 29. This means that it is very difficult to add and subtract large numbers and thus limits mathematical calculations (a higher mental function) in that culture.

Stages in the development of thinking

In one of the relatively few empirical studies that he carried out, Vygotsky (1987) studied the process of concept formation in children. Children were given wooden blocks of varying height and shape, with each block labelled with a nonsense symbol (e.g. 'ZAT' was used to label tall and square blocks). The child's task

Table 10.4	Vygotsky's stages of concept formation	
1	*Vague syncretic stage:*	Largely trial and error without understanding.
2	*Complexes stage:*	Some appropriate strategies are used but the main attributes are not identified.
3	*Potential concept stage:*	One attribute only (e.g. tall) can be dealt with at a time.
4	*Mature concept stage:*	The child is able to deal with several attributes simultaneously (e.g. tall and square).

was to work out what these labels meant. Vygotsky observed that children went through three stages before achieving mature concepts (see Table 10.4).

One of Vygotsky's central interests was in the relationship between language and thought, and this produced another set of developmental stages (see Table 10.5). In Vygotsky's view, language and thought are separate functions in children under the age of two. Vocal activity, or pre-intellectual language, is a form of social interaction and emotional expression. At the same time, children use prelinguistic thought, mental activities such as problem-solving which do not use verbal operations. This is a period of practical intelligence, when elementary functions are developing.

After the age of two, the child begins to use external symbols or signs, such as language or other cultural tools, to assist in problem-solving. It is this sign-using behaviour which transforms elementary functions into higher functions. A young child will often talk out loud when solving problems, a kind of egocentric speech. After the age of 7, this self-talk becomes silent (inner speech) and differs in form from social speech. Inner dialogues continue to be used as a means of developing and reflecting on problems.

Throughout life, language serves a dual purpose: for thought and for social communication. Social processes shape language and also shape thought. (See Chapter 9 for a discussion of the relationship between language and thought, including Vygotsky's views.)

The zone of proximal development (ZPD)

The role of experts and of culture is further elaborated in Vygotsky's concept of the zone of proximal

development (though perhaps 'zone of potential development' would be a more useful translation). The ZPD is the distance between a child's current and potential abilities at any moment in time, i.e. the area between what children can do with no assistance and what they can do with expert guidance. This zone is critical in leading cognitive development, and the concept explains how children become what they are not yet. Instruction 'wakens a whole series of functions that are in a stage of maturation lying in the zone of proximal development' (Vygotsky 1987, p. 212). This is the key difference between individual construction (Piaget's view) and social construction (Vygotsky's view). Social influences 'waken' abilities that might or would otherwise stay dormant if the child is left untutored. A study by McNaughton and Leyland (1990) (see *In Focus*) demonstrated the ZPD in action.

In summary, Vygotsky argued strongly that the child's cognitive development took place as the result of social interactions between the child and other people. Vygotsky's theory centred on the social construction of knowledge. The infant has elementary mental functions. This kind of thinking is not dissimilar to that of other primates. Around the age of 2, the use of language and other cultural symbols transforms a child's rudimentary abilities into more sophisticated cognitive abilities. These symbols are learned from others (experts) and are therefore external. In time they become internalized. The child learns to make sense of the world through the 'shared meanings' of others.

Criticisms of Vygotsky's theory

For many years there was very little empirical support for Vygotsky's theory, but this is now growing,

Table 10.5	The development of language and thought	
Speech stage	*Age*	*Function*
Pre-intellectual, social speech	0–3	Language serves a social function. At the same time thought is prelinguistic.
Egocentric speech	3–7	Language is used to control one's own behaviour, but is often spoken aloud.
Inner speech	7+	Self-talk becomes silent. The child also uses speech for social purposes.

in focus

'Scaffolding'

McNaughton and Leyland (1990) conducted a study to demonstrate the process of 'scaffolding', a metaphor first used by Wood *et al.* (1976) to explain how a tutor or expert can advance a child's thinking by providing a framework within which a child can develop. In the study by McNaughton and Leyland, children were given a variety of progressively more difficult jigsaw puzzles to work on with the assistance of their mothers. The highest level of difficulty was recorded. A week later the children returned and worked on new jigsaws, this time unaided. The level of jigsaw difficulty reached was lower for most children.

The difference between the two sessions enabled McNaughton and Leyland to define the child's ZPD. The child's unaided performance indicated their current *ability*, whereas aided performance represented their potential *capability*.

The researchers found that there were three types of scaffolding given by the mothers, which were related to task difficulty. When the children were doing puzzles which were too easy (below the child's ZPD), the mothers were mainly concerned with keeping the child on task. At the second level (within the child's ZPD), the mothers focused at helping the children solve the puzzle for themselves. At the third level (beyond the child's ZPD), the emphasis was on completing the puzzle by whatever means. At this latter level, the mother (expert) has recognized that little or no learning will take place because it is beyond the child's capabilities, therefore she takes over. At the level below, the mother guides learning through the use of 'shared meanings'. Vygotsky predicted that the greatest teaching input would occur at the *edge* of the ZPD, the point at which the child can still cope.

as interest in the theory has increased. Part of the reason for the lack of empirical study is that the theory focuses on the *process* of cognitive development rather than the outcome, and this is harder to test.

Similarly, because empirical support for the theory has only slowly become available, there is limited negative criticism of it. On the positive side, the theory has found successful applications in education, as we will see later in this chapter.

Evaluation of Vygotsky's theory

◆ Vygotsky's ideas on cognitive development have had considerable influence.

◆ Expert intervention and the mediation of language (signs) are crucial to cognitive development. Without them the child would not maximize their ZPD.

◆ Although Vygotsky produced very little direct empirical evidence, other researchers have provided support for his ideas and their application.

◆ Glassman (1999) argues that it is wrong to see Piaget and Vygotsky as opposites, that in fact the two theories are remarkably similar especially at their central core. Piaget focused on the natural laws of intellectual development while Vygotsky concentrated on the impact of social processes and culture. An integration of both views might therefore be highly productive

The information-processing approach

An information-processing theory is essentially one which uses concepts drawn from computer technology – input, output, storage, programs, routines and so on. Such theories view cognitive activity as the taking in and processing of information. These theories are common in cognitive psychology (see Chapter 8), and information-processing theories of cognitive development overlap considerably with research in areas like memory and attention, as we will see.

As a developmental approach, information-processing assumes that, if adults think differently and more successfully than children, this is because the adults can process more information. Several specific information-processing theories of development can be termed 'neo-Piagetian', because they use information-processing ideas to reinterpret aspects of Piaget's theory. We shall consider one such theory now, from Robbie Case. Case began studying how children think because he wanted to improve the early learning opportunities of economically disadvantaged students and other learners with special needs.

Case's concept of mental space

Case (1985, 1992) suggested that greater efficiency in information-processing ability occurs as children become able to use their mental space more effectively. Mental space (or M space) is a concept rather similar to 'working memory'. It is roughly equivalent to short-term memory and describes that area of the brain where information is stored during processing. There is a limit to the amount of information that can be held in M space at any one time. However, the amount of data that can be processed increases with age because of the following factors:

◆ Brain maturation, especially changes in the myelin sheath (a fatty protective layer around the nerves which increases), lead to faster neural transmission rates.

◆ Strategies become more automatic with practice and so need less conscious attention, thus freeing M-space for other work.

◆ Once schemes are sufficiently automatic, they can become 'central conceptual structures', allowing children to think about their experience in more advanced ways and to develop more efficient ways to solve problems – in effect to move to a new stage of development.

◆ Metacognitive skills (thinking about thinking) are especially important.

Case suggested that cognitive activity could be described in terms of various 'schemes'. 'Figurative' schemes are concepts – patterns of stimulation that have been experienced on several occasions and are recognized as a discrete unit. 'Operative' schemes represent strategies or rules that can be used to transform figurative schemes. 'Executive' schemes are representations of how to use figurative and operative schemes to achieve a goal. In other words, executive schemes serve to organize the other two kinds of schemes. Figurative schemes are equivalent to Piaget's schemas and operative schemes are equivalent to Piaget's concept of operations. Case's model differs from Piaget's because of the addition of an executive 'agent' to coordinate all cognitive activity.

A further similarity with Piaget's theory was Case's four stages of development: sensorimotor, representational, logical and formal operations. Case suggested that the shift between stages occurs when the executive structures enable a qualitatively different kind of thought, and this in turn is related to changes in M space.

Activity 2: Children at play

Observe a child engaged in any game, e.g. skipping or hide and seek, and think about the various demands being made on the child's perception, memory and attention. Consider how these may change as the child becomes better at the game.

Empirical support

Chi (1978) gave children and adults the task of trying to recall chess board positions. The children were relative experts at chess whereas the adults were novices at the game. Research typically finds that people's ability to recall digits after hearing them only once improves with age (adults can usually recall about seven digits). In Chi's study, however, it was the children who could recall more. This finding must be due to experience which led to greater automation and the ability to process more information.

Experience also leads to 'chunking' of information, an efficient information-processing or metacognitive strategy. Lange (1973) showed how older children and adults have increased memory spans because they use chunking. If words are presented in categorized form (e.g. apples, oranges, bananas, shirt, trousers, hat) or an uncategorized form (e.g. desk, arm, tree, apples, hat), young children perform equally well on both kinds of task, whereas older children can remember more of the categorized lists. This is presumably because younger children have not yet developed strategies for organizing material and increasing memory efficiency.

Evaluation of the information-processing approach

◆ The information-processing approach offers a more detailed account of cognitive development by identifying the specific component skills required in a task and studying how these develop. The emphasis on strategies means development can be measured, for example, in terms of the number of items a child can recall.

◆ Information-processing models can easily be related to the physical basis of thought, i.e. the brain, which may be useful in understanding brain damage.

◆ Information-processing models can account for cognitive development across the entire life span.

◆ Case's account is not qualitatively different from Piaget's; both theories rely on information-processing concepts and can be accused of being mechanistic and reductionist. Like Piaget, Case fails to take account of cultural and emotional influences.

Practical applications in education

The ultimate test of any theory is the extent to which it can inform practice. In the case of theories of cognitive development, the major practical application is to advise educational practice. The essential advice based on the three theoretical approaches for education is:

◆ Piaget claimed that children do not need to be taught. They learn because they are drawn into experiences. If a child is taught something prematurely that they could have discovered for themselves, this prevents them from ever completely understanding it. It is a child-centred approach.

◆ Vygotsky suggested that the desire to learn is an *outcome* of learning rather than being a prerequisite for learning. Vygotsky also felt that expert guidance is needed to move the child through the ZPD, and that without active intervention the child learns less. This is a more teacher-centred approach.

◆ Case suggested that learning relies on experience – therefore practising strategies and building up more complex routines will advance cognitive development.

It is as well to remember that learning doesn't just take place at school, but also at home, with parents and siblings, and many of the applications considered below can be adapted for use either at home or in school.

Piaget: Discovery learning

The first outcome of Piaget's theory for educational practice is the view that children learn by constructing their own knowledge when placed in novel situations. The teacher should provide materials which moderately challenge current schemas, leading to disequilibrium, accommodation and the construction of new schemas. The teacher does not make the discrepancies explicit, but stands back and allows the child to work it out for him or herself. Peers are also important in presenting conflict and breaking down egocentrism.

A further outcome from Piaget's theory is linked with his view that logic is not an innate mental process, rather it is the outcome of cognitive development. Therefore logic, mathematics and science should be taught in primary schools because they will facilitate cognitive development. However, these concepts can only be taught when the child is 'ready' because otherwise the child won't fully understand them. When Einstein asked Piaget when it might be appropriate to teach children about time and velocity, the answer was 'in the stage of concrete operations'.

A further implication of Piaget's theory for the school curriculum is the use of concrete materials in teaching young children. He believed that it is vital for students to have the chance to manipulate concrete objects when they are first learning abstract principles. This philosophy underpinned the Nuffield Secondary Science project as well as the Montessori approach to teaching preschool children. Maria Montessori (1912) advised teachers to allow preschool children to work on simple tasks at their own level, such as using physical apparatus to develop their understanding of concepts, and that this would be self-motivating.

Vygotsky: The social context

Vygotsky did not accept that teachers should wait for the child to be ready to learn and claimed that 'what a child can do with assistance today he/she can do by him/herself tomorrow'. The social context enables learning. This can be seen in scaffolding (see *In Focus*, 'Scaffolding' on p. 255) and peer tutoring (see *In Focus*, 'Peer tutoring' on p. 258).

There are a number of studies that demonstrate the success of scaffolding. For example, Wood *et al.* (1976) observed mothers and children (aged 4 to 5 years) working together. They found that the most efficient strategy was a combined approach of both general and specific instructions. When the learner runs into difficulty, the instructor gives specific instructions; when the learner is coping well, only general encouragement is needed. The learner is given a scaffold by those who are more expert and it enables them to achieve more. In time, we all learn to scaffold ourselves (self-instruction). The process of scaffolding is outlined in Table 10.6.

Activity 3: Helping children

Observe an adult or an older child helping a young child with some activity (e.g. doing a jigsaw). How does the adult or older child help? Does the help seem to fit the child's needs? How does the help offered change as the child becomes more skilled at the task?

Table 10.6: The stages involved in scaffolding

1 Recruitment: gaining the child's interest.

2 Reduction of degrees of freedom: breaking the task down into manageable steps.

3 Direction maintenance: encouraging and motivating the child until they have become self-motivating.

4 Marking critical features: drawing attention to aspects of the problem which will help further progress.

5 Demonstration: the tutor finishes the task off so that the learner can imitate this back in a better form.

Source: adapted from Wood *et al.* (1976, p. 98)

in focus

Peer tutoring (Blaye *et al.* 1991)

The introduction of computers into classrooms has often resulted in children working in pairs or small groups. Blaye and colleagues studied 11 year olds, to see whether co-working could be shown to benefit individual development. Some children worked in pairs while others worked alone, trying to solve problems presented in the context of a computer adventure game. The tasks were difficult and very few succeeded. In fact, no individuals managed to do them all and only some pairs were successful.

In a second session, there was a degree of improvement in performance. About 50 per cent of the pairs of children working together were successful, compared to less than 20 per cent of children working alone.

In their third and final session, all children worked individually on a variation of the task. What was interesting is that there was some transfer from having worked as a member of a pair. Over 70 per cent of children who had previously worked in pairs were successful, compared with only 30 per cent of children who had previously worked individually.

There were, however, individual differences, because not all of those who had worked in pairs were successful and some of those who worked individually were successful. However, the result does suggest some advantage to working in pairs, both while the child was a member of the pair and when they subsequently worked individually. One might presume that the discussions which took place between pair members enhanced their development through the zone of proximal development. In other words, they benefited from peer tutoring.

Peers can also be experts, and peer tutoring was seen by Vygotsky as an effective form of learning. He advocated cooperative group work: small groups of children working together and discussing what they are doing. Bennett and Dunne (1991) found that children who were engaged in cooperative group work were less competitive, less concerned with status and more likely to show evidence of logical thinking than those who worked alone. A study by Blaye *et al.* (1991) shows the advantages that can come from children working in pairs (see *In Focus*). But not all children benefit in such situations. Benefit appears to be related to their status within the group and their ability; higher status and more able children benefit most.

Developing skills and strategies

At a very general level, all the theories we have considered reflect aspects of information-processing within them. But the information-processing approach has its own quite distinctive contribution to make to educational practice. Whilst information-processing theorists agree with Piaget that children actively explore their world, they are closer to Vygotsky in their recommendations that teachers should take a direct role in instructing children.

Information-processing research tries to identify what cognitive abilities and strategies are needed for good performance on a task and how these develop. They also try to find out the difference between 'good' and 'poor' learners. They then try to devise teaching procedures that will improve children's learning. Table 10.7 summarizes some general guidelines for teachers that have been derived from information-processing research. Brown and Burton (1978) show how the information-processing approach can lead to new teaching applications (see *In Focus* at the top of the next page).

Table 10.7 Implications of information-processing for teachers

1 Know what information is needed and what has to be done with it to be successful.

2 Do not overload short-term memory.

3 Try to find out what rule the child is using if consistent errors are being made.

4 Encourage 'metacognitive' knowledge about strategies and their usefulness (e.g. 'Why does summarizing in your own words help?').

Brown and Burton (1978)

A study by Brown and Burton (1978) shows how some of the guidelines based on the information-processing approach can be applied to the study of children's errors in arithmetic tasks. In computer science, a 'bug' refers to an error in a computer programme. Brown and Burton used the term to apply to an error in a child's arithmetic rules. A bug leads to systematic errors, but still implies some understanding, although imperfect. The examples below illustrate the errors that can arise when a subtraction procedure has not quite been applied correctly. In each case, the smaller number has been consistently subtracted from the larger number, regardless of which is on the top line.

$$
\begin{array}{r}
625 \\
-\ 478 \\
\hline
253
\end{array}
\qquad
\begin{array}{r}
444 \\
-\ 363 \\
\hline
121
\end{array}
$$

Once they had identified such 'bugs', Brown and Burton set up two computerized games to train teachers to recognize and correct these bugs. The games, 'Buggy' and 'Debuggy', give the teacher examples of the bug and the teacher tries to identify the bug. Two benefits have been shown:

◆ Teachers become more skilful at detecting bugs (i.e. faulty rules used by children).

◆ Teachers realize that children's errors may be due to the use of systematic, but imperfect rules that can be corrected, rather than due to carelessness.

In conclusion, the current popularity of Vygotsky's work is at least in part due to its emphasis on the importance of social influences on education. He argued that it is educationally more valuable to know what children can do with some assistance, rather than what they can do unaided. This means that his theory offers the potential for making greater use of instructors. On the other hand, if Piaget is right, by using expert intervention we are stifling creativity and complete understanding. It may be possible to combine all approaches successfully as in the CAP project (see *In Focus* below).

Cognitive acceleration program (CAP) in science

◆ *Piagetian* – The programme was designed to develop abstract logical thought at the stage of formal operations.

◆ *Vygotskian: cognitive* – Conflict was recognized as a key to promoting learning. Learning took place in a social context because children were encouraged to discuss their approaches to problem-solving with each other.

◆ *Information-processing* – Emphasis on metacognitive skills (central conceptual structures) allowing children to develop more efficient ways to solve problems.

The aim of the programme was to develop abstract thinking at an age when many children have not yet reached this stage (or may never reach it). The children were given real-life problems such as how to organize food in a larder or how to predict the force needed to raise a heavy load, and are encouraged to ask 'what if?' questions.

Adey and Shayer (1993) tested the short- and long-term effects of the programme. A group of students, aged 11 to 12 years had special lessons every two weeks over a period of two years. A control group had no special lessons. Although the intervention was set within the context of science learning, the effects were found in science, mathematics, and English. In terms of long-term effects, Adey and Shayer found that schools running CAP significantly increased their GCSE results in Science, Mathematics and even English. For example, the number of C grades or above in Science was 18.8 per cent higher in schools running CAP than in the control schools.

Exam summary: Development of thinking

The AQA examination will test your understanding of the following areas:

◆ theories of cognitive development (including those of Piaget and Vygotsky) and information-processing approaches (pp. 247–56)

◆ applications of these theories (pp. 256–9).

Example question

The question below should take you 30 minutes to answer.

◆ Describe one theory of cognitive development and assess the empirical evidence that has been used to support it. *(24 marks)*

Suggested answer structure

We have covered three theories of cognitive development in this first section. Piaget (pp. 247–53) suggested that cognitive development takes place as a result of experiences which force the child to accommodate new information, creating new schemas and occasionally leading to a qualitatively different kind of thinking – moving from one stage to the next. However, these stage changes also depend on 'readiness'. Vygotsky (pp. 253–5) placed emphasis on the importance of social context in transforming elementary into higher mental functions, and the role of the ZPD in understanding how this transformation takes place. Case's information-processing approach (pp. 255–6) saw cognitive development as the increasingly efficient use of M space through the automation of schemes and metacognitive skills.

This question asks you to describe just one of these theories for the AO1 component of the question, and to assess the empirical evidence that has been used to support it (the AO2 component). Although this looks a very straightforward question (as indeed it is), it merits very careful reading. First of all, you have to be realistic about how much descriptive detail you can reproduce in 15 minutes writing time. Taking Piaget's theory as an example, we have looked at the structure of the intellect (p. 248), stages in development (pp. 248–52) as well as the qualitative differences in children's thought (such as object permanence, egocentricity and conservation) that we have covered along the way. This means that you have to be fairly selective about what you include and what you leave out. It would be important, for example, to include a description of the processes of assimilation and accommodation (p. 248), and an explanation of some of the qualitative differences between the different stages of development. What you could not, and should not, do is to describe every last detail of each stage, or try and illustrate the exact procedures used in all the different types of conservation experiments. Being able to extract the gist of a theory such as this requires practice and understanding (a point that Piaget himself made about learning), hence the careful reading of both question and content. Remember, in some questions you might be asked to 'outline two theories ...', in the same 15 minutes, which would require even more of a précis of this theory.

When addressing the AO2 component of this question, remember that you are being asked to assess the evidence used to support your chosen theory. This means putting it under close critical scrutiny rather than just describing it alongside the theory.

The development of measured intelligence

Activity 4: Measuring intelligence

Think of as many examples as you can of activities or behaviours that you consider reflect 'intelligence'. Then consider the following questions:

◆ How do you think that intelligence might be measured?

◆ What kinds of test could be used?

◆ How might 'intelligence' be measured in very young children?

You may be asking why this section is entitled 'the development of *measured* intelligence'. This neatly side steps the question 'what is intelligence?' which may be one of the most challenging concepts in psychology. When you tried doing Activity 4, did you find that you produced a range of ideas about intelligence? You may not be surprised to discover that psychologists have not agreed on one definition of intelligence either. They even disagree on whether there is one general kind of intelligence or several different kinds. Although there are a variety of definitions of intelligence, there is, however, considerable agreement that it refers to differences in the ability to acquire information, to think and reason well, and to deal effectively and adaptively with the environment.

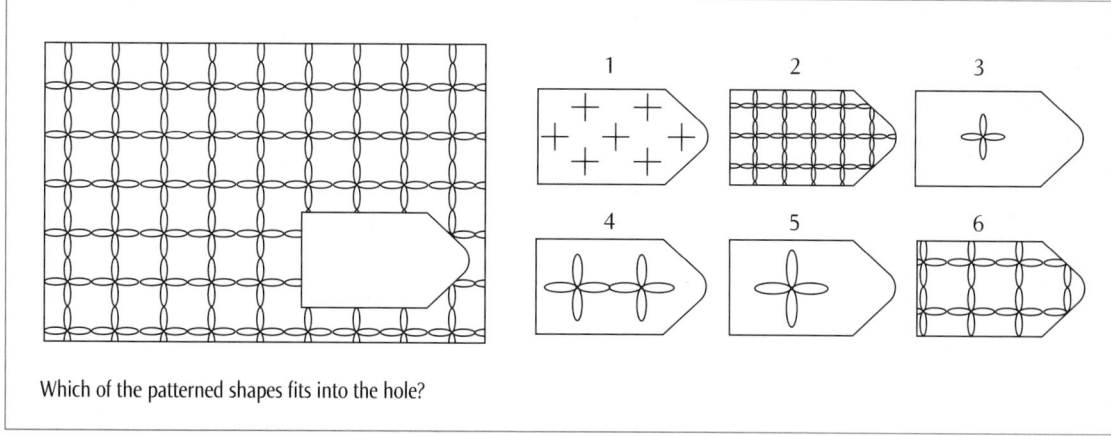

Which of the patterned shapes fits into the hole?

Figure 10.3 An example taken from the Raven Progressive Matrices Test. *Source:* Raven (1958)

However, we need not concern ourselves with what intelligence is and instead will focus only on one aspect of intelligence – the intelligence test.

Intelligence tests

The issue of assessing children's intelligence was first tackled by Binet in 1905. The French government had asked Binet to develop a way of identifying pupils who needed special remedial education. Binet and his colleague Simon developed a test of 'general mental ability' consisting of a range of items which varied in difficulty. Binet and Simon determined at what age the average child would succeed with each item by giving the tests to many school children. In this way, they could then identify those pupils who were performing below average. (These were the tests that Piaget worked on when he noticed the consistent errors that children of certain ages were making.) Binet's developmental approach was so successful in predicting school performance that it became the basis for many other intelligence tests. The Stanford–Binet test is based on the original model and is still used today.

IQ

In many intelligence tests, the score is given as an 'intelligence quotient' (IQ). This score enables one individual's performance to be compared with the performance of others. Following Binet, the general principle for calculating IQ has been to establish the child's 'mental age'. A child will have a mental age of, say, 8 if that child passes the test items that average 8 year olds pass, but does not pass the tests that average 9 year olds pass. If a child's mental age is divided by the child's actual age (their 'chronological age' or CA), and multiplied by 100 (to remove fractions), then the result is the child's IQ. This means a child of average ability will have an IQ of 100. Scores above or below 100 indicate a child of greater or less than average intelligence.

Types of IQ test

No doubt you will have taken an intelligence test at some time in your life, even if you didn't realize it. Often IQ tests are given to groups although some of them require one-to-one testing. There are also different kinds of test items. Some are verbal items (e.g. 'Choose the word which is opposite in meaning to the word in capital letters PARTISAN: (a) commoner, (b) neutral, (c) ascetic, (d) pacifier'). Some are non-verbal, such as asking a child to arrange pictures in an order so they tell a story or Raven's Progressive Matrices (shown in Figure 10.3). Some non-verbal tests are called 'culture-fair' because people from all over the world should be just as able to understand them, whereas verbal tests or even telling a story with pictures may be tasks that simply wouldn't make sense to people outside a particular culture.

Factors that affect intelligence test performance

In this section we shall look at what is known about the factors that can affect children's scores on IQ tests. Psychological research has identified quite a number of such factors, such as:

◆ *Genetic factors:* Your intelligence is more or less fixed from the moment you are conceived. It is determined by your genes and inherited from your parents.

◆ *Environmental and cultural factors:* Your life experiences affect the extent to which your intelligence 'grows'. Life 'experiences' include such things as diet and education.

◆ *Test factors:* IQ performance also depends on how highly motivated you are or whether the test is appropriate for your life experiences.

◆ *Race:* Do different ethnic or racial groups differ in their intelligence?

Genetic factors

The long-standing controversy about the relative contributions of genetic factors ('nature') versus environmental factors ('nurture') has been prominent in the debate about IQ differences. It is now accepted that it is not simply a 'nature versus nurture' debate, but a question of 'how much' each contributes. There have been a variety of research designs used to study genetic factors:

◆ kinship studies

◆ adoption studies

◆ genetic research.

Kinship studies look at the correlation in IQ scores between pairs of individuals who are genetically related to varying degrees. This includes looking at twins, siblings, and parents and offspring. Much of the early research considered the differences between identical twins and non-identical twins, and those reared apart or together. Identical twins share the same genetic material and are monozygotic (MZ) – they come from the same egg (one zygote). Non-identical twins are as similar as any two siblings are because they came from two separate eggs (dizygotic, DZ). In fact, DZ twins are a little more similar than siblings are because they also shared the same experiences before birth. And MZ twins are less identical than was once thought; even individuals with the exact same genetic material have small differences because experience interacts with development (which means that no clone can ever be exactly like the original).

What did the early studies find? A classic study was conducted by Shields (1962) who, by advertising on the television, managed to find 44 pairs of MZ twins who had been reared apart. He found that these individuals had quite similar IQs (a correlation of 0.77) and that this was the same for MZ twins reared together. This suggested that environment had very little influence on the development of their IQ and appears to support the view that genetic factors are of greater importance. However, major criticisms have been levelled at Shields' research, most notably by Kamin (1977) who pointed out that, in reality, the twins had actually spent a substantial amount of time together and many were raised by relatives and lived quite close by. Therefore, they were not truly raised in different environments. A second problem is that the evidence is correlational and so does not show that genetic factors *caused* IQ; it could be that identical twins have a similar effect on

people around them, which leads to self-fulfilling prophecy and similar academic achievements. Ceci (1990) re-analysed some of the data from early studies and found that if one looked only at pairs of twins who lived in rural areas, then the correlations were massively reduced to around 0.27. The same was true if one looked only at twins from urban areas. This suggests that when the environmental factor is held constant, the correlations are low, indicating a more minimal role for genetics.

Twin studies have continued. For example, the Swedish Adoption/Twin Study of Ageing (SATSA) (Pederson *et al.* 1992) has followed DZ and MZ twins, half of whom were separated before the age of one. The correlations obtained are similar to Shields' study: MZ twins reared together 0.80 and DZ twins reared apart 0.32.

The results from many of the studies plus those of other relations (siblings and parents) were analysed jointly in a classic article by Bouchard and McGue (1981). A summary of their findings is shown in Table 10.8. The findings support the genetic view because the closer two individuals are related, the higher the correlation. The correlation for MZ twins reared apart (0.72) is higher than for DZ twins reared together (0.60). This indicates that genetic factors are at least partially responsible for differences in IQ scores. However, comparison of three other sets of correlations in Table 10.8 indicates considerable environmental effects:

◆ The correlation of MZ twins reared apart (0.72) is lower than that of MZ twins reared together (0.86).

◆ The correlation for DZ twins reared together (0.60) is higher than that for siblings reared together (0.47).

◆ The correlation for siblings reared together (0.47) is higher than that for siblings reared apart (0.24).

On the basis of this kind of evidence, it seems that about half of the variation in IQ scores may be due to individual differences in heredity. This is a far more

Table 10.8 Summarized IQ correlations	
Kinship pair	*Average correlation*
Identical twins reared together	0.86
Identical twins reared apart	0.72
Fraternal twins reared together	0.60
Siblings reared together	0.47
Siblings reared apart	0.24

Source: Buchard and McGue (1981, p. 1056)

The Texas Adoption Project (Horn 1983)

The Texas Adoption Project was made possible by the data from a large private adoption agency in Texas. The agency had given IQ tests to the unmarried mothers of some 469 children who were adopted after birth by 300 adoptive families. The IQs of the adoptive mothers were also available. The correlation of the adopted children's IQ with their biological mother's IQ was 0.28 and with their adoptive mother's IQ 0.15. While these figures show some genetic contribution, the difference between the correlations is very small. Other research has produced similar results. In statistical terms, the small correlations indicate that the IQ scores of the biological mothers explain 8 per cent of the differences in the adopted children's IQ scores, whilst the IQ scores of the adoptive mothers explain 2 per cent of the differences in the adopted children's scores. Assuming that biological and adoptive fathers contributed similarly, there is still about 80 per cent of the variation in children's IQ scores to be accounted for by individual environmental experiences outside the shared home, such as school. One intriguing possibility here is that genes may influence development by their effect on how a child reacts to particular experiences.

Horne also studied the adopted children of two groups of biological mothers with widely different IQ scores, those with IQs above 120 and those with IQs below 95. When tested in middle childhood, the average IQ of children of biological mothers with lower IQs was 102, but the average IQ of the children of the high-IQ biological mothers was 118. This study clearly shows that both environment and heredity contribute substantially to IQ.

moderate estimate than the controversial claims made by 'hereditarians' such as Jensen (1969).

Adoption studies allow researchers to compare the IQ correlations of children with both their biological and their adoptive parents. Early adoption studies often suffered from a methodological limitation – selective placement may have taken place. This means that children's adoptive families were 'matched' as closely as possible with their biological parents. When this has occurred, genetic and environmental influences cannot be separated. There are, however, more recent adoption studies where selective placement has been minimal (see *In Focus*, 'The Texas Adoption Project').

In their transracial adoption study, Scarr and Weinberg (1976, 1983) looked at Black American children adopted by White families. The adoptive families had higher educational status and income than the children's biological families. They found that the average IQ of the adopted Black children was 106 (those who had been adopted within twelve months of birth averaged 110), whereas the average IQ of Black American children with similar genetic backgrounds, but who were not brought up in a middle-class environment was 90. Scarr and Weinberg conclude that the typically lower IQ scores of Black children in low-income Black communities must be due to environment.

Most recently, *genetic research* has looked at another source of evidence – locating the actual genes involved in intelligence. Plomin claims to have identified the first gene related to intelligence, called IGF2R (see Chorney *et al.* 1998). Since many genes determine intelligence (i.e. it is polygenic), it is likely that high intelligence will

be determined by having a variety of high quality genes. A person who has a lot of these 'plus genes' will have high IQ, whereas those who have a mixture of pluses and minuses would have average IQ. If, therefore, one compared the genes from individuals with high IQs ('super-brights') with those of average intelligence, one should be able to single out genes which are associated with brightness. This is what Plomin and his co-workers did and they found that IGF2R was present in 33 per cent of the 'super-brights', but in only 17 per cent of the average group. This one gene would only contribute a small amount to the individual's IQ, perhaps just 4 IQ points, but a series of pluses will add up to 'super-bright'. The fact that not all the super-brights had the gene is understandable because you only need a lot of the 'bright' genes to be bright – you don't need to have them all.

Environmental and cultural factors

We have seen that kinship research supported the influence of both genetic and environmental factors, and some studies (e.g. Scarr and Weinberg 1976, 1983) were more supportive of environmental influences. Recent studies of environmental factors have tried to find which specific aspects of the environment contribute to children's IQ scores, and by how much.

Cultural factors are embedded in environmental evidence insofar as their influence is transmitted through members of one's social group. The term 'culture' refers to the rules, morals and methods of interaction that bind a group of people and which are determined through the process of socialization.

Table 10.9 Environmental factors affecting IQ scores

1 The mother has a history of mental illness.

2 The mother has serious anxiety.

3 The mother has rigid attitudes, beliefs and values about her child's development.

4 There are few positive interactions between mother and infant.

5 The main earner in the household has a semi-skilled job.

6 The mother did not go to High School.

7 The child is from a minority group.

8 The father does not live with the family.

9 The family has suffered more than 20 stressful events, such as divorce or separation, before the child was aged 4.

10 There are four or more children in the family.

Source: Sameroff and Seifer (1983)

Socialization is achieved largely through parents, school and peers, as well as members of one's culture in general. IQ may be influenced by these individuals, as described in the following sections. Cultural factors are also apparent in differences in the desire to succeed, which is considered later.

Specific cultural and environmental factors have been studied:

◆ home background

◆ parental involvement

◆ enrichment programmes.

In an investigation into *home background*, the Rochester Longitudinal Study (Sameroff *et al.* 1993) that began in the 1970s has followed several hundred children from birth to adolescence. It has identified 10 environmental factors that were found to affect the children's IQ (see Table 10.9). The more factors a child had, the lower their IQ. In fact, IQ decreased at a rate of about 4 IQ points per factor, and together the factors were found to account for almost half the variability in children's IQ scores. However, we again should note that these data are correlational. It may be that low parental IQ was the cause of the risk factors (e.g. 'mother did not go to high school') and also the cause of low IQ in the child (child inherited low IQ).

Focusing on *parental involvement,* Hart and Risley (1995) also conducted a long-term investigation of children's development. They looked in particular at the verbal interactions between parents and children, analysing tape recordings taken during the children's first three years. All the children started speaking at about the same time, but by the age of three there were significant differences in vocabulary which were

associated with home background. Children from professional families had about 1,100 words, children from working-class homes had 750 words and those from families on welfare had just above 500 words. These differences were related to language use in parents. Hart and Risley identified five parent behaviours that were strongly related to vocabulary development in children. These were: using a wide vocabulary, high rates of approval, language with a high information content, asking children about things rather than being directive, and responding to children. Furthermore, there was a correlation of 0.78 between IQ at age 3 and these parenting behaviours.

Caldwell and Bradley (1978) have developed a checklist of items to use when gathering information about the quality of children's home lives, called the Home Observation for Measurement of the Environment (HOME). There are versions of HOME for infancy, preschool and middle childhood. Each has subscales that relate to aspects of the child's environment. Almost all the items have some relation to later achievement. HOME scores can correlate 0.5 with later IQ scores. Low scores in infancy can predict a reduction in IQ scores of up to 20 points. For the preschool scales, Bradley and Caldwell (1984) found that children who score well on IQ tests are generally from families who:

◆ are emotionally responsive and involved with the child

◆ provide appropriate play materials and opportunities to explore and learn

◆ expect their child to learn and achieve.

The correlation between HOME scores and IQ is lower for middle childhood, probably because by then children are spending time in other environments such as school. While these results using HOME scores are consistent with much other research, they are based on correlational data and again can say nothing conclusive about causation, especially as these results come from children raised by their biological parents. A longitudinal study by Yeates *et al.* (1979) helps here. They measured the IQ scores of 112 mothers and their children at ages 2, 3 and 4 years and their HOME scores. The best predictor of a child's IQ at age 2 was the mother's IQ, as genetic causes would suggest, but by the age of 4, HOME scores were the best predictors of a child's IQ. Home environment is therefore important.

The debate about whether it is nature or nurture which has greatest influence in the development of measured intelligence has important practical implications and none more so than in terms of compensatory education or *enrichment programmes.* If intelligence were entirely genetic, then school

The benefits of better diet

A rather remarkable study by Benton and Cook (1991) found that when vitamin and mineral supplements were given to 6-year-old children their IQs increased by an average of 7.6 points. It was astonishing that it occurred at all, but particularly as the experiment took place over a six-week period. The results might be explained in terms of expectations – perhaps the children came to believe that the supplements would improve their performance and this increased their desire to do better. However, the experiment was well controlled. There were two experimental groups: one group was given the supplements whereas the other children received a placebo (i.e. they thought they were also receiving the supplements). The experiment was also double blind. Neither the experimenters nor the children knew who was receiving the actual supplements. Moreover, the IQ of the placebo group decreased by 1.7 points. This suggests that the vitamins must have had some beneficial effect.

Such findings are supported by Lynn's (1986) observation that average IQ scores are increasing worldwide. In one decade, the scores increased by 1.7, 3.0 and 7.7 in the UK, US and Japan respectively. Lynn suggests that such change is unlikely to be genetic, but is more likely to be due to improved diet and also improved education (which is also an environmental effect).

programmes designed to give disadvantaged children a boost should not be effective. Head Start is the name given to the largest enrichment programme that has ever been conducted. It was designed to reverse the effects of what was seen as social disadvantage in the United States by providing intensive preschool education (compensatory education). This was sometimes accompanied by the extra provision of social services, medicine and nutritional advice, as well as involving the children's families in care and education. When children in the preschool programme entered school, they showed more advanced cognitive and social behaviour than children who were not involved in the programme (Lee *et al.* 1990). The initial positive effects disappeared in the years following entry, but later research showed a 'sleeper effect'. When the children were older they had higher arithmetic and reading skills, greater feelings of competence, and were more likely to go to college (Lazar and Darlington 1982). There have been some criticisms of the Head Start programme, however, such as the fact that the choice of the control groups of children was not strictly random.

In the Head Start program, enrichment wasn't simply given in terms of mental stimulation. The children were also offered improved physical care. It may be possible to enrich IQ through improved diet (see *In Focus*, 'The benefits of better diet').

Test factors

We have seen that children from certain families (lower social class or 'inferior' genetic stock) perform less well on IQ tests. It is supposed that this indicates that they have lower intelligence. However, it could be that the problem lies within the tests themselves, in areas such as:

◆ test content and criteria

◆ familiarity with test materials

◆ motivation.

IQ tests are designed to predict success in a particular culture. Items on IQ tests may be biased because other cultures use *different criteria*. Luria (1971) gives a clear example. When presented with a classification task involving the four items: axe, log, shovel and saw, and asked to identify which one is the odd one out, 'log' is considered to be the odd one out because it is not a tool. 'Log' is, therefore, the 'correct answer' because our culture values the ability to classify. However, Luria found that unskilled Russian peasants chose 'shovel' because it wasn't needed when cutting up the log with the axe and the saw. Cole *et al.* (1971) found that the Kpelle in Nigeria persistently grouped pictures of objects according to their use until they were asked to sort them in the way a stupid person would do. They then used the categories preferred by Europeans!

Attempts to produce 'culture-free' or 'culture-fair' tests, such as Raven's Progressive Matrices, have had mixed success. There is evidence that even these tests are affected by general experience and culture. For example, Flynn (1987) found that scores on Raven's matrices have increased by about 20 points in the last 30 years. This large increase is unlikely to be due to genetic or environmental change. It may be that our use of more visually-based technologies has improved our abilities to do these particular tests, and this supports the view that such tests are not assessing a universal skill, but one that is learned.

Performance on some IQ test items may depend on particular opportunities to learn prior to the test and hence on *familiarity with test materials*. Dirks (1982) found that children's performance on an IQ test item requiring the child to rearrange wooden blocks to copy a design quickly, was related to their experience of a popular, but expensive game that made very similar demands. Heath (1989) found that the mothers of Black American children typically asked their children 'real' questions, that is questions that did not have one correct, short answer already known by the mother. Such questions helped the children to develop complex verbal skills, but did not prepare them for the kinds of questions they met in the classroom or in IQ tests.

IQ scores can improve if the child is familiar with the tester, is given praise for success, and has some test experience, especially of giving correct answers. Zigler *et al.* (1973) found that preschool children from impoverished backgrounds could gain up to ten IQ points if they had a short play session with the tester beforehand, or were tested a second time. By comparison, middle-class children's scores increased by only three IQ points.

Motivation can also be explained in terms of expectations. The better you are expected to do, the more motivated you are likely to be. A classic study by Rosenthal and Jacobsen (1968), called 'Pygmalion in the classroom', showed how high expectations can lead to large increases in IQ test performance. Some pupils were randomly selected to be 'bloomers'. This information was passed to the teachers with the explanation that the 'bloomers' were children who were not currently performing well academically, but who had the potential to do much better. After a year, some of the younger children who had been identified as bloomers showed very large IQ gains compared with the control group (one child gained 40 IQ points). This gave support to the idea of the self-fulfilling prophecy, i.e. one person's beliefs about another can be realized as a direct result of those beliefs.

Intelligence and race

The most controversial issue in this area of psychology is the extent to which differences in IQ can be related to race. Jensen (1969) sparked off an emotional and political controversy when he published results of research that showed that on average Black Americans scored 15 points below White Americans. He claimed that this showed that Black people were genetically inferior to White people. Such research is extremely dangerous because of the potential support it gives to racist prejudices. But it is especially dangerous because it is flawed in a number of ways.

◆ The concept of 'race' is misleading. In reality, people with apparently similar biological heritage come from a range of different cultural backgrounds and experiences.

◆ Bodmer (1972) pointed out that average differences between genetically different populations must be environmental. Figure 10.4 illustrates this.

◆ Tyler (1965) found that Black people from the northern parts of America did better than those from the southern states. These differences must be due to environment, which in turn suggests that Black/White differences must also be environmental.

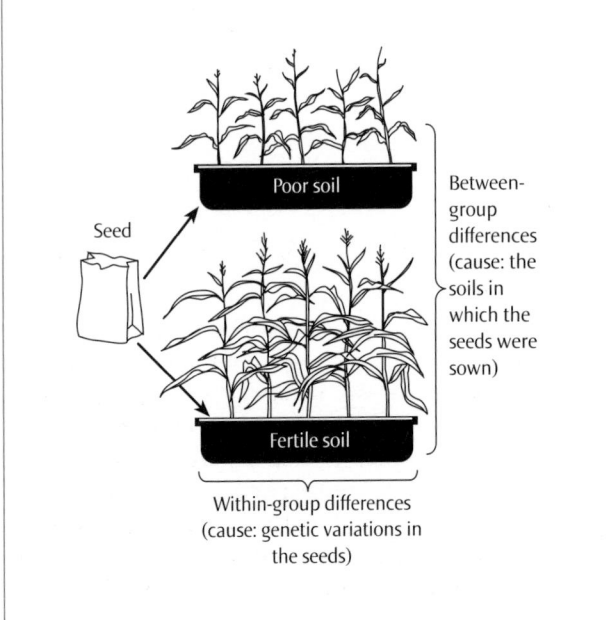

Figure 10.4
If the same seeds are planted in two different environments, we find large average differences *between the groups*. The most logical explanation is that the differences are due to the environment. *Within each group* there are also differences. Since all group members share the same environment, the within-group differences must be due to genetic differences.

We can apply this to differences between different groups of people. A group of children living in a city slum will have a lower *average* IQ than those in middle-class suburbs. Within each of these groups there will be some variation, and this will be down to their genetic differences. The same principle can be applied to differences between racial groups.

Source: adapted from Colby *et al.* (1983)

◆ Scarr and Weinberg's research (described earlier) showed that Black children adopted into White homes developed IQs equivalent to their White peers. This again supports the environmental argument.

◆ Most IQ tests are designed by middle-class Americans. It is likely that other social and ethnic groups will do less well. Williams (1972) designed BITCH (Black Intelligence Test of Cultural Homogeneity) to show that one could produce a test which would advantage American Black children, while White children would do less well by comparison.

It seems clear that conclusions about innate racial differences are unlikely to be correct and, at best, can only serve to perpetuate extremely damaging prejudices.

The development of measured intelligence is due to an interaction between nature and nurture. Perhaps this is best expressed in Gottesman's (1963) concept of a 'reaction range'. He proposed that we are all born with genetic potentials for height, weight, creativity, intelligence and so on. There is a theoretical minimum and maximum. The environments we experience determine the extent to which we reach the maximum of our own particular range. However, the limit of each person's range does not matter. What does matter is that we try to maximize every individual's abilities whatever their limit.

Exam summary: Development of measured intelligence

The AQA examination will test your understanding of the following areas:

◆ research into the role of genetic factors in development of intelligence test performance (pp. 261–3, 521–3)

◆ research into the role of cultural differences in development of intelligence test performance (pp. 263–7).

Example question

The question below should take you 30 minutes:

◆ Critically consider the role of genetic factors in the development of measured intelligence. *(24 marks)*

Suggested answer structure

The role of genetic factors in the development of measured intelligence test performance is covered on pp. 261–3. Measured intelligence results from an interaction between both genetic and environmental factors. The best current estimates suggest that each contribute about 50 per cent of the variability between test scores. Research into the role of genetic factors has focused on kinship studies (p. 262), including twin studies which typically show that the correlation for MZ (identical) twins reared apart is higher than for DZ (nonidentical) twins reared together (p. 262). Adoption studies allow researchers to compare the IQ correlations of children with both biological and adoptive parents. Although studies like the Texas Adoption Project (p. 263) have shown closer correlations between children and their biological parents than children and their adoptive parents, the differences between these correlations tend to be relatively small. More recently, attention has switched to attempts to locate the genes involved in intelligence. It is likely, given the primary findings of early research, that intelligence might be determined more by having a variety of high quality genes, such as the IGF2R gene (p. 263).

Although this question is specifically concerned with genetic factors in the development of intelligence, it would be quite acceptable to include discussion of research that shows the importance of environmental factors. The more that variability in intelligence can be attributed to environmental factors, the weaker the case for inherited factors. Look at Chapter 19, pp. 521–3, for a discussion of the ways in which genes and environment may interact together, useful for the AO2 content of your answer. A good way of closing your essay would be to present Gottesman's concept of a 'reaction range' for intelligence (p. 267).

The development of moral understanding

What is moral development?

Moral development is concerned with the rules about the rightness and wrongness of certain behaviours and how people should behave in relation to others. Moral behaviour is related to prosocial behaviour because both promote social relationships. Traditionally, psychologists have studied three aspects of moral development:

◆ how children *think* and *reason* about moral issues

◆ how children actually *behave* when required to exercise judgement

◆ how children *feel* about moral issues – for example, feelings of guilt.

Cognitive developmental theories, such as those of Piaget and Kohlberg, have looked at *thinking* and *reasoning* about moral issues. Some of the learning theories such as classical and operant conditioning, and social learning theories, have been concerned with actual moral *behaviour*, and the psychodynamic theories of Freud and Erikson have shed some light on *feelings* about ethical and moral matters. In this chapter we are going to focus on the development of moral understanding.

Table 10.10 Comparing Piaget's stages of cognitive development and stages in the development of moral understanding			
Age (approx)	Stage	Characteristics	Equivalent stage of cognitive development
0–5	Premoral judgement	Rules not understood	Pre-operational, egocentric
5–9	Moral realism	Heteronomous morals (controlled by others) Rules exist as 'things' (realism) Actions evaluated in terms of consequences Punishment should be by atonement	Intuitive, inability to conserve
7+	Moral relativity	Autonomous morals (controlled by oneself) Rules can be changed by consent (relativism) Actions evaluated in terms of intentions Punishment should fit the crime (reciprocity)	Concrete → formal operations

Note that there is an overlap between the stages. Piaget believed that the age from 7–9 was a period of transition between the two stages and that children in this age range will show evidence of features from both.

Piaget's theory of moral understanding

Moral understanding is a mental activity and therefore it is no surprise to find that Piaget applied his ideas on cognitive development to the specific area of moral development. Piaget's theory of the development of moral understanding followed similar principles to his stage theory of cognitive development, as you can see in Table 10.10. At each stage of the child's development, the way that they are able to think about right and wrong is related to their cognitive abilities generally. So, for example, preschool children are likely to be 'premoral' because they cannot as yet use abstract rules and their egocentricity makes it hard for them to understand the intentions of others.

Piaget considered that equal-status contact with peers was critical in enabling the child to understand the perspective of others and develop socially and morally. When children go to nursery or to school for the first time, they begin to engage more in social situations without adult involvement. They have to learn to handle inevitable conflicts over who should have a turn first or what game to play. Because peers have equal status, they must work out means of reaching a compromise in order to function as a group. In doing this they gradually begin to see that rules are social contracts achieved in relation to context. It is critical that adults are not involved because they only serve to reinforce the child's respect for authority and inflexible rules.

Piaget's research

Piaget (1932) based his theory on two lines of investigation. First of all he observed groups of children aged between 3 and 12 playing games of marbles and asked them questions about the rules of the game. He found that the youngest children used no rules at all. By the age of 5 the children were using rules, but these were seen as absolute law, fixed and unchangeable. Rules must also be obeyed, and failure to obey a rule automatically results in punishment (imminent justice), based on the idea that someone in authority instantly punishes wrongdoing. According to Piaget, this is the stage of heteronomous morality or moral realism. Children of 10 had moved on to the next stage of 'moral relativism' because of their greater cognitive maturity. They now realized that the rules could be changed, as long as everyone agreed. Piaget called this the stage of autonomous morality or morality of reciprocity. Children are now more flexible in their thinking and can adopt alternative ways of looking at things.

Piaget's second kind of investigation involved pairs of 'moral stories' (see In Focus, 'Piaget's stories'). In each pair there was one story where the child had good intentions, but accidentally caused considerable damage, whereas in the other story there was less damage, but the child's intentions were also less good (the child behaved without due care and attention). Piaget asked children, 'Which of the characters was the naughtier and who should be punished the most?' Piaget was interested in the reasons the children gave for their answers rather than just the answers themselves, and whether they used consequences or intentions as the basis for their moral judgement. Children in the stage of moral realism focused on the *consequences* of the action rather than the *intent*. Older children were able to take intention into consideration when considering the morality of an action, thereby refraining from making judgements that are purely based on the outcome or *consequences* of an action.

Piaget's stories

Pairs of stories used by Piaget in studies of young children's moral development.

Story 1: A little boy who is called John is in his room. He is called to dinner. He goes into the dining room. But behind the door there was a chair, and on the chair there was a tray with 15 cups on it. John couldn't have known that there was all this behind the door. He goes in, the door knocks against the tray, 'bang' to the 15 cups and they all get broken!

Story 2: Once there was a little boy whose name was Henry. One day when his mother was out he tried to get some jam out of the cupboard. He climbed up on a chair and stretched out his arm. But the jam was too high up and he couldn't reach it and have any. But while he was trying to get it, he knocked over a cup. The cup fell down and broke.

Below is a characteristic response for a child in the stage of moral realism:

Questioner:	'What did the first boy do?'
Child:	'He broke 15 cups.'
Questioner:	'And the second one?'
Child:	'He broke a cup by moving roughly.'
Questioner:	'Is one of the boys naughtier than the other?'
Child:	'The first one is because he knocked over 15 cups.'
Questioner:	'If you were the daddy, which one would you punish most?'
Child:	'The one who broke 15 cups.'
Questioner:	'Why did he break them?'
Child:	'The door shut too hard and knocked them over. He didn't do it on purpose.'
Questioner:	'And why did the other boy break a cup?'
Child:	'Because he was clumsy. When he was getting the jam the cup fell down.'
Questioner:	'Why did he want to get the jam?'
Child:	'Because he was alone. Because the mother wasn't there.'

Source: Piaget (1932, p. 122 and p. 129)

We can see that the child in the stage of moral realism regards John as being the naughtier of the two, because the outcome of his behaviour was that 15 cups were broken, although the child recognizes that this was unintentional. Henry only broke one cup, while he was trying to *deceive* his mother, but because the consequences of the action were less in the child's eyes, he is seen as less naughty. According to Piaget, an older child would say that Henry was the naughtier because he wanted to take the jam without his mother's permission. This child is then considering intentions and would deny that it mattered that John broke more cups because he did not do it deliberately.

Evaluation of Piaget's research on moral development

The first question is whether we consider games of marbles to be an appropriate test of morality. Turiel (1983) suggested that people do use social-conventional rules as a way of making moral judgements and therefore it would be reasonable to suggest a scheme of moral development based on the use and understanding of such rules. However, Turiel also pointed out that there are other social rules, such as those related to etiquette and games. Marbles would be an example of the latter and therefore not fully representative of moral behaviour.

The 'moral story' evidence has also been criticized. It is possible that the reason the younger children made judgements on the basis of consequences rather than intentions was because the consequences were much easier to identify. When intentions are made clearer, even younger children appear to be able to make decisions based on them. For example, Chandler *et al.* (1973) found that when the format of these stories was changed from a verbal to a videotaped presentation, then 6 year olds recognized the intentions of the actor just as well as older children did. Likewise, Feldman *et al.* (1976) found that young children were able to make judgements based on intention when the intentions of the characters in the stories were evaluated separately from the outcomes, whereas in Piaget's original stories, the intent of the child was always confused with the consequences of the action.

On the other hand, there has been some support for Piaget. Armsby (1971) manipulated moral stories so that there was either a small amount of deliberate damage or a large amount of accidental damage. Younger children did take intention into account, but had difficulty weighing up the relative importance of value and intention, which meant that they ended up making judgements in terms of outcome alone, as Piaget had found. The conclusion must be that younger children rely *more* on consequences than intentions when judging right and wrong, but that moral behaviour does not follow a simple formula.

An important feature of Piaget's theory is his claim that the moral stages are innate and universal. This would lead us to expect cross-cultural support for his stages. Linaza (1984), for example, found the same sequence of development in Spanish children. However, we should note that where researchers have used the same research methods as Piaget, they might well find the same results because of the methodological flaws described above. Not all cross-cultural evidence has not been as supportive.

Piaget also claimed that peer interaction would be important in the development of moral understanding, in the same way as he suggested that cognitive challenges lead to the accommodation of existing schema. Moreover, he suggested that adult interaction would be less valuable. Kruger (1992) found support for the peer participation hypothesis. In this experiment, female participants (average age 8 years) were paired either with a friend of the same age or with their mother. Prior to the experiment, each girl was questioned to determine her stage of moral development. Then each pair was asked to reach an agreement about two moral stories. All individuals were again assessed on a moral reasoning task, and it was found that those girls working with peers showed a greater increase in moral maturity than those working with their mothers. Presumably, the more appropriate discussions between peers assisted moral understanding, even within this short space of time.

Overall, more recent research suggests that Piaget may have underestimated the complexity of moral reasoning. A more complex approach to the study of moral reasoning is reflected in the work of Kohlberg.

Kohlberg's theory of moral understanding

Both Piaget and Kohlberg's theories are cognitive developmental and have certain common characteristics:

◆ They suggest that moral development proceeds through a sequence of innately determined stages which follow an invariant sequence.

◆ Each stage is defined by the kind of thought (cognition) used to make moral judgements.

◆ They focus more on *how* people think rather than *what* they think.

◆ There is an underlying assumption that moral principles are linked to moral behaviour.

Lawrence Kohlberg's theory built on Piaget's ideas and extended them to cover adolescence and adulthood. The basis for the theory was a set of 10 moral dilemmas (see *In Focus*), with accompanying questions, which reflected the fact that in real life there often is no single 'correct' answer. The key factor is how people explain their decision rather than the decision itself. Kohlberg's first study using these dilemmas was cross-sectional, interviewing 72 boys aged between 10 and 16. Each interview lasted two hours. Kohlberg analysed the responses to these dilemmas, resulting in his classification scheme of three levels of moral reasoning, subdivided into six stages (see Table 10.11).

For each dilemma Kohlberg decided what stage of moral reasoning best described the individual's responses. For example, in the case of Heinz, a person might say that 'He should steal the drug for his wife because people would think he was bad if he let her die'. This would be classed as Stage 3 because it shows a sense of living up to other people's expectations.

Kohlberg found that each individual tended to have one dominant category of reasoning, in other words their reasoning on each dilemma might be at a different level, but overall they showed a tendency to one particular stage of reasoning. The original sample was followed for a further 26 years (Colby *et al.* 1983). The boys and men were tested six times in all, at three-yearly intervals. The graph in Figure 10.5 shows how moral reasoning developed. At age 10 the children displayed mainly Stage 2 reasoning, but there were examples of Stages 1 and 3. By the age of 22, no one used Stage 1 reasoning, and Stages 3 and 4 were predominant. By the age of 36, and the end of the study, there was still very little evidence of Stage 5 reasoning (about 5 per cent).

Empirical support

Walker *et al.* (1987) developed a modified set of nine stages to allow for the fact that reasoning often falls between two of Kohlberg's stages. They found general agreement with Kohlberg, for example that the equivalent of Stage 2-type reasoning dominates at age 10 and Stage 3 at age 16.

Kohlberg's moral dilemmas

One of the most famous of Kohlberg's dilemmas concerns that of Heinz, described below.

In Europe, a woman was near death from a particular kind of cancer. There was one drug that the doctors thought might save her. It was a form of radium that a chemist in the same town had recently discovered. The drug was expensive to make, but the chemist was charging ten times what the drug cost him to make. He paid $200 for the radium and charged $2,000 for a small dose of the drug. The sick woman's husband, Heinz, went to everyone he knew to borrow the money, but he could only get together about $1,000 which is half of what it cost. He told the chemist that his wife was dying, and asked him to sell it cheaper or let him pay later. But the chemist said: 'No, I discovered the drug and I'm going to make money from it.' So Heinz got desperate and broke into the man's store to steal the drug for his wife.

After hearing the story, the individual is asked a series of questions, such as:

◆ Should Heinz steal the drug? Why or why not?

◆ Is it actually right or wrong for him to steal the drug? Why is it right or wrong?

◆ What if Heinz didn't love his wife? Would that change anything?

◆ What if the person dying was a stranger? Should Heinz steal the drug for a stranger?

◆ It is against the law for Heinz to steal? Does that make it morally wrong?

Source: Colby and Kohlberg (1987)

Table 10.11 Stages of moral development (Kohlberg 1976)

Level 1: Preconventional morality

Stage 1: Punishment and obedience orientation
The child decides what is wrong on the basis of what is punished. Obedience is not valued for its own sake; the child obeys because adults have superior power.

Stage 2: Individualism, instrumental purpose and exchange
The child follows rules when it is in his immediate interest. What is good is what brings pleasant results. Right is also what is fair, what is an equal exchange, a deal or an agreement.

Level 2: Conventional morality

Stage 3: Mutual interpersonal expectations, relationships and interpersonal conformity
The family or small group to whom the child belongs becomes important. Moral actions are those that live up to others' expectations. 'Being good' becomes important for its own sake, and the child generally values trust, loyalty, respect, gratitude and keeping mutual relationships.

Stage 4: Social system and conscience (law and order)
A shift in focus from family and close groups to the larger society. Good is fulfilling duties one has agreed to; laws are to be upheld except in extreme cases. Contributing to society is also seen as good.

Level 3: Principled or postconventional morality

Stage 5: Social contract or utility and individual rights
Acting so as to achieve the 'greatest good for the greatest number'. The child is aware that there are different views and values, that values are relative. Laws and rules should be upheld in order to preserve the social order, but they can be changed. Still, there are some basic nonrelative values, such as the importance of each person's life and liberty that should be upheld no matter what.

Stage 6: Universal ethical principles
The person develops and follows self-chosen ethical principles in determining what is right. Since laws usually conform to those principles, laws should be obeyed, but when there is a difference between law and conscience, conscience dominates. At this stage, the ethical principles followed are part of an articulated, integrated, carefully thought-out and consistently followed system of values and principles.

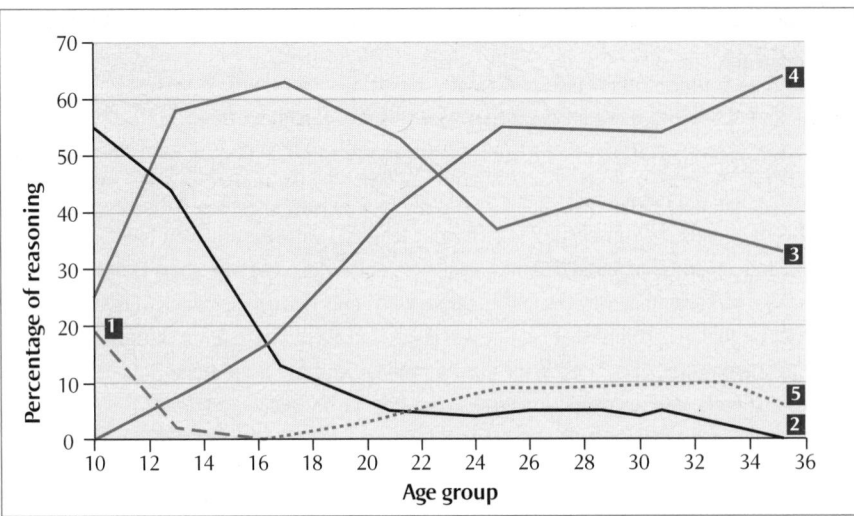

Figure 10.5
Use of Kohlberg's moral stages at ages 10 to 36 by male participants studied longitudinally over a 20-year period
Source: Gleitman (1991)

In order to demonstrate that his moral stages were universal, Kohlberg (1969) studied the moral reasoning of children in other countries – Britain, Mexico, Taiwan, Turkey, USA and Yucatan – and found the same pattern of development. He also found that development tended to be slower in non-industrialized countries. Colby and Kohlberg (1987) reported longitudinal studies in Turkey and Israel that produced similar results. Snarey *et al.* (1985) listed 44 different cross-cultural studies in 26 countries that found a progression from Stages 1 to 4 at about the same ages. Very few studies found any Stage 5 reasoning and where it occurred it was likely to be in urban areas. Eckensberger (1983) reviewed over 50 studies again lending support to the invariant progression of Kohlberg's stages.

How does moral understanding develop?

Like Piaget, Kohlberg felt that social interactions were important. Moral understanding develops not from being *told* what is right or wrong, but through experiencing situations that demand moral responses. In support of this Hartshorne and May (1928) found that children who attended Sunday school were less rather than more likely to be honest! More seriously, Berkowitz and Gibbs (1983) suggested that the key to moral progression lay in 'transactive interactions'. These are discussions where each participant engages in cognitive operations on the discussion, such as saying 'Have you considered what would happen if ...'? This supports Kohlberg's view that cognitive challenges to one's current thoughts promote moral growth, *but* only if the person is 'cognitively ready'.

Evaluation of Kohlberg's research

What are the strengths of Kohlberg's theory of moral understanding? It acknowledged the fact that people do not operate on just one level of moral reasoning.

Activity 5: Investigating moral understanding

Try interviewing individuals using either Piaget's or Kohlberg's moral dilemmas. Spend time designing a good range of questions to use with participants in order to collect a variety of data. You must be sensitive about conducting research with children and might prefer to focus on young or even older adults. Even with adults you should consider ethical guidelines and discuss your plans with your teacher. It might be interesting to compare people of different ages, and also interview boys and girls.

What problems arise in conducting interviews? What questions worked well and which ones didn't? What conclusions can you draw?

Instead, Kohlberg suggested that people vary in different situations, although one kind of reasoning will tend to dominate at different ages. In addition, the theory may have useful practical applications. Fodor (1972) found that the development of moral reasoning can be related to antisocial behaviour. His research showed that delinquents tended to operate at a much lower level on the Kohlberg scales than nondelinquents. The dilemmas could be used in working with delinquents and/or identifying those who are less morally mature.

However, there have been a number of criticisms. Firstly, Stage 6 is probably a moral ideal rarely reached and the same is largely true for Stage 5. In fact, Colby and Kohlberg (1987) performed a more careful analysis of the original data and found only 15 per cent reached Stage 5 and that there was no evidence whatsoever of Stage 6 judgements. Universal ethical principles (Stage 6) may characterize only a handful of people such as

Martin Luther King or Gandhi, and even then it is probable that they do not function at this level in all areas of their lives. Nevertheless, Stage 6 represents the ideal state of moral development.

Secondly, the point has been made that the dilemmas (like Piaget's stories) are rather artificial tests of morality understanding. They are perhaps tests of moral ideals. When people are questioned in real-life situations, their moral reasoning may reflect different criteria for making judgements. Gilligan (1982) interviewed women who were facing the dilemma of whether or not to have an abortion. The results produced a stage theory (described on p. 275) quite different to Kohlberg's, although this may be because the participants were women.

This brings us to the third criticism, that Kohlberg's theory was gender-biased. Kohlberg claimed that women had a less developed sense of moral reasoning. However, the original participants were all males and it is possible that Kohlberg produced a scheme of male morality. Gilligan (who was Kohlberg's student) proposed that women have quite a different sense of moral understanding to men. She suggested that women operate an 'ethic of care' whereas men base their moral judgements on notions of justice. We will examine the evidence for this later, in the section on individual differences. If Gilligan is right, it means that Kohlberg's theory is not universally applicable.

And this brings us to the fourth criticism. Does Kohlberg's theory apply beyond our Western culture? The cross-cultural evidence cited earlier appears to indicate that Kohlberg's stages are universal, but there is some question about whether people in other cultures could truly understand dilemmas drawn from Western culture. The dilemmas and Kohlberg's stage descriptions are typical of urban, individualistic, middle-class Western Europeans, i.e. a society where the needs of the individual are considered to be of greater importance than the needs of the community. In other cultures, meeting family obligations and submitting to the authority of elders is regarded as reflecting the highest of moral principles, and yet would be scored at lower levels according to Kohlberg's theory (Snarey *et al.* 1985). It may be that participants in cross-cultural studies were responding to subtle experimenter cues or other demand characteristics (the features of an experiment which 'invite' participants to behave in a particular way). Shweder (1991, cited in Durkin 1995, p. 498) launched a particularly strong attack on Kohlberg, arguing that 'his research strategies leave him methodologically doomed to impose stage classifications upon informants from other cultures that both distort the meaning of what they have to say, and fail to take account of implicit structures in their views of their own social order'. In other words, Kohlberg's

stages inevitably impose a structure on what research participants have to say.

Finally, we should mention that some of the same criticisms which have been mentioned in relation to Piaget, apply equally to Kohlberg – chiefly the fact that they both overlook the strong emotional component in moral decisions, which is a part of the next account of moral development.

Einsenberg's theory of prosocial reasoning

Nancy Eisenberg (sometimes referred to as Eisenberg-Berg) felt that Kohlberg's emphasis on justice and fairness overlooked a key aspect of morality, that of 'prosocial' moral reasoning. This refers to that area of thinking concerned with helping or comforting others possibly at a personal cost (see also Chapter 3 which discusses prosocial behaviour). Like Piaget and Kohlberg, Eisenberg believed that changes take place in moral reasoning in parallel with the maturation of general cognitive abilities. Eisenberg particularly emphasized the growth of role-taking skills – the ability to assume the perspective and take the part of another person. These skills in turn assist in the growth of empathy and thus prosocial moral reasoning.

Eisenberg also used dilemmas in her research (see *In Focus*). Her dilemmas focused on situations where there was conflict between the child's own needs and those of others, and were set in a context where the role of laws, rules, punishments or formal obligations were minimized. Each dilemma involved a situation where the central character has to decide whether or not to comfort someone when this prosocial act would be at some personal cost to the giver (i.e. to behave altruistically).

Eisenberg-Berg and Hand (1979) found that the responses of preschool children to these stories tended to be 'hedonistic' and self-centred. For example, they might say that Mary should go on to the party so she wouldn't miss out. In contrast, older children were better able to take the feelings of the other person into account. By adolescence, some of the children interviewed expressed the view that they would lose their own self-respect if they ignored the needs of the other person.

The same children were tested with various different dilemmas and, like Kohlberg, the researchers found that moral understanding was not consistent. For example, some preschool children mentioned their own feelings as well as the needs of others, displaying the characteristics of their own level and some of the next level of prosocial moral development. When the children were tested a year and a half later, there was evidence of development –

Eisenberg's dilemmas

Eisenberg, like Piaget and Kohlberg, also used dilemmas to investigate the development of moral understanding. It is ethically difficult to do anything else, especially when conducting research with children.

Eisenberg's dilemmas looked at individual conflicts in prosocial situations. The dilemmas were designed for use with young children. Here is one version used with girls:

> 'One day a girl called Mary was going to a friend's birthday party. On her way she saw a girl who had fallen down and hurt her leg. The girl asked Mary to go to her house and get her parents so the parents could come and take her to a doctor. But if Mary did run and get the child's parents, she would be late to the party and miss the ice cream, cake, and all the games. What should Mary do? Why?'

Boys were given the same story with the characters changed to Eric and another boy. All the stories were accompanied by illustrations and the interviewer amplified any parts of the story not understood by the child.

fewer hedonistic justifications and an increase in altruistic ones. Eisenberg *et al.* (1983) started a longitudinal study that has followed a group of children from age 4 through to adolescence (Eisenberg *et al.* 1987, 1991) asking them questions about the stories. They have found continuing support for the stage or 'levels' theory outlined in Table 10.12.

Empathy and role-taking

Eisenberg *et al.* (1987) have suggested that the ability to empathize is a key feature of being able to develop higher forms of prosocial moral reasoning. Empathy is a person's ability to experience the emotions of another. One way to learn this is through taking on the roles of others and seeing the world through another's eyes. The games that young children play often involve the practice of these role-taking skills that may be vital to their moral development.

As empathy grows, children become capable of experiencing compassion or 'sympathetic distress'. There is a distinction between the cognitive understanding of the other person's condition and a younger child's more primitive empathetic distress displayed when they are with someone who is suffering. Cognitive awareness leads the child to go to the assistance of others, whereas distress on its own does not. Caplan and Hay (1989) found that children aged between 3 and 5 were often upset by another child's distress, but rarely offered to help. The children said it was because an adult was available to help. This suggests that their cognitive interpretation was that, in times of distress, an adult will aid the victim. Older children come to realize that it doesn't have to be the adult.

Table 10.12 Levels of prosocial reasoning

Level		Brief description	Age range
1	Hedonistic (self-centred)	Prosocial behaviour most likely when it will benefit self in some way.	Preschool and early primary.
2	Needs oriented	Will consider needs of others, but not much evidence of sympathy or guilt.	A few preschoolers, mainly primary.
3	Approval oriented	Prosocial behaviour in return for approval and praise from others; understanding of what is appropriate.	Primary and some secondary.
4	Empathetic or transitional	Evidence of sympathy and guilt; vague reference to abstract principles, duties and values.	Older primary and secondary school pupils.
5	Strongly internalized	Strong sense of internalized principles which are important to self-respect.	A small number of secondary and perhaps a few primary.

Source: adapted from Eisenberg *et al.* (1983)

Practical applications for child rearing

Eisenberg's research has been used to make specific recommendations about what parents can do to encourage their children to be more altruistic.

1 Create a warm and loving family environment.

2 Explain why and give rules. Clear rules about what to do and what not to do are important, but it also helps to explain why the consequences of an action matter.

3 Provide prosocial attributions. It is better to praise a child for being a prosocial person, such as saying 'What a helpful child'. This makes them see themselves as prosocial and will encourage such behaviour in the future.

4 Get children doing helpful things, such as looking after pets and younger siblings, and giving toys away. It will be counterproductive if you have to force children to do these things.

5 Act as a model of helpful and prosocial behaviour. Rosenhan (1970) found that children imitated their parents if the parents not only subscribed to good causes, but also engaged actively in helping such causes.

Source: adapted from Bee (1999)

Evaluation of Eisenberg's approach

Eisenberg's theory offers a different perspective on the development of moral understanding. It emphasizes the importance of emotional factors and focuses on prosocial reasoning rather than issues of wrongdoing. Nevertheless, there are strong parallels between this theory and Kohlberg's stage account, and therefore it can be seen as a broadening of Kohlberg's original approach (Bee 1995).

Eisenberg's approach can be adapted to give useful advice to parents, and others involved with children, about how to raise children who are helpful and altruistic (see *In Focus*).

Individual and cultural variations

One of the main criticisms of Kohlberg's theory was that it may apply mainly to males and to Western culture. We will now consider the evidence related to individual and cultural differences.

Gender differences

Gilligan (1982) believed that Kohlberg's theory reflected a male view of morality and ignored the rather different view that women take towards moral issues: one concerned more with care than with justice. Gilligan compiled her own stage theory of moral development based on the interviews she conducted with women. She observed that the least mature individuals reasoned in terms of self-interest (Stage 1). The next stage was 'self-sacrifice', where an individual sacrifices her own concerns to the welfare of others. The final stage was a post-conventional one of 'nonviolence' where an

individual tries to avoid hurting anyone. These stages represent a morality of care as opposed to justice. Gilligan found further evidence for gender differences in a later study (Gilligan and Attanucci 1988) where both men and women were rated on moral dilemmas. They found that, *overall*, men favoured a justice orientation and women favoured a care orientation, though most people displayed elements of both moralities.

Gilligan used her research to explain why Kohlberg found that women were 'morally inferior' to men. If women's responses were based around *caring* and *personal relationships*, they would be classified as Stage 3 responses according to Kohlberg's coding system. Men are more likely to respond to moral dilemmas along the lines of *justice* and *fairness*, which would normally place them at Stage 5 or even beyond. Using Gilligan's stage system men might appear morally 'inferior'.

The basis for these gender differences does seem to reflect somewhat stereotypical ideas about the reasoning of males and females. Other researchers have also emphasized that *both* males and females consider issues related to both caring and justice in their moral reasoning (e.g. Galotti 1989). In fact, a review by Walker (1984) found no consistent gender differences in relation to the scoring on Kohlberg's dilemmas, and some research by Funk (1986) has found women scoring higher than men.

On the other hand, Eisenberg *et al.* (1987) found gender differences similar to Gilligan's: girls between the ages of 10 and 12 tended to give more caring empathetic responses than boys of the same age. However, this may be because girls mature more quickly than boys, while boys catch up later in adolescence. It may also be a result of demand characteristics within the research (remember that demand characteristics describe those features of an experiment which 'invite' particular behaviours from participants). Eisenberg and Lennon (1983) found that, when researchers were known to be looking at empathetic behaviour, women portrayed themselves in line with their stereotypically nurturant and empathetic role. When the aim of the study was less apparent, gender differences disappeared.

Overall, we are presented with a confusing picture, but nevertheless Gilligan's work has been instrumental in raising the important issue of a possible gender bias and thereby highlighting gender issues in the context of research into the development of moral reasoning.

Culture

We have already noted that Kohlberg's dilemmas are based on situations typical of middle-class Western culture. The difference between Western culture and other cultures has sometimes been described as individualistic versus collectivistic culture. An individualistic culture is one that emphasizes individuality, individual needs and independence. Collectivistic cultures involve sharing tasks and belongings, possibly living in large family groups, and valuing interdependence. It would be reasonable to expect differences between such different societies in terms of moral and prosocial attitudes, since morals are a way of governing social relationships. We would expect individualistic societies to be more competitive and collectivistic societies to be more altruistic. Indeed, Whiting and Whiting (1975) found that 100 per cent of Kenyan children behaved altruistically, whereas only 8 per cent of American children did. Eisenberg and Mussen (1989) found that children living on Israeli kibbutzim (communal farming communities) were more cooperative than North-Americans. However, Hedge and Yousif (1992) did not find differences in helpfulness when comparing British and Sudanese people.

We can also consider culture in terms of rural versus urban societies, with the former tending to be more helpful or altruistic. For example, Korte and Kerr (1975) found that stamped-addressed letters left lying in the street were more likely to be placed in a post box if the street was in a rural rather than an urban location. And when Hedge and Yousif (1992) compared British and Sudanese people they did find urban/rural differences in helpfulness in both countries.

Exam summary: Development of moral understanding

The AQA examination will test your understanding of the following areas:

- ◆ Theories of moral understanding and prosocial reasoning (pp. 267–75)
- ◆ Influence of gender (p. 273, pp. 275–6) and cultural variations (p. 273 and p. 276) on development of moral understanding.

Example question

The question below is typical of one drawn from the material above, and should take you 30 minutes to answer.

(a) Describe one theory of moral understanding.
(12 marks)

(b) Evaluate this theory in terms of alternative theories and/or psychological studies.
(12 marks)

Suggested answer structure

This question requires you to describe (part a) and evaluate (part b) one theory of moral understanding. All three of the theories covered in this section would be appropriate choices for this question. Cognitive developmental theories have identified stages in the process of the development of moral understanding. Piaget (pp. 268–70) linked his stages to cognitive development generally, although his evidence was based on rather superficial social rules. Kohlberg's stages (pp. 270–3) went beyond childhood and reflected more of the ambiguity in moral decisions. This theory has been criticized for gender and culture bias. Eisenberg's theory (pp. 273–5) looked at the role of empathy and role-taking skills in the development of prosocial understanding.

The AO2 component can be addressed in one of two ways. The question allows for a critical examination of the degree of research support and/or the contrasting views of other theorists. For example, Fodor (1972) found that delinquents operated at a lower level on Kohlberg's stages compared with nondelinquents (p. 272), whereas Gilligan's study of women facing the dilemma of having an abortion (pp. 273 and 275) produced results that were quite different to those predicted by Kohlberg's theory.

Both gender and cultural variations are a problem for any theory because it seems that moral standards vary, for example, between men and women, and between individualistic and collectivistic societies. For example, Gilligan believed that Kohlberg's theory 'reflected a male view of morality and ignored the rather different view that women take towards moral issues...' (p. 275). The differences between individualistic and collectivistic cultures (e.g. attitude to sharing tasks and independence versus interdependence) are such that we might expect differences between such societies in terms of their moral attitudes (p. 276). This is supported in some studies but not in others. For more information about cultural differences in helping behaviour, you might like to read the appropriate section in Chapter 3.

If you take the approach of using other theories to evaluate your chosen theory (e.g. Kohlberg to evaluate Piaget, or Eisenberg to evaluate Kohlberg), it is important that you use these, rather than merely describing one theory as an alternative point of view. Using another theory in this way may involve drawing out points of agreement or disagreement, reasons why one offers a more acceptable explanation of moral understanding than the other, or perhaps even pointing out that one fits the research evidence better than the other.

Chapter summary

- **Theories of cognitive development** have enriched our understanding of children's thinking. **Piaget's** theory focused on maturational stages and adaptation of schemas as a result of experience. **Vygotsky's** theory centred on the social construction of knowledge and the role of experts, language and culture. **Information-processing theories,** such as Case's, explain cognitive development in terms of acquiring more efficient strategies and metacognitive skills.

- There are both differences of emphasis (e.g. in the role of language, or the use of strategies) and considerable overlap (e.g. in the importance of experience) between the theories.

- All three theories have been successfully applied to **education**.

- Intelligence is measured using **IQ tests**. Both **genetic** and **environmental factors** can contribute substantially to IQ scores, although there are methodological difficulties in assessing the exact contributions of each.

- Great caution is needed when interpreting IQ scores, particularly those of children from different social and cultural (**racial**) backgrounds.

- Two cognitive developmental theories of the **development** of **moral understanding** are examined. Both **Piaget** and **Kohlberg** used moral stories or dilemmas to produce stage theories. Kohlberg's theory is more elaborate, but has been criticized for being culture-bound and possibly gender-biased.

- An alternative way of looking at moral development has been investigated by **Eisenberg** in her theory of prosocial reasoning, which focuses on the importance of empathy.

- **Individual and cultural differences** are important considerations in relation to moral understanding. **Gilligan** highlighted the difference between the ethics of caring and of justice. She portrayed women as having a 'different voice' towards moral issues, which is not synonymous with being morally 'deficient'. Individualistic and collectivistic societies are likely to have different views of moral principles.

Further resources

Donaldson, M. (1978) *Children's Minds,* London: Fontana.

An influential yet readable critique of Piaget.

Durkin, K. (1995) *Developmental Social Psychology,* Oxford: Blackwell.

A really excellent text with detailed chapters on moral development.

Smith, P.K., Cowie, H. and Blades, M. (1998) *Understanding Children's Development* (3rd edn), Oxford: Blackwell.

The latest edition of this standard developmental text includes a nice feature of studies reported in detail.

Websites

The Piaget Society: **http://www.piaget.org/index.html**

The Montessori Method: **http://www.cs.cmu.edu/~mmbt/women/montessori /method/method.html**

Chapter 11

Social and personality development

Cara Flanagan

Preview

In this chapter we shall be looking at:

◆ personality development, including psychodynamic and social learning explanations of personality development

◆ gender development, including explanations of the development of gender identity and gender roles in terms of social learning theory, cognitive–developmental and gender schema theories

◆ adolescence and research into social development in adolescence, including the formation of identity, relationships with peers and parents, and a consideration of cultural differences.

Introduction

The common thread running through this chapter is social development. We are going to explain human behaviour from the social development perspective. 'Social' refers to any situation involving two or more members of the same species. In terms of social development, this means we are going to focus on those aspects of development which affect our social relationships, and which are also affected by our social relationships. These social relationships include friends and peers; siblings, parents and grandparents; teachers; and other members of our community including pop stars, people on television, and authors of books.

The development of personality, gender and adolescence all involve an interaction between nature and nurture. We are born with certain elements of our character predetermined, but probably the greater contribution to our adult personalities comes from life experiences, especially social experiences. The first part of this chapter examines two theories that explain how social factors influence personality development. We then move on to gender development. Genes determine the sex of boys and girls, which is a biological fact. However, the extent to which an individual behaves in a masculine or feminine manner is a feature of their gender, rather than of their sex, and gender is related to their social experiences and cultural influences.

In the final part of this chapter we focus on adolescence – a stage of development which is triggered by biology in the form of puberty. There are major psychological changes at this time and many of these can be related to social influences.

Personality development

What is personality?

'Personality' is a term we all use. You might describe someone as being 'clever but with no personality', referring to the fact that a person lacked certain socially attractive qualities. Psychologists use the term in a more formal sense and have tried to identify the key characteristics of the concept:

◆ Personality refers to a *characteristic set of behaviours*, attitudes, interests and capabilities.

◆ These characteristics are relatively *stable*. A 'kind' person is someone who generally behaves in a kind manner.

◆ These characteristics are useful for *predicting future behaviour*. We have expectations that a kind person will behave in a kind fashion.

◆ The characteristic set of behaviours has some *coherence*. We don't just possess a list of characteristics, but they all combine somehow into a 'personality'.

◆ Personality is a means of distinguishing between people; it is an *individual difference*.

Psychologists have presented various theories to explain the development of personality. We will look first at a psychodynamic explanation and then at two social learning theory approaches. Finally, we will briefly consider an alternative approach to social explanations: the biological approach.

The psychodynamic approach

A psychodynamic explanation is one which tries to explain what drives or motivates development (hence the use of the word 'dynamic'). Many psychological explanations of development aim to identify what causes behaviour, but few of them look of the dynamics of this cause. The best-known psychodynamic approach is Freud's psychoanalytic theory. He suggested that the individual is driven to satisfy biological urges and these motives cause us to interact with the environment in certain ways so that early experience plays a critical role. As we will see, biological drives and early experience are the cornerstones of Freud's theory.

Freud's personality theory

Sigmund Freud (1856–1939) spent most of his life in Vienna, though he fled from there just before the Second World War and spent his last years in London. He initially trained in medicine and was interested in neurology (the study of the nervous system); his first paper was on the development of the spinal cord in primitive fish. He moved from neurology to the study of neurotic illness, which led him to develop his ideas about the causation and treatment of such illnesses. Until then, it was thought that neurotic (or psychological) illnesses had physical causes. Freud proposed a radical new theory and therapy:

psychoanalytic theory describes the development of personality and psychoanalysis is the therapy derived from psychoanalytic theory. Both seek to explain human development in terms of an interaction between innate drives and early experience. Wordsworth expressed it poetically as 'The child is father of the man'.

The first year of life

In the early months of life, an infant's behaviour is driven by the pleasure principle. This means that infants do things that produce pleasure or gratification, and they also avoid pain. In fact, in Freudian terms, it is not the infant that is motivated in this way, but rather it is the part of the infant's personality called the 'id'. The id is described as the primitive, instinctive part of the personality that demands immediate satisfaction.

During development, the individual seeks gratification through different organs of the body. In the first year, the focus is on the mouth and pleasure is gained by, for example, eating and sucking. Therefore this stage of development is called the oral stage. This drive for oral satisfaction would clearly be a useful drive for a young infant, to direct its attention towards gaining food.

Thus we have the three strands of Freud's personality theory: the driving force (pleasure), the personality structure (the id), and the organ-focus (on the mouth). As children get older, they pass through other stages, each of which focuses on a different organ. These stages, known as 'psychosexual stages, are summarized in Table 11.1.

The phallic stage of development

Around the age of 3, a boy becomes aware of his genital area. Freud called the events that followed the 'Oedipus conflict'. In Greek mythology Oedipus fell in love with his mother and killed his father, only later realizing who they actually were. Freud suggested that when a young boy first becomes sexually aware, he unconsciously begins to desire his mother, and sees his father as a rival. This leads the boy to wish to get rid of his father so he can have his mother all to himself. He then fears that his father will discover his true feelings and this leads to feelings of anxiety. Eventually the complex is resolved when the boy comes to identify with his father. Identification is important for both moral and gender development.

But how then does one explain girls' moral and gender development? Jung, a follower of Freud, proposed that a similar sequence of events happens. He called this the 'Electra complex'. Electra was another Greek figure. Her mother and her mother's lover killed her father. Electra encouraged her brother to kill her mother. In Jung's analysis, a young girl feels desire for her father and rejects her mother.

Freud explained it somewhat differently. He suggested that, during the genital stage, girls come to recognize that they don't have a penis and blame their mother for this. The girl's father now becomes her love-object and she substitutes her 'penis envy' with a wish to have a child. This leads to a kind of resolution and ultimate identification with her same-gender parent. Freud concluded that girls never develop quite as strong a sense of justice as boys because they do not experience quite as strong a resolution of their genital conflicts.

Table 11.1 Freud's psychosexual stages and their consequences

Stage in development	Description	Personality structure	Fixations	Effects on adult personality
The oral stage (0–18 months)	The infant's main source of pleasure is the mouth.	The id	Fixations may be caused by insufficient breastfeeding or too much pleasure at the breast.	The oral receptive personality is very trusting and dependent on others whereas the oral aggressive personality is dominating. Orally fixated individuals may seek gratification through smoking, thumb-sucking and pencil chewing.
The anal stage (18–36 months)	Pleasure is derived from expelling and/or withholding faeces.	The ego	Fixations may be caused by strict toilet training, or by intense pleasure associated with, for example, smearing faeces on the wall.	The anal-retentive character wants to make a terrible mess and therefore builds up defences against this such as being very orderly, rigid and hating waste. Other associated traits include stinginess, punctuality, possessiveness. The anal-expulsive character is very generous and may also be creative and productive.
The phallic stage (3–6 years)	Children focus on their genitals and, initially, on the opposite-gender parent. Resolution is by identifying with the same-gender parent.	The superego	Fixations are caused by a lack of identification with an adult.	A fixation at this stage results in the phallic personality type who is self-assured, vain and impulsive. Conflicts may result in homosexuality, authority problems, and rejection of appropriate gender roles.
Latency stage	Little development takes place. Boys and girls do not interact much.			
The genital stage (Puberty)	The main source of pleasure is again the genitals. Focus is also on the development of independence.		If some issues remain unresolved, the individual can't shift focus from their immediate needs to larger responsibilities involving others.	

Other personality structures

In addition to the id, there is the ego or, as Freud called it the 'I'. The ego develops during the first two years of life as a consequence of the infant's experiences of the world. The force that motivates the ego is the reality principle, which makes the child accommodate to the demands of the environment. The ego is equivalent to our rational mind, which must modify the demands of the id.

The superego (or 'above-I') emerges around the age of 5. This embodies the child's conscience and sense of right and wrong. Freud proposed that children enter the phallic stage around the age of 3 (see *In Focus*).

At this time their id derives satisfaction from the genital region, in the same way that the young infant gained pleasure from its mouth. This coincides with the age when children are first becoming aware of their gender, and also aware of a three-way conflict between themselves and their parents. Initially, the child rejects the same-gender parent and the opposite-gender parent becomes the love-object. This conflict is resolved differently in boys and girls (see *In Focus*, 'The phallic stage of development'), but for both sexes resolution leads to identification with the same-gender parent. Identification results in taking on the attitudes and ideas of that other person, including their notions of right and wrong. Thus the superego is born.

Handling conflict

The id, ego and superego are inevitably in conflict. Conflicts are perhaps most common between the id and the superego, because the id's demands for instant gratification clash with the superego's moral standards. Conflicts cause the individual to experience anxiety. In order to reduce this anxiety, the ego uses 'defence mechanisms', such as those described in Table 11.2. These ego defences are unconscious and are a key dynamic of the personality.

Let's consider one example. A small child does something wrong, such as spilling milk all over the sofa. In order for them to 'defend their ego', they may deal with this event by repressing it – forgetting that it happened – so that when their mother asks what happened, the child genuinely says 'I don't know'. As well as repressing, the child might project and blame the mother for spilling the milk, deny guilt, adopt a highly self-righteous attitude towards others who spill their milk, kick the cat or intellectualize the accident by informing the mother about the effects of gravity! Each of these is an example of the ego defences listed in Table 11.2.

In the long term, ego defences may cause abnormal personality development because they exert pressure through unconsciously motivated behaviour. Freud's case history of Anna O. illustrates this (see *In Focus*).

The notion of the unconscious was another key element of Freud's theory. He proposed that there are three levels of the mind: the conscious, the preconscious, and the unconscious. The conscious consists of those thoughts that are currently the focus of attention. The preconscious consists of information and ideas that could be retrieved easily from memory and brought into consciousness. The unconscious consists of information that is either very hard or almost impossible to bring into conscious awareness.

Stages of psychosexual development

Table 11.1 shows the five stages of psychosexual development. Freud believed that an individual's libido or sexual drive is fixated on a part of the body during particular periods of a child's life. The 'choice' of body region is related to phases of development. The mouth is important in the early months, the anal region becomes important during toilet training, and the genitals are an obvious focus during gender identity development.

Freud's use of the term 'sexual' may be slightly misleading. He did not mean that the satisfaction is sexual in the adult sense of the word, but more as a source of physical pleasure; sensual perhaps rather than sexual.

If a child experiences severe problems or excessive pleasure at any stage of development, this leads to fixation. This means that the individual's libido becomes attached to that stage. Later in life, when in a stressful situation, an adult tends to regress (move back) to the psychosexual stage upon which they had previously fixated. The result would be that they behave as they

---

Table 11.2 Defence mechanisms for handling conflicts between the id, ego and superego

The main defence mechanisms that protect the ego are:

1	*Repression*	A painful or guilt-provoking thought is kept out of the conscious mind. For example, you might forget that a favourite pet had died because you forgot to feed it.
2	*Projection*	Unknowingly displacing one's own unacceptable feelings onto someone else. For instance, you might suspect others of cheating in an exam because that is what you did.
3	*Denial*	Simply denying the existence of something that is threatening. However, denying the existence of the thing does not make it go away. An example of this would be an Elvis Presley fan who believes Elvis didn't really die, but that there is a conspiracy behind it.
4	*Reaction formation*	Adopting an attitude diametrically opposed to one's real feelings. The classic example is in homophobia, in which people who worry that they might have homosexual feelings deal with the resulting anxiety by adopting a harsh antihomosexual attitude that helps convince themselves of their heterosexuality.
5	*Displacement*	Unconsciously redirecting an emotion from the person who has caused it onto a third party. For example, you might shout at a friend after someone had told you off. Displacement is used to explain a possible cause of prejudiced behaviour – redirecting feelings of frustration on to a scapegoat.
6	*Intellectualization*	Coping with a threatening event by removing the emotion from it. For example, dealing with the diagnosis of a terminal illness by reading all the books on the disorder. This may well be a useful response, but the individual has not dealt with the related emotional issues.

The case history of Anna O.

The observations Freud made of his patients formed the basis for his ideas about the dynamics of personality. One of the best known was his observations of Anna O. He presented this case history when he was first invited to speak in America in 1909.

'The patient was a girl of 21, of a high degree of intelligence. Her illness first appeared while she was caring for her father, whom she tenderly loved, during the severe illness that led to his death. The patient had a severe paralysis of both right extremities, disturbance of eye-movements, an intense nausea when she attempted to take nourishment, and at one time for several weeks a loss of the power to drink, in spite of tormenting thirst. She occasionally became confused or delirious and mumbled several words to herself. If these same words were later repeated to her when she was in a hypnotic state, she engaged in deeply sad, often poetically beautiful, day dreams, we might call them, which commonly took as their starting point the situation of a girl beside the sick-bed of her father. The patient jokingly called this treatment "chimney sweeping". Dr Breuer [Freud's colleague] soon hit upon the fact that through such cleansing of the soul more could be accomplished than a temporary removal of the constantly recurring mental "clouds".

During one session, the patient recalled an occasion when she was with her governess, and how that lady's little dog, that she abhorred, had drunk out of a glass. Out of respect for the conventions the patient had remained silent, but now under hypnosis she gave energetic expression to her restrained anger, and then drank a large quantity of water without trouble, and woke from hypnosis with the glass at her lips. The symptom thereupon vanished permanently.

Permit me to dwell for a moment on this experience. No one had ever cured an hysterical symptom by such means before, or had come so near understanding its cause. This would be a pregnant discovery if the expectation could be confirmed that still other, perhaps the majority of symptoms, originated in this way and could be removed by the same method.

Such was indeed the case, almost all the symptoms originated in exactly this way, as we were to discover. The patient's illness originated at the time when she was caring for her sick father, and her symptoms could only be regarded as memory symbols of his sickness and death. While she was seated by her father's sick bed, she was careful to betray nothing of her anxiety and her painful depression to the patient. When, later, she reproduced the same scene before the physician, the emotion which she had suppressed on the occurrence of the scene burst out with especial strength, as though it had been pent up all along.

In her normal state she was entirely ignorant of the pathogenic scenes and of their connection with her symptoms. She had forgotten those scenes. When the patient was hypnotized, it was possible, after considerable difficulty, to recall those scenes to her memory, and by this means of recall the symptoms were removed.'

Source: adapted from Freud (1910)

would have done at that age. Both fixation and regression are forms of ego defence. Freud described various personality traits that are the result of early fixations. These are shown in Table 11.1.

Activity 1: Identifying ego defences

Think of an emotionally 'threatening' situation, such as the example of spilling milk given above. Suggest how the different forms of ego defence might deal with this so that your ego is left feeling unthreatened.

Summary of the main points of Freud's theory

Freud proposed that the dynamics of personality development come from several sources.

◆ The pleasure and reality principles drive the id and ego.

◆ The libido motivates the individual to focus on specific body regions during stages of development.

◆ Conflict between personality structures creates ego defences, leading to personality characteristics.

◆ Early fixations result in further enduring personality traits.

Adult personality is the product of early experience and is motivated by unconscious ego defences.

It is probably important to realize that Freud did not intend the idea of personality structures (id, ego and superego) to suggest real entities, 'he was not literally dividing the mind into three parts, but describing the *experience* of being pulled in different directions by conflicting influences' (Jarvis in press).

It is also important to recognize that Freud did not intend the five stages of psychosexual development to be seen as abrupt transitions.

Empirical evidence

A theory is based on empirical data (observations made in the real world). Freud's empirical data were the observations he made of patients undergoing psychoanalysis. He never made any notes during a therapeutic session, feeling that any lack of attention during therapy would interfere with its progress and believed that he would be able to record all the important details afterwards. His expectations and selective recall may have introduced bias into these notes. Freud recorded only a few case histories (see *In Focus*, 'The case history of Anna O.').

There is other evidence that supports some aspects of Freud's research. The concept of repression is of interest to memory researchers and you have already looked at the evidence to support it during your AS course. One line of evidence comes from the study of 'repressors', for example Myers and Brewin (1994). They tested the personality of a number of people and identified various subgroups in terms of their trait anxiety (how likely one is to become anxious) and defensiveness (the tendency to protect oneself from anxiety). Repressors are low on trait anxiety and high on defensiveness, i.e. they lack anxiety but are very defensive – it may well be that their low anxiety is due

to effective ego defence. Myers and Brewin found that repressors took much longer to recall negative childhood memories than other personality types. This suggests that there is a link between the personality type and the tendency to suppress anxiety-provoking memories. Furthermore, Myers and Brewin found that the 'repressors' actually reported *more* painful memories, which suggests that individuals with anxiety-provoking memories are more likely to repress such memories.

Another area of cognitive psychology that has drawn on Freud's ideas is that of perceptual defence – the concept that things are likely to be ignored if they are unpleasant or emotionally threatening. McGinnies (1949) demonstrated this in a classic study where participants were shown lists of words. The presentation time for each word was increased until the participant was able to correctly identify the word. McGinnies found that emotionally threatening words such as 'raped' and 'penis' required longer exposure time than words such as 'apple' and 'dance'.

In your AS studies you may also have considered Freud's contribution to the theory of attachment, the psychodynamic approach to the treatment of abnormal behaviour, and psychodynamic explanations of eating disorders. Research in all of these areas tends to lack objectivity. It is an interpretation of the facts from one particular perspective – that of the psychoanalyst.

Evaluation of Freud's theory

There are many positive features of Freud's theory. Perhaps the greatest confirmation of its validity lies in the fact that it remains one of the most pervasive theories in psychology, and beyond. Hall and Lindzey (1970) put this down to the fact that Freud's conception of human nature was both 'broad and deep'. The use of

---

in focus   The Freudian slip

People often say things, or write them, which are muddled up, such as saying 'I'm going to kiss my teacher' when they meant to say 'kick'. Freud suggested that such errors were not simple accidents, but the result of unconscious intrusions into behaviour that revealed a person's true feelings. Freud (1920) gave an example of this. A British Member of Parliament referred to his colleague as 'the honourable member from Hell' instead of from Hull.

Cognitive psychologists have been interested in such unintentional slips because they are an important feature of many accidents – when people switch on the 'automatic pilot' and cease to attend to what they are doing. Reason (1979) studied these 'action slips' and concluded that this automatic processing has clear advantages because it frees the conscious mind to deal with other processing activities. Reason suggested that action slips occur when mental control should, but doesn't, return to the activity that is being processed automatically. Freud would suggest that, at this time, the unconscious, automated activity is left 'prey' to other unconscious thoughts and there is then an opportunity for these to be expressed.

picturesque language and mythological allusions gives his work an exciting literary quality, and the fact that he was not a rigorous scientist is balanced by the meticulous observations that he made.

Jarvis (in press) identifies the most significant feature of Freudian theory as the notion that the human personality has more than one aspect: '... we reveal this when we say things like "part of me wants to do it, but part of me is afraid to...".' Freud's introduction of the unconscious permits us to explain how someone can be both rational and irrational, and this can account for many aspects of behaviour, such as the fact that people predict they will behave in one way and actually do something quite different.

On the other hand, there are serious criticisms to be considered. Perhaps the most crucial problem with Freud's personality theory is that it was based on the study of *abnormal* individuals. This can perhaps be justified in that one of the main applications of personality theory is in the treatment of abnormality.

In addition, however, his experience largely centred on a very limited sample: White, Viennese, middle-class, women. It is unlikely that we can generalize from this to all human nature. For example, Freud's overemphasis on sex may be due to the fact that he wrote at a time of great sexual repression. This may have caused sex to be something that *was* repressed in many minds at that time, but may not apply to development now or in other cultures.

A third criticism was that he studied adults and based his theory of childhood on the *recollections* of childhood. This is not likely to be reliable.

Subsequent psychologists, called neo-Freudians, have adapted Freud's theory to try to incorporate social influences and address the rather unreasonable way that he dealt with women. To some extent these later theories are reinterpretations of what Freud meant. For instance, Lacan (1966) suggested penis envy was envy of the penis only insofar as the penis is a symbol of male dominance. This was a reasonable conclusion in nineteenth-century society, but may be less true in our age of more equal opportunity.

Social learning approaches

Learning theory

Learning theory is based on the principles of classical and operant conditioning. The development of personality is probably best explained in terms of the latter, operant conditioning. This can be described as follows: an animal is placed in a cage where food will be delivered if it presses a lever. At first the animal presses the lever accidentally and is rewarded by receiving food. This increases the probability that the behaviour (lever pressing) will be repeated. The food or *reward* is *reinforcing*. If the lever press results in an electric shock this will decrease the probability of the response being repeated.

This can explain how any behaviour is acquired, including the behaviour we are interested in – the acquisition of personality characteristics. For example, individuals might acquire the personality trait of friendliness because they are rewarded when displaying such behaviour (operant conditioning). This would increase the likelihood of such behaviour being repeated.

Social learning theory

Albert Bandura felt that learning theory was not sufficient to explain *all learning*; it would simply take too long to learn everything through trial and error, reward and punishment. He formulated an extension of learning theory, which would incorporate the social context. He suggested that reinforcement or punishment could take place *indirectly*. If an individual sees someone else being rewarded, they are likely to imitate that behaviour. This is called *vicarious reinforcement*.

Bandura's classic study showed that children do acquire new behaviours by imitating the behaviour of others. Simply watching the behaviour of another may lead to the imitation of that behaviour. However, behaviour is more likely to be imitated if:

◆ the model is rewarded for their actions, such as being praised

◆ the observer identifies with the model, e.g. they are the same gender or the same age

◆ the observer admires the model, such as when watching a television hero or person of higher social status

◆ the observer has low self-esteem or is highly dependent on others.

The more direct the reinforcement, the stronger the influence. Children respond most to direct reward, next to seeing a model in action and least to a filmed model, especially a cartoon character (Bandura *et al.* 1963).

The most obvious source of imitation for a child is their parents, but there is also the media (television, pop songs, books, magazines), other adults (teachers, grandparents, neighbours) and peers (friends, siblings).

Acquiring personality through social learning

Bandura and Walters (1963) developed a theory of personality development based on the principles of social learning theory. According to this view *all* aspects of personality are learned. A child may learn novel behaviours through direct or indirect reinforcement or punishment. Subsequently, personality characteristics

The effects of modelling on behaviour

Walters and Thomas (1963) recruited participants for a study on the effects of punishment on learning. The participants worked in pairs, one was supposedly learning a task (this person was actually a confederate of the experimenters). The 'true' participant was told to give the learner a shock following each error that was made. After each error, the participant was given the opportunity to select the level of shock to use for the next trial. Prior to the experiment all participants had been shown a film. Those participants who watched a violent scene were found to select higher shock intensities than those who watched a nonviolent movie scene.

This is an example of *disinhibition*. The participants observed socially unacceptable behaviour in the film and this *weakened* the prosocial behaviours they had previously learned. In other words, their tendency to behave prosocially was disinhibited or unlearned as a result of modelling.

that are in the child's repertoire may be strengthened or weakened depending on whether the child is directly or indirectly rewarded or punished. A study by Walters and Thomas (see *In Focus*) shows how socially desirable behaviour may be *reduced* by social modelling.

To explain personality development further, Bandura introduced two important concepts. One is *reciprocal determinism*. Both learning theory and social learning theory portray the individual as being controlled by their environment. Things happen to the individual, which increase or decrease the likelihood of any future behaviour. However, Bandura recognized that learning is not merely passive – it is reciprocal. He suggested that individuals are controlled by and also control their environment. As the individual acts, this changes the environment, thus affecting subsequent behaviour. For example, if you watch your mother baking a cake and then start to imitate her, this modifies her behaviour and subsequently affects you. Individuals are also capable of reinforcing themselves. They are capable of making their own choices and this ultimately affects what they imitate.

The second important concept is *self-efficacy*. Bandura (1977) claimed that a person's sense of their own effectiveness (or efficacy) influences what they ultimately achieve. If you believe that you cannot jump over a two-metre hurdle, this will affect the way you approach the task and thus what you achieve. Your sense of self-efficacy is an important personality trait. It is derived from experience.

Evaluation of Bandura's theory

Bandura's account of personality development is based on the premise that the principles of learning and social learning are sufficient to account for the development of that behaviour. Social learning theory explains how novel behaviours are acquired and how existing behaviour is modified. It also accounts for self-

determination rather than being a passive recipient of one's environment.

However, as an account of personality development, social learning theory has never been very successful because it lacks detail and cohesiveness. It is rather sketchy on the details of *how* we influence our environment and make choices. There is no doubt that social learning explains aspects of personality development, but usually as an addition to other perspectives.

Situationalism

The situationalist view is a departure from all personality theories because it suggests that personality is not an enduring trait. At the very core of all personality theories is the notion that the traits we possess are lasting and that in some way these traits have unity. Walter Mischel made the radical suggestion that personality is not consistent at all. He argued that, in reality, people are only consistent in the *same situations*, but their behaviour varies from one situation to another. You might be shy in class but quite the opposite when alone with your friends.

Mischel (1968) pointed out that the reason we may think that personality is consistent is because we tend to see people in similar situations, and offer excuses for occasional lapses, 'She is usually reliable, but when her boyfriend is home you simply can't rely on her at all'. One advantage of Mischel's theory, therefore, is that it can explain personality inconsistency. Mischel and Peake (1982) confirmed this inconsistency in a study where various individuals were asked to rate the behaviour of 63 students in various situations. The observers were asked to focus on their conscientiousness, and included family and friends of the students plus unknown observers. Mischel and Peake found almost zero correlation between the different situations.

A further reason why we think of personality as being consistent is because that is the way our minds are organized. The notion of consistency is a useful tool for organizing our perceptions about others and ourselves, and it allows us to be able to make predictions about subsequent behaviour. We all intuitively recognize the situational element whenever we say, 'She is never late except when her children are ill'.

Evaluation of Mischel's theory

Mischel's theory is an example of the social learning approach because it suggests that we learn through *selective* reinforcement – we learn that certain behaviours are most appropriate or successful in certain situations. This leads us to behave in the same way in those situations, but not in the same way in other situations.

One objection to this account is that it denies free will. Situationalism suggests that we are controlled by situations. There is also counter-evidence that people are consistent across situations. For example, Small *et al.* (1983) found consistency in terms of dominance and prosocial behaviours in adolescents in a number of different situations while on a camping trip.

A biological view

One way of evaluating the social learning theory approach is to consider the alternative view that personality may have little to do with social factors, but rather it may be the product of your biology. The Greeks suggested that there were four personality types and these were related to the presence of certain bodily fluids or 'humours'. We still use the words which were coined in Medieval times, from the Greek and Latin, to describe the humours: *sanguine* individuals had too much blood (from 'sanguis' meaning blood in Latin); *melancholics* had too much black bile, *choleric* types had too much bile, and *phlegmatic* individuals had too much phlegm.

In fact, Freud's theory had a biological element to it, but Hans Eysenck's (1963) Type theory was even more rooted in biology. According to this theory, there are three personality dimensions: introvert–extrovert, neurotic–stable, and normality–psychoticism. Each of us can be located somewhere on each of the three dimensions and this expresses our personality type; for example, you are either more inclined to be extrovert or more inclined to be introvert. Eysenck suggested that these types have a biological basis. Extroverts have lower cortical arousal than introverts, which means that their brains operate at a generally lower level of arousal. Therefore, they require greater external stimulation in order to feel the same levels of excitement as introverts. This would explain why extroverts tend to be more outward going and enjoy

risky pastimes. Introverts shy away from too much excitement and are easier to condition, which would explain why they are more likely to behave in a socially acceptable manner.

Thomas provides another approach to the biology of personality development. He worked as a child psychiatrist and questioned why he rarely saw two children from the same family, despite the fact that they must often have shared similar life experiences. This led him and his colleagues to embark on a long-term study of infants that demonstrated that individuals are born with certain characteristic patterns of emotional response or temperament (Thomas and Chess 1977, 1980). Children are undemanding, or slow to warm up, and these traits tend to endure throughout life. Temperament interacts with life experience to produce adult personality.

Exam summary: Personality development

The AQA examination will test your understanding of the following areas:

◆ psychodynamic explanations of personality development (pp. 280–5)

◆ social learning approaches to personality development (pp. 285–7).

Example question

The question below is typical of one drawn from the material above, and should take you 30 minutes to answer.

(a) Outline and evaluate **one** theory of personality development based on the psychodynamic approach. *(12 marks)*

(b) Outline and evaluate **one** theory of personality development based on the social learning approach. *(12 marks)*

Suggested answer structure

Freud's psychodynamic (or psychoanalytic) theory (pp. 280–5) suggests that biological forces interact with early experience to produce adult personality. Conflicts are dealt with by ego defences and expressed unconsciously. Freud's empirical evidence (p. 284) has been criticized, but his theory remains highly influential. The social learning approach can be seen in Bandura's personality theory (pp. 285–6), which used the principles of social learning theory to explain how novel behaviours are acquired and existing behaviours are modified. Bandura also used the concepts of reciprocal determinism and self-efficacy. Mischel's situationalist theory (pp. 286–7) proposed that we are selectively reinforced so that we behave in one way in one situation (where we were previously rewarded), but a different way in another situation (where we had not previously received rewards). This leads us to behave consistently in the same situations.

A question like this makes very specific requests that must be adhered to carefully to ensure the maximum 'catch' of the marks available. First of all, there are two parts, each being worth 12 marks. Second, within each of those two parts of the question, there are two skills to be addressed (AO1 and AO2). This means that each of these four *chunks* will take about 7.5 minutes of writing time, and about 150 words. This is a lot more difficult than it sounds, particularly when describing Freud's theory. You must practise being able to describe theories such as this in a concise yet sufficiently detailed form. With practice, you will be able to offer a coherent yet concise account of Freudian theory in the time slot available in this question. As a test of the difficulty of this task, ask your teacher to summarize Freudian theory in 150 words – then sit back and look smug!

Gender development

What is gender?

Gender refers to the psychological characteristics associated with being male or female. Your gender identity is a fundamental part of your self-concept – 'I am a boy' or 'I am a girl'. Gender identity generates gender behaviour – behaving like a boy or a girl. But such behaviour depends on knowledge of gender roles. A gender role is a set of expectations that prescribe how males and females should think, act and feel. In this section we will be concerned with gender identity, gender behaviour and knowledge of gender roles.

There are various approaches to explaining gender development, which are not mutually exclusive. The ultimate account is likely to be a mix of:

◆ the effects of socialization, i.e. your parents and your culture – this is *social learning theory*

◆ the changes in the way a child thinks – this is the *cognitive–developmental approach*

◆ biological factors – this includes the *psychoanalytic* and *evolutionary* approaches.

We will now consider each of these theoretical approaches in turn.

Social learning theory

In the previous section of this chapter on personality development, the basic principles of social learning theory were explained. We can apply these same principles to an understanding of how gender is learned – through direct and indirect reinforcement.

Direct reinforcement

Children learn gender-appropriate and gender-inappropriate behaviours through the application of reward and punishment. For example, parents may encourage more traditional feminine behaviour in their daughter by saying, 'You do look pretty when you wear a dress, instead of jeans', or discourage the same in their sons, 'You look like a girl in that shirt'. Praise and teasing can either encourage or discourage gender-appropriate behaviour.

Much direct reinforcement is unconscious, as illustrated by the following experiment. Smith and Lloyd (1978) videotaped women playing with a 4-month-old baby. The baby was dressed either as a boy or a girl and was introduced with an appropriate name. There were seven toys present: a squeaky hammer and stuffed rabbit in trousers (masculine); a doll and squeaky Bambi (feminine); a squeaky pig, a ball and a rattle (neutral). They found that each woman's choice of toy varied with the perceived gender of the infant. The women also responded differently to gross motor activity from boys than girls. In other words, the women were reinforcing gender stereotypes, probably with very little conscious thought. It is possible that the women behaved in this way as a demand characteristic of the experiment – they had only the one clue to guide their behaviour, which was the apparent gender of the infant. With children they knew, they might have behaved in a less stereotyped fashion.

Peers are also important in this process of gender-behaviour reinforcement. Lamb and Roopnarine (1979) observed a group of nursery schoolchildren during free play periods and found that the children generally reinforced peers for gender-appropriate play (by giving them more attention or imitating them) and were quick to criticize gender-inappropriate play. Interestingly, the children responded more readily to reinforcement by same-gender rather than opposite-gender peers.

Indirect or vicarious reinforcement

You may learn gender-appropriate behaviour by being rewarded or punished yourself (as we have just seen), but you can also learn it vicariously by observing other people being rewarded or punished for their feminine or masculine activity. The media is a very potent source of such indirect reinforcement – remember that 'the media' includes magazines and books, computer games and films as well as TV.

Gender stereotypes portrayed in the media have a powerful influence on all of us, but especially children who are acquiring their gender identity. A stereotype is a fixed, often simplistic picture of a group of people. Cultural attitudes are communicated through stereotypes; for example, the image of a woman doing the washing-up is a stereotype that communicates an expectation about gender roles in our society. Our society has many persistent gender stereotypes (a typical male is assertive, independent, good at maths, while a typical female is dependent, relatively passive, good at verbal tasks). Stereotypes that are rewarded are more likely to be imitated, but even in the absence of rewards, a stereotype can act as a model.

Evidence on the effects of stereotypes comes from Williams (1985) who recorded the effects of television in an unusual natural experiment. The residents of a small Canadian town were going to receive television for the first time. He called the town 'Notel' and used a control town nearby ('Multitel') to assess the impact of TV on local behaviour. Behaviour was observed over a period of two years. One of the findings was that the Notel children's gender-role attitudes became more traditional and gender-stereotyped. Williams suggested that American television portrays men and women in traditional roles and this influenced the gender-role attitudes of the children. He felt that the effects of television were stronger in developing countries where children have relatively less information to influence their attitudes, whereas children in the developed world would be less influenced by television stereotypes.

Leary et al. (1982) found that children who watched television frequently were more likely to hold stereotypical ideas about gender and more likely to conform to gender-role preferences of a culturally appropriate nature. The fact that these data are correlational means that we cannot be sure whether the TV programmes made the children more gender-stereotyped or that gender-stereotyped children watch more TV.

Other studies have looked at stereotypes in children's books. For example, Crabb and Bielawski (1994) compared children's books from 1938 and 1989 in terms of how they represented the way men and women use equipment such as washing machines, lawn mowers, and so on, and found relatively little change. Such stereotypes act as social representations of our culture. They reflect the way that society thinks, but they also shape the way people continue to think.

Counter-stereotypes

One way to reverse gender stereotypes is to use counter-stereotypes, such as female doctors or men looking after children. The effectiveness of such indirect stereotypes in the media may depend on real-life experience – when children have exposure to stereotypes which contradict what they see on television, they will be most affected by their direct experience. For example, if one never encounters a woman in a professional job, it is unlikely that exposure to counter-stereotypes on television will have much effect. People also feel more comfortable with information that confirms their stereotypes. This is called a 'confirmatory bias', i.e. the tendency to recall information consistent with stereotypes. Cohen (1981) found that adults tended to remember information in a video about a librarian if it was consistent with their stereotype whereas inconsistent information was less well recalled.

However, stereotypes do tend to have some basis. Jacklin and Maccoby (1978) found support for the existence of biological gender differences in a study where they introduced unfamiliar 2-year-olds to each other and dressed them in neutral clothing. They found that interactions were most lively and positive with same-gender pairs. This may well reflect an early incompatibility between girls and boys, partly based on biological differences such as boisterousness and partly due to learned preferences for toys and certain activities.

The influence of culture

A particular strength of the social learning approach is that it explains cultural differences. There are many cultural differences in gender behaviours. Whiting and Edwards (1988) examined 11 different cultures and concluded that 'we are the company we keep'. This view of *cultural determinism* can only be explained in terms of different child-rearing practices and different cultural attitudes. However, there is also evidence for *cultural relativism* (see *In Focus*, p. 290).

Evaluation of social learning theory and gender behaviour

Social factors clearly influence the development of gender behaviour. Social learning theory explains how children learn behaviour appropriate for their gender and their culture. At the same time, there are some biological gender differences and therefore social learning theory is not a sufficient explanation on its own.

There is evidence which conflicts with some of the empirical data outlined above. For example, Jacklin and Maccoby's (1978) finding that boys and girls are not treated differently in terms of the kinds of gender reinforcements they receive. Also, Smith and Daglish (1977) found that parents who exhibited more gender stereotypical behaviour (i.e. behaved in a particularly masculine or feminine fashion) did not necessarily have

Gender determinism and relativism

Mead's (1935) classic study of societies in New Guinea showed that there were both similarities and differences in gender roles across societies. In one society – the Mundugumour – both males and females behaved in what we would regard as a masculine fashion – aggressive, ruthless and strongly sexual. In contrast, the Arapesh were warm, emotional and nonaggressive, regardless of their gender. The ideal in their society was equivalent to our ideas of femaleness. However, within each society the men were always more aggressive than the women. The fact that there were cultural differences supports the view of *cultural determinism* – that gender-role behaviours are *determined* by our culture. On the other hand, the fact that there were the same differences between men and women within each culture supports *cultural relativism*, i.e. that relative to each other there are always the same differences between men and women.

Other research has supported these findings. Williams and Best (1982) explored gender stereotypes in 30 different national cultures. In each country, 100 male and female students were asked to look at a list of adjectives and state whether they were associated with men or women, or both, in their culture. Williams and Best found that there were many similarities across the various cultures. Men were seen as more dominant, aggressive and autonomous, whereas women were more nurturing, deferential and interested in affiliation. However, Williams and Best (1992) found that such consensus was strongest in collectivistic societies and weaker in individualistic societies where gender equality is more influential. This again suggests a cultural difference – the effect of different socialization practices.

children who were equally gender-stereotyped, whereas social learning theory would predict such a link.

The social learning approach traditionally portrays the child as a passive part of the process whereas there is evidence that individual motivation, self-regulation and cognitive processes play a crucial role in gender identity development, as we shall see in the cognitive–developmental accounts which follow. Taking the example mentioned earlier, if 'looking pretty' does not matter to the girl in question, then rewarding her for such behaviour will have no effect.

However, recently, Bandura and colleagues have adapted traditional social learning theory to allow for the mediating effect of cognitive and motivational factors. This is called social cognitive theory (Bussey and Bandura 1992). They regard one important mediating factor in gender-role development to be the child's ability to regulate his or her own activities according to the rules relating to gender-appropriate behaviour. This indicates a shift from parental control over this process to a more independent self-evaluation of how children themselves feel when engaged in either gender-appropriate or cross-gender play (see *In Focus*).

Cognitive–developmental theories

You may be familiar with some cognitive–developmental theories from other chapters in this book, especially Chapter 10, which explored Piaget's theory of cognitive development. The cognitive–

A study to test the relative importance of self-evaluation and gender constancy

Bussey and Bandura (1992) asked preschoolers to decide whether they would feel 'real great' or 'real awful' if they played with a variety of same-gender or opposite-gender toys. The results showed that between 3 and 4 years, both boys and girls indicated self-approval for same-gender behaviour and disapproval for opposite-gender behaviour. Boys felt great about playing with dump trucks and robots, but were not comfortable with kitchen sets and baby dolls. Girls showed the opposite preferences.

These results were particularly interesting because the researchers had arranged things so the children thought they were registering their responses anonymously. This means that the results cannot be explained easily in terms of demand characteristics, i.e. that they choose the toys because they thought they were expected to do this.

Bussey and Bandura concluded that children learn early in life that there are sanctions against cross-gender behaviour, and they start to regulate their own behaviour accordingly.

developmental approach focuses on how children's thinking changes as they get older.

The development of gender identity

Kohlberg (1966) proposed a stage theory of gender identity and gender-role development (see Table 11.3), predicting that as cognition matures, so does the child's understanding of gender. This means that children can only acquire gender concepts when they have reached an appropriate age and are 'ready' to acquire this knowledge. Once children have acquired a gender concept, this leads them to identify with members of the same gender and actively seek information about gender-appropriate behaviour. In other words, they further their gender development.

There are parallels between this gender development and that of cognitive development generally (see Chapter 10).

Empirical evidence

Slabey and Frey (1975) conducted research with children. If children over the age of 2 are shown a picture of a young boy and girl and asked 'Which one are you?', they can give an appropriate response. This is the stage of *gender identity*, the recognition of being a boy or a girl. The next stage is *gender stability*. Slabey and Frey asked children, 'Were you a little boy or a little girl when you were a baby?' and 'When you grow up, will you be a mummy or a daddy?'. Children do not recognize that their gender is constant until they are about 3 or 4 years old.

The final stage is *gender constancy*, the recognition that your gender doesn't change even when external features are changed, such as growing your hair long or having it cut. This occurs around the age of 7, which, according to Piaget, is about the same time as children

are capable of conservation (described in Chapter 10). It is not surprising that Piaget predicted that children will acquire the concept of gender constancy during the same stage as they acquire conservation, simply because the same logic is involved. The child has to be able to infer that something remains the same, although it *looks* different

Kohlberg predicted that, only once children reach the stage of constancy, would they start to acquire gender-appropriate behaviours. Slabey and Frey (1975) showed preschool children a film with men on one side and women on the other. Those children who had previously been rated as having greater gender consistency watched more same-gender models. This shows that children at this stage of development are more focused on same-gender models who will provide them with information about gender-appropriate behaviour. It also suggests that gender consistency is the cause, rather than the effect, of identification.

As with all stage theories, there is some disagreement about the actual ages when these changes take place, although the sequence is not contested. Age discrepancies may be due to the methods used to test the children's understanding. For example, when preschool children were shown *drawings* where gender-inappropriate changes in hairstyle or dress have been made to a boy or girl, very few of them were able to recognize that gender remains the same despite the changes (Emmerlich *et al.* 1977). However, if they were shown *photographs* of real children, first in the nude with sexual anatomy visible, and then dressed in gender-inappropriate clothing, almost half the 3- to 5-year-olds knew that the child's gender had not changed in line with the change in clothing (Bem 1989). An additional finding is that when

---

Table 11.3   Kohlberg's stages in the development of gender identity

Kohlberg suggests that children go through the following stages in developing an understanding of gender:

Approx. age	Stage of understanding of gender	Description
2–3 years	Gender identity	The child recognizes that he/she is a boy or a girl.
3–7 years	Gender stability	Awareness that gender is fixed. The child accepts that males remain male and females remain female. Little boys no longer think they might grow up to be a mummy and little girls give up their hopes of becoming Batman.
7–12 years	Gender consistency	Children recognize that superficial changes in appearance or activities do not alter gender. Even when a girl wears jeans or plays football, or when a boy has long hair or a burning interest in needlepoint, the child's gender remains constant.

Source: Kohlberg (1966), cited in Hetherington and Parke (1993, p. 547)

preschoolers are asked whether they *themselves* would change gender if they wore gender-inappropriate dress, almost all of them realized that they would remain the same (Martin and Halverson 1983). It seems that children grasp this concept earlier when applied to themselves, than when applied to others (Wehren and DeLisi 1983).

The sequence of gender development appears to be universal. Munroe *et al.* (1984) observed the same sequence of identity, stability and constancy in children of many different cultures. This suggests that the sequence is biologically controlled (which is the view that cognitive–developmental theorists take) because people in different cultures will have different social experiences, therefore any similarities must be due to our genetic make-up.

Evaluation of Kohlberg's theory

This account differs from the social learning approach because it suggests that gender development leads to identification rather than vice versa. It also emphasizes the child's active role. Kohlberg suggested that the child is self-socializing and uses adult rewards and punishments as clues about what is acceptable or not. Thus the child is the agent in the socialization process rather than being socialized by others through reward and punishment.

Gender schema theory

Martin and Halverson (1983) proposed an alternative cognitive–developmental approach. The key difference between gender schema theory and Kohlberg's view lies in the stage at which the child is motivated to acquire knowledge about their gender. In Kohlberg's theory, children must recognize the permanence of gender before they can begin to imitate same-gender models. In gender schema theory, gender schema begin to be formed as soon as the child recognizes that there is a difference between men and women. The term 'schema' refers to 'concept clusters' that a child acquires in relation to gender, such as gender stereotypes. Children develop schema or 'theories' about gender-appropriate behaviour which help them to organize and interpret their experience. It is the readiness to categorize gender information that drives the development of gender.

Empirical evidence

The fundamental feature of this theory is that gender stereotype precedes gender concept. This has been supported by a number of studies. For instance, Martin and Little (1990) found that preschool children had only very rudimentary gender understanding, yet they had strong gender stereotypes about what boys and girls were permitted to do.

The concept of androgyny

The concepts of masculinity and femininity are central to our self-identity. If children are asked to describe themselves, one of the first things they are likely to say is 'I am a boy' (or a girl). Small children are strong advocates of their gender and avoid behaving like the opposite sex (Mike says to Paul, 'You can't do *that* – it's for *girls*!'). In the past, psychologists have suggested that healthy psychological development is related to a strong sense of gender identity and that it is 'unhealthy' to be in a state of gender confusion, which could explain why boys and girls cling tenaciously to their gender identity.

Psychologists have also suggested that individuals should be either masculine or feminine, but not both. It would be psychologically 'unhealthy' or maladjusted to be a feminine male or masculine female. Good psychological adjustment comes from modelling yourself on your sex stereotype (the image of femininity or masculinity in your society).

Bem (1974) proposed an alternative view of a healthy gender concept. She argued that narrow gender concepts inevitably limit a person's repertoire of behaviours. A man who feels strongly that he must behave in a masculine fashion is more limited in terms of his behaviour than a man who is less rigid about doing things that might be regarded as feminine. Bem suggested that individuals who are less gender-stereotyped are freer to do things which are appropriate for a situation, rather than being tied to behaving in a manner appropriate to their gender.

Bem used the term 'androgyny' to describe this mixture of feminine and masculine behaviour. Individuals who mix feminine and masculine behaviours according to the situation are 'androgynous'. She thought that such people might be better adjusted than those who are more rigidly gender stereotyped.

Source: Flanagan and Marshall (1999)

There is also support for the way that stereotypes help children to organize their gender concepts. Liben and Signorella (1993) showed young children pictures of adults engaged in stereotypical opposite-gender activity (such as a male nurse). They found that the children disregarded the information, missed the point, or forgot it completely, insisting that the nurse was a woman. This supports the notion that children only notice information which is consistent with their existing stereotypes and underlines the importance of stereotypes in acquiring further knowledge. This is again the 'confirmatory bias' – the tendency to recall information consistent with stereotypes.

Further support for the role of gender schema comes from the evidence presented earlier, that children are more receptive to same-gender reinforcement. A key feature of the gender schema approach is that it explains why boys are not influenced by female teachers or influenced by men trying to reinforce feminine-type behaviours – it is because the child is actively processing the information which is consistent with his or her gender schema. Only this view can explain how children, who are exposed to a multiplicity of stereotypes, select the ones appropriate for them. Empirical support for this comes from Fagot (1985) who showed that teachers tend to reinforce 'feminine' behaviours in both boys and girls, such as quiet, sedentary activities. However, both display different behaviours, suggesting that the boys' gender schema overrides the reinforcement.

Evaluation of gender schema theory

Gender schema theorists take the view that rigid, early gender stereotyping is the starting place for gender development. Children are searching for rules and trying to make sense of the world around them. Children need to construct rules, apply these rigidly at first and then adapt them to their circumstances. Gender schema theory offers a valuable perspective in emphasizing the role of active construction of gender. It explains how gender stereotypes persist in terms of how people are more likely to remember information that is consistent with their schemas. Gender schema theory also explains how gender behaviours occur before gender identity.

One criticism of the theory stems from the fact that research has failed to find anything but very weak connections between gender awareness and gender-typed behaviour (Bee 1999), whereas gender schema theory would predict a close relationship. Strong differences between boys and girls have also been found, with girls tending to have more flexible gender concepts and a greater tendency to engage in opposite-gender activities (Archer 1989). Such findings are not consistent with the theory.

Activity 2: The development of gender constancy

Compare the responses of a 2- to 3-year-old child and a 5- to 6-year-old child whom you know well, to the kinds of questions that you think will assess gender constancy. Here are some examples, but add some of your own, after close consultation with your teacher.

◆ Are you a boy or a girl?

◆ When you are grown up will you be a man or a woman?

◆ (To a boy) If you grow your hair really long, would you be a girl?

◆ (To a girl) If you cut your hair really short, would you be a boy?

When working with young children, you should be especially aware of the issue of informed consent.

Biological theories

We should finally consider the possibility that some aspects of our gender behaviour are biologically rather than socially or cognitively determined. We have seen evidence to support this view, from cross-cultural studies and also from Jacklin and Maccoby (1978).

Psychodynamic theories

Freud's theory of psychosexual development suggested that gender development, like the whole of personality development, is related to biological drives which interact with the environment. Freud's conception was that gender identity is formed as a result of identification with one's same-gender parent during the phallic stage. Interestingly, the age he gave for this stage fits in with cognitive–developmental theories.

One difficulty with this view is that children are able to acquire gender-appropriate behaviour in single-parent families, even though the same-gender role model may not be present. Presumably, when developing his theory, Freud had no concept of anything other than the nuclear family consisting of mother, father and children.

A more recent, alternative perspective within the psychodynamic framework comes from object-relations theorists (Chodorow 1978). These theorists suggest that early relationships, particularly with the mother (because she is *usually* the main caretaker), establish a template for how to relate to other people. As they develop, females do not necessarily have to deviate from this template as it is based on women like themselves. As a result, they see femininity and closeness in relationships as inextricably linked. In contrast, males have to distance themselves from the nurturing mother figure in order to develop their masculinity, which in turn becomes defined in terms of a *lack* of closeness in relationships.

Evolutionary accounts

A current, popular view is that many of our gender-role behaviours can be shown to have adaptive value. The theory of evolution is discussed in Chapter 15. The essential principle is that any behaviour which increases an individual's survival and reproduction is desirable and 'adaptive'. Any gender behaviour that promotes survival is likely to be retained in an animal's repertoire. For example, we might suppose that if females stay 'at home' to look after infants while men gather food this would promote the survival of offspring. This might explain certain differences in male and female behaviours – males are more aggressive and like hunting, whilst females enjoy nurturing and cooking!

The influence of hormones

Finally, there is also some evidence that females who are exposed to male hormones during prenatal development show more masculine behaviours. Beach (1974) found that female dogs that were exposed perinatally to male hormones were subsequently likely to urinate in the manner of males. Similarly, Young *et al.* (1964) found that female monkeys exposed to male hormones during the critical prenatal period were more likely to engage in rough-and-tumble play in their early years. There is also some evidence for the same effects on human behaviour. At one time mothers who were liable to miscarry were treated with male hormones to prevent this. This treatment was stopped when it became apparent that the mothers gave birth to genetic females with male genitals. The girls received corrective surgery, but appeared to behave in a more tomboyish fashion when assessed later in childhood (Money and Ehrhardt 1972).

Exam summary: Gender development

The AQA examination will test your understanding of the following area:

◆ explanations of the development of gender identity and gender roles (pp. 288–94).

Example question

The question below is typical of one drawn from the material above, and should take you 30 minutes.

◆ Discuss psychological research into the factors that influence gender roles. *(24 marks)*

Suggested answer structure

The AQA *Glossary of Terms* defines 'research' as '...*the process of gaining knowledge and understanding either through theory construction and examination, or through empirical data collection*'. This tells us that insights from *theories* of the development of gender role are as relevant in answering this question as are the findings from research *studies* (i.e. empirical data collection). This therefore gives you a wide choice of material from which to construct your response.

Gender refers to the psychological characteristics associated with being male or female. A gender *role* is a set of expectations that prescribe how males and females should think, act and feel. Social learning theory (pp. 288–90) stresses the importance of reinforcement, observational learning, modelling and imitation. Important influences in shaping gender-role behaviour include parents, peers, media, and stereotypes generally. The social learning approach can explain cultural differences, but not why children respond differently to reinforcement. A recent modification, called social cognitive theory, does allow for self-regulation in gender development.

Cognitive-developmental theories (e.g. Kohlberg, pp. 290–2) suggest that gender development is the result of a biologically determined sequence: gender identity, stability and constancy. Kohlberg suggested that gender development leads to identification rather than vice-versa, as in social learning theory, and that a child must recognize the permanence of gender before they can begin to imitate same-sex models. Gender schema theory (pp. 292–3) proposes that gender-stereotype precedes gender concept and is able to explain why children are more receptive to same-sex reinforcement.

The biological view includes psychodynamic theories of biological drives (p. 293), evolutionary accounts that some gender behaviours have adaptive value (p. 294), and the influence of hormones during development (p. 294). An understanding of gender development can best be achieved by combining all three approaches described above. The influence of each factor will vary from individual to individual.

Note that the inclusion of biological explanations should be done carefully. The question asks for *psychological,* rather than biopsychological, or evolutionary research. This does not mean they are irrelevant to this question, but rather that they might provide a useful contrast to research that stresses the role of psychological factors, such as cognition or observational learning. It is important not to be too ambitious in the amount of material you can deal with in 30 minutes. High marks come from a compromise between breadth and depth.

Adolescence

What is adolescence?

Adolescence is a transitional period between childhood and adulthood. Biologically, this period begins when the individual enters puberty and ends on reaching sexual maturity. Psychologically, there are a number of levels on which the individual makes the transition to adulthood (e.g. social, emotional and cognitive) which do not have clear beginnings and ends.

There are many questions about adolescence.

◆ What psychological development takes place during adolescence, especially in terms of identity?

◆ Is adolescence necessarily a time of conflict?

◆ What relationships are important during adolescence?

◆ To what extent are there cultural differences?

Changes during adolescence: identity

Chapter 10 describes how children's minds develop as they get older. Piaget reported an important biological change about the time of puberty, namely that the child moves from the stage of concrete operations to the stage of formal operations, and becomes capable of abstract thinking and systematic rational thought. Such intellectual changes have many important consequences: they enable the adolescent to reach a higher level of moral development, to tackle complex academic subjects, to become critical of existing philosophical systems and to define a new identity. Earlier in this chapter, we saw that Freud also saw adolescence as a time of identity formation.

Blos' psychoanalytic view

Blos (1967) took up Freud's ideas and suggested that adolescence was like a second period of individuation. The first took place when the infant became a self-reliant toddler. In adolescence the individual is again achieving independence ('reindividuation'). Adolescents may typically overreact to parental authority and be at pains to assert their individuality. This separation from parents results in an emotional emptiness that is satisfied by group experiences. The striving for independence may also lead to regression, which Blos regarded as a healthy and necessary response. Regression may be to a more infantile state in order to receive substitute parenting, or regression may take the form of hero worship that can act as a substitute parent. Blos also believed that rebellion was important as a means of ego defence in order to prevent adolescents becoming dependent on their parents again.

There is some empirical support for Blos' view of reindividuation. For example, Steinberg and Silverberg (1986) measured emotional autonomy, which is the degree of emotional independence adolescents feel from their parents. In a large sample of American 10- to 16-year-olds, they found that, as autonomy increased so did peer dependence and that this was strongest between the ages of 11 and 13. This would seem to support Blos, although Ryan and Lynch (1989) suggested that the findings could be interpreted differently. It could be argued that those children who engage most in peer relations do so because they have failed to get adequate emotional satisfaction at home.

Erikson's account of psychosocial development

The main theme in all psychodynamic accounts is that the child is presented with new conflicts at each stage of development and these must be resolved successfully for healthy psychological development to occur. Erikson (1968) suggested that these conflicts were psycho*social* rather than Freud's psycho*sexual* crises – resolving social rather than physical conflicts. Across the lifespan, Erikson identified eight crises or stages of personality development, though only the fifth one – from age 12 to 18 – need concern us here. A crisis is a conflict, such as between independence and dependence, which needs to be resolved in order for the individual to move on to the next developmental stage. The task for adolescents is to resolve the conflict between *identity* and *role confusion* and thus establish 'a subjective sense of an invigorating sameness and continuity' (Erikson 1968, p.19). (All eight stages are outlined in Chapter 12 on adulthood, and the final three stages are discussed there).

Prior to adolescence the child has established a sense of identity, but this is challenged by the physical changes of puberty and the child's new intellectual abilities. The adolescent experiences role confusion: what job do I want to do, what religious and political beliefs should I hold, what kind of person do I want to be, and so on. Erikson felt that the route to a fully developed adult personality lay in making a commitment to a set of roles in life.

Erikson also introduced the idea of a *psychosocial moratorium*, i.e. a temporary suspension of activity. Adolescents would use this time to adopt certain attitudes or occupations temporarily in order to decide which suited them best. Role sampling is a way of establishing one's own identity, the dominant task for this age group. Resolution of this role confusion results in formation of an adult identity.

The importance of identity lies in the way that it enables the individual to cope well with the demands

<table>
<tr><td>in focus</td><td>**Erikson's stage of identity vs role confusion**</td></tr>
</table>

Erikson (1968) predicted that failure to resolve the psychosocial crisis of identity versus role confusion would result in a lack of personal identity (i.e. role confusion). This may result in one of four kinds of behaviour:

◆ *Negative identity* – One way of coping with the failure to resolve one's identity crisis is to adopt an extreme identity, such as taking on the role of a delinquent or a drug abuser. The individual can gain some sense of control and is asserting their independence from others, especially parents.

◆ *Intimacy* – The adolescent avoids being involved in close relationships because they fear losing their own fragile sense of identity. This may result in the formation of rather stereotyped relationships, or ones that are inappropriate, or the individual may prefer isolation. An example might be the kind of pop star worship which is characteristic of some teenagers.

◆ *Time perspective* – The role-confused adolescent avoids making plans for the future because such plans mean thinking about the future and the complexities of being an adult, all of which provoke feelings of anxiety.

◆ *Industry* – Adolescents find it difficult to get their level of 'industry' right. They either compulsively overwork or they find it hard to concentrate.

of life and, importantly, to be able to form adult relationships. Failure to resolve this crisis results in a lack of identity (see *In Focus*, 'Erikson's stage of identity vs role confusion').

However, Erikson's conception that identity formation is related to role decisions may be dated. The notion of finding a 'job for life' may be less true today than it was 40 years ago.

Marcia's theory

Erikson's ideas were largely theoretical and others, such as Marcia (1966), have reformulated them so they could be tested empirically. Marcia used an interview technique to assess 'identity status' in areas such as occupation, religion, politics and attitudes about sex.

For example, he would ask: 'Have you ever had any doubts about your religious beliefs?' The answers to such questions were categorized as representing one of four outcomes of adolescence, as outlined in Table 11.4.

The most likely route for an adolescent would be to start at identity diffusion, proceed to moratorium, possibly via foreclosure, and end with identity achievement. Marcia (1980) argued that adolescent identity formation involves both crisis and commitment. Crisis occurs through having to re-evaluate previous choices and values. Commitment happens after this re-evaluation, when the individual takes on a set of roles and ideologies. The four stages of adolescent development can be categorized in terms of commitment and crisis (see Table 11.5).

Table 11.4	Four identity statuses proposed by Marcia (1980)	
1	*Identity diffusion or confusion*	In this stage the individual hasn't even started to think about the issues. They might respond, 'My parents are churchgoers, but I've never given it any thought'.
2	*Identity foreclosure*	An individual in this stage has prematurely formed an opinion that is not based on individual consideration. For example, they may have unquestioningly taken on conventional attitudes, which is a means of avoiding the uncertainties of thinking for themselves.
3	*Identity moratorium*	This is similar to Erikson's concept of a stage when decisions about identity are put on hold while the adolescent may 'try on' various possibilities, such as becoming a Quaker for a while.
4	*Identity achievement*	This occurs when an adolescent has been through the period of confusion or crisis, and achieved their own identity. For example, 'I've thought a lot about alternative religions and feel most in tune with the Far Eastern beliefs'. This is seen as the most mature status.

Table 11.5 Four identity statuses proposed by Marcia (1980)		
	High degree of crisis	*Low degree of crisis*
High degree of commitment to a particular role or value	**Identity achievement status** (crisis is past)	**Foreclosure status** (crisis not gone through, but commitment made)
Low degree of commitment to a particular role or value	**Moratorium status** (in the midst of the crisis and no commitment made)	**Identity diffusion status** (not in crisis and no commitment made, perhaps because in pre- or post-crisis)

Empirical evidence for Marcia's theory

Marcia's approach was developed in order to enable adolescence to be studied empirically, and many researchers have done this. Meilman (1979) looked at 12- to 24-year-old males and found that the percentage of individuals rated as identity achievers rose steadily after the age of 15. However, at age 24, only 50 per cent were classed as identity achievers, which means that a lot of people had not resolved this stage. Waterman (1985) used data from several cross-sectional studies of 11- to 21-year-olds. He found a decrease in diffusion status and an increase in identity achievement with age. Moratorium was quite uncommon at all ages, and a total of 33 per cent were in foreclosure. Identity achievement occurred somewhat later than Erikson predicted, but this is probably explained by the fact that most of the participants studied were college students who tend to postpone adult status.

Other studies have looked at various social influences. Waterman (1982) reviewed a number of studies that looked at the relationship between parenting styles and identity development. He concluded that domineering parenting is associated with identity foreclosure, whereas moratorium and identity achievement are connected with a more warm, democratic style. Noller and Callan (1991) suggested that this is because democratic parents impose less rigid moral standards which allow their children to explore alternative identities.

On a more critical note, some studies have questioned the extent to which Marcia's stages are universal. A study by Waterman and Waterman (1975) found that there may be cohort effects, in other words that people during particular historical periods behave differently. They studied fathers and sons and found that the sons were mainly classed as identity moratorium or identity diffusion, whereas the fathers were in identity foreclosure. It is possible that the fathers, who grew up in the prewar period, were encouraged to achieve this kind of adult identity. This suggests a flaw in both Erikson's and Marcia's theories – that they are relevant to a historical period and a particular culture.

Evaluation of the psychosocial approach

Marcia's approach was an extension of Erikson's original scheme, which aimed to make it a more empirical and therefore useful approach. Research has supported the theory, suggesting that confusion does decline through adolescence and that identity achievement is important to future development. However, as we have seen, the scheme may be culture- and gender-biased, supported by studies largely of male, middle-class Americans.

In addition, in contrast to Erikson and Marcia, other researchers have claimed that identity remains fairly stable in adolescence. Coleman (1974), for example, suggested that adolescents have two identities, one for the present and one for the future. The present one is fairly stable, but the future one becomes increasingly confused and conflicting as the adolescent grows and sees ever-increasing choices of identity in the future.

A further issue to consider is the extent to which identity and identity-achievement is a unitary concept. Archer (1982) used Marcia's interview technique and found that only 5 per cent of those interviewed were classed in the same identity status for occupational choice, gender role, religious values and political ideology; 90 per cent were in two or three different stages across all four areas. For example, someone might be in 'identity confusion' as regards their sexual attitudes, but be in 'identity achievement' in terms of their occupational choice. This suggests that Marcia and Erikson's views offer an oversimplified account of a more complex picture.

Storm and stress – or not?

The theories we have examined so far all describe adolescence as a period of crisis. G. Stanley Hall (1904) suggested that adolescence is a time of 'storm and stress' during which the child must experience the turbulent history of the human race in order to reach maturity. This so-called 'recapitulation theory' has little real foundation. Nevertheless Hall's concept of 'storm and stress' (a translation of the German *Sturm und Drang*, the name of a literary and artistic movement

Rutter *et al.* (1976) on adolescent turmoil

In a study of 2,303 14- to 15-year-olds on the Isle of Wight, Rutter and colleagues (1976) looked for evidence of increased conflict between adolescents and their parents. Parents and teachers answered questionnaires about the teenagers' behaviour, and various subsamples of teenagers were selected for interviews and psychiatric assessment.

In one part of the research, 200 randomly selected teenagers were compared with 304 others who had scored high on measures of deviancy. These two groups were compared in terms of the amount of conflict between themselves and their parents and in terms of evidence of inner turmoil expressed through their behaviour or the presence of psychiatric disorder. In the 'deviant' group, conflict was generally three times more common and showed itself more often in these teenagers' communications with their parents and in their behaviour (e.g. withdrawal from the family).

Concerning conflict, 1 in 6 of the parents reported arguments with their sons or daughters about their conduct and 1 in 3 complained about their teenagers' hairstyle or clothing. The teenagers themselves perceived a higher frequency of conflict, but rarely reported serious disagreements or criticized their parents. The general picture was one of good relationships between parents and their teenage children with growing mutual trust and appreciation.

On the subject of inner turmoil, clinical depression was rarely found, although 1 in 5 reported often feeling miserable or depressed, leading Rutter *et al.* to query whether adolescence is any different from other stages of life in this respect. To test this idea, the incidence of psychiatric disorder in a group of 10-year-olds was compared with that in 14- to 15-year-olds and this showed only a modest increase in the teenagers (from about 11 per cent of 10-year-olds to 13 per cent of 14- to 15-year-olds).

Rutter *et al.* concluded that 'adolescent turmoil is a fact, not a fiction, but that its psychiatric importance has probably been overestimated in the past'.

characterized by the expression of emotional unrest) has had a lasting influence on both popular culture and psychological theories. There is some support for this view. For example, MacFarlane (1964) conducted interviews with 30-year-olds about their life experiences and found that many remembered their adolescent years as a time of confusion and despair.

But is adolescence necessarily accompanied by conflict and inner turmoil? The study by Rutter *et al.* (1976) (see *In Focus*) suggests that it isn't.

Activity 3: Your adolescent years

Reflect for a few minutes on your own adolescent years. Do you feel you experienced conflict or inner turmoil relating to your sense of identity, rate of maturation or family relationships?

Do you expect other periods in your life to be more, less or equally demanding when compared with the adolescent phase? Discuss your answers with a person of a similar age to yourself.

Cross-cultural evidence

One useful source of evidence in this area is cross-cultural research that can show us whether adolescent turmoil is universal. Margaret Mead's classic book, *Coming of age in Samoa* (1928), described how boys and girls growing up on the South Sea Island of Samoa experienced a relatively easy passage from childhood to adulthood. She noted that, in that culture, sexuality was dealt with in an open, casual manner and children were therefore spared the guilt, anxiety and confusion that many Western children experience. She suggested that the turmoil that some adolescents experience may be due to the pressures of growing up in an industrialized society where they are faced with a large choice of opportunities and decisions. In a small, rural community there are very few choices to be made and this may explain why there is no identity crisis. Mead's advice was that we should recognize the stress that is caused by life choices and prepare adolescents more carefully.

It is important to be somewhat cautious when considering cross-cultural research because it is prone to many difficulties. Freeman (1983) criticized

Mead's conclusions, arguing that she was not sufficiently closely involved with the Samoan people and that she saw only what she wanted to see. He argued that she may not have established sufficient trust with the Samoan people to expect total honesty from them. For example, one woman told Freeman that she had not been honest with Mead about her sexual experiences. It is hard to know whether Mead or Freeman provides the more accurate account. Mead studied women, while Freeman's research was based on studying males. In addition, these two studies took place at different times – the influence of Western ideas on the Samoans from Christian missionaries and American air-base staff might have brought about change.

Bronfenbrenner (1974) compared child-rearing patterns in the USSR and the USA, and found that Russian adolescents showed more prosocial behaviour and less of the antisocial behaviour common in the American adolescents. One reason for this finding could be that Russian youths had more opportunities to integrate with adult society early on, whereas the American youths tended to be segregated and discouraged from entering adulthood. The greater degree of conflict shown by the American youths could, therefore, have resulted from the development of a youth subculture distinguishing itself from adults by adopting a different set of values and norms.

The conclusion appears to be that 'storm and stress', where it does occur in any society, may be due to the way adults handle adolescence rather than as a consequence of the stage of transition itself.

Explanations of the factors which might lead to 'storm and stress'

If 'storm and stress' is due to the way in which our society handles adolescence, then what are the difficulties we, as a society, impose?

Eccles *et al.* (1993) suggested that the reason many adolescents experience stress is because of the mismatch between their developing needs and the opportunities afforded to them by their social environments. Indeed, in some Western cultures, adolescents would appear to be held in a state of moratorium by laws that block access to the adult world, such as the minimum school-leaving age and minimum voting age.

A further cause of 'storm and stress' may be the lack of recognition that we give adolescence. In other cultures, such as Samoa, there are 'rites of passage' to celebrate the arrival of adulthood. Jews hold a *bar mitzvah* for boys when they reach puberty. In many ways, Western culture does the opposite of celebration – by withholding adult privileges and failing to recognize events of puberty as a cause for celebration.

Another possible explanation is in terms of parental responses. It may be that the stress of adolescence is a reflection of the problem that parents are having. For example, Gecas and Seff (1990) found that over 60 per cent of parents find adolescence a stressful period. Parents have to cope with a physically and psychologically different person and also with the conflicts of dependence and independence. This in turn may lead to anxiety for children.

Coleman's focal theory of adolescence

An attempt to draw together the conflicting findings about adolescence and to offer an explanation for them has been made by Coleman (1974). The main tenet of his argument was that, in reality, most adolescents do not experience severe difficulties. Instead, he suggested that they cope with the changes which take place during adolescence by 'focusing on' (thus 'focal theory') and dealing with different issues at different times. This strategy means that they are likely to experience little stress. Coleman agreed with Erikson's concept of changing roles and of psychological and social adjustments which need to be made, but he did not agree that crisis was both inevitable and healthy. Instead, it may well be that those adolescents who experience crisis have other ongoing problems that make the adjustment more difficult. This view was supported by Coleman's own research (see *In Focus*, 'Empirical support for focal theory').

If Coleman is right, then why does the view continue to be perpetuated that adolescence is a troubled time? One reason may be that some psychological theories have been developed by psychiatrists who have based their ideas on the biased samples of troubled adolescents with whom they worked. A second reason may be 'media amplification'. Certain adolescent behaviours, such as vandalism and drug taking, are often reported sensationally in the media and this creates an exaggerated picture of the problem in the eyes of the general public.

Evaluation of focal theory

In general, focal theory offers a more reasonable view than Erikson and Marcia' identity crisis, and one that is supported by empirical data. Many, if not most, adolescents experience few difficulties and these would not always be characterized as crises. Therefore there is no reason to suppose that adolescence is necessarily a time of storm and stress or that such crises need to be weathered for healthy personality development. At the same time, it is clear that adolescents do have adjustments to make to their physical and psychological identities.

in focus

Empirical support for focal theory

Coleman and Hendry (1990) interviewed 800 boys and girls aged 11 to 17. The respondents were asked about topics that were anxiety provoking, such as self-image, being alone, occupational choice, and peer, sexual and parental relationships. The results showed that each issue seemed to have a different distribution curve, peaking in importance over a particular age. Concerns about peer relations, for example, peaked earlier than occupational choice. In addition, some adolescents came to these issues earlier than normal and others experienced them later. Adolescent life, therefore, can be seen as a mixture of stability and adjustment in different areas of life at different times. The coincidence of a number of important issues all peaking at once could cause problems, but generally, adolescents navigate carefully through this stage of life, choosing whether to engage with particular issues immediately or later. In this way, they manage their own life stage and are generally successful in coming through unscathed.

This supported Coleman's focal theory that adolescents focus on only a few particular issues at any one time. There appeared to be no specific pattern for any age.

Adolescent relationships

The theories we have examined so far suggest that there are many sources of social influence during adolescence, such as the media, parents and peers. One view of adolescent social development is that it is a time of transition from 'parent orientation' to 'peer orientation'.

Parental relationships

Do adolescents rely less on their parents? According to Blos (1967), the stage of reindividuation involves separation from parents and finding substitute parents. Wade and Tavris (1993) suggest that this 'traditional' view that separation is necessary for healthy development may be outdated. In many cultures, continuing love and connection between parent and child is the norm. Apter (1990) studied 65 mother–daughter pairs in the US and in Britain and found that most of the adolescent girls said that the person they felt closest to was their mother. They may have minor quarrels, but these might be best understood as attempts to change the power balance of the parent–child relationship from a one-sided one of parental authority to a more equal adult relationship, rather than a major rift.

Paikoff and Brooks-Gunn (1991) found that the number of arguments over topics such as dress, dating, curfews and tidiness does increase during adolescence. However, such arguments are usually mild. This again supports the 'healthy' nature of adolescent–parent rows as a means of achieving individuation.

Peer relationships

According to Erikson, each life crisis is resolved through psychosocial interactions. In adolescence it is the peer group that is especially significant. As we have seen, peer relations are an important ego defence against role confusion. This may result in overidentification with peers, which results in the kind of cliques, in- and out-groups of adolescents.

Blos (1967) also offered an explanation for the importance of the peer group. He suggested that peers provide a 'way-station' on the road to achieving separation and individuation because they help the adolescent to avoid feelings of loneliness without having to make any commitment. Kirchler *et al.* (1991) have pointed out that adolescents who do not develop peer relationships and who stick to their families may have trouble establishing their autonomy and engaging in adult relationships. The peer group in adolescence can therefore be seen to play an important role.

There may be some individual differences. For example, Fulini and Eccles (1993) questioned nearly 2,000 11-year-olds, and found that peer orientation was higher in adolescents who rated their parents as more authoritarian and where adolescents felt they had few opportunities to be involved in decision making. Adolescents who experience a democratic parenting style may rely less on their peers.

Culture

If we take a strictly biological approach we would expect the experience of adolescence to be universal. It isn't. The fact that the decade between 10 and 20 is also a time of many other changes or transitions in our culture – leaving school, getting a job, going to university, leaving home, experiencing love and/or sex for the first time – suggests that the experience of adolescence needs to be explained in terms of more than biology alone.

We have already considered cross-cultural research related to the question of whether 'storm and stress' is created by our culture. We will now consider some other cultural issues.

Historical change

Shaffer (1993) claimed that adolescence is an 'invention' of the twentieth century. He argued that when it became illegal to employ children, this created a new section of the population, an 'adolescent peer culture' which was isolated from those who were younger and older. They were not able to identify with younger children and were now kept separate from the adult working population. Until this time there was no 'adolescent' phase. It was G. Stanley Hall, writing at the beginning of the twentieth century, who first identified this period of development. According to Gross (1996), the concept of a 'teenager' is even more recent, being coined in the 1950s. Adolescence is therefore historically a new conception and it is also culturally specific.

Adolescence in other societies

Shaffer (1993) also reported that in some cultures there still is no adolescent period. For example, the St Lawrence Eskimos have no prolonged phase of development; instead, there is just a moment of change when a boy becomes a man and a girl becomes a woman. Mead's studies of Samoan children (discussed above) showed a trouble-free transition, quite different from the picture often painted for our culture.

Jensen (1999) reviewed recent research related to the 'storm and stress hypothesis' and concluded that there might be a link between transitional difficulties and living in an individualistic society. The quest for autonomy and individuation may be unique to individualistic societies (a type of culture which values individual needs and independence) as contrasted with collectivistic societies where individuals share tasks, belongings and income, and value interdependence.

Exam summary: Adolescence

The AQA examination will test your understanding of the following area:

◆ research into social development, including formation of identity (pp. 295–9)

◆ research into relationships with parents and peers (pp. 298–300)

◆ cultural differences in adolescent behaviour (pp. 298–9 and p. 301).

Example question

The question below is typical of one drawn from the material above, and should take you 30 minutes to answer.

(a) Outline **one** theory of social development in adolescence. *(12 marks)*

(b) Assess the effects that relationships with parents and peers have on adolescent development.
(12 marks)

Suggested answer structure

We have covered a number of theories of social development in adolescence, all of which would be suitable as a response for the first part of this question. These are: *Blos's* psychoanalytic view of adolescence (p. 295), *Erikson's* psychosocial theory (pp. 295–6), *Marcia's* theory (pp. 296–7) and *Coleman's* focal theory of adolescence (pp. 299–300).

Blos believed that adolescence was like a second period of individuation, where the adolescent achieves independence from their parents. Rebellion is seen as an important part of this process, as it prevents adolescents becoming dependent on their parents again. Erikson suggested that the crisis for adolescence was identity. A good resolution of this stage would be identity formation, an unhealthy outcome would be role confusion. The path to this goal may involve a 'moratorium', during which various role possibilities are tried out. Marcia further developed Erikson's theory so that it could be tested empirically. There is some support for Marcia's four outcomes of adolescence (identity diffusion, foreclosure, moratorium and identity achievement), suggesting that confusion does decline, but both Marcia and Erikson may have simplified a more complex picture.

The term *outline* requires only a summary description of one theory (the AO1 component of the question), it does *not* require an evaluation of this theory. This is an important point to stress, as many students believe that *all* questions require a description and evaluation of some common material. In this question, the AO2 component in the second part of the question requires something quite different to this, an assessment of the effects that parents and peers have on adolescent development. The material for this second part of the question can be found on pp. 298 and 300. Remember that you are *assessing* the effects that parents and peers have on adolescent development, so you should consider the research support for the contention that they *do* have an important effect. The popular stereotype is that parents and adolescents clash, but psychological research suggests that this is not true. Parental relationships may remain important for many adolescents. Some children rely on peer relationships as substitutes during transition. This may be related to authoritarian parenting.

Chapter summary

◆ **Explanations of personality development** provide us with an understanding of how we come to be who we are. **Freud**'s psychoanalytic theory (a **psychodynamic** approach) combines biological drives with early experience to explain the unconscious factors that motivate adult behaviour.

◆ **Social learning approaches** include **Bandura**'s social learning theory of observational learning and **Mischel**'s situational approach that relies on selective reinforcement.

◆ There is evidence to support both psychodynamic and social learning approaches, although Freud's data may lack objectivity since they were collected during clinical interviews and recorded retrospectively.

◆ **Gender identity** and **gender roles** develop to some extent as a consequence of **social learning**, through identification with role models and exposure to stereotypes. This model suggests that it is a passive process.

◆ **Cognitive–developmental theories** suggest that gender development leads to identification rather than vice versa. Having a gender concept leads a child actively to acquire gender-role knowledge. **Gender schema theory** suggests that this active information-seeking takes place even before gender identity starts to form. Children develop schema or 'theories' about gender-appropriate behaviour.

◆ Social explanations may be insufficient on their own; there are also biological explanations of gender behaviour.

◆ A key task for the **social development of adolescence** is the **formation of identity**. One explanation comes from **Marcia** who developed Erikson's concept of identity crisis and moratorium. Blos described identity formation in terms of reindividuation.

◆ Adolescence as a period of 'storm and stress' is a cultural stereotype, which is not consistently supported by research. Coleman's focal theory proposes that stress can be avoided if problems are focused on one at a time.

◆ **Relationships with parents and peers** are a key part of the individuation process, although **cultural differences** suggest that this may be unique to individualistic cultures.

Further resources

Hall, C.S., Lindzey, G. and Campbell, J.B. (1997) *Theories of Personality*, New York: John Wiley.

This latest revision of a classic textbook on personality theory includes some excellent descriptions of relevant research, although much more detail than is required for A-level studies.

Kroger, J. (1996) *Identity in Adolescence*, London: Routledge.

Part of the Routledge series on 'adolescence and society' edited by John Coleman.

Smith, P.K., Cowie, H. and Blades, M. (1998) *Understanding Children's Development* (3rd edn), Oxford: Blackwell.

This clearly written text contains some useful material on gender development and adolescence.

Website

http://www.spsp.org/

The website of the Society for Personality and Social Psychology.

Chapter 12

Adulthood

Alison Wadeley

Preview

In this chapter, we shall be looking at definitions, contexts and methodological issues surrounding adulthood and ageing. In particular, we shall look at:

◆ early and middle adulthood, including evidence for the existence of crises and transitions

◆ family and relationships in adulthood, including research into factors associated with marriage and partnering, divorce and parenthood

◆ late adulthood – stage theories and life events.

Introduction

In a song for his son, John Lennon wrote 'Life is what happens to you while you're busy making other plans' and Woody Allen once remarked 'Life is hard and then you die'. Until the latter half of the twentieth century, psychologists had little more to say about development over the entire course of life than this. Adulthood, in particular, which for many of us could last for over 50 years, was relatively ignored. In fact, Levinson (1978) remarked that adulthood was 'one of the best kept secrets in our society...' (p. ix).

Why has the growth of a developmental psychology of the lifespan been so slow? There are at least two important reasons for this. One is the undoubted influence of such prominent figures as Freud

(1856–1939), Piaget (1896–1980) and Bowlby (1907–90), all of whom emphasized the importance of the early years of life. Another concerns the practical and methodological difficulties of studying the entire lifespan. Psychologists have attempted to deal with these obstacles in various ways and some considerable progress is now being made.

This chapter takes adulthood as its main theme and presents a selection of the existing theories and research in this vast area. In this opening section we will begin by clarifying some of the terminology and considering some of the methodological problems faced in studying adulthood. In later sections we will consider theories of lifespan development, the impact of a selection of specific life events on adults and some of the cognitive changes that accompany ageing.

Adulthood, ageing and methodological issues

A general definition of the term 'adulthood' is 'to have matured or to have grown to full size and strength'. In psychology, some theorists have focused their definitions on specific aspects of development. Freud, for example, thought that adults were in the 'genital stage' of personality development, while Piaget suggested that adults had reached the 'formal operational stage' of intellectual development. Others prefer more general definitions. To them, adulthood is not an unchanging

---

in focus

Transitions to adulthood

How do we know when someone has reached adulthood? Many cultures mark the onset of puberty in recognition that childhood is drawing to a close and the transition to adulthood has begun. Many tribal and village cultures have highly ritualized procedures, e.g. following girls' first menstrual period or attainment of a particular age. The role of the adolescent may then change quite markedly. In certain religions there may be ceremonies such as the Jewish bar mitzvah (for boys) or Christian confirmation (for either sex) but the roles played by these adolescents may not change in any perceptible way. In the UK, there is a variety of legally defined transitions which adolescents make according to age, e.g. the right to marry, to vote, to buy and consume alcohol and cigarettes, to drive or leave school. The eighteenth birthday is often a critical point, but in the absence of clear guidelines, adulthood in many western cultures is conferred imperceptibly.

state or even just a steady decline to death. Baltes and Baltes (1990), for example, prefer to see adulthood as a time of, often positive, development and change with gains and losses along the way. This development and change occurs on many different fronts and these work together to affect the whole person (see *In Focus*, p. 303).

Ageing measured in terms of time (e.g. in years) is known as *chronological* age and so starts from the moment of conception, but this type of ageing becomes a less useful concept for understanding development once we have matured. There are three additional types of ageing we should consider:

◆ *biological ageing* – changes in bodily functions and in bodily tissues and organs

◆ *psychological ageing* – mental reactions to growing older and how one sees oneself

◆ *social ageing* – how individuals relate to society as they grow older. Neugarten (1968) used the term 'social clock' to describe society's timetable mapping out what we should do at different times of life (e.g. have children, retire). Successful social ageing may depend on whether we are in time with the social clock, as well as on whether society reveres or rejects its older members.

These four types of ageing may synchronize with each other or be out of step; either way, they exert an important influence on how we cope with adulthood.

The usual way of studying age-related changes is to employ either a longitudinal or cross-sectional research design. The first of these repeatedly studies the *same* group at different points in time, whilst the second studies a number of *different* age groups all at the same time. They answer essentially the same research questions about the effects of ageing, but in different ways. See Table 12.1 for some examples of more elaborate research designs.

A central problem in cross-sectional research is in controlling, or accounting for, cohort differences, whereas longitudinal studies are especially affected by the historical time of testing. A cohort consists of a group of individuals, or 'generation', who were born during the same time interval and who will, therefore,

age together. Each cohort is of a specific size and will generally decline in number, usually with a shift to there being more females (who tend to outlive males). A cohort occupies a unique historical niche that usually means that it differs from other cohorts in important ways. Think of the impact of the motor car, World Wars I and II, television, the contraceptive pill, the AIDS epidemic and advances in communications and information technology. Any conclusions we try to draw about adult development must always be evaluated in the light of the historical context of the cohort since chronological age alone is only part of the picture.

Activity 1: Your cohort

Spend a few minutes listing the main social, cultural, historical and other influences on people born in the same year as you. If you can, compare your list with those of people from other cohorts.

Using these methods, some psychologists have succeeded in formulating developmental theories of the entire lifespan whilst others have focused on specific stages or phases of life, such as old age. Still others have chosen to approach adulthood through studying reactions to the kinds of life events that many adults experience, such as marrying or becoming a parent; Neugarten (1980) advocates this latter approach. As we will see, stage theories of adult personality development have the disadvantage of playing down individual differences. The life events approach does overcome this drawback to some extent. The strengths and weaknesses of different approaches need to be borne in mind when assessing research findings and the theories that arise from them.

In summary, various definitions of adulthood and ageing have been put forward by psychologists, taking into account to varying degrees, biological, social, personality and cognitive factors. Development at any stage of life is often positive, although there will inevitably be gains and losses. A number of research

Table 12.1 Some research designs for studying age-related change

◆ *The cohort-sequential design* — Two or more cohorts are taken and studied longitudinally, each over the same age range. Comparison of the cohorts allows us to separate out cohort effects from age effects.

◆ *The time-sequential design* — Two or more cross sections covering the same age range are taken at different testing times. Comparisons allow us to separate age effects from historical time of testing effects.

◆ *The cross-sequential design* — Two or more cohorts covering different age ranges are taken for comparison and tested at two or more times.

designs are available to developmental psychologists; these are broadly based around cross-sectional and longitudinal methods. Research into any stage of the lifespan must take account of cohort effects that introduce many variables and influence psychologists'

conclusions about the effects of age on behaviour. Because of the methodological difficulties presented by attempting to integrate widely differing patterns of adult development, some psychologists prefer to study the impact of life events on adult development.

Early and middle adulthood

Three stage theories of adult personality development are considered in this section. All of them extend beyond early and middle adulthood, but they are presented in their entirety here in order to show the context in which this stage of development occurs.

Activity 2: Lifelines

Take a large piece of paper and draw a straight line across it from left to right. Label the left end of the line 'my birth' and the right end 'my death' and add a rough scale to show age in years. Using the line to indicate 'average', plot and label the past highs and lows of your life so far, so that you have something that looks like a temperature chart. Now project forward and plot the highs and lows that you expect to experience in future years. Are any periods of life:

◆ 'busier' than others?
◆ more low than high, or vice versa?

Can cognitive, social, physiological, financial, work or other influences account for the patterns on your lifeline? Ask a friend to do the same so that you can compare your two lifelines.

Three theories of development

Erikson's 'Eight ages of man'

Erikson's psychodynamic approach to personality development was built up over about 30 years (Erikson 1980). He agreed with several key ideas from Sigmund Freud's psychoanalytic theory, but disagreed with others. For example, he accepted that personality developed in stages and that it consisted of an id, ego and superego, but he disagreed that personality was largely laid down in childhood. Instead, he thought that it continued to develop throughout adulthood. He also saw social forces as far more important in shaping personality then sexual ones (hence his approach is known as a psychosocial theory of personality development). In addition, Erikson's theory is more flexible than Freud's, in that he saw greater possibilities for change.

Erikson saw personality development as advancing through eight invariant stages (see Table 12.2) rather like sensitive periods, in that certain aspects of personality development are best dealt with at particular stages in life. Nevertheless, problems not resolved earlier on can be revisited later in life and worked through more positively. On the other hand, healthy development can be undone by later experiences. Each stage, which is roughly age related, presents the individual with a specific psychosocial 'crisis' to be worked through. This means that the individual faces, and must resolve, a series of psychological conflicts relating to their interactions with others in increasingly wider social settings. The crisis takes place in a particular social setting and if decisions are made which mean that it is dealt with successfully, the individual develops a certain virtue or psychological strength.

For the purposes of this section, the final three stages in Table 12.2 are the most relevant. However, it is important to note that the outcomes of the earlier stages will be carried forward into adulthood (e.g. basic trust is seen as the cornerstone of a healthy personality). Some stages (such as identity vs role confusion or intimacy vs isolation) may have to be dealt with repeatedly, especially in times of rapid social change. The final stage (ego integrity vs despair) involves an integration of all that has gone before in the previous stages.

In adulthood, the first major crisis is that of intimacy vs isolation. The main task is to develop a close, meaningful, caring relationship, usually with one other person and to avoid the isolation that may result from failing to do so. At the same time, individuals need to retain some independence and freedom rather than totally immersing themselves in someone else. In middle adulthood, the main crisis surrounds generativity vs stagnation. Generativity refers to the need to be productive, creative and caring with regard to one's own and future generations. Child rearing and career may be two avenues for generativity to be satisfied. A feeling of stagnation may lie behind the 'midlife crisis', when an adult may feel their current life pattern has little purpose or meaning. In later adulthood, the individual faces the ego integrity vs despair crisis. The end of life is approaching and it is a

| Table 12.2 Erikson's psychosocial stages of personality development ||||
Approximate age	Quality to be developed	Social focus	Virtue
0 to 1 year (infancy)	Basic trust vs mistrust	Maternal person	Hope (an optimistic trust that the world will meet one's needs)
2 to 3 years (early childhood)	Autonomy vs shame and doubt	Parental persons	Will (the ability to exercise self-restraint and choice)
4 to 5 years (play age)	Initiative vs guilt	Basic family	Purpose (a sense of goal-directedness)
6 to 12 years (school age)	Industry vs inferiority	Neighbourhood, school	Competence (a sense of confidence in one's own abilities)
13 to 18 years	Identity vs role confusion	Peer groups	Fidelity (the ability freely to pledge loyalty to others)
19 to 25 years	Intimacy vs isolation	Friendships	Love (both romantic and erotic and including the ability to commit oneself to others and maintain the commitment through degrees of compromise and self-denial)
26 to 40 years	Generativity vs stagnation	The household	Care (a sense that certain things in life have meaning and importance, leading one to be productive in life)
41 years +	Ego integrity vs despair	Humankind	Wisdom (a sense that life has been worthwhile, arrived at by integrating the outcomes of previous stages)

time to reflect on how one's life has been. A sense of time well spent during a productive and meaningful life will lead to a sense of ego integrity, while a sense of bitterness, opportunities missed and time wasted may lead to despair.

Ego development does not progress in the same way for everyone and therefore it is difficult to provide evidence for a theory such as Erikson's. In addition, present-day life styles are changing rapidly. People's life experiences differ so much that the three adult goals of intimacy, generativity and ego integrity may not necessarily be achieved in an orderly fashion, if at all. Today, adults are faced with a more uncertain future as concepts such as 'marriage for life' or 'a job for life' change. This makes it harder to achieve intimacy through marriage or identity through work. There is also an increasing tendency for adults to delay commitment to an intimate relationship and to delay having children. A possible consequence of this is that they may well be dealing with all three adult goals simultaneously. This does not necessarily invalidate Erikson's ideas, but it does highlight the influence of the historical niche in which they were developed.

Evidence for transitions and crises 'out of time' comes from a number of sources. In a book entitled *New Passages*, Sheehy (1996) suggests that, in the industrialized world, people are increasingly delaying the responsibilities of adulthood as well as striving to maintain their youth in other ways. Earlier research by Sangiuliano (1978, cited in Bee and Mitchell 1984) pointed out differences in timing for men and women, where women tended to achieve intimacy before identity. Women seemed to commit themselves to family responsibilities at first, but by middle age, were able to attend to identity development. For men, the achievement of identity through work came earlier. This traditional pattern may still hold in certain pockets of society, but there is strong evidence to suggest that women's work patterns are changing (Office for National Statistics 1999) and this will alter their opportunities for ego development. Future research needs to take into account the impact of sociocultural, socioeconomic and gender differences.

Evaluation of Erikson's theory

◆ Erikson's theory has been very influential in establishing the lifespan approach to human development.

◆ The theory has face validity because it appeals to intuition and common experience, at least in a traditional pattern of adulthood.

◆ Erikson has shown the importance of social influences in personality development, although some see this as a weakness since successful development is not just restricted to those who conform to the social clock and is still possible in individuals who are 'out of step' with society's expectations.

◆ There are some problems with testing a theory such as Erikson's. We would have to depend on extensive self-report, clinical interviews and questionnaires with all their attendant problems. In addition, many of Erikson's ideas are difficult to put into a testable form. These problems mean that there is a lack of sound empirical evidence for the theory. The exception, perhaps, is his own cross-cultural research with the Sioux and Yurok Indians, in which he compared different child-rearing practices and the responses of these people to rapid social change (Erikson 1980). He claimed parents themselves must be fully integrated into their own society and thus be able to instil in their children a deep sense of purpose and meaning in their actions. If the parents' social order is breaking up around them, this becomes an increasingly difficult task.

◆ Erikson's proposed order of ego development is increasingly challenged as a result of changes in modern life style, but there is still evidence that transitions occur even though the timing might vary.

Activity 3: Midlife crisis

Before you read on, pause for a moment to reflect on the idea of 'midlife crisis'. Why do you think it occurs? How do you think such a crisis would manifest itself?

Daniel Levinson's 'Seasons of a man's life'

In 1969, Levinson selected a sample of 40 men, aged from 35 to 45 years, from a variety of occupational groups. Over a period of two to three months, each participant had between five and ten biographical interviews each lasting one to two hours.

A central idea in this theory is the *life structure* defined as the 'underlying pattern or design of a person's life at any given time' (1978, p. 41). The life structure changes over the lifespan and we build it primarily around our relationships and work. Using transcriptions of the detailed interview material, Levinson was able to illustrate that the life structure evolves through a series of alternating stable (structure building) and transitional (structure changing or crisis) phases. These he called *the seasons of a man's life*. An outline of these is given in Table 12.3. The lifespan is seen as covering four eras of pre-, early, middle and late adulthood, each with specific tasks to be mastered. Where the eras overlap, we experience transitions lasting roughly five years. The ages given in Figure 12.1 are approximate, as there is some variation around them although it is not thought to be much more than five or six years.

A key feature of Levinson's theory is the concept of the structure-changing, midlife transition or crisis – an idea that has essential validity for some, especially those following the traditional pattern of adult life. Levinson even viewed this crisis as necessary and inevitable. He claimed that 80 per cent of his sample had experienced moderate or severe crisis in midlife and that those who had not were likely to pay the price later. Durkin (1995) questions whether the inevitable ups and downs of life are particularly acute in midlife and concludes that they are not. In fact, some studies (e.g. Farrell and Rosenberg 1981) showed that only about 12 per cent of people experience midlife as unusually

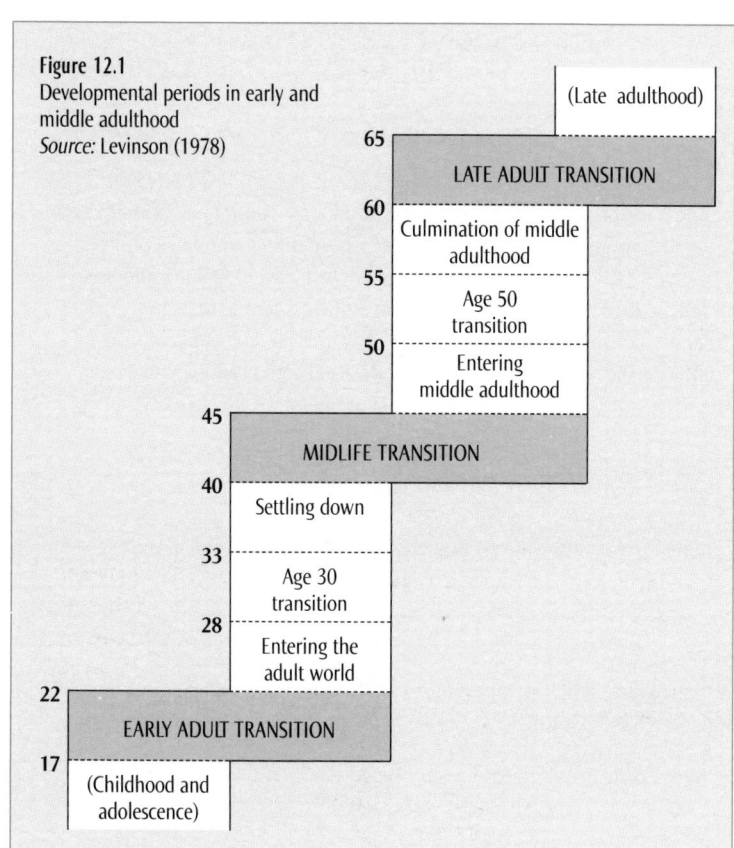

Figure 12.1
Developmental periods in early and middle adulthood
Source: Levinson (1978)

(Late adulthood)

65
LATE ADULT TRANSITION
60
Culmination of middle adulthood
55
Age 50 transition
50
Entering middle adulthood
45
MIDLIFE TRANSITION
40
Settling down
33
Age 30 transition
28
Entering the adult world
22
EARLY ADULT TRANSITION
17
(Childhood and adolescence)

Table 12.3   The seasons of a man's life

Pre-adulthood (0–17 years)

In this phase, the individual grows from dependent baby to early adulthood.

Early adult transition (18–22 years)

This involves separating oneself from pre-adulthood through increasing moves towards all kinds of independence, e.g. financial, emotional. The individual is able to explore some of life's possibilities in terms of, say, occupational choice and personal identity without yet making firm commitments. It is, as with other transitions, a time of reappraisal.

Early adulthood (22–40 years)

This can be one of the most dynamic, challenging and stressful periods of adult life. Initially, individuals forge firmer links between themselves and the adult world. Possibilities are still being explored, but this is the time to make some choices and commitments to begin to give the life more structure (although it is important still to leave open possibilities for change). It may now be possible to fulfil some of the 'dreams' of youth, perhaps establishing a home and family, qualifying in one's chosen career and finding a way to balance them all. A keener sense of time passing by means important decisions about the life structure must be made before it is too late, so there may be some readjustments from time to time. The individual will hopefully settle on a few key choices, find a 'niche' in the adult world, and from its security continue to grow through contributing constructively to aspects of personal, home and working life. The later part of this phase has been dubbed 'becoming one's own man' or BOOM.

Midlife transition (40–45 years)

The sense of passing time and one's own mortality become even more pressing as the physical signs of ageing become more obvious and as the deaths of older relatives and one's contemporaries occur. Initial dreams and plans may or may not be realized and for some (not all) this can be a period of 'midlife crisis' in which changes must be made in order to avoid extreme disappointment. In this transition, however, BOOM is completed and, with luck, individuals emerge from it wiser and able to be more loving, caring and reflective rather than isolated and stagnated.

Middle adulthood (45–60 years)

During this stage, illusions of immortality and eternal youth will usually disappear and it is a time to build on choices and decisions made during the midlife transition. For some, this may mean a new occupation, perhaps new key relationships. For others, the change may be more subtle so that the existing occupation and relationships remain, but the person's attitude to them changes. Typically, adults in this stage are less inward looking and are more concerned with the generations that follow. They have the power, authority and wisdom to make an important and lasting impact on the world and others around them. In a small way, this could mean acting as a mentor to others or becoming more of a family person. On a larger scale the individual could become involved in world politics. For many people, successful progress through this era could make it one of the most satisfying, positive and productive phases of life.

Late adult transition (60–65 years)

The signs of physical decline are now becoming increasingly obvious and one is now becoming 'old' in the eyes of one's culture.

Late adulthood (65 years to the end of life)

A final acceptance that life is finite is now unavoidable and it is important to find a way of accepting and living with how one's life has been, what it is like now, and what the future can realistically hold. Again for some, this is a time of crisis, for others a period of calm and reflection and making the most of life.

Source: Levinson (1978)

critical and that most experience it as positive. Findings such as these emphasize how varied people's life courses are and how important the coincidence of any stage of life with other events is. For example, at midlife, some adults are emptying the nest of children, whilst others might have a 'crowded nest' full of offspring unwilling or unable to move out. Still other adults might become parents for the first time or start a second family.

Levinson's original work was rather androcentric and this has prompted others to ask whether the findings for men have relevance for women. Roberts and Newton (1987) reported on studies involving female interviewers and 39 female interviewees. Although women's lives appeared to be more complex than men's lives, some broad similarities in development were found. Early adulthood involved transition, with age 30 being particularly critical. The concept of a 'dream' was also central for females although this, too, was more complex, often involving success of husband and family relationships rather than personal career. In general, it appears that in spite of using a framework developed with male interviewees,

there is evidence for 'seasons' in women's lives as well. However, an important difference for women is that their investment in others as part of their lives' dreams puts them at greater risk of disappointment.

Evaluation of Levinson's work

◆ There are few quantitative data to support the ideas of Levinson because the information collected was in the form of clinical interview reports. Some would see this as a strength because of the richness of the qualitative data. Others regard it as a weakness.

◆ Most of the interviewees in the study had not reached the age of 45. In fact, information was only gathered for 15 participants after the age of 45. Consequently, the evidence for the later eras is sketchy, being based on a very small group of adults.

◆ The original sample studied by Levinson was limited in age and occupational background, as well as being all male. Although further research has been carried out, there is still a need for further work involving females and across cultures.

Table 12.4 False assumptions to be dealt with in adulthood (Gould 1978, 1980)	
Age in years	*False assumption and its components*
Late teens to early twenties	I will always belong to my parents and believe in their world. ◆ If I get any more independent, it will be a disaster. ◆ I can only see the world through my parents' assumptions. ◆ Only they can guarantee my safety. ◆ They must be my only family. ◆ I don't own my body.
Twenties	Doing it my parents' way with willpower and perseverance will probably bring results. But when I am too frustrated, confused or tired, or am simply unable to cope, my parents will step in and show me the way. ◆ Rewards will come automatically if we do what we are supposed to do. ◆ There is only one right way to do things. ◆ My loved ones are able to do for me what I haven't been able to do for myself. ◆ Rationality, commitment and effort will always prevail over other forces.
Late twenties to early thirties	Life is simple and controllable. There are no significant coexisting contradictory forces within me. ◆ What I know intellectually, I know emotionally. ◆ I am not like my parents in ways I don't want to be. I can see the reality of those close to me quite clearly. ◆ Threats to my security aren't real.
Mid-thirties to fifty	There is no evil in me or death in the world. The sinister has been expelled. ◆ My work (for men) or my relationship with men (for women) grants me immunity from death and danger. ◆ There is no life beyond this family. ◆ I am innocent.

◆ Levinson's theory highlights the importance of taking into account the sociocultural and historical setting when describing adult development.

◆ The theory also acknowledges the centrality of others in our development.

Roger Gould's 'Evolution of adult consciousness'

Gould's (1978, 1980) ideas stem from his work as a psychiatrist. They are based on medical students' ratings of taped therapy sessions from which a questionnaire was devised. This questionnaire was sent to 524 white, middle-class 16- to 50-year-olds who were not clinical patients. From their responses, Gould identified seven age-related stages of adult development. He proposed that, as we move through these stages, we progress from childhood to adult consciousness and we do this by facing and leaving behind four major false emotional assumptions. While we hold these assumptions they give us an illusion of safety and serve to protect us from anxiety, which is why giving them up can be both difficult and painful. Gould thought that our forties could be a particularly difficult period because passing time and a greater sense of our own mortality make facing our false assumptions all the more pressing. The assumptions we have to face and discard are shown in detail in Table 12.4.

By the time we are in our 50s, we should have given up our illusions and developed what Gould calls a sense of 'me' and a feeling of autonomy – that 'I own myself'. There is a contact with one's 'inner core' which gives us a sense of meaning and the personal strength to deal with whatever life still has to bring. We should have dealt with the separation anxiety of childhood, freed ourselves from illusions of absolute safety, and learned to stand alone. Individuals who do not reach this stage may feel rootless and that life lacks meaning.

Ultimately, adult development is about coming to realize that we are creators of our own lives and are not constrained by the false assumptions of earlier stages in life. An important factor in this is a changing sense of time with age. Before young adulthood, the future is nebulous and there is a sense of time stretching endlessly ahead. As we progress through life, we should have a sense of moving along a fairly well-defined time-line, especially if we have chosen a particular career path. By our thirties and forties, there is an growing sense that time is not unlimited and that choices must therefore be made. This increasing urgency is also fuelled by a sense of our own mortality, so that what we do with the available time matters more and more. The modern phenomenon called 'downshifting' provides some anecdotal evidence for this. Downshifters are people who, in midlife, find themselves leading a pressurized life style with long working hours and many demands on time. They make a conscious choice to simplify their life style and settle for less in monetary terms in order to improve their quality of life.

Evaluation of Gould's theory

◆ Gould's theory is based on the evaluations of taped patient interviews from only eight medical students. Their relatively inexperienced evaluations were then used as a basis for the questionnaire and this calls its validity into question.

◆ The 524 questionnaire respondents were white, middle-class adults which tells us little about other adult groups.

◆ There were no attempts to assess the reliability of the questionnaire.

◆ The detail about life after 60 is sketchy, but this is hardly surprising given the age range of Gould's questionnaire respondents.

◆ As with other adulthood theories, Gould's analysis does seem to have some face validity, but it must take into account sociocultural and gender differences.

Activity 4: Analysing your lifeline

Take your lifeline from Activity 2 and, using three different coloured pens for clarity, superimpose the stages suggested by Erikson, Levinson and Gould. How well do they 'fit' your life course? Can you relate the events you expect to experience to the stages or phases suggested by these theories?

Conclusions about stage theories of development

Although Erikson, Levinson and Gould have described adult development using different terminology, there is some general agreement about the overall trends in adulthood (e.g. finding an identity in adolescence, establishing intimacy, making career choices, becoming generative and, finally, looking for a meaning to life and facing death). The forces behind these trends differ in each theory, but they share an emphasis on phases or stages that all adults can be expected to move through with varying degrees of success.

These three approaches offer a much-needed framework for understanding certain aspects of adulthood, but there are some important limitations to bear in mind:

◆ In each case there are some doubts about the soundness of the research on which the ideas are based, particularly with regard to the number and type of participants used and the methods of data collection.

The Social Readjustment Rating Scale

One major attempt to classify and measure the effects of life events was made by Holmes and Rahe (1967). They studied 5,000 patient records and listed 43 life events that had occurred in the months preceding illness. With the help of 100 judges, who rated each event in terms of how much change it would entail, they developed the Social Readjustment Rating Scale (SRRS). On this scale, each event has a value indicating 'life change units' or LCUs. Individuals can be asked to check off all the events that have affected them in, say, the previous year and add the LCUs to arrive at a grand total. See Table 12.5. Links between these scores (which indicate the amount of stress experienced) and stress-related illness can then be researched.

◆ Some critics think there is a rather negative overemphasis on crisis, particularly in midlife, and that this could be because of the nature of the cohorts used.

◆ We cannot be sure how well the three approaches apply to different individuals, societies and cohorts. Possible variation within these is well worth further investigation.

◆ We must also remember that the changes described in these theories go on against a background of many other age-related changes (e.g. physiological and cognitive/intellectual), that individuals are having to cope with at the same time. (Cognitive changes are considered later in this chapter. For a discussion of other changes, see Bee 1998 or Berk 1998.)

◆ Some researchers think that there is little convincing evidence for stages in adult development and prefer instead to focus on specific life events that affect many adults. We will return to this in the next section. The Social Readjustment Rating Scale (see *In Focus*) is one attempt to assess the effect of life events.

Exam summary: Early and middle adulthood

The AQA examination will test your understanding of the following areas:

◆ theories of development in early and middle adulthood (pp. 305–11)

◆ evidence for the existence of crises and transitions (pp. 305–10).

Example question

The question below should take you 30 minutes:

◆ Outline and evaluate **two** theories of development in early and middle adulthood. *(24 marks)*

Suggested answer structure

The first thing you should do with any exam question is to take it apart in order to discover exactly what is required. This is all the more vital with questions such as this, where there is a requirement to cover two

theories, and to produce descriptive and evaluative content for them both. The question has used the term *outline* to tell you that only a summary outline is required, but that is not particularly helpful if you can't précis to save your life. Before we begin planning what might be an effective response to this question, it is best we put your mind at ease over one thing. Although the question asks for two theories of early and middle adulthood, this is not a requirement for you to write two early adulthood theories and two middle adulthood theories. You are merely asked to include two theories that deal with the periods of early and middle adulthood. All the theories included in this first section do just that.

As this question asks for two theories, you should divide up your time equally between the two, and as the AO1 and AO2 components of each theory are likewise equally weighted, your time and effort can be further subdivided. In 'strategic' terms, that would give you an essay plan something like this:

◆ outline description of theory 1 = 7.5 minutes or (approximately) 150 words

◆ evaluation of theory 1 = 7.5 minutes or 150 words

◆ outline description of theory 2 = 7.5 minutes or 150 words

◆ evaluation of theory 2 = 7.5 minutes or 150 words.

The only decision that remains is for you to read the section again and decide which two theories you feel confident to write about in this way.

The stage theories of Erikson (pp. 305–7), Levinson (pp. 307–10) and Gould (pp. 309–10) offer explanations of development over the entire lifespan or for specific periods in adulthood. There are broad areas of agreement in these theories, although they explain the 'pushes' and 'pulls' of development differently. All of them recognize that there are transitions, and sometimes crises that demand major reorientation and adjustment. Their own research, the resulting theories and the work of others provide evidence for this. Methodological criticisms have been raised about all three approaches and all are open to cohort effects. Nevertheless, they have given us some much-needed frameworks within which to view development in adulthood.

Family and relationships in adulthood

Bearing in mind the many variables that can affect how individuals react to life events, can we make any general statements about the effects of specific life events? To address this question, this section focuses on three key events affecting many adults – marriage (or partnering), parenthood and divorce. Two further events, retirement and bereavement, are considered later in the chapter. But before reading on, you might like to complete Activity 5 which asks you to identify which of the life events listed by Holmes and Rahe (1967) in the Social Readjustment Rating Scale are currently affecting your own life.

Activity 5: Your score on the SRRS scale

Analyse your own situation, using the SRRS scale shown in Table 12.5.

◆ How many of the life events listed have you experienced in the last year?

◆ How appropriate is it for this stage in your life?

◆ Project ahead 10 years, then 20 years. Does the scale seem more appropriate now?

◆ Do you think there are stages in life where the listed events are likely to cluster together?

Marriage (or partnering)

Western-style, voluntary heterosexual marriage is only one of several forms of adult intimate living arrangement and, according to figures from the Office for National Statistics (1999), it is in decline. In 1996, there were 185,000 first-time marriages, but this is less than half the number recorded in 1970 when first-time UK marriages peaked. In 1997, there were 9,000 fewer marriages than in 1996, the lowest rate since 1917. Not surprisingly, there is a corresponding increase in cohabitation, but the most common reason for cohabitation ending is still marriage. In spite of the relatively high risk of divorce or separation, many

Table 12.5 The Social Readjustment Rating Scale

Rank	Life event	Mean value	Rank	Life event	Mean value
1	Death of spouse	100	22	Change in responsibilities at work	29
2	Divorce	73	23	Son or daughter leaves home	29
3	Marital separation	65	24	Trouble with in-laws	29
4	Jail term	63	25	Outstanding personal achievement	28
5	Death of a close family member	63	26	Spouse begins or stops work	26
6	Personal illness or injury	53	27	Begin or end school	26
7	Marriage	50	28	Change in living conditions	25
8	Fired at work	47	29	Revision of personal habits	24
9	Marital reconciliation	45	30	Trouble with boss	23
10	Retirement	45	31	Change in work hours or conditions	20
11	Change in health of family member	44	32	Change in residence	20
12	Pregnancy	40	33	Change in schools	20
13	Sex difficulties	39	34	Change in recreation	19
14	Gain of new family member	39	35	Change in church activities	19
15	Business readjustment	39	36	Change in social activities	18
16	Change in financial status	38	37	Moderate mortgage or loan	17
17	Death of close friend	37	38	Change in sleeping habits	16
18	Change to different line of work	36	39	Change in number of family get-togethers	15
19	Change in number of arguments with spouse	35	40	Change in eating habits	15
20	Heavy mortgage repayments	31	41	Vacation	13
21	Foreclosure of mortgage or loan	30	42	Christmas	12
			43	Minor violations of the law	11

Source: adapted from Holmes and Rahe (1967)

Activity 6: Your views on marriage and partnering

For many adults in the Western world, marriage (or partnering) is voluntarily entered into. Why do you think that people seek such relationships? Do you consider that marriage and cohabitation are different? If so, how?

Parenthood is also something that can be planned. What do you think people's reasons are for having children?

people still opt for marriage or some other form of long-term, partnered, living arrangement and most psychological research is still focused on marriage. What can it tell us about why people marry and what they can expect from marriage? Try Activity 6 now.

On a practical level, marriage fulfils basic needs for companionship and security. It is an overt sign of adult status and provides a legitimate unit within which to rear children. In Erikson's (1980) terms, marriage is one way to solve the psychosocial crisis of intimacy vs isolation. Through making a commitment to another person, we develop the ego quality of being able to love (even if this means some self-denial and compromise) and avoid emotional isolation. With time, the initial passionate and erotic love that can draw two people together may deepen into a more profound and secure attachment that stands the test of time and the inevitable rough patches in life.

The U-shaped curve

Clearly some relationships wear better than others. To try to understand why, psychologists have studied the quality of marital relationships at different stages in the marriage and come up with conflicting views. One of the more persistent findings (Bee 1998) concerns the 'U-shaped' curve of marital satisfaction which occurs because satisfaction declines after marriage, reaches a low when children are at school and then rises steadily to peak in retirement. A major problem to consider, apart from difficulties with developing valid measures of marital satisfaction, is that such findings are based on the cross-sectional method and, as time goes on, unsatisfactory marriages may have ended and consequently been lost from the samples of 'older' marriages. This would lead to an artificial impression of growing satisfaction with time. Indeed, Vaillant and Vaillant's (1993) 40-year study of marriages in 169 Lebanese college men and women suggests that the U-curve may be an illusion created by using a retrospective approach (asking people to look back over time). When a prospective approach is used

(people are monitored as they go along), marital satisfaction appears to remain fairly stable.

Cross-cultural comparisons of marriage

Comparisons of marital satisfaction in men and women persistently show that Western women are less satisfied with their marriages than men (e.g. Schumm et al. 1998), but cross-culturally, the criteria for judging such satisfaction may vary. In a comparison of American and Japanese spouses, Kamo (1993) discovered that the quality of marital interactions was regarded as important in both cultures. However, he also found that age and satisfaction were negatively related in the USA, but not in Japan, and that husband's income mattered more for Japanese wives than for American wives. In a study of 11 cultures (India, Pakistan, Thailand, Mexico, Brazil, Japan, Hong Kong, the Philippines, Australia, England and the US), Levine et al. (1995) reported that, in cultures which emphasize individualism, greater importance was assigned to love in marriage than was the case in collectivist cultures. They also found that love mattered in cultures with higher standards of living, higher marriage and divorce rates, and lower fertility rates.

Marital status, gender difference and mental health

With regard to the link between marital status and health, Bee (1998) showed that, compared with never-married individuals, married people enjoy better physical health and markedly better mental health. Single men are worst off in these respects and married men fare best, with married and single women falling between these two extremes. Argyle and Henderson (1985) argue that it is the quality of the relationship that seems to contribute most to this effect – a close confiding relationship matters more than simply living in the same house or having a sexual relationship. One reason why marriage seems to favour men could be that women are better confidantes for their husbands than their husbands are for them. In other respects, in spite of changes in attitudes towards women's role, marriage for them may be less satisfactory, not only because of possibly greater domestic and work role conflict, but also because the arrival of children requires a relatively greater adjustment for women than it does for most men.

So can psychologists offer any general advice to people contemplating marriage about how to give themselves the best chance in the decades to come? Berk (1998) and Bee (1994) summarize a number of factors that correlate with marital quality and stability. See Table 12.6 on p. 314, but be warned – this evidence is correlational so there is no guarantee of success no matter how many factors are present!

Table 12.6 Factors that correlate with marital quality and stability

◆ length of courtship at least six months

◆ homogamy in family background, e.g. similarity in age, religion, social class

◆ individuals come from high social class and have more education

◆ higher levels of self-esteem

◆ more leisure time spent together

◆ partners like each other and consider their spouse their best friend

◆ approval from others such as friends and family

◆ first pregnancy after first year of marriage

◆ stable marital patterns in extended family

◆ secure financial and employment status

◆ perceived similarity in both interests and personal qualities

◆ more positive than negative interactions with each other

◆ effective communication with each other

◆ role fit, i.e. each partner fits the other's expectations.

Source: adapted from Berk (1998) and Bee (1998)

Parenthood

Parenthood, like other life events, can be both stressful and rewarding. Unlike some other life events, such as marriage, it is irrevocable. In our culture, there may be little preparation for parenthood and little support, other than from a number of, often contradictory, child-care books. Increasingly, children in the UK are being born outside marriage – in 1997 this was true for one third of all live births – but four-fifths of these births were registered by both parents, with three-quarters of these registrations showing that parents shared the same address (*Social Trends* 1999). This leaves substantial numbers of parents coping with lone parenthood with widely varying degrees of support from others.

Cultural differences in parenthood

The arrival of a child is also one of the most abrupt transitions experienced by adults in the Western world regardless of whether they are partnered or single. Contrast this with a Mexican American family ritual, *La cuarentena* (see *In Focus*), which lasts 40 days after the birth of the first child, and is aimed at supporting the parents in their new role and establishing them and their child within their new family structure. In less well-developed cultures, such as that of the Amazonian Penare Indians or the nomadic Wodabe of Western Sudan, newborns are welcomed into a tight system of social support where parents are not isolated in their new role.

Western parenthood calls for major readjustments in life style and is accompanied by practical issues, such as general fatigue, as well as physical changes (for the mother) and the emotional changes that accompany coming to terms with suddenly being entirely responsible for a helpless and vulnerable baby. Within couples, the roles of the new father and mother may initially become more traditional and polarized, and the preparenthood balance and quality of the relationship will probably never return. This pattern seems to be generally true in developed Western culture. Nickel *et al.* (1995), for example, showed a general decrease in marital satisfaction after the birth of children in Germany, the USA, Austria and Korea. However, in non-Western cultures, where parenthood is highly valued, motherhood confers high status and the extended family is supportive, the decline in satisfaction levels is

---

in focus

La cuarentena

In certain regions of Mexico, pregnancy and childbirth are seen as part of the normal life course, and the intervention of medical authorities is minimal, although there is usually a midwife who is important during both pregnancy and birth. A special period of 40 days called *la cuarentena*, is observed after the birth of a child. This does not involve isolation as in true 'quarantine' but, instead, is a time when grandmothers, friends or mothers-in-law play a vital role. These women help with household chores and other aspects of the mother's usual work. The role of the women, primarily the mother, is recognized as central during *la cuarentena* and they are the primary caregivers in these situations. The father generally participates very little. However, mothers are usually positive about this and protect the male's image. This opinion may be influenced by the financial help that males provide but also by the belief that men do not know how to, and do not have the ability to, participate in the child-rearing process. This culturally prescribed pattern of behaviour helps to aid the recovery of the mother after birth and the survival of her infant while easing both the mother and the father into their new roles as parents.

Table 12.7 Reasons for choosing parenthood	
Ego expansion	a sense of importance and purpose
Creativity	a sense of achievement (or what Erikson would call successful resolution of the generativity crisis)
Status and conformity satisfaction	fulfilling the expectations of your culture
Control and authority	over your dependants
Love and affection	both given and received
Happiness and security	through the creation of a stable family unit

Source: Turner and Helms (1983)

less marked (Berk 1998). Whatever the circumstances, parenthood exerts a powerful pull. Turner and Helms (1983) suggest a number of reasons why adults choose parenthood (see Table 12.7). These remain remarkably consistent across cultures, although Barnes (1995) adds that, in some cultures, the child's ability to work and/or contribute to the family's income is critical.

Stages of parenthood

Within marriage, the arrival of children is typically associated with the early years. At that time there may be additional pressures such as low income and high job pressure whilst the parents establish themselves at work. By the time the children are at school, parents may find themselves under the greatest pressure in their career (especially if they are competing with keen, younger, childless colleagues who are also cheaper to employ). Parents with adolescent children seemed to be under even greater strain. Bee (1994) reported that the happiest parents were young couples with few financial pressures. In spite of this, 80 to 90 per cent of couples with children said they were very happy and that parenthood had improved their relationship. This was especially true just before the 'empty nest' phase when children were about to be launched into the adult world. For many parents, the 'empty nest' phase was particularly good, being marked by an increase in energy and zest for life and much satisfaction in the adult offspring.

Parenthood and gender roles

How is the impact of parenthood on women and men different? Sadly, traditional male–female roles appear to hinder both genders in their capacity as parents. Women still carry the brunt of domestic and parenting tasks even when both partners work outside the home (Berk 1998), and the adjustments they are required to make are considerably greater. Women also have to battle with idealized ideas about 'mother love' and 'maternal instinct' and the 'good mother's role' and these may be difficult to reconcile with other needs such as career fulfilment. Those who have established identities outside motherhood may find a constant conflict of interests between career and parenting, while those who immerse themselves in motherhood may have identity problems when the children become less dependent or leave home.

Men may initially be more involved in practical aspects of child care, and just as immersed in their newborns as women, but they are typically less well-prepared for parenthood and may feel left out or unequal to meeting the demands of being provider, household help and nurturer. Both sexes have to adjust to sharing their time and affection differently within the family but, initially, this can be harder for the father, particularly if he is less involved than the mother in the daily care of the infant. Indeed, some studies (e.g. Terry *et al.* 1991) show that marital satisfaction after transition to parenthood is greater when the woman perceives that her spouse is contributing fairly to the performance of household tasks. A Scandinavian study (Olsson *et al.* 1998) found that new parents agreed that the metaphor of the spider's web described the tension in their changed relationship – the mother is the spider carrying the baby on her back, and the father only enters the web on her terms. Levine (1976) suggests that the roles of both fathers and mothers need to be redefined and revitalized so that more of the satisfactions of parenthood are open to men and women (as well as more of the strains).

Lugo and Hershey (1979) believe that careful preparation and greater understanding of the different effects on males and females could reduce many of the negative aspects of the parenthood crisis. Much influenced by Maslow's (1968) 'hierarchy of human needs', they advise that we prepare for parenthood by building a unit that meets our physical and psychological needs, i.e. for survival, security, love, esteem and understanding. If we work on this, parenthood can be a step forward on the road to personal growth and even help us towards self-actualization.

Divorce

Next to the death of a spouse, divorce is the most difficult life crisis we are ever likely to experience. Bee (1998) notes that divorce is more likely in those: who marry younger or older than average; who are childless; whose parents had an unhappy marriage; or who married because of an unplanned pregnancy. Overall, the divorce rate in the UK is high. The number of divorces more than doubled between 1970 and 1996. Figures from 1996 show that nine per cent of marriages ended within the first three years, peaking at 28 per cent between five and nine years (Office for National Statistics 1999). Durkin (1995) suggests that increasing freedom to enter into or terminate relationships in general has led to higher and idealized expectations of the married relationship and what it is required to provide in terms of exclusivity, fulfilment and love. For example, both partners expect to fulfil their life's dreams (Levinson 1978) and if their marriage is only allowing one of them to do that, it may be at risk.

On the positive side, divorce can be good for you. It may mark the end of a long period of unhappiness and lack of personal growth but, even if the eventual outcome is good, divorce is nearly always traumatic and the weight of the evidence suggests that a long and difficult period of coping and adjustment is necessary. Bohannon (1970) suggested six stages in the divorce process. These are shown in Table 12.8.

Stages in the divorce process

Each of the stages may be accompanied by a conflicting range of emotions including pervasive feelings of failure, ambivalence towards the partner, grief, relief, loneliness and excitement. There may be greater anxiety, loss of self-esteem, reduced productivity at work and greater vulnerability to mental and physical illness. In a review of relevant research, Gottman (1998) links divorce with increased incidence of physical illness, suicide, violence, homicide, suppressed immunity and mortality from diseases.

It is during the divorce process itself that both parties seem to suffer most acutely. The degree of trauma seems to be associated with:

◆ length of marriage

◆ the age of the spouses

◆ the number and ages of any children

◆ who suggested the divorce

◆ how it went.

For both men and women, disorganization is a feature of the year following divorce. Both men and women experience a drop in income, but women generally seem to suffer more financially from a divorce, especially if they assumed their major role would be as a home-maker, or if they took a career break in order to rear children and their earnings fell behind. Indeed, employed women seem to suffer less loss of self-esteem and distress than women without a clear work identity (Bisagni and Eckenrode 1995). There is some evidence (e.g. Berk 1998) that divorcees over the age of 50 find adjustment harder than do younger ones. The older age group seems to feel they have fewer options open to them and find their social life is more difficult. Older men in particular have difficulty envisaging what the future would hold.

Parents and children in divorce

Divorcees with children have to deal with their own distress as well as that of their children. In addition, they have to take sole responsibility for discipline and may find it hard to be consistent, so the children's behaviour may deteriorate. Another great source of conflict concerns access rights to children. Whilst Berk (1998) points out that divorce is never 'good for the children', she says that its effects are less likely to cause serious, long-term damage if there is plenty of frequent and satisfactory contact between the child and both parents, coupled with a

Table 12.8 Stages in the divorce process	
The emotional divorce	The marriage collapses, there is conflict and antagonism.
The legal divorce	The marriage contract is dissolved.
The economic divorce	Decisions are made over money and property.
The co-parental divorce	Custody of and access to children is decided.
The community divorce	Relationships with friends and family are adjusted.
The psychic divorce	There is adjustment to singlehood and autonomy is regained.

Source: Bohannon (1970)

minimum disruption to the child's life style and daily routine. Naturally, children of different ages react differently to divorce, and understanding this can help parents to cope better with both the child's unhappiness and their own worries about the child's unhappiness. There is also some evidence that boys become more unruly following divorce and that their schoolwork suffers more than it does for girls, possibly because they receive less overt emotional support (Berk 1998). Some parents cope by arranging for their families to become 'blended', i.e. where step and biological parents both take responsibility for the children's welfare. Difficult though this can be, it does help to maintain contact between divorced parents and their children and lessen the pressure on both.

Cultural differences and similarities in divorce

Existing research does seem to show that at least two years of turmoil is extremely likely following divorce. For adults, divorce-related disorganization tends to decline after two years depending on the degree of financial pressure, number and age of children, and the emotional support available. Interestingly, in a study of divorcees in Israeli kibbutzim, Kaffman (1993) found that, because of their life style, the legal, parenting and economic obstacles that usually exacerbate stress in divorce were relatively minor considerations. This meant that life after divorce held fewer sources of conflict for them than it did for non-kibbutz dwellers. What remained for kibbutz dwellers was something Kaffman called the 'authentic emotional divorce'. However, when he compared the emotional impact of divorce on kibbutz and non-kibbutz dwellers, he found that it was similar in both samples, pointing to what he calls 'the ubiquitousness of the human experience' (p. 117). In other words, divorce feels pretty much the same to everyone regardless of the practical and material issues that accompany it.

Exam summary: Family and relationships in adulthood

The AQA examination will test your understanding of the following areas:

◆ research into factors in marriage/partnering (pp. 312–13), parenthood (pp. 314–15) and divorce (pp. 316–17)

◆ gender and cultural differences (pp. 313–15, 317).

Example question

The question that follows is typical of one drawn from the material above, and should take you 30 minutes.

◆ Discuss research into factors associated with marriage (partnering). *(24 marks)*

Suggested answer structure

This question asks for a 'discussion of research into factors...'. The term 'research' is defined (see Table 21.2 on p. 552) as:

'The process of gaining knowledge and understanding either through theory construction and examination, or through empirical data collection.'

This allows you, therefore, to include insights from theories about marriage, as well as insights gained from 'empirical data collection' (i.e. research studies). Both of these are part of the 'cycle of scientific enquiry' (see p. 517).

We have examined various aspects of research into factors associated with marriage. In general, this research tells us that marriage fulfils different needs, that it affects men and women differently, and that there are differences across cultures.

One of the major and most persistent of findings is that marriage satisfaction follows the pattern of a U-shaped curve, with satisfaction being highest shortly after marriage and at retirement, with a low whilst children are at school, then rising steadily to a peak at retirement (p. 313). This finding is confounded by the use of the cross-sectional method (unsuccessful marriages might have been 'lost' from the sample) and the use of retrospective methods. The use of prospective methods appear to show patterns of marital satisfaction that are fairly stable over time.

Cross-cultural comparisons of marital happiness tend to show that Western women are less satisfied with their marriages than men, although the criteria for judging satisfaction may vary across different cultures. Individualistic cultures place more importance on love as a criterion for happiness in marriage, whereas this was assigned less importance in collectivist cultures (p. 313).

Some research has examined the proposition that married people enjoy better physical and mental health (p. 313). This appears to be more a question of the quality of the relationship rather than the mere physical presence of a marriage partner. There is some evidence (Table 12.6 on p. 314) concerning the factors that correlate with marital quality and stability, although these are only correlational (i.e. they accompany marital quality and stability rather than necessarily causing it).

Cognitive changes in late adulthood

Three theories of successful ageing are described here, emphasizing the social context of ageing in later life. The related critical life event of retirement is also considered in this context. We then go on to consider possible cognitive changes in later life and finish with a consideration of the impact of one further critical life event, bereavement.

Three explanations of adjustment to old age

Social disengagement theory

Social disengagement theory (Cumming and Henry 1961) sees ageing as a gradual and mutual process of separation between individuals and their social roles and interests. As people age, their activity levels tend to decrease and they may become freer of family and work responsibilities. This is a natural, and often positive, process whereby, in later life, the ageing person becomes more reflective and self-sufficient and less absorbed in other people and events. They generally bring this about themselves, but other events, such as loss of spouse and retirement, also encourage disengagement to happen.

Cumming and Henry (1961) described three phases in the process of disengagement:

1 There is *shrinkage of life space* brought about by fewer interactions with others and the relinquishing of some of our roles.

2 There is *increased individuality*, as the individual becomes more flexible in the way in which the remaining roles are expressed.

3 There is *acceptance* of these life changes. This is not meant to imply that the individual is resigned to disengagement. Instead, acceptance leads to the person becoming more inward and self-reliant as though preparing for death.

Of course, this is a culturally specific view in which society is seen as withdrawing itself from the person. In some tribal and village cultures, elders may become pivotal in the life of the community and valued for their wisdom and advice. The problems with this theory must, therefore, be considered in the light of cultural differences:

◆ People who apparently disengage may simply be embracing a life style that they prefer but were prevented from adopting before. This has to do with personality rather than advancing age. In a follow-up study of some of the original sample of Cumming and Henry (1961), Havighurst and colleagues identified different personality types. There were some called *disengaged* whose activity, but not contentment levels, had fallen. By contrast there were *reorganizers* whose activity levels had not dropped. They had simply changed.

◆ There are plenty of examples of people who actively resist disengagement and who are unhappy when social forces require them to. There are others whose culture actively discourages disengagement. Those who remain actively socially engaged are often happier than those not so engaged (Havighurst *et al.* 1968). This calls into question whether disengagement really is 'natural' and inevitable.

◆ People may disengage from a wider social circle, but replace a larger number of more superficial contacts with a smaller number of high-quality, more rewarding contacts (see the account of selectivity theory below).

◆ There may be a cohort effect that gives a false impression of disengagement. Later generations of elderly people may be healthier, more financially secure, generally better catered for socially and so have greater choice. If this proves to be the case 'disengagement' may disappear (Bromley 1988).

Activity theory

In direct contrast to disengagement theory, activity theory (Havighurst *et al.* 1968) sees individuals as preferring to remain active and productive in later life, even resisting disengagement from society, although, sadly, social barriers to continued activity can make resistance difficult. Where some disengagement is inevitable (e.g. through children leaving home, statutory retirement, reduction in income and changes in physical capabilities), the individual is less likely to be demoralized if they are well prepared and have plenty of substitute activities. However, the quality of these activities is important for life satisfaction. Activities that simply maintain frequency of social contact are a poor substitute for roles and relationships that are meaningful and worthwhile to the individual. It is likely that this theory, like disengagement theory, oversimplifies the issues.

Selectivity theory

A newer approach (Field and Minkler 1988, Lang and Carstensen 1994) focuses on the way in which social relationships, and the needs they fulfil, change with age. In our younger years we may select relationships, not just for companionship, but also for guidance, information and affirmation. The older, wiser person also selects relationships for companionship, but less so for other things. Older people appear to disengage from unrewarding relationships and select those that are primarily emotionally supportive and pleasant. It is the quality of these, rather than the quantity, that matters when a person feels that the time they have left is limited.

In comparing these theories it is immediately obvious that there is some value in all of them but no one theory is sufficient on its own. People vary considerably in the degree to which they wish to be active or disengaged or selective and in how much control they have over these things. In fact, successful ageing would appear to result from achieving a balance that suits the individual concerned. We should also consider many other variables (such as health, income, place of residence, sense of control, social support systems, marital status and family) when assessing a person's life satisfaction. Indeed, we would probably find that later life is no more or less satisfying than any other stage of life once we take into account all the ways in which people differ.

Effects of retirement

Retirement in the Western world is a relatively modern creation, made possible by the promise of at least some financial support (in the form of pensions) for those who are retired, although the traditional concept of a 'job for life' until the age of 65 is also changing rapidly. Changes in the nature of work and in the working patterns of men and women mean that cohort effects are particularly salient when considering research about retirement. Both men and women now retire at a variety of ages and for different reasons. For many, the transition to retirement is abrupt, whilst for others it is blurred as they disengage gradually from work or

become 'unretired–retired' having never completely stopped working at all.

As health care and longevity improve, many of us can anticipate long years of retirement, but is this always a welcome prospect? In a cross-cultural study, Gee and Baillie (1999) questioned 183 Australian and British men and women in employment who were aged 40 and over about their expectations for retirement. Their main finding was that most participants regarded retirement optimistically as a 'new beginning', but expected to undertake some active preparation to help them to adapt to the changes they would have to face. Research bears out their intuition that retirement is not so much a single event as a process of adaptation. For example, Atchley (1982, 1988) identified five periods of adjustment that people who retire in the traditional sense, but not all, may experience to varying degrees. These are shown in Table 12.9.

Findings such as Atchley's, while informing potential retirees of what they could expect, do not apply to everyone. Schaie and Willis (1991) comment that most people adjust well to retirement, but that problems are least likely amongst those who retired voluntarily and who enjoy financial security and good health. Furthermore, people who report high personal involvement in their jobs, or whose leisure time is unsatisfactory, feel the greatest disruption to their lives following retirement; some of these will cope by retaining a foothold in their occupation for as long as possible. Those who do not judge their self-worth primarily in terms of their job, and who engage in a variety of activities outside their work, tend to adjust to retirement more easily. Particular problems of adjustment may be apparent for couples whose preretirement relationship conformed to the stereotypical domesticated woman/working man pattern. In these cases, although both need to adjust to

Table 12.9 Five periods of adjustment to retirement	
Honeymoon period	A period of relative enjoyment and euphoria (more common for voluntary retirees who are financially secure). There may be a feeling of being on holiday and of being able to busy oneself with things that there was no time for while at work. Extensive travel and/or house moves are possible.
Rest and relaxation period	A time to rest and take stock after the initial activity of the honeymoon phase.
Disenchantment period	A period thought to affect only a small proportion of retirees. Expectations may have been unrealistic or unmet because of bereavement and/or physical and mental health problems. Support may be reduced if social networks have been disrupted.
Reorientation period	Another opportunity to take stock and adjust expectations in line with the more clearly understood reality of the situation.
Routine period	A stable and satisfying routine is established giving structure and meaning to retirement.

Source: Atchley (1982, 1988)

the changed situation, the male may have more to do in adapting to a domain which is more familiar to, and dominated by, his partner.

An Australian study by Sharpley and Layton (1998) supports some of these ideas. They questioned 349 males and 385 females, aged between 44 and 90 years old, for the first five years after retirement from full-time work. A key finding was that men and women who had retired voluntarily were significantly less anxious, depressed and stressed than those who had retired because of ill health or redundancy. Furthermore, with regard to physical health, males who retired earlier fared better than later retirees, but no such pattern emerged for women. A better understanding of this particular life event has led to the recognition that it can be made easier to manage if preretirement education is given. Importantly, Sharpley and Layton's findings suggested that preretirement education which addressed social, health, personal, relationship and, of course, financial aspects of the retirement could help to reduce some of the psychological distress which is sometimes part of this phase of life. In this respect forewarned is forearmed.

Cognitive processing changes in late adulthood

While it is true that certain diseases associated with ageing can lead to a reduction in cognitive functioning, the rather negative stereotype of inevitable intellectual decline in late adulthood is something of a myth. Cultural context is also important here. In China, government ministers in their 70s might be regarded as youngsters and prone to hot-headedness, whereas in the UK or USA they might be seen as wiser than younger people, but might also be stereotyped as being prone to senility (Durkin 1995).

There is some evidence to suggest that older people generally perform less well on tasks that require mental processing speed. Berk (1998) suggests that this could be due to deterioration in neural networks as neurons in the brain die. Alternatively, or perhaps as a result, it could be because information is lost as an ageing system takes longer to move it through the various processing stages. However, research has identified a number of variables that should be considered before jumping to the conclusion that slowing down is inevitable. First, a decline in processing speed may be accounted for by the fact that older people have more experience than younger ones and may be able to consider more, and more complex, strategies for solving a problem (e.g. Stuart-Hamilton 2000). In certain cases, this might enable them to arrive at a better solution, albeit more slowly.

A second problem concerns cohort effects. When we compare mental abilities in different generations, we must take account of their different educational experiences. Younger people may be more familiar with being tested in particular ways and so have developed strategies that help them to succeed. Younger people may also be more recently practised, so to compare them with unpractised older people is unfair. However, Schaie and Hertzog (1983) showed that both age and cohort effects matter in tests of mental ability. They compared Americans born in different decades and found differences for age and cohort effects were equally strong.

Care should also be taken over what is meant by 'intellectual ability'. Psychologists generally agree that 'intelligence' is multi-faceted. For example, a distinction can be drawn between 'crystallized' and 'fluid' intelligence. Crystallized intelligence is 'the ability to store and manipulate learned information' (Durkin 1995, p. 645) while fluid intelligence is a general, problem-solving ability that we bring to bear on novel or unfamiliar problems. Baltes and Baltes (1990) claim that crystallized intelligence increases with age, but that there is a general decline in fluid intelligence. This difference could quite simply be accounted for by practice. Crystallized intelligence is maintained on a daily basis while fluid intelligence may be more frequently exercised in younger people.

Bee (1998) points out that there is little decline in intellectual functioning until about the last five years of life (a phenomenon referred at as the 'terminal drop'). Because each cohort contains more and more people within this range (we live in an ageing society), it looks as if the whole cohort is declining intellectually.

A further aspect of the negative stereotype about older people is that their memories become unreliable but, as with intelligence, we need to define the term with care, as there are many different kinds of memory. Typically, tests of recall show a decline with age (although there is immense variation between individuals) while tests of recognition show no such decline. Older adults may recall lists less efficiently than younger ones, although they can often recall the gist of a passage of prose equally well. Older adults may process certain information less deeply than younger ones, but training in memory strategies can eliminate this difference (Schaie and Willis 1991).

An example of research in this area is a study by Laursen (1997) involving 711 participants from four cohorts born in 1922, 1932, 1942 and 1952 and followed up over 11 years between 1982–3 and 1993–4. Laursen carried out a variety of tests of cognitive functioning and found, amongst other things, a decline in:

- *non-verbal* learning and memory
- *retention* of verbal memory
- concentration and reaction time which could underpin performance on other tests.

Further analysis of the data led Laursen to the general conclusion that such abilities become more scattered with age such that there is more variability in older generations than in younger ones. However, this study also underlines the problems inherent in such research and it is important to take these into account when interpreting the findings. For example, Laursen began with over 1,000 participants, but lost over 300. The greatest loss of participants (attrition) was found amongst those with only primary schooling and low social status and amongst the oldest participants. Other factors contributing to attrition concerned health status and occupational activity. The sample that remained, although large, was inevitably self-selected. In addition, Laursen found that there were specific generation effects in the sample that complicated comparison across groups. Both of these factors could account for the apparent increase in variability of participants' abilities.

Finally, a study by Levy and Langer (1994) provides an interesting twist on the issue of ageing and cognition. In their study they found that a person's attitudes towards ageing can actually affect how well they perform on specific cognitive tasks (see *In Focus*).

Coping with bereavement

For Erikson, the final life crisis of 'integrity vs despair' is at least partly triggered by anticipation of one's own death. Although death can occur at any age, it is, perhaps, more in our thoughts as we grow older and as our peers begin to die. The loss we feel is thus on two fronts: for ourselves and for others.

Elizabeth Kübler-Ross' (1969) pioneering work into how people who are terminally ill and those who are dying cope with impending death has helped considerably in enabling us to understand and support both the person who is dying and their bereaved relatives. Her clinical interviews led to a well-known stage theory of dying, although she warns against thinking of these stages as universal or invariant in order. She recommends that the defences of the dying person are not undermined and that no attempt should be made to 'push' the dying person to Stage 5. A sense of control for the individual is central. Weisman (1972) argues that the person should be helped towards an 'appropriate death' that fulfils their expectations and ideals so that they can 'die well'. In cases where death can be anticipated, Fulton (1970) described four stages of grieving in the person facing bereavement. Murray-Parkes (1972) then described stages of coping with the death of someone close. The various stages suggested by Kübler-Ross, Fulton and Murray-Parkes are shown in Table 12.10 on p. 322.

Stereotypes of old age and memory function

The stereotype that intellectual capacities decline with age may be, at least partly, in the mind. Levy and Langer (1994) investigated the impact of negative stereotypes about ageing on memory. Their participants were drawn from three groups:

- hearing American adults
- Americans with profound hearing disability
- Chinese adults.

They further subdivided the groups into younger (15- to 30-year-old) and older (59- to 91-year-old) participants. They reasoned that hearing disabled Americans would be insulated from dominant cultural messages about ageing and that the Chinese participants would also be protected from negative stereotypes as a result of the veneration enjoyed by elderly Chinese people. They measured participants' memory on a series of tests. They also recorded participants' stereotypical views about the elderly.

They found that the Chinese and hearing-disabled Americans had more positive stereotypes about the elderly. In addition, elderly participants (but not the young ones) in these two groups out-performed the elderly hearing American group on the memory tasks. Also, the correlation between performance and attitude in the elderly was positive while in younger participants it was negative. Findings such as these point to the role of psychological factors, as well as age-associated physiological ones, in determining cognitive ability.

Table 12.10 Stages of coping with dying, facing bereavement and dealing with bereavement

Stages of dying (Kübler-Ross 1969)

Denial	The person resists facing death and may seek other professional opinions or reassurance from religion.
Anger	The person asks 'Why me?' and may feel hostile, resentful and envious of others. There may also be a strong feeling of frustration over unfinished business.
Bargaining	When 'Why me?' is not answered, bargains may be struck with God or fate. Many bargains will be made and broken.
Depression	Denial becomes impossible. Hospitalization may be necessary. There may be physical deterioration and a great sense of loss as well as guilt and worry about letting others down.
Acceptance	In this 'final rest before the long journey', the dying person may feel devoid of feelings, weak and resolute, although not happy.

Stages of grieving in the person facing bereavement (Fulton 1970)

Depression	Accompanied by extreme upset and anticipatory grief.
Heightened concern	For the ill person, accompanied by the need to deal with unfinished business and discuss things with the dying person. Caring well for them at this point can help to obviate guilt when the person dies.
Rehearsals for the death	Developing coping strategies.
Adjustment to the consequences	New coping strategies along with those developed at stage three can help here.

Stages of grieving after the death has occurred (Murray-Parkes 1972)

Initial response	Shock, disbelief, extreme sorrow, numbness, coldness and emptiness.
Coping	Anxiety and fear about breaking down completely. The person may turn to tranquillizers, sleeping pills or alcohol, and may show a number of physical and psychological symptoms. These will become more sporadic in the first year or so.
Intermediate phase	Characterized by obsessional reviews ('I could have done more'), trying to explain the loss ('It was God's will') and searching for the presence of the deceased through reminiscing and revisiting certain places.
Recovery phase	In about the second year, a more positive attitude may develop, even pride at having survived the crisis and grown through it.

Mourning rituals and support

Mourning rituals seem to fulfil two major functions – to allow us to draw on social support and to allow time for healing. The social function enables us to develop or reaffirm networks with others and to share feelings about the person who has died. It allows us to express emotions in a supportive atmosphere and acknowledge the reality of the loss. It also allows others to affirm the new status of the bereaved person. It seems the degree of social change demanded by this new status is a crucial factor. Berk (1998), for example, proposes that widows who had previously had their own roles, independent of their husbands, felt least disruption to their life style. In fact, recent research by Lindstrøm (1999) in Norway found that women who had adopted a modern feminine gender role coped better with the loss of a spouse than women who had adopted a traditional role.

One social group that might fulfil support functions is the 'convoy' (Kahn and Antonucci 1980). This consists of friends, family and others who accompany us through life providing emotional and practical aid. Evidence suggests that those with a complete convoy that meets their needs cope with bereavement more effectively, but those who lack a convoy are more prone to illness, emotional disturbance and death following bereavement. Indeed, bereaved members of close-knit communities, with accessible family networks, seem to fare better than their counterparts in less supportive circumstances. Littlewood (1992) suggests that close community ties were one reason why residents of Aberfan (where so many children and adults tragically lost their lives when a coal-tip engulfed their school and neighbouring buildings in 1963) were able to cope with relatively little outside help.

The healing power of time is widely recognized and different mourning rituals seem to have evolved to fit the needs of particular cultures. All the major religions have rituals which give death meaning and 'shape' the process of mourning. Orthodox Jews, for example, have highly structured rituals and phases of mourning traditionally lasting for one year. These are thought to be amongst the healthiest and most supportive forms of mourning in existence. Their customs seem to fit the proposed stages particularly well, suggesting that mourning rituals may have evolved quite naturally to give the right kind of support at the right time. Contrast this with the indigenous American Maya Indians whose mourning period is limited to just four days!

Life styles around the world differ enormously, so the form of mourning is, to a large extent, shaped by practicalities. Where day-to-day survival is not assured, and death from natural causes is commonplace, a period of non-productivity is a luxury and swift return to everyday life is essential. In the wealthier Western world where survival is more assured, we can take time over mourning. Medical advances also mean that most of us can hope to live long and healthy lives and to die of old age. Untimely death from disease, or other conditions, now tends to be seen as a theoretically avoidable defeat for medical science and, therefore, a reason for much personal anguish.

Stroebe and Stroebe (1987) are convinced that, whatever form they take, 'following culturally prescribed rituals aids recovery from bereavement' (p. 51). Unfortunately, it seems that increasingly secularized Western cultures in particular lack clear guidelines about mourning and so seem to be at the greatest loss about how to deal with a person who is bereaved. It is here, perhaps, that a better understanding of the functions of mourning could help. To end your work on this section, try Activity 7 on p. 324.

Exam summary: Cognitive changes in late adulthood

The AQA examination will test your understanding of the following areas:

◆ explanations of adjustment to old age (pp. 318–19)

◆ effects of retirement (pp. 319–20)

◆ cognitive changes (pp. 320–1)

◆ coping with bereavement (pp. 321–3)

◆ cultural differences in coping with bereavement (pp. 322–3).

Mourning rituals across cultures

in focus

Within cultures, differing religious beliefs and ideas about the afterlife also affect the pattern of mourning. A striking contrast in recent times is provided by the Muslim and Church of England ceremonies following the deaths of Dodi Al Fayed and Princess Diana in 1997. Dodi's faith dictated that the funeral should take place within 24 hours of his death. Diana's was a much lengthier affair.

The Hopi Indians of Arizona fear and dislike the dead. They do their best, through ritual, to break the bonds between the living and the dead. Funerals are short and perfunctory and, afterwards, the bereaved work hard to forget. For the Kota of southern India, expressions of grief are more protracted. Shortly after death, a 'green' funeral is held while the loss is still 'fresh'. This is followed by a 'dry' funeral, which takes place at annual intervals, lasts for 11 days and includes remembrance of others who have died in the previous year. Further expressions of grief are encouraged as various rituals are enacted but, at the end of this phase, the sombre mood ends abruptly to be replaced by an atmosphere of celebration. There are more rituals (including sexual intercourse for the widowed, preferably with a sibling of the dead person), all intended to return the bereaved to normal life.

In Japanese Shintoism and in Buddhism, the dead become ancestors. Small shrines, or altars, in Japanese homes allow continued contact with ancestors and provide a place where food, drink and treats can be left for them. Christians also believe in the afterlife and see no harm in commemorating the dead in various ways. Some people believe that dying is simply a point in the continuous cycle of life and death that affects all living organisms and that the dead should not be embalmed but simply returned to the earth in biodegradable coffins thus causing as little contamination as possible.

Activity 7: Highs and lows of life

Ask a few people of very different ages to identify the three major highs and three major lows of their lives to date. Deliberately leave the question open ended. Ask them to mark on the diagram given here the extent to which they saw each event as positive or negative and how much change was involved.

◆ Do people mention the kinds of life event listed in the SRRS (see Table 12.5 on p. 312)?

◆ Do the positions of these events on the diagram correspond to the ranking of events on the SRRS?

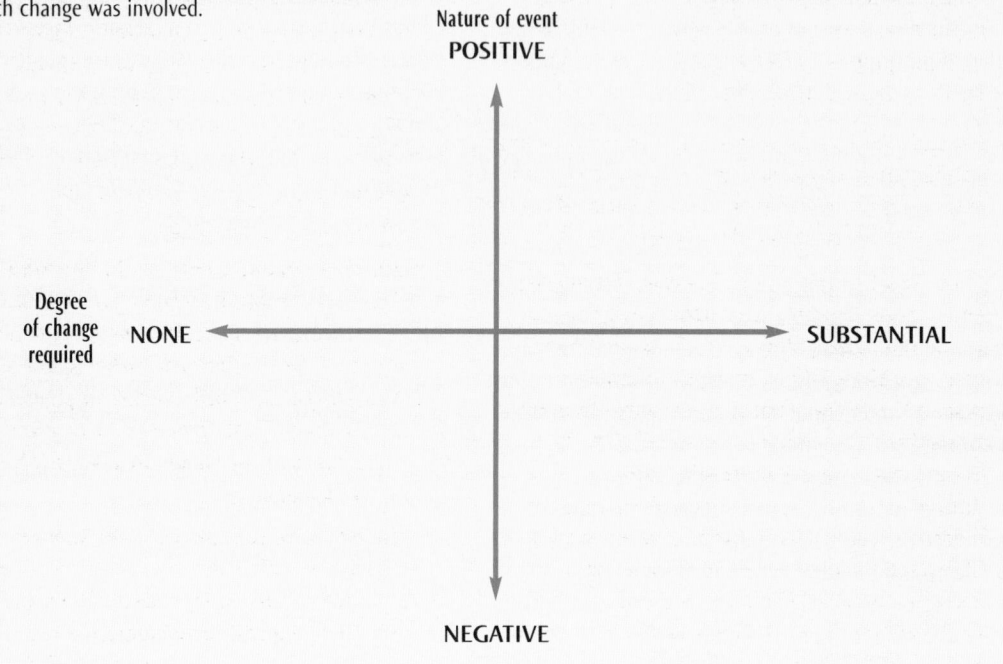

Example question

The question below is typical of one drawn from the material above, and should take you 30 minutes to answer.

◆ Discuss the impact of either retirement or bereavement in late adulthood.   *(24 marks)*

Suggested answer structure

This question gives you the choice of discussing the impact of one of these life events in late adulthood. You should not try to cover both of these, as only one would count towards the mark you would receive. Retirement (pp. 319–20) is an increasingly nebulous concept – it seems to be a generally positive experience if entered into willingly. The impact of this is mediated by a number of variables. Bereavement (pp. 321–3) is probably the most traumatic life event of all. Individual and cultural differences are important in how, and how well, people cope.

The AO1 content for the impact of retirement is well covered in this section. This might include a description of Atchley's five periods of adjustment to retirement (honeymoon, rest and relaxation, disenchantment,

reorientation and routine) which many, if not all people experience to varying degrees (p. 319). Also relevant in this context is Gee and Baillie's cross-cultural study of retirement in Britain and Australia, which found that most people perceived retirement optimistically as a 'new beginning'. The AO2 component might be approached by considering whether these findings are universal. Schaie and Willis suggest that although most people adjust well to retirement, other factors tend to determine how successful and satisfying this transition really is (pp. 319–20).

The AO1 content for the impact of bereavement is also well covered in this section. This might include a description of the stages of dying (Kübler-Ross), the stages of grieving in the person facing bereavement (Fulton) and the stages of grieving after death has occurred (Murray-Parkes). These are summarized in Table 12.10 on p. 322. Also relevant is the role of mourning rituals and support (pp. 322–3). These allow people to draw upon social support and also give time for healing. The AO2 component might include an examination of the research support for these claims. For example, evidence suggests that those with a complete 'convoy' (social support) that meets their needs cope with bereavement more effectively than those who lack a convoy (p. 322). Alternatively, you might assess the extent of cultural differences in mourning rituals (*In Focus*, p. 323). This demonstrates that the process of death and mourning might have quite different significance in different cultures.

Chapter summary

◆ Psychologists have taken a variety of approaches to studying the relatively neglected area of lifespan psychology with some producing overarching theories, while others focus on particular stages of life or on specific life events.

◆ The study of the lifespan is dogged by methodological difficulties, especially those concerning cohort effects and the inherent problems associated with cross-sectional or longitudinal research.

◆ **Theories of development in early and middle adulthood** proposed by **Erikson**, **Levinson** and **Gould** offer different views of the nature of these phases of life. All three theories are built on **research evidence** that suggests that important **transitions** occur during adulthood. They also acknowledge the **existence of crises in adulthood**, which require that adjustments are made, but which vary in the relative emphasis placed upon these. Some critics argue that adulthood is no more critical than any other life phase, while others question whether 'crisis' is an artefact created by cohort effects.

◆ The impact of the three life events of **marriage (or partnering)**, **parenthood** and **divorce** are commonly experienced during early and middle adulthood. There are gender and cultural differences in the nature and **effects of such events on the individual** although all seem to require considerable adjustment. The timing of these life events within the lifespan and their co-occurrence with other events are additional factors that can affect their impact.

◆ **Explanations of adjustment to old age** offer differing views about the social forces operating in the later phases of life. Some individuals seem to disengage (**social disengagement theory**), while others prefer to remain active. Selectivity theory suggests that as we grow older we simply become more particular about who and what we choose to engage or disengage with (health and circumstances permitting).

◆ Studies of **cognitive changes in late adulthood** yield mixed results depending on the type of ability being measured. In some cases there appears to be a decline associated with age, but these can be explained in many ways, including neurophysiological degeneration, changes in strategies, or even changes in a person's beliefs about their abilities.

◆ **The effects of retirement** are becoming increasingly nebulous as more and more people retire early and/or keep aspects of their working life going. **Coping with bereavement** is regarded as one of the most distressing life events of all. Although some of the immediate emotional reactions seem to be universal, there are **cultural differences** in patterns of coping which seem to serve the same basic purpose of allowing grief to take its course and to activate social support systems.

◆ **Kübler-Ross's** pioneering work into how people who are terminally ill or dying cope with their impending death has helped in understanding and supporting both the person who is dying and their bereaved relatives.

Further resources

Bee, H. (1998) *Lifespan Development* (2nd edn), New York: Longman.

A very readable survey of psychological development from birth to death.

Berk, L.E. (1998) *Development through the Lifespan*, London: Allyn & Bacon.

An interactive text covering lifespan development and which features case studies of real people and much useful information on cultural issues.

Durkin, K. (1995) *Developmental Social Psychology*, Oxford: Blackwell.

An excellent, detailed, general text focusing on lifespan developmental psychology.

Website

www.nlm.nih.gov/medlineplus/bereavement.html

An intresting collection of resources on the topic of bereavement in both adults and children.

Part 5: Comparative Psychology

A2

DETERMINANTS OF ANIMAL
BEHAVIOUR

Mike Cardwell

ANIMAL COGNITION

Mike Cardwell

EVOLUTIONARY EXPLANATIONS
OF HUMAN BEHAVIOUR

John Cartwright

Chapter 13

Determinants of animal behaviour

Mike Cardwell

Preview

In this chapter we shall be looking at:

◆ evolutionary explanations for the behaviour of animals, including biological explanations for apparent altruism

◆ classical and operant conditioning and their role in the behaviour of nonhuman animals

◆ explanations and research studies relating to social learning in nonhuman animals, including evidence for intelligence in nonhuman animals.

Introduction

It is useful to make clear right from the start that the question of whether learning or evolution underlie any given behaviour is meaningless. Any behaviour, however simple or complex, has both an element of inheritance and learning about it. The only point of debate is over the relative importance of the contributions made to a behaviour by phylogeny and ontogeny.

The term *phylogeny* refers to the inheritance of species-specific behaviour patterns, e.g. the arching of a cat's back when it is threatened. *Ontogeny* refers to behaviour which has been acquired during the lifetime of the individual and is not shared with every member of the species. For instance, some cats learn how to open doors by pulling downwards on the handle. Similarly, some blue tits learn how to tear into the caps of milk bottles left on the doorstep. Whenever a behaviour is seen in all members of a species the strength of inheritance is clear. However, the occurrence of a behaviour in just one or two individuals does not necessarily mean it is '100 per cent learned'. This is because some forms of behaviour are only slight modifications of natural forms. For instance, the opening of the milk-bottle top by blue tits involves similar actions to those they undertake when stripping the bark from trees to reach insects underneath. The influence of inheritance in this case is still very strong, and the actions an animal may perform associated with a particular aim, such as to obtain food, are often composed of variations on a theme. As we shall see, disentangling the contribution of nature and nurture with respect to animal behaviour is not as straightforward as we might like to think.

Evolutionary explanations of animal behaviour

'I have called this principle, by which each slight variation, if useful, is preserved, by the term Natural Selection.' (Charles Darwin, 1859, *The Origin of Species*)

Darwin's theory of evolution has four main parts:

◆ Organisms have changed over time. Those living today are different from those that have lived in the past. The world is not constant, but changing, and organisms must constantly adapt to these changes.

◆ All organisms are derived from common ancestors. Over time, populations split into different species which are related because of this common ancestry. This explains the similarities of organisms that are classified together – they are similar because of shared traits inherited from their common ancestors.

◆ Change is gradual and slow, taking place over a long time (this is now contested by the view that evolution takes place through a process of rapid change and long periods of stability (stasis), known as *punctuated equilibrium*.)

◆ The mechanism by which this change takes place is known as *natural selection*, a process that occurs over successive generations.

Darwin's theory of the process of evolution was as much shaped by his observations of the selective breeding of domesticated animals as it was by his field studies of natural selection. Species of horse, cattle, dogs and other household pets have been bred to accentuate certain of their features which humans either exploit or else find aesthetically pleasing. For instance, horses bred for racing are lighter, leaner and weaker than those bred for farm work. Working horses are tougher, stronger, have more stamina and are less 'temperamental' than those bred to win races. You may own a dog or cat yourself (whether a pedigree or not) which has features that are the result of hundreds of generations of selective breeding. These features may be physical (such as long ears, thick coat, large eyes or drooping jaw) or behavioural (such as running ability, a placid or aggressive temperament, or tracking, hunting or retrieving ability). These diverse breeds possess such qualities as a result of humans systematically mating females with males over many generations in order to produce the most exaggerated forms of the required characteristics. The different breeds become genetically altered from the original, and this is the basis of the 'purity' (i.e. pedigree), of each breed.

Darwin himself became an avid breeder of pigeons so as to study the process by which this type of selection is achieved. His opinion was that the means by which evolution works in bringing about changes in appearance and behaviour of species is similar to the selective breeding of animals which he witnessed at first hand. The pressures on animals that happen in a natural environment bring about adaptations, i.e. those individuals having the best means of overcoming an extreme circumstance such as climatic change, floods, predation, competition for scarce resources, and so on, are those more likely to survive.

Natural selection

The logic behind the process of natural selection is as follows (see Fig. 13.1):

1 All organisms are capable of 'over-reproducing'. If all the offspring that organisms were able to produce were to survive and reproduce, they would very quickly overpopulate the planet.

2 As a consequence, there is a 'struggle' to survive and reproduce, in which only a proportion of individuals succeed in leaving progeny (offspring).

3 Organisms show variation in characteristics that influence their success in this struggle for existence.

4 Offspring tend to resemble their parents, particularly in terms of those characteristics that influence success in the struggle to survive and reproduce.

5 Organisms that possess certain traits that enable them to survive and reproduce will contribute disproportionately to the offspring that make up the next generation.

6 Because offspring resemble their parents, the population in the next generation will contain a higher proportion of individuals that possess whatever adaptation enabled their parents to survive and reproduce.

Natural selection will only occur if there is some heritable variation for the trait in question, and if there is differential survival and reproduction associated with the possession of that trait. For example, some individuals are faster than others because of differences in their genes. If their predators, however, were that very much faster, then speed differences in the prey

Figure 13.1 Components of natural selection

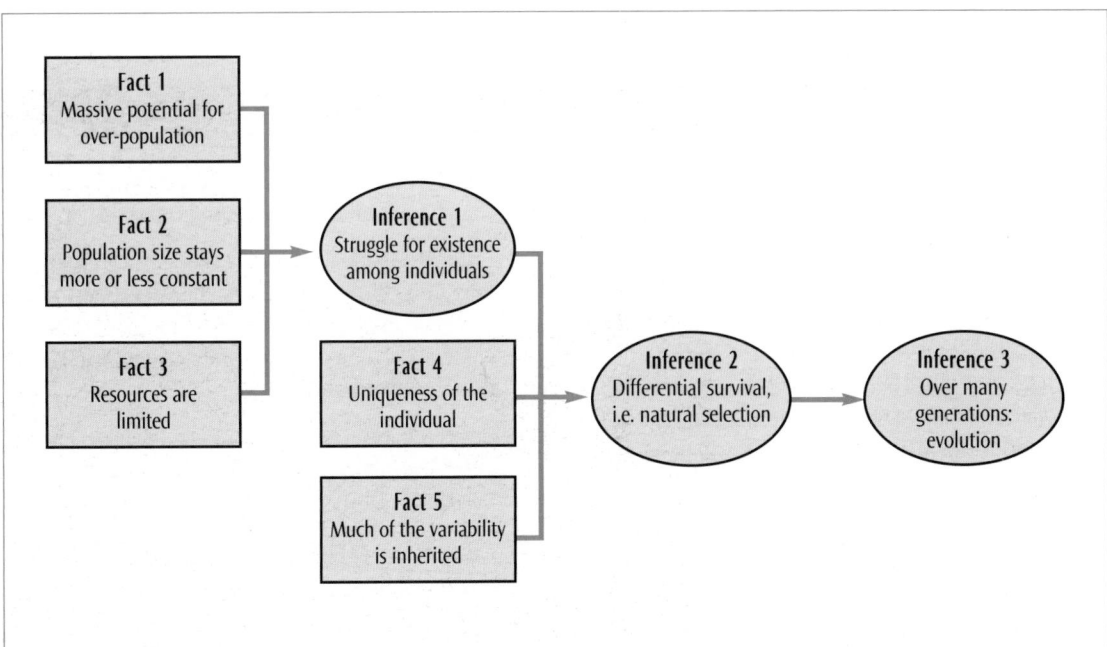

species would make little difference to their survival and so evolution of that trait would not take place (e.g. if cheetahs hunted snails). Natural selection can only occur among existing variations in a population. It may well be profitable for polar bears to have white noses, but as the genes for white noses do not exist in the existing population of polar bears, this development cannot happen. Variants do not arise because they are needed. They arise by random processes that are governed by the laws of genetics.

Survival of the fittest

The idea that evolution is a process of selecting out the weakest and least competitive animals, often referred to as 'the survival of the fittest', is usually thought to be all that Darwin had to say. This basic misunderstanding is quite common even today. In fact, the very expression 'survival of the fittest' was not even written by Darwin himself, but by a political economist called Herbert Spencer, when advocating the 'naturalness' of market-place economics. Darwin regarded physical endurance as only one quality that animals must show in their struggle to survive.

In Darwin's theory, *fitness* is not a quality that individuals possess, such as muscular physique, physical durability or a state of good health. Bodily strength and physical fitness themselves do not guarantee the survival of individuals in an evolutionary sense, however useful these qualities may be in competition with other conspecifics (members of the same species) for scarce resources. In terms of evolution, fitness is linked with *reproductive success*. It is individuals who leave the most surviving offspring who have the greatest chance of evolutionary success. Darwin took for granted that differential reproductive success was at the centre of the process of evolution. In addition to differences in the relative success of individuals to reproduce is the fitness and survival prospects of their progeny (generally referred to as *fecundity*). Now do Activity 1.

Evaluation of evolutionary explanations of animal behaviour

Darwin was very aware that his theory of evolution was in many respects contradicted by observable fact. The problems with the 1859 version of this theory were twofold:

◆ Despite the emphasis on selfishness as the basis of evolutionary success, *apparent altruism* is commonly seen in animal societies.

Activity 1: Adam and Eve

At the start, a couple (let's call them Adam and Eve) have just three children. When these children grow, they in turn will each have three children, as will their own (nine) children, and so on into the future. Remember, a couple having three children are only adding to the population by one surplus individual. For the purpose of this calculation, assume that the only reason for death is old age. Therefore, each child in one generation becomes a parent in the next, followed by becoming a grandparent in the next. Each generation will therefore consist of children, parents and grandparents. We shall fix the point of natural death at the age of grandparents, so in no generation will great-grandparents be alive. The task is to calculate how many direct descendants from Adam and Eve there will be alive after 12 generations. (Assuming there to be three generations per century, this time-scale will be approximately 300 years.) Carry out your own calculations on this problem before referring to Fig. 13.2 on p. 332.

◆ There are examples of animal behaviour and *morphology* (body structure and physiology) which seem to confer no advantage upon the individual. The most often cited instance of this is the tail of the peacock. Peacocks have such long tails (or, more accurately, trains) that their flight and general mobility is impaired. Even more serious is the observation that predators are more able to catch them by grabbing at these long feathers. In this case, what seems to be a *sub-optimal* evolutionary strategy is seen to become *predominant*.

Indian peacock (*Pavo cristatus*)

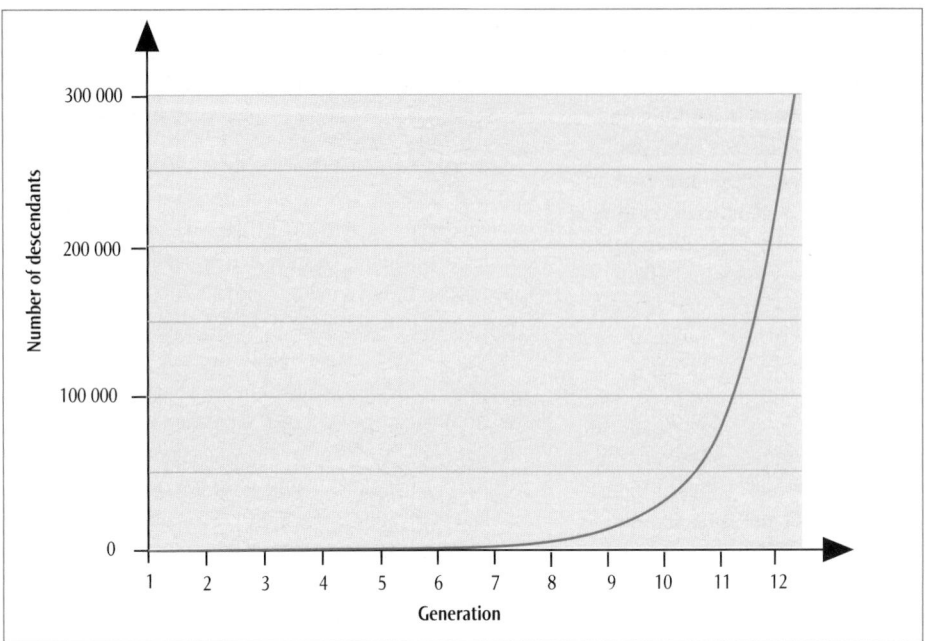

Figure 13.2
Number of descendants of Adam and Eve after 300 years

Evolutionary theory has now solved the riddles posed by these two problems. Regarding the first of these, Darwin himself saw no solution and it perplexed him for the rest of his days. The behaviour of social insects, where individuals behave suicidally by attacking aggressive and larger intruders to the nest or hive, seemed inexplicable in terms of *natural selection*. Individuals who pay any cost (calculated in terms of reducing their reproductive potential) for the benefit of others should receive such a heavy penalty in evolutionary terms that such behaviour would be strongly selected against. This would ultimately lead to extinction, i.e. there would be no descendants left of individuals who acted in this way. Compare this with others acting selfishly. They would pay no costs, obtain most benefits, and thereby gain more reproductive potential. In short, selfishness should outrun altruism in no time at all in the evolutionary race.

Even more problematic for Darwin's (1859) version of the theory is that there are castes in social insect societies which forego reproductive effort altogether – these individuals (such as worker honey bees) spend their entire lives in caring for the brood of others, usually the single queen of the colony. Such examples of ultimate self-sacrifice were neither understood nor seemingly explicable until a century later, as we shall see.

The second problem outlined above, that of how structures such as the peacock's train could evolve, was more or less successfully tackled by Darwin (1871) in his book entitled *The Descent of Man, and Selection in Relation to Sex*. Briefly, a feature will evolve by sexual selection if one sex is attracted to individuals of the opposite sex who possess this feature. In this case, the feature will serve to facilitate the mating prospects of its bearer. The exact reason why such a preference exists when choosing a mate did not seem to matter very much, since it was evident to naturalists of Darwin's day that mates were selected on a nonrandom (or 'assortative') basis, i.e. some are more *attractive* than others. It could simply be that some features are aesthetically more pleasing, in the same way for animals as for humans. Therefore, despite being a physical burden to its owner, a large and spectacular train enables the peacock to be selected by the peahen as her mate. Consequently, those males with the larger and more

Worker honey bees (*Apis mellifera*) overseeing the brood chambers

gorgeous trains will have greater mating success, leaving greater numbers of descendants who are also endowed with large, attractive trains.

The tendency to choose males with such features will endure in subsequent generations as males are faced with ongoing competition for larger and grander trains. The peahens in their turn continue to accept or reject suitors on the basis of these sexually attractive features. As long as the females continue to find long-tailed males as most attractive, evolution will ensure that tail length (or any other sexually selected feature) will prevail. The basis of so-called *sexual selection* is discussed in detail in Chapter 15.

Darwin's difficulties resolved

The difficulties arising from these elements of Darwin's theory of evolution were not fully resolved until many decades after his death in 1882. Part of the problem in resolving them was the then lack of knowledge about mechanisms of inheritance, i.e. genetics. Among Darwin's misconceptions was the idea that characteristics were passed between generations by a process of blending, i.e. if a dark-coated female mates with a light-coated male then their offspring will have a coat of intermediate shade. Second, and perhaps crucially, Darwin's reasoning was occurring at the wrong 'level', i.e. he believed that individuals live to reproduce. It is more accurate to consider evolution in terms of the transmission of life's units (i.e. genes) from one generation to the next. Darwin's 'insuperable problem' of the caste system of social insects can be explained in this way. Among these social insects the high degree of genetic relatedness among sisters means that it is more productive (in terms of increased fitness) for them to help each other than it would be to have their own offspring.

Challenging the theory of evolution

We should, perhaps clarify what we mean by a 'theory'. The term is used in science to describe 'A collection of inter-related general principles that is put forward as an explanation of a set of known facts and empirical findings' (Reber 1995). Dismissing the theory of evolution as 'simply a theory' rests on a confusion over what is a theory in the scientific sense and what is a 'theory' in the more popular use of the term. In this latter context, the term appears to refer to 'any reasonable set of ideas or principles that are deemed dismissible or suspect' (Reber 1995). Being a scientific theory implies self-consistency, agreement with observations and usefulness. Lack of proof isn't a weakness, either. The more evidence we have for something, the more certainty we assign to it. When we have enough evidence about something, we call it a fact but nothing in the scientific world has ever been proved beyond all doubt. Evolution is supported by a good deal of observational evidence, in the fields of genetics, animal behaviour, palaeontology, and so on. In challenging the *theory* of evolution, it is necessary to address that evidence.

Biological explanations for apparent altruism

In the previous section, we looked at how Darwin was puzzled by the prevalence of apparently altruistic behaviour in the animal world. The point is that in any given circumstance an animal ought (i.e. 'ought' in terms of increasing its fitness, or reproductive success) to behave selfishly. The reason for this is that altruism, in comparison with a strategy that is selfish, would be less successful and therefore would not evolve in competition with nonaltruism.

However, Darwin's paradox was resolved by the work of Hamilton (1963, 1964) who showed in his *Kin selection theory* that evolution does not operate directly on individual organisms but upon their genetic make-up. In other words, any one individual may pass on genes to future generations not just by means of their own reproductive success but also by facilitating the reproductive potential of their relatives (who, by definition, share some genetic material). In theory, the closer this genetic relationship is then the greater the cooperation and altruism each should show towards the other. Hamilton coined the term 'inclusive fitness' to describe the effect of genetic relatedness in determining how individuals would behave altruistically towards one another.

For instance, Sherman (1981) showed that in Belding's ground squirrel the females who are close relatives (such as mother–daughter or sister–sister) do not fight over burrow sites or over the use of resources within a territory, though their behaviour towards other, unrelated females was highly aggressive. The related females not only show little antagonism to one another but often actively help each other in defending their young from attack by predators or intruders. Related females were seen to give alarm calls at the sight of a predator to warn one another, a behaviour observed only when they were in one another's company; they remained silent at other times.

Altruism can be defined as an act of helping which increases the (reproductive) fitness of the individual who is helped, at some cost to the fitness of the helper. The *cost* of helping is essential to this definition, to understanding both what is being contributed by the helper as well as what is the important gain made by being helped. In both cases, the essential cost and benefit is fitness, which is a measure of reproductive success, i.e. the total contribution made to the gene pool by an individual, including their own offspring and those succoured by all those individuals to whom they are genetically related. Helping a close relative or one of their offspring can therefore be considered to be an example of a selfish commitment to maximizing this inclusive fitness. But altruism is not confined to acts of helping between related individuals. Before reading any further, look at Activity 2.

Activity 2: Apparent altruism in animals

Consider the following examples of apparent altruism in animals. What reasons can you suggest explaining why these apparently altruistic behaviours occur? After you have done this, return to the chapter and compare your ideas with the explanations given there.

◆ A lamb becomes alarmed by the sight of a dog and rushes to its mother who allows it to suckle.

◆ A juvenile male chimpanzee wrestles with a larger male but their play turns more aggressive. A second young male intervenes, and both chase off the larger male.

◆ A grouper fish remains motionless with its mouth agape while a tiny fish swims in and out of its mouth collecting morsels of food from inside.

◆ An ant returning to its nest having fed encounters a beetle larva near the entrance. The larva prods at the ant's mouth parts, and receives a meal of regurgitated food.

According to the definition given above, each of the behaviours listed in Activity 2 qualifies as altruism, though the costs and benefits to helper and helped are not the same throughout. Let us examine them one by one.

Kin recognition and selection

It might seem 'natural' for a parent to care for its young by providing food and protection. Clearly, there are common interests between two related individuals, and in this case, the mother will usually place herself between the dog and her lamb. The lamb's alarm response of suckling enables her to achieve this. But the lamb is also allowed to suckle from the mother even without the dog being there, and this is also altruistic since it is costly by depleting her own food reserves. Though the lamb may be at a stage when it can graze successfully for itself the mother still does not reject its suckling, and especially when the lamb is in a state of alarm, such as caused by seeing the dog. However, any lamb straying away from its mother will obtain no help from other mothers in the same field. However hard the lamb may try, other mothers will only offer protection and

milk to their own lambs. They recognize their own offspring by a combination of sound and body smell.

Clearly, then, this form of altruism is based upon kinship, i.e. individuals act favourably towards others to whom they are related. But, without a language to express relationship, how could an animal 'know' they are related to another. The exact way in which animals come to favour relatives over nonrelatives has raised some controversy (Grafen 1982,1990), but there are a number of mechanisms by which this could occur (Stuart 1991). To give just two examples:

◆ spatial proximity (family groups tend to stay together)

◆ phenotype matching (related individuals have certain characteristics such as smell, appearance or behaviour in common).

In gregarious species which spend time with nonrelatives (such as in the case of lambs playing together), kin recognition becomes important. For instance, ground-nesting birds usually recognize their own eggs soon after laying them, whereas tree-nesters are unable to do so (and this makes such species more prone to *brood parasitism*, as we shall see later). In species where the young have a period of dependency (often referred to as 'infancy') the parents and young often form early 'bonds', in which each learns to recognize the other by some salient feature, such as odour or visual cue. This 'natural' mechanism is often exploited by farmers when a sheep in their flock dies giving birth. The farmer brings the surviving lamb to a sheep who has herself just lambed. In the minutes after giving birth herself, the foster mother is allowed to sniff and lick the second lamb as if it were her own. After a few minutes together they will act as mother and offspring for life.

Evaluation of kin selection explanations of apparent altruism

Evidence for the importance of phenotype matching in kin selection comes from studies of Belding's ground squirrels. Because females may mate with more than one male, litters may contain both full siblings and half siblings. It is possible for researchers to ascertain who is who by DNA 'fingerprinting', and this can be matched to the pattern of altruism shown by the offspring. Females raised with full and half sisters consistently show more altruistic behaviour (e.g. defence against predators and in territorial disputes) towards their full sisters than their half sisters (Holmes and Sherman 1982).

Studies of mate choice in different strains of inbred mice have supported the claim that genetically similar individuals share distinctive odours that serve both to elicit altruistic behaviour, and also prevent inbreeding. These strains differ primarily in a group of genes called the *Major Histocompatibility Complex (MHC)*. These genes are responsible for the recognition of tissue as 'self' or 'not self'. The MHC differs in otherwise genetically identical mice. Male mice prefer to mate with females of a different MHC to themselves, and this ability is based on the ability to discriminate female odours (Boyse *et al.* 1991).

There are a number of reasons why it is important for an individual to respond differently to kin and non-kin:

◆ Parents who fails to recognize their own offspring would waste resources on another's young. This does sometimes occur in what is known as 'brood parasitism', discussed shortly.

◆ If the young are to be protected by the parent they will need to recognize one another quickly so that help can be provided.

◆ Related individuals who collaborate are more likely to fend off aggression from others who are nonrelatives.

◆ At the time of reaching sexual maturity, it is important that individuals avoid mating with relatives to ensure diversity of genetic material occurs between generations. In addition to this reason, inbreeding itself is believed to have disadvantages which would affect the fitness of offspring.

This raises the question of whether the *exact* relatedness between individuals matters in this argument: that is, does it matter whether an individual is helping a sister or a cousin? The answer is that it does indeed matter. In addition to the above, helping a distant relative has much less benefit, in terms of inclusive fitness, than does helping a sibling (brother or sister). Remember that any measure of relatedness is also an inverse measure of *unrelatedness*. For instance, stating that you share half your genes with one parent means that half of the genes are not shared, i.e. are unrelated. With a distant relative the majority of your genes are not common to you both. In fact, relationships more distant than siblings means you have much more unshared than shared genetic material.

Reciprocal altruism

This particular explanation for apparently altruistic behaviour was proposed by Trivers (1971). Trivers argued that one animal might show altruistic behaviour towards another if the recipient of this favour reciprocated some time in the future. In a sense then, this involves a 'loan' that will be repaid on some future occasion. In Activity 2, the behaviour of the second young chimp could be explained in this

way. Who knows when he may need a similar favour? Such reciprocating arrangements are not unusual in the animal kingdom. For instance, Wilkinson (1984) found that unrelated vampire bats regurgitate food for one another on their return to the nesting site. While in many instances the recipient of the meal was a relative of the altruist, often they were not. However, the unrelated animals were usually roosting neighbours of the altruist, and Wilkinson went on to show experimentally that the exchanges taking place between unrelated individuals were reciprocated, i.e. they had built up a relationship based upon mutual exchanges of favour. Theoretically, in such a social climate, a cheating strategy (i.e. take the favour but don't return it) would gain more than an honest one. But within the community of vampire bats the cost of being denied a meal having once cheated is very high, since on cold nights an individual going hungry rarely survives.

Trivers was aware of the possibilities of cheating in such arrangements and suggested that reciprocal altruism would only evolve in species where individuals could recognize each other, and apply sanctions to those who refused to reciprocate. But if cheating is so potentially profitable for an individual, why is it not more common? To solve this problem, Axelrod and Hamilton (1981) turned to game theory analysis (see *In Focus,* 'The prisoner's dilemma' on p. 336).

As a result of the analysis of the strategies used in games such as the prisoner's dilemma, Axelrod and Hamilton put forward a beguilingly simple strategy that would reward cooperation and discourage defection. The strategy, tit for tat, called for one animal to cooperate with another (in this discussion, to display altruistic behaviour to another) who would then return the favour. If one party simply returns whatever happened in the previous interaction between the two animals, cooperation would be met with cooperation, defection with return defection. In this way, a cooperative alliance could be formed between two animals that would jointly benefit both. This simple explanation of how cheating is controlled in reciprocal altruism has two major advantages. First, it is retaliatory. Potential defection is discouraged because it would be met with mutual defection and the defecting animal would lose the long-term benefits of cooperation. Second, it is conciliatory, in that animals do not miss out on the future benefits of cooperation by holding a grudge against an animal that had once defected.

Evaluation of reciprocal altruism explanations

The example of the vampire bats quoted earlier would fit nicely into this model of reciprocal altruism for the following reasons (Manning and Dawkins 1998).

The prisoner's dilemma

Two suspects are arrested by the police and held in separate cells where they cannot communicate with each other. Each is told by the interviewing officer that they only have a weak case against him, and that this would result in only a short prison sentence. However, each is encouraged to inform on the other, with the result that the other prisoner would be given a long prison sentence and the informer would be set free. If, however, both inform on each other, they would both be sent to prison for a moderate sentence. The rewards and costs of each alternative (expressed as a numerical value) for Prisoner A are shown in Fig. 13.3.

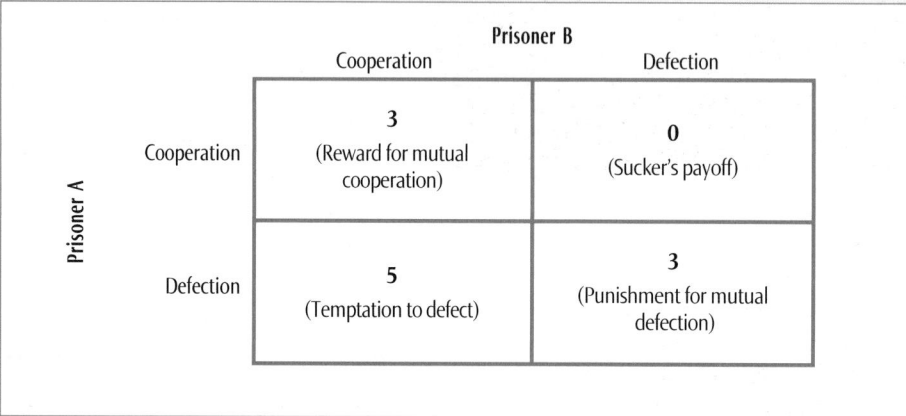

Figure 13.3 The rewards and costs of informing

As you might expect, the normal response is for both prisoners to 'squeal' on the other. If prisoner A informs on prisoner B whilst he stays silent the payoff is maximized. Even if prisoner B also informs, it is better to mutually inform (i.e. defect on any cooperative arrangement) than be caught with the 'sucker's payoff', that is to stay silent whilst someone is informing on you.

Axelrod and Hamilton argued that if this situation were repeated time and time again with the same players, it would soon become apparent that the most profitable arrangement for the players would be to cooperate.

♦ These bats return to the same roost day after day and associate with particular individuals over long periods of time, remembering benefits given and received. This means that they are able to detect cheating in bats who do not reciprocate.

♦ Bats are sensitive to whether another individual is starving or well fed, and are able to help a starving bat without too much cost to themselves. A starving bat loses weight at a much higher rate than a well-fed bat so giving of a blood meal provides the recipient with more time until starvation than the donor loses.

♦ Failing to obtain a feed can happen to any of the bats, so all bats benefit from the 'insurance policy' of being fed by others in times of need.

A problem with explaining how this form of altruism has evolved concerns the time period between giving and receiving. The term *delayed* reciprocal altruism is often used to focus on just this fact. Until the altruist

has been repaid, the altruist has gained nothing. In fact, it is worse off than if it had done nothing. This may well explain why documented cases of reciprocal altruism are rare (Manning and Dawkins 1998). It is more common to find examples where there is mutual and immediate co-operation between animals, and it is to this we turn next.

Mutualism, or return effects

Some cooperative relationships may even involve individuals from differing species, such as cleaner fish (see photo on p. 337) who survive by removing either skin parasites from other fish or even, in the case of the grouper, food particles which could harbour bacteria inside the mouth of the host fish. The grouper not only refrains from eating the small fish, but occasionally closes its mouth with it inside when danger looms to threaten the safety of its small companion. Sometimes individuals will cooperate and help one another because, as a team, they can

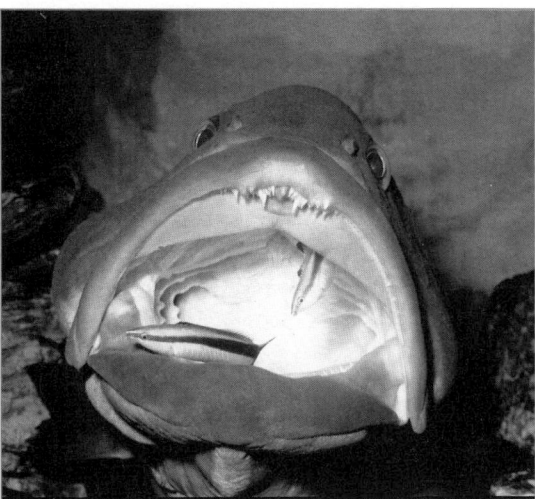

Cleaner fish wrasse (*Labroides dimidiatus*) inside cod's mouth

achieve more than by working alone. For instance, lionesses will hunt together in bringing down a wildebeest and other large ungulates (hoofed mammals) which they could not tackle safely alone. Having killed the prey the lionesses will then share it, though not necessarily equally (Caraco and Wolf 1975).

Some mutualistic relationships involve human beings and animals. The greater honeyguide has such a relationship with humans in parts of Africa. The bird leads people to honeybee hives in trees, rock crevices and termite mounds (Grier and Burk 1992). When the humans break into the hive to get the honey, they leave bee larvae and wax which the birds consume. The humans and birds have developed, through evolution or learning, elaborate interspecific communication signals. The people, such as the Borans of Kenya, use loud whistle sounds to attract the birds. The birds fly close to the people and emit their own special call to indicate their presence, then use a combination of flight and perching patterns to indicate the direction and distance to the hive. A three-year field study by Isack and Reyer (1989) confirmed the validity of this relationship. By observing from camouflaged positions, the researchers were able to gain considerable insight into the birds' behaviour. For example, the birds would visit the hives shortly after dawn when the bees where docile, peering inside presumably to check the status of each hive. Isack and Reyer found that when guided by these birds, the Boran people were able to find hives much more quickly than when they were unguided. The benefits of this relationship to the birds were twofold. First, they had much greater access to hives with human help, and second, the use of smoke to clear the hives reduced the chances of the birds being stung by the bees.

Induced (manipulated) altruism

Some strategies that solicit help from others can be regarded as ploys which are aimed at cheating. This *induced altruism* is sometimes referred to as 'manipulation' or 'social parasitism'. Such behaviour would include the laying of eggs in another bird's nest ('brood parasitism'). This is practised by the cuckoo (see *In Focus*, p. 338) and a number of other species, as well as the example of the beetle grub 'begging' for food from the passing ant – Hölldobler (1971) found that the larva of the *Atemelles* beetle mimics the begging behaviour of ants so as to obtain food from passing workers. Wickler (1968) found a similar instance of deception shown in *Aspidontus*, a fish whose appearance mimics the cleaner fish *Labroides*. However, rather than clean the host fish, *Aspidontus* individuals approach it and then bite into its flesh, making off with a morsel of food.

Exam summary: Evolutionary explanations of animal behaviour

The AQA examination will test your understanding of the following areas:

◆ evolutionary explanations for the behaviour of nonhuman animals (pp. 329–33)

◆ biological explanations for apparent altruism (pp. 333–8).

Example question

The question below is typical of one drawn from the material above, and should take you 30 minutes to answer.

◆ Outline and evaluate two biological explanations for apparent altruism in nonhuman animals.

(24 marks)

Suggested answer structure

Questions such as this can be quite difficult to answer in 30 minutes, as there are four distinct 'chunks'. This can, however, be useful to you when planning your response, as it gives you a ready-made structure to your essay. If we 'deconstruct' this essay title, we get the following (using the examples of kin selection and reciprocal altruism as the two chosen explanations):

◆ outline description of one biological explanation for apparent altruism (e.g. kin selection) – this should take 7.5 minutes of writing time and be approximately 150 words in length

◆ evaluation of kin selection as an explanation for apparent altruism – 7.5 minutes and approximately 150 words

in focus

The cost of recognition

The European cuckoo is probably best known as the bird that lays its eggs in other birds' nests (such as the reed warbler and dunnock). When the young cuckoo hatches, it pushes the eggs of the host bird out of the nest. In this way it monopolizes the parental effort of the host bird while reducing the reproductive success of the host to zero. It would seem reasonable that the smaller song birds typically parasitized by cuckoos would recognize their own eggs and/or offspring and discriminate against cuckoos. However, cuckoos' eggs are very good mimics of their host's eggs with cuckoos 'specializing' in different host species and laying eggs that closely resemble those of the host. The host thus faces a problem, and its behaviour can be understood in terms of the costs and benefits of accepting or rejecting unusual eggs in the nest (Davies *et al.* 1996). If the host bird rejects one egg from its nest, it may break others in the process, and there is always the possibility that it may be rejecting one of its own eggs. If the probability of parasitism is low, then it probably benefits the host species to be fairly lax about rejecting eggs. When the potential for parasitism is high, however, the benefits of rejecting eggs outweighs the costs, and host birds should discriminate more strongly against possible 'deviant' eggs. Exposing reed warblers to a stuffed cuckoo on the edge of their nest increases the likelihood that they will reject a model cuckoo egg (Davies *et al.* 1996).

Cuckoo (*Cuculus candrus*) being fed by a dunnock (*Prunella modularis*)

Why do host birds not reject the cuckoo *after* it has been born? This supposes that the parent bird knows what its offspring should look like in the first place. On average, birds that accept any offspring in the nest have more reproductive success overall compared to birds that learn what their offspring look like from the first brood, and reject in the future any offspring that look different (Lotem 1993). In the case of the cuckoo, any host bird that was parasitized might learn to accept cuckoos and reject any future young of its own. This is clearly not in the host bird's best interests. This is one occasion where learning is more costly than not learning.

◆ outline description of second biological explanation for apparent altruism (e.g. reciprocal altruism) – 7.5 minutes and approximately 150 words

◆ evaluation of reciprocal altruism as an explanation for apparent altruism – 7.5 minutes and approximately 150 words.

We have covered four explanations for apparent altruism in this section. Note that this is referred to as *apparent* altruism because each of these explains 'altruistic' behaviours in terms of the selfish motivation of the altruist (except in the special case of induced altruism where this behaviour is *manipulated* by other animals). Kin selection theory (pp. 333–5) explains altruistic behaviour in terms of the increased *fitness* that can be achieved by helping those with whom we share genes. Explanations of reciprocal altruism (pp. 335–6) see altruism as part of a reciprocal arrangement between individual animals. Animals may help each other if the favour is returned some time in the future. Reciprocal arrangements tend to be restricted to animals that live in close proximity to each other, and where consequently the likelihood of the favour being returned is high. Sometimes animals will cooperate and help each other because they are able to achieve more as a team than by working alone (pp. 336–7). Some of these mutualistic relationships may involve partnerships between animals and humans. A special example of apparent altruism is *induced* altruism (pp. 337–8), where a parasitic organism (such as the cuckoo) subverts some natural behaviour of the host (and therefore the altruist) to their own ends.

Classical and operant conditioning

Classical (Pavlovian) conditioning

Classical conditioning was first described in detail by the Russian physiologist Ivan Pavlov (1927). Pavlov was investigating the salivatory reflex in dogs, a response which occurs automatically when food is placed on the animal's tongue. He observed that his animals salivated not just in response to this stimulus (which is the basic reflex action itself), but also in response to anything else which was regularly coinciding with the feeding routine, such as the presence of the food dish, or the person who regularly fed them. All animals are born with a host of reflexes, which may be either simple, such as a constriction of the pupil of the eye when strong light is seen, or complex, such as the righting reflex of the cat when it falls to the ground. The whole point about natural reflexes such as these is that:

◆ they are innate, i.e. they are present in the animal at, or soon after, birth

◆ they are triggered consistently and automatically by the occurrence of one kind of stimulus

◆ once such a response is triggered, it is not normally altered for its duration by subsequent events

◆ experience does little to alter the time course or pattern of the response.

We can now turn our attention to the processes involved in classical conditioning.

Acquisition

In a typical classical conditioning experiment the researcher selects one naturally occurring reflex of an animal and then deliberately and consistently presents an artificial stimulus (that is, one which does not normally trigger the reflex itself) prior to the natural stimulus (the one which does normally trigger off that reflex). Imagine for the purpose of this description this artificial stimulus to be the sound of a buzzer.

In his description of the procedure involved, Pavlov used a particular terminology to define these different components. The natural stimulus for any reflex (e.g. food touching the tongue, in the case of salivation) is referred to as an 'unconditioned stimulus' (UCS), where the term 'conditioning' may be read as 'training'. In other words, an unconditioned stimulus is one which produces a response that is innate, or 'untrained'. When our eyes blink as an

object approaches them at speed, this is not a trained response but one which we are born with. When the reflex is described as an *unconditioned response* (UCR), it means it occurs after an unconditioned stimulus. Before training takes place, the artificial stimulus is referred to as the *neutral stimulus*, and after training it is referred to as a *conditioned stimulus* (CS).

At the start the CS does *not* bring about a reflex response by itself. However, after many pairings of the neutral stimulus (NS) followed by the UCS, the situation changes. The animal's salivation reflex begins at the onset of the buzzer and now works even though the dog's tongue is not stimulated. The neutral stimulus (NS) has now acquired the ability to produce the response in question and is now a conditioned stimulus (CS) – see Fig. 13.4. Pavlov realized that the salivation which occurs in response to the buzzer still has the properties of a reflex, but now happens as a learned response. Furthermore, the range of stimuli which can act as a CS seemed potentially infinite – being anything audible, visible, tactile or of any sensory modality which the subject (in this case, the dog) can detect.

Timing

The precise timing of the NS (CS) – UCS pairing has a considerable influence on whether the NS will become a reliable CS, leading to a predictable CR. As we have seen, a dog initially only salivates when presented with the food (UCS), but gradually the buzzer (NS) begins to elicit salivation, and after a number of trials the dog salivates as soon as it hears the buzzer. The relative timing of this period between the onset of the NS and the UCS is crucial to the success of conditioning. Table 13.1 shows some of the different timings and their consequences.

Figure 13.4 The process of classical conditioning

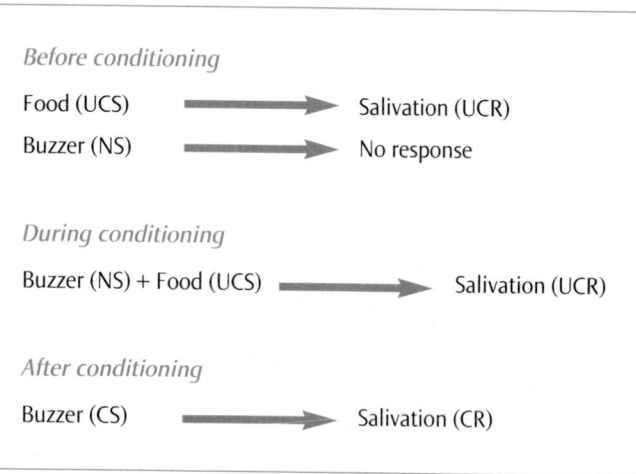

Before conditioning

Food (UCS) ⟶ Salivation (UCR)

Buzzer (NS) ⟶ No response

During conditioning

Buzzer (NS) + Food (UCS) ⟶ Salivation (UCR)

After conditioning

Buzzer (CS) ⟶ Salivation (CR)

Table 13.1   The conditioning outcomes of different time intervals between the NS and the UCS

Time interval between NS and UCS	Conditioning outcomes
Standard (forward) pairing– NS precedes UCS but overlaps with it	Conditioning effects are strong with this pairing
	Response elicited by UCS extends backwards as it becomes associated with NS
Delayed pairing – NS precedes UCS	As above, but the longer the delay, the weaker the strength of conditioning
Simultaneous pairing – NS and UCS occur together	Conditioning tends to fail – NS cannot be used to *predict* the onset of the UCS
Backward pairing – UCS precedes NS	Conditioning tends to be ineffective – as UCS has already elicited a response, therefore the response is not dependent on a relationship between NS and UCS

Extinction and spontaneous recovery

In the case of innate reflexes it has already been stated that they are almost permanent features of the animal's behaviour repertory, however young or old the animal may be, and that they show little or no change over the lifespan. Pavlov examined the nature of the conditioned reflex to compare it with these aspects of the UCR. Unlike the UCR, he found that the CR is *labile,* i.e. does not become permanently established as a response. On the contrary, the CR does not long outlast the removal of the UCS. So, for instance, although the dog may have been trained to salivate to the buzzer sound, if the buzzer is continually sounded without being followed by the food stimulus on the tongue, then salivation to the buzzer rapidly diminishes. This dying out of the CR when the CS is no longer paired with the UCS is referred to as a process of *extinction.* Experimentally, extinction is brought about by *unpaired* presentations of the CS. The extinction process can be seen by measuring the CR over experimental trials, with the response gradually diminishing until it eventually seems to disappear altogether (see Fig. 13.5). Figure 13.5 shows what happens when the trials proceed as with training, except that the UCS no longer follows the presentation of the CS. By the second presentation, the CR remains nearly the same as the last CS–UCS pairing, but by the tenth trial, the CR is now only one-half what it originally was. Likewise, by the twentieth trial the CR has further diminished, this time to the point where it is virtually 'extinct'.

However, Pavlov found that extinction is not like a process of forgetting. The unique thing about a CR that has become extinct is that is always liable to reappear suddenly, under the right conditions. This sudden reappearance is referred to as *spontaneous recovery,* and there are two main situations which bring it about:

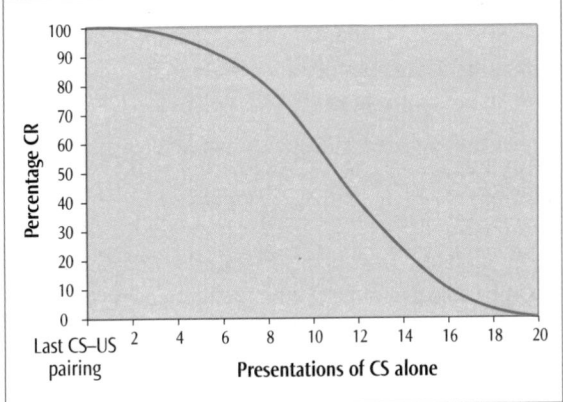

Figure 13.5 Extinction of CR when US no longer paired with CS

◆ a postponement of training (i.e. a time lapse between one extinction trial and another), which is sufficient to reinstate the CR

◆ the subject being startled (e.g. any sudden event, such as loud noise, which occurs during the process of extinction training may bring back the CR, however transiently).

There is one more reason to doubt that extinction is analogous to forgetting. When the subject is retrained by using the original CS–UCS pairings, the CR is quickly reinstated. This reinstatement occurs much faster than the original conditioning, which implies that the CR was not really 'lost'. To explain the process of response extinction, Pavlov described the CR as being *inhibited,* much like the energy that may be maintained in a coil spring by keeping your hand pressed down upon it. When the inhibition is removed, the response returns (in the metaphor of the coil spring, it rebounds into shape when your hand pressure is removed).

It is as though the nervous system has the property of being able to hold back a learned response until some 'releasing' event takes place. What was known about the generally inhibitory action of the cerebral cortex (see Chapter 4) suggested to Pavlov, and other neurophysiologists of his time, that much of the brain in complex animals was designed for suppressing learned responses until the occasion was right for their 'release'.

Stimulus generalization

Pavlov also introduced a term called *stimulus generalization*, which occurs when a stimulus is presented which is similar to the CS, but not identical to it. For instance, if conditioned to salivate at the sound of one buzzer, will the response occur when a *different* buzzer sound is played? The more similar the new buzzer is to the CS then the greater will be the similarity between the responses to this new sound and to the original one. For instance, if the salivatory response is measured in millilitres (ml) per minute, then the original CS will evoke the most saliva in that time. However, a similar-sounding buzzer will also evoke a similar amount, more so than a less-similar sounding buzzer, and so on. When plotted graphically, the effect is a bell-shaped curve, illustrated in Fig. 13.6. As this figure shows, stimuli at positions –1 and +1 are similar to the CS in their ability to evoke a CR – in fact each produces over 80 per cent of the response which the CS produces. In practice, the stimulus at position –1 might be a buzzer with a sound of slightly lower pitch that the CS itself, and the one at +1 might have a slightly higher pitch. On the other hand, a stimulus at position –4 might be markedly lower in pitch to the CS, and as the graph shows, this stimulus produces only a small fraction (about 3 per cent) of the response which the CS evokes.

So, despite the fact that conditioning has involved only the use of one stimulus (CS), the response itself may be generalized to others. This is an important point to bear in mind in the application of this theory to psychological medicine. Where people experience a strong fear (phobia) of one stimulus, such as a spider, this may be generalized to most crawling insects.

Stimulus discrimination

In contrast to generalized responses, Pavlov found that conditioning can bring about discrimination of response to the CS. When discrimination occurs the learned reflex can only be evoked by the CS, i.e. the typically generalized responses to other, similar stimuli are absent. Consider the effect illustrated in Fig. 13.7.

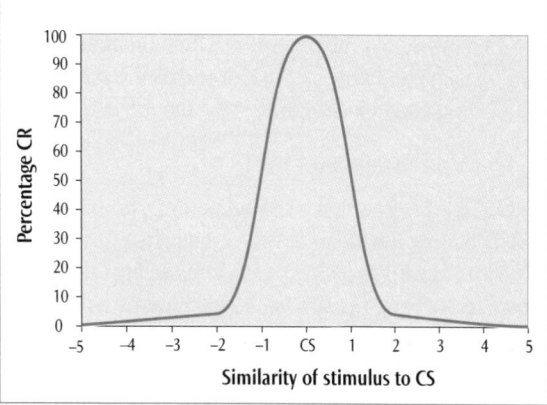

Figure 13.7 Discrimination of CR to CS

The response to stimuli other than the CS is now curtailed. For example, whereas the CR to stimuli at positions –2 and +2 were previously (see Fig. 13.6) over 20 per cent of the response to the CS, now these stimuli evoke less than 5 per cent of the CR.

The way in which discrimination training has been carried out is as follows. During the original conditioning, where the CS–UCS pairings were made, there needs to be a number of occasions when other stimuli, similar to the CS, are introduced. These other stimuli, however, are never paired with the UCS. The end result of this form of training is that the response which is conditioned to the CS is very specific to it. Now, the responses to almost all other stimuli are removed, with the CR being evoked by the CS and little else. For example, during the procedure to condition a dog to salivate (CR) to a black square (CS+), a grey square (CS-) is introduced intermittently. However, the grey square is never paired with food (UCS). Initially, the dog will sometimes salivate to the grey square but gradually it will learn to discriminate between the two squares and will salivate (CR) only when the black square (CS+) is presented.

You may notice from Fig. 13.7 that the stimuli at positions –1 and +1 do still evoke a considerable proportion of the CR (about 60 per cent of it). This is because in practice the difference between the pitch of buzzer (in the example given here) of the stimulus at –1 and the CS, or +1 and the CS, is extremely slight. These

Figure 13.6 Generalization of CR to stimuli similar to CS

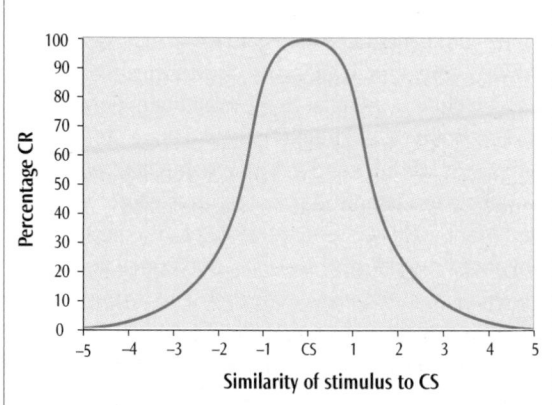

differences in pitch may even be extremely difficult for the human ear to discern. The discrimination training can proceed until highly similar stimuli to the CS do not evoke much CR. In fact, Pavlov reported in his experiments that if such training persists so that the distinction between stimuli is so fine that the subject's senses are hardly able to detect them, a condition of 'experimental neurosis' may arise in the subject being conditioned. In this case the subject's performance may break down altogether, with unpleasant consequences for their behaviour and general health. For instance, self-immolation may occur, where the animal may bite its own paws during the procedure. Discrimination training taken to this degree therefore, has the potential for inflicting psychological distress on the subject.

Higher order conditioning

It is possible to condition a second neutral stimulus (NS) by pairing it with an already established CS, a procedure known as *higher order conditioning* (also known as *second-order conditioning*). Suppose a dog has learned to salivate to the sound of a buzzer. A bell can be rung just before the buzzer. With repeated pairings of the bell and buzzer, the dog may learn to salivate to the sound of the bell although the light will elicit less salivation than does the buzzer. It is possible that higher-order conditioning works in the same way as normal classical conditioning (also known as *first-order conditioning*), with the second CS (CS_2) activating a representation of the first CS (CS_1) which then activates a representation of the UCS and so elicits a CR. An alternative view is that CS_2 does not lead to a representation of CS_1 but rather becomes associated with the response elicited by CS_1. According to Rescorla (1980) the former explanation is more likely when CS_1 and CS_2 are very similar, but when they are very different then the latter explanation is more likely.

The role of classical conditioning in animal behaviour

The importance of classical conditioning to animals lies primarily in their ability to learn that one thing (the CS) predicts the coming of something else (the UCS). Earlier in this chapter we discussed how animal behaviour might be influenced by evolutionary factors. It makes sense to examine classical conditioning from this perspective. One possibility is that the display of conditional responses (CRs) gives animals a selective advantage in some way.

Foraging and hunting behaviour

In their foraging behaviour, animals may learn that some flavours will be followed by illness, whereas others have more beneficial consequences. The importance of the relationship between the CS and CR in feeding was demonstrated dramatically in a conditioned taste-aversion study by Garcia *et al.* (1977). In a taste-aversion study, an animal is conditioned to avoid a particular food which has been associated with some painful outcome or toxic reaction. The animal learns to avoid that food because of a conditioned aversion response to its smell or taste (Reber 1995). In Garcia *et al.*'s study, coyotes and wolves were made ill by feeding them mutton wrapped in raw sheep hide and laced with a toxic substance, lithium chloride. The effects of this conditioning episode were then tested by allowing the animals to approach live sheep. Rather than attacking the sheep as they normally would, the coyotes sniffed their quarry and turned away, some of them retching. The wolves initially charged the sheep and made oral contact on their target's flank. They immediately released their prey. During the next half hour, the sheep became increasingly dominant and the wolves withdrew like submissive pups (Garcia *et al.* 1977). These responses are evidence that the CS (the taste and smell of sheep) paired with illness was sufficient to change the behaviour (CR) of the predators towards their prey. In the natural world, learning to avoid food that makes you ill is a valuable lesson.

Behaviour towards conspecifics

Research with male blue gourami fish (*Trichogaster trichopterous*) lends some support to the prediction that animals who change their behaviour in response to conditioned stimuli have a selective advantage. In one study by Hollis (1984), male gouramis were trained to expect an aggressive encounter with another male following the lighting of a red panel on the side of their tank. The fish showed evidence of having learned the relationship between the CS (red light) and the UCS (rival male's arrival) by beginning their aggressive display during the CS. When control males (who had not been conditioned to the CS) and conditioned males were allowed to fight each other, the conditioned males directed more bites, showed more aggressive displays and invariably won.

In many species, males who hold territories behave aggressively towards any animal approaching their territory, even females. Mating would be facilitated if males could anticipate the approach of a female and inhibit aggression towards her (Shettleworth 1998). Using techniques similar to the experiment described earlier, Hollis (1990) found that conditioned males directed fewer bites and more courtship behaviour towards a test female than did controls. More importantly, this behaviour translates into spectacularly enhanced reproductive success. Conditioned males fathered, on average, over one thousand young whereas control males (where the CS had not been paired with a female) fathered, on average, less than one hundred young (Hollis *et al.* 1997).

Evaluation of classical conditioning

Insights from classical conditioning research have clearly led to some striking discoveries about animal behaviour. The appealing simplicity of Pavlov's views have come under attack in recent decades as psychologists have discovered certain constraints, or limitations, on the generality of findings regarding classical conditioning (Zimbardo *et al.* 1995).

Different animals face different challenges in order to survive in their particular ecological niche. As a result of this, different species may well have different capabilities for learning in a given situation. Therefore, we might expect some relationships between CS and UCS to be more difficult for some species to learn than for others. To accommodate this possibility, Seligman (1970) proposed the concept of *preparedness* as follows:

◆ Animals are *prepared* to learn associations that are significant in terms of their survival needs

◆ Animals are *unprepared* to learn associations that are not significant in this respect

◆ Animals are *contraprepared* to learn any association that in some way runs contrary to any naturally occurring behavioural predisposition.

An example of an association for which animals might be biologically *prepared* is taste-aversion learning. Research on taste-aversion learning (as discussed earlier) poses particular problems for Pavlovian conditioning. Recall that an animal may eat poisoned food, and later become ill (but survive). After just one experience, and despite a long interval between the CS (tasting the food) and UCS (becoming ill), the animal learns to avoid all foods with that taste. What's more, this learned association is remarkably resistant to extinction. This form of learning challenges the assumptions of Pavlov's view of classical conditioning in three ways:

◆ *Number of trials* – classical conditioning, as we have seen, is a gradual process, requiring many associations between the NS and the UCS. In taste-aversion, learning takes place after just one trial. This phenomenon is known as *one-trial learning*.

◆ *Delay between NS and UCS* – the longer the delay between the neutral stimulus (NS) and the UCS, the less likely is a learned association between the two. In taste-aversion, conditioning takes place *despite* several hours between the two.

◆ *Extinction* – in classical conditioning, the withdrawal of the UCS means that extinction sets in rapidly. Yet in taste-aversion, the time period before extinction is prolonged way beyond what we might expect.

It is clear that species differ in terms of their motives, motor and cognitive capacities and certainly in the degree to which their natural style of life depends on learning. We must, therefore, be cautious about generalizing from one species to another. Each species' genetic endowment places limitations on their learning abilities. These biological constraints suggest that the principles of classical conditioning cannot be universally applied across all species or situations. Some aspects of classical conditioning clearly depend on the way an animal is genetically predisposed toward stimuli in its environment. What any organism can and cannot readily learn appears to be as much a product of its evolutionary history as its learning opportunities.

Operant conditioning

'Operant conditioning ... resembles a hundred million years of natural selection or a thousand years of the evolution of a culture compressed into a very short period of time.' (Skinner 1981, p. 502)

Although the title of 'founding father of behaviour analysis' is attributed to B.F. Skinner (dating from the publication in 1938 of his book *The Behaviour of Organisms*), the roots of this approach go back at least to the nineteenth century. Skinner himself acknowledged the influence of Thorndike on his early work, especially Thorndike's (1911) description of a *law of effect*. The law of positive effect states that any behaviour that leads to a positive outcome, such as a successful solution to a problem, or a state of 'satisfaction' in the organism, will tend to be retained and repeated in future. The increasing frequency of this behaviour by an organism will be reinforced by each further successful outcome that behaviour brings about.

Reinforcement

In terms of Thorndike's 'law of (positive) effect', the outcome of a behaviour will act so as to strengthen, or reinforce, that behaviour.

In Thorndike's view, behaviour is *reinforced* and maintained by its consequences. Therefore, any behaviour that fails to bring about a successful outcome, will be unreinforced and should not appear as frequently when the animal is placed in similar circumstances. Thorndike demonstrated the law of effect by giving animals problems to solve. For instance, a cat placed in a box from which it could only escape by operating a latch, would learn to do so eventually. Before learning the successful strategy the cat would have tried numerous other, unsuccessful behaviours, such as scratching and biting, and these would not have brought about its escape. Escape is itself a reinforcing outcome for the action of operating the latch and so, on being returned to the box again, the latch would become the focus of the cat's behaviour and actions directed at it would be those most in evidence.

Skinner devised an easier measurement technique for investigating how reinforcement acts upon behaviour. The Skinner Box was designed by him to reward the subject, not by allowing escape, but by providing food pellets. In this circumstance the animal (usually a rat or a pigeon) would also initially show only escape-seeking behaviour in the box. However, one of these actions, such as pressing downwards on a lever, would bring about a food reinforcer (see Fig. 13.8).

This action would bring about reinforcement in the form of a food pellet delivered automatically from the hopper. This is much the same mechanism which delivers a chocolate bar from a machine when a coin is inserted. In the Skinner Box the subject's actions are easily (and automatically) recorded by measuring the number of food items obtained in a given interval of time. For instance, if twenty-five pellets of food were dispensed from the hopper in the first hour, and one hundred and fifty in the second hour, then the threefold increase in the subject's response rate is easy to monitor and record.

By using the Skinner Box arrangement, many interesting insights were gained regarding how reinforcement comes to control a subject's responses. For instance, the delivery of one food item for every lever press might seem to be the optimal way of ensuring the response is learned and maintained. But that is not what Skinner discovered. His greatest insight was in showing that reinforcement exerts subtle (though nonetheless predictable) effects on behaviour depending upon how the reinforcer is made contingent (i.e. dependent) upon the response.

As in classical conditioning, the time interval between two elements of the conditioning process (in this case the response and the reinforcer) is crucial. If the reinforcer follows immediately after the response, conditioning is more effective than if they are separated by a delay (Pearce 1997). This does not mean that

conditioning is impossible when this time interval is extended. Lattal and Gleeson (1990) showed that the rate of lever pressing in rats increased steadily over 20 sessions of training, even when the delay between response and reinforcer was as long as 30 seconds.

Schedules of reinforcement

If a food-reinforcer is not dispensed for every single response (e.g. lever press), but is arranged according to a predetermined 'schedule', such as one food pellet for every fifth lever press, then different response patterns arise depending upon the exact relationship between response and reinforcement.

There are four ways in which reinforcement may be scheduled:

◆ as a ratio of the number of responses, such as the 1:5 example above, or

◆ as a result of a time-base or time-interval criterion. For instance, this might mean the delivery of a food pellet at the end of, say, one minute *provided that the subject has responded in that interval* (and not otherwise).

In addition to the above two forms of schedule, in which reinforcement may occur by either a time- or response-based criterion, reinforcement may also be applied in either a fixed or a variable schedule.

◆ A *fixed* schedule dispenses reinforcement on a reliable basis, e.g. in a 1:5 fixed-ratio (FR5) schedule the reinforcer is delivered after every fifth lever press. Similarly, a fixed-interval schedule of one minute (FI1) will deliver reinforcement at the end of every minute, provided that the subject has made the required response (e.g. lever pressing) in that time.

◆ *Variable* schedules dispense food on an erratic basis, e.g. a variable ratio schedule of 1:5 (VR5) will deliver food *on average* once every five responses, but during any one trial that number may vary from 5. Only over a large number of trials will the schedule be seen to have averaged one reinforcer per five responses. On a variable interval schedule of one minute (VI1) the interval is varied around the period of one minute, though this interval alters from trial to trial so that only over the long run does the one minute average become apparent.

Some schedules, such as a low-fixed ratio, tend to bring about rapid initial learning of the required response, but the response rate itself does not accelerate as rapidly as it does with, say, a variable-interval schedule. The 'extinction' rates also differ markedly between schedules, i.e. extinction being the rate at which the conditioned response (such as lever-pressing in the

Figure 13.8 The Skinner Box

Skinner Box) diminishes in frequency when the reinforcement is stopped altogether. Typically, a subject working on a VI schedule which has a relatively long interval will maintain their response rate far longer than will a subject working on one of the fixed-schedule types (i.e. FR or FI).

Because the above schedules all reinforce the subject for some, but not all, of their responses, they are referred to generally as 'partial reinforcement', to distinguish them from 'continuous reinforcement' (CRF), in which reinforcement is dispensed after every correct response. Typically, CRF schedules will induce rapid initial learning, a slower overall response rate, and rapid extinction. By comparison, partial reinforcement schedules generally induce slower initial learning, overall faster rates of responding, and slower extinction rates, though each of the four forms of partial schedule will vary in their effects on these aspects of learning, as has been pointed out above.

Activity 3: Reinforcement schedules

Which type or which combination of reinforcement schedules do you think would be most effective in training a young dog to obey its owner, e.g. to come when called, to stay, to lie down?

Punishment and negative reinforcement

In Thorndike's original formulation there was also a law of negative effect. By this he meant that if a subject's actions led to unwanted or unpleasant outcomes ('annoyers', as he called them), then those actions would diminish over time, i.e. the subject would become less likely on future occasions to reproduce those actions. This contingency between a behaviour and negative consequences is, however, less clear than that, as Thorndike himself found. One reason for this is that unpleasant outcomes may arise in a variety of ways, such as from:

◆ a failure to obtain a reward which was an expected consequence of some action the subject carried out

◆ a failure to avoid an unpleasant stimulus by taking appropriate avoiding action

◆ a direct consequence of the action itself.

For instance, a cat may be lying behind a door when she hears the rattle of keys outside. If the cat remains behind the door when it opens against her she would be hurt. Her inaction brings about a negative consequence – had she moved in response to the rattle of keys she would not have been hurt. On subsequent

occasions the sound of keys may be sufficient to prompt her into moving from the area. This key sound leads to avoidance behaviour. This is an example of *negative* reinforcement in that failure to make the correct response will lead to an unpleasant outcome, whereas making the correct response (moving out of the way) will lead to a desirable outcome (i.e. not getting hurt).

Consider another situation where a dog is reaching up to a table by leaning against a stool, and the stool topples under its weight. The pain is felt this time as a consequence of the dog's actions, rather than inaction, and has the effect of *punishing* the behaviour which preceded it.

Negative reinforcement has been generally regarded as being more effective than punishment in bringing about learning because it aims to activate a desired response rather to deactivate an unwanted one. Part of the problem with attempting to eradicate an undesirable behaviour is that it does not necessarily follow that a desired one will arise in its place. For instance, having learned not to reach to the table by leaning against the stool the dog may then embark upon an even more risky or undesirable behaviour, such as jumping straight on to the table. There is also the view that punishment fails to do more than just suppress a behaviour while the punishing agent is present, a view that has tended to prevail in institutions such as prisons, where sustained vigilance is required.

In negative reinforcement procedures the subject has actively to avoid the unpleasant event. The event itself, say, a mild electric shock delivered to the feet in a Skinner Box, has its onset signalled by the occurrence of a warning event such as a light or a buzzer. The shock is an aversive event and therefore the subject will soon learn to avoid it if possible, in much the same way as learning to obtain food or water by pressing a lever. The activity required of pressing the lever when, say, the buzzer plays, enables the subject to avoid the shock altogether. Failure to respond appropriately to the buzzer will bring about the aversive event. In a 'Sidman avoidance' schedule the subject is placed in a box which has two compartments. Shortly after the warning the subject has to move from one section of the box to another in order to avoid the aversive event (hence the name 'shuttle' box is sometimes used to describe this apparatus). See Table 13.2 for a summary of types of reinforcement.

The theoretical question which negative reinforcement poses is: what is the reinforcer? For instance, when the subject responds to the lever so as to obtain a pellet the reinforcement is the food item itself. But in negative-reinforcement procedures the outcome is the avoidance of, not the contact with the reinforcer. To explain this conundrum some

Table 13.2 Types of reinforcement		
	Primary reinforcer *(unlearned)*	*Secondary reinforcer* *(learned by process of classical* *conditioning)*
Positive reinforcement (presentation increases preceding response)	e.g. food, water	e.g. praise, money
Negative reinforcement (removal increases preceding response)	e.g. removal of pain	e.g. removal of feared stimulus (e.g. a light that signals onset of electric shock)

Note: both positive and negative reinforcement, by definition, always increase the probability of the response that precedes them. Punishment, on the other hand, has the opposite effect, decreasing the probability of the response that precedes it.

behaviourists reasoned that reinforcement of both positive and negative types acts upon 'drive reduction' mechanisms. A 'drive' is like a biological instinct – for instance, the experience of hunger is accompanied by a drive or motivation to find food in order to satisfy that hunger. To experience fear when expecting a shock to happen motivates or 'drives' the response of seeking safety so as to reduce that fear.

However, when shock is made unavoidable in a shuttle box, the subject will soon not only fail to attempt to avoid at all, but will also be less likely to learn an avoidance routine in future situations where the shock (or other aversive event) *is* avoidable. This situation has become known as 'learned helplessness'.

The role of operant conditioning in animal behaviour

Unpredictable environmental changes during an animal's lifetime cannot be anticipated by pre-programmed forms of behaviour. The individual animal must rely upon its own resources in adapting to any such changes. The ability to modify behaviour in the light of unpredictable environmental changes is clearly a sign of intelligence, and gives such animals a clear selective advantage. Although most of the work on operant conditioning has taken place in the laboratory, there are clear examples of natural behaviour that utilize the principles of operant conditioning.

An example of operant conditioning 'in action' comes from a study of the mating behaviour of cowbirds. Cowbirds are brood parasites and therefore young males do not hear the songs of adults of their species during the early part of their life. West and King (1988) studied the origins of two geographical 'accents' in cowbirds in the United States. They discovered that rather than being less complex, the songs of males reared in isolation were *more* complex than normally reared males. Male cowbirds appear to have the

elements of both dialects, but through the process of operant conditioning, males narrow down their song pattern so that it matches the 'preference' of the local females. When the male sings particular elements from his repertoire, the female responds with a brief 'wing-stroking' display, similar to the copulation invitation found in many types of passerine (nesting) birds. The male responds by increasing the frequency with which he produces the rewarded elements of his song, eliminating those that have no effect on the female.

Evaluation of operant conditioning

The principles of operant conditioning have been used in many different experimental settings and in many different applications, often with spectacular success. But how universal is operant conditioning, and can we truly teach anything to anyone using these techniques? Breland and Breland (1951) had used operant conditioning techniques to train animals of many different species to perform many diverse behaviours. The Brelands believed that the principles of operant conditioning derived from laboratory research could be applied successfully to the control of animal behaviour outside the laboratory.

After their training, however, some of the Brelands' animals no longer performed the 'tricks' they had learned using operant conditioning techniques. For example, a racoon was trained to pick up coins which it would deposit in a 'piggy' bank for a food reinforcement. The racoon eventually refused to give up the coins, rubbing them together in its paws, and 'dipping' them into the piggy bank before taking them out again. This is not surprising if we consider the fact that this is how racoons behave naturally, rubbing crayfish together to remove their shells and then washing them. The Brelands believed that even after conditioning, behaviours drift back towards instinct after a time. They called this process *instinctive drift*

(Breland and Breland 1951). The racoon's behaviour could not be explained by the simple relationship between stimulus – behaviour – consequence, but *was* understandable if we consider the species-specific tendencies of racoons. These tendencies override the temporary changes that are brought about by operant conditioning – the animals' inherited behaviour pattern being incompatible with the operant conditioning task (Zimbardo *et al.* 1995).

Attempts to teach totally arbitrary responses in the laboratory (such as bar pressing in rats or disc pecking in pigeons) may come undone because of the incompatibility of these arbitrary responses with the consummatory responses related to the animals' motivational state (e.g. the hungry racoon 'washing' the coins). In this case the required operant response of releasing the coins (to obtain food as a reinforcement) is incompatible with the classically conditioned consummatory response of rubbing them together as if they *were* food.

One of the main assumptions of operant conditioning is that the consequences of a behaviour determine the likelihood of its future occurrence. Pigeons have been carefully trained to peck a small illuminated disc on the wall of a Skinner box in order to obtain the reward of food. The delivery of food was contingent on the response of pecking the illuminated disc. However, if the key is merely illuminated for a few seconds prior to the delivery of food *regardless of the pigeons' behaviour*, the birds end up pecking the disc as vigorously as they would if their pecking behaviour had been previously reinforced. However, the relationship is simply one between the *stimulus* and the *reinforcer*, with the response of the pigeon being irrelevant to the delivery of the food. The classically conditioned association between light and food is sufficient to generate the high rate of pecking behaviour, the pigeons' consummatory response to food. This has led some commentators to conclude that *classical* conditioning is responsible for much of what researchers have been recording as *operant* behaviour (Mackintosh 1981).

Exam summary: Classical and operant conditioning

The AQA examination will test your understanding of the following areas:

◆ classical conditioning and its role in the behaviour of nonhuman animals (pp. 339–43)

◆ operant conditioning and its role in the behaviour of nonhuman animals (pp. 343–7).

Example question

The question below is typical of one drawn from the material above, and should take you 30 minutes to answer.

◆ Describe the nature of classical conditioning, and assess the role of this type of learning in the behaviour of nonhuman animals. *(24 marks)*

Suggested answer structure

A piece of advice that we keep making in these exam summaries is the reminder that except for the questions in Unit 5 (Chapters 16 to 18), all other questions in the A2 examination must be answered in 30 minutes. This may not be the case if you are writing a coursework essay using the question above, but in an examination, 30 minutes is your lot. It pays, therefore, to get used to the very tight time restrictions of examination questions, and to practice responding to their requirements in a very cost-effective and focused way. Questions on classical conditioning are very much a case in point. There is potentially a massive amount of procedural detail that you could write in response to the instruction 'Describe the *nature* of classical conditioning...', but you only have 15 minutes (as this is the AO1 component of the question) to do it.

We have covered a number of key aspects of classical conditioning in this section. These are: acquisition procedures (p. 339), timing (pp. 339–40), extinction and spontaneous recovery (pp. 340–1), stimulus generalization (p. 341), stimulus discrimination (pp. 341–2) and higher order conditioning (p. 342). Each of these is important, but probably they are ranked in importance as they appear here. If you look at the assessment criteria in Table 21.4 on p. 558, you will see that the higher mark bands require both breadth *and* depth in the AO1 content, with the highest marks coming from answers that show a balance between the two.

The AO2 component of this question requires an assessment of the role of classical conditioning in the behaviour of nonhuman animals. As most of the work on classical conditioning has taken place in the rather artificial environment of the laboratory, we might question whether this type of learning has any relevance to the natural behaviour of animals in the wild. We have covered two areas where classical conditioning has been used to explain a learning experience. The first of these is related to foraging behaviour, where animals have been found to develop aversions to poisoned food through the process of classical conditioning (p. 342). The second area relates to behaviour towards conspecifics (members of an animal's own species), which demonstrates the importance of classically conditioned behaviours in intrasexual aggression and intersexual reproductive behaviour (p. 342).

Social learning in nonhuman animals

In the previous section, we concentrated on what animals could learn on their own. However, as many animals live in groups, it would benefit them to be able to copy what other members of the group have learned through trial and error (Pearce 1997). Copying others may lead an individual animal to avoid poisonous food, or to choose a nutritious food item, or possibly they may learn how to avoid predators by observing the behaviour of other animals in the group. Social learning clearly has great potential, but is it widespread among animals? It is to this question that we now turn.

Explanations and research studies

Imitation

If a problem is particularly difficult to solve, it might take animals a considerable amount of time before they come up with the solution. Once they have done that, however, it would benefit other members of their species to be able to imitate the behaviour of the successful animal. Imitation would, theoretically, be of considerable value to many different species. Evidence for imitation in nonhuman species is, however, relatively rare. From her work on imitation in rats, Hayes (1993) suggested that the difference between imitation and other forms of social learning was represented by what the animal learned as a result of its observations. Non-imitative social learning involves learning about a particular stimulus or event (e.g. that a particular food is good to eat), whereas imitation involves an animal learning about specific responses or behaviours. Imitation therefore implies that the animal understands, as a result of observing another, that a particular behaviour or action has a specific relationship with an outcome.

There have been many experiments designed to explore imitation in nonhuman species. Bugnyar and Huber (1997) studied marmosets (*Callithrix jacchus*) who were required to either push or pull a pendulum door to get a food reward inside a box. After they had learned these behaviours, the researchers exposed 'observer' monkeys to one of the two behaviours for one daily session over a period of three days. None of the observer monkeys imitated the specific strategies for getting the reward that they had been observing over the previous three days, although they were able to acquire some simple motor skills as a result of observing the demonstrator monkeys.

A field study of rehabilitated orang utans (*Pongo pygmaeus*) in Borneo provided some evidence of imitation in a more natural setting (Russon and Galdikas 1995), although instances of imitative

behaviour were comparatively rare. Where imitation did take place, the researchers noted a preference for models with whom the observer had an established relationship. For hand-reared orang-utans, this preference was for human models, and this preference gradually transferred to other orang-utans as these relationships developed. Status was also important, with subordinate animals seeming to imitate dominant animals.

A study that did provide clear evidence for imitation was carried out by Nagell *et al.* (1993). They studied the abilities of mother-reared chimpanzees, enculturated chimpanzees (those raised in close contact with humans) and children. These three groups were tested on simple, complex and delayed imitative tasks using a human model. For the simple and complex tasks, mother-reared chimps performed more poorly than both the enculturated chimpanzees and the human children. In the delayed task, however, where there was a 48-hour time period between the demonstration and the opportunity to imitate, the enculturated chimpanzee group outperformed each of the other two groups.

One of the most famous examples of apparent imitation in animals is the incidence of sweet potato washing in Japanese macaque monkeys. A colony of macaques on Koshima Island was fed with sweet potatoes, and in 1953, a young female, Imo, was first seen taking her sand-covered potato to the stream and washing it before eating. This habit spread quickly to other members of the colony, apparently a clear case of imitative behaviour. There are reasons, however, for believing that such behaviour does not involve imitation. Nagell *et al.* (1993) have suggested that the spread of this habit is more likely to be due to *stimulus enhancement*, i.e. as a result of watching another animal, the observer's attention is drawn towards whatever they are doing. The attention of a naïve monkey may be drawn to a potato when it sees another monkey pick one up. The naïve monkey may pick up its own potato, and for social reasons follow the first monkey into the water, thus learning by accident the benefits of placing the potato in the water. The advantage of this explanation, however contrived, is that it relies on processes already known to exist rather than suggesting that such animals are willing imitators (Pearce 1997).

Foraging

Norwegian rats (*rattus norvegicus*), the common laboratory rat, are colonial omnivores – they will eat almost anything that does not poison them

(Shettleworth 1998). This means that young rats have lots of potential food to learn about – vital if they are to know which foods they may eat safely. When the young rats leave the nest to forage, they prefer to go where other rats are feeding or have recently been feeding. Combined with a preference for familiar flavours, this ensures that they eat only what will not harm them. Research by Galef and Wigmore (1983) tested the feeding preferences of rats exposed to the food preferences of other rats. They paired rats together in cages, and fed them normal laboratory rat food. They then removed one of each pair (the *demonstrator*) who was put in another cage, deprived of food for 24 hours, then fed *either* cinnamon-flavoured or cocoa-flavoured food. Each demonstrator was then returned to its previous companion (the *observer* rat) and the two were allowed to interact for 15 minutes. The demonstrator rat was then removed again, and for the next 24 hours, the observer rat had a choice of two bowls of food, cinnamon and cocoa flavoured. The observer rat showed a distinct preference for whatever food the demonstrator rat had been fed on. This can be seen in Figure 13.9, where it can be seen that the observer rat shows a clear preference for the cinnamon-flavoured food, the same flavour as the food given to its companion. These findings suggest that a rat colony could serve as a centre where rats could exchange information about nearby food sources. Rats behave in a way that facilitates this type of learning, as when they meet they engage in mouth-to-mouth contact and sniffing.

Figure 13.9 Design and results of experiments establishing social transmission of food preferences in Norwegian rats
Source: Shettleworth (1998) after Galef and Wigmore (1983)

Culturally transmitted behaviour? Maybe not.

An intriguing example of behaviour that we have already encountered in this chapter is the tearing of milk bottle tops by blue tits who then feed off the thick layer of cream at the top of the bottle. This bottle opening behaviour became common in localized areas of Britain, rather than being found more randomly spread across the country as a whole. This suggested that the behaviour was being culturally transmitted, i.e. being transferred from one bird to another. However, there are other explanations for this phenomenon that do not require the process of social learning. First, the act of tearing and pecking at a bottle top is clearly not imitation as pecking and tearing at bark are an important part of the blue tits' natural foraging behaviour (Shettleworth 1998). Second, blue tits that encountered open bottles (the results of another bird's work) would come to associate the opened bottle with food. Coming across an unopened bottle, they would engage in food-related behaviours like pecking and

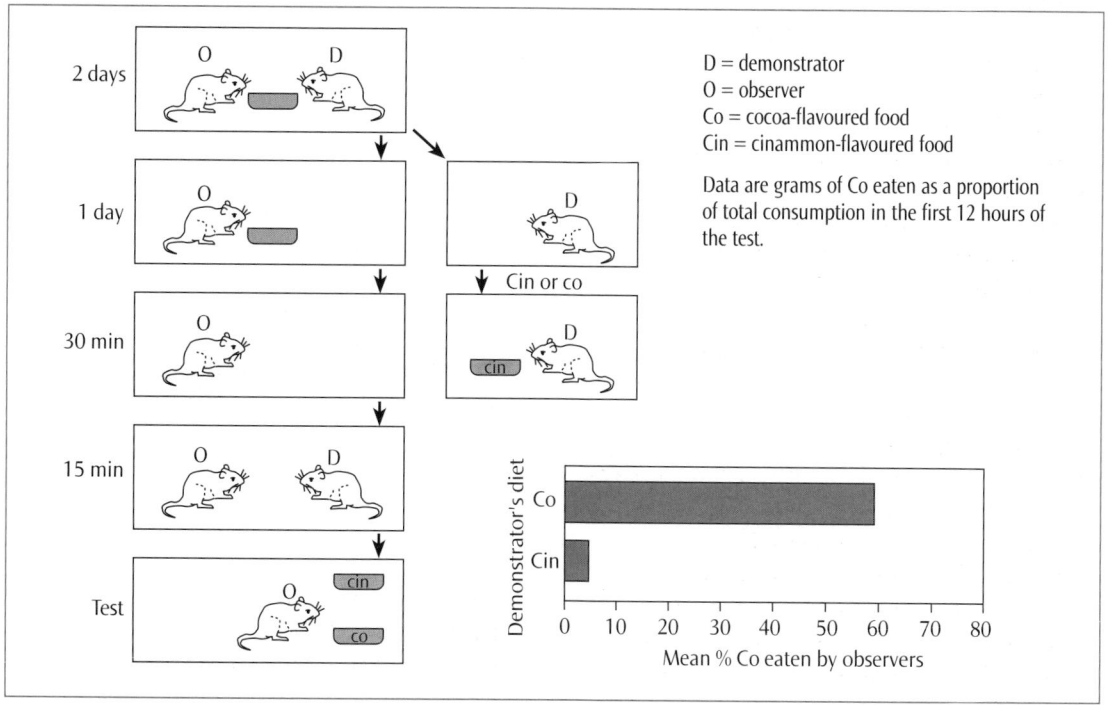

tearing, which would then be reinforced (Hinde and Fisher 1951). Quite why these birds began opening the bottles in the first place is somewhat of a mystery. Sherry and Galef (1990) reported that caged naïve birds were unlikely to open a foil-covered container of cream when they were in isolation. However, if they could see another bird in an adjacent cage they would begin to peck at the foil until they were eventually able to open it. The reasons for this *social facilitation* effect are not clear, but it is possible that the sight of the other bird reduced fear or in some way encouraged foraging responses (Pearce 1997). What *is* clear, however, is that this skill is unlikely to have been learned through imitation.

Do animals teach others?

To be classified as 'teacher', an animal has to modify its behaviour in some way, when in the presence of naïve individuals, so as to facilitate their learning (Caro and Hauser 1992). The teacher will incur some short-term cost, but for teaching to evolve, the teacher should reap some benefit in the long term, perhaps in terms of increased inclusive fitness. In a number of species adults can be observed apparently teaching their young what foods to eat, or how to catch them. Domestic cats will first bring back dead birds and mice (prey that are usually difficult to catch) to the nest and present them to the kittens. Later the mother will bring back live prey and allow the kittens to play with it. Finally, the kittens are able to capture prey by themselves without any help from the mother. In this example, there is an immediate cost to the mother of delayed feeding (sometimes the prey escapes and is lost) while the inexperienced offspring interact clumsily with the prey she has brought. However, this also has two potential advantages to her. First, she will be able to reduce the time she has to spend finding food for her offspring, as they quickly become more efficient foragers. Second, in the longer term, the offspring may increase her inclusive fitness by becoming more efficient foragers and producing more grandchildren for the teacher.

There is also evidence of certain aspects of tool-use in chimpanzees being 'taught' in this way. Boesch (1991) observed hundreds of cases where chimpanzee mothers 'stimulated' or 'facilitated' their infants coula nut-cracking behaviour. *Stimulation* consisted of leaving a stone 'hammer' near an 'anvil' block, and *facilitation* involved providing both hammers and nuts for infants at or near the anvils. Although stimulation and facilitation were fairly common, direct teaching was less common. In two cases observed by Boesch, however, chimpanzee mothers actively intervened when their infants were unsuccessful at breaking open the nuts because either nut or hammer was misoriented. In these cases the mother positioned either the nut or the hammer correctly for the infant. In contrast to these findings there was no evidence found

of either teaching or imitative learning in chimpanzees in another part of West Africa (Inoue-Nakamura and Matsuzawa 1997). Although there is some evidence of animals behaving in a way that is instructional to their offspring, it is not clear that it is the mothers' *intention* to teach their offspring. There are two particular problems in trying to ascertain whether the mother does intend to teach her offspring. First, it is virtually impossible for us to *measure* the mother's intention. Second, there is little evidence that the mothers understand what knowledge another animal possesses, a capacity referred to as having a *theory of mind*. We will explore this more in the next section.

Intelligence in nonhuman animals

Animal intelligence is a notoriously difficult concept. It may be seen as a hierarchy of learning processes, with habituation, the most basic form of learning, being shared by all species. As we move 'up' the phylogenetic hierarchy, animals acquire the ability to learn by association (classical and operant conditioning), complex learning abilities such as problem-solving and learning sets, and finally, the acquisition of language (considered unique to humans). However, this view of intelligence is criticized by many comparative psychologists as being unacceptably narrow. If intelligence is seen as the ability to solve problems that have ecological relevance in the animal's own environment then all species must be seen as equally intelligent in their own ways. There has been considerable comparative interest in species differences in self-recognition and theory of mind, although the relevance of such cognitive abilities to animals is still uncertain. Intelligence may simply be a product of brain size, which present humans and the cetaceans (marine mammals) as among the most intelligent species. Relative brain size (i.e. brain size relative to body size) is considered to be a better indicator of animal intelligence, although such a view also has problems (see *In Focus*, 'The Intelligence of cetaceans').

Self-recognition

Mirror self-recognition is usually seen as reflecting a state of self-awareness in animals, though even human beings need some practice at using mirrors. Congenitally blind people who have had their sight restored and young children who have never seen a mirror before both act as though they were seeing another person the first time they are confronted by their own reflection in a mirror. This reaction, however, is quickly replaced by self-recognition (Povinelli *et al.* 1993). Gallup (1970) first demonstrated that chimpanzees were able to recognize themselves in a mirror. After they were accustomed to using mirrors (chimpanzees typically use them to inspect their anal-

The intelligence of cetaceans

'The brain size of whales is much larger than that of humans. Their cerebral cortexes are as convoluted. They are at least as social as humans. Anthropologists believe that the development of human intelligence has been critically dependent upon these three factors: brain volume, brain convolutions, and social interactions among individuals. Here we find a class of animals where the three conditions leading to human intelligence may be exceeded, and in some cases greatly exceeded.' Sagan (1973)

It is widely believed that whales and other cetaceans (such as dolphins and porpoises) are highly intelligent. The basis for this belief appears to be partly the size and complex surface appearance of cetacean brains (Klinowska 1994). The brain of a mature male sperm whale does weigh in at a whopping 7.8 kg (compared to the human equivalent of 1.5 kg), but as a percentage of brain size to body weight, the sperm whale returns a miserly 0.02%. The degree of convolutions (or folds) of the cerebral cortex has also been seen as an indicator of intelligence. Ridgway (1986) provides evidence that bottlenose dolphins have a much higher degree of folding than humans, but the neocortex of cetacean brains is relatively thin, (about half that of humans), giving an average dolphin neocortical volume that is about 80% of that of humans. Dolphin brains are still relatively large – so is that an indication of high intelligence? Crick and Mitchison's (1983) theory of dream sleep may provide an alternative explanation for such large brains. They propose that REM sleep (see Chapter 5) acts to remove undesirable interactions in networks of cells in the cerebral cortex. They call this process 'reverse learning'. Animals that cannot use this system must have another way to avoid overloading the neural network, for example having bigger brains. The spiny anteater and dolphins are the only

mammals so far tested which do not have REM sleep (Mukhametov 1984), and *they* have disproportionately large brains. If we follow this line of reasoning, spiny anteaters and dolphins have large brains because they cannot dream.

The behaviour of dolphins and other cetaceans is also cited as evidence of high intelligence. Many of us have been amazed by the performance of captive dolphins and killer whales in *Sea World* centres and other marine parks, but many other animals, from elephants to fleas can achieve such feats. The complexity of cetacean 'societies' is also quoted as evidence for a highly intelligent species, but ants and bees, which have indisputably complex societies, are not usually described as 'intelligent' because of this. Although we still know little about the cetaceans' 'sophisticated communication abilities', they appear to be extremely rudimentary compared with the sophistication of human language. Although cetaceans appear able to communicate information about 'what', 'where' and 'who', there is no substantive evidence that they are able to transmit information about 'when', 'how' or 'why' (Gaskin 1982). As Margaret Klinowska puts it, 'With respect to Kipling's (1902) "six honest serving men" of learning and intellect, cetaceans appear to be three servants short' (Klinowska 1994).

genital area and other 'hidden' parts of their bodies), they were anaesthetized and a red mark placed on their foreheads and ears. After recovering from the anaesthetic, none of the subjects showed any interest in the marks until they saw themselves in a mirror, whereupon they touched the red marks on their own faces. The chimpanzees appeared to be using the mirror to direct responses towards their own body.

Using this criterion, a wide range of species have been tested with the mark test, and the results show successful performance by all four great ape species (chimpanzees, bonobos, orang-utans and gorillas), and failure by the numerous monkey species tested.

Although there is still some debate about what the mark test really does reflect in terms of cognitive abilities, the data overwhelmingly support a division between the great apes and humans versus other species on performance on this task.

The reason why some animals demonstrate self-recognition of themselves in mirrors and others do not is not clear. One suggestion is that self-recognition is confined to those species that can make use of information provided by mirrors. However, studies by Pepperberg *et al.* (1995) with parrots and Povinelli (1989) with elephants, have shown that some species can use mirrors but show no evidence of self-recognition.

in focus

Dogs – man's best friend?

Because human beings and dogs evolved together, scientists believe that we share certain patterns of thought that allow us to live together. Vilmos Csányi (cited in Douglas, 2000) believes that dogs and their owners are clearly emotionally attached. Researchers from Csányi's lab in Budapest gave dogs the 'Strange Situation test', originally devised to test the attachment that exists between an infant and its primary caregiver. A securely attached infant behaves in a characteristic way in a strange situation. So long as the mother is nearby, the infant shows little fear and is happy to explore a new environment. If the mother leaves, the infant becomes distressed. When she returns they are eager to greet her. Topál and Miklósi (1998) tested how 51 dogs responded to a similar strange situation. The dogs were keen to play and explore a familiar room as long as their owner was there. When the owner left the dogs became distressed, and greeted them enthusiastically on their return.

The researchers believe that the attachment to people might explain why dogs sometimes appear stupid. In 1980, researchers from the University of Michigan described how a wolf learned to manipulate a complicated door catch simply by watching another wolf open it. Dogs, on the other hand, couldn't master the catch even after years of watching the door open and close. During their domestication, dogs appear to have become obedient and trainable while losing some of their cognitive abilities such as problem-solving. Topál and Miklósi point out that dogs understand object permanence, that things don't cease to exist just because they can't see them, and are about the same level as apes in this respect. One area where human contact has enhanced the mental capacity of dogs is communication. Topál and Miklósi showed that dogs could respond to a range of subtle human gestures. They were able to retrieve hidden food items when prompted to do so by their owner pointing, nodding or even glancing towards the hiding place. In this study, the distance between gesture and reward did not affect the dogs' success.

Most researchers accept that only animals who can recognize themselves in a mirror are self-aware, allowing them to empathize and attribute intent and emotions in others. Dogs do not pass this test. As dogs have no sense of self, they are unable, for example, to use their own experience of pain to attribute painful experiences to others.

The more intimate the bond between dog and owner, the more dependent the dog, and the worse their problem-solving abilities. This is not always the case, however, as in the case of guide dogs, the best problem-solving dogs are those that are strongly attached to their blind owners. Once a guide dog develops a bond with its owner, it hands over the decision-making only to step in when the need arises. Prior to this discovery, only humans were supposed to be capable of this kind of sophisticated cooperation, where the initiative shifts constantly between two parties.

The remarkable social skills of dogs are understandable given that they are adapted to the same environment as their human masters. Csányi argues that communication, social bonding and cooperation have evolved in people *and* dogs so that both species can cope with their common environment. Dogs have been part of our evolutionary environment just as we have been part of theirs. The intriguing possibility is that there may just have been mutual influences (Douglas 2000).

A different explanation for why only a few species seem to be able to recognize themselves in a mirror comes from Gallup (1983), who believes that the use of mirrors for self-recognition depends on self-awareness. A chimpanzee is presumed to be able to use a mirror to locate a red spot on its forehead because it is self-aware, i.e. it *knows* it is looking at its own reflection. This view is not shared by all researchers. Heyes (1998) argues that there is little reliable evidence that any nonhuman primates are able to use a mirror to derive information about their own bodies, and even if there were, that this would indicate the possession of a self-concept, or any other aspect of self-awareness. As mentioned, in the original procedures carried out by Gallup (1970), animals with some experience of mirrors are anaesthetized and marked on their forehead with red dye. Several hours later, the frequency with which the animal touches the marks on its head is measured first in the absence of the mirror and then with the mirror present. Chimpanzees typically touch the marked areas of their head more in the mirror condition than in the mirror-absent condition. Heyes suggests that there is an alternative explanation for this finding – the *anaesthetic artefact hypothesis*. In the mirror-present condition (which occurs second) the animals would have had time to recover from the anaesthetic, therefore would be more active than in the previous, mirror-absent condition (Heyes 1998). Even if there were evidence that some primates *did* have the capacity implied by mirror self-recognition tasks, it would not, according to Heyes (1995) imply that the animal was 'self-aware'. To use a mirror as a source of information about its own body, an animal must be able to distinguish sensory inputs resulting from its own body and those inputs originating elsewhere. If an animal could learn that when it is standing in front of a mirror the input it receives correlates with inputs from its own body, it might be said to possess a 'body concept'. The fact that the humble pigeon can learn to use a mirror to detect paper dots attached to its feathers (Epstein *et al.* 1981), yet few would argue that pigeons possess a self-concept or are self-aware.

Theory of mind

We (i.e. human beings) possess a 'theory of mind' which we use to explain our behaviour by referring to mental states (e.g. 'I made that mistake because I was tired'). Our theory of mind not only allows us to explain our own behaviour, but also to make inferences about the intentions, desires, knowledge, and states of mind of other animals (Pearce 1997). Premack and Woodruff (1978) were the first researchers to experimentally address the possibility of a theory of mind in chimpanzees. They presented Sarah, an adult female chimpanzee, with a series of videotape sequences showing a human experiencing some sort of 'problem'. In one sequence, the human was seen shivering violently while standing next to an unplugged heater. As each video reached the point where the human would be likely to come up with a solution, the tape was stopped. Sarah was then given several photographs and was required to choose one. In the example given, Sarah chose the photograph with the heater plugged in, inferring, we presume, that heat would thus be provided and the human would be warm. As a result of this original research study, Premack and Woodruff asked the question whether chimpanzees, and other apes,

really do have a 'theory of mind'. Two kinds of research evidence have been used to address this question.

Deception

If an animal can understand that the actions of other animals can be influenced by the knowledge that they have, this leads us to the intriguing possibility that one animal might deliberately manipulate the information that the second animal receives. Woodruff and Premack (1979) tested this possibility in a study designed to see if chimpanzees really were capable of deception. In this study, chimpanzees, studied individually, observed a laboratory trainer hiding some food under one of two containers. The chimpanzee was then placed where it could see the containers but could not reach them. Another trainer then came into the room, and (depending on the condition) could either *help* the chimpanzee get the food if the animal pointed at the right container (the *co-operative trainer* condition) or *keep* it for himself (the *competitive assistant* condition). Some of the chimpanzees were able to earn food under both conditions, suggesting they had learned to direct the 'competitive' trainer to the wrong container, thus keeping the food in the other container for themselves. If the chimpanzees *knew* that the trainer would act on their false information, this would clearly be evidence for a theory of mind. This would be understandable, as in times of food shortage, if would benefit animals living in social groups (such as chimpanzees) to be secretive about food so that it is not stolen by another member of the group (Pearce 1997).

Although findings such as this are intriguing, for such behaviour to be a product of a 'theory of mind' a complicated line of reasoning would be required. First, the animals must understand that the trainer intended to steal the food. Second, they must understand that it is possible to convey false information about the location of the food by pointing to the wrong container. Finally, they must believe that this knowledge would hinder the assistant in his quest for the hidden food. As yet, there is little evidence that apes are capable of such sophisticated reasoning and Premack and Woodruff's findings are more easily explained in terms of learned discrimination between different responses and their outcomes. In other words, when one trainer is in the room, pointing at the right container becomes associated with the reward. When the other trainer is in the room, pointing also at the wrong container produces the desired outcome.

Attributions to others

A much simpler way of testing whether chimpanzees have a theory of mind is to test whether they are capable of attributing knowledge to another animal. Povinelli *et al.* (1990) explored this possibility with a study designed to see if chimpanzees could understand the very different knowledge states of *seeing* and *knowing*. In this study, two experimenters were initially present with their chimpanzee subject. One of the experimenters left the room and while they were out, the second experimenter hid a piece of food under one of four cups behind a low screen. The chimpanzee could see that food was being hidden under one of the cups, but was unable to see which one it was. When the absent experimenter returned, both experimenters pointed to a cup. The experimenter who had hidden the food (the 'knower') always pointed to the right cup, but the other experimenter (the 'guesser') always pointed to a wrong cup. Four of the five chimpanzees were eventually able to reliably choose the right cup on the basis of this information.

There are two interpretations of this finding. The interpretation that is consistent with a theory of mind explanation is that the chimpanzees were able to attribute *knowledge* to the assistant who had stayed in the room and knew that the assistant who had left the room lacked this knowledge. An alternative explanation is that the chimpanzees had learned a much simpler rule: picking the person who had stayed in the room leads to a reward; picking the other person does not lead to a reward. Extensions to this design, for example having the 'guesser' stay in the room but with his head in a bag, have produced ambiguous results and have led Heyes (1998) to conclude that plausible as these arguments are, they are based on fairly weak experimental evidence. To assume that chimpanzees must possess a theory of mind simply because they are developmentally close to young children is an assumption that has yet to be supported by reliable experimental evidence.

Social intelligence

Another aspect of intelligence may also be how animals solve social problems as well as physical problems, a form of intelligence that social psychologists call *social cognition*. Primates that form large and stable social groups are assumed to have the most highly developed social cognition of all animals. Repeated interactions over a prolonged period allow these animals to learn each other's identity and to build up altruistic or antagonistic relationships. According to evolutionary psychologists, reasoning ability evolved largely out of the need to detect cheaters in social relationships (i.e. animals which take the benefits of a social relationship must also pay a cost), a cognitive adaptation for social exchange.

Observations of vervet monkeys suggest that they know a great deal about their social world, but are less impressive in their understanding of their physical world (Cheney and Seyfarth 1990). For example, vervets appear to know many of the characteristics of their own group

and neighbouring groups, such as their voices, their relationships and where they might be found. Their knowledge of aspects of their physical environment is considerably less detailed. For example, leopards and snakes are two common vervet predators. However, although vervets react to the *presence* of these predators, they appear unable to recognize the signs that such dangers are nearby (e.g. a dead antelope over a tree or snake trails in the dust). This fairly simple example of 'learning by association' might be expected in an 'intelligent' species yet is absent in vervet monkeys. Vervets, according to Cheney and Seyfarth (1990) appear to be good social psychologists but poor naturalists.

Activity 4: Intelligent behaviour?

Use your own observations and examples given you by friends or family to make a list of animal behaviours that seem to indicate that the animal is behaving *intelligently*. From your reading of this chapter, can you find alternative explanations (such as conditioning) to explain any of these observed behaviours?

Exam summary: Social learning in nonhuman animals

The AQA examination will test your understanding of the following areas:

◆ explanations and research studies of social learning in nonhuman animals (pp. 348–50)

◆ evidence for intelligence in nonhuman animals (pp. 350–4).

Example question

The question below is typical of one drawn from the material above, and should take you 30 minutes to answer.

◆ Describe and evaluate evidence for intelligence in nonhuman animals. *(24 marks)*

Suggested answer structure

We have seen that intelligence in nonhuman animals is a notoriously difficult concept to define, and comparisons across different species with respect to intelligence may be meaningless if we take the view that each species is of equal intelligence as it has adapted to its ecological niche with equal success.

It is widely believed that whales and other cetaceans are highly intelligent, yet this may be somewhat illusory. There is reason for believing that the size and organization of cetacean brains reflects less their high

Is 'natural selection' still at work?

Perhaps it is no accident that the word 'generation' could also be read as 'gene-ration'. We, the individual animals who make up the natural world, are merely the carriers of genes, even though in different species we package them in relatively unique ways (Dawkins 1976, 1982). In each living organism the genetic material comes to it having survived a tortuous voyage down aeons of time by use of temporary time-travelling vehicles, of which we are merely the latest designs. Many multitudes of genes and gene combinations have fallen by the wayside on this incredible journey through time. On a global scale, perhaps more of these carriers are failing by way of extinction in recent times than ever before (Wilson 1992). There have been disasters on a epic scale in earlier times, such as the decline and fall of the dinosaur empire and the massive extinctions evident in the Burgess Shale, a fossil bed located in the Canadian Rockies (Gould 1989).

But that does not mean that natural selection has stopped functioning. Humans have created new rules for selection involving themselves and most other organisms on the planet today, with the new conditions including overpopulation, environmental pollutants, deforestation, factory-style agricultural production, pesticides, antibiotics, greenhouse gases, nuclear fallout, over-fishing, and a host of other threats to nature's balance. Natural selection will act upon genotypes with as much vigour as it ever did, and take directions which are as unpredictable as ever in the game of evolutionary chance (Gould 1994).

The conditions of life may be much harsher in the future, but it is still likely that genes will survive in carriers in some form or other. They may not continue to build life forms of the kind we are used to seeing today, but that has always been the way of evolution. In terms of evolutionary time, humans have been an extremely recent addition to this planet, and we have still not had as much impact on the world as did the dinosaurs. However mightily they once ruled the planet, they are merely fossils today. That fate doubtlessly awaits us

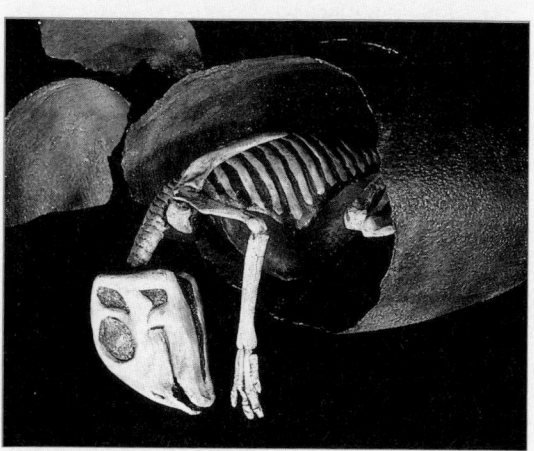

too. We might hope to last some of the hundreds of millions of years which they enjoyed on this planet. If recent history is anything to go by, the odds are stacked against our achieving anything like that.

Just to mention one reason for this gloomy prediction, the world now holds a human population of around five and half billion people. If the current growth rate of 1.7 per cent per year continues for another 400 years, the population would swell to five and a half *trillion* people. This figure would permit each person to occupy an area on this planet just a little larger than an average living room of a modern house (Cohen 1995).

intelligence, but more an evolutionary adaptation to their lifestyle and evolutionary niche (pp. 350–1). There is also reason to believe that the intelligence of our own domestic dogs may in some way reflect the dependent relationship that dogs have developed with their owners. Contrary to popular belief, the domestication of dogs has resulted in a loss of certain of their cognitive abilities (p. 352). Two related areas that have attracted a great deal of research interest and generated a great deal of controversy in the animal intelligence debate are self-recognition (pp. 350–3) and theory of mind (pp. 353–4). Chimpanzees appear able to recognize themselves in a mirror, whereas monkeys (and dogs) cannot. The significance of this is not yet clear, and no

satisfactory explanation has yet been provided why chimpanzees should have this advantage over other primates (with the exception of the other great apes). Research evidence on theory of mind in nonhuman animals has been divided in whether nonhumans have this facility. There is some research evidence that chimpanzees are capable of deception (i.e. deliberately misleading another animal), although critics claim that there is little evidence that apes are capable of such sophisticated reasoning (pp. 353–4). Finally there is evidence that nonhuman animals may also differ in their social cognition (p. 354), a particularly important skill in communities that rely on established patterns of reciprocal relationships.

Chapter summary

◆ **Animal behaviour** evolves through the process of natural selection. Not all behaviour has evolved because it confers an adaptive advantage on animals. The essence of Darwin's theory of evolution is that organisms attempt to maximize their reproductive output. **Evolution** is now seen not as occurring to benefit an individual animal, but to benefit its genes.

◆ Animals sometimes behave in **apparently altruistic** ways that increase the reproductive fitness of the individual that is helped at some cost to the helper. However, there may be a **biological explanation** for this. As a result of this self-sacrificing behaviour, animals may increase their inclusive fitness and are therefore displaying selfishness at a genetic level (kin selection). In reciprocal altruism, animals may help one another but have the favour returned sometime in the future. Some animals will cooperate and help one another because as a team they can achieve more than by working alone.

◆ In **classical conditioning**, a naturally occurring reflex (the UCS–UCR reflex) is associated with another stimulus (the CS) that is not typically capable of producing the response in question. Following consistent association with the UCS, the new stimulus is able to trigger the original behaviour. If the UCS is no longer paired with the UCR, however, the CR is extinguished. The CR might reappear under certain conditions in a procedure known as spontaneous recovery. When a stimulus is presented which is similar to the CS, the response might generalize to it dependent on the degree of similarity. If other stimuli are never paired with the UCS, however, the organism will discriminate between them and only respond to the original CS.

◆ **Operant conditioning** refers to learning that is dependent on the outcome of a behaviour. If behaviour is reinforced in some way, that behaviour will reappear more frequently in the future. This reinforcement may be positive, a pleasant event, or negative avoiding or escaping from an unpleasant event. Reinforcement can also be presented in various schedules. These might be continuous or partial. Continuous reinforcement schedules produce more rapid initial learning but also more rapid extinction rates. Partial reinforcement results in slower extinction rates. If a behaviour produces unpleasant consequences (punishment) it is less likely to be produced in the future.

◆ Many animals live in groups. Therefore, it would benefit them to be able to copy what other members of the group have learned. **Imitation would**, theoretically, be of considerable value to many different species, yet evidence for imitation in nonhuman species is relatively rare. Some animals learn about **foraging** and preferred food sources by associating with conspecifics.

◆ **Animal intelligence**, a difficult concept, may be seen as a hierarchy of learning processes, with the most basic forms of learning being shared by all species and 'higher' levels being associated with the more 'intelligent' species. There has been considerable comparative interest in **social learning in nonhuman animals** especially in species differences in **self-recognition** and **theory of mind**, although the relevance of such cognitive abilities to animals is still uncertain. **Intelligence** may also be seen as a product of how animals solve social problems as well as physical problems, a process known as social cognition.

Further resources

Manning, A. and Dawkins, M.S. (1998)
An Introduction to Animal Behaviour (5th edn), Cambridge: Cambridge University Press.

A very readable and beautifully illustrated text dealing with most of the issues in this chapter.

Pearce, J.M. (1997) *Animal Learning and Cognition* (2nd edn), Hove: Psychology Press.

A very comprehensive account of all aspects of animal learning (described in this chapter) and animal cognition (described in Chapter 14).

Websites

http://ccp.uchicago.edu/~jyin/evolution.html

Evolution and behaviour. A massive site that acts as a jumping off place to explore all the aspects of evolution covered in this chapter.

http://www.behavior.org/

The Cambridge Center for Behavioural Studies, providing information resources about the practical applications of behavioural technology. The Behaviour Analysis Webring links together the major Internet resources in this field around the world.

Chapter 14

Animal cognition

Mike Cardwell

Preview

In this chapter we shall be looking at:

- explanations and research into animal navigation
- explanations of the use of signalling systems in nonhuman animals and research into animal language
- explanations and research into memory in nonhuman animals.

Introduction

Our interest in the cognitive abilities of animals may be fuelled partly by academic interest, but also it is born out of a sense of wonder about our natural world. Anecdotes about the amazing feats of domestic pets, the spectacular navigational skills of homing pigeons or the haunting song of the humpback whale have all contributed to the feeling that animals may be a lot smarter than we imagine. The study of animal cognition is one way we can apply the principles of scientific psychology to this most fascinating area of animal behaviour.

To move between parts of their habitat (subhabitats) efficiently and safely, animals must travel in the right direction, to the right distance, at the right time (Waterman 1989). Navigation enables animals to find their way from one place to another. A good navigator

must be able to sense direction, distance, and time. Sometimes this is over vast distances, as in the migration of the arctic tern from the Antarctic ice pack half way around the world to its feeding grounds on the coast of Greenland. Sometimes this is more localized, with animals trying to find their way back home after a morning's foraging. Some animals navigate by sight, some use the sun and the stars as a celestial 'map', and some, such as whales, follow the contours of coastlines. Some animals use senses far different from ours, as in the case of echolocation in dolphins.

Animal communication and human language have fundamental differences in both their structure and also their function. The intriguing possibility that nonhumans might be able to learn human language has led to a flurry of research projects which have explored the linguistic capacities of chimpanzees, gorillas, dolphins, and even the parrot. The claim that these animals are demonstrating *language* is one of the most hotly contested assertions in comparative psychology.

The study of animal memory is concerned with how information acquired at one time can influence behaviour in the future. In species which store food in order to retrieve it at a later date, a good spatial memory is vital. If we establish that animals can indeed retain information about past events, then we begin to ask questions about the sort of information they might retain, how much they might be able to remember, and for how long.

Animal navigation

'Our everyday experience is full of animals and people on the move.' (Waterman 1989)

Homing behaviour

A fundamental distinction between plant and animal life is the ability to move at will around the environment. Most plant life acts like a chemical factory, making up and breaking down chemicals into

nutrient and waste products, and using one of a number of reproductive mechanisms to germinate and reproduce. Animals tend to move around in search of food (*foraging*), whether obtained from plants or other animal life (though some plants are also highly effective hunters and trappers of animals, too). Animal species that build or otherwise manufacture a home (e.g. a nest, burrow or shelter) that is used by them more than once, do not only need to have some way of remembering where the home is, but also need to have some form of navigational or direction-finding protocol for locating it from a distance. The means by which animals locate their home range from afar can be very impressive, with some species able to do so as part of a migratory pattern which may take them many thousands of miles each year (MacFarland 1993). The albatross is able to home successfully after trips of over 4,000 miles! Animals use a variety of different strategies for homing. We will consider each of these in turn.

The use of landmarks

Tinbergen and Kruyt (1938) demonstrated how the digger wasp uses the main features around its burrow to locate its home when returning from a foraging flight. The wasp makes its home by burrowing a short distance into soft dirt and, just prior to leaving each time, makes a hovering flight overhead, seemingly 'taking in' any changes in the environment in the vicinity of the burrow entrance. Tinbergen and Kruyt carried out an ingenious experiment by altering the position of landmarks (pine cones they had set out themselves) after the wasp had flown out of sight. When the resident wasp returned, it was deceived by the new placement of cones into searching for its burrow entrance in the wrong place entirely.

The impressive ability of pigeons to find their home loft after release from the loft is largely dependent on their ability to learn prominent landmarks in the area. If they are released within sight of these landmarks, they can use them to find their way home. When they are released from more distant locations, their journey time improves with successive journeys, suggesting an increasing reliance on landmarks as they become more familiar with their terrain (Pearce 1997). However, there are sound reasons for not believing that pigeons

make exclusive use of landmarks for navigation. Pigeons that are taken a considerable distance from their home loft are still able to find their way home, despite the fact that they have never seen any of the landmarks before. In other words, in the absence of familiar landmarks, pigeons appear to be capable of *true navigation* (see below), not just finding their way home from a familiar starting point (as in the case of the digger wasp described earlier). They must use at least one other form of navigation. We will examine the possibility of 'true' navigational skills in pigeons next.

Homing using true *navigation*

To test whether birds are capable of true navigation (i.e. have the ability to reach their goal regardless of their starting point) or simply show a compass orientation (always heading in one specific compass direction regardless of the 'correct' direction), a group of scientists carried out an ingenious experiment (cited in Ridley 1995). They captured *young* starlings on their annual migration from their breeding grounds around the Baltic Sea to their wintering sites in southern England, Belgium and northern France. After tagging, the birds were taken, by aeroplane, to Switzerland, where they were released. After release, the birds continued on the same heading as before (south-west) despite the fact they had been displaced by nearly 500 miles from their original route! Instead of ending up in southern England, many of the birds arrived in northern Spain (see right hand picture in Fig. 14.1).

Interestingly, *adult* birds that were captured and released in the same way compensated for the displacement and headed north-west, the proper direction for their usual wintering grounds. The juveniles, it appears, were relying on compass

Figure 14.1 Results of experiment to detect whether birds use compass orientation or true navigation

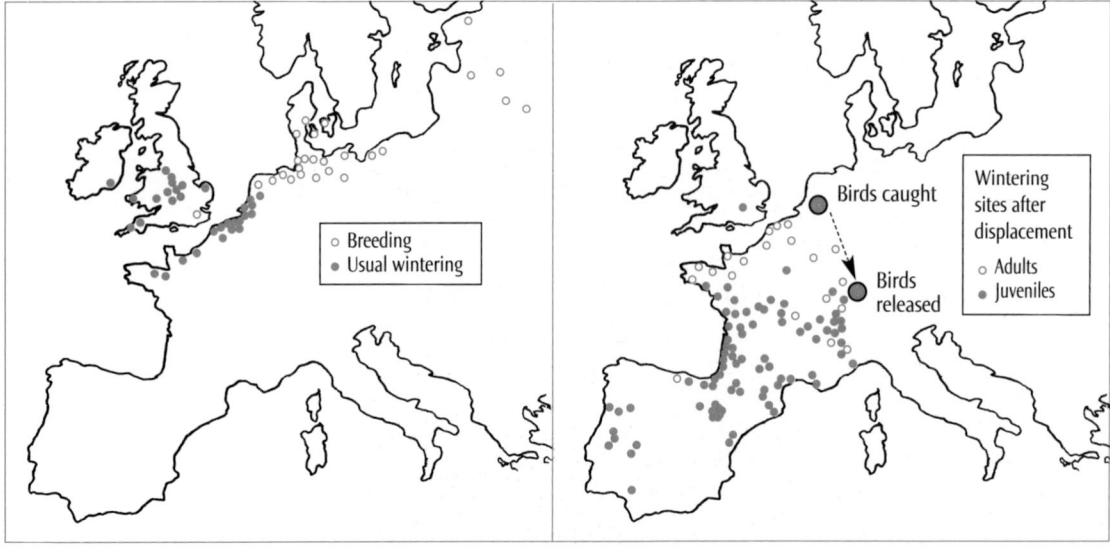

orientation, the adults on true navigation. The theory of true navigation in pigeons has been unanimously supported by the research literature, and is often referred to as 'map and compass' navigation. It is so called because in order to find its way home, the pigeon must be able to work out its map position, and then from this position must orient itself in the home direction via some sort of compass mechanism. The evidence seems to suggest that the map component is based on olfactory, magnetic and visual cues, while the compass sense appears to be guided by the sun and magnetic information (Wallraff 1990).

The sun compass

It has long been believed that pigeons use the position of the sun to help them navigate. Kramer (1952) trained pigeons to locate food using the sun as a directional cue. When he deflected the image of the sun with mirrors, he found that the orientation of the birds shifted correspondingly. The sun compass is presumed to operate in the following way. When a pigeon is released, it observes the position of the sun and compares it with its internal body clock. If a pigeon is released at noon (according to its body clock) then it would expect the sun to be directly overhead. If the sun appears to be lower in the sky then the pigeon should be able to compute the direction it should take to return to its home loft. This is a complex calculation, but clock-shifting experiments suggest it is not beyond the capabilities of pigeons.

An animal's internal clock is set according to the light–dark cycle (see Chapter 5). If pigeons are kept in an artificial environment with a light–dark cycle that is out of sync with the external light–dark cycle, it should be possible to alter the birds' internal clock, and therefore the accuracy of the sun compass. In a typical clock-shift experiment, the birds are kept in conditions where the lights might be switched on at midnight and off at midday, with all external cues removed. After a few days, it is possible to have shifted the birds' internal clock forward 6 hours (dawn is actually at 6 a.m., but the birds' internal clock tells them it is midday). If a bird is then released at 9 a.m., its internal clock tells it that it is actually 3 p.m.; this leads the bird to infer that the sun should be in the south-west (where it *should* be at 3 p.m.) whereas it is actually in the south-east. The bird should then make its computations based on this information, and fly at right angles to the actual direction home. A number of experiments (e.g. Keeton 1969) have confirmed these predictions, and thus confirm the importance of the sun compass in homing.

However Keeton (1969) also suggested that pigeons must be using another system apart from the sun compass to determine directional information. For example, on overcast days, when the sun isn't visible, pigeons are still able to home successfully. Interestingly enough, he found that clock-shifted pigeons deviated from normal pigeons only on sunny days. On overcast days, however, both clock-shifted and normal pigeons homed successfully and there appeared to be no difference in performance between the two groups. From this finding, Keeton concluded that the sun is only used for directional information when it is visible, but at other times pigeons must make use of another, secondary, compass sense.

Magnetic cues

Keeton suggested that pigeons may also have the ability to detect the earth's magnetic field. To investigate this possibility, he glued small magnets onto the heads of the birds and then released them from unfamiliar sites. The magnets had the effect of disrupting any detection of the magnetic field of the earth, and should, therefore, make successful homing impossible on overcast days. As predicted, he found that these birds experienced no difficulty homing on sunny days, but were unable to

Pigeons appear able to use a variety of navigational strategies to find their way home

find their way back to their home loft on overcast days (Keeton 1971). Keeton concluded that pigeons appear to use two compass systems during navigation. The primary system relies on the position of the sun, and the secondary system on the earth's magnetic field. Keeton also found that young, inexperienced pigeons were often disoriented when wearing the magnets, even in sunny conditions. He suggested that this was an indication that the magnetic compass was innate and was used to calibrate the sun compass as a result of homing experience. These inexperienced birds were unable to use the information provided by the sun because of their inexperience, and could not use the earth's magnetic field because of the magnet.

The magnetic map hypothesis has been criticized on several grounds:

◆ Attempts to train pigeons to respond to a change in the magnetic field have failed. These experiments are based on the assumption that if pigeons can detect a change in the magnetic field, it should be possible to train them to respond to such a change. Kreithen (1975) tested 97 pigeons for their ability to detect changes in the magnetic field using a classically conditioned increase in heart rate as the conditioned response (see Chapter 13 for an explanation of classical conditioning). The birds were first exposed to an experimentally induced change in the magnetic field followed by a weak electric shock which caused the pigeon's heart rate to increase. After several trials, if the bird was able to detect a change in the magnetic field, it would be able to anticipate the electric shock after sensing the change in the magnetic field, and its heart rate would increase. No such response was found. Although this might indicate some problem with the laboratory method, a more likely explanation is that the pigeon was simply unable to sense such changes.

◆ It has also been suggested that the effects of magnetic treatments during pigeon navigation are not a direct result of the magnetic treatments themselves, but rather their side-effects on the pigeon's nervous system (Papi *et al.* 1992), in particular the opioid system (which controls sensitivity to pain). Papi and colleagues found that birds given an opiate antagonist (which blocks the action of natural opiates) were more likely to become disoriented when released at unfamiliar sites. Likewise, birds subjected to an oscillating magnetic field were found to have a lower concentration of opiate receptors in the brain. Papi suggested that the disorientation effects of the magnetic treatment are therefore attributable to stress caused by the experimental procedures rather than the disruption caused by the magnets.

We will finish this section by examining one of the most controversial explanations of the homing behaviour of pigeons – that of olfactory navigation.

Olfactory cues

Research on homing pigeons, the only bird to have been thoroughly investigated with respect to olfactory navigation, suggests that they may rely on local odours for their homeward orientation (Papi 1991). Experiments to test this hypothesis fall into two categories – those which attempt to remove the odours that are supposedly used for navigation, and those which attempt to disrupt the pigeons' olfactory map. A relatively simple prediction that arises from the first of these categories of research is that anosmic pigeons (i.e. those prevented from receiving olfactory information) should not be able to home. Various methods are used for creating this condition, including plugging nostrils, local anaesthetic and surgically cutting the olfactory nerves. Numerous concerns have been raised about the procedures used to induce anosmia and their bearings on the findings of research investigations. Some critics have suggested that the behavioural side-effects of anosmia (e.g. motivational and learning difficulties) might affect the pigeons' motivation or ability to process navigational information correctly. The existing evidence does not support a motivational deficit. Wallraff (1988) showed that anosmic pigeons flew distances comparable to controls, but in random directions. This suggests that they were similarly motivated to home, but did not know the right direction (Able 1996).

Overall, the results from experiments in which pigeons are prevented from acquiring olfactory information en route to and at the release site, tend to support the olfactory hypothesis. Although there remain concerns that the procedures used to create anosmia may in some way affect the results, there is, as yet, no evidence to support this assertion.

The second method involves manipulating the olfactory 'map' used by pigeons. This has the advantage of producing a predictable effect on the orientation of the pigeons, rather than a general disorientation in the case of the anosmic pigeons. Experiments using this technique have focused on three aspects of homing. First, experimenters have attempted to alter the odours experienced at the loft, so that pigeons would receive a predictably altered olfactory 'map' of their home loft. Second, as pigeons are known to use olfactory information acquired on their transport to the release point, attempts have been made to mislead them by providing false information during their journey. Third, attempts have been made to manipulate the odours at the release site in order to fool the pigeons in a predictable way.

Most attention has been focused on manipulations at the home loft. The olfactory hypothesis states that pigeons learn an odour 'map' by associating odours perceived at the home loft with the directions they are carried by winds (Able 1996). Disrupting these by reversing the movement of air (and with it the movement of odours) should make birds fly in the opposite direction (compared to controls) when released. This is exactly what happens. Research by Ioalè *et al.* (1990) used fans to blow an air current carrying the scent of the chemical benzaldehyde. By experimentally manipulating the direction of the air current, Ioalè and colleagues were able to reverse the direction of the natural air currents at the loft. When both experimental and control group pigeons (who had not experienced the reversal) were exposed to benzaldehyde during the transport to the release site, the controls headed in a homeward direction, and the experimental group pigeons vanished in the opposite direction.

One of the major problems in universally accepting that pigeons make exclusive use of olfactory navigation for homing is the difficulty in replicating research in other parts of the world. Different results in different

---

in focus

Olfactory nest recognition

Olfaction may play an important role in the order of birds known as *procellariiformes*. These birds are more commonly known as the 'tubenoses' because of the large tubes located on the top of their bills. These tubes allow them to drain salt from their bodies while drinking seawater. Most birds do not drink seawater because it adds too much salt to their bodies, but these birds must drink seawater as they are oceanic travelers who remain at sea except during nesting periods. Procellariiformes such as the storm petrel (*Hydrobates pelagicus*) have a well-developed olfactory system, and experiments with other birds of this order suggest that they might use this to guide their navigation to colony sites (Grubb 1973).

Mínguez (1997) studied storm petrels in their nesting sites along the coast of Benidorm. Only one chick is raised in each brood, and this fledges about 60 days after hatching. For much of these 60 days, however, the chick is left on its own, the parent only returning to feed the bird in the nest, lodged inside crevices in the rocky coastline. Mínguez noted that as the birds became older, they became more active, venturing away from the nest, but always returning to the right nest for feeding. In order to test whether the birds were using their olfactory sense to guide them back to the nest, Mínguez took 11 storm petrel chicks and removed them from their nest (storm petrels are an endangered species in Spain, so the number used was minimized). He carefully blocked the nares (to prevent olfactory information) of six of these chicks and tested their ability to find their way back to the nest from varying distances. He then tested the other five,

manipulating them in the same way, but without blocking their nares. Two days later he reversed the conditions for the same 11 chicks. None of the chicks with blocked nares found their nest, whereas all those with unblocked nares did so successfully. At the end of the experiments, all blockages were removed and all chicks placed back on the right nests.

A chick's ability to find its way back to its own nest would be crucial if parental feeding only took place there. Mínguez observed where feeding took place, and found that chicks were always on the nest when they received food. If adults (who have no parent-offspring recognition) simply feed any young that happen to be in the nest, then why

Procellariiformes, such as this fork-tailed storm petrel, have large tubes at the top of their bills, part of a well-developed olfactory system

doesn't the chick find the nearest nest and feed there? The answer seems to lie in the fact that resident chicks are fiercely territorial and are very much more aggressive towards unrelated chicks than are their parents. Therefore nest parasitism may well be unprofitable, and even dangerous, for the petrel chick and the pressure should be strong for a petrel chick to recognize its own nest and stay in it (Mínguez 1997).

parts of the world appear to reflect either the different rearing procedures employed, or aspects of the local environment around the loft. The degree to which pigeons rely on olfactory navigation appears to be determined by how and where they are raised and housed. When pigeons are raised in lofts that are sheltered from winds (thus making it difficult to form a reliable olfactory map) they appear largely unaffected by anosmic procedures and home successfully, suggesting that they possess some other navigational capability (Able 1996).

Activity 1: How do humans navigate?

Think of some of the different ways in which human beings navigate around their surroundings *without* the use of technological assistance (e.g. using the sun, stars, wind direction, etc.).

Do you know anyone who is a scuba diver? Ask them how they can navigate under water without using their compass.

Is there evidence for natural navigational skills in human beings? How would you test to see if human beings had a magnetic sense?

Wildebeest crossing the Mara River in Kenya on migration

Migration

Migration is a generic term which usually describes the mass movement of members of a species from one location to another. The trigger for this behaviour may be seasonal changes in weather, air temperature or day length, or in response to fluctuations in the environment, such as food supply. For instance, wildebeest on the African savannah move towards rain when they sense it during the dry season. They seem to be able to read the signs, such as darkened clouds or cool winds emanating from the direction of the rains.

The distance over which animals migrate may range from one to two metres (e.g. the vertical movements of zooplankton in a lake, moving to different depths according to time of day) to several thousand miles, such as the albatross or the monarch butterfly. Usually these are return migrations, but not always. For instance, adult Atlantic salmon migrate from the Sargasso Sea (South Atlantic) to the lakes and rivers of Europe where they themselves were spawned. After spawning near the site of their own birthplace, they perish, leaving the next generation to fight their way along the freshwater pathways back to the sea.

Birds which migrate over large distances are able to use a range of environmental cues to guide them, such as the smell of the sea while following a continental coastline, the sight of mountains or other landmarks, or by using the earth's magnetic field. The use of such landmarks is not confined to migratory journeys,

---

The monarch butterfly

The monarch butterfly lives mainly in North America. When the temperatures begin to fall, these large, strikingly coloured insects begin their amazing migration south to winter in the southern United States and Mexico. Although not all monarchs migrate south in this way, those who do, do so at astonishing speeds – with some tagged monarchs covering more than 80 miles in a single day. Although they may continue their free-living existence following this migration, when the weather turns colder, the butterflies aggregate into dense groups to keep warm. As they are cold blooded, it appears that this seasonal migration is driven by the need to be in a place warm enough for them still to maintain an active life.

however, since many animals utilize knowledge of their environment (a so-called 'cognitive map') to navigate during their daily forays from home.

The migration of birds

When the terrain allows it, birds often migrate in stages. Their overall migration may, therefore, be made up of a series of relatively short steps punctuated by rest stops. These are necessary to replenish the body resources needed to travel such long distances. Most small song birds stop to feed each day during their migration, with their migratory flights normally taking place at night. If they are crossing a large body of water or desert, these birds may fly for a full 24 hours at a time. Other birds (such as storks) make use of the rising air currents to make long flights during the day. Soarers such as the stork depend on thermal updrafts for their migration, and appear loath to fly over water if they cannot see land on the other side (because of the absence of the rising warm air necessary to soar).

First-time migrators frequently travel without more experienced adults. As they leave either before or after the adults, their navigation cannot be guided by them. There is evidence that experienced birds are better able to navigate direct routes than juveniles and therefore reach their destination first. Successful navigation also depends on the effects of wind and weather. Computer modelling has shown that birds migrating from North America to the Eastern Caribbean islands or to South America in the autumn may be aided by strong seasonal prevailing winds. Shortly after a strong cold front with its brisk north-west winds, birds head south-east out to sea in great numbers. If they fly at their most efficient sustained speed, they generally make landfall in three to four days. This model indicates that in such instances, successful navigation would not require a precise compass heading, nor a specific place of leaving, nor, even, a specific altitude or air speed. As long as typical weather conditions prevail, a high degree of success would be expected without any elaborate navigational control. Without the right weather pattern, however, mass disaster would ensue. Weather is, of course, notoriously unpredictable, but it does have some major reliable features that can be exploited in migration. The steady westerly gales that blow at high southerly latitudes propel the wandering albatross around the world in its yearly circuit. Between 30° and 60° north of the equator, south-westerly winds prevail, while north-westerlies blow between 30° and 60° south (Waterman 1989).

Aquatic migration

Many aquatic animals migrate over vast distances. In the Bahamas, spiny lobsters that spend the summer in shallow water move during the autumn to deeper water. They typically form a 'queue' in columns of up to 60 individuals, and walk to their new home, perhaps 50 to 60 kilometres away. The queuing may serve to reduce the drag of the water on each individual, and thus save energy. Adult wool-handed crabs live in rivers such as the Yangtze and the Rhine, but migrate downstream as far as 1200 kilometres to release their eggs in the sea.

Navigating underwater is quite different from navigating in air because of the extremely poor visibility and the underwater currents. Visual piloting is therefore of limited usefulness underwater. Many species do have well-developed visual systems, however, and these must be primarily important for prey detection, and to a lesser extent for orientation and navigation. Visual functioning in the absence of daylight is also possible because of bioluminescence (the production of light by organisms themselves) which is widespread in the sea. Water currents are in many ways similar to winds. They are generally much slower than winds, but then swimming is much slower than flying. As winds can help or hinder the migration of birds, so currents can help or hinder the migration of aquatic organisms. Winds and tides supply most of the energy for ocean currents although, typically, currents reach only about 2 per cent of the driving wind's speed (Waterman 1989).

One of the most closely studied migrating fish is the salmon. Typically, immature fish descend from the streams in which they were born, to spend part of their life at sea. This urge to migrate varies according to the species. In some salmon species it is rare, in others it is common. In the first phase of migration, the juvenile salmon live in fresh water. At the right time, these juveniles swim downstream towards the sea. For some species this is days after their birth, in others (such as the Atlantic salmon) this can be as long as 7 years after their birth. During the 1 to 5 years that salmon spend in the ocean, they feed extensively and achieve most of

---

Activity 2: Observing migration in birds

If you live close to a Wildfowl and Wetlands Trust site (such as Slimbridge in Gloucestershire or Welney in Norfolk), visit between October and December to see the migrating Bewick swans at the end of their 4,000 km migration from Arctic Russia.

Alternatively, visit the following website to learn more about the migratory behaviour of these birds:

http://www.bbc.co.uk/education/archive/ heading_south/

Table 14.1 Numbers of coho salmon released and later recaptured in two rivers in Washington state, with and without their olfactory sense impaired				
Stream of origin		Number released	Number recaptured	
			Issaquah	East Fork
Issaquah	Controls	121	46	0
	Nose plugged	145	39	12
East Fork	Controls	38	8	19
	Nose plugged	38	16	3

their growth. During this second phase they must find food and avoid predators.

In the third phase, salmon return as adults to the mouths of their native rivers. The different populations sort themselves out and navigate successfully to their own home stream. In the fourth phase, the salmon must swim against the current (for some, a distance of 4,000 kilometres) often ascending a long river. At every fork in the river, the fish must make the correct navigational decision. It seems certain that chemical cues are used to recognize both the home estuary and also the precise spawning area. This hypothesis is supported by research carried out by Wisby and Hasler (cited in Harden-Jones 1968). Wisby and Hasler plugged the noses of salmon which then homed less accurately than untreated controls. The results of this experiment can be seen in Table 14.1.

The navigation of these fish is clearly tied to specific geographical objectives, because individual fish return exactly to their parents' spawning site. Breeding experiments show clearly that precise navigation depends on both genetic factors and juvenile learning.

The advantages of migration

Though such migration may seem rather a pointless activity, the benefits are usually that the individuals exploit the best breeding or feeding conditions in both places. The seasonal changes which affect latitudes at some distance from the equator mean that the climate, food or other resources fluctuate greatly with the seasons. Southern latitudes experience considerably better winter weather than we have in Europe, and during our summer much of the southern latitudes are covered in snow and ice. Insectivores (insect eaters) and frugivores (fruit eaters) are able, by moving south, to find food that they would never be able to find in a harsh winter environment. Many of the birds that remain in the north forage on seeds which remain available throughout the winter. Northern summers also tend to have much longer days for birds to forage.

Tropical days tend to be around 12 hours long, whereas days in a northern summer may be as long as 16 hours. This is particularly important during the breeding season when parent birds have to feed nestlings that will increase to 50 times their hatching weight in 13 days. A final advantage of migration is that it diminishes at least some of the predatory pressures on migratory species. Predators that specialize in hunting one particular bird species cannot evolve, as their prey are not around as a food source full time.

The impetus to migrate may not be a *decision* left to individual animals – the so-called 'migration *instinct*' can markedly affect an animal's behaviour at the close of a season. On the other hand, many individuals of bird species seem to *decide* not to migrate in a given year (though of course, no 'reasoning' is implied here – the response may simply be one where the environmental cues have not been sufficiently strong to trigger off the behaviour seen in others of the species).

Exam summary: Animal navigation

The AQA examination will test your understanding of the following areas:

◆ explanations and research into animal navigation (pp. 357–64).

Example question

The question below is typical of one drawn from the material above, and should take you 30 minutes to answer.

◆ Critically consider two explanations of animal navigation. *(24 marks)*

Suggested answer structure

Before attempting this question, you should turn to Table 21.1 on p. 551. You will see that the injunction *Critically consider* has a very specific requirement.

It requires you to show your knowledge and understanding (the AO1 content – in this case your knowledge and understanding of two explanations of animal navigation) and the *strengths and limitations* (the AO2 content) of these explanations. To accomplish this you might look at research that supports these explanations and research that challenges them or alternatively examine the advantages and disadvantages of each method of navigation. While you are in Chapter 21, turn to Table 21.3 on p. 554. You will see that in the AO2 Assessment Criteria, there are six bands. Failure to address both the strengths *and* the limitations of these two explanations would restrict you to a maximum mark in Band 2 (top). Examiners call this *partial performance*. It is a general rule – if you are asked to do two things and you only do one, that is partial performance, and now you know what the penalty is!

This section has covered two main areas of animal navigation, homing and migration. You might choose two explanations from homing, two from migration, or one from each. An acceptable (if overly ambitious) interpretation of the question is to take *homing* and *migration* as your two chosen explanations. This would produce a difficult and potentially very superficial trawl through the various theoretical explanations that make up these aspects of navigation, therefore it is not recommended. We have considered the following explanations of homing behaviour – the use of landmarks (p. 358), the sun compass (p. 359), magnetic cues (pp. 359–60) and olfactory cues (pp. 360–2). We have also studied different explanations of migration (pp. 362–4). In this context, the *explanations* are slightly different, in that they are explanations of different groups of animals (birds and aquatic organisms).

One way of illustrating the strengths and limitations of a particular explanation is to examine the balance of research evidence that either supports or challenges its assumptions. For example, although there is research evidence to support the claim that pigeons make extensive use of the sun compass in their homing, there is also evidence that they must be using another navigational system as well (p. 359). We have also seen that overall, experiments testing the olfactory hypothesis have tended to support its predictions. However, these findings are not confirmed in all areas of the world, suggesting that the degree to which pigeons rely on olfactory navigation appears to be determined by how and where they are raised and housed (p. 362).

Animal communication and language

Signalling systems in nonhuman animals

Language is a system of communication in which messages are conveyed between people. But are the elements of human language present in other species? The question of whether language is unique to humans remains controversial.

The propensity of humans to use spoken language stems from the fact that our brain is designed in many important and unique ways for dealing with auditory communication within a given frequency range corresponding to the human voice (about 1 to 5 kHz). There have been numerous attempts to teach animals to understand human language, but the most productive approach to studying animal communication has been to try to learn the secrets of how *their* communication systems work.

Communication channels

Any communication system involves a *signaller* and a *receiver*. The means by which signals are communicated will depend partially upon the properties of the modality through which the signal is transmitted. For instance, the fabulous display of the peacock is both visual and auditory (the feathers make a fluttering sound during full display), but the effectiveness of colour and movement depends upon the peahen (as receiver) attending to the peacock at the time. To bring about, or to retain, her interest in him, the peacock often has to strut around in front of her, or encircle her so as to intercept her gaze whenever she turns away.

The female, in this instance, is able to some extent to ignore the visual information provided by the male. But other forms of communication are less easily switched on and off by the receiver. For instance, the bellowing sound made by a band of howler monkeys as they patrol the boundary of their arboreal territory echoes around the South American forests like a foghorn. Only a stone-deaf individual would fail to receive the warning message from such a troup.

Ants use a chemical signal to communicate sources of food. For instance, the fire ant scout lays a scent trail which excites workers to follow it, eventually leading them towards the food source. In their turn, workers lay their own scent trails so as to maintain the 'pathway' until that food supply has been exhausted. We can now look at each of these 'channels' of communication in more detail.

The evolution of visual signals

Many communication systems become ritualized during evolution, that is, the behaviour may become rigidly automatic and will have taken on a new function from that for which it was originally designed. For instance, during courtship, the mandarin drake uses its bill to tap against the brightly coloured markings on its wing tips. This gesture is believed to originate from a preening movement, but now serves to impress the female by emphasizing its wing markings.

Many visual displays are ritualized like this, particularly those occurring during courtship and conflict encounters. A ritualized display is one where two (or more) conspecifics (members of the same species) engage in stereotypical sequences of action, each one's responses serving as a stimulus or trigger for the further responses of the other. For instance, the stickleback male engages in a zig-zag dance in front of a pregnant female (carrying a bellyful of unfertilized eggs). His dance may induce her to deposit her eggs in his nest – a shallow pit dug in a stream or river bed, usually under the cover of some light vegetation. After she lays the eggs he swims over and fertilizes them. Each action in this sequence depends upon the previous actions of the other. If the female shows little interest in the male's dance, or she does not approach his nest, the ritual may come to an abrupt end (Tinbergen 1951).

Such ritualization in behaviour sequences serves to 'tune in' each individual to the responsiveness of the other. During courtship rituals, this process enables *sexual selection* to occur (described in Chapter 15) where individuals are able to assess the qualities of the other. Furthermore, the existence of the stereotypical behaviour patterns which occur during visual displays serves to prevent crossbreeding between closely related species. The appropriate responses to any one behaviour in such a sequence would only be made by a conspecific – individuals of other species making no such response. This is believed to be important because hybrids arising from crossbreeding are rarely as viable as purebred offspring, and are therefore costly errors for parents to make.

Another reason for the evolution of stereotypical, ritualized behaviour patterns is that they create a system which is difficult to infiltrate or exploit by others. A system which is difficult to counterfeit makes it less open to outsiders or cheats to exploit (a process which is referred to as dishonest signalling) (Zahavi 1979). As an analogy, consider how only the very best of forgers are able to reproduce the complex configuration found in a banknote. That is not to say,

however, that some forgers and cheats do not get through the system – just that if the task were easier, then more of us might be making paper money!

In conflict situations, too, ritualized bouts enable visual signalling to precede actual combat. This enables an opponent to withdraw when they make the assessment that the other is stronger or bigger than themselves. To learn of this after a fight has started may prove to be immensely costly, adding injury to defeat.

Finally, there is a well-known example of visual communication discussed by Tinbergen and Perdeck (1950). They demonstrated (by means of some ingenious experiments) that the orange spot which appears on the mandible of the herring gull bill, serves as a 'target' for the chick's pecking. When the chick pecks at this spot on the parent's bill, it triggers the adult to regurgitate food into the nest for the young to eat.

Advantages and disadvantages of visual communication

Grier and Burk (1992) list four main advantages of visual communication:

◆ It may be transmitted instantaneously (as in the arching of a cat's back or the flash of bright plumage).

◆ It can carry a large amount of information (about sex, status, breeding condition, and so on).

◆ It is highly directional, permitting the source to be detected easily.

◆ Some aspects, such as body coloration, are permanent, and after the initial expenditure of energy to produce them require little further energy to maintain. (The use of visual *displays*, however, such as the courtship display of the peacock, may involve a considerable amount of energy to bring such structures to the attention of others.)

The main disadvantages of visual communication are:

◆ It cannot be used over great distances, being limited by obstructions (such as dense undergrowth, poor visibility or the limited visual acuity of the receiver).

◆ It requires light or the production of light and, therefore, is of little use in the dark. As we saw in the previous section on migration, some animals are capable of generating their own light, a process known as *bioluminescence*.

Auditory communication

Sound signals are potentially capable of immense variety. They can be varied in terms of pitch, loudness and in timing. Humpback whales, for example, span the whole range of human hearing (and probably beyond), resembling a deep rumbling cathedral organ at one end of the scale, and a piercing bat at the other (Dawkins 1981). The song of the humpback whale is so loud that it could, theoretically at least, be heard by other whales on the far side of the world.

Birds, like mammals, also produce 'songs'. Singing appears to serve two main functions in birds, defending territories, and attracting females to mate. The mobbing call found in many species of songbird is used to attract companions to help in harassing a predator that may pose a potential threat. You may well have heard a blackbird using such a call in the presence of a neighbourhood cat. The alarm calls of many species share the same acoustic properties, thus making it difficult to detect the exact location of the caller. This makes a lot of sense, as calling in the presence of a predator might attract unwanted attention and act as a beacon for the predator. Dawkins (1981) suggests that alarm calls signal 'Danger', rather than 'Danger over here', for just that reason.

The songs of male birds may also stimulate female reproductive behaviour. Female canaries who are played recordings of the artificially reduced repertoires of male canaries, tend to build nests at a lower rate (Kroodsma, cited in Ridley 1995). Males in polygamous species tend to have more complex songs than males in monogamous species, suggesting that as competition is greater in polygamous species, females use complexity of song as an important criterion for mate selection.

Advantages and disadvantages of auditory communication

Grier and Burk (1992) suggest the following advantages for auditory communication:

◆ Auditory signals can go around obstacles and through dense vegetation, and can be used in the dark.

◆ Auditory signals are much quicker to transmit than chemical signals.

◆ Auditory communication is much more flexible than other types of signal and allows for longer and more complex messages. Many monkey species (such as the titi monkeys and gibbons) produce long and complex 'songs' made up of much smaller elements. These can be used for courtship and to give information about sex, rank and even 'marital status' (Cowlishaw 1992).

As for disadvantages, Grier and Burk (1992) suggest the following:

◆ Sound is subject to interference (e.g. from other elements of the acoustic environment) and attenuation (fading with distance).

◆ A major disadvantage of auditory signals is that they require considerable energy to produce and must be produced repeatedly. This means they are often easy for predators to 'overhear'.

Chemical communication

Chemical signals (*pheromones*) are particularly well developed in insects and mammals. Some chemical signals are very short lived, very volatile and have low molecular weights. The chemicals used by ants to signal alarm would fall into this category. If these signals were not short lived, it would be impossible to change the signal quickly in the event of a new danger. These signals disperse quickly over fairly localized ranges, but are virtually undetectable after a minute or so. Many moths use chemical signals to attract mates. In some cases, such as the silkworm moth, the receivers are so sensitive to the airborne chemical message that just one or two molecules are sufficient to trigger a response.

On the other hand, some other chemical signals are extremely long lasting. This has the tremendous advantage of allowing the signal to persist in the absence of the signaller. Territory markers need to be persistent for just this reason, and therefore require a fairly high molecular weight (Manning and Dawkins 1998). If the territory is fairly small, scent markers are placed along the territorial boundary. If the territory is large, and it is impossible to keep the boundary fully scented, pheromones and

Humpback whales off the coast of Alaska

Activity 3: Chemical communication in ants

1 Find a trail of active ants (preferably on an outside flat surface).

2 Put a heaped teaspoon of honey about 60 to 75 cm to the side of the trail.

3 Surround the honey with four pieces of overlapping, H-shaped card, as shown.

4 Once the ants have discovered the honey, observe their behaviour for 10 minutes.

5 After 10 minutes, swap the piece of card over which the ants have made a trail with the one directly opposite it.

6 Observe their behaviour for a further 10 minutes. What does this tell you about ants' use of chemical communication?

Source: based on an original idea by Michael Dockery of the Association for the Study of Animal Behaviour

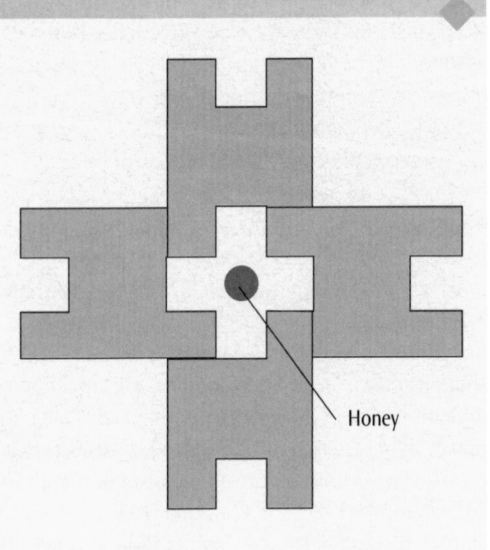

Honey

---

faeces are deposited at strategic points within the territory to inform others that the territory is occupied.

Advantages and disadvantages of chemical communication

Greir and Burk (1992) suggest a number of advantages and disadvantages for chemical communication.

The main advantages are:

◆ It transmits through darkness and around obstacles.

◆ It has the greatest potential range (sharks are known to detect the smell of blood from many kilometres away).

◆ It may be stable and long lasting, as in the boundary marking of territorial animals, and may be transmitted 'into the future', so that the signaller does not have to be constantly present.

◆ Chemical signals are relatively 'private', in that receivers must have specific receptors to receive them. This makes it hard for predators to 'eavesdrop'.

The main disadvantages are:

◆ Chemical signals may be slow to transmit (the larger the molecule, the slower the transmission).

◆ Chemical signals may fade too quickly, or may not fade quickly enough and so interfere with subsequent messages.

Deception in communication

In some encounters between pairs of animals, individuals may engage in disputes that could escalate into actual combat. In such a case, one or both individuals may initially signal their determination to fight in order to bluff the other that they mean serious business. Conversely, a weakening in the resolve to fight may be 'leaked' in their body language, signalling to the other that victory is about to be conceded. Under such circumstances, the message may be either reliable (an 'honest' signal) or else deceptive. For instance, an individual hoping to win a dispute by any means (short of actual combat) may rely heavily upon bluff, perhaps by appearing to be more aggressive or stronger than may be true. This strategy will involve dishonest signalling to the opponent.

Animals may also signal dishonestly when faced with a predator. For instance, many prey species inflate their body or 'stand tall' when threatened, in order to look like formidable opposition. On the other hand, appearing carefree in front of an opponent or predator may also send a useful signal. For example, Thompson's gazelles show a pronounced escape gait known as 'stotting' or 'pronking', in which they leap by 'bouncing' along on all four legs a metre or two into the air (see the photo of a springbok).

The whole countenance of a gazelle while stotting seems to be one of nonchalance, or even arrogance. This behaviour appears in the presence of some of its many predators, but not all. Most of the big cats which prey upon gazelle are able to catch them if the chase is over a short distance. Gazelles, not surprisingly, do not stott in front of the big cats. However, when pack predators such as African hunting dogs approach, stotting is seen in many of the herd members. It is believed that this gait signals to the predator that this individual is both strong and fast, and unlikely to be caught if chased. This interpretation is based upon the observation that few of the stotting gazelles are singled out by the dogs, implying that stotting is a clear signal of an

Springbok (*Antidorcas marsupialis*) 'stotting'

partridge feigns a broken wing in order to lead a predator such as a fox away from the location of their nest. Recent interest in deceitfulness in animal communication has been stimulated by the controversy over whether animals have conscious awareness (Griffin 1984, 1991). Some argue that in order to deceive others, an individual must have a 'Machiavellian' intent to fool them (Byrne and Whiten 1988). In plain language, animals able to 'lie' must presume that those they are deceiving have 'minds' which can be misled (see Chapter 13 for a discussion of 'theory of mind' in nonhuman animals).

Animal language

One of the most provocative debates over recent years has been concerned with whether language is an ability that is unique to humans. Research evidence from studies of chimpanzees and gorillas has begun to challenge this assumption of language being 'species-specific', although the debate has been looked upon with amusement by some scientists, and with intense emotion by others.

individual's ability to escape (Fitzgibbon and Fanshawe 1988), but it is by no means clear whether all the stotting males are signalling honestly.

Sometimes a signal to a predator may take the form of outright bluff, like when a crane or a

Table 14.2   Hockett's design features of language

1	Vocal/auditory	Sounds are transmitted from one person to another.
2	Broadcast/directional	Sounds are 'broad' cast, although the listener can determine the direction of their origin.
3	Rapid fading	The signal fades away rapidly.
4	Total feedback	Speakers can hear what they themselves are saying.
5	Interchangeability	A sender can receive signals as well as transmit.
6	Specialization	Language has a special communication function – it is not a by-product of some other behaviour.
7	Semanticity	Language has meaning.
8	Arbitrariness	The use of arbitrary units (e.g. words) means that they do not need to resemble physically the event they represent.
9	Traditional transmission	Language can be passed from one generation to the next.
10	Learnability	New forms of language can be learnt.
11	Discreteness	Language can be organized into discrete units (e.g. words) and the meaning of a communication determined by the organization of these units (e.g. sentences).
12	Duality of patterning	Language has more than one level of organization. Speech sounds can be organized into words and words can be organized into sentences.
13	Displacement	The speaker is able to refer to things that are not present in space (e.g. out of sight) or time (e.g. yesterday).
14	Productivity	A language user can produce an infinite variety of novel utterances.
15	Prevarication	Language can be used to deceive, to talk about things that are not true.
16	Reflexiveness	Language enables users to talk about themselves, to describe their own experiences.

Before we take a critical look at some of these projects, it would make sense to have a look at what is actually *meant* by language. This then gives us some criteria against which to assess whether, in fact, these researchers have succeeded in teaching language *per se*, or some other nonlinguistic behaviour. One of the first major attempts to construct criteria for language were the 'design features' of language published by Hockett (1959). Hockett's sixteen features that define 'language' can be seen in Table 14.2.

Dance language of the honeybee

Language clearly includes the ability to speak of things that are not present or that have not yet happened. This immediately appears to rule out just about all animal language. Or does it? Lindauer (1955) and von Frisch (1967) studied the remarkable communication system in honey bees, known as 'dance language'. Honey bee scouts scour the countryside around the hive looking for sources of nectar. When one scout locates a source it will return to the hive and engage in an excited 'waggle dance', which signals to the workers both the direction (within ±25 degrees) and distance (within ±15 per cent) of the source from the hive. This dance is thought to provide information via sight, sound, vibration and odour, about the quality and location of the food, and is effective even when danced within the darkness of the hive. The waggle dance system is used not just for conveying information about food source, but is also used in other circumstances. For instance, during a swarm, in which a new colony is founded, the dancers seem to convey information about sites they have found which may be suitable for establishing the new hive.

Although it has been suggested by a number of commentators that the bees are merely responding automatically to the stimulus of movement and sounds produced by the returning scouts, there is evidence that the workers make decisions about whether or not to follow up the information they are provided with. For instance, Gould (1986, 1992) led a captive scout to a nectar source he had placed in a boat in the middle of a lake, and then released the bee. Despite the scout's dancing on returning to the hive, very few workers left the hive to investigate. Not only do bees dislike flying over water, but the prospect of finding food in the middle of a lake must seem remote. This seems a reasonable deduction, because when Gould next took the captive scout fully across the lake to the opposite shore, the scout was able to recruit workers by the waggle dance when it returned to the hive. The basis of the honey bee's dance is believed to be even more complex than was first thought, since it contains an amalgam of interacting signals (Kirchner and Towne 1994).

This appears to challenge one of the most basic assumptions of language, that nonhumans are unable to show *displacement* in their communication (i.e. the ability to 'talk' of things that are removed in time or space). We will come back to these design features of language later as we assess whether these projects have succeeded in demonstrating the acquisition of 'language'.

Natural animal language

There is a traditional belief that humans are unique organisms. With the advent of Darwinian theory, however, the case for some sort of massive evolutionary discontinuity separating us from other animals has become more tenuous. Attempts to identify uniquely human behavioural traits have been concerned with a number of issues, including the incidence of tool use, the killing of members of one's own species (conspecifics), and the possession of language. Since the first two of these have been documented in a number of nonhuman species, language has become the major focus of research.

Language is dependent on such a complex package of cognitive and anatomical features that, at first, it seems to be the exception to the otherwise clear pattern of continuity between humans and other animals, particularly the higher primates. It is, however, possible to isolate the different functional attributes of language (e.g. Hockett 1960) and then search for these in the cognitive and communicative abilities of other animals. Any such research is immediately faced with a considerable hurdle, which is the lack of a common communicative system between the human researchers and their animal subjects.

Beginning in the 1960s, a series of projects has documented the behaviour of chimpanzees and marine mammals that have been trained to respond to American sign language or to arbitrary symbols, often in complex sentences. Research of this kind has revealed much about the cognitive abilities of animals and particularly about their ability to solve logical problems. We will focus on this approach to the study of animal language in a later section.

A second approach has been to focus on the natural communicative systems of nonhuman animals. A major goal of this approach is to determine whether the signals employed by other species have evolved properties in common with human language. Research in this area has searched for three types of cognitive ability:

◆ Are animals, like humans, able to partition the structure of sound into discrete categories (i.e. *words*)?

◆ Can animal signals be reasonably considered to describe external objects or environmental events?

in focus

How animals communicate danger

Cheyney and Seyfarth (1990) recorded the sounds made by vervet monkeys in response to the sight of an eagle, leopard and snake. The grunting noises they produce in these situations seem all the same to the untrained human ear. But during playback of these same sounds to the monkeys, it was found that their responses were appropriate to the signal being sent (Seyfarth and Cheyney 1992). For instance, vocal signals made when a leopard was seen caused the vervets to run up trees – a sanctuary beyond the reach of any big cat. Playback of the vocalizations made in the presence of a snake caused them to rear up on their hind limbs and stare around them into the undergrowth from where a snake might approach. Vocalizations made in response to an eagle caused the vervets to rush into thicket, a place where a large-winged bird could not enter. There is also evidence that vervet monkeys respond to the alarm calls emitted by starlings, a warning sound which may also be in response to the approach of an eagle (Hauser 1988). In detail, an eagle call sounds like a two-syllable cough, whereas a snake evokes a chuttering sound from the vervets.

The leopard call is also found to be different when made by males and females. The male gives a loud bark whereas the female gives a high-pitched 'chirrup' when a leopard is seen.

◆ Does the production of animal signals show a sensitivity to the presence of appropriate receivers?

Research in these three areas has revealed that the parallels between animal communication and human language are more extensive than is commonly supposed.

The categorical perception of sounds

When human beings are presented with tape-recorded syllables made up of single consonant-vowel combinations (such as 'da' or 'ta'), they are reliably able to detect where one ends and the other begins. This ability to perceive these phonemes categorically is generally believed to indicate our possession of a specialized decoder, a cognitive device that has evolved for processing speech sounds. We might, therefore, expect the categorical perception of phonemes such as 'da' and 'ta' to be uniquely human. This appears not to be the case. Experiments using chinchillas have shown that they are able to discriminate between sounds in much the same way as humans, i.e. they are able to recognize *phonetic boundaries* between different speech categories (Kuhl 1981). Perhaps this is an ability, if not unique to humans, that might be unique to mammals? This too proves not to be the case, with budgerigars also able to be trained to learn the 'da' and 'ta' categories and discriminate accurately between them when presented with novel examples (Dooling *et al.* 1987).

The referential nature of animal signals

Until recently, there was little reason to believe that animal signals might be *referential*, i.e. that they might provide information about the event that elicited the signal. The first evidence to the contrary came from the study of vervet monkeys in Amboseli national park in Kenya. Vervets live in social groups and have a large vocal repertoire that includes a variety of calls that are used in social interactions, and several types of alarm calls (see *In Focus*). Vervets are not the only primates that have this ability. Ring-tailed lemurs give different types of alarm calls in response to aerial and terrestrial predators. Playback experiments have shown that these different types of call produce qualitatively different and adaptive responses in conspecifics (Macedonia 1990).

The social context of animal signals

Animal signalling is generally assumed to be essentially *reflexive*: that is, when a stimulus sufficient to elicit antipredator behaviour is presented (e.g. a hawk to a chicken), then alarm calls will necessarily be produced (Evans and Marler 1995). Bickerton (1990) suggests that the capacity to control the production of vocal signals independently of other reactions to a stimulus was an essential element in the evolution of language. Research by Gyger *et al.* (1986), however, was the first to challenge this assumption. Male chickens were confined in a wire cage, with a second cage next to them on the floor. The male chickens were presented with a hawk stimulus in the presence of either a female chicken, a female bobwhite quail, or an empty cage. The male chickens gave significantly more alarm calls with the hen present than with either the bobwhite quail or the empty cage. The likelihood of calling did not interfere with other antipredator behaviour, such as crouching down, fixating upon the stimulus or remaining immobile. This selective calling is generally referred to as an example of *audience effect*, and casts doubt on the claim that animal signals are purely reflexive.

Nonhuman animals have also shown an ability to engage in precisely timed vocal interactions, of which duets are the most striking example. In some species, there is evidence of 'turn-taking' reminiscent of that which occurs during human conversations, suggesting that there are rules determining when call production is appropriate (Chaiken 1990). Experiments using interactive playbacks have demonstrated that both birds (McGregor *et al.* 1992) and frogs (Schwartz 1991) are sensitive to the timing relationship between their signals and those that are broadcast to them.

Further parallels between animal communication and human language are suggested by studies of song learning in birds, which reveal the existence of a sensitive period early in life and the importance of auditory feedback (Marler 1991). Song learning thus provides evidence of Hockett's language criterion of *traditional transmission* (i.e. transmission from one generation to the next). This vocal learning process also gives rise to geographical variation in structure which is analogous to linguistic dialects. In addition, production of learned song, like human speech, is controlled by anatomically distinct regions on one side of the brain. Research with primates, especially the Japanese macaque, has shown an enhanced ability to discriminate species-specific calls when they are presented to the right ear (and hence the left hemisphere).

Evaluation of 'natural' animal language research

Although these parallels between the functional properties of animal communication and those of human language are extensive, there are no animal signalling systems that have all the characteristics just described. There is, for example, no evidence of vocal learning in nonhuman primates. Animal calls that have so far been studied appear to provide information about the approach of potential predators (Seyfarth and Cheney 1980) or the discovery of food. There is no evidence, however, that animals are capable of describing abstract concepts, nor evidence that animal calls have anything that corresponds to the grammatical items (e.g. big, over, many) that allow humans to encode information about relative properties such as size, position and number, as well as indicating tense.

The most dramatic contrast between animal communication and human language is provided by syntax. The rule-based nature of syntax gives rise to the property of *productivity* (Hockett 1960), the ability to generate an essentially infinite variety of meaningful new utterances using a relatively small set of basic components. Despite the extraordinary flexibility conferred by productivity, studies of animal signals provide no evidence of the evolution of such an ability in nonhuman species.

Teaching language to animals

There have been many different research projects that have attempted to demonstrate language ability in nonhuman species and these have taken one of two major approaches. Some researchers, such as Gardner and Gardner (1969) in their work with the chimpanzee, Washoe, have attempted to teach their subjects a form of sign language known as American Sign Language (ASL). This same approach was taken by Patterson (1978) with her gorilla Koko, and by Terrace *et al.* (1979) with their chimpanzee Nim (an abbreviated form of its full name, Neam Chimpsky – not totally unlike the name of a famous psycholinguist, Noam Chomsky).

Gardner and Gardner (1969) taught their female chimp Washoe how to use ASL, a sign language used in the USA by deaf people. The Gardners used a variety of techniques, such as moulding Washoe's hands into the correct shape for a particular sign, modelling the sign themselves, and reinforcing her whenever she used an appropriate sign. Washoe showed herself to be a very able pupil. The Gardners devised a number of procedures to test whether she was using signs accurately or in a more random manner. In one situation, Washoe was shown a series of pictures and was required to respond with the appropriate signs. She signed correctly in 72 per cent of the trials. Washoe showed other evidence of Hockett's design criteria for language. When a small doll was placed in her drinking cup, Washoe made the signs for 'Baby in my cup'. In this way she was demonstrating Hockett's criterion of *productivity*, in that she was combining signs to produce a novel sentence. There was even evidence of *displacement* in her signing, at times she would refer to things that were not physically present (Gardner and Gardner 1969). Evidence of displacement was also found by Patterson (1979) when she 'conversed' with Koko the gorilla. In the following sequence, Penny Patterson and Koko are 'discussing' an incident that had happened some days earlier, in which Koko had bitten Patterson.

Patterson:	What did you do to Penny?
Koko:	Bite.
Patterson:	You admit it?
Koko:	Sorry, bite, scratch. Wrong bite.
Patterson:	Why bite?
Koko:	Because mad.
Patterson:	Why mad?
Koko:	Don't know.

The greatest setback to this type of research came with the publication, in 1979, of the results of Terrace's investigation with the chimpanzee, Nim. Not only did

Activity 4: Koko.org – The Gorilla Foundation

Pay a visit to the Gorilla Foundation and find out more about Koko. This site includes a gallery of artwork produced by Koko and other gorillas, as well as videos and an online book written by Penny Patterson about her work with Koko.

http://www.koko.org/

Terrace find that Nim's linguistic abilities were far short of a child of equivalent age (for example, he seemed not to be able to move beyond two word utterances), but also Nim seemed less interested in initiating conversation than in copying the signs made by his trainers. From films of other signing chimps, Terrace was able to show that they too were simply responding to the signs made by their trainers rather than using language spontaneously. Even Washoe's famous 'baby in my cup' sentence, claimed Terrace, was produced as a response to signs made an instant before by Washoe's trainers. Terrace suggested that what appeared to be sentence construction by chimpanzees such as Washoe may well be a result of the apes responding to subtle and unconscious cueing by the trainers (Terrace *et al.* 1979). Terrace believed that the Washoe phenomenon was a modern version of the 'Clever Hans effect'. Clever Hans was the name given to a supposed wonder horse that lived at the turn of the century. Hans was able to respond to mathematical problems by tapping out the answers with his hoof. It was subsequently discovered by the psychologist Oskar Pfungst that Hans could only perform these miraculous feats when his trainer also knew the question. Without his trainer knowing the question (the so-called 'double blind procedure') Hans was unable to perform in the same way. Without realizing it, his trainer had been unconsciously cueing Hans when to stop tapping. Terrace believed that this same explanation was appropriate for the signing apes as well.

In response to Terrace's criticisms, researchers such as Roger Fouts have claimed that Terrace's own failures with Nim could be attributed to the use of untrained and incompetent volunteers in Nim's training. Nim's environment was undoubtedly quite different from those of the other signing chimps, and possibly not as conducive to learning. Fouts believed that Terrace had drilled Nim by the application of operant conditioning and, as a result, Nim had become passive and inactive, producing only those behaviours that had previously been reinforced, rather than spontaneously generating new utterances. Claims that Washoe was merely responding to unconscious social cueing are also contradicted by the many successful double-blind experiments carried out by Gardner and Gardner.

An alternative approach to the study of ape language has been to use external objects such as keyboards and plastic signs that are associated with words. In these studies, the animal is first taught a set of names for familiar objects, persons and actions, by pairing the symbol with these objects and actions. After the association is learned, the researcher can note the ape's ability to use the symbol in an appropriate and spontaneous manner. The most recent, and indeed impressive example of this approach has been in Sue Savage-Rumbaugh's work with a pygmy chimpanzee (bonobo) called Kanzi (see *In Focus*).

Kanzi's impressive linguistic performance (which is seen as equivalent to that of a two-year old child) suggests a possible species difference between bonobos and chimpanzees, that somehow predisposes the former species to language more so than the latter species. Savage-Rumbaugh (1986) discovered, for example, that like young children, Kanzi was able to acquire many of his English comprehension skills through observation, just as young children typically comprehend much more than they can produce. Although other bonobos have been similarly studied, and do indeed appear to have a greater propensity to acquire comprehension of spoken English than do chimpanzees (Rumbaugh *et al.* 1994), the reasons for this difference are not clear.

Is it really language?

Part of the controversy surrounding attempts to teach language to animals seems to revolve around whether these animals really can show linguistic competence (i.e. showing evidence of syntax, reference and so on) or whether they are merely showing the product of conditioning (see Chapter 13). Shettleworth (1998) suggests this is paradoxical. While the experience of conditioning procedures is increasingly being said to lead to complex and subtle representations of the world, it is proposed that interpreting an animal's communicative behaviour as being the result of associative learning somehow robs it of any interesting cognitive content.

Many of the criticisms of these ape studies have revolved around the fact that they do not demonstrate some, or all of the features that are found in *human* language. Perhaps this is the wrong way to go about this type of evaluation. Reynolds (1981) argues that we should evaluate a species' *linguistic* competence in the light of its other cognitive and behavioural capacities. Terrace's claim that apes are not really inclined to comment spontaneously on conversation topics introduced by others, says Reynolds, is consistent with other aspects of ape behaviour. In their use of tools and

Kanzi

One of the most exciting research projects in the area of ape language has been that carried out with Kanzi, a pygmy chimpanzee (or bonobo) by Savage-Rumbaugh and her colleagues (Savage-Rumbaugh 1988). Kanzi was born in captivity in Atlanta in 1980. Right from the start, the project was designed with all the criticisms from previous ape studies in mind, so that the same criticisms could not be made about Kanzi's language abilities. For example, all the work was video-taped, and there were other careful control procedures to rule out any unconscious cueing from Kanzi's trainers.

Kanzi can communicate with his trainers by touching a symbol on a keyboard, which in turn is connected to a speech synthesizer so that the appropriate word is produced. To communicate with Kanzi, his trainers can use spoken English. In her 1988 publication concerning Kanzi's progress, Savage-Rumbaugh claimed that he had responded correctly 100 per cent of the time to 109 out of 194 spoken test words, and 75 per cent to another 40 test words. He also responded appropriately to 105 out of 107 action-object sentences ('Kanzi, go get me a coke'). Kanzi also appears to have some syntactic ability, since he responds differently to a word depending on the way it is used in a sentence.

Unlike many of the earlier studies in this area which concentrated solely on the production of language, research with Kanzi has also focused on the comprehension of language. Is this ape acquiring language? Savage-Rumbaugh believes that he is.

---

in other social behaviours, chimpanzees and other apes rarely show evidence of the coordination of individual actions to produce a common product. The fact that their sign language also lacks these features does not, therefore, seem surprising. These discrepancies do not prove that chimpanzees and gorillas lack language, but that they lack language as it is used by human beings in their everyday social interactions. Whether, then, the differences between humans and nonhumans in the use of language is a quantitative or qualitative divide is not clear. What is clear, however, is that *human* language is much more than the type of language displayed by apes and other animals. Human language has shaped our species and is an integral part of our own consciousness. We might ask whether it is profitable to attempt to teach animals to use a language system for which they are not adapted. A more profitable endeavour, it would seem, might be to learn more about the communication systems that they themselves use.

Exam summary: Animal communication and language

The AQA examination will test your understanding of the following areas:

◆ explanations of the use of different signalling systems in nonhuman animals (pp. 365–70)

◆ research into animal language (pp. 369–74).

Example question

The question below is typical of one drawn from the material above, and should take you 30 minutes to answer.

◆ Describe and evaluate research into animal language. *(24 marks)*

Suggested answer structure

The specification uses two examples of research into animal language – attempts to teach language to nonhuman animals and studies of natural animal language. These are just examples, and there is no requirement for you to cover both in your response to this question. It *is* important, however, not to confuse animal *communication* with animal *language* as topics, although some of the material that is relevant to one (e.g. the dance 'language' of bees) would also be relevant to the other.

We have covered *natural* animal language on pp. 370–2, and *teaching language to animals* on pp. 372–4. Research into natural animal language has tended to focus on three significant aspects of animal communication that might satisfy the requirements to be called *language*. These are the categorical perception of sounds (p. 371), the referential nature of animal signals (p. 371), and the social context of animal signals (pp. 371–2). Although research has found evidence of all three of these criteria in the natural communication of animals, there are no animal signalling systems that have all three of these characteristics.

Research that has attempted to teach human language to animals has occupied a very controversial place in comparative psychology. Early studies of chimps such as Washoe (p. 372) were highly criticized for the methodological problems inherent in their design. Using Hockett's 'design features of language' (Table 14.2 on p. 369), it has been possible to show evidence of displacement (the ability to communicate about things removed in time and space) in Koko the gorilla (pp. 372–3). More recently, studies have concentrated on the impressive language skills of bonobos (pygmy chimpanzees). Savage-Rumbaugh's work with Kanzi (pp. 373–4) has shown that his language skills are on a par with those of a 2-year-old child.

Critics of these research studies have suggested that they are not really showing evidence of *language*, but of conditioning (i.e. reproducing behaviours that are associated with reward – p. 373). We may also question whether it is profitable to attempt such interventions rather than trying to find out more about the communication systems that animals use naturally.

Memory in nonhuman animals

In order for learning to occur, information must be retained from one occasion to the next – that is, it must be *remembered*. The study of memory in nonhuman animals poses particular problems for the researcher. Subjects cannot be asked *what* they remember, so researchers must find other ways of testing this. As in the study of human subjects, we must keep in mind the distinction between *performance* in a task and the proposed cognitive mechanisms that underlie that performance. Two areas that have attracted a great deal of attention, and attendant controversy, are the use of memory in navigation (and, in particular, the proposition that somehow animals can construct and remember a *cognitive map* of their immediate area), and the relationship between spatial memory and the specialist behaviour of food caching in birds.

Memory and navigation

Honeybees and other nesting animals face the problem of finding their way between nest sites and distant feeding sites. To set and maintain their course, animals must first determine their position relative to their goal, and then choose the appropriate direction of travel, using features of the environment that are detectable at their starting point and along the way. For insects moving about a large foraging range, an important source of navigational information appears to be celestial cues (the sun and sun-linked patterns of polarized light). These celestial cues provide a true compass for insects and so compensate for the sun's movement relative to other landmarks on the ground. If the sun's position is to be used effectively for navigation, bees must be able to compare the position of the sun and their inbuilt time sense (which is determined by the light–dark cycle – see Chapter 5). Research studies (e.g. Dyer and Dickinson 1994) have suggested that bees are equipped with an innate template that charts the sun's position throughout the day, and that this is modified by further experience.

The importance of landmarks in navigation has been covered in a previous section, but it is worth looking at some of the earlier research again. You may recall how digger wasps use landmarks (such

Birds' memory for songs

Many birds learn the songs they sing, but in some species the songs that are learned in the summer are not sung until the next spring. This means that these songs must be remembered until they are first sung, some eight months later (Marler and Peters 1981). Birds can also use song memory to recognize their neighbours. This makes a good deal of adaptive sense, as birds that learn who their neighbours are spend less time and energy repelling only unfamiliar conspecifics from their territory. These memories can be very long lasting. Male hooded warblers who return in the spring recognize the songs of old neighbours that they have not heard singing for eight months (Godard 1991). In a field study of great tits, the long-term retention of memories for former neighbours appeared to create proactive interference, i.e. interfered with learning the songs of new neighbours (McGregor and Avery 1986).

as rows of trees) near the nest to guide their final approach (Tinbergen and Kruyt 1938). Baerends also studied digger wasps, and found that they also use landmarks (e.g. rows of trees) to set a homeward course when neither the nest nor landmarks in its vicinity can be seen (Baerends 1941). As a result of this and related findings, Baerends proposed a relatively simple explanation for these abilities. As the wasp travels through the environment, it memorizes the sequence of visual images that lead it to food and back again. When a homing wasp finds itself on one of these routes, it compares what it sees with what it has previously memorized and sets an appropriate course. Baerends found that wasps were able to learn more than one route connecting their nest to other parts of their habitat, but were unable to connect these up into a more global spatial representation of the different routes.

This view was challenged in the 1980s with the suggestion that honeybees do form such cognitive 'maps' that chart the relative positions of familiar locations (Gould 1986).

Cognitive mapping

The ability to learn a relationship among widely separated sites would certainly be impressive, as it implies that an animal could memorize spatial relationships that it had experienced over time simply as a result of its movement through the environment. It would be difficult enough to 'draw' a picture mentally of the landscape from directly above it, but imagine how difficult this would be if one were the size of a bee, flying at the height of only a few metres above ground.

Experienced bees appear to be able to use both landmarks and celestial cues independently to obtain directional and positional information during flight. That is, they can use the sun as a celestial compass to find their way even when in unfamiliar terrain, and by using landmarks they can find their way even on cloudy days. Whether bees can use a memorized relationship between landmarks and the celestial compass for navigation is less clear. The ability to exploit a memorized relationship between landmarks and celestial cues would be especially useful when landmarks provide ambiguous information by themselves (e.g. encountering a landmark that has similar aspects from all sides). However, according to Dyer (1996), bees have a very limited ability to exploit the relationship between celestial cues and large-scale features of their environment for navigation. This suggests that they lack the ability to organize their memory of large-scale landmarks in the way proposed by Gould (1986). The apparent

simplicity of the bee's spatial memory may well be advantageous because it imposes low computational demands on an animal whose capacity for processing information is presumably constrained by its small nervous system. These simple representational systems may have another advantage, in that they may allow more rapid learning of useful navigational information than mechanisms that encode more complex representations of the environment (Dyer 1996). Mechanisms that allow rapid development of spatial memory would be clearly advantageous for a species which collects food for only about 10 days before it dies.

Although the suggestion that bees and other insects possess cognitive maps has been more or less discarded, the view that mammals might have cognitive mapping abilities has been harder to shift. In fact, although there is considerable evidence that mammals process and store large amounts of information about the environment, their ability to demonstrate more global 'view from above' navigation has not been demonstrated in the wild. When a wild mammal shows its ability to navigate straight to a goal within its home range, one cannot assess whether it has relied on a cognitive map or some simpler orientation mechanism (Benhamou 1996).

Memory and foraging

Food-storing birds have the ability to retrieve food that they have hidden over many hundreds of square metres after various periods of time. Some species can even successfully retrieve food stored the season before. In order to accomplish this impressive feat, food-storing species would need to possess a large spatial memory capacity, or at least larger than that of non-food-storing species. Research has generally demonstrated this fact. It has also been shown that food-storing species tend to remember spatial cues with greater accuracy than nonspatial cues, and that the increased memory capacity necessary for this behaviour has a neuroanatomical representation. A general hypothesis that would explain this is that the selective pressure of filling a food-storing niche within a given ecosystem caused the food-storing species of birds to evolve specialized brain structures that would give them the necessary memory ability (Clayton and Krebs 1995).

The most impressive of the food-storing species is Clark's nutcracker. These birds collect many thousands of pine seeds every autumn and then bury them in shallow holes (caches). Forming a small hole with the bill and then depositing a few seeds and covering them with soil makes each cache. The seeds

The spatial memory of grey and red squirrels

Field experiments under naturalistic conditions have shown that grey squirrels are capable of relocating buried food with considerable accuracy. After burying a number of food items, squirrels were removed for a period of 20 days and then replaced into the original site. Food sites were relocated to within 5 cm in 62.5% of all attempts. Some recall was also evident after much longer periods of 43 and 62 days. Researchers used the same methods on a population of red squirrels, which are less reliant on stored food, but found they were less successful in retrieval of the stored food sites, having a much shorter retention period for stored food. This research suggests that grey squirrels have a spatial memory which is accurate enough to support the storage and retrieval of food sites, and that this is a product of adaptive (evolutionary) specialization (MacDonald 1997).

are retrieved throughout the winter and spring. The birds are believed to store the caches in over 3,000 different locations. Balda and Kamil (1992) allowed captive birds to form caches in a large room with suitable holes drilled in the floor. The birds where then excluded from the room for varying periods. Even after periods as long as 40 weeks, the birds sought out the correct locations far better than by chance. Close relations of food-storing species (such as the great tit or the jackdaw) tend to store very little, if any, food. What is interesting is that these species perform less well in tasks involving spatial memory (Manning and Dawkins 1998). This difference in spatial memory has a neuroanatomical correlate in that the hippocampus (a part of the brain thought to be significant in learning and memory) is larger in food-storing species of birds than in their non food-storing relatives (Krebs *et al.* 1989). Similar differences in the relative size of the hippocampus have been found between mammals which hold territories (and therefore require a good spatial memory), such as the gibbon, and those which do not (Sherry *et al.* 1992). Comparisons of this type, which try to relate brain proportions in different species, are not without problems, as we cannot be certain that we are comparing like with like. However, there has been rapid co-evolution of brain and behaviour in food-storing species and some evidence of the same type of specialization in mammals as well.

An evolutionary explanation requires that the relationship between spatial memory and food-storing behaviour be evident in other species as well. The prediction that food-storing species have better spatial memory than other species has been tested with other birds and with titmice, but the pattern of results has not been consistent with the proposition that spatial memory varies with dependence on stored food (Shettleworth 1995).

Exam summary: Memory in nonhuman animals

The AQA examination will test your understanding of the following areas:

◆ Explanations and research studies into memory in nonhuman animals (pp. 375–7).

Example question

The question below is typical of one drawn from the material above, and should take you 30 minutes to answer.

◆ Outline and evaluate explanations and research studies relating to memory in nonhuman animals.

(24 marks)

Suggested answer structure

This is a friendly question in that it taps into the exact content of this section. However, it is quite a demanding question, as it asks for an *outline* (i.e. a summary description) and an *evaluation* of both explanations *and* research studies. This question would benefit from very careful 'deconstruction' (i.e. taking apart) in order to make sure that you are dealing with all the required components in the time available. If we do that, we come up with the following:

◆ an outline description of at least *two* explanations of memory in nonhuman animals.

◆ an evaluation of these explanations.

◆ an outline description of at least *two* research studies relating to memory in nonhuman animals

◆ an evaluation of these research studies.

This is quite a task in 30 minutes, and this question has been included here just to show that sometimes you can be really stretched when answering questions in such a short time, so it benefits you to engage in very careful planning. Each of the bullet points above would occupy about 7.5 minutes writing time, which is equivalent to about 150 words.

We have examined two main areas of research into animal memory – memory and navigation (pp. 375–6), and memory and foraging (pp. 376–7). The *In Focus* on p. 375 also presents an explanation (and associated research evidence) on birds' memory for songs. An important issue in the topic of memory and navigation, is whether animals can use cognitive maps (p. 376), i.e. do they have the

ability to learn a relationship between widely separated sites. This debate will certainly provide you with the essential ingredients of your response to this question – explanation, research and evaluation.

Much of the research concerned with the use of memory in foraging has been focused on the spatial ability of food-storing species such as Clark's nutcracker (pp. 376–7). Research has generally found that those species that rely heavily on stored food for their survival tend to have better spatial memory, and a more highly developed hippocampus, the area of the brain thought to be important in learning and memory (p. 377).

Chapter summary

◆ The **homing** ability of animals has been the subject of considerable debate. Some animals are able to home using landmarks, whereas others (such as pigeons) appear to be capable of true **navigation**. Pigeons make use of the sun as a primary navigational aid, but on overcast days when the sun is not visible, they may switch to a secondary system, such as the use of a magnetic sense. There is some disagreement over whether pigeons make use of olfactory information in their homing behaviour, although this is generally accepted to be of key importance in the **migratory** behaviour of salmon.

◆ Animals migrate from one location to another for a variety of reasons, such as seasonal changes or fluctuations in the food supply. The benefits of migration are that individuals exploit the best breeding or feeding conditions in both locations. Many migrating birds make use of the prevailing winds in their migration, whereas others use the thermal air currents.

◆ **Communication** occurs when one animal (the signaller) signals to another (the receiver) in such a way that it changes the behaviour of the receiver in some way. The environment and lifestyle of an animal determine the type of sensory channel that it most often uses.

◆ **Visual** displays are often instantaneous, require little energy and contain a large amount of information (especially for mating). However, they can only be transmitted at close range. **Auditory** signals can be used in the dark and travel long distances, but they use up a lot of energy and can be intercepted. **Olfactory** and chemical

communication have the greatest range and are private – often used for marking territory.

◆ **Signals** have frequently become ritualized over time so that their current function has little in common with their original function. Deceptive communications have the advantage of manipulating the behaviour of another animal to the signaller's advantage.

◆ Debates over whether animals possess **language** have focused primarily on studies of apes. Early attempts to **teach language** using sign language, e.g. with Washoe and Nim, have been criticized because of the possibility of methodological weaknesses in the testing procedures. Later research, particularly with Kanzi, has produced more convincing evidence that apes do, in fact, have the ability both to produce and understand some form of language. In studies of **natural animal language**, e.g. in vervet monkeys, the discovery that ape language is deficient compared to human language is seen as a characteristic of the general behaviour of the species, rather than as a deficiency in the ability to learn and use some form of **language**.

◆ The study of animal **memory** has failed to demonstrate that either insects such as honeybees, or mammals, show evidence of utilizing a cognitive map. Research on honeybees has shown that these insects, although able to use a sun compass and the information provided by terrestrial landmarks to **navigate**, are unable to integrate information from both these to provide a more global representation of their habitat.

◆ Research on **foraging** has shown that birds that are keen food-storers also tend to have well-developed **spatial memories**. The behavioural specialization of these species appears to be reflected in the neural specialization that accompanies it. Birds that are adept at **food caching** and retrieval tend to have relatively more neurons in the hippocampus, an area of the brain that has important functions in learning and memory.

Further resources

Shettleworth, S.J. (1998) *Cognition, Evolution and Behaviour*, New York: Oxford University Press.

A fairly advanced text, but a wonderfully comprehensive account of research in this area.

Website

http://www.cccturtle.org/

The sea turtle migration tracking program – track your favourite turtle on its annual migration!

http://www.dolphin-institute.com/

The Dolphin Institute – dedicated to dolphins and whales through education, research and conservation.

http://www.santefe.edu/~johnson/articles.chimp. html

A New York Times article on the chimp language debate.

Chapter 15

Evolutionary explanations of human behaviour

John Cartwright

Preview

In this chapter we shall be looking at:

◆ the relationship between human reproductive behaviour and sexual selection, including evolutionary explanations of sex differences in parental investment

◆ evolutionary explanations of human mental disorders, including depression and anxiety disorders

◆ the evolution of human intelligence, including the relationship between brain size and intelligence.

Introduction

The renowned evolutionary psychologist Martin Daly once said that 'the reason why psychologists have wandered down so many garden paths is not that their subject is resistant to the scientific method but that it has been inadequately informed by selectionist thought' (Daly 1997, p. 2). Such is the complaint made by evolutionary psychology against mainstream psychology: that it neglects the unifying paradigm that evolution could supply. In this chapter, we will examine the potential of selectionist thought to account for human sexual behaviour, mental disorders and the evolution of brain size. The first section will show how the sexual behaviour of humans can be interpreted in terms of strategies designed to maximize reproductive success. Males and females differ physically in the demands of childbearing. It is no surprise to find then that men and women have slightly different strategies.

Evolutionary psychology also helps to throw light on mental disorders. By viewing the mind as a series of tools adapted to ancestral environments, we are in a better position to understand why some of these tools fail.

Finally, one of the most difficult yet important questions in the life sciences is understanding why humans evolved high intelligence. In the final section, we will examine some of the theories that attempt to address this question.

Human reproductive behaviour

The mechanism of Darwinian evolution by natural selection

The essence of Darwinism can be summarized in terms of three principles:

◆ variation

◆ selection

◆ inheritance.

Variation is to be found among individuals of sexually reproducing species such as humans, because children never exactly resemble their parents. They differ because sexual reproduction serves to stir up the genes of each parent and present a whole new combination to each offspring. In addition, variation is enriched by the occurrence of spontaneous but random novelty. Genes often suffer damage or mutations and a feature may appear that was not present in previous generations or present to a different degree. Most mutations are harmful and all animals have chemical screening techniques to root them out. Occasionally, however, such changes may bring about some benefit.

Selection occurs because resources required by organisms to thrive and reproduce, such as food, shelter and access to mates, are not infinite. Competition must inevitably arise and some organisms will leave fewer offspring than others. Some of the variations discussed above may confer an advantage on their possessors in terms of access to these resources and hence in terms of leaving offspring.

Physical and behavioural characteristics are products of information to be found in the genome of individuals acting in concert with environmental influences. Individuals *inherit* their DNA from the previous generation and pass their own DNA on to the next generation. Those variants that leave more offspring will tend to be preserved and gradually become the norm. If the departure from the original ancestor is sufficiently radical, new species may form and natural selection will have brought about evolutionary change.

As a consequence of natural selection, organisms will eventually become adapted to their environments and their mode of life. In the broad sense, this means being well suited to the essential processes of life, such as obtaining food, avoiding predation, finding mates, competing with rivals for limited resources, and so on. As a result of Darwinian evolution, both the human body and the mind can be expected to be structured in ways that helped our ancestors to survive and reproduce. Hominids have been on the planet for about five million years and, consequently, human behaviour, at least to the degree that it is under genetic influence, should be geared towards reproductive success.

Sex and parental investment

Sexual reproduction involves the fusion of two gametes, sperm from the male and an ovum from the female. Ova are about 100 times larger than sperm and it is clear that for each gamete produced, a female makes a heavier investment (in terms of the supply of biomass) than does the male. But the investment of the female is not over once she has produced an ovum. The female must carry the developing embryo and foetus to full term. Even after birth, the infants of early humans (before the invention of bottle milk) would have been dependent on mother's milk for one or two years. All this adds up to a huge asymmetry in the parental investment each sex makes in the rearing of offspring, and this has left its mark on the mating strategies employed by human males and females.

Parental investment and reproductive rates

In 1972, the evolutionary biologist Robert Trivers defined parental investment as 'any investment by the parent in an individual offspring that increases the offspring's chance of surviving (and hence reproductive success) at the cost of the parent's ability to invest in other offspring' (Trivers 1972).

When Trivers advanced this concept, it seemed to promise a coherent and plausible way of examining the relationship between parental investment, sexual selection and mating behaviour. The sex that invests least will compete over the sex that invests most, and the sex that invests most will have more to lose by a poor match and so will be choosier over its choice of partner.

Using this definition, Trivers concluded that the optimum number of offspring for each parent would be

different. In the case of many mammals, a low-investing male will have the potential to sire more offspring than a single female could produce. A male will therefore increase his reproductive success by increasing the number of his copulations. It turned out that measuring 'investment' was not easy. More recently, evolutionary biologists have adopted the concept of reproductive rate as a more reliable predictor of mating behaviour.

Potential reproductive rates: humans and other animals

Clutton-Brock and Vincent (1991) have suggested that a fruitful way of understanding mating behaviours is to focus on the potential offspring production rate of males and females. These authors suggest that it is important to identify the sex which is acting as a 'reproductive bottleneck' for the other. In mammals, it is the involvement in gestation and nurturing that places limitations on the reproductive output of females.

Humans are a special case in point in that, although the range of parental investment possible by a male ranges from near zero (if the male deserts), to equal or more than that of the female; a male is capable of siring more offspring than a single female could bear (see *In Focus*, 'Prolific parents'). With this in mind, it is probably true to say that in *Homo sapiens* the limiting factor in reproduction resides marginally with the female. This by itself would predict competition between males over access to females. This is part of the phenomenon of sexual selection examined later in this chapter.

Describing mating behaviour: systems and strategies

As noted earlier, at the microscopic level, sexual reproduction is basically simple: the fusion of a large gamete supplied by the female with a smaller one supplied by the male. It is the prelude to this that is complicated. The social arrangements to facilitate this fusion are known as mating systems. Table 15.1 shows a simple classification of some common mating systems.

The obvious question is: to what category do humans belong? This is an extremely difficult question to answer. The law in Western countries prescribes monogamy, but this may not be the ancestral system to which we are adapted. There is also a more fundamental problem with the idea of a system. Species in themselves do not behave as a single entity; it is the behaviour of individuals that is the raw material for evolution. A better approach might be to focus on strategies pursued by individuals in their attempt to maximize their fitness in any given context. The most common behaviour of individuals may then allow us loosely to apply the label 'system' to the species as a matter of descriptive convenience.

Prolific parents

The record often claimed for the largest number of children from one parent is 888 for a man and 69 for a woman. The father was Ismail the Bloodthirsty (1672–1727), an Emperor of Morocco. The mother was a Russian lady who experienced 27 pregnancies with a high number of twins and triplets. You are probably more astonished by the female record than the male.

The figure of 888 looks extreme compared to most cases of fatherhood but would, prima facie, seem to be a practical possibility. Ismail died at the age of 55 and could have enjoyed a period of fertility of 40 years. Over this time he could have had sex with his concubines once or twice daily. The record claimed for Ismail has recently been questioned, however, by Dorothy Einon of University College London (Einon 1998). She analysed the mathematical probability of conception by members of his harem. The problem for a man such as Ismail with access to a large number of women is twofold. First, he is uncertain when each is ovulating. The fact that ovulation takes place between 14 and 18 days before the next menstruation was not known until 1920. Copulating with a woman once every day would only give a probability of hitting the right day for any one woman of about 10 per cent. This could be raised to 15 per cent if days of menstruation are avoided. Second, only half of all menstrual cycles are fertile. Further reductions then have to be made for probabilities of conception, implantation and miscarriage. The end result becomes that if Ismail had coitus three times per week, without interruption due to illness or exhaustion, he would have produced a lifetime total of 79 children, and with coitus 14 times per week a total of 368 children.

Factors affecting human mating strategies

As a result of the asymmetries in both parental investment and potential reproductive rates noted earlier, if the mammalian male is to optimize his reproductive success his best strategy would be to divert more effort into mating than to parenting; in other words to pursue polygyny. A female, on the other hand, will be more disposed towards monogamy (or monandry – having only one male partner) since the bottleneck to her reproductive success is not the number of impregnations from amorous males that she can solicit, but the resources she is able to accumulate for gestation and nurture.

Cultural distribution of mating systems

A broad sweep of different human societies reveals that in many, the sexual behaviour observed departs from the monogamy advocated (at least in a legal sense) in most Western cultures (Fig. 15.1).

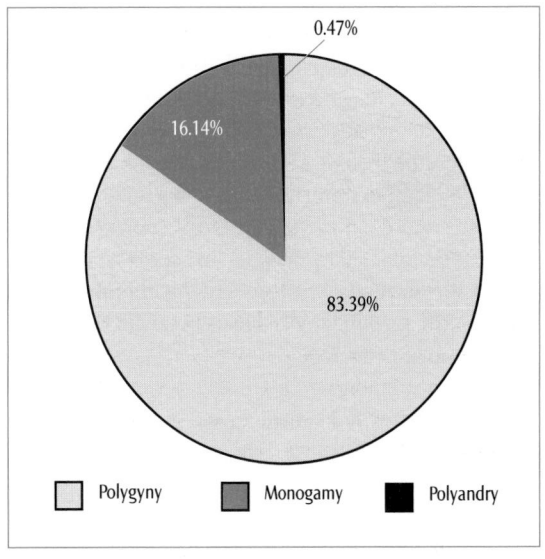

Figure 15.1 Human mating systems in traditional cultures prior to Western influence. *Source*: Smith (1984)

Table 15.1 Simple classification of mating systems

System	Definition in terms of mating exclusivity and/or pair bond character
Monogamy	Copulation and bonding with only one partner
Annual	Pair bond formed with a new individual each year
Perennial	Pair bond formed for life
Polygamy	One sex copulates with more than one member of the other sex
Polygyny	Males mate with several females; females only with one male
Polyandry	One female mates with several males; males with only one female

Figure 15.1 shows that the most common mating system found in traditional cultures is polygyny. It is also instructive to examine hunter-gathering societies, since for most of our time on this planet humans have lived in this mode of existence. Studies, such as those by Howell (1979) on the !Kung San people, tend to reveal a pattern of mild polygyny. The males have a slightly higher variance in reproductive success than females as a result of serial polygyny arising from remarriage, or simultaneous polygyny.

It turns out that food supply and the role of hunting in obtaining food are important factors in understanding the mating strategies of hunter-gatherers. It is very likely that a foraging way of life, especially where hunting produced an important part of the diet, never really sustained a high degree of polygyny. The reasons are basically twofold and fairly simple. First, hunting large animals is risky and needs a combination of cooperation and luck. Given the prolonged period of gestation and nurturing for human infants, hunting is carried out by males, while the cooperation needed means that male rivalry must be kept within strict limits. Following a kill, the meat must be shared between all those that helped and also with other unsuccessful groups. If a high degree of polygyny prevailed in such groups, sexual rivalry would militate against such sharing. In fact, the equitable sharing of hunted food is characteristic of hunter-gatherers. Second, even if there were a surplus after sharing, meat is difficult to store. It is hard to see how, in a foraging culture, sufficient wealth or resources could ever be accumulated by one man to support a sizeable harem. Predictably, in the few hunter-gathering societies left, only mild polygyny is observed, with men having one or two wives.

Polyandry amongst humans is very rare. At first sight, both males and females linked polyandrously would appear to gain little. From the female's perspective, sperm from one male is sufficient to fertilize all her eggs, so why bother to mate with more than one male? From the male perspective it is even worse: if a male is forced to supply some parental care, then the last thing he should want is to share his mate with another male and face the prospect of rearing offspring that are not his own.

Consequently, there are very few polyandrous human societies. One of the best documented is the Tre-ba people of Tibet, where two brothers may share a wife. One reason for this arrangement seems to be as a means of avoiding the split of a family landholding in a harsh environment where a family unit must be of a certain minimum size and where the tax system weighs against the division of property. However, this is not simply a reversal of polygyny: men are socially dominant over women and the younger brother's ambition is to obtain his own wife (Crook and Crook 1988). Moreover, when a Tre-ba family has daughters but not sons, then polygyny is practised whereby the daughters share a husband and the family holding is passed on through them.

Sexual selection

Natural selection and sexual selection

Darwin's idea of natural selection was that animals should end up with physical and behavioural characteristics that allow them to perform well in competition with their rivals. Most features of plants and animals should therefore have some adaptive function in the struggle for existence. Nature should allow no extravagance or waste. So what about the peacock's train? It does not help a peacock fly any faster or better. It would seem to be a magnificent irrelevance, a positive encumbrance that should have been eliminated by natural selection long before now. Yet the tail of the peahen is a far more sensible and modest affair, her overall coloration is also less gaudy and ostentatious than that of the male.

When males and females differ like this in some physical characteristic, they are said to be sexually dimorphic (literally: two shapes). Sexual dimorphism is found to varying degrees in the animal kingdom. Humans are moderately dimorphic: men are, on average, taller than women and more muscular, and grow more facial hair. Now some of these differences could in principle be due to natural selection: males and females may exploit different food resources and female mammals are generally adapted to provide more care to offspring than males. But however ingeniously we work to apply the principle of natural selection, we are drawn back to the peacock's tail. With characteristic insight and determination, by 1871 Darwin had provided the answer to this seeming paradox. In his *Descent of Man and Selection in relation to Sex* (1871), he gave the explanation that is still accepted (with refinements) today. The force of natural selection is complemented by the force of sexual selection: individuals possess features which make them attractive to members of the opposite sex or help them compete with members of the same sex for access to mates. The tail of the peacock has been shaped for the delectation of the peahen. Darwin also argued that sexual selection was bound to favour the evolution of a variety of special adaptations, such as weapons, defensive organs, sexual differences in size and shape and a whole range of subtle devices to threaten or deter rivals. The importance of size is illustrated by a number of seal species. During the breeding season, bull elephant seals (*Mirounga angustirostris*) rush towards each other and engage in a contest of head butting.

Such fighting has led to a strong selection pressure in favour of size, and consequently male seals are several times larger than females. Natural and sexual selection then form the twin pillars of Darwin's adaptationist paradigm.

Intersexual and intrasexual selection

We should really distinguish between two types of sexual selection: intrasexual and intersexual (see Fig. 15.2). Where conditions favour polygyny, males must compete with other males, this leads to *intrasexual* selection (*intra* = within). On the other hand, a female investing heavily in offspring, or only capable of raising a few offspring in a season or lifetime, needs to make sure she has made the right choice. There will probably be no shortage of males, but the implications of a wrong choice for the female are graver than for the male, who may be seeking other partners anyway. Females under these conditions can afford to be choosy. This leads to *intersexual* selection (inter = between). Among humans, both males and females have a highly developed sense of male and female beauty. Both sexes are discriminating in their choice of partners, and this aesthetic sensibility is consistent with a high degree of maternal and paternal investment. It serves to remind us of the fact that, although in principle a human male could desert his mate and continue to impregnate other women, human infants need prolonged periods of care from both parents. This means that if a male wishes to ensure the survival of his offspring, he needs to stay around and perform his share of caring and nurturing. The next section examines the intersexual selection that results from competition before copulation.

Intersexual selection

Darwin had difficulty in explaining in adaptationist language, why females find certain male features attractive. Numerous ancillary theories have emerged over the last 20 years to address this problem and they tend to fall into two schools: the *good-sense* school and the *good-taste* school. These are summarized in Table 15.2.

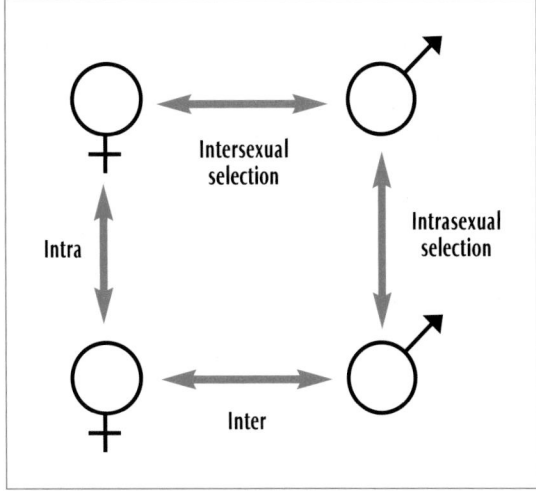

Figure 15.2 Inter- and intrasexual selection

The good-taste school of thought stems largely from the ideas of Fisher, who tackled the problem in the 1930s. Fisher argued that a female preference for a particular feature, once started, could lead to a runaway effect. The original preference may once have been made on sensible criteria, a long tail for example may have indicated status or freedom from parasite infections, but once the fashion took hold, it would become despotic and self-reinforcing. The overall effect would be to saddle males with increasingly longer tails, until the sheer expense of producing them outweighs any benefit in attracting females. But since attracting females is fundamental, very long tails indeed could be produced by this process. In this Fisherian view, tail length need serve no other purpose than a simple fashion accessory to delight the senses of the opposite sex.

The good-sense view suggests that an animal is responding to, and estimating the quality of, the genotype of a prospective mate through the signals he or she sends out prior to mating. Or alternatively, that a judgement is made on the level of resources a mate is likely to be able to provide.

The good-genes dimension of good sense would explain why, in polygynous mating systems, females share a mate with many other females, even though

Table 15.2 Mechanisms of intersexual competition

Category	Mechanism
Good taste (Fisherian runaway process)	Initial female preference becomes self-reinforcing, a runaway effect results in elaborate and often dysfunctional (in terms of natural selection) appendages, e.g. peacock's train.
Good sense (genes)	Female may use signals from male to estimate his genetic fitness.
Good sense (resources)	Female may inspect resources held by male and willingness to invest resources (potential for good behaviour). This could also serve as indication of genetic quality.

there may be plenty of males without partners, and despite the fact that males contribute nothing in the way of resources or parental care. Females are, in effect, looking for good genes. The fact that the male is donating them to all and sundry is of no concern to her. It is suggested that the female is able to judge the quality of the male's genotype from the 'honest signals' he is forced to send. So, for example, size, bodily condition, symmetry, and social status are all signals providing the female with information about the potential of her mate. Human females find some men sexually attractive, even though they know he may be unreliable, philandering and something of a cad.

Males and females can send signals about their health and reproductive status in a variety of ways. One time-honoured principle of fashion is that 'if you have it, flaunt it – if you haven't, hide it'. This applies to cosmetics as much as clothes, and leads to a distinction between honest and dishonest signals. An honest signal is when the appearance of a male or a female is a reliable guide to their genetic fitness. A dishonest signal is when the signal bears little relationship to the true genetic worth of the signalling individual.

Activity 1: Signals people send each other

Compile a table showing the honest and dishonest signals that human males and females send each other. You may like to consider fashion, wealth and cosmetics. Devise the table to show whether the signal is honest or dishonest, and speculate on what the message is trying to say.

Good resources and good behaviour

Humans show sexual dimorphism in a range of traits such as muscularity, body size, facial hair and risk-taking behaviour, and it is likely that many of these are the results of sexual selection. The fact that human infants need prolonged care would ensure that females were alert to the abilities of males to provide resources. In addition, the fact that a female invests considerably in each offspring would make mistakes (in the form of weak or sickly offspring that are unlikely to reproduce) very expensive. It has been estimated that human females of the Stone Age would have raised only two or three children successfully to adulthood. Females would therefore be on the look out for males who showed signs of being genetically fit and healthy and who were able to provide resources. Both these attributes, genetic and material, would ensure that her offspring received a good start in life.

Human females, therefore, expect males to bring something to mating in addition to their DNA. A female may only consent to mating once she has judged the ability of the male to provide resources before and after copulation. In the case of humans, resources could be indicated by the social and financial status of a male, and, just as importantly, his willingness to donate them in a caring relationship. This could of course be one of the functions of courtship in human societies. It seems more than likely that courtship enables each sex to 'weigh up' their prospective partner in terms of their commitment to a relationship and the resources they are likely to bring, both genetic and material.

In human hunter-gathering societies there is evidence that food is often exchanged for sex, and that wealthy men are able to secure more partners.

Table 15.3 Physical characteristics of the great apes in relation to mating and reproduction

Species	Male body weight (kg)	Female body weight (kg)	Dimorphism M/F (ratio of male size to female size)	Mating system	Weight of testes (g)	Weight of testes as % of body weight	Approx number of sperm per ejaculate (x 10^7)
Humans (Homo sapiens)	70	63	1.1	Monogamy and polygyny	25–50	0.04–0.08	25
Common chimps (Pan troglodytes)	40	30	1.3	Multimale in promiscuous groups	120	0.3	60
Orang-utan (Pongo pymaeus)	84	38	2.2	Unimale temporary liaisons	35	0.05	7
Gorilla (Gorilla gorilla)	160	89	1.8	Unimale polygyny	30	0.02	5

Data from Standen and Foley (1989) and other sources

Testis size and bodily dimorphism applied to humans

Jared Diamond (1991) has called the theory of testis size and sperm competition 'one of the triumphs of modern physical anthropology' (p. 62).

Table 15.3 shows some key data on testis size and bodily dimorphism for chimps, gorillas, orang-utans and humans. The fact that men are slightly heavier than women could reflect a number of features of our evolutionary ancestry. It could indicate the protective role of men in open savannah environments; it could be the result of food-gathering specialization, whereby men hunted and women gathered; or it could reflect male competition for females in unimale or multimale groups. The dimorphism for humans is mild, however, compared to that for gorillas. This would indicate that *Homo sapiens* did not evolve in a system of unimale harem mating. Also, if early humans did routinely compete to control groups of females, we would not only expect a higher level of body size dimorphism but also smaller testes. The testes of gorillas relative to body size are less than half the average for humans. On the other hand, if early humans had behaved like chimpanzees – in multimale groups – then we would expect larger testes. In fact, if human males had the same relative size of testes as chimps they would roughly be as large as medium-sized oranges.

In modern societies, the phenomenon of the 'sugar daddy' is well known. Rich and powerful men seem to be able to attract younger and highly attractive females as their partners.

Physical comparisons of humans with other primates

Mating behaviour has left its mark on the physical characteristics of primates such as chimps, gorillas and humans. As already noted, the males of species where there is intense competition for females can be expected to be larger than the females. We can also expect the size of a male's testes to vary in a species-typical manner in relation to sexual selection. In some species, such as chimpanzees, females may mate with several males in one day. The result of this is that her vaginal tract may contain the sperm of more than one male. This has led to a selective pressure on males to increase the number of sperm at each ejaculate in order that sperm can compete effectively with rival sperm. This is known as sperm competition. The significance of testis size is that it indicates the degree of sperm competition in the species. In the 1970s, the biologist R.V. Short suggested that the differences in testis size for primates could be understood in terms of the intensity of sperm competition.

To obtain reliable indicators, testis size has to be controlled for body weight, since larger mammals will generally have larger testes to produce the required volume of ejaculate to counter the dilution effect of the larger reproductive tract of the female. When these effects are controlled for, and relative testis size measured, the results support Short's suggestion that relatively larger testes are selected for in multimale groups, such as chimpanzees, where sperm competition will take place in the reproductive tract of the female. In contrast, a single male gorilla in a harem (sometimes called a unimale group) does not need to produce as

Activity 2: Human sexual dimorphism

Human males and females are sexually dimorphic. On average, males have:

◆ greater upper-body strength
◆ more facial and bodily hair
◆ greater height and mass
◆ deeper voices
◆ riskier life histories and higher juvenile mortality
◆ later sexual maturity
◆ earlier death
◆ broader and more prominent chins
◆ lower levels of fat deposited on buttocks and hips.

Decide whether you think each of these characteristics is the result of inter- or intrasexual selection.

much sperm as a male in a multimale group; for him, the battle has already been won by intrasexual selection with other males, and rival sperm are unlikely to be a threat. The testes of human males are relatively smaller than those of chimpanzees, but larger than those of gorillas. From a comparison of human testis size with other primates, Short concludes that we are not 'inherently monogamous ... neither are we adapted to a multimale promiscuous mating system'. His view is that 'we are basically a polygynous primate in which the polygyny usually takes the form of serial monogamy' (Short 1994, p. 13).

Evidence that both males and females make considerable investment in a relationship comes from the fact that both sexes have a highly refined sense of sexual attractiveness. We do not mate at random; we choose our partners carefully. Coupled with this, there is strong agreement on what features are attractive in males and females. This is the subject of the next section.

The evolutionary basis of sexual desire and mate choice

Male and female attractiveness – some expectations and approaches

Darwinians view attractiveness in terms of reproductive fitness. Features that are positive indicators of reproductive fitness in a potential mate should be viewed as attractive by males and females. In this sense, beauty is more than skin deep – it is to be found in the 'eye' of the genes. Despite the mild degree of polygyny indicated by the evidence presented earlier, and the few cases of opportunistic extreme polygyny found in harems, it is clear that in most relationships, men and women make an appreciable investment of time and energy. Consequently, both sexes should be choosy about future partners, but in different ways.

Of all the features used in appraising a potential mate, two in particular have produced robust empirical findings that reveal inherent differences between male and female taste. They are physical attractiveness and the status of males. In the case of male status, the application of the principles established earlier predict that, since females make a heavy investment in raising young, and since biparental care is needed following birth, females will be attracted to males who show signs of being able to bring resources to the relationship. If females respond to indicators of potential provisioning and status, then males should be attracted to females who appear fecund and physically capable of caring for children. Since the period of female fertility (roughly 13 to 45) occupies a narrower

age band than that of the male (13 to 65), we would also expect the age of prospective partners to be evaluated differently by each sex. Men should be fussier about age and hence rate physical features that correlate with youth and fertility higher on a scale of importance.

To test these expectations, we can examine human preferences using data from at least two sources:

◆ what people say about their desires in response to questionnaires

◆ what people look for when they advertise for a partner.

Questionnaire approaches: cross-cultural comparisons

The use of a questionnaire on sexual desire in one culture lays itself open to the objection that responses reflect cultural practices and the norms of socialization, rather than universal constants of human nature. In an effort to circumvent this problem, David Buss (1989) conducted a questionnaire survey of men and women in 37 different cultures across Africa, Europe, North America and South America, and hence across a wide diversity of religious, ethnic, racial and economic groups. As might be expected, numerous problems were encountered with collecting such data. However, Buss' work remains one of the most comprehensive attempts so far to examine the sensitivity of expressed mating preferences to cultural variation. From the general considerations noted above, Buss tested several hypotheses (Table 15.4).

The results in terms of the number of cultures where there was a significant ($p < 0.05$) difference between the qualities addressed in each hypothesis are shown in Table 15.5.

There are clearly problems with many studies based on questionnaires, particularly when unselective

Table 15.4 Predictions on mate choice preferences tested cross-culturally by Buss (1989)	
Prediction	*Functional (adaptive) significance*
Women, more than men, should rate earning potential in a mate more highly	The fitness of a woman's offspring can be increased by allocation of resources
Men, more than women, should rate physical attractiveness highly	The fitness and reproductive potential of a female is more heavily influenced by age than for a man.
Men will on the whole prefer women younger than themselves	Men reach sexual maturity later than women do. Also as above.
Men, more than women, will value chastity	'Mummy's babies, daddy's maybes'. For a male to have raised a child not his own would have been, and still is, highly damaging to his reproductive fitness.
Women, more than men, should regard ambition and drive positively	Ambition and drive are linked to the ability to secure resources and offer protection, both of which would be fitness-enhancing to a woman.

Table 15.5 Number of cultures supporting, or otherwise, hypotheses on gender differences in mate preference

Hypothesis	Number of cultures supporting hypothesis	per cent of total	Number of cultures contrary (con) to hypothesis or result not significant (ns)	per cent of total
Women, more than men, value earning potential	36	97	1 ns	3
Men, more than women, value physical attributes	34	92	3 ns	8
Women, more than men, value ambition and industriousness	29	78	3 con	8
			5 ns	13
Men, more than women, value chastity	23	62	14 ns	38
Men prefer women younger than themselves	37	100	0	0

(data from Buss 1989)

samples are used. Nevertheless, the findings tend to be in agreement with evolutionary expectations. If, as social science critics would say, responses are conditioned by social norms, then we still have the problem of explaining why so many social norms correspond with evolutionary predictions.

The use of published advertisements

An intriguing way to gather information on mating preferences is to inspect the content of 'lonely hearts' advertisements in the personal column of newspapers and magazines. A typical advertisement is shown in Fig. 15.3.

Notice that the advertisement offers information about the advertiser as well as his preferences for a mate. Such information carries some advantages over questionnaire response surveys, in that it is less intrusive and less subject to the well-known phenomenon that interviewees will tend to comply with what they take to be the expectations of the questioner. Moreover, the data is 'serious' in that it represents the attempts of real people to secure real partners. Against this must be placed the fact that the data is selective and probably does not represent a survey across the entire population profile. Figure 15.4 gives details of the findings from a survey by Dunbar (1995).

The results are consistent with the questionnaire surveys of Buss and others, and the following conclusions emerge:

◆ Women, more than men, seek cues to financial security.

◆ Men, more than women, offer financial security.

◆ Women, more than men, advertise traits of physical appearance.

◆ Men, more than women, seek indications of physical appearance.

Figure 15.3 Typical ad in the 'personal column' of a newspaper

SINGLE PROFESSIONAL male, 29, graduate, homeowner, nonsmoker, GSOH, seeks younger, slim woman for friendship and romance.

Figure 15.4 Features of 'lonely hearts' advertisements
Source: adapted from Dunbar (1995)

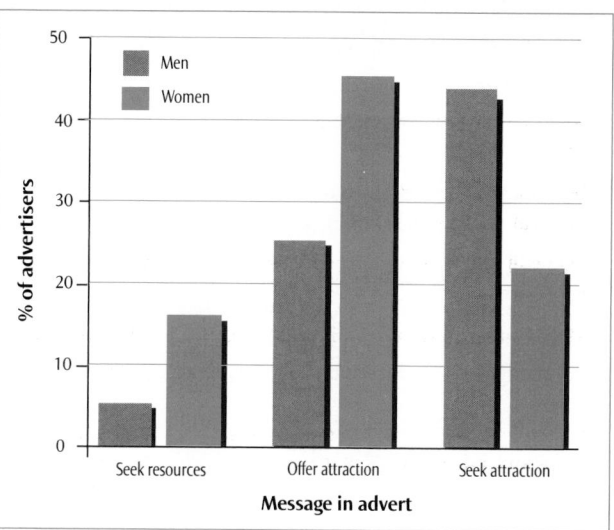

Activity 3: **Survey of personal columns**

Studies such as those carried out by Dunbar are relatively easy to perform. Carry out your own survey of the personal columns in a local newspaper. Since you know what to expect, pay particular attention to whether an advertisement is offering attraction or resources. You could ask someone else to judge this and then analyse the data yourself.

Variations on this theme include looking at personal columns in gay newspapers or journals. Try to formulate some hypotheses about what gay men and women should desire in a partner, and test them.

Another variation is to look at mate advertisements by age group. Once women and men are over 50, they are probably not looking to produce children. In addition, there are more women over 60 than there are men. Both these points may lead to different expectations about patterns of desire.

Origin of mate-choice preferences – evolutionary psychology or structural powerlessness

Studies on expressed preferences reveal nothing about the origin of those preferences. Some social scientists have proposed an alternative to adaptive explanations, termed by Buss and Barnes (1986) the 'structural powerlessness and sex role socialization hypothesis'. This suggests that since in patriarchal societies women have less access to power and wealth than men, then the chief way a woman can attain status and acquire resources is to marry up the social ladder (hypergamy) and trade looks for status. The hypothesis fails on the first count, however, of explaining why preferences are remarkably similar across a wide range of cultures. If it is argued that all these cultures share the same features of patriarchy, we then need an even grander theory to explain this. A more serious problem is that the structural powerlessness model makes a prediction at variance with the facts. If women seek high status males to advance their own standing, then it follows that women should be less selective with regard to status and wealth as their own premarital wealth and power increases. The evidence, however, suggests otherwise. High-status women still value high-status men. Buss (1994) found that women with high incomes tend to value the financial status of men even more than women on lower incomes do.

Marriage as a reproductive contract: control of female sexuality

Marriage is a cross-cultural phenomenon, and although ceremonies differ in their details, and marriage law varies across cultures, in virtually all societies it has a set of predictable features. Marriage entails or confers:

◆ mutual obligations between husband and wife

◆ rights of sexual access that are usually, but not always, exclusive of others

◆ legitimization of children

◆ an expectation that marriage will last.

Viewed through Darwinian eyes, marriage begins to look like a reproductive contract. This is seen at its clearest when fears arise that the contract has been breached, such as when one male is cuckolded by another. In reproductive terms, the consequences of cuckoldry are more serious for the male than the female. The male risks donating parental investment to offspring that are not his own. This male predicament is reflected in laws dealing with the response of a man to incidents where he finds his partner has been unfaithful. In the United States, a man who kills another caught in the act of adultery with his wife is often given a more lenient sentence of manslaughter rather than murder. The law carries the assumption that under these circumstances a reasonable man cannot be held totally responsible for his actions.

Jealousy and violence

In the light of selectionist thinking, the emotion of jealousy in men is an adaptive response to the risk that past and future parental investment may be 'wasted' on offspring that are not his biological progeny. Men also lose the maternal investment they would otherwise gain for their offspring, since this is directed at a child who is not the true offspring of the male. In females, given the certainty of maternity, jealousy should be related to the fact that a male partner may be expending resources elsewhere when they could be devoted to herself and her offspring. It is to be expected then that jealousy and its consequences will be asymmetrically distributed between the sexes. We should also expect it to be a particularly strong emotion in men, since humans show higher levels of paternal investment than any other of the 200 species of primates. In a near monogamous mating system, men have more to lose than women do.

Sex differences in jealousy

To test for sexual differences in the experience of jealousy, Buss *et al.* (1992) issued questionnaires to undergraduates at the University of Michigan, asking them to rank the level of distress caused by either the sexual or emotional infidelity of a partner. The result suggested that men tend to be more concerned about sexual infidelity and women more about emotional infidelity.

The same effect was observed when subjects were 'wired up' and tested for physiological responses to the suggestion that they imagine their partner behaving unfaithfully either sexually or emotionally. The difference was less marked for women, but men consistently and significantly showed heightened distress to thoughts of sexual infidelity compared to emotional.

Such effects are what would be predicted from an evolutionary model of the emotions. Men tend to be more concerned about the sexual activity of their partners, since it is through extrapair sex that a male's investment is threatened. Women, on the other hand, should not be so concerned about the physical act of sex per se, but rather emotional ties that may lead her partner and his investment away from herself.

Activity 4: Investigating jealousy

Devise a questionnaire to investigate sex differences in the experience of jealousy among your own age group. Consider, as Buss did, both emotional and physical infidelity. Make predictions at the onset and then examine whether your data supports or refutes your predictions.

Exam summary: Human reproductive behaviour

The AQA examination will test your understanding of the following areas:

- the relationship between sexual selection and human reproductive behaviour (pp. 384–91)
- evolutionary explanations of sex differences in parental investment (pp. 382–4).

Example question

The question below should take you 30 minutes to answer.

- Discuss the relationship between sexual selection and human reproductive behaviour.   *(24 marks)*

Suggested answer structure

Although this question asks for the relationship between sexual selection and *human* reproductive behaviour, it is appropriate for you to explain what is meant by sexual selection in *nonhuman* terms (e.g. by drawing upon the insights about the peacock's tail). Be careful, however, that your answer does not dwell

too long on sexual selection in nonhuman animals, you are merely setting the scene and clarifying concepts by using nonhuman examples.

This question allows you to choose any aspects of this first chapter – all are relevant to the question. However, you should aim for a balance of 'fundamental' information (such as an explanation of sexual selection and how this might impact on human beings), and more 'elective' content, where it is very much up to you which aspects of the section you feel are worth including. Given that you only have 30 minutes for this response, it pays not to be over-ambitious at this stage. You might plan your essay as six 100 word paragraphs, with the equivalent of three paragraphs being AO1 content and three AO2 content.

One route through the demands of this question is as follows:

- explanation of the nature of sexual selection (pp. 384–5)
- intersexual selection in humans (pp. 385–6)
- good resources and good behaviour (pp. 386–7)
- consequences of sexual selection in humans – testis size and bodily dimorphism in humans (pp. 386–8)
- support for predictions from sexual selection (pp. 388–90)
- consequences of sexual selection in humans – jealousy and violence (pp. 390–1).

The first three of these points deal with the AO1 component of the question, and the last three deal with the AO2 component. This is just one way of answering this question. You might like to read the section again and decide how best you might answer this question using the advice given above.

Evolutionary explanations of mental disorders

If we accept, and it is difficult not to do so, the Darwinian view that natural and sexual selection have shaped our bodies and minds, we can begin to ask questions about the adaptive value of having emotions and expressing them. A plausible start would be to see emotions as acting like other physiological responses, such as pain, hunger and sexual arousal. With these, it is easy to see how they function to ensure that the organism avoids danger, thrives and sexually reproduces. From this perspective, emotions regulate our behaviour to ensure that our genes survive. This is the point made by Nesse and Williams in their influential book *Evolution and Healing*:

> '*Just as the capacity for experiencing fatigue has evolved to protect us from overexertion, the capacity for sadness may have evolved to prevent additional losses.*' (Nesse and Williams 1995, p. 209)

In other words, when we are hopelessly losing, it is best to quit; sadness provides the trigger. In this sense, depression is akin to pain that makes us stop eating sour fruit or prodding a wasp's nest. When you are in a hole, it's best to stop digging.

Mental disorders

So far, we have seen how emotions that we find distressing, such as sadness, fear and anxiety, may be responses that are, or at least once were, useful to us. We still have a lot of explaining to do, however, since the responses of some people are so extreme, irrational and destructive that they can only be labelled disorders.

The fact that evolution has provided us with an emotional system that, by and large, regulates our behaviour towards our best reproductive interests, does not mean that the system will always function perfectly. By analogy, the human immune system is a wonderful piece of physiological precision engineering sculpted by hard-fought battles with parasites and disease over millions of years. For most of us, most of the time, it does a sterling job of keeping infections and disease at bay. Yet for some people, it is prone to malfunctioning. It can become too active and attacks the body's own tissues causing disorders such as rheumatoid arthritis. Possibly, in a similar way, anxiety disorders represent an overactive anxiety system. Such an approach may be on the right lines, but as it stands, is too vague to be of much use or capable of testing. As with physical disease states, mental disorders probably have a wide range of causes. The evolutionary approach has generated a number of plausible hypotheses for mental abnormalities. Two are reviewed below.

Adam and Eve banished from Paradise by Tommaso Masaccio (1401–28), The Brancacci Chapel, Santa Maria del Carmine, Florence

The Bridgeman Art Library

The Genesis myth of the expulsion from Eden may also contain a grain of poetic truth for evolutionary psychology. It has been suggested that many modern mental disorders result ultimately from the abandonment of a hunter-gatherer lifestyle.

1 Exiles from Eden

Over the last 10,000 years, roughly since the invention of agriculture, humans have transformed their way of life so that for the majority of the world's 6 billion people, conditions are now vastly different to the *environment of evolutionary adaptation* or the EEA – roughly that period between 2 million and 100,000 years before the present, when the basic building blocks of the human genome were laid down. Could this transformation be the cause of many of today's psychiatric problems? Perhaps humans have trapped themselves in an air-conditioned zoo, showing many of the symptoms of caged animals. This view, sometimes called the 'genome lag' or 'exile from Eden' hypothesis, has attracted numerous adherents (see *In Focus*). Freud explored this general idea in his *Civilisation and its Discontents* (1930) and Jung in his *Modern Man in Search of Soul* (1933). The notion has a superficial plausibility: by abandoning the hunter-gatherer lifestyle to which we are optimally adapted, and moving to live in cities where some, the powerful few, accumulate fantastic power and wealth, we have set our genes and culture on a collision course. We have stone age genes and minds forced to live in a space-age culture.

2 Inclusive fitness theories

Inclusive fitness is a term that came into use after groundbreaking work by the theoretical biologist William Hamilton in 1964. For Darwin, fitness was a

Mate choice, self-esteem and the genome lag

One area where the genome lag hypothesis may be fruitful is mate choice and estimations of self-worth. In choosing a mate an individual takes into account a number of factors, but two essential ones are the attractiveness (fitness) of a potential spouse (judged by, amongst other things, physical signs of fecundity heath, resistance to disease and so on), coupled with some estimation of one's own sexual appeal. In pairing up, humans estimate their own relative attractiveness and circumstances before deciding what minimum level of attractiveness will suffice in a partner. In ancestral environments, where humans ranged in groups of about 100 to 150, such assessments were probably reasonably accurate. There would, for example, be very few extremely attractive or extremely wealthy people. The problem with modern culture is that people are now frequently exposed to images of highly desirable men and women in the form of fashion models, actors and actresses. The overall effect may be to bias our perception of the true frequency of such people in our social group. Men may become dissatisfied with their partners, thinking they have settled for someone too low down on the attractiveness scale; women may underrate their own attractiveness and take drastic actions such as cosmetic surgery or crash-dieting to improve their appearance (Buss 1996). In short, our ability to beam images of beautiful people around the globe may lead many to experience low self-esteem.

This approach may have some merit, but more work needs to be done. The problem is that despite abandoning the EEA, humans are thriving as never before. Compare the global population of *Homo sapiens* at 6 billion with that of our nearest relative, the common chimp (*Pan troglodytes*) at a few hundred thousand. Moreover, some psychiatric disorders, such as schizophrenia, seem to be present in all societies and are even found amongst the few genuine hunter-gatherer cultures left.

property of an organism (which included physical and behavioural features) that helped itself and its offspring survive. Hence, a mother will behave kindly towards her children at great expense to herself because children represent her genetic investment. Expressed in the gene-centred language and formulation preferred by Dawkins and others, we should say that the genes for nurturing survive by directing their efforts towards individuals that contain copies of those genes. One thing a human mother is assured of, albeit experienced in emotional rather than intellectual terms, is that 50 per cent of her genes are to be found in any of her children. What Hamilton did is to realize that copies of our genes are also to be found in other relatives. It would follow that individuals should also be kind to brothers, sisters and cousins, since they too will contain copies of some of our genes. The chance of any one gene picked at random being found in another individual is called the coefficient of genetic relatedness ('r'). The r-value between you and a brother or sister by the same parent is 0.5; between yourself and a cousin 0.125; between yourself and an identical twin 1.0. The importance of inclusive fitness was first glimpsed by the English biologist Haldane in the 1930s when he amusingly told his friends whilst drinking in a London pub that he would lay down his life for at least an identical twin or eight cousins.

Insights from inclusive fitness have been used to tackle a number of human behavioural patterns. One of them is suicide. The evolutionary psychologist Denys de Catanzaro has suggested that humans commit suicide when they are unable to contribute anymore to their own inclusive fitness. If an individual ever reaches the sorry state where they are acting as a burden to nearby kin and actively reducing inclusive fitness by remaining alive (e.g. by diverting resources from the family group), then it makes genetic sense for them to end their own life and allow their genes to prosper in others. By conducting a survey on a wide variety of people, Cantazaro looked at correlations between *suicidal ideation* (a measure of the intent of people in the sample ever to commit suicide) and events in their own life. He found that suicidal intent was positively correlated with the perceived burden on the individual's family and negatively correlated with measures of sexual success, such as number of children or frequency of sexual activity (de Cantazaro 1995). In other words, when individuals are performing badly in the heterosexual market, or are a drain on the resources of kin, they are more likely to entertain suicidal thoughts. More work remains to be done in this area, but it is likely that, at best, inclusive fitness provides only a partial explanation of suicide. Suicide also correlates with other social variables that are harder to explain by evolutionary reasoning.

Anxiety disorders and adaptive value

Anxiety is often useful. A bit of anxiety before an exam may persuade you to revise more thoroughly. Anxiety in the face of danger, such as walking through a field with a bull in it, may ensure you keep your distance or,

Table 15.6 Types of fear and their adaptive origins

Type of Fear	Adaptive origin
Fear of snakes	Poisonous snakes have been a threat to primates and hominids for the last few million years.
Fear of heights (Acrophobia)	Humans are relatively large animals and falling has always posed a grave danger. Significantly, acrophobia usually provokes a freezing reaction, making it less likely that a person will fall.
Claustrophobia	In a small confined space humans are vulnerable since escape is difficult.
Stranger anxiety (Xenophobia)	Harm from unfamiliar humans, especially males has always been seen as a potential threat.
Agoraphobia	Risks lie beyond the familiar territory of the home.

more sensibly, avoid the field altogether. We should at this point distinguish between fears and phobias. Fears are natural human emotions that bear some relationship to the source of danger. Phobias are fears wildly out of proportion to the actual hazards faced. Fears are adaptive whereas phobias can lead to maladaptive behaviour.

If fear and moderate anxiety represent evolved responses, then it could be that some of our innermost and recurring fears represent ancestral memories of hazards encountered in the EEA. Fear of the dark, for example, is clearly understandable in these terms: humans are vulnerable at night from attack by predators with better night vision or from humans with ill intent. Table 15.6 shows how we could, in principle, map specific fears to the adaptive memory they represent.

The fears shown in Table 15.6 are ingrained to some degree in the human psyche. It is significant that more city dwellers go to psychiatrists with excessive fears of snakes and strangers, than with fears of cars or electrical sockets (Buss 1999). Yet for modern urban humans, electricity and cars represent statistically a far greater risk than snakes or strangers.

Children's fear towards strangers is not altogether surprising. It is likely that infanticide represented a real risk for our primate ancestors. In polygynous mating groups of several animal species, when the dominant male is displaced by another, the new male sets about killing the infants by his previous rival. This has the effect

of bringing the females back into oestrus and also ensuring that neither he nor his new mates waste energy on raising infants that are not his own. This brutal side of our past may have left its mark on modern humans. The evolutionary psychologists Margo Wilson and Martin Daly have found that the risk of infanticide for a stepchild is 100 times higher than for a child with natural parents (Daly and Wilson 1988). The fearful and often tearful reaction of a 1-year-old child when a strange male approaches may be a relic of our brutal past. In fact, such a reaction has been documented in a number of cultures (Smith 1979).

Depression

Evolutionary explanations of mental disorders have to confront the fact that some disorders seem to run in families and, although environmental influences in specific families also play a role, the evidence points towards at least a partial genetic basis. We know from human genetics that deleterious genes can persist almost indefinitely in the gene pool if their defects are matched by some other advantage. This whole area provides another possible evolutionary basis for mental disorders.

Unipolar depression

The term unipolar refers to the fact that in people who suffer from this condition there is one abnormal state, that of depression with all its associated symptoms. It is sometimes thought that there are two discrete categories of unipolar depression: reactive and endogenous. Reactive depression is a response to some painful event such as loss of a loved one, redundancy at work or an instance of personal failure. Endogenous depression arises from inside the person and is usually more serious. These terms are not used in the DSM (see Chapter 16), but instead we find major depressive disorder (MDD) which is a severe but short lived, and dysthymic disorder, which is less acute but may last for much longer.

Activity 2: Modern fears

Consider the following thought experiment. Imagine a tree that grew on the African plains during the EEA which bore berries that were digestible, but had a contraceptive effect. Speculate on what the reaction of modern humans would be to these trees.

Bipolar depression

As the term bipolar indicates, in this condition there are two states, often called *mania* and *depression*. People afflicted by this condition (many of whom in history have been talented and creative people) experience violent mood swings, ranging from mania, with its typical frantic activity, irritability, recklessness and increase in sexual energy, to depression itself.

There is evidence of some genetic basis to bipolar depression but little for unipolar depression. Studies on twins by Price (1968) found that both monozygotic twins (MZ) were much more likely to suffer from manic depression if either one of them did, than were nonidentical or dizygotic (DZ) twins. Significantly, this was observed even if the monozygotic twins were reared apart. Studies on children adopted by healthy couples have also shown that an individual is far more predisposed to manic depression if their biological parents also suffered from the disorder.

The adaptive value of genetically based disorders.

Evolutionary psychiatry now faces a big problem. If there is a genetic basis to such disorders as bipolar depression, albeit only as a contributing factor, what are such genes doing remaining in the gene pool? We would expect that a maladaptive gene would have been 'weeded out' by natural selection long ago. Yet the fact that it is widely distributed in human populations suggests that it is not a recent arrival, awaiting eradication by the reduced fertility of depressives, but that it has been around for a very long time.

There are two types of standard response to this conundrum. The first is to suggest that the gene for the maladaptive trait in question is linked in some ways to other genes that enhance fitness. People prone to manic depression, for example, may also be highly creative. This could have helped our ancestors find solutions to tricky environmental problems in our past. Finding novel ways to obtain food, build shelters or escape predators would have been extremely valuable aids during our evolution. The second type of response is to argue that the same genes that cause depression in some people give rise to different effects that increase fertility by some means or other, in others. This is an argument that has been applied to explain the possible genetic basis of male homosexuality. A gene for male homosexuality could thrive in the gene pool if, when found in the sisters of homosexuals, it increases their fertility.

A major indication that the depressive and manic responses found in bipolar depression have some adaptive function is the fact that they are found almost universally in all human societies in response to some characteristic life events (Stevens and Price 1996). The 'characteristic life events' which trigger either a depressive or a manic reaction tend to be those which involve the experience of one of two types of outcomes – loss or gain. Events that are perceived as a 'gain' in the short-term at least, would include promotion, childbirth, or financial security (such as winning the lottery). A loss might involve the death of a parent, redundancy or financial insecurity. In the long-term, these gains and losses amount to gains and losses in the resources needed for reproductive success.

From an evolutionary perspective, it would appear that these extremes of mood evolved as a means of adapting to alterations in one's resource-holding power and chances of reproductive success (Stevens and Price 1996). This position is summed up most succinctly by Nesse and Williams (1995), who comment: 'If there is little chance of a payoff, it is best to sit tight rather than waste energy.'

The rank theory of depression

This theory proposes that depression is an adaptive response to losing rank in a status conflict and seeing oneself as a loser. According to this theory, such a response is adaptive because it helps the individual adjust to the fact that they have lost and must now occupy a subordinate position in the dominance hierarchy. The purpose of the depression is to prevent the loser from risking further injury by continuing the conflict, and to preserve the relative stability of the social group. In defeat, an involuntary process comes into operation which both prevents the individual from continuing to compete, but also reduces their level of aspiration. This involuntary process results in the loss of energy, depressed mood and loss of confidence, which are typical characteristics of depression.

An important contribution of rank theory is that it offers an explanation of how depression might have evolved – it emerged as the yielding component (i.e. the *yielding subroutine*) of a status conflict between two individual animals. This yielding following defeat is important for two reasons. First, it ensures that the loser really does yield and does not make any attempt at a comeback, and second, it shows the winner that they really have won, so that they break off with no further damage to the loser. In this way, social harmony is restored. Rank theory also offers the hypothesis that mania evolved as the winning component of a status conflict. Again, the adaptive function is twofold. First, it makes clear to the loser that any attempt at a comeback will be successfully resisted, and second, it ensures that, should the loser attempt to re-open the conflict, the winner has the confidence, strength and other resources necessary to repel them. The object of the losing strategy is thus *damage limitation,* whilst the object of the winning strategy is *status preservation* (Stevens and Price 1996).

When humans interact together, the question of dominance may not arise initially. However, after working or living in close proximity for some time, conflict may arise, perhaps over leadership of the group or over access to resources (such as promotion). Over the course of time, the depressive response may also become triggered by other situations that do not necessarily involve the loss of rank, but involve a loss of some other sort (perhaps the ending of a close relationship). In such circumstances, a response that has been selected by natural selection because it *is* adaptive, is activated in situations that make it psychologically maladaptive. As Allen (1995) puts it: 'It is the depressed mood state that has been selected by evolution, whereas the clinically depressed state is a pathological aberration based on this adaptive emotional mechanism.'

Schizophrenia

Schizophrenia is a complex condition involving disturbances to cognition, emotions and behaviour. The range of these symptoms is such that various attempts have been made to classify schizophrenia into a number of types. The DSM lists three:

◆ paranoid, involving hallucinations and delusions

◆ disorganized, involving poorly coordinated speech and disorganized behaviour

◆ catatonic, involving apathy and lack of drive.

Schizophrenia usually strikes men in their late teens or early twenties, and women in their late twenties. It can blight what seem to be promising careers and, although drugs can ameliorate the symptoms, there is no known cure. The prevalence in populations has been estimated from different studies to between 0.2 to 2.0 per cent. This is often approximated to an incidence of 1 per cent across all populations.

Like bipolar depression, there seems to be a genetic component. Table 15.7 uses the concept of *r*-value discussed earlier to tabulate the probability of developing

Table 15.7	Probability of developing schizophrenia	
Relationship	r-value	Probability of developing schizophrenia if relative has the condition (concordance)
MZ twins	1	0.48
DZ twins	0.5	0.17
Siblings	0.5	0.09
Grandchildren of a grandparent	0.25	0.05

(Note that the average probability for any person is 0.01)

schizophrenia if another relative has the condition. We should note that no studies have shown concordance levels of 100 per cent. This indicates that although there may be a genetic component to schizophrenia, environmental influences are also at work. Both the onset of schizophrenia and the course that it takes may be strongly influenced by the social dynamic of family life.

Schizophrenia: the group-splitting hypothesis

Stevens and Price have proposed a novel hypothesis for the persistence of schizophrenia. They suggest that schizoid personalities have acted in the past to perform the valuable function of dividing human groups when they become too large. All groups have their optimum size. As the size of a group increases, so more eyes and brains become available to watch out for predators and to find food. However, beyond a certain size, characteristic of the species and the environment in which it lives, negative effects begin to outweigh the disadvantages. Food may be more easily spotted, but then there are more mouths to feed and the share for each is reduced. This means that the group must travel over a greater home range to find food of sufficient quantity. As the travel distance increases, so does the energy used in finding food, and so do the risks from predators. It follows that as a group grows in size through reproduction, or the movement in of outsiders, there comes a point when the optimum group size is exceeded and fission will increase the fitness of each individual. Stevens and Price maintain that it is the symptoms of a schizoid personality, such as cognitive dissonance, mood changes, bizarre beliefs, hallucinations and delusions of grandeur that would have induced others, already discontented by the conditions prevailing in a group beginning to exceed its optimum size, to follow and form a new community.

Evaluation of evolutionary explanations of mental disorders

The evolutionary approach to mental disorders is still at an embryonic stage, or at best in its infancy. Against this immaturity, however, we should also remember that contemporary mainstream psychiatry is still nowhere near the stage of established medicine as a discipline or series of approaches based on a coherent body of evidence and theory. Nesse and Williams (1995) criticize most current psychiatry for putting the cart before the horse, for 'trying to find the flaws that cause the disease without understanding normal functions of the mechanisms'. As an analogy, they consider coughing. The traditional psychiatric approach, parodied by these authors, would be to describe and catalogue coughing; study the neural mechanisms at work when coughing takes place and identify the cough-control centre in the brain.

Psychiatrists would then proceed to observe how certain substances, like codeine, suppress coughing, leading to speculations that coughing may be the result of a lack of natural codeine-like substances in the body. Amidst all this, how much clearer it becomes when we know that coughing is a natural defensive reaction of the body to expel foreign matter from the lungs, the oesophagus or the mouth. The analogy is of course an oversimplification. However, it is a powerful one when taken as a more general reminder that the best way to progress in understanding the mind is to establish the purposes for which it was designed. In this respect evolutionary psychology, even if it never fulfils its claim to provide a unifying base for the whole of psychology, will have much to offer.

Exam summary: Evolutionary explanations of mental disorders

The AQA examination will test your understanding of the following areas:

◆ evolutionary explanations of human mental disorders including depression and anxiety disorders (pp. 392–7).

Example question

The question should take you 30 minutes to answer.

◆ Outline and evaluate evolutionary explanations of two human mental disorders.   *(24 marks)*

Suggested answer structure

The specification entry for this topic prescribes *depression* and *anxiety disorders,* although this question is more general and allows you to select which disorders you would like to write about. Although that is the case in *this* question, another time the question might stipulate which disorders you should write about. We have covered three types of mental disorders in this

chapter: anxiety disorders (pp. 393–4), depression (pp. 394–6) and schizophrenia (p. 396). Anxiety is seen as having some adaptive value, particularly in terms of specific types of fear (such as fear of snakes and fear of strangers – see Table 15.6). Fear of strangers, for example, might be linked to the fear of infanticide among our ancestors (p. 394).

One of the major assumptions of evolutionary explanations of mental disorders with some genetic basis is that genes can persist in the gene pool if their defects are matched by some other advantage. A major indication that this is the case in bipolar depression comes from the finding that the depressive and manic responses found in bipolar depression are present in all human societies in response to characteristic life events (p. 395). One explanation for the adaptive nature of depression is *rank theory* (p. 395) which claims that the depressive response has evolved to prevent the loser in a status conflict from risking further injury by continuing the conflict. Rank theory explains that the mania response likewise evolved as the winning component of a status conflict, i.e. status preservation.

Like bipolar depression, schizophrenia appears to have a genetic component. Stevens and Price have proposed the *group-splitting hypothesis* (p. 396) to explain the persistence of this disorder. They suggest that schizoid personalities have acted in the past to perform the valuable function of dividing human groups when they become too large for the resources available locally.

As well as the AO1 content detailed above, this question also requires an AO2 component in equal measure. You might include comments on each individual explanation, e.g. 'It is the depressed mood state that has been selected by evolution, whereas the clinically depressed state is a pathological aberration based on this adaptive emotional mechanism' (p. 396). Alternatively, you may include some of the more generic criticisms of evolutionary explanations of mental disorders found on pp. 396–7.

The evolution of intelligence

Brain size in humans and other mammals

Since the nineteenth century, there have been numerous attempts to establish which features of the human brain, if any, confer upon humans their unique qualities. It is tempting to think that we simply have bigger brains than other mammals, but even a cursory examination of the evidence rules this out. Elephants have brains four times the size of our own and there are species of whales with brains five times larger than the average human brain. We should expect this of course – larger bodies need larger brains to operate them. The

next step would be to compare the relative size of brains amongst mammals (i.e. brain mass/body mass). The results are unedifying: we are now outclassed by such modest primates as the mouse lemur (*Microcebus murinus*) which has a relative brain size of 3 per cent compared to 2 per cent for humans.

We can find some reassurance, however, in the phenomenon of *allometry*: as an organism increases in size, there is no reason to expect the dimensions of its parts, such as limbs or internal organs, to increase in proportion to mass or volume. If we simply magnified a mouse to the size of an elephant, its legs would still be thinner in proportion to its body than those of an elephant. This happens in primates too: the bones of large primates are thicker, relatively speaking, than the bones of smaller primates. In fact, there is a fairly predictable relationship between brain and body size in mammals:

Brain size = C (Body size)^k
where C and k are constants (Equation 1)

The constant C represents the brain weight of a hypothetical adult animal weighing 1g. The constant k indicates how the brain scales with increasing body size and seems to depend upon the taxonomic group in question. Much of the pioneering work in developing these equations was done by Jerison (1973), who concluded that for the entire class of mammals k was about 0.67 and C about 0.12. There is much discussion about the precise values for these constants, and even within primate groups k varies from 0.66 to 0.88. Later revisions of Jerison's works suggest k may be 0.75 for most primates.

If we plot a graph of brain size against body weight for mammals on linear scales, a curve results, showing that brain size grows more slowly than body size (see Fig. 15.5).

Figure 15.5
Growth of brain size in relation to body size for mammals

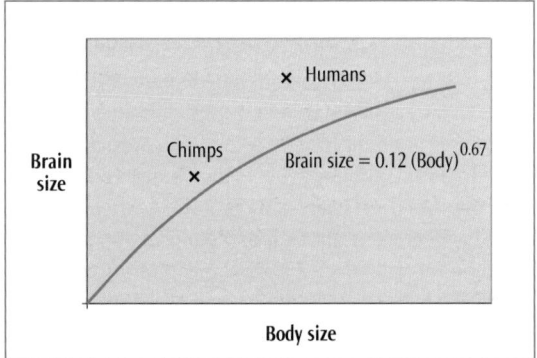

An animal occupying a point above the line is said to be encephalized, that is, it has a brain larger than expected for an animal of its body mass.

Equation 1 and Fig. 15.5 start to give an indication of what makes humans so special: we lie well above the allometric line for other mammals. If we insert a value of 60 kg as a typical body mass for humans into equation 1, our brains should weigh about 191 grams. If we use the equation for primates and take k as 0.75, we get a prediction of 460 grams. In fact, the real figure for humans is nearly 1300 grams. Our brains are at least seven times larger than expected for a mammal of our size and about three times larger than expected for a primate of our size.

Ancestral brains

A reasonable estimation of the size of the brains of our early ancestors can be obtained by taking endocasts of the cranial cavity in fossil skulls. Results indicate that about 2 million years ago, the brains of hominids underwent a rapid expansion. Australopithecines possessed brains of a size to be expected from typical primates of their stature, but *Homo sapiens* now have brains about three times larger than a primate of equivalent body build. The departure of brain size from the allometric line is known as the encephalization quotient (EQ). Some values for the great apes and early hominids are shown in Table 15.8.

Large brains are expensive to run. A chimp devotes 8 per cent of its basal metabolic rate (BMR) to maintaining a healthy brain, whereas for humans the figure is 22 per cent, even though the human brain represents only about 2 per cent of body mass. Larger brains require better sources of nourishment. To develop a large brain through evolutionary time, a fairly stable environment is needed where energy-rich foods can reliably be obtained. In fact, the initial increase in brain size about 2 million years ago does seem to correlate

Table 15.8 Body weights, brain weights and encephalization quotients for selected apes and hominids

Species	Body weight (g)	Brain weight (g)	Jerison EQ*
Orang-utan (*Pongo pygmaeus*)	53,000	413	2.35
Gorilla (*Gorilla gorilla*)	126,500	506	1.61
Common chimp (*Pan troglodytes*)	36,350	410	3.01
Homo habilis	40,500	631	4.30
Homo erectus	58,600	826	4.40
Homo sapiens	60,000	1250	6.55

* Calculated from: EQ = $\dfrac{\text{Actual Brain Weight}}{\text{Predicted Brain weight from } 0.12 \, (\text{Body Weight})^{0.67}}$

Source: data from Boaz and Almquist (1997) and other sources

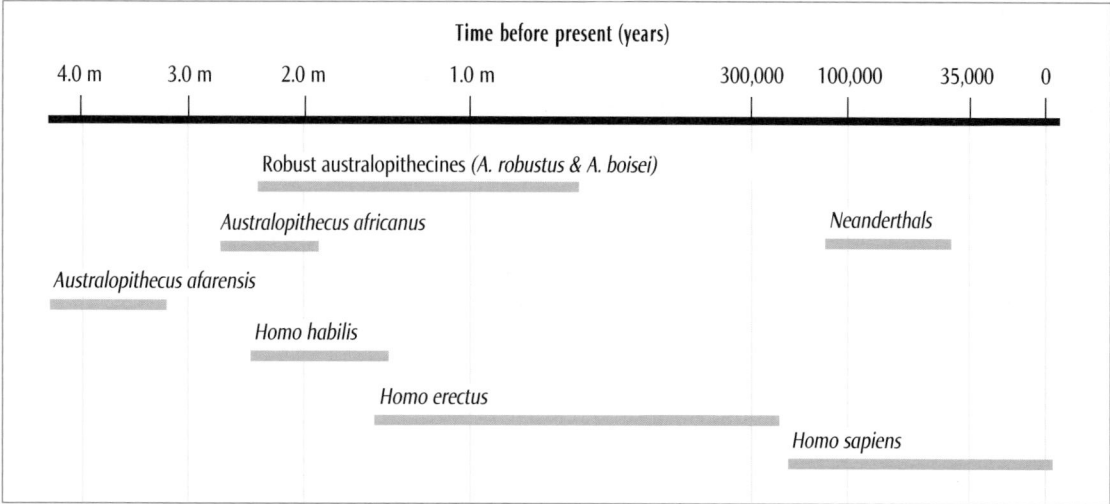

Figure 15.6 Time chart of early hominids
Note that due to the uncertainties of hominid phylogeny, no branching sequences are given to link hominids

with a switch from a largely vegetation-based diet of Australopithecines, to a diet with a higher percentage of meat, as found with *Homo habilis.* Figure 15.6 shows a time chart for the hominids.

Exactly why we developed such large brains is a disputed subject. The rapid growth of the human brain, which for about 1.5 million years remained at about 750 cc, and then in the last 0.5 million years doubled to its present volume, has led some, such as Miller (1996), to suggest that a runaway sexual selection process must have been at work. Whatever the cause, an increase in brain size posed at least two problems for early hominids: how to obtain enough nourishment to support energetically expensive neural tissue, and how to give birth to human babies with large heads. The first of these problems, as noted above, was probably solved by an earlier switch to a meat-eating diet about 2 million years ago. The second problem was solved by bringing about what is, in effect, the premature birth of all human babies. One way to squeeze a large-brained infant through a pelvic canal is to allow the brain to continue to grow after birth. In nonhuman primates, the rate of brain growth slows relative to body growth after birth. Nonhuman primate mothers have a relatively easy time and birth is usually over in a few minutes. Human mothers suffer hours of childbirth pains and the brain of the infant still continues to grow at prebirth rates for about another 13 months. Measured in terms of brain weight development, if we were like other primates, a full term for a human pregnancy would be about 21 months, by which time the head of the infant would be too large to pass through the pelvic canal. As in so many other ways, natural selection has forced a compromise between the benefits of bipedalism (requiring a small pelvis) and the risks to mother and child during and after childbirth.

Human infants are born, effectively, 12 months premature. Even then, the risks of childbirth are high for both women and their babies. Before modern technology, death during labour was not an infrequent occurrence. Evolution has exacted a demanding price for our large heads. In the book of Genesis, God's punishment for Eve was that 'In sorrow thou shalt bring forth children'.

The premature birth of human infants required a different social system for its support than the unimale groups of our distant Australopithecine ancestors. As brain size grew, so infants became more dependent on parental care. Women would have used strategies to ensure that care was extracted from males. This would lead to a more monogamous mating pattern emerging, since a single male could not provision many females. It is significant that body size sexual dimorphism of hominids during the australopithecine phase was such that males were sometimes 50 per cent larger than females. This dimorphism was probably selected by intra sexual selection as males fought with males to control sizeable harems. By the time of *Homo sapiens,* this had reduced to 10 to 20 per cent, signalling a move away from polygyny towards monogamy. Women probably ensured male care and provisioning for offspring by the evolution of concealed ovulation. The concealment of ovulation means that a male is never sure when the female is ovulating. The only way he can then be sure of fathering a child is to engage in sexual activity throughout the ovarian cycle. The continual sexual receptivity of the female and the low probability of conception per act of intercourse ensured that males remained attentive. If this reasoning is correct, and many now agree it to be extremely plausible, then we have established a link between human sexuality and brain size. Put simply, the increase in brain size of early hominids drove them to frequent sexual activity. As brain size grew, so sex became even more fun.

The problem remains why such a risky organ should have evolved to the proportions that it has. There are two related questions that quickly arise, and answering the first helps with the second. The first is why primates evolved larger brains than other mammals. The second is why among our own ancestors did brain size increase well beyond that typical of other primates.

Origins of primate intelligence

There are two popular theories at present that address the problem of why primates are vastly more intelligent than most mammals. One is that the environment of primates poses special problems in terms of the mental capacity needed to gather food. The other is that group living for primates requires considerable mental skill and complexity.

In recent years, there have emerged several related hypotheses that suggest that it may be the demands on the social world, rather than the problem of finding food, that have been the main determinant of the growth in primate intelligence. Whitten and Byrne (1988) developed these theories and labelled them together as the 'Machiavellian intelligence hypothesis' – named after the Renaissance politician and author Nicolo Machiavelli. The essence of the Machiavellian intelligence hypothesis is that primate intelligence allows an individual to serve his or her own interests by interacting with others, either cooperatively or manipulatively, without disturbing the overall social cohesion of the group.

We can picture a primate group as a product of centripetal forces resulting from predatory pressures tending to keep the group together and centrifugal forces emanating from tension and conflict in the group tending to push the group apart. Predation from without and conflict from within both act negatively on the reproductive fitness of an individual, so we can expect evolution to have come up with ways of mitigating these. With regard to conflict, chimps and other primates seem to have hit upon grooming as an effective mechanism to reduce intragroup tensions and so enhance group cohesion. Grooming involves one individual picking through the fur of another, removing bits of plant material, fleas or scabs. It is a form of altruism of the 'you scratch my back and I'll scratch yours' variety. There is now general agreement that grooming serves a more subtle and sophisticated function than simple fur hygiene. A pair of primates that regularly groom each other are more likely to provide assistance to each other when one is threatened, than nongrooming partners. Grooming seems to serve to maintain friendships, cement alliances, and is used to effect reconciliation after a fight.

To test the idea that brain enlargement was a result of the cognitive demand of the social world, we obviously need some way of measuring two things: first, the level of social complexity set by group size and group dynamics, and second, the level of intelligence possessed by species that forage and live in groups.

The social complexity of a group is indicated to some degree by the mean size of the group: the larger the group the more relationships there are to keep track of, the higher the levels of stress, and the greater the all-round level of harassment. Measuring group size is fairly easy, and reliable data exist for a range of primate species. We need to be careful, however, since it does not follow that stress is linearly related to group size.

The assumptions made in measuring social and environmental complexity begin to look reasonable compared to those we face when estimating the intelligence of an animal. Given the controversy surrounding the construction of a fair and culture-neutral IQ test for humans, it is not surprising that there is considerable disagreement over the creation of a 'species fair' behavioural measure of intelligence.

As long ago as 1970, Maclean argued that the human brain can be divided into three main sections: a primitive core that we have inherited from our reptile-like ancestors, a midsection that contains areas concerned with sensory perception and integrating bodily functions, and finally an outer layer or cortex that is distinctive to mammals. The word cortex comes from the Latin for bark, and it is this crinkly outer layer that lies like a sheet over the cerebrum. It consists largely of nerve cell bodies and unmyelinated fibres (i.e. fibres without a white myelin sheath) giving it a grey appearance – hence the phrase 'grey matter' to distinguish it from the white matter beneath. The cortex is only about 3 mm deep in humans. In nonprimate mammals it accounts for about 35 per cent of the total brain volume. In primates, this proportion rises to about 50 per cent for the prosimians and to about 80 per cent for humans. If we desire some objective measure of animal intelligence, it could be the cortex that we need to focus on. The cortex surrounding the cerebellum is often more specifically referred to as the neocortex, to distinguish it from other cortical areas of the brain, such as the pyriform cortex and the hippocampal cortex.

If we accept that it may be the neocortex that is the advanced region of the brain, concerned with conscious-ness and thought, then it is this region of the brain that should correlate with whatever feature has driven the increase in intelligence in humans and other primates.

To test the Machiavellian theory of neocortex enlargement, Dunbar (1993) plotted the ratio of the volume of neocortex to the rest of the brain against various measures of environmental complexity and also against group size. The results were fairly conclusive.

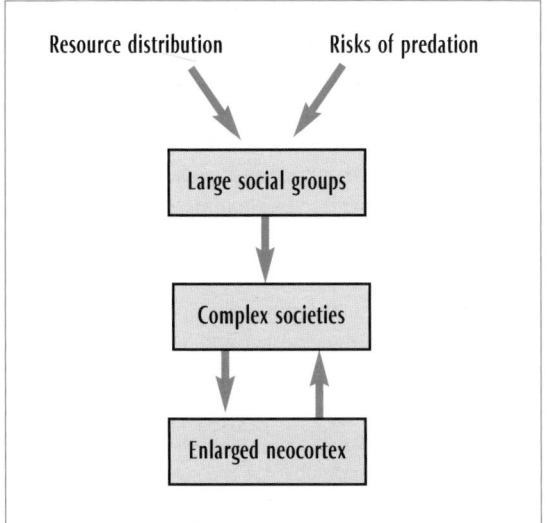

Figure 15.7 Predictions from the Machiavellian intelligence hypothesis

He found no relationship between neocortex volume and environmental complexity, but a strong correlation between the size of the neocortex and group size. Dunbar's work is important because it lends support to the theory that the complexity of the human cortex is due more to the demands of our social environment than the demands of our physical environment.

Exam summary: The evolution of intelligence

The AQA examination will test your understanding of the following areas:

◆ evolutionary factors in the development of human intelligence (pp. 397–401)

◆ the relationship between brain size and intelligence (pp. 397–400).

Example question

The question below should take you 30 minutes.

◆ Discuss evolutionary factors in the development of human intelligence. *(24 marks)*

Suggested answer structure

This question gives you the opportunity to draw on any of the material in this section. The specification entry for this topic *includes* the relationship between brain size and intelligence (second bullet point above), therefore this is also legitimate content in response to this question.

There is no mention of *explanations* or *research studies* in this question. This is a direct response to the wording in the AQA specification ('Evolutionary factors in...'), so it is reassuring that questions are set so closely to the wording of the specification entry. This certainly makes revision more systematic, and removes the problem of the unexpected question on exam papers in this subject.

The word *factors* is just about as friendly as you can get in an exam question. It is effectively asking you to write about any of the ways that evolution might be involved in the development of human intelligence. We have covered the nature of ancestral brains (pp. 398–400) which explains why, although large and expensive to run, human brains may have evolved to be so much larger than the brains of other primates. The two major theories (pp. 400–1) why human intelligence evolved as it did are as follows:

◆ The first theory is that the environment of primates poses special problems (e.g. foraging over large distances) and larger brains were necessary to cope with these demands.

◆ The Machiavellian intelligence hypothesis, on the other hand, suggested that the complexity of human intelligence evolved because of the demands of the human social environment, which allowed individuals to serve their own interests through their interactions with others, without disturbing the overall social cohesion of the group.

Although both views are hypothetical; in nature, recent evidence seems to favour the 'social' hypothesis over the 'environmental' hypothesis as the most likely explanation for the evolution of human intelligence in its present form.

Chapter summary

◆ An evolutionary approach to human sexuality helps us to understand **human reproductive behaviour**, as pursued by ancestral and contemporary males and females.

◆ **Sexual selection** results when individuals compete for mates. The fact that men are slightly larger than women tends to suggest some degree of intrasexual competition among males for mates, with selection

pressures favouring size and strength. Men's testes are too large however to point to a unimale mating system, such as found among gorillas, and too small to be consistent with multimale and multifemale 'promiscuous' mating groups such as found among chimps.

◆ Individuals of one sex also compete with each other to satisfy the requirements laid down by the other sex. An individual may require, for example, some demonstration or signal of genetic fitness or ability to gather and provide resources. Selective pressure resulting from the choosiness of one sex for the other is known as intersexual selection.

◆ The precise form that mating competition takes (such as which sex competes for the other) is related to the **sex differences in parental investments** and the ratio of fertile males to females. If females, for example, by virtue of their heavy investments in offspring or by their scarcity, act as reproductive bottlenecks for males, then males will compete with males for access to females, and females can be expected to be discriminating in their choice of mates.

◆ Evolutionary considerations would predict that females look for high status males who are good providers, while males look for young, healthy and fertile females who are good child-bearers.

◆ The **evolutionary approach** to **mental disorders** is still in its infancy. The finding that some mental disorders such as **bipolar depression** and schizophrenia are linked with heredity suggests that these conditions have at least a partial genetic basis. The fact that natural selection has not yet eradicated these genes points towards the possibility that they are linked with traits that confer some reproductive advantage to the individuals concerned, or their relatives, or the group to which they belong.

◆ Some disorders, such as **depression** and **anxiety disorder**, could result from the fact that we are not optimally adapted to living in a twenty-first-century technological culture. Whatever the future potential of evolutionary psychiatry, it seems almost certain that a better understanding of human emotions, such as fear and anxiety, will result from knowing what adaptive purposes these emotions once served.

◆ Large brains, their metabolic requirements and the consequent need for prolonged infant care would have favoured increasingly monogamous sexual relationships between our ancestors in the Pleistocene. It is likely that environmental and social factors were responsible for the selective pressure that led to large brains. The role of social factors in the evolution of primate and **human intelligence** is increasingly receiving support as part of the 'machiavellian intelligence hypothesis'.

◆ The work of such people as Dunbar, Byrne and Whitten suggests that it is the social complexity of primate life that may have demanded an increase in brain size (which we now know has a direct, if complex, **relationship to intelligence**). We may reasonably infer that this was also probably a powerful factor in driving up the size of brains in early hominids. From a gene's eye view, brain tissue is expensive and risky, but probably worth the effort given the potential benefits.

Further resources

Cartwright, J. (2000) *Evolution and Human Behaviour*, Macmillan.

A good overview of evolutionary theory applied to numerous aspects of human behaviour.

Buss, D.M. (1999) *Evolutionary Psychology*, Needham Heights: Allyn & Bacon.

An excellent discussion of male and female mating strategies

Dunbar, R.I.M. (1996) *Grooming, Gossip and the Evolution of Language*, London: Faber & Faber.

A readable and popular account of the evolution of brain size and its possible causes.

Short, R. and Potts, M. (1999) *Ever Since Adam and Eve: The Evolution of Human Sexuality*, Cambridge: Cambridge University Press.

Superbly illustrated and authoritative work. A humane account of the evolution and significance of human sexuality.

Stevens, A. and Price, J. (1996) *Evolutionary Psychiatry*, London: Routledge.

One of the few books available that considers the evolutionary approach to mental disorders.

Website

http://www.psych.ucsb.edu/research/cep/new.html

A website devoted to the Centre for Evolutionary Psychology – serious surfing for serious students.

Part 6: Individual Differences

ISSUES IN THE CLASSIFICATION AND DIAGNOSIS OF PSYCHOLOGICAL ABNORMALITY

Paul Humphreys
Roger Cocks
Pamela Prentice

PSYCHOPATHOLOGY

Pamela Prentice

TREATING MENTAL DISORDERS

Pamela Prentice

Chapter 16

Issues in the classification and diagnosis of psychological abnormality

Paul Humphreys, Roger Cocks, Pamela Prentice

Preview

In this chapter we shall be looking at:

◆ the classification and diagnosis of mental disorders, including the current versions of ICD, as a classification-only system, and DSM, as a classification and diagnostic system

◆ multiple-personality disorder (dissociative identity disorder), and research into multiple-personality disorder as a spontaneous or iatrogenic (created by the therapist) phenomenon

◆ culture-bound syndromes, and arguments for and against their existence.

Introduction

In your AS-level Psychology course you will have learned about different attempts which have been made to define abnormality (e.g. statistical infrequency, deviation from social norms, failure to function adequately and deviation from ideal mental health) and the limitations of such attempts. You will also have looked at biological and psychological models of abnormality (e.g. psychodynamic, behavioural and cognitive models) and the implications of these for treatment. But how do we recognize abnormal behaviour? How do we classify different types of abnormality? How do we diagnose certain individuals as being mentally ill? These are the major concerns of the first section of this chapter.

Classificatory systems

Describing mental disorder

The current edition (1994) of the *Diagnostic Statistical Manual of Mental Disorders* – DSM-IV – published by the American Psychiatric Association, offers the following description of mental disorder:

'In DSM-IV, each of the mental disorders is conceptualized as a clinically significant behavioural or psychological syndrome or pattern that occurs in an individual and that is associated with present distress (e.g. a painful symptom) or disability (i.e. impairment in one or more important areas of functioning) or with a significantly increased risk of suffering death, pain, disability or an important loss of freedom. In addition, this syndrome or pattern must not be merely an expectable and culturally sanctioned response to a particular event, for example the death of a loved one. Whatever its original cause, it must currently be considered a manifestation of a behavioural, psychological or biological dysfunction in the individual. Neither deviant behaviour (e.g. political, religious or sexual) nor conflicts that are primarily between the individual and society are mental disorders unless the deviance or conflict is a symptom of a dysfunction in the individual, as described above' (pp. xxi–xxii).

Describing mental disorder is one thing, but devising systems to classify and diagnose different forms of mental disorder is quite another.

'Botanists would never have advanced their field without a clear taxonomy for classifying plants. Mere "plant" and "not plant" would not be very fruitful. So, too, we need to have a system that allows us to identify the different types of disorders which fall under the rubric of "abnormality".' (State University of New York at Buffalo, *Abnormal Psychology*, Lecture 2, hereafter referred to as SUNYB2 1999)

Before we proceed any further, we need to be clear about the distinction between classification and diagnosis. *Classification* is what botanists do when they differentiate between types of flowers (for example, roses and orchids) and variations within those categories (e.g. different kinds of roses). *Diagnosis* is when botanists look at one particular flower and decide that its characteristics identify it as a rose (as opposed to a tulip, etc.). Classification is deciding what schizophrenia is (as opposed to depression, for example) and what the characteristics of the different types of schizophrenia are. Diagnosis is the clinical judgement that a particular person is suffering from schizophrenia.

The major classification system currently in use is the ICD-10, and the major classification and diagnosis system is the DSM-IV.

The classification of mental disorders

The major classification system is the ICD (formerly the International statistical Classification of Diseases and related health problems). Its history dates back to 1893 with the Bertillon Classification or International List of Causes of Death. It is published by the World Health Organization (WHO), and the current version (ICD-10) was published in 1993. It is a large work consisting of three volumes running to over 2,000 pages. The primary function of the ICD is to facilitate the collection of basic health statistics. Mental disorders were not included until the sixth revision in 1952 (ICD-6). Various countries have developed their own classification systems, such as the American Psychiatric Association – Diagnostic and Statistical Manual of Mental Disorders (DSM) and the Chinese Classification of Mental Disorders (CCMD).

The main purpose of classification systems, in particular the ICD, is to initiate consensus or agreement on a universal definition for specific disorders or syndromes. This helps to ensure that whenever research is undertaken on a disorder with a particular set of symptoms, the disorder can be universally recognized. Without agreed definitions (labels), it would be difficult for researchers and clinicians to communicate. An additional purpose of the DSM classification system is to assist clinicians to diagnose a person's problem (or set of symptoms) as a particular disorder. This may also enable a clinician to use available information on a given disorder to decide upon an appropriate course of treatment.

A robust classification system must satisfy the following criteria (SUNYB2 1999):

◆ It should provide an exhaustive system that includes all types of abnormal behaviours.

◆ The classificatory categories should be mutually exclusive, i.e. the boundaries between different categories should not be 'fuzzy', and it should be clear what disorder(s) a particular person is suffering from.

◆ It should be valid. Davison and Neale (1997) outline three kinds of validity in relation to classification systems – aetiological, concurrent and predictive:

 – *Aetiological validity* is met when the same causal factors for a particular disorder are found in all people with that disorder (e.g. if a disorder is thought to be genetically determined, then there should be a family history of that disorder in all who suffer from it).

 – *Concurrent validity* is met when other symptoms, that are not part of the disorder itself, are nevertheless characteristic of those with the disorder (e.g. finding that most people with schizophrenia have difficulties in personal relationships).

 – *Predictive validity* means that classification categories should predict the prognosis, or outcome, of a disorder.

◆ It should be reliable: the consistency with which clinicians agree on a diagnosis for a particular set of symptoms is known as inter-rater reliability. For a classification system to be useful, those using it must be able to agree when a person should or should not be given a particular diagnosis.

The ICD

ICD-10 offers 11 general categories of mental disorders:

◆ organic, including symptomatic, mental disorders (e.g. dementia in Alzheimer's disease)

◆ mental and behavioural disorders due to psychoactive substance abuse (e.g. those arising from alcohol abuse)

◆ schizophrenia, schizotypal and delusional disorders

◆ mood (affective) disorders (e.g. recurrent depressive disorder)

◆ neurotic, stress-related and somatoform disorders (e.g. anxiety disorders)

◆ behavioural syndromes associated with physiological disturbances and physical factors (e.g. anorexia nervosa)

◆ disorders of adult personality and behaviour (e.g. paranoia)

◆ mental retardation

◆ disorders of psychological development (e.g. childhood autism)

◆ behavioural emotional disorders with onset usually occurring in childhood or adolescence (e.g. conduct disorders)

◆ unspecified mental disorder mental/disorders not specified elsewhere.

Critical issues in classification

Two important issues need to be borne in mind when considering the usefulness of any classificatory system.

1 One has to assume that the categories of mental illness are 'real' and 'out there' and that each disorder is a distinct entity. It may be, however, that they are simply perceptual categories that we *impose* on the world to make it orderly and that enable us to understand it. They may merely be 'figments of scientists' imaginations!' (SUNYB2 1999).

2 Terms used in psychology, including clinical psychology, have a variety of meanings and can refer to different things. When using terms such as 'anxiety' or 'depression', how confident can we be that we are talking about the same thing? These are inevitably subjective judgements. Moreover, it is all too easy to reify the terms we use:

'The words we use to describe people, such as anxious, depressed and so on, were meant for just that: to describe them. However, there is the danger that those terms will be turned around to explain people's behavior: "Why does she act that way?", "Because she is depressed". The description becomes the explanation – a circular and thus meaningless explanation is set up. The description is used to explain itself!' (SUNYB2 1999, pp. 7–8)

The classification and diagnosis of mental disorders

The American Psychiatric Association (APA) first published the DSM in 1952 as a variant of the mental disorders section of ICD-6 because there was some disagreement about the taxonomy (i.e. classification) of mental disorders.

The current edition of DSM is DSM-IV, which was published in 1994. Table 16.1 lists the major categories of mental disorder listed in DSM-IV.

In order to diagnose a problem, assessment procedures are required. These usually include some or all of the following:

◆ clinical interview (to ascertain information from the client/patient regarding their problem)

◆ careful observation of the client's behaviour, mood states, etc. (usually during an interview)

◆ medical records

◆ psychometric tests.

Psychometric tests include intelligence (IQ) tests, which are often used to differentiate between mental retardation and mental disorder. Cognitive tests that engage verbal, spatial and problem-solving abilities are used to test for cognitive impairments.

Using DSM-IV, classification and diagnosis are made according to a multi-axial assessment, consisting of five axes (see Table 16.2). The first two involve classification according to symptoms, whilst the remainder relate to

Table 16.1 The major categories of mental disorder listed in DSM-IV

Clinical disorders	Personality disorders
Schizophrenia and other psychotic disorders	Antisocial personality disorder
Mood disorders	Paranoid personality disorder
Anxiety disorders	Schizoid personality disorder
Somatoform disorders	Schizotypal personality disorder
Factitious disorders	Borderline personality disorder
Dissociative disorders	Narcissistic personality disorder
Sexual and gender identity disorder	Avoidant personality disorder
Sleep disorders	Dependent personality disorder
Eating disorders	Obsessive-compulsive personality disorder
Impulse-control disorders	
Adjustment disorders	**Mental retardation**
Disorders first diagnosed in infancy, childhood or adolescence	
Delirium, dementia and amnesic and other cognitive disorders	

Table 16.2 Multi-axial assessment in DSM-IV

Axis I: 'Clinical disorders' and Axis II: 'Personality disorders' and 'Mental retardation'

Classification is defined according to a set of symptoms that have been identified as present in a particular disorder. Diagnosis is made according to a symptom count from the defined list. The greater the number of symptoms, the more likely the diagnosis.

Axis III: 'General medical conditions'

These might be relevant to the understanding or management of the disorder. It may be that the mental disorder is a consequence of a physiological condition (e.g. pregnancy complications or infectious diseases).

Axis IV: 'Psychosocial and environmental problems'

These are taken into consideration when making a diagnosis. Such problems might include bereavement, marital discord, unemployment, poverty, illiteracy, sexual or physical abuse.

Axis V: 'Global assessment of functioning scale'

Psychological, social and occupational functioning is considered on a hypothetical continuum of mental illness, from (100) superior functioning in a wide range of activities, to (70) some mild symptoms, to (50) some serious symptoms, to (1) persistent danger of seriously hurting self or others.

other factors that are taken into consideration when making a diagnosis.

Research into the reliability and validity of classification and diagnosis

Psychiatric diagnosis is notoriously unreliable, and studies have shown that even very experienced psychiatrists only agree about 50 per cent of the time (see Spitzer and Williams 1985 for a review of the process of diagnosis). In the 1960s and 1970s there was a great deal of concern that psychiatrists too readily gave a diagnosis of schizophrenia. There was even greater concern that many people were being admitted to mental hospitals when they were not mentally ill, and once admitted they were detained and given treatment without their informed consent. This was supported in a well-known, classic study by Rosenhan (1973) (see *In Focus*).

An attempt to improve reliability and validity of the DSM is the Composite International Diagnostic Interview (CIDI) described by Andrews and Peters (1997). Patients work through a fully structured interview via a computer program (currently CIDI 2.1), working either on their own or with an assistant. They answer questions about psychiatric disorders, and their

in focus

On being sane in insane places (Rosenhan 1973)

A classic study was carried out in which nine healthy people were admitted to psychiatric hospitals. The data from one of these 'pseudopatients' (as Rosenhan called them) was discounted because he falsified details about his personal history, which the other eight did not. The pseudopatients (Rosenhan was one himself) were three psychologists, a paediatrician, a psychiatrist, a psychology graduate student, a housewife and a painter (five men, three women). The eight gained admission to twelve different hospitals after contacting them for appointments and then said that they were hearing voices, often unclear, but saying things such as 'empty', 'hollow' and 'thud'. The pseudopatients said that the voices were unfamiliar, but were of the same gender as themselves. Although they falsified their names and jobs, all other information given was true. As soon as they were admitted to the psychiatric wards all eight stopped simulating any symptoms of abnormality. All except one were diagnosed as schizophrenic.

The pseudopatients were never detected and were eventually discharged with the diagnosis of schizophrenia in remission. Length of hospitalization ranged from 7 to 52 days (average 19). Perhaps most interestingly though is the fact that several fellow patients (35 out of 118 in the first three hospitalizations, when detailed records were kept by the pseudopatients) 'detected their sanity'. One said, 'You're not crazy. You're a journalist, or a professor (referring to the constant note taking by the pseudopatients). You're checking up on the hospital.'

responses determine which questions from the pool they are subsequently given and which are skipped. If sufficient symptoms are endorsed and they occur in certain patterns or clusters, a clinical diagnosis is made. All of this is carried out automatically by the computer program. A study by Griest *et al.* (1987) shows that not only did patients who took part in the study find this method of analysis and diagnosis acceptable, many said they felt more comfortable answering the questions on a computer than to an interviewer. Many said that it provided them with an opportunity to reveal symptoms about which they had never been asked before.

Andrews and Peters (1997) report that both reliability and validity are high and conclude that CIDI:

> 'provides the opportunity for improving diagnostic accuracy in routine clinical practice. This computerized interview could be used in psychiatry as laboratory tests are used in other branches of medicine. Improved diagnostic accuracy should lead to better treatment and thus, to more effective patient outcomes' (p.6).

Accusations have been made (e.g. Fernando 1991, Rack 1982, Ussher 1992) that there are biases in diagnosis, such that social class, race and gender have a large bearing on the likelihood of someone being diagnosed as being mentally ill. We will conclude this section by examining some relevant evidence.

Social class

A study by Umbenhauer and DeWitte (1978) investigated the effects of social class on the attitudes of mental health professionals. They found that upper-class people received more favourable clinical judgements and were more likely to be offered

psychotherapy than working-class people. Johnstone (1989) pointed to studies showing that, regardless of symptoms, more serious diagnoses were given to working-class patients. They were more likely to spend longer periods in hospital and more likely to be considered as having a poorer prognosis. Working-class patients were more likely to be prescribed physical treatments, such as ECT and drugs, and less likely to be offered psychotherapy. Johnstone asserted that health professionals justify this by claiming that working-class patients were less able to benefit from verbal therapies because they were less articulate. She concluded that working-class patients, who were the least powerful and who experienced the most social and economic hardship, ended up receiving 'disabling' rather than 'empowering' psychiatric treatments. This served to deprive them even further of any remaining autonomy and independence, and also served to 'diffuse legitimate protest' about the likely social origins of their problems, such as unemployment and poverty.

Race

Fernando (1988) claims that stereotyped ideas about race are inherent in British psychiatry. For example, there are stereotypes of Black violence and the belief that Black people cannot 'use' help and are not therefore suitable for open hospitals. Table 16.3 lists some British research on ethnicity and mental health.

Research has shown that the compulsory detaining of African-Caribbean patients in secure hospitals is higher than for any other group. Ineichen *et al.* (1984) examined hospital admissions in Bristol and found that non-White groups (West Indians plus other non-Whites) accounted for 32 out of 89 compulsory admissions, but only 30 out of 175 voluntary

Table 16.3 Research studies on ethnicity and mental health (Fernando 1988, p. 74)

1 Over-diagnosis of schizophrenia in:
- West Indian and Asian immigrant in-patients (Cochrane 1977, Carpenter and Brockington 1980, Dean *et al.* 1981)
- patients of West Indian ethnicity admitted compulsorily in Bristol (Harrison *et al.* 1984) and in Birmingham (McGovern and Cope 1987).

2 Excess of compulsory admission of:
- patients of West Indian ethnicity in Bristol (Harrison *et al.* 1984) and in Birmingham (McGovern and Cope 1987).

3 Excessive transfer to locked wards of:
- West Indian, Indian and African patients (Bolton 1984).

4 Excessive admission of 'offender patients' of:
- people of West Indian ethnicity in Birmingham (McGovern and Cope 1987).

5 Overuse of ECT for:
- Asian in-patients in Leicester (Shaikh 1985)
- Black immigrant patients in East London (Littlewood and Cross 1980).

admissions. In a survey conducted by McGovern and Cope (1987) on hospital-detained psychotic patients in Birmingham, it was found that two-thirds were African-Caribbean (both migrants and British born), whilst the remaining one-third were White and Asian.

Culture 'blindness' in diagnosis

Cochrane and Sashidharan (1995) point out that it is a common assumption that the behaviours of the White population are normative and that any deviation from this by another ethnic group reveals some racial or cultural pathology. Conversely, as Rack (1982) points out, if a member of a minority ethnic group exhibits a set of symptoms that is similar to that of a White British-born patient, then they are assumed to be suffering from the same disorder, which may not actually be the case. For example, within the culture of one ethnic group, it might be regarded as normal to see or hear a deceased relative during the bereavement period. Under DSM-IV criteria, this behaviour might be misdiagnosed as a symptom of a psychotic disorder. Cochrane and Sashidharan (1995) suggest that practitioners are almost forced into assuming that mental illnesses such as schizophrenia, depression and neurosis, which are commonly found in European patients, are also found in non-European patients. Moreover, they claim that the system does not easily allow for other disorders to be identified, which do not conform to those recognized in White patients, because British psychiatry is 'shot through with Eurocentric bias'. They claim that so-called 'culture-bound syndromes' receive academic discussion, but they are doubtful that this influences clinical practices in GP surgeries or busy hospitals.

Gender

Mental health statistics indicate that certain mental disorders are diagnosed more frequently in men, while others are diagnosed more frequently in women. It has been suggested that this can be explained through biological differences. However, those who claim that the differences merely reflect stereotyped judgements among mental health professionals have challenged this view.

Broverman *et al.* (1981) thought that since certain behavioural characteristics have traditionally been ascribed to either male or female gender, it is likely that clinical diagnosis of mental disorders will reflect these distinctions. They conducted an important study on gender-role stereotypes and clinical judgements and found that clinicians have different concepts of health for men and women and that these differences do tend to parallel the gender-role stereotypes prevalent in our society. They asked 46 male and 33 female mental health professionals (clinically trained psychologists,

Activity 1: Whose disorder?

Read the following statements and decide whether you think each one is true or false.

1   Regardless of how we define psychological disorders, men are more likely to have problems than women are.

2   Women are more likely to suffer from social phobias or excessive fear of social situations than men are.

3   Females constitute around 95 per cent of people who have specific fears (e.g. fear of snakes or fear of the dark).

4   Men are more likely than women to suffer from an alcohol-related disorder.

5   Women are more likely to be diagnosed with obsessive–compulsive personality disorder.

6   Men are more likely to be diagnosed with antisocial personality disorder.

(The answers are given at the end of the chapter)

psychiatrists and social workers) to rate the characteristics of the healthy man, the healthy woman and the healthy adult. They found that the healthy adult and the healthy man were rated in a similar way as assertive, decisive and relatively independent. The healthy woman was regarded as more submissive, dependent and emotional than the healthy man.

In the light of their study, Broverman and colleagues suggest that a double standard of mental health exists within clinical diagnosis, with certain behavioural characteristics thought to be pathological in members of one gender, but not in the opposite gender. It is generally believed that health consists of good adjustment to one's environment. Men and women are trained from birth to fulfil different social roles, and therefore healthy adjustment for a woman is to accept the behavioural norms for her gender, even though these behaviours may be considered less healthy for the generalized healthy adult. If the 'adjustment' notion of health is accepted, then it would be maladaptive for a woman to exhibit characteristics that are considered to be 'healthy' for men, but not for women. One of the dangers of mental health professionals adopting the adjustment notion of health is that they actively reinforce and perpetuate gender-role stereotypes.

Gender and the environment

Howell (1981) points out that women's experience in this culture predisposes them to depression, and clinicians are therefore diagnosing a *situation* rather than a *person*. Cochrane (1995) explains that

Table 16.4 DSM-IV diagnostic description for personality disorders more prevalent in males or females

◆ *Histrionic personality disorder* (diagnosed more frequently in females)

A pervasive pattern of excessive emotionality and attention seeking.

◆ *Dependent personality disorder* (diagnosed more frequently in females)

A pervasive and excessive need to be taken care of that leads to submissive and clinging behaviour and fears of separation.

◆ *Narcissistic personality disorder* (diagnosed more frequently in males)

A pervasive pattern of grandiosity (in fantasy or behaviour), need for admiration and lack of empathy.

◆ *Obsessive-compulsive personality disorder* (diagnosed more frequently in males)

A pervasive pattern of preoccupation with orderliness, perfectionism and mental and interpersonal control, at the expense of flexibility, openness and efficiency.

depression can be related to the long-term effects of child abuse and also to gender-role socialization, which produces increased female vulnerability. He points out the adverse effects on women of power relationships and gender discrimination. Despite the vast amount of evidence that relates women's depression to sociocultural factors, clinicians continue to ignore environmental circumstances and convey the message that the problem lies in the person's illness (Johnstone 1989). Johnstone believes that this also applies to men. She points out that unemployed men have a high rate of psychiatric breakdown, and that by labelling the problem as a mental disorder, not only does the person have the stigma of a psychiatric label, but the problem is seen only in individual terms, rather than in the wider political and social context. Bennett (1995) believes that the socialization of men in industrialized societies has created masculine stereotypes that alienate men from seeking help for psychological problems.

Gender bias in DSM-IV

Gender differences are particularly marked in the prevalence rates for specific personality disorders (see Table 16.4). It has been suggested that this differential diagnosis may reflect gender bias in the diagnostic system, rather than actual differences. In a study by Hamilton *et al.* (1986), clinicians were given client descriptions consistent with the symptoms of Histrionic Personality Disorder (as described in Table 16.4), which has traditionally been diagnosed more frequently in women than in men.

In the study by Hamilton and colleagues, the gender of the client was varied, but the symptoms were identical. Clinicians consistently rated female clients as more histrionic than males. Narcissistic Personality Disorder (see Table 16.4), on the other hand, is diagnosed more frequently in males, but does this

statistic truly reflect the prevalence of the disorder in males? The diagnostic symptom criteria in DSM-IV list behaviours that reflect stereotypical male gender roles much more than female – for example, 'shows arrogance', 'has a sense of entitlement', 'has a grandiose sense of self-importance' (see *In Focus* on p. 412 for an examination of sexism in assessment and diagnosis of patients).

Exam summary: Classificatory systems

The AQA examination will test your understanding of the following areas:

◆ current version of ICD (p. 406)

◆ current version of DSM (pp. 405–8)

◆ research into reliability and validity of classification and diagnosis (pp. 408–12).

Example question

The question below is typical of one drawn from the material above, and should take you 45 minutes to answer:

(a) Outline the main features of the ICD and DSM approaches to the classification of psychological abnormality. *(15 marks)*

(b) Assess the extent to which such classification systems might be considered both reliable and valid. *(15 marks)*

Suggested answer structure

There a number of features that sets questions in this chapter apart from the other questions that we have discussed throughout the A2 part of this book (you should refer to Chapter 21 for a more detailed account of these differences). The main differences are as follows:

In Focus: Sexism in assessment and diagnosis

Worell and Remer (1992) claim that sexism occurs in assessment and diagnosis in four ways:

1 *Disregarding environmental context*

Assessment and diagnosis focus primarily on traits and behaviours of the individual without due regard to the environmental context such as poverty, patriarchy and powerlessness. Judgements are often made without taking into account the person's response to the environment. Consequently, if the clinician holds strong, stereotypical views on gender roles, behaviour can either be dismissed as an overreaction or regarded as abnormal or pathological.

2 *Differential diagnosis based on gender*

If female and male clients present the same symptoms, but different diagnoses are made, then gender bias is occurring. This is most likely to happen if symptoms mirror traditional gender role stereotypes and if diagnostic classifications use descriptions such as 'dependent' or 'submissive', which are more likely to be associated with a female stereotype.

3 *Therapist misjudgement*

Because of sex-role stereotyping, therapists may have preconceived ideas about particular symptoms and may therefore perceive those symptoms more readily in either males or females. Because people are often unaware that they hold stereotypical beliefs, therapists may be unaware that they are making these assumptions.

4 *Theoretical orientation gender bias*

Diagnosis is often made on the basis of the therapist's own theoretical orientation. If that orientation is gender-biased, then it is more likely that the assessment made by the therapist will also be biased.

◆ Questions in the *Individual Differences* section of the specification are worth 30 marks rather than 24.

◆ The time allowance for these questions is 45 minutes rather than 30 minutes.

◆ These questions have a *synoptic* element (see p. 553), and are marked on a different set of marking criteria (see Table 21.3 on p. 554). By including both ICD *and* DSM in this question, you are given the opportunity to show your critical awareness of the breadth of approaches relevant to the classification of mental disorders.

The question above is in two parts, and merits very careful reading. The first part requires a summary description (the definition of the injunction *outline*) of both ICD *and* DSM approaches. We have looked at the ICD classification approach on p. 406, and the DSM approach on pp. 405, 407–8. DSM identifies a number of characteristics, such as personal distress, disability and dysfunction, when defining mental disorders. It is important to distinguish between *classification* (categorizing the individual characteristics of a disorder) and *diagnosis* (identifying these characteristics in a particular individual). The ICD classification (currently in its tenth edition), deals with classification, whereas

the DSM (currently in its fourth edition – DSM-IV), deals with classification and diagnosis. The ICD offers 11 general categories of mental disorders, whereas the DSM makes an assessment on a multi-axial basis.

The second part of this question constitutes the AO2 component, therefore you should ensure that when you include material in this second part of your response, you are using it to *assess* whether classification systems such as ICD and DSM really are reliable and valid instruments. One effective way to do this is to examine the results of research that has attempted to answer these questions, and consider what this tells us about these issues.

We have covered issues of reliability and validity on pp. 406, 408–11. The reliability and validity of any system of classification or diagnosis is very important when considering its usefulness. Rosenhan's (1973) classic study (*In Focus*, p. 408) demonstrated how problematic the validity of diagnosis can be in practice, but a new technique developed by Andrews and Peters (1997) – known as the Composite International Diagnostic Interview (CIDI) – promises improved reliability and validity (pp. 408–9). There is also considerable empirical evidence to suggest that psychiatric diagnosis has been influenced by class, race and gender bias (pp. 409–12).

Multiple-personality disorder (dissociative identity disorder)

As the case studies in this section illustrate, one of the most interesting examples of mental disorder is what was, until recently, called 'multiple-personality disorder'. If you have seen the film *Sybil*, you could hardly have failed to have been intrigued. We will examine what underlies this disorder and examine the argument that it is *iatrogenic* (i.e. induced unintentionally by therapeutic practice), rather than *spontaneous*.

Case studies of dissociative identity disorder (DID)

A total of four short case studies have been included in this section of the chapter to help you understand some of the features associated with dissociative identity disorders (DID). We start with descriptions of George and Eve (see *In Focus* below and on p. 414), with descriptions of Sybil and Ken following later.

The DSM-IV distinguishes four major subtypes of dissociative disorders:

1   dissociative amnesia

2   dissociative fugue (a dreamlike, altered state of consciousness)

3   dissociative identity disorder (multiple-personality disorder)

4   depersonalization disorder.

All of the above, except depersonalization disorder, involve important personal events which cannot be recalled or where one's current identity is lost. This is why, in the DSM-IV, multiple-personality disorder is now called dissociative identity disorder, to signal some of the commonalities with other conditions. Since DSM-IV uses the term dissociative identity disorder, rather than 'multiple-personality disorder', this is the term we will use in this chapter.

Dissociative identity disorder has existed under a variety of names, but despite this it has been subject to few experimental investigations. Indeed, it has been treated sceptically by some researchers in the field. For example, Spanos (1994) suggests that DIDs are created by role-play. He asserts that patients are influenced by their therapist's goals and expectations, much like an actor who loses all sense of perspective and eventually believes the role they are playing to be real. Gleaves (1996) notes that although the disorder does occur in other cultures, it is extremely rare in Europe and Japan, leading some, like Mersky (1992), to call it nothing more than a North American 'diagnostic fad' caused by the power of suggestion. Writing in the *Journal of Abnormal and Social Psychology*, Thigpen and Cleckey (1954) also admit that the relatively few cases reported (e.g. by William James 1890 and Morton Prince 1906) were treated sceptically by psychologists such as McDougal (1908), who is reported to have said that such cases may have been 'moulded in their development to a degree that cannot be determined'. This was said because the therapy was mostly based on hypnosis. On the other hand, Thigpen and Cleckey (1957) seemed totally convinced: 'A thousand alterations of manner, gesture, expression, posture, of nuances in reflex or instinctive reaction, of glance, of eyebrow tilting and eye movement all argued that this could only be another woman ...'. Furthermore, they say: ' We think it unlikely that someone consciously acting could over a period of months avoid even one telling error or imperfection. But it is not impossible.'

Case study 1: George

George lost his short-term memory and it was a strange experience seeing him and then meeting him again, just five minutes later, when he behaved as if the first meeting had not occurred. The sheer bewilderment on his face as he tried to cope in this new, but alien, world signified the importance of the loss. One feature of his behaviour concerned the battle to order and sequence events in his life by attempting to make a written diary to keep track of, by extraordinary means, the happenings in his life. Without the continuity that memory brings to us, life would lack coherence and meaning. We would not have a sense of who we are without our memory. Our expectations, values and goals in life could not possibly develop without memory. People with dissociative disorders are described in the DSM-IV as having an alteration in the integrative functions of consciousness, identity or motor behaviour. 'Dissociation refers to a disruption in memory where a separation of one part of a person's identity from another occurs'. The disruption referred to occurs in the absence of an identifiable physical cause.

Case study 2: The three faces of Eve

Of all the personalities typical of dissociative identity disorder, the most famous is probably *The Three Faces of Eve*, described in a book by Thigpen and Cleckey (1957) and also made into a film. Eve was a mother within a troubled marriage who sought psychotherapy. During therapy she complained of hearing an imaginary voice. Although she had blackouts, these did not disturb her. During therapy, the authors of the book describe the birth of a new personality: 'after a tense moment of silence, there was a quick reckless smile and in a bright voice that sparkled, she said "Hi there, Doc!". A new personality emerged, Eve Black, a happy-go-lucky, flirtatious personality who did not like Eve White, the mother and primary personality. During therapy a third personality, Jane, revealed herself. Hypnosis was used to reconcile the characters. The therapist tried to allow one character, the calmer Jane, to dominate, and treatment ended with one character in control. This character was like Jane, but she labelled herself Evelyn White. 'Chris Sizemoore' was Eve's real name. Historically, psychologists believed that multiple-personality disorder usually involved two or three subpersonalities, but according to the American Psychiatric Association, the average is nearer 15 and, although Eve had three faces, she claimed that she had 22 personalities, but they always appeared in groups of three. In a book that she wrote after her therapy was complete, she insisted that her identities were not a result of role-play or mood, but were separate identities with different appetites, handwriting, skills, IQ, facial expressions and dress codes.

As can be seen in the case study of Eve, a person with dissociative identity disorder displays two or more distinct personalities, often called subpersonalities, each with a unique set of behaviours, emotions and thoughts. At any given time, one of the subpersonalities dominates the person's consciousness and interactions with other people.

Theoretical explanations of dissociative identity disorder

Psychodynamic explanation

Repression is a defence mechanism described by Freud in his ideas about human motivation. The purpose of defence mechanisms is to prevent the occurrence of anxiety by preventing painful thoughts and memories from reaching consciousness. All of us employ such defences, but in some cases the process results in the application of the defence repression in an extreme way that prevents normal functioning. This is one explanation of dissociative amnesia and fugue. Psychodynamic theorists suggest that hurtful experiences, such as a parent's extreme reaction to expressions of id impulses, especially unacceptable infantile sexual desires in the oedipal stage, can lead to massive repression where a person unconsciously blocks the memory of emotionally charged situations.

In dissociative identity disorder, individuals are seen by psychodynamic theorists as using different identities to cope by escaping elsewhere. Theorists also point to extremely traumatic childhood experiences, especially childhood abuse, as being central to the occurrence of DID. This is graphically illustrated by Schreiber (1973) in the case of 'Sybil' (whose story has also been made into a film). Sybil's mother took delight in suspending her upside down from the ceiling and filling her bladder with cold water through an enema. According to psychodynamic theorists, children such as Sybil fear for their existence in what to them seems a very cruel and dangerous world. Their only escape is to live in the world of another person, thus rendering them an observer from afar. Sybil's therapist, Dr Wilbur, described Sybil as seeking rescue from those around her, but after recognizing the futility of the search she turned inwards to seek refuge from within, amongst her multiple personalities (see also *In Focus*, 'Case study 3: Sybil', p. 416).

There is some evidence in support of the role of abuse. Kluft (1984) suggests that in 97 per cent of cases, there have been instances of physical and/or sexual abuse. One problem with this position is that child abuse has an occurrence far greater than the number of instances of DID would suggest. Dissociative identity disorders are regarded as relatively rare. One hundred cases were reported in 1970, but a huge increase to 1000s of cases were reported by the mid-1980s. According to Mersky (1992), at least some of the increase may be attributed to iatrogenic causes.

Behavioural explanation

In the behaviourist's view, the basis of dissociation is an acquired response learned through the mechanism of Skinner's operant conditioning, with the reinforcement being the relief from anxiety that occurs when one's mind drifts to more neutral subjects. In this respect, the behavioural view bears some similarity to the psychodynamic view, where trauma and anxiety avoidance are the central elements. Behaviourists, however, believe that dissociations occur by chance and that subtle reinforcement processes are at the heart of keeping the person unaware that the personality is using dissociation as an escape. Evidence for both positions comes largely from case histories. Comer (1999) points out that behavioural theory does not explain why more people do not develop dissociative disorders. As mentioned earlier, there are far more cases of abuse in children than there are DIDs. This criticism, however, is one that reflects an outdated view of the general process view of learning, where all stimuli are viewed as having an equal ability to elicit responses in all individuals. Researchers in the field of biological constraints, such as Seligman (1971), have recently produced evidence that have tempered claims of the extreme environmentalists. On their evidence, one could explain the selective nature of DID as a predisposition in some individuals' make-up to respond in particular ways. Seligman has also used predisposition in people's make-up to explain the selective nature of phobias. We will return to the issue of prevalence later.

State-dependent learning

Bower (1990) demonstrated that a person's particular state can affect their learning and memory. Memories acquired in a sad emotional state are better remembered in that same state. In the case of DIDs, experiences occurring in a dissociated state are more likely to be remembered in that state. Somehow, and this is not yet fully understood, different states represent different levels of arousal, so that memories acquired at one level of arousal will be forgotten in another level of arousal. Clusters of distinct memories develop and these are the subpersonalities. This seems plausible because it explains how personality transitions occur rapidly and in stressful circumstances, because in stressful circumstances large changes in arousal levels can occur. There is, however, no clear agreement between theorists on the relationship between arousal and memory.

Self-hypnosis

As an observer of hypnosis in various entertainment contexts, the author of this chapter noted the behaviour of a volunteer in the hypnosis process. The individual who was hypnotized left the stage at the interval to join friends for a discussion. It was clear that while he could hold a conversation with his friends, he could not recall his own or his friends' names. On stage after the interval, he was put into a state of regression. He was told to behave as if he were 6 years old and was ordered to play with imaginary toys. The display was very convincing and appeared to be more than simply role-play. Phenomena observed in hypnosis have led some to believe that some form of self-hypnosis could induce people to forget unpleasant events. Self-hypnosis has also been used to explain DID. The proponents of such explanations suggest that children are highly suggestible and that in traumatic circumstances children would escape to fulfil a wish to be someone else. There are, however, too many puzzles about the nature of hypnosis to be certain about the relationship between it and DID.

There is disagreement over whether hypnosis is a special trance-like state or whether it can be explained by normal social, attentional and cognitive processes (Miller and Bowers 1986). If the latter is the case then this has implications for whether DID is a less remarkable state than some would claim.

DID as a spontaneous or iatrogenic phenomenon

The explanations given for DID in the above-mentioned theories are not particularly convincing, and little research has been undertaken in relation to DID. When DID is described as iatrogenic, this implies that it has been induced unintentionally by therapeutic practice. The therapists create multiple identities or personalities by suggesting their existence during therapy or eliciting them by hypnotic suggestion. By looking for such identities/personalities, the therapist is believed to reinforce certain patterns of behaviour by becoming more interested when their clients exhibit symptoms of dissociation. DID can also occur spontaneously in the absence of iatrogenic factors.

Thus there are two views of the nature of DID (Lilienfield et al. 1999). These are sometimes referred to as the *post-traumatic model* (PTM) and the *sociocognitive model* (SCM). In the post-traumatic model, DID is seen as a distinct condition that is best conceptualized as a defensive response to early trauma, as illustrated in the case of Sybil (see *In Focus*, p. 416). To cope with the pain, individuals partition their experience into separate personalities (or alters) and this allows the person to pretend that the abuse is happening to someone else. In this, dissociative identity disorder is regarded as a spontaneous disorder.

SCM, on the other hand, is seen as 'a syndrome that consists of rule-governed and goal-directed experiences, and displays of multiple enactment that have been created, legitimized and maintained by social reinforcement ... these are synthesized by drawing on a wide variety of sources including broadcast media, cues provided by therapists, personal experiences and observations of individuals who have enacted multiple identities' (Lilienfield et al. 1999).

<table>
<tr><td>

in focus

Case study 3: Sybil

In the 1980s, Sybil became a well-known example of someone suffering from DID. It was clear to most observers that Sybil was troubled and eager for help. She was not, however, aware of her identities/personalities until her therapist introduced her to them. In a *Horizon* programme broadcast on BBC television in 1999, clips of the film *Sybil* were shown to illustrate that the therapist tries quite hard to convince her that the personalities exist. *Horizon* then interviews Professor Hubert Spiegel, who explains his doubts about the authenticity of DID as a genuine disorder. He claimed that when Dr Wilbur needed to be out of town, she had asked Professor Spiegel to stand in as a locum. In therapy, Sybil was reported to have asked Professor Spiegel: 'Do you want me to be Helen?' He replied that it was not necessary, but if she wanted to then she should feel free to do so. Sybil replied that if it was not necessary, she would prefer not to. He got the impression that she was being cued to live experiences as she recalled them, but as if she was someone else. With Professor Spiegel, however, she did not experience alters (separate identities/personalities). As mentioned above, Sybil was troubled and eager for help and was willing to do anything. The *Horizon* programme makers suggested that Dr Wilbur was the answer to Sybil's willingness to please. At the time DID (or multiple-personality disorder) was almost unknown as a condition, yet almost overnight most therapists had clients with DID on their couches. Professor Spiegel called the clinics 'training schools', where therapists learned to uncover DIDs. This would fit rather well with a behavioural reinforcement view of DID.

During the *Horizon* programme, Professor Spiegel's son, who is also a therapist, was interviewed. Talking about a particular client whom he had known for many years and who had undergone hundreds of therapy sessions, Professor Spiegel's son seemed totally convinced that his client was a genuine case of DID and was not an example of an iatrogenic phenomenon.

</td></tr>
</table>

According to SCM, iatrogenic and sociocultural factors play a substantial role in the occurrence of DID. This model fits quite well with Spiegel's 'training school' accusation mentioned above, and given the recent explosion of cases (from 80 in 1979 to 6000 in 1986), many writers, such as Boor (1992), refer to an 'epidemic'.

Gleaves (1996) criticizes the SCM, arguing that no disorder can be due solely to iatrogenic factors. Although iatrogenic factors may be a common cause of DID, the disorder can also occur spontaneously in their absence. For instance, DID occurs in societies where the involvement of mental health professionals is minimal. Individual differences in personality may therefore operate in conjunction with personal and sociocultural factors to predispose people to DID. For example, a study by Scroppo *et al.* (1998) suggests that people suffering from DID showed an increased projective and imaginative activity, a diminished ability to integrate mental contents, a complex and driven cognitive style, and a highly unconventional view of reality. So even supporters of the SCM do not deny that 'much of the psychopathological raw material from which DID is sculpted exists prior to professional intervention' (Lilienfield *et al.* 1999). In other words, iatrogenesis may contribute to DID, but no more so than many other social influences.

Simulation of DID

Case study 4 illustrates concerns about DID showing itself as a response simply because it is rewarding to do so. Gleaves (1996) suggests that this is a key assumption behind the sociocultural model. However, the SCM carefully distinguishes between role enactment and role simulation. In the latter, behaviour is spontaneous and occurs without conscious effort. It is admitted, however, that in some instances DID may be feigned to avoid culpability for criminal actions or to obtain attention. Such problems have fuelled debates about its existence. Proponents of the SCM claim that there is confusion about existence and aetiology. Proponents of the SCM do not claim that DID is not a 'real' phenomenon, in the sense that there are individuals who show all the signs of DID. They do, however, wonder if the condition is best described as a response to trauma (the notion behind the post-traumatic model) or as a 'socially influenced product that unfolds largely in response to the shaping influences of therapeutic practices, culturally based scripts, and social expectations' (Lilienfield *et al.* 1999).

What about those who claim that DID is hypnotically induced and can be brought about through self-hypnosis and is, therefore, a product of iatrogenesis? Coons (1989) did a survey in which he indicated that most DID patients had never been in focus **Case study 4: Ken Bianchi**

Davison and Neale (1997) report on the case of Ken Bianchi, the hillside strangler, who attempted a defence of insanity for his serial killings. However, the court decided that he was faking DID to avoid punishment. During the trial, Spanos (1985), who was highly sceptical of the existence of DID, managed to elicit another personality in Ken during a pretrial meeting. In the interview the therapist said, 'I've talked to Ken, but I think there is another part of Ken that I have not spoken to'. Eventually Steve emerged. Steve hated Ken for being nice and Steve admitted that he murdered a number of women. The jury however remained unconvinced.

In Spanos' (1985) study, undergraduate students role-played second personalities. This was done so well that the personalities being acted out even scored differently on a personality test, indicating that when the situation demands it, people can adopt another personality. This only indicates that convincing role-play is possible and *not* that DID is no more than role-play, as Spanos argues.

hypnotized. So, hypnosis may not play as important a role as some would suggest. Certainly, the sociocultural model suggests that hypnotism is not a special case of facilitating responses to suggestions. Leading interviews and suggestive questions are equally likely to induce multiple roles.

The motivation for developing DID

Gleaves (1996) maintains that the intense suffering experienced by individuals with DID suggests that processes like reinforcement are perhaps not involved in the causes or maintenance of the condition. This is an uninformed view of reinforcement. A reinforcer is anything that increases the probability of occurrence of behaviour. Take the case of the child who is placed in detention for being late, but whose subsequent behaviour leads to greater tardiness. In this case, what appears to be a punishment is technically a reinforcer because a reinforcer is defined by its resulting effects on the frequency of behaviour. This 'punishment' has led to an increase in the frequency of tardy behaviour and is therefore, by definition, acting as a reinforcer, not as a punishment, as a lay person may view it. Mowrer (1948) called this the neurotic paradox. With this in mind, it is possible to view the suffering as iatrogenically induced. Indeed, it is clear that distressing behaviour – even maladaptive behaviour – may not appear reinforcing to an outside observer, but may be very reinforcing to clients with poor home support and who become dependent on their therapists. In fact, socially deprived individuals are said to find negative attention more reinforcing than no attention at all.

As Scroppo and colleagues (1998) point out (see *In Focus* on p. 418), the study of DID reminds

Activity 2: Repression and dissociation

Go to http://www.jimhopper.com/memory/ and locate the page headed 'Recovered memories of sexual abuse: scientific and scholarly resources'.

Scroll down this page to Chris Brewin's contribution. Summarize his concerns about the terms repression and dissociation as explanations of forgetting.

If you have the opportunity, discuss the issues with classmates.

us that, although therapy is generally effective, we need to remember that 'the clinician qua diagnostician and treatment provider can be the creator as well as the discoverer of psychopathology'.

Exam summary: Multiple-personality disorder (dissociative identity disorder)

The AQA examination will test your understanding of the following areas:

◆ case studies of multiple personality disorder (pp. 413–17)

◆ research into multiple personality disorder (pp. 414–18).

Example question

The question that follows on p. 418 is typical of one drawn from the material above, and should take you 45 minutes to answer:

Scroppo's caution

Scroppo *et al.* (1998) describe the controversy surrounding the great increase in numbers of DIDs. They point out that the sceptics maintain that iatrogenesis is the reason for the increase in numbers. Furthermore, the sceptics also insist that DID patients do not share in any consistent etiological or psychological processes. On the other hand, those who maintain that dissociation occurs because of the effects of severe trauma, point to other factors which may account for the increase in numbers, e.g. more rigorous diagnostic criteria and wider awareness of DID.

A study by Scroppo and colleagues involved 21 DID patients and 21 non-DID patients. Their findings showed that DID patients exhibited fairly consistent patterns of behaviour over a wide range of 'domains'. They claim that 'the chronic and relatively severe history of psychological impairment found amongst their DID participants' argues against an entirely iatrogenic aetiology. They conclude that, apart from the consistent patterns referred to above, DID patients exhibited a distinctive and theoretically consistent set of perceptual and cognitive characteristics that differentiated them from controls and related clinical groups, such as those suffering from post-traumatic stress disorder. They conclude that, 'although DID is a controversial diagnosis, there is reason to believe that genuine, distinctive and theoretically consonant psychological processes underlie the disorder'.

◆ Critically consider the extent to which dissociative identity (multiple-personality) disorders have been shown to be iatrogenic (i.e. manufactured by the therapist). *(30 marks)*

Suggested answer structure

As with all questions, this one requires careful reading. The AO1 requirement is for you to show your knowledge and understanding of the arguments for the origins of DID, and the AO2 requirement is for you to weigh up the strengths and limitations of each of these different perspectives. You should be able to do that from the material in this chapter, but it pays to see what people more intimately involved with the field are writing about this disorder. The two websites below offer arguments for and against the existence of DID as a real disorder. Be wary, however, about the difference between personal conviction and informed psychology when reading this material.

http://mentalhelp.net/guide/dissoc.htm

http://www.iatrogenic.org

In DSM-IV, four distinguishing subtypes of dissociative disorder are identified. In dissociative identity disorder (DID) a person displays two or more distinct personalities with a unique set of behaviours, emotions and thoughts. The wide publication of famous cases such as 'the three faces of Eve' has led to the conjecture that this condition may actually be manufactured by therapists during therapy sessions through the act of suggestion to people who are vulnerable and eager to please. The process of therapeutically induced behaviours is known as iatrogenesis. Although there are many psychological explanations for DID, including psychodynamic, behavioural, state-dependent learning, and self-hypnosis, none seems very convincing. Current opinion is divided as to how far dissociative identity disorder is therapeutically induced.

The theories mentioned above would serve as a useful background to your discussion of the iatrogenic nature of dissociative identity disorder. These theories also serve the useful purpose of increasing the breadth of explanations that you are discussing (therefore satisfying the synoptic element of this question). If psychological theories cannot provide a satisfactory explanation for this phenomenon, it raises the possibility that it is a *manufactured* condition rather than a condition that exists prior to therapy. The post-traumatic model (pp. 414–16) sees DID as a distinct condition that is a defensive response to early trauma (as in the case of Sybil – *In Focus*, p. 416). The sociocognitive model (pp. 415–16), on the other hand, sees the interaction of many different factors as being responsible for the emergence of the disorder. Dissociative identity disorder is assumed to result from influences such as broadcasting media, therapists' suggestions, personal experiences, observations of others displaying the symptoms of the disorder, social reinforcement and a host of other sociocultural factors (see also 'Scroppo's caution' – *In Focus* on p. 418). As with the earlier inclusion of different theories that have attempted to explain this disorder, the systematic critical examination of the different factors that might combine to produce the experience of DID would contribute effectively to the synoptic element of this question.

Culture-bound syndromes

As we have already seen, both the ICD and DSM aim to be universal and scientific, i.e. they aim to offer a set of classificatory (and, in the case of the DSM, diagnostic) 'clusters' of mental disorders which can be applied worldwide and which are not dependent on any particular theories of abnormality, such as those you will have met in your AS-level psychology course.

However, culture-bound syndromes (CBSs) raise a serious challenge to both of these aims. In this section, we will look at what CBSs are, including a categorization system and an exhaustive list of CBSs currently recognized. Finally, we will examine the crucial question of whether CBSs really are 'unique ways of being mad' (Gross 1996), or whether they are merely localized manifestations of DSM/ICD illnesses.

A definition of culture-bound syndromes

The ICD-10 states that CBSs share two principal features:

◆ They are not easily accommodated by the categories in established and internationally used psychiatric classifications.

◆ They were first described in, and subsequently closely associated with, a particular population or cultural area.

DSM-IV defines CBSs as 'recurrent, locality-specific patterns of aberrant behavior and troubling experience that may or may not be linked to a specific DSM-IV diagnostic category. Many of these patterns are indigenously considered to be "illnesses", or at least afflictions, and most have local names' (p. 844).

The term *indigenous* is central to the concept of the CBS. What does it mean? Kim and Berry (1993) define it as something which develops within a particular culture (i.e. it has not been 'imported' into it) and serves a function for that culture. So, for example, although Coca-Cola is consumed across most of the globe, it is indigenous only to the USA.

The DSM-IV definition of CBSs is not, however, without its problems. Humphreys (1999) raises the following points:

◆ 'locality-specific patterns' – several CBSs are found in quite a large number of cultures; does this weaken their right to be called a CBS?

◆ 'aberrant' – by whose criteria?

◆ 'troubling' – to whom?

◆ 'indigenously considered to be an illness' – does this mean that if the local people do not consider it to be an illness, but rather acceptable, normal behaviour, that it does not count as a CBS?

---

in focus

The role of culture in psychology

It has been estimated that 90 per cent of all psychologists who have ever lived, and about 90 per cent of the psychological literature, originated in the Western world (Sam 1996). This has considerable consequences for our examination of abnormality, and our classification and diagnosis of mental disorders. As Sam (1996, pp. 1–2) argues:

'The inability of many psychological theories to account for behavioural expressions in certain cultural societies (e.g. culture-bound syndromes like *Brain fag* in West Africa, *Amok* in South Eastern Asia and *Susto* found among children dwelling in the Andes*) can no longer be denied, thus acquiring modern psychology a description of being "culture-bound and culture-blind". This view concedes psychology as being too rooted in one society, and as not paying enough attention to other cultural societies and ethnic groups...

The culture-blindness of psychology stems from the fact that psychology has not significantly taken into account a great variety of factors like differences in value systems, and differences in ways of diagnosing diseases found in other cultures that influence the behavior of millions of other people ...

The point is not to suggest that modern psychology, as we know it, is useless, but to point out that any serious study of human psychology must include cultural and ethnic variation.'

This provides a strong justification for the exploration of cultural differences in the classification and diagnosis of abnormal behaviours or mental disorders.

* These specific CBSs are described on pp. 421–4.

◆ what may appear to outsiders to be 'aberrant behavior and troubling experiences', may be quite logical in the context of a particular culture (see the example of *pa-feng* later in this section).

You should bear these points in mind as you read the rest of this section.

Closely allied to the concept of culture-bound syndromes is that of folk illness, and the way in which a folk illness is treated through folk medicine (Neff, undated). These, too, are concepts of illness which are held by localized (indigenous) groups of people. Bell's (1999) Folk Illness Glossary, for example, includes five CBSs out of a total of 21 illnesses. The principal difference between the two is that the majority of folk illnesses do not relate to mental disorders, but to what Pfeiffer (1982) refers to as 'concrete' illnesses. So, for example, *Masuk angin*, found in Indonesia, means 'wind enters' and refers to bloated stomach (ascribed to standing in windy places and staying out after dark).

Looking for patterns

Before focusing on specific CBSs, we need to address one further issue. There is a danger that we may degenerate into considering CBSs as a list of exotic or quaint illnesses in far-away places. This would undervalue their significance entirely. We need to view them in the light of what patterns of commonality and difference we can discern. Pfeiffer (1982) argues that it is impossible to have a single classificatory category called culture-bound syndromes (in the way the ICD-10 has neurotic disorders and personality disorders, for example), because they are too diverse and, perhaps most importantly, only make sense in terms of the values of the cultures within which they occur. As he puts it:

> 'Even when one views the culture-bound syndromes separately, it is not possible to arrange them according to a uniform system. This is because cultural influences contribute differentially to the causation, formation, and interpretation of psychopathological syndromes.' (p. 202)

However, this is not to say that we cannot endeavour to impose some form of organization upon them. One of the most prolific writers on CBSs in recent times , Hall (1998a, 1998b, 1998c, 1998d), categorizes CBSs in the following way (Hall 1998a):

1. a psychiatric illness (not organically caused) which is locally recognized as an illness and which does not correspond to a recognized Western category (e.g. *amok**)

2. a psychiatric illness (not organically caused) which is locally recognized as an illness and does resemble a Western category, but may be lacking some symptoms that are regarded as important in many cultures (e.g. *taijin kyofusho**)

3. a psychiatric illness not yet recognized in the West (e.g. *kuru**)

4. a psychiatric illness (which may or may not be organically caused) that is found in many cultures, but only seen as an illness in one or a few (e.g. *koro**)

5. culturally accepted idioms of illness which would not be regarded as acceptable in mainstream Western medicine (e.g. *evil eye**)

6. a syndrome allegedly occurring in a given culture, but which does not, in fact, exist, e.g. *windigo**, which is used to justify the expulsion or execution of an outcast in the same way that witchcraft was.

* These specific CBSs are described on pp. 421–4.

Case studies of syndromes apparently bound by culture

Where in the world do they exist?

Hall offers a number of categorizations of CBSs – alphabetically, by symptoms and by geographical locality. Since we are exploring whether or not psychiatric illnesses can be classified globally, we will list and describe CBSs in terms of where in the world they are found. This arrangement also emphasizes that CBSs *do* exist in the homeland of the DSM and the ICD (i.e. North America and Western Europe).

The descriptions of specific CBSs given in Tables 16.5 to 16.11 are taken from DSM-IV (pp. 845–9), Berry *et al.* (1992), Hall (1998b, 1998d) and Humphreys (1999). A total of 36 different CBSs have been noted across the globe. When preparing for the A-level examination, you would only need to be able to refer to a small sample of these to illustrate your answers.

Activity 3: Eating disorders

Currently two of the most prevalent disorders in the Western world are anorexia nervosa and bulimia nervosa. Well-known cases of figures in the public arena, such as the late Princess Diana, have highlighted its profile.

Hall (1998b) contends that anorexia nervosa and bulimia nervosa in their classic forms are CBSs, specific to the USA and Western Europe (although related syndromes have existed in other times and places, e.g. anorexia mirabilis in medieval Europe, and both anorexia and bulimia are now reported in Westernizing countries).

If he is right, what factors do you think put people under such intense pressure to be thin?

Table 16.5   Culture-bound syndromes: East Asia

China

Koro	The belief that the penis (or, more rarely, the vulva or the nipples) is retracting into the body and that when it is fully retracted, death will result. Panic attempts to keep the penis from retracting can lead to severe physical damage. Koro occasionally occurs in local epidemics. Also found in Assam and Thailand. Found in isolated cases in the USA and Europe.
Pa-feng	A phobic fear of the wind. Suffers fear an excess of yin (negative energy) from exposure to the wind and wrap up in warm clothing and eat hot foods.
Qi-gong psychotic reaction	An acute, short-term episode characterized by dissociative, paranoid or nonpsychotic symptoms that occur after taking part in a particular Chinese folk health-enhancing practice.
Shenjian shuairuo	Symptoms include physical and mental fatigue, dizziness, headaches and other pains, difficulty in concentrating, sleep disturbance and memory loss. Many cases would fit the DSM-IV criteria for major depressive disorder or anxiety disorder.
Shenkui	Anxiety or panic symptoms sometimes with physical complaints for which no cause can be found. Symptoms include dizziness, backache, fatigue, general weakness, insomnia, frequent dreams and sexual dysfunction such as premature ejaculation or impotence. The condition is attributed to excessive semen loss from frequent intercourse, masturbation or nocturnal emission. The men fear semen loss because it represents the loss of their vital essence and can thereby be life-threatening.

Taiwan

Hsieh-ping	A brief trance state in which the person is possessed by an ancestral ghost who often attempts to communicate to other members of the family. Symptoms include tremor, disorientation, delirium and hallucinations.

Japan

Imu	Imitative behaviour (usually amongst women) that seems beyond control. Movements and speech are copied and individuals in this state are compliant to commands to do things that they ordinarily would not (for example, uttering obscenities).
Shinkeishitsu	A syndrome marked by obsessions, perfectionism, ambivalence and social withdrawal.
Taijin kyofusho	Intense fear that one's body, body parts or bodily functions are displeasing, embarrassing or offensive to other people.

Korea

Hwa-byung	Anger syndrome. Symptoms are attributed to suppression of anger and include insomnia, fatigue, panic, fear of impending death, indigestion, anorexia and palpitations.
Shin-byung	Characterized by anxiety and somatic complaints (such as weakness and dizziness) followed by dissociation and possession by ancestral spirits.

Other East Asian and Siberian groups

Amurakh, irkunii, ikota, olan, myriachit and menkeiti (see *imu*, Japan*)

* *Indicates similarity of symptoms, although they may not be identical.*

Table 16.6   Culture-bound syndromes: South and Southeast Asia

Assam

Jinjinia bemar	(see *koro*, China, Table 16.5)*

India

Dhat or jiryan	Semen-loss syndrome (see *shenkui*, China)*.

Indonesia

Latah (see *imu*, Japan)*	Also occurs in Malaysia where it is more frequent in middle-aged women.

Malaysia

Amok	Usually found in males. A period of brooding followed by short-duration, wild, aggressive behaviour, in which there are outbursts of violent, aggressive, destructive and even homicidal behaviour. (The term 'running amok' is in common usage in the West.)
Koro	(see China)*

Phillipines

Mali-mali, silok	(see *imu*, Japan)*

Sri Lanka

Sukra prameha	Semen-loss syndrome (see *shenkui*, China)*

Thailand

Rok-joo	(see *koro*, China)*
Bah-tschi, bah-tsi, baah-ji	(see *imu*, Japan)*

* *Indicates similarity of symptoms, although they may not be identical.*

Table 16.7   Culture-bound syndromes: Africa

North Africa

Zar	Experience of spirit. Symptoms include laughing, shouting, hitting the head against walls, singing or weeping. Sufferers may show apathy and withdrawal, refuse to eat or carry out everyday tasks, or may develop a long-term relationship with the possessing spirit. This behaviour is often not considered abnormal locally.

Sub-Saharan Africa

Brain fag or brain fog (West Africa)	A condition experienced by students. Symptoms include difficulties in concentrating, remembering and thinking. Symptoms centre on the head and neck and include pain, pressure, tightness, blurring of vision, heat or burning.
Boufee deliriante (West Africa and Haiti)	Sudden outburst of agitated and aggressive behaviour, marked confusion and psychomotor excitement, sometimes accompanied by visual and auditory hallucinations.

Table 16.8 Culture-bound syndromes: The Mediterranean and Middle East	
Greece	
Nerva	Distress. It refers to a general state of vulnerability to stressful life experiences. There are many symptoms including emotional distress, headaches, irritability, digestive and sleep disturbances, nervousness, an inability to concentrate and tingling sensations.
Portuguese Cape Verdeans	
Sangue dormido	This literally means sleeping blood. Symptoms include pain, numbness, tremor, paralysis, convulsions, blindness, heart attack and infection.
Spain	
Mal de ojo	The 'evil eye'. Occurs as a common form of disease, misfortune and social disruption throughout the Mediterranean, Latin America and the Muslim world.

Table 16.9 Culture-bound syndromes: Latin America and the Caribbean	
The Caribbean (also Southern USA)	
Falling out or blacking out	Episodes are characterized by sudden collapse, either without warning or preceded by feelings of dizziness. The sufferer's eyes are open, but they claim they cannot see. He or she usually hears and understands what is occurring around them, but feels unable to move.
Latin America	
Ataque de nervios	A form of distress principally found amongst Latinos from the Caribbean, but also amongst many Latin American and Latin Mediterranean groups. Symptoms include uncontrollable shouting, attacks of crying, trembling, heat in the chest rising to the head, and verbal and/or physical aggression. It frequently occurs as a result of a stressful family event, especially the death of a relative, but also possibly a divorce or disagreement with a family member.
Bilis or colera	Part of a general Latin American form of distress and explanation of physical or mental illness as a result of extreme emotion, which upsets the humours (described in terms of hot and cold). Bilis and colera specifically implicate anger in the cause of illness. (See Neff [undated] for an elaboration as a folk illness amongst American Hispanic groups.)
Locura	A severe, chronic psychosis attributed to an inherited vulnerability, the effect of multiple life difficulties, or a combination of the two. Symptoms include incoherence, agitation, auditory and visual hallucinations, inability to follow rules of normal social interaction, unpredictability and possible violence.
Mal de pelea (Puerto Rico)	(see *amok*, Malaysia)*
Mal do ojo	(see Spain)*
Mal puesto or brujeria	Illness caused by witchcraft.
Nervios	(similar to *nerva*, Greece)*
Susto	An illness attributed to a frightening event that causes the soul to leave the body leading to symptoms of unhappiness and sickness. These may occur months or even years after the supposedly precipitating event.

* Indicates similarity of symptoms, although they may not be identical.

Table 16.10 Culture-bound syndromes: Native Americans, Arctic and Polynesia

Native Americans

Cafard/cathard (Polynesia)	(see *amok*, Malaysia)*
Iich'aa (Navaho)	(see *amok*, Malaysia)*
Ghost sickness (American Indian groups)	Preoccupation with death and the deceased, sometimes associated with witchcraft. Symptoms may include bad dreams, weakness, feelings of danger, loss of appetite, fainting, fear, anxiety, hallucinations, loss of consciousness, confusion, feelings of futility and a sense of suffocation.
Grisi siknis (Miskito Indians)	Symptoms include headaches, anxiety, anger and aimless running; some similarities to *pibloktoq*.
Hi-Wa itck (Mohave Indians)	Symptoms include insomnia, depression and loss of appetite. It is sometimes associated with unwanted separation from a loved one.
Kuru (New Guinea)	A progressive psychosis and dementia indigenous to cannibalistic tribes in the region. It results from an aberrant protein that is capable of replicating itself by deforming other proteins in the brain. It has been identified with a form of Creuzfeldt-Jacob Disease (CJD).
Pibloktoq or *Arctic hysteria* (Greenland Eskimos and Arctic)	An abrupt dissociative episode accompanied by extreme excitement of up to 30 minutes duration and frequently followed by convulsive seizures and coma lasting up to 12 hours. The individual may be withdrawn or mildly irritable for a period of hours or days before the attack and will typically report complete amnesia for the attack. During the attack, the individual may tear off their clothes, break furniture, shout obscenities, eat faeces, flee from protective shelters, or perform other irrational or dangerous acts. This syndrome is found throughout the Arctic with varying local names.
Windigo or *witiko* (Algonkian Indians, Northeast USA; Eastern Canada)	This involves distaste for ordinary food and feelings of depression and anxiety leading to possession by a giant man-eating monster, often resulting in homicide and cannibalism. If a cure is not attained the sufferer often pleads for death to be spared their cannibalistic desires.

* Indicates similarity of symptoms, although they may not be identical.

Table 16.11 Culture-bound syndromes: USA and Western Europe

Anorexia mirabilis or holy anorexia (medieval Europe)	Severe restriction of food intake, associated with experience of religious devotion. Often not considered pathological within the culture.
Anorexia nervosa (North America, Western Europe)	Severe restriction of food intake, associated with morbid fear of obesity. Other methods may also be used to lose weight, including excessive exercise. May overlap with bulimia nervosa.
Bulimia nervosa (North America, Western Europe)	Binge eating followed by purging through self-induced vomiting, laxatives or diuretics. A morbid fear of obesity; may overlap with anorexia nervosa.
Involutional paraphrenia (Germany; Spain)	A paranoid disorder occurring in midlife.
Rootwork (Southern USA)	A set of cultural interpretations that explain illness as the results of hexing, witchcraft, voodoo or the influence of the evil eye.
Spell (Southern USA)	A trance state in which individuals 'communicate' with deceased relatives or with spirits. At times this is associated with brief periods of personality change.
Tabanka (Trinidad)	Depression associated with a high rate of suicide. Found in men abandoned by their wives.

Arguments for and against the existence of culture-bound syndromes

The first, and perhaps most obvious, question to ask is whether or not CBSs exist at all. The comprehensive list given above would seem to suggest that they do. However, some may be increasingly historical 'curiosities' as the world shrinks due to technological developments, specifically those relating to travel and communication. In particular, we should point to what has been called the Americanization of the world: that is, the increasing influence of American culture in the world today. Pfeiffer (1982, p. 216) argues:

> 'The universal spread of technical civilization and of the scientific medicine pertaining to it, has caused the disappearance of well-defined syndromes that are specific to a certain culture ... This does not mean, however, that the dimensions of cultural influence ... have lost their meaning. They have merely become harder to recognize now that the contrast between folk medicine and scientific medicine is missing.'

The answer to our first question would, then, appear to be that CBSs do exist, although several may be harder to find than, say, 50 years ago.

Another key question, to which we now turn our attention, is whether, in the context of classification and diagnosis, the CBSs are really 'unique ways of being mad', or whether they could be assimilated within those classificatory and diagnostic clusters of, for example, the DSM. The ICD-10 states:

> 'The status of these disorders is controversial: many researchers argue that they differ only in degree from disorders already included in existing psychiatric classifications, such as anxiety disorders and reactions to stress, and that they are therefore best regarded as local variations of disorders that have long been recognized. Their exclusive occurrence in specific population or cultural areas has also been questioned.' (Chapter V(F), p. 1)

However, before we can begin to address this, there is an even more fundamental question we must pose, which is: are the CBSs classifiable at all? Certainly not as a single, coherent entity, as both Arieti and Meth (1959) and Pfeiffer (1982) have convincingly argued. They are simply too disparate and can only be understood when viewed through the values of the different cultures in which they are used to make sense of certain symptoms. Hall (1998c) argues, however, that we should not merely regard the list of CBSs above as 36 entities. Rather, we can see that many of them share common symptoms or characteristics. A 10-item index of symptoms is shown in Table 16.12.

Table 16.12 Index of symptoms of CBSs

General symptom(s)	Illustrative CBS
Startle matchin (e.g. the influence of sudden fright)	Imu
Genital retraction	Koro
Sudden mass assault	Amok
Running	Pibloktoq
Semen loss	Dhat
Spiritual possession	Zar
Obsession with the deceased	Hsieh-ping
Exhaustion	Brain fag
Suppressed rage	Hwa-byung
Food restriction	Anorexia nervosa

Source: Simons and Hughes (1985)

If CBSs cannot be accommodated within a single individual category, can the various forms of CBSs be accommodated in the DSM and ICD classification and diagnostic systems? In examining cross-cultural analysis of psychopathology, Berry *et al.* (1992) argue that three positions can be taken in relation to abnormalities, mental disorders, etc. These are:

◆ *absolute* – unchanging in all studied cultures in terms of origin, symptoms, etc.

◆ *universal* – found in all cultures, but affected by cultural influences in terms of what brings them out, what forms they take, etc.

◆ *culturally relative* – unique to some cultures and understandable only in terms of values and concepts held within those cultures.

Since CBSs clearly do not fit the 'absolute' position, do they fit either the second or third categories listed above? Are they mental disorders which are found in most, if not all, cultures, but which are triggered by different factors in different cultures and take somewhat different 'forms'? Or are they really unique to certain cultures?

A chief proponent for the 'universal' view is probably Pow-Meng Yap (1974). Two of the key points made by Yap are:

◆ Human mental disorders have an essentially supracultural nature (broad and spanning all cultures). So, for example, the dopamine hypothesis has been put forward as a biopsychological explanation for schizophrenia (see Chapter 17). Thus, it could be argued that symptoms are something which emerge from within the individual and these symptoms cluster together to form discrete categories of mental illnesses. This was exactly the starting point of contemporary psychiatry with the early writings of Kraeplin in the late nineteenth century.

◆ A comparative psychiatry endeavours to establish common links across cultures in a similar way to that in which comparative psychology explores links between behaviours in different species. CBSs are seen as culturally specific expressions of common human problems and disorders that are addressed by the ICD and DSM. Yap argues, for example, that *latah* is a local cultural expression of 'primary fear reaction', *amok* is a 'rage reaction', and *windigo* is a 'possession state'.

Wolfgang Pfeiffer counters this position. Pfeiffer (1982) agrees with Yap that the manifestations of illnesses, the human behaviours (what he calls the 'concrete' aspect) may indeed be 'a universally human character'. But this is only one part of the issue. His argument is that the diagnostic and classificatory systems of the West (universal and scientific) are so qualitatively different in nature to the folk illnesses and medicines that are specific to particular cultures that they cannot be integrated except by distortion. He writes:

'The individual case of illness can usually be integrated into the international psychiatric (classificatory) system without any particular problems. In spite of this, the attempt to bring the culture-bound syndromes into a psychiatric diagnostic system is doomed to failure because the symptoms in the two spheres are selected and ordered from qualitatively disparate points of view.' (Pfeiffer 1982, p. 214)

By way of illustration, he argues that CBSs must be viewed at the level of the individual culture, rather than at the home of the American Psychological Association in Washington, DC, because they are specific in the following four aspects:

◆ Culture-specific areas of stress – Cultures differ in what puts unbearable stress on people. In one, it may be work and status; in another, it may be family relations.

◆ Culture-specific shaping of conduct – Different cultures 'allow' and 'debar' certain expressions and behaviours. What might be permitted as a culturally acceptable release mechanism in certain cultures (for example, violent behaviour in particular prescribed activities), may not be in others. So, for example, *bilis* (distress caused by extreme emotion that has upset the balance of bodily fluids) is treated by Hispanics in Southwestern USA by encouraging the expression of one's emotions and the drinking of teas of bitter herbs such as estafiate or warm water.

◆ Culture-specific interpretations – The great English psychologist Bartlett once observed that 'all human life is effort after meaning'. A behaviour is one thing, what we take that to mean, and what sense we make of it, is entirely another. Think of how certain women were 'discovered' (sic) to be witches because of certain, culturally specific interpretations of their behaviours (Ussher 1992).

Do CBSs indicate that the classificatory systems are Western and White?

Humphreys (1999, pp. 16–17) has pointed out that the very conception of a culture-bound syndrome indicates that the ICD and DSM are ethnocentric (i.e. bound in one culture and supporting the prominence of that culture):

'The ICD and DSM have arisen out of the experiences and concerns of the (dominant) West and anything ... that has arisen elsewhere and is not found in the West is seen as exotic and "other". Furthermore, because of this dominance, the psychopathologies of the West are – paradoxically – regarded as normal (sic) with no need for recourse to explanations emphasizing the cultures in which these people live.'

Fernando (1991, pp. 79–80) also supports this position:

'When a "new" condition is noticed in a non-Western society ... the syndrome is perceived as alien ... something exotic, unclassifiable, culture-reactive, etc. ... The fact that they occur quite frequently makes no difference; if they are limited – or apparently limited – to other cultures, they are not admitted into the mainstream of psychiatric illness ... The concept of a CBS is therefore one that has been generated by Western psychiatry: psychopathology in the West is seen as culturally neutral and psychopathology that is distinctly different (from that seen in the West) as "culture-bound".'

'When culture "distorts" a syndrome beyond a certain point, a CBS is identified. Practitioners go along with this approach seeing symptom constellations in the West as standard and those in other cultures as anomalies.'

◆ Culture-specific interventions – We have not explored the variety of culture-specific ways of treating disorders, but folk medicine is a particularly good example of the ways in which indigenous peoples treat their illnesses.

To conclude, Hall (1999) argues:

'The matter is very complicated and turns on a number of very deep questions about the nature of mental illness. Some [of the CBSs] do indeed turn out to be variants of more familiar disorders (or, conversely, the "typical" presentation in a Western setting is our particular variation on the world-wide theme).

'... Universal symptoms ... may tie in to a folk medical theory that elaborates this into a commonly believed-in condition, rather than an individual idiosyncrasy, and therefore makes it available as an illness for many members of a given culture.

'... The DSM is artificially designed to give clear diagnosis for research purposes; for better or worse, folk taxonomies don't do this.'

Therefore, if CBSs are a form of folk-illness to be treated by folk medicine, then they are, as Pfeiffer observed, qualitatively inconsistent with the aims and purposes of the ICD and DSM as universal and scientific.

Exam summary: Culture-bound syndromes

The AQA examination will test your understanding of the following areas:

◆ case studies of apparently culture-bound syndromes (pp. 420–24)

◆ evaluation of evidence for culture-bound syndromes (pp. 425–7).

Example question

The question should take you 45 minutes to answer:

◆ 'Culture-bound syndromes are merely exotic expressions of mental illnesses encompassed within the DSM and ICD. They have no independent existence of their own.' Discuss.   *(30 marks)*

Suggested answer structure

The question starts with a quotation, and as the question amounts to a single word ('Discuss'), it is evident that you should engage with the content of this quotation during your answer.

The material for this question can be found on pp. 419–27. This section has looked at how the ICD-10 and DSM-IV define culture-bound syndromes (CBSs) and you may have noted that CBSs might be seen as a challenge to the universal and scientific positions taken by the ICD and DSM systems. Tables 16.5 to 16.11 give extensive coverage of disorders considered to be CBSs – including their principal symptoms – arranged by geographical regions of the world. You should not attempt to include all of these in your answer, just sufficient to illustrate the CBSs found in different regions of the world. Interestingly, anorexia nervosa and bulimia nervosa might be seen as CBSs, although they are increasingly being recognized in Westernizing countries.

Although two classificatory systems for CBSs have been created, it is important to recognize that their variety and cultural specificity mean that they cannot be configured into a separate entity in a classificatory system in their own right. In particular, it was argued that they make sense as 'folk illnesses' with 'folk medicine' treatments, only in terms of the values and belief systems of the particular culture in which they are found (p. 427).

Yap and Pfeiffer present contrasting views on whether or not CBSs can be assimilated into current classificatory and diagnostic systems such as the DSM and the ICD (pp. 425–7). It was concluded that although this may be possible for some CBSs, because there is often commonality of symptoms, the experience of the CBSs can only be fully understood by viewing them in terms of the values of the cultures to which they are indigenous. The discussion of CBSs acknowledge the influence of cultural diversity of mental disorders – this contributes to the *synoptic* element of this question.

Chapter summary

◆ The **ICD** and the **DSM** offer clinical means of **classifying** and **diagnosing mental disorders**. The ICD is a classification-only tool, whereas the DSM provides both classification and diagnosis. The World Health Organization in Europe produces the ICD and the American Psychiatric Association in the USA produces the DSM. Both the ICD and DSM have been revised on several occasions.

◆ The ICD comprises 11 categories of mental disorder including mood (affective) disorders, behavioural syndromes and mental retardation. Assessment on the DSM involves five axes: clinical disorders; personality disorders and mental retardation; general medical conditions; psychosocial and environmental problems; and global assessment of functioning scale.

◆ The issues of **reliability** and **validity** are critical in the classification and diagnosis of mental disorders as **Rosenhan's** (1973) classic study clearly demonstrates. Davison and Neale (1997) suggest that three kinds of validity are important when assessing any classification system: aetiological, concurrent and predictive validity. A relatively new technique for diagnosis developed in Australia, the Composite International Diagnostic Interview or CIDI, that involves patient/computer interaction, seems promising in terms of improved validity and reliability.

◆ There is considerable empirical evidence to suggest that there is diagnostic bias relating to race, class and gender. For example, there is evidence of overdiagnosis of schizophrenia in West Indian immigrant in-patients in Britain; upper-class people have been found to receive more favourable clinical judgements than working-class people. Worell and Remer (1992) contend that gender influences diagnosis in four ways: disregarding the environmental context; differential diagnosis based on gender; therapist misjudgement; and theoretical orientation gender bias.

◆ The clinical disorder **dissociative identity disorder** (or **multiple-personality disorder**, as it is often more commonly known) is well illustrated by the **case studies** of George, Eve (documented by **Thigpen and Cleckey** 1957), Sybil and Ken. It has, however, been subject to few experimental investigations. In 1970, only 100 cases had been reported, but by the mid-1980s this had risen to well over 1,000. Mersky (1992) argues that many of these are **iatrogenic** (i.e. they have been 'manufactured' by the therapist), rather than being **spontaneous**.

◆ A number of explanations for dissociative identity disorder (DID) have been put forward, including a psychodynamic explanation, a behavioural explanation, and state-dependent learning and self-hypnosis. Two views of DID have become dominant: the post-traumatic model (PTM) and the sociocognitive model (SCM). The former views DID as a response to a particular trauma (as in the case study of Sybil), whereas the latter sees it as cognitions arising out of social reinforcements. SCM accords a larger role to iatrogenesis than does PTM. Scroppo *et al.* (1998) investigated the huge increase in the reporting of DID and the associated iatrogenesis controversy. They conclude that DID is associated with genuine, distinctive and theoretically consonant processes.

◆ **Culture-bound syndromes** (CBSs) are included in the latest editions of both the ICD and DSM. Thirty-six CBSs (e.g. **koro, dhat**) have currently been identified and described. They are often listed by the geographical region in the world where they occur.

◆ The **existence of CBSs** offers a clear illustration of the importance of cultural factors in psychiatric classification and diagnosis. However, Pfeiffer (1982) argues that it is not possible to have a single classificatory system, because CBSs are too diverse and only make sense within their cultural setting.

◆ There is considerable **controversy** about whether or not CBSs **exist** (i.e. whether they have the same clinical status as other pathologies listed in the ICD and DSM) or are merely 'exotic' manifestations of pathologies that are already included. The former position is supported by Pfeiffer (1982) whilst Yap (1974) advocates the latter position. Hall (1999) contends that many CBSs do not fit easily into the Western classificatory and diagnostic systems and are qualitatively inconsistent with the aims of the purposes of the ICD and DSM (for example, a scientific and universal approach).

Further resources

Johnstone, L. (1989) *Users and Abusers of Psychiatry: A Critical Look at Traditional Psychiatric Practice*, London: Routledge.

A highly readable account of some of the biases that have occurred in psychiatric classification and diagnosis. This account is more even-handed and balanced than most of the more passionate accounts.

Simons, R.C. and Hughes, C.C. (eds) (1985) *The Culture-Bound Syndromes: Folk Illnesses of Psychiatric and Anthropological Interest*, Dordrecht: D. Reidel.

This book is generally regarded as the classic text in the field of culture-bound syndromes. Now out of print, but it is well worth the trouble of tracking down a copy, perhaps through the interlibrary loan system.

synoptic issues See the *Checklist of synoptic issues* (pp. 645–50) for ideas about how to use issues in this chapter for synoptic assessment.

Answer to Activity 2

1 False	3 True	5 False
2 False	4 True	6 True

Chapter 17

Psychopathology

Pamela Prentice

Preview

In this chapter we shall be looking at:

◆ anxiety disorders, including phobias, post-traumatic stress disorder and obsessive–compulsive disorder

◆ depression, including its clinical characteristics, and biological and psychological explanations of it

◆ schizophrenia, including its clinical characteristics, and biological and psychological explanations of it.

Note that these topics appear in a different order in the AQA Psychology A specification.

Introduction

The medical profession and the psychology profession have long been trying to understand the causes of mental disorders, not least in order to provide suitable treatment for their alleviation. This chapter will look at the psychopathology of mental disorders, outlining briefly the specific disorders mentioned in the preview.

The main purpose of this chapter is to examine different views, or theories, of the aetiology (explanation of cause) for each of the disorders. A number of different aetiological theories have been postulated and researched and these tend to be split into two major groupings.

◆ The first represents the *medical model* which views mental disorders as an 'illness' or a 'disease'. Researchers in this field attempt to examine whether the mental disorder can be explained by neurological damage to the brain or by a dysfunction in the action of neurotransmitters (brain chemicals). In addition, the medical model seeks to establish whether a particular mental disorder is inherited through a genetic predisposition.

◆ The second grouping represents the view that mental disorders are a problem of *psychological dysfunction*, relating to the interaction between individuals and their environment. These explanations include views of the behaviourists (learning theory), cognitive–behavioural theories, psychodynamic theories and social learning theories. In addition, there is a theory known as the 'diathesis-stress model' which examines the interaction of social factors with other vulnerability factors.

You will find that some explanations seem more plausible than others for some types of disorder, but not for others. As yet, no one aetiology has been accepted as the complete explanation for any single mental disorder, and an open mind on a combination of aetiologies seems more appropriate.

Anxiety disorders

Phobias

Phobias are classified as anxiety disorders in DSM-IV (see Chapter 16) and are the most common of all anxiety disorders. We all have aversions to certain things or situations, which can make us feel a little squeamish or anxious – or even fearful – when we encounter them. This is quite normal. It is only when the aversion becomes an excessive and unreasonable fear that it is classified as a phobia. Even then many people adapt their life in order to avoid or cope with

their extreme fears. When someone cannot do this, however, and the fear or anxiety becomes so severe that it interferes with their life to such a degree that their behaviour becomes dysfunctional, then the phobia is classified as a mental disorder. Phobias are often accompanied by fainting and mild depression.

Phobias have been categorized into three main types:

◆ specific (isolated) phobias

◆ social phobias

◆ agoraphobia.

Onset appears to be earliest for animal phobias, followed by other specific phobias and social phobia, with the latest onset being for agoraphobia (Kendler *et al.* 1992a). The likelihood of a person developing a phobia during their lifetime is 11.3 per cent for specific phobias, 13.3 per cent for social phobia and 6.7 per cent for agoraphobia (Magee *et al.* 1996), and females outnumber males by two to one (Eaton *et al.* 1991).

Clinical characteristics of phobias

Specific (isolated) phobias are, as the term implies, fears relating to something specific. Earlier versions of DSM, prior to DSM-IV (1994), called these 'simple' phobias, although they are far from simple. Almost everyone has aversions to certain things, the most common being spiders, snakes, rodents or heights. Four major subtypes of specific phobia have been identified:

◆ animal type

◆ situational type (e.g. planes, lifts, enclosed spaces)

◆ natural environment type (e.g. heights, storms, water)

◆ blood-injection-injury type.

There is also a fifth category of 'other' for those that do not fit one of the four major types. Table 17.1 lists some

specific phobias. The average age of onset for specific phobias is around 7 to 9 years. Most people who suffer from phobias tend to have more than one of the same type and some people even have multiple phobias of several types. With the increase in air travel, fear of flying is becoming one of the most common phobias and many airlines now offer therapy programmes based on systematic desensitization (see Chapter 18, *Treating mental disorders*).

Social phobia is an excessive fear of social situations. Most people are nervous about public speaking, but someone with a social phobia is afraid of any activity performed in public, such as eating in public or going into a public lavatory. It has been suggested that social phobia is merely a case of excessive shyness, but this is not so because, for example, there are many actors and athletes who perform in public yet are excessively shy, and their shyness does not usually extend to, say, eating in public. The age of onset tends to be around 15 years and is most prevalent in people aged 18 to 29 years.

Agoraphobia is a fear of public places. It is especially debilitating because it can result in people being afraid to go out of their home. This means they are unable to go to work or even to shop for provisions. For these reasons it is thought to be the most serious of all phobias. Many people with agoraphobia are also prone

---

Table 17.1 Specific (simple) phobias

Animal type		Situational type	
Arachnophobia	spiders	Aerophobia	flying
Ophidiophobia	snakes	Tachophobia	speed
Helminthophobia	worms	Claustrophobia	enclosed spaces
Hippophobia	horses	Ochlophobia	crowds
Musophobia	mice	Autophobia	being alone
Apiphobia	bees	Kenophobia	empty rooms
Ailurophobia	cats	Necrophobia	death
Cynophobia	dogs	Ergasiophobia	work
Androphobia	men	Scholionophobia	school
Gynophobia	women	Bibliophobia	books
Pediophobia	children	Graphophobia	writing
Xenophobia	strangers		
		Natural environment type	
Blood-injection-injury type		Acrophobia	heights
Algophobia	pain	Keraunophobia	thunder
Spermophobia	germs	Astraphobia	lightning
Hematophobia	blood	Hydrophobia	water
Belonophobia	sharp objects	Pyrophobia	fire
Nosemaphobia	illness	Homichlophobia	fog
Trypanophobia	injections	Phengophobia	daylight
Toxiphobia	poison	Sciophobia	shadows
		Achluophobia	darkness

Source: extracted from Melville (1978)

to panic attacks when they venture into public places. Agoraphobia is closely associated with *panic disorder*, as people with panic disorder fear public places because they are likely to induce a panic attack. Indeed, DSM-IV classifies two types of panic disorder: with and without agoraphobia. However, agoraphobia can continue even if the person has not had a panic attack in years. Onset of agoraphobia is generally in early adulthood and is most common in females.

Genetic explanations of phobic anxiety disorders

When we talk of a genetic predisposition, we are looking at whether something is hereditary, i.e. whether it runs in families. However, a genetic predisposition does not necessarily mean that someone will definitely develop a particular disorder, although it does indicate those who may be more at risk for developing a particular disorder.

To determine a genetic link for any disorder in humans, research focuses on three main areas of study:

◆ *Family history studies* examine the recurrence of a particular disorder between and within generations. One of the major problems with family history studies is that they usually rely on interviews with the family members of someone already diagnosed with a particular disorder. This means that accounts are retrospective and subjective, and do not have the benefit of diagnostic criteria. Some studies have examined medical records, but these would exclude anyone suffering from a disorder who did not present for treatment.

◆ *Adoption studies* look at the occurrence of a disorder when a child with affected biological parents is adopted at an early age by 'healthy' parents.

◆ *Twin studies* examine the rate of concordance of a disorder (i.e. whether both twins are affected). A comparison is made between monozygotic (MZ) twins, who have identical genetic make-up, and dizygotic (DZ) twins, who are no more genetically alike than any other siblings.

The rationale behind both adoption and twin studies is an attempt to separate genetic factors from environmental factors.

Fear and anxiety have evolutionary advantages for survival, because they trigger our 'fight or flight' mechanisms, i.e. the release of certain brain chemicals which give us a spurt of energy in threatening or dangerous situations either to attack or to escape faster. We know, therefore, that fear and anxiety are part of the genetic make-up of many species, including humans. However, not all humans develop such extreme fears that they become phobias and most phobias are related to things which are not potentially harmful. Genetic

research, therefore, is attempting to establish whether there is a familial genetic link – whether the tendency to develop phobias is hereditary. Research into phobias has focused mainly on family studies with first-degree relatives (parents, children, siblings) and, in a few studies, with second-degree relatives (aunts, uncles, nieces, nephews). There have been a small number of twin studies and virtually no adoption studies.

Family history studies have focused mainly on agoraphobia. A study by Solyom et al. (1974) of 47 phobic patients found a family history of psychiatric disorder in 45 per cent of the cases (with 30 per cent of their mothers having phobias), in contrast to only 19 per cent in families of a non-phobic control group of patients. Noyes et al. (1986) found a higher-than-normal rate of agoraphobia (11.6 per cent) and panic disorder (17.3 per cent) in first-degree relatives, using the family interview method. Another family interview study by Fyer et al. (1990) of 49 first-degree relatives of people with a specific phobia found that 31 per cent of relatives were also diagnosed with phobias, but only two people had the same type. Reich and Yates (1988) found a 6.6 per cent rate for relatives of people with social phobia compared with 2.2 per cent in controls. When categorizing people into those with animal-types of phobias and those with non-animal types of phobias, they found a much higher frequency of the same type of phobia in relatives compared with controls.

A twin study by Slater and Shields (1969) found 41 per cent concordance in 17 MZ twin pairs versus 4 per cent in 28 DZ twin pairs, for any type of anxiety disorder. A more recent study conducted by Torgersen (1983) found 31 per cent concordance in 13 MZ twin pairs for panic disorder and agoraphobia versus zero concordance in 16 DZ twin pairs, although none of the concordant twins shared the same phobia. Kendler et al. (1992a) interviewed 722 female twins with a lifetime history of phobia. They found that MZ twins have significantly lower rates of agoraphobia than DZ twins, which goes against the genetic hypothesis, although they suggest it may reflect a protective effect of the close emotional bond between MZ twins. For specific phobias they found that a shared environment was a much more likely explanation than genetic.

Most of the family studies show that the relatives of those with phobias are more likely to suffer phobias themselves compared with relatives of non-phobic controls. However, there are methodological difficulties with family studies, the main problem being that in most instances family members share the same environment and could equally therefore have learnt the behaviour. Twin studies offer more reliable data to test the genetic hypothesis, but unfortunately very few have been conducted. The lack of empirical research, particularly in recent years, is an indication that there is very little support for the genetic transmittance of anxiety disorders.

in focus

Case study of a phobia

Eddie had always been terrified of travelling in cars and had managed to avoid this for most of her life by using buses or trains. For some reason she was not afraid to travel by these methods.

Eddie finished her degree and got a good job with an advertising agency. They told her she would need to drive in order to visit clients and would have access to the pool car. Eddie knew she would have to overcome her fear and arranged driving lessons. To her surprise she did not find this as frightening as she had expected and passed on the second attempt. The first time she used the pool car, however, she tried to reverse out of a parking space and hit the adjacent car, doing considerable damage to both cars. The car park attendant told her the other car belonged to the Managing Director. Eddie lost her nerve and went straight home, resigning from her job immediately.

After that Eddie stayed at home, refusing to go out socially or to find another job, even one which did not involve driving. Eddie was referred for treatment by her general practitioner (GP). She knew that her recent anxiety was related to the car accident, but she had no idea why she had been terrified of cars since she was a young child. She could not recall a car accident in her past.

Neurological explanations of phobias

Neurological theories are based on the functioning of the autonomic nervous system. Research indicates that people who develop phobias are those who generally maintain a high level of physiological arousal which makes them particularly sensitive to their external environment. This suggests an interaction between arousal level and conditioning, but the question is whether high arousal levels are the cause, or the consequence, of the phobia. Asso and Beech (1975) favour the former argument, suggesting that a high level of physiological arousal makes it easier to acquire a conditioned response. However, Lader and Mathews (1968) found that high levels of arousal are more significant only in the cases of agoraphobia and social phobia, whereas conditioning is more significant in the case of specific phobias. (See next section for a more detailed account of the conditioning of phobias.)

Behavioural theory (conditioning)

The *classical conditioning* explanation for phobias proposes that first a panic attack occurs, in response, for instance, to being trapped in a lift. This results in an association being established between anxiety and that lift. Subsequently, this anxiety becomes generalized to all lifts. Consequently, the person will actively avoid using lifts in the future. In terms of operant conditioning, avoidance of lifts is further reinforced by the reduction in anxiety experienced when the person adopts alternative strategies, such as using the stairs.

The conditioning explanation for phobias has been extensively researched and is supported by early studies on humans and animals that would now be regarded as unethical. In a now classic study, Watson and Raynor (1920) apparently conditioned a 10-month-old boy,

named Little Albert, into developing a phobia towards a white rat, using classical conditioning techniques. Although there has been considerable support for the behaviourist explanation of phobias, more recent studies have failed to replicate their findings, including an attempt by Watson and Raynor themselves. Munjack (1984) took a group of people with driving phobia and found that only 50 per cent of them had actually had a frightening experience in a car. Added to this, it was found that 50 per cent of the control group who did not have a phobia had had a frightening experience in a car, many of these involving an accident.

A traditional view within the field of psychology was a link between *personality* and *anxiety*. Hans Eysenck (1970) put forward a theory of personality in which people could be measured on three dimensions of extroversion/introversion, neuroticism and psychoticism. Eysenck claimed that people who scored high on neuroticism and also high on introversion are more likely to develop anxiety disorders. As a behaviourist, Eysenck linked this to conditioning. He claimed that introverted people are more susceptible to punishment cues and less susceptible to reward cues, as well as being prone to greater physiological arousal, all of which, according to him, make them more easily conditioned. The theory was well researched in the 1970s, but interest began to wane as studies proved inconclusive. However, there has been a recent resurgence of interest. For example, Gershuny and Sher (1998) tested the theory with 466 undergraduate students and found that those with high scores on neuroticism and introversion had suffered from either anxiety or depression at a three-year follow-up.

Some phobic reactions are more common than others and this has been accounted for by the suggestion that there are *species-specific biological predispositions* to fear certain stimuli, dating back to our ancestors. This has been researched by Seligman (1971) who proposed the concept of biological 'preparedness'. The suggestion is that all species are innately 'prepared' to avoid certain stimuli because they are potentially dangerous. A classic study by Garcia and Koelling (1966) showed that rats could easily be conditioned to avoid life-threatening stimuli, such as shocks or toxic liquids, but not to avoid stimuli which carried no adverse consequences, such as flashing lights. Human phobias, such as fear of the dark or fear of heights, are consistent with this theory. However, this does not necessarily lend support for biological preparedness.

The ease with which certain phobias can develop could equally be accounted for in *social learning* terms, that is through modelling our behaviour on others and, in particular, on our parents. If certain stimuli are potentially dangerous, then from an early age we observe others avoiding these. In the same way, we also learn that certain stimuli are commonly avoided within a given culture, which can explain apparent phobias for stimuli that are not necessarily life-threatening – for example, snakes and large spiders, most of which are not dangerous. Further criticism of the theory of 'biological preparedness' comes from a study by McNally and Steketee (1985). They found that in 91 per cent of cases of snake and spider phobias, the cause for concern was not a fear of being harmed, but rather a fear of having a panic attack. The exception was in the case of dog phobias, where most people were afraid of being bitten.

Rotter (1966) suggested that the development of a phobia, or any other anxiety disorder, relates to the extent to which a person feels in *control of events* in their life. Rotter suggested that some people have a higher degree of internal control and are therefore better able to cope with external events because they can exert a degree of control over the impact of these events. Rotter called this 'internal locus of control'. Conversely, he suggested that some people have an 'external locus of control', which means they believe that events are beyond their control and they cannot exert any influence. Rotter maintained that the origins of internal and external locus of control lie in the contingencies of reinforcement experienced in early life. For example, those who were reinforced in a consistent way in early life grow up to trust in the stability of cause-and-effect relationships and in their own judgements. Those whose reinforcement was inconsistent, i.e. they were rewarded or punished on some occasions and not on others for the same behaviour, have learnt that the world is unpredictable and they cannot trust in their own judgements. Studies (e.g. Emmelkamp and Cohen-Kettenis 1975) have supported this theory in that the extent of fear

experienced by people with agoraphobia correlates with the extent to which the person externalizes the situation.

Cognitive–behavioural explanations of phobias

The cognitive–behavioural explanation for phobias extends the behavioural view of the conditioning of physiological reflexes to the cognitive domain of 'thinking'. Leading theorists in this field, such as Albert Ellis (1962) and Aaron Beck (1963), suggest that catastrophic thoughts and irrational beliefs contribute to the development of a phobia. For example, an experience of feeling 'hemmed in' in a crowded lift might be maintained later on by thoughts and beliefs such as 'I might suffocate if I were trapped in a lift'. This then turns into a fear of lifts, which is then generalized to other similar situations, resulting in the onset of claustrophobia. Therefore, it is not only an initial exposure to a fearful situation that initiates the phobia, as proposed by conditioning theory; rather it is also the person's irrational thoughts about the future possibility of a fearful situation. In a series of studies, Mathews (1989) found that threatening stimuli were perceived more quickly than positive or neutral stimuli in people with phobias compared with controls.

According to Beck, people with phobias have a belief system whereby they know at a rational level that danger is minimal, yet they also truly believe that their feared object or situation will cause them physical or psychological harm. Beck *et al.* (1985) found that danger beliefs are activated when the person is in close proximity to the phobic stimuli, but at a distance they may state that the probability of harm is almost zero. The 'odds' then gradually change as the person comes closer and the sense of danger increases until they are actually in the feared situation, when the fear becomes 100 per cent. Beck and colleagues (1985) also found that people with phobias are more preoccupied with their 'fear of fear' than the actual object or situation itself.

Williams *et al.* (1997) examined this concept by subjecting people with agoraphobia to a hierarchy of increasingly scary tasks, whilst monitoring their thoughts throughout. Their results supported Beck *et al.*, in that participants' statements, which were tape-recorded, were mainly a preoccupation with their current anxiety rather than their safety. However, it may be that their danger thoughts were simply not expressed out loud. Even in situations where there is a good outcome, people with phobias tend to view the outcome in a negative way. A study conducted by Wallace and Alden (1997) on social phobia examined this concept. They manipulated a social situation to be successful or unsuccessful, with participants rating their ability, perceptions of others' standards, social goals and emotional responses, both before and after the interaction. They found that people diagnosed with social phobia produced negative responses, even in the successful situation; for example, success meant that others would expect more of them in the future.

Negative self-appraisal appears to be a key feature in social phobia, together with a sense of perfectionism. A study by Bieling and Alden (1997) found that people with social phobia scored significantly higher than controls on perfectionism and they also had lowered perceptions of their social ability. The cognitive–behavioural explanation has found considerable support from numerous studies and cognitive–behavioural therapy is very effective in reducing phobic anxiety. However, it is difficult to ascertain whether irrational thoughts are the cause of phobias, or merely a symptom of the disorder.

Psychodynamic explanations of phobias

The psychodynamic view is that the anxiety expressed towards an object or situation is a displacement of internal underlying anxiety. The *psychoanalytic view* (Freudian) is that phobias are associated with unconscious sexual fears (or 'id' impulses) and that they operate through the defence mechanisms of *repression* and *displacement*. The original source of the fear is repressed into the unconscious and the fear is then displaced onto some other person, object or situation. Thus the fear appears to be irrational because there is no conscious explanation for it. Freud's theory of phobias rests on his 1909 case study of a boy named Little Hans who developed a fear of horses (Freud 1909). Freud believed that the boy's phobia was directly related to his unconscious fear of his father, associated with the Oedipal phase. Although there is no empirical evidence to support Freud's theory directly, cross-cultural studies (e.g. Whiting 1966) do indicate that anxieties and phobias are more common in cultures characterized by strict upbringing and punishment.

Activity 1: Little Hans and Little Albert

Find out what you can about the two studies of Little Hans (Freud 1909) and Little Albert (Watson and Raynor 1920). Which do you think offers the most plausible explanation of phobias?

Bowlby (1973) suggested that phobias can be explained by his theory of 'attachment and separation'. For instance, agoraphobia is said to relate to a fear of losing someone to whom the person has become attached (most often the mother).

He maintained that the origins lie with 'separation anxiety' in early childhood, particularly where parents are overprotective. However, with respect to phobias, studies tend to show a lack of consistency. For example, Parker (1979) found that being overprotected during early childhood correlated with the development of social phobias later on. On the other hand, the development of agoraphobia was found to correlate with having parents who had tended to display a lack of affection. Many studies indicate no relationship at all between parental rearing styles and types of anxiety disorders. In more general psychodynamic theories, phobias are an outward expression of inner underlying fears and anxiety that have their origins in earlier traumatic or distressing experiences.

Activity 2: Your fears and phobias?

First identify any of your own fears and phobias. Now think about the most likely explanation, taking account of all the above aetiological theories.

Diathesis-stress model explanation of phobias

Major life events have long been regarded as a major contributing factor in all anxiety disorders, including phobias. Holmes and Rahe (1967) explained the cumulative effects of major life events, and the work of Kobasa (1979) highlighted the effects of everyday minor hassles. Kleiner and Marshall (1987) found that in a group of agoraphobics, 84 per cent had experienced family problems prior to the onset of their first panic attack and this finding has been confirmed by a number of other studies. However, the difficulty with the life-events theory is that many people who experience the most adverse life events do not develop an anxiety disorder.

The diathesis-stress model proposes an interaction between various factors and may explain individual differences in susceptibility to stress and anxiety. It is suggested that we all have our own individual tolerance thresholds which form a predisposition to stress; this is known as our *diathesis* or *vulnerability* factor. The origin of this predisposition to vulnerability is not certain. It may be genetically inherited, or alternatively it may be acquired through early experience; explanations include psychodynamic, behavioural and cognitive ones. The interaction between this vulnerability factor and the degree of life stress a person encounters (major life events and/or minor hassles) is thought to determine the likelihood that anxiety will reach a degree where it becomes

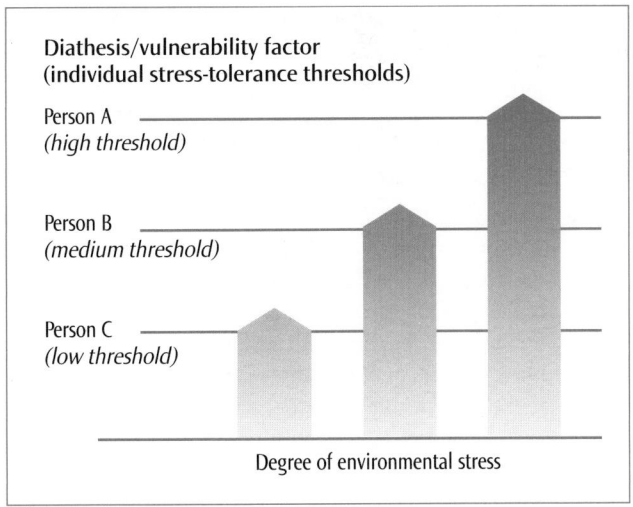

Figure 17.1 Diathesis-stress model

When environmental stressors (illustrated by the shaded arrows) penetrate the tolerance threshold for an individual, this results in physical or mental symptoms (illustrated by the darker shaded areas).

◆ A small number of stressors, such as minor ailments or failing a driving test, may penetrate the stress tolerance of person C (who has a low threshold).

◆ Additional stressors may penetrate the stress tolerance threshold of both person C and person B (who has a medium threshold).

◆ The cumulative effect of many stressors, or one significant or life-threatening event, may penetrate the stress-tolerance threshold of persons C and B and even of person A (who has a high threshold).

Figure 17.2
Various explanations of the development of a phobia

Genetic predisposition (medical)	Physiological vulnerability to anxiety	Environmental stress	**P**
Biological preparedness (behavioural)	Conditioning	Experience of fearful event	**H**
Early-life experience (psychodynamic)	Psychological vulnerability	Environmental stress	**O**
Negative ways of thinking (cognitive–behavioural)	Psychological vulnerability	Environmental stress	**B I A**

dysfunctional (see Fig. 17.1), and from this phobias may develop.

There is some evidence for genetic factors in the development of phobias, but this is more likely to be a tendency to inherit a physiological predisposition towards anxiety in general, rather than being specific to phobias.

There is some evidence to support the behavioural view of conditioning and, indeed, many people with specific phobias do report a fearful experience as the onset of the phobia. However, many people have a similar experience and do not develop a phobia, which suggests that other vulnerability factors play a part and lends support for the diathesis-stress model.

The vulnerability factor is, therefore, the key to the aetiology of phobias. This could be a physiological vulnerability, or a deeper underlying problem that is expressing itself in a phobia or in negative ways of thinking. It should be remembered, however, that we all have fears and anxieties; they only become a mental disorder when they are so extreme that the person's life has become dysfunctional.

Figure 17.2 summarizes explanations of the development of phobias.

Post-traumatic stress disorder (PTSD)

Anxiety disorders are usually associated with objects and events which most people do not find threatening. There are, however, some events that would be threatening for almost everyone, such as an aeroplane crash or an earthquake. People who encounter a very traumatic experience usually suffer from *acute stress disorder*, which is a temporary reaction, and most people recover within a short while and continue with their lives. However, some people do not recover and go on to develop the pathological disorder known as *post-traumatic stress disorder* (PTSD).

Although PTSD was not listed in DSM until 1980, it is not a new disorder. It was noted in the First World War that armed combat could produce symptoms known as 'shell shock', but it was not until after the Vietnam War that PTSD was classified as a specific disorder. Since then, PTSD has been associated with exposure to any extremely traumatic event, such as a natural disaster, fire, serious accident, violent personal assault, kidnapping, terrorist attack, being diagnosed with a terminal illness, or being a witness to a serious accident or crime. PTSD can appear immediately after the trauma, or its onset can be delayed for several months or even years. According to DSM-IV, children are as susceptible to PTSD as adults and there appear to be no gender, age or cultural differences in susceptibility to PTSD. Certain traumatic events are, however, more likely to occur in one group than another – for example, sexual assault and armed combat are more likely to be gender-specific.

Symptoms of PTSD include the persistent re-experiencing of the event through frightening dreams and flashback episodes, which are usually triggered by cues that are associated with or resemble the traumatic event. The person persistently avoids any thing, place or person associated with the trauma, and there may even be an inability to recollect the traumatic event. There may also be changes in the person's general behaviour in that they may lack concentration and become easily startled, irritable and angry. There is also a loss of interest in activities, a detachment from others and an inability to experience feelings of love. The case study (see *In Focus*) should give you some idea of the experience of post-traumatic stress disorder.

The very term, post-traumatic stress disorder, implies that the disorder is caused by the stressful exposure to a traumatic event, which would appear to rule out alternative explanations. Certainly the reason for the onset of the disorder is clear: it follows a traumatic event, even when there has been a delayed onset of six months or more. Risk factors for PTSD have been identified, such as the level of severity of the traumatic event and/or how great the exposure was to the traumatic event. However, this does not explain why some people recover quickly from a traumatic event, regardless of its level of severity or the length of exposure, and why other people develop PTSD.

Neurological explanations of PTSD

The view of endrocrinology is that trauma causes long-term alterations and abnormalities in specific brain systems. The suggestion is that exposure to an extremely traumatic event has an adverse effect on the normal physiological stress reaction of autonomic arousal which triggers the release of adrenaline and serotonin in order to prepare for 'fight' or 'flight'. Van der Kolk (1988) suggests that there is an absence of resilience in those suffering from PTSD, as if autonomic arousal is no longer a preparation for an emergency, but a precipitant of responses that bear no relationship to the present stimulus. He reaches this conclusion from laboratory studies on survivors of extreme stress, including Vietnam War veterans, which showed that when exposed to trauma cues (visual, auditory and imaginary), there was a consistently higher physiological reactivity (e.g. in heart rate, temperature, pulse, respiration) than in controls. One suggestion is that the experience of the trauma damages the noradrenergic system, which then raises levels of noradrenaline, making the person more prone to being startled and to express emotion. Evidence for this position comes from Kosten *et al.* (1987) who found higher than normal levels of noradrenaline in PTSD hospital patients.

In the case of prolonged stressful events over a long period of time, the suggestion is that the persistent secretion of neurotransmitters leads to a diminished supply of noradrenaline, which makes the person less resilient even to minor stressful events. 'Noradrenergic burnout' is accompanied by a decrease in learning ability, memory functions and motivation. In addition to human studies, support also comes from animal conditioning studies on 'learned helplessness', which showed that when animals were exposed to

---

in focus

Case study of post-traumatic stress disorder

Susan, a 23-year-old clerical worker, had always been happy and carefree. She enjoyed her work, had lots of friends and was engaged to be married. Recently, however, she had become morose and distant. She no longer wanted to go out with friends and she was unable to concentrate at work. Her friends noticed that she had begun to cry a lot and was easily startled. She was also frequently angry with her boyfriend for no apparent reason. She began to withdraw from relationships with people and called off her engagement. Susan eventually went to see a counsellor, to whom she revealed that, six months before, she had been raped by her boss one evening when she was working late. He was married and had warned her not to tell anyone or she would be fired. Afterwards, at home in her flat, Susan had tried to scrub away the effects of the rape in the shower. For several days she felt dirty and cheap, but couldn't tell anyone, especially her boyfriend, because she was worried that he wouldn't believe her. She even began to doubt herself, believing that maybe she had in some way 'asked for it'. She resolved to put it behind her and get on with her life. This she managed to do quite well for over two months, but then she began having nightmares about being stalked by someone who wanted to harm her. Even when awake, she was often overcome by violent images that would intrude on her thoughts.

inescapable shock there were deficits in motivation, learning ability and memory, that are characteristic of depression in humans. Van der Kolk (1988) found significant excretions of dopamine and noradrenaline in parts of the brain and changes in cortisol and adrenaline levels. When there was prolonged exposure to the shock, there was an eventual depletion of noradrenaline. More recent studies have found damage to the hippocampus, for example with combat-related PTSD (Gurvits *et al.* 1996).

Whilst new discoveries in neuro-endocrinology are providing answers for specific symptoms of PTSD, they still cannot explain individual differences in susceptibility to the disorder. For this reason, research has also focused on the psychological aspects of stress.

Behavioural explanations of PTSD

The more traditional *behavioural* account for PTSD is based on Pavlov's theory of *classical conditioning* (Pavlov 1927, 1941). Pavlov found that, over a period of time, repeated dosages of overwhelming excitation mobilized innate reflexive responses in the form of a defensive reaction (fear response). These primary responses were then linked by association to cues in the environment. The cues then became the *conditioned stimuli*, which would by themselves elicit a *conditioned response*. Pavlov called this *traumatic mental imprinting*.

In *cognitive psychology,* PTSD can be explained in terms of 'state- or situation-dependent memory'. Anything which elicits a fearful, emotional response, or any situation which resembles the original traumatic event, can trigger the memory of the actual event. With PTSD it is as if everything exposed to every one of our senses (sight, smell, etc.) at the time of the original trauma, is somehow imprinted alongside the original trauma, much like a whirlpool or a hurricane sucking in everything within its reach. In cognitive–behavioural terms, people who experience a traumatic event often feel that life is no longer predictable. This, in turn, produces a belief that they are no longer in control of any aspect of their life. Irrational thoughts develop – for example, that the disaster was somehow their own fault. This results in faulty coping methods such as avoidance, blaming, catastrophizing, isolation from others and the abuse of drugs and alcohol. Lazarus (1991) maintains that these inadequate coping strategies fail to reduce the effects of the traumatic event and can actually increase the experience of the stress, which in turn leads to PTSD.

Psychodynamic explanations of PTSD

The growing recognition of PTSD has generated a resurgence of interest in the *psychodynamic* view. This view explains the often delayed onset of PTSD; for example, the studies of Archibald *et al.* (1963) on survivors of the Normandy campaign, showed that the onset of PTSD had been delayed by 15 years in some people. Horowitz (1975) suggested that the traumatic event was suppressed or dissociated because it was too painful for the conscious mind to contemplate, but there remained an internal struggle to integrate the trauma into the person's existing beliefs about themselves and the world.

A more recent application of the psychodynamic approach to PTSD proposes that someone who has experienced emotional trauma in childhood is more vulnerable to trauma in later life. This would explain individual differences in the effects of exposure to the same traumatic events. There is support for this in that, for example, rape victims are more likely to develop PTSD if they had psychological problems prior to the traumatic event (Sales *et al.* 1984). Bremner *et al.* (1993) have shown that PTSD is also more prevalent in those who in childhood experienced poverty, parental separation or divorce, physical or sexual abuse, mental illness in a family member, or any other catastrophic event. They suggest that abused children tend to dissociate themselves from the memory of the abuse and that this becomes a habitual way of dealing with any difficult or traumatic event in life, which then sets the stage for the development of PTSD. However, it could equally be argued from a psychodynamic perspective that such people should be less susceptible because they have built up strong defence mechanisms.

Diathesis-stress model explanation of PTSD

A more pragmatic view is that psychological factors interact with environmental factors in a cumulative fashion. A person who is more vulnerable because of past experiences is more likely to be affected by stressful events. This vulnerability increases with the intensity and duration of the traumatic event, increasing the likelihood of PTSD. A person's level of vulnerability could also be explained in terms of the strength of available social support systems, since it has been found that those who have a strong support system, who are loved and cared for, are more likely to recover from a traumatic experience, such as rape. Conversely, it was found that Vietnam war veterans with a weak social support system were more likely to develop PTSD.

Early DSM criteria for PTSD stated that the person must have experienced an event which was 'beyond the range of usual human experience', but this has been deleted from DSM-IV because many such events are now becoming more usual. Parson (1993) regards PTSD as a public-health problem deriving from the increase in aircraft and railroad incidents, drug-instigated violence, terrorist activity, child abuse (physical and

Figure 17.3
Percentages of victims of rape and attempted rape who later developed symptoms of PTSD and percentages of those who later attempted suicide *Source:* adapted from study by Kilpatrick *et al.* (1985), cited in Comer (1995, p. 224)

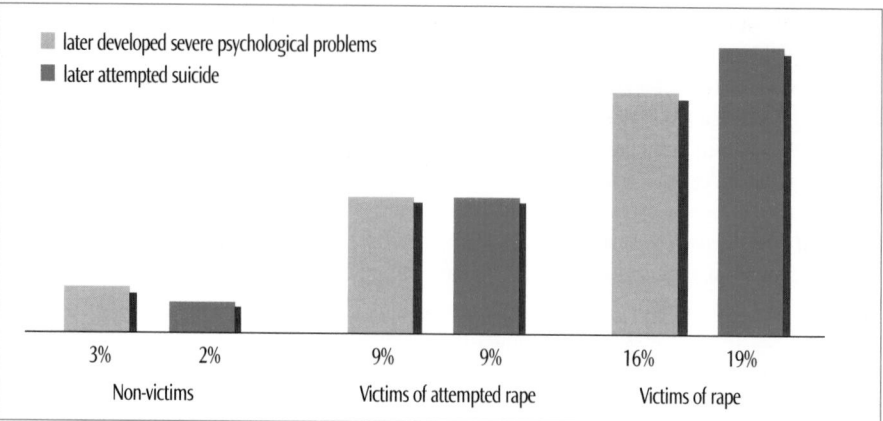

sexual) and brutal rape – which, he says, is the fastest growing crime in the United States of America. Figure 17.3 shows the extent of the psychological effects of rape. DSM-IV now states that the person must have experienced, witnessed, or been confronted with an event or events that involved actual or threatened death or serious injury, or a threat to the physical integrity of self or others.

Evaluation of explanations of PTSD

To search for a cause of post-traumatic stress disorder is probably the wrong way to try to understand PTSD. Certainly a traumatic event precipitates the disorder, which may trigger neurochemical malfunction, but if this were the sole cause, then everyone experiencing the same traumatic event would develop PTSD. Psychological and sociocultural factors do not in themselves cause the disorder, but they may play an important role in the person's vulnerability to develop the disorder. However, Scott and Stradling (1994) suggest that PTSD can occur without a trauma. They cite clinical case examples of people who have all the symptoms of PTSD in the absence of a single, acute dramatic trauma of any kind. An explanation could be that PTSD can occur, not only from trauma, but also through prolonged exposure to stressors.

Obsessive–compulsive disorder

Most of us have obsessional thoughts at times, often related to fears, and on occasions have a compulsion or impulse to act in ways that are strange and out of character. Most of us have certain ritualistic or routine ways of doing things, like always putting on our clothes in a particular order and many of us have certain superstitious beliefs. For someone with *obsessive–compulsive disorder* (OCD), these are so invasive and taken to such an extreme, and are accompanied by such severe anxiety, that the person cannot function effectively in their daily life. OCD is probably the most severe of all anxiety disorders and found to be one of the most difficult to treat.

Obsessions are persistent and recurrent thoughts, images, beliefs and impulses which enter the mind apparently uninvited and which cannot be removed. The 'compulsive' element of OCD is the compulsion to perform behaviours that follows on from obsessions. Examples are given below:

◆ Obsessional cleanliness – An obsession with dirt and contamination leads to compulsive behaviours such as repeated hand-washing, whereby a person can scrub their hands raw. There is also continual scrubbing and bleaching of surroundings, especially sinks, toilets and doorknobs.

◆ Obsessional rituals – These are specific ways or orders of doing things that are totally fixed and rigid, yet accompanied by an urge to resist.

◆ Obsessional doubts – These are usually related to safety concerns: for example, doubting whether they have switched off the gas hob or locked the door when leaving the house.

◆ Compulsive checking – This follows on from obsessional doubts. Here the person will have a compulsion to check and double-check continually and is often unable to leave the house because they cannot stop checking.

◆ Obsessional ruminations – These are internal debates which are endlessly reviewed, the person presenting arguments for and against even the simplest of actions.

◆ Obsessional impulses – These are strong urges to perform acts of an embarrassing, dangerous or violent nature, such as jumping in front of a car or blaspheming in church.

The age of onset for OCD is usually in late teens and early twenties, and it affects around 2 per cent of the population (American Psychiatric Association 1994). People with OCD are generally aware that their obsessional thoughts and behaviours are illogical, but they are powerless to overcome them. Often they attempt to hide them from others. People with OCD suffer severe anxiety, which is thought to precipitate the symptoms. However, the obsessions and compulsions do not appear to alleviate the initial anxiety, rather they create additional anxieties as a consequence. People with OCD also tend to suffer from severe depression, which is an understandable reaction.

Biological explanations of obsessive–compulsive disorder

As far as *biological explanations* are concerned, there is tentative evidence to support OCD as a genetically inherited disorder. Family history studies report a prevalence of up to 10 per cent in first-degree relatives (e.g. Carey and Gottesman 1981) and twin studies (e.g. Hoaker and Schnurr 1980) indicate a concordance rate of between 50 and 60 per cent. In all these studies, however, these people shared the same environment, suggesting that environmental factors may have a stronger influence. It has been suggested (e.g. Rapoport 1989) that obsessions and compulsions result from fixed action patterns in the brain that have evolutionary significance for survival. In stressful and dangerous situations, certain action patterns are triggered, but most people cease to perform actions when their purpose has been completed. For people with OCD, the fixed action patterns are inappropriately triggered by their own perceptions of danger.

Some links have been found with biochemical imbalance. Positron emission tomography (PET) scan studies have shown that people diagnosed with OCD have increased metabolic activity in the frontal regions of the brain (e.g. Rauch *et al.* 1994). Support for the biochemical explanation comes from the effectiveness of medication, in particular drugs which inhibit the re-uptake of serotonin – which have been found beneficial for up to 60 per cent of patients with OCD (Zohar *et al.* 1996). The symptoms recur, however, when medication is ceased (Lydiard *et al.* 1996) indicating that medication is not a cure. Added to this, Baxter *et al.* (1992) found that both treatment with drugs and treatment with behaviour therapy were equally effective in addressing abnormalities found in the orbitofrontal cortex and in the caudate nucleus, indicating that changes in metabolic activity may be the result of, rather than the cause of, OCD. From studies such as this, it seems likely that psychological factors are associated with OCD, either in addition to, or as an alternative explanation to biological ones.

Behavioural explanations of OCD

The *behavioural explanation* is that OCD is an extreme form of *learned avoidance behaviour*. An initial event is associated with anxiety or fear, and avoidance behaviour initially alleviates this fear, subsequently becoming a conditioned response. The behavioural explanation falls down, however, in that the symptoms of OCD, such as avoidance behaviour, themselves create

anxiety. Nevertheless, the behavioural view is supported by the effectiveness of behavioural therapies (see Chapter 18), such as graded exposure and flooding. Studies, such as the one by Baxter *et al.* (1992) and Schwartz *et al.* (1996), have found that behavioural therapies not only reduce symptoms of OCD, but also effect changes in biochemical activity. Marks (1981) found behavioural therapy to be very effective in treating obsessive cleaning and checking behaviour, but not so effective for obsessional thoughts. Cognitive–behavioural explanations of OCD are that the disorder is a consequence of faulty and irrational ways of thinking taken to an absolute extreme, and cognitive–behavioural therapies (see Chapter 18) have been shown to be effective (e.g. Emmelkamp *et al.* 1988). Neither medication nor psychological therapies, however, appear to offer a long-term solution to OCD, and it remains a very difficult disorder to understand and treat effectively.

Exam summary: Anxiety disorders

The AQA examination will test your understanding of the following areas:

◆ clinical characteristics of one disorder (phobias, pp. 430–1; post-traumatic stress disorder, pp. 435–6; obsessive–compulsive disorder, pp. 438–9)

◆ biological explanations (including evidence) of chosen disorder (phobias, pp. 431–32; PTSD, pp. 436–7; OCD, p. 439)

◆ psychological explanations (including evidence) of chosen disorder (phobias, pp. 432–5; PTSD, pp. 437–8; OCD, p. 439).

Example question

The question below should take you 45 minutes:

◆ Describe and evaluate two or more explanations of the development of phobias. *(30 marks)*

Suggested answer structure

This question is different from other questions that you may have encountered elsewhere in these A2 chapters. It differs in a number of important ways:

◆ Questions in the *Individual Differences* section of the specification are worth 30 marks rather than 24.

◆ The time allowance for these questions is 45 minutes rather than 30 minutes. This extra time allows for a more detailed *description* of two theories than has been the case in Unit 4 questions (where the *outline* injunction has been used in such cases).

◆ These questions have a *synoptic* element (see p. 553), and are marked on a different set of marking criteria (see Table 21.3 on p. 554).

◆ The question uses the instruction *two or more* to allow for a more detailed account of two explanations or a less detailed account of more than two.

You should not include description of the clinical characteristics of phobias in your answer. Sometimes questions will ask you to do this, but not this one.

This section has covered the following explanations of phobias: genetic (p. 431), neurological (p. 432), behavioural (pp. 432–3), cognitive–behavioural (pp. 433–4), psychodynamic (p. 434) and the diathesis-stress model (pp. 434–5).

There is some evidence for genetic factors in the development of phobias, but this is more likely to be a tendency to inherit a physiological predisposition towards anxiety in general, rather than being specific to phobias. There is also some evidence to support the behavioural view of conditioning and, indeed, many people with

specific phobias do report a fearful experience as the onset of the phobia. However, many people have a similar experience and do not develop a phobia, which suggests that other vulnerability factors play a part and lends support for the diathesis-stress model. The vulnerability factor is, therefore, the key to the aetiology of phobias. This could be a physiological vulnerability, or a deeper, underlying problem that is expressing itself in a phobia or in negative ways of thinking.

It is a good idea, when choosing material with which to answer this question, to bear the synoptic requirement of the question in mind. There are a number of different views of phobias expressed in this chapter, but there are also a number of different investigative methods used in research relating to this topic. These include twin studies (p. 431), experimental studies (p. 432), case studies (p. 434) and psychometric tests (pp. 434–5).

Depression (unipolar disorder)

Clinical characteristics

The term *unipolar* distinguishes the mental disorder of depression from the quite different disorder of manic-depression, which is known as a 'bipolar' disorder because of the two extremes of mania and depression. This section is concerned only with depression: a unipolar disorder.

We all feel depressed from time to time and this is quite normal. Usually this is short-lived and does not interfere too much with our everyday functioning; we carry on going to work, school or college, even though we might not feel much like socializing. This is not depression in the clinical sense. Clinical depression is when everyday functioning is seriously impaired.

Depression is an *affective* (mood) disorder, characterized by feelings of sadness and a general withdrawal from those around us. The degree of impairment varies and can range from mild to severe

such that it causes an inability to feed or dress or maintain personal hygiene. Depression can be so serious that it leads to suicide. Table 17.2 lists some of the main symptoms of depression.

It has long been thought that there are two quite discrete categories of depression – *reactive* and *endogenous* – with quite different aetiologies. Reactive, as the term implies, is a reaction to stressful events outside ourselves, such as the death of someone close, or redundancy, or even failing exams, whereas endogenous depression is thought to arise from within the person, independent of external events. Whilst reactive depression can range from mild to quite serious, endogenous depression is usually very severe.

Although the categories of reactive and endogenous are in common use by clinicians, they are not contained in either ICD10 or DSM-IV (see Chapter 16), which only serves to emphasize the difficulties associated with classification and diagnosis.

Table 17.2 Symptoms of depression

Cognitive	Behavioural	Emotional	Physical
Low self-esteem	Decrease in sexual activity	Sadness	Loss of weight
Guilt	Loss of appetite	Irritability	Loss of energy
Self-dislike	Disordered sleep patterns	Apathy (no interest or pleasure in activities)	Aches and pains
Loss of libido (no interest in sex)	Poor care of self and others		Sleep disturbance
Negative thoughts	Suicide attempts		Menstrual changes
Suicidal thoughts			
Poor memory			
Lack of ability to think and concentrate			

DSM-IV lists two sub-types of depressive disorder, *major depressive disorder* (MDD), which is severe but can be short-lived, and *dysthymic disorder* (DD), which may be less severe but is more chronic, i.e. it has a longer duration. If the depressive episode has lasted for two consecutive years with less than two months without symptoms, then dysthymic disorder is diagnosed. Major depression can become a psychotic illness when very severe, with symptoms such as delusions or hallucinations.

Explanations of depression

Genetic explanation of depression

Does depression run in families? There is some evidence for genetic transmission although studies generally show mixed results. There have been a number of twin studies comparing MZ (identical twins) with DZ (non-identical) twins, which provide the most convincing evidence for genetic links. For example McGuffin *et al.* (1996) found 46 per cent concordance in MZ twins compared to 20 per cent in DZ twins in a total of 109 twin pairs, with no evidence of the effect of shared environment.

An Australian study of 2,662 twin pairs by Bierut *et al.* (1999) reported a heritability factor of between 36 per cent and 44 per cent, but claim that environmental factors played a larger role. They also found gender differences indicating lifetime prevalence of 31 per cent for females and 19 per cent for males

(DSM-IV major depressive disorders). A similar study conducted in Virginia by Kendler and Prescott (1999) with 3,790 twin pairs found a heritability factor of 39 per cent, with the remaining 61 per cent environmental and no difference between males and females. However, a study with a sub-group of adolescents from the Virginia study (Silberg *et al.* 1999) found a heritability factor of 28 per cent, with 72 per cent environmental factors and a much higher incidence of depression in girls than boys. Kendler *et al.* (1992b), in a female twin study, suggest that there is a genetic predisposition and that the same genes influence both major depression and generalized anxiety disorder, with whichever developing as a result of environmental experience.

DSM-IV states that there is a high incidence of unipolar depression in the offspring of those with bipolar (manic) depression. However, that may be a reaction to living with a parent with manic-depression. Whilst there appears to be some degree of genetic evidence for depression, in most cases those diagnosed share the same environment, which means it may equally be a learned behaviour. Alternatively, there may be a genetic component operating as a predisposing factor, with additional precipitating causes.

Biochemical explanations of depression

The biochemical theory of depression emerged in the 1950s, when it was discovered that a certain class of drugs, known as Tricyclic drugs, was effective in treating depression. Since then it has been proposed that depression is linked to a disturbance of amine metabolism (brain chemistry). Three specific neurotransmitters are thought to be involved:

- noradrenaline (closely linked to adrenaline)
- serotonin (a brain substance which can be interfered with by hallucinogenic compounds such as LSD and magic mushrooms)
- dopamine.

Activity 3: Case study of Jonathan

- What symptoms of major depression are shown in Jonathan's behaviour?

- What information would you need in order to determine whether Jonathan's depression is endogenous or reactive?

Case study of major depression

Jonathan is a 37-year-old building worker who was brought to the psychiatric clinic by his wife. Although Jonathan had been functioning normally for the past several years, he suddenly became severely disturbed and depressed. At the time of admission, Jonathan was agitated and suicidal, even going so far as buying a gun to kill himself. He had lost his appetite and had developed insomnia during the preceding two weeks. He had become hypersensitive in his dealings with neighbours, co-workers and family, insisting that others were being over-critical of him. This was the second such episode in Jonathan's history, the first having occurred five years earlier following the loss of his job because of a massive layoff in his business.

Source: Halgin and Whitbourne (1993)

It is thought that tricyclic drugs increase noradrenergic function which is thought to be reduced in people with depression, but so far there is no conclusive evidence to support such a view. Postmortems of depressed patients have not revealed an abnormality of noradrenaline concentration (Cooper 1988). Serotonin serves to modulate neural activity and is thought to regulate emotional reactions. If the level of serotonin is too low, then it allows wild fluctuations in other neural activity, producing symptoms of depression. However, it cannot be ruled out that the serotonin levels fluctuate as a result of decreased motor activity in a state of depression. Advances in technology have enabled health-care professionals to measure the action of neurotransmitters through PET scans). Mann *et al.* (1996) found impaired serotonergic transmission in people with depression. Dopamine is thought to be especially involved in depression in old age, because the dopamine content of the brain diminishes considerably over the age of 45. However, the synthetic drug L-dopa (which replicates the action of dopamine) has no specific antidepressant effect.

Another biological explanation has emerged from endocrinology. Levels of the hormone cortisol are found to be high in those suffering from depression and techniques known to suppress cortisol secretion

have been found to be successful in depressive patients (Carroll 1982). This suggests that there is overactivity in the hypothalamic-pituitary-adrenal cortex. However, this may be due to the stress of being ill, because

---

Activity 4: Mood changes in relation to the weather

Perhaps you have noticed your own mood changes in relation to weather? You can test this easily in the UK because our weather changes so frequently. Draw up a table using or adapting the example below. Record what your mood is on particular days, and what the temperature and weather are like on those days. To what extent does your mood change with changes in the weather?

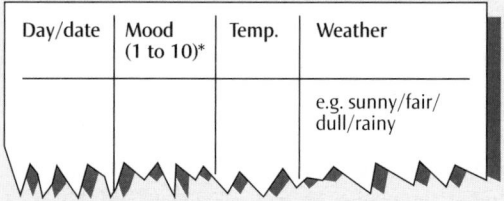

Day/date	Mood (1 to 10)*	Temp.	Weather
			e.g. sunny/fair/ dull/rainy

* estimate this on a scale of 0 to 10 (0 = very miserable, 10 = very happy)

Seasonal Affective Disorder (SAD)

Depression can be seasonal: that is, the person suffers a regular period of depression at a specific time of year. Winter depression is the most common. One explanation is that this relates to changes in the number of daylight hours and that either the person is not exposed to enough natural light, or they are adversely affected by too much artificial light. Special daylight light bulbs can now be purchased and appear to be effective for those suffering from this type of depression.

More recently, four environmental variables have been related to SAD which are:

◆ photoperiod (hours from sunrise to sunset)

◆ daily hours of sunshine

◆ mean daily temperature

◆ total daily solar radiation.

Young *et al.* (1997) tested each of these and found that only a short photoperiod related to the onset of SAD. Attempts have been made to ascertain the reason for SAD and there is some evidence for links with brain chemicals, particularly seratonin and noradrenaline. It has been found that treatment with antidepressant drugs which contain serotonin are effective, whereas those drugs containing noradrenaline have no effect (Lam *et al.* 1996). They concluded that SAD may be related to serotonergic mechanisms. However, the relationship cannot be causal because treatment does not cure the problem, which returns when drug treatment is ceased. Perhaps there is a genetic component. Although not a great deal of research has yet been conducted, some evidence is emerging for a genetic predisposition. For example, Madden *et al.* (1996) report a significant genetic influence in winter-pattern SAD. Their data were collected from 4,639 adult twins in Australia via a mailed questionnaire. However, it has been found that people do not always answer such questionnaires truthfully.

increased cortisol secretion is a function of the stress response. A study by Nemeroff *et al.* (1992), however, has shown that there is marked adrenal gland enlargement in those suffering from major depression which is not found in controls.

Endocrine (hormonal) changes could account for dysthymic depression relating to premenstrual, post-natal and menopausal phases. These types of depression can be very serious indeed, leading to suicide attempts. In the case of postnatal depression, psychotic elements often appear, such as fantasies and loss of contact with reality. Some mothers with severe postnatal depression may harm or even kill their newborn child. Cooper (1988), however, found little difference between the number of women suffering from depression immediately after childbirth and a control group of non-pregnant women of a similar age. Premenstrual depression occurs in the week prior to menstruation and 25 per cent of women are seriously affected, although most are not of diagnosable severity. An oestrogen–progesterone imbalance has been suggested (Dalton 1964), oestrogen levels being too high and progesterone levels too low. At menopause, oestrogen levels drop. Hormone replacement therapy appears to be reasonably effective for treating many (but not all) women who suffer from menopausal depression. Both oestrogen and progesterone increase greatly during pregnancy and then fall rapidly after childbirth, which may account for postnatal depression. However, research evidence for these hormone-imbalance theories is inconclusive (Clare 1985).

Nevertheless, if hormonal changes are not implicated, then it is difficult to explain why these depressive states occur more frequently during periods of hormonal change. One of the problems in trying to ascertain hormonal links with depression is that there are invariably social changes occurring at the same time. A possible explanation is that hormonal changes interact with a genetic predisposition to depression, together with excessive tiredness and a stressful domestic situation.

Psychodynamic explanations of depression

The Freudian psychoanalytic view relates depression in adulthood to the individual's early relationship with parents. Hostile feelings towards parent(s), it is claimed, are redirected towards the self in the form of self-accusation or self-hatred. These feelings may arise from a lack of love and care, support and safety, or from child abuse. In general terms, the psychodynamic view relates to the repression of early trauma that re-emerges in adulthood in the form of an anxiety disorder or depression. The case study of Robert (see *In Focus*) is an example of the longer-term effects of early trauma.

In his theory of 'attachment and separation', John Bowlby (1973) suggested that separation from or loss of the mother in early childhood could result in severe depression in adulthood. Support for this view comes from carefully conducted studies by Hinde (1977), who examined the effects of separating infant rhesus monkeys from their mother. These monkeys (both mother and child) very quickly displayed behaviours similar to the symptoms of depression in humans. However, Paykel (1981) subsequently reviewed fourteen studies and found the evidence inconclusive because seven studies supported the hypothesis and seven did not support the hypothesis. It should also be borne in mind that it may be unwise to use studies of primates to support aetiological theories of disorders in humans.

Stressful life events

Major life events such as bereavement, unemployment, divorce and serious illness are thought to be significant precipitating factors in reactive depression, though not in endogenous depression. In 1978, Brown and Harris published a very influential book, entitled *The Social Origins of Depression*, the result of a major study of depression among houswives in Camberwell, London. They identified two types of *precipitating factors* for depression:

---

in focus

Case study of Robert

Robert is in his early twenties and suffers from severe clinical depression. He was a small, thin child and from the start of junior school he was bullied by a group of boys. Pleas to his parents and to the school did not resolve the problem and he became more and more withdrawn. He felt abandoned and learned not to trust anyone. His fear of being bullied also became an obsession and he began to ruminate in his head almost all of the time: for example, 'Will the bullies be waiting round the corner?', 'What would happen if I took another route?', 'Will I be able to escape?' These ruminations completely took over his thoughts and became an integral part of his personality, such that as an adult he now cannot cease to ruminate upon every single aspect of daily activity. These ruminations, together with his inability to trust others, are at the root of his depression.

A2 Individual Differences

◆ severe life events

◆ long-term difficulties.

These factors came into play when the person also experienced *vulnerability factors*, such as lack of paid employment outside the home, two or more children under the age of five, early loss of mother and, especially, the lack of a close confiding relationship.

Brown and Harris originally identified people who were already depressed. However, they have continued to research their life-events theory to incorporate early-life experiences. They conducted a study in Islington with 404 women with vulnerability factors in that they were working-class, single mothers living in an inner city area. An eight-year follow-up (Brown and Harris 1993) found that early-life experience was a strong predictor of adult depression. The childhood adversities they found most significant were parental indifference and physical or sexual abuse. Early loss of mother was not found to be significant unless it increased the chances of negative experiences. A prospective study by Bifulco *et al.* (1998) confirms this theory. They gathered data on 105 working-class mothers with vulnerability factors, but who were not depressed. Their vulnerability factors included ongoing psychosocial factors, such as negative close relationships, and adverse early-life experiences. They found that over a period of 14 months, 37 per cent of these women became depressed and, of these, two-thirds had experienced childhood neglect or abuse. They also found that early loss of a parent was not significant, provided that subsequent care had been good, which does not support Bowlby's theory of the effects of early separation mentioned in the previous section.

Parker *et al.* (1998) propose a 'lock and key' hypothesis of depression, which posits that early adverse experiences establish locks that are activated by keys mirroring the earlier adverse experience which, in turn, induces depression. They interviewed 270 severely clinically depressed patients and found 'lock and key' links in almost one-third of their sample (see Table 17.3

for examples). These cases were predominantly in the endogenous category of diagnosis, with the remaining two-thirds being predominantly diagnosed with 'reactive' depression, suggesting that the 'lock and key' hypothesis relates to those with more severe chronic depression.

Veijola *et al.* (1998) conducted a study on gender differences in adult depression and found that adverse early-life experiences predisposed females to depression in adulthood, especially sexual and physical abuse. They only found a weak association between parental loss, through death or divorce, and adult depression. They found no significant relationship between early-life experience and adult depression in males and suggested that, in males, early adverse experiences were more likely to be expressed in antisocial personality and alcoholism.

The life events theory has received a great deal of support and is now incorporated into the DSM diagnostic criteria under Axis IV, where social and environmental circumstances are assessed. However, it does not explain why many patients do not report critical life events at the onset of their depression or why many people have ongoing psychosocial stressors yet do not become clinically depressed.

The diathesis-stress model (see Fig. 17.1 on p. 435) provides a solution: life events may be precipitating factors that interact with other vulnerability factors, which may be a genetic predisposition, personality factors, or adverse early-life experience.

Behavioural theories of depression

Traditional conditioning theory relates to social reinforcement. Lewinsohn (1974) suggested that depression is a consequence of a reduction in positive reinforcement. For example, if someone experiences bereavement, or loss of job, then there is less opportunity for enjoying pleasant experiences and receiving positive reinforcement. Depression may then occur. There is also a secondary gain, in that the depressive behaviour may be positively reinforced by others in the form of sympathy and concern. However,

Table 17.3 Examples of patients' 'lock and key' links to depression	
Lock	*Key*
Death of both parents when 11; children split up and fostered out	Loss of job and loss of identity
Forced into boarding school at young age – no choice	Triple bypass operation – no choice
Mother left, put into orphanage	Marital separation, husband left
Two siblings died as children	Son married, Crohn's disease diagnosed
Physical and sexual abuse by father	Physical illness

Source: Parker et al. (1998)

this cannot explain why the depression does not cease long after sympathy from others has waned.

Seligman (1974) put forward a behavioural theory of *learned helplessness* to explain reactive depression. In the course of investigating the effects of Pavlovian fear conditioning in dogs, Seligman found that, when placed in an inescapable and unavoidable stressful situation, the dog failed to initiate escape behaviour in another stressful situation where escape was possible. Seligman suggested that people are generally able to influence many aspects of their environment, but sometimes things just happen, irrespective of their own behaviour. If this occurs too often, then people lose their motivation and just give up, because they have learned that they are helpless in life situations.

Maier and Seligman (1976) tested this theory with humans, subjecting people to inescapable noise, shock and insoluble problems, and found that they later failed to escape from similar situations where escape was possible. These results were not always replicated, however, and some studies showed that helplessness actually facilitated subsequent performance (Wortman and Brehm 1975).

Like many of the behavioural theories, learned helplessness was seen to be inadequate as a complete explanation because it did not take cognitions into account. Allied to this, gender differences were found in studies involving insoluble problems, the predominant female response being depression and the predominant male response being anger.

In view of the inadequacy of the learned helplessness account, Seligman later reformulated his theory in *cognitive, attributional* terms calling this the *hopelessness theory of depression* (Abramson *et al.* 1978). This was in response to the term 'hopelessness' previously being used by Beck (e.g. Beck 1963) to describe a system of negative expectancies concerning the person and their future. Hopelessness has been identified as one of the core characteristics of depression, particularly in suicide. Beck developed a 'Hopelessness Scale' in order to measure and quantify levels of hopelessness (Beck *et al.* 1974). The hopelessness theory suggested that

when people experience failure, they usually try and attribute a cause to that failure. Causal explanations operate on three dimensions of judgement:

- ◆ internal–external (personal or environmental)
- ◆ stable–unstable (always so, or just on this occasion)
- ◆ global–specific (all encompassing, or specific to this situation).

A maladaptive style is to attribute all negative events to internal, stable, global causes. These causal explanations can then lead to expectations, which in turn can lead to symptoms of depression (see Fig. 17.4). Research in support of the hopelessness theory comes from studies using the *Attributional Style Questionnaire*, devised by Seligman (1974), which gives scores for internality, stability and globality of an individual's expectations. A study, conducted on grade aspirations in college students, showed that most of those with poor results were depressed after the exams. Two days later, however, those who made unstable, specific attributions about their failure had recovered, whereas those who had made stable, global attributions remained depressed. However, most of Seligman's studies were conducted on college students, rather than on clinically depressed patients. Furthermore, one of the key elements of the hopelessness theory is that depressed people believe they have little control over their lives; yet Ford and Neale (1985) found that depressed students did not underestimate their degree of control. What is not clear is whether hopelessness is a cause of depression, or whether it is a side effect of becoming depressed. If it is the cause, then it would have to precede the onset of depression. A five-year longitudinal study of children by Nolen-Hoeksema *et al.* (1992) found no connection between attributional style and depression in young children, but they did as the children grew older, suggesting that attributional styles may develop over a number of years.

Abramson *et al.* (1989) further reformulated their theory of hopelessness, to include the role of expectancy. They outlined a sequence of events which they claimed leads to hopelessness. This begins with a negative event which interacts with

Figure 17.4 An example of attributional judgements leading to depression

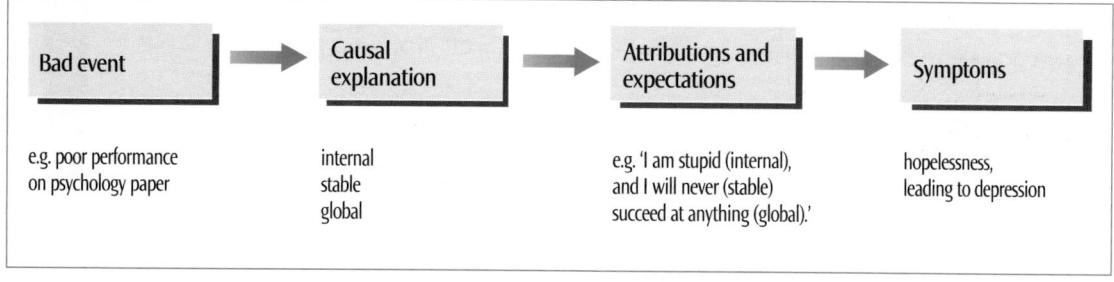

the person's already-held negative schemas, and a stable and global attribution is made of the event's occurrence. These beliefs lead to hopelessness expectancy for the future which then results in hopelessness depression. Abramson and colleagues have even suggested *hopelessness depression* as a subtype of depression. A study by DeVellis and Blalock (1992) tested the claim that *hopelessness expectancy* is a sufficient cause for depression in a longitudinal study of 57 adults. They found support for the link between expectancy and depression, but as a moderating, rather than mediating factor, i.e. that it does not by itself cause the depression, merely the degree.

Cognitive–behavioural explanations of depression

Beck (1967) developed his cognitive–behavioural theory of depression quite separately from Seligman and Abramson's hopelessness theory. He suggested that depression is the result of negative thinking and catastrophizing, which he called 'cognitive errors'. Beck (1991) maintains that there are three components to depression, which he called the 'cognitive triad':

1 negative views of the self as worthless and helpless

2 negative views of the world as full of obstacles and a negative view of one's ongoing experience of the world

3 negative views about the future as continuing in much the same way.

As these three components interact, they interfere with normal cognitive processing, leading to impairments in perception, memory and problem-solving abilities, with the person becoming completely obsessed with automatic negative thoughts, or schemas, such as 'I am worthless' and 'I can't ever do anything right'. These faulty cognitions can, in turn, lead to depression. Beck maintained that there is strong evidence that stable temperament and behavioural tendencies are present

at birth, based on the evolutionary strategies of fight, flight, freeze, or faint as alternative reactions to threat. Beck claimed that inherited strategies can be strengthened or weakened by the environment. He also claimed that negative schemas may be acquired in childhood as a result of traumatic events and/or negative treatment. Gotlib and Macleod (1997) suggest that negative schemas are deep-seated belief systems which develop early in life as the result of a series of negative events.

Exam summary: Depression (unipolar disorder)

The AQA examination will test your understanding of the following areas:

◆ clinical characteristics of depression (pp. 440–1)

◆ biological explanations (including evidence) of depression (pp. 441–3)

◆ psychological explanations (including evidence) of depression (pp. 443–6).

Example question

The question below is typical of one drawn from the material above, and should take you 45 minutes to answer:

◆ Critically consider the view that depression has psychological origins. *(30 marks)*

Suggested answer structure:

As with the previous question, you should not include description of the clinical characteristics of depression in your answer. There is an understandable temptation to do this, but examination questions are quite precise in their requirements, and the golden rule is that if it isn't asked for, don't give it (unless relevant and likely to get marks, which is not the case here).

It is also important to choose material that answers the question set. There is an argument that even genetic and biochemical explanations are, in

Figure 17.5 Explanations for the development of depression

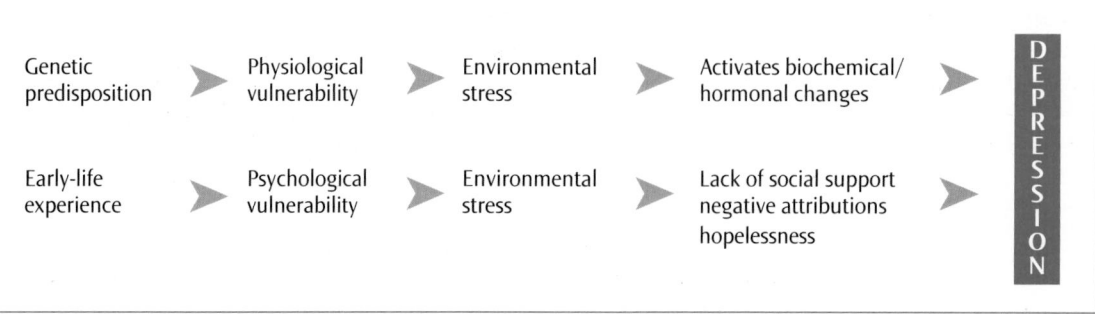

essence, psychological, representing *biological* and *physiological* psychology respectively. However, the specification does distinguish between *biological* and *psychological* explanations in a quite deliberate way, so it is prudent to follow this division in your answer. This does not make these biological explanations redundant in this answer, however, as they can be used as part of the AO2 component of the answer. If they are to be used in this way, it is important that they form part of a coherent critical argument rather than simply 'being there'.

This section has covered the following psychological explanations of depression – psychodynamic explanations (p. 443), stressful life events (pp. 443–4), behavioural theories (pp. 444–6) and cognitive-behavioural explanations (p. 446). Psychological and social factors appear to provide the most plausible accounts for reactive depression. The diathesis-stress model explains how factors within the individual can interact with external environmental factors, accounting for individual differences in susceptibility to depression. The vulnerability element may be inherited temperament,

or vulnerability may develop through adverse life experience, conditioning, or negative ways of thinking. Figure 17.5 summarizes explanations of the development of depression.

It is a good idea, when choosing material with which to answer this question, that you bear the synoptic requirement of the question in mind. There are a number of different psychological explanations of depression expressed in this chapter, but there are also a number of different investigative methods used in research relating to this topic. These include animal studies (p. 443), longitudinal studies (pp. 444 and 445), retrospective case studies (p. 444), experimental studies (p. 445) and questionnaires (p. 445).

Presenting an alternative biological view to depression need not be restricted to a discussion of the importance of biochemistry or genetics, but might also include discussion of the adaptive nature of depression, particular of bipolar depression. This is covered on pp. 440–6. If you don't get carried away, but use this material to make a succinct critical point, it will be effective for the synoptic element of the question.

Schizophrenia

Clinical characteristics

Schizophrenia is the condition most often associated with the term 'madness'. It is not a split personality; rather it is a group of psychotic disorders that are characterized by a loss of contact with reality. Symptoms are mainly disturbances of thought processes, but also extend to disturbances of emotion and behaviour. There are two major symptom categories, one of which relates to *acute* schizophrenia, characterized by what are known as *positive* symptoms, such as hallucinations and delusions. The other relates to *chronic* schizophrenia, characterized by what are known as *negative* symptoms, such as apathy and withdrawal.

A further distinction has been made between Type I (positive/acute) as a *functional* disorder and Type II (negative/chronic) as an *organic* disorder. DSM-IV has now moved away from these definitions and classified schizophrenia into three main sub-types: *paranoid, disorganized* and *catatonic.* Table 17.4 incorporates symptoms from both the traditional distinctions and DSM-IV classifications.

Schizophrenia is a serious psychotic disorder. DSM-IV (1994) states that estimates of prevalence vary in different studies and have ranged from 0.2 per cent to 2.0 per cent and that these rates are similar throughout the world. Although it can emerge later in life, the onset of schizophrenia for men is usually in

the late teens or early twenties and for women onset is usually in the late twenties. It can suddenly strike, for example, a young person at university or just starting a career with a bright future. Around one-third have a single episode, or just a few brief acute episodes, and recover fully, whilst around another third have an episodic pattern of acute symptoms throughout life, maintaining a reasonable level of functioning whilst in remission. For the remaining third there is an unremitting course which deteriorates from acute to chronic symptoms. Treatment can reduce the effects of acute symptoms and some people recover spontaneously, but, as yet, there is no known cure for schizophrenia, despite the vast amount of money spent on research worldwide. (See *In Focus*, p. 449, for three case studies of schizophrenia.)

Explanations of schizophrenia

Neurological explanations of schizophrenia

It has long been believed that schizophrenia is a disease of the brain. This view was held by Kraepelin towards the end of the last century, who was the first to identify and label 'schizophrenia'. He believed that schizophrenia resulted from a process of brain degeneration. The medical profession at the time attempted to understand this by conducting postmortems. Brain abnormalities have been detected

Table 17.4 Symptoms of acute and chronic schizophrenia incorporating DSM-IV types

DSM-IV	Type I – functional Acute (positive) symptoms	Type II – organic Chronic (negative) symptoms
Paranoid type	Delusions of grandeur Delusions of persecution Auditory hallucinations	
Disorganized type		Disorganized speech Disorganized behaviour Inappropriate affect Flat emotions
Catatonic type		Apathy Loss of drive Cataleptic stupor and bizarre postures Excessive motor activity Echolalia

Explanation of symptoms

Delusions of grandeur:	Beliefs that they are someone grand or famous, such as The Messiah, Albert Einstein or Elvis Presley, or beliefs that they have special magical powers.
Delusions of persecution:	Beliefs that people are plotting against them, that they are being spied upon, talked about by strangers or deliberately victimized.
Auditory hallucinations:	Voices heard in the absence of external stimuli, which are often critical, warning of danger or giving commands.
Disorganized speech:	Inappropriate speech, for example: 'It's raining... fruit trees in summer... acts of Jupiter in a sea of haze... I should go and get my coats and hats... cosmic laws interjecting with... apples, oranges, pears...'
Disorganized behaviour:	Severe disruption in the ability to perform daily living activities, such as showering, dressing, preparing meals.
Inappropriate affect:	Silliness and laughter which are out of context, e.g. laughing when hearing terrible news.
Flat emotions:	No emotional response can be elicited to any stimulus; face is immobile, eyes are lifeless, speech is toneless, often staring vacantly.
Apathy:	Loss of interest in normal goals.
Loss of drive:	Feeling drained of energy and unable to initiate or complete a course of action.
Cataleptic stupor:	Standing motionless like a statue in bizarre postures.
Excessive motor activity:	Moving in odd and disturbing ways (e.g. sudden movement, odd gestures, strange grimaces) that are apparently purposeless and not influenced by external stimuli.
Echolalia:	Repetitive echoing of words spoken by others, or the accentuated imitation of the mannerisms of other people.

Activity 5: Case studies of schizophrenia

Answer the following questions after reading the *In Focus* case studies on the next page.

1   What type of catatonic behaviour is shown by Maria's staring and mutism?

2   What behaviours shown by Joshua suggest that he has disorganized schizophrenia?

3   What behaviours of Esther's would lead you to consider her as having paranoid schizophrenia?

Three case studies of schizophrenia

Catatonic schizophrenia

Maria is a 19-year-old college student who has been psychiatrically hospitalized for more than a month. For days prior to her admission, and for the weeks since her arrival in the hospital, Maria has been mute. Rigidly posturing her body and staring at the ceiling, she spends most of the day in a trance-like state that seems impenetrable. Her family and college acquaintances have been mystified. In trying to sort out why and when she began showing such odd behaviour, the only incident that could be recalled was Maria's ranting and raving, just prior to going into the catatonic state, that one of her lecturers was a 'demon'.

Disorganized schizophrenia

Joshua is a 43-year-old man who can be found daily standing near the steps of a local bank on a busy street corner. Every day he wears a yellow T-shirt, worn-out hiking shorts and orange trainers. Rain or shine, day in and day out, Joshua maintains his 'post' at the bank. Sometimes he can be seen 'conversing' with imaginary people. Without provocation he sobs miserably, and at other times he explodes into shrieks of laughter. Police and social workers keep taking him to shelters for people who are homeless, but Joshua manages to get out and be back on the street before he can be treated.

Paranoid schizophrenia

Esther is a 31-year-old unmarried woman who lives with her elderly mother. A belief that the outside world is filled with radio waves that will insert evil thoughts into her head keeps Esther from leaving the house. The windows in her bedroom are 'protected' with aluminium foil that 'deflects the radio waves'. She often hears voices that comment on these radio signals. For example, one comment was the slow, deep voice of an elderly man who angrily stated, 'We're going to get these thoughts into your head. Give up the fight!'

Source: adapted from Halgin and Whitbourne (1993, pp. 280–1)

in people diagnosed with schizophrenia, but it was not possible to ascertain whether these abnormalities had caused the schizophrenia or whether the schizophrenia had caused the brain damage.

Recent advances in technology have enabled the medical profession to examine the live brains of people with schizophrenia. Magnetic resonance imaging (MRI) has been a tremendous breakthrough because it provides a picture of the brain. MRI studies show quite definite structural abnormalities in the brains of many patients with schizophrenia. Brown *et al.* (1986) found decreased brain weight and enlarged ventricles, which are the cavities in the brain that hold cerebrospinal fluid. Flaum *et al.* (1995) also found enlarged ventricles, along with smaller thalamic, hippocampal and superior temporal volumes. Buchsbaum (1990) found abnormalities in the frontal and prefrontal cortex, the basal ganglia, the hippocampus and the amygdala.

Young *et al.* (1991), using MRI, found a number of structural brain differences between people diagnosed with schizophrenia and controls, particularly in the asymmetry of the brain. For example, in controls the amygdala was smaller on the left than the right, but in the schizophrenia group, asymmetry was absent.

Young and colleagues found that the degree of abnormality correlated with the severity of the symptoms. Whilst MRI studies appear to provide conclusive evidence of structural abnormalities, it is worth noting that they do not always agree on the regions of the brain affected. For example, Flaum *et al.* (1995) found no abnormalities in the temporal lobe regions, whereas Woodruff *et al.* (1997) found quite significant reductions in the temporal lobe, compared with controls. Structural abnormalities have been found more often in those with negative/chronic symptoms, rather than positive/acute symptoms, lending support to the belief that there are two types of schizophrenia: Type I (acute) as a 'functional' disorder and Type II (chronic) as an 'organic' disorder. An argument against this is that many people with acute symptoms of schizophrenia later go on to develop chronic symptoms, which could indicate a further degeneration of the brain rather than two distinct types of schizophrenia.

Evidence for progressive brain degeneration comes from Rapoport *et al.* (1997) who looked at childhood onset schizophrenia in a sample who were seriously ill at the age of eight. They found marked ventricular enlargement in these children, compared to controls, which continued to increase progressively into adolescence. They claim that this is an indication that ventricular enlargement cannot be a trigger for schizophrenia, since the enlargement could only be sustained over a limited number of years, otherwise the enlargements would be too improbable. This explains why many researchers, for example Nopoulos et al. (1997), have found no difference between ventricular enlargement (the most significant structural difference) and duration of illness. Nopoulos and colleagues also examined gender differences, finding similar patterns of structural abnormalities in males and females, although males appear to manifest greater severity, especially with regard to ventricular enlargement. Their review of evidence concludes that female brains are generally more resistant to a variety of disease processes which leads to less severe illness. Cannon et al. (1994a) found that ventricular enlargement was greater in those who were genetically high risk and had also experienced birth complications.

As more MRI studies are being undertaken, more abnormalities are being identified. For example, Goldstein et al. (1999) have found a number of cortical abnormalities, Velakoulis et al. (1999) found smaller hippocampal volumes which are present from the onset of the illness and Kwon et al. (1999) report a reduction by 28 per cent of the volume of grey matter (so-called because of its pinkish-grey colour) in the left planum temporale. The evidence for structural brain abnormalities really does appear to confirm Kraepelin's belief held more than a century ago. However, the critical period for the onset of schizophrenia is not usually before adolescence. Therefore, if brain abnormalities precede the onset of clinical symptoms, this would confirm the view that schizophrenia is a developmental disorder. Weinberger (1988) claims that, despite the wealth of research, the evidence is still inconclusive as to whether there are progressive structural brain changes prior to the initial onset of schizophrenia. This means that the causal direction of the hypothesis is still in question – whether structural abnormalities predispose to schizophrenia, or whether the onset of clinical symptoms cause structural changes.

One of the main problems in trying to understand the causal direction is that, so far, brain imaging in relation to schizophrenia has mainly been restricted to people who have already been diagnosed. A study on teenage monkeys by Castner et al. (1998) may shed some light on this debate. They subjected the monkeys to brain-damaging X-rays during fetal development and found that they showed no ill effects during childhood, compared to the control group, but at puberty they developed symptoms of schizophrenia, such as hallucinations. It is difficult, however, to link behaviour in monkeys to symptoms of schizophrenia that have been identified in humans and there are, of course, ethical issues associated with animal research of this kind.

Neurochemical explanations of schizophrenia

Research into schizophrenia has also focused on neurochemical abnormalities. The rationale behind the biochemical theory is that if schizophrenia can be transmitted genetically, then either structural or biochemical abnormalities should be detectable in the brains of those diagnosed for schizophrenia. Research into neurochemical functioning has focused on serotonin and noradrenaline, but results have been inconclusive.

More convincing evidence has come from research on dopamine receptors. Interest in dopamine arose when it was found that phenothiazines (neuroleptic, anti-psychotic drugs which reduce the symptoms of schizophrenia) serve to inhibit dopamine activity and that L-dopa (a synthetic dopamine-releasing drug) can induce symptoms resembling paranoid (acute) schizophrenia in non-psychotic people. An interesting corollary concerning Parkinson's disease and schizophrenia has been noted. Symptoms of Parkinson's disease, such as shaking of the limbs, are common side effects of anti-psychotic medication and Parkinson's disease is known to be associated with low levels of dopamine (see Fig. 17.6).

Studies on amphetamines have provided further support for the dopamine hypothesis. The symptoms of amphetamine psychosis are similar to paranoid schizophrenia and one of the actions of amphetamines is the release of dopamine at central synapses. Amphetamines have also been shown to worsen the

Figure 17.6
Dopamine links with schizophrenia and Parkinson's disease

Disorder	Symptoms	Drug	Action	Effect
Schizophrenia	Disordered thought and behaviour	Phenothiazine	Decreases dopamine	Reduces disordered thought and behaviour Causes stiffness and tremors
Parkinson's disease	Stiffness and tremors	L-dopa	Increases dopamine	Reduces stiffness and tremors

symptoms of schizophrenia. In a study by Randrup and Munkvad (1966), behaviour similar to that found in those suffering from schizophrenia was induced in rats by administering amphetamines and the effects were then reversed by neuroleptic drugs. Further support comes from postmortems of patients with schizophrenia, which have revealed a specific increase of dopamine in the left amygdala (Falkai *et al.* 1988) and increased dopamine receptor density in the caudate nucleus putamen (Owen *et al.* 1978).

Given the findings from postmortems, and assuming that dopamine is the important factor in the action of antipsychotic drugs, then it would be expected that dopamine metabolism is abnormal in patients with schizophrenia. With the development of PET scans, metabolic activity can now be monitored in live brains. PET scan research conducted by Wong *et al.* (1986) revealed that dopamine receptor density in the caudate nuclei is indeed greater in those with schizophrenia than in controls. However, this has not been supported in subsequent studies. According to Iacono *et al.* (1988), dopamine deficiency may be the cause of ventricular enlargement, which is one of the most notable structural abnormalities. Yet despite extensive research on dopamine receptors in the brains of schizophrenia patients, no consensus has yet been reached.

Unfortunately, neither postmortems nor PET scans can reveal whether increased dopaminergic activity causes schizophrenia, or whether schizophrenia interferes with dopamine metabolism. It is possible that the inconclusive findings in dopamine studies merely reflect the two subtypes of schizophrenia, because amphetamines are known to worsen positive symptoms associated with acute schizophrenia and lessen negative symptoms associated with chronic schizophrenia, whilst phenothiazines (antipsychotic drugs) alleviate positive symptoms, but are not so effective with negative symptoms. A final point is that dopamine is unlikely to be the only factor in schizophrenia because it has also been implicated in mania and a number of other mental disorders which have quite different symptoms. Each of these disorders is alleviated by quite different drugs, yet the main evidence for the dopamine link in schizophrenia is the effectiveness of phenothiazines in alleviating symptoms.

Adolescent/early adulthood onset of schizophrenia occurs mainly in males, whereas there are no gender differences in late-age onset. According to Seeman (1997) in her review of the literature, estrogens are thought to be neuroprotective with regard to neural degeneration and susceptibility to toxins. Therefore, if schizophrenia is associated with brain degeneration this would explain gender differences in diagnosis of early onset but not late onset, because oestrogen levels drop at menopause. It has also been found that females

---

Activity 6: Schizophrenia and dopamine

Based on information given in the previous paragraphs, which of the following statements seem more likely to be correct?

a) High levels of dopamine cause schizophrenia.
b) High levels of dopamine induce symptoms of schizophrenia.
c) Schizophrenia causes high levels of dopamine to be produced.
d) There is no connection at all between schizophrenia and dopamine activity.

---

respond more favourably and quickly than males to neuroleptic (antipsychotic) drugs and again oestrogens are thought to be implicated.

There is now quite convincing evidence for both structural abnormalities and neurochemical abnormalities in the brains of people with schizophrenia, but there are conflicting views as to whether these abnormalities result from a genetic defect, or from birth complications leading to brain damage. A longitudinal study by Dalman *et al.* (1999) found significant links between birth complications and later development of schizophrenia, with pre-eclampsia being the most significant risk factor. However, it is unlikely that problems such as pre-eclampsia could be the sole cause of schizophrenia, because this is a common birth complication and not all such infants go on to develop schizophrenia. It may be that birth complications interact in some way with a genetic predisposition.

Genetic explanation for schizophrenia

Family history studies have been conducted since the 1900s in an attempt to identify a genetic link with schizophrenia. Of the more recent studies, Kendler *et al.* (1985) have shown that first-degree relatives of those with schizophrenia are 18 times more at risk than the general population. A study in Roscommon, a county in the West of Ireland, by Kendler *et al.* (1993) further supports a familial link, especially in siblings and slightly less in parents. They found, however, that the familial link was not necessarily specific to schizophrenia, since increased rates of schizophrenia were found in relatives of those with schizoaffective disorder, schizotypal personality disorder and other psychotic disorders. This study was, of course, conducted in one specific geographical location and it may not be possible to generalize this to other populations. Family studies have specific methodological limitations. In this study, Kendler and colleagues used mainly interview data, although they did check with hospital records for confirmation of psychotic diagnosis in relatives. A study on 109 sibling pairs in the UK diagnosed with schizophrenia or schizoaffective disorder was conducted by Cardno *et al.* (1998) to try to ascertain whether they shared the same schizophrenic symptoms, which might be expected if the behaviour was environmentally learned. The expression of symptoms was so different between the siblings that they concluded the study offered no support for shared environmental factors contributing to the cause of schizophrenia. However, they were also sceptical about genetic links.

Family studies are generally inconclusive because they are conducted retrospectively, in that they are comparing a cross section of people who have already been diagnosed. A prospective (longitudinal) study can provide more reliable data and a number of large-scale projects have been undertaken in different parts of the world.

The *Copenhagen High-Risk Study* in Denmark, begun by Kety and colleagues in 1962, identified 207 offspring of mothers diagnosed with schizophrenia along with a matched control of 104 children with 'healthy' mothers (low-risk). The children were aged between 10 and18 years at the start of the study and were matched on age, gender, parental socio-economic status and urban/rural residence. Follow-up of the children has been conducted in 1974 and in 1989, when the mean age of the children was 42 years and through the risk period for onset of schizophrenia. Results published by Parnas *et al.* (1993) strongly support a familial link with two psychotic disorders, with schizophrenia diagnosis in 31 (16.2 per cent) of the high-risk group compared to two (1.9 per cent) in the low-risk group (in the low-risk group, the mother of one person was diagnosed with schizophrenia a few years into the study) and schizotypal personality disorder diagnosis in 36 (18.8 per cent) of the high-risk group compared to five (5.0 per cent) in the low-risk group. Although these percentages may not seem very high, they were both significant to $p < 0.0001$ (see Chapter 23 for an explanation of p). Combining the figures for the two disorders, the percentages are 35 per cent high-risk compared to 6.9 per cent low-risk. Another prospective study with offspring of patients with schizophrenia – the *New York High-Risk Project* – has reported similar findings at a 25-year follow-up (Erlennmeyer-Kimling *et al.* 1997). The main difficulty with family studies is that they cannot differentiate between genetic and environmental influences because the individuals share the same environment.

The *Israeli High-Risk Study*, begun by Marcus and colleagues in 1967, attempted to separate out genetic from environmental factors. They identified 50 high-risk children (where one or both parents had been diagnosed with schizophrenia) and 50 matched control children (similar age and background, but neither parent had been diagnosed with schizophrenia, or any other mental disorder). Within each group, half were raised on a kibbutz (where all the children are reared together and separate from their parents) and half in a traditional family setting. The age range of children at the start of the study was 8.1 to 14.8 years. At a 13-year follow-up, 22 of the high-risk group had been diagnosed with schizophrenia and only four of the control group. Sixteen of those diagnosed were from the kibbutz and ten from traditional families (Marcus *et al.* 1987). A more recent update on the Israeli study (Fish *et al.* 1992) reports cognitive dysfunctioning at around age 10 in approximately half of the high-risk children, compared to 15 per cent in the low-risk group, along with birth complications or low birth weights.

The *Finnish Adoption study*, which Tienari began in 1969, identified adopted-away offspring of biological mothers who had been diagnosed with schizophrenia (112 index cases), plus a matched control group of 135 adopted-away offspring of mothers who had not been diagnosed with any mental disorder. Adoptees ranged from 5 to 7 years at the start of the study and all had been separated from their mother before the age of 4. The study reported that 7 per cent of the index adoptees developed schizophrenia, compared to 1.5 per cent of the controls (Tienari *et al.* 1987).

The *Danish Adoption Study*, reported by Kety *et al.* (1994), taking a national sample from across Denmark, found high rates of diagnosis for chronic schizophrenia in adoptees whose biological parents had the same diagnosis, even though they had been adopted by 'healthy' parents.

All the above prospective studies are still ongoing. Whilst there has been an update on the Danish study, more recent follow-ups are awaited from the Israeli and Finnish studies, since many of the people in the sample had not passed through the critical period for the onset of schizophrenia at the last major follow-ups. The data they have provided so far, however, indicate a strong genetic link for schizophrenia. A major problem in these longitudinal studies, however, is that diagnostic criteria for schizophrenia are continually being updated and changed.

Twin studies offer perhaps the best means of establishing genetic links, by comparing the difference in concordance rates for MZ and DZ twins. Both share the same environment, but only the MZ twins have identical genetic make-up. Many studies have been conducted and they all show a much higher concordance rate in MZ than in DZ twins. To separate out genetics conclusively from the environment, researchers have sought out MZ twins reared apart where at least one twin has been diagnosed with schizophrenia. Obviously they are few in number and

Figure 17.7
Genetic risk of
developing
schizophrenia
Source: Zimbardo
et al. 1995

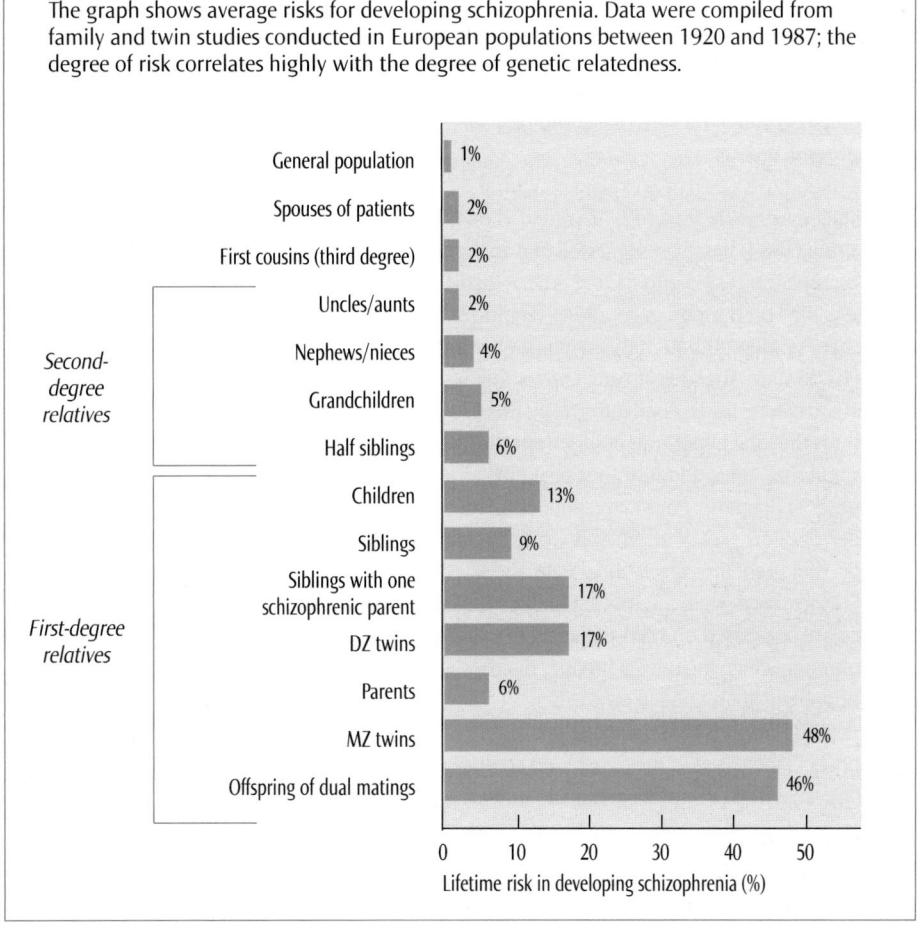

The graph shows average risks for developing schizophrenia. Data were compiled from family and twin studies conducted in European populations between 1920 and 1987; the degree of risk correlates highly with the degree of genetic relatedness.

General population — 1%
Spouses of patients — 2%
First cousins (third degree) — 2%

Second-degree relatives
Uncles/aunts — 2%
Nephews/nieces — 4%
Grandchildren — 5%
Half siblings — 6%

Children — 13%
Siblings — 9%
Siblings with one schizophrenic parent — 17%

First-degree relatives
DZ twins — 17%
Parents — 6%
MZ twins — 48%
Offspring of dual matings — 46%

Lifetime risk in developing schizophrenia (%)
0   10   20   30   40   50

an added problem is that one of the reasons for separation may have been a problem in the family. Gottesman and Shields (1982) used the Maudsley twin register and found 58 per cent (seven out of twelve MZ twin pairs reared apart) were concordant for schizophrenia. If the genetic hypothesis is correct, then the offspring of a non-affected discordant MZ twin should still be high-risk. A study by Fischer (1971) found that 9.4 per cent of such offspring developed schizophrenia, which is a much higher incidence than in the general population (approximately 1 per cent). A study in London using the Maudsley Twin Register by Cardno *et al.* (1999) found a 40 per cent concordance rate in MZ twins, compared to 5.3 per cent in DZ twins. Dworkin (1987) separated twin data into positive (acute) symptoms and negative (chronic) symptoms, and found a stronger genetic component for negative symptoms.

Twin, adoption and family studies continue to provide reliable evidence that the degree of risk increases with the degree of genetic relatedness (see Fig. 17.7). However, no twin study has yet shown 100 per cent concordance in MZ twins, which would provide the most conclusive evidence for genetic links alone.

Season of birth explanation for schizophrenia

Other avenues of research have been explored for alternatives to the genetic view of schizophrenia as a developmental disorder. Since the late 1920s, it has been noticed that an overwhelmingly high proportion of people diagnosed with schizophrenia were born in the winter and early spring (Hope-Simpson 1981). Bradbury and Miller (1985) conducted a review of the evidence and found that this was borne out in most countries in the northern hemisphere. A recent study in England and Wales shows that this has remained consistent over the latter half of this century (Procopio and Marriott 1998).

A number of viral infections, such as measles, scarlet fever, polio, diphtheria and pneumonia and, in particular, the virus Influenza A, have been suggested as an explanation (Torrey *et al.* 1988, Torrey *et al.* 1996). Influenza A is most prevalent in the winter and if implicated in some way could explain the high proportion of winter births in those diagnosed with schizophrenia. The suggestion is that if the mother is infected during pregnancy there is pre-birth exposure to the Influenza A virus. It is thought that the 25- to 30-week foetus is most vulnerable because of accelerated growth in the cerebral cortex at this time (Mednick *et al.* 1988). It is hypothesized that the viral infection enters the brain and gestates until it is activated by hormonal changes in puberty. Alternatively, there may be a gradual degeneration of the brain which eventually becomes so severe that symptoms of schizophrenia emerge.

This hypothesis could also explain structural abnormalities in the brain which are revealed on MRI scans. Crow (1984) has even suggested that the virus could become integrated into the genome, which could then be passed on through generations, lending support for the genetic view. Although this seems highly unlikely, Weiss (1978) states that it is already known that retroviruses can be transcribed into DNA. Further support for the viral hypothesis comes from the observation that, throughout history, peaks in schizophrenia diagnosis have corresponded with major flu epidemics (Torrey *et al.* 1988). It is worth noting, however, that these are correlational data and so caution should be observed when attempting to infer causation. The data are also based on DSM-II diagnostic criteria for schizophrenia, which included a broader diagnostic range of patients than DSM-III onwards.

Hare (1983) reports that the incidence of schizophrenia increased in the nineteenth century with urbanization, which precipitated many infectious diseases. However, with urbanization came more hospitals and in turn more detected cases of illnesses in general, so the figures may simply reflect diagnostic statistics, rather than more actual cases of schizophrenia. A recent study by Marcelis *et al.* (1998) in the Netherlands reports, a high positive correlation between urban birth and later development of schizophrenia, and that this is a linear association with the degree of urbanicity. They make no claims, however, that this is associated with increased risk of viral infections, but rather suggest an association with social factors such as stress, divorce, noise, pollution and crime.

Torrey *et al.* (1988) claimed that the link between viral infection and schizophrenia only occurs in those who are already genetically predisposed. If that were the case, however, 100 per cent concordance would be expected in MZ twins and perhaps in DZ twins, because they are in the uterus together and are both therefore exposed to the same viruses.

Activity 7: Aetiologies of schizophrenia

Taking the preceding evidence into account, do you think that the three biological aetiologies (genetic, biochemical and neurological) are mutually exclusive? Or can you suggest how they might fit together to explain schizophrenia?

Dysfunctional families

In the 1950s and 1960s it was thought that people suffering from schizophrenia were from *dysfunctional* families. There was even a strong belief that schizophrenia was caused by a dysfunction of communication within the family. The term 'schizophrenogenic families' (coined by Fromm-Reichmann 1948) was used to describe families with high emotional tension, with many secrets, close alliances and conspiracies. An associated suggestion was the double-bind situation, where children are given conflicting messages from parents who express care, yet at the same time appear critical (Bateson *et al.* 1956). It was thought that this led to confusion, self-doubt and eventual withdrawal. This theory went into decline because of a failure to replicate findings across studies. Another reason for the loss of interest in it in the 1970s was the convincing evidence appearing for a genetic predisposition in schizophrenia.

The main problem, however, was that families were studied retrospectively, long after the person's mental disorder may have affected the family system. Living with someone who is suffering from schizophrenia is difficult and distressing for the whole family. Routines are disrupted, often with one parent having to give up paid employment to care for the person. As families struggle to cope with schizophrenia, to suggest that they have caused the disorder is at least unhelpful and at most highly destructive.

Expressed emotion

By the mid-1970s, psychologists had become more interested in the part the family might play in the *course,* rather than the *cause,* of schizophrenia. Vaughn and Leff, working at the Medical Research Council in London, published a paper in 1976 suggesting that the extent of expressed emotion within a family was a strong predictor of relapse rates among discharged patients. Their research was stimulated by an earlier study by Brown (1972) showing that patients with schizophrenia who returned to homes where a high level of emotion was expressed (high EE) – such as hostility, criticism, over-involvement and over-concern – showed a greater tendency to relapse than those returning to low-EE homes. Vaughn and Leff (1976) found similar results, with 51 per cent relapse in those in high-EE homes and only 13 per cent relapse in those in low-EE homes. Vaughn and Leff included in their study the amount of time spent in face-to-face contact with relatives after discharge and found that relapse rates increased as face-to-face contact increased with high-EE relatives. The study also included data on whether or not the patient was on medication and it was found that the relapse rate increased to 92 per cent

Table 17.5   Results of prospective studies of expressed emotion (EE)

Author	Location	No. of subjects	Follow-up	Relapse rate High EE	Relapse rate Low EE
Vaughn and Leff (1976)	S. London	37	9 months	50%	12%
Leff and Vaughn (1981)*	S. London	36	2 years	62%	20%
Vaughn et al. (1984)	Los Angeles	54	9 months	56%	28%
Macmillan et al. (1986)	N. London	67	2 years	63%	39%
Leff et al. (1987)	Chandigargh (India)	76	1 year	33%	14%
Budzyna-Dawidowski	Cracow (Poland)	36	1 year	32%	9%
et al. (1989)			2 years	72%	18%
Cazzullo et al. (1989)	Milan (Italy)	45	9 months	58%	21%
Barrelet et al. (1990)	Geneva	41	9 months	32%	0%

* Follow-up of same patients as Vaughn and Leff (1976)

Source: extracted from Bebbington and Kuipers (1992), cited in Kavanagh (1992)

in high-EE homes with increased contact coupled with no medication. It should be noted, however, that no study has since replicated these particular results relating to medication.

A point worth considering is that *under*stimulation is believed to increase negative symptoms in schizophrenia (e.g. withdrawal and apathy) and *over*stimulation is believed to precipitate positive symptoms (e.g. hallucinations, delusions and restlessness). In relating this to 'expressed emotion' it might therefore be expected that both low and high EE would precipitate a relapse, dependent upon whether the schizophrenic condition is either chronic or acute. However, since remission periods are more frequent in acute schizophrenia, it may not be possible to test this hypothesis.

Twenty years on, EE has now become a well-established 'maintenance' model of schizophrenia and many prospective studies have been conducted which support the expressed-emotion hypothesis across many cultures (see Table 17.5). So well accepted has this model become, that treatment programmes for schizophrenia usually include education and training for family members in controlling levels of EE.

However, despite the widely held acceptance of the EE model, it is not without its critics. First, many patients with schizophrenia are either estranged from their families or have minimal contact, and yet there is no evidence that such people are less prone to relapse (Goldstein 1988). There is no reason why this should negate the model, however, because presumably any social involvement could be regarded as high or low EE. Adopting this view is less accusing to families, suggesting that they are more in focus simply because they are usually the first and most frequent point of contact. Added to this, it has been suggested that high

EE may well develop as a response to the burdens of living with schizophrenia.

The EE model has become so widely accepted that research is now focusing on relatives of those with schizophrenia in order to understand better which aspects of high and low EE relate to relapse. Weisman et al. (1998) have examined the attributions of relatives in order to offer an explanation as to why people with negative symptom schizophrenia are more likely to relapse than those with positive symptoms. They found that relatives tend to attribute positive symptoms (e.g. hallucinations and delusions) to the person's mental illness and therefore do not hold them accountable for this behaviour. On the other hand, relatives tend to attribute negative symptoms (e.g. apathy and social withdrawal) to the person's personality characteristics and tend to become angry and critical in an attempt to change those behaviours, because they are perceived as controllable. This study was supported by Lopez et al. (1999), who found much higher relapse rates in families characterized by negative affect (criticism) than in those with positive affect (warmth). In particular, this was related to the degree to which the patient's behaviour was viewed to be controllable or uncontrollable. They conclude that since families play an important role in the course of schizophrenia, they need to learn all they can about the disorder in order to prevent attributions of controllability and subsequent criticism.

Diathesis-stress model explanation for schizophrenia

Since the 1980s the diathesis-stress model (see Fig. 17.1 on p. 435) has been applied to schizophrenia. The reasoning behind this theory is that those individuals who develop schizophrenia may be genetically predisposed. In addition, however, the research on

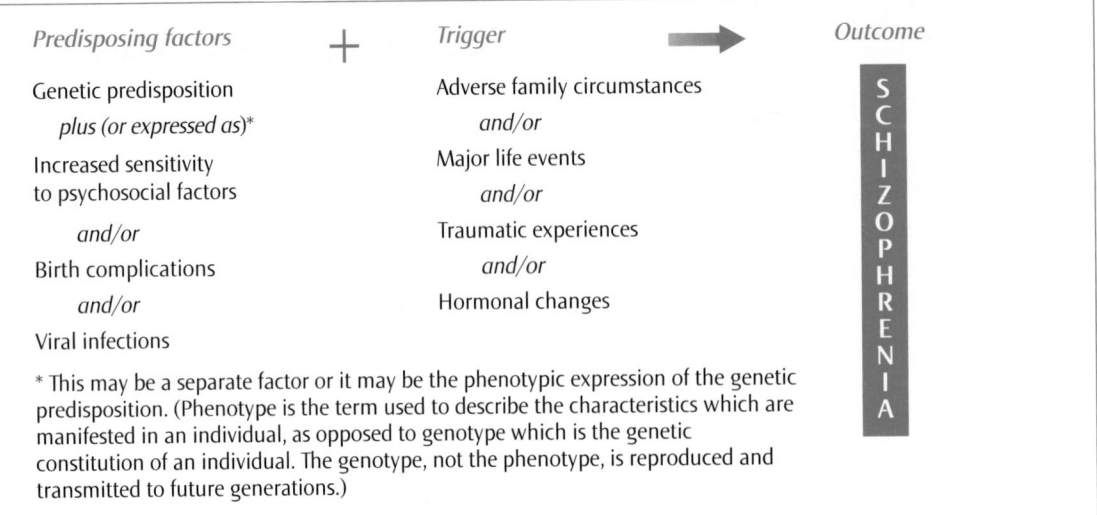

Figure 17.8 An integrative model of the aetiology of schizophrenia

'expressed emotion' has revealed that they are also extremely sensitive to psychosocial elements in their environment. Therefore, stressful events in the environment, such as major life events, traumatic experiences, or dysfunctional families, may act as a 'trigger' in a high-risk individual (see Fig. 17.8).

Support for the 'diathesis-stress' model also comes from prospective longitudinal studies. As research gathered further evidence for genetic factors, it was also becoming clear that schizophrenia did not always develop in those thought to be genetically vulnerable. This led researchers back to the environment in the search for precipitating factors.

The Finnish Adoption Study undertaken by Tienari (1987) also investigated environmental factors by assessing the quality of parenting through a battery of tests and interviews. All of the reported cases of schizophrenia occurred in families rated as 'disturbed'. Furthermore, where the rearing environments were rated as 'healthy' in the high-risk sample, the occurrence of schizophrenia was well below general population rates. However, this cannot be seen as evidence for a purely environmental aetiology because low-risk children from 'disturbed' families did not develop schizophrenia.

The Israeli High Risk Study (Marcus 1987) investigated environmental factors by assessing the parents on hostility, inconsistency and over-involvement. All the reported cases of schizophrenia had poor parenting ratings. However, all of these cases also showed signs of neuropsychological abnormalities at the time of initial assessment (13 years previously), which raises the question of whether these abnormalities had influenced the parent–child interaction.

These studies are ongoing and many of the children have not yet passed through the critical period for the onset of schizophrenia. However, the evidence so far strongly supports the diathesis-stress model.

Cognitive explanations of schizophrenia

Cognitive psychologists examine the cognitive functioning of people with schizophrenia, bearing in mind that schizophrenia is a 'thought' disorder. Cognitive psychologists have been focusing on perception and attentional processes, memory and problem-solving. The cognitive view accepts that there are almost certainly physiological abnormalities associated with schizophrenia and that these are transcribed into cognitive malfunctioning. In addition to this, cognitive psychologists are attempting to find evidence for genetic links by examining whether malfunctioning cognitive processing is a family trait, expressed in the phenotype (see explanation in Fig. 17.8), albeit to a lesser degree of severity in non-schizophrenic family members.

Park et al. (1995) identified working memory deficits in people with schizophrenia and in their first degree non-schizophrenic relatives, a study that has been supported by Faraone et al. (1999), who also found impairments in auditory attention. Faraone and colleagues claim that these memory and attention impairments are a manifestation of the genetic predisposition to schizophrenia and are even bold enough to claim that these are the cause of schizophrenia. They admit, however, that their data cannot explain why some relatives do not develop schizophrenia, even though they have the predisposing genes. They suggest that further work is needed to establish whether some people have a low 'dose' of the genes, or, alternatively, whether they have not been exposed to any environmental agents that may trigger the disorder. Cannon et al. (1994b) who also identified verbal memory and attention, but not visual memory deficits, in people with schizophrenia and their non-schizophrenic siblings, suggested that the mediating factors that determine the expression of these genes are birth complications.

Attentional mechanisms have been studied in relation to 'eye-tracking' dysfunctions (ETD) and these have been identified in people with schizophrenia (e.g. Levy *et al.* 1993). Dysfunctions are detected by a procedure of following a moving target in a horizontal plane whereby the colour changes randomly and the participant must count the number of changes. A study by Kinney *et al.* (1999) has identified an ETD in people with schizophrenia and also in their non-schizophrenic relatives. They suggest that this is a genetic defect. They were also investigating season of birth and found no evidence of dysfunction in eye-tracking in those diagnosed with schizophrenia who were winter births. They conclude that genetic and environmental factors associated with severe-weather births are quite separate aetiological factors in schizophrenia. Cognitive impairments can result from brain injury resulting from, say, a stroke or an accident, but these rarely result in a mental disorder. Cognitive impairments thought to have a genetic origin have, however, been implicated in a number of different mental disorders, for example Attention Deficit Hyperactivity Disorder. As an explanation for schizophrenia, this is a new area of research and as yet it is not possible to evaluate the validity of such a link.

Exam summary: Schizophrenia

The AQA examination will test your understanding of the following areas:

◆ clinical characteristics of schizophrenia (p. 447)

◆ biological explanations (including evidence) of schizophrenia (pp. 447–54)

◆ psychological explanations (including evidence) of schizophrenia (pp. 454–7).

Example question

The question below is typical of one drawn from the material above, and should take you 45 minutes to answer:

◆ Discuss the view that schizophrenia is a genetic disorder.   *(30 marks)*

Suggested answer structure:

This question is slightly more focused than the previous one. The question does not focus on one particular *perspective* (such as *biological* explanations), but instead asks for discussion of one aspect of that – i.e. *genetic* explanations. These are covered on pp. 451–3 of this section. Note that this question does not require description of the clinical characteristics of schizophrenia, although other questions might ask explicitly for just that. Other explanations of schizophrenia (e.g. neurochemical or environmental explanations) may also be used in this answer as part of the AO2 component of the answer. If they are to be used in this way, it is important that they form part of a coherent critical argument rather than simply 'being there'.

The current view of schizophrenia holds that genetic influence predisposes, or renders a person vulnerable (high risk) to the disorder, with biochemical and neurological factors being expressions of the predisposition. No twin study has yet shown 100 per cent concordance. However, this may be because there is a lifetime genetic risk and the disorder has not yet been expressed in undiagnosed identical twins. A more likely alternative is that there are environmental factors that interact with a genetic predisposition, or operate as a trigger. These could be birth complications, viral infections or social/family factors. There may even be environmental factors that mitigate against the expression of a schizophrenia, or alternatively there may be a number of quite separate causes for schizophrenia.

It is a good idea, when choosing material with which to answer this question, that you bear the synoptic requirement of the question in mind. As well as the genetic explanations of schizophrenia discussed in this section, there are also a number of different investigative methods used in research relating to this topic. These include *family history studies* such as the Copenhagen High-Risk Study in Denmark (p. 452), *adoption studies* such as the Finnish Adoption Study (p. 452) and *twin studies*, such as Cardno *et al.*'s study using the Maudsley Twin Register (p. 453).

A useful way to keep up to date in this topic area, as well as developing your knowledge and understanding of schizophrenia and its causes, is to use the websites listed at the end of this chapter.

Chapter summary

◆ This chapter has looked at different types of mental disorders: **phobic anxiety disorders**, **unipolar depression** and **schizophrenia**. There are many explanations of the causes of specific disorders and some have been supported by **empirical evidence** more strongly than others. However, this does not inevitably make these explanations more correct.

◆ **Twin, adoption** and **family studies** continue to provide strong, although not yet conclusive, evidence for a genetic link with schizophrenia.

◆ There is some evidence for a **genetic link** with unipolar depression, although this has not been firmly established, and evidence for a genetic link with phobias is weak. It may be that the genetic tendency is to be more sensitive to the environment and, as such, more susceptible to certain types of mental disorder, such as depression and anxiety.

◆ A **genetic predisposition** merely predisposes someone to developing a disorder, i.e. they are more or less at risk depending upon the degree of relatedness; it does *not* mean that someone who is at risk will automatically develop the disorder.

◆ **Neurological research** has highlighted possible **structural brain abnormalities** linked with schizophrenia, which could be a genetic defect, or caused through brain complications or viral infections. The structural abnormalities could even be caused by having schizophrenia, since it is still not clear whether they precede the onset of the disorder.

◆ There is no evidence for structural brain abnormalities in depression and anxiety disorders, such as phobias. There is evidence for **biochemical involvement** in both schizophrenia and depression, although it is still not clear whether this is implicated in the cause, or a physical symptom of the disorder.

◆ There is very little evidence for **social/psychological explanations of** schizophrenia, other than levels of expressed emotion, which could act as a trigger, or affect the length of remission between acute episodes. The **psychodynamic**, **behavioural** and **cognitive** approaches offer plausible psychological explanations of depression and phobias, but not for schizophrenia.

◆ The **diathesis-stress model** offers an explanation which accounts for individual differences, by suggesting a predisposition to vulnerability which interacts with environmental factors, such as stressful life events.

Further resources

Comer, R.J. (1997) *Abnormal Psychology*, New York: Freeman. Chapters 6, 8, 12 and 15.

Davison, G.C. and Neale, J.M. (1997) *Abnormal Psychology* (7th edn), New York: John Wiley.

> These two books both provide readable, comprehensive accounts of the disorders discussed in this chapter.

Oltmanns, T.F., Neale, J.M. and Davison, G.C. (1995) *Case Studies in Abnormal Psychology* (4th edn), New York: John Wiley.

> This book provides extended, detailed case studies to illustrate mental disorders.

Websites

www.artvt.com/expressed_emotion.htm

> *A short, but highly readable, essay from the Harvard Medical School on expressed emotion and the schizophrenic patient.*

http://www.mentalhealth.com/main.html

> *A major source of information about all aspects of mental health, and links to other relevant sites.*

http://www.schizophrenia.com/

> *A non-profit-making information, support and education centre focused specifically on schizophrenia.*

synoptic issues See the *Checklist of synoptic issues* (pp. 645–50) for ideas about how to use issues in this chapter for synoptic assessment.

Chapter 18

Treating mental disorders

Pamela Prentice

Preview

In this chapter we shall be looking at:

◆ biological (somatic) therapies

◆ behavioural therapies

◆ alternatives to biological and behavioural therapies, including cognitive–behavioural therapies, psychodynamic therapies and humanistic therapies.

Introduction

A number of different therapies and treatments for mental disorders will be outlined, each one based on a particular theoretical orientation regarding the basis of human nature and the causes of psychological problems. You will already be familiar with these orientations or models of mental disorder from your studies of individual differences at AS level and you may wish to refresh yourself on these before starting this chapter, as this background knowledge is essential to an understanding of therapies.

This chapter will explain the use and mode of action of each type of treatment, followed by an account of attempts made to assess the effectiveness of the treatment. There are considerable ethical issues involved with therapy and intervention. These are of particular concern to those involved in mental health, whether recipients or practitioners. Some of these issues will also be considered in this chapter.

Biological (somatic) therapies

Biological treatments follow from biological explanations for abnormal behaviour; that is, mental disorder viewed as illness and resulting mainly from a biochemical imbalance. Biological treatments are, therefore, designed to redress biochemical imbalance. This is achieved through the administration of chemical drugs and, in some cases, electro-convulsive therapy (ECT). The term 'somatic' is often used to describe biological therapies, somatic meaning 'related to the body'.

Use and mode of action of chemotherapy (drug treatments)

Medication believed to be beneficial for mental disorders are psychotropic drugs and are classified into four main types, all of which operate on the central nervous system.

◆ *Anti-anxiety drugs:* These are known as benzodiazepines and are minor tranquillizers designed to reduce levels of anxiety. Benzodiazepines such as Librium and Valium, were introduced in the 1950s and 1960s and soon became the most prescribed drugs in the world. They are sedatives which inhibit the nervous system and produce muscle relaxation and an overall calming effect. They bind to receptor sites, which produce a natural tranquillizer, and also increase the activity of the neurotransmitter GABA that alters the activity of other neurotransmitters, such as noradrenaline, producing an inhibitory effect on the brain.

◆ *Antidepressant drugs:* These are stimulants designed to alleviate depressive symptoms. Antidepressant drugs fall into three categories: tricyclics, serotonin re-uptake inhibitors and monoamine-oxidase inhibitors (MAOIs), which were the first antidepressants on the market. MAOIs are stimulants designed to alleviate depressive symptoms. They block the enzyme monoamine-oxidase preventing the breaking down of norepinephrine and serotonin, which then pool in the synapse, leading to desensitization. Tricyclics, such as Tofranil, operate in a similar way, but are milder antidepressants and, although they are slower acting, have fewer severe side effects. Prozac is the newest of the antidepressant drugs, which selectively inhibits the re-uptake of serotonin. The neurotransmitter, serotonin, is thought to play a part in mood regulation, inducing relaxation and controlling aggression.

◆ *Antipsychotic drugs:* These are neuroleptic drugs used in the treatment of schizophrenia and other psychotic disorders. Neuroleptics are major tranquillizers, the most notable being pheno-thiazines, which sedate the person and ameliorate symptoms of psychosis, such as delusions and hallucinations. An excess of the neurotransmitter dopamine has been linked with schizophrenia (see Chapter 17) and one of the actions of phenothiazine drugs is that they bind to dopamine receptors and block the build up of dopamine.

◆ *Antimanic drugs:* These are lithium salts used to control the mania in those suffering from manic-depression. They were discovered through the work of John Cade, an Australian physician. He conducted lithium carbonate tests on guinea pigs, after inducing mania by injecting urine from manic patients. Cade then tested his lithium preparation on manic patients and found that their manic euphoria had calmed within a few days. By the 1970s lithium carbonate had become the routine treatment for manic-depression.

Appropriateness and effectiveness of chemotherapy

Drug treatments have been especially beneficial in restoring faith in the medical profession as the front line for treating mental disorders, after Freud had cast a shadow of doubt on the physical origins of mental problems. Outcome studies indicate that drugs are reasonably effective for treating certain mental disorders and they are readily available, easily administered and cost-effective. However, they have considerable side effects. Table 18.1 lists general levels of effectiveness, along with potential side effects. A more detailed analysis of effectiveness is outlined in the following paragraphs.

Anti-anxiety drugs

Benzodiazepines have been found to be effective in reducing symptoms of anxiety and panic. For example, Gelernter *et al.* (1991) found them to be more effective than a placebo for social phobia and Lecrubier *et al.*

Table 18.1 Effectiveness and side effects of drug treatments

Drug treatment	Disorder	Effectiveness	Side effects
Anti-anxiety			
◆ Benzodiazepines	anxiety specific phobias panic	short-term improvement little improvement some improvement	*become less potent over time as the body builds up tolerance and requires larger dosages, which can lead to physical dependency on the drug.*
Antidepressants			
◆ Tricyclics	depression agoraphobia	moderate improvement moderate improvement	*cardiac problems, tremor, rash, mania, confusion, weight gain, memory loss, fatigue.*
◆ Serotonin re-uptake inhibitors (e.g. Prozac)	depression	moderate improvement	*nausea, nervousness, anxiety, insomnia, fever, convulsions, diarrhoea, sexual dysfunction, mania, suicidal morbidity.*
◆ MAO inhibitors	depression social phobia agoraphobia	moderate improvement moderate improvement moderate improvement	*hypertension, dizziness, fatigue, tremors, nervousness, convulsions, rashes, weight gain, mania, hallucinations, toxicity, may be fatal if taken with other antidepressants.*
Antimanic			
◆ Lithium salts	manic-depression	substantial improvement	*cardiac problems, vomiting, convulsions, tremors, gastrointestinal problems, toxicity.*
Antipsychotic			
◆ Phenothiazines	schizophrenia	partial improvement	*irregular heartbeat, low blood pressure, immobility of face, uncontrolled fidgeting, tremors, spasms, impotence, epileptic seizures, tardive dyskinesia.*

(1997) found that around 60 per cent of patients with panic disorder remained free of panic whilst on medication.

Benzodiazepines were taken up eagerly by GPs when they were first introduced because they offered a safe way to alleviate anxieties in patients. They did not lead to fatality when taken in overdose, unlike opioids, such as morphine and laudanum. These were the only drugs previously available and doctors were loath to prescribe them because of the dangers of addiction, severe side effects, overdose and potential fatality. These new drugs offered a quick and easy solution for GPs who could write a prescription rather than engage in counselling (for which few GPs are trained), thereby reducing patient consultation time. Unfortunately, benzodiazepines did not prove to be such a magic solution after all because they created dependence on the drug, sometimes for many years after the initial problem had been resolved. The frequency and willingness with which GPs prescribed benzodiazepines in the 1960s and 1970s has led to the recent development of self-help groups for people trying to overcome their long-term dependence. Most GPs are now careful to restrict such drugs to short courses. Benzodiazepines also create tolerance, which means that the dosage needs to be increased over time to produce the same beneficial effects. Dependence also leads to physical withdrawal symptoms, such as tremors, irritability and insomnia. However, Linden et al. (1998) found that neither the dosage (high or low) or length of treatment (long- or short-term) were major factors in dependence on benzodiazepines. They found that when patients were asked to take a three-week drug holiday programme, withdrawal occurred before the programme began, indicating that the dependency was psychological, rather than physical.

One of the main problems with anti-anxiety drugs is that they only treat the physical symptoms and not the cause of the anxiety. This is illustrated by the statistics that there is around a 90 per cent relapse rate when benzodiazepine medication is ceased (Fyer et al. 1987).

Antidepressants

Antidepressants have been tested in trials with placebos (e.g. Prien 1988) and found to be effective in reducing symptoms of severe depression in around 65 to 75 per cent of cases, compared to around 33 per cent for placebos. Spiegel (1989) found that around 65 per cent of depressed patients improved with tricyclics, although there are potential side effects, the most serious being cardiac problems. MAO inhibitors are equally effective and have the same side effects. The first MAOI was Iproniazid, and its antidepressant effect was discovered by accident when it was tried as a new drug for tuberculosis and found to induce euphoria. It was widely used as a treatment for depression in the late 1950s, but it was found to have a toxic effect if combined with other drugs and certain foods and drinks. It was quickly superseded by the tricyclics, such as Tofranil, which operate in a similar way, but are milder antidepressants and, although they are slower acting, have fewer severe side effects. MAOIs are still prescribed, but only with extreme caution in that they can be fatal if taken with other forms of medication. A study by Jarrett et al. (1999) found that MAOIs were much more effective than tricyclics for severe depression and Thase et al. (1991) claimed that they might be the only recourse for treating depressive episodes in manic-depression.

Prozac was hailed as the 'wonder drug' for depression when it was first introduced in the late 1980s and is currently the most frequently prescribed of all antidepressants. However, it has recently become a media target because there have been so many anecdotal reports of serious side effects, including a preoccupation with violence and suicide (Steiner 1991). Antidepressants are not so effective with children, but have been found to be very effective with older people, although with more side effects than with younger people. More recently, the natural herb hypericum, commonly known as St John's Wort, has been found in clinical trials to have antidepressant qualities with very few side effects (Holden 1997). It is thought that the herb alters serotonin function in some way.

Antipsychotic drugs

Antipsychotic drugs have provided a breakthrough in treating the symptoms of schizophrenia, such as delusions and hallucinations. Prior to the introduction of phenothiazines in the 1950s, schizophrenia was considered untreatable and patients were interned in mental institutions. As Rosenhan and Seligman (1995) vividly explain, the back wards of mental hospitals were called 'snake pits', filled with inmates who were unreachable or mutely catatonic, or were wild with delusions and straitjacketed, or were 'giggling out' unrelated words. All previous attempts to treat schizophrenia, such as insulin shock, ECT and drugs, had failed, until the introduction of phenothiazines. The American Psychiatric Association (1997) reports that phenothiazines are effective with 60 per cent of patients. These drugs have enabled many patients to live a reasonably normal life in the community. Community care has, however, proved inadequate for many people with schizophrenia, one of the problems being poor compliance with medication. Research indicates that if antipsychotic drugs are stopped abruptly and too soon, then symptoms recur (Davis et al. 1993). This has led to the 'revolving door syndrome' of continual discharge into the community and readmission into hospital.

It is estimated that around 7 per cent of people diagnosed with schizophrenia refuse to take phenothiazines (Hoge *et al.* 1990), perhaps because they have considerable side effects. They operate on dopamine receptors and, when administered to psychotic patients, can induce symptoms similar to those in Parkinson's disease, such as stiffness, immobility and tremors. The most serious side effect is tardive dyskinesia, which includes uncontrollable, frog-like sucking and smacking of the lips. It is thought that phenothiazines destroy a part of the brain and, once begun, this process is irreversible. It occurs in around 30 per cent of those taking the drug and the risk increases with prolonged usage (Gualtieri 1991). A note of optimism is that newer types of neuroleptics, such as Clozapine and Risperidone (introduced in 1990) are reported to have far fewer side effects (American Psychiatric Association 1997). However, other studies (e.g. Umbricht and Kane 1996) have found side effects that may be potentially life-threatening. Despite side effects, drugs continue to be the main form of treatment for psychotic disorders because other forms of therapy, such as psychotherapy, have traditionally been thought to have little effect.

Antimanic drugs

Lithium salts (e.g. lithium carbonate) have been found to be effective for around 80 per cent of patients with manic-depression (Rosenhan and Seligman 1995). Prior to their introduction, 15 per cent of manic-depressives committed suicide and a large proportion were unable to function properly in daily life because of their extreme mood swings. Many patients, however, are loath to take medication because they like being in a euphoric state (Johnson *et al.* 1989) and because lithium carbonate has side effects. It is toxic and can lead to gastrointestinal and cardiac problems, and even death. Another problem is that if a person starts on lithium and then discontinues it, its future use can increase the risk of manic-depressive episodes (Suppes *et al.* 1991). Although lithium has been found to be effective for mania, studies (e.g. Gitlin *et al.* 1995) in a five-year prospective study) indicate that around 70 per cent of people relapse whilst on medication.

General evaluation of chemotherapy

There has traditionally been a good deal of criticism levelled at the use of chemotherapy for psychological problems, particularly in mental institutions where patients have no choice. Are they administered to alleviate suffering in the patient, or to sedate patients so they are more compliant with institutional regimes? As a result of such criticism, there has recently been greater emphasis on voluntary agreement and the right to refuse treatment. There are, however, two sides to this debate – the right to refuse versus the consequences of non-compliance. For example, some patients with schizophrenia are genuinely very dangerous unless sedated with major tranquillizers. Ensuring that such patients stay on their regime of drugs was not too difficult in the days of mental institutions, but in the current climate of civil rights and care in the community, this is not so straightforward. Issues of compliance with medication have become high profile in recent years after some innocent bystanders have been attacked by schizophrenia outpatients (see *In Focus*, 'Fatal stabbing by schizophrenia patient'). Compliance with medication can, however, have adverse effects if drugs have not been accurately prescribed. For example, neuroleptic drugs can produce the symptoms of schizophrenia in people without a psychotic disorder (see *In Focus*, 'It was the drugs that made me mad').

Combining drugs and psychological treatments

It has now become clear that drugs do not necessarily offer a long-term cure, because in many cases symptoms recur when the drugs are no longer taken. It is believed by many psychologists that biochemical imbalance is the result of, rather than the cause of, mental disorders. This leads to the claim that drugs merely treat the symptoms (e.g. the anxiety or depression), but do not address the cause of the problem (e.g. why the person is anxious or depressed). Consequently, they can only provide short-term alleviation. Given that there are also numerous side effects from drugs, as shown in Table 18.1, one wonders whether the benefits could ever outweigh the costs, particularly if the initial problems still remain.

Fatal stabbing by schizophrenia patient

In Torquay in September 1993, Andrew Robinson stabbed a nurse in the face and neck. She remained conscious, but paralysed, and died five days later. Robinson suffered from paranoid schizophrenia and had a 15-year history of violence. This led to a government inquiry into community care, which recommended new powers of supervision for mental patients in the community and legal powers to enforce compliance with medication. The National Association for Mental Health (MIND) expressed concern that the government might use this one isolated case as a basis for an overhaul in the law.

'It was the drugs that made me mad'

In a report in *The Independent* (4.10.94), Adam Sandall reported on a 43-year-old woman who was anorexic and who had been prescribed drugs which had nightmare effects for 22 years. Jane was a top student at school, in academics and in sports and drama and she had lots of boyfriends. Unfortunately she felt that everything she did was for others and when she started slimming, she felt that this was for herself. However, her health quickly started to deteriorate and she was referred to a London hospital. There she was treated with ECT and neuroleptic drugs. They did not help her condition and her anorexia continued. She was then diagnosed as manic-depressive and later as schizophrenic. When she left hospital, she could not hold down a job and began living rough. Her weight continued to drop until it was below four stone and she was admitted to a psychiatric hospital. There she put on weight, left hospital and married.

Several years later, still on medication, Jane had another breakdown, believing that her husband was interfering with her brain and feeling that she was getting madder. This time Jane was referred to a different psychiatrist who suggested she cease taking the drugs. She went through a two-year period of withdrawal, which she said was 'hell' and included bizarre physical symptoms, panic attacks and insomnia. Eventually, she started to feel better and actually began to laugh again. Jane is convinced that she was suffering from 'toxic psychosis' – the effect of the drugs she had been prescribed for so many years. Her new psychiatrist explained that, whilst neuroleptic drugs are effective in treating schizophrenia, the side effects can mimic psychotic symptoms in people who are not schizophrenic. Adapting to her new life has not been easy for Jane, but she is finding that drawing is helping her tremendously as she tries to forget the past 22 years.

Activity 1: Benefits vs side effects of drugs

Do you think the potential benefits (effectiveness) of drug treatment outweigh the potential costs (side effects), described in Table 18.1? Remember, if you, or a member of your family, were suffering from a mental disorder, you might think differently.

Many people, however, prefer drugs. This may be because taking medicine is a familiar activity, whereas psychological treatment is unfamiliar territory and many people feel cautious, or even threatened, by the thought of it.

For psychological therapies to be effective, the client or patient must have some insight, in so much as they must recognise that they have a problem. Some people suffering from chronic psychotic disorders have little or no insight and therefore psychological treatment is difficult, although for many psychotic patients insight is regained during periods of remission from acute psychotic episodes. With the assistance of phenothiazines, which reduce psychotic symptoms such as delusions and hallucinations, psychotic patients can be 'more available' to psychological therapies, such as insight therapies and family therapy. Short courses of antidepressant drugs can be worthwhile in cases of severe clinical depression, because without these drugs, patients often have no motivation to engage in psychological treatment. Antidepressants may even be essential, as a first line of treatment for severe clinical depression, because of the high risk of suicide. These examples illustrate ways that somatic treatment and psychological treatment can work together, rather than as alternative forms of treatment.

Use and mode of action of electro-convulsive therapy (ECT)

ECT was originally developed by Cerletti and tested as a treatment for schizophrenia in 1938. It was found to be ineffective in reducing psychotic symptoms, but very effective in alleviating severe depression in some people. ECT involves the passage of electrical current through the brain by the application of between 70 and 130 volts which induces a convulsion or epileptic seizure. The convulsion is thought to act upon neurochemical transmission in a way that improves the person's mood state. The original procedure was bilateral, i.e. the current passed through both cerebral hemispheres of the brain. The patient was awake prior to the seizure. The contortions of the body produced by the original procedure have now been minimized by a newer procedure, where a strong muscle relaxant and an anaesthetic are given prior to treatment.

The procedure used now is also unilateral, passing the current through the non-dominant hemisphere only (Abrams *et al.* 1991).

Appropriateness and effectiveness of ECT

ECT is a controversial treatment, not least because the medical profession is still unsure of how it works – an analogy has been drawn with kicking the side of the television set to make it work. ECT has, however, been successful in treating severe depression in patients where all other methods have failed and many argue that this is sufficient justification for its use, especially if it prevents suicide. It is a quick form of treatment, in contrast to drugs or psychological therapies, and Klerman (1988) maintains that ECT may be the optimal treatment for severe depression. Studies indicate that 60 to 70 per cent of patients improve with ECT (e.g. Sackeim 1988), although a large proportion of these become depressed again the following year (Sackeim *et al.* 1993). ECT should only be administered if antidepressant drugs have no effect and if there is a risk that the person will commit suicide. ECT has been found to be beneficial to those who have not responded to antidepressant drugs, although it has been found that the relapse rate is high if it is followed by the same ineffective antidepressant drugs (Sackeim *et al.* 1990). With acute mania, ECT has been found to be effective in around 80 per cent of people who had not responded to medication (Mukherjee *et al.* 1994).

When ECT was first introduced, there were dangerous side effects, such as bone fractures, memory loss and confusion. There are no detectable changes in brain structure with the newer unilateral procedure and, as the technique is continually improved, side effects are being reduced. Studies examining cognitive side effects have confirmed this. For example, Devanand *et al.* (1994) found no evidence of long-term memory loss or any other longer-term cognitive changes. Nevertheless, ECT remains controversial; it requires consent from the patient or a close relative and is only used when other methods have failed. Although techniques are improving, there continues to be a decline in the use of ECT. Comer (1995) suggests three reasons for this:

◆ Applying an electrical current to the brain is a frightening and forceful form of intervention and even with the newer techniques there are still side effects, especially with repeated use.

◆ ECT has a history of abuse, being used as a means of punishing or controlling people in mental hospitals, with some people having received hundreds of ECT treatments.

◆ Effective antidepressant drugs now provide a more attractive alternative.

Use and mode of action of psychosurgery

Psychosurgery is an extreme form of biological treatment. It involves the cutting of neural tissue in the brain and was designed to alter the symptoms of severe psychological disorders. The first technique was the *lobotomy*, developed in the 1940s by Egas Moniz, a Portuguese neurologist, as a cure for schizophrenia. This involved severing the connection between the frontal cortex and the lower centres of the brain. Moniz was awarded the 1949 Nobel Prize for medicine, along with Walter Hess. In the 1960s this procedure was replaced by the *prefrontal leukotomy*, thought to be less extreme, which involved drilling two holes in either side of the skull and inserting a pointed instrument to sever nerve fibres. A more recent procedure is the *cingulotomy*, where a tiny cut is made in the cingulum nerve fibres, using an electrode needle which is guided by magnetic resonance imaging, making the procedure far more precise.

Psychosurgery continues to be regarded as the most controversial of all treatments for mental disorders. The procedure is irreversible because neural tissue has been destroyed and there is no guarantee that the procedure will have a beneficial effect. Significant detrimental effects were found with the earlier lobotomy operation, such as withdrawal, stupors, seizures and even death. The more recent leukotomy procedure is less severe, but there are still dangers involved. According to Beck and Cowley (1990), the procedure is beneficial in some cases of severe anxiety, depression and obsessive-compulsive disorders. Nowadays, psychosurgery is performed only in extreme cases when all other forms of treatment have failed and where, because of the disorder, the person is likely to cause harm to themselves or to others.

Appropriateness and effectiveness of psychosurgery

Psychosurgery has come under attack more than any other treatment for mental disorders. Comer (1995) explains that psychosurgery was performed on tens of thousands of people in the 1950s as a response to overcrowding in mental institutions and the absence of effective treatments for many serious mental disorders. Comer (1995) also explains that there was concern in the US about the suspected use of psychosurgery to control perpetrators of violent crimes. The lobotomy also became a civil rights issue with claims that it was being used as a means of silencing political activists and of controlling difficult mental patients in institutions. Disturbing films, such as *One Flew over the Cuckoo's Nest*, based on Ken Kesey's book and released in 1975, have provided a vivid portrait of the consequences of enforced biological treatment, culminating in psychosurgery. In addition, accusations levelled at the medical profession by the antipsychiatry movement in the 1960s, have instilled doubts about the true purpose of surgical treatments for mental disorders.

A particularly controversy with biological treatments has been the issue of informed consent to treatment. Certain people, including children, those with learning impairments and people with psychotic disorders, may not be able to give informed consent for treatment owing to a lack of insight into their problem and, in the case of psychosis, a loss of contact with reality. For this reason, it has been possible for clinicians to administer biological treatments, in the form of medication, ECT and even psychosurgery, without informed consent from the patient. This is particularly so in the case of treatment administered to someone who has been detained under sectioning laws, where it is usually decided by the consultant psychiatrist. However, the Mental Health Act for England and Wales 1983 states that the patient's consent is now required for psychosurgery, along with a second opinion by an independent doctor.

Exam summary: Biological (somatic) therapies

The AQA examination will test your understanding of the following areas:

◆ use and mode of action of: chemotherapy (pp. 459–60), ECT (pp. 463–4), psychosurgery (p. 464)

◆ issues surrounding use of: chemotherapy (pp. 460–3), ECT (p. 464), psychosurgery (p. 464–5).

Example question

The question below is typical of one drawn from the material above, and should take you 45 minutes:

(a) Outline the use and mode of action of two biological (somatic) therapies. *(15 marks)*

(b) Assess the issues surrounding the use of these two therapies. *(15 marks)*

Suggested answer structure

This question is different from other questions that you may have encountered elsewhere in these A2 chapters. It differs in a number of important ways:

◆ Questions in the *Individual Differences* section of the specification are worth 30 marks rather than 24.

◆ Questions in the *Individual Differences* section and the *Perspectives* section (Assessment Unit 5) are marked on a different set of marking criteria (see Table 21.3 on p. 554).

◆ The time allowance for these questions is 45 minutes rather than 30 minutes. This means that the

average length of an answer is closer to 800 words rather than the average of 600 words for questions from Assessment Unit 4.

◆ This extra time allowance is to allow for the synoptic element of the question (see p. 553).

This section has covered the use and mode of action of three types of biological therapy – chemotherapy (pp. 459–60), electroconvulsive therapy (pp. 463–4) and psychosurgery (p. 464). The question asks for *two* of these. In case you are tempted, there is absolutely nothing to be gained by outlining more than the two required. As you have approximately 22 minutes for this part of the question, that gives you about 11 minutes for each outline. For example, if you chose to outline the use and action of chemotherapy, you might describe the different classes of drugs used in the treatment of mental disorders:

◆ anti-anxiety drugs (such as the benzodiazepines Librium and Valium)

◆ antidepressant drugs (such as the selective serotonin re-uptake inhibitor (SSRI) Prozac)

◆ antipsychotic drugs (neuroleptic drugs such as the phenothiazines)

◆ antimanic drugs (such as lithium carbonate).

For the second part of the question, you are required to assess (i.e. point out both the strengths *and* limitations of) your two chosen therapies. You will find the page references for your two chosen therapies at the beginning of this exam summary. Chemotherapy has been found to be effective for mental disorders, although there may be considerable side effects associated with drug treatments. A criticism levelled at chemotherapy is that drugs only treat biological symptoms and not the cause of many mental disorders, which may have social or psychological origins rather than physical ones. Drugs are a less expensive method of treating mental disorders than psychological treatment, although if they are not dealing with the underlying cause, then symptoms may return when medication is ceased. A further problem with chemotherapy is that drugs used in the treatment of mental disorders create dependence.

ECT has been used effectively in the treatment of depression, although it does not work for everyone and, although the newer methods have minimized physical side effects, there are still potential cognitive side effects, such as memory impairments.

Psychosurgery is now rarely conducted, except in extreme circumstances where a person's life may be in danger. Full, informed consent is now required for both ECT and psychosurgery.

Behavioural therapies

Behavioural therapies emerged in the 1950s and are a logical extension to behaviourism as applied to the field of psychopathology. The main assumption of the behavioural view is that abnormal behaviour, and even mental disorders, are acquired in the same way as normal behaviour, through the principles of classical and operant conditioning, and social learning theory. Therefore, just as it is learned, the behaviour can equally be unlearned.

Use and mode of action of behavioural therapies

Over the past 30 or 40 years, a number of therapeutic techniques have been developed out of the learning paradigm, with the overall aim of encouraging adaptive strategies to enable the person to function more effectively in the environment. The first stage in behavioural therapy is a 'functional analysis' to assess the person's level of functioning, identify the stimulus antecedents to maladaptive responses, and to decide upon the most appropriate treatment techniques. Techniques derived from classical conditioning and operant conditioning are described below.

Behavioural therapies based on classical conditioning

◆ *Systematic desensitization:* This technique, devised by Wolpe (1958), was developed specifically to counter-condition fears, phobias and anxieties. The therapist works with the client to compile a hierarchical list of feared situations, starting with those that arouse minimal anxiety, progressing to those that are the most frightening. The person is first encouraged to relax and then to progress through graded exposure from the least fearful situation to the more difficult situations over a number of sessions. The principle behind this technique is to replace the conditioned fear response with one of relaxation. It is the pairing of relaxation with the feared stimulus that induces the desensitization effect. This technique can either be conducted either *in vitro* (through imagined imagery) or *in vivo* (real-life).

◆ *Flooding* (also known as 'implosion'): Quicker and often thought to be more effective than systematic desensitization, the philosophy is that if someone refuses to face up to their fear, that fear will never be overcome and may even grow in strength. Flooding is a technique whereby the person is asked to remain with the fear, experiencing the full impact of their anxiety state. Physiologically, it is

Activity 2: Tackling fears

In pairs or small groups, think about a specific fear that one of you has. Write down a hierarchy of graded exposure in line with systematic desensitization, starting with the least fearful situation relating to the specific fear, through a number of systematic steps of increasing fearfulness, and ending with the most frightening situation.

not possible to maintain a state of high anxiety for a very long period, and so eventually it will subside. This transition through the anxiety shows the person that they are still safe and that nothing dreadful has happened to them. Thus the fear should be extinguished. For ethical reasons, this technique is conducted mainly in *vitro* and the therapist should first ensure that the person is in good physical health.

◆ *Aversion therapy:* This was developed from studies with animals which showed that the pairing of an unpleasant stimulus, such as an electric shock, with a neutral stimulus can produce negative reactions, or 'aversion' to the neutral stimulus. This has formed the basis of 'aversion therapy', which was developed to deal with habits and addictions. Here the therapist attempts to attach negative feelings to stimuli that are considered inappropriate. An example of this is smoking. This is achieved through pairing the taste of tobacco with a feeling of nausea, for example by inserting a nausea-inducing substance into cigarettes. The major problem with this technique is that it is doubtful that aversion will continue once the negative pairing has been discontinued.

Appropriateness and effectiveness of techniques based on classical conditioning

Behavioural therapies based on classical conditioning are considered to be very appropriate methods of treatment for anxiety disorders, such as phobias and post-traumatic stress disorder, and for addictions, although they are not regarded as suitable for psychotic disorders such as schizophrenia. These methods are widely adopted by clinical psychologists within the NHS and are relatively quick, usually taking just a few months, in contrast to psychodynamic therapies that usually last several years. They are also very effective in group therapy. The treatment is structured, the goals are clear, and clinical progress is measurable.

The efficacy of behavioural techniques has been shown to be quite high. McGrath *et al.* (1990) claimed that systematic desensitization is effective for around 75 per cent of people with specific phobias. Comer (1995) cites an interesting study on 'flooding', conducted by Hogen and Kirchner (1967). Twenty-one people with a phobia for rats were asked to imagine themselves having their fingers nibbled and being clawed by rats. After treatment, 20 were able to open a rat's cage and 14 could actually pick up the rat. *In vivo* techniques are found to be more effective for specific phobias than *in vitro* (Menzies and Clarke 1993). Agoraphobia is one of the most difficult phobias to treat, yet systematic desensitization has facilitated improvement for between 60 and 80 per cent of cases (Craske and Barlow 1993). However, improvements are shown to be only partial and in 50 per cent of cases relapses occur. Barlow and Lehman (1996) reviewed evidence for the effectiveness of behavioural therapies. They report that for specific phobias, graded exposure (systematic desensitization) was very effective and the preferred choice of patients. They also report that for blood-injection-injury types of phobias (see Table 17.1 on p. 430), 90 per cent of patients are cured in around five sessions of graded exposure. These are people who might previously have avoided receiving necessary health and dental care. Ost *et al.* (1991) conducted a study whereby the whole hierarchy of feared stimuli were presented in a single session over several hours. This was with 20 patients with spider phobias and Ost and colleagues found that, no matter how severe the phobia, 90 per cent were much improved or completely recovered at a four-year follow-up. Ost *et al.* (1992) repeated their results in a further study with blood phobia patients. Of course, it should be borne in mind that reported recovery might not have been a direct consequence of the one session of behavioural therapy received four years earlier.

A number of studies comparing different types of therapy have found systematic desensitization to be equally effective for phobias when administered alone, or in combination with other treatments, such as medication or cognitive–behavioural therapy (e.g. Burke *et al.* 1997). A study conducted by Beurs *et al.* (1995) compared systematic desensitization with cognitive–behavioural therapy (see next section) and also included pharmacological treatment, plus a placebo group. Their sample comprised 96 patients diagnosed with panic disorder with agoraphobia, randomly assigned into the four groups:

◆ medication followed by graded exposure

◆ placebo medication followed by graded exposure

◆ cognitive–behavioural therapy (in the form of panic management), followed by graded exposure

◆ graded exposure alone.

They were all given 12 weekly treatment sessions. Beurs and colleagues found all four treatments to be effective in decreasing agoraphobic avoidance, but the combination of medication and systematic desensitization was twice as effective as the other three, which were all about equal.

Critics of behaviourist methods point out that quite often people with phobias have no recollection of any traumatic experience involving the object of their fear. Psychoanalytic theorists (see later in this chapter) claim that this is because the phobia is merely a symptom, a conscious manifestation of the underlying cause, a signal from the unconscious that something is wrong. Bandura (1969) argued that if underlying is defined as 'not immediately obvious', then behaviour therapists do indeed look for underlying causes. The task is for the therapist to work with the client to find the most significant causes.

Behavioural therapies based on operant conditioning

◆ *Token economy:* This is a behaviour modification programme based on Skinner's (1953) principle of behaviour shaping through positive reinforcement. In exchange for desirable behaviour, the person will receive rewards in the form of tokens, which can be exchanged for goods, outings or privileges. Token economy has been applied extensively in institutions, mainly with psychotic patients, and with people who have severe learning difficulties. Although it has been claimed that it is difficult to sustain the modified behaviour beyond the institution, the intention is that positive reinforcement will be elicited naturally from others in the environment as a consequence of correct behaviour.

◆ *Social skills training:* Bandura's (1969) 'social learning theory' is an extension of operant conditioning, to include learning through observing and modelling the behaviour of others. Originally, Bandura applied the concept of 'modelling' as a treatment for phobias, but more recently, modelling has been applied widely in the development of social skills training, particularly in assertiveness and interpersonal skills training. The technique involves behaviour rehearsal in the form of role-play and feedback. People are encouraged to practise appropriate responses to replace maladaptive responses in the safety of a role-play situation. Skills training is thought to be particularly helpful for people with low self-esteem, for those who are anxious in social situations and for those who are often exploited by others.

Appropriateness and effectiveness of techniques based on operant conditioning

According to social learning theory, phobias can develop through observing those fears in significant others and modelling behaviour upon those observations. Bandura supported the effectiveness of using modelling in the treatment of phobias in a clinical study of 48 nursery children with dog phobias (Bandura and Menlove 1968) and with adults with snake phobias (Bandura *et al.* 1969), claiming a 90 per cent success rate.

When agreeing to a particular therapy, the patient or client, and to some degree the therapist, cannot always anticipate what may occur during the course of therapy. This has been a major criticism of behavioural therapies, in particular the technique of 'flooding'. Even when conducted *in vitro* (using imagination or video films) rather than *in vivo* (real life), there may be dangerous consequences of hyperventilation, raised blood pressure or heart attacks. As such, this procedure should not be undertaken without adequate training and proper medical supervision. Aversion therapy has also come under attack because it breaches ethical guidelines in its use of induced pain or nausea as aversive stimuli.

Programmes of behaviour modification, such as token economy programmes do not offer a cure for mental disorders; they are merely intended to enable patients to 'fit' better into their social world. For example, chronic psychiatric patients often have no motivation to maintain personal hygiene and therefore tokens can be earned for washing, brushing hair, etc. The intention is to give the person back some dignity. The natural rewards that will eventually replace the tokens to reinforce the behaviour are that others will be more sympathetic towards them. Token economy has been widely adopted in psychiatric institutions with psychotic patients and found to be very effective in reducing inappropriate behaviour (Emmelkamp 1994). It has been suggested, however, that the so-called success of this therapy may have more to do with its requirement for closer interaction between patient and nurse, suggesting that it is the attention that is therapeutic rather than the technique. Behavioural methods have provided an opportunity for nursing staff to become far more involved in treatment, which may have increased their investment in helping the patient.

Token economy has been widely administered in institutions, but has been open to criticism with regard to the choice of goals, which may actually go against the patient's wishes. What is regarded as desirable behaviour is often designed to serve the institution on the pretext of serving the recipient. Whenever goals are imposed by others, then desirable behaviour is inevitably influenced by personal or institutional bias, even when the goal is truly believed to be for the client's own good. One of the major criticisms of token economy is that, in order to be effective, important reinforcements need to be controlled, which may violate basic human rights, such as restrictions on food, privacy and freedom of movement. Comer (1995) explains that boundaries have now been set on basic rights that clinicians cannot violate, but this may reduce the impact of token economy programmes. One of the saddest consequences of token economy programmes is that people become dependent on the regime and find it very difficult to think for themselves when outside the institutional setting. This has been the case with many people who have recently found themselves back in the community after prolonged institutional care.

Exam summary: Behavioural therapies

The AQA examination will test your understanding of the following areas:

◆ use and mode of action of therapies based on classical conditioning (p. 466) and on operant conditioning (p. 467)

◆ issues surrounding the use of therapies based on classical conditioning (pp. 466–7) and on operant conditioning (p. 468).

Example question

The question below is typical of one drawn from the material above, and should take you 45 minutes to answer:

(a) Outline the use and mode of action of two behavioural therapies. *(15 marks)*

(b) Assess the issues surrounding the use of behavioural therapies (e.g. appropriateness and effectiveness). *(15 marks)*

Suggested answer structure

This question is very similar to the question at the end of the previous section, therefore most of the comments there also apply here. We have examined two classes of behavioural therapies. These are therapies based on *classical conditioning* and therapies based on *operant conditioning*. The page references for each of these are detailed above. Therapies based on classical conditioning that are covered here are:

◆ systematic desensitization – the conditioned fear response is replaced by one of relaxation

◆ flooding – the person faces up to the feared situation, and because nothing happens, the fear is eventually extinguished

◆ aversion therapy – the therapist attempts to attach negative feelings to stimuli that are considered to be inappropriate.

Therapies based on operant conditioning that are covered here are:

◆ token economy – in exchange for desirable behaviour, the person will receive rewards in the form of tokens, which can be exchanged for various privileges

◆ social skills training – the person learns desirable behaviours by observing them in others.

From this choice of five different therapies, you are required to select two and outline why they are *used*, and how they work (*mode of action*). This first part of the question constitutes the AO1 component.

In the second part of this question, you are required to *assess* the issues surrounding the use of behavioural therapies. Two examples of appropriate issues are given in the question (i.e. appropriateness and effectiveness), but these are only examples – the choice is yours.

Systematic desensitization has been found to be very effective in the treatment of anxieties and phobias, although critics claim that this method only treats the symptoms and not the cause of the problems. Indeed, it has been shown that quite often symptoms recur at a later date, sometimes in a different form. However, for some it does work effectively and it offers a quick way of being able to function better on a daily basis. Aversion therapy has not been found to be effective in the longer term. Social skills training has been applied successfully in a number of contexts and token economy programmes are still widely employed in institutions. However, these have been criticized on the grounds of basic human rights.

A particular disadvantage of behavioural therapies is that they only deal with behavioural symptoms, and theorists of other orientations claim that thinking and emotions have a large role in mental disorders.

Alternatives to biological and behavioural therapies

Use and mode of action of cognitive–behavioural therapies

Cognitive–behavioural therapies began in the 1960s. Albert Ellis (1962) founded *rational-emotive therapy* (RET) which he subsequently renamed *rational-emotive-behaviour* therapy (REBT). Aaron Beck (1976) developed a cognitive therapy for depression and Donald Meichenbaum (1975) developed a cognitive–behavioural therapy for stress management. The rationale for all cognitive–behavioural therapies is that thoughts (cognitions) interact with, and have an enormous influence on, emotions and behaviour. When these thoughts are persistently negative and irrational, they can result in maladaptive behaviour. Ellis (1962) maintained that people can become habituated to their disturbed thoughts and this results in problems such as anxiety and depression. Ellis (1991) devised the ABC model (see Fig. 18.1 on p. 470) to illustrate how irrational, self-defeating thoughts can lead to maladaptive behaviour. Although cognitive–behavioural therapists do not disregard what has happened in the past, the focus of therapy is on the person's current state of functioning.

Cognitive–behavioural therapy is *active* and *directive,* and it involves a collaborative enterprise between therapist and client. The aim of therapy is to help the client to identify their negative, irrational thoughts and to replace these with more positive, rational ways of thinking. A therapy session includes both cognitive and behavioural elements, with homework between sessions.

◆ *Cognitive element:* The therapist encourages the client to become aware of beliefs which contribute to anxiety or depression, or are associated with a general dysfunction in daily life. This involves direct Socratic questioning, such as: 'Tell me what you think about ...'. The therapist does not comment upon the irrational or biased nature of these beliefs, instead they are treated as hypotheses and examined for validity. Diagrams (such as the ABC model) can be used to help the client understand better where their faulty cognitions are leading them. The therapist and client also conduct a cost–benefit analysis, examining the advantages and disadvantages of particular beliefs.

◆ *Behavioural element:* The therapist and client decide together how these hypotheses can be reality-tested through experimentation. Experiments can be conducted through role-play during the session or better still through homework assignments. The aim is that by actively testing out possibilities, clients will themselves come to recognize the consequences of their faulty cognitions. The therapist and client then work together to set new goals for the client in order that more realistic and rational beliefs are incorporated into ways of thinking. These are usually in graded stages of difficulty so that clients can build upon their own success.

As a cognitive–behavioural theorist, Meichenbaum (1972) suggested that it is not a situation itself which causes anxiety, but the negative way that we talk to ourselves in relation to a situation. Meichenbaum developed 'stress inoculation therapy' (SIT), which he

Figure 18.1
An example of the ABC model in action
Source: Prentice (1995), adapted from Ellis (1991)

A: Activating event

Linda gets a low mark in her mock exam for A level psychology.

B: Beliefs (about A)

Rational thoughts
Linda tells herself that she could have done better, but did not put in enough revision.

Irrational thoughts
Linda tells herself that she should have done well and this means she will fail in her final exams.

C: Consequences (of B)

Desirable emotions
Linda feels disappointed with her own efforts.

Undesirable emotions
Linda feels that she must be awful at psychology.

Desirable behaviour
Linda resolves to put in more effort for her final exams.

Undesirable behaviour
Linda decides to give up college.

Activity 3: An activating event

Think about a recent activating event (A). Did you follow the rational or the irrational route, as illustrated in Fig. 18.1?

---

also called 'self-instructional training' (again SIT). This therapy has been extensively developed within stress management training and has been widely adopted in industry (see *In Focus*).

Appropriateness and effectiveness of cognitive–behavioural therapies

Like the older behavioural therapies, cognitive–behavioural therapies are structured, with clear goals and measurable outcomes. They are increasingly becoming the most widely employed therapy by clinical psychologists in the National Health Service (NHS), not least because they are short-term and therefore economic.

Meichenbaum has concentrated on stress management and his techniques have been widely used in industry and education. Meichenbaum (1975) evaluated his model with anxious college students before exams. He compared his own cognitive modification methods with traditional systematic

desensitization, plus a third group of waiting list controls. Students were given eight therapy sessions, evaluated through test performance and self-reports obtained immediately after treatment and at a one-month follow-up. The cognitive modification methods were found to be the most effective, followed by the systematic desensitization group, with controls remaining just as anxious.

Cognitive–behavioural therapies appeal to clients who find insight therapies (which delve into inner emotional conflicts) too threatening. Although they are subject to the criticism that they do not address underlying causes, cognitive–behavioural therapies attempt to empower clients by educating them into self-help strategies. However, despite this, many clients do become dependent upon their therapist.

Ellis (1980) maintains that REBT is appropriate for any kind of psychological problem, such as anxiety disorders, sexual problems and depression, but not for severe mental disturbance, where the person cannot be treated with talking therapies. He maintains that REBT helps clients to 'cure' themselves in an elegant way because it can be incorporated into their way of life. Haaga and Davison (1989) found REBT to be effective for anger, aggression, depression and antisocial behaviour, although not as effective as systematic desensitization in reducing anxiety. Engels *et al.* (1993) examined quantitative data from 28 controlled studies which showed REBT to be superior to placebo and no

Meichenbaum's 'stress inoculation therapy'

Meichenbaum's 'stress inoculation therapy' is based upon the belief we are often unaware of the negative way that we talk to ourselves and it is this, rather than a given situation itself, that causes anxiety. Negative self-speech, or what Meichenbaum calls 'self-defeating internal dialogue', such as anticipating failure and minimizing strengths, creates anxiety, which in turn produces a self-fulfilling prophesy, because high levels of anxiety lead to poor performance. The aim of stress management training is to redirect self-speech into something more positive and confidence building. The Meichenbaum Model consists of three phases:

Phase 1: Identifying the problem

This first phase is often called the 'educational phase', the aim being to identify and examine faulty internal dialogues which lead to inadequate behaviour, e.g. 'In the exams I will forget everything I know', leads to 'I will forget, therefore I am going to fail'. This in turn leads to maladaptive behaviour, e.g. dizziness, fainting, mental blanks, which then leads to a self-fulfilling prophesy of failure.

Phase 2: Acquiring coping skills

The aim now is to examine these self-defeating dialogues for validity (it is usually found that negative statements are rarely based in reality). The next step is to re-structure thinking by converting these negative self-dialogues into positive self-statements – what Meichenbaum calls 'preparation statements', e.g. 'I'm going to do better than I thought' or 'I've coped with situations like this before'.

Phase 3: Practising coping responses

Having devised a number of preparation statements, the final phase is to practise these continually until they become automatic and replace the previous self-defeating dialogues.

treatment, but only equally effective when compared with systematic desensitization or combination therapies (those combining REBT with some form of behaviour therapy). A more recent appraisal by Haaga and Davison (1993) suggests that there are difficulties in evaluating the effectiveness of REBT because of the difficulty in defining and measuring 'irrational beliefs'.

Beck's work has centred mainly on depression. He devised the 'Beck Depression Inventory', which is an assessment scale for depression, and from this many more have been devised, such as the 'Suicide Intent Scale'. These scales have been widely adopted by clinical psychologists to monitor depression in clients, and employed by researchers for outcome studies. Beck has subsequently applied his techniques to phobias and anxieties (Beck et al. 1985) and to personality disorders (Beck et al. 1990). The concept of irrational beliefs has been tested and supported empirically (e.g. Beck 1991). In outcome studies on depression, cognitive–behavioural therapies have been found to be equally or more effective than drugs (e.g. Hollon et al. 1992). Long-term follow-up studies have also shown that the relapse rate is lower in those who received cognitive–behavioural therapy (Evans et al. 1992).

Cognitive–behavioural therapy (CBT) is thought to be particularly effective for depression and anxiety disorders and sexual problems. It has also been widely employed in stress management. A number of studies have compared this therapy with traditional chemotherapy (antidepressant drugs) in the treatment of major depression. Some have found CBT to be more effective (e.g. Seligman et al. 1979) whilst others have not. The predominance of studies find both types of therapy equally effective although, of course, cognitive–behavioural therapies have no physical side effects. A study by Jarrett et al. (1999) found CBT and MAOI antidepressant drugs to be equally effective with 108 patients with severe depression in a 10-week trial. Hollon et al. (1992) found no difference between cognitive–behavioural therapy and treatment with tricyclics (antidepressant drugs) with 107 patients over a 12-week trial. They also found no difference between CBT alone and CBT combined with antidepressant drugs. Hollon and colleagues claimed that relapse often occurs when people cease medication; however, with CBT the effect is maintained beyond the termination of therapy. They point out, however, that only about 40 per cent of those who begin treatment – either drugs or psychological therapy – will complete it. One of the difficulties with studies of this kind is that they are generally undertaken with small samples and over too short a period of time to assess the longer-term effectiveness. Another difficulty is that a control group (no treatment) is essential and these people often exert their right to withdraw in order to seek treatment themselves.

A number of studies have compared traditional behavioural, graded exposure treatment (systematic desensitization) with CBT and graded exposure combined. Burke et al. (1997) hypothesized that graded exposure would be more effective if the rationale was related in cognitive terms (i.e. by presenting this as an opportunity to challenge negative thoughts), rather than a strictly behavioural rationale. They tested this with two groups of females with agoraphobia, balanced for age, severity and duration of the phobia, and the presence of panic. One group was given the cognitive rationale for graded exposure, with prior CBT whereby they were taught to identify and challenge negative thoughts; the other group was given only a behavioural rationale. Each group was given 10 sessions, and was assessed at the end of the sessions and six months later. Burke and colleagues found that both groups had improved equally, with no significant difference six months after treatment. They concluded that CBT does not add to the effectiveness of graded exposure in the treatment of agoraphobia. However, the sample size was very small – they started with 39 people and 13 dropped out. Burke and colleagues themselves also point out that a six-month follow-up may not have been long enough to test whether CBT is more effective in preventing relapse. A similar study was conducted with people diagnosed with agoraphobia by Beurs et al. (1995). They found that CBT combined with graded exposure was not superior to graded exposure alone. Although CBT was found to be effective in a number of comparative studies, it has not been found to add to the effectiveness of behavioural treatments for phobic disorders. It should be borne in mind, however, that these studies did not test CBT alone versus graded exposure alone.

In a review of behavioural versus cognitive–behavioural therapy for anxiety disorders, Barlow and Lehman (1996) found CBT to be the most effective for generalized anxiety disorder and social phobia, but behavioural therapy was found to be more effective for specific phobias and obsessive-compulsive disorder. A study by Brent et al. (1997) with 107 adolescents diagnosed with major depression, compared individual CBT, systematic behaviour family therapy and individual supportive therapy (see 'Humanistic therapy' later in this chapter). They found CBT to be the most effective, with a more rapid and complete treatment response. Brent and colleagues felt that the rapidity of improvement was an important factor because a significant proportion of severely depressed adolescents commit suicide in their first episode of depression. They

also view rapidity as an economic advantage for both patients and the health service.

A difficulty in assessing the effectiveness of therapy for depression, according to Senra and Polaino (1998), is the measurement scale used to monitor the effects of treatment. They assessed 52 patients with major depression with the Beck Depression Inventory, the Hamilton Rating Scale and the Zung Self-Rating Depression Scale (Beck et al. 1961, Hamilton 1960 and Zung 1965, respectively). Depending which scale they used, they got different measures of improvement, which makes evaluation of therapy very difficult.

A number of studies have reported that one session of behavioural, graded exposure, treatment has been sufficient to effect improvement (see previous section). A study by Thorpe and Salkovskis (1997) reports significant improvement in patients with spider phobia after just one session of CBT compared to no therapy.

In the main, cognitive–behavioural therapies are thought to be appropriate only for those who have developed good problem-solving skills and are capable of gaining reasonable insight into their problems. However, both Beck and Meichenbaum see a role for CBT with psychotic patients. Hole, Rush and Beck (1979) worked with chronic schizophrenia patients encouraging them to reality-test their delusions, and they found that in half of the patients they could reduce the pervasive nature of delusions. One of the major symptoms of acute schizophrenia is 'inner speech' and this is usually of a controlling nature (telling the person what to do). Meichenbaum and Cameron (1973) developed a programme wherein patients are trained to develop more adaptive controlling statements in their 'inner speech'. Cognitive–behavioural techniques for schizophrenia are continually being developed and refined (e.g. Kingdon and Turkington 1994) and although they do not offer a cure for schizophrenia, they are effective in 'normalizing' symptoms.

Use and mode of action of psychodynamic therapies

The aim of psychodynamic therapy is not to 'cure' the patient's psychological problems in the same way that the medical profession might hope to find a cure for cancer. Rather, the aim is to enable the person to cope better with inner emotional conflicts that are causing disturbance. The purpose of therapy is to uncover unconscious conflicts and anxieties that have their origins in the past, in order to gain insight into the causes of psychological disturbance. After bringing these conflicts into consciousness, the client is encouraged to work through them by examining and dealing with them in the safety of the consulting room, and, in so doing, release the power they exert over behaviour – a process known as *catharsis*. An important aspect of this is that confusing or traumatic childhood experiences can be better understood with the benefit of adult knowledge.

In psychodynamic therapy, a variety of techniques are employed to facilitate the process of catharsis, including the following:

◆ *Free association*: The client is asked to recline on a chair or couch (with the therapist out of sight) and allow the free flow of feelings, thoughts or images. As these come to mind, clients express them in words, without censorship. The analyst must listen, suspending their own values and judgements and interrupting from time to time to ask the client to reflect upon the significance of associations. The reasoning is that associations should arise from, and therefore reflect, internal dynamic conflict.

◆ *Word association:* The client is read a list of words one at a time and asked to reply with whatever comes instantly to mind. The analyst pays particular attention to unusual responses, hesitations and mental blanks, which may indicate repression. (You may like to try Activity 4 now.)

Activity 4: Word association

Try the word association test in pairs, with one person responding and the other speaking the words and noting the responses. Devise your own list of around eight words such as:

Dark	Mother	Earth	Death
Child	Home	Water	Moon

◆ *Dream analysis:* Freud believed that our unconscious drives are expressed uncensored in dreams, although they are disguised in symbolic form in order to protect the conscious mind. The role of the analyst is to help the client interpret the significance of their dreams. In Freudian psychoanalysis, dreams are interpreted as wish-fulfilment, usually of a sexual or aggressive nature. In Adlerian therapy, dreams are viewed as an attempt to avoid feelings of inferiority, the most common dreams being of flying or falling. In Jungian analysis, dreams are an attempt to solve particular problems or to anticipate the future.

◆ *Transference*: This occurs when the client redirects feelings (e.g. of hostility) towards the therapist, that are unconsciously directed towards a significant person in their life (usually a parent), but which have been censored from the conscious mind. Transference is important because it indicates that repressed conflict is coming very close to conscious awareness. Transference must occur naturally, however, and the therapist must neither encourage nor prevent it. The aim is to identify the source (person) of the transference and the circumstances surrounding the repression.

◆ *Projective tests:* There are many types of projective test, the most well-known being the Rorschach Ink Blot (see Fig. 18.2) and the Thematic Apperception Test (see Fig. 18.3). The client is asked to describe what they see in the ink blot or to tell a story around the picture. These are used as tools to uncover recurrent themes that may reveal the unconscious needs and motives of the person. Try Activity 5 and see what these projective tests reveal to you about yourself.

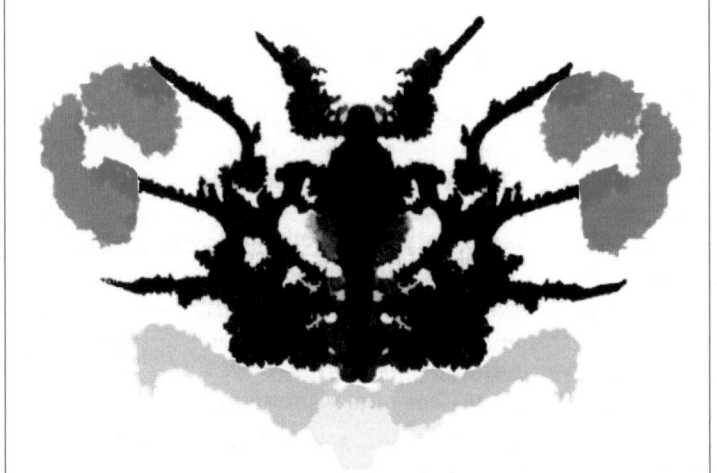

Figure 18.2
Projective test: Rorschach Ink Blot

Figure 18.3 Projective test: Picture from the Thematic Apperception Test, introduced in 1935 by Henry Murray and his associates at the Harvard Psychological Clinic. Like the Rorschach Ink Blot, this projective test is designed to reveal unconscious thoughts and concerns

Appropriateness and effectiveness of psychodynamic therapies

Psychodynamic therapy is generally conducted over a number of years, which makes it expensive, and this has restricted its availability. More modern, brief psychodynamic therapies have emerged, however, and their focus has been much more on current, rather than past, concerns. Psychodynamic therapy has been regarded as appropriate for psychological problems traditionally labelled as 'neuroses', such as anxiety disorders, depression and eating disorders, although its use may be limited with depression because patients are generally apathetic and fatigued. Comer (1995) cites the American Psychiatric Association's concern about 'transference' with patients suffering from depression, because of their tendency towards extreme dependency on important people in their lives. Comer also points out that psychodynamic techniques may be detrimental to the treatment of obsessive–compulsive disorder, because 'free association' may inadvertently increase the person's tendency to ruminate and overinterpret. Psychodynamic therapy was traditionally believed to be of little benefit for patients with schizophrenia, because their loss of contact with reality would prevent them from using insight therapy. With the introduction of phenothiazines, however, patients with schizophrenia can now be much more 'available' to psychotherapy and it has been shown to be beneficial (Boker 1992).

Probably the most-quoted indictment against psychodynamic therapy came from Eysenck (1952) who claimed that it simply does not work. He reviewed two outcome studies, incorporating waiting list controls, which showed that 66 per cent of the control group improved spontaneously, whereas only 44 per cent of psychoanalysis patients improved. Eysenck's papers were reviewed by Bergin (1971). He reported that patients in one of the control groups were in fact hospitalized and those in the other group were being treated by their GP. He also found that by selecting

different outcome criteria, improvement in the psychoanalysis group increased to 83 per cent and the control groups dropped to 30 per cent. Interestingly, Eysenck was still defending his attack on psychotherapy in an interview in 1996 with Colin Feltham at Sheffield Hallam University (Feltham 1996). Eysenck referred to a meta-analysis published in 1991 (40 years after his initial indictment) conducted by Svartberg and Stiles. Of 19 studies comparing psychoanalysis and no treatment, there was no difference in outcome one year after the end of treatment. Eysenck said: 'Clearly there was no evidence that psychoanalysis or psychotherapy did any good'. However, other studies have been more supportive of psychotherapy.

A meta-analysis of six studies with a total of 595 patients diagnosed with major depressive disorder, conducted by Thase et al. (1997) examined the effectiveness of psychotherapy combined with pharmacological treatment (antidepressants) compared to psychotherapy alone. (Meta-analysis is a statistical technique for combining the data from a number of experiments.) They report that, over a 12-week period, with less severe patients, there was no significant difference in the outcome of psychotherapy with or without additional medication (37 per cent versus 48 per cent showing a marked improvement in their clinical condition), indicating that improvement was due to psychotherapy alone. However, with more severe patients, the combined psychotherapy and medication patients showed a much greater improvement than with psychotherapy alone (25 per cent versus 43 per cent). This suggests that if the disorder is more severe, it is advisable to combine medication with therapy. However, Persons et al. (1996) argued that the American Psychiatric Association (APA), in its guidelines for the treatment of severe depression, understates the value of psychotherapy alone and overvalues combined psychotherapy–pharmacology regimes. They claim that the APA has not taken sufficient account of empirical evidence in support of psychotherapy for severe depression.

Mufson et al. (1999) conducted a 12-week clinical trial with 48 adolescents diagnosed with major depression, aged between 12 and 18 years and randomly assigned to a psychotherapy group or a control group (with no therapy, but fortnightly assessment of functioning). After 12 weeks there was a notably greater decrease in depressive symptoms and increase in social functioning and problem-solving skills in 75 per cent of the psychotherapy group compared to 46 per cent of the control group. It should be borne in mind, however, that both the above studies were conducted over a 12-week period. As a long-term therapy, it may not be possible to test the effectiveness of psychotherapy over such a short period.

Because psychotherapy is a long-term treatment, it is not widely available on the NHS, on the grounds of cost-effectiveness. However, there have been some recent developments in 'brief psychotherapy', which can produce some quick improvements in functioning. Guthrie *et al.* (1999) subjected brief psychotherapy to clinical trials with non-psychotic outpatients at two mental health centres in Manchester. The patients had been unresponsive over six months of routine medication treatment. Patients were randomly assigned either to brief psychotherapy for eight weekly sessions, or remaining with their existing drug treatment. During the eight-week trial, treatment costs were the same for both types of treatment. Over the six months following the trial, however, health care utilization was significantly reduced in the brief psychotherapy group, resulting in significant reductions in health care costs.

Corsini and Wedding (1995) claim that, depending on the criteria involved, 'cures' range from 30 to 60 per cent. The concept of 'cure' is, however, inappropriate, and Bolger (1989) makes the point that much of the evaluative research is based on the medical model of problem behaviour that assumes that a psychological disorder follows a course similar to that of a disease. It is now generally accepted that there are methodological difficulties in evaluating the effectiveness of psychodynamic therapy. It generally spans several years and the point at which it is assessed may be crucial to a measurement of efficacy. Corsini and Wedding (1995) also explain that there are too many variables involved to enable a controlled and statistically valid outcome study. Comparisons may be made between symptoms at the beginning and termination of treatment, but during the course of

therapy other complications may arise as a direct result of insight during therapy. Because treatment is over such a long period, there may also be other factors occurring in the client's life during the course of therapy which impact upon the outcome. Life may have been favourable for some clients and unfavourable for others.

Effectiveness is a subjective concept, measurable only by the extent to which clients feel that their condition has improved. Freud himself was quite modest about the therapeutic claims of psychoanalysis (Freud 1937). A study by Hardy *et al.* (1995) found that improvement correlated highly with prior expectation of psychotherapy. Despite difficulties in evaluation, psychodynamic therapies continue to thrive and the newer brief therapies have made this type of therapy more accessible and affordable.

Criticism has been levelled at psychodynamic therapies in relation to emotional rather than physical harm (as with medical treatments). For example, a psychoanalyst may guide a client towards an insight that may prove emotionally distressing, yet is necessary for recovery from their current problem. The distress surrounding the new insight may prove to be greater than the distress of the current problem. Psychotherapists abiding by a professional code of ethics should warn their clients of this danger before engaging in therapy, and therapists should never work beyond their competence in dealing with what may arise in therapy. Recovered memories of child abuse have been the subject of much debate and legal wrangling over the past few years, in discussions of what has become known as *false memory syndrome* (see *In Focus*). Supporters of false memory syndrome

---

in focus

False memory syndrome (FMS)

Many patients have claimed they have uncovered traumatic memories during therapeutic sessions. The debate over whether recovered memories during therapy are accurate representations of events that have happened in childhood is one of modern psychology's most contentious issues. Is it possible to recover previously forgotten memories of childhood trauma and what might be the consequences of such recollections? Critics of the notion of recovered memories have cast doubt on their validity on two counts. Firstly, they point to the somewhat bizarre or unlikely nature of many of the recollections and, secondly, they question the use of techniques such as suggestion and hypnotic regression to extract these memories. The consequences of either side of the FMS argument pose ethical problems for the therapist. First, if these are false memories (often about sexual abuse), then there is concern over the consequences of parents being falsely accused of abusing their children. Second, if these are true memories, there may be harmful effects on the people who have actually been abused in childhood in not being believed (Andrews et al. 1995).

A further ethical issue is now emerging as a direct result of the proliferation of media articles on 'false memory syndrome' over the past few years. These have created a climate of disbelief about the credibility of disclosures of child sexual abuse to the extent that adult survivors are now discouraged from disclosing and seeking help for themselves (Toon et al. 1996).

(FMS) have suggested that a client may succumb to the belief because the suggestions come from an authority figure. Toon *et al.* (1996) report that FMS supporters accuse therapists in private practice of even inducing false memories for financial gain, because the therapy will take longer. Toon and colleagues point out, however, that there is no clear-cut evidence, as yet, to demonstrate the existence of therapist-induced false memories.

Psychodrama

Psychodrama was developed by J.L. Moreno in the early 1920s. Moreno was a psychiatrist working in Vienna at the same time as Sigmund Freud. However, he rejected Freud's methods of psychoanalysis for two main reasons:

◆ He believed that people could be better helped through groupwork, rather than individual one-to-one therapy.

◆ He believed that therapy should be an active experience rather than based on talking alone.

Moreno observed the therapeutic effects of role-playing within children's play and believed this could be extended to adults through drama. Problems and anxieties can be expressed or 'acted out' in a role-play situation within the safety of an understanding and supportive therapy group. Incidentally, Moreno coined the terms 'roles' and 'role-play'. Moreno believed that every human being is an actor in that they perform their own personal drama. He gave as an example that women play many roles, such as wife, mother, sister, daughter, nurse and teacher. A psychologically healthy person can switch roles easily, but problems emerge when people are rigidly fixed within a specific role or when one role dominates the person. However, Moreno was firmly convinced that everyone is capable of being their own saviour. In 1922, Moreno began to combine professional theatre with therapy by presenting personal dramas on stage, whereby the actors would improvise roles and a psychodrama would emerge. The purpose was that people in the audience, as well as the actors on stage, could identify and engage with the drama in a therapeutic way. Moreno thought that role reversal was an important part of this process and actors were encouraged to try out roles that were the opposite of their usual roles.

Although Moreno lived close to Freud in Vienna, they met only once when Moreno attended a lecture by Freud. On this occasion Freud asked him about his work and Moreno replied: 'Well Dr Freud, I start where you leave off. You meet people in the artificial setting of your office; I meet them on the street and in their homes, in their natural surroundings. You analyse their dreams; I try to give them the courage to dream again.' (Moreno 1970, p.6).

Moreno moved to the USA in 1925 and founded the Moreno Institute, where he developed psychodrama further into a structured therapy. It was not until 1965, however, that the first set of rules for psychodrama were published and this was by his wife Zerka (Moreno 1965). Psychodrama takes place within a group setting and group sizes vary, but are usually between 10 and 15 people. A single session can span several hours, whereby one member of the group will elect to play out a chosen scenario, or drama, from a problem area in their life. Everyone in the group will then be assigned a role from the following:

◆ *The director* – the person who will direct the drama, including the preparation and planning. The director will monitor the drama as it unfolds, intervene where necessary to change the direction, or focus, offer clarification and provide a summary at the end. The director can also facilitate the playing out of a future event. The director is the therapist who is a specialist trained in the use and techniques of psychodrama.

◆ *The protagonist* – the volunteer who is electing to play out his or her drama. The chosen scenario should be an event from the past or present that can be re-enacted 'on stage'. The director can at any point ask the protagonist to engage in a soliloquy where he or she is asked to think out loud.

◆ *The auxiliary egos* – significant people within the drama, such as a parent or spouse and can include people who are alive or dead. The protagonist chooses the actors for these roles from within the group. At any point the director can ask the protagonist to move into the role of one of the auxiliary egos in order to experience the drama from that perspective.

◆ *The double* – the inner voice of the protagonist whose role is to move the action to a deeper level in order to enable the protagonist to access his or her unconscious. The double will mirror the actions and words of the protagonist, who can then observe aspects of his or her own self of which he or she had previously been unaware.

◆ *The audience* – the remaining members of the group. Their role is to observe and give feedback at the end in general discussion. They are also able to benefit therapeutically from the experience by themselves identifying with the emerging drama.

◆ *The stage* – where the action takes place and where the protagonist, assisted by the director, will arrange some basic furniture to form a stage set.

The action takes place as if it were happening now, even though the chosen scenario may be from the past, present or future. In replaying a past event, often what is important is what didn't happen rather than what did happen. In this case, the director can direct the drama to examine alternative scenarios.

Appropriateness and effectiveness of psychodrama

Psychodrama is a very powerful therapy because of its experiential nature and the experience can be quite traumatic, which is why it is important for every member of the group to be sensitive and supportive. The therapy is effective in addressing past events that have never been addressed, for example re-experiencing a childhood trauma in the safety of a therapeutic environment. It is particularly useful when trying to deal with problems from the past, especially when a person is no longer around in the protagonist's life, for example a significant person has died and issues had not been resolved before that person's death.

Psychodrama is also useful in testing out scenarios involving people whom it would be difficult to address in real life. It is also useful for learning new skills and ways of interacting with others through the experience of playing roles in other people's dramas and the feedback discussions. Karp (1995) found psychodrama effective for people with psychosomatic disorders. Hugh (1998) cites Dayton (1994), who found it useful for people with addictions, in order to explore emerging situations better within a holding environment. She also cites Corey (1995) who found it useful with people whose second language is English, in that by adopting their first language they can become much more expressive and able to get in touch with their emotions.

Karp (1995) maintained that psychodrama is suitable for those who are able and willing to engage in role-play with an audience. However, there are some people who might find this difficult and would not wish to explore their problems in such a dramatic and public way. Perls (1992) said that one of the problems with psychodrama is that participants may introduce their own perceptions and interpretations of events and as such may 'contaminate' the drama. Davies (1993) explained that psychodrama is not acting and there is always the danger that participants may seek to put on a 'performance'. He explains that psychodrama is not a panacea and that it requires a great deal of risk-taking and, therefore, many people may prefer the safer, more traditional, one-to-one psychotherapies. Moreno's work has precipitated the wider use of groupwork within therapy, without the drama element, recognising the value of working through problems within a supportive group. These include self-help groups and facilitated groups for specific problems, such as addictions or eating disorders, and with specific groups of people such as abusers or victims of abuse. Working with those who share the same experience helps them feel less alone, or 'different', and enables them to more readily and openly address their problems.

Use and mode of action of humanistic therapy

Humanistic therapy is based on the main premise of humanistic theory that people have a natural tendency towards growth and development (an 'actualizing tendency') and will themselves seek to resolve problems in their life, rather than succumbing to them.

Humanistic therapy is better known as 'person-centred therapy' and originated largely from the work of Carl Rogers (1951). Rogers did not hold with the interventionist techniques of the psychodynamic or behaviourist schools. He believed they created dependence upon the therapist and was convinced that the major element of concern in the therapeutic relationship was the distribution of power. He introduced the term 'person-centred' to underline the fact that this approach was first and foremost a means to access the personal power of individual clients to become more autonomous, spontaneous and confident in themselves.

Like psychodynamic therapy, humanistic person-centred therapy is an insight therapy in that it involves delving into deeper emotions. Rogers, however, believed that therapy should focus on the present, rather than on the past, because it is now that the person is grappling with problems. Although he does not dispute that events in the past have a huge influence on our behaviour, he was more concerned with what is happening in clients' lives now and how therapy can trigger changes by encouraging people to recognize and value their capacity to direct their own life. Rogers believed that for this to occur, therapy needs the right climate, which rests not on techniques, but on the relationship between the therapist and the client. Rogers proposed three core conditions that he claimed are both necessary and sufficient for this relationship. These three core conditions – warmth, genuineness and empathy – are qualities that should be exhibited and communicated by the therapist. When experienced by clients to a significant degree, clients should be able to discover the resources needed within themselves to effect personal change and re-integration. According to Rogers, interventions by a therapist, however well intentioned, run counter to person-centred therapy.

- *Warmth*: The first condition is 'warmth' (or 'unconditional positive regard'), which means that the therapist must have respect for the client and display complete acceptance of the person in his or her own right at that moment in time. This must also be accompanied by a non-judgemental attitude towards the client.

- *Genuineness*: The second and most important condition is, according to Rogers, 'genuineness', meaning that the therapist must show that they are a 'real' person, with thoughts and feelings, which should be expressed where appropriate. This is enhanced by 'self-disclosure', which would be deemed totally inappropriate in psychoanalytic therapy, where the therapist must remain 'blank' in order to facilitate 'transference'. Rogers adopts quite the opposite view in that he believes that the client must feel that the therapist is emotionally involved and completely transparent.

- *Empathy*: The third condition is 'empathic understanding'. By this Rogers meant that the therapist must enter the client's inner world. He suggested that this could be achieved through genuine, attentive listening and by restating what the client says, in order to clarify its emotional significance. Rogers believed this required intense concentration on the part of the therapist, along with an ability to be sensitive to what is currently going on for the client just below the level of awareness. The therapist must sense the pleasure and the hurt of the client as if they were their own.

Appropriateness and effectiveness of humanistic therapies

Humanistic theorists, such as Rogers, recognized that most people need help at some time or other in their life, although they would not regard their condition as pathological. Humanistic therapy, therefore, took the monopoly on therapy away from the arena of 'specialist expertise', such as clinical psychologists, psychiatrists and psychotherapists, and made therapy much more accessible. Client-centred therapy is now strongly represented within 'counselling' and is probably the most widely adopted therapy in both the UK and the United States of America. Counsellors adopting a basically Rogerian approach are increasingly employed in sectors such as social services, the National Health Service, industry, commerce and education, as well as the voluntary agencies such as those counselling on marriage, bereavement, drugs, HIV, and so on. The growth of person-centred counselling could be seen to vouch for its own effectiveness, or at the very least, the growing need for a therapy that is less intrusive and that is non-interventionist.

Like all insight therapies, person-centred counselling is difficult to evaluate for effectiveness because there are too many variables to take into account. Most of the early research was focused on Rogers' insistence that the three core conditions are both necessary and sufficient for an effective therapeutic outcome. For example, Mitchell (1977) found that 'genuineness' was of central importance, but on further analysis realized that it was not genuineness *per se* which correlated with a positive client outcome, but rather a 'lack of genuineness' which mitigated against a positive client outcome, by interfering with the helpful effects of 'warmth' and 'empathy'.

Studies have also focused on a range of different settings. For example, Dryden *et al.* (1989) cite studies by Rose and Marshall (1974) who evaluated counselling for truancy and delinquency in a number of schools and found that pupils responded favourably. A survey of HIV counselling services in a London hospital by Du Plessis *et al.* (1995) found that 57 per cent of users thought the service was good or excellent and 66 per cent said they would use the service again. A number of studies have found counselling in medical general practice to be effective. A survey conducted by Monach and Monro (1995) reported that counselling in general practice surgeries and health centres has expanded rapidly in response to perceived increases in mental health problems and pressure for more financial efficiency. If the measure of effectiveness is financial efficiency, then counselling is probably more effective than most other treatments for certain types of psychological problems, such as mild depression or anxiety, because psychiatric and clinical psychology services are expensive to run. The only cheaper alternative is short-term, GP-prescribed pharmacological treatment, such as benzodiazepines, but many GPs are reluctant to prescribe these longer term because of dependence. Many GPs are now also reluctant to diagnose someone with a mental disorder, and referral for counselling avoids this because counsellors do not require a 'label' in order to offer assistance.

One of the major difficulties in assessing the effectiveness of counselling is that there is a huge discrepancy in the amount of training and competency among counsellors. Currently, there are no statutory regulations governing the qualifications or length of training necessary to practise, although the British Association for Counselling has attempted to address this by introducing terms of accreditation. Government legislation is also in the pipeline. With counselling now being available in such diverse settings and for such a diversity of problems, training is also becoming specialized. For example, there is specialist training for HIV, drugs and alcohol, marital, rape, suicide, bereavement and stress management counselling, along with counselling for amputee patients, people awaiting kidney transplants, and so on. Assessing the effectiveness of these services is extremely difficult, not least because there are no truly viable comparisons or objective assessment measures. Effectiveness is 'in the eye of the beholder', in other words it is a subjective concept which can be measured only by whether an individual believed that counselling had been helpful. The growth of counselling around the world is testimony to its perceived effectiveness.

One of the benefits of person-centred counselling is that it emphasizes the role of choice and self-direction. Devine and Fernald (1973) demonstrated that the role of choice and commitment to a particular type of treatment hugely influenced the therapeutic outcome. Clients with snake phobias were shown films of four types of treatment. The clients were then split into three groups:

◆ The first group were allowed to select their preferred treatment.

◆ The second group were randomly assigned to a treatment.

◆ The third group were required to undergo a non-preferred treatment.

The most successful therapeutic experience was found in the first group, who were given the treatment of their choice. Devine and Fernald concluded that this was because a sense of control had been exercised over the therapeutic process. In contrast, clients who were forced into a nonpreferred treatment merely complied without any real commitment.

There are limitations to the scope of counselling, however. Counselling is best suited to those clients who are able to discuss their emotional concerns in detail and who are motivated to focus on their subjective experience. As Rogers himself pointed out, person-centred therapy may not be very effective for severe mental disorders, such as schizophrenia. However, counselling may be useful for someone with schizophrenia, for example, along with their family, in providing support and guidance for coping with such a severe mental disorder. *Milieu therapy* is an innovative humanistic approach,

designed specifically for institutionalized chronic psychiatric patients and appears to have met with some success (see *In Focus* on p. 480).

Activity 6: Case study

Read the following case study of Peter and consider how each of the treatment therapies mentioned in this chapter would approach Peter's problems. Then decide which, in your opinion, might be the most effective.

Peter is attending college and just coming up to his A-level exams. Over the past month or so he has been suffering from severe anxiety, is unable to eat or sleep and his mind is in turmoil. He has now developed a phobia for examination halls and gets palpitations if he goes near that part of the college building. When his teachers talk about the exams he goes into a cold sweat. He knows he must get good grades, but is unable to concentrate on revision and his mind often goes blank. When his mind isn't blank, it is running on overtime, thinking that he is useless and a failure.

His father had set his heart on Peter becoming an engineer, which is something he had always dreamed of himself, but didn't get the opportunity for a university education. Peter thinks he will enjoy university, but he is not sure that engineering is the right choice for him. He is taking science A levels, but his real interest is in literature and he is particularly fond of analysing poetry. His father says this is a 'girl's' subject and was quite dismissive when Peter suggested A-level English two years earlier.

Over the past week or so, Peter has been preoccupied with recollections from childhood. He remembers an occasion when his father took him to the swimming pool for the first time and threw him in at the deep end. Peter was terrified and still has nightmares about it, even though he is now quite a good swimmer. He recalls that his father said he must 'plunge into life' and take all the opportunities he can. Peter knows that his father loves him and wants a good life for him. He also knows how disappointed his father will be if he doesn't get the grades required for engineering, yet at the moment he is unable to function well enough even to sit the exams.

Milieu therapy

Milieu therapy, pioneered by Maxwell Jones (1953), is based on the idea that if psychiatric patients are to make clinical progress, then the social milieu of institutions must change. In milieu therapy, a therapeutic community is created in psychiatric wards, where people are not treated as patients, but 'residents'. Each person is valued as an individual and participates alongside staff on institutional planning in an atmosphere of mutual respect. The purpose is not to offer a 'cure' for disorders such as chronic schizophrenia but rather to promote independence and responsibility, and to restore self-respect. Milieu therapy has been introduced in many psychiatric institutions in Britain and the US, and is an effective 'halfway house' for patients who are to be discharged into the community.

Exam summary: Alternatives to biological and behavioural therapies

The AQA examination will test your understanding of the following areas:

◆ use and mode of action of *either*

   – psychodynamic-based therapies (p. 472–3 and pp. 476–7)

   or

   – cognitive–behavioural therapies (pp. 469–71)

◆ issues surrounding the use of *either*

   – psychodynamic-based therapies (pp. 474–6 and p. 477)

   or

   – cognitive–behavioural therapies (pp. 470–2).

Example question

The question below is typical of one drawn from the material above, and should take you 45 minutes to answer:

◆ Discuss the use of one or more psychodynamic therapies in the treatment of mental disorders.

(30 marks)

Suggested answer structure

The wording of this question invites a description and evaluation of the *use* of one or more psychodynamic therapies. First of all, you decide what counts as a *psychodynamic* therapy, as distinct from any other type of therapy. We have examined two types of psychodynamic therapy, Freudian psychoanalysis (pp. 472–6), and psychodrama (pp. 476–7). The use of the expression *one or more* indicate that you could discuss one of these therapies in depth, or both in less depth. If you look at Table 21.4 on p. 558, you will see that the higher mark bands require *both* breadth *and* depth, so this

should be a factor in your choice of strategy. Although the word 'use' is prominent in this question, this also implies that you could discuss the issues that surround the use of this form of therapy. Critical discussion of these issues (e.g. is the therapy *appropriate* and is it *effective*) would constitute the AO2 component of your answer. One of the most outspoken critics of psychodynamic therapies was Hans Eysenck (p. 474). The website address below gives you his original paper, so you can follow his arguments for yourself.

http://www.yorku.ca/dept/psych/classics/Eysenck/psychotherapy.htm

Psychodynamic therapies are designed to address underlying causes of mental disorders, which usually have their origins in the past. Unlike behavioural and cognitive–behavioural therapies, psychodynamic therapies are difficult to test for effectiveness because they are not dealing with outward behavioural symptoms, but inner emotional conflicts, and improvement is a subjective concept.

Psychotherapy has been the subject of much criticism over the years, but nevertheless it is a thriving profession which is an indication that many people believe in its effectiveness. Psychotherapy generally spans several years and as such is a more costly therapy than chemotherapy, or behavioural methods. For this reason, it is not widely available on the NHS.

It is a good idea, when choosing material with which to answer this question, that you bear the synoptic requirement of the question in mind. There are a number of different aspects of psychodynamic therapies discussed in this chapter (techniques, research support, etc.), but we have also covered many of the wider issues such as the concept of 'cure' and the debate over false memory syndrome. Inclusion of these wider issues will contribute positively towards your synoptic overview in this question.

Chapter summary

◆ Each of the therapies outlined in this chapter offers quite different methods of treatment for mental disorders, based upon their respective model of abnormality.

◆ **Biological (somatic) treatments** address physical symptoms of mental disorder. They consist mainly of drugs (**chemotherapy**), which are prescribed to redress biochemical imbalance. They are reasonably effective in the short term, although there are numerous adverse side effects. Dependence can be created if drugs are taken over a long period of time.

◆ With severe depression, **ECT** has been found to be effective for some patients, but again there are adverse side effects. **Psychosurgery** continues to be regarded as a controversial and extreme form of therapy, even with the newer procedure of cingulotomy, largely because it involves permanent damage to the neural tissue.

◆ **Behavioural therapies** attempt to identify maladaptive learning and to modify it into more adaptive behavioural strategies. Techniques such as systematic desensitization are thought to be effective for phobias. Behaviour modification programmes have been subjected to ethical scrutiny on the grounds that the goals are set by the institution and may not serve the interests of the recipient.

◆ **Cognitive–behavioural therapies** extend the behavioural model to the realms of thinking and attempt to replace distorted irrational thoughts with more rational ways of thinking. It has been found to be effective for coping with anxiety. Beck's cognitive–behavioural therapy has been found to be more effective than any other therapy for depression.

◆ **Psychodynamic (insight) therapies** attempt to uncover unconscious anxieties and conflicts in order to disable their power over behaviour. Although their success is difficult to test empirically, they are thought to be very effective for certain disorders, such as anxiety and depression.

◆ **Humanistic (person-centred) therapy** aims to improve perceptions of self-worth and to enhance the human capacity to realize full potential. The growth of person-centred counselling in education, voluntary agencies and industry vouches for its usefulness.

◆ Some therapies are easier than others to test for **effectiveness**, but this does not necessarily mean that they are more effective. Many therapists nowadays take an eclectic approach. They are trained in a number of different therapies and draw on whichever they feel to be most appropriate for a particular client.

◆ Since therapists deal with people who are disturbed and distressed, there are inevitably **ethical issues** to be taken into consideration. Some of these issues have been considered in relation to particular therapies.

Further resources

Corsini, R.J. and Wedding, D. (1995) *Current Psychotherapies* (5th edn), Illinois: FE Peacock Publishers.

An American text which covers traditional, along with more recent, theories and applications of therapy. Suitable for undergraduates and those with a special interest in therapy.

Dryden, W. (1996) *Individual Therapy: A Handbook*, Milton Keynes: Open University Press.

A British text with a chapter for each therapy written by different authors. The chapters are slim and most, but not all, are written in a clear style that is interesting and informative. The latest edition was published in 1996.

Nelson-Jones, R. (1995) *The Theory and Practice of Counselling* (2nd edn), London: Cassell.

This British text has recently been revised. It provides well-written accounts of a variety of theories and how they are developed in practice. Self-assessment questions are included. It is especially suited to those wishing to pursue a career in counselling.

continued on p. 482

Websites

www.nsf.org.uk

Site for National Schizophrenia Fellowship. It offers advice and support to people with severe mental illness.

www.cochranelibrary.com/ccweb/cochrane/revabstr/ab000088.htm

An informative abstract of Steiner's study (1999) of family psychosocial interventions in community settings for the care of those with schizophrenia.

http://www.epub.org.br/cm/history_i.htm

History of neurosciences – includes two excellent articles on the history of psychosurgery and the history of shock therapy (lots of pictures!).

http://apsa.org/

The American Psychoanalytic Association – a huge and informative site that is even interactive!

http://www.antipsychiatry.org

A comprehensive site full of articles criticizing the use of traditional psychiatric techniques.

| synoptic issues | See the *Checklist of synoptic issues* (pp. 645–50) for ideas about how to use issues in this chapter for synoptic assessment. |

Part 7: Perspectives

ISSUES AND DEBATES
IN PSYCHOLOGY

Mike Cardwell

APPROACHES IN PSYCHOLOGY

Phil Banyard

Issues and debates in psychology

Mike Cardwell

Preview

In this chapter we shall be looking at:

◆ gender bias in theory and research

◆ cultural bias in theory and research

◆ ethical issues in research

◆ the ethics of socially sensitive research

◆ the use of nonhuman animals in research

◆ free will and determinism in psychology

◆ reductionism in theory and research

◆ psychology as science

◆ nature–nurture in theory and research.

Introduction

The aim of this chapter is to introduce you to some of the major issues and debates that concern psychologists. Although gender and cultural biases have existed since the early days of psychological research, it is only in the latter part of the twentieth century that efforts have been made to address these issues. It will be obvious to you that ethical issues should be a major concern within psychology and

indeed they are. It is not only in research using human participants, but also where nonhuman animals are used as subjects, that ethical issues arise. This latter area of enquiry raises a commendable amount of concern and debate among students and a good deal of entrenched opinion that often defies counter argument.

Socially sensitive research poses special ethical difficulties for research psychologists. For example, research into gender differences or race often carries significant consequences not only for those who take part in the research, but also members of the social groups they represent. Psychologists need to be aware that their research can be manipulated and exploited for bad as well as good purposes.

The debates around free will versus determinism, reductionism versus holism, and nature versus nurture have a long pedigree. Few psychologists adhere rigidly to only one side in these debates, ignoring blindly all arguments proffered by the other point of view. Increasingly, psychologists seem to be resolving these issues by adopting a more interactionist approach. The debate over whether psychology is – or should even try to be – a science is still a contentious issue, one that gets to the very heart of what psychology is about and how it should conduct its investigations.

Gender bias in psychological theory and research

Traditional views of men and women

Start this section by trying Activity 1 on p. 486.

Gender bias is not a new thing. For centuries we have accepted assumptions about the differences between the sexes. Even though the conditions under which these ideas were originally formed have changed, these outdated notions have tended to remain. For the psychologist who is trying to understand these ideas, it is necessary to understand their origin. However, that isn't too hard to do, and we don't have to look very far to find representations of men and women that appear as old as time itself.

Both Aristotle and Plato wrote extensively about the role of women. Of the two, Aristotle (384–322 BC) was the more negative. He saw women's inferiority as being biologically based. 'We should look upon the female,' he said, 'as being a deformity, though one which occurs in the ordinary course of nature.' In Aristotle's philosophical writings, women are portrayed as not possessing fully developed rationality. Men, therefore, must both rule them and be responsible for them. Aristotle, it might be claimed, was also the perpetrator of that modern legacy, the gender stereotype. Women are frequently 'pathologized' because of their physical differences from men, for example their 'irrationality' or

Activity 1: Self-assessment – Beliefs about women

For each of the statements listed below, circle the number to the right of the statement that describes your response to it. Your responses can range from strongly disagree (1) to strongly agree (5). Bear your responses in mind as you read through this first section – they will be commented on later.

| | Disagree | | Neutral | Agree | |
	Strongly	Somewhat		Somewhat	Strongly
1 Women are less decisive than men.	1	2	3	4	5
2 Women are less dominating than men.	1	2	3	4	5
3 Women are more passive than men.	1	2	3	4	5
4 Women have more emotional insight than men.	1	2	3	4	5
5 Women are more interpersonal than men.	1	2	3	4	5
6 Women are less career-interested than men.	1	2	3	4	5
7 Women are more vulnerable than men.	1	2	3	4	5
8 Women are less intelligent than men.	1	2	3	4	5
9 Women are less sexual than men.	1	2	3	4	5
10 Women are more appearance-conscious than men.	1	2	3	4	5
11 Women are sexual teases.	1	2	3	4	5
12 Women are more moral than men.	1	2	3	4	5
13 Women act sillier than men do.	1	2	3	4	5
14 Menstruation debilitates women.	1	2	3	4	5

We will return to this assessment later, but for now it may be profitable to take a look at where some of these ideas may have come from in the first place.

Source: adapted from: Belk and Snell (1986)

their emotionality is often attributed to premenstrual syndrome or to menopausal symptoms. In other words, their pathology is seen as inescapably connected to their femaleness.

Psychological theories and gender bias

'Throughout history people have knocked their heads against the riddle of femininity.' (Freud 1931)

Within psychology there have been two main approaches to gender-related characteristics: there are the theories that ignore the differences between men and women, and those which exaggerate them. Hare-Mustin and Marecek (1988) describe these as showing *beta bias* and *alpha bias* respectively.

Alpha bias

Alpha bias theories assume real and enduring differences between men and women. Sometimes alpha bias theories heighten the value of women, as in Chodorow's conception of women as more relational and caring (Chodorow 1978), while sometimes they are used to devalue women. Within sociobiology, for example, differences in male and female behaviour may

be attributed to genetic determinism. Thus, male social dominance or sexual promiscuity might be seen as a product of their evolutionary history.

Beta bias

Beta bias theories and research have traditionally ignored or minimized sex differences. They have done this either by ignoring questions about the lives of women, or by assuming that findings from studies of males apply equally well to females. Such approaches, at best misguided, at worst arrogant, have resulted in what is essentially an *androcentric* view of human behaviour (based on and concerning males), rather than offering insights into what is essentially one half of the human race.

These are not the only types of bias that lurk within the study of psychology. Worell and Remer (1992) identified six other biases that also have their origins partly in outdated assumptions about men and women.

Androcentric

Androcentric theories tend to offer an interpretation of women based on an understanding of the lives of men. Ideas of 'normal' behaviour may be drawn exclusively from studies of the development of males. A well-known example of an androcentric theory is Freud's account of male identity development, in which the young boy's identification with his father leads to the formation of a superego and of high moral standards. Girls, on the other hand, who do not experience the same Oedipal conflict as boys, cannot, it appears, develop their superego (and thus their moral standards) to the same degree as boys.

Gendercentric

Gendercentric theories see male and female development as following separate paths. Freud's theory can thus be seen as being both androcentric and gendercentric. Other theories that might be regarded as gendercentric do not devalue women in the way that androcentric theories might. Theories that might be described as gendercentric display an alpha bias, in that they emphasize how males and females differ, rather than how their characteristics might intersect.

Ethnocentric

Ethnocentric theories assume that development and interaction are the same across cultures and races. Such theories are often characterized by an Anglo-European orientation, and as such may offer quite fixed sets of assumptions about 'normal' patterns of family functioning, and appropriate roles for males and females within the family structure.

Heterosexist

Most traditional theories of psychological development view heterosexual orientation as normal and therefore view orientation toward partners of the same sex as abnormal. In Freud's psychoanalytic theory, for example, a homosexual orientation was interpreted as a failure to achieve a normal gender identity, and was therefore treated as if it were a personality disorder. Homosexuality was diagnosed as a category of mental illness by the American Psychiatric Association up until 1973, when it was finally removed from the diagnostic classification system DSM-II.

Intrapsychic

Intrapsychic theories tend to attribute all behaviour of an individual to factors within themselves. These theories tend to minimize the role of external influences, thus leading to the inevitable consequence of 'blaming' the victim for whatever happens to them. An example of an intrapsychic theory would be Nancy Chodorow's (1978) object relations theory, where a later behaviour may be attributed to an earlier developmental failure. For example, a woman who stays in an abusive and unsatisfying marriage may be seen as the product of an earlier failure to separate herself from her own mother.

Deterministic

These theories assume that patterns of behaviour have developed as a result of past events and are thus more or less fixed. The consequence of this would be that ideas of gender role become an inflexible aspect of one's personality and are thus relatively unchangeable at a later stage of development.

Bias-free theories

There are a number of ways that psychological theories can avoid the biases described above. Worell and Remer (1992) offer four criteria by which theories might be evaluated in order to overcome the often detrimental models of women that develop from more traditional nonfeminist models.

Gender-free

Gender-free theories see men and women as similar in their psychological make-up. Such theories avoid stereotypes or any labels that imply that one sex may be more valued than the other. Cast your mind back to Activity 1 at the beginning of this section. If you gave answers that were anything other than a 3 (neutral), you have stereotypes about women, and as such your conceptions of male and female behaviour are not gender-free. A gender-free theory attempts to avoid sexist and stereotyped concepts of the broader culture.

Flexible

A flexible theory uses ideas that can apply equally to individuals or groups of any age, race, gender or sexual orientation. Such theories emphasize within-sex differences in behaviour, as well as between-sex differences. These theories thereby offer a range of satisfying and fulfilling life styles for both men and women, rather than devaluing one or the other as less mature, incomplete or unhealthy due to some preconceived notions of what might be considered normal or healthy (and therefore linked to one sex, age, etc., rather than another).

Interactionist

For a theory to be considered interactionist, it should recognize the interaction between a range of individual-centred factors (including affective, cognitive and behavioural factors) and those which are more environmental (other people, institutions, etc.). Interactionist theories would recognize multiple influences on a person's behaviour, and accept that an individual could not be properly understood without consideration of all relevant factors. Gender is thus seen as only one contributing factor in a person's behaviour.

Lifespan

The essential ingredient of a lifespan approach to development is the belief that behaviour changes can occur at any time during an individual's lifetime, rather than being restricted to specific periods that exert powerful influences on later behaviour. When applied to gender-related behaviour, such theories suggest that these behaviours are not fixed in people but may always be open to change. Individuals develop within a particular social-historical environment and, as such, experience a range of influences that are specific to that time, but nevertheless remain capable of choice and thus self-determined change.

Gender bias in psychological research

'An experiment typically consists of a brief encounter among strangers in an unfamiliar setting, often under the eye of a psychologist. The question is whether this context is a valid one from which to make generalizations about behaviour.' (Riger 1992)

The main source of discontent with psychological research and its bias against women has centred around the use of traditional scientific methods, most notably the use of the laboratory experiment. This technique has dominated psychological research and has become the normative research method in much of 'mainstream' psychology. In the eyes of the outsider, the laboratory experiment is the essence of scientific 'proof' about human behaviour. For some reason, there is more credibility and prestige associated with the results of laboratory experiments than there is with other methods in psychology.

So, why is this a problem, and why is the experiment seen as being so gender biased?

Nicolson (1995) identifies two main problems with this adherence to an experimental science of psychology.

◆ The experiment takes the *behaviour* of an individual research participant as the unit of study rather than the participant herself. This ignores the social, personal and cultural context in which the behaviour is enacted. In this way, psychologists discover 'truths' about gender differences that are attributed to the characteristics of the participant rather than the characteristics of the research context.

◆ Experimental psychology characteristically disadvantages women. Stripped of their social power and knowledge, they are placed in a 'strange' environment, where they are expected to respond to the requirements of a (usually) male experimenter. Female participants are thus forced into a position of subordination in their interaction with a man who is in charge of the experiment.

As a result of 'scientific' research, women have been labelled as irrational, inappropriately volatile and easily depressed for no reason. They are accused of having more lapses of attention than men, and of generally performing worse on both simple and complex cognitive tasks. Women are thus portrayed as being intellectually and emotionally deficient in relation to men. They have been pathologized through the use of the labels *premenstrual syndrome, postnatal depression* and *menopausal symptoms.* These have been identified by the medical profession and by psychologists as conditions, and therefore as incontestable facts.

Women and the menstrual cycle

Feminist psychologists have identified that women's 'deficiencies' in behavioural, cognitive and emotional functioning are due to the conceptualization of the research question and the flaws in the methodologies used. Nowhere is this more noticeable than in the study of premenstrual syndrome (PMS). One extreme outcome of research in this area has been the attempts to use PMS as a legal defence to plead 'diminished responsibility'. PMS was seen as giving a woman an excuse for anything, including murder, while making her 'not responsible for herself'. What is the evidence for such a belief? Claims by scientists concerning the menstrual cycle are inevitably more to do with the male-dominated culture in which scientific enquiry is embedded, than with the experiences and concerns of women themselves. Women are caught in the contradictions of the dominant culture which sees them as both biologically and psychologically inferior. A woman who does not display the characteristic qualities to suit her to the 'feminine role' is seen to be in need of treatment. Thus women are led to seek attributions for their 'unsatisfactory condition'. A medicalized concept such as PMS represents an appealing explanation to women themselves and to others. It serves to justify women's oppression and lack of achievement compared to men.

Source: adapted from Nicolson (1995)

The *In Focus* illustrates the problems of applying this kind of reasoning in psychological research.

As well as criticizing the general experimental approach to psychology, feminists have shown that bias can appear at every stage of the experimental design, from formulating the research question to the interpretation of the data. Some examples of this research bias are given below:

◆ *Formulating the research question* – Gross (1995) points out that topics that are studied in psychological research frequently reflect the prevalent gender stereotypes of the culture. For example, leadership is often defined by researchers in terms of dominance, aggression and other characteristics that are stereotyped as typically male characteristics.

◆ *Selection of research participants* – Social psychologists, for example, have typically developed theories from white, male undergraduates. This is then represented as 'human behaviour' (Fine and Gordon 1989). You might like to consider how some of the classic social psychology experiments mentioned in Chapters 1 to 3 have addressed this problem.

Alternative research strategies

If science is gender-biased and androcentric, what criteria should be considered when carrying out a study?

Worell (1992) suggests a number of research criteria that are particularly important to ensure non-gender-biased research investigations:

◆ *using alternative methods of inquiry* – expanding the boundaries of accepted scientific methodology to explore the personal lives of women

◆ *looking at meaningful contexts* – considering women in the natural settings in which they function

◆ *collaborating with research participants* – entering into a partnership with participants to explore personally relevant variables

◆ *soliciting diverse samples* – looking at women who vary by age, socio-economic class, partner preference, minority or ethnic group, etc.

Exam summary: Gender bias in psychological theory and research

The AQA examination will test your understanding of the following areas:

◆ gender bias in psychological theory (pp. 486–8)

◆ gender bias in psychological research (pp. 488–9).

Example question

The question below is typical of one drawn from the material above, and should take you 45 minutes:

◆ With reference to two psychological theories, discuss the view that psychology presents a gender-biased view of human behaviour. *(30 marks)*

Suggested answer structure

The wording of this question invites a fairly general discursive response, but it does require you to support your argument through reference to two psychological theories. There are a number of ways that you might address the AO1 requirement of the question. As the question does not require you to embed your whole response within the two chosen theories, you might begin by *describing* (the AO1 component of the injunction *discuss*) some of the different forms of gender bias found in psychological explanations of human behaviour (pp. 486–7). Chodorow's object relations theory and Freud's theory of psychoanalysis are included here as examples of the *alpha bias* and the *androcentric bias* respectively. Given the wording of this question, it is quite appropriate to include reference to these two theories to illustrate the bias in question. You may also include reference to theories from elsewhere in the book (e.g. Kohlberg's theory of moral understanding, pp. 270–3 or Levinson's *Seasons of a man's life*, pp. 307–10) to illustrate your discussion of the biased nature of psychology. You don't need a very detailed account of your chosen theories, just sufficient to support your description of (in this case) the different gender biases.

As is the case with all questions, there is an AO2 requirement which cannot be overlooked here. This could be satisfied by considering the extent to which the claims made about the two theories are justified, or perhaps by taking a critical look at the way in which psychological research also demonstrates a gender bias. This must, it is suggested (See *In Focus*, p. 488) shape our conceptions of the differences between men and women. Alternatively, you might examine the possibility of developing theories that are *gender-free* (pp. 487–8), or of adopting research methods that avoid the pitfalls identified by Nicolson on p. 488.

It is important to remember that there is a *synoptic* element (see p. 553 for an explanation) to the assessment of this question. To demonstrate your 'understanding and critical appreciation of the breadth of theoretical and methodological approaches, issues and debates in psychology', your theories should be drawn from different sections of the specification (e.g. *Developmental Psychology* and *Individual Differences*).

Cultural bias in psychological theory and research

What do we mean by culture? 'Culture refers to the collective programming of the mind which distinguishes members of one group from another.' (Hofstede 1980)

In attempting to distinguish one culture from another, we are attempting to draw definitive lines in terms of what is generally a characteristic in one culture but not, perhaps, a characteristic of another. Smith and Bond (1998) identify two major problems with this:

◆ Behaviour differences between any two countries may also be found between different subcultures within the same country.

◆ We assume that cultures are free from conflict and dissent in the behaviour of their members. It is clear that within any culture, there will be a great deal of divergence in the experiences of individuals that make up that culture.

A useful distinction between national cultures has been made by Hofstede (1980). He proposed that cultures could be classified in a number of ways, including their position on the dimension of *individualism–collectivism*. This measures whether an individual's identity is more defined by personal achievement and independence, or by collective achievement and interdependence.

Hofstede studied 50 national cultures and three regions, and ranked them in terms of their scores on the individualism–collectivism dimension. Examples of his findings can be seen in Table 19.1. Note that a high rank denotes a high *individualism* score; a low rank denotes a high *collectivism* score. Under this system, the United States would be the most individualist national culture and Guatemala the most collectivist.

In making this distinction between cultures, Hofstede was careful to avoid what is known as the *ecological fallacy*. This would be the (mistaken) belief that if two cultures differ in terms of their individualist or collectivist

bias, then any two individuals taken at random from those cultures would also differ in that way.

Hofstede's work is not without its problems. It would be tempting, for example, to use these ideas as causal explanations of an individual's behaviour. If individuals are socialized within a collectivist culture, does that mean that they would always behave in a characteristic way? Clearly this would not be the case. Second, the techniques used to gather these data (a series of questionnaires) and the dimensions proposed to explain the results demonstrate a cultural bias specific to western scientific values (see previous section on the problems of using a scientific approach).

Cultural bias in psychology

The emic–etic distinction

This distinction, usually attributed to Berry (1969), focuses on the differences in our analysis of human behaviour:

◆ *Etic* analyses focus on the universals of human behaviour. For example, the theory of moral development proposed by Kohlberg (see Chapter 10) sees moral development as a universal process. That is, all individuals, regardless of culture, would experience the same developmental processes.

◆ An *emic* analysis of behaviour, on the other hand, would focus on the varied ways in which activities and development could be observed in any specific cultural setting.

Berry makes the point that psychology frequently involves an 'imposed etic', in that attempts to explain human behaviour in different parts of the world often involve using theories and research studies that have been developed within (predominantly) the USA. This imposed etic makes the assumption that whatever measures have been used in one cultural context (in this case the USA), will have the same meaning when applied in a different cultural context. Smith and Bond (1998) give the example of the F scale, a measure of authoritarianism that was developed by Adorno *et al.* (1950) in the USA. People who scored highly on this scale invariably showed greater prejudice against minority group members. However, using the same scale with white South African participants, Pettigrew (1958) found that scores on the F scale did not correlate with anti-black prejudice. The *In Focus* on 'Obedience to authority' shows the difficulty of drawing direct comparisons across cultures with respect to one of the most controversial areas of social psychological research, obedience to authority.

Table 19.1 Examples of individualism–collectivism rankings for national cultures	
Country	*Ranking*
United States	1
Australia	2
Great Britain	3
France	10
India	21
Jamaica	25
Hong Kong	37
Pakistan	47
Guatemala	53

Source: Hofstede (1980)

Obedience to authority and the problem of cross-cultural replication

In Milgram's study of obedience to authority (Milgram 1963), he found that 65 per cent of his American participants obeyed orders from an authority figure to give 'fatal' shocks to another person as part of an experiment on learning (You probably looked at Milgram's research in your studies for AS level.) Although no shocks were actually given, the procedures used were convincing and participants were clearly under the impression that they had been giving real shocks.

Despite the outcry in the USA about the ethics of this research, at least eight studies were carried out in other countries after Milgram's results had been published. Extracts from these results are summarized below:

Study	Country	Participants	Percentage obedience
Milgram (1963)	USA	Males general population	65
Mantell (1971)	Germany	Males general population	85
Kilham and Mann (1974)	Australia	Male students	40
		Female students	16
Burley and McGuiness (1977)	UK	Male students	50
Shanab and Yahya (1978)	Jordan	Students	62
Meeus and Raaijmakers (1986)	Holland	General population	92

Source: adapted from Smith and Bond (1993)

Although these studies *appear* to show quite pronounced national differences in the degree of obedience, there are a number of reasons why we should not read too much into the results of this research.

◆ The experiments themselves varied in the way that they were carried out, and also in the type of 'victims' used in the research. For example, in Milgram's study the victims were all men, whereas in the Australian study (Kilham and Mann 1974), the female students were required to give shocks to a female victim. In the Dutch study (Meeus and Raaijmakers 1986), no shocks were given but the 'teacher' was instructed to harass and criticize the victim instead.

◆ With the exception of the study carried out in Jordan (Shanab and Yahya 1978), all of these studies were carried out in advanced industrial countries, so we are unable to conclude unequivocally that this is a universal aspect of human social behaviour.

This discussion demonstrates some of the difficulties in replicating studies exactly across different cultures. In fact, we might argue that exact replication is rarely possible, particularly in areas such as social and developmental psychology. Many of the studies quoted throughout this book have been carried out as a result of a study in another country (usually the USA) becoming well known, and researchers attempting to see if they could get similar results in their own

country. Failure to ensure that participants and procedures are equivalent in different studies means that alternative explanations of the research findings (known as *plausible rival hypotheses*) must be addressed. Some of the problems of establishing equivalence in cross-cultural research are as follows (adapted from Smith and Bond 1998).

◆ *Translation* – Participants are instructed by spoken or written word and their verbal or written responses often constitute the main findings of the research. These instructions and responses must be faithfully translated for the purposes of comparison.

◆ *Manipulation of variables* – The operationalization of variables (see later in this chapter) and the impact of any manipulation must be the same in each cultural group being studied. For example, the expression of happiness might be different in different groups, and the impact of a specific independent variable (such as an insult) dramatically different depending on the way it is interpreted by those involved in the study.

◆ *Participants* – Although these may be taken from similar social groups (university students, schoolchildren, etc.), they may have quite different social backgrounds and experiences in different cultural groups. To gain access to a university in some cultures, for example, does not involve the same criteria as it does in the West.

◆ *The research tradition* – In many cultures, people grow up being used to the idea of scientific research and respond positively to participation in this tradition. Inherent in this positive attitude is the belief that their responses will remain confidential. This trust in the whole research process cannot be taken for granted in all other cultures where psychological research may be rare, if practised at all.

Activity 2: Identifying biases

Turn to Chapter 10 and read about Kohlberg's theory of moral development. Which gender and cultural biases are characteristic of this theory?

Exam summary: Cultural bias in psychological theory and research

The AQA examination will test your understanding of the following areas:

◆ cultural bias in psychological theory (p. 490)

◆ cultural bias in psychological research (pp. 490–2).

Example question

The question below is typical of one drawn from the material above, and should take you 45 minutes to answer:

◆ Discuss the view that research practices in psychology are culturally biased. *(30 marks)*

Suggested answer structure

The term 'research practice' is sufficiently broad to allow you to include both research *studies* (e.g. attempts to replicate Milgram's obedience research in other cultures) and *theoretical* insights (e.g. *economic* theories of relationships – see Chapter 2) to illustrate your answer. The question is asking you to *discuss* the view that research in psychology is *culturally biased*. First of all, you should consider what you understand by the term 'culturally biased' and how this might apply to psychology (pp. 490–2). For example, we have made the point that psychology may be guilty of displaying an *imposed etic*, attempting to explain human behaviour in one part of the world (e.g. China) using theories and research studies that have been developed within another (e.g. USA).

You need to think carefully about what is and what is not relevant to this question. For example, although this section starts with an explanation of the difference between *individualist* and *collectivist* cultures (p. 490), it would not be a good use of your time to write a detailed account explaining how this distinction was developed by Hofstede. It may well be helpful, on the other hand, to include some discussion of how the diversity of these cultural influences may cause our Western ideas of 'normal' behaviour to be inappropriate when explaining the behaviour of the members of other cultures. Examples to illustrate this might well include cultural differences in *bereavement* (see Chapter 12) and *culture-bound syndromes* (see Chapter 16).

As in other questions in this section, this has both an AO2 (as well as the AO1) and a *synoptic* requirement. You can satisfy the latter by describing a breadth of explanations or research methods that demonstrate cultural bias. To address the AO2 requirement of the question, you might consider some of the difficulties that psychologists face when trying to *understand* and *explain* cultural diversity in behaviour. For example, helping others has different meanings in different cultures (see Chapter 1), and attempts to replicate research such as Milgram's often founders because of the difficulties of cross-cultural replication (pp. 491–2).

Ethical issues in research with human participants

The ethical issues of psychological research are based on a number of fundamental moral principles. These are rules or standards that can be justified from a variety of theoretical perspectives. Most psychologists would endorse some version of the following principles.

◆ *Nonmalificence* – Do not harm other people (harm encompasses physical and psychological harm).

◆ *Beneficence* – Help or benefit other people.

◆ *Autonomy* – Allow moral agents to make their own decisions and act on them. This principle implies freedom of thought, expression, and action.

◆ *The Harm Principle* – Autonomy may be limited in order to prevent people from harming each other.

◆ *Utility* – Maximize good consequences and minimize bad consequences for all people.

◆ *Honesty* – Do not lie or deceive other people. Do not manipulate the truth.

◆ *Privacy* – Respect personal privacy and confidentiality.

◆ *Fidelity* – Keep your promises and agreements; be trustworthy.

On a distinction between *ethics* and *morality*

There may at first appear to be no clear-cut distinction between the terms 'ethics' and 'morality', and indeed, many writers use these terms interchangeably. When writing about *theories* of ethics and/or morality, writers tend not to make a distinction between the two, whereas when writing about the *practice* of ethics, the distinction between them becomes more apparent.

It is possible to make a useful distinction between the terms if we use the term 'ethics' to refer to professional, work-related issues, and the term 'morality' in the more personal context of living one's own life (Jones 1999). In this way, work becomes a rule-governed and disciplined activity designed to accomplish some specific task. The overriding value which penetrates the entire activity of work is called 'competence'. Historically, the role of ethics has been in the promotion and maintenance of competence in a particular discipline or activity. Ethics thus fosters the wellbeing of a particular line of work such as medicine, law or psychology. What these three disciplines have in common is that they contain the three basic elements necessary in order for ethics to have a role. They require the acquisition of specialised knowledge, they have standards of competence, and they have well-defined sets of practices that allow the knowledge and standards of competence to be utilized. One consequence of these qualities is that such professions tend to produce a body of rules to promote the long-term welfare of the work. These rules are called 'ethics'.

◆ *Integrity* – Make your actions reflect your moral commitments, principles, beliefs and virtues; do not make decisions based on whimsy, selfishness, or moral cowardice.

◆ *Justice* – Treat people justly, fairly; promote just or fair social institutions; fight injustice.

These moral principles underlie the issues that arise in psychological research with human participants. In the sections that follow, we will examine some of these issues both in terms of why they are important in psychological research and also in terms of the potential impact when these issues are ignored.

Being a research psychologist then, requires an appreciation not only of how to deal with the immediate concerns and rights of our research participants, but also of the more fundamental question of why the research is being carried out in the first place.

Deception

Kimmel (1996) suggests that the effective use of deception in psychological research depends on a number of important methodological assumptions, including the following:

◆ The level of naivete among participants should be high.

◆ The experimental procedure should not produce cues that might be interpreted by participants as indicating that deception is taking place.

◆ Participants' suspiciousness of deception should not alter the experimental effect.

The effectiveness of deception in research assumes a naive participant population. One way of assessing the effectiveness of any research manipulation is to examine its experimental realism, i.e. the degree to which the investigation appears realistic to participants and is taken seriously by them. When deception is employed, investigators take special care that their 'cover story' (how they introduce the investigation to participants) is convincing enough for participants to accept it.

Many of the critics of Milgram's research on obedience have argued that this study lacked experimental realism as participants were able to see through the deception. Orne and Holland (1968), in their description of a replication of Milgram's work supported this claim. In postexperimental interviews, participants claimed not to have believed the deception used by the researcher. This is in contrast to the results of Milgram's own postexperimental interviews, where participants claimed not to have seen through the deception and believed that they had been really delivering painful electric shocks. Orne and Holland explain this apparent inconsistency by claiming that it is consistent with the role of a 'good participant' who may prefer to conceal the fact that they have seen through a deception so as not to compromise the value of the investigation in which they are a participant.

The impact of deception

Baumrind (1985) suggests the following as consequences of deception:

◆ It may decrease the number of naive participants available for future research.

◆ It may reduce support for psychological research in general (e.g. in the media and within the general population).

◆ It may undermine the commitment of researchers always to tell the truth.

Probably the most serious consequence of deception is that it removes the ability of research participants to give their fully informed consent to take part in an investigation. If we don't tell participants everything that is going on in an investigation, then how can they really make a fully informed decision about whether they should take part? This does create dilemmas for the researcher, especially since complete openness may decrease the effectiveness of the investigation.

There are alternatives to deception however, with deception only being used if such alternatives are considered inappropriate. We may, for example, take a random sample of the population to be studied and introduce them to the research design, including knowledge of the deception to be used. If they agree that they would still have given their voluntary informed consent had they known the true aim of the investigation, then we may assume that they represent the views of the rest of their population group.

Informed consent

The essence of the principle of informed consent is that the human subjects of research should be allowed to agree or refuse to participate in the light of comprehensive information concerning the nature and purpose of the research (Homan 1991).

Homan suggests that there are two issues implied in the 'informed' part of informed consent and two involved in the 'consent' part.

To be *informed* means:

◆ all pertinent aspects of what is to happen and what *might* happen are disclosed to the participant

◆ the participants should also be able to understand this information.

If someone volunteers to take part in a study, we might believe that they are doing so because they know exactly what is going to happen to them. Unfortunately, this is not always the case. Epstein and Lasagna (1969) discovered that only one third of participants volunteering for an experiment really understood what was involved.

To give *consent* means:

◆ the participant must be competent to make a rational and mature judgement

◆ the agreement to participate should be voluntary, free from coercion and undue influence.

Some participants may initially give their consent to take part in a study, but if they later realize that they would like to withdraw that consent (for whatever reason), they are free to do so, even if they have previously accepted payment for their participation. The issues of consent and withdrawal may appear compromised by the payment of participants. After all, we live in a society where people who accept payment are seen as entering into a contract to provide services. If a shopkeeper changed his mind about handing over your groceries after he had taken your money, you would be justifiably aggrieved.

It is sometimes difficult to know how much information is appropriate in a particular research investigation. Professional bodies such as the BPS acknowledge the rights of human participants to know about any likely risks, the fact that their participation is voluntary, and the magnitude of their commitment. Most professional organizations such as the BPS either offer explicit guidance concerning informed consent, or put in its place a more general commitment to respect and consideration for participants. The Canadian Psychological Association (CPA), for example, places 'respect for the dignity of persons' above all other values in psychological research.

The rights of the participant are not the only justification of the principle of informed consent. It benefits psychological researchers to be open and honest in their research, as this is more likely to generate public respect and support than more covert and secretive practices. Even those researchers who claim to have obtained informed consent may sometimes be selective in how much they have told their participants. The issue is not between telling the truth and telling lies, but about where one draws the line to decide how much information is sufficient (Homan 1991). A general rule is that the greater the risk, the more meticulous should be the operation of informing potential participants (Homan 1991).

Even if researchers have sought and obtained informed consent, that does not guarantee that participants really do understand what they have let themselves in for. As Schuler (1982) points out, many designs are unintelligible to professional colleagues, let alone participants! Another problem is the requirement for the researcher to point out any likely benefits and risks of participation.

Researchers are not always able to predict accurately the risks of taking part in a study. Stanley Milgram has claimed that he could not have foreseen the severity of the stress experienced by his participants (Milgram 1974).

The issue of informed consent is slightly different when we consider research that takes place in more naturalistic settings (i.e. *field* research). The major obstacle to obtaining informed consent in field research is that it is often simply not feasible, or may be detrimental to the interests of the research (Kimmel 1996). If participants are aware that they are part of a research project, it may defeat the purpose of the research. It is generally accepted that in situations where behaviour is public (such as in shopping malls and at football matches), and the procedures used do not significantly affect participants' lives and do not pose any risk for them, then informed consent is cumbersome and unnecessary (Kimmel 1996). In such situations, obtaining informed consent may be seen as ethically and methodologically undesirable *provided* other measures have been taken to safeguard the interests of the participants (e.g. to ensure their anonymity and to minimize invasions of privacy).

Privacy

Although informed consent may not be such a central issue in field research, privacy most certainly is. When a researcher decides to carry out field research, people are frequently unaware that they are acting as research participants and that a study is taking place.

According to Kimmel (1996), the desire for privacy is balanced against the desire for disclosure and personal communication with others. Webb *et al.* (1981) suggest a continuum of situations by which we can judge whether privacy has been unacceptably violated. At one end of this continuum, those figures who are in the public eye (footballers, politicians, etc.) are aware that their every move, comment or action is constantly under close public scrutiny. On the other hand, figures who are not under the spotlight of public and media attention may well be unaware of the possibility that their behaviour is being observed. These people might be offended to find that strangers were observing them and taking notes on their behaviour.

At the other extreme, people may be 'spied' on in situations where they would clearly expect their behaviour not to be observed (for example, in their own homes, offices, or changing rooms). Although the degree of privacy possible in these settings varies from time to time, there is still general agreement that these are areas where an invasion of privacy

would be inappropriate. Four dimensions are used to determine where a particular piece of research lies on the privacy continuum, and therefore how acceptable observation is under such circumstances.

◆ *How public the setting is* – People can less reasonably expect privacy in shopping malls or football grounds than in the private settings of their own homes.

◆ *The publicness of the person* – Public personalities are regularly subject to observation and reporting that would be considered an invasion of privacy for a less public individual.

◆ *The degree of anonymity provided* – Privacy is maintained when the link between an individual and the information obtained is severed.

◆ *The nature of the information disclosed* – Certain information (e.g. about sexual practices or benefit fraud) is considered more sensitive and poses a greater risk to participants than does other information. Ethical judgements are used to take into consideration the possibility that obtaining such sensitive information would be seen as an invasion of privacy.

Ethics and social responsibility

Some of the more notorious social psychology experiments, such as Milgram's experiments on obedience to authority and Piliavin's research on bystander intervention in emergencies (see p. 70), illustrate the ethically thin ice that many psychologists have chosen to skate upon. But is this the one-sided affair that it might at first appear? Social psychologists such as the late Stanley Milgram and Irving Piliavin have an ethical responsibility to society as a whole, and we might argue that they would not be fulfilling that responsibility if they did not carry out such important research to the best of their ability. Elliot Aronson (1999) suggests that psychologists face a particularly difficult dilemma when their wider responsibility to society conflicts with their more specific responsibilities to each individual research participant. This conflict is greatest when the issues under investigation are issues of great social importance.

Is it just a coincidence that social psychological studies of obedience and bystander behaviour have attracted such adverse reactions from the public? It appears that the more important the issue and the more potential benefit a study might have for society, the more likely it is that the individual participant may experience some degree of discomfort or anxiety. Perhaps we are too short-sighted in sometimes condemning research for the more immediate impact that it has on the people that take part.

Socially sensitive research

Trying to define anything in psychology creates problems and 'socially sensitive research' is no different. Indeed, we might argue that all research is potentially 'socially' sensitive in some way, rather than trying to isolate certain research areas as being potentially more sensitive than others. In fact, few textbooks use this term at all, although many acknowledge the special problems that social researchers face in their work. Sieber and Stanley (1988) offer the following definition of 'socially sensitive research.

> '... studies in which there are potential social consequences or implications, either directly for the participants in research or the class of individuals represented by the research.' (Sieber and Stanley 1988, p. 49)

The essence of this definition is that much of what we study in psychology has a *social* impact. This isn't to say that all research doesn't have that potential, but it is a little harder to imagine the social impact of, for example, research into perceptual illusions or short-term memory. Research about the genetic basis of criminality, on the other hand, has a potential for profound social consequences (compulsory genetic testing, imprisonment of genetically influenced criminals, and so on). One of the problems of any research that comes under this definition is that it is likely to attract a good deal of attention, not only from other psychologists, but also from the media and the public (Wadeley *et al.* 1997). Whilst this is not necessarily a bad thing, given that the results of psychological research should be more available to a wider audience, it does open up research practices to a wider (and sometimes ill-informed) critical scrutiny.

The sorts of research that would come under the heading of socially sensitive research include research into racial differences, gender-related abilities, sexual orientation, and so on. Not only does this type of research have implications for the people that take part (see previous sections on the ethics of laboratory and field research), but also for the wider social group that they represent. If, for example, researchers carried out research that demonstrated differences in the mathematical abilities of boys and girls, this might well have implications far beyond the very small percentage of participants that had actually been tested. This may take the form of lowered expectations for one sex

compared with the other, self-fulfilling prophecies, occupational discrimination, and so on. Such research is, therefore, 'sensitive' and because of that, as soon as it is exposed to public scrutiny and commentary, it becomes controversial.

Ethical guidelines may protect the immediate needs of research participants, but may not deal with all the possible ways in which research may inflict harm on a group of people or section of society. The Canadian Psychological Association (1991), for example, advises its members to 'analyse likely short-term, ongoing, and long-term risks and benefits of each course of action on the individual(s)/group(s) involved or likely to be affected.'

Psychologists are cautioned that some aspects of human behaviour are beyond the scope of psychological research, although it is largely left to individual psychologists as to how this caution is interpreted. This has resulted in some researchers avoiding sensitive areas altogether, and those who do pursue such areas often risk criticism from colleagues and others outside the discipline.

Of course, we could avoid the controversies associated with this kind of research by restricting our research interests to those areas that attract very little attention from the media and from peers outside of our special area of interest. This is not really the answer, as much of the research that takes place in socially sensitive areas has important and potentially beneficial effects for certain sections of society. What we should be most concerned about, however, is the possibility that the results of such research might also offer the possibility of abuse and discrimination or, as Sieber and Stanley suggest, offer some scientific credibility to the prevailing prejudice (Sieber and Stanley 1988).

Carrying out research in socially sensitive areas (such as racial and gender-related research) raises difficult ethical issues (see Table 19.2) and should focus psychologists more clearly on the implications of their findings. Ignoring these important areas of research, however, would amount to an abdication of what Aronson (1999) refers to as the 'social responsibilities' of the psychological researcher.

Activity 3: Ethical investigations

Look at some of the research carried out in different areas of psychology that you are studying. To what extent would these investigations be considered 'ethical' if they were carried out now?

Table 19.2   Ten ethical issues in socially sensitive research

1   Privacy

During the research process, a skilled investigator may extract more information from participants than they intended to give. Some research (e.g. AIDS research) may lead to social policies that are an invasion of people's private lives (e.g. through compulsory antibody testing and quarantine).

2   Confidentiality

In some areas of research, questions may reveal information of a sensitive nature (such as sexual habits or drug use). In such situations confidentiality is paramount. Otherwise, participants would be less willing to divulge this information in the future and further research in this area would have been compromised.

3   Sound and valid methodology

Some of the controversies that arise from socially sensitive research can be attributed to poorly designed or executed studies or inappropriate interpretations of the findings. Although other scientists may be aware of these problems, the media and the public may not, and thus poor studies might shape important social policy to the detriment of those groups represented by the research.

4   Deception

Deception refers to causing a person to believe that which is not true. This may not only involve deceiving others, but also self-deception. Claims about women's lack of mathematical ability or of racial differences in intelligence both present situations that might be self-deceiving for those who read about these alleged deficiencies.

5   Informed consent

It is important to ensure that when research is reported in the scientific literature, as well as the popular media, it is done so in such a way that people are not misled or coerced into acting in a way that is not in their best interests. Respectful communication between scientist and society is both assumed and essential.

6   Justice and equitable treatment

It is important that during the research all participants are treated in an equitable manner, and that resources which are vital to the participants' wellbeing (e.g. educational opportunities) are not withheld from one group whilst being available to another. Likewise, ideas that create prejudicial treatment of one sector of society are seen as unfair

and therefore unacceptable. Freud's ideas of the 'deficient' nature of women were instrumental in their treatment as second-class citizens in the early part of this century.

7   Scientific freedom

It is the role of the researcher to carry out scientific research. This freedom to pursue scientific research is balanced against the obligation to protect those who take part or the sectors of society that they represent. Censorship of scientific activity is generally regarded as unacceptable, but some careful monitoring of the research process is seen as necessary.

8   Ownership of data

The question of who 'owns' research data is a very complex one. Some of the problems with determining ownership involve the sponsorship of the research (e.g. a university department, military unit or commercial organization) and the public accessibility of the data. A major concern in the interpretation and application of research findings in psychology is that they may be used for reasons other than those for which they were originally intended. Kelman (1965) suggests that it is the responsibility of all researchers to consider in advance the ways in which their research might be used. This is in sharp contrast to the view taken by many scientists, that knowledge is 'ethically neutral'.

9   Values and epistemology of social scientists

There is no such thing as a value-free science. Inevitably, the researchers themselves have values concerning the nature of human beings that might differ from those of the recipients of their research findings. Some researchers take the view that all research should be for the betterment of human beings, whilst others stress the importance of scientific truth and rigorous methodology. The late Hans Eysenck was very much a proponent of the latter, whilst his controversial views were frequently criticized by those who subscribed more to the former.

10 Risk/benefit ratio

Whilst we might argue that the goal of all psychological research is ultimately beneficial, there are often accompanying side effects that may be risky for those who take part or those who are represented in the research. When this is the case, it is necessary to take steps to minimize the possible costs of the research.

Source: adapted from Sieber and Stanley (1988)

Exam summary: Ethical issues in research with human participants

The AQA examination will test your understanding of the following areas:

◆ ethical issues in research with human participants (pp. 492–5)

◆ the ethics of socially sensitive research (pp. 496–7).

Example question

The question below is typical of one drawn from the material above, and should take you 45 minutes to answer:

◆ Discuss the ethics of socially sensitive research.

(30 marks)

Suggested answer structure

This question merits careful reading. There is an alarming tendency for many students not to see the words 'socially sensitive' and to write about more general ethical issues. This is not to say that issues such as deception, confidentially and privacy are not relevant to socially sensitive research – they clearly are. However, it is all too easy to slip into answering the wrong question, particularly during the stress of an examination. On a more general note, it is quite appropriate to discuss the use of ethical guidelines in psychological research. These are, after all, the main way that researchers deal with the ethical issues discussed in this section. (You should have looked at these in your AS level studies.) Remember, however, when answering questions on ethical issues that the *guidelines* are not the *issues*, but ways of resolving them. As we have seen, however (p. 497), ethical guidelines may not deal with all the possible ways in which research may inflict harm on a group of people or section of society.

It is an interesting exercise, although perhaps a little distracting when trying to write an essay, to see how professional psychologists deal with the sensitive issues of research. You will have read about the Canadian Psychological Association's approach to this issue (p. 497), but you can read about this in more detail on their website: http://www.cpa.ca

It is often difficult, in discursive questions such as this, to remember that you must include AO2 material (in this case an *evaluation*) as well as *describing* what the particular issues might be (the AO1 content). Your response should, therefore, be planned extremely carefully. As in all the questions in this section, there is also a requirement to display a *breadth* of theories, methods, etc. that might be appropriate for the *synoptic* part of the assessment

for this question. You should take every opportunity to demonstrate the breadth of your critical understanding of socially sensitive research issues. Part of the synoptic requirement of questions such as this is that they span more than one area of psychology, so remember to draw your examples from different sections of the specification, such as *Social Psychology, Individual Differences*, and so on.

To address the AO1 component (which requires a *description* of the issues of socially sensitive research), it is wise to begin with a definition (p. 496), and then move on to give some examples of socially sensitive research drawn from different areas of psychology (to fulfil the synoptic component). You may, for example, describe the particular problems associated with research into gender differences, or research into the genetic basis of criminality (p. 496). It is important, even when giving examples, that you illustrate *why* such research is socially sensitive, rather than just suggesting that it is. Research becomes socially sensitive when the impact of a study extends beyond the people taking part and has significant social consequences for the group that they represent.

The table on p. 497 illustrates ten of the most important issues in socially sensitive research (e.g. privacy, scientific freedom, risk/benefit ratio). You should not attempt to include *all* of these, this would make your response far too superficial (see Table 21.3 on p. 554 to understand the consequences of this). Select *some* of these issues and elaborate them as in the table, possibly using the rest of this book to search out actual examples of research that illustrate the issue in question (again, this helps with the synoptic assessment of the question).

For the AO2 part of the question, try to examine some of the judgmental issues associated with this type of research. For example, you might consider the *adequacy* of existing ethical guidelines for dealing with socially sensitive research (p. 496) or how psychologists might deal constructively with the issues that such research raises (again the CPA approach to ethics is a good example of this). Does it have potentially positive consequences for society, or does it merely 'add scientific credibility to the prevailing prejudice' (p. 496)?

A good way to finish your response to a question on socially sensitive research is to remind the reader of Elliot Aronson's point about the 'social responsibilities' of the psychological researcher that need to be offset against the particular problems of socially sensitive research.

The use of nonhuman animals in research

As psychology is, you might imagine, the study of *human* behaviour, why then do we bother studying *nonhuman* animals? There are several reasons why psychologists may choose to expend their research efforts on nonhuman animals.

Why psychologists study nonhuman animals

◆ Animals may be studied simply because they are fascinating in their own right. The development of *ethology* (the study of behaviour in its natural environment) has arisen for this very reason, although some of the methods used are also open to ethical concerns (see p. 501).

◆ Animals offer the opportunity for greater control and objectivity in research procedures. Given the interest in and value of scientific methods in psychology, greater opportunities for experimental control exist with animals than with humans. Much of behaviourist theory was established using animal studies for just this reason. Objectivity is more easily

attained with nonhuman than human animals, simply because it is difficult to remain completely objective when studying our own species. We may have expectations, biases and stereotypes of members of our own species that are not as evident when we work with another species.

◆ We may use animals when we can't use humans. Animals have been exposed to various procedures and events that would simply not be possible with human beings. Harlow's deprivation work with rhesus monkeys (Harlow 1962; see *In Focus*) could not have been carried out on humans. Often the need to establish cause and effect relationships in psychological research involves participants in procedures that they would not consent to take part in. This does, of course, raise the moral question of why we might expose animals to research procedures that we could not justify with human participants. We will return to this thorny question later.

◆ Human beings and nonhuman animals have sufficient of their physiology and evolutionary past in common to justify conclusions drawn from the

---

in focus

Contact, comfort and attachment (Harlow 1962)

An important factor in the development of the attachment bond between infant and caregiver is the physical contact that exists between them. The research that first established this fact was carried out by Harry Harlow in the early 1960s. Harlow's original intention was not to explore the role of physical contact in attachment, but rather to look at the effects of brain damage on learning. This was not the sort of experiment it would have been possible to carry out with human subjects. In order to maintain a sample of young rhesus monkeys free from disease, Harlow raised them alone, away from their mothers. He noticed that these motherless monkeys formed strong attachments to small pieces of cloth in their cages and would protest loudly when they were removed. This led Harlow to wonder whether his infant monkeys needed physical contact with something soft for their normal development.

In an experiment to find out, he constructed artificial or 'surrogate' mothers. One of these was a bare wire frame, whilst the other one was covered in a soft terry towelling material. The motherless infants could only obtain milk from the 'wire' mother. The infants spent most of their time, however, clinging to the soft towelling mother and only went to the wire mother when they needed to drink. In subsequent research (Harlow and Harlow 1966), infant rhesus monkeys were exposed to various forms of rejection from their surrogate mothers. These included expelling strong jets of air and metal spikes that appeared from inside the towelling and pushed the monkey away. None of these seemed to have any lasting effects on the attachment of the infant to the surrogate mother, as they merely waited for the rejection episode to stop, then moved back onto the mother.

From findings such as these, Harlow concluded that at least in part, a monkey's attachment to its mother depends on the contact comfort that she provides. Evidence for such effects in human infants is mixed but does seem to suggest that they, too, have a need for contact, and the cuddling that is an integral part of the parent–infant relationship plays an important role in the formation of a lasting attachment bond.

one being applied to the other. Behaviourists such as Skinner saw sufficient similarity between rats and humans to warrant a special interest in rats as research subjects. Apparent similarities in the way rats and humans learn led Skinner to establish laws of learning based almost entirely on the study of rats (and other nonhuman animals) in controlled environments.

Changing trends in animal research

There has long been a tradition of using animals in psychology. Knowledge derived from this research has been instrumental in the development of many psychological theories and practices. Despite this long tradition, the popularity of animal research, particularly within the UK has diminished dramatically over the last fifteen years. The decrease in the use of animals has in part been due to the tightening of legislation concerning the use of animals. This is a direct result of the Animals (Scientific Procedures) Act of 1986, and also a result of the decrease in numbers of students choosing to follow psychology degree options that make significant use of nonhuman animals. This latter reason has inevitable consequences for the postgraduate interests of psychology students, and ultimately the research interests of psychology departments. The legislative changes surrounding the use of animals in research have also made university research review bodies more wary of the financial and moral constraints that underlie this avenue of research interest.

Table 19.3 contains the results of a survey carried out by Thomas and Blackman (1991) which compared the types and overall numbers of animals used in research in UK psychology departments for the academic years 1976–7 and 1988–9. It is clear from these results that there has been a significant decline in:

◆ the overall numbers of animals used

◆ the number of different species used

◆ the number of different procedures used.

It is significant that the only increase in any category is in the nonexperimental research projects, such as those involving the observation of animals. The annual number of animal experiments has fallen by over two and a half million over the last 20 years. This is due to higher standards of animal welfare, scientific advances and stricter controls (see *In Focus* on p. 502). Although there are sometimes small rises, such as in 1994 and 1996, the overall trend is downwards. A change in the law in 1986 led to 'procedures', rather than 'experiments', being reported. The definition of procedures is somewhat broader, including the use of animals to produce natural products for research or treatment.

---

in focus **Some significant moments in the history of animal research**

1859 Charles Darwin publishes his *Theory of Evolution by Natural Selection*.

Darwin's theory provided a scientific rationale for using animals to learn about humans. Darwin also believed in an emotional and behavioural continuum between humans and animals, and was thus aware of the suffering that experimentation might cause.

1959 William Russell and Rex Burch publish the 'three Rs'.

In *The Principles of Humane Experimental Technique*, Russell and Birch set out three goals for the conscientious researcher. These were: replacement of animals by other methods, reduction of numbers of animals used by more sophisticated statistical techniques, and refinement of experimental techniques to cause less suffering.

1975 Peter Singer publishes *Animal Liberation* and coins the term 'speciesism'.

Singer believed that the total benefits (to both humans and animals) of research should be weighed against the total suffering caused in the process. Singer did not believe that the interests of humans and animals had equal weight, but believed that ignoring the interests of an animal just because it was not human was to commit speciesism.

1986 Animals (Scientific Procedures) Act is passed.

This act safeguards laboratory animal welfare while allowing important research to continue. At the heart of this act is a cost-benefit analysis which must be applied before any research project involving animals can go ahead. The costs, in terms of potential animal suffering, must be weighed against the potential benefits of the research.

Table 19.3 Number of animals in 1988/9 academic year subjected to various types of research procedures

	Non-experi-mental	Food/water deprivation	Other deprivation	Drugs	Surgery	Electric shock	Other exp.	Total 1989	Total 1977	1989 total as % of 1977
Monkey	146				11		2	159	364	44
Cat									32	0
Rabbit									600	0
Rat	608	3495	355	3990	1431	490	403	10772	35560	30
Guinea pig									100	0
Gerbil									140	0
Mouse	600		30	610			262	1502	2614	57
Other mammals	50							50	221	23
Pigeon	40	621		48	61			770	1062	73
Chick									1600	0
Other birds	32							32	710	5
Reptiles	1							1	4	25
Fish									189	0
Total 1989	1477	4116	385	4648	1503	490	667	13286		
Total 1977	1174	8980	5916	6851	4761	3929	11585		43196	
1989 total as % of 1977 Standard	126	46	7	68	32	12	6			31

(adapted from Thomas and Blackman 1991)

Activity 4: Ethical investigations?

Look through the book and identify some studies using animals in laboratory settings. What ethical issues arise from these studies? Do you think the findings in these studies sufficiently important to justify the use of animals?

Field experiments in animal research

Ethical concern about the use of animals is normally focused on laboratory research with animals. This is due to the belief that animal research in the field involves discreet observation and noninterference with the animals being studied. A steady diet of BBC natural history programmes tends to reinforce such a view.

However, field experiments (i.e. manipulating some part of the animal's natural habitat) have been an important part of ethological research since the beginning of this discipline. It is important to consider the ethical concerns of this area of research for three major reasons:

◆ Ethologists are in a unique position to comment on how animals react to stress and suffering; their insights are, therefore, vital if animals are to be used in psychological research.

◆ Ethological research tends not to be of any direct benefit to human beings. If the justification of research is determined purely on that basis, then ethological research would be considered to be very low priority.

◆ By their very nature, field experiments alter the natural environment of the animal in some way. This tampering with nature in order to understand it places great responsibilities on the researcher to ensure that the disruptive effects of any manipulation are kept to a minimum.

Cuthill (1991), in an analysis of over 930 research papers published in the journal *Animal Behaviour* between the years 1986 and 1990, calculated 46 per

A case-study in animal experimentation

Aims of the study

To demonstrate, using an animal model of anxiety, that the drug clonidine has a specific anti-anxiety action.

Methods

The elevated plus maze is a + shaped maze raised about a metre off the floor. Two opposite arms are enclosed by walls and two are open. Effective anti-anxiety drugs such as librium and valium increase the time rats spend on the open arms relative to the time spent in the enclosed arms. This piece of apparatus is therefore often used to screen new drugs to see if they may have clinical anti-anxiety potential.

Rats were injected with one of several doses of clonidine, and 20 minutes later given a 10-minute exposure to the plus maze. There were ten rats in each dosage group and a nondrugged control group. Time spent on open arms and in enclosed arms was recorded.

Results

Low doses of clonidine increased the time spent on open arms relative to the time spent in enclosed arms, in a similar manner to librium. At higher doses, there was a clear sedative (tranquillizing) action. The conclusion was that, at low doses, clonidine has a significant anti-anxiety action.

Ethical issues

◆ Source of animals and housing – rats were supplied by an animal breeding company accredited by the Home Office. All laboratories engaged in animal work have their housing and testing facilities checked by Home Office inspectors. Checks include cage sizes, lighting, temperature, humidity, security and day-to-day care and management. There are regular visits by Home Office inspectors and accredited vets. All animal housing facilities are now custom-built to Home Office regulations.

◆ Experimental work – all studies with animals have to be licensed by the Home Office under the Animals (Scientific Procedures) Act 1986. Every researcher has to apply for a personal licence, demonstrating that they have the necessary skills and experience to work with animals. Often, these licences restrict the researcher to certain techniques and a certain species, and they must not stray beyond those restrictions. Then the researcher applies for a project licence. This details the aims and methods of the proposed research project, including the procedures to be used, numbers of animals, level of stress involved, and justification for the research in terms of its implications, e.g. for the development of more effective clinical drugs. The application is assessed by experts in the field and will only be approved if the stress experienced by the animals (e.g. drug injection, exposure to stressful situations such as the plus maze) is justified by the benefits of the research; if the number of animals is the minimum necessary for valid results; and if there are no alternative procedures which could achieve the same ends without using animals.

Source: Green and Vale (1995)

cent (426) to be field studies. Of these 426 papers, one-third involved experimental manipulations. The main methods are broken down by percentage of papers in Figure 19.1.

Major types of experimental manipulation in field research

1 *Dummies* – This involves the presence of a stuffed dummy predator. Although the appearance of a predator is within the normal experience of an animal, its presence can cause distress and in some cases, abandonment of its young.

2 *Nontrivial handling* – Repeated trappings in order for procedures such as radio tagging to take place can lead to distress both from capture and also from the increased energy expenditure which is necessary for smaller animals (such as birds) to carry the transmitting device.

3 *Playback* – As used in studies of alarm calls (such as Seyfarth *et al.*'s study of vervet monkeys 1980) playback of recorded signals can cause some distress. In extreme cases, the habituation that may develop to signals in the absence of a predator, may

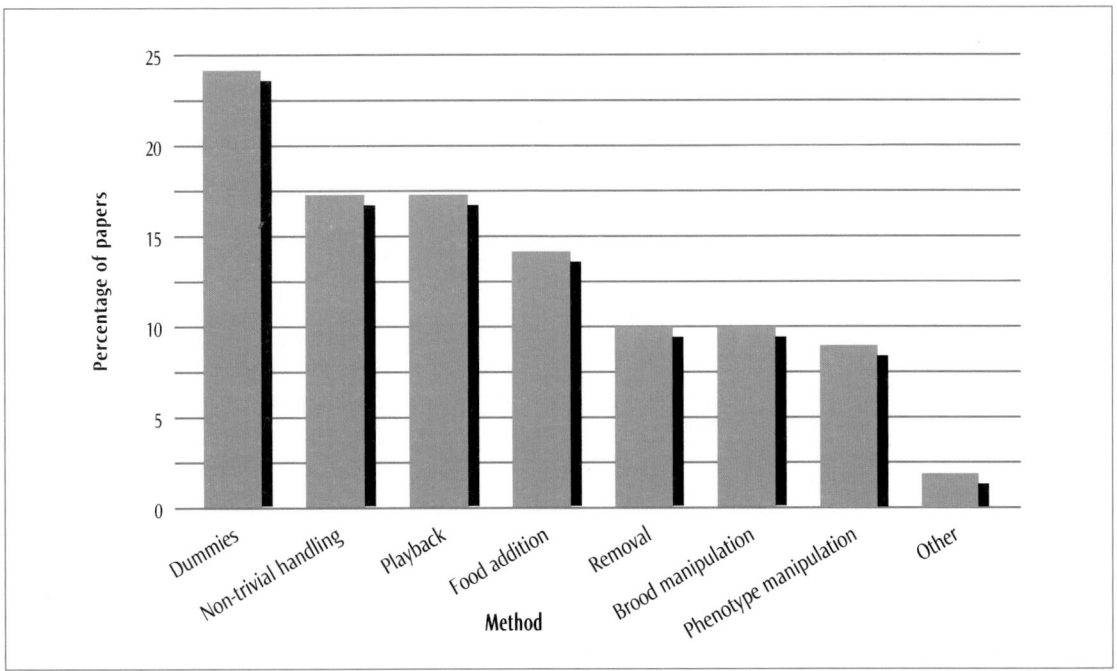

Figure 19.1 Methods employed in papers involving field experiments, published in Animal Behaviour from 1986 to 1990
Source: Cuthill (1991)

put the animals in danger should they fail to respond to alarm calls involving real predators.

4 *Food addition* – If food is provided to provoke territorial disputes or dominance encounters, there is a risk of injury from the aggression that this might cause. The artificial provision of extra food also upsets the natural ecology of the area, and leaves animals without the food on which they have come to depend once the experiment is over.

5 *Removal* – This may involve the temporary removal of an animal (e.g. the removal of one parent in studies of biparental care) or the release of an animal elsewhere from its normal territory. This may impair the survival chances of the animal on release, or may lead to an increased chance of starvation in the young that are left behind.

6 *Brood manipulation* – This is largely restricted to studies involving birds. It enables investigators to study the optimum clutch size in different species of birds, by looking at the effects of brood manipulation upon the increased mortality through starvation. By interfering with the ecological conditions under which birds must survive, the investigator takes responsibility for the effects of any alteration.

7 *Phenotype manipulation* – By altering characteristics of certain animals (e.g. through altering plumage in some way, such as artificially extending tail length) it is possible to investigate the effects of specific characteristics on reproductive success. It is difficult to assess the possible stressful effects that such

alterations might have on the animals concerned. Males that are given extra plumage might find themselves the victims of aggression from other males who respond to the new adornment as if it were a 'badge of rank'.

Field experiments involving animals may create problems that persist long after the experiment is concluded. In order to minimize the disruptive effects of these studies, a number of procedures are necessary to assess the potential impact of the study. First, the use of pilot studies might go some way towards assessing the potential impact of the study. Second, animals that are not directly a part of the study should be monitored to check whether they are being affected by the manipulation. Finally, it is important to carry out follow-up studies to assess (and minimize) the disruptive effects of the experiment.

Arguments for animal research

'Animal liberators need to accept that animal research is beneficial to humans. And animal researchers need to admit that if animals are close enough to humans that their bodies, brains and even psyches are good models for the human condition, then ethical dilemmas surely arise in using them. But the moral burden is not for scientists alone to bear. All of us who use modern medicine and modern consumer products need to acknowledge the debt we owe to our fellow creatures and support science in its quest to do better by the animals.' (Barbara Orlans 1997)

The arguments most commonly used in *defence* of animal research are summarized by Kimmel (1996).

◆ Animal research has produced many benefits to humans and to animals.

◆ Researchers are sensitive to the pain and suffering experienced by animals and use procedures that ensure animals are humanely treated.

◆ Researchers have developed alternative procedures which have led to a reduction in the use of animals. Therefore animals are only used when no other suitable procedure is available.

Traditional defence of the use of animals (for whatever purposes) has centred around the philosophical notion that humans and nonhumans can be differentiated, in that nonhumans do not possess a soul, and are therefore not capable of moral choice or, indeed, any other feelings and emotions that are peculiarly human. Despite increasing research evidence that animals are, in fact, capable of experiencing a whole range of emotions and feelings, this view of animals as 'mechanical systems' or 'renewable resources' is a hard one to shake off.

Even within the utilitarian argument (see *In Focus*, p. 506), research with animals would be tolerated if it produced considerable benefits for humanity. This has led to the most well developed of the pro-animal research arguments. Experimentation with animals, it is claimed, has produced considerable improvements in the lives of human beings. Conditioning techniques derived from work on animals are now in regular use within therapeutic contexts. Likewise, early views about the nature and causes of stress and the modifiability of involuntary behaviour have been shown to be incorrect as a result of animal research (Weiss 1972).

This position is still open to criticism from those who argue that the pro-animal research lobby has a tendency to overemphasize the benefits and play down the suffering that produced those benefits. Some of the major arguments justifying animal research, together with their critical counterpoints, are presented in Table 19.4.

Arguments against animal research

'Even granting that we [humans] face greater harm than laboratory animals presently endure if... research on these animals is stopped, the animal rights view will not be satisfied with anything less than total abolition.'

(Tom Regan: *The Case For Animal Rights* 1983)

'If abandoning animal research means that there are some things we cannot learn, then so be it ...

We have no basic right...not to be harmed by those natural diseases we are heir to.'

(Tom Regan: *The Case for Animal Rights* 1983)

We can usefully divide the arguments against animal research into two separate types. There are those that object to the use of animals in research on *scientific* grounds, and those that object to such research on *ethical* grounds.

Scientific objections

The essence of a scientific argument against the use of animals is that animal experiments would tell us nothing of any value about human behaviour because of the dissimilarities between humans and nonhumans. Whilst it is true that some research is carried out on animals to discover facts about animals, the majority of animal studies in psychology are comparative, i.e. animals are being used because they may give us important insights into human behaviour.

If animals are to be used to tell us something about human behaviour, then it follows that there should be sufficient similarity between the brains and behaviour of humans and nonhuman animals. If this were not so, then the case for studying animals to gain insights into human behaviour would be very weak indeed. Critics of animal research often assert that these assumed similarities just do not exist. Green (1994) argues otherwise: the basic physiology of the brain and nervous systems of all mammals is essentially the same. Although the human brain might be more highly developed, its similarity to the brains of nonhuman mammals is far greater than critics of this approach would have us believe. Similarly, the basic classifications of behaviour (affective, cognitive and motivational) are evident in all mammalian species.

Ethical objections

The second type of argument is an ethical one. We may take an extreme ethical stance over the issue of animal research, contending that pain or distress is never justifiable in animal research, regardless of the benefits to humankind. This position owes much to the work of people such as Peter Singer and Tom Regan (Regan and Singer 1976). Singer saw discrimination against animals as logically parallel to any other form of discrimination. In the same way that we would argue against racism and sexism as being morally indefensible, Singer suggests that 'speciesism' (discrimination against one species for the benefits of another) is also unacceptable. Regan, a champion of the animal rights movement, makes the point that current legislation does not go far enough in protecting the subjects of animal research. What is needed, he claims, is not larger, cleaner cages, but empty cages (Regan 1983).

Table 19.4	Justifying animal research

Arguments for animal research	Counterpoints
1 Experiments on animals have made an important contribution to advances in medicine and psychology that have brought major improvements in the health and wellbeing of human beings *and* animals.	1 These contributions have often been accomplished at considerable expense in terms of animal suffering. Although adopting a costs-benefits analysis of individual research projects should ensure that the costs (in terms of animal suffering) and the benefits (in terms of significant medical and scientific advancements) are predictable, neither of these is certain prior to a study commencing. By calculating the benefits to *humankind*, but the costs to *animals*, we might be committing speciesism.
2 Rights arise as a result of implicit contracts between members of society, and imply duties. Animals have no such responsibilities, cannot reciprocate and therefore have no rights.	2 Animals have rights by virtue of their 'inherent value'. These rights include the right to be treated with respect and not to be harmed. The traditional scientific position on animal research treats animals as 'renewable resources', rather than as organisms of value whose rights we must respect. If we fail to recognize the rights of other species, we would be violating the principle of respect. Also, infants and the mentally ill might not be able to fulfil their obligations to society, but are not denied rights within it.
3 Evolution has placed human beings 'on top' of the phylogenetic tree, so it is natural for us to make use of 'lower animals' for our own ends. If, by using animals, we can ease human suffering, then we are morally obliged to do so.	3 This is known as the *naturalistic fallacy*. David Hume (a philosopher writing in the eighteenth century), said that 'what *is* cannot dictate what *ought* to be'. Natural history may well have provided us with an understanding of why our morals have evolved into their present form, but we can *transcend* our nature. Not using other species for our own ends may be seen as the next step in that evolution.
4 A number of less invasive procedures have been developed and are being used in animal research. This minimizes animal suffering and provides a moral justification for animal research.	4 If researchers were not allowed to use animals in research, they would have to develop other techniques (such as clinical and epidemiological studies) to take the place of animal research. CAT, PET and MRI scans, and in-depth computer modelling are among the modern approaches that are available as very real alternatives to animal research. If we were to adopt a model based on animal 'rights' then animals would have the right not to be used by humans for research *regardless* of how 'noninvasive' the research procedures, or how potentially beneficial the consequences for human beings.
5. There are strict laws (e.g. the 1986 Use of Animals Act) and codes of conduct (e.g. BPS and ASAB guidelines) that protect animals that are used in research.	5 Most ethical guidelines are based on a 'costs-benefits' model, where the recipients of costs (i.e. the animals) and benefits (i.e. humans) tend to be different, and which ignore the substantive rights of animals in favour of practical, utilitarian considerations.

In defence of the use of animals in research, the British Association for the Advancement of Science produced a Declaration on Animals in Research (1990), which includes the statement:

'Continued research involving animals is essential for the conquest of many unsolved medical problems, such as cancer, AIDS, other infectious diseases, and genetic, developmental, neurological and psychiatric conditions'.

Criteria for assessing research on animals

Medical research has as its goal outcomes which are directly beneficial to human beings. The use of animals

in such research is usually justified to the public because it contributes directly to the relief of human suffering. Developing a cure for a disease such as cancer or Alzheimer's disease can offset much of the terrible physical, social and economic suffering that inevitably accompanies such conditions. But how could *psychologists* justify the use of animals? One justification proposed is that the study of animals helps us to understand natural principles (such as those involved in learning) because they are a convenient way of developing and testing such principles.

As mentioned earlier, some people may hold the opinion that it is morally wrong to inflict any kind of pain or suffering upon nonhuman animals. If we are to

Some philosophical views on animal research

Singer's utilitarian view of animal research

The main focus of the utilitarian argument is that what is ethically acceptable is that which produces the greatest pleasure and happiness (relative to pain and suffering) for the greatest number of people. According to this argument, no one person's happiness is more important than any other's. Peter Singer's book *Animal Liberation*, published in 1975, extends this utilitarian argument to include all sentient (capable of sensation) creatures. His 'principle of equality' holds that all such creatures have an equal interest in avoiding pain and suffering.

Consistent with this principle of equality is the belief that we have no moral basis for elevating the interests of one species (e.g. humans) over those of other species. To do so would be to commit speciesism, which is logically parallel to other forms of discrimination such as racism and sexism. Speciesism, according to Singer, is the result of a prejudiced attitude, which sets the interests of our own species above those of other species.

Research on animals might be permitted under some circumstances, but only when the potential benefits of the research are high and the research could also be carried out using human subjects.

Regan's animals' rights argument

The fundamental belief of the animal rights position is that all animals have rights that are based on their inherent value. These rights include the right to be treated with respect and not to be harmed. A consequence of this position is that animals have the right *not* to be used by humans for research, regardless of any potential benefits for humans that might arise from such research.

The traditional scientific position on animal research, claim proponents of this position, treats animals as 'renewable resources' rather than as organisms of value whose rights we must respect. If we fail to recognize the rights of other species, according to this argument, we would be violating the principle of respect.

Tom Regan, a champion of this position, believes that we cannot justify animal research by quoting benefits for human beings or even improvements to research conditions. Unlike the utilitarian position, animal research would not be tolerated under any conditions. Cost-benefit considerations are insufficient justification for animal research.

---

find an acceptable way of using animals in research, what kinds of criteria, over and above those covered by the Animals Act (1986) (outlined in Table 19.5), should be considered? In 1986, Professor Patrick Bateson, Secretary of the Ethical Committee of the Association for the Study of Animal Behaviour, proposed a system that would allow such criteria to be applied. Bateson's decision cube (see Fig. 19.2) assesses proposed research on three criteria.

The three criteria used to assess proposed research with animals are:

◆ the quality of the research
◆ the degree of animal suffering
◆ the certainty of benefit.

Quality of the research

Although determining the quality of research may appear to be very subjective, there is actually a great deal of agreement among psychologists about what constitutes high-quality research. The difficulties of obtaining research funding, together with the sheer expense of animal research, means that institutional committees are likely to award research grants only to animal research of the highest quality (in terms of design and procedures).

Degree of animal suffering

It is, of course, difficult to put oneself inside the mind of an animal and assess the degree to which a particular animal is or is not suffering as a result of the procedures to which we expose it. Some animals when threatened by danger remain rigid and silent because that is the safest thing to do. We may not recognize such behaviour as being a state of stress. As we increase our knowledge of how animals behave, we become more aware of what is and what is not likely to be stressful for a particular species.

Table 19.5 Guidelines for the Use of Animals in Research: Extracts from the Animals (Scientific Procedures) Act 1986

1 The law

Within the United Kingdom there are specific laws protecting the rights of animals. Failure to comply with these laws leads to prosecution.

2 Ethical considerations

If animals are to be constrained, harmed or stressed in any way, investigators must consider whether the knowledge to be gained justifies the procedure. Alternatives to animal experiments should be considered wherever possible.

3 Species

If the research procedures used are likely to cause pain or discomfort, the investigator should bear in mind that some species may be less likely to suffer than others. Investigators should, therefore, have knowledge of a species' natural history as well as its special needs.

4 Number of animals

Laboratory studies should use the smallest number of animals necessary. Careful thought in the design of an experiment as well as the statistical analysis used can reduce the number of animals necessary in any given study.

5 Endangered species

Members of endangered species should not be collected or manipulated in the wild except as a serious attempt at conservation.

6 Caging and social environment

Caging conditions should take into account the social behaviour of the species. An acceptable density of one species may constitute overcrowding for a different species. In social animals caging in isolation may have undesirable effects.

7 Motivation

When arranging schedules of deprivation, the experimenter should consider the animal's normal eating and drinking habits and its metabolic requirements. However, differences between species must also be borne in mind. A short period of deprivation for one species may be unacceptably long for another.

8 Aversive stimuli and stressful procedures

Procedures that cause pain or distress to animals are illegal in the UK unless the experimenter holds a Home Office Licence and the relevant certificates. The investigator should be satisfied that there are no alternative ways of conducting the experiment without the use of aversive stimulation.

If alternatives are not available, the investigator has the responsibility of ensuring that any suffering is kept to a minimum and that it is justified by the expected scientific contribution of the experiment. Any stressful procedures to be used have to be assessed and licensed by the Home Office.

Figure 19.2
Bateson's decision cube

A cube for deciding whether a research project should proceed (clear space) or it should not (solid space) (from Bateson 1986). The most obvious case for proceeding is when the amount of suffering is negligible, the quality of the research is high and the benefit is certain. At the other extreme, the clearest case where research should not be done is when the suffering is likely to be great, the quality of the work and the benefit uncertain.

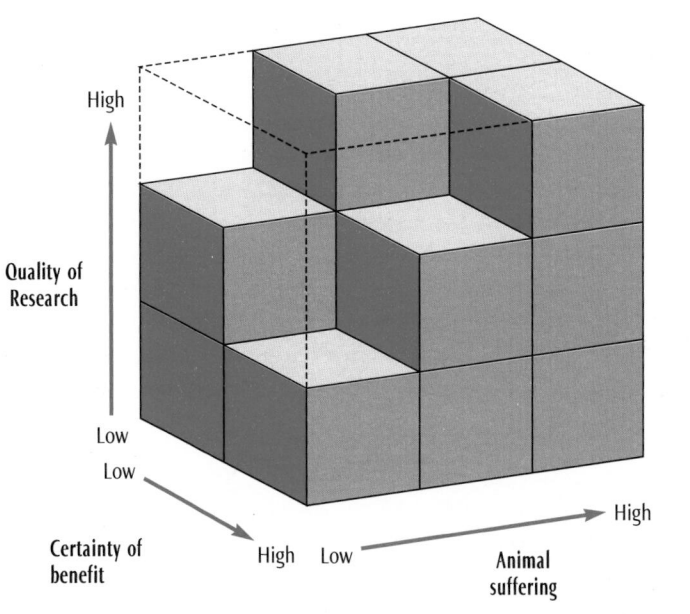

Certainty of benefit

In the minds of many, if not most, people great human suffering is felt to be worse than the possibility of moderate discomfort inflicted on an animal in the course of research. The funding of high-quality psychological research may not always be seen in that light by its critics. It is difficult to predict exactly what the benefits of such research might be to the lives of humans and other animals. The *In Focus* on Alzheimer's disease presents such an avenue of research. You might like to ask yourself, as you read this, whether in such cases the ends really can justify the means.

Comments on the Bateson model

This model provides an indication of when animal research may be tolerated and when it can not. When the quality of the research and the certainty of benefit are both high, the likelihood of animal research being considered acceptable is a great deal higher than when these are both low. It is also obvious that certain levels of animal suffering cannot be tolerated regardless of the quality of the research or the probability of benefit. The model would also permit research which has no direct benefit, yet was of high scientific quality and involved little animal suffering.

The effectiveness of a model such as that proposed by Bateson depends on any evaluation of quality,

benefit and suffering being accurate. This is not as straightforward as it might appear.

◆ Evaluating the quality of the research – This should pose little or no problem to the scientist who should be aware of what constitutes high or not so high quality research. It is a routine part of any research application that it is assessed along these lines.

◆ Measurement of animal suffering – Different species react differently to stress, and these reactions may be very different to those that might cause human beings to react in an avoidant manner. Dawkins (1985) suggests that three factors can be used to measure animal suffering:

Activity 5: Reviewing Harlow's study

Imagine you are part of a committee reviewing proposals for research involving animals. You receive an application for the Harlow study described earlier (see p. 499). How would you review it? What suggestions would you make to the researcher in the light of the Bateson model just outlined, and how would you justify your decision to turn the proposal down or to allow it to go ahead?

in focus   Alzheimer's disease

One of the major social problems of the 1990s and onwards will be the increasing numbers, relative to the whole population, of old people. A proportion of these will suffer from senile dementia, the commonest form of which is Alzheimer's disease. In its severest form, Alzheimer's produces severe memory loss, confusion, loss of the sense of self-identity, and double incontinence. Caring for sufferers is usually a family affair, 24 hours a day every day of the year, and involves watching your husband or wife, father or mother, degenerating in front of you.

There is as yet no cure for Alzheimer's disease. It is not linked to immoral behaviour or physical self-abuse of any sort, so lifestyle changes do not prevent it. We know from the brain changes seen at postmortem that there is a particular pattern of damage to brain circuits, and we know from animal studies that these circuits are also involved in memory in rats and monkeys. Damage to these circuits in animals produces memory loss, and this model of Alzheimer's disease is being used to develop possible treatments. These include new drugs to restore brain function, and the use of grafts of brain cells to replace cells that have died. These latter techniques have already been used in the treatment of Parkinson's disease, a progressive movement disorder which is also caused by damage to a specific brain circuit. Animal research is also helping to reveal the biochemical abnormalities responsible for producing the brain damage.

There are encouraging signs that a treatment for Alzheimer's disease may emerge, which will have depended absolutely on the use of animal testing for its development. If successful, it would have a dramatic impact, improving the quality of life for both those with Alzheimer's and those who would otherwise sacrifice their lives in caring for them. Is this potential benefit sufficient to justify the use of animals in psychological research?

Source: Green (1994)

The future of animal research – the 'three Rs'

In 1990, The British Association for the Advancement of Science produced a Declaration on Animals in Medical Research – *Animals and the Advancement of Science.*

> 'The comprehensive legislation governing the use of animals in scientific research must be strictly adhered to. Those involved must respect animal life, using animals only when essential and as humanely as possible, and they should adopt alternative methods as soon as they are proved to be reliable.'

Reduction

The reduction alternative involves using methods that obtain the same amount of information from fewer animals, or more information from the same number of animals. Improved experimental designs and a better understanding of statistical techniques would help to reduce the number of animals used in research.

Replacement

This is an area that has probably advanced the least. It involves, for example, the increased use of brain imaging and scanning procedures (such as MRI and PET scans) in humans; the use of computer simulations and mathematical models of human behaviour.

Refinement

This involves using procedures that minimize stress and enhance animal wellbeing. Ethological research has shown a strong connection between environment and behaviour. Research has shown that purely utilitarian environments tend to reduce social behaviour (such as grooming and scent marking) in captive animals. Stress reduction through manipulation of the lab environment also has advantages for researchers. They can more easily justify their research, and the reduction in stress means that animals are more likely to behave 'naturally'.

---

an animal's state of physical health, signs of stress and the animal's behaviour.

◆ Evaluating the benefits that might be derived from the research – This is a more difficult judgement to make. The aims of a particular piece of research should go beyond what is essentially curiosity about gaining real understanding.

Exam summary: The use of nonhuman animals in research

The AQA examination will test your understanding of the following areas:

◆ the use of nonhuman animals in psychological research (pp. 499–503)

◆ constraints on the use of nonhuman animals (pp. 505–9)

◆ arguments (scientific and ethical) for and against the use of nonhuman animals in research (pp. 503–5).

Example question

The question below is typical of one drawn from the material above, and should take you 45 minutes to answer:

◆ Describe and evaluate arguments for and against the use of nonhuman animals in psychological research. *(30 marks)*

Suggested answer structure

This question is set from the third of the bullet points above. It is more usual for students to think of arguments for and against something as being entirely *evaluative*. This is not the case. I may have a number of arguments why my football team is better than yours (they have prettier coloured shirts and nicer names...). You might quite rightly point out that my arguments are pretty weak because they have very little to do with footballing ability, and are based on a number of bizarre assumptions about the importance of footballers' names and the colour of their shirts. In AQA terms, my arguments here would be the AO1 component, and your riposte would be the evaluation (the AO2 component).

You should restrict yourself to a discussion of these arguments (the use of animals, not the relevance of footballers' names). These are covered explicitly in Table 19.4 (p. 505), although there are a number of other places in this section where these arguments appear. For example, on pp. 499–500, you will find a discussion of the reasons *why* psychologists study animals – clearly these are perceived advantages of the use of nonhumans in psychological research. Remember though, that you should be evaluating each of the arguments (either for or against) that you are describing. You may, for example, include the point (p. 499) that 'Animals offer the opportunity for greater control and objectivity in research procedures'. This can then be evaluated using the scientific objections covered on p. 504.

For a more searching and comprehensive coverage of the arguments for and against the use of animals in research, try the second of the website references given at the end of this chapter. Do remember, though, that the question asks for the arguments surrounding *psychological* research, not cosmetic or medical research. Some medical research clearly *is* relevant to a question such as this (e.g. research on Alzheimer's disease or the testing of psychotherapeutic drugs) but other research (e.g. research on cancer) is less relevant in this context.

Free will versus determinism

Free will

The idea that we are able to have some choice in how we act is fundamental in most common-sense theories of psychology. The notion of 'free will' allows us to separate out what is clearly the *intention* of an individual from what has been *caused* by some internal or external event. In the sense that we are freed from the causal influences of past events (e.g. of instinct or of our past reinforcement history), the concept of free will is of fundamental importance when explaining human behaviour. The idea of free will is inconsistent with the opposite idea of determinism, because under the latter view of human behaviour, individuals act as a result of some prior cause.

Part of the scientific perspective in psychology is a belief in this causal determinism. Free will, therefore, would appear to be incompatible with the goals of scientific psychology. This is not, however, necessarily the case. If we examine the meaning of the term 'free will', we may find that the concept of human intention and planning is not that far removed from the ideas of scientific determinism. The term 'free' is taken to mean that a person or their behaviour is independent from the causal determinism of past events. The term 'will' refers to the idea that people make decisions about the goals they are seeking to achieve. This view that human beings behave 'for the sake of their intentions' can be seen as a form of 'final causal determinism'. In other words, the final goals (getting an A level, finding a birthday present for a friend) determine a person's present actions. This apparent contradiction need not be so. When most people talk about determinism, they are, in fact, talking about *efficient causality*, a definition of causality originally put forward by the philosopher David Hume (1951). To say that one event has been determined by another, wrote Hume, meant that:

◆ the two events must be highly correlated (i.e. when one occurs, so does the other)

◆ they must appear in a certain chronological order (i.e. one after the other)

◆ they must be located near to one another (Slife and Williams 1995).

Although, as Hume admitted, the presence of these three criteria does not *necessarily* imply a cause–effect relationship, this belief in the importance of efficient causality has been enough to convince many scientists that the only appropriate way of determining the cause of events is to examine events in the past.

Activity 6: Cause and effect

Try to recall events that were related in the three ways described above. Did this necessarily mean that one of these events had caused the other?

If we accept this view of behaviour, that it is something that has been caused by events in the past, it becomes clear that we cannot accept the notion of free will. Free will, as Slife and Williams (1995) point out, enables people to choose a path that is inconsistent with their past. If we do not accept that we are bound to the past, but accept that we have the capacity to formulate plans and goals and act accordingly (a philosophical position known as *human teleology*), we are proposing the existence and influence of free will. As we have seen, the notion of free will is not inconsistent with the notion of determinism. A goal that is the product of our own free will can be responsible for our current thoughts and actions. For example, if I decide that I want to learn to play the piano, I might seek out a piano teacher, buy myself a piano and start practising. All these actions are clearly the product of my own conscious planning (i.e. my free will) but are determined by my final goal, that of being able to play the piano. Indeed, anyone who knew of my intention to learn to play the piano could very probably predict those very same actions mentioned above.

The concept of free will is therefore not only compatible with a wider view of determinism, but is

'The DNA made me do it, M'lud...'

'Crime, and the fear of crime and violence, dominate much of politics in the US and Britain, stimulating a search for simple explanations and simple ways of dealing with the problem. One of the most heated debates is over claims that genetics and biology can help to explain the causes of crime and violence.

'What is the evidence linking biology to crime? A widely cited piece of research (van Dusen *et al.* 1983) is a Danish study of 14,427 people adopted as children by unrelated families. The theory is that if the biological parents have a heritable predisposition to crime, they might transmit these characteristics to their offspring. The research showed that as the 'criminality' of the biological parent increases from having no convictions on court records to three or more convictions, the proportion of adopted sons who are subsequently convicted themselves steadily increases from about 13 per cent to 25 per cent. This genetic predisposition is apparently for property crimes rather than violent crimes, and it is difficult to see how there could be a 'gene for theft'. Moreover, the findings are not clearly duplicated by a similar Swedish adoption study.

'The first problem with studies linking biology and crime is that most simply fail to demonstrate an association between the two, let alone a meaningful cause. The second flaw is that where a link is made, it is quite illegitimate to extrapolate these results to the population at large, even if the claims are hedged with qualifications about biology only 'predisposing' individuals to crime. The consequences of arguing that crime has a genetic component can only be authoritarian. The legal and moral implications are likely to be greater calls for authorities to contain and control those deemed to be genetically unfit or dangerous.'

Toby Andrew, *The Independent*, 23 January 1996

also very important if we are to view individuals as being morally responsible for their own actions. If our actions are merely the product of some past event or of our biological 'programming', then we cannot be held responsible for our behaviours. This is a view that has concerned many psychologists and politicians, and is illustrated by the *In Focus*.

Determinism

One of the major debates within psychological thinking is the degree to which our behaviour is determined by factors over which we have no control. Some approaches tend to see the source of this determinism as being *outside* the individual, a position known as 'environmental determinism', whilst others propose the source of this determinism as coming from *inside* the organism, e.g. in the form of unconscious motivation or genetic determinism – a position known as 'biological determinism'. The position taken on this issue will have an important effect on the way that we explain human nature.

The psychodynamic approach

In his psychoanalytic theory, Freud believed that we are controlled by unconscious forces over which we have no control and are largely unaware. An essential part of this theory is a belief in 'psychic determinism', the view that events do not occur by chance, they are purposeful, being related to unconscious processes.

This view of humans as being unable to choose their course of action was in stark contrast to the previously held belief that we were rational, thinking beings, fully in control of our own actions. Because of this control by internal forces, and the belief that any perceived freedom of choice is in fact illusory, this theory is an example of biological determinism (see Chapter 20 for more about the psychodynamic approach).

The behavioural approach

Behaviourists believe that our behaviour is a product of the reinforcement provided by the environment. Within our own reinforcement history, we have been conditioned into behaving in specific ways. Although most of us accept that such conditioning clearly takes place, we still cling to the belief that we are free to plan our own actions. Skinner (1971) suggested that most human beings somehow believe that we are both free to choose and are controlled at the same time. For behaviourists, however, the position is much clearer: we have *no* freedom to choose our actions. They are determined by factors in our environment which, directly or indirectly, mould our behaviour. This approach is an example of environmental determinism (see Chapter 20 for more about the behaviourist approach).

The humanistic approach

The antithesis of the two previous approaches, this approach believes that human beings are free to plan their own actions, and ultimately their own destiny.

People are seen as struggling to grow and to make difficult decisions that will profoundly affect their lives (Rogers 1974). As a result of these decisions, each of us becomes unique and responsible for our own behaviour. Humanistic therapies such as person-centred therapy are based on the assumption of free will. The therapist helps clients to exercise free will in such a way as to maximize the rewards in their lives.

Determinism and science

The notion of current events being determined by something in the past is fundamental to scientific psychology. Indeed, we might argue that discovering the determinants of behaviour is the ultimate goal of psychology. When we speak of the determinants of an action, we are implying that the action has been caused by some specific past event. This, of course, has the inevitable consequence that, as scientists, we focus almost exclusively on past events. This is bound to be the case, we might argue, because causality can only work in this direction. Such a linear view of determinism is so deeply ingrained in scientific thinking that any other view of causality would seem inconceivable. Even theorists who differ fundamentally in their perspectives on human behaviour seem to share a common belief that we need to study past events in order to understand the present. Indeed, the essence of the experimental method in psychology is that we measure a behaviour before and after an experimental procedure in order to explore the relationship between cause and effect. There is, however, a need for a broader view of causality that takes into account intention and decision-making. This is not incompatible with the idea of behaviour being caused, only with the traditional scientific view of behaviour being caused by past events.

Behavioural scientists who accept this view of humans being guided by their own conscious planning have embraced a less radical view of determinism. This 'soft' determinism view proposes that people act consistently with their character. It is less difficult to reconcile this view of determinism with the idea of free will than it is with the 'hard' determinism view that behaviour is caused by environmental or biological factors.

Activity 7: Causes of mental disorders

Turn to Chapter 18 on treating mental disorders. How deterministically do each of these therapies represent the causes of the psychological disorders they are treating?

Exam summary: Free will versus determinism

The AQA examination will test your understanding of the following areas:

◆ definitions of the terms free will and determinism (pp. 510–12)

◆ arguments for and against their existence (pp. 510–12)

◆ assumptions concerning free will and determinism in psychological theory and research (pp. 511–12).

Example question

The question below is typical of one drawn from the material above, and should take you 45 minutes to answer:

(a) Explain what is meant by the terms free will and determinism. *(15 marks)*

(b) Assess the free will versus determinism debate as it applies to two psychological theories. *(15 marks)*

Suggested answer structure:

The first part of this question invites more than a simple definition. As it gives you 15 marks, and allows 22 minutes of writing time, it gives you the opportunity for a fairly searching examination of the concepts of free will and determinism. The main points of free will and determinism are covered on pp. 510–11. The notion of free will involves an individual acting solely as a result of their own *intention*, whereas the notion of determinism sees behaviour as being *caused* by factors over which we have little or no control. It is worthwhile to consider the different *types* of determinism such as *environmental* and *biological* determinism (p. 511).

The second part of this question (also providing the synoptic assessment in this question) asks you to *assess* (i.e. make a considered appraisal of...) the free will versus determinism debate as it applies to two psychological theories. You have read about three of these (the psychodynamic, behavioural and humanistic approaches) on pp. 511–12, although it would also benefit you to read Phil Banyard's extended coverage of each of these approaches in Chapter 20. To what extent do each of these advocate free will or a determinist position? For example, Freud's psychoanalytic theory sees behaviour as being a product of unconscious forces. The humanistic approach believes that human beings are free to plan their own actions, making difficult decisions that will 'profoundly affect their lives' (p. 512).

You are not, of course, restricted to the approaches that we have covered in this section, but you can use any theory that you feel presents a clear position on the free will versus determinism debate. For example, the rank theory of depression (p. 395–6) presents an evolutionary perspective on depression that explains this as an adaptive and inevitable response to loss of status. On the other hand, Maslow's theory of self-actualization (pp. 142–3) presents a view that emphasizes the richness and complexity of human motivation.

Reductionism

One of the notable developments in scientific thinking in the behavioural sciences has been the notion that the simplest explanations of events are generally the best. Sometimes known as 'Occam's razor' (after William of Occam, 1290–1349), this view has been with us for centuries as an important criterion for deciding which explanations are best. The essence of Occam's razor is that unnecessary constructs and levels of explanation can be cut away in order to find the simple explanation that lurks underneath. A more recent, but similar idea was suggested by Morgan (1852–1936). Morgan's law of parsimony states that we have no need to explain behaviour in terms of complex psychological processes when it can adequately be explained in terms of much simpler processes.

This tendency to simplify human behaviour to more biological or mechanical processes has persisted since then, with psychologists frequently reducing explanations to their simplest level. This has become known as *reductionism*. Following a reductionist line of thinking, we can suggest that we should always look for something more basic underneath whatever it is we are trying to explain – that is, the real cause of the event we are experiencing.

Physiological reductionism

Because human beings are biological organisms, it should be possible to reduce even complex behaviours to their constituent neurophysiological components. There is a clear advantage to this, as it leads to the application of concise and concrete terms which are then susceptible to scientific methods of research (Wadeley *et al.* 1997). For example, scientists interested in the causes of schizophrenia (see Chapter 17) have found evidence that excess activity of the biochemical neurotransmitter dopamine is a characteristic of schizophrenia. Evidence for the importance of dopamine in schizophrenia comes, in part, from the discovery that antipsychotic drugs that reduce dopamine activity in the brain may also reduce the symptoms of the disorder. This discovery has led to the hope that schizophrenia might be eradicated by controlling the brain chemistry of schizophrenics by the administration of antipsychotic drugs. Such a 'biochemical' theory of schizophrenia would effectively de-emphasize the importance of environmental factors in the development of the disorder.

Evaluation of physiological reductionism

The view that disorders such as schizophrenia can be neatly explained in terms of biochemical deficiencies may be changing. Investigators have discovered that research suggests that different types of schizophrenia may represent different disorders, each with a distinct course, distinct biological, genetic and even psychological origins, and a distinct response to treatment. Most theorists now agree that schizophrenia is probably 'caused' by a combination of factors. Genetic and biological factors may establish a predisposition to develop the disorder; psychological factors such as personal or familial stress help to bring the disorder to fruition; and other psychological and sociocultural factors, such as individual misinterpretations or societal labelling, help maintain and in some cases worsen the symptoms (Comer 1995).

Examples such as schizophrenia show us that complex phenomena cannot easily be explained simply by reference to a physiological imbalance. The influence of these brain chemicals is indisputable, but to argue that they *cause* schizophrenia is to neglect all other potential influences in the course of this disorder. Increasingly, the treatment of complex disorders such as schizophrenia has moved away from a 'drugs only' culture to a combination of drugs, psychotherapy and community care (see Chapters 17 and 18 for a fuller discussion of the causes and treatment of schizophrenia).

Biological reductionism

One of the most important influences on Western thought has been Darwin's theory of evolution. Darwin's theory offered a reductionist explanation of all the complex living phenomena in our world. All this had come about, he argued, through the principles of natural selection (see Chapter 13). Together with the principles (unknown to Darwin at the time he was writing) of Mendelian genetics, this provided a way of explaining how species change and how such variety is possible within the natural world.

In this theory, behaviours that can be shown to arise from genetic factors must have some 'survival value'. It is possible that many human behaviours have also evolved because of their survival value, or more generally, their ability to increase an individual's opportunities for passing on their genes. This view – that evolution has bred into us a tendency to act in such a way as to maximize our chances of passing on our genes – has been championed by sociobiologists, a group of scientists who are interested in the evolution of social behaviours. The principles of kin selection suggest that in helping biological relatives, with whom we share genes, we are also ensuring the survival of our own genetic code. This, according to Wilson (1975), is the primary motivation behind much of human social behaviour from altruism (concern for others) to xenophobia (fear of strangers) (quoted in Tavris and Wade 1995). According to sociobiologists, nature 'selects' certain psychological traits and social customs (such as kinship bonds and taboos against female adultery) because they help to ensure the transmission of an individual's genes.

Evolutionary theory also claims that species have a point of 'common origin' – that is, differences between species are not seen as *qualitative* (i.e. implying differences in kind) but rather as *quantitative*, in that different species have evolved further than others along the evolutionary path. If, it is supposed, the forces of evolution work in the same way for all species, then it makes sense that we must share a number of natural processes with other species as well. Based on this idea of evolutionary continuity, behaviourists have chosen to study simpler species in order to understand more about these processes in a more basic form. An essential belief within behaviourism is the fact that all organisms learn and behave in essentially the same way, and therefore the processes of learning and conditioning must be the same in all species. This fact, suggest Slife and Williams (1995), provides the justification for studying subhuman species and then generalizing to human beings.

Evaluation of biological reductionism

Tavris and Wade (1995) suggest three errors that people typically make when accepting biological explanations for complex behaviour.

1 *Drawing premature conclusions*: Because dramatic breakthroughs in research make better headlines, the media may leap to conclusions on the basis of only limited studies. For example, research on the biological origins of schizophrenia has led to almost universal acceptance that this is a disease with physical origins. Research has implicated abnormalities in the biochemical transmitter dopamine, whilst there have even been claims that exposure to the influenza virus during prenatal development might be the main culprit. Twin and adoption studies have suggested an important genetic influence in the disorder and current interest in chromosome mapping reflects the search for a 'schizophrenia gene'. Enticing though these explanations might be, no one explanation can account for all cases and all types of schizophrenia.

2 *Drawing unwarranted conclusions about cause and effect*: Although we commonly think of our biology as affecting the way we experience the world, the opposite may also be true. There are many studies that have shown how a stimulating environment can change the structure of an animal's brain (a concept known as 'neural plasticity'). Tavris and Wade also quote evidence from PET (positive emission tomography) scan studies showing that during certain intellectual tasks, the brains of high performers appear less active and metabolize glucose more slowly than the brains of lower performers. The suggestion that an efficient brain is the *result* of superior performance rather than the cause of it is supported in research by Haier *et al.* (1992). In this study, participants who were allowed to play a computer game for a period of several weeks showed a slower glucose metabolism rate (i.e. they were more neurologically efficient) than a control group who did not play the computer game.

3 *Exaggerating the power of genes*: When we read about the role of genetics in a particular behaviour, we might assume that genes are the cause and the *only* cause. Even the words that we use to describe genetic influence, such as 'control' and 'determine' imply an inevitability that may not actually exist (Tavris and Wade 1995).

Recent research on the origins of homosexuality has proposed a genetic link in homosexuality (Hamer *et al.* 1993). By studying 40 pairs of gay brothers, Hamer showed that 33 of the 40 pairs shared a common stretch of DNA on their X chromosomes. This research has created a great deal of interest, given that other psychological perspectives have failed to find the origins of homosexuality. Previous attempts to discover the biological origins of homosexuality (such as hormonal deficiencies or levels of testosterone) also appear to have been unsuccessful. However, Hamer is quick to point out that 'sexual orientation is too complex to be determined by a single gene. The main value of this work is that it opens a window into understanding how genes, the brain and the environment interact to mould human behaviour' (Hamer 1993, quoted in Tavris and Wade 1995).

Wilson (1978) argues that genes hold culture on a leash, but the problem, according to Gould (1987) is in determining the length of the leash. If it is only a foot long, then society has very little room to manoeuvre and change, but if the leash is ten feet long, biology would only establish a broad range of possibilities. To sociobiologists, the leash is short and human nature inevitable; to many psychologists, however, given the enormous variation between cultures and individuals, the leash is long and flexible (Tavris and Wade 1995).

Environmental reductionism

If you have read about behaviourism, you may have reached the conclusion that people are constantly being controlled by forces outside their control, and that, in the words of John Watson, given the right environment, anybody can be made into anything. The application of behaviourist principles in behaviour modification programmes can have considerable success, e.g. in training severely disturbed adults and those with severe learning difficulties to earn a living in the community. But is it all as simple as it sounds? Can we reduce everything to environmental influences in the way that behaviourists suggest?

In recent years, psychologists have become more aware of the biological constraints on learning and have incorporated these considerations into their theories of the way in which organisms learn. These genetic dispositions and biological characteristics place limits on what individuals and species can learn. Of particular importance is the finding that all organisms appear to be *biologically prepared* to learn some responses more easily than others. Conditioning procedures that capitalize on these inborn tendencies are more likely to be successful than those which do not. When two psychologists turned animal trainers attempted to train animals to carry out actions for which they were not biologically prepared (i.e. the behaviour had no specific relevance in their evolutionary past and therefore they had no inborn tendency to learn it), they soon encountered problems (Breland and Breland 1961). In one example, a pig was trained to drop large wooden coins into a 'piggy bank'. The animal was then reinforced for its performance by being given food. The Brelands found that, after a while, the pig started to drop the 'coins' on the ground and push them along with its snout. As this delayed the onset of the reinforcer (which was given when the animal deposited the coin in the piggy bank), it posed a problem for a simple conditioning explanation. Breland and Breland explained this behaviour as 'instinctive drift', a reversion to an instinctive

behaviour more usually associated with gaining food. In this case, the pig was reverting to its rooting instinct where it uses its snout to uncover edible roots.

Evaluation of environmental reductionism

The importance of biological preparedness is also evident in human behaviour. Research has demonstrated that many organisms (including human beings) are biologically prepared to associate sickness with a particular taste and develop a consequent food aversion (Garcia and Koelling 1966). We have all been in the situation where we think we have become sick shortly after eating something, regardless of the real cause of the sickness. As a result, we carefully avoid the associated food or drink for quite a while afterwards. This phenomenon can also explain why children undergoing chemotherapy treatment (who may experience feelings of nausea as a result of their treatment) often develop food aversions at the same time (Bernstein 1985).

This is actually part of a larger problem within behaviourism. Restricting ourselves to the study of only one influence at a time may make perfect sense within the context of a laboratory science, but we may miss the complexity of influences on any one behaviour. These influences interact in complicated ways and it can be frustratingly difficult trying to ascertain which, if any, of them really is causing the behaviour in question.

This oversimplification problem also applies when we adopt behaviourist principles in the real world. In a world dominated by either reinforcement or punishment, it might appear that the only way to motivate people is with the 'carrot and the stick'. Kohn (1993) argues that this sort of 'pop behaviourism' distracts us from asking whether the behaviour being reinforced is worthwhile in the first place. Skinner never believed that life should be reduced to the mindless use of extrinsic reinforcers that were merely 'bribes in disguise'.

'Too rarely are people reinforced for creativity, risk, participation, taking gambles. Too rarely are they given an opportunity to take pride in the products of their work, or to exercise initiative in their choice of pleasures.' (Skinner 1987)

Activity 8: Implications of reductionist thinking

Try to find examples of reductionist thinking in the explanations of behaviour offered in the chapters of this book. What do you feel are the implications of accepting these explanations?

Exam summary: Reductionism

The AQA examination will test your understanding of the following areas:

◆ reductionism as an explanation of behaviour (pp. 513–15)

◆ examples of reductionism in theory and research (pp. 513–15)

◆ arguments for and against reductionist explanations (pp. 513–15).

Example question

The question below is typical of one drawn from the material above, and should take you 45 minutes to answer:

◆ Describe and evaluate reductionist explanations of two areas of psychology. *(30 marks)*

Suggested answer structure

This question is a lot more friendly that it might appear on first reading. It asks you to apply the concept of reductionism (reducing explanations to their simplest level) to two areas of psychology. It all depends, we might imagine, on what is meant by an *area* of psychology. An area might be an entire perspective (such as *physiological* explanations or

environmental explanations), or it might be more localized (such as explanations of *schizophrenia* or *learning*). This section has been written to allow for either of these interpretations.

If we adopt the latter interpretation (i.e. schizophrenia and learning), we can present a physiological explanation of the former (p. 513) and an environmentally reductionist explanation of the latter (p. 515). Schizophrenia has many levels of explanation, but neurochemical explanations (such as the influence of dopamine) are a good example of a reductionist line of thought. You may like to read the section on neurochemical explanations of schizophrenia on pp. 450–1 before you construct your response to this part of the question. Evaluation of this explanation can be found on p. 513. Remember that you are evaluating this as a *reductionist* explanation, not evaluating the dopamine hypothesis per se. It is important to keep this fact firmly in mind as you read elsewhere in the book. The same argument is true for your discussion of learning. Behaviourists argue that much of what we learn is simply a product of conditioning (see Chapter 13), but reducing complex behaviour down to such mechanical relationships clearly presents problems, not least of which are the often complicated ways in which conditioning, cognition and biology interact together (p. 515).

Psychology as science

What is science? At first examination this may seem a fairly trivial question. We all know what science is, but what does it really mean to describe something as 'scientific', and can psychology really be considered scientific in the same way that the natural sciences are considered scientific.

The word 'science' comes from a Latin word which literally means 'knowledge'. Science can, therefore, be seen as concerned with what we *know* to be true, rather than what we *believe* to be true. Because of this, we attach considerable importance to science as a way of distinguishing what is true and real from what is not. In the contemporary use of the term, science is often seen as both a body of knowledge that we accept as being trustworthy, and also the method for attaining that knowledge (i.e. the *scientific method*).

The characteristics of science

Probably the most fundamental characteristic of science is its reliance on *empirical methods* of observation and investigation, i.e. observation through sensory experience rather than a reliance on thoughts

and ideas. All scientific ideas must, at some point, be subjected to empirical investigation through careful observation of perceivable events or phenomena. Science has emerged as a trusted approach to the acquisition of knowledge because of this reliance on sensory experience. This does not mean, however, that science is purely empirical in nature. For science to 'make sense', it is necessary to explain the results of empirical observation. That means constructing theories, which in turn can be tested and refined through further empirical observation. This cycle of scientific enquiry is shown in Fig. 19.3.

Slife and Williams (1995) identify a number of further attributes that characterize science.

◆ Scientific observation is made under *objective* conditions. In other words, observation is not influenced by factors such as bias or expectation, or the particular cultural values of the scientist.

◆ Scientific observation takes place under *controlled* conditions. This is often accomplished in the context of the experiment, where scientists can control the conditions under which they make their observations.

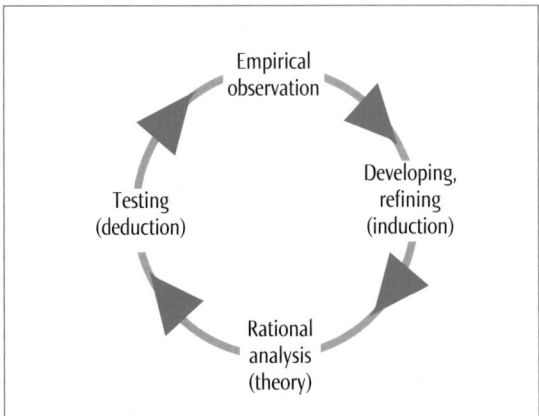

Figure 19.3 The cycle of scientific enquiry

◆ Science involves making *predictions* about what is expected to happen under specified conditions. In this way, the scientist is able to *validate* or *falsify* whatever theory or hypothesis led to the observations being made. This ability to control and predict behaviour in experimental settings gives us the expectation that we will also be able to control and predict behaviour in real-life settings. It is this expectation that drives psychology towards science as a chosen route to knowledge, and towards the establishment of a *technology* of behaviour.

◆ Scientific investigations are open to public scrutiny, i.e. the methods and results of scientific investigations are there for all to see and to check. Confidence in results is increased when investigations can be *replicated,* and the results repeated.

The emergence of scientific psychology

The *science* of psychology has a fairly short history – just over 100 years. Prior to that, psychology had been considered simply a branch of philosophy. The German physiologist and psychologist Wilhelm Wundt founded the first laboratory for experimental psychology in Leipzig in 1879. Wundt stressed the use of scientific methods in psychology, particularly through the use of introspection (the process by which a person looks inward at their own mental processes to gain insight into how they work). Although the value of introspective reports was dubious, this approach did stress the need for precise subjective observations that contrasted with the poorly controlled observations of earlier studies in related fields. Although Wundt is generally regarded as the founding father of experimental psychology, he did not believe that it was applicable to all areas of human behaviour. Wundt's main contribution was to present psychology as an independent scientific discipline, equivalent in many ways to more traditional 'scientific' disciplines such as anatomy and physiology. While Wundt's

background and training was in these disciplines, he did not believe that human behaviour was reducible to them.

Is psychology scientific?

There are two underpinnng views of science that might help us to decide whether psychology constitutes a science.

Science as knowledge

Science is a body of knowledge that explains the nature of the world. Viewed from this perspective, scientific knowledge has two main characteristics:

◆ Scientific explanations reject, and are preferred to, other explanations of naturally occurring phenomena (such as magic or other supernatural explanations).

◆ Scientific explanations are often stated as laws or general principles about the relationship between different events. Because of the regularity of the way in which these events occur together, it then becomes possible to control and predict them.

Although most psychologists have certainly rejected the role of supernatural phenomena in determining human behaviour, it is perhaps a little hopeful to claim that psychology has led to the development of universal laws of human behaviour. However, although most psychologists accept the idea that behaviour tends to be determined, the inability to control all the myriad human variables that underlie behaviour means that accurate control and prediction is almost impossible.

Science as method

The second way of characterizing science is to see it as a method of studying phenomena. Scientific investigation involves empirical observation and the development of theories that in turn are constantly tested and refined in the light of further observation. When viewed from this perspective, it is clear that psychology probably *does* qualify as a science, because scientific methods are the preferred method of investigation for most psychologists. Indeed, the laboratory experiment has probably become the dominant mode of investigation in psychology, and therefore offers the psychologist opportunities for control and prediction that are absent in less 'scientific' methods. This raises various issues:

◆ Is the use of scientific methods sufficient cause for labelling psychology a 'science'? Slife and Williams quote the example of parapsychology (the study of paranormal phenomena) as an area that has been subjected to rigorous scientific study, yet few psychologists would accept parapsychology as 'scientific'.

◆ Would we accept that the traditional scientific methods as used in the natural sciences are necessarily the best means of studying human behaviour? We will return to this question later.

Problems of scientific psychology

Maintaining objectivity

We saw earlier that objectivity was an important characteristic of scientific enquiry. By that we mean that there is an assumption that any subjective influences (such as the values and expectations of the investigator) are excluded from the investigation. In this way, we can be sure that the results are not distorted because of the subjectivity of the investigator. Thomas Kuhn (1970) believed that total objectivity is never possible. The view that any particular scientist holds about the world (in Kuhn's terms, their 'paradigm') makes them think about the world in a specific way. This influences what they investigate, the methods they use to investigate it, and the sorts of explanations that they see as acceptable for the results obtained. This is important if psychology is to be considered scientific according to the first perspective of science outlined earlier (i.e. the need for observations to be made under objective conditions). As all scientific knowledge emerges from within a specific set of influences (the paradigm), and these lead scientists to think about a problem in their own special way, it is questionable whether it is possible to establish *universal* laws of human behaviour.

Operationalization

To carry out a scientific test, we must be able to observe whatever it is we are investigating. This may seem a straightforward requirement, but it is not always so. For example, there are many events (such as motivation or fear) that we cannot observe directly. Instead, we observe something else that we feel represents the thing we are really interested in. For example, we may choose to define fear in terms of some physiological change (such as pupil dilation), or motivation in terms of questionnaire responses. The trouble with these operational definitions is that they are not necessarily measurements of the thing we were originally interested in. The consequence of this is that psychologists often explore the relationship between two things (e.g. love and happiness) without ever being able to measure either of these directly. Instead, as is the case with many investigations in psychology, our observations are always one step removed from the phenomenon (e.g. fear) that we are really interested in studying.

Activity 9: Definitions

Think how you might define each of the following in order to investigate it:

◆ love
◆ happiness
◆ hunger
◆ satisfaction.

Consider whether your operational definitions would really do them justice.

Establishing causality

It is generally accepted in scientific psychology that the only way of establishing causality is by carrying out an experiment. Experiments are often contrasted with correlational designs because in the latter, the researcher merely observes that the two variables (e.g. amount of revision and examination success) are related, while in the former, the researcher is able to manipulate one variable systematically (the *independent variable*) in order to see its effect on another (the *dependent variable*). In order to be confident that any change in the dependent variable had been caused by the manipulation of the independent variable, the researcher would need to control everything else that could possibly have a causal effect on the dependent variable. Clearly this is impossible when we are dealing with human beings. We have no way of knowing all the possible ways in which any one individual might be influenced to behave at any given time. Although this appears to make statements of causality redundant, it is, however, possible to observe that when X is manipulated in some way, Y tends to occur. In this way, we might *approach* the cause of a behaviour rather than being confident we *know* how it was caused.

Verification and falsification

One of the classic problems in verifying hypotheses (i.e. showing that they are true) is the logical fallacy of *affirming the consequent*. Think about the following statements:

'If this hypothesis is true then X will be observed.'

'X is observed (affirming the consequent), therefore the hypothesis is true.'

In this example, the hypothesis (e.g. that watching violent videos makes children violent) is described as the antecedent, and the outcome (in this case a measurement of violence) is the consequent. If X is observed, then the consequent is said to be affirmed and we could conclude that watching violent videos does indeed make children violent.

It can be argued that empirical studies can only ever affirm the consequent, i.e. they can only show that the hypothesis given *might* explain the results of the investigation, but then so might many other possible explanations. Thus data cannot *prove* that a hypothesis is correct, nor can they indicate which of a range of possible alternative explanations is the most likely. Affirming the consequent thus always leads to a logically invalid conclusion (see 'Problem-solving' in Chapter 9).

As scientists have considerable problems validating their hypotheses (i.e. proving that they are true), they may instead attempt to *falsify* them. According to Popper (1959), if we can prove things to be false, then we can rule them out as explanations and thus arrive at the truth by a process of elimination. The way in which scientists can falsify hypotheses is by *negating the consequent:*

'If this hypothesis is true, then X will be observed.'

'X is not observed, therefore the hypothesis is not true.'

In this way, the consequent (the observation of X) was not evident, therefore it follows that the antecedent (the hypothesis) is false.

Alternative views on the science–psychology relationship

We have been exploring the issue of whether science can establish 'truth' about human behaviour with any degree of certainty. This raises the question not about whether psychology might be considered scientific, but whether it *should* be scientific. It should be clear that some aspects of human behaviour might be more accessible than others to this type of empirical proof. For example, it may be a fairly straightforward endeavour to explore mundane issues such as the short-term memory span using scientific methods. However, psychology is concerned with human behaviour in all its richness and complexity, and scientific methods may not be the best route to investigating this area.

Slife and Williams (1995) present three positions on whether a science of human behaviour is possible or even desirable.

◆ Scientific methods might be seen as essential because of the need for empirical validation. All theories should be subject to rigorous tests to show that they are internally consistent (i.e. they make sense) and that they can explain a wide range of events consistent with the predictions of the

theory. It is also important that the claims of a particular theory can be demonstrated through actual, observable behaviour.

◆ The study of human experience requires the development of methods that are quite different from those used in the study of the natural world. Scientists studying humans would place a great deal of importance on the experience of their participants as a way of understanding their behaviour. The use of qualitative methods avoids the measurement and quantification of behaviour, allowing participants to describe their own experiences within their own linguistic style. The role of the qualitative researcher would be to question, describe and interpret this experience.

◆ The study of human behaviour and experience requires *methodological pluralism.* Researchers attempt to make sense of the world around them, and must make their choice of method based on the nature of the problem they are investigating. All methods open the door to knowledge in one way, but close it in another. On the basis of this, no one method might be considered superior to another.

Exam summary: Psychology as science

The AQA examination will test your understanding of the following areas:

◆ the characteristics of science (pp. 516–17)

◆ the development of scientific psychology (p. 517)

◆ arguments for and against the claim that psychology is a science (pp. 517–19).

Example question

The question below is typical of one drawn from the material above, and should take you 45 minutes to answer:

◆ Discuss the view that psychology is not, and should not strive to be, a science. *(30 marks)*

Suggested answer structure

This question covers the third of the above bullet points, but also relies on information from the first (i.e. the *characteristics* of science, and scientific psychology in particular). A suitable structure for this answer would be to examine what is meant by science and whether psychology might be classified as a science under these criteria. For example, we have seen that most psychologists accept the view that behaviour is *determined* in some way (p. 512) and that scientific explanations which explain the causal relationship between different events are the aim of scientific psychology (p. 517). Most psychologists still subscribe to the use of scientific *methods*, with the laboratory experiment still a dominant force in the subject. This account of the nature of science and psychology's place in it would be the AO1 part of your response, therefore should account for approximately half your writing time and space.

For the AO2 part of the question, you might consider how successful psychology has been in achieving its scientific status. For example, although most psychologists *do* accept the idea that much of our behaviour is determined, the inability to control all the 'myriad human variables that underlie behaviour' makes accurate control and prediction impossible (p. 517). Also relevant to this part of the question are the specific problems of scientific psychology, such as the problems of maintaining objectivity, and establishing causality (p. 518). The question also contains a reference to whether psychology should 'strive' to be a science. Given the attendant difficulties of 'scientific' psychology, a discussion of some of the alternatives (p. 519) would demonstrate a 'breadth of different methodological approaches' in psychology, and would serve the added function of extending the synoptic element of your response.

Nature and nurture

'In the sixteenth century, the Mogul emperor Akbar, a descendant of Genghis Khan, reared children in isolation to discover whether their natural religion would be Hinduism, the Christian faith, or some other creed. But this experiment was a failure: it only produced deaf mutes. The implicit assumption in this so-called experiment was that environment contributes more than inheritance to human talents: experience has the power to hide the inborn nature of an individual.' (Kimble 1993)

History of the nature–nurture debate

In the early days of psychology (around the turn of the twentieth century), there was an almost inevitable tension between those who favoured a view of behaviour as a product of heredity (*nature*) and those who favoured the greater influence of environment (*nurture*). Those who adopted the former viewpoint were called *nativists* and those who adopted the latter point of view were called *empiricists*. In order for the new science of psychology to be useful, it would have to have applications to everyday living. If behaviour was to be changed for the better, it made sense that only environmental intervention would accomplish this. However, at the time, the dominant view of human behaviour was fundamentally hereditarian, seeing it as a product of biological influences and therefore implying that environmental influences were, at best, limited. The nature versus nurture issue remained one of the major divisions in psychology throughout the early stages of the subject. The two sides of the debate made different *assumptions*. Those psychologists who saw their role as interventionist also tended to believe that the environment had a dominant influence on behaviour, whereas those psychologists concerned more with description and diagnosis have tended to be more 'nativist' in their view of behaviour (Richards 1996).

Learning and instinct

Midway through the last century, there were two dominant schools of thought concerning human behaviour. American behavourists, as a result of extensive laboratory work with animals, concluded that all behaviour was the product of trial and error learning. What's more, this process was considered to be so universal that differences between species were regarded as irrelevant: learning applied to all species, including humans (de Waal 1999). In contrast to this extreme environmentalist position, the ethological school in Europe focused on natural behaviour. According to this position, animals are born with a number of 'fixed-action patterns' that are little changed by the environment. These fixed-action patterns are the result of evolutionary adaptations. We do not need to learn how to laugh or cry, these are innate signals, universally used and understood.

Although behaviourists accepted that evolution had some relevance in human behaviour, this was merely to acknowledge the continuity between humans and other animals. Humans shared a great deal with other animals, which made the study of the latter both understandable and justifiable. As Skinner bluntly put it: 'Pigeon, rat, monkey, which is which? It doesn't matter.' However, although evolution implies continuity between species, it also implies diversity, each animal being adapted to a specific way of life in a specific environment (de Waal 1999). Behaviourists were gradually forced to adopt some of the ideas of evolutionary biology, especially with the discovery that learning is not the same for all species and across all species. Animals are specialized learners, and will more easily learn associations that are important for survival.

Ethologists also ran into problems explaining some aspects of animal and human behaviour. Behavioural traits, such as the inhibition of aggression, or altruistic behaviour, were seen as being 'for the benefit of the species'. This may well be true, but animals are inclined to inhibit aggression or display altruistic behaviour for more fundamentally selfish reasons. These early ideas have now been replaced by theories of how an action benefits the animals concerned and its genetic relatives.

Nature–nurture and intelligence

Until the middle of the twentieth century, intelligence was widely regarded as mainly biologically determined. The 'amount' of intelligence possessed by an individual was present at birth and would remain the same throughout life, regardless of experience or training (the *nature* view). A consequence of this perspective was the belief that it was intelligence that gave individuals their potential for life success. If intelligence, and therefore potential, was inherited, there seemed little one could do for individuals of low intelligence. A different perspective, the origins of which stretch back as far as the seventeenth century, proposed that intelligence was largely a product of experience and was, within limits, completely malleable (the *nurture* view).

In the early 1950s, the predominant view concerning the origins of intelligence had shifted from the 'nature' to the 'nurture' side of the argument. Supporters of this view put forward arguments that intelligence was not genetically determined, but was due to the nature of an individual's experience. It was argued that intelligence was particularly malleable in early childhood. This led to the development of a number of compensatory education programmes, such as the *Head Start* programme in the USA, which were part of a wider 'War on Poverty' initiative.

A developmental model of intelligence which cast doubts on a strict environmental view of intelligence also became influential in the 1950s. Jean Piaget's theory (see Chapter 10) is significant in two respects. First, it bridges the gap between 'nature' and 'nurture', by arguing that biologically given structures unfold when placed in a nurturing environment. Second, he proposed four mechanisms of cognitive development (maturation, experience, social transmission, and equilibrium) through which the environment interacts with the internal structures of the individual. In Piaget's theory, the individual is the main focus, whereas the role of the environment is merely to facilitate the automatic unfolding of biological, cognitive structures. What was particularly significant about this theory, in terms of its position in the nature–nurture debate, was that it emphasized the potential that was available to all children with the right environmental events to bring it about. The *interaction* of nature and nurture (or genes and environment) are central in Piaget's theory.

The Bell Curve

Arguments about the basis of intelligence have always been controversial, but this debate reached, in the words of one commentator, 'incendiary' proportions with the publication of an American book *The Bell Curve* (Herrnstein and Murray 1994). In this book, Herrnstein and Murray argued for substantial individual and group differences in intelligence, claiming that these differences profoundly influence a social and occupational meritocracy based on cognitive ability, and they could not easily be overcome. The *Bell Curve* presents powerful arguments that cognitive ability has become a more important determinant of social status than social class of origin, and that differences in cognitive ability are in part due to differences in genetic endowment. Herrnstein and Murray claim that the downward pressures in US national intelligence have been caused by the large number of children born to 'low-IQ women'. They also argue that the US government 'subsidises births among poor women (through social security support) who are disproportionately at the low end of the intelligence distribution'.

Herrnstein and Murray's book is a classic example of the dark side of the nature–nurture debate. Critics point to the fact that the work contains many inaccuracies and unqualified assumptions and relies heavily on data from other research studies that are equally questionable. What is significant about *The Bell Curve*, however, is that it demonstrates that the nature–nurture debate is more than an academic position. It can also be used to support political agendas – people will always depict human nature one way or another for their own purposes (de Waal 1999) (see Chapter 10 for a discussion of the role of genetics and cultural factors affecting performance on intelligence tests).

Methodological difficulties in the nature–nurture debate

There is no agreement about how we might define or measure the environment in which a person grows up. There are no standard units of environment by which we might compare one environment against another. At best, the efforts to manipulate environmental variables focus on gross dimensions; at worst, the efforts to define and manipulate the environment are laden with value judgements about good and bad environments that have minimal empirical support (Horowitz 1993). Researchers using animals have, for obvious reasons, been much more successful in defining and manipulating environmental variables. It is this kind of research that emphasizes that much of behavioural development that was taken to be 'innate' (and therefore effectively unalterable) is subject to environmental influence. Trying to understand how such environmental variables would affect human behavioural development is a much more complex issue. It is at the cultural level that this difficulty becomes most pronounced, yet it is probably at the level of cultural influences that the most powerful and subtle environmental variables may well operate (Horowitz 1993).

Gene–environment interactions

When we say that a behavioural trait such as intelligence or depression is inherited, all we mean is that *part* of its variability is explained by genetic factors. This means that the environment accounts for the rest of the variability. This interaction between genes and environment is proving far more complex than scientists originally imagined. For example, the balance between genetic and environmental influences on a particular behaviour appears to change as a person ages. The genetic influence on many traits appears to *increase* as people get older (Plomin 1994). The Colorado Adoption Project, for example, found that the correlation for general cognitive ability between adopted children and their biological parents increased dramatically from the age of 3 to 16. In contrast, although there was a small correlation early on between adopted children and their adoptive parents,

this faded with age. At age 16, there was no relationship between the IQ of adopted children and their adoptive parents, indicating that the general rearing environment has little impact on the development of IQ (Plomin *et al.* 1988).

Genes may not only influence behaviour, they may also influence the environment itself. In other words, our experiences may be influenced in part by our genetic make-up – people may react differently to us because of some inherited aspect of our personality. Likewise, we may choose certain experiences because they fit best with our innate preferences. Research has suggested three types of gene–environment relationships (Azar 1997).

◆ A *passive* relationship between genes and environment may occur because parents transmit genes that promote a certain trait and also construct the rearing environment. For example, if we assume that musical ability is genetic, then musically gifted children may be assumed to have parents who are musically inclined and who provide both the genes and the environment that promotes the development of musical ability.

◆ An *evocative* relationship between genes and environment may occur because genetically distinct individuals may evoke different reactions in those around them. For example, a musically gifted child may be chosen for special training and

The incest taboo – nature or nurture?

At the beginning of this century, there were two distinctly opposite explanations of the incest taboo (which serves to suppress sexual urges between family members). Freud believed that the 'earliest sexual excitations of human beings were invariably incestuous'. The incest taboo was, therefore, evidence of the victory of culture over nature. In contrast, Edward Westermarck, a fervent Darwinian, argued that early familiarity between mother and child, and between siblings, kills sexual desire. This, he claimed, was an evolutionary mechanism to prevent the harmful effects of inbreeding.

In what is the largest-scale study of its type, Wolf (1995) examined the marital histories of 14,400 women as part of a natural experiment carried out in Taiwan. In some regions of Taiwan, families used to adopt and raise future daughters-in-law, which meant that they and their future husbands were raised together from an early age. Wolf compared these marriages with others where the bride and groom did not meet until the day of the wedding. Using divorce and fertility rates as measures of marital happiness and sexual activity, Wolf found strong evidence for the 'Westermarck effect' – that early associations appear to compromise marital compatibility. Nonhuman primates are subject to the same mechanism. In many primate species, inbreeding is avoided through migration of one sex or the other at puberty.

The Westermarck effect is important because it rests on a combination of nature *and* nurture. It includes an innate component (the effect of early familiarity), a developmental component (learned sexual aversion), a cultural component (most societies have family arrangements that lead to sexual inhibitions among relatives), an evolutionary reason (suppression of inbreeding) and direct parallels with animal behaviour (de Waal 1999).

Activity 10: Perceptual development

Go to Chapter 8. Read the section that deals with explanations for perceptual development. Note the evidence given for each side of the nature–nurture debate as regards perceptual development.

How would you sum up the nature–nurture debate in this area?

---

opportunities by teachers or may produce reactions of awe from their peers.

◆ An *active* relationship between genes and environment may occur because individuals actively select experiences that fit in with their genetically influenced preferences. For example, musically gifted children may seek out musical friends and opportunities.

Exam summary: Nature and nurture

The AQA examination will test your understanding of the following areas:

◆ definitions of the terms nature and nurture (p. 520)

◆ assumptions made about nature and nurture in theory and research (pp. 520–1)

◆ different views about the relationship between nature and nurture (pp. 522–3).

Example question

The question below is typical of one drawn from the material above, and should take you 45 minutes to answer:

(a) Outline the assumptions made about nature and nurture in two areas of psychological theory or research. *(15 marks)*

(b) Evaluate the concept of nature versus nurture in terms of the possible relationship between the two. *(15 marks)*

Suggested answer structure:

On first reading, this question appears quite tricky. It should not be if handled carefully. The question spans two of the above bullet points, therefore your content will come mostly from the pages indicated. Do remember, however, that the function of this *Perspectives* section is to test your overview of psychology, therefore the content in this chapter is *illustrative* rather than *definitive*. This means you should be constantly referring to other material you have covered elsewhere in the book. This both elaborates your understanding of debates such as nature versus nurture, but it also provides a synoptic element in your answers (see Chapter 21), and for that you will be richly rewarded.

As with the reductionism question discussed earlier, you can either turn to major *perspectives* (see Chapter 20), or different topic areas, such as *intelligence* (p. 521) or *depression* (pp. 394–6 and 441–6). In this chapter, we have looked in some detail at how the nature–nurture debate has 'evolved' within the field of intelligence, while in the latter set of page references, you can see some quite different accounts of depression that stress the *adaptive* nature of the depressive response (pp. 394–6) versus the influence of psychological events in its development (pp. 441–6).

The second part of this question asks for an evaluation of the nature/nurture debate in terms of a possible relationship between the two. You might begin this response by considering how difficult it is to separate out the influences of nature and nurture (p. 522), and then how, for example, the influences of genes and environment might interact together (pp. 522–3).

Chapter summary

◆ **Gender bias** is embedded both in psychology and in history. Philosophers such as Aristotle saw sex differences in behaviour as being biologically based. In more contemporary **theories** of psychology, there have been two main approaches to gender-related characteristics. Theories that ignore the differences between men and women have a **beta bias**, and those that exaggerate the differences an **alpha bias**. Such biases lead to an **androcentric** view of human behaviour. There are a number of ways in which psychology can avoid these biases, by avoiding

gender stereotypes and considering the constant interaction between individual and environmental influences in a person's development.

◆ Psychological **research** appears to disadvantage women through its reliance on experimental research. The construction of knowledge concerning female deficiency has typically been created within such a context. Alternative research strategies would move away from rigid experimental manipulations towards a consideration of the experiences of women in their own lives.

◆ **Cultural biases** in psychology may be evident through the '**imposed etic**' whereby theories and research from one culture are used to explain the behaviour and experiences of members of another culture. Attempts to reproduce psychological studies in different cultures are rarely straightforward. Failure to ensure equivalence in these studies means that alternative explanations of the research findings often have to be considered. Psychological theories have also been used to impose or to bolster particular social or political beliefs and practices.

◆ **Ethical issues** in psychological research **using human participants** are based on a number of fundamental moral principles. Deception is seen as unacceptable because it removes the participant's ability to give their informed consent to take part in research. Informed consent requires the full disclosure of what might happen in an investigation to potential participants, who are in turn competent to make rational judgements based on this information. The issue of privacy is of particular importance in field research, particularly in conditions where it might be expected by the participants involved.

◆ **Socially sensitive research** are those studies in which there are potential social consequences either for the participants themselves or the class of individuals represented by the research. Carrying out research in socially sensitive areas raises difficult ethical issues and should focus psychologists more on the implications of their findings.

◆ The notion of **free will** allows us to separate out what is the intention of an individual from what has been caused by some internal or external event. If we accept that behaviour is something that has been caused by events in the past, it becomes clear that we cannot accept the notion of free will. If we do not accept that we are bound to our past, but rather have the capacity to formulate plans and act accordingly, we are proposing the existence and influence of free will. The view that human beings might also behave for the sake of their intentions can be seen as a form of final causal determinism.

◆ The concept of free will is not only compatible with a wider view of **determinism**, but is also important if we are to view individuals as being morally responsible for their own actions. If our actions are merely the product of some past event or our biological 'programming', then we cannot be held responsible for our behaviours.

◆ **Freud's** psychoanalytic theory provides an example of biological determinism. Behaviourists (such as **Skinner**) explain behaviour in terms of environmental determinism. Humanistic psychologists stress the importance of free will.

◆ The subject of **nonhuman animal research** is unquestionably one of the most controversial issues within psychology. Heated arguments for and against using animals involve both **ethical** and **scientific** dimensions. Some psychologists believe that the public outcry against the abuse of animals has often blinded us to the potential advantages of high-quality research that both minimizes animal suffering yet provides clear scientific benefits. Legislation concerning animal research appears to be focused more directly on laboratory studies, but is less clearly defined in field experiments that may also involve adverse effects on the subjects involved.

◆ One of the most significant positions in scientific thinking is the notion that the simplest **explanations** are usually the best. The tendency to reduce human behaviour to simple biological or **mechanical** processes has become known as **reductionism**. According to this line of thinking, we should attempt to find the simple principles that inevitably underlie more complex behaviours. Biological reductionism includes the influence of genes on human behaviour. Sociobiologists believe that human beings behave according to the pressures of natural selection and act in such a way as to maximize the transmission of their genes. Behaviourist explanations of behaviour in terms of stimulus, response and reinforcement must be tempered by the knowledge that organisms are biologically prepared to learn some things more readily than others, particularly those things that have some survival value.

◆ **Science** is concerned with the acquisition of knowledge that is considered trustworthy. The scientific method is the process by which explanatory theories are established through empirical observation and **objectivity**, and are constantly refined and updated in the same way. Although most psychologists embrace the aims and methods of science there are some doubts (e.g. raised by **Kuhn**'s concept of the scientist's **paradigm**) over whether its subject matter and methods enable us to consider **psychology** as truly scientific. Recent developments in psychology have placed greater emphasis on the subjective experience of research participants than on **experimental methods** and restricting the collection of information to the gathering of numerical data.

◆ There has been a **history** of tension between those who favour a view of behaviour as a product of heredity (**nature**) and those who favour the greater influence of environment (**nurture**). Behaviourists concluded that all behaviour was the product of learning. In contrast, ethologists focused on natural behaviour, believing that animals are born with a number of 'fixed-action patterns' that are little changed by the environment. Behaviourists have been forced to adopt some of the ideas of evolutionary biology, especially with the discovery that learning is not the same for all species and across all species. Views of the development of intelligence (such as **Piaget's theory**) also reflect the nature–nurture debate. Psychologists disagree over how much of intelligence can be changed as a result of environmental influences (i.e. the **gene–environment interaction**). This debate over the determination of intelligence has pushed the issue into the political arena, most notably since the publication of *The Bell Curve*.

Further resources

Kimmel, **A.J.** (1996) *Ethical Issues in Behavioural Research: A Survey*, Cambridge, MA: Blackwell.

A comprehensive account of the ethical issues of psychological research with nonhuman and human participants.

Sieber, **J.E. and Stanley**, **B.** (1988) 'Ethical and professional dimensions of socially sensitive research', *American Psychologist*, 43 (1), pp. 49–55.

Well worth reading if you can get hold of a copy. A detailed account of the issues of socially sensitive research as well as discussion of the ways of dealing with these issues.

Slife, **B.D. and Williams**, **R.N.** (1995) *What's Behind the Research? Discovering Hidden Assumptions in the Behavioural Sciences*, Thousand Oaks: Sage.

A clearly written and authoritative text that covers most of the issues in this chapter.

Websites

http://www.yorku.ca/dept/psych/classics/

A wonderful site that gives access to articles charting the historical development of psychology and many of the most significant shaping influences.

http://www.sciam.com/0297issue/0297forum.html

The benefits and ethics of animal research. Three articles from Scientific American *on the importance (or not) of animal research.*

synoptic issues

See the *Index of synoptic issues* (pp. 645–50) for ideas about how to use issues in this chapter for synoptic assessment.

Chapter 20

Approaches in psychology

Phil Banyard

Preview

In this chapter we will look at what is meant by 'approaches' in psychology. We will then look in detail at the following five approaches:

◆ the biological approach

◆ the evolutionary approach

◆ the psychodynamic approach

◆ the behavioural approach

◆ the cognitive approach.

Introduction

When sitting in the bath trying to think of a reason not to get out, we are sometimes moved to consider the great questions of life: Who am I? What's it all for? How did I come to be like this? These questions have been the cause of many debates since people first had the ability to think, and will no doubt continue to be debated as long as people live on this planet. These are the big questions that psychology sets out to answer, and although much of the psychological research you read about appears to be quite detailed and narrow, the ultimate aim is to discover more about who and what we are.

Psychologists offer many different explanations for human behaviour and experience. The type of explanation offered depends upon the approach (perspective) adopted by the psychologist. Inevitably this means that we sometimes come across different explanations for the same event. This does not mean that only one explanation is right and all the rest are wrong, but rather that the explanations are affected by the context (approach) used.

In psychology, there are a number of contrasting contexts in which we choose to view people. Each one of them adds to our overall understanding of what makes people behave and experience the world in the way that they do, but none of these contexts is able to give us the whole story. These contexts are sometimes referred to as 'perspectives' or 'approaches' or 'paradigms'. Whatever we choose to call them, they are made up of the same components:

◆ a set of assumptions about what the basic influences on behaviour and experience are

◆ a metaphor (or story) about how people operate or function

◆ evidence that supports the metaphor and adds to our overall understanding of people.

The approaches outlined in this chapter are different from each other and you may wonder how such different approaches can exist within the same subject. However, two things unite them: their subject matter (the behaviour and experience of individual people) and their attempts to obtain evidence systematically in order to enhance our understanding of human beings.

Approaches in psychology

We will consider five of the traditional approaches used by psychologists. They focus on different aspects of behaviour and experience:

◆ what we *are made of* (the *biological* approach)

◆ how we *evolved* (the *evolutionary* approach)

◆ what we *feel* (the *psychodynamic* approach)

◆ what we *do* (the *behavioural* approach)

◆ what we *think* (the *cognitive* approach).

This is by no means an exhaustive list, but it should allow us to consider some of the big themes in psychological debate. For each of the five approaches we will consider the basic ideas and assumptions, the metaphor used, some key names and key evidence, some examples of what the approach explains and some limitations of the approach. One chapter cannot do full justice to each of these approaches, but it will give you a basic framework so that you can draw on examples from other parts of the book, identify the approach that is being used and evaluate the evidence accordingly.

The biological approach *(looking at what we are made of)*

In order to understand how the biological approach to psychology began, we need to consider the views of the French scientist and philosopher, René Descartes (1596–1650). He proposed that human beings are made up of two principal components: a body and a soul (or mind). He argued that a person without a soul would be no more than an automaton, controlled entirely by external stimuli and internal chemistry. According to Descartes, the mind of a human being is quite separate from the body, a notion referred to as *dualism*. Descartes believed that the mind (soul) came from God and is immortal, whereas the body is like a machine and eventually it wears out (dies). Extreme dualists believe that there is no interaction between the mind and the body. Descartes, however, thought the mind could influence the body via the pineal gland (a structure at the base of the brain). This hypothesis is not taken seriously nowadays but, nevertheless, Descartes' idea of a one-way influence of mind over body has been highly influential. This concept of the mind being located somewhere within (but separate from) the body has been described as 'a ghost in the machine' (Ryle 1949). Unlike Descartes, other philosophers believed that the body (machine) had an effect on the mind and thence on behaviour. This is a major assumption of the biological approach in psychology: that the physical body, especially the brain, exerts an important influence on experience and behaviour.

We now know that the control centre of the 'machine' is the brain, but the brain did not become the main focus of study until the nineteenth century. The German doctor Franz Josef Gall (1758–1828) carried out convincing demonstrations of the importance of the brain for higher human functions, though he blotted his copybook by developing the bogus science of phrenology which attempted to read a person's personality through an analysis of the shape of their skull. The French scientist Pierre Flourens (1794–1867), who systematically removed parts of animals' brains in order to observe the effects, enhanced understanding of the way certain functions are localized in regions of the brain. In the following quote, he describes how a series of ablations (operations to remove brain tissue) had an effect on an animal:

'I removed the cerebellum in a young but vigorous dog by a series of deeper and deeper slices. The animal lost gradually the faculty of orderly and regular movement. Soon he could walk only by staggering in zigzags. He fell back when he wanted to advance; when he wanted to turn to the right, he turned to the left. .... He had all his intellectual faculties, all his senses; he was only deprived of the faculty of coordinating and regularizing his movements.' (quoted in Fancher 1990, p. 82)

One early example of evidence for the localization of cognitive functions in the brain came from the work of Paul Broca (1824–1880). He was able to show that a small area of the brain is responsible for the production of speech. Damage to this area renders a person speechless even though they can still understand the spoken word. This area is still referred to as Broca's area. Since that time it has been possible to identify a number of regions of the brain that, if damaged, have specific effects on the way we think or the way we behave or the way we feel. Some of the work into localization of function, however, has been disappointing. For example, Karl Lashley (1890–1959) tried to find the part of the brain responsible for memory by systematically removing parts of rats' brains to observe the effects. He was unable, however, to find a specific site. He eventually proposed the Law of Mass Action. This states that the decline in performance of the animal is related to the amount of brain tissue that is removed rather than which bit is removed.

More recently, the work of Canadian neurosurgeon Wilder Penfield (1891–1976) has provided more information about localized brain function. He was interested in providing relief for people with epilepsy. He had observed that just before an epileptic seizure, people often experienced peculiar warning signs, called auras, that are very personal to the individual. To cut a long story short, Penfield exposed the brains of his fully conscious volunteer patients and then stimulated various parts with an electrode in an attempt to create the aura artificially. Once he had found the part of the brain that stimulated the aura, he surgically removed it in an attempt to stop the source of the epileptic attacks. The operations had a degree of success. The work also provided a lot of information about the localized functions of the brain, including areas for movement and areas for interpreting stimuli.

The biological-machine metaphor

Biological psychology explores human behaviour and experience by looking at people as if they are biological machines. This idea has some value because it is clear that our biology affects our behaviour and experience. On a simple level, we know certain foodstuffs such as coffee or alcoholic drinks will affect the way we see the world and the way we behave. Also, it has been known for a long time that damage to the brain and nervous system can have an effect on behaviour and experience.

Therefore, the structure and biochemistry of the nervous system are two important aspects of biological psychology. However, the real issue is how much our biology affects our behaviour and experience and to what extent other factors intervene. As we shall see later, there are some occasions when the biological-machine metaphor cannot explain all behaviour and experience.

What can the biological approach explain?

Brain structure

As already mentioned, certain areas of the brain are known to be responsible for certain specific behaviours. Traditional methods, such as studying people who have had brain surgery or those who have sustained brain damage through strokes or accidents, have produced a lot of information about the relationship between sites in the brain and our experience and behaviour. In addition, modern techniques (such as PET scans) for investigating the brain non-invasively (without surgery) have increased our understanding even further (see Chapter 4).

This approach of mapping out brain structures and identifying which behaviours they are responsible for fits well with the machine metaphor. It has enabled us to identify, for example, pleasure centres in the hypothalamus (Olds and Milner 1954) which give us some clues about the factors that motivate our behaviour, and the areas in the cerebral cortex that process visual information (Hubel and Wiesel 1968). A recent study on London taxi drivers (Maguire *et al.* 1997) has even identified an area of the hippocampus that appears to be involved in the drivers' recall of their routes around the capital. Sadly, they were unable to find the part of the brain that stimulates their unique style of conversation.

Brain chemistry

The last thirty years have seen a dramatic growth in our knowledge about the way that chemicals affect our behaviour and experience. The centre of the action is the synapse which is the gap between nerve cells that is bridged by the release and uptake of neurochemicals (see Chapter 4). It has been found, for example, that morphine and other opium-based drugs attach themselves to specific receptor sites at some synapses. They are able to do this because they resemble one class of neurochemicals (Snyder 1984). In brief, opiates bring pain relief because they stimulate the relevant nervous system pathways.

It is possible to bring relief from a number of disorders by changing the levels of neurotransmitters in the brain. For example, the symptoms of Parkinson's disease, such as shaking of the limbs, are known to be associated with lowered levels of the neurochemical dopamine. It is possible to raise the level of dopamine through medication or through transplants, and so alleviate the symptoms. Unfortunately, taking dopamine-enhancing drugs like L-DOPA produces a number of unpleasant side effects as well as the desired reduction in uncontrolled movements. The side effects include nausea, restlessness and occasionally hallucinations and delusions. These last two are particularly important because of the connection made between dopamine and the mental states we refer to as schizophrenia. It is believed that people in schizophrenic states have enhanced levels of dopamine and are therefore given drugs that are meant to reduce these dopamine levels. Unfortunately, they also have a range of unpleasant side effects including giving the patients some of the symptoms of Parkinson's disease.

In the popular scientific press, neurochemicals are often referred to as the main factor in psychological disorders. For example, low levels of serotonin are commonly described as the cause of depressed moods, and people take medications such as Prozac to boost the levels of active serotonin in the nervous system (see also the sections on drug treatments of mental disorders in Chapter 18). As with antischizophrenic medications, people can experience a wide variety of serious side effects which suggests that the chemistry of the brain is very complex.

In summary, it is clear that our behaviour is structured to some extent by the nuts and bolts of our brains and the neurochemical messengers that operate within them. But how far can we take the mechanical metaphor before it breaks down? The next section looks at some of the issues arising from this approach.

Evaluation of the biological approach

We will now look at the some of the practical, theoretical and philosophical issues related to the biological approach.

Practical issues

One of the practical issues concerns the way that the mechanical model of the brain is applied. The most infamous technique to change behaviour through brain surgery is the frontal lobotomy. This was stimulated by the research of Fulton and Jacobsen (1935). They observed that after they had removed the frontal lobes of a truculent female chimpanzee she became passive. Within a year of this report, the Portuguese surgeon Moniz attempted the first operations on people. The operation was enthusiastically taken up as a means of pacifying people and also of relieving obsessive and compulsive symptoms. Over the next 30 years, tens of thousands of operations were carried out, and Moniz was given a Nobel prize for his work, although, by a strange irony, his career ended prematurely when he was disabled by a lobotomized patient who shot him.

The lobotomy operation is rarely performed now because it did not have the desired effects. There are a number of practical difficulties in trying to change behaviour through brain surgery. These include:

◆ The so-called structures of the brain are not as separate as textbooks suggest and some of them are no more than a slight thickening of the tissue. This means it may be difficult to identify accurately and remove a particular piece.

◆ Each individual brain is different and this uniqueness further confuses the search for the appropriate bit.

◆ A range of brain structures that interact with each other affects many behavioural and cognitive functions. Consequently, removing one piece may not bring about the change wanted and may bring about a number of changes not wanted.

Theoretical issues

The mechanical model of the brain breaks down in some exceptional circumstances. An example of this comes from the case studies of adult survivors of childhood hydrocephalus made by neurosurgeon John Lorber (1981). This research made use of the new scanning methods for investigating the brain. Adults with larger than average heads were chosen because the size of their head might be related to childhood hydrocephalus (water in the head). Investigations found a number of people with unusual brain structures, including one man with most of his brain missing. This man did not have the basic structures that occur in most brains, but just had a smearing of brain about 3 mm thick around the skull. He had no visual cortex yet he had 20-20 vision, and he had none of the structures associated with intellectual activity, yet he had a degree. There is no simple explanation for these phenomena, but they provide a major challenge to the machine description of the brain.

A further problem with the biological approach comes from the issue of causation. Just because two things change at the same time, it does not mean that one causes the other. Take, for example, the changes in dopamine that occur in schizophrenic states as described above. Does the increase in dopamine cause the schizophrenic state or does the mental state of schizophrenia cause a change in dopamine levels? We are aware that mental events can have physical consequences. For example, I can induce the physiological changes associated with anger just by making myself have angry thoughts. When we use drugs, therefore, to reduce dopamine levels, some

people think that we may not be treating the cause of schizophrenia but rather its consequence.

Philosophical issues

The mind–body distinction proposed by Descartes is still being debated to this day. Some claim that a machine alone is not capable of intelligent thought (e.g. Searle 1980, see the cognitive approach on p. 545). Others seek to explain how mental events can affect physical events, or in other words how a ghost can operate the machine (e.g. Eccles 1987).

A more immediate issue concerns the view of people that the biological model gives us. Look at the following quote from physiological psychologist Peter Milner:

'I am interested in organisms as pieces of machinery, and I would like to know much the same about them as I once wanted to know about the gadgets I saw around me: first, what happens when the controls or inputs are manipulated and, a little later, how it happens.' (Milner 1970, p. 1)

The idea of regarding people as objects in scientific study means that people might be treated as objects in everyday life. When objects breakdown we may fix them (e.g. by brain surgery) or when they are beyond repair we may discard them and view them as useless. It is difficult not to be shocked at such a brutal approach to people and at such a pessimistic vision of human behaviour and experience.

Summary: The biological approach

In brief, the biological approach views people as being like biological machines. The approach argues that brain chemistry and brain structures are the major causes of behaviour and experience. It examines the changes in the brain that accompany changes in behaviour and experience. It proposes physical interventions to bring about psychological changes. It argues that there is no ghost (soul or mind) in the machine.

Activity 1: Applying the biological approach
One way of exploring how common the biological approach is in our everyday explanations is to look at the way we describe daily activities. Make a list of the things that we do that have some biological assumptions behind them. Just to get you started, what about having a cup of coffee in the morning to help us get going. It assumes (largely correctly) that the chemicals in coffee will give us a lift. What sort of biological explanations are sometimes given to explain some aggressive behaviours?

The evolutionary approach *(looking at where we came from)*

If you had to pick one scientific idea that has had the greatest effect on modern thought, then you might well pick the theory of evolution. This theory has transformed the way we look at ourselves and continues to exert an influence on psychology, particularly with the growing interest in genetic explanations of behaviour. Many readers of this book might be encouraged to discover that the author of the theory, Charles Darwin (1809-82), did not do very well at school, and in his autobiography he said of his education that 'Nothing could have been worse for the development of my mind ...' (Darwin, 1869, p. 27). Darwin eventually recovered from his schooling and wrote *The Origin of Species*, published in 1859. The book presented an argument for the development of species over time through the process of natural selection. The book was mainly about plants and non-human animals, but it did contain a brief paragraph about human development that accurately predicted future scientific discoveries:

> 'In the distant future I see open fields for far more important researches. Psychology will be based on a new foundation, that of necessary acquirement of each mental power and capacity for gradation. Light will be thrown on the origin of man and history.' (Darwin 1859, p. 488)

In later publications, Darwin argued that human beings were descended from animal ancestors. He demonstrated the similarities in the physical structures of people and animals, including similarities in the structure of the brain. He then went on to argue that there was no fundamental difference between the mental abilities of humans and those of animals. To say these ideas were controversial understates the effect they had at the time. A society that believed it had been fashioned by God was being told that it was fashioned by the environment. The controversy abated during Darwin's lifetime, and when he died the Church authorities, who had so vigorously opposed his theories, consented to his being buried in Westminster Abbey.

Before we go on to look at the implications of evolutionary theory for psychology, we need to consider briefly the process of natural selection – the way that evolution works. According to Darwin's account of evolution, natural selection is the way that species change over time and become more adaptive to their environment. The key features of this are:

◆ Individuals have unique genetic characteristics.

◆ Some individuals survive and breed while others die before they breed.

◆ The genetic characteristics of the survivors are retained.

◆ The genetic characteristics of those who do not breed are lost.

What this means is that the characteristics that enable some individuals to survive and reproduce are likely to be passed on to the next generation. The species then develops through a process of selective breeding – selected by the environment. The key ideas of Darwin's theory are *genetic variation* (in individuals in each generation) and *natural selection* (some individuals live and some die depending on how well adapted they are to their environment). Of course, if a species (like ourselves) is able to tamper with natural selection (e.g. by developing medicine that keeps unhealthy people alive until they can breed), then this might have an effect on how the species develops.

Social Darwinism

The issue for psychology raised by evolutionary theory is not about whether the structure of our bodies evolved through natural selection, but whether the ways that we behave and experience the world have also evolved in the same way. Darwin's cousin, Francis Galton (1822–1911), who was an explorer, statistician, inventor and scientist who made many contributions to science, enthusiastically took up this issue. Among his diverse interests, he studied fingerprints, beauty, word association, paranoia, cuckoos and animal hearing. He is most famous in psychology for his work on statistics and mental testing.

Galton was impressed by Darwin's work and proposed to apply it to people. In his 1869 book, *Hereditary Genius*, he wrote:

> 'I propose to show in this book that a man's natural abilities are derived from inheritance, under exactly the same limitations as are the form and physical features of the whole organic world.' (Galton 1869, reproduced in Fancher 1990, p. 220)

Galton offered three types of evidence to support his case, all of which are still used today:

◆ *The distribution of abilities*

At the time Galton wrote his book, it had already been observed that if one collected measures of weight or height from a large population, the

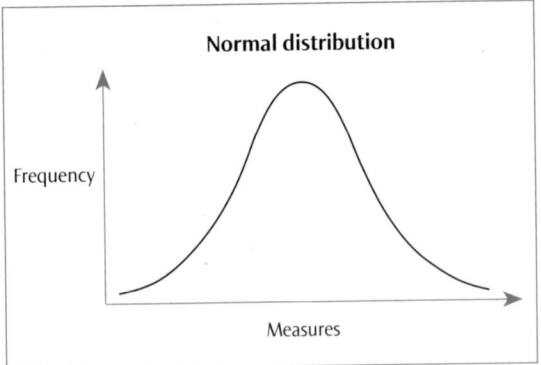

Normal distribution

Frequency

Measures

Figure 20.1 Distribution of abilities

measures fell into a bell-shaped normal distribution (see Fig. 20.1). It was noted that these characteristics were mainly structured by inheritance. According to Galton, perhaps the normal distribution was itself an indication of inheritance. Since several psychological characteristics, such as intellectual ability, seemed to be normally distributed in the general population, he thought they were largely determined by inheritance.

◆ The way that *eminence appeared to run in families*

Galton examined the family trees of twelve different groups of eminent people such as judges, military commanders, writers, scientists and wrestlers, and made two observations:

– if a family member of the eminent person was also eminent then they were likely to be close family rather than distant family

– there was a tendency for relatives to excel in the same field.

◆ A comparison of *adoptive versus biological relatives*

It is possible to look at people brought up in the same home environment and compare those who are biologically related with those who are not. Galton claimed to have found greater similarity between those who were biologically related than among those who had no biological ties. Although Galton's study had its weaknesses, the principal idea was sound and this method has been developed and used ever since.

Galton was trying to establish how much of our behaviour and experience is due to inheritance and how much is due to the environment we are brought up in. In his writings, he used the phrase 'nature and nurture' to describe the two possible sources of influence, and this phrase has circumscribed the subsequent debate. The side that you choose to come down on affects the way you will see society. Galton, along with many of his contemporaries, believed that

the massive social and economic divisions in Victorian society were there because some people were superior to others. He sought to provide a scientific explanation for this by establishing the heritability of psychological characteristics.

In 1884 Galton created a mental testing laboratory in the Natural History Museum in London where he collected measurements on such things as visual acuity, strength of grip, colour vision, hearing acuity and hand preference, from the visitors to the museum who, incidentally, paid Galton for the privilege. He hoped to use these measures to estimate people's hereditary intelligence. These tests, inappropriate as they might seem, marked the start of intelligence testing and the attempt to show that the variation between people in their psychological abilities is under genetic control.

Eugenics

It has been argued that Galton's work was driven by one major concern – how to manipulate the forces of evolution to the advantage of the human race. The idea is expressed in *Hereditary Genius*:

'As it is easy ... to obtain by careful selection a permanent breed of dogs or horses gifted with peculiar powers of running, or of doing anything else, so would it be quite practicable to produce a highly-gifted race of men by judicious marriages during several consecutive generations.' (Galton 1869, reproduced in Fancher 1990, p. 228)

Galton later coined the term *eugenics* to describe his project of improving the race through selective breeding. This project has consistently attracted the attention of scientists ever since and the recent work on the human genetic code has provided it with some added momentum. Clearly, such a project has a down side and we will consider that later on in this section. For now, we are going to take a brief look at a more recent evolutionary account.

Sociobiology

It has become clear that it is not possible to explain successfully the development of human behaviour using the principles of Social Darwinism. For example, the issue of altruism presents a major problem (see Chapter 13). However, the sentiments of Social Darwinism – and hence eugenics – have found a new home in the modern theory of sociobiology. This theory (e.g. Wilson 1975, Dawkins 1976) attempts to explain our behaviour using genetic principles and produces entertaining, plausible, though, some argue, fundamentally flawed accounts. One of the more controversial claims by some sociobiologists is the idea that it is 'natural' for males to be sexually promiscuous so that they can maximize their chances of passing on their genes to the next generation. (For a review of sociobiology, see Hayes 1995.)

The phrase 'the selfish gene' (Dawkins 1976) has become part of everyday explanations of behaviour. The notion of 'the selfish gene' refers to the idea that the driving force behind evolution is the gene rather than the individual organism. According to this theory, individuals act in order to see as many as possible of their genes passed on to the next generation. That might mean producing offspring, but it might also mean looking after the offspring of close relatives since they share a significant number of one's genes. The pressures, therefore, are to maximize genetic survival rather than individual survival.

Sociobiologists present a range of examples from the animal world to support their argument, though it is difficult to see the similarity between, for example, wasp society and human society. Iit is also worth noting that they offer relatively few examples of mammal behaviour to support their theory. One of the problems with the selective use of animal evidence is that animal behaviour is very varied. Even quite similar species can have dramatically different patterns of behaviour. So, for every example that supports the sociobiological approach, it is possible to find another that contradicts it.

The evolutionary metaphor

The evolutionary metaphor is that we are just slightly more complex animals, and that our behaviour has developed in the same way that our bodies have. The features that have been most fit (adaptive to the environment) have been passed on. The evolutionary account views human behaviour in the context of general animal behaviour. It also explains our behaviour as having a biological cause, and suggests we are what we are because that is the way evolution shaped it. The evolutionary account also suggests that differences between people are largely due to genetic variation and can therefore be affected by genetic engineering.

Evaluation of the evolutionary approach

We will now look at the some of the practical, theoretical and moral issues related to the evolutionary approach.

Practical issues

One practical issue concerns the attempt to measure the relative effects of nature and nurture on any psychological characteristic. The traditional technique of family studies (e.g. where we look at how the

degree of genetic similarity can be used to predict behavioural similarity) has a central problem – how to quantify the environment and how to control for variations within it. For example, just because two children are brought up in the same home does not mean they have the same environment. One of them might have been supported and encouraged, while the other might have been labelled as a 'no hoper' from an early age and therefore developed under the adult expectation that they would not amount to much.

Theoretical issues

Among the many theoretical issues are the following:

◆ The problem of *mapping genes to behaviour*

In his sociobiological descriptions of behaviour, Dawkins refers to the gene as the unit of natural selection. This is a clever play with words because it allows him to describe certain behaviours in genetic terms. The biological reality is that behaviour cannot be directly inherited. Our inheritance comes in the form of biological structures that will then have an influence on behaviour. It is this gap between biology and behaviour that poses the challenge for sociobiologists.

◆ The relationship between *animal* and *human behaviour*

Just because behaviour looks the same in animals and people, it does not mean that it has the same cause. It is a popular misreading of behaviour to see animal characteristics in people and human characteristics in animals. This latter error is referred to as *anthropomorphism*, an example of which is the popular idea that lemmings commit suicide. This is not the case. Suicide is a decision that people take to end their own lives. It cannot be argued that lemmings wake up one day, consider the pointlessness of their existence and decide to throw themselves off a cliff.

In psychology, we commonly use evidence derived from animals to make generalizations about human conditions, e.g. the work on learned helpless in dogs (Seligman and Maier 1967) or the work on pleasure centres (Olds and Milner 1954). The latter work describes responses in rats as being pleasurable, but do rats experience pleasure, and if they do, how would we know?

◆ The difficulty in *defining and measuring psychological characteristics*

In order for something to be inherited, it has to exist. Obvious as this might sound, it is the issue that challenges a number of 'hereditary' arguments.

Take the issue of intelligence. We know that individuals vary widely in how they perform on different tests of mental ability. They may be good at maths but poor at pattern recognition or word manipulation. The concept of intelligence relies on the idea that there is an underlying quality that affects our performance on all mental tests. If this underlying quality does not exist, then it is impossible to inherit it and so the debate on the inheritance of intelligence collapses. Some evidence supports the existence of an underlying 'general intelligence' characteristic and some challenges it (see Gould 1981).

Moral issues

The big moral issue arising from the evolutionary approach is that of eugenics. The Social Darwinists noticed that better health care and social conditions meant that not so many people were dying at a young age and they feared that the effect of natural selection was being blunted. In other words, if the weak survived then they would pass on their weak genes to the next generation. They proposed, therefore, that breeding better members of the species should be engineered to improve society and eventually remove people who would weaken the human species. The principle of eugenics had some powerful supporters who put forward views that make our hair stand on end today. For example, Francis Galton wrote:

'There exists a sentiment for the most part quite unreasonable against the gradual extinction of an inferior race.' (Galton 1883, cited in Rose *et al.* 1984, p. 30)

History is witness to the many attempts by one group of people to slaughter another. Some examples of mass murder, at least partly justified in the name of eugenics, include Native Americans by immigrant settlers, Aborigines by Australian settlers and Jews, Gypsies and homosexuals by the Nazis. These are extreme examples of how eugenics may be implemented and they would find few apologists or supporters in modern society.

There is, however, another aspect to eugenics that will challenge us more and more as our knowledge increases. It is now possible to know some details about a baby before it is born, such as its gender or whether it might have some genetic disability like deafness or spina bifida. In some societies, parents have the choice to engage in their own eugenics programmes by deciding to terminate pregnancies of children with unwanted characteristics. As our knowledge increases, how will parents decide whether to continue with a pregnancy or not? What are the ethics of these choices? One might accept the termination of 'handicapped' pregnancies (though many people do not), but what about terminating a pregnancy because the baby will be female, or ugly or blonde?

A further moral issue is raised by the way that sociobiology seems to concentrate on the negative and competitive aspects of human behaviour and ignore the positive and cooperative ones. In fact Dawkins writes:

'We must expect lies and deceit, selfish exploitation of communication to arise whenever the interests of the genes of different individuals converge ... [so] ... we must expect that children will deceive their parents, that husbands will cheat on wives, and that brother will lie to brother.' (Dawkins 1976, p. 149)

This depressing vision of social behaviour is perhaps not one that you wish to subscribe to. In human history, alongside the brutality there have been many movements that have inspired people to acts of kindness, selfless behaviour and cooperative endeavour (e.g. some religious and charitable organizations). These movements are likely to continue, challenging the stark evolutionary explanations of behaviour.

Summary: The evolutionary approach

In brief, the evolutionary approach considers human beings in terms of their evolutionary development from more primitive states. It argues that the differences between people in their abilities are largely due to genetic factors. It views animal behaviour as just a simpler version of human behaviour. Evolutionary arguments have been associated with eugenics (the attempt to breed superior people).

Activity 2: Applying the evolutionary approach

Try to use the evolutionary approach to explain some aspect of our behaviour and experience. For example, you might have observed that newborn babies have a very strong grip. If they ever get hold of your hair you know about it. This gripping behaviour might well have had some advantage when their mothers carried young animals around. Those who managed to hold on to her body hair were more likely to survive than those who did not manage. What about our anxiety/fear responses, or our delight in dancing, or our pleasure in good food? How might the evolutionary approach attempt to explain why older men marry younger women more often than older women marry younger men?

The psychodynamic approach *(looking at how we feel)*

When people are asked to name the most famous figure in the history of psychology, they usually come up with the name of Sigmund Freud. Freud's approach to understanding human behaviour, known as psychoanalysis, has had a profound effect within psychology, yet his approach is one of many that share some common assumptions, whilst differing fundamentally in others. Contemporaries of Freud, such as Carl Jung and Alfred Adler, despite being inspired by Freudian theory, emphasized different issues in human development and experience. This wider theoretical framework is known as the psychodynamic approach.

Educated in Vienna, Freud spent most of his life there before fleeing Austria for London after the German invasion in 1938. Freud trained as a doctor, specializing in neurological disorders. In 1885, he won a six-month fellowship to study with Jean Charcot, a French doctor whose interests in hysteria (physical symptoms that appear to have no physical cause) had a profound effect on Freud's own theories. He began writing about psychoanalysis, as he called his theory, shortly after. In 1919, he was given the title of professor at the University of Vienna. He became a prolific writer on psychology despite a long series of battles with cancer that he was eventually to lose at the age of 83.

Freud's theory of psychoanalysis

Freud believed that the human mind had both conscious and unconscious areas. The unconscious part of the mind was seen as being dominated by the 'id', a primitive part of the personality that pursues only pleasure and gratification. The id is not concerned with social rules but only with self-gratification. This disregard for the consequences of a behaviour is referred to as 'primary process thinking'. The second area is the 'ego',

which dominates the conscious mind. This is the part of our mind that is in contact with the outside world, the part that considers the consequences of an action, and as such carries out 'secondary process thinking'.

The third part of the mind is the 'superego'. This develops as we become more aware of the rules and conventions of society and specifically of our parents. It contains our social conscience, and through the experience of guilt and anxiety when we do something wrong, it guides us towards socially acceptable behaviour. According to Freud, the ego and the superego dwell largely in the conscious mind, while the id is in the unconscious area of our mind.

One of the more controversial aspects of Freud's theory, and the one that probably caused the greatest problem for his contemporaries, was his ideas of the sexual instinct and its importance in the development of the individual. According to Freud, human beings experience a cycle of arousal in their sexual instinct. When this cycle is at a high point, the id demands gratification and determines to carry out behaviours that will result in sexual gratification. In most civilized societies, however, sexual gratification is not something that can be achieved without a consideration of social morality. The superego may, therefore, *oppose* gratification with the result that the ego is caught between two conflicting demands: the id demands immediate gratification, while the superego demands conformity to the moralistic conventions of the society. The ego struggles to maintain a balance between these conflicting demands. How successful it is in achieving this goal ultimately determines both our everyday behaviour and also our mental health.

Another of the key aspects of Freud's theory is the claim that people move through a series of developmental stages (see Table 20.1). Each of the stages described in Table 20.1 is characterized by different demands for sexual gratification and different ways of achieving that gratification. If we do not receive the right amount of gratification, receiving either too much or too little, we become fixated in a particular stage; that is, we continue to have the same demand for gratification that we had at that stage throughout the rest of our life. This condition is thought to produce a variety of neurotic behaviours depending on the type of fixation. Freud believed that to deal with fixation at any particular stage (the fixation point), we must go back, or 'regress', to that stage and resolve the issues that led to the fixation.

To Freud, how well we deal with the demands of each of these developmental stages, and whether or not we receive the optimal amount of gratification, determines how psychologically healthy we are as an adult.

Sigmund Freud

Table 20.1 Freud's psychosexual stages of development

Oral stage (birth to about 15 months)	The newborn child is governed only by its drives. Only the id is present at this stage and so the infant seeks immediate gratification, achieved through its mouth (i.e. through feeding, crying and oral exploration of its world).
Anal stage (15 months to about 3 years)	The focus of gratification shifts from the mouth to the anus. The child experiences pleasure from the elimination of faeces. This brings the child into conflict with their parents. Random elimination (as demanded by the id) incurs parental displeasure, yet withholding elimination (as requested by the parents) is denying the demands of the id, which until this point has been the source of all motivation. The resolution of this conflict requires the development of the ego, and as such has important implications for personality in later life.
Phallic stage (3 years to about 5 years)	The focus of gratification is now on the genitals, although this gratification is not the same as experienced by adults. Children take an increasing interest in their own genitals, and show a curiosity about other people's bodies. The major conflict that children face during this stage is the Oedipal conflict, the resolution of which should result in the attachment to the parents, most notably the same sex parent and the development of a superego. The idea of the Oedipal conflict is central to Freudian theory (see *In Focus*).
Latency stage (around 5 years until puberty)	The drives that have been responsible for gratification in the previous stages appear relatively inactive (hence the reference to them being latent). This is partly due to the repression of sexual drives that is accomplished during the Oedipal stage. These repressed drives may be redirected into other activities, such as the formation of friendships, or hobbies.
Genital stage (puberty onwards)	With puberty, there is a re-emergence of the earlier drives. Drive energy is focused on the genitals once more, but this time with an adult expression of sexuality. Although the term 'genital' suggests that gratification during this stage must inevitably be sexual, Freud emphasized the importance of secondary process thinking as a form of symbolic gratification in this stage. Thus, forming loving relationships or assuming the responsibilities of adult life may all be seen as symbolic ways of satisfying the drive energy of this stage.

The psychoanalytic 'iceberg' metaphor

Freud's ideas about the mind have been likened to an *iceberg* with the area above water being the conscious mind and the part under the water the unconscious mind (see Fig. 20.2). In this image, the id lurks below the surface of conscious awareness and cannot be seen (i.e. we are not aware of its influence). As with an iceberg, the majority of the mass of the mind (and hence its greatest potential influence) is under the surface. This analogy should not be overworked, but it does illustrate the relationship between consciousness and Freud's three aspects of the mind.

Another metaphor used to describe the psychoanalytic explanation of how the mind works is that of a *dramatic conflict* between different forces struggling for control. The best known example of this is Freud's account of the Oedipal conflict.

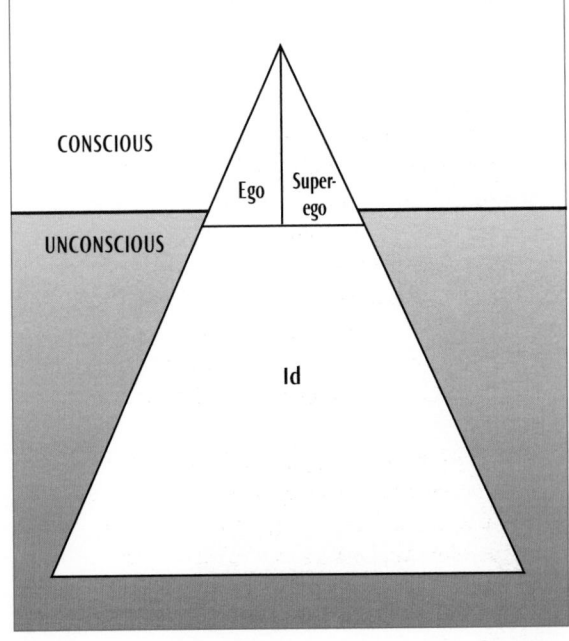

Figure 20.2 The iceberg representation of the human mind

The Oedipal conflict

The major conflict in the Freudian view of development is the Oedipal conflict. This is named after the Greek tragedy in which Oedipus unwittingly kills his own father and marries his own mother. The term was first used by Freud to describe the incestuous feelings that a young boy develops towards his mother, coupled with a jealousy and rivalry with his father for the affections of the mother. As the son comes to realize that the father is more powerful than he is, he begins to fear punishment, specifically that his father might castrate him for his incestuous feelings towards the mother. When the castration anxiety becomes intense, he represses his feelings for the mother and identifies with his father in a process called 'identification with the aggressor'. This lessens the chances of being castrated as the father will no longer see him as a rival. In this way, the boy will attempt to emulate his father, and in so doing he will internalize the father's moral standards, and so develop a superego.

In the female version of the Oedipus conflict, girls between the ages of 4 and 6 envy their father for possessing the penis that they have been denied. When the girl discovers that she lacks a penis, she is thought to blame the mother, and thus transfers her affections from the mother to the father. Because (according to Freud) both boys and girls value the penis, daughters choose their fathers as their primary love object. As they realize the unequal struggle to possess the father, they must renounce these feelings and identify with their mother. This is the fundamental problem. Boys renounce their feelings for the mother because of the fear of castration, yet Freud suggested this would not be the case with girls, who had already been 'castrated' by their mother. Freud suggested that this conflict would simply fade away as girls realized they would never possess their father. Because the threat of punishment through castration is not present for girls, they would not be under the same pressure to renounce these feelings and identify with the moral standards of the mother.

Freud claimed that this conflict is forced (repressed) into the unconscious mind and, as a result, we are no longer aware of the feelings that we had previously experienced. This is commonly referred to as 'childhood amnesia' and explains why, other than a few fragmentary memories, we remember very little of our life before the age of 5.

Source: adapted from Cardwell (1996)

Contributions of the psychodynamic approach

Probably the most significant contribution of the psychodynamic approach has been in the development of psychotherapy. In Freud's psychoanalytic theory, neurotic problems in adulthood were seen as the result of unresolved conflicts from childhood. These had been repressed because the immature ego was unable to deal with them at the time. The aims of psychoanalytic therapy are to create the right kind of conditions so that the patient is able to bring these conflicts into the conscious mind where they can be addressed and dealt with.

The psychodynamic approach is also used to explain various unconscious anxieties which can be expressed in different ways. Skal (1993) suggests that the attraction of horror films can be explained using psychodynamic concepts. The appeal of these films, argues Skal, is that they reflect unconscious anxieties about specific conditions in our own lives. By watching horror movies, we can displace our own anxieties onto the movies themselves and overcome them. Skal supports his argument by pointing out that specific kinds of horror movies are popular at specific times in our history. After the First World War, films such as *The Phantom of the Opera* reflected the mutilation of many who lived through the war. After the Second World War, films about the horrors of the atomic bomb and about alien invasions (e.g. *Invasion of the Body Snatchers*) became widespread.

Tavris and Wade (1995) suggest that the most important contribution of the psychodynamic approach may well be in showing us that because of unconscious patterns and needs, individuals tend to be the last to know the reasons for their own behaviour. There is an old joke about two psychoanalysts who meet in the corridor. 'You're all right', says the first psychoanalyst, 'How am I?'

Explanations based on the psychodynamic approach account for the unpredictability in our behaviour, the unwanted negative moods that arise for apparently no reason, and the emotional overreaction to innocent remarks (Tavris and Wade 1995).

Evaluation of the psychodynamic approach

The psychodynamic approach has many supporters and many critics. The debates that have ensued raise a number of practical and theoretical issues:

Practical issues

One of the most important implications of adopting this view of human behaviour is its reliance on the concept of an unconscious mind which influences our thinking and behaviour in ways about which we are unaware. If we are unaware of the forces that guide us, then it follows that we are not capable of intervening to change or go against them (Slife and Williams 1995).

According to Freud, we are in large part a legacy of our past. Our adult life is shaped by the way in which we have charted our stages of development and dealt with the conflicts presented in each. As Slife and Williams (1995) point out, this view of development makes us very much 'victims of our past'. In psychoanalytic theory, not only are early experiences important, but they also influence and shape our present experience and behaviour. As all this is happening unconsciously, we are not only victims of our past, but are also totally unaware of these influences.

Because we are essentially trapped in the past, this poses real problems for an individual trying to escape from early repressive influences. If we are controlled by the past, then how do we manage to exert any sort of control over our lives? Psychoanalytic theorists take it for granted that a person can be freed from such influences through psychoanalytic therapy. Whether or not such therapy is effective in resolving psychological problems is a matter of intense debate. The relationship between how a person's problems might be defined and explained within the theory itself, and how they might be helped by psychoanalytic therapy is not always that clear. The problems associated with psychoanalytic therapy are dealt with more fully in Chapter 18.

Theoretical issues

Of key importance in Freudian theory is the belief that all our behaviour is influenced in a causal way by an underlying sexual instinct. Freud felt that such was the power of the sexual instinct that it acted as the motivating force behind all our behaviours. The implication of this point of view is that our social behaviour, including our relationships with others, is ultimately connected with the fulfilment of sexual gratification, and a desire for pleasure. Other psychodynamic theorists such as Jung and Adler disagreed with Freud about the idea of such a pervasive sexual instinct, and proposed their own ideas of what motivated human behaviour.

Related to this theory of the underlying sexual instinct is the belief that sexual motivation arises from the body, yet affects the mind, which must find ways of seeking gratification. While this might seem a fairly simple concept, the mind–body relationship (as we saw in the previous sections) is far from simple and has never been fully resolved.

In order to be accepted as a scientific theory, we should be able to conceive of circumstances where the theory might be proved wrong. In other words, if we have no way of showing that a theory might be wrong, then we have no grounds for accepting that it might be right. Such a theory would lack 'falsifiability'. Freud's theory is often criticized for lacking this criterion of falsifiability. There are a number of reasons for this. First, much of Freudian theory makes use of concepts or processes (such as the superego or the Oedipal conflict) that cannot be observed directly, but can only be inferred. This makes them more difficult to validate. Second, although offering a persuasive description of human behaviour, the theory fails to make predictions about behaviour that can be tested through use of scientific methods.

Summary: The psychodynamic approach

The psychodynamic approach explains behaviour in terms of the unconscious processes operating in the mind, with an emphasis on the notion of motivation and of past experience.

In Freud's psychoanalytic theory, behaviour is seen as a product of the constant interplay between the three parts of the personality: the id, ego and superego. Freud believed that people developed through five stages of development: the oral, anal, phallic, latent and genital. Each stage is marked by its own developmental conflict, but the most important of these, in terms of its impact on later development, is the Oedipal conflict. Failure to receive the correct amount of gratification in any of these stages may result in a fixation, with the individual later needing to regress to that stage in order to resolve the issues that were unresolved at the time.

The behavioural approach *(looking at what we do)*

Behaviourism was one of the great intellectual movements of the twentieth century and it continues to have a far-reaching effect on the way that we see ourselves and the ways that we deal with people. The term 'behaviourism' was first used by John B. Watson (1878–1958) in a paper written in 1913 in which he outlined a plan for the conduct of psychology that was to dominate the subject for the next fifty years. Surprisingly, Watson left psychology in 1920 having been forced to resign his university post over a personal matter, and despite his international acclaim he was unable to obtain another academic post. The most likely cause was class prejudice against Watson (he came from the poor side of the tracks), but psychology's loss was commerce's gain because Watson went on to have a successful career in advertising, introducing his scientific methods of behavioural analysis to the study of the consumer.

Reasons for the rise of behaviourism

The ideas first proposed by Watson captured the scientific and public imagination for a number of reasons:

◆ *The failure of analytical introspection*

The favoured method in psychology before behaviourism was analytical introspection: looking inwards to examine and report one's own mental experience (see the cognitive approach). Experimenters used themselves as subjects to analyse their sensations and perceptions. The obvious drawback to this is that a dispute between two scientists is difficult to resolve since none of their data is open to scrutiny. At the start of the twentieth century, scientific arguments about the nature of thought, sensation and perception appeared to have stalled.

◆ *The success of other sciences*

At the same time that psychology appeared to have stalled, the other sciences were making giant strides forward. At the end of the nineteenth century, for example, medical scientists such as Pasteur were discovering how germs caused diseases and how to develop techniques for dealing with them. Neuroscientists such as Broca were starting to map the brain, chemists had developed the periodic table of elements, and physicists had discovered the atomic nature of matter. It was a time of dramatic breakthroughs in science and a change in the way we saw our place in the universe.

◆ *The theory of evolution*

Darwin's work on evolution (see above) sent shock waves through the Western world. It challenged the way we looked at ourselves and at animals. Traditional beliefs had sought to explain the complex behaviour of animals in terms of instinct – in-built behaviour patterns without thought or reason. On the other hand, human behaviour was thought to be driven by another factor – the soul, that gave us reason and the opportunity to carve out our own personal destiny. The central idea of evolution, that animals, including humans, have developed over generations under the pressures of natural selection, challenged this distinction. Could it be that animals might learn, and that humans might have some instincts?

◆ *Research on animal behaviour*

Animal research was providing a number of insights into the nature of habits and learning. For example, Jacques Loeb (1859–1924) introduced the concept of tropism to refer to actions that followed as a direct response to a stimulus (like a moth being drawn to a bright light). Of particular importance in the development of behaviourism was the work of Russian physiologist Ivan Pavlov (1849–1936) who explored the learned reflex and what came to be known as classical conditioning (see Chapter 13).

This climate of rapidly developing scientific ideas created a need for change in psychology if it was going to make a contribution to twentieth-century science.

Watson and behaviourism

In his writings on behaviourism, Watson (1913) proposed the following:

◆ The rejection of introspection as a method of study in psychology, and the adoption of experimental and objective techniques.

◆ The rejection of consciousness and the mind as the main focus of study. He proposed that we should study behaviour, as this could be observed and verified.

◆ A belief that human behaviour is the result of conditioning. In particular, he proposed that we are born a blank slate (a *tabula rasa*), and develop our personality, intelligence, and other attributes through our experiences in life. As Watson put it: 'There is no such thing as an inheritance of capacity, talents, temperament, mental condition and characteristics. These things depend on training.'

◆ The difference between animals and humans is quantitative rather than qualitative. We can study animals, therefore, as a way of understanding the basic principles of human behaviour.

◆ The aim of psychology should not only be to observe and record human activity but also to develop techniques that can control and alter human behaviour.

At the time, Watson's ideas struck a chord in the public imagination. A central theme of the behavioural argument is that nearly all behaviour is learnt and not innate. This challenged the very structure of society at the time, where power and success were more dependent on your family's social position than on your ability. The scientists of the time explained class divisions in terms of biological inheritance. People who had status, wealth and power were commonly thought to come from superior stock (see the section on Social Darwinism above). The ideas of behaviourism, on the other hand, claimed that all people are born equal and that the differences between them developed from their life experiences. This fitted in well with part of the opening lines of the American Declaration of Independence, which stated that 'all men are born equal' and also with the newly formed communist government in Russia that was committed to equality. The Western world of the 1920s was starting to give power to ordinary people, and the new science of behaviourism gave weight to these popular aspirations.

Watson is usually mentioned in psychology textbooks for his infamous study on Little Albert (Watson and Rayner 1920 – see In Focus) in which he demonstrated that fear could be learnt by a child under the age of 1. His research work, however, was very wide ranging and took in a number of social issues where he tried to make a positive contribution to our understanding of human behaviour. For example, he was employed by the US military during the First World War (1914–18) to measure the effectiveness of health education films that sought to reduce the incidence of venereal disease (Lashley and Watson 1921). Although Watson left psychology in 1920, his ideas survived and were developed by a number of psychologists, most famously B.F. Skinner.

Thorndike, Skinner and operant conditioning

Around the turn of the twentieth century, American psychologist Edward Lee Thorndike (1874–1949) investigated how animals learn. In one series of observations he placed a cat in a 'puzzle box' and measured the time it took to escape. Over a number of trials, the time taken to escape decreased. From his observations he developed the Law of (positive) Effect. This states that any behaviour that leads to a positive outcome will tend to be repeated in similar circumstances. This provided a description of animal behaviour that did not require concepts such as consciousness or thought.

Thorndike's work was developed by the behaviourists including B.F. Skinner (1904–90). These psychologists explored the principles of learning using behaviour as the main focus of their study. A key concept in behaviourism is reinforcement, commonly defined in terms of its effect on behaviour. Reinforcement increases the likelihood that an action will be repeated in the future. Punishment, on the other hand, reduces the likelihood that an action will be repeated. This is an important point because some things that might appear to punish, for example shouting at a child who is behaving in an irritating way, might in fact lead to the behaviour appearing more frequently. The shouting, therefore, has to be seen as reinforcing (e.g. by providing attention) rather than punishing.

---

in focus

Classical conditioning – the case of Albert

Albert was a placid 11-month-old boy. Watson and Rayner gave him a live white rat to play with. He showed no fear of his new pet. The two researchers next established that Albert did not like loud noises.

By striking a metal bar behind his head with a hammer, Albert was made to cry. When they next presented the child with the rat, they struck the bar at the same time. Albert fell onto the mat and started to cry. After repeated presentations of the rat and the loud noise together, the rat was presented without the accompanying loud noise. Albert cried and tried to crawl away. He had become conditioned to fear the rat, which had become a conditioned stimulus for his fear.

Unfortunately, Watson and Rayner were unable to try removing Albert's fear because his mother withdrew him from their 'care'. See Chapter18 for more information on the processes involved in desensitization (a technique used to help people suffering from phobias).

Source: Watson and Rayner (1920)

The principles of operant conditioning are further described in Chapter 13. Skinner believed it was unnecessary to look for any underlying causes of behaviour. He explained all behaviour with reference to the reinforcement contingencies that could be used to change it.

The behavioural metaphor

The behaviourists believed that we can understand an animal or a person by thinking of it as a machine, and looking at what goes into the machine (stimulus or inputs) and measuring what comes out (responses or outputs). In this view, animals or people are like puppets who respond to stimuli with no more control than one has over a reflex action like a knee jerk. Put like this, the approach sounds harsh and simplistic but it has led to a number of effective applications.

Uses of behaviourism

The techniques of behaviourism have been used to study and *train animal behaviour* and to show how seemingly complex behaviours can be influenced by simple means. By using simple reinforcements like food, animals have been trained to run mazes, play ping-pong and use simple communication devices. Also, and perhaps more remarkably, Skinner was able to demonstrate that he could train pigeons how to operate the guidance system of missiles. So successful was the work that during the Second World War (1939–45) the US military created some prototype missiles for the pigeons to fly (Skinner 1960), though they eventually decided not to commission them.

Therapeutic techniques based on the behavioural approach are still commonly used in treating a range of psychiatric disorders. Classical conditioning techniques include aversion therapy, flooding and systematic desensitization. Operant conditioning techniques include the use of token economies and time outs (see Chapter 18 for more details).

Behavioural techniques are also used in a variety of other situations such as in *classroom management*. Wheldall and Merrett (1983) used conditioning techniques to modify the behaviour of disruptive children. Children who were disruptive in class were rewarded for any evidence of attentiveness and general good behaviour. Prior to this time, these children spent a good deal of their time out of their seats and had this behaviour reinforced by their teacher who was forced to pay them attention because of it. As a result of this change of reinforcement patterns, the amount of disruptive behaviour dropped and the children spent a much greater amount of their time engaged in quiet and productive class work.

Skinner (1958) pioneered the idea of self-paced individual instruction, with every child being taught by a 'teaching' machine that presented small amounts of information, asked questions and gave out reinforcement for correct answers. Later versions of this basic idea included programmes that could deliver remedial instructional loops so that the learner could go back over steps that they had not successfully accomplished. By presenting information only one bit at a time, the learner was more likely to experience constant success rather than constant failure.

Evaluation of the behavioural approach

Behaviourism is not without its critics. A full critique of behaviourism would take too long, but a few moral, philosophical, practical and theoretical issues will be looked at here.

Moral and philosophical issues

One of the main moral issues surrounding behaviourism relates to its ideas about control. What control do we have over ourselves and who should be allowed to control whom?

A fundamental belief in behavioural theory is the belief that human behaviour does not just happen, but rather it is caused by environmental events that we cannot control. In other words, behaviourism is strongly deterministic (see Chapter 19 for discussion of free will versus determinism). The consequence of adopting this deterministic position is to say that we do not control our own actions and therefore cannot be held responsible for them. Furthermore, it becomes possible for others to control behaviour by manipulating environmental events. Watson stated:

> 'The interest of the behaviorist in man's doings is more than the interest of the spectator – he wants to control man's reactions as physical scientists want to control and manipulate other natural phenomena. It is the business of behaviourist psychology to be able to predict and to control human activity.' (Watson 1913, p. 11)

Watson, therefore, is clear that psychology's ambition should be to control people. Furthermore, he is also clear about who should have the control:

> 'If psychology would follow the plan I suggest, the educator, the physician, the jurist, and the business man could utilize our data in a practical way, as soon as we are able, experimentally, to obtain them.' (Watson 1913, reprinted in Benjamin 1988, p. 406)

This may sound ethically questionable, but both Watson and Skinner believed that they could use the techniques of behaviourism to create better people and a better world.

> 'I should like to go one step further now and say, "Give me a dozen healthy infants, well-formed, and my own specified world to bring them up in and I'll guarantee to take any one at random and train him to become any type of specialist I might select – doctor, lawyer, artist, merchant-chief and, yes, even beggarman and thief – regardless of his talents, penchants, tendencies, abilities, vocations, and race of his ancestors." I am going beyond my facts and I admit it, but so have the advocates of the contrary and they have been doing it for thousands of years.' (Watson 1913, p. 104)

> 'The real issue is the effectiveness of techniques of control. We shall not solve the problems of alcoholism and juvenile delinquency by increasing the sense of responsibility. It is the environment which is "responsible" for the objectionable behaviour, and it is the environment, not some attribute in the individual which must be changed.' (Skinner 1973, pp. 6-7)

Let us return to the view of a person as a ghost in a machine – the problem was always how to define and find this ghost. The behaviourists solve this very easily by saying there is no ghost, just the machine, ready to be conditioned by the environment. This view, not surprisingly, attracts a lot of criticism because it seems to be denying the very thing that we think makes each one of us special. It seems to be abolishing the person and replacing him or her with a robot. Skinner is quite clear about this and says,

> 'His abolition has long been overdue. Autonomous man is a device used to explain what we cannot explain in any other way. He has been constructed from our ignorance, and as our understanding increases, the very stuff of which he is composed vanishes.' (Skinner 1973, p. 195)

Practical issues

Does behaviourism work at a practical level? The answer is yes and no. It is clear that many people get help from behavioural therapies, but it is far from clear whether they might not also get as much help from non-behavioural therapies (see Chapter 18). A review of therapies by Smith and Glass (1977) compared the improvement rates for patients who received a wide variety of treatments. They found that any treatment was at least marginally better than no treatment but that most of the popular treatments, including behavioural therapies, had very similar improvement rates.

Theoretical issues

A human psychological ability that poses a challenge for the behavioural approach is language. If children learned to speak by the principles of operant and classical conditioning, then they would learn by trial and error, and trial and success. In other words, correct words or phrases would be rewarded, and consequently would be more likely to be repeated. Children quite clearly do not learn language like this. One example will highlight the problem. When they are first learning to speak, children commonly copy adult speech and so you might well hear a young child say 'I went'. This is grammatically correct and will be rewarded with adult approval. However, our language is structured by rules and the most common rule for making a past tense is to add '-ed' to a word, e.g. 'walked', 'climbed' or 'cooked'. If we observe the child who first said 'I went', we will see that she later learns the general rule for the past tense and then says 'I goed'. The rule is right but the application (generalization) of the rule by the young child to all verbs leads to the amusing errors that adults enjoy so much. The problem for behaviourism is that the correct response (which was rewarded) is replaced by an incorrect response. These rule-based errors are common in the development of child language (Slobin 1971).

The general problem for behaviourism is that it oversimplifies explanations for people's behaviour and experiences. It considers situational stimuli and observable responses but it does not pay much attention to the processes that go on inside the mind of the person (sometimes called 'the black box'). Cognitive psychologists took up the study of what happens inside the black box. We shall look at the cognitive approach in the next section.

Activity 3: Applying the behavioural approach

Behaviourists attempt to explain all our behaviour in terms of reinforcement and punishment. We could reasonably explain how we learn to ride a bike in terms of trial and error. Someone tells us what to do, but basically we get on the bike and try a range of activities until we find one that will keep us on the bike and allow us to move forwards. Can we use this type of analysis for all behaviours though? Try and give a behavioural explanation for the following:

(a) learning to: swim, solve mathematical puzzles, paint a picture, chat up a girl or boy friend

(b) becoming hooked on gambling or computer games

(c) behaving aggressively.

Summary: The behavioural approach

In brief, the behavioural approach studies people in terms of the stimuli that elicit and control behavioural responses. The role of reinforcement is paramount in conditioning behaviour.

This approach emphasizes the importance of environment (as opposed to genetics) in shaping how people behave. Animal behaviour is seen as a simpler version of human behaviour. Some behaviourists have advocated the view that we should find the best ways to control people so that we can build a better society.

The cognitive approach *(looking at how we process information)*

The cognitive approach is the dominant approach in modern psychology. The approach became popular in psychology departments once the problems with the behavioural approach could not be ignored any longer. As described above, the behaviourists viewed the mind of people as a 'black box', and they studied what impinged on the black box (stimuli) and what came out of the black box (responses), but they did not pay attention to what went on inside the black box. As we are all well aware, quite a lot goes on inside our heads and much of our behaviour can be affected by mental events.

Cognitive psychology views people as being like machines but is prepared to admit that the machinery is very complicated. As such, the cognitive approach is really neobehavioural, or to put it in other words, is a reworking of the ideas of Watson and Skinner, but with a twist. Let us first look at the beginnings of cognitive psychology in the nineteenth century.

Psychophysics

The study of the physical world and the mental world and the differences between them was the starting point for cognitive psychology. In some early experiments, Gustav Fechner (1801–87) was able to demonstrate some of these differences. For example, he investigated how much louder a sound had to be, compared with an original sound, before a person would perceive it as twice as loud. Fechner discovered that the louder sound had to be approximately 8 times greater in its physical intensity than the quieter sound before it was perceived (subjectively experienced) as twice as loud. Obviously, the physical sensations created by stimuli impinging on the sense organs are only the first steps in how we come to experience our world. Some of Fechner's experiments involved sticking compass points simultaneously into a person to determine how close the two points had to be before people experienced them as a single point.

The first psychology laboratory

In 1879 Wilhelm Wundt (1823–1920), who like Darwin failed many of his school courses, set up the first psychological laboratory in Leipzig, and brought together the traditions of physiology and philosophy to make them into the new science of psychology. According to Wundt, psychology was the study of immediate experience, and that excluded any consideration of cultural or social interpretations. He tried to create experiences in his laboratory that could be repeated and independently verified by others. The main method in the laboratory was introspection, that is an experiential form of self-observation. The introspective judgements in Wundt's laboratory were largely quantitative and dealt mainly with sensory dimensions such as intensity and duration. About half the work carried out in Wundt's laboratory was on sensory processes and perception, though it also looked at reaction time, associative learning, attention and emotion. Eventually the approach of Wundt was replaced and the method of introspection was largely discarded, but Wundt had set the grand plan for psychology; it should be experimental and it should be laboratory based.

Although Wundt's work was sidelined for a number of years, it is possible to argue that several trends in modern psychology are developments of research from the Leipzig laboratory (Blumenthal 1975). For example:

◆ In the area of language, the issues debated in the 1960s about Chomsky's transformational grammar (see Chapter 9) were very similar to the debates at the turn of the century.

◆ One of Wundt's students was Emil Kraepelin. His early theory of schizophrenia (1919) proposed that the problem came from cognitive processes that could be observed in abnormalities of attention.

◆ Wundt proposed a theory of emotion that had three bipolar factors: pleasant vs unpleasant, high arousal vs low arousal, and concentrated attention vs relaxed attention. Later work using more complex statistical techniques has also suggested these three factors.

◆ Selective attention attracted some interest in cognitive psychology during the second half of the twentieth century, and the ground breaking work of Sperling on sensory memory (1960) took inspiration from Wundt's research.

Modern cognitive psychology

Modern cognitive psychology gained momentum in the second half of the twentieth century and has become the dominant approach in psychology up to the present day. Early proponents of this approach (such as Miller *et al.* 1960) pointed out that behavioural accounts were inadequate because they said nothing about how people process information. Cognitive psychologists, on the other hand, went on to propose models of human thought and problem-solving (e.g. Newell and Simon 1972). These advances continue today as attempts are made, for example, to produce better and better chess-playing computers. One of the defining books was Ulric Neisser's (born 1928) *Cognitive Psychology* (1967). For Neisser, cognitive psychology was the study of how people learn, structure, store and use knowledge. Topics studied in cognitive psychology include perception (see Chapter 8), attention (see Chapter 7), memory (covered at AS level), thinking and problem-solving (see Chapter 9). Cognitive psychology has helped explain many aspects of everyday behaviour and experience, e.g. why we forget things, why eyewitness testimony is often inaccurate, and why we experience visual illusions. By applying knowledge from cognitive psychology, we can improve our performance in many areas. This may include developing techniques to improve study skills, designing user-friendly equipment (e.g. instrument panels on aircraft), and devising interview techniques to help people recollect accurately what they have seen.

The cognitive metaphor

The cognitive approach is mechanistic and depends on the development of technology as to which machine is used as the metaphor. In the 1950s and 60s the information-processing models tried to model human thought processes on a telephone exchange (e.g. Broadbent 1958). The arrival of the microchip made this metaphor redundant and cognitive psychologists now model the human mind on the most complex technology available to date – the computer.

The approach looks at the inputs (the stimuli) to the machine and the outputs (what it does). In addition, however, the cognitive approach also looks at the various processes that occur between the input and the output. Nevertheless, it still views these as mechanistic processes. In keeping with Wundt's study of immediate experience, the issues of cultural or social influence are largely ignored.

Social cognition

One of the weaknesses of the cognitive approach as described above is its failure to address everyday behaviour and experience. In the last quarter of the twentieth century, social psychologists have made some contributions to bridge this gap. Under the general label of social cognition, they explored how we interpret what is going on around us. The way we make assumptions about people and the way we attribute causes to people's behaviour and the way we assess risk, for example, will all contribute to how we make sense of and behave in the social world. You will find work on social cognition discussed in Chapter 1.

Evaluation of the cognitive approach

We will now look at the some of the practical, theoretical and philosophical issues arising from the cognitive approach.

Practical and theoretical issues

Many of the issues relating to the cognitive approach arise from the way that the evidence is collected. These include:

◆ The use of *introspection*

As we have seen above, there are some problems with the introspective method. The method has moved on a lot since the days of Wundt but it remains controversial. On the one hand, we have to rely on the accuracy and honesty of people who are describing their experiences, as well as assuming that we mean the same things by the same words. The problem is that I might be able to describe an experience of pain, for example, using words that you understand, but this does not mean that you have the same experience when you feel pain. On the other hand, if we disregard people's introspective reports then we have very little to record other than observations of overt behaviour.

◆ The use of *laboratories*

A large proportion of research in cognitive psychology is conducted in laboratories using very controlled tasks. Participants are commonly asked to respond to simple tasks presented on a monitor. The methodological question is whether the simple task actually mirrors any meaningful part of everyday cognitive functioning. If it does not, then the results might just be a response to the experimental procedure and tell us little or nothing about how we think in real-life situations.

◆ The concept of *memory*

An example of the type of problem found with the cognitive approach is demonstrated by the concept of memory. It is clear that we are able to record information, store it and recall it at a later date, but there is no evidence that we have a 'thing' called a memory. We memorize information but there does not appear to be a physical slot in the brain where we store it. Furthermore, there has been a lengthy debate about the existence of and distinction between long-term memory and short-term memory. The evidence amounts to little more than that we remember some things for longer than we remember other things. This, however, did not stop cognitive psychologists exploring the idea of two memory stores for many years.

◆ *Social and cultural differences*

Wundt set the agenda for ignoring social and cultural variables, and although some cognitive psychologists have shown the importance of these variables (e.g. Bartlett 1932, Deregowski 1972), they do not form part of the general debate in cognitive psychology. A recent review of mainstream British psychology journals (Banyard and Hunt 2000) found that very few articles considered issues of culture, social class or sexual orientation. This is not to say that these variables will affect all research issues in cognitive psychology, but it is not reasonable to assume they will affect none of them.

Philosophical issues

If the brain can be legitimately conceived of as a computer, then it should be possible eventually to build a computer that does what a human brain can do. Does a computer merely perform some functions in a similar way to a person, or does it, in fact, actually 'think' like a person? This question summarizes the key issue for the cognitive metaphor, and is debated in the field known as Artificial Intelligence (AI). The aim of those who work in this field is to build and programme computers to behave 'intelligently'. One area of AI has focused on programming computers to 'understand' natural language inputs. There have been a number of attempts to write programmes that respond to natural language including Weizenbaum's ELIZA (1966). ELIZA, programmed to act as a non-directive psychotherapist, was able to respond to a user's inputs. But the question that springs to mind in relation to all of these programmes is: 'Do they really understand the language?'

Searle (1980) addressed this question in his famous description of the Chinese Room thought experiment. One of the targets of Searle's experiment was the Turing test (Turing 1950), proposed as a hallmark test of whether a computer could think and understand. In the Turing test, a participant communicates via a computer keyboard with two 'people' who are hidden from view; one of these people is a real person, and the other is a computer programme. If the participant cannot reliably identify which is the computer and which is the person, then the computer programme has passed the test and can be said to be able to think and understand like a person.

Searle was able to demonstrate, however, that the ability to make responses in a language indistinguishable from those of a native speaker is not, in itself, sufficient to demonstrate understanding. Under certain circumstances ELIZA can pass the Turing test. But when it is revealed how the programme works, it becomes clear that its use of rather unintelligent pattern-matching strategies in no sense amounts to understanding. Or to put it another way, just because it walks like a duck and quacks like a duck, it does not mean that it really is a duck. There is more to being a duck than walking and quacking. Therefore, to date, the computer metaphor remains an inadequate way of modelling human cognitive processes.

Summary: The cognitive approach

The cognitive approach is the dominant approach in modern psychology. It views human beings as information-processing machines and employs a computer metaphor to model human thinking. Most work using the cognitive approach is carried out in laboratories. Little attention is paid to social and cultural factors.

Activity 4: Applying the cognitive approach

At the heart of the cognitive approach is the computer metaphor. But what are the similarities and differences between people and computers? Make a list of some cognitive activities and consider how they are similar and different in people and computers? For example, you might like to think about how a person's culture or mood could affect their ability to think or remember. Start with memory and problem-solving and then move on to any other examples of cognition that you can think of.

Other approaches in psychology *(a do-it-yourself guide)*

The above accounts of the major perspectives in psychology are not exhaustive. It is possible to identify a number of different perspectives with which to view the behaviour and experience of people. Some of these are covered elsewhere in this book: for example, the developmental approach is discussed in Chapters 10, 11 and 12. When considering any approach in psychology you need to look at:

◆ the assumptions the approach makes about people

◆ some history of how the approach developed

◆ some evidence that supports it, including any useful applications

◆ some issues that challenge it.

Activity 5: Summary activity

Read the following true story and give at least **two** explanations that use different approaches in psychology. The most obvious one to start with is the biological approach, but it cannot explain everything that went on.

In 1966, Charles Whitman, a responsible family man, murdered his mother and his wife and then packed up a supply of guns, ammunition and food, and climbed to the top of an observation tower at the University of Texas. From there he shot at anyone he could see, killing 14 and

injuring 31 before he was eventually shot dead by police. Prior to the shooting he had been seeking psychiatric help for headaches and thoughts of violence, and he left a note asking for an autopsy to be carried out on his brain. This autopsy was inconclusive, though it did find some evidence of a tumour in the areas of the amygdala. Whitman had expressed distress at the separation of his parents and also expressed anger towards his father. Throughout the notes he made just before his death, he attempted to make sense of his environment and explain his behaviour. Why did he behave in that way?

Chapter summary

◆ Psychology has been trying to describe and explain human behaviour and experience for about 150 years. During that time a number of **approaches** has emerged, including the biological, evolutionary, psychodynamic, behavioural and cognitive approaches.

◆ The **biological** approach looks at the relationship between biology (the physiological systems in the body) and behaviour. This approach has applications, for example, in the fields of psychopathology and therapies.

◆ The **evolutionary** approach examines how evolutionary ideas, such as natural selection, help explain human behaviour. This approach has recently become popular as a way of explaining certain behaviours, such as male sexual promiscuity.

◆ The **psychodynamic** approach focuses on how unconscious motives influence behaviour. This has been a popular approach for many years in the field of psychotherapy.

◆ The **behavioural** approach attempts to explain behaviour in terms of conditioning. It emphasizes the role of reinforcement in learning and maintaining behaviours. This approach has been applied widely and has been used, for example, to modify the behaviour of disruptive children and to treat anxiety disorders such as phobias.

◆ The **cognitive** approach tries to explain how cognitive processes such as attention, perception, memory and thinking work. This approach has been applied to help us, for example, to improve our memories and to develop artificial intelligence systems.

◆ These approaches have developed a number of techniques for systematically investigating behaviour and experience. Some empirical evidence supports all the approaches.

◆ No single approach, however, can offer a complete explanation of the complexity of human behaviour and experience, though all are able to add something to our understanding.

Further resources

Miller, G.A. (1966) *Psychology: The Science of Mental Life*, Harmondsworth: Penguin.

This book gives an interesting account of the history of psychological ideas and gives brief biographies of some of the major figures.

Fancher, R.E. (1990) *Pioneers of Psychology* (2nd edn), New York: W.W. Norton.

This describes how psychological ideas have developed over the last 200 years. Although the material may seem quite old, the ideas are nevertheless often contemporary.

Benjamin, L.T. (ed.) (1988) *A History of Psychology: Original Sources and Contemporary Research*, New York: McGraw-Hill.

A series of original writings by the great and the good in psychology, accompanied by comments from the editor.

Benjafield, J.G. (1996) *A History of Psychology*, Boston: Allyn & Bacon.

This book presents the ideas of significant individuals in psychology, also showing how cultural context shaped the dominant ideas of different times..

Part 8: Exam Preparation and Coursework

PREPARING FOR THE A2
EXAMINATION

Mike Cardwell

COURSEWORK

Graham Davies

STATISTICAL ANALYSIS FOR
COURSEWORK

Graham Davies

Preparing for the A2 examination

Mike Cardwell

Preview

In this chapter we shall be looking at the following aspects of the examination process:

◆ examination preparation

◆ examination performance

◆ examination marking.

Introduction

Examinations are generally among the most feared times in our lives. The stress of the lead-up period, the pressure to do well, the impenetrable questions and those awful two months when we fear that examiners are doing their level best to undo our best efforts. As they say in the songs, it doesn't have to be that way. Like an athlete training for the Olympics, a student training for an A-level examination simply needs to know how to harness all that good intent in the most cost-effective way possible. The pressure? Well much of that is self-imposed anyway, and perhaps we all need to be reminded that in the great scheme of things, examination success is relatively unimportant compared to some of the more significant aspects of our lives. Unlike some of those, you can always take your examination again.

The examination process is no longer a closely guarded secret, with questions and marking schemes for previous examinations being readily available from AQA. Everything else is as predictable as a wet day at Wimbledon. And what does happen to your examination paper after you emerge from the examination hall, your job done and the long wait for the results about to begin? This chapter takes you through the A2 examination process, and should ensure that all the good psychology from the rest of this book doesn't get wasted because of poor preparation or inadequate examination technique. Read on ...

Examination preparation

Revision strategies

'How do I revise for the exam?' This is probably one of the questions most often asked by students coming up to this or any examination. You will have already developed your own revision strategies for the AS examination, so we will focus here on some points of specific relevance to the A2 examination.

1 Revise carefully

The number of hours spent staring at a book is not directly proportional to examination success. There are, however, a number of useful things you can do with your time. Take a look at the AQA psychology specification. The specification is split into a number of options (*Social, Developmental, Individual Differences,* etc.). You will also see that each of these options is split into a number of subsections (represented by the chapters in this book). Now for the good news. The Assessment and Qualifications Alliance (your examination board, thankfully shortened to AQA) guarantee one question from each of these subsections. When planning what to revise, you should take this into account. It certainly has the effect of making your revision less stressful.

A word of warning though. If you do decide to concentrate your revision on certain subsections of the specification, make sure you cover *everything* in that subsection rather than just concentrating on the bits you like. This book has been constructed with this type of approach in mind. Each chapter should stand alone for revision purposes. In other words, if you read and absorb Chapter 1, you should be able to answer any question set on the Social Cognition subsection of the *Social Psychology* part of the specification.

The other important aspect of careful revision is to check what you are revising against the requirements of the specification. Can you do what the specification asks you to do? If you can, then there should be no problem. If you went for your driving test, you would only expect to be tested on three-point turns, emergency braking and so on. The examiner is hardly likely to turn around suddenly and say "I've got this Challenger tank out in the back, let's see how you get on with that then!"

2 Revise actively

Merely reading material in textbooks is not necessarily the most productive way of using your time. In the A2 examination you will not be asked to 'write everything you can remember about perception'. Instead, you will be given a specific set of instructions which tell you what you should write about and which specific skills you should demonstrate in your answer. Students often do far worse than they deserve to do in examinations because they do not address the second of these points. They can often describe in great detail theories of perception or research on bystander behaviour, but cannot provide any evaluative commentary on that material. It is an inescapable fact in A2 level psychology, that you will always be asked to provide narrative content (description, explanation, etc.) and commentary (evaluation, analysis, etc.) *in equal measures.* You should make a point in your notes of highlighting those points that are part of the narrative and those that are part of your commentary. In the sections that follow, you should become more familiar with how to play this 'skills' game more successfully.

3 Organizing your revision

None of us has enough time for all the things we plan to do and, as the exams get closer, that precious time seems to become scarcer than ever. It is never too early to plan your revision.

Decide (realistically) just how much of the specification you are going to revise and make a plan of what you are going to revise and when. Read the A2 Introduction again (at the start of the book) and you will get more of an idea of the way that the specification is put together, and what you are expected to do in your revision. It is certainly permissible (perhaps even advisable) to concentrate on certain areas of the specification at this stage. If you find you are spending hours and hours dealing with the complexities of one particular subsection of the specification, then it might be worth taking a deep breath and dumping it in favour of a subsection where you feel more confident of doing well. When you plan your revision, remember that the heading 'Perception –

Figure 21.1 Revision timetable for 'Perception' subsection

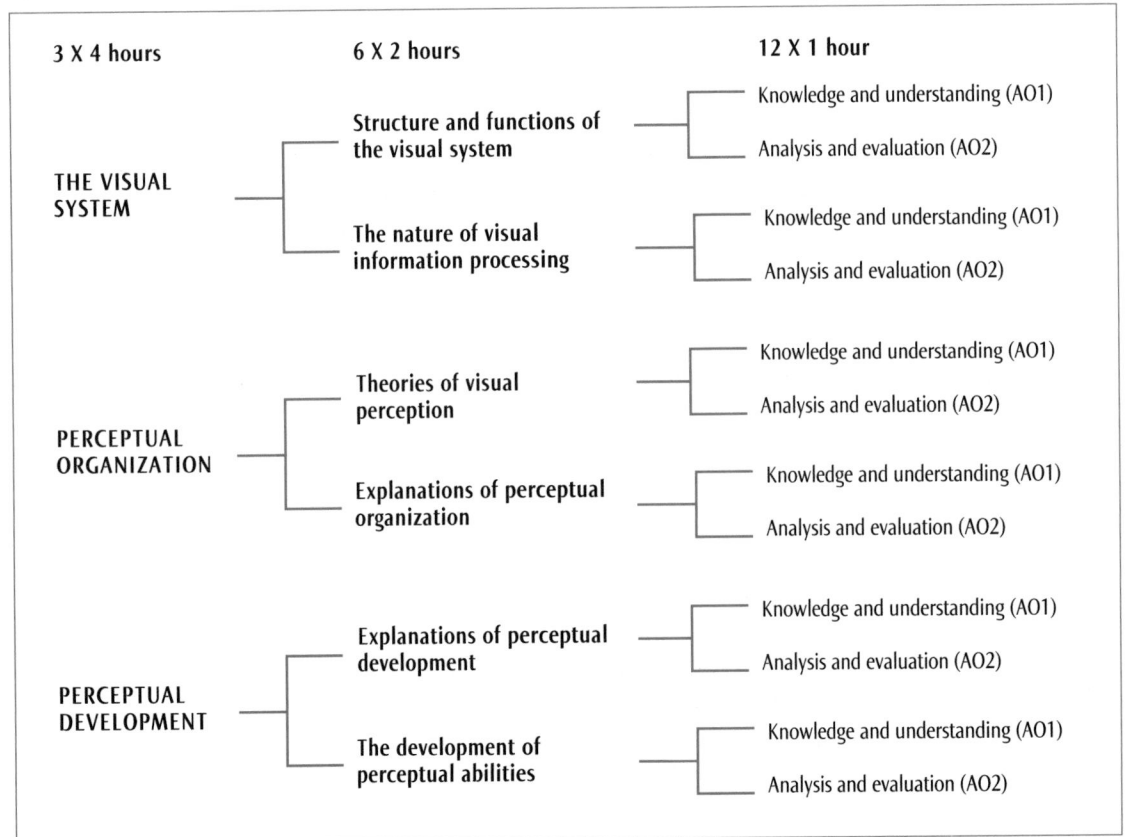

12 hours' on a piece of paper doesn't really help you when it comes down to spending those 12 hours profitably. Instead, you might divide your revision time for the perception subsection as shown in Fig 21.1.

Above all, remember you are studying psychology, and try to use all those relevant bits of psychology to help you make this a profitable time. For example, don't cram too much into one session (*maximum span of attention*), nor expect to remember everything perfectly immediately after the revision session (*the reminiscence effect*). Reward yourself when you have had a productive session (*positive reinforcement*), and don't spend time worrying about what you *should* be doing, just do it and congratulate yourself on a job well done (*positive feedback*).

AO1 and AO2

The AQA examination tests your ability in two main skill areas. These are known as AO1 and AO2. Every examination question tests both of these skills and they are equally weighted in the marking schemes. You should have already met these terms at AS level, and will be familiar with them in practice, but what do we mean by AO1 and AO2 in the context of an A2 exam?

The best way of thinking about them is to see AO1 as a *narrative* (i.e. giving information and showing understanding) and AO2 as a *commentary* (i.e. being able to offer some comments about the narrative, such as evaluating the points made or showing how they fit into a wider body of knowledge). Each question might ask you to offer a slightly different form of AO1 and AO2, depending on the requirements of the question.

The 'instructions' on how to answer questions are contained in the terms used in the question wording itself, which are published by the AQA in the document *Glossary of Terms*. A simplified version of this *Glossary of Terms* is presented in Table 21.1.

It is well worth your while learning the differences between the different terms, particularly which are AO1 terms, which are AO2, and which require a mixture of AO1 + AO2.

Let's take a look at this in the context of a specific examination question:

◆ Discuss **one** theory of moral understanding.

(24 marks)

The 'instruction' in this question is *discuss*, which we can translate as requiring a *description* (the AO1 requirement) and an *evaluation* (the AO2 requirement)

Table 21.1   AO1 and AO2 terms

AO1 terms

Consider	show knowledge and understanding of the topic area.
Define	explain what is meant by a particular term.
Describe	show knowledge of the topic area.
Examine	present a detailed descriptive consideration of the topic area.
Explain	show understanding of a topic in a coherent and intelligible way.
Outline/State	offer a brief description (in summary form) of the topic area.

AO2 terms

*Analyse/Critically analyse**	demonstrate understanding through a consideration of the different components of the topic area.
*Assess/Critically assess**	present a considered appraisal of the topic area through a judgement of the strengths and limitations of the information presented.
Criticize	evaluate in terms of the strengths and weaknesses of the topic area.
*Evaluate/Critically evaluate**	make an informed judgement of the value of a topic area.

AO1 + AO2 terms

Compare and contrast	consider both the similarities and differences between the topic areas.
Critically consider	show knowledge and understanding of a topic area, plus the strengths and limitations of the material used.
Distinguish between	consider the differences between two topic areas.
Discuss	describe and evaluate a topic area.

These terms are used interchangeably and have the same meaning as each other.

Source: adapted from the *Glossary of Terms*, AQA

of one theory of moral development. This would mean that you must describe *and* evaluate to gain maximum marks. This does raise another question. What is meant by a 'theory' and how does it differ from a 'model' or indeed from 'research'? The AQA *Glossary of Terms* also offers a translation of these terms (see Table 21.2) so that you can be quite sure what an examination question is asking you to do. As we shall see later, all A2 questions (with the exception of questions set in *Individual Differences* and *Perspectives*) require answers to be written in 30 minutes. Examination questions will reflect this, so an alternative version of the question set above might be:

◆ Outline and evaluate **two** theories of moral understanding. *(24 marks)*

The major difference between these two questions is that the latter one requires coverage of *two* theories, although in less depth. It is worth remembering this examination-setting strategy and being in a position to respond to it constructively. For example, in responding to the first

question, you might well be able to sustain a discussion of Kohlberg's theory, but in what way would your account of this theory be different if you were responding to the second question? The skill of précis is a skill worth developing, and the A2 examination will give you plenty of opportunity to put this skill into practice.

Question-setting

When the Chief or Principal Examiners sit down to write an examination paper, they have to follow a number of basic rules and guidelines. The main guidelines are as follows:

◆ All questions must be drawn from the specification, with similar wording wherever possible.

◆ One question is set on each subsection of the specification (i.e. three from *Social Psychology*, three from *Cognitive Psychology,* and so on).

◆ All questions have an equal weighting of AO1 (12 marks) and AO2 (12 marks). No matter how many parts there are to a question, 12 marks will always be given for AO1 and 12 for AO2. This is slightly different for the *Perspectives* questions – we will come to this later.

◆ Specification content which is preceded by the words 'should include' or 'including' can be specified in an examination question. Content which is preceded by the words 'for example' cannot be specified in a question.

◆ There are no rules regarding repetition of questions. The fact that a topic area is examined one year does not mean it will not be examined the next. Similarly, the fact that a particular topic hasn't been examined for a year or two doesn't mean that it will automatically be examined soon.

Activity 1: Practising AO1 and AO2 skills

Using the information in Chapter 10, pp. 270–2, construct a 300-word *description* of Kohlberg's theory of moral understanding (this is equivalent to the AO1 component of the first question).

Now try and précis this material into 150 words (this is equivalent to the AO1 component of one of the two requested theories in the second question). You might then like to repeat this exercise using the equivalent AO2 material for the same theory (pp. 272–3).

Table 21.2   Other terms used in AQA examination questions

Applications	actual or possible ways of using psychological knowledge in an applied or practical setting
Concept(s)	an idea or group of ideas that are often the basic units of a psychological theory
Evidence	material drawn either from investigations or from theories in order to support or contradict an argument or theory
Findings	the outcome of a research investigation
Insights	perceptions from either investigations or theories that help us to understand or appraise a topic area
Methods	the different ways in which research investigations can be carried out
Model	used synonymously with 'theory', although it may be less elaborate or complex
Research	the process of gaining knowledge and understanding either through theory construction and examination, or through empirical data collection
Studies	empirical investigations
Theory	a set of interrelated ideas or principles that can be used to explain observed phenomena

When examination questions are set, the AQA employ a *Reviser* whose job is to check that the questions are appropriate in terms of standard and complexity, and could be answered within the time given. The Reviser must also check that the 'rules' outlined above are adhered to. For example, a question such as the following would be rejected by the Reviser:

◆ Describe and evaluate Freud's explanation of personality development.   *(24 marks)*

This would not be an appropriate question because, although Freud's name does appear under the appropriate subsection of the *Developmental Psychology* specification (personality development), it is included merely as an *example* of a psychodynamic explanation that might be considered. It is not a prescription that Freud must be studied, therefore questions cannot be asked specifically on this theorist. If you look through the specification, you will see that sometimes theories or ideas are introduced as 'for example', and sometimes as 'including' or 'should include'. In the former case, they cannot be specified in the examination question; in the latter two cases, they can.

Activity 2: Improper exam questions

Each of the following questions would be rejected by a Reviser. Can you work out why? (Answers at the end of the chapter.)

1 Describe any two theories of moral understanding.   *(24 marks)*

2 Critically consider the use of flooding and token economies as therapies.   *(30 marks)*

3 (a) Describe any one theory of human aggression.   *(12 marks)*

   (b) Reflect upon the insights that might be gathered from this theory in order to reduce aggression.   *(12 marks)*

Synoptic assessment

From September 2000, AQA – as with all examination boards – will include a synoptic component in their assessment at A2 level. This form of assessment will test your understanding of the subject as a whole. This will always take place at the end of your course, and accounts for 20% of the total marks awarded for this A level. By placing this part of the assessment at the end of the examination process, it gives students a chance to develop an *overview* of the subject that would be impossible earlier in the course.

In the AQA examinations, most of the synoptic assessment comes in Unit 5, *Individual Differences*, and *Perspectives*. Because of this extra requirement, questions in this assessment unit are answered in 45 minutes, unlike questions in Unit 4, which are answered in 30 minutes. This extra time allowance is reflected in the extra marks available for this part of the exam. Each question in Unit 5 is worth 30 marks (15 marks for AO1 and 15 marks for AO2). A simplified version of the marking criteria for this part of the exam can be seen in Table 21.3.

What counts as synoptic assessment?

The AQA requirement is that you gain an understanding and critical appreciation of the 'breadth of theoretical and methodological approaches, issues and debates in psychology'. This can be demonstrated in a variety of ways, including the following:

◆ a demonstration of different explanations or perspectives relating to the topic area (for example, schizophrenia can be explained from many different perspectives; different perspectives also have different positions in the nature–nurture and free will versus determinism debates)

◆ a demonstration of different methods used to study the topic area (for example, the nature and origins of psychopathological conditons might be studied using twin studies, chromosomal mapping, cross-cultural studies, and so on)

◆ overarching issues relating to the topic area (for example, the use of biological therapies might be discussed in terms of the issue of reductionism, nature–nurture, or ethics)

◆ a demonstration of links with other areas of the specification (for example, depression might be seen as having an adaptive role within human evolution; Freud's views of personality development might demonstrate a gender bias).

Approaches in psychology

In this section of the examination, you will be required to apply your knowledge of any two theoretical approaches in psychology to a novel situation which will be presented within the stimulus material. You should try and develop a good working knowledge of the different approaches in psychology, their methods, strengths and limitations, and those areas of behaviour where you feel they offer a plausible explanation. An example of a 'spider diagram' for evolutionary explanations is shown in Fig. 21.2. You might like to elaborate on this by considering each of its points (see Chapters 15 and 19), and then repeating the exercise for as many other approaches as you are able.

Table 21.3   Marking criteria for synoptic assessment questions

AO1 Assessment Criteria

Band	Marks	Content (knowledge, description and understanding	Synopticity	Construction and organization	Breadth and depth
5	13–15	Accurate and well detailed	Clear evidence of a range of methods and/or perspectives	Presented coherently	Substantial evidence of both and appropriate balance
4	10–12	Slightly limited: accurate and reasonably detailed	Slightly limited evidence of different methods and/or perspectives	Coherent	Evidence of breadth and depth but imbalanced
3	7–9	Limited, although accurate and reasonably detailed	Limited evidence of different methods and/or perspectives	Reasonable	Evidence of breadth and/or depth
2	4–6	Basic and lacking in detail	Little evidence of different methods and/or perspectives	Sometimes focused	
1	0–3	Just discernible/ anecdotal/inaccurate	Little or no evidence of different methods and/or perspectives	Muddled and incomplete	

AO2 Assessment Criteria

Band	Marks	Commentary	Synopticity	Use of material	Elaboration
5	13–15	Informed and thorough	Clear critical commentary on different methods and/or perspectives	Highly effective	Evidence of appropriate selection and coherent elaboration
4	10–12	Informed but slightly limited	Slightly limited critical commentary on different methods and/or perspectives	Effective	Evidence of coherent elaboration
3	7–9	Reasonable but limited	Limited critical commentary on different methods and/or perspectives	Reasonably effective	Some evidence of elaboration
2	4–6	Minimal, superficial and rudimentary	Minimal critical commentary on different methods and/or perspectives	Minimally effective	Little evidence of elaboration
1	0–3	Weak, muddled and/or incomplete	Little or no critical commentary on different methods and/or perspectives	Ineffective	Muddled and incomplete

The questions will not specify which approaches you should use, so this is your opportunity to be creative. Although this sounds quite daunting, the friendly part of these questions is the fact that the questions themselves will always be the same, only the stimulus material and its associated topic area will change.

Questions will ask you to do the following:

(a) Describe how two different approaches might explain this phenomenon. *(12 marks)*

(b) Assess the strengths and limitations of one of these explanations. *(6 marks)*

(c) Analyse how the phenomenon might be investigated by one of these explanations. *(6 marks)*

(d) Evaluate the use of this method for investigating this phenomenon. *(6 marks)*

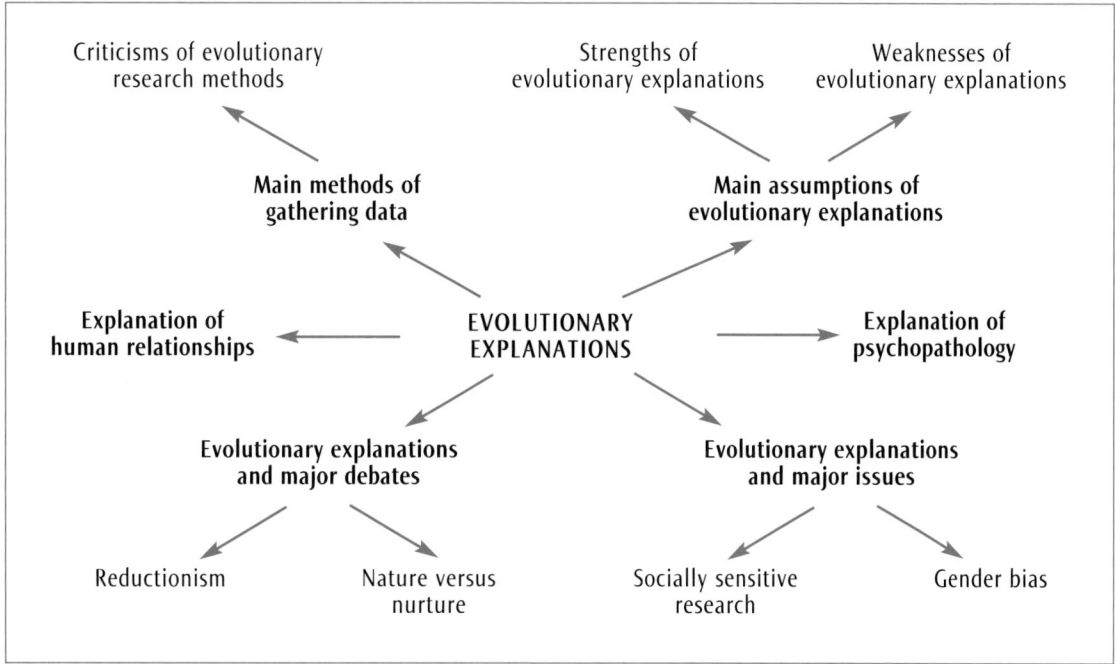

Figure 21.2 Spider diagram of 'evolutionary explanations'

The stimulus material for these questions may be drawn from almost any area of human functioning, so it does not give you an advantage to have studied one area of psychology rather than another. See *In Focus* for an example of an *Approaches* question.

The question in the *In Focus* can be answered in a number of ways. You may choose to explain this relationship from the viewpoint of one of the major *perspectives* in psychology. For example, the behaviourist perspective might explain this relationship in terms of juvenile crime being rewarding for children (status, access to resources, etc.). Alternatively, the psychodynamic perspective might explain this relationship in terms of a deficient superego (and hence a less well-developed sense of guilt or shame). You are

not restricted to using the major perspectives identified in the specification. You might, for example, explain the relationship in terms of children's exposure to the *discourses* of a deviant subculture, which helps to construct a pattern of deviant behaviour in adulthood that they see as normal (a social constructionist perspective). Note that this last explanation may appear more sociological than psychological. This does not matter, as students are encouraged to explore insights into human behaviour that can be derived from other disciplines such as sociology, philosophy, and so on. Once you have picked your two approaches and have constructed how you think they might explain this novel situation, you can then move on to the other questions. Bear in mind that you should focus your

---

in focus

An example of an 'Approaches' question

The findings of research into childhood predictors of adult offending suggest that a range of adverse features in early life are associated with social difficulties and the onset of antisocial behaviour and later criminal behaviour. The intensity and severity of such disadvantage appear to be predictive of chronic offending in later life.

(a) Describe how two different approaches might explain this relationship between childhood experience and later adult offending. *(12 marks)*

(b) Assess the strengths and limitations of one of these explanations. *(6 marks)*

(c) Analyse how the relationship between childhood experience and later adult offending might be investigated by one of these explanations. *(6 marks)*

(d) Evaluate the use of this method for investigating the relationship between childhood experiences and later adult offending. *(6 marks)* responses on the subject matter of the stimulus material at all times, rather than slipping into a more general account of the approach in question or its methods of investigation. It is important (and comforting) to remember that you are not meant to *know* how each of these approaches explains the phenomenon in the stimulus material (it may never

have been studied by that perspective), but simply to be able to *speculate* how your knowledge of these approaches might be applied in its explanation.

It is worth practising doing just that, explaining every novel behaviour you read about from as many different psychological viewpoints as possible (you will soon become a liability to your friends ...).

Examination performance

Reading questions

One of the most elusive (it seems) skills for students in examinations is for them to interpret what is actually required from a particular question. This should not be as difficult as it might appear, given what you now know about the way that questions are actually set. We have included examples of examination questions in each chapter, together with an interpretation and suggested route through the answer. There is no substitute for practice in this respect, so get hold of as many past papers as possible and 'deconstruct' the questions into their constituent skills and parts. When you are skilled at working out exactly what is required in each question, you are ready to move on to the next stage – planning an effective response.

Activity 3: Working out what skills are needed

What specific skills are required in each of the following questions? (Answers are given on p. 560.)

1 (a) Explain what is meant by the terms prejudice and discrimination. *(6 marks)*

   (b) Outline any two strategies for the reduction of prejudice or discrimination. *(6 marks)*

   (c) Critically assess the effectiveness of such techniques. *(12 marks)*

2 Critically consider the use of any two different signalling systems used by nonhuman animals. *(24 marks)*

3 (a) Consider any one approach to the classification of mental disorders. *(15 marks)*

   (b) Evaluate the use of such classification systems in terms of their reliability and validity. *(15 marks)*

Time management

Having mastered the art of unravelling the requirements of the questions, the next hurdle is for you to manage your time effectively in the examination. This involves both time management *between* questions and *within* questions. The first of these really should present no problems to the well-prepared student. Each question is worth 30 minutes (except for Unit 5, where the questions are allocated 45 minutes each), so if you extend the time you give to one question, you are effectively stealing it from another. You should also remember that this 30 minutes includes thinking time, pencil-sharpening and all those other time-consuming activities that we must do in an examination. This does mean that, in reality, you tend only to have around 25 or so minutes of writing time for each question. There is no real reason, therefore, why you should spend more than 30 minutes on any one question. Imagine the following two scenarios involving Unit 4:

A Time (mins) per essay	Mark	B Time (mins) per essay	Mark
40	18	30	16
40	18	30	16
10	6	30	16
Total:	**42**	Total:	**48**

This is based on the reasoning that it is very much easier to push a mark up from 10 to 16, than it is to push it from 16 to 20. It is rarely cost-effective to extend any one individual essay beyond the 30 minutes allocated to it, within the confines of a one-and-a-half-hour examination.

The second problem is to manage your time within a question, so that all the different aspects and requirements of the question are covered.

Let us take a typical question as an example:

◆ Describe and evaluate research into the influence of the media on antisocial behaviour. *(24 marks)*

With only 30 minutes to answer this question, you may be tempted to start writing straight away and run the risk of only getting half or two-thirds through the whole question when the 30 minutes is up. To perform effectively and maximize your marks for any particular question, you need a strategy. There are many such strategies, but a particularly effective one is as follows:

◆ Decide *exactly* what is required in each question, or part of a question.

◆ Calculate how much time should be allocated to each aspect of the question.

◆ Divide the answer into about six paragraphs, about 5 minutes per paragraph.

◆ Plan what will go into each paragraph.

◆ Finally, stick to that plan, and don't go over the allocated time span.

This strategic method has a number of advantages. First, it makes sure that you are answering all parts of the question (provided your planning is appropriate). Second, it ensures that you do not get caught short of time before you have made significant progress into the question. Finally, it makes the whole process of writing an essay less daunting. Writing a series of preplanned 100 word chunks is much easier than writing one 600 word essay. If the thought of writing 100 words worries you, you may be interested to know that there are exactly 100 words in this paragraph!

Activity 4: Planning an essay

Take one of the example questions given earlier, or any other question in this chapter, and plan an essay according to the six paragraphs system just proposed.

Examination marking

Although this part of the examination process may not appear to be something that students can actively take part in, a knowledge of the vagaries of examination marking can certainly help you in your quest for the highest marks possible. The AQA uses a separate marking grid for AO1 and AO2, but they work in the same way. A simplified version of these marking grids can be seen in Table 21.4.

Contrary to popular opinion, examiners are not in the business of trying to find ways to award the lowest marks possible, but neither can they award 'sympathy' marks for essays that are good psychology yet not particularly relevant to the question set. There is a lot involved in examining at this level, but some of the basic rules are as follows:

◆ All answers are marked at the level of a notional 18-year-old who is writing for 30 (or 45 if Unit 5) minutes under examination conditions. What this means in practice is that examiners do not look for the 'perfect' answer, and are realistic in what they can expect a student to write in 30 (or 45) minutes.

◆ Examiners engage in a process known as positive marking. This means that they do not look for opportunities to take marks off (because of errors), but rather for opportunities to add marks on (for correct and appropriate material). If you write something that is wrong, the examiner effectively ignores it, and looks for content that can be credited under the terms of the question.

◆ There are no right or prescriptive answers. One of the features of this subject is that there are many ways to approach questions, and many different perspectives to take in answering them. Students often worry that they might be answering a question in the 'wrong' way. Provided that their answer is relevant to the question, it will be credited by the examiner. Examiners often learn things from students, so it is gratifying to know that your work is being marked by an appreciative audience.

◆ Examiners do not mark with ideas of pass and fail in their mind, nor of the grades they think an answer might be worth. Examiners will award marks according to the marking guidelines illustrated in Table 21.4, together with any special requirements of the question (for example, have the candidates included two theories if asked to do so?).

◆ Names and dates are not perhaps as important as you might imagine. Students spend a great deal of their time revising as many names and dates as they can, perhaps under the impression that it is the weight of such detail that gets the high marks. This impression is bolstered when you read learned academic journals, which appear top heavy with research names and dates. In this guise, they do serve an important function, but they are less important in A-level examinations. Including a researcher's name or the date of the research certainly helps to place the research in context, but as long as a piece of research is recognizable and is described in a way that is both accurate and relevant to the question, it will gain as many marks as if it were anchored to a name and date.

◆ Quality of written communication: each examination script is assessed as a whole, and up to four marks awarded for the quality of written communication used. This involves the accurate expression of ideas, the precise use of specialist terms, and good grammar, punctuation and spelling.

Table 21.4 Marking criteria used in AQA A2 level psychology

AO1 Assessment Criteria

Band	Marks	Content (knowledge, description and understanding)	Relevance	Construction and organization	Breadth and depth
3 (top)	11–12	Accurate and well detailed		Presented coherently	Substantial evidence of both and appropriate balance
3 (bottom)	9–10	Slightly limited: accurate and well detailed		Presented coherently	Evidence of both but imbalanced
2 (top)	7–8	Limited: accurate and reasonably detailed		Reasonable	Some evidence of breadth and/or depth
2 (bottom)	5–6	Limited, generally accurate but lacking in detail		Reasonable	Some evidence of breadth and/or depth
1 (top)	3–4	Basic, rudimentary, sometimes flawed	Sometimes irrelevant	Sometimes focused	
1 (bottom)	1–2	Just discernible/ anecdotal/inaccurate	Wholly or mainly irrelevant	Muddled and incomplete	

AO2 Assessment Criteria

Band	Marks	Commentary	Use of material	Elaboration
3 (top)	11–12	Informed and thorough	Highly effective	Evidence of appropriate selection and coherent elaboration
3 (bottom)	9–10	Informed	Effective	Evidence of appropriate selection and coherent elaboration
2 (top)	7–8	Reasonable, although slightly limited	Effective	Evidence of coherent elaboration
2 (bottom)	5–6	Reasonable, although limited	Reasonably effective	Some evidence of elaboration
1 (top)	3–4	Restricted, superficial and rudimentary	Restricted	Minimal
1 (bottom)	1–2	Just discernible although weak, muddled and/or incomplete	Wholly or mainly irrelevant	

Quality of Written Communication (QoWC) Assessment Criteria

Band	Marks	Expression of ideas	Use of specialist terms	Grammar, punctuation and spelling
5	4	Accurate and clear	Precise and broad	Only minor errors
4	3	Reasonably accurate	Good range	Few errors
3	2	Coherent	Some	Reasonable
2	1	Adequate	Reasonable range	Adequate
1	0	Poor	Limited range	Poor

Activity 5: Mark your own essays!

The next time you write an essay, mark it yourself according to the marking guidelines given in Table 21.4. Try to place your answer in an appropriate mark band descriptor for each of the two skills (AO1 and AO2).

When you have done that, try to assess whether your answer is best described by the 'top' or 'bottom' criteria for that band.

From there, it should be fairly straightforward to give yourself an appropriate mark. Next, you should justify the mark you have given. If you are not in the top band, why not? What would you have needed to gain a mark in the top band? If you get used to doing this, and following the guidance from your teachers, you will effectively become an examiner for your own work. It is hard to go backwards after that!

Activity 6: Test your knowledge of the *Glossary of Terms*

Knowing your AO1 instructions from your AO2 instructions is a vital part of examination success. Many students come unstuck in an examination simply because they respond inappropriately to the words in a question.

The list on the right contains a number of these terms. Some are AO1 terms, some AO2 and some AO1 + AO2. These are mixed in with some bogus terms that are not in the *Glossary of Terms*. Can you identify which are AO1, AO2, AO1+AO2, and which are bogus? (Clue: There are four of each.)

Check your answers against those on p. 560.

Admire	Critically consider	Distinguish between
Analyse	Critically evaluate	Examine
Appraise		Inspect
Assess	Criticize	Outline
Compare and contrast	Describe	Slag off
Consider	Discuss	

Chapter summary

◆ Effective revision is more than good intentions and lots of time. It is more a question of being aware of the skills and topics of the specification, and structuring your revision in a way that is most likely to bring maximum rewards. This means knowing *what* to revise, *how* to revise and *when* to revise. Given that examinations are both predictable and fair, poor performance is often due to poor preparation.

◆ It is important to read the questions properly, looking in particular for the 'instructions' contained in the Glossary terms such as Describe, Assess and Critically consider. It is also important to respond to instructions about the type of material required (e.g. theories, research findings) and the number of theories, research findings, etc.

◆ The examination also assesses candidates in terms of their understanding and critical appreciation of the breadth of theoretical and methodological approaches in psychology. This might be achieved by demonstrating different explanations or perspectives relating to the topic area; demonstrating different methods used to study the topic area; overarching issues relating to the topic area; links with other areas of the specification.

◆ Examiners are guided by a set of guidelines that underlie all A-level examination marking. There are no prescriptive answers, nor do examiners mark in terms of pass or fail. Examiners engage in positive marking, looking for opportunities to give marks for appropriate material rather than knocking them off for material that is wrong or inappropriate.

Answers to activities

Activity 2

1 This question is only assessing AO1 (through the instruction *describe*). The Reviser might suggest that an appropriate AO2 term such as *evaluate* is added.

2 The terms 'flooding' and 'token economies' do appear on the specification, but only as examples of behaviour therapies. This means that a question setter cannot specify them in a question (although they may appear as illustrative examples).

3 The second part of this question uses a term that is not in the *Glossary of Terms*, nor is it clear exactly what is required (as the specification does not include a reference to the reduction of aggression). As the first part of the question is all AO1, the second part should be all AO2. It is not clear how a student would present AO2 material on the reduction of aggression without first describing those insights (an AO1 requirement).

Activity 3

1 (a) AO1 – showing your *understanding* of the terms prejudice and discrimination

(b) AO1 – a brief description (in summary form) of two strategies for the reduction of prejudice or discrimination

(c) AO2 – a judgement of the strengths and limitations of each of these techniques.

2 AO1 + AO2 – *knowledge and understanding* of the use of two signalling systems (AO1) plus the *strengths and limitations* of these systems (AO2).

3 (a) AO1 – *knowledge and understanding* of one approach to the classification of mental disorders

(b) AO2 – make an *informed judgement* about the value of classification systems based on their reliability and validity.

Activity 6

AO1 terms
Consider
Describe
Examine
Outline

AO2 terms
Analyse
Assess
Critically evaluate
Criticize

AO1 + AO2 terms
Compare and contrast
Critically consider
Discuss
Distinguish between

Bogus terms
Admire
Appraise
Inspect
Slag off

Chapter 22

Coursework

Graham Davies

Preview

In this chapter we will be looking at the different aspects of producing coursework for your A-level psychology course, including:

◆ the support documents available from the exam board

◆ how to write a project brief

◆ how coursework should be organized and presented

◆ the ethical constraints which you will need to consider

◆ how to write up a coursework report.

Introduction

The aim of this chapter is to help you gain maximum benefit from your A-level psychology coursework. For A2, Module 6, of the A-level psychology course, you are required to submit a project brief and the report of one coursework investigation. This can be either experimental in nature or non-experimental, but must contain an analysis of results which employs inferential statistics – in other words, you will need to

apply a statistical test to the data you obtain. Your research method must be selected from one of the following:

◆ experiment (laboratory or field)

◆ natural experiment

◆ survey

◆ observational study

◆ an investigation using correlational analysis.

The coursework investigation you conduct must be supervised by a teacher and be on a topic which is contained in the AQA AS or A2 psychology specification. It will account for 15 per cent of your final mark, so it is worth doing well.

You are likely to look to your teacher, parents/guardians or others for help. This is not a problem as long as the report you produce is your own work. However, you must acknowledge *all* sources of help that you receive while carrying out your coursework investigation. Remember also that your psychology coursework presents you with many opportunities if you are attempting a key skills qualification.

Exam board documents

The AQA produces a series of specification support documents to help you with your coursework reporting. You should have copies of, or access to, the following:

◆ *Notes for Guidance to Candidates (A Level Psychology)*

This document provides guidance on the examination requirements and on how coursework should be presented. It also contains the ethical guidelines for carrying out coursework produced by the Association for the Teaching of Psychology (ATP 1992). You will need to familiarize yourself with these.

◆ *Project Brief Proposal Form*

This will help you with the planning of your coursework and forms part of the overall assessment. A copy of this is also available in the Appendix of the AQA specification.

◆ Candidate Record Form

You will need to attach one of these, with the appropriate sections completed, to the front of your report when it is submitted for marking.

◆ *Assessment Criteria for Coursework*

This is an important source of guidance. If you study the highest mark bands carefully, you can gain considerable insight into what is required for higher marks.

◆ *Malpractice in Coursework*
This document outlines the action that is taken for claiming that someone else's work is your own or for copying from textbooks or other candidates (plagiarism). It is not a nice thing to mention, but all A-level students are advised to read this document carefully, noting the contents.

Although it is aimed at teachers, you might also like to look at Psychology A level: *Specification Support Materials for AS/A2 Psychology*. This book contains a number of marked examples of A-level psychology coursework (of varying standards), together with notes provided by the Principal Coursework Moderator on their various strengths and weaknesses. Ask your teacher or lecturer if you can see a copy.

The project brief

The function of the project brief is to help you clarify your thinking and plan your coursework in the most efficient way. This reduces the danger of making mistakes with your method. You will find it helpful to submit the project brief to your teacher so that you can be given approval for your planned project before you begin data collection. Your brief is marked as part of your coursework assessment and needs to include the following:

◆ the aim of the research and a statement of the hypotheses

◆ an explanation of why a directional (one-tailed) or non-directional (two-tailed) hypothesis has been proposed

◆ identification of the research method and the design employed

◆ an explanation of the strengths and weaknesses of your chosen research method/design

◆ identification of potential sources of bias

◆ identification of potential confounding variables

◆ a strategy for dealing with the sources of bias and confounding variables that you have identified

◆ explanation of the minimum level of statistical significance used for any statistical test that you have employed to analyse your results

◆ identification of relevant ethical issues and your strategy for dealing with these.

Organizing and presenting your coursework report

The maximum length for your coursework report is 2,000 words (exclusive of project brief, tables, graphs, charts, references or appendices). Remember that conciseness is an important report-writing skill. Reports should be submitted on A4 paper, preferably secured by treasury tags or in a plastic document file. Avoid using bulky ring files, paper clips or plastic wallets from which the work has to be removed before it can be read – moderators dislike these!

The write-up of your investigation needs to be organized and produced in a manner appropriate for a scientific report. There is no single correct way of doing this, but the approach outlined here is one that is widely used. The following tips may be useful:

◆ Avoid using the first person singular or plural ('I' or 'we'). Opinions differ on this point, but many students comment that they find it easier to write reports using the third person in the passive voice (i.e. 'The investigation was carried out' rather than 'I carried out an investigation').

◆ Keep to the past tense. Your coursework is reporting what has taken place, rather than what you are about to do. Therefore you will find it much easier if you use the past tense, otherwise you might find yourself stringing together phrases such as 'The participants were about to have been able to have been...'

◆ Label all pieces of paper connected with a particular investigation with the report title – it can be hard to work out later on what odd fragments of data are if you do not do this.

◆ Write your report up as soon as you have completed the investigation. It is much harder if you leave it and return to it later on.

◆ Leave yourself enough time to write your report. It will probably take longer than you think, and rushed work often leads to careless errors. Don't forget that credit is given to the quality of your written expression.

Ethical considerations

In your AS level psychology, you will have already looked at ethical issues, but they warrant further discussion here as they arise whenever research is carried out in the name of psychology. It is vitally important that you are familiar with ethical guidelines *before* you carry out your coursework investigation. You should familiarize yourself with both the ethical guidelines produced for practising psychologists by the British Psychological Society (BPS 1993) and those produced for students at pre-degree levels by the Association for the Teaching of Psychology (ATP 1992).

You will need to address ethical issues on your project brief. If you are an AQA A-level psychology candidate you should have your own copy of the ATP ethical guidelines as they form part of the *Notes for Guidance to Candidates* published by the AQA.

Any work that you carry out for your psychology coursework *must* be on a topic checked and approved by your examination centre *before* you start work on it. If you go ahead without this approval, the examination centre may refuse to accept it for marking. Ask your teacher or lecturer for advice.

The key ethical issues are laid out in Table 22.1.

'Psychological research can be fun, but it should not be carried out just for fun.' (ATP 1992)

Some psychological research is fun to do, but may involve costs to participants' rights or feelings that are unjustifiable (e.g. in terms of potential discomfort or embarrassment). The fact that research has been carried out in the past by qualified psychologists does not mean that it is automatically an appropriate topic for study by A-level psychology candidates. For example, research on bystander behaviour, conformity or personal space may involve levels of deception or discomfort which make such work inappropriate for A-level students. In such cases, do something else.

Table 22.1 Ethical considerations when carrying out psychological research

General issues

◆ Should the study be carried out at all?

◆ Is it being carried out in the most ethical way?

◆ Do the ends justify the means?

◆ What are the 'costs' and 'benefits' of the work?

Consent

◆ Informed consent should be given by participants wherever possible.

◆ Deception of participants should be avoided.

◆ Debriefing of participants should take place.

◆ Participants have the right to withdraw from an investigation at any time.

◆ Participants completing an investigation have the right to refuse the use of their data.

◆ Participants may see a researcher as being in a position of power, so pressure should not be placed on people to continue to take part when they do not wish to do so.

◆ Right to privacy should be respected.

◆ Some participants may not be in a position to give informed consent themselves (these include children, some elderly people and those with special needs).

Conduct

◆ Safety of self, those in the investigator's care and others the investigator comes into contact with must be maintained at all times.

◆ Physiological and psychological discomfort to others should be avoided.

◆ Act within the law.

◆ Do not copy data, copyright materials or other people's wording.

◆ Participants should leave the research situation in at least as good a psychological state as they entered it.

Competence

◆ Researchers should be sufficiently qualified to carry out the work undertaken.

Confidentiality

◆ Maintain confidentiality of data at all times.

◆ Do not name participants (numbers or pseudonyms may be used).

Source: Davies (1994)

Psychology has many fascinating possibilities for studies to be carried out which involve neither deception nor physical or psychological discomfort.

You should not exploit others simply for your own interests. It is particularly important that you consider the rights of those who may not be in a position to give their full informed consent, for example those with special needs and people who are mentally ill. Children represent another vulnerable group – if you are studying them, you must obtain informed consent from their parents, and it is also courteous to ask the children themselves. Remember that you will probably have to produce a simple and jargon-free way of doing this.

Sometimes, the fact that debriefing of participants takes place is seen as removing any risks that result from deception. You need to think carefully about this – sometimes deception can even enter into the debriefing process, e.g. when participants ask 'how they did', as illustrated in the cartoon. If you feel that answering such questions honestly might upset your participants, then you should not embark on the study in the first place.

The following scenarios could come from genuine psychological investigations, but how would *you* feel if...

◆ ... you are a parent with your children in the park. You see someone watching your children and making notes on their behaviour.

◆ ... you carry out a survey involving questions on activities such as under-age drinking or the taking of illegal drugs. Legitimate authorities (e.g. a head teacher, college principal or the police) then question you about your sources of information. In such circumstances you have no legal right to keep your participants' identities confidential.

Before carrying out any investigation as part of your psychology coursework, you should ask yourself the questions shown in Table 22.2 (derived from the Association for the Teaching of Psychology ethical guidelines). If you are in any doubt about the ethical aspects of your investigation, do not go ahead with it.

Table 22.2   Questions to ask before carrying out investigations

◆ Should I be conducting this kind of study at all?

◆ What is the most ethical way of carrying it out?

◆ Am I sufficiently competent to carry it out?

◆ Have I informed the participants of all that they need and would expect to know before taking part?

◆ Have they willingly agreed to take part?

◆ How do I ensure that all research records are confidential and anonymous, and will remain so?

◆ How do I ensure that my research is carried out professionally and in a way that protects the rights of those involved?

Source: ATP (1992)

Writing up a coursework report

The following pages provide detailed guidance on what you might consider including in the different sections of a coursework report. Always remember that the report is being written for someone who is unfamiliar with the investigation that you have carried out. Can this person replicate your work from the description provided?

Activity 2: Research reports

Obtain two or three examples of research reports from journals or textbooks. As you read the suggestions for layout outlined here, review these in terms of good or poor practice.

The title

Selecting an informative title isn't always as easy as it seems. Avoid a general title which gives the reader little information on the nature of the investigation, e.g. 'Short-term memory'. At the same time avoid a title which is overcomplicated. A useful way of thinking about titles is to consider the key variables involved in the investigation, for example, 'The relationship between health and stress levels', or 'The effect of imagery on encoding'.

The abstract

The aim of writing an abstract is to summarize the complete investigation briefly and clearly so that someone new to the topic being investigated can gain an idea of what actually happened. This should not be more than a paragraph or two long and merits careful writing – composing an abstract is a skill which needs to be practised if you are to perfect it. Within this short section you should provide information on:

◆ the background idea of the investigation (e.g. the previous research that it was based on)

◆ the aim(s) and/or hypothesis(-es)

◆ the research method/design

◆ the sample of participants

◆ the results of the investigation (including the statistical conclusion, where appropriate)

◆ how the findings were interpreted.

Given the short length of this section you have no more than a sentence or two on each of the above points. Although this section will appear at the beginning of your report, you will probably find it easier to write it last as it summarizes the whole investigation.

Activity 3: Writing abstracts

Read one of the major studies for your A level psychology course (or a detailed report of it). Try to write an abstract for this study.

The introduction

The introduction section aims to provide a rationale for the investigation that has been undertaken. It should contain relevant previous research or background material, developing logically into a discussion of the reasoning behind the current study, and end with a clear statement of the investigation's aim(s) and hypotheses. Your writing should progress smoothly and avoid sudden changes in direction. Coolican (1999) provides a helpful way of thinking about this process, suggesting that the introduction to an experimental report should be like a funnel – see Fig. 22.1 (a) on p. 566.

A good way to start an introduction is to outline briefly in broad terms the area that you are investigating. Once you have completed this, you should continue by discussing any previous research that has taken place on the topic in question. The key point here is to make sure that the research you are quoting is focused on the topic that is being investigated. You should not treat the introduction as an opportunity to write a general essay on the area concerned. Try not to fall into the trap of writing absolutely everything that you can find on the topic – if you produce an introduction of excessive length then you are unlikely to obtain full marks for this section. Remember that the introduction can be regarded as a funnelling down process – as you write it, you move closer and closer to the specific aspect of the topic that you are investigating. So, end this part of your introduction with a description of the research that is closest to the area that you are investigating. Remember to ensure that you are using your own wording – the unacknowledged use of text from books or other media is regarded as plagiarism.

Once you have reviewed relevant previous research, it is time to move on to develop the rationale behind your own investigation. How did your ideas develop from the previous research that has been outlined? Why was this considered to be an interesting area for investigation? What were the aims of your study? How did you formulate your hypothesis(-es)? It is very important to state clearly any null/alternative hypotheses investigated. These should be written in an operationalized form (i.e. one that is precisely testable) – a common problem with the phrasing of hypotheses in completed coursework reports is that they often read more like general aims.

If you re-read your introduction you should be able to see the logical flow of ideas from research topic through to aim(s) and hypothesis(-es).

Some students include 'Aim(s) and hypothesis(-es)' as a separate subsection of the report. Whether you choose to do this is up to you. Select the approach that suits you best.

The method section

In the method section you will need to state precisely how your investigation was carried out. A key aim to keep in mind here is *replicability* – that you should be able to give your report to someone unfamiliar with the investigation concerned, who could replicate it precisely from your description. You will probably find writing this section easier if you divide it into subsections. There is no single correct way of doing this – what follows is a common 'tried and tested' format. Each of these subsections of the method section may well be only one or two paragraphs in length.

Figure 22.1 (a) Coolican's concept of the introduction as a funnel compared to some less successful approaches, e.g. Fig. 22.1 (b) and (c)

Start with the general psychological subject area. Discuss theory and research work which is relevant to the research topic. Move from the general area to the particular hypotheses to be tested via a coherent and logical argument as to why specific predictions have been made. State the specific HYPOTHESIS

Figure 22.1 (b)

Sometimes, however, the general topic area remains broad and the discussion is not focused specifically on the research topic in question. There is no real attempt to formulate the hypotheses and a sudden break in continuity occurs before the specific hypothesis is stated.

Figure 22.1 (c)

Another approach which fails to achieve the funnelling down achieved in Fig. 22.1 (a) is one in which general information on the research area in question occurs in various places throughout the introduction. Research studies on the area of interest are included, but not presented in a logical order, which makes the development of ideas hard to follow. Again, a break in continuity occurs before the specific hypothesis is stated.

Design

In the design subsection you will need to state the research method used (e.g. naturalistic observation or experiment). The best students will elaborate this and justify why this method was used. You should then go on to outline and justify the actual design used. For example, if your report is based on an experiment using a repeated measures design, you might briefly outline what the experimental conditions were and state why this design was used in preference to independent measures. Don't forget to mention such things as the number of participants per group or how many trials participants undertook. This is also the place to tell the reader what your key variables were. For example, in an experiment it is useful to report the independent and dependent variables here, remembering to avoid vague phrasing.

Participants

In this subsection you should state the number of participants that you have used. You might also report their age range and gender (but only if these are relevant to the investigation). You should also state the sampling method used to select your participants together with the population from which they were drawn. A common misconception here concerns random samples. Remember that taking every tenth person or using anyone that is available are *not* random techniques (although they may result in a representative sample) as every participant does not stand an equal chance of selection. Don't forget to say how your participants were allocated to different groups or conditions.

Apparatus and/or materials

The actual title of this subsection can be varied to meet the needs of the investigation concerned (e.g. many involve materials but no apparatus as such). This is a subsection where many students fail to do themselves full justice. Here you should report the details of any apparatus or materials used. If materials are in written form, then you may well find it useful to include a copy in an appendix at the end of your report. Also, you might find it helpful to refer to scoresheets or standardized instructions to participants here – it is vital to include the latter as this helps to ensure that the investigation that you are describing is fully replicable. However, don't include trivial details such as makes of pens or pencils, and remember that it is unnecessary to include every single response sheet or questionnaire – a specimen included in an appendix is usually sufficient.

Procedure

The procedure is the place to report exactly how the investigation was carried out. The key issue here is replicability. So if, for example, you are carrying out an observational study, you will need to report it in such a way that someone else could carry out a similar study after reading your description. If it is an experiment, then you will need to say what the participants had to do. If you test each participant individually, you will probably find it easier to report the procedure for one participant and then state that this procedure was repeated *x* times. Some students prefer to present their standardized instructions to participants here. Alternatively, you may like to include them as an appendix, but if you do, remember to refer to them here.

The results section

Coursework assessors are often surprised by the indifferent quality of results sections when compared to the other sections of reports. Results sections often appear to have had less time and effort spent upon them. Once again, there is no single correct way of writing up this section. Alternative approaches are possible, all capable of earning full marks, so adopt the way that suits you best. For example, some candidates divide their material into two sections, headed 'results' and 'treatment of results' respectively, whereas others prefer to use a single section headed 'results'.

Organization

Whichever approach you decide to adopt, it is important to organize it in such a way that there is a logical flow of information presented to the reader (as with the rest of your report, it is important to express everything clearly, assuming that the reader is unfamiliar with the piece of work that you have undertaken).

First of all, decide which information you are going to present in your results section, and which you are going to place in an appendix. Items which are best placed in an appendix are those which interrupt the flow of the text. For example, tables of raw data, specimen scoresheets, completed questionnaires or statistical computations. This does not mean that they cannot be mentioned in this section – it is good practice for every appendix to be referred to at some point in the text.

The best A-level students produce a results section which includes a text that guides the reader through the various elements of the results, and this greatly improves the accessibility of this section for the reader (remember that your examiner may be unfamiliar with the investigation undertaken). The results section might include the following:

◆ statement of how data have been obtained (for example, how questionnaires or observational studies have been scored – students frequently omit this, which means that it is difficult to achieve full marks for replicability)

◆ reference to a table containing the raw data which should be included as an appendix to the report (e.g. 'A table showing the numbers of words recalled correctly by participants in the imagery and random list conditions can be found in Appendix 2')

◆ an appropriate summary table of results – this table should also be referred to in the text of the results section

◆ reference to any graphs and/or charts which have been used to summarize the data

◆ the full reasons for using the inferential statistical test(s) that you have used

◆ the results of the application of the test(s).

A *summary table* might include appropriate descriptive statistics. For example, relevant measures of central tendency (such as mean or median) or of dispersion (e.g. range or standard deviation) can often be used to good effect. Select the measures which are most appropriate for the particular investigation, and remember to state what these statistics actually tell us about the results of the investigation.

A good *graph* or *chart* can add greatly to the clarity of reporting your findings. It is useful to remember here that selectivity of the techniques employed is important. An appropriate technique for a particular investigation might be a scattergraph (in a study involving correlational analysis), a bar chart, histogram or frequency polygon. This is not meant to be an exhaustive list, and many students use other specialized techniques which are appropriate in the context of the investigation concerned. The key factor is to assess your requirements before you begin to produce your illustrations; it is, unfortunately, quite common for candidates to include beautifully drawn graphs or charts which show little that is relevant in terms of the original aims and hypotheses of the investigation. Computer drawn graphics are sometimes a problem here. Simply because a graph can be produced on a computer does not guarantee that an appropriate technique is being used. Two things which you should try to avoid are:

- graphs or charts with 'Participant number' on their x-axes – these rarely show useful information, and indeed can sometimes lead to potentially bizarre interpretations (e.g. 'participant 7.8 recalled 9.1 words')

- unnecessary repetition – you are very unlikely to gain extra marks for presenting the same information in several different ways (e.g. on a pie chart, frequency polygon and histogram).

Keep in mind that the specific aim of your illustrations is to add to the clarity (and quality) of your results. Your graphs or charts should, therefore, show something that can be related directly to the aims and hypotheses of your investigation. For example, they might compare the distributions of scores in the different conditions of an experiment, or show the relationship between sets of data which are being correlated. Add a comment on what these graphs/charts show.

The best coursework reports provide reasoned explanations for the choice of any inferential statistical test, with students basing their reasons for selection on the nature of the data that they have obtained and what they are trying to demonstrate from its application. It may be useful, for example, to state whether the analysis is aiming to find a difference, correlation or association, as well as to provide comments on the nature of the data obtained (e.g. whether the statistical test is going to treat it as being at a nominal, ordinal, interval or ratio level of measurement). The results section is not the place to include your statistical calculations. They can be referred to here, but actual calculations should be consigned to an appendix. You can report the results of your statistical test(s) by adapting the phrasing used with the worked examples of statistical tests (see Chapter 23).

You should always report the results of the inferential statistical test(s) you have used. It is important here that you have adopted an appropriate minimum level of statistical significance and reported the level of statistical significance actually achieved. Was your null hypothesis rejected or retained at your chosen level of significance?

Presentation of results

Care taken in the presentation of the results section can be rewarding. When drawing graphs or charts, it is helpful to use a sharp pencil or an appropriate pen (not an elderly felt tip or blobby ball-point). Alternatively, if you know that this is one of your weak areas, use computer-generated graphics. Try to think of appropriate titles for each of your graphs, charts or tables – you should aim to produce something which makes it immediately clear what the illustration is showing, without having to refer to the text. For

example, 'results' or 'data' would be insufficient. 'Table showing the mean number of words recalled in the imagery and random list conditions' would be much more informative. Some students head their tables with terms such as 'Condition A' or 'Condition B' – but this does not make it easy for the reader (such as your coursework moderator) who has not been involved directly with the study to understand what is happening. It is also important to ensure that labelling of graphs, charts and tables is carried out to a high standard. You should ensure that, for example, headings of columns of data and labels on axes of graphs are meaningful, with the relevant units of measurement given wherever appropriate. It is helpful to number graphs, charts and tables so that they can be referred to more easily in the text.

Discussion section

The discussion section often seems to be the place where, perhaps more than on any other section of the coursework report, the good candidate will score well and the weaker candidate poorly. With careful planning and by logically sequencing your ideas, it is possible to maximize your marks. It is useful to try and answer the following six questions in your reports.

1 What do your results actually mean?

Ideally, this first part of the discussion section will follow on logically from the end of your results section. In fact, a good way to start your discussion is to state the main findings that you obtained. How do these results fit in with the aims and/or hypotheses that you proposed at the start of your study? This is also the place to discuss, if necessary, any individual results, e.g. any atypical data that may have affected the outcome of your study. Be careful with your interpretation, keep in mind the nature of your sample of participants and that you should not generalize results inappropriately.

2 How do your results fit in with previous research?

In your introduction section you will have discussed the background research or theory relevant to the investigation that you have undertaken. In your discussion, you should now move on to consider the ways in which your research supports or fails to support this previous background material. Weaker candidates here will merely state that 'the results support the findings of research by...'. Better candidates, on the other hand, will be able to go on to compare the data obtained from previous investigations with those from their own study, discussing any similarities or differences. As mentioned previously, selectivity of material is very important in the introduction sections of your coursework reports. If you have written an introduction which is suitably selective, this should benefit you here as you will be linking your results to those from appropriate theory or research.

If, however, your results do not fit in with those obtained from any previous research, then this is the place to suggest possible reasons why this might be so. You may need to examine any differences in methodology carefully if you are to do this well.

Remember that you should not need to introduce background studies into the discussion section that have not been mentioned previously in the introduction. If you find that you are doing this, then your selection of studies made in the introduction may need revising. Also, avoid making statements which are demonstrably untrue. Such statements might claim, for example, that your results 'prove the work of Bower to be wrong'.

3 What are the methodological limitations of your study?

This is your opportunity to criticize constructively the method that you have used in your study. It is important here that you confine yourself to factors which really are likely to have affected the outcome and not descend into trivia. The possible effects of any serious design weaknesses should be addressed here, for example, a failure to counterbalance in a repeated measures design or problems with observer reliability in a naturalistic observational study. Try to avoid potentially trivial points such as using a random sample instead of an opportunist one (when this is unlikely to have affected the results anyway), using more participants (when plenty were used), or minor issues such as time of day, light levels or room temperature. These should only be mentioned if you really do feel that they may have affected your results.

4 If you did the investigation again, how could you improve it?

You now have the opportunity to suggest how the problems that you have identified could be overcome if you were to undertake the investigation again. The suggestions that you make here should be both practical and ethical.

5 What are the wider implications of your results?

This is your opportunity to step back and assess the wider practical or theoretical implications of your findings. You might also review any ethical issues which arose in your investigation. It is difficult to give precise guidance here as the implications are often specific to a particular study, but you might consider whether, for example, there are implications for society, education, specific psychological theories or equal opportunities policies.

6 Can you suggest any follow-up studies?

You could now move on to suggest the possible direction for any further research. Given your findings, where could you go from here? What other research proposals could you make? How would you carry these out? Avoid simply stating the general area that might be investigated, try and go a bit further and suggest the method or design that might be used to achieve your proposal.

Conclusion

Although it is not credited separately, it is useful to provide a conclusion section which summarizes briefly your main findings. These need to be described without the use of statistical notation.

References

You will need to include references for:

◆ all studies that you have quoted in your coursework report

◆ any books, journals, internet sites or other sources of information that you obtained information from

◆ any computer packages that you have used.

References should be given in alphabetical order of author. For a book reference you will need to give the author (including the initials), date of publication, title of the book, edition number (if there is more than one edition), place of publication and publisher. For example:

Coolican, H. (1999) *Research Methods and Statistics in Psychology* (3rd edn), London: Hodder and Stoughton.

References for journal articles should provide the author and title of the article, name of the journal concerned, volume number and relevant page numbers, thus:

Kendler, K.S. and Prescott, C.A. (1999) 'A population-based twin study of lifetime major depression in men and women', *Archives of General Psychiatry*, 56, pp. 39-44.

Occasionally you may need to give the reference for an article in a book that has been edited by someone else. This can be done as follows:

Gotlib, I.H. and Macleod, C. (1997) 'Information processing in anxiety and depression: a cognitive-developmental perspective', in J. Burack and J. Enns (eds) *Attention, Development and Psychopathology*, New York: Guildford Press.

There are conventions about how to present references:

◆ Titles of books and journals are normally italicized or, if you are writing your coursework by hand, underlined.

◆ Titles of articles or chapters in books are in Roman (ordinary) letters, but are put inside quotation marks. These can be either single or double marks – it's up to you to choose, but once you have made your choice, use the same kind of quotation marks throughout.

◆ You can choose whether or not to include full stops after authors' initials. Again, be consistent – either put them all in or none at all.

◆ Internet sites can be referenced by giving the address of the site concerned together with the title of the material obtained.

Activity 4: Writing references

Practise giving references in the ways outlined above when you carry out your essay work. Developing the habit of providing good accurate references will stand you in good stead if you continue your studies into higher education.

Decide what conventions you will use to present references. You may find it useful to spend a few minutes looking at the list of references at the back of this book and working out what conventions have been used for this text.

Appendices

An appendix is the proper location for material that interrupts the readability of your report. For example, appendices might contain stimulus materials, diagrams of research layouts, tally charts from observational studies, specimen questionnaire surveys, raw data tables or statistical calculations. Do not, however, treat them as a repository for rough notes – remember that everything you place in your report will be marked. If you are including specimen response sheets or questionnaires, you will not need to include every single copy – a specimen is normally quite sufficient.

Final checks

When you have finished writing your report:

◆ Carefully check that you have included everything necessary. You may like to use the checklist in the chapter summary to help you do this.

◆ Check your English (including the spelling). Don't forget that marks are awarded for quality of language.

◆ Complete a candidate record form as far as possible and attach it securely to the front of your report.

◆ Add your completed project brief.

◆ Remember to photocopy your report if you are likely to want to look at it again before you have completed your course. This is a good idea anyway as the exam board sometimes retains reports for grading and archive purposes.

Further resources

Your key sources are likely to be the support materials produced by the Exam Board. However, you will find the following useful:

Association for the Teaching of Psychology (1992) *Ethics in Psychological Research: Guidelines for Students at Pre-degree Level*, Leicester: Association for the Teaching of Psychology.

British Psychological Society (1993) *Code of Conduct, Ethical Principles and Guidelines*, Leicester: British Psychological Society. They are available on the Internet at **http://www.bps.org.uk/Charter/Codeofcon.htm**

These sets of ethical guidelines are essential reading for any student undertaking coursework.

Coolican, H. (1999) *Research Methods and Statistics in Psychology* (3rd edn), London: Hodder and Stoughton.

Coolican, H. (1996) *Introduction to Research Methods and Statistics in Psychology* (2nd edn), London: Hodder and Stoughton.

These two textbooks provide valuable reference texts which give detailed information on the research methods that you are likely to be using in your coursework. The first text provides the greater detail, the second is briefer and more condensed.

Searle, A. (1999) *Introducing Research and Data in Psychology*, London: Routledge.

A pocket-size volume aimed at those who find research methods and statistics a daunting prospect.

Chapter summary

Checklist: A-level psychology practicals

The checklist on the next two pages is designed to help you maximize your marks for practical work based on experimentation or correlational analysis. With a little ingenuity you can also adapt it for observational studies. Using the checklist as a starting point, create your own master copy which you can use for your own coursework (and any practice reports that you may produce). Remember, though, that not every question will apply to every study.

Name: **Title of practical work:**

Project brief

Have you:

- ☐ stated your aim and hypotheses?
- ☐ explained why a directional (one-tailed) or non-directional (two-tailed) hypothesis has been used?
- ☐ identified your research method and design?
- ☐ explained why this research method/design has been used?
- ☐ identified possible sources of bias and confounding variables?
- ☐ stated how possible sources of bias and confounding variables have been dealt with?
- ☐ explained your minimum level of statistical significance?
- ☐ stated your strategy for dealing with any ethical issues?

Abstract (summary)

Have you stated:

- ☐ the topic area studied?
- ☐ the aim/hypothesis?
- ☐ brief details of the method used?
- ☐ the principal findings?
- ☐ the main implications of your findings?

Introduction, aims and hypotheses

Have you:

- ☐ stated the general area of your study?
- ☐ referred to relevant and carefully selected background studies?
- ☐ reported your reasons for studying this topic?
- ☐ clearly stated your aim(s)?
- ☐ precisely stated: (a) the alternative hypothesis(-es) (b) the null hypothesis(-es)?
- ☐ stated whether the alternative hypotheses are directional (1-tailed) or non-directional (2-tailed)?
- ☐ reported how you arrived at these aims/hypotheses?
- ☐ organized your introduction in a logical way?

Method

Have you: ☐ divided this section into suitable subsections?

Have you stated:

- ☐ the design used?
- ☐ the nature of any experimental groups/conditions?
- ☐ the nature of any control groups/conditions?
- ☐ the IV and DV or the variables correlated?
- ☐ stated the minimum level of statistical significance you will accept?
- ☐ your number of participants?
- ☐ the population from which participants were drawn?

Method *continued*

Have you stated:
- ☐ how participants were selected/sampled?
- ☐ how participants were allocated to experimental groups/conditions?
- ☐ relevant characteristics of participants, e.g. age range, sex?
- ☐ details of all apparatus and materials used?
- ☐ any standardized instructions given to participants?
- ☐ the procedure followed in such a way that someone else could replicate it precisely using your description?

Results

Have you:
- ☐ provided a summary table of results?
- ☐ provided titles for all graphs, charts and data tables?
- ☐ labelled all axes and columns of your graphs, charts and data tables?
- ☐ used appropriate descriptive/inferential statistical techniques?
- ☐ stated full reasons why a particular statistical test was selected to analyse your data?
- ☐ reported appropriately your observed and critical values?
- ☐ reported your level of statistical significance?
- ☐ reported the outcome of your study in terms of the hypotheses tested?

Discussion

Have you stated:
- ☐ the results that you obtained?

Have you discussed:
- ☐ what your results mean in terms of your aims/hypotheses?
- ☐ your findings with reference to the studies quoted in your introduction?
- ☐ the limitations of your study?
- ☐ how improvements could be made to the study if it were to be done again?
- ☐ suggestions for follow-up studies?
- ☐ any wider implications of your findings?

Conclusion

Have you:
- ☐ briefly summarized your main findings?

References:

Have you:
- ☐ provided full references for all sources used and quoted by namet?
- ☐ written references in a conventional style?

Appendices

Have you:
- ☐ provided copies of such things as stimulus materials and experimental layouts which are referred to in the text but not included elsewhere?
- ☐ provided a table of raw data?
- ☐ included specimen statistical calculations?
- ☐ provided appropriate titles and labelling for all appendices?

Presentation

Have you:
- ☐ written your report in a concise scientific style?
- ☐ structured your report logically into sections?
- ☐ avoided unnecessary repetition or irrelevancy?
- ☐ provided a contents page and numbered your pages?
- ☐ presented your report in such a way that someone else could precisely replicate the study from your description?
- ☐ linked all graphs, charts and data tables into your text?
- ☐ acknowledged all sources of help with your coursework?

Chapter 23

Statistical analysis for coursework

Graham Davies

Preview

In this chapter we shall be looking at:

◆ calculation of the standard deviation

◆ an introduction to inferential statistics

◆ the concept of statistical significance

◆ some of the inferential statistical tests which may be used to analyse your coursework data, including:

  – tests of difference

  – tests of correlation

  – tests of association.

Introduction

This chapter will look at some of the ways in which you can statistically analyse your coursework data. You have already met some of the descriptive statistical techniques for data analysis when you completed the research methods component of your AS level course. In this, you were introduced to descriptive statistical techniques such as measures of central tendency, measures of dispersion and the production of graphs and charts. Look back at your AS textbook and/or notes, if you need to refresh your memory on these.

This chapter will extend your knowledge of how to analyse data by showing you how to calculate the most important of the measures of dispersion, standard deviation.

The concept of statistical significance will be introduced and you will be shown how to calculate some of the inferential statistical tests which you might use to analyse and draw conclusions from your coursework data.

Calculating the standard deviation

As you will remember from your AS level psychology (Module 3, *Research Methods*), measures of dispersion enable us to examine the variability within our data sets and help us to understand whether scores in a given set of data are similar to or very different from each other. The standard deviation is one such measure of dispersion, being a measure of the variability (i.e. of the typical deviation) of a given sample of scores from its mean. You will find it helpful to refresh your memory by re-reading your AS level notes for Unit 3. Before calculating the standard deviation, you need to remember that for standard deviation to be an accurate measure, you need to have data that are approximately normally distributed. You also require data that are measured on an *interval scale* or a *ratio scale*. Levels of measurement are an important concept in statistics (see *In Focus* on p. 574).

Calculation of the standard deviation involves working out the deviation of all the individual values in the sample of data concerned from the sample mean – in other words, we have to find the differences between each of these individual values and their mean.

The standard deviation can be calculated using the formulae in Fig. 23.1. This is the first time in this book that we have met statistical formulae. If you don't like maths, please do not panic! The calculation is simple, and remember that you will not be asked to carry out any statistical calculations under examination conditions. Most computer statistical packages will calculate standard deviation for you, as will most scientific calculators, so now is the time to learn how to use them!

The statistical symbols used in the formulae form part of a standard notation that will occur elsewhere, so it is worth the effort getting to know what these symbols mean.

Now for a few words on when to use the two different formulae. In order to explain this, we need to refer to the concepts of population and sample – if you are not sure what these mean, refer back to your AS level textbook/notes.

in
focus

Levels of measurement

The quantitative measurements that psychologists obtain from their research investigations can be made at different levels of measurement. These vary in terms of their precision and in how they can be used. The four most common levels of measurement will be discussed here.

The nominal level

Nominal level data provide the weakest level of measurement available to the psychologist, and are sometimes referred to as categorized or frequency count data. Data can be allocated into categories by counting frequency of occurrence within particular categories. An example might be the placing of research participants into categories based on their gender and the frequency with which they interpret a stimulus in different ways. For example:

	Interpretation A	Interpretation B
Female	25	15
Male	20	20

The ordinal level

Ordinal level data are capable of being placed into rank order (i.e. from highest value to lowest value or vice versa). This means the researcher can meaningfully compare scores with each other, although the extent of meaningful comparison is limited. It is possible to state that one value is higher than another, but it is not possible to assume more than this. For example, it is reasonable to assume that if children's helpfulness is rated on an eleven-point scale (with high numbers = high helpfulness) a child with a rating of 10 has been observed as being more helpful than a child with a rating of 5. However, it is unreasonable to conclude that the child with a rating of 10 is twice as helpful as the one with a rating of 5, as the points on such a rating scale are at intervals which are (or may be) arbitrary or unequal. It is impossible to tell precisely how much the points on the scale really differ, i.e. we cannot say that the difference between ratings of 1 and 2 and ratings of 9 and 10 are exactly equal. The most that we can achieve is the relative ranking of the children concerned.

Interval and ratio levels

The interval and ratio levels of measurement are more precise – they consist of data which are measured in fixed units with equal distances between all the points on the scale concerned (e.g. the difference between 10°C and 11°C is the same as the difference between 20°C and 21°C). The key difference between interval and ratio scales lies in how zero values can be interpreted. Well-known examples of the interval level of measurement include temperature measured in degrees C or degrees F. In both of these cases 0 degrees is not meaningful because neither 0°C nor 0°F can be interpreted as a baseline for no temperature. Minus values are possible, and proportions are meaningless if calculated with zero as the baseline.

Ratio scales provide the strongest level of measurement of those discussed here, and on such scales zero really does provide a baseline which can be used for calculating proportions. Examples of data measured on ratio scales are distance in centimetres and time in seconds.

There is debate between statisticians about the interpretation of these levels of measurement. For example, some people treat numbers of words recalled in a memory task as interval data, whereas others treat such data as ordinal on the grounds that all words are not equally easy to recall. This raises the important point that data do not arrive with a label signifying the level of measurement attached to them – the researcher needs to decide the appropriate level at which data are to be treated.

For example, let us assume we have a series of times, such as the times taken for rats to run a particular maze (all times are in seconds):

   20 28 29 30 30 31 34 40 42 44 46 47

These data consist of times – fixed units of measurement which we could treat, correctly, as being on a ratio scale. However, we could allocate rank orders to these scores, thereby treating our data as being on an ordinal scale. Alternatively, we could group the scores into categories such as 'number of rats running the maze in less than 40 seconds' and 'number of rats taking 40 seconds or more to run the maze'. In this case, we are now treating our data as nominal.

Formula 1: $S = \sqrt{\dfrac{\Sigma d^2}{N}}$

Formula 2: $s = \sqrt{\dfrac{\Sigma d^2}{N-1}}$

where:

S or s = standard deviation
(the statistic we are aiming to calculate)

$\sqrt{}$ = square root

Σ = sum of (ie add up)

d^2 = the squared deviation of each value from the mean

N = the number of scores

Figure 23.1
Formulae used for calculating standard deviation

◆ *Formula 1* is used for obtaining the standard deviation of values from a population where the whole population has been sampled. For example, when we are interested in, say, the data obtained from a psychology class and do not wish to say anything about any larger population.

◆ *Formula 2* is used for obtaining the standard deviation of values from a sample which constitutes part of a total population which you wish to say something about. This formula gives you an estimate of the standard deviation of the population – the difference between the two formulae allows for any sampling errors. It is most likely that you will need to use formula 2 since psychologists are most often interested in making inferences about a wider population.

A specimen calculation, using formula 2, is shown in Fig. 23.2. Notice that the formulae involve squaring values – the function of this is to remove any minus signs (remember that when you multiply a minus by a minus the result is a plus). Later in the calculation a square root is calculated, which serves to restore the original units of measurement.

The interpretation of a standard deviation value was introduced at AS level. In addition, knowing the standard deviation of a given sample of data allows us to calculate a standard score (also known as a *z score*) which is the number of standard deviations a given value is away from its mean. Once a standard score is known, then it is possible to calculate the proportion of individuals between that standard score and the mean (see Appendix 1 at the end of this chapter for an explanation and example).

Calculate the standard deviation of the following data:

85 86 94 95 96 107 108 108 109 112

These data could represent, for example, the psychology test scores of a sample of 10 students.

1 Calculate the mean of the data.

Mean = $\dfrac{85 + 86 + 94 + 95 + 96 + 107 + 108 + 108 + 109 + 112}{10}$

Mean = $\dfrac{1000}{10}$

Mean = 100

2 Place your data into the first column of a table organized as follows:

Psychology test scores	d	d^2
85	−15	225
86	−14	196
94	−6	36
95	−5	25
96	−4	16
107	7	49
108	8	64
108	8	64
109	9	81
112	12	144
		$\Sigma d^2 = 900$

3 Find the difference (d) between each of the values in the table and the mean (see d column in table above).

4 Square all the values of d (see d^2 column in table above).

5 Find the sum of all the values of d^2 (see Σd^2 above). $\Sigma d^2 = 900$.

6 Substitute in the formula: $s = \sqrt{\dfrac{\Sigma d^2}{N-1}}$

$s = \sqrt{\dfrac{900}{10-1}}$ $s = \sqrt{\dfrac{900}{9}}$

$s = \sqrt{100}$ $s = 10$

Figure 23.2
Calculation of the standard deviation (using formula 2)

Inferential statistics

Describing data in the ways covered at AS level are not the only statistical techniques available to the investigator. The use of *inferential statistics* enables a researcher to draw conclusions about the wider population from which a particular sample has been drawn. By using such inferential techniques, the researcher can, on the basis of data obtained from a particular sample, make statements of probability about the likelihood of obtaining a particular set of results by chance. Through such statements, reasoned conclusions can be reached by the researcher as to whether a null hypothesis can be retained or rejected, and following on from this, whether an alternative hypothesis may be accepted.

Activity 1: Understanding hypotheses

Write down what you understand by the terms null hypothesis and alternative hypothesis. Compare what you have written down with the explanation of these terms given in your AS level textbook.

Statistical significance

The concept of *statistical significance* is central to inferential statistics. A statistically significant result is one which is unlikely to have occurred through chance. In practice, we can never be 100 per cent certain that chance has not played a part. When, however, the likelihood of obtained results having occurred through chance is only slim, then researchers will prefer to reject their null hypothesis and accept their alternative hypothesis.

Level of significance

How do we know when to reject a null hypothesis and when to retain it? The answer to this question lies in the concept of *level of significance*, which can be defined as an arbitrary value used as a criterion for ascertaining whether a particular set of data differs from that which would be expected if only chance factors operate.

Significance levels may be written as percentages or in decimals. For example:

◆ The *5% level of significance* is also written as $p = 0.05$ (where p = the probability of the results being due to chance).

◆ The *1% level of significance* is also written as $p = 0.01$.

Be careful that you do not mix up the different ways of expressing levels of significance – a quite common error is for students to add a percentage symbol onto the end of a decimal version (e.g. $p = 0.05\%$ is a very different value to $p = 0.05$). In practice, the normal way of expressing significance levels is to use the symbol $\leq$, which means less than or equal to. Thus, for example, the expression $p \leq 0.05$ refers to achieving a significance level of at least 5% – i.e. the probability of results such as these occurring through chance is no greater than 0.05 (or 5%).

As mentioned earlier, the choice of significance level is largely arbitrary. However, the 5% level of significance is regarded as being the minimum level which is acceptable for deciding results are significant. If the 5% level of significance is achieved (i.e. $p \leq 0.05$), this means that the likelihood of the results obtained having occurred through chance is one in 20 or less (i.e. such results are likely to occur 5% or less of the time). When this level of significance is used in experimental research, we are stating that any difference between sets of scores is so large that it is unlikely to have arisen due to chance. The researcher will conclude that the results are unlikely to have occurred because the null hypothesis is true and, provided some other unwanted variable has not intervened, that they are due to the effects of the independent variable. The alternative hypothesis can, therefore, be accepted.

The 5% level of significance is by no means the only one which is used. Less stringent levels (such as 10%) are occasionally employed, but it is sometimes important that more stringent levels of statistical significance are used, e.g. when we need to be even more certain that the results obtained are not due to chance.

Activity 2: Levels of significance

Can you think of situations in which you would want to use more stringent levels of statistical significance?

More stringent levels of statistical significance are likely to be needed when a 5% risk of results occurring through chance would be unacceptable. Such a situation might be where harm might occur to participants as a result, for example, in some medical research. Examples of more stringent levels include the 1% level of significance (or $p \leq 0.01$), where the null hypothesis would only be rejected if the likelihood of the results obtained occurring through chance is 1% or less. Even more stringent levels are the 0.5% ($p \leq 0.005$) or 0.1% ($p \leq 0.001$).

Type I and Type II errors

Why has the 5% level of significance become the one which is conventionally used by psychologists? This significance level represents a reasonable balancing point between the chances of making a Type I error and a Type II error.

◆ A *Type I error* is said to occur when a null hypothesis is rejected when in fact it is true, and the likelihood of making such an error is equal to the level of significance employed. For example, at $p \leq 0.05$ the risk of making a Type I error is one in twenty or less. This type of error can occur when an insufficiently stringent significance level is adopted.

◆ A *Type II error* occurs when a null hypothesis is retained when in fact it is false, i.e. there is a failure to detect a difference or relationship that is really there. This can occur when significance levels are made too stringent.

It is often considered preferable to run a higher risk of making a Type II error rather than make a Type I error, because it is better scientific practice to err on the side of caution. Before reading on, try Activity 3.

If you used a 10% level of significance, you would be more likely to make a Type I error. You would be rejecting your null hypothesis if the likelihood of results such as these occurring through chance was 10% or less. If you used a 1% level of significance, a Type II error would be more likely, as the null hypothesis

---

Activity 3: Understanding Type I and Type II errors

What type of error would you be more likely to make if you were to use the following levels of significance instead of the 5% level ($p \leq 0.05$)?

◆ a 10% level of significance ($p \leq 0.1$)
◆ a 1% level of significance ($p \leq 0.01$)

---

would be rejected only if you were at least 99% certain that results obtained were not due to chance.

Using and interpreting inferential statistical tests

In order to obtain the probability level of a particular set of results occurring through chance, we need to select and apply an appropriate *inferential statistical test*. To select the correct test, we need to know the answers to certain questions concerning the nature of the data obtained (see *In Focus*, 'Selecting a statistical test'). These questions concern whether data are being tested for differences, relationships or associations, the level of measurement of the data and the design of the study. Look back at the *In Focus* on p. 574 if you need to refresh your memory of levels of measurement and at your AS level textbook for information on different experimental designs.

---

in focus

Selecting a statistical test

The following table shows the factors involved in choosing the correct statistical test.

Level of measurement	Two sample tests of difference		Two sample tests of correlation
	Independent data	*Related data*	
Nominal	Chi-squared Test for Independent Samples (χ^2) (see p. 579)	Sign Test (see p. 582)	—
Ordinal, interval or ratio	Mann-Whitney U Test (see p. 578)	Wilcoxon Matched Pairs Signed Ranks Test (see p. 581)	Spearman's Rank Order Correlation Coefficient (r_s) (p. 583)

More powerful tests may be used when data are measured on an interval or ratio scale and certain other requirements are met. These tests include t tests and Pearson's Product Moment Correlation Coefficient. These are beyond the requirements of the AQA A-level specification, but if you would like to find out more about the alternatives, you are directed to more detailed texts, such as those by Coolican (1999) and Dyer (1995) (see 'Further resources' at the end of the chapter).

The Mann-Whitney U Test

The Mann-Whitney U Test is a *test of difference* that is suitable for use with independent data. It can be used when at least an ordinal level of measurement has been achieved. It can therefore be used with data on an interval or ratio level of measurement which is converted to an ordinal level for the purposes of the test. Two versions of this test will be discussed here. The first is used when the larger of the two samples under investigation contains no more than twenty observations or when the size of each sample is equal, with up to a maximum of twenty observations in each. (See your AS level textbook for information about independent data and *In Focus* p. 574 for a discussion of levels of measurement.)

Specimen calculation

Below is a specimen calculation of the Mann Whitney U test (where there are no more than twenty observations in each condition), using data obtained from a memory experiment.

	Condition 1			Condition 2	
Participant no.	*No. of words recalled (control condition)*	*Rank order*	*Participant no.*	*No. of words recalled (experimental condition)*	*Rank order*
1	7	2	10	20	19
2	6	1	11	14	11
3	8	3.5	12	14	11
4	12	8	13	18	17
5	9	5	14	15	13
6	14	11	15	17	16
7	8	3.5	16	13	9
8	11	7	17	16	14.5
9	10	6	18	19	18
			19	16	14.5
		47 = Σ ranks for Condition 1	(Σ = sum of)		

1 Place the data to be analysed into the appropriate columns of a table drawn up in a similar way to the one shown.

2 Rank the data, from the lowest value (allocated rank one) to the highest value (rank N). *Notice that both data sets are ranked in a single sequence and that the ranks are shared for any scores which are the same.*

See Appendix 2 for how to rank your data.

3 Calculate the sum of the ranks for the smaller of the two samples and call this value T. If both samples contain the same number of observations, calculate the sum of the ranks for either sample.

In the example provided, $T = 47$.

4 Substitute in the following formula:

$$U = N_1 N_2 + \frac{N_1 (N_1 + 1)}{2} - T$$

Here, U = the observed (i.e. the calculated) value of the Mann-Whitney statistic.

N_1 = the number of values in the smaller sample (or in the sample for which the sum of the ranks has been calculated if both are the same size).

N_2 = the number of values in the larger sample (or in the sample for which the sum of the ranks has not been calculated if both are the same size).

Here, $U = (9 \times 10) + \dfrac{9(9 + 1)}{2} - 47$

$U = 90 + \dfrac{90}{2} - 47$

$U = 90 + 45 - 47 = 88$

$U = 88$. This is the observed value of U.

5 Substitute in the following formula:

$U' = N_1 N_2 - U$

Here, $U' = (9 \times 10) - 88$

$U' = 90 - 88$

$U' = 2$. This is the observed value of U'.

6 Select the smaller value of U and U'. In this example, U' has the smaller value of 2. Whichever is the smallest value becomes the value of U.

7 Consult the table in Appendix 3 to obtain the critical values of U (a critical value of U is the maximum value of U that is significant at a given level of significance). (Statistical significance is discussed earlier in this chapter.) In order to obtain this you need to know:

(a) The values of N_1 and N_2 (in this case 9 and 10 respectively)

(b) Whether a one-tailed or two-tailed test is required (in this case, let us assume a one-tailed test).

(The concept of directional and non-directional hypotheses is covered in AS Module 3.)

Take the smaller of the observed values of U and U'. In this case the smaller is U', which = 2. If this value is equal to or less than the critical value for a given level of significance, the null hypothesis can be rejected.

(Levels of significance are discussed on p. 576. Null and alternative hypotheses are covered in AS Module 3.)

A minimum significance level of $p \leq 0.05$ will be assumed in this case. From Appendix 3, table 4, the critical value of U for $N_1 = 9$ and $N_2 = 10$ for a one-tailed test at $p = 0.05$ is 24. As the observed value of U (2) is less than the critical value (24) the probability of these results occurring through chance is less than 5%.

In this case, the null hypothesis could be rejected in favour of the alternative hypothesis.

Note: If the observed value had been greater than the critical value, then the probability of these results occurring through chance would have been greater than 5%. In this case the null hypothesis would not have been rejected.

Formula

The formula for the calculation of the Mann Whitney U test where one or more of the samples has more than twenty observations is shown below.

$$z = \frac{U - \dfrac{N_1 N_2}{2}}{\sqrt{\left(\left[\dfrac{N_1 N_2}{N(N-1)} \right] \times \left[\dfrac{N^3 - N}{12} - \Sigma T \right] \right)}}$$

This formula provides the researcher with a z score. (See Appendix 1 for how to interpret z scores.)

The Chi-squared Test for Independent Samples (χ^2)

The Chi-squared Test for Independent Samples (χ^2) is a *test of association* for use with independent data which are measured at a nominal level (in the form of frequencies). It tests for differences by examining the association which exists between data categorized into rows and columns. It compares observed frequencies (those actually obtained) with expected frequencies (the average frequencies which would be observed if the null hypothesis were true). (See *In Focus*, p. 574 for a discussion of levels of measurement and your AS level textbook for information about the null hypothesis.)

You need to be aware of some cautions on the use of the Chi-squared test:

◆ The Chi-squared test should only be employed in situations where each observation is included in one category only. No overlap between categories is permissible.

◆ The observations used in the test must be actual frequencies of occurrence. Data such as averages, percentages or proportions should not be used.

◆ No individual participant should contribute more than one unit to a category. An exception to this is where all data relate to the same participant.

◆ The probability of making a type one error is increased when there are expected frequencies of less than 5, especially when the total sample size is small (i.e. less than 20). It is, however, possible to employ the Chi-squared test in such situations, although the potential for error increases with very small samples or an increase in the number of expected frequencies less than 5. This potential problem can be minimized by the use of a larger sample size. (Type one errors are discussed earlier in this chapter.)

Specimen calculation

Below is a specimen calculation of the Chi-squared Test for Independent Samples using data from an investigation into children's thinking.

1 Place the observed values to be analysed into the appropriate boxes of a table drawn up in a similar way to the table shown at the top of the next page. This kind of table is called a contingency table – in this case it is a 2 × 2 contingency table as there are two rows of data and two columns. Other numbers of rows and columns are possible using this same test.

	No. of children able to solve problem	No. of children unable to solve problem	Row total
4-year-old children	Cell 1 8	Cell 2 12	RT1 20
5-year-old children	Cell 3 17	Cell 4 3	RT2 20
Column total	CT1 25	CT2 15	GT 40

where   RT1 and RT2 are row totals,
CT1 and CT2 are column totals and
GT is the grand total.

2 Calculate the expected frequency for each cell, using the formula:

$$\text{Expected frequency } (E) = \frac{RT \times CT}{GT}$$

For cell 1: $E = \dfrac{20 \times 25}{40} = \dfrac{500}{40} = 12.5$

For cell 2: $E = \dfrac{20 \times 15}{40} = \dfrac{300}{40} = 7.5$

For cell 3: $E = \dfrac{20 \times 25}{40} = \dfrac{500}{40} = 12.5$

For cell 4: $E = \dfrac{20 \times 15}{40} = \dfrac{300}{40} = 7.5$

3 Subtract the expected frequency (E) from the observed frequency (O) for each cell:

Cell 1: $O - E = 8 - 12.5 = -4.5$
Cell 2: $O - E = 12 - 7.5 = 4.5$
Cell 3: $O - E = 17 - 12.5 = 4.5$
Cell 4: $O - E = 3 - 7.5 = -4.5$

4 Calculate $(O - E)^2$ for each cell:

Cell 1: $-4.5^2 = 20.25$
Cell 2: $4.5^2 = 20.25$
Cell 3: $4.5^2 = 20.25$
Cell 4: $-4.5^2 = 20.25$

5 Calculate $\dfrac{(O - E)^2}{E}$ for each cell:

Cell 1: $20.25 \div 12.5 = 1.62$
Cell 2: $20.25 \div 7.5 = 2.7$
Cell 3: $20.25 \div 12.5 = 1.62$
Cell 4: $20.25 \div 7.5 = 2.7$

6 Add the answers to stage 5 to obtain the observed value of χ^2:

$1.62 + 2.7 + 1.62 + 2.7 = 8.64$.

This is the observed value of χ^2.

Note: Stages 2 to 6 can be represented by the following formula:

$$\chi^2 = \sum \left(\frac{(O - E)^2}{E} \right)$$

7 Calculate the number of degrees of freedom using the formula:

Degrees of freedom (df)
= (No. of rows – 1) (No. of columns – 1).

(Degrees of freedom are the number of cell values which are free to vary, given that row totals and column totals are known.)

In the example above

$df = (2 - 1)(2 - 1)$

$df = 1$.

8 Consult the table in Appendix 4 to obtain the critical values of χ^2 (a critical value of χ^2 is the minimum value of χ^2 that is significant at a given level of significance). (Statistical significance is discussed earlier in this chapter.) In order to obtain this you need to know:

(a) the number of degrees of freedom (in this case $df = 1$).

(b) whether a one-tailed test or two-tailed test is required.

You should note that a one-tailed test should only be employed with a 2 × 1 contingency table and a directional hypothesis. Directional hypotheses and non-directional hypotheses are covered in AS Module 3.

If the observed value of χ^2 is equal to or greater than the critical value for a given level of significance, the null hypothesis can be rejected. (Levels of significance are discussed on p. 576; null and alternative hypotheses are covered in AS Module 3.)

A minimum significance level of $p \leq 0.05$ will be assumed in this case. From Appendix 4, the critical value of χ^2 for $df = 1$ and a two-tailed test at $p = 0.05$ is 3.84. As the observed value of χ^2 (8.64) is greater than the critical value (3.84) the likelihood of these results occurring through chance is less than 5%.

In this case, the null hypothesis could be rejected in favour of the alternative hypothesis.

Note: If the observed value had been less than the critical value then the probability of results such as these occurring through chance would have been greater than 5%. In this case, the null hypothesis would not have been rejected.

The Wilcoxon Matched Pairs Signed Ranks Test

The Wilcoxon Matched Pairs Signed Ranks Test is a *test of difference* that is suitable for use with related data. It can be used when at least an ordinal level of measurement has been achieved. It can therefore be used with data on an interval or ratio level of measurement which is converted to an ordinal level for the purposes of the test. Two versions of this test will be discussed here. The first is used when there is a maximum of 25 pairs of observations. (See your AS level textbook for information about independent data, and the *In Focus* on p. 574 for a discussion of levels of measurement.)

Specimen calculation

Below is a specimen calculation of the Wilcoxon Matched Pairs Signed Ranks Test where there is a maximum of 25 pairs of observations, using data obtained from a memory experiment.

Participant no.	No. of words recalled (control condition)	No. of words recalled (experimental condition)	Difference	Rank order
1	17	20	−3	4
2	12	14	−2	2.5
3	16	14	+2	2.5
4	12	19	−7	9
5	16	15	+1	1
6	14	19	−5	6
7	13	13	0	(omitted)
8	11	16	−5	6
9	13	19	−6	8
10	11	16	−5	6

1 Place the data to be analysed into the appropriate columns of a table drawn up in a similar way to that in the table, which represents the data obtained from a memory experiment.

2 Calculate the difference between each pair of scores (see the 'Difference' column in the table). Note that it is essential that the direction of any differences is recorded.

3 Rank the data in the difference column, from the lowest value (allocated rank one) to the highest value (rank N). Notice that:

(a) any zero differences are disregarded

(b) positive and negative signs are disregarded

(c) the ranks are shared for any scores which are tied.

(See Appendix 2, p. 589, for how to rank your data.)

4 Calculate the sum of the ranks which correspond to:

(a) the differences with the + sign, and

(b) the differences with the − sign.

Call the smaller of these values T. In the example provided:

Sum of the ranks which correspond to the differences with the + sign = 2.5 + 1 = 3.5.

Sum of the ranks which correspond to the differences with the − sign
$$= 4 + 2.5 + 9 + 6 + 6 + 8 + 6 = 41.5$$

The smallest sum of ranks is T.

Therefore, the observed value of $T = 3.5$.

5 Consult the table in Appendix 5 to obtain the critical values of T (a critical value is the maximum value of T that is significant at a given level of probability).

(Statistical significance is discussed earlier in this chapter.)

In order to obtain this you need to know:

(a) The value of N (the number of pairs of scores). NB. Note that pairs of scores with a difference of zero are not included. In this example, the number of pairs of scores = 9.

(b) Whether a one-tailed or two-tailed test is required. In this example, let us assume two-tailed.

(The concept of directional and non-directional hypotheses is covered in AS Module 3.)

If the observed value of T is equal to or less than the critical value for a given level of significance, the null hypothesis can be rejected. (Null and alternative hypotheses are covered in AS Module 3.)

A minimum significance level of $p \le 0.05$ will be assumed in this case. From Appendix 5, the critical value of T for $N = 9$ for a two-tailed test at $p = 0.05$ is 5. As the observed value of T (3.5) is less than the critical value (5) the likelihood of the results occurring through chance is less than 5%.

In this case, the null hypothesis could be rejected in favour of the alternative hypothesis.

Note: If the observed value had been greater than the critical value, then the likelihood of results such as these occurring through chance would have been greater than 5%. In this case the null hypothesis would not have been rejected.

Formula

The formula for the calculation of the Wilcoxon Matched Pairs Signed Ranks Test when there are more than 25 pairs of scores is given below:

$$z = \frac{N(N+1) - 4T}{\sqrt{\left(\dfrac{2N(N+1)(2N+1)}{3}\right)}}$$

This formula provides the researcher with a z score (see Appendix 1).

The Sign Test

The Sign Test is a test of difference that is suitable for use with related data, which is measured at a nominal level of measurement. The test examines the direction of any difference between pairs of scores.

1 The example that follows uses data obtained from an investigation which set out to discover whether the perceptions of psychology held by students changed after following a GCSE psychology course. Place the data to be analysed into the appropriate columns of a table drawn up in a similar way to that in the table that follows.

Participant no.	Attitude	Direction of difference
1	More favourable	+
2	More favourable	+
3	No change	omitted
4	Less favourable	−
5	More favourable	+
6	More favourable	+
7	More favourable	+
8	No change	omitted
9	More favourable	+
10	More favourable	+

Note: It is perfectly possible to derive the direction of difference from numerical values (e.g. if actual ratings had been used in the example above, before and after taking a GCSE psychology course).

2 Enter a plus sign or a minus sign to indicate the direction of difference for each participant (see direction of difference column in the table above).

3 Add the number of times the less frequent sign occurs, and call this s. In the example above, the less frequent sign is the minus sign, which occurs once. Therefore the observed value of $s = 1$.

4 Consult the table in Appendix 6 to obtain the critical values of s. A critical value is the maximum value of s that is significant at a given level of probability. In order to obtain this you need to know:

(a) The value of N (the number of pairs of scores).

Note that pairs of scores with no + or − sign are not included. In this case, the number of pairs of scores = 8.

(b) Whether a one-tailed or two-tailed test is required (in this case, let us assume two-tailed). (The concept of directional and non-directional hypotheses is covered in AS Module 3.)

If the observed value of s is equal to or less than the critical value for a given level of significance, the null hypothesis can be rejected. (Null and alternative hypotheses are covered in AS Module 3.)

A minimum significance level of $p \leq 0.05$ will be assumed in this case. From Appendix 6, the critical value of s for $N = 8$ for a two-tailed hypothesis at $p = 0.05$ is 0. As the observed value of s (1) is greater than the critical value (0), the probability of results such as these occurring through chance is greater than 5%. In this case, the null hypothesis cannot be rejected.

Note: If the observed value had been less than or equal to the critical value, then the likelihood of results such as these occurring through chance would have been less than 5%. In this case the null hypothesis would have been rejected.

Spearman's Rank Order Correlation Coefficient (r_s)

Spearman's Rank Order Correlation Coefficient (r_s) is a *test of correlation* that is suitable for use with pairs of scores. It can be used when at least an ordinal level of measurement has been achieved. It can therefore be used with data on an interval or ratio level of measurement which is converted to an ordinal level for the purposes of the test.

The example below uses data obtained from an investigation which set out to investigate the possible correlation between psychology test scores and biology test scores from a group of participants studying both subjects.

Participant no.	Psychology test score	Rank order	Biology test score	Rank order	d	d^2
1	95	10	92	9	1	1
2	27	2	36	2	0	0
3	47	4	40	3	1	1
4	68	7	57	5	2	4
5	50	5	61	6	−1	1
6	94	9	91	8	1	1
7	33	3	41	4	−1	1
8	26	1	35	1	0	0
9	93	8	93	10	−2	4
10	59	6	70	7	−1	1
						$\Sigma d^2 = 14$

1 Draw a scattergraph of the data sets that you wish to correlate. This is important as this technique measures only straight-line relationships, and drawing a scattergraph can help you to decide if this is the case.

2 Place the data to be analysed into the appropriate columns of a table drawn up in a similar way to that in the table.

3 Rank each set of scores separately, giving the lowest score rank 1 and the highest score rank N.

Note: Accuracy is diminished if this test is used when ranks are shared for any scores which are tied. In such cases, the appropriate procedure is to carry out the calculation for Pearson's Product-moment Correlation Coefficient on the two sets of ranks. This test is covered in more advanced texts such as Coolican 1999 and Dyer 1995) However, unless

there are large numbers of ties, the effects on the outcome are likely to be very small.

(If the test is carried out where ranks are tied, then see Appendix 2, for how to rank your data.)

4 Find the difference (d) between each pair of rank order scores (see d column in above table).

5 Square each of the d values (see d^2 column in above table).

6 Calculate the sum of the d^2 values. This is the value described as Σd^2 in the above table. (The symbol Σ means 'sum of'.)

7 Substitute in the following formula:

$$r_s = 1 - \left(\frac{6\Sigma d^2}{N(N^2 - 1)} \right)$$

Here, r_s = the observed (i.e. calculated) value of Spearman's correlation coefficient

Σd^2 = the sum of the squared differences

N = the number of pairs of scores being correlated.

Here:

$$r_s = 1 - \left(\frac{84}{10(100-1)} \right)$$

$$= 1 - \left(\frac{84}{10 \times 99} \right)$$

$$= 1 - \frac{84}{990}$$

$$= 1 - 0.0848$$

$$= 0.9152$$

This is the observed value of r_s.

8 Consult the table in Appendix 7 to obtain the critical values of r_s (a critical value is the minimum value of r_s that is significant at a given level of probability). In order to obtain this you need to know:

(a) the value of N (the number of pairs of scores)

(b) whether a one-tailed or two-tailed test is required (in this case, let us assume one-tailed).

(The concept of directional and non-directional hypotheses is covered in AS Module 3.)

If the observed value of r_s is equal to or greater than the critical value for a given level of significance, the null hypothesis can be rejected. (Null and alternative hypotheses are covered in AS Module 3.)

A minimum significance level of $p \leq 0.05$ will be assumed in this case. From Appendix 7, when $N = 10$, the critical value of r_s for a one-tailed hypothesis at $p = 0.05$ is 0.564. As the observed value of r_s (0.9152) is greater than the critical value (0.564), the likelihood of results such as these occurring through chance is less than 5%. In this case, the null hypothesis can be rejected.

Note: If the observed value had been less than the critical value, then the likelihood of results such as these occurring through chance would have been greater than 5%. In this case the null hypothesis would not have been rejected.

Summary: Inferential statistics

Inferential statistical techniques enable researchers to draw conclusions about the populations from which their samples have been drawn. By using these techniques, the researcher may reach reasoned conclusions concerning whether to retain or reject their null hypotheses. Reaching these conclusions is based on the probability of such results occurring through chance.

The decision concerning which inferential statistical test to use is based on factors which include the level of measurement of the data, whether data are related or independent, and whether the researcher seeks to establish a difference, correlation or association.

Chapter summary

◆ The **standard deviation** is a measure of dispersion suitable for use with normally distributed data that are at an ordinal or ratio level of measurement. Calculation allows us to make statements of probability about how likely (or unlikely) a given value is to occur.

◆ **Inferential statistical techniques** enable researchers to draw conclusions about the **populations** from which their samples have been drawn. By using these techniques, the researcher may reach reasoned conclusions concerning whether to retain or reject their **null hypotheses.** Reaching these conclusions is based on the probability of such results occurring through chance. The decision concerning which inferential

statistical test to use is based on factors which include the **level of measurement** of the data, whether data are **related** or **independent**, and whether the researcher seeks to establish a **difference, correlation** or **association**.

◆ **Significance levels** are used as criteria for ascertaining whether a particular set of data differs from what would be expected if chance factors operated.

◆ **Inferential statistical tests** can be used to calculate the **probability level** of the obtained results occurring by chance. Tests may measure **differences**, **associations** or **correlations** between sets of data.

Further resources

Coolican, H. (1999) *Research Methods and Statistics in Psychology*, London: Hodder & Stoughton.

> *A clearly written text that covers the inferential statistical techniques that you are likely to encounter.*

Coolican, H. (1995) *Introduction to Research Methods and Statistics in Psychology*, London: Hodder & Stoughton.

> *A condensed version of the Coolican text above.*

Dyer, C. (1995) *Beginning Research in Psychology: A Practical Guide to Research Methods and Statistics*, Oxford: Blackwell.

> *A detailed text which covers the statistical tests included in this chapter.*

Foster, J.J. and Parker, I. (1995) *Carrying out Investigations in Psychology: Methods and Statistics*, Leicester: BPS Books.

> *A detailed and advanced text which is of use for reference purposes.*

Searle, A. (1999) *Introducing Research and Data in Psychology*, London: Routledge.

> *Contains a user-friendly introduction to statistical methods.*

Appendix 1: Standard scores

The table provided below gives the area beneath the normal distribution curve between the mean and any given standard score (i.e. *z* score). These values are therefore also the probabilities of finding a value within the area concerned.

◆ Column A gives the positive z score.

◆ Column B gives the area between the mean and *z* (see diagram below left). Since the curve is symmetrical, areas for negative *z* scores are the same as for positive ones.

◆ Column C gives the area that is beyond *z* (see diagram below right).

To find the proportion of individuals between a given standard score and the mean:

1 Calculate the mean and the standard deviation for the sample concerned.

2 Calculate the standard score (or *z* score, i.e. the number of standard deviations a given score is away from its mean). For example, if a sample of test scores has a mean of 100 and a standard deviation of 10, then a test score of 80 would have a standard score of 2 (two standard deviations below the mean). Similarly, a test score of 107 would have a standard score of 0.7 (and so on).

3 Look up this standard score in the left-hand column of the table (Column A) and read off the corresponding value in Column B. This is the probability of a score occurring between the mean and the standard score.

4 If a percentage is required, the value obtained should be multiplied by 100. If a probability is required for a score occurring between the same number of standard scores either side of the mean, then the value obtained should be doubled.

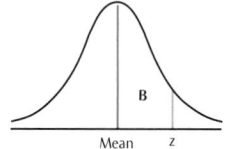

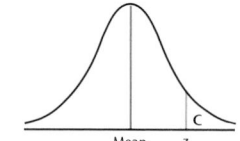

Areas under the normal distribution

A z	B Area between mean and z	C Area beyond z	A z	B Area between mean and z	C Area beyond z	A z	B Area between mean and z	C Area beyond z
0.00	.0000	.5000	0.20	.0793	.4207	0.40	.1554	.3446
0.01	.0040	.4960	0.21	.0832	.4168	0.41	.1591	.3409
0.02	.0080	.4920	0.22	.0871	.4129	0.42	.1628	.3372
0.03	.0120	.4880	0.23	.0910	.4090	0.43	.1664	.3336
0.04	.0160	.4840	0.24	.0948	.4052	0.44	.1700	.3300
0.05	.0199	.4801	0.25	.0987	.4013	0.45	.1736	.3264
0.06	.0239	.4761	0.26	.1026	.3974	0.46	.1772	.3228
0.07	.0279	.4721	0.27	.1064	.3936	0.47	.1808	.3192
0.08	.0319	.4681	0.28	.1103	.3897	0.48	.1844	.3156
0.09	.0359	.4641	0.29	.1141	.3859	0.49	.1879	.3121
0.10	.0398	.4602	0.30	.1179	.3821	0.50	.1915	.3085
0.11	.0438	.4562	0.31	.1217	.3783	0.51	.1950	.3050
0.12	.0478	.4522	0.32	.1255	.3745	0.52	.1985	.3015
0.13	.0517	.4483	0.33	.1293	.3707	0.53	.2019	.2981
0.14	.0557	.4443	0.34	.1331	.3669	0.54	.2054	.2946
0.15	.0596	.4404	0.35	.1368	.3632	0.55	.2088	.2912
0.16	.0636	.4364	0.36	.1406	.3594	0.56	.2123	.2877
0.17	.0675	.4325	0.37	.1443	.3557	0.57	.2157	.2843
0.18	.0714	.4286	0.38	.1480	.3520	0.58	.2190	.2810
0.19	.0753	.4247	0.39	.1517	.3483	0.59	.2224	.2776

A z	B Area between mean and z	C Area beyond z	A z	B Area between mean and z	C Area beyond z	A z	B Area between mean and z	C Area beyond z
0.60	.2257	.2743	1.05	.3531	.1469	1.50	.4332	.0668
0.61	.2291	.2709	1.06	.3554	.1446	1.51	.4345	.0655
0.62	.2324	.2676	1.07	.3577	.1423	1.52	.4357	.0643
0.63	.2357	.2643	1.08	.3599	.1401	1.53	.4370	.0630
0.64	.2389	.2611	1.09	.3621	.1379	1.54	.4372	.0618
0.65	.2422	.2578	1.10	.3643	.1357	1.55	.4394	.0606
0.66	.2454	.2546	1.11	.3665	.1335	1.56	.4406	.0594
0.67	.2486	.2514	1.12	.3686	.1314	1.57	.4418	.0582
0.68	.2517	.2483	1.13	.3708	.1292	1.58	.4429	.0571
0.69	.2549	.2451	1.14	.3729	.1271	1.59	.4441	.0559
0.70	.2580	.2420	1.15	.3749	.1251	1.60	.4452	.0548
0.71	.2611	.2389	1.16	.3770	.1230	1.61	.4463	.0537
0.72	.2642	.2358	1.17	.3790	.1210	1.62	.4474	.0526
0.73	.2673	.2327	1.18	.3810	.1190	1.63	.4484	.0516
0.74	.2704	.2296	1.19	.3830	.1170	1.64	.4495	.0505
0.75	.2734	.2266	1.20	.3849	.1151	1.65	.4505	.0495
0.76	.2764	.2236	1.21	.3869	.1131	1.66	.4515	.0485
0.77	.2794	.2206	1.22	.3888	.1112	1.67	.4525	.0475
0.78	.2823	.2177	1.23	.3907	.1093	1.68	.4535	.0465
0.79	.2852	.2148	1.24	.3925	.1075	1.69	.4545	.0455
0.80	.2881	.2119	1.25	.3944	.1056	1.70	.4554	.0446
0.81	.2910	.2090	1.26	.3962	.1038	1.71	.4564	.0436
0.82	.2939	.2061	1.27	.3980	.1020	1.72	.4573	.0427
0.83	.2967	.2033	1.28	.3997	.1003	1.73	.4582	.0418
0.84	.2995	.2005	1.29	.4015	.0985	1.74	.4591	.0409
0.85	.3023	.1977	1.30	.4032	.0968	1.75	.4599	.0401
0.86	.3051	.1949	1.31	.4049	.0951	1.76	.4608	.0392
0.87	.3078	.1922	1.32	.4066	.0934	1.77	.4616	.0384
0.88	.3106	.1894	1.33	.4082	.0918	1.78	.4625	.0375
0.89	.3133	.1867	1.34	.4099	.0901	1.79	.4633	.0367
0.90	.3159	.1841	1.35	.4115	.0885	1.80	.4641	.0359
0.91	.3186	.1814	1.36	.4131	.0869	1.81	.4649	.0351
0.92	.3212	.1788	1.37	.4147	.0853	1.82	.4656	.0344
0.93	.3238	.1762	1.38	.4162	.0838	1.83	.4664	.0336
0.94	.3264	.1736	1.39	.4177	.0823	1.84	.4671	.0329
0.95	.3289	.1711	1.40	.4192	.0808	1.85	.4678	.0322
0.96	.3315	.1685	1.41	.4207	.0793	1.86	.4686	.0314
0.97	.3340	.1660	1.42	.4222	.0778	1.87	.4693	.0307
0.98	.3365	.1635	1.43	.4236	.0764	1.88	.4699	.0301
0.99	.3389	.1611	1.44	.4251	.0749	1.89	.4706	.0294
1.00	.3413	.1587	1.45	.4265	.0735	1.90	.4713	.0287
1.01	.3438	.1562	1.46	.4279	.0721	1.91	.4719	.0281
1.02	.3461	.1539	1.47	.4292	.0708	1.92	.4726	.0274
1.03	.3485	.1515	1.48	.4306	.0694	1.93	.4732	.0268
1.04	.3508	.1492	1.49	.4319	.0681	1.94	.4738	.0262

A	B	C	A	B	C	A	B	C
z	Area between mean and z	Area beyond z	z	Area between mean and z	Area beyond z	z	Area between mean and z	Area beyond z
1.95	.4744	.0256	2.40	.4918	.0082	2.85	.4978	.0022
1.96	.4750	.0250	2.41	.4920	.0080	2.86	.4979	.0021
1.97	.4756	.0244	2.42	.4922	.0078	2.87	.4979	.0021
1.98	.4761	.0239	2.43	.4925	.0075	2.88	.4980	.0020
1.99	.4767	.0233	2.44	.4927	.0073	2.89	.4981	.0019
2.00	.4772	.0228	2.45	.4929	.0071	2.90	.4981	.0019
2.01	.4778	.0222	2.46	.4931	.0069	2.91	.4982	.0018
2.02	.4783	.0217	2.47	.4932	.0068	2.92	.4982	.0018
2.03	.4788	.0212	2.48	.4934	.0066	2.93	.4983	.0017
2.04	.4793	.0207	2.49	.4936	.0064	2.94	.4984	.0016
2.05	.4798	.0202	2.50	.4938	.0062	2.95	.4984	.0016
2.06	.4803	.0197	2.51	.4940	.0060	2.96	.4985	.0015
2.07	.4808	.0192	2.52	.4941	.0059	2.97	.4985	.0015
2.08	.4812	.0188	2.53	.4943	.0057	2.98	.4986	.0014
2.09	.4817	.0183	2.54	.4945	.0055	2.99	.4986	.0014
2.10	.4821	.0179	2.55	.4946	.0054	3.00	.4987	.0013
2.11	.4826	.0174	2.56	.4948	.0052	3.01	.4987	.0013
2.12	.4830	.0170	2.57	.4949	.0051	3.02	.4987	.0013
2.13	.4834	.0166	2.58	.4951	.0049	3.03	.4988	.0012
2.14	.4838	.0162	2.59	.4952	.0048	3.04	.4988	.0012
2.15	.4842	.0158	2.60	.4953	.0047	3.05	.4989	.0011
2.16	.4846	.0154	2.61	.4955	.0045	3.06	.4989	.0011
2.17	.4850	.0150	2.62	.4956	.0044	3.07	.4989	.0011
2.18	.4854	.0146	2.63	.4957	.0043	3.08	.4990	.0010
2.19	.4857	.0143	2.64	.4959	.0041	3.09	.4990	.0010
2.20	.4861	.0139	2.65	.4960	.0040	3.10	.4990	.0010
2.21	.4864	.0136	2.66	.4961	.0039	3.11	.4991	.0009
2.22	.4868	.0132	2.67	.4962	.0038	3.12	.4991	.0009
2.23	.4871	.0129	2.68	.4963	.0037	3.13	.4991	.0009
2.24	.4875	.0125	2.69	.4964	.0036	3.14	.4992	.0008
2.25	.4878	.0122	2.70	.4965	.0035	3.15	.4992	.0008
2.26	.4881	.0119	2.71	.4966	.0034	3.16	.4992	.0008
2.27	.4884	.0116	2.72	.4967	.0033	3.17	.4992	.0008
2.28	.4887	.0113	2.73	.4968	.0032	3.18	.4993	.0007
2.29	.4890	.0110	2.74	.4969	.0031	3.19	.4993	.0007
2.30	.4893	.0107	2.75	.4970	.0030	3.20	.4993	.0007
2.31	.4896	.0104	2.76	.4971	.0029	3.21	.4993	.0007
2.32	.4898	.0102	2.77	.4972	.0028	3.22	.4994	.0006
2.33	.4901	.0099	2.78	.4973	.0027	3.23	.4994	.0006
2.34	.4904	.0096	2.79	.4974	.0026	3.24	.4994	.0006
2.35	.4906	.0094	2.80	.4974	.0026	3.30	.4995	.0005
2.36	.4909	.0091	2.81	.4975	.0025	3.40	.4997	.0003
2.37	.4911	.0089	2.82	.4976	.0024	3.50	.4998	.0002
2.38	.4913	.0087	2.83	.4977	.0023	3.60	.4998	.0002
2.39	.4916	.0084	2.84	.4977	.0023	3.70	.4999	.0001

Appendix 2: Method for ranking data in statistical tests

1 Organize data into ascending order of values (see specimen data below).

2 Allocate rank 1 to the lowest value.

3 Allocate ranks to the remaining values, averaging the ranks for any tied scores (see below).

Scores	Rank	Notes
10	1	
12	2.5	*Both scores of 12 are given the average rank of positions 2 and 3.*
12	2.5	*Note that the next score is rank 4, not 3.*
15	4	
17	5	
18	7	
18	7	*Three scores of 18 are given the average rank of positions 6, 7 and 8.*
18	7	*Note that the next score is rank 9, not 8.*
20	9	
25	10	

Appendix 3: The critical values of U

**Table 1: Critical values of U for a one-tailed test at $p = 0.005$;
two-tailed test at $p = 0.01^*$ (Mann-Whitney)**

N_2		1	2	3	4	5	6	7	8	9	10	11	12	13	14	15	16	17	18	19	20
	1	–	–	–	–	–	–	–	–	–	–	–	–	–	–	–	–	–	–	–	–
	2	–	–	–	–	–	–	–	–	–	–	–	–	–	–	–	–	–	–	0	0
	3	–	–	–	–	–	–	–	–	0	0	0	1	1	1	2	2	2	2	3	3
	4	–	–	–	–	–	0	0	1	1	2	2	3	3	4	5	5	6	6	7	8
	5	–	–	–	–	0	1	1	2	3	4	5	6	7	7	8	9	10	11	12	13
	6	–	–	–	0	1	2	3	4	5	6	7	9	10	11	12	13	15	16	17	18
	7	–	–	–	0	1	3	4	6	7	9	10	12	13	15	16	18	19	21	22	24
	8	–	–	–	1	2	4	6	7	9	11	13	15	17	18	20	22	24	26	28	30
	9	–	–	0	1	3	5	7	9	11	13	16	18	20	22	24	27	29	31	33	36
	10	–	–	0	2	4	6	9	11	13	16	18	21	24	26	29	31	34	37	39	42
	11	–	–	0	2	5	7	10	13	16	18	21	24	27	30	33	36	39	42	45	48
	12	–	–	1	3	6	9	12	15	18	21	24	27	31	34	37	41	44	47	51	54
	13	–	–	1	3	7	10	13	17	20	24	27	31	34	38	42	45	49	53	56	60
	14	–	–	1	4	7	11	15	18	22	26	30	34	38	42	46	50	54	58	63	67
	15	–	–	2	5	8	12	16	20	24	29	33	37	42	46	51	55	60	64	69	73
	16	–	–	2	5	9	13	18	22	27	31	36	41	45	50	55	60	65	70	74	79
	17	–	–	2	6	10	15	19	24	29	34	39	44	49	54	60	65	70	75	81	86
	18	–	–	2	6	11	16	21	26	31	37	42	47	53	58	64	70	75	81	87	92
	19	–	0	3	7	12	17	22	28	33	39	45	51	56	63	69	74	81	87	93	99
	20	–	0	3	8	13	18	24	30	36	42	48	54	60	67	73	79	86	92	99	105

N_1

Table 2: Critical values of U for a one-tailed test at $p = 0.01$; two-tailed test at $p = 0.02$* (Mann-Whitney)

	N_1																			
N_2	1	2	3	4	5	6	7	8	9	10	11	12	13	14	15	16	17	18	19	20
1	–	–	–	–	–	–	–	–	–	–	–	–	–	–	–	–	–	–	–	–
2	–	–	–	–	–	–	–	–	–	–	–	0	0	0	0	0	0	0	1	1
3	–	–	–	–	–	–	0	0	1	1	1	2	2	2	3	3	4	4	4	5
4	–	–	–	–	0	1	1	2	3	3	4	5	5	6	7	7	8	9	9	10
5	–	–	–	0	1	2	3	4	5	6	7	8	9	10	11	12	13	14	15	16
6	–	–	–	1	2	3	4	6	7	8	9	11	12	13	15	16	18	19	20	22
7	–	–	0	1	3	4	6	7	9	11	12	14	16	17	19	21	23	24	26	28
8	–	–	0	2	4	6	7	9	11	13	15	17	20	22	24	26	28	30	32	34
9	–	–	1	3	5	7	9	11	14	16	18	21	23	26	28	31	33	36	38	40
10	–	–	1	3	6	8	11	13	16	19	22	24	27	30	33	36	38	41	44	47
11	–	–	1	4	7	9	12	15	18	22	25	28	31	34	37	41	44	47	50	53
12	–	–	2	5	8	11	14	17	21	24	28	31	35	38	42	46	49	53	56	60
13	–	0	2	5	9	12	16	20	23	27	31	35	39	43	47	51	55	59	63	67
14	–	0	2	6	10	13	17	22	26	30	34	38	43	47	51	56	60	65	69	73
15	–	0	3	7	11	15	19	24	28	33	37	42	47	51	56	61	66	70	75	80
16	–	0	3	7	12	16	21	26	31	36	41	46	51	56	61	66	71	76	82	87
17	–	0	4	8	13	18	23	28	33	38	44	49	55	60	66	71	77	82	88	93
18	–	0	4	9	14	19	24	30	36	41	47	53	59	65	70	76	82	88	94	100
19	–	1	4	9	15	20	26	32	38	44	50	56	63	69	75	82	88	94	101	107
20	–	1	5	10	16	22	28	34	40	47	53	60	67	73	80	87	93	100	107	114

Table 3: Critical values of U for a one-tailed test at $p = 0.025$; two-tailed test at $p = 0.05$* (Mann-Whitney)

	N_1																			
N_2	1	2	3	4	5	6	7	8	9	10	11	12	13	14	15	16	17	18	19	20
1	–	–	–	–	–	–	–	–	–	–	–	–	–	–	–	–	–	–	–	–
2	–	–	–	–	–	–	–	0	0	0	0	1	1	1	1	1	2	2	2	2
3	–	–	–	–	0	1	1	2	2	3	3	4	4	5	5	6	6	7	7	8
4	–	–	–	0	1	2	3	4	4	5	6	7	8	9	10	11	11	12	13	13
5	–	–	0	1	2	3	5	6	7	8	9	11	12	13	14	15	17	18	19	20
6	–	–	1	2	3	5	6	8	10	11	13	14	16	17	19	21	22	24	25	27
7	–	–	1	3	5	6	8	10	12	14	16	18	20	22	24	26	28	30	32	34
8	–	0	2	4	6	8	10	13	15	17	19	22	24	26	29	31	34	36	38	41
9	–	0	2	4	7	10	12	15	17	20	23	26	28	31	34	37	39	42	45	48
10	–	0	3	5	8	11	14	17	20	23	26	29	33	36	39	42	45	48	52	55
11	–	0	3	6	9	13	16	19	23	26	30	33	37	40	44	47	51	55	58	62
12	–	1	4	7	11	14	18	22	26	29	33	37	41	45	49	53	57	61	65	69
13	–	1	4	8	12	16	20	24	28	33	37	41	45	50	54	59	63	67	72	76
14	–	1	5	9	13	17	22	26	31	36	40	45	50	55	59	64	67	74	78	83
15	–	1	5	10	14	19	24	29	34	39	44	49	54	59	64	70	76	80	85	90
16	–	1	6	11	15	21	26	31	37	42	47	53	59	64	70	75	81	86	92	98
17	–	2	6	11	17	22	28	34	39	45	51	57	63	67	75	81	87	93	99	105
18	–	2	7	12	18	24	30	36	42	48	55	61	67	74	80	86	93	99	106	112
19	–	2	7	13	19	25	32	38	45	52	58	65	72	78	85	92	99	106	113	119
20	–	2	8	13	20	27	34	41	48	55	62	69	76	83	90	98	105	112	119	127

**Table 4: Critical values of U for a one-tailed test at $p = 0.05$;
two-tailed test at $p = 0.10^*$ (Mann-Whitney)**

		N_1																		
		1	2	3	4	5	6	7	8	9	10	11	12	13	14	15	16	17	18	19	20
N_2	1	–	–	–	–	–	–	–	–	–	–	–	–	–	–	–	–	–	–	0	0
	2	–	–	–	–	0	0	0	1	1	1	1	2	2	2	3	3	3	4	4	4
	3	–	–	0	0	1	2	2	3	3	4	5	5	6	7	7	8	9	9	10	11
	4	–	–	0	1	2	3	4	5	6	7	8	9	10	11	12	14	15	16	17	18
	5	–	0	1	2	4	5	6	8	9	11	12	13	15	16	18	19	20	22	23	25
	6	–	0	2	3	5	7	8	10	12	14	16	17	19	21	23	25	26	28	30	32
	7	–	0	2	4	6	8	11	13	15	17	19	21	24	26	28	30	33	35	37	39
	8	–	1	3	5	8	10	13	15	18	20	23	26	28	31	33	36	39	41	44	47
	9	–	1	3	6	9	12	15	18	21	24	27	30	33	36	39	42	45	48	51	54
	10	–	1	4	7	11	14	17	20	24	27	31	34	37	41	44	48	51	55	58	62
	11	–	1	5	8	12	16	19	23	27	31	34	38	42	46	50	54	57	61	65	69
	12	–	2	5	9	13	17	21	26	30	34	38	42	47	51	55	60	64	68	72	77
	13	–	2	6	10	15	19	24	28	33	37	42	47	51	56	61	65	70	75	80	84
	14	–	2	7	11	16	21	26	31	36	41	46	51	56	61	66	71	77	82	87	92
	15	–	3	7	12	18	23	28	33	39	44	50	55	61	66	72	77	83	88	94	100
	16	–	3	8	14	19	25	30	36	42	48	54	60	65	71	77	83	89	95	101	107
	17	–	3	9	15	20	26	33	39	45	51	57	64	70	77	83	89	96	102	109	115
	18	–	4	9	16	22	28	35	41	48	55	61	68	75	82	88	95	102	109	116	123
	19	–	4	10	17	23	30	37	44	51	58	65	72	80	87	94	101	109	116	123	130
	20	–	4	11	18	25	32	39	47	54	62	69	77	84	92	100	107	115	123	130	138

* Dashes in the body of the table indicate that no
decision is possible at the stated level of
significance. For any N_1 and N_2, the observed value
of U is significant at a given level of significance if
it is equal to or less than the critical values shown.

Source: Runyon and Haber (1976)

Appendix 4: Critical values of χ^2

Level of significance for a one-tailed test

df	0.10	0.05	0.025	0.01	0.005	0.0005
1	1.64	2.71	3.84	5.41	6.64	10.83

Level of significance for a two-tailed test

df	0.20	0.10	0.05	0.02	0.01	0.001
1	1.64	2.71	3.84	5.41	6.64	10.83
2	3.22	4.60	5.99	7.82	9.21	13.82
3	4.64	6.25	7.82	9.84	11.34	16.27
4	5.99	7.78	9.49	11.67	13.28	18.46
5	7.29	9.24	11.07	13.39	15.09	20.52
6	8.56	10.64	12.59	15.03	16.81	22.46
7	9.80	12.02	14.07	16.62	18.48	24.32
8	11.03	13.36	15.51	18.17	20.09	26.12
9	12.24	14.68	16.92	19.68	21.67	27.88
10	13.44	15.99	18.31	21.16	23.21	29.59
11	14.63	17.28	19.68	22.62	24.72	31.26
12	15.81	18.55	21.03	24.05	26.22	32.91
13	16.98	19.81	22.36	25.47	27.69	34.53
14	18.15	21.06	23.68	26.87	29.14	36.12
15	19.31	22.31	25.00	28.26	30.58	37.70
16	20.46	23.54	26.30	29.63	32.00	39.29
17	21.62	24.77	27.59	31.00	33.41	40.75
18	22.76	25.99	28.87	32.35	34.80	42.31
19	23.90	27.20	30.14	33.69	36.19	43.82
20	25.04	28.41	31.41	35.02	37.57	45.32
21	26.17	29.62	32.67	36.34	38.93	46.80
22	27.30	30.81	33.92	37.66	40.29	48.27
23	28.43	32.01	35.17	38.97	41.64	49.73
24	29.55	33.20	36.42	40.27	42.98	51.18
25	30.68	34.38	37.65	41.57	44.31	52.62
26	31.80	35.56	38.88	42.86	45.64	54.05
27	32.91	36.74	40.11	44.14	46.96	55.48
28	34.03	37.92	41.34	45.42	48.28	56.89
29	35.14	39.09	42.69	46.69	49.59	58.30
30	36.25	40.26	43.77	47.96	50.89	59.70
32	38.47	42.59	46.19	50.49	53.49	62.49
34	40.68	44.90	48.60	53.00	56.06	65.25
36	42.88	47.21	51.00	55.49	58.62	67.99
38	45.08	49.51	53.38	57.97	61.16	70.70
40	47.27	51.81	55.76	60.44	63.69	73.40
44	51.64	56.37	60.48	65.48	68.71	78.75
48	55.99	60.91	65.17	70.20	73.68	84.04
52	60.33	65.42	69.83	75.02	78.62	89.27
56	64.66	69.92	74.47	79.82	83.51	94.46
60	68.97	74.40	79.08	84.58	88.38	99.61

Calculated value of χ^2 must **equal** or **exceed** the table (critical) values for significance at the level shown.

Source: abridged from Fisher and Yates (1974)

Appendix 5: Critical values of T for the Wilcoxon Matched Pairs Signed Ranks Test

Level of significance for a two-tailed test

0.10	0.05	0.02	0.01

Level of significance for one-tailed test

N	0.05	0.025	0.01	0.005
5	0			
6	2	0		
7	3	2	0	
8	5	3	1	0
9	8	5	3	1
10	10	8	5	3
11	13	10	7	5
12	17	13	9	7
13	21	17	12	9
14	25	21	15	12
15	30	25	19	15
16	35	29	23	19
17	41	34	27	23
18	47	40	32	27
19	53	46	37	32
20	60	52	43	37
21	67	58	49	42
22	75	65	55	48
23	83	73	62	54
24	91	81	69	61
25	100	89	76	68

Values of T that are equal to or less than the tabled value are significant at, or beyond, the level indicated.

Source: taken from Table 1 of McCormack (1965)
With permission of the publishers.

Appendix 6: Critical values of *s* in the Sign Test

Level of significance for one-tailed test

N	0.05	0.025	0.01	0.005	0.0005

Level of significance for two-tailed test

	0.10	0.05	0.02	0.01	0.001
5	0	–	–	–	–
6	0	0	–	–	–
7	0	0	0	–	–
8	1	0	0	0	–
9	1	1	0	0	–
10	1	1	0	0	–
11	2	1	1	0	0
12	2	2	1	1	0
13	3	2	1	1	0
14	3	2	2	1	0
15	3	3	2	2	1
16	4	3	2	2	1
17	4	4	3	2	1
18	5	4	3	3	1
19	5	4	4	3	2
20	5	5	4	3	2
25	7	7	6	5	4
30	10	9	8	7	5

The observed value of *s* is significant at a given level of significance
if it is equal to or less than the critical value shown.

Appendix 7: Critical values of Spearman's Rank Order Correlation Coefficient (r_s)

Level of significance for a two-tailed test

	0.10	0.05	0.02	0.01

Level of significance for one-tailed test

N	0.05	0.025	0.01	0.005
4	1.000			
5	.900	1.000	1.000	
6	.829	.886	.943	1.000
7	.714	.786	.893	.929
8	.643	.738	.833	.881
9	.600	.700	.783	.833
10	.564	.648	.745	.794
11	.536	.618	.709	.755
12	.503	.587	.671	.727
13	.484	.560	.648	.703
14	.464	.538	.622	.675
15	.443	.521	.604	.654
16	.429	.503	.582	.635
17	.414	.485	.566	.615
18	.401	.472	.550	.600
19	.391	.460	.535	.584
20	.380	.447	.520	.570
21	.370	.435	.508	.556
22	.361	.425	.496	.544
23	.353	.415	.486	.532
24	.344	.406	.476	.521
25	.337	.398	.466	.511
26	.331	.390	.457	.501
27	.324	.382	.448	.491
28	.317	.375	.440	.483
29	.312	.368	.433	.475
30	.306	.362	.425	.467

Values of r_s that equal or exceed the tabled value are significant at, or below the level indicated.

Source: Zar (1972)
With permission of the author and publisher.

A2

GLOSSARY

REFERENCES

CHECKLIST OF SYNOPTIC ISSUES

INDEX

Glossary

Ablation: surgical removal of brain tissue.

Abnormality: *see* **Psychological abnormality**.

Accommodation: the process of changing existing schemas when new information cannot be assimilated.

Action slips: a form of absent-mindedness where a person performs an action that was not intended; caused by not paying attention to what is going on.

Activity theory: proposition that individuals prefer to remain active and productive in later life, even resisting disengagement from society – contrasts with social disengagement theory.

Actor/observer biases (in attribution): these refer to the tendency for (a) actors to explain their own behaviour in situational terms and (b) observers to explain the behaviour of others in dispositional (person) terms.

Adaptation: a feature of an organism that has been shaped by natural selection so that it enhances the fitness of its possessor.

Adolescence: a transitional period of development between puberty and adulthood. The concept of a distinct developmental period of adolescence has often been seen as a Westernized phenomenon, with progression from childhood to adulthood in other cultures being more abrupt and marked by rituals and 'rites of passage'.

Adoption studies: investigations that compare correlations, e.g. of children's IQ scores with both their biological and adoptive parents.

Adrenocorticotropic hormone (ACTH): released by the anterior pituitary during stressful situations. ACTH, in turn, triggers the release of corticosteroids (another type of hormone). Corticosteroids produce many of the effects of the stress response.

Adulthood: the period when one has matured or grown to full size and strength. May be arbitrarily defined in the UK as the period between 16 or 18 years, and death.

Agency theory: theory developed by Milgram to explain why people obey orders that go against conscience. When people see themselves as mere agents of another person, they will obey that person's orders, feeling themselves free of individual responsibility.

Aggression: an action or a series of actions where the aim is to cause harm to another person or object.

Aims: when used in the context of psychological investigations, this refers to the general investigative purpose of the study.

Alpha/beta bias: alpha bias refers to theories and research which assume real and enduring differences between men and women. Sometimes alpha bias theories heighten the value of women, and sometimes they are used to devalue women. Beta bias theories and research have traditionally ignored or minimized differences between men and women. They have done this either by ignoring questions about the lives of women or by assuming that findings from studies of men apply equally well to women.

Altruism (animal): an animal is considered to be engaging in altruistic behaviour when by so doing it increases the survival chances of another animal whilst decreasing its own.

Altruism (human): as with animal altruism, this involves some cost to the altruist and some benefit to the recipient. Unlike animal altruism, there is often evidence of 'kindly intent' on the part of the altruist.

Anal stage: the second stage of psychosexual development (according to psychoanalytic theory) when the child's main source of pleasure is the anus and the expelling or withholding of faeces.

Analyse/Critically analyse: show understanding by examining the different components of a topic area.

Androcentrism: refers to the tendency of some theories to offer an interpretation of women based on an understanding of the lives of men (*see also* **Alpha/beta bias**).

Animal language: as an area of research, this refers to either (a) attempts

to teach nonhuman animals to speak, or (b) studies of animals' 'natural' language in their own natural environment.

Anorexia nervosa: (literally, a nervous loss of appetite) a disorder characterized by the pursuit of extreme thinness and by an extreme loss of weight.

Anticonformity: refers to behaviour carried out in order to oppose the norms of the group.

Antisocial behaviour: this is a general term used to refer to any behaviour that harms or offends another person. Common examples are aggression and discrimination.

Anxiety disorders: the most common of adult mental disorders, characterized by severe anxiety. Phobias are probably the most familiar of these disorders.

AO1 (Assessment Objective 1): the demonstration of knowledge and understanding through clear and effective communication.

AO2 (Assessment Objective 2): analysis and evaluation.

AO3 (Assessment Objective 3): design, conduct and report.

Applications: actual or possible ways of using psychological knowledge in an applied or practical setting.

Arousal: refers to the body's level of alertness and activation as reflected in certain physiological responses such as heart rate or muscle tension.

Assess/Critically assess: a considered appraisal of an area through a review of the strengths and weaknesses of the information presented.

Assimilation: the process of fitting new information into existing schemas.

Association areas: parts of the cortex that receive input from more than one sensory system.

Attachment: this refers to the result of a bonding process between two individuals (usually the mother and her offspring), characterized by mutual involvement and the desire to remain close to each other.

Attention: a focused concentration of mental activity (*see also* **Focused attention** and **Divided attention**).

Attenuation theory of attention: Treisman's proposal that, instead of selecting one channel and blocking the others, the filtering mechanism (a) selects one channel and passes it on for semantic analysis, and (b) allows the unattended channels through for processing but in weakened (attenuated) form.

Attribution (of causality): the way in which we infer the causes of our own or another person's behaviour according to a set of cognitive rules and biases. As a result of these strategies we decide whether a person's behaviour is caused by their own stable characteristics, or whether it is a result of situational influences.

Attributional biases: the tendency to depart from the normal rules of attribution and make biased attributions about the behaviour of others or ourselves.

Authoritarian personality: personality style strongly associated with prejudiced attitudes, where the person is intolerant of ambiguity or uncertainty, submissive to those in authority and dismissive or arrogant towards those perceived to be of lower social status.

Autokinetic effect: an optical illusion experienced when a person in a totally dark room sees a stationary spot of light appearing to move.

Automatic processing: a type of mental operation that is normally rapid; does not require conscious awareness; does not interfere with other mental activities; is usually a result of prolonged practice.

Autonomic nervous system (ANS): part of the nervous system that maintains the normal functioning of the body's inner environment. The ANS has two subdivisions: (a) the *sympathetic division* whose activity mobilizes energy resources and prepares the body for action, and (b) the *parasympathetic division* whose activity tends to conserve the body's energy resources and restore inner calm.

Availability heuristic: a rule of thumb used to make decisions about frequencies of events based on how easily relevant examples can be remembered – a cognitive short cut.

Aversion therapy: a behavioural treatment that aims to rid the individual of an undesirable habit (e.g. smoking) by pairing the habit with unpleasant (aversive) consequences.

Bar chart: a way of graphically representing scores on a discrete variable such as the number of cats in the UK belonging to different breeds.

Behavioural model of abnormality: the view that abnormal behaviours are maladaptive learned responses to the environment which can be replaced by more adaptive behaviours.

Behaviourism: one of the major orientations in psychology that concentrates on overt (observable) events rather than covert (unobservable) mental processing. Behaviours are seen as being acquired through the processes of learning.

Behaviour therapies: therapeutic techniques of changing behaviour that are based on the principles of classical conditioning. The term 'behaviour modification' is more usually used for techniques derived from operant conditioning.

Biofeedback: a technique that provides physiological feedback to a person about some bodily process (e.g. heart rate, muscle tension) of which the person is usually unaware.

Biological psychology: the study of the relationship between the physiological systems in the body and behaviour.

Biological rhythms: cycles of activity that occur with some regularity in an organism. *Infradian* rhythms occur less than once a day (e.g. human menstrual cycle), *circadian* rhythms repeat themselves every 24 hours (e.g. sleep/waking cycle), and *ultradian* rhythms more than once a day (e.g. stages of sleep during one night).

Biological (somatic) therapies: an approach to the treatment of mental disorders that relies on the use of physical or chemical methods.

Bipolar depression/disorder (manic depressive disorder): a mood disorder characterized by extremes of mania and depression.

Black English Vernacular (BEV): an English dialect spoken by Black people in both America and the UK, commonly referred to as 'Black English'.

Bonding: the process whereby the young of a species form a bond with their parent(s). In the bonding process, parents also bond with their offspring and thus safeguard them from abuse or abandonment.

Bottom-up processing: processing of information (stimulus) that is determined solely by aspects of the stimulus.

Broca's area: the area of the inferior prefrontal cortex of the left hemisphere of the brain, hypothesized by Broca to be the centre of speech production.

Buffers: term used in social influence research to refer to any aspect of a situation that protects people from having to confront the consequences of their actions.

Bulimia nervosa: characterized by secret binge eating followed by vomiting, misuse of laxatives, diuretics, excessive exercise, etc., in order to lose weight.

Bystander behaviour: the behaviour shown by those who witness an emergency. This is often referred to as 'bystander *apathy*' because of the tendency of bystanders to ignore the emergency when in the company of others.

Capacity models/ resource allocation models (of divided attention): those models proposing that we have a pool of processing resources that we can allocate according to the demands of the task and environmental factors.

Cardiovascular system: consists of two parts, the heart and the blood vessels. It is a system for distributing oxygen and nutrients to the organs in the body. Heart rate, blood pressure and local blood volume are three measures of cardiovascular activity commonly used in research by psychophysiologists.

CAT (computed axial tomography) scans: a noninvasive, multiple X-ray procedure for creating images of the brain.

Categorization: a short cut used when processing information. A category is a set of items perceived to have at least one feature in common. In interpersonal perception, categories such as young–old and male–female are used.

Central tendency: a single value which is representative of a set of numbers by indicating the most typical value. Three measures of central tendency are the *mean, median* and *mode*.

Cerebral cortex: an area of the brain resembling a folded sheet of grey tissue that covers the rest of the brain. It is associated with 'higher functions', such as language and reasoning.

Chemotherapy: treatment by using drugs.

Chi-square test: an inferential test of association for independent data at a nominal level.

Chunking: combining individual letters or numbers into larger meaningful units.

Circadian rhythms: *see* **Biological rhythms**.

Classical conditioning: a basic form of learning – the procedure whereby a neutral stimulus is paired with a stimulus that automatically produces a response. Consequently the neutral stimulus comes to elicit the response.

Cocktail party phenomenon: refers to (a) a person's ability to concentrate on just one conversation although others are going on all around and (b) the way a person engaged in (attending to) one conversation will nevertheless hear their own name if it is mentioned in a nearby conversation.

Cognitive–behavioural therapies: techniques that involve helping clients to identify their negative, irrational thoughts and to replace these with more positive, rational ways of thinking.

Cognitive development: the growth of cognitive (thinking) abilities. This may be studied by examining changes in the form and structure of children's thinking as they get older, or by looking at individual differences in the power of children's thinking as measured, e.g. by IQ tests.

Cognitive interview: an interview technique designed to be used by police investigators to help elicit accurate information from eyewitnesses.

Cognitive labelling theory: Schachter and Singer's theory that it is the combination of physiological arousal and cognitive appraisal that leads to the experience of emotion.

Cognitive model of abnormality: the view that stresses the role of cognitive problems (such as illogical thought processes) in abnormal functioning.

Cognitive psychology: research field in psychology that focuses on mental processes used to acquire, store, retrieve and use knowledge.

Cohort: a group of individuals who were born during the same time interval, i.e. a 'generation'.

Collectivistic cultures: cultures that value group loyalty, prefer group to individual decisions and where the needs of the group outweigh the concerns of the individual.

Colour processing/vision: refers to the ability to see chromatic colours (hues) such as yellow, green and blue. Two theories have been proposed – trichromatic and opponent-process – but no satisfactory complete explanation exists.

Companionate love: the emotional state that combines feelings of affection and attachment characterized by mutual concern for each other – less intense than romantic love.

Compare and contrast: consider both the similarities and the differences between two topic areas.

Compliance: the act of publicly conforming but privately maintaining one's own views.

Concept(s): an idea or group of ideas that might be used as the basis for a psychological theory.

Confidentiality: the ethical concern that information gathered during psychological research or therapy should not be divulged to others unless otherwise agreed in advance or unless there is a legal requirement to disclose it.

Conformity: a type of social influence expressed through exposure to the views of a majority and our submission to those views.

Confounding variable: uncontrolled variable that produces an unwanted effect on the dependent variable. It obscures the effect of the independent variable.

Consent: *see* **Informed consent**

Consider/Critically consider: show knowledge and understanding of the topic area, as well as the strengths and limitations of the material presented.

Constructivist theories (of perception): top-down (or concept-driven) theories that emphasize the need for several sources of information in order to construct our perception of the world. In addition to information available in the sensory stimulus, we need to use higher cognitive processes, according to this theory, to interpret the information appropriately.

Contact hypothesis: suggestion that prejudice can be reduced if members of different groups are brought into contact with each other.

Content analysis: an investigative technique where people are not studied directly but through the artefacts that they produce, e.g. the analysis of documents, messages and verbal discourse.

Contrast processing: term used in the study of visual perception to describe the ability to differentiate between brightness levels in adjoining areas.

Control (psychological): the sense that one can anticipate events that occur in one's environment – a feeling that one can accomplish things and is not at the mercy of forces beyond one's control. Types of control include: informational, decisional, behavioural, cognitive and retrospective.

Control group: in an experimental design, the group used as a baseline against which to compare the performance of the experimental group.

Controlled (attentional) processing: a mental operation that is conscious, relatively slow and easily interrupted.

Correlation: the degree of relatedness between two sets of scores. If two sets of scores are correlated, it enables researchers to predict (with varying degrees of certainty) the approximate value of one score if they know the value of the other. A *positive correlation* exists when high values on one variable are associated with high values on another variable. A *negative correlation* exists when high values on one variable are associated with low values on another variable.

Correlational analysis: a type of analysis used to measure the extent of

relationship between variables that are thought likely to co-vary.

Correlation coefficient: a statistic that expresses the strength of a correlation. The closer the coefficient is to +1 or −1 the stronger the correlation (relationship).

Cortical activity: neural activity in the cortex of the brain.

Corticosteroids: *see* **Adrenocorticotropic hormone (ACTH)**.

Counterbalancing: an experimental technique where the sequence in which different conditions are presented is varied to overcome any effect caused by the order of presentation.

Co-variation model of attribution: Kelley's theory that people decide on the cause of a behaviour by weighing up how *consistent* and *distinctive* the behaviour is and how much *consensus* there is about it.

Crisis: a psychological conflict which needs to be resolved if the individual is to move on to the next stage of development.

Critical period: a crucial period in a person's or animal's development when certain experiences must happen for normal development to proceed. Today it is more common to use the term *sensitive period* to describe the optimum period for certain experiences to happen.

Criticize: evaluate a topic area in terms of its strengths and weaknesses.

Crowding: the feeling that is induced if our expectations about the use of space are violated by the presence of others.

Cultural bias: a tendency in psychological theory and research to ignore the differences between cultures and impose understanding based on the study of one culture alone.

Cultural identity: the influence of one's culture on the development of identity. Individualist cultures stress the importance of personal achievement and independence, while collectivist cultures stress the importance of collective achievement and dependence.

Culture: the enduring attitudes and behaviours, etc., shared by a large group of people and passed on from one generation to another.

Culture-bound syndromes: according to DSM-IV, these are recurrent, locality-specific patterns of aberrant behaviour and troubling experience – many are considered to be 'illnesses' and most have local names.

Debriefing: an ethical requirement in studies where participants are aware that they have taken part in an investigation. Debriefing is carried out after the data have been collected and involves providing information to participants and discussing their experience of the research.

Decay theory: refers to memory traces fading away with time until they can no longer be retrieved.

Decision-making: kind of reasoning that involves making choices and sometimes taking risks.

Defence mechanism: according to psychoanalytic theory, an unconscious strategy used to protect the ego from anxiety by falsifying, distorting or denying reality.

Define: explain what is meant by a particular term.

Deindividuation: process that occurs when one loses one's sense of individual identity so that social, moral and societal constraints on behaviour are loosened.

Demand characteristics: the tendency for experimental participants to adjust their behaviour according to their own interpretation of the aims of the experiment.

Dependent variable: in experimental investigations, this refers to the variable that it assumed to be affected by the independent variable – it is the variable measured at the end of the experimental procedure (*see also* **Independent variable**).

Depression (unipolar disorder): a type of mood disorder where the person experiences feelings of great sadness, worthlessness and guilt, and finds the challenges of life overwhelming.

Deprivation: the loss of something. The term is most often used in the field of maternal deprivation, where the child is deprived of the love of the primary attachment figure.

Depth/distance (visual) perception: the ability to experience the world in three dimensions by using monocular and binocular cues to assess depth, and distance between objects.

Describe: show knowledge of a topic area.

Descriptive statistics: techniques used to describe or characterize obtained data.

Diagnostic and Statistical Manual (DSM): a classification, definition and description of over 200 mental health disorders which groups disorders in terms of their common features.

Diathesis-stress model (of mental disorders): general model of disorders postulating that people develop mental disorders when they possess both a constitutional vulnerability (diathesis) and are exposed to stressful events.

Directional (one-tailed) hypothesis: a predictive statement that specifies the direction of the relationship or difference that will be found in a set of results, for example that participants in one condition will perform *better* than those

in another, or that a correlation will be *positive* rather than negative.

Direct theories of perception: bottom-up (or data-driven) theories proposing that there is sufficient information in the sensory stimulus to allow us to make sense of our environment without the involvement of stored knowledge or problem-solving skills.

Discrimination: a way of behaving towards members of a categorized group such that all members of that group are treated in the same (usually unfair) way, i.e. the behavioural expression of prejudice.

Discuss: describe and evaluate a topic area.

Displacement: occurs when material in short-term memory is pushed out by new, incoming information before it has been sufficiently processed to pass on to long-term memory.

Dissociation model of minority influence: refers to the claim that minority ideas are assimilated into the majority viewpoint without people remembering where they came from.

Dissolution of relationships: refers to the study of how and why relationships break down.

Distinguish between: consider the differences between two topic areas.

Distributed functions: refers to the proposition that high level cognitive functions are distributed across large areas of the cortex.

Divided attention: the ability to divide our attentional processing between more than one task.

Dizygotic (fraternal) twins: twins that develop from different zygotes (eggs) and are no more likely to be similar than any pair of siblings.

Dreaming: a stage of sleep characterized by the experience of visual imagery and rapid eye movements (REM).

Drive reduction theory (of motivation): Hull's thesis that all behaviour is motivated and that all motivation originates in the satisfaction of homeostatic drives such as hunger and thirst. The stimuli that reduce the drives (e.g. food and water) serve to reinforce the behaviour that led to them.

Dual process theory: Moscovici's theory that explains minority social influence as a different psychological process to that involved in majority social influence. Majority social influence is seen as producing no more than compliance, but minority social influence is seen as causing a process of conversion.

Early selection theories (of attention): those theories (e.g. Broadbent's) which place the filtering mechanism that selects some inputs and rejects others early on in the attentional process,

before analysis for meaning occurs (*see also* **Late selection theories**).

Eating disorders: a serious disruption of healthy eating habits or appetite.

Ecological theory of sleep: the hypothesis that sleep has evolved to keep animals inconspicuous and safe from predators at times when normal activities like feeding are impossible.

Ecological validity: the degree to which the findings from a study can be generalized beyond the context of the investigation.

EEG: electroencephalogram, a noninvasive recording of the electrical activity of the brain, using electrodes fixed to the scalp.

Ego: according to psychoanalytic theory, the part of the personality responsible for decision making and dealing with reality.

Egocentrism: a feature of thinking in the young child, characterized by an inability to take the perspective of another person.

Elaborated code: speech that is not context-bound; it uses more complex grammatical structures and more abstract vocabulary than restricted code.

Electrical self-stimulation of the brain (ESB): the technique used by Olds and Milner of implanting an electrode in the hypothalamus (area of the brain) of a living animal, so that when the animal performs a specified task it receives stimulation there.

Electroconvulsive therapy (ECT): a treatment involving passing an electrical current through the brain by the application of between 70 and 130 volts which induces a convulsion or epileptic seizure.

Emotion: a complex set of physiological and cognitive interactions that people describe in subjective terms such as happiness, fear or anger.

Empathy-altruism hypothesis: altruistic behaviour is explained as a consequence of empathy, i.e. being able to imagine how the person who needs help feels.

Empirical study: almost any form of investigation where the aim is to collect some form of data based on observation or experience.

Encoding: changing sensory input into a form or code to be processed by the memory system.

Endogenous pacemakers (biological clocks): internal timing mechanisms that enable biological rhythms to continue in the absence of obvious external cues (*see also* **Exogenous zeitgebers** and **Biological rhythms**).

Enrichment: attempts either to accelerate early learning ('hothousing') or to overcome early deprivation through the provision of compensatory education programmes.

Equity theory: proposition that people stay in relationships as long as they perceive them to be fair. Equity is not the same as equality. If one partner gives more in a relationship but also benefits more than the other person does, then the relationship may still be equitable.

Ethical guidelines: prescriptive guidance on the conduct of psychologists in research and practice. These represent the key issues that face psychologists in their work with humans and animals and are regularly updated by the organizations that issue them.

Ethics: a branch of philosophy that is concerned with what is right or acceptable in the pursuit of a given goal.

Ethnocentrism: the term used to describe the belief in the superiority of one's own ethnic and cultural group.

Evaluate/Critically evaluate: make an informed judgement as to the value of an argument, theory or piece of research.

Evidence: material that might be drawn from theories or investigations and is used to support or contradict an argument or theory.

Evolution: the change over successive generations in the genetic make-up of a particular group or species. The dominant force in this change is natural selection.

Evolutionary psychology: the study of how evolutionary ideas, such as natural selection, help explain human behaviour.

Examine: give a detailed descriptive account of a topic area.

Exogenous *zeitgebers* ('time givers'): external events that play a role in rhythmic activities (*see also* **Endogenous pacemakers** and **Biological rhythms**).

Expectancy/incentive approaches: in the study of motivation, these approaches investigate the *incentives* that elicit goal-directed behaviour.

Experiment: an investigative technique which involves the manipulation of an independent variable in order to see its effect on a dependent variable.

Experimental/alternative hypothesis: a testable statement made at the start of an investigation which serves as a prediction of events should statistical analysis dismiss the role of chance factors.

Experimental design: a procedure used within an experiment to control the influence of participant variables that might otherwise influence the outcome of the experiment.

Experimental group: the group of participants given the treatment whose effect is being investigated. The performance of these participants is compared with the performance of those in the control group.

Experimental validity: a measure of whether the experimental procedures actually worked, i.e. were the conclusions justified?

Experimenter effects: aspect of the experimenter's behaviour or characteristics that influence participants and cause them to change their behaviour as a result.

Explain: show understanding of a topic through coherent and intelligible explanation.

Extinction: the procedure, after classical or operant conditioning, of repeatedly presenting the conditioned stimulus without any reinforcement until the conditioned response ceases to be produced.

Eyewitness testimony: the study of the accuracy of memory following an accident or crime, and the types of errors that are commonly made in such situations.

Family systems theory: the view of the family as a set of interacting and inter-dependent parts. In family systems therapy, the therapist will meet all members of a family, point out problem interactions and help the whole family to change.

Feature detection theory: an explanation for pattern recognition; the proposal that we process images in terms of their constituent parts and then match the features of a pattern to those features stored in memory.

Feature processing: term used in the study of visual perception to describe the ability to detect contours, essential for the recognition of objects.

Field experiment: an experimental manipulation of an independent variable that takes place in a natural setting rather than in the more artificial setting of the laboratory.

Findings: the outcome of a research investigation.

Fitness: term used in evolutionary psychology, can be measured by number of offspring an individual leaves compared to other individuals of the same species. *Inclusive fitness* is measured by the number of copies of one's genes that appear in current or subsequent generations in offspring and nonoffspring.

Flashbulb memory: a detailed, vivid, long-lasting memory of a highly significant event.

Flooding: a behavioural technique used to treat phobias. The phobic person is exposed to the feared situation for an extended period with no opportunity to escape.

Focal theory (of adolescence): the argument that adolescents deal with changes that occur by focusing on different issues at different times. Consequently, they are likely to experience little stress. This theory contrasts with the view of adolescence as inevitably a period of 'storm and stress'.

Focused (selective) attention: where a person manages to focus on one thing at a time to the exclusion of other competing stimuli.

Foraging: the different ways in which animals satisfy their nutritional requirements.

Forgetting: the loss of the ability to recall or recognize something that has previously been learned.

Free will vs determinism: the debate between those who believe that behaviour is determined by external or internal factors acting on the individual (determinism), and those who believe that people respond actively to events around them (free will).

Frequency polygon: a frequency distribution that shows the peaks of each of the class intervals.

Fundamental attribution error: a tendency to see the behaviour of others as being due to their stable personality characteristics rather than the influence of situational factors.

Gender: term sometimes used to refer to the psychological characteristics of being male and female (as opposed to 'sex' which refers to purely biological characteristics). However, many psychologists use the terms interchangeably.

Gender bias: the treatment of men and women in psychological research and/or theory in a way which offers a view of behaviour and experience that might not fully represent the characteristics of both genders.

Gender role: a set of expectations that describe how males and females should think, act and feel.

Gender schema theory: the cognitive-developmental approach that claims children develop gender schema (concept clusters such as stereotypes) as soon as they recognize that there is a difference between men and women.

General Adaptation Syndrome (GAS): a model, described by Hans Selye, of how the body reacts during stressful situations. There are three stages: (a) *alarm* stage when an arousal response is activated (body prepared to expend energy, e.g. to fight or flee); (b) *resistance* stage when body is apparently coping with the stressor; (c) *exhaustion* stage if stress continues for too long – may lead to physical symptoms such as stomach ulcers.

Generalizability: the ability of researchers to offer a justifiable extension of their findings beyond the actual sample of participants used to a wider population of people.

Genetics: the part of biological science concerned with the study of heredity and the role of genes throughout one's life.

Genital stage: the final stage of psychosexual development (according to psychoanalytic theory) when the main source of pleasure is the genitals.

Gestalt approach: in problem-solving this refers to the need for structural understanding, i.e. the ability to understand how all parts of the problem fit together to meet the goal.

Hardiness: personality factors (control, commitment and challenge) identified by Kobasa that provide defence against negative effects of stress.

Hassles and Uplifts Scales: scales devised by Lazarus and Kanner to measure the role of minor stressful events and everyday pleasant events on health and illness.

Helping: a general term for giving assistance to another person.

Hemisphere asymmetries: refers to the fact that some functions of the cortex are located in one hemisphere only, rather than being symmetrically organized across both hemispheres.

Heuristic: a problem-solving strategy that involves taking the most likely option – a rule of thumb – a cognitive short cut.

Histogram: a type of frequency distribution chart or diagram where continuous data are divided into proportional intervals.

Homeostasis: the stability of an organism's internal environment.

Homeostatic drive theory (of eating and drinking): refers to the proposition that eating and drinking are controlled by an internal homeostatic mechanism. For example, the body's need for food is conveyed to the brain, from where messages are sent to initiate eating to restore homeostasis.

Homing behaviour: refers to the ability of animals to navigate towards a target that is normally their home range.

Hormones: chemicals released by the endocrine system into general circulation.

Humanistic model of abnormality: abnormality seen in terms of blocks and frustrations to an individual's self-growth and development.

Humanistic psychology: a view of human beings that sees every person as unique and possessing an innate potential for positive growth.

Humanistic therapy: a treatment where the therapist tries to see the world through the client's eyes and endeavours to encourage the client to exercise free will and decide on their own life course.

Hypothalamus: area of brain located just below the thalamus (the large, two-lobed structure at the top of the brain stem). It plays an important role in the regulation of some motivated behaviours (*see also* **Limbic system**).

Hypothesis: a specific, testable statement that enables a researcher to predict the results of a study.

Iatrogenic disorder: a disorder that has been unintentionally induced by therapeutic practice.

Id: according to psychoanalytic theory, the part of the personality present at birth, the mental representation of biological drives.

Ideal mental health: the basis for optimal living as described by Jahoda, comprising positive attitudes to self, self-actualization, resistance to stress, autonomy, accurate perceptions and adaptation to the environment.

Identification: (a) in the area of social influence, this refers to the process of adopting the views of a group because one wants to be with or be liked by the group. Such views may not be maintained if the group is no longer present; (b) in Freud's theory of psychosexual development, the process when the child incorporates the qualities and ideas of the parent of the same sex.

Identity formation: the process, according to Erikson, whereby a person achieves a sense of integrity and continuity. Failure to achieve a sense of identity may result in role confusion. Marcia named four stages in this process: identity confusion, identity foreclosure, identity moratorium and identity achievement.

Illusions: perceptual experiences that are not true representations of the physical event that is experienced through the senses. A *visual illusion* is an image that 'tricks' the perceptual system so that one 'sees' things they way they aren't.

Illusory correlations: relationships that appear to exist between two events where, in fact, none exist.

Imaging techniques: *see* **CAT, MEG, MRI** and **PET** scans.

Imitation: copying another person's behaviour.

Immune system: system that protects the body against infection; a network of cells and chemicals that seek out and destroy invading particles.

Imposed etic: term that refers to the assumption that research questions or procedures used in one culture will have the same meaning for participants when applied in another culture and that consequently their responses will mean the same in the new culture.

Imprinting: a type of early learning where a young animal forms an attachment to another animal that is difficult to change with subsequent experience (*filial imprinting*) or where they learn the characteristics of their own species (or a foster species) for later courtship and mating (*sexual imprinting*).

Incentive: a stimulus that elicits goal-directed behaviour.

Independent behaviour: behaviour where a person resists the social influence imposed by those around them (e.g. by displaying *non*conformity, or disobedience to authority).

Independent groups: a type of experimental design where participants are randomly allocated to the different conditions of the experiment.

Independent variable: in experimental investigations, this refers to the variable deliberately manipulated by the researcher in an attempt to change the performance of participants on the dependent variable.

Individualistic cultures: cultures where self-interest and individual rights are promoted, rather than the needs and interests of others.

Individuation: refers to the desire to be distinguished from others.

Inferential statistics: the techniques (tests) used to analyse the data from samples to enable us to infer or draw conclusions about the population from which the sample is drawn. Such tests include Chi-square, Binomial Sign, Wilcoxon Matched Pairs, Mann-Whitney *U*, and Spearman's *Rho*.

Informational social influence: occurs when we look to others for guidance about what to do or believe. Based on a desire to be right, it is the influence that occurs when one accepts information from others as evidence about reality.

Information processing approach: a reference to the belief that the processing of sensory information takes place in a series of stages. In developmental psychology, this approach assumes that if adults think more successfully than children do, it is because they can process more information than children can.

Informed consent: an ethical requirement that participants or clients should have sufficient information about an experiment or therapeutic intervention to enable them to make an informed judgement about whether or not to take part.

Infradian rhythms: *see* **Biological rhythms**.

In-group: a group of which one perceives oneself a member (in contrast to the out-group).

Insights: perceptions from theories or investigations that enable us to understand or appraise a topic area.

Intelligence: an underlying ability which enables an individual to adapt to and function effectively within a given environment.

Intelligence test: a type of assessment that purports to measure intelligence.

Interference theory: refers to the process that occurs when memory traces are disrupted or obscured by other incoming information.

Internalization: a social influence process that results in a true and enduring change of views.

International Classification of Disorders (ICD): a classification of physical and psychological disorders published and regularly updated by the World Health Organization.

Interval level data: *see* **Levels of measurement**.

Interview: any face-to-face situation where one person (the interviewer) asks questions of another (the respondent).

Investigator effects: arise when a researcher's behaviour or characteristics influence the results of an investigation.

IQ (Intelligence quotient): *see* **Measured intelligence**.

James-Lange theory of emotion: the idea that the perception of an emotion-arousing stimulus leads to a behavioural response. This response involves changes in the body's physiology which are detected by the brain and interpreted as an emotion.

Kin selection/ kin altruism: refers to behaviour that increases the chances that an animal's close genetic relatives will survive and reproduce. The closer the genetic relationship, the greater the co-operation and altruism animals show towards each other.

Kinship (family) studies: investigations which look at the correlation in some characteristic or quality (e.g. intelligence) between pairs of individuals who are genetically related to varying degrees.

Labelling theory: the view that serious mental illness is caused by society's reactions to unusual behaviour, e.g. diagnostic labels may result in self-fulfilling prophecies, so that the labelled person comes to behave in a way that justifies the label.

Laboratory experiment: an investigative technique where the experimental manipulation of the independent variable takes place within such conditions that careful control of extraneous variables is possible.

Language acquisition: the processes by which children acquire or develop human language.

Language Acquisition Device (LAD): an innate mechanism that is programmed to recognize grammatical structure and therefore makes it easy for children to acquire language.

Lateralization of function: *see* **Hemisphere asymmetries**.

Late selection theories (of attention): those theories (e.g. Deutsch and Deutsch's) claiming that both attended and unattended inputs are analysed for meaning before one input is selected and reaches consciousness. Selection depends on the pertinence of the input (*see also* **Early selection theories**).

Law of effect: Thorndike's theory that reinforced behaviour is more likely to be repeated and unreinforced behaviour is likely to die out.

Learned helplessness: a psychological state produced as a result of being exposed to uncontrollable events. Observed in people who give up trying to cope because previous attempts have been frustrated and led to failure.

Lesioning: injuring brain tissue, e.g. by heating the tip of an implanted electrode so that a small area of tissue is destroyed.

Levels of measurement: types of data. Four levels (scales) of data are commonly encountered in psychology. The *nominal level* is the weakest level and deals with frequency count data, e.g. the number of students who gained grade A in their History exam. *Ordinal level* data can be placed in rank order, i.e. from the highest to the lowest value, e.g. names and positions of top five contestants in a general knowledge competition. *Interval level* data has all the properties of the ordinal scale but it also has equal intervals between adjacent units on the scale, e.g. the Celsius temperature scale. The highest level of measurement is called a *ratio scale*. It has the properties of an interval scale but also has an absolute zero point, e.g. the Kelvin temperature scale where 0 degree is the complete absence of heat.

Levels of processing: refers to Craik and Lockhart's proposal that the more deeply information is processed, the better it is remembered.

Life changes (and events): *see* **Social Readjustment Rating Scale**, **Life Experiences Survey** and **Hassles and Uplifts Scales**.

Life Experiences Survey: devised by Sarason et al., and a modified version of the SRRS, this scale provides respondents with a score for the amount of positive and negative life changes they have experienced. A high score for negative life changes is positively correlated with stress-related health problems.

Limbic system: collections of nuclei and tracts in the brain that border the thalamus; plays a role in emotion (*see also* **Hypothalamus**).

Linguistic relativity hypothesis: theory that the language we use is responsible for shaping our thoughts about the world. The *weak* version states that language *influences* thinking, whereas the *strong* version states that language *determines* the way we think.

Localization of function: the principle that psychological functions are located in specialized areas of the brain.

Locus of control: refers to how much someone perceives that they have personal control over their lives. Individuals with an *internal locus* are more likely than those with an *external locus* to believe that they are responsible for what happens in their lives.

Longitudinal study: an investigation where participants are studied over an extended period of time.

Long-term memory: part of memory system that holds large amounts of information for long periods of time (*see also* **Short-term memory**).

Maintaining relationships: refers to the study of the strategies people use to prevent relationships breaking down.

Mann-Whitney *U* test: an inferential test of difference for independent groups when at least ordinal level data have been obtained.

Matched participants (matched pairs): a type of experimental design where pairs of participants are matched on relevant variables and then the members of each pair allocated randomly to conditions.

Matching hypothesis: proposal that people tend to select partners who are alike in terms of physical attractiveness, background, etc.

Mean: the arithmetic average that is calculated by dividing the sum of all scores by the number of items or participants.

Means-end analysis: a problem-solving strategy that involves breaking problems down into their constituent parts, which are then solved in turn until the solution (goal) is reached.

Measured intelligence: refers to the score achieved on taking an intelligence test. This is sometimes called an intelligence quotient (IQ).

Measures of dispersion: a measurement of the spread or variability in a set of scores.

Media influences: the way in which the media (e.g. television, Internet) might cause changes in behaviour in those who are exposed to it. Much of the debate concerning media influences has focused on its effects on aggressive behaviour.

Median: the middle value in a set of scores when they are arranged in rank order.

Medical model of abnormality: a view of abnormality that sees mental disorders as being caused by abnormal physiological processes such as genetic and biochemical factors. Abnormality, according to this model, is seen as an illness or disease.

MEG (magnetoenecephalography): noninvasive technique for visualizing (imaging) the brain by recording tiny magnetic fields produced by active neurons.

Membership group: a group of people who are members because of their *presence* in the group.

Memory: the mental processes involved in registering, storing and retrieving information.

Mental disorder: *see* **Psychological disorder**.

Methods: the different ways that research investigations can be carried out.

Migration: term usually used to describe the mass movement of members of a species from one location to another (e.g. seasonal migrations of birds).

Minority influence: the effect when a persuasive minority exerts pressure to change the attitudes, beliefs or behaviours of the majority. Minorities are most influential when they appear consistent and principled.

Mode: the most frequently occurring score in a set of data.

Model: a term that is used synonymously with 'theory', although it may refer to something that is less elaborate or complex.

Modelling: the term used by Bandura to describe observational learning.

Models of memory: different explanations concerning the nature of memory and the processes involved in remembering and retrieving information.

Modular theories (of divided attention): propose that humans possess several different processing mechanisms (modules) of attention that specialize in handling particular tasks.

Monotropy: an infant's tendency, according to Bowlby, to become attached to one individual. This attachment is seen as qualitatively different from subsequent attachments.

Monozygotic (identical) twins: twins that develop from the same zygote (egg) and are therefore genetically identical.

Moral development: the process by which children come to internalize standards of right and wrong, and ultimately make their own decisions concerning moral issues.

Motivation: literally, why organisms act in the way that they do, i.e. the study of what arouses and directs behaviour.

Movement perception: refers to our ability to perceive accurately the movement of people and objects.

MRI (magnetic resonance imaging): a noninvasive technique for picturing (imaging) the brain (or other soft tissue of the body) by subjecting it to a sequence of pulsed radio waves while the head (or other body part) is held in a powerful magnetic field.

Multiple personality disorder (Dissociative identity disorder): a disorder where a disruption in memory causes a separation of one part of a person's identity from another.

Multistore model of memory: based on the information-processing approach, the model characterizes memory as a flow of information through a set of stages in a fixed sequence.

Nativist theory: in the area of language development, the proposition that children are biologically equipped to acquire language (*see also* **Language Acquisition Device**).

Natural experiment: an example of a 'quasi-experiment' where the allocation of participants to the different experimental conditions is outside the control of the investigator, but rather is manipulated fortuitously by some outside agency.

Naturalistic observation: an observational technique where behaviour is observed in its natural context without intrusion by the person doing the observing.

Natural selection: the part of Darwin's theory that states that those animals that are well adapted to their environment will leave behind more offspring than those animals who are less well adapted.

Nature–nurture debate: the controversy about the relative contributions of genetic factors (nature) versus environmental factors (nurture) in determining a person's characteristics and abilities, e.g. their level of intelligence.

Navigation (in nonhuman animals): the ability to reach a goal regardless of starting point (in contrast to simply showing compass orientation – always heading in one specific compass direction regardless of the 'correct' direction).

Negative reinforcement: *see* **Reinforcement**.

Negative-state relief model: theory that we help others in order to feel better ourselves, e.g. to improve our mood.

Neonate research: investigations carried out using newborn infants.

Nominal level data: *see* **Levels of measurement**.

Non-directional (two-tailed) hypothesis: a statement made at the outset of a research study where a relationship or difference is predicted but the direction of the relationship or difference is not.

Noninvasive procedures: in studies of brain function, these procedures (e.g. PET scans) for imaging the brain do not require direct interference with brain tissue.

Normal distribution: a bell-shaped, continuous distribution, symmetrical about its midpoint.

Normality thesis: refers to Milgram's claim that anyone is capable of obedience to a malevolent authority, given certain circumstances.

Normative social influence: occurs when we conform because we wish to be liked by others.

NREM sleep: stages of sleep where no rapid eye movements are found.

Null hypothesis: a statement that attributes the results obtained within a research investigation to chance or to some other event that is not covered by the research hypothesis under test.

Obedience: a type of social influence where an individual acts according to the orders of some authority figure. It is normally assumed that without such an order the person would not have carried out that behaviour.

Object permanence: the knowledge that things that are out of sight actually still exist.

Observational studies: *see* **Naturalistic observation**.

Observer reliability: a measure of consistency between observers, i.e. how much two or more observers' ratings (or codings) are in agreement.

Obsessive–compulsive disorder: an anxiety disorder in which the individual is plagued with uncontrollable thoughts (obsessions) and performs seemingly senseless rituals (compulsive behaviours).

Operant conditioning: an explanation of learning that sees the consequences of a behaviour as being of vital importance to the future appearance of that behaviour. If a behaviour is followed by a desirable consequence, it becomes more frequent; if it is followed by an undesirable consequence, it becomes less frequent.

Operationalization: the process whereby a variable is defined in terms of the steps or behaviours necessary to measure it. For example, using the behaviour 'laughing' as a measure of 'happiness' or the maximum number of digits a person can recall immediately after learning as a measure of short-term memory capacity.

Operation Headstart: an enrichment intervention programme set up for preschool children in the US in the 1960s. It was designed to reverse the effects of social disadvantage.

Optimal arousal: the term refers to the claim that a major motivation for animals is to maintain an optimal level of alertness and activation (arousal) that is neither too high nor too low.

Oral stage: the first stage of psychosexual development (according to psychoanalytic theory) when the infant's main source of pleasure is the mouth.

Ordinal level data: *see* **Levels of measurement**.

Out-group: a group of which one is not a member (in contrast to the in-group).

Outline/State: offer a summary description of the topic area.

Parental investment: actions that increase the survival chances of one set of offspring but at the expense of the parent procuring more offspring.

Participant reactivity: the tendency for participants in a research investigation to alter their behaviour because of the presence of the observer.

Participants: those people who are studied and contribute data in a research investigation.

Pattern recognition: the process by which we transform and organize the raw information provided by our sensory receptors into a meaningful whole.

Perception: the process by which we transform sensory information from the environment into the experience of objects, sounds, movement, etc.

Perceptual constancies: the tendency for objects to provide the same perceptual experience despite changes in the viewing conditions.

Perceptual development: the systematic change of perceptual abilities and processes that develop as a result of maturation and experience.

Perceptual organization: the ability of an organism to organize the information that arrives via the senses into some meaningful perceptual experience.

Personality: a relatively stable, characteristic set of behaviours, attitudes, interests and capabilities, sometimes used as a means of distinguishing between people – an individual difference.

PET (positron emission tomography) scans: a noninvasive technique for visualizing (imaging) the activity in the brain by measuring the accumulation of a radioactive substance in various regions of the brain. A battery of detectors scans the brain after the radioactive substance has been injected into the bloodstream.

Phallic stage: the third stage of psychosexual development (according to psychoanalytic theory) when the child focuses on the genitals and initially on the opposite gender parent. Crisis at this stage is resolved by identifying with the same gender parent.

Phobic disorder: a type of anxiety disorder where there is a persistent and unreasonable fear of an object or situation.

Piaget, Jean: a Swiss psychologist whose major contribution to psychology was the theory that intelligence was the product of a natural and inevitable sequence of developmental stages and processes.

Pilot study: a small-scale preliminary investigation carried out before the main study to detect any problems or ambiguities so that adjustments can be made.

Pituitary: a gland in the skull cavity just below the surface of the brain, responsible for releasing a number of hormones into the bloodstream.

Post-traumatic stress disorder: a type of anxiety disorder that arises as a result of some traumatic event. The symptoms begin shortly after the event and may last for years.

Precocial species: animals that can move about, feed and generally look after themselves shortly after birth.

Prejudice: prejudging individuals on the basis of their membership of a particular category or group.

Primary motor area: area of the cortex, in the frontal lobe, where sensorimotor signals converge and depart.

Privation: refers to a situation where, for example, there is a lack (rather than a loss) of an attachment.

Proactive interference: occurs when an old memory trace interferes with learning and retrieval of new information.

Probability: a numerical measure of the chance that something will happen.

Problem-solving: a complex skill used whenever we need to reach a goal that is not readily available.

Prosocial behaviour: an act that benefits others but may appear to have no direct benefit for the person performing it.

Prosocial reasoning: the area of thinking concerned with helping or comforting others, possibly at a personal cost.

Protection of participants: an ethical requirement that researchers have a duty of care towards their participants. Normally, the risk of harm to participants should be no greater than they would expect to meet in ordinary life.

Prototype theory: an explanation for pattern recognition; the proposal that we match incoming information against an abstract model in long-term memory that embodies the most typical features of an object or pattern.

Psychoanalysis: therapeutic method in which a person is given insights into the unconscious psychological conflicts that are seen as the cause of their symptoms.

Psychodrama: therapeutic technique in which clients work in groups to gain insight into their problems by 'acting out' chosen scenarios from problem areas in their lives.

Psychodynamic approach: the study of how unconscious motives influence behaviour.

Psychodynamic models of abnormality: models that view abnormal behaviour as being caused by underlying psychological forces of which the individual is probably unaware.

Psychodynamic theories: theories that emphasize change and development in the individual and where 'drive' is a central concept in the process of development.

Psychodynamic therapies: treatments that help clients to uncover past traumatic events and the conflicts that have resulted from them. These conflicts can then be resolved so that the client is able to restore an adaptive level of functioning.

Psychological abnormality: behaviour and psychological functioning that is considered different from the 'normal'. Usually called 'mental disorder'.

Psychological disorder: a term used synonymously with 'mental disorder', it refers to a level of functioning that is harmful or distressing to the individual or to those around them. Psychological disorders are usually defined and described according to some current classification system such as DSM IV.

Psychology as science: the use of scientific methods to establish a body of psychological knowledge that is considered trustworthy and verifiable.

Psychometric testing: the testing of individuals on items that have been shown to measure competence in some area of functioning, e.g. intelligence, personality or special aptitudes.

Psychopathology: the study of the origins and course of psychological disorders such as schizophrenia and depression.

Psychopathology thesis: in social influence research the suggestion that people who commit atrocities are psychologically impaired and different to most people (in contrast to Milgram's 'normality thesis').

Psychosomatic illness: an illness with physical symptoms but thought to be caused by the continual mobilization of the autonomic nervous system (ANS) under stress.

Psychosurgery: cutting brain tissue in order to alleviate the symptoms of severe psychological disorder.

Punishment: that which decreases the probability of the response that preceded it, the opposite of reinforcement.

Qualitative data: information in non-numerical form, e.g. speech, written words, pictures.

Quantitative data: information in numerical form, e.g. number of students in a class, average scores on a quiz.

Quasi-experiment: a type of research that is broadly similar in approach to an experiment but in which the investigator does not directly allocate participants to the different research conditions but makes use of divisions that already exist in terms of the conditions of interest.

Questionnaire surveys: a technique, using a structured set of questions, for asking a large sample of people about their views and behaviours, etc. Questionnaire surveys may be conducted in person, by telephone, by post, etc.

Randomization: a way of overcoming order effects by randomizing the order in which participants tackle the different conditions in an experiment.

Random sampling: a technique for selecting members from a population such that every member of the population has an equal chance of being chosen.

Range: a measure of dispersion within a set of scores, this refers to the distance between the lowest and the highest score.

Rational-emotive behaviour therapy: a form of psychotherapy, based on the work of Ellis, where the therapist actively confronts clients about their irrational thinking.

Ratio scale: see **Levels of measurement**.

Reactance: a psychological boomerang effect, causing people to do the opposite of what has been asked. Occurs when attempts to restrict freedom are made too blatantly.

Realistic conflict theory: an explanation for prejudice and discrimination proposing that inter-group hostility develops when groups are competing for scarce resources.

Recognition-by-components theory (RBC): proposition that an object can be recognized when we have identified its constituent geons (basic three-dimensional shapes) and how these are spatially related.

Reconstructive memory: refers to Bartlett's view of memory – an imaginative construction influenced by schemas.

Reductionism: the tendency to reduce human behaviour to simpler levels of analysis, such as the effects of genes or environmental reinforcement.

Reference group: refers to a group with whom we *identify*.

Reinforcement: the process by which a response is strengthened. This can be *positive*, when a response produces a pleasant outcome or *negative* when the response leads to the removal of something unpleasant. Each outcome strengthens the response it follows.

Relative deprivation: the state that people experience when they perceive a gap between what others have and what they have themselves, i.e. others are seen as relatively better off.

Reliability: the degree to which a description or score is consistent over time or across different observers. If the findings of research are consistently replicable then they can be called reliable.

REM (rapid eye movement) sleep: sometimes called paradoxical sleep; the stage of sleep characterized by rapid eye movements, loss of muscle tone and a waking EEG pattern. The stage of sleep strongly associated with dreaming.

Repeated measures: a type of experimental design where the same participants are used in all conditions of the experiment.

Representative sample: a selected group from a target population that reflects the characteristics of the population, e.g. same proportions of people in different social classes or in different age groups.

Repression: (a) defence mechanism (unconscious process) in which a distressing memory or impulse is excluded from conscious awareness; (b) a theory of forgetting.

Research: the process of gaining knowledge, either by an examination of appropriate theories or through empirical data collection.

Resource allocation models (of attention): see **Capacity models**.

Restoration (recuperation) theory of sleep: the hypothesis that the purpose of sleep is to restore the body to its full waking capacity. Therefore, sleep acts to repair the damage wrought by wakefulness.

Restricted code: a pattern of speech that uses fairly basic vocabulary, contains mainly concrete description and can usually only be understood when set in context (*see also* **Elaborated code**).

Retina: the light sensitive part of the eye, where light is changed into a neural response to be passed to the brain via the optic nerve. It consists of three layers of neural tissue including a layer of photoreceptors called rods and cones.

Retroactive interference: occurs when new information interferes with the ability to retrieve old information from memory.

Rewards-cost model: theory by Piliavin that bystanders decide whether or not to help a victim in distress by weighing up the rewards and costs of helping and not helping.

Role ambiguity: with reference to the workplace, a lack of clarity about the requirements of one's work role. This sometimes results from having no clear (or contradictory) guidelines or standards of performance – a major factor contributing to work-related stress.

Romantic (passionate) love: an intensely emotional state characterized by physical longing when object of passion is absent, joy when relationship is going well and anguish when it goes wrong.

Scaffolding: a term coined by Wood *et al.* to explain how a tutor can advance a child's thinking by providing a framework within which the child can develop.

Scattergraph (or scattergram): a graphical representation of the correlation between two sets of measurements.

Schemas: knowledge packages built up through experience of the world. In theories of memory and thinking, the term 'schema' refers to a cognitive structure which can be used to interpret information.

Schizophrenia: a serious mental disorder that is characterized by severe disruptions in psychological functioning and a loss of contact with reality.

Seasonal affective disorder (SAD): a mood disorder related to changes in season. A period of depression in winter is the most common.

Selection: the differential survival of organisms or genes in a population as a result of some selective force.

Selective attention: see **Focused attention**.

Self-categorization theory: states that people are most likely to be influenced by those perceived to be like themselves (members of their in-groups).

Self-recognition: the ability to look in a mirror and recognize the image as belonging to oneself.

Self-serving bias: a type of attributional bias where people attribute failure to factors outside their control and success to their own ability or effort.

Sensitive period: *see* **Critical period**.

Sensory adaptation: term refers to (a) the temporary decrease in sensitivity that happens when a sensory system is exposed to a particular stimulus for a period of time, and (b) the temporary increase in sensitivity that occurs when a sensory system is not stimulated for a time.

Sensory and motor processes: those physiological or psychological processes which relate to the senses (sensory) or to the actions (motor) of an organism.

Sensory memory: storage system that holds information in relatively unprocessed form for fractions of a second after the physical stimulus is no longer available.

Separation anxiety: distress shown by infants when separated from their main caregiver.

Sexual selection: term refers to the observation that individuals possess features that make them attractive to members of the opposite sex (intersexual selection), or help them to compete with members of the same sex for access to mates (intrasexual selection)

Shadowing: in studies of focused attention, this refers to repeating back a message that is heard in one ear.

Short-term memory: system for storing information for short periods of time (*see also* **Long-term memory**).

Signalling: term refers to what happens when one animal indirectly causes another animal to change its behaviour because it perceived the signal through its sense organs. Examples of signalling systems include bird song and the release of pheromones (smell signals) by moths and ants.

Sign (Binomial sign) test: an inferential test of difference for use with related data, measured at a nominal level.

Sleep: a loss of consciousness which is characterized by specific behavioural and physiological effects. Sleep can be non-REM (NREM) or REM which is associated with dreaming.

Sociability: a child's willingness to interact with others and to seek their attention or approval.

Social class: term used to describe the broad variations in economic and social positions within a society.

Social cognition: the area of social psychology concerned with how people think about other individuals or other groups of people.

Social constructionism: theory that knowledge is relative, socially constructed and 'facts' are not permanent realities.

Social development: refers to the growth of social behaviours, such as the ability to form attachments, develop healthy self-esteem and form appropriate relationships.

Social disengagement theory: proposition that healthy ageing is a gradual and mutual process of separation between individuals and their social roles and interests (*see also* **Activity theory**).

Social drift theory (hypothesis): the attempt to explain the relationship between social class and serious mental illness by proposing that those who are seriously mentally ill 'drift' down the socio-economic scale.

Social exchange theory: an explanation of why some relationships continue while others end, based on the notion that people remain in relationships as long as the rewards of staying outweigh the costs.

Social identity theory: proposition that human beings categorize themselves and others into in-groups and out-groups. Because of the need to maintain a positive social identity, unfavourable comparisons are made between the two and competition and discrimination develop.

Social impact theory: a social influence theory proposing that influence effects depend upon the number of people exerting influence, their status and their immediacy.

Social influence: the process by which a person's attitudes, beliefs or behaviours are modified by the presence or actions of others.

Socialization: the process by which an individual's behaviour and characteristics are shaped to be acceptable to the society in which he or she lives.

Social learning theory: an explanation of the way in which people learn through observing and imitating the behaviour of others.

Socially sensitive research: any research that may have direct social consequences for those taking part in the study or the class of people who are represented.

Social norms: the rules for behaviour established by a society.

Social Readjustment Rating Scale (SRRS): a rating scale, devised by Holmes and Rahe, that scores major life events and life changes according to their psychological impact, proposing that higher scores on the SRRS increase the chances of stress-related health breakdown.

Social relationship: an encounter with another person (or people) that endures through time.

Social releasers: social behaviours that elicit a caregiving reaction (e.g. smiling) from another person.

Social representations: the ways in which ordinary people represent the world around them. These enable people to turn the unfamiliar into the familiar and the complex into the more easily understood.

Social support: people and/or services one can turn to when in need. May take the form of tangible support (actual goods and services), information (e.g. advice) or emotional support (e.g. reassurance that one is cared for).

Sociobiological theory: the explanation of social behaviour in evolutionary terms – e.g. that aggressive behaviour has evolved as a means of protecting one's genes.

Somatic therapies: *see* **Biological therapies**.

Spearman's Rank Order Correlation Coefficient (Rho): an inferential test of correlation suitable for use with pairs of scores when at least ordinal levels of measurement have been obtained.

Species: a set of organisms that possess similar inherited characteristics and have the potential to interbreed to produce fertile offspring.

Split brain: the cutting of the corpus callosum resulting in the effective separation of the two hemispheres of the brain.

Spontaneous recovery: the phenomenon in classical conditioning observed by Pavlov: when the process of extinction is completed and the animal is later replaced in the experimental situation, it may well spontaneously produce the previously conditioned behaviour. This finding demonstrates that extinction is not the same as forgetting, but rather is a process of inhibition.

Standard deviation: a statistical measure of the variation from the mean in a set of scores.

Statistically infrequent behaviour: behaviour that occurs rarely.

Statistical significance: a conclusion drawn from the data collected in a research study that the results are unlikely to have been caused by chance, and can therefore be attributed to the particular relationship under study.

Stereotypes: a fixed and often simplistic generalization about a group or class of people. Stereotypes are frequently unflattering and may *underlie* prejudice and discrimination.

Stimulus discrimination: in classical conditioning, this refers to the situation where one conditioned stimulus (CS) is paired with an unconditioned stimulus while another conditioned stimulus is left unpaired. In this case, only the paired CS will evoke the conditioned response (CR).

Stimulus generalization: in conditioning, this refers to the finding that once a response to a given stimulus has been learned, the response may also be evoked by other similar stimuli.

Strange situation: A laboratory-based structured observation method of assessing how securely or insecurely attached an infant is to its caregiver.

Stress: three ways of defining stress: (a) as *a response or reaction* to something in the environment; (b) as a *stimulus or stressor* – a feature of the environment that produces a 'stress' response; (c) as a *lack of fit* between the perceived demands of the environment and the perceived ability to cope with those demands. This *transactional model* of stress is the most popular among psychologists.

Stress-inoculation training: a cognitive-behavioural strategy used in stress management. It has three phases: *Conceptualization* – client relives stressful event and analyses its features to achieve a more realistic understanding of the demand being made; *Skills training and practice* – to help overcome key elements causing stress; *Real-life application* – put training to test in real-life situations.

Stress reduction: techniques used by an individual to cope with stress and reduce its adverse effects.

Stroop effect: refers to how colour name words have an interfering effect on the time taken to name the ink colours of nonmatching colours.

Studies: usually these refer to empirical investigations, although in a general sense they refer to any attempt to study a person or persons (or any other organism) in order to find out something about them.

Subcultural differences: those differences found within a particular culture, society or country, e.g. differences between social classes, or between men and women.

Superego: according to psychoanalytic theory, the part of the personality that acts as the conscience.

Survey: a method of obtaining information by questioning a large sample of people.

Synoptic assessment: in psychology this term applies to the assessment of the candidate's understanding and appreciation of the breadth of theoretical and methodological approaches, issues and debates in psychology (AQA).

Systematic desensitization: a behavioural therapy used to treat phobias and anxieties. After being trained in relaxation techniques, the phobic person is gradually exposed to situations that are more and more anxiety provoking until the fear response is replaced by one of relaxation.

Temperament: refers to a person's typical energy level or characteristic mood. Temperament is usually viewed as a genetic predisposition because of the wide differences seen in new-borns in terms of their reactivity to stimulation and general mood.

Template theory: an explanation for pattern recognition; the proposal that we match incoming information against miniature copies (templates) of patterns that we have stored in long-term memory.

Theory: a set of interrelated ideas or principles that can be used to explain observed phenomena.

Theory of mind: the ability to understand that someone may have different thoughts from one's own.

Token economies: a behaviour modification programme where a person receives rewards in the form of tokens for desirable behaviour. Tokens can be exchanged later for goods or privileges.

Top-down processing: processing that is guided by expectations, stored knowledge and context (*see also* **Bottom-up processing**).

Transference: a process that occurs during psychoanalysis when a client redirects feelings towards the therapist that are unconsciously directed towards a significant person in their life.

Type A behaviour: a behaviour pattern characterized by impatience, competitiveness, constant time pressure, etc. Some correlation found between Type A behaviour and coronary heart disease.

Type I error: the error that occurs when a null hypothesis is wrongly rejected.

Type II error: the error that occurs when a null hypothesis is retained when it is in fact false.

Ultradian rhythms: *see* **Biological rhythms**.

Understudied relationships: refers to those relationships that have, until recently, received little attention by researchers, e.g. gay relationships, relationships formed via the Internet.

Unipolar depression/disorder: *see* **Depression**.

Validity: the degree to which a test, measurement or experimental manipulation is doing the job it has been designed to do.

Variable: something that alters or can be changed.

Variation: term used to describe the differences found among individuals of sexually reproducing species (because offspring do not exactly resemble either parent).

Visual pathways: refers to the routes by which nerve impulses pass from the retina to the visual areas of the brain. The most studied pathway is the *retina-geniculate-striate pathway* that conducts signals to the primary visual cortex via the lateral geniculate nuclei of the thalamus.

Visual perception: the process by which we transform sensory information from the eyes to produce an experience of depth, distance, colour, etc.

Voluntary and involuntary relationships: voluntary relationships are those entered into freely, while involuntary relationships are those where the partners (or participants) have no choice (e.g. some arranged marriages).

Vygotsky: a Russian psychologist who believed that cognitive development was founded on social interaction, with a child's understanding of the world being derived from collaboration with others.

Weapon focus: refers to the finding that eyewitnesses to a crime who see a weapon are distracted by it and less able to identify the perpetrator of the crime later on.

Wernicke's area: area of left temporal cortex hypothesized by Wernicke to be the centre where language is comprehended.

Westermark effect: refers to the finding that children who are reared closely together before the age of six avoid sexual relationships later.

Wilcoxon Matched Pairs Signed Ranks test: an inferential test of difference suitable for use with related data when at least ordinal level data have been obtained.

Withdrawal from investigation: an ethical requirement of psychological research that participants have the right to withdraw at any time from the investigation.

Working memory: a model of memory formulated by Baddeley and Hitch to replace the concept of short-term memory. It proposes a multicomponent, flexible system concerned with active processing and short-term storage of information.

Work overload: having too much work to do in the time available.

Yerkes-Dodson Law: performance increases along with arousal up to an optimum point, after which further increases in arousal are associated with decrements in performance.

Zone of proximal development (ZPD): the distance between a child's current abilities (when working unassisted) and their potential abilities or what they can do under expert guidance.

Abèles, R.D. (1976) 'Relative deprivation, rising expectations, and black militancy', *Journal of Social Issues*, 32, pp.119-37.

Able, K.P. (1996) 'The debate over olfactory navigation by homing pigeons', *The Journal of Experimental Biology*, 199, pp.121-4.

Abramov, I., Gordon, J., Hendrickson, A., Hainline, L., Dobson, V. and LaBosserie, E. (1982) 'The retina of the newborn human infant', *Science*, 217, pp.265-7.

Abrams, R., Swartz, C.M. and Vedak, C. (1991) 'Antidepressant effects of high dose right unilateral electroconvulsive therapy', *Archives of General Psychiatry*, 48, pp.746-8.

Abramson, L.Y., Metalsky, G.I. and Alloy, L.B. (1989) 'Hopelessness depression: a theory-based subtype of depression', *Psychological Review*, 96, pp.358-72.

Abramson, L.Y., Seligman, M.E.P. and Teasdale, J.D. (1978) 'Learned helplessness in humans: critique and reformulation', *Journal of Abnormal Psychology*, 87, pp.49-74.

Adams, R.J. (1995) 'Further exploration of human neonatal chromatic achromatic discrimination', *Journal of Experimental Child Psychology*, 60, pp.344-60.

Adey, P. and Shayer, M. (1993) 'An exploration of long-term far-transfer effects following an extended intervention program in the high school science curriculum', *Cognition and Instruction*, 11(1), pp.1- 29.

Adorno, T.W., Frenkey-Brunswick, E., Levinson, D.J. and Sanford, R.N. (1950) *The Authoritarian Personality*, New York: Harper & Row.

Aglioti, S.A., DeSouza, J. and Goodale, M. (1994) 'Size contrast illusions deceive the eye but not the hand', *Curr. Biol.*, 5, pp.679-85.

Akiyama, M.M. (1984) 'Are language acquisition strategies universal?', *Developmental Psychology*, 20, pp.219-28.

Allen, N. (1995) 'Towards a computational theory of depression', *ASCAP, The Newsletter of the Society for Sociophysiological Integration*, 8 (7), pp.3-12.

Alloy, L.B. and Tabachnik, N. (1984) 'Assessment of covariation by humans and animals: the joint influence of prior expectations and current situational information', *Psychological Review*, 91, pp.112-49.

Allport, D.A. (1980) 'Attention and performance', in G. Claxton (ed.) *Cognitive Psychology: New Directions*, London: Routledge and Kegan Paul.

Allport, D.A. (1989) 'Visual attention', in M.I. Posner (ed.) *Foundations of Cognitive Science*, Cambridge, MA: MIT Press.

Allport, D.A., Antonis, B. and Reynolds, P. (1972) 'On the division of attention: a disproof of the single channel hypothesis', *Quarterly Journal of Experimental Psychology*, 24, pp.225-35.

Allport, G. (1954) *The Nature of Prejudice*, New York: Double-Day Anchor.

American Psychiatric Association (1994) *Diagnostic and Statistical Manual of Mental Disorders* (4th edn), Washington, DC: American Psychiatric Association.

American Psychiatric Association (1997) 'Practice guidelines for the treatment of patients with schizophrenia', *The American Journal of Psychiatry*, 154(4), Supplement, pp.1-63.

Ammar, H. (1954) *Growing up in an Egyptian Village: Silwa, Province of Aswan*, London: Routledge & Paul.

Anand, B.K. and Brobeck, J.R. (1951) 'Hypothalamic control of food intake in rats and cats', *Yale Journal of Biological Medicine*, 24, pp.123-40.

Anderson, C.A. (1989) 'Temperature and aggression: the ubiquitous effects of heat on the occurrence of human violence', *Psychological Bulletin*, 106, pp.74-96.

Andrews, B., Morton, J., Bekerian, D.A., Brewin, C.R., Davies, G.M. and Mollon, P. (1995) 'The recovery of memories in clinical practice', *The Psychologist*, 8 (5), pp.209-14.

Andrews, G. and Peters, L. (1997) 'The CIDI-Auto: A computerised diagnostic interview for psychiatry', http://www.unsw.edu.au/ clients/crufad/cidi/discuss.htm

Antin, J., Gibbs, J. and Smith, G.P. (1978) 'Intestinal satiety requires pregastric food stimulation', *Physiology and Behavior*, 20, pp.67-70.

Apter, T. (1990) *Altered Loves: Mothers and Daughters during Adolescence*, New York: St. Martin's Press.

Archer, J. (1989) 'Childhood gender roles: structure and development', *The Psychologist*, 12, pp.367-70.

Archer, S.L. (1982) 'The lower age boundaries of identity development', *Child Development*, 53, pp.1551-6.

Archibald, H.C.D., Long, D.M., Miller, C. and Tuddenham, R.D. (1963) 'Gross stress reactions in combat', *American Journal of Psychiatry*, 119, p. 317.

Argyle, M. (1988) 'Social relationships', in M. Hewstone, W. Stroebe, J.P. Codol and G.M. Stephenson (eds) *Introduction to Social Psychology*, Oxford: Blackwell.

Argyle, M. (1992) *The Social Psychology of Everyday Life*, London: Routledge.

Argyle, M. (1994) *The Psychology of Interpersonal Behaviour*, Harmondsworth: Penguin.

Argyle, M. and Henderson, M. (1985) *The Anatomy of Relationships*, London: Penguin.

Arieti, S. and Meth, J. (1959) 'Rare, unclassifiable, collective, exotic syndromes', in S. Arieti (ed.) *American Handbook of Psychiatry*, Vol. 1, New York: Basic Books, pp.546-63.

Armsby, R.E. (1971) 'A re-examination of the development of moral judgement in children', *Child Development*, 42, pp.1241-8.

Arnold, M. (1960) *Emotion and Personality*, Vol. I, *Psychological Aspects*, New York: Columbia University Press.

Aronson, E. (1984 [4th edn], 1988 [5th edn], 1995 [7th edn], 1999 [8th edn]) *The Social Animal*, New York: W.H. Freeman.

Aronson, E., Stephan, C., Sikes, J., Blaney, N. and Snapp, M. (1978) *The Jigsaw Classroom*, Beverley Hills: Sage.

Aserinsky, E. and Kleitman, N. (1953) 'Regularly occurring periods of eye mobility and concomitant phenomena during sleep', *Science*, 118, p.273.

Aslin, R.N. (1987) 'Motor aspects of visual development in infancy', in P. Salapatek and L. Cohen (eds) *Handbook of Infant Perception,* Vol. 1, *From Sensation to Perception,* Orlando: Academic Press.

Asso, D. and Beech, H.R. (1975) 'Susceptibility to the acquisition of a conditioned response in relation to the menstrual cycle', *Journal of Psychosomatic Research,* 19, pp.337-44.

Association for the Teaching of Psychology (1992) *Ethics in Psychological Research: Guidelines for Students at Pre-degree Level,* Leicester: Association for the Teaching of Psychology.

Atchley, R.C. (1982) 'Retirement as a social institution', *Annual Review of Sociology,* 8, pp.263-87.

Atchley, R.C. (1988) *Social Forces and Aging,* Belmont, CA: Wadsworth.

Atkin, C.K., Greenberg, B.S., Korzenny, F. and McDermott, S. (1979) 'Selective exposure to televised violence', *Journal of Broadcasting,* 23, pp.5-13

Au, T.K. (1983) 'Chinese and English counterfactuals: the Sapir-Whorf hypothesis revisited', *Cognition,* 15, pp.155-87.

Augoustinos, M. and Walker, I. (1995) *Social Cognition: An Integrated Introduction,* London: Sage.

Averill, J.R. and Boothroyd, P. (1977) 'On falling in love in conformance with the romantic ideal', *Motivation and Emotion,* 1, pp.235-47.

Axelrod, R. and Hamilton, W.D. (1981) 'The evolution of coop-eration', *Science,* 211, pp.1390-6.

Ayres, J. (1983) 'Strategies to maintain relationships: their identification and usage', *Communication Quarterly,* 31, pp.207-25.

Azar, B. (1997). 'Nature, nurture: not mutually exclusive', *APA Monitor* at http://www.apa.org/monitor/may97/twinstud.html

Baddeley, A.D. (1986) *Working Memory,* Oxford: Oxford University Press.

Baerends, G.P. (1941) 'Fortpflanzungsverhalten und Orientierung der Grabwaspe *Ammophila campestris',* Jur. Tijdscher. Ent. Deel, 84, pp.268-75.

Baggaley, J. (1991) 'Media health campaigns: not just what you say, but the way you say it', in World Health Organisation, *AIDS Prevention through Health Promotion: Facing Sensitive issues,* Geneva: World Health Organisation.

Balda, R.P. and Kamil, A.C. (1992) 'Long-term spatial memory in Clark's nutcracker *Nucifraga columbiana', Animal Behaviour,* 44, pp.761-9

Baltes, P.B. and Baltes, M.M. (eds) (1990) *Successful Aging: Perspectives from the Behavioural Sciences,* Cambridge: Cambridge University Press.

Bandura, A. (1965) 'Influence of a model's reinforcement contin-gencies on the acquisition of imitative responses', *Journal of Personality and Social Psychology,* 1, pp.589-95.

Bandura, A. (1969) *Principles of Behaviour Modification,* New York: Holt, Rinehart & Winston.

Bandura, A. (1977) 'Self-efficacy: toward a unifying theory of behaviour change', *Psychological Review,* 84, pp.191-215.

Bandura, A. (1986) *Social Foundations of Thought and Action: A Social Cognitive Theory,* Englewood Cliffs, NJ: Prentice Hall.

Bandura, A. and Menlove, F.L. (1968) 'Factors determining vicarious extinction of avoidance behaviour through symbolic modelling', *Journal of Personality and Social Psychology,* 8, pp.99-108.

Bandura, A. and Walters, R.H. (1963) *Social Learning and Personality Development,* New York: Holt, Rinehart & Winston.

Bandura, A., Blanchard, E.B. and Ritter, B. (1969) 'Relative efficacy of desensitization and modelling approaches for inducing behavioural, affective and attitudinal changes', *Journal of Personality and Social Psychology,* 13, pp.173-99.

Bandura, A., Ross, D. and Ross, S.A. (1963) 'Imitation of film-mediated aggressive models', *Journal of Abnormal and Social Psychology,* 66, pp.3-11.

Banks, W.P. and Krajicek, D. (1991) 'Perception', *Annual Review of Psychology,* 42, pp.305-31.

Banyard, P. and Hunt, N. (2000) 'Reporting research: something missing?', *The Psychologist,* 13, pp.68-71.

Barash, D. (1979)*The Whisperings Within,* New York: Harper & Row.

Barlow, D.H. and Lehman, C.L. (1996) 'Advances in the psychosocial treatment of anxiety disorders', *Archives of General Psychiatry,* 53, pp.727-35.

Barlow, G. and Hill, T. (1985) *Video Violence and Children,* London: Hodder & Stoughton.

Barnes, P.E. (1995) *Personal, Social and Emotional Development of Children,* Oxford: Blackwell.

Baron, R.A. and Bell, P.A. (1976) 'Aggression and heat: mediating effect of prior provo-cation and exposure to an aggressive model', *Journal of Personality and Social Psychology,* 31, pp.825-32.

Baron, R.A. and Byrne, D. (1997) *Social Psychology* (8th edn), London: Allyn & Bacon.

Baron, R.A. and Richardson, D.R. (1994) *Human Aggression* (2nd edn), New York: Plenum.

Bartlett, F.C. (1932) *Remembering,* Cambridge: Cambridge University Press.

Basso, K. (1979) *Portraits of 'The Whiteman',* Cambridge University Press.

Bates, E., O'Connell, B. and Shore, C. (1987) 'Language and communication in infancy', in J.D. Osofsky (ed.) *Handbook of Infant Development* (2nd edn), New York: Wiley.

Bates, E., Thal, D. and Janowsky, J.S. (1992) Early language development and its neural correlates', in I. Rapin and S. Segalowitz (eds) *Handbook of Neuropsychology,* Vol. 6, Amsterdam: Elsevier.

Bateson, G., Jackson, D.D., Haley, J. and Weakland, J. (1956) 'Toward a theory of schizo-phrenia', *Behavioural Science,* 1, pp.251-64.

Bateson, P. (1986) 'When to experiment on animals', *New Scientist,* 109, pp.30-2.

Batson, C.D. and Oleson, K.C. (1991) 'Current status of the empathy-altruism hypothesis', in M.S. Clark (ed.) *Prosocial Behaviour,* Newbury Park, CA: Sage.

Batson, C.D., Duncan, B.D., Ackerman, P., Buckley, T. and Birch, K. (1981) 'Is empathic emotion a source of altruistic motivation?', *Journal of Personality and Social Psychology,* 40, pp.290-302.

Batson, C.D., O'Quin, K., Fultz, J., Vanderplas, M. and Isen, A.M. (1983) 'Influence of self-reported distress and empathy on egoistic versus altruistic motivation to help', *Journal of Personality and Social Psychology,* 45, pp.706-18.

Batson, C.D., Dyck, J.L., Brandt, J.R., Batson, J.G., Powell, A.L., McMaster, M.R. and Griffitt, C. (1988) 'Five studies testing two new egoistic alternatives to the empathy-altruism hypothesis', *Journal of Personality and Social Psychology,* 55, pp.52-77.

Baumrind, D. (1985) 'Research using intentional deception: ethical issues revisited', *American Psychologist,* 40, pp.165-74.

Baxter, L.R., Schwartz, J.M., and Bergman, K.S. (1992) 'Caudate glucose metabolic rate changes with both drug and behaviour therapy for obsessive–compul-sive disorder', *Archives of General Psychiatry,* 49, p. 681.

Beach, F.A. (1974) 'Effects of gonadal hormones on urinary behaviour in dogs', *Physiology and Behaviour,* 12, pp.1005-13.

Beall, A.E. and Sternberg, R.J. (1995) *The Psychology of Gender,* New York: Guilford Press.

Bebbington P. and Kuipers, L. (1992) 'Life events and social factors', in D.J. Kavanagh (ed.) *Schizophrenia: An Overview and Practical Handbook,* London: Chapman & Hall.

Beck, A.T. (1963) 'Thinking and depression', *Archives of General Psychiatry,* 9, pp.324-33.

Beck, A.T. (1976) *Cognitive Therapy and the Emotional Disorders,* New York: Penguin Books.

Beck, A.T. (1991) 'Cognitive therapy: a 30-year retrospective', *American Psychologist*, 46 (4), pp.368-75.

Beck, A.T. and Cowley, G. (1990) 'Beyond lobotomies', *Newsweek*, 26 March 1990, p.44.

Beck, A.T., Emery, G. and Greenberg, R.L. (1985) *Anxiety Disorders and Phobias: A Cognitive Perspective*, New York: Basic Books.

Beck, A.T., Freeman, A. and Associates (1990) *Cognitive Therapy of Personality Disorders*, New York: Guildford Press.

Beck, A.T., Ward, C.H., Mendelson, M., Mock, J. and Erlbaugh, J. (1961) 'An inventory for measuring depression', *Archives of General Psychiatry*, 4, pp.561-71.

Beck, A.T., Weissman, A., Lester, D. and Trexler, L. (1974) 'The measurement of pessimism: the hopelessness scale', *Journal of Consulting and Clinical Psychology*, 42 (6), pp.861-5.

Beck, W.H., Ward-Hull, C.I. and McLear, P.M. (1976) 'Variables related to women's somatic preferences of the male and female body', *Journal of Personality and Social Psychology*, 34, pp.1200-10.

Bee, H.L. (1998) *Lifespan Development* (2nd edn), New York: Longman.

Bee, H.L. (1999) *The Developing Child* (9th edn), Boston: Allyn & Bacon.

Bee, H.L. and Mitchell, S.K. (1984) *The Developing Person: A Life-Span Approach* (2nd edn), New York: Harper & Row.

Belk, S.S. and Snell, W.E. (1986) 'Beliefs about women: components and correlates', *Personality and Social Psychology Bulletin*, 12, pp.403-13.

Bell, B. (1999) 'The Folk Illness Glossary (FIG)', http://ihs2.unn.ac.uk:8080/figtab.htm

Bellugi, U. (1970) 'Learning the language', *Psychology Today*, 4, pp.32-5.

Bellugi, U., Bihrle, A., Jernigan, T., Trauner, D. and Doherty, S. (1991) 'Neuropsychological, neurological and neuroanatomical profile of Williams

syndrome', *American Journal of Medical Genetics Supplement*, 6, pp.115-25.

Belson, W. (1978) *Television Violence and the Adolescent Boy*, Franborough: Teakfield.

Bem, S.L. (1974) 'The measurement of psychological androgyny', *Journal of Consulting and Clinical Psychology*, 42, pp.155-62.

Bem, S.L. (1989) 'Genital knowledge and gender constancy in pre-school children', *Child Development*, 60, pp.649-62.

Benhamou, S. (1996) 'No evidence for cognitive mapping in rats', *Animal Behaviour*, 52, pp.201-12.

Benjafield, J.G. (1996) *A History of Psychology*, Boston: Allyn & Bacon.

Benjamin, L.T. (ed.) (1988) *A History of Psychology*, New York: McGraw-Hill.

Bennett, M. (1995) Why don't men come to counselling? Some speculative theories, *Counselling*, 6 (4), pp.310–13.

Bennett, N. and Dunne, E. (1991) 'The nature and quality of talk in co-operative classroom groups', *Learning and Instruction*, 1(2), pp.103-18.

Benton, D. and Cook, R. (1991) 'Vitamin and mineral supplements improve intelligence scores and concentration', *Personality and Individual Differences*, 12(11), pp.1151-8.

Berbaum, K. and Lenel, J.C. (1983) 'Objects in the path of apparent motion', *American Journal of Psychology*, 96, pp.491-501.

Bergin, A.E. (1971) 'The evaluation of therapeutic outcomes', in A.E. Bergin and S.L. Garfield (eds) *Handbook of Psychotherapy and Behaviour Change: An Empirical Analysis*, New York: Wiley.

Berglas, S. and Jones, E.E. (1978) 'Drug choice as an externalization strategy in response to noncontingent success', *Journal of Personality and Social Psychology*, 36, pp.405-17.

Berk, L.E. (1998) *Development through the Lifespan*, London: Allyn & Bacon.

Berkowitz, L. (1972) 'Frustrations, comparisons, and other sources of emotional arousal as

contributors to social unrest', *Journal of Social Issues*, 28, pp.77-91.

Berkowitz, L. (1984) 'Some effects of thoughts on anti- and prosocial influences of media events: a cognitive neoassociation analysis', *Psychological Bulletin*, 95, pp.410-27.

Berkowitz, L. (1989) 'Frustration–aggression hypothesis: examination and reformulation', *Psychological Bulletin*, 106, pp.59-73.

Berkowitz, M.W. and Gibbs, J.C. (1983) 'Measuring the developmental features of moral discussion', *Merill-Palmer Quarterly*, 29, pp.299-410.

Berlin, B. and Kay, P. (1969) *Basic Colour Terms: Their Universality and Evolution*, Berkeley & Los Angeles: University of California Press.

Bernard, C. (1856) 'Lecons de physiologie expérimentale appliquée à la médecine', *Cours du Semestre d'Eté*, 1855, 2, pp.49-52.

Bernstein, B. (1971) *Classes, Codes and Control*,Vol. 1, London: Routledge & Kegan Paul.

Bernstein, I.L. (1985) 'Learning food aversions in the progression of cancer and treatment', *Annals of the New York Academy of Sciences*, 443, pp.365-80.

Berry, J. (1969) 'On cross-cultural comparability', *International Journal of Psychology*, 4, pp.119-28.

Berry, J. (1971) 'Müller-Lyer susceptibility: culture, ecology, or race?', *International Journal of Psychology*, 6, pp.193-7.

Berry, J., Poortinga, Y.H., Segall, M.H. and Dasen, P.R. (1992) *Cross Cultural Psychology: Research and Applications*, Cambridge, MA: Cambridge University Press.

Best, B.J. (1973) *Classificatory Development in Deaf Children: Research on Language and Cognitive Development*, Occasional Paper No. 15, Research Development and Demonstration Center in Education of Handicapped Children, University of Minnesota.

Bettencourt, B.A., Brewer, M.B., Croak, M.R. and Miller, N. (1992) 'Co-operation and the

reduction of intergroup bias: the role of reward structure and social orientation', *Journal of Experimental Social Psychology*, 28, pp.301-9.

Betzig, L.L. (1996) *Human Nature: A Critical Reader*, Oxford: Oxford University Press.

Beurs, E., van Balkom, A.J.L.M., Lange, A., Keole, P. and van Dyck, R. (1995) 'Treatment of panic disorder with agoraphobia', *American Journal of Psychiatry*, 152, pp.683-91.

Bhavnani, K.K. and Phoenix, A. (1994) *Shifting Identities, Shifting Racism: A Feminism and Psychology Reader*, London: Sage.

Bickerton, D. (1984) 'The language bioprogram hypothesis', *Behavioural and Brain Sciences*, 7, pp.173-221.

Bickerton, D. (1990) *Language and Species*, Chicago: University of Chicago Press.

Bickman, L. (1972) 'Social influence and diffusion of responsibility in an emergency', *Journal of Experimental Social Psychology*, 8, pp.438-45.

Biederman, I. (1987) 'Recognition-by-components: a theory of human image understanding', *Psychological Review*, 94, pp.115-47.

Biederman, I. (1990) 'Higher-level vision', in E.N. Osherson, S.M. Kosslyn and J.M. Hollerbach (eds) *An Invitation to Cognitive Science*, Vol. 2, Cambridge, MA: MIT Press, pp.41-72.

Bieling, P.J. and Alden, L.E. (1997) 'The consequences of perfectionism for patients with social phobia', *British Journal of Clinical Psychology*, 36, pp.589-97.

Bierbrauer, G. (1979) 'Why did he do it? Attribution of obedience and the phenomenon of dispositional bias', *European Journal of Social Psychology*, 9, pp.67-84.

Bierhoff, H.W., Klein, R. and Kramp, P. (1991) 'Evidence for the altruistic personality from data on accident research', *Journal of Personality*, 59, pp.263-80.

Bierut, L.J., Heath, A.C., Bucholz, K.K., Dinwiddie, S.H., Madden, P.A.F., Statham, D.J., Dunne, M.P. and Martin, N.G. (1999) 'Major depressive disorder in a community-based twin sample',

Archives of General Psychiatry, 56, pp.557-63.

Bifulco, A., Brown, G.W., Moran, P., Ball, C. and Campbell, C. (1998) 'Predicting depression in women: the role of past and present vulnerability', *Psychological Medicine*, 28, pp.30-50.

Billig, M. (1985) 'Prejudice, categorisation and particularisation: from a perceptual to a rhetorical approach', *European Journal of Social Psychology*, 15, pp.79-104.

Binkley, S. (1979) 'A timekeeping enzyme in the pineal gland', *Scientific American*, 240, pp.66-71.

Bisagni, G.M. and Eckenrode, J. (1995) 'The role of work identity in women's adjustment to divorce', *American Journal of Orthopsychiatry*, 65 (4), pp.574-83.

Blau, P.M. (1964) *Exchange and Power in Social Life*, New York: Wiley.

Blaye, A., Light, P., Joiner, R. and Sheldon, S. (1991) 'Collaboration as a facilitor of planning and problem solving on a computer based task', *British Journal of Educational Psychology*, 61, pp.471-83.

Blehar, M.C. and Rosenthal, N.E. (1989) 'Seasonal affective disorders and phototherapy. Report of a National Institute of Mental Health-sponsored workshop', *Archives of General Psychiatry*, 46, pp.469-74.

Bloom, A.H. (1981) *The Linguistic Shaping of Thought: A Study on the Impact of Language on Thinking in China and the West*, Hillsdale, NJ: Erlbaum.

Bloom, L. (1993) *The Transition from Infancy to Language: Acquiring the Power of Expression*, Cambridge: Cambridge University Press.

Blos, P. (1967) 'The second individuation process of adolescence', *Psychoanalytic Study of the Child*, 22, pp.162-86.

Blos, P. (1967) *On Adolescence: A Psychoanalytic Interpretation*, New York: Free Press.

Blumenthal, A.L. (1975) 'A reappraisal of Wilhelm Wundt', *American Psychologist*, 30, pp.1081-8.

Boaz, N.T. and Almquist, J. (1997) *Biological Anthropology*, Englewood Cliffs, NJ: Prentice-Hall.

Bodmer, W.F. (1972) 'Race and IQ: the genetic background', in K. Richardson and D. Spears (eds) *Race, Culture and Intelligence*, Harmondsworth, Middlesex: Penguin.

Boesch, C. (1991) 'Teaching among wild chimpanzees', *Animal Behaviour*, 41A, pp.530-2.

Bohannon, P. (1970) *Divorce and After*, New York: Doubleday.

Boker, W. (1992) 'A call for partnership between schizophrenic patients, relatives and professionals', *British Journal of Psychiatry*, 161 (Suppl. 18), pp.10-12.

Bolger, T. (1989) 'Research and evaluation in counselling', in W. Dryden, D. Charles-Edwards and R. Woolfe (eds) *Handbook of Counselling in Britain*, London: Routledge.

Bolles, R.C. (1967) *Theory of Motivation*, New York: Harper & Row.

Bolton, P. (1984) 'Management of compulsorily admitted patients to a high security unit', *International Journal of Social Psychiatry*, 30, pp.77-84.

Bond, M.H. (1988) 'Finding universal dimensions of individual variation in multicultural studies of values', *Journal of Personality and Social Psychology*, 55, pp.1009-15.

Bonda, E., Petrides, M., Ostry, D. and Evans, A. (1996) 'Specific involvement of human parietal systems and the amygdala in the perception of biological motion', *Journal of Neuroscience*, 161, pp.3737-44.

Boor, N. (1992) The multiple personality epidemic: additional cases and inferences regarding diagnosis, etiology, dynamics and treatment, *Journal of Nervous and Mental Disease*, 170, pp.302-304.

Boring, E.G. (1950) *A History of Experimental Psychology* (2nd edn), New York: Appleton-Century-Crofts.

Borke, H. (1975) 'Piaget's Mountains revisited. Changes in the egocentric landscape', *Developmental Psychology*, 11, pp.240-3.

Bornstein, M.H., Tamis-LeMonda, C.S., Tal, J., Ludermann, P., Toda, S., Rahn, C.W., Pecheux, M., Azuma, H. and Vardi, D. (1992) 'Maternal responsiveness to infants in three societies: the United States, France and Japan', *Child Development*, 63, pp.808-21.

Bornstein, S. (1985) 'On the development of colour naming in young children: data and theory', *Brain and Language*, 26, pp.72-93.

Bouchard, T.J. and McGue, M. (1981) 'Familial studies of intelligence: a review', *Science*, 22, pp.1055-9.

Bower, G. (1990) 'Awareness, the unconscious and repression: an experimental psychologist's perspective', in J. Singer (ed.) *Repression and Dissociation*, Chicago: University of Chicago Press, pp.209-32.

Bower, T.G.R. (1965) 'Stimulus variables determining space perception in infants', *Science*, 149, pp.88-9.

Bower, T.G.R. (1966) 'The visual world of infants', *Scientific American*, 215, pp.80-92.

Bower, T.G.R. (1981) 'Cognitive development' in M. Roberts and J. Tamburrini (eds) *Child Development 0-5*, Edinburgh: Holmes McDougall.

Bower, T.G.R. (1982) *Development in Infancy* (2nd edn), San Francisco: W.H. Freeman.

Bowlby, J. (1973) *Attachment and Loss*, Vol. 2, *Separation, Anxiety and Anger*, New York, Basic Books.

Boyden, T., Carroll, J.S. and Maier, R.A. (1984) 'Similarity and attraction in homosexual males: the effects of age and masculinity–feminity', *Sex Roles*, 10, pp.939-48.

Boyse, E.A., Beauchamp, G.K., Yamazaki, K. and Bard. J. (1991) 'Genetic components of kin recognition in mammals', in P.G. Hepper (ed.), *Kin Recognition*, Cambridge: Cambridge University Press.

Boysen, S.T. and Himes, G.T. (1999) 'Current issues and emerging theories in animal cognition', *Annual Review of Psychology*, 50, pp.683-705.

Bradbury, T.N. and Miller, G.A. (1985) 'Season of birth in schizophrenia: a review of evidence, methodology and etiology', *Psychological Bulletin*, 98, pp.569-94.

Bradley, R.H. and Caldwell, B.M. (1984) '174 Children: a study of the relationships between the home environment and cognitive development during the first five years', in A.W. Gottfried (ed.) *Home Environment and Early Cognitive Development: Longitudinal Research*, New York: Academic Press.

Bradshaw, J.L. and Wallace, G. (1971) 'Models for the processing and identification of faces', *Perception and Psychophysics*, 9, pp.443-8.

Bradshaw, S.D. (1998) 'I'll go if you will: do shy persons utilize social surrogates?', *Journal of Social and Personal Relationships*, 15, pp.651-69.

Braine, M.D.S. (1971) 'On two types of models of the internalisation of grammars', in D.L. Slobin (ed.) *The Ontogenesis of Grammar*, New York: Academic Press.

Brearley, H.C. (1932) *Homicide in the United States*, Montclair, NJ: Patterson-Smith.

Brehm, S. S. and Kassin, S. M. (1996) *Social Psychology* (3rd edn), Boston, MA: Houghton Mifflin.

Breland, K. and Breland, M. (1951) 'A field of applied animal psychology', *American Psychologist*, 6, pp.202-4.

Breland, K. and Breland, M. (1961) 'The misbehaviour of organisms', *American Psychologist*, 16, pp.681-4.

Bremner, J.D., Southwick, S.M., Johnson, D.R., Yehoda, R. and Charney, D.S. (1993) 'Childhood physical abuse and combat-related post-traumatic stress disorder in Vietnam Veterans', *American Journal of Psychiatry*, 150 (2), pp.235-39.

Brent, D.A., Holder, D., Kolko, D., Birmaher, B., Baugher, M., Roth, C., Iyengar, S. and Johnson, B.A. (1997) 'Clinical psychotherapy trial for adolescent depression comparing cognitive, family and supportive therapy', *Archives of General Psychiatry*, 54, pp.877-85.

Brewer, M.B. and Campbell, D.T. (1976) *Ethnocentrism and Intergroup Attitudes: East*

African Evidence, New York: Sage.

Brewer, M.B. and Miller, N. (1984) 'Beyond the contact hypothesis: theoretical perspectives on desegregation', in N. Miller and M.B. Brewer (eds) *Groups in Contact: The Psychology of Desegregation*, New York: Academic Press.

Brewin, C.R. and Andrews, B. (1998) 'Recovered memories of trauma: phenomenology and cognitive mechanisms', *Clinical Psychology Review*, 4, pp.949-70.

British Association for the Advancement of Science (1990) *Animals and the Advancement of Science*, London.

British Psychological Society (1993) *Code of Conduct, Ethical Principles and Guidelines*, Leicester: BPS.

Broadbent, D.E. (1954) 'The role of auditory localization in attention and memory span', *Journal of Experimental Psychology*, 47, pp.191-6.

Broadbent, D.E. (1958) *Perception and Communication*, Oxford: Pergamon.

Broadbent, D.E. (1982) 'Task combination and selective intake of information', *Acta Psychologica*, 50, pp.253-90.

Broca, P. (1861) 'Remarques sur le siège de la faculté du langage articulé, suivées d'une observation d'aphémie', *Bulletin de la Société Anatomique* (Paris), 6, pp.330-57.

Brodbar-Nemzer, J.Y. (1986) 'Divorce and group commitment: the case of the Jews', *Journal of Marriage and the Family*, 48, pp.329-40.

Bromley, D.B. (1988) *Human Ageing: An introduction to Gerontology* (3rd edn), Harmondsworth: Penguin.

Bronfenbrenner, U. (1974) 'The origins of alienation', *Scientific American*, 231, pp.53-61.

Broverman, I.K., Broverman D.M., Clarkson, F.E., Rosencrantz, P.S. and Vogel, S.R. (1981) 'Sex role stereotypes and clinical judgements of mental health', in E. Howell and M. Bayes (eds) *Women and Mental Health*, New York: Basic Books.

Brown, G.W. (1972) 'Influence of family life on the course of

schizophrenic disorders: a replication', *British Journal of Psychiatry*, 121, pp.241-8.

Brown, G.W. and Harris, T.O. (1978) *The Social Origins of Depression*, London: Tavistock.

Brown, G.W. and Harris, T.O. (1993) 'Aetiology of anxiety and depressive disorders in an inner-city population. 1. Early adversity', *Psychological Medicine*, 23, pp.143-154.

Brown, J.S. and Burton, R.D. (1978) 'Diagnostic model for procedural bugs in basic mathematical skills', *Cognitive Science*, 2, pp.155-92.

Brown, K. and Pennell, A. (1998) *The Effects of Video Violence on Young Offenders*, Home Office Research and Statistics Directorate, Research Findings No. 65.

Brown, R. (1958) *Words and Things*, New York: Free Press.

Brown, R. (1965) *Social Psychology*, London: Collier McMillan.

Brown, R. (1973) *A First Language: The Early Stages*, Cambridge, MA: Harvard University Press.

Brown, R. (1995) *Prejudice: Its Social Psychology*, Oxford: Blackwell.

Brown, R. and Bellugi, U. (1964) 'Three processes in the child's acquisition of syntax', *Harvard Educational Review*, 34, pp.133-51.

Brown, R. and Hanlon, C. (1970) 'Derivational complexity and order of acquisition in child speech', in J.R. Hayes (ed.) *Cognition and the Development of Language*, New York: John Wiley & Sons.

Brown, R. and Lenneberg, E.H. (1954) 'A study in language and cognition', *Journal of Abnormal and Social Psychology*, 49, pp.454-62.

Brown, R., Colter, N. and Corsellis, J.A.N. (1986) 'Post-mortem evidence of structural brain changes in schizophrenia: differences in brain weight, temporal brain area, and parahippocampal gyrus compared with affective disorder', *Archives of General Psychiatry*, 43, pp.36-42.

Bruce, V. (1995) 'Perceiving and recognising faces', in I. Roth and V. Bruce (eds) *Perception*

and Representation: Current Issues (2nd edn), Buckingham: Open University Press.

Bruce, V. and Green, P.R. (1990) *Visual Perception: Physiology, Psychology and Ecology* (2nd edn), Hove: Lawrence Erlbaum.

Bruce, V. and Young, A.W. (1986) 'Understanding face recognition', *British Journal of Psychology*, 77, pp.305-27.

Bruce, V., Burton, A.M., Hanna, E., Healey, P., Mason, O., Coombes, A., Fright, R. and Linney, A. (1993) 'Sex discrimination: how do we tell the difference between male and female faces', *Perception*, 22, pp.131-52.

Bruner, J.S. (1983) *Child's Talk: Learning to Use Language*, New York: Norton.

Bryan, J.H. and Bryan, N.H. (1970) 'Preaching and practising self-sacrifice: children's actions and reactions', *Child Development*, 41, pp.329-53.

Bryan, J.H. and Test, M.A. (1967) Models and helping: naturalistic studies in aiding behavior', *Journal of Personality and Social Psychology*, 6, pp.400-7.

Bryant, P.E. and Trabasso, T. (1971) 'Transitive inferences and memory in young children', *Nature*, 232, pp.456-8.

Buchsbaum, M.S. (1990) 'The frontal lobes, basal ganglia, and temporal lobes as sites for schizophrenia', *Schizophrenia Bulletin*, 16, pp.379-89.

Buckingham, D. (1996) *Moving Images: Understanding Children's Emotional Responses to Television*, Manchester: Manchester University Press.

Bugnyar, T. and Huber, L. (1997) 'Push or pull: an experimental study on imitation in marmosets', *Animal Behaviour*, 54, pp.817-31.

Burch, R. and Russell, W. (1959) *The Principles of Humane Experimental Technique*, Methuen: London.

Burke, M., Drummond, L.M. and Johnston, D.W. (1997) 'Treatment choice for agoraphobic women: exposure or cognitive-behavioural therapy?', *British Journal of Clinical Psychology*, 36, pp.409-19.

Burling, R. (1973) *English in Black and White*, New York: Holt, Rinehart & Winston.

Burton, A.M. and Bruce, V. (1993) 'Naming faces and naming names', *Memory*, 1, pp.457-80.

Burton, A.M., Bruce, V. and Johnston, R.A. (1990) 'Understanding face recognition with an interactive activation model', *British Journal of Psychology*, 81, pp.361-80.

Buss, D. (1989) 'Sex differenecs in human mate preferences', *Behavioural and Brain Sciences*, 12, pp.1-49.

Buss, D. (1994) *The Evolution of Desire*, New York: HarperCollins.

Buss, D. (1994) 'The strategies of human mating', *American Scientist*, 82, pp.238-49.

Buss, D. (1996) 'Sexual conflict: evolutionary insights into feminism and the battle of the sexes', in D.M. Buss and N.M. Malamuth *Sex, Power and Conflict: Evolutionary and Feminist Perspectives*, New York: Oxford University Press.

Buss, D. (1999) *Evolutionary Psychology*, Needham Heights, MA: Allyn & Bacon.

Buss, D. and M. Barnes (1986) 'Preferences in human mate selection', *Journal of Personality and Social Psychology*, 50, pp.559-70.

Buss, D., Larsen, R., Westen, D. and Semmelroth, J. (1992) 'Sex differences in jealousy', *Psychological Science*, 3, pp.251-5.

Bussey, K. and Bandura, A. (1992) 'Self-regulatory mechanisms governing gender-development', *Child Development*, 63, pp.1236-50.

Butler, R.A. (1953) 'Discrimination learning by Rhesus monkeys to visual-exploration motivation', *Journal of Comparative and Physiological Psychology*, 46, pp.95-8.

Byrne, R.W. and Whiten, A. (1988) *Machiavellian Intelligence: Social Expertise and the Evolution of Intellect in Monkeys, Apes and Humans*, Oxford: Oxford University Press.

Caldwell, B.M. and Bradley, R.M. (1978) *Home Observation for Measurement of the*

Environment, Little Rock: University of Arkansas.

Cameron, C., Oskamp, S. and Sparks, W. (1977) 'Courtship American style: newspaper ads', *Family Coordinator,* 26, pp.27-30.

Campbell, S.S. and Murphy, P.J. (1998) 'Extraocular circadian phototransduction in humans', *Science,* 279, pp.396-9.

Campos, J.J., Langer, A. and Krowitz, A. (1970) 'Cardiac response on the cliff in pre-locomotor human infants', *Science,* 170, pp.196-7.

Cannon, T.D., Mednic, S.A., Parnas, J., Schulsinger, F., Praestholm J. and Vestergaard, A. (1994a) 'Developmental brain abnormalities in the offspring of schizophrenic mothers', *Archives of General Psychiatry,* 51, 955-962.

Cannon, T.D., Zorrilla, L.E., Shtasel, D., Gur, R.E., Gur, R.C., Marco, E.J., Moberg, P. and Price, R.A. (1994b) 'Neuropsychological func-tioning in siblings discordant for schizophrenia and healthy volunteers', *Archives of General Psychiatry,* 51, pp.651-61.

Cannon, W.B. (1929) *Bodily Changes in Pain, Hunger, Fear and Rage,* New York: Appleton-Century-Crofts.

Cannon, W.B. (1932) *The Wisdom of the Body,* New York: Norton.

Cannon, W.B. and Washburn, A.L. (1912) 'An explanation of hunger', *American Journal of Physiology,* 29, pp.441-54.

Cano, I., Hopkins, N. and Islam, M.R. (1991) 'Memory for stereotype-related material – a replication study with real-life groups', *European Journal of Social Psychology,* 21, pp.349-57.

Caplan, M.Z. and Hay, D.F. (1989) 'Preschoolers' responses to peer distress and beliefs about bystander intervention', *Journal of Child Psychology and Psychiatry,* 30, pp.231-42.

Caraco, T. and Wolf, L.L. (1975) 'Ecological determinants of group size of foraging lions', *American Naturalist,* 109, pp.343-52.

Cardno, A.G., Jones, L.A., Murphy, K.C., Sanders, R.D., Asherson, P., Owen, M.J. and McGuffin, P. (1998) 'Sibling pairs with schiz-ophrenia or schizoaffective disorder: associations of subtypes, symptoms and demo-graphic variables', *Psychological Medicine,* 28, pp.815-23.

Cardno, A.G., Marshall, E.J., Coid, B., Macdonald, A.M., Ribchester, T.R., Davies, N.J., Venturi, P., Jones, L.A., Lewis, S.W., Sham, P.C., Gottesman I.I., Farmer, A.E., McGuffin, P., Reveley, A.M. and Murray R.M. (1999) 'Heritability estimates for psychotic disorders', *Archives of General Psychiatry,* 56 (4), pp.162-8.

Cardwell, M.C. (1996) *The Complete A-Z of Psychology,* London: Hodder & Stoughton.

Carey, G. and Gottesman, I. (1981) 'Twin and family studies of anxiety, phobic, and obsessive disorders', in D. Klein and J. Rabkin (eds) *Anxiety: New Research and Changing Concepts,* New York: Raven Press.

Carlson, N.R. (1994) *Physiology of Behavior* (5th edn), Boston: Allyn & Bacon.

Carmichael, L., Hogan, H.P. and Walter, A.A. (1932) 'An experi-mental study of the effect of language on the reproduction of visually presented forms', *Journal of Experimental Psychology,* 15, pp.73-86.

Caro, T.M. and Hauser, M.D. (1992) 'Is there teaching in non-human animals?', *Quarterly Review of Biology,* 67, pp.151-74.

Carpenter, L. and Brockington, I.F. (1980) 'A study of mental illness in Asians, West Indians and Africans living in Manchester', *British Journal of Psychiatry,* 137, pp.201-5.

Carroll, B.J. (1982) 'The dexam-ethasone suppression test for melancholia', *British Journal of Psychiatry,* 140, pp.292-304.

Carroll, J.B. and Casagrande, J.B. (1958) 'The function of language classifications in behaviour', in E.E. Maccoby, T.M. Newcombe and E.L. Hartley (eds) *Readings in Social Psychology* (3rd edn), New York: Holt, Rinehart & Winston.

Cartwright, R. (1984) 'Broken dreams: a study of the effects of divorce and separation on dream content', *Journal for the Study of Interpersonal Processes,* 47, pp.251-9.

Case, R. (1985) *Intellectual Development: Birth to Adulthood,* New York: Academic Press.

Case, R. (1992) 'Neo-Piagetian theories of intellectual develop-ment', in H. Beilin and P.B. Pufall (eds) *Piaget's Theory: Prospects and Possibilities,* Hillsdale, New Jersey: Erlbaum.

Caspi, A. and Herbener, E.S. (1990) 'Continuity and change: assortative marriage and the consistency of personality in adulthood', *Journal of Personality and Social Psychology,* 58, pp.250-8.

Castner, S.A., Algan, O., Findlay, H.A., Rakic, P. and Goldman-Rakie, P.S. (1998) 'Fetal X-irradiation in monkeys impairs working memory after but not prior to puberty', *Society of Neuroscience,* 24, Part 1, p.225.

Cave, C.B. and Kosslyn, S.M. (1993) 'The role of parts and spatial relations in object iden-tification', *Perception,* 22, pp.229-48.

Ceci, S. (1990) *On Intelligence ... More or Less: A Bio-ecological Theory of Intellectual Development,* New York: Prentice Hall.

Centerwall, B.S. (1989) 'Exposure to television as a cause of violence', in G. Comstock (ed.) *Public Communication and Behaviour,* 2, Orlando: Academic.

Cha, J.-H. (1994) 'Aspects of indi-vidualism and collectivism in Korea', in U. Kim, H.C. Triadis, C. Kagiticibasi, S.-C. Choi and G. Yoon (eds) *Individualism and Collectivism: Theory, Method and Applications,* Newbury Park: Sage.

Chaiken, M. (1990) 'The ontogeny of antiphonal calling in European starlings', *Developmental Psychobiology,* 23, pp.233-46.

Chandler, M.J., Greenspan, S. and Barenboim, C. (1973) 'Judgements of intentionality in response to videotaped and verbally presented moral dilemmas: the medium is the message', *Child Development,* 44, pp.315-320.

Chapman, G.B. and Johnson, E.J. (1994) 'The limits of anchoring', *Journal of Behavioural Decision Making,* 7, pp.223-42.

Chen, H., Yates, B.T. and McGinnies, E. (1988) 'Effects of involvement on observers' estimates of consensus, distinc-tiveness, and consistency', *Personality and Social Psychology Bulletin,* 14, pp.468-78.

Cheng, P.W. (1985) 'Restructuring versus automaticity: alternative accounts of skills acquisition', *Psychological Review,* 92, pp.414-23.

Cherny, L. (1998) Paper submitted to the SIGGRAPH 1998 committee.

Cherry, E.C. (1953) 'Some experi-ments on the recognition of speech with one and two ears', *Journal of the Acoustical Society of America,* 25, pp.975-9.

Cheyney, D.L. and Seyfarth, R.M. (1990) *How Monkeys See the World,* Chicago: University of Chicago Press.

Chi, M.T. (1978) 'Knowledge structures and memory devel-opment', in R.S. Siegler (ed.) *Child Thinking: What develops?* Hillsdale, NJ: Erlbaum.

Chodorow, N. (1978) *The Reproduction of Mothering,* Berkeley: University of California Press.

Chomsky, N. (1957) *Syntactic Structures,* The Hague: Mouton.

Chomsky, N. (1968) *Language and Mind,* New York: Harcourt Brace.

Chomsky, N. (1981) *Lectures on Government and Binding,* Dordrecht: Foris.

Chorney, M.J., Chorney, K., Seese, N., Owen, M.J., Daniels, J., McGuffin, P., Thompson, L.A., Detterman, D.K., Benbow, C.P., Lubinski, D., Eley, T.C. and Plomin, R. (1998) 'A quantita-tive trait locus (QTL) associated with cognitive ability in children', *Psychological Science,* 9, pp.159-66.

Churchland, P.S. and Ramachandran, V.S. (1996) 'Filling in: why Dennett is wrong', in K. Atkins (ed.) *Perception,* Oxford: Oxford University Press.

Cialdini, R.B., Borden, R.J., Thorne, A., Walker, M.R., Freeman, S. and Sloan, L.R. (1976) 'Basking in reflected glory: three (football) field studies', *Journal of Personality* and Social Psychology, 34, pp.366-374.

Cialdini, R.B., Kenrick, D.T. and Bauman, D.J. (1982) 'Effects of mood on pro-social behaviour in children and adults', in N. Eisenberg Berg (ed.) *Development of Prosocial Behaviour*, New York: Academic Press.

Cialdini, R.B., Reno, R.R. and Kallgren, C.A. (1990) 'A focus theory of normative conduct: recycling the concept of social norms to reduce littering in public places', *Journal of Personality and Social Psychology*, 58, pp.1015-26.

Cialdini, R.B., Schaller, M., Honlainhan, D., Arps, H., Fultz, J. and Beaman, A.L. (1987) 'Empathy-based helping: is it selflessly or selfishly motivated?', *Journal of Personality and Social Psychology*, 52, pp.749-58.

Clahsen, H. (1992) 'Learnability theory and the problem of development in language acquisition', in J. Weissenborn, H. Goodluck and T. Roeper (eds) *Theoretical Issues in Language Acquisition*, Hillsdale, NJ: Erlbaum.

Clare, A.W. (1985) 'Hormones, behaviour and the menstrual cycle', *Journal of Psychosomatic Research*, 29, pp.225-33.

Clark, E.V. (1993) *The Lexicon in Acquisition*, Cambridge: Cambridge University Press.

Clark, H.H. (1991) 'Words, the world and their possibilities', in G.R. Lockhead and J.R. Pomerantz (eds) *The Perception of Structure*, Washington, DC: American Psychological Association.

Clark, M.S. and Mills, J. (1979) 'Interpersonal attraction and communal relationships', *Journal of Personality and Social Psychology*, 37, pp.12-24.

Clark, R.D. and Word, L.E. (1974) 'Where is the apathetic bystander? Situational characteristics of the emergency', *Journal of Personality and Social Psychology*, 29, pp.279-87.

Clayton, C. and Krebs, J.R. (1995) 'Memory in food-storing birds: from behaviour to brain', *Current Opinion in Neurobiology*, 5 (2), pp.149-54.

Clutton-Brock, T.H. and Vincent, A.C.J. (1991) 'Sexual selection and the potential reproductive rates of males and females', *Nature*, 351, pp.58-60.

Cochrane, R. (1977) Mental illness in immigrants to England and Wales: an analysis of mental hospital admissions, 1971, *Social Psychiatry*, 12, pp.25-35.

Cochrane, R. (1995) Women and depression, *Psychology Review*, 2 (1), pp.20-4.

Cochrane, R. and Sashidharan, S.P. (1995) 'Mental health and ethnic minorities: a review of the literature and implications for services', Paper presented to the Birmingham and Northern Birmingham Health Trust.

Cohen, C. (1981) 'Person categories and social perception: testing some boundaries of the processing effects of prior knowledge', *Journal of Personality and Social Psychology*, 40, pp.441-52.

Cohen, C. (1987) 'Nuclear language', *Bulletin of the Atomic Scientist*, June 1987, pp.17-24.

Cohen, J.E. (1995) 'The uniqueness of present human population growth', in J. Brockman and K. Matson (eds) *How Things Are: A Science Tool-Kit for the Mind*, London: Weidenfeld and Nicolson.

Colby, A. and Kohlberg, L. (1987) *The Measurement of Moral Judgement*, Cambridge: Cambridge University Press.

Colby, A., Kohlberg, L., Gibbs, J. and Liebermann, M. (1983) 'A longitudinal study of moral development', *Monographs of the Society for Research in Child Development*, 48(1-2), No. 200.

Cole, M., Gay, J., Glick, J. and Sharp, D.W. (1971) *The Cultural Content of Learning and Thinking*, New York: Basic Books.

Coleman, J.C. (1974) *Relationships in Adolescence*, London: Routledge & Kegan Paul.

Coleman, J.C. and Hendry, L. (1990) *The Nature of Adolescence*, London: Routledge.

Collett, P. and O'Shea, G. (1976) 'Pointing the way to a fictional place, a study of direction

giving in England and Iran', *European Journal of Social Psychology*, 6, pp.447-58.

Comer, R.J. (1995 [2nd edn, 1999 [3rd edn]) *Abnormal Psychology*, New York: W.H. Freeman.

Comstock, G. (1989) *The Evolution of American Television*, Newbury Park: Sage.

Conel, J.L. (1951) *The Postnatal Development of the Cerebral Cortex* (Vol. 3), Cambridge: Harvard University Press.

Cook, M. (1978) *Perceiving Others*, London: Routledge.

Coolican, H. (1999) *Research Methods and Statistics in Psychology* (3nd edn), London: Hodder & Stoughton.

Coons, P. (1989) 'Iatrogenic factors in the misdiagnosis of multiple personality disorder', *Dissociation*, 2, pp.70-6.

Cooper, P.J. (1988) 'Non-psychotic psychiatric disorder after childbirth: a prospective study of prevalence, incidence, course and nature', *British Journal of Psychiatry*, 152, pp.799-806.

Cooper, R.P. and Aslin, R.N. (1994) 'Developmental differences in infant attention to the spectral properties of infant directed speech', *Child Development*, 65, pp.1663-77.

Coren, S. (1996) *Sleep Thieves*, New York: Free Press.

Coren, S., Ward, L.M. and Enns, J.T. (1999) *Sensation and Perception* (5th edn), Orlando: Harcourt Brace.

Corey, G. (1995) *Theory and Practice of Group Counselling*, California: Brookes/Cole.

Corrigan, R. (1978) 'Language development as related to stage 6 object permanence development', *Journal of Child Language*, 5, pp.173-89.

Corsini, R.J. and Wedding, D. (1995) *Current Psychotherapies* (5th edn), Illinois: F.E. Peacock Publishers.

Corteen, R.S. and Dunn, D. (1973) 'Shock associated words in a non-attended message: a test for momentary awareness', *Journal of Experimental Psychology*, 102, pp.1143-4.

Corteen, R.S. and Wood, B. (1972) 'Autonomous response to shock associated words in an unattended channel',

Journal of Experimental Psychology, 94, pp.308-13.

Courage, M.L. and Adams, J. (1996) 'Infant peripheral vision: the development of monocular visual acuity in the first three months of postnatal life', *Vision Research*, 36, pp.1207-15.

Cowlishaw, G. (1992) 'Song function in gibbons', *Behaviour*, 121, pp.131-53.

Crabb, P.B. and Bielawski, D. (1994) 'The social representation of material culture in children's books', *Sex Roles*, 30 (1/2), pp.69-79.

Craske, M.G. and Barlow, D.H. (1993) 'Panic disorder and agoraphobia', in D.H. Barlow (ed.) *Clinical Handbook of Psychological Disorders: A Step-by-Step Treatment Manual* (2nd edn), New York: Guildford.

Crawford, C. (1998) 'Environment and Adaptations: Then and Now', in C. Crawford and D. L. Krebs (eds) *Handbook of Evolutionary Psychology*, Mahwah, NJ: Lawrence Erlbaum.

Cray, E. (1995) 'Teaching about racism', *Psychology Teaching*, 4, Association for the Teaching of Psychology, Leicester: British Psychological Society.

Crick, F. and Mitchison, G. (1983) 'The function of dream sleep', *Nature*, 304, pp.111-14.

Crocker, J. and Major, B. (1989) 'Social stigma and self-esteem: the self-protective properties of stigma', *Psychological Review*, 96, pp.608-30.

Crook, J.H. and Crook, S.J. (1988) 'Tibetan polyandry', in L. Betzig, Borgehoff-Mulder and P. Turke (eds) *Human Reproductive Behaviour*, Cambridge: Cambridge University Press.

Crooke, C. (1992) 'Cultural artefacts in social development: the case of computers', in H. McGurk (ed.) *Childhood Social Development: Contemporary Perspectives*, Hove: Erlbaum.

Crow, T.J. (1984) 'A re-evaluation of the viral hypothesis: is psychosis the result of retroviral integration at the site to the cerebral dominance gene?', *British Journal of Psychiatry*, 145, pp.243-53.

Cumberbatch, G. (1994) 'Legislating mythology: video

violence and children', *Journal of Mental Health*, 3, pp.485-94.

Cumberbatch, G. (1997) 'Media violence: science and common sense', *Psychology Review*, April 1997, pp.2-7.

Cumming, E., and Henry, W.E. (1961) *Growing Old*, New York: Basic Books.

Cunningham, M.R. (1988) 'Does happiness mean friendliness? Induced mood and hetero-sexual disclosure', *Personality and Social Psychology Bulletin*, 14, pp.283-97.

Cuthill, I. (1991) 'Field experiments in animal behaviour', *Animal Behaviour*, 42, pp.1007-14.

Czeisler, C.A., Moore-Ede, M.C. and Coleman, R.M. (1982) 'Rotating shift work schedules that disrupt sleep are improved by applying circadian principles', *Science*, 217, pp.460-3.

Dalman, C., Allebeck, P., Cullberg, J., Grunewald, C. and Koster, M. (1999) 'Obstetric complications and the risk of schizophrenia: a longitudinal study of a national birth cohort', *Archives of General Psychiatry*, 56 (3), pp.234-40.

Dalton, K. (1964) *The Premenstrual Syndrome*, London: Heinemann.

Daly, M. (1997) 'Introduction', in G. R. Bock and G. Cardew, *Characterising Human Psychological Adaptations*, Chichester: John Wiley.

Daly, M. and Wilson, M. (1988) *Homicide*, Belmont: Wadsworth.

Dana, C.L. (1921) 'The anatomic seat of the emotions: a discussion of the James-Lange Theory', *Archives of Neurology and Psychiatry (Chicago)*, 6, pp.634-9.

Danner, F.W. and Day, M.C. (1977) 'Eliciting formal operations', *Child Development*, 48, pp.1600-6.

Darley, J. and Latané, B. (1968) 'Bystander intervention in emergencies', *Journal of Personality and Social Psychology*, 8, pp.377-83.

Darwin, C. (1859) *On the Origin of Species by Means of Natural Selection, or the Preservation of Favoured Races in the Struggle for Life*, London: Murray.

Darwin, C. (1871) *The Descent of Man and Selection in relation to Sex*, London: John Murray. For a general source book of Darwin's original writings, see Porter, D.M. and Graham, P.W. (eds) (1993) *The Portable Darwin*, Harmondsworth: Penguin Books.

Darwin, C. (1969) *The Autobiography of Charles Darwin*, New York: Norton.

Davenport, G.C. (1994) *An Introduction to Child Development* (2nd edn), London: HarperCollins.

Davenport, W.H. (1965) 'Sexual patterns and their regulation in a society of the Southwest Pacific', in F.A. Beach (ed.), *Sex and Behavior*, New York: Wiley.

Davies, G. (1994) 'Ethical considerations', *Psychology Review*, 1(1), pp.13-15.

Davies, M.H. (1993) 'Psychodrama group therapy', in M. Aveline and W. Dryden (eds) *Group Therapy in Britain*, Milton Keynes: Open University Press.

Davies, N.B., Brooke, M. de L. and Kacelnik, A. (1996) 'Recognition errors and probability ability of parasitism determine whether reed warblers should accept or reject mimetic cuckoo eggs', *Proceedings of the Royal Society of London B*, 263, pp.925-31.

Davis, J.D., Kane, J.M., Marder, S.R., Brauzer, B., Gierl, B., Schooler, N., Casey, D.E. and Hassan, M. (1993) 'Dose response of prophylatic antipsychotics', *Journal of Clinical Psychiatry*, 54 (3), pp.24-30.

Davison, G.C. and Neale, J.M. (1997) *Abnormal Psychology* (7th edn), New York: John Wiley & Sons.

Dawkins, M.S. (1985) 'The scientific basis for assessing suffering in animals', in P. Singer *Defence of Animals*, Oxford: Blackwell.

Dawkins, R. (1976) *The Selfish Gene*, Oxford: Oxford University Press.

Dawkins, R. (1981) 'Communication', in D. McFarland (ed.) *The Oxford Companion to Animal Behaviour*, Oxford: Oxford University Press, pp.78-91.

Dawkins, R. (1982) *The Extended Phenotype*, London: W.H. Freeman.

Dawson, M.E. and Schell, A.M. (1983) 'Lateral asymmetries in electrodermal responses to non-attended stimuli: a reply to Walker and Ceci', *Journal of Experimental Psychology: Human Perception and Performance*, 9, pp.148-50.

Day, R.H. (1990) 'The Bourdon illusion in haptic space', *Perception and Psychophysics*, 47, pp.400-4.

Dayton, T. (1994) *The Drama Within*, Florida: Health Communications Inc.

Deacon, T. W. (1992) 'The human brain', in S. Jones, R. Martin and D. Pilbeam (eds) *The Cambridge Encyclopedia of Human Evolution*, Cambridge: Cambridge University Press.

Dean, G., Walsh, D., Downing, H. and Shelley, E. (1981) 'First admissions of native-born and immigrants to psychiatric hospitals in South-East England, 1970', *British Journal of Psychiatry*, 139, pp.506-12.

Deaux, K. (1976) *The Behaviour of Women and Men*, Monterey, CA: Brooks/Cole.

Deaux, K., Dane, F.C. and Wrightsman, L.S. (1993) *Social Psychology in the '90s* (6th edn), Pacific Grove, CA: Brooks/Cole.

de Cantazaro, D. (1995) 'Reproductive status, family interactions, and suicidal ideation: surveys of the general public and high risk groups', *Ethology and Sociobiology*, 16, pp.385-94.

DeLucia, P. and Hochberg, J. (1991) 'Geometrical illusions in solid objects under ordinary viewing conditions', *Perception and Psychophysics*, 50, pp.547-54 .

Dement, W. and Kleitman, N. (1957) 'Cyclic variations in EEG during sleep and their relation to eye movements, body motility and dreaming', *Electroencephalography and Clinical Neurophysiology*, 9, pp.673-90.

Deregowski, J. (1972) 'Pictorial perception and culture', *Scientific American*, 227, pp.82-8.

Deregowski, J. (1980) 'Illusions, patterns and pictures: a cross-cultural perspective', London: Academic Press.

Deutsch, J.A. and Deutsch, D. (1963) 'Attention, some theoretical considerations', *Psychological review*, 70, pp.80-90.

Deutsch, J.A., Young, G.W. and Kalogeris, T.J. (1978) 'The stomach signals satiety', *Science*, 201, pp.165-7.

Deutsch, M. and Collins, M.E. (1951) *Interracial Housing: A Psychological Evaluation of a Social Experiment*, Minneapolis: University of Minneapolis Press.

DeValois, R.L. and DeValois, K.K. (1980) 'Spatial vision', *Annual Review of Psychology*, 31, pp.309-41.

Devanand, D.P., Dwork, A.J., Hutchinson, E.R., Bolwig, T.G. and Sackeim, H.A. (1994) 'Does ECT alter brain structure?', *American Journal of Psychiatry*, 151, pp.957-70.

DeVellis, B.M. and Blalock, S.J. (1992) 'Illness attributions and hopeless depression: the role of hopelessness expectancy', *Journal of Abnormal Psychology*, 101, pp.257-64.

de Villiers, P.A. and de Villiers, J.G. (1992) 'Language development', in M.H. Bornstein and M.E. Lamb (eds) *Developmental Psychology: An Advanced Textbook* (3rd edn), Hillsdale, NJ: Erlbaum.

Devine, P.A. and Fernald, P.S. (1973) 'Outcome effects of receiving a preferred, randomly assigned or non-preferred therapy', *Journal of Consulting and Clinical Psychology*, 41 (1), pp.104-7.

de Waal, F.B.M. (1999) 'The end of nature versus nurture', *Scientific American*, 281, 6, pp.56-61.

Diamond, J.M. (1991) *The Rise and Fall of the Third Chimpanzee*, London: Radius.

Diener, E. (1980) 'Deindividuation: the absence of self-awareness and self-regulation in group members', in P. Paulus (ed.) *The Psychology of Group Influence*, Hillsdale, NJ: Lawrence Erlbaum.

Dindia, K. and Baxter, L.A. (1987) 'Maintenance and repair strategies in marital relationships',

Journal of Social and Personal Relationships, 4, pp.143-58.

Dion, K.K. and Dion, K.L. (1993) 'Individualistic and collectivistic perspectives on gender and the cultural context of love and intimacy', *Journal of Social Issues*, 49, pp.53-69.

Dirks, J. (1982) 'The effect of a commercial game on children's Block Design scores on the WISC-R test', *Intelligence*, 6, pp.109-23.

Doise, W. (1986) *Levels of Explanation in Social Psychology*, Cambridge: Cambridge University Press.

Donaldson, M. (1978) *Children's Minds*, London: Fontana.

Donnerstein, E. and Wilson, D.W. (1976) 'The effects of noise and perceived control upon ongoing and subsequent aggressive behaviour', *Journal of Personality and Social Psychology*, 34, pp.774-81.

Dooling, R.J., Soli, S.D., Kline, R.M., Park, T.J., Hue, C. and Bunnell, T. (1987) 'Perception of synthetic speech sounds by the budgerigar (*Melopsittacus undulatus*)', *Bulletin of the Psychonomic Society*, 25, pp.139-42.

Douglas, K. (2000) 'Mind of a dog', *New Scientist*, 165, pp.22-27.

Dryden, W., Charles-Edwards, D. and Woolfe, R. (1989) *Handbook of Counselling in Britain*, London: Routledge.

Duck, S. (1981) 'Toward a research map for the study of relationship breakdown', in S. Duck and R. Gilmour (eds) *Personal Relationships*, Vol. 3, *Personal Relationships in Disorder*, London: Academic Press.

Duck, S. (1988) *Relating to Others*, Milton Keynes: Open University Press.

Duck, S. (1999a) *Relating to Others* (2nd edn), Buckingham: Open University Press.

Duck, S. (1999b) 'Relationships, social psychology and everyday life', Paper presented to the BPS (Social Section) Conference, University of Lancaster, September 1999.

Dunbar, R. (1993) 'Coevolution of neocortical size, group size and language in humans',

Behavioural and Brain Sciences, 16, pp.681-735.

Dunbar, R. (1995) 'Are you lonesome tonight?', *New Scientist*, 11 February, pp.26-31.

Dunbar, R. (1996) *Grooming, Gossip and the Evolution of Language*, London, Faber & Faber.

Duncan, H.F., Gourlay, N. and Hudson, W. (1973) 'A study of pictorial representation among the Bantu and white primary school children in South Africa', Johannesburg: Witwatersrand University Press.

Duncker, K. (1945/35) 'On problem solving', *Psychological Monographs*, 58, pp.1-113 (originally published in German in 1935).

Du Plessis, P., Bor, R., Slack, D., Swash, E. and Corbell, D. (1995) 'Assessment of HIV counselling and social care services in a London hospital', *British Journal of Guidance and Counselling*, 23, pp.45-51.

Durkheim, E. (1898) 'Representations individuelles et representations collectives', *Revue de Metaphysique*, 6, pp.274-302 (in D.F. Pocock (trans.) *Sociology and Philosophy*, New York: Free Press, 1953).

Durkin, K. (1995) *Developmental Social Psychology*, Oxford: Blackwell.

Dutton, D.C. and Aron, A.P. (1974) 'Some evidence for heightened sexual attraction under conditions of high anxiety', *Journal of Personality and Social Psychology*, 30, pp.510-17.

Dworkin, B.R. (1987) 'Genetics and the phenomenology of schizophrenia' in P.D. Harvey and E.F. Walker (eds) *Positive and negative symptoms of psychosis*, Hillsdale, New York: Erlbaum.

Dyer, C. (1995) *Beginning Research in Psychology: A Practical Guide to Research Methods and Statistics*, Oxford: Blackwell.

Dyer, F.C. (1996) 'Spatial memory and navigation by honeybees on the scale of the foraging range', *The Journal of Experimental Biology*, 199, pp.147-54.

Dyer, F.C. and Dickinson, J.A. (1994) 'Development of sun compensation by honey bees: how partially experienced bees estimate the sun's course', *Proceedings of the National Academy of Sciences USA*, 91, pp.4471-4.

Eagley, A.H. and Crowley, M. (1986) 'Gender and helping behaviour: a meta-analytic review of the social psychological literature', *Psychological Review*, 100, pp.283-308.

Eaton, W.W., Dryman, A. and Weissman, M.M. (1991) 'Panic and phobia', in L.N. Robins and D.A. Reiger (eds) *Psychiatric Disorders in America*, New York: The Free Press.

Eccles, J. (1987) 'Brain and Mind, Two or One?' in C. Blakemore and S. Greenfield (eds) *Mindwaves*, London: Blackwell.

Eccles, J.S., Midgley, C., Wigfield, A. and Buchanan, C.M. (1993) 'Development during adolescence: the impact of stage-environment fit on young adolescents' experiences in schools and in families', *American Psychologist*, 48, pp.90-101.

Eckensberger, L.H. (1983) 'Research on moral development', *German Journal of Psychology*, 7(3), pp.195-244.

Egrise, D., Rubinstein, M., Schoutens, A., Cantraine, F. and Mendlewicz, J. (1986) 'Seasonal variation of platelet serotonin uptake and 3H-imipramine binding in normal and depressed subjects', *Biological Psychiatry*, 21, pp.283-92.

Einon, D. (1998) 'How many children can one man have?', *Evolution and Human Behaviour*, 19, pp.413-26.

Eisenberg, N. and Lennon, R. (1983) 'Sex differences in empathy and related capacities', *Psychological Bulletin*, 94(1), pp.100-31.

Eisenberg, N. and Mussen, P.H. (1989) *The Roots of Prosocial Behaviour in Children*, Cambridge: Cambridge University Press.

Eisenberg, N., Lennon, R. and Roth, K. (1983) 'Prosocial development: a longitudinal study', *Developmental Psychology*, 19, pp.846-55.

Eisenberg, N., Miller, P.A., Shell, R., McNalley, S. and Shea, C.

(1991) 'Prosocial development in adolescence: a longitudinal study', *Developmental Psychology*, 27, pp.849-57.

Eisenberg, N., Shell, R., Paternak, J., Lennon, R., Beller, R. and Mathy, R.M. (1987) 'Prosocial development in middle childhood: a longitudinal study', *Developmental Psychology*, 23, pp.712-718.

Eisenberg-Berg, N. and Hand, M. (1979) 'The relationship of preschoolers' reasoning about prosocial moral conflicts to prosocial behaviour', *Child Development*, 50, pp.356-63.

Ekman, P. (1973) *Darwin and Facial Expression: A Century of Research in Review*. New York: Academic Press.

Ekman, P. (1992) 'Facial expressions of emotions: new findings, new questions', *Psychological Science*, 3, pp.34-8.

Elliott, J. (1977) 'The power and pathology of prejudice', in P.G. Zimbardo and F.L. Ruch, *Psychology and Life* (9th edn), Diamond Printing, Glenview, Illinois: Scott, Foresman.

Elliott, J. (1990) in *Discovering Psychology*, Program 20 [PBS video series], Washington, DC: Annenberg/CPB Program.

Ellis, A. (1962) *Reason and Emotion in Psychotherapy*, New York: Citadel.

Ellis, A. (1980) 'Discomfort anxiety: a new cognitive-behavioural construct. Part 2', *Rational Living*, 15 (1), pp.25-30.

Ellis, A. (1991) 'The revised ABCs of rational-emotive therapy', *Journal of Rational-Emotive and Cognitive-Behaviour Therapy*, 9, pp.139-92.

Ellis, H.D. (1986) 'Processes underlying face recognition', in R. Bruyer (ed.) *The Neuropsychology of Face Perception and Facial Expression*, Hove: Laurence Elbaum Associates.

Emmelkamp, P.M. (1994) 'Behaviour therapy with adults', in A.E. Bergin and S.L. Garfield (eds) *Handbook of Psychotherapy and Behaviour Change* (4th edn), New York: Wiley.

Emmelkamp, P.M. and Cohen-Kettenis, P. (1975) 'Relationship

of locus of control to phobic anxiety and depression', *Psychological Reports*, 36(2), p.390.

Emmelkamp, P.M., Visser, S. and Hoekstra, R.J. (1988) 'Cognitive therapy vs exposure in the treatment of obsessive compulsives', *Cognitive Therapy Research*, 12 (1), pp.103-14.

Emmerlich, W., Goldmann, K., Kirsh, K. and Sharabany, R. (1977) 'Evidence for a transitional phase in the development of gender constancy', *Child Development*, 48, pp.930-6.

Engel, M., Nechglin, H. and Arkin, A.M. (1975) 'Aspects of mothering: correlates of the cognitive development of black male infants in the second year of life', in A. Davids (ed.) *Child Personality and Psychopathology: Current Topics*, Vol. 2, New York: Wiley.

Engels, G.I., Garnefski, N. and Diekstra, R.F.W. (1993) 'Efficacy of rational–emotive therapy: a quantitative analysis', *Journal of Consulting and Clinical Psychology*, 61(6), pp.1083-90.

Epstein, A.N., Fitzsimons, J.T. and Rolls, B.J. (1970) 'Drinking induced by injection of angiotensin into the brain of the rat', *Journal of Physiology* (London), 210, pp.457-74.

Epstein, L.C. and Lasagna, L. (1969) 'Obtaining informed consent', *Archives of Internal Medicine*, 123, pp.682-8.

Epstein, R., Lanza, R.P. and Skinner, B.F. (1981) '"Self-awareness" in the pigeon', *Science*, 212, pp.695-6.

Erikson, E.H. (1968) *Identity: Youth and Crisis*, London: Faber.

Erikson, E.H. (1980) *Identity and the Life Cycle*, New York: Norton.

Erlennmeyer-Kimling, L., Adamo, U.H., Rock, D., Roberts, S.A., Bassett, A.S., Squires-Wheeler, E., Cornblat, B.A., Endicott, J., Pape, S. and Gottessman, I.I. (1997) 'The New York High-Risk Project', *Archives of General Psychiatry*, 54, pp.1096-1102.

Eron, L.D., Huesmann, L.R., Lefkowitz, M.M., and Walder, L.O. (1972) 'Does television violence cause aggression?',

American Psychologist, 27, pp.253-63.

Eron, L.D. (1992) 'The impact of televised violence', Testimony on behalf of the American Psychological Association before the Senate Committee on Governmental Affairs, June 18.

Ervin-Tripp, S. (1964) 'An analysis of the interaction of language, topic and listener' *American Anthropologist*, 66, pp.94-100.

Ervin-Tripp, S., Guo, J. and Lampert, M. (1990) 'Politeness and persuasion in children's control acts', *Journal of Pragmatics*, 14, pp.307-31.

Evans, C.S. and Marler, P. (1995) 'Language and animal communication: Parallels and contrasts', in H.L. Roitblat and J.-A. Meyer (eds) *Comparative Approaches to Cognitive Science*, Cambridge, MA: MIT Press.

Evans, G., Bullinger, M. and Hygger, S. (1998) 'The effects of chronic exposure to aircraft noise', *Psychological Science*, 9(1), pp.75-7.

Evans, M.D., Hollon, S.D., DeRubeis, R.J. and Associates (1992) 'Differential relapse following cognitive therapy and pharmacotherapy for depression', *Archives of General Psychiatry*, 49, pp.802-8.

Everson, C.A., Bergmann, B.M. and Rechstaffen, A. (1989) 'Sleep deprivation in the rat: III. Total sleep deprivation', *Sleep*, 12, pp.13-21.

Eysenck, H.J. (1952) 'The effects of psychotherapy: an evaluation', *Journal of Consulting Psychology*, 16, pp.319-24.

Eysenck, H.J. (1963) 'Biological basis of personality', *Nature*, 199, pp.1031-4.

Eysenck, H.J. *The Structure of Human Personality* (3rd edn), London: Methuen.

Eysenck, M.W. and Keane, M.T. (1995) *Cognitive Psychology: A Student's Handbook* (3rd edn), Hove: Lawrence Erlbaum Associates.

Fagot, B.I. (1985) 'Beyond the reinforcement principle: another step toward understanding sex role development', *Developmental Psychology*, 21, pp.1097-1104.

Falkai, P., Bogerts, B., and Rozumek, M. (1988) 'Limbic pathology in schizophrenia', *Proceedings of the National Academy of Science, USA*, 2, pp.560-3.

Fancher, R. (1990) *Pioneers of Psychology* (2nd edn), New York: W.W. Norton.

Fantz, R.L. (1961) 'The origin of form perception', *Scientific American*, 204 (5), pp.66-72.

Faraone, S.V., Seidman, L.J., Kremen, W.S., Toomey, R. and Pepple, J.R. (1999) 'Neuropsychological functioning among the nonpsychotic relatives of schizophrenic patients: a four-year follow-up study', *Journal of Abnormal Psychology*, 108, pp.176-81.

Farr, R. (1977) 'Heider, Harré and Herzlich on health and illness: some observations on the structure of 'représentations collectives', *European Journal of Social Psychology*, 7, pp.491-504.

Farrell, M.P. and Rosenberg, S.D. (1981) *Men at Midlife*, Boston: Auburn House.

Fechner, G.T. (1966) *Elements of Psychophysics* (Vol. 1), New York: Holt, Rinehart & Winston (original work published in 1860)

Feldman, N.S., Klosson, E.C., Parsons, J.E., Knoles, W.S. and Ruble, D.N. (1976) 'Order of information presentation and children's moral judgements', *Child Development*, 47, pp.556-9.

Feldman, R. (1968) 'Responses to compatriots and foreigners who seek assistance', *Journal of Personality and Social Psychology*, 10, pp.202-14.

Felson, R.B. (1996) 'Mass media effects on violent behaviour', *Annual Review of Sociology*, 22, pp.103-28.

Feltham, C. (1996) 'Psychotherapy's staunchest critic: an interview with Hans Eysenck', *British Journal of Guidance and Counselling*, 24, pp.423-35.

Fenson, L., Dale, P.S., Resnick, J.S., Bates, E., Thal, D.J. and Pethick, S.J. (1994) 'Variability in early communicative development', *Monographs of the Society for Research in Child development*, 59 (5, Serial No. 242).

Fenson, L., Dale, P.S., Resnick, S., Thal, D.J., Bates, E., Hartung, J., Pethick, S. and Reilly, J. (1991) *The MacArthur Communicative Development Inventories: Technical Manual*, San Diego, CA: San Diego State University.

Fernando, S. (1988) *Race and Culture in Psychiatry*, London: Croom Helm.

Fernando, S. (1991) *Mental Health, Race and Culture*, London: Macmillan/Mind.

Festinger, L., Schachter, S. and Back, K.W. (1950) *Social Pressures in Informal Groups*, New York: Harper.

Fiedler, K. (1982) 'Causal schemata: review and criticism of research on a popular construct', *Journal of Personality and Social Psychology*, 42, pp.1001-13.

Fiedler, K. (1996) 'Processing social information for judgements and decisions', in M. Hewstone, W. Stroebe and G.M. Stephenson (eds) *Introduction to Social Psychology* (2nd edn), Oxford: Blackwell.

Field, D. and Minkler, (1988) 'Continuity and change in social support between young-old, old-old and very old adults', *Journal of Gerontology*, 43, pp.100-6.

Fine, M. and Gordon, S.M. (1989) 'Feminist transformations of/despite psychology' in M. Crawford and M. Gentry (eds) *Gender and Thought: Psychological Perspectives*, New York: Springer-Verlag.

Fischer, M. (1971) 'Psychosis in the offspring of schizophrenic monozygotic twins and their normal co-twins', *British Journal of Psychiatry*, 118, pp.43-52.

Fish, B., Marcus, J., Hans, S.L., Auerbach, J.G. and Perdue, S. (1992) 'Infants at risk for schizophrenia: sequelae of a genetic neurointegrative defect', *Archives of General Psychiatry*, 49, pp.221-37.

Fishbein, M. and Ajzen, L. (1975) *Belief, Attitude, Intention and Behaviour: An Introduction to Theory and Research*, Reading, MA: Addison-Wesley.

Fisher, A.E. and Coury, J.N. (1962) 'Cholinergic tracing of a central neural circuit underlying the thirst drive', *Science*, 138, pp.691-3.

Fisher, R.A. and Yates, F. (1974) *Statistical Tables for Biological, Agricultural and Medical Research* (6th edn), Harlow: Longman Group Ltd.

Fiske, A.P. (1991) 'The cultural relativity of selfish individualism: anthropological evidence that humans are inherently sociable', in M.S. Clark (ed.) *Prosocial Behaviour*, Newbury Park, CA: Sage.

Fiske, S.T. (1989) 'Interdependence and stereotyping: from the laboratory to the Supreme Court (and back)', Invited address, American Psychological Association: New Orleans.

Fiske, S.T. and Neuberg, S.L. (1990) 'A continuum model of impression formation, from category based to individuating processes: influence of information and motivation on attention and interpretation', in M.P. Zanna (ed.) *Advances in Experimental Social Psychology*, Vol. 23, New York: Academic Press.

Fiske, S.T. and Taylor, S. (1992) *Social Cognition*, Reading, MA: Addison-Wesley.

Fitzgibbon, C.D. and Fanshawe, J.H. (1988) 'Stotting in Thompson's gazelles: an honest signal of condition', *Behavioural Ecology and Sociobiology*, 23, pp.69-74.

Flanagan, C. (1999) *Early Socialisation*, London: Routledge.

Flanagan, C. and Marshall, M. (1999) *OCR AS Pack*, Crewe, Cheshire: Hartshill Press.

Flanagan, C. (2000) 'New insights into aggression', *Psychology Review*, 6, (3), pp.12-13.

Flaum, M., Swayze II, V.W., O'Leary, D.S., Yuh, W.T.C., Ehrhardt, J.C., Arndt, S.V. and Andreasen, N.C. (1995) 'Effects of diagnosis, laterality and gender on brain morphology in schizophrenia', *American Journal of Psychiatry*, 152 (2), pp.704-14.

Flavell, J.H. (1985) *Cognitive Development* (2nd edn), Englewood Cliffs, NJ: Prentice Hall.

Flynn, J.P. (1976) 'Neural basis of threat and attack', in R.G. Grenell and S. Gabay (eds) *Biological Foundations of Psychiatry*, New York: Raven Press.

Flynn, J.R. (1987) 'Massive IQ gains in 14 nations: what IQ tests really measure', *Psychological Bulletin*, 101, pp.271-91.

Foa, U.G. and Foa, E.B. (1975) *Resource Theory of Social Exchange*, Morristown, USA: General Learning Press.

Fodor, E.N. (1972) 'Delinquency and susceptibility to social influence among adolescents as a function of level of moral development', *Journal of Social Psychology*, 86, pp.257-60.

Fong, G.T., Krantz, D.H. and Nisbett, R.E. (1986) 'The effects of statistical training on thinking about everyday problems', *Cognitive Psychology*, 18, pp.253-92.

Ford, C. and Neale, J.M. (1985) 'Effects of a helplessness induction on judgements of control', *Journal of Personality and Social Psychology*, 49, pp.1330-6.

Ford, C.S. and Beach, F.A. (1951) *Patterns of Sexual Behavior*, New York: Harper & Row.

Fowler, H. (1965) *Curiosity and Exploratory Behaviour*, New York: Macmillan.

Franzoi, S.L. and Herzog, M.E. (1987) 'Judging physical attractiveness: what body aspects do we use?', *Personality and Social Psychology Bulletin*, 13, pp.34-44.

Freeman, D. (1983) *Margaret Mead and Samoa: The Making and Unmaking of an Anthropological Myth*, Cambridge, MA: Harvard University Press.

French, C.C. and Richards, A. (1993) 'Clock this! An everyday example of a schema-driven error in memory', *British Journal of Psychology*, 84, pp.249-53.

Freud, S. (1910) 'The origin and development of psychoanalysis', *American Journal of Psychology*, 21, pp.181-218.

Freud, S. (1920) *A General Introduction to Psychoanalysis*, New York: Washington Square Press.

Freud, S. (1931, translated by J. Strachey 1977) *Three Essays on the Theory of Sexuality*, London: Hogarth Press.

Freud, S. (1933) *New Introductory Lectures on Psychoanalysis*, London, Hogarth Press.

Freud, S. (1937) 'Analysis terminable and interminable', in J. Strachey (ed.) *The Complete Psychological Works of Sigmund Freud*, London: Hogarth Press.

Freud, S. (1955) *The Interpretation of Dreams*, New York: Basic Books.

Freud, S. (1990, original work published in 1909) 'Case study of Little Hans' in *Sigmund Freud 8, Case Histories I*, London: Penguin Books.

Friedman, S.L. and Stevenson, M. (1975) 'Developmental changes in understanding of implied motion in two-dimensional pictures', *Child Development*, 46, pp.773-8.

Friedman, S.L. and Stevenson, M. (1980) 'Perception of movements in pictures', in M. Hagen (ed.) *Perception of Pictures*, Vol. 1, *Albert's Model: The Projective Model of Pictorial Information*, New York: Academic Press.

Friedrich, L.K. and Stein, A.H. (1973) 'Aggressive and prosocial television programs and the natural behavior of preschool children', *Monographs of the Society for Research in Child Development*, 38 (4), Serial No. 151.

Friedrich-Cofer, L.K., Huston-Stein, A., Kipnis, D.M., Susman, E.J. and Clewett, A.S. (1979) 'Environmental enhancement of prosocial television content: effects on interpersonal behavior, imaginative play and self-regulation in a neutral setting', *Developmental Psychology*, 15, pp.637-746.

Fromm-Reichmann, F. (1948) 'Notes on the development of treatment of schizophrenics by psychoanalytic psychotherapy', *Psychiatry*, 11, pp.263-73.

Fuld, K., Wooten, B.R. and Whalen, J.J. (1981) 'The elemental hues of short-wave and extraspectral lights', *Perception and Psychophysics*, 29, pp.317-22.

Fulton, J.F. and Jacobsen, C.F. (1935) 'Fonctions des lobes frontaux; étude comparée chez l'homme et les singes chimpanzes', Paper presented at the International Neurological Congress, London.

Fulton, R. (1970) 'Death, grief and social recuperation', *Omega: Journal of Death and Dying*, 1, pp.23-8.

Fultz, J., Batson, C.D., Fortenbach, V.A., McCarthy, P.M. and Varney, L.L. (1986) 'Social evaluation and the empathy-altruism hypothesis', *Journal of Personality and Social Psychology*, 50, pp.761-9.

Funk, J.L. (1986) 'Gender differences in the moral reasoning of conventional and postconventional adults', Unpublished doctoral dissertation, University of Texas.

Fyer, A., Leibowitz, M., Gorman, J., Compeas, R., Levin, A., Davies, S., Goetz, D. and Klein, D. (1987) 'Discontinuation of alprazolam treatment in panic patients', *American Journal of Psychiatry*, 144, pp.303-8.

Fyer, A.J., Mannuzza, S., Gallops, M.S., Martin, L.Y., Aaronson, C., Gorman, J.M., Liebowitz, M.R. and Klein, D.F. (1990) 'Familial transmission of simple fears and phobias', *Archives of General Psychiatry*, 40, pp.1061-4.

Gaertner, S.L. and Dovidio, J.F. (1977) 'The subtlety of white racism, arousal and helping behaviour', *Journal of Personality and Social Psychology*, 35, pp.691-707.

Gaertner, S.L., Mann, J., Murrell, A.J. and Pomere, M. (1990) 'How does co-operation reduce intergroup bias?', *Journal of Personality and Social Psychology*, 59, pp.692-704.

Gaertner, S.L., Dovidio, J.F., Anastasio, P.A., Bachevan, B.A. and Rust, M.C. (1993) 'The common ingroup identity model: recategorization and the reduction of intergroup bias', in W. Stroebe and M. Hewstone (eds) *European Review of Social Psychology*, 4, Chichester: John Wiley.

Galef, B.G. Jr and Wigmore, S.W. (1983) 'Transfer of information concerning distant foods: a laboratory investigation of the "Information-centre" hypothesis', *Animal Behaviour*, 31, pp.748-58.

Gallup, G.G. (1970) 'Chimpanzees: self-recognition', *Science*, 167, pp.86-7.

Gallup, G.G. (1983) 'Toward a comparative psychology of mind', in R.E. Mellgren, *Animal Cognition and Behaviour*, New York: Elsevier.

Galotti, K.M. (1989) 'Gender differences in self-reported moral reasoning: a review and new evidence', *Journal of Youth and Adolescence*, 18, pp.475-88.

Garcia, J. and Koelling, R.A. (1966) 'Relation of cue to consequence in avoidance learning', *Psychonomic Science*, 4, pp.123-4.

Garcia, J., Rusiniak, K.W. amd Brett, L.P. (1977) 'Conditioning food-illness in wild animals: *Caveant canonici*', in H. Davis and H.M.B. Hurwitz (eds), *Operant-Pavlovian Interactions*, Hillsdale, NJ: Lawrence Erlbaum Associates pp.273-316.

Gardner, B.T. and Gardner, R.A. (1969) 'Teaching sign language to a chimpanzee', *Science*, 165, pp.664-72.

Garland, H.A., Hardy, A. and Stephenson, L. (1975) 'Information search as affected by attribution type and response category', *Personality and Social Psychology Bulletin*, 1, pp.612-15.

Garner, W.R. (1979) 'Letter discrimination and identification', in A.D. Pick (ed.) *Perception and Its Development: A Tribute to Eleanor Gibson*, Hillsdale, NJ: Erlbaum.

Garnets, L. and Kimmel, D. (1991) 'Lesbian and gay male dimensions in the psychological study of human diversity', in J. Goodchilds (ed.) *Psychological Perspectives on Human Diversity in America: Master Lectures*, Washington DC: American Psychological Association.

Gaskin, D.E. (1982) *The Ecology of Whales and Dolphins*, London: Honeymoon.

Gauntlett, D. (1997) *Video Critical: Children, the Environment and Media Power*, Luton: John Libbey Media.

Gauntlett, D. (1998) 'Ten things wrong with the 'effects model', in R. Dickinson, R. Harindranath and O. Linné (eds) *Approaches to Audiences – A Reader*, London: Arnold.

Gecas, V. and Seff, M.A. (1990) 'Families and adolescents:

A review of the 1980s', *Journal of Marriage and the Family*, 52, pp.941-58.

Gee, S. and Baillie, J. (1999) 'Happily ever after? An exploration of retirement expectations', *Educational Gerontology*, 25 (2), pp.109-28.

Geen, R.G. (1990) *Human Aggression*, Milton Keynes: Open University Press.

Geer, J.H. and Jarmecky, L. (1973) 'The effect of being responsible for reducing another's pain on subjects' response and arousal', *Journal of Personality and Social Psychology*, 26, pp.232-7

Gelernter, C.S., Uhde, T.W. and Cimbolic, P. (1991) 'Cognitive–behavioural and pharmacological treatments of social phobia – a controlled study', *Archives of General Psychiatry*, 49, p. 938.

Gelfand, D.M., Hartmann, D.P., Walder, P. and Page, B. (1973) 'Who reports shoplifters? A field-experimental study', *Journal of Personality and Social Psychology*, 25, pp.276-85.

Gerbner, G. (1994) 'The politics of media violence: some reflections', in O. Linné and C. J. Hamelink (eds) *Mass Communication Research: On Problems and Policies: The Art of Asking the Right Questions*, Norwood, NJ: Ablex Publishing.

Gergen, K.J., Morse, S.J. and Gergen, M.M. (1980) 'Behavior exchange in cross-cultural perspective', in H.C. Triandis and R.W. Brislin (eds) *Handbook of Cross-cultural Psychology: Social Psychology*, Boston, MA: Allyn & Bacon.

Gerkema, M.P. and Dann, S. (1985) 'Ultradian rhythms in behavior: the case of the common vole (microtus arvalis)', in H. Schulz and P.Lavie (eds), *Ultradian Rhythms in Physiology and Behavior*, Berlin: Springer Verlag.

Gershuny, B.S. and Sher, K.J. (1998) 'The relation between personality and anxiety: findings from a three-year prospective study', *Journal of Abnormal Psychology*, 107, pp.252-62.

Ghuman, P. (1994) *Coping with Two Cultures: British Asian and Indo-Canadian Adolescents*, Clevedon: Multilingual Matters.

Gibson, E.J. (1969) *Principles of Perceptual Learning and Development*, New York: Prentice-Hall.

Gibson, E.J. and Spelke, E.S. (1983) 'The development of perception', in J.H. Flavell and E.M. Markman (eds) *Handbook of Child Psychology*, Vol. 3, *Cognitive Development*, New York: Wiley.

Gibson, E.J. and Walk P.D. (1960) 'The visual cliff', *Scientific American*, 202, pp.64-71.

Gibson, J.J. (1950) *The Perception of the Visual World*, Boston: Houghton Mifflin.

Gibson, J.J. (1966) *The Senses Considered as Perceptual Systems*, Boston: Houghton Mifflin.

Gibson. J.J. (1979) *The Ecological Approach to Visual Perception*, Boston: Houghton Mifflin.

Gilligan, C. (1982) *In a Different Voice: Psychological Theory and Women's Development*, Cambridge, Massachusetts: Harvard University Press.

Gilligan, C. and Attanucci, J. (1988) 'Two moral orientations: gender differences and similarities', *Merrill-Plamer Quarterly*, 34, pp.223-37.

Gillin, J.C., Sitaram, N., Janowsky, D., Risch, C., Huey, L. and Storch, F. (1985) 'Cholinergic mechanisms in REM sleep', in A. Wauquier, J.M. Gaillard, J. Monti and M. Radulovacki (eds) *Sleep: Neurotransmitters and Neuromodulators*, New York: Raven Press.

Gitlin, M.J., Swendsen, J., Heller, T.L. and Hammen, C. (1995) 'Relapse and impairment in bipolar disorder', *American Journal of Psychiatry*, 152, pp.1635-40.

Glassman, N. (1999) 'All things being equal: the two roads of Piaget and Vygotsky', in P. Lloyd and C. Fernyhough (eds), *Lev Vygotsky: Critical Assessments: Vygotsky's Theory*, Vol. I (pp.282-310), New York, NY: Routledge.

Gleason, J.B. and Ratner, N.B. (1993) 'Language development in children', in J.B. Gleason and N.B. Ratner (eds) *Psycholinguistics*, Fort Worth, TX: Harcourt Brace Jovanovich.

Gleaves, D. (1996) 'The socio-cognitive model of dissociative

identity disorder: a re-examination of the evidence', *Psychological Bulletin*, 120, pp.42-59.

Gleitman, H. (1991) *Psychology* (3rd edn), London: W.W. Norton & Co.

Godard, R. (1991) 'Long-term memory of individual neighbours in a migratory song-bird', *Nature*, 350, pp.228-9.

Goldstein, E.B. (1999) *Sensation and Perception* (5th edn), Pacific Grove: Brooks/Cole Publishing.

Goldstein, J.M., Goodman, J.M., Seidman, L.J., Kennedy, D.N., Markris, N., Lee, H., Tourville, J., Caviness, V.S., Faraone, S.V. and Tsuang, M.T. (1999) 'Cortical abnormalities in schizophrenia identified by structural magnetic resonance imaging', *Archives of General Psychiatry*, 56, pp.537-47.

Goldstein, M.J. (1988) 'The family and psychotherapy', *Annual Review of Psychiatry*, 39, pp.283-99.

Gombrich, E.H. (1972) 'The mask and the face. The perception of physiognomic likeness in life and in art', in E.H. Gombrich, J. Hochberg and M. Black (eds) *Art, Perception and Reality*, Baltimore: Johns Hopkins Press.

Gonsiorek, J. and Weinrich, J. (1991) 'The definition and scope of sexual orientation', in J. Gonsiorek and J. Weinrich (eds), *Homosexuality: Research Implications for Public Policy*, Newbury Park: Sage.

Goodwin, R. (1999) *Personal Relationships Across Cultures*, London: Routledge.

Goodwin, R. and Findlay, C. (1997) 'We were just fated together. Chinese love and the concept of yuan in Hong Kong and England', *Personal Relationships*, 4, pp.85-92.

Goodwin, R., Adatia, K., Sinhal, H., Cramer, D. and Ellis, P. (1997) *Social Support and Marital Well-being in an Asian Community*, York: Joseph Rowntree Foundation.

Gopnik, M. and Crago, M.B. (1991) 'Familial aggregation of a developmental language disorder', *Cognition*, 29, pp.1-50.

Gordon, J.C.B. (1981) *Verbal Deficit: A Critique*, London: Croom Helm.

Gotlib, I.H. and Macleod, C. (1997) 'Information processing in anxiety and depression: a cognitive-developmental perspective', in J. Burack and J. Enns (eds), *Attention, Development and Psychopathology*, New York: Guildford Press.

Gottesman, I.I. (1963) 'Heritability of personality: a demonstration', *Psychological Monographs*, 77 (Whole no. 572).

Gottesman, I.I. and Shields, J. (1982) *Schizophrenia: The Epigenetic Puzzle*, Cambridge: Cambridge University Press

Gottman, J.M. (1998) 'Psychology and the study of marital processes', *Annual review of Psychology*, 49, pp.169-97.

Gould, J.L. (1986) 'The locale map of honey bees: do insects have cognitive maps?' *Science*, 207, pp.545-7.

Gould, J.L. (1992) 'Honey bee cognition', in C.R. Gallistel (ed) *Animal Cognition*, Cambridge, Massachusetts: MIT Press.

Gould, R.L. (1978) *Transformations: Growth and change in adult life*, New York: Simon & Schuster.

Gould, R.L. (1980) 'Transformation tasks in adulthood', in *The Course of Life*, Vol. 3, Adulthood and Aging Processes, Bethesda MD: National Institute of Mental Health.

Gould, S.J. (1981) *The Mismeasure of Man*, London: Penguin.

Gould, S.J. (1987) *An Urchin in the Storm*, New York: W.W. Norton.

Gould, S.J. (1989) *Wonderful Life: the Burgess Shale and the Nature of History*, Harmondsworth: Penguin.

Gould, S.J. (1994) 'The evolution of life on earth', *Scientific American*, 271, pp.63-9.

Grafen, A. (1982) 'How not to measure inclusive fitness', *Nature*, 298, pp.425-6.

Grafen, A. (1990) 'Do animals really recognize kin?', *Animal Behaviour*, 2, pp.42-54.

Gray, J.A. and Wedderburn, A.A. (1960) 'Grouping strategies with simultaneous stimuli', *Quarterly Journal of Experimental Psychology*, 12, pp.180-4.

Gredler, M. (1992) *Learning and Instruction Theory into Practice*, New York: Macmillan Publishing Company.

Green, S. (1994) *Principles of Biopsychology*, Hove: Erlbaum.

Green, S. and Vale, A. (1995) 'Differential effects of clonidine in two animal models of anxiety', *Journal of Psychopharmacology*, 9, p. A31.

Greene, B. (1994) 'Lesbian and gay sexual orientations', in B. Green and G.M. Herek (eds), *Lesbian and Gay Psychology: Theory, Research and Clinical Applications*, London: Sage.

Greeno, J.G. (1974) 'Hobbits and Orcs: Acquisition of a sequential concept', *Cognitive Psychology*, 6, pp.270-92.

Greeno, J.G. (1994) 'Gibson's affordances', *Psychological Review*, 101, pp.336-42.

Gregory, R.L. (1966) *Eye and Brain*, New York: McGraw Hill.

Gregory, R.L. (1973) *Eye and Brain* (2nd edn), New York: World Universities Library.

Gregory, R.L. (1990) *Eye and Brain* (4th edn), London: Weidenfeld & Nicholson.

Grier, J.W and Burk, T. (1992) *Biology of Animal Behaviour*, St Louis: Mosby.

Griest, J.H., Klein, M.H., Erdman H.P., Bires, J.K., Bass, S.M., Machtinger, P.E. and Kresge, D.G. (1987) 'Comparison of computer- and interviewer-administered versions of the Diagnostic Interview Schedule', *Hospital and Community Psychiatry*, 38, pp.1304-11.

Griffin, D.R. (1984) *Animal Thinking*, Cambridge, Massachusetts: Harvard University Press.

Griffin, D.R. (1991) *Animal Minds*, Chicago: Chicago University Press.

Griffiths, M. (1998) 'Violent video games – are they harmful?', *Psychology Review*, 4:4, pp.28-9.

Gross, R.D. (1992) *Psychology: The Science of Mind and Behaviour* (2nd edn), London: Hodder & Stoughton.

Gross, R.D. (1995) *Themes, Issues and Debates in Psychology*, London: Hodder & Stoughton.

Gross, R.D. (1996) *Psychology: The Science of Mind and Behaviour* (3rd edn), London: Hodder & Stoughton.

Gross, R.D., Humphreys, P.W. and Petkova, B. (1997) *Challenges in Psychology*, London: Hodder & Stoughton.

Grubb, T.C. (1973) 'Colony location by Leach's Petrel', *Auk*, 90, pp.78-82.

Grudin, J.T. (1983) 'Error patterns in novice and skilled transcription typing', in W.E. Cooper (ed.) *Cognitive Aspects of Skilled Typewriting*, New York: Springer.

Grusec, J.E. (1991) 'The socialisation of altruism', in M.S. Clark (ed.) *Prosocial Behaviour*, Newbury Park, CA: Sage.

Gualtieri, C. (1991) *Neuropsychiatry and Behavioural Pharmacology*, New York: Springer-Verlag.

Gunter, B. (1994) 'The question of media violence', in J. Bryant and D. Zillman (eds) *Media Effects: Advances in Theory and Research*, Hillsdale: Lawrence Erlbaum.

Gunter, B. and McAleer, J. (1997) *Children and Television*, London: Routledge.

Gupta, G.R. (1976) 'Love, arranged marriage and the Indian social structure', *Journal of Comparative Family Studies*, 7 pp.75-85.

Gurvits, T.V., Shenton, M.E., Hokama, H., Ohta, H., Lasko, N.B., Gilbertson, M.W., Orr, S.P., Kikinis, R., Jolesz, F.A., McCarley, R.W. and Pitman, R.K. (1996) 'Magnetic resonance imaging study of hippocampal volume in chronic combat-related posttraumatic stress disorder', *Biological Psychiatry*, 40, pp.1091-9.

Guthrie, E., Moorey, J., Margison, F., Barker, H., Palmer, S., McGrath, G., Tomenson, B. and Creed, F. (1999) 'Cost-effectiveness of brief psychodynamic interpersonal therapy in high utilizers of psychiatric services', *Archives of General Psychiatry*, 56, pp.519-26.

Gyger, M., Karakashian, S., and Marler, P. (1986) 'Avian alarm calling: Is there an audience effect?', *Animal Behaviour*, 34, pp.1570-2.

Haaga, D.A. and Davison, G.C. (1989) 'Outcome studies of rational–emotive therapy', in M.E. Bernard and R.D. DiGiuseppe (eds) *Inside Rational–Emotive Therapy*, San Diego, California: Academic Press.

Haaga, D.A. and Davison, G.C. (1993) 'An appraisal of rational–emotive therapy', *Journal of Consulting and Clinical Psychology*, 61(2), pp.215-20.

Haeger, G. (1993) 'Social and temporal comparisons in a European context', Unpublished MSc thesis: University of Kent.

Hagell, A. and Newburn, T. (1994) *Young Offenders and the Media: Viewing Habits and Preferences*, London: Policy Studies Institute.

Hagen, M. and Jones, R. (1978) 'Cultural effects on pictorial perception: how many words is one picture really worth?', in R. Walk and H. Pick (eds) *Perception and Experience*, New York: Plenum Press.

Haier, R.J., Siegel, B.V. Jr., Nuechterlein, A. and Soderling, E. (1992) 'Regional glucose metabolic changes after learning a complex visuospatial/motor task: a positron emission tomographic study', *Brain Research*, 570, pp.134-43.

Haith, M.M. (1990) *Rules that Babies Look By*, Hillsdale, NJ: Erlbaum.

Halaas, J.J., Gajiwala, K.S., Maffei, M., Cohen, S.L., Chait, B.T., Rabinowitz, D., Lallone, R.L., Burley, S.K. and Friedman, J.M. (1995) 'Weight-reducing effects of the plasma protein encoded by the obese gene', *Science*, 269, pp.543-6.

Halgin, R.P. and Whitbourne, S.K. (1993) *Abnormal Psychology* (International edition), Orlando, Florida: Harcourt Brace Jovanovich, Inc.

Hall, C.S. and Lindzey, G. (1970) *Theories of Personality*, London: Wiley.

Hall, G.S. (1904) *Adolescence*, New York: Appleton-Century-Crofts.

Hall, T.M. (1998a) 'Culture-bound syndromes', http://weber.ucsd.edu~thall/cbs_intro.html

Hall, T.M. (1998b) 'Glossary of culture-bound syndromes', http://weber.ucsd.edu~thall/cbs_glos.html

Hall, T.M. (1998c) 'Index of culture-bound syndromes by symptoms', http://weber.ucsd.edu~thall/cbs_sxs.html

Hall, T.M. (1998d) 'Index of culture-bound syndromes by culture', http://weber.ucsd.edu~thall/cbs_cul.html

Hall, T.M. (1999) personal communication, 10 December 1999.

Halpern, D. (1995) *More than Bricks and Mortar? Mental Health and the Built Environment*, London: Taylor and Francis.

Hamer, D., Hu, S. and Magnuson, V.L. (1993) 'A linkage between DNA markers on the X chromosome and male sexual orientation', *Science*, 261, pp.321-7.

Hamilton, D.L. (1981) 'Illusory correlation and stereotyping', in D.L. Hamilton (ed.) *Cognitive Processes in Stereotyping and Intergroup Behaviour*, Hillsdale, New Jersey: Erlbaum.

Hamilton, D.L. and Gifford, R.K. (1976) 'Illusory correlation in interpersonal perception: a cognitive basis of stereotypic judgements', *Journal of Experimental Social Psychology*, 12, pp.392-407.

Hamilton, D.L. and Sherman, J.W. (1994) 'Stereotypes', in R.S. Wyer Jr and T.K. Srull (eds), *Handbook of Social Cognition* (2nd edn), Vol. 2, Hillsdale, NJ: Erlbaum.

Hamilton, M. (1960) 'A rating scale for depression', *Journal of Neurology, Neurosurgery and Psychiatry*, 23, pp.56-62.

Hamilton, S., Rothbart, M. and Dawes, R.M. (1986) 'Sex bias, diagnosis, and DSM-III', *Sex Roles*, 15, pp.269-74.

Hamilton, W.D. (1963) 'The evolution of altruistic behaviour', *The American Naturalist*, 97, pp.354-6.

Hamilton, W.D. (1964) 'The genetic evolution of social behaviour I and II', *Journal of Theoretical Biology*, 7, pp.1-52.

Hampson, P.J. and Morris, P.E. (1996) *Understanding Cognition*, Oxford: Blackwell.

Hapkiewitz, W.G. and Roden, A.H. (1971) 'The effect of aggressive cartoons on children's interpersonal play', *Child Development*, 42, pp.1583-5.

Harden-Jones, F.R. (1968) *Fish Migration*, Edward Arnold: London.

Hardy, G.E., Barkham, M., Shapiro, D.A., Reynolds, S., Rees, A. and Stiles, W.B. (1995) 'Credibility and outcome of cognitive–behavioural and psychodynamic–interpersonal psychotherapy', *British Journal of Clinical Psychology*, 34, pp.555-69.

Hare, E.H. (1983) 'Was insanity on the increase?', *British Journal of Psychiatry*, 142, pp.439-55.

Hare-Mustin, R.T. and Marecek, J. (1988) 'The meaning of difference: gender theory, postmodernism, and psychology', *American Psychologist*, 43, pp.455-64.

Harley, T.A. (1995) *The Psychology of Language: from Data to Theory*, Hove: Erlbaum (UK), Taylor & Francis.

Harlow, H.F. (1950) 'Learning and satiation of response in intrinsically motivated complex puzzle performance by monkeys', *Journal of Comparative and Physiological Psychology*, 43, pp.289-94.

Harlow, H.F. (1962) 'Heterosexual affectional system in monkeys', *American Psychologist*, 17, pp.1-9.

Harlow, H.F. and Harlow, M.K. (1966) 'Learning to love', *American Psychologist*, 54, pp.244-72.

Harris, M.J., Milich, R., Corbitt, E.M., Hoover, D.W. and Brady, M. (1992) 'Self-fulfilling effects of stigmatising information on children's social interactions', *Journal of Personality and Social Psychology*, 63, pp.41-50.

Harrison, A.A. and Saeed, L. (1977) 'Let's make a deal: an analysis of revelations and stipulations in lonely hearts advertisements', *Journal of Personality and Social Psychology*, 35, pp.257-64.

Harrison, G, Ineichen, B., Smith, J. and Morgan, H.G. (1984) 'Psychiatric hospital admissions in Bristol. 2. Social and clinical aspects of compulsory admission', *British Journal of Psychiatry*, 145, pp.605-11.

Hart, B. and Risley, T. (1995) *Meaningful Differences in the Everyday Experiences of Young American Children*, Baltimore: Paul Brooks Publishing Company.

Hart, C.W.M. and Pillig, R. (1960) *The Tiwi of North Australia*, New York: Holt, Reinhart & Winston.

Hartline, H.K., Wagner, H.G. and Ratliff, F. (1956) 'Inhibition in the eye of Limulus', *Journal of General Physiology*, 39, pp.651-73.

Hartshorne, H. and May, M.S. (1928) *Moral Studies in the Nature of Character: Studies in the Nature of Character*, New York: Macmillan.

Haslam, N. (1994) 'The mental representations of social relationships: dimensions, laws or categories', *Journal of Personality and Social Psychology*, 67, pp.575-84.

Hatfield, E. (1987) 'Love' in R.J. Corsini (ed.), *Concise Encyclopaedia of Psychology*, New York: Wiley.

Hatfield, E. and Walster, G.W. (1981) *A New Look at Love*, Reading, MA: Addison-Wesley.

Hatfield, E., Utne, M.K. and Traupmann, J. (1979) 'Equity theory and intimate relationships', in R.L. Burgess and T.L. Huston (eds) *Exchange Theory in Developing Relationships*, New York: Academic Press.

Havighurst, R.J., Neugarten, B.L. and Tobin, S.S. (1968) 'Disengagement and patterns of aging', in B. L. Neugarten (ed.) *Middle Age and Aging*, Chicago: University of Chicago Press.

Hawkins, P.R. (1973) 'Social class, the nominal group and reference', in B. Bernstein (ed.) *Class, Codes and Control*, Vol. 2, London: Routledge & Kegan Paul.

Hay, D.C. and Young, A.W. (1982) 'The human face', in A.W. Ellis (ed.) *Normality and Pathology in Cognitive Functions*, London: Academic Press.

Hayes, N. (1993) *Principles of Social Psychology*, Hove: Erlbaum.

Hayes, N. (1995) *Psychology in Perspective*, London: Macmillan.

Hays, R.B. (1985) 'A longitudinal study of friendship development', *Journal of Personality and Social Psychology*, 48, pp.909-24.

Healy, A.F. (1976) 'Detection errors on the word "the": evidence for reading units larger than letters', *Journal of Experimental Psychology: Human Perception and Performance*, 2 (2), pp.235-42.

Hearold, S. (1986) 'A synthesis of 1,043 effects of television on social behaviour', in G. Comstock (ed.) *Public Communications and Behaviour*, Vol. I, New York: Academic Press.

Heath, S.B. (1989) 'Oral and literate traditions among black Americans living in poverty', *American Psychologist*, 44, pp.367-73.

Hebb, D.O. (1958) *A Textbook of Psychology*, Philadelphia: W.B. Saunders.

Hedge, A. and Yousif, Y.H. (1992) 'The effect of urban size, cost and urgency on helpfulness: a cross-cultural comparison between the United Kingdom and the Sudan', *Journal of Cross-Cultural Psychology*, 23, pp.107-15.

Heider, E.R. (1972) 'Universals in colour naming and memory', *Journal of Experimental Psychology*, 93, pp.10-20.

Heider, K.G. (1976) 'Dani sexuality: a low energy system', *Man*, 11, pp.188-201.

Helmholtz, H.L.F. von (1896) *Vorträge und Reden*, Braunschweig: Vieweg und Sohn.

Hendrick, C. and Hendrick, S. (1986) 'A theory and method of love', *Journal of Personality and Social Psychology*, 50, pp.392-402.

Hendrick, S.S. and Hendrick, C. (1992) *Liking, Loving and Relating* (2nd edn), Pacific Grove, CA: Brooks/Cole.

Hennigan, K.M., Heath, L., Wharton, J.D., Del Rosario, M.L., Cook, T.D. and Calder, B.J. (1982) 'Impact of the introduction of television on crime in the United States: empirical findings and theoretical implications', *Journal of Personality and Social Psychology*, 42, pp.461-77.

Herek, G.M. (1989) 'Gay and lesbian youth', *Journal of Homosexuality*, 17, pp.1-4.

Hering, E. (1964) *Outlines of a Theory of the Light Sense* (trans. L. Hurvich and D. Jameson) Cambridge, MA: Harvard University Press (original work published in 1878).

Herrnstein, R.J. and Murray, C. (1994) *The Bell Curve: Intelligence and Class Structure in American Life*, New York: The Free Press.

Herzlich, C. (1973) *Health and Illness: A Social Psychological Analysis*, London: Academic Press.

Hetherington, A.W. and Ranson, S.W. (1942) 'The relation of various hypothalamic lesions to adiposity in the rat', *Journal of Comparative Neurology*, 76, pp.475-99.

Hetherington, E.M. and Parke, R.D. (1993) *Child Psychology: A Contemporary Viewpoint* (4th edn), New York: McGraw-Hill.

Hewstone, M., Jaspars, J. and Lalljee, M. (1982) 'Social representations, social attribution and social identity: the intergroup images of 'public' and 'comprehensive' schoolboys', *European Journal of Social Psychology*, 12(3), pp.241-69.

Hewstone, M., Wolfgang, S. and Stephenson, G.M. (1996) *Introduction to Social Psychology*, Oxford: Blackwell.

Heyes, C.M. (1995) 'Self-recognition in primates: further reflections create a hall of mirrors', *Animal Behaviour*, 50, pp.1533-42.

Heyes, C.M. (1998) 'Theory of mind in nonhuman primates', *Behavioural and Brain Sciences*, 21 (1), pp.101-34.

Hilgard, E.R., Irvine, R.P. and Whipple, J.E. (1953) 'Rote memorization, understanding and transfer: an extension of Katona's card trick experiment', *Journal of Experimental Psychology*, 46, pp.288-92.

Hill, E. and Williamson, J. (1998) 'Choose six numbers, any

numbers', *The Psychologist*, 11, pp.17-21.

Hill, R. (1970) *Family Development in Three Generations*, Cambridge, MA: Schenkman.

Hilton, D.J. and Slugoski, B.R. (1986) 'Knowledge-based causal attribution: the abnormal conditions focus model', *Psychological Review*, 93, pp.75-88.

Hinde, R.A. (1977) 'Mother–infant separation and the nature of inter-individual relationships: experiments with rhesus monkeys', *Proceedings of the Royal Society of London* (B), 196, pp.29-50.

Hinde, R.A. and Fisher, J. (1951) 'Further observations on the opening of milk bottles by birds', *British Birds*, 44, pp.392-96.

Hladik, E.G. and Edwards, H.T. (1984) 'A comparative analysis of mother–father speech in the naturalistic home environment', *Journal of Psycholinguistic Research*, 13, pp.321-32.

Hoaker, P. and Schnurr, R. (1980) 'Genetic factors in obsessive–compulsive neurosis', *Canadian Journal of Psychiatry*, 25, pp.167-72.

Hobson, J.A. (1988) *The Dreaming Brain*, New York: Basic Books.

Hockett, C.F. (1959) 'Animal "languages" and human language', *Human Biology*, 31, pp.32-9.

Hockett, C.F. (1960) 'Logical considerations in the study of animal communication', in W.E. Lanyon and W.N. Tavolga (eds) *Animal Sounds and Communication*, Washington, DC: American Institute of Biological Sciences. McFarland, D. (1993) *Animal Behaviour* (2nd edn), Harlow: Addison Wesley Longman.

Hoffman, C., Lau, I. and Johnson, D.R. (1986) 'The linguistic relativity of person cognition', *Journal of Personality and Social Psychology*, 51, pp.1097-1105.

Hofstede, G. (1980) *Culture's Consequences: International Differences in Work-related Values*, Beverley Hills, California: Sage.

Hofstede, G. (1983) 'Dimensions of national cultures in fifty cultures and three regions', in J.B. Annis, R.C. Deregowski and S. Dziurawiec (eds) *Expiscations in Cross-cultural Psychology*, Lisse: Swets and Zweitlinger.

Hofstede, G. (1994) *Cultures and Organizations: Software of the Mind*, London: Harper-Collins.

Hoge, S.K., Appelbaum, P.S., Lawler, T., Beck, J.C., Litman, R., Greer, A., Gutheil, T.G. and Kaplan, E. (1990) 'A prospective, multicenter study of patient's refusal of antipsychotic medication', *Archives of General Psychiatry*, 47, pp.949-56.

Hogen, R.A. and Kirchner, J.H. (1967) 'A preliminary report of the extinction of learned fears via a short term implosive therapy', *Journal of Abnormal Psychology*, 72, pp.106-11.

Hogg, M.A. and Vaughan, G.M. (1995 [1st edn], 1998 [2nd edn]) *Social Psychology*, Hemel Hempstead: Prentice Hall/Harvester Wheatsheaf.

Hohmann, G.W. (1966) 'Some effects of spinal cord lesions on experimental emotional feelings', *Psychophysiology*, 3, pp.143-56.

Holden, C. (1997) 'National Institute of Health to explore St John's Wort', *Science*, 278, p. 391.

Hole, R.W., Rush, A.J. and Beck, A.T. (1979) 'A cognitive investigation of schizophrenic delusions', *Psychiatry*, 42, pp.312-19.

Hölldobler, B. (1971) 'Communication between ants and their guests', *Scientific American*, 224, pp.86-93.

Hollis, K.L. (1984) 'The biological function of Pavlovian conditioning: the best offence is a good defence', *Journal of Experimental Psychology: Animal Behaviour Processes*, 10, pp.413-25.

Hollis, K.L. (1990) 'The role of Pavlovian conditioning in territorial aggression and reproduction', in D.A. Dewsbury (ed.) *Contemporary Issues in Comparative Psychology*, Sunderland, MA: Sinaur Associates.

Hollis, K.L., Pharr, V.L., Dumas, M.J., Britton, G.B. and Field, J. (1997) 'Classical conditioning

provides paternity advantage for territorial male blue gouramis (*Trichogaster trichopterous*)', *Journal of Comparative Psychology*, 111, pp.219-25.

Hollon, S.D., DeRubeis, R.J., Evans, M.D., Wiemer, M.J., Garvey, M.J., Grove, W.M. and Tuason, V.B. (1992) 'Cognitive therapy and pharmacotherapy for depression: singly and in combination', *Archives of General Psychiatry*, 49, pp.774-809.

Holmes, T.H. and Rahe, R.H. (1967) 'The social readjustment rating scale', *Journal of Psychosomatic Research*, 11, pp.213-18.

Holmes, W.G. and Sherman, P.W. (1982) 'The ontogeny of kin recognition in two species of ground squirrels', *Animal Behaviour*, 34, pp.38-47.

Holtgrave, D.R., Tinsley, B.J. and Kay, L.S. (1994) 'Heuristics, biases and environmental health risk analysis', in L. Heath, R.S. Tindale, J. Edwards, E.J. Posovac, F.B. Bryant, E. Henderson-King, Y. Suarez-Balcazar and J. Myers (eds) *Applications of Heuristics and Biases to Social Issues*, New York: Plenum.

Homan, R. (1991) *Ethics of Social Research*, Harlow: Longman.

Homans, G.C. (1961, 1974 revised edition) *Social Behaviour: Its Elementary Forms*, New York: Harcourt Brace Jovanovich.

Hope-Simpson, R.E. (1981) 'The role of season in the epidemiology of schizophrenia', *Journal of Hygiene*, 86, pp.35-47.

Horn, J.L. (1994) 'Crowding', in R. Corsini (ed.) *Encyclopedia of Psychology*, Vol. 1 (2nd edn), New York: John Wiley.

Horn, J.M. (1983) 'The Texas Adoption Project: adopted children and their intellectual resemblance to biological and adoptive parents', *Child Development*, 54, pp.266-75.

Horne, J. (1978) 'A review of the biological effects of total sleep deprivation in man', *Biological Psychology*, 7, pp.55-102.

Horne, J. (1988) *Why We Sleep*, Oxford: Oxford University Press.

Horowitz, F.D. (1993) 'The need for a comprehensive new environmentalism', in R. Plomin and G.E. McClearn (1993) (eds) *Nature, Nurture and Psychology*, Washington, DC: American Psychological Association.

Horowitz, M.J. (1975) 'Intrusive and repetitive thoughts after experimental stress', *Archives of General Psychiatry*, 32, pp.223-8.

Howell, E. (1981) 'The influence of gender on diagnosis and psychopathology', in E. Howell, and M. Bayes (eds) *Women and Mental Health*, New York: Basic Books.

Howell, N. (1979) *Demography of the Dobe area !Kung*, New York: Academic Press.

Hubel, D.H. (1963) 'The visual cortex of the brain', *Scientific American*, 209, pp.54-62.

Hubel, D.H. and Wiesel, T.N. (1959) 'Receptive fields of single neurons in the cat's visual cortex', *Journal of Physiology*, 148, pp.574-91.

Hubel, D.H. and Wiesel, T.N. (1962) 'Receptive fields, binocular interaction and functional architecture in the cat's visual cortex', *Journal of Physiology*, 160, pp.106-54.

Hubel, D.H. and Wiesel, T.N. (1968) 'Receptive fields and functional architecture of monkey striate cortex', *Journal of Physiology*, 195, pp.215-43.

Hubel, D.H. and Wiesel, T.N. (1979) 'Brain mechanisms of vision', *Scientific American*, 82, pp.84-97.

Huber, V.L., Neale, M.A. and Northcraft, G.B. (1987) 'Decision bias and personnel selection strategies', *Organizational Behaviour and Human Decision Processes*, 40, pp.136-47.

Huesmann, L.R. (1982) 'Television and aggressive behaviour', in D. Pearl, L. Bouthilet and J. Lazar (eds) *Television and Behaviour: Ten Years of Scientific Progress and Implications for the Eighties.* Vol. 2: *Technical Reviews*, Rockville, MD: National Institute of Mental Health.

Huesmann, L.R. (1988) 'An information processing model for the development of aggression', *Aggressive Behaviour*, 14, pp.13-24.

Huesmann, L.R., Lagerspetz, K., and Eron, L.D. (1984) 'Intervening variables in the TV violence-aggression relation: evidence from two countries', *Developmental Psychology*, 20, pp.746-75.

Hugh, M. (1998) *Counselling Skills and Theory*, London: Hodder & Stoughton.

Hull, C.L. (1943) *Principles of Behavior*, New York: Appleton-Century-Crofts.

Hume, D. (1951) cited in L.A. Selby-Bigge (ed.) *Inquiries concerning the Human Understanding and concerning the Principles of Morals*, London: Oxford University Press.

Humphreys, P.W. (1997) 'Social, cultural and subcultural differences in the determination of (ab)normality', *Psychology Review*, 3 (4), pp.10-15.

Humphreys, P.W. (1999) 'Culture-bound syndromes', *Psychology Review*, 6 February, pp.14-18.

Hunt, E. and Agnoli, F. (1991) 'The Whorfian hypothesis: a cognitive psychological perspective', *Psychological Review*, 98, pp.377-89.

Hurvich, L. and Jameson, D. (1957) 'An opponent-process theory of colour vision', *Psychological Review*, 64, pp.384-404.

Huston, T.L. (1973) 'Ambiguity of acceptance, social desirability and dating choice', *Journal of Experimental Psychology*, 9, pp.32-42.

Iacono, W.G., Bassett., A.S. and Jones, B.D. (1988) 'Eye tracking dysfunction is associated with partial trisomy of chromosome 5 and schizophrenia', *Archives of General Psychiatry*, 45, pp.1140-1.

Ineichen, B., Harrison, G. and Morgan, H.G. (1984) 'Psychiatric hospital admissions in Bristol: 1. Geographical and ethnic factors', *British Journal of Psychiatry*, 145, pp.600-4.

Ingoldsby, B.B. (1995) 'Mate selection and marriage', in B.B. Ingoldsby and S. Smith (eds) *Families in Multicultural Perspective*, New York: Guilford.

Inoue-Nakamura, N. and Matsuzawa, T. (1997) 'Development of stone tool use by wild chimpanzees (*Pan troglodytes*)', *Journal of Comparative Psychology*, 111, pp.159-73.

Ioalè, P., Nozzolini, M. and Papi, F. (1990) 'Homing pigeons do extract directional information from olfactory stimuli', *Behavioural Ecology Sociobiology*, 26, pp.301-5.

Irwin, A.R and Gross, A.M. (1995) 'Cognitive tempo, violent video games, and aggressive behaviour in young boys', *Journal of Family Violence*, 10, pp.337-50.

Isack, H.A. and Reyer, H.U. (1989) 'Honeyguides and honey gatherers: interspecific communication in a symbiotic relationship', *Science*, 243, pp.1343-6.

Isen, A.M. (1984) 'Toward understanding the role of affect in cognition', in R.S. Wyer and T.K. Krull (eds) *Handbook of Social Cognition*, Hillsdale, New Jersey: Erlbaum.

Islam, M.R. and Hewstone, M. (1993) 'Dimensions of contact as predictors of intergroup anxiety, perceived outgroup variability and outgroup attitude: an integrative model', *Personality and Social Psychology Bulletin*, 19, pp.700-10.

Jacklin, C.N. and Maccoby, E.E. (1978) 'Social behaviour at 33 months in same-sex and mixed-sex dyads', *Child Development*, 49, pp.557-69.

Jacobsen, E. (1932) 'The electrophysiology of mental activities', *American Journal of Psychology*, 44, pp.677-94.

Jahoda, G. (1971) 'Retinal pigmentation, illusion perceptibility and space perception', *International Journal of Psychology*, 6, pp.199-208.

James, W. (1884) 'What is an emotion?', *Mind*, 19, pp.188-205.

James, W. (1890) cited in Thigpen, C. and Cleckey, H. (1954) 'A case of multiple personality disorder', *Journal of Abnormal and Social Psychology*, 49, pp.135-51.

Jarrett, R.B., Schaffer, M., McIntire, D., Witt-Browder, A., Kraft, D. and Risser, R.C. (1999) 'Treatment of atypical depression with cognitive therapy or phenalzine: a double-blind placebo-controlled trial', *Archives of General Psychiatry*, 56, pp.431-7.

Jarvis, M. (In press) *Perspectives in Psychology*, London: Routledge.

Jennings, H.H. (1950) *Leadership and Isolation*, New York: Longman.

Jensen, A.J. (1999) 'Adolescent storm and stress, reconsidered', *American Psychologist*, 54 (5), pp.317-26.

Jensen, A.R. (1969) 'How much can we boost IQ and scholastic achievement?', *Harvard Educational Review*, 39, pp.1-123.

Jerison, H.J. (1973) *Evolution of Brain and Intelligence*, New York: Academic Press.

Jobanputra, S. (1995) 'Psychology and racism: views from the inside', *Psychology Teaching*, 4, Association of Teachers in Psychology, Leicester: British Psychological Society.

Johansson, G. (1975) 'Visual motion perception', *Scientific American*, 232, pp.76-89.

Johnson, H., Olafsson, K., Anderson, J. and Pledge, P. (1989) 'Lithium every second day', *American Journal of Psychiatry*, 146, p. 557.

Johnson, J.R. and Ramsted, V. (1983) 'Cognitive development in preadolescent language impaired children', *British Journal of Disorders of Communication*, 18, pp.49-55.

Johnson, R.D. (1987) 'Making judgements when information is missing: inferences, biases and framing effects', *Acta Psychologica*, 66, pp.69-72.

Johnson, T.J., Feigenbaum, R. and Weiby, C.R. (1964) 'Some determinants and consequences of the teacher's perception of causality', *Journal of Educational Psychology*, 55, pp.237-46.

Johnston, A., DeLuca, D., Murtaugh, K. and Diener, E. (1977) 'Validation of a laboratory play measure of child aggression', *Child Development*, 48, pp.324-7.

Johnston, J. and Ettema, J. (1986) 'Using television to best advantage: Research for prosocial television', in J. Bryant and D. Zillmann (eds) *Perspectives on Media Effects*,

Hillsdale, NJ: Lawrence Erlbaum Associates.

Johnston, W.A. and Heinz, S.P. (1978) 'Flexibility and capacity demands of attention', *Journal of Experimental Psychology: General*, 107, pp.420-35.

Johnston, W.A. and Heinz, S.P. (1979) 'Depth of non-target processing in an attention task', *Journal of Experimental Psychology*, 5, pp.168-175.

Johnstone, L. (1989) *Users and Abusers of Psychiatry: A Critical Look at Traditional Psychiatric Practice*, London: Routledge.

Jolicoeur, P. and Landau, M.J. (1984) 'Effects of orientation on the identification of simple visual patterns', *Canadian Journal of Psychology*, 38, pp.80-93.

Jones, E.E. and Nisbett, R.E. (1971) *The Actor and the Observer; Divergent Perceptions of the Causes of Behaviour*. Morristown, NJ: General Learning Press.

Jones, J. (1999) *On the Distinction between Ethics and Morality*, Department of Philosophy, Raritan Valley Community College.

Jones, M. (1953) *The Therapeutic Community*, New York: Basic Books.

Jost, J.T. and Banaji, M.R. (1994) 'The role of stereotyping in system-justification and the production of false conscious-ness', *British Journal of Social Psychology*, 33, pp.1-27.

Kaffman, M. (1993) 'Divorce in the Kibbutz: lessons to be drawn', *Family Process*, 32 (1), pp.117-33.

Kahn, R.L. and Antonucci T.C. (1980) 'Convoys over the life course: attachments, roles and social support', in P.B. Baltes and O.G. Brim, Jr (eds) *Life-span Development and Behaviour* (Vol. 3), New York: Academic Press.

Kahneman, D. (1973) *Attention and Effort*, Englewood Cliffs, NJ: Prentice Hall.

Kahneman, D. and Tversky, A. (1972) 'Subjective probability: a judgement of representative-ness', *Cognitive Psychology*, 3, pp.430-54.

Kahneman, D. and Tversky, A. (1973) 'On the psychology of

prediction', *Psychological Review*, 80 (4), pp.237-51.

Kamin, L.J. (1977) *The Science and Politics of IQ*, Harmondsworth, Middlesex: Penguin.

Kamo, Y. (1993) 'Determinants of marital satisfaction: a compar-ison of the United States and Japan', *Journal of Social and Personal Relationships*, 10 (4), pp.551-68.

Karlins, M., Coffman, T.L. and Walters, G. (1969) 'On the fading of social stereotypes: studies in three generations of college students', *Journal of Personality and Social Psychology*, 13, pp.1-16.

Karni, A., Tanne, D., Rubinstein, B.S., Askenasy, J.J. and Sagi, D. (1994) 'Dependence on REM sleep of overnight improve-ment of a perceptual skill', *Science*, 265, pp.679-82.

Karp, M. (1995) 'An introduction to psychodrama counselling', *Journal of the British Association of Counselling*, 6(4), pp.294-8.

Katz, D. and Braly, K.W. (1933) 'Racial stereotypes of 100 college students', *Journal of Abnormal and Social Psychology*, 28, pp.280-90.

Kavanagh, D.J. (1992) *Schizophrenia: An Overview and Practical Handbook*, London: Chapman & Hall.

Kaya, N. and Erkíp, F. (1999) 'Invasion of personal space under the condition of short-term crowding: a case study on an automatic teller machine', *Journal of Environmental Psychology*, 19, pp.183-9.

Kaye, K.L. and Bower, T.G.R. (1994) 'Learning and inter-modal transfer of information in new-borns', *Psychological Science*, 5, pp.286-88.

Keeton, W.T. (1969) 'Orientation by pigeons: is the sun necessary?', *Science*, 165, pp.922-8.

Keeton, W.T. (1971) 'Magnets interfere with pigeon homing', *Proceedings of the National Academy of Sciences*, 68 (1), pp.102-6.

Kelley, H.H. (1967) 'Attribution theory in social psychology', in D. Levine (ed.) *Nebraska Symposium on Motivation*, Vol.

15, Lincoln, NE: Nebraska University Press.

Kelley, H.H. (1971) 'Attribution in social interaction', in E.E. Jones *et al.* (eds) *Attribution: Perceiving the Causes of Behaviour*, Morristown, NJ: General Learning Press.

Kelley, H.H. (1972) 'Causal schemata and the attribution process', in E.E. Jones *et al.* (eds) *Attribution: Perceiving the Causes of Behaviour*, Morristown, NJ: General Learning Press.

Kelley, H.H. (1973) 'The process of causal attribution', *American Psychologist*, 28, pp.107-28.

Kelley, H.H., Berscheid, E., Christensen, A., Harvey, J.H., Huston, T.L., Levinger, G., McClintock, E., Pellau, L.A. and Peterson, D.R. (1983) *Close Relationships*, New York: W.H. Freeman.

Kelman, H.C. (1965) 'Manipulation of human behaviour: an ethical dilemma for the social scientist', *Journal of Social Issues*, 21, pp.31-46.

Kendler, K.S. and Prescott, C.A. (1999) 'A population-based twin study of lifetime major depression in men and women', *Archives of General Psychiatry*, 56, pp.39-44.

Kendler, K.S. Masterson, C.C. and Davis, K.L. (1985) 'Psychiatric illness in first degree relatives of patients with paranoid psychosis, schizophrenia and medical controls', *British Journal of Psychiatry*, 147, pp.524-31.

Kendler, K.S., Neale, M.C., Kessler, R.C., Heath, A.C. and Eaves, L.J. (1992a) 'Major depression and generalized anxiety disorder', *Archives of General Psychiatry*, 49, pp.716-22.

Kendler, K.S., Neale, M.C., Kessler, R.C., Heath, A.C. and Eaves, L.J. (1992b) 'The genetic epidemi-ology of phobias in women', *Archives of General Psychiatry*, 49, pp.273-81.

Kendler, K.S., McGuire, M., Gruenberg, A.M., O'Hare, A., Spelling, M. and Walsh, D. (1993) 'The Roscommon Family Study: methods, diagnosis, and risk of schizo-phrenia in relatives', *Archives of General Psychiatry*, 50, pp.527-40.

Kenrick, D.T. and MacFarlane, S.W. (1986) 'Ambient tempera-ture and horn honking: a field study of the heat/aggression relationship', *Environment and Behaviour*, 18, pp.179-91.

Kerckhoff, A.C. and Davis, K.E. (1962) 'Value consensus and need complementarity in mate selection', *American Sociological Review*, 27, pp.250-95.

Kerr, P. (1982, Sept 16) 'Now, computerized bulletin boards', *New York Times*, pp.Cl, C7.

Kety, S.S., Wender, P.H., Jacobsen, B., Ingraham, L.J., Jansson, L., Faber, B. and Kinney, D.K. (1994) 'Mental illness in the biological and adoptive relatives of schizophrenia adoptees', *Archives of General Psychiatry*, 51, pp.442-55.

Kilham, W. and Mann, L. (1974) 'Level of destructive obedience as a function of transmitter and executant roles in the Milgram obedience paradigm', *Journal of Personality and Social Psychology*, 29, pp.696-702.

Kiloh, L.G., Gye, R.S., Rushworth, R.G., Bell, D.S. and White, R.T. (1974) 'Stereotactic amyg-daloidotomy for aggressive behavior', *Journal of Neurology, Neurosurgery, and Psychiatry*, 37, pp.437-44.

Kilpatrick, D.G. *et al.* (1985) 'Mental health correlates of criminal victimization: a random community survey', *Journal of Consulting and Clinical Psychology*, 53, pp.866-73.

Kim, U. and Berry, J.W. (1993) *Indigenous Psychologies: Research and Experience in Cultural Context (Cross-Cultural Research and Methodology*, Vol. 17), London: Sage.

Kimble, G.A. (1993) 'Evolution of the nature-nurture issue in the history of psychology', in R. Plomin and G.E. McClearn (1993) (eds) *Nature, Nurture and Psychology*, Washington DC: American Psychological Association.

Kimmel, A.J. (1996) *Ethical Issues in Behavioural Research: A Survey*, Cambridge, MA: Blackwell.

Kingdon, D.G. and Turkington, D. (1994) *Cognitive-Behavioural*

Therapy of Schizophrenia, Hove: Erlbaum.

Kinney, D.K., Levy. D.L., Yurgelun-Todd, D.A., Lajonchere, C.M. and Holzman, P.S. (1999) 'Eye-tracking dysfunction and birth-month weather in schizophrenia', *Journal of Abnormal Psychology,* 108, pp.359-62.

Kipling, R. (1902) *Just-So Stories,* London: Macmillan.

Kirchler, E., Pombeni, M.L. and Palmonari, A. (1991) 'Sweet sixteen ... Adolescents' problems and the peer group as a source of support', *European Journal of Psychology and Education,* 6, pp.393-410.

Kirchner, W.H. and Towne, W.F. (1994) 'The sensory basis of the honey bee's dance language', *Scientific American,* (June) 270, pp.52-9.

Kleiner, L. and Marshall, W.L. (1987) 'Interpersonal problems and agoraphobia', *Journal of Anxiety Disorders,* 1, pp.313-23.

Kleinginna, P.R.Jr. and Kleinginna, A.M. (1981) 'A categorised list of emotional definitions, with suggestions for a consensual definition', *Motivation and Emotion,* 5, pp.345-79.

Klerman, G.L. (1988) 'Depression and related disorders of mood (affective disorders)', in A.M. Nicholi Jr (ed.) *The New Harvard Guide to Psychiatry,* Cambridge, Massachussets: Harvard University Press.

Klinowska, M. (1994) 'Brains, behaviour and intelligence in cetaceans', *11 Essays on Whales and Man* (2nd edn), High North Alliance.

Kluft, R.P. (1984) 'Introduction to multiple personality disorder', *Psychiatric Annals,* 14, pp.19-24.

Kluver, H. and Bucy, P. (1939) 'Preliminary analysis of functions of the temporal lobes in monkeys', *Archives of Neurology and Psychiatry,* 42, pp.979-1000.

Kobasa, S.C. (1979) 'Stressful life events, personality, and health: an enquiry into hardiness', *Journal of Personality and Social Psychology,* 37, pp.1-11.

Koestner, R. and Wheeler, L. (1988) 'Self presentation in personal advertisements: the influence of implicit notions of attraction and role expecta-tions', *Journal of Social and Personality Psychology,* 5, pp.149-60.

Kohlberg, L. (1966) 'A cognitive-developmental analysis of children's sex-role concepts and attitudes', in E.E. Maccoby (ed.), *The Development of Sex Differences,* Stanford, CA: Stanford University Press.

Kohlberg, L. (1969) *Stages in the Development of Moral Thought and Action,* New York: Holt.

Kohlberg, L. (1976) 'Moral stages and moralization', in T. Likona (ed.), *Moral Development and Behaviour,* New York: Holt, Rinehart & Winston.

Kohler, W. (1925) *The Mentality of Apes,* New York: Harcourt Brace Jovanovich.

Kohn, A. (1993) *Punished by Rewards,* Boston: Houghton Mifflin.

Kolota, G. (1987) 'Associations or rules in learning languages?', *Science,* 237, pp.113-14.

Korte, C. and Kerr, N. (1975) 'Response to altruistic opportu-nities in urban and nonurban settings', *Journal of Social Psychology,* 95, pp.183-4.

Kosten, T.R., Mason, J.W., Giller, E.L., Ostroff, R. and Harkness, I. (1987) 'Sustained urinary norepinephrine and epineph-rine elevation in post-traumatic stress disorder', *Psycho-neuroendocrinology,* 12, pp.13-20.

Kraepelin, E. (1919) *Dementia Praecox and Paraphrenia,* New York: Robert E. Krieger.

Kramer, G. (1952) 'Experiments on bird orientation', *Ibis,* 94, pp.265-85.

Krantz, S.E. and Rude, S. (1984) 'Depressive attributions: selection of difference causes or assignment of different meanings?', *Journal of Personality and Social Psychology,* 47, pp.103-203.

Krebs, J.R., Sherry, D.F., Healy, S.D., Perry, V.H. and Vaccarino, A.L. (1989) 'Hippocampal specialisation of food-storing birds', *Proceedings of the National Academy of Sciences USA,* 86, pp.1388-92.

Kreithen, M.L. (1975) 'Effects of magnetism, barometric pressure and polarized light on the homing pigeon', Thesis: Cornell University

Kruger, A.C. (1992) 'The effect of peer and adult-child transactive discussions on moral reasoning', *Merill-Palmer Quarterly,* 38, pp.191-211.

Kübler-Ross, E. (1969) *On Death and Dying,* New York: Macmillan.

Kuczaj, S.A. (1977) 'The acquisi-tion of regular and irregular past tense forms', *Journal of Verbal Learning and Verbal Behaviour,* 16, pp.589-600.

Kuhl, P. (1981) 'Discrimination of speech by nonhuman animals: basic auditory sensitivities conducive to the perception of speech-sound categories', *Journal of the Acoustical Society of America,* 70, pp.340-9.

Kuhn, T.S. (1970) *The Structure of Scientific Revolutions* (2nd edn), Chicago: University of Chicago Press.

Kunda, Z. and Nisbett, R.E. (1986) 'The psychometrics of everyday life', *Cognitive Psychology,* 18, pp.195-224.

Kwon, J.S., McCarley, R.W., Hirayasu, Y., Anderson, J.E., Fischer, I.A., Kikinis, R., Jolesz, F.A. and Shenton, M.E. (1999) 'Left planum temporale volume reduction in schizophrenia', *Archives of General Psychiatry,* 56, pp.142-8.

Labov, W. (1970) 'The logic of non-standard English', in J.E. Alatis (ed.) *20th Annual Round Table,* Washington, DC: Georgetown University Press.

Labov, W. (1972) *Language in the Inner City: Studies in the Black English Vernacular,* Philadelphia: University of Pennsylvania Press.

Lacan, J. (1966) 'Function et champ de la parole et du language en psychoanalyse', *Ecrits,* Paris: Seuil.

Lader, M.H. and Mathews, A.M. (1968) 'A physiological model of phobic anxiety and desensiti-zation', *Behaviour Research and Therapy,* 6, pp.411-21.

Lam, R.W., Zis, A.P., Grewal, A., Delgado, P.L., Charney, D.S. and Krystal, J.H. (1996) 'Effects of rapid tryptophan depletion in patients with seasonal affective disorder in remission after light therapy', *Archives of General Psychiatry,* 53, pp.41-4.

Lamb, M.E. and Roopnarine, J.L. (1979) 'Peer influences on sex-role development in preschoolers', *Child Development,* 50, pp.1219-22.

Lang, F.R. and Carstensen, L.L. (1994) 'Close emotional rela-tionships in later life: further support for proactive aging in the social domain', *Psychology and Aging,* 9, pp.315-24.

Lange, C.G. (1885) *The Emotions* (English translation 1922), Baltimore: Williams & Wilkins.

Lange, G. (1973) 'The develop-ment of conceptual and rote recall skills among school age children', *Journal of Experimental Child Psychology,* 15(3), pp.394-406.

Langer, E.J., Bashner, R.S. and Chanowitz, B. (1985) 'Decreasing prejudice by increasing discrimination', *Journal of Personality and Social Psychology,* 49, pp.113-20.

Langlois, J.H., Ritter, J.M., Roggman, L.A. and Vaughn, L.S. (1991) 'Facial diversity and infant perception for attractive faces', *Developmental Psychology,* 27, pp.79-84.

Lantz, D. and Stefflre, V. (1964) 'Language and cognition revisited', *Journal of Abnormal Psychology,* 69, pp.472-81.

Lashley, K. and Watson, J.B. (1921) 'A psychological study of motion pictures in relation to venereal disease', *Social Hygiene,* 7, pp.181-219.

Lashley, K.S. (1929) *Brain Mechanisms and Intelligence,* Chicago: University of Chicago Press.

Latané, B. and Darley, J.M. (1970) *The Unresponsive Bystander: Why Doesn't He Help?',* New York: Appleton Century Crofts.

Latané, B. and Nida, S. (1981) 'Ten years of research on group size and helping', *Psychological Bulletin,* 89, pp.308-24.

Latané, B., Williams, K. and Hawkins, S. (1979) 'Many hands make light work: the causes and consequences of social loafing', *Journal of Personality and Social Psychology,* 37, pp.822-32.

Lattal, K.A. and Gleeson, S. (1990) 'Response acquisition with delayed reinforcement', *Journal of Experimental*

Psychology: Animal Behaviour Processes, 16, pp.27-39.

Lau, R.R. and Russell, D. (1980) 'Attributions in the sports pages', *Journal of Personality and Social Psychology,* 39, pp.29-38.

Laursen, P. (1997) 'The impact of aging on cognitive functioning: an 11 year follow-up study of four age cohorts', *Acta Neurologica Scandinavica,* 96, No. S172.

Laws, G., Davies, L. and Andrews, C. (1995) 'Linguistic structure and non-linguistic cognition: English and Russian blues compared', *Language and Cognitive Processes,* 10, pp.59-94.

Lazar, I. and Darlington, R. (1982) 'Lasting effects of early education: a report from the Consortium of Longitudinal Studies', *Monographs of the Society for Research in Child Development,* 47(2-3), Serial No. 195.

Lazarus, R.S. (1984) 'On the primacy of cognition', *American Psychologist,* 39, pp.124-9.

Lazarus, R.S. (1991) *Emotion and Adaptation,* New York: Oxford University Press.

Lea, M. and Duck, S. (1982) 'A model for the role of similarity of values in friendship development', *British Journal of Social Psychology,* 21, pp.301-10.

Leary, M.A., Greer, D. and Huston, A.C. (1982) 'The relation between TV viewing and gender roles', Paper presented at the Southwestern Society for Research in Human Development, Galveston, Texas.

Lecrubier, Y., Baker, A., and Dunbar, G. (1997) 'Long term evaluation of paroxetine, clomiphramine and placebo in panic disorder', *Acta Psychiatrica Scandinavica,* 95, pp.153-60.

Lee, J.A. (1973) *The Colors of Love: An Exploration of the Ways of Loving,* Don Mills, Ontario: New Press.

Lee, V.E., Brookes-Gunn, J., Schnur, E. and Liaw, F. (1990) 'Are Head Start effects sustained? A longitudinal follow-up comparison of disadvantaged children attending Head Start, no preschool, and other preschool programs',

Child Development, 61, pp.495-507.

Lefkowitz, M., Eron, L., Walder, L. and Huesmann, L.R. (1972) 'Television violence and child aggression: a follow-up study', in G.A. Comstock and E.A. Rubenstein (eds) *Television and Social Behaviour,* Vol. 3, *Television and Adolescent Aggressiveness,* Washington, DC: United States Government Printing Office.

LeMagnen, J. (1981) 'The metabolic basis of dual periodicity of feeding in rats', *The Behavioral and Brain Sciences,* 4, pp.561-607.

Lenneberg, E.H. and Roberts, J.M. (1956) *The Language of Experience,* Memoir 13, Indiana University Publications in Anthropology and Linguistics.

Leung, K. and Bond, M.H. (1984) 'The impact of cultural collectivism on reward allocation', *Journal of Personality and Social Psychology,* 47, pp.793-804.

Levine, J. (1976) 'Real kids versus the average family', *Psychology Today,* June, pp.14-15.

Levine, R., Sato, S., Hashimoto, T. and Verma, J. (1995) 'Love and Marriage in 11 cultures', *Journal of Cross-cultural Psychology,* 26 (5), pp.554-71.

Levinson, D.J. (1978) *The Seasons of a Man's Life,* New York: Knopf.

Levy, B. and Langer, E. (1994) 'Aging free from negative stereotypes: successful memory in China and among the American deaf', *Journal of Personality and Social Psychology,* 66, pp.989-97.

Levy, D.L., Holzman, P.S., Matthysse, S. and Mendell, N.R. (1993) 'Eye tracking dysfunction and schizophrenia: a critical perspective', *Schizophrenia Bulletin,* 19, pp.461-536.

Lewinsohn, P.M. (1974) 'A behavioural approach to depression', in R.J. Friedman and M.M. Katz (eds) *The Psychology of Depression: Contemporary Theory and Research,* Washington, DC: Winston Wiley.

Lewinsohn, P.M., Mischel, W., Chaplin, W. and Barton, R. (1980) 'Social competence and depression: the role of illusory

self-perceptions', *Journal of Abnormal Psychology,* 89, pp.203-12.

Lewis, C.S. (1960) *The Four Loves,* New York: Harcourt Brace Jovanovich.

Lewis, J.L. (1970) 'Semantic processing of unattended messages using dichotic listening', *Journal of Experimental Psychology,* 85, pp.225-8.

Liben, L.S. and Signorella, M.L. (1993) 'Gender-schematic processing in children: the role of initial interpretations of stimuli', *Developmental Psychology,* 29, pp.141-9.

Liebert, R.M. and Baron, R.A. (1972) 'Short term effects of television aggression on children's aggressive behaviour', in J.P. Murray, E.A. Rubenstein, and G.A. Comstock (eds) *Television and Social Behaviour,* Vol. 2, *Television and Social Learning,* Washington, DC: United States Government Printing Office.

Liebowitz, M. (1983) *The Chemistry of Love,* New York: Berkley Books.

Lieven, E.V.M. (1994) 'Crosslinguistic and crosscultural aspects of language addressed to children', in C. Gallaway and B.J. Richards (eds) *Input and Interaction in Language Acquisition,* Cambridge: Cambridge University Press.

Lilienfield, S., Lyn, S., Kirsch, T., Chaves, J., Sarbin, T., Gammaway, G. and Powell, R. (1999) 'Dissociative identity disorder and the sociocognitive model: recalling the lessons of the past', *Psychological Bulletin,* 125 (5), pp.507-23.

Linaza, J. (1984) 'Piaget's marbles: The study of children's games and their knowledge of rules', *Oxford Review of Education,* 10, pp.271-4.

Lindauer, M. (1955) cited in D.R. Griffin (1992) *Animal Minds,* Chicago: Chicago University Press.

Linden, M., Bar, T. and Geisellmann, B. (1998) 'Patient treatment insistence and medication craving in long-term low-dosage benzodiazepine prescriptions', *Psychological Medicine,* 28, pp.721-9.

Lindstrøm, T.C. (1999) 'Coping with bereavement in relation to different feminine gender roles', *Scandinavian Journal of Psychology,* 40 (1), pp.33-41.

Lippmann, W. (1922) *Public Opinion,* New York: Harcourt, Brace & World.

Liss, M.B. and Reinhardt, L.C. (1979) 'Behavioral and attitudinal responses to prosocial programs', Paper presented at the meeting of the Society for Research in Child Development, San Francisco, CA.

Littlefield, C.H. and Rushton, J.P. (1986) 'When a child dies: the sociology of bereavement', *Journal of Personality and Social Psychology,* 51 (4), pp.797-802.

Littlewood, J. (1992) *Aspects of Grief: Bereavement in Adult Life,* London: Tavistock/Routledge.

Littlewood, R. and Cross, S. (1980) 'Ethnic minorities and psychiatric services', *Sociology of Health and Illness,* 2, pp.194-201.

Litton, I. and Potter, J. (1985) 'Social representations in the ordinary explanation of a 'riot', *European Journal of Social Psychology,* 15, pp.371-88.

Liu, L.G. (1985) 'Reasoning counterfactually in Chinese: are there any obstacles?', *Cognition,* 21, pp.239-70.

Logothetis, N.K. and Pauls, J. (1995) 'Psychophysical and physiological evidence for viewer-centred object representaions in the primate', *Cerebral Cortex,* 5, pp.270-88.

Lombroso, C. (1911) *Crime: Its Causes and Remedies,* Boston: Little, Brown.

Loo, C. (1978) 'The effects of spatial density on children: fishing with a net rather than a pole', in A. Baum and Y. Epstein (eds) *Human Response to Crowding,* Hillsdale, NJ: Lawrence Erlbaum.

Lopez, S.R., Nelson, K.A., Snyder, K.S. and Mintz, J. (1999) 'Attributions and affective reactions of family members and course of schizophrenia', *Journal of Abnormal Psychology,* 108, pp.307-14.

Lorber, J. (1981) 'Is your brain really necessary?',*Nursing Mirror,* 30 April, 152 (18), pp.29-30.

Lord, C.G. (1997) *Social Psychology*, Fort Worth: Harcourt Brace College.

Lotem, A. (1993) 'Learning to recognise nestlings is maladaptive for cuckoo (*Cuculus canorus*) hosts', *Nature*, 362, pp.743-5.

Lott, B.E. (1994) *Women's Lives: Themes and Variations in Gender Learning*, Pacific Grove, CA: Brooks Cole.

Lovelace, V. and Huston, H.C. (1983) 'Can television teach prosocial behaviour?', *Prevention in Human Services*, 2, pp.93-106.

Lucas, K. and Lloyd, B. (1999) 'Starting smoking: girls' explanations of the influence of peers', *Journal of Adolescence*, 22, pp.647-55

Luchins, A.S. (1942) 'Mechanization in problem-solving', *Psychological Monographs*, 54 (6), Whole No. 248.

Lugo, J.O. and Hershey, G.L. (1979) *Lifespan Development* (2nd edn), London: Macmillan.

Lujansky, H. and Mikula, G. (1983) 'Can equity theory explain the quality and stability of romantic relationships?', *British Journal of Social Psychology*, 22, pp.101-12.

Lukes, S. (1975) *Emile Durkheim, His Life and Work: A Historical and Critical Study*, Harmondsworth: Penguin.

Luria, A.R. (1971) 'Towards the problem of the historical nature of psychological processes', *International Journal of Psychology*, 6, pp.259-72.

Lydiard, R.B., Brawman-Mintzer, O. and Ballenger, J.C. (1996) 'Recent developments in the psychopharmacology of anxiety disorders', *Journal of Consulting and Clinical Psychology*, 64, pp.660-8.

Lynch, P. (1994) 'Type A behaviour, hostility, and cardio-vascular function at rest after playing video games in teenagers', *Psychosomatic Medicine*, 56, p. 152.

Lynn, R. (1986) 'The rise of national intelligence: Evidence from Britain, Japan and the USA', *Personality and Individual Differences*, 7(1), pp.23-32.

McArthur, L.Z. and Post, D.L. (1977) 'Figural emphasis and

person perception', *Journal of Experimental Social Psychology*, 13, pp.520-35.

McClelland, D.C. (1961) *The Achieving Society*, Princeton, New Jersey: Van Nostrand.

McCormack, R.L. (1965) 'Extended tables of the Wilcoxon matched pair signed rank statistic', *Journal of the American Statistical Association*, 60, pp.864-71.

McCune-Nicolich, L. (1981) 'The cognitive bases of relational words in the single word period', *Journal of Child Language*, 8, pp.15-34.

MacDonald, I.M.V. (1997) 'Field experiments on duration and precision of grey and red squirrel spatial memory', *Animal Behaviour*, 54, pp.879-91.

McDougall, W. (1908) *Introduction to Social Psychology*, cited by Thigpen, C. and Cleckey, H. (1954) 'A case of multiple personality disorder', *Journal of Abnormal and Social Psychology*, 49, pp.135-51.

Macedonia, J.M. (1990) 'What is communicated in the antipredator calls of lemurs: evidence from antipredator call playbacks to ringtailed and ruffed lemurs', *Ethology*, 86, pp.177-90.

MacFarlane, J.W. (1964) 'Perspectives on personality consistency and change from the guidance study', *iVita Humana*, 7, pp.115-26.

McGarrigle, J. and Donaldson, M. (1974) 'Conservation accidents', *Cognition*, 3, pp.341-50.

McGinnies, E. (1949) 'Emotionality and perceptual defence', *Psychological Review*, 56, pp.244-51.

McGovern, D. and Cope, R. (1987) 'The compulsory detention of males of different ethnic groups, with special reference to offender patients', *British Journal of Psychiatry*, 150, pp.505-12.

McGovern, L.P. (1976) 'Dispositional social anxiety and helping behaviour under three conditions of threat', *Journal of Personality*, 44, pp.84-97.

McGrath, T., Tsui, E., Humphries, S. and Yule, W. (1990)

'Successful treatment of a noise phobia in a nine-year-old girl with systematic desensitization *in vivo*', *Educational Psychology*, 10(1), pp.79-83.

McGregor, P.K. and Avery, M.I. (1986) 'The unsung songs of great tits (*Parus major*): learning neighbours' songs for discrimination', *Behavioural Ecology and Sociobiology*, 18, pp.311-6.

McGregor, P.K., Dabelsteen, T., Shepherd, M. and Pedersen, S.B. (1992) 'The signal value of matched singing in great tits: evidence from interactive playback experiments', *Animal Behaviour*, 43, pp.987-98.

McGuffin, P., Katz, R., Watkins, S. and Rutherford, J. (1996) 'A hospital-based twin register of the heritability of DSM-IV unipolar depression', *Archives of General Psychiatry*, 53, pp.129-36.

McHugh, P.R. and Moran, T.H. (1985) 'The stomach: a conception of its dynamic role in satiety', *Progress in Psychobiology and Physiological Psychology*, 11, pp.197-232.

MacKay, D.G. (1973) 'Aspects of the theory of comprehension, memory and attention', *Quarterly Journal of Experimental Psychology*, 25, pp.22-40.

McKenry, P.C. and Price, S.J. (1995) 'Divorce: a comparative perspective', in B.B. Ingoldsby and S. Smith (eds) *Families in Multicultural Perspective*, New York: Guilford Press.

Mackintosh, N.J. (1981) 'Learning', in D. McFarland (ed.) *The Oxford Companion to Animal Behaviour*. Oxford: Oxford University Press.

MacLean, P.D. (1949) 'Psychosomatic disease and the "visceral brain": Recent developments bearing on the Papez theory of emotion', *Psychosomatic Medicine*, 11, pp.338-53.

MacLean, P.D. (1970) 'The triune brain, emotion, and scientific bias', in F.O. Schmitt (ed.) *The Neurosciences*, New York: Rockefeller University.

MacLeod, C. and Campbell, L. (1992) 'Memory accessibility and probability judgements: an experimental evaluation of the availability heuristic', *Journal of*

Personality and Social Psychology, 63, pp.890-902.

McNally, R.J. and Steketee, G.S. (1985) 'The etiology and maintenance of severe animal phobias', *Behaviour Research and Therapy*, 23(4), pp.431-5.

McNaughton, S. and Leyland, J. (1990) 'Maternal regulation of children's problem-solving behaviour and its impact on children's performance, *Child Development*, 61, pp.113-126.

McNeil, B.J., Pauker, S.G., Sox, H.C. and Tversky, A. (1982) 'On the elicitation of preferences for alternative therapies', *New England Journal of Medicine*, 306, pp.1259-62.

McNeil, J.D. (1966) *The ABC Learning Activity: Language of Instruction*, New York: American Book.

McNeil, J.D., Pauker, S.G. and Tversky, A. (1988) 'On the framing of medical decisions', in D.E. Bell, H. Raiffa and A. Tversky (eds) *Decision Making: Descriptive, Normative and Prescriptive Interactions*, New York: Cambridge University Press.

McTear, M.F. (1985) *Children's Conversations*, Oxford: Ellis Horwood.

Madden, P.A.F., Heath, A., Rosenthal, N.E. and Martin, N.E. (1996) 'Seasonal changes in mood and behaviour', *Archives of General Psychiatry*, 53, pp.47-55.

Magee, W.J., Eaton, W., Wittchen, H.U., McGonagle, K.A. and Kessler, R.C. (1996) 'Agoraphobia, simple phobia and social phobia in the national comorbidity survey', *Archives of General Psychiatry*, 53 (2), pp.159-68.

Magnusson, A. and Stefansson, J.G. (1993) 'Prevalence of seasonal affective disorder in Iceland', *Archives of General Psychiatry*, 50, pp.941-6.

Maguire, E.A., Frackowiak, R.S.J. and Frith, C.D. (1997). 'Recalling routes around London: activation of the right hippocampus in taxi drivers', *The Journal of Neuroscience*, 17(18), pp.7103-10.

Maier, N.R.F. (1931) 'Reasoning in humans 1: On direction', *Journal of Comparative Psychology*, 10, pp.115-43.

Maier, S.J. and Seligman, M.E.P. (1976) 'Learned helplessness: theory and evidence', *Journal of Experimental Psychology: General,* 105, pp.2-46.

Malamuth, N.M. and Check, J.V.P. (1981) 'The effects of mass media exposure on acceptance of violence against women: a field experiment', *Journal of Research in Personality,* 15, pp.436-46.

Malotki, E. (1983) *Hopi Time: A Linguistic Analysis of Temporal Concepts in the Hopi Language,* Berlin: Mouton.

Mann, J.J., Malone, K.M., Diehl, D.J., Perel, J., Cooper, T.B. and Mintun, M.A. (1996) 'Demonstration in vivo of reduced serotonin responsivity in the brain of untreated depressed patients', *American Journal of Psychiatry,* 153, pp.174-82.

Mann, L. (1981) 'The baiting crowd in episodes of threatened suicide', *Journal of Personality and Social Psychology,* 41, pp.703-9.

Manning, A. and Dawkins, M.S. (1998) *A Introduction to Animal Behaviour* (2nd edn), Cambridge: Cambridge University Press.

Manstead, A.S.R. and Hewstone, M. (1995) *The Blackwell Encyclopaedia of Social Psychology.,* Oxford: Blackwell.

Manstead, A.S.R., Hewstone, M., Fiske, S.T., Hogg, M.A., Reis, H.T. and Gün, R.S. (1995) *The Blackwell Encyclopedia of Social Psychology,* Oxford: Blackwell.

Maranon, G. (1924) 'Contribution à l'étude de l'action émotive de l'adrénaline', *Revue Française d'Endocrinologie,* 2, pp.301-25.

Marcelis, M., Navarro-Mateu, R., Murray, R., Selten, J.P. and J. Van Os (1998) 'Urbanization and psychosis: a study of 1942–1978 birth cohorts in The Netherlands', *Psychological Medicine,* 28, pp.871-9.

Marcia, J. (1966) 'Development and validation of ego identity status', *Journal of Personality and Social Psychology,* 3, pp.551-8.

Marcia, J. (1980) 'Identity in adolescence', in J. Adelson (ed.) *Handbook of Adolescent Psychology,* New York: Wiley.

Marcus, J., Hans, S.L., Nagier, S., Auerbach, J.G., Mirsky, A.F. and Aubrey, A. (1987) 'Review of the NIMH Israeli Kibbutz-City and the Jerusalem infant development study', *Schizophrenia Bulletin,* 13, pp.425-38.

Marie-Claire (1993) 'Hi-tech sex', *Marie-Claire* (London edn), May, pp.22-5.

Markowitz, L.M. (1991) 'Homosexuality: are we still in the dark?', *The Family Therapy Networker,* January pp.26-29; February pp.31-35.

Marks, I.M. (1981) 'Review of behavioural psychotherapy: obsessive–compulsive disorders', *American Journal of Psychiatry,* 138, pp.584-92.

Markus, H. and Kitayama, S. (1991) 'Culture and the self: Implications for cognition, emotion and motivation', *Psychological Review,* 98, pp.224-53.

Marler, P. (1991) 'Song-learning behaviour: the interface with neuroethology', *Trends in Neurosciences,* 14, pp.199-206.

Marler, P. and Peters, S. (1981) 'Sparrows learn adult song and more from memory', *Science,* 213, pp.780-2.

Marsh, P., Rosser, E. and Harre, R. (1978) *The Rules of Disorder,* London: Routledge.

Marshall, G.D. and Zimbardo, P.G. (1979) 'Affective consequences of inadequately explained physiological arousal', *Journal of Personality and Social Psychology,* 37, pp.970-88.

Martin, C. and Halverson, C. (1983) 'Gender constancy: a methodological and theoretical analysis', *Sex Roles,* 9, pp.775-90.

Martin, C. and Little, J.K. (1990) 'The relation of gender understanding to children's sex-typed preferences and gender stereotypes', *Child Development,* 61, pp.1427-39.

Maruyama, G., Fraser, S.C. and Miller, N. (1982) 'Personal responsibility and altruism in children', *Journal of Personality and Social Psychology,* 42 (4), pp.658-64.

Maslach, C. (1979) 'Negative emotional biasing of unexplained arousal', *Journal of Personality and Social Psychology,* 37, pp.953-69.

Maslow, A.H. (1954) *Motivation and Personality,* New York: Harper & Row.

Maslow, A.H. (1968) *Towards a Psychology of Being,* New York: Van Nostrand.

Masterson, J.F. (1967) *The Psychiatric Dilemma of Adolescence,* Boston: Little Brown.

Mathews, A. (1989) 'Cognitive aspects of the aetiology and phenomenology of anxiety disorders', in P.M.G. Emmelkamp, W.T.A.M. Everaerd, F. Kraimat and M.J.M.van Son (eds) *Annual Series of European Research in Behaviour Therapy. Vol. IV: Fresh perspectives on anxiety disorders,* Amsterdam: Swets and Zeitlinger.

Matlin, M.W. (1998) *Cognition* (4th edn), Orlando: Harcourt Brace College Publishers.

May, J.L. and Hamilton, P.A. (1980) 'Effects of musically evoked affect on women's interpersonal attraction and perceptual judgements of physical attractiveness of men', *Motivation and Emotion,* 4, pp.217-28.

Mead, M. (1928) *Coming of Age in Samoa,* New York: Morrow.

Mead, M. (1935) *Sex and Temperament in Three Primitive Societies,* New York: Morrow.

Meddis, R. (1979) 'The evolution and function of sleep', in D.A. Oakley and H.C. Plotkin (eds) *Brain, Behaviour and Evolution,* London: Methuen.

Mediascope Inc. (1996) *National Television Violence Study: Executive Summary: 1994-95,* Los Angeles, CA: Mediascope Inc.

Mednick, S.A., Machon, R.A., Huttunen, M.O. and Bonett, D. (1988) 'Adult schizophrenia following prenatal exposure to an influenza epidemic', *Archives of General Psychiatry,* 45 (2), pp.189-92.

Meeus, W.H.J. and Raaijmakers, O.A.W. (1986) 'Administrative obedience: carrying out orders to use psychological-administrative violence', *European Journal of Social Psychology,* 16, pp.311-24.

Meichenbaum, D.H. (1972) 'Cognitive modification of test anxious college students', *Journal of Consulting and Clinical Psychology,* 39 (3), pp.370-80.

Meichenbaum, D.H. (1975) 'Self-instructional methods', in F.H. Kanfer and A.P. Goldstein (eds) *Helping People Change: A Textbook of Methods,* New York: Pergamon.

Meichenbaum, D.H. and Cameron, R. (1973) 'Training schizophrenics to talk to themselves: a means of developing attentional controls', *Behaviour Therapy,* 4, pp.515-34.

Meilman, P.W. (1979) 'Cross-sectional age changes in ego identity status during adolescence', *Developmental Psychology,* 15, pp.230-1.

Meloen, J.D., Hagendoorn, L., Raaijmakers, Q. and Visser, L. (1988) 'Authoritarianism and the revival of political racism: reassessments in the Netherlands of the reliability and validity of the concepts of authoritarianism used by Adorno et al.', *Political Psychology,* 9, pp.413-29.

Melville, J. (1978) *Phobias and Obsessions,* New York: Penguin.

Menzies, R.G. and Clarke, J.C. (1993) 'A comparison of *in vivo* and vicarious exposure in the treatment of childhood water phobia', *Behavioural Research Therapy,* 31 (1), pp.9-15.

Mersky, H. (1992) 'The manufacture of multiple personality disorder', *British Journal of Psychiatry,* 160, pp.327-40.

Messenger-Davies, M. (1989) *Television is Good for Your Kids,* London: Hilary Shipman.

Messer, D. (1999) 'The development of communication and language', in D. Messer and S. Millar (eds) *Exploring Developmental Psychology,* London: Arnold.

Messner, S.F. (1986) 'Television violence and violent crime: an aggregate analysis', *Social Problems,* 33, pp.218-35.

Middleton, R. (1976) 'Regional differences in prejudice', *American Sociological Review,* 41, pp.94-117.

Milavsky, J.R., Kessler, R.C., Stipp, H.H. and Rubens, W.S. (1982) *Television and Aggression: A Panel Study,* New York: Academic Press.

Milgram, S. (1963) 'Behavioural study of obedience', *Journal of Abnormal and Social Psychology*, 67, pp.371-8.

Milgram, S. (1965) 'Some conditions of obedience and disobedience to authority', *Human Relations*, 18, pp.57-76.

Milgram, S. (1970) 'The experience of living in cities', *Science*, 167, pp.1461-8.

Milgram, S. (1974) *Obedience to Authority*, New York: Harper & Row.

Milgram, S. (1977) *The Individual in a Social World*, Reading, MA: Addison-Wesley.

Miller, D.T. and Ross, M. (1975) 'Self-serving biases in the attribution of causality: fact or fiction?', *Psychological Bulletin*, 82, pp.213-25.

Miller, G. (1996) 'Sexual selection in human evolution', in C. Crawford and D.L. Krebs (eds) *Evolution and Human Behaviour*, Mahwah: Lawrence Erlbaum.

Miller, G.A. (1966) *Psychology: The Science of Mental Life*, Harmondsworth: Penguin.

Miller, G.A. and McNeill, D. (1969) 'Psycholinguistics', in G. Lindzey and E. Aronson (eds) *The Handbook of Social Psychology*, Vol. 3, Reading, MA: Addison-Wesley.

Miller, G.A., Galanter, E.H. and Pribram, K.H. (1960) *Plans and the Structure of Behaviour*, New York: Holt, Rhinehart & Winston.

Miller, J.G. (1984) 'Culture and the development of everyday social explanation', *Journal of Personality and Social Psychology*, 46, pp.961-78.

Miller, J.G. and Bersoff, D.M. (1994) 'Cultural differences on the moral status of reciprocity and the discounting of endogenous motivation', *Personality and Social Psychology Bulletin*, 20, pp.592-602.

Miller, J.G. and Bersoff, D.M. (1998) 'The role of liking in perceptions of the moral responsibility to help: a cultural perspective', *Journal of Experimental Social Psychology*, 34, pp.443-69.

Miller, L.C., Lechner, R.E. and Rugs, D. (1985) 'Development of conversational responsiveness: preschoolers' use of responsive listener cues and relevant comments', *Developmental Psychology*, 21, pp.473-80.

Miller, M. and Bowers, K. (1986) 'Hypnotic analgesia and stress inoculation in the reduction of pain', *Journal of Abnormal Psychology*, 95, pp.6-14.

Milner, P. (1970) *Physiological Psychology*, London: Holt, Rhinehart & Winston.

Minai, N. (1981) *Women in Islam: Tradition and Transition in the Middle East*, New York: Seaview Books.

Mínguez, E. (1997) 'Olfactory nest recognition by British storm petrel chicks', *Animal Behaviour*, 53, pp.701-7.

Mischel, W. (1968) *Personality and Assessment*, New York: Wiley.

Mischel, W. and Peake, P.K. (1982) 'Beyond déja vu in the search for cross-situational consistency', *Psychological Review*, 89, pp.730-55.

Mitchell, K.M. (1977) 'A reappraisal of the therapeutic effectiveness of accurate empathy, nonpossessive warmth and genuineness', in A.S. Gurman and A.M. Razin (eds) *Effective Psychotherapy: A Handbook of Research*, New York: Pergamon.

Mitchell, P.R. and Kent, R.D. (1990) 'Phonetic variation in multi-syllable babbling', *Journal of Child Language*, 17, pp.247-65.

Moffitt, A., Kramer, M. and Hoffman, R. (1993) *The Function of Dreams*, New York: State University of New York Press.

Moghaddam, F.M. (1998) *Social Psychology: Exploring Universals across Cultures*, New York: W.H. Freeman.

Moghaddam, F.M., Taylor, D.M. and Wright, S.C. (1993) *Social Psychology in Cross-Cultural Perspective*, New York: W.H. Freeman.

Monach, J. and Monro, S. (1995) 'Counselling in general practice: issues and opportunities', *British Journal of Guidance and Counselling*, 23, pp.313-25.

Money, J. (1988) *Gay, Straight and In-between: The Sexology of Erotic Orientation*, New York: Oxford University Press.

Money, J. and Ehrhardt, A.A. (1972) *Man and Woman, Boy and Girl*, Baltimore: John's Hopkins University Press.

Montessori, M. (1912) *The Montessori Method: A Scientific Pedagogy as Applied to Child Education in the 'Children's Houses'*, translated from the Italian by A.E. George, New York: Frederick A. Stokes Co.

Moore, C. and Frye, D. (1986) 'The effect of the experimenter's intention on the child's understanding of conservation', *Cognition*, 22, pp.283-98.

Moray, N. (1959) 'Attention in dichotic listening: affective cues and the influence of instructions', *Quarterly Journal of Experimental Psychology*, 11, pp.56-60.

Moreno, J.L. (1965) 'Psychodynamic rules, techniques and adjunctive methods', *Group Psychotherapy*, Vol. 23, Washington, DC: Heldref Publications.

Moreno, J.L. (1970) *Psychodrama I, II, III*, Boston, MA: Beacon Press.

Moscovici, S. (1961) *La Psychoanalyse, Son Image et Son Public*, Paris: Presses Universitaires de France.

Moscovici, S. (1981) 'On social representations', in J.P. Forgas (ed.) *Social Cognition: Perspectives in Everyday Understanding*, London: Academic Press.

Moscovici, S. (1985) 'The myth of the lonely paradigm: a rejoinder', *Social Research*, 51, pp.939-67.

Mowrer, O.H. (1948) 'Learning theory and the neurotic paradox', *American Journal of Orthopsychiatry*, 18, pp.571-610

Mufson, L., Weissman, M.M., Moreau, D. and Garfinkel, R. (1999) 'Efficacy of interpersonal psychotherapy for depressed adolescents', *Archives of General Psychiatry*, 56, pp.573-9.

Mukhametov, L.M. (1984) 'Sleep in marine mammals', in A.Borbely and J-L. Valatax (eds) *Sleep Mechanisms. Experimental Brain Research*, Suppl. 8, Berlin: Springer-Verlag, pp.227-37.

Mukherjee, S., Sackeim, H.A. and Schnur, D.B. (1994) 'Electroconvulsive therapy of acute manic episodes: a review of fifty years experience', *American Journal of Psychiatry*, 151, pp.169-76.

Munjack, D.J. (1984) 'The onset of driving phobias', *Journal of Behaviour Therapy and Experimental Psychiatry*, 15, pp.305-8.

Munroe, R.H., Shimmin, H.S. and Munroe, R.L. (1984) 'Gender understanding and sex role preference in four cultures', *Developmental Psychology*, 20, pp.673-82.

Murray, H.A. (ed.) (1938) *Explorations in Personality*, New York: Oxford University Press.

Murray-Parkes, C. (1972) *Bereavement: Studies of Grief in Adult Life*, New York: International Universities Press.

Murstein, B.I. (1972) 'Physical attractiveness and marital choice', *Journal of Personality and Social Psychology*, 22 (1), pp.8-12.

Mwamwenda, T.S. and Monyooe, L.A. (1997) 'Status of bridewealth in an African culture', *Journal of Social Psychology*, 137, pp.269-71.

Myers, L.B. and Brewin, C.R. (1994) 'Recall of early experiences and the repressive coping style', *Journal of Abnormal Psychology*, 103, pp.288-92.

Nadler, A. (1986) 'Help seeking as a cultural phenomenon: differences between city and kibbutz dwellers', *Journal of Personality and Social Psychology*, 51, pp.976-82.

Nadler, A. (1993) Personal communication, in R.A. Baron and D. Byrne (1994) *Social Psychology: Understanding Human Interaction* (7th edn), Boston, MA: Allyn & Bacon.

Nagell, K., Olguin, R.S. and Tomasello, M. (1993) 'Processes of social learning in the tool use of chimpanzees (*Pan troglodytes*) and human children (*Homo sapiens*)', *Journal of Comparative Psychology*, 107, pp.174-86.

Neff, N. (undated) 'Folk Medicine in Hispanics in the Southwestern United States', http://www-sbp.bcm.tmc.edu/HispanicHealth/Courses/mod7/amod7.html

Neisser, U. (1964) 'Visual search', *Scientific American*, 210, pp.94-102.

Neisser, U. (1967) *Cognitive Psychology*, New York: Appleton-Century-Crofts.

Neisser, U. (1976) *Cognition and Reality*, San Francisco: W.H. Freeman.

Nemeroff, C.B., Krishnan, R.R., Reed, D., Leder, R., Beam, C. and Dunnick, N.R. (1992) 'Adrenal gland enlargement in major depression', *Archives of General Psychiatry*, 49, pp.384-7.

Nesse, M. and Williams, C. (1995) *Evolution and Healing. The New Science of Darwiniam Medicine*, London: Weidenfield & Nicolson.

Neugarten, B.L. (1968) *Personality in Middle and Late Life* (2nd edn), New York: Atherton Press.

Neugarten, B.L. (1980) 'Act your age: must everything be a midlife crisis?', in *Annual Editions: Human Development, 1980/1981*, Guilford, CT: Dushkin Publishers, pp.289-90.

Newcomb, T.M. (1961) *The Acquaintance Process*, New York: Holt, Rinehart & Winston.

Newell, A. and Simon, H.A. (1972) *Human Problem-solving*, Englewood Cliffs, NJ: Prentice Hall.

Newell, A., Shaw, J.C. and Simon, H.A. (1958) 'Elements of a theory of general problem-solving', *Psychological Review*, 65, pp.151-66.

Newson, E. (1994) 'Video violence and the protection of children', *Psychology Review*, 1(2), pp.2-5.

Nickel, H., Quaiserpohl, C., Rollett, B., Vetter, J. and Werneck, H. (1995) 'Changing marital satisfaction during the transition to parenthood: cross cultural studies in four countries', *Psychologie in Erziehung und Unterricht*, 42(1), pp.40-53.

Nicolson, P. (1995) 'The menstrual cycle, science and femininity: assumptions underlying menstrual cycle research', *Soc. Sci. Med.*, 41, pp.779-84.

Nisbett, R.E. (1972) 'Hunger, obesity and the ventro–medial hypothalamus', *Psychological Review*, 79, pp.433-53.

Nisbett, R.E. and Ross, L. (1980) *Human Inference Strategies and Shortcomings of Social Judgement*, Englewood Cliffs, NJ: Prentice Hall.

Nolen-Hoeksema, S. (1990) *Sex Differences in Depression*, Stanford, CA: Stanford University Press.

Nolen-Hoeksema, S., Girgus, S., and Seligman, M.E.P. (1992) 'Predictors and consequences of childhood depressive symptoms: a five-year longitudinal study', *Journal of Abnormal Psychology*, 101, pp.405-22.

Noller, P. and Callan, V. (1991) *The Adolescent in the Family*, London: Routledge.

Nopoulos, P., Flaum, M.D. and Andreasen, N.C. (1997) 'Sex differences in brain morphology in schizophrenia', *American Journal of Psychiatry*, 154, pp.1648-54.

Norman, D.A. (1968) 'Towards a theory of memory and attention', *Psychological Review*, 75, pp.522-36.

Norman, D.A. (1981) 'Categorization of action slips', *Psychological Review*, 88, pp.1-15.

Norman, D.A. and Bobrow, D.T. (1975) 'On data-limited and resource-limited processes', *Cognitive Psychology*, 7, pp.44-64.

Norman, D.A. and Shallice, T. (1986) 'Attention to action: willed and automatic control of behaviour', in R. Davison, G. Schwartz and D. Shapiro (eds) *Consciousness and Self-regulation: Advances in Research and Theory*, New York: Plenum.

Northcraft, G.B and Neale, M.A. (1987) 'Experts, amateurs and real estate: an anchoring-and-adjustment perspective on property pricing decisions', *Organizational Behavior and Human Decision Processes*, 39(1), pp.84-97.

Novick, L.R. (1988) 'Analogical transfer, problem similarity and expertise', *Journal of Experimental Psychology*, 14, pp.510-20.

Novick, L.R. and Holyoak, K.J. (1991) 'Mathematical problem-solving by analogy', *Journal of Experimental Psychology: Learning, Memory and Cognition*, 17, pp.398-415.

Nowakowski, R.S. (1987) 'Basic concepts of CNS development', *Child Development*, 58, pp.568-95.

Noyes, R., Crowe, R.R., Harris, E.L., Hamra, B.J., McChesney, C.M. and Chaudhry, D.R. (1986) 'Relationship between panic disorder and agoraphobia: a family study', *Archives of General Psychiatry*, 43, pp.227-32.

O'Callaghan, E., Gibson, T., Colohan, H.A., Walshe, D., Buckley, P., Larkin, C. and Waddington, J.L. (1991) 'Season of birth in schizophrenia: evidence for confinement of an excess of winter births to patients without a family history of mental disorder', *British Journal of Psychiatry*, 158, pp.764-9.

Office for National Statistics (Great Britain) (1999) *Social Trends 29*, J. Matheson and J. Pullinger (eds), London: The Stationery Office.

Ojemann, G.A. (1983) 'The intra-hemispheric organisation of human language, derived from electrical stimulation techniques', *Trends in Neurosciences*, 6, pp.184-9.

O'Keefe, J. and Nadel, L. (1978) *The Hippocampus as a Cognitive Map*, Oxford: Clarendon Press.

Olds, J. and Milner, P. (1954) 'Positive reinforcement produced by electrical stimulation of the septal area and other regions of the rat brain', *Journal of Comparative and Physiological Psychology*, 47, pp.419-27.

Oller, D.K. (1981) 'Infant vocalisations: exploration and reflectivity', in R.E. Stark (ed.) *Language Behaviour in Infancy and Early Childhood*, New York: Elsevier/North Holland.

Olson, S.L., Bayles, K. and Bates, J.E. (1986) 'Mother–child interaction and children's speech progress: a longitudinal study of the first two years', *Merrill-Palmer Quarterly*, 32, pp.1-20.

Olsson, P., Jansson, L. and Norberg, A. (1998) 'Parenthood as talked about in Swedish ante- and postnatal midwifery consultations: a qualitative study of 58 video-recorded consultations', *Scandinavian Journal of Caring Sciences*, 12 (4), pp.205-14.

Olton, D.S. (1976) 'Spatial memory', *Scientific American*, 236, pp.82-98.

Orlans, B. (1997) 'Ethical decision making about animal experiments', in K.D. Pimple, F.B. Orlans and J.P. Gluck (1997) 'Ethical issues in the use of animals in research', *Ethics and Behaviour*, 7 (2).

Orne, M.T. and Holland, C.C. (1968) 'On the ecological validity of laboratory deceptions', *International Journal of Psychiatry*, 6 (4), pp.282-93.

Ost, L.G., Hellstrom, K. and Kaver, A. (1992) 'One vs five sessions of exposure in the treatment of injection phobia', *Behavior Therapy*, 23, pp.263-82.

Ost, L.G., Salkovskis, P.M. and Hellstrom, K. (1991) 'One-session therapist-directed exposure vs self-exposure in the treatment of spider phobia', *Behavior Therapy*, 22, pp.407-22.

Oswald, I. (1980) *Sleep* (4th edn), Harmondsworth: Penguin Books.

Owen, F., Cross, A.J., Crow, T.J. and Poulter, M. (1978) 'Increased dopamine receptor sensitivity in schizophrenia', *Lancet*, 2, pp.223-6

Paikoff, R.L. and Brooks-Gunn, J. (1991) 'Do parent–child relationships change during adolescence?', *Psychological Bulletin*, 110, pp.47-66.

Palmer, S.E. (1975) 'The effects of contextual scenes on the identification of objects', *Memory and Cognition*, 3, pp.519-26.

Papez, J.W. (1937) 'A proposed mechanism of emotion', *Archives of Neurology and Psychiatry (Chicago)*, 38, pp.725-43.

Papi, F. (1991) 'Orientation in birds: olfactory navigation', *EXS*, 60, pp.52-85.

Papi, F., Luschi, P. and Limonta, P. (1992) 'Orientation-disturbing magnetic treatment affects the pigeon opioid system', *The Journal of Experimental Biology*, 166, pp.169-79.

Park, S., Holtzman, P.S. and Goldman-Rakic, P.S. (1995) 'Spatial working memory deficits in the relatives of schizophrenic patients', *Archives of*

General Psychiatry, 52, pp.821-8.

Parke, R.D., Berkowitz, L., Leyens, J.P., West, S. and Sebastian, R.J. (1977) 'Some effects of violent and nonviolent movies on the behaviour of juvenile delinquents', in L. Berkowitz (ed.) *Advances in Experimental Psychology*, 10, New York: Academic Press.

Parker, G. (1979) 'Reported parental characteristics of agoraphobics and social phobics', *British Journal of Psychiatry*, 135, pp.555-60.

Parker, G., Gladstone, G., Roussos, J., Wilhelm, K., Mitchell, P., Hadzi-Pavlovic, D., Austin, M.P. and Hickie, I. (1998) 'Qualitative and quantitative analyses of a "lock and key" hypothesis of depression', *Psychological Medicine*, 28, pp.1263-73.

Parker, I. (1987) 'Social representations: social psychology's (mis)use of sociology', *Journal for the Theory of Social Behaviour*, 17, pp.447-69.

Parnas, J., Cannon, T.D., Jacobsen, B., Schulsinger, H., Schulsinger, F. and Medick, S.A. (1993) 'Lifetime DSM-III-R diagnostic outcomes in the offspring of schizophrenic mothers: results from the Copenhagen High-Risk Study', *Archives of General Psychiatry*, 50, pp.707-14.

Parson, E.R. (1993) 'Children of community trauma: Inner city violence, images of the media and therapists' perceptions and response', in J.P. Wilson and J. Lindy (eds) *Countertransference in the Treatment of Post-traumatic Stress Disorder*, New York: Guildford Press.

Parsons, R., Tassinary, L.G., Ulrich, R.S., Hebl, M.R. and Grossman-Alexander, M. (1998) 'The view from the road: the calming effects of the roadside environment', *Journal of Environmental Psychology*, 18, 2, pp.113-40.

Pascalis, O., deSchonen, S., Morton, J., Deruelle, C. and Fabre-Grenet, M. (1995) 'Mother's face recognition by neonates: a replication and an extension', *Infant Behaviour and Development*, 18, pp.79-85.

Patterson, F. (1978) 'The gestures of a gorilla: sign language acquisition in another pongid

species', *Brain and Language*, 5, pp.72-97.

Patterson, F. (1979) 'Conversation with a gorilla', *National Geographic*, 154(4), pp.438-65.

Paulson, F.L. (1974) 'Teaching co-operation on television: an evaluation of Sesame Street social goals programs', *Audio-Visual Communication Review*, 22, pp.229-46.

Paulus, P.B. (1977) *Crowding in the Laboratory and its Relation to Social Facilitation*, Paper presented at the meeting of the Midwestern Psychological Association, Chicago.

Pavlov, I.P. (1927) *Conditioned Reflexes*, Oxford: Oxford University Press.

Pavlov, I.P. (1941) *Conditioned Reflexes and Psychiatry*, New York: International Publishers.

Paykel, E.S. (1981) 'Have multivariate statistics contributed to classification?', *British Journal of Psychiatry*, 139, pp.357-62.

Pearce, J.M. (1997) *Animal Learning and Cognition* (2nd edn), Hove: Psychology Press.

Pearson, G. (1984) *Hooligan: A History of Respectable Fears*, London: Macmillan.

Pederson, N.L., Plomin, R., Nesselroade, J.R. and McClearn, G.E. (1992) 'A quantitative genetic analysis of cognitive abilities during the second half of the life span', *Psychological Science*, 3(6), pp.346-53.

Penfield, W. (1958) 'Functional localization in temporal and deep Sylvian areas', *Research Publications of the Association for Research into Nervous and Mental Disease*, 36, pp.210-26.

Pennington, D., Gillen, K. and Hill, P. (1999) *Social Psychology*, London: Arnold.

Penrod, S. (1983) *Social Psychology*, Englewood Cliffs, New Jersey: Prentice-Hall.

Peplau, L.A. (1991) 'Lesbian and gay relationships', in J. Gonsiorek and J. Weinrich (eds), *Homosexuality: Research Implications for Public Policy*, Newbury Park: Sage.

Pepperberg, I.M., Garcia, S.E., Jackson. E.C. and Marconi, S. (1995) 'Mirror-use by African Grey parrots (*Psittacus erithacus*)', *Journal of Comparative Psychology*, 109, pp.182-95.

Perls, F.S. (1992) *Gestalt Therapy Verbatim*, New York: The Centre for Gestalt Development.

Persons, J.B., Thase, M.E. and Crits-Christoph, P. (1996) 'The role of psychotherapy in the treatment of depression', *Archives of General Psychiatry*, 53, pp.283-93.

Pettigrew, T.F. (1958) 'Personality and sociocultural factors in intergroup attitudes: a cross-national comparison', *Journal of Conflict Resolution*, 2, pp.29-42.

Pettigrew, T.F. (1959) 'Regional differences in anti-negro practice', *Journal of Abnormal and Social Psychology*, 59, pp.28-56.

Pettigrew, T.F. (1979) 'The ultimate attribution error: extending Allport's cognitive analysis of prejudice', *Personality and Social Psychology Bulletin*, 5, pp.461-76.

Pfeiffer, W.M. (1982) 'Culture-Bound Syndromes', in I. Al-Issa (ed.) *Culture and Psychopathology*, Baltimore, Maryland: University Park Press.

Phillips, D.P. (1983) 'The impact of mass media violence on US homicides', *American Sociological Review*, 48, pp.560-8.

Pi-Sunyer, X., Kissileff, H.R., Thornton, J. and Smith, G.P. (1982) 'C-terminal octapeptide of cholecystokinin decreases food intake in obese men', *Physiology and Behavior*, 29, pp.627-30.

Piaget, J. (1926) *The Language and Thought of the Child*, New York: Harcourt Brace Jovanovich.

Piaget, J. (1932) *The Moral Judgement of the Child*, Harmondsworth: Penguin.

Piaget, J. (1954) *The Construction of Reality in the Child*, New York: Basic Books.

Piaget, J. (1960) *Psychology of Intelligence*, Paterson, NJ: Littlefield, Adams.

Piaget, J. and Inhelder, B. (1956) *The Child's Conception of Space*, London: Routledge & Kegan Paul.

Pick, H.L. (1987) 'Information and the effects of early perceptual experience', in N.

Eisenberg (ed.) *Contemporary Topics in Developmental Psychology*, New York: Wiley.

Piliavin, I., Rodin, J. and Piliavin, J. (1969) 'Good Samaritanism: an underground phenomenon?', *Journal of Personality and Social Psychology*, 13, pp.289-99.

Piliavin, J.A. and Chang, H. (1990) 'Altruism: a review of recent theory and research', *Annual Review of Sociology*, 16, pp.27-65.

Piliavin, J.A., Dovidio, J.F., Gaertner, S.L. and Clark, R.D. (1981) *Emergency Intervention*, New York: Academic Press.

Pilleri, G. (1979) 'The blind Indus dolphin', *Platanista indi. Endeavour*, 3, pp.48-56.

Pinker, S. (1989) *Learnability and Cognition*, Cambridge, MA: MIT Press.

Pinker, S. (1990) 'Language Acquisition', in D.N. Osherson and H. Lasnik (eds) *Language: An Invitation to Cognitive Science*, Vol. 1, Cambridge, MA: MIT Press.

Pinker, S. (1994) *The Language Instinct*, Harmondsworth: Allen Lane.

Pirchio, M., Spinelli, D., Fiorentini, A. and Maffei, L. (1978) 'Infant contrast sensitivity evaluated by evoked potentials', *Brain Research*, 141, pp.179-84.

Pitz, G.F. and Sachs, N.J. (1984) 'Judgement and decision: theory and application', *Annual Review of Psychology*, 35, pp.139-63.

Plomin, R. (1994) *Genetics and Experience: The Interplay between Nature and Nurture*, Thousand Oaks, CA: Sage.

Plomin, R., DeFries, J.C. and Fulker, D.W. (1988) *Nature and Nurture during Infancy and Early Childhood*, New York: Academic Press.

Pollack, R.H. (1963) 'Contour detectability thresholds as a function of chronological age', *Perceptual and Motor Skills*, 17, pp.411-17.

Pollack, R.H. and Silvar, S.D. (1967) 'Magnitude of the Müller-Lyer illusion in children as a function of pigmentation of the Fundus oculi', *Psychonomic Science*, 8, pp.83-4.

Poltrock, S.E., Lansman, M. and Hunt, E. (1982) 'Automatic and controlled attention processes in auditory target detection', *Journal of Experimental Psychology: Human Perception and Performance*, 8, pp.37-45.

Pomerantz, J.R. (1981) 'Perceptual organisation in information processing', in M. Kubovy and J.R. Pomerantz (eds) *Perceptual Organisation*, Hillsdale, NJ: Erlbaum.

Popper, K. (1959) *The Logic of Scientific Discovery*, New York: Basic Books.

Posner, M. and Keele, S.W. (1968) 'On the genesis of abstract ideas', *Journal of Experimental Psychology*, 77, pp.353-63.

Posner, M. and Snyder, C.R.R. (1975) 'Facilitation and inhibition in the processing of signals', in P.M.A. Rabbitt and S. Dornic (eds) *Attention and Performance*, London: Academic Press.

Potter, J. and Litton, I. (1985) 'Some problems underlying the theory of social representations', *British Journal of Social Psychology*, 24, pp.81-90.

Povinelli, D.J. (1989) 'Failure to find self-recognition in Asian elephants (*Elephas maximusi*) in contrast to their use of mirror cues to discover hidden food', *Journal of Comparative Psychology*, 103, 122-31.

Povinelli, D.J., Nelson, K.E. and Boyson, S.T. (1990) 'Inferences about guessing and knowing by chimpanzees (*Pan troglodytes*)', *Journal of Comparative Psychology*, 104, pp.203-10.

Povinelli, D.J., Rulf, A.B., Landau, K.R. and Bierschwale, D.T. (1993) 'Self-recognition in chimpanzees: distribution, ontogeny and patterns of emergence', *Journal of Comparative Psychology*, 107, pp.347-72.

Premack, D. and Woodruff, G. (1978) 'Does the chimpanzee have a theory of mind?', *Behavioural and Brain Sciences*, 4, pp.515-26.

Prentice, P. (1995) 'Rational–emotive therapy', *Psychology Review*, 2(2), pp.28-31.

Prentice-Dunn, S. and Rogers, R.W. (1989) 'Deindividuation and the self-regulation of behaviour', in P. Paulus (ed.) *The Psychology of Group Influence*, Hillsdale, NJ: Lawrence Erlbaum.

Price, L.H. (1968) 'The genetics of depressive behaviour', in A. Coppen and S. Walk (eds) *Recent Developments in Affective Disorders*, British Journal of Psychiatry Special Publication No. 2.

Prien, R.F. (1988) 'Somatic treatment of unipolar depressive disorder', in A.J. Frances and R.E. Hales (eds) *Review of Psychiatry*, Washington, DC: American Psychiatric Press.

Prince, M. (1906) *The Dissolution of a Personality*, New York: Longman, cited in R. Gross (1990) *Key Studies in Psychology*, London: Hodder & Stoughton.

Procopio, M. and Marriott, P.K. (1998) 'Is the decline in diagnosis of schizophrenia caused by the disappearance of a seasonal aetiological agent? An epidemiological study in England and Wales', *Psychological Medicine*, 28, pp.367-73.

Przybyla, D.P.J. (1985) *The Facilitating Effects of Exposure to Erotica on Male Prosocial Behaviour*, Doctoral Dissertation, State University of New York at Albany.

Rack, P. (1982) *Race, Culture and Mental Disorder*, London: Tavistock.

Ramachandran, V.S. (1992) 'Blind spots', *Scientific American*, pp.102-9.

Ramachandran, V.S. and Blakeslee, S. (1999) *Phantoms in the Brain*, London: Fourth Estate.

Randrup, A. and Munkvad, I. (1966) 'On the role of dopamine in the amphetamine excitatory response', *Nature*, 211, p. 540.

Rapoport, J.L. (1989) 'The biology of obsessions and compulsions', *Scientific American*, 260, pp.83-9.

Rapoport, J.L., Giedd, J., Kumra. S., Jacobsen, L., Smith, A., Lee, P., Nelson, J. and Hamburger, S. (1997) 'Childhood-onset schizophrenia', *Archives of General Psychiatry*, 54, pp.897-903.

Rauch, S.L., Jenike, M.A. and Alpert, N.M. (1994) 'Regional cerebral blood flow measured during symptom provocation in obsessive–compulsive disorder using oxygen 15-labeled carbon dioxide and positron emission tomography', *Archives of General Psychiatry*, 51, pp.62-70.

Raven, J.C. (1958) *Raven's Standard Progressive Matrices*, London: K.K.Lewis & Co. Ltd.

Reason, J. (1979) 'Actions not as planned: the price of automatization', in G. Underwood and R. Stephens (eds) *Aspects of Consciousness*, Vol.1, London: Academic Press.

Reason, J. (1992) 'Cognitive underspecification: its variety and consequences', in B.J. Baars (ed.) *Experimental Slips and Human Error: Exploring the Architecture of Volition*, New York: Plenum Press.

Reber, A.S. (1995) *Penguin Dictionary of Psychology* (2nd edn), London: Penguin.

Rechtien, J.G. and Fiedler, E. (1988) 'Contributions to psychohistory: XIII. Courtly love today: romance and socialization in interpersonal scripts', *Psychological Reports*, 63, pp.683-95.

Reed, S. (1972) 'Pattern recognition and categorisation', *Cognitive Psychology*, 3, pp.382-407.

Regan, T. (1983) *The Case for Animal Rights*.

Regan, T. and Singer, P. (eds) (1976) *Animal Rights and Human Obligations*, Englewood Cliffs, NJ: Prentice-Hall.

Reich, J. and Yates, W. (1988) 'Family history of psychiatric disorders in social phobia', *Comprehensive Psychiatry*, 29, pp.72-5.

Reid, E. (1998) 'The Self and the Internet: variations on the illusion of one self', in J. Gackenbach (ed.) *Psychology and the Internet*, San Diego: Academic Press.

Rescorla, R.A. (1980) *Pavlovian Second-order Conditioning*, Hillsdale, NJ: Lawrence Erlbaum Associates.

Revelle, W. (1993) 'Individual differences in personality and motivation: "Non-cognitive" determinants of cognitive performance', in A.D. Baddeley and I. Weiskrantz (eds) *Attention: Awareness, Selection and Control*, Oxford: Oxford University Press.

Reynolds, P.C. (1981) *On the Evolution of Human Behaviour*, Berkeley and Los Angeles: University of California Press.

Rholes, W.S. and Pryor, J.B. (1982) 'Cognitive accessibility and causal attributions', *Personality and Social Psychology Bulletin*, 8, pp.719-27.

Richards, G. (1996) *Putting Psychology in its Place*, London: Routledge.

Ridgway, S.H. (1986) 'Dolphin brain size', in M.M. Bryden and R.J. Harrison (eds) *Research on Dolphins*, Oxford: Clarendon Press, pp.59-70.

Ridley, M. (1995) *Animal Behaviour* (2nd edn), Oxford: Blackwell.

Riesen, A.H. (1965) 'Effects of early deprivation of photic stimulation', in S. Osler and R. Cooke (eds) *The Biosocial Basis of Mental Retardation*, Baltimore: John Hopkins University Press.

Riger, S. (1992) 'Epistemological debates, feminist voices: science, social values, and the study of women', *American Psychologist*, 47, p. 730.

Roberts, P. and Newton, P.M. (1987) 'Levinsonian studies of women's adult development', *Psychology and Aging*, 2, pp.154-63.

Robinson, J.P. and Bachman, J.G. (1972) 'Television viewing habits and aggression', in G.A. Comstock and E.A. Rubinstein (eds) *Television and Social Behavior*, Vol. 3, *Television and Adolescent Aggressiveness*, Washington, DC: United States Government Printing Office.

Rock, I. (1983) *The Logic of Perception*, Cambridge, MA: MIT Press.

Rock, I. (1995) *Perception*, New York: Scientific American Library.

Rockman, S. (1980) *On the Level: Final Report on Formative Evaluation*, Bloomington, IN: Agency for Instructional Television.

Rogers, C.R. (1951) *Client-centred Therapy*, Boston: Houghton Mifflin.

Rogers, C.R. (1974) 'In retrospect: forty-six years', *American Psychologist*, 29, pp.115-23.

Rokeach, M. (1956) 'Political and religious dogmatism: an alternate to the authoritarian personality', *Psychological Monographs*, 70, No. 18.

Romaine, S. (1984) *The Language of Children and Adolescents: The Acquisition of Communicative Competence*, Oxford: Basil Blackwell.

Rose, G. and Marshall, T.F. (1974) *Counselling and School Social Work: An Experimental Study*, London: Wiley.

Rose, S., Kamin, L.J. and Lewontin, R.C. (1984) *Not in Our Genes: Biology, Ideology and Human Nature*, Harmondsworth: Penguin.

Rose, S.A. and Blank, M. (1974) 'The potency of context in childrens' cognition: an illustration through conservation', *Child Development*, 45, pp.499-502.

Rosenblatt, P.C. and Anderson, R.M. (1981) 'Human sexuality in cross-cultural perspective', in M. Cook (ed.) *The Bases of Human Sexual Attraction*, London: Academic Press.

Rosenhan, D.L. (1970) 'The natural socialisation of altruistic autonomy', in J.L. Macaulay and L. Berkowitz (eds) *Altruism and Helping Behaviour*, New York: Academic Press.

Rosenhan, D.L. (1973) 'On being sane in insane places', *Science*, 179, pp.250-8.

Rosenhan, D.L. and Seligman, M.E.P. (1995) *Abnormal Psychology* (3rd edn), New York: Norton.

Rosenthal, R. and Jacobsen, L. (1968) *Pygmalion in the Classroom*, New York: Holt, Rinehart & Winston.

Rosenwasser, A.M., Boulos, Z. and Ternan, M. (1981) 'Circadian organisation of food intake and meal patterns in the rat', *Physiology and Behavior*, 27, pp.33-39.

Rosenzweig, M.R., Leiman, A.L. and Breedlove, S.M. (1999) *Biological Psychology* (2nd edn), Sunderland, MA: Sinauer Associates, Inc.

Ross, L.D. (1977) 'The intuitive psychologist and his shortcomings: distortions in the attribution process', in L. Berkowitz (ed.) *Advances in Experimental Social Psychology*, Vol. 10, New York: Academic Press.

Ross, L.D., Amabile, T.M. and Steinmetz, J.L. (1977) 'Social roles, social control, and biases in social perception: biased attributional processes in the debriefing paradigm', *Journal of Personality and Social Psychology*, 35, pp.485-94.

Roth, I. and Bruce, B. (1995) *Perception and Representation. Current Issues* (2nd edn), Buckingham: Open University Press.

Rotter, J.B. (1966) 'Generalized expectancies for internal versus external control of reinforcement', *Psychological Monographs*, 80, pp.1-28.

Rubin, Z. (1973) *Liking and Loving: An Invitation to Social Psychology*, New York: Holt, Rinehart & Winston.

Rubin, Z., Hill, C.T., Peplau, L.A. and Dunkel-Schetter, C. (1980) 'Self-disclosure in dating couples: Sex roles and the ethic of openness', *Journal of Marriage and the Family*, 42, pp.305-17.

Rumbaugh, D.M., Savage-Rumbaugh, E.S. and Sevcik, R.A. (1994) 'Biobehavioural roots of language: a comparative perspective of chimpanzee, child and culture', in R.W. Wrangham, W.C. McGrew, F.B.M. de Waal, P.G. Heltne and L.A. Marquardt (eds) *Chimpanzee Cultures*, Cambridge, MA: Harvard University Press, pp.319-34.

Rumelhart, D.E. and Norman, D.A. (1983) 'Representation in memory', in R.C. Atkinson, R.J. Herrnstein, G. Lindsey and R.D. Luce (eds) *Handbook of Experimental Psychology*, Chichester: Wiley.

Runciman, W.G. (1966) *Relative Deprivation and Social Justice*, London: Routledge & Kegan Paul.

Runyon, R. and Haber, A. (1976) *Fundamentals of Behavioural Statistics* (3rd edn), Reading, MA: McGraw Hill.

Rusak, B. and Zucker, I. (1975) 'Biological rhythms and animal behavior', *Annual Review of Psychology*, 26, 137-71.

Rusbult, C.E. (1983) 'A longitudinal study of the investment model: the development and deterioration of satisfaction and commitment in heterosexual involvements', *Journal of Personality and Social Psychology*, 45, pp.101-17.

Rusbult, C.E. and Martz, J.M. (1995) 'Remaining in an abusive relationship: an investment model analysis of nonvoluntary dependence', *Personality and Social Psychology Bulletin*, 21, pp.558-71.

Rushton, J.P. and Owen, D. (1975) 'Immediate and delayed effects of TV modelling and preaching on children's generosity', *British Journal of Social and Clinical Psychology*, 14, pp.309-10.

Russon, A.E. and Galdikas, B.M.F. (1995) 'Constraints on great apes' imitation: model and action selectivity in rehabilitant orangutan (*Pongo pygmaeus*) imitation', *Journal of Comparative Psychology*, 109, pp.5-17.

Rutlidge, L.L. and Hupka, R.B. (1985) 'The facial feedback hypothesis: methodological concerns and new supporting evidence', *Motivation and Emotion*, 9, pp.219-40.

Rutter, M., Graham, P., Chadwock, O. and Yule, W. (1976) 'Adolescent turmoil: fact or fiction?', *Journal of Child Psychology and Psychiatry*, 7, pp.35-56.

Ryan, R.M. and Lynch, J.H. (1989) 'Emotional autonomy versus detachment: revisiting the vicissitudes of adolescence and young adulthood', *Child Development*, 60, pp.34-64.

Ryle, G. (1949) *The Concept of Mind*, New York: Barnes & Noble.

Sachs, J., Bard, B. and Johnson, M.L. (1981) 'Language with restricted input: case studies of two hearing children of deaf parents', *Applied Psycholinguistics*, 2, pp.33-54.

Sackeim, H.A. (1988) 'The efficacy of electroconvulsive therapy', *Ann. NY Academic Science*, 462, pp.70-5.

Sackeim, H.A., Nordlie, J.W. and Gur, R.C. (1993) 'Effects of stimulus intensity and electrode replacement on the efficacy of the effects of electroconvulsive therapy', *New England Journal of Medicine*, 328, pp.839-46.

Sackeim, H.A., Prudic, J. and Devanand, D.P. (1990) 'The impact of medication resistance and continuation of pharmacotherapy following response to electroconvulsive therapy in major depression', *Journal of Clinical Pharmacology*, 10, pp.96-104.

Saegert, S., Swap, W. and Zajonc, R.B. (1973) 'Exposure, contact and interpersonal attraction', *Journal of Personality and Social Psychology*, 25, pp.234-42.

Sagan, C. (1973) *The Cosmic Connection*, New York: Doubleday.

Sales, E., Baum, M. and Shore, B. (1984) 'Victim readjustment following assault', *Journal of Social Issues*, 37, pp.5-27 and 40 (1), pp.117-36.

Sam, D.L. (1996) 'Culture: a missing link in the psychological science of human behavior', http://www.calstatela.edu/academiclpsych/lg/su96sam.htm

Sameroff, A. and Seifer, R. (1983) 'Familial role and child competence', *Child Development*, 54, pp.1254-68.

Sameroff, A., Seifer, R., Baldwin, A. and Baldwin C. (1993) 'Stability of intelligence from preschool to adolescence: the influence of social and family risk factors', *Child Development*, 64, pp.80-97.

Sandell, A. (1994) 'It was the drugs that made me mad', *The Independent*, 4 October 1994.

Sapir, E. (1921) *Language*, New York: Harcourt, Brace & World.

Satow, K.L. (1975) 'Social approval and helping', *Journal of Experimental Social Psychology*, 62, pp.356-63.

Savage-Rumbaugh, E.S. (1986) *Ape Language from Conditioned Response to Symbol*, New York: Columbia University Press.

Savage-Rumbaugh, E.S. and Lewin, R. (1994) *Kanzi: The Ape at the Brink of the Human Mind*, London: Doubleday.

Savage-Rumbaugh, S. (1988) 'A new look at ape language: comprehension of vocal speech and syntax', *Nebraska*

Symposium on Motivation, 35, pp.201-55.

Scarr, S. and Weinberg, R.A. (1976) 'IQ test performance of black children adopted by white families', *American Psychologist*, 31, pp.726-39.

Scarr, S. and Weinberg, R.A. (1983) 'The Minnesota adoption studies: generation differences and malleability', *Child Development*, 54, pp.260-7.

Schachter, S. (1971) 'Some extraordinary facts about obese humans and rats', *American Psychologist*, 26, pp.129-44.

Schachter, S. and Singer, J.E. (1962) 'Cognitive, social, and physiological determinants of emotional state', *Psychological Review*, 69, pp.379-99.

Schaie, K.W. and Hertzog, C. (1983) 'Fourteen-year cohort-sequential analysis of adult intellectual development', *Developmental Psychology*, 19, pp.531-43.

Schaie, K.W. and Willis, S.L. (1991) *Adult Development and Aging*, New York: Harper Collins.

Schank, R. and Abelson, R. (1977) *Scripts, Plans, Goals and Understanding: An Enquiry into Human Knowledge*, New Jersey: Erlbaum.

Schettino, A.P. and Borden, R.J. (1975) 'Group size versus group density: where is the affect?', *Personality and Social Psychology Bulletin*, 2, pp.67-70.

Schneider, B.H., Smith, A., Poisson, S.E. and Kwan, A.B. (1997) 'Cultural dimensions of children's peer relations', in S. Duck (ed.) *Handbook of Personal Relationships: Theory, Research and Interventions* (2nd edn), Chichester: John Wiley.

Schreiber, F.R (1973) *Sybil*, New York: Warner.

Schuler, H. (1982) *Ethical Problems in Psychological Research*, New York: Academic Press.

Schumm, W.R., Webb, F.J. and Bullman, S.R. (1998) 'Gender and marital satisfaction: data from a national survey of families and households', *Psychological Reports*, 83 (1), pp.319-27.

Schuster, B., Fosterling, F. and Weiner, B. (1989) 'Perceiving the causes of success and failure: a cross-cultural examination of attributional concepts', *Journal of Cross-Cultural Psychology*, 20, pp.191-213.

Schwartz, J.J. (1991) 'Why stop calling? A study of unison bout singing in a neotropical treefrog', *Animal Behaviour*, 42, pp.565-77.

Schwartz, J.M., Stoessel, P.W., Baxter, L.R., Martin, K.M. and Phelps, M.E. (1996) 'Systematic changes in cerebral glucose metabolic rate after successful behaviour modification treatment of obsessive–compulsive disorder', *Archives of General Psychiatry*, 53, pp.109-13.

Schwartz, S. (1994) 'Beyond individualism-collectivism: new cultural dimensions of values', in U. Kim, H.C. Triadis, C. Kagitcibasi, S.-C. Choi and G. Yoon (eds) *Individualism and Collectivism: Theory, Method and Application*, Newbury Park: Sage.

Schwartz, S. (1997) 'Values and Culture', in D. Munro, S. Carr and J. Schumaker (eds) *Motivation and Culture*, New York: Routledge.

Schwartz, S.H. and David, T.B. (1976) 'Responsibility, norms and helping in an emergency', *Journal of Personality and Social Psychology*, 16, pp.299-310.

Scott M.J. and Stradling, S.G. (1994) 'Post-traumatic stress disorder without the trauma', *British Journal of Clinical Psychology*, 33, pp.71-4.

Scroppo, J., Weinberger, J., Drob, S. and Eagle, P. (1998) 'Identifying dissociative identity disorder: a self-report and projective study', *Journal of Abnormal Psychology*, 92, pp.272-84.

Searle, J. (1980) 'Minds, brains and programs', *The Behavioural and Brain Sciences*, 3, pp.417-57.

Sears, O.D., Peplau, A. and Freedman, J. (1988) *Social Psychology*, Englewood Cliffs, NJ: Prentice Hall.

Seeman, M.V. (1997) 'Psychopathology in women and men: focus on female hormones', *American Journal of Psychiatry*, 154, pp.1641-7.

Segal, S.J. and Fusella, V. (1970) 'Influence of imaged pictures and sounds on the detection of visual and auditory signals', *Journal of Experimental Psychology*, 83, pp.458-64.

Segall, M.H., Campbell, D.T. and Herskovits, M.J. (1963) 'Cultural differences in the perception of geometric illusions', *Science*, 193, pp.769-71.

Segall, M.H., Campbell, D.T. and Herskovits, M.J. (1966) *The Influence of Culture on Visual Perception*, Indianapolis: Bobbs-Merrill.

Segall, M.H., Dasen, P.R., Berry, J.W. and Poortinga, Y.H. (1990) *Human Behaviour in Global Perspective: An Introduction to Cross-cultural Psychology*, New York: Pergamon Press.

Selfridge, O.G. (1959) 'Pandemonium: a paradigm for learning', in *Symposium on the Mechanisation of Thought Processes*, London: HMSO.

Seligman, M.E.P. (1970) 'On the generality of the laws of learning', *Psychological Review*, 77, pp.406-18.

Seligman, M.E.P. (1971) 'Phobias and preparedness', *Behaviour Therapy*, 2, pp.307-20.

Seligman, M.E.P. (1974) 'Depression and learned helplessness', in R.J. Friedman and M.M. Katz (eds) *The Psychology of Depression: Contemporary Theory and Research*, Washington, DC: Winston Wiley.

Seligman, M.E.P. and Maier, S.F. (1967) 'Failure to escape traumatic shock', *Journal of Experimental Psychology*, 74, pp.1-9.

Seligman, M.E.P., Abramson, L.Y., Semmell, A. and von Baeyer, C. (1979) 'Depression and attributional style', *Journal of Abnormal Psychology*, 88, pp.242-7.

Senra, C. and Polaino, A. (1998) 'Assessment of treatment outcome in depressed patients: concordance of methods', *British Journal of Clinical Psychology*, 37, pp.217-27.

Sergent, J. (1984) 'An investigation into component and configural processes underlying face recognition', *British Journal of Psychology*, 75, pp.221-42.

Sergent, J. and Signoret, J.L. (1992) 'Functional and anatomical decomposition of face processing: evidence from prosopagnosia and PET study of normal subjects', in V. Bruce, A. Cowey, A.W. Ellis and D.I. Perrett (eds) *Processing the Facial Image*, Oxford: Clarendon Press.

Seyfarth, R.M. and Cheney, D.L. (1980) 'The ontogeny of vervet monkey calling: a preliminary report', *Zeitschrift für Tierpsychologie*, 54, pp.37-56.

Seyfarth, R.M. and Cheyney, D.L. (1992) 'Meaning and mind in monkeys', *Scientific American*, 267, pp.122-8.

Shaffer, D.R. (1993) *Developmental Psychology: Childhood and Adolescence* (3rd edition), Pacific Grove, CA: Brooks/Cole Publishing Co.

Shaffer, L.H. (1975) 'Multiple attention in continuous verbal tasks', in P.M.A. Rabbitt and S. Dornic (eds) *Attention and Performance*, London: Academic Press.

Shaikh, A. (1985) 'Cross-cultural comparison: psychiatric admission of Asian and indigenous patients in Leicestershire', *International Journal of Social Psychiatry*, 31, p. 3-11.

Shanab, M.E. and Yahya, K.A. (1978) 'A cross-cultural study of obedience', *Bulletin of the Psychonomic Society*, 11, pp.267-9.

Shapley, R. and Lennie, P. (1985) 'Spatial frequency analysis in the visual system', *Annual Review of Neuroscience*, 8, pp.547-83.

Sharpley, C.F. and Layton, R. (1998) 'Effects of age of retirement, reason for retirement, and pre-retirement training on psychological and physical health during retirement', *Australian Psychologist*, 33(2), pp.119-24.

Shatz, M. and Gelman, R. (1973) 'The development of common skills: modifications in the speech of young children as a function of the listener', *Monograph of the Society for Research in Child Development*, 152.

Shaw, D.F. (1997) 'Gay men and computer communication: a

discourse of sex and identity in cyberspace', in S.G. Jones (ed.) *Virtual Culture: Identity and Communication in Cybersociety*, Thousand Islands: Sage.

Sheehy, G. (1996) *New Passages*, New York: Harper Collins.

Shephard, R.N. and Zare, S.L. (1983) 'Path-guided apparent motion', *Science*, 220, pp.632-4.

Sherif, M. (1966) *Group Conflict and Co-operation: Their Social Psychology*, London: Routledge & Kegan Paul.

Sherif, M. and Sherif, C.W. (1953) *Groups in Harmony and Tension: An Integration of Studies on Intergroup Relations*, New York: Octagon.

Sherif, M., Harvey, O.J., White, B.J., Hood, W.R. and Sherif, C.W. (1961) *Intergroup Conflict and Cooperation: The Robber's Cave Experiment*, Norman, Oklahoma: University of Oklahoma.

Sherman, P.W. (1981) 'Kinship, demography and Belding's ground squirrel nepotism', *Behavioral Ecology and Sociobiology*, 8, pp.251-9.

Sherry, D. F. and Galef, B.G. Jr. (1990) 'Social learning without imitation: more about milk bottle opening by birds', *Animal Behaviour*, 40, pp.987-9.

Sherry, D., Jacobs, L.F. and Gaulin, S.J.C. (1992) 'Spatial memory and adaptive specialisation of the hippocampus', *Trends in Neurosciences*, 15, pp.298-303.

Shettleworth, S.J. (1995) 'Comparative studies of memory in food storing birds: From the field to the Skinner box', in E. Alleva, A. Fasolo, H.P. Lipp, L. Nadel, and L. Ricceri (eds) *Behavioural Brain Research in Naturalistic and Semi-Naturalistic Settings*, Dordrecht: Kluwer Academic Press.

Shettleworth, S.J. (1998) *Cognition, Evolution and Behavior*, New York: Oxford University Press.

Shields, J. (1962) *Monozygotic Twins Brought Up Apart and Brought up Together*, London: Oxford University Press.

Shiffrin, R.M. and Schneider, W. (1977) 'Controlled and automatic human information processing: perceptual learning,

automatic attending and a general theory', *Psychological Review*, 84, pp.127-90.

Shiloh, S. (1994) 'Heuristics and biases in health decision making: their expression in genetic counselling', in L. Heath, R.S. Tindale, J. Edwards, E.J. Posavac, F.B. Bryant, E. Henderson-King, Y. Suarez-Balcazar and J. Myers (eds) *Applications of Heuristics and Biases to Social Issues*, New York: Plenum.

Short, R.V. (1994) 'Why sex', in R.V. Short and E. Balaban (eds)*The Differences between the Sexes*, Cambridge: Cambridge University Press.

Shotland, R.L. and Huston, T.L. (1979) 'Emergencies: what are they and do they influence bystanders to intervene?', *Journal of Personality and Social Psychology*, 37 (10), pp.1822-34.

Sieber, J.E. and Stanley, B. (1988) 'Ethical and professional dimensions of socially sensitive research', *American Psychologist*, 43 (1), pp.49-55.

Silberg, J., Pickles, A., Rutter, M., Hewitt, J., Simonoff E., Maes, H., Carbonneau, R., Murrelle, L., Foley, D. and Eaves, L. (1999) 'The influence of genetic factors and life stress on depression among adolescent girls', *Archives of General Psychiatry*, 56, pp.225-32.

Silvar, S.D. and Pollack, R.H. (1967) 'Racial differences in pigmentation of the Fundus oculi', *Psychonomic Science*, pp.159-60.

Simmel, G. (1971) *On Individuality and Social Forms*, Chicago: University of Chicago Press.

Simon, P. (1968) *Save the Life of My Child*, Sony Music Entertainment Inc.

Simon, R.W., Eder, D. and Evans, C. (1992) 'The development of feeling norms underlying romantic love among adolescent females', *Social Psychology Quarterly*, 55(1), pp.29-46.

Simons, R.C. and Hughes, C.C. (eds) (1985) *The Culture-Bound Syndromes: Folk Illnesses of Psychiatric and Anthropological Interest*, Dordrecht: D. Reidel.

Simpson, J.A., Campbell, B. and Berscheid, E. (1986) 'The association between romantic love

and marriage: Kephart (1967) twice revisited', *Personality and Social Psychology Bulletin*, 12, pp.363-72.

Sinclair-de-Zwart, H. (1969) 'Developmental psycholinguistics', in D. Elkind and J. Flavell (eds), *Studies in Cognitive Development*, New York: Oxford University Press.

Singer, P. (1975) *Animal Liberation*, New York: Avon.

Skal, D.J. (1993) *The Monster Show: A Cultural History of Horror*, New York: Norton.

Skinner, B.F. (1938) *The Behavior of Organisms*, New York: Appleton-Century-Crofts.

Skinner, B.F. (1948) 'Superstition in the pigeon', *Journal of Experimental Psychology*, 38, pp.168-72.

Skinner, B.F. (1953) *Science and Human Behavior*, New York: Macmillan.

Skinner, B.F. (1957) *Verbal Behaviour*, New York: Appleton-Century-Crofts.

Skinner, B.F. (1958) 'Teaching Machines', *Science*, 128, pp.969-77.

Skinner, B.F. (1960) 'Pigeons in a pelican', *American Psychologist*, 15, pp.28-37.

Skinner, B.F. (1971) *Beyond Freedom and Dignity*, New York: Knopf.

Skinner, B.F. (1973) *Beyond Freedom and Dignity*, Harmondsworth: Penguin.

Skinner, B.F. (1981) 'Selection by consequences', *Science*, 213, pp.501-4.

Skinner, B.F. (1987) 'What is wrong with daily life in the Western world?', in B.F. Skinner *Upon Further Reflection*, Englewood Cliffs, NJ: Prentice-Hall.

Slabey, R.G. and Frey, K.G. (1975) 'Development of gender constancy and selective attention to same-sex models', *Child Development*, 46, pp.849-56.

Slater, A. and Morrison, V. (1985) 'Shape constancy and slant perception at birth', *Perception*, 14, pp.337-44.

Slater, E. and Sheilds, J. (1969) 'Genetic aspects of anxiety', *British Journal of Psychiatry*, 3, pp.62-71.

Slobin, D.I. (1971) *Psycholinguistics*, Illinois: Scott Foresman.

Slobin, D.I. (1985) 'Crosslinguistic evidence for the language-making capacity', in D.I. Slobin (ed.), *The Crosslinguistic Study of Language Acquisition*, Vol. 2, *Theoretical Issues*, Hillsdale, NJ: Erlbaum.

Slovic, P., Fischoff, B. and Lichtenstein, S. (1982) 'Facts versus fears: understanding perceived risk', in D. Kahneman, P. Slovic and A. Tversky (eds) *Judgement under Uncertainty: Heuristics and Biases*, New York: Cambridge University Press.

Slugoski, B. (1998) *Social Cognition*, Leicester: BPS Books.

Small, S.A., Zeldin, R.S. and Savin-Williams, R.C. (1983) 'In search of personality traits: a multi-method analysis of naturally occurring prosocial and dominance behaviour', *Journal of Personality*, 51, pp.1-16.

Smith, C. (1999) Quoted in 'Perchance to learn', *New Scientist*, 2205, pp.26-30.

Smith, C. and Lloyd, B. (1978) 'Maternal behaviour and perceived sex of infant: revisited', *Child Development*, 49, pp.1263-5.

Smith, E. and Mackie, D. (2000) *Social Psychology*, Philadelphia, PA: Psychology Press.

Smith, J.F. and Kida, T. (1991) 'Heuristics and biases: expertise and task realism in auditing', *Psychological Bulletin*, 109, pp.472-89.

Smith, M.L. and Glass, G.V. (1977) 'Meta-analysis of psychotherapy outcome studies', *American Psychologist*, 32, pp.752-60.

Smith, P. and Bond, M.H. (1993) *Social Psychology Across Cultures: Analysis and Perspectives*, Harvester Wheatsheaf: New York.

Smith, P. and Bond, M.H. (1998) *Social Psychology Across Cultures* (2nd edn), Hemel Hemstead: Prentice Hall.

Smith, P.K. (1979) 'The ontogeny of fear in children', in W. Sluckin (ed.) *Fear in Animals and Man*, London, Van Nostrand.

Smith, P.K. and Daglish, L. (1977) 'Sex differences in parent and infant behaviour in the home', *Child Development*, 48, pp.1250-4.

Smith, P.K., Cowie, H. and Blades, M. (1998) *Understanding Children's Development* (3nd edn), Oxford: Blackwell.

Smith, R.L. (1984) 'Human sperm competition', in R.L. Smith (ed.) *Sperm Competition and the Evolution of Animal Mating Systems*, Orlando: Academic Press.

Smith, S.M., Brown, H.O., Thomas, J.E.P. and Goodman, L.S. (1947) 'The lack of cerebral effects of d-tubocurarine', *Anesthesiology*, 8, pp.1-14.

Snarey, J.R., Reimer, J. and Kohlberg, L. (1985) 'Development of social-moral reasoning among kibbutz adolescents: a longitudinal cross-cultural study', *Developmental Psychology*, 21, pp.3-17.

Snow, C.E. (1994) 'Beginning from baby talk: twenty years of research on input and interaction', in C. Gallaway and B. Richards (eds) *Input and Interaction in Language Acquisition*, Cambridge: Cambridge University Press.

Snyder, S.H. (1977) 'Opiate receptors and internal opiates', *Scientific American*, 236, pp.44-56.

Snyder, S.H. (1984) 'Drug and neurotransmitter receptors in the brain', *Science*, 224, pp.22-31.

Solso, R. and McCarthy, J.E. (1981) 'Prototype formation of faces: a case for pseudomemory', *British Journal of Psychology*, 72, pp.499-503.

Solyom, L., Beck, P., Solyom, C. and Hugel, R. (1974) 'Some etiological factors in phobic neurosis', *Canadian Psychiatric Association Journal*, 21, pp.109-13.

Spanos, N. (1994) 'Multiple identity enactments and multiple personality disorder: a socio-cognitive perspective', *Psychological Bulletin*, 116, pp.143-165.

Spanos, N., Weekes, J. and Bertrand, L . (1985) 'Multiple personality: a social psychological perspective,' *Journal of Abnormal Psychology*, 94, pp.362-376.

Spelke, E.S., Hirst W. and Neisser, U. (1976) 'Skills of divided attention', *Cognition*, 4, pp.215-30.

Sperling, G. (1960) 'The information available in brief visual presentation', *Psychological Monographs*, 74, pp.1-29.

Sperry, R.W. (1982) 'Some effects of disconnecting the cerebral hemispheres', *Science*, 217, pp.1223-6.

Spiegel, R. (1989) *Psychopharmacology* (2nd edn), New York: Wiley.

Spiegel, T.A. (1973) 'Caloric regulation of food intake in man', *Journal of Comparative and Physiological Psychology*, 84, pp.24-37.

Spitzer, R.L. and Williams, J.B.W. (1985) 'Classification in psychiatry', in H.I. Kaplan and B.J. Sadock (eds) *Comprehensive Textbook of Psychiatry* (4th edition), Baltimore: Williams and Wilkins.

Sprafkin, J.N., Liebert, R.M. and Poulos, R.W. (1975) 'Effects of a prosocial televised example on children's helping', *Journal of Experimental Child Psychology*, 20, pp.119-26.

Sprecher, S., Sullivan, Q. and Hatfield, E. (1994) 'Mate selection preferences: gender differences examined on a national scale', *Journal of Personality and Social Psychology*, 66, pp.1074-80.

Standen, V. and Foley, R.A. (eds) (1989) *Comparative Socioecology: The Behavioural Ecology of Humans and Other Mammals*, in Special Publication of the British Ecological Society, No. 8, Oxford: Blackwell Scientific .

State University of New York at Buffalo (1999) *Abnormal Psychology*, lecture 2: http://ub-counseling.buffalo. edu/Abpsy/lecture2.html

Steele, C.M. (1997) 'A threat in the air: how stereotypes shape intellectual identity and performance', *American Psychologist*, 52, pp.613-29.

Steele, C.M. and Southwick, L. (1985) 'Alcohol and social behaviour. I. The psychology of drunken excess', *Journal of Personality and Social Psychology*, 48, pp.18-34.

Stein, A.H. and Friedrich, L.K. (1972) 'Television content and young children's behavior', in J.P. Murray, E.A. Rubinstein and G.A. Comstock (eds) *Television and social learning*, Washington: U.S. Government Printing Office.

Steinberg, L. and Silverberg, S.B. (1986) 'The vicissitudes of autonomy in early adolescence', *Child Development*, 57, pp.84-51.

Steiner, W. (1991) 'Fluoxetine-induced mania in a patient with obsessive-compulsive disorder', *American Journal of Psychiatry*, 148, pp.1403-4.

Stephens, W. (1963) *The Family in Cross-cultural Perspective*, New York: Holt, Rhinehart & Winston.

Stern, W.C. and Morgane, P.J. (1974) 'Theoretical view of REM sleep: maintenance of catecholamine systems in the central nervous system', *Behavioral Biology*, 11, pp.1-32.

Sternberg, R.J. (1986) 'A triangular theory of love', *Psychological Review*, 93, pp.119-35.

Sternberg, R.J. (1988) *The Triangle of Love*, New York: Basic Books.

Stevens, A. and Price, J. (1996) *Evolutionary Psychiatry*, London: Routledge.

Stewart, V.M. (1973) 'Tests of the "carpentered world" hypothesis by race and environment in America and Zambia', *International Journal of Psychology*, 8, pp.83-94.

Stickgold, R. (1998) 'Sleep: Offline memory reprocessing', *Trends in Cognitive Sciences*, 2, pp.484-7.

Stokols, D. (1976) 'The experience of crowding in primary and secondary environments', *Environment and Behaviour*, 8, pp.49-86.

Stokols, D., Rall, M., Pinner, B. and Schopler, J. (1973) 'Physical, social and personal determinants of the perception of crowding', *Environment and Behaviour*, 5, pp.87-117.

Stouffer, S.A., Suchman, E.A., DiVinney, L.C., Starr, S.A. and Williams, R.M. (1949) *The American Soldier: Adjustment during Army Life*, Vol. 1,

Princeton: Princeton University Press.

Strachan, T. and Read, A.P. (1996) *Human Molecular Genetics*. Oxford: Bios Scientific.

Strack, F., Martin, L.L. and Stepper, S. (1988) 'Inhibiting and facilitating conditions of the human smile: a non-obtrusive test of the facial feedback hypothesis', *Journal of Personality and Social Psychology*, 54, pp.768-77.

Stratton, P. and Hayes, N. (1993) *A Student's Dictionary of Psychology* (2nd edn), London: Edward Arnold.

Stroebe, W. and Stroebe, M.S. (1987) *Bereavement and Health*, Cambridge: Cambridge University Press.

Strongman, K.T. (1987) *The Psychology of Emotion* (3rd edn), Chichester: Wiley.

Stroop, J.R. (1935) 'Studies of interference in serial-verbal reaction', *Journal of Experimental Psychology*, 18, pp.643-62.

Stuart, R.J. (1991) 'Kin recognition as a functional concept', *Animal Behaviour*, 41, pp.1093-4.

Stuart-Hamilton, I. (2000) 'Aging and intelligence', *Psychology Review*, 6 (4) (in press).

Styles, E.A. (1997) *The Psychology of Attention*, Hove: Psychology Press.

Suggs, R.C. (1966) *Marquesan Sexual Behavior*, New York: Harcourt, Brace & World.

Suppes, T., Baldessarini, R.J. and Faedda, G.L. (1991) 'Risk of recurrence following discontinuation of lithium treatment in bipolar disorder', *Archives of General Psychiatry*, 48, pp.1082-7.

Svartberg, M. and Stiles, T.C. (1991) *Comparative Effects of Psychotherapy*, Baltimore, MD: Johns Hopkins University Press.

Tajfel, H. (1970) 'Experiments in intergroup discrimination', *Scientific American*, 223, pp.96-102.

Tajfel, H. (ed.) (1978) *Differentiation between Social Groups: Studies in the Social Psychology of Intergroup Relations*, London: Academic Press.

Tajfel, H. (1981) *Human Groups and Social Categories,* Cambridge: Cambridge University Press.

Tajfel, H. (1982) 'Social psychology of intergroup relations', *Annual Review of Psychology, 33,* pp.1-30.

Tajfel, H., Flament, C., Billig, M.G. and Bundy, R.P. (1971) 'Social categorisation and intergroup behaviour', *European Journal of Social Psychology,* 1, pp.149-78.

Tanaka, J.W. and Farah, M.J. (1993) 'Parts and wholes in face recognition', *Quarterly Journal of Experimental Psychology,* 46A, pp.225-45.

Tannen, D. (1990) *You Just Don't Understand: Women and Men in Conversation,* New York: William Morrow, Ballantine.

Tannen, D. (1993) *Framing in Discourse,* Oxford: Oxford University Press.

Tannen, D. (1995) *Talking from 9 to 5,* London: Virago Press.

Tapp, J.T. (1969) 'Activity, reactivity and the behaviour-directing properties of stimuli', in J.T. Tapp (ed.) *Reinforcement and Behavior,* New York: Academic Press.

Tavris, C. and Wade, C. (1995) *Psychology in Perspective,* New York: HarperCollins.

Taylor, S.E., Fiske, S.T., Etcoff, N.I. and Ruderman, A.J. (1978) 'Categorical and contextual bases of person memory and stereotyping', *Journal of Personality and Social Psychology,* 36, pp.778-93.

Terrace, H.S., Petitto, L.A., Sanders, R.J. and Bever, T.G. (1979) 'Can an ape create a sentence?', *Science,* 206, pp.891-902.

Terry, D.J., McHugh, T.A. and Noller, P. (1991) 'Role dissatisfaction and the decline of marital quality across the transition to parenthood', *Australian Journal of Psychology,* 43 (3), pp.129-32.

Tesser, A. and Paulhus, D.L. (1976) 'Toward a casual model of love', *Journal of Personality and Social Psychology,* 34, pp.1095-l05.

Thase, M.E., Frank, E. and Kupfer, D.J. (1991) 'Biological processes in major depression', in E.E. Beckham and W.R. Leber (eds) *Handbook of Depression,*

Homewood, Illinois: Dorsey Press.

Thase, M.E., Greenhouse, J.B., Frank, E., Reynolds, C.F., Pilconis, P.A., Hurley, K., Grochocinski, V. and Kupfer, D.J. (1997) 'Treatment of major depression with psychotherapy or psychotherapy-pharmacotherapy combinations', *Archives of General Psychiatry,* 54, pp.1009-15.

Thibaut, J.W. and Kelley, H.H. (1959) *The Social Psychology of Groups,* New York: Wiley.

Thigpen, C. and Cleckey, H. (1954) 'A case of multiple personality disorder', *Journal of Abnormal and Social Psychology,* 49, pp.135-51.

Thigpen, C. and Cleckey, H. (1957) *The Three Faces of Eve,* New York: McGraw Hill.

Thomas and Blackman (1991) 'Are animal experiments on the way out?', *The Psychologist,* 4 (5), pp.208-12.

Thomas, A. and Chess, S. (1977) *Temperament and Development,* New York: Brunner-Mazel.

Thomas, A. and Chess, S. (1980) *The Dynamics of Psychological Development,* New York: Brunner-Mazel.

Thomas, J.C. (1974) 'An analysis of behaviour in the hobbits-orcs problem', *Cognitive Psychology,* 6, pp.257-69.

Thorndike, E.L. (1911) *Animal Intelligence: Experimental Studies,* New York: Macmillan.

Thorpe, S.J. and Salkovskis, P.M. (1997) 'The effect of one-session treatment for spider phobia on attentional bias and beliefs', *British Journal of Clinical Psychology,* 36, pp.225-41.

Tienari, P., Sorri, A., Lahti, I. and Naarala, M. (1987) 'Genetic and psychosocial factors in schizophrenia: The Finnish adoptive family study', *Schizophrenia Bulletin,* 13, pp.477-84.

Tinbergen, N. (1951) *The Study of Instinct,* Oxford: Oxford University Press.

Tinbergen, N. and Kruyt (1938) cited in Tinbergen N. (1951) *The Study of Instinct,* Oxford: Oxford University Press.

Tinbergen, N. and Perdeck, A.C. (1950) 'On the stimulus

situation releasing the begging response in the newly hatched herring gull chick', *Behaviour,* 3, pp.1-38.

Tizard, B. and Hughes, M. (1984) *Young Children Learning,* London: Fontana.

Tolman, E.C. (1948) 'Cognitive maps in rats and men', *Psychological Review,* 55, pp.189-208.

Tomarken, A. J., Mineka, S., *et al.* (1989) 'Fear-relevant selective associations and covariation bias', *Journal of Abnormal Psychology* 98, pp.381-94.

Tomasello, M. and Farrar, M.J. (1986) 'Object permanence and relational words: a lexical training study', *Journal of Child Language,* 13, pp.495-505.

Tomasello, M. and Mannle, S. (1985) 'Pragmatics of sibling speech to one-year-olds', *Child Development,* 56, pp.911-17.

Toon, F., Fraise, J., McFetridge, M. and Alwin, N. (1996) 'Memory or mirage? The FMS debate', *The Psychologist,* 9 (2), pp.73-77.

Topál, J. and Miklósi, A. (1998) 'Attachment behaviour in dogs', *Journal of Comparative Psychology,* 112.

Tordoff, M.G., Novin, D. and Russek, M. (1982) 'Effects of hepatic denervation on the anorexic response to epinephrine, amphetamine, and lithium chloride: a behavioral identification of glucostatic afferents', *Journal of Comparative and Physiological Psychology,* 96, pp.361-75.

Torgersen, S. (1983) 'Genetic factors in anxiety disorders', *Archives of General Psychiatry,* 40, pp.1085-9.

Torrey, E.F., Rawlings, R. and Waldman, I.N. (1988) 'Schizophrenia births and viral diseases in two states', *Schizophrenia Research,* 1, pp.73-7.

Torrey, E.F., Rawlings, R.R., Ennnis, J.M., Merrill, D.D. and Flores, D.S. (1996) 'Birth seasonality in bipolar disorder, schizophrenia, schizoaffective disorder and stillbirths', *Schizophrenia Research,* 21 (3), pp.141-9.

Tovee, M.J., Rolls, E.T. and Azzopardi, P. (1994) 'Translation invariance in the responses to

faces of single neurons in the temporal visual cortex areas of the alert macaque', *Journal of Neurophysiology,* 72, pp.1049-60.

Tower, R.K., Kelly, C. and Richards, A. (1997) 'Individualism, collectivism and reward allocation: a cross-cultural study in Russia and Britain', *British Journal of Social Psychology,* 36, pp.331-45.

Treisman, A.M. (1960) 'Contextual cues in selective listening', *Quarterly Journal of Experimental Psychology,* 12, pp.242-8.

Treisman, A.M. (1964) 'Verbal cues, language and meaning in selective attention', *American Journal of Psychology,* 77, pp.206-19.

Treisman, A.M. and Geffen, G. (1967) 'Selective attention: perception or response?', *Quarterly Journal of Experimental Psychology,* 19, pp.1-18.

Trivers, R. (1971) 'The evolution of reciprocal altruism', *Quarterly Review of Biology,* 46, pp.35-57.

Trivers, R. (1972) 'Parental investment and sexual selection', in B. Campbell (ed.) *Sexual Selection and the Descent of Man,* Chicago: Aldine de Gruyter.

Turiel, E. (1983) *The Development of Social Knowledge: Morality and Social Convention,* Cambridge: Cambridge University Press.

Turing, A.M. (1950) 'Computing machinery and intelligence', *Mind,* 59, pp.433-60.

Turnbull, C. (1961) 'Some observations regarding the experiences and behaviour of the Bambuti', *American Journal of Psychology,* 74, pp.153-63.

Turner, J.C. (1982) 'Towards a cognitive redefinition of the social group', in H. Tajfel (ed.) *Social Identity and Intergroup Relations,* Cambridge: Cambridge University Press.

Turner, J.S. and Helms, D.B. (1983) *Lifespan Development,* New York: Holt, Rinehart & Winston.

Tversky, A. and Kahneman, D. (1971) 'Belief in the law of small numbers', *Psychological Bulletin,* 76, pp.105-110.

Tversky, A. and Kahneman, D. (1973) Availability: a heuristic for judging frequency and probability', *Cognitive Psychology*, 5, pp.207-32.

Tversky, A. and Kahneman, D. (1974) 'Judgement under uncertainty: heuristics and biases', *Science*, 815, pp.1124-31.

Tversky, A. and Kahneman, D. (1982) 'Judgement under uncertainty: heuristics and biases', in D. Kahneman, P. Slovic and A. Tversky (eds) *Judgement under Uncertainty: Heuristics and Biases*, New York: Cambridge University Press.

Tversky, A. and Kahneman, D. (1987) 'Rational choice and the framing of decisions', in R. Hogarth and M. Reder (eds) *Rational Choice: The Contrast between Economics and Psychology*, Chicago: University of Chicago Press.

Tyerman, A. and Spencer, C. (1983) 'A critical test of the Sherifs' robbers cave experiments: intergroup competition and co-operation between groups of well acquainted individuals', *Small Group Behaviour*, 14, pp.515-31.

Tyler, C.W. (1997) 'Analysis of human receptor density', in V. Lakshminarayanan (ed.) *Basic and Clinical Applications of Vision Science*, Norwell, MA: Kluwer Academic.

Tyler, L.E. (1965) *The Psychology of Human Differences* (3rd edn), New York: Appleton-Century-Crofts.

Umbenhauer, S.L. and DeWitte, L.L. (1978) 'Patient race and social class: attitudes and decisions among three groups of mental health professionals', *Comprehensive Psychiatry*, 19 (6), pp.509-15.

Umbricht, D. and Kane, J.M. (1996) 'Medical complications of new antipsychotic drugs', *Schizophrenia Bulletin*, 22, pp.475-83.

Umilta, C., Simion, F. and Valeuza, E. (1996) 'Newborn's preference for faces', *European Psychologist*, 1, 3, pp.200-5.

Underwood, G. (1974) 'Moray vs. the rest: the effects of extended shadowing practice', *Quarterly Journal of Experimental Psychology*, 26, pp.368-72.

Ussher, J. (1989) *The Psychology of the Female Body*, London: Routledge.

Ussher, J. (1992) *Women's Madness: Misogyny or Mental Illness?* Hemel Hempstead: Harvester Wheatsheaf.

Vaillant, C.O. and Vaillant, G.E. (1993) 'Is the U-curve of marital satisfaction an illusion? A 40-year study of marriage', *Journal of Marriage and the Family*, 55 (1), pp.230-9.

Valenstein, E.S. (1967) 'Selection of nutritive and non-nutritive solutions under different conditions of need', *Journal of Comparative and Physiological Psychology*, 63, pp.429-33.

Van de Castle, R. (1994) *Our Dreaming Mind*, New York: Ballantine.

Van der Kolk, B. (1988) 'The trauma spectrum: the interaction of biological and social events in the genesis of the trauma response', *Journal of Traumatic Stress*, 1, pp.273-90.

Van Dusen, K.T., Mednick, S.A., Gabrielli, W.F. and Hutchings, B. (1983) 'Social class and crime in an adoption cohort', *Journal of Criminal Law and Criminology*, 74, pp.249-69.

Van Gelder, L. (1985) 'The strange case of the electronic lover', *Ms.*, October, pp.94-124.

Van Yperen, N.W. and Buunck, B.P. (1990) 'A longitudinal study of equity and satisfaction in intimate relationships', *European Journal of Social Psychology*, 20, pp.287-310.

Varner, D., Cook, J.E., Schneck, M.E., McDonald, M. and Teller, D.Y. (1985) 'Tritan discriminations by 1- and 2-month old human infants', *Vision Research*, 25, pp.821-31.

Vaughn, C.E. and Leff, J.P. (1976) 'The influence of family and social factors on the course of psychiatric illness. A comparison of schizophrenia and depressed neurotic patients', *British Journal of Psychiatry*, 129, pp.125-37.

Veijola, J., Puukka, P., Lehtinen, V., Moring, J., Lindholm, T. and Vaisanen, E. (1998) 'Sex differences in the association between childhood experiences and adult depression', *Psychological Medicine*, 28, pp.21-7.

Velakoulis, D., Pantelis, C., McGorry, P.D., Dudgeon, P., Brewer, W., Cook, M., Desmond, P., Bridle, N., Tierney, P., Murrie, V., Singh, B. and Copolov, D. (1999) 'Hippocampal volume in first-episode psychosis and chronic schizophrenia', *Archives of General Psychiatry*, 56, pp.133-41.

Vivian, J. and Brown, R. (1995) 'Prejudice and intergroup conflict', in M. Argyle and A.M. Colman (eds) *Social Psychology*, Harlow: Longman.

von Frisch, K. (1967) *The Dance Language and Orientation of Bees*, Cambridge, Massachusetts: Harvard University Press.

Von-Neumann, J. and Morgenstern, O. (1947) *Theory of Games and Economic Behavior* (2nd edn), Princeton: Princeton University Press.

Vygotsky, L.S. (1934) *Thought and Language*, edited and translated by E. Hanfmann and G. Vakar (1962), Cambridge, MA: MIT Press.

Vygotsky, L.S. (1987) 'The development of scientific concepts in childhood', in R.W. Rieber and A.S. Carton (eds) *The Collected Works of L.S. Vygotsky*, Vol. 1, New York: Plenum Press.

Wade, C. and Tavris, C. (1993) *Psychology*, New York: Harper Collins.

Wadeley, A., Birch, A. and Malim, T. (1997) *Perspectives in Psychology* (2nd edn), London: Macmillan.

Walace, S.T. and Alden, L.E. (1997) 'Social phobia and positive social events: the price of success', *Journal of Abnormal Psychology*, 106, pp.416-24.

Walker, I. and Mann, L. (1987) 'Unemployment, relative deprivation, and social protest', *Personality and Social Psychology Bulletin*, 13, pp.275-83.

Walker, L. (1984) 'Sex differences in the development of moral reasoning: a critical review', *Child Development*, 55, pp.677-91.

Walker, L.J., deVries, B. and Trevethan, S.D. (1987) 'Moral stages and moral orientations in real-life and hypothetical dilemmas', *Child Development*, 58, pp.842-58.

Walker, W.D., Rowe, R.C. and Quinsey, V.L. (1993) 'Authoritarianism and sexual aggression', *Journal of Personality and Social Psychology*, 65, pp.1036-45.

Wallraff, H.G. (1988) 'Navigation mit Duftkarte und Sonnenkompass: das Heimfindevermögen der Brieftauben', *Naturwissenschaften*, 75, pp.380-92.

Wallraff, H.G. (1990) 'Navigation by homing pigeons', *Ethology, Ecology and Evolution*, 2, pp.81-115.

Walster, E. and Piliavin, J.A. (1972) 'Equity and the innocent bystander', *Journal of Social Issues*, 28 (3), pp.165-89.

Walster, E.H. and Walster, G.W. (1969) 'The matching hypothesis', *Journal of Personality and Social Psychology*, 6, pp.248-53.

Walster, E.H., Aronson, E., Abrahams, D. and Rottman, L. (1966) 'Importance of physical attractiveness in dating behavior', *Journal of Personality and Social Psychology*, 4, pp.325-42.

Walster, E.H., Walster, G.W. and Berscheid, E. (1978) *Equity Theory and Research*, Boston, Massachusetts: Allyn and Bacon.

Walters, R.H. and Thomas, L. (1963) 'Enhancement of punitiveness by visual and audiovisual displays', *Canadian Journal of Psychology*, 16, pp.244-55.

Walton. G.E., Bower, N.J.A. and Bower, T.G.R. (1992) 'Recognition of familiar faces by newborns', *Infant Behaviour and Development*, 15, pp.265-9.

Warr, P.B. (1965) 'Proximity as a determinant of positive and negative sociometric choice', *British Journal of Social and Clinical Psychology*, 4, pp.104-9.

Waterman, A.S. (1982) 'Identity development from adolescence to adulthood: an extension of theory and a review of research', *Developmental Psychology*, 18, pp.341-58.

Waterman, A.S. (1985) 'Identity in the context of adolescent psychology', *New Directions for Child Development*, 30, pp.5-24.

Waterman, C.K. and Waterman, A.S. (1975) 'Fathers and sons: a study of ego-identity across two generations', *Journal of Youth and Adolescence*, 4, pp.331-8.

Waterman, T.H. (1989) *Animal Navigation*, New York: Scientific American Library.

Watson, J.B. (1913) 'Psychology as the behaviourist views it', *Psychological Review*, 20, pp.158-78.

Watson, J.B. and Rayner, R. (1920) 'Conditioned emotional responses', *Journal of Experimental Psychology*, 63, pp.575-82.

Webb, E.J., Campbell, D.T., Schwartz, R.D., Sechrest, L. and Grove, J.B. (1981) *Nonreactive Measures in the Social Sciences* (2nd edn), Boston: Houghton Mifflin.

Weber, E.U., Bockenholt, U., Hilton, D.J. and Wallace, B. (1993) 'Determinants of diagnostic hypothesis generation: effects of information, base rates and experience', *Journal of Experimental Psychology: Learning, Memory and Cognition*, 19, pp.1131-64.

Wehren, A. and DeLisi, R. (1983) 'The development of gender understanding: judgements and explanations', *Child Development*, 54, pp.1568-78.

Weinberger, D.R. (1988) 'Premorbid neuropathology in schizophrenia', *Lancet*, 2, pp.959-60.

Weiner, B. (1979) 'A theory of motivation for some classroom experiences', *Journal of Educational Psychology*, 71, pp.3-25.

Weiner, B. (1986) *An Attributional Theory of Motivation and Emotion*, New York: Springer-Verlag.

Weisberg, R., Dicamillo, M. and Phillips, D. (1978) 'Transferring of associations to new situations: a nonautomatic process', *Journal of Verbal Learning and Behaviour*, 17, pp.219-28.

Weisman, A.D. (1972) *On Dying and Denying: A Psychiatric Study of Terminality*, New York: Behavioural Publications.

Weisman, A.G., Nuechterlein, K.H., Goldstein, M.J. and Snyder K.S. (1998) 'Expressed emotion, attributions, and schizophrenia symptom dimen-

sions', *Journal of Abnormal Psychology*, 107, pp.355-9.

Weiss, J.M. (1972) 'Influence of psychological variables on stress-induced pathology', in J. Knight and R. Porter (eds), *Physiology, Emotion and Psychosomatic Illness*, Amsterdam: Elsevier.

Weiss, R.A. (1978) 'Why cell biologists should be aware of genetically transmitted viruses', *National Cancer Institute Monograph*, 48, pp.183-9.

Weissman, M.M., Bruce, M.L., Leaf, P.J., Florio, L.P. and Holzer, C. (1991) 'Affective disorders', in L.N. Robins and D.A. Regier (eds) *Psychiatric Disorders in America: The Epidemiologic Catchment Area Study*, New York: Free Press.

Weizenbaum, J. (1966) 'ELIZA: a computer program for the study of natural language communication between man and machine', *Communications of the Association for Computing Machinery*, 9, pp.36-45.

Wells, G. (1985) 'Preschool literacy-related activities and success in school', in D.R. Olson, N. Torrance and A. Hildyard (eds) *Literacy, Language and Learning*, Cambridge: Cambridge University Press, pp.229-55.

Werker, J.F. and Tees, R.C. (1984) 'Cross language speech development: evidence for perceptual reorganisation during the first year of life', *Infant Behaviour and Development*, 7, pp.49-63.

Wernicke, C. (1874) *Der Aphasische Symptomenkomplex*, Breslau: Cohn & Weigert.

Wertheimer, M. (1945) *Productive Thinking*, New York: Harper & Row.

West, M.J. and King, A.P. (1988) 'Female visual displays affect the development of male song in the cowbird', *Nature*, 334, pp.244-6.

Wetherell, M. and Potter, J. (1992) *Mapping the Language of Racism: Discourse and the Legitimation of Exploitation*, London and New York: Harvester Wheatsheaf and Columbia University Press.

Wheldall, K. and Merritt, F. (1983) 'Good behaviour', *The*

Times Educational Supplement, 25 November 1983, in H. Coolican *et al.* (1996) *Applied Psychology*, London: Hodder & Stoughton.

Whiting, B. and Edwards, C. (1988) *Children of Different Worlds: The Formation of Social Behaviour*, Cambridge, MA: Harvard University Press.

Whiting, B.B. and Whiting, J.W.M. (1975) *Children of Six Cultures*, Cambridge, MA: Harvard University Press.

Whiting, J.W. (1966) *Six Cultures Series 1: Field Guide for a Study of Socialization*, New York: Wiley.

Whitten, A. and Byrne, R. (1988) 'Tactical deception in primates', *Behavioural and Brain Sciences*, 11, pp.233-44.

Whorf, B.L. (1956) *Language, Thought and Reality*, Cambridge, MA: MIT Press.

Wickler, W. (1968) *Mimicry in Plants and Animals*, New York: McGraw-Hill.

Wilkins, H. (1991) 'Computer talk: long distance conversations by computer', *Written Communcation*, 8, pp.56-78.

Wilkinson, G.S. (1984) 'Reciprocal food sharing in the vampire bat', *Nature*, 308, pp.181-4.

Williams, J.E. and Best, D.L. (1982) *Measuring Sex Stereotypes: A Thirty-Nation Study*, Beverly Hills, CA: Sage.

Williams, J.E. and Best, D.L. (1992) 'Psychological factors associated with cross-cultural differences in individualism–collectivism', in S. Iwawaki, Y. Kashima and K. Leung (eds) *Innovations in Cross-Cultural Psychology*, Amsterdam: Swets & Zeitlinger.

Williams, J.H. (1987) *Psychology of Women* (3rd edition), London: W.W. Norton & Co.

Williams, R.L. (1972) *The BITCH Test (Black Intelligence Test of Cultural Homogeneity)*, St. Louis: Washington University.

Williams, S.L., Kinney, P.J., Harap, S.T. and Liebmann, M. (1997) 'Thoughts of agoraphobic people during scary tasks', *Journal of Abnormal Psychology*, 106, pp.511-20.

Williams, T.M. (1985) 'Implications of a natural experiment in the developed world for research on television

in the developing world. Special issue: Television in the developing world', *Journal of Cross Cultural Psychology*, 16 (3), pp.263-287.

Williams, T.M. (1986) *The Impact of Television: A Natural Experiment in Three Communities*, New York: Academic Press.

Wills, T.A. (1992) 'The helping process in the context of personal relationships', in S. Spacaman and S. Oskamp (eds) *Helping and Being Helped: Naturalistic Studies*, Newbury Park, CA: Sage.

Wilson, E.O. (1975) *Sociobiology, The New Synthesis*, Cambridge, MA: Harvard University Press.

Wilson, E.O. (1978) *On Human Nature*, Cambridge, MA: Harvard University Press.

Wilson, E.O. (1992) *The Diversity of Life*, Harmondsworth: Penguin.

Winson, J. (1997) 'The meaning of dreams', *Scientific American*, Special Issue, 7, pp.58-67.

Wispe, L.G. (1972) 'Positive forms of social behaviour: an overview', *Journal of Social Issues*, 28 (3), pp.1-19.

Wittchen, H.U., Nelson, C.B. and Lachner, G. (1998) 'Prevalence of mental disorders and psychosocial impairments in adolescents and young adults', *Psychological Medicine*, 28, pp.109-26.

Wolf, A.P. (1995) *A Chinese Brief for Edward Westermarck*, Stanford: Stanford University Press.

Wolpe, J. (1958) *Psychotherapy by Reciprocal Inhibition*, Stanford, California: Stanford University Press.

Wong, D.F., Wagner, H.N., Tune, L.E., Dannals, R.F., Pearlson, G.D. and Links, J.M. (1986) 'Positron emission tomography reveals elevated D2 dopamine receptors in drug-naive schizophrenics', *Science*, 234, pp.1558-62.

Wood, D.J., Bruner, J.S. and Ross, G. (1976) 'The role of tutoring in problem-solving', *Journal of Child Psychology and Psychiatry*, 17, pp.89-100.

Wood, N. and Cowan, N. (1995) 'The cocktail party phenomenon revisited: how frequent are attention shifts to one's name in an irrelevant auditory channel?', *Journal of Experimental Psychology: Human Perception and Performance*, 16, pp.135-49.

Wood, W., Wong, F.Y. and Chachere, J.G. (1991) 'Effects of media violence on viewers' aggression in unconstrained social interaction', *Psychological Bulletin*, 109, pp.371-83.

Woodruff, G. and Premack, D. (1979) 'Intentional communication in the chimpanzee: the development of deception', *Cognition*, 7, pp.333-62.

Woodruff, P.W.R., Wright, I.C., Shuriquie, N., Russouw, H., Rushe, T., Howard, R.J., Graves, M., Bullmore, E.T. and Murray, R.M. (1997) 'Structural brain abnormalities in male schizophrenics reflect fronto-temporal dissociation', *Psychological Medicine*, 27, pp.1257-66.

Worell, J. (1992) 'Feminist journals: academic empowerment or professional liability?', in J. Williams (ed.) *Gender in Academe*, Tampa: University of South Florida Press.

Worell, J. and Remer, P. (1992) *Feminist Perspectives in Therapy*, Chichester: Wiley.

World Health Organization (1993) *The ICD-10 Classification of Mental and Behavioural Disorders: Diagnostic Criteria for Research*, Geneva: WHO.

Wortman, C.B. and Brehm, J.W. (1975) 'Responses to uncontrollable outcomes: an integration of the reactance theory and the learned helplessness model', in L. Berkowitz (ed.) *Advances in Social Psychology*, New York: Academic Press.

Yamada, J.E. (1990) *Laura: A Case for the Modularity of Language*, Cambridge, MA: MIT Press.

Yang, M.M. (1994) *Gifts, Favors, and Banquets: The Art of Social Relationships in China*, Ithaca, NY: Sage.

Yap, P.-M. (1974) *Comparative Psychiatry: A Theoretical Framework*, Toronto: University of Toronto Press.

Yarkin, K.L., Town, J.P. and Wallston, B.S. (1982) 'Blacks and women must try harder: stimulus person's race and sex attributions of causality', *Personality and Social*

Psychology Bulletin, 8, pp.21-24.

Yates, B.L. (1999) *Modeling Strategies for Prosocial Television: A Review*, Paper presented to the Open Paper Competition, AEJMC Southeast Colloquium, Lexington, Kentucky, March 4-6, 1999.

Yeates, K.O., MacPhee, D., Campbell, F.A. and Ramey, G.T. (1979) 'Maternal IQ and home environment as determinants of early childhood intellectual competence: a developmental analysis', *Developmental Psychology*, 15, pp.731-9.

Yerkes, R.M. and Dodson, J.D. (1908) 'The relation of strength of stimuli to rapidity of habit-formation', *Journal of Comparative Neurology and Psychology*, 18, 459-82.

Yin, R.K. (1969) 'Looking at upside-down faces', *Journal of Experimental Psychology*, 81, pp.141-5.

Yonas, A. (1981) 'Infants' responses to optical information for collision', in R.N. Aslin, J.R. Alberts and M.R. Peterson (eds) *Development of Perception: Psychobiological Perspectives*, Vol. 2, *The Visual System*, New York: Academic Press.

Yonas, A. and Owsley, C. (1987) 'Development of visual space perception', in P. Salapatek and L. Cohen (eds) *Handbook of Infant Perception*, Vol. 2, *From Perception to Cognition*, Orlando: Academic Press.

Young, A.H., Blackwood, D.H.R., Roxborough, H., McQueen, J.K., Martin, M.J. and Kean, D. (1991) 'A magnetic resonance imaging study of schizophrenia: brain structure and clinical symptoms', *British Journal of Psychiatry*, 158, pp.158-64.

Young, A.W., Hay, D.C. and Ellis, A.W. (1987) 'The faces that launched a thousand slips: everyday difficulties and errors in recognising people', *British Journal of Psychology*, 76, pp.495-523.

Young, A.W., Newcombe, F., deHaan, E.H.F., Small, M. and Hau, D.C. (1993) 'Face perception after brain injury', *Brain*, 116, pp.941-59.

Young, M.A., Meaden, P.M., Fogg, L.F., Cherrin, E.A. and Eastman,

C.I. (1997) 'Which environment variables are related to the onset of seasonal affective disorder?', *Journal of Abnormal Psychology*, 106, pp.554-62.

Young, W.C., Goy, R.W. and Phoenix, C.H. (1964) 'Hormones and sexual behaviour', *Science*, 143, pp.212-8.

Zahavi, A. (1979) 'Ritualisation and the evolution of movement signals', *Behaviour*, 72, pp.77-81.

Zajonc, R.B. (1968) 'Attitudinal effects of mere exposure', *Journal of Personality and Social Psychology*, 9, pp.1-27.

Zajonc, R.B. (1984) 'On the primacy of affect', *American Psychologist*, 39, pp.117-23.

Zar, J.H. (1972) 'Significance testing of the Spearman Rank Correlation Coefficient', *Journal of the American Statistical Association*, 67, pp.578-80.

Zhang, Y., Proenca, R., Maffei, M., Barone, M., Leopold, L. and Friedman, J.M. (1994) 'Positional cloning of the mouse gene and its human homologue', *Nature*, 372, pp.425-32.

Zigler, E.F., Abelson, W.D. and Seitz, V. (1973) 'Motivational factors in the performance of economically disadvantaged children on the Peabody Picture Vocabulary Test', *Child Development*, 44, pp.294-303.

Zihl, J., von Cramon, D. and Mai, N. (1983) 'Selective disturbance of movement vision after bilateral posterior damage', *Brain*, 106, pp.313-40.

Zimbardo, P. (1969/1970) 'The human choice: individuation, reason and order versus deindividuation, impulse and chaos', in W.J. Arnold and D. Levine (eds) *Nebraska Symposium on Motivation*, Vol. 17, Lincoln, Nebraska: University of Nebraska Press.

Zimbardo, P., McDermott, M., Jansz, J. and Metaal, N. (1995) *Psychology: A European Text*, London: HarperCollins.

Zohar, J., Judge, R. and the OCD paroxetine study investigators (1996) 'Paroxetine vs. clomipremine in the treatment of obsessive–compulsive disorder', *British Journal of Psychiatry*, 169, pp.468-74.

Zucker, I., Boshes, M. and Dark, J.S. (1983) 'Suprachiasmatic nuclei influence circannual and circadian rhythms of ground squirrels', *American Journal of Physiology*, 244, pp.R472-80.

Zung, W.W.K. (1965) 'A self-rating depression scale', *Archives of General Psychiatry*, 12, pp.63-70.

Checklist of synoptic issues

Introduction

In Chapter 29, you will have read about the nature of synopticity which is an important aspect of Unit 5 assessment: 'An understanding and critical appreciation of the breadth of theoretical and methodological approaches, issues and debates in psychology'. What follows is not intended to be an exhaustive catalogue of synoptic opportunities for each chapter, merely an illustration of some of the ways in which you might respond to this aspect of the assessment. This includes different explanations or perspectives that might be applied to a particular topic, different methods that

have been used to study it, the overarching issues relating to that topic (ethical, scientific, philosophical, etc.) and a demonstration of the links that might be made between this topic and other areas of the specification (or even other disciplines).

Remember that the synoptic aspect of your assessment is not simply an invitation to present a long list of points that might reflect synopticity, but a chance to discuss these within the context of your answer. The following references could be used as a starting point to demonstrate your 'understanding and critical appreciation' of the topic under discussion.

Chapter 16 Classification and diagnosis of psychological abnormality

Classificatory systems

407 Different methods – Effective diagnosis requires the use of several different assessment procedures.

408 Psychology as science – Assessing the reliability and validity of classificatory systems.

408 Ethical concerns – People are occasionally detained without their informed consent.

409 Biases in diagnosis – Social class, race and gender may determine the likelihood of a person being diagnosed as mentally ill.

Multiple-personality disorder (dissociative identity disorder)

413 Cultural differences – The disorder is rare in Europe and Japan, and has been described as a North American 'diagnostic fad'.

414 Theoretical explanations – There are a range of different theoretical perspectives on the origins of this disorder. These include psychodynamic, behavioural and cognitive explanations.

416 Free will versus determinism – In some instances the behaviour associated with this disorder may be spontaneous yet in others it

may be feigned to avoid culpability for criminal actions.

417 The neurotic paradox – Even apparently 'maladaptive behaviour' may bring rewards for the person who displays it.

Culture-bound syndromes

419 Cultural diversity – Culture-bound syndromes are 'recurrent, locality-specific patterns of aberrant behaviour ... that may or may not be linked to a specific DSM-IV diagnostic category'.

420 Reductionism – Culture-bound syndromes cannot be reduced to a single classificatory category because they are too diverse: they only make sense in terms of the values of the cultures in which they occur.

420 Eating disorders – These may be seen as culture-bound syndromes as they are specific to the USA and Western Europe and other Westernizing countries.

426 Cultural bias – The concept of a culture-bound syndrome is one generated by Western psychiatry; psychopathology in the West is seen as culturally neutral and psychopathology that is distinctively different is seen as 'culture-bound'.

Chapter 17 Psychopathology

Anxiety disorders

431– Different perspectives – Anxiety disorders can
438 be explained from different perspectives, including biological, evolutionary, cognitive, behavioural and psychodynamic.

431 Nature–nurture – Family and twin studies suggest that there is a genetic predisposition to phobic anxiety disorders.

431– Different methods – A variety of different
438 investigative methods have been used to study the development of anxiety disorders, including family history studies, twin studies, adoption studies, psychometric tests and experiments.

434 Links to developmental psychology – Phobic anxiety disorders can be linked to early attachment and separation experiences.

437 Links to physiological psychology – Prolonged exposure to stress (PTSD) may lead to the depletion of the neurotransmitter noradrenaline.

439 Links to physiological psychology – The use of positron emission tomography (PET) scanning has found that people diagnosed with obsessive–compulsive disorder have increased metabolic activity in the frontal regions of the brain.

Depression

441 Nature-nurture – Twin studies suggest that there is a genetic predisposition to depression.

441 Biological (somatic) therapies – Insights from drug treatments of depression have led to the suggestion that specific neurotransmitters are involved in depression.

442 Links to physiological psychology – Research suggests that depressives may experience overactivity in the hypothalamic-pituitary-adrenal cortex and adrenal gland enlargement.

443 Animal research – Studies of rhesus monkeys separated from their mothers suggest that both mothers and babies develop symptoms similar to depression in humans.

445 Animal research – Seligman's studies of dogs led to the suggestion that reactive depression may be a product of learned helplessness.

445 Links to social psychology – Depression may be explained in terms of the tendency for depressives to attribute all negative events to internal, stable, global causes.

Schizophrenia

449 Links to physiological psychology – Magnetic resonance imaging (MRI) has shown structural abnormalities in the brains of many patients with schizophrenia.

450 Links to other disciplines – The study and treatment of Parkinson's disease has highlighted the importance of dopamine for Parkinson's *and* schizophrenia.

451 Nature-nurture – Twin, family and adoption studies have demonstrated the importance of a genetic predisposition for schizophrenia.

453 Reductionism – Although twin studies have provided evidence for a genetic predisposition to schizophrenia, none has shown 100 per cent concordance in MZ twins. Research on 'expressed emotion' has shown that schizophrenics are also extremely sensitive to psychosocial elements in their environment.

454 Role of cultural factors – Schizophrenia has historically been linked with increased urbanization and with major flu epidemics.

456 Links to cognitive psychology – Cognitive psychologists have identified cognitive impairments that may also be present in the families of schizophrenics.

Chapter 18 Treating mental disorders

Biological (somatic) therapies

459– Biological therapies come in a variety of forms,
465 including drug treatments, electroconvulsive therapy (ECT) and psychosurgery.

459– Links to physiological psychology – Biological
462 explanations of abnormal behaviour implicate the important role of neurotransmitters such as *serotonin* and *dopamine*. Drugs alter the neurochemistry of the brain, and may modify the action of these neurotransmitters.

462 Ethical issues – The use of some drug regimes, such as the prolonged use of *phenothiazines* in the treatment of schizophrenia, may lead to irreversible damage of parts of the brain.

462 Links to contemporary events – Based on a fatal stabbing incident in 1993, the government was prompted into recommending enforced medication for mental patients living in the community.

464–5 Ethical issues – The use of ECT or psychosurgery as treatments requires that a person (or close relative) give their *informed consent* before they are given these forms of treatment.

464–5 Therapy or social control? – The use of psychosurgery has been criticized as a form of social control. Members of the antipsychiatry movement have doubted the true purpose of surgical treatments for mental disorders.

Behavioural therapies

466–8 Behavioural therapies come in several forms (e.g. systematic desensitization, flooding, token economy and social skills training) and serve a variety of different functions (e.g. the treatment of phobias, shaping desirable behaviours, modelling appropriate social behaviour).

468 Ethical issues – Aversion therapy is seen as breaching ethical guidelines in its use of induced pain or nausea as aversive stimuli.

468 Therapy or social control? – When 'desirable behaviour' is determined by the institution, this may be designed to serve the institution on the pretext of serving the recipient.

468 Free will versus determinism – In token economy programmes, people may become dependent on the regime and find it very difficult to think for themselves when outside the institutional setting.

Alternatives to biological and behavioural therapies

469 Links to physiological psychology – Cognitive–behavioural therapy is commonly used as a form of *stress management* (e.g. Meichenbaum's 'stress-inoculation therapy').

471 Comparison with other therapies – A number of studies have compared the effectiveness of cognitive–behavioural treatment with drug (particularly antidepressant drugs) treatment and with behavioural treatments.

474 Psychodynamic therapy is regarded as appropriate for a range of different neuroses, including anxiety disorders, eating disorders and, to a lesser extent, depression.

475 Comparison with other therapies – Studies have compared the effectiveness of psychoanalytic treatment with drug treatment.

475 Psychology as science – It is difficult to measure the effectiveness of psychoanalytic treatment because there are too many variables involved to enable a controlled and statistically valid outcome study.

475 Links to contemporary events – The 'discovery' of traumatic memories during therapeutic sessions has led to a debate over whether these are 'real' memories or 'false' memories. This also creates *ethical issues* for the therapist and in some cases lengthy legal battles ensue.

477 Free will versus determinism – Unlike the psychodynamic and behaviourist approaches, humanistic therapies attempt to access the personal power and autonomy of the client.

478 Person-centred counselling is used in a wide variety of settings, including truancy, bereavement and HIV counselling.

479 Psychology as science – Testing the effectiveness of humanistic therapies using traditional scientific methods is difficult because it can be measured only by whether an individual believed that counselling had been helpful.

Chapter 19 Issues and debates in psychology

Gender bias in psychological theory and research

486–7 Gender bias comes in many different forms, such as alpha bias (assuming real differences between men and women) and beta bias (minimizing sex differences) and may be compounded by cultural and sexual biases.

487 Free will versus determinism – Deterministic theories (such as psychoanalysis) assume that patterns of behaviour (e.g. gender role behaviour) develop as a result of past events (e.g. socialization) and are more or less fixed.

488 Links to contemporary issues – Studies of premenstrual syndrome (PMS) have resulted in

claims that such research reflects the male-dominated culture of scientific enquiry rather than the experiences of women themselves.

488–9 Different topics, different methods – Traditional experimental studies are seen as ignoring the social, personal and cultural context in which behaviour typically happens. Feminist psychologists advocate the use of methods that ensure non-gender-biased investigations.

Cultural bias in psychological theory and research

426 Cultural bias – The concept of a culture-bound syndrome is one generated by Western psychiatry; psychopathology in the West is seen as culturally neutral and psychopathology that is distinctively different as 'culture-bound'.

490 Free-will versus determinism – If individuals are socialized within a particular *type* of culture (i.e. individualist or collectivist), this does not mean they will always behave in a characteristic way.

490–1 Cultural bias is evident in a variety of psychological theories and research studies, including Kohlberg's theory of moral understanding, Adorno's theory of the authoritarian personality and Milgram's research on obedience to authority.

491–2 Psychology as science – Smith and Bond (1998) claim that there are problems of establishing equivalence in cross-cultural research, including the manipulation of variables, the nature of participants and the research tradition in the culture being studied.

Ethical issues in research with human participants

492 The ethical issues of psychological research are informed by a number of underlying moral principles, including *nonmalificence* (not harming others), *honesty* (not lying or deceiving others) and *privacy* (respecting personal privacy and confidentiality).

493 Links to other disciplines – Medicine, law and psychology all contain the same basic elements for ethics to have a role: the acquisition of specialized knowledge, standards of competence and well-defined sets of practices that allow knowledge and competence to be utilized.

494 Free-will versus determinism – The use of deception removes the ability of research participants to *choose* whether to take part in research based on full knowledge of their role in the investigation.

495 Links to research methods – Some ethical issues may have different significance depending on the setting of the investigation. The need for *informed consent* may be different in naturalistic studies, and the requirement for *privacy* is determined by the nature of the observation and its setting.

496 The issues of socially sensitive research underlie many different areas of psychological research, including research into drug and sexual habits, gender and racial differences.

497 Links to research methods – Some of the controversies that arise from socially sensitive research can be attributed to poorly designed studies or inappropriate interpretations of the findings.

497 Psychology as science – The freedom to pursue scientific research is balanced against the obligation to protect those who take part or the sectors that they represent. Some researchers take the view that all research should be for the betterment of human beings, whilst others stress the importance of scientific truth and rigorous methodology.

514 Reductionism – Searching for genetic links to 'explain' homosexuality raises a number of sensitive ethical issues such as the right for privacy and the potential abuse of research findings.

521 Nature and nurture – As demonstrated in *The Bell Curve* (Herrnstein and Murray, 1994), the nature-nurture debate can also be used to support political agendas that may disadvantage certain groups of people.

The use of nonhuman animals in research

443 Individual differences – Studies of rhesus monkeys separated from their mothers suggest that both mothers and babies develop symptoms similar to depression in humans.

445 Individual differences – Seligman's studies of dogs led to the suggestion that reactive depression may be a product of learned helplessness.

499 Psychology as science – Animals offer the opportunity for greater control and objectivity in research procedures. Objectivity is more easily attained with nonhuman than human animals.

499 Links with approaches – Greater opportunities for experimental control exist with animals than with humans. Much of behaviourist theory was established using animal studies for just this reason.

499 Links with developmental psychology – Harlow's research established that a monkey's attachment to its mother depends on the contact comfort that she provides. Evidence for such effects in human infants indicates that they too have a need for contact, and that this is important in the formation of a lasting attachment bond.

501–3 Links to comparative psychology – Ethical issues also arise in animal research in the field, particularly in field experiments, where part of an animal's natural habitat is manipulated in some way.

504–7 Links to other disciplines – Many of the objections to animal research (such as Singer's utilitarian argument and Regan's animal rights position) are formulated on *philosophical* premises.

508 Links to contemporary issues – Animal research may have considerable value in helping to find treatments for major diseases such as Alzheimer's disease.

Free will versus determinism

416 Individual differences – In some instances the behaviour associated with multiple-personality disorder may be spontaneous yet in others it may be feigned to avoid culpability for criminal actions.

468 Individual differences – In token economy programmes, people may become dependent on the regime and find it very difficult to think for themselves when outside the institutional setting.

477 Individual differences – Unlike the psychodynamic and behaviourist approaches, humanistic therapies attempt to access the personal power and autonomy of the client.

487 Gender bias in theory and research – Deterministic theories (such as psychoanalysis) assume that patterns of behaviour develop (e.g. gender-role behaviour) as a result of past events and are more or less fixed.

490 Cultural bias in theory and research – If individuals are socialized within a particular *type* of culture (i.e. individualist or collectivist), this does not mean they will always behave in a characteristic way.

494 Ethical issues in research with human participants – The use of deception removes the ability of research participants to *choose* whether to take part based on full knowledge of their role in the investigation.

510/ 512 Psychology as science – The scientific perspective in psychology is based on a belief in *causal determinism*. The notion of free will and the goals of scientific psychology *appear* to be incompatible.

511 Links to contemporary issues – Claims for the genetic basis of criminality are hotly disputed. Crime, it is argued, may contain a genetic component, which would change our assumptions about responsibility for a criminal act.

512 Reductionism – Attempts to explain crime and other social problems in terms of genetics and biology are indicative of a search for simple explanations and simple ways of dealing with such problems.

511–2 Different approaches to psychology (e.g. the *psychodynamic, behavioural* and *humanistic* approaches) have different perspectives on the free-will versus determinism debate. The position that these approaches take in this debate has an important effect on the way that we explain human nature.

Reductionism

420 Individual differences – Culture-bound syndromes cannot be reduced to a single classificatory category because they are too diverse and only make sense in terms of the values of the cultures in which they occur.

453 Individual differences – Although twin studies have provided evidence for a genetic predisposition to schizophrenia, none has shown 100% concordance in MZ twins. Research on 'expressed emotion' has shown that schizophrenics are also extremely sensitive to psychosocial elements in their environment.

512 Free-will versus determinism – Attempts to reduce crime and other social problems to explanations based on genetics and biology are indicative of a search for simple explanations and simple ways of dealing with such problems.

513 Links to individual differences and physiological psychology – Reductionist explanations of schizophrenia have highlighted the role of the neurotransmitter dopamine. This has led to the hope that schizophrenia might be eradicated by controlling the brain chemistry of schizophrenics by the administration of antipsychotic drugs.

513–4 Links to comparative psychology – Attempts to explain human behaviour using evolutionary concepts is an example of biological reductionism.

514 Links to contemporary issues – Despite claims for a genetic link in homosexuality, it is likely that sexual orientation is too complex to be determined by a single gene.

514 Ethical issues in socially sensitive research – Searching for genetic links to 'explain' homosexuality raises a number of sensitive ethical issues such as the right for privacy and the potential abuse of research findings.

515 Links to contemporary issues – Research on biological preparedness has explained why children undergoing chemotherapy treatment often develop food aversions at the same time.

515 Psychology as science – Reducing our research focus to the study of only one influence at a time may miss the complexity of influences on a behaviour at any given time.

Psychology as science

408 Individual differences – Assessing the reliability and validity of classificatory systems.

475 Individual differences – It is difficult to measure the effectiveness of psychoanalytic treatment because there are too many variables involved to enable a controlled and statistically valid outcome study.

479 Individual differences – Testing the effectiveness of humanistic therapies using traditional scientific methods is difficult because it can be measured only by whether an individual believed that counselling had been helpful.

491–2 Social psychology – Smith and Bond (1998) claim that there are problems of establishing equivalence in cross-cultural research, including the manipulation of variables, the nature of participants and the research tradition in the culture being studied.

497 Ethical issues in research with human participants – The freedom to pursue scientific research is balanced against the obligation to protect those who take part or the sectors that they represent. Some researchers take the view that all research should be for the betterment of human beings, whilst others stress the importance of scientific truth and rigorous methodology.

499 The use of nonhuman animals in research – Animals offer the opportunity for greater control and objectivity in research procedures. Objectivity is more easily attained with nonhuman than human animals.

510/ Free will versus determinism – The scientific
512 perspective in psychology is based on a belief in *causal determinism*. The notion of free will and the goals of scientific psychology *appear* to be incompatible.

515 Reductionism – Reducing our research focus to the study of only one influence at a time may miss the complexity of influences on a behaviour at any given time.

521–2 Nature and nurture – Adopting a strict scientific approach is problematic when investigating the contributions of nature and nurture, due to the difficulties of manipulating and measuring the necessary variables.

Nature and nurture

431 Individual differences – Family and twin studies suggest that there is a genetic predisposition to phobic anxiety disorders.

441 Individual differences – Twin studies suggest that there is a genetic predisposition to depression.

451 Individual differences – Twin, family and adoption studies have demonstrated the importance of a genetic predisposition for schizophrenia.

520–1 Links to different approaches – The nature versus nurture debate is exemplified in the contrasting views of *ethology* and *behaviourism*.

521 Links to developmental psychology – The nature versus nurture argument has been particularly fierce in debates about the origins of *intelligence* and in the effectiveness of compensatory education programmes such as *Head Start*.

521 Ethics of socially sensitive research – As demonstrated in *The Bell Curve* (Herrnstein and Murray 1994), the nature-nurture debate can also be used to support political agendas that may disadvantage certain groups of people.

521–2 Psychology as science – Adopting a strict scientific approach is problematic when investigating the contributions of nature and nurture, due to the difficulties of manipulating and measuring the necessary variables.

A

abnormal conditions focus model 3–4
abnormality
  classification and diagnosis 405–28
abstracts 565
accommodation 187
achievement attribution 4–6
action potential 92, 94
action slips 169–73, 284
activity theory of old age 318
actor/observer biases 7–8
adolescence 295–301
  cross-cultural variations 298–9, 301
  focal theory 299–300
  historical aspects 301
  identity formation 295–7
  moratorium during 295
  parental relationships 300
  peer relationships 300
  'storm and stress' 297–8, 299
adoption studies 262–3, 452
Adorno, T.W. 19, 490
adulthood 303–25
  cognitive changes 318–23
  defined 303–4
  relationships during 312–17
  stage theories 305–11
aerial perspective 200
affect-centred model of attraction 34
affordances 197
ageing, types of 304
aggression 55–64
  defined 55
  environmental factors 61–3
  theories 56–60
agoraphobia 430–1, 467
aha! phenomenon 235
Ajzen, L. 18
alcohol consumption and helping behaviour 71
alexia 103
algorithms 237

allometry 397
Allport, D.A. 164, 167
Allport, F.H. 198
alpha bias 486
alpha rhythm 94
altruism 65–9
  in animals 333–7
  defined 65, 333
  induced 337
  reciprocal 335–6
Alzheimer's disease 95, 508
amnesia, childhood, 537
anaesthetic artefact hypothesis 353
analogy 238
anchoring 15
anchoring and adjustment heuristic 242
androcentric theories 486–7
androgyny 292
angular gyrus 103
animals
  altruism 333–7
  communication 365–75
  deception 353, 368–9
  foraging 342, 348–9, 376–7
  imitation by 348
  intelligence 350–4
  language of 369–72
  language teaching to 372–4
  memory 375–7
  migration 362–5
  navigation 357–65, 375–6
  in research 499–510
  self-recognition 350–3
  social cognition 354
  teaching others 350
  theory of mind 353
Anna O. 283
ant communication 365
anthropomorphism 533
anti-anxiety drugs 459, 460–1
antidepressants 459–60, 461
antimanic drugs 460, 462
antipsychotics 460, 461–2
antisocial behaviour 55–64
  environmental factors 61–3

media influences 57, 80–6
anxiety disorders 429–40
  cognitive–behavioural therapy 472
  drug treatment 459, 460–1
  evolutionary theory 393–4
  genetic factors 431, 439
  and personality 432
AO1/AO2 skills 551–2
aphasia 101
apraxias 103
aquatic migration 363–4
Argyle, M. 34, 35, 39, 48
Aristotle 485
Arnold, M. 144
Aron, A.P. 150
Aronson, E. 495
arousal
  optimal 139
arousal:cost-reward model 73–5
Artificial Intelligence (AI) 545
association cortex 99, 101–4
attention
  divided 155, 164–73
  focus of 8
  focused 155, 156–63
  slips of 169–73, 284
attenuator theory 159–61
attraction 30–6
attribution 1–10
  biases 2, 6–9
  dispositional 2
  situational 2
  theories 1, 2–6
attributional retraining 9
audience effect 371
auditory communication 366–7
auditory cortex 100
augmentation principle 4
Augoustinos, M. 8, 12, 13, 15
authoritarian personality 19
autokinetic effect 201
automatic versus controlled processing 168–9
availability heuristic 11, 241
aversion therapy 466

axons 91

B

Balda, R.P. 376
Baltes, M.M. 304, 320
Baltes, P.B. 304, 320
Bandura, A. 56, 57, 81, 84, 85, 285, 467
basal ganglia 101
base-rate fallacy 241
Bateson, P. 506
bats 335–5
Batson, C.D. 65, 66, 67, 68, 69, 75
Baumrind, D. 493
Baxter, L.A. 36
'beaker problem' 251–2
Beck, A.T. 433, 446, 469, 471
bee
  cognitive maps 376
  waggle dance 370
behavioural theories 539–43
  anxiety disorders 432–3
  depression 444–6
  obsessive–compulsive disorder 439
  post-traumatic stress disorder 437
behavioural therapy 466–9
  see also cognitive–behavioural therapy
Bell Curve, The 521
Belson, W. 83
benzene ring 126
benzodiazepines 459, 460–1
bereavement 321–3
Berger, H. 94
Berkowitz, L. 56, 84
Bernstein, B. 225
Berry, J. 490
beta bias 486
Bhavnani, K.K. 18
Bianchi, Ken 417
bias-free theories 487–8
Biederman, I. 177
bilinguals 222
Binet, A. 261
binocular depth cues 200
binocular disparity 200
biological clocks 115–17

biological reductionism 513–15
biological rhythms 113–18
    types of 114–15
biological theories 528–30
    altruism 333–7
    gender development 293–4
    personality development 287
biological therapies 459–65
birds
    brood parasitism 337, 338
    egg recognition 334, 338
    foraging 349–50
    memory 375, 376
    migration 363
    mutualistic relationships with man 337
    navigation 358–61, 363
    nest recognition 361
    song 346, 367, 372, 375
Black English Vernacular 226
blind spot 188
blood glucose 135
Bloom, L. 224
Blos, P. 295, 300
blue tits 349–50
Bobo doll 56
body shape 31
body weight set-point 135–6
Boesch, C. 350
Bond, M.H. 30, 46, 490, 491
bottom-up processing 178, 193–4
Bower, T.G.R. 211, 212
Bowlby, J. 434, 443
brain
    chemical stimulation and recording 95–6
    cortex 99–101, 400–1
    electrical stimulation and recording 94–5, 176, 192
    lesion studies 96
    scanning 96–8
    self-stimulation 140–1
    size 397–400
    surgery 145–6, 464–5, 529–30
brain function
    and gender 110
    lateralization 105–10
    localization 99–104
    studying 94–8
Braly, K.W. 12
Breland, K. 346–7, 515
Breland, M. 346–7, 515
bride-price 47
brief psychotherapy 475
Broadbent, D.E. 157, 158, 164
Broca's aphasia 101
Broca's area 102, 528
Bronfenbrenner, U. 299

Brown, K. 84
Brown, R. 19, 20, 21, 22
Bruce, V. 180, 181, 182
Bruner, J.S. 233
Bucy, P. 145
Burk, T. 366, 367, 368
Buss, D. 388, 390, 391, 393, 394
butterfly 362
Byrne, R. 400
bystander behaviour 64–5, 69–75

C

Cannon, W.B. 133, 146
Cannon–Bard theory 147
capacity models of attention 165–7
Cardwell, M.K. 31, 33
carpentered world 213
Cartwright, R. 127
Case, R. 255
Caspi, A. 32
CAT scans 96
categorization 11
cats 350
causal schemata 4
causality 1
Centerwall, B.S. 83
cerebellum 101
cetaceans 351, 356–7
chemical communication 367–8
chemotherapy 459–63
Cherry, E.C. 156
Cheyney, D. 371, 372
Chi-squared test 579–81, 592
child directed speech 231
child-rearing 278
childhood amnesia 537
children, record number of 383
chimpanzees 398
    deception by 353
    imitation by 348
    reproduction 386
    self-recognition 350–3
    teaching each other 350
    teaching language to 372–4
    theory of mind 353, 354
Chinese Room 545
Chodorow, N. 486, 487
cholecystokinin 135
Chomsky, N. 231, 232
chromosomes 91
Cialdini, R.B. 68, 69
CIDI 408–9
cingulotomy 464
circadian rhythms 114
circannual rhythms 114–15
Clark, E.V. 228
Clark, H.H. 228
classical conditioning 339–43

classification systems 405–12
Clayton, C. 376
cleaner fish 336, 337
Cleckey, H. 413, 414
client-centred therapy 477–9
Clozapine 462
Clutton-Brock, T.H. 382
cocktail party problem 156
cognitive acceleration programme 259
cognitive appraisal 147
cognitive–behavioural theory
    depression 446
    phobias 433–4
cognitive–behavioural therapy 469–72
    see also behavioural therapy, cognitive therapy
cognitive development 247–77
cognitive expense 3
cognitive functions 99, 101–4
    in old age 320–1
cognitive labelling 147–8
cognitive misers, 1, 3, 11
cognitive neuropsychology 100
cognitive psychology 544
cognitive theory 543–5
    depression 446
    language acquisition 233
    schizophrenia 456–7
cognitive triad 446
cohort 304
Coleman J.C. 297, 299, 300
collective representation 14
collective unconscious 128
collectivistic/individualistic cultures 45–6, 75–7, 276
colour coding 221–2
colour constancy 203
colour vision 191–2, 208
commissurotomy 105
communication 365–75
    see also language
complex cells 176, 192
Composite International Diagnostic Interview (CIDI) 408–9
computer dance study 31
computer-mediated communication 50–2
computerized axial tomography 96
concept-driven processing 179, 194
concrete operations 248, 250–1
conditioning
    classical 339–43
    first-order 342
    higher-order (second-order) 342
    operant 343–7

cones 187–8
confirmatory bias 11
conflicting cues theory 205
Confucian dynamism 46
conjugation fallacy 241
conscious 282, 535
consensus 2, 3
conservation 250
consistency 2, 3
constructivism 197–9
contact hypothesis 24–6
contention scheduling 170
context and recognition 178–9
continuity hypothesis 232
contrast perception 190–1, 208
control
    locus of 433
controlled versus automatic processing 168–9
convergence 200
Coolican, H. 577
Coren, S. 117
cornea 186
corpus callosum 105
correlational analysis 583–4
cortex 99–101, 400–1
cortical cells 176, 192
cortical organization 99–104
    crossed/uncrossed pathways 101
    laws of 99
    topographic maps 100
cortisol 442
counselling 478–9
counter-stereotypes 289
couples, types of 39
coursework 561–72
co-variation model 2–4
cowbirds 346
crab migration 363
Crick, F. 125
cross-cultural research 48–9
cross-cultural variations
    adolescence 298–9, 301
    divorce 317
    helping behaviour 77
    love 43–4
    marriage 47–8, 313
    mate preferences 388–9
    mating systems 383–4
    morality 276
    mourning rituals 323
    parenthood 314–15
    perception 213–16
    prosocial behaviour 75–7
    relationships 45–9
    self-serving bias 9
crowd behaviour 58–9
crowding and aggression 62–3
cuckoos 337, 338
cultural bias 490–2

cultural determinism 289
culture-bound syndromes 410, 419–27
cultures
    classification 45–7
    defined 45
Cumberbatch, G. 80
cytoplasm 91
Czeisler, C.A. 117

D

Daly, M. 394
dark adaptation 190
Darley, J. 69, 70, 72
Darwin, C. 329–30, 384, 531
data-driven processing 179, 193–4
Dawkins, M.S. 335, 336, 355, 367, 377
Dawkins, R. 532, 533, 534
de Waal, F.B.M. 520, 522
death 321–3
Deaux, K. 58
decategorization 26
deception
    in animals 353, 368–9
    in research 493–4
decision-making 238–42
defence mechanisms 282
deindividuation 58–9
delta waves 119
Dement, W. 118
dendrites 91
denial 282
depression 440–7
    attributional style 9
    behavioural theory 444–6
    biochemical factors, 441–3
    bipolar 395
    cognitive–behavioural therapy 471–2
    cognitive triad 446
    drug therapy 459–60, 461
    dysthymic disorder 441
    endogenous 394
    evolutionary theory 394–6
    genetic factors 441
    hopelessness theory 445–6
    life events 443–4
    lock and key hypothesis 444
    major depressive disorder 441
    postnatal 443
    psychodynamic theory 443
    psychodynamic therapy 474
    rank theory 395–6
    reactive 394
    symptoms 440
    unipolar 394, 440
depth perception 199–200, 208, 213–14
Descartes, R. 528

desensitization 466
determinism 487, 511–12
Deutsch, D. 161
Deutsch, J.A. 161, 134 ••????•
Deutsch–Norman model 161–2
diagnosis of mental disorders 407–11
Diagnostic Statistical Manual of Mental Disorders (DSM-IV) 405, 406, 407, 411
diathesis-stress model
    phobias 434–5
    post-traumatic stress disorder 437–8
    schizophrenia 455–6
dichotic listening 108–9, 156
diet and intelligence 265
diffusion of responsibility 69–70
digger wasps 358, 375–6
dimorphism 384, 387
Dindia, K. 36
Dion, K.K. 43
direct perception 185, 194–7
disconnection syndrome 107
discounting principle 4
discrimination 18
    see also prejudice
disengagement in old age 318
displacement 282
dissociative identity disorder, 413–18
distinctiveness 2–3
divided attention 155, 164–73
divided field experiments 106–7, 108
divorce 47–8, 316–17
dogmatism 19
dogs 322
Doise, W. 30
dolphins 351
Donaldson, M. 250
dopamine 450–1
dowries 47
dreams 124–30
    analysis of 127–30, 473
    functions of 125–6
    and learning 126–7
    and problem-solving 127
drive-reduction 141
drug treatment 459–63
DSM-IV 405, 406, 407, 411
dual tasks 164–5
dualism 528
Duck, S. 29, 31, 32, 37
Dunbar, R. 33
Duncker, K. 235
Dutton, D.C. 150
Dyer, F.C. 375, 376

E

ecological theory 194
economic exchange theories 38–40

education 256–9, 541
    and prejudice reduction 23–4
ego 281, 535
ego defence 282
ego justification 14
egocentrism 249
Egrise, D. 115
eight ages of man 305–6
Eisenberg, N. 273–5, 276
Ekman, P. 149
elaborated code 225
Electra complex 280
electrical brain stimulation and recording 94, 95, 140–1, 176, 192
electroconvulsive therapy 463–4
electroencephalography (EEG) 94, 95, 118–19
electronic friendships 50–2
ELIZA 545
Elliot, J. 24
Ellis A. 433, 469, 470
emic-etic distinction 490
emotion 144–50
    brain activity 144–6
    theories 146–50
empathic understanding 478
empathy 65–6, 274
empathy-altruism hypothesis 65–8
enduring dispositions 167
engrams 99
enrichment programmes 264–5
environment of evolutionary adaptation 392
environmental factors and aggression 261–3
environmental reductionism 515
epilepsy 105
equity theory 38
Erikson, E.H. 295, 296, 305–7
Eron, L. 86
Ervin-Tripp, S. 229
Eskimos 220
ethical issues 492–8, 563–4
ethnocentrism 21–2, 487
eugenics 534
event-related potentials (ERPs) 94, 95
evolutionary theories 531–4
    of behaviour 329–38
    gender development 294
    intelligence 397–401
    mental disorders 392–7
    reproductive behaviour 381–91, 393
examination board documents 561–2
examinations
    marking schemes 554, 557–9

performance 556–9
preparation for 549–56
question-setting 552–3
questions, reading 556
synoptic assessment 553–6
time management 556–7
expressed emotion 454–5
extinction 340
extra-cellular fluid 91
eye 186–8
eye movements in infants 208
Eysenck, H.J. 287, 432, 474
Eysenck, M.W. 165, 171, 173

F

F scale 19
face recognition 180–2, 209
facial expression 149
false consensus bias 11
false memory syndrome 475–6
family relationships 312–17
    schizophrenia 454–5
Fantz, R.L. 209
fear 394
feature detection 175–7, 192
Fechner, G. 543
fecundity 331
Felson, R.B. 83
Fiedler, K. 4, 11
field experiments 501–3
figuration 15
filter model of attention 157–9
filter theory of mate selection 32
first-order conditioning 342
fish
    migration 363–4
    mutual relationships between 336, 337
    visual communication 366
Fishbein, M. 18
Fiske, S.T. 7, 10, 25
fitness 331, 388, 392–3
Flavell, J.H. 209
flexible theory 487
flooding 466, 467
flow patterns 196–7, 201
focal colour 222
focal theory of adolescence 299–300
focus of attention 8
focused attention 155, 156–63
folk illness 420
football hooligans 59
foraging 342, 348–50, 376–7
formal operations 248, 251–2
fovea 187–8
framing effect 239
free association 473
free will 510–11

Freud, S. 127, 129, 280–5, 443, 473, 535–7
Freudian slips 284
Friedrich, L.K. 79, 82
frontal lobe syndrome 103
functional fixedness 235
fundamental attribution error 6–7
fusion 200

G

Gaertner, S.L. 26
Gage, Phineas 103
Gallup, G.G. 350, 352, 353
Galton, F. 531–2, 534
galvanic skin response 162
gambler's fallacy 240
Ganzfeld 195
Garcia, J. 515
Gardner, B.T. 372
Gardner, R.A. 372
Gardner, Randy 120
Gauntlett, D. 86
gay relationships 49–50, 51
gazelle 368–9
gender bias 485–9
gender determinism 290
gender development 288–94
    cognitive-developmental theory 290–2
    evolutionary theory 294
    and hormones 294
    identity formation 291–2
    media influences 289
    peer influences 288
    psychodynamic theory 293–4
    social learning 288–90
gender-free theories 487
gender identity 291–2
gender-related variations
    hemispheric asymmetries 110
    jealousy 390–1
    language use 227
    mental disorder diagnosis 410–11, 412
    morality 275–6
gender relativism 290
gender schema 292–3
gender stereotypes 289
gendercentric theories 487
General Problem Solver 237
genetic factors
    anxiety disorders 431, 439
    depression 441
    intelligence 262–3
    schizophrenia 451–3
genetic relatedness, coefficient of 393
genome lag 392, 393
Genovese, Kitty 65, 69–70
genuineness 478
'George' 413

Gestaltism 234–6
Gibson, E.J. 210, 211
Gibson, J.J. 185, 194, 195
Gifford, R.K. 13
Gilligan, C. 275
glucose levels 135
good-sense/good-taste 385–6
Goodwin, R. 43, 45, 46, 47, 48
gorillas 386, 398, 372
Gould, J.L. 370, 376
Gould, R.L. 309, 310
Gould, S.T. 355
'grain of truth' hypothesis 13
Green, S. 504
Greene, B. 49, 50
Gregory, R.L. 179, 198, 199, 204
Grier, J.W. 366, 367, 368
grooming 400
ground squirrel 333
group justification 14
groups, intergroup conflict 20

H

habituation 207
Hamer, D. 514
Hamilton, D.L. 10, 13
Hamilton, W.D. 392
handedness 109–10
Harris, M.J. 23
Hatfield, E. 39, 40, 41
Headstart 264–5
heat and aggression 61–2
Helmholtz, H.L.F. von 179, 198
helping 65
    cross-cultural variations in 77
    factors affecting 71–2
    and personality 71
hemispheric asymmetries 105–10
    and gender 110
Hendrick, C. 42, 43
Hendrick, S. 42, 43
Herbener, E.S. 32
heterosexist theory 487
heuristics 11, 237, 240–2
Hewstone, M. 11
Heyes, C.M. 353
hierarchy of needs 142–3
higher-order conditioning 342
Hobbits-and-Orcs problem 237–8
Hobson, J.A. 125
Hockett, C.F. 369, 370, 372
Hofstede, G. 45, 46, 490
Holland, C.C. 493
Holmes T. 311, 312, 434
holophrase 228
Homan, R. 494
HOME 264
homeostasis/homeostatic drive 133–4, 138–41
homing 357–62

homosexuality 49–50, 51
honeyguide 337
hopelessness theory of depression 445–6
horizon ration 196
hormones 294, 442, 443
Horne, J. 120, 121
Hubel, D.H. 176, 178, 192
hue 191
Huesmann, L.R. 57, 84
Hull, C.L. 141
humanistic therapy 477–9
hunger 134–6
hunting 342
hydrocephalus 530
hypercomplex cells 176, 192
hypothalamus 135–6
hypovolemic thirst 137–8

I

iatrogenesis 415–16, 418
ICD-10 406
'iceberg' metaphor 536
id 280, 535
illusory correlation 13
imitation 348
impression management 9
incentives 139–40
incest 522
indigenous 419
individualistic/collectivistic cultures 45–6, 75–7, 276
infanticide 394
information processing 178–9, 193–4, 236–7, 255–6, 258–9
informed consent 494–5
infradian rhythms 114
insight 235
instinctive drift 346–7
intellectualization 282
intelligence and intelligence testing 260–7
    of animals 350–4
    and culture 263–5
    and diet 265
    and environment 263–5
    evolutionary approach 397–401
    genetic factors 262–3
    in old age 320
    and race 266–7
    test factors 265–6
intelligence quotient (IQ) 261
intelligent perception 185, 198
interactionist theory 487
intergroup conflict 20
International Statistical Classification of Disease (ICD-10) 406
interpersonal relationships see relationships

intersexual selection 385–6
interval scales 574
intrapsychic theories 487
intrasexual perception 385
investment model 39
ions 91
Iproniazid 461
IQ 261
iris 187

J

Jacobsen, E. 219
Jacobsen, L. 266
James–Lange theory 146
jealousy 390–1
Jennings, H.H. 34
jet lag 116
'jigsaw' technique 23, 24
Jones, J. 493
Jung, C.G. 128

K

Kahneman, D. 166, 167, 173, 239, 240, 241, 242
Kamil, A.C. 376
Kanizsa triangle 204
Katz, D. 12
Keane M.T. 165, 171, 173
Keaton, W.T. 359, 360
Kekule (chemist) 126
Kelley, H.H. 2, 4, 38
Kimmel, A.J. 493, 495
kin selection 333–4
kinship studies 262–3, 431, 441, 451–3
Kleiginna, A.M. 144
Kleiginna, P.R. 144
Kleitman, N. 118
Kluver, H. 145
Kohlberg, L. 270–3, 291
Kohler, W. 235
Krebs, J.R. 376, 377
Kübler-Ross, E. 321, 322
Kuhn, T. 518

L

la cuarentena 314
Labov, W. 226
language
    acquisition 228–34
    in animals 369–74
    cultural aspects 226–7
    and gender 227
    processing 101–2, 103, 104
    social aspects 225–6
    and thought 219–27, 254
language acquisition device 231
language acquisition socialization system 233
Lashley, K.S. 99, 528
Latané, B. 69, 70, 72
lateral geniculate nucleus 188

lateral inhibition 190–1
law of effect 343
law of equipotentiality 99
law of mass action 99
Lazarus, R.S. 437
learned helplessness 445
learning
    state-dependent 415
Lee, J.A. 43
leptin 136
lesbian relationships 49–50
levels of measurement 574
Levinson, D.J. 303, 307–10, 316
Lewinsohn, P.M. 9
libido 282
life events 434, 443–4
life structure 307
lifespan approach 488
light 115–16, 185
light adaptation 190
lightness constancy 203
limbic system 103–4, 145
linear perspective 200
linguistic relativity hypothesis 220–4
lithium salts 460, 462
Little Albert 432, 540
Little Hans 434
Litton, I. 17
Lloyd, B. 16
lobotomy 145–6, 464, 529–30
lobster migration 363
lock and key hypothesis 444
locus of control 433
Lord, C.G. 34, 40
love 40–4
Lucas, K. 16
Luchins, A.S. 236

M

M space 255–6
Machiavellian intelligence hypothesis 400
MacLean, P.D. 145
magnetic navigation 359–60
magnetic resonance imaging (MRI) 96–7
magnetoencephalography (MEG) 97–8
Magnusson, A. 114
major histocompatibility complex 335
manipulation 337
Mann, L. 58
Mann-Whitney test 578–9, 589–81
Manning, A. 335, 336, 367, 377
Manstead, A.S.R. 4, 13
Manstead, S.R. 57, 59, 62, 74
MAOIs 459, 460, 461
Marcia, J. 296–7
marking schemes 554, 557–9

marmosets 348
marriage 47, 312–14, 390
    dissolution 47–8, 316–17
Maslow, A.H. 142
matching hypothesis 31
mate selection 32, 388–90, 393
mating systems 382–4
McClelland, D.C. 142
McKenry, P.C. 48
Mead, M. 290, 298
means-end analysis 237–8
measurement levels 574
Meddis, R. 122
media influences
    and antisocial behaviour 57, 80–6
    gender stereotypes 289
    and prosocial behaviour 78–80
medical model 429
MEG (magnetoencephalography) 97–8
Meichenbaum, D.H. 469, 470, 471, 472
melatonin 114–15, 116
memory
    of animals 375–7
    of childhood 537
    in old age 320–1
    recovered 475–6
mental age 261
mental disorders 429–58
    classification 405–12
    diagnosis 407–11
    evolutionary approach 392–7
    treatment
        see treatment methods
        see also abnormality and specific conditions
mental space 255–6
migration 362–5
Milgram, S. 491, 495
milieu therapy 479
Milner, P. 140, 529, 533
Mínguez, E. 361
minimal groups 22, 23
mirror self-recognition 350–3
Mischel, W. 286
Mitchison, G. 125
mob behaviour 58–9
modelling 285–6
modularity 167–8
Moghaddam, F.M. 6, 7, 8, 14, 30, 32, 40, 45, 61, 62, 75, 77
momentary intentions 167
monarch butterfly 362
monkey
    communication 371
    imitation by 348
    social cognition 354

monoamine-oxidase inhibitors (MAOIs) 459, 460, 461
monocular depth cues 200, 215
Montessori, Maria 257
mood state and helping behaviour 71
moral dilemmas 271, 274
moral panics 80
morality
    and culture 276
    development 267–75
    and gender 275–6
Moray, N. 156, 158
Morgenstern, O. 239
Moscovici, S. 14, 15
motherese 231
motion agnosia 201
motion parallax 200
motion perception 200–2
motivation 133–44
    brain mechanisms 133–8
    theories 138–43
motor cortex 100–1
motor functions 99, 100
mourning rituals 322–3
MRI (magnetic resonance imaging) 96–7
Müller–Lyer illusion 204–5, 213, 214
multiple necessary causes 4
multiple-personality disorder 413–18
multiple sufficient causes 4
Murray, H.A. 141
Murray-Parkes, C. 321, 322
Murstein, B.I. 31
mutualism 336–7
myelin sheaths 92

N

nativism 231–3
natural selection 329, 330–1, 355, 381–2, 384
nature–nurture 206, 211, 520–3
Necker cube 199
needs 141–3
    hierarchy of 142–3
    need for achievement (nAch) 142
negative-state relief model 68–9
neglect 103
Neisser, U. 169, 176
neocortex 400–1
neonates
    speech perception 228
    visual perception 206–12
nerve impulses 92, 94
Neugarten, B.L. 304
Neumann, J. von 239
neurons 91–4
neurotic paradox 417

neurotoxins 96
neurotransmitters 93, 94, 529
    measurement of 95
Newcomb, T.M. 32
Newell, A. 236, 237
Newson, E. 80
Nicolson, P. 488
nightmares 124–5
Nisbett, R.E. 135
nodes of Ranvier 92
noise and aggression, 62
nominal level data 574
noradrenaline 436–7
Norman, D.A. 169, 170, 172
nutcracker 376–7

O

obedience
    Milgram's studies 491, 495
obesity 136
object permanence 249
objectification 15
observational learning 56
obsessive–compulsive disorder 438–40
Occam's razor 513
occipital lobe 104
Oedipus conflict 280, 537
offspring, record number of 383
Ojemann, G.A. 104
old age 318–23
Olds, J. 140, 529, 533
olfactory navigation 360–2
ontologizing 15
operant conditioning 343–7
Operation Headstart 264–5
opponent process theory 191–2
optic array 194
optic chiasm 188
optic flow 196–7, 201
optic tract 188
orang-utans 398
    imitation by 348
    reproduction 386
ordinal level data 574
Orne, M.T. 493
osmoreceptors 137
Oswald, I. 120, 124, 125
out-groups 20
overcrowding 62–3
overlap 200
overregularization 228–9

P

pacemakers 115–17
panic disorder 431
Papez, J.W. 145
Papi, F. 360
parental investment 382–4
parenthood 314–15
parietal lobe 103, 189
Parke, R.D. 82

Parker, I. 17
Parkinson's disease 529
participants in research
consent from 494–5
protection of 495
partnering 312–14
pattern recognition 155,
174–83
Patterson, F. 372
Pavlov, I.P. 339, 340, 341, 437,
539
payoff matrices 38
peacocks 331, 365, 384
Pearce, J.M. 344, 353, 358
peer relationships 288, 300
peer tutoring 258
Penfield, W. 94, 528
Pennell, A. 84
Penrose triangle 204
perception 185–218
cross-cultural variations
213–16
development of 206–16
theories 193–206
perceptual set, 198
person-centred therapy 477–9
personal columns 31, 33,
389–90
personal distress 66
personality development
279–88
psychodynamic theory
280–5, 305–7
situation theory 286–7
social learning theory
285–6
Type theory 287
personification 15
perspective taking 66
PET scans 97
Pettigrew, T.F. 490
phenothiazines 460, 462
pheromones 367–8
phi phenomenon 201–2
phobias 429–35
and arousal 432
behavioural therapy 467,
468
cognitive–behavioural
theory 433–4
cognitive–behavioural
therapy 472
and conditioning 432
diathesis-stress model
434–5
evolutionary theory 394
genetic factors 431
psychodynamic theory
434
social 430
social learning 433
specific 430
Phoenix, A. 18
photopic system 188

photopigments 190
photoreceptors 187–8, 190
physical attractiveness 31–2
physiological reductionism
513
Piaget, J. 224, 247–53,
268–70
pictorial cues 200, 215
pictorial images 214–16
pigeon homing 358, 359–62
Piliavin, I. 70, 71, 73, 74
pineal gland 115–16
point light walkers 201
polyandry 384
polygyny 384
Ponzo illusion 204
Popper, K. 519
positron emission tomography
97
postcentral gyrus 100
postnatal depression 443
post-traumatic stress disorder
435–40
behavioural theory 437
diathesis-stress model
437–8
and noradrenaline 436–7
psychodynamic theory
437
Potter, J. 17
Povinelli, D.J. 350, 351, 353
power-distance 46
pragmatics 229
precentral gyrus 100
preconscious 282
preferential looking 207
prefrontal leukotomy 464
prejudice 12, 18–23
reducing 23–6
pre-linguistic phase 228
Premack, D. 353
premenstrual syndrome 58,
488
pre-operational thought 248,
249–50
preparedness 343, 433
Price, S.J. 48
prisoner's dilemma 336
probability 239–42
problem solving 234–8
problem space 237
project brief 562
projection 282
projective tests 473
propagation 92
prosocial behaviour 64–77
cross-cultural variations
75–7
defined 65
media influences 78–80
prosocial reasoning 273–5
prototype theories 175
Prozac 459, 461
pseudopatients 408

psychodrama 476–7
psychodynamic theory 535–8
depression 443
gender formation 293–4
personality formation
280–5, 305–7
phobias 434
post-traumatic stress
disorder 437
psychodynamic therapy
472–6
psychological abnormality
see abnormality
psychological analysis levels
30
psychology, as a science
516–20
psychosexual development
280, 281, 282–3, 535–6
psychosurgery 145–6, 464–5,
529–30
punctuated equilibrium 329
punishment 345–6
pupil 187
pure word blindness 103

R
race
and intelligence 266–7
and language use 226–7
and mental disorder
diagnosis 409–10
racism 18
Rahe, R. 311, 312, 434
rank ordering 589
rank theory of depression
395–6
rapid eye movement sleep
119, 121–2, 124
rat foraging 348–9
ratio scales 574
Rational-Emotive Behaviour
Therapy 469–71
Raynor, R. 432
reaction formation 282
realistic conflict theory 20–1
Reason, J. 170, 171
recapitulation theory 297
recategorization 26
receptors 93
reciprocal determinism 286
recognition-by-components
177–8
recovered memory 476–7
reductionism 513–16
reference citation 569–70
Regan, T. 504
reindividuation 295
reinforcement 343–4
negative 345–6
positive 346
schedules 344–5
vicarious 285, 288–9
relationships 29–54, 312–17

cross-cultural variations
45–9
dissolution 37, 38–40,
47–8, 316–17
formation 30–6
maintenance 36–40
and social class 48
relative deprivation theory 60
relative height and size 200
REM sleep 119, 121–2, 124
Remer, P. 486, 487
report writing 564–70
representativeness heuristic
11, 240
repression 282, 284, 414
reproductive behaviour
381–91, 393
reproductive fitness 388
reproductive rate 382
reproductive success 331
research
on animals 499–710
deception in 493–4
ethical issues 492–8,
563–4
socially sensitive 496–7
research participants
consent from 494–5
protection of 495
research reports 564–70
responsibility, diffusion of
69–70
resting potential 92
restricted code 225
results presentation 567–8
retina 187–8
retirement 319–20
revision 549–51
Ridley, M. 358, 367
Risperidone 462
Robber's Cave 20
Rock, I. 198, 202
rods 187, 188
Rogers, C.R. 477, 478, 512
Rokeach, M. 19
role playing 476
Rorschach Ink Blot test 473
Rosenhan, D.L. 408
Rosenthal R., 266
Ross, L.D. 6, 7
Rubin, Z. 32
Rusbult, C.E. 39
Rutter, M. 298

S
Sagan, C. 351
saltatory conduction 92
Sander illusion 214
Sapir, E. 220
Sapir–Whorf hypothesis 220
saturation 191
scaffolding 255, 257
Schacter, S. 147
schema theory 10–11, 172–3

schizophrenia 447–57
  brain abnormalities 447, 449–50
  cognitive theory 456–7
  diathesis-stress model 455–6
  and dopamine 450–1
  drug treatment 460, 461–2
  evolutionary theory 396
  expressed emotion 454–5
  eye-tracking dysfunction 457
  family relationships 454–5
  genetic factors 451–3
  group splitting hypothesis 396
  season of birth 453–4
  symptoms 448
Schneider, W. 168, 169
science 516–20
scotopic system 188
script schemata 10
scripts 57
seals 384–5
seasonal affective disorder 114–15, 442
seasons of a man's life 307–10
second-order conditioning 342
selective (focused) attention 155, 156–63
selectivity theory of old age 318–19
self-awareness 58
self-efficacy 286
self-enhancing bias 8
self-handicapping 9
self-hypnosis 415
self-instructional training 470
self-protecting bias 8
self-recognition 350–3
self-serving bias 8–9
self-stimulation of brain 140–1
'selfish gene' 533
Selfridge, O.G. 175
Seligman, M.E.P. 445
senile dementia 95
sensorimotor stage 248, 249
sensory adaptation 189–90
sensory functions 99, 100
serotonin 115, 441, 442
serotonin re-uptake inhibitors 459–60
sex-role socialization 390
sexual desire 388–90
sexual dimorphism 384, 387
sexual reproduction 382–4
sexual selection 384–8
Seyfarth, R. 371, 372
shadows 200
Shallice, T. 169, 170
shape constancy 203, 211

Shaw, D.F. 49, 51
sheep 334
Sherif, M. 20
Sherry, D. 377
Shettleworth, S.J. 373, 375
Shiffrin, R.M. 20, 168, 169
shift work 116–17
Siffre, Michel 116
Sign Test 582–3, 594
Simon, H.A. 237
Simon, R.W. 41
Simon, T. 261
simple cells 176, 192
simultaneous lightness contrast 190
Sinclair-de-Zwart, H. 225, 253
Singer, E. 147
situation theory 197
situationalism 286–7
size constancy 202–3, 211, 212, 213–14
skill AO1/AO2 551–2
Skinner, B.F. 229, 343, 540, 541, 542
Skinner box 344, 345
sleep 118–24
  deprivation 120–2
  functions of 119–23
  paradoxical 119
  REM 119, 121–2, 124
  slow-wave 119
  stages 118–19
Slife, B.D. 510, 514, 516, 519
Slobin, D.I. 233
small-sample fallacy 240–1
Smith, P. 30, 490, 491
smoking 16
social ageing 304
social change 22
social class 48, 225–6, 409
social cognition 1–28, 354, 544–5
social creativity 22
social Darwinism 531–2
social disengagement 318
social exchange theory 38
social facilitation 350
social identity theory 21–3
social interactionist theory 233–4
social learning theory
  aggression 56–8
  gender development 288–9
  personality development 285–6
  phobias 433
social loafing 70
social parasitism 337
social perception 10–18
social phobia 430
Social Readjustment Rating Scale 311, 312
social relationships 30
  see also relationships

social representations 1, 14–17
social schemata 10–11
social skills training 467
socially sensitive research 496–7
sociobiology 33, 532–3
  of attraction 33–4
somatosensory cortex 100
Spearman's Rank Order Correlation Coefficient 583–4, 595
specific language impairment 233
speech
  see language
sperm competition 387
Sperry, R. 105
Spiegel, T.A. 134
split-brains 105–8
split-span procedure 157, 158, 159
spontaneous recovery 340
squirrel memory 377
stage theories 291–2, 305–11, 321, 322
standard deviation 573, 575
standard scores 586–8
state-dependent learning 415
state-dependent memory 437
statistical methods 573–85
  selection of 577
statistical significance 576–7
statistical tables 586–95
Stefansson, J.G. 114
Stein, A.H. 79, 82
stereotype threat 14
stereotyping 1, 10–14, 289, 321, 409
Sternberg, R.J. 42
stickleback 366
stimulus discrimination 341–2
stimulus generalization 341
stimulus overload 72
'storm and stress' 297–8, 299
stotting 368–9
Stouffer, S.A. 60
stress inoculation training 469, 471
  see also post-traumatic stress disorder
Strongman, K.T. 150
Stroop effect 168
structural powerlessness 390
sucking rate 207
suicide 393
sun compass 359
superego 281, 535
supervisory attentional system 169–70
suprachiasmatic nucleus 115–16
survival of the fittest 331
'Sybil' 414, 416
symbolic descriptions 186

synapses 93–4
synoptic assessment 553–6
system justification 14
systematic desensitization 466

T
Tajfel, H. 21, 22
tardive dyskinesia 462
Tavris, C. 514, 515
Taylor S.E. 7, 10, 12
telegraphic speech 228
television
  and antisocial behaviour 57, 80–6
  and gender stereotyping 289
  and prosocial behaviour 78–80
  violence on 80–4
temperature and aggression 61–2
template theory 174
temporal lobe 103, 189
Terrace, H.S. 372, 373
testis size 386, 387
Texas Adoption project 263
texture gradient 195–6, 200
Thematic Apperception Test 141, 473
theory of mind 353, 354
Thibaut, J.W. 38
Thigpen, C. 413, 414
thirst 136–8
Thorndike, E.L. 343, 540
Three Faces of Eve 414
three mountains tasks 249
Tinbergen, N. 358, 366, 376
token economy 467, 468
top-down processing 179, 194
transference 473
transformational grammar 232
treatment methods, 459–81
  behavioural 466–9
  cognitive–behavioural 469–72
  combining 462–3
  counselling 478–9
  drugs 459–63
  electroconvulsive 463–4
  humanistic (person-centred) 477–9
  psychodrama 476–7
  psychodynamic 472–6
  psychosurgery 145–6, 464–5, 529–30
triangle theory of love 42
trichromatic theory 191
tricyclic antidepressants 459, 460, 461
Triesman, A.M. 159, 160, 162
Trivers, R. 382
tubenoses 361

Turing, A.M. 545
Tversky, A. 239, 240, 241, 242
twin studies 262, 431, 441,
    452–3
Type I/II errors 577
Type theory 287

U

ultimate attribution error 7
ultradian rhythms 114
uncertainty avoidance 46
unconditional positive regard
    478
unconscious 282, 535
utility theory 239

V

vampire bats 335–6
verbal labels 221
veridical perception 204
Verona High School 23
vesicles 93
vicarious reinforcement 285,
    288–9
video games 85
Vincent, A.C.J. 382
visual acuity 208
visual cliff 210
visual communication 366
visual constancies 202–3, 211,
    212, 213–14
visual contrast 190–1
visual cortex 100, 104, 176,
    188–9, 192
visual illusions 203–5, 213,
    214
visual information processing
    189–92
visual pathway 105–6, 188–9
visual pattern recognition
    155, 174–83
visual perception 185–218
    cross-cultural variations
        213–16
    development of 206–16
    theories 193–206
visual system 104, 185–93
Vygotsky, L.S. 225, 253–5,
    257–8

W

Wade, C. 514, 515
Walk, P.D. 210
Walker, I. 8, 12, 13, 15
Walster, E.H. 31
Walster, G.W. 31
wasp navigation 358, 375–6
water jar problem 236
Waterman, T.H. 357, 363
Watson, J.B. 219, 432,
    539–40, 541
Weiner, B. 4, 5
Wernicke's aphasia 101
Wernicke's area 102

Wertheimer, M. 235
Westermarck effect 522
whales 351, 366–7
Whitten, A. 400
Whorf, B.L. 220, 221
Wiesel, T.N. 176, 178, 192
Wilcoxon Matched Pairs Test
    581–2, 593
Wilkinson, G.S., 335
Williams, R.N. 510, 514, 516,
    519
Williams, T.M. 82
Wilson, M. 394
Winson, J. 127
Wolpe, J. 466
Woodruff, G. 353
word association 473
Worell, J. 486, 487, 489
Wundt, W. 543

Y

Yerkes–Dodson law 167
yielding subroutine 395
Young, A.W. 180, 181, 182
Young–Helmholtz theory 191

Z

zeitgebers 114, 115, 116
Zhang, Y. 166
Zimbardo, P.G. 18, 58
zone of proximal development
    254